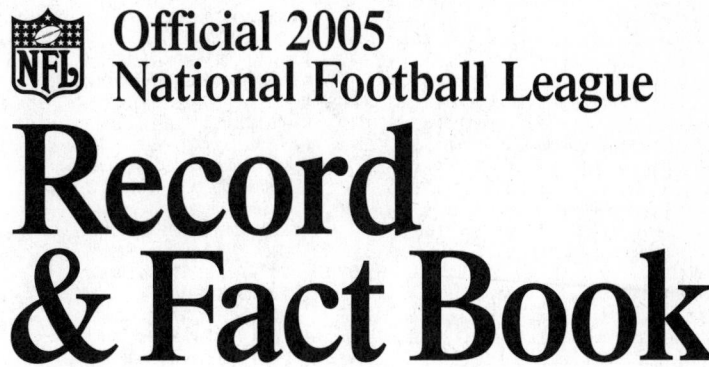

Official 2005
National Football League
Record
& Fact Book

T0204351

NATIONAL FOOTBALL LEAGUE
280 Park Avenue, New York, N.Y. 10017 (212) 450-2000. NFL Internet Address: http://www.NFL.com

Printed in the United States of America.

A National Football League Book.

Compiled by the NFL Communications Department and Seymour Siwoff, Elias Sports Bureau.
Statistics by Elias Sports Bureau.

Edited by Randall Liu, NFL Communications Department, and Matt Marini. Layout by William Tham. Cover design by Michael Rupich.
Produced by NFL Communications Department.

Cover photograph of the Super Bowl XXXIX champion New England Patriots by John Iacono/SPORTS ILLUSTRATED.

Time Inc.
HOME ENTERTAINMENT
Time Inc. Home Entertainment
1271 Avenue of the Americas, New York, N.Y. 10020
Manufactured in the United States of America.
First printing, July 2005.
10 9 8 7 6 5 4 3 2 1

A National Football League Book
Time Inc. Home Entertainment

All times local, except American Bowl in Tokyo, which is EDT. Dates and times subject to change.
Nationally televised games indicated by network in parentheses.

Saturday, August 6	American Bowl at Tokyo, Japan	
	Atlanta _____ vs. Indianapolis _____	(ESPN2) 5:00 A.M.
Monday, August 8	Hall of Fame Game at Canton, Ohio	
	Chicago _____ vs. Miami _____	(ABC) 7:00

PRESEASON/WEEK 1

Thursday, August 11	San Diego _____ at Green Bay _____	(ESPN) 7:00
Friday, August 12	Detroit _____ at New York Jets _____	7:00
	New England _____ at Cincinnati _____	7:30
	Chicago _____ at St. Louis _____	7:00
	Kansas City _____ at Minnesota _____	7:00
	Seattle _____ at New Orleans _____	7:00
	Tampa Bay _____ at Tennessee _____	7:00
Saturday, August 13	Baltimore _____ at Atlanta _____	7:30
	Miami _____ at Jacksonville _____	7:30
	Buffalo _____ at Indianapolis _____	7:00
	Denver _____ at Houston _____	7:00
	New York Giants _____ at Cleveland _____	8:00
	Washington _____ at Carolina _____	8:00
	Dallas _____ at Arizona _____	7:00
	Oakland _____ at San Francisco _____	7:00
Monday, August 15	Philadelphia _____ at Pittsburgh _____	(ESPN) 8:00

PRESEASON/WEEK 2

Thursday, August 18	New Orleans _____ at New England _____	(FOX) 8:00
Friday, August 19	Minnesota _____ at New York Jets _____	(CBS) 8:00
	Tennessee _____ at Atlanta _____	7:30
	Cincinnati _____ at Washington _____	8:00
Saturday, August 20	Cleveland _____ at Detroit _____	1:00
	Green Bay _____ at Buffalo _____	6:00
	Jacksonville _____ at Tampa Bay _____	7:30
	Miami _____ at Pittsburgh _____	7:30
	Carolina _____ at New York Giants _____	8:00
	Chicago _____ at Indianapolis _____	7:00
	Oakland _____ at Houston _____	7:00
	Philadelphia _____ at Baltimore _____	8:00
	Arizona _____ at Kansas City _____	7:30
	San Francisco _____ at Denver _____	7:00
Sunday, August 21	St. Louis _____ at San Diego _____	1:00
Monday, August 22	Dallas _____ at Seattle _____	(ABC) 5:00

PRESEASON/WEEK 3

Thursday, August 25	Atlanta _____ at Jacksonville _____	(ESPN) 8:00
Friday, August 26	Pittsburgh _____ at Washington _____	(FOX) 8:00
	Cincinnati _____ at Philadelphia _____	7:30
	Baltimore _____ at New Orleans _____	7:00
	Buffalo _____ at Chicago _____	7:00
	Carolina _____ at Cleveland _____	8:00
	New England _____ at Green Bay _____	7:00
	New York Jets _____ at New York Giants _____	8:00
	San Diego _____ at Minnesota _____	7:00
	Arizona _____ at Oakland _____	6:30
	Tennessee _____ at San Francisco _____	7:00
Saturday, August 27	Indianapolis _____ at Denver _____	(CBS) 6:00
	Tampa Bay _____ at Miami _____	7:30
	Houston _____ at Dallas _____	7:00
	Seattle _____ at Kansas City _____	7:30
Monday, August 29	St. Louis _____ at Detroit _____	(ABC) 8:00

PRESEASON/WEEK 4

Thursday, September 1
Atlanta _____ at Miami _____		7:30
Houston _____ at Tampa Bay _____		7:30
New York Jets _____ at Philadelphia _____		7:30
Cleveland _____ at Chicago _____		7:00
Green Bay _____ at Tennessee _____		7:00
Jacksonville _____ at Dallas _____		7:00
New York Giants _____ at New England _____		8:00
Pittsburgh _____ at Carolina _____		8:00
Washington _____ at Baltimore _____		8:00
New Orleans _____ at Oakland _____		6:00
San Francisco _____ at San Diego _____		7:00

Friday, September 2
Detroit _____ at Buffalo _____	7:00
Indianapolis _____ at Cincinnati _____	7:30
Kansas City _____ at St. Louis _____	7:00
Minnesota _____ at Seattle _____	6:00
Denver _____ at Arizona _____	7:00

FIRST WEEKEND

Thursday, September 8	Oakland _____ at New England _____	(ABC) 9:00
Sunday, September 11	Houston _____ at Buffalo _____	1:00
FOX-TV National Weekend	New Orleans _____ at Carolina _____	1:00
	Cincinnati _____ at Cleveland _____	1:00
	Seattle _____ at Jacksonville _____	1:00
	New York Jets _____ at Kansas City _____	12:00
	Denver _____ at Miami _____	1:00
	Tampa Bay _____ at Minnesota _____	12:00
	Tennessee _____ at Pittsburgh _____	1:00
	Chicago _____ at Washington _____	1:00
	Green Bay _____ at Detroit _____	4:15
	Arizona _____ at New York Giants _____	4:15
	Dallas _____ at San Diego _____	1:15
	St. Louis _____ at San Francisco _____	1:15
	Indianapolis _____ at Baltimore _____	(ESPN) 8:30
Monday, September 12	Philadelphia _____ at Atlanta _____	(ABC) 9:00

SECOND WEEKEND

Sunday, September 18	New England _____ at Carolina _____	1:00
CBS-TV National Weekend	Detroit _____ at Chicago _____	12:00
	Minnesota _____ at Cincinnati _____	1:00
	Pittsburgh _____ at Houston _____	12:00
	Jacksonville _____ at Indianapolis _____	12:00
	New York Giants _____ at New Orleans _____	12:00
	San Francisco _____ at Philadelphia _____	1:00
	Buffalo _____ at Tampa Bay _____	1:00
	Baltimore _____ at Tennessee _____	12:00
	St. Louis _____ at Arizona _____	1:05
	Atlanta _____ at Seattle _____	1:05
	San Diego _____ at Denver _____	2:15
	Cleveland _____ at Green Bay _____	3:15
	Miami _____ at New York Jets _____	4:15
	Kansas City _____ at Oakland _____	(ESPN) 5:30
Monday, September 19	Washington _____ at Dallas _____	(ABC) 8:00

THIRD WEEKEND
Open Dates:
Baltimore, Detroit, Houston, Washington

Sunday, September 25	Atlanta _____ at Buffalo _____	1:00
CBS-TV National Weekend	Cincinnati _____ at Chicago _____	12:00
	Tampa Bay _____ at Green Bay _____	12:00
	Cleveland _____ at Indianapolis _____	12:00
	Carolina _____ at Miami _____	1:00
	New Orleans _____ at Minnesota _____	12:00
	Jacksonville _____ at New York Jets _____	1:00
	Oakland _____ at Philadelphia _____	1:00
	Tennessee _____ at St. Louis _____	12:00
	Dallas _____ at San Francisco _____	1:05
	Arizona _____ at Seattle _____	1:05
	New England _____ at Pittsburgh _____	4:15
	New York Giants _____ at San Diego _____	(ESPN) 5:30
Monday, September 26	Kansas City _____ at Denver _____	(ABC) 7:00

FOURTH WEEKEND
Open Dates:
Chicago, Cleveland, Miami, Pittsburgh

Sunday, October 2
FOX-TV National Weekend

Houston _____ at Cincinnati _____	1:00
Denver _____ at Jacksonville _____	1:00
Philadelphia _____ at Kansas City _____	12:00
San Diego _____ at New England _____	1:00
Buffalo _____ at New Orleans _____	12:00
St. Louis _____ at New York Giants _____	1:00
Detroit _____ at Tampa Bay _____	1:00
Indianapolis _____ at Tennessee _____	12:00
Seattle _____ at Washington _____	1:00
New York Jets _____ at Baltimore _____	4:05
Minnesota _____ at Atlanta _____	4:15
Dallas _____ at Oakland _____	1:15
San Francisco _____ at Arizona (Mexico) _____	(ESPN) 7:30
Monday, October 3 Green Bay _____ at Carolina _____	(ABC) 9:00

FIFTH WEEKEND
Open Dates:
Kansas City, Minnesota, New York Giants, Oakland

Sunday, October 9
FOX-TV National Weekend

New England _____ at Atlanta _____	1:00
Miami _____ at Buffalo _____	1:00
Chicago _____ at Cleveland _____	1:00
Baltimore _____ at Detroit _____	1:00
New Orleans _____ at Green Bay _____	12:00
Tennessee _____ at Houston _____	12:00
Tampa Bay _____ at New York Jets _____	1:00
Seattle _____ at St. Louis _____	12:00
Indianapolis _____ at San Francisco _____	1:05
Carolina _____ at Arizona _____	1:15
Philadelphia _____ at Dallas _____	3:15
Washington _____ at Denver _____	2:15
Cincinnati _____ at Jacksonville _____	(ESPN) 8:30
Monday, October 10 Pittsburgh _____ at San Diego _____	(ABC) 6:00

SIXTH WEEKEND
Open Dates:
Arizona, Green Bay, Philadelphia, San Francisco

Sunday, October 16
CBS-TV National Weekend

Cleveland _____ at Baltimore _____	1:00
Minnesota _____ at Chicago _____	12:00
New York Giants _____ at Dallas _____	12:00
Carolina _____ at Detroit _____	1:00
Washington _____ at Kansas City _____	12:00
Atlanta _____ at New Orleans _____	12:00
Jacksonville _____ at Pittsburgh _____	1:00
Miami _____ at Tampa Bay _____	1:00
Cincinnati _____ at Tennessee _____	12:00
New York Jets _____ at Buffalo _____	4:15
New England _____ at Denver _____	2:15
San Diego _____ at Oakland _____	1:15
Houston _____ at Seattle _____	(ESPN) 5:30
Monday, October 17 St. Louis _____ at Indianapolis _____	(ABC) 8:00

SEVENTH WEEKEND
Open Dates:
Carolina, Jacksonville, New England, Tampa Bay

Sunday, October 23
CBS-TV National Weekend

Pittsburgh _____ at Cincinnati _____	1:00
Detroit _____ at Cleveland _____	1:00
Indianapolis _____ at Houston _____	12:00
Kansas City _____ at Miami _____	1:00
Green Bay _____ at Minnesota _____	12:00
San Diego _____ at Philadelphia _____	1:00
New Orleans _____ at St. Louis _____	12:00
San Francisco _____ at Washington _____	1:00
Dallas _____ at Seattle _____	1:05
Tennessee _____ at Arizona _____	1:15
Baltimore _____ at Chicago _____	3:15
Denver _____ at New York Giants _____	4:15
Buffalo _____ at Oakland _____	1:15
Monday, October 24 New York Jets _____ at Atlanta _____	(ABC) 9:00

2005 SCHEDULE AND NOTE CALENDAR

EIGHTH WEEKEND
Open Dates:
Atlanta, Indianapolis, New York Jets, Seattle

Sunday, October 30
FOX-TV National Weekend

Matchup	Time
Minnesota _____ at Carolina _____	1:00
Green Bay _____ at Cincinnati _____	1:00
Arizona _____ at Dallas _____	12:00
Chicago _____ at Detroit _____	1:00
Cleveland _____ at Houston _____	12:00
Miami _____ at New Orleans _____	12:00
Washington _____ at New York Giants _____	1:00
Jacksonville _____ at St. Louis _____	12:00
Oakland _____ at Tennessee _____	12:00
Kansas City _____ at San Diego _____	1:05
Philadelphia _____ at Denver _____	2:15
Tampa Bay _____ at San Francisco _____	1:15
Buffalo _____ at New England _____	(ESPN) 8:30

Monday, October 31 Baltimore _____ at Pittsburgh _____ — (ABC) 9:00

NINTH WEEKEND
Open Dates:
Buffalo, Dallas, Denver, St. Louis

Sunday, November 6
CBS-TV National Weekend

Matchup	Time
Cincinnati _____ at Baltimore _____	1:00
Tennessee _____ at Cleveland _____	1:00
Houston _____ at Jacksonville _____	1:00
Oakland _____ at Kansas City _____	12:00
Atlanta _____ at Miami _____	1:00
Detroit _____ at Minnesota _____	12:00
Chicago _____ at New Orleans _____	12:00
San Diego _____ at New York Jets _____	1:00
Carolina _____ at Tampa Bay _____	1:00
Seattle _____ at Arizona _____	2:05
New York Giants _____ at San Francisco _____	1:05
Pittsburgh _____ at Green Bay _____	3:15
Philadelphia _____ at Washington _____	(ESPN) 8:30

Monday, November 7 Indianapolis _____ at New England _____ — (ABC) 9:00

TENTH WEEKEND
Open Dates:
Cincinnati, New Orleans, San Diego, Tennessee

Sunday, November 13
FOX-TV National Weekend

Matchup	Time
Kansas City _____ at Buffalo _____	1:00
San Francisco _____ at Chicago _____	12:00
Arizona _____ at Detroit _____	1:00
Houston _____ at Indianapolis _____	1:00
Baltimore _____ at Jacksonville _____	1:00
New England _____ at Miami _____	1:00
Minnesota _____ at New York Giants _____	1:00
Washington _____ at Tampa Bay _____	1:00
New York Jets _____ at Carolina _____	4:05
Denver _____ at Oakland _____	1:05
Green Bay _____ at Atlanta _____	4:15
St. Louis _____ at Seattle _____	1:15
Cleveland _____ at Pittsburgh _____	(ESPN) 8:30

Monday, November 14 Dallas _____ at Philadelphia _____ — (ABC) 9:00

ELEVENTH WEEKEND

Sunday, November 20
CBS-TV National Weekend

Matchup	Time
Tampa Bay _____ at Atlanta _____	1:00
Carolina _____ at Chicago _____	12:00
Indianapolis _____ at Cincinnati _____	1:00
Miami _____ at Cleveland _____	1:00
Detroit _____ at Dallas _____	12:00
New Orleans _____ at New England _____	1:00
Philadelphia _____ at New York Giants _____	1:00
Arizona _____ at St. Louis _____	12:00
Jacksonville _____ at Tennessee _____	12:00
Oakland _____ at Washington _____	1:00
Seattle _____ at San Francisco _____	1:05
Pittsburgh _____ at Baltimore _____	4:15
New York Jets _____ at Denver _____	2:15
Buffalo _____ at San Diego _____	1:15
Kansas City _____ at Houston _____	(ESPN) 7:30

Monday, November 21 Minnesota _____ at Green Bay _____ — (ABC) 8:00

TWELFTH WEEKEND	**Thursday, November 24**	Atlanta _____ at Detroit _____	(FOX) 12:30
		Denver _____ at Dallas _____	(CBS) 3:15
	Sunday, November 27	Carolina _____ at Buffalo _____	1:00
	FOX-TV National Weekend	Baltimore _____ at Cincinnati _____	1:00
		St. Louis _____ at Houston _____	12:00
		New England _____ at Kansas City _____	12:00
		Cleveland _____ at Minnesota _____	12:00
		Chicago _____ at Tampa Bay _____	1:00
		San Francisco _____ at Tennessee _____	12:00
		San Diego _____ at Washington _____	1:00
		Jacksonville _____ at Arizona _____	2:05
		Miami _____ at Oakland _____	1:05
		Green Bay _____ at Philadelphia _____	4:15
		New York Giants _____ at Seattle _____	1:15
		New Orleans _____ at New York Jets _____	(ESPN) 8:30
	Monday, November 28	Pittsburgh _____ at Indianapolis _____	(ABC) 9:00
THIRTEENTH WEEKEND	**Sunday, December 4**	Houston _____ at Baltimore _____	1:00
	CBS-TV National Weekend	Atlanta _____ at Carolina _____	1:00
		Green Bay _____ at Chicago _____	12:00
		Jacksonville _____ at Cleveland _____	1:00
		Minnesota _____ at Detroit _____	1:00
		Tennessee _____ at Indianapolis _____	1:00
		Buffalo _____ at Miami _____	1:00
		Tampa Bay _____ at New Orleans _____	12:00
		Dallas _____ at New York Giants _____	1:00
		Cincinnati _____ at Pittsburgh _____	1:00
		Washington _____ at St. Louis _____	3:05
		Arizona _____ at San Francisco _____	1:05
		Denver _____ at Kansas City _____	3:15
		New York Jets _____ at New England _____	4:15
		Oakland _____ at San Diego _____	(ESPN) 5:30
	Monday, December 5	Seattle _____ at Philadelphia _____	(ABC) 9:00
FOURTEENTH WEEKEND	**Sunday, December 11**	New England _____ at Buffalo _____	1:00
	CBS-TV National Weekend	Tampa Bay _____ at Carolina _____	1:00
		Cleveland _____ at Cincinnati _____	1:00
		Indianapolis _____ at Jacksonville _____	1:00
		St. Louis _____ at Minnesota _____	12:00
		Oakland _____ at New York Jets _____	1:00
		Chicago _____ at Pittsburgh _____	1:00
		Houston _____ at Tennessee _____	12:00
		Washington _____ at Arizona _____	2:05
		New York Giants _____ at Philadelphia _____	4:05
		San Francisco _____ at Seattle _____	1:05
		Kansas City _____ at Dallas _____	3:15
		Baltimore _____ at Denver _____	2:15
		Miami _____ at San Diego _____	1:15
		Detroit _____ at Green Bay _____	(ESPN) 7:30
	Monday, December 12	New Orleans _____ at Atlanta _____	(ABC) 9:00
FIFTEENTH WEEKEND	**Saturday, December 17**	Tampa Bay _____ at New England _____	(FOX) 1:30
		Kansas City _____ at New York Giants _____	(CBS) 5:00
		Denver _____ at Buffalo _____	(ESPN) 8:30
	Sunday, December 18	Arizona _____ at Houston _____	12:00
	FOX-TV National Weekend	San Diego _____ at Indianapolis _____	1:00
		San Francisco _____ at Jacksonville _____	1:00
		New York Jets _____ at Miami _____	1:00
		Pittsburgh _____ at Minnesota _____	12:00
		Carolina _____ at New Orleans _____	12:00
		Seattle _____ at Tennessee _____	12:00
		Dallas _____ at Washington _____	1:00
		Cincinnati _____ at Detroit _____	4:05
		Cleveland _____ at Oakland _____	1:05
		Philadelphia _____ at St. Louis _____	3:15
		Atlanta _____ at Chicago _____	(ESPN) 7:30
	Monday, December 19	Green Bay _____ at Baltimore _____	(ABC) 9:00

SIXTEENTH WEEKEND

Saturday, December 24	Dallas _____ at Carolina _____	1:00
CBS-TV National Weekend	Buffalo _____ at Cincinnati _____	1:00
	Pittsburgh _____ at Cleveland _____	1:00
	Jacksonville _____ at Houston _____	12:00
	San Diego _____ at Kansas City _____	12:00
	Tennessee _____ at Miami _____	1:00
	Detroit _____ at New Orleans _____	12:00
	San Francisco _____ at St. Louis _____	12:00
	Atlanta _____ at Tampa Bay _____	1:00
	New York Giants _____ at Washington _____	1:00
	Philadelphia _____ at Arizona _____	2:05
	Oakland _____ at Denver _____	2:15
	Indianapolis _____ at Seattle _____	1:15
Sunday, December 25	Chicago _____ at Green Bay _____	(FOX) 4:00
	Minnesota _____ at Baltimore _____	(ESPN) 8:30
Monday, December 26	New England _____ at New York Jets _____	(ABC) 9:00

SEVENTEENTH WEEKEND

Saturday, December 31	Denver _____ at San Diego _____	(CBS) 1:30
	New York Giants _____ at Oakland _____	(ESPN) 5:00
Sunday, January 1	Carolina _____ at Atlanta _____	1:00
FOX-TV National Weekend	Baltimore _____ at Cleveland _____	1:00
	Arizona _____ at Indianapolis _____	1:00
	Cincinnati _____ at Kansas City _____	12:00
	Chicago _____ at Minnesota _____	12:00
	Miami _____ at New England _____	1:00
	Buffalo _____ at New York Jets _____	1:00
	Detroit _____ at Pittsburgh _____	1:00
	New Orleans _____ at Tampa Bay _____	1:00
	Tennessee _____ at Jacksonville _____	4:05
	Houston _____ at San Francisco _____	1:05
	Seattle _____ at Green Bay _____	3:15
	Washington _____ at Philadelphia _____	4:15
	St. Louis _____ at Dallas _____	(ESPN) 7:30

**Wild Card Playoff Games
Site Priorities**

Two Wild Card teams (division non-champions with best two records) from each conference and the division champions with the third and fourth-best record in each conference will enter the first round of the playoffs. The division champion with the third-best record will play host to the Wild Card team with the second-best record. The division champion with the fourth-best record will play host to the Wild Card team with the best record. There are no restrictions on intra-division games.

Saturday, January 7, 2006 American Football Conference

_____ at _____ (ABC)

National Football Conference

_____ at _____ (ABC)

Sunday, January 8, 2006 American Football Conference

_____ at _____ (CBS)

National Football Conference

_____ at _____ (FOX)

**Divisional Playoff Games
Site Priorities**

In each conference, the two division champions with the highest won-lost-tied percentage during the regular season will play host to the Wild Card winners. The division champion with the best record in each conference is assured of playing the lowest seeded Wild Card survivor. There are no restrictions on intra-division games.

Saturday, January 14, 2006 American Football Conference

_____ at _____ (CBS)

National Football Conference

_____ at _____ (FOX)

Sunday, January 15, 2006 American Football Conference

_____ at _____ (CBS)

National Football Conference

_____ at _____ (FOX)

Championship Games
Site Priorities for
Championship Games
The home teams will be the surviving playoff winners with the best won-lost-tied percentage during the regular season. A Wild Card team cannot play host unless two Wild Card teams are in the game, in which case the Wild Card team that was seeded highest in the first round of the playoffs will be the home team.

Sunday, January 22, 2006 American Football Conference

_____ at _____ (CBS)

National Football Conference

_____ at _____ (FOX)

Super Bowl XL **Sunday, February 5, 2006** Super Bowl XL at Ford Field, Detroit, Michigan

_____ vs. _____ (ABC)

AFC-NFC Pro Bowl **Sunday, February 12, 2006** AFC-NFC Pro Bowl at Aloha Stadium, Honolulu, Hawaii

AFC_____ vs. NFC _____ (ESPN)

POSTSEASON GAMES

Saturday, January 7	AFC and NFC Wild Card Playoffs (ABC)
Sunday, January 8	AFC and NFC Wild Card Playoffs (CBS and FOX)
Saturday, January 14	AFC and NFC Divisional Playoffs (CBS and FOX)
Sunday, January 15	AFC and NFC Divisional Playoffs (CBS and FOX)
Sunday, January 22	AFC and NFC Championship Games (CBS and FOX)
Sunday, February 5	Super Bowl XL at Ford Field, Detroit (ABC)
Sunday, February 12	AFC-NFC Pro Bowl in Honolulu, Hawaii (ESPN)

2005 NATIONALLY TELEVISED GAMES AT A GLANCE

All times ET.

Thursday, September 8	Oakland at New England (ABC)	9:00 P.M.
Sunday, September 11	Dallas at San Diego (FOX)	1:15 P.M.
	Indianapolis at Baltimore (ESPN)	8:30 P.M.
Monday, September 12	Philadelphia at Atlanta (ABC)	9:00 P.M.
Sunday, September 18	Cleveland at Green Bay (CBS)	3:15 P.M.
	Kansas City at Oakland (ESPN)	5:30 P.M.
Monday, September 19	Washington at Dallas (ABC)	8:00 P.M.
Sunday, September 25	New England at Pittsburgh (CBS)	4:15 P.M.
	New York Giants at San Diego (ESPN)	5:30 P.M.
Monday, September 26	Kansas City at Denver (ESPN)	7:00 P.M.
Sunday, October 2	Dallas at Oakland (FOX)	1:15 P.M.
	San Francisco at Arizona (Mexico) (ESPN)	7:30 P.M.
Monday, October 3	Green Bay at Carolina (ABC)	9:00 P.M.
Sunday, October 9	Philadelphia at Dallas (FOX)	3:15 P.M.
	Cincinnati at Jacksonville (ESPN)	8:30 P.M.
Monday, October 10	Pittsburgh at San Diego (ABC)	6:00 P.M.
Sunday, October 16	New England at Denver (CBS)	2:15 P.M.
	Houston at Seattle (ESPN)	5:30 P.M.
Monday, October 17	St. Louis at Indianapolis (ABC)	8:00 P.M.
Sunday, October 23	Denver at New York Giants (CBS)	4:15 P.M.
Monday, October 24	New York Jets at Atlanta (ABC)	9:00 P.M.
Sunday, October 30	Philadelphia at Denver (FOX)	2:15 P.M.
	Buffalo at New England (ESPN)	8:30 P.M.
Monday, October 31	Baltimore at Pittsburgh (ABC)	9:00 P.M.
Sunday, November 6	Pittsburgh at Green Bay (CBS)	3:15 P.M.
	Philadelphia at Washington (ESPN)	8:30 P.M.
Monday, November 7	Indianapolis at New England (ABC)	9:00 P.M.
Sunday, November 13	Green Bay at Atlanta (FOX)	4:15 P.M.
	Cleveland at Pittsburgh (ESPN)	8:30 P.M.
Monday, November 14	Dallas at Philadelphia (ABC)	9:00 P.M.
Sunday, November 20	New York Jets at Denver (CBS)	2:15 P.M.
	Kansas City at Houston (ESPN)	7:30 P.M.
Monday, November 21	Minnesota at Green Bay (ABC)	8:00 P.M.
Thursday, November 24	Atlanta at Detroit (FOX)	12:30 P.M.
	Denver at Dallas (CBS)	3:15 P.M.
Sunday, November 27	Green Bay at Philadelphia (FOX)	4:15 P.M.
	New Orleans at New York Jets (ESPN)	8:30 P.M.
Monday, November 28	Pittsburgh at Indianapolis (ABC)	9:00 P.M.
Sunday, December 4	New York Jets at New England (CBS)	4:15 P.M.
	Oakland at San Diego (ESPN)	5:30 P.M.
Monday, December 5	Seattle at Philadelphia (ABC)	9:00 P.M.
Sunday, December 11	Kansas City at Dallas (CBS)	3:15 P.M.
	Detroit at Green Bay (ESPN)	7:30 P.M.
Monday, December 12	New Orleans at Atlanta (ABC)	9:00 P.M.
Saturday, December 17	Tampa Bay at New England (FOX)	1:30 P.M.
	Kansas City at New York Giants (CBS)	5:00 P.M.
	Denver at Buffalo (ESPN)	8:30 P.M.
Sunday, December 18	Philadelphia at St. Louis (FOX)	3:15 P.M.
	Atlanta at Chicago (ESPN)	7:30 P.M.
Monday, December 19	Green Bay at Baltimore (ABC)	9:00 P.M.
Saturday, December 24	Oakland at Denver (CBS)	1:15 P.M.
Sunday, December 25	Chicago at Green Bay (FOX)	4:00 P.M.
	Minnesota at Baltimore (ESPN)	8:30 P.M.
Monday, December 26	New England at New York Jets (ABC)	9:00 P.M.
Saturday, December 31	Denver at San Diego (CBS)	1:30 P.M.
	New York Giants at Oakland (ESPN)	5:00 P.M.
Sunday, January 1	Seattle at Green Bay (FOX)	3:15 P.M.
	St. Louis at Dallas (ESPN)	7:30 P.M.

2005

July 5	Claiming period of 24 hours begins in waiver system.
Mid-July	Preseason training camps open. Clubs not permitted to open official preseason camp earlier than July 5. Veteran players cannot be required to report earlier than 15 days prior to club's first preseason game.
July 22#	Signing period ends at 4 P.M., New York time, for Unrestricted Free Agents to whom a June 1 tender was made by Old Club, and for Transition Players. After this date and through 4 P.M., New York time, on November 15, Old Club has exclusive negotiating rights to these players.
	#or the first scheduled day of the first NFL training camp, whichever is later.
August 6-8	Hall of Fame Weekend.
August 8	Pro Football Hall of Fame Game, Canton, Ohio: Chicago vs. Miami
August 9	If a Drafted Rookie has not signed with his club by this date, he may not be traded to any other club in 2005.
August 9	Deadline for players under contract to report to earn a season of free-agency credit.
August 11-15	First Preseason Weekend.
August 13-17	Deadline for club to provide written notice to certain unsigned players and the NFLPA of its intent to place them on the Exempt List if they fail to report no later than one day prior to the club's second preseason game. Any player who fails to report prior to the deadline will be ineligible to play or receive compensation for at least three games (preseason or regular season) from the time that he reports.
August 30	Roster cut-down to maximum of 65 players on Active List by 4 P.M., New York time.
August 31	All tryouts on this date and for the remainder of the season must be reported to the League office.
September 4	Roster cut-down to maximum of 53 players on Active/Inactive List by 4 P.M., New York time. Clubs may dress minimum of 42 and maximum of 45 players and Third Quarterback for each regular-season and postseason game.
September 4	Simultaneously with the cut-down to 53, clubs that have players in the categories of Active/Physically Unable to Perform or Active/Non-Football Injury or Illness must take one of the following options: place player on Reserve/Physically Unable to Perform or Reserve/Non-Football Injury or Illness, whichever is applicable; ask waivers; terminate; trade; or continue to count him on Active List.
September 5	After 12 noon, New York time, clubs may establish a Practice Squad of eight players by signing free agents who do not have an accrued season of free-agency credit or who were on the 45-player Active List for less than nine regular-season games during their only Accrued Season(s). A player cannot
	participate on the Practice Squad for more than two seasons.
September 6	All clubs are required to file a personnel (injury) report with their conference Director of Information by 1 P.M., New York time, on this Tuesday and thereafter on each Wednesday before a regular-season game. Such report is to be updated by 1 P.M., New York time, each Thursday. An update must also be reported if there is any change in a player's condition after Thursday.
September 7	Beginning at 4 P.M., New York time, Team Salary includes all players receiving compensation under their 2005 contracts. Top 51 rule is no longer in effect.
September 8-12	Regular Season opens.
September 8-12	Beginning on these dates vested veterans terminated from the Active List or Inactive List (and from Reserve/Injured if the player is placed on Reserve/Injured after the beginning of the regular season) are entitled to receive, after the end of the regular-season schedule, Termination Pay pursuant to the terms of the 1993 CBA.
September 27	Priority on multiple waiver claims is now based on the current season's standing.
October 18	Beginning the day after the conclusion of the sixth regular-season weekend and continuing through the day after the conclusion of the ninth regular-season weekend, clubs are permitted to begin practicing players on Reserve/Physically Unable to Perform and Reserve/Non-Football Injury or Illness for a period not to exceed 21 days. Players may be activated during the 21-day practice period or until 4 P.M., New York time, on the day after the conclusion of the 21-day period.
October 18	All trading ends at 4 P.M., New York time.
October 19	Players with at least four previous pension-credited seasons are subject to the waiver system for the remainder of the regular season and postseason.
November 7	Deadline at 4 P.M., New York time, for an increase in a player's 2005 Salary to be counted as Salary for the current year. Any notice of an increase in a player's 2005 Salary received by the NFLMC after this deadline will be treated as a Signing Bonus.
November 15	Signing period ends at 4 P.M., New York time, for Franchise Players who are eligible to receive Offer Sheets.
November 15	Deadline for clubs to sign by 4 P.M., New York time, their unsigned Franchise and Transition Players, including Franchise Players who were eligible to receive Offer Sheets until this date. If still unsigned after this date, such players are prohibited from playing in NFL in 2005.
November 15	Deadline for clubs to sign by 4 P.M., New York time, their Unrestricted Free Agents to whom June 1 tender was made. If still unsigned after this date, such players are prohibited from playing in NFL in 2005.

November 15	Deadline for clubs to sign by 4 P.M., New York time, their Restricted Free Agents to whom June 1 tender was made. If such players remain unsigned, they are prohibited from playing in NFL in 2005.
November 15	Deadline for clubs to sign Drafted players by 4 P.M., New York time. If such players remain unsigned, they are prohibited from playing in NFL in 2005.
December 2	Deadline for reinstatement of players in Reserve List categories of Retired, Did Not Report, and Exclusive Rights, and of players who were placed on Reserve/Left Squad in a previous season.
December 30	Deadline for waiver requests in 2005, except for "special waiver requests," which have a 10-day claiming period, with termination or assignment delayed until after the Super Bowl.
January 2	Clubs may begin signing free-agent players for the 2006 season.

2006

January 7-8	Wild Card Playoff Games.
January 14-15	Divisional Playoff Games.
January 22	AFC and NFC Championship Games.
February 5	Super Bowl XL, Ford Field, Detroit, Michigan.
February 12	AFC-NFC Pro Bowl, Honolulu, Hawaii.

2007

| February 4 | Super Bowl XLI, Dolphins Stadium, Miami, Florida. |

2008

| February 3 | Super Bowl XLII, Cardinals Stadium, Glendale, Arizona. |

2009

| February 1* | Super Bowl XLIII, Raymond James Stadium, Tampa, Florida. |

*Tentative date

The NFL is online to provide fans and media quick and easy access to all the latest professional football information.

NFL.COM—(http://NFL.com or AOL Keyword: NFL.com)
NFL.com, the league's year-round home page on the Internet, enters its ninth season in cyberspace. The site provides NFL information during the regular season, postseason, and offseason, including:

NEWS/STATS: Up-to-the-minute news from around the league, plus game previews, injury reports, and player and team stats.

TEAM AREAS: Customized areas for all 32 clubs, featuring updated rosters, depth carts, and all the latest news from the teams.

GAMEDAY COVERAGE: Live game coverage with play-by-play, scores, and statistics, including graphical drive charts and comprehensive scoreboard that does not require reloading to get the latest information.

VIDEO HIGHLIGHTS: The site showcases NFL Films video highlights of the previous week's games as well as upcoming matchups. Video also supports feature stories and team highlight clips from every game last season.

SUPERBOWL.COM—(http://SuperBowl.com)
Look for SuperBowl.com in late December for complete coverage of the playoffs and Super Bowl XL. The multimedia site follows all postseason action and features audio and video clips of past Super Bowls.

During the week leading up to Super Bowl XL, the site will go 'live' from Detroit, providing coverage of events, press conferences, and chats with Super Bowl players and coaches.

On Super Bowl Sunday, SuperBowl.com will showcase a live Internet cybercast, complete with online commentators calling the action. The site also features digital photos from the game, live public address audio and press-box announcements, and live audio from foreign broadcasts.

NFLEUROPE.COM—(http://NFLEurope.com)
The official site of NFL Europe League provides in-depth information on the six teams and their players, and weekly video highlights of game action. In addition, the site includes weekly player diaries from NFL allocated players, as well as a complete league stats package.

NFLYOUTHFOOTBALL.COM—(http://nflyouthfootball.com)
NFLyouthfootball.com is the NFL's official youth football website. Boys and girls ages 6-18 can be a part of something big by getting involved nationwide with one of the NFL's Youth Football programs. Coaches, parents, and youth organizations can learn how to host their own local NFL Punt, Pass, and Kick event and can learn how to get children involved with an NFL FLAG league in their local community. Our website is also a resource for coaches and parents to help them promote a positive experience for all youth participants. The NFL's youth football programs follow our Seven Guiding Principles, which are posted on our website, and were developed from feedback from kids, parents, and coaches.

PLAYFOOTBALL.COM—(http://playfootball.com)
Play Football is the NFL's official Website for kids. It offers boys and girls an interactive sports destination where kids and their families can get actively involved with the NFL. Youths can find profiles on NFL players and people behind the scenes of the NFL, vote on weekly MVPs and Plays of the Week, play challenging games, and learn about football strategy and skill.

NFLHS.COM—(http://NFLHS.com)
The League's Website dedicated to high school football. NFLHS.com covers high school football on a nation-wide basis and also looks into the high school careers of current and former NFL players and coaches. NFLHS.com goes behind the scenes at major NFL events, such as the Super Bowl and the Draft, and provides coverage from a high school perspective. The site is packed with tips and drills, health and safety information, academic tips and news on the NFL's and its teams' efforts in the community. Whatever you are looking for regarding high school football, we've got it!

JOINTHETEAM.COM—(http://JoinTheTeam.com)
JointheTeam.com is the official Website dedicated to the off-the-field community work of the NFL and the member clubs. The site provides news and information regarding how the NFL gives back and serves as a useful tool for individuals who are looking for a way to make a difference in their communities. As part of the NFL's Join The Team platform, the site encourages people to unite with NFL teams, players and partners to give back to communities across America. Join The Team is a "call to action" —a way for everyone to come together and make a difference through community involvement.

PROFOOTBALLHOF.com—(http://profootballhof.com)
Profootballhof.com is the official site of the Pro Football Hall of Fame in Canton, Ohio. In addition to a complete visitor's guide to the Hall, the site features bios, stories and Q & A's with Hall of Fame inductees, a detailed archive of football history, and information on appearances by members of the Hall.

OFFICIAL NFL TEAM SITES
In addition to a dedicated area on NFL.com, all 32 teams have their own Websites, which have separate URLs, and are linked from NFL.com.

Arizona Cardinals (www.azcardinals.com)
Atlanta Falcons (www.atlantafalcons.com)
Baltimore Ravens (www.baltimoreravens.com)
Buffalo Bills (www.buffalobills.com)
Carolina Panthers (www.panthers.com)
Chicago Bears (www.chicagobears.com)
Cincinnati Bengals (www.bengals.com)
Cleveland Browns (www.clevelandbrowns.com)
Dallas Cowboys (www.dallascowboys.com)
Denver Broncos (www.denverbroncos.com)
Detroit Lions (www.detroitlions.com)
Green Bay Packers (www.packers.com)
Houston Texans (www.houstontexans.com)
Indianapolis Colts (www.colts.com)
Jacksonville Jaguars (www.jaguars.com)
Kansas City Chiefs (www.kcchiefs.com)
Miami Dolphins (www.miamidolphins.com)
Minnesota Vikings (www.vikings.com)
New England Patriots (www.patriots.com)
New Orleans Saints (www.neworleanssaints.com)
New York Giants (www.giants.com)
New York Jets (www.newyorkjets.com)
Oakland Raiders (www.raiders.com)
Philadelphia Eagles (www.philadelphiaeagles.com)
Pittsburgh Steelers (www.steelers.com)
St. Louis Rams (www.stlouisrams.com)
San Diego Chargers (www.chargers.com)
San Francisco 49ers (www.sf49ers.com)
Seattle Seahawks (www.seahawks.com)
Tampa Bay Buccaneers (www.buccaneers.com)
Tennessee Titans (www.titansonline.com)
Washington Redskins (www.redskins.com)

NFL Network provides fans with a network to call their own.

Seven days a week, 24 hours a day, 365 days a year, fans turn to NFL Network to receive information and insight straight from team headquarters, league offices and wherever else the NFL is making news.

NFL Network gives fans unprecedented year-round access to all NFL events, including the preseason, regular season, playoffs, Super Bowl, Pro Bowl, Scouting Combine, league meetings, the playing schedule, NFL Draft, mini-camps and training camps.

NFL Network is available on cable and satellite television through your local service provider. DirecTV carries NFL Network nationally to all its subscribers on Channel 212. In addition, four of the top five cable providers—Comcast, Cox, Charter and Adelphia—also carry NFL Network. Heading into the 2005 season, NFL Network is available to 57 million U.S homes, plus to viewers in Canada and Mexico. If your provider doesn't currently offer NFL Network, please call (866) NFL-NETWORK to make them aware of your interest in receiving it.

KEY PROGRAMMING

NFL TOTAL ACCESS
NFL Network's signature show is THE football show of record. NFL Total Access is uniquely structured to see the game through the participants' eyes, airing at 7:00 PM ET/PT every Monday through Saturday and hosted by Rich Eisen.

Covering all 32 teams, *NFL Total Access* features interviews with players, coaches and other key league personnel. Providing the latest news in an informative and entertaining way, NFLTA is the only show to telecast from all key league events. Using the most advanced technology, *NFL Total Access* has the ability to go live to any NFL team headquarters at any time.

PLAYBOOK
The foremost Xs and Os show on television is *Playbook*, featuring a breakdown of coaches tapes to analyze how each game was won and lost and to project how each team will fare in their upcoming match-up. *Playbook* airs five days a week. On Tuesdays, *Playbook*-Look Back spends an hour at 8:00 PM ET/PT dissecting the games from the prior weekend. On Wednesdays, Thursdays and Fridays, *Playbook* is a 30-minute show each night at 8:30 PM ET/PT that analyzes the upcoming weekend games. On Saturday night, *Playbook* at 8:00 PM ET/PT is a 60-minute show that gives you all the information you need heading into the weekend's action. *Playbook* is hosted by former University of Iowa quarterback Paul Burmeister, alongside several analysts.

NFL NETWORK GAME OF THE WEEK
Every Wednesday and Thursday current NFL games are featured on *NFL Network Game of the Week,* a 60-minute condensed version of a full-game airing at 9:00 PM ET/PT.

The series takes fans inside an NFL game, in a way they do not see on a weekend broadcast. Using unique NFL Films camera angles, microphones on the field and in the locker room, GOTW tells the story of the game from the inside out.

During the season, *NFL Network Game of the Week* enables fans to relive Sunday's most interesting game(s). In the off-season the series will showcase match-ups from years past. This show is available in High Definition format.

IN THEIR OWN WORDS
In a stark departure from classic documentary style, NFL Network lets the NFL's most successful and intriguing coaches and players tell their own stories on a show called *In Their Own Words,* airing Friday's at 9 PM ET/PT.

The series uses rare interviews, archival action footage and exclusive sound captured on the field, on the sidelines and in the locker room, to let the subject tell a story in his own words, without the use of a host or narration.

In Their Own Words gives fans unprecedented access to NFL personalities as they reveal their intensity, humor, competitiveness and humanity in each one-hour episode.

LIVE PRESS CONFERENCES
NFL Network endeavors to go live as often as possible to cover league and team press conferences. During the football season, on Mondays, from 2:30-5:30 PM ET, NFL Total Access whips around the league showing live press conferences from head coaches. On Wednesdays, when key players such as quarterbacks hold their media availability, NFL Total Access will bounce from club to club from 3:00-5:00 PM ET to cover these press conferences. In addition, any time special press conferences are called by teams, tune to NFL Network, where these breaking news events will likely be covered.

OTHER PROGRAMMING HIGHLIGHTS

PRESEASON GAMES: NFL Network is the only place on television where fans can view the majority of NFL preseason games. NFL Network televises every game that does not appear on the four NFL broadcast partners (ABC, CBS, FOX, and ESPN) during the preseason, more than 50 games each summer.

NFL EUROPE: From April to June, pro football fans can watch young players compete for a World Bowl championship on NFL Network, which televises two primetime games each week during the NFL Europe season, 22 games in all.

Log on to www.NFL.com/NFLnetwork for more information on NFL Network.

The NFL expanded to 32 teams in 2002 with the addition of the Houston Texans. In addition, the NFL realigned for the first time since 1970—into eight divisions of four teams each—and the scheduling formula that was introduced guarantees for the first time that all teams play each other on a regular, rotating basis. Although the number of teams has increased to 32, the number of playoff teams remains the same at 12.

Under the NFL scheduling formula, every team within a division plays 16 games as follows:

- Home and away against its three division opponents (6 games).
- The four teams from another division within its conference on a rotating three-year cycle (4 games).
- The four teams from a division in the other conference on a rotating four-year cycle (4 games).
- Two intraconference games based on the prior year's standings (2 games). These games will match a first-place team against the first-place teams in the two same-conference divisions the team is not scheduled to play that season. The second-place, third-place, and fourth-place teams in a conference will be matched in the same way each year.

"The scheduling formula is one of the most positive aspects of realignment," says NFL Commissioner Paul Tagliabue. "The formula guarantees that NFL fans will see every team play each other on a regular, rotating basis. The formula will eliminate the many aberrations of the past in which teams either did not play for long periods of time or did not play in another team's stadium for many years."

The schedule format takes each team through a cycle of games—home and away—against every other team in the league. From 2002-2009, every team will play every other team at least twice—once home and once away. After the 2009 season, a decision will be made on whether to continue with the same rotation or modify it.

In determining how to begin the divisional rotation in 2002, the displacement of teams from their old divisions in the new alignment was taken into account. Preference was given to scheduling games with former division rivals and other regional opponents for clubs realigned from otherwise intact divisions.

The scheduling format includes the following elements:

- There is an increased common-opponent emphasis with every team in a division playing against 14 common opponents.
- All teams play each other on a regular basis, home and away, for a more consistent presentation of attractive games, eliminating the many schedule aberrations of the past.
- Teams are guaranteed to play all non-division opponents in their conference at least once every three years, and at home at least once every six years.
- Every AFC team plays every NFC team once every four years, and at home once every eight years.
- A team's record from the previous year has less of a bearing on its schedule, with only two (rather than four) opponents being based on the previous year's standing. Thus, the so-called "easy" fifth-place schedules are eliminated.
- The division in which a team resides is less of a factor in a team's won-loss record with 10 of 16 games each year being against non-division teams.

FUTURE SCHEDULING ROTATION

		2005	2006	2007	2008	2009
AFC EAST	Intraconference	AFCW	AFCS	AFCN	AFCW	AFCS
	Interconference	NFCS	NFCN	NFCE	NFCW	NFCS
AFC NORTH	Intraconference	AFCS	AFCW	AFCE	AFCS	AFCW
	Interconference	NFCN	NFCS	NFCW	NFCE	NFCN
AFC SOUTH	Intraconference	AFCN	AFCE	AFCW	AFCN	AFCE
	Interconference	NFCW	NFCE	NFCS	NFCN	NFCW
AFC WEST	Intraconference	AFCE	AFCN	AFCS	AFCE	AFCN
	Interconference	NFCE	NFCW	NFCN	NFCS	NFCE
NFC EAST	Intraconference	NFCW	NFCS	NFCN	NFCW	NFCS
	Interconference	AFCW	AFCS	AFCE	AFCN	AFCW
NFC NORTH	Intraconference	NFCS	NFCW	NFCE	NFCS	NFCW
	Interconference	AFCN	AFCE	AFCW	AFCS	AFCN
NFC SOUTH	Intraconference	NFCN	NFCE	NFCW	NFCN	NFCE
	Interconference	AFCE	AFCN	AFCS	AFCW	AFCE
NFC WEST	Intraconference	NFCE	NFCN	NFCS	NFCE	NFCN
	Interconference	AFCS	AFCW	AFCN	AFCE	AFCS

AFC EAST NON-DIVISIONAL OPPONENTS 2005-2009

BUFFALO BILLS

	2005 Home	Away	2006 Home	Away	2007 Home	Away
Intraconference by Division	DEN	OAK	JAX	HOU	BALT	CLE
	KC	SD	TENN	IND	CIN	PITT
Interconference by Division	ATL	NO	GB	CHI	DALL	PHIL
	CAR	TB	MINN	DET	NYG	WASH
Intraconference by Position	AFCS	AFCN	AFCW	AFCN	AFCW	AFCS

	2008 Home	Away	2009 Home	Away
Intraconference by Division	OAK	DEN	HOU	JAX
	SD	KC	IND	TENN
Interconference by Division	SF	ARIZ	NO	ATL
	SEA	STL	TB	CAR
Intraconference by Position	AFCN	AFCS	AFCN	AFCW

MIAMI DOLPHINS

	2005 Home	Away	2006 Home	Away	2007 Home	Away
Intraconference by Division	DEN	OAK	JAX	HOU	BALT	CLE
	KC	SD	TENN	IND	CIN	PITT
Interconference by Division	ATL	NO	GB	CHI	DALL	PHIL
	CAR	TB	MINN	DET	NYG	WASH
Intraconference by Position	AFCS	AFCN	AFCW	AFCN	AFCW	AFCS

	2008 Home	Away	2009 Home	Away
Intraconference by Division	OAK	DEN	HOU	JAX
	SD	KC	IND	TENN
Interconference by Division	SF	ARIZ	NO	ATL
	SEA	STL	TB	CAR
Intraconference by Position	AFCN	AFCS	AFCN	AFCW

NEW ENGLAND PATRIOTS

	2005 Home	Away	2006 Home	Away	2007 Home	Away
Intraconference by Division	OAK	DEN	HOU	JAX	CLE	BALT
	SD	KC	IND	TENN	PITT	CIN
Interconference by Division	NO	ATL	CHI	GB	PHIL	DALL
	TB	CAR	DET	MINN	WASH	NYG
Intraconference by Position	AFCS	AFCN	AFCW	AFCN	AFCW	AFCS

	2008 Home	Away	2009 Home	Away
Intraconference by Division	DEN	OAK	JAX	HOU
	KC	SD	TENN	IND
Interconference by Division	ARIZ	SF	ATL	NO
	STL	SEA	CAR	TB
Intraconference by Position	AFCN	AFCS	AFCN	AFCW

NEW YORK JETS

	2005 Home	Away	2006 Home	Away	2007 Home	Away
Intraconference by Division	OAK	DEN	HOU	JAX	CLE	BALT
	SD	KC	IND	TENN	PITT	CIN
Interconference by Division	NO	ATL	CHI	GB	PHIL	DALL
	TB	CAR	DET	MINN	WASH	NYG
Intraconference by Position	AFCS	AFCN	AFCW	AFCN	AFCW	AFCS

	2008 Home	Away	2009 Home	Away
Intraconference by Division	DEN	OAK	JAX	HOU
	KC	SD	TENN	IND
Interconference by Division	ARIZ	SF	ATL	NO
	STL	SEA	CAR	TB
Intraconference by Position	AFCN	AFCS	AFCN	AFCW

AFC NORTH NON-DIVISIONAL OPPONENTS 2005-2009

BALTIMORE RAVENS

	2005 Home	2005 Away	2006 Home	2006 Away	2007 Home	2007 Away
Intraconference by Division	HOU	JAX	OAK	DEN	NE	BUFF
	IND	TENN	SD	KC	NYJ	MIA
Interconference by Division	GB	CHI	ATL	NO	ARIZ	SF
	MINN	DET	CAR	TB	STL	SEA
Intraconference by Position	AFCE	AFCW	AFCE	AFCS	AFCS	AFCW

	2008 Home	2008 Away	2009 Home	2009 Away
Intraconference by Division	JAX	HOU	DEN	OAK
	TENN	IND	KC	SD
Interconference by Division	PHIL	DALL	CHI	GB
	WASH	NYG	DET	MINN
Intraconference by Position	AFCW	AFCE	AFCS	AFCE

CINCINNATI BENGALS

	2005 Home	2005 Away	2006 Home	2006 Away	2007 Home	2007 Away
Intraconference by Division	HOU	JAX	OAK	DEN	NE	BUFF
	IND	TENN	SD	KC	NYJ	MIA
Interconference by Division	GB	CHI	ATL	NO	ARIZ	SF
	MINN	DET	CAR	TB	STL	SEA
Intraconference by Position	AFCE	AFCW	AFCE	AFCS	AFCS	AFCW

	2008 Home	2008 Away	2009 Home	2009 Away
Intraconference by Division	JAX	HOU	DEN	OAK
	TENN	IND	KC	SD
Interconference by Division	PHIL	DALL	CHI	GB
	WASH	NYG	DET	MINN
Intraconference by Position	AFCW	AFCE	AFCS	AFCE

CLEVELAND BROWNS

	2005 Home	2005 Away	2006 Home	2006 Away	2007 Home	2007 Away
Intraconference by Division	JAX	HOU	DEN	OAK	BUFF	NE
	TENN	IND	KC	SD	MIA	NYJ
Interconference by Division	CHI	GB	NO	ATL	SF	ARIZ
	DET	MINN	TB	CAR	SEA	STL
Intraconference by Position	AFCE	AFCW	AFCE	AFCS	AFCS	AFCW

	2008 Home	2008 Away	2009 Home	2009 Away
Intraconference by Division	HOU	JAX	OAK	DEN
	IND	TENN	SD	KC
Interconference by Division	DALL	PHIL	GB	CHI
	NYG	WASH	MINN	DET
Intraconference by Position	AFCW	AFCE	AFCS	AFCE

PITTSBURGH STEELERS

	2005 Home	2005 Away	2006 Home	2006 Away	2007 Home	2007 Away
Intraconference by Division	JAX	HOU	DEN	OAK	BUFF	NE
	TENN	IND	KC	SD	MIA	NYJ
Interconference by Division	CHI	GB	NO	ATL	SF	ARIZ
	DET	MINN	TB	CAR	SEA	STL
Intraconference by Position	AFCE	AFCW	AFCE	AFCS	AFCS	AFCW

	2008 Home	2008 Away	2009 Home	2009 Away
Intraconference by Division	HOU	JAX	OAK	DEN
	IND	TENN	SD	KC
Interconference by Division	DALL	PHIL	GB	CHI
	NYG	WASH	MINN	DET
Intraconference by Position	AFCW	AFCE	AFCS	AFCE

AFC SOUTH NON-DIVISIONAL OPPONENTS 2005-2009

HOUSTON TEXANS

	2005 Home	Away	2006 Home	Away	2007 Home	Away
Intraconference by Division	CLE	BALT	BUFF	NE	DEN	OAK
	PITT	CIN	MIA	NYJ	KC	SD
Interconference by Division	ARIZ	SF	PHIL	DALL	NO	ATL
	STL	SEA	WASH	NYG	TB	CAR
Intraconference by Position	AFCW	AFCE	AFCN	AFCW	AFCE	AFCN

	2008 Home	Away	2009 Home	Away
Intraconference by Division	BALT	CLE	NE	BUFF
	CIN	PITT	NYJ	MIA
Interconference by Division	CHI	GB	SF	ARIZ
	DET	MINN	SEA	STL
Intraconference by Position	AFCE	AFCW	AFCW	AFCN

INDIANAPOLIS COLTS

	2005 Home	Away	2006 Home	Away	2007 Home	Away
Intraconference by Division	CLE	BALT	BUFF	NE	DEN	OAK
	PITT	CIN	MIA	NYJ	KC	SD
Interconference by Division	ARIZ	SF	PHIL	DALL	NO	ATL
	STL	SEA	WASH	NYG	TB	CAR
Intraconference by Position	AFCW	AFCE	AFCN	AFCW	AFCE	AFCN

	2008 Home	Away	2009 Home	Away
Intraconference by Division	BALT	CLE	NE	BUFF
	CIN	PITT	NYJ	MIA
Interconference by Division	CHI	GB	SF	ARIZ
	DET	MINN	SEA	STL
Intraconference by Position	AFCE	AFCW	AFCW	AFCN

JACKSONVILLE JAGUARS

	2005 Home	Away	2006 Home	Away	2007 Home	Away
Intraconference by Division	BALT	CLE	NE	BUFF	OAK	DEN
	CIN	PITT	NYJ	MIA	SD	KC
Interconference by Division	SF	ARIZ	DALL	PHIL	ATL	NO
	SEA	STL	NYG	WASH	CAR	TB
Intraconference by Position	AFCW	AFCE	AFCN	AFCW	AFCE	AFCN

	2008 Home	Away	2009 Home	Away
Intraconference by Division	CLE	BALT	BUFF	NE
	PITT	CIN	MIA	NYJ
Interconference by Division	GB	CHI	ARIZ	SF
	MINN	DET	STL	SEA
Intraconference by Position	AFCE	AFCW	AFCW	AFCN

TENNESSEE TITANS

	2005 Home	Away	2006 Home	Away	2007 Home	Away
Intraconference by Division	BALT	CLE	NE	BUFF	OAK	DEN
	CIN	PITT	NYJ	MIA	SD	KC
Interconference by Division	SF	ARIZ	DALL	PHIL	ATL	NO
	SEA	STL	NYG	WASH	CAR	TB
Intraconference by Position	AFCW	AFCE	AFCN	AFCW	AFCE	AFCN

	2008 Home	Away	2009 Home	Away
Intraconference by Division	CLE	BALT	BUFF	NE
	PITT	CIN	MIA	NYJ
Interconference by Division	GB	CHI	ARIZ	SF
	MINN	DET	STL	SEA
Intraconference by Position	AFCE	AFCW	AFCW	AFCN

AFC WEST NON-DIVISIONAL OPPONENTS 2005-2009

DENVER BRONCOS

	2005 Home	Away	2006 Home	Away	2007 Home	Away
Intraconference by Division	NE	BUFF	BALT	CLE	JAX	HOU
	NYJ	MIA	CIN	PITT	TENN	IND
Interconference by Division	PHIL	DALL	SF	ARIZ	GB	CHI
	WASH	NYG	SEA	STL	MINN	DET
Intraconference by Position	AFCN	AFCS	AFCS	AFCE	AFCN	AFCE

	2008 Home	Away	2009 Home	Away
Intraconference by Division	BUFF	NE	CLE	BALT
	MIA	NYJ	PITT	CIN
Interconference by Division	NO	ATL	DALL	PHIL
	TB	CAR	NYG	WASH
Intraconference by Position	AFCS	AFCN	AFCE	AFCS

KANSAS CITY CHIEFS

	2005 Home	Away	2006 Home	Away	2007 Home	Away
Intraconference by Division	NE	BUFF	BALT	CLE	JAX	HOU
	NYJ	MIA	CIN	PITT	TENN	IND
Interconference by Division	PHIL	DALL	SF	ARIZ	GB	CHI
	WASH	NYG	SEA	STL	MINN	DET
Intraconference by Position	AFCN	AFCS	AFCS	AFCE	AFCN	AFCE

	2008 Home	Away	2009 Home	Away
Intraconference by Division	BUFF	NE	CLE	BALT
	MIA	NYJ	PITT	CIN
Interconference by Division	NO	ATL	DALL	PHIL
	TB	CAR	NYG	WASH
Intraconference by Position	AFCS	AFCN	AFCE	AFCS

OAKLAND RAIDERS

	2005 Home	Away	2006 Home	Away	2007 Home	Away
Intraconference by Division	BUFF	NE	CLE	BALT	HOU	JAX
	MIA	NYJ	PITT	CIN	IND	TENN
Interconference by Division	DALL	PHIL	ARIZ	SF	CHI	GB
	NYG	WASH	STL	SEA	DET	MINN
Intraconference by Position	AFCN	AFCS	AFCS	AFCE	AFCN	AFCE

	2008 Home	Away	2009 Home	Away
Intraconference by Division	NE	BUFF	BALT	CLE
	NYJ	MIA	CIN	PITT
Interconference by Division	ATL	NO	PHIL	DALL
	CAR	TB	WASH	NYG
Intraconference by Position	AFCS	AFCN	AFCE	AFCS

SAN DIEGO CHARGERS

	2005 Home	Away	2006 Home	Away	2007 Home	Away
Intraconference by Division	BUFF	NE	CLE	BALT	HOU	JAX
	MIA	NYJ	PITT	CIN	IND	TENN
Interconference by Division	DALL	PHIL	ARIZ	SF	CHI	GB
	NYG	WASH	STL	SEA	DET	MINN
Intraconference by Position	AFCN	AFCS	AFCS	AFCE	AFCN	AFCE

	2008 Home	Away	2009 Home	Away
Intraconference by Division	NE	BUFF	BALT	CLE
	NYJ	MIA	CIN	PITT
Interconference by Division	ATL	NO	PHIL	DALL
	CAR	TB	WASH	NYG
Intraconference by Position	AFCS	AFCN	AFCE	AFCS

NFC EAST NON-DIVISIONAL OPPONENTS 2005-2009

DALLAS COWBOYS

	2005 Home	Away	2006 Home	Away	2007 Home	Away
Intraconference by Division	ARIZ	SF	NO	ATL	GB	CHI
	STL	SEA	TB	CAR	MINN	DET
Interconference by Division	DEN	OAK	HOU	JAX	NE	BUFF
	KC	SD	IND	TENN	NYJ	MIA
Intraconference by Position	NFCN	NFCS	NFCN	NFCW	NFCW	NFCS

	2008 Home	Away	2009 Home	Away
Intraconference by Division	SF	ARIZ	ATL	NO
	SEA	STL	CAR	TB
Interconference by Division	BALT	CLE	OAK	DEN
	CIN	PITT	SD	KC
Intraconference by Position	NFCS	NFCN	NFCW	NFCN

NEW YORK GIANTS

	2005 Home	Away	2006 Home	Away	2007 Home	Away
Intraconference by Division	ARIZ	SF	NO	ATL	GB	CHI
	STL	SEA	TB	CAR	MINN	DET
Interconference by Division	DEN	OAK	HOU	JAX	NE	BUFF
	KC	SD	IND	TENN	NYJ	MIA
Intraconference by Position	NFCN	NFCS	NFCN	NFCW	NFCW	NFCS

	2008 Home	Away	2009 Home	Away
Intraconference by Division	SF	ARIZ	ATL	NO
	SEA	STL	CAR	TB
Interconference by Division	BALT	CLE	OAK	DEN
	CIN	PITT	SD	KC
Intraconference by Position	NFCS	NFCN	NFCW	NFCN

PHILADELPHIA EAGLES

	2005 Home	Away	2006 Home	Away	2007 Home	Away
Intraconference by Division	SF	ARIZ	ATL	NO	CHI	GB
	SEA	STL	CAR	TB	DET	MINN
Interconference by Division	OAK	DEN	JAX	HOU	BUFF	NE
	SD	KC	TENN	IND	MIA	NYJ
Intraconference by Position	NFCN	NFCS	NFCN	NFCW	NFCW	NFCS

	2008 Home	Away	2009 Home	Away
Intraconference by Division	ARIZ	SF	NO	ATL
	STL	SEA	TB	CAR
Interconference by Division	CLE	BALT	DEN	OAK
	PITT	CIN	KC	SD
Intraconference by Position	NFCS	NFCN	NFCW	NFCN

WASHINGTON REDSKINS

	2005 Home	Away	2006 Home	Away	2007 Home	Away
Intraconference by Division	SF	ARIZ	ATL	NO	CHI	GB
	SEA	STL	CAR	TB	DET	MINN
Interconference by Division	OAK	DEN	JAX	HOU	BUFF	NE
	SD	KC	TENN	IND	MIA	NYJ
Intraconference by Position	NFCN	NFCS	NFCN	NFCW	NFCW	NFCS

	2008 Home	Away	2009 Home	Away
Intraconference by Division	ARIZ	SF	NO	ATL
	STL	SEA	TB	CAR
Interconference by Division	CLE	BALT	DEN	OAK
	PITT	CIN	KC	SD
Intraconference by Position	NFCS	NFCN	NFCW	NFCN

NFC NORTH NON-DIVISIONAL OPPONENTS 2005-2009

CHICAGO BEARS

	2005		2006		2007	
	Home	Away	Home	Away	Home	Away
Intraconference by Division	ATL	NO	SF	ARIZ	DALL	PHIL
	CAR	TB	SEA	STL	NYG	WASH
Interconference by Division	BALT	CLE	BUFF	NE	DEN	OAK
	CIN	PITT	MIA	NYJ	KC	SD
Intraconference by Position	NFCW	NFCE	NFCS	NFCE	NFCS	NFCW

	2008		2009	
	Home	Away	Home	Away
Intraconference by Division	NO	ATL	ARIZ	SF
	TB	CAR	STL	SEA
Interconference by Division	JAX	HOU	CLE	BALT
	TENN	IND	PITT	CIN
Intraconference by Position	NFCE	NFCW	NFCE	NFCS

DETROIT LIONS

	2005		2006		2007	
	Home	Away	Home	Away	Home	Away
Intraconference by Division	ATL	NO	SF	ARIZ	DALL	PHIL
	CAR	TB	SEA	STL	NYG	WASH
Interconference by Division	BALT	CLE	BUFF	NE	DEN	OAK
	CIN	PITT	MIA	NYJ	KC	SD
Intraconference by Position	NFCW	NFCE	NFCS	NFCE	NFCS	NFCW

	2008		2009	
	Home	Away	Home	Away
Intraconference by Division	NO	ATL	ARIZ	SF
	TB	CAR	STL	SEA
Interconference by Division	JAX	HOU	CLE	BALT
	TENN	IND	PITT	CIN
Intraconference by Position	NFCE	NFCW	NFCE	NFCS

GREEN BAY PACKERS

	2005		2006		2007	
	Home	Away	Home	Away	Home	Away
Intraconference by Division	NO	ATL	ARIZ	SF	PHIL	DALL
	TB	CAR	STL	SEA	WASH	NYG
Interconference by Division	CLE	BALT	NE	BUFF	OAK	DEN
	PITT	CIN	NYJ	MIA	SD	KC
Intraconference by Position	NFCW	NFCE	NFCS	NFCE	NFCS	NFCW

	2008		2009	
	Home	Away	Home	Away
Intraconference by Division	ATL	NO	SF	ARIZ
	CAR	TB	SEA	STL
Interconference by Division	HOU	JAX	BALT	CLE
	IND	TENN	CIN	PITT
Intraconference by Position	NFCE	NFCW	NFCE	NFCS

MINNESOTA VIKINGS

	2005		2006		2007	
	Home	Away	Home	Away	Home	Away
Intraconference by Division	NO	ATL	ARIZ	SF	PHIL	DALL
	TB	CAR	STL	SEA	WASH	NYG
Interconference by Division	CLE	BALT	NE	BUFF	OAK	DEN
	PITT	CIN	NYJ	MIA	SD	KC
Intraconference by Position	NFCW	NFCE	NFCS	NFCE	NFCS	NFCW

	2008		2009	
	Home	Away	Home	Away
Intraconference by Division	ATL	NO	SF	ARIZ
	CAR	TB	SEA	STL
Interconference by Division	HOU	JAX	BALT	CLE
	IND	TENN	CIN	PITT
Intraconference by Position	NFCE	NFCW	NFCE	NFCS

NFC SOUTH NON-DIVISIONAL OPPONENTS 2005-2009

ATLANTA FALCONS

	2005 Home	2005 Away	2006 Home	2006 Away	2007 Home	2007 Away
Intraconference by Division	GB	CHI	DALL	PHIL	SF	ARIZ
	MINN	DET	NYG	WASH	SEA	STL
Interconference by Division	NE	BUFF	CLE	BALT	HOU	JAX
	NYJ	MIA	PITT	CIN	IND	TENN
Intraconference by Position	NFCE	NFCW	NFCW	NFCN	NFCE	NFCN

	2008 Home	2008 Away	2009 Home	2009 Away
Intraconference by Division	CHI	GB	PHIL	DALL
	DET	MINN	WASH	NYG
Interconference by Division	DEN	OAK	BUFF	NE
	KC	SD	MIA	NYJ
Intraconference by Position	NFCW	NFCE	NFCN	NFCW

CAROLINA PANTHERS

	2005 Home	2005 Away	2006 Home	2006 Away	2007 Home	2007 Away
Intraconference by Division	GB	CHI	DALL	PHIL	SF	ARIZ
	MINN	DET	NYG	WASH	SEA	STL
Interconference by Division	NE	BUFF	CLE	BALT	HOU	JAX
	NYJ	MIA	PITT	CIN	IND	TENN
Intraconference by Position	NFCE	NFCW	NFCW	NFCN	NFCE	NFCN

	2008 Home	2008 Away	2009 Home	2009 Away
Intraconference by Division	CHI	GB	PHIL	DALL
	DET	MINN	WASH	NYG
Interconference by Division	DEN	OAK	BUFF	NE
	KC	SD	MIA	NYJ
Intraconference by Position	NFCW	NFCE	NFCN	NFCW

NEW ORLEANS SAINTS

	2005 Home	2005 Away	2006 Home	2006 Away	2007 Home	2007 Away
Intraconference by Division	CHI	GB	PHIL	DALL	ARIZ	SF
	DET	MINN	WASH	NYG	STL	SEA
Interconference by Division	BUFF	NE	BALT	CLE	JAX	HOU
	MIA	NYJ	CIN	PITT	TENN	IND
Intraconference by Position	NFCE	NFCW	NFCW	NFCN	NFCE	NFCN

	2008 Home	2008 Away	2009 Home	2009 Away
Intraconference by Division	GB	CHI	DALL	PHIL
	MINN	DET	NYG	WASH
Interconference by Division	OAK	DEN	NE	BUFF
	SD	KC	NYJ	MIA
Intraconference by Position	NFCW	NFCE	NFCN	NFCW

TAMPA BAY BUCCANEERS

	2005 Home	2005 Away	2006 Home	2006 Away	2007 Home	2007 Away
Intraconference by Division	CHI	GB	PHIL	DALL	ARIZ	SF
	DET	MINN	WASH	NYG	STL	SEA
Interconference by Division	BUFF	NE	BALT	CLE	JAX	HOU
	MIA	NYJ	CIN	PITT	TENN	IND
Intraconference by Position	NFCE	NFCW	NFCW	NFCN	NFCE	NFCN

	2008 Home	2008 Away	2009 Home	2009 Away
Intraconference by Division	GB	CHI	DALL	PHIL
	MINN	DET	NYG	WASH
Interconference by Division	OAK	DEN	NE	BUFF
	SD	KC	NYJ	MIA
Intraconference by Position	NFCW	NFCE	NFCN	NFCW

NFC WEST NON-DIVISIONAL OPPONENTS 2005-2009

ARIZONA CARDINALS

	2005 Home	Away	2006 Home	Away	2007 Home	Away
Intraconference by Division	PHIL	DALL	CHI	GB	ATL	NO
	WASH	NYG	DET	MINN	CAR	TB
Interconference by Division	JAX	HOU	DEN	OAK	CLE	BALT
	TENN	IND	KC	SD	PITT	CIN
Intraconference by Position	NFCS	NFCN	NFCE	NFCS	NFCN	NFCE

	2008 Home	Away	2009 Home	Away
Intraconference by Division	DALL	PHIL	GB	CHI
	NYG	WASH	MINN	DET
Interconference by Division	BUFF	NE	HOU	JAX
	MIA	NYJ	IND	TENN
Intraconference by Position	NFCN	NFCS	NFCS	NFCE

ST. LOUIS RAMS

	2005 Home	Away	2006 Home	Away	2007 Home	Away
Intraconference by Division	PHIL	DALL	CHI	GB	ATL	NO
	WASH	NYG	DET	MINN	CAR	TB
Interconference by Division	JAX	HOU	DEN	OAK	CLE	BALT
	TENN	IND	KC	SD	PITT	CIN
Intraconference by Position	NFCS	NFCN	NFCE	NFCS	NFCN	NFCE

	2008 Home	Away	2009 Home	Away
Intraconference by Division	DALL	PHIL	GB	CHI
	NYG	WASH	MINN	DET
Interconference by Division	BUFF	NE	HOU	JAX
	MIA	NYJ	IND	TENN
Intraconference by Position	NFCN	NFCS	NFCS	NFCE

SAN FRANCISCO 49ERS

	2005 Home	Away	2006 Home	Away	2007 Home	Away
Intraconference by Division	DALL	PHIL	GB	CHI	NO	ATL
	NYG	WASH	MINN	DET	TB	CAR
Interconference by Division	HOU	JAX	OAK	DEN	BALT	CLE
	IND	TENN	SD	KC	CIN	PITT
Intraconference by Position	NFCS	NFCN	NFCE	NFCS	NFCN	NFCE

	2008 Home	Away	2009 Home	Away
Intraconference by Division	PHIL	DALL	CHI	GB
	WASH	NYG	DET	MINN
Interconference by Division	NE	BUFF	JAX	HOU
	NYJ	MIA	TENN	IND
Intraconference by Position	NFCN	NFCS	NFCS	NFCE

SEATTLE SEAHAWKS

	2005 Home	Away	2006 Home	Away	2007 Home	Away
Intraconference by Division	DALL	PHIL	GB	CHI	NO	ATL
	NYG	WASH	MINN	DET	TB	CAR
Interconference by Division	HOU	JAX	OAK	DEN	BALT	CLE
	IND	TENN	SD	KC	CIN	PITT
Intraconference by Position	NFCS	NFCN	NFCE	NFCS	NFCN	NFCE

	2008 Home	Away	2009 Home	Away
Intraconference by Division	PHIL	DALL	CHI	GB
	WASH	NYG	DET	MINN
Interconference by Division	NE	BUFF	JAX	HOU
	NYJ	MIA	TENN	IND
Intraconference by Position	NFCN	NFCS	NFCS	NFCE

TOP ACTIVE PASSERS
1,000 or more attempts

		Yrs.	Att.	Comp.	Pct. Comp.	Yards	TD	Pct. TD	Had Int.	Pct. Int.	Ratings Pts.
1.	Kurt Warner, Ariz.	7	1,965	1,295	65.9	16,501	108	5.5	69	3.5	95.7
2.	Chad Pennington, NYJ	5	1,091	718	65.8	8,091	53	4.9	27	2.5	93.7
3.	Daunte Culpepper, Minn.	6	2,391	1,539	64.4	18,598	129	5.4	74	3.1	93.2
4.	Peyton Manning, Ind.	7	3,880	2,464	63.5	29,442	216	5.6	120	3.1	92.3
5.	Marc Bulger, St.L.	3	1,231	795	64.6	9,635	57	4.6	42	3.4	89.7
6.	Trent Green, K.C.	7	2,822	1,705	60.4	21,607	133	4.7	82	2.9	87.9
7.	Tom Brady, N.E.	5	2,018	1,243	61.6	13,925	97	4.8	52	2.6	87.5
8.	Brett Favre, G.B.	14	7,003	4,306	61.5	49,734	376	5.4	226	3.2	87.4
9.	Jeff Garcia, Det.	6	2,612	1,593	61.0	18,139	123	4.7	65	2.5	87.2
10.	Brian Griese, T.B.	7	2,144	1,351	63.0	15,208	96	4.5	71	3.3	85.3
11.	Rich Gannon, Oak.	16	4,206	2,533	60.2	28,743	180	4.3	104	2.5	84.7
12.	Brad Johnson, Minn.	11	3,504	2,166	61.8	23,913	143	4.1	98	2.8	84.0
13.	Donovan McNabb, Phil.	6	2,586	1,507	58.3	16,926	118	4.6	57	2.2	83.9
14.	Mark Brunell, Wash.	11	3,880	2,314	59.6	26,987	151	3.9	92	2.4	83.9
15.	Matt Hasselbeck, Sea.	6	1,756	1,048	59.7	12,466	72	4.1	48	2.7	83.7
16.	Steve McNair, Tenn.	10	3,395	2,013	59.3	23,980	140	4.1	92	2.7	83.4
17.	Drew Brees, S.D.	4	1,309	802	61.3	8,772	56	4.3	38	2.9	83.2
18.	Jake Delhomme, Car.	4	1,068	626	58.6	7,739	51	4.8	36	3.4	83.0
19.	Aaron Brooks, N.O.	5	2,340	1,323	56.5	16,274	107	4.6	67	2.9	81.5
20.	Jeff George, Chi.	12	3,967	2,298	57.9	27,602	154	3.9	113	2.8	80.4
21.	Chris Chandler, *	17	4,005	2,328	58.1	28,484	170	4.2	146	3.6	79.1
22.	Jeff Blake, *	12	3,232	1,819	56.3	21,656	133	4.1	99	3.1	77.9
23.	Jay Fiedler, NYJ	7	1,704	1,000	58.7	11,737	68	4.0	66	3.9	76.9
24.	Charlie Batch, Pitt.	7	1,334	747	56.0	9,063	49	3.7	40	3.0	76.8
25.	Drew Bledsoe, Dall.	12	6,049	3,449	57.0	39,808	221	3.7	181	3.0	76.7
26.	Doug Flutie, S.D.	11	2,141	1,172	54.7	14,686	86	4.0	68	3.2	76.4
27.	Gus Frerotte, Mia.	11	2,141	1,169	54.6	15,097	77	3.6	66	3.1	76.1
28.	Jon Kitna, Cin.	8	2,808	1,650	58.8	18,160	108	3.8	102	3.6	75.7
29.	Vinny Testaverde, *	18	6,420	3,631	56.6	44,475	268	4.2	255	4.0	75.4
30.	Jim Miller, NYG	6	1,046	610	58.3	6,387	36	3.4	31	3.0	75.2

TOP ACTIVE SCORERS
(number in parantheses represents 2-point conversions scored)

		Yrs.	TD	FG	PAT	TP
1.	Gary Anderson, *	23	0	538	820	2,434
2.	Morten Andersen, *	23	0	520	798	2,358
3.	John Carney, N.O.	17	0	365	442	1,537
4.	Matt Stover, Balt.	14	0	350	431	1,481
5.	Steve Christie, *	15	0	336	468	1,476
6.	Jason Elam, Den.	12	0	317	491	1,442
7.	Jason Hanson, Det.	13	0	308	412	1,336
8.	Jerry Rice, Den.	20	208	0	(4)	1,256
9.	John Kasay, Car.	14	0	284	332	1,184
10.	Jeff Wilkins, St.L.	11	0	224	399	1,071
11.	Adam Vinatieri, N.E.	9	0	243	327 (1)	1,058
12.	Ryan Longwell, G.B.	8	0	206	346	964
13.	Todd Peterson, Atl.	11	0	212	303	939
14.	Doug Brien, Chi.	11	0	206	287	905
15.	Mike Vanderjagt, Ind.	7	0	194	292	874
16.	Olindo Mare, Mia.	8	0	194	258	840
17.	Marshall Faulk, St.L.	11	135	0	(6)	822
18.	John Hall, Was.	8	0	182	244	790
19.	Tim Brown, *	17	105	0	(1)	632
20.	David Akers, Phil.	7	0	139	201	618
21.	Marvin Harrison, Ind.	9	98	0	(5)	598
22.	Martín Gramatica, *	6	0	137	181	592
23.	Terrell Owens, Phil.	9	97	0	(2)	586
24.	Curtis Martin, NYJ	10	95	0	(3)	576
25.	Kris Brown, Hou.	6	0	132	177	573
26.	Joe Nedney, S.F.	9	0	127	191	572
27.	Randy Moss, Oak.	7	91	0	(3)	552
28.	Sebastian Janikowski, Oak.	5	0	118	197	551
29.	Priest Holmes, K.C.	8	87	0	0	522
30.	Jerome Bettis, Pitt.	12	85	0	(3)	516

TOP ACTIVE RUSHERS

		Yrs.	Att.	Yards	TD
1.	Curtis Martin, NYJ	10	3,298	13,366	85
2.	Jerome Bettis, Pitt.	12	3,369	13,294	82
3.	Marshall Faulk, St.L.	11	2,771	11,987	100
4.	Eddie George, *	9	2,865	10,441	68
5.	Corey Dillon, N.E.	8	2,210	9,696	57
6.	Garrison Hearst, *	12	1,831	7,966	30
7.	Edgerrin James, Ind.	6	1,828	7,720	51
8.	Priest Holmes, K.C.	8	1,615	7,584	80
9.	Fred Taylor, Jax.	7	1,637	7,580	48
10.	Stephen Davis, Car.	9	1,725	7,326	53
11.	Ahman Green, G.B.	7	1,528	7,177	49
12.	Charlie Garner, T.B.	11	1,537	7,097	39
13.	Tiki Barber, NYG	8	1,533	6,927	41
14.	Warrick Dunn, Atl.	8	1,690	6,905	36
15.	Antowain Smith, N.O.	7	1,618	6,222	51
16.	Shaun Alexander, Sea.*	5	1,347	5,937	62
17.	LaDainian Tomlinson, S.D.	4	1,363	5,899	54
18.	Jamal Lewis, Balt.	4	1,239	5,763	33
19.	Duce Staley, Pitt.	8	1,392	5,637	23
20.	Tyrone Wheatley, *	10	1,270	4,962	40
21.	Dorsey Levens, *	11	1,243	4,955	36
22.	Mike Alstott, T.B.	9	1,265	4,837	49
23.	Clinton Portis, Wash.	3	906	4,414	34
24.	Michael Pittman, T.B.	7	1,128	4,340	19
25.	Deuce McAllister, N.O.	4	961	4,194	31
26.	Travis Henry, Buff.	4	963	3,849	27
27.	Anthony Thomas, Dall.	4	858	3,332	21
28.	Steve McNair, Tenn.	10	582	3,300	35
29.	Kevan Barlow, S.F.	4	715	3,033	21
30.	Kordell Stewart, *	10	556	2,850	38

*Free agent; subject to developments.

TOP ACTIVE PASS RECEIVERS

	Yrs.	No.	Yards	TD
1. Jerry Rice, Den.	20	1,549	22,895	197
2. Tim Brown, *	17	1,094	14,934	100
3. Marvin Harrison, Ind.	9	845	11,185	98
4. Jimmy Smith, Jax.	11	792	11,264	61
5. Issac Bruce, St.L.	11	777	11,753	74
6. Keenan McCardell, S.D.	13	755	9,763	53
7. Marshall Faulk, St.L.	11	723	6,584	35
8. Rod Smith, Den.	10	712	9,772	59
9. Keyshawn Johnson, Dall.	9	673	8,917	54
10. Terrell Owens, Phil.	9	669	9,772	95
11. Ricky Proehl, Car.	15	641	8,407	50
12. Johnnie Morton, K.C.	11	603	8,431	43
13. Curtis Conway, *	12	594	8,230	52
Eric Moulds, Buff.	8	594	8,280	44
15. Muhsin Muhammad, Chi.	9	578	7,751	44
16. Randy Moss, Oak.	7	574	9,142	90
17. Tony Gonzalez, K.C.	8	570	6,905	54
18. Wayne Chrebet, NYJ	10	565	7,212	41
19. Torry Holt, St.L.	6	517	8,156	45
20. Hines Ward, Pitt.	7	505	6,055	41
21. Joe Horn, N.O.	9	490	7,168	52
22. Troy Brown, *	12	475	5,516	25
23. Tiki Barber, NYG	8	474	4,188	10
24. Amani Toomer, NYG	9	469	7,113	37
25. Joey Galloway, T.B.	10	467	7,214	54
26. Terry Glenn, Dall.	9	461	6,640	31
27. Curtis Martin, NYJ	10	460	3,211	10
28. Derrick Mason, Balt.	8	453	6,114	37
29. Charlie Garner, T.B.	11	419	3,711	12
30. Eddie Kennison, K.C.	9	414	6,282	32

TOP ACTIVE INTERCEPTORS

	Yrs.	No.	Yards	TD
1. Aeneas Williams, *	14	55	807	9
2. Deion Sanders, *	13	51	1,274	9
3. Terrell Buckley, *	13	50	793	6
4. Ray Buchanan, *	12	47	827	4
5. Troy Vincent, Buff.	13	43	633	3
6. Ashley Ambrose, *	13	42	512	3
7. Donnie Abraham, NYJ	9	38	468	3
8. Ty Law, *	10	36	583	6
Darren Sharper, Minn.	8	36	677	5
10. Aaron Glenn, Dall.	11	35	515	5
Sammy Knight, K.C.	8	35	594	4
12. Rodney Harrison, N.E.	11	31	357	2
Brock Marion, *	12	31	527	3
Dewayne Washington, *	11	31	569	5
15. Tory James, Cin.	8	30	328	0
16. Sam Madison, Mia.	8	29	476	2
Patrick Surtain, K.C.	7	29	298	2
18. Dexter McCleon, K.C.	8	28	160	0
Tony Parrish, S.F.	7	28	636	1
20. Willie Williams, Pitt.	12	26	302	4
21. Brian Dawkins, Phi.	9	25	427	2
Shawn Springs, Wash.	8	25	352	2
Duane Starks, N.E.	7	25	245	2
24. Brent Alexander, NYG	11	24	208	0
Aaron Beasley, *	9	24	487	2
Jay Bellamy, N.O.	11	24	286	1
Dre' Bly, Det.	6	24	443	5
Dale Carter, Balt.	12	24	256	1
Marcus Coleman, Hou.	9	24	470	2
John Lynch, Den.	12	24	202	0

TOP ACTIVE PUNT RETURNERS
40 or more punt returns

	Yrs.	No.	Yards	Avg.	TD
1. Rod Smith, Den.	10	52	645	12.4	1
2. Santana Moss, Wash.	4	88	1,052	12.0	2
3. Az-Zahir Hakim, *	7	131	1,513	11.5	3
4. Dante Hall, K.C.	5	119	1,366	11.5	4
5. Eddie Drummond, Det.	3	54	605	11.2	4
6. Michael Lewis, N.O.	4	122	1,363	11.2	1
7. David Allen, Jax.	2	42	468	11.1	0
8. Phillip Buchanon, Hou.	3	72	790	11.0	3
9. Allen Rossum, Atl.	7	190	2,084	11.0	3
10. Reggie Swinton, Hou.	4	90	977	10.9	2
11. Wes Welker, Mia.	1	43	464	10.8	0
12. Troy Brown, *	12	237	2,524	10.6	3
13. Dennis Northcutt, Cle.	5	139	1,469	10.6	2
14. Jimmy Williams, N.O.	4	55	576	10.5	1
15. B.J. Sams, Balt.	1	55	575	10.5	2
16. Bobby Engram, Sea.	9	100	1,044	10.4	2
17. Deion Sanders, *	13	212	2,199	10.4	6
18. Hank Poteat, N.E.	4	76	788	10.4	1
19. Tim Brown, *	17	326	3,320	10.2	3
20. Deltha O'Neal, Cin.	5	135	1,358	10.1	2
21. Karl Williams, *	9	255	2,565	10.1	5
22. Eddie Kennison, K.C.	9	141	1,413	10.0	3
23. Tim Dwight, N.E.	7	130	1,300	10.0	3
24. Nate Clements, Buff.	4	57	565	9.9	2
25. Lamont Brightful, NYG	3	69	681	9.9	1
26. Joey Galloway, T.B.	10	136	1,332	9.8	5
27. Peter Warrick, Cin.	5	54	526	9.7	2
28. Amani Toomer, NYG	9	109	1,060	9.7	3
29. Tiki Barber, NYG	8	122	1,181	9.7	1
30. Justin McCareins, NYJ	4	51	491	9.6	1

TOP ACTIVE KICKOFF RETURNERS
40 or more kickoff returns

	Yrs.	No.	Yards	Avg.	TD
1. Bethel Johnson, N.E.	2	71	1,863	26.2	2
2. Terrence McGee, Buff.	2	60	1,530	25.5	3
3. Eddie Drummond, Det.	3	102	2,600	25.5	2
4. Tim Brown, *	17	49	1,235	25.2	1
5. Reuben Droughns, Cle.	4	46	1,153	25.1	0
6. Dominic Rhodes, Ind.	3	78	1,955	25.1	2
7. Jerry Azumah, Chi.	6	87	2,180	25.1	1
8. Steve Smith, Car.	4	93	2,311	24.8	2
9. Michael Lewis, N.O.	4	198	4,852	24.5	3
10. Rodney Harrison, N.E.	5	242	5,877	24.3	5
11. Kevin Kasper, *	4	77	1,869	24.3	0
12. Deuce McAllister, N.O.	4	45	1,091	24.2	0
13. Duce Staley, Pitt.	8	48	1,158	24.1	0
14. Aaron Stecker, N.O.	5	118	2,845	24.1	1
15. Jonathan Carter, NYJ	4	44	1,060	24.1	1
16. Brock Marion, *	12	123	2,951	24.0	0
17. Chad Morton, Wash.	5	174	4,172	24.0	3
18. Reggie Swinton, Hou.	4	145	3,463	23.9	2
19. Kevin Mathis, Atl.	8	51	1,216	23.8	0
20. Chris Cole, Jax.	5	89	2,105	23.7	0
21. Ladell Betts, Wash.	3	54	1,277	23.6	0
22. ReShard Lee, *	1	41	964	23.5	0
23. Jamal Robertson, Car.	3	42	982	23.4	0
24. Tim Dwight, N.E.	7	192	4,473	23.3	2
25. Aaron Glenn, Dall.	11	111	2,578	23.2	1
26. Wes Welker, Mia.	1	61	1,415	23.2	1
27. Josh Scobey, Ariz.	2	105	2,407	22.9	1
28. James Thrash, Wash.	8	113	2,586	22.9	1
29. Brandon Bennett, *	6	117	2,675	22.9	1
30. Kevin Faulk, N.E.	6	150	3,426	22.8	2

TOP ACTIVE PUNTERS
50 or more punts

		Yrs.	No.	Avg.	LG
1.	Shane Lechler, Oak.	5	360	45.9	73
2.	Todd Sauerbrun, Den.	10	760	44.0	73
3.	Tom Rouen, Car.	12	749	43.6	76
4.	Darren Bennett, Minn.	9	828	43.5	66
5.	Chris Hanson, Jax.	5	274	43.5	69
6.	Tom Tupa, Wash.	16	873	43.4	73
7.	Hunter Smith, Ind.	6	373	43.2	69
8.	Mitch Berger, N.O.	10	639	43.2	75
9.	Mike Scifres, S.D.	2	69	43.1	60
10.	Brian Moorman, Buff.	4	308	42.9	84
11.	Chris Gardocki, Pitt.	14	1,045	42.9	72
12.	Rodney Williams, N.O.	1	91	42.9	90
13.	Craig Hentrich, Tenn.	11	818	42.9	78
14.	Josh Miller, N.E.	9	628	42.8	75
15.	Leo Araguz, Sea.	7	304	42.8	64
16.	Scott Player, Ari.	7	575	42.7	67
17.	Mat McBriar, Dall.	1	75	42.4	68
18.	Matt Turk, Mia.	10	790	42.4	77
19.	Brad Maynard, Chi.	8	741	42.2	75
20.	Kyle Larson, Cin.	1	83	42.2	66
21.	Bryan Barker, *	15	1,082	42.1	83
22.	Jeff Feagles, NYG	17	1,364	41.6	77
23.	Andy Lee, S.F.	1	96	41.6	81
24.	Micah Knorr, NYJ	5	329	41.4	66
25.	Josh Bidwell, T.B.	5	390	41.4	68
26.	Toby Gowin, Atl.	8	629	41.2	72
27.	Dirk Johnson, Phil.	3	159	41.2	62
28.	Kyle Richardson, Cle.	8	494	41.1	67
29.	Dave Zastudil, Balt.	3	243	41.0	67
30.	Chad Stanley, Hou.	6	441	40.8	70

TOP ACTIVE QUARTERBACK SACKERS

		Yrs.	No.
1.	Michael Strahan, NYG	12	118.0
2.	Simeon Rice, T.B.	9	105.0
3.	Kevin Carter, Mia.	10	86.0
4.	Jason Taylor, Mia.	8	80.5
5.	Hugh Douglas, Phil.	10	80.0
	Jason Gildon, *	11	80.0
7.	Warren Sapp, Oak.	10	79.5
8.	Chad Brown, N.E.	12	78.0
9.	Willie McGinest, N.E.	11	72.0
10.	Bryant Young, S.F.	11	69.5
11.	La'Roi Glover, Dall.	9	68.5
12.	Peter Boulware, *	8	67.5
13.	Marco Coleman, Den.	13	64.5
14.	Lance Johnstone, Minn.	9	62.5
15.	Trevor Pryce, Den.	8	60.0
16.	Javon Kearse, Phil.	6	55.0
17.	Leonard Little, St.L.	7	51.5
	Dan Wilkinson, Det.	11	51.5
19.	Ellis Johnson, *	10	51.0
	Junior Seau, Mia.	15	51.0
21.	Kabeer Gbaja-Biamila, G.B.	5	50.5
22.	Duane Clemons, Cin.	9	47.5
23.	Raylee Johnson, Den.	11	47.0
	Patrick Kerney, Atl.	6	47.0
25.	Chidi Ahanotu, *	12	46.5
26.	Phillip Daniels, Wash.	9	45.5
	Gary Walker, Hou.	10	45.5
28.	Grant Wistrom, Sea.	7	45.0
29.	Greg Ellis, Dall.	7	44.0
	Marcellus Wiley, Jax.	8	44.0

ACTIVE COACHES' CAREER RECORDS (Order Based on Career Victories)
Start of 2005 Season

Coach	Team(s)	Yrs.	Regular Season Won	Lost	Tied	Pct.	Postseason Won	Lost	Pct.	Career Won	Lost	Tied	Pct.
Marty Schottenheimer	Cleveland Browns, Kansas City Chiefs, Washington Redskins, San Diego Chargers	19	177	117	1	.602	5	12	.294	182	129	1	.585
Bill Parcells	New York Giants, New England Patriots, New York Jets, Dallas Cowboys	17	154	116	1	.570	11	7	.611	165	123	1	.573
Joe Gibbs	Washington Redskins	13	130	70	0	.650	16	5	.762	146	75	0	.661
Bill Cowher	Pittsburgh Steelers	13	130	77	1	.627	8	9	.471	138	86	1	.616
Mike Holmgren	Green Bay Packers, Seattle Seahawks	13	125	83	0	.601	9	8	.529	134	91	0	.596
Mike Shanahan	Los Angeles Raiders, Denver Broncos	12	109	71	0	.606	7	4	.636	116	75	0	.607
Dick Vermeil	Philadelphia Eagles, St. Louis Rams, Kansas City Chiefs	14	110	103	0	.516	6	5	.545	116	108	0	.518
Dennis Green	Minnesota Vikings, Arizona Cardinals	11	103	72	0	.589	4	8	.333	107	80	0	.572
Bill Belichick	Cleveland Browns, New England Patriots	10	89	71	0	.556	10	1	.909	99	72	0	.579
Jeff Fisher	Tennessee Titans	10	93	73	0	.560	5	4	.556	98	77	0	.560
Tony Dungy	Tampa Bay Buccaneers, Indianapolis Colts	9	88	56	0	.611	5	7	.412	93	63	0	.596
Tom Coughlin	Jacksonville Jaguars, New York Giants	9	74	70	0	.514	4	4	.500	78	74	0	.513
Andy Reid	Philadelphia Eagles	6	64	32	0	.667	7	5	.583	71	37	0	.657
Steve Mariucci	San Francisco 49ers, Detroit Lions	8	68	60	0	.531	3	4	.429	71	64	0	.526
Jon Gruden	Oakland Raiders, Tampa Bay Buccaneers	7	62	50	0	.554	5	2	.714	67	52	0	.563
Brian Billick	Baltimore Ravens	6	56	40	0	.583	5	2	.714	61	42	0	.592
Mike Sherman	Green Bay Packers	5	53	27	0	.663	2	4	.333	55	31	0	.640
Norv Turner	Washington Redskins, Oakland Raiders	8	54	70	1	.436	1	1	.500	55	71	1	.437
Mike Martz	St. Louis Rams	5	51	29	0	.638	3	4	.429	54	33	0	.621
Dom Capers	Carolina Panthers, Houston Texans	7	46	66	0	.411	1	1	.500	47	67	0	.412
Jim Haslett	New Orleans Saints	5	42	38	0	.525	1	1	.500	43	39	0	.524
Herman Edwards	New York Jets	4	35	29	0	.547	2	3	.400	37	32	0	.536
John Fox	Carolina Panthers	3	25	23	0	.521	3	1	.750	28	24	0	.538
Mike Tice	Minnesota Vikings	4	23	26	0	.469	1	1	.500	24	27	0	.471
Marvin Lewis	Cincinnati Bengals	2	16	16	0	.500	0	0	.000	16	16	0	.500
Jack Del Rio	Jacksonville Jaguars	2	14	18	0	.438	0	0	.000	14	18	0	.438
Jim Mora	Atlanta Falcons	1	11	5	0	.688	1	1	.500	12	6	0	.667
Mike Mularkey	Buffalo Bills	1	9	7	0	.563	0	0	.000	9	7	0	.563
Lovie Smith	Chicago Bears	1	5	11	0	.313	0	0	.000	5	11	0	.313
Romeo Crennel	Cleveland Browns	0	0	0	0	.000	0	0	.000	0	0	0	.000
Mike Nolan	San Francisco 49ers	0	0	0	0	.000	0	0	.000	0	0	0	.000
Nick Saban	Miami Dolphins	0	0	0	0	.000	0	0	.000	0	0	0	.000

COACHES WITH 100 CAREER VICTORIES (Order Based on Career Victories)
Start of 2005 Season

Coach	Team(s)	Yrs.	Regular Season				Postseason			Career			
			Won	Lost	Tied	Pct.	Won	Lost	Pct.	Won	Lost	Tied	Pct.
Don Shula	Baltimore Colts, Miami Dolphins	33	328	156	6	.677	19	17	.528	347	173	6	.666
George Halas	Chicago Bears	40	318	148	31	.682	6	3	.667	324	151	31	.682
Tom Landry	Dallas Cowboys	29	250	162	6	.607	20	16	.556	270	178	6	.603
Earl (Curly) Lambeau	Green Bay Packers, Chicago Cardinals, Washington Redskins	33	226	132	22	.631	3	2	.600	229	134	22	.631
Chuck Noll	Pittsburgh Steelers	23	193	148	1	.566	16	8	.667	209	156	1	.572
Dan Reeves	Denver Broncos, New York Giants, Atlanta Falcons	23	190	165	2	.535	11	9	.550	201	174	2	.536
Chuck Knox	Los Angeles Rams, Buffalo Bills, Seattle Seahawks	22	186	147	1	.558	7	11	.389	193	158	1	.550
Marty Schottenheimer	Cleveland Browns, Kansas City Chiefs, Washington Redskins, San Diego Chargers	19	177	117	1	.602	5	12	.294	182	129	1	.585
Paul Brown	Cleveland Browns, Cincinnati Bengals	21	166	100	6	.624	4	8	.333	170	108	6	.612
Bud Grant	Minnesota Vikings	18	158	96	5	.621	10	12	.455	168	108	5	.608
Bill Parcells	New York Giants, New England Patriots, New York Jets, Dallas Cowboys	17	154	116	1	.570	11	7	.611	165	123	1	.573
Marv Levy	Kansas City Chiefs, Buffalo Bills	17	143	112	0	.561	11	8	.579	154	120	0	.562
Steve Owen	New York Giants	23	151	100	17	.602	2	8	.200	153	108	17	.586
Joe Gibbs	Washington Redskins	13	130	70	0	.650	16	5	.762	146	75	0	.661
Bill Cowher	Pittsburgh Steelers	13	130	77	1	.627	8	9	.471	138	86	1	.616
Hank Stram	Kansas City Chiefs, New Orleans Saints	17	131	97	10	.574	5	3	.625	136	100	10	.576
Mike Holmgren	Green Bay Packers, Seattle Seahawks	13	125	83	0	.601	9	8	.529	134	91	0	.596
Weeb Ewbank	Baltimore Colts, New York Jets	20	130	129	7	.502	4	1	.800	134	130	7	.508
Mike Ditka	Chicago Bears, New Orleans Saints	14	121	95	0	.560	6	6	.500	127	101	0	.557
Jim Mora	New Orleans Saints, Indianapolis Colts	15	125	106	0	.541	0	6	.000	125	112	0	.527
George Seifert	San Francisco 49ers, Carolina Panthers	11	114	62	0	.648	10	5	.667	124	67	0	.649
Sid Gillman	Los Angeles Rams, Los Angeles-San Diego Chargers, Houston Oilers	18	122	99	7	.552	1	5	.167	123	104	7	.542
George Allen	Los Angeles Rams, Washington Redskins	12	116	47	5	.712	2	7	.222	118	54	5	.686
Mike Shanahan	Los Angeles Raiders, Denver Broncos	12	109	71	0	.606	7	4	.636	116	75	0	.607
Dick Vermeil	Philadelphia Eagles, St. Louis Rams, Kansas City Chiefs	14	110	103	0	.516	6	5	.545	116	108	0	.518
Don Coryell	St. Louis Cardinals, San Diego Chargers	14	111	83	1	.572	3	6	.333	114	89	1	.561
John Madden	Oakland Raiders	10	103	32	7	.759	9	7	.563	112	39	7	.739
Ray (Buddy) Parker	Chicago Cardinals, Detroit Lions, Pittsburgh Steelers	15	104	75	9	.581	3	1	.750	107	76	9	.585
Dennis Green	Minnesota Vikings, Arizona Cardinals	11	103	72	0	.589	4	8	.333	107	80	0	.572
Vince Lombardi	Green Bay Packers, Washington Redskins	10	96	34	6	.739	9	1	.900	105	35	6	.750
Tom Flores	Oakland-Los Angeles Raiders, Seattle Seahawks	12	97	87	0	.527	8	3	.727	105	90	0	.538
Bill Walsh	San Francisco 49ers	10	92	59	1	.609	10	4	.714	102	63	1	.617

Active coaches in bold.

The **New England Patriots** have won two consecutive Super Bowls and can become the first team in NFL history to win three Super Bowls in a row.

The Patriots need one playoff victory to pass the Green Bay Packers (9, 1961-62, 1965-67) for the most consecutive postseason victories in NFL history. New England has won nine playoff games in a row.

The **Philadelphia Eagles** have played in four consecutive Championship Games and can become the second team (Oakland, 1973-77) in NFL history to appear in five Championship Games in a row.

The **Pittsburgh Steelers** have won 14 consecutive regular season games and need five wins in a row for the longest regular-season winning streak in NFL history (New England Patriots, 18).

The **Chicago Bears** need four regular season victories to become the first team with 650 regular season victories.

The **New York Giants** need seven victories to become the third team (Chicago Bears, 660 and Green Bay Packers, 636) with 600 total victories.

The **Oakland Raiders** need 10 regular season victories to reach 400 regular season victories.

Marty Schottenheimer, San Diego, needs 10 regular season victories to pass Chuck Knox (186) into seventh place all-time in regular season victories and needs 12 victories to pass Knox (193) into seventh place all-time in career victories. In 19 seasons, Schottenheimer has 177 regular season victories and 182 career victories.

Bill Parcells, Dallas, needs six victories to pass Bud Grant (168) and Paul Brown (170) into eighth place all-time in career victories. In 17 seasons, Parcells has 165 career victories.

Bill Belichick, New England, needs one victory to reach 100 career victories and needs 11 regular season victories to reach 100 regular season victories. In 10 seasons, Belichick has 99 career victories and 89 regular season victories.

Jeff Fisher, Tennessee, needs two victories to reach 100 career victories and needs seven regular season victories to reach 100 regular season victories. In 10 seasons, Fisher has 98 career victories and 93 regular season victories.

Tony Dungy, Indianapolis, needs seven victories to reach 100 career victories and needs 12 regular season victories to reach 100 regular season victories. In nine seasons, Dungy has 93 career victories and 88 regular season victories.

Brett Favre, Green Bay, needs 266 passing yards to join Dan Marino (61,361) and John Elway (51,475) as the only players in NFL history with 50,000 passing yards. Favre needs 1,742 passing yards to pass Elway to move into second place all-time. In 14 seasons, Favre has passed for 49,734 yards.

Favre has passed for 3,000 yards in a season 13 times in his 14-year career and can pass Dan Marino (13) for first all-time with his next 3,000-yard passing season. Favre holds the record for most consecutive seasons with 3,000 passing yards with 13 (active).

Favre has passed for 376 touchdowns and needs 24 to join Dan Marino (420) as the only players in NFL history with 400 touchdown passes.

Favre has led the league in touchdown passes four times in his 14-year career and can pass Johnny Unitas, Len Dawson, and Steve Young (4) for the most seasons leading the league in touchdown passes.

Favre needs 20 touchdown passes to extend his NFL-best streak to 12 consecutive seasons with 20 touchdown passes. Favre has thrown for 20 touchdowns in 11 consecutive seasons, the longest streak in NFL history.

Favre needs three touchdown passes at Lambeau Field for the single-stadium NFL record. Favre has thrown 178 touchdown passes at Lambeau Field and only trails John Elway's mark of 180 at Mile High Stadium.

Favre needs 14 wins to pass John Elway (147) and Dan Marino (148) for the most wins by a quarterback. In 14 seasons, Favre has won 135 games.

Favre needs 248 passing attempts to pass John Elway (7,250) to move into second place all-time. In 14 seasons, Favre has 7,003 passing attempts.

Vinny Testaverde needs 2,528 passing yards to pass Fran Tarkenton (47,003) to move into fifth place all-time. In 18 seasons, Testaverde has passed for 44,475 yards.

Testaverde has thrown 268 touchdown passes in 18 seasons and needs 24 to pass Joe Montana (273), Johnny Unitas (290), and Warren Moon (291) to move into fifth place all-time.

Testaverde needs 56 completions to pass Fran Tarkenton (3,686) to move into fifth place all-time (see Bledsoe note). In 18 seasons, Testaverde has completed 3,631 passes.

Drew Bledsoe, Dallas, needs 192 passing yards to become the 10th player in NFL history to pass for 40,000 yards. In 12 seasons, Bledsoe has 39,808 passing yards.

Bledsoe needs 238 completions to pass Vinny Testaverde (3,631) and Fran Tarkenton (3,686) to move into fifth place all-time (see Testaverde note). In 12 seasons, Bledsoe has completed 3,449 passes.

Peyton Manning, Indianapolis, needs 4,000 passing yards to become the first player in NFL history with seven consecutive 4,000-yard passing seasons. Manning is the only player to pass for 4,000 yards in six consecutive seasons. Manning needs 4,000 passing yards to pass Dan Marino (6) for the most career 4,000-yard passing seasons.

Manning needs 25 touchdown passes to become the first player in NFL history with eight consecutive seasons having 25 touchdown passes. Manning is the only player to have seven consecutive seasons with 25 touchdown passes.

Manning has thrown 82 touchdown passes to wide receiver Marvin Harrison and the duo needs four touchdowns to pass Steve Young-Jerry Rice (85) for the most touchdowns by an NFL quarterback-receiver tandem.

Manning and Harrison have combined for 702 completions and 9,410 yards. The duo owns the NFL record for the most completions by a tandem and needs 129 yards to pass Jim Kelly-Andre Reed (9,538) for the most yardage by teammates in NFL history.

Daunte Culpepper, Minnesota, needs 3,000 passing yards and 400 rushing yards this season to become the first quarterback in NFL history with five seasons with 3,000 passing yards and 400 rushing yards. Culpepper is the only player to accomplish the feat in four seasons.

Curtis Martin, New York Jets, needs 1,000 rushing yards to become the first player in NFL history to rush for 1,000 yards in each of his first 11 seasons. Martin is tied with Barry Sanders for the all-time mark with 10.

Martin needs 1,000 rushing yards to join Emmitt Smith (11) as the only players to rush for 1,000 yards in 11 consecutive seasons. Martin can also tie Smith for first place all-time with 11 seasons with 1,000 rushing yards.

Martin has rushed for 13,366 yards in 10 seasons. Martin needs 1,634 rushing yards to become the fourth player in NFL history with 15,000 rushing yards (see Bettis note).

Martin needs 250 carries to become the second player in NFL history (Emmitt Smith, 12) to record 11 consecutive seasons with 250 rushing attempts. Martin needs 250 carries to become the first player in NFL history to begin his career with 11 consecutive seasons with 250 rushing attempts.

Jerome Bettis, Pittsburgh, has rushed for 13,294 yards in 12 seasons. Bettis needs 1,706 rushing yards to become the fourth player in NFL history with 15,000 rushing yards (see Martin note).

Bettis needs 1,000 rushing yards to move into sole possession of fifth place all-time in career 1,000-yard seasons. In 12 seasons, Bettis has rushed for 1,000 yards eight times, tied with Tony Dorsett, Franco Harris, and Thurman Thomas.

Marshall Faulk, St. Louis, needs 11 touchdowns to pass Marcus Allen (145) to move into third place all-time. In 11 seasons, Faulk has scored 135 touchdowns.

Faulk has rushed for 100 touchdowns in his 11-year career and needs 11 rushing touchdowns to pass John Riggins (104), Jim Brown

(106) and Walter Payton (110) to move into third place all-time.

Faulk needs 1,429 total yards from scrimmage to become the fourth player in NFL history with 20,000 scrimmage yards. In 11 seasons, Faulk has gained 18,571 total yards from scrimmage.

Faulk has gained 2,000 scrimmage yards four times in his career, tied for the most in NFL history. With one more 2,000-scrimmage yard season, Faulk will pass Eric Dickerson (4) and Walter Payton (4) for the most all-time.

Faulk needs 1,393 combined yards to become the fifth player in NFL history with 20,000 combined yards (see Brown note). In 11 seasons, Faulk has gained 18,607 combined yards.

Faulk has gained 2,000 combined yards four times in his career, tied for the most in NFL history. Faulk needs one more season with 2,000 combined yards to pass Eric Dickerson (4), Brian Mitchell (4), and Walter Payton (4) for the most all-time.

Faulk needs 13 rushing yards and 416 receiving yards to become the first player in NFL history with 12,000 rushing yards and 7,000 receiving yards. In 11 seasons, Faulk has 11,987 rushing yards and 6,584 receiving yards.

LaDainian Tomlinson, San Diego, has scored a rushing touchdown in 12 consecutive games and needs a rushing touchdown in each of his next two games to pass John Riggins (1982-83) and George Rogers (1985-86) for the longest streak in NFL history (13).

Tomlinson needs 10 rushing touchdowns to extend his streak of consecutive seasons to begin a career with 10 rushing touchdowns to five, the most in NFL history.

Tomlinson has rushed for 200 yards in a game four times in his four-year career. Tomlinson needs one 200-yard rushing game to pass Jim Brown (4), Earl Campbell (4), and Barry Sanders (4) to move into sole possession of second place all-time and needs two to tie O.J. Simpson (6) for the NFL record.

Edgerrin James and Marvin Harrison, Indianapolis, have registered 100-yard rushing and receiving performances in the same game 19 times and need two such games to pass Emmitt Smith-Michael Irvin (20) for the most in NFL history.

Jerry Rice, Denver, needs three receiving touchdowns to become the first player in NFL history with 200 career touchdown receptions. In 20 seasons, Rice has 197 touchdown receptions, the most in NFL history.

Rice has 1,549 receptions in his 20-year career, the most in NFL history, and needs 51 to become the first player with 1,600 career receptions.

Rice needs 105 receiving yards to become the first player in NFL history with 23,000 receiving yards. Rice has gained an NFL-best 22,895 receiving yards in 20 seasons.

Rice has led the league in receiving yards six times in his 20-year career and can tie Don Hutson (7) for the most seasons leading the league in receiving yards.

Rice needs one 200-yard receiving game to tie Lance Alworth (5) for most career 200-yard receiving games. In 20 seasons, Rice has four 200-yard receiving games.

Rice needs 1,454 combined yards to become the first player in NFL history with 25,000 combined yards. In 20 seasons, Rice has gained an NFL-record 23,546 combined yards.

Rice needs 1,460 total yards from scrimmage to become the first player in NFL history to reach 25,000 scrimmage yards. In 20 seasons, Rice has gained an NFL-record 23,540 total yards from scrimmage.

Tim Brown needs eight receptions to pass Cris Carter (1,101) to move into second place all-time. Brown has 1,094 receptions in 17 seasons.

Brown needs 66 receiving yards to become the second player in NFL history (Jerry Rice, 22,895) with 15,000 career receiving yards. In 17 seasons, Brown has 14,934 receiving yards.

Brown has 100 touchdown receptions in 17 seasons and needs one to pass Steve Largent (100) to move into sole possession of third place all-time.

Brown needs 318 combined yards to become the fifth player in NFL history with 20,000 combined yards (see Faulk note). In 17

seasons, Brown has gained 19,682 combined yards.

Randy Moss, Oakland, needs 1,000 receiving yards to become the first player in NFL history with 1,000 receiving yards in each of his first eight seasons. Moss is the only player in NFL history with 1,000 receiving yards in each of his first seven seasons.

Marvin Harrison, Indianapolis, needs 100 receptions to pass Jerry Rice (4) to become the first player in NFL history with five 100-catch seasons. In nine seasons, Harrison has four seasons with 100 receptions.

Harrison has 845 career receptions in his first nine seasons and already has more catches than any player in NFL history had in their first 10.

Harrison needs 96 receptions to pass Irving Fryar (851) and Art Monk (940) to move into fifth place all-time. In nine seasons, Harrison has 845 receptions.

Harrison has three 1,500-receiving yard seasons in his nine-year career and needs 1,500 receiving yards to tie Jerry Rice (4) for the most 1,500-receiving yard seasons.

Harrison has 47 100-yard receiving games in nine seasons and needs four to pass Michael Irvin (47) and Don Maynard (50) to move into second place all-time.

Harrison needs three touchdown receptions to pass Tim Brown (100) and Steve Largent (100) to move into third place all-time (see Brown and Owens notes). In nine seasons, Harrison has 98 touchdown receptions.

Terrell Owens, Philadelphia, needs six touchdown receptions to pass Marvin Harrison (98), Tim Brown (100), and Steve Largent (100) to move into third place all-time (see Brown and Harrison notes). In nine seasons, Owens has 95 touchdown receptions.

Jimmy Smith, Jacksonville, needs 1,000 receiving yards to pass Cris Carter and Steve Largent (8) to move into a second place tie with Tim Brown in 1,000-yard receiving seasons. In 12 seasons, Smith has eight 1,000-yard seasons.

Tony Gonzalez, Kansas City, needs nine touchdowns to pass Wesley Walls (54), Jerry Smith (60), and Shannon Sharpe (62) to become the all-time leader in touchdowns by a tight end in NFL history. In eight seasons, Gonzalez has 54 touchdowns.

Dante Hall, Kansas City, has five kickoff-return touchdowns in his five-year career. Hall needs one kickoff-return touchdown to tie Mel Gray (6), Ollie Matson (6), Gale Sayers (6) and Travis Williams (6) for the most in NFL history.

Hall needs one kick return touchdown (kickoff or punt) to pass Mel Gray (9), Ollie Matson (9) and Deion Sanders (9) to move into sole possession of third place all-time. In five seasons, Hall has nine combined kick return touchdowns.

Hall needs 2,000 combined net yards to join Marshall Faulk (1998-2001) as the only players to post 2,000 combined net yards in four consecutive seasons.

Aeneas Williams needs one interception return for a touchdown to pass Ken Houston (9) and Deion Sanders (9) to move into second place all-time (see Sanders note). In 14 seasons, Williams has nine interception returns for touchdowns.

Deion Sanders needs one interception return for a touchdown to pass Ken Houston (9) and Aeneas Williams (9) to move into second place all-time (see Williams note). In 13 seasons, Sanders has nine interception returns for touchdowns.

Jason Elam, Denver, has scored 100 points in each of his first 12 seasons, the longest streak all-time. Elam needs 100 points to become the first player in NFL history with 100 points in each of his first 13 seasons.

Adam Vinatieri, New England, has scored 100 points in each of his first nine seasons and needs 100 points to become the second player (Jason Elam, 12) in NFL history with 100 points in each of his first 10 seasons.

Ryan Longwell, Green Bay, has scored 100 points in each of his first eight seasons and needs 100 points to become the third player (Jason Elam, 12 and Adam Vinatieri, 9) in NFL history with 100 points in each of his first nine seasons.

70th Annual NFL Draft, April 23-24, 2005
*Denotes Compensatory Selection

ARIZONA CARDINALS
1. Antrel Rolle—8, DB, Miami
2. J.J. Arrington—44, RB, California
3. Eric Green—75, DB, Virginia Tech
   Darryl Blackstock—95, LB, Virginia, from New England
4. Elton Brown—111, G, Virginia
5. Lance Mitchell—168, LB, Oklahoma, from New England
7. LeRon McCoy—226, WR, Indiana (Pa.)

ATLANTA FALCONS
1. Roddy White—27, WR, Alabama-Birmingham
2. Jonathan Babineaux—59, DT, Iowa
3. Jordan Beck—90, LB, Cal Poly-San Luis Obispo
4. Chauncey Davis—128, DE, Florida State
5. Michael Boley—160, LB, Southern Mississippi,
   from Denver
   Frank Omiyale—163, T, Tennessee Tech
6. DeAndra Cobb—201, RB, Michigan State
7. Darrell Shropshire—241, DT, South Carolina

BALTIMORE RAVENS
1. Mark Clayton—22, WR, Oklahoma
2. Dan Cody—53, LB, Oklahoma
   Adam Terry—64, T, Syracuse, from New England
4. Jason Brown—124, C, North Carolina
5. Justin Green—158, RB, Montana
6.* Derek Anderson—213, QB, Oregon State
7. Mike Smith—234, LB, Texas Tech

BUFFALO BILLS
2. Roscoe Parrish—55, WR, Miami
3. Kevin Everett—86, TE, Miami
4. Duke Preston—122, C, Illinois
5. Eric King—156, DB, Wake Forest
6. Justin Geisinger—197, G, Vanderbilt
7. Lionel Gates—236, RB, Louisville

CAROLINA PANTHERS
1. Thomas Davis—14, DB, Georgia
2. Eric Shelton—54, RB, Louisville, from Seattle
3. Evan Mathis—79, G, Alabama
   Atiyyah Ellison—89, DT, Missouri, from Green Bay
4. Stefan LeFors—121, QB, Louisville, from Seattle
5. Adam Seward—149, LB, Nevada-Las Vegas
   Geoff Hangartner—169, T, Texas A&M
   * Ben Emanuel—171, DB, UCLA
6. Jovan Haye—189, DE, Vanderbilt
   Joe Berger—207, T, Michigan Tech

CHICAGO BEARS
1. Cedric Benson—4, RB, Texas
2. Mark Bradley—39, WR, Oklahoma
4. Kyle Orton—106, QB, Purdue
5. Airese Currie—140, WR, Clemson
6. Chris Harris—181, DB, Louisiana-Monroe
7. Rodriques Wilson—220, LB, South Carolina

CINCINNATI BENGALS
1. David Pollack—17, LB, Georgia
2. Odell Thurman—48, LB, Georgia
3. Chris Henry—83, WR, West Virginia
4. Eric Ghiaciuc—119, C, Central Michigan
5. Adam Kieft—153, T, Central Michigan
6. Tab Perry—190, WR, UCLA
7. Jonathan Fanene—233, DE, Utah

CLEVELAND BROWNS
1. Braylon Edwards—3, WR, Michigan
2. Brodney Pool—34, DB, Oklahoma
3. Charlie Frye—67, QB, Akron
4. Antonio Perkins—103, DB, Oklahoma
5. David McMillan—139, LB, Kansas
6. Nick Speegle—176, LB, New Mexico
   Andrew Hoffman—203, DE, Virginia,
   from San Diego through Tampa Bay
7. Jon Dunn—217, T, Virginia Tech

DALLAS COWBOYS
1. Demarcus Ware—11, DE, Troy
   Marcus Spears—20, DE, Louisiana State, from Buffalo
2. Kevin Burnett—42, LB, Tennessee
4. Marion Barber—109, RB, Minnesota
   Chris Canty—132, DE, Virginia, from Philadelphia
6.* Justin Beriault—208, DB, Ball State
   * Rob Petitti—209, T, Pittsburgh
7. Jay Ratliff—224, DT, Auburn

DENVER BRONCOS
2. Darrent Williams—56, DB, Oklahoma State
3. Karl Paymah—76, DB, Washington State,
   from Washington
   * Domonique Foxworth—97, DB, Maryland
   * Maurice Clarett—101, RB, Ohio State
6. Chris Myers—200, T, Miami
7. Paul Ernster—239, K, Northern Arizona

DETROIT LIONS
1. Mike Williams—10, WR, Southern California
2. Shaun Cody—37, DT, Southern California,
   from Tennessee
3. Stanley Wilson—72, DB, Stanford
5. Dan Orlovsky—145, QB, Connecticut
6. Bill Swancutt—184, DE, Oregon State
   Johnathan Goddard—206, LB, Marshall, from New England

GREEN BAY PACKERS
1. Aaron Rodgers—24, QB, California
2. Nick Collins—51, DB, Bethune-Cookman,
   from New Orleans
   Terrence Murphy—58, WR, Texas A&M
4. Marviel Underwood—115, DB, San Diego State,
   from Carolina
   Brady Poppinga—125, LB, Brigham Young
5. Junius Coston—143, C, North Carolina A&T,
   from Oakland
   Michael Hawkins—167, DB, Oklahoma, from Philadelphia
6. Mike Montgomery—180, DE, Texas A&M, from Oakland
   Craig Bragg, Craig—195, WR, UCLA,
   from Baltimore through New England
7. Kurt Campbell—245, DB, Albany (N.Y.), from Philadelphia
   William Whitticker—246, G, Michigan State,
   from New England

HOUSTON TEXANS
1. Travis Johnson—16, DE, Florida State, from New Orleans
3. Vernand Morency—73, RB, Oklahoma State, from Dallas
4. Jerome Mathis—114, WR, Hampton
5. Drew Hodgdon—151, C, Arizona State
6. C.C. Brown—188, DB, Louisiana-Lafayette
7. Kenneth Pettway—227, LB, Grambling

INDIANAPOLIS COLTS
1. Marlin Jackson—29, DB, Michigan
2. Kelvin Hayden—60, DB, Illinois
3. Vincent Burns—92, DE, Kentucky
4. Dylan Gandy—129, G, Texas Tech
  * Matt Giordano—135, DB, California
5. Jonathan Welsh—148, DE, Wisconsin,
     from Dallas through Philadelphia
   Rob Hunt—165, C, North Dakota State
  * Tyjuan Hagler—173, LB, Cincinnati
6. Dave Rayner—202, K, Michigan State
7. Anthony Davis—243, RB, Wisconsin

JACKSONVILLE JAGUARS
1. Matt Jones—21, WR, Arkansas
2. Khalif Barnes—52, T, Washington
3. Scott Starks—87, DB, Wisconsin
4. Alvin Pearman—127, RB, Virginia, from New York Jets
5. Gerald Sensabaugh—157, DB, North Carolina
6. Chad Owens—185, KR, Hawaii,
     from Dallas through Oakland and New York Jets
   Patrick Thomas—194, LB, North Carolina State
7. Chris Roberson—237, DB, Eastern Michigan

KANSAS CITY CHIEFS
1. Derrick Johnson—15, LB, Texas
3.* Dustin Colquitt—99, P, Tennessee
4. Craphonso Thorpe—116, WR, Florida State
5. Boomer Grigsby—138, LB, Illinois State, from Miami
   Alphonso Hodge—147, DB, Miami (Ohio), from Detroit
6. Will Svitek—187, T, Stanford
   Khari Long—199, DE, Baylor, from Green Bay
7. James Kilian—229, QB, Tulsa
   Jeremy Parquet—238, T, Southern Mississippi,
     from Green Bay

MIAMI DOLPHINS
1. Ronnie Brown—2, RB, Auburn
2. Matt Roth—46, DE, Iowa, from Kansas City
3. Channing Crowder—70, LB, Florida, from Chicago
4. Travis Daniels—104, DB, Louisiana State
5. Anthony Alabi—162, T, TCU,
     from Green Bay through Kansas City
7. Kevin Vickerson—216, DT, Michigan State

MINNESOTA VIKINGS
1. Troy Williamson—7, WR, South Carolina, from Oakland
   Erasmus James—18, DE, Wisconsin
2. Marcus Johnson—49, G, Mississippi
3. Dustin Fox—80, DB, Ohio State
4. Ciatrick Fason—112, RB, Florida, from Washington
6. C.J. Mosley—191, DT, Missouri
7. Adrian Ward—219, DB, Texas-El Paso, from Oakland

NEW ENGLAND PATRIOTS
1. Logan Mankins—32, G, Fresno State
3. Ellis Hobbs—84, DB, Iowa State, from Baltimore
  * Nick Kaczur—100, T, Toledo
4. James Sanders—133, DB, Fresno State
5. * Ryan Claridge—170, LB, Nevada-Las Vegas
7. Matt Cassel—230, QB, Southern California,
     from Minnesota through New York Jets and Oakland
  * Andy Stokes—255, TE, William Penn

NEW ORLEANS SAINTS
1. Jammal Brown—13, T, Oklahoma, from Houston
2. Josh Bullocks—40, DB, Nebraska, from Washington
3. Alfred Fincher—82, LB, Connecticut
4. Chase Lyman—118, WR, California
5. Adrian McPherson—152, QB, Florida State
6. Jason Jefferson—193, DT, Wisconsin
7. Jimmy Verdon—232, DE, Arizona State

NEW YORK GIANTS
2. Corey Webster—43, DB, Louisiana State
3. Justin Tuck—74, DE, Notre Dame
4. Brandon Jacobs—110, RB, Southern Illinois
6. Eric Moore—186, DE, Florida State

NEW YORK JETS
2. Mike Nugent—47, K, Ohio State,
     from Houston through Oakland
   Justin Miller—57, DB, Clemson
3. Sione Pouha—88, DT, Utah
4. Kerry Rhodes—123, DB, Louisville, from Jacksonville
5. Andre Maddox—161, DB, North Carolina State
6. Cedric Houston—182, RB, Tennessee,
     from Arizona through Oakland
   Joel Dreessen—198, TE, Colorado State
7. Harry Williams—240, WR, Tuskegee

OAKLAND RAIDERS
1. Fabian Washington—23, DB, Nebraska, from Seattle
2. Stanford Routt—38, DB, Houston
3. Andrew Walter—69, QB, Arizona State
   Kirk Morrison—78, LB, San Diego State, from Houston
6. Anttaj Hawthorne—175, DT, Wisconsin,
     from San Francisco through Philadelphia, Green Bay,
     and New England
  * Ryan Riddle—212, LB, California
  * Pete McMahon—214, T, Iowa

PHILADELPHIA EAGLES
1. Mike Patterson—31, DT, Southern California
2. Reggie Brown—35, WR, Georgia, from Miami
   Matt McCoy—63, LB, San Diego State
3. Ryan Moats—77, RB, Louisiana Tech, from Kansas City
4. Sean Considine—102, DB, Iowa, from San Francisco
   Todd Herremans—126, T, Saginaw Valley State,
     from Denver through Cleveland, Seattle, Carolina,
     and Green Bay
5. Trent Cole—146, LB, Cincinnati, from Washington
  * Scott Young—172, G, Brigham Young
6. * Calvin Armstrong—211, T, Washington State
7. * Keyonta Marshall—247, DT, Grand Valley State
  * David Bergeron—252, LB, Stanford

PITTSBURGH STEELERS
1. Heath Miller—30, TE, Virginia
2. Bryant McFadden—62, DB, Florida State
3. Trai Essex—93, T, Northwestern
4. Fred Gibson—131, WR, Georgia
5. Rian Wallace—166, LB, Temple
6. Chris Kemoeatu—204, G, Utah
7. Shaun Nua—228, DE, Brigham Young, from Carolina
   Noah Herron—244, RB, Northwestern

ST. LOUIS RAMS
1. Alex Barron—19, T, Florida State
2. Ronald Bartell—50, DB, Howard
3. Oshiomogho Atogwe—66, DB, Stanford, from Miami
   Richie Incognito—81, G, Nebraska
4. Jerome Carter—117, DB, Florida State
   * Claude Terrell—134, G, New Mexico
5. Jerome Collins—144, TE, Notre Dame,
   from New York Giants through San Diego and Tampa Bay
6. Dante Ridgeway—192, WR, Ball State
   * Reggie Hodges—210, P, Ball State
7. * Ryan Fitzpatrick—250, QB, Harvard
   * Madison Hedgecock—251, RB, North Carolina

SAN DIEGO CHARGERS
1. Shawne Merriman—12, LB, Maryland,
   from New York Giants
   Luis Castillo—28, DT, Northwestern
2. Vincent Jackson—61, WR, Northern Colorado
4. Darren Sproles—130, RB, Kansas State
5. Wesley Britt—164, T, Alabama
6. Wes Sims—177, G, Oklahoma, from Miami
7. Scott Mruczkowski—242, C, Bowling Green

SAN FRANCISCO 49ERS
1. Alex Smith—1, QB, Utah
2. David Baas—33, G, Michigan
3. Frank Gore—65, RB, Miami
   Adam Snyder—94, T, Oregon, from Philadelphia
5. Ronald Fields—137, DT, Mississippi State
   * Rasheed Marshall—174, WR, West Virginia
6. Derrick Johnson—205, DB, Washington, from Philadelphia
7. Daven Holly—215, DB, Cincinnati
   Marcus Maxwell—223, WR, Oregon, from Detroit
   * Patrick Estes—248, TE, Virginia
   * Billy Bajema—249, TE, Oklahoma State

SEATTLE SEAHAWKS
1. Chris Spencer—26, C, Mississippi,
   from New York Jets through Oakland
2. Lofa Tatupu—45, LB, Southern California, from Carolina
3. David Greene—85, QB, Georgia
   * LeRoy Hill—98, LB, Clemson
4. Ray Willis—105, T, Florida State, from Oakland
5. Jeb Huckeba—159, DE, Arkansas
6. Tony Jackson—196, RB, Iowa
7. Cornelius Wortham—235, LB, Alabama
   * Doug Nienhuis—254, G, Oregon State

TAMPA BAY BUCCANEERS
1. Carnell Williams—5, RB, Auburn
2. Barrett Ruud—36, LB, Nebraska
3. Alex Smith—71, TE, Stanford
   Chris Colmer—91, T, North Carolina State, from San Diego
4. Dan Buenning—107, G, Wisconsin
5. Donte Nicholson—141, DB, Oklahoma
   Larry Brackins—155, WR, Pearl River J.C., from St. Louis
6. Anthony Bryant—178, DT, Alabama
7. Rick Razzano—221, RB, Mississippi
   Paris Warren—225, WR, Utah, from New York Giants
   Hamza Abdullah—231, DB, Washington State,
   from St. Louis
   * J.R. Russell—253, WR, Louisville

TENNESSEE TITANS
1. Adam Jones—6, DB, West Virginia
2. Michael Roos—41, T, Eastern Washington, from Detroit
3. Courtney Roby—68, WR, Indiana
   * Brandon Jones—96, WR, Oklahoma
4. Vincent Fuller—108, DB, Virginia Tech
   David Stewart—113, T, Mississippi State, from Detroit
   * Roydell Williams—136, WR, Tulane
5. Damien Nash—142, RB, Missouri
   Daniel Loper—150, T, Texas Tech, from Kansas City
6. Bo Scaife—179, TE, Texas
7. Reynaldo Hill—218, DB, Florida

WASHINGTON REDSKINS
1. Carlos Rogers—9, DB, Auburn
   Jason Campbell—25, QB, Auburn, from Denver
4. Manuel White—120, RB, UCLA, from Minnesota
5. Robert McCune—154, LB, Louisville, from Minnesota
6. Jared Newberry—183, LB, Stanford
7. Nehemiah Broughton—222, RB, Citadel

NUMBER OF PLAYERS DRAFTED—2005

BY POSITION:

Defensive Backs	50
Linebackers	36
Wide Receivers	30
Tackles	26
Running Backs	26
Defensive Ends	20
Defensive Tackles	15
Guards	15
Quarterbacks	14
Tight Ends	9
Centers	8
Kickers	3
Punters	2
Kick Returner	1

BY COLLEGE:

Oklahoma	11
Florida State	9
Virginia	7
Wisconsin	7
Georgia	6
Louisville	6
Stanford	6
Auburn	5
California	5
Iowa	5
Miami	5
Southern California	5
Utah	5
Alabama	4
Michigan State	4
Nebraska	4
UCLA	4
Arizona State	3
Ball State	3
Brigham Young	3
Cincinnati	3
Clemson	3
Florida	3
Louisiana State	3
Michigan	3
Mississippi	3
Missouri	3
North Carolina	3
North Carolina State	3
Northwestern	3
Ohio State	3
Oklahoma State	3
Oregon State	3
San Diego State	3
South Carolina	3
Tennessee	3
Texas	3
Texas A&M	3
Texas Tech	3
Virginia Tech	3
Washington State	3
West Virginia	3
Arkansas	2
Central Michigan	2
Connecticut	2
Fresno State	2
Illinois	2
Maryland	2
Mississippi State	2
Nevada Las-Vegas	2
New Mexico	2
Notre Dame	2
Oregon	2
Southern Mississippi	2
Vanderbilt	2
Washington	2
Akron	1
Alabama-Birmingham	1
Albany (N.Y.)	1
Baylor	1
Bethune-Cookman	1
Bowling Green	1
Cal Poly-San Luis Obispo	1
Citadel	1
Colorado State	1
Eastern Michigan	1
Eastern Washington	1
Grambling	1
Grand Valley State	1
Hampton	1
Harvard	1
Hawaii	1
Houston	1
Howard	1
Illinois State	1
Indiana	1
Indiana (Pa.)	1
Iowa State	1
Kansas	1
Kansas State	1
Kentucky	1
Louisiana-Lafayette	1
Louisiana-Monroe	1
Louisiana Tech	1
Marshall	1
Miami (Ohio)	1
Michigan Tech	1
Minnesota	1
Montana	1
North Carolina A&T	1
North Dakota State	1
Northern Arizona	1
Northern Colorado	1
Pearl River J.C.	1
Pittsburgh	1
Purdue	1
Saginaw Valley State	1
Southern Illinois	1
Syracuse	1
TCU	1
Temple	1
Tennessee Tech	1
Texas-El Paso	1
Toledo	1
Troy	1
Tulane	1
Tulsa	1
Tuskegee	1
Wake Forest	1
William Penn	1

BY CONFERENCE:

Southeastern	37
Atlantic Coast	36
Big 12	34
Pacific 10	33
Big Ten	30
Mountain West	16
Conference USA	15
Mid-American	11
Big East	8
Western Athletic	6
Mid-Eastern Athletic	4
Big Sky	3
Great Lakes Intercollegiate Athletic	3
Great West Football	3
Sun Belt	3
Gateway Football	2
Independent	2
Ivy League	1
Mid-States Football Association	1
Mississippi C.C. Athletic Association	1
Northeast	1
Ohio Valley	1
Pennsylvania State Athletic	1
Southern	1
Southern Intercollegiate Athletic	1
Southwestern Athletic	1

UNDERCLASSMEN IN THE DRAFT

Year	Entered	Drafted	In Top 10
1989	25	12	3
1990	38	18	5
1991	33	22	2
1992	48	25	5
1993	46	24	5
1994	43	26	6
1995	42	22	2
1996	46	21	4
1997	44	27	7
1998	41	20	3
1999	42	27	5
2000	31	20	4
2001	54	31	5
2002	43	26	5
2003	54	32	5
2004	44	35	5
2005	57	38	4

WAIVERS

The waiver system is a procedure by which player contracts or NFL rights to players are made available by a club to other clubs in the League. During the procedure, the 31 other clubs either file claims to obtain the players or waive the opportunity to do so—thus the term "waiver." Claiming clubs are assigned players on a priority based on the inverse of won-and-lost standing. The claiming period is three business days from the beginning of the League Year through the last business day before July 4, and 24 hours after July 4 through the conclusion of the regular season. If a player passes through waivers unclaimed, he becomes a free agent. All waivers are no recall and no withdrawal. Under the Collective Bargaining Agreement, from the beginning of the waiver system each year through the trading deadline (October 18, 2005), any veteran who has acquired four years of pension credit is not subject to the waiver system if the club desires to release him. After the trading deadline, such players are subject to the waiver system.

ACTIVE/INACTIVE LIST

The Active/Inactive List is the principal status for players participating for a club. It consists of all players under contract who are eligible for preseason, regular-season, and postseason games. Teams are permitted to open training camp with no more than 80 players under contract and thereafter must meet two mandatory roster reductions prior to the season opener. Teams will be permitted an Active List of 45 players and an Inactive List of eight players for each regular-season and postseason game. Provided that a club has two quarterbacks on its 45-player Active List, a third quarterback from its Inactive List is permitted to dress for the game, but if he enters the game during the first three quarters, the other two quarterbacks are thereafter prohibited from playing. Teams also are permitted to establish Practice Squads of up to eight players who are eligible to participate in practice, but these players remain free agents and are eligible to sign with any other team in the league.

August 30	Roster reduction to 65 players
September 4	Roster reduction to 53 players
September 5	Teams establish a Practice Squad of up to eight players

In addition to the squad limits described above, the overall roster limit of 80 players remains in effect throughout the regular season and postseason. The overall limit is applicable to players on a team's Active, Inactive, and certain Exempt Lists, players on the Practice Squad, and players on the Reserve List as Injured, Physically Unable to Perform, Non-Football Illness/Injury, and Suspended by Club.

RESERVE LIST

The Reserve List is a status for players who, for reasons of injury, retirement, military service, or other circumstances, are not immediately available for participation with a club. Players on Reserve/Injured are not eligible to practice or return to the Active/Inactive List in the same season that they are placed on Reserve. Players in the category of Reserve/Retired, Reserve/Did Not Report, Reserve/Exclusive Rights, and players who were placed in the category of Reserve/Left Squad in a previous season may not be reinstated during the period from 30 days before the end of the regular season through the postseason.

TRADES

Unrestricted trading between the AFC and NFC is allowed in 2005 through October 18, after which trading will end until 2006.

ANNUAL ACTIVE PLAYER LIMITS

NFL

Year(s)	Limit
1991-2005	45**
1985-90	45
1983-84	49
1982	45†-49
1978-81	45
1975-77	43
1974	47
1964-73	40
1963	37
1961-62	36
1960	38
1959	36
1957-58	35
1951-56	33
1949-50	32
1948	35
1947	35*-34
1945-46	33
1943-44	28
1940-42	33
1938-39	30
1936-37	25
1935	24
1930-34	20
1926-29	18
1925	16

** 45 plus a third quarterback
† 45 for first two games
* 35 for first three games

AFL

Year(s)	Limit
1966-69	40
1965	38
1964	34
1962-63	33
1960-61	35

NFL FREE AGENCY MOVEMENT

The following chart details veteran free agents who signed with new teams:

	Unrestricted	Restricted	Transition	Franchise	TOTALS
1993	100	8	4	1	113
1994	101	0	4	0	105
1995	154	6	2	0	162
1996	100	4	2	0	106
1997	86	2	2	0	90
1998	112	4	1	2	119
1999	115	2	1	0	118
2000	107	4	0	0	111
2001	93	4	0	0	97
2002	130	1	0	0	131
2003	111	5	1	0	117
2004	124	1	1	0	126

The following procedures will be used to break standings ties for postseason playoffs and to determine regular-season schedules.

Note: Tie games count as one-half win and one-half loss for both clubs.

TO BREAK A TIE WITHIN A DIVISION

If, at the end of the regular season, two or more clubs in the same division finish with the best won-lost-tied percentage, the following steps will be taken until a champion is determined:

TWO CLUBS

1. Head-to-head (best won-lost-tied percentage in games between the clubs.)
2. Best won-lost-tied percentage in games played within the division.
3. Best won-lost-tied percentage in common games.
4. Best won-lost-tied percentage in games played within the conference.
5. Strength of victory.
6. Strength of schedule.
7. Best combined ranking among conference teams in points scored and points allowed.
8. Best combined ranking among all teams in points scored and points allowed.
9. Best net points in common games.
10. Best net points in all games.
11. Best net touchdowns in all games.
12. Coin toss.

THREE OR MORE CLUBS

(Note: If two clubs remain tied after a third club is eliminated during any step, tie-breaker reverts to Step 1 of the two-club format.)

1. Head-to-head (best won-lost-tied percentage in games among the clubs.)
2. Best won-lost-tied percentage in games played within the division.
3. Best won-lost-tied percentage in common games.
4. Best won-lost-tied percentage in games played within the conference.
5. Strength of victory.
6. Strength of schedule.
7. Best combined ranking among conference teams in points scored and points allowed.
8. Best combined ranking among all teams in points scored and points allowed.
9. Best net points in common games.
10. Best net points in all games.
11. Best net touchdowns in all games.
12. Coin toss.

TO BREAK A TIE FOR THE WILD-CARD TEAM

If it is necessary to break ties to determine the two Wild Card clubs from each conference, the following steps will be taken:

A. If all the tied clubs are from the same division, apply division tie-breaker.

B. If the tied clubs are from different divisions, apply the following steps:

TWO CLUBS

1. Head-to-head, if applicable.
2. Best won-lost-tied percentage in the games played within the conference.
3. Best won-lost-tied percentage in common games, minimum of four.
4. Strength of victory.
5. Strength of schedule.
6. Best combined ranking among conference teams in points scored and points allowed.
7. Best combined ranking among all teams in points scored and points allowed.
8. Best net points in conference games.
9. Best net points in all games.
10. Best net touchdowns in all games.
11. Coin toss.

THREE OR MORE CLUBS

1. Apply division tie-breaker to eliminate all but highest ranked club in each division prior to proceeding to Step 2. The original seeding within a division upon application of the division tie-breaker remains the same for all subsequent applications of the procedure that are necessary to identify the Wild Card participants.
2. Head-to-head sweep (apply only if one club has defeated each of the others or one club has lost to each of the others).
3. Best won-lost-tied percentage in games played within the conference.
4. Best won-lost-tied percentage in common games, minimum of four.
5. Strength of victory.
6. Strength of schedule.
7. Best combined ranking among conference teams in points scored and points allowed.
8. Best combined ranking among all teams in points scored and points allowed.
9. Best net points in conference games.
10. Best net points in all games.
11. Best net touchdowns in all games.
12. Coin toss.

When the first Wild Card team has been identified, the procedure is repeated to name the second Wild Card (i.e., eliminate all but the highest ranked club in each division prior to proceeding to Step 2.) In situations where three teams from the same division are involved in the procedure, the original seeding of the teams remains the same for subsequent applications of the tie-breaker if the top-ranked team in that division qualifies for a Wild Card berth.

OTHER TIE-BREAKING PROCEDURES

1. Only one club advances to the playoffs in any tie-breaking step. Remaining tied clubs revert to the first step of the applicable division or Wild Card tie-breakers. As an example, if two clubs remain tied in any tie-breaker step after all other clubs have been eliminated, the procedure reverts to Step 1 of the two-club format to determine the winner. When one club wins the tie-breaker, all other clubs revert to Step 1 of the applicable two-club or three-club format.
2. In comparing records against common opponents among tied teams, the best won-lost-tied percentage is the deciding factor since teams may have played an unequal number of games.
3. To determine home-field priority among division-titlists, apply Wild Card tie-breakers.
4. To determine home-field priority for Wild Card qualifiers, apply division tie-breakers (if teams are from the same division) or Wild Card tie-breakers (if teams are from different divisions).

TIE-BREAKING PROCEDURE FOR SELECTION MEETING

If two or more clubs are tied in the selection order, the strength-of-schedule tie-breaker is applied, subject to the following exceptions for playoff clubs:

1. The Super Bowl winner is last and the Super Bowl loser next-to-last.
2. Any non-Super Bowl playoff club involved in a tie shall be assigned priority within its segment below that of non-playoff clubs and in the order that the playoff club exited from the playoffs. Thus, within a tied segment a playoff club that loses in the Wild Card game will have priority over a playoff club that loses in the Divisional playoff game, which in turn will have priority over a club that loses in the Conference Championship game. If two tied clubs exited the playoffs in the same round, the tie is broken by strength of schedule.

If any ties cannot be broken by strength of schedule, the divisional or conference tie-breakers, whichever are applicable, are applied. Any ties that still exist are broken by a coin flip.

For the 2004-08 seasons, the NFL will continue to employ a system of Referee Replay Review to aid officiating.

Prior to the two-minute warning of each half, a Coaches' Challenge System will be in effect. After the two-minute warning, and throughout any overtime period, a Referee Review will be initiated by a Replay Assistant from a Replay Booth.

The following procedures will be used:

REVIEWS BY REFEREE: All Replay Reviews will be conducted by the Referee on a field-level monitor after consultation with the other covering official(s), prior to review. A decision will be reversed only when the Referee has *indisputable visual evidence* available to him that warrants the change.

COACHES' CHALLENGE: In each game, a team will be permitted two challenges that will initiate Referee Replay reviews. Each challenge will require the use of a team time out. If a challenge is upheld, the time out will be restored to the challenging team. If both challenges are upheld, a third challenge will be awarded to the challenging team. No challenges will be recognized from a team that has exhausted its time outs.

REPLAY ASSISTANT'S REQUEST FOR REVIEW: After the two-minute warning of each half, and throughout any overtime period, any review will be initiated by a Replay Assistant. There is no limit to the number of reviews that may be initiated by the Replay Assistant. His ability to initiate a review will be unrelated to the number of time outs that either team has remaining, and no time out will be charged for any review initiated by the Replay Assistant.

TIME LIMIT: Each review will be a maximum of 90 seconds in length, timed from when the Referee begins his review of the replay at the field-level monitor.

REVIEWABLE PLAYS: The Replay System will cover the following play situations only:

A) **PLAYS GOVERNED BY SIDELINE, GOAL LINE, END ZONE, AND END LINE:**
1. Scoring plays, including a runner breaking the plane of the goal line.
2. Pass complete/incomplete/intercepted at sideline, goal line, end zone, and end line.
3. Runner/receiver in or out of bounds.
4. Recovery of loose ball in or out of bounds.

B) **PASSING PLAYS:**
1. Pass ruled complete/incomplete/intercepted in the field of play.

2. Touching of a forward pass by an ineligible receiver.
3. Touching of a forward pass by a defensive player.
4. Quarterback (Passer) forward pass or fumble.
5. Illegal forward pass beyond line of scrimmage.
6. Illegal forward pass after change of possession.
7. Forward or backward pass thrown from behind line of scrimmage.

C) **OTHER DETECTABLE INFRACTIONS:**
1. Runner ruled not down by defensive contact.
2. Forward progress with respect to first down.
3. Touching of a kick.
4. Number of players on the field.

INSTANT REPLAY HISTORY

From 1986-1991, a limited system of Instant Replay was used on a year-by-year basis. Replay also was experimented with during the 1996 and 1998 preseasons. For the 1999 season, the NFL introduced a system of Referee Replay Review to aid officiating. That system was extended on a one-year basis for the 2000 season and and then approved for the next three years through 2003. In March 2004, the system was extended for five seasons through 2008.

Following are the results of the different systems:

REGULAR SEASON, 1986-1991

Year	Games	Plays Closely Reviewed	Reversals
1986	224	374	38
1987	210	490	57
1988	224	537	53
1989	224	492	65
1990	224	504	73
1991	224	570	90
TOTAL	1,330	2,967	376

PRESEASON, 1996, 1998

Year	Games	Challenges	Reversals
1996	10	13	3
1998	10	10	3
TOTAL	20	23	6

REGULAR SEASON, 1999-2004

Year	Games	Total Replay Reviews	Challenges	Reversals
1999	248	195	133	57
2000	248	247	179	84
2001	248	258	191	89
2002	256	294	208	94
2003	256	255	184	66
2004	256	283	233	88
TOTAL	1,512	1,532	1,128	478

The AFC

American Football Conference
North Division
Team Colors: Black, Purple, and Metallic
Gold
1 Winning Drive
Owings Mills, Maryland 21117
Telephone: (410) 701-4000

2005 SCHEDULE
PRESEASON
Aug. 13 at Atlanta.............................7:30
Aug. 20 **Philadelphia** 8:00
Aug. 26 at New Orleans..................7:00
Sept. 1 **Washington** 8:00

REGULAR SEASON
Sept. 11 **Indianapolis**.......................8:30
Sept. 18 at Tennessee 12:00
Sept. 25 Open Date
Oct. 2 **New York Jets** 4:05
Oct. 9 at Detroit 1:00
Oct. 16 **Cleveland** 1:00
Oct. 23 at Chicago.........................3:15
Oct. 31 at Pittsburgh (Mon.) 9:00
Nov. 6 **Cincinnati** 1:00
Nov. 13 at Jacksonville...................1:00
Nov. 20 **Pittsburgh**.........................4:15
Nov. 27 at Cincinnati 1:00
Dec. 4 **Houston** 1:00
Dec. 11 at Denver............................2:15
Dec. 19 **Green Bay** (Mon.) 9:00
Dec. 25 **Minnesota** 8:30
Jan. 1 at Cleveland 1:00

Stadium: M&T Bank Stadium
(opened in 1998)
•**Capacity:** 69,084
1101 Russell Street
Baltimore, Maryland 21230
Playing Surface: Sportexe Momentum
Training Camp: McDaniel College
2 College Hill
Westminster, Maryland
21157

M&T BANK STADIUM

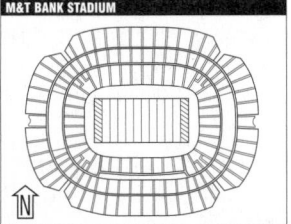

CLUB OFFICIALS
Owner: Steve Bisciotti
President: Dick Cass
Executive Vice President/General
Manager: Ozzie Newsome
Senior Vice President/Public and
Community Relations: Kevin Byrne
Senior Vice President/Business Ventures:
Dennis Mannion
Vice President of Football Administration:
Pat Moriarty
Senior Director of Operations: Bob Eller
Director of Publications/Assistant
Director of Public Relations:
Francine Lubera
Director of Pro Personnel: George Kokinis
Director of College Scouting:
Eric DeCosta
Director of Player Development:
O.J. Brigance
Assistant Director of Pro Personnel:
Vince Newsome
Scouts: Chad Alexander, Joe Douglas,
Joe Hortiz, Daniel Jeremiah,
Lionel Vital, Jeremiah Washburn,
Andrew Weidel
Head Trainer: Bill Tessendorf
Equipment Manager: Ed Carroll
Video Director: Jon Dubé
Senior Director, Finance: Jeff Goering
Senior Director, Business Development:
Mark Burdett
Senior Director, Information Technology:
Bill Jankowski
Senior Director, Ticket Sales and
Operations: Baker Koppelman
Senior Director, Stadium Operations:
Roy Sommerhof
Senior Director of Broadcasting:
Larry Rosen
Director of Premium Services/Suites:
Theresa Abato
Director, Community Relations:
Kenny Abrams
Director, Corporate Partnerships:
Ed Burchell
Director, Marketing: Lisa Dixon
Director, Corporate Sales: Kevin Rochlitz
Director, Security: Darren Sanders
Director, Corporate Sales Administration:
Erin Stewart

COACHING HISTORY
(77-73-1)
Records include postseason games
1996-98   Ted Marchibroda 16-31-1
1999-2004 Brian Billick...............61-42-0

ATTENDANCE
Home 550,783   Away 557,431
Total 1,108,214
Single-game home record,
69,924 (11/21/04)
Single-season home record, 550,783
(2004)

2005 DRAFT CHOICES
Round	Name	Pos.	College
1	Mark Clayton	WR	Oklahoma
2	Dan Cody	LB	Oklahoma
	Adam Terry	T	Syracuse
4	Jason Brown	C	North Carolina
5	Justin Green	RB	Montana
6	Derek Anderson	QB	Oregon State
7	Mike Smith	LB	Texas Tech

2004 TEAM RECORD

PRESEASON (3-1)

Date	Result	Opponent
8/12	W 24-0	Atlanta
8/20	L 17-26	at Philadelphia
8/28	W 17-6	Detroit
9/2	W 27-17	at N.Y. Giants

REGULAR SEASON (9-7)

Date	Result	Opponent	Att.
9/12	L 3-20	at Cleveland	73,068
9/19	W 30-13	Pittsburgh	69,859
9/26	W 23-9	at Cincinnati	65,575
10/4	L 24-27	Kansas City	69,827
10/10	W 17-10	at Washington	90,287
10/24	W 20-6	Buffalo	69,809
10/31	L 10-15	at Philadelphia	67,715
11/7	W 27-13	Cleveland	69,781
11/14	W 20-17	at N.Y. Jets (OT)	77,826
11/21	W 30-10	Dallas	69,924
11/28	L 3-24	at New England	68,756
12/5	L 26-27	Cincinnati	69,695
12/12	W 37-14	N.Y. Giants	69,856
12/19	L 10-20	at Indianapolis	57,240
12/26	L 7-20	at Pittsburgh	64,227
1/2	W 30-23	Miami	69,843

(OT) Overtime

SCORE BY PERIODS

Ravens	63	89	75	87	3 —	317
Opponents	46	59	57	106	0 —	268

2004 TEAM STATISTICS

	Ravens	Opp.
Total First Downs	260	273
Rushing	103	88
Passing	135	158
Penalty	22	27
3rd Down: Made/Att	81/231	75/218
3rd Down Pct.	35.1	34.4
4th Down: Made/Att	4/15	2/8
4th Down Pct.	26.7	25.0
Possession Avg.	29:36	30:24
Total Net Yards	4375	4803
Avg. Per Game	273.4	300.2
Total Plays	991	1009
Avg. Per Play	4.4	4.8
Net Yards Rushing	2063	1681
Avg. Per Game	128.9	105.1
Total Rushes	491	469
Net Yards Passing	2312	3122
Avg. Per Game	144.5	195.1
Sacked/Yards Lost	35/247	39/264
Gross Yards	2559	3386
Att./Completions	465/258	501/276
Completion Pct.	55.5	55.1
Had Intercepted	11	21
Punts/Average	97/40.6	94/40.1
Net Punting Avg.	97/34.6	94/33.1
Penalties/Yards	94/894	101/798
Fumbles/Ball Lost	26/12	23/13
Touchdowns	33	27
Rushing	11	9
Passing	13	14
Returns	9	4

2004 INDIVIDUAL STATISTICS

PASSING	Att.	Comp.	Yds.	Pct.	TD	Int.	Tkld.	Rate
Boller	464	258	2,559	55.6	13	11	35/247	70.9
Hymes	1	0	0	0.0	0	0	0/0	39.6
Ravens	465	258	2,559	55.5	13	11	35/247	70.7
Opponents	501	276	3,386	55.1	14	21	39/264	68.0

SCORING	TD R	TD P	TD Rt	PAT	FG	Saf	PTS
Stover	0	0	0	30/30	29/32	0	117
J. Lewis	7	0	0	0/0	0/0	0	42
Moore	0	4	0	0/0	0/0	0	26
Heap	0	3	0	0/0	0/0	0	18
Sams	1	0	2	0/0	0/0	0	18
Hymes	0	2	0	0/0	0/0	0	12
McAlister	0	0	2	0/0	0/0	0	12
Reed	0	0	2	0/0	0/0	0	12
C. Taylor	2	0	0	0/0	0/0	0	12
Boller	1	0	0	0/0	0/0	0	6
Dinkins	0	1	0	0/0	0/0	0	6
J. Johnson	0	0	1	0/0	0/0	0	6
K. Johnson	0	1	0	0/0	0/0	0	6
Jones	0	1	0	0/0	0/0	0	6
Sanders	0	0	1	0/0	0/0	0	6
Wilcox	0	1	0	0/0	0/0	0	6
Williams	0	0	1	0/0	0/0	0	6
Ravens	11	13	9	30/30	29/32	0	317
Opponents	9	14	4	24/24	26/31	1	268

2-Pt. Conversions: Moore.
Ravens 1-3, Opponents 1-3.

RUSHING	Att.	Yds.	Avg.	LG	TD
J. Lewis	235	1,006	4.3	75t	7
C. Taylor	160	714	4.5	47	2
Boller	53	189	3.6	19	1
White	14	62	4.4	16	0
M. Smith	12	48	4.0	13	0
Ricard	10	36	3.6	14	0
Sams	4	19	4.8	8	1
K. Johnson	1	0	0.0	0	0
Stewart	1	-1	-1.0	-1	0
Sanders	1	-10	-10.0	-10	0
Ravens	491	2,063	4.2	75t	11
Opponents	469	1,681	3.6	35t	9

RECEIVING	No.	Yds.	Avg.	LG	TD
K. Johnson	35	373	10.7	35	1
T. Taylor	34	421	12.4	47	0
C. Taylor	30	184	6.1	23	0
Heap	27	303	11.2	37	3
Hymes	26	323	12.4	57t	2
Wilcox	25	219	8.8	20	1
Moore	24	293	12.2	52	4
Jones	20	152	7.6	19	1
Ricard	11	39	3.5	8	0
J. Lewis	10	116	11.6	46	0
Dinkins	9	94	10.4	18	1
White	2	4	2.0	6	0
M. Smith	2	31	15.5	25	0
Darling	2	5	2.5	4	0
Sams	1	2	2.0	2	0
Ravens	258	2,559	9.9	57t	13
Opponents	276	3,386	12.3	76t	14

INTERCEPTIONS	No.	Yds.	Avg.	LG	TD
Reed	9	358	39.8	106t	1
Williams	3	156	52.0	94	1
Sanders	3	87	29.0	48t	1
McAlister	1	51	51.0	51t	1
Baxter	1	33	33.0	33	0
Thomas	1	8	8.0	8	0
J. Johnson	1	6	6.0	6t	1
Weaver	1	1	1.0	1	0
Demps	1	0	0.0	0	0
Ravens	21	700	33.3	106t	5
Opponents	11	172	15.6	71	0

PUNTING	No.	Yds.	Avg.	In 20	LG
Zastudil	73	2,948	40.4	26	61
Murphy	18	777	43.2	6	54
Stewart	5	177	35.4	2	42
Stover	1	33	33.0	0	33
Ravens	97	3,935	40.6	34	61
Opponents	94	3,767	40.1	24	59

PUNT RETURNS	No.	FC	Yds.	Avg.	LG	TD
Sams	55	12	575	10.5	78t	2
Sanders	5	0	41	8.2	23	0
Ravens	60	12	616	10.3	78t	2
Opponents	36	21	281	7.8	18	0

KICKOFF RETURNS	No.	Yds	Avg	LG	TD
Sams	59	1,251	21.2	64	0
Dinkins	1	7	7.0	7	0
J. Johnson	1	6	6.0	6	0
Ravens	61	1,264	20.7	64	0
Opponents	65	1,509	23.2	95t	2

FIELD GOALS	1-19	20-29	30-39	40-49	50+
Stover	2/2	9/9	7/8	9/10	2/3
Ravens	2/2	9/9	7/8	9/10	2/3
Opponents	1/1	13/13	3/4	8/10	1/3

SACKS	No.
Suggs	10.5
Thomas	8.0
Douglas	5.5
Weaver	4.0
Demps	2.5
Baxter	2.0
Reed	2.0
Williams	2.0
Gregg	1.5
R. Lewis	1.0
Ravens	39.0
Opponents	35.0

RECORD HOLDERS
INDIVIDUAL RECORDS—CAREER

Category	Name	Performance
Rushing (Yds.)	Jamal Lewis, 2000-04	5,763
Passing (Yds.)	Vinny Testaverde, 1996-97	7,148
Passing (TDs)	Vinny Testaverde, 1996-97	51
Receiving (No.)	Travis Taylor, 2000-04	204
Receiving (Yds.)	Qadry Ismail, 1999-2001	2,819
Interceptions	Ed Reed, 2002-04	21
Punting (Avg.)	Greg Montgomery, 1996-97	43.2
Punt Return (Avg.)	Jermaine Lewis, 1996-2001	11.8
Kickoff Return (Avg.)	Corey Harris, 1998-2001	24.0
Field Goals	Matt Stover, 1996-2004	242
Touchdowns (Tot.)	Jamal Lewis, 2000-04	34
Points	Matt Stover, 1996-2004	1,001

INDIVIDUAL RECORDS—SINGLE SEASON

Category	Name	Performance
Rushing (Yds.)	Jamal Lewis, 2003	2,066
Passing (Yds.)	Vinny Testaverde, 1996	4,177
Passing (TDs)	Vinny Testaverde, 1996	33
Receiving (No.)	Michael Jackson, 1996	76
Receiving (Yds.)	Michael Jackson, 1996	1,201
Interceptions	Ed Reed, 2004	9
Punting (Avg.)	Kyle Richardson, 1998	43.9
Punt Return (Avg.)	Jermaine Lewis, 2000	16.1
Kickoff Return (Avg.)	Corey Harris, 1998	27.6
Field Goals	Matt Stover, 2000	35
Touchdowns (Tot.)	Michael Jackson, 1996	14
	Jamal Lewis, 2003	14
Points	Matt Stover, 2000	135

INDIVIDUAL RECORDS—SINGLE GAME

Category	Name	Performance
Rushing (Yds.)	Jamal Lewis, 9-14-03	*295
Passing (Yds.)	Vinny Testaverde, 10-27-96	429
Passing (TDs)	Tony Banks, 9-10-00	5
Receiving (No.)	Priest Holmes, 10-11-98	13
Receiving (Yds.)	Qadry Ismail, 12-12-99	268
Interceptions	Many times	2
	Last time by Deion Sanders, 10-24-04	
Field Goals	Matt Stover, 9-21-97, 12-26-99, 10-28-00	5
Touchdowns (Tot.)	Marcus Robinson, 11-23-03	4
Points	Marcus Robinson, 11-23-03	24

*NFL Record

2005 VETERAN ROSTER

No.	Name	Pos.	Ht.	Wt.	Birthdate	NFL Exp.	College	Hometown	How Acq.	'04 Games/ Starts
12	Abney, Derek	WR/RS	5-9	180	12/19/80	2	Kentucky	Scholfield, Wis.	D7a-'04	0*
7	Boller, Kyle	QB	6-3	220	6/17/81	3	California	Newhall, Calif.	D1b-'03	16/16
77	Brown, Orlando	T	6-7	360	12/12/70	10	South Carolina State	Washington, D.C.	FA-'03	14/13
24	Carter, Dale	CB	6-1	194	11/28/69	12	Tennessee	Covington, Ga.	FA-'04	0*
81	Darling, Devard	WR	6-1	215	4/16/82	2	Washington State	Houston, Texas	D3-'04	3/0
47	Demps, Will	S	6-0	205	11/7/79	4	San Diego State	Palmdale, Calif.	FA-'02	16/16
87	Dinkins, Darnell	TE	6-2	255	1/20/77	4	Pittsburgh	Pittsburgh, Pa.	FA-'04	10/4
93	Edwards, Dwan	DT	6-3	315	5/16/81	2	Oregon State	Columbus, Mont.	D2-'04	4/0
62	Flynn, Mike	C	6-3	305	6/15/74	8	Maine	Springfield, Mass.	FA-'97	9/5
91	Franklin, Aubrayo	DT	6-1	320	8/27/80	3	Tennessee	Johnson City, Tenn.	D5a-'03	6/0
54	Green, Roderick	LB	6-2	250	4/26/82	2	Central Missouri State	Brenham, Texas	D5-'04	9/0
97	Gregg, Kelly	DT	6-0	310	11/1/76	6	Oklahoma	Edmond, Okla.	FA-'00	14/14
86	Heap, Todd	TE	6-5	252	3/16/80	5	Arizona State	Mesa, Ariz.	D1-'01	6/5
80	Hymes, Randy	WR	6-3	211	8/7/79	4	Grambling	Hitchcock, Texas	FA-'02	14/7
95	Johnson, Jarret	DE	6-3	285	8/14/81	3	Alabama	Chiefland, Fla.	D4a-'03	16/0
11	Johnson, Patrick	WR	5-10	196	8/10/76	7	Oregon	Redlands, Calif.	FA-'05	0*
82	Jones, Terry	TE	6-3	260	12/3/79	4	Alabama	Tuscaloosa, Ala.	D5-'02	15/10
92	Kemoeatu, Maake	DT	6-5	340	1/10/79	4	Utah	Kahuku, Hawaii	FA-'02	14/3
31	Lewis, Jamal	RB	5-11	245	8/29/79	6	Tennessee	Atlanta, Ga.	D1a-'00	12/12
52	Lewis, Ray	LB	6-1	245	5/15/75	10	Miami	Lakeland, Fla.	D1b-'96	15/15
59	Maese, Joe	LS	6-0	245	12/2/78	5	New Mexico	Phoenix, Ariz.	D6-'01	15/0
85	Mason, Derrick	WR	5-10	192	1/17/74	9	Michigan State	Detroit, Mich.	FA-'05	16/16*
21	McAlister, Chris	CB	6-1	206	6/14/77	7	Arizona	Pasadena, Calif.	D1-'99	15/14
84	Moore, Clarence	WR	6-6	211	9/24/82	2	Northern Arizona	Buena Park, Calif.	D6-'04	15/6
34	Mughelli, Ovie	FB	6-1	255	6/10/80	3	Wake Forest	Charleston, S.C.	D4b-'03	3/0*
64	Mulitalo, Edwin	G	6-3	345	9/1/74	7	Arizona	Daly City, Calif.	D4b-'99	15/15
56	Nelson, Jim	LB	6-1	234	4/16/75	7	Penn State	Waldorf, Md.	UFA(Ind)-'05	15/1*
4	Norton, Zach	CB	5-11	183	11/19/81	2	Cincinnati	Lloyd, Fla.	FA-'04	0*
75	Ogden, Jonathan	T	6-9	345	7/31/74	10	UCLA	Washington, D.C.	D1a-'96	12/12*
71	Ogden, Marques	G/T	6-3	300	11/15/80	2	Howard	Washington, D.C.	FA-'04	0*
79	Pashos, Tony	T	6-6	337	8/3/80	3	Illinois	Lock Port, Ill.	D5b-'03	6/0
50	Polley, Tommy	LB	6-3	240	1/18/78	5	Florida State	Baltimore, Md.	UFA(StL)-'05	15/13*
20	Reed, Ed	S	5-11	200	9/11/78	4	Miami	St. Rose, La.	D1-'02	16/16
39	Ricard, Alan	FB	5-11	237	1/17/77	5	Northeast Louisiana	Amite, La.	FA-'00	16/9
69	Rimpf, Brian	G	6-5	319	2/11/81	2	East Carolina	Raleigh, N.C.	D7b-'04	1/0
22	Rolle, Samari	CB	6-0	175	8/10/76	8	Florida State	Miami, Fla.	FA-'05	11/11*
36	Sams, B.J.	RB	5-10	185	10/29/80	2	McNeese State	Mandeville, La.	FA-'04	16/1
57	Scott, Bart	LB	6-2	235	8/18/80	4	Southern Illinois	Detroit, Mich.	FA-'02	13/0
32	Smith, Musa	RB	6-0	232	5/31/82	3	Georgia	West Perry, Pa.	D3-'03	9/0
88	Smith, Trent	TE	6-5	245	9/15/79	3	Oklahoma	Clinton, Okla.	D7a-'03	0*
3	Stover, Matt	K	5-11	178	1/27/68	16	Louisiana Tech	Dallas, Texas	PB(NYG)-'91	16/0
55	Suggs, Terrell	LB	6-3	260	10/11/82	3	Arizona State	Chandler, Ariz.	D1a-'03	16/16
63	Szalay, Thatcher	C	6-4	303	1/18/79	2	Montana	Whitefish, Mont.	FA-'04	0*
29	Taylor, Chester	RB	5-11	213	9/22/79	4	Toledo	River Rouge, Mich.	D6c-'02	16/4
96	Thomas, Adalius	LB	6-2	270	8/18/77	6	Southern Mississippi	Equality, Ala.	D6a-'00	16/16
68	Vincent, Keydrick	G	6-5	325	4/13/78	5	Mississippi	Bartow, Fla.	UFA(Pitt) -'05	16/16*
98	Weaver, Anthony	DE	6-3	290	7/28/80	4	Notre Dame	Saratoga Springs, N.Y.	D2-'02	16/15
83	Wilcox, Daniel	TE	6-1	245	3/23/77	4	Appalachian State	Atlanta, Ga.	FA-'04	16/5
49	Williams, Chad	S	5-9	207	1/22/79	4	Southern Mississippi	Birmingham, Ala.	D6d-'02	16/1
2	Wright, Anthony	QB	6-1	215	2/14/76	7	South Carolina	Vanceboro, N.C.	FA-'02	0*
15	Zastudil, Dave	P	6-3	215	10/26/78	4	Ohio University	Bay Village, Ohio	D4a-'02	13/0
70	Zielinski, Matt	DT	6-2	302	12/2/80	2	Duke	Amherst, N.Y.	FA-'04	0*

* Abney missed '04 season because of injury; Carter missed '04 season because of injury; P. Johnson last active with Cincinnati in '03; Mason played 16 games with Tennessee in '04; Nelson played 15 games with Indianapolis; Norton missed '04 season because of injury; M. Ogden inactive for 16 games with Jacksonville in'03; Polley played 15 games with St. Louis; Rolle played 11 games with Tennessee in '04; T. Smith missed '04 season because of injury; Szalay inactive for 1 game with Cincinnati in'03; Vincent played 16 games with Pittsburgh; Wright inactive for 7 games; Zielinski missed '04 season because of injury;

Players lost through free agency (8): T/G Bennie Anderson (Buff; 16 games in '04); CB Gary Baxter (Cle; 16); DE Marques Douglas (SF; 16); LB Edgerton Hartwell (Atl; 16); C Casey Rabach (Wash; 16); WR Travis Taylor (Minn; 11); CB Raymond Walls (Ariz; 16); RB Jamel White (Det; 13).

Also played with Ravens in '04—T Ethan Brooks (14), LB Cornell Brown (13), CB Corey Fuller (14), FB Harold Morrow (15), K Wade Richey (12), LB T.J. Slaughter (14), QB Kordell Stewart (2).

2005 FIRST-YEAR ROSTER

Name	Pos.	Ht.	Wt.	Birthdate	College	Hometown	How Acq.
Abiamiri, Rob	TE	6-2	240	12/21/82	Maryland	Randallstown, Md.	FA
Alford, Bill	CB	5-9	175	10/30/81	Vanderbilt	Brunswick, Ga.	FA
Anderson, Derek	QB	6-6	245	6/15/83	Oregon State	Scappoose, Ore.	D6
Brown, Jason	T/G	6-3	315	5/5/83	North Carolina	Henderson, N.C.	D4
Brown, Lester	T	6-4	304	10/18/82	Louisiana Tech	Compton, Calif.	FA
Burnell, Keith (1)	RB	5-11	201	1/7/79	Delaware	Chesapeake, Va.	FA
Carlyle, Calvin (1)	CB/S	5-11	186	9/12/79	Oregon State	Los Angeles, Calif.	FA-'04
Caylor, Drew (1)	C/LS	6-5	291	9/12/79	Stanford	Bethesda, Md.	FA-'04
Clay, Joe	DT	6-1	270	11/26/81	Houston	San Angelo, Texas	FA
Clayton, Mark	WR	5-10	195	7/2/82	Oklahoma	Arlington, Texas	D1
Cody, Dan	LB	6-5	255	12/1/81	Oklahoma	Ada, Okla.	D2a
Curry, Walter	DT/DE	6-4	284	6/18/81	Albany State	Crescent City, Fla.	FA
Durant, Darian	QB	5-11	221	8/19/82	North Carolina	Florence, S.C.	FA
Gibson, Gary	DT	6-3	285	5/5/82	Rutgers	Jamesville, N.Y.	FA
Goodpaster, Patrick	DE	6-2	288	3/15/82	Colorado State	Carson, Calif.	FA
Green, Justin	FB	5-11	251	4/30/82	Montana	San Diego, Calif.	D5
Hawkins, Phil	G	6-4	310	2/26/82	Houston	Chicago, Ill.	FA
Johnson, Jarvis	S	5-10	195	11/22/82	Rutgers	Miami, Fla.	FA
Katula, Matt	LS	6-6	280	8/22/82	Wisconsin	Brookfield, Wis.	FA
Lloyd, Rhys	K	5-11	231	6/5/82	Minnesota	Dover, England	FA
Manus, Tommy	WR	6-4	222	10/10/81	Morgan State	Dallas, Texas	FA
Mouton, Cash	CB	6-0	193	11/10/82	Louisiana-Monroe	Lafayette, La.	FA
Ohliger, Jesse (1)	P	6-4	224	10/23/80	Murray State	Wilmington, Del.	FA
Redmon, Tellis (1)	RB	5-10	210	12/19/78	Minnesota	Fort Worth, Texas	FA-'04
Sinclair, Matt	LB	6-1	244	7/24/82	Illinois	St. Louis, Mo.	FA
Smith, Mike	LB	6-1	240	9/2/81	Texas Tech	Lubbock, Texas	D7
Smith, Tyson	LB	6-2	237	10/9/81	Iowa State	Des Moines, Iowa	FA
Stamps, Fred (1)	WR	6-1	184	12/10/80	Louisiana-Lafayette	New Orleans, La.	FA-'04
Terry, Adam	T	6-8	330	9/1/82	Syracuse	Queensbury, N.Y.	D2b
Williams, Curtis	WR	6-2	204	4/26/82	Maryland	Huntington Station, N.Y.	FA
Winborne, Jamaine (1)	CB/S	5-10	202	12/26/80	Virginia	Chesapeake, Va.	FA-'04

The term NFL Rookie is defined as a player who is in his first season of professional football and has not been on the roster of another professional football team for any regular-season or postseason games. A Rookie is designated by an "R" on NFL rosters. Players who have been active in another professional football league or players who have NFL experience, including either preseason training camp or being on an Active List or Inactive List, or on Reserve/Injured or Reserve/Physically Unable to Perform for fewer than six regular-season games, are termed NFL First-Year Players. An NFL First-Year Player is designated by a "1" on NFL rosters. Thereafter, a player is credited with an additional year of experience for each season in which he accumulates six games on the Active List or Inactive List, or on Reserve/Injured or Reserve/Physically Unable to Perform.

Log on to www.baltimoreravens.com for an up-to-date roster.

COACHING STAFF

Head Coach,
Brian Billick

Pro Career: Entering his seventh season, Brian Billick is tied for fourth in longevity in the NFL. Billick and Philadelphia's Andy Reid trail only Pittsburgh's Bill Cowher (14), Tennessee's Jeff Fisher (11) and Denver's Mike Shanahan (11). Has posted four winning seasons in six years. Billick has taken his team to the playoffs in three of the last five years, earning a Super Bowl championship in his second season (2000). Baltimore defeated the New York Giants, 34-7, in Super Bowl XXXV. Billick's Ravens returned to the playoffs in 2001, earning a 10-6 record and winning a Wild Card playoff game at Miami. In 2003, Billick led Baltimore to its first division title, the AFC North, with a 10-6 record and was the youngest team in the playoffs. Prior to becoming the Ravens' head coach, Billick spent seven seasons (1992-98) with the Minnesota Vikings, including the last five years as their offensive coordinator. In 1998, the Vikings' offense scored an NFL single-season record 556 points. In 2000, Billick's Ravens allowed the fewest points in NFL history (165) in a 16-game season. Billick was named the second head coach in Ravens history on January 19, 1999. Career record: 61-42.

Background: Billick was an honorable mention All-America in 1976 as a tight end at Brigham Young. Played linebacker at Air Force as a freshman before transferring to BYU. Drafted by the 49ers in the eleventh round of the 1977 draft, was released, and had a brief stint with the Dallas Cowboys, but did not play. Coached collegiately at Redlands (1977), Brigham Young (1978), San Diego State (1981-85), Utah State (1986-88), and Stanford (1989-1991). Billick's NFL career started with the 49ers, where he was assistant director of public relations from 1979-1980.

Personal: Born February 28, 1954 in Fairborn, Ohio. He and his wife, Kim, have two daughters—Aubree and Keegan. Billick has co-authored two books: *Competitive Leadership: Twelve Principles for Success* (with Dr. James A. Peterson) and *Finding the Winning Edge* with Pro Football Hall of Fame coach Bill Walsh.

ASSISTANT COACHES

Clarence Brooks, defensive line; born May 20, 1951, New York, N.Y. Guard Massachusetts 1970-73. No pro playing experience. College coach: Massachusetts 1976-1980, Syracuse 1981-89, Arizona 1990-92. Pro coach: Chicago Bears 1993-98, Cleveland Browns 1999, Miami Dolphins 2000-04, joined Ravens in 2005.

Jim Fassel, offensive coordinator; born August 31, 1949, Anaheim, Calif. Quarterback Fullerton College 1967-68, Southern California 1969-1972. No pro game experience. College coach: Fullerton College 1973, Utah 1976, 1985-89, Weber State 1977-78, Stanford 1979-1983. Pro coach: Hawaii Hawaiians (World League) 1974, New Orleans Breakers (USFL) 1984, New York Giants 1991-92, Denver Broncos 1993-94, Oakland Raiders 1995, Arizona Cardinals 1996, New York Giants 1997-2003 (head coach), joined Ravens in 2004.

John Fassel, coaching assistant; born January 10, 1974, Anaheim, Calif. Wide receiver/quarterback Pacific 1994-95, Weber State 1996-98. No pro playing experience. College coach: Bucknell 1999, 2001, Idaho State 2000, New Mexico Highlands 2002-03. Pro coach: Amsterdam Admirals (NFLE) 2000, joined Ravens in 2005.

Jedd Fisch, offensive assistant; born May 5, 1976, Livingston, N.J. Attended Florida. No college or pro playing experience. College coach: Florida 1999-2000. Pro coach: Houston Texans 2001-2003, joined Ravens in 2004.

Jeff FitzGerald, linebackers; born April 18, 1960, Burbank, Calif. Linebacker Oregon State 1980. No pro playing experience. College coach: Cincinnati 1985-86, Alabama 1987-89, San Diego State 1994-97. Pro coach: Tampa Bay Buccaneers 1990-93, Washington Redskins 1998-99, Arizona Cardinals 2000-2003, joined Ravens in 2004.

Chris Foerster, offensive line/asst. head coach; born October 12, 1961, Milwaukee, Wis. Center Colorado State 1979-1982. No pro playing experience. College coach: Colorado State 1983-87, Stanford 1988-1991, Minnesota 1992. Pro coach: Minnesota Vikings 1993-95, Tampa Bay Buccaneers 1996-2001, Indianapolis Colts 2002-03, Miami Dolphins 2004, joined Ravens in 2005.

Jeff Friday, strength and conditioning; born October 11, 1966, Milwaukee, Wis. Attended Wisconsin-Milwaukee. No college or pro playing experience. College coach: Illinois State 1991-92, Northwestern 1992-95. Pro coach: Minnesota Vikings 1996-98, joined Ravens in 1999.

Wade Harman, tight ends/asst. offensive line; born October 1, 1963, Corydon, Iowa. Linebacker Drake 1985, Utah State 1986. No pro playing experience. College coach: Utah State 1987-1991, Pacific 1992-95, Morningside 1996. Pro coach: Minnesota Vikings 1997-98, joined Ravens in 1999.

Johnnie Lynn, secondary; born December 19, 1956, Los Angeles. Defensive back UCLA 1975-78. Pro defensive back New York Jets 1979-1986. College coach: Arizona 1988-1993. Pro coach: Tampa Bay Buccaneers 1994-95, San Francisco 49ers 1996, New York Giants 1997-2003, joined Ravens in 2004.

Rick Neuheisel, quarterbacks; born February 7, 1961, Madison, Wis. Quarterback UCLA 1979-1983. Pro quarterback San Antonio Gunslingers (USFL) 1984-85, San Diego Chargers 1987, Tampa Bay Buccaneers 1987. College coach: UCLA 1988-1994, Colorado 1995-98 (head coach), Washington 1999-2002 (head coach). Pro coach: Joined Ravens in 2005.

Mike Pettine, outside linebackers; born September 25, 1966, Doylestown, Pa. Safety Virginia 1984-87. No pro playing experience. College coach: Pittsburgh 1993-94. Pro coach: Joined Ravens in 2002.

Paul Ricci, asst. strength and conditioning; born November 15, 1969, Elmer, N.J. Offensive lineman Penn State 1988-89. Pro coach: Seattle Seahawks 1993, Philadelphia Eagles 1995-96, Arizona Cardinals 1996-97, joined Ravens in 2002.

Rex Ryan, defensive coordinator; born December 13, 1962, Ardmore, Okla. Defensive end Southwest Oklahoma State 1983-86. No pro playing experience. College coach: Eastern Kentucky 1987-88, New Mexico Highlands 1989, Morehead State 1990-93, Cincinnati 1996-97, Oklahoma 1998. Pro coach: Arizona Cardinals 1994-95, joined Ravens in 1999.

David Shaw, receivers; born July 31, 1972, San Diego. Wide receiver Stanford 1990-94. No pro playing experience. College coach: Western Washington University 1995-96. Pro coach: Philadelphia Eagles 1997, Oakland Raiders 1998-2001, joined Ravens in 2002.

Matt Simon, running backs; born December 6, 1953, Akron, Ohio. Linebacker Eastern New Mexico 1972-75. No pro playing experience. College coach: Washington 1982-1991, New Mexico 1992-93, North Texas 1994-97 (head coach). Pro coach: Denver Broncos 1998, joined Ravens in 1999.

Bennie Thompson, asst. special teams; born February 10, 1963, New Orleans. Safety Grambling State 1981-84. Pro safety New Orleans 1989-1991, Kansas City Chiefs 1992-93, Cleveland Browns 1994-95, Baltimore Ravens 1996-99. Pro coach: Joined Ravens in 2000.

Dennis Thurman, secondary; born April 13, 1956, Santa Monica, Calif. Safety Southern California 1974-77. Pro defensive back Dallas Cowboys 1978-1985, St. Louis Cardinals 1986. College coach: Southern California 1993-2000. Pro coach: Phoenix Cardinals 1988-89, joined Ravens in 2002.

Gary Zauner, special teams coordinator; born November 2, 1950, Milwaukee, Wis. Punter Wisconsin-La Crosse 1968-1972. No pro playing experience. College coach: Brigham Young 1979-1980, San Diego State 1981-86, New Mexico 1987-88, Long Beach State 1990-91. Pro coach: Minnesota Vikings 1994-2001, joined Ravens in 2002.

American Football Conference
East Division
Team Colors: Dark Navy, Red, Royal,
and Nickel
One Bills Drive
Orchard Park, New York 14127-2296
Telephone: (716) 648-1800

2005 SCHEDULE
PRESEASON
Aug. 13	at Indianapolis	7:00
Aug. 20	**Green Bay**	6:00
Aug. 26	at Chicago	7:00
Sept. 2	**Detroit**	7:00

REGULAR SEASON
Sept. 11	**Houston**	1:00
Sept. 18	at Tampa Bay	1:00
Sept. 25	**Atlanta**	1:00
Oct. 2	at New Orleans	12:00
Oct. 9	**Miami**	1:00
Oct. 16	**New York Jets**	4:15
Oct. 23	at Oakland	1:15
Oct. 30	at New England	8:30
Nov. 6	Open Date	
Nov. 13	**Kansas City**	1:00
Nov. 20	at San Diego	1:15
Nov. 27	**Carolina**	1:00
Dec. 4	at Miami	1:00
Dec. 11	**New England**	1:00
Dec. 17	**Denver** (Sat.)	8:30
Dec. 24	at Cincinnati (Sat.)	1:00
Jan. 1	at New York Jets	1:00

Stadium: Ralph Wilson Stadium
(opened in 1973)
• **Capacity:** 73,967
One Bills Drive
Orchard Park, New York
14127-2296
Playing Surface: AstroPlay
Training Camp: St. John Fisher College
Rochester, New York
14618

RALPH WILSON STADIUM

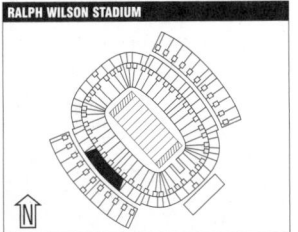

CLUB OFFICIALS
Owner: Ralph C. Wilson, Jr.
President/General Manager:
Tom Donahoe
Assistant General Manager: Tom Modrak
Corporate V.P.: Linda Bogdan
Treasurer: Jeffrey C. Littman
Vice President/Communications:
Scott Berchtold
Vice President/Business Development
and Marketing: Russ Brandon
Vice President/Operations: Bill Munson
Vice President/Business Administration:
Jim Overdorf
Director of Pro Personnel: John Guy
Consultant: Christy Wilson Hofmann
Executive Director/Marketing:
Marc Honan
Executive Director/Corporate Sales:
Pete Guelli
Executive Director/Business
Development: Karen Marsch
Director of Merchandise: Tim Kehoe
Director of Ticket Operations and
Customer Service: David Wheat
Director of Archives: Denny Lynch
Director of Community Relations:
Gretchen Geitter
Director of Player Programs:
Paul Lancaster
Director of Information Technology:
Dan Evans
Director of Stadium Operations:
Joe Frandina
Director of Security: Bill Bambach
Director of Business Operations:
Don Purdy
Controller: Frank Wojnicki
Equipment Manager: Dave Hojnowski
Asst. Equipment Manager:
Randy Ribbeck
Coordinator/Strength and Conditioning:
Brad Roll
Strength and Conditioning Assistant:
John Allaire
Athletic Trainers: Bud Carpenter,
Chris Fischetti, Shone Gipson,
Greg McMillen
Video Director: Henry Kunttu
Asst. Video Director: Greg Estes
Scouts: Brad Forsyth, Joe Haering,
Shawn Heinlen, David Hinson,
Doug Majeski, Marc Ross, Bob Ryan,
George (Chink) Sengal,
David G. Smith, David W. Smith,
Terry Wooden

COACHING HISTORY
(336-361-8)
Records include postseason games
1960-61	Buster Ramsey	11-16-1
1962-65	Lou Saban	38-18-3
1966-68	Joe Collier*	13-17-1
1968	Harvey Johnson	1-10-1
1969-1970	John Rauch	7-20-1
1971	Harvey Johnson	1-13-0
1972-76	Lou Saban**	32-29-1
1976-77	Jim Ringo	3-20-0
1978-1982	Chuck Knox	38-38-0
1983-85	Kay Stephenson***	10-26-0
1985-86	Hank Bullough****	4-17-0
1986-1997	Marv Levy	123-78-0
1998-2000	Wade Phillips	29-21-0
2001-03	Gregg Williams	17-31-0
2004	Mike Mularkey	9-7-0

*Released after two games in 1968
**Resigned after five games in 1976
***Released after four games in 1985
****Released after nine games in 1986

ATTENDANCE
Home 563,330   Away 533,376
Total 1,096,706
Single-game home record,
80,368 (10/4/92)
Single-season home record,
635,889 (1991)

2005 DRAFT CHOICES
Round	Name	Pos.	College
2	Roscoe Parrish	WR	Miami
3	Kevin Everett	TE	Miami
4	Duke Preston	C	Illinois
5	Eric King	DB	Wake Forest
6	Justin Geisinger	G	Vanderbilt
7	Lionel Gates	RB	Louisville

2004 TEAM RECORD

PRESEASON (1-3)

Date	Result	Opponent
8/15	W 16-6	Denver
8/21	L 15-16	Tennessee
8/28	L 17-30	at Indianapolis
9/2	L 17-20	at Detroit

REGULAR SEASON (9-7)

Date	Result	Opponent	Att.
9/12	L 10-13	Jacksonville	72,389
9/19	L 10-13	at Oakland	53,610
10/3	L 17-31	New England	72,698
10/10	L 14-16	at N.Y. Jets	77,976
10/17	W 20-13	Miami	72,714
10/24	L 6-20	at Baltimore	69,809
10/31	W 38-14	Arizona	65,887
11/7	W 22-17	N.Y. Jets	72,574
11/14	L 6-29	at New England	68,756
11/21	W 37-17	St. Louis	72,393
11/28	W 38-9	at Seattle	66,271
12/5	W 42-32	at Miami	73,084
12/12	W 37-7	Cleveland	72,330
12/19	W 33-17	at Cincinnati	65,378
12/26	W 41-7	at San Francisco	63,248
1/2	L 24-29	Pittsburgh	73,414

SCORE BY PERIODS

Bills	89	101	80	125	0	—	395
Opponents	78	100	12	94	0	—	284

2004 TEAM STATISTICS

	Bills	Opp.
Total First Downs	271	258
Rushing	102	79
Passing	149	150
Penalty	20	29
3rd Down: Made/Att	77/215	77/214
3rd Down Pct.	35.8	36.0
4th Down: Made/Att	10/21	11/15
4th Down Pct.	47.6	73.3
Possession Avg.	30:21	29:39
Total Net Yards	4691	4228
Avg. Per Game	293.2	264.3
Total Plays	982	978
Avg. Per Play	4.8	4.3
Net Yards Rushing	1874	1604
Avg. Per Game	117.1	100.3
Total Rushes	483	447
Net Yards Passing	2817	2624
Avg. Per Game	176.1	164.0
Sacked/Yards Lost	38/215	45/319
Gross Yards	3032	2943
Att./Completions	461/262	486/261
Completion Pct.	56.8	53.7
Had Intercepted	17	24
Punts/Average	78/43.1	79/40.7
Net Punting Avg.	78/36.5	79/33.0
Penalties/Yards	121/1047	120/865
Fumbles/Ball Lost	26/12	31/15
Touchdowns	46	29
Rushing	15	6
Passing	21	20
Returns	10	3

2004 INDIVIDUAL STATISTICS

PASSING	Att.	Comp.	Yds.	Pct.	TD	Int.	Tkld.	Rate
Bledsoe	450	256	2,932	56.9	20	16	37/215	76.6
Losman	5	3	32	60.0	0	1	1/0	39.2
Matthews	3	2	44	66.7	1	0	0/0	149.3
Moorman	3	1	24	33.3	0	0	0/0	63.2
Bills	461	262	3,032	56.8	21	17	38/215	76.7
Opponents	486	261	2,943	53.7	20	24	45/319	65.2

SCORING	TD R	TD P	TD Rt	PAT	FG	Saf	PTS
Lindell	0	0	0	45/45	24/28	0	117
McGahee	13	0	0	0/0	0/0	0	78
Evans	0	9	0	0/0	0/0	0	54
Campbell	0	5	0	0/0	0/0	0	30
Moulds	0	5	0	0/0	0/0	0	30
McGee	0	0	3	0/0	0/0	0	18
Clements	0	0	2	0/0	0/0	0	12
Euhus	0	2	0	0/0	0/0	0	12
Spikes	0	0	2	0/0	0/0	0	12
S. Williams	2	0	0	0/0	0/0	0	12
P. Williams	0	0	1	0/0	0/0	1	8
Peters	0	1	0	0/0	0/0	0	6
J. Smith	0	0	1	0/0	0/0	0	6
Bills	15	21	10	45/45	24/28	1	395
Opponents	6	20	3	27/27	27/32	0	284

2-Pt. Conversions: None.
Bills 0-1, Opponents 1-2.

RUSHING	Att.	Yds.	Avg.	LG	TD
McGahee	284	1,128	4.0	41	13
Henry	94	326	3.5	19	0
S. Williams	42	167	4.0	27t	2
Evans	5	85	17.0	48	0
Burns	20	73	3.7	21	0
Bledsoe	22	37	1.7	17	0
Moorman	2	23	11.5	34	0
Moulds	5	19	3.8	12	0
Losman	2	15	7.5	10	0
J. Smith	2	11	5.5	8	0
Reed	2	-1	-0.5	6	0
Matthews	2	-3	-1.5	-1	0
Greer	1	-6	-6.0	-6	0
Bills	483	1,874	3.9	48	15
Opponents	447	1,604	3.6	58	6

RECEIVING	No.	Yds.	Avg.	LG	TD
Moulds	88	1,043	11.9	49	5
Evans	48	843	17.6	69t	9
McGahee	22	169	7.7	16	0
Campbell	17	203	11.9	27	5
Shelton	17	114	6.7	24	0
Reed	16	153	9.6	20	0
Aiken	11	148	13.5	54	0
Euhus	11	98	8.9	17	2
Henry	10	45	4.5	10	0
Neufeld	6	61	10.2	29	0
Shaw	5	59	11.8	20	0
Trafford	3	25	8.3	10	0
J. Smith	3	21	7.0	11	0
S. Williams	3	19	6.3	10	0
Thomas	1	24	24.0	24	0
Burns	1	7	7.0	7	0
Bills	262	3,032	11.6	69t	21
Opponents	261	2,943	11.3	51t	20

INTERCEPTIONS	No.	Yds.	Avg.	LG	TD
Clements	6	77	12.8	35	1
Spikes	5	122	24.4	62t	2
McGee	3	21	7.0	21	0
Milloy	2	20	10.0	11	0
Reese	1	33	33.0	33	0
Baker	1	26	26.0	26	0
P. Williams	1	20	20.0	20t	1
Vincent	1	8	8.0	8	0
Kelsay	1	3	3.0	3	0
Posey	1	3	3.0	3	0
Adams	1	0	0.0	0	0
Stamer	1	0	0.0	0	0
Bills	24	333	13.9	62t	4
Opponents	17	357	21.0	94	1

PUNTING	No.	Yds.	Avg.	In 20	LG
Moorman	77	3,325	43.2	17	80
Lindell	1	37	37.0	0	37
Bills	78	3,362	43.1	17	80
Opponents	79	3,218	40.7	18	69

PUNT RETURNS	No.	FC	Yds.	Avg.	LG	TD
Clements	35	10	327	9.3	86t	1
J. Smith	9	0	157	17.4	70t	1
Reed	1	0	7	7.0	7	0
S. Williams	1	0	0	0.0	0	0
Bills	46	10	491	10.7	86t	2
Opponents	37	6	315	8.5	34	0

KICKOFF RETURNS	No.	Yds.	Avg.	LG	TD
McGee	52	1,370	26.3	104t	3
Fletcher	4	86	21.5	23	0
Shelton	2	25	12.5	15	0
Clements	1	14	14.0	14	0
Kelsay	1	14	14.0	14	0
Moulds	1	2	2.0	2	0
Neufeld	1	3	3.0	3	0
J. Smith	1	28	28.0	28	0
Bills	63	1,542	24.5	104t	3
Opponents	77	1,406	18.3	65	0

FIELD GOALS	1-19	20-29	30-39	40-49	50+
Lindell	0/0	13/14	10/11	1/3	0/0
Bills	0/0	13/14	10/11	1/3	0/0
Opponents	2/2	11/12	8/9	6/7	0/2

SACKS	No.
Schobel	8.0
Adams	5.0
Kelsay	4.5
Edwards	4.0
Milloy	4.0
Fletcher	3.5
Denney	3.0
Spikes	3.0
P. Williams	2.5
McGee	2.0
Greer	1.0
Posey	1.0
Thomas	1.0
Vincent	1.0
Wire	1.0
Clements	0.5
Bills	45.0
Opponents	38.0

RECORD HOLDERS
INDIVIDUAL RECORDS—CAREER

Category	Name	Performance
Rushing (Yds.)	Thurman Thomas, 1988-1999	11,938
Passing (Yds.)	Jim Kelly, 1986-1996	35,467
Passing (TDs)	Jim Kelly, 1986-1996	237
Receiving (No.)	Andre Reed, 1985-1999	941
Receiving (Yds.)	Andre Reed, 1985-1999	13,095
Interceptions	George (Butch) Byrd, 1964-1970	40
Punting (Avg.)	Brian Moorman, 2001-04	42.9
Punt Return (Avg.)	Clifford Hicks, 1990-92	12.2
Kickoff Return (Avg.)	O.J. Simpson, 1969-1977	30.0
Field Goals	Steve Christie, 1992-2000	234
Touchdowns (Tot.)	Andre Reed, 1985-1999	87
	Thurman Thomas, 1988-1999	87
Points	Steve Christie, 1992-2000	1,011

INDIVIDUAL RECORDS—SINGLE SEASON

Category	Name	Performance
Rushing (Yds.)	O.J. Simpson, 1973	2,003
Passing (Yds.)	Drew Bledsoe, 2002	4,359
Passing (TDs)	Jim Kelly, 1991	33
Receiving (No.)	Eric Moulds, 2002	100
Receiving (Yds.)	Eric Moulds, 1998	1,368
Interceptions	Billy Atkins, 1961	10
	Tom Janik, 1967	10
Punting (Avg.)	Paul Maguire, 1969	44.5
Punt Return (Avg.)	Keith Moody, 1977	13.1
Kickoff Return (Avg.)	Ed Rutkowski, 1963	30.2
Field Goals	Steve Christie, 1998	33
Touchdowns (Tot.)	O.J. Simpson, 1975	23
Points	Steve Christie, 1998	140

INDIVIDUAL RECORDS—SINGLE GAME

Category	Name	Performance
Rushing (Yds.)	O.J. Simpson, 11-25-76	273
Passing (Yds.)	Drew Bledsoe, 9-15-02	463
Passing (TDs)	Jim Kelly, 9-8-91	6
Receiving (No.)	Andre Reed, 11-20-94	15
Receiving (Yds.)	Jerry Butler, 9-23-79	255
Interceptions	Many times	3
	Last time by Nate Clements, 10-20-02	
Field Goals	Steve Christie, 10-20-96	6
Touchdowns (Tot.)	Cookie Gilchrist, 12-8-63	5
Points	Cookie Gilchrist, 12-8-63	30

2005 VETERAN ROSTER

No.	Name	Pos.	Ht.	Wt.	Birthdate	NFL Exp.	College	Hometown	How Acq.	'04 Games/ Starts
95	Adams, Sam	DT	6-4	335	6/13/73	12	Texas A&M	Houston, Texas	FA-'03	16/16
89	Aiken, Sam	WR	6-2	204	12/14/80	3	North Carolina	Kenansville, N.C.	D4b-'03	16/0
66	Anderson, Bennie	T/G	6-5	345	2/17/77	5	Tennessee State	Atlanta, Ga.	FA-05	16/12*
77	Anderson, Tim	DT	6-3	304	11/22/80	2	Ohio State	Clyde, Ohio	D3-'04	3/0
26	Baker, Rashad	S	5-10	198	2/22/82	2	Tennessee	Camden, N.J.	FA-'04	14/3
97	Bannan, Justin	DT	6-3	305	4/18/79	4	Colorado	Organerale, Calif.	D5-'02	11/0
30	Brown, Dante	RB	6-1	215	7/28/80	2	Memphis	Cincinnati, Ohio	FA-'04	1/0
35	Burns, Joe	RB	5-9	215	9/15/79	4	Georgia Tech	Thomasville, Ga.	FA-'02	16/0
84	Campbell, Mark	TE	6-6	255	12/6/75	7	Michigan	Clawson, Mich.	T(Cle)-'03	12/12
22	Clements, Nate	CB	6-0	209	12/12/79	5	Ohio State	Shaker Heights, Ohio	D1-'01	16/16
55	Crowell, Angelo	LB	6-1	235	8/16/81	3	Virginia	Winston-Salem, N.C.	D3-'03	16/0
92	Denney, Ryan	DE	6-7	275	6/15/77	4	Brigham Young	Thornton, Colo.	D2b-'02	16/6
47	Dorenbos, Jon	LS	6-0	250	7/21/80	3	Texas-El Paso	Garden Grove, Calif.	FA-'03	13/0
98	Edwards, Ron	DT	6-3	320	7/12/79	5	Texas A&M	Houston, Texas	D3a-'01	16/2
87	Euhus, Tim	TE	6-5	249	10/2/80	2	Oregon State	Eugene, Ore.	D4-'04	12/5
83	Evans, Lee	WR	5-10	197	3/11/81	2	Wisconsin	Bedford, Ohio	D1a-'04	16/11
59	Fletcher, London	LB	5-10	245	5/19/75	8	John Carroll	Cleveland, Ohio	FA-'02	16/16
69	Gandy, Mike	T/G	6-4	310	1/3/79	4	Notre Dame	Dallas, Texas	FA-'04	5/5*
33	Greer, Jabari	CB	5-11	169	2/11/82	2	Tennessee	Jackson, Tenn.	FA-'04	12/1
86	Haddad, Drew	WR	5-11	187	8/15/78	2	Buffalo	Westlake, Ohio	FA-'04	1/0
53	Haggan, Mario	LB	6-3	248	3/3/80	3	Mississippi State	Clarksdale, Miss.	D7-'03	16/0
20	Henry, Travis	RB	5-9	215	10/29/78	5	Tennessee	Frostproof, Fla.	D2b-'01	10/5
10	Holcomb, Kelly	QB	6-2	212	7/9/73	9	Middle Tennessee State	Fayetville, Tenn.	UFA(Cle)-'05	4/2*
90	Kelsay, Chris	DE	6-4	275	10/31/79	3	Nebraska	Auburn, Neb.	D2-'03	16/11
9	Lindell, Rian	K	6-3	235	1/20/77	6	Washington State	Vancouver, Wash.	FA-'03	16/0
7	Losman, J.P.	QB	6-2	217	3/12/81	2	Tulane	Venice, Calif.	D1b-'04	4/0
6	Matthews, Shane	QB	6-3	199	6/1/70	12	Florida	Pascagoula, Miss.	FA-'04	3/0
79	McFarland, Dylan	T	6-5	290	7/11/80	2	Montana	Kalispell, Mont.	D7a-'04	2/0
21	McGahee, Willis	RB	6-0	228	10/21/81	2	Miami	Miami, Fla	D1-'03	16/11
24	McGee, Terrence	CB	5-9	195	10/14/80	3	Northwestern State	Athens, Texas	D4a-'03	16/13
36	Milloy, Lawyer	S	6-0	190	11/14/73	10	Washington	Tacoma, Wash.	FA-'03	11/11
8	Moorman, Brian	P	6-0	175	2/5/76	5	Pittsburg State	Sedgwick, Kan.	FA-'01	16/0
80	Moulds, Eric	WR	6-2	210	7/17/73	10	Mississippi State	Lucedale, Miss.	D1-'96	16/16
88	Neufeld, Ryan	TE	6-4	250	11/22/75	5	UCLA	Morgan Hill, Calif.	FA-'03	16/5
71	Peters, Jason	T	6-4	328	1/22/82	2	Arkansas	Queen City, Texas	FA-'04	5/1
96	Posey, Jeff	LB	6-4	241	8/14/75	8	Southern Mississippi	Bassfield, Miss.	FA-'03	16/15
82	Reed, Josh	WR	5-10	208	5/1/80	4	Louisiana State	Rayne, La.	D2a-'02	12/1
91	Ritzmann, Constantin	DE	6-3	254	12/20/79	2	Tennessee	Berlin, Germany	FA-'04	0*
93	Sape, Lauvale	DT	6-1	296	8/29/80	2	Utah	Leilehua, Hawaii	D6-'03	0*
94	Schobel, Aaron	DE	6-4	262	9/1/77	5	Texas Christian	Columbus, Texas	D2a-'01	16/16
31	Shelton, Daimon	FB	6-0	262	9/15/72	8	Sacramento State	Duarte, Calif.	FA-'04	16/12
19	Smith, Jonathan	WR	5-10	194	11/28/81	2	Georgia Tech	Argyle, Ga.	D7b-'04	9/0
72	Smith, Lawrence	G	6-3	295	8/16/79	2	Tennessee State	Atlanta, Ga.	FA-'04	16/8
64	Sobieski, Ben	T/G	6-5	315	5/3/79	2	Iowa	Mahtomedi, Minn.	D5-'03	0*
51	Spikes, Takeo	LB	6-2	242	12/17/76	8	Auburn	Sandersville,Ga.	FA-'03	16/16
57	Stamer, Josh	LB	6-2	238	10/11/77	3	South Dakota	Sutherland, Iowa	FA-'03	16/0
70	Teague, Trey	C	6-5	300	12/27/74	8	Tennessee	Jackson, Tenn.	FA-'02	12/12
28	Thomas, Kevin	CB	6-0	182	7/28/78	4	Nevada-Las Vegas	Sacramento, Calif.	D6-'02	16/1
81	Trafford, Rod	TE	6-3	250	11/28/78	2	South Carolina	Morristown, N.J.	FA-'04	4/0
65	Tucker, Ross	T/G	6-4	316	3/2/79	5	Princeton	Wyomissing, Pa.	W(Dall)-'03	16/12
58	Villarrial, Chris	G	6-3	318	6/9/73	10	Indiana (PA)	Hershey, Pa.	FA-'04	16/16
23	Vincent, Troy	CB	6-1	200	6/8/71	14	Wisconson	Trenton, N.J.	FA-'04	7/7
68	Williams, Mike	T	6-6	360	1/11/80	4	Texas	The Colony, Texas	D1-'02	15/15
40	Williams, Shaud	RB	5-7	193	10/2/80	2	Alabama	Andrews, Texas	FA-'04	4/0
27	Wire, Coy	S	6-0	205	11/7/78	4	Stanford	Camp Hill, Pa.	D3-'02	13/3
2	Woodbury, Tory	QB	6-2	208	7/12/78	3	Winston Salem	Winston-Salem, N.C.	FA-'05	0*

* Anderson played 16 games with Baltimore in '04; Gandy played 5 games with Chicago; Holcomb played 4 games with Cleveland; Ritzmann missed '04 season because of injury; Sape last active with Buffalo in '03; Sobieski last active with Buffalo in '03; Woodbury last active with N.Y. Jets in '02.

Players lost through free agency (2): T Jonas Jennings (SF; 14 games in '04), DT Pat Williams (Minn; 16).

Also played with Bills in '04—TE Brad Banta (3 games), QB Drew Bledsoe (16), T Marcus Price (14), S Pierson Prioleau (16), G Mike Pucillo (2), S Izell Reese (9), WR Bobby Shaw (4).

2005 FIRST-YEAR ROSTER

Name	Pos.	Ht.	Wt.	Birthdate	College	Hometown	How Acq.
Brown, LaWaylon	DT	6-5	305	6/12/80	Oklahoma State	Whitehouse, Texas	FA
Brown, Tony	WR	6-2	199	5/29/81	Tennessee	Lauderdale Lakes, Fla.	FA
Cieslak, Brad	TE	6-3	262	7/1/82	Northern Illinois	Long Grove, Ill.	FA
Esposito, Jasen	G	6-4	305	6/14/81	Kutztown	Reading, Pa.	FA-'04
Everett, Kevin	TE	6-4	241	2/5/82	Miami	Kilgore, Texas	D3
Ezekiel, Liam	LB	6-0	249	10/30/82	Northeastern	Arlington, Mass.	FA
Fontenot, Therrian	CB	5-10	187	6/28/81	Fresno State	Lawndale, Fla.	FA
Gates, Lionel	RB	6-0	233	3/13/82	Louisville	Jacksonville, Fla.	D7
Gause, George	DE	6-4	275	6/20/82	South Carolina	Conway, S.C.	FA
Geisinger, Justin	T/G	6-3	322	5/24/82	Vanderbilt	Pittsburgh, Pa.	D6
Goldsberry, Jon	FB	6-1	246	12/4/81	Purdue	Santa Claus, Ind.	FA
Gudmundsen, Geir	G	6-5	302	6/29/82	Albany	Saugerties, N.Y.	FA
Hill, Kahlil	WR	6-2	200	8/15/78	Iowa	Iowa City, Iowa	FA-'04
Hunter, Wendell	LB	6-0	228	4/19/82	California	Carson, Calif.	FA
King, Eric	CB	5-10	185	5/10/82	Wake Forest	Woodstock, Md.	D5
Lee, Rob	CB	6-0	193	2/11/81	Northern Illinois	Port Washington, Wis.	FA
Leger, Daniel	S	6-0	213	1/31/83	Colorado School of Mines	Arvada. Colo.	FA
Leonhard, Jim	S	5-8	190	10/27/82	Wisconsin	Tony, Wis.	FA
Oglesby, Evan	CB	5-10	185	12/18/81	North Alabama	Taccoa, Ga.	FA
Osunde, Uyi	DE	6-3	255	2/28/82	Connecticut	Bloomsburg, Pa.	FA-'04
Parrish, Roscoe	WR	5-9	168	7/16/82	Miami	Miami, Fla.	D2
Peoples, Will	WR	6-0	200	9/6/81	Oklahoma	Humble, Texas	FA
Preston, Duke	T/G	6-5	311	6/12/82	Illinois	San Diego, Calif.	D4
Pruce, David	T/G	6-8	328	6/1/78	Buffalo	Chardon, Ohio	FA-'04
Rheem, Joe	K	6-0	211	7/1/82	Kansas State	Wichita, Kan.	FA
Sverchek, Tom	DT	6-2	288	1/30/82	California	San Luis Obispo, Calif.	FA
Towns, Daryl	LB	6-0	236	9/21/82	Nevada	Pasadena, Calif.	FA-'04
Ward, Marvin	CB	5-11	208	8/7/82	Northwestern	Landover, Md.	FA
Wilson, George	WR	6-0	210	3/14/81	Arkansas	Paducah, Ky.	FA-'04

The term NFL Rookie is defined as a player who is in his first season of professional football and has not been on the roster of another professional football team for any regular-season or postseason games. A Rookie is designated by an "R" on NFL rosters. Players who have been active in another professional football league or players who have NFL experience, including either preseason training camp or being on an Active List or Inactive List, or on Reserve/Injured or Reserve/Physically Unable to Perform for fewer than six regular-season games, are termed NFL First-Year Players. An NFL First-Year Player is designated by a "1" on NFL rosters. Thereafter, a player is credited with an additional year of experience for each season in which he accumulates six games on the Active List or Inactive List, or on Reserve/Injured or Reserve/Physically Unable to Perform.

Log on to www.buffalobills.com for an up-to-date roster.

COACHING STAFF
Head Coach,
Mike Mularkey
Pro Career: Enters his second season with the Bills after being named as the thirteenth coach in franchise history on January 14, 2004. In his first season as head coach, the Bills rallied from an 0-4 to finish with a 9-7 record. The 1992 San Diego Chargers (11-5) are the only team in NFL history to finish with a better record after an 0-4 start. Mularkey also became only the third coach in Bills history to win nine or more games in his first season. Mularkey captained a team that showed toughness and fight in 2004, as well as the ability of all three units to combine to form one successful unit on the field. In his first season, Mularkey's Bills increased their win total by three games from 2003 and increased their point output by 152. During a six-game winning streak late in the season, the Bills averaged 38 points per game. With a renewed focus on attacking opponents with a physical style of play, the Bills improved their rushing yardage output by 210 yards and gave up their lowest sack total in five years with 38 sacks allowed. The team's defense ranked second in the NFL and in the top five in numerous categories while leading the league in takeaways with 39. The special teams unit ranked first in the NFL and tied a league record with 5 combined kickoff and punt return touchdowns. Mularkey came to Buffalo with 10 years experience as an NFL assistant coach and another nine as an NFL player. He spent three seasons (2001-03) as the offensive coordinator for the Pittsburgh Steelers, who ranked among the NFL's top five overall offenses in two of those three years. In 2001, Mularkey's first as coordinator, Pittsburgh had the league's number one-ranked rushing attack and the third-ranked overall offense. That year, the Steelers posted a 13-3 regular season record, won the AFC Central title, and advanced to the AFC Championship Game. The next year, Pittsburgh had the league's fifth-ranked overall offense and again won the division crown as well as a first-round playoff game before falling 34-31 in overtime to Tennessee in a Divisional Playoff game. Mularkey was named Pittsburgh's offensive coordinator on January 5, 2001 after five seasons as Pittsburgh's tight ends coach. He broke into coaching at Concordia College (Minn.) in 1993 before spending the next two seasons as an assistant with the Tampa Bay Buccaneers. Mularkey was the Buccaneers' quality control coach in 1994, and tight ends coach in 1995. He was selected in the ninth round of the 1983 draft by the San Francisco 49ers and went on to spend nine seasons as an NFL tight end with the Minnesota Vikings (1983-88) and Pittsburgh Steelers (1989-91). His career statistics include 102 catches for 1,222 yards and 9 touchdowns. Career record: 9-7.

Background: Played collegiately at Florida and finished his Gator career with 55 catches for 628 yards and 3 touchdowns. He later earned a dual degree in kinesiology and sociology from Minnesota.

Personal: Born November 19, 1961 in Fort Lauderdale, Fla. He and his wife, Betsy, have two sons, Shane and Patrick.

ASSISTANT COACHES
Bobby April, special teams coordinator; born April 15, 1963, New Orleans. Linebacker/defensive end Nicholls State 1972-75. No pro playing experience. College coach: Southern Mississippi 1978, Tulane 1979, Arizona 1980-86, Southern California 1987-1990. Pro coach: Atlanta Falcons 1991-93, Pittsburgh Steelers 1994-95, New Orleans Saints 1996-99, St. Louis Rams 2001-02, joined Bills in 2004.

Don Blackmon, linebackers; born March 14, 1958, Pompano Beach, Fla. Linebacker Tulsa 1977-1980. Pro linebacker New England Patriots 1981-87. Pro coach: New England Patriots 1988-1990, Cleveland Browns 1991-92, New York Giants 1993-96, Atlanta Falcons 1997-2001, joined Bills in 2003.

Tom Clements, offensive coordinator; born June 18, 1953, McKees Rocks, Pa. Quarterback Notre Dame 1972-74. Pro quarterback Ottawa Rough Riders (CFL) 1975-78, Hamilton Tiger-Cats (CFL) 1979, 1981-82, Kansas City Chiefs 1980, Winnipeg Blue Bombers (CFL) 1983-87, College coach: Notre Dame 1992-95. Pro coach: New Orleans Saints 1997-99, Kansas City Chiefs 2000, Pittsburgh Steelers 2001-03, joined Bills in 2004.

Jerry Gray, defensive coordinator; born December 16, 1962, Lubbock, Texas. Safety Texas 1981-84. Pro defensive back Los Angeles Rams 1985-1991, Houston Oilers 1992, Tampa Bay Buccaneers 1993. College coach: Southern Methodist 1995-96. Pro coach: Tennessee Titans 1997-2000, joined Bills in 2001.

Tim Krumrie, defensive line; born May 20, 1960, Menomonie, Wis. Defensive tackle Wisconsin 1979-1982. Pro defensive tackle Cincinnati Bengals 1983-1994. Pro coach: Cincinnati Bengals 1995-2002, joined Bills in 2003.

Chuck Lester, defensive assistant; born May 18, 1955, Chicago. Linebacker Oklahoma 1974. No pro playing experience. College coach: Iowa State 1980-81, Oklahoma 1982-84. Pro coach: Kansas City Chiefs 1984-86 (scout), joined Bills in 1987.

Jim McNally, offensive line; born December 13, 1943, Buffalo. Guard Buffalo 1961-65. No pro playing experience. College coach: Buffalo 1966-1970, Marshall 1971-74, Boston College 1975-77, Wake Forest 1978-79. Pro coach: Cincinnati Bengals 1980-94, Carolina Panthers 1995-98, New York Giants 1999-2003, joined Bills in 2004.

Mike Miller, tight ends; born April 9, 1970, Plum Borough, Pa. No college or pro playing experience. College coach: Robert Morris 1997-98. Pro coach: Pittsburgh Steelers 1999-2003, joined Bills in 2004.

Brad Roll, strength & conditioning; born July 4, 1958, Houston. Center Blinn (Tex.) J.C. 1976-77, Stephen F. Austin 1978-79. No pro playing experience. College coach: Stephen F. Austin 1980, Southwestern Louisiana 1981-86, Kansas 1987-88, Miami 1989-1992. Pro coach: Tampa Bay Buccaneers 1993-95, Miami Dolphins 1996-2003, joined Bills in 2004.

Eric Studesville, running backs; born May 29, 1967, Madison, Wis. Defensive back Wisconsin-Whitewater 1985-88. No pro playing experience. College coach: Wingate 1994, Kent State 1995-96. Pro coach: Chicago Bears 1997-2000, New York Giants 2001-03, joined Bills in 2004.

Steve Szabo, defensive backs; born September 11, 1943, Chicago. Halfback-defensive back Navy 1961-64. No pro playing experience. College coach: Johns Hopkins 1969, Toledo 1970, Iowa 1971-73, Syracuse 1974-76, Iowa State 1977-78, Ohio State 1979-1981, Western Michigan 1982-84, Edinboro 1985-87 (head coach), Northern Iowa 1988, Colorado State 1989-1990, Boston College 1991-93. Pro coach: Jacksonville 1995-2002, joined Bills in 2004.

Tyke Tolbert, wide receivers; born September 15, 1967, Conroe, Texas. Wide receiver Louisiana State 1988-90. No pro playing experience. College coach: Louisiana-Monroe 1994-97, Auburn 1998, Louisiana-Lafayette 1999-2001, Florida 2002. Pro coach: Arizona Cardinals 2003, joined Bills in 2004.

Frank Verducci, offensive line; born March 17, 1957, Glen Ridge, N.J. Tight end/fullback U.S. Merchant Marine Academy-Kings Point 1975. No pro playing experience. College coach: Colorado State 1980, Maryland 1981-83, Northern Illinois 1984, Iowa 1985-86, 1989-1998, Northwestern 1987-88. Pro coach: Cincinnati Bengals 1999-2001, Dallas Cowboys 2002, joined Bills in 2004.

Sam Wyche, quarterbacks; born January 5, 1945, Atlanta. Quarterback Furman 1963-65. Pro quarterback Cincinnati Bengals 1968-1970, Washington Redskins 1971-73, Detroit Lions 1974, St. Louis Cardinals 1976, Buffalo Bills 1976. College coach: South Carolina 1967, Indiana 1983 (head coach). Pro coach: San Francisco 49ers 1979-1982, Cincinnati Bengals 1984-1991 (head coach), Tampa Bay Buccaneers 1992-95 (head coach), joined Bills in 2004.

**American Football Conference
North Division**
Team Colors: Black, Orange, and White
One Paul Brown Stadium
Cincinnati, Ohio 45202-3492
Telephone: (513) 621-3550
Ticket Office (513) 621-TDTD (8383)

2005 SCHEDULE
PRESEASON
Aug. 12 **New England** 7:30
Aug. 19 at Washington 8:00
Aug. 26 at Philadelphia..................7:30
Sept. 2 **Indianapolis**........................7:30

REGULAR SEASON
Sept. 11 at Cleveland 1:00
Sept. 18 **Minnesota** 1:00
Sept. 25 at Chicago........................12:00
Oct. 2 **Houston** 1:00
Oct. 9 at Jacksonville...................8:30
Oct. 16 at Tennessee 12:00
Oct. 23 **Pittsburgh**..........................1:00
Oct. 30 **Green Bay**.........................1:00
Nov. 6 at Baltimore........................1:00
Nov. 13 Open Date
Nov. 20 **Indianapolis**......................1:00
Nov. 27 **Baltimore**...........................1:00
Dec. 4 at Pittsburgh......................1:00
Dec. 11 **Cleveland** 1:00
Dec. 18 at Detroit 4:05
Dec. 24 **Buffalo** (Sat.) 1:00
Jan. 1 at Kansas City 12:00

Stadium: Paul Brown Stadium
(opened in 2000)
• **Capacity:** 65,326
One Paul Brown Stadium
Cincinnati, Ohio 45202-3492
Playing Surface: Synthetic
Training Camp: Georgetown College
Georgetown, Kentucky
40324

PAUL BROWN STADIUM

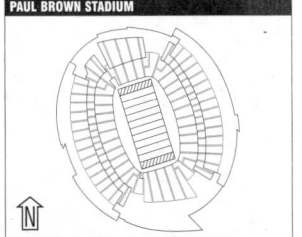

CLUB OFFICIALS
President: Mike Brown
Senior Vice President: Pete Brown
Executive Vice President: Katie Blackburn
Vice President: Paul Brown
Vice President: John Sawyer
Business Development: Troy Blackburn
Business Manager: Bill Connelly
Chief Financial Officer: Bill Scanlon
Director of Development—Paul Brown
Stadium: Bob Bedinghaus
Controller: Johanna Kappner
Managing Director of Paul Brown
Stadium: Eric Brown
Director of Technology: Jo Ann Ralstin
Bengals.com Editor: Geoff Hobson
Director of Sales and Public Affairs:
Jeff Berding
Director of Corporate Sales and
Marketing: Vince Cicero
Ticket Manager: Tim Kelly
Director of Ticket Sales: Kevin Lane
Director of Player Relations: Eric Ball
Director of Football Operations:
Jim Lippincott
Director of Player Personnel: Duke Tobin
Public Relations Director: Jack Brennan
Athletic Trainer: Paul Sparling
Equipment Manager: Rob Recker
Video Director: Travis Brammer

COACHING HISTORY
(247-328-1)
Records include postseason games
1968-1975	Paul Brown	55-59-1
1976-78	Bill Johnson*	18-15-0
1978-79	Homer Rice	8-19-0
1980-83	Forrest Gregg	34-27-0
1984-1991	Sam Wyche	64-68-0
1992-96	Dave Shula**	19-52-0
1996-2000	Bruce Coslet***	21-39-0
2000-02	Dick LeBeau	12-33-0
2003-04	Marvin Lewis	16-16-0

* Resigned after five games in 1978
** Released after seven games in 1996
*** Resigned after three games in 2000

ATTENDANCE
Home 512,498   Away 571,717
Total 1,084,215
Single-game home record,
65,362 (12/28/03)
Single-season home record, 512,498
(2004)

2005 DRAFT CHOICES
Round	Name	Pos.	College
1	Pollack, David	LB	Georgia
2	Odell Thurman	LB	Georgia
3	Chris Henry	WR	West Virginia
4	Eric Ghiaciuc	C	Central Michigan
5	Adam Kieft	T	Central Michigan
6	Tab Perry	WR	UCLA
7	Jonathan Fanene	DE	Utah

2004 TEAM RECORD

PRESEASON (2-2)

Date	Result		Opponent
8/14	L	6-20	at Tampa Bay
8/21	W	31-3	New England
8/28	L	10-37	at Atlanta
9/3	W	16-13	Indianapolis

REGULAR SEASON (8-8)

Date	Result		Opponent	Att.
9/12	L	24-31	at N.Y. Jets	77,230
9/19	W	16-13	Miami	65,705
9/26	L	9-23	Baltimore	65,575
10/3	L	17-28	at Pittsburgh	62,402
10/17	L	17-34	at Cleveland	73,263
10/25	W	23-10	Denver	65,806
10/31	L	20-27	at Tennessee	68,932
11/7	W	26-3	Dallas	65,721
11/14	W	17-10	at Washington	87,786
11/21	L	14-19	Pittsburgh	65,780
11/28	W	58-48	Cleveland	65,677
12/5	W	27-26	at Baltimore	69,695
12/12	L	28-35	at New England	68,756
12/19	L	17-33	Buffalo	65,378
12/26	W	23-22	N.Y. Giants	64,606
1/2	W	38-10	at Philadelphia	67,074

SCORE BY PERIODS

Bengals	69	108	96	101	0	—	374
Opponents	75	117	82	98	0	—	372

2004 TEAM STATISTICS

	Bengals	Opp.
Total First Downs	286	303
Rushing	93	123
Passing	172	158
Penalty	21	22
3rd Down: Made/Att	88/219	80/218
3rd Down Pct.	40.2	36.7
4th Down: Made/Att	6/12	5/15
4th Down Pct.	50.0	33.3
Possession Avg.	29:20	30:40
Total Net Yards	5140	5365
Avg. Per Game	321.3	335.3
Total Plays	1004	1031
Avg. Per Play	5.1	5.2
Net Yards Rushing	1839	2062
Avg. Per Game	114.9	128.9
Total Rushes	437	474
Net Yards Passing	3301	3303
Avg. Per Game	206.3	206.4
Sacked/Yards Lost	31/219	37/257
Gross Yards	3520	3560
Att./Completions	536/324	520/313
Completion Pct.	60.4	60.2
Had Intercepted	22	20
Punts/Average	84/41.7	79/41.9
Net Punting Avg.	84/35.5	79/35.7
Penalties/Yards	103/810	106/887
Fumbles/Ball Lost	17/10	40/16
Touchdowns	42	41
Rushing	14	11
Passing	23	23
Returns	5	7

2004 INDIVIDUAL STATISTICS

PASSING	Att.	Comp.	Yds.	Pct.	TD	Int.	Tkld.	Rate
Palmer	432	263	2,897	60.9	18	18	25/178	77.3
Kitna	104	61	623	58.7	5	4	6/41	75.9
Bengals	536	324	3,520	60.4	23	22	31/219	77.0
Opponents	520	313	3,560	60.2	23	20	37/257	79.5

SCORING	TD R	TD P	TD Rt	PAT	FG	Saf	PTS
Graham	0	0	0	41/41	27/31	0	122
R. Johnson	12	0	0	0/0	0/0	0	72
C. Johnson	0	9	0	0/0	0/0	0	54
Houshmandzadeh	0	4	0	0/0	0/0	0	24
Schobel	0	4	0	0/0	0/0	0	24
Washington	0	3	0	0/0	0/0	0	18
Geathers	0	0	1	0/0	0/0	0	6
J. Johnson	0	1	0	0/0	0/0	0	6
Kaesviharn	0	0	1	0/0	0/0	0	6
Larson	1	0	0	0/0	0/0	0	6
O'Neal	0	0	1	0/0	0/0	0	6
Palmer	1	0	0	0/0	0/0	0	6
Simmons	0	0	1	0/0	0/0	0	6
Stewart	0	1	0	0/0	0/0	0	6
Watson	0	1	0	0/0	0/0	0	6
M. Williams	0	0	1	0/0	0/0	0	6
Bengals	14	23	5	41/41	27/31	0	374
Opponents	11	23	7	40/40	28/31	1	372

2-Pt. Conversions: None.
Bengals 0-1, Opponents 0-1.

RUSHING	No.	Yds	Avg	LG	TD
R. Johnson	361	1,454	4.0	52	12
Watson	26	161	6.2	25	0
Houshmandzadeh	6	51	8.5	16	0
Palmer	18	47	2.6	14	1
Kitna	10	42	4.2	15	0
C. Johnson	4	39	9.8	18	0
Russell	3	15	5.0	13	0
Warrick	2	14	7.0	8	0
Larson	1	11	11.0	11t	1
J. Johnson	3	5	1.7	4	0
Perry	2	1	0.5	1	0
Washington	1	-1	-1.0	-1	0
Bengals	437	1,839	4.2	52	14
Opponents	474	2,062	4.4	75t	11

RECEIVING	No.	Yds	Avg	LG	TD
C. Johnson	95	1,274	13.4	53t	9
Houshmandzadeh	73	978	13.4	62	4
Washington	31	378	12.2	28	3
Watson	25	171	6.8	21	1
Schobel	21	201	9.6	76t	4
J. Johnson	16	53	3.3	9	1
Kelly	15	85	5.7	14	0
R. Johnson	15	84	5.6	30	0
Warrick	11	127	11.5	30	0
Stewart	10	48	4.8	9	1
Walter	8	67	8.4	18	0
Perry	3	33	11.0	13	0
Russell	1	21	21.0	21	0
Bengals	324	3,520	10.9	76t	23
Opponents	313	3,560	11.4	99t	23

INTERCEPTIONS	No.	Yds	Avg	LG	TD
James	8	66	8.3	23	0
O'Neal	4	60	15.0	31t	1
M. Williams	3	51	17.0	51t	1
Simmons	2	61	30.5	50t	1
Geathers	1	36	36.0	36t	1
Herring	1	0	0	0	0
Powell	1	-2	-2.0	-2	0
Bengals	20	272	13.6	51t	4
Opponents	22	446	20.3	62t	4

PUNTING	No.	Yds.	Avg.	In 20	LG
Larson	83	3,499	42.2	21	66
Bengals	84	3,499	41.7	21	66
Opponents	79	3,309	41.9	23	69

PUNT RETURNS	Ret	FC	Yds	Avg	LG	TD
Ratliff	17	5	207	12.2	49	0
Houshmandzadeh	11	7	88	8.0	28	0
O'Neal	7	6	33	4.7	17	0
Bengals	35	18	328	9.4	49	0
Opponents	51	10	378	7.4	63	0

KICKOFF RETURNS	No.	Yds	Avg	LG	TD
Russell	39	872	22.4	40	0
Watson	13	240	18.5	32	0
Houshmandzadeh	10	227	22.7	32	0
Stewart	3	20	6.7	10	0
Kelly	1	14	14.0	14	0
Lan. Moore	1	15	15.0	15	0
O'Neal	1	15	15.0	15	0
Bengals	68	1,403	20.6	40	0
Opponents	80	1,573	19.7	41	0

FIELD GOALS	1-19	20-29	30-39	40-49	50+
Graham	0/0	7/7	10/12	7/8	3/4
Bengals	0/0	7/7	10/12	7/8	3/4
Opponents	0/0	13/13	8/8	7/10	0/0

SACKS	No.
J. Smith	8.0
Clemons	6.5
Hardy	4.0
Geathers	3.5
Thornton	3.0
L. Johnson	2.0
Powell	2.0
M. Williams	2.0
Lan. Moore	1.0
O'Neal	1.0
Simmons	1.0
Webster	1.0
Bengals	37.0
Opponents	31.0

RECORD HOLDERS
INDIVIDUAL RECORDS—CAREER

Category	Name	Performance
Rushing (Yds.)	Corey Dillon, 1997-2003	8,061
Passing (Yds.)	Ken Anderson, 1971-1986	32,838
Passing (TDs)	Ken Anderson, 1971-1986	197
Receiving (No.)	Carl Pickens, 1992-99	530
Receiving (Yds.)	Isaac Curtis, 1973-1984	7,101
Interceptions	Ken Riley, 1969-1983	65
Punting (Avg.)	Dave Lewis, 1970-73	43.8
Punt Return (Avg.)	Mike Martin, 1983-89	9.9
Kickoff Return (Avg.)	Lemar Parrish, 1970-77	24.7
Field Goals	Jim Breech, 1980-1992	225
Touchdowns (Tot.)	Pete Johnson, 1977-1983	70
Points	Jim Breech, 1980-1992	1,151

INDIVIDUAL RECORDS—SINGLE SEASON

Category	Name	Performance
Rushing (Yds.)	Rudi Johnson, 2004	1,454
Passing (Yds.)	Boomer Esiason, 1986	3,959
Passing (TDs)	Ken Anderson, 1981	29
Receiving (No.)	Carl Pickens, 1996	100
Receiving (Yds.)	Chad Johnson, 2003	1,355
Interceptions	Ken Riley, 1976	9
Punting (Avg.)	Dave Lewis, 1970	46.2
Punt Return (Avg.)	Lemar Parrish, 1974	18.8
Kickoff Return (Avg.)	Tremain Mack, 1999	27.1
Field Goals	Doug Pelfrey, 1995	29
Touchdowns (Tot.)	Carl Pickens, 1995	17
Points	Shayne Graham, 2004	122

INDIVIDUAL RECORDS—SINGLE GAME

Category	Name	Performance
Rushing (Yds.)	Corey Dillon, 10-22-00	278
Passing (Yds.)	Boomer Esiason, 10-7-90	490
Passing (TDs)	Boomer Esiason, 12-21-86	5
	Boomer Esiason, 10-29-89	5
Receiving (No.)	Carl Pickens, 10-11-98	13
Receiving (Yds.)	Eddie Brown, 11-6-88	216
Interceptions	Many times	3
	Last time by David Fulcher, 12-17-89	
Field Goals	Doug Pelfrey, 11-6-94	6
Touchdowns (Tot.)	Larry Kinnebrew, 10-28-84	4
	Corey Dillon, 12-4-97	4
Points	Larry Kinnebrew, 10-28-84	24
	Corey Dillon, 12-4-97	24

2005 VETERAN ROSTER

No.	Name	Pos.	Ht.	Wt.	Birthdate	NFL Exp.	College	Hometown	How Acq.	'04 Games/ Starts
53	Abdullah, Khalid	LB	6-2	227	3/6/79	3	Mars Hill	Jacksonville Beach, Fla.	D5-'03	0*
71	Anderson, Willie	T	6-5	340	7/11/75	10	Auburn	Whistler, Ala.	D1-'96	16/16
79	Andrews, Stacy	T	6-7	346	6/2/81	2	Mississippi	Camden, Ark.	D4c-'04	1/0
96	Askew, Matthias	DT	6-5	308	7/1/82	2	Michigan State	Ft. Lauderdale, Fla.	D4a-'04	5/0
21	Bauman, Rashad	CB	5-8	184	5/7/79	4	Oregon	Phoenix, Ariz.	W(Wash)-'04	4/0
74	Braham, Rich	C	6-4	305	11/6/70	12	West Virginia	Morgantown, W. Va.	W(Ariz)-'94	10/10
4	Bramlet, Casey	QB	6-4	225	4/2/81	2	Wyoming	Wheatland, Wyo.	D7-'04	0*
27	Brooks, Greg	CB	5-11	177	12/16/80	2	Southern Mississippi	New Orleans, La.	D6-'04	0*
13	Broussard, Jamall	WR	5-9	172	8/19/81	2	San Jose State	Kingwood, Texas	FA-'05	8/0*
92	Clemons, Duane	DE	6-5	275	5/23/74	10	California	Riverside, Calif.	FA-'03	14/14
67#	Fontenot, Jerry	C	6-3	300	11/21/66	17	Texas A&M	Lafayette, La.	FA-'04	11/6
91	Geathers, Robert	DE	6-3	271	8/11/83	2	Georgia	Georgetown, S.C.	D4b-'04	14/1
17	Graham, Shayne	K	6-0	197	12/9/77	5	Virginia Tech	Dublin, Va.	W(Car)-'03	16/0
22	Herring, Kim	S	6-0	212	9/10/75	9	Penn State	Solon, Ohio	FA-'04	12/10
84	Houshmandzadeh, T.J.	WR	6-1	197	9/26/77	5	Oregon State	Barstow, Calif.	D7-'01	16/13
20	James, Tory	CB	6-2	192	5/18/73	10	Louisiana State	New Orleans, La.	FA-'03	16/16
73	Johnson, Belton	T	6-6	303	7/23/80	2	Mississippi	Coffeeville, Miss.	FA-'04	0*
85	Johnson, Chad	WR	6-1	192	1/9/78	5	Oregon State	Miami, Fla.	D2-'01	16/16
31	Johnson, Jeremi	FB	5-11	265	9/4/80	3	Western Kentucky	Louisville, Ky.	D4b-'03	16/6
59	Johnson, Landon	LB	6-2	227	3/13/81	2	Purdue	Lubbock, Texas	D3b-'04	16/11
32	Johnson, Rudi	HB	5-10	220	10/1/79	5	Auburn	Ettrick, Va.	D4-'01	16/16
76	Jones, Levi	T	6-5	310	8/24/79	4	Arizona State	Eloy, Ariz.	D1-'02	16/16
34	Kaesviharn, Kevin	S	6-1	194	8/29/76	5	Augustana (S.D.)	Lakewood, Calif.	FA-'01	15/6
82	Kelly, Reggie	TE	6-4	255	2/22/77	7	Mississippi State	Aberdeen, Miss.	UFA(Atl)-'03	16/15
3	Kitna, Jon	QB	6-2	220	9/21/72	9	Central Washington	Tacoma, Wash.	UFA(Sea)-'01	4/3
75	Kooistra, Scott	G	6-6	320	10/14/80	3	North Carolina State	Cary, N.C.	D7a-'03	16/0
19	Larson, Kyle	P	6-1	204	9/2/80	2	Nebraska	Funk, Neb.	FA-'04	16/0
94	Martin, Terrance	DT	6-2	323	7/6/79	3	North Carolina State	Toano, Va.	FA-'04	2/0
58	Miller, Caleb	LB	6-3	225	9/3/80	2	Arkansas	Sulphur Springs, Texas	D3a-'04	13/3
81	Milons, Freddie	WR	5-11	193	6/27/80	3	Alabama	Starkville, Miss.	FA-'05	0*
42	Mitchell, Anthony	S	6-1	198	12/13/74	6	Tuskegee	Atlanta, Ga.	FA-'04	12/0
60	Moore, Langston	DT	6-1	303	7/17/81	3	South Carolina	Charleston, S.C.	FA-'03	15/8
50	Moore, Larry	G/C	6-3	300	6/1/75	8	Brigham Young	San Diego, Calif.	FA-'04	13/1
37	Myles, Reggie	CB	5-11	185	10/10/79	4	Alabama	Pascagoula, Miss.	FA-'02	16/0
24	O'Neal, Deltha	CB	5-11	190	1/30/77	6	California	Milpitas, Calif.	T(Den)-'04	12/10
9	Palmer, Carson	QB	6-5	230	12/27/79	3	Southern California	Mission Viejo, Calif.	D1-'03	13/13
77	Patterson, Elton	DE	6-2	271	6/3/81	3	Central Florida	Tallahassee, Fla.	FA-'05	8/0*
23	Perry, Chris	HB	6-0	224	12/27/81	2	Michigan	Advance, N.C.	D1-'04	2/0
72	Powell, Carl	DE	6-2	285	1/4/74	7	Louisville	Detroit, Mich.	UFA(Wash)-'03	10/2
25	Ratliff, Keiwan	CB	5-11	190	4/19/81	2	Florida	Columbus, Ohio	D2a-'04	16/5
30	Roberts, Terrell	CB	5-10	197	4/7/81	3	Oregon State	Richmond, Calif.	FA-'03	11/1
98	Robinson, Bryan	DT	6-4	296	6/22/74	9	Fresno State	Toledo, Ohio	UFA(Mia)-'05	16/13*
88	Russell, Cliff	WR	5-11	186	2/8/79	4	Utah	Fayetteville, N.C.	FA-'04	13/1
48	St. Louis, Brad	LS/TE	6-3	247	8/19/76	6	Southwest Missouri State	Belton, Mo.	D7-'00	16/0
89	Schobel, Matt	TE	6-5	257	11/4/78	4	Texas Christian	Columbus, Texas	D3-'02	16/1
93	Scott, Greg	DT	6-4	293	10/2/79	3	Hampton	Courtland, Va.	FA-'04	1/0
28	Shabazz, Siddeeq	S	5-11	200	2/5/81	3	New Mexico State	Anthony, N.M.	W(Atl)-'05	15/0*
56	Simmons, Brian	LB	6-3	244	6/21/75	8	North Carolina	New Bern, N.C.	D1b-'98	15/15
90	Smith, Justin	DE	6-4	270	9/30/79	5	Missouri	Holt's Summit, Mo.	D1-'01	16/16
66	Smith, Shaun	DT	6-2	320	8/19/81	2	South Carolina	Brooklyn, N.Y.	W(NO)-'04	8/2*
65	Steinbach, Eric	G/T	6-6	297	4/4/80	3	Iowa	Lockport, Ill.	D2-'03	16/5
95	Stevens, Larry	LB	6-2	241	1/22/82	2	Michigan	Tacoma, Wash.	FA-'04	9/0
86	Stewart, Tony	TE	6-5	260	8/9/79	5	Penn State	Allentown, Pa.	W(Phil)-'02	16/9
62	Sulfsted, Alex	T	6-3	320	12/21/77	4	Miami (OH)	Cincinnati, Ohio	FA-'04	4/0
97	Thornton, John	DT	6-3	297	10/2/76	7	West Virginia	Philadelphia, Pa.	UFA(Tenn)-'03	16/16
83	Walter, Kevin	WR	6-3	218	8/4/81	3	Eastern Michigan	Libertyville, Ill.	FA-'03	16/0
80	Warrick, Peter	WR	5-11	192	6/19/77	6	Florida State	Bradenton, Fla.	D1-'00	4/1
87	Washington, Kelley	WR	6-3	218	8/21/79	3	Tennessee	Stephens City, Va.	D3-'03	16/2
33	Watson, Kenny	HB	5-11	218	3/13/78	4	Penn State	Harrisburg, Pa.	FA-'03	16/0
52	Webster, Nate	LB	6-0	235	11/29/77	6	Miami	Miami, Fla.	UFA(TB)-'04	3/3
55	Wilkins, Marcus	LB	6-2	235	1/2/80	4	Texas	Austin, Texas	W(Ariz)-'04	16/16
63	Williams, Bobbie	G	6-4	330	9/25/76	6	Arkansas	Jefferson, Texas	UFA(Phil)-'04	16/16
40	Williams, Madieu	S	6-1	193	10/18/81	2	Maryland	Lanham, Md.	D2b-'04	16/13

* Abdullah missed '04 season because of injury; Bramlet did not play in 3 games and was inactive for 13 games; Brooks was inactive for 1 game; Broussard played 8 games with Carolina in '04; B. Johnson missed '04 season because of injury; Milons last active with Pittsburgh in '03; Patterson played 6 games with Jacksonville and 2 games with Cincinnati; Robinson played 16 games with Miami; Shabazz played 15 games with Atlanta; S. Smith played 5 games with New Orleans and 3 games with Cincinnati.

\# Unrestricted free agent; subject to developments.

Players lost through free agency (3): LB Frank Chamberlin (Hou; 0 games in '04), P Kyle Richardson (Cle; 0), DT Tony Williams (Jax; 6).

Also played with Bengals in '04—S Rogers Beckett (7 games), LB Kevin Hardy (16), FB James Lynch (1).

2005 FIRST-YEAR ROSTER

Name	Pos.	Ht.	Wt.	Birthdate	College	Hometown	How Acq.
Anderson, Lyonel	TE	6-3	253	8/20/82	Kansas	Rochester, N.Y.	FA
Augustin, Allen (1)	LB	6-0	227	6/12/81	Florida State	Miami, Fla.	FA
Body, Patrick	S/CB	6-2	192	1/17/82	Toledo	Pittsburgh, Pa.	FA
Cherry, Matt (1)	WR	6-1	203	12/14/81	Akron	Chicago, Ill.	W(Jax)-'04
Cockheran, Jeremiah (1)	WR	6-0	191	1/11/81	Hawaii	Fontana, Calif.	FA
Crawford, Derrick (1)	DE	6-3	270	9/13/78	Texas A&M-Commerce	Avon Park, Fla.	FA
Demers, Rich	FB	6-0	250	4/25/81	Massachusetts	East Boston, Mass.	FA
Dickerson, Kori (1)	TE	6-4	240	12/6/78	Southern California	Los Angeles, Calif.	W(Wash)
Easlick, Doug (1)	FB	5-11	243	12/4/80	Virginia Tech	Marlton, N.J.	FA
Fanene, Jonathan	DE	6-4	291	3/19/82	Utah	Pago Pago, American Samoa	D7
Ghent, Ronnie (1)	TE	6-2	253	1/5/80	Louisville	Lakeland, Fla.	FA
Ghiaciuc, Eric	C	6-4	302	5/28/81	Central Michigan	Oxford, Mich.	D4
Haldi, Josh	QB	6-2	215	7/10/82	Northern Illinois	Madison, Ohio	FA
Henry, Chris	WR	6-4	197	5/17/83	West Virginia	Belle Chasse, La.	D3
Jones, Herana-Daze	S	5-11	211	4/15/82	Indiana	Louisville, Ky.	FA
Key, Sale	WR	6-4	226	11/3/81	Idaho State	Citrus Heights, Calif.	FA
Kieft, Adam	T	6-7	337	8/21/82	Central Michigan	Rockford, Mich.	D5
Lougheed, Pete (1)	T	6-5	300	11/5/79	Purdue	Fort Wayne, Ind.	W(Cin)-'04
Perry, Tab	WR	6-3	229	1/20/82	UCLA	Milpitas, Calif.	D6
Pollack, David	LB	6-2	265	6/19/82	Georgia	Snellville, Ga.	D1
Sullivan, Cedric	LB	6-2	248	2/4/83	Troy	Houston, Texas	FA
Thomas, Jeremy	FB	5-11	245	11/23/81	Georgia	Loganville, Ga.	FA
Thurman, Odell	LB	6-0	233	7/9/83	Georgia	Monticello, Ga.	D2
Vieira, Steven	G	6-6	311	1/22/82	UCLA	Carlsbad, Calif.	FA
Wilkerson, Ben	C	6-4	300	11/22/82	Louisiana State	Hemphill, Texas	FA
Williams, Brandon (1)	CB	5-11	186	11/17/80	Michigan	Omaha, Neb.	FA
Wilson, Quincy (1)	HB	5-9	225	4/26/81	West Virginia	Weirton, W. Va.	W(Atl)-'04
Young, James	S	6-1	214	7/2/82	Georgia Southern	Tampa, Fla.	FA

The term NFL Rookie is defined as a player who is in his first season of professional football and has not been on the roster of another professional football team for any regular-season or postseason games. A Rookie is designated by an "R" on NFL rosters. Players who have been active in another professional football league or players who have NFL experience, including either preseason training camp or being on an Active List or Inactive List, or on Reserve/Injured or Reserve/Physically Unable to Perform for fewer than six regular-season games, are termed NFL First-Year Players. An NFL First-Year Player is designated by a "1" on NFL rosters. Thereafter, a player is credited with an additional year of experience for each season in which he accumulates six games on the Active List or Inactive List, or on Reserve/Injured or Reserve/Physically Unable to Perform.

COACHING STAFF
Head Coach,
Marvin Lewis

Pro Career: After establishing himself as a record-setting NFL defensive coordinator, Lewis was named the ninth head coach in Bengals history on January 14, 2003. In two seasons, he has re-established the Bengals as a playoff contender with clubs that have attracted record fan support. Cincinnati has posted consecutive 8-8 records under Lewis, winning as many games in the last two seasons as it did in the previous four. In 2004, with a quarterback (Carson Palmer) seeing his first NFL playing time and with five rookie or first-year defenders frequently on the field at the same time, the Bengals again finished 8-8 and sold out every regular season home game for the first time since 1992. The 2004 club set a total attendance record for the second consecutive year. In 2003, the Bengals were the NFL's most improved team (six-game increase), and Lewis finished second in *Associated Press* voting for NFL Coach of the Year while also being named Rookie Coach of the Year by *Football Digest*. Prior to his arrival, Lewis directed the NFL's fifth-ranked defensive unit with the Washington Redskins (2002), serving as assistant head coach in addition to his coordinator's role. He spent six seasons (1996-2001) as defensive coordinator with the Baltimore Ravens, a tenure that included a Super Bowl victory following the 2000 season. In the 2000 regular season, Lewis' Baltimore defense set the NFL record for fewest points allowed in a 16-game campaign (165). Lewis' 2000 defensive unit has been widely considered as one of the best NFL defenses of all time. The 970 rushing yards allowed was the fewest in NFL history for a 16-game season. The Ravens' four shutouts were the most in the NFL since 1976. Prior to joining Baltimore, he spent four seasons (1992-95) with Pittsburgh as linebackers coach, guiding Pro Bowl players Kevin Greene, Chad Brown, Levon Kirkland, and Greg Lloyd. Career record: 16-16.

Background: Lewis earned All-Big Sky Conference honors as a linebacker at Idaho State for three years (1978-1980), and he also saw action at quarterback and free safety. He received his bachelor's degree in physical education from Idaho State in 1981, and earned his Master's degree in athletic administration from the school in 1982. He was inducted into Idaho State's Hall of Fame in 2001. Lewis began his coaching career at his alma mater, Idaho State (1981-84). The team finished 12-1 during Lewis' first season and won the NCAA Division I-AA championship. Lewis was also a linebackers coach at Long Beach State (1985-86), New Mexico (1987-89), and Pittsburgh (1990-91).

Personal: Born Sept. 23, 1958, McDonald, Pa. Lewis and his wife, Peggy, have two children—Whitney and Marcus.

ASSISTANT COACHES

Paul Alexander, asst. head coach/offensive line; born February 12, 1960, Rochester, N.Y. Tackle Cortland State 1979-1981. No pro playing experience. College coach: Penn State 1982-84, Michigan 1985-86, Central Michigan 1987-1991. Pro coach: New York Jets 1992-93, joined Bengals in 1994.

Jim Anderson, running backs; born March 27, 1948, Harrisburg, Pa. Linebacker/defensive end California Western 1967-69. No pro playing experience. College coach: California Western 1970-71, Scottsdale (Ariz.) C.C. 1973, Nevada-Las Vegas 1974-75, Southern Methodist 1976-1980, Stanford 1981-83. Pro coach: Joined Bengals in 1984.

Bob Bratkowski, offensive coordinator; born December 2, 1955, San Angelo, Texas. Wide receiver Washington State 1975-77. No pro playing experience. College coach: Missouri 1978-1980, Weber State 1981-85, Wyoming 1986, Washington State 1987-88, Miami 1989-1991. Pro coach: Seattle Seahawks 1992-98, Pittsburgh Steelers 1999-2000, joined Bengals in 2001.

Chuck Bresnahan, defensive coordinator; born September 8, 1960, Springfield, Mass. Linebacker Navy 1979-1982. No pro playing experience. College coach: Navy 1983, 1986, Georgia Tech 1987-1991, Maine 1992-93. Pro coach: Cleveland Browns 1994-95, Indianapolis Colts 1996-97, Oakland Raiders 1998-2003, joined Bengals in 2004.

Louie Cioffi, asst. defensive backs; born September 21, 1973, Greenlawn, N.Y. Attended SUNY-Stony Brook. No college or pro playing experience. College coach: C.W. Post 1995-96. Pro coach: New York Jets 1993-94, joined Bengals in 1997.

Kevin Coyle, defensive backs; born January 14, 1956, Staten Island, N.Y. Defensive back Massachusetts 1975-77. No pro playing experience. College coach: Cincinnati 1978-79, Arkansas 1980, U.S. Merchant Marine Academy 1981, Holy Cross 1982-1990, Syracuse 1991-93, Maryland 1994-96, Fresno State 1997-2000. Pro coach: Joined Bengals in 2001.

Paul Guenther, staff assistant; born December 22, 1971, Richboro, Pa. Linebacker Ursinus College 1990-93. No pro playing experience. College coach: Western Maryland 1994-95, Ursinus College 1996, 1997-2001 (head coach 1997-2001), Jacksonville 1997. Pro coach: Washington Redskins 2002-03, joined Bengals in 2005.

Jay Hayes, defensive line; born March 3, 1960, South Fayette, Pa. Defensive end Idaho 1978-1981. Pro defensive end/linebacker Michigan Panthers (USFL) 1984, Memphis Showboats (USFL) 1985. College coach: Notre Dame 1988-1991, California 1992-94, Wisconsin 1995-98. Pro coach: Pittsburgh Steelers 1999-2001, Minnesota Vikings 2002, joined Bengals in 2003.

Jonathan Hayes, tight ends; born Aug. 11, 1962, South Fayette, Pa. Linebacker/tight end Iowa 1981-84. Pro tight end Kansas City Chiefs 1985-1993, Pittsburgh Steelers 1994-96. College coach: Oklahoma 1999-2002. Pro coach: Joined Bengals in 2003.

Ricky Hunley, linebackers; born November 11, 1961, Petersburg, Va. Linebacker Arizona 1980-83. Pro linebacker Denver Broncos 1984-87, Los Angeles Raiders 1989-1990. College coach: Southern California 1992-93, Missouri 1994-2000, Florida 2001. Pro coach: Washington Redskins 2002, joined Bengals in 2003.

Hue Jackson, wide receivers; born October 22, 1965, Los Angeles. Quarterback Pacific 1985-86. No pro playing experience. College coach: Pacific 1987-89, Cal State-Fullerton 1990, Arizona State 1992-95, California 1996, Southern California 1997-2000. Pro coach: London Monarchs (WFL) 1991, Washington Redskins 2001-03, joined Bengals in 2004.

Chip Morton, strength and conditioning; born November 27, 1962, Hamden, Conn. Attended North Carolina. No college or pro playing experience. College coach: Ohio State 1985-86, Penn State 1987-1991. Pro coach: San Diego Chargers 1992-94, Carolina Panthers 1995-98, Baltimore Ravens 1999-2001, Washington Redskins 2002, joined Bengals in 2003.

Ray Oliver, asst. strength and conditioning; born June 6, 1961, Cincinnati. Defensive back Ohio State 1980-81. College coach: Pittsburgh 1985-88, Kentucky 1989-1991, South Carolina 1993-95, Memphis 2001-03. Pro coach: Tampa Bay Buccaneers 1992, New Jersey Nets (NBA) 1996-97, joined Bengals in 2004.

Darrin Simmons, special teams; born April 9, 1973, Elkhart, Kan. Punter Kansas 1993-95. No pro playing experience. College coach: Kansas 1996, Minnesota 1997. Pro coach: Baltimore Ravens 1998, Carolina Panthers 1999-2002, joined Bengals in 2003.

Bob Surace, offensive assistant; born April 25, 1968, Harrisburg, Pa. Center Princeton 1987-89. No pro playing experience. College coach: Springfield College 1990-91, Maine Maritime Academy 1992-93, Rensselaer Polytechnic Institute 1995, Western Connecticut State 1996-2001 (head coach 2000-01). Pro coach: Shreveport Pirates (CFL) 1994, joined Bengals in 2002.

Ken Zampese, quarterbacks; born July 19, 1967, Santa Maria, Calif. Wide receiver San Diego 1985-88. No pro playing experience. College coach: San Diego 1989, Southern California 1990-91, Northern Arizona 1992-95, Miami (Ohio) 1996-97. Pro coach: Philadelphia Eagles 1998, Green Bay Packers 1999, St. Louis Rams 2000-02, joined Bengals in 2003.

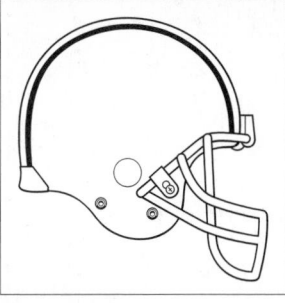

American Football Conference
North Division
Team Colors: Brown, Orange, and White
76 Lou Groza Blvd.
Berea, Ohio 44017
Telephone: (440) 891-5000

2005 SCHEDULE
PRESEASON
Aug. 13 **New York Giants** 8:00
Aug. 20 at Detroit 1:00
Aug. 26 **Carolina**...........................8:00
Sept. 1 at Chicago..........................7:00

REGULAR SEASON
Sept. 11 **Cincinnati** 1:00
Sept. 18 at Green Bay 3:15
Sept. 25 at Indianapolis 12:00
Oct. 2 Open Date
Oct. 9 **Chicago** 1:00
Oct. 16 at Baltimore.......................1:00
Oct. 23 **Detroit** 1:00
Oct. 30 at Houston 12:00
Nov. 6 **Tennessee** 1:00
Nov. 13 at Pittsburgh......................8:30
Nov. 20 **Miami**................................1:00
Nov. 27 at Minnesota 12:00
Dec. 4 **Jacksonville**.......................1:00
Dec. 11 at Cincinnati 1:00
Dec. 18 at Oakland 1:05
Dec. 24 **Pittsburgh** (Sat.) 1:00
Jan. 1 **Baltimore**...........................1:00

Stadium: Cleveland Browns Stadium
(opened in 1999)
• **Capacity:** 73,300
100 Alfred Lerner Way
Cleveland, Ohio 44114
Playing Surface: Grass
Headquarters/Training Camp:
76 Lou Groza Boulevard
Berea, Ohio 44017

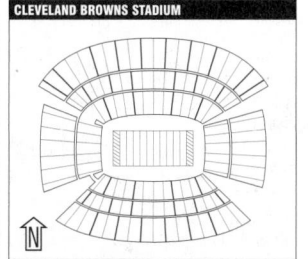
CLEVELAND BROWNS STADIUM

CLUB OFFICIALS
Owner: Randy Lerner
President and Chief Executive Officer:
John Collins
Senior Vice President and General
Manager: Phil Savage
Head Coach: Romeo Crennel
Executive Vice President and Chief
Financial Officer: Doug Jacobs
Executive Vice President and Chief
Operating Officer: Lew Merletti
Vice President of Communications:
Bill Bonsiewicz
Vice President of New Media and
Publishing: Vic Carucci
Vice President of Administration:
Diane Downing
Vice President of Security, Logistics and
Information Technology: Carl Meyer
President of the Cleveland Browns
Foundation: Jakki Nance
Vice President of Event and Stadium
Operations: Don Renzulli
Vice President of Broadcasting and
Production: George Veras
Director of Business Development:
Lorne Novick
Director of Corporate Sales and
Partnership Marketing: Brett Reynolds
Director of Direct Marketing and
Customer Service: John Schulze
Manager, Publicity/Media Relations:
Ken Mather
Head Athletic Trainer: Mike Colello
Equipment Manager: TBA
Video Director: Pat Dolan
Head Groundskeeper: Chris Powell

COACHING HISTORY
(415-352-10)
Records include postseason games
1950-1962 Paul Brown 115-49-5
1963-1970 Blanton Collier.............79-38-2
1971-74 Nick Skorich 30-26-2
1975-77 Forrest Gregg* 18-23-0
1977 Dick Modzelewski 0-1-0
1978-1984 Sam Rutigliano** 47-52-0
1984-88 Marty Schottenheimer ..46-31-0
1989-1990 Bud Carson*** 12-14-1
1990 Jim Shofner....................1-6-0
1991-95 Bill Belichick 37-45-0
1999-2000 Chris Palmer 5-27-0
2001-04 Butch Davis****........24-36-0
2004 Terry Robiskie 1-4-0
*Resigned after 13 games in 1977
**Released after eight games in 1984
***Released after nine games in 1990
****Resigned after 11 games in 2004

ATTENDANCE
Home 567,060   Away 549,592
Total 1,116,652
Single-game home record,
85,073 (9/21/70)
Single-season home record, 620,496
(1980)

2005 DRAFT CHOICES

Round	Name	Pos.	College
1	Braylon Edwards	WR	Michigan
2	Brodney Pool	DB	Oklahoma
3	Charlie Frye	QB	Akron
4	Antonio Perkins	DB	Oklahoma
5	David McMillan	LB	Kansas
6	Nick Speegle	LB	New Mexico
	Andrew Hoffman	DE	Virginia
7	Jon Dunn	T	Virginia Tech

2004 TEAM RECORD

PRESEASON (3-1)

Date	Result	Opponent
8/14	L 3-24	at Tennessee
8/21	W 17-10	Detroit
8/28	W 21-19	at Kansas City
9/3	W 24-10	Chicago

REGULAR SEASON (4-12)

Date	Result	Opponent	Att.
9/12	W 20-3	Baltimore	73,068
9/19	L 12-19	at Dallas	63,119
9/26	L 10-27	at N.Y. Giants	78,521
10/3	W 17-13	Washington	73,348
10/10	L 23-34	at Pittsburgh	63,609
10/17	W 34-17	Cincinnati	73,263
10/24	L 31-34	Philadelphia (OT)	73,394
11/7	L 13-27	at Baltimore	69,781
11/14	L 10-24	Pittsburgh	73,703
11/21	L 7-10	N.Y. Jets	72,547
11/28	L 48-58	at Cincinnati	65,677
12/5	L 15-42	New England	73,028
12/12	L 7-37	at Buffalo	72,330
12/19	L 0-21	San Diego	72,489
12/26	L 7-10	at Miami	73,169
1/2	W 22-14	at Houston	70,724

(OT) Overtime

SCORE BY PERIODS

Browns	67	62	55	92	0 —	276
Opponents	107	107	72	101	3 —	390

2004 TEAM STATISTICS

	Browns	Opp.
Total First Downs	245	307
Rushing	94	141
Passing	125	144
Penalty	26	22
3rd Down: Made/Att	59/203	78/216
3rd Down Pct.	29.1	36.1
4th Down: Made/Att	7/16	7/16
4th Down Pct.	43.8	43.8
Possession Avg.	28:03	31:57
Total Net Yards	4481	5215
Avg. Per Game	280.1	325.9
Total Plays	921	1024
Avg. Per Play	4.9	5.1
Net Yards Rushing	1657	2314
Avg. Per Game	103.6	144.6
Total Rushes	441	532
Net Yards Passing	2824	2901
Avg. Per Game	176.5	181.3
Sacked/Yards Lost	41/252	32/190
Gross Yards	3076	3091
Att./Completions	439/251	460/277
Completion Pct.	57.2	60.2
Had Intercepted	21	15
Punts/Average	85/40.0	85/41.6
Net Punting Avg.	85/35.4	85/33.9
Penalties/Yards	115/854	109/890
Fumbles/Ball Lost	32/19	20/13
Touchdowns	29	45
Rushing	6	22
Passing	21	17
Returns	2	6

2004 INDIVIDUAL STATISTICS

PASSING	Att.	Comp.	Yds.	Pct.	TD	Int.	Tkld.	Rate
Garcia	252	144	1,731	57.1	10	9	24/99	76.7
McCown	98	48	608	49.0	4	7	12/122	52.6
Holcomb	87	59	737	67.8	7	5	5/31	96.8
Echemandu	1	0	0	0.0	0	0	0/0	39.6
F. Jackson	1	0	0	0.0	0	0	0/0	39.6
Browns	439	251	3,076	57.2	21	21	41/252	74.9
Opponents	460	277	3,091	60.2	17	15	32/190	79.0

SCORING	TD R	TD P	TD Rt	PAT	FG	Saf	PTS
Dawson	0	0	0	28/28	24/29	0	100
Heiden	0	5	0	0/0	0/0	0	32
Bryant	0	4	0	0/0	0/0	0	24
Shea	0	4	0	0/0	0/0	0	24
Morgan	0	3	0	0/0	0/0	0	18
Suggs	2	1	0	0/0	0/0	0	18
André Davis	0	2	0	0/0	0/0	0	12
Garcia	2	0	0	0/0	0/0	0	12
Green	2	0	0	0/0	0/0	0	12
Northcutt	0	2	0	0/0	0/0	0	12
Alston	0	0	1	0/0	0/0	0	6
Crocker	0	0	1	0/0	0/0	0	6
Browns	6	21	2	28/28	24/29	0	276
Opponents	22	17	6	44/44	24/28	1	390

2-Pt. Conversions: Heiden.
Browns 1-1, Opponents 1-1.

RUSHING	No.	Yds	Avg	LG	TD
Suggs	199	744	3.7	39	2
Green	163	585	3.6	46	2
Garcia	35	169	4.8	21	2
J. Jackson	12	81	6.8	38	0
Echemandu	8	25	3.1	6	0
McCown	6	25	4.2	11	0
Northcutt	8	19	2.4	8	0
Smith	4	9	2.3	4	0
F. Jackson	1	4	4.0	4	0
Frost	1	1	1.0	1	0
Holcomb	3	-2	-0.7	0	0
André Davis	1	-3	-3.0	-3	0
Browns	441	1,657	3.8	46	6
Opponents	532	2,314	4.3	52	22

RECEIVING	No.	Yds	Avg	LG	TD
Northcutt	55	806	14.7	58t	2
Bryant	42	546	13.0	55t	4
Heiden	28	287	10.3	30	5
Shea	26	252	9.7	35	4
Suggs	20	178	8.9	59t	1
André Davis	16	416	26.0	99t	2
Green	14	84	6.0	17	0
F. Jackson	13	168	12.9	24	0
Morgan	9	144	16.0	46t	3
Smith	7	39	5.6	16	0
J. Jackson	6	22	3.7	13	0
Winslow	5	50	10.0	21	0
King	5	49	9.8	16	0
Echemandu	3	25	8.3	19	0
Mustard	1	9	9.0	9	0
Heinrich	1	1	1.0	1	0
Browns	251	3,076	12.3	99t	21
Opponents	277	3,091	11.2	72t	17

INTERCEPTIONS	No.	Yds	Avg	LG	TD
Henry	4	83	20.8	51	0
Andra Davis	3	35	11.7	30	0
Sanders	2	36	18.0	24	0
McCutcheon	2	0	0.0	2	0
Gardner	1	30	30.0	30	0
Little	1	28	28.0	28	0
Crocker	1	20	20.0	20t	1
Griffith	1	18	18.0	18	0
Browns	15	250	16.7	51	1
Opponents	21	232	11.0	106t	2

PUNTING	No.	Yds.	Avg.	In 20	LG
Frost	85	3,404	40.0	24	54
Browns	85	3,404	40.0	24	54
Opponents	85	3,537	41.6	21	62

PUNT RETURNS	Ret	FC	Yds	Avg	LG	TD
Northcutt	36	12	432	12.0	44	0
Browns	36	12	432	12.0	44	0
Opponents	48	10	313	6.5	49	0

KICKOFF RETURNS	No.	Yds	Avg	LG	TD
Alston	46	1,016	22.1	93t	1
D. Brown	13	243	18.7	30	0
King	5	95	19.0	24	0
F. Jackson	4	70	17.5	22	0
J. Jackson	2	39	19.5	23	0
Mustard	2	13	6.5	9	0
Shea	2	19	9.5	13	0
Sanders	1	9	9.0	10	0
Browns	75	1,504	20.1	93t	1
Opponents	59	1,336	22.6	93t	1

FIELD GOALS	1-19	20-29	30-39	40-49	50+
Dawson	0/0	11/11	6/8	6/9	1/1
Browns	0/0	11/11	6/8	6/9	1/1
Opponents	0/0	7/8	9/9	6/9	2/2

SACKS	No.
Ekuban	8.0
Lang	7.0
Warren	4.0
McKinley	3.0
Thompson	2.5
Crocker	2.0
Rogers	1.5
Griffith	1.0
Myers	1.0
Roye	1.0
Andra Davis	0.5
Holdman	0.5
Browns	32.0
Opponents	41.0

RECORD HOLDERS
INDIVIDUAL RECORDS—CAREER

Category	Name	Performance
Rushing (Yds.)	Jim Brown, 1957-1965	12,312
Passing (Yds.)	Brian Sipe, 1974-1983	23,713
Passing (TDs)	Brian Sipe, 1974-1983	154
Receiving (No.)	Ozzie Newsome, 1978-1990	662
Receiving (Yds.)	Ozzie Newsome, 1978-1990	7,980
Interceptions	Thom Darden, 1972-74, 1976-1981	45
Punting (Avg.)	Horace Gillom, 1950-56	43.8
Punt Return (Avg.)	Greg Pruitt, 1973-1981	11.8
Kickoff Return (Avg.)	Greg Pruitt, 1973-1981	26.3
Field Goals	Lou Groza, 1950-59, 1961-67	234
Touchdowns (Tot.)	Jim Brown, 1957-1965	126
Points	Lou Groza, 1950-59, 1961-67	1,349

INDIVIDUAL RECORDS—SINGLE SEASON

Category	Name	Performance
Rushing (Yds.)	Jim Brown, 1963	1,863
Passing (Yds.)	Brian Sipe, 1980	4,132
Passing (TDs)	Brian Sipe, 1980	30
Receiving (No.)	Ozzie Newsome, 1983	89
	Ozzie Newsome, 1984	89
Receiving (Yds.)	Webster Slaughter, 1989	1,236
Interceptions	Thom Darden, 1978	10
	Anthony Henry, 2001	10
Punting (Avg.)	Gary Collins, 1965	46.7
Punt Return (Avg.)	Leroy Kelly, 1965	15.6
Kickoff Return (Avg.)	Billy Lefear, 1975	31.7
Field Goals	Matt Stover, 1995	29
Touchdowns (Tot.)	Jim Brown, 1965	21
Points	Jim Brown, 1965	126

INDIVIDUAL RECORDS—SINGLE GAME

Category	Name	Performance
Rushing (Yds.)	Jim Brown, 11-24-57	237
	Jim Brown, 11-19-61	237
Passing (Yds.)	Brian Sipe, 10-25-81	444
Passing (TDs)	Frank Ryan, 12-12-64	5
	Bill Nelsen, 11-2-69	5
	Brian Sipe, 10-7-79	5
	Kelly Holcomb, 11-28-04	5
Receiving (No.)	Ozzie Newsome, 10-14-84	14
Receiving (Yds.)	Ozzie Newsome, 10-14-84	191
Interceptions	Many times	3
	Last time by Anthony Henry, 11-18-01	
Field Goals	Don Cockroft, 10-19-75	5
	Matt Stover, 10-29-95	5
	Phil Dawson, 1-2-05	5
Touchdowns (Tot.)	Dub Jones, 11-25-51	*6
Points	Dub Jones, 11-25-51	36

*NFL Record

2005 VETERAN ROSTER

No.	Name	Pos.	Ht.	Wt.	Birthdate	NFL Exp.	College	Hometown	How Acq.	'04 Games/ Starts
89	Alston, Richard	WR	5-11	215	11/20/80	2	East Carolina	Warrenton, N.C.	FA-'04	9/0
63	Andruzzi, Joe	T/G	6-3	312	8/23/75	9	Southern Connecticut St.	Staten Island, N.Y.	UFA(NE)-'05	16/16*
24	Baxter, Gary	CB/S	6-2	204	11/24/78	5	Baylor	Tyler, Texas	UFA(Balt)-'05	16/16*
28	Bodden, Leigh	CB/S	6-1	200	9/24/81	3	Duquesne	Upper Marlborough, Md.	FA-'03	8/1
78	Bogle, Phil	T/G	6-3	332	9/27/79	2	New Haven	Spring Valley, N.Y.	FA-'05	0*
20	Boyd, James	CB/S	5-11	208	10/17/77	2	Penn State	Chesapeake, Va.	FA-'05	0*
52	Boyer, Brant	LB	6-1	240	6/27/71	12	Arizona	Ogden, Utah	UFA(Jax)-'01	0*
47	Brooks, Jamal	LB	6-2	240	11/9/76	4	Hampton	Greneda Hills, Calif.	FA-'05	0*
81 t-	Bryant, Antonio	WR	6-2	188	3/9/81	4	Pittsburgh	Miami, Fla.	T(Dall)-'04	15/8*
35	Carter, Dyshod	CB/S	5-10	195	6/18/78	3	Kansas State	Denver, Colo.	FA-'04	5/0
65	Chambers, Kirk	T/G	6-7	313	3/19/79	2	Stanford	Provo, Utah	D6-'04	6/0
57	Coates, Sherrod	LB	6-2	242	12/22/78	2	Western Kentucky	Boynton Beach, Fla.	FA-'04	5/0
60	Coleman, Cosey	T/G	6-4	322	10/27/78	6	Tennessee	New Orleans, La.	UFA(TB)-'05	16/16*
75	Collins, Javiar	T/G	6-6	322	4/13/78	5	Northwestern	St. Paul, Minn.	FA-'04	0*
25	Crocker, Chris	CB/S	5-11	194	3/9/80	3	Marshall	Chesapeake, Va.	D3-'03	12/5
54	Davis, Andra	LB	6-1	255	12/23/78	4	Florida	Live Oak, Fla.	D5-'02	11/11
87	Davis, Andre'	WR	6-1	195	6/12/79	4	Virginia Tech	Niskayuna, N.Y.	D2-'02	7/7
4	Dawson, Phil	K	5-11	200	1/23/75	7	Texas	Dallas, Texas	FA-'99	16/0
70	DeMar, Enoch	T/G	6-4	320	9/7/80	3	Indiana	Indianapolis, Ind.	FA-'03	15/11
8 t-	Dilfer, Trent	QB	6-4	234	3/13/72	12	Fresno State	Aptos, Calif.	T(Sea)-'05	5/2*
34 t-	Droughns, Reuben	RB	5-11	220	8/21/78	6	Oregon	Chicago, Ill.	T(Den)-'05	16/15*
74	Eason, Nick	DE/DT	6-3	301	5/29/80	3	Clemson	Lyons, Ga.	FA-'04	1/0
23	Echemandu, Adimchinobe	RB	5-10	226	11/21/80	2	California	Lagos, Nigeria	D7-'04	4/0
50	Faine, Jeff	T/G	6-3	300	4/6/81	3	Notre Dame	Milwaukee, Ore.	D1-'03	13/13
95	Fisk, Jason	DT	6-3	295	9/4/72	11	Stanford	Davis, Calif.	UFA(SD)-'05	15/1*
67	Fowler, Melvin	T/G	6-3	305	3/31/79	4	Maryland	Wheatley Heights, N.Y.	D3-'02	15/3
3	Frost, Derrick	P	6-4	210	11/25/80	2	Northern Iowa	St. Louis, Mo.	FA-'03	16/0
94	Gordon, Amon	DE/DT	6-2	305	10/13/81	2	Stanford	San Diego, Calif.	D5-'04	6/0
29	Grant, William	DB	6-1	205	7/10/80	2	Mars Hill	Asheville, N.C.	FA-'04	0*
31	Green, William	RB	6-0	215	12/17/79	4	Boston College	Atlantic City, N.J.	D1-'02	15/13
71	Harris, Sterling	T/G	6-6	305	8/17/81	2	Southern Methodist	Dallas, Texas	FA-'04	0*
82	Heiden, Steve	TE	6-5	265	9/21/76	7	South Dakota State	Rushford, Minn.	T(SD)-'02	13/13
49	Heinrich, Keith	TE	6-5	260	3/19/79	4	Sam Houston State	Tomball, Texas	FA-'03	7/0
90	Jackson, Corey	DE/DT	6-6	255	11/6/78	2	Nevada	Cassatt, S.C.	FA-'03	1/0
19	Jackson, Frisman	WR	6-3	220	6/12/79	4	Western Illinois	Chicago, Ill.	FA-'04	10/0
22	Jameson, Michael	CB/S	5-11	205	7/14/79	5	Texas A&M	Killeen, Texas	D6-'01	16/0
85	Jones, C.J.	WR	5-11	195	9/20/80	2	Iowa	Boynton Beach, Fla.	FA-'03	0*
26	Jones, Sean	CB/S	6-1	215	3/2/82	2	Georgia	Atlanta, Ga.	D2-'04	0*
56	Kurpeikis, Justin	LB	6-3	254	7/17/77	3	Penn State	Pittsburgh, Pa.	FA-'05	5/0*
96	Lang, Kenard	DE/DT	6-3	280	1/31/75	9	Miami	Orlando, Fla.	UFA(Wash)-'02	16/15
39	Lehan, Michael	CB/S	6-0	190	11/25/79	3	Minnesota	Hopkins, Minn.	D5b-'03	10/2
33	McCutcheon, Daylon	CB/S	5-10	190	12/9/76	7	Southern California	La Puente, Calif.	D3a-'99	12/10
97	McKinley, Alvin	DE/DT	6-3	310	6/9/78	6	Mississippi State	Jackson, Miss.	FA-'01	16/2
40	Miller, Ben	FB	6-3	265	8/18/79	2	Air Force	Columbia Station, Ohio	FA-'02	0*
86	Northcutt, Dennis	WR	5-11	175	12/22/77	6	Arizona	Los Angeles, Calif.	D2-'00	16/11
62	Osika, Craig	T/G	6-3	318	12/4/79	3	Indiana	Valparaiso, Ind.	FA-'04	0*
64	Pontbriand, Ryan	LS	6-2	255	10/1/79	3	Rice	Houston, Texas	D5a-'03	16/0
73	Randall, Greg	T/G	6-5	322	6/23/78	5	Michigan State	Galveston, Texas	FA-'05	0*
10	Richardson, Kyle	P	6-2	210	3/2/73	8	Arkansas State	Farmington, Mo.	UFA(Cin)-'05	0*
99	Roye, Orpheus	DE/DT	6-4	320	1/21/73	10	Florida State	Carrol City, Fla.	UFA(Pitt)-'00	15/14
27	Russell, Brian	CB/S	6-2	204	2/5/78	4	San Diego State	West Covina, Calif.	RFA(Minn)-'05	16/16*
83	Shea, Aaron	TE	6-3	255	12/5/76	6	Michigan	Ottawa, Ill.	D4b-'00	15/8
42	Smith, Terrelle	FB	6-0	255	3/12/78	6	Arizona State	West Covina, Calif.	UFA(NO)-'04	16/9
55	Stewart, Matt	LB	6-3	232	8/31/79	5	Vanderbilt	Columbus, Ohio	UFA(Atl)-'05	16/15*
44	Suggs, Lee	RB	6-0	210	8/11/80	3	Virginia Tech	Roanoke, Va.	D4-'03	10/3
58	Taylor, Ben	LB	6-2	245	8/31/78	4	Virginia Tech	Bellaire, Ohio	D4b-'02	3/2
51	Thompson, Chaun	LB	6-2	250	5/22/80	3	West Texas A&M	Mt. Pleasant, Texas	D2-'03	16/13
72	Tucker, Ryan	T/G	6-6	320	6/12/75	9	Texas Christian	Midland, Texas	UFA(StL)-'02	7/7
53	Unck, Mason	LB	6-3	235	3/30/80	2	Arizona State	Ogden, Utah	FA-'04	1/0
77	Verba, Ross	T/G	6-4	305	10/31/73	9	Iowa	Des Moines, Iowa	UFA(GB)-'01	16/16
36	Williams, Renauld	LB	6-0	211	2/23/81	2	Hofstra	Westbury, N.Y.	W(Mia)-'05	2/0*
80	Winslow, Kellen	TE	6-4	250	7/21/83	2	Miami	San Diego, Calif.	D1-'04	2/2

* Andruzzi played 16 games with New England in '04; Baxter played 16 games with Baltimore; Bogle inactive for 2 games with San Diego; Boyd last active with Jacksonville in '02; Boyer missed '04 season because of injury; Brooks inactive for 6 games with Dallas; Bryant played 5 games with Dallas and 10 games with Cleveland; Coleman played 16 games with Tampa Bay; Collins inactive for 9 games; Dilfer played 5 games with Seattle; Droughns played 16 games with Denver; Fisk played 15 games with San Diego; Grant missed '04 season because of injury; Harris missed '04 season because of injury; C.J. Jones inactive for 11 games in '03; S. Jones missed '04 season on Physically Unable to Perform list; Kurpeikis played 5 games with New England; Miller missed '04 season because of injury; Osika inactive for 3 games; Randall last active with Houston in '03; Richardson missed '04 season with Cincinnati because of injury; Russell played 16 games with Minnesota; Stewart played 16 games with Atlanta; Williams played 2 games with Miami.

t- Browns traded for Bryant (Dall), Dilfer (Sea), Droughns (Den).

Traded—DE Ebenezer Ekuban (Den; 16 games in '04), QB Luke McCown (TB; 5), WR Quincy Morgan (Dall; 15), DT/DE Michael Myers (Den; 16), DT Gerard Warren (Den; 13).

Players lost through free agency (6): G Daimon Cook (Mia; 15 games in '04), LB Barry Gardner (NYJ; 14), CB Anthony Henry (Dall; 15), QB Kelly Holcomb (Buff; 4), LB Warrick Holdman (Wash; 16), CB Lewis Sanders (Hou; 16).

Also played with Browns in '04—LB Kevin Bentley (16 games), DE Courtney Brown (2), QB Jeff Garcia (11), G Kelvin Garmon (8), T/G Joaquin Gonzalez (16), S Robert Griffith (16), RB James Jackson (4), WR Andre King (9), S Earl Little (16), TE Chad Mustard (7), DE Tyrone Rogers (14), LB Eric Westmoreland (16), G Paul Zukauskas (14)

2005 FIRST-YEAR ROSTER

Name	Pos.	Ht.	Wt.	Birthdate	College	Hometown	How Acq.
Burt, Larry	DE/DT	6-2	304	11/10/81	Miami (OH)	Warrensville Heights, Ohio	FA
Byrd, Charles	CB/S	5-11	202	6/24/81	Morehead State	Oxford, Ohio	FA
Campbell, Lang	QB	6-1	199	9/25/81	William & Mary	Winchester, Va.	FA
Carberry, Kevin	DE/DT	6-4	269	5/19/83	Ohio	Oak Lawn, Ill.	FA
Chavez, Bradley	WR	6-0	195	4/21/82	Alabama-Birmingham	Satsuma, Ala.	FA
Cribbs, Josh	WR	6-1	192	6/9/83	Kent State	Washington, D.C.	FA
Dawson, Lewis (1)	T/G	6-5	320	2/25/81	Citadel	Fayetteville, N.C.	FA-'04
Dunn, Jonathon	T	6-7	328	12/12/81	Virginia Tech	Norfolk, Va.	D7
Edwards, Braylon	WR	6-3	211	2/21/83	Michigan	Detroit, Mich.	D1
Flowers, Bill	WR	6-0	183	12/16/80	Mississippi	Pelham, Ala	FA
Fraley, Justin	CB/S	5-11	204	12/8/81	Minnesota	Cleveland, Ohio	FA
Fraser, Simon	DE/DT	6-6	288	3/27/83	Ohio State	Upper Arlington, Ohio	FA
Frye, Charlie	QB	6-4	217	8/28/81	Akron	Willard, Ohio	D3
Harris, Josh (1)	QB	6-1	238	9/9/82	Bowling Green	Westerville, Ohio	FA-'04
Harrison, Kevin	LB	6-0	245	12/24/81	Eastern Michigan	Belleville, Mich.	FA
Hoffman, Andrew	DT	6-4	296	2/15/82	Virginia	Fairfax, Va.	D6b
Irons, Paul	TE	6-2	242	12/23/83	Florida State	New Orleans, La.	FA
Johnson, Jamall	CB/S	6-1	210	10/12/82	Northwestern State (LA)	LaPlace, La.	FA
King, James	CB/S	6-0	211	1/14/82	Central Michigan	Southfield, Mich.	FA
Mahl, Eric	LB	6-2	245	4/29/83	Kent State	Monroeville, Ohio	FA
McCullough, Sultan (1)	RB	6-0	197	2/20/80	Southern California	Pasadena, Calif.	FA-'04
McIntyre, Corey (1)	FB	6-0	245	1/25/79	West Virginia	Stuart, Fla.	FA-'04
McMillan, David	DE	6-3	262	9/20/81	Kansas	Killeen, Texas	D5
Moore, Ellery	DE/DT	6-1	300	9/28/82	Kentucky	Massillon, Ohio	FA
Moore, Lance	WR	5-9	177	8/31/83	Toledo	Westerville, Ohio	FA
Parker, J'Vonne	DE/DT	6-4	325	6/7/82	Rutgers	Newark, N.J.	FA
Perkins, Antonio	CB/S	5-11	188	1/9/82	Oklahoma	Lawton, Okla.	D4
Pool, Brodney	CB/S	6-2	208	5/24/84	Oklahoma	Houtson, Texas	D2
Rideau, Brandon	WR	6-3	200	10/18/82	Kansas	Beaumont, Texas	FA
Scott, Chad	RB	5-8	195	6/11/81	North Carolina	Plant City, Fla.	FA
Speegle, Nick	LB	6-6	250	11/29/81	New Mexico	Albuquerque, N.M.	D6a
Stickdorn, Clint	T/G	6-5	307	4/30/82	Cincinnati	Toledo, Ohio	FA

The term NFL Rookie is defined as a player who is in his first season of professional football and has not been on the roster of another professional football team for any regular-season or postseason games. A Rookie is designated by an "R" on NFL rosters. Players who have been active in another professional football league or players who have NFL experience, including either preseason training camp or being on an Active List or Inactive List, or on Reserve/Injured or Reserve/Physically Unable to Perform for fewer than six regular-season games, are termed NFL First-Year Players. An NFL First-Year Player is designated by a "1" on NFL rosters. Thereafter, a player is credited with an additional year of experience for each season in which he accumulates six games on the Active List or Inactive List, or on Reserve/Physically Unable to Perform.

Log on to www.clevelandbrowns.com for an up-to-date roster.

COACHING STAFF
Head Coach,
Romeo Crennel
Pro Career: Named head coach of the Browns on Feb. 8, 2005, becoming the eleventh full-time head coach in franchise history. Crennel, who returns to Cleveland after serving as the Browns defensive coordinator in 2000, most recently crafted the defense for the New England Patriots that won the Super Bowl in three of the last four seasons (2001, 2003-04). Crennel has 35 years of coaching experience, including 24 seasons in the NFL, and has appeared in six Super Bowls, with five Super Bowl rings. In 2004, Crennel's defense played an integral role in the Patriots' 24-21 win over the Philadelphia Eagles in Super Bowl XXXIX, as the defense forced 4 turnovers and registered 4 sacks. In 2004, his defensive unit was tied for third in the NFL with 45 sacks and tied for second with 260 points allowed (16.3 ppg.) despite using 10 different starting lineups. In 2003, he was recognized by the Pro Football Writers of America as the NFL's Assistant Coach of the Year. The New England defense was among the best units in NFL history, propelling the Patriots to a 15-game winning streak that culminated with a 32-29 victory over Carolina in Super Bowl XXXVIII. New England allowed a league-low and franchise-record 14.9 points per game, including 3 shutouts, while also leading the league with 29 interceptions. In 2001, the Patriots' defense surrendered just 272 points (17.0 ppg), ranking sixth in the league for fewest points allowed, as the Patriots won Super Bowl XXXVI for the first title in club history. Crennel seved a season as the defensive coordinator with the Cleveland Browns (2000) and coached for the New York Jets (1997-99). His first tenure in New England (1993-96) as defensive line coach ended with an appearance in Super Bowl XXXI. While an assistant coach with the New York Giants (1981-1992), the Giants won two Super Bowl titles (XXI and XXV) and reached the postseason six times. Career record: 0-0.
Background: Crennel coached collegiately at Western Kentucky (1970-74), Texas Tech (1975-77), Mississippi (1978-79), and Georgia Tech (1980). Crennel was a four-year starter (1966-69) as a defensive lineman at Western Kentucky, earning team MVP honors his senior year after moving to offensive tackle.
Personal: Born June 18, 1947 in Lynchburg, Va. Earned his bachelor's degree in physical education and Master's degree from Western Kentucky. Crennel and his wife, Rosemary, have three daughters—Lisa Tulley, Tiffany Crennel, and Kristin Cullinane.

ASSISTANT COACHES
Dave Atkins, running backs; born May 18, 1949, Victoria, Texas. Running back Texas El-Paso 1970-72. Pro running back San Francisco 49ers 1973, Honolulu Hawaiians (WFL) 1974, San Diego Chargers 1975. College coach: Texas El-Paso 1979-1980, San Diego State 1981-85. Pro coach: Philadelphia Eagles 1986-1992, New England Patriots 1993, Arizona Cardinals 1994-95, New Orleans Saints 1996, 2000-04, Minnesota Vikings 1997-99, joined Browns in 2005.
Maurice Carthon, offensive coordinator; born April 24, 1961, Chicago. Running back Arkansas State 1979-1982. Pro running back New Jersey Generals (USFL) 1983-85, N.Y. Giants 1985-1991, Indianapolis Colts 1992. Pro coach: New England Patriots 1994-96, N.Y. Jets 1997-2000, Detroit Lions 2001-02, Dallas Cowboys 2003-04, joined Browns in 2005.
Ben Coates, tight ends; born Aug. 16, 1969, Greenwood, S.C. Tight end Livingstone College 1987-1990. Pro tight end New England Patriots 1991-99, Baltimore Ravens 2000. College coach: Livingstone College 2001-04. Pro coach: Joined Browns in 2005.
Carl Crennel II, offensive quality control; born Sept. 7, 1974, Montreal, Quebec, Canada. Attended Robert Morris. No college or pro playing experience. College coach: Robert Morris 1998-2000, Duquesne 2002, West Virginia Tech 2003-04. Pro coach: Erie Invaders (IFL) 2000, Jacksonville Tomcats (AFL2) 2001, joined Browns in 2005.
Jeff Davidson, offensive line; born Oct. 3, 1967 in Akron, Ohio. Offensive lineman Ohio State 1986-89. Pro offensive lineman Denver Broncos 1990-92, New Orleans Saints 1994. Pro coach: New Orleans Saints 1995-96, New England Patriots 1997-2004, joined Browns in 2005.
Todd Grantham, defensive coordinator; born Sept. 13, 1966, Pulaski, Va. Offensive lineman Virginia Tech 1984-88. No pro playing experience. College coach: Virginia Tech 1990-95, Michigan State 1996-98. Pro coach: Indianapolis Colts 1999-2001, Houston Texans 2002-04, joined Browns in 2005.
Mike Haluchak, linebackers; born Nov. 28, 1949, Concord, Calif. Linebacker Southern California 1967-1970. No pro playing experience. College coach: Southern California 1976-77, Cal State-Fullerton 1978, Pacific 1979-1980, California 1981, North Carolina State 1982. Pro coach: Oakland Invaders (USFL) 1983-85, San Diego Chargers 1986-1991, Cincinnati Bengals 1992-93, Washington Redskins 1994-96, New York Giants 1997-99, St. Louis Rams 2000-02, Jacksonville Jaguars 2003-04, joined Browns in 2005.
John Lott, strength and conditioning; born May 9, 1964, Denton, Texas. Offensive lineman North Texas 1983-86. Pro offensive lineman Pittsburgh Steelers 1987. College coach: North Texas 1990, Houston 1991-96. Pro coach: New York Jets 1997-2004, joined Browns in 2005.
Randy Melvin, defensive line; born April 3, 1959, Aurora, Ill. Defensive line Eastern Illinois 1978-1981. No pro playing experience. College coach: Eastern Illinois 1988-1994, Wyoming 1995-96, Purdue 1997-99, Rutgers 2002-04, Illinois 2005. Pro coach: New England 2000-01, joined Browns in 2005.
Terry Robiskie, wide receivers; born Nov. 12, 1954, New Orleans. Running back Louisiana State 1973-76. Pro running back Oakland Raiders 1977-79, Miami Dolphins 1980-81. Pro coach: Los Angeles Raiders 1982-1993, Washington Redskins 1994-2000 (interim head coach 2000), joined Browns in 2001 (interim head coach 2004).
Jerry Rosburg, special teams coordinator; born Nov. 24, 1955, Fairmont, Minn. Linebacker North Dakota State 1974-77. No pro playing experience. College coach: Northern Michigan 1981-86, Western Michigan 1987-1991, Cincinnati 1992-95, Minnesota 1996, Boston College 1997-98, Notre Dame 1999-2000. Pro coach: Joined Browns in 2001.
Rip Scherer, quarterbacks; born Aug. 3, 1952. Quarterback William & Mary 1970-74. No pro playing experience. College coach: Penn State 1974-75, North Carolina State 1976, Hawaii 1977-78, Virginia 1979, Georgia Tech 1980-86, Alabama 1987, Arizona 1988-1990, James Madison 1991-94, Memphis 1995-2000, Kansas 2001, Southern Mississippi 2003-04. Pro coach: Joined Browns in 2005.
Bob Trott, defensive assistant; born March 19, 1954, Concord, N.C. College safety North Carolina 1973-75. No pro playing experience. College coach: North Carolina 1976-77, Air Force 1978-1983, Arkansas 1984-89, Clemson 1990, Duke 1996-2001, Baylor 2002, Louisiana-Monroe 2003-04. Pro coach: New York Giants 1991-92, New England Patriots 1993-95, joined Browns in 2005.
Mel Tucker, secondary; born Jan. 4, 1972, Cleveland. College defensive back Wisconsin 1992-95. No pro playing experience. College coach: Michigan State 1997, Miami (Ohio) 1998-99, Louisiana State 2000, Ohio State 2001-04. Pro coach: Joined Browns in 2005.
Jeff Uhlenhake, asst. offensive line; born Jan. 28, 1966, Newark, Ohio. College offensive lineman Ohio State 1985-88. Pro offensive lineman Miami Dolphins 1989-1993, New Orleans Saints 1994-96, Washington Redskins 1996-99. College coach: Ohio State 2003, Cincinnati 2004. Pro coach: Joined Browns in 2005.
Cory Undlin, defensive quality control; born June 29, 1971, St. Cloud, Minn. Safety California Lutheran 1990-94. No pro playing experience. College coach: California Lutheran 1998-2002, Fresno State 2002-03. Pro coach: New England 2004, joined Browns in 2005.

**American Football Conference
West Division
Team Colors:** Orange, Broncos Navy
Blue, and White
**13655 Broncos Parkway
Englewood, Colorado 80112
Telephone:** (303) 649-9000

**2005 SCHEDULE
PRESEASON**
Aug. 13 at Houston 7:00
Aug. 20 **San Francisco** 7:00
Aug. 27 **Indianapolis** 6:00
Sept. 2 at Arizona........................7:00

REGULAR SEASON
Sep. 11 at Miami..........................1:00
Sep. 18 **San Diego** 2:15
Sep. 26 **Kansas City** (Mon.)............7:00
Oct. 2   at Jacksonville 1:00
Oct. 9   **Washington** 2:15
Oct. 16 **New England** 2:15
Oct. 23 at New York Giants..........4:15
Oct. 30 **Philadelphia** 2:15
Nov. 6   Open Date
Nov. 13 at Oakland.......................1:05
Nov. 20 **New York Jets** 2:15
Nov. 24 at Dallas (Thu.) 3:15
Dec. 4   at Kansas City.................3:15
Dec. 11 **Baltimore** 2:15
Dec. 17 at Buffalo (Sat.)...............8:30
Dec. 24 **Oakland** (Sat.) 2:15
Dec. 31 at San Diego (Sat.)...........1:30

Stadium: INVESCO Field at Mile High
    (opened in 2001)
    •**Capacity:** 76,125
    1701 Bryant Street
    Denver, Colorado 80204
Playing Surface: Grass (PAT)
Training Camp: 13655 Broncos Parkway
    Englewood, Colorado
    80112

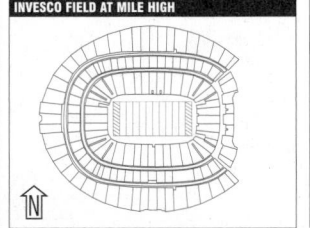

INVESCO FIELD AT MILE HIGH

CLUB OFFICIALS
President-Chief Executive Officer:
    Pat Bowlen
Executive Vice President of Football
    Operations/ Head Coach:
    Mike Shanahan
Executive Vice President of Business
    Operations: Joe Ellis
FOOTBALL STAFF
General Manager: Ted Sundquist
Director of Pro Scouting: Rick Smith
Director of College Scouting:
    Jim Goodman
Coordinator of Football Administration:
    Mike Bluem
Trainer: Steve Antonopulos
Equipment Manager: Chris Valenti
Video Director: Kent Erickson
BUSINESS STAFF
General Counsel/Senior Vice President of
    Administration: Rich Slivka
Vice President of Public Relations:
    Jim Saccomano
Vice President of Ticket Operations/
    Business Development: Rick Nichols
Vice President of Marketing: Greg Carney
Vice President of Finance: Jim Barlow
Vice President of Community
    Development: Cindy Galloway-Kellogg
STADIUM MANAGEMENT COMPANY
Vice President and General Manager:
    Mac Freeman

**COACHING HISTORY
(365-331-10)**
Records include postseason games
1960-61   Frank Filchock...............7-20-1
1962-61   Jack Faulkner* 9-22-1
1964-66   Mac Speedie**.............6-19-1
1966   Ray Malavasi 4-8-0
1967-1971 Lou Saban*** 20-42-3
1971   Jerry Smith 2-3-0
1972-76   John Ralston..............34-33-3
1977-1980 Robert (Red) Miller......42-25-0
1981-1992 Dan Reeves..............117-79-1
1993-94   Wade Phillips 16-17-0
1995-2004 Mike Shanahan 108-63-0
    *Released after four games in 1964
    **Resigned after two games in 1966
    ***Resigned after nine games in 1971

ATTENDANCE
Home 589,534   Away 525,858
Total 1,115,392
Single-game home record,
    76,643 (11/11/00)
Single-season home record, 594,813
    (2000)

2005 DRAFT CHOICES

Round	Name	Pos.	College
2	Darrent Williams	DB	Oklahoma State
3	Karl Paymah	DB	Washington St.
	Domonique Foxworth	DB	Maryland
	Maurice Clarett	RB	Ohio State
6	Chris Myers	T	Miami
7	Paul Ernster	K	Northern Arizona

2004 TEAM RECORD

PRESEASON (2-3)

Date	Result	Opponent
8/9	L 17-20	vs. Washington at Canton, OH
8/15	L 6-16	at Buffalo
8/21	W 19-3	at Seattle
8/27	W 31-17	Houston
9/2	L 21-33	Arizona

REGULAR SEASON (10-6)

Date	Result	Opponent	Att.
9/12	W 34-24	Kansas City	75,939
9/19	L 6-7	at Jacksonville	69,127
9/26	W 23-13	San Diego	74,533
10/3	W 16-13	at Tampa Bay	65,341
10/10	W 20-17	Carolina	75,072
10/17	W 31-3	at Oakland	62,507
10/25	L 10-23	at Cincinnati	65,806
10/31	L 28-41	Atlanta	75,083
11/7	W 31-13	Houston	74,292
11/21	W 34-13	at New Orleans	64,900
11/28	L 24-25	Oakland	75,936
12/5	L 17-20	at San Diego	65,395
12/12	W 20-17	Miami	75,027
12/19	L 17-45	at Kansas City	77,702
12/25	W 37-16	at Tennessee	68,809
1/2	W 33-14	Indianapolis	75,149

POSTSEASON (0-1)

Date	Result	Opponent	
1/9	L 24-49	at Indianapolis	56,609

SCORE BY PERIODS

Broncos	102	138	50	91	0	—	381
Opponents	68	121	67	48	0	—	304

2004 TEAM STATISTICS

	Broncos	Opp.
Total First Downs	351	235
Rushing	127	83
Passing	184	130
Penalty	40	22
3rd Down: Made/Att	78/206	65/209
3rd Down Pct.	37.9	31.1
4th Down: Made/Att	7/14	5/14
4th Down Pct.	50.0	35.7
Possession Avg.	32:38	27:23
Total Net Yards	6332	4459
Avg. Per Game	395.8	278.7
Total Plays	1070	918
Avg. Per Play	5.9	4.9
Net Yards Rushing	2333	1512
Avg. Per Game	145.8	94.5
Total Rushes	534	396
Net Yards Passing	3999	2947
Avg. Per Game	249.9	184.2
Sacked/Yards Lost	15/90	38/266
Gross Yards	4089	3213
Att./Completions	521/303	484/272
Completion Pct.	58.2	56.2
Had Intercepted	20	12
Punts/Average	70/40.5	95/44.7
Net Punting Avg.	70/34.3	95/38.2
Penalties/Yards	93/880	120/1062
Fumbles/Ball Lost	23/9	24/8
Touchdowns	42	35
Rushing	13	16
Passing	27	17
Returns	2	2

2004 INDIVIDUAL STATISTICS

PASSING

	Att.	Comp.	Yds.	Pct.	TD	Int.	Tkld.	Rate
Plummer	521	303	4,089	58.2	27	20	15/90	84.5
Broncos	521	303	4,089	58.2	27	20	15/90	84.5
Opponents	484	272	3,213	56.2	17	12	38/266	78.0

SCORING

	TD R	TD P	TD Rt	PAT	FG	Saf	PTS
Elam	0	0	0	42/42	29/34	0	129
Droughns	6	2	0	0/0	0/0	0	48
Lelie	0	7	0	0/0	0/0	0	42
Smith	0	7	0	0/0	0/0	0	42
Hape	0	4	0	0/0	0/0	0	24
Bell	3	0	0	0/0	0/0	0	18
Griffin	2	1	0	0/0	0/0	0	18
K. Johnson	0	2	0	0/0	0/0	0	12
Putzier	0	2	0	0/0	0/0	0	12
Carswell	0	1	0	0/0	0/0	0	6
Hearst	1	0	0	0/0	0/0	0	6
E. Johnson	0	0	1	0/0	0/0	0	6
Plummer	1	0	0	0/0	0/0	0	6
Watts	0	1	0	0/0	0/0	0	6
Wilson	0	0	1	0/0	0/0	0	6
Broncos	13	27	2	42/42	29/34	0	381
Opponents	16	17	2	31/32	21/26	0	304

2-Pt. Conversions: None.
Broncos 0-0, Opponents 0-3.

RUSHING

	No.	Yds	Avg	LG	TD
Droughns	275	1,240	4.5	51t	6
Bell	75	396	5.3	29	3
Griffin	85	311	3.7	47t	2
Plummer	62	202	3.3	22	1
Hearst	20	81	4.1	11	1
Smith	5	33	6.6	14	0
Watts	5	33	6.6	10	0
Sapp	4	32	8.0	18	0
Lelie	3	5	1.7	8	0
Broncos	534	2,333	4.4	51t	13
Opponents	396	1,512	3.8	44	16

RECEIVING

	No.	Yds	Avg	LG	TD
Smith	79	1,144	14.5	85t	7
Lelie	54	1,084	20.1	58	7
Putzier	36	572	15.9	39	2
Droughns	32	241	7.5	23t	2
Watts	31	385	12.4	28	1
Carswell	22	198	9.0	20	1
Griffin	10	68	6.8	22	1
K. Johnson	9	126	14.0	31	2
Jackson	8	73	9.1	20	0
Hape	8	35	4.4	11	4
Luke	6	52	8.7	12	0
Bell	5	80	16.0	58	0
Hearst	2	20	10.0	15	0
Bailey	1	11	11.0	11	0
Broncos	303	4,089	13.5	85t	27
Opponents	272	3,213	11.8	71t	17

INTERCEPTIONS

	No.	Yds	Avg	LG	TD
Bailey	3	0	0.0	0	0
Herndon	2	17	8.5	15	0
Wilson	2	17	8.5	10	1
Hayward	1	76	76.0	76	0
E. Johnson	1	32	32.0	32t	1
K. Kennedy	1	21	21.0	21	0
Williams	1	10	10.0	10	0
Lynch	1	2	2.0	2	0
Broncos	12	175	14.6	76	2
Opponents	20	344	17.2	97	1

PUNTING

	No.	Yds.	Avg.	In 20	LG
Knorr	54	2,243	41.5	12	66
Baker	15	591	39.4	7	48
Broncos	70	2,834	40.5	19	66
Opponents	95	4,250	44.7	36	65

PUNT RETURNS

	Ret	FC	Yds	Avg	LG	TD
Smith	22	8	223	10.1	30	0
Luke	19	8	135	7.1	21	0
Adams	2	1	42	21.0	39	0
Broncos	43	17	400	9.3	39	0
Opponents	32	11	295	9.2	50	0

KICKOFF RETURNS

	No.	Yds	Avg	LG	TD
R. Alexander	19	386	20.3	32	0
Luke	15	306	20.4	32	0
Droughns	14	344	24.6	48	0
Griffin	4	52	13.0	21	0
Sapp	1	34	34.0	34	0
Broncos	53	1,122	21.2	48	0
Opponents	68	1,635	24.0	97t	1

FIELD GOALS

	1-19	20-29	30-39	40-49	50+
Elam	0/0	10/10	7/8	9/12	3/4
Broncos	0/0	10/10	7/8	9/12	3/4
Opponents	0/0	6/6	7/8	3/5	5/7

SACKS

	No.
Hayward	10.5
E. Johnson	3.0
Palepoi	3.0
Coleman	2.5
Fatafehi	2.5
Wilson	2.5
Elliss	2.0
K. Kennedy	2.0
Lynch	2.0
Williams	2.0
Chukwurah	1.0
Herndon	1.0
R. Johnson	1.0
Middlebrooks	1.0
Pope	1.0
Spragan	1.0
Broncos	38.0
Opponents	15.0

RECORD HOLDERS
INDIVIDUAL RECORDS—CAREER

Category	Name	Performance
Rushing (Yds.)	Terrell Davis, 1995-2001	7,607
Passing (Yds.)	John Elway, 1983-1998	51,475
Passing (TDs)	John Elway, 1983-1998	300
Receiving (No.)	Rod Smith, 1995-2004	712
Receiving (Yds.)	Rod Smith, 1995-2004	9,772
Interceptions	Steve Foley, 1976-1986	44
Punting (Avg.)	Jim Fraser, 1962-64	45.2
Punt Return (Avg.)	Darrien Gordon, 1997-98	12.5
Kickoff Return (Avg.)	Abner Haynes, 1965-66	26.3
Field Goals	Jason Elam, 1993-2004	317
Touchdowns (Tot.)	Terrell Davis, 1995-2001	65
Points	Jason Elam, 1993-2004	1,442

INDIVIDUAL RECORDS—SINGLE SEASON

Category	Name	Performance
Rushing (Yds.)	Terrell Davis, 1998	2,008
Passing (Yds.)	Jake Plummer, 2004	4,089
Passing (TDs)	John Elway, 1997	27
	Jake Plummer, 2004	27
Receiving (No.)	Rod Smith, 2001	113
Receiving (Yds.)	Rod Smith, 2000	1,602
Interceptions	Goose Gonsoulin, 1960	11
Punting (Avg.)	Tom Rouen, 1998	46.9
Punt Return (Avg.)	Floyd Little, 1967	16.9
Kickoff Return (Avg.)	Bill Thompson, 1969	28.5
Field Goals	Jason Elam, 1995, 2001	31
Touchdowns (Tot.)	Terrell Davis, 1998	23
Points	Terrell Davis, 1998	138

INDIVIDUAL RECORDS—SINGLE GAME

Category	Name	Performance
Rushing (Yds.)	Mike Anderson, 12-3-00	251
Passing (Yds.)	Jake Plummer, 10-31-04	499
Passing (TDs)	Frank Tripucka, 10-28-62	5
	John Elway, 11-18-84	5
	Gus Frerotte, 11-19-00	5
Receiving (No.)	Rod Smith, 9-23-01	14
Receiving (Yds.)	Shannon Sharpe, 10-20-02	214
Interceptions	Goose Gonsoulin, 9-18-60	*4
	Willie Brown, 11-15-64	*4
	Deltha O'Neal, 10-7-01	*4
Field Goals	Gene Mingo, 10-6-63	5
	Rich Karlis, 11-20-83	5
	Jason Elam, 9-3-95, 10-13-02	5
Touchdowns (Tot.)	Clinton Portis, 12-7-03	5
Points	Clinton Portis, 12-7-03	30

*NFL Record

2005 VETERAN ROSTER

No.	Name	Pos.	Ht.	Wt.	Birthdate	NFL Exp.	College	Hometown	How Acq.	'04 Games/ Starts
81	Adams, Charlie	WR	6-2	190	10/23/79	3	Hofstra	Mechanicsburg, Pa.	FA-'04	4/0
69	Alexander, P.J.	G	6-4	297	12/23/78	3	Syracuse	Tallahassee, Fla.	FA-'03	5/0
45	Alexander, Roc	CB	5-10	186	9/23/81	2	Washington	Colorado Springs, Colo.	FA-'04	16/1
82	Alexander, Stephen	TE	6-4	250	11/7/75	8	Oklahoma	Chickasha, Okla.	UFA(Det)-'05	16/15*
38	Anderson, Mike	RB	6-0	230	9/21/73	6	Utah	Winnsboro, S.C.	D6-'00	0*
24	Bailey, Champ	CB	6-0	192	6/22/78	7	Georgia	Folkston, Ga.	T(Wash)-'04	16/16
26	Bell, Tatum	RB	5-11	213	3/2/81	2	Oklahoma State	Dallas, Texas	D2a-'04	14/0
42	Brandon, Sam	S	6-2	200	7/5/79	4	Nevada-Las Vegas	Riverside, Calif.	D4-'02	9/0
98	Brown, Courtney	DE	6-4	290	2/14/78	6	Penn State	Alvin, S.C.	FA-'05	2/2
51	Burns, Keith	LB	6-2	235	5/16/72	12	Oklahoma State	Alexandria, Va.	UFA(TB)-'05	16/0*
65	Carlisle, Cooper	G/T	6-5	295	8/11/77	6	Florida	McComb, Miss.	D4b-'00	16/3
89	Carswell, Dwayne	TE	6-3	290	1/18/72	12	Liberty	Jacksonville, Fla.	FA-'94	15/14
55	Chukwurah, Patrick	LB	6-1	250	3/1/79	5	Wyoming	Irving, Texas	FA-'04	14/0
70	Clabo, Tyson	G	6-6	314	10/17/81	2	Wake Forest	Knoxville, Tenn.	FA-'04	0*
	Clement, Anthony	T	6-8	337	4/10/76	8	Louisiana-Lafayette	Cecilia, La.	FA-'05	16/8*
92	Coleman, Marco	DE	6-3	270	12/18/69	14	Georgia Tech	Dayton, Ohio	UFA(Phil)-'04	16/16
96	Davis, Dorsett	DT	6-5	305	1/24/79	4	Mississippi State	Cleveland, Miss.	D3-'02	0*
33	Dayne, Ron	RB	5-10	245	3/14/78	6	Wisconsin	Berlin, N.J.	UFA(NYG)-'05	14/2
91 t-	Ekuban, Ebenezer	DE	6-3	275	5/29/76	7	North Carolina	Bowie, Md.	T(Cle)-'05	16/11*
1	Elam, Jason	K	5-11	200	3/8/70	13	Hawaii	Ft. Walton Beach, Fla.	D3b-'93	16/0
94	Elliss, Luther	DT	6-5	318	3/22/73	11	Utah	Mancos, Colo.	FA-'04	8/0
68	Fatafehi, Mario	DT	6-2	300	1/27/79	5	Kansas State	Honolulu, Hawaii	FA-'03	16/16
25	Ferguson, Nick	S	5-11	201	11/27/74	6	Georgia Tech	Miami, Fla.	FA-'03	16/1
72	Foster, George	T	6-5	338	6/9/80	3	Georgia	Macon, Ga.	D1-'03	16/16
	Gold, Ian	LB	6-0	223	8/23/78	6	Michigan	Belleville, Mich.	FA-'05	16/13*
74	Green, Cornell	T	6-6	315	8/25/76	6	Central Florida	St. Petersburg, Fla.	UFA(TB)-'04	0*
53	Green, Louis	LB	6-3	228	9/23/79	2	Alcorn State	Vicksburg, Miss.	FA-'03	6/0
21	Griffin, Quentin	RB	5-7	195	1/12/81	3	Oklahoma	Houston, Texas	D4a-'03	6/4
50	Hamilton, Ben	G/C	6-3	283	8/18/77	5	Minnesota	Minneapolis, Minn.	D4a-'01	16/16
86	Hape, Patrick	TE	6-4	262	6/6/74	9	Alabama	Killen, Ala.	UFA(TB)-'01	16/5
14	Jackson, Nate	WR	6-3	223	6/4/79	3	Menlo	San Jose, Calif.	T(SF)-'03	12/0
12	Johnson, B.J.	WR	5-11	207	8/4/82	2	Texas	Grand Prairie, Texas	FA-'04	0*
39	Johnson, Kyle	FB	6-0	242	12/15/78	3	Syracuse	Woodbridge, N.J.	FA-'03	14/3
99	Johnson, Raylee	DE	6-3	272	6/1/70	13	Arkansas	Fordyce, Ark.	FA-'04	14/1
13	Kanell, Danny	QB	6-3	218	11/21/73	8	Florida State	Fort Lauderdale, Fla.	FA-'03	0*
83	Leach, Mike	TE/LS	6-2	245	10/18/76	6	William & Mary	Jefferson Township, N.J.	FA-'02	16/0
85	Lelie, Ashley	WR	6-3	200	2/16/80	4	Hawaii	Honolulu, Hawaii	D1-'02	16/16
78	Lepsis, Matt	T	6-4	290	1/13/74	9	Colorado	Conroe, Texas	FA-'97	16/16
31	LeSueur, Jeremy	CB	6-0	197	10/5/80	2	Michigan	Holly Springs, Miss.	D3-'04	0*
87	Luke, Triandos	WR	5-10	189	12/24/81	2	Alabama	Phenix City, Ala.	D6a-'04	10/0
47	Lynch, John	S	6-2	220	9/25/71	13	Stanford	Del Mar, Calif.	FA-'04	15/15
19	Mattos, Grant	WR	6-2	200	3/12/81	2	Southern California	Mountain View, Calif.	FA-'04	0*
8	Mauck, Matt	QB	6-1	213	2/12/79	2	Louisiana State	Jasper, Ind.	D7a-'04	0*
23	Middlebrooks, Willie	CB	6-1	200	2/12/79	5	Minnesota	Homestead, Fla.	D1-'01	12/2
48	Miree, Brandon	RB	5-11	237	4/14/81	2	Pittsburgh	Cincinnati, Ohio	D7b-'04	0*
76 t-	Myers, Michael	DT	6-2	300	1/20/76	8	Alabama	Vicksburg, Miss.	T(Cle)-'05	16/7*
66	Nalen, Tom	C	6-3	286	5/13/71	12	Boston College	Foxboro, Mass.	D7c-'94	16/16
90	Nwokorie, Chukie	DE	6-3	285	7/10/75	6	Purdue	West Lafayette, Ind.	FA-'05	0*
95	Palepoi, Anton	DE	6-3	283	1/19/78	4	Nevada-Las Vegas	Salt Lake City, Utah	FA-'04	11/0
58	Pierce, Terry	LB	6-1	251	6/21/81	3	Kansas State	Fort Worth, Texas	D2-'03	15/0
16	Plummer, Jake	QB	6-2	212	12/19/74	9	Arizona State	Boise, Idaho	UFA(Ariz)-'03	16/16
75	Pope, Monsanto	DT	6-3	300	1/27/78	4	Virginia	Hopewell, Va.	D7b-'02	16/15
93	Pryce, Trevor	DE	6-5	295	8/3/75	9	Clemson	Winter Park, Fla.	D1-'97	2/1
88	Putzier, Jeb	TE	6-4	256	1/20/79	4	Boise State	Eagle, Idaho	D6-'02	16/5
	Rice, Jerry	WR	6-2	200	10/13/62	21	Mississippi Valley State	Crawford, Miss.	FA-'05	17/14*
37	Sapp, Cecil	RB	5-11	229	12/23/78	3	Colorado State	Miami, Fla.	FA-'03	5/0
10 t-	Sauerbrun, Todd	P	5-10	215	1/4/73	11	West Virginia	Garden City, N.Y.	FA-'01	16/0*
28	Shoate, Jeff	CB	5-10	189	3/23/81	2	San Diego State	San Diego, Calif.	D5-'04	7/0
80	Smith, Rod	WR	6-0	200	5/15/70	11	Missouri Southern	Texarkana, Ark.	FA-'94	16/16
59	Steele, Markus	LB	6-3	240	7/24/79	4	Southern California	Bedford, Ohio	FA-'05	0*
63	Stuber, Tim	G	6-5	315	2/2/78	3	Colorado State	Northglenn, Colo.	FA-'04	0*
97	Sykes, Jashon	LB	6-2	236	9/25/79	3	Colorado	Los Angeles, Calif.	FA-'02	3/0
97	Veal, Demetrin	DT	6-2	288	8/11/81	4	Tennessee	Paramount, Calif.	FA-'04	0*
35	Walls, Lenny	CB	6-4	192	9/26/79	4	Boston College	San Francisco, Calif.	FA-'02	7/1
61 t-	Warren, Gerard	DT/DE	6-4	325	7/25/78	5	Florida	Raiford, Fla.	T(Cle)-'05	13/13*

No.	Name	Pos.	Ht.	Wt.	NFL Birthdate	Exp.	College	Hometown	'04 Games/ How Acq.	Starts
17	Watts, Darius	WR	6-2	188	12/19/81	2	Marshall	Atlanta, Ga.	D2b-'04	16/2
52	Williams, D.J.	LB	6-1	242	7/20/82	2	Miami	Concord, Calif.	D1-'04	16/14
56	Wilson, Al	LB	6-0	240	6/21/77	7	Tennessee	Jackson, Tenn.	D1-'99	16/16
32	Young, Chris	S	6-0	210	1/23/80	3	Georgia Tech	Senoia, Ga.	D7a-'02	10/0

* Alexander played 16 games with Detroit in '04; Anderson missed '04 season because of injury; Brown played 2 games with Cleveland; Burns played 16 games with Tampa Bay; Clabo inactive for 2 games; Clement played 16 games with Arizona; Davis missed '04 season because of injury; Dayne played 14 games with N.Y. Giants; Ekuban played 16 games with Cleveland; Gold played 16 games with Tampa Bay; C. Green did not play in 3 games; B.J. Johnson missed '04 season because of injury; Kanell did not play in 16 games; LeSueur missed '04 season because of injury; Mattos last active with San Diego in '03; Mauck inactive for 2 games; Miree missed '04 season because of injury; Myers played 16 games with Cleveland; Nwokorie last active with Green Bay in '03; Rice played 6 games with Oakland and 11 with Seattle; Sauerbrun played 16 games with Carolina; Steele was last active with Dallas in '03; Stuber inactive for 2 games; Veal inactive for 3 games; Warren played 13 games with Cleveland.

t- Broncos traded for Ekuban (Cle), Myers (Cle), Sauerbrun (Car), Warren (Cle).

Traded—RB Reuben Droughns (16 games in '04) to Cleveland, P/K Jason Baker (Car; 10).

Players lost through free agency (4): DE Reggie Hayward (Jax; 16 games in '04), CB Kelly Herndon (Sea; 16), S Kenoy Kennedy (Det; 16), LB Donnie Spragan (Mia; 16).

Also played with Broncos in '04—DT Darius Holland (2 games), RB-Garrison Hearst (7), DT Ellis Johnson (13), P/K Micah Knorr (12), G Dan Neil (14 games).

2005 FIRST-YEAR ROSTER

Name	Pos.	Ht.	Wt.	Birthdate	College	Hometown	How Acq.
Briggs, Kris (1)	RB	5-11	242	4/17/81	Southern Methodist	Carthage, Texas	FA
Browner, Brandon	CB	6-4	221	8/2/84	Oregon State	Sylmar, Calif.	FA
Clarett, Maurice	RB	5-11	234	10/29/83	Ohio State	Youngstown, Ohio	D3c
Cox, Curome (1)	CB	6-1	199	2/28/81	Maryland	Washington, D.C.	FA-'04
Crenshaw, Romar (1)	WR	6-0	185	9/22/80	Southeastern Oklahoma St.	Broken Bow, Okla.	FA-'04
Crowell, Jeff (1)	P/K	6-1	195	8/4/73	Portland State.	Morgan Hill, Calif.	FA
Devoe, Todd (1)	WR	6-2	198	4/5/80	Central Missouri State	Fort Lauderdale, Fla.	FA
Duke, Wesley	TE	6-5	225	6/21/81	Mercer	Norcross, Ga.	FA
Ernster, Paul	P/K	6-0	217	1/26/82	Northern Arizona	Glendale, Ariz.	D7
Foxworth, Domonique	CB	5-11	178	3/27/83	Maryland	Catonsville, Md.	D3b
Fredrickson, Tyler (1)	P/K	6-3	220	2/26/81	California	Goleta, Calif.	FA
Garner, Randy (1)	DE	6-4	285	11/28/77	Arkansas	Atlanta, Texas	FA
Hicks, Reese (1)	G	6-6	318	2/14/80	Georgetown (KY)	Levanon, Ohio	FA
Hunt, Aaron (1)	DE	6-2	265	6/19/80	Texas Tech	Denison, Texas	FA
Myers, Chris	G/T	6-4	300	9/15/81	Miami	Miami, Fla.	D6
Paymah, Karl	CB	6-0	200	11/29/82	Washington State	Culver City, Calif.	D3a
Pears, Erik	T	6-8	315	6/25/82	Colorado State	Denver, Colo.	FA
Pinkard, Mike (1)	TE	6-4	259	12/27/79	Arizona State	Thornton, Colo.	FA
Renteria, D.J.	DT	6-3	300	1/15/81	New Mexico	Roswell, N.M.	FA-'04
Sewell, Josh (1)	C/G	6-2	300	7/26/81	Nebraska	Lincoln, Neb.	D6b-'04
Van Pelt, Bradlee (1)	QB	6-2	225	7/3/80	Colorado State	Santa Barbara, Calif.	D7c-'04
Williams, Darrent	CB	5-8	188	9/27/82	Oklahoma State	Fort Worth, Texas	D2

The term NFL Rookie is defined as a player who is in his first season of professional football and has not been on the roster of another professional football team for any regular-season or postseason games. A Rookie is designated by an "R" on NFL rosters. Players who have been active in another professional football league or players who have NFL experience, including either preseason training camp or being on an Active List or Inactive List, or on Reserve/Injured or Reserve/Physically Unable to Perform for fewer than six regular-season games, are termed NFL First-Year Players. An NFL First-Year Player is designated by a "1" on NFL rosters. Thereafter, a player is credited with an additional year of experience for each season in which he accumulates six games on the Active List or Inactive List, or on Reserve/Injured or Reserve/Physically Unable to Perform.

Log on to www.denverbroncos.com for an up-to-date roster.

COACHING STAFF

Head Coach,
Mike Shanahan

Pro Career: Became the eleventh head coach in Broncos history on January 31, 1995. Mike Shanahan led the Broncos to back-to-back Super Bowl championships in 1997 and 1998, becoming just the fifth head coach to accomplish that feat, and is the only coach to win seven consecutive postseason games in a two-year period. No NFL head coach has won more game than Mike Shanahan's 108 victories since the start of the 1995 season. During his NFL career, Shanahan has been a part of teams that have played in nine conference championship games and six Super Bowls. In 27 seasons as a pro and college coach, Shanahan's teams have participated in postseason or bowl games 22 times. Under Shanahan's guidance, Denver has set and NFL record by posting the most victories in both a two-year (33, 1997-98) and three-year (46, 1996-98) period. In the last twelve years (nine with Denver and three as offensive coordinator with the San Francisco 49ers), Shanahan's offenses have finished number one in the NFL four times, second twice, and third twice. Shanahan was an assistant with Denver (1984-87, 1989-1991) and San Francisco (1992-94). Returned to Denver as quarterbacks coach on October 16, 1989, after posting 8-12 record as the Los Angeles Raiders' head coach. Career record: 116-75.

Background: Shanahan coached at Oklahoma (1975-76), Northern Arizona (1977), Eastern Illinois (1978), Minnesota (1979), and Florida (1980-83).

Personal: Born in Oak Park, Illinois, on August 24, 1952. He was a wishbone quarterback-defensive back at Eastern Illinois. Mike and his wife, Peggy, have two children—Kyle and Krystal.

ASSISTANT COACHES

Ronnie Bradford, special teams; born October 1, 1970, Minot, N.D. Defensive back Colorado 1989-1992. Pro defensive back Denver Broncos 1993-95, Arizona Cardinals 1996, Atlanta Falcons 1997-2001, Minnesota Vikings 2002. Pro coach: Joined Broncos in 2003.

Tim Brewster, tight ends; born October 13, 1960, Phillipsburg, N.J. Tight End Illinois 1980-1983. No pro playing experience. College coach: Purdue 1986, North Carolina 1989-1997, Texas 1998-2001. Pro coach: San Diego Chargers 2002-04, joined Broncos in 2005.

Jacob Burney, defensive line/ends; born January 24, 1959, Chattanooga, Tenn. Defensive tackle Tennessee-Chattanooga 1977-1980. No pro playing experience. College coach: New Mexico 1983-86, Tulsa 1987, Mississippi State 1988, Wisconsin 1989, UCLA 1990-92, Tennessee 1993. Pro coach: Cleveland Browns/Baltimore Ravens 1994-98,

Carolina Panthers 1999-2001, joined Broncos in 2002.

Troy Calhoun, asst. to head coach; born September 26, 1966, McMinnville, Ore. Quarterback Air Force 1986-89. No pro playing experience. College coach: Air Force 1989, 1993-94, Ohio University 1994-2000, Wake Forest 2001-02. Pro coach: Joined Broncos in 2003.

Larry Coyer, defensive coordinator; born April 19, 1943, Huntington, W. Va. Linebacker Marshall 1962-64. No pro playing experience. College coach: Marshall 1965-67, Iowa 1974-77, Oklahoma State 1978, Iowa State 1979-1983, 1995-96, UCLA 1987-89, Houston 1990, Ohio State 1991-92, East Carolina 1993, Pittsburgh 1997-99. Pro coach: Michigan Panthers (USFL) 1984-85, Memphis Showboats (USFL) 1986, New York Jets 1994, joined Broncos in 2000.

Rick Dennison, offensive line; born June 22, 1958, in Kalispell, Mont. Tight end Colorado State 1976-79. Pro linebacker Denver Broncos 1982-1990. Pro coach: Joined Broncos in 1995.

Kirk Doll, linebackers; born September 24, 1951, Wichita, Kan. Defensive end-tackle East Carolina 1971-72. No pro playing experience. College coach: Wichita State 1975-76, Iowa State 1979, Tulsa 1980-84, Arizona State 1985-87, Texas A&M 1988-1994, Notre Dame 1994-2001, Louisiana State 2002-03. Pro coach: Joined Broncos in 2004.

Gary Kubiak, offensive coordinator; born August 15, 1961, Houston, Texas. Quarterback Texas A&M 1979-1982. Pro quarterback Denver Broncos 1983-1991. College coach: Texas A&M 1992-93. Pro coach: San Francisco 49ers 1994, joined Broncos in 1995.

Thomas McGaughey, special teams assistant; born May 8, 1973, Chicago. Safety Houston 1991-95. Pro safety Philadelphia Eagles 1996, Barcelona Dragons (NFLE) 1997. College coach: Houston 1997, 2003-04. Pro coach: Scottisch Claymores (NFLE) 2002, Kansas City Chiefs 2002, joined Broncos in 2005.

Pat McPherson, quarterbacks; born April 15, 1969, Santa Clara, Calif. Linebacker Santa Clara 1991-92. No pro playing experience. Pro coach: Joined Broncos in 1998.

Andre Patterson, defensive line/tackles; born June 12, 1960, Camdon, Ark. Offensive lineman Contra Costa (Calif.) J.C. 1978-1980, Montana 1981. No pro playing experience. College coach: Montana 1982, Weber State 1988, Cornell 1990-91, Washington State 1992-93, Cal Poly-San Luis Obispo 1994-96. Pro coach: New England Patriots 1997, Minnesota Vikings 1998-99, Dallas Cowboys 2000-02, Cleveland Browns 2003-04, joined Broncos in 2005.

Jim Ryan, defensive assistant; born May 18, 1957, Bellmawr, N.J.. Linebacker

William & Mary 1974-1978. Linebacker Denver Broncos 1979-1988. Pro coach: Joined Broncos in 2005.

Greg Saporta, asst. strength and conditioning; born February 2, 1957, New York, N.Y. Wide receiver Buffalo State 1977-79. No pro playing experience. College coach: Florida 1981-88, 1993-94, North Carolina 1989-1992. Pro coach: Joined Broncos in 1995.

Cedric Smith, asst. strength and conditioning; born May 27, 1968, Enterprise, Ala. Running back Florida 1986-89. Pro fullback Minnesota Vikings 1990, New Orleans Saints 1991, Washington Redskins 1994-95, Arizona Cardinals 1996-98. Pro coach: Joined Broncos in 2001.

Bob Slowik, defensive backs; born May 16, 1954, Pittsburgh. Defensive back Delaware 1973-76. No pro playing experience. College coach: Delaware 1977-78, Florida 1979-1982, Drake 1983, Rutgers 1984-89, East Carolina 1990-91. Pro coach: Dallas Cowboys 1992, Chicago Bears 1993-98, Cleveland Browns 1999, Green Bay Packers 2000-04, joined Broncos in 2005.

Ryan Slowik, defensive assistant; born Dec. 27, 1980, Chicago. Safety Wisconsin-Oshkosh 2002-03. No pro playing experience. College coach: Wisconsin-Oshkosh 2004. Pro coach: Joined Broncos in 2005.

Jimmy Spencer, asst. defensive backs; born March 29, 1969, Manning, S.C. Cornerback Florida 1988-1990. Pro cornerback Washington Redskins 1991, New Orleans Saints 1992-95, Cincinnati Bengals 1996-97, San Diego Chargers 1998-99, Denver Broncos 2000-current. Pro coach: Joined Broncos in 2003.

Bobby Turner, running backs; born May 6, 1949, East Chicago, Ind. Defensive back Indiana State 1968-1971. No pro playing experience. College coach: Indiana State 1975-1982, Fresno State 1983-88, Ohio State 1989-1990, Purdue 1991-94. Pro coach: Joined Broncos in 1995.

Rich Tuten, strength and conditioning; born December 30, 1953, Columbia, S.C. Nose guard Clemson 1976-78. No pro playing experience. College coach: Florida 1979-1988, 1993-94, North Carolina 1989-1992. Pro coach: Joined Broncos in 1995.

Steve Watson, wide receivers; born May 28, 1957, Baltimore. Wide receiver Temple 1975-78. Pro wide receiver Denver 1979-1987. Pro coach: Joined Broncos in 2001.

**American Football Conference
South Division**
Team Colors: Deep Steel Blue, Battle
Red, and Liberty White
Two Reliant Park
Houston, Texas 77054
Telephone: (832) 667-2000

2005 SCHEDULE
PRESEASON
Aug. 13 **Denver**...............................7:00
Aug. 20 **Oakland**............................7:00
Aug. 27 at Dallas.............................7:00
Sept. 1 at Tampa Bay 7:30

REGULAR SEASON
Sept. 11 at Buffalo 1:00
Sept. 18 **Pittsburgh**.......................12:00
Sept. 25 Open Date
Oct. 2 at Cincinnati 1:00
Oct. 9 **Tennessee** 12:00
Oct. 16 at Seattle...........................5:30
Oct. 23 **Indianapolis**...................12:00
Oct. 30 **Cleveland** 12:00
Nov. 6 at Jacksonville...................1:00
Nov. 13 at Indianapolis 1:00
Nov. 20 **Kansas City** 7:30
Nov. 27 **St. Louis** 12:00
Dec. 4 at Baltimore.......................1:00
Dec. 11 at Tennessee 12:00
Dec. 18 **Arizona** 12:00
Dec. 24 **Jacksonville** (Sat.)...........12:00
Jan. 1 at San Francisco................1:05

Stadium: Reliant Stadium
(opened in 2002)
•**Capacity:** 71,054
Houston, Texas 77054
Playing Surface: Grass
Training Camp: Reliant Park Practice
Facility

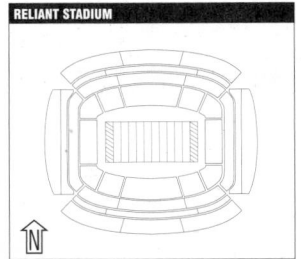

RELIANT STADIUM

CLUB OFFICIALS
Chairman and CEO: Robert C. McNair
Vice Chairman: Philip Burguieres
Senior Vice President and General
Manager/Football Operations:
Charley Casserly
Senior Vice President/Chief Sales &
Marketing Officer: Jamey Rootes
Senior Vice President/Treasurer and Chief
Financial Officer: Scott Schwinger
Senior Vice President/General Counsel
and Chief Administrative Officer:
Suzie Thomas
Vice President/Ticket Operations:
John Schriever
Vice President/Communications:
Tony Wyllie
Vice President/Corporate Sales:
John Vidalin
Vice President of Marketing: Kim Babiak
Controller: Marilan Logan
Director of Negotiations: Dan Ferens
Director of Pro Scouting: Chuck Banker
Associate Directors of Pro Scouting:
Bobby Grier, Miller McCalmon
Pro Scout: Rob Kisiel
Coordinator of College Scouting:
Mike Maccagnan
National Scout: George Saimes
College Scouts: Larry Bryan,
Eugene Armstrong, Pete Russell,
Dave Sears, Rob Lohman,
Tom Throckmorton
Pro and College Scouting Administrator:
Brian Hudspeth
Director of Operations: Barry Asimos
Director of Corporate Sales: Ted Major
Director of Security: Ryan Reichert
Director of Community Relations:
Regina Woolfolk
Director of Internet Services &
Publications: Carter Toole
Media Relations Manager:
Rocky Harris
Director of Player Programs:
Marcus Heard
Director of Information Technology:
Nick Ignatiev
Executive Director, Houston Texans
Foundation: Joanie Haley
Human Resources Administrator:
Glenda Morrison
Head Athletic Trainer: Kevin Bastin
Coordinator of Rehabilitation: Tom Colt
Assistant Athletic Trainer: John Ishop
Director of Equipment Services:
Jay Brunetti
Assistant Equipment Manager:
Matt Grupp, Christian Snell
Video Director: Ken Sparacino
Assistant Video Director: Joe Malota
Video Assistant: Robert Wells

COACHING HISTORY
(16-32-0)
2002-03   Dom Capers.................16-32-0

ATTENDANCE
Home 555,421   Away 533,147
Total 1,088,568
Single-game home record,
70,758 (12/21/03)
Single-season home record,
555,421 (2004)

2005 DRAFT CHOICES
Round	Name	Pos.	College
1	Travis Johnson	DE	Florida State
3	Vernand Morency	RB	Oklahoma State
4	Jerome Mathis	WR	Hampton
5	Drew Hodgdon	C	Arizona State
6	C.C. Brown	DB	Louisiana-Lafayette
7	Kenneth Pettway	LB	Grambling

HOUSTON TEXANS

2004 TEAM RECORD
PRESEASON (1-3)

Date	Result		Opponent
8/14	W	18-0	Dallas
8/21	L	3-38	at Pittsburgh
8/27	L	17-31	at Denver
9/2	L	9-17	Tampa Bay

REGULAR SEASON (7-9)

Date	Result		Opponent	Att.
9/12	L	20-27	San Diego	70,255
9/19	L	16-28	at Detroit	61,465
9/26	W	24-21	at Kansas City	77,433
10/3	W	30-17	Oakland	70,741
10/10	L	28-34	Minnesota (OT)	70,718
10/17	W	20-10	at Tennessee	68,932
10/31	W	20-6	Jacksonville	70,502
11/7	L	13-31	at Denver	74,292
11/14	L	14-49	at Indianapolis	56,511
11/21	L	13-16	Green Bay	70,769
11/28	W	31-21	Tennessee	70,721
12/5	L	7-29	at New York Jets	77,875
12/12	L	14-23	Indianapolis	70,762
12/19	W	24-5	at Chicago	62,122
12/26	W	21-0	at Jacksonville	66,227
1/2	L	14-22	Cleveland	70,724

(OT) Overtime

SCORE BY PERIODS

Texans	33	101	60	115	0	—	309
Opponents	61	105	85	82	6	—	339

2004 TEAM STATISTICS

	Texans	Opp.
Total First Downs	300	304
Rushing	103	89
Passing	174	194
Penalty	23	21
3rd Down: Made/Att	81/211	89/205
3rd Down Pct.	38.4	43.4
4th Down: Made/Att	13/21	1/6
4th Down Pct.	61.9	16.7
Possession Avg.	29:59	30:01
Total Net Yards	5128	5458
Avg. Per Game	320.5	341.1
Total Plays	1001	971
Avg. Per Play	5.1	5.6
Net Yards Rushing	1882	1843
Avg. Per Game	117.6	115.2
Total Rushes	481	417
Net Yards Passing	3246	3615
Avg. Per Game	202.9	225.9
Sacked/Yards Lost	49/301	24/161
Gross Yards	3547	3776
Att./Completions	471/286	530/344
Completion Pct.	60.7	64.9
Had Intercepted	14	22
Punts/Average	73/41.2	69/41.7
Net Punting Avg.	73/35.7	69/36.4
Penalties/Yards	106/928	123/979
Fumbles/Ball Lost	22/11	22/8
Touchdowns	37	39
Rushing	16	4
Passing	16	32
Returns	5	3

2004 INDIVIDUAL STATISTICS

PASSING

PASSING	Att.	Comp.	Yds.	Pct.	TD	Int.	Tkld.	Rate
Carr	466	285	3,531	61.2	16	14	49/301	83.5
Gaffney	3	0	0	0.0	0	0	0/0	39.6
Banks	2	1	16	50.0	0	0	0/0	77.1
Texans	471	286	3,547	60.7	16	14	49/301	83.0
Opponents	530	344	3,776	64.9	32	22	24/161	88.7

SCORING

SCORING	TD R	TD P	TD Rt	PAT	FG	Saf	PTS
K. Brown	0	0	0	34/34	17/24	0	85
Davis	13	1	0	0/0	0/0	0	84
Johnson	0	6	0	0/0	0/0	0	36
Wells	3	2	0	0/0	0/0	0	32
Bradford	0	3	0	0/0	0/0	0	18
Gaffney	0	2	0	0/0	0/0	0	12
C. Anderson	0	0	1	0/0	0/0	0	6
Armstrong	0	1	0	0/0	0/0	0	6
Coleman	0	0	1	0/0	0/0	0	6
Faggins	0	0	1	0/0	0/0	0	6
Miller	0	1	0	0/0	0/0	0	6
Peek	0	0	1	0/0	0/0	0	6
Sharper	0	0	1	0/0	0/0	0	6
Texans	16	16	5	34/34	17/24	0	309
Opponents	4	32	3	37/37	22/29	1	339

2-Pt. Conversions: Wells.
Texans 1-3, Opponents 0-1.

RUSHING

RUSHING	No.	Yds	Avg	LG	TD
Davis	302	1,188	3.9	44	13
Carr	73	299	4.1	24	0
Wells	82	299	3.6	14	3
Hollings	11	47	4.3	13	0
Gaffney	4	30	7.5	10	0
Johnson	4	12	3.0	14	0
Stanley	1	5	5.0	5	0
Baxter	2	1	0.5	1	0
Simmons	1	1	1.0	1	0
Norris	1	0	0.0	0	0
Texans	481	1,882	3.9	44	16
Opponents	417	1,843	4.4	55t	4

RECEIVING

RECEIVING	No.	Yds	Avg	LG	TD
Johnson	79	1,142	14.5	54t	6
Davis	68	588	8.6	38	1
Gaffney	41	632	15.4	69	2
Armstrong	29	415	14.3	44	1
Bradford	27	399	14.8	47	3
Miller	17	178	10.5	27	1
Wells	11	79	7.2	28	2
Hollings	5	46	9.2	27	0
Bruener	4	52	13.0	27	0
Norris	4	13	3.3	7	0
Baxter	3	3	3.0	3	0
Texans	286	3,547	12.4	69	16
Opponents	344	3,776	11.0	80t	32

INTERCEPTIONS

INTERCEPTIONS	No.	Yds	Avg	LG	TD
Robinson	6	146	24.3	61	0
Glenn	5	40	8.0	23	0
Faggins	3	47	15.7	43t	1
Wong	3	0	0.0	0	0
Coleman	2	116	58.0	102t	1
McCree	1	24	24.0	24	0
Peek	1	20	20.0	20	0
Simmons	1	0	0.0	0	0
Texans	22	393	17.9	102t	2
Opponents	14	157	11.2	77t	1

PUNTING

PUNTING	No.	Yds.	Avg.	In 20	LG
Stanley	73	3,009	41.2	19	57
Texans	73	3,009	41.2	19	57
Opponents	69	2,880	41.7	24	64

PUNT RETURNS

PUNT RETURNS	Ret	FC	Yds	Avg	LG	TD
Moses	36	13	309	8.6	27	0
Glenn	4	0	22	5.5	18	0
Robinson	0	0	-2	—	-2	0
Texans	40	13	329	8.2	27	0
Opponents	30	24	265	8.8	46	0

KICKOFF RETURNS

KICKOFF RETURNS	No.	Yds	Avg	LG	TD
Moses	59	1,303	22.1	49	0
Gaffney	2	31	15.5	27	0
Norris	2	25	12.5	15	0
Washington	2	27	13.5	16	0
Wells	2	27	13.5	18	0
Hollings	1	23	23.0	23	0
Starling	1	14	14.0	14	0
Texans	69	1,450	21.0	49	0
Opponents	60	1,386	23.1	99t	1

FIELD GOALS

FIELD GOALS	1-19	20-29	30-39	40-49	50+
K. Brown	0/0	7/7	3/5	6/9	1/3
Texans	0/0	7/7	3/5	6/9	1/3
Opponents	0/0	7/7	3/7	10/13	2/2

SACKS

SACKS	No.
Wong	5.5
Babin	4.0
Robinson	3.0
Payne	2.0
Peek	2.0
Sharper	2.0
Smith	2.0
Polk	1.0
Wright	1.0
G. Walker	0.5
Texans	24.0
Opponents	49.0

RECORD HOLDERS
INDIVIDUAL RECORDS—CAREER

Category	Name	Performance
Rushing (Yds.)	Domanick Davis, 2003-04	2,219
Passing (Yds.)	David Carr, 2002-04	8,136
Passing (TDs)	David Carr, 2002-04	34
Receiving (No.)	Andre Johnson, 2003-04	145
Receiving (Yds.)	Andre Johnson, 2003-04	2,118
Interceptions	Aaron Glenn, 2002-04	11
Punting (Avg.)	Chad Stanley, 2002-04	41.2
Punt Return (Avg.)	Avion Black, 2002	13.4
Kickoff Return (Avg.)	J.J. Moses, 2003-04	22.7
Field Goals	Kris Brown, 2002-04	52
Touchdowns (Tot.)	Domanick Davis, 2003-04	22
Points	Kris Brown, 2002-04	233

INDIVIDUAL RECORDS—SINGLE SEASON

Category	Name	Performance
Rushing (Yds.)	Domanick Davis, 2004	1,188
Passing (Yds.)	David Carr, 2004	3,531
Passing (TDs)	David Carr, 2004	16
Receiving (No.)	Andre Johnson, 2004	79
Receiving (Yds.)	Andre Johnson, 2004	1,142
Interceptions	Marcus Coleman, 2003	7
Punting (Avg.)	Chad Stanley, 2003	41.5
Punt Return (Avg.)	Avion Black, 2002	13.4
Kickoff Return (Avg.)	J.J. Moses, 2003	23.4
Field Goals	Kris Brown, 2003	18
Touchdowns (Tot.)	Domanick Davis, 2004	14
Points	Kris Brown, 2004	85

INDIVIDUAL RECORDS—SINGLE GAME

Category	Name	Performance
Rushing (Yds.)	Domanick Davis, 12-26-04	158
Passing (Yds.)	David Carr, 10-10-04	372
Passing (TDs)	David Carr, 10-10-04	3
Receiving (No.)	Andre Johnson, 10-10-04	12
Receiving (Yds.)	Andre Johnson, 10-10-04	170
Interceptions	Aaron Glenn, 12-8-02	2
	Marcus Coleman, 9-7-03	2
	Kenny Wright, 9-28-03	2
	Dunta Robinson, 10-3-04	2
Field Goals	Kris Brown, 9-7-03	5
Touchdowns (Tot.)	Many times	2
	Last time by Domanick Davis, 11-14-04	
Points	Kris Brown, 9-7-03	15

2005 VETERAN ROSTER

No.	Name	Pos.	Ht.	Wt.	Birthdate	NFL Exp.	College	Hometown	How Acq.	'04 Games/ Starts
50	Anderson, Charlie	LB	6-4	243	12/8/81	2	Mississippi	Jackson, Miss.	D6c-'04	15/0
27	Anderson, Jason	RB	6-0	205	4/29/80	2	South Dakota	Palmdale, Calif.	FA-'04	0*
88	Armstrong, Derick	WR	6-2	206	4/2/79	3	Arkansas-Monticello	Dallas, Texas	FA-'03	14/2
93	Babin, Jason	LB	6-2	259	5/24/80	2	Western Michigan	Kalamazoo. Mich.	D1b-'04	16/16
12	Banks, Tony	QB	6-4	229	4/5/73	10	Michigan State	San Diego, Calif.	FA-'02	5/0
47	Baxter, Jarrod	FB	6-1	243	3/9/79	4	New Mexico	Albuquerque, N.M.	D5a-'02	9/1
75	Beasley, Chad	T	6-5	305	11/13/78	3	Virginia Tech	Gate City, Va.	FA-'05	0*
33	Bell, Jason	CB	6-0	186	4/1/78	5	UCLA	Long Beach, Calif.	W(Dall)-'02	9/0
85	Bradford, Corey	WR	6-1	201	12/8/75	8	Jackson State	Clinton, La.	UFA(GB)-'02	15/10
3	Brown, Kris	K	5-11	205	12/23/76	7	Nebraska	Southlake, Texas	RFA(Pitt)-'02	16/0
67	Brown, Milford	G	6-4	331	8/15/80	4	Florida State	Montgomery, Ala.	SD6-'02	2/2
87	Bruener, Mark	TE	6-4	258	9/16/72	11	Washington	Olympia, Wash.	UFA(Pitt)-'04	16/11
31 t-	Buchanon, Phillip	CB	5-10	185	9/19/80	4	Miami	Ft. Meyers, Fla.	T(Oak)-'05	14/14*
8	Carr, David	QB	6-3	220	7/21/79	4	Fresno State	Bakersfield, Calif.	D1-'02	16/16
59	Chamberlin, Frank	LB	6-1	238	1/2/78	5	Boston College	Mahwah, N.J.	UFA(Cin)-'05	0*
42	Coleman, Marcus	S	6-2	206	5/24/74	10	Texas Tech	Dallas, Texas	ED(NYJ)-'02	12/12
37	Davis, Domanick	RB	5-9	221	10/1/80	3	Louisiana State	Breaux Bridge, La.	D4-'03	15/15
95	DeLoach, Jerry	DE	6-2	335	7/17/77	5	California	Valley, Calif.	T(Wash)-'02	15/3
26	Earl, Glenn	S	6-1	215	6/10/81	2	Notre Dame	Naperville, Ill.	D4-'04	12/9
54	Evans, Troy	LB	6-1	237	12/3/77	4	Cincinnati	Cincinnati, Ohio	FA-'02	13/0
38	Faggins, Demarcus	CB	5-10	180	6/13/79	4	Kansas State	Irving, Texas	D6a-'02	16/2
86	Gaffney, Jabar	WR	6-1	205	12/1/80	4	Florida	Jacksonville, Fla.	D2-'02	16/12
56	Greenwood, Morlon	LB	6-0	238	7/17/78	5	Syracuse	Freeport, N.Y.	UFA(Mia)-'05	16/15*
62	Harrison, Tyreo	LB	6-2	238	5/15/80	2	Notre Dame	Sulpher Springs, Texas	FA-'05	0*
25	Hollings, Tony	RB	5-10	218	12/1/81	3	Georgia Tech	Jeffersonville, Ga.	SD2-'03	7/0
94	Ioane, Junior	DT	6-4	332	7/21/77	6	Arizona State	Mt. Pleasant, Utah	W(Oak)-'03	3/0
80	Johnson, Andre	WR	6-3	219	7/11/81	3	Miami	Miami, Fla.	D1-'03	16/16
73	Jones, Garrick	T	6-5	323	12/2/78	3	Arkansas State	Little Rock, Ark.	W(KC)-'03	16/0
83	Joppru, Bennie	TE	6-4	260	1/5/80	3	Michigan	Minnetonka, Minn.	D2-'03	0*
20	Lord, Jammal	S	6-2	222	1/10/82	2	Nebraska	Bayonne, N.J.	D6b-'04	1/0
76	McKinney, Steve	C	6-4	302	10/15/75	8	Texas A&M	Friendswood, Texas	UFA(Ind)-'02	16/16
82	Miller, Billy	TE	6-3	245	4/24/77	7	Southern California	Westlake Village, Calif.	FA-'02	16/9
57	Monk, Quincy	LB	6-3	250	1/30/79	4	North Carolina	Jacksonville, N.C.	FA-'04	2/0
63	Moreno, Zeke	LB	6-2	235	10/1/78	5	Southern California	Chula Vista, Calif.	UFA(SD)-'05	9/0*
84	Moses, J.J.	WR	5-6	175	9/12/79	4	Iowa State	Waterloo, Iowa	FA-'03	15/0
81	Murphy, Matt	TE	6-5	268	2/23/80	3	Maryland	New Haven, Mich.	FA-'03	11/1
44	Norris, Moran	FB	6-1	254	6/16/78	5	Kansas	Houston, Texas	W(NO)-'02	12/4
53	Orr, Shantee	LB	6-0	241	5/28/81	3	Michigan	Detroit, Mich.	FA-'03	4/0
91	Payne, Seth	DT	6-4	315	2/12/75	9	Cornell	Victor, N.Y.	ED(Jax)-'02	16/12
98	Peek, Antwan	LB	6-3	238	10/29/79	3	Cincinnati	Cincinnati, Ohio	D3a-'03	14/1
48	Pittman, Bryan	LS	6-3	275	1/20/77	3	Washington	Auburn, Wash.	FA-'03	16/0
69	Pitts, Chester	G	6-4	329	6/26/79	4	San Diego State	Inglewood, Calif.	D2-'02	16/16
51	Polk, DaShon	LB	6-2	240	3/13/77	6	Arizona	Pacoima, Calif.	UFA(Buff)-'04	16/4
4	Ragone, Dave	QB	6-3	225	10/3/79	3	Louisville	Middleberg, Ohio	D3c-'03	0*
23	Robinson, Dunta	CB	5-10	174	4/11/82	2	South Carolina	Athens, Ga.	D1a-'04	16/16
21	Sanders, Lewis	CB	6-1	210	6/22/78	6	Maryland	Staten Island, N.Y.	UFA(Cle)-'05	16/5*
92	Sears, Corey	DE	6-4	314	4/15/73	7	Mississippi State	Converse, Texas	FA-'02	15/0
30	Simmons, Jason	S	5-9	199	3/30/76	8	Arizona State	Lawndale, Calif.	UFA(Pitt)-'02	10/6
99	Smith, Robaire	DE	6-4	328	11/15/77	6	Michigan State	Flint, Mich.	UFA(Tenn)-'04	16/16
7	Stanley, Chad	P	6-3	216	9/28/71	6	Stephen F. Austin	Ore City, Texas	FA-'02	16/0
17	Starling, Kendrick	WR	6-0	193	1/29/76	2	San Jose State	Marshall, Texas	FA-'04	8/0
64	Stewart, Daleroy	DT	6-4	298	12/27/79	4	Southern Mississippi	Vero Beach, Fla.	FA-'05	11/0*
89	Swinton, Reggie	WR	6-0	182	7/24/75	5	Murray State	Little Rock, Ark.	UFA(Det)-'05	13/1*
2	Symons, B.J.	QB	6-1	215	11/19/80	2	Texas Tech	Cypress, Texas	D7c-'04	0*
71	Wade, Todd	T	6-8	317	10/30/76	6	Mississippi	Jackson, Miss.	UFA(Mia)-'04	14/13
96	Walker, Gary	DE	6-2	324	2/28/73	11	Auburn	Royston, Ga.	ED(Jax)-'02	15/15
22	Walker, Ramon	S	6-0	212	11/8/79	4	Pittsburgh	Akron, Ohio	D5b-'02	0*
78	Wand, Seth	T	6-7	330	8/6/79	3	Northwest Missouri State	Springfield, Mo.	D3b-'03	16/16
77	Washington, Todd	C	6-3	317	7/19/76	8	Virginia Tech	Melfa, Va.	FA-'03	15/0
70	Weary, Fred	G	6-4	308	9/30/77	4	Tennessee	Montgomery, Ala.	D3a-'02	2/1
32	Wells, Jonathan	RB	6-1	252	7/21/79	4	Ohio State	River Ridge, La.	D4-'02	16/1
72	Wiegert, Zach	G	6-5	305	8/16/72	11	Nebraska	Fremont, Neb.	UFA(Jax)-'03	13/13
52	Wong, Kailee	LB	6-2	246	5/23/76	7	Stanford	Eugene, Ore.	UFA(Minn)-'02	16/16

* J. Anderson missed '04 season because of injury; Beasley last played with Cleveland in '03; Buchanon played 14 games with Oakland in '04; Chamberlin missed '04 season with Cincinnati because of injury; Greenwood played 16 games with Miami; Harrison last played with Philadelphia in '03; Joppru missed '04 season because of injury; Moreno played 9 games with San Diego; Ragone inactive for 16 games; Sanders played 16 games with Cleveland; Stewart played 11 games with San Francisco; Swinton played 13 games with Detroit; Symons missed '04 season because of injury; R. Walker missed '04 season because of injury.

t- Texans traded for Buchanan (Oak).

Players lost through free agency (2): S Marlon McCree (Car; 16 games in '04), CB Kenny Wright (Jax; 16 games in '04)

Also played with Texans in '04—S Eric Brown (13 games), LB Jay Foreman (11), CB Aaron Glenn (16), LB Jamie Sharper (16), T Marcus Spears (16).

2005 FIRST-YEAR ROSTER

Name	Pos.	Ht.	Wt.	Birthdate	College	Hometown	How Acq.
Acholonu, D.D. (1)	LB	6-3	230	10/17/80	Washington State	Seattle, Wash.	W(Buff)-'04
Brown, C.C.	S	6-0	208	1/28/83	Louisiana-Lafayette	Greenwood, Miss.	D6
Brown, Tim	T	6-5	313	5/12/80	West Virginia	Harrisburg, Pa.	FA
Cheatwood, Tim (1)	LB	6-4	258	5/11/78	Ohio State	Cleveland, Ohio	FA
Davis, Jason (1)	DE	6-3	320	9/12/80	West Virginia	Ft. Lauderdale, Fla.	FA-'03
Dunn, Anthony (1)	LB	6-2	246	7/1/80	Northern Colorado	Denver, Colo.	FA-'03
Evans, Brandon (1)	G	6-4	356	12/27/81	Houston	Houston, Texas	FA-'04
Halterman, Aaron	TE	6-5	255	3/31/82	Indiana	Greenwood, Ind.	FA
Hodgdon, Drew	C	6-3	309	11/15/81	Arizona State	Palo Alto, Calif.	D5
Johnson, Chris	T	6-3	330	3/14/82	Arizona	Houston, Texas	FA
Johnson, Travis	DE	6-3	305	4/26/82	Florida State	Sherman Oaks, Calif.	D1
Lightbody, Sam	T	6-9	314	4/22/81	Washington State	Huntington Beach, Calif.	FA
Malone, Alfred	DE	6-5	303	2/21/82	Troy	Frisco City, Ala.	FA
Mathis, Jerome	WR	5-11	181	6/26/83	Hampton	Petersburg, Va.	D4
Matthews, Adam (1)	RB	5-11	205	10/3/81	Northern Colorado	Northglenn, Colo.	FA
McKenzie, Chris	CB	5-8	182	3/17/82	Arizona State	Queens, N.Y.	FA
Morency, Vernand	RB	5-9	212	2/4/80	Oklahoma State	Miami, Fla.	D3
Moretti, David (1)	LB	6-1	235	6/25/81	Oregon	San Jose, Calif.	FA
Narcisse, Nick (1)	WR	5-10	178	12/24/80	Tulane	Slidell, La.	FA
Parsons, Preston (1)	QB	6-4	236	2/19/79	Northern Arizona	Portland, Ore.	FA
Pettway, Kenneth	LB	6-3	236	11/13/82	Grambling State	Gilmer, Texas	D7
Pitts, Devin	WR	6-3	206	5/2/81	San Diego State	Carson, Calif.	FA
Scates, Cody (1)	P	6-1	205	12/8/81	Texas A&M	Tyler, Texas	FA
Simon, Jonathon	DT	6-6	299	5/28/81	Colorado State	Watauga, Texas	FA
Smith, Myniya	T	6-6	343	7/21/81	Southern	New Orleans, La.	FA
Snyder, Chris (1)	K	6-0	190	11/7/81	Montana	Meade, Wash.	FA
Suber, Allen (1)	WR	5-9	189	10/21/81	Bethune-Cookman	Tampa, Fla.	FA-'04
Thomas, Sloan (1)	WR	6-1	203	12/22/81	Texas	Klein, Texas	D7b-'04
Williams, Carlos	DE	6-4	295	10/16/82	Arizona	Denver, Colo.	FA
Williams, Cedrick	CB	5-9	170	10/1/79	Kansas State	Boca Raton, Fla.	FA
Wishom, Jerron	CB	5-11	199	3/1/82	Louisiana Tech	Lutcher, La.	FA
Young, David (1)	S	6-1	211	5/17/79	Georgia Southern	Columbia, S.C.	FA-'04

The term NFL Rookie is defined as a player who is in his first season of professional football and has not been on the roster of another professional football team for any regular-season or postseason games. A Rookie is designated by an "R" on NFL rosters. Players who have been active in another professional football league or players who have NFL experience, including either preseason training camp or being on an Active List or Inactive List, or on Reserve/Injured or Reserve/Physically Unable to Perform for fewer than six regular-season games, are termed NFL First-Year Players. An NFL First-Year Player is designated by a "1" on NFL rosters. Thereafter, a player is credited with an additional year of experience for each season in which he accumulates six games on the Active List or Inactive List, or on Reserve/Injured or Reserve/Physically Unable to Perform.

Log on to www.houstontexans.com for an up-to-date roster.

COACHING STAFF

Head Coach,
Dom Capers

Pro Career: The Texans introduced Capers as their first head coach on January 21, 2001. In 2004, the Texans posted their best season with seven victories, posted back-to-back victories—a feat they turned on three occasions—for the first time in club history, and improved for the third consecutive season. In 2004, the Texans were 5-11. The 2002 Texans finished 4-12, tied for the second-most victories by an expansion team (Jacksonville, 1995). Capers previously spent four seasons (1995-98) as head coach of the Carolina Panthers, guiding that expansion franchise from its infancy to a playoff berth in its second season. Capers compiled a 31-35 record in four seasons as the Panthers' head coach. In 1995, the Panthers' 7-9 record set an NFL mark for most victories by an expansion team. Carolina also posted the first four-game winning streak in expansion history, the first winning home record by an expansion club, and the first win over a defending Super Bowl champion (San Francisco) in expansion annals. In 1996, Capers won coach of the year as the Panthers posted a 12-4 record and won the NFC West title. Carolina then defeated defending Super Bowl champion Dallas in the divisional playoffs before losing to Green Bay in the NFC Championship Game. Capers has been a professional assistant coach for the USFL's Philadelphia/Baltimore Stars (1984-85), New Orleans Saints (1986-1991), Pittsburgh Steelers (1992-94), and Jacksonville Jaguars (1999-2000). Career record: 47-67.

Background: Capers played safety and linebacker at Mount Union College (1968-1971). Capers coached collegiately at Kent State (1972-74), Hawaii (1975-76), San Jose State (1977), California (1978-79), Tennessee (1980-81), and Ohio State (1982-83).

Personal: Born August 7, 1950 in Cambridge, Ohio. He and his wife Karen live in Houston.

ASSISTANT COACHES

Kippy Brown, wide receivers; born March 6, 1955, Sweetwater, Tenn. Quarterback Memphis State 1974-77. No pro playing experience. College coach: Memphis State 1978-1980, Louisville 1982, Tennessee 1983-89, 1993-94. Pro coach: New York Jets 1990-92, Tampa Bay Buccaneers 1995, Miami Dolphins 1996-99, Green Bay Packers 2000, Memphis Maniax (XFL, head coach) 2001, joined Texans in 2002.

Vic Fangio, defensive coordinator; born August 22, 1958, Dunmore, Pa. Attended East Stroudsburg State. No pro playing experience. College coach: North Carolina 1983. Pro coach: Philadelphia/Baltimore Stars (USFL) 1984-85, New Orleans Saints 1986-1994, Carolina Panthers 1995-98, Indianapolis Colts 1999-2001, joined Texans in 2002.

Chick Harris, running backs; born September 21, 1945, Durham, N.C. Running back Northern Arizona 1966-69. No pro playing experience. College coach: Colorado State 1970-71, Long Beach State 1972-73, Washington 1975-1980. Pro coach: Detroit Wheels (WFL) 1974, Buffalo Bills 1981-82, Seattle Seahawks 1983-1991, Los Angeles Rams 1992-94, Carolina Panthers 1995-2001, joined Texans in 2002.

Jon Hoke, defensive backs; born January 24, 1957, Kettering, Ohio. Defensive back Ball State 1976-1979. Pro defensive back Chicago Bears 1980. College coach: Bowling Green 1983-86, San Diego State 1987-88, Kent State 1989-1993, Missouri 1994-98, Florida 1999-2001. Pro coach: Joined Texans in 2002.

Mike London, defensive line; born October 9, 1960, West Point, N.Y. Defensive back Richmond 1979-1982. No pro playing experience. College coach: Richmond 1988-89, William & Mary 1990-93, Richmond 1994-96, Boston College 1997-2000, Virginia 2001-04. Pro coach: Joined Texans in 2005.

Joe Marciano, special teams coordinator; born February 10, 1954, Dunmore, Pa. Quarterback Temple 1972-75. No pro playing experience. College coach: East Stroudsburg State 1977, Rhode Island 1978-79, Villanova 1980, Penn State 1981, Temple 1982. Pro coach: Philadelphia/Baltimore Stars (USFL) 1983-85, New Orleans Saints 1986-1995, Tampa Bay Buccaneers 1996-2001, joined Texans in 2002.

Tony Marciano, tight ends; born June 14, 1956, Scranton, Pa. Offensive line Indiana University (Pa.) 1975-77. No pro playing experience. College coach: Texas Christian 1978-1980, Southern Methodist 1981-86, Brown 1987-88, Richmond 1989-1990, Kent State 1991-92. Pro coach: Toronto Argonauts (CFL) 1994, Calgary Stampeders (CFL) 1995-97, Indianapolis Colts 1998-2001, joined Texans in 2002.

Steve Marshall, offensive line (tackles); born June 20, 1956, Hartford, Conn. Guard-tight end Louisville 1976-78. No pro playing experience. College coach: Plymouth State 1979, Tennessee 1980-81, Marshall 1982-83, Louisville 1984, Murray State 1985-86, Virginia Tech 1987-1992, Tennessee 1993-95, UCLA 1996, Texas A&M 1997, North Carolina 1998-99, Colorado 2000-2001. Pro coach: Joined Texans in 2002.

Tony Oden, defensive assistant/asst. defensive backs; born June 30, 1973, Cleveland. Linebacker Baldwin-Wallace College 1991-95. No pro playing experience. College coach: Millersville (Pa.) 1996, Boston College 1997, Army 1998-

99, East Carolina 2000-02, Eastern Michigan 2003. Pro coach: Joined Texans in 2004.

Tom Olivadotti, linebackers; born September 22, 1945, Long Beach, N.J. Defensive back/wide receiver Upsala College 1963-66. No pro playing experience. College coach: Princeton 1976-77, Boston College 1978-79, Miami 1980-83. Pro coach: Washington Federals (USFL) 1984, Cleveland Browns 1985-86, Miami Dolphins 1987-1995, Minnesota Vikings 1996-99, New York Giants 2000-03, joined Texans in 2004.

Chris Palmer, offensive coordinator; born September 23, 1949, Brewster, N.Y. Quarterback Southern Connecticut State 1968-1971. No pro playing experience. College coach: Connecticut 1972-74, Lehigh 1975, Colgate 1976-1982, New Haven 1986-87 (head coach), Boston 1988-89 (head coach). Pro coach: Montreal Concordes (CFL) 1983, New Jersey Generals (USFL) 1984-85, Houston Oilers 1990-92, New England Patriots 1993-96, Jacksonville Jaguars 1997-98, Cleveland Browns 1999-2000 (head coach), joined Texans in 2001.

Joe Pendry, offensive line (centers-guards); born August 5, 1947, Welch, W. Va. Tight end West Virginia 1965-66. No pro playing experience. College coach: West Virginia 1969-1974 1976-77, Kansas State 1975, Pittsburgh 1978-79, Michigan State 1980-81, Southwest Missouri State 2003. Pro coach: Philadelphia Stars (USFL) 1983, Pittsburgh Maulers (USFL) 1984, Cleveland Browns 1985-88, Kansas City Chiefs 1989-1992, Chicago Bears 1993-94, Carolina Panthers 1995-97, Buffalo Bills 1998-2000, Washington Redskins 2001, joined Texans in 2004.

Dan Riley, strength and conditioning; born October 19, 1949, Syracuse, N.Y. Attended Keene State. No college or pro playing experience. Pro coach: Army 1974-77, Penn State 1977-1981. Pro coach: Washington Redskins 1982-2000, joined Texans in 2001.

Greg Roman, quarterbacks; born August 19, 1972, Atlantic City, N.J. Defensive line-linebacker John Carroll 1990-94. No pro playing experience. Pro coach: Carolina Panthers 1995-2001, joined Texans in 2002.

Eric Sutulovich, asst. special teams; born February 28, 1974, Kansas City, Kan. Tight end Louisiana Tech 1993-95. No pro playing experience. College coach: Louisiana Tech 1997-99, Pittsburgh 2000, Fort Scott 2001. Pro coach: Joined Texans in 2002.

Ray Wright, asst. strength and conditioning; born December 30, 1971, Cleveland. Running back-wide receiver Duke 1990-95. No pro playing experience. College coach: Cornell 1999, Maryland 2001. Pro coach: Joined Texans in 2002.

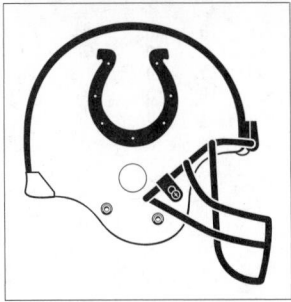

American Football Conference
South Division
Team Colors: Royal Blue and White
P.O. Box 535000
Indianapolis, Indiana 46253
Telephone: (317) 297-2658

2005 SCHEDULE
PRESEASON

Aug. 6	vs. Atlanta in Tokyo, Japan	6:00
Aug. 13	**Buffalo**	7:00
Aug. 20	**Chicago**	7:00
Aug. 27	at Denver	6:00
Sept. 2	at Cincinnati	7:30

REGULAR SEASON

Sept. 11	at Baltimore	8:30
Sept. 18	**Jacksonville**	12:00
Sept. 25	**Cleveland**	12:00
Oct. 2	at Tennessee	12:00
Oct. 9	at San Francisco	1:05
Oct. 17	**St. Louis** (Mon.)	8:00
Oct. 23	at Houston	12:00
Oct. 30	Open Date	
Nov. 7	at New England (Mon.)	9:00
Nov. 13	**Houston**	1:00
Nov. 20	at Cincinnati	1:00
Nov. 28	**Pittsburgh** (Mon.)	9:00
Dec. 4	**Tennessee**	1:00
Dec. 11	at Jacksonville	1:00
Dec. 18	**San Diego**	1:00
Dec. 24	at Seattle (Sat.)	1:15
Jan. 1	**Arizona**	1:00

Stadium: RCA Dome (opened in 1983)
    •Capacity: 55,506
    100 South Capitol Avenue
    Indianapolis, Indiana 46225
Playing Surface: FieldTurf
Training Camp: Rose-Hulman Institute
    5500 Wabash Avenue
    Terre Haute, IN 47803

RCA DOME

CLUB OFFICIALS
Owner and CEO: James Irsay
President: Bill Polian
Head Coach: Tony Dungy
Senior Executive Vice President:
  Pete Ward
Executive Vice President: Bob Terpening
Senior Vice President-Business
  Development: Tom Zupancic
Vice President of Football Operations:
  Chris Polian
Assistant General Manager/Scouting:
  Dom Anile
Vice President-Finance: Kurt Humphrey
Vice President-Ticket Operations:
  Larry Hall
Vice President-Public Relations:
  Craig Kelley
Director of Pro Player Personnel:
  Clyde Powers
Director of College Scouting: Mike Butler
Director of Player Development:
  Steve Champlin
Executive Director of Administration:
  Bill Brooks
Executive Director of Sponsorship Sales:
  Jay Souers
Director of Ticket Sales/Marketing:
  Greg Hylton
Director of Community
  Relations/Marketing: Nicole Duncan
Equipment Manager: Jon Scott
Video Director: Marty Heckscher
Head Trainer: Hunter Smith
Assistant Director of Public Relations:
  Vernon Cheek
Assistant Equipment Managers:
  Mike Mays, Sean Sullivan,
  Brian Seabrooks
Assistant Trainers: Dave Hammer,
  Dave Walston, Bryant Baugh
Assistant Video Director: John Starliper
Purchasing Administrator: Dave Filar

COACHING HISTORY
Baltimore 1953-1983
(389-390-7)
Records include postseason games

1953	Keith Molesworth	3-9-0
1954-1962	Weeb Ewbank	61-52-1
1963-69	Don Shula	73-26-4
1970-72	Don McCafferty*	26-11-1
1972	John Sandusky	4-5-0
1973-74	Howard Schnellenberger**	4-13-0
1974	Joe Thomas	2-9-0
1975-79	Ted Marchibroda	41-36-0
1980-81	Mike McCormack	9-23-0
1982-84	Frank Kush***	11-28-1
1984	Hal Hunter	0-1-0
1985-86	Rod Dowhower****	5-24-0
1986-1991	Ron Meyer#	36-36-0
1991	Rick Venturi	1-10-0
1992-95	Ted Marchibroda	32-35-0
1996-97	Lindy Infante	12-21-0
1998-2001	Jim Mora	32-34-0
2002-04	Tony Dungy	37-17-0

  *Released after five games in 1972
  **Released after three games in 1974
  ***Resigned after 15 games in 1984
  ****Released after 13 games in 1986
  #Released after five games in 1991

ATTENDANCE
Home 442,756   Away 547,836
Total 990,592
Single-game home record,
  61,139 (10/20/97)
Single-season home record, 481,305
  (1984)

2005 DRAFT CHOICES

Round	Name	Pos.	College
1	Marlin Jackson	DB	Michigan
2	Kelvin Hayden	DB	Illinois
3	Vincent Burns	DE	Kentucky
4	Dylan Gandy	G	Texas Tech
	Matt Giordano	DB	California
5	Jonathan Welsh	DE	Wisconsin
	Rob Hunt	C	North Dakota St.
	Tyjuan Hagler	LB	Cincinnati
6	Dave Rayner	K	Michigan State
7	Anthony Davis	RB	Wisconsin

2004 TEAM RECORD
PRESEASON (2-2)

Date	Result	Opponent
8/14	W 21-17	at San Diego
8/21	L 7-31	N.Y. Jets
8/28	W 30-17	Buffalo
9/3	L 13-16	at Cincinnati

REGULAR SEASON (12-4)

Date	Result	Opponent	Att.
9/9	L 24-27	at New England	68,756
9/19	W 31-17	at Tennessee	68,932
9/26	W 45-31	Green Bay	57,280
10/3	W 24-17	at Jacksonville	73,114
10/10	W 35-14	Oakland	57,230
10/24	L 24-27	Jacksonville	56,615
10/31	L 35-45	at Kansas City	78,312
11/8	W 31-28	Minnesota	57,307
11/14	W 49-14	Houston	56,511
11/21	W 41-10	at Chicago	61,908
11/25	W 41-9	at Detroit	63,107
12/5	W 51-24	Tennessee	57,278
12/12	W 23-14	at Houston	70,762
12/19	W 20-10	Baltimore	57,240
12/26	W 34-31	San Diego (OT)	57,330
1/2	L 14-33	at Denver	75,149

(OT) Overtime

POSTSEASON (1-1)

1/9	W 49-24	Denver	56,609
1/16	L 3-20	at New England	68,756

SCORE BY PERIODS

Colts	120	157	118	124	3	—	522
Opponents	78	102	73	98	0	—	351

2004 TEAM STATISTICS

	Colts	Opp.
Total First Downs	379	331
Rushing	94	103
Passing	238	209
Penalty	47	19
3rd Down: Made/Att	70/164	91/217
3rd Down Pct.	42.7	41.9
4th Down: Made/Att	4/7	9/28
4th Down Pct.	57.1	32.1
Possession Avg.	28:40	31:20
Total Net Yards	6475	5929
Avg. Per Game	404.7	370.6
Total Plays	968	1042
Avg. Per Play	6.7	5.7
Net Yards Rushing	1852	2037
Avg. Per Game	115.8	127.3
Total Rushes	427	440
Net Yards Passing	4623	3892
Avg. Per Game	288.9	243.3
Sacked/Yards Lost	14/109	45/340
Gross Yards	4732	4232
Att./Completions	527/353	557/364
Completion Pct.	67.0	65.4
Had Intercepted	10	19
Punts/Average	54/45.2	52/42.7
Net Punting Avg.	54/36.8	52/37.9
Penalties/Yards	106/801	116/877
Fumbles/Ball Lost	19/7	36/17
Touchdowns	66	39
Rushing	10	12
Passing	51	26
Returns	5	1

2004 INDIVIDUAL STATISTICS
PASSING

	Att.	Comp.	Yds.	Pct.	TD	Int.	Tkld.	Rate
Manning	497	336	4,557	67.6	49	10	13/101	121.1
Sorgi	29	17	175	58.6	2	0	1/8	99.1
Saturday	1	0	0	0.0	0	0	0/0	39.6
Colts	527	353	4,732	67.0	51	10	14/109	119.7
Opponents	557	364	4,232	65.4	26	19	45/340	89.5

SCORING

	TD R	TD P	TD Rt	PAT	FG	Saf	PTS
Vanderjagt	0	0	0	59/60	20/25	0	119
Harrison	0	15	0	0/0	0/0	0	90
Wayne	0	12	0	0/0	0/0	0	72
Stokley	0	10	0	0/0	0/0	0	60
James	9	0	0	0/0	0/0	0	56
Pollard	0	6	0	0/0	0/0	0	36
Clark	0	5	0	0/0	0/0	0	30
Mungro	0	3	0	0/0	0/0	0	18
Rhodes	1	0	1	0/0	0/0	0	12
David	0	0	1	0/0	0/0	0	6
Hutchins	0	0	1	0/0	0/0	0	6
Morris	0	0	1	0/0	0/0	0	6
Sanders	0	0	1	0/0	0/0	0	6
Bryant	0	0	0	5/5	0/1	0	5
Colts	10	51	5	64/65	20/26	0	522
Opponents	12	26	1	36/36	25/31	0	351

*2-Pt. Conversions: James.
Colts 1-1, Opponents 3-3.*

RUSHING

	No.	Yds	Avg	LG	TD
James	334	1,548	4.6	40	9
Rhodes	53	254	4.8	55	1
Manning	25	38	1.5	19	0
Mungro	5	19	3.8	8	0
Smith	1	2	2.0	2	0
Wayne	1	-4	-4.0	-4	0
Sorgi	8	-5	-0.6	2	0
Colts	427	1,852	4.3	55	10
Opponents	440	2,037	4.6	47	12

RECEIVING

	No.	Yds	Avg	LG	TD
Harrison	86	1,113	12.9	59	15
Wayne	77	1,210	15.7	71t	12
Stokley	68	1,077	15.8	69t	10
James	51	483	9.5	56	0
Pollard	29	309	10.7	31	6
Clark	25	423	16.9	80t	5
Mungro	7	36	5.1	16	3
Hartsock	4	33	8.3	17	0
Rhodes	2	24	12.0	20	0
Pyatt	2	12	6.0	7	0
Moorehead	1	7	7.0	7	0
Walters	1	5	5.0	5	0
Colts	353	4,732	13.4	80t	51
Opponents	364	4,232	11.6	79t	26

INTERCEPTIONS

	No.	Yds	Avg	LG	TD
David	4	36	9.0	34t	1
Harper	3	12	4.0	12	0
June	2	71	35.5	71	0
Doss	2	32	16.0	32	0
Brackett	2	2	1.0	2	0
Hutchins	1	77	77.0	77t	0
Morris	1	17	17.0	17	0
Thornton	1	5	5.0	5	0
Bacon	1	0	0.0	0	0
Jefferson	1	0	0.0	0	0
Nelson	1	0	0.0	0	0
Colts	19	252	13.3	77t	1
Opponents	10	191	19.1	65	0

PUNTING

	No.	Yds.	Avg.	In 20	LG
Smith	54	2,443	45.2	21	62
Colts	54	2,443	45.2	21	62
Opponents	52	2,220	42.7	16	64

PUNT RETURNS

	Ret	FC	Yds	Avg	LG	TD
David	8	4	50	6.3	13	0
Pyatt	8	5	47	5.9	13	0
Walters	7	6	40	5.7	14	0
Moorehead	1	0	34	34.0	34	0
Colts	24	15	171	7.1	34	0
Opponents	29	13	395	13.6	91t	1

KICKOFF RETURNS

	No.	Yds	Avg	LG	TD
Rhodes	48	1,188	24.8	88t	1
Pyatt	10	230	23.0	32	0
Mungro	7	111	15.9	24	0
Walters	1	16	16.0	16	0
Peko	0	0	—	—	0
Colts	66	1,545	23.4	88t	1
Opponents	92	1,960	21.3	71	0

FIELD GOALS

	1-19	20-29	30-39	40-49	50+
Vanderjagt	0/0	6/6	9/11	5/7	0/1
Bryant	0/0	0/0	0/0	0/1	0/0
Colts	0/0	6/6	9/11	5/8	0/1
Opponents	0/0	6/6	7/9	9/11	3/5

SACKS

	No.
Freeney	16.0
Mathis	10.5
Brock	6.5
Reagor	5.0
Morris	3.0
Scioli	2.0
Doss	1.0
Thomas	1.0
Colts	45.0
Opponents	14.0

RECORD HOLDERS
INDIVIDUAL RECORDS—CAREER

Category	Name	Performance
Rushing (Yds.)	Edgerrin James, 1999-2004	7,720
Passing (Yds.)	Johnny Unitas, 1956-1972	39,768
Passing (TDs)	Johnny Unitas, 1956-1972	287
Receiving (No.)	Marvin Harrison, 1996-2004	845
Receiving (Yds.)	Marvin Harrison, 1996-2004	11,185
Interceptions	Bob Boyd, 1960-68	57
Punting (Avg.)	Chris Gardocki, 1994-98	44.8
Punt Return (Avg.)	Ron Gardin, 1970-71	13.5
Kickoff Return (Avg.)	Jim Duncan, 1969-1971	32.5
Field Goals	Mike Vanderjagt, 1998-2004	194
Touchdowns (Tot.)	Lenny Moore, 1956-1967	113
Points	Mike Vanderjagt, 1998-2004	874

INDIVIDUAL RECORDS—SINGLE SEASON

Category	Name	Performance
Rushing (Yds.)	Edgerrin James, 2000	1,709
Passing (Yds.)	Peyton Manning, 2004	4,557
Passing (TDs)	Peyton Manning, 2004	*49
Receiving (No.)	Marvin Harrison, 2002	*143
Receiving (Yds.)	Marvin Harrison, 2002	1,722
Interceptions	Tom Keane, 1953	11
Punting (Avg.)	Rohn Stark, 1985	45.9
Punt Return (Avg.)	Clarence Verdin, 1989	12.9
Kickoff Return (Avg.)	Jim Duncan, 1970	35.4
Field Goals	Mike Vanderjagt, 2003	37
Touchdowns (Tot.)	Lenny Moore, 1964	20
Points	Mike Vanderjagt, 2003	157

INDIVIDUAL RECORDS—SINGLE GAME

Category	Name	Performance
Rushing (Yds.)	Edgerrin James, 10-15-00	219
Passing (Yds.)	Peyton Manning, 10-31-04	472
Passing (TDs)	Peyton Manning, 9-28-03, 11-25-04	6
Receiving (No.)	Marvin Harrison, 12-26-99, 11-17-02	14
Receiving (Yds.)	Raymond Berry, 11-10-57	224
Interceptions	Many times	3
	Last time by Mike Prior, 12-20-92	
Field Goals	Many times	5
	Last time by Mike Vanderjagt, 12-7-03	
Touchdowns (Tot.)	Many times	4
	Last time by Eric Dickerson, 10-31-88	
Points	Many times	24
	Last time by Eric Dickerson, 10-31-88	

*NFL Record

2005 VETERAN ROSTER

No.	Name	Pos.	Ht.	Wt.	Birthdate	NFL Exp.	College	Hometown	How Acq.	'04 Games/ Starts
26	Bacon, Waine	CB/S	5-10	191	4/11/79	2	Alabama	Ft. Washington, Md.	FA-'04	11/0
58	Brackett, Gary	LB	5-11	235	5/23/80	3	Rutgers	Glassboro, N.J.	FA-'03	15/1
79	Brock, Raheem	DE	6-4	274	6/10/78	4	Temple	Philadelphia, Pa.	FA-'02	16/16
5	Brown, Travis	QB	6-3	215	7/17/77	6	Northern Arizona	Phoenix, Ariz.	FA-'04	0*
35	Carthon, Ran	RB	6-0	218	2/10/81	2	Florida	Key West, Fla.	FA-'05	0*
44	Clark, Dallas	TE/FB	6-3	252	6/12/79	3	Iowa	Livermore, Iowa	D1-'03	15/13
42	David, Jason	CB/S	5-8	172	6/12/82	2	Washington State	Covina, Calif.	D4c-'04	16/11
71	Diem, Ryan	T	6-6	331	7/1/79	5	Northern Illinois	Carol Stream, Ill.	D4-'01	16/16
20	Doss, Mike	CB/S	5-10	207	3/24/81	3	Ohio State	Canton, Ohio	D2-'03	10/9
93	Freeney, Dwight	DE	6-1	268	2/19/80	4	Syracuse	Hartford, Conn.	D1-'02	16/16
76	Freitas, Makoa	T	6-4	307	11/23/79	3	Arizona	Honolulu, Hawaii	D6c-'03	16/0
51	Gardner, Gilbert	LB	6-1	228	5/9/82	2	Purdue	Angleton, Texa	D3b-'04	11/0
78	Glenn, Tarik	T	6-5	332	5/25/76	9	California	Oakland, Calif.	D1-'97	16/16
74	Gonzalez, Joaquin	G/T	6-5	315	9/7/79	3	Miami	Miami, Fla.	FA-'05	16/11
10	#Gramatica, Martin	K	5-8	170	11/27/75	7	Kansas State	LaBelle, Fla.	FA-'04	15/0*
25	Harper, Nick	CB/S	5-10	182	9/10/74	5	Ft. Valley State	Baldwin, Ga.	FA-'01	14/14
88	Harrison, Marvin	WR	6-0	175	8/25/72	10	Syracuse	Philadelphia, Pa.	D1-'96	16/16
80	Hartsock, Ben	TE	6-4	262	7/5/80	2	Ohio State	Chillicothe, Ohio	D3a-'04	16/3
57	Houchin, Thomas	LB	6-3	254	10/7/80	2	Kansas State	Sanger, Texas	FA-'04	0*
27	Hutchins, Von	CB/S	5-9	181	2/14/81	2	Mississippi	Natchez, Miss.	D6a-'04	16/1
61	Hutton, Trevor	G	6-5	305	2/28/80	2	Utah State	Santa Maria, Calif.	FA-'04	4/0
32	James, Edgerrin	RB	6-0	214	8/1/78	7	Miami	Immokalee, Fla.	D1-'99	16/16
29	Jefferson, Joseph	CB/S	6-1	202	2/15/80	4	Western Kentucky	Adairville, Ky.	D3-'02	9/3
59	June, Cato	LB	6-0	227	11/18/79	3	Michigan	Washington, D.C.	D6a-'03	16/16
65	Lilja, Ryan	G	6-2	285	10/15/81	2	Kansas State	Shawnee, Kan.	W(KC)-'04	7/6
18	Manning, Peyton	QB	6-5	230	3/24/76	8	Tennessee	New Orleans, La.	D1-'98	16/16
98	Mathis, Robert	DE	6-2	235	2/26/81	3	Alabama A&M	Atlanta, Ga.	D5a-'03	16/1
85	Moorehead, Aaron	WR	6-3	200	11/5/80	3	Illinois	Deerfield, Ill.	FA-'03	7/0
94	#Morris, Rob	LB	6-2	243	1/18/75	6	Brigham Young	Nampa, Idaho	D1-'00	15/14
23	Mungro, James	RB	5-9	214	2/13/78	4	Syracuse	East Stroudsburg, Pa.	W(Det)-'02	15/0
55	Pope, Kendyll	LB	6-1	220	5/9/81	2	Florida State	Fort White, Fla.	D4a-'04	2/0
84	Pyatt, Brad	WR	5-11	195	4/16/80	3	Northern Colorado	Arvada, Colo.	FA-'03	8/0
90	Reagor, Montae	DT	6-3	285	6/29/77	7	Texas Tech	Waxahachie, Texas	UFA(Den)-'03	16/16
33	Rhodes, Dominic	RB	5-9	203	1/17/79	5	Midwestern State (TX)	Abilene, Texas	FA-'01	16/0
97	Rogers, Nick	DE	6-2	250	5/31/79	4	Georgia Tech	East Point, Ga.	W(GB)-'04	11/0
21	Sanders, Bob	CB/S	5-8	206	2/24/81	2	Iowa	Erie, Pa.	D2b-'04	6/4
38	Sapp, Gerome	CB/S	6-1	216	2/8/81	3	Notre Dame	Houston, Texas	FA-'04	13/0
63	Saturday, Jeff	C	6-2	295	6/8/75	7	North Carolina	Tucker, Ga.	FA-'99	14/14
73	Scott, Jake	G	6-5	280	4/16/81	2	Idaho	Lewiston, Idaho	D5a-'04	12/9
17	Smith, Hunter	P	6-2	209	8/9/77	7	Notre Dame	Sherman, Texas	D7a-'99	16/0
48	Snow, Justin	TE	6-3	240	12/21/76	6	Baylor	Abilene, Texas	FA-'00	16/0
12	Sorgi, Jim	QB	6-5	196	12/3/80	2	Wisconsin	Fraser, Mich.	D6b-'04	4/0
83	Stokley, Brandon	WR	5-11	197	6/23/76	7	Southwestern Louisiana	Dallas, Texas	UFA(Balt)-'03	16/3
30	Strickland, Donald	CB/S	5-10	187	11/24/80	3	Colorado	Redwood City, Calif.	D3-'03	4/4
91	Thomas, Josh	DE	6-5	271	6/26/81	2	Syracuse	Orchard Park, N.Y.	FA-'04	11/0
50	Thornton, David	LB	6-2	230	11/1/78	4	North Carolina	Goldsboro, N.C.	D4-'02	16/15
75	Tripplett, Larry	DT	6-2	295	1/18/79	4	Washington	Los Angeles, Calif.	D2-'02	16/0
47	Utecht, Ben	TE	6-6	251	6/30/81	2	Minnesota	Hastings, Minn.	FA-'04	0*
13	Vanderjagt, Mike	K	6-5	211	3/24/70	8	West Virginia	Oakville, Ontario, Canada	FA-'98	15/0
86	Walters, Troy	WR	5-7	172	12/15/76	6	Stanford	College Station, Texas	W(Minn)-'02	5/0
87	Wayne, Reggie	WR	6-0	198	11/17/78	5	Miami	New Orleans, La.	D1b-'01	16/16
52	Whiteside, Keyon	LB	6-0	229	1/31/80	3	Tennessee	Forest City, N.C.	D3-'02	7/0
96	Williams, Josh	DT	6-3	285	8/9/76	6	Michigan	Houston, Texas	D4-'00	16/15

* Brown did not play in 2 games in '04; Carthon inactive for 7 games; Gramatica played 11 games with Tampa Bay, 4 games with Indianapolis; Houchin missed '04 season because of injury; Utecht missed '04 season on Physically Unable to Perform list.

#Unrestricted free agent, subject to developments.

Players lost through free agency (3): CB/S Idrees Bashir (Car; 13 games in '04); G Rick DeMulling (Det; 11); LB Jim Nelson (Balt; 15).

Also played with Colts in '04—P Jason Baker (4 games), CB/S Cory Bird (13), K Matt Bryant (1), RB Carey Davis (1), CB/S Anthony Floyd (11), RB Tom Lopienski (2), LB Jim Nelson (15), G Tupe Peko (11), TE Marcus Pollard (13), DE Brad Scioli (9).

2005 FIRST-YEAR ROSTER

Name	Pos.	Ht.	Wt.	Birthdate	College	Hometown	How Acq.
Adibi, Nathaniel (1)	DE	6-3	249	1/25/81	Virginia Tech	Hampton, Va.	FA
Arth, Tom (1)	QB	6-4	220	5/11/81	John Carroll	Westlake, Ohio	FA
Baaqee, Mikal	LB	5-10	225	10/20/81	Virginia Tech	Columbia, Md.	FA
Brown, Justin	DE	6-2	260	4/16/82	East Central (OK)	Fletcher, Okla.	FA
Burns, Vincent	DT	6-2	260	6/21/81	Kentucky	Valdosta, Ga.	D3
Campbell, Cody	G	6-4	305	9/29/81	Texas Tech	Lubbock, Texas	FA
Chart, Lee	G	6-2	290	7/3/81	Southern Utah	Park City, Utah	FA
Culton, Montiese	WR	6-2	180	1/18/82	Tulsa	Duncanville, Texas	FA
Davis, Anthony	RB	5-7	200	5/21/82	Wisconsin	Plainfield, N.J.	D7
Dennis, Jerome	CB/S	6-1	192	12/6/81	Utah State	Los Angeles, Calif.	FA
Dixon, Daryl (1)	CB/S	5-10	193	9/6/80	Florida	New Smyrna Beach, Fla.	FA
Fletcher, Bryan (1)	TE	6-5	238	3/23/79	UCLA	St. Louis, Mo.	FA
Ford, Willie (1)	CB/S	6-2	200	5/12/78	Syracuse	Falmouth, Mass.	FA
Fowlkes, Davon	WR	5-7	165	2/8/82	Appalachian St.	Fort Wayne, Ind.	FA
Gandy, Dylan	C/G	6-3	302	3/8/82	Texas Tech	Harlingen, Texas	D4a
Giordano, Matt	CB/S	5-11	192	10/16/82	California	Fresno, Calif.	D4b
Hagler, Tyjuan	LB	6-0	236	12/3/81	Cincinnati	Kankakee, Ill.	D5c
Hannah, Nick	LB	6-1	220	10/3/81	Eastern Oregon	East Wenetchee, Wash.	FA
Hawkins, Joey	TE	6-9	252	12/16/81	Texas Tech	Gilmer, Texas	FA
Hayden, Kelvin	CB/S	6-0	195	7/23/83	Illinois	Chicago, Ill.	D2
Hill, Eric (1)	CB/S	6-0	190	5/22/80	Colorado State	Denver, Colo.	FA
Humphrey, Tory	TE	6-3	253	1/20/83	Central Michigan	Saginaw, Mich.	FA
Hunt, Rob	C/G	6-3	298	3/3/81	North Dakota State	Cavalier, N.D.	D5b
Jackson, Marlin	CB/S	6-0	196	6/30/83	Michigan	Sharon, Pa.	D1
Laskowski, Chris	LB	5-9	210	9/12/81	Florida Atlantic	Melbourne, Fla.	FA
Lobel, Blake	DT	6-3	265	7/6/82	San Diego State	Upland, Calif.	FA
Lombardo, Lou	T	6-5	308	5/19/82	Maryland	Baltimore, Md.	FA
Lynch, Brandon (1)	CB/S	5-11	192	1/31/82	Middle Tennessee State	Augusta, Ga.	FA
Mays, Jermaine (1)	CB/S	5-11	198	7/13/79	Minnesota	Miami, Fla.	FA
Portis, Marico (1)	T/G	6-2	315	11/29/79	Alabama	Prichard, Ala.	FA
Rayner, Dave	K	6-2	205	10/26/82	Michigan State	Oxford, Mich.	D6
Reid, Darrell	DE	6-2	288	6/20/82	Minnesota	Freehold, N.J.	FA
Russell, Jason	G	6-5	300	6/23/82	Central Arkansas	Blytheville, Ariz.	FA
Scaldaferri, Stephen (1)	K	5-10	200	9/18/79	Kentucky	Silver Spring, Md.	FA
Sims, Dominique	LB	6-1	230	2/25/82	Minnesota	Minneapolis, Minn.	FA
Sommersell, Andre (1)	LB	6-2	230	6/26/80	Colorado State	Fountain Valley, Calif.	FA
Standeford, John (1)	WR	6-4	206	4/15/82	Purdue	Monrovia, Ind.	FA
Stewart, Jason (1)	DT	6-1	285	11/14/80	Fresno State	Bakersfield, Calif.	FA-'04
Thomas, Levon	WR	6-0	195	7/7/83	Georgia Tech	College Park, Ga.	FA
Toles, Deryck (1)	LB	5-11	224	12/30/80	Penn State	Warren, Ohio	FA
Ulrich, Matt	G	6-2	309	12/30/81	Northwestern	Streamwood, Ill.	FA
Wall, J.T. (1)	RB	6-0	250	9/12/79	Georgia	Milledgeville, Ga.	FA
Weaver, Jarrell (1)	LB	6-3	205	12/28/80	Miami	Miami, Fla.	FA
Welsh, Jonathan	DE	6-4	228	6/9/82	Wisconsin	Houston, Texas	D5a
Williams, Marcus	RB	5-10	230	10/22/83	Maine	Amherst, Mass.	FA
Wright, Kerry	WR	5-9	175	7/30/81	Middle Tennessee State	East Point, Ga.	FA

The term NFL Rookie is defined as a player who is in his first season of professional football and has not been on the roster of another professional football team for any regular-season or postseason games. A Rookie is designated by an "R" on NFL rosters. Players who have been active in another professional football league or players who have NFL experience, including either preseason training camp or being on an Active List or Inactive List, or on Reserve/Injured or Reserve/Physically Unable to Perform for fewer than six regular-season games, are termed NFL First-Year Players. An NFL First-Year Player is designated by a "1" on NFL rosters. Thereafter, a player is credited with an additional year of experience for each season in which he accumulates six games on the Active List or Inactive List, or on Reserve/Injured or Reserve/Physically Unable to Perform.

Log on to www.colts.com for an up-to-date roster.

COACHING STAFF

Head Coach,
Tony Dungy

Pro Career: Tony Dungy enters his fourth season as head coach of the Indianapolis Colts. Dungy was named head coach of the club on January 22, 2002. This season marks Dungy's tenth as an NFL head coach. He is the NFL's winningest head coach from 1999-2004 with a mark of 64-32 (30-18 with Tampa Bay, 34-14 with Colts). He has directed the Colts to 10-6, 12-4 and 12-4 records, joining Ted Marchibroda (1975-77) as the only coaches in club history to produce 10-plus victories and playoff berths in the first three seasons with the team. In 2004, Dungy led the Colts to their second consecutive divisional title, the fourth for the franchise in its 21-year Indianapolis era. Dungy helped produce the fourteenth 10-plus-victory season in franchise history. Dungy has directed seven of his nine Colts and Buccaneers teams to the playoffs, twice being a conference finalist. Dungy has six career double-digit victory seasons and stands as the only NFL head coach to defeat all 32 NFL teams. Dungy held a 54-42 record as head coach with Tampa Bay from 1996-2001, qualifying for the playoffs four times in six seasons. Dungy produced some of the NFL's stingiest defenses during his years at Tampa Bay. His units ranked no lower than 11th in his six seasons. At 25, Dungy was the NFL's youngest assistant coach when hired by the Pittsburgh Steelers in 1981. In 1982, he was promoted from defensive assistant to defensive backs coach, before becoming the league's youngest defensive coordinator in 1984 at age 28. He served as defensive backs coach at Kansas City (1989-1991) and as defensive coordinator at Minnesota (1992-95). Dungy signed with Pittsburgh as a free agent in 1977 and played safety for two seasons. He had nine interceptions in 30 games for Pittsburgh and played in the club's Super Bowl XIII victory over Dallas. He was traded to San Francisco in 1979 and played 15 games for the 49ers. Career record: 93-63.
Background: Starred as a quarterback at University of Minnesota from 1973-76. Finished career as school's all-time leader in attempts, completions, passing yards, and touchdown passes. Two-time team most valuable player, played in Hula Bowl, East-West Shrine Game and Japan Bowl.
Personal: Born October 6, 1955, in Jackson, Mich. Tony and his wife Lauren have five children—daughters Tiara and Jade, and sons James, Eric and Jordan.

ASSISTANT COACHES

Jim Caldwell, asst. head coach/quarterbacks; born January 16, 1955, Beloit, Wis. Defensive back Iowa 1973-76. No pro playing experience. College coach: Iowa 1977, Southern Illinois 1978-1980, Northwestern 1981, Colorado 1982-84, Louisville 1985, Penn State 1986-1992, Wake Forest 1993-2000. Pro coach: Tampa Bay Buccaneers 2001, joined Colts in 2002.

Clyde Christensen, wide receivers; born January 28, 1958, Covina, Calif. Quarterback Fresno (Calif.) J.C. 1975, North Carolina 1976-78. No pro playing experience. College coach: Mississippi 1979, East Tennessee State 1980-82, Temple 1983-85, East Carolina 1986-88, Holy Cross 1989-1990, South Carolina 1991, Maryland 1992-93, Clemson 1994-95. Pro coach: Tampa Bay Buccaneers 1996-2001, joined Colts in 2002.

Leslie Frazier, defensive assistant; born April 3, 1959, Columbus, Miss. Defensive back Alcorn State 1979-1980. Pro defensive back Chicago Bears 1981-86. College coach: Trinity (Ill.) College 1988-1996 (head coach), Illinois 1997-98. Pro coach: Philadelphia Eagles 1999-2002, Cincinnati Bengals 2003-04, joined Colts in 2005.

Richard Howell, asst. strength and conditioning; born February 19, 1972, Bladenboro, N.C. Quarterback Davidson 1990-93. No pro playing experience. College coach: Davidson 1994-98, North Carolina 1998-99. Pro coach: Barcelona Dragons (NFLE) 1999, joined Colts in 2000.

Gene Huey, running backs; born July 20, 1947, Uniontown, Pa. Defensive back-wide receiver Wyoming 1965-68. Pro running back San Diego Chargers 1969. College coach: Wyoming 1970-73, New Mexico 1974-76, Nebraska 1977-1986, Arizona State 1987, Ohio State 1988-1991. Pro coach: Joined Colts in 1992.

Ron Meeks, defensive coordinator; born August 27, 1954, Jacksonville. Defensive back Arkansas State 1972-76. Pro defensive back Hamilton Tiger-Cats (CFL) 1977-79, Ottawa Rough Riders (CFL) 1979, Toronto Argonauts (CFL) 1980-81. College coach: Arkansas State 1984-85, Miami 1986-87, New Mexico State 1988, Fresno State 1989-1990. Pro coach: Dallas Cowboys 1991, Cincinnati Bengals 1992-96, Atlanta Falcons 1997-99, Washington Redskins 2000, St. Louis Rams 2001, joined Colts in 2002.

Pete Metzelaars, offensive quality control; born May 24, 1960, Three Rivers, Mich. Tight end Wabash College 1978-1981. Pro tight end Seattle Seahawks 1982-84, Buffalo Bills 1985-1994, Carolina Panthers 1995, Detroit Lions 1996-97. College coach: Wingate 2003. Pro coach: Barcelona Dragons (NFLE) 2003, joined Colts in 2004.

Tom Moore, offensive coordinator; born November 7, 1938, Owatonna, Minn. Quarterback Iowa 1957-1960. No pro playing experience. College coach: Iowa 1961-62, Dayton 1965-68, Wake Forest 1969, Georgia Tech 1970-71, Minnesota 1972-73, 1975-76. Pro coach: New York Stars (WFL) 1974, Pittsburgh Steelers 1977-1989, Minnesota Vikings 1990-93,

Detroit Lions 1994-96, New Orleans Saints 1997, joined Colts in 1998.

Howard Mudd, offensive line; born February 10, 1942, Midland, Mich. Guard Hillsdale (Mich.) College 1960-63. Pro offensive lineman San Francisco 49ers 1964-69, Chicago Bears 1969-1971. College coach: California 1972-73. Pro coach: San Diego Chargers 1974-76, San Francisco 49ers 1977, Seattle Seahawks 1978-1982, 1993-97, Cleveland Browns 1983-88, Kansas City Chiefs 1989-1992, joined Colts in 1998.

Mike Murphy, linebackers; born September 25, 1944, New York, N.Y. Guard-linebacker Huron (S.D.) 1963-66. No pro playing experience. College coach: Vermont 1970-73, Idaho State 1974-76, Western Illinois 1977-78. Pro coach: Saskatchewan Rough Riders (CFL) 1979-1983, Chicago Blitz (USFL) 1984, Detroit Lions 1985-89, Arizona Cardinals 1990-93, Seattle Seahawks 1995-97, joined Colts in 1998.

Russ Purnell, special teams; born June 12, 1948, Chicago. Center Orange Coast (Calif.) J.C. 1966-67, Whittier College 1968-69. No pro playing experience. College coach: Whittier College 1970-71, Southern California 1982-85. Pro coach: Seattle Seahawks 1986-1994, Tennessee Oilers/Titans 1995-98, Baltimore Ravens 1999-2001, joined Colts in 2002.

Diron Reynolds, defensive quality control; born February 23, 1971, Aiken, S.C. Linebacker Wake Forest 1989-1993. No pro playing experience. College coach: Wake Forest 1997-2000; Indiana 2001. Pro coach: Joined Colts in 2002.

John Teerlinck, defensive line; born April 9, 1951, Rochester, N.Y. Defensive lineman Western Illinois 1970-73. Pro defensive tackle San Diego Chargers 1974-77. College coach: Iowa Lakes J.C. 1977, Eastern Illinois 1978-79, Illinois 1980-82. Pro coach: Chicago Blitz (USFL) 1983-84, Arizona Wranglers/Outlaws (USFL) 1985-86, Cleveland Browns 1989-1990, Los Angeles Rams 1991, Minnesota Vikings 1992-94, Detroit Lions 1995-96, Denver Broncos 1997-2001, joined Colts in 2002.

Ricky Thomas, tight ends; born March 29, 1965, London, England. Safety Alabama 1983-86. College coach: Kentucky 1996, Gardner-Webb 1997. Pro coach: Tampa Bay Buccaneers 1997-2001, joined Colts in 2002.

Jon Torine, strength and conditioning; born November 16, 1973, Livingston, N.J. Linebacker Springfield (Mass.) College 1991. No pro playing experience. Pro coach: Buffalo Bills 1995-97, joined Colts in 1998.

Alan Williams, defensive assistant; born November 4, 1969, Norfolk, Va. Running back William & Mary 1988-1991. No pro playing experience. College coach: William & Mary 1996-2000. Pro coach: Tampa Bay Buccaneers 2001, joined Colts in 2002.

American Football Conference
South Division
Team Colors: Teal, Black, and Gold
ALLTEL Stadium
One ALLTEL Stadium Place
Jacksonville, Florida 32202
Telephone: (904) 633-6000

2005 SCHEDULE
PRESEASON
Aug. 13	**Miami**	7:30
Aug. 20	at Tampa Bay	7:30
Aug. 25	**Atlanta**	8:00
Sept. 1	at Dallas	7:00

REGULAR SEASON
Sept. 11	**Seattle**	1:00
Sept. 18	at Indianapolis	12:00
Sept. 25	at New York Jets	1:00
Oct. 2	**Denver**	1:00
Oct. 9	**Cincinnati**	8:30
Oct. 16	at Pittsburgh	1:00
Oct. 23	Open Date	
Oct. 30	at St. Louis	12:00
Nov. 6	**Houston**	1:00
Nov. 13	**Baltimore**	1:00
Nov. 20	at Tennessee	12:00
Nov. 27	at Arizona	2:05
Dec. 4	at Cleveland	1:00
Dec. 11	**Indianapolis**	1:00
Dec. 18	**San Francisco**	1:00
Dec. 24	at Houston (Sat.)	12:00
Jan. 1	**Tennessee**	4:05

Stadium: ALLTEL Stadium
(opened in 1995)
•**Capacity:** 67,164
One ALLTEL Stadium Place
Jacksonville, Florida 32202
Playing Surface: Grass
Training Camp: ALLTEL Stadium
One ALLTEL Stadium Place
Jacksonville, Florida 32202

ALLTEL STADIUM

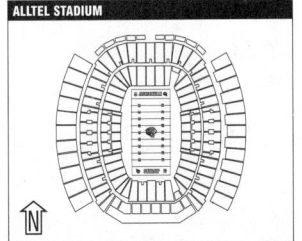

CLUB OFFICIALS
Chairman and Chief Executive Officer:
Wayne Weaver
Senior Vice President/Football
Operations: Paul Vance
Senior Vice President/Chief Financial
Officer: Bill Prescott
Senior Vice President/Business
Development: Tim Connolly
Vice President/Player Personnel:
James Harris
Vice President/Communications and
Media: Dan Edwards
Executive Director of Ticket Sales and
Marketing: Scott Loft
Executive Director of Corporate
Sponsorship: Macky Weaver
Executive Director of Football Operations:
Skip Richardson
Executive Director of Information
Technology: Bruce Swindell
Director of Pro Personnel: Charles Bailey
Director of College Scouting: Gene Smith
Director of Ticket Operations: Tim Bishko
Director of Special Events and
Promotions: Tim Beach
Director of Marketing: Jennifer Perkins
Director of Broadcasting: Chris Sinclair
Associate General Counsel: Joe Pierce
Head Athletic Trainer: Michael Ryan
Video Director: Mike Perkins
Equipment Manager: Drew Hampton
Assistant Director of Pro Personnel:
Louis Clark
Executive Scouts: Terry McDonough,
Tim Mingey
Regional Scouts: Andy Dengler,
Chris Driggers, Art Perkins
BLESTO Representative: Kadar Hamilton
Scouts: Marty Miller, Larry Wright
Scouting Assistant: Chris Prescott
Coordinator, Communications:
Hunter Robinson
Executive Assistant to VP,
Communications and Media:
Alisa Abbott
Chair & Chief Executive Officer, Jaguars
Foundation: Delores Barr Weaver
Executive Director: Peter Racine

COACHING HISTORY
(86-82-0)
Records include postseason games
1995-2002	Tom Coughlin	72-64-0
2003-04	Jack Del Rio	14-18-0

ATTENDANCE
Home 512,717	Away 488,168
Total 1,000,885
Single-game home record,
74,143 (12/28/98)
Single-season home record, 561,472
(1998)

2005 DRAFT CHOICES
Round	Name	Pos.	College
1	Matt Jones	WR	Arkansas
2	Khalif Barnes	T	Washington
3	Scott Starks	DB	Wisconsin
4	Alvin Pearman	RB	Virginia
5	Gerald Sensabaugh	DB	North Carolina
6	Chad Owens	KR	Hawaii
	Patrick Thomas	LB	North Carolina St.
7	Chris Roberson	DB	Eastern Michigan

2004 TEAM RECORD
PRESEASON (3-1)

Date	Result	Opponent
8/14	L 5-16	at Miami
8/20	W 14-6	Tampa Bay
8/27	W 9-7	Green Bay
9/2	W 31-0	at New England

REGULAR SEASON (9-7)

Date	Result	Opponent	Att.
9/12	W 13-10	at Buffalo	72,389
9/19	W 7-6	Denver	69,127
9/26	W 15-12	at Tennessee	68,932
10/3	L 17-24	Indianapolis	73,114
10/10	L 21-34	at San Diego	52,101
10/17	W 22-16	Kansas City	66,413
10/24	W 27-24	at Indianapolis	56,615
10/31	L 6-20	at Houston	70,502
11/14	W 23-17	Detroit (OT)	66,431
11/21	L 15-18	Tennessee	69,703
11/28	L 16-27	at Minnesota	64,004
12/5	L 16-17	Pittsburgh	76,877
12/12	W 22-3	Chicago	67,572
12/19	W 28-25	at Green Bay	70,437
12/26	L 0-21	Houston	66,227
1/2	W 13-6	at Oakland	41,112

(OT) Overtime

SCORE BY PERIODS

Jaguars	35	75	56	89	6 —	261
Opponents	61	86	34	99	0 —	280

2004 TEAM STATISTICS

	Jaguars	Opp.
Total First Downs	279	290
Rushing	88	83
Passing	161	181
Penalty	30	26
3rd Down: Made/Att	80/217	84/205
3rd Down Pct.	36.9	41.0
4th Down: Made/Att	10/18	5/10
4th Down Pct.	55.6	50.0
Possession Avg.	30:28	29:32
Total Net Yards	5009	5134
Avg. Per Game	313.1	320.9
Total Plays	991	972
Avg. Per Play	5.1	5.3
Net Yards Rushing	1850	1777
Avg. Per Game	115.6	111.1
Total Rushes	446	438
Net Yards Passing	3159	3357
Avg. Per Game	197.4	209.8
Sacked/Yards Lost	32/156	37/217
Gross Yards	3315	3574
Att./Completions	513/305	497/306
Completion Pct.	59.5	61.6
Had Intercepted	11	16
Punts/Average	84/42.8	74/44.1
Net Punting Avg.	84/35.5	74/35.1
Penalties/Yards	109/940	118/966
Fumbles/Ball Lost	23/11	30/12
Touchdowns	26	31
Rushing	9	7
Passing	17	18
Returns	0	6

2004 INDIVIDUAL STATISTICS

PASSING

PASSING	Att.	Comp.	Yds.	Pct.	TD	Int.	Tkld.	Rate
Leftwich	441	267	2,941	60.5	15	10	25/114	82.2
Garrard	72	38	374	52.8	2	1	6/35	71.2
Toefield	0	0	0	—	0	0	1/7	—
Jaguars	513	305	3,315	59.5	17	11	32/156	80.7
Opponents	497	306	3,574	61.6	18	16	37/217	82.0

SCORING

SCORING	TD R	TD P	TD Rt	PAT	FG	Saf	PTS
Scobee	0	0	0	21/21	24/31	0	93
J. Smith	0	6	0	0/0	0/0	0	36
G. Jones	3	0	0	0/0	0/0	0	18
Taylor	2	1	0	0/0	0/0	0	18
Wilford	0	2	0	0/0	0/0	0	14
Hankton	0	2	0	0/0	0/0	0	12
Leftwich	2	0	0	0/0	0/0	0	12
R. Williams	0	1	0	0/0	0/0	0	10
B. Jones	0	1	0	0/0	0/0	0	8
Brady	0	1	0	0/0	0/0	0	6
T. Edwards	0	1	0	0/0	0/0	0	6
Fuamatu-Ma'afala	1	0	0	0/0	0/0	0	6
Garrard	1	0	0	0/0	0/0	0	6
Toefield	0	1	0	0/0	0/0	0	6
Wrighster	0	1	0	0/0	0/0	0	6
Favors	0	0	0	0/0	0/0	1	2
D. Smith	0	0	0	0/0	0/0	1	2
Jaguars	9	17	0	21/21	24/31	2	261
Opponents	7	18	6	27/28	21/28	0	280

2-Pt. Conversions: R. Williams 2, B. Jones, Wilford.
Jaguars 4-4, Opponents 2-3.

RUSHING

RUSHING	No.	Yds	Avg	LG	TD
Taylor	260	1,224	4.7	46	2
Toefield	51	169	3.3	16	0
G. Jones	62	162	2.6	12	3
Leftwich	39	148	3.8	17	2
Garrard	12	76	6.3	12	1
Fuamatu-Ma'afala	20	69	3.5	10	1
T. Edwards	2	2	1.0	2	0
Jaguars	446	1,850	4.1	46	9
Opponents	438	1,777	4.1	47	7

RECEIVING

RECEIVING	No.	Yds	Avg	LG	TD
J. Smith	74	1,172	15.8	65	6
T. Edwards	50	533	10.7	36	1
Taylor	36	345	9.6	64t	1
Toefield	28	151	5.4	16	1
R. Williams	27	268	9.9	26	1
Wilford	19	271	14.3	46	2
Yoder	14	157	11.2	56	0
Brady	14	103	7.4	21	1
Wrighster	10	69	6.9	12	1
Hankton	9	81	9.0	14t	2
M. Edwards	7	41	5.9	15	0
B. Jones	6	87	14.5	26t	1
Fuamatu-Ma'afala	4	19	4.8	8	0
G. Jones	3	13	4.3	9	0
Allen	2	8	4.0	5	0
Lewis	1	4	4.0	4	0
Leftwich	1	-7	-7.0	-7	0
Jaguars	305	3,315	10.9	65	17
Opponents	306	3,574	11.7	54	18

INTERCEPTIONS

INTERCEPTIONS	No.	Yds	Avg	LG	TD
Darius	5	80	16.0	37	0
Mathis	5	42	8.4	21	0
Grant	2	4	2.0	4	0
Washington	2	0	0.0	0	0
Cooper	1	0	0.0	0	0
D. Smith	1	0	0.0	0	0
Jaguars	16	126	7.9	37	0
Opponents	11	163	14.8	43t	1

PUNTING

PUNTING	No.	Yds.	Avg.	In 20	LG
Hanson	84	3,592	42.8	28	69
Jaguars	84	3,592	42.8	28	69
Opponents	74	3,265	44.1	19	80

PUNT RETURNS

PUNT RETURNS	Ret	FC	Yds	Avg	LG	TD
Lewis	23	7	227	9.9	50	0
Allen	15	2	144	9.6	32	0
T. Edwards	3	1	26	8.7	14	0
Mathis	1	0	8	8.0	8	0
Jaguars	42	10	405	9.6	50	0
Opponents	38	13	429	11.3	83t	2

KICKOFF RETURNS

KICKOFF RETURNS	No.	Yds	Avg	LG	TD
Lewis	21	386	18.4	26	0
T. Edwards	15	335	22.3	45	0
Allen	11	210	19.1	25	0
G. Jones	5	90	18.0	23	0
Toefield	3	43	14.3	19	0
Brady	1	15	15.0	15	0
M. Edwards	1	8	8.0	8	0
Jaguars	57	1,087	19.1	45	0
Opponents	50	995	19.9	52	0

FIELD GOALS

FIELD GOALS	1-19	20-29	30-39	40-49	50+
Scobee	0/0	10/10	8/11	5/7	1/3
Jaguars	0/0	10/10	8/11	5/7	1/3
Opponents	0/0	9/9	7/10	5/8	0/1

SACKS

SACKS	No.
Favors	5.5
Henderson	5.5
Peterson	5.0
Stroud	4.5
McCray	3.5
Gildon	3.0
Ayodele	2.0
D. Smith	2.0
Barnes	1.0
Cooper	1.0
Grant	1.0
Patterson	1.0
Meier	0.5
Ransom	0.5
Jaguars	37.0
Opponents	32.0

RECORD HOLDERS
INDIVIDUAL RECORDS—CAREER

Category	Name	Performance
Rushing (Yds.)	Fred Taylor, 1998-2004	7,580
Passing (Yds.)	Mark Brunell, 1995-2003	25,698
Passing (TDs)	Mark Brunell, 1995-2003	144
Receiving (No.)	Jimmy Smith, 1995-2004	792
Receiving (Yds.)	Jimmy Smith, 1995-2004	11,264
Interceptions	Aaron Beasley, 1996-2001	15
Punting (Avg.)	Chris Hanson, 2001-04	43.5
	Bryan Barker, 1995-2000	43.5
Punt Return (Avg.)	Chris Hudson, 1995-98	10.9
Kickoff Return (Avg.)	Reggie Barlow, 1997-2000	23.3
Field Goals	Mike Hollis, 1995-2001	175
Touchdowns (Tot.)	Jimmy Smith, 1995-2004	63
Points	Mike Hollis, 1995-2001	764

INDIVIDUAL RECORDS—SINGLE SEASON

Category	Name	Performance
Rushing (Yds.)	Fred Taylor, 2003	1,572
Passing (Yds.)	Mark Brunell, 1996	4,367
Passing (TDs)	Mark Brunell, 1998	20
Receiving (No.)	Jimmy Smith, 1999	116
Receiving (Yds.)	Jimmy Smith, 1999	1,636
Interceptions	Aaron Beasley, 1999	6
	Marlon McCree, 2002	6
Punting (Avg.)	Bryan Barker, 1998	45.0
Punt Return (Avg.)	Reggie Barlow, 1998	12.9
Kickoff Return (Avg.)	Reggie Barlow, 1998	24.9
Field Goals	Mike Hollis, 1997, 1999	31
Touchdowns (Tot.)	Fred Taylor, 1998	17
Points	Mike Hollis, 1997	134

INDIVIDUAL RECORDS—SINGLE GAME

Category	Name	Performance
Rushing (Yds.)	Fred Taylor, 11-19-00	234
Passing (Yds.)	Mark Brunell, 9-22-96	432
Passing (TDs)	Mark Brunell, 11-29-98	4
Receiving (No.)	Keenan McCardell, 10-20-96	16
Receiving (Yds.)	Jimmy Smith, 9-10-00	291
Interceptions	Many times	2
	Last time by Donovin Darius, 1-2-05	
Field Goals	Mike Hollis, 12-1-96, 11-30-97, 9-10-00	5
Touchdowns (Tot.)	James Stewart, 10-12-97	5
Points	James Stewart, 10-12-97	30

2005 VETERAN ROSTER

No.	Name	Pos.	Ht.	Wt.	Birthdate	NFL Exp.	College	Hometown	How Acq.	'04 Games/ Starts
32	Allen, David	RB	5-9	195	2/9/78	2	Kansas State	Liberty, Mo.	FA-'04	5/0
51	Ayodele, Akin	LB	6-2	251	9/17/79	4	Purdue	Irving, Texas	D3-'02	16/16
80	Brady, Kyle	TE	6-6	278	1/14/72	11	Penn State	New Cumberland, Pa.	UFA(N.Y.J.)-'99	11/8
78	Chase, Martin	DT	6-2	310	12/19/74	8	Oklahoma	Lawton, Okla.	UFA(N.Y.G.)-'05	0*
81	Cole, Chris	WR	6-0	195	11/12/77	5	Texas A&M	Littleton, Colo.	FA-'05	0*
77	Compton, Mike	T/G	6-6	310	9/18/70	13	West Virginia	Richlands, Va.	FA-'04	13/0
35	Cooper, Deke	S	6-2	210	10/18/77	4	Notre Dame	Evansville, Ind.	FA-'03	16/0
58	Cordova, Jorge	LB/DE	6-1	241	9/25/81	2	Nevada	Murrieta, Calif.	D3-'04	0*
21	Cousin, Terry	CB	5-9	185	4/11/75	9	South Carolina	Miami, Fla.	FA-'05	16/5*
20	Darius, Donovin	S	6-1	225	8/12/75	8	Syracuse	Camden, N.J.	D1b-'98	16/16
16	Edwards, Troy	WR	5-10	195	4/7/77	7	Louisiana Tech	Shreveport, La.	FA-'03	16/4
55	Favors, Greg	LB	6-1	244	9/30/74	8	Mississippi State	Atlanta, Ga.	UFA(Car)-'04	15/11
68	Fletcher, Derrick	G	6-6	350	9/9/75	4	Baylor	Houston, Texas	FA-'04	0*
45	Fuamatu-Ma'afala, Chris	RB	6-0	252	3/4/77	8	Utah	Honolulu, Hawaii	FA-'03	7/1
9	Garrard, David	QB	6-1	244	2/14/78	4	East Carolina	Durham, N.C.	D4a-'02	4/2
50	Gilbert, Tony	LB	6-0	244	10/16/79	3	Georgia	Macon, Ga.	W(Ariz)-'03	16/0
37	Grant, Deon	S	6-2	210	3/14/79	6	Tennessee	Augusta, Ga.	UFA(Car)-'04	16/16
5	Gray, Quinn	QB	6-3	246	5/21/79	2	Florida A&M	Fort Lauderdale, Fla.	FA-'03	0*
85	Hankton, Cortez	WR	6-0	200	1/20/81	3	Texas Southern	New Orleans, La.	FA-'03	12/0
2	Hanson, Chris	P	6-2	223	10/25/76	5	Marshall	Senoia, Ga.	FA-'01	16/0
97	Hayward, Reggie	DE	6-5	270	3/14/79	5	Iowa State	Dolton, Ill.	UFA(Den)-'05	16/15*
98	Henderson, John	DT	6-7	328	1/9/79	4	Tennessee	Nashville, Tenn.	D1-'02	16/16
12	Hybl, Nate	QB	6-4	222	5/1/80	2	Oklahoma	Hazelhurst, Ga.	FA-'05	0*
86	Jones, Brian	TE	6-3	235	8/23/81	2	Arkansas-Pine Bluff	Bastrop, La.	FA-'04	16/0
33	Jones, Greg	RB	6-1	250	4/4/81	2	Florida State	Beaufort, S.C.	D2b-'04	16/3
7	Leftwich, Byron	QB	6-5	245	1/14/80	3	Marshall	Washington, D.C.	D1-'03	14/14
67	Manuwai, Vince	G	6-2	312	7/12/80	3	Hawaii	Honolulu, Hawaii	D3-'03	16/16
6	Marler, Seth	K	6-1	200	3/27/81	3	Tulane	Lilburn, Ga.	FA-'03	0*
27	Mathis, Rashean	CB	6-1	200	8/27/80	3	Bethune-Cookman	Jacksonville, Fla.	D2-'03	16/16
93	McCray, Bobby	DE	6-6	251	8/8/81	2	Florida	Miami, Fla.	D7-'04	16/7
63	Meester, Brad	C	6-3	300	3/23/77	6	Northern Iowa	Parkersburg, Iowa	D2-'00	16/16
92	Meier, Rob	DT	6-5	293	8/29/77	6	Washington State	W. Vancouver, B.C., Canada	D7b-'00	11/8
65	Naeole, Chris	G	6-3	320	12/25/74	9	Colorado	Kaaava, Hawaii	UFA(NO)-'02	16/16
62	Norman, Dennis	C	6-5	312	1/26/80	4	Princeton	Marlton, N.J.	FA-'04	0*
72	Pearson, Mike	T	6-7	297	8/22/80	4	Florida	Seffner, Fla.	D2-'02	4/4
54	Peterson, Mike	LB	6-1	230	6/17/76	7	Florida	Gainesville, Fla.	UFA(Ind)-'03	16/16
90	Ransom, Derrick	DT	6-3	307	9/13/76	8	Cincinnati	Indianapolis, Ind.	FA-'04	10/0
26	Richardson, David	CB	6-0	202	9/9/81	2	Cal Poly-San Luis Obispo	Los Angeles, Calif.	FA-'04	2/0
66	Romberg, Brett	C	6-2	293	10/10/79	3	Miami	Windsor, Ontario, Canada	FA-'03	0*
76	Salaam, Ephraim	T	6-7	295	6/19/76	8	San Diego State	Sacramento, Calif.	FA-'04	15/12
10	Scobee, Josh	K	6-1	190	6/23/82	2	Louisiana Tech	Longview, Texas	D5a-'04	16/0
73	Smith, Brent	G/T	6-5	305	11/21/73	9	Mississippi State	Pontotoc, Miss.	FA-'05	4/1*
52	Smith, Daryl	LB	6-2	234	4/14/82	2	Georgia Tech	Albany, Ga.	D2a-'04	15/13
82	Smith, Jimmy	WR	6-1	208	2/9/69	13	Jackson State	Jackson, Miss.	FA-'95	16/16
41	Sorensen, Nick	S	6-3	210	7/31/78	5	Virginia Tech	Vienna, Va.	FA-'03	16/0
95	Spicer, Paul	DE	6-4	287	8/18/75	6	Saginaw Valley State	Indianapolis, Ind.	FA-'00	2/2
99	Stroud, Marcus	DT	6-6	312	6/25/78	5	Georgia	Barney, Ga.	D1-'01	16/16
28	Taylor, Fred	RB	6-1	234	1/27/76	8	Florida Belle	Glade, Fla.	D1a-'98	14/14
24	Thomas, Kiwaukee	CB	5-11	192	6/19/77	6	Georgia Southern	Perry, Ga.	D5-'00	16/2
29	Thompson, Chris	CB	6-0	187	5/19/82	2	Nicholls State	New Orleans, La.	D5b-'04	0*
22	Toefield, LaBrandon	RB	5-11	232	9/24/80	3	Louisiana State	Independence, La.	D4b-'03	14/0
57	Wayne, Nate	LB	6-0	237	1/12/75	8	Mississippi	Macon, Ga.	FA-'05	9/7*
75	Wiley, Marcellus	DE	6-4	275	11/30/74	9	Columbia	Santa Monica, Calif.	FA-'05	16/15*
19	Wilford, Ernest	WR	6-4	223	1/14/79	2	Virginia Tech	Richmond, Va.	D4b-'04	15/3
74	Williams, Maurice	T	6-5	310	1/26/79	5	Michigan	Detroit, Mich.	D2-'01	16/16
11	Williams, Reggie	WR	6-4	223	5/17/83	2	Washington	Tacoma, Wash.	D1-'04	16/15
94	Williams, Tony	DT	6-2	296	7/9/75	9	Memphis	Memphis, Tenn.	UFA(Cin)-'05	6/6*
87	Wrighster, George	TE	6-3	260	4/1/81	3	Oregon	Van Nuys, Calif.	D4a-'03	4/3
25	Wright, Kenny	CB	6-1	207	9/14/77	7	Northwestern State	Ruston, La.	UFA(Hou)-'05	16/0*
83	Yoder, Todd	TE	6-4	250	3/18/78	6	Vanderbilt	New Palestine, Ind.	UFA(TB)-'04	16/8
88	Zelenka, Joe	TE/LS	6-3	270	3/9/76	7	Wake Forest	Cleveland, Ohio	FA-'01	16/0

* Chase missed '04 season with Giants because of injury; Cole last active with Denver in '03; Cordova missed '04 season because of injury; Cousin played 16 games with N.Y. Giants in '04; Fletcher inactive for 2 games; Gray did not play in 2 games; Hayward played 16 games with Denver; Hybl last active with Cleveland in '03; Marler missed '04 season because of injury; Norman inactive for 4 games; Romberg did not play in 6 games; B. Smith played 4 games with N.Y. Jets; Thompson inactive for 16 games; Wayne played 9 games with Philadelphia; Wiley played 16 games with Dallas; T. Williams played 6 games with Cincinnati; Wright played 16 games with Houston.

Players lost through free agency (1): T Bob Whitfield (NYG; 10 games in '04).

Also played with Jaguars in '04—DT Willie Blade (5 games), CB Juran Bolden (13), FB Marc Edwards (13), DE Jason Gildon (9), DE Brandon Green (3), LB Tommy Hendricks (15), WR Jermaine Lewis (13), LB Jimmy McClain (1), DE Elton Patterson (6).

2005 FIRST-YEAR ROSTER

Name	Pos.	Ht.	Wt.	Birthdate	College	Hometown	How Acq.
Alexis, Rich (1)	RB	6-0	213	3/6/81	Washington	Coral Springs, Fla.	FA-'04
Allmond, Marcell (1)	CB	6-0	209	5/28/81	Southern California	Anaheim, Calif.	FA-'04
Barnes, Khalif	T	6-5	305	4/21/82	Washington	Spring Valley, Calif.	D2
Connolly, Daniel	G	6-4	311	9/2/82	Southeast Misssouri State	St. Louis, Mo.	FA
Davis, Jim	DE	6-3	270	10/4/81	Virginia Tech	Highland Springs, Va.	FA
Economos, Andrew	LS	6-1	250	6/24/82	Georgia Tech	Atlanta, Ga.	FA
Enzor, Jamar	LB	6-1	237	12/28/81	Cincinnati	Havana, Fla.	FA
Franklin, Julius	G	6-3	316	4/26/82	Bethune-Cookman	Orlando, Fla.	FA
Hand, Omari (1)	DE	6-4	265	7/3/80	Tennessee	Tallahassee, Fla.	FA-'04
Jones, Matt	WR	6-6	242	4/22/83	Arkansas	Fort Smith, Ark.	D1
Kinney, James	LB	6-1	244	6/5/82	Missouri	Kankakee, Ill.	FA
Maddox, Anthony (1)	DT	6-1	295	11/22/78	Delta State	Funston, Ga.	D4a-'04
Mitchell, Jason	WR	6-0	193	7/19/81	Southern California	Los Angeles, Calif.	FA
Owens, Chad	WR/KR	5-7	183	4/3/82	Hawaii	Honolulu, Hawaii	D6a
Pearman, Alvin	RB	5-10	210	8/10/82	Virginia	Charlotte, N.C.	D4
Perryman, Ray	S	5-11	195	11/27/78	Northern Arizona	Phoenix, Ariz.	FA
Roberson, Chris	CB	5-11	185	6/3/83	Eastern Michigan	Farmington Hills, Mich.	D7
Sensabaugh, Gerald	S	6-0	210	6/13/83	North Carolina	Kingsport, Tenn.	D5
Starks, Scott	CB	5-9	180	6/27/83	Wisconsin	St. Louis, Mo.	D3
Tate, Joe (1)	G	6-5	291	12/30/80	Michigan State	Southfield, Mich.	FA-'04
Thomas, Benard	DE	6-4	263	4/10/81	Nebraska East	Palo Alto, Calif.	FA
Thomas, Pat	LB	6-2	237	1/26/83	North Carolina State	Miami, Fla.	D6b
Webb, Lee	FB	5-11	240	11/3/81	Southern California	Inglewood, Calif.	FA
Whittaker, Huey (1)	WR	6-4	234	6/19/81	South Florida	Springhill, Fla.	FA-'04
Wimbush, Derrick	RB	6-1	211	8/26/80	Fort Valley State	Mauk, Ga.	FA

The term NFL Rookie is defined as a player who is in his first season of professional football and has not been on the roster of another professional football team for any regular-season or postseason games. A Rookie is designated by an "R" on NFL rosters. Players who have been active in another professional football league or players who have NFL experience, including either preseason training camp or being on an Active List or Inactive List, or on Reserve/Injured or Reserve/Physically Unable to Perform for fewer than six regular-season games, are termed NFL First-Year Players. An NFL First-Year Player is designated by a "1" on NFL rosters. Thereafter, a player is credited with an additional year of experience for each season in which he accumulates six games on the Active List or Inactive List, or on Reserve/Injured or Reserve/Physically Unable to Perform.

Log on to www.jaguars.com for an up-to-date roster.

COACHING STAFF

Head Coach,
Jack Del Rio

Pro Career: Jack Del Rio was named head coach of the Jaguars on January 17, 2003, becoming the second head coach in franchise history. At 42, Del Rio is the second-youngest head coach in the NFL (Jon Gruden is the youngest). In 2004, the Jaguars registered a 9-7 record for the franchise's first winning season since 1999. In 2003, six of the Jaguars' eleven losses were by seven points or less. Del Rio was the defensive coordinator for the Carolina Panthers in 2002, and the team's defense ranked second in the league after finishing thirty-first in 2001. From 1999-2001, he was the linebackers coach for the Baltimore Ravens, helping the team win Super Bowl XXXV. Del Rio previously coached in New Orleans (1997-98). He previously spent 11 years as an NFL linebacker. In 1985, he was a third-round choice of the New Orleans Saints and was named to the NFL's All-Rookie team. Del Rio also played for the Kansas City Chiefs (1987-88), Dallas Cowboys (1989-1991), and Minnesota Vikings (1992-95). He played in the Pro Bowl following the 1994 season. Career record: 14-18.

Background: Four-year starter at linebacker from 1981-84 at Southern California, where he earned consensus All-America honors as a senior and was runner-up for the Lombardi Award. He was co-MVP of the 1985 Rose Bowl. Drafted by baseball's Toronto Blue Jays in 1981, Del Rio batted .340 while playing catcher on USC's baseball team. He has a political science degree from Kansas.

Personal: Born April 4, 1963 in Castro Valley, Calif. Jack and his wife, Linda, live in Jacksonville, and have three daughters, Lauren, Hope, and Aubrey, and a son, Luke.

ASSISTANT COACHES

Ken Anderson, quarterbacks; born February 15, 1949, Batavia, Ill. Quarterback Augustana (Ill.) 1967-1970. Pro quarterback Cincinnati Bengals 1971-1986. Pro coach: Cincinnati Bengals 1992-2002, joined Jaguars in 2003.

Mark Asanovich, strength and conditioning; born May 20, 1959, Duluth, Minn. Attended St. Cloud State. No college or pro playing experience. College coach: Ohio State 1984-85, The Citadel 1986. Pro coach: Minnesota Vikings 1995, Tampa Bay Buccaneers 1996-2001, Baltimore Ravens 2002, joined Jaguars in 2003.

Paul Boudreau, offensive line; born December 30, 1949, Arlington, Mass. Offensive lineman Boston College 1971-73. No pro playing experience. College coach: Boston College 1974-75, Maine 1976-78, Dartmouth 1979-1981, Navy 1982. Pro coach: Edmonton Eskimos (CFL) 1983-86, New Orleans Saints 1987-1993, Detroit Lions 1994-96, New England Patriots 1997-98, Miami

Dolphins 1999-2000, Carolina Panthers 2001-02, joined Jaguars in 2003.

Dave Campo, asst. head coach/secondary; born July 18, 1947, Groton, Conn. Defensive back Central Connecticut State 1967-1970. No pro playing experience. College coach: Central Connecticut State 1971-72, Albany 1973, Bridgeport 1974, Pittsburgh 1975, Washington State 1976, Boise State 1977-79, Oregon State 1980, Weber State 1981-82, Iowa State 1983, Syracuse 1984-86, Miami 1987-88. Pro coach: Dallas Cowboys 1989-2002 (head coach 2000-2002), Cleveland Browns 2003-2004, joined Jaguars in 2005.

Les Ebert, asst. strength and conditioning; born October 1, 1972, Brainerd, Minn. Attended Minnesota-Duluth. No college or pro playing experience. Pro coach: Tampa Bay Buccaneers 1999-2002, joined Jaguars in 2003.

Ray Hamilton, defensive line; born January 20, 1951, Omaha, Neb. Nose tackle Oklahoma 1969-1972. Pro defensive lineman New England Patriots 1973-1981. College coach: Tennessee 1992. Pro coach: New England Patriots 1985-89, Tampa Bay Buccaneers 1991, Los Angeles Raiders 1993-94, New York Jets 1994-96, 2000, New England Patriots 1997-99, Cleveland Browns 2001-02, joined Jaguars in 2003.

Andy Heck, asst. offensive line; born January 1, 1967, Fargo, N.D. Tackle Notre Dame 1985-88. Pro tackle Seattle 1989-1993, Chicago 1994-98, Washington 1999-2000. College coach: Virginia 2001-03. Pro coach: Joined Jaguars in 2003.

Todd Howard, asst. defensive line; born February 18, 1965, Bryan, Texas. Linebacker Texas A&M 1983-86. Pro linebacker Kansas City Chiefs 1987-88, Barcelona Dragons (WLAF) 1991-92. College coach: Texas A&M 1991-93, Grinnell 1994-97, Louisiana Tech 2000-02. Pro coach: St. Louis Rams 1998-99, joined Jaguars in 2003.

Mark Michaels, asst. special teams; born August 15, 1963, Kingston, Pa. Defensive lineman Connecticut 1983-86. No pro playing experience. College coach: New Haven 1987-1990, Brown 1993-97, Massachusetts 1998. Pro coach: Helsinki Roosters (Finnish Maple League) 1991, Utah Pioneers (Professional Spring Football League) 1992, Cleveland Browns 1999-2000, Seattle Seahawks 2001-2004, joined Jaguars in 2005.

Kennedy Pola, running backs; born November 22, 1963, Pago, Pago, American Samoa. Fullback Southern California 1982-85. No pro playing experience. College coach: UCLA 1992-93, San Diego State 1994-96, Colorado 1997-98, San Diego State 1999, Southern California 2000-2003. Pro coach: Cleveland Browns 2004, joined Jaguars in 2005.

Alvin Reynolds, defensive backs; born June 24, 1959, Pineville, La. Safety Indiana State 1978-1981. No pro playing

experience. College coach: Indiana State 1982-1992. Pro coach: Denver Broncos 1993-95, Baltimore Ravens 1996-98, Carolina Panthers 1999-2002, joined Jaguars in 2003.

Alfredo Roberts, tight ends; born March 17, 1965, Fort Lauderdale, Fla. Tight end Miami 1983-87. Pro tight end Kansas City Chiefs 1988-1990, Dallas Cowboys 1991-93. College coach: Florida Atlantic 1999-2002. Pro coach: Joined Jaguars in 2003.

Pete Rodriguez, special teams coordinator; born July 25, 1940, Chicago. Guard-linebacker Denver 1959-1960, Western State (Colo.) 1961-63. College coach: Arizona 1968-69, Western Illinois 1970-73, 1979-1982 (head coach 1979-1982), Florida State 1974-75, Iowa State 1976-78, Northern Iowa 1986. Pro coach: Michigan Panthers (USFL) 1983-84, Denver Gold (USFL) 1985, Jacksonville Bulls (USFL) 1986, Ottawa Rough Riders (CFL) 1987, Los Angeles Raiders 1988-89, Phoenix Cardinals 1990-93, Washington Redskins 1994-97, Seattle Seahawks 1998-2003, joined Jaguars in 2004.

Carl Smith, offensive coordinator; born April 28, 1948, Wasco, Calif. Quarterback Bakersfield College 1966-67, defensive back Cal-Poly San Luis Obispo 1969-70. No pro playing experience. College coach: Colorado 1972-73, Southwestern Louisiana 1974-78, Lamar 1979-1981, North Carolina State 1982, Southern California 2004. Pro coach: Philadelphia/Baltimore Stars (USFL) 1983-85, New Orleans Saints 1986-1996, New England Patriots 1997-2000, Cleveland Browns 2001-2003, joined Jaguars in 2005.

Mike Smith, defensive coordinator; born November 30, 1959, Chicago. Linebacker East Tennessee 1977-1981. Pro linebacker Winnipeg Blue Bombers (CFL) 1982. College coach: San Diego State 1982-85, Morehead State (Ky.) 1986, Tennessee Tech 1987-1998. Pro coach: Baltimore Ravens 1999-2002, joined Jaguars in 2003.

Brian VanGorder, linebackers; born April 17, 1959, Jackson, Mich. Linebacker Wayne State 1979-1980. No pro playing experience. College coach: Grand Valley State 1989-1991, Wayne State 1992-94 (head coach), Central Florida 1995-97, Central Michigan 1998-99, Western Illinois 2000, Georgia 2001-2004. Pro coach: Joined Jaguars in 2005.

Steve Walters, wide receivers; born June 16, 1948, Jonesboro, Ark. Quarterback-defensive back Arkansas 1967-1970. No pro playing experience. College coach: Tampa 1973, Northeastern Louisiana 1974-75, Morehead State 1976, Tulsa 1977-78, Memphis State 1979, Southern Methodist 1980-81, Alabama 1985. Pro coach: New England Patriots 1982-84, 1997-98, New Orleans Saints 1986-1996, Tennessee Titans 1999-2004, joined Jaguars in 2005.

American Football Conference
West Division
Team Colors: Red, Gold, and White
One Arrowhead Drive
Kansas City, Missouri 64129
Telephone: (816) 920-9300

2005 SCHEDULE
PRESEASON
Aug. 12   at Minnesota 7:00
Aug. 20   **Arizona** 7:30
Aug. 27   **Seattle** 7:30
Sept. 2   at St. Louis.........................7:00

REGULAR SEASON
Sept. 11   **New York Jets** 12:00
Sept. 18   at Oakland..........................5:30
Sept. 26   at Denver (Mon.) 7:00
Oct. 2   **Philadelphia** 12:00
Oct. 9   Open Date
Oct. 16   **Washington** 12:00
Oct. 23   at Miami.............................1:00
Oct. 30   at San Diego 1:05
Nov. 6   **Oakland** 12:00
Nov. 13   at Buffalo 1:00
Nov. 20   at Houston 7:30
Nov. 27   **New England** 12:00
Dec. 4   **Denver**..............................3:15
Dec. 11   at Dallas.............................3:15
Dec. 17   at New York Giants (Sat.)....5:00
Dec. 24   **San Diego** (Sat.) 12:00
Jan. 1   **Cincinnati** 12:00

Stadium: Arrowhead Stadium
      (opened in 1972)
      •**Capacity:** 79,451
      One Arrowhead Drive
      Kansas City, Missouri 64129
Playing Surface: Grass
Training Camp: University of
      Wisconsin-River Falls
      River Falls, Wisconsin
      54022

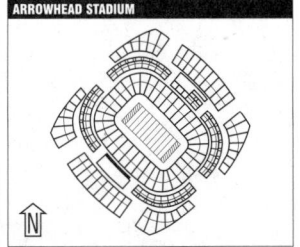

ARROWHEAD STADIUM

CLUB OFFICIALS
Founder: Lamar Hunt
Chairman of the Board: Clark Hunt
Vice Chairman of the Board:
   Jack Steadman
President: Carl Peterson
Executive Vice President/Assistant
   General Manager: Dennis Thum
Vice President of Football
   Operations/Player Personnel: Lynn Stiles
Senior Vice President of Administration:
   Bill Newman
Secretary: Jim Seigfreid
Director of Finance/Treasurer: Dale Young
Vice President of Sales and Marketing:
   Wallace Bennett
Vice President of Pro Personnel:
   Bill Kuharich
Director of College Scouting: Chuck Cook
Director of Public Relations: Bob Moore
Associate Director of Public Relations:
   Pete Moris
Director of Stadium Operations:
   Steve Schneider
Director of Development: Ken Blume
Director of Corporate Sponsorship:
   Anita Bailey
Director of Sales: Gary Spani
Director of Player Development:
   Lamonte Winston
Director of Community Relations:
   Brenda Sniezek
Director of Ticket Operations:
   Doug Hopkins
Director of Special Events:
   Annette Teson
Equipment Manager: Mike Davidson
Asst. Equipment Managers: Allen Wright,
   Chris Shropshire
Administrative Trainer: Dave Kendall
Athletic Trainer: Bud Epps
Assistant Athletic Trainer and Director of
   Rehabilitation: Keith Abrams
Director of Video Operations: Mike Portz
Video Assistants: Todd Weger,
   Andrew Hearne

COACHING HISTORY
Dallas Texans 1960-62
(364-320-12)
Records include postseason games
1960-1974 Hank Stram 129-79-10
1975-77   Paul Wiggin* 11-24-0
1977   Tom Bettis 1-6-0
1978-1982 Marv Levy 31-42-0
1983-86   John Mackovic 30-35-0
1987-88   Frank Gansz...................8-22-1
1989-1998 Marty Schottenheimer...104-65-1
1999-2000 Gunther Cunningham ...16-16-0
2001-04   Dick Vermeil..................34-31-0
*Released after seven games in 1977

ATTENDANCE
Home 623,264   Away 515,419
Total 1,138,683
Single-game home record,
   82,893* (10/2/00)
Single-season home record,
   629,569 (1999)
*Arrowhead Stadium attendance: 78,502;
 Kauffman Stadium attendance: 4,391

2005 DRAFT CHOICES

Round	Name	Pos.	College
1	Derrick Johnson	LB	Texas
3	Dustin Colquitt	P	Tennessee
4	Craphonso Thorpe	WR	Florida State
5	Boomer Grigsby	LB	Illinois State
	Alphonso Hodge	DB	Miami (Ohio)
6	Will Svitek	T	Stanford
	Khari Long	DE	Baylor
7	James Kilian	QB	Tulsa
	Jeremy Parquet	T	So. Mississippi

2004 TEAM RECORD
PRESEASON (1-3)

Date	Result	Opponent
8/13	L 24-34	at N.Y. Giants
8/23	W 24-7	St. Louis
8/28	L 19-21	Cleveland
9/2	L 20-24	at Dallas

REGULAR SEASON (7-9)

Date	Result	Opponent	Att.
9/12	L 24-34	at Denver	75,939
9/19	L 17-28	Carolina	78,136
9/26	L 21-24	Houston	77,433
10/04	W 27-24	at Baltimore	69,827
10/17	L 16-22	at Jacksonville	66,413
10/24	W 56-10	Atlanta	78,260
10/31	W 45-35	Indianapolis	78,312
11/7	L 31-34	at Tampa Bay	65,495
11/14	L 20-27	at New Orleans	64,900
11/22	L 19-27	New England	78,431
11/28	L 31-34	San Diego	77,447
12/5	W 34-27	at Oakland	51,292
12/13	W 49-38	at Tennessee	68,932
12/19	W 45-17	Denver	77,702
12/25	W 31-30	Oakland	77,289
1/2	L 17-24	at San Diego	64,920

SCORE BY PERIODS

Chiefs	113	137	93	140	0	—	483
Opponents	81	152	73	129	0	—	435

2004 TEAM STATISTICS

	Chiefs	Opp.
Total First Downs	398	327
Rushing	138	97
Passing	228	190
Penalty	32	40
3rd Down: Made/Att	91/193	71/185
3rd Down Pct.	47.2	38.4
4th Down: Made/Att	4/14	5/16
4th Down Pct.	28.6	31.3
Possession Avg.	32:14	27:46
Total Net Yards	6,695	6,037
Avg. Per Game	418.4	377.3
Total Plays	1,089	960
Avg. Per Play	6.1	6.3
Net Yards Rushing	2,289	1,834
Avg. Per Game	143.1	114.6
Total Rushes	496	397
Net Yards Passing	4,406	4,203
Avg. Per Game	275.4	262.7
Sacked/Yards Lost	32/227	41/250
Gross Yards	4,633	4,453
Att./Completions	561/370	522/312
Completion Pct.	66.0	59.8
Had Intercepted	17	13
Punts/Average	55/39.5	64/42.2
Net Punting Avg.	55/31.5	64/35.8
Penalties/Yards	117/963	117/957
Fumbles/Ball Lost	20/10	23/8
Touchdowns	62	53
Rushing	31	18
Passing	27	32
Returns	4	3

2004 INDIVIDUAL STATISTICS

PASSING

	Att.	Comp.	Yds.	Pct.	TD	Int.	Tkld.	Rate
Green	556	369	4,591	66.4	27	17	32/227	95.2
Collins	5	1	42	20.0	0	0	0/0	62.1
Chiefs	561	370	4,633	66.0	27	17	32/227	94.9
Opponents	522	312	4,453	59.8	32	13	41/250	97.5

SCORING

	TD R	TD P	TD Rt	PAT	FG	Saf	PTS
Tynes	0	0	0	58/60	17/23	0	109
Holmes	14	1	0	0/0	0/0	0	90
Johnson	9	2	0	0/0	0/0	0	66
Blaylock	8	1	0	0/0	0/0	0	54
Kennison	0	8	0	0/0	0/0	0	50
Gonzalez	0	7	0	0/0	0/0	0	42
Dunn	0	3	0	0/0	0/0	0	18
Morton	0	3	0	0/0	0/0	0	18
Hall	0	0	2	0/0	0/0	0	12
Horn	0	1	0	0/0	0/0	0	6
Mitchell	0	0	1	0/0	0/0	0	6
Parker	0	1	0	0/0	0/0	0	6
Warfield	0	0	1	0/0	0/0	0	6
Chiefs	31	27	4	58/60	17/23	0	483
Opponents	18	32	3	50/51	21/27	0	435

2-Pt. Conversions: Kennison.
Chiefs 1-2, Opponents 2-2.

RUSHING

	No.	Yds	Avg	LG	TD
Holmes	196	892	4.6	33t	14
Johnson	120	581	4.8	46t	9
Blaylock	118	539	4.6	24	8
Green	25	85	3.4	13	0
Hall	8	56	7.0	17	0
Richardson	12	56	4.7	13	0
Morton	7	43	6.1	14	0
Kennison	2	15	7.5	15	0
Horn	1	12	12.0	12	0
Gonzalez	1	5	5.0	5	0
Collins	1	4	4.0	4	0
Easy	4	1	0.3	4	0
Cheek	1	0	0.0	0	0
Chiefs	496	2,289	4.6	46t	31
Opponents	397	1,834	4.6	78t	18

RECEIVING

	No.	Yds	Avg	LG	TD
Gonzalez	102	1,258	12.3	32	7
Kennison	62	1,086	17.5	70t	8
Morton	55	795	14.5	52	3
Blaylock	25	246	9.8	30	1
Hall	25	230	9.2	22	0
Johnson	22	278	12.6	40	2
Holmes	19	187	9.8	52	1
Richardson	19	118	6.2	22	0
Dunn	17	120	7.1	17	3
Horn	15	178	11.9	30	1
Parker	9	137	15.2	48t	1
Chiefs	370	4,633	12.5	70t	27
Opponents	312	4,453	14.3	65	32

INTERCEPTIONS

	No.	Yds	Avg	LG	TD
Wesley	4	92	23.0	65	0
Warfield	4	49	12.3	43t	1
McCleon	2	23	11.5	23	0
Barber	1	10	10.0	10	0
Sapp	1	0	0.0	0	0
Beisel	1	-1	-1.0	-1	0
Chiefs	13	173	13.3	65	1
Opponents	17	244	14.4	102t	1

PUNTING

	No.	Yds.	Avg.	In 20	LG
Cheek	42	1,643	39.1	8	55
Murphy	4	189	47.3	1	58
Baker	9	340	37.8	3	52
Chiefs	55	2,172	39.5	12	58
Opponents	64	2,703	42.2	23	66

PUNT RETURNS

	Ret	FC	Yds	Avg	LG	TD
Hall	23	17	232	10.1	46	0
Harts	1	0	0	0.0	0	0
Chiefs	24	17	232	9.7	46	0
Opponents	24	13	301	12.5	75t	2

KICKOFF RETURNS

	No.	Yds	Avg	LG	TD
Hall	68	1,718	25.3	97t	2
Horn	4	44	11.0	17	0
Blaylock	1	22	22.0	22	0
Kennison	1	36	36.0	36	0
Stills	1	0	0.0	0	0
Chiefs	75	1,820	24.3	97t	2
Opponents	85	1,908	22.4	44	0

FIELD GOALS

	1-19	20-29	30-39	40-49	50+
Tynes	0/0	5/5	7/8	3/6	2/4
Chiefs	0/0	5/5	7/8	3/6	2/4
Opponents	1/1	6/7	5/5	8/9	1/5

SACKS

	No.
Allen	9.0
Hicks	5.0
Browning	4.5
Fujita	4.5
Dalton	4.0
Beisel	2.5
Stills	2.5
Sims	2.0
Bartee	1.5
Barber	1.0
Mitchell	1.0
Siavii	1.0
Woods	1.0
Wilkerson	0.5
Chiefs	41.0
Opponents	32.0

RECORD HOLDERS

INDIVIDUAL RECORDS—CAREER

Category	Name	Performance
Rushing (Yds.)	Priest Holmes, 2001-04	5,482
Passing (Yds.)	Len Dawson, 1962-1975	28,507
Passing (TDs)	Len Dawson, 1962-1975	237
Receiving (No.)	Tony Gonzalez, 1997-2004	570
Receiving (Yds.)	Otis Taylor, 1965-1975	7,306
Interceptions	Emmitt Thomas, 1966-1978	58
Punting (Avg.)	Jerrel Wilson, 1963-1977	43.4
Punt Return (Avg.)	Dante Hall, 2000-04	11.5
Kickoff Return (Avg.)	Noland Smith, 1967-69	26.8
Field Goals	Nick Lowery, 1980-1993	329
Touchdowns (Tot.)	Priest Holmes, 2001-04	76
Points	Nick Lowery, 1980-1993	1,466

INDIVIDUAL RECORDS—SINGLE SEASON

Category	Name	Performance
Rushing (Yds.)	Priest Holmes, 2002	1,615
Passing (Yds.)	Trent Green, 2004	4,591
Passing (TDs)	Len Dawson, 1964	30
Receiving (No.)	Tony Gonzalez, 2004	102
Receiving (Yds.)	Derrick Alexander, 2000	1,391
Interceptions	Emmitt Thomas, 1974	12
Punting (Avg.)	Jerrel Wilson, 1965	45.4
Punt Return (Avg.)	Dante Hall, 2003	16.3
Kickoff Return (Avg.)	Dave Grayson, 1962	29.7
Field Goals	Nick Lowery, 1990	34
Touchdowns (Tot.)	Priest Holmes, 2003	*27
Points	Priest Holmes, 2003	162

INDIVIDUAL RECORDS—SINGLE GAME

Category	Name	Performance
Rushing (Yds.)	Barry Word, 10-14-90	200
Passing (Yds.)	Elvis Grbac, 11-5-00	504
Passing (TDs)	Len Dawson, 11-1-64	6
Receiving (No.)	Tony Gonzalez, 1-2-05	14
Receiving (Yds.)	Stephone Paige, 12-22-85	309
Interceptions	Bobby Ply, 12-16-62	*4
	Bobby Hunt, 10-4-64	*4
	Deron Cherry, 9-29-85	*4
Field Goals	Many times	5
	Last time by Nick Lowery, 9-20-93	
Touchdowns (Tot.)	Abner Haynes, 11-26-61	5
Points	Abner Haynes, 11-26-61	30

*NFL Record

2005 VETERAN ROSTER

No.	Name	Pos.	Ht.	Wt.	Birthdate	NFL Exp.	College	Hometown	How Acq.	'04 Games/ Starts
69	Allen, Jared	DE	6-6	265	4/3/82	2	Idaho State	Los Gatos, Calif.	D4b-'04	15/10
59	Barber, Shawn	LB	6-2	240	1/14/75	8	Richmond	Richmond, Va.	UFA(Phil)-'03	8/8
24	Bartee, William	CB	6-1	200	6/25/77	6	Oklahoma	Daytona Beach, Fla.	D2-'00	14/9
26	Battle, Julian	CB	6-2	205	7/11/81	3	Tennessee	West Palm Beach, Fla.	D3-'03	12/1
99	Bell, Kendrell	LB	6-1	234	7/2/78	5	Georgia	Augusta, Ga.	UFA(Pitt)-'05	3/0*
65	Black, Jordan	T	6-5	304	1/28/80	3	Notre Dame	Mesquite, Texas	D5-'03	16/4
67	Bober, Chris	C/T	6-5	310	12/24/76	6	Nebraska-Omaha	Omaha, Neb.	UFA(NYG)-'04	12/2
85	Boerigter, Marc	WR	6-3	220	5/4/78	4	Hastings	Hastings, Neb.	FA-'02	0*
38	Brown, Dee	RB	5-10	210	5/12/78	3	Syracuse	Lake Brantley, Fla.	FA-'05	5/0*
93	Browning, John	DT	6-5	297	9/30/73	10	West Virginia	Miami, Fla.	D3-'96	16/7
52	Caver, Quinton	LB	6-4	241	8/22/78	5	Arkansas	Anniston, Ala.	FA-'03	16/4
15	Collins, Todd	QB	6-4	228	11/5/71	11	Michigan	Walpole, Mass.	W(Buff)-'98	2/0
75	Dalton, Lional	DT	6-1	315	2/21/75	8	Eastern Michigan	Detroit, Mich.	FA-'04	16/13
89	Dunn, Jason	TE	6-6	274	11/15/73	9	Eastern Kentucky	Harrodsburg, Ky.	FA-'00	16/0
97	Fox, Keyaron	LB	6-3	235	1/24/82	2	Georgia Tech	Atlanta, Ga.	D3-'04	12/0
51	Fujita, Scott	LB	6-5	250	4/28/79	4	California	Rio Mesa, Calif.	D5-'02	16/16
83	Gammon, Kendall	TE	6-4	255	10/23/68	14	Pittsburg State	Rose Hill, Kan.	UFA(NO)-'00	16/0
88	Gonzalez, Tony	TE	6-5	251	2/27/76	9	California	Huntington Beach, Calif.	D1-'97	16/16
10	Green, Trent	QB	6-3	217	7/9/70	12	Indiana	St. Louis, Mo.	T(StL)-'01	16/16
92 t-	Hall, Carlos	DE	6-4	259	1/16/79	4	Arkansas	Marianna, Ark.	T(Tenn)-'05	14/14*
82	Hall, Dante	WR	5-8	187	9/20/78	6	Texas A&M	Houston, Texas	D5a-'00	16/6
42	Harts, Shaunard	S	6-0	210	8/4/78	4	Boise State	Pittsburg, Calif.	D7a-'01	16/6
98	Hicks, Eric	DE	6-6	280	6/17/76	8	Maryland	Erie, Pa.	FA-'98	16/16
9	Hill, Darrell	WR	6-2	187	6/19/79	4	Northern Illinois	Chicago, Ill.	FA-'05	14/0*
39	Holcombe, Robert	FB	5-11	220	12/11/75	8	Illinois	Mesa, Ariz.	FA-'05	16/8*
31	Holmes, Priest	RB	5-9	213	10/7/73	9	Texas	San Antonio, Texas	UFA(Balt)-'01	8/8
81	Horn, Chris	WR	5-11	195	7/13/77	3	Rocky Mountain	Notus, Idaho	FA-'04	14/0
11	Huard, Damon	QB	6-3	212	7/9/73	9	Washington	Puyallup, Wash.	FA-'04	0*
66	Ingram, Johnathan	C	6-2	300	9/20/80	2	San Diego State	La Quinta, Calif.	FA-'04	0*
64	Issa, Jabari	DE	6-5	296	4/18/78	3	Washington	San Mateo, Calif.	FA-'05	0*
27	Johnson, Larry	RB	6-1	230	11/19/79	3	Penn State	State College, Pa.	D1-'03	10/3
87	Kennison, Eddie	WR	6-1	201	1/20/73	10	Louisiana State	Lake Charles, La.	FA-'01	14/14
29	Knight, Sammy	S	6-1	205	9/10/75	9	Southern California	Riverside, Calif.	UFA(Mia)-'05	16/16*
57	Maslowski, Mike	LB	6-2	243	7/11/74	7	Wisconsin–La Crosse	Thorp, Wis.	FA-'99	0*
22	McCleon, Dexter	CB	5-10	195	10/9/73	9	Clemson	Meridian, Miss.	FA-'03	13/6
50	Mitchell, Kawika	LB	6-1	253	10/10/79	3	South Florida	Lake Howell, Fla.	D2-'03	15/12
80	Morton, Johnnie	WR	6-0	185	10/7/71	12	Southern California	Torrance, Calif.	FA-'02	13/12
18	Parker, Samie	WR	5-11	190	3/25/81	2	Oregon	Long Beach, Calif.	D4a-'04	4/0
35	Pile, Willie	S	6-2	206	5/25/80	2	Virginia Tech	Alexandria, Va.	FA-'04	16/5
49	Richardson, Tony	FB	6-1	238	12/17/71	11	Auburn	Daleville, Ala.	FA-'95	16/16
77	Roaf, Willie	T	6-5	320	4/18/70	13	Louisiana Tech	Pine Bluff, Ark.	T(NO)-'02	16/16
79	Sampson, Kevin	T	6-4	312	6/19/81	2	Syracuse	Westwood, N.J.	D7-'04	6/0
20	Sapp, Benny	CB	5-9	190	1/20/81	2	Northern Iowa	Ft. Lauderdale, Fla.	FA-'04	15/1
91	Scanlon, Rich	LB	6-2	249	12/23/80	2	Syracuse	Oradell, N.J.	FA-'04	6/0
61	Sharpe, Montique	DT	6-2	296	3/10/80	2	Wake Forest	Washington, D.C.	D7a-'03	0*
68	Shields, Will	G	6-3	320	9/15/71	13	Nebraska	Lawton, Okla.	D3-'93	16/16
94	Siavii, Junior	DT	6-5	336	11/14/78	2	Oregon	Pago Pago, American Samoa	D2a-'04	12/0
90	Sims, Ryan	DT	6-4	315	5/4/80	4	North Carolina	Spartanburg, S.C.	D1-'02	15/13
55	Stills, Gary	DE	6-2	250	7/11/74	7	West Virginia	Valley Forge, Pa.	D3a-'99	16/0
23 t-	Surtain, Patrick	CB	5-11	192	6/19/76	8	Southern Mississippi	New Orleans, La.	T(Mia)-'05	15/15*
1	Tynes, Lawrence	K	6-1	202	5/3/78	2	Troy State	Milton, Fla.	FA-'04	16/0
44	Warfield, Eric	CB	6-0	200	3/3/76	8	Nebraska	Texarkana, Ark.	D7a-'98	16/16
54	Waters, Brian	G	6-3	318	2/18/77	6	North Texas	Waxahachie, Texas	FA-'00	16/16
76	Welbourn, John	G/T	6-5	310	3/30/76	7	California	Rolling Hills, Calif.	T(Phil)-'04	10/10
25	Wesley, Greg	S	6-2	206	3/19/78	6	Arkansas-Pine Bluff	England, Ark.	D3-'00	12/11
62	Wiegmann, Casey	C	6-2	285	7/20/73	10	Iowa	Parkersburg, Iowa	UFA(Chi)-'01	16/16
96	Wilkerson, Jimmy	DE	6-2	280	1/4/81	3	Oklahoma	Omaha, Texas	D6-'03	15/0
74	Williams, Brett	T	6-5	321	5/2/80	3	Florida State	Kissimmee, Fla.	D4-'03	5/0
84	Wilson, Kris	TE	6-2	251	8/22/81	2	Pittsburgh	Lancaster, Pa.	D2b-'04	3/0
21	Woods, Jerome	S	6-3	205	3/17/73	10	Memphis	Memphis, Tenn.	D1-'96	10/10

* Bell played 3 games with Pittsburgh in '04; Boerigter missed '04 season because of injury; Brown played 5 games with Cleveland; C. Hall played 14 games with Tennessee; Hill played 14 games with Tennessee; Holcombe played 16 games with Tennessee; Huard inactive for 15 games; Ingram inactive for 6 games in '04; Issa last active with Arizona in '01; Knight played 16 games with Miami; Maslowski missed '04 season because of injury; Sharpe last active with Kansas City in '03; Surtain played 15 games with Miami.

t-   Chiefs traded for C. Hall (Tenn) and Surtain (Mia).

Players lost through free agency (2): LB Monty Beisel (NE; 11 games in '04), RB Derrick Blaylock (NYJ; 12).

Also played with Chiefs in '04—P Jason Baker (2 games), P Steve Cheek (12), FB Omar Easy (15), DE Vonnie Holliday (9), LB Fred Jones (16).

2005 FIRST-YEAR ROSTER

Name	Pos.	Ht.	Wt.	Birthdate	College	Hometown	How Acq.
Barnett, Thomas (1)	T	6-4	314	10/21/78	Kansas State	Oklahoma City, Okla.	FA
Booth, John (1)	WR	6-0	199	7/22/82	Mid-America Nazarene	Bradenton, Fla.	FA
Canonico, Eddie (1)	S	6-1	180	9/17/78	Sacramento State	Las Vegas, Nev.	FA
Clausen, Casey (1)	QB	6-3	218	1/9/81	Tennessee	Mission Hills, Calif.	FA
Colquitt, Dustin	P	6-1	191	5/6/82	Tennessee	Knoxville, Tenn.	D3
Connot, Scott (1)	S	6-3	216	6/24/81	South Dakota State	Spencer, Neb.	FA-'04
Crouch, Eric (1)	S	6-0	195	11/16/78	Nebraska	Omaha, Neb.	FA
Cruz, Ronnie (1)	RB	6-0	237	6/11/81	Northern State	Lakeport, Calif.	FA
Curry, Nathaniel	WR	5-10	196	3/11/82	Georgia Tech	Miami, Fla.	FA
Dixon, Arrion	DT	6-4	308	10/21/81	Arkansas	Wynne, Ark.	FA
Gado, Sam	RB	5-11	210	11/13/82	Liberty	Columbia, S.C.	FA
Griffin, Kris	LB	6-3	232	5/27/81	Indiana (PA)	Rochester, Pa.	FA
Grigsby, James	LB	5-11	249	11/15/81	Illinois State	Canton, Ill.	D5a
Hall, Joe (1)	FB	6-2	318	11/3/79	Kansas State	Lakewood, Calif.	FA
Helms, Gabriel	CB	5-10	221	3/25/80	Northwest Missouri State	St. Louis, Mo.	FA
Hodge, Alphonso	CB	5-10	203	5/30/82	Miami (OH)	Lakewood, Ohio	D5b
Johnson, Aaron (1)	G	6-4	293	9/6/77	Ball State	Cloquet, Minn.	FA
Johnson, Derrick	LB	6-3	242	11/22/82	Texas	Waco, Texas	D1
Johnson, Mike	C	6-3	296	3/26/82	Kansas State	Boulder, Colo.	FA
Jones, Darius	DT	6-2	304	2/19/82	Wisconsin	Beloit, Wis.	FA
Kilian, James	QB	6-3	218	10/24/80	Tulsa	Medford, Okla.	D7a
Long, Khari	DE	6-3	257	5/23/82	Baylor	Wichita Falls, Texas	D6b
McIntyre, Jeris (1)	WR	6-0	203	7/4/81	Auburn	Tampa, Fla.	D6-'04
Miller, Matt (1)	G	6-4	321	2/15/81	Louisiana College	Lafayette, La.	FA
Moore, Chazz (1)	S	6-0	209	4/20/78	Cal State-Northridge	Portland, Ore.	FA
Murphy, Nick (1)	P	5-11	191	10/22/79	Arizona State	Desert Mountain, Ariz.	FA-'04
Parquet, Jeremy	T	6-6	321	4/11/82	Southern Mississippi	Norco, La.	D7b
Perkins, Justin	CB	5-10	186	7/9/82	Connecticut	Sunrise, Fla.	FA
Smith, McKenzie (1)	RB	5-8	196	10/19/81	Washington State	Pasadena, Calif.	FA
Smith, Richard (1)	WR	5-10	191	7/16/80	Arkansas	Shreveport, La.	FA-'04
Svitek, Will	T	6-6	300	1/8/82	Stanford	Newbury, Calif.	D6a
Thompson, Edwin	TE	6-4	260	8/4/81	Idaho State	Los Lunas, N.M.	FA
Thorpe, Craphonso	WR	6-0	187	6/27/83	Florida State	Tallahassee, Fla.	D4
Vance, Forest (1)	G	6-4	298	4/16/81	UC Davis	Colfax, Calif.	FA
Ville, Zach	DE	6-1	291	4/24/82	Missouri	Miami, Fla.	FA
Walden, Willie	TE	6-7	278	10/18/81	Montana	Vancouver, Wash.	FA
Walker, Demetrios (1)	DE	6-2	254	4/21/81	Middle Tennessee State	Kansas City, Mo.	FA

The term NFL Rookie is defined as a player who is in his first season of professional football and has not been on the roster of another professional football team for any regular-season or postseason games. A Rookie is designated by an "R" on NFL rosters. Players who have been active in another professional football league or players who have NFL experience, including either preseason training camp or being on an Active List or Inactive List, or on Reserve/Injured or Reserve/Physically Unable to Perform for fewer than six regular-season games, are termed NFL First-Year Players. An NFL First-Year Player is designated by a "1" on NFL rosters. Thereafter, a player is credited with an additional year of experience for each season in which he accumulates six games on the Active List or Inactive List, or on Reserve/Injured or Reserve/Physically Unable to Perform.

Log on to www.kcchiefs.com for an up-to-date roster.

COACHING STAFF

Head Coach,
Dick Vermeil

Pro Career: Dick Vermeil was named the ninth head coach in Chiefs franchise history on January 12, 2001. Vermeil joins Bill Parcells, Dan Reeves, and Don Shula as the only coaches in NFL history to guide two different teams to the Super Bowl. In 1999, he led St. Louis to a win in Super Bowl XXXIV and guided Philadelphia to Super Bowl XV after the 1980 season. Was head coach of the Philadelphia Eagles from 1976-1982. Named NFL coach of the year in 1980 and 1999. Entered league as the first special teams coach in NFL history with the L.A. Rams (1969). Career record: 116-108.
Background: Vermeil played quarterback at San Jose State (1956-57) after transferring from Napa (Calif.) J.C. Was named "Coach of the Year" on four levels: high school, junior college, NCAA Division I, and the NFL. Is the only coach to post victories in the Super Bowl (Rams, XXXIV) and the Rose Bowl (UCLA, Jan. 1976). Was head coach at UCLA from 1974-75.
Personal: Born October 30, 1936 in Calistoga, Calif. Vermeil and his wife Carol have three children and 11 grandchildren.

ASSISTANT COACHES

Gunther Cunningham, defensive coordinator; born June 19, 1946, Munich, Germany. Linebacker-placekicker Oregon 1966-68. No pro playing experience. College coach: Oregon 1969-1971, Arkansas 1972, Stanford 1973-76, California 1977-1980. Pro coach: Hamilton Tiger-Cats (CFL) 1981, Baltimore/Indianapolis Colts 1982-84, San Diego Chargers 1985-1990, L.A. Raiders 1991-94, Kansas City Chiefs 1995-2000 (head coach 1999-2000), Tennessee Titans 2001-03, rejoined Chiefs in 2004.
Vernon Dean, asst. defensive backs; born May 5, 1959, Houston. Cornerback Los Angeles Valley J.C. 1977-78, U.S. International 1979, San Diego State 1980-81. Pro cornerback Washington Redskins 1982-87, Seattle Seahawks 1988. College coach: Georgetown 1990-93, Western Oregon 2000-01, Western Illinois 2002. Pro coach: Joined Chiefs in 2003.
Irv Eatman, asst. offensive line; born January 1, 1961, Birmingham, Ala. Defensive end-offensive tackle UCLA 1979-1982. Pro offensive tackle Philadelphia/Baltimore Stars (USFL) 1983-85, Kansas City Chiefs 1986-1990, New York Jets 1991-92, L.A. Rams 1993, Atlanta Falcons 1994, Houston Oilers 1995-96. Pro coach: Green Bay Packers 1999, Pittsburgh Steelers 2000, joined Chiefs in 2001.
Frank Gansz, Jr., special teams; born August 8, 1962, Greenville, S.C. Defensive back The Citadel 1981-84. No pro playing experience. College coach: Kansas 1987, Pittsburgh 1988-89, Army 1990-91, Houston 1993-97. Pro coach: New York-

New Jersey Knights (WLAF) 1992, Oakland Raiders 1998-99, joined Chiefs in 2001.
Peter Giunta, defensive backs; born August 11, 1956, Salem, Mass. Running back-defensive back Northeastern 1974-77. No pro playing experience. College coach: Penn State 1981-83, Brown 1984-87, Lehigh 1988-1990. Pro coach: Philadelphia Eagles 1991-94, N.Y. Jets 1995-96, St. Louis Rams 1997-2000, joined Chiefs in 2001.
Carl Hairston, defensive line; born December 15, 1952, Martinsville, Va. Defensive end Maryland-Eastern Shore 1972-75. Pro defensive end Philadelphia Eagles 1976-1983, Cleveland Browns 1984-89, Phoenix Cardinals 1990. Pro coach: Kansas City Chiefs 1995-96, St. Louis Rams 1997-2000, rejoined Chiefs in 2001.
Jeff Hurd, strength and conditioning; born April 24, 1958, Pomona, Calif. Attended Fort Hays State. No college or pro playing experience. College coach: Fort Hays State 1984, Delta State 1985-86, Clemson 1986-87, Western Michigan 1987-1992, Tulsa 1994. Pro coach: Jacksonville Jaguars 1995-97, joined Chiefs in 1998.
Charlie Joiner, receivers; born October 14, 1947, Many, La. Wide receiver Grambling State 1965-68. Pro defensive back-wide receiver Houston Oilers 1969-1972, Cincinnati Bengals 1972-75, San Diego Chargers 1976-1986. Inducted into Pro Football Hall of Fame 1996. Pro coach: San Diego Chargers 1987-1991, Buffalo Bills 1992-2000, joined Chiefs in 2001.
Bob Karmelowicz, defensive line; born July 22, 1949, New Britain, Conn. Nose tackle Bridgeport 1968-1971. No pro playing experience. College coach: Arizona State 1975-79, Massachusetts 1980, Texas-El Paso 1981, Nevada-Las Vegas 1982, Illinois 1983-86, Washington State 1987-88, Miami 1989-1991. Pro coach: Cincinnati Bengals 1992-93, Washington Redskins 1994-96, joined Chiefs in 1997.
Billy Long, asst. strength and conditioning; born June 23, 1959, Phenix City, Ala. College coach: Alabama State 1981-86, Arkansas-Pine Bluff 1987-1991, Southern 1992-2000. Pro coach: Joined Chiefs in 2001.
Chad O'Shea, asst. special teams; born Dec. 18, 1972, Houston. Quarterback Marshall 1991-93, Houston 1994-95. No pro playing experience. College coach: Houston 1996-99, Southern Mississippi 2000-02. Pro coach: Joined Chiefs in 2004.
Fred Pagac, linebackers; born April 26, 1952, Richeyville, Penn. Tight end Ohio State 1971-73. Pro tight end Chicago Bears 1974, Tampa Bay Buccaneers 1976. College coach: Ohio State 1978-2000. Pro coach: Oakland Raiders 2001-03, joined Chiefs in 2004.
Al Saunders, asst. head coach/offensive coordinator; born February 1, 1947, London, England. Wide receiver-defensive back San Jose State 1966-68. No pro play-

ing experience. College coach: Southern California 1970-71, Missouri 1972, Utah State 1973-75, California 1976-1981, Tennessee 1982. Pro coach: San Diego Chargers 1983-88 (head coach 1986-88), Kansas City Chiefs 1989-1998, St. Louis Rams 1999-2000, rejoined Chiefs in 2001.
Bob Saunders, offensive assistant/quality control; born Nov. 21, 1976, Walnut Creek, Calif. Wide receiver-defensive back Southern Methodist 1995. No pro playing experience. Pro coach: Joined Chiefs in 2004.
James Saxon, running backs; born March 23, 1966, Beaufort, S.C. Running back American River (S.C.) J.C. 1985, San Jose State 1986-87. Pro running back Kansas City Chiefs 1988-1991, Miami Dolphins 1992-94, Philadelphia Eagles 1995. College coach: Rutgers 1997-98, Menlo College 1999. Pro coach: Buffalo Bills 2000, joined Chiefs in 2001.
Terry Shea, quarterbacks; born June 12, 1946, San Mateo, Calif. Quarterback Oregon 1965-67. No pro playing experience. College coach: Oregon 1968-69; Mt. Hood (Ore) J.C. 1970-75, Utah State 1976-1981, San Jose State 1984-86, 1990-91 (head coach 1990-91), California 1987-89, Stanford 1992-94, Rutgers 1996-2000 (head coach). Pro coach: British Columbia Lions (CFL) 1995, Kansas City Chiefs 2001-03, Chicago Bears 2004, re-joined Chiefs in 2005.
Mike Solari, offensive line; born January 16, 1955, Daly City, Calif. Offensive lineman San Diego State 1975-76. No pro playing experience. College coach: Mira Vista (Calif.) J.C. 1978, U.S. International 1979, Boise State 1980, Cincinnati 1981-82, Kansas 1983-85, Pittsburgh 1986, Alabama 1990-91. Pro coach: Dallas Cowboys 1987-88, Phoenix Cardinals 1989, San Francisco 49ers 1992-96, joined Chiefs in 1997.
Jason Verduzco, tight ends; born April 3, 1970, Walnut Creek, Calif. Quarterback Illinois 1989-1992. Pro quarterback: British Columbia Lions (CFL) 1993. College coach: Hamilton College (N.Y.) 1994-96, Illinois 1997-99. Pro coach: Washington Redskins 2000, joined Chiefs in 2001.
Darvin Wallis, defensive assistant/quality control; born February 14, 1949, Ft. Branch, Ind. Defensive end Arizona 1970-71. No pro playing experience. College coach: Adams State 1976-77, Tulane 1978-79, Mississippi 1980-81. Pro coach: Cleveland Browns 1982-88, joined Chiefs in 1989.
Mike White, director of football administration; born January 4, 1936, Berkeley, Calif. Offensive end California 1955-57. No pro playing experience. College coach: California 1958-1963, 1972-77 (head coach 1972-77), Stanford 1964-1971, Illinois 1980-87 (head coach). Pro coach: San Francisco 49ers 1978-79, Los Angeles-Oakland Raiders 1990-96 (head coach 1995-96), St. Louis Rams 1997-99, joined Chiefs in 2001.

**American Football Conference
East Division**
Team Colors: Aqua, Coral, Blue, and
White
7500 S.W. 30th Street
Davie, Florida 33314
Telephone: (954) 452-7000

2005 SCHEDULE
PRESEASON
Aug. 8   vs. Chicago at Canton, OH..7:00
Aug. 13 at Jacksonville....................7:30
Aug. 20 at Pittsburgh.......................7:30
Aug. 27 **Tampa Bay**........................7:30
Sept. 1 **Atlanta**..............................7:30

REGULAR SEASON
Sept. 11 **Denver**...............................1:00
Sept. 18 at New York Jets 4:15
Sept. 25 **Carolina**...........................1:00
Oct. 2   Open Date
Oct. 9   at Buffalo 1:00
Oct. 16 at Tampa Bay 1:00
Oct. 23 **Kansas City** 1:00
Oct. 30 at New Orleans.................12:00
Nov. 6   **Atlanta**...............................1:00
Nov. 13 **New England** 1:00
Nov. 20 at Cleveland 1:00
Nov. 27 at Oakland 1:05
Dec. 4   **Buffalo**..............................1:00
Dec. 11 at San Diego 1:15
Dec. 18 **New York Jets** 1:00
Dec. 24 **Tennessee** (Sat.)...............1:00
Jan. 1   at New England 1:00

Stadium: Dolphins Stadium
            (opened in 1987)
           •**Capacity:** 75,192
            2269 Dan Marino Blvd.
            Miami, Florida 33056
Playing Surface: Grass (PAT)
Training Camp: Nova Southeastern Univ.
            7500 S.W. 30th Street
            Davie, Florida 33314

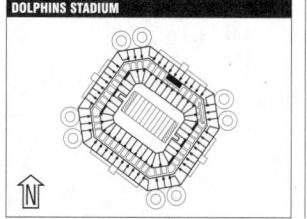

DOLPHINS STADIUM

CLUB OFFICIALS
Owner/Chairman of the Board:
  H. Wayne Huizenga
Chief Executive Officer, Dolphin
  Enterprises: Joe Bailey
Head Coach: Nick Saban
Executive Vice President & Chief
  Operating Officer: Bryan Wiedmeier
Senior Vice President-Finance &
  Administration: Jill R. Strafaci
Senior Vice President-Operations:
  Bill Galante
Senior Vice President-Media Relations:
  Harvey Greene
Senior Vice President-Sales & Marketing:
  Jim Ross
General Manager: Rick Spielman
Coordinator of Football Operations/
  Assistant to the Head Coach:
  Scott O'Brien
Director of Pro Personnel: George Paton
Director of College Scouting:
  Ron Labadie
Staff Counsel: Matt Thomas
Senior Director of Ticket Operations:
  Andy Major
Senior Director of Internet & Publications:
  Scott Stone
Director of Player Programs & Alumni:
  Jamie Allen
Director of Media Relations: Neal Gulkis
Director of Operations: Rhett Ticconi
Director of Information Technology:
  Tery Howard
Director of Cheerleaders & Event
  Entertainment: Dorie Grogan
Director of Special Events & Television
  Programming: Jeff Griffith
Director of Records & Archives:
  Kristin Hingston
Head Athletic Trainer: Kevin O'Neill
Equipment Manager: Tony Egues
Video Director: Dave Hack
Team Security Investigator:
  Stuart Weinstein

COACHING HISTORY
(373-254-4)
Records include postseason games
1966-69   George Wilson.............15-39-2
1970-1995 Don Shula 274-147-2
1996-99   Jimmy Johnson...........38-31-0
2000-04   Dave Wannstedt* 43-33-0
2004   Jim Bates.........................3-4-0
*Resigned after nine games in 2004

ATTENDANCE
Home 580,808   Away 556,787
Total 1,137,595
Single-game home record,
  75,283 (10/27/96)
Single-season home record, 592,161
  (1999)

2005 DRAFT CHOICES
Round	Name	Pos.	College
1	Ronnie Brown	RB	Auburn
2	Matt Roth	DE	Iowa
3	Channing Crowder	LB	Florida
4	Travis Daniels	DB	Louisiana St.
5	Anthony Alabi	T	Texas Christian
7	Kevin Vickerson	DT	Michigan St.

2004 TEAM RECORD
PRESEASON (2-2)

Date	Result		Opponent
8/14	W	16-5	Jacksonville
8/21	L	0-17	Washington
8/28	L	10-17	at Tampa Bay
9/3	W	20-19	at New Orleans

REGULAR SEASON (4-12)

Date	Result		Opponent	Att.
9/11	L	7-17	Tennessee	69,987
9/19	L	13-16	at Cincinnati	65,705
9/26	L	3-13	Pittsburgh	72,225
10/3	L	9-17	N.Y. Jets	73,157
10/10	L	10-24	at New England	68,756
10/17	L	13-20	at Buffalo	72,714
10/24	W	31-14	St. Louis	72,945
11/1	L	14-41	at N.Y. Jets	78,216
11/7	L	23-24	Arizona	72,612
11/21	L	17-24	at Seattle	66,644
11/28	W	24-17	at San Francisco	66,156
12/5	L	32-42	Buffalo	73,084
12/12	L	17-20	at Denver	75,027
12/20	W	29-28	New England	73,629
12/26	W	10-7	Cleveland	73,169
1/2	L	23-30	at Baltimore	69,843

SCORE BY PERIODS

Dolphins	79	59	34	103	0	—	275
Opponents	79	88	95	92	0	—	354

2004 TEAM STATISTICS

	Dolphins	Opp.
Total First Downs	267	281
Rushing	71	107
Passing	165	139
Penalty	31	35
3rd Down: Made/Att	80/232	72/223
3rd Down Pct.	34.5	32.3
4th Down: Made/Att	8/16	8/11
4th Down Pct.	50.0	72.7
Possession Avg.	28:20	31:40
Total Net Yards	4404	4894
Avg. Per Game	275.3	305.9
Total Plays	1022	1009
Avg. Per Play	4.3	4.9
Net Yards Rushing	1339	2302
Avg. Per Game	83.7	143.9
Total Rushes	384	539
Net Yards Passing	3065	2592
Avg. Per Game	191.6	162.0
Sacked/Yards Lost	52/326	36/223
Gross Yards	3391	2815
Att./Completions	586/309	434/244
Completion Pct.	52.7	56.2
Had Intercepted	26	15
Punts/Average	99/41.5	102/41.0
Net Punting Avg.	99/36.9	102/33.3
Penalties/Yards	112/852	107/852
Fumbles/Ball Lost	42/16	22/10
Touchdowns	31	42
Rushing	10	12
Passing	19	20
Returns	2	10

2004 INDIVIDUAL STATISTICS

PASSING

	Att.	Comp.	Yds.	Pct.	TD	Int.	Tkld.	Rate
Feeley	356	191	1,893	53.7	11	15	23/136	61.7
Fiedler	190	101	1,186	53.2	7	8	25/165	67.1
Rosenfels	39	16	264	41.0	1	3	3/16	41.0
Booker	1	1	48	100.0	0	0	0/0	118.8
Morris	0	0	0	—	0	0	1/9	—
Dolphins	586	309	3,391	52.7	19	26	52/326	62.5
Opponents	434	244	2,815	56.2	20	15	36/223	76.9

SCORING

	TD R	TD P	TD Rt	PAT	FG	Saf	PTS
Mare	0	0	0	18/18	12/16	0	54
Chambers	0	7	0	0/0	0/0	0	44
Morris	6	0	0	0/0	0/0	0	36
McMichael	0	4	0	0/0	0/0	0	26
Thompson	0	4	0	0/0	0/0	0	24
Minor	3	0	0	0/0	0/0	0	18
Bryant	0	0	0	7/7	3/3	0	16
Welker	0	0	1	1/1	1/1	0	10
B. Gramatica	0	0	0	0/1	3/3	0	9
Booker	0	1	0	0/0	0/0	0	6
Feeley	1	0	0	0/0	0/0	0	6
Gilmore	0	1	0	0/0	0/0	0	6
Konrad	0	1	0	0/0	0/0	0	6
Lee	0	1	0	0/0	0/0	0	6
Pope	0	0	1	0/0	0/0	0	6
Knight	0	0	0	0/0	0/0	1	2
Dolphins	10	19	2	26/27	19/23	1	275
Opponents	12	20	10	42/42	20/28	0	354

2-Pt. Conversions: Chambers, McMichael.
Dolphins 2-4, Opponents 0-0.

RUSHING

	No.	Yds	Avg	LG	TD
Morris	132	523	4.0	35t	6
Minor	109	388	3.6	34	3
Henry	46	141	3.1	53	0
Chambers	9	76	8.4	24	0
Gordon	35	64	1.8	11	0
Fiedler	12	59	4.9	26	0
Forsey	19	53	2.8	15	0
Konrad	2	18	9.0	15	0
Feeley	14	13	0.9	7t	1
King	4	9	2.3	3	0
Turk	1	3	3.0	3	0
Booker	1	-8	-8.0	-8	0
Dolphins	384	1,339	3.5	53	10
Opponents	539	2,302	4.3	62	12

RECEIVING

	No.	Yds	Avg	LG	TD
McMichael	73	791	10.8	42t	4
Chambers	69	898	13.0	76t	7
Booker	50	638	12.8	45	1
Thompson	23	359	15.6	36	4
Morris	22	124	5.6	24	0
Gilmore	15	206	13.7	37	1
Lee	13	110	8.5	15t	1
Minor	13	75	5.8	20	0
Gordon	13	74	5.7	20	0
Konrad	8	69	8.6	20t	1
Martin	4	15	3.8	7	0
Henry	3	12	4.0	7	0
Bellamy	1	8	8.0	8	0
King	1	8	8.0	8	0
Easlick	1	4	4.0	4	0
Dolphins	309	3,391	11.0	76t	19
Opponents	244	2,815	11.5	69t	20

INTERCEPTIONS

	No.	Yds	Avg	LG	TD
Freeman	4	59	14.8	47	0
Knight	4	32	8.0	32	0
Surtain	4	2	0.5	2	0
Ayanbadejo	1	2	2.0	2	0
J. Williams	1	0	0.0	0	0
Taylor	1	-3	-3.0	-3	0
Dolphins	15	92	6.1	47	0
Opponents	26	464	17.8	66t	8

PUNTING

	No.	Yds.	Avg.	In 20	LG
Turk	98	4,088	41.7	29	67
Mare	1	19	19.0	0	19
Dolphins	99	4,107	41.5	29	67
Opponents	102	4,177	41.0	30	63

PUNT RETURNS

	Ret	FC	Yds	Avg	LG	TD
Welker	43	12	464	10.8	71	0
Brightful	9	2	89	9.9	36	0
Gilmore	0	0	11	—	11	0
Dolphins	52	14	564	10.8	71	0
Opponents	45	19	258	5.7	24	0

KICKOFF RETURNS

	No.	Yds	Avg	LG	TD
Welker	57	1,313	23.0	95t	1
Brightful	5	126	25.2	32	0
Gilmore	5	114	22.8	53	0
Morris	1	27	27.0	27	0
Poole	1	22	22.0	22	0
Wyrick	1	58	58.0	58	0
Dolphins	70	1,660	23.7	95t	1
Opponents	51	1,114	21.8	104t	1

FIELD GOALS

	1-19	20-29	30-39	40-49	50+
Mare	0/0	1/2	6/7	3/4	2/3
Bryant	0/0	1/1	0/0	2/2	0/0
B. Gramatica	0/0	2/2	1/1	0/0	0/0
Welker	0/0	1/1	0/0	0/0	0/0
Dolphins	0/0	5/6	7/8	5/6	2/3
Opponents	2/2	5/5	4/7	6/11	3/3

SACKS

	No.
Taylor	9.5
D. Bowens	7.0
Zgonina	5.0
Romero	3.5
Pope	2.0
Thomas	2.0
J. Williams	2.0
Ahanotu	1.0
Edwards	1.0
Poole	1.0
Seau	1.0
Surtain	1.0
Dolphins	36.0
Opponents	52.0

RECORD HOLDERS
INDIVIDUAL RECORDS—CAREER

Category	Name	Performance
Rushing (Yds.)	Larry Csonka, 1968-1974, 1979	6,737
Passing (Yds.)	Dan Marino, 1983-1999	*61,361
Passing (TDs)	Dan Marino, 1983-1999	*420
Receiving (No.)	Mark Clayton, 1983-1992	550
Receiving (Yds.)	Mark Duper, 1982-1992	8,869
Interceptions	Jake Scott, 1970-75	35
Punting (Avg.)	John Kidd, 1994-97	44.2
Punt Return (Avg.)	Jeff Ogden, 2000-01	13.7
Kickoff Return (Avg.)	Mercury Morris, 1969-1975	26.5
Field Goals	Olindo Mare, 1997-2004	194
Touchdowns (Tot.)	Mark Clayton, 1983-1992	82
Points	Olindo Mare, 1997-2004	840

INDIVIDUAL RECORDS—SINGLE SEASON

Category	Name	Performance
Rushing (Yds.)	Ricky Williams, 2002	1,853
Passing (Yds.)	Dan Marino, 1984	*5,084
Passing (TDs)	Dan Marino, 1984	48
Receiving (No.)	O.J. McDuffie, 1998	90
Receiving (Yds.)	Mark Clayton, 1984	1,389
Interceptions	Dick Westmoreland, 1967	10
Punting (Avg.)	John Kidd, 1996	46.3
Punt Return (Avg.)	Jeff Ogden, 2000	17.0
Kickoff Return (Avg.)	Duriel Harris, 1976	32.9
Field Goals	Olindo Mare, 1999	*39
Touchdowns (Tot.)	Mark Clayton, 1984	18
Points	Olindo Mare, 1999	144

INDIVIDUAL RECORDS—SINGLE GAME

Category	Name	Performance
Rushing (Yds.)	Ricky Williams, 12-1-02	228
Passing (Yds.)	Dan Marino, 10-23-88	521
Passing (TDs)	Bob Griese, 11-24-77	6
	Dan Marino, 9-21-86	6
Receiving (No.)	Jim Jensen, 11-6-88	12
Receiving (Yds.)	Mark Duper, 11-10-85	217
Interceptions	Dick Anderson, 12-3-73	*4
Field Goals	Olindo Mare, 10-17-99	6
Touchdowns (Tot.)	Paul Warfield, 12-15-73	4
	Mark Ingram, 11-27-94	4
Points	Paul Warfield, 12-15-73	24
	Mark Ingram, 11-27-94	24

*NFL Record

2005 VETERAN ROSTER

No.	Name	Pos.	Ht.	Wt.	Birthdate	NFL Exp.	College	Hometown	How Acq.	'04 Games/ Starts
36	Akins, Chris	S	5-11	200	11/29/76	7	Arkansas-Pine Bluff	Little Rock, Ark.	UFA(NE)-'04	0*
50	Ayanbadejo, Brendon	LB	6-1	230	9/6/76	3	UCLA	Santa Cruz, Calif.	FA-'03	16/2
37	Bell, Yeremiah	S	6-1	200	3/3/78	2	Eastern Kentucky	Winchester, Ky.	D6c-'03	13/0
86	Booker, Marty	WR	6-0	212	7/31/76	7	Louisiana-Monroe	Jonesboro, La.	T(Chi)-'04	15/15
96	Bowens, David	DE	6-3	260	7/3/77	6	Western Illinois	Detroit, Mich.	FA-'01	16/15
95	Bowens, Tim	DT	6-4	325	2/7/73	12	Mississippi	Okolona, Miss.	D1-94	2/2
22	Bua, Tony	S	5-11	212	2/11/80	2	Arkansas	River Ridge, La.	D5-'04	7/0
72	Carey, Vernon	T	6-5	333	7/31/81	2	Miami	Miami, Fla.	D1-'04	14/2
93	Carter, Kevin	DE	6-5	290	9/21/73	11	Florida	Tallahassee, Fla.	FA-'05	16/16*
84	Chambers, Chris	WR	5-11	210	8/12/78	5	Wisconsin	Cleveland, Ohio	D2-'01	15/15
64	Chester, Larry	DT	6-2	325	10/17/75	8	Temple	Hammond, La.	UFA(Car)-'02	2/2
76	Cook, Damion	G	6-5	320	4/16/79	5	Bethune-Cookman	Ft. Lauderdale, Fla.	UFA(Cle)-'05	15/6*
20	Edwards, Mario	CB	6-0	200	12/1/75	6	Florida State	Pascagoula, Miss.	FA-'05	15/3*
44	Evans, Heath	FB	6-0	245	12/30/78	5	Auburn	West Palm Beach, Fla.	UFA(Sea)-'05	15/0*
7	Feeley, A.J.	QB	6-3	225	5/16/77	5	Oregon	Ontario, Ore.	T(Phil)-'04	11/8
79	Flemons, Ronald	DE	6-6	276	10/20/79	4	Texas A&M	San Antonio, Texas	FA-'04	1/0
11	Frerotte, Gus	QB	6-3	235	7/31/71	12	Tulsa	Ford City, Pa.	UFA(Minn)-'05	16/0*
82	Gilmore, Bryan	WR	6-0	195	1/21/78	5	Midwestern State	Lufkin, Texas	W(Ariz)-'04	16/2
30	Gordon, Lamar	RB	6-1	228	1/7/80	4	North Dakota State	Milwaukee, Wis.	T(StL)-'04	3/2
66	Hadnot, Rex	C	6-2	323	1/28/82	2	Houston	Lufkin, Texas	D6-'04	15/7
91	Holliday, Vonnie	DE	6-5	290	12/11/75	8	North Carolina	Camden, S.C.	FA-'05	9/3*
25	Howard, Reggie	CB	6-0	190	5/17/77	6	Memphis	Memphis, Tenn.	UFA(Car)-'04	15/2
78	James, Jeno	G	6-3	310	1/12/77	6	Auburn	Montgomery, Ala.	UFA(Car)-'04	14/14
57	Jenkins, Corey	LB	6-0	222	8/25/76	3	South Carolina	Columbia, S.C.	D6a-'03	7/0*
24	Jones, Tebucky	S	6-2	220	10/6/74	8	Syracuse	New Britain, Conn.	FA-'05	16/16*
85	Lee, Donald	TE	6-3	255	8/31/80	3	Mississippi State	Maben, Miss.	D5a-'03	16/10
29	Madison, Sam	CB	5-11	185	4/23/74	9	Louisville	Monticello, Fla.	D2-'97	16/16
16	Mann, Maurice	WR	6-2	191	9/14/82	2	Nevada	Monterey, Calif.	FA-'04	0*
10	Mare, Olindo	K	5-10	190	6/6/73	9	Syracuse	Cooper City, Fla.	FA-'97	11/0
32	Martin, Jamar	FB	5-11	256	4/12/80	4	Ohio State	Canton, Ohio	W(Dall)-'04	9/1
73	McDougle, Stockar	T	6-6	335	1/11/77	6	Oklahoma	Deerfield Beach, Fla.	UFA(Det)-'05	16/16*
77	McIntosh, Damion	T	6-4	325	3/25/77	6	Kansas State	Hollywood, Fla.	UFA(SD)-'04	14/14
68	McKinney, Seth	C	6-3	305	6/12/79	4	Texas A&M	Austin, Texas	D3-'02	16/16
81	McMichael, Randy	TE	6-3	260	6/28/79	4	Georgia	Fort Valley, Ga.	D4-'02	16/16
28	Minor, Travis	RB	5-10	205	6/30/79	5	Florida State	Baton Rouge, La.	D3a-'01	11/4
58	Moore, Eddie	LB	6-0	230	7/5/80	3	Tennesssee	S. Pittsburg, Tenn.	D2-'03	13/4
31	Morris, Sammy	RB	6-0	220	3/23/77	6	Texas Tech	San Antonio, Texas	UFA(Buff)-'04	13/9
82	Newson, Kendall	WR	6-1	198	3/5/80	3	Middle Tennessee State	Decatur, Ga.	FA-'03	0*
89	Perry, Ed	TE	6-4	265	9/1/74	10	James Madison	Richmond, Va.	D6d-'97	16/0
40	Poole, Will	CB	5-10	193	7/24/81	2	Southern California	Queens, NY	D4-'04	15/1
33	Pope, Derrick	LB	5-11	233	5/4/82	2	Alabama	Galveston, Texas	D7b-'04	16/3
94	Romero, Dario	DT	6-3	305	4/13/78	4	Eastern Washington	Spokane, Wash.	FA-'02	14/1
18	Rosenfels, Sage	QB	6-4	222	3/6/78	5	Iowa State	Maquoketa, Iowa	T(Wash)-'02	3/1
45	Roundtree, Alphonso	S	6-0	190	7/7/77	2	Tulane	Bradenton, Fla.	FA-'03	0*
70	St. Clair, John	T	6-4	315	7/31/78	6	Virginia	Roanoke, Va.	UFA(StL)-'04	14/14
55	Seau, Junior	LB	6-3	250	1/19/69	16	Southern California	Seaside, Calif.	T(SD)-'03	8/8
75	Shaw, Josh	DT	6-2	290	9/7/79	3	Michigan State	Ft. Lauderdale, Fla.	FA-'05	5/0
74	Smith, Wade	T	6-4	300	4/26/81	3	Memphis	Dallas, Texas	D3a-'03	6/2
59	Spragan, Donnie	LB	6-3	240	7/12/79	5	Stanford	Union City, Calif.	UFA(Den)-'05	16/14*
99	Taylor, Jason	DE	6-6	255	9/1/74	9	Akron	Pittsburgh, Pa.	D3a-'97	16/16
61	Thomas, Jason	G	6-3	310	6/10/77	3	Hampton	Savannah, Ga.	FA-'05	0*
54	Thomas, Zach	LB	5-11	230	9/1/73	10	Texas Tech	Pampa, Texas	D5c-'96	13/13
88	Thompson, Derrius	WR	6-2	220	7/5/77	7	Baylor	Cedar Hill, Texas	UFA(Wash)-'03	16/3
26	Tillman, Travares	S	6-1	190	10/8/77	5	Georgia Tech	Lyons, Ga.	UFA(Car)-'05	6/1*
1	Turk, Matt	P	6-5	250	6/16/68	11	Wisconsin-Whitewater	Greenfield, Wis.	FA-'03	16/0
97	Walters, Matt	DE	6-5	270	8/22/79	2	Miami	Melbourne, Fla.	FA-'05	0*
83	Welker, Wes	WR	5-9	190	5/1/81	2	Texas Tech	Oklahoma City, OK	FA-'04	15/0*
69	Whitley, Taylor	G	6-4	315	2/21/80	3	Texas A&M	Sudan, Texas	D3b-'03	16/11
8	Williams, Quintin	S	5-11	204	9/24/82	2	Wake Forest	Goldsboro, N.C.	FA-'04	6/0
62	Wilson, Eric	G	6-3	290	1/30/72	2	Michigan State	Monroe, Mich.	FA-'04	0*
35	#Wyrick, Jimmy	CB	5-9	170	12/31/76	6	Minnesota	DeSoto, Texas	FA-'04	14/0
90	Zgonina, Jeff	DT	6-2	285	5/24/70	13	Purdue	Mundelein, Ill.	UFA(StL)-'03	16/14

* Akins missed '04 season because of injury; Carter played 16 games with Tennessee in '04; Cook played 9 games with Baltimore and 6 with Cleveland; Edwards played 15 games with Tampa Bay; Evans played 15 games with Seattle; Frerotte played 16 games with Minnesota; Holliday played 9 games with Kansas City; Jenkins played 4 games with Chicago, 3 with Miami; Jones played 16 games with New Orleans; Mann inactive for 7 games; McDougle played 16 games with Detroit; Newson missed '04 season because of injury; Roundtree missed '04 season because of injury; Spragan played 16 games with Denver; J. Thomas last active with Baltimore in '03; Tillman played 6 games with Carolina; Walters last active with N.Y. Jets in '03; Welker played 1 game with San Diego and 14 with Miami; Wilson missed '04 season because of injury.

#Unrestricted free agent, subject to developments.

Traded—CB Patrick Surtain (15 games in '04) to Kansas City.

Players lost through free agency (3): LB Morlon Greenwood (Hou; 16 games in '04), S Sammy Knight (KC; 16); DT Bryan Robinson (Cin; 16).

Also played with Dolphins in '04—DT Chidi Ahanotu (5 games), K Matt Bryant (3), KR LaMont Brightful (2), FB Doug Easlick (3), S Antuan Edwards (8), QB Jay Fiedler (8), RB Brock Forsey (7), S Arturo Freeman (16), K Bill Gramatica (1), RB Leonard Henry (7), G Greg Jerman (1), FB Rob Konrad (10), DT Mario Monds (5), DE Jay Williams (16), LB Renauld Williams (2).

2005 FIRST-YEAR ROSTER

Name	Pos.	Ht.	Wt.	Birthdate	College	Hometown	How Acq.
Alabi, Anthony	TE	6-5	310	2/16/81	Texas Christian	San Antonio, Texas	D5
Bellamy, Ronald (1)	WR	6-0	200	12/28/81	Michigan	New Orleans, La.	FA-'04
Berlin, Brock	QB	6-0	213	7/4/81	Miami	Shreveport, La.	FA
Bigby, Atari	S	5-11	210	9/19/81	Central Florida	Miami, Fla.	FA
Brown, Ronnie	RB	6-0	233	12/12/81	Auburn	Cartersville, Ga.	D1
Brown, Van	DE	6-5	265	5/18/81	Northwestern Oklahoma St.	Alhambra, Calif.	FA
Crowder, Channing	LB	6-2	252	12/2/83	Florida	Atlanta, Ga.	D3
Curry, Derek	LB	6-1	236	9/5/81	Notre Dame	Sealy, Texas	FA
Daniels, Travis	CB	6-1	194	9/8/82	Louisiana State	Holloywood, Fla.	FA
Davis, Josh	WR	6-0	191	12/11/80	Marshall	York, S.C.	FA
Delahoussaye, William (1)	LS	6-2	242	5/7/80	Louisiana-Lafayette	Crowley, La.	FA-'04
Denney, John	DE	6-5	275	12/13/78	Brigham Young	Thornton, Colo.	FA
Eiland, Deandre	CB/S	5-11	202	6/4/82	South Carolina	Tupelo, Miss.	W(Minn)-'04
Elam, Abram	S	6-0	205	10/15/81	Kent State	Riveria Beach, Fla.	FA
Harris, Kay-Jay	RB	6-0	229	3/27/79	West Virginia	Tampa, Fla.	FA
Haw, Brandon (1)	CB/S	6-0	200	9/24/80	Rutgers	Cheverly, Md.	FA
Holmes, Alex	TE	6-2	265	8/22/82	Southern California	Sherman Oaks, Calif.	FA
Huggins, Luther	WR	5-9	190	1/20/82	Central Florida	Miami, Fla.	FA
Hunt, Jack	S	6-1	200	11/30/81	Louisiana State	Ruston, La.	FA
Madison, Tony	WR	6-1	204	3/16/82	Kansas State	Florisant, Mo.	FA
Meeks, Bobby	G	6-2	300	4/8/81	Florida State	Houston, Texas	FA
Mitchell, Shirdonya	CB	5-11	190	5/16/82	Missouri	Arlington, Texas	FA
Moa, Ben (1)	FB	6-2	256	4/22/81	Utah	Ogden, Utah	FA
Munson, Joe	TE	6-3	235	5/23/83	Troy State	Chico, Calif.	FA
Pape, Tony (1)	T	6-6	324	9/29/81	Michigan	Clarendon Hills, Ill.	D7a-'04
Reed, Rodney (1)	G	6-4	280	8/17/80	Louisiana State	West Monroe, La.	FA
Roth, Matt	DE	6-4	278	10/14/82	Iowa	Villa Park, Ill.	D2
Sesay, Victor	TE	6-5	279	11/19/80	Missouri	Washington, D.C.	FA
Solomona, Chris	DE	6-4	285	9/3/82	Oregon	San Pedro, Calif.	FA
Strother, Billy (1)	LB	6-0	230	1/8/82	New Mexico	Evansville, Ind.	FA-'04
Taylor, Winston (1)	LB	6-1	241	10/10/81	Illinois	Decatur, Ill.	FA
Thompson, Orrin	DT	6-5	315	11/11/82	Duke	Charlotte, N.C.	FA
Turner, Lionel	LB	6-2	258	2/21/82	Louisiana State	Walker, La.	FA
Vickerson, Kevin	DT	6-5	310	1/8/83	Michigan State	Detroit, Mich.	D7

The term NFL Rookie is defined as a player who is in his first season of professional football and has not been on the roster of another professional football team for any regular-season or postseason games. A Rookie is designated by an "R" on NFL rosters. Players who have been active in another professional football league or players who have NFL experience, including either preseason training camp or being on an Active List or Inactive List, or on Reserve/Injured or Reserve/Physically Unable to Perform for fewer than six regular-season games, are termed NFL First-Year Players. An NFL First-Year Player is designated by a "1" on NFL rosters. Thereafter, a player is credited with an additional year of experience for each season in which he accumulates six games on the Active List or Inactive List, or on Reserve/Injured or Reserve/Physically Unable to Perform.

Log on to www.miamidolphins.com for an up-to-date roster.

COACHING STAFF

Head Coach,
Nick Saban

Pro Career: Signed a five-year contract on December 27, 2004 to become the sixth coach in Dolphins history. Joins the Dolphins following a 10-year stint as a collegiate head coach, including the last five at Louisiana State where he led the Tigers to a composite record of 48-16 and a national championship following the 2003 season. Prior to his tenure at LSU, Saban guided Michigan State to a five-year record of 35-24-1 (1995-99). Began his NFL career as defensive backs coach with the Houston Oilers from 1988-89. After one year (1990) as head coach at Toledo, was named defensive coordinator with the Cleveland Browns in 1991, and spent four years (1991-94) on Bill Belichick's staff. Career record: 0-0.

Background: Saban served as an assistant at the collegiate level at Kent State (1973-76), Syracuse (1977), West Virginia (1978-79), Ohio State (1980-81), Navy (1982) and Michigan State (1983-87). Saban lettered three seasons (1970-72) as a defensive back at Kent State, where he also played shortstop on the school's baseball team.

Personal: Born October 31, 1951 in Fairmont, West Virginia. He and his wife, Terry, have a son, Nicholas, and a daughter, Kristen.

ASSISTANT COACHES

Keith Armstrong, special teams; born December 15, 1963, Trenton, N.J. Running back/defensive back Temple 1983-86. No pro playing experience: College coach: Temple 1987, Miami 1988, Akron 1989, Oklahoma State 1990-92, Notre Dame 1993. Pro coach: Atlanta Falcons 1994-96, Chicago Bears 1997-2000, joined Dolphins in 2001.

Charlie Baggett, asst. head coach/wide receivers; born January 21, 1953, Fayetteville, N.C. Quarterback Michigan State 1972-75. No pro playing experience. College coach: Bowling Green 1977-1980, Minnesota 1981-82, Michigan State 1983-1992, 1995-98. Pro coach: Houston Oilers 1993-94, Green Bay Packers 1999, Minnesota Vikings 2000-04, joined Dolphins in 2005.

Tim Davis, asst. offensive line; born June 17, 1958. Tackle Utah 1978-1980. No pro playing experience. College coach: Wisconsin 1983-86, Arizona 1987, Walla Walla (Wash.) C.C. 1988, Idaho State 1989, Utah 1990-96, Wisconsin 1997-2001, Southern California 2002-04. Pro coach: Joined Dolphins in 2005.

Derek Dooley, tight ends; born June 10, 1968, Athens, Ga. Wide receiver Virginia 1987-1990. No pro playing experience. College coach: Georgia 1996, Southern Methodist 1997-99, Louisiana State 2000-04. Pro coach: Joined Dolphins in 2005.

George Edwards, linebackers; born January 16, 1967, Siler City, N.C. Linebacker Duke 1985-89. No pro playing experience. College coach: Florida 1990-91, Appalachian State 1992-95, Duke 1996, Georgia 1997. Pro coach: Dallas Cowboys 1998-2001, Washington Redskins 2002-03, Cleveland Browns 2004, joined Dolphins in 2005.

Eric Fears, asst. strength and conditioning; born December 12, 1960, Tallahassee, Fla. Running back Virginia 1981-83. No pro playhing experience. College coach: Virginia 1984-86, 1994-95, The Citadel 1987, South Carolina 1988-1992, Washington State 1993, Georgia 1996-2003. Pro coach: Joined Dolphins in 2004.

John Gamble, strength and conditioning; born June 26, 1957, Richmond, Va. Linebacker Hampton Institute 1975-78. No pro playing experience. College coach: Virginia 1982-1993. Pro coach: Joined Dolphins in 2004.

Jason Garrett, quarterbacks; born March 28, 1966, Abington, Pa. Quarterback Princeton 1987-88. Pro quarterback Ottawa Rough Riders (CFL) 1991, Dallas Cowboys 1993-99, New York Giants 2000-03, Tampa Bay Buccaneers 2004, Miami Dolphins 2004. Pro coach: Joined Dolphins in 2005.

Judd Garrett, offensive quality control; born June 25, 1967, Abington, Pa. Running back Princeton 1987-89. Pro running back London Monarchs (WLAF) 1991-92, Dallas Cowboys 1993, Las Vegas Posse (CFL) 1994, San Antonio Texans (CFL) 1995. College coach: Princeton 1990. Pro coach: New Orleans Saints 1997-99, joined Dolphins in 2000.

Bert Hill, associate strength & conditioning; born January 25, 1958, Montgomery, Ala. Linebacker Marion (Ala.) Military Institute 1976-77, Wichita State 1978. No pro playing experience. College coach: Nicholls State 1981, Auburn 1982, Texas A&M 1983-87, 1989, Ohio State 1988. Pro coach: Detroit Lions 1990-2000, joined Dolphins in 2005.

Hudson Houck, offensive line; born January 7, 1943, Los Angeles. Center Southern California 1962-64. No pro playing experience. College coach: Southern California 1970-72, 1976-82, Stanford 1973-75. Pro coach: Los Angeles Rams 1983-91, Seattle Seahawks 1992, Dallas Cowboys 1993-2001, San Diego Chargers 2002-04, joined Dolphins in 2005.

Travis Jones, asst. defensive line; born June 6, 1972, Milledgville, Ga. Linebacker Georgia 1991-94. Pro linebacker Baltimore Stallions (CFL) 1995. College coach: Georgia 1997, Appalachian State 1998-2000, Kansas 2001-02, Louisiana State 2003-04. Pro coach: Joined Dolphins in 2005.

Scott Linehan, offensive coordinator; born September 17, 1963, Sunnyside,

Wash. Quarterback Idaho 1982-86. No pro playing experience. College coach: Idaho 1988-90, Nevada-Las Vegas 1991, Idaho 1992-93, Washington 1994-98, Louisville 1999-2001. Pro Coach: Minnesota Vikings 2002-04, joined Dolphins in 2005.

Will Muschamp, asst. head coach/defense; born August 3, 1971, Rome, Ga. Linebacker Georgia 1991-94. No pro playing experience. College coach: Auburn 1995-97, West Georgia 1998, Eastern Kentucky 1999, Valdosta State 2000, Louisiana State 2001-04. Pro coach: Joined Dolphins in 2005.

Mel Phillips, secondary; born January 6, 1942, Shelby, N.C. Defensive back/running back North Carolina A&T 1964-65. Pro defensive back San Francisco 49ers 1966-1977. Pro coach: Detroit Lions 1980-84, joined Dolphins in 1985.

Glenn Pires, defensive quality control; born September 13, 1958, New Bedford, Mass. Offensive lineman Springfield College 1976-79. No pro playing experience. College coach: Dartmouth 1985-88, Syracuse 1989-1994, Michigan State 1995. Pro coach: Arizona Cardinals 1996-2000, Detroit Lions 2001-02, joined Dolphins in 2003.

Dan Quinn, defensive line; born September 11, 1970, Orange, N.J. Defensive lineman Salisbury State 1990-93. No pro playing experience. College coach: William & Mary 1994, Virginia Military Institute 1995, Hofstra 1997-2000. Pro coach: San Francisco 49ers 2001-04, joined Dolphins in 2005.

Richard Smith, defensive coordinator; born October 17, 1955, Los Angeles. Offensive lineman Rio Hondo (Calif.) J.C. 1975-76, Fresno State 1977-78. No pro playing experience. College coach: Rio Hondo (Calif.) J.C. 1979-1980, Cal State-Fullerton 1981-83, California 1984-86, Arizona 1987. Pro coach: Houston Oilers 1988-1992, Denver Broncos 1993-96, San Francisco 49ers 1997-2002, Detroit Lions 2003-04, joined Dolphins in 2005.

Bobby Williams, running backs; born November 21, 1958, St. Louis, Mo. Running back/defensive back Purdue 1978-1981. No pro playing experience. College coach: Purdue 1982, Ball State 1983-84, Eastern Michigan 1985-89, Michigan State 1990-2002 (head coach, 2000-02), Louisiana State 2004. Pro coach: Detroit Lions 2003, joined Dolphins in 2004.

American Football Conference
East Division
Team Colors: Blue, Red, Silver, and White
Gillette Stadium
One Patriot Place
Foxborough, Massachusetts 02035
Telephone: (508) 543-8200

2005 SCHEDULE
PRESEASON

Aug. 12	at Cincinnati	7:30
Aug. 18	**New Orleans**	8:00
Aug. 26	at Green Bay	7:00
Sept. 1	**New York Giants**	8:00

REGULAR SEASON

Sept. 8	**Oakland** (Thu.)	9:00
Sept. 18	at Carolina	1:00
Sept. 25	at Pittsburgh	4:15
Oct. 2	**San Diego**	1:00
Oct. 9	at Atlanta	1:00
Oct. 16	at Denver	2:15
Oct. 23	Open Date	
Oct. 30	**Buffalo**	8:30
Nov. 7	**Indianapolis** (Mon.)	9:00
Nov. 13	at Miami	1:00
Nov. 20	**New Orleans**	1:00
Nov. 27	at Kansas City	12:00
Dec. 4	**New York Jets**	4:15
Dec. 11	at Buffalo	1:00
Dec. 17	**Tampa Bay** (Sat.)	1:30
Dec. 26	at New York Jets (Mon.)	9:00
Jan. 1	**Miami**	1:00

Stadium: Gillette Stadium
(opened in 2002)
 •**Capacity:** 68,756
 One Patriot Place
 Foxborough, Massachusetts 02035
Playing Surface: Grass
Training Camp: Gillette Stadium
 Foxborough,
 Massachusetts 02035

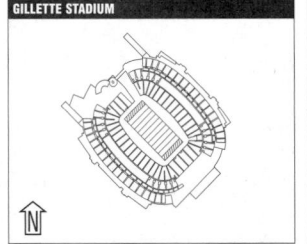

GILLETTE STADIUM

CLUB OFFICIALS
CEO and Chairman: Robert K. Kraft
Vice Chairman: Jonathan A. Kraft
Vice President, Community Affairs and
 Corporate Philanthropy: Rena Clark
Vice President, Finance: Jim Hausmann
Vice President, Chief Marketing Officer:
 Lou Imbriano
Vice President, Player Personnel:
 Scott Pioli
Chief Administrative Counsel:
 Jack Mula
Executive Director of Marketing
 Operations: Jennifer Ferron
Executive Director of Media Relations:
 Stacey James
Executive Director of Corporate
 Development: David Pearlstein
Director of Suite Services:
 Melissa Aghjayan
Director of Pro Personnel: Nick Caserio
Director of College Scouting:
 Thomas Dimitroff
Director of Retail Operations:
 Ken Flanders
Director of Entertainment and Broadcast
 Production: Gary Grodecki
Director of Ticketing: Maryruth Hughey
Director of Sales: Murray Kohl
Director of Sales: Jon Levy
Director of Sales: Joe Mariani
Director of Research: Richard Miller
Director of Premium Seating Services:
 Bill Nelsen
Director of Human Resources:
 Joanne Nichols
Director of Cheerleaders: Tracy Sormanti
Director of Football Development and
 Promotions for Community Affairs:
 Andre Tippett
Director of Customer and Sponsor
 Services: Gail Titus
Director of Finance: Jim Wilson
Equipment Manager: Don Brocher
Video Director: Jimmy Dee
Head Athletic Trainer: Jim Whalen
Kraft Group, Vice President of
 Information Technology: Pat Curley
Gillette Stadium, Vice President of
 Security and Front of House
 Operations: Mark Briggs
Gillette Stadium, Vice President of
 Business Development and External
 Affairs: Dan Murphy
Gillette Stadium, Vice President of
 Operations: Jim Nolan

COACHING HISTORY
Boston 1960-1970
(344-349-9)
Records include postseason games

1960-61	Lou Saban*	7-12-0
1961-68	Mike Holovak	53-47-9
1969-1970	Clive Rush**	5-16-0
1970-72	John Mazur***	9-21-0
1972	Phil Bengtson	1-4-0
1973-78	Chuck Fairbanks****	46-41-0
1978	Hank Bullough-Ron Erhardt#	0-1-0
1979-1981	Ron Erhardt	21-27-0
1981-84	Ron Meyer##	18-16-0
1984-89	Raymond Berry	51-41-0
1990	Rod Rust	1-15-0
1991-92	Dick MacPherson	8-24-0
1993-96	Bill Parcells	34-34-0
1997-99	Pete Carroll	28-23-0
2000-04	Bill Belichick	62-27-0

Records include postseason games
 *Released after five games in 1961
 **Released after seven games in 1970
 ***Resigned after nine games in 1972
 ****Suspended for final regular-season game in 1978
 #Co-coaches
 ##Released after eight games in 1984

ATTENDANCE
Home 558,532   Away 550,025
Total 1,108,557
Single-game home record,
 70,262 (12/12/04)
Single-season home record,
 558,532 (2004)

2005 DRAFT CHOICES

Round	Name	Pos.	College
1	Logan Mankins	G	Fresno State
3	Ellis Hobbs	DB	Iowa State
	Nick Kaczur	T	Toledo
4	James Sanders	DB	Fresno State
5	Ryan Claridge	LB	Nevada-Las Vegas
7	Matt Cassel	QB	Southern California
	Andy Stokes	TE	William Penn

2004 TEAM RECORD

PRESEASON (1-3)

Date	Result	Opponent
8/13	W 24-6	Philadelphia
8/21	L 3-31	at Cincinnati
8/28	L 17-20	at Carolina
9/2	L 0-31	Jacksonville

REGULAR SEASON (14-2)

Date	Result	Opponent	Att.
9/9	W 27-24	Indianapolis	68,756
9/19	W 23-12	at Arizona	51,557
10/3	W 31-17	at Buffalo	72,698
10/10	W 24-10	Miami	68,756
10/17	W 30-20	Seattle	68,756
10/24	W 13-7	N.Y. Jets	68,756
10/31	L 20-34	at Pittsburgh	64,737
11/7	W 40-22	at St. Louis	66,107
11/14	W 29-6	Buffalo	68,756
11/22	W 27-19	at Kansas City	78,431
11/28	W 24-3	Baltimore	68,756
12/5	W 42-15	at Cleveland	73,028
12/12	W 35-28	Cincinnati	68,756
12/20	L 28-29	at Miami	73,629
12/26	W 23-7	at N.Y. Jets	77,975
1/2	W 21-7	San Francisco	68,756

(OT) Overtime

POSTSEASON (3-0)

Date	Result	Opponent	
1/10	W 20-3	Indianapolis	68,756
1/18	W 41-27	at Pittsburgh	65,242
2/1	W 24-21	vs. Philadelphia	78,125
		at Jacksonville	

SCORE BY PERIODS

Patriots	87	159	102	89	0	—	437
Opponents	55	94	45	66	0	—	260

2004 TEAM STATISTICS

	Patriots	Opp.
Total First Downs	344	290
Rushing	120	83
Passing	193	177
Penalty	31	30
3rd Down: Made/Att	93/206	81/209
3rd Down Pct.	45.1	38.8
4th Down: Made/Att	4/10	13/30
4th Down Pct.	40.0	43.3
Possession Avg.	31:22	28:38
Total Net Yards	5,722	4,972
Avg. Per Game	357.6	310.8
Total Plays	1,035	988
Avg. Per Play	5.5	5.0
Net Yards Rushing	2134	1572
Avg. Per Game	133.4	98.3
Total Rushes	524	405
Net Yards Passing	3,588	3,400
Avg. Per Game	224.3	212.5
Sacked/Yards Lost	26/162	45/311
Gross Yards	3,750	3,711
Att./Completions	485/293	538/315
Completion Pct.	60.4	58.6
Had Intercepted	14	20
Punts/Average	56/42.0	69/41.5
Net Punting Avg.	56/33.7	69/36.8
Penalties/Yards	101/822	118/1014
Fumbles/Ball Lost	24/13	31/16
Touchdowns	49	31
Rushing	15	9
Passing	29	18
Returns	5	4

2004 INDIVIDUAL STATISTICS

PASSING	Att.	Comp.	Yds.	Pct.	TD	Int.	Tkld.	Rate
Brady	474	288	3,692	60.8	28	14	26/162	92.6
Davey	10	4	54	40.0	0	0	0/0	57.9
Vinatieri	1	1	4	100.0	1	0	0/0	122.9
Patriots	485	293	3,750	60.4	29	14	26/162	92.5
Opponents	538	315	3,711	58.6	18	20	45/311	75.3

SCORING	TD R	TD P	TD Rt	PAT	FG	Saf	PTS
Vinatieri	0	0	0	48/48	31/33	0	141
Dillon	12	1	0	0/0	0/0	0	80
Graham	0	7	0	0/0	0/0	0	42
Patten	0	7	0	0/0	0/0	0	42
Branch	0	4	0	0/0	0/0	0	24
Faulk	2	1	0	0/0	0/0	0	18
Givens	0	3	0	0/0	0/0	0	18
Fauria	0	2	0	0/0	0/0	0	12
B. Johnson	0	1	1	0/0	0/0	0	12
Vrabel	0	2	0	0/0	0/0	0	12
Abdullah	1	0	0	0/0	0/0	0	6
Brown	0	1	0	0/0	0/0	0	6
Gay	0	0	1	0/0	0/0	0	6
Green	0	0	1	0/0	0/0	0	6
Samuel	0	0	1	0/0	0/0	0	6
Seymour	0	0	1	0/0	0/0	0	6
Patriots	15	29	5	48/48	31/33	0	437
Opponents	9	18	4	23/23	15/18	0	260

2-Pt. Conversions: Dillon.
Patriots 1-1, Opponents 3-8.

RUSHING	No.	Yds	Avg	LG	TD
Dillon	345	1,635	4.7	44	12
Faulk	54	255	4.7	20	2
Pass	39	141	3.6	19	0
Cobbs	22	50	2.3	13	0
Brady	43	28	0.7	10	0
Abdullah	13	13	1.0	5	1
B. Johnson	2	8	4.0	11	0
Patten	1	5	5.0	5	0
Izzo	1	0	0.0	0	0
Davey	4	-1	-0.2	3	0
Patriots	524	2,134	4.1	44	15
Opponents	405	1,572	3.9	34	9

RECEIVING	No.	Yds	Avg	LG	TD
Givens	56	874	15.6	50	3
Patten	44	800	18.2	48t	7
Branch	35	454	13.0	26t	4
Graham	30	364	12.1	48	7
Pass	28	215	7.7	22	0
Faulk	26	248	9.5	31t	1
Brown	17	184	10.8	22	1
Fauria	16	195	12.2	25	2
Dillon	15	103	6.9	20	1
B. Johnson	10	174	17.4	48	1
Weaver	8	93	11.6	25	0
Klecko	3	18	6.0	11	0
Watson	2	16	8.0	14	0
Vrabel	2	3	1.5	2t	2
Abdullah	1	9	9.0	9	0
Patriots	293	3,750	12.8	50	29
Opponents	315	3,711	11.8	65t	18

INTERCEPTIONS	No.	Yds	Avg	LG	TD
Wilson	4	51	12.8	24	0
Bruschi	3	70	23.3	36	0
Brown	3	22	7.3	17	0
Gay	2	23	11.5	13	0
Harrison	2	12	6.0	12	0
Samuel	1	34	34.0	34t	1
McGinest	1	27	27.0	27	0
Phifer	1	26	26.0	26	0
Poole	1	21	21.0	21	0
Banta-Cain	1	4	4.0	4	0
Law	1	0	0.0	0	0
Patriots	20	290	14.5	36	1
Opponents	14	242	17.3	65	1

PUNTING	No.	Yds.	Avg.	In 20	LG
Jo. Miller	56	2,350	42.0	19	69
Patriots	56	2,350	42.0	19	69
Opponents	69	2,866	41.5	21	63

PUNT RETURNS	Ret	FC	Yds	Avg	LG	TD
Faulk	20	11	133	6.7	16	0
Brown	12	3	83	6.9	23	0
B. Johnson	4	1	8	2.0	6	0
Poole	2	0	6	3.0	6	0
Branch	1	0	0	0.0	0	0
Gay	1	0	0	0.0	0	0
Patriots	40	15	230	5.8	23	0
Opponents	31	7	365	11.8	71	1

KICKOFF RETURNS	No.	Yds	Avg	LG	TD
B. Johnson	41	1,016	24.8	93t	1
Pass	6	115	19.2	24	0
Faulk	4	73	18.3	24	0
Kasper	3	61	20.3	21	0
Banta-Cain	1	21	21.0	21	0
Patten	1	16	16.0	16	0
Klecko	0	0	0.0	0	0
Patriots	56	1,302	23.3	93t	1
Opponents	86	2,003	23.3	98t	1

FIELD GOALS	1-19	20-29	30-39	40-49	50+
Vinatieri	0/0	13/13	7/7	11/12	0/1
Patriots	0/0	13/13	7/7	11/12	0/1
Opponents	1/1	5/5	5/6	2/3	2/3

SACKS	No.
McGinest	9.5
Vrabel	5.5
Colvin	5.0
Seymour	5.0
Green	4.0
Bruschi	3.5
Warren	3.5
Harrison	3.0
Wilfork	2.0
Banta-Cain	1.5
Phifer	1.5
T. Johnson	1.0
Patriots	45.0
Opponents	26.0

RECORD HOLDERS

INDIVIDUAL RECORDS—CAREER

Category	Name	Performance
Rushing (Yds.)	Sam Cunningham, 1973-79, 1981-82	5,453
Passing (Yds.)	Drew Bledsoe, 1993-2001	29,657
Passing (TDs)	Steve Grogan, 1975-1990	182
Receiving (No.)	Stanley Morgan, 1977-1989	534
Receiving (Yds.)	Stanley Morgan, 1977-1989	10,352
Interceptions	Raymond Clayborn, 1977-1989	36
	Ty Law, 1995-2004	36
Punting (Avg.)	Tom Tupa, 1996-98	44.7
Punt Return (Avg.)	Mack Herron, 1973-75	12.0
Kickoff Return (Avg.)	Allen Carter, 1975-76	27.2
Field Goals	Adam Vinatieri, 1996-2004	243
Touchdowns (Tot.)	Stanley Morgan, 1977-1989	68
Points	Gino Cappelletti, 1960-1970	1,130

INDIVIDUAL RECORDS—SINGLE SEASON

Category	Name	Performance
Rushing (Yds.)	Corey Dillon, 2004	1,635
Passing (Yds.)	Drew Bledsoe, 1994	4,555
Passing (TDs)	Vito (Babe) Parilli, 1964	31
Receiving (No.)	Troy Brown, 2001	101
Receiving (Yds.)	Stanley Morgan, 1986	1,491
Interceptions	Ron Hall, 1964	11
Punting (Avg.)	Tom Tupa, 1997	45.8
Punt Return (Avg.)	Mack Herron, 1974	14.8
Kickoff Return (Avg.)	Raymond Clayborn, 1977	31.0
Field Goals	Tony Franklin, 1986	32
Touchdowns (Tot.)	Curtis Martin, 1996	17
Points	Gino Cappelletti, 1964	155

INDIVIDUAL RECORDS—SINGLE GAME

Category	Name	Performance
Rushing (Yds.)	Tony Collins, 9-18-83	212
Passing (Yds.)	Drew Bledsoe, 11-13-94	426
Passing (TDs)	Vito (Babe) Parilli, 11-15-64	5
	Vito (Babe) Parilli, 10-15-67	5
	Steve Grogan, 9-9-79	5
Receiving (No.)	Troy Brown, 9-22-02	16
Receiving (Yds.)	Terry Glenn, 10-3-99	214
Interceptions	Many times	3
	Last time by Roland James, 10-23-83	
Field Goals	Gino Cappelletti, 10-4-64	6
Touchdowns (Tot.)	Many times	3
	Last time by Antowain Smith, 11-3-02	
Points	Gino Cappelletti, 12-18-65	28

2005 VETERAN ROSTER

No.	Name	Pos.	Ht.	Wt.	Birthdate	NFL Exp.	College	Hometown	How Acq.	'04 Games/ Starts
	#Abdullah, Rabih	RB	6-0	235	4/27/75	8	Lehigh	Roselle, N.J.	FA-'04	9/0
68	Ashworth, Tom	T	6-6	305	10/10/77	4	Colorado	Englewood, Colo.	FA-'01	6/6
96	Bailey, Rodney	DT/DE	6-3	305	10/7/79	5	Ohio State	Cleveland, Ohio	RFA(Pitt)-'04	0*
48	Banta-Cain, Tully	LB	6-2	250	8/28/80	3	California	Sunnyvale, Calif.	D7b-'03	16/0
44	Beisel, Monty	LB	6-3	238	8/20/78	5	Kansas State	Douglass, Kan.	UFA(KC)-'05	11/9*
12	Brady, Tom	QB	6-4	225	8/3/77	6	Michigan	San Mateo, Calif.	D6b-'00	16/16
83	Branch, Deion	WR	5-9	193	7/18/79	4	Louisville	Albany, Ga.	D2-'02	9/9
	Brown, Chad	LB	6-2	245	7/12/70	13	Colorado	Altadena, Calif.	FA-'05	7/7*
	#Brown, Troy	WR	5-10	196	7/2/71	13	Marshall	Blackville, S.C.	D8-'93	12/0
54	Bruschi, Tedy	LB	6-1	247	6/9/73	10	Arizona	Roseville, Calif.	D3-'96	16/16
41	Charlton, Ike	CB	5-11	199	10/6/77	5	Virginia Tech	Orlando, Fla.	FA-'05	7/2*
58	Chatham, Matt	LB	6-4	250	6/28/77	6	South Dakota	Sioux City, Iowa	W(StL)-'00	5/0
	#Cherry, Je'Rod	CB/S	6-1	210	5/30/73	10	California	Berkeley, Calif.	FA-'01	12/0
34	Cobbs, Cedric	RB	6-0	225	1/9/81	2	Arkansas	Little Rock, Ark.	D4b-'04	4/0
59	Colvin, Rosevelt	LB	6-3	250	9/5/77	7	Purdue	Indianapolis, Ind.	UFA(Chi)-'03	16/1
6	Davey, Rohan	QB	6-2	245	4/14/78	4	Louisiana State	Miami, Fla.	D4a-'02	4/0
51	Davis, Don	LB	6-1	235	12/17/72	10	Kansas	Olathe, Kan.	UFA(StL)-'03	16/2
28	Dillon, Corey	RB	6-1	225	10/24/74	9	Washington	Seattle, Wash.	T(Cin)-'04	15/14
86	Dwight, Tim	WR	5-8	180	7/13/75	8	Iowa	Iowa City, Iowa	FA-'05	12/0*
33	Faulk, Kevin	RB	5-8	202	6/5/76	7	Louisiana State	Carencro, La.	D2-'99	11/1
88	Fauria, Christian	TE	6-4	250	9/22/71	11	Colorado	Encino, Calif.	UFA(Sea)-'02	16/10
2	Flutie, Doug	QB	5-10	180	10/23/62	12	Boston College	Natick, Mass.	FA-'05	2/1*
21	Gay, Randall	CB	5-11	186	5/5/82	2	Louisiana State	Brusly, La.	FA-'04	15/9
87	Givens, David	WR	6-0	215	8/16/80	4	Notre Dame	Humble, Texas	D7b-'02	15/12
76	Gorin, Brandon	T	6-6	308	7/17/78	4	Purdue	Muncie, Ind.	FA-'03	14/10
82	Graham, Daniel	TE	6-3	257	11/16/78	4	Colorado	Denver, Colo.	D1-'02	14/14
97	Green, Jarvis	DE/DT	6-3	290	1/12/79	4	Louisiana State	Donaldsonville, La.	D4b-'02	16/1
37	Harrison, Rodney	S	6-1	220	12/15/72	12	Western Illinois	Chicago, Ill.	FA-'03	16/16
91	Hill, Marquise	DE	6-6	300	8/7/82	2	Louisiana State	New Orleans, La.	D2-'04	1/0
71	Hochstein, Russ	G	6-4	305	10/7/77	5	Nebraska	Hartington, Neb.	FA-'03	16/2
53	Izzo, Larry	LB	5-10	228	9/26/74	10	Rice	Houston, Texas	UFA(Mia)-'01	16/0
18	James, Cedric	WR	6-1	197	3/19/79	4	Texas Christian	Fort Worth, Texas	FA-'04	0*
81	Johnson, Bethel	WR	5-11	200	2/11/79	3	Texas A&M	Corsicana, Texas	D2b-'03	13/1
52	Johnson, Ted	LB	6-4	253	12/4/72	11	Colorado	Alameda, Calif.	D2-'95	16/15
	#Kasper, Kevin	WR	6-1	202	12/23/77	5	Iowa	Hinsdale, Ill.	FA-'04	8/0
99	Kelley, Ethan	DT/DE	6-2	310	2/12/80	2	Baylor	Sugar Land, Texas	D7c-'03	1/0
90	Klecko, Dan	DT/LB	5-11	275	1/12/81	3	Temple	Colts Neck, N.J.	D4a-'03	6/2
67	Koppen, Dan	C	6-2	296	9/12/79	3	Boston College	Whitehall, Pa.	D5-'03	16/16
	Leyva, Victor	T	6-4	307	12/18/77	4	Arizona State	Porterville, Colo.	FA-'05	0*
72	Light, Matt	T	6-4	305	6/23/78	5	Purdue	Greenville, Ohio	D2-'01	16/16
45	Mallard, Wesly	LB	6-1	230	11/21/78	4	Oregon	Columbus, Ga.	FA-'05	4/0*
55	McGinest, Willie	LB	6-5	270	12/11/71	12	Southern California	Long Beach, Calif.	D1-'94	16/16
8	Miller, Josh	P	6-4	225	7/14/70	10	Arizona	Rockaway, N.Y.	FA-'04	16/0
64	Mruczkowski, Gene	G/C	6-2	305	6/6/80	3	Purdue	Cleveland, Ohio	FA-'03	10/0
61	Neal, Stephen	G	6-4	305	10/9/76	4	Cal State-Bakersfield	San Diego, Calif.	FA-'01	16/14
65	Nimmo, Lance	T	6-4	303	9/13/79	2	West Virginia	New Castle, Pa.	FA-'04	0*
35	Pass, Patrick	FB	5-10	217	12/31/77	6	Georgia	Tucker, Ga.	D7b-'00	14/4
66	Paxton, Lonie	LS	6-2	260	3/13/78	6	Sacramento State	Corona, Calif.	FA-'00	16/0
38	Poole, Tyrone	CB	5-8	188	2/3/72	10	Fort Valley State	LaGrange, Ga.	UFA(Den)-'03	5/4
31	Poteat, Hank	CB	5-10	192	8/30/77	4	Pittsburgh	Harrisburg, Pa.	FA-'04	0*
7	Redman, Chris	QB	6-3	223	7/7/77	5	Louisville	Louisville, Ky.	FA-'05	0*
42	Reid, Dexter	S	5-11	203	3/18/81	2	North Carolina	Norfolk, Va.	D4a-'04	13/2
62	Roehl, Jeff	T	6-4	300	5/18/80	2	Northwestern	Evergreen Park, Ill.	FA-'05	0*
14	Sam, P.K.	WR	6-3	210	2/26/83	2	Florida State	Buford, Ga.	D5-'04	3/0
22	Samuel, Asante	CB	5-10	185	1/6/81	3	Central Florida	Ft. Lauderdale, Fla.	D4b-'03	13/8
17	Schifino, Jake	WR	6-1	201	11/15/79	3	Akron	Pittsburgh, Pa.	FA-'05	1/0*
30	Scott, Chad	CB	6-1	202	9/6/74	9	Maryland	Capitol Heights, Md.	FA-'05	7/7*
29	Scott, Guss	S	5-10	205	5/21/82	2	Florida	Jacksonville, Fla.	D3-'04	0*
93	Seymour, Richard	DT/DE	6-6	310	10/6/79	5	Georgia	Gadsden, S.C.	D1-'01	15/15
23	t-Starks, Duane	CB	5-10	174	5/23/74	8	Miami	Miami, Fla.	T(Ariz)-'05	15/8*
10	Terrell, David	WR	6-3	212	3/13/79	5	Michigan	Richmond, Va.	FA-'05	16/15*
4	Vinatieri, Adam	K	6-0	202	12/28/72	10	South Dakota State	Rapid City, S.D.	FA-'96	16/0
50	Vrabel, Mike	LB	6-4	261	8/14/75	9	Ohio State	Akron, Ohio	UFA(Pitt)-'01	16/15
94	Warren, Ty	DT/DE	6-5	300	2/6/81	3	Texas A&M	Bryan, Texas	D1-'03	16/16
84	Watson, Benjamin	TE	6-3	253	12/18/80	2	Georgia	Rock Hill, S.C.	D1b-'04	1/1

85	Weaver, Jed	TE	6-4	258	8/11/76	7	Oregon	Redmond, Ore.	FA-'04	10/1
75	Wilfork, Vince	DT/DE	6-2	325	11/4/81	2	Miami	Boynton Beach, Fla.	D1a-'04	16/6
26	Wilson, Eugene	S/CB	5-10	195	8/17/80	3	Illinois	Merrillville, Ind.	D2a-'03	15/14
74	Yates, Billy	G	6-2	305	4/15/80	2	Texas A&M	Fort Worth, Texas	FA-'04	0*

* Bailey missed '04 season because of injury; Beisel played 11 games with Kansas City in '04; C. Brown played 7 games with Seattle; Charlton played 7 games with N.Y. Giants; Dwight played 12 games with San Diego; Flutie played 2 games with San Diego; James last active with Minnesota in '02; Leyva last active with Cincinnati in '03; Mallard played 4 games with N.Y. Giants; Nimmo last active with N.Y. Jets in '03; Poteat played 3 postseason games; Redman last active with Baltimore in '03; Roehl last active with N.Y. Giants in '03; Schifino played 1 game with Tennessee; C. Scott played 7 games with Pittsburgh; G. Scott missed '04 season because of injury; Starks played 15 games with Arizona; Terrell played 16 games with Chicago; Yates on roster for 1 postseason game.

\# Unrestricted free agent; subject to developments.

t- Patriots traded for Starks (Ariz).

Players lost through free agency (4): G Joe Andruzzi (Cle; 16 games in '04), T Adrian Klemm (GB; 2), QB Jim Miller (NYG; 0), WR David Patten (Wash; 16).

Also played with Patriots in '04—LB Eric Alexander (3 games), LB Justin Kurpeikis (5), CB Ty Law (7), CB Omare Lowe (3), S Shawn Mayer (3), CB Earthwind Moreland (9), LB Roman Phifer (13), NT Keith Traylor (16).

2005 FIRST-YEAR ROSTER

Name	Pos.	Ht.	Wt.	Birthdate	College	Hometown	How Acq.
Alexander, Eric (1)	LB	6-2	240	2/8/82	Louisiana State	Port Arthur, Texas	FA-'04
Bartosic, Mark (1)	WR	6-0	195	10/30/80	Susquehanna	Sunbury, Pa.	FA
Birmingham, DeCori	RB	5-10	210	11/22/82	Arkansas	Atlanta, Texas	FA
Bryant, Ricky (1)	WR	6-0	185	3/24/81	Hofstra	Detroit, Mich.	FA-'04
Cassel, Matt	QB	6-4	222	5/17/82	Southern California	Northridge, Calif.	D7a
Chapman, Kory (1)	RB	6-1	202	7/13/80	Jacksonville State	Batesville, Miss.	FA-'04
Charles, Earl	RB	6-1	215	9/11/82	Marshall	Brooklyn, N.Y.	FA
Claridge, Ryan	LB	6-2	254	4/12/81	Nevada-Las Vegas	Almont, Mich.	D5
Conway, Travis	LS	6-5	252	6/3/82	Virginia Tech	Richmond, Va.	FA
Eckel, Kyle	FB	5-11	244	12/30/81	Navy	Haverford, Pa.	FA
Gould, Robbie	K	6-1	181	12/6/82	Penn State	Lock Haven, Pa.	FA
Hobbs, Ellis	CB	5-9	188	5/16/83	Iowa State	DeSoto, Texas	D3a
Jacobs, Joel (1)	TE	6-3	250	10/28/80	Nebraska-Kearney	Mullen, Neb.	FA
Kaczur, Nick	T	6-4	319	7/28/79	Toledo	Brantford, Ontario, Canada	D3b
Kopp, Rhett (1)	P	5-10	167	5/14/77	Carson-Newman	Athens, Ga.	FA
Krug, Ryan	G	6-4	304	6/7/82	Connecticut	Pine Beach, N.J.	FA
Lorenz, Mike	T	6-5	315	8/26/81	Wisconsin	Manitowoc, Wis.	FA
Mankins, Logan	T/G	6-4	307	3/10/82	Fresno State	Catheys Valley, Calif.	D1
McGrew, Michael	WR	6-2	201	5/17/82	Virginia	Birmingham, Ala.	FA
McNeil, DeMarco (1)	DT/DE	6-1	301	12/15/79	Auburn	Eight Mile, Ala.	FA
Sanders, James	S	5-10	207	11/11/83	Fresno State	Porterville, Calif.	D4
Steen, Grant (1)	LB	6-2	240	10/22/80	Iowa	Emmetsburg, Iowa	FA
Stokes, Andy	TE	6-5	245	6/2/81	William Penn	St. George, Utah	D7b
Thomas, Santonio	DT/DE	6-4	308	7/2/81	Miami	Belle Glade, Fla.	FA
Torrey, Andre	LB	6-4	245	1/28/82	Arizona	Alameda, Calif.	FA
Ventrone, Raymond	S	5-10	200	10/21/82	Villanova	Pittsburgh, Pa.	FA
Wright, Mike	DT/DE	6-4	295	3/1/82	Cincinnati	Cincinnati, Ohio	FA

The term NFL Rookie is defined as a player who is in his first season of professional football and has not been on the roster of another professional football team for any regular-season or postseason games. A Rookie is designated by an "R" on NFL rosters. Players who have been active in another professional football league or players who have NFL experience, including either preseason training camp or being on an Active List or Inactive List, or on Reserve/Injured or Reserve/Physically Unable to Perform for fewer than six regular-season games, are termed NFL First-Year Players. An NFL First-Year Player is designated by a "1" on NFL rosters. Thereafter, a player is credited with an additional year of experience for each season in which he accumulates six games on the Active List or Inactive List, or on Reserve/Injured or Reserve/Physically Unable to Perform.

Log on to www.patriots.com for an up-to-date roster.

COACHING STAFF
Head Coach,
Bill Belichick

Pro Career: Bill Belichick is in his 31st season as an NFL coach and is the only head coach in league history to win three Super Bowl championships in a four-year span. Hired by Patriots owner Robert Kraft on Jan. 27, 2000, Belichick is in his sixth season as Patriots head coach and last season moved ahead of Vince Lombardi to claim the best postseason record in NFL history (10-1). He is the winningest head coach in the league over the last four seasons, a period during which his teams have delivered three Super Bowl championships. He is the Patriots' all-time leader in victories (62) and winning percentage (.697). Since 2001, Belichick has directed the Patriots to a 57-16 (.781) record—the most successful run in franchise history—including a perfect 9-0 postseason mark. Since 1986, Belichick's contributions as an assistant coach and as a head coach have led to five Super Bowl titles, six conference championships and eight division titles. Over the last two seasons, Belichick has directed the Patriots through the most prosperous two-year period in NFL history, netting back-to-back Super Bowl victories and consecutive 17-2 campaigns. The team's 2003-04 total of 34 victories marked the highest two-year win total in the NFL's 85-year history, and a record winning streak of 21 consecutive games spanned the two seasons. The 2004 season saw the Patriots tie the best regular-season record by a defending Super Bowl champion (14-2), as Belichick joined Mike Ditka as the only head coaches in NFL history to enjoy back-to-back seasons of 14 or more regular-season wins. New England capped off the 2004 season with a victory over the Philadelphia Eagles in Super Bowl XXXIX. In 2003, Belichick led the Patriots to a 17-2 mark that culminated in a victory over the Carolina Panthers in Super Bowl XXXVIII. That season, the Patriots became the first team in 31 years and just the second club ever to win 15 consecutive games en route to the championship. Only the 1972 Miami Dolphins won more consecutive games in a single season. By 2001, just his second season at the helm in New England, he had reversed the course of the team and returned it to NFL prominence. The Patriots closed out the 2001 season by winning nine consecutive games, including a victory in Super Bowl XXXVI against the St. Louis Rams to claim the first league championship in franchise history. Now entering his 31st season as an NFL coach, Belichick has spent more seasons in the league than any other NFL head coach and is one of just two coaches in league history (George Seifert) to win multiple Super Bowls as a head coach and as an assistant coach. He launched

his career in 1975 as a special assistant with the Baltimore Colts, then became an assistant special teams coach with Detroit (1976-77) and Denver (1978). In 1979, he joined the New York Giants and contributed to Super Bowl championships with the team in 1986 and 1990 as the team's defensive coordinator. Following Super Bowl XXV, Belichick was named head coach of the Cleveland Browns in 1991, becoming the youngest head coach in the NFL at age 37. By 1994, Belichick brought the Browns back to the playoffs, finishing 11-5 and advancing to the second round of the playoffs, while allowing a league-low 204 total points. In 1996, Belichick joined New England and was a key contributor to the team's rebound from a 6-10 season in 1995 to an 11-5 season and the team's first division title in 10 years en route to Super Bowl XXXI against Green Bay. Belichick then spent three seasons with the New York Jets from 1997 to 1999, helping New York improve from a 1-15 season in 1996 to an appearance in the AFC Championship Game in 1998. Career record: 99-72.

Background: Belichick was a center/tight end at Wesleyan 1971-74.

Personal: Born April 16, 1952, Nashville. Bill and his wife, Debby, have three children—Amanda, Stephen, and Brian.

ASSISTANT COACHES

Joel Collier, asst. secondary; born December 25, 1963, Buffalo. Linebacker Northern Colorado 1984-87. No pro playing experience. College coach: Syracuse 1988-89. Pro coach: Tampa Bay Buccaneers 1990, New England Patriots 1991-93, Miami Dolphins 1994-2004, rejoined Patriots in 2005.

Brian Daboll, wide receivers; born Welland, Ontario. Safety Rochester 1994-96. No pro playing experience. College coach: William & Mary 1997, Michigan State 1998-99. Pro coach: Joined Patriots in 2000.

Ivan Fears, running backs; born November 15, 1954, Portsmouth, Va. Running back William & Mary 1973-75. No pro playing experience. College coach: William & Mary 1977-1980, Syracuse 1981-1990. Pro coach: New England Patriots 1991-92, Chicago Bears 1993-98, rejoined Patriots in 1999.

Pepper Johnson, defensive line; born July 29, 1964, Detroit. Linebacker Ohio State 1982-85. Pro linebacker New York Giants 1986-1992, Cleveland Browns 1993-95, Detroit Lions 1996, New York Jets 1997-98. Pro coach: Joined Patriots in 2001.

Eric Mangini, defensive coordinator; born January 10, 1971, Hartford, Conn. Nose tackle Wesleyan (Conn.) 1989-1990, 1992-93. No pro playing experience. Pro coach: Cleveland Browns 1995, Baltimore Ravens 1996, New York Jets 1997-99, joined Patriots in 2000.

Pete Mangurian, tight ends; born June

17, 1955, Los Angeles. Defensive lineman Louisiana State 1975-78. No pro playing experience. College coach: Southern Methodist 1979-1980, New Mexico State 1981, Stanford 1982-83, Louisiana State 1984-87, Cornell 1998-2000 (head coach). Pro coach: Denver Broncos 1988-1992, New York Giants 1993-96, Atlanta Falcons 1997, 2001-03, joined Patriots in 2005.

Josh McDainels, quarterbacks; born April 22, 1976, Canton, Ohio. Wide receiver John Carroll 1995-98. No pro playing experience. College coach: Michigan State 1999-2000. Pro coach: Joined Patriots in 2001.

Harold Nash, asst. strength and conditioning; born May 5, 1970, New Orleans. Defensive back Louisiana-Lafayette 1988-1993. Pro defensive back Shreveport Pirates (CFL) 1994-95, Montreal Alouettes (CFL) 1996-99, Winnipeg Blue Bombers (CFL) 1999-2003, Edmonton Eskimos (CFL) 2004. Pro coach: Joined Patriots in 2005.

Matt Patricia, asst. offensive line; born Sept. 13, 1974. Center-guard Rensselaer 1992-96. No pro playing experience. College coach: Rensselaer 1996, Amherst 1999-2000, Syracuse 2001-03. Pro coach: Joined Patriots in 2004.

Dean Pees, linebackers; born September 4, 1949, Dunkirk, Ohio. Attended Bowling Green. No college or pro playing experience. College coach: Findlay 1979-1982, Miami (Ohio) 1983-86, Navy 1987-89, Toledo 1990-93, Notre Dame 1994, Michigan State 1995-97, Kent State 1998-2003. Pro coach: Joined Patriots in 2004.

Dante Scarnecchia, asst. head coach-offensive line; born February 15, 1948, Los Angeles. Center-guard California Western (now U.S. International) 1968-1970. No pro playing experience. College coach: California Western 1970-72, Iowa State 1973-74, Southern Methodist 1975-76, 1980-81, Pacific 1977-78, Northern Arizona 1979. Pro coach: New England Patriots 1982-88, Indianapolis Colts 1989-1990, rejoined Patriots in 1991.

Brad Seely, special teams; born September 6, 1956, Vinton, Iowa. Tackle-guard South Dakota State 1974-77. No pro playing experience. College coach: Colorado State 1980, Southern Methodist 1981, North Carolina State 1982, Pacific 1983, Oklahoma State 1984-88. Pro coach: Indianapolis Colts 1989-1993, New York Jets 1994, Carolina Panthers 1995-98, joined Patriots in 1999.

Mike Woicik, strength and conditioning; born September 26, 1956, Baltimore. Attended Boston College. No college or pro playing experience. College coach: Springfield College 1978-79, Syracuse 1980-89. Pro coach: Dallas Cowboys 1990-96, New Orleans Saints 1997-99, joined Patriots in 2000.

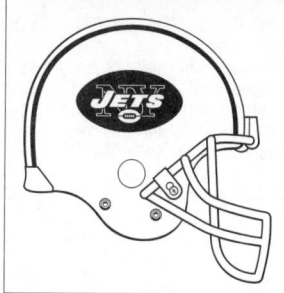

American Football Conference
East Division
Team Colors: Green and White
1000 Fulton Avenue
Hempstead, New York 11550
Telephone: (516) 560-8100

2005 SCHEDULE
PRESEASON
Aug. 12	**Detroit**	7:00
Aug. 19	**Minnesota**	8:00
Aug. 26	at New York Giants	8:00
Sept. 1	at Philadelphia	7:30

REGULAR SEASON
Sept. 11	at Kansas City	12:00
Sept. 18	**Miami**	4:15
Sept. 25	**Jacksonville**	1:00
Oct. 2	at Baltimore	4:05
Oct. 9	**Tampa Bay**	1:00
Oct. 16	at Buffalo	4:15
Oct. 24	at Atlanta (Mon.)	9:00
Oct. 30	Open Date	
Nov. 6	**San Diego**	1:00
Nov. 13	at Carolina	4:05
Nov. 20	at Denver	2:15
Nov. 27	**New Orleans**	8:30
Dec. 4	at New England	4:15
Dec. 11	**Oakland**	1:00
Dec. 18	at Miami	1:00
Dec. 26	**New England** (Mon.)	9:00
Jan. 1	**Buffalo**	1:00

Stadium: Meadowlands
(opened in 1976)
• **Capacity:** 79,466
East Rutherford, New Jersey
07073
Playing Surface: FieldTurf
Training Camp: 1000 Fulton Avenue
Hempstead, New York
11550

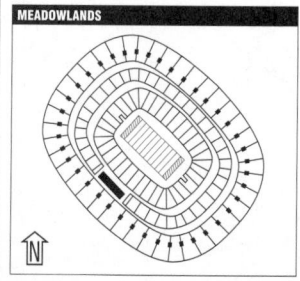

MEADOWLANDS

CLUB OFFICIALS
Chairman and CEO:
  Robert Wood Johnson IV
President: Jay Cross
Executive Vice President/General
  Manager: Terry Bradway
Senior V.P., Football Operations/Asst. GM:
  Mike Tannenbaum
Senior V.P., Stadium Development:
  Bill Senn
Senior V.P., Sales and Marketing:
  Lee Stacey
V.P., Public Relations: Ron Colangelo
V.P., Finance: Michael Gerstle
V.P., Strategic Planning: Matt Higgins
V.P., Design & Construction: Bob Jordan
V.P., Operations: Michael Kensil
V.P., Business Operations: Robert Parente
V.P., Corporate Sales & Marketing:
  Marc Riccio
V.P., Development: Thad Sheely
V.P., Player Development: Kevin Winston
Director, Pro Personnel: JoJo Wooden
Senior Director, Football Administration:
  Dawn Aponte
Pro Personnel Assistant: Tom Frawley
Pro Personnel Assistant/Salary Cap
  Analyst: Megan Rogers
Senior Director, College Scouting:
  Jesse Kaye
National Scout: Joey Clinkscales
Coordinator, College Scouting:
  John Griffin
Personnel Scouts: Jeff Bauer,
  Matt Bazirgan, Joe Bommarito,
  Ron Brockington, Jim Cochran,
  Michael Davis, Sid Hall,
  Brendan Prophett, Gary Smith
Scouting Consultant: Dick Haley
Assistant, College Scouting:
  Kirwan Watson
College Scouting Assistant: Kerri Stork
Head Athletic Trainer/Senior Director of
  Sports Medicine and Rehabilitation:
  Dave Price
Assistant Athletic Trainer: John Mellody,
  Jimmy Ntelekos
Controller: Mike Minarczyk
Director, Public & Media Relations:
  Douglas Miller
Senior Director IT/Video: Tom Murphy
Manager, Community Relations:
  Jesse Linder
Senior Director of Security: Steve Yarnell
Equipment Manager: Clay Hampton
Assistant Equipment Manager:
  Gus Granneman
Director, Internet & Publications:
  Ken Ilchuk
Director, Ticket Operations:
  John Buschhorn

COACHING HISTORY
New York Titans 1960-62
(312-374-8)
Records include postseason games
1960-61	Sammy Baugh	14-14-0
1962	Clyde (Bulldog) Turner	5-9-0
1963-1973	Weeb Ewbank	73-78-6
1974-75	Charley Winner*	9-14-0
1975	Ken Shipp	1-4-0
1976	Lou Holtz**	3-10-0
1976	Mike Holovak	0-1-0
1977-1982	Walt Michaels	41-49-1
1983-89	Joe Walton	54-59-1
1990-93	Bruce Coslet	26-39-0
1994	Pete Carroll	6-10-0
1995-96	Rich Kotite	4-28-0
1997-99	Bill Parcells	30-20-0
2000	Al Groh	9-7-0
2001-04	Herman Edwards	37-32-0

*Released after nine games in 1975
**Resigned after 13 games in 1976

ATTENDANCE
Home 622,985   Away 505,467
Total 1,128,452
Single-game home record,
  78,920 (11/10/02)
Single-season home record,
  628,773 (2002)

2005 DRAFT CHOICES
Round	Name	Pos.	College
2	Mike Nugent	K	Ohio State
	Justin Miller	DB	Clemson
3	Sione Pouha	DT	Utah
4	Kerry Rhodes	DB	Louisville
5	Andre Maddox	DB	North Carolina St.
6	Cedric Houston	RB	Tennessee
	Joel Dreessen	TE	Colorado State
7	Harry Williams	WR	Tuskegee

2004 TEAM RECORD

PRESEASON (3-1)

Date	Result	Opponent
8/13	L 13-23	at New Orleans
8/21	W 31-7	at Indianapolis
8/27	W 17-10	N.Y. Giants
9/3	W 28-27	Philadelphia

REGULAR SEASON (10-6)

Date	Result	Opponent	Att.
9/12	W 31-24	Cincinnati	77,230
9/19	W 34-28	at San Diego	57,310
10/3	W 17-9	at Miami	73,157
10/10	W 16-14	Buffalo	77,976
10/17	W 22-14	San Francisco	78,189
10/24	L 7-13	at New England	68,756
11/1	W 41-14	Miami	78,216
11/7	L 17-22	at Buffalo	72,574
11/14	L 17-20	Baltimore (OT)	77,826
11/21	W 10-7	at Cleveland	72,547
11/28	W 13-3	at Arizona	35,820
12/5	W 29-7	Houston	77,875
12/12	L 6-17	at Pittsburgh	63,581
12/19	W 37-14	Seattle	77,894
12/26	L 7-23	New England	77,975
1/2	L 29-32	at St. Louis (OT)	65,877

POSTSEASON (1-1)

Date	Result	Opponent	
1/8	W 20-17	at San Diego (OT)	67,536
1/15	L 17-20	at Pittsburgh (OT)	64,915

(OT) Overtime

SCORE BY PERIODS

Jets	51	94	95	93	0 —	333
Opponents	34	104	34	83	6 —	261

2004 TEAM STATISTICS

	Jets	Opp.
Total First Downs	313	282
Rushing	135	87
Passing	163	169
Penalty	15	26
3rd Down: Made/Att	91/214	79/208
3rd Down Pct.	42.5	38.0
4th Down: Made/Att	4/8	5/13
4th Down Pct.	50.0	38.5
Possession Avg.	31:51	28:09
Total Net Yards	5438	4878
Avg. Per Game	339.9	304.9
Total Plays	996	966
Avg. Per Play	5.5	5.0
Net Yards Rushing	2388	1566
Avg. Per Game	149.3	97.9
Total Rushes	527	432
Net Yards Passing	3050	3312
Avg. Per Game	190.6	207.0
Sacked/Yards Lost	31/181	37/220
Gross Yards	3231	3532
Att./Completions	438/282	497/289
Completion Pct.	64.4	58.1
Had Intercepted	11	19
Punts/Average	80/38.2	89/40.1
Net Punting Avg.	80/33.5	89/34.8
Penalties/Yards	91/693	86/720
Fumbles/Ball Lost	19/5	29/14
Touchdowns	38	30
Rushing	15	8
Passing	19	21
Returns	4	1

2004 INDIVIDUAL STATISTICS

PASSING

	Att.	Comp.	Yds.	Pct.	TD	Int.	Tkld.	Rate
Pennington	370	242	2,673	65.4	16	9	18/103	91.0
Q. Carter	58	35	498	60.3	3	1	12/70	98.2
Bollinger	9	5	60	55.6	0	0	1/8	76.2
Jordan	1	0	0	0.0	0	1	0/0	0.0
Jets	438	282	3,231	64.4	19	11	31/181	90.5
Opponents	497	289	3,532	58.1	21	19	37/220	78.3

SCORING

	TD R	TD P	TD Rt	PAT	FG	Saf	PTS
Brien	0	0	0	33/34	24/29	0	105
Martin	12	2	0	0/0	0/0	0	84
Moss	0	5	0	0/0	0/0	0	30
Baker	0	4	0	0/0	0/0	0	24
McCareins	0	4	0	0/0	0/0	0	24
D. Abraham	0	0	2	0/0	0/0	0	12
Jordan	2	0	0	0/0	0/0	0	12
Becht	0	1	0	0/0	0/0	0	6
J. Carter	0	1	0	0/0	0/0	0	6
Chrebet	0	1	0	0/0	0/0	0	6
Cotchery	0	0	1	0/0	0/0	0	6
Pennington	1	0	0	0/0	0/0	0	6
Sowell	0	1	0	0/0	0/0	0	6
Vilma	0	0	1	0/0	0/0	0	6
Jets	15	19	4	33/34	24/29	0	333
Opponents	8	21	1	29/29	16/19	1	261

2-Pt. Conversions: None.
Jets 0-4, Opponents 1-1.

RUSHING

	No.	Yds	Avg	LG	TD
Martin	371	1,697	4.6	25t	12
Jordan	93	479	5.2	33	2
Pennington	34	126	3.7	16	1
Sowell	2	28	14.0	19	0
Askew	6	23	3.8	14	0
Q. Carter	12	20	1.7	9	0
Moss	6	18	3.0	12	0
Bollinger	1	2	2.0	2	0
McCareins	2	-5	-2.5	-2	0
Jets	527	2,388	4.5	33	15
Opponents	432	1,566	3.6	53	8

RECEIVING

	No.	Yds	Avg	LG	TD
McCareins	56	770	13.8	43	4
Moss	45	838	18.6	69t	5
Sowell	45	342	7.6	34	1
Martin	41	245	6.0	22	2
Chrebet	31	397	12.8	35t	1
Baker	18	182	10.1	23	4
Jordan	15	112	7.5	25	0
Becht	13	100	7.7	19	1
J. Carter	10	173	17.3	46t	1
Cotchery	6	60	10.0	18	0
Askew	2	12	6.0	11	0
Jets	282	3,231	11.5	69t	19
Opponents	289	3,532	12.2	65	21

INTERCEPTIONS

	No.	Yds	Avg	LG	TD
Coleman	4	43	10.8	37	0
Vilma	3	58	19.3	38t	1
Buckley	3	30	10.0	18	0
D. Abraham	2	66	33.0	66t	1
Barrett	2	14	7.0	14	0
McGraw	2	0	0.0	0	0
Tongue	1	23	23.0	23	0
Barton	1	7	7.0	7	0
Hobson	1	2	2.0	2	0
Jets	19	243	12.8	66t	2
Opponents	11	332	30.2	78	0

PUNTING

	No.	Yds.	Avg.	In 20	LG
Gowin	80	3,057	38.2	22	58
Jets	80	3,057	38.2	22	58
Opponents	89	3,571	40.1	26	64

PUNT RETURNS

	Ret	FC	Yds	Avg	LG	TD
Moss	27	7	225	8.3	46	0
McCareins	14	6	88	6.3	26	0
Jets	41	13	313	7.6	46	0
Opponents	34	14	221	6.5	25	0

KICKOFF RETURNS

	No.	Yds	Avg	LG	TD
J. Carter	17	374	22.0	40	0
Jordan	14	284	20.3	40	0
Cotchery	13	362	27.8	94t	1
Askew	2	18	9.0	13	0
Jets	46	1,038	22.6	94t	1
Opponents	72	1,557	21.6	87t	1

FIELD GOALS

	1-19	20-29	30-39	40-49	50+
Brien	0/0	9/10	4/6	10/11	1/2
Jets	0/0	9/10	4/6	10/11	1/2
Opponents	0/0	9/9	5/6	2/3	0/1

SACKS

	No.
Ellis	11.0
J. Abraham	9.5
Ferguson	3.5
Robertson	3.0
Barton	2.5
Coleman	2.0
Reed	2.0
Vilma	2.0
Thomas	1.5
Jets	37.0
Opponents	31.0

RECORD HOLDERS
INDIVIDUAL RECORDS—CAREER

Category	Name	Performance
Rushing (Yds.)	Curtis Martin, 1998-2004	8,473
Passing (Yds.)	Joe Namath, 1965-1976	27,057
Passing (TDs)	Joe Namath, 1965-1976	170
Receiving (No.)	Don Maynard, 1960-1972	627
Receiving (Yds.)	Don Maynard, 1960-1972	11,732
Interceptions	Bill Baird, 1963-69	34
Punting (Avg.)	Tom Tupa, 1999-2001	43.1
Punt Return (Avg.)	Dick Christy, 1961-63	16.2
Kickoff Return (Avg.)	Chad Morton, 2001-02	25.0
Field Goals	Pat Leahy, 1974-1991	304
Touchdowns (Tot.)	Don Maynard, 1960-1972	88
Points	Pat Leahy, 1974-1991	1,470

INDIVIDUAL RECORDS—SINGLE SEASON

Category	Name	Performance
Rushing (Yds.)	Curtis Martin, 2004	1,697
Passing (Yds.)	Joe Namath, 1967	4,007
Passing (TDs)	Vinny Testaverde, 1998	29
Receiving (No.)	Al Toon, 1988	93
Receiving (Yds.)	Don Maynard, 1967	1,434
Interceptions	Dainard Paulson, 1964	12
Punting (Avg.)	Curley Johnson, 1965	45.3
Punt Return (Avg.)	Dick Christy, 1961	21.3
Kickoff Return (Avg.)	Bobby Humphery, 1984	30.7
Field Goals	Jim Turner, 1968	34
Touchdowns (Tot.)	Art Powell, 1960	14
	Don Maynard, 1965	14
	Emerson Boozer, 1972	14
	Curtis Martin, 2004	14
Points	Jim Turner, 1968	145

INDIVIDUAL RECORDS—SINGLE GAME

Category	Name	Performance
Rushing (Yds.)	Curtis Martin, 12-3-00	203
Passing (Yds.)	Joe Namath, 9-24-72	496
Passing (TDs)	Joe Namath, 9-24-72	6
Receiving (No.)	Clark Gaines, 9-21-80	17
Receiving (Yds.)	Don Maynard, 11-17-68	228
Interceptions	Many times	3
	Last time by Marcus Coleman, 10-23-00	
Field Goals	Jim Turner, 11-3-68	6
	Bobby Howfield, 12-3-72	6
Touchdowns (Tot.)	Wesley Walker, 9-21-86	4
Points	Wesley Walker, 9-21-86	24

2005 VETERAN ROSTER

No.	Name	Pos.	Ht.	Wt.	Birthdate	NFL Exp.	College	Hometown	How Acq.	'04 Games/ Starts
29	Abraham, Donnie	CB	5-10	192	10/8/73	10	East Tennessee State	Orangeburg, S.C.	UFA(TB)-'02	16/16
94	Abraham, John	WE	6-4	256	5/6/78	6	South Carolina	Lamar, S.C.	D1b-'00	12/12
35	Askew, B.J.	FB	6-3	233	8/19/80	3	Michigan	Cincinnati, Ohio	D3-'03	16/0
86	Baker, Chris	TE	6-3	258	11/18/79	4	Michigan State	Queens, N.Y.	D3-'02	16/0
36	Barrett, David	CB	5-10	195	12/22/77	6	Arkansas	Osceola, Ark.	UFA(Ariz)-'04	16/16
50	Barton, Eric	LB	6-2	245	9/29/77	7	Maryland	Alexandria, Va.	UFA(Oak)-'04	16/16
23	Blaylock, Derrick	RB	5-9	205	8/23/79	5	Stephen F. Austin	Atlanta, Texas	UFA(KC)-'05	12/5*
5	Bollinger, Brooks	QB	6-1	205	11/15/79	3	Wisconsin	Grand Forks, N.D.	D6-'03	1/0
55	Brown, Mark	LB	6-0	238	5/19/80	2	Auburn	Germantown, Tenn.	FA-'03	11/6
84	Carter, Jonathan	WR	6-0	180	3/20/79	3	Troy State	Lineville, Ala.	W(NYG)-'02	13/1
77	Cavka, Marko	T	6-7	294	4/4/81	2	Sacramento State	Cypress, Calif.	D6-'04	0*
45	Celestin, Oliver	S	6-0	207	2/25/81	2	Texas Southern	New Orleans, La.	FA-'04	8/0
80	Chrebet, Wayne	WR	5-10	188	8/14/73	11	Hofstra	Garfield, N.J.	FA-'95	16/1
26	Coleman, Erik	S	5-10	200	5/6/82	2	Washington State	Spokane, Wash.	D5-'04	16/16
87	t-Coles, Laveranues	WR	5-11	193	12/29/77	6	Florida State	Jacksonville, Fla.	T(Wash)-'05	16/16*
89	Cotchery, Jerricho	WR	6-0	207	6/16/82	2	North Carolina State	Birmingham, Ala.	D4a-'04	12/0
22	Davison, Andrew	CB	5-11	185	1/22/77	3	Kansas	Detroit, Mich.	FA-'05	0*
85	Dearth, James	TE/LS	6-4	270	1/22/76	5	Tarleton State	Scurry, Texas	FA-'01	16/0
92	Ellis, Shaun	DE	6-5	285	6/24/77	6	Tennessee	Anderson, S.C.	D1a-'00	15/15
69	Fabini, Jason	T	6-7	304	8/25/74	8	Cincinnati	Ft. Wayne, Ind.	D4-'98	16/16
9	Fiedler, Jay	QB	6-2	225	12/29/71	10	Dartmouth	Oceanside, N.Y.	UFA(Mia)-'05	8/7*
53	Gardner, Barry	LB	6-1	245	12/13/76	7	Northwestern	Harvey, Ill.	UFA(Cle)-'05	14/5*
78	Goodwin, Jonathan	G	6-3	318	12/2/78	4	Michigan	Columbia, S.C.	D5-'02	15/4
98	Harper, Alan	DT	6-1	285	9/6/79	4	Fresno State	Fontana, Calif.	FA-'03	11/0
54	Hobson, Victor	LB	6-0	252	2/3/80	3	Michigan	Mt. Laurel, N.J.	D2-'03	12/11
97	Johnson, Trevor	WE	6-4	260	2/26/81	2	Nebraska	Lincoln, Neb.	D7b-'04	16/0
88	t-Jolley, Doug	TE	6-4	250	1/2/79	4	Brigham Young	Sandy, Utah	T(Oak)-'05	16/13*
79	Jones, Adrian	T	6-4	296	6/10/81	2	Kansas	Dallas, Texas	D4b-'04	12/0
30	Joyce, Delvin	RB	5-7	190	9/21/78	2	James Madison	Martinsville, Va.	FA-'05	0*
66	Kendall, Pete	G	6-5	280	7/9/73	10	Boston College	Weymouth, Mass.	FA-'04	15/15
4	Knorr, Micah	P	6-2	208	1/9/75	6	Utah State	Anaheim, Calif.	FA-'05	12/0*
70	Legree, Lance	DE/DT	6-1	300	12/22/77	5	Notre Dame	St. Stephens, S.C.	UFA(NYG)-'05	15/7*
28	Martin, Curtis	RB	5-11	210	5/1/73	11	Pittsburgh	Pittsburgh, Pa.	RFA(NE)-'98	16/16
68	Mawae, Kevin	C	6-4	289	1/23/71	12	Louisiana State	Leesville, La.	UFA(Sea)-'98	16/16
81	McCareins, Justin	WR	6-2	215	12/11/78	5	Northern Illinois	Naperville, Ill.	T(Tenn)-'04	16/16
57	McClover, Darrell	LB	6-2	226	8/25/81	2	Miami	Ft. Lauderdale, Fla.	D7a-'04	16/0
38	McGraw, Jon	S	6-3	206	4/2/79	4	Kansas State	Manhattan, Kan.	D2-'02	12/0
24	Mickens, Ray	CB	5-8	180	1/4/73	10	Texas A&M	El Paso, Texas	D3-96	0*
65	Moore, Brandon	G	6-3	295	6/3/80	3	Illinois	Gary, Ind.	FA-'03	13/13
20	Pagel, Derek	S	6-1	208	10/24/79	3	Iowa	Plainfield, Iowa	D5a-'03	5/0
10	Pennington, Chad	QB	6-3	225	6/26/76	6	Marshall	Knoxville, Tenn.	D1c-'00	13/13
93	Reed, James	DT	6-0	286	2/3/77	5	Iowa State	Saginaw, Mich.	D7a-'01	16/0
63	Robertson, Dewayne	DT	6-1	317	10/16/81	3	Kentucky	Memphis, Tenn.	D1-'03	16/16
33	Sowell, Jerald	FB	6-0	237	1/21/74	9	Tulane	Baker, La.	W(GB)-'97	16/16
21	Strait, Derrick	CB	5-11	189	8/27/80	2	Oklahoma	Austin, Texas	D3-'04	5/0
99	Thomas, Bryan	DE	6-4	266	6/7/79	4	Alabama-Birmingham	Birmingham, Ala.	D1-'02	14/5
25	Tongue, Reggie	S	6-0	204	4/11/73	10	Oregon State	Baltimore, Md.	UFA(Sea)-'04	16/16
51	Vilma, Jonathan	LB	6-1	230	4/16/82	2	Miami	South Miami, Fla.	D1-'04	16/14
42	Washington, Rashad	S	6-1	217	3/15/80	2	Kansas State	Wichita, Kan.	D7d-'04	7/0
52	Wright, Kenyatta	LB	6-0	240	2/19/78	5	Oklahoma State	Vian, Okla.	FA-'03	16/0
64	Yovanovits, Dave	G	6-3	294	3/6/81	3	Temple	Stanhope, N.J.	D7-'03	4/0

* Blaylock played 12 games with Kansas City in '04; Cavka inactive for 16 games; Coles played 16 games with Washington; Davison last active with Dallas in '03; Fiedler played 8 games with Miami; Gardner played 14 games with Cleveland; Jolley played 16 games with Oakland; Joyce last active with N.Y. Giants in '03; Knorr played 12 games with Denver; Legree played 15 games with N.Y. Giants in '04; Mickens missed '04 season because of injury.

t- Jets traded for Coles (Wash), Jolley (Oak).

Traded—LB Sam Cowart (9 games in '04) to Minnesota, WR Santana Moss (15) to Washington.

Retired—Josh Evans, 10-year defensive tackle, 1 game in '04.

Players lost through free agency (5): TE Anthony Becht (TB, 16 games in '04), DT Jason Ferguson (Dall; 16), P Toby Gowin (Atl; 16), RB LaMont Jordan (Oak; 16), T Kareem McKenzie (NYG; 16).

Also played for Jets in '04—K Doug Brien (16 games), CB Roderick Bryant (12), CB Terrell Buckley (16), QB Quincy Carter (7), LB Jason Glenn (10).

2005 FIRST-YEAR ROSTER

Name	Pos.	Ht.	Wt.	Birthdate	College	Hometown	How Acq.
Beitia, Xavier	K	5-10	198	11/23/82	Florida State	Tampa, Fla.	FA
Chila, Matthew (1)	TE	6-3	250	9/10/81	Villanova	Somers Point, N.J.	FA
Davis, Josh (1)	RB	5-10	200	10/11/80	Nebraska	Loveland, Colo.	FA-'04
Davis, Mondoe	LB	6-1	225	3/19/82	Delaware	Newport News, Va.	FA
Dreessen, Joel	TE/LS	6-4	260	7/26/82	Colorado State	Fort Morgan, Colo.	D6b
Eakin, Kevin (1)	QB	6-1	225	6/22/81	Fordham	St. Paul, Minn.	FA
Evans, Joey (1)	DE	6-4	279	8/22/79	North Carolina	Fayetteville, N.C.	FA-'04
Gessner, Chas (1)	WR	6-4	215	8/17/81	Brown	Hyattsville, Md.	FA-'04
Graham, Benjamin	P	6-4	220	11/2/73	Deakin (Australia)	Geelong, Victoria, Australia	FA
Haley, Dennis	LB	6-1	247	2/18/82	Virginia	Roanoke, Va.	FA
Houston, Cedric	RB	6-0	220	6/28/82	Tennessee	Clarendon, Ark.	D6a
Jackson, Eddie	WR	6-4	225	3/21/81	West Virginia	Columbus, Ohio	FA
Johnson, Darrien	DB	5-11	215	5/3/80	Iowa	Chicago, Ill.	FA
Kearney, Carl	WR	6-1	213	2/16/81	Georgia Southern	Griffin, Ga.	FA-'04
King, Michael	G	6-3	298	6/15/82	Northwestern State	Natchitoches, La.	FA
Lockhart, Radell (1)	DL	6-3	275	5/11/79	Catawba College	Charlotte, N.C.	FA
Maddox, Andre	S	6-1	200	10/8/82	North Carolina State	Miami, Fla.	D5
McGill, Tim (1)	DT	6-2	330	6/24/79	Illinois	Chicago, Ill.	FA-'04
Miller, Justin	CB	5-10	202	2/14/84	Clemson	Owensboro, Ky.	D2b
Missant, Charles	C	6-3	295	4/23/81	Western Michigan	Grosse Pointe, Mich.	FA
Myers, Ryan (1)	LB	6-2	245	2/27/80	Akron	Wellington, Ohio	FA
Nerys, Jason (1)	G	6-3	305	6/16/81	Delaware	Waldwick, N.J.	FA-'04
Nugent, Mike	K	5-9	182	3/2/82	Ohio State	Centerville, Ohio	D2a
Nwabuisi, Austine	FB	6-1	235	8/23/82	Kansas	Houston, Texas	FA
Pickens, John	LB	6-2	240	2/13/83	Northwestern	Franklin Lakes, N.J.	FA
Pouha, Sione	DT	6-3	325	2/3/79	Utah	Salt Lake City, Utah	D3
Ralph, Brock (1)	WR	6-2	185	7/16/80	Wyoming	Raymond, Alberta, Canada	FA-'04
Rhodes, Kerry	S	6-3	210	8/2/82	Louisville	Bessemer, Ala.	D4
Snell, Isaac	T	6-6	288	11/4/81	North Dakota State	Piperstone, Minn.	FA
Stubbs, Terrence (1)	WR	5-11	190	3/25/80	Temple	Chesapeake, Va.	FA
Tellis, Henry	T	6-6	308	12/15/80	Troy State	Montgomery, Ala.	FA
Thomas, Charles (1)	T	6-5	315	11/26/78	Troy State	Nashville, Tenn.	FA
Williams, Harry, Jr.	WR	6-3	185	8/10/82	Tuskegee	Birmingham, Ala.	D7-'04
Witherspoon, Jovan	WR	6-3	210	8/13/81	Central Michigan	Fort Wayne, Ind.	FA

The term NFL Rookie is defined as a player who is in his first season of professional football and has not been on the roster of another professional football team for any regular-season or postseason games. A Rookie is designated by an "R" on NFL rosters. Players who have been active in another professional football league or players who have NFL experience, including either preseason training camp or being on an Active List or Inactive List, or on Reserve/Injured or Reserve/Physically Unable to Perform for fewer than six regular-season games, are termed NFL First-Year Players. An NFL First-Year Player is designated by a "1" on NFL rosters. Thereafter, a player is credited with an additional year of experience for each season in which he accumulates six games on the Active List or Inactive List, or on Reserve/Injured or Reserve/Physically Unable to Perform.

Log on to www.newyorkjets.com for an up-to-date roster.

COACHING STAFF

Head Coach,
Herman Edwards

Pro Career: On January 28, 2001, Edwards was named the Jets' thirteenth full-time head coach. Edwards previously served as the assistant head coach-defensive backs coach for Tampa Bay (1996-2000). Last season, Edwards guided the Jets to the postseason for the third time in his four seasons at the helm. He is the only coach in Jets history with three trips to the postseason. In 2002, the Jets won the AFC East and posted the biggest postseason victory (41-0) in club history. In 2001, he led the Jets to a 10-6 regular-season mark and became the first head coach in team history to make the playoffs in his first season. Before joining Tampa Bay, Edwards worked for the Kansas City Chiefs for six seasons (1990-95) in several different roles. He began his pro coaching career as a participant of the NFL's Minority Coaching Fellowship program with the Kansas City Chiefs in the summer of 1989. Career record: 37-32.

Background: Played cornerback collegiately for California (1972, 1974), Monterey Peninsula (Calif.) J.C. (1973), and San Diego State (1975-76). Played in NFL for Philadelphia Eagles (1977-1985), Los Angeles Rams (1986), and Atlanta Falcons (1986). He was defensive backs coach at San Jose State (1987-89).

Personal: Born April 27, 1954, Monmouth, N.J. Edwards and his wife Lia have one son, Marcus.

ASSISTANT COACHES

Sal Alosi, asst. director of physical development; born May 11, 1977, Massapequa, N.Y. Linebacker Hofstra 1996-2000. No pro playing experience. College coach: Hofstra 2001. Pro coach: Joined Jets in 2002.

Jeremy Bates, quarterbacks; born August 27, 1976, Manhattan, Kan. Quarterback Tennessee 1995, Rice 1996-99. No pro playing experience. Pro coach: Tampa Bay 2002-04, joined Jets in 2005.

Tim Berbenich, offensive assistant; born December 19, 1979, Huntington, N.Y. Wide receiver Hamilton College 1998-2001. No pro playing experience. Pro coach: Joined Jets in 2003.

Corwin Brown, defensive backs; born April 25, 1970, Chicago. Safety Michigan 1989-1992. Pro safety New England Patriots 1993-96, New York Jets 1997-98, Detroit Lions 1999-2000. College coach: Virginia 2001-03. Pro coach: Joined Jets in 2004.

Dick Curl, asst. to the head coach/running backs; born May 4, 1940, Chester, Pa. Quarterback Richmond 1959-1962. No pro playing experience. College coach: Trenton State 1973-74 (head coach 1974), Rutgers 1975-79, 1982-88, Virginia 1980-81, Boston College 1989-1990. Pro coach: Barcelona Dragons

(NFLEL) 1991-97, Frankfurt Galaxy (NFLEL) 1998-99 (head coach), joined Jets in 2003.

Pep Hamilton, wide receivers; born September 19, 1974, Charlotte. Quarterback Howard 1993-96. No pro playing experience. College coach: Howard 1997-2002. Pro coach: Joined Jets in 2003.

Mike Heimerdinger, offensive coordinator, born October 13, 1952, DeKalb, Ill. Wide receiver Eastern Illinois 1970-74. No pro playing experience. College coach: Florida 1980, Air Force 1981, North Texas State 1982, Florida 1983-87, Cal State-Fullerton 1988, Rice 1989-1993, Duke 1994. Pro coach: Denver Broncos 1995-99, Tennessee Titans 2000-04, joined Jets in 2005.

Donnie Henderson, defensive coordinator; born May 17, 1957, Baltimore. Defensive back Utah State 1978-79. No pro playing experience. College coach: Utah State 1983-88, Idaho 1989-90, California 1992-97, Houston 1998. Pro coach: Baltimore Ravens 1999-2003, joined Jets in 2004.

Denny Marcin, defensive line; born April 24, 1942, Cleveland. Defensive-offensive lineman Miami (Ohio) 1961-64. No pro playing experience. College coach: Miami (Ohio) 1974-77, North Carolina 1978-1987, Illinois 1988-1996. Pro coach: New York Giants 1997-2003, joined Jets in 2004.

Doug Marrone, offensive line; born July 25, 1964, Bronx, N.Y. Offensive lineman Syracuse 1982-86. Pro offensive lineman Miami Dolphins 1987, New Orleans Saints 1989, London Monarchs (NFLE) 1992. College coach: Cortland State 1992, U.S. Coast Guard 1993, Northeastern 1994, Georgia Tech 1995-99, Georgia 2000, Tennessee 2001. Pro coach: Joined Jets in 2002.

Chris Mattura, defensive assistant; born February 2, 1960, New York City. Attended SUNY Regents. No college or pro playing experience. College coach: Hofstra 1985, Fordham 1989-1991, C.W. Post 1992-95. Pro coach: Joined Jets in 2002.

Markus Paul, director of physical development; born April 1, 1966, Orlando, Fla. Safety Syracuse 1984-88. Pro safety Chicago Bears 1989-1993, Tampa Bay Buccaneers 1993. Pro coach: New Orleans Saints 1998-99, New England Patriots 2000-04, joined Jets in 2005.

Bob Sutton, linebackers; born January 28, 1951, Ypsilanti, Mich. Attended Eastern Michigan. No college or pro playing experience. College coach: Michigan 1972-73, Syracuse 1974, Western Michigan 1975-76, 1980-81, Illinois 1977-79, North Carolina State 1982, Army 1983-1999 (head coach 1991-99). Pro coach: Joined Jets in 2000.

Nate Wainwright, asst. coach; born July 28, 1975, Iowa City, Iowa. Attended Iowa.

No college or pro playing experience. Pro coach: Joined Jets in 2001.

Mike Westhoff, asst. head coach/special teams coordinator; born January 10, 1948, Pittsburgh. Center/linebacker Wichita State 1967-69. No pro playing experience. College coach: Indiana 1974-75, Dayton 1976, Indiana State 1977, Northwestern 1978-1980, Texas Christian 1981. Pro coach: Baltimore/Indianapolis Colts 1982-84, Arizona Outlaws (USFL) 1985, Miami Dolphins 1986-2000, joined Jets in 2001.

John Zernhelt, tight ends, born January 4, 1954, Pottsville, Pa. Offensive lineman Maryland 1974-77. No pro playing experience. College coach: Ferrum 1977-1980, Marshall 1981, East Carolina 1982-86, Maryland 1987-1991, Rice 1992-93, Duke 1994-95, South Carolina 1996-98, James Madison 1999-2002, The Citadel 2003-04. Pro coach: Joined Jets in 2005.

American Football Conference
West Division
Team Colors: Silver and Black
1220 Harbor Bay Parkway
Alameda, California 94502
Telephone: (510) 864-5000

2005 SCHEDULE
PRESEASON
Aug. 13 at San Francisco 7:00
Aug. 20 at Houston 7:00
Aug. 26 **Arizona**. 6:30
Sept. 1 **New Orleans**. 6:00

REGULAR SEASON
Sept. 8 at New England (Thu.) . . . 9:00
Sept. 18 **Kansas City** 5:30
Sept. 25 at Philadelphia. 1:00
Oct. 2 **Dallas**. 1:15
Oct. 9 Open Date
Oct. 16 **San Diego** 1:15
Oct. 23 **Buffalo** 1:15
Oct. 30 at Tennessee. 12:00
Nov. 6 at Kansas City. 12:00
Nov. 13 **Denver** 1:05
Nov. 20 at Washington. 1:00
Nov. 27 **Miami**. 1:05
Dec. 4 at San Diego 5:30
Dec. 11 at New York Jets 1:00
Dec. 18 **Cleveland** 1:05
Dec. 24 at Denver (Sat.). 2:15
Dec. 31 **New York Giants** (Sat.) . . . 5:00

Stadium: McAfee Coliseum
    (opened in 1966)
    •**Capacity:** 63,132
    7000 Coliseum Way
    Oakland, CA 94621-1917
Playing Surface: Grass
Training Camp: Napa Valley Marriott
           Napa, California 94558

McAFEE COLISEUM

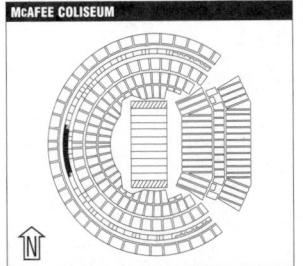

CLUB OFFICIALS
Owner: Al Davis
Chief Executive: Amy Trask
Personnel Executive: Michael Lombardi
Legal: Jeff Birren, Dan Ventrelle
Finance: Marc Badain, Tom Blanda,
  Derek Person, Ed Villanueva
Special Projects: Jim Otto
Senior Executive: John Herrera
Public Relations: Mike Taylor,
  Zac Emmons
Ticket Operations: Peter Eiges
Multi-Cultural Initiatives: Patty Herrera,
  Elena Valenzuela
Internet: Jerry Knaak
Suites: Andrea Stamps, Rachel Venrick
Marketing: Morris Bradshaw,
  Dawn French, Craig Purcell
Community Relations: Scott Fink
Youth Initiatives: Rosie Bone
Raiderettes: Karen Kovac
Trainers: H. Rod Martin, Mark Mayer,
  Scott Touchet
Equipment: Bob Romanski,
  Richard Romanski, Danny Molina
Video Operations: Dave Nash, Jim Otten,
  John Otten

COACHING HISTORY
Oakland 1960-1981
Los Angeles 1982-1994
(415-293-11)
Records include postseason games

1960-61	Eddie Erdelatz*	6-10-0
1961-62	Marty Feldman**	2-15-0
1962	Red Conkright	1-8-0
1963-65	Al Davis	23-16-3
1966-68	John Rauch	35-10-1
1969-1978	John Madden	112-39-7
1979-1987	Tom Flores	91-56-0
1988-89	Mike Shanahan***	8-12-0
1989-1994	Art Shell	56-41-0
1995-96	Mike White	15-17-0
1997	Joe Bugel	4-12-0
1998-2001	Jon Gruden	40-28-0
2002-03	Bill Callahan	17-18-0
2004	Norv Turner	5-11-0

  *Released after two games in 1961
 **Released after five games in 1962
***Released after four games in 1989

ATTENDANCE
Home 391,329   Away 548,634
Total 939,963
Single-game home record,
  62,660 (11/3/02)
Single-season home record,
  471,151 (2002)

2005 DRAFT CHOICES
Round	Name	Pos.	College
1	Fabian Washington	DB	Nebraska
2	Stanford Routt	DB	Houston
3	Andrew Walter	QB	Arizona State
	Kirk Morrison	LB	San Diego State
6	Anttaj Hawthorne	DT	Wisconsin
	Ryan Riddle	LB	California
	Pete McMahon	T	Iowa

2004 TEAM RECORD
PRESEASON (3-1)

Date	Result	Opponent
8/14	W 33-30	at San Francisco
8/21	L 20-21	Dallas
8/28	W 17-16	at Arizona
9/2	W 28-24	St. Louis

REGULAR SEASON (5-11)

Date	Result	Opponent	Att.
9/12	L 21-24	at Pittsburgh	60,147
9/19	W 13-10	Buffalo	53,610
9/26	W 30-20	Tampa Bay	60,874
10/3	L 17-30	at Houston	70,741
10/10	L 14-35	at Indianapolis	57,230
10/17	L 3-31	Denver	62,507
10/24	L 26-31	New Orleans	45,337
10/31	L 14-42	at San Diego	66,210
11/7	W 27-24	at Carolina	73,518
11/21	L 17-23	San Diego	46,905
11/28	W 25-24	at Denver	75,936
12/5	L 27-34	Kansas City	51,292
12/12	L 10-35	at Atlanta	70,616
12/19	W 40-35	Tennessee	44,299
12/25	L 30-31	at Kansas City	77,289
1/2	L 6-13	Jacksonville	41,112

SCORE BY PERIODS

Raiders	51	121	60	88	0 —	320
Opponents	68	155	89	130	0 —	442

2004 TEAM STATISTICS

	Raiders	Opp.
Total First Downs	275	367
Rushing	75	115
Passing	176	210
Penalty	24	42
3rd Down: Made/Att	71/200	101/213
3rd Down Pct.	35.5	47.4
4th Down: Made/Att	7/14	7/15
4th Down Pct.	50.0	46.7
Possession Avg.	26:47	33:13
Total Net Yards	5153	5936
Avg. Per Game	322.1	371.0
Total Plays	939	1072
Avg. Per Play	5.5	5.5
Net Yards Rushing	1295	2012
Avg. Per Game	80.9	125.8
Total Rushes	327	537
Net Yards Passing	3858	3924
Avg. Per Game	241.1	245.3
Sacked/Yards Lost	30/161	25/182
Gross Yards	4019	4106
Att./Completions	582/330	510/315
Completion Pct.	56.7	61.8
Had Intercepted	22	9
Punts/Average	73/46.7	68/41.3
Net Punting Avg.	73/37.2	68/37.3
Penalties/Yards	134/1013	102/837
Fumbles/Ball Lost	23/13	14/9
Touchdowns	35	56
Rushing	10	21
Passing	24	30
Returns	1	5

2004 INDIVIDUAL STATISTICS

PASSING

	Att.	Comp.	Yds.	Pct.	TD	Int.	Tkld.	Rate
Collins	513	289	3,495	56.3	21	20	25/144	74.8
Gannon	68	41	524	60.3	3	2	5/17	86.9
Curry	1	0	0	0.0	0	0	0/0	39.6
Raiders	582	330	4,019	56.7	24	22	30/161	76.1
Opponents	510	315	4,106	61.8	30	9	25/182	99.4

SCORING

	TD R	TD P	TD Rt	PAT	FG	Saf	PTS
Janikowski	0	0	0	31/32	25/28	0	106
Porter	0	9	0	0/0	0/0	0	54
Curry	0	6	0	0/0	0/0	0	36
Wheatley	4	0	0	0/0	0/0	0	24
Zereoue	3	0	0	0/0	0/0	0	18
Whitted	0	2	0	0/0	0/0	0	14
Crockett	2	0	0	0/0	0/0	0	12
Gabriel	0	2	0	0/0	0/0	0	12
Te. Johnson	0	2	0	0/0	0/0	0	12
Jolley	0	2	0	0/0	0/0	0	12
C. Anderson	0	1	0	0/0	0/0	0	6
Buchanon	0	0	1	0/0	0/0	0	6
Fargas	1	0	0	0/0	0/0	0	6
Raiders	10	24	1	31/32	25/28	1	320
Opponents	21	30	5	53/54	17/25	0	442

2-Pt. Conversions: Whitted.
Raiders 1-3, Opponents 1-2.

RUSHING

	No.	Yds	Avg	LG	TD
Zereoue	112	425	3.8	55t	3
Wheatley	85	327	3.8	60	4
Crockett	48	232	4.8	47	2
Fargas	35	126	3.6	15	1
Redmond	21	119	5.7	18	0
Collins	16	36	2.3	8	0
Gannon	5	26	5.2	20	0
Gabriel	2	7	3.5	4	0
Hetherington	1	4	4.0	4	0
Curry	1	-3	-3.0	-3	0
Porter	1	-4	-4.0	-4	0
Raiders	327	1,295	4.0	60	10
Opponents	537	2,012	3.7	34	21

RECEIVING

	No.	Yds	Avg	LG	TD
Porter	64	998	15.6	52	9
Curry	50	679	13.6	63	6
Zereoue	39	284	7.3	13	0
Gabriel	33	551	16.7	58t	2
Redmond	32	233	7.3	22	0
Jolley	27	313	11.6	34t	2
Crockett	16	87	5.4	11	0
Wheatley	15	78	5.2	20	0
C. Anderson	13	175	13.5	28	1
Fargas	11	68	6.2	21	0
Whitted	9	227	25.2	57	2
Te. Johnson	9	131	14.6	25	2
Rice	5	67	13.4	18	0
J. Stone	3	80	26.7	55	0
Hetherington	3	28	9.3	14	0
Morant	1	20	20.0	20	0
Raiders	330	4,019	12.2	63	24
Opponents	315	4,106	13.0	85t	30

INTERCEPTIONS

	No.	Yds	Avg	LG	TD
Buchanon	3	69	23.0	37	1
D. Walker	1	45	45.0	45	0
Buchanan	1	27	27.0	27	0
Woodson	1	25	25.0	25	0
Brayton	1	24	24.0	24	0
M. Anderson	1	23	23.0	23	0
Ti. Johnson	1	8	8.0	8	0
Raiders	9	221	24.6	45	1
Opponents	22	356	16.2	61	3

PUNTING

	No.	Yds.	Avg.	In 20	LG
Lechler	73	3,409	46.7	22	67
Raiders	73	3,409	46.7	22	67
Opponents	68	2,808	41.3	21	63

PUNT RETURNS

	Ret	FC	Yds	Avg	LG	TD
Buchanon	21	7	121	5.8	18	0
Gabriel	2	2	7	3.5	7	0
Woodson	1	0	4	4.0	4	0
Raiders	24	9	132	5.5	18	0
Opponents	35	10	413	11.8	50	0

KICKOFF RETURNS

	No.	Yds	Avg	LG	TD
Gabriel	53	1,140	21.5	64	0
Francis	14	259	18.5	33	0
Redmond	8	153	19.1	31	0
Curry	4	63	15.8	25	0
Hetherington	1	23	23.0	23	0
Porter	1	6	6.0	6	0
J. Stone	1	20	20.0	20	0
Whitted	1	36	36.0	36	0
Raiders	83	1,700	20.5	64	0
Opponents	62	1,458	23.5	50	0

FIELD GOALS

	1-19	20-29	30-39	40-49	50+
Janikowski	1/1	7/7	7/8	8/10	2/2
Raiders	1/1	7/7	7/8	8/10	2/2
Opponents	1/1	5/5	7/7	4/10	0/2

SACKS

	No.
Kelly	4.0
Washington	3.0
Brayton	2.5
Sapp	2.5
Woodson	2.5
Clark	2.0
Grant	2.0
Asomugha	1.0
Cooper	1.0
Gbaja-Biamila	1.0
Hamilton	1.0
Irons	1.0
Ti. Johnson	0.5
Raiders	25.0
Opponents	30.0

RECORD HOLDERS
INDIVIDUAL RECORDS—CAREER

Category	Name	Performance
Rushing (Yds.)	Marcus Allen, 1982-1992	8,545
Passing (Yds.)	Ken Stabler, 1970-79	19,078
Passing (TDs)	Ken Stabler, 1970-79	150
Receiving (No.)	Tim Brown, 1988-2003	1,070
Receiving (Yds.)	Tim Brown, 1988-2003	14,734
Interceptions	Willie Brown, 1967-1978	39
	Lester Hayes, 1977-1986	39
Punting (Avg.)	Shane Lechler, 2000-04	45.9
Punt Return (Avg.)	Claude Gibson, 1963-65	12.6
Kickoff Return (Avg.)	Jack Larscheid, 1960-61	28.4
Field Goals	Chris Bahr, 1980-88	162
Touchdowns (Tot.)	Tim Brown, 1988-2003	104
Points	George Blanda, 1967-1975	863

INDIVIDUAL RECORDS—SINGLE SEASON

Category	Name	Performance
Rushing (Yds.)	Marcus Allen, 1985	1,759
Passing (Yds.)	Rich Gannon, 2002	4,689
Passing (TDs)	Daryle Lamonica, 1969	34
Receiving (No.)	Tim Brown 1997	104
Receiving (Yds.)	Tim Brown, 1997	1,408
Interceptions	Lester Hayes, 1980	13
Punting (Avg.)	Shane Lechler, 2003	46.9
Punt Return (Avg.)	Claude Gibson, 1964	14.4
Kickoff Return (Avg.)	Harold Hart, 1975	30.5
Field Goals	Jeff Jaeger, 1993	35
Touchdowns (Tot.)	Marcus Allen, 1984	18
Points	Jeff Jaeger, 1993	132

INDIVIDUAL RECORDS—SINGLE GAME

Category	Name	Performance
Rushing (Yds.)	Napoleon Kaufman, 10-19-97	227
Passing (Yds.)	Cotton Davidson, 10-25-64	427
Passing (TDs)	Tom Flores, 12-22-63	6
	Daryle Lamonica, 10-19-69	6
Receiving (No.)	Tim Brown, 12-21-97	14
Receiving (Yds.)	Art Powell, 12-22-63	247
Interceptions	Many times	3
	Last time by Rod Woodson, 9-29-02	
Field Goals	Jeff Jaeger, 12-11-94	5
	Sebastian Janikowski, 10-29-00	5
Touchdowns (Tot.)	Art Powell, 12-22-63	4
	Marcus Allen, 9-24-84	4
	Harvey Williams, 11-16-97	4
Points	Art Powell, 12-22-63	24
	Marcus Allen, 9-24-84	24
	Harvey Williams, 11-16-97	24

2005 VETERAN ROSTER

No.	Name	Pos.	Ht.	Wt.	Birthdate	NFL Exp.	College	Hometown	How Acq.	'04 Games/ Starts
83	Anderson, Courtney	TE	6-7	270	11/19/80	2	San Jose State	Richmond, Calif.	D7-'04	9/4
23	Anderson, Marques	S	5-11	210	5/26/79	4	UCLA	Long Beach, Calif.	T(GB)-'04	14/0
21	Asomugha, Nnamdi	CB	6-2	210	7/6/81	3	California	Los Angeles, Calif.	D1-'03	16/7
70	Badger, Brad	G	6-4	320	1/11/75	9	Stanford	Corvallis, Ore.	UFA(Minn)-'02	16/12
91	Brayton, Tyler	DE/LB	6-6	280	11/20/79	3	Colorado	Pasco, Wash.	D1-'03	15/15
58	Burgess, Derrick	DE	6-2	260	8/12/78	5	Mississippi	Greenbelt, Md.	UFA(Phil)-'05	12/11*
55	Clark, Danny	LB	6-2	245	5/9/77	6	Illinois	Blue Island, Ill.	UFA(Jax)-'04	16/16
5	Collins, Kerry	QB	6-5	245	12/30/72	11	Penn State	Lebanon, Pa.	FA-'04	14/13
40	Cooper, Jarrod	S	6-1	215	3/31/78	5	Kansas State	Pearland, Texas	FA-'04	15/0*
32	Crockett, Zack	FB	6-2	240	12/2/72	11	Florida State	Pompano Beach, Fla.	UFA(Jax)-'99	16/9
89	Curry, Ronald	WR	6-2	210	5/28/79	3	North Carolina	Hampton, Va.	D7-'02	12/3
38	Curtis, Kevin	S	6-2	215	7/28/80	2	Texas Tech	Lubbock, Texas	FA-'05	0*
20	Fargas, Justin	RB	6-1	220	1/25/80	3	Southern California	Sherman Oaks, Calif.	D3-'03	12/0
53	Foreman, Jay	LB	6-2	240	2/18/76	7	Nebraska	Eden Prairie, Minn.	FA-'05	11/11
10	Francis, Carlos	WR	5-10	190	1/3/81	2	Texas Tech	Fort Worth, Texas	D4-'04	5/0
85	Gabriel, Doug	WR	6-2	215	8/27/80	3	Central Florida	Orlando, Fla.	D5-'03	16/5
76	Gallery, Robert	T	6-7	325	7/26/80	2	Iowa	Masonville, Iowa	D1-'04	16/15
12	Gannon, Rich	QB	6-3	210	12/20/65	18	Delaware	Philadelphia, Pa.	UFA(KC)-'99	3/3
94	Gbaja-Biamila, Akbar	DE/LB	6-5	270	5/6/79	3	San Diego State	Los Angeles, Calif.	FA-'03	14/0
36	Gibson, Derrick	S	6-2	215	3/22/79	5	Florida State	Miami, Fla.	D1-'01	0*
59	Grant, DeLawrence	LB	6-3	280	11/18/79	5	Oregon State	Compton, Calif.	D3-'01	9/9
64	Grove, Jake	C	6-4	300	1/22/80	2	Virginia Tech	Forest, Va.	D2-'04	9/8
98	Hamilton, Bobby	DE	6-5	285	7/1/71	11	Southern Mississippi	Columbus, Miss.	UFA(NE)-'04	16/15
44	Hetherington, Chris	FB	6-3	245	11/27/72	10	Yale	North Branford, Conn.	FA-'04	5/2
79	Hicks, Robert	T	6-7	330	11/17/74	4	Mississippi State	Atlanta, Ga.	FA-'05	0*
22	Hill, Renaldo	CB	5-11	190	11/12/78	4	Michigan State	Detroit, Mich.	UFA(Ariz)-'05	13/10*
71	Hulsey, Corey	G	6-4	325	7/26/77	4	Clemson	Gainesville, Ga.	FA-'04	3/0
96	Irons, Grant	DE/LB	6-6	285	7/7/79	4	Notre Dame	The Woodlands, Texas	FA-'03	8/2
11	Janikowski, Sebastian	K	6-2	250	3/2/78	6	Florida State	Daytona Beach, Fla.	D1-'00	16/0
82	Johnson, Teyo	TE	6-6	260	11/29/81	3	Stanford	San Diego, Calif.	D2-'03	8/1
51	Johnson, Tim	LB	6-0	245	2/7/78	4	Youngstown State	Fairfield, Ala.	FA-'03	16/0
34	Jordan, LaMont	RB	5-10	230	11/11/78	5	Maryland	Suitland, Md.	UFA(NYJ)-'05	16/0*
93	Kelly, Tommy	DT	6-6	300	12/27/80	2	Mississippi State	Jackson, Miss.	FA-'04	10/3
9	Lechler, Shane	P	6-2	225	8/7/76	6	Texas A&M	East Bernard, Texas	D5-'00	16/0
19	Morant, Johnnie	WR	6-4	220	12/7/81	2	Syracuse	Parsippany, N.J.	D5-'04	4/0
18	t-Moss, Randy	WR	6-4	215	2/13/77	8	Marshall	Rand, W. Va.	T(Minn)-'05	13/13*
42	Nash, Keyon	S	6-3	215	3/11/79	2	Albany State	Colquit, Ga.	D6-'02	2/0
39	Niklos, J.R.	FB	6-2	240	6/19/79	2	Western Illinois	Worthington, Ohio	FA-'05	0*
47	Norman, Josh	TE	6-2	240	7/27/80	3	Oklahoma	Midland, Texas	FA-'05	0*
84	Porter, Jerry	WR	6-2	220	7/14/78	6	West Virginia	Washington, D.C.	D2-'00	16/16
90	Sands, Terdell	DT	6-7	335	10/31/79	3	Tennessee-Chattanooga	Chattanooga, Tenn.	FA-'03	15/0
99	Sapp, Warren	DT	6-2	300	12/19/72	11	Miami	Apopka, Fla.	UFA(TB)-'04	16/16
30	Schweigert, Stuart	S	6-1	210	6/21/81	2	Purdue	Saginaw, Mich.	D3-'04	16/3
65	Sims, Barry	T	6-5	300	12/1/74	7	Utah	Park City, Utah	FA-'99	16/16
78	Slaughter, Chad	T	6-8	340	6/4/78	5	Alcorn State	Dallas, Texas	FA-'02	10/0
97	Smith, Kenny	DT	6-4	300	9/8/77	4	Alabama	Meridian, Miss.	UFA(NO)-'05	0*
	Smith, Marquis	LB	6-2	240	1/13/75	4	California	San Diego, Calif.	FA-'05	0*
56	Smith, Travian	LB	6-4	240	8/26/75	8	Oklahoma	Tatum, Texas	D5-'98	8/4
15	Stone, John	WR	5-11	180	7/7/79	2	Wake Forest	Linwood, N.J.	FA-'03	4/0
67	Stone, Ron	G	6-5	325	7/20/71	13	Boston College	Boston, Mass.	UFA(SF)-'04	5/5
	Thomas, Edward	LB	6-1	325	9/27/75	4	Georgia Southern	Atlanta, Ga.	FA-'05	0*
62	Treu, Adam	C	6-5	300	6/24/74	9	Nebraska	Lincoln, Neb.	D3-'97	16/16
8	Tuiasosopo, Marques	QB	6-1	220	3/22/79	5	Washington	Woodinville, Wash.	D2-'01	0*
50	Tuitele, Maugaula	LB	6-1	250	5/26/78	2	Colorado State	Torrance, Calif.	FA-'04	1/0
25	Walker, Denard	CB	6-1	190	8/9/73	9	Louisiana State	Dallas, Texas	FA-'04	16/5
66	Walker, Langston	T	6-8	345	9/3/79	4	California	Oakland, Calif.	D2-'02	16/1
46	Ware, Kevin	TE	6-3	260	9/30/80	3	Washington	San Diego, Calif.	FA-'05	5/0*
92	Washington, Ted	DT	6-5	365	4/13/68	14	Louisville	Tampa, Fla.	UFA(NE)-'04	16/16
87	Whitted, Alvis	WR	6-0	185	9/4/74	8	North Carolina State	Hillsborough, N.C.	FA-'02	11/5
29	Williams, Brock	CB	5-10	195	8/11/79	2	Notre Dame	Hammond, La.	FA-'04	2/0
54	Williams, Sam	LB	6-5	265	7/28/80	3	Fresno State	Clayton, Calif.	D3-'03	9/4
24	Woodson, Charles	CB	6-1	200	10/7/76	8	Michigan	Fremont, Ohio	D1-'98	13/12
95	Word, Mark	DE	6-5	295	11/23/75	4	Jacksonville State	Miami, Fla.	FA-'05	0*

* Burgess played 12 games with Philadelphia; Cooper played 6 games with Carolina, 9 games with Oakland; Curtis missed '02 season with San Francisco because of injury; Gibson missed '04 season because of injury; Hicks last active with Buffalo in '00; Hill played 13 games with Arizona; Jordan played 16 games with N.Y. Jets; Moss played 13 games with Minnesota; Niklos inactive for 12 games with St. Louis in '02; Norman last active with San Diego in '03; K. Smith missed '04 season with New Orleans because of injury; M. Smith last active with Cleveland in '01; Thomas last active with Jacksonville in '02; Tuiasosopo did not play in 13 games; Ware played 5 games with San Francisco; Word last active with Cleveland in '03.

t- Raiders traded for Moss (Minn).

Traded—CB Phillip Buchanan (Hou; 14 games in '04), LB Napoleon Harris (Minn; 16), TE Doug Jolley (NYJ; 16).

Also played with Raiders in '04—S Ray Buchanan (16 games), G Frank Middleton (7), DT John Parrella (16), RB J.R. Redmond (16), WR Jerry Rice (6), S David Terrell (16), RB Tyrone Wheatley (8), TE Roland Williams (12), RB Amos Zereoue (15).

2005 FIRST-YEAR ROSTER

Name	Pos.	Ht.	Wt.	Birthdate	College	Hometown	How Acq.
Adkisson, James (1)	WR	6-5	230	1/11/80	South Carolina	St. Louis, Mo.	FA-'04
Bonner, Cedric (1)	WR	6-0	170	12/14/78	Texas A&M Commerce	Dallas, Texas	FA
Brooks, C.J.	G	6-5	310	8/21/82	Maryland	Morrow, Ga.	FA
Carr, Chris	CB	5-9	185	4/30/83	Boise State	Reno, Nev.	FA
Carter, Vince	C	6-2	300	12/5/82	Oklahoma	Waco, Texas	FA
Douglas, Ivan	T	6-6	325	3/17/80	Ohio State	Cincinnati, Ohio	FA
Engemann, Brett (1)	QB	6-5	235	12/7/77	Brigham Young	Provo, Utah	FA-'04
Foschi, John Paul (1)	TE	6-4	270	5/19/82	Georgia Tech	Atlanta, Ga.	FA
Green, DeJuan (1)	RB	5-11	205	5/13/80	South Florida	Jacksonville, Fla.	FA-'04
Green, Rod	G/T	6-5	290	6/23/82	Arkansas-Pine Bluff	El Dorado, Ark.	FA
Hawthorne, Anttaj	DT	6-3	310	11/15/81	Wisconsin	Hamden, Conn.	D6a
Hicks, Jordan	DE/LS	6-4	265	12/13/81	Georgetown (KY)	Lebanon, Ohio	FA
Lekkerkerker, Brad (1)	T	6-7	330	5/8/78	UC Davis	Chino, Calif.	FA-'04
McMahon, Pete	T	6-8	330	10/15/81	Iowa	Debuque, Iowa	D6c
Morrison, Kirk	LB	6-2	240	2/19/82	San Diego State	Oakland, Calif.	D3b
Riddle, Ryan	LB	6-2	255	7/5/81	California	Culver City, Calif.	D6b
Rivers, David (1)	QB	6-3	220	9/1/77	Western Carolina	Augusta, Ga.	FA-'04
Rose, Shaun (1)	T	6-5	310	7/17/80	East Carolina	Wilson, N.C.	FA
Routt, Stanford	CB	6-1	195	7/26/83	Houston	Austin, Texas	D2
Walter, Andrew	QB	6-6	230	5/11/82	Arizona State	Grand Junction, Colo.	D3a
Ward, LaShaun (1)	WR	6-0	200	9/22/80	California	Pasadena, Calif.	FA
Washington, Fabian	CB	5-11	185	6/9/83	Nebraska	Bradenton, Fla.	D1
Washington, Maurice	WR	6-1	210	2/15/81	Texas A&M-Kingsville	Oakland, Calif.	FA

The term NFL Rookie is defined as a player who is in his first season of professional football and has not been on the roster of another professional football team for any regular-season or postseason games. A Rookie is designated by an "R" on NFL rosters. Players who have been active in another professional football league or players who have NFL experience, including either preseason training camp or being on an Active List or Inactive List, or on Reserve/Injured or Reserve/Physically Unable to Perform for fewer than six regular-season games, are termed NFL First-Year Players. An NFL First-Year Player is designated by a "1" on NFL rosters. Thereafter, a player is credited with an additional year of experience for each season in which he accumulates six games on the Active List or Inactive List, or on Reserve/Injured or Reserve/Physically Unable to Perform.

Log on to www.raiders.com for an up-to-date roster.

COACHING STAFF
Head Coach,
Norv Turner

Pro career: Norv Turner became the fourteenth head coach in Raiders history on January 26, 2004. Turner was head coach of the Washington Redskins from 1994-2000. Turner posted a winning record in four of his seven seasons with the Redskins. His 1999 Redskins claimed their first NFC Eastern Division title since 1991. Washington defeated Detroit, 27-13, in an NFC first-round playoff game. That season, the Redskins' offense finished the year as the league's second-ranked unit. Turner spent the 2002-03 seasons as assistant head coach/offensive coordinator for the Miami Dolphins. In 2001, Turner was the assistant head coach/offensive coordinator with the San Diego Chargers. Turner was offensive coordinator for Dallas from 1991-93, and helped lead the Cowboys to two straight Super Bowl titles (XXVII and XXVIII). Turner began his NFL coaching career as an assistant with the Los Angeles Rams (1985-1990). Career record: 55-71-1.

Background: Turner was a three-year letterman (1972-74) as a quarterback at the Oregon, spending two seasons behind NFL Hall of Fame quarterback Dan Fouts. Turner coached collegiately at Oregon (1975) and Southern California (1976-1984), where the Trojans won four Rose Bowl games and claimed the 1978 National Championship.

Personal: Born in LeJeune, N.C. on May 17, 1952. Turner and his wife, Nancy, have three children—Scott, Stephanie, and Drew.

ASSISTANT COACHES

Joe Avezzano, special teams; born November 17, 1943, Yonkers, N.Y. Guard Florida State 1961-65. Pro center Boston Patriots 1966. College coach: Florida State 1968, Iowa State 1969-1972, Pittsburgh 1973-76, Tennessee 1977-79, Oregon State 1980-84 (head coach), Texas 1985-88. Pro coach: Dallas Cowboys 1990-2002, Dallas Desperados (AFL) 2002-03 (head coach), joined Raiders in 2004.

Martin Bayless, specials teams asst.; born October 11, 1962, Dayton, Ohio. Defensive back Bowling Green 1981-83. Pro defensive back St. Louis Cardinals 1984, Buffalo Bills 1984-86, San Diego Chargers 1987-1991, Kansas City Chiefs 1992-93, 1995-96, Washington Redskins 1994. College coach: North Carolina 2001 Pro coach: Amsterdam Admirals (NFLE) 2002-03, Carolina Panthers 2003, joined Raiders in 2004.

Fred Biletnikoff, wide receivers; born February 23, 1943, Erie, Pa. Receiver Florida State 1962-64. Pro wide receiver Oakland Raiders 1965-1978, Montreal Alouettes (CFL) 1980. Inducted into Pro Football Hall of Fame in 1988. College coach: Palomar (Calif.) J.C. 1983, Diablo Valley (Calif.) J.C. 1984, 1986. Pro coach: Oakland Invaders (USFL) 1985, Calgary Stampeders (CFL) 1987-88, joined Raiders in 1989.

Willie Brown, squad development; born December 2, 1940, Yazoo City, Miss., Defensive back Grambling State 1959-1962. Pro defensive back Denver Broncos 1963-66, Oakland Raiders 1967-1978. Inducted into Pro Football Hall of Fame in 1984. College coach: Long Beach State 1990-91 (head coach 1991). Pro coach: Oakland/Los Angeles Raiders 1979-1988, rejoined Raiders in 1995.

Sam Clancy, defensive line; born May 29, 1958, Pittsburgh. No college playing experience. Pro defensive lineman Seattle Seahawks 1982-83, Pittsburgh Maulers (USFL) 1984-85, Cleveland Browns 1985-88, Indianapolis Colts 1989-1993. Pro coach: Barcelona Dragons (NFLE) 1995-99, New Orleans Saints 2000-03, joined Raiders in 2004.

Jim Colletto, offensive line; born October 2, 1944, San Francisco. Fullback/linebacker UCLA 1964-67. No pro playing experience. College coach: UCLA 1967-68, Brown 1969, Xavier 1970-71, Pacific 1972-74, Cal State Fullerton 1975-79 (head coach), UCLA 1980-81, Purdue 1982-84, Arizona State 1985-87, Ohio State 1988-1990, Purdue 1991-96 (head coach), Notre Dame 1997-98. Pro coach: Baltimore Ravens 1999-2004, joined Raiders in 2005.

Jeff Fish, strength & conditioning; born June 6, 1966, Ithaca, N.Y. Wide receiver Western Carolina 1986-88. No pro playing experience. College coach: Clemson 1991-92, Kent State 1993-94, Tulsa 1995-96, Missouri 2001-02. Pro coach: Tampa Bay Buccaneers 1997, Kansas City Chiefs 1998-2000, joined Raiders in 2004.

Chris Griswold, quality control, defense; born February 23, 1973, Hornell, N.Y. Defensive lineman Hobart College 1992-96. No pro playing experience. College coach: Allegheny 1998, Princeton 1999-2001. Pro coach: Joined Raiders in 2002.

Pat Jones, outside linebackers; born November 4, 1947, Memphis, Tenn. Nose guard Arkansas Tech 1965, linebacker/nose guard Arkansas 1966-1967. No pro playing experience. College coach: Arkansas 1974-75, Southern Methodist 1976-77, Pittsburgh 1978, Oklahoma State 1979-1994 (head coach 1984-1994). Pro coach: Miami Dolphins 1996-2003, joined Raiders in 2004.

Clayton Lopez, defensive backs; born May 26, 1971, Los Angeles. Safety Nevada 1991-94. No pro playing experience. College coach: Nevada 1995-98. Pro coach: Seattle Seahawks 1999-2003, joined Raiders in 2004.

Don Martindale, inside linebackers; born May 19, 1963, Dayton, Ohio. Linebacker Defiance College 1984-86. No pro playing experience. College coach: Defiance 1987, Notre Dame 1994-95, Cincinnati 1996-98, Western Illinois 1999, Western Kentucky 2000-02. Pro coach: Joined Raiders in 2004.

Keith Millard, asst. defensive line; born March 18, 1962, Pleasanton, Calif. Defensive lineman Washington State 1980-84. Pro defensive lineman Minnesota Vikings 1985-1991, Seattle Seahawks 1992, Green Bay Packers 1992, Philadelphia Eagles 1993. College coach: Fort Lewis 1996, Menlo College 1997-2000. Pro coach: San Francisco Demons (XFL) 2001, Denver Broncos 2002-04, joined Raiders in 2005.

Chuck Pagano, defensive assistant; born October 2, 1960, Boulder, Colo. Safety Wyoming 1980-83. No playing experience. College coach: Southern California 1984-85, Miami 1986, Boise State 1987-88, East Carolina 1989, Nevada-Las Vegas 1990-91, East Carolina 1992-94, Miami 1995-2000. Pro coach: Cleveland Browns 2001-04, joined Raiders in 2005.

Skip Peete, running backs; born January 30, 1963, Mesa, Ariz. Wide receiver Arizona 1981-82, Kansas 1984-85. Pro wide receiver New York Jets 1987. College coach: Pittsburgh 1988-1992, Michigan State 1993-94, Rutgers 1995, UCLA 1996-97. Pro coach: Joined Raiders in 1998.

Jimmy Raye, offensive coordinator; born March 26, 1946, Fayetteville, N.C. Quarterback Michigan State 1965-67. Pro defensive back Philadelphia Eagles 1969. College coach: Michigan State 1971-75, Wyoming 1976. Pro coach: San Francisco 49ers 1977, Detroit Lions 1978-79, Atlanta Falcons 1980-82, 1987-89, Los Angeles Rams 1983-84, 1991, Tampa Bay Buccaneers 1985-86, New England Patriots 1990, Kansas City Chiefs 1992-2000, Washington Redskins 2001, New York Jets 2002-03, joined Raiders in 2004.

Rob Ryan, defensive coordinator; born December 13, 1962, Ardmore, Okla. Linebacker Oklahoma State 1984, Southwestern Oklahoma State 1985-86. No pro playing experience. College coach: Western Kentucky 1987, Ohio State 1988, Tennessee State 1989-1993, Hutchinson (Kan.) C.C. 1996, Oklahoma State 1997-99. Pro coach: Arizona Cardinals 1994-95, New England Patriots 2000-03, joined Raiders in 2004.

John Shoop, quarterbacks; born August 1, 1969, Pittsburgh. Quarterback University of South 1987-1990. No pro playing experience. College coach: Dartmouth 1991, Vanderbilt 1992-94. Pro coach: Carolina Panthers 1995-98, Chicago Bears 1999-2003, Tampa Bay Buccaneers 2004, joined Raiders in 2005.

Chris Turner, offensive assistant; born February 28, 1969, Fairfield, Calif. No pro playing experience. College coach: San Jose State 1993, Notre Dame 1994, Bucknell 1995-2001. Pro coach: Joined Raiders in 2002.

**American Football Conference
North Division**
Team Colors: Black and Gold
3400 South Water Street
Pittsburgh, Pennsylvania 15203
Telephone: (412) 432-7800

2005 SCHEDULE
PRESEASON
Aug. 15 **Philadelphia** 8:00
Aug. 20 **Miami** 7:30
Aug. 26 at Washington 8:00
Sept. 1 at Carolina.........................8:00

REGULAR SEASON
Sept. 11 **Tennessee** 1:00
Sept. 18 at Houston 12:00
Sept. 25 **New England** 4:15
Oct. 2 Open Date
Oct. 10 at San Diego (Mon.) 6:00
Oct. 16 **Jacksonville**.......................1:00
Oct. 23 at Cincinnati......................1:00
Oct. 31 **Baltimore** (Mon.) 9:00
Nov. 6 at Green Bay 3:15
Nov. 13 **Cleveland** 8:30
Nov. 20 at Baltimore......................4:15
Nov. 28 at Indianapolis (Mon.)........9:00
Dec. 4 **Cincinnati** 1:00
Dec. 11 **Chicago** 1:00
Dec. 18 at Minnesota...................12:00
Dec. 24 at Cleveland (Sat.) 1:00
Jan. 1 **Detroit** 1:00

Stadium: Heinz Field (opened in 2001)
 • **Capacity:** 64,350
  100 Art Rooney Avenue
  Pittsburgh, Pennsylvania 15212
Playing Surface: DD GrassMaster
Training Camp: St. Vincent College
  Latrobe, Pennsylvania
  15650

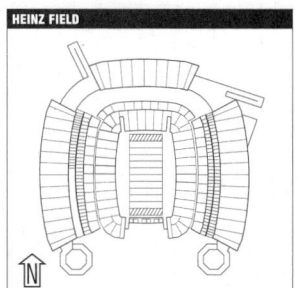

HEINZ FIELD

CLUB OFFICIALS
Chairman: Daniel M. Rooney
President: Arthur J. Rooney II
Vice President: John R. McGinley
Vice President: Arthur J. Rooney Jr.
Administration Advisor: Charles H. Noll
Director of Business: Mark Hart
Business Operations: Omar Khan
Director of Football Operations:
 Kevin Colbert
College Scouting Coordinator:
 Ron Hughes
Pro Scouting Coordinator: Doug Whaley
Head Athletic Trainer: John Norwig
Director of Marketing: Tony Quatrini
Communications Coordinator: TBD
Public Relations/Media Manager:
 Dave Lockett
Director of Stadium Management:
 Jim Sacco
Video Coordinator: Bob McCartney
Human Relations/Office Coordinator:
 Geraldine Glenn
Ticket Manager: Ben Lentz

COACHING HISTORY
**Pittsburgh Pirates 1933-1940
(508-498-21)**
Records include postseason games
1933   Forrest (Jap) Douds 3-6-2
1934   Luby DiMelio 2-10-0
1935-36   Joe Bach.......................10-14-0
1937-39   Johnny (Blood) McNally* ..6-19-0
1939-1940 Walt Kiesling 3-13-3
1941   Bert Bell** 0-2-0
          Aldo (Buff) Donelli*** 0-5-0
1941-44   Walt Kiesling**** 13-20-2
1945   Jim Leonard 2-8-0
1946-47   Jock Sutherland.............13-10-1
1948-1951 Johnny Michelosen 20-26-2
1952-53   Joe Bach.......................11-13-0
1954-56   Walt Kiesling 14-22-0
1957-1964 Raymond (Buddy) Parker .51-48-6
1965   Mike Nixon 2-12-0
1966-68   Bill Austin.....................11-28-3
1969-1991 Chuck Noll 209-156-1
1992-2004 Bill Cowher.................138-86-1
     *Released after three games in 1939
    **Resigned after two games in 1941
   ***Released after five games in 1941
****Co-coach with Earle (Greasy) Neale in
     Philadelphia-Pittsburgh merger in 1943 and
     with Phil Handler in Chicago Cardinals-
     Pittsburgh merger in 1944

ATTENDANCE
Home 508,984   Away 561,115
Total 1,070,099
Single-game home record,
 64,046 (12/26/04)
Single-season home record,
 508,984 (2004)

2005 DRAFT CHOICES
Round	Name	Pos.	College
1	Heath Miller	TE	Virginia
2	Bryant McFadden	DB	Florida State
3	Trai Essex	T	Northwestern
4	Fred Gibson	WR	Georgia
5	Rian Wallace	LB	Temple
6	Chris Kemoeatu	G	Utah
7	Shaun Nua	DE	Brigham Young
	Noah Herron	RB	Northwestern

2004 TEAM RECORD
PRESEASON (2-2)

Date	Result	Opponent
8/14	L 21-27	at Detroit
8/21	W 38-3	Houston
8/26	W 27-21	at Philadelphia
9/2	L 13-16	Carolina

REGULAR SEASON (15-1)

Date	Result	Opponent	Att.
9/12	W 24-21	Oakland	60,147
9/19	L 13-30	at Baltimore	69,859
9/26	W 13-3	at Miami	72,225
10/3	W 28-17	Cincinnati	62,402
10/10	W 34-23	Cleveland	63,609
10/17	W 24-20	at Dallas	64,162
10/31	W 34-20	New England	64,737
11/7	W 27-3	Philadelphia	64,975
11/14	W 24-10	at Cleveland	73,703
11/21	W 19-14	at Cincinnati	65,780
11/28	W 16-7	Washington	63,707
12/5	W 17-16	at Jacksonville	76,877
12/12	W 17-6	N.Y. Jets	63,581
12/18	W 33-30	at N.Y. Giants	78,836
12/26	W 20-7	Baltimore	64,227
1/2	W 29-24	at Buffalo	73,414

POSTSEASON (1-1)

Date	Result	Opponent	
1/15	W 20-17	N.Y. Jets (OT)	64,915
1/23	L 27-41	New England	62,242

(OT) Overtime

SCORE BY PERIODS

Steelers	123	90	47	112	0	— 372
Opponents	79	42	66	64	0	— 251

2004 TEAM STATISTICS

	Steelers	Opp.
Total First Downs	310	248
Rushing	134	79
Passing	147	146
Penalty	29	23
3rd Down: Made/Att	94/219	63/193
3rd Down Pct.	42.9	32.6
4th Down: Made/Att	7/12	7/13
4th Down Pct.	58.3	53.8
Possession Avg.	34:00	26:01
Total Net Yards	5184	4134
Avg. Per Game	324.0	258.4
Total Plays	1012	882
Avg. Per Play	5.1	4.7
Net Yards Rushing	2464	1299
Avg. Per Game	154.0	81.2
Total Rushes	618	357
Net Yards Passing	2720	2835
Avg. Per Game	170.0	177.2
Sacked/Yards Lost	36/250	41/225
Gross Yards	2970	3060
Att./Completions	358/228	484/269
Completion Pct.	63.7	55.6
Had Intercepted	13	19
Punts/Average	67/43.0	79/42.7
Net Punting Avg.	67/37.4	79/36.3
Penalties/Yards	99/837	104/875
Fumbles/Ball Lost	20/8	28/13
Touchdowns	41	26
Rushing	16	8
Passing	20	14
Returns	5	4

2004 INDIVIDUAL STATISTICS

PASSING

PASSING	Att.	Comp.	Yds.	Pct.	TD	Int.	Tkld.	Rate
Roethlisberger	295	196	2,621	66.4	17	11	30/213	98.1
Maddox	60	30	329	50.0	1	2	6/37	58.3
Bettis	1	1	10	100.0	1	0	0/0	147.9
Randle El	1	1	10	100.0	1	0	0/0	147.9
St. Pierre	1	0	0	0.0	0	0	0/0	39.6
Steelers	358	228	2,970	63.7	20	13	36/250	93.2
Opponents	484	269	3,060	55.6	14	19	41/225	68.0

SCORING

SCORING	TD R	TD P	TD Rt	PAT	FG	Saf	PTS
Reed	0	0	0	40/40	28/33	0	124
Bettis	13	0	0	0/0	0/0	0	78
Burress	0	5	0	0/0	0/0	0	30
Ward	1	4	0	0/0	0/0	0	30
Randle El	0	3	0	0/0	0/0	0	18
Tuman	0	3	0	0/0	0/0	0	18
Haynes	0	2	0	0/0	0/0	0	12
Riemersma	0	2	0	0/0	0/0	0	12
Farrior	0	0	1	0/0	0/0	0	6
Harrison	0	0	1	0/0	0/0	0	6
Kreider	0	1	0	0/0	0/0	0	6
Polamalu	0	0	1	0/0	0/0	0	6
Roethlisberger	1	0	0	0/0	0/0	0	6
Staley	1	0	0	0/0	0/0	0	6
Stuvaints	0	0	1	0/0	0/0	0	6
Townsend	0	0	1	0/0	0/0	0	6
Steelers	16	20	5	40/40	28/33	1	372
Opponents	8	14	4	24/24	23/27	0	251

2-Pt. Conversions: None.
Steelers 0-1, Opponents 1-2.

RUSHING

RUSHING	No.	Yds	Avg	LG	TD
Bettis	250	941	3.8	29	13
Staley	192	830	4.3	38	1
Haynes	55	272	4.9	18	0
Parker	32	186	5.8	58	0
Roethlisberger	56	144	2.6	20	1
Randle El	8	34	4.3	12	0
Ward	7	25	3.6	16t	1
Kreider	4	18	4.5	6	0
Maddox	9	15	1.7	10	0
Brown	1	2	2.0	2	0
St. Pierre	4	-3	-0.7	2	0
Steelers	618	2,464	4.0	58	16
Opponents	357	1,299	3.6	35	8

RECEIVING

RECEIVING	No.	Yds	Avg	LG	TD
Ward	80	1,004	12.6	58	4
Randle El	43	601	14.0	39	3
Burress	35	698	19.9	48	5
Haynes	18	142	7.9	26	2
Kreider	10	75	7.5	13	1
Mays	9	137	15.2	46	0
Tuman	9	89	9.9	26	3
Riemersma	7	82	11.7	26t	2
Staley	6	55	9.2	21	0
Bettis	6	46	7.7	20	0
Parker	3	16	5.3	12	0
Cushing	1	17	17.0	17	0
Morey	1	8	8.0	8	0
Steelers	228	2,970	13.0	58	20
Opponents	269	3,060	11.4	58t	14

INTERCEPTIONS

INTERCEPTIONS	No.	Yds	Avg	LG	TD
Polamalu	5	58	11.6	26t	1
Farrior	4	113	28.3	41	1
Townsend	4	54	13.5	39t	1
Hope	1	41	41.0	41	0
Scott	1	23	23.0	23	0
Porter	1	3	3.0	3	0
Foote	1	1	1.0	1	0
I. Taylor	1	0	0.0	0	0
Williams	1	0	0.0	0	0
Steelers	19	293	15.4	41	3
Opponents	13	190	14.6	51t	3

PUNTING

PUNTING	No.	Yds	Avg	In 20	Lg
Gardocki	67	2,879	43.0	24	61
Steelers	67	2,879	43.0	24	61
Opponents	79	3,375	42.7	26	63

PUNT RETURNS

PUNT RETURNS	Ret	FC	Yds	Avg	LG	TD
Randle El	42	13	347	8.3	60	0
Colclough	1	0	13	13.0	13	0
Haynes	1	0	5	5.0	5	0
Steelers	44	13	365	8.3	60	0
Opponents	34	8	252	7.4	33	0

KICKOFF RETURNS

KICKOFF RETURNS	No.	Yds	Avg	LG	TD
Colclough	26	566	21.8	48	0
Randle El	21	527	25.1	41	0
I. Taylor	11	184	16.7	22	0
Cushing	3	45	15.0	20	0
Kirschke	1	13	13.0	13	0
Steelers	62	1,335	21.5	48	0
Opponents	74	1,595	21.6	91t	1

FIELD GOALS

FIELD GOALS	1-19	20-29	30-39	40-49	50+
Reed	1/1	8/9	12/13	5/8	2/2
Steelers	1/1	8/9	12/13	5/8	2/2
Opponents	0/0	7/8	11/12	5/6	0/1

SACKS

SACKS	No.
A. Smith	8.0
Porter	7.0
Haggans	6.0
Townsend	4.0
Farrior	3.0
Foote	3.0
Colclough	1.5
Harrison	1.0
Hoke	1.0
Kirschke	1.0
Polamalu	1.0
von Oelhoffen	1.0
Williams	1.0
Kriewaldt	0.5
Steelers	41.0
Opponents	36.0

RECORD HOLDERS
INDIVIDUAL RECORDS—CAREER

Category	Name	Performance
Rushing (Yds.)	Franco Harris, 1972-1983	11,950
Passing (Yds.)	Terry Bradshaw, 1970-1983	27,989
Passing (TDs)	Terry Bradshaw, 1970-1983	212
Receiving (No.)	John Stallworth, 1974-1987	537
Receiving (Yds.)	John Stallworth, 1974-1987	8,723
Interceptions	Mel Blount, 1970-1983	57
Punting (Avg.)	Bobby Joe Green, 1960-61	45.7
Punt Return (Avg.)	Bobby Gage, 1949-1950	14.9
Kickoff Return (Avg.)	Lynn Chandnois, 1950-56	29.6
Field Goals	Gary Anderson, 1982-1994	309
Touchdowns (Tot.)	Franco Harris, 1972-1983	100
Points	Gary Anderson, 1982-1994	1,343

INDIVIDUAL RECORDS—SINGLE SEASON

Category	Name	Performance
Rushing (Yds.)	Barry Foster, 1992	1,690
Passing (Yds.)	Terry Bradshaw, 1979	3,724
Passing (TDs)	Terry Bradshaw, 1978	28
Receiving (No.)	Hines Ward, 2002	112
Receiving (Yds.)	Yancey Thigpen, 1997	1,398
Interceptions	Mel Blount, 1975	11
Punting (Avg.)	Bobby Joe Green, 1961	47.0
Punt Return (Avg.)	Bobby Gage, 1949	16.0
Kickoff Return (Avg.)	Lynn Chandnois, 1952	35.2
Field Goals	Norm Johnson, 1995	34
Touchdowns (Tot.)	Louis Lipps, 1985	15
Points	Norm Johnson, 1995	141

INDIVIDUAL RECORDS—SINGLE GAME

Category	Name	Performance
Rushing (Yds.)	John Fuqua, 12-20-70	218
Passing (Yds.)	Tommy Maddox, 11-10-02	473
Passing (TDs)	Terry Bradshaw, 11-15-81	5
	Mark Malone, 9-8-85	5
Receiving (No.)	Courtney Hawkins, 11-1-98	14
Receiving (Yds.)	Plaxico Burress, 11-10-02	253
Interceptions	Jack Butler, 12-13-53	*4
Field Goals	Gary Anderson, 10-23-88	6
	Jeff Reed, 12-1-02	6
Touchdowns (Tot.)	Ray Mathews, 10-17-54	4
	Roy Jefferson, 11-3-68	4
Points	Ray Mathews, 10-17-54	24
	Roy Jefferson, 11-3-68	24

*NFL Record

2005 VETERAN ROSTER

No.	Name	Pos.	Ht.	Wt.	Birthdate	NFL Exp.	College	Hometown	How Acq.	'04 Games/ Starts
16	Batch, Charlie	QB	6-2	216	12/5/74	8	Eastern Michigan	Pittsburgh, Pa.	FA-'02	0*
49	Battaglia, Marco	TE	6-3	250	1/25/73	9	Rutgers	Queens, N.Y.	FA-'05	0*
36	Bettis, Jerome	RB	5-11	255	2/16/72	13	Notre Dame	Detroit, Mich.	T(StL)-'96	15/6
72	Brooks, Barrett	T	6-4	325	5/5/72	10	Kansas State	Florissant, Mo.	FA-'03	5/0
23	Carter, Tyrone	S	5-8	190	3/31/76	6	Minnesota	Pompano Beach, Fla.	FA-'04	9/0
21	Colclough, Ricardo	CB	5-11	186	4/18/82	2	Tusculum	Sumter, S.C.	D2-'04	16/0
48	Cushing, Matt	FB	6-4	251	7/2/75	7	Illinois	Chicago, Ill.	FA-'03	16/0
66	Faneca, Alan	G	6-5	307	12/7/76	8	Louisiana State	New Orleans, La.	D1-'98	16/16
51	Farrior, James	LB	6-2	243	1/6/75	9	Virginia	Ettrick, Va.	UFA(NYJ)-'02	16/16
50	Foote, Larry	LB	6-0	239	6/12/80	4	Michigan	Detroit, Mich.	D4-'02	16/16
17	Gardocki, Chris	P	6-1	192	2/7/70	15	Clemson	Stone Mountain, Ga.	UFA-'04	16/0
53	Haggans, Clark	LB	6-4	243	1/10/77	6	Colorado State	Torrance, Calif.	D5a-'00	13/13
98	Hampton, Casey	DT	6-1	325	9/3/77	5	Texas	Galveston, Texas	D1-'01	6/6
92	Harrison, James	LB	6-0	242	5/4/78	2	Kent State	Akron, Ohio	FA-'04	16/4
64	Hartings, Jeff	C	6-3	299	9/7/72	10	Penn State	St. Henry, Ohio	UFA(Det)-'01	16/16
34	Haynes, Verron	RB	5-9	222	2/17/79	4	Georgia	Bronx, N.Y.	D5-'02	13/0
76	Hoke, Chris	DT	6-3	296	4/6/76	5	Brigham Young	Long Beach, Calif.	FA-'02	14/10
28	Hope, Chris	S	5-11	206	9/29/80	4	Florida State	Rock Hill, S.C.	D3-'02	16/16
29	Iwuoma, Chidi	CB	5-8	184	2/19/78	5	California	Pasadena, Calif.	FA-02	14/0
95	Jackson, Alonzo	LB	6-4	268	9/15/80	3	Florida State	Americus, Ga.	D2-'03	7/0
74	Jones, Jim	G	6-3	319	1/27/78	2	Notre Dame	Chicago, Ill.	FA-'04	0*
99	Keisel, Brett	DE	6-5	285	9/19/78	4	Brigham Young	Greybull, Wyo.	D7b-'02	13/0
90	Kirschke, Travis	DT	6-3	298	9/6/74	9	UCLA	Highland Ranch, Colo.	UFA(SF)-'04	16/1
88	Kranchick, Matt	TE	6-7	260	12/13/79	2	Penn State	Carlisle, Pa.	D6b-'04	2/0
35	Kreider, Dan	FB	5-11	255	3/11/77	6	New Hampshire	Mount Joy, Pa.	FA-'00	16/9
57	Kriewaldt, Clint	LB	6-1	248	3/16/76	7	Wisconsin-Stevens Point	Shiocton, Wis.	UFA(Det)-'03	15/0
31	Logan, Mike	CB/S	6-1	211	9/15/74	9	West Virginia	Pittsburgh, Pa.	UFA(Jax)-'01	3/0
8	Maddox, Tommy	QB	6-4	219	9/2/71	9	UCLA	Hurst, Texas	FA-'01	4/3
89	Mays, Lee	WR	6-2	193	9/18/78	4	Texas-El Paso	Houston, Texas	D6-'02	16/1
81	Morey, Sean	WR	5-11	200	2/26/76	4	Brown	Marshfield, Mass.	FA-'04	16/0
56	Okobi, Chukky	C/G	6-1	318	10/18/78	5	Purdue	Pittsburgh, Pa.	D5-'01	16/0
39	Parker, Willie	RB	5-10	209	11/11/80	2	North Carolina	Clinton, N.C.	FA-'04	8/0
43	Polamalu, Troy	S	5-10	212	4/19/81	3	Southern California	Roseburg, Ore.	D1-'03	16/16
55	Porter, Joey	LB	6-3	250	3/22/77	7	Colorado State	Bakersfield, Calif.	D3a-'99	15/15
82	Randle El, Antwaan	WR	5-10	192	8/17/79	4	Indiana	Markham, Ill.	D2-'02	16/7
87	Rasby, Walter	TE	6-3	252	9/7/72	11	Wake Forest	Washington, N.C.	FA-'04	4/2
3	Reed, Jeff	K	5-11	232	4/9/79	4	North Carolina	Charlotte, N.C.	FA-'02	16/0
7	Roethlisberger, Ben	QB	6-5	241	3/2/82	2	Miami (OH)	Findlay, Ohio	D1-'04	14/13
54	Schneck, Mike	LS	6-0	237	8/4/77	7	Wisconsin	Whitefish Bay, Wis.	FA-'99	16/0
73	Simmons, Kendall	G	6-3	319	3/11/79	4	Auburn	Ripley, Miss.	D1-'02	0*
91	Smith, Aaron	DE	6-5	298	4/9/76	7	Northern Colorado	Colo. Springs, Colo.	D4-'99	16/15
77	Smith, Marvel	T	6-5	321	8/6/78	6	Arizona State	Oakland, Calif.	D2-'00	16/16
2	St. Pierre, Brian	QB	6-2	220	11/28/79	3	Boston College	Danvers, Mass.	D5-'03	1/0
22	Staley, Duce	RB	5-11	242	2/27/75	9	South Carolina	Columbia, S.C.	UFA(Phil)-'04	10/10
78	Starks, Max	T	6-8	337	1/10/82	2	Florida	Orlando, Fla.	D3-'04	10/0
33	Stuvaints, Russell	S	6-0	210	8/28/80	3	Youngstown State	Mckeesport, Pa.	FA-'04	15/0
24	Taylor, Ike	CB	6-1	191	5/5/80	3	Louisiana-Lafayette	Gretna, La.	D4-'03	13/1
26	Townsend, Deshea	CB	5-10	190	9/8/75	8	Alabama	Batesville, Miss.	D4a-'98	15/15
84	Tuman, Jerame	TE	6-4	253	3/24/76	7	Michigan	Liberal, Kan.	FA-'03	16/16
67	von Oelhoffen, Kimo	DT/DE	6-4	299	1/30/71	12	Boise State	Kaunakakai, Hawaii	UFA(Cin)-'00	16/15
86	Ward, Hines	WR	6-0	215	3/8/76	8	Georgia	Forest Park, Ga.	D3b-'98	16/16
27	Williams, Willie	CB	5-9	194	12/26/70	13	Western Carolina	Columbia, S.C.	FA-'04	16/10
80	Wilson, Cedrick	WR	5-10	183	12/17/78	5	Tennessee	Memphis, Tenn.	UFA(SF)-'05	15/15*
18	Young, Walter	WR	6-4	220	12/7/79	2	Illinois	Park Forest, Ill.	FA-'04	0*

* Batch missed '04 because of injury; Battaglia did not play in 1 game; Jones did not play in 1 game; Simmons did not play in 1 game; Wilson played 15 games with San Francisco in '04; Young did not play in 1 game.

Players lost through free agency (5): LB Kendrell Bell (KC; 3 games), WR Plaxico Burress (NYG; 11), NT Kendrick Clancy (NYG; 8), T Oliver Ross (Ariz; 16), G Keydrick Vincent (Balt; 16).

Also played with Steelers in '05—TE Jay Riemersma (11 games), CB Chad Scott (7).

2005 FIRST-YEAR ROSTER

Name	Pos.	Ht.	Wt.	Birthdate	College	Hometown	How Acq.
Barr, Mike (1)	P	6-3	230	12/8/78	Rutgers	Lynchburg, Va.	FA
Booker, Ulish (1)	T	6-6	309	8/14/79	Michigan State	West Haven, Conn.	FA
Bowman, Grant (1)	DT	6-1	300	5/13/80	Michigan	Columbus, Ohio	FA-'04
Burr, Josh (1)	T	6-9	320	9/8/76	South Dakota	Dubuque, Iowa	FA-'02
Capers, Tavaris	WR	5-8	174	2/15/82	Central Florida	Miami, Fls.	FA
Claxton, Ben (1)	C	6-2	288	7/30/80	Mississippi	Dublin, Ga.	FA
Cobb, Zamir (1)	WR	5-11	182	6/11/82	Temple	Washington, D.C.	FA-'04
Collins, Chris (1)	WR	6-1	201	8/16/82	Mississippi	Gloster, Miss.	FA
Davis, Morgan	T	6-6	313	8/7/80	Wisconsin	Barron, Wis.	FA
Duff, Vontez (1)	CB	5-11	204	3/8/82	Notre Dame	Copperas Cove, Texas	FA-'04
Dzvonick, Bob (1)	DT	6-1	280	6/30/78	Buffalo	Pittsburgh, Pa.	FA
Essex, Trai	T	6-4	324	12/5/82	Northwestern	Fort Wayne, Ind.	D3
Farrior, Matt (1)	LB	6-1	230	8/6/81	Florida	Peterson, Va.	FA
Frazier, Andre	LB	6-5	234	6/29/82	Cincinnati	Cincinnati, Ohio	FA
Frieser, John (1)	TE	6-4	260	12/10/81	Colgate	Endwell, N.Y.	FA
Gibson, Fred	WR	6-4	202	10/26/81	Georgia	Waycross, Ga.	D4
Harris, Elliott	DT	6-3	285	10/29/81	Arkansas	Marianna, Ark.	FA
Harrison, Arnold	LB	6-3	236	9/20/82	Georgia	Augusta, Ga.	FA
Herron, Noah	RB	5-11	224	4/3/82	Northwestern	Mattawan, Mich.	D7b
Iorio, Joe (1)	C	6-3	308	7/7/81	Penn State	Toledo, Ohio	FA
Israel, Ron (1)	S	6-0	204	1/5/78	Notre Dame	Hadden Heights, N.J.	FA
Kemoeatu, Chris	G	6-3	344	1/4/83	Utah	Kahuka, Hawaii	D6
Kuhn, John	RB	6-0	255	9/9/82	Shippensburg	York, Pa.	FA
McFadden, Bryant	CB	5-11	190	11/21/81	Florida State	Hollywood, Fla.	D2
Miller, Heath	TE	6-5	256	10/22/82	Virginia	Swords Creek, Va.	D1
Nua, Shaun	DE	6-5	280	5/22/81	Brigham Young	Pago Pago, American Samoa	D7a
Patten, Janssen (1)	S	5-11	191	4/15/82	Bowling Green	Stone Mountain, Ga.	FA
Roper, Dedrick (1)	LB	6-2	245	7/31/81	Northwood	Detroit, Mich.	FA
Stanley, Ronald	LB	6-0	244	3/6/83	Michigan State	Saginaw, Mich.	FA
Suisham, Shaun	K	6-0	199	12/29/81	Bowling Green	Wallaceburg, Ontario, Canada	FA
Taylor, Eric (1)	DE	6-2	305	12/14/81	Memphis	Winchester, Tenn.	FA
Tuiasosopo, Zach	FB	6-2	249	12/19/81	Washington	Woodinville, Wash.	FA
Vandermade, Lenny (1)	G	6-2	291	1/3/81	Southern California	Santa Ana, Calif.	FA-'04
Verstraete, Jake	G	6-6	313	6/5/82	Northern Illinois	Atkinson, Ill.	FA
Wallace, Rian	LB	6-2	243	5/24/82	Temple	Pottstown, Pa.	D5
Warren, Greg	LS	6-3	252	10/18/81	North Carolina	Goldsboro, N.C.	FA
Washington, Nate	WR	6-1	185	8/28/83	Tiffin	Toledo, Ohio	FA
Wilson, Travis (1)	FB	6-3	256	5/31/81	Kansas State	Farmington Hills, Mich.	FA

The term NFL Rookie is defined as a player who is in his first season of professional football and has not been on the roster of another professional football team for any regular-season or postseason games. A Rookie is designated by an "R" on NFL rosters. Players who have been active in another professional football league or players who have NFL experience, including either preseason training camp or being on an Active List or Inactive List, or on Reserve/Injured or Reserve/Physically Unable to Perform for fewer than six regular-season games, are termed NFL First-Year Players. An NFL First-Year Player is designated by a "1" on NFL rosters. Thereafter, a player is credited with an additional year of experience for each season in which he accumulates six games on the Active List or Inactive List, or on Reserve/Injured or Reserve/Physically Unable to Perform.

Log on to www.steelers.com for an up-to-date roster.

COACHING STAFF
Head Coach,
Bill Cowher

Pro Career: Became the fifteenth head coach in Steelers history when he replaced Chuck Noll on January 21, 1992. In 1995, at age 38, he became the youngest coach to lead his team to a Super Bowl. Cowher is only the second coach in NFL history to lead his team to the playoffs in each of his first six seasons as head coach, joining Pro Football Hall of Fame member Paul Brown. During Cowher's 20-year coaching career, teams he has been associated with have made the postseason 15 times. Began his NFL career as a free-agent linebacker with the Philadelphia Eagles in 1979, and then signed with the Cleveland Browns the following year. Cowher played three seasons (1980-82) in Cleveland before being traded back to the Eagles, where he played two more years (1983-84). Cowher began his coaching career in 1985 at age 28 under Marty Schottenheimer with the Browns. He was the Browns' special teams coach in 1985-86 and secondary coach in 1987-88 before following Schottenheimer to the Kansas City Chiefs in 1989 as defensive coordinator. Career record: 138-86-1.

Background: Excelled in football, basketball, and track for Carlynton High in Crafton, Pa. Was a three-year starter at linebacker for North Carolina State, serving as captain and earning team MVP honors as a senior. Graduated in 1979 with education degree.

Personal: Born in Pittsburgh, on May 8, 1957. His wife Kaye, also a North Carolina State graduate, played professional basketball for the New York Stars of the Women's Professional Basketball League with twin sister Faye. Bill and Kaye live in Pittsburgh and have three daughters—Meagan Lyn, Lauren Marie, and Lindsay Morgan.

ASSISTANT COACHES

Bruce Arians, wide receivers; born October 3, 1952, Paterson, N.J. Quarterback Virginia Tech 1970-74. No pro playing experience. College coach: Virginia Tech 1975-77, Mississippi State 1978-1980, Alabama 1981-82, Temple 1983-88 (head coach), Mississippi State 1993-95, Alabama 1997. Pro coach: Kansas City Chiefs 1989-1992, New Orleans Saints 1996, Indianapolis Colts 1998-2000, Cleveland Browns 2001-03, joined Steelers in 2004.

Keith Butler, linebackers; born May 16, 1956, Anniston, Ala. Linebacker Memphis 1974-77. Pro linebacker Seattle Seahawks 1978-1987. College coach: Memphis 1990-97, Arkansas State 1998. Pro coach: Cleveland Browns 1999-2002, joined Steelers in 2003.

James Daniel, tight ends; born January 17, 1953, Wetumpka, Ala. Guard Alabama State 1970-73. No pro playing experience. College coach: Auburn 1981-1992. Pro coach: New York Giants 1993-96, Atlanta Falcons 1997-2003, joined Steelers in 2004.

Russ Grimm, offensive line; born May 2, 1959, Scottdale, Pa. Center Pittsburgh 1977-1980. Pro guard Washington Redskins 1981-1991. Pro coach: Washington Redskins 1992-2000, joined Steelers in 2001.

Dick Hoak, running backs; born December 8, 1939, Jeannette, Pa. Halfback-quarterback Penn State 1958-1960. Pro running back Pittsburgh Steelers 1961-1970. Pro coach: Joined Steelers in 1972.

Ray Horton, asst. defensive backs; born April 12, 1960, Tacoma, Wash. Defensive back Washington 1979-1982. Pro defensive back Cincinnati Bengals 1983-88, Dallas Cowboys 1989-1992. Pro coach: Washington Redskins 1994-96, Cincinnati Bengals 1997-2001, Detroit Lions 2002-03, joined Steelers in 2004.

Dick LeBeau, defensive coordinator; born September 9, 1937, London, Ohio. Defensive back Ohio State 1955-58. Pro cornerback Detroit Lions 1959-1972. Pro coach: Philadelphia Eagles 1973-75, Green Bay Packers 1976-79, Cincinnati Bengals 1980-1991, 1997-2002 (head coach 2000-02), Pittsburgh Steelers 1992-96, Buffalo Bills 2003, re-joined Steelers in 2004.

John Mitchell, defensive line; born October 14, 1951, Mobile, Ala. Defensive end Eastern Arizona J.C. 1969-1970, Alabama 1971-72. No pro playing experience. College coach: Alabama 1973-76, Arkansas 1977-1982, Temple 1986, Louisiana State 1987-1990. Pro coach: Birmingham Stallions (USFL) 1983-85, Cleveland Browns 1991-93, joined Steelers in 1994.

Darren Perry, asst. defensive backs; born December 29, 1968, Chesapeake, Va. Safety Penn State 1987-1991. Pro safety Pittsburgh Steelers 1992-98, New Orleans Saints 2000. Pro coach: Cincinnati Bengals 2002, joined Steelers in 2003.

Kevin Spencer, special teams; born November 2, 1953, Queens, N.Y. Outside linebacker Springfield College 1971. No pro playing experience. College coach: SUNY-Cortland 1975-76, Cornell 1979-1980, Ithaca 1981-86, Wesleyan 1978-1991. Pro coach: Cleveland Browns 1991-94, Oakland Raiders 1995-97, Indianapolis Colts 1998-2001, joined Steelers in 2002.

Mark Whipple, quarterbacks; born April 1, 1957, Tarrytown, N.Y. Quarterback Brown 1976-78. No pro playing experience. College coach: St. Lawrence 1980, Union College 1981-82, Brown 1983, New Hampshire 1986-87, New Haven 1988-1993 (head coach), Brown 1994-97 (head coach), Massachusetts 1998-2003 (head coach). Pro coach: Arizona Wranglers 1984 (USFL), joined Steelers in 2004.

Ken Whisenhunt, offensive coordinator; born February 28, 1962, Atlanta. Tight end-quarterback Georgia Tech 1980-84. Pro tight end Atlanta Falcons 1985-88, Washington Redskins 1989-1990, New York Jets 1991-93. College coach: Vanderbilt 1995-96. Pro coach: Baltimore Ravens 1997-98, Cleveland Browns 1999, New York Jets 2000, joined Steelers in 2001.

American Football Conference
West Division
Team Colors: Navy Blue, White, and Gold
P.O. Box 609609
San Diego, California 92160-9609
Telephone: (858) 874-4500

2005 SCHEDULE
PRESEASON
Aug. 11	at Green Bay	7:00
Aug. 21	**St. Louis**	1:00
Aug. 26	at Minnesota	7:00
Sept. 1	**San Francisco**	7:00

REGULAR SEASON
Sept. 11	**Dallas**	1:15
Sept. 18	at Denver	2:15
Sept. 25	**New York Giants**	5:30
Oct. 2	at New England	1:00
Oct. 10	**Pittsburgh** (Mon.)	6:00
Oct. 16	at Oakland	1:15
Oct. 23	at Philadelphia	1:00
Oct. 30	**Kansas City**	1:05
Nov. 6	at New York Jets	1:00
Nov. 13	Open Date	
Nov. 20	**Buffalo**	1:15
Nov. 27	at Washington	1:00
Dec. 4	**Oakland**	5:30
Dec. 11	**Miami**	1:15
Dec. 18	at Indianapolis	1:00
Dec. 24	at Kansas City (Sat.)	12:00
Dec. 31	**Denver** (Sat.)	1:30

Stadium: Qualcomm Stadium
(opened in 1967)
• Capacity: 70,000
9449 Friars Road
San Diego, California 92108
Playing Surface: Grass
Training Camp: Chargers Park
4020 Murphy Canyon Rd.
San Diego, CA 92123

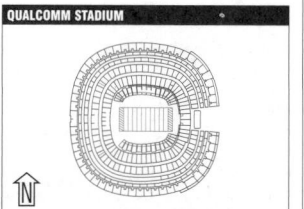

QUALCOMM STADIUM

CLUB OFFICIALS
Owner: Alex G. Spanos
President/CEO: Dean A. Spanos
Executive Vice President:
Michael A. Spanos
Executive Vice President & General
Manager: A.J. Smith
Executive Vice President & Chief
Operating Officer: Jim Steeg
Executive Vice President-Finance:
Jeremiah T. Murphy
Vice President of Football Operations:
Ed McGuire
Vice President-Chief Financial &
Administrative Officer: Jeanne M. Bonk
Vice President & Chief Marketing Officer:
Ken Derrett
Assistant General Manager & Director of
Player Personnel: Buddy Nix
Director of College Scouting:
Jimmy Raye
Director of Pro Scouting: Fran Foley
Assistant Director of Pro Scouting:
Dennis Abraham
Head Athletic Trainer: James Collins
Director of Video Operations:
Brian Duddy
Equipment Manager: Bob Wick
Director of Player Development:
Arthur Hightower
Senior Director of Marketing
Partnerships: Dennis O'Leary
Senior Director of Ticket Sales and
Service: Todd Poulsen
Director of Marketing Programs and
Business Development: A.G. Spanos
Director of Business Operations:
John Hinek
Director of Public Relations: Bill Johnston
Director of Public Affairs &
Corporate/Community Relations:
Kimberley Layton
Director of Security: Dick Lewis
Director of Stadium Operations & Events:
Sean O'Connor
Controller: Marsha Wells
Director of Ticket Operations:
Michael L. Dougherty
Director of Guest Services:
David Anderson

COACHING HISTORY
Los Angeles 1960
(327-357-11)
Records include postseason games
1960-69	Sid Gillman*	83-51-6
1969-1970	Charlie Waller	9-7-3
1971	Sid Gillman**	4-6-0
1971-73	Harland Svare***	7-17-2
1973	Ron Waller	1-5-0
1974-78	Tommy Prothro****	21-39-0
1978-1986	Don Coryell#	72-60-0
1986-88	Al Saunders	17-22-0
1989-1991	Dan Henning	16-32-0
1992-96	Bobby Ross	50-36-0
1997-98	Kevin Gilbride	6-16-0
1998	June Jones	3-7-0
1999-2001	Mike Riley	14-34-0
2002-04	Marty Schottenheimer	24-25-0

*Retired after nine games in 1969
**Resigned after 10 games in 1971
***Resigned after eight games in 1973
****Resigned after four games in 1978
#Resigned after eight games in 1986
##Released after six games in 1998

ATTENDANCE
Home 501,351   Away 530,689
Total 1,032,040
Single-game home record,
69,288 (11/7/99)
Single-season home record,
546,533 (1999)

2005 DRAFT CHOICES
Round	Name	Pos.	College
1	Shawne Merriman	LB	Maryland
	Luis Castillo	DT	Northwestern
2	Vincent Jackson	WR	No. Colorado
4	Darren Sproles	RB	Kansas State
5	Wesley Britt	T	Alabama
6	Wes Sims	G	Oklahoma
7	Scott Mruczkowski	C	Bowling Green

2004 TEAM RECORD
PRESEASON (2-2)

Date	Result	Opponent
8/14	L 17-21	Indianapolis
8/21	W 38-13	at Arizona
8/27	L 20-26	Seattle
9/2	W 31-15	at San Francisco

REGULAR SEASON (12-4)

Date	Result	Opponent	Att.
9/12	W 27-20	at Houston	70,255
9/19	L 28-34	N.Y. Jets	57,310
9/26	L 13-23	at Denver	74,533
10/3	W 38-17	Tennessee	54,006
10/10	W 34-21	Jacksonville	52,101
10/17	L 20-21	at Atlanta	70,187
10/24	W 17-6	at Carolina	73,096
10/31	W 42-14	Oakland	66,210
11/7	W 43-17	New Orleans	59,662
11/21	W 23-17	at Oakland	46,905
11/28	W 34-31	at Kansas City	77,447
12/5	W 20-17	Denver	65,395
12/12	W 31-24	Tampa Bay	65,858
12/19	W 21-0	at Cleveland	72,489
12/26	L 31-34	at Indianapolis (OT)	57,330
1/2	W 24-17	Kansas City	64,920

POSTSEASON (0-1)

Date	Result	Opponent	
1/8	L 17-20	N.Y. Jets (OT)	67,536

(OT) Overtime

SCORE BY PERIODS

Chargers	92	138	106	110	0 —	446
Opponents	37	97	52	124	3 —	313

2004 TEAM STATISTICS

	Chargers	Opp.
Total First Downs	328	320
Rushing	131	79
Passing	160	200
Penalty	37	41
3rd Down: Made/Att	97/208	69/196
3rd Down Pct.	46.6	35.2
4th Down: Made/Att	5/8	13/24
4th Down Pct.	62.5	54.2
Possession Avg.	31:30	28:30
Total Net Yards	5542	5360
Avg. Per Game	346.4	335.0
Total Plays	996	991
Avg. Per Play	5.6	5.4
Net Yards Rushing	2185	1307
Avg. Per Game	136.6	81.7
Total Rushes	525	355
Net Yards Passing	3357	4053
Avg. Per Game	209.8	253.3
Sacked/Yards Lost	21/149	29/142
Gross Yards	3506	4195
Att./Completions	450/288	607/372
Completion Pct.	64.0	61.3
Had Intercepted	8	23
Punts/Average	69/43.1	64/42.4
Net Punting Avg.	69/38.4	64/37.0
Penalties/Yards	108/875	109/940
Fumbles/Ball Lost	27/10	19/10
Touchdowns	55	36
Rushing	24	15
Passing	29	19
Returns	2	2

2004 INDIVIDUAL STATISTICS

PASSING	Att.	Comp.	Yds.	Pct.	TD	Int.	Tkld.	Rate
Brees	400	262	3,159	65.5	27	7	18/131	104.8
Flutie	38	20	276	52.6	1	0	1/7	85.0
Rivers	8	5	33	62.5	0	0	1/10	110.9
Tomlinson	2	1	38	50.0	0	0	1/1	95.8
McCardell	1	0	0	0.0	0	0	0/0	39.6
Scifres	1	0	0	0.0	0	1	0/0	0.0
Chargers	450	288	3,506	64.0	29	8	21/149	102.0
Opponents	607	372	4,195	61.3	19	23	29/142	76.6

SCORING	TD R	TD P	TD Rt	PAT	FG	Saf	PTS
Kaeding	0	0	0	54/55	20/25	0	114
Tomlinson	17	1	0	0/0	0/0	0	108
Gates	0	13	0	0/0	0/0	0	78
Parker	0	4	0	0/0	0/0	0	24
Caldwell	0	3	0	0/0	0/0	0	18
Chatman	3	0	0	0/0	0/0	0	18
Brees	2	0	0	0/0	0/0	0	12
Dwight	0	1	1	0/0	0/0	0	12
Flutie	2	0	0	0/0	0/0	0	12
Osgood	0	2	0	0/0	0/0	0	12
Peelle	0	2	0	0/0	0/0	0	12
D. Edwards	0	0	1	0/0	0/0	0	6
Floyd	0	1	0	0/0	0/0	0	6
Krause	0	1	0	0/0	0/0	0	6
McCardell	0	1	0	0/0	0/0	0	6
Chargers	24	29	2	54/55	20/25	1	446
Opponents	15	19	2	33/34	20/27	0	313

2-Pt. Conversions: None.
Chargers 0-0, Opponents 2-2.

RUSHING	No.	Yds	Avg	LG	TD
Tomlinson	339	1,335	3.9	42	17
Chatman	65	392	6.0	52	3
Turner	20	104	5.2	30	0
Brees	53	85	1.6	22	2
Dwight	4	54	13.5	48	0
Neal	16	53	3.3	8	0
Parker	4	53	13.3	38	0
Caldwell	4	45	11.3	20	0
Flutie	5	39	7.8	20	2
Pinnock	9	26	2.9	11	0
McCardell	1	3	3.0	3	0
Shaw	1	1	1.0	1	0
Rivers	4	-5	-1.2	-1	0
Chargers	525	2,185	4.2	52	24
Opponents	355	1,307	3.7	26	15

RECEIVING	No.	Yds	Avg	LG	TD
Gates	81	964	11.9	72t	13
Tomlinson	53	441	8.3	74t	1
Parker	47	690	14.7	79t	4
McCardell	31	393	12.7	31	1
Caldwell	18	310	17.2	58t	3
Osgood	15	308	20.5	65	2
Neal	13	66	5.1	12	0
Peelle	10	84	8.4	17t	2
Krause	5	81	16.2	29	1
Turner	4	8	2.0	7	0
Floyd	3	49	16.3	27	1
Pinnock	3	26	8.7	14	0
Dwight	2	31	15.5	23t	1
Chatman	2	17	8.5	17	0
Brees	1	38	38.0	38	0
Chargers	288	3,506	12.2	79t	29
Opponents	372	4,195	11.3	50	19

INTERCEPTIONS	No.	Yds	Avg	LG	TD
D. Edwards	5	49	9.8	30t	1
Florence	4	54	13.5	40	0
Wilson	3	12	4.0	12	0
Kiel	2	31	15.5	31	0
Foley	2	4	2.0	4	0
Hart	1	13	13.0	13	0
Jammer	1	12	12.0	12	0
Davis	1	4	4.0	4	0
Dingle	1	1	1.0	1	0
Fletcher	1	0	0.0	0	0
Phillips	1	0	0.0	0	0
Wilhelm	1	0	0.0	0	0
Chargers	23	180	7.8	40	1
Opponents	8	66	8.3	25	0

PUNTING	No.	Yds.	Avg.	In 20	LG
Scifres	69	2,974	43.1	29	60
Chargers	69	2,974	43.1	29	60
Opponents	64	2,713	42.4	13	59

PUNT RETURNS	Ret	FC	Yds	Avg	LG	TD
Parker	27	10	237	8.8	32	0
Dwight	1	5	6	6.0	6	0
Florence	1	0	0	0.0	0	0
Chargers	29	15	243	8.4	32	0
Opponents	23	23	164	7.1	38	0

KICKOFF RETURNS	No.	Yds	Avg	LG	TD
Dwight	50	1,222	24.4	87t	1
Chatman	4	89	22.3	35	0
Welker	4	102	25.5	33	0
Butler	2	35	17.5	24	0
Neal	1	12	12.0	12	0
Turner	1	18	18.0	18	0
Chargers	62	1,478	23.8	87t	1
Opponents	83	1,846	22.2	96t	2

FIELD GOALS	1-19	20-29	30-39	40-49	50+
Kaeding	1/1	9/11	2/2	5/6	3/5
Chargers	1/1	9/11	2/2	5/6	3/5
Opponents	0/0	11/11	6/9	2/6	1/1

SACKS	No.
Foley	10.0
Phillips	4.0
Williams	4.0
Godfrey	2.0
Leber	2.0
Scott	1.5
Dingle	1.0
D. Edwards	1.0
Fisk	1.0
Kiel	1.0
Olshansky	1.0
Cesaire	0.5
Chargers	29.0
Opponents	21.0

RECORD HOLDERS
INDIVIDUAL RECORDS—CAREER

Category	Name	Performance
Rushing (Yds.)	LaDainian Tomlinson, 2001-04	5,899
Passing (Yds.)	Dan Fouts, 1973-1987	43,040
Passing (TDs)	Dan Fouts, 1973-1987	254
Receiving (No.)	Charlie Joiner, 1976-1986	586
Receiving (Yds.)	Lance Alworth, 1962-1970	9,585
Interceptions	Gill Byrd, 1983-1992	42
Punting (Avg.)	Darren Bennett, 1995-2003	43.8
Punt Return (Avg.)	Darrien Gordon, 1993-96	13.6
Kickoff Return (Avg.)	Leslie (Speedy) Duncan, 1964-1970	25.3
Field Goals	John Carney, 1990-2000	261
Touchdowns (Tot.)	Lance Alworth, 1962-1970	83
Points	John Carney, 1990-2000	1,076

INDIVIDUAL RECORDS—SINGLE SEASON

Category	Name	Performance
Rushing (Yds.)	LaDainian Tomlinson, 2002	1,683
Passing (Yds.)	Dan Fouts, 1981	4,802
Passing (TDs)	Dan Fouts, 1981	33
Receiving (No.)	LaDainian Tomlinson, 2003	100
Receiving (Yds.)	Lance Alworth, 1965	1,602
Interceptions	Charlie McNeil, 1961	9
Punting (Avg.)	Darren Bennett, 2000	46.2
Punt Return (Avg.)	Leslie (Speedy) Duncan, 1965	15.5
Kickoff Return (Avg.)	Keith Lincoln, 1962	28.4
Field Goals	John Carney, 1994	34
Touchdowns (Tot.)	Chuck Muncie, 1981	19
Points	John Carney, 1994	135

INDIVIDUAL RECORDS—SINGLE GAME

Category	Name	Performance
Rushing (Yds.)	LaDainian Tomlinson, 12-28-03	243
Passing (Yds.)	Dan Fouts, 10-19-80, 12-11-82	444
Passing (TDs)	Dan Fouts, 11-22-81	6
Receiving (No.)	Kellen Winslow, 10-7-84	15
Receiving (Yds.)	Wes Chandler, 12-20-82	260
Interceptions	Many times	3
	Last time by Dwayne Harper, 11-27-95	
Field Goals	John Carney, 9-5-93, 9-18-93	6
	Greg Davis, 10-5-97	6
Touchdowns (Tot.)	Kellen Winslow, 11-22-81	5
Points	Kellen Winslow, 11-22-81	30

2005 VETERAN ROSTER

No.	Name	Pos.	Ht.	Wt.	Birthdate	NFL Exp.	College	Hometown	How Acq.	'04 Games/ Starts
96	Ball, Dave	DE	6-5	277	1/4/81	2	UCLA	Dixon, Calif.	D5a-'04	6/0
97	Bingham, Ryon	DT	6-3	303	6/6/81	2	Nebraska	Sandy, Utah	D7a-'04	0*
50	Binn, David	LS	6-3	223	2/6/72	12	California	San Mateo, Calif.	FA-'94	16/0
65	Brandt, David	C	6-4	311	9/25/77	4	Michigan	Jenison, Mich.	FA-'03	3/0
9	Brees, Drew	QB	6-0	209	1/15/79	5	Purdue	Austin, Texas	D2-'01	15/15
49	Brewer, Sean	TE	6-4	255	10/5/77	4	San Jose State	Riverside, Calif.	FA-'05	0*
82	Caldwell, Reche	WR	6-0	215	3/28/79	4	Florida	Tampa, Fla.	D2b-'02	6/6
74	Cesaire, Jacques	DE	6-2	295	8/30/80	3	Southern Connecticut St.	Gardner, Mass.	FA-'03	16/12
24	Chatman, Jesse	RB	5-8	247	9/22/79	4	Eastern Washington	Seattle, Wash.	FA-'02	15/0
54	Cooper, Stephen	LB	6-1	235	6/19/79	3	Maine	Wareham, Mass.	FA-'03	16/2
22	Davis, Sammy	CB	6-0	195	4/8/80	3	Texas A&M	Humble, Texas	D1-'03	12/10
68	Dielman, Kris	G	6-4	310	2/3/81	3	Indiana	Troy, Ohio	FA-'03	15/0
90	Dingle, Adrian	DE	6-3	296	6/25/77	7	Clemson	Holly Hill, S.C.	D5a-'99	10/2
59	Edwards, Donnie	LB	6-2	227	4/6/73	10	UCLA	Chula Vista, Calif.	UFA(KC)-'02	16/16
25	Fletcher, Jamar	CB	5-10	186	8/28/79	5	Wisconsin	St. Louis, Mo.	T(Mia)-'04	16/0
29	Florence, Drayton	CB	6-0	195	12/19/80	3	Tuskegee	Ocala, Fla.	D2a-'03	13/5
53	Foley, Steve	LB	6-4	265	9/11/75	8	Northeast Louisiana	Little Rock, Ark.	UFA(Hou)-'04	16/16
77	Fonoti, Toniu	G	6-4	350	11/26/81	4	Nebraska	Hauula, Hawaii	D2a-'02	16/16
28	Galloway, Ahmad	RB	5-11	223	3/10/80	2	Alabama	Millington, Tenn.	FA-'04	0*
85+	Gates, Antonio	TE	6-4	260	6/18/80	3	Kent State	Detroit, Mich.	FA-'03	15/15
58	Godfrey, Randall	LB	6-2	245	4/6/73	10	Georgia	Valdosta, Ga.	UFA(Sea)-'04	15/15
79	Goff, Mike	G	6-5	311	1/6/76	8	Iowa	Peru, Ill.	UFA(Cin)-'04	16/16
62	Hallen, Bob	C-G	6-3	295	3/9/75	8	Kent State	Mentor, Ohio	FA-'04	2/0
61	Hardwick, Nick	C	6-4	295	9/12/81	2	Purdue	Indianapolis, Ind.	D3b-'04	14/14
42	Hart, Clinton	S	6-0	205	7/20/77	3	Central Florida C.C.	Bushnell, Fla.	W(Phil)-'04	14/0
23	Jammer, Quentin	CB	6-0	204	6/19/79	4	Texas	Angleton, Texas	D1-'02	16/16
75	Jordan, Leander	T	6-4	316	9/15/77	6	Indiana (PA)	Pittsburgh, Pa.	UFA(Jax)-'04	5/0
27	Jue, Bhawoh	S	6-0	200	5/24/79	5	Penn State	Chantilly, Va.	UFA(GB)-'05	16/4*
10	Kaeding, Nate	K	6-0	187	3/26/82	2	Iowa	Coralville, Iowa	D3a-'04	16/0
48	Kiel, Terrence	S	5-11	207	11/24/80	3	Texas A&M	Lufkin, Tex.	D2b-'03	16/16
89	Krause, Ryan	TE	6-3	256	6/16/81	2	Nebraska-Omaha	Omaha, Neb.	D6-'04	1/1
51	Leber, Ben	LB	6-3	244	12/7/78	4	Kansas State	Vermillion, S.D.	D3-'02	16/16
12	Lemon, Cleo	QB	6-2	215	8/16/79	2	Arkansas State	Greenwood, Miss.	FA-'03	0*
87 t-	McCardell, Keenan	WR	6-1	191	1/6/70	14	Nevada-Las Vegas	Houston, Texas	T(TB)-'04	7/6
31	Milligan, Hanik	S	6-3	200	11/3/79	3	Houston	Coconut Creek, Fla.	D6-'03	14/0
41	Neal, Lorenzo	FB	5-11	255	12/27/70	13	Fresno State	Hanford, Calif.	UFA(Cin)-'03	16/10
72	Oben, Roman	T	6-4	305	10/9/72	10	Louisville	Washington D.C.	T(TB)-'04	16/16
70	Olivea, Shane	T	6-3	312	10/7/81	2	Ohio State	Long Beach, N.Y.	D7b-'04	16/16
99	Olshansky, Igor	DE	6-6	309	5/3/82	2	Oregon	San Francisco, Calif.	D2-'04	16/16
81	Osgood, Kassim	WR	6-5	209	5/20/80	3	San Diego State	Salinas, Calif.	FA-'03	16/7
88	Parker, Eric	WR	6-0	180	4/14/79	4	Tennessee	Shorewood, Ill.	FA-'02	15/13
84	Peelle, Justin	TE	6-4	255	3/15/79	4	Oregon	Dublin, Calif.	D4-'02	16/4
95	Phillips, Shaun	LB	6-3	262	5/13/81	2	Purdue	Willingboro, N.J.	D4-'04	16/0
34	Pinnock, Andrew	FB	5-10	250	3/12/80	3	South Carolina	Bloomfield, Conn.	D7-'03	1/0
52	Polk, Carlos	LB	6-2	262	2/22/77	5	Nebraska	Rockford, Ill.	D4-'01	1/0
17	Rivers, Philip	QB	6-5	228	12/8/81	2	North Carolina State	Athens, Ala.	T(NYG)-'04	2/0
5	Scifres, Mike	P	6-2	236	10/8/80	3	Western Illinois	Destrehan, La.	D5-'03	16/0
78	Scott, DeQuincy	DE	6-1	260	3/5/78	4	Southern Mississippi	LaPlace, La.	FA-'01	14/2
21	Tomlinson, LaDainian	RB	5-10	221	6/23/79	5	Texas Christian	Waco, Texas	D1-'01	15/15
33	Turner, Michael	RB	5-10	237	2/13/82	2	Northern Illinois	North Chicago, Ill.	D5b-'04	14/1
71	Van Buren, Courtney	T	6-6	350	2/22/80	3	Arkansas-Pine Bluff	St. Louis, Mo.	D3-'03	1/0
56	Wilhelm, Matt	LB	6-2	254	2/2/81	3	Ohio State	Elryia, Ohio	D4-'03	7/0
76	Williams, Jamal	DT	6-3	348	4/28/76	8	Oklahoma State	Washington, D.C.	D2(Supp)-'98	15/15
20	Wilson, Jerry	FS	5-11	190	7/17/73	10	Southern	Lake Charles, La.	FA-'02	16/16

* Bingham missed '04 season because of injury; Brewer last active with Atlanta in '03; Galloway missed '03 season with Denver because of injury; Jue played 16 games with Green Bay in '04; Lemon inactive for 16 games.

+ Exclusive Rights free agent; subject to developments.

t Chargers traded for McCardell (TB).

Players lost through free agency (1): LB Zeke Moreno (Hou; 9 games in '04).

Also played with Chargers in '04—DT Eric Downing (3 games), WR Tim Dwight (12), DT Jason Fisk (15), QB Doug Flutie (2), WR Bobby Shaw (7).

2005 FIRST-YEAR ROSTER

Name	Pos.	Ht.	Wt.	Birthdate	College	Hometown	How Acq.
Britt, Wesley	T	6-8	314	11/21/81	Alabama	Cullman, Ala.	D5
Butler, Robb (1)	S	6-0	217	9/14/81	Robert Morris	Pittsburgh, Pa.	FA-'04
Cage, Jemelle	DE	6-1	284	6/1/81	Louisiana Tech	New Orleans, La.	FA
Camarillo, Greg	WR	6-1	190	4/18/82	Stanford	Menlo Park, Calif.	FA
Castillo, Luis	DT/DE	6-3	303	8/4/83	Northwestern	Garfield, N.J.	D1b
Cox, Jonathan (1)	CB	5-10	185	2/16/82	Georgia Tech	Chicago, Ill.	FA-'04
Curry, Markus	CB	5-11	181	4/7/81	Michigan	Detroit, Mich.	FA
Duckett, Adell	DE	6-3	270	10/7/81	Texas Tech	Mineral Wells, Texas	FA
Elimimian, Abraham	CB	5-9	193	3/2/82	Hawaii	Los Angeles, Calif.	FA
Farmer, Robby	LB	6-2	240	12/18/81	Troy State	Hayden, Ala.	FA
Floyd, Malcom (1)	WR	6-5	201	9/8/81	Wyoming	Sacramento, Calif.	FA-'04
Franklin, Gabe	CB	5-10	188	6/28/82	Boise State	Hayward, Calif.	FA
Fuga, Lui	DT	6-1	304	1/25/80	Hawaii	Oahu, Hawaii	FA
Harris, Marques	LB	6-1	231	9/20/81	Southern Utah State	Grand Junction, Colo.	FA
Hodges, Howard (1)	LB	6-2	255	5/29/81	Iowa	Copperas Cove, Texas	FA-'04
Jackson, Vincent	WR	6-5	241	1/14/83	Northern Colorado	Colorado Springs, Colo.	D2
Johnson, Chase	C	6-2	295	12/12/81	Texas Christian	Shawnee Mission, Kan.	FA
Joseph, Carlos (1)	T	6-6	342	7/14/80	Miami	Miami, Fla.	D7c-'04
Leach, Jason	S	5-11	203	7/21/82	Southern California	La Puente, Calif.	FA
Lekkerkerker, Cory	T	6-7	323	7/25/81	California-Davis	Chino, Calif.	FA
Martin, Ruvell (1)	WR	6-5	220	8/10/2	Saginaw Valley State	Muskegon, Mich.	FA
McCarty, Cody	TE	6-4	263	1/2/82	Texas Christian	Bishop, Texas	FA
Merriman, Shawne	LB	6-4	272	5/25/84	Maryland	Upper Marlboro, Md.	D1a
Morris, Carl (1)	WR	6-3	213	3/3/81	Harvard	Sterling, Va.	FA-'04
Mruczkowski, Scott	C	6-5	318	4/5/82	Bowling Green	Garfield Heights, Ohio	D7
Murray, Calvin (1)	RB	5-10	198	4/19/81	Miami (OH)	Dublin, Ohio	FA-'04
Ochs, Craig	QB	6-2	211	8/20/81	Montana	Boulder, Colo.	FA
Perkins, Ray	RB	5-10	205	11/6/82	Southeastern Louisiana	Ft. Lauderdale, Fla.	FA
Pollard, Jonathan	LB	6-1	247	11/19/81	Oregon State	Las Vegas, Nev.	FA
Pollard, Robert (1)	DE	6-2	278	6/28/81	Texas Christian	Beaumont, Texas	FA-'04
Quinnie, Willie (1)	WR	6-2	180	10/2/80	Alabama-Birmingham	Theodore, Ala.	FA-'04
Robinson, Derreck	DE	6-4	289	3/3/82	Iowa	Minneapolis, Minn.	FA
Ross, Isaiah (1)	C	6-3	315	11/6/81	Nevada	Elk Grove, Calif.	FA
Sims, Wes	G	6-4	317	4/8/81	Oklahoma	Weatherford, Okla.	D6
Sproles, Darren	RB/KR	5-6	181	6/20/83	Kansas State	Olathe, Kan.	D4
Tant, Matthew	FB	5-10	231	3/14/83	Vanderbilt	Pegram, Tenn.	FA
Young, Danny (1)	TE/LS	6-5	265	1/13/82	North Carolina State	San Diego, Calif.	FA

The term NFL Rookie is defined as a player who is in his first season of professional football and has not been on the roster of another professional football team for any regular-season or postseason games. A Rookie is designated by an "R" on NFL rosters. Players who have been active in another professional football league or players who have NFL experience, including either preseason training camp or being on an Active List or Inactive List, or on Reserve/Injured or Reserve/Physically Unable to Perform for fewer than six regular-season games, are termed NFL First-Year Players. An NFL First-Year Player is designated by a "1" on NFL rosters. Thereafter, a player is credited with an additional year of experience for each season in which he accumulates six games on the Active List or Inactive List, or on Reserve/Injured or Reserve/Physically Unable to Perform.

Log on to www.chargers.com for an up-to-date roster.

COACHING STAFF
Head Coach,
Marty Schottenheimer

Pro Career: Marty Schottenheimer is entering his fourth season as the head coach of the San Diego Chargers. He was named the NFL Coach of the Year by the *Associated Press* in 2004 after leading the Chargers to a 12-4 record and their first AFC West title since 1994. In 18 full seasons as a head coach in the NFL, Schottenheimer has led his teams to 13 winning seasons. He is eighth on the NFL's all-time list with 177 regular-season wins. Schottenheimer is 24-25, including playoffs, in three seasons as head coach of the Chargers. He spent 2001 as the Washington Redskins head coach and director of football operations. In his 10 years as head coach of the Kansas City Chiefs (1989-1998), he had a record of 104-65-1 and advanced to the playoffs seven times. The Cleveland Browns went to the playoffs all four seasons (1985-88) he was the head coach. In 1986, Schottenheimer was the consensus AFC coach of the year. He coached with the Portland Storm (WFL) in 1974, New York Giants (1975-77), and Detroit Lions (1978-79), and Cleveland Browns (1980-84). In 1984, he took over as the Browns' head coach midway through the season. Played linebacker for Buffalo (1965-68) and Boston Patriots (1969-1970). Career record: 182-129-1.

Background: Schottenheimer was an All-America linebacker at Pittsburgh (1962-64). After leaving the Chiefs in 1998, he joined ESPN as a pro football analyst.

Personal: Born September 23, 1943 in Canonsburg, Pa. Marty and his wife Patricia have one daughter, Kristen, one son, Brian, who is the Chargers' quarterbacks coach, and one grandchild, Brandon.

ASSISTANT COACHES

Cam Cameron, offensive coordinator; born February 6, 1961, Chapel Hill, N.C. Quarterback Indiana 1980-83. No pro playing experience. College coach: Michigan 1984-1993, Indiana 1997-2001 (head coach). Pro coach: Washington Redskins 1994-96, joined Chargers in 2002.

Pete Carmichael Jr., asst. wide receivers/quality control; born October 6, 1971, Farmingham, Mass. Attended Boston College. No college or pro playing experience. College coach: New Hampshire 1994, Louisiana Tech 1995-99. Pro coach: Cleveland Browns 2000, Washington Redskins 2001, joined Chargers in 2002.

Rob Chudzinski, tight ends; born May 12, 1968, Toledo, Ohio. Tight end Miami 1986-1990. No pro playing experience. College coach: Miami 1994-2003. Pro Coach: Cleveland Browns 2004, joined Chargers in 2005.

Steve Crosby, special teams; born July 3, 1950, Great Bend, Kan. Running back Fort Hayes State 1970-73. Pro running back New York Giants 1974-76. College coach: Vanderbilt 1998-2001. Pro coach: Miami Dolphins 1979-1982, Atlanta Falcons 1983-84, 1986-89, Cleveland Browns 1985, 1991-95, New England Patriots 1990, joined Chargers in 2002.

Albert Lewis, asst. secondary; born October 6, 1960, Mansfield, La. Cornerback Grambling State 1979-1982. Pro cornerback Kansas City Chiefs 1983-1993, Oakland Raiders 1994-98. Pro coach: Joined Chargers in 2004.

James Lofton, wide receivers; born July 5, 1956, Fort Ord, Calif. Wide receiver Stanford 1975-77. Pro wide receiver Green Bay Packers 1978-1986, Los Angeles Raiders 1987-88, Buffalo Bills 1989-1992, Los Angeles Rams 1993, Philadelphia Eagles 1993. Pro coach: Joined Chargers in 2002.

Greg Manusky, linebackers; born August 12, 1966, Wilkes-Barre, Pa. Linebacker Colgate 1983-87. Pro linebacker Washington Redskins 1988-1990, Minnesota Vikings 1991-93, Kansas City Chiefs 1994-99. Pro coach: Washington Redskins 2001, joined Chargers in 2002.

Carl Mauck, offensive line; born July 7, 1947, McLeansboro, Ill. Linebacker/center Southern Illinois 1966-68. Pro center Baltimore Colts 1969, Miami Dolphins 1970, San Diego Chargers 1971-74, Houston Oilers 1975-1981. Pro coach: New Orleans Saints 1982-85, Kansas City Chiefs 1986-88, Tampa Bay Buccaneers 1991, San Diego Chargers 1992-95, Arizona Cardinals 1996-97, Buffalo Bills 1998-2000, Detroit Lions 2001-03, re-joined Chargers in 2005.

Wayne Nunnely, defensive line; born March 29, 1952, Los Angeles. Fullback Nevada-Las Vegas 1972-75. No pro playing experience. College coach: Nevada-Las Vegas 1976, 1982-89 (head coach 1986-89), Cal Poly-Pomona 1977-78, Cal State-Fullerton 1979, Pacific 1980-81, Southern California 1991-92, UCLA 1993-94. Pro coach: New Orleans Saints 1995-96, joined Chargers in 1997.

John Pagano, asst. linebackers/quality control; born March 30, 1967, Boulder, Colo. Linebacker Mesa State College 1985-88. No pro playing experience. College coach: Mesa State College 1989, Nevada-Las Vegas 1990-91, Louisiana Tech 1994, Mississippi 1995. Pro coach: New Orleans Saints 1996-97, Indianapolis Colts 1998-2001, joined Chargers in 2002.

Wade Phillips, defensive coordinator; born June 21, 1947, Orange, Texas. Linebacker Houston 1966-68. No pro playing experience. College coach: Houston 1969, Oklahoma State 1973-74, Kansas 1975. Pro coach: Houston 1976-1980, New Orleans 1981-85 (head coach of last four games in 1985), Philadelphia

1986-88, Denver 1989-1994 (head coach 1993-94), Buffalo 1995-2000 (head coach 1998-2000), Atlanta 2002-03 (head coach last three games of 2003), joined Chargers in 2004.

Dave Redding, strength and conditioning; born June 14, 1952, North Platte, Neb. Defensive end Nebraska 1972-75. No pro playing experience. College coach: Nebraska 1976, Washington State 1977, Missouri 1978-1981. Pro coach: Cleveland Browns 1982-88, Kansas City Chiefs 1989-1997, Washington Redskins 2001, joined Chargers in 2002.

Matt Schiotz, asst. strength and conditioning; born June 8, 1971, Menomonie, Wis. Attended Wisconsin-La Crosse. No college or pro playing experience. College coach: Kansas 1995-96, Southern California 1998-2000. Pro coach: Kansas City Chiefs 1997, Washington Redskins 2001, joined Chargers in 2002.

Brian Schottenheimer, quarterbacks; born October 16, 1973, Denver. Quarterback Kansas 1992, Florida 1993-96. No pro playing experience. College coach: Syracuse 1999, Southern California 2000. Pro coach: St. Louis Rams 1997, Kansas City Chiefs 1998, Washington Redskins 2001, joined Chargers in 2002.

Clarence Shelmon, running backs; born September 17, 1952, Bossier City, La. Running back Houston 1971-75. No pro playing experience. College coach: Army 1978-1980, Indiana 1981-83, Arizona 1984-86, Southern California 1987-1990. Pro coach: Los Angeles Rams 1991, Seattle Seahawks 1992-97, Dallas Cowboys 1998-2001, joined Chargers in 2002.

Brian Stewart, secondary; born December 4, 1964, San Diego. Cornerback Northern Arizona 1983, 1986-87, Santa Monica City College 1984-85. No pro playing experience. College coach: Cal Poly-San Luis Obispo 1993-94, Northern Arizona 1995, Missouri 1996, 1999-2000, San Jose State 1997-98, Syracuse 2001. Pro coach: Houston 2002-03, joined Chargers in 2004.

John Wuehrmann, coaching administrator; born January 21, 1956, Chicago. Attended Wyoming. No college or pro playing experience. Pro coach: Joined Chargers in 2003.

**American Football Conference
South Division**
Team Colors: Navy, Titans Blue, Red, Silver
**460 Great Circle Road
Nashville, Tennessee 37228
Telephone: (615) 565-4000**

2005 SCHEDULE
PRESEASON
Aug. 12	**Tampa Bay**	7:00
Aug. 19	at Atlanta	7:30
Aug. 26	at San Francisco	7:00
Sept. 1	**Green Bay**	7:00

REGULAR SEASON
Sept. 11	at Pittsburgh	1:00
Sept. 18	**Baltimore**	12:00
Sept. 25	at St. Louis	12:00
Oct. 2	**Indianapolis**	12:00
Oct. 9	at Houston	12:00
Oct. 16	**Cincinnati**	12:00
Oct. 23	at Arizona	1:15
Oct. 30	**Oakland**	12:00
Nov. 6	at Cleveland	1:00
Nov. 13	Open Date	
Nov. 20	**Jacksonville**	12:00
Nov. 27	**San Francisco**	12:00
Dec. 4	at Indianapolis	1:00
Dec. 11	**Houston**	12:00
Dec. 18	**Seattle**	12:00
Dec. 24	at Miami (Sat.)	1:00
Jan. 1	at Jacksonville	4:05

Stadium: The Coliseum
(opened in 1999)
• **Capacity:** 68,809
One Titans Way
Nashville, Tennessee 37213
Playing Surface: Natural Grass
Training Camp: Baptist Sports Park
460 Great Circle Road
Nashville, Tennessee
37228

THE COLISEUM

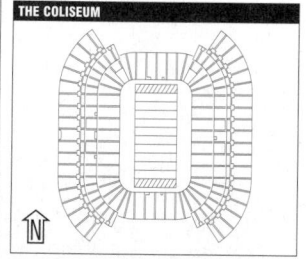

CLUB OFFICIALS
Owner/Chairman of the Board/CEO/
President: K.S. (Bud) Adams, Jr.
Executive V.P./General Manager and
Director Of Football Operations:
Floyd Reese
Executive V.P. of Administration/Facilities:
Don MacLachlan
Executive V.P./General Counsel:
Steve Underwood
Asst. General Counsel: Elza Bullock
Vice President/Finance:
Robert McBurnett
Vice President/Community Affairs:
Bob Hyde
Director of Player Personnel:
Rich Snead
Director of College Scouting:
Mike Ackerley
Director of Sales and Operations:
Stuart Spears
Asst. Director of Sales and Operations:
Brent Akers
Director of Broadcasting: Mike Keith
Director of Marketing: Ralph Ockenfels
Controller: Jenneen Kaufman
Director of Information Systems:
Russ Hudson
Director of Internet
Operations/Publications: Gary Glenn
Director of Media Relations:
Robbie Bohren
Asst. Director of Media Relations:
Dwight Spradlin
Director of Security: Steve Berk
Director of Ticket Operations:
Marty Collins
Director of Pro Personnel: Al Smith
Director of Player Development:
Marcus Robertson
Director of Cheerleading: Stacie Kinder
Director of Suite and Club Services:
Bill Wainwright
Head Athletic Trainer: Brad Brown
Assistant Athletic Trainers:
Don Moseley, Geoff Kaplan
Equipment Manager: Paul Noska
Video Director: Anthony Pastrana

COACHING HISTORY
**Houston 1960-1996
(342-359-6)**
Records include postseason games
1960-61	Lou Rymkus*	12-7-1
1961	Wally Lemm	10-0-0
1962-63	Frank (Pop) Ivy	17-12-0
1964	Sammy Baugh	4-10-0
1965	Hugh Taylor	4-10-0
1966-1970	Wally Lemm	28-40-4
1971	Ed Hughes	4-9-1
1972-73	Bill Peterson**	1-18-0
1973-74	Sid Gillman	8-15-0
1975-1980	O.A. (Bum) Phillips	59-38-0
1981-83	Ed Biles***	8-23-0
1983	Chuck Studley	2-8-0
1984-85	Hugh Campbell****	8-22-0
1985-89	Jerry Glanville	35-35-0
1990-94	Jack Pardee#	44-35-0
1994-2004	Jeff Fisher	98-77-0

* Released after five games in 1961
** Released after five games in 1973
*** Resigned after six games in 1983
**** Released after 14 games in 1985
\# Released after 10 games in 1994

ATTENDANCE
Home 535,329	Away 490,774

Total 1,026,103
Single-game home record,
68,809, many times (last: 12/28/03)
Single-season home record,
537,496 (2001)

2004 DRAFT CHOICES
Round	Name	Pos.	College
1	Adam Jones	DB	West Virginia
2	Michael Roos	T	Eastern Washington
3	Courtney Roby	WR	Indiana
	Brandon Jones	WR	Oklahoma
4	Vincent Fuller	DB	Virginia Tech
	David Stewart	T	Mississippi State
	Roydell Williams	WR	Tulane
5	Damien Nash	RB	Missouri
	Daniel Loper	T	Texas Tech
6	Bo Scaife	TE	Texas
7	Reynaldo Hill	DB	Florida

2004 TEAM RECORD
PRESEASON (3-1)

Date	Result	Opponent
8/14	W 24-3	Cleveland
8/21	W 16-15	at Buffalo
8/30	L 17-20	at Dallas
9/3	W 27-7	Green Bay

REGULAR SEASON (5-11)

Date	Result	Opponent	Att.
9/11	W 17-7	at Miami	69,987
9/19	L 17-31	Indianapolis	68,932
9/26	L 12-15	Jacksonville	68,932
10/3	L 17-38	at San Diego	54,006
10/11	W 48-27	at Green Bay	70,420
10/17	L 10-20	Houston	68,932
10/24	L 3-20	at Minnesota	64,108
10/31	W 27-20	Cincinnati	68,932
11/14	L 17-19	Chicago (OT)	68,932
11/21	W 18-15	at Jacksonville	69,703
11/28	L 21-31	at Houston	70,721
12/5	L 24-51	at Indianapolis	57,278
12/13	L 38-49	at Kansas City	68,932
12/19	L 35-40	at Oakland	44,299
12/25	L 16-37	Denver	68,809
1/2	W 24-19	Detroit	68,809

(OT) Overtime

SCORE BY PERIODS

Titans	106	111	49	78	0 —	344
Opponents	76	117	99	145	2 —	439

2004 TEAM STATISTICS

	Titans	Opp.
Total First Downs	308	318
Rushing	85	99
Passing	200	189
Penalty	23	30
3rd Down: Made/Att	74/217	62/186
3rd Down Pct.	34.1	33.3
4th Down: Made/Att	12/27	9/12
4th Down Pct.	44.4	75.0
Possession Avg.	31:40	28:20
Total Net Yards	5487	5724
Avg. Per Game	342.9	357.8
Total Plays	1053	977
Avg. Per Play	5.2	5.9
Net Yards Rushing	1871	1917
Avg. Per Game	116.9	119.8
Total Rushes	420	421
Net Yards Passing	3616	3807
Avg. Per Game	226.0	237.9
Sacked/Yards Lost	44/317	32/220
Gross Yards	3933	4027
Att./Completions	589/356	524/333
Completion Pct.	60.4	63.5
Had Intercepted	19	18
Punts/Average	79/42.9	74/43.6
Net Punting Avg.	79/38.2	74/38.8
Penalties/Yards	110/923	95/774
Fumbles/Ball Lost	33/12	22/12
Touchdowns	41	52
Rushing	12	18
Passing	27	29
Returns	2	5

2004 INDIVIDUAL STATISTICS

PASSING	Att.	Comp.	Yds.	Pct.	TD	Int.	Tkld.	Rate
Volek	357	218	2,486	61.1	18	10	30/216	87.1
McNair	215	129	1,343	60.0	8	9	13/95	73.1
Johnson	12	6	68	50.0	0	0	1/6	67.4
Hentrich	4	2	10	50.0	0	0	0/0	56.3
Bennett	1	1	26	100.0	1	0	0/0	158.3
Titans	589	356	3,933	60.4	27	19	44/317	82.1
Opponents	524	333	4,027	63.5	29	18	32/220	91.2

SCORING	TD R	TD P	TD Rt	PAT	FG	Saf	PTS
Anderson	0	0	0	37/37	17/22	0	88
Bennett	0	11	0	0/0	0/0	0	66
Mason	0	7	0	0/0	0/0	0	42
Brown	6	0	0	0/0	0/0	0	36
A. Smith	4	0	0	0/0	0/0	0	24
Kinney	0	3	0	0/0	0/0	0	18
Fleming	0	2	0	0/0	0/0	0	12
Meier	0	2	0	0/0	0/0	0	12
McNair	1	0	0	0/0	0/0	0	8
Berlin	0	1	0	0/0	0/0	0	6
Bulluck	0	0	1	0/0	0/0	0	6
Thompson	0	0	1	0/0	0/0	0	6
Troupe	0	1	0	0/0	0/0	0	6
Volek	1	0	0	0/0	0/0	0	6
Elling	0	0	0	2/2	1/2	0	5
Hentrich	0	0	0	0/0	1/3	0	3
Titans	12	27	2	39/39	19/27	0	344
Opponents	18	29	5	50/50	23/28	3	439

2-Pt. Conversions: McNair.
Titans 1-2, Opponents 1-2.

RUSHING	No.	Yds	Avg	LG	TD
Brown	220	1,067	4.9	52	6
A. Smith	137	509	3.7	43	4
McNair	23	128	5.6	23	1
Holcombe	17	62	3.6	20	0
Volek	11	50	4.5	14	1
Fleming	7	40	5.7	13	0
Bennett	1	12	12.0	12	0
Hentrich	1	8	8.0	8	0
Johnson	2	-2	-1.0	-1	0
Mason	1	-3	-3.0	-3	0
Titans	420	1,871	4.5	52	12
Opponents	421	1,917	4.6	55	18

RECEIVING	No.	Yds	Avg	LG	TD
Mason	96	1,168	12.2	37t	7
Bennett	80	1,247	15.6	48t	11
Troupe	33	329	10.0	33	1
Kinney	25	193	7.7	21	3
Meier	25	127	5.1	29	2
A. Smith	22	169	7.7	31	0
Berlin	20	278	13.9	31	1
Brown	20	147	7.4	21	0
Fleming	19	164	8.6	37	2
Holcombe	11	60	5.5	9	0
McAddley	2	38	19.0	36	0
Calico	2	13	6.5	9	0
Volek	1	0	0.0	0	0
Titans	356	3,933	11.0	48t	27
Opponents	333	4,027	12.1	62	29

INTERCEPTIONS	No.	Yds	Avg	LG	TD
Dyson	6	135	22.5	44	0
Thompson	4	77	19.3	37t	1
Bulluck	2	25	12.5	25	0
Woolfolk	1	25	25.0	25	0
Ta. Williams	1	13	13.0	13	0
McGarrahan	1	11	11.0	11	0
Rolle	1	0	0.0	0	0
Waddell	1	0	0.0	0	0
Gardner	1	-1	-1.0	-1	0
Titans	18	285	15.8	44	1
Opponents	19	306	16.1	51t	2

PUNTING	No.	Yds.	Avg.	In 20	LG
Hentrich	73	3,117	42.7	20	64
Elling	6	272	45.3	1	58
Titans	79	3,389	42.9	21	64
Opponents	74	3,223	43.6	24	66

PUNT RETURNS	Ret	FC	Yds	Avg	LG	TD
Mason	24	12	93	3.9	13	0
Waddell	9	3	54	6.0	18	0
Berlin	7	1	26	3.7	13	0
Titans	40	16	173	4.3	20	0
Opponents	31	26	195	6.3	75t	1

KICKOFF RETURNS	No.	Yds	Avg	LG	TD
McAddley	38	849	22.3	45	0
Fleming	18	316	17.6	30	0
Waddell	17	342	20.1	33	0
Holcombe	3	26	8.7	14	0
Bennett	1	-8	-8.0	-8	0
Kinney	1	21	21.0	21	0
Schobel	1	12	12.0	12	0
Titans	79	1,558	19.7	45	0
Opponents	69	1,389	20.1	35	0

FIELD GOALS	1-19	20-29	30-39	40-49	50+
Anderson	0/0	4/5	4/4	9/12	0/1
Hentrich	0/0	0/0	0/0	0/0	1/3
Elling	0/0	1/1	0/1	0/0	0/0
Titans	0/0	5/6	4/5	9/12	1/4
Opponents	0/0	12/12	5/7	3/6	3/3

SACKS	No.
Carter	6.0
Bulluck	5.0
Long	5.0
Starks	4.5
LaBoy	3.5
Hall	2.5
Odom	2.0
Haynesworth	1.0
Schulters	1.0
Ta. Williams	1.0
McGarrahan	0.5
Titans	32.0
Opponents	44.0

RECORD HOLDERS
INDIVIDUAL RECORDS—CAREER

Category	Name	Performance
Rushing (Yds.)	Eddie George, 1996-2003	10,009
Passing (Yds.)	Warren Moon, 1984-1993	33,685
Passing (TDs)	Warren Moon, 1984-1993	196
Receiving (No.)	Ernest Givins, 1986-1994	542
Receiving (Yds.)	Ernest Givins, 1986-1994	7,935
Interceptions	Jim Norton, 1960-68	45
Punting (Avg.)	Greg Montgomery, 1988-1993	43.6
Punt Return (Avg.)	Billy Johnson, 1974-1980	13.2
Kickoff Return (Avg.)	Bobby Jancik, 1962-67	26.5
Field Goals	Al Del Greco, 1991-2000	246
Touchdowns (Tot.)	Eddie George, 1996-2003	74
Points	Al Del Greco, 1991-2000	1,060

INDIVIDUAL RECORDS—SINGLE SEASON

Category	Name	Performance
Rushing (Yds.)	Earl Campbell, 1980	1,934
Passing (Yds.)	Warren Moon, 1991	4,690
Passing (TDs)	George Blanda, 1961	36
Receiving (No.)	Charley Hennigan, 1964	101
Receiving (Yds.)	Charley Hennigan, 1961	1,746
Interceptions	Fred Glick, 1963	12
	Mike Reinfeldt, 1979	12
Punting (Avg.)	Craig Hentrich, 1998	47.2
Punt Return (Avg.)	Billy Johnson, 1977	15.4
Kickoff Return (Avg.)	Ken Hall, 1960	31.3
Field Goals	Al Del Greco, 1998	36
Touchdowns (Tot.)	Earl Campbell, 1979	19
Points	Al Del Greco, 1998	136

INDIVIDUAL RECORDS—SINGLE GAME

Category	Name	Performance
Rushing (Yds.)	Billy Cannon, 12-10-61	216
	Eddie George, 8-31-97	216
Passing (Yds.)	Warren Moon, 12-16-90	527
Passing (TDs)	George Blanda, 11-19-61	*7
Receiving (No.)	Charley Hennigan, 10-13-61	13
	Haywood Jeffires, 10-13-91	13
	Drew Bennett, 12-19-04	13
Receiving (Yds.)	Charley Hennigan, 10-13-61	272
Interceptions	Many times	3
	Last time by Samari Rolle, 12-26-99	
Field Goals	Roy Gerela, 9-28-69	5
	Al Del Greco, 12-3-00	5
Touchdowns (Tot.)	Billy Cannon, 12-10-61	5
Points	Billy Cannon, 12-10-61	30

*NFL Record

2005 VETERAN ROSTER

No.	Name	Pos.	Ht.	Wt.	Birthdate	NFL Exp.	College	Hometown	How Acq.	'04 Games/ Starts
64	Amano, Eugene	C	6-3	295	8/1/82	2	Southeast Missouri State	San Diego, Calif.	D7b-'04	15/2
58	Amato, Ken	LB/LS	6-2	245	5/18/77	3	Montana State	Miami, Fla.	FA-'03	16/0
24	Beckham, Tony	CB	6-1	187	10/1/78	4	Wisconsin-Stout	Ocala, Fla.	D4b-'02	5/1
60	Bell, Jacob	G/T	6-4	306	3/2/81	2	Miami (OH)	Cleveland, Ohio	D5a-'04	15/14
83	Bennett, Drew	WR	6-5	206	8/26/78	5	UCLA	Orinda, Calif.	FA-'01	16/16
50	Boiman, Rocky	LB	6-4	236	1/24/80	4	Notre Dame	Cincinnati, Ohio	D4c-'02	7/6
29	Brown, Chris	RB	6-3	219	4/17/81	3	Colorado	Naperville, Ill.	D3-'03	11/11
53	Bulluck, Keith	LB	6-3	235	4/4/77	6	Syracuse	New City, N.Y.	D1-'00	16/16
87	Calico, Tyrone	WR	6-4	222	11/9/80	3	Middle Tennessee State	Memphis, Tenn.	D2-'03	1/0
54	Calmus, Rocky	LB	6-3	238	8/1/79	4	Oklahoma	Jenks, Okla.	D3-'02	4/3
96	Clauss, Jared	DT	6-4	294	4/7/81	2	Iowa	West Des Moines, Iowa	D7a-'04	14/1
44	Fleming, Troy	FB	6-0	230	10/1/80	2	Tennessee	Franklin, Tenn.	D6-'04	16/0
30	Gardner, Rich	CB	5-10	199	2/1/81	2	Penn State	Chicago, Ill.	D3b-'04	15/1
77	Hartwig, Justin	C	6-4	305	11/21/78	4	Kansas	West Des Moines, Iowa	D6-'02	15/15
92	Haynesworth, Albert	DT	6-6	320	6/17/81	4	Tennessee	Hartsville, S.C.	D1-'02	10/10
15	Hentrich, Craig	P/K	6-3	213	5/18/71	12	Notre Dame	Alton, Ill.	UFA(GB)-'98	16/0
72	Hopkins, Brad	T	6-3	305	9/5/70	13	Illinois	Moline, Ill.	D1-'93	11/11
55	Kassell, Brad	LB	6-3	242	1/7/80	4	North Texas	Llano, Texas	FA-'02	15/14
88	Kinney, Erron	TE	6-5	275	7/28/77	6	Florida	Ashland, Va.	D3a-'00	9/9
91	LaBoy, Travis	DE	6-3	253	8/10/81	2	Hawaii	San Rafael, Calif.	D2b-'04	13/2
99	Long, Rien	DT	6-6	300	8/7/81	3	Washington State	Anacortes, Wash.	D4-'03	15/4
9	McNair, Steve	QB	6-2	235	2/14/73	11	Alcorn State	Mt. Olive, Miss.	D1-'95	8/8
23	Nickey, Donnie	S	6-3	215	4/25/80	3	Ohio State	Plain City, Ohio	D5-'03	15/5
98	Odom, Antwan	DE	6-4	277	9/24/81	2	Alabama	Bayou La Batre, Ala.	D2c-'04	16/7
75	Olson, Benji	G	6-4	320	6/5/75	8	Washington	Port Orchard, Wash.	D5-'98	15/15
69	Piller, Zach	G	6-5	321	5/2/76	7	Florida	Tallahassee, Fla.	D3-'99	1/1
51	Reynolds, Robert	LB	6-3	242	5/20/81	2	Ohio State	Bowling Green, Ky.	D5b-'04	14/1
40	Sandy, Justin	S	6-0	214	2/22/82	2	Northern Iowa	Sioux City, Iowa	FA-'04	1/0
95	Schobel, Bo	DE	6-5	264	3/24/81	2	Texas Christian	Columbus, Texas	D4a-'04	5/2
31	Schulters, Lance	S	6-2	202	5/27/75	8	Hofstra	Brooklyn, N.Y.	UFA(SF)-'02	3/3
59	Sirmon, Peter	LB	6-2	237	2/18/77	6	Oregon	Walla Walla, Wash.	D4b-'00	0*
56	Spencer, Cody	LB	6-2	245	6/1/81	2	North Texas	Port Lavaca, Texas	FA-'04	7/0
90	Starks, Randy	DT	6-3	307	12/14/83	2	Maryland	Waldorf, Md.	D3a-'04	14/8
28	Thompson, Lamont	S	6-1	220	7/30/78	4	Washington State	Richmond, Calif.	FA-'03	16/13
84	Troupe, Ben	TE	6-4	262	9/1/82	2	Florida	Augusta, Ga.	D2a-'04	14/7
93	Vanden Bosch, Kyle	DE	6-4	278	11/17/78	5	Nebraska	Larchwood, Iowa	UFA(Ariz)-'05	16/1*
7	Volek, Billy	QB	6-2	214	4/28/76	6	Fresno State	Fresno, Calif.	FA-'00	10/8
36	Waddell, Michael	CB	5-10	187	1/9/81	2	North Carolina	Ellerbe, N.C.	D4b-'04	16/4
25	Williams, Tank	S	6-3	223	6/30/80	4	Stanford	Bay St. Louis, Miss.	D2-'02	9/9
78	Williams, Todd	T/G	6-5	330	4/9/78	3	Florida State	Bradenton, Fla.	D7-'03	6/0
26	Woolfolk, Andre	CB	6-2	197	1/26/80	3	Oklahoma	Denver, Colo.	D1-'03	10/2

* Sirmon missed '04 season because of injury; Vanden Bosch played 16 games with Arizona.

Traded—DE Carlos Hall (KC; 14 games in '04).

Players lost through free agency (4): WR Eddie Berlin (Chi; 16 games in '04); CB Andre Dyson (Sea; 16); TE Shad Meier (NO; 14), RB Antowain Smith (NO; 13).

Also played with Titans in '04—K Gary Anderson (15 games), DE Kevin Carter (16), K Aaron Elling (1), LB Justin Ena (16), FB-RB Robert Holcombe (16), QB Doug Johnson (2), LB Jordan Kramer (4), WR Derrick Mason (16), T Jason Mathews (11), S Scott McGarrahan (16), T Fred Miller (16), G Marico Portis (1), CB Samari Rolle (11), WR Jake Schifino (1), DE Juqua Thomas (10).

2005 FIRST-YEAR ROSTER

Name	Pos.	Ht.	Wt.	Birthdate	College	Hometown	How Acq.
Anderson, Jason	WR	6-3	195	6/25/82	Wake Forest	Charlotte, N.C.	FA
Anthony, Charles	RB	5-11	210	1/31/83	Tennessee State	Orlando, Fla.	FA
Atkinson, Brian	LB	6-1	225	2/28/82	Northern Illinois	Chicago, Ill.	FA
Bates, Todd	DE	6-4	252	3/12/81	Alabama	Heflin, Ala.	FA
Boyd, Shane	QB	6-1	235	9/18/82	Kentucky	Lexington, Ky.	FA
Bush, Chris	WR	6-1	193	7/22/81	Tulane	LaPlace, La.	FA
Cartwright, Vincent	WR	6-3	208	12/31/81	Sam Houston State	Shelbyville, Texas	FA
Dabdoub, Brandon	DT	6-1	290	10/6/81	Colorado	Metairie, La.	FA
Debrow, Ellis	WR	6-4	230	3/20/81	Delta State	Pensacola, Fla.	FA
Dixon, Jimmy	FB	6-1	230	4/26/82	Georgia Tech	Arlington, Texas	FA
Douglas, Robert	FB	6-2	235	7/25/82	Memphis	St. Louis, Mo.	FA
Eldridge, Nigel	LB	6-1	225	3/14/82	Alabama-Birmingham	Montgomery, Ala.	FA
Erickson, Mike	G/T	6-4	304	5/8/82	Nebraska	Omaha, Neb.	FA
Fuller, Vincent	S	6-1	190	8/3/82	Virginia Tech	Baltimore, Md.	D4a
Guidugli, Gino	QB	6-4	230	3/13/83	Cincinnati	Ft. Thomas, Ky.	FA
Hall, Ben	TE	6-5	265	7/27/82	Clemson	Wellford, S.C.	FA
Harris, Antoine	CB	5-10	190	4/8/82	Louisville	Columbus, Ohio	FA
Harris, Travis	LB	6-2	241	8/2/81	Florida	Decatur, Ala.	FA
Haugabrook, Sidney	S	5-10	190	3/11/82	Delaware	Atlanta, Ga.	FA
Herrell, Ben (1)	T	6-7	316	7/28/80	Miami (OH)	Middleton, Wis.	FA
Hill, Reynaldo	CB	5-11	185	8/28/82	Florida	Ft. Lauderdale, Fla.	D7
Jackson, Jamacia	S	6-1	225	9/19/81	South Carolina	Sumter, S.C.	FA
Jackson, Terry	RB	5-10	195	3/3/82	Southern Illinois	Saginaw, Mich.	FA
Johnson, Earvin	WR	6-3	192	12/13/82	Nevada-Las Vegas	Southgate, Calif.	FA
Johnson, Shawn (1)	DE	6-5	275	3/21/80	Delaware	Rochester, N.Y.	FA
Jones, Brandon	WR	6-1	212	10/6/82	Oklahoma	Texarkana, Texas	D3b
Jones, Pacman	CB	5-10	187	9/30/83	West Virginia	Atlanta, Ga.	D1
Kimrin, Ola (1)	K	6-3	230	2/29/72	Texas-El Paso	Malmo, Sweden	FA
Larkins, Corey	RB	5-7	200	10/23/81	Tennessee	Opelika, Ala.	FA
LeJeune, Norman (1)	S	6-0	200	5/10/80	Louisiana State	Brusly, La.	FA
Loper, Daniel	T	6-6	320	1/15/82	Texas Tech	Houston, Texas	D5b
Massey, Sam (1)	CB	6-2	205	3/17/81	Morgan State	Camden, Ga.	FA
Nash, Damien	RB	5-10	215	4/14/82	Missouri	St. Louis, Mo.	D5a
Neal, Karlton	DE	6-4	253	11/5/82	Tennessee	Chicago, Ill.	FA
Nix, Alonzo	WR	5-10	190	2/5/83	Tennessee-Chattanooga	Laurel, Miss.	FA
Payton, Jarrett (1)	RB	6-0	220	12/26/80	Miami	Arlington, Ill.	FA
Randall, Marcus	QB	6-2	221	3/14/82	Louisiana State	Baton Rouge, La.	FA
Reyes, Walter	RB	5-10	210	5/22/81	Syracuse	Girard, Ohio	FA
Roby, Courtney	WR	6-0	189	1/10/83	Indiana	Indianapolis, Ind	D3a
Rodgers, Stefan	T	6-4	305	11/3/81	Lambuth	Jacksonville, Ark.	FA
Rodriguez, Joel	C	6-3	304	6/27/82	Miami	Miami, Fla.	FA
Rodriguez, Robert	LB	6-0	240	12/25/81	Texas-El Paso	El Paso, Texas	FA
Rogers, Will	G	6-4	320	10/18/81	Mississippi State	Atlanta, Ga.	FA
Roos, Michael	T	6-7	315	10/5/82	Eastern Washington	Vancouver, Wash.	D2
St. Louis, Jimmy	TE	6-5	265	12/2/81	Murray State	Pensacola, Fla.	FA
Scaife, Bo	TE	6-3	249	1/6/81	Texas	Denver, Colo.	D6
Small, O.J.	WR	6-1	230	8/18/82	Florida	Jacksonville, Fla.	FA
Smith, Joe (1)	RB	6-1	224	8/26/79	Louisiana Tech	Cleveland, Texas	FA
Smith, Kenneth	DE	6-2	267	6/6/81	Benedict College	Simpsonville, S.C.	FA
Stewart, David	T	6-7	318	8/28/82	Mississippi State	Moulton, Ala.	D4b
Strong, Derrick (1)	DE	6-4	261	4/16/82	Illinois	Chicago, Ill.	FA
Swaggert, Brent (1)	T	6-4	293	4/7/81	Montana State	Buffalo, Minn.	FA
Timothee, Kevin	CB	5-11	191	11/30/81	Florida International	Ft. Lauderdale, Fla.	FA
White, Jason	QB	6-2	226	6/19/80	Oklahoma	Tuttle, Okla.	FA
White, Marcus	DT	6-5	310	11/13/81	Murray State	Theodore, Ala.	FA
Williams, Roydell	WR	6-0	187	3/14/81	Tulane	New Orleans, La.	D4c
Wright, Alton	DE	6-4	240	1/3/81	Miami	Houston, Texas	FA

The term NFL Rookie is defined as a player who is in his first season of professional football and has not been on the roster of another professional football team for any regular-season or postseason games. A Rookie is designated by an "R" on NFL rosters. Players who have been active in another professional football league or players who have NFL experience, including either preseason training camp or being on an Active List or Inactive List, or on Reserve/Injured or Reserve/Physically Unable to Perform for fewer than six regular-season games, are termed NFL First-Year Players. An NFL First-Year Player is designated by a "1" on NFL rosters. Thereafter, a player is credited with an additional year of experience for each season in which he accumulates six games on the Active List or Inactive List, or on Reserve/Injured or Reserve/Physically Unable to Perform.

Log on to www.titansonline.com for an up-to-date roster.

COACHING STAFF
Head Coach,
Jeff Fisher

Pro Career: Officially became the franchise's fifteenth head coach on January 5, 1995, after closing his first campaign with the Oilers as head coach/defensive coordinator. He replaced Jack Pardee on November 14, 1994, coaching the remaining six games as head coach. Fisher holds the franchise mark for wins with 98 over his 10-year coaching career and ranks third among NFL head coaches (Dungy and Reid) with 61 victories since 1999. Last year he became the fourth youngest coach (46) since 1960 to reach 90 regular-season victories (John Madden, Don Shula, and Bill Cowher). Over the last six seasons, Fisher has led the Titans to four playoff appearances, two AFC Championship Games, two division titles and a berth in Super Bowl XXXIV. In 2000, Fisher became only the fifth coach in NFL history to lead his team to consecutive 13-win seasons, joining Mike Holmgren, George Seifert, Marv Levy, and Mike Ditka. Fisher originally joined the Oilers in 1994 as the defensive coordinator, after serving as defensive backs coach for the San Francisco 49ers (1992-93). Prior to heading up the 49ers secondary, Fisher served as the defensive coordinator for the Los Angeles Rams (1991). He began his coaching career with the Philadelphia Eagles in 1986, where he handled defensive backs until becoming the NFL's youngest defensive coordinator in 1988. Drafted by Chicago in seventh round in 1981, he spent five seasons as a cornerback and kick returner for the Bears (1981-85). Assisted defensive coordinator Buddy Ryan in Bears' 1985 Super Bowl championship season after being placed on injured reserve with ankle injury. Career record: 98-77.

Background: Played at Southern California (1977-1980) for John Robinson in a star-studded defensive backfield that included Ronnie Lott, Dennis Smith, and Joey Browner. Member of the USC team that won the national championship in 1978. Also served as the Trojans' backup placekicker and was a Pac-10 All-Academic selection in 1980.

Personal: Born February 25, 1958, in Culver City, Calif. Jeff and his wife, Juli, have three children, sons Brandon and Trenton, and daughter Tara.

ASSISTANT COACHES

Chuck Cecil, asst. coach/safeties and nickel backs; born November 8, 1964, Red Bluff, Calif. Defensive back Arizona 1983-87. Pro safety Green Bay Packers 1988-1992, Phoenix Cardinals 1993, Houston Oilers 1995. Pro coach: Joined Titans in 2001.

Norm Chow, offensive coordinator; born May 3, 1946, Honolulu, Hawaii. Guard Utah 1965-67. No pro playing experience. College coach: Brigham Young 1973-1999, North Carolina State 2000, Southern California 2001-04. Pro coach: Joined Titans in 2005.

Marty Galbraith, asst. special teams; born February 3, 1950, Joplin, Mo. Defensive back Missouri Southern 1971-73. No pro playing experience. College coach: Purdue 1977, Wake Forest 1978-1982, Louisiana State 1987-88, Wake Forest 1989-1990, Pittsburgh 1991, Georgia Tech 1992-93, Marshall 1998-99, North Carolina State 2000-02, Duke 2004. Pro coach: Tampa Bay Bandits (USFL) 1983-84, Kansas City Chiefs 1985, Arizona Outlaws (USFL) 1986, Arizona Cardinals 2003, joined Titans in 2005.

George Henshaw, asst. head coach; born January 22, 1948, Richmond, Va. Defensive tackle West Virginia 1967-69. No pro playing experience. College coach: West Virginia 1970-75, Florida State 1976-1982, Alabama 1983-86, Tulsa 1987 (head coach). Pro coach: Denver Broncos 1988-1992, New York Giants 1993-96, joined Titans/Oilers in 1997.

Ned James, offensive assistant/quality control; born January 18, 1964, Syracuse, N.Y. Quarterback New Mexico 1985-86. Pro quarterback Dallas Texans (Arena League) 1990. College coach: Arizona State 1987, Long Beach State 1988, Texas Christian 1989-1990, Winona State 1992-94, Indiana 2000, New Mexico 2001. Pro coach: London Monarchs (WLAF) 1992, Seattle Seahawks 1995-97, New Orleans Saints 1998-99, New Jersey Gladiators (Arena League) 2001, joined Titans in 2002.

Craig Johnson, quarterbacks; born March 3, 1960, Rome, N.Y. Quarterback Wyoming 1978-1982. No pro playing experience. College coach: Wyoming 1983, Arkansas 1984, Army 1985, Rutgers 1986-88, Virginia Military Institute 1989-1991, Northwestern 1992-96, Maryland 1997-99. Pro coach: Joined Titans in 2000.

Alan Lowry, special teams; born November 21, 1950, Miami, Okla. Defensive back-quarterback Texas 1970-72. No pro playing experience. College coach: Virginia Tech 1974, Wyoming 1975, Texas 1977-1981. Pro coach: Dallas Cowboys 1982-1990, Tampa Bay Buccaneers 1991, San Francisco 49ers 1992-95, joined Titans/Oilers in 1996.

Dave McGinnis, linebackers; born August 7, 1951, Independence, Kan. Defensive back Texas Christian 1970-72. No pro playing experience. College coach: Texas Christian 1973-74, 1982, Missouri 1975-77, Indiana State 1978, 1980-81, Kansas State 1983-85. Pro coach: Chicago Bears 1986-1995, Arizona Cardinals 1996-2003 (head coach 2000-2003), joined Titans in 2004.

Mike Munchak, offensive line; born March 5, 1960, Scranton, Pa. Guard-tackle Penn State 1979-1981. Pro guard Houston Oilers 1982-1993. Inducted into Pro Football Hall of Fame 2001. Pro coach: Joined Titans/Oilers in 1994.

Jim Schwartz, defensive coordinator; born June 2, 1966, Baltimore. Linebacker Georgetown 1984-88. No pro playing experience. College coach: Maryland 1989, Minnesota 1990, North Carolina Central 1991, Colgate 1992. Pro coach: Cleveland Browns/Baltimore Ravens 1995-98, joined Titans in 1999.

Ray Sherman, wide receivers; born November 27, 1951, Berkeley, Calif. Wide receiver Laney (Calif.) J.C. 1969-1970, Fresno State 1971-72. No pro playing experience. College coach: San Jose State 1974, California 1975, 1981, Michigan State 1976-77, Wake Forest 1978-1980, Purdue 1982-85, Georgia 1986-87. Pro coach: Houston Oilers 1988-89, Atlanta Falcons 1990, San Francisco 49ers 1991-93, New York Jets 1994, Minnesota Vikings 1995-97, 1999, Pittsburgh Steelers 1998, Green Bay Packers 2000-04, re-joined Titans in 2005.

Sherman Smith, running backs; born November 1, 1954, Youngstown, Ohio. Quarterback Miami (Ohio) 1972-75. Pro running back Seattle Seahawks 1976-1982, San Diego Chargers 1983-84. College coach: Miami (Ohio) 1990-91, Illinois 1992-94. Pro coach: Joined Titans/Oilers in 1995.

Jim Washburn, defensive line; born December 2, 1949, Shelby, N.C. Offensive lineman Gardner-Webb 1973-76. No pro playing experience. College coach: Southern Methodist 1976, Lees McRae (N.C.) J.C. 1977-78, Livingston 1979, New Mexico 1980-82, South Carolina 1983-88, Purdue 1989, Arkansas 1994-97, Houston 1998. Pro coach: London Monarchs (WLAF) 1991, Charlotte Rage (AFL) 1993, joined Titans in 1999.

Steve Watterson, strength and rehabilitation; born November 27, 1956, Newport, R.I. Attended Rhode Island. No college or pro playing experience. Pro coach: Philadelphia Eagles 1984-85, joined Titans/Oilers in 1986.

Everett Withers, defensive backs; born June 15, 1963, Charlotte. Defensive back Appalachian State 1981-85. No pro playing experience. College coach: Austin Peay 1988-1990, Tulane 1991, Southern Mississippi 1992-93, Louisville 1995-97, Texas 1998-2000. Pro coach: New Orleans Saints 1994, joined Titans in 2001.

The NFC

**National Football Conference
West Division**
Team Colors: Cardinal Red, Black, and
White
P.O. Box 888
Phoenix, Arizona 85001-0888
Telephone: (602) 379-0101

2005 SCHEDULE
PRESEASON
Aug. 13 **Dallas** 7:00
Aug. 20 at Kansas City 7:30
Aug. 26 at Oakland 6:30
Sept. 2 **Denver** 7:00

REGULAR SEASON
Sept. 11 at New York Giants 4:15
Sept. 18 **St. Louis** 1:05
Sept. 25 at Seattle 1:05
Oct. 2 **San Francisco** (Mexico) 7:30
Oct. 9 **Carolina** 1:15
Oct. 16 Open Date
Oct. 23 **Tennessee** 1:15
Oct. 30 at Dallas 12:00
Nov. 6 **Seattle** 2:05
Nov. 13 at Detroit 1:00
Nov. 20 at St. Louis 12:00
Nov. 27 **Jacksonville** 2:05
Dec. 4 at San Francisco 1:05
Dec. 11 **Washington** 2:05
Dec. 18 at Houston 12:00
Dec. 24 **Philadelphia** (Sat.) 2:05
Jan. 1 at Indianapolis 1:00

Stadium: Sun Devil Stadium
(opened in 1958)
• **Capacity:** 73,014
Fifth Street
Tempe, Arizona 85287
Playing Surface: Grass
Training Camp: Northern Arizona University
Flagstaff, Arizona 86011

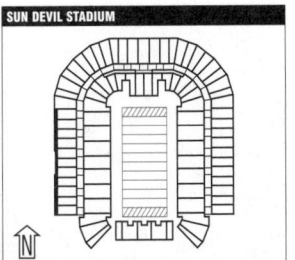

SUN DEVIL STADIUM

CLUB OFFICIALS
President: William V. Bidwill
Vice President/General Counsel:
Michael Bidwill
Vice President: William V. Bidwill, Jr.
Vice President-Football Operations:
Rod Graves
Vice President-Sales and Marketing:
Ron Minegar
Senior Director of Football Operations:
John Idzik
Treasurer and Chief Financial Officer:
Charley Schlegel
Video Director: Benny Greenberg
Director of Media Relations: Mark Dalton
Senior Director of Marketing and
Promotions: Lisa Manning
Senior Director of Business
Development: Steve Ryan
Director of Players Programs:
Anthony Edwards
Director of Community Relations:
Luis Zendejas
Director of Cardinals Charities:
Pat Tankersley
Information Services Director: Mark Feller
Broadcast Manager/Executive Producer:
Tom Hanny
Director of Ticketing: Steve Bomar
Director of Ticket Sales: Jamie Brandt
Director of Cheerleading: Heather Shrake
Head Trainer: John Omohundro
Assistant Trainers:
Jim Shearer, Jeff Herndon,
Freddie Carbajal
Equipment Manager: Mark Ahlemeier
Assistant Equipment Managers:
Steve Christensen, Chris Collins

COACHING HISTORY
**Chicago 1920-1959, St. Louis 1960-1987
(448-642-39)**
Records include postseason games

1920-22	John (Paddy) Driscoll	17-8-4
1923-24	Arnold Horween	13-8-1
1925-26	Norman Barry	16-8-2
1927	Guy Chamberlin	3-7-1
1928	Fred Gillies	1-5-0
1929	Dewey Scanlon	6-6-1
1930	Ernie Nevers	5-6-2
1931	LeRoy Andrews*	0-1-0
1931	Ernie Nevers	5-3-0
1932	Jack Chevigny	2-6-2
1933-34	Paul Schissler	6-15-1
1935-38	Milan Creighton	16-26-4
1939	Ernie Nevers	1-10-0
1940-42	Jimmy Conzelman	8-22-3
1943-45	Phil Handler**	1-29-0
1946-48	Jimmy Conzelman	27-10-0
1949	Phil Handler-Buddy Parker***	2-4-0
1949	Raymond (Buddy) Parker	4-1-1
1950-51	Earl (Curly) Lambeau****	7-15-0
1951	Phil Handler-Cecil Isbell#	1-1-0
1952	Joe Kuharich	4-8-0
1953-54	Joe Stydahar	3-20-1
1955-57	Ray Richards	14-21-1
1958-1961	Frank (Pop) Ivy##	15-31-2
1961	Chuck Drulis-Ray Prochaska- Ray Willsey###	2-0-0
1962-65	Wally Lemm	27-26-3
1966-1970	Charley Winner	35-30-5
1971-72	Bob Hollway	8-18-2
1973-77	Don Coryell	42-29-1
1978-79	Bud Wilkinson####	9-20-0
1979	Larry Wilson	2-1-0
1980-85	Jim Hanifan	39-50-1
1986-89	Gene Stallings@	23-34-1
1989	Hank Kuhlmann	0-5-0
1990-93	Joe Bugel	20-44-0
1994-95	Buddy Ryan	12-20-0
1996-2000	Vince Tobin@@	29-44-00
2000-03	Dave McGinnis	17-40-0
2004	Dennis Green	6-10-0

* Resigned after one game in 1931
** Co-coach with Walt Kiesling in Chicago
Cardinals-Pittsburgh merger in 1944
*** Co-coaches for first six games in 1949
**** Resigned after 10 games in 1951
\# Co-coaches
\#\# Resigned after 12 games in 1961
\#\#\# Co-coaches
\#\#\#\# Released after 13 games in 1979
@ Released after 11 games in 1989
@@ Released after seven games in 2000

ATTENDANCE
Home 286,674   Away 528,672
Total 815,346
Single-game home record,
73,025 (9/19/93)
Single-season home record, 497,330
(1994)

2005 DRAFT CHOICES
Round	Name	Pos.	College
1	Antrel Rolle	DB	Miami
2	J.J. Arrington	RB	California
3	Eric Green	DB	Virginia Tech
	Darryl Blackstock	LB	Virginia
4	Elton Brown	G	Virginia
5	Lance Mitchell	LB	Oklahoma
7	LeRon McCoy	WR	Indiana, Pa.

2004 TEAM RECORD
PRESEASON (1-3)

Date	Result		Opponent
8/14	L	6-23	at Minnesota
8/21	L	13-38	San Diego
8/28	L	16-17	Oakland
9/2	W	33-21	at Denver

REGULAR SEASON (6-10)

Date	Result		Opponent	Att.
9/12	L	10-17	at St. Louis	65,538
9/19	L	12-23	New England	51,557
9/26	L	3-6	at Atlanta	70,534
10/3	W	34-10	New Orleans	28,109
10/10	L	28-31	at San Francisco (OT)	62,836
10/24	W	25-17	Seattle	35,695
10/31	L	14-38	at Buffalo	65,887
11/7	W	24-23	at Miami	72,612
11/14	W	17-14	N.Y. Giants	42,297
11/21	L	10-35	at Carolina	72,796
11/28	L	3-13	N.Y. Jets	35,820
12/5	L	12-26	at Detroit	62,262
12/12	L	28-31	San Francisco (OT)	35,069
12/19	W	31-7	St. Louis	40,070
12/26	L	21-24	at Seattle	65,825
1/2	W	12-7	Tampa Bay	31,650

(OT) Overtime

SCORE BY PERIODS

Cardinals	40	78	57	109	0	—	284
Opponents	64	100	63	89	6	—	322

2004 TEAM STATISTICS

	Cardinals	Opp.
Total First Downs	280	282
Rushing	86	101
Passing	152	153
Penalty	42	28
3rd Down: Made/Att	84/241	66/209
3rd Down Pct.	34.9	31.6
4th Down: Made/Att	5/12	8/14
4th Down Pct.	41.7	57.1
Possession Avg.	30:53	29:07
Total Net Yards	4550	5141
Avg. Per Game	284.4	321.3
Total Plays	1047	993
Avg. Per Play	4.3	5.2
Net Yards Rushing	1668	2105
Avg. Per Game	104.3	131.6
Total Rushes	475	450
Net Yards Passing	2882	3036
Avg. Per Game	180.1	189.8
Sacked/Yards Lost	39/320	38/229
Gross Yards	3202	3265
Att./Completions	533/299	505/271
Completion Pct.	56.1	53.7
Had Intercepted	18	15
Punts/Average	99/42.7	97/41.9
Net Punting Avg.	99/36.4	97/35.8
Penalties/Yards	124/948	139/1121
Fumbles/Ball Lost	34/11	32/15
Touchdowns	31	35
Rushing	15	12
Passing	14	18
Returns	2	5

2004 INDIVIDUAL STATISTICS

PASSING

	Att.	Comp.	Yds.	Pct.	TD	Int.	Tkld.	Rate
McCown	408	233	2,511	57.1	11	10	31/263	74.1
S. King	84	47	502	56.0	1	4	6/42	57.7
Navarre	40	18	168	45.0	1	4	1/8	25.8
E. Smith	1	1	21	100.0	1	0	0/0	158.3
Fitzgerald	0	0	0	—	0	0	1/7	—
Cardinals	533	299	3,202	56.1	14	18	39/320	68.5
Opponents	505	271	3,265	53.7	18	15	38/229	73.2

SCORING

	TD R	TD P	TD Rt	PAT	FG	Saf	PTS
Rackers	0	0	0	28/28	22/29	0	94
E. Smith	9	0	0	0/0	0/0	0	54
Fitzgerald	0	8	0	0/0	0/0	0	48
Ayanbadejo	3	1	0	0/0	0/0	0	24
McCown	2	0	0	0/0	0/0	0	14
Hambrick	1	1	0	0/0	0/0	0	12
Jones	0	2	0	0/0	0/0	0	12
Boldin	0	1	0	0/0	0/0	0	6
Johnson	0	1	0	0/0	0/0	0	6
Starks	0	0	1	0/0	0/0	0	6
Wilson	0	0	1	0/0	0/0	0	6
Cardinals	15	14	2	28/28	22/29	1	284
Opponents	12	18	5	29/30	25/26	0	322

2-Pt. Conversions: McCown.
Cardinals 1-3, Opponents 4-5.

RUSHING

	Att.	Yds.	Avg.	LG	TD
E. Smith	267	937	3.5	29t	9
Hambrick	63	283	4.5	62	1
Ayanbadejo	30	122	4.1	23	3
McCown	36	112	3.1	12	2
Scobey	27	89	3.3	10	0
Croom	29	76	2.6	20	0
S. King	9	30	3.3	16	0
Fitzgerald	8	14	1.8	10	0
Williams	2	6	3.0	3	0
Boldin	1	3	3.0	3	0
Anderson	1	2	2.0	2	0
Johnson	2	-6	-3.0	1	0
Cardinals	475	1,668	3.5	62	15
Opponents	450	2,105	4.7	74	12

RECEIVING

	No.	Yds	Avg	LG	TD
Fitzgerald	58	780	13.4	48	8
Boldin	56	623	11.1	31t	1
Johnson	49	537	11.0	40	1
Jones	45	426	9.5	40	2
Ayanbadejo	19	171	9.0	21t	1
Williams	18	197	10.9	33	0
Scobey	18	191	10.6	42	0
E. Smith	15	105	7.0	18	0
Poole	5	70	14.0	24	0
Edwards	5	51	10.2	19	0
Hambrick	4	16	4.0	9	1
Diamond	3	19	6.3	8	0
Croom	2	16	8.0	8	0
Newhouse	1	5	5.0	5	0
McCown	1	-5	-5.0	-5	0
Cardinals	299	3,202	10.7	48	14
Opponents	271	3,265	12.0	75t	18

INTERCEPTIONS

	No.	Yds	Avg	LG	TD
Macklin	4	18	4.5	16	0
Wilson	3	62	20.7	27	0
Starks	3	46	15.3	41t	1
Darling	1	65	65.0	65	0
Dockett	1	20	20.0	20	0
Dansby	1	2	2.0	2	0
Hill	1	2	2.0	2	0
Harris	1	-1	-1.0	-1	0
Cardinals	15	214	14.3	65	1
Opponents	18	263	14.6	76	1

PUNTING

	No.	Yds.	Avg.	In 20	LG
Player	98	4,230	43.2	32	57
Cardinals	99	4,230	42.7	32	57
Opponents	97	4,064	41.9	25	68

PUNT RETURNS

	Ret	FC	Yds	Avg	LG	TD
Williams	42	12	286	6.8	38	0
Starks	7	1	43	6.1	15	0
Boldin	0	1	0	—	—	0
Cardinals	49	14	329	6.7	38	0
Opponents	56	16	486	8.7	71t	1

KICKOFF RETURNS

	No.	Yds	Avg	LG	TD
Scobey	32	723	22.6	71	0
Croom	16	314	19.6	35	0
Johnson	6	135	22.5	47	0
Ayanbadejo	3	50	16.7	21	0
Edwards	3	40	13.3	14	0
Hayes	3	6	2.0	6	0
Vanden Bosch	1	7	7.0	7	0
Williams	1	18	18.0	18	0
Cardinals	65	1,293	19.9	71	0
Opponents	46	1,017	22.1	87t	1

FIELD GOALS

	1-19	20-29	30-39	40-49	50+
Rackers	0/0	6/6	5/7	6/7	5/9
Cardinals	0/0	6/6	5/7	6/7	5/9
Opponents	0/0	13/13	7/7	3/4	2/2

SACKS

	No.
Berry	14.5
Dansby	5.0
Pace	4.5
Dockett	3.5
Zellner	2.0
Darling	1.0
R. Davis	1.0
Harris	1.0
Hill	1.0
Kolodziej	1.0
Starks	1.0
Thompson	1.0
Wilson	1.0
Macklin	0.5
Cardinals	38.0
Opponents	39.0

RECORD HOLDERS
INDIVIDUAL RECORDS—CAREER

Category	Name	Performance
Rushing (Yds.)	Ottis Anderson, 1979-1986	7,999
Passing (Yds.)	Jim Hart, 1966-1983	34,639
Passing (TDs)	Jim Hart, 1966-1983	209
Receiving (No.)	Larry Centers, 1990-98	535
Receiving (Yds.)	Roy Green, 1979-1990	8,497
Interceptions	Larry Wilson, 1960-1972	52
Punting (Avg.)	Jerry Norton, 1959-1961	44.9
Punt Return (Avg.)	Charley Trippi, 1947-1955	13.7
Kickoff Return (Avg.)	Ollie Matson, 1952, 1954-58	28.5
Field Goals	Jim Bakken, 1962-1978	282
Touchdowns (Tot.)	Roy Green, 1979-1990	70
Points	Jim Bakken, 1962-1978	1,380

INDIVIDUAL RECORDS—SINGLE SEASON

Category	Name	Performance
Rushing (Yds.)	Ottis Anderson, 1979	1,605
Passing (Yds.)	Neil Lomax, 1984	4,614
Passing (TDs)	Charley Johnson, 1963	28
	Neil Lomax, 1984	28
Receiving (No.)	Larry Centers, 1995	101
	Anquan Boldin, 2003	101
Receiving (Yds.)	David Boston, 2001	1,598
Interceptions	Bob Nussbaumer, 1949	12
Punting (Avg.)	Jerry Norton, 1960	45.6
Punt Return (Avg.)	John (Red) Cochran, 1949	20.9
Kickoff Return (Avg.)	Ollie Matson, 1958	35.5
Field Goals	Greg Davis, 1995	30
Touchdowns (Tot.)	John David Crow, 1962	17
Points	Jim Bakken, 1967	117
	Neil O'Donoghue, 1984	117

INDIVIDUAL RECORDS—SINGLE GAME

Category	Name	Performance
Rushing (Yds.)	LeShon Johnson, 9-22-96	214
Passing (Yds.)	Boomer Esiason, 11-10-96 (OT)	522
Passing (TDs)	Jim Hardy, 10-2-50	6
	Charley Johnson, 9-26-65, 11-2-69	6
Receiving (No.)	Sonny Randle, 11-4-62	16
Receiving (Yds.)	Sonny Randle, 11-4-62	256
Interceptions	Bob Nussbaumer, 11-13-49	*4
	Jerry Norton, 11-20-60	*4
	Kwamie Lassiter, 12-27-98	*4
Field Goals	Jim Bakken, 9-24-67	*7
Touchdowns (Tot.)	Ernie Nevers, 11-28-29	*6
Points	Ernie Nevers, 11-28-29	*40

*NFL Record

2005 VETERAN ROSTER

No.	Name	Pos.	Ht.	Wt.	Birthdate	NFL Exp.	College	Hometown	How Acq.	'04 Games/ Starts
76	Allen, Ian	T	6-4	313	7/22/78	4	Purdue	Atlanta, Ga.	FA-'05	4/0*
20	Anderson, Damien	RB	5-11	211	7/17/79	4	Northwestern	Wilmington, Ill.	FA-'04	4/0
30	Ayanbadejo, Obafemi	FB	6-2	233	3/5/75	7	San Diego State	Santa Cruz, Calif.	UFA(Mia)-'04	16/5
92	Berry, Bertrand	DE	6-3	277	8/15/75	8	Notre Dame	Houston, Texas	UFA(Den)-'04	16/16
81	Boldin, Anquan	WR	6-1	220	10/3/80	3	Florida State	Pahokee, Fla.	D2-'03	10/9
73	Bridges, Jeremy	G	6-4	323	4/19/80	3	Southern Mississippi	McComb, Miss.	W(Phil)-'04	14/8
91	Bryant, Wendell	DT	6-5	308	9/12/80	4	Wisconsin	St. Louis, Mo.	D1-'02	3/0
32	Croom, Larry	RB	5-10	205	10/29/81	2	Nevada-Las Vegas	Long Beach, Calif.	FA-'04	6/1
41	Curry, Clarence	CB	6-1	210	12/7/81	2	Villanova	Parsippany, N.J.	FA-'04	1/0
58	Dansby, Karlos	LB	6-4	243	11/3/81	2	Auburn	Birmingham, Ala.	D2-'04	15/11
51	Darling, James	LB	6-1	247	12/29/74	9	Washington State	Kettle Falls, Wash.	UFA(NYJ)-'03	15/15
75	Davis, Leonard	T	6-6	366	9/5/78	5	Texas	Wortham, Texas	D1-'01	15/15
98	Davis, Russell	DT	6-4	306	3/28/75	7	North Carolina	Fayetteville, N.C.	W(Chi)-'00	16/16
82	Diamond, Lorenzo	TE	6-3	255	12/15/79	2	Auburn	Biloxi, Miss.	FA-'03	5/4
90	Dockett, Darnell	DT	6-4	293	5/27/81	2	Florida State	Burtonsville, Md.	D3-'04	16/15
83	Edwards, Eric	TE	6-5	257	8/4/80	2	Louisiana State	Monroe, La.	FA-'04	16/1
11	Fitzgerald, Larry	WR	6-3	221	8/31/83	2	Pittsburgh	Minneapolis, Minn.	D1-'04	16/16
34	Griffith, Robert	S	6-0	200	11/30/70	12	San Diego State	San Diego, Calif.	UFA(Cle)-'05	16/16*
64	Haayer, Adam	T	6-6	311	2/22/77	4	Minnesota	Forest Lake, Minn.	FA-'05	4/1*
22	Hambrick, Troy	RB	6-1	249	11/6/76	6	Savannah State	Pasco, Fla.	T(Oak)-04	10/0
84	Hamilton, Lawrence	WR	6-3	205	8/31/80	3	Stephen F. Austin	Marshall, Texas	W(NYJ)-04	1/0
29	Harris, Quentin	S	6-1	213	1/26/77	4	Syracuse	Wilkes-Barre, Pa.	FA-'02	16/4
54	Hayes, Gerald	LB	6-1	247	10/10/80	3	Pittsburgh	Paterson, N.J.	D3-'03	16/1
48	Hodel, Nathan	LS	6-2	248	11/12/77	4	Illinois	Fairview Heights, Ill.	FA-'01	16/0
42	Hodgins, James	FB	6-1	264	4/30/77	7	San Jose State	San Jose, Calif.	UFA(StL)-'03	0*
57	Huff, Orlando	LB	6-3	250	8/14/78	5	Fresno State	Upland, Calif.	UFA(Sea)-'05	14/2*
59	Joe, Leon	LB	6-1	225	10/26/81	2	Maryland	Fort Washington, Md.	W(Chi)-'04	4/0
80	Johnson, Bryant	WR	6-3	214	3/7/81	3	Penn State	Baltimore, Md.	D1a-'03	16/11
53	Keys, Isaac	LB	6-3	247	6/6/78	2	Morehouse	St. Louis, Mo.	FA-'04	3/0
95	King, Kenny	DT	6-4	291	4/23/81	3	Alabama	Daphne, Ala.	D5-'03	0*
72	Kolodziej, Ross	DT	6-3	292	5/11/78	5	Wisconsin	Plover, Wis.	FA-'04	13/4
60	Leckey, Nick	C	6-3	298	3/12/82	2	Kansas State	Grapevine, Texas	D6-'04	16/0
27	Macklin, David	CB	5-10	200	7/14/78	6	Penn State	Newport News, Va.	UFA(Ind)-'04	16/16
37	Mayes, Adrian	S	6-1	215	11/17/80	2	Louisiana State	Houston, Texas	FA-'04	4/0
12	McCown, Josh	QB	6-4	213	7/4/79	4	Sam Houston State	Jacksonville, Texas	D3a-'02	14/13
16	Navarre, John	QB	6-6	251	9/9/80	2	Michigan	Cudahy, Wis.	D7-'04	1/1
38	Nelson, Rhett	CB	6-0	198	2/16/80	3	Colorado State	Littleton, Colo.	W(Minn)-'05	4/0*
87	Newhouse, Reggie	WR	6-1	211	2/16/81	2	Baylor	Dallas, Texas	FA-'03	3/0
25	Ohalete, Ifeanyi	S	6-2	221	5/22/79	5	Southern California	Los Alimitos, Calif.	W(Wash)-'04	16/13
56	Okeafor, Chike	DE	6-5	265	3/27/76	7	Purdue	Grand Rapids, Mich.	UFA(Sea)-'05	16/16*
97	Pace, Calvin	DE	6-4	270	10/28/80	3	Wake Forest	Douglasville, Ga.	D1b-'03	14/0
10	Player, Scott	P	6-1	211	12/17/69	8	Florida State	St. Augustine, Fla.	FA-98	16/0
1	Rackers, Neil	K	6-1	207	8/16/76	6	Illinois	St. Louis, Mo.	FA-'03	16/0
66	Reuber, Alan	G	6-6	314	1/26/81	2	Texas A&M	Plano, Texas	W(Minn)-'04	3/0
78	Ross, Oliver	T	6-5	324	9/27/74	7	Iowa State	Los Angeles, Calif.	UFA(Pitt)-'05	16/16*
33	Scobey, Josh	RB	6-0	220	12/11/79	4	Kansas State	Oklahoma City, Okla.	D6-'02	12/0
70	Shelton, L.J.	T	6-6	354	3/21/76	7	Eastern Michigan	Rochester Hills, Mich.	D1b-'99	12/9
31	Shipp, Marcel	RB	5-11	225	8/8/78	5	Massachusetts	Paterson, N.J.	FA-'01	0*
71	Stepanovich, Alex	C	6-4	304	9/25/81	2	Ohio State	Berea, Ohio	D4-'04	16/16
26	Tate, Robert	CB	5-11	192	10/19/73	8	Cincinnati	Harrisburg, Pa.	FA-'04	14/0
79	Wakefield, Fred	T	6-7	312	9/17/78	5	Illinois	Tuscola, Ill.	FA-'01	0*
23	Walls, Raymond	CB	5-10	189	7/24/79	5	Southern Mississippi	Kentwood, La.	UFA(Balt)-'05	16/1*
13	Warner, Kurt	QB	6-2	219	6/22/71	8	Northern Iowa	Cedar Rapids, Iowa	UFA(NYG)-'05	10/9*
74	Wells, Reggie	G	6-4	320	11/8/80	3	Clarion (PA)	Library, Pa.	D6a-'03	16/16
24	Wilson, Adrian	S	6-3	230	10/12/79	5	North Carolina State	High Point, N.C.	D3-'01	16/16
94	Zellner, Peppi	DE	6-6	286	3/14/75	7	Fort Valley State	Forsythe, Ga.	T(Oak)-'04	16/14

* Allen played 4 games with Philadelphia in '04; Griffith played 16 games with Cleveland; Haayer played 4 games with Minnesota; Hodgins missed '04 season because of injury; Huff played 14 games with Seattle; King missed '04 season because of injury; Nelson played 4 games with Minnesota; Okeafor played 16 games with Seattle; Ross played 16 games with Pittsburgh; Shipp missed '04 season because of injury; Wakefield missed '04 season because of injury; Walls played 16 games with Baltimore; Warner played 10 games with New York Giants.

Traded—CB Duane Starks (16 games in '04) to New England.

Players lost through free agency (4): CB Renaldo Hill (Oak; 13 games in '04), TE Freddie Jones (Car; 16), CB Michael Stone (StL; 14), DE Kyle Vanden Bosch (Tenn; 16).

Also played with Cardinals in '04—CB Dyshod Carter (6 games), T Anthony Clement (16), LB Ronald McKinnon (16), QB Shaun King (3), DT John Nix (1), WR Nathan Poole (9), RB Emmitt Smith (15), G Cameron Spikes (16), LB Ray Thompson (11), WR Karl Williams (15), LB LeVar Woods (14).

2005 FIRST-YEAR ROSTER

Name	Pos.	Ht.	Wt.	Birthdate	College	Hometown	How Acq.
Arrington, J.J.	RB	5-9	214	1/23/83	California	Nashville, N.C.	D2
Bergen, Adam	TE	6-4	263	9/3/83	Lehigh	Seaford, N.Y.	FA
Blackstock, Darryl	LB	6-3	240	5/30/83	Virginia	Newport News, Va.	D3b
Blizzard, Bobby (1)	TE	6-4	272	3/22/80	North Carolina	Hampton, Va.	FA-'04
Bronson, John	TE	6-3	260	7/8/82	Penn State	Kent, Wash.	FA
Brown, Elton	G	6-4	339	5/22/82	Virginia	Hampton, Va.	D4
Bulman, Tim	DT	6-3	290	10/31/82	Boston College	Milton, Mass.	FA
Cantu, Rolando (1)	G	6-5	361	2/25/81	ITESM Monterey	Monterey, Mexico	FA-'04
Chang, Tim	QB	6-1	207	10/9/81	Hawaii	Honolulu, Hawaii	FA
Davis, Fabian (1)	WR	5-11	199	12/7/78	Wake Forest	Greenville, S.C.	FA-'04
Ekejiuba, Isaiah	LB	6-4	219	10/5/81	Virginia	Chestnut Ridge, N.Y.	FA
Fordyce, Mat (1)	K	6-0	196	9/21/80	Fordham	Mentor, Ohio	FA
Francisco, Aaron	CB	6-2	212	7/5/83	Brigham Young	Laie, Hawaii	FA
Golliday, Aaron (1)	TE	6-4	279	12/3/79	Nebraska	York, Neb.	FA
Green, Eric	CB	5-11	188	3/16/82	Virginia Tech	Clewiston, Fla.	D3a
Hardy, Jermaine	CB	5-10	213	3/20/82	Virginia	Roanoke, Va.	FA
Holiday, Carlyle	WR	6-3	217	10/4/81	Notre Dame	San Antonio, Texas	FA
King, Tyler	DE	6-5	266	9/5/80	Connecticut	Attleboro, Mass.	FA
Lewis, Chris (1)	QB	6-3	215	12/13/80	Stanford	Long Beach, Calif.	FA-'04
McCoy, LeRon	WR	6-1	205	1/24/82	Indiana (PA)	Harrisburg, Pa.	D7
Mitchell, Lance	LB	6-2	250	10/9/81	Oklahoma	Los Banos, Calif.	D5
Moore, Casey (1)	FB	6-2	246	7/26/80	Stanford	St. Petersburg, Fla.	FA-'04
Newton, Jim (1)	T	6-10	338	10/13/78	Utah State	Newbury Park, Calif.	FA-'04
Powell, Luke (1)	WR-PR	5-8	178	2/22/81	Stanford	Smyrna, Tenn.	FA
Reid, Lamont	CB	6-0	187	5/4/82	North Carolina State	Concord, N.C.	FA
Robinson, Roger	RB	5-10	199	4/22/82	Northern Arizona	Apple Valley, Calif.	FA
Rolle, Antrel	CB	6-0	206	12/16/82	Miami	Homestead, Fla.	D1
Sanders, Tyrone (1)	CB	5-10	173	2/22/81	Texas Christian	Dallas, Texas	FA-'04
Shazor, Ernest	S	6-4	231	7/4/83	Michigan	Detroit, Mich.	FA
Sheldon, Dan	WR	5-11	173	5/23/82	Northern Illinois	Burlington, Ill.	FA
Smith, Antonio (1)	DE	6-4	272	10/21/81	Oklahoma State	Oklahoma City, Okla.	D5-'04

The term NFL Rookie is defined as a player who is in his first season of professional football and has not been on the roster of another professional football team for any regular-season or postseason games. A Rookie is designated by an "R" on NFL rosters. Players who have been active in another professional football league or players who have NFL experience, including either preseason training camp or being on an Active List or Inactive List, or on Reserve/Injured or Reserve/Physically Unable to Perform for fewer than six regular-season games, are termed NFL First-Year Players. An NFL First-Year Player is designated by a "1" on NFL rosters. Thereafter, a player is credited with an additional year of experience for each season in which he accumulates six games on the Active List or Inactive List, or on Reserve/Injured or Reserve/Physically Unable to Perform.

Log on to www.azcardinals.com for an up-to-date roster.

COACHING STAFF
Head Coach, Dennis Green

Pro Career: Named the thirty-third head coach of the Arizona Cardinals on January 7, 2004. Posted 101-70 (.591) composite record in 10 seasons (1992-2001) as head coach of the Minnesota Vikings. Led club to eight postseason berths (four NFC Central Division titles) and two NFC championship games. Green is one of four NFL coaches to achieve a 15-victory season (15-1 in 1998), joining Bill Walsh (San Francisco, 1984), Mike Ditka (Chicago, 1985) and Bill Cowher (Pittsburgh, 2004), and is one of just eight coaches in NFL history to lead his team to the playoffs in each of his first three seasons (1992-94) as an NFL head coach. Green's eight postseason appearances with the Vikings were accomplished with seven different quarterbacks—Sean Salisbury (1992), Jim McMahon (1993), Warren Moon (1994), Brad Johnson (1996), Randall Cunningham (1997-98), Jeff George (1999), and Daunte Culpepper (2000). The Vikings were the only NFL team to qualify for the playoffs each season from 1996-2000 and posted the NFL's best winning percentage (.639, 92-52) from 1992-2000. Green's first professional coaching opportunity came as special teams coach for San Francisco in 1979. Career record: 107-80.

Background: Green was an all-Pennsylvania running back at John Harris High School in Harrisburg, Pa. before attending Iowa where he started for one season as a flanker (1968) followed by two at running back (1969-70 where he was honorable mention all-Big Ten both years) for the Hawkeyes. Green played defensive back briefly for the British Columbia Lions of the Canadian Football League in 1971. Green was a college assistant coach at Iowa (1972, 1974-76), Dayton (1973), and Stanford (1977-78, 1980). During his six seasons (1981-85) as head coach at Northwestern, he was named Big Ten Conference coach-of-the-year in 1982. As head coach at Stanford from 1989-1991, Green led the Cardinal to the 1991 Aloha Bowl.

Personal: Born February 17, 1949 in Harrisburg, Pa., Green earned his degree in recreation from Iowa. He and his wife, Marie, have a daughter, Vanessa, and son, Zachary. Green also has a daughter, Patti, and a son, Jeremy.

ASSISTANT COACHES

Frank Bush, linebackers; born January 10, 1963, Athens, Ga. Linebacker North Carolina State 1981-84. Pro linebacker Houston Oilers 1985-86. Pro coach: Houston Oilers 1987-1991 (scout), 1992-94, Denver Broncos 1995-2003, joined Cardinals in 2004.

Ryan Capretta, asst. strength and conditioning; born June 25, 1977, Westlake Village, Calif. Wide receiver Santa Barbara C.C. 1995-96, Indiana State 1997-99. No pro playing experience. College coach: Indiana State 1999, Stanford 2002-03. Pro coach: Baltimore Ravens 2000-01, joined Cardinals in 2003.

Rick Courtright, defensive quality control; born Jan. 4, 1961, Miami. Linebacker Wheaton College 1980-83. No pro playing experience. College coach: Washington 1991-92, Minnesota-Morris 1993, Ohio 1994, Idaho State 1995, Idaho 1996-99, Murray State 2000, Western Illinois 2001-03. Pro coach: Joined Cardinals in 2004.

Carl Hargrave, tight ends; born November 8, 1954, Frankfurt, Germany. Defensive back Upper Iowa 1972-75. No pro playing experience. College coach: Upper Iowa 1977-1980, Northwestern 1981-85, Pittsburgh 1986, Houston 1987-1991, Iowa 1992-93, Lindenwood 2002-03. Pro coach: Minnesota Vikings 1994-2001, joined Cardinals in 2004.

Bill Khayat, offensive quality control; born March 26, 1973, York, Pa. Tight end Duke 1992-95. Pro tight end Kansas City Chiefs 1996, Carolina Panthers 1997, Barcelona Dragons (NFLE) 1998. College coach: Tennessee State 2000-03. Pro coach: Joined Cardinals in 2004.

Mike Kruczek, quarterbacks; born March 15, 1953, Washington, D.C. Quarterback Boston College 1973-75. Pro quarterback Pittsburgh Steelers 1976-79, Washington Redskins 1980. College coach: Florida State 1982-83 Central Florida 1985-2003 (head coach 1998-2003). Pro coach: Jacksonville Bulls (USFL) 1984, joined Cardinals in 2004.

Daryl Lawrence, asst. strength and conditioning; born October 20, 1965, Chicago Heights, Ill. Attended Illinois State. No college or pro playing experience. College coach: Illinois State 1995-96, Army 1998-99. Pro coach: Minnesota Vikings 1997, 2000-03, joined Cardinals in 2004.

Everett Lindsay, offensive line; born September 18, 1970, Burlington, Iowa. Tackle Mississippi 1989-1992. Pro tackle/guard Minnesota Vikings 1993-98, 2001-2003, Baltimore Ravens 1999, Cleveland Browns 2000. Pro coach: Joined Cardinals in 2004.

Kevin O'Dea, special teams; born June 9, 1960, Williamsport, Pa. Wide receiver-defensive back Lock Haven 1983-85. No pro playing experience. College coach: Lock Haven 1986, Cornell 1987, Virginia 1988-1990, Penn State 1991-93. Pro coach: San Diego Chargers 1994-95, Tampa Bay Buccaneers 1996-2001, Detroit Lions 2002-03, joined Cardinals in 2004.

Clancy Pendergast, defensive coordinator; born November 29, 1967, Phoenix. Attended Arizona. No college or pro playing experience. College coach: Mississippi State 1991, Southern California 1992, Oklahoma 1993-94, Alabama-Birmingham 1995. Pro coach: Houston Oilers 1995, Dallas Cowboys 1996-2002, Cleveland Browns 2003, joined Cardinals in 2004.

Donald 'Deek' Pollard, defensive line; born September 16, 1939, Roodhouse, Ill. Defensive back Western Illinois 1957-1961. No pro playing experience. College coach: Western Illinois 1971-73, Florida State 1974-75, Oklahoma State 1976-78, Central Florida 1990-93, Boston College 1994, Syracuse 1998-99. Pro coach: New York Giants 1979-1981, Denver Gold (USFL) 1983, Arizona Wranglers (USFL) 1984-85, Cleveland Browns 1989, St. Louis Rams 1995-96, joined Cardinals in 2004.

Keith Rowen, offensive coordinator; born September 2, 1952, New York, N.Y. Tackle Stanford 1972-74. No pro playing experience. College coach: Stanford 1975-76, Long Beach State 1977-78, Arizona 1979-1982. Pro coach: Boston/New Orleans Breakers (USFL) 1983-84, Cleveland Browns 1984, Indianapolis Colts 1985-88, New England Patriots 1989, Atlanta Falcons 1990-93, Minnesota Vikings 1994-96, Oakland Raiders 1997-98, Kansas City Chiefs 1999-2004, joined Cardinals in 2005.

Richard Solomon, defensive backs; born December 8, 1949, New Orleans. Running back-defensive back Iowa 1970-72. No pro playing experience. College coach: Dubuque 1973-75, Southern Illinois 1976, Iowa 1977-78, Syracuse 1979, Illinois 1980-86, Western Illinois 2003. Pro coach: New York Giants 1987-1991 (scout), Minnesota Vikings 1992-2001, joined Cardinals in 2004.

Steve Wetzel, strength and conditioning; born May 11, 1963, Washington, D.C. Attended Slippery Rock. No college or pro playing experience. College coach: Maryland 1985-89, George Mason 1990. Pro coach: Washington Redskins 1990-91, Minnesota Vikings 1991-2003, joined Cardinals in 2004.

Kirby Wilson, running backs; born August 24, 1961, Los Angeles, Calif. Running back-wide receiver Pasadena (Calif.) C.C. 1979-1980, Illinois 1981-82. Pro cornerback Winnipeg Blue Bombers (CFL) 1983, Toronto Argonauts (CFL) 1984. College coach: Pasadena (Calif.) C.C. 1989-1990, Southern Illinois 1991-92, Wyoming 1993-94, Iowa State 1995-96, Southern California 2001. Pro coach: New England Patriots 1997-99, Washington Redskins 2000, Tampa Bay Buccaneers 2002-03, joined Cardinals in 2004.

Mike Wilson, wide receivers; born December 19, 1958, Los Angeles, Calif. Wide receiver Washington State 1978-1980. Pro wide receiver San Francisco 49ers 1981-1990. College coach: Stanford 1992-94, Southern California 1997-2000. Pro coach: Oakland Raiders 1995-96, joined Cardinals in 2004.

National Football Conference
South Division
Team Colors: Black, Red, Silver, and White
4400 Falcon Parkway
Flowery Branch, Georgia 30542
Telephone: (770) 965-3115

2005 SCHEDULE
PRESEASON
Aug. 6	vs. Indianapolis (Tokyo)	6:00
Aug. 13	**Baltimore**	7:30
Aug. 19	**Tennessee**	7:30
Aug. 25	at Jacksonville	8:00
Sept. 1	at Miami	7:30

REGULAR SEASON
Sep. 12	**Philadelphia** (Mon.)	9:00
Sep. 18	at Seattle	1:05
Sep. 25	at Buffalo	1:00
Oct. 2	**Minnesota**	4:15
Oct. 9	**New England**	1:00
Oct. 16	at New Orleans	12:00
Oct. 24	**New York Jets** (Mon.)	9:00
Oct. 30	Open Date	
Nov. 6	at Miami	1:00
Nov. 13	**Green Bay**	4:15
Nov. 20	**Tampa Bay**	1:00
Nov. 24	at Detroit (Thu.)	12:30
Dec. 4	at Carolina	1:00
Dec. 12	**New Orleans** (Mon.)	9:00
Dec. 18	at Chicago	7:30
Dec. 24	at Tampa Bay (Sat.)	1:00
Jan. 1	**Carolina**	1:00

Stadium: Georgia Dome
(opened in 1992)
• **Capacity:** 71,228
One Georgia Dome Drive
Atlanta, Georgia 30313
Playing Surface: FieldTurf
Training Camp: Atlanta Falcons
4400 Falcon Parkway
Flowery Branch, GA 30542

CLUB OFFICIALS
Owner & CEO: Arthur M. Blank
President-General Manager: Rich McKay
Executive Vice President-Head Coach:
Jim Mora
Executive Vice President-Chief
Administrative Officer: Ray Anderson
Executive Vice President-Marketing:
Dick Sullivan
Executive Vice President-People &
Organization Development:
Wayne Luke
Vice President of Player Personnel:
Ron Hill
Vice President & CFO: Greg Beadles
Controller: Wallace Norman
Vice President of Corporate
Development: Tommy Nobis
Logistics Manager: Spencer Treadwell
Vice President of Communications and
Community Relations: Susan Bass
Vice President of Information
Technology: Danny Branch
Vice President of Football
Communications: Reggie Roberts
Vice President of Marketing: Jim Smith
Senior Director of Media Relations:
Frank Kleha
Director of Ticket Operations:
Jack Ragsdale
Director of Ticket Sales: Dave Cohen
Coordinator-Program Development/
Player Outreach: Chris Demos
Director of Player Programs:
Billy (White Shoes) Johnson
Director of Football Administration:
Brian Xanders
Director of Pro Personnel: Les Sneed
Director of College Scouting: Phil Emery
Area Scouts: Matt Berry, Boyd Dowler,
Bob Harrison, Taylor Morton,
Mark Olson, Alex Page (Asst.),
Bruce Plummer
Pro Scouts: Ray Farmer
Head Athletic Trainer: Ron Medlin
Assistant Athletic Trainers: Harold King,
Thomas Reed
Video Director: Mike Crews
Video Assistants: Rocky Sabbatini,
Aaron Vik
Equipment Manager: Brian Boigner
Senior Equipment Director/Gameday
Coordinator: Horace Daniel
Executive Director—Atlanta Falcons
Youth Foundation: Shawn Huff
Director of Event Marketing and
Entertainment: Roddy White
Football Communications Manager:
Ted Crews
Football Communications Coordinator:
Ryan Moore

COACHING HISTORY
(243-357-6)
Records include postseason games
1966-68	Norb Hecker*	4-26-1
1968-1974	Norm Van Brocklin**	37-49-3
1974-76	Marion Campbell***	6-19-0
1976	Pat Peppler	3-6-0
1977-1982	Leeman Bennett	47-44-0
1983-86	Dan Henning	22-41-1
1987-89	Marion Campbell****	11-32-0
1989	Jim Hanifan	0-4-0
1990-93	Jerry Glanville	28-38-0
1994-96	June Jones	19-30-0
1997-2003	Dan Reeves#	52-61-1
2003	Wade Phillips	2-1-0
2004	Jim Mora	12-6-0

*Released after three games in 1968
**Released after eight games in 1974
***Released after five games in 1976
****Retired after 12 games in 1989
#Released after 13 games in 2003

ATTENDANCE
Home 547,674   Away 560,049
Total 1,107,180
Single-game home record,
70,891 (11/23/03)
Single-season home record,
553,979 (1992)

2005 DRAFT CHOICES
Round	Name	Pos.	College
1	Roddy White	WR	Ala.-Birmingham
2	Jonathan Babineaux	DT	Iowa
3	Jordan Beck	LB	Cal Poly-SLO
4	Chauncey Davis	DE	Florida State
5	Michael Boley	LB	So. Mississippi
	Frank Omiyale	T	Tennessee Tech
6	DeAndra Cobb	RB	Michigan State
7	Darrell Shropshire	DT	South Carolina

ATLANTA FALCONS

2004 TEAM RECORD

PRESEASON (2-2)

Date	Result		Opponent
8/12	L	0-24	at Baltimore
8/20	W	27-24	Minnesota
8/28	W	37-10	Cincinnati
9/3	L	0-27	at Washington

REGULAR SEASON (11-5)

Date	Result		Opponent	Att.
9/12	W	21-19	at San Francisco	65,584
9/19	W	34-17	St. Louis	70,882
9/26	W	6-3	Arizona	70,534
10/3	W	27-10	at Carolina	73,461
10/10	L	10-17	Detroit	70,434
10/17	W	21-20	San Diego	70,187
10/24	L	10-56	at Kansas City	78,260
10/31	W	41-28	at Denver	75,083
11/14	W	24-14	Tampa Bay	70,810
11/21	W	14-10	at N.Y. Giants	78,793
11/28	W	24-21	New Orleans	70,521
12/5	L	0-27	at Tampa Bay	65,556
12/12	W	35-10	Oakland	70,616
12/18	W	34-31	Carolina (OT)	70,845
12/26	L	13-26	at New Orleans	64,900
1/2	L	26-28	at Seattle	66,740

(OT) Overtime

POSTSEASON (1-1)

Date	Result		Opponent	
1/15	W	47-17	St. Louis	70,709
1/23	L	10-27	at Philadelphia	67,717

SCORE BY PERIODS

Falcons	71	118	42	106	3	—	340
Opponents	57	105	76	99	0	—	337

2004 TEAM STATISTICS

	Falcons	Opp.
Total First Downs	284	310
Rushing	133	107
Passing	120	183
Penalty	31	20
3rd Down: Made/Att	73/201	72/200
3rd Down Pct.	36.3	36.0
4th Down: Made/Att	10/18	10/16
4th Down Pct.	55.6	62.5
Possession Avg.	29:10	30:50
Total Net Yards	5084	5207
Avg. Per Game	317.8	325.4
Total Plays	969	999
Avg. Per Play	5.2	5.2
Net Yards Rushing	2672	1681
Avg. Per Game	167.0	105.1
Total Rushes	524	434
Net Yards Passing	2412	3526
Avg. Per Game	150.8	220.4
Sacked/Yards Lost	50/280	48/312
Gross Yards	2692	3838
Att./Completions	395/217	517/328
Completion Pct.	54.9	63.4
Had Intercepted	16	19
Punts/Average	76/40.6	80/43.3
Net Punting Avg.	76/36.9	80/36.4
Penalties/Yards	109/905	129/900
Fumbles/Ball Lost	26/14	24/13
Touchdowns	41	41
Rushing	20	20
Passing	15	19
Returns	6	2

2004 INDIVIDUAL STATISTICS

PASSING

	Att.	Comp.	Yds.	Pct.	TD	Int.	Tkld.	Rate
Vick	321	181	2,313	56.4	14	12	46/266	78.1
Schaub	70	33	330	47.1	1	4	4/14	42.0
Mohr	3	2	24	66.7	0	0	0/0	91.0
Price	1	1	25	100.0	0	0	0/0	118.8
Falcons	395	217	2,692	54.9	15	16	50/280	72.0
Opponents	517	328	3,838	63.4	19	19	48/312	82.8

SCORING

	TD R	TD P	TD Rt	PAT	FG	Saf	PTS
Feely	0	0	0	40/40	18/23	0	94
Dunn	9	0	0	0/0	0/0	0	54
Duckett	8	0	0	0/0	0/0	0	48
Crumpler	0	6	0	0/0	0/0	0	36
Price	0	3	0	0/0	0/0	0	18
Vick	3	0	0	0/0	0/0	0	18
Finneran	0	2	0	0/0	0/0	0	12
Mathis	0	0	2	0/0	0/0	0	12
White	0	2	0	0/0	0/0	0	12
Coleman	0	0	1	0/0	0/0	0	6
Griffith	0	1	0	0/0	0/0	0	6
D. Hall	0	0	1	0/0	0/0	0	6
Pritchett	0	1	0	0/0	0/0	0	6
Rossum	0	0	1	0/0	0/0	0	6
Smith	0	0	1	0/0	0/0	0	6
Falcons	20	15	6	40/40	18/23	0	340
Opponents	20	19	2	39/39	16/18	1	337

2-Pt. Conversions: None.
Falcons 0-1, Opponents 1-2.

RUSHING

	Att.	Yds.	Avg.	LG	TD
Dunn	265	1,106	4.2	60	9
Vick	120	902	7.5	58	3
Duckett	104	509	4.9	35	8
Griffith	9	39	4.3	10	0
Price	3	34	11.3	16	0
Schaub	8	26	3.3	11	0
Pritchett	6	18	3.0	8	0
White	3	14	4.7	26	0
Layne	1	12	12.0	12	0
Wright	3	10	3.3	8	0
Jenkins	1	2	2.0	2	0
Rossum	1	0	0.0	0	0
Falcons	524	2,672	5.1	60	20
Opponents	434	1,681	3.9	29	20

RECEIVING

	No.	Yds.	Avg.	LG	TD
Crumpler	48	774	16.1	49t	6
Price	45	575	12.8	50	3
White	30	370	12.3	54	2
Dunn	29	294	10.1	59	0
Finneran	23	258	11.2	26	2
Griffith	22	220	10.0	62	1
Jenkins	7	119	17.0	46	0
Blakley	4	35	8.8	13	0
Duckett	3	15	5.0	11	0
McCrary	2	23	11.5	14	0
Pritchett	2	5	2.5	4	1
Layne	1	6	6.0	6	0
Feely	1	-2	-2.0	-2	0
Falcons	217	2,692	12.4	62	15
Opponents	328	3,838	11.7	80t	19

INTERCEPTIONS

	No.	Yds	Avg	LG	TD
Beasley	4	115	28.8	85	0
Brooking	3	41	13.7	27	0
Mathis	2	101	50.5	66t	2
D. Hall	2	50	25.0	48t	1
Rossum	2	22	11.0	14	0
Coleman	1	39	39.0	39t	1
Draft	1	33	33.0	33	0
Scott	1	22	22.0	22	0
Webster	1	18	18.0	18	0
Smith	1	1	1.0	1	0
Kerney	1	0	0.0	0	0
Falcons	19	442	23.3	85	4
Opponents	16	201	12.6	75	0

PUNTING

	No.	Yds.	Avg.	In 20	LG
Mohr	76	3,082	40.6	19	56
Falcons	76	3,082	40.6	19	56
Opponents	80	3,466	43.3	20	67

PUNT RETURNS

	No.	FC	Yds.	Avg.	LG	TD
Rossum	37	14	457	12.4	75t	1
Finneran	0	3	0	—	—	0
Falcons	37	17	457	12.4	75t	1
Opponents	33	21	134	4.1	25	0

KICKOFF RETURNS

	No.	Yds.	Avg.	LG	TD
Rossum	58	1,250	21.6	49	0
Griffith	1	31	31.0	31	0
D. Hall	1	48	48.0	48	0
Pritchett	1	2	2.0	2	0
Falcons	61	1,331	21.8	49	0
Opponents	56	1,117	19.9	96t	1

FIELD GOALS

	1-19	20-29	30-39	40-49	50+
Feely	1/1	7/7	7/9	3/6	0/0
Falcons	1/1	7/7	7/9	3/6	0/0
Opponents	0/0	7/7	4/5	2/3	3/3

SACKS

	No.
Kerney	13.0
Coleman	11.5
Smith	6.0
T. Hall	3.0
Brooking	2.5
Scott	2.5
Williams	2.5
Jasper	2.0
Stewart	1.5
Beasley	1.0
Glymph	1.0
Rossum	1.0
D. Hall	0.5
Falcons	48.0
Opponents	50.0

RECORD HOLDERS
INDIVIDUAL RECORDS—CAREER

Category	Name	Performance
Rushing (Yds.)	Gerald Riggs, 1982-88	6,631
Passing (Yds.)	Steve Bartkowski, 1975-1985	23,468
Passing (TDs)	Steve Bartkowski, 1975-1985	154
Receiving (No.)	Terance Mathis, 1994-2001	573
Receiving (Yds.)	Terance Mathis, 1994-2001	7,349
Interceptions	Rolland Lawrence, 1973-1980	39
Punting (Avg.)	Rick Donnelly, 1985-89	42.6
Punt Return (Avg.)	Darrien Gordon, 2001	14.1
Kickoff Return (Avg.)	Darrick Vaughn, 2000-01	25.7
Field Goals	Morten Andersen, 1995-2000	139
Touchdowns (Tot.)	Terance Mathis, 1994-2001	57
Points	Morten Andersen, 1995-2000	620

INDIVIDUAL RECORDS—SINGLE SEASON

Category	Name	Performance
Rushing (Yds.)	Jamal Anderson, 1998	1,846
Passing (Yds.)	Jeff George, 1995	4,143
Passing (TDs)	Steve Bartkowski, 1980	31
Receiving (No.)	Terance Mathis, 1994	111
Receiving (Yds.)	Alfred Jenkins, 1981	1,358
Interceptions	Scott Case, 1988	10
Punting (Avg.)	Billy Lothridge, 1968	44.3
Punt Return (Avg.)	Darrien Gordon, 2001	14.1
Kickoff Return (Avg.)	Darrick Vaughn, 2000	27.7
Field Goals	Jay Feely, 2002	32
Touchdowns (Tot.)	Jamal Anderson, 1998	16
Points	Jay Feely, 2002	138

INDIVIDUAL RECORDS—SINGLE GAME

Category	Name	Performance
Rushing (Yds.)	Gerald Riggs, 9-2-84	202
Passing (Yds.)	Steve Bartkowski, 11-15-81	416
Passing (TDs)	Wade Wilson, 12-13-92	5
Receiving (No.)	William Andrews, 11-15-81	15
Receiving (Yds.)	Terance Mathis, 12-13-98	198
Interceptions	Many times	2
	Last time by Ashley Ambrose, 11-18-01	
Field Goals	Norm Johnson, 11-13-94	6
Touchdowns (Tot.)	T.J. Duckett, 12-12-04	4
Points	T.J. Duckett, 12-12-04	24

2005 VETERAN ROSTER

No.	Name	Pos.	Ht.	Wt.	Birthdate	NFL Exp.	College	Hometown	How Acq.	'04 Games/ Starts
88	Anelli, Mark	TE	6-3	265	6/5/79	4	Wisconsin	Addison, Ill.	FA-'05	0*
80	Beverly, Eric	TE	6-3	300	3/28/74	9	Miami (OH)	Cleveland, Ohio	UFA(Det)-'04	13/3
64	Bibla, Martin	G	6-3	306	10/4/79	4	Miami	Mountaintop, Pa.	D4-'02	11/0
85	Blakley, Dwayne	TE	6-4	257	8/10/79	2	Missouri	St. Joseph, Mo.	W(Tenn)-'04	15/1
56	Brooking, Keith	LB	6-2	245	10/30/75	8	Georgia Tech	Senoia, Ga.	D1-'98	16/16
55	Brown, Michael	LB	5-10	220	1/16/80	2	Louisville	Louisville, Ky.	FA-'05	2/0*
29	Carpenter, Keion	S	5-11	205	10/31/77	7	Virginia Tech	Baltimore, Md.	UFA(Buff)-'02	0*
26	Coady, Rich	S	6-1	210	1/26/76	7	Texas A&M	Dallas, Texas	UFA(StL)-'05	16/5*
75	Coleman, Rod	DT	6-2	285	8/16/76	7	East Carolina	Vicksburg, Miss.	UFA(Oak)-'04	13/13
83	Crumpler, Alge	TE	6-2	262	12/23/77	5	North Carolina	Wilmington, N.C.	D2-'01	14/14
39	Davis, Carey	FB	5-10	225	3/27/81	2	Illinois	St. Louis, Mo.	FA-'04	1/0
14	Detmer, Ty	QB	6-0	189	10/30/67	14	Brigham Young	San Antonio, Texas	UFA(Det)'04	0*
72	Draper, Shawn	T	6-3	275	4/5/79	2	Alabama	Huntsville, Ala.	FA-'05	0*
45	Duckett, T.J.	RB	6-0	254	2/17/81	4	Michigan State	Kalamazoo, Mich.	D1-'02	13/0
28	Dunn, Warrick	RB	5-9	180	1/5/75	9	Florida State	Baton Rouge, La.	UFA(TB)-'02	16/16
86	Finneran, Brian	WR	6-5	210	1/31/76	7	Villanova	Mission Viejo, Calif.	FA-'00	12/1
65	Forney, Kynan	G	6-3	307	9/8/78	5	Hawaii	Nacogdoches, Texas	D7b-'01	16/16
93	Glymph, Junior	DE	6-5	270	4/13/81	2	Carson-Newman	Hackensack, N.J.	FA-'04	3/0
4	Gowin, Toby	P	5-10	167	3/30/75	9	North Texas	Jacksonville, Texas	UFA(NYJ)-'05	16/0*
33	Griffith, Justin	FB	6-1	232	4/13/81	3	Mississippi State	Magee, Miss.	D4-'03	12/11
72	Grigsby, Otis	DE	6-3	260	11/19/80	2	Kentucky	San Antonio, Texas	FA-'05	0*
21	Hall, DeAngelo	CB	5-10	197	11/19/83	2	Virginia Tech	Chesapeake, Va.	D1a-'04	10/9
50	Hartwell, Edgerton	LB	6-1	250	5/27/78	5	Western Illinois	Las Vegas, Nev.	UFA(Balt)-'05	16/16*
38	Heard, Ronnie	S	6-2	215	10/5/76	6	Mississippi	Bay City, Texas	UFA(SF)-'05	16/14*
73	Herndon, Steve	G	6-4	292	5/25/77	5	Georgia	LaGrange, Ga.	FA-'04	15/1
90	Herron, Anthony	DE	6-3	280	9/24/79	3	Iowa	Boiling Brook, Ill.	FA-'04	0*
12	Jenkins, Michael	WR	6-4	217	6/18/82	2	Ohio State	Tampa, Fla.	D1b-'04	16/0
47	Joyce, Eric	CB	5-10	193	1/21/78	2	Tennessee State	Nashville, Tenn.	FA-'05	0*
97	Kerney, Patrick	DE	6-5	273	12/30/76	7	Virginia	Newtown, N.J.	D1-'99	16/16
66	King, Austin	C	6-5	303	4/11/81	2	Northwestern	Cincinnati, Ohio	FA-'04	4/0
53	Kramer, Jordan	LB	6-1	230	12/7/79	3	Idaho	Parma, Idaho	FA-'05	4/0*
96	Lake, Antwan	DE	6-4	308	7/10/79	4	West Virginia	Seaford, Del.	FA-'03	16/2
94	Lavalais, Chad	DT	6-1	293	4/15/79	2	Louisiana State	Marksville, La.	D5-'04	16/5
61	Lehr, Matt	G	6-2	304	4/25/79	5	Virginia Tech	Jacksonville, Fla.	UFA(StL)-'05	7/2*
23	Mathis, Kevin	CB	5-9	185	4/29/74	9	Texas A&M-Commerce	Gainesville, Texas	FA-'02	15/12
39	Mayer, Shawn	S	6-0	202	3/4/79	3	Penn State	Hillsborough, N.J.	FA-'05	3/0*
25	McCadam, Kevin	S	6-1	219	3/6/79	4	Virginia Tech	Lakeside, Calif.	D5a-'02	16/2
62	McClure, Todd	C	6-1	286	2/16/77	6	Louisiana State	Baton Rouge, La.	D7-'99	16/16
44	McCrary, Fred	FB	6-0	247	9/19/72	11	Mississippi State	Naples, Fla.	FA-'04	3/2
92	Mitchell, Brandon	DT	6-3	290	6/19/75	9	Texas A&M	Abbeville, La.	UFA(Sea)-'05	15/0*
67	Moore, Michael	G	6-2	318	11/1/76	5	Troy State	Fayette, Ala.	FA-'03	1/1
30	Morton, Christian	CB	6-0	180	4/28/81	2	Illinois	St. Louis, Mo.	FA-'04	2/0
71	Peck, Jared	T	6-5	290	5/6/79	2	North Dakota State	Bloomington, Minn.	FA-'03	1/0
2	Peterson, Todd	K	5-11	180	2/4/70	12	Georgia	Washington, D.C.	UFA(SF)-'05	16/0*
81	Price, Peerless	WR	5-11	190	10/27/76	7	Tennessee	Dayton, Ohio	T(Buff)-'03	16/15
42	Pruitt, Etric	S	6-0	196	8/16/81	2	Southern Mississippi	Theodore, Ala.	FA-'04	3/0
48	Rackley, Derek	TE	6-4	250	7/18/77	6	Minnesota	Apple Valley, Minn.	FA-'00	16/0
98	Reese, Ike	LB	6-2	222	10/16/73	8	Michigan State	Jacksonville, N.C.	UFA(Phil)-'05	16/1*
20	Rossum, Allen	CB	5-8	178	10/22/75	8	Notre Dame	Dallas, Texas	UFA(GB)-'02	16/1
8	Schaub, Matt	QB	6-5	237	6/25/81	2	Virginia	Westchester, Pa.	D3-'04	6/1
24	Scott, Bryan	S	6-1	219	4/13/81	3	Penn State	Warrington, Pa.	D2-'03	16/16
76	Shaffer, Kevin	T	6-5	290	3/2/80	4	Tulsa	Leola, Pa.	D7b-'02	15/15
91	Smith, Brady	DE	6-5	274	6/5/73	10	Colorado State	Barrington, Ill.	UFA(NO)-'00	16/16
79	Stokes, Barry	T	6-4	310	12/20/73	8	Eastern Michigan	Flint, Mich.	UFA(NYG)-'05	0*
99	Vaughn, Khaleed	DE	6-4	270	5/20/81	2	Clemson	Atlanta, Ga.	FA-'04	3/0
7	Vick, Michael	QB	6-0	215	6/26/80	5	Virginia Tech	Newport News, Va.	D1-'01	15/15
36	Webster, Jason	CB	5-9	187	9/8/77	6	Texas A&M	Houston, Texas	UFA(SF)-'04	10/9
74	Weiner, Todd	T	6-4	297	9/16/75	8	Kansas State	Coral Springs, Fla.	UFA(Sea)-'02	16/16
89	White, Dez	WR	6-1	215	8/23/79	6	Georgia Tech	Jacksonville, Fla.	UFA(Chi)-'04	16/15
51	Williams, Demorrio	LB	6-0	232	7/6/80	2	Nebraska	Beckville, Texas	D4-'04	16/1
35	Wright, Jason	RB	5-10	210	7/12/82	2	Northwestern	Diamond Bar, Calif.	FA-'04	2/0

* Anelli did not play in 1 game with Chicago in '04; Brown played 2 games with Washington in '04; Carpenter missed '04 season because of injury; Coady played 16 games with St. Louis; Detmer did not play 1 game; Draper did not play in 1 game with New Orleans in '04; Gowin played 16 games with N.Y. Jets; Grigsby did not play in 1 game with Miami; Hartwell played 16 games with Baltimore; Heard played 16 games with San Francisco; Herron spent '02 season with Detroit on Physically Unable to Perform (PUP) list; Joyce last active with Chicago in '02; Kramer played 4 games with Tennessee; Lehr played 7 games with St. Louis; Mayer played 3 games with New England; Mitchell played 15 games with Seattle; Peterson played 16 games with San Francisco; Reese played 16 games with Philadelphia; Stokes last active with N.Y. Giants in '03.

Players lost through free agency (3): K Jay Feely (NYG; 16 games in '04), G Roberto Garza (Chi; 16), T Matt Stewart (Cle; 16).

Also played with Falcons in '04—CB Aaron Beasley (14 games), LB Chris Draft (14), LB Jamie Duncan (4), WR Jimmy Farris (14), DE Travis Hall (15), DT Ed Jasper (12), LB Eric Johnson (16), FB George Layne (2), LB Terrence Melton (1), P Chris Mohr (16), FB Stanley Pritchett (14), DE Karon Riley (1), TE Darnell Sanders (2), S Siddeeq Shabazz (15), LB Artie Ulmer (16).

2005 FIRST-YEAR ROSTER

Name	Pos.	Ht.	Wt.	Birthdate	College	Hometown	How Acq.
Archie, Adrian (1)	LB	5-11	233	7/30/80	Richmond	Alexandria, Va.	FA-'04
Babineaux, Jonathan	DT	6-2	286	10/12/81	Iowa	Port Arthur, Texas	D2
Bady, Lawrence	WR	5-10	189	11/17/82	Boise State	Vacaville, Calif.	FA
Beck, Jordan	LB	6-2	233	4/18/83	Cal Poly-San Luis Obispo	Santa Cruz, Calif.	D3
Boley, Michael	LB	6-3	236	8/24/82	Southern Mississippi	Athens, Ala.	D5a
Bratton, Brian	WR	5-10	186	7/31/82	Furman	Wheeling, W. Va.	FA
Bryant, Romby (1)	WR	6-1	181	12/21/79	Tulsa	Oklahoma City, Okla.	FA
Buhl, Jonte	CB	5-10	175	4/4/82	Texas A&M	Pflugerville, Texas	FA
Casey, Brian	TE	6-6	271	9/17/81	Kansas State	Gladstone, Mo.	FA
Cash, Antoine	LB	6-1	223	3/5/82	Southern Mississippi	Anguilla, Miss.	FA
Cobb, DeAndra	RB	5-10	196	5/18/81	Michigan State	Las Vegas, Nev.	D6
Cucci, Steve	TE	6-5	268	5/4/81	Houston	Bradenton, Fla.	FA
Davis, Chauncey	DE	6-2	277	1/27/83	Florida State	Auburndale, Fla.	D4
Dudley, Kevin	FB	6-0	238	1/2/82	Michigan	Brookville, Ind.	FA
Flinn, Ryan (1)	P	6-5	205	2/14/80	Central Florida	Fort Myers, Fla.	FA
Johnson, Kerry	WR	6-3	200	3/6/82	Mississippi	Oxford, Miss.	FA
Jones, Byron	CB	5-10	182	7/28/83	Texas A&M	Bay City, Texas	FA
Koenen, Michael	P	5-11	195	7/13/82	Western Washington	Ferndale, Wash.	FA
Leake, John (1)	LB	6-0	228	8/28/81	Clemson	Plano, Texas	FA
Mabry, Mike (1)	C	6-1	295	4/26/80	Central Florida	Houston, Texas	FA
Magner, Cole	WR	6-2	196	11/11/82	Bowling Green	Ojai, Calif.	FA
McLendon, T.A.	RB	5-10	235	2/21/84	North Carolina State	Albemarle, N.C.	FA
Mosley, Kendrick (1)	WR	6-2	197	7/21/81	Western Michigan	Pahokee, Fla.	FA-'04
Newton, Cam	S	6-1	203	5/19/82	Furman	Darlington, S.C.	FA
Nyenhuis, Gabe (1)	DE	6-3	269	6/26/81	Colorado	St. Charles, Ill.	FA
Omiyale, Frank	T	6-4	310	11/23/82	Tennessee Tech	Nashville, Tenn.	D5b
Pearson, Dave (1)	T	6-3	297	3/29/81	Michigan	Brighton, Mich.	FA-'04
Randall, Bryan	QB	6-0	222	8/16/83	Virginia Tech	Williamsburg, Va.	FA
Shropshire, Darrell	DT	6-2	301	3/18/83	South Carolina	Kershaw, S.C.	D7
Thomas, Hannibal	WR	6-3	205	4/6/83	Cincinnati	Atlanta, Ga.	FA
Tinsley, Derrick	WR	6-0	200	10/30/82	Tennessee	Marietta, Ga.	FA
White, Roddy	WR	6-0	208	11/2/81	Alabama-Birmingham	James Island, S.C.	D1

The term NFL Rookie is defined as a player who is in his first season of professional football and has not been on the roster of another professional football team for any regular-season or postseason games. A Rookie is designated by an "R" on NFL rosters. Players who have been active in another professional football league or players who have NFL experience, including either preseason training camp or being on an Active List or Inactive List, or on Reserve/Injured or Reserve/Physically Unable to Perform for fewer than six regular-season games, are termed NFL First-Year Players. An NFL First-Year Player is designated by a "1" on NFL rosters. Thereafter, a player is credited with an additional year of experience for each season in which he accumulates six games on the Active List or Inactive List, or on Reserve/Physically Unable to Perform.

Log on to www.atlantafalcons.com for an up-to-date roster.

COACHING STAFF

Executive Vice President/Head Coach, Jim Mora

Pro Career: Second-year head coach Jim Mora was hired by the Falcons on January 9, 2004. Set franchise record for the most wins by a first year head coach and became eleventh rookie head coach in NFL history to capture a division title. Directed team to second NFC championship game in franchise history. Led the NFL in rushing offense (167 yards per game) and quarterback sacks (48). In 2003, in his fifth season as defensive coordinator of the San Francisco 49ers, Mora's unit finished fourth in the NFC in total defense and ninth in the NFL in rushing defense. San Francisco's 42 quarterback sacks finished tied for fourth in the NFL. Despite a rash of injuries, the 49ers gave a solid effort on defense in 2002, finishing seventh in the NFL against the run and 14th in total defense. The 49ers defense was truly a team effort as four starters earned NFC Player-of-the-Week honors during the season. In 2001, the defense ranked sixth in the NFL in scoring defense, allowing only 16.3 points per game. The team also registered three shutouts, the most in 49ers history. Mora served as the 49ers' secondary coach (1997-98). He was named as the secondary coach for the Saints in 1992. During his five years in New Orleans (1992-96), the team twice led the NFL in fewest passing yards allowed (1992-93). Mora spent seven seasons in the Chargers' organization as a member of the pro personnel department (1985), defensive assistant in the secondary (1986-88), and defensive backs coach (1989-1991). Career record: 12-6.

Background: Mora played defensive back for Washington (1980-83), appearing in two Rose Bowls. He served as an assistant for one season (1984) on Don James' staff, helping the squad earn a berth in the Orange Bowl.

Personal: Born November 19, 1961 in Los Angeles. Mora attended Interlake High in Bellevue, Wash. He is the son of former NFL head coach Jim Mora. He and his wife, Shannon, have four children: Cole (1-7-95), Lillia (8-19-96), Ryder (1-11-99), and Trey (10-4-02).

ASSISTANT COACHES

Dennis Allen, defensive assistant; born September 22, 1972, Hurst, Texas. Safety Texas A&M 1992-95. No pro playing experience. College coach: Texas A&M 1996-99, Tulsa 2000-01. Pro coach: Joined Falcons in 2002.

Clancy Barone, tight ends; born July 26, 1963, San Andreas, Calif. Attended Cal State-Sacramento. No college or pro playing experience. College coach: American River (Calif.) J.C. 1987-1989, Cal State-Sacramento 1990-92, Texas A&M 1993, Eastern Illinois 1994-96, Wyoming 1997-

1999, Houston 2000-02, Texas State 2003. Pro coach: Joined Falcons in 2004.

Chris Beake, linebackers; born September 10, 1972, Kansas City, Mo. Attended Air Force. No college or pro playing experience. College coach: Air Force 1994-95. Pro coach: San Francisco 49ers 1999-2003, joined Falcons in 2004.

Rocky Colburn, asst. strength and conditioning; born May 24, 1963, Dallas, Ore. Safety Alabama 1981-83. No pro playing experience. College coach: Alabama 1984, 1987-1992, Samford 1986. Pro coach: Joined Falcons in 1999.

Chris Dalman, offensive assistant; born March 15, 1970, Salinas, Calif. Guard/center Stanford 1989-1992. Pro center San Francisco 49ers 1993-2000. Pro coach: Joined Falcons in 2005.

Joe DeCamillis, special teams coordinator; born June 29, 1965, Arvada, Colo. Attended Wyoming. No college or pro playing experience. College coach: Wyoming 1988. Pro coach: Denver Broncos 1989, Miami Dolphins 1990, New York Giants 1993-96, joined Falcons in 1997.

Ed Donatell, defensive coordinator; born February 4, 1957, Akron, Ohio. Defensive back Glenville (W. Va.) State 1975-78. College coach: Kent State 1979-1980, Washington 1981-82, Pacific 1983-85, Idaho 1986-88, Cal State-Fullerton 1989. Pro coach: New York Jets 1990-94, Denver Broncos 1995-99, Green Bay Packers 2000-03, joined Falcons in 2004.

Alex Gibbs, consultant/offensive line; born February 22, 1941 Morganton, N.C. Running back-defensive back Davidson College 1959-1963. No pro playing experience. College coach: Duke 1969-1970, Kentucky 1971-72, West Virginia 1973-74, Ohio State 1975-78, Auburn 1979-1981, Georgia 1982-83. Pro coach: Denver Broncos 1984-87, Oakland Raiders 1988-89, San Diego Chargers 1990-91, Indianapolis Colts 1992, Kansas City Chiefs 1993-94, Denver Broncos 1995-2003, joined Falcons in 2004.

Jeff Jagodzinski, offensive line; born October 12, 1963, Milwaukee, Wis. Fullback Wisconsin-Whitewater 1981-84. No pro playing experience. College coach: Wisconsin-Whitewater 1985, Northern Illinois 1986, Louisiana State 1987-88, East Carolina 1989-1996, Boston College 1997-98. Pro coach: Green Bay Packers 1999-2003, joined Falcons in 2004.

Bill Johnson, defensive line; born June 23, 1955, Monroe, La. Defensive lineman Northwestern (La.) State 1976-79. No pro playing experience. College coach: Northwestern (La.) State 1980-81, McNeese State 1985-86, Miami 1987, Louisiana Tech 1988-89, Arkansas 1990-91, 2000, Texas A&M 1992-99. Pro coach: Joined Falcons in 2001.

Mike Johnson, quarterbacks; born May 2, 1967, Los Angeles. Quarterback Arizona State 1985-86, Akron 1988-89. Pro quar-

terback Arizona Cardinals 1990, San Antonio Riders (World League) 1991-92, British Columbia Lions (CFL) 1992-93, Shreveport Pirates (CFL) 1994-95. College coach: Oregon State 1997-99. Pro coach: San Diego Chargers 2000-01, joined Falcons in 2002.

Greg Knapp, offensive coordinator; born March 5, 1963, Long Beach, Calif. Quarterback Cal State-Sacramento 1982-85. No pro playing experience. College coach: Cal State-Sacramento 1986-1994. Pro coach: San Francisco 49ers 1995-2003, joined Falcons in 2004.

Brett Maxie, defensive backs; born January 13, 1962, Dallas. Safety Texas Southern 1982-85. Pro safety New Orleans Saints 1985-1993, Atlanta Falcons 1994, Carolina Panthers 1995-96, San Francisco 49ers 1997. Pro coach: Carolina Panthers 1998, San Francisco 49ers 1999-2003, joined Falcons in 2004.

Al Miller, strength and conditioning; born August 29, 1947, El Dorado, Ark. Wide receiver Northeast Louisiana 1965-69. No pro playing experience. College coach: Northwestern State (La.) 1974-78, Mississippi State 1980, Northeast Louisiana 1981, Alabama 1982-84. Pro coach: Denver Broncos 1987-92, New York Giants 1993-96, joined Falcons in 1997.

Robert Prince, offensive assistant; born May 8, 1965, Okinawa, Japan. Attended Humboldt State. No college or pro playing experience. College coach: Humboldt State 1989-1990, Montana State 1991, Cal State-Sacramento 1992-93, Fort Lewis College 1994-95, Recruit Seagulls (X League Japan) 1996-97, Portland State 1998-2000, Boise State 2001-03. Pro coach: Joined Falcons in 2004.

George Stewart, wide receivers; born December 29, 1958, Little Rock, Ark. Guard Arkansas 1977-1980. No pro playing experience. College coach: Minnesota 1984-85, Notre Dame 1986-88. Pro coach: Pittsburgh Steelers 1989-1991, Tampa Bay Buccaneers 1992-95, San Francisco 49ers 1996-2002, joined Falcons in 2003.

Emmitt Thomas, senior defensive assistant/secondary; born June 3, 1943, Angleton, Texas. Quarterback-receiver Bishop (Texas) College 1963-65. Pro defensive back Kansas City Chiefs 1966-1978. College coach: Central Missouri State 1979-1980. Pro coach: St. Louis Cardinals 1981-85, Washington Redskins 1986-1994, Philadelphia Eagles 1995-98, Green Bay Packers 1999, Minnesota Vikings 2000-01, joined Falcons in 2002.

Ollie Wilson, running backs; born March 3, 1951, Worcester, Mass. Wide receiver Springfield 1971-73. No pro playing experience. College coach: Springfield 1975, Northeastern 1976-1982, California 1983-1990. Pro coach: Atlanta Falcons 1991-96, San Diego Chargers 1997-2001, rejoined Falcons in 2002.

National Football Conference
South Division
Team Colors: Black, Panther Blue, and
Silver
800 South Mint Street
Charlotte, North Carolina 28202-1502
Telephone: (704) 358-7000

2005 SCHEDULE
PRESEASON
Aug. 13 **Washington** 8:00
Aug. 20 at New York Giants 8:00
Aug. 26 at Cleveland 8:00
Sept. 1 **Pittsburgh** 8:00

REGULAR SEASON
Sept. 11 **New Orleans**......................1:00
Sept. 18 **New England** 1:00
Sept. 25 at Miami.............................1:00
Oct. 3 **Green Bay** (Mon.) 9:00
Oct. 9 at Arizona..........................1:15
Oct. 16 at Detroit 1:00
Oct. 23 Open Date
Oct. 30 **Minnesota** 1:00
Nov. 6 at Tampa Bay 1:00
Nov. 13 **New York Jets** 4:05
Nov. 20 at Chicago......................12:00
Nov. 27 at Buffalo 1:00
Dec. 4 **Atlanta**..............................1:00
Dec. 11 **Tampa Bay**.......................1:00
Dec. 18 at New Orleans................12:00
Dec. 24 **Dallas** (Sat.) 1:00
Jan. 1 at Atlanta...........................1:00

Stadium: Bank of America Stadium
(opened in 1996)
• **Capacity:** 73,298
Charlotte, North Carolina
28202-1502
Playing Surface: Grass
Training Camp: Wofford College
Spartanburg,
South Carolina 29303

BANK OF AMERICA STADIUM

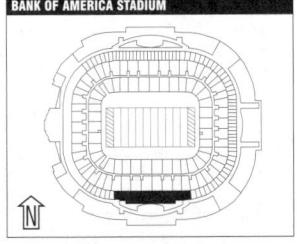

CLUB OFFICIALS
Owner/Founder: Jerry Richardson
President, Panthers Football LLC:
Mark Richardson
President Panthers Stadium LLC:
Jon Richardson
General Manager: Marty Hurney
General Counsel: Richard Thigpen
Chief Financial Officer: Dave Olsen
Controller: Mike Dudan
Director of Pro Scouting: Mark Koncz
Pro Scouts: Hal Hunter, Trent Kirchner,
Tag Ribary, Brandon Taylor
Director of College Scouting: Tony Softli
College Scouts: Brian Adams,
Bucky Brooks, Ryan Cowden,
Khary Darlington, Jeff Morrow,
Joe Schoen, Mike Szabo,
Gerald Williams
Director of Communications:
Charlie Dayton
Communications Assistant:
Bruce Speight
Public Relations Assistant: Deedee Mills
Media Relations Assistant:
Steven Drummond
Director of Ticket Operations:
Phil Youtsey
Director of Player Relations: Donnie Shell
Director of Community Relations and
Cheerleader/Mascot Programs:
Riley Fields
Cheerleader/Mascot Program Manager:
Tina Neely
Director of Sales and Sponsor Services:
Kyle Caddell
Director of Broadcast Administration:
Henry Thomas
Executive Producer-Television:
Greg Brannon
Executive Producer-Radio: David Langton
Director of Information Systems:
Mason Vincent
Salary Cap Analyst/Negotiatior:
Rob Rogers
Video Director: Mark Hobbs
Assistant Video Director: Jeff Mueller
Head Trainer: Ryan Vermillion
Assistant Trainers: Mark Shermansky,
Reggie Scott
Equipment Manager: Jackie Miles
Assistant Equipment Manager: Don Toner
Director of Security: Gene Brown
Stadium Operations Manager: Scott Paul
Director of Entertainment and
Panthervision: Kyle Ritchie
Facilities Manager: Matthew Getz
Head Groundskeeper: Tom Vaughan
Human Resources/Office Manager:
Tracy Rivers

COACHING HISTORY
(75-91-0)
Records include postseason games
1995-98   Dom Capers 31-35-0
1999-2001 George Seifert 16-32-0
2002-04   John Fox....................28-24-0

ATTENDANCE
Home 577,019   Away 536,514
Total 1,113,533
Single-game home record,
76,136 (12/10/95)
Single-season home record, 577,019
(2004)

2005 DRAFT CHOICES

Round	Name	Pos.	College
1	Thomas Davis	DB	Georgia
2	Eric Shelton	RB	Louisville
3	Evan Mathis	G	Alabama
	Atiyyah Ellison	DT	Missouri
4	Stefan LeFors	QB	Louisville
5	Adam Seward	LB	Nevada-Las Vegas
	Geoff Hangartner	T	Texas A&M
	Ben Emanuel	DB	UCLA
6	Jovan Haye	DE	Vanderbilt
	Joe Berger	T	Michigan Tech

2004 TEAM RECORD

PRESEASON (4-0)

8/14	W	23-20	at Washington
8/19	W	27-20	N.Y. Giants
8/28	W	20-17	New England
9/2	W	16-13	at Pittsburgh

REGULAR SEASON (7-9)

Date	Result	Opponent	Att.
9/13	L	14-24	Green Bay	73,656
9/19	W	28-17	at Kansas City	78,136
10/3	L	10-27	Atlanta	73,461
10/10	L	17-20	at Denver	75,072
10/17	L	8-30	at Philadelphia	67,707
10/24	L	6-17	San Diego	73,096
10/31	L	17-23	at Seattle	66,214
11/7	L	24-27	Oakland	73,518
11/14	W	37-27	at San Francisco	63,618
11/21	W	35-10	Arizona	72,796
11/28	W	21-14	Tampa Bay	73,124
12/5	W	32-21	at New Orleans	58,878
12/12	W	20-7	St. Louis	73,306
12/18	L	31-34	at Atlanta (OT)	70,845
12/26	W	37-20	at Tampa Bay	65,380
1/2	L	18-21	New Orleans	73,302

(OT) Overtime

SCORE BY PERIODS

Panthers	78	90	62	125	0	—	355
Opponents	80	79	92	85	3	—	339

2004 TEAM STATISTICS

	Panthers	Opp.
Total First Downs	308	307
Rushing	85	98
Passing	192	177
Penalty	31	32
3rd Down: Made/Att	83/206	99/215
3rd Down Pct.	40.3	46.0
4th Down: Made/Att	3/8	6/12
4th Down Pct.	37.5	50.0
Possession Avg.	29:56	30:04
Total Net Yards	5225	5382
Avg. Per Game	326.6	336.4
Total Plays	991	1021
Avg. Per Play	5.3	5.3
Net Yards Rushing	1582	1904
Avg. Per Game	98.9	119.0
Total Rushes	422	474
Net Yards Passing	3643	3478
Avg. Per Game	227.7	217.4
Sacked/Yards Lost	33/246	34/225
Gross Yards	3889	3703
Att./Completions	536/311	513/303
Completion Pct.	58.0	59.1
Had Intercepted	15	26
Punts/Average	79/43.1	64/41.1
Net Punting Avg.	79/36.9	64/37.9
Penalties/Yards	123/1020	117/1078
Fumbles/Ball Lost	23/11	29/12
Touchdowns	42	40
Rushing	10	19
Passing	29	18
Returns	3	3

2004 INDIVIDUAL STATISTICS

PASSING	Att.	Comp.	Yds.	Pct.	TD	Int.	Tkld.	Rate
Delhomme	533	310	3,886	58.2	29	15	33/246	87.3
Peete	1	1	3	100.0	0	0	0/0	79.2
Proehl	1	0	0	0.0	0	0	0/0	39.6
Smith	1	0	0	0.0	0	0	0/0	39.6
Panthers	536	311	3,889	58.0	29	15	33/246	87.0
Opponents	513	303	3,703	59.1	18	26	34/225	72.0

SCORING	TD R	TD P	TD Rt	PAT	FG	Saf	PTS
Muhammad	0	16	0	0/0	0/0	0	96
Kasay	0	0	0	27/28	19/22	0	84
Goings	6	1	0	0/0	0/0	0	42
Colbert	0	5	0	0/0	0/0	0	32
Mangum	0	3	0	0/0	0/0	0	18
Seidman	0	2	0	0/0	0/0	0	14
Foster	2	0	0	0/0	0/0	0	12
Hoover	0	2	0	0/0	0/0	0	12
Peppers	0	0	2	0/0	0/0	0	12
Chandler	0	0	0	8/8	0/2	0	8
Sauerbrun	0	0	0	4/4	1/1	0	7
Bennett	1	0	0	0/0	0/0	0	6
Delhomme	1	0	0	0/0	0/0	0	6
Moorehead	0	0	1	0/0	0/0	0	6
Panthers	10	29	3	39/40	20/25	0	355
Opponents	40	19	18	39/39	20/28	0	339

2-Pt. Conversions: Colbert, Seidman.
Panthers 2-2, Opponents 0-1.

RUSHING	Att.	Yds.	Avg.	LG	TD
Goings	217	821	3.8	57t	6
Foster	59	255	4.3	71	2
Hoover	68	246	3.6	16	0
Davis	24	92	3.8	12	0
Delhomme	25	71	2.8	13	1
Harris	15	53	3.5	19	0
Bennett	6	17	2.8	11	1
Muhammad	3	15	5.0	13	0
Proehl	1	9	9.0	9	0
Smart	3	4	1.3	3	0
Peete	1	-1	-1.0	-1	0
Panthers	422	1,582	3.7	71	10
Opponents	474	1,904	4.0	71	19

RECEIVING	No.	Yds.	Avg.	LG	TD
Muhammad	93	1,405	15.1	51	16
Colbert	47	754	16.0	63	5
Goings	45	394	8.8	37	1
Proehl	34	497	14.6	34	0
Mangum	34	323	9.5	26	3
Hoover	21	161	7.7	34	2
Seidman	13	123	9.5	27	2
Foster	9	76	8.4	42	0
Smith	6	60	10.0	15	0
Gaines	4	34	8.5	14	0
Davis	2	32	16.0	22	0
Hankton	2	25	12.5	20	0
Smart	1	5	5.0	5	0
Panthers	311	3,889	12.5	63	29
Opponents	303	3,703	12.2	75t	18

INTERCEPTIONS	No.	Yds.	Avg.	LG	TD
Gamble	6	15	2.5	13	0
Witherspoon	4	48	12.0	25	0
Manning	4	46	11.5	30	0
Branch	3	79	26.3	76	0
Peppers	2	143	71.5	97	1
Morgan	2	20	10.0	11	0
Allen	1	21	21.0	21	0
Moorehead	1	17	17.0	17t	1
Fields	1	14	14.0	14	0
Hawkins	1	9	9.0	9	0
Buckner	1	8	8.0	8	0
Panthers	26	420	16.2	97	2
Opponents	15	321	21.4	64t	3

PUNTING	No.	Yds.	Avg.	In 20	LG
Sauerbrun	76	3,351	44.1	25	65
Kasay	2	51	25.5	0	34
Panthers	79	3,402	43.1	25	65
Opponents	64	2,630	41.1	21	67

PUNT RETURNS	No.	FC	Yds.	Avg.	LG	TD
Broussard	10	8	43	4.3	13	0
Gamble	9	2	69	7.7	16	0
Baker	8	3	49	6.1	18	0
Hawkins	1	0	4	4.0	4	0
Smith	0	1	0	—	—	0
Panthers	28	14	165	5.9	18	0
Opponents	38	12	303	8.0	34	0

KICKOFF RETURNS	No.	Yds.	Avg.	LG	TD
Broussard	24	555	23.1	49	0
Bennett	8	177	22.1	43	0
Smart	8	169	21.1	33	0
Robertson	6	180	30.0	49	0
Proehl	3	64	21.3	27	0
Baker	2	39	19.5	23	0
Colbert	2	30	15.0	19	0
Foster	2	16	8.0	14	0
Hoover	2	30	15.0	16	0
Seidman	2	20	10.0	12	0
Rasmussen	1	12	12.0	12	0
Wesley	1	15	15.0	15	0
Panthers	61	1,307	21.4	49	0
Opponents	69	1,477	21.4	66	0

FIELD GOALS	1-19	20-29	30-39	40-49	50+
Kasay	0/0	11/11	4/4	1/2	3/5
Chandler	0/0	0/0	0/2	0/0	0/0
Sauerbrun	0/0	0/0	1/1	0/0	0/0
Panthers	0/0	11/11	5/7	1/2	3/5
Opponents	1/1	5/7	7/10	7/9	0/1

SACKS	No.
Peppers	11.0
Fields	4.0
Buckner	3.5
Rucker	3.5
Witherspoon	3.0
Minter	2.0
Moorehead	2.0
Morgan	2.0
Jenkins	1.0
Jordan	1.0
Wallace	1.0
Panthers	34.0
Opponents	33.0

RECORD HOLDERS
INDIVIDUAL RECORDS—CAREER

Category	Name	Performance
Rushing (Yds.)	Tshimanga Biakabutuka, 1996-2001	2,530
Passing (Yds.)	Steve Beuerlein, 1996-2000	12,690
Passing (TDs)	Steve Beuerlein, 1996-2000	86
Receiving (No.)	Muhsin Muhammad, 1996-2004	578
Receiving (Yds.)	Muhsin Muhammad, 1996-2004	7,751
Interceptions	Eric Davis, 1996-2000	25
Punting (Avg.)	Todd Sauerbrun, 2001-04	45.5
Punt Return (Avg.)	Winslow Oliver, 1996-98	10.7
Kickoff Return (Avg.)	Michael Bates, 1996-2000	25.7
Field Goals	John Kasay, 1995-2004	202
Touchdowns (Tot.)	Wesley Walls, 1996-2002	44
	Muhsin Muhammad, 1996-2004	44
Points	John Kasay, 1995-2004	843

INDIVIDUAL RECORDS—SINGLE SEASON

Category	Name	Performance
Rushing (Yds.)	Stephen Davis, 2003	1,444
Passing (Yds.)	Steve Beuerlein, 1999	4,436
Passing (TDs)	Steve Beuerlein, 1999	36
Receiving (No.)	Muhsin Muhammad, 2000	102
Receiving (Yds.)	Muhsin Muhammad, 2004	1,405
Interceptions	Doug Evans, 2001	8
Punting (Avg.)	Todd Sauerbrun, 2001	47.5
Punt Return (Avg.)	Winslow Oliver, 1996	11.5
Kickoff Return (Avg.)	Michael Bates, 1996	30.2
Field Goals	John Kasay, 1996	37
Touchdowns (Tot.)	Muhsin Muhammad, 2004	16
Points	John Kasay, 1996	145

INDIVIDUAL RECORDS—SINGLE GAME

Category	Name	Performance
Rushing (Yds.)	Stephen Davis, 10-26-03	178
Passing (Yds.)	Steve Beuerlein, 12-12-99	373
Passing (TDs)	Steve Beuerlein, 1-2-00	5
Receiving (No.)	Muhsin Muhammad, 12-18-99, 11-27-00	11
Receiving (Yds.)	Muhsin Muhammad, 9-13-98	192
Interceptions	Deon Grant, 9-22-02	3
Field Goals	John Kasay, 12-5-04	6
Touchdowns (Tot.)	Many times	3
	Last time by Nick Goings, 11-21-04	
Points	Fred Lane, 11-2-97	18
	Tshimanga Biakabutuka, 10-3-99	18
	Muhsin Muhammad, 12-18-99, 11-14-04	18
	Steve Smith, 12-8-02	18
	Nick Goings, 11-21-04	18

2005 VETERAN ROSTER

No.	Name	Pos.	Ht.	Wt.	Birthdate	NFL Exp.	College	Hometown	How Acq.	'04 Games/ Starts
59#	Armstead, Jessie	LB	6-1	237	10/26/70	13	Miami	Dallas, Texas	FA-'04	0*
80	Baker, Eugene	WR	6-2	183	3/18/76	3	Kent State	Monroeville, Pa.	FA-'05	3/0
t-	Baker, Jason	P/K	6-2	205	5/17/78	5	Iowa	Fort Wayne, Ind.	W(Ind)-'04	10/0*
33	Bashir, Idrees	S	6-2	198	12/7/78	5	Memphis	Decatur, Ga.	UFA(Ind)-'05	13/13*
36#	Bennett, Brandon	RB	5-11	220	2/3/73	7	South Carolina	Taylors, S.C.	FA-'04	8/0
28	Branch, Colin	S	5-11	205	3/2/80	3	Stanford	Carlsbad, Calif.	D4-'03	16/15
99	Buckner, Brentson	DT	6-2	310	9/30/71	12	Clemson	Columbus, Ga.	UFA(SF)-'01	15/15
67	Carstens, Jordan	DT	6-5	300	1/22/81	2	Iowa State	Bagley, Iowa	FA-'04	12/1
18	Carter, Drew	WR	6-2	200	9/5/81	2	Ohio State	Solon, Ohio	D5-'04	0*
6	Cheek, Steve	P	6-4	205	4/18/77	2	Humboldt State	Westfield, N.J.	FA-'05	12/0*
50	Ciurciu, Vinny	LB	6-0	235	5/2/80	3	Boston College	Paramus, N.J.	FA-'03	16/4
83	Colbert, Keary	WR	5-10	193	5/21/82	2	Southern California	Oxnard, Calif.	D2-'04	15/15
49	Cramer, Casey	FB	6-2	250	1/5/82	2	Dartmouth	Middleton, Wis.	FA-'04	6/1
48	Davis, Stephen	RB	6-0	230	3/1/74	10	Auburn	Spartanburg, S.C.	FA-'03	2/2
17	Delhomme, Jake	QB	6-2	215	1/10/75	7	Louisiana-Lafayette	Lafayette, La.	UFA(NO)-'03	16/16
52	Draft, Chris	LB	5-11	232	2/26/76	7	Stanford	Placentia, Calif.	FA-'05	14/13*
64	Ferrario, Bill	T/G	6-2	315	9/22/78	4	Wisconsin	Scranton, Pa.	FA-'04	0*
78	Fordham, Todd	T	6-5	319	10/9/73	9	Florida State	Atlanta, Ga.	T(Pitt)-'04	15/7
26	Foster, DeShaun	RB	6-0	222	1/10/80	4	UCLA	Tustin, Calif.	D2-'02	4/3
23#	Fuller, Curtis	S	5-10	188	7/25/78	5	Texas Christian	Fort Worth, Texas	W(GB)-'04	6/0
84	Gaines, Michael	TE	6-3	280	3/30/80	2	Central Florida	Tallahassee, Fla.	D7-'04	15/6
20	Gamble, Chris	CB	6-1	181	3/11/83	2	Ohio State	Sunrise, Fla.	D1-'04	16/16
37	Goings, Nick	RB	6-0	225	1/26/78	5	Pittsburgh	Dublin, Ohio	FA-'01	16/8
69	Gross, Jordan	T	6-4	300	7/20/80	3	Utah	Fruitland, Idaho	D1-'03	16/16
31	Hampton, William	S	5-10	190	3/7/75	4	Murray State	Little Rock, Ark.	FA-'03	4/0
88	Hankton, Karl	WR	6-2	202	7/24/70	7	Trinity College (IL)	New Orleans, La.	FA' 00	15/0
25	Harris, Joey	RB	5-10	205	12/18/80	2	Purdue	Tomball, Texas	FA-'04	4/0
45	Hoover, Brad	FB	6-0	245	11/11/76	6	Western Carolina	Thomasville, N.C.	FA-'00	14/9
34	Jackson, Eddie	CB	6-0	190	12/19/80	2	Arkansas	Richardson, Texas	FA-'04	10/0
77	Jenkins, Kris	DT	6-4	335	8/3/79	5	Maryland	Ypsilanti, Mich.	D2-'01	4/4
85	Jones, Freddie	TE	6-4	265	9/16/74	9	North Carolina	Landover, Md.	UFA(Ariz)-'05	16/15*
91	Jordan, Omari	DT	6-4	315	4/15/78	2	Buffalo	Cleveland, Ohio	FA-'04	5/0
61	Kadela, Dave	T	6-6	304	5/6/78	4	Virginia Tech	Dearborn, Mich.	FA-'04	1/0
4	Kasay, John	K	5-10	198	10/27/69	15	Georgia	Athens, Ga.	UFA(Sea)-'95	14/0
59	Knight, Bryan	LB	6-2	238	1/22/79	3	Pittsburgh	Buffalo, N.Y.	FA '05	0*
56	Kyle, Jason	LB	6-3	242	5/12/72	11	Arizona State	Tempe, Ariz.	UFA(SF)-'01	16/0
23	Lucas, Ken	CB	6-0	205	1/23/79	5	Mississippi	Cleveland, Miss.	UFA(Sea)-'05	16/16*
86	Mangum, Kris	TE	6-4	252	8/15/73	8	Mississippi	Magee, Miss.	D7 '97	15/10
24	Manning Jr., Ricky	CB	5-8	185	11/18/80	3	UCLA	Fresno, Calif.	D3b-'03	16/16
27	McCree, Marlon	S	5-11	202	3/17/77	5	Kentucky	Daytona Beach, Fla.	UFA(Hou)-'05	16/1*
30	Minter, Mike	S	5-10	195	1/15/74	9	Nebraska	Lawton, Okla.	D2 '97	16/16
60	Mitchell, Jeff	C	6-4	300	1/29/74	9	Florida	Dallas, Texas	UFA(Balt)-'01	16/16
94	Moorehead, Kindal	DT	6-2	285	10/14/78	3	Alabama	Memphis, Tenn.	D5-'03	14/12
55	Morgan, Dan	LB	6-2	245	12/19/78	5	Miami	Coral Springs, Fla.	D1-'01	12/12
72	Nelson, Bruce	G	6-5	301	5/12/79	3	Iowa	Emmetsburg, Iowa	D2-'03	0*
66	Peko, Tupe	G/T	6-4	305	9/19/78	4	Michigan State	Whittier, Calif.	W(Ind)-'05	11/8*
90	Peppers, Julius	DE	6-6	283	1/18/80	4	North Carolina	Bailey, N.C.	D1-'02	16/16
62	Pinkney, Cleveland	DT	6-1	300	9/14/77	3	South Carolina	Sumter, S.C.	W(Atl)-'04	2/0
92#	Pittman, Kavika	DE	6-6	273	10/9/74	10	McNeese State	Frankfurt, Germany	FA-'03	0*
81	Proehl, Ricky	WR	6-0	190	3/7/68	16	Wake Forest	Hillsborough, N.J.	UFA(StL)-'03	16/3
97	Rasmussen, Kemp	DE	6-3	265	5/25/79	4	Indiana	Hadley, Mich.	FA-'02	12/0
76	Reyes, Tutan	OL	6-3	305	10/28/77	6	Mississippi	Queens, N.Y.	W(TB)-'02	14/12
39#	Richardson, Damien	S	6-1	210	4/3/76	8	Arizona State	Fresno, Calif.	D6 '98	0*
22	Robertson, Jamal	RB	5-10	210	1/10/77	4	Ohio Northern	Washington, D.C.	FA-'04	5/0
11	Ross, Micah	WR	6-2	219	1/13/76	4	Jacksonville	Jacksonville, Fla.	FA-'04	10/0
8	Rouen, Tom	P	6-3	225	6/9/68	13	Colorado	Littleton, Colo.	UFA(Sea)-'05	4/0*
93	Rucker, Micheal	DE	6-5	275	2/28/75	7	Nebraska	St. Joseph, Mo.	D2b '99	16/16
82	Seidman, Mike	TE	6-4	261	2/11/81	3	UCLA	Westlake Village, Calif.	D3a-'03	16/6
53	Short, Brandon	LB	6-3	253	7/11/77	6	Penn State	McKeesport, Pa.	UFA(NYG)-'04	16/2
32	Smart, Rod	RB	5-11	201	1/9/77	5	Western Kentucky	Lakeland, Fla.	W(Phil)-'02	3/0
89	Smith, Steve	WR	5-9	185	5/12/79	5	Utah	Lynwood, Calif.	D3-'01	1/0
19	Tolver, J.R.	WR	6-1	200	1/13/80	2	San Diego State	San Diego, Calif.	FA-'05	0*
57	Tufts, Sean	LB	6-3	236	3/26/82	2	Colorado	Eglewood, Colo.	D6-'04	3/0
65#	Tylski, Rich	G	6-4	305	2/27/71	8	Utah Statae	San Diego, Calif.	FA-'04	16/1
68	Wahle, Mike	G	6-6	304	3/29/77	8	Navy	Lake Arrowhead, Calif.	FA-'05	16/16*

96	Wallace, Al	DE	6-5	275	3/25/74	6	Maryland	W. Palm Beach, Fla.	T(Mia)-'02	16/0
16	Weinke, Chris	QB	6-4	232	7/31/72	5	Florida State	St. Paul, Minn.	D4-'01	0*
21	Wesley, Dante	CB	6-0	211	4/5/79	4	Arkansas-Pine Bluff	Pine Bluff, Ark.	D4-'02	13/0
70	Wharton, Travelle	T	6-4	312	5/19/81	2	South Carolina	Simpsonville, .SC.	D3-'04	11/11
71#	Willig, Matt	T	6-8	315	1/21/69	14	Southern California	Santa Fe Springs, Calif.	FA-'03	16/9
54	Witherspoon, Will	LB	6-1	231	8/19/80	4	Georgia	Panama City, Fla.	D3-'02	16/16

* Armstead missed '04 season because of injury; J. Baker played 2 games with Kansas City, 4 games with Indianapolis, and 4 games with Denver; Bashir played 13 games with Indianapolis in '04; D. Carter mmissed '04 season on Physically Unable to Perform list; Cheek played 12 games with Kansas City; Draft played 14 games with Atlanta; Freeman last active with Kansas City in '03; C. Hill inactive for 1 game with Chicago in '03; M. Hill last active with Seattle in '03; Hunter missed '03 season with Baltimore because of injury; Jones played 16 games for Arizona; Knight last active with Chicago in '03; Lucas played 16 games with Seattle; McCree played 16 games with Houston; Nelson missed '04 season because of injury; Peko played 11 games with Indianapolis; Pittman missed '04 season because of injury; Richardson missed '04 season because of injury; Rouen played 4 games with Seattle; J. Smith last active with St. Louis in '03; Tolver last active with Miami in '03; Wahle played 16 games with Green Bay; Weinke inactive for 16 games.

\# Unrestricted free agent, subject to developments.

t- Panthers traded for J. Baker (Den).

Traded—P Todd Sauerbrun (Den; 16 games in '04).

Retired—Rodney Peete, 16-year quarterback, 1 game in '04.

Players lost through free agency (2): LB Brian Allen (Wash; 14 games in '04), S Travares Tillman (Mia; 6).

Also played with Carolina in '04—WR Jamall Broussard (8 games), G Doug Brzezinski (8), K Jeff Chandler (2), S Jarrod Cooper (6), DT Damane Duckett (2), LB Mark Fields (14), CB Artrell Hawkins (14), WR Muhsin Muhammad (16).

2005 FIRST-YEAR ROSTER

Name	Pos.	Ht.	Wt.	Birthdate	College	Hometown	How Acq.
Alexander, Lorenzo	DT	6-1	301	5/31/83	California	Berikley, Calif.	FA
Berger, Joseph	G	6-5	303	5/25/82	Michigan Tech	Newaygo, Mich.	D6b
Burns, Antoine (1)	WR	6-0	195	10/31/79	Minnesota	Milwaukee, Wis.	FA-'04
Davis, Thomas	S/LB	6-0	231	3/22/83	Georgia	Shellman, Ga.	D1
Doty, Jonathan	T	6-7	307	3/8/82	Kansas State	West Des Moines, Iowa	FA
Ellison, Atiyah	DT	6-3	303	9/29/81	Missouri	St. Louis, Mo.	D3b
Emanuel, Ben	S	6-2	213	6/18/82	UCLA	Friendswood, Texas	D5c
Farley, Scott (1)	S	6-0	212	4/24/80	Williams (MA)	Williamston, Mass.	FA-'04
Hangartner, Geoff	C	6-5	301	4/22/82	Texas A&M	New Braunfels, Texas	D5b
Haye, Jovan	DE	6-2	284	6/21/82	Vanderbilt	Fort Lauderdale, Fla.	D6a
Hill, Efrem	WR	6-0	179	7/23/83	Samford	Atlanta, Ga.	FA
Johnson, Adam (1)	TE	6-5	213	11/11/79	Buffalo	Alta Loma, Calif.	FA-'04
Lawrence, Marcus	LB	6-0	236	6/21/82	South Carolina	Aiken, S.C.	FA
LeFors, Stefan	QB	6-0	201	6/7/81	Louisville	Baton Rouge, La.	D4
Maddox, Nick (1)	RB	5-11	215	12/11/80	Florida State	Kannapolis, N.C.	FA-'04
Mathis, Evan	G	6-5	304	11/1/81	Alabama	Homewood, Ala.	D3a
McPherson, Lornell	CB	5-9	180	6/24/81	Nebraska	Omaha, Neb.	FA
Rutherford, Rod (1)	QB	6-2	223	12/12/80	Pittsburgh	Pittsburgh, Pa.	FA-'04
Seward, Adam	LB	6-2	248	6/15/82	Nevada-Las Vegas	Las Vegas, Nev.	D5a
Shelton, Eric	RB	6-1	246	6/23/83	Louisville	Lexington, Ky.	D2
Stubblefield, Taylor	WR	5-11	174	1/21/82	Purdue	Yakima, Wash.	FA
Watson, Michael	T	6-4	316	10/6/82	West Virginia	Pasadena, Calif.	FA

The term NFL Rookie is defined as a player who is in his first season of professional football and has not been on the roster of another professional football team for any regular-season or postseason games. A Rookie is designated by an "R" on NFL rosters. Players who have been active in another professional football league or players who have NFL experience, including either preseason training camp or being on an Active List or Inactive List, or on Reserve/Injured or Reserve/Physically Unable to Perform for fewer than six regular-season games, are termed NFL First-Year Players. An NFL First-Year Player is designated by a "1" on NFL rosters. Thereafter, a player is credited with an additional year of experience for each season in which he accumulates six games on the Active List or Inactive List, or on Reserve/Injured or Reserve/Physically Unable to Perform.

Log on to www.panthers.com for an up-to-date roster.

COACHING STAFF

Head Coach,
John Fox

Pro Career: Became third coach in Carolina Panthers history on January 25, 2002. In 2004, directed Carolina team that overcame a 1-7 record to end the regular season with mark of 7-9. Of the 28 NFL teams that began season with 1-7 record since 1990, Panthers became only third team to finish season with seven victories. In 2003, guided Panthers to Super Bowl XXXVIII two years after inheriting team that won one game in 2001. Joined Vince Lombardi and Bill Parcells as the only coaches in NFL history to inherit a one-win team and guide it to the playoffs in their second season. In 2002, engineered a six-game turn-around that ranks second for rookie head coaches since the NFL went to 16-game schedule in 1978. In 2002, the Panthers became the only team since the NFL merger to improve from thirty-first to second in total defense in one season. Prior to joining Carolina he served as the defensive coordinator for the New York Giants (1997-2001). In 2000, Fox helped the Giants reach Super Bowl XXXV. In the NFC Championship Game, the Giants' 41-0 victory over Minnesota was the first shutout in a conference title game since 1986. Before joining the Giants, Fox was a consultant for the Rams (1996), defensive coordinator for the Raiders (1994-95), and defensive backs coach for the Chargers (1992-93) and Steelers (1989-1991). Career record: 28-24.

Background: Defensive back at San Diego State (1976-77). Coached at San Diego State (1978), U.S. International (1979) Boise State (1980), Long Beach State (1981), Utah (1982), Kansas (1983), Iowa State (1984), and Pittsburgh (1986-88). Fox entered the pro ranks in 1985 as the secondary coach for the Los Angeles Express (USFL). Received bachelor's degree in physical education and earned a teaching credential from San Diego State.

Personal: Born February 8, 1955, in Virginia Beach, Va. He and his wife, Robin, have four children—Mathew, Mark, Cody, and Halle.

ASSISTANT COACHES

Danny Crossman, special teams; born January 17, 1967, El Paso, Texas. Defensive back Kansas 1985, Pittsburgh 1987-89. Pro defensive back Washington Redskins 1990, Detroit Lions 1991-92. College coach: U.S. Coast Guard Academy 1993, Western Kentucky 1994-96, Central Florida 1997-98, Georgia Tech 1999-2001, Michigan State 2002. Pro coach: Joined Panthers in 2003.

Paul Ferraro, special teams assistant; born April 30, 1959, Ridgewood, N.J. Defensive back Springfield College 1980-82. No pro playing experience. College coach: Massachusetts 1982, Syracuse 1983, Villanova 1984-86, Dartmouth 1987, Catholic 1988, Maine 1989, Ohio 1990, Bowling Green 1991-98, Georgia Tech 1999-2000, Rutgers 2001-04. Pro coach: Joined Panthers in 2005.

Ken Flajole, linebackers; born October 4, 1954, Seattle. Linebacker Wenatchee Valley (Wash.) C.C. 1973-74, Pacific Lutheran 1975-76. No pro playing experience. College coach: Pacific Lutheran 1977-78, Washington 1979, Montana 1980-85, Texas-El Paso 1986-88, Missouri 1989-1993, Richmond 1994, Hawaii 1995, Nevada 1996-97. Pro coach: Green Bay Packers 1998, Seattle Seahawks 1999-2002, joined Panthers in 2003.

Mike Gillhamer, defensive asisstant/secondary; born February 20, 1956, Oakland. Defensive back Carroll College 1972, Wenatchee (Wash.) J.C. 1973, Humboldt State 1974-75. No pro playing experience. College coach: College of the Sequoias 1979-1983, Weber State 1984, Utah 1985-89, San Jose State 1990-93, Nevada 1994-95, Oregon 2001-02, Louisville 2003. Pro coach: New York Giants 1997-2000, joined Panthers in 2004.

Dan Henning, offensive coordinator; born June 21, 1942, Bronx, N.Y. Quarterback William & Mary 1962-64. Pro quarterback San Diego Chargers 1964, 1966-67. College coach: Florida State 1968-1970, 1974, Virginia Tech 1971, 1973, Boston College 1994-96 (head coach). Pro coach: Houston Oilers 1972, New York Jets 1976-78, 1998-2000, Miami Dolphins 1979-1980, Washington Redskins 1981-1982, 1987-88, Atlanta Falcons 1983-86 (head coach), San Diego Chargers 1989-1991 (head coach), Detroit Lions 1992-93, Buffalo Bills 1997, joined Panthers in 2002.

David Magazu, tight ends; born June 10, 1957, Taunton Mass. Defensive tackle Springfield College 1976-79. No pro playing experience. College coach: Ithaca 1980, Western Michigan 1981, Michigan 1982, Michigan 1983, Northern Illinois 1984, Ball State 1985-86, Navy 1987-89, Indiana State 1990-91, Colorado State 1992-94, Kentucky 1995-96, Memphis 1997-98, Boston College 1999-2002. Pro coach: Joined Panthers in 2003.

Mike Maser, offensive line; born March 2, 1947, Clayton N.Y. Guard Buffalo 1967-1970. No pro playing experience. College coach: Marshall 1973, Bluefield State College 1974-78, Maine 1979-1980, Boston College 1981-1993. Pro coach: Jacksonville Jaguars 1995-2002, joined Panthers in 2003.

Mike McCoy, quarterbacks/offensive assistant; born April 1, 1972, San Francisco. Quarterback Long Beach State 1990-91, Utah 1992-94. Pro quarterback Amsterdam Admirals (NFLE) 1997, Calgary Stampeders (CFL) 1999. Pro coach: Joined Panthers in 1999.

Rod Perry, secondary; born September 11, 1953, Fresno, Calif. Defensive back Colorado 1972-74. Pro cornerback Los Angeles Rams 1975-1982, Cleveland Browns 1983-84. College coach: Columbia 1985, Fresno C.C. 1986, Fresno State 1987-88. Pro coach: Seattle Seahawks 1989-1991, Los Angeles Rams 1992-94, Houston Oilers 1995-96, San Diego Chargers 1997-2001, joined Panthers in 2002.

Jerry Simmons, strength and conditioning; born June 15, 1954, Elkhart, Kan. Linebacker Fort Hays State 1976-77. No pro playing experience. College coach: Fort Hays State 1978, Clemson 1980, Rice 1981-82, Southern California 1983-87. Pro coach: New England Patriots 1988-1990, Cleveland Browns/Baltimore Ravens 1991-98, joined Panthers in 1999.

Jim Skipper, running backs; born January 23, 1949, Breaux Bridge, La. Defensive back Whittier College 1971-72. No pro playing experience. College coach: Cal Poly-Pomona 1974-76, San Jose State 1977-78, Pacific 1979, Oregon 1980-82. Pro coach: Philadelphia/Baltimore Stars (USFL) 1983-85, New Orleans Saints 1986-1995, Arizona Cardinals 1996, New York Giants 1997-2000, San Francisco Demons (XFL) 2001 (head coach), joined Panthers in 2002.

Sal Sunseri, defensive line; born August 1, 1959, Pittsburgh. Linebacker Pittsburgh 1979-1981. College coach: Pittsburgh 1985-1992, Iowa Wesleyan 1993, Louisville 1995-97, Alabama A&M 1998-99, Louisiana State 2000, Michigan State 2001. Pro coach: Joined Panthers in 2002.

Mike Trgovac, defensive coordinator; born February 27, 1959, Youngstown, Ohio. Defensive lineman Michigan 1977-1980. No pro playing experience. College coach: Michigan 1984-85, Ball State 1986-88, Navy 1989, Colorado State 1990-91, Notre Dame 1992-94. Pro coach: Philadelphia Eagles 1995-98, Green Bay Packers 1999, Washington Redskins 2000-01, joined Panthers in 2002.

Richard Williamson, wide receivers; born April 13, 1941, Ft. Deposit, Ala. Receiver Alabama 1961-62. No pro playing experience. College coach: Alabama 1963-67, 1970-71, Arkansas 1968-69, 1972-74, Memphis State 1975-1980 (head coach). Pro coach: Kansas City Chiefs 1983-86, Tampa Bay Buccaneers 1987-1991 (interim head coach 1990, head coach 1991), Cincinnati Bengals 1992-94, joined Panthers in 1995.

**National Football Conference
North Division**
Team Colors: Navy Blue, Orange, and
White
**Halas Hall at Conway Park
1000 Football Drive
Lake Forest, Illinois 60045
Telephone:** (847) 295-6600

2005 SCHEDULE
PRESEASON
Aug. 8   vs. Miami at Canton, OH.....7:00
Aug. 12   at St. Louis........................7:00
Aug. 20   at Indianapolis...................7:00
Aug. 26   **Buffalo**...............................7:00
Sept. 1   **Cleveland**..........................7:00

REGULAR SEASON
Sept. 11 at Washington 1:00
Sept. 18 **Detroit** 12:00
Sept. 25 **Cincinnati** 12:00
Oct. 2   Open Date
Oct. 9   at Cleveland 1:00
Oct. 16   **Minnesota** 12:00
Oct. 23   **Baltimore**..........................3:15
Oct. 30   at Detroit 1:00
Nov. 6   at New Orleans.................12:00
Nov. 13   **San Francisco** 12:00
Nov. 20   **Carolina**..........................12:00
Nov. 27   at Tampa Bay 1:00
Dec. 4   **Green Bay**......................12:00
Dec. 11   at Pittsburgh......................1:00
Dec. 18   **Atlanta**..............................7:30
Dec. 25   at Green Bay 4:00
Jan. 1   at Minnesota 12:00

Stadium: Soldier Field
          (opened in 1924)
          •**Capacity:** 61,500
          1410 S. Museum Campus Dr.
          Chicago, Illinois 60605
Playing Surface: Natural Grass
Training Camp: Olivet-Nazarene Univ.
               Bourbonnais, Illinois
               60901

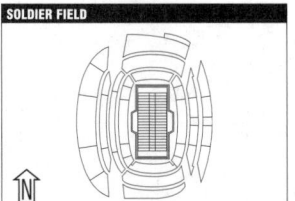

SOLDIER FIELD

CLUB OFFICIALS
Chairman of the Board:
   Michael B. McCaskey
Secretary: Virginia H. McCaskey
President and CEO: Ted Phillips
General Manager: Jerry Angelo
Vice President: Tim McCaskey
Senior Director of Administration:
   John Bostrom
Senior Director of Corporate
   Communications: Scott Hagel
Senior Director of Corporate Sales &
   Marketing: Dave Greeley
Senior Director of Business Development
   & Alumni Relations: Brian McCaskey
Senior Director of Ticket Operations:
   George McCaskey
Senior Director of Finance & Treasurer:
   Karen Murphy
Director of Pro Personnel: Bobby DePaul
Director of College Scouting:
   Greg Gabriel
Director of Player Contracts and Legal
   Affairs: Cliff Stein
Assistant Director of Pro Personnel:
   Morocco Brown
Director of Player Development:
   Bobbie Howard
Director of Special Projects:
   Pat McCaskey
Director of Community Relations:
   Caroline Guip
Director of Broadcasting: Greg Miller
Media Services Manager: Jim Christman
Media Information Manager:
   Roger Hacker
Media Relations Assistant: Brian Hardin
Video Director: Dean Pope
Assistant Video Directors:
   Dave Hendrickson, Dan Tuohy
Head Athletic Trainer: Tim Bream
Assistant Trainers: Reggie Barnes,
   Chris Hanks
Director of Rehabilitation: Bobby Slater
Strength and Conditioning Coordinator:
   Rusty Jones
Head Equipment Manager: Tony Medlin
Assistant Equipment Managers:
   Carl Piekarski, Brad Camp
Scouts: Chris Ballard, Marty Barrett,
   Rex Hogan, Ted Monago,
   Mark Sadowski, Jeff Shiver

COACHING HISTORY
**Decatur Staleys 1920,
Chicago Staleys 1921
(660-489-42)**
Records include postseason games
1920-29	George Halas	84-31-19
1930-32	Ralph Jones	24-10-7
1933-1942	George Halas*	88-24-4
1942-45	Hunk Anderson-Luke Johnsos**	24-12-2
1946-1955	George Halas	76-43-2
1956-57	John (Paddy) Driscoll	14-10-1
1958-1967	George Halas	76-53-6
1968-1971	Jim Dooley	20-36-0
1972-74	Abe Gibron	11-30-1
1975-77	Jack Pardee	20-23-0
1978-1981	Neill Armstrong	30-35-0
1982-1992	Mike Ditka	112-68-0
1993-98	Dave Wannstedt	41-57-0
1999-2003	Dick Jauron	35-46-0
2004	Lovie Smith	5-11-0

*Retired after five games to enter U.S. Navy
**Co-coaches

ATTENDANCE
Home 485,429   Away 529,885
Total 1,015,314
Single-game home record,
   66,900 (9/5/93)
Single-season home record, 527,769
   (1999)

2005 DRAFT CHOICES
Round	Name	Pos.	College
1	Cedric Benson	RB	Texas
2	Mark Bradley	WR	Oklahoma
4	Kyle Orton	QB	Purdue
5	Airese Currie	WR	Clemson
6	Chris Harris	DB	Louisiana-Monroe
7	Rod Wilson	LB	South Carolina

2004 TEAM RECORD
PRESEASON (2-2)

Date	Result	Opponent
8/12	W 13-10	at St. Louis
8/21	W 20-13	San Francisco
8/27	L 13-17	New Orleans
9/3	L 10-24	at Cleveland

REGULAR SEASON (5-11)

Date	Result	Opponent	Att.
9/12	L 16-20	Detroit	61,535
9/19	W 21-10	at Green Bay	70,688
9/26	L 22-27	at Minnesota	64,163
10/3	L 9-19	Philadelphia	61,894
10/17	L 10-13	Washington	61,945
10/24	L 7-19	at Tampa Bay	65,550
10/31	W 23-13	San Francisco	62,054
11/7	W 28-21	at N.Y. Giants	78,786
11/14	W 19-17	at Tennessee (OT)	68,932
11/21	L 10-41	Indianapolis	61,908
11/25	L 7-21	at Dallas	64,026
12/5	W 24-14	Minnesota	62,051
12/12	L 3-22	at Jacksonville	67,572
12/19	L 5-24	Houston	62,122
12/26	L 13-19	at Detroit	61,924
1/2	L 14-31	Green Bay	62,197

(OT) Overtime

SCORE BY PERIODS

Bears	34	80	36	79	2	—	231
Opponents	78	117	50	86	0	—	331

2004 TEAM STATISTICS

	Bears	Opp.
Total First Downs	230	302
Rushing	84	109
Passing	121	165
Penalty	25	28
3rd Down: Made/Att	56/223	67/220
3rd Down Pct.	25.1	30.5
4th Down: Made/Att	6/19	4/15
4th Down Pct.	31.6	26.7
Possession Avg.	28:20	31:40
Total Net Yards	3816	5390
Avg. Per Game	238.5	336.9
Total Plays	967	1046
Avg. Per Play	3.9	5.2
Net Yards Rushing	1624	2050
Avg. Per Game	101.5	128.1
Total Rushes	430	496
Net Yards Passing	2192	3340
Avg. Per Game	137.0	208.8
Sacked/Yards Lost	66/449	35/173
Gross Yards	2641	3513
Att./Completions	471/249	515/287
Completion Pct.	52.9	55.7
Had Intercepted	16	17
Punts/Average	110/42.6	92/40.4
Net Punting Avg.	110/38.3	92/32.0
Penalties/Yards	124/956	120/914
Fumbles/Ball Lost	35/21	21/12
Touchdowns	26	36
Rushing	10	9
Passing	9	23
Returns	7	4

2004 INDIVIDUAL STATISTICS

PASSING	Att.	Comp.	Yds.	Pct.	TD	Int.	Tkld.	Rate
Hutchinson	161	92	903	57.1	4	3	23/160	73.6
Krenzel	127	59	718	46.5	3	6	23/158	52.5
Quinn	98	51	413	52.0	1	3	15/109	53.7
Grossman	84	47	607	56.0	1	3	5/22	67.9
Edinger	1	0	0	0.0	0	1	0/0	0.0
Bears	471	249	2,641	52.9	9	16	66/449	61.7
Opponents	515	287	3,513	55.7	23	17	35/173	78.1

SCORING	TD R	TD P	TD Rt	PAT	FG	Saf	PTS
Edinger	0	0	0	22/22	15/24	0	67
T. Jones	7	0	0	0/0	0/0	0	42
Berrian	0	2	0	0/0	0/0	0	12
B. Johnson	0	2	0	0/0	0/0	0	12
McKie	0	2	0	0/0	0/0	0	12
McQuarters	0	0	2	0/0	0/0	0	12
Thomas	2	0	0	0/0	0/0	0	12
Azumah	0	0	1	0/0	0/0	0	6
Briggs	0	0	1	0/0	0/0	0	6
M. Brown	0	0	1	0/0	0/0	0	6
Clark	0	1	0	0/0	0/0	0	6
Grossman	1	0	0	0/0	0/0	0	6
Haynes	0	0	1	0/0	0/0	0	6
Lyman	0	1	0	0/0	0/0	0	6
Terrell	0	1	0	0/0	0/0	0	6
Vasher	0	0	1	0/0	0/0	0	6
Krenzel	0	0	0	0/0	0/0	0	2
Ogunleye	0	0	0	0/0	0/0	1	2
Bears	10	9	7	22/22	15/24	3	231
Opponents	9	23	4	35/35	26/36	1	331

2-Pt. Conversions: Krenzel
Bears 1-4, Opponents 0-1.

RUSHING	Att.	Yds.	Avg.	LG	TD
T. Jones	240	948	4.0	54	7
Thomas	122	404	3.3	41t	2
Wade	12	76	6.3	14	0
Grossman	11	48	4.4	8	1
Krenzel	18	41	2.3	12	0
Quinn	3	35	11.7	23	0
Berrian	8	28	3.5	25	0
Peterson	6	19	3.2	13	0
Hutchinson	6	14	2.3	11	0
Terrell	3	10	3.3	20	0
McKie	1	1	1.0	1	0
Bears	430	1,624	3.8	54	10
Opponents	496	2,050	4.1	40	9

RECEIVING	No.	Yds.	Avg.	LG	TD
T. Jones	56	427	7.6	45	0
Terrell	42	699	16.6	63	1
Wade	42	481	11.5	40	0
Clark	24	282	11.8	31	1
Thomas	17	132	7.8	30	0
Berrian	15	225	15.0	49t	2
B. Johnson	14	55	3.9	14	2
McKie	13	70	5.4	15t	2
Gage	12	156	13.0	32	0
Lyman	11	73	6.6	13	1
Peterson	2	30	15.0	30	0
Gilmore	1	11	11.0	11	0
Bears	249	2,641	10.6	63	9
Opponents	287	3,513	12.2	69	23

INTERCEPTIONS	No.	Yds.	Avg.	LG	TD
Vasher	5	177	35.4	71t	1
Azumah	4	128	32.0	70t	1
McQuarters	2	85	42.5	45t	1
Green	2	0	0.0	0	0
Haynes	1	45	45.0	45t	1
Urlacher	1	42	42.0	42	0
Briggs	1	38	38.0	38t	1
Gray	1	31	31.0	31	0
Bears	17	546	32.1	71t	5
Opponents	16	222	13.9	45	1

PUNTING	No.	Yds.	Avg.	In 20	LG
Maynard	108	4,638	42.9	34	58
Edinger	2	53	26.5	1	30
Bears	110	4,691	42.6	35	58
Opponents	92	3,713	40.4	18	57

PUNT RETURNS	No.	FC	Yds.	Avg.	LG	TD
McQuarters	44	13	435	9.9	75t	1
Berrian	2	2	10	5.0	12	0
Gage	0	0	56	—	56	0
Gray	0	0	9	—	9	0
Bears	46	15	510	11.1	75t	1
Opponents	57	21	380	6.7	29	0

KICKOFF RETURN	No.	Yds.	Avg.	LG	TD
Azumah	42	924	22.0	73	0
Berrian	17	385	22.6	41	0
D. Jones	6	112	18.7	23	0
McKie	3	65	21.7	25	0
Peterson	3	57	19.0	22	0
McQuarters	2	46	23.0	37	0
B. Johnson	1	18	18.0	18	0
Bears	74	1,607	21.7	73	0
Opponents	54	1,160	21.5	43	0

FIELD GOALS	1-19	20-29	30-39	40-49	50+
Edinger	0/0	6/7	2/5	4/7	3/5
Bears	0/0	6/7	2/5	4/7	3/5
Opponents	0/0	11/11	6/8	7/11	2/6

SACKS	No.
A. Brown	6.0
Urlacher	5.5
Ogunleye	5.0
Harris	3.5
Boone	2.5
Hillenmeyer	2.5
Haynes	2.0
Scott	2.0
Azumah	1.5
Green	1.5
Idonije	1.0
Worrell	1.0
Briggs	0.5
Ta. Johnson	0.5
Bears	35.0
Opponents	66.0

RECORD HOLDERS
INDIVIDUAL RECORDS—CAREER

Category	Name	Performance
Rushing (Yds.)	Walter Payton, 1975-1987	16,726
Passing (Yds.)	Sid Luckman, 1939-1950	14,686
Passing (TDs)	Sid Luckman, 1939-1950	137
Receiving (No.)	Walter Payton, 1975-1987	492
Receiving (Yds.)	Johnny Morris, 1958-1967	5,059
Interceptions	Gary Fencik, 1976-1987	38
Punting (Avg.)	George Gulyanics, 1947-1952	44.5
Punt Return (Avg.)	George McAfee, 1940-41, 1945-1950	*12.8
Kickoff Return (Avg.)	Gale Sayers, 1965-1971	*30.6
Field Goals	Kevin Butler, 1985-1995	243
Touchdowns (Tot.)	Walter Payton, 1975-1987	125
Points	Kevin Butler, 1985-1995	1,116

INDIVIDUAL RECORDS—SINGLE SEASON

Category	Name	Performance
Rushing (Yds.)	Walter Payton, 1977	1,852
Passing (Yds.)	Erik Kramer, 1995	3,838
Passing (TDs)	Erik Kramer, 1995	29
Receiving (No.)	Marty Booker, 2001	100
Receiving (Yds.)	Marcus Robinson, 1999	1,400
Interceptions	Mark Carrier, 1990	10
Punting (Avg.)	Bobby Joe Green, 1963	46.5
Punt Return (Avg.)	Harry Clark, 1943	15.8
Kickoff Return (Avg.)	Gale Sayers, 1967	37.7
Field Goals	Kevin Butler, 1985	31
Touchdowns (Tot.)	Gale Sayers, 1965	22
Points	Kevin Butler, 1985	144

INDIVIDUAL RECORDS—SINGLE GAME

Category	Name	Performance
Rushing (Yds.)	Walter Payton, 11-20-77	275
Passing (Yds.)	Johnny Lujack, 12-11-49	468
Passing (TDs)	Sid Luckman, 11-14-43	*7
Receiving (No.)	Jim Keane, 10-23-49	14
Receiving (Yds.)	Harlon Hill, 10-31-54	214
Interceptions	Many times	3
	Last time by Mark Carrier, 12-9-90	
Field Goals	Roger LeClerc, 12-3-61	5
	Mac Percival, 10-20-68	5
Touchdowns (Tot.)	Gale Sayers, 12-12-65	*6
Points	Gale Sayers, 12-12-65	36

*NFL Record

2005 VETERAN ROSTER

No.	Name	Pos.	Ht.	Wt.	Birthdate	NFL Exp.	College	Hometown	How Acq.	'04 Games/ Starts
68	Anderson, Bryan	G	6-4	330	3/30/80	2	Pittsburgh	Philadelphia, Pa.	D7-'03	4/0
23	Azumah, Jerry	CB	5-10	192	9/1/77	7	New Hampshire	Worcester, Mass.	D5c-'99	12/8
86	Berlin, Eddie	WR	5-11	195	1/14/78	5	Northern Iowa	Urbandale, Iowa	UFA(Tenn)-'05	16/1*
80	Berrian, Bernard	WR	6-1	185	12/27/80	2	Fresno State	Winton, Calif.	D3-'04	16/1
70	Boone, Alfonso	DT	6-4	318	1/11/76	5	Mt. San Antonio (CA) J.C.	Saginaw, Mich.	FA-'00	12/2
10	Brien, Doug	K	6-0	185	11/24/70	12	California	Bloomfield, N.J.	FA-'05	16/0*
55	Briggs, Lance	LB	6-1	238	11/12/80	3	Arizona	Sacramento, Calif.	D3-'03	16/16
96	Brown, Alex	DE	6-3	262	6/4/79	4	Florida	White Springs, Fla.	D4-'02	16/16
30	Brown, Mike	S	5-10	212	2/13/78	6	Nebraska	Scottsdale, Ariz.	D2-'00	2/2
74	Brown, Ruben	G	6-3	300	2/13/72	11	Pittsburgh	Lynchburg, Va.	FA-'04	9/9
58	Cain, Jeremy	LB	6-1	235	4/24/80	2	Massachusetts	Ft. Lauderdale, Fla.	FA-'04	5/0
88	Clark, Desmond	TE	6-3	254	4/20/77	7	Wake Forest	Lakeland, Fla.	UFA(Mia)-'03	15/13
75	Colombo, Marc	T	6-8	325	10/8/78	4	Boston College	Bridgewater, Mass.	D1-'02	8/2
79	Edwards, Steve	T	6-5	330	2/20/79	3	Central Florida	Chicago, Ill.	FA-'03	15/8
14	Elliott, Jamin	WR	5-11	195	10/5/79	3	Delaware	Portsmouth, Va.	D6b-'02	0*
87	Gage, Justin	WR	6-4	210	1/25/81	3	Missouri	Jefferson City, Mo.	D5b-'03	16/2
63	Garza, Roberto	T/G	6-2	296	3/26/79	5	Texas A&M-Kingsville	Rio Hondo, Texas	UFA(Atl)-'05	15/15*
85	Gilmore, John	TE	6-4	262	9/21/79	4	Penn State	West Lawn, Pa.	FA-'02	16/1
25	Gray, Bobby	S	6-0	210	4/30/78	4	Louisiana Tech	Aldine, Texas	D5a-'02	10/4
43	Green, Mike	S	6-0	195	12/6/76	6	Northwestern State (LA)	Ruston, La.	D7b-'00	16/16
8	Grossman, Rex	QB	6-1	218	8/23/80	3	Florida	Bloomington, Ind.	D1b-'03	3/3
91	Harris, Tommie	DT	6-3	300	4/29/83	2	Oklahoma	Killeen, Texas	D1-'04	16/16
97	Haynes, Michael	DE	6-3	274	9/13/80	3	Penn State	Columbus, N.J.	D1a-'03	16/4
92	Hillenmeyer, Hunter	LB	6-4	238	10/28/80	3	Vanderbilt	Nashville, Tenn.	FA-'03	16/11
9	Hutchinson, Chad	QB	6-5	237	2/21/77	4	Stanford	Encinitas, Calif.	FA-'04	5/5
71	Idonije, Israel	DT	6-7	290	11/17/80	2	Manitoba	Brandon, Manitoba, Canada	FA-'03	15/0
47	Johnson, Bryan	FB	6-1	242	1/18/78	5	Boise State	Pocatello, Idaho	T(Wash)-'04	12/6
11	Johnson, Ron	WR	6-2	218	5/23/80	3	Minnesota	Detroit, Mich.	FA-'05	0*
99	Johnson, Tank	DT	6-3	300	12/7/81	2	Washington	Tempe, Ariz.	D2-'04	16/1
35	Johnson, Todd	S	6-1	200	12/18/78	2	Florida	Sarasota, Fla.	D4a-'03	16/10
20	Jones, Thomas	RB	5-10	220	8/19/78	6	Virginia	Big Stone Gap, Va.	FA-'04	14/14
94	Kashama, Alain	DE	6-4	270	12/8/79	2	Michigan	Montreal, Quebec, Canada	FA-'04	3/0
15	Kittner, Kurt	QB	6-2	211	1/23/80	2	Illinois	Schaumburg, Ill.	FA-'05	0*
10	Krenzel, Craig	QB	6-4	228	7/1/81	2	Ohio State	Sterling Heights, Mich.	D5-'04	6/5
57	Kreutz, Olin	C	6-2	292	6/9/77	8	Washington	Honolulu, Hawaii	D3-'98	16/16
89	Lyman, Dustin	TE	6-4	254	8/5/76	6	Wake Forest	Boulder, Colo.	D3b-'00	16/10
65	Mannelly, Patrick	T/LS	6-5	265	4/18/75	8	Duke	Atlanta, Ga.	D6b-'98	16/0
31	Marshall, Alfonso	CB	6-0	188	1/17/81	2	Miami	Clewiston, Fla.	D7-'04	7/0
4	Maynard, Brad	P	6-1	186	2/9/74	9	Ball State	Sheridan, Ind.	UFA(NYG)-'01	16/0
37	McKie, Jason	FB	5-11	240	5/22/80	4	Temple	Gulf Breeze, Fla.	FA-'03	15/2
26	McMillon, Todd	CB	5-11	188	9/26/74	6	Northern Arizona	Bellflower, Calif.	FA-'00	14/1
21	McQuarters, R.W.	CB	5-10	195	12/21/76	8	Oklahoma State	Tulsa, Okla.	T(SF)-'00	16/14
60	Metcalf, Terrence	G/T	6-3	318	1/28/78	4	Mississippi	Clarksdale, Miss.	D3-'02	13/5
69	Miller, Fred	T	6-7	320	2/6/73	10	Baylor	Aldine, Texas	FA-'05	16/16*
72	Mitchell, Qasim	T	6-6	355	12/3/79	3	North Carolina A&T	Jacksonville, N.C.	FA-'03	16/14
87	Muhammad, Muhsin	WR	6-2	217	5/5/73	10	Michigan State	Lansing, Mich.	FA-'05	16/16*
59	Odom, Joe	LB	6-1	235	12/14/79	3	Purdue	Bethalto, Ill.	D6a-'03	16/5
93	Ogunleye, Adewale	DE	6-4	260	8/9/77	5	Indiana	Staten Island, N.Y.	T(Mia)-'04	12/12
82	Owens, John	TE	6-3	270	1/10/80	4	Notre Dame	Hyattsville, Md.	W(Det)-'04	2/0
29	Peterson, Adrian	RB	5-10	210	7/1/79	4	Georgia Southern	Alachua, Fla.	D6a-'02	14/0
98	Pierson, Shurron	DE	6-2	250	5/31/82	3	South Florida	Wildwood, Fla.	T(Oak)-'04	6/0
36	Pippens, Jerrell	S	6-3	205	7/30/80	2	Nebraska	Philadelphia, Pa.	W(SD)-'04	2/0
52	Reese, Marcus	LB	6-1	233	6/15/81	3	UCLA	San Jose, Calif.	FA-'03	11/2
48	Reid, Gabe	TE	6-4	260	5/28/77	3	Brigham Young	American Samoa	FA-'03	0*
83	Sanders, Darnell	TE	6-6	270	3/16/79	4	Ohio State	Warrensville Heights, Ohio	W(Atl)-'05	2/0*
95	Scott, Ian	DT	6-2	305	11/8/81	3	Florida	Gainesville, Fla.	D4b-'03	14/13
76	Tait, John	T	6-6	315	1/26/75	7	Brigham Young	Tempe, Ariz.	RFA(KC)-'04	13/13
33	Tillman, Charles	CB	6-1	196	2/23/81	3	Louisiana-Lafayette	Copperas Cove, Texas	D2-'03	8/7
54	Urlacher, Brian	LB	6-4	258	5/25/78	6	New Mexico	Lovington, N.M.	D1-'00	9/9
31	Vasher, Nathan	CB	5-10	180	11/17/81	2	Texas	Texarkana, Texas	D4-'04	16/7
84	Wade, Bobby	WR	5-10	192	2/25/81	3	Arizona	Phoenix, Ariz.	D5a-'03	16/14
62	Woods, LeVar	LB	6-3	245	3/15/78	5	Iowa	Larchwood, Iowa	FA-'05	14/2*
24	Worrell, Cameron	S	5-11	199	12/14/79	3	Fresno State	Chowchilla, Calif.	FA-'03	13/0

* Berlin played 16 games with Tennessee in '04; Elliott last active with New England in '03; Garza played 15 games with Atlanta; R. Johnson last active with Baltimore in '03; Kittner last active with Atlanta in '03; Miller played 16 games with Tennessee; Muhammad played 16 games with Carolina; Reid missed '04 season because of injury; Sanders played 2 games with Atlanta; Woods played 14 games with Arizona.

Players lost through free agency (1): RB Anthony Thomas (Dall; 12 games in '04).

Also played with Bears in '04—K Paul Edinger (16 games), G Mike Gandy (5), T Aaron Gibson (4), LB Corey Jenkins (4), LB Leon Joe (1), WR Daryl Jones (2), QB Jonathan Quinn (5), WR David Terrell (16), RB Anthony Thomas (12), G Rex Tucker (6).

2005 FIRST-YEAR ROSTER

Name	Pos.	Ht.	Wt.	Birthdate	College	Hometown	How Acq.
Abron, Zack (1)	RB	5-8	229	2/3/80	Missouri	Lake St. Louis, Mo.	FA
Ballard, Derrick (1)	S	6-1	215	12/8/81	Memphis	Madison, Ga.	FA
Belton, Keith (1)	FB	6-0	232	6/1/81	Syracuse	West Charlotte, N.C.	W(Det)-'04
Benson, Cedric	RB	5-10	222	12/28/82	Texas	Midland, Texas	D1
Bradley, Mark	WR	6-1	201	1/29/82	Oklahoma	Pine Bluff, Ark.	D2
Campbell, Darrell (1)	DT	6-4	290	7/6/81	Notre Dame	South Holland, Ill.	FA
Currie, Airese	WR	5-10	186	11/16/82	Clemson	Columbia, S.C.	D5
Dinwiddie, Ryan (1)	QB	6-1	190	11/27/80	Boise State	Elk Grove, Calif.	FA
Dorsey, Quinn (1)	DE	6-4	260	4/1/80	Oregon	Denver, Colo.	T(NE)-'04
Droege, Rob (1)	T	6-6	315	2/15/81	Missouri	St. Louis, Mo.	FA
Ford, Carl (1)	WR	6-0	183	10/8/80	Toledo	Monroe, Mich.	W(GB)-'04
Harris, Chris	S	6-1	206	8/6/82	Louisiana-Monroe	Little Rock, Ark.	D6
Jackson, Jonathan	DE	6-3	250	10/17/82	Oklahoma	Houston, Texas	FA
Johnson, Ben (1)	T	6-7	325	4/7/80	Wisconsin	Brussels, Wis.	FA
Jones, Tyler	K	6-1	198	10/17/82	Boise State	Boise, Idaho	FA
Kelly, Kareem (1)	WR	6-0	186	4/1/81	Southern California	Long Beach, Calif.	W(Balt)-'04
Lacy, Bo (1)	G/T	6-4	300	11/22/80	Arkansas	New Port, Ark.	W(Pitt)-'04
Larsen, Stephen	LB	6-1	235	4/13/82	San Diego State	Chandler, Ariz.	FA
McGhghy, Matt	G	6-3	296	1/26/82	Northern Illinois	Keokuk, Iowa	FA
McGowan, Brandon	S	6-0	190	9/16/83	Maine	Jersey City, N.J.	FA
Novak, Nick	K	6-0	186	8/21/81	Maryland	Charlottesville, Va.	FA
Orton, Kyle	QB	6-4	226	11/14/82	Purdue	Runnels, Iowa	D4
Pauly, Greg	DT	6-6	295	3/23/82	Notre Dame	Waukesha, Wis.	FA
Poole, Sean	T	6-7	290	7/7/82	Michigan State	Flint, Mich.	FA
Ricker, A.J. (1)	C	6-4	300	3/29/80	Missouri	Klein, Texas	FA-'04
Russell, Fred (1)	RB	5-7	191	9/14/80	Iowa	Romulus, Mich.	W(Mia)-'04
Setta, Nick (1)	K	5-11	204	5/6/81	Notre Dame	Lockport, Ill.	FA
Shivers, Jason (1)	S	6-0	201	11/4/82	Arizona State	Phoenix, Ariz.	W(StL)-'04
Smith, Leroy	CB	5-10	190	12/26/81	Florida State	Quincy, Fla.	FA
Washburn, Cliff (1)	DE	6-5	285	1/25/80	Citadel	Shelby, N.C.	W(NYG)-'03
White, Greg (1)	DE	6-3	268	7/25/79	Minnesota	Newark, N.J.	FA
Wigfall, Walter (1)	G/T	6-3	375	10/5/79	Texas A&M-Kingsville	Katy, Texas	FA
Wilson, Rod	LB	6-2	217	11/12/81	South Carolina	Cross, S.C.	D7
Wise, Talib	CB	6-0	200	8/13/82	Nevada	Chicago, Ill.	FA

The term NFL Rookie is defined as a player who is in his first season of professional football and has not been on the roster of another professional football team for any regular-season or postseason games. A Rookie is designated by an "R" on NFL rosters. Players who have been active in another professional football league or players who have NFL experience, including either preseason training camp or being on an Active List or Inactive List, or on Reserve/Injured or Reserve/Physically Unable to Perform for fewer than six regular-season games, are termed NFL First-Year Players. An NFL First-Year Player is designated by a "1" on NFL rosters. Thereafter, a player is credited with an additional year of experience for each season in which he accumulates six games on the Active List or Inactive List, or on Reserve/Injured or Reserve/Physically Unable to Perform.

Log on to www.chicagobears.com for an up-to-date roster.

COACHING STAFF

Head Coach,
Lovie Smith

Pro Career: Named the thirteenth head coach in Chicago Bears history on January 15, 2004. Smith instilled his defensive tenacity into the Bears in his first season while leading the squad to a 5-11 record. Chicago set a franchise record with 6 defensive touchdowns and matched another with 3 safeties en route to leading the NFC in defensive scoring. The Bears also posted a sack total in 2004 that was nearly double that from the previous season (35 to 18) while also forcing 9 more turnovers than they did in 2003. Showing consistent in-game defensive improvement from the first half to the second half throughout Smith's inaugural season as a head coach, Chicago's defense held six opponents to 3 points or less in the second half while limiting five opponents to less than 100 yards of total offense after halftime. The Bears' defense also led the NFL in third-down efficiency and paced the NFC (fourth in NFL) in red-zone defense. Smith came to Chicago from St. Louis where he engineered a dramatic turnaround as the defensive coordinator of the Rams (2001-03). In Smith's first season as an NFL defensive coordinator with St. Louis, he helped the Rams return to the Super Bowl after missing the playoffs the previous season. Smith has coached on playoff teams in four of the last six campaigns. Smith previously coached the linebackers for the Tampa Bay Buccaneers (1996-2000). Known for his attacking style on defense, Smith orchestrated one of the NFL's most productive units in takeaways, defensive touchdowns, and sacks in 2003. St. Louis led the NFL with 46 takeaways while tying for fourth with 24 interceptions and leading the NFL with 22 fumble recoveries. The 46 takeaways for the Rams equals the 1999 Eagles for the second-highest single-season total in the NFL since 1993. While in Tampa Bay, he helped improve a Buccaneers' defense that had not ranked above twentieth in the NFL in the four seasons prior to Smith's arrival under head coach Tony Dungy and defensive coordinator Monte Kiffin. However, the Buccaneers ranked eleventh in 1996, third in 1997, second in 1998, third in 1999, and ninth in 2000. Career record: 5-11.

Background: Played at Tulsa (1976-79), where he was a linebacker as a freshman before being switched to strong safety. Smith was a two-time All-America and three-time All-Missouri Conference defensive back. Attended high school in Big Sandy, Texas, where the Wildcats won three state championships and he earned all-state honors three years as an end and linebacker. Smith has spent 22 years in coaching at the collegiate and professional levels. He began his coaching career at his hometown high school in 1980 before moving to Cascia Hall Prep in Tulsa the following year. Two years later Smith began coaching collegiately at Tulsa (1983-86), Wisconsin (1987), Arizona State (1988-91), Kentucky (1992), Tennessee (1993-94), and Ohio State (1995).

Personal: Born May 8, 1958, Gladewater, Texas. Lovie and his wife MaryAnne have three sons—Mikal, Matthew and Miles and twin grandsons—Malachi and Noah.

ASSISTANT COACHES

Bob Babich, linebackers; born February 20, 1961, Aliquippa, Pa. Linebacker Mesa (Colo.) C.C. 1979-1980, Tulsa 1981-82. No pro playing experience. College coach: Tulsa 1984-87, 1990, Wisconsin 1988-89, Bowling Green 1991, East Carolina 1992-93, Pittsburgh 1994-96, North Dakota State 1997-2002 (head coach). Pro coach: St. Louis Rams 2003, joined Bears in 2004.

Mike Bajakian, offensive quality control; born August 4, 1974, River Vale, N.J. Quarterback Williams College 1993-96. No pro playing experience. College coach: Rutgers 1998-99, Sacred Heart 2000, Michigan 2000-01, Central Michigan 2002-03. Pro coach: Joined Bears in 2004.

Rob Boras, tight ends; born September 30, 1970, Glen Ellyn, Ill. Center DePauw 1988-1991. No pro playing experience. College coach: DePauw 1992-93, Texas 1994-97, Benedictine 1998 (head coach), Nevada-Las Vegas 1999-2003. Pro coach: Joined Bears in 2004.

Charlie Coiner, asst. special teams; born Waynesboro, Va. Attended Catawba College, Appalachian State. No college or pro playing experience. College coach: Appalachian State 1983-86, Minnesota 1987, Louisville 1995-97, Tennessee-Chattanooga 1998, Louisiana State 1999, Texas Southern 2000. Pro coach: Joined Bears in 2001.

Darryl Drake, wide receivers; born December 11, 1956, Louisville, Ky. Wide receiver Western Kentucky 1975-78. Pro wide receiver Washington Redskins 1979, Ottawa Rough Riders (CFL) 1981, Cincinnati Bengals 1983. College coach: Western Kentucky 1983-1991, Georgia 1992-96, Baylor 1997, Texas 1998-2003. Pro coach: Joined Bears in 2004.

Perry Fewell, defensive backs; born September 7, 1962, Gastonia, N.C. Defensive back Lenoir-Rhyne 1981-84. No pro playing experience. College coach: North Carolina 1985-86, Army 1987, 1992-94, Kent State 1988-1991, Vanderbilt 1995-97. Pro coach: Jacksonville Jaguars 1998-2002, St. Louis Rams 2003-04, joined Bears in 2005.

Harold Goodwin, asst. offensive line; born November 14, 1973, Columbia, S.C. Offensive lineman Michigan 1992-94. No pro playing experience. College coach: Eastern Michigan 1998-99, Central Michigan 2000-03. Pro coach: Joined Bears in 2004.

Torrian Gray, asst. defensive backs; born March 18, 1974, Lakeland, Fla. Safety Virginia Tech 1993-96. Pro safety Minnesota Vikings 1997-2000. College coach: Maine 2000-01, Connecticut 2002-03. Pro coach: Joined Bears in 2004.

Harry Hiestand, offensive line; born November 19, 1958, Malvern, Pa. Offensive lineman Springfield College 1978-79, East Stroudsburg 1980. No pro playing experience. College coach: East Stroudsburg 1981-85, Pennsylvania 1986, Southern California 1987, Toledo 1988, Cincinnati 1989-93, Missouri 1994-96, Illinois 1997-2004. Pro coach: Joined Bears in 2005.

Lloyd Lee, defensive quality control; born August 10, 1976, Minneapolis. Safety Dartmouth 1994-97. Pro safety San Diego Chargers 1998-99. Pro coach: Tampa Bay Buccaneers (scout) 2001-03 , joined Bears in 2004.

Ron Rivera, defensive coordinator; born January 7, 1962, Fort Ord, Calif. Linebacker California 1980-83. Pro linebacker Chicago Bears 1984-1992. Pro coach: Chicago Bears 1997-98, Philadelphia Eagles 1999-2003, re-joined Bears in 2004.

Tim Spencer, running backs; born December 10, 1960, Martin Ferry, Ohio. Running back Ohio State 1979-1982. Pro running back Chicago Blitz (USFL) 1983, Arizona Wranglers (USFL) 1984, Memphis Showboats (USFL) 1985, San Diego Chargers 1985-1990. College coach: Ohio State 1994-2003. Pro coach: Joined Bears in 2004.

Dave Toub, special teams coordinator; born June 1, 1962, Ossining, N.Y. Offensive lineman Springfield College 1980-81, Texas-El Paso 1983-84. No pro playing experience. College coach: Texas El-Paso 1987-89, Missouri 1989-2000. Pro coach: Philadelphia Eagles 2001-03, joined Bears in 2004.

Ron Turner, offensive coordinator; born December 5, 1953, Martinez, Calif. Wide receiver Diablo Valley (Calif.) C.C. 1973-74, Pacific 1975-76. No pro playing experience. College coach: Pacific 1977, Arizona 1978-1980, Northwestern 1981-82, Pittsburgh 1983-84, Southern California 1985-87, Texas A&M 1988, Stanford 1989-1991, San Jose State 1992 (head coach), Illinois 1997-2004 (head coach). Pro coach: Chicago Bears 1993-96, re-joined Bears in 2005.

Wade Wilson, quarterbacks; born February 1, 1959, Commerce, Texas. Quarterback East Texas State 1977-1980. Pro quarterback Minnesota Vikings 1981-1991, Atlanta Falcons 1992, New Orleans Saints 1993-94, Dallas Cowboys 1995-97, Oakland Raiders 1998-99. Pro coach: Dallas Cowboys 2000-02, joined Bears in 2004.

**National Football Conference
East Division**
Team Colors: Royal Blue, Metallic Silver
Blue, and White
Cowboys Center
One Cowboys Parkway
Irving, Texas 75063
Telephone: (972) 556-9900

2005 SCHEDULE
PRESEASON
Aug. 13 at Arizona...........................7:00
Aug. 22 at Seattle............................5:00
Aug. 27 **Houston** 7:00
Sept. 1 **Jacksonville**........................7:00

REGULAR SEASON
Sept. 11 at San Diego 1:15
Sept. 19 **Washington** (Mon.)..........8:00
Sept. 25 at San Francisco.................1:05
Oct. 2   at Oakland..........................1:15
Oct. 9   **Philadelphia** 3:15
Oct. 16   **New York Giants** 12:00
Oct. 23   at Seattle............................1:05
Oct. 30   **Arizona** 12:00
Nov. 6   Open Date
Nov. 14 at Philadelphia (Mon.).........9:00
Nov. 20 **Detroit** 12:00
Nov. 24 **Denver** (Thu.) 3:15
Dec. 4   at New York Giants 1:00
Dec. 11 **Kansas City** 3:15
Dec. 18 at Washington 1:00
Dec. 24 at Carolina (Sat.) 1:00
Jan. 1   **St. Louis** 7:30

Stadium: Texas Stadium (opened in 1971)
•**Capacity:** 65,529
2401 E. Airport Freeway
Irving, Texas 75062
Playing Surface: Sportfield Realgrass
Training Camp: Marriott Residence Inn
Oxnard, California 93030

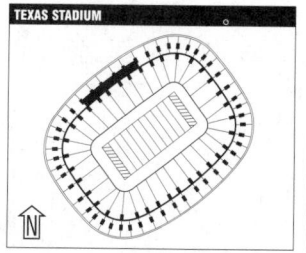

TEXAS STADIUM

CLUB OFFICIALS
Owner/President/General Manager:
Jerry Jones
Chief Operating Officer/Executive Vice
President-Player Personnel:
Stephen Jones
Vice President/Director of Charities and
Special Events: Charlotte Anderson
Chief Sales and Marketing Officer/Vice
President: Jerry Jones Jr.
CFO: George Mitchell
Vice President of College and Pro
Scouting: Jeff Ireland
General Counsel: Alec Scheiner
Director of Public Relations:
Rich Dalrymple
Director of Corporate Communications:
Brett Daniels
Director of Community Relations:
Emily Robbins
Assistant Director of College Scouting:
Tom Ciskowski
Assistant Director of Pro Scouting:
Bryan Broaddus
Director of Operations: Bruce Mays
Director of Player Development:
Steve Carichoff
Chief Human Resources and Diversity
Officer: Vincent Thompson
Director of Information Technology:
Peter Walsh
Director of Broadcasting: Scott Purcel
Internet Director: Derek Eagleton
Director of Ticket Operations:
Carol Padgett
Director of Sales, Promotions and
Advertising: Joel Finglass
Head Athletic Trainer: Jim Maurer
Equipment Manager: Mike McCord
Video Director: Robert Blackwell
Cheerleader Director: Kelli Finglass

COACHING HISTORY
(415-307-6)
Records include postseason games
1960-1988 Tom Landry 270-178-6
1989-1993 Jimmy Johnson 51-37-0
1994-97   Barry Switzer 45-26-0
1998-99   Chan Gailey 18-16-0
2000-02   Dave Campo................15-33-0
2003-04   Bill Parcells 16-17-0

ATTENDANCE
Home 497,256   Away 566,426
Total 1,063,682
Single-game home record,
65,180 (11/12/95)
Single-season home record,
518,167 (1995)

2005 DRAFT CHOICES
Round	Name	Pos.	College
1	Demarcus Ware	DE	Troy
	Marcus Spears	DE	Louisiana St.
2	Kevin Burnett	LB	Tennessee
4	Marion Barber	RB	Minnesota
	Chris Canty	DE	Virginia
6	Justin Beriault	DB	Ball State
	Rob Petitti	T	Pittsburgh
7	Jay Ratliff	DT	Auburn

DALLAS COWBOYS

2004 TEAM RECORD
PRESEASON (3-1)

Date	Result	Opponent
8/14	L 0-18	at Houston
8/21	W 21-20	at Oakland
8/30	W 20-17	Tennessee
9/2	W 24-20	Kansas City

REGULAR SEASON (6-10)

Date	Result	Opponent	Att.
9/12	L 17-35	at Minnesota	64,105
9/19	W 19-12	Cleveland	63,119
9/27	W 21-18	at Washington	90,367
10/10	L 10-26	N.Y. Giants	64,018
10/17	L 20-24	Pittsburgh	64,162
10/24	L 20-41	at Green Bay	70,679
10/31	W 31-21	Detroit	63,616
11/7	L 3-26	at Cincinnati	65,721
11/15	L 21-49	Philadelphia	64,190
11/21	L 10-30	at Baltimore	69,924
11/25	W 21-7	Chicago	64,026
12/6	W 43-39	at Seattle	68,093
12/12	L 13-27	New Orleans	64,056
12/19	L 7-12	at Philadelphia	67,723
12/26	W 13-10	Washington	63,705
1/2	L 24-28	at N.Y. Giants	78,500

SCORE BY PERIODS

Cowboys	63	82	72	76	0 —	293
Opponents	47	120	83	155	0 —	405

2004 TEAM STATISTICS

	Cowboys	Opp.
Total First Downs	296	297
Rushing	101	88
Passing	171	180
Penalty	24	29
3rd Down: Made/Att	78/214	75/192
3rd Down Pct.	36.4	39.1
4th Down: Made/Att	9/17	2/7
4th Down Pct.	52.9	28.6
Possession Avg.	30:37	29:23
Total Net Yards	5197	5285
Total Plays	1004	960
Avg. Per Play	5.2	5.5
Net Yards Rushing	1769	1764
Avg. Per Game	110.6	110.3
Total Rushes	449	425
Net Yards Passing	3428	3521
Avg. Per Game	214.3	220.1
Sacked/Yards Lost	36/208	33/197
Gross Yards	3636	3718
Att./Completions	519/308	502/310
Completion Pct.	59.3	61.8
Had Intercepted	23	13
Punts/Average	76/42.3	78/41.8
Net Punting Avg.	76/35.1	78/35.8
Penalties/Yards	105/867	104/879
Fumbles/Ball Lost	26/14	20/9
Touchdowns	33	49
Rushing	14	14
Passing	19	31
Returns	0	4

2004 INDIVIDUAL STATISTICS

PASSING

PASSING	Att.	Comp.	Yds.	Pct.	TD	Int.	Tkld.	Rate
Testaverde	495	297	3,532	60.0	17	20	34/182	76.4
Henson	18	10	78	55.6	1	1	2/26	61.8
K. Johnson	2	0	0	0.0	0	1	0/0	0.0
Anderson	1	1	26	100.0	1	0	0/0	158.3
Crayton	1	0	0	0.0	0	1	0/0	0.0
Glenn	1	0	0	0.0	0	0	0/0	39.6
McBriar	1	0	0	0.0	0	0	0/0	39.6
Cowboys	519	308	3,636	59.3	19	23	36/208	74.5
Opponents	502	310	3,718	61.8	31	13	33/197	94.2

SCORING

SCORING	TD R	TD P	TD Rt	PAT	FG	Saf	PTS
Cundiff	0	0	0	31/31	20/26	0	91
J. Jones	7	0	0	0/0	0/0	0	42
Witten	0	6	0	0/0	0/0	0	38
K. Johnson	0	6	0	0/0	0/0	0	36
George	4	0	0	0/0	0/0	0	24
Glenn	0	2	0	0/0	0/0	0	12
Robinson	0	2	0	0/0	0/0	0	12
Anderson	1	0	0	0/0	0/0	0	6
Barnes	0	1	0	0/0	0/0	0	6
Copper	0	1	0	0/0	0/0	0	6
Crayton	0	1	0	0/0	0/0	0	6
Lee	1	0	0	0/0	0/0	0	6
Testaverde	1	0	0	0/0	0/0	0	6
Cowboys	14	19	0	31/31	20/26	1	293
Opponents	14	31	4	44/45	21/23	0	405

2-Pt. Conversions: Witten.
Cowboys 1-2, Opponents 2-4.

RUSHING

RUSHING	No.	Yds	Avg	LG	TD
J. Jones	197	819	4.2	53	7
George	132	432	3.3	24	4
Anderson	57	246	4.3	27	1
Lee	27	128	4.7	14	1
Testaverde	21	38	1.8	10	1
Coakley	1	33	33.0	33	0
Morgan	2	23	11.5	24	0
K. Johnson	2	13	6.5	13	0
Ra. Williams	1	13	13.0	13	0
Ward	1	11	11.0	11	0
Barnes	5	10	2.0	8	0
Henson	1	7	7.0	7	0
Copper	1	-1	-1.0	-1	0
Glenn	1	-3	-3.0	-3	0
Cowboys	449	1,769	3.9	53	14
Opponents	425	1,764	4.2	90t	14

RECEIVING

RECEIVING	No.	Yds	Avg	LG	TD
Witten	87	980	11.3	42t	6
K. Johnson	70	981	14.0	39	6
Anderson	26	207	8.0	28	0
Glenn	24	400	16.7	48	2
Morgan	22	260	11.8	53	0
J. Jones	17	109	6.4	37	0
Bryant	16	266	16.6	48	0
Crayton	12	162	13.5	39t	1
Barnes	10	59	5.9	14	1
George	9	83	9.2	28	0
Copper	7	84	12.0	22	1
Campbell	2	16	8.0	9	0
Robinson	2	2	1.0	1t	2
Ra. Williams	1	14	14.0	14	0
Ward	1	5	5.0	5	0
Lee	1	4	4.0	4	0
Polite	1	4	4.0	4	0
Cowboys	308	3,636	11.8	53	19
Opponents	310	3,718	12.0	76t	31

INTERCEPTIONS

INTERCEPTIONS	No.	Yds	Avg	LG	TD
Newman	4	31	7.8	21	0
Nguyen	3	19	6.3	19	0
Ro. Williams	2	53	26.5	33	0
Frazier	2	2	1.0	2	0
Hunter	1	2	2.0	2	0
Scott	1	2	2.0	2	0
Cowboys	13	109	8.4	33	0
Opponents	23	526	22.9	101t	4

PUNTING

PUNTING	No.	Yds.	Avg.	In 20	LG
McBriar	75	3,182	42.4	22	68
Cundiff	1	34	34.0	1	34
Cowboys	76	3,216	42.3	23	68
Opponents	78	3,260	41.8	22	58

PUNT RETURNS

PUNT RETURNS	Ret	FC	Yds	Avg	LG	TD
Frazier	24	9	229	9.5	55	0
Ward	14	6	114	8.1	13	0
Crayton	4	1	34	8.5	17	0
Newman	2	0	13	6.5	7	0
Cowboys	44	16	390	8.9	55	0
Opponents	39	16	410	10.5	43	0

KICKOFF RETURNS

KICKOFF RETURNS	No.	Yds	Avg	LG	TD
Lee	41	964	23.5	62	0
Copper	16	307	19.2	39	0
Reeves	13	199	15.3	27	0
N. Jones	2	43	21.5	25	0
Morgan	2	25	12.5	19	0
B. Thornton	2	43	21.5	24	0
Lehr	1	9	9.0	9	0
Pierce	1	13	13.0	13	0
Cowboys	78	1,603	20.6	62	0
Opponents	62	1,083	17.5	34	0

FIELD GOALS

FIELD GOALS	1-19	20-29	30-39	40-49	50+
Cundiff	1/1	6/6	4/4	9/13	0/2
Cowboys	1/1	6/6	4/4	9/13	0/2
Opponents	1/1	6/6	4/4	7/8	3/4

SACKS

SACKS	No.
Ellis	9.0
Glover	7.0
Ogbogu	4.5
Dixon	3.0
Wiley	3.0
Coleman	1.0
Hunter	1.0
N. Jones	1.0
Nguyen	1.0
Scott	1.0
T. Williams	1.0
Carson	0.5
Cowboys	33.0
Opponents	36.0

RECORD HOLDERS
INDIVIDUAL RECORDS—CAREER

Category	Name	Performance
Rushing (Yds.)	Emmitt Smith, 1990-2002	*17,162
Passing (Yds.)	Troy Aikman, 1989-2000	32,942
Passing (TDs)	Troy Aikman, 1989-2000	165
Receiving (No.)	Michael Irvin, 1988-1999	750
Receiving (Yds.)	Michael Irvin, 1988-1999	11,904
Interceptions	Mel Renfro, 1964-1977	52
Punting (Avg.)	Toby Gowin, 1997-99, 2003	41.7
Punt Return (Avg.)	Deion Sanders, 1995-99	13.3
Kickoff Return (Avg.)	Mel Renfro, 1964-1977	26.4
Field Goals	Rafael Septien, 1978-1986	162
Touchdowns (Tot.)	Emmitt Smith, 1990-2002	164
Points	Emmitt Smith, 1990-2002	986

INDIVIDUAL RECORDS—SINGLE SEASON

Category	Name	Performance
Rushing (Yds.)	Emmitt Smith, 1995	1,773
Passing (Yds.)	Danny White, 1983	3,980
Passing (TDs)	Danny White, 1983	29
Receiving (No.)	Michael Irvin, 1995	111
Receiving (Yds.)	Michael Irvin, 1995	1,603
Interceptions	Everson Walls, 1981	11
Punting (Avg.)	Sam Baker, 1962	45.4
Punt Return (Avg.)	Bob Hayes, 1968	20.8
Kickoff Return (Avg.)	Mel Renfro, 1965	30.0
Field Goals	Richie Cunningham, 1997	34
Touchdowns (Tot.)	Emmitt Smith, 1995	25
Points	Emmitt Smith, 1995	150

INDIVIDUAL RECORDS—SINGLE GAME

Category	Name	Performance
Rushing (Yds.)	Emmitt Smith, 10-31-93	237
Passing (Yds.)	Don Meredith, 11-10-63	460
Passing (TDs)	Many times	5
	Last time by Troy Aikman, 9-12-99	
Receiving (No.)	Lance Rentzel, 11-19-67	13
Receiving (Yds.)	Bob Hayes, 11-13-66	246
Interceptions	Many times	3
	Last time by Terance Newman, 12-14-03	
Field Goals	Chris Boniol, 11-18-96	*7
	Billy Cundiff, 9-15-03	*7
Touchdowns (Tot.)	Many times	4
	Last time by Emmitt Smith, 9-4-95	
Points	Many times	24
	Last time by Emmitt Smith, 9-4-95	

*NFL Record

2005 VETERAN ROSTER

No.	Name	Pos.	Ht.	Wt.	Birthdate	NFL Exp.	College	Hometown	How Acq.	'04 Games/ Starts
76	Adams, Flozell	T	6-7	343	5/18/75	8	Michigan State	Bellwood, Ill.	D2-'98	16/16
73	Allen, Larry	G	6-3	325	11/27/71	12	Sonoma State	Compton, Calif.	D2-'94	16/16
36	Barnes, Darian	FB	6-2	241	2/29/80	4	Hampton	Toms River, N.J.	T(TB)-'04	16/10
34	Bickerstaff, Erik	RB	6-0	230	7/25/80	2	Wisconsin	Waukesha, Wis.	FA-'03	0*
11	Bledsoe, Drew	QB	6-5	238	2/14/72	13	Washington State	Ellensburg, Wash.	FA-'05	16/16*
86	Campbell, Dan	TE	6-5	262	4/13/76	7	Texas A&M	Glen Rose, Texas	UFA(NYG)-'03	3/2
91	Carson, Leonardo	DT	6-2	292	2/11/77	6	Auburn	Mobile, Ala.	FA-'03	15/15
95	#Claybrooks, DeVone	DT	6-3	310	9/15/77	5	East Carolina	Bassett, Va.	FA-'04	8/0
93	Coleman, Kenyon	DE	6-5	284	4/10/79	4	UCLA	Alta Loma, Calif.	T(Oak)-'03	12/0
18	Copper, Terrance	WR	6-0	201	3/12/82	2	East Carolina	Washington, N.C.	FA-'04	10/0
84	Crayton, Patrick	WR	6-0	200	4/7/79	2	Northwestern Oklahoma St.	DeSoto, Texas	D7b-'04	8/0
3	Cundiff, Billy	K	6-1	207	3/30/80	4	Drake	Harlan, Iowa	FA-'02	16/0
	Dantzler, Woody	S	5-10	209	10/4/79	3	Clemson	Orangeburg, S.C.	FA-'05	0*
29	Davis, Keith	S	5-10	198	12/30/78	3	Sam Houston	Italy, Texas	FA-'04	15/0
24	#Dixon, Tony	S	6-1	210	6/18/79	5	Alabama	Reform, Ala.	D2b-'01	16/7
98	Ellis, Greg	DE	6-6	271	8/14/75	8	North Carolina	Wendell, N.C.	D1-'98	16/16
95	Ferguson, Jason	DT	6-3	305	11/28/74	9	Georgia	Nettleton, Miss.	UFA(NYJ)-'05	16/15*
27	Finley, Clint	S	6-0	210	3/27/77	2	Nebraska	Andrews, Texas	FA-'05	0*
55	Fowler, Ryan	LB	6-3	243	5/20/82	2	Duke	Redington Shores, Fla.	FA-'04	2/0
30	Frazier, Lance	CB	5-10	183	2/23/81	2	West Virginia	Delray Beach, Fla.	FA-'04	12/8
20	Glenn, Aaron	CB	5-9	185	7/16/72	12	Texas A&M	Humble, Texas	FA-'05	16/16*
83	Glenn, Terry	WR	5-11	193	7/23/74	10	Ohio State	Columbus, Ohio	T(GB)-'03	6/6
97	Glover, La'Roi	DT	6-2	282	7/4/74	10	San Diego State	San, Diego, Calif.	UFA(NO)-'02	16/16
65	Gurode, Andre	G	6-4	314	3/6/78	4	Colorado	Houston, Texas	D2a-'02	14/13
42	Henry, Anthony	CB	6-1	205	11/3/76	5	South Florida	Fort Myers, Fla.	UFA(Cle)-'05	15/14*
7	Henson, Drew	QB	6-4	233	2/13/80	2	Michigan	Brighton, Mich.	T(Hou)-'04	7/1
47	Hunter, Pete	CB	6-2	208	5/25/80	4	Virginia Union	Atlantic City, N.J.	D5-'02	3/3
56	James, Bradie	LB	6-2	245	1/17/81	3	Louisiana State	Monroe, La.	D4-'03	16/2
52	Johnson, Al	C	6-5	296	1/27/79	2	Wisconsin	Brussels, Wis.	D2-'03	16/15
19	Johnson, Keyshawn	WR	6-4	214	7/22/72	10	Southern California	Los Angeles, Calif.	T(TB)-'04	16/16
21	Jones, Julius	RB	5-10	205	8/14/81	2	Notre Dame	Big Stone Gap, Va.	D2a-'04	8/7
33	Jones, Nathan	CB	5-10	184	6/13/82	2	Rutgers	Scotch Plains, N.J.	D7a-'04	16/1
1	McBriar, Mat	P	6-1	210	7/8/79	2	Hawaii	East Brighton, Australia	FA-'04	16/0
10	Merritt, Ahmad	WR	5-10	195	2/5/77	4	Wisconsin	Chicago, Ill.	FA-'05	0*
81	t- Morgan, Quincy	WR	6-1	215	9/23/77	5	Kansas State	Garland, Texas	T(Cle)-'04	15/12*
41	Newman, Terence	CB	5-11	190	9/4/78	3	Kansas State	Salina, Kan.	D1-'03	16/16
59	Nguyen, Dat	LB	5-11	238	9/25/75	7	Texas A&M	Rockport, Texas	D3-'99	16/16
60	Noll, Ben	G	6-4	300	11/14/81	2	Pennsylvania	Wildwood, Mo.	W(StL)-'04	1/1
54	O'Neil, Keith	LB	6-0	235	8/26/80	3	Northern Arizona	Amherst, N.Y.	FA-'03	16/0
90	Ogbogu, Eric	DE	6-4	269	7/18/75	8	Maryland	Irvington, N.Y.	FA-'03	15/1
72	Peterman, Stephen	G	6-4	318	1/11/82	1	Louisiana State	Waveland, Miss.	D3-'04	0*
88	Pierce, Brett	TE	6-5	250	1/7/81	2	Stanford	Vancouver, Wash.	FA-'04	8/1
35	Reeves, Jacques	CB	5-11	190	10/8/82	2	Purdue	Lancaster, Texas	D7c-'04	15/1
62	Rivera, Marco	G	6-4	310	4/26/72	10	Penn State	Elmont, N.Y.	UFA(GB)-'05	16/16*
85	Robinson, Jeff	TE	6-4	250	2/20/70	13	Idaho	Spokane, Wash.	UFA(StL)-'02	16/0
75	Rogers, Jacob	T	6-6	305	8/17/81	2	Southern California	Oxnard, Calif.	D2-'04	2/0
9	Romo, Tony	QB	6-2	219	4/21/80	3	Eastern Illinois	Burlington, Wis.	FA-'03	6/0
80	Ryan, Sean	TE	6-5	257	3/27/80	2	Boston College	Buffalo, N.Y.	FA-'04	6/1
38	Scott, Lynn	S	6-0	211	6/23/77	5	Northwestern Oklahoma St.	Turpin, Okla.	FA-'01	16/9
58	Shanle, Scott	LB	6-2	237	11/23/79	3	Nebraska	St. Edward, Neb.	W(StL)-'03	16/3
51	Singleton, Al	LB	6-2	236	8/7/75	9	Temple	Irvington, N.J.	UFA(TB)-'03	13/12
87	Smith, Zuriel	WR	5-11	166	1/15/80	2	Hampton	Mechanicsville, Va.	FA-'05	0*
32	Thomas, Anthony	RB	6-2	228	11/11/77	5	Michigan	Winnfield, La.	UFA(Chi)-'05	11/2*
25	Thornton, Bruce	CB	5-10	198	1/31/80	2	Georgia	LaGrange, Ga.	D4-'04	1/0
53	Thornton, Kalen	LB	6-3	240	5/12/82	2	Texas	Dallas, Texas	FA-'04	16/0
77	Tucker, Torrin	T	6-6	315	12/25/79	3	Southern Mississippi	Meridian, Miss.	FA-'03	13/13
78	Vollers, Kurt	T	6-7	300	4/4/79	4	Notre Dame	Whittier, Calif.	FA-'02	13/3
71	Walter, Tyson	G/C	6-4	303	3/17/78	4	Ohio State	Bainbridge, Ohio	D6a-'02	13/1
31	Williams, Roy	S	6-0	226	8/14/80	4	Oklahoma	Union City, Calif.	D1-'02	16/16
82	Witten, Jason	TE	6-5	261	5/6/82	3	Tennessee	Elizabethton, Tenn.	D3-'03	16/15

* Bickerstaff missed '04 season because of injury; Bledsoe played 16 games with Buffalo; Dantzler last active with Atlanta in '03; Ferguson played 16 games with N.Y. Jets; Finley last active with Kansas City in '03; A. Glenn played 16 games with Houston; Henry played 15 games with Cleveland; Merritt last active with Chicago in '03; Morgan played 6 games with Cleveland and 9 games with Dallas; Peterman missed '04 season because of injury; Rivera played 16 games with Green Bay; Smith last active with Dallas in '03; Thomas played 11 games with Chicago.

t- Cowboys traded for Morgan (Cle).

Traded—WR Antonio Bryant (5 games in '04) to Cleveland.

Retired—Emmitt Smith, 15-year running back, 15 games with Arizona in '04.

\# Unrestricted free agent; subject to developments.

Also played with Cowboys in '04—RB Richie Anderson (12 games), LB Dexter Coakley (16), DT Chris Cooper (2), DT Chad Eaton (6), RB Eddie George (13), RB ReShard Lee (14), G/C Matt Lehr (7), DT Daleroy Stewart (1), QB Vinny Testaverde (16), WR Dedric Ward (8), DE Marcellus Wiley (16), WR Randal Williams (2), CB Tyrone Williams (3).

2005 FIRST-YEAR ROSTER

Name	Pos.	Ht.	Wt.	Birthdate	College	Hometown	How Acq.
Barber, Marion	RB	6-0	212	6/10/83	Minnesota	Wayzata, Minn.	D4a
Beriault, Justin	S	6-3	204	8/23/81	Ball State	Indianapolis, Ind.	D6a
Brooks, Jermaine (1)	DT	6-3	290	4/11/79	Arkansas	Pasadena, Calif.	FA-'04
Burnett, Kevin	LB	6-3	230	12/24/82	Tennessee	Carson, Calif.	D2
Canty, Chris	DE	6-7	280	11/10/82	Virginia	Charlotte, N.C.	D4b
Condo, Jon	LB	6-3	244	8/26/81	Maryland	Philipsburg, Pa.	FA
Cooper, Roger	LB	6-2	239	6/4/81	Montana State	Port Orchard, Wash.	FA
Crowder, Tom (1)	WR	6-1	207	1/21/81	Arkansas	Camden, Ark.	FA-'04
Curtis, Tony	TE	6-5	269	2/11/83	Portland State	Seaside, Calif.	FA
Dahl, Harvey	T	6-6	299	6/24/81	Nevada	Fallon, Nev.	FA
DeRonde, Kevin (1)	LB	6-5	259	8/15/78	Iowa State	Pella, Iowa	FA
Evans, Jonathan	FB	6-0	240	10/10/81	Baylor	Duncanville, Texas	FA
Goolsby, Mike	LB	6-3	244	9/10/82	Notre Dame	Joliet, Ill.	FA
Greathouse, Clinton (1)	P	5-10	221	5/28/80	Texas Tech	Artesia, N.M.	FA
Harrell, Reggie	WR	6-3	214	1/28/81	Texas Christian	Arlington, Texas	FA
Johnson, Thomas	DT	6-2	294	6/24/81	Middle Tennessee State	Memphis, Tenn.	FA
Kincade, Keylon (1)	RB	5-11	204	8/20/82	Southern Methodist	Troup, Texas	FA
Love, Reggie (1)	LB	6-4	224	4/29/82	Duke	Charlotte, N.C.	FA
Petitti, Rob	T	6-6	340	5/21/82	Pittsburgh	Rumson, N.J.	D6b
Polite, Lousaka (1)	FB	6-0	246	9/14/81	Pittsburgh	Woodland Hills, Pa.	FA-'04
Price, Dominique	S	6-0	215	12/16/82	Northwestern	Louisville, Ky.	FA
Ratliff, Jay	DE	6-4	293	8/29/81	Auburn	Valdosta. Ga.	FA
Rector, Jamaica	WR	5-10	189	8/10/81	Northwest Missouri State	Celeste, Texas	FA
Reid, Duncan	TE	6-6	231	1/29/82	Fresno State	Glendora, Calif.	D5-'04
Spears, Marcus	DE	6-4	307	3/8/83	Louisiana State	Baton Rouge, La.	D1b
Tarullo, Matthew	G/C	6-5	314	8/13/82	Syracuse	Albany, N.Y.	FA
Thompson, Tyson	RB	6-1	215	5/21/81	San Jose State	Irving, Texas	FA
Tickles, Marlon	DT/LS	6-2	288	5/15/81	Tulane	Mableton, Ga.	FA
Visintainer, Brett	K	6-1	211	7/19/82	Fresno State	San Ramon, Calif.	FA
Ware, Demarcus	DE	6-4	251	7/31/82	Troy State	Auburn, Ala.	D1a
Wilder, Sam	T	6-5	303	1/10/82	Colorado	Dallas, Texas	FA
Williams, Lenny (1)	CB	5-10	190	12/16/81	Southern	Lake Charles, La.	FA-'04

The term NFL Rookie is defined as a player who is in his first season of professional football and has not been on the roster of another professional football team for any regular-season or postseason games. A Rookie is designated by an "R" on NFL rosters. Players who have been active in another professional football league or players who have NFL experience, including either preseason training camp or being on an Active List or Inactive List, or on Reserve/Injured or Reserve/Physically Unable to Perform for fewer than six regular-season games, are termed NFL First-Year Players. An NFL First-Year Player is designated by a "1" on NFL rosters. Thereafter, a player is credited with an additional year of experience for each season in which he accumulates six games on the Active List or Inactive List, or on Reserve/Injured or Reserve/Physically Unable to Perform.

Log on to www.dallascowboys.com for an up-to-date roster.

COACHING STAFF
Head Coach,
Bill Parcells
Pro Career: Named head coach on January 2, 2003, Parcells has accumulated a 165-123-1 record, including two Super Bowl victories (XXI and XXV with the Giants) and another Super Bowl appearance (XXXI with New England) in 17 seasons as an NFL head coach. His 165 career victories make him the second winningest active coach in the NFL, trailing only Marty Schottenheimer (182). Parcells has guided his teams to 11 winning seasons, nine playoff berths, and posted an 11-7 postseason record. Parcells-led teams have finished in either first or second place in their division ten times. With the Cowboys' postseason appearance in 2003, Parcells became the first coach in NFL history to lead four different teams to the playoffs. He is one of only four coaches (Don Shula, Reeves, and Dick Vermeil) in NFL history to have led two separate teams to the Super Bowl. Parcells, Denver's Mike Shanahan, Washington's Joe Gibbs, and New England's Bill Belichick are the only active coaches to have claimed two-or-more Super Bowl titles, and he is one of just eight active coaches to have ever won a Super Bowl title. In his first season at the helm in Dallas, Parcells took a team that had posted three consecutive 5-11 seasons and posted a 10-6 mark in the regular season, as well as an NFC Wild Card playoff berth. In 2004, the Cowboys posted a 6-10 record in his second season. Under his direction, the N.Y. Jets (1997-99)—who won a combined four games the two seasons prior to his arrival—improved to 9-7 his first season and 12-4 with a trip to the AFC Championship Game his second season. This success marked the first time in NFL history that a team had won one game and within two years was playing for a conference championship. He took over the New England Patriots (1993-96) following a 2-14 season by the Patriots. Within two years, Parcells coached the team to a 10-6 mark and its first playoff game in eight years. In his fourth year, the Patriots went 11-5 and advanced to Super Bowl XXXI against Green Bay. Parcells began his NFL head coaching career with the N.Y. Giants (1983-1990), who had posted one winning season in its previous 10 years. After an initial campaign of 3-12-1, he improved the club's victory total to 9, 10, 14, 10, 12, and 13 between 1984 and 1990. In the process, the Giants were able to win two Super Bowl titles—Super Bowl XXI over Denver and Super Bowl XXV over Buffalo. During his time at the Giants helm, the club won two Super Bowls, three division titles, and had only one losing season. For his accomplishment, Parcells was honored with NFL Coach of the Year honors in both 1986

and 1989. Career record: 165-123-1.
Background: Played linebacker at Wichita State 1961-63. Served as college coach at: Hastings (Neb.) 1964, Wichita State 1965, Army 1966-69, Florida State 1970-72, Vanderbilt 1973-74, Texas Tech 1975-77, and was head coach at Air Force in 1978.
Personal: Born August 22, 1941, in Englewood, N.J. Parcells resides in Irving, Texas. He has three daughters—Suzy, Jill, and Dallas.

ASSISTANT COACHES
Todd Bowles, defensive backs; born November 18, 1963, Elizabeth, N.J. Defensive back Temple 1982-85. Pro defensive back Washington Redskins 1986-1990, 1992-93, San Francisco 49ers 1991. College coach: Morehouse College 1997, Grambling State 1998-99. Pro coach: New York Jets 2000, Cleveland Browns 2001-04, joined Cowboys in 2005.
Bruce DeHaven, special teams; born September 6, 1948, Trousdale, Kan. Attended Southwestern (Kan.) College. No pro playing experience. College coach: Kansas 1979-1981, New Mexico State 1982. Pro coach: New Jersey Generals (USFL) 1983, Pittsburgh Maulers (USFL) 1984, Orlando Renegades (USFL) 1985, Buffalo Bills 1987-1999, San Francisco 49ers 2000-02, joined Cowboys in 2003.
Gary Gibbs, linebackers; born August 13, 1952, Beaumont, Texas. Linebacker Oklahoma 1972-74. No pro playing experience. College coach: Oklahoma 1975-1994 (head coach 1989-1994), Georgia 2000, Louisiana State 2001. Pro coach: Joined Cowboys in 2002.
Todd Haley, wide receivers; born February 28, 1967, Atlanta. Attended Florida and Miami. No college or pro playing experience. Pro coach: New York Jets 1996-2000, Chicago Bears 2001-2003, joined Cowboys in 2004.
Joe Juraszek, strength and conditioning; born June 8, 1958, Chicago. Linebacker/defensive end New Mexico 1976-1980. No pro playing experience. College coach: Oklahoma 1981-86, 1993-96, Texas Tech 1987-1992. Pro coach: Joined Cowboys in 1997.
David Lee, quarterbacks/offensive quality control; born July 2, 1953, Cape Girardeau, Mo. Quarterback Vanderbilt 1971-74. No pro playing experience. College coach: Tennessee-Martin 1975-76, Vanderbilt 1977, Mississippi 1978-1982, New Mexico 1983, Arkansas 1984-88, 2001-02, Texas-El Paso 1989-1993 (head coach), Rice 1994-2000. Pro coach: Joined Cowboys in 2003.
Anthony Lynn, running backs; born December 21, 1968, McKinney, Texas. Fullback Texas Tech 1987-1990. Pro fullback Denver Broncos 1993, 1997-1999, San Francisco 49ers 1995-96. Pro coach: Denver Broncos 2000-02, Jacksonville

Jaguars 2003-2004, joined Cowboys in 2005.
Mike MacIntyre, asst. secondary/defensive quality control; born March 14, 1965, Miami. Safety Vanderbilt 1985-86, Georgia Tech 1987-88. No pro playing experience. College coach: Georgia 1990-91, Davidson 1992, Tennessee-Martin 1993-96, Temple 1997-98, Mississippi 1999-2002. Pro coach: Joined Cowboys in 2003.
Paul Pasqualoni, tight ends; born August 16, 1949, New Haven, Conn. Linebacker Penn State 1968-1971. No pro playing experience. College coach: Southern Connecticut State 1976-1981, Western Connecticut 1982-86 (head coach), Syracuse 1987-2004 (head coach 1991-2004). Pro coach: Joined Cowboys in 2005.
Sean Payton, asst. head coach/passing game coordinator; born December 29, 1963, San Mateo, Calif. Quarterback Eastern Illinois 1982-86. Pro quarterback Ottawa Rough Riders (CFL) 1987, Chicago Bears 1987. College coach: San Diego State 1988-89, 1992-93, Indiana State 1990-91, Miami (Ohio) 1994-95, Illinois 1996. Pro coach: Philadelphia Eagles 1997-98, New York Giants 1999-2002, joined Cowboys in 2003.
Kacy Rodgers, defensive line; born June 24, 1969, Humboldt, Tenn. Linebacker/defensive end Tennessee 1988-1991. Pro linebacker Shreveport Pirates (CFL) 1994. College coach: Tennesse-Martin 1994-97, Louisiana-Monroe 1998, Middle Tennessee State 1999-2001, Arkansas 2002. Pro coach: Joined Cowboys in 2003.
Tony Sparano, running game coordinator/offensive line; born October 7, 1961, West Haven, Conn. Center New Haven 1978-1981. No pro playing experience. College coach: New Haven 1984-87, 1994-98 (head coach 1994-98), Boston University 1988-1993. Pro coach: Cleveland Browns 1999-2000, Washington Redskins 2001, Jacksonville Jaguars 2002, joined Cowboys in 2003.
Mike Zimmer, defensive coordinator; born June 5, 1956, Peoria, Ill. Quarterback/linebacker Illinois State 1974-76. No pro playing experience. College coach: Missouri 1979-1980, Weber State 1981-88, Washington State 1989-1993. Pro coach: Joined Cowboys in 1994.

National Football Conference
North Division
Team Colors: Honolulu Blue and Silver
Detroit Lions Practice &
Training Facility
222 Republic Drive
Allen Park, Michigan 48101
Telephone: (313) 216-4000

2005 SCHEDULE
PRESEASON
Aug. 12 at New York Jets.................7:00
Aug. 20 Cleveland 1:00
Aug. 29 **St. Louis** 8:00
Sept. 2 at Buffalo 7:00

REGULAR SEASON
Sept. 11 **Green Bay**........................4:15
Sept. 18 at Chicago.......................12:00
Sept. 25 Open Date
Oct. 2 at Tampa Bay 1:00
Oct. 9 **Baltimore**..........................1:00
Oct. 16 **Carolina**.............................1:00
Oct. 23 at Cleveland 1:00
Oct. 30 **Chicago** 1:00
Nov. 6 at Minnesota 12:00
Nov. 13 **Arizona** 1:00
Nov. 20 at Dallas...........................12:00
Nov. 24 **Atlanta** (Thu.) 12:30
Dec. 4 **Minnesota** 1:00
Dec. 11 at Green Bay 7:30
Dec. 18 **Cincinnati** 4:05
Dec. 24 at New Orleans (Sat.) 12:00
Jan. 1 at Pittsburgh......................1:00

Stadium: Ford Field (opened in 2002)
   •**Capacity:** 64,500
   2000 Brush Street
   Detroit, Michigan 48226
Playing Surface: FieldTurf
Training Camp: 222 Republic Drive
   Allen Park, Michigan
   48101

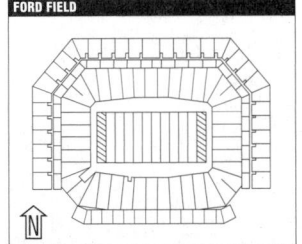

CLUB OFFICIALS
Chairman and Owner: William Clay Ford
Vice Chairman: William Clay Ford, Jr.
President and CEO: Matt Millen
Executive Vice President/COO:
   Tom Lewand
Senior Vice President & Assistant GM:
   Martin Mayhew
Senior Vice President: Bill Keenist
Senior Vice President/CFO: Tom Lesnau
Secretary: David Hempstead
Director of Pro Personnel: Sheldon White
Director of College Scouting:
   Scott McEwen
Scouts: Russ Bolinger, Bob Beers,
   Chad Henry, Silas McKinnie,
   Dennis Murphy, Lance Newmark,
   Dave Uyrus, Dennis Gentry
Senior Director of Community Affairs:
   Tim Pendell
Director of Media Relations:
   Matt Barnhart
Director of Broadcasting and
   Production: Bryan Bender
Director of Ticket Operations:
   Mark Graham
Head Athletic Trainer: Al Bellamy
Equipment Manager: Tim O'Neill
Video Director: Robert Yanagi

COACHING HISTORY
Portsmouth Spartans 1930-33
(480-530-32)
Records include postseason games
1930   Hal (Tubby) Griffen 5-6-3
1931-36   George (Potsy) Clark ...49-20-6
1937-38   Earl (Dutch) Clark 14-8-0
1939   Elmer (Gus) Henderson ...6-5-0
1940   George (Potsy) Clark 5-5-1
1941-42   Bill Edwards* 4-9-1
1942   John Karcis 0-8-0
1943-47   Charles (Gus) Dorais ..20-31-2
1948-1950 Alvin (Bo) McMillin 12-24-0
1951-56   Raymond (Buddy) Parker..50-24-2
1957-1964 George Wilson.............55-45-6
1965-66   Harry Gilmer.................10-16-2
1967-1972 Joe Schmidt 43-35-7
1973   Don McCafferty 6-7-1
1974-76   Rick Forzano** 15-17-0
1976-77   Tommy Hudspeth 11-13-0
1978-1984 Monte Clark 43-63-1
1985-88   Darryl Rogers*** 18-40-0
1988-1996 Wayne Fontes..............67-71-0
1997-2000 Bobby Ross****........27-32-0
2000   Gary Moeller...................4-3-0
2001-02   Marty Mornhinweg 5-27-0
2003-04   Steve Mariucci............11-21-0
   *Released after three games in 1942
   **Resigned after four games in 1976
   ***Released after 11 games in 1988
****Resigned after nine games in 2000

ATTENDANCE
Home 499,224   Away 531,330
Total 1,030,554
Single-game home record,
   80,444 (12/20/81)
Single-season home record, 644,904
   (1980)

2005 DRAFT CHOICES
Round	Name	Pos.	College
1	Mike Williams	WR	Southern California
2	Shaun Cody	DT	Southern California
3	Stanley Wilson	DB	Stanford
5	Dan Orlovsky	QB	Connecticut
6	Bill Swancutt	DE	Oregon State
	Johnathan Goddard	LB	Marshall

2004 TEAM RECORD
PRESEASON (2-2)

Date	Result	Opponent
8/14	W 27-21	Pittsburgh
8/21	L 10-17	at Cleveland
8/28	L 6-17	at Baltimore
9/2	W 20-17	Buffalo

REGULAR SEASON (6-10)

Date	Result	Opponent	Att.
9/12	W 20-16	at Chicago	61,535
9/19	W 28-16	Houston	61,465
9/26	L 13-30	Philadelphia	62,472
10/10	W 17-10	at Atlanta	70,434
10/17	L 10-38	Green Bay	62,938
10/24	W 28-13	at N.Y. Giants	78,841
10/31	L 21-31	at Dallas	63,616
11/7	L 10-17	Washington	62,657
11/14	L 17-23	at Jacksonville (OT)	66,431
11/21	L 19-22	at Minnesota	64,156
11/25	L 9-41	Indianapolis	63,107
12/5	W 26-12	Arizona	62,262
12/12	L 13-16	at Green Bay	70,497
12/19	L 27-28	Minnesota	62,337
12/26	W 19-13	Chicago	61,924
1/2	L 19-24	at Tennessee	68,809

(OT) Overtime

SCORE BY PERIODS

Lions	60	97	45	94	0 —	296
Opponents	86	80	92	86	6 —	350

2004 TEAM STATISTICS

	Lions	Opp.
Total First Downs	263	320
Rushing	92	118
Passing	142	167
Penalty	29	35
3rd Down: Made/Att	66/210	98/231
3rd Down Pct.	31.4	42.4
4th Down: Made/Att	6/16	7/19
4th Down Pct.	37.5	36.8
Possession Avg.	28:03	31:57
Total Net Yards	4693	5401
Avg. Per Game	293.3	337.6
Total Plays	949	1071
Avg. Per Play	4.9	5.0
Net Yards Rushing	1777	1887
Avg. Per Game	111.1	117.9
Total Rushes	407	498
Net Yards Passing	2916	3514
Avg. Per Game	182.3	219.6
Sacked/Yards Lost	37/208	38/222
Gross Yards	3124	3736
Att./Completions	505/285	535/328
Completion Pct.	56.4	61.3
Had Intercepted	13	14
Punts/Average	93/40.5	84/43.5
Net Punting Avg.	93/34.2	84/36.9
Penalties/Yards	121/1000	114/976
Fumbles/Ball Lost	12/7	20/10
Touchdowns	32	43
Rushing	7	10
Passing	19	29
Returns	6	4

2004 INDIVIDUAL STATISTICS

PASSING

PASSING	Att.	Comp.	Yds.	Pct.	TD	Int.	Tkld.	Rate
Harrington	489	274	3,047	56.0	19	12	36/196	77.5
McMahon	15	11	77	73.3	0	1	1/12	56.8
Williams	1	0	0	0.0	0	0	0/0	39.6
Lions	505	285	3,124	56.4	19	13	37/208	76.7
Opponents	535	328	3,736	61.3	29	14	38/222	89.4

SCORING

SCORING	TD R	TD P	TD Rt	PAT	FG	Saf	PTS
Hanson	0	0	0	28/28	24/28	0	100
Williams	0	8	0	0/0	0/0	0	48
Jones	5	1	0	0/0	0/0	0	36
Drummond	0	0	4	0/0	0/0	0	24
Hakim	0	3	0	0/0	0/0	0	18
Schlesinger	0	3	0	0/0	0/0	0	18
Pinner	2	0	0	0/0	0/0	0	12
Streets	0	1	0	0/0	0/0	0	8
Alexander	0	1	0	0/0	0/0	0	6
Bly	0	0	1	0/0	0/0	0	6
Kircus	0	1	0	0/0	0/0	0	6
Swinton	0	1	0	0/0	0/0	0	6
Bra. Walker	0	0	1	0/0	0/0	0	6
Redding	0	0	0	0/0	0/0	1	2
Lions	7	19	6	28/28	24/28	1	296
Opponents	10	29	4	37/38	17/20	1	350

2-Pt. Conversions: Streets.
Lions 1-4, Opponents 1-4.

RUSHING

RUSHING	No.	Yds	Avg	LG	TD
Jones	241	1,133	4.7	74	5
Bryson	50	264	5.3	28	0
Harrington	48	175	3.6	17	0
Pinner	57	174	3.1	14	2
McMahon	2	18	9.0	14	0
Drummond	1	9	9.0	9	0
Schlesinger	4	7	1.8	2	0
Swinton	1	3	3.0	3	0
Williams	1	1	1.0	1	0
Hakim	1	0	0.0	0	0
Harris	1	-7	-7.0	-7	0
Lions	407	1,777	4.4	74	7
Opponents	498	1,887	3.8	43	10

RECEIVING

RECEIVING	No.	Yds	Avg	LG	TD
Williams	54	817	15.1	46	8
Bryson	44	322	7.3	30	0
Alexander	41	377	9.2	30	1
Hakim	31	533	17.2	39t	3
Streets	28	260	9.3	22	1
Jones	28	180	6.4	34	1
Swinton	18	213	11.8	28	1
Pinner	11	72	6.5	26	0
Fitzsimmons	10	103	10.3	27	0
Schlesinger	10	91	9.1	30	3
Trejo	4	37	9.3	18	0
Kircus	3	68	22.7	50t	1
Vines	3	51	17.0	26	0
Lions	285	3,124	11.0	62	19
Opponents	328	3,736	11.4	82t	29

INTERCEPTIONS

INTERCEPTIONS	No.	Yds	Avg	LG	TD
Bly	4	107	26.8	55t	1
Marion	3	43	14.3	24	0
Lewis	1	33	33.0	33	0
Hall	1	30	30.0	30	0
K. Smith	1	2	2.0	2	0
Lehman	1	1	1.0	1	0
Cash	1	0	0.0	0	0
Goodman	1	0	0.0	0	0
Bra. Walker	1	0	0.0	0	0
Lions	14	216	15.4	55t	1
Opponents	13	194	14.9	43	2

PUNTING

PUNTING	No.	Yds.	Avg.	In 20	LG
Harris	92	3,765	40.9	32	60
Lions	93	3,765	40.5	32	60
Opponents	84	3,658	43.5	25	64

PUNT RETURNS

PUNT RETURNS	Ret	FC	Yds	Avg	LG	TD
Drummond	24	8	316	13.2	83t	2
Swinton	16	9	104	6.5	18	0
Lions	40	17	420	10.5	83t	2
Opponents	46	24	441	9.6	56	0

KICKOFF RETURNS

KICKOFF RETURNS	No.	Yds	Avg	LG	TD
Drummond	41	1,092	26.6	99t	2
Swinton	18	410	22.8	43	0
Bryson	2	27	13.5	14	0
Trejo	2	12	6.0	10	0
Curry	1	-1	-1.0	-1	0
DeVries	1	5	5.0	5	0
Schlesinger	1	23	23.0	23	0
Lions	66	1,568	23.8	99t	2
Opponents	54	1,058	19.6	52	0

FIELD GOALS

FIELD GOALS	1-19	20-29	30-39	40-49	50+
Hanson	0/0	9/9	10/11	5/8	0/0
Lions	0/0	9/9	10/11	5/8	0/0
Opponents	1/1	6/8	5/5	4/4	1/2

SACKS

SACKS	
Hall	11.5
Edwards	4.5
S. Rogers	4.0
Davis	3.5
DeVries	3.0
Redding	3.0
Bell	2.0
Lewis	2.0
Wilkinson	1.5
Lehman	1.0
Pritchett	1.0
Bra. Walker	1.0
Lions	38.0
Opponents	37.0

RECORD HOLDERS

INDIVIDUAL RECORDS—CAREER

Category	Name	Performance
Rushing (Yds.)	Barry Sanders, 1989-1998	15,269
Passing (Yds.)	Bobby Layne, 1950-58	15,710
Passing (TDs)	Bobby Layne, 1950-58	118
Receiving (No.)	Herman Moore, 1991-2001	670
Receiving (Yds.)	Herman Moore, 1991-2001	9,174
Interceptions	Dick LeBeau, 1959-1972	62
Punting (Avg.)	Yale Lary, 1952-53, 1956-1964	44.3
Punt Return (Avg.)	Jack Christiansen, 1951-58	12.8
Kickoff Return (Avg.)	Pat Studstill, 1961-67	25.7
Field Goals	Jason Hanson, 1992-2004	308
Touchdowns (Tot.)	Barry Sanders, 1989-1998	109
Points	Jason Hanson, 1992-2004	1,336

INDIVIDUAL RECORDS—SINGLE SEASON

Category	Name	Performance
Rushing (Yds.)	Barry Sanders, 1997	2,053
Passing (Yds.)	Scott Mitchell, 1995	4,338
Passing (TDs)	Scott Mitchell, 1995	32
Receiving (No.)	Herman Moore, 1995	123
Receiving (Yds.)	Herman Moore, 1995	1,686
Interceptions	Don Doll, 1950	12
	Jack Christiansen, 1953	12
Punting (Avg.)	Yale Lary, 1963	48.9
Punt Return (Avg.)	Pat Studstill, 1962	15.8
Kickoff Return (Avg.)	Mel Gray, 1994	28.4
Field Goals	Jason Hanson, 1993	34
Touchdowns (Tot.)	Barry Sanders, 1991	17
Points	Jason Hanson, 1995	132

INDIVIDUAL RECORDS—SINGLE GAME

Category	Name	Performance
Rushing (Yds.)	Barry Sanders, 11-13-94	237
Passing (Yds.)	Charlie Batch, 11-18-01	436
Passing (TDs)	Gary Danielson, 12-9-78	5
Receiving (No.)	Herman Moore, 12-4-95	14
Receiving (Yds.)	Cloyce Box, 12-3-50	302
Interceptions	Don Doll, 10-23-49	*4
Field Goals	Garo Yepremian, 11-13-66	6
	Jason Hanson, 10-17-99	6
Touchdowns (Tot.)	Dutch Clark, 10-22-34	4
	Cloyce Box, 12-3-50	4
	Barry Sanders, 11-24-91	4
Points	Dutch Clark, 10-22-34	24
	Cloyce Box, 12-3-50	24
	Barry Sanders, 11-24-91	24

*NFL Record

2005 VETERAN ROSTER

No.	Name	Pos.	Ht.	Wt.	Birthdate	NFL Exp.	College	Hometown	How Acq.	'04 Games/ Starts
76	Backus, Jeff	T	6-5	305	9/21/77	5	Michigan	Norcross, Ga.	D1-'01	16/16
97	Bailey, Boss	LB	6-3	235	10/14/79	3	Georgia	Folkston, Ga.	D2-'03	0*
94	Bell, Marcus	DT	6-2	326	6/1/79	4	Memphis	Memphis, Tenn.	UFA(Ariz)-'04	16/0
32	Bly, Dré	CB	5-10	185	5/22/77	7	North Carolina	Chesapeake, Va.	UFA(StL)-'03	13/13
25	Bryant, Fernando	CB	5-11	175	3/26/77	7	Alabama	Murfeesboro, Tenn.	UFA(Jax)-'04	10/10
24	Bryson, Shawn	RB	6-1	230	11/30/76	7	Tennessee	Franklin, N.C.	UFA(Buff)-'03	16/1
79	Butler, Kelly	T	6-7	324	7/24/82	2	Purdue	Grand Rapids, Mich.	D6-'04	0*
29	Cash, Chris	CB	5-10	185	7/13/80	4	Southern California	Stockton, Calif.	D6-'02	11/5
55	Curry, Donté	LB	6-1	240	7/22/78	4	Morris Brown	College Park, Ga.	W(Wash)-'02	12/0
52	Davis, James	LB	6-1	240	4/26/79	3	West Virginia	Stuart, Fla.	D5b-'03	16/15
64	DeMulling, Rick	G	6-4	304	7/21/77	5	Idaho	Cheney, Wash.	UFA(Ind)-'05	11/11*
95	DeVries, Jared	DE	6-4	275	6/11/76	7	Iowa	Aplington, Iowa	D3-'99	15/0
18	Drummond, Eddie	WR	5-9	190	4/12/80	4	Penn State	Pittsburgh, Pa.	FA-'02	11/1
39	Echols, Michael	CB	5-10	185	10/13/78	3	Wisconsin	Youngstown, Ohio	W(Minn)-'04	0*
98	Edwards, Kalimba	DE	6-6	265	12/26/79	4	South Carolina	Atlanta, Ga.	D2-'02	16/0
82	FitzSimmons, Casey	TE	6-4	258	10/10/80	3	Carroll College	Helena, Mont.	FA-'03	16/3
36	Fox, Vernon	S	5-10	200	10/9/79	4	Fresno State	Las Vegas, Nev.	FA-'04	14/0
5	Garcia, Jeff	QB	6-1	200	2/24/70	7	San Jose State	Gilroy, Calif.	FA-'05	11/10*
35	Goodman, André	CB	5-10	185	8/11/78	4	South Carolina	Greenville, S.C.	D3-'02	11/4
96	Hall, James	DE	6-2	280	2/4/77	6	Michigan	New Orleans, La.	FA-'00	16/16
4	Hanson, Jason	K	5-11	190	6/17/70	14	Washington State	Spokane, Wash.	D2b-'92	16/0
3	Harrington, Joey	QB	6-4	220	10/21/78	4	Oregon	Portland, Ore.	D1-'02	16/16
2	Harris, Nick	P	6-2	218	7/23/78	5	California	Avondale, Ariz.	W(Cin)-'03	16/0
50	Holmes, Earl	LB	6-2	242	4/28/73	10	Florida A&M	Tallahassee, Fla.	UFA(Cle)-'03	16/14
42	Holt, Terrence	S	6-2	208	3/5/80	3	North Carolina State	Raleigh, N.C.	D5a-'03	16/0
68	Hopson, Tyrone	G/C	6-2	294	5/28/76	4	Eastern Kentucky	Owensboro, Ky.	FA-'04	11/0
85	Johnson, Kevin	WR	5-11	195	7/15/76	7	Syracuse	Hamilton West, N.J.	FA-'05	16/5*
34	Jones, Kevin	RB	6-0	225	8/21/82	2	Virginia Tech	Chester, Pa.	D1b-'04	15/14
26	Kennedy, Kenoy	S	6-1	215	11/15/77	6	Arkansas	Terrell, Texas	UFA(Den)-'05	16/16*
87	Kircus, David	WR	6-2	190	2/19/80	3	Grand Valley State	Imlay City, Mich.	D6-'03	7/0
69	Kosier, Kyle	T	6-5	309	11/27/78	4	Arizona State	Phoenix, Ariz.	RFA(SF)-'05	16/16*
54	Lehman, Teddy	LB	6-1	240	11/18/81	2	Oklahoma	Fort Gibson, Okla.	D2-'04	16/16
59	Lewis, Alex	LB	6-0	235	6/11/81	2	Wisconsin	Delran, N.J.	D5-'04	15/1
57	Littleton, Jody	LB	6-1	240	10/23/74	3	Baylor	Brighton, Colo.	FA-'03	8/0
62	Loverne, David	G	6-3	299	5/22/76	7	San Jose State	Concord, Calif.	UFA(StL)-'04	15/3
67	Muhlbach, Don	LS	6-5	262	8/17/81	2	Texas A&M	Newark, Ohio	FA-'04	8/0
21	Pinner, Artose	RB	5-10	235	1/5/78	3	Kentucky	Hopkinsville, Ky.	D4-'03	9/2
81	Pollard, Marcus	TE	6-3	247	2/8/72	11	Bradley	Valley, Ala.	FA-'05	13/13*
58	Rainer, Wali	LB	6-2	240	4/19/77	7	Virginia	Rockingham, N.C.	UFA(Jax)-'03	16/0
51	Raiola, Dominic	C	6-1	295	12/30/78	5	Nebraska	Honolulu, Hawaii	D2a-'01	16/16
78	Redding, Cory	DE	6-4	290	11/15/80	3	Texas	Austin, Texas	D3-'03	16/16
80	Rogers, Charles	WR	6-3	220	5/23/81	3	Michigan State	Saginaw, Mich.	D1-'03	1/1
92	Rogers, Shaun	DT	6-4	345	3/12/79	5	Texas	LaPorte, Texas	D2b-'01	16/16
71	Rogers, Victor	T	6-6	330	11/10/78	4	Colorado	Federal Way, Wash.	D7c-'02	1/0
30	Schlesinger, Cory	FB	6-0	247	6/23/72	11	Nebraska	Duncan, Neb.	D6b-'95	13/11
38	Smith, Keith	CB	5-11	191	3/20/80	2	McNeese State	Leesville, La.	D3-'04	15/2
27	Smith, Paul	RB	5-11	234	1/31/78	6	Texas-El Paso	El Paso, Texas	UFA-'03	0*
10	Vines, Scottie	WR	6-2	220	4/17/79	2	Wyoming	Alexander City, Ala.	FA-'04	13/11
28	Walker, Bracy	S	6-0	202	10/28/70	12	North Carolina	Lake Villa, Ill.	UFA(KC)-'02	16/16
23	White, Jamel	RB	5-9	222	2/11/78	6	South Dakota	Palmdale, Calif.	UFA(Balt)-'05	13/0*
72	Wilkinson, Dan	DT	6-4	335	3/13/73	12	Ohio State	Dayton, Ohio	UFA(Wash)-'03	16/16
11	Williams, Roy	WR	6-3	212	12/20/81	2	Texas	Odessa, Texas	D1a-'04	14/11
65	Woody, Damien	G	6-3	325	11/3/77	7	Boston College	Beaverdam, Va.	UFA(NE)-'04	16/16

* Bailey missed '04 season because of injury; Butler inactive for 15 games; DeMulling played 11 games with Indianapolis in '04; Echols inactive for 2 games; Garcia played 11 games with Cleveland; Johnson played 16 games with Baltimore; Kennedy played 16 games with Denver; Kosier played 16 games with San Francisco; Pollard played 13 games with Indianapolis; P. Smith missed '04 season because of injury; White played 13 games with Baltimore.

Players lost through free agency (4): TE Stephen Alexander (Den; 16 games in '04), T Stockar McDougle (Mia; 16), QB Mike McMahon (Phil; 1), WR Reggie Swinton (Hou; 13).

Also played with Lions in '04—CB Rod Babers (2 games), WR Az-Zahir Hakim (12), T Matt Joyce (12), CB Chris Kern (2), S Brock Marion (16), DT Kelvin Pritchett (16).

2005 FIRST-YEAR ROSTER

Name	Pos.	Ht.	Wt.	Birthdate	College	Hometown	How Acq.
Anderson, Adam	P	6-0	188	6/28/81	Western Michigan	Grand Rapids, Mich.	FA
Battle, Andrew (1)	LB	6-4	235	7/21/81	Indiana (PA)	Allentown, Pa.	FA-'04
Bubin, Sean (1)	T	6-6	306	1/26/81	Illinois	Houston, Texas	W(Jax)-'04
Cody, Shaun	DT	6-4	292	1/22/83	Southern California	Hacienda Heights, Calif.	D2
Cox, Chip	S	5-9	185	6/24/83	Ohio	Columbus, Ohio	FA
Curry, Kentrell (1)	S	6-1	202	5/11/81	Georgia	Toccoa, Ga.	FA-'04
Genord, Scott (1)	LB	6-2	245	7/28/81	Fullerton (CA) J.C.	Detroit, Mich.	FA-'04
Goddard, Johnathan	LB	6-0	238	5/11/81	Marshall	Jacksonville, Fla.	D6b
Guman, Andrew	S	6-3	208	8/25/82	Penn State	Allentown, Pa.	FA
Hamilton, Paris	WR	6-1	195	7/26/81	Minnesota	Katy, Texas	FA
Hanoian, Greg	FB	6-2	255	12/9/81	Syracuse	Providence, R.I.	FA
Hennessey, Rory	G	6-5	300	9/8/82	Yale	Strongsville, Ohio	FA
Herzing, Adam (1)	WR	6-2	202	9/23/80	Cal Poly-San Luis Obispo	San Jose, Calif.	FA
Jackson, Howard	RB	5-10	160	9/24/82	Texas El-Paso	Freeport, Texas	FA
Jasmin, Marcus	DT	6-5	307	11/15/82	Texas A&M	New Orleans, La.	FA
Johnson, Cliff (1)	S	6-0	211	1/8/81	Morgan State	Baltimore, Md.	FA
Kaleita, Tom	T	6-6	318	5/29/83	Eastern Michigan	Ypsilanti, Mich.	FA
Kennedy, Brandon (1)	DT	5-10	350	10/21/81	North Texas	Terrell, Texas	FA
Killeen, Ryan	K	5-11	185	7/11/83	Southern California	Norco, Calif.	FA
Lingruen, Blake	C	6-4	282	8/19/81	Wake Forest	Liberty Center, Ohio	FA
Martinez, Glenn (1)	WR	6-1	183	11/30/81	Saginaw Valley State	Tampa, Fla.	FA
Matthews, Will	FB	6-3	250	4/30/81	Texas	Austin, Texas	FA
McCoy, Matt (1)	T	6-7	290	8/13/81	Ferris State	Charlotte, Mich.	FA-'04
Mortensen, Todd	QB	6-4	225	7/12/79	San Diego	Tempe, Ariz.	FA
Newton, Levi	G	6-4	310	6/30/83	South Florida	Jacksonville, Fla.	FA
Orlovsky, Dan	QB	6-4	238	8/18/83	Connecticut	Shelton, Conn.	D5
Payne, Brandon	CB	6-0	183	2/10/81	New Mexico	Dayton, Texas	FA
Procter, Cory	G	6-4	295	10/18/82	Montana	Missoula, Mont.	FA
Randall, Jason	TE	6-5	269	12/26/82	Michigan State	Muskegon Heights, Mich.	FA
Sanchez, Jeff (1)	CB	5-9	182	1/21/81	Tulane	New Orleans, La.	FA
Savoy, Steve	WR	5-11	191	2/27/82	Utah	Washington, D.C.	FA
Stephens, Leonard (1)	TE	6-3	242	7/9/78	Howard	Brooklyn, N.Y	FA-'04.
Swancutt, Bill	DE	6-4	264	9/4/82	Oregon State	Salem, Ore.	D6a
Valenzuela, Robbie	DE	6-2	310	2/14/83	Oregon	Modesto, Calif.	FA
Williams, Mike	WR	6-5	229	1/4/84	Southern California	Tampa, Fla.	D1
Wilson, Stanley	CB	5-11	189	11/5/82	Stanford	Carson, Calif.	D3

The term NFL Rookie is defined as a player who is in his first season of professional football and has not been on the roster of another professional football team for any regular-season or postseason games. A Rookie is designated by an "R" on NFL rosters. Players who have been active in another professional football league or players who have NFL experience, including either preseason training camp or being on an Active List or Inactive List, or on Reserve/Injured or Reserve/Physically Unable to Perform for fewer than six regular-season games, are termed NFL First-Year Players. An NFL First-Year Player is designated by a "1" on NFL rosters. Thereafter, a player is credited with an additional year of experience for each season in which he accumulates six games on the Active List or Inactive List, or on Reserve/Injured or Reserve/Physically Unable to Perform.

Log on to www.detroitlions.com for an up-to-date roster.

COACHING STAFF
Head Coach,
Steve Mariucci

Pro Career: Named the Lions' twenty-second head coach February 4, 2003, and has compiled a 71-64 career coaching record. Joined the Lions after spending six years as the head coach for San Francisco 49ers (1997-2002). He compiled a 60-43 (.583) record, while his teams earned playoff berths four times (1997, 1998, 2001, and 2002). One of thirteen head coaches since the NFL-AFL merger in 1970 to lead his team to a division title in his first season. He established an NFL mark for consecutive wins by a rookie head coach with an 11-game winning streak. He served as quarterbacks coach for the Green Bay Packers (1992-95). His first pro position was in 1985 when he was a receivers coach for the USFL's Orlando Renegades. Later that fall, he had a brief stint with the Los Angeles Rams as quality control coach. Career record: 71-64.

Background: Three-time All-America quarterback at Northern Michigan. Began his coaching career at his alma mater (1978-79), and moved to Cal State-Fullerton (1980-82), and Louisville (1983-84). Joined the Southern California staff in 1986, then moved to California in 1987. In 1990-91, he served as the Bears' offensive coordinator. Became the head coach at California in 1996 and guided the squad to a 5-0 start and a berth in the Aloha Bowl.

Personal: Born November 4, 1955, in Iron Mountain, Mich. He and his wife, Gayle, have four children—Tyler, Adam, Stephen, and Brielle.

ASSISTANT COACHES

Jason Arapoff, strength and conditioning; born July, 8 1965, Weymouth, Mass. Defensive back Springfield College 1985-88. No college or pro playing experience. Pro coach: Washington Redskins 1992-2000, joined Lions in 2001.

Malcolm Blacken, asst. strength and conditioning; born October 12, 1965, Richmond, Va. Running back Virginia Tech 1984-88. No pro playing experience. College coach: South Carolina 1990-91, George Mason 1992-94, Virginia 1995. Pro coach: Washington Redskins 1996-2000, joined Lions in 2001.

Larry Brooks, defensive line; born June 10, 1950, Prince George, Va. Defensive lineman Virginia State 1968-1971. Pro defensive tackle Los Angeles Rams 1972-1982. College coach: Virginia State 1992-93. Pro coach: Los Angeles Rams 1983-1990, Green Bay Packers 1994-98, Seattle Seahawks 1999-2002, Chicago Bears 2003, joined Lions in 2004.

George Catavolos, defensive backs; born May 8, 1945, Chicago. Defensive back Purdue 1964-67. No pro playing experience. College coach: Purdue 1967-68,

1971-76, Middle Tennessee State 1969, Louisville 1970, Kentucky 1977-1981, Tennessee 1982-83. Pro coach: Indianapolis Colts 1984-1994, 1998-2001, Carolina Panthers 1995-97, Washington Redskins 2002-03, joined Lions in 2004.

Don Clemons, defensive assistant/quality control; born February 15, 1954, Newark, N.J. Defensive end Muhlenberg (Pa.) 1973-76. No pro playing experience. College coach: Kutztown State 1977-78, New Mexico 1979, Arizona State 1980-84. Pro coach: Joined Lions in 1985.

Fred Graves, wide receivers; born March 2, 1950, Los Angeles. Halfback/split end Utah 1968-1970. Pro wide receiver Chicago Bears 1971. College coach: Northeast Missouri State 1975-76, Western Illinois 1977-78, New Mexico State 1979-1981, Utah 1982-2000. Pro coach: Buffalo Bills 2001-2003, Cleveland Browns 2004, joined Lions in 2005.

Johnny Holland, linebackers; born March 11, 1965, Belleville, Texas. Linebacker Texas A&M 1983-86. Pro linebacker Green Bay Packers 1987-1993. Pro coach: Green Bay Packers 1995-99, Seattle Seahawks 2000-02, joined Lions in 2003.

Dick Jauron, defensive coordinator; born October 7, 1950, Peoria, Ill. Running back Yale 1970-72. Pro defensive back Detroit Lions 1973-77, Cincinnati Bengals 1978-1980. Pro coach: Buffalo Bills 1985, Green Bay Packers 1986-1994, Jacksonville Jaguars 1995-98, Chicago Bears 1999-2003 (head coach), joined Lions in 2004.

Sean Kugler, asst. offensive line/tight ends; born August 9, 1966, Lockport, N.Y. Offensive lineman Texas-El Paso 1985-88. Pro offensive lineman Sacramento Surge (WLAF) 1991. College coach: Texas-El Paso 1993-2000. Pro coach: Joined Lions in 2001.

Stan Kwan, special teams assistant/offensive assistant; born November 2, 1967, Phoenix. Attended South Mountain (Ariz.) C.C., San Diego State. No college or pro playing experience. Pro coach: San Diego Chargers 1991-96, Detroit Lions 1997-2000, Arizona Cardinals 2001-2003, re-joined Lions in 2004.

Pat Morris, offensive line; born April 7, 1954, Cleveland. Offensive lineman Southern California 1972-75. No pro playing experience. College coach: Southern California 1976-77, 1983-86, Northern Arizona 1978, Minnesota 1979-1982, Michigan State 1987-1994, Stanford 1995-96. Pro coach: San Francisco 49ers 1997-2003, joined Lions in 2004.

Greg Olson, quarterbacks; born March 1, 1963, Richland, Wash. Quarterback Central Washington 1983-86. No pro playing experience. College coach: Washington State 1987-89, Central Washington 1990-93, Idaho 1994-96, Purdue 1997-2000, 2002. Pro coach: San

Francisco 49ers 2001, Chicago Bears 2003, joined Lions in 2004.

Chuck Priefer, special teams; born July 26, 1944, Cleveland. Attended John Carroll. No college or pro playing experience. College coach: Miami (Ohio) 1977, North Carolina 1978-1983, Kent State 1986, Georgia Tech 1987-1991. Pro coach: Green Bay Packers 1984-85, San Diego Chargers 1992-96, joined Lions in 1997.

Tom Rathman, running backs; born October 7, 1962, Grand Island, Neb. Running back Nebraska 1983-85. Pro running back San Francisco 49ers 1986-1993, Los Angeles Raiders 1994. College coach: Menlo College 1996. Pro coach: San Francisco 49ers 1997-2002, joined Lions in 2003.

Phil Snow, defensive assistant; born December 22, 1955, Woodland, Calif. Quarterback Sacramento City College 1974-75, Cal State Hayward 1977-78. No pro playing experience. College coach: Laney (Calif.) College 1979-1981, Boise State 1982-86, California 1987-1991, Arizona State 1992-2000, UCLA 2001-2002, Washington 2003-2004. Pro coach: Joined Lions in 2005.

Andy Sugarman, tight ends; born May 23, 1972, San Francisco. Attended California. No college or pro playing experience. College coach: California 1990-1997. Pro coach: San Francisco 49ers 1998-2002, joined Lions in 2003.

Ted Tollner, offensive coordinator; born May 29, 1940, San Francisco. Quarterback Cal Poly-San Luis Obispo 1959-1961. No pro playing experience. College coach: College of San Mateo 1971-72 (head coach), San Diego State 1973-1980, 1994-2001 (head coach 1994-2001), Brigham Young 1981, Southern California 1982-86 (head coach 1983-86). Pro coach: Buffalo Bills 1987-88, San Diego Chargers 1989-1991, San Francisco 2002-2004, joined Lions in 2005.

National Football Conference
North Division
Team Colors: Dark Green, Gold, and White
Lambeau Field Atrium
1265 Lombardi Avenue
Green Bay, Wisconsin 54304
Telephone: (920) 569-7500

2005 SCHEDULE
PRESEASON
Aug. 11 **San Diego** 7:00
Aug. 20 at Buffalo 6:00
Aug. 26 **New England** 7:00
Sept. 1 at Tennessee 7:00

REGULAR SEASON
Sept. 11 at Detroit 4:15
Sept. 18 **Cleveland** 3:15
Sept. 25 **Tampa Bay**.....................12:00
Oct. 3 at Carolina (Mon.) 9:00
Oct. 9 **New Orleans**...................12:00
Oct. 16 Open Date
Oct. 23 at Minnesota 12:00
Oct. 30 at Cincinnati 1:00
Nov. 6 **Pittsburgh**........................3:15
Nov. 13 at Atlanta 4:15
Nov. 21 **Minnesota** (Mon.) 8:00
Nov. 27 at Philadelphia...................4:15
Dec. 4 at Chicago........................12:00
Dec. 11 **Detroit** 7:30
Dec. 19 at Baltimore (Mon.) 9:00
Dec. 25 **Chicago** 4:00
Jan. 1 **Seattle**.............................3:15

Stadium: Lambeau Field (opened in 1957)
  • **Capacity:** 72,601
    1265 Lombardi Avenue
    Green Bay, Wisconsin 54304
Playing Surface: Grass
Training Camp: St. Norbert College
    De Pere, Wisconsin 54115

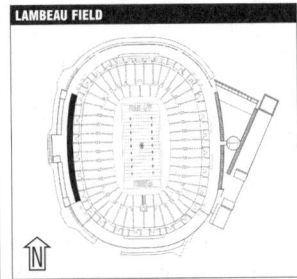

LAMBEAU FIELD

CLUB OFFICIALS
President and CEO: Bob Harlan
Vice President: John Fabry
Secretary: Peter Platten
Treasurer: Larry Weyers
Executive Vice President/General
  Manager/Director of Football
  Operations: Ted Thompson
Executive Vice President/Head Coach:
  Mike Sherman
Executive Vice President and Chief
  Operating Officer: John Jones
Vice President of Player Finance/General
  Counsel: Andrew Brandt
Dir. of College Scouting: John Dorsey
Dir. of Pro Personnel: Reggie McKenzie
Personnel Analyst to General Manager:
  John Schneider
Assistant to GM/Director of Football
  Administration: Bruce Warwick
Director of Player Development:
  Turner Gill
Director of Public Relations: Jeff Blumb
Assistant Director of Public Relations-
  Broadcasting/Corporate
  Communications: Aaron Popkey
Assistant Director of Public Relations-
  Football Communications: Zak Gilbert
Public Relations Coordinators:
  Sarah Quick, Adam Woullard
Ticket Director: Mark Wagner
Director of Marketing and Corporate
  Sales: Craig Benzel
Director of Premium Guest Services:
  Jennifer Ark
Director of Atrium Business
  Development: Steve Klegon
Director of Retail Operations:
  Kate Hogan
Team Historian: Lee Remmel
Director of Administrative Affairs:
  Mark Schiefelbein
Director of Finance:
  Vicki Vannieuwenhoven
Director of Information Technology:
  Wayne Wichlacz
Director of Facility Operations:
  Ted Eisenreich
Director of Corporate Security:
  Jerry Parins
Assistant Director of Security:
  Doug Collins
Corporate Counsel: Jason Wied
Salary Cap Analyst: Melanie Maroh
Manager of Community Relations:
  Cathy Dworak
Assistant Director of College Scouting:
  Shaun Herock
College Scouts: Lee Gissendaner,
  Brian Gutekunst, Alonzo Highsmith,
  Lenny McGill, Sam Seale,
  Jon-Eric Sullivan
Scouting Coordinator: Danny Mock
Pro Personnel Assistants: Tim Terry,
  Eliot Wolf
Director of Research and Development:
  Mike Eayrs
Video Director: Bob Eckberg
Head Trainer: Pepper Burruss
Equipment Manager: Gordon (Red) Batty

COACHING HISTORY
(636-494-36)
Records include postseason games
1921-1949 Earl (Curly) Lambeau .212-106-21
1950-53   Gene Ronzani* 14-31-1
1953   Hugh Devore-
           Ray (Scooter) McLean**..0-2-0
1954-57   Lisle Blackbourn...........17-31-0
1958   Ray (Scooter) McLean....1-10-1
1959-1967 Vince Lombardi 98-30-4
1968-1970 Phil Bengtson 20-21-1
1971-74   Dan Devine 25-28-4
1975-1983 Bart Starr 53-77-3
1984-87   Forrest Gregg 25-37-1
1988-1991 Lindy Infante................24-40-0
1992-98   Mike Holmgren 84-42-0
1999   Ray Rhodes....................8-8-0
2000-04   Mike Sherman 55-31-0
  *Resigned after 10 games in 1953
**Co-coaches

ATTENDANCE
Home 564,344   Away 538,984
Total 1,103,328
Single-game home record,
  70,688 (9/19/04)
Single-season home record,
  564,344 (2004)

2005 DRAFT CHOICES
Round	Name	Pos.	College
1	Aaron Rodgers	QB	California
2	Nick Collins	DB	Bethune-Cookman
	Terrence Murphy	WR	Texas A&M
4	Marviel Underwood	DB	San Diego State
	Brady Poppinga	LB	Brigham Young
5	Junius Coston	C	North Carolina A&T
	Mike Hawkins	DB	Oklahoma
6	Mike Montgomery	DE	Texas A&M
	Craig Bragg	WR	UCLA
7	Kurt Campbell	DB	Albany, N.Y.
	Will Whitticker	G	Michigan State

2004 TEAM RECORD
PRESEASON (1-3)

Date	Result		Opponent
8/16	L	3-21	Seattle
8/21	W	19-14	New Orleans
8/27	L	7-9	at Jacksonville
9/3	L	7-27	at Tennessee

REGULAR SEASON (10-6)

Date	Result		Opponent	Att.
9/13	W	24-14	at Carolina	73,656
9/19	L	10-21	Chicago	70,688
9/26	L	31-45	at Indianapolis	57,280
10/3	L	7-14	New York Giants	70,623
10/11	L	27-48	Tennessee	70,420
10/17	W	38-10	at Detroit	62,938
10/24	W	41-20	Dallas	70,679
10/31	W	28-14	at Washington	89,295
11/14	W	34-31	Minnesota	70,671
11/21	W	16-13	at Houston	70,769
11/29	W	45-17	St. Louis	70,385
12/5	L	17-47	at Philadelphia	67,723
12/12	W	16-13	Detroit	70,497
12/19	L	25-28	Jacksonville	70,437
12/24	W	34-31	at Minnesota	64,311
1/2	W	31-14	at Chicago	62,197

POSTSEASON (0-1)

Date	Result		Opponent	Att.
1/9	L	17-31	Minnesota	71,075

SCORE BY PERIODS

Packers	57	146	107	114	0	—	424
Opponents	82	147	58	93	0	—	380

2004 TEAM STATISTICS

	Packers	Opp.
Total First Downs	354	307
Rushing	98	92
Passing	228	181
Penalty	28	34
3rd Down: Made/Att	98/207	69/197
3rd Down Pct.	47.3	35.0
4th Down: Made/Att	8/14	5/9
4th Down Pct.	57.1	55.6
Possession Avg.	30:28	29:32
Total Net Yards	6357	5541
Avg. Per Game	397.3	346.3
Total Plays	1053	967
Avg. Per Play	6.0	5.7
Net Yards Rushing	1908	1878
Avg. Per Game	119.3	117.4
Total Rushes	441	409
Net Yards Passing	4449	3663
Avg. Per Game	278.1	228.9
Sacked/Yards Lost	14/101	40/280
Gross Yards	4550	3943
Att./Completions	598/382	518/314
Completion Pct.	63.9	60.6
Had Intercepted	19	8
Punts/Average	66/40.1	81/39.2
Net Punting Avg.	66/33.4	81/34.6
Penalties/Yards	116/950	112/942
Fumbles/Ball Lost	22/10	17/7
Touchdowns	50	47
Rushing	9	12
Passing	36	33
Returns	5	2

2004 INDIVIDUAL STATISTICS

PASSING

	Att.	Comp.	Yds.	Pct.	TD	Int.	Tkld.	Rate
Favre	540	346	4,088	64.1	30	17	12/93	92.4
Nall	33	23	314	69.7	4	0	2/8	139.4
Pederson	23	11	120	47.8	0	2	0/0	27.4
Fisher	1	1	8	100.0	1	0	0/0	139.6
Green	1	1	20	100.0	1	0	0/0	158.3
Packers	598	382	4,550	63.9	36	19	14/101	93.8
Opponents	518	314	3,943	60.6	33	8	40/280	99.1

SCORING

	TD R	TD P	TD Rt	PAT	FG	Saf	PTS
Longwell	0	0	0	48/48	24/28	0	120
Walker	0	12	0	0/0	0/0	0	72
Driver	0	9	0	0/0	0/0	0	56
Green	7	1	0	0/0	0/0	0	48
Franks	0	7	0	0/0	0/0	0	42
Henderson	0	3	0	0/0	0/0	0	18
Sharper	0	0	3	0/0	0/0	0	18
Davenport	2	0	0	0/0	0/0	0	12
Fisher	0	2	0	0/0	0/0	0	12
Ferguson	0	1	0	0/0	0/0	0	8
Carroll	0	0	1	0/0	0/0	0	6
Chatman	0	1	0	0/0	0/0	0	6
Hawthorne	0	0	1	0/0	0/0	0	6
Packers	9	36	5	48/48	24/28	0	424
Opponents	12	33	2	47/47	17/25	0	380

2-Pt. Conversions: Driver, Ferguson.
Packers 2-2, Opponents 0-0.

RUSHING

	No.	Yds	Avg	LG	TD
Green	259	1,163	4.5	90t	7
Davenport	71	359	5.1	40t	2
Fisher	65	224	3.4	24	0
W. Williams	6	42	7.0	28	0
Chatman	4	36	9.0	18	0
Favre	16	36	2.3	17	0
Luchey	10	24	2.4	4	0
Pederson	2	15	7.5	9	0
Nall	3	7	2.3	9	0
Driver	3	4	1.3	14	0
O'Sullivan	2	-2	-1.0	-1	0
Packers	441	1,908	4.3	90t	9
Opponents	409	1,878	4.6	54	12

RECEIVING

	No.	Yds	Avg	LG	TD
Walker	89	1,382	15.5	79t	12
Driver	84	1,208	14.4	50	9
Green	40	275	6.9	48	1
Fisher	38	277	7.3	25	2
Franks	34	361	10.6	29	7
Henderson	34	239	7.0	38t	3
Ferguson	24	367	15.3	48	1
Chatman	22	246	11.2	21	1
Martin	5	88	17.6	35	0
Steele	4	42	10.5	27	0
Davenport	4	33	8.3	12	0
Luchey	2	20	10.0	11	0
Thurman	2	12	6.0	9	0
Packers	382	4,550	11.9	79t	36
Opponents	314	3,943	12.6	68t	33

INTERCEPTIONS

	No.	Yds	Avg	LG	TD
Sharper	4	97	24.3	43t	2
Harris	1	29	29.0	29	0
Jue	1	23	23.0	23	0
Barnett	1	16	16.0	16	0
Carroll	1	0	0.0	0	0
Packers	8	165	20.6	43t	2
Opponents	19	166	8.7	31	1

PUNTING

	No.	Yds.	Avg.	In 20	LG
Barker	66	2,644	40.1	16	64
Packers	66	2,644	40.1	16	64
Opponents	81	3,176	39.2	31	58

PUNT RETURNS

	Ret	FC	Yds	Avg	LG	TD
Chatman	32	27	245	7.7	28	0
Sharper	1	0	9	9.0	9	0
Packers	33	27	254	7.7	28	0
Opponents	34	10	301	8.9	40	0

KICKOFF RETURNS

	No.	Yds	Avg	LG	TD
Chatman	25	565	22.6	59	0
Ferguson	21	526	25.0	71	0
Davenport	14	286	20.4	27	0
Thurman	3	59	19.7	28	0
Carroll	2	31	15.5	16	0
Henderson	2	16	8.0	10	0
Whitley	2	33	16.5	20	0
Peterson	1	6	6.0	6	0
Packers	70	1,522	21.7	71	0
Opponents	79	1,594	20.2	58	0

FIELD GOALS

	1-19	20-29	30-39	40-49	50+
Longwell	0/0	8/8	8/9	6/8	2/3
Packers	0/0	8/8	8/9	6/8	2/3
Opponents	0/0	5/5	5/8	7/12	0/0

SACKS

	No.
Gbaja-Biamila	13.5
Jenkins	4.5
Kampman	4.5
Roman	3.5
Barnett	3.0
Truluck	2.5
Carroll	2.0
Hunt	2.0
Diggs	1.0
G. Jackson	1.0
Lee	1.0
C. Williams	1.0
Navies	0.5
Packers	40.0
Opponents	14.0

RECORD HOLDERS
INDIVIDUAL RECORDS—CAREER

Category	Name	Performance
Rushing (Yds.)	Jim Taylor, 1958-1966	8,207
Passing (Yds.)	Brett Favre, 1992-2004	49,734
Passing (TDs)	Brett Favre, 1992-2004	376
Receiving (No.)	Sterling Sharpe, 1988-1994	595
Receiving (Yds.)	James Lofton, 1978-1986	9,656
Interceptions	Bobby Dillon, 1952-59	52
Punting (Avg.)	Craig Hentrich, 1994-97	42.8
Punt Return (Avg.)	Desmond Howard, 1996, 1999	13.8
Kickoff Return (Avg.)	Travis Williams, 1967-1970	26.7
Field Goals	Ryan Longwell, 1997-2004	206
Touchdowns (Tot.)	Don Hutson, 1935-1945	105
Points	Ryan Longwell, 1997-2004	964

INDIVIDUAL RECORDS—SINGLE SEASON

Category	Name	Performance
Rushing (Yds.)	Ahman Green, 2003	1,883
Passing (Yds.)	Lynn Dickey, 1983	4,458
Passing (TDs)	Brett Favre, 1996	39
Receiving (No.)	Sterling Sharpe, 1993	112
Receiving (Yds.)	Robert Brooks, 1995	1,497
Interceptions	Irv Comp, 1943	10
Punting (Avg.)	Craig Hentrich, 1997	45.0
Punt Return (Avg.)	Billy Grimes, 1950	19.1
Kickoff Return (Avg.)	Travis Williams, 1967	*41.1
Field Goals	Chester Marcol, 1972	33
	Ryan Longwell, 2000	33
Touchdowns (Tot.)	Ahman Green, 2003	20
Points	Paul Hornung, 1960	*176

INDIVIDUAL RECORDS—SINGLE GAME

Category	Name	Performance
Rushing (Yds.)	Ahman Green, 12-28-03	218
Passing (Yds.)	Lynn Dickey, 10-12-80	418
Passing (TDs)	Many times	5
	Last time by Brett Favre, 9-27-98	
Receiving (No.)	Don Hutson, 11-22-42	14
Receiving (Yds.)	Billy Howton, 10-21-56	257
Interceptions	Bobby Dillon, 11-26-53	*4
	Willie Buchanon, 9-24-78	*4
Field Goals	Chris Jacke, 11-11-90, 10-14-96	5
	Ryan Longwell, 9-24-00	5
Touchdowns (Tot.)	Paul Hornung, 12-12-65	5
Points	Paul Hornung, 10-8-61	33

*NFL Record

2005 VETERAN ROSTER

No.	Name	Pos.	Ht.	Wt.	Birthdate	NFL Exp.	College	Hometown	How Acq.	'04 Games/ Starts
56	Barnett, Nick	LB	6-2	232	5/27/81	3	Oregon State	Fontana, Calif.	D1-'03	16/16
71	Barry, Kevin	T	6-4	332	7/20/79	4	Arizona	Racine, Wis.	FA-'02	13/3
72	Bedell, Brad	T/G	6-4	318	2/12/77	5	Colorado	Arcadia, Calif.	T(Mia)-'04	4/0
28	Carroll, Ahmad	CB	5-10	190	8/4/83	2	Arkansas	Atlanta, Ga.	D1-'04	14/11
83	Chatman, Antonio	WR/KR	5-9	183	2/12/79	3	Cincinnati	Los Angeles, Calif.	FA-'03	16/2
76	Clifton, Chad	T	6-5	330	6/26/76	6	Tennessee	Martin, Tenn.	D2-'00	16/16
90	Cole, Colin	DT	6-2	325	6/24/80	2	Iowa	Ft. Lauderdale, Fla.	FA-'04	3/1
69	Curtin, Brennan	T	6-9	335	6/30/80	3	Notre Dame	Palm Beach, Fla.	D6-'03	0*
44	Davenport, Najeh	RB	6-1	250	2/8/79	4	Miami	Miami, Fla.	D4-'02	11/1
60	Davis, Rob	LS	6-3	284	12/10/68	10	Shippensburg	Greenbelt, Md.	FA-'97	16/0
59	Diggs, Na'il	LB	6-4	240	7/8/78	6	Ohio State	Los Angeles, Calif.	D4a-'00	14/14
80	Driver, Donald	WR	6-0	190	2/2/75	7	Alcorn State	Houston, Texas	D7b-'99	16/11
4	Favre, Brett	QB	6-2	225	10/10/69	15	Southern Mississippi	Kiln, Miss.	T(Atl)-'92	16/16
89	Ferguson, Robert	WR	6-1	210	12/17/79	5	Texas A&M	Houston, Texas	D2-'01	13/5
40	Fisher, Tony	RB	6-1	222	10/12/79	4	Notre Dame	Euclid, Ohio	FA-'02	16/0
58	Flanagan, Mike	C	6-5	301	11/10/73	10	UCLA	Sacramento, Calif.	D3a-'96	3/3
88	Franks, Bubba	TE	6-6	265	1/6/78	6	Miami	Big Spring, Texas	D1-'00	16/14
29	Franz, Todd	S	6-0	205	4/12/76	4	Tulsa	Weatherford, Okla.	FA-'05	16/0*
35	Freeman, Arturo	S	6-0	200	10/27/76	6	South Carolina	Orangeburg, S.C.	FA-'05	16/11*
94	Gbaja-Biamila, Kabeer	DE	6-4	250	9/24/77	6	San Diego State	Los Angeles, Calif.	FA-'00	16/15
30	Green, Ahman	RB	6-0	218	2/16/77	8	Nebraska	Omaha, Neb.	T(Sea)-'00	15/15
31	Harris, Al	CB	6-1	185	12/7/74	8	Texas A&M-Kingsville	Pompano Beach, Fla.	T(Phil)-'03	16/16
33	Henderson, William	FB	6-1	252	2/19/71	11	North Carolina	Chester, Va.	D3b-'95	16/8
26	Horton, Jason	CB	6-0	190	2/16/80	2	North Carolina A&T	Ahoskie, N.C.	FA-'04	14/0
97	Hunt, Cletidus	DT	6-4	310	1/2/76	7	Kentucky State	Memphis, Tenn.	D3b-'99	16/14
75	Jackson, Grady	DT	6-2	345	1/21/73	9	Knoxville	Greensboro, Ala.	W(NO)-'03	10/10
77	Jenkins, Cullen	DE/DT	6-3	290	1/20/81	2	Central Michigan	Belleville, Mich.	FA-'04	16/6
37	Johnson, Chris	CB	5-11	198	9/25/79	3	Louisville	Longview, Texas	D7a-'03	0*
74	Kampman, Aaron	DE	6-4	284	11/30/79	4	Iowa	Parkersburg, Iowa	D5a-'02	16/16
70	Klemm, Adrian	G	6-4	318	5/21/77	6	Hawaii	Santa Monica, Calif.	UFA(NE)-'05	2/0*
48	Leach, Vonta	FB	6-0	250	11/6/81	2	East Carolina	Rowland, N.C.	FA-'04	6/0
64	Lee, James	DT	6-5	323	3/12/80	3	Oregon State	Salem, Ore.	D5a-'03	9/1
53	Lenon, Paris	LB	6-2	240	11/26/77	4	Richmond	Lynchburg, Va.	FA-'02	16/4
21	Little, Earl	S	6-0	202	3/10/73	8	Miami	Miami, Fla.	FA-'05	16/11*
8	Longwell, Ryan	K	6-0	200	8/16/74	9	California	Bend, Ore.	W(SF)-'97	16/0
22	Luchey, Nick	FB	6-2	273	3/30/77	7	Miami	Farmington Hills, Mich.	UFA(Cin)-'03	16/6
87	Martin, David	TE	6-4	265	3/13/79	5	Tennessee	Norfolk, Va.	D6-'01	9/3
78	Morley, Steve	T/G	6-7	330	8/18/81	2	St. Mary's (Canada)	Halifax, Nova Scotia, Canada	FA-'04	0*
16	Nall, Craig	QB	6-3	230	4/21/79	4	Northwestern State (LA)	Alexandria, La.	D5b-'02	5/0
50	Navies, Hannibal	LB	6-3	245	7/19/77	7	Colorado	Berkeley, Calif.	UFA(Car)-'03	15/14
73	O'Dwyer, Matt	G	6-4	325	9/1/72	11	Northwestern	Lincolnshire, Ill.	UFA(TB)-'05	4/0*
7 t-	O'Sullivan, J.T.	QB	6-2	227	8/25/79	2	UC Davis	Carmichael, Calif.	T(NO)-'04	1/0
98	Peterson, Kenny	DT/DE	6-3	285	11/21/78	3	Ohio State	Canton, Ohio	D3-'03	9/0
23	Roman, Mark	S	5-11	201	3/26/77	6	Louisiana State	New Iberia, La.	UFA(Cin)-'04	16/15
67	Ruegamer, Grey	C/G	6-4	305	6/11/76	6	Arizona State	Las Vegas, Nev.	UFA(NE)-'03	15/11
11	Sander, B.J.	P	6-4	218	7/29/80	2	Ohio State	Cincinnati, Ohio	D3c-'04	0*
82	Steele, Ben	TE	6-5	260	5/27/78	2	Mesa State	Palisade, Colo.	FA-'04	15/0
65	Tauscher, Mark	T	6-4	315	6/17/77	6	Wisconsin	Auburndale, Wis.	D7a-'00	16/16
24	Thomas, Joey	CB	6-1	190	8/29/80	2	Montana State	Seattle, Wash.	D3a-'04	14/0
55	Thompson, Ray	LB	6-3	232	11/21/77	6	Tennessee	New Orleans, La.	FA-'05	11/3*
91	Truluck, R-Kal	DE	6-4	255	9/30/74	4	SUNY Cortland	Rockland County, N.Y.	T(KC)-'04	14/1
84	Walker, Javon	WR	6-3	215	10/14/78	4	Florida State	Lafayette, La.	D1-'02	16/12
95	Washington, Donnell	DT	6-6	328	2/6/81	2	Clemson	Beaufort, S.C.	D3b-'04	0*
63	Wells, Scott	C	6-2	304	1/17/81	2	Tennessee	Brentwood, Tenn.	FA-'04	5/2
99	Williams, Corey	DT/DE	6-4	313	8/17/80	2	Arkansas State	Camden, Ark.	D6-'04	12/0
32	Williams, Walt	RB	6-1	217	9/8/77	3	Grambling State	Brusly, La.	FA-'04	1/0

* Curtin missed '04 season because of injury; Franz played 16 games with Washington in '04; Freeman played 16 games with Miami; C. Johnson inactive for 8 games; Klemm played 2 games with New England; Little played 16 games with Cleveland; Morley inactive for 16 games; O'Dwyer played 4 games with Tampa Bay; Sander inactive for 16 games; Thompson played 11 games with Arizona; Washington missed '04 season because of injury.

t- Packers traded for O'Sullivan (NO).

Traded—CB Mike McKenzie (1 game in '04) to New Orleans.

Retired—Doug Pederson, 12-year quarterback; 4 games in '04.

Players lost through free agency (2): CB/S Bhawoh Jue (SD; 16 games in '04), G Marco Rivera (Dall; 16).

Also played with Packers in '04—P Bryan Barker (16 games), S Curtis Fuller (1), S/CB Michael Hawthorne (16), RB James Jackson (1), LB Steve Josue (4), LB Torrance Marshall (9), LB Nick Rogers (10), S Darren Sharper (15), DT Larry Smith (3), G Mike Wahle (16), S James Whitley (6).

2005 FIRST-YEAR ROSTER

Name	Pos.	Ht.	Wt.	Birthdate	College	Hometown	How Acq.
Barnard, Brooks (1)	P	6-3	205	11/4/79	Maryland	Annapolis, Md.	FA
Benekos, Bryce	P	6-5	222	6/8/83	Texas-El Paso	Chino Hills, Calif.	FA
Bragg, Craig	WR/KR	6-1	195	3/15/82	UCLA	San Jose, Calif.	D6b
Breeden, Sam (1)	WR	6-4	206	7/12/79	Northwestern Oklahoma St.	Rockingham, N.C.	FA
Butler, Vince	WR	6-0	185	5/9/81	Northwestern Oklahoma St.	Tampa, Fla.	FA
Campbell, Kurt	LB	6-1	227	7/30/82	Albany	Kingston, Jamaica	D7a
Collins, Nick	S/CB	5-11	200	8/16/83	Bethune-Cookman	Cross City, Fla.	D2a
Coston, Junius	G/C	6-3	317	11/5/83	North Carolina A&T	Raleigh, N.C.	D5a
Cross, Garrett	TE	6-4	245	11/30/82	California	Chico, Calif.	FA
Curry, Julius (1)	S	6-0	195	5/17/79	Michigan	Harper Woods, Mich.	FA
Day, Chris (1)	CB	5-11	178	1/22/82	Grambling State	Birmingham, Ala.	FA
Dendy, Patrick	CB	6-0	190	3/10/82	Rice	Austin, Texas	FA
Garrett, John (1)	LB	6-1	250	7/4/81	Baylor	Mart, Texas	FA
Hawkins, Mike	CB	6-1	180	7/15/83	Oklahoma	Carrollton, Texas	D5b
Hayes, Joe (1)	G	6-4	304	6/15/81	San Jose State	Vallejo, Calif.	FA
Herrion, Atlas (1)	G/T	6-4	313	12/3/80	Alabama	Daphne, Ala.	FA
Jones, Jamal (1)	WR/KR	6-0	214	4/24/81	North Carolina A&T	Hyattsville, Md.	FA
Kight, Kelvin (1)	WR/KR	6-0	209	7/2/82	Florida	Lithonia, Ga.	FA
Lacey, Chonn (1)	S	6-1	217	5/15/79	Temple	Pottstown, Pa.	FA
Lindsay, A.J.	DT	6-3	315	6/10/83	Temple	Kokomo, Ind.	FA
Manning, Roy	LB	6-2	245	12/4/81	Michigan	Saginaw, Mich.	FA
McBrien, Scott (1)	QB	6-0	189	2/14/80	Maryland	Hyattsville, Md.	FA
McHugh, Sean (1)	TE	6-5	265	5/27/82	Penn State	Chagrin Falls, Ohio	FA-'04
McNeil, Nick (1)	LB	6-2	245	8/19/81	Western Carolina	Leland, N.C.	FA
Montgomery, Michael	DE	6-5	275	8/18/83	Texas A&M	Center, Texas	D6a
Morgan, Shawn	LB	6-2	235	11/6/78	Fayetteville State	Havelock, N.C.	FA
Murphy, Terrence	WR/KR	6-1	196	12/15/82	Texas A&M	Tyler, Texas	D2b
Poppinga, Brady	LB	6-3	245	9/21/79	Brigham Young	Evanston, Wyo.	D4b
Quinn, Joe	G/C	6-4	290	6/1/80	Minnesota	Glenwood City, Wis.	FA
Robertson, Chris (1)	RB	6-1	235	4/30/80	Houston	Denison, Texas	FA
Rodgers, Aaron	QB	6-2	223	12/2/83	California	Chico, Calif.	D1
Samp, Chris	WR	6-3	217	7/12/80	Winona State	Green Bay, Wis.	FA
Sims, Doug (1)	DT	6-1	344	10/20/79	Hawaii	Albany, Calif.	FA
Smith, Art (1)	CB/S	6-1	204	10/18/81	Northeastern	Hamilton, N.J.	FA
Thurman, Andrae (1)	WR	5-11	185	10/25/80	Southern Oregon	Avondale, Ariz.	FA-'04
Torrence, Leigh	CB	5-11	185	1/4/82	Stanford	Atlanta, Ga.	FA
Underwood, Marviel	S	5-10	197	2/17/82	San Diego State	San Leandro, Calif.	D4a
White, Chris	G	6-2	285	2/28/83	Southern Mississippi	Winona, Miss.	FA
Whitticker, Will	G	6-5	338	8/2/82	Michigan State	Marion, Ind.	D7b
Williams, Chaz	RB	5-9	210	7/9/82	Georgia Southern	Apopka, Fla.	FA
Williams, Seante (1)	DE	6-6	252	9/16/81	Jacksonville State	Pensacola, Fla.	FA
Williams, Wendell (1)	S	6-1	215	10/20/81	Louisiana-Lafayette	Baton Rouge, La.	FA
Woodfin, Zac	LB	6-1	235	3/19/83	Alabama-Birmingham	Prattville, Ala.	FA

The term NFL Rookie is defined as a player who is in his first season of professional football and has not been on the roster of another professional football team for any regular-season or postseason games. A Rookie is designated by an "R" on NFL rosters. Players who have been active in another professional football league or players who have NFL experience, including either preseason training camp or being on an Active List or Inactive List, or on Reserve/Injured or Reserve/Physically Unable to Perform for fewer than six regular-season games, are termed NFL First-Year Players. An NFL First-Year Player is designated by a "1" on NFL rosters. Thereafter, a player is credited with an additional year of experience for each season in which he accumulates six games on the Active List or Inactive List, or on Reserve/Injured or Reserve/Physically Unable to Perform.

Log on to www.packers.com for an up-to-date roster.

COACHING STAFF

Executive Vice President/Head Coach, Mike Sherman

Pro Career: Named the thirteenth head coach in Packers history January 18, 2000. Also served as general manager from 2001-04. Sherman has led Green Bay to five consecutive winning seasons and three straight division titles. Joins Pro Football Hall of Fame members Curly Lambeau and Vince Lombardi, along with Mike Holmgren, as the only head coaches in team history to post a winning record. Previously had served as Green Bay's tight ends coach (1997-98) before following Holmgren to Seattle in 1999 to serve as the Seahawks' offensive coordinator/tight ends coach. Career record: 55-31.

Background: Played guard, tackle, and linebacker at Central Connecticut State (1974, 1976-77), where he holds a bachelor's degree in English. Coached high school football (1978-1980) before collegiately coaching at Pittsburgh (1981-82), Tulane (1983-84), Holy Cross (1985-88), Texas A&M (1989-1993, 1995-96), and UCLA (1994).

Personal: Born December 19, 1954, in Norwood, Mass. He and his wife, Karen, have five children—Sarah, Emily, Matthew, Benjamin, and Selena.

ASSISTANT COACHES

Joe Baker, secondary/safeties; born June 29, 1969, Glen Ridge, N.J. Wide receiver Princeton 1987-1990. No pro playing experience. College coach: East Stroudsburg 1991, Samford 1993, Wisconsin 1999. Pro coach: Birmingham Fire (WLAF) 1992, Jacksonville Jaguars 1994-98, New Orleans Saints 2000-04, joined Packers in 2005.

Jim Bates, defensive coordinator; born May 31, 1946, Pontiac, Mich. Linebacker Tennessee 1964-67. No pro playing experience. College coach: Tennessee 1968, Southern Mississippi 1972, Villanova 1973-74, Kansas State 1975-76, West Virginia 1977, Texas Tech 1978-1983, Tennessee 1989, Florida 1990. Pro coach: San Antonio Gunslingers (USFL) 1984-85 (head coach 1985), Arizona Outlaws (USFL) 1986, Detroit Drive (AFL) 1988, Cleveland Browns 1991-93, 1995, Atlanta Falcons 1994, Dallas Cowboys 1996-99, Miami Dolphins 2000-04 (interim head coach 2004), joined Packers in 2005.

Larry Beightol, offensive line; born November 21, 1942, Pittsburgh. Guard/linebacker Catawba College 1960-63. No pro playing experience. College coach: William & Mary 1968-1971, North Carolina State 1972-75, Auburn 1976, Arkansas 1977-78, 1980-82, Louisiana Tech 1979 (head coach), Missouri 1983-84. Pro coach: Atlanta Falcons 1985-86, Tampa Bay Buccaneers 1987-88, San Diego Chargers 1989, New York Jets 1990-94, Houston Oilers 1995, Miami Dolphins 1996-98, joined Packers in 1999.

Edgar Bennett, running backs; born February 15, 1969, Jacksonville. Running back Florida State 1987, 1989-1991. Pro running back Green Bay Packers 1992-96, Chicago Bears 1998-99. Pro coach: Joined Packers in 2001.

Darrell Bevell, quarterbacks; born January 6, 1970, Yuma, Ariz. Quarterback Northern Arizona 1989, Wisconsin 1992-95. No pro playing experience. College coach: Westmar 1996, Iowa State 1997, Connecticut 1998-99. Pro coach: Joined Packers in 2000.

John Bonamego, special teams coordinator; born August 14, 1963, Waynesboro, Pa. Wide receiver/quarterback Central Michigan 1985-86. No pro playing experience. College coach: Maine 1988-1991, Lehigh 1992, Army 1993-98. Pro coach: Jacksonville Jaguars 1999-2002, joined Packers in 2003.

James Campen, asst. offensive line/quality control; born June 11, 1964, Sacramento, Calif. Center Sacramento City (Calif.) J.C. 1982-83, Tulane 1984-85. Pro center New Orleans Saints 1987-88, Green Bay Packers 1989-1993. Pro coach: Joined Packers in 2004.

Mark Duffner, linebackers; born July 19, 1953, Annandale, Va. Defensive lineman William & Mary 1972-74. No pro playing experience. College coach: Ohio State 1975-76, Cincinnati 1977-1980, Holy Cross 1981-1991 (head coach 1986-1991), Maryland 1992-96 (head coach). Pro coach: Cincinnati Bengals 1997-2002, joined Packers in 2003.

James Franklin, wide receivers; born February 2, 1972, Bristol, Pa. Quarterback East Stroudsburg 1991-94. No pro playing experience. College coach: Kutztown 1995, East Stroudsburg 1996, James Madison 1997, Washington State 1998, Idaho State 1999, Maryland 2000-04. Pro coach: Joined Packers in 2005.

Charlie Jackson, defensive quality control; November 4, 1976, Vienna, Ga. Defensive back Air Force Academy 1997-99. No pro playing experience. College coach: UCLA 2002-03, Air Force Academy 2004. Pro coach: Joined Packers in 2005.

Brad Miller, asst. special teams; born May 30, 1963, Pasadena, Calif. Tight end/safety Oregon State 1981-84. No pro playing experience. College coach: Riverside (Calif.) C.C. 1986-1993, Portland State 1994. Pro coach: Birmingham Barracudas (CFL) 1995, Edmonton Eskimos (CFL) 1996-2000, joined Packers in 2001.

Robert Nunn, defensive tackles; born June 10, 1965, Apache, Okla. Linebacker Oklahoma State 1983-84, 1986-87. No pro playing experience. College coach: Northeastern Oklahoma 1988, Tennessee 1989-1990, Georgia Military College 1991-99 (head coach 1992-99). Pro

coach: Miami Dolphins 2000-02, 2004, Washington Redskins 2003, joined Packers in 2005.

Joe Philbin, tight ends/asst. offensive line; born July 2, 1961, Springfield, Mass. Tight end Washington & Jefferson 1980. No pro playing experience. College coach: Tulane 1984-85, Worcester Tech 1986-87, U.S. Merchant Marine Academy 1988-89, Allegheny 1990-93, Ohio University 1994, Northeastern 1995-96, Harvard 1997-98, Iowa 1999-2002. Pro coach: Joined Packers in 2003.

Tom Rossley, offensive coordinator; born August 9, 1946, Painesville, Ohio. Wide receiver Cincinnati 1966-68. No pro playing experience. College coach: Arkansas 1972, Rice 1976, 1978-1981, Cincinnati 1977, Holy Cross 1986-87, Southern Methodist 1988-89, 1991-96 (head coach 1991-96). Pro coach: Montreal Concorde (CFL) 1982-84, San Antonio Gunslingers (USFL) 1985, Denver Dynamite (AFL) 1987, Atlanta Falcons 1990, Chicago Bears 1997-98, Kansas City Chiefs 1999, joined Packers in 2000.

Barry Rubin, strength and conditioning; born June 25, 1957, Monroe, La. Running back/punter Louisiana State 1976-77, tight end/punter Northwestern (La.) State 1978-1980. No pro playing experience. College coach: Northeast Louisiana 1981-83, 1987-1990, 1994, Louisiana State 1984-85. Pro coach: Joined Packers in 1995.

Bob Sanders, defensive line/defensive ends; born December 5, 1953, Jacksonville, N.C. Linebacker Davidson College 1973-75. No pro playing experience. College coach: Georgia Tech 1978, East Carolina 1980-82, Richmond 1983-84, Duke 1985-89, Florida 1990-2000. Pro coach: Miami Dolphins 2001-04, joined Packers in 2005.

Lionel Washington, defensive nickel package/cornerbacks; born October 21, 1960, New Orleans. Defensive back Tulane 1979-1982. Pro defensive back St. Louis Cardinals 1983-86, Los Angeles/Oakland Raiders 1987-1994, 1997, Denver Broncos 1995-96. Pro coach: Joined Packers in 1999.

National Football Conference
North Division
Team Colors: Purple, Gold, and White
9520 Viking Drive
Eden Prairie, Minnesota 55344
Telephone: (952) 828-6500

2005 SCHEDULE
PRESEASON
Aug. 12 **Kansas City** 7:00
Aug. 19 at New York Jets.................8:00
Aug. 26 **San Diego**..........................7:00
Sept. 2 at Seattle............................6:00

REGULAR SEASON
Sept. 11 **Tampa Bay**.......................12:00
Sept. 18 at Cincinnati 1:00
Sept. 25 **New Orleans**...................12:00
Oct. 2 at Atlanta...........................4:15
Oct. 9 Open Date
Oct. 16 at Chicago......................12:00
Oct. 23 **Green Bay**......................12:00
Oct. 30 at Carolina.........................1:00
Nov. 6 **Detroit** 12:00
Nov. 13 at New York Giants 1:00
Nov. 21 at Green Bay (Mon.) 8:00
Nov. 27 **Cleveland** 12:00
Dec. 4 at Detroit 1:00
Dec. 11 **St. Louis** 12:00
Dec. 18 **Pittsburgh**......................12:00
Dec. 25 at Baltimore......................8:30
Jan. 1 **Chicago** 12:00

Stadium: Hubert H. Humphrey Metrodome
(opened in 1982)
•**Capacity:** 64,121
500 11th Avenue South
Minneapolis, Minnesota 55415
Playing Surface: FieldTurf
Training Camp: Minnesota State-Mankato
Mankato, Minnesota
56001

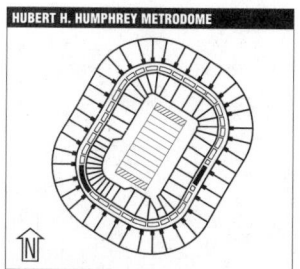

HUBERT H. HUMPHREY METRODOME

CLUB OFFICIALS
Owner: Zygmunt Wilf
Vice President of Football Operations:
Rob Brzezinski
Vice President of Sales and Marketing:
Steve LaCroix
Vice President of Finance: Steve Poppen
Director of Football Administration:
Dave Blando
Director of Pro Scouting: Paul Wiggin
Director of College Scouting:
Scott Studwell
Senior Consultant/Player Personnel:
Frank Gilliam
Director of Public Relations: Bob Hagan
Director of Community Relations:
Brad Madson
Director of Research and Development:
Chad Ostlund
Director of Operations: Breck Spinner
Director of Ticket Sales: Phil Huebner
Director of Video: Bob Marcus
Equipment Manager: Dennis Ryan
Head Athletic Trainer: Chuck Barta
Senior Consultant/Medical Services:
Fred Zamberletti

COACHING HISTORY
(380-315-9)
Records include postseason games
1961-66   Norm Van Brocklin 29-51-4
1967-1983 Bud Grant 161-99-5
1984   Les Steckel 3-13-0
1985   Bud Grant 7-9-0
1986-1991 Jerry Burns...............55-46-0
1992-2001 Dennis Green* 101-70-0
2001-04   Mike Tice 24-27-0
*Resigned after 15 games in 2001

ATTENDANCE
Home 499,369   Away 538,522
Total 1,037,891
Single-game home record,
64,482 (11/2/03)
Single-season home record,
510,741 (1998)

2005 DRAFT CHOICES
Round	Name	Pos.	College
1	Troy Williamson	WR	South Carolina
	Erasmus James	DE	Wisconsin
2	Marcus Johnson	G	Mississippi
3	Dustin Fox	DB	Ohio State
4	Ciatrick Fason	RB	Florida
6	C.J. Mosley	DT	Missouri
7	Adrian Ward	DB	Texas-El Paso

2004 TEAM RECORD

PRESEASON (2-2)

Date	Result	Opponent
8/14	W 23-6	Arizona
8/20	L 24-27	at Atlanta
8/27	W 23-10	at San Francisco
9/2	L 21-23	at Seattle

REGULAR SEASON (8-8)

Date	Result	Opponent	Att.
9/12	W 35-17	Dallas	64,105
9/20	L 16-27	at Philadelphia	67,676
9/26	W 27-22	Chicago	64,163
10/10	W 34-28	at Houston (OT)	70,718
10/17	W 38-31	at New Orleans	64,900
10/24	W 20-3	Tennessee	64,108
10/31	L 13-34	N.Y. Giants	64,012
11/8	L 28-31	at Indianapolis	57,307
11/14	L 31-34	at Green Bay	70,671
11/21	W 22-19	Detroit	64,156
11/28	W 27-16	Jacksonville	64,004
12/5	L 14-24	at Chicago	62,051
12/12	L 23-27	Seattle	64,110
12/19	W 28-27	at Detroit	62,337
12/24	L 31-34	Green Bay	64,311
1/2	L 18-21	at Washington	76,876

(OT) Overtime

POSTSEASON (1-1)

1/9	W 31-17	at Green Bay	71,075
1/16	L 14-27	at Philadelphia	67,722

SCORE BY PERIODS

Vikings	54	136	73	136	6	—	405
Opponents	78	135	54	128	0	—	395

2004 TEAM STATISTICS

	Vikings	Opp.
Total First Downs	351	350
Rushing	98	110
Passing	225	220
Penalty	28	20
3rd Down: Made/Att	102/195	90/196
3rd Down Pct.	52.3	45.9
4th Down: Made/Att	6/10	10/16
4th Down Pct.	60.0	62.5
Possession Avg.	30:02	29:58
Total Net Yards	6339	5905
Avg. Per Game	396.2	368.9
Total Plays	985	1018
Avg. Per Play	6.4	5.8
Net Yards Rushing	1823	2006
Avg. Per Game	113.9	125.4
Total Rushes	387	435
Net Yards Passing	4516	3896
Avg. Per Game	282.3	243.5
Sacked/Yards Lost	46/238	39/234
Gross Yards	4754	4130
Att./Completions	552/380	544/338
Completion Pct.	68.8	62.1
Had Intercepted	12	11
Punts/Average	57/39.3	59/42.2
Net Punting Avg.	57/35.3	59/36.2
Penalties/Yards	117/884	110/974
Fumbles/Ball Lost	20/9	25/11
Touchdowns	50	46
Rushing	8	15
Passing	39	30
Returns	3	1

2004 INDIVIDUAL STATISTICS

PASSING	Att.	Comp.	Yds.	Pct.	TD	Int.	Tkld.	Rate
Culpepper	548	379	4,717	69.2	39	11	46/238	110.9
Moss	2	1	37	50.0	0	1	0/0	56.3
Frerotte	1	0	0	0.0	0	0	0/0	39.6
Moore	1	0	0	0.0	0	0	0/0	39.6
Vikings	552	380	4,754	68.8	39	12	46/238	109.8
Opponents	544	338	4,130	62.1	30	11	39/234	95.5

SCORING	TD R	TD P	TD Rt	PAT	FG	Saf	PTS
Andersen	0	0	0	45/45	18/22	0	99
Moss	0	13	0	0/0	0/0	0	78
Burleson	0	9	1	0/0	0/0	0	62
Robinson	0	8	0	0/0	0/0	0	48
O. Smith	2	2	0	0/0	0/0	0	26
Wiggins	0	4	0	0/0	0/0	0	24
M. Williams	3	1	0	0/0	0/0	0	24
Culpepper	2	0	0	0/0	0/0	0	14
M. Bennett	1	1	0	0/0	0/0	0	12
Campbell	0	1	0	0/0	0/0	0	6
Claiborne	0	0	1	0/0	0/0	0	6
K. Williams	0	0	1	0/0	0/0	0	6
Vikings	8	39	3	45/45	18/22	0	405
Opponents	15	30	1	43/43	24/27	1	395

2-Pt. Conversions: Burleson, Culpepper, O. Smith.

Vikings 3-4, Opponents 1-3.

RUSHING	No.	Yds	Avg	LG	TD
O. Smith	124	544	4.4	38	2
Culpepper	88	406	4.6	16	2
Moore	65	379	5.8	33	0
M. Bennett	70	276	3.9	25	1
M. Williams	30	161	5.4	49	3
Burleson	6	49	8.2	11	0
Campbell	3	4	1.3	16	0
Russell	1	4	4.0	4	0
Vikings	387	1,823	4.7	49	8
Opponents	435	2,006	4.6	53	15

RECEIVING	No.	Yds	Avg	LG	TD
Wiggins	71	705	9.9	39	4
Burleson	68	1,006	14.8	68t	9
Moss	49	767	15.7	82t	13
Robinson	47	657	14.0	50t	8
O. Smith	36	394	10.9	63t	2
Moore	27	238	8.8	26	0
M. Williams	21	233	11.1	28	1
M. Bennett	21	207	9.9	38t	1
Campbell	19	364	19.2	61	1
Berton	9	78	8.7	14	0
Owens	8	69	8.6	18	0
Kleinsasser	2	24	12.0	18	0
Ned	1	9	9.0	9	0
Howry	1	3	3.0	3	0
Vikings	380	4,754	12.5	82t	39
Opponents	338	4,130	12.2	62	30

INTERCEPTIONS	No.	Yds	Avg	LG	TD
Winfield	3	89	29.7	56	0
B. Williams	2	14	7.0	14	0
Russell	1	41	41.0	41	0
Shaw	1	22	22.0	22	0
R. Smith	1	19	19.0	19	0
Claiborne	1	15	15.0	15t	1
K. Williams	1	7	7.0	7	0
Chavous	1	0	0.0	0	0
Vikings	11	207	18.8	56	1
Opponents	12	207	17.3	52	0

PUNTING	No.	Yds.	Avg.	In 20	LG
D. Bennett	57	2,240	39.3	18	61
Vikings	57	2,240	39.3	18	61
Opponents	59	2,488	42.2	24	55

PUNT RETURNS	Ret	FC	Yds	Avg	LG	TD
Burleson	25	9	214	8.6	91t	1
Moore	4	1	28	7.0	17	0
Howry	2	3	33	16.5	21	0
Moss	0	1	0	—	—	0
Vikings	31	14	275	8.9	91t	1
Opponents	26	15	169	6.5	15	0

KICKOFF RETURNS	No.	Yds	Avg	LG	TD
Campbell	35	760	21.7	55	0
Moore	20	386	19.3	33	0
O. Smith	9	155	17.2	24	0
Burleson	2	51	25.5	29	0
Howry	2	45	22.5	24	0
Ross	2	33	16.5	19	0
Berton	1	3	3.0	3	0
Davis	1	15	15.0	15	0
Johnson	1	0	0.0	0	0
Vikings	73	1,448	19.8	55	0
Opponents	75	1,869	24.9	92t	1

FIELD GOALS	1-19	20-29	30-39	40-49	50+
Andersen	1/1	8/8	5/7	4/6	0/0
Vikings	1/1	8/8	5/7	4/6	0/0
Opponents	0/0	5/5	10/12	7/7	2/3

SACKS	No.
K. Williams	11.5
Johnstone	11.0
Udeze	5.0
Newman	3.5
Mixon	2.5
Hovan	1.5
Claiborne	1.0
Henderson	1.0
Johnson	1.0
Martin	0.5
Thomas	0.5
Vikings	39.0
Opponents	46.0

RECORD HOLDERS
INDIVIDUAL RECORDS—CAREER

Category	Name	Performance
Rushing (Yds.)	Robert Smith, 1993-2000	6,818
Passing (Yds.)	Fran Tarkenton, 1961-66, 1972-78	33,098
Passing (TDs)	Fran Tarkenton, 1961-66, 1972-78	239
Receiving (No.)	Cris Carter, 1990-2001	1,004
Receiving (Yds.)	Cris Carter, 1990-2001	12,383
Interceptions	Paul Krause, 1968-1979	53
Punting (Avg.)	Harry Newsome, 1990-93	43.8
Punt Return (Avg.)	David Palmer, 1994-2000	9.4
Kickoff Return (Avg.)	Charlie West, 1968-1973	25.5
Field Goals	Fred Cox, 1963-1977	282
Touchdowns (Tot.)	Cris Carter, 1990-2001	110
Points	Fred Cox, 1963-1977	1,365

INDIVIDUAL RECORDS—SINGLE SEASON

Category	Name	Performance
Rushing (Yds.)	Robert Smith, 2000	1,521
Passing (Yds.)	Daunte Culpepper, 2004	4,717
Passing (TDs)	Daunte Culpepper, 2004	39
Receiving (No.)	Cris Carter, 1994, 1995	122
Receiving (Yds.)	Randy Moss, 2003	1,632
Interceptions	Paul Krause, 1975	10
Punting (Avg.)	Bobby Walden, 1964	46.4
Punt Return (Avg.)	David Palmer, 1995	13.2
Kickoff Return (Avg.)	John Gilliam, 1972	26.3
Field Goals	Gary Anderson, 1998	35
Touchdowns (Tot.)	Chuck Foreman, 1975	22
Points	Gary Anderson, 1998	164

INDIVIDUAL RECORDS—SINGLE GAME

Category	Name	Performance
Rushing (Yds.)	Chuck Foreman, 10-24-76	200
Passing (Yds.)	Tommy Kramer, 11-2-86	490
Passing (TDs)	Joe Kapp, 9-28-69	*7
Receiving (No.)	Rickey Young, 12-16-79	15
Receiving (Yds.)	Sammy White, 11-7-76	210
Interceptions	Many Times	3
	Last time by Brian Williams, 11-23-03	
Field Goals	Rich Karlis, 11-5-89	*7
Touchdowns (Tot.)	Chuck Foreman, 12-20-75	4
	Ahmad Rashad, 9-2-79	4
Points	Chuck Foreman, 12-20-75	24
	Ahmad Rashad, 9-2-79	24

*NFL Record

2005 VETERAN ROSTER

No.	Name	Pos.	Ht.	Wt.	Birthdate	NFL Exp.	College	Hometown	How Acq.	'04 Games/ Starts
86	Angulo, Richard	TE	6-8	270	11/13/80	3	Western New Mexico	Albuquerque, N.M.	W(StL)-'03	0*
2	Bennett, Darren	P	6-5	235	1/9/65	11	No College	Perth, Australia	UFA(SD)-'04	15/0
23	Bennett, Michael	RB	5-9	209	8/13/78	5	Wisconsin	Milwaukee, Wis.	D1-'01	11/7
44	Berton, Sean	TE	6-4	263	10/31/79	3	North Carolina State	Greensburg, Pa.	FA-'03	14/7
78	Birk, Matt	C	6-4	309	7/23/76	8	Harvard	St. Paul, Minn.	D6-'98	12/11
33	Brown, Ralph	CB	5-10	185	9/16/78	5	Nebraska	LaPuenta, Calif.	FA-'04	12/0
81	Burleson, Nate	WR	6-0	192	8/19/81	3	Nevada	Seattle, Wash.	D3-'03	16/15
16	Campbell, Kelly	WR	5-10	173	7/23/80	4	Georgia Tech	Atlanta, Ga.	FA-'05	16/3
21	Chavous, Corey	S	6-1	205	1/5/76	8	Vanderbilt	Aiken, S.C.	UFA(Ariz)-'02	16/16
1	Cortez, Jose	K	5-11	200	5/27/75	5	Oregon State	Van Nuys, Calif.	FA-'04	8/0
55 t-	Cowart, Sam	LB	6-2	245	2/26/75	8	Florida State	Jacksonville, Fla.	T(NYJ)-'05	9/2*
11	Culpepper, Daunte	QB	6-4	264	1/28/77	7	Central Florida	Ocala, Fla.	D1a-'99	16/16
50	Davis, Rod	LB	6-2	239	4/2/81	2	Southern Mississippi	Gulfport, Miss.	D5-'04	14/0
71 #	Dixon, David	G	6-5	343	1/5/69	12	Arizona State	Auckland, New Zealand	FA-'94	16/16
5	Dorsch, Travis	P	6-6	221	9/4/79	2	Purdue	Bozeman, Mont.	FA-'04	0*
65	Dorsey, Nat	T	6-7	322	9/9/83	2	Georgia Tech	New Orleans, La.	D4a-'04	13/7
83	Dugan, Jeff	TE	6-4	258	4/8/81	2	Maryland	Pittsburgh, Pa.	D7-'04	14/2
	Edinger, Paul	K	5-8	175	1/17/78	6	Michigan State	Lakeland, Fla.	FA-'05	16/0*
8	Elling, Aaron	K	6-2	201	5/31/78	3	Wyoming	Lander, Wyo.	FA-'03	7/0
73	Goldberg, Adam	G	6-7	310	8/12/80	2	Wyoming	Edina, Minn.	FA-'03	13/6
58 t-	Harris, Napoleon	LB	6-2	255	2/25/79	4	Northwestern	Harvey, Ill.	T(Oak)-'05	14/9*
56	Henderson, E.J.	LB	6-1	245	8/3/80	3	Maryland	Aberdeen, Md.	D2-'03	14/14
67	Herrera, Anthony	G	6-2	315	6/14/80	2	Tennessee	Naples, Fla.	FA-'04	0*
13	Hill, Shaun	QB	6-3	226	1/9/80	4	Maryland	Parsons, Kan.	FA-'02	0*
82	Howry, Keenan	WR	5-10	172	6/17/81	3	Oregon	Los Alamitos, Calif.	D7-'03	3/0
22	Irvin, Ken	CB	5-11	182	7/11/72	11	Memphis	Lindale, Ga.	UFA(NO)-'03	0*
14	Johnson, Brad	QB	6-5	226	9/13/68	14	Florida State	Black Mountain, N.C.	FA-'05	4/4*
97	Johnson, Spencer	DT	6-3	286	12/12/81	2	Auburn	Silas, Ala.	FA-'04	9/7
51	Johnstone, Lance	DE	6-4	250	6/11/73	10	Temple	Philadelphia, Pa.	FA-'01	16/1
31	Jones, Rushen	S	5-10	194	4/4/80	3	Vanderbilt	Memphis, Tenn.	FA-'03	5/0
40	Kleinsasser, Jim	TE	6-3	272	1/31/77	7	North Dakota	Carrington, N.D.	D2-'99	1/1
76	Liwienski, Chris	G	6-5	325	8/2/75	7	Indiana	Sterling Heights, Mich.	FA-'99	16/16
46	Loeffler, Cullen	LS	6-5	241	1/27/81	2	Texas	Ingram, Texas	FA-'04	16/0
90	Martin, Steve	DT	6-4	320	5/31/74	10	Missouri	Jefferson City, Mo.	UFA(Hous)-'04	12/0
74	McKinnie, Bryant	T	6-8	335	9/23/79	4	Miami	Woodbury, N.J.	D1-'02	16/16
30	Moore, Mewelde	RB	5-11	209	7/24/82	2	Tulane	Baton Rouge, La.	D4b-'04	10/3
52	Newman, Keith	LB	6-2	248	1/9/77	7	North Carolina	Tampa, Fla.	FA-'04	15/14
24	Offord, Willie	S	6-1	216	12/22/78	4	South Carolina	Palatka, Fla.	D3-'02	16/0
89	Owens, Richard	TE	6-4	273	11/4/80	2	Louisville	Middleburg, Fla.	FA-'04	7/2
87	Robinson, Marcus	WR	6-3	215	2/27/75	9	South Carolina	Fort Valley, Ga.	UFA(Balt)-'04	16/7
75	Rosenthal, Mike	T	6-7	318	6/10/77	7	Notre Dame	Mishawaka, Ind.	UFA(NYG)-'03	2/2
98	Scott, Darrion	DE	6-3	289	10/25/81	2	Ohio State	Charleston, W. Va.	D3-'04	12/0
42	Sharper, Darren	S	6-2	210	11/3/75	9	William & Mary	Richmond, Va.	FA-'05	15/13*
32	Smith, Onterrio	RB	5-10	214	12/8/80	3	Oregon	Sacramento, Calif.	D4-'03	11/6
57	Smith, Raonall	LB	6-2	241	10/22/78	4	Washington State	Gig Harbor, Wash.	D2-'02	7/3
27	Smoot, Fred	CB	5-11	178	4/17/79	5	Mississippi State	Jackson, Miss.	UFA(Wash)-'05	15/15*
59	Stewart, Quincy	LB	6-1	234	3/27/78	4	Louisiana Tech	Tyler, Texas	FA-'05	0*
89	Taylor, Travis	WR	6-1	210	3/30/78	6	Florida	Jacksonville, Fla.	UFA(Balt)-'05	11/9*
54	Thomas, Dontarrious	LB	6-2	241	9/2/80	2	Auburn	Perry, Ga.	D2-'04	16/5
95	Udeze, Kenechi	DE	6-3	281	3/5/83	2	Southern California	Los Angeles, Calif.	D1-'04	16/5
85	Wiggins, Jermaine	TE	6-2	260	1/18/75	6	Georgia	East Boston, Mass.	UFA(Car)-'04	14/13
91	Wiley, Grant	LB	6-0	229	3/11/81	2	West Virginia	Trappe, Pa.	FA-'04	0*
29	Williams, Brian	CB	5-11	198	7/2/79	4	North Carolina State	High Point, N.C.	D4a-'02	16/16
93	Williams, Kevin	DT	6-5	311	8/16/80	3	Oklahoma State	Fordyce, Ark.	D1-'03	16/16
20	Williams, Moe	RB	6-1	205	7/26/74	10	Kentucky	Columbus, Ga.	UFA(Balt)-'02	14/1
94	Williams, Pat	DT	6-3	317	10/24/72	9	Texas A&M	Monroe, La.	UFA(Buff)-'05	16/15*
26	Winfield, Antoine	CB	5-9	180	6/24/77	7	Ohio State	Akron, Ohio	UFA(Buff)-'04	14/12
60	Withrow, Cory	C	6-2	287	4/5/75	6	Washington State	Spokane, Wash.	FA-'99	12/5

* Angulo missed '04 season because of injury; Cowart played 9 games with N.Y. Jets in '04; Dorsch last active with Cincinnati in '02; Edinger played 16 games with Chicago; Harris played 14 games with Oakland; Herrera inactive for 7 games; Hill inactive for 16 games; Irvin missed '04 season because of injury; Johnson played 4 games with Tampa Bay; Sharper played 15 games with Green Bay; Smoot played 15 games with Washington; Stewart last active with N.Y. Jets in '03; Taylor played 11 games with Baltimore; Wiley missed '04 season because of injury; P. Williams played 15 games with Buffalo.

t- Vikings traded for Cowart (NYJ), Harris (Oak).

Traded—WR Randy Moss (13 games in '04) to Oakland.

Players lost through free agency (4): LB Chris Claiborne (StL; 12 games in '04), QB Gus Frerotte (Mia; 16), DT Chris Hovan (TB; 13), S Brian Russell (Cle; 16).

Also played with Vikings in '04—K Morten Andersen (16 games), C Billy Conaty (8), G Adam Haayer (6), DE Kenny Mixon (14), LB Mike Nattiel (16), RB Larry Ned (16), CB Rhett Nelson (4), CB Derek Ross (9), CB Terrance Shaw (15), DE Chuck Wiley (5), LB Max Yates (1).

2005 FIRST-YEAR ROSTER

Name	Pos.	Ht.	Wt.	Birthdate	College	Hometown	How Acq.
Bamiro, David	LB	6-2	220	7/7/83	Stony Brook	Central Islip, N.Y.	FA
Benoit, Sarth	LB	6-2	250	2/6/79	Southern Connecticut State	New City, N.Y.	FA
Bowenkamp, John	QB	6-5	227	3/1/81	North Dakota	Lakeville, Minn.	FA
Coleman, Eric	DT	6-5	300	8/6/82	Clemson	Charlottesville, Va.	FA
Cooper, Ira	LB	6-2	230	9/30/81	Nebraska	Omaha, Neb.	FA
Cottrell, T.J. (1)	TE	6-5	245	5/3/82	Buffalo State	Buffalo, N.Y.	FA
Edwards, Dovonte	CB	6-0	182	10/17/82	North Carolina State	Chapel Hill, N.C.	FA
Farwell, Heath	LB	6-0	235	12/31/81	San Diego State	Corona, Calif.	FA
Fason, Ciatrick	RB	6-0	207	10/29/82	Florida	Jacksonville, Fla.	D4
Fife, Jason (1)	QB	6-3	222	1/23/81	Oregon	Lake Elsinore, Calif.	FA
Fox, Dustin	S	5-11	190	10/8/82	Ohio State	Canton, Ohio	D3
Fulton, Skyler (1)	WR	6-0	200	6/17/82	Arizona State	Olympia, Wash.	FA
Gallishaw, Laroni	CB	6-0	190	4/4/81	Murray State	Lakeland, Fla.	FA
Harley, David	DT	6-1	330	6/23/82	Rutgers	Tallahassee, Fla.	FA
Hoag, Ryan (1)	WR	6-2	200	11/23/79	Gustavus Adolphus	Minneapolis, Minn.	FA
Hosack, Aaron (1)	WR	6-2	210	11/28/81	Minnesota	Chino, Calif.	FA
Hunter, Will (1)	S	5-10	190	3/24/79	Syracuse	Chester, Pa.	FA
Jahnke, Chris	T	6-5	310	12/4/81	Indiana	Louisville, Ky.	FA
James, Erasmus	DE	6-4	266	11/4/82	Wisconsin	Hollywood, Fla.	D1b
Johnson, Marcus	G	6-6	321	12/1/81	Mississippi	Coffeeville, Miss.	D2
Jones, Christopher	WR	6-3	203	7/17/82	Jackson State	Shuqualak, Miss.	FA
Melander, Rian	T	6-7	295	12/21/81	Minnesota	St. Paul, Minn.	FA
Mosley, C.J.	DT	6-2	314	8/6/83	Missouri	Waynesville, Mo.	D6
Nelson, Ben (1)	WR	6-2	185	8/21/79	St. Cloud State	Anoka, Minn.	FA
Newton, Brandon (1)	G	6-2	308	4/1/81	Hofstra	Lauderdale Lakes, Fla.	FA
Nichols, Jonathan	K	5-11	182	9/28/81	Mississippi	Greenwood, Miss.	FA
Obeng, William	T	6-6	307	4/14/83	San Jose State	Chicago, Ill.	FA
Pinderhughes, Brandon (1)	CB	6-0	204	8/21/82	Nebraska-Omaha	St. Paul, Minn.	FA
Ross, Matt	TE	6-6	244	1/23/83	Texas Lutheran	San Antonio, Texas	FA
Schmitt, Kyle	C	6-4	295	8/12/81	Maryland	Latrobe, Pa.	FA
Snell, Shannon (1)	G	6-2	310	4/27/82	Florida	Tampa, Fla.	FA
Wallace, Butchie (1)	RB	5-10	205	12/24/80	Marshall	Myrtle Beach, S.C.	FA
Ward, Adrian	CB	5-10	170	7/1/82	Texas-El Paso	Hayward, Calif.	D7
Williamson, Troy	WR	6-1	203	4/30/82	South Carolina	Aiken, S.C.	D1a

The term NFL Rookie is defined as a player who is in his first season of professional football and has not been on the roster of another professional football team for any regular-season or postseason games. A Rookie is designated by an "R" on NFL rosters. Players who have been active in another professional football league or players who have NFL experience, including either preseason training camp or being on an Active List or Inactive List, or on Reserve/Injured or Reserve/Physically Unable to Perform for fewer than six regular-season games, are termed NFL First-Year Players. An NFL First-Year Player is designated by a "1" on NFL rosters. Thereafter, a player is credited with an additional year of experience for each season in which he accumulates six games on the Active List or Inactive List, or on Reserve/Injured or Reserve/Physically Unable to Perform.

Log on to www.vikings.com for an up-to-date roster.

COACHING STAFF
Head Coach,
Mike Tice

Pro Career: Named the Vikings' sixth head coach on January 10, 2002. In 2004, led the team to first playoff berth and first postseason victory since 2000. Guided the team to a nine-game winning streak in 2002-03, tied for third-best in team history. Led the team to three consecutive wins to end the 2002 season and a 6-0 start in 2003. Tice has been associated with the team since 1992, playing tight end from 1992-93 and 1995, coaching the tight ends in 1996 and the offensive line from 1997-2001. Tice added the title of assistant head coach for the 2001 season and was made the interim head coach for the Vikings' last regular season game of the 2001 season against Baltimore. Tice is the first Vikings alumni player to hold the title of the franchise's head coach. In five seasons coaching the offensive line, Tice guided five different players—Matt Birk, Jeff Christy, Randall McDaniel, Todd Steussie, Korey Stringer—to 10 Pro Bowl appearances. In 1998, the offensive line paved the way for numerous NFL and Vikings records including a League record for points scored in a season (556) and set Vikings records for total yards (6,264) and fewest sacks allowed in a 16-game season (25). Career record: 24-27.
Background: Played quarterback at the University of Maryland from 1977-1980. Tice completed 71 of 140 passes for 928 yards with 5 touchdowns as a senior and 896 yards and 5 touchdowns as a junior. Over his 14-year NFL career, Tice caught 107 passes for 894 yards and 11 touchdowns and blocked for running backs that rushed for over 1,000 yards in a season five times. Tice played three seasons with the Vikings (1992-93, 1995), 10 years with the Seattle Seahawks (1981-88, 1990-91), and one season with the Washington Redskins (1989) and made 109 starts in 177 games played.
Personal: Born February 2, 1959 in Bayshore, N.Y. Attended Central Islip High School on Long Island. He and wife Diane have two children, Adrienne and Nathan.

ASSISTANT COACHES
Brian Baker, defensive line; born June 20, 1962, Baltimore. Linebacker Maryland 1980-83. No pro playing experience. College coach: Maryland 1984-85, Army 1986, Georgia Tech 1987-1995. Pro coach: San Diego Chargers 1996, Detroit Lions 1997-2000, joined Vikings in 2001.
Pete Bercich, linebackers; born December 23, 1971, Joliet, Ill. Linebacker Notre Dame 1990-93. Pro linebacker Minnesota Vikings 1994-2000. Pro coach: Joined Vikings in 2002.
Wes Chandler, wide receivers; born August 22, 1956, New Smyrna Beach, Fla. Wide receiver Florida 1974-77. Pro wide receiver New Orleans Saints 1978-1981, San Diego Chargers 1981-87, San Francisco 49ers 1988. College coach: Central Florida 1994-95. Pro coach: Orlando Thunder (NFLE) 1991-92, Rhein Fire (NFLE) 1995-97, Frankfurt Galaxy (NFLE) 1998, Berlin Thunder (NFLE) 1999 (head coach), Dallas Cowboys 2000-02, joined Vikings in 2005.
Ted Cottrell, defensive coordinator/asst. head coach; born June 13, 1947, Chester, Pa. Linebacker Delaware Valley College 1966-68. Pro linebacker Atlanta Falcons 1969-1970, Winnipeg Blue Bombers (CFL) 1971. College coach: Rutgers 1973-1980, 1983. Pro coach: Kansas City Chiefs 1981-82, New Jersey Generals (USFL) 1983-84, Buffalo Bills 1986-89, 1995-2000, Arizona Cardinals 1990-94, New York Jets 2001-03, joined Vikings in 2004.
Dean Dalton, running backs; born July 27, 1963, Platteville, Wis. Defensive back Air Force Academy 1981-82, Western Illinois 1983-84. No pro playing experience. College coach: Western Illinois 1984-85, Wisconsin 1986-87, Texas Southern 1988-89, Purdue 1990. Pro coach: Joined Vikings in 1999.
Mark Ellis, asst. strength and conditioning; born December 18, 1969, Littlefield, Texas. Defensive back Temple 1990-91. College coach: Lackawanna (Pa.) J.C. 1993, Navarro College 1994, Fort Scott (Kan.) C.C. 1995. Pro coach: Joined Vikings in 2004.
Randy Hanson, offensive assistant/asst. quarterbacks; born January 17, 1968, Sacramento, Calif. Quarterback Pacific 1990-92. No pro playing experience. College coach: Eastern Washington 1993-95, 1998-99, Washington 1996-97, Portland State 2000-02. Pro coach: Joined Vikings in 2003.
Chuck Knox Jr., coverage coordinator; born February 19, 1965, Englewood, N.J. Running back Arizona 1984-88. No pro playing experience. Pro coach: Los Angeles Rams 1993-94, Philadelphia Eagles 1995-98, Green Bay Packers 1999, joined Vikings in 2000.
Steve Loney, offensive coordinator/offensive line; born April 26, 1952, Marshalltown, Iowa. Offensive line Iowa State 1970-73. No pro playing experience. College coach: Missouri Western College 1975-76, Moorhead State 1979-1983, The Citadel 1984-86, Colorado State 1989-1992, Connecticut 1994, Iowa State 1995-97, 2000-01, Minnesota 1998-99. Pro coach: Phoenix Cardinals 1993, joined Vikings in 2002.
Rich Olson, quarterbacks; born July 7, 1948, Los Angeles. Quarterback/safety Washington State 1968-69. No pro playing experience. College coach: Washington State 1970, Fresno State 1971, 1984-1991, Southern California 1977, Southern Methodist 1978-1980, Arkansas 1981-83, Miami 1992-94. Pro coach: Seattle Seahawks 1995-98, Washington Redskins 1999-2000, Arizona Cardinals 2001-02, San Francisco 49ers 2004, joined Vikings in 2005.
Jim Panagos, asst. defensive line/asst. special teams; born March 23, 1971, Brooklyn, N.Y. Defensive line Maryland 1989-1992. No pro playing experience. College coach: Maryland 1993. Pro coach: Joined Vikings in 2002.
Kevin Ross, asst. secondary; born January 16, 1962, Camden, N.J. Defensive back Temple 1980-83. Pro defensive back Kansas City Chiefs 1984-1993, 1997, Atlanta Falcons 1994-95, San Diego Chargers 1996. Pro coach: Joined Vikings in 2003.
Kurtis Shultz, strength and conditioning; born March 10, 1972, Baltimore. Attended Maryland. No college or pro playing experience. College coach: Loyola (Md.) 1995-97, Maryland and Johns Hopkins 1999-2002. Pro coach: Cincinnati Bengals 2003, joined Vikings in 2004.
John Tice, tight ends/asst. offensive line; born June 22, 1960, Bayshore, N.Y. Tight end Maryland 1978-1982. Pro tight end New Orleans Saints 1983-1992. Pro coach: Joined Vikings in 1999.
Rusty Tillman, special teams coordinator; born February 27, 1946, Beloit, Wis. Tight end-linebacker-defensive end-punter Northern Arizona 1967-69. Pro linebacker Washington Redskins 1970-77. Pro coach: Seattle Seahawks 1979-1994, Tampa Bay Buccaneers 1995, Oakland Raiders 1996-97, Indianapolis Colts 1998, New York/New Jersey Hitmen (XFL) 2001 (head coach), joined Vikings in 2003.

National Football Conference
South Division
Team Colors: Old Gold, Black, and White
5800 Airline Drive
Metairie, Louisiana 70003
Telephone: (504) 733-0255

2005 SCHEDULE
PRESEASON
Aug. 12	**Seattle**	7:00
Aug. 18	at New England	8:00
Aug. 26	**Baltimore**	7:00
Sept. 1	at Oakland	6:00

REGULAR SEASON
Sept. 11	at Carolina	1:00
Sept. 18	**New York Giants**	12:00
Sept. 25	at Minnesota	12:00
Oct. 2	**Buffalo**	12:00
Oct. 9	at Green Bay	12:00
Oct. 16	**Atlanta**	12:00
Oct. 23	at St. Louis	12:00
Oct. 30	**Miami**	12:00
Nov. 6	**Chicago**	12:00
Nov. 13	Open Date	
Nov. 20	at New England	1:00
Nov. 27	at New York Jets	8:30
Dec. 4	**Tampa Bay**	12:00
Dec. 12	at Atlanta (Mon.)	9:00
Dec. 18	**Carolina**	12:00
Dec. 24	**Detroit** (Sat.)	12:00
Jan. 1	at Tampa Bay	1:00

Stadium: Louisiana Superdome
(opened in 1975)
• **Capacity:** 64,900
1500 Poydras Street
New Orleans, Louisiana 70112
Playing Surface: Sportexe Momentum
Training Camp: New Orleans Saints
Training Facility

LOUISIANA SUPERDOME

CLUB OFFICIALS
Owner: Tom Benson
Owner/Executive: Rita Benson LeBlanc
Executive Vice President/General
  Manager: Mickey Loomis
Executive Vice President/Administration:
  Arnold D. Fielkow
Executive Vice President/Chief Financial
  Officer: Dennis Lauscha
Director of Player Personnel:
  Rick Mueller
Senior Football Administrator: Russ Ball
Director of Operations: James Nagaoka
Director of College Scouting:
  Rick Reiprish
College Scouting Coordinator:
  Rick Thompson
Pro Scouts: Mike Baugh, Ryan Pace
Area Scouts: Bill Quinter,
  James Jefferson
Combine Scout: Barrett Wiley
Player Personnel Assistant:
  Terry Fontenot
Equipment Manager: Dan Simmons
Assistant Equipment Manager:
  Glennon (Silky) Powell
Equipment Assistants: Nolan Castex,
  Eddie Falgout
Head Athletic Trainer: Scottie B. Patton
Assistant Athletic Trainers:
  Duane Brooks, Kevin Mangum
Training Assistant: Reggie Stone
Video Director: Dave Desposito
Director of Player Development:
  Ricky Porter
Defensive Assistant/Special Projects:
  Joe Alley
Offensive Assistant/Asst. to the Head
  Coach: Josh Constant
Director of Media & Public Relations:
  Greg Bensel
Assistant Director of Media & Public
  Relations: Ricky Zeller
Media & Public Relations Manager:
  Justin Macione
Media & Public Relations Assistant:
  Nicholas Karl
Director of Security: Geoff Santini
Director of Photography:
  Michael C. Hebert
Director of Community Affairs/Director of
  Business Public Relations: Paul Corliss
Senior Director of Marketing & Business
  Development: Conrad Kowal
Director of Ticket Sales & Operation
  Services: Michael Stanfield
Director of New Media: Chris Pika
Director of Information Technologies:
  Jeff Huffman
Facilities Manager: Terry Ashburn

COACHING HISTORY
(235-344-5)
Records include postseason games
1967-70	Tom Fears*	13-34-2
1970-72	J.D. Roberts	7-25-3
1973-75	John North**	11-23-0
1975	Ernie Hefferle	1-7-0
1976-77	Hank Stram	7-21-0
1978-80	Dick Nolan***	15-29-0
1980	Dick Stanfel	1-3-0
1981-85	O.A. (Bum) Phillips****	27-42-0
1985	Wade Phillips	1-3-0
1986-96	Jim Mora#	93-78-0
1996	Rick Venturi	1-7-0
1997-99	Mike Ditka	15-33-0
2000-04	Jim Haslett	43-39-0

*Released after seven games in 1970
**Released after six games in 1975
***Released after 12 games in 1980
****Resigned after 12 games in 1985
#Resigned after eight games in 1996

ATTENDANCE
Home 497,045   Away 462,678
Total 959,723
Single-game home record,
  70,940 (9/2/79)
Single-season home record,
  548,728 (1992)

2005 DRAFT CHOICES
Round	Name	Pos.	College
1	Jammal Brown	T	Oklahoma
2	Josh Bullocks	DB	Nebraska
3	Alfred Fincher	LB	Connecticut
4	Chase Lyman	WR	California
5	Adrian McPherson	QB	Florida State
6	Jason Jefferson	DT	Wisconsin
7	Jimmy Verdon	DE	Arizona State

2004 TEAM RECORD

PRESEASON (2-2)

Date	Result	Opponent
8/13	W 23-13	N.Y. Jets
8/21	L 14-19	at Green Bay
8/27	W 17-13	at Miami
9/3	L 19-20	Chicago

REGULAR SEASON (8-8)

Date	Result	Opponent	Att.
9/12	L 7-21	Seattle	64,900
9/19	W 30-27	San Francisco	64,900
9/26	W 28-25	at St. Louis (OT)	65,856
10/3	L 10-34	at Arizona	28,109
10/10	L 17-20	Tampa Bay	64,900
10/17	L 31-38	Minnesota	64,900
10/24	W 31-26	at Oakland	45,337
11/7	L 17-43	at San Diego	59,662
11/14	W 27-20	Kansas City	64,900
11/21	L 13-34	Denver	64,900
11/28	L 21-24	at Atlanta	70,521
12/5	L 21-32	Carolina	58,878
12/12	W 27-13	at Dallas	64,056
12/19	W 21-17	at Tampa Bay	65,075
12/26	W 26-13	Atlanta	64,900
1/2	W 21-18	at Carolina	73,302

(OT) Overtime

SCORE BY PERIODS

Saints	29	132	83	101	3	—	348
Opponents	117	110	70	108	0	—	405

2004 TEAM STATISTICS

	Saints	Opp.
Total First Downs	291	343
Rushing	82	118
Passing	177	193
Penalty	32	32
3rd Down: Made/Att	70/210	80/210
3rd Down Pct.	33.3	38.1
4th Down: Made/Att	9/18	6/7
4th Down Pct.	50.0	85.7
Possession Avg.	28:18	31:42
Total Net Yards	5193	6141
Avg. Per Game	324.6	383.8
Total Plays	989	1067
Avg. Per Play	5.3	5.8
Net Yards Rushing	1606	2253
Avg. Per Game	100.4	140.8
Total Rushes	406	485
Net Yards Passing	3587	3888
Avg. Per Game	224.2	243.0
Sacked/Yards Lost	41/223	37/207
Gross Yards	3810	4095
Att./Completions	542/309	545/324
Completion Pct.	57.0	59.4
Had Intercepted	16	13
Punts/Average	85/43.6	71/40.8
Net Punting Avg.	85/39.0	71/34.5
Penalties/Yards	129/1141	119/965
Fumbles/Ball Lost	23/10	31/20
Touchdowns	40	44
Rushing	15	16
Passing	21	24
Returns	4	4

2004 INDIVIDUAL STATISTICS

PASSING	Att.	Comp.	Yds.	Pct.	TD	Int.	Tkld.	Rate
Brooks	542	309	3,810	57.0	21	16	41/223	79.5
Saints	542	309	3,810	57.0	21	16	41/223	79.5
Opponents	545	324	4,095	59.4	24	13	37/207	87.7

SCORING	TD R	TD P	TD Rt	PAT	FG	Saf	PTS
Carney	0	0	0	38/38	22/27	0	104
Horn	0	11	0	0/0	0/0	0	68
McAllister	9	0	0	0/0	0/0	0	54
Stallworth	0	5	0	0/0	0/0	0	30
Brooks	4	0	0	0/0	0/0	0	24
Stecker	2	0	1	0/0	0/0	0	18
B. Williams	0	2	0	0/0	0/0	0	12
Bockwoldt	0	0	1	0/0	0/0	0	6
Conwell	0	1	0	0/0	0/0	0	6
Hall	0	1	0	0/0	0/0	0	6
Lewis	0	0	1	0/0	0/0	0	6
Mitchell	0	0	1	0/0	0/0	0	6
Pathon	0	1	0	0/0	0/0	0	6
Bryant	0	0	0	0/0	0/0	1	2
Saints	15	21	4	38/38	22/27	1	348
Opponents	16	24	4	42/42	31/35	1	405

2-Pt. Conversions: Horn.
Saints 1-2, Opponents 2-2.

RUSHING	No.	Yds	Avg	LG	TD
McAllister	269	1,074	4.0	71	9
Stecker	58	244	4.2	42t	2
Brooks	58	173	3.0	15	4
McAfee	2	54	27.0	53	0
Stallworth	6	37	6.2	26	0
Carter	10	17	1.7	8	0
Karney	3	7	2.3	4	0
Saints	406	1,606	4.0	71	15
Opponents	485	2,253	4.6	60	16

RECEIVING	No.	Yds	Avg	LG	TD
Horn	94	1,399	14.9	57	11
Stallworth	58	767	13.2	45	5
Pathon	34	581	17.1	38	1
McAllister	34	228	6.7	20	0
B. Williams	33	362	11.0	22	2
Stecker	29	174	6.0	26	0
Conwell	10	102	10.2	28	1
Lewis	8	127	15.9	30	0
Karney	6	42	7.0	17	0
Gardner	1	23	23.0	23	0
Hall	1	4	4.0	4t	1
Brooks	1	1	1.0	1	0
Saints	309	3,810	12.3	57	21
Opponents	324	4,095	12.6	59	24

INTERCEPTIONS	No.	Yds	Avg	LG	TD
McKenzie	5	19	3.8	14	0
Ambrose	3	19	6.3	19	0
Brown	2	0	0.0	0	0
Jones	1	55	55.0	55	0
Ch. Grant	1	8	8.0	8	0
Ruff	1	0	0.0	0	0
Saints	13	101	7.8	55	0
Opponents	16	260	16.3	76	1

PUNTING	No.	Yds.	Avg.	In 20	LG
Berger	85	3,704	43.6	28	63
Saints	85	3,704	43.6	28	63
Opponents	71	2,896	40.8	17	60

PUNT RETURNS	Ret	FC	Yds	Avg	LG	TD
Lewis	34	11	382	11.2	53	0
Stallworth	6	1	6	1.0	4	0
Saints	40	12	388	9.7	53	0
Opponents	43	25	310	7.2	59t	1

KICKOFF RETURNS	No.	Yds	Avg	LG	TD
Lewis	51	1,215	23.8	96t	1
Stecker	18	469	26.1	98t	1
McAfee	8	137	17.1	26	0
Hall	3	20	6.7	8	0
Ruff	1	9	9.0	9	0
W. Smith	1	17	17.0	17	0
Whitehead	1	12	12.0	12	0
Saints	83	1,879	22.6	98t	2
Opponents	74	1,710	23.1	63	0

FIELD GOALS	1-19	20-29	30-39	40-49	50+
Carney	0/0	3/3	12/15	5/6	2/3
Saints	0/0	3/3	12/15	5/6	2/3
Opponents	0/0	10/10	9/10	8/10	4/5

SACKS	No.
Howard	11.0
Ch. Grant	10.5
W. Smith	7.5
Young	2.5
Bryant	2.0
Watson	2.0
Bockwoldt	1.0
Sullivan	0.5
Saints	37.0
Opponents	41.0

RECORD HOLDERS
INDIVIDUAL RECORDS—CAREER

Category	Name	Performance
Rushing (Yds.)	George Rogers, 1981-84	4,267
Passing (Yds.)	Archie Manning, 1971-1982	21,734
Passing (TDs)	Archie Manning, 1971-1982	115
Receiving (No.)	Eric Martin, 1985-1993	532
Receiving (Yds.)	Eric Martin, 1985-1993	7,854
Interceptions	Dave Waymer, 1980-89	37
Punting (Avg.)	Mark Royals, 1997-98	45.7
Punt Return (Avg.)	Mel Gray, 1986-88	13.4
Kickoff Return (Avg.)	Walter Roberts, 1967	26.3
Field Goals	Morten Andersen, 1982-1994	302
Touchdowns (Tot.)	Dalton Hilliard, 1986-1993	53
Points	Morten Andersen, 1982-1994	1,318

INDIVIDUAL RECORDS—SINGLE SEASON

Category	Name	Performance
Rushing (Yds.)	George Rogers, 1981	1,674
Passing (Yds.)	Jim Everett, 1995	3,970
Passing (TDs)	Aaron Brooks, 2002	27
Receiving (No.)	Joe Horn, 2000, 2004	94
Receiving (Yds.)	Joe Horn, 2004	1,399
Interceptions	Dave Whitsell, 1967	10
Punting (Avg.)	Mark Royals, 1997	45.9
Punt Return (Avg.)	Mel Gray, 1987	14.7
Kickoff Return (Avg.)	Don Shy, 1969	27.9
	Mel Gray, 1986	27.9
Field Goals	Morten Andersen, 1985	31
	John Carney, 2002	31
Touchdowns (Tot.)	Dalton Hilliard, 1989	18
Points	John Carney, 2002	130

INDIVIDUAL RECORDS—SINGLE GAME

Category	Name	Performance
Rushing (Yds.)	George Rogers, 9-4-83	206
Passing (Yds.)	Aaron Brooks, 12-3-00	441
Passing (TDs)	Billy Kilmer, 11-2-69	6
Receiving (No.)	Tony Galbreath, 9-10-78	14
Receiving (Yds.)	Wes Chandler, 9-2-79	205
Interceptions	Tommy Myers, 9-3-78	3
	Dave Waymer, 10-6-85	3
	Reggie Sutton, 10-18-87	3
	Gene Atkins, 12-22-91	3
	Sammy Knight, 9-9-01	3
Field Goals	Many times	5
	Last time by John Carney, 9-26-04	
Touchdowns (Tot.)	Joe Horn, 12-14-03	4
Points	Joe Horn, 12-14-03	24

2005 VETERAN ROSTER

No.	Name	Pos.	Ht.	Wt.	Birthdate	NFL Exp.	College	Hometown	How Acq.	'04 Games/ Starts
50	Allen, James	LB	6-2	245	11/11/79	4	Oregon State	Portland, Ore.	D3-'02	16/10
48	Banks, Mike	TE	6-4	261	11/5/79	3	Iowa State	Mason City, Iowa	FA-'05	0*
20	Bellamy, Jay	S	5-11	200	7/8/72	12	Rutgers	Aberdeen, N.J.	UFA(Sea)-'01	16/16
65	Bentley, LeCharles	G/C	6-2	313	11/7/79	4	Ohio State	Cleveland, Ohio	D2-'02	16/16
17	Berger, Mitch	P	6-4	228	6/24/72	11	Colorado	Karnloops, B.C., Canada	UFA(StL)-'03	16/0
57	Bockwoldt, Colby	LB	6-1	237	4/14/81	2	Brigham Young	Sunset, Utah	D7-'04	16/7
4	Bouman, Todd	QB	6-2	226	8/1/72	8	St. Cloud State	Ruthton, Minn.	T(Minn)-'03	16/0
2	Brooks, Aaron	QB	6-4	220	3/24/76	7	Virginia	Newport News, Va.	T(GB)-'00	16/16
35	Brown, Fakhir	CB	5-11	192	9/21/77	6	Grambling State	Mansfield, La.	FA-'02	16/10
92	Bryant, Tony	DE	6-6	282	9/3/76	6	Florida State	Marathon, Fla.	FA-'03	16/0
3	Carney, John	K	5-11	185	4/20/64	16	Notre Dame	West Palm Beach, Fla.	UFA(SD)-'01	16/0
85	Conwell, Ernie	TE	6-2	255	8/17/72	10	Washington	Kent, Wash.	UFA(StL)-'03	16/10
21	Craft, Jason	CB	5-10	187	2/13/76	7	Colorado State	Denver, Colo.	T(Jax)-'04	14/0
54	Fisher, Levar	LB	6-2	240	7/2/79	3	North Carolina State	Beaufort, N.C.	FA-'05	0*
71	Folau, Spencer	T	6-5	310	4/5/73	9	Idaho	Redwood City, Calif.	UFA(Mia)-'02	16/3
72	Gandy, Wayne	T	6-4	315	2/10/71	12	Auburn	Haines City, Fla.	UFA(Pitt)-'03	16/16
88	Gardner, Talman	WR	6-1	210	3/10/80	3	Florida State	New Orleans, La.	D7-'03	11/1
37	Gleason, Steve	S	5-11	212	3/19/77	5	Washington State	Gonzaga, Calif.	FA-'01	15/0
94	Grant, Charles	DE	6-3	290	9/3/78	4	Georgia	Colquitt, Ga.	D1b-'02	16/16
58	Grant, Cie	LB	6-0	235	11/27/79	3	Ohio State	New Philadelphia, Ohio	D3-'03	0*
95	Green, Howard	DT	6-2	320	1/12/79	3	Louisiana State	Donaldsonville, La.	FA-'03	14/12
89	Hall, Lamont	TE	6-4	260	11/16/74	6	Clemson	Clover, S.C.	FA-'04	16/2
19	Henderson, Devery	WR	5-11	200	3/26/82	2	Louisiana State	Opelousas, La.	D2a-'04	1/0
81	Hilton, Zachary	TE	6-8	268	7/2/80	3	North Carolina	Silver Springs, Md.	FA-'03	0*
52	Hodge, Sedrick	LB	6-4	246	9/13/78	5	North Carolina	Atlanta, Ga.	D3a-'01	9/6
61	Holland, Montrae	G	6-2	322	5/21/80	3	Florida State	Ore City, Texas	D4-'03	13/13
87	Horn, Joe	WR	6-1	213	1/16/72	10	Itawamba (MS) J.C.	Fayetteville, N.C.	UFA(KC)-'00	16/16
47	Houser, Kevin	LS	6-2	252	8/23/77	6	Ohio State	Westlake, Ohio	D7-'00	16/0
93	Howard, Darren	DE	6-3	275	11/19/76	6	Kansas State	St. Petersburg, Fla.	D2-'00	13/12
41	Isom, Jasen	FB	6-0	240	1/7/77	2	Western Illinois	Wheatley Heights, N.Y.	FA-'05	5/1*
64	Jacox, Kendyl	G	6-2	325	6/10/75	8	Kansas State	Dallas, Texas	UFA(SD)-'02	13/13
44	Karney, Mike	FB	5-11	258	7/6/81	2	Arizona State	Kent, Wash.	D5b-'04	16/8
53	Knight, Roger	LB	6-0	245	10/11/78	4	Wisconsin	Brooklyn, N.Y.	FA-'01	15/0
69	Ledford, Dwayne	G	6-4	300	11/2/76	3	East Carolina	Morgantown, N.C.	FA-'05	0*
77	Leisle, Rodney	DT	6-3	315	2/5/81	2	UCLA	Bakersfield, Calif.	D5a-'04	2/0
84	Lewis, Michael	WR	5-8	173	11/14/71	5	No College	New Orleans, La.	FA-'01	14/1
75	Mayberry, Jermane	G	6-4	325	8/29/73	10	Texas A&M-Kingsville	Floresville, Texas	UFA(Phil)-'05	12/12*
25	McAfee, Fred	RB	5-10	193	6/20/68	14	Mississippi College	Philadelphia, Miss.	FA-'04	11/0
26	McAllister, Deuce	RB	6-1	232	12/27/78	5	Mississippi	Lena, Miss.	D1-'01	14/14
34 t-	McKenzie, Mike	CB	6-0	194	4/26/76	7	Memphis	Miami, Fla.	T(GB)-'04	11/10*
80	Meier, Shad	TE	6-4	255	6/7/78	5	Kansas State	Pittsburg, Kan.	UFA(Tenn)-'05	14/6*
51	Melton, Terrence	LB	6-1	235	1/1/77	2	Rice	Houston, Texas	FA-'04	3/0
40	Mitchell, Mel	S	6-1	222	2/10/79	4	Western Kentucky	Rockledge, Fla	D5-'02	15/0
67	Nesbit, Jamar	G	6-4	328	12/17/76	7	South Carolina	Summersville, S.C.	UFA(Jax)-'04	16/4
59	Rodgers, Derrick	LB	6-0	230	10/14/71	9	Arizona State	New Orleans, La.	T(Mia)-'03	8/8
56	Ruff, Orlando	LB	6-3	253	9/28/76	7	Furman	Winnsboro, S.C.	UFA(SD)-'03	14/8
32	Smith, Antowain	RB	6-2	232	3/14/72	9	Houston	Miami, Fla.	UFA(Tenn)-'05	13/4*
24	Smith, Dwight	S	5-10	201	8/13/78	5	Akron	Detroit, Mich.	UFA(TB)-'05	16/16*
91	Smith, Will	DE	6-3	282	7/4/81	2	Ohio State	Utica, N.Y.	D1-'04	16/4
83	Stallworth, Donte'	WR	6-0	196	11/10/80	4	Tennessee	Sacramento, Calif.	D1a-'02	16/9
27	Stecker, Aaron	RB	5-10	213	11/13/75	6	Western Illinois	Green Bay, Wis.	UFA(TB)-'04	16/3
78	Stinchcomb, Jon	T	6-5	315	8/27/79	3	Georgia	Lilburn, Ga.	D2-'03	4/0
97	Sullivan, Johnathan	DT	6-3	315	1/21/81	3	Georgia	Griffin, Ga.	D1-'03	7/4
22	Thomas, Fred	CB	5-9	185	9/11/73	10	Tennessee-Martin	Bruce, Miss.	UFA(Sea)-'00	15/7
55	Watson, Courtney	LB	6-1	246	9/18/80	2	Notre Dame	Sarasota, Fla.	D2b-'04	12/8
98	Whitehead, Willie	DE	6-3	300	1/26/73	7	Auburn	Tuskegee, Ala.	FA-'99	8/0
82	Williams, Boo	TE	6-4	265	6/22/79	5	Arkansas	Tallahassee, Fla.	FA-'01	16/8
28	Williams, Jimmy	CB	5-11	190	3/10/79	5	Vanderbilt	Baton Rouge, La.	UFA(SF)-'05	12/6*
6	Williams, Rodney	P	6-1	198	4/25/77	2	Georgia Tech	Decatur, Ga.	FA-'05	0*
66	Young, Brian	DT	6-2	298	7/8/77	6	Texas-El Paso	El Paso, Texas	UFA(StL)-'04	15/15

* Banks last active with Arizona in '03; Fisher inactive for 1 game with Arizona in '04; Cie Grant missed '04 season because of injury; Hilton inactive for 6 games; Isom played 5 games with San Francisco; Ledford did not play in 2 games with San Francisco; Mayberry played 12 games with Philadelphia; McKenzie played 1 game with Green Bay and 10 with New Orleans; Meier played 14 games with Tennessee; A. Smith played 13 games with Tennessee; D. Smith played 16 games with Tampa Bay; J. Williams played 12 games with San Francisco; R. Williams last active with N.Y. Giants in '01.

t- Saints traded for McKenzie (GB).

Traded—QB J.T. O'Sullivan (0 games in '04) to Green Bay.

Players lost through free agency (2): T Victor Riley (Hou; 16 games in '04), DT Kenny Smith (Oak; 0).

Also played with Saints in '04—CB Ashley Ambrose (9 games), RB Ki-Jana Carter (2), S Deveron Harper (5), S Tebucky Jones (16), CB Monty Montgomery (5), WR Jerome Pathon (15), LB Darrin Smith (3), DT Shaun Smith (5).

2005 FIRST-YEAR ROSTER

Name	Pos.	Ht.	Wt.	Birthdate	College	Hometown	How Acq.
Anderson, Thyron (1)	WR	6-4	202	8/28/79	Grambling State	Jonesboro, Ga.	FA
Archibald, Ben (1)	T	6-3	320	8/26/78	Brigham Young	Tacoma, Wash.	FA
Beveridge, Scott	WR	5-11	189	9/3/81	Peru State	Reno, Nev.	FA
Booker, Fred (1)	CB	5-9	199	6/4/78	Louisiana State	Independence, La.	FA
Brown, Jammal	T	6-6	313	3/30/81	Oklahoma	Lawton, Okla.	D1
Bullocks, Josh	S	6-1	207	2/28/83	Nebraska	Chattanooga, Tenn.	D2
Clark, Matthew	CB	5-8	180	1/18/83	UCLA	Pacoima, Calif.	FA
Davis, Tramissian	WR	6-0	195	11/24/80	Louisiana Tech	Monroe, La.	FA
Ellick, Dwight	CB	5-10	182	9/30/82	Notre Dame	Tampa, Fla.	FA
Fincher, Alfred	LB	6-1	238	8/15/83	Connecticut	Norwood, Mass.	D3
Finlen, Chris (1)	QB	6-3	200	5/19/79	Northern Illinois	Roscoe, Ill.	FA
Fiske, Nate (1)	K	5-9	195	8/11/81	UCLA	Anaheim, Calif.	FA
Garrison, Jeremiah (1)	LB	6-1	233	8/1/82	South Carolina	Belton, S.C.	FA
Hafford, Brent (1)	S	6-0	190	9/20/81	Stephen F. Austin	Jasper, Texas	FA
Henry, Keron	WR	6-1	218	8/20/82	Connecticut	Brooklyn, N.Y.	FA
Hoffmann, Augie (1)	G	6-2	315	2/23/81	Boston College	Park Ridge, N.J.	FA
Jefferson, Jason	DT	6-1	310	12/20/81	Wisconsin	Chicago, Ill.	D6
Joseph, Keith	RB	6-2	249	12/9/81	Texas A&M	Houston, Texas	FA
Kingsbury, Kliff (1)	QB	6-4	210	8/9/79	Texas Tech	New Braunfels, Texas	FA
Ladouceur, L.P.	LS	6-4	257	3/13/81	California	Montreal, Quebec, Canada	FA
Lyman, Chase	WR	6-4	210	9/4/82	California	Los Altos Hills, Calif.	D4
McPherson, Adrian	QB	6-3	218	5/8/83	Florida State	Bradenton, Fla.	D5
Ndukwe, Ikechuku	G	6-3	330	7/17/82	Northwestern	Powell, Ohio	FA
Poli-Dixon, Brian (1)	WR	6-5	218	4/21/79	UCLA	Tucson, Ariz.	FA
Rabe, Russel	LB	6-2	228	6/21/82	Minnesota-Duluth	Lake Holcombe, Wis.	FA
Rohloff, Cabel	LB	6-4	250	10/22/80	Northern Colorado	Bailey, Colo.	FA
Schurman, Nate (1)	FB	6-2	247	11/8/81	Southwest Missouri State	St. Joseph, Mo.	FA
Setterstrom, Chad (1)	G	6-3	309	6/13/80	Northern Iowa	Northfield, Minn.	FA
Steitz, Nick	G	6-3	312	8/18/82	Oregon	Los Banos, Calif.	FA
Vance, Chris (1)	WR	6-2	190	9/13/80	Ohio State	Fort Myers, Fla.	FA
Verdon, Jimmy	DE	6-3	280	11/4/81	Arizona State	Ponoma, Calif.	D7

The term NFL Rookie is defined as a player who is in his first season of professional football and has not been on the roster of another professional football team for any regular-season or postseason games. A Rookie is designated by an "R" on NFL rosters. Players who have been active in another professional football league or players who have NFL experience, including either preseason training camp or being on an Active List or Inactive List, or on Reserve/Injured or Reserve/Physically Unable to Perform for fewer than six regular-season games, are termed NFL First-Year Players. An NFL First-Year Player is designated by a "1" on NFL rosters. Thereafter, a player is credited with an additional year of experience for each season in which he accumulates six games on the Active List or Inactive List, or on Reserve/Injured or Reserve/Physically Unable to Perform.

Log on to www.neworleanssaints.com for an up-to-date roster.

COACHING STAFF
Head Coach,
Jim Haslett
Pro Career: Named the thirteenth head coach in Saints history on February 3, 2000. Owns second-best winning percentage (.524) in club history and in 2000 earned NFL coach of the year honors, won a division title, and led Saints to their first-ever playoff victory. In 2004, guided the Saints to four consecutive victories to conclude the season, keeping the club in playoff contention into the final weekend. Joined the Saints after three-year stint as defensive coordinator of the Pittsburgh Steelers (1997-99). Previously coached with the Saints (1995-96), Los Angeles Raiders (1993-94), and NFL Europe's Sacramento Surge (1991-92). Career record: 43-39.
Background: Four-time defensive end All-America at Indiana University (Penn.) from 1975-78, and was inducted into College Football Hall of Fame in 2001. Second-round pick of the Buffalo Bills and was voted as *Associated Press* defensive rookie of the year (1979) and as an All-Pro in 1981. Played nine NFL seasons (Buffalo 1979-1986, N.Y. Jets 1987). Began his coaching career at the University of Buffalo (1988-1990).
Personal: Born December 9, 1955 in Pittsburgh. He and his wife Beth, have three children—Kelsey, Elizabeth, and Chase.

ASSISTANT COACHES
Adam Bailey, asst. strength and conditioning; born March 30, 1976, Tyler, Texas. Attended University of Louisville. No college or pro playing experience. College coach: Missouri 2002-2003. Pro coach: New Orleans VooDoo (AFL) 2004-2005, joined Saints in 2005.
Chip Beake, offensive assistant/quality control; born May 27, 1969, Kansas City, Mo. Quarterback South Carolina 1990-1992. No pro playing experience. College coach: Kentucky 1993-94, MacPherson College (Kan.) 1998, Colorado School of Mines 1999. Pro coach: Barcelona Dragons (NFLE) 1995-2000, joined Saints in 2000.
Greg Brown, defensive assistant/cornerbacks; born October 10, 1957, Denver. Defensive back Glendale (Ariz.) C.C. 1976-77, Texas-El Paso 1978-79. No pro playing experience. College coach: Wyoming 1987-88, Purdue 1989-1990, Colorado 1991-93. Pro coach: Tampa Bay Buccaneers 1984-86, Atlanta Falcons 1994, San Diego Chargers 1995-96, Tennessee Oilers 1997-98, San Francisco 49ers 1999, Atlanta Falcons 2000-01, joined Saints in 2002.
Al Everest, special teams coordinator; born August 22, 1950, Santa Barbara, Calif. Safety Southern Methodist 1970-71. No pro playing experience. College coach: Southern Methodist 1972, North Texas State 1973-74, Cameron (Okla.) 1974-

75, U.S. International 1981-87. Pro coach: Arkansas Miners (PSFL) 1991-92, Birmingham Barracudas (CFL) 1995, Arizona Cardinals 1996-99, joined Saints in 2000.
Rock Gullickson, strength and conditioning; born April 11, 1955, Moorhead, Minn. Guard Moorhead (Minn.) State 1973-76. No pro playing experience. College coach: Moorhead State 1978, Mayville (N.D.) State 1979-1980, South Dakota State 1981, Montana State 1982-89, Rutgers 1990-92, Texas 1993-97, Louisville 1998-99. Pro coach: Joined Saints in 2000.
John (Jack) Henry, associate head coach/running game coordinator; born March 14, 1946, Wilmerding, Pa. Linebacker Penn State 1964-65, guard Indiana (Pa.) 1967-68. No pro playing experience. College coach: West Virginia 1970, 1978-79, Edinboro 1973, Louisville 1974, Millersville 1975-76, Southern Illinois 1977, Appalachian State 1980, Wake Forest 1981-85, Indiana (Pa.) 1986-89, Pittsburgh 1993-95. Pro coach: Pittsburgh Steelers 1990-91, San Diego Chargers 1996, Detroit Lions 1997-99, joined Saints in 2000.
Ty Knott, defensive assistant/quality control; born December 9, 1965, Los Angeles, Defensive back Oregon Tech 1988-89. No pro playing experience. College coach: Whittier College 1994-95, Indiana University (Pa.) 1997-99, Mt. San Antonio (Calif.) J.C. 2000, Greenville 2001. Pro coach: Jacksonville Jaguars 2002, joined Saints in 2003.
Winston Moss, linebackers; born December 24, 1965, Miami. Linebacker Miami 1983-86. Pro linebacker Tampa Bay Buccaneers 1987-1990, Los Angeles Raiders 1991-94, Seattle Seahawks 1995-97. Pro coach: Seattle Seahawks 1998, joined Saints in 2000.
Bob Palcic, tight ends; born July 2, 1948, Gownada, N.Y. Linebacker Dayton 1968-1970. No pro playing experience. College coach: Dayton 1974-75, Ball State 1976-77, Wisconsin 1978-1981, Arizona 1984-85, Ohio State 1986-1991, Southern California 1992, UCLA 1993. Pro coach: Atlanta Falcons 1994-96, Detroit Lions 1997-98, Cleveland Browns 1999, joined Saints in 2000.
John Pease, defensive line; born October 14, 1943, Pittsburgh. Wingback Utah 1963-64. No pro playing experience. College coach: Fullerton (Calif.) J.C. 1970-73, Long Beach State 1974-76, Utah 1977, Washington 1978-1983. Pro coach: Philadelphia/Baltimore Stars (USFL) 1983-85, New Orleans Saints 1986-94, Jacksonville Jaguars 1995-2002, re-joined Saints in 2004.
Jim Pyne, asst. offensive line; born November 23, 1971, Milford, Mass. Center Virginia Tech 1990-93. Pro center/guard Tampa Bay Buccaneers 1994-97, Detroit Lions 1998, Cleveland Browns

1999-2000, Philadelphia Eagles 2001. Pro coach: Tampa Bay Buccaneers 2003-2004, joined Saints in 2005.
Jimmy Robinson, wide receivers; born January 3, 1953, Atlanta. Wide receiver Georgia Tech 1972-74. Pro wide receiver Atlanta Falcons 1975, New York Giants 1976-79, San Francisco 49ers 1980, Denver Broncos 1981. College coach: Georgia Tech 1986-89. Pro coach: Memphis Showboats (USFL) 1984-85, Atlanta Falcons 1990-93, Indianapolis Colts 1994-97, New York Giants 1998-2003, joined Saints in 2004.
Willy Robinson, senior defensive assistant/secondary; born February 10, 1956, Ft. Carson, Colo. Defensive back Fresno State 1976-77. College coach: Fresno State 1978, 1980-1993, San Jose State 1979, Miami 1994, Oregon State 1999. Pro coach: Seattle Seahawks 1995-98, Pittsburgh Steelers 2000-03, San Francisco 49ers 2004, joined Saints in 2005.
Johnny Roland, running backs; born May 21, 1943, Corpus Christi, Texas. Running back Missouri 1961-65. Pro running back St. Louis Cardinals 1966-1972, New York Giants 1973. College coach: Notre Dame 1975. Pro coach: Green Bay Packers 1974, 2004, Philadelphia Eagles 1976-78, Chicago Bears 1983-1992, New York Jets 1993-94, St. Louis Rams 1995-96, Arizona Cardinals 1997-2003, joined Saints 2005.
Turk Schonert, quarterbacks; born January 15, 1957, Torrance, Calif. Quarterback Stanford 1975-79. Pro quarterback Cincinnati Bengals 1980-85, Atlanta Falcons 1986, Cincinnati Bengals 1987-89. Pro coach: Tampa Bay Buccaneers 1992-95, Buffalo Bills 2000, Carolina Panthers 2001, New York Giants 2003, joined Saints 2005.
Mike Sheppard, offensive coordinator; born October 29, 1951, Tulsa, Okla. Wide receiver Cal Lutheran 1969-1972. No pro playing experience. College coach: Cal Lutheran 1974-76, Brigham Young 1977-78, U.S. International 1979, Idaho State 1980-81, Long Beach State 1982, 1984-86, Kansas 1983, New Mexico 1987-1991, California 1992. Pro coach: Cleveland Browns 1993-95, Baltimore Ravens 1996, San Diego Chargers 1997-98, Seattle Seahawks 1999-2000, Buffalo Bills 2001, joined Saints in 2002.
Rick Venturi, defensive coordinator; born February 23, 1946, Taylorville, Ill. Quarterback/defensive back Northwestern 1965-67. No pro playing experience. College coach: Northwestern 1968-1972, 1978-1980 (head coach 1978-1980), Purdue 1973-76, Illinois 1977. Pro coach: Hamilton Tiger-Cats (CFL) 1981, Indianapolis Colts 1982-1993 (interim head coach for final 11 games of 1991), Cleveland Browns 1994-95, joined Saints in 1996 (interim head coach for final eight games of 1996).

National Football Conference
East Division
Team Colors: Blue, Red, and White
Giants Stadium
East Rutherford, New Jersey 07073
Telephone: (201) 935-8111

2005 SCHEDULE
PRESEASON
Aug. 13	at Cleveland	8:00
Aug. 20	**Carolina**	8:00
Aug. 26	**New York Jets**	8:00
Sept. 1	at New England	8:00

REGULAR SEASON
Sept. 11	**Arizona**	4:15
Sept. 18	at New Orleans	12:00
Sept. 25	at San Diego	5:30
Oct. 2	**St. Louis**	1:00
Oct. 9	Open Date	
Oct. 16	at Dallas	12:00
Oct. 23	**Denver**	4:15
Oct. 30	**Washington**	1:00
Nov. 6	at San Francisco	1:05
Nov. 13	**Minnesota**	1:00
Nov. 20	**Philadelphia**	1:00
Nov. 27	at Seattle	1:15
Dec. 4	**Dallas**	1:00
Dec. 11	at Philadelphia	4:05
Dec. 17	**Kansas City** (Sat.)	5:00
Dec. 24	at Washington (Sat.)	1:00
Dec. 31	at Oakland (Sat.)	5:00

Stadium: Giants Stadium (opened in 1976)
  •**Capacity:** 80,242
  East Rutherford, New Jersey
  07073
Playing Surface: FieldTurf
Training Camp: University at Albany
  1400 Washington Avenue
  Albany, New York 12222

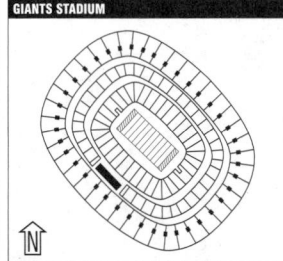

GIANTS STADIUM

CLUB OFFICIALS
President/Co-CEO: Wellington T. Mara
Chairman/Co-CEO: Preston Robert Tisch
Executive Vice President and Chief
  Operating Officer/General Counsel:
  John K. Mara, Esq.
Treasurer: Jonathan Tisch
Senior Vice President-General Manager:
  Ernie Accorsi
Vice President-Player Evalutions:
  Chris Mara
Vice President-Chief Financial Officer:
  Christine Procops
Vice President-Marketing: Rusty Hawley
Vice President-Medical Services:
  Ronnie Barnes
Vice-President-Communications:
  Pat Hanlon
Assistant General Manager:
  Kevin Abrams
Director of Player Personnel: Jerry Reese
Director of Pro Player Personnel:
  David Gettleman
Assistant Director of Pro Player
  Personnel: Ken Sternfeld
Director of College Scouting: Jerry Shay
Director of Research and Development:
  Raymond J. Walsh, Jr.
Director of Player Development:
  Charles Way
Director of Marketing Partnerships:
  Glenn Todd
Pro Personnel Assistants: Geoff Mazza,
  Tom Polifroni
Director of Promotions: Frank Mara
Ticket Manager: John Gorman
Director of Administration: Jim Phelan
Controller: Steven Hamrahi
Director of Community Relations:
  Allison Stangeby
Director of Creative Services:
  Doug Murphy
Director of Public Relations:
  Peter John-Baptiste
Assistant Director of Communications:
  Avis Roper
Head Athletic Trainer: Ronnie Barnes
Assistant Athletic Trainers: John
  Johnson, Steve Kennelly,
  Byron Hansen
Equipment Manager: Ed Wagner, Jr.
Assistant Equipment Managers:
  Joseph Skiba, Ed Skiba, Tim Slaman
Video Director: Dave Maltese
Assistant Video Directors: Carmen
  Pizzano, Ed Triggs
Community Relations Coordinator:
  Ethan Medley
Broadcast Production Manager:
  Stephen Venditti
Director of Information Technology:
  Jon Berger
Director of Marketing Services & Youth
  Partnerships: Beth Roche

COACHING HISTORY
(593-508-33)
Records include postseason games
1925	Bob Folwell	8-4-0
1926	Joe Alexander	8-4-1
1927-28	Earl Potteiger	15-8-3
1929-1930	LeRoy Andrews*	24-5-1
1930	Benny Friedman-Steve Owen	2-0-0
1931-1953	Steve Owen	153-108-17
1954-1960	Jim Lee Howell	55-29-4
1961-68	Allie Sherman	57-54-4
1969-1973	Alex Webster	29-40-1
1974-76	Bill Arnsparger**	7-28-0
1976-78	John McVay	14-23-0
1979-1982	Ray Perkins	24-35-0
1983-1990	Bill Parcells	85-52-1
1991-92	Ray Handley	14-18-0
1993-96	Dan Reeves	32-34-0
1997-2003	Jim Fassel	60-56-1
2004	Tom Coughlin	6-10-0

  *Released after 15 games in 1930
  **Released after seven games in 1976

ATTENDANCE
Home 629,874   Away 522,143
Total 1,152,017
Single-game home record,
  78,907 (9/15/03)
Single-season home record,
  629,874 (2004)

2005 DRAFT CHOICES
Round	Name	Pos.	College
2	Corey Webster	DB	Louisiana State
3	Justin Tuck	DE	Notre Dame
4	Brandon Jacobs	RB	Southern Illinois
6	Eric Moore	DE	Florida State

2004 TEAM RECORD
PRESEASON (1-3)

Date	Result	Opponent
8/13	W 34-24	Kansas City
8/19	L 20-27	at Carolina
8/27	L 10-17	at N.Y. Jets
9/2	L 17-27	Baltimore

REGULAR SEASON (6-10)

Date	Result	Opponent	Att.
9/12	L 17-31	at Philadelphia	67,532
9/19	W 20-14	Washington	78,767
9/26	W 27-10	Cleveland	78,521
10/3	W 14-7	at Green Bay	70,623
10/10	W 26-10	at Dallas	64,018
10/24	L 13-28	Detroit	78,841
10/31	W 34-13	at Minnesota	64,012
11/7	L 21-28	Chicago	78,786
11/14	L 14-17	at Arizona	42,297
11/21	L 10-14	Atlanta	78,793
11/28	L 6-27	Philadelphia	78,830
12/5	L 7-31	at Washington	87,872
12/12	L 14-37	at Baltimore	69,856
12/18	L 30-33	Pittsburgh	78,836
12/26	L 22-23	at Cincinnati	64,606
1/2	W 28-24	Dallas	78,500

SCORE BY PERIODS

Giants	72	79	55	97	0	—	303
Opponents	72	114	71	90	0	—	347

2004 TEAM STATISTICS

	Giants	Opp.
Total First Downs	281	310
Rushing	105	112
Passing	143	170
Penalty	33	28
3rd Down: Made/Att	56/190	87/208
3rd Down Pct.	29.5	41.8
4th Down: Made/Att	4/19	6/14
4th Down Pct.	21.1	42.9
Possession Avg.	28:52	31:08
Total Net Yards	4722	5187
Avg. Per Game	295.1	324.2
Total Plays	951	1005
Avg. Per Play	5.0	5.2
Net Yards Rushing	1904	2157
Avg. Per Game	119.0	134.8
Total Rushes	424	498
Net Yards Passing	2818	3030
Avg. Per Game	176.1	189.4
Sacked/Yards Lost	52/279	40/250
Gross Yards	3097	3280
Att./Completions	475/269	467/292
Completion Pct.	56.6	62.5
Had Intercepted	13	14
Punts/Average	77/40.1	77/38.9
Net Punting Avg.	77/34.4	77/33.8
Penalties/Yards	118/977	120/1007
Fumbles/Ball Lost	29/11	27/14
Touchdowns	34	41
Rushing	18	13
Passing	12	28
Returns	4	0

2004 INDIVIDUAL STATISTICS

PASSING

	Att.	Comp.	Yds.	Pct.	TD	Int.	Tkld.	Rate
Warner	277	174	2,054	62.8	6	4	39/196	86.5
Manning	197	95	1,043	48.2	6	9	13/83	55.4
Feagles	1	0	0	0.0	0	0	0/0	39.6
Giants	475	269	3,097	56.6	12	13	52/279	73.5
Opponents	467	292	3,280	62.5	28	14	40/250	90.9

SCORING

	TD R	TD P	TD Rt	PAT	FG	Saf	PTS
Christie	0	0	0	33/33	22/28	0	99
Barber	13	2	0	0/0	0/0	0	90
Shockey	0	6	0	0/0	0/0	0	36
Cloud	3	0	0	0/0	0/0	0	18
Carter	0	1	0	0/0	0/0	0	6
Dayne	1	0	0	0/0	0/0	0	6
Green	0	0	1	0/0	0/0	0	6
Ponder	0	0	1	0/0	0/0	0	6
Rivers	0	1	0	0/0	0/0	0	6
Shiancoe	0	1	0	0/0	0/0	0	6
Tyree	0	1	0	0/0	0/0	0	6
Umenyiora	0	0	1	0/0	0/0	0	6
Ward	0	0	1	0/0	0/0	0	6
Warner	0	0	0	0/0	0/0	0	0
Giants	18	12	4	33/33	22/28	0	303
Opponents	13	28	0	37/37	20/25	0	347

2-Pt. Conversions: None.
Giants 0-1, Opponents 2-4.

RUSHING

	No.	Yds	Avg	LG	TD
Barber	322	1,518	4.7	72t	13
Dayne	52	179	3.4	15	1
Cloud	21	90	4.3	26	3
Manning	6	35	5.8	15	0
I. Hilliard	3	34	11.3	17	0
Warner	13	30	2.3	13	1
Carter	2	23	11.5	15	0
Finn	3	7	2.3	5	0
Ponder	1	-4	-4.0	-4	0
Taylor	1	-8	-8.0	-8	0
Giants	424	1,904	4.5	72t	18
Opponents	498	2,157	4.3	50	13

RECEIVING

	No.	Yds	Avg	LG	TD
Shockey	61	666	10.9	38	6
Barber	52	578	11.1	62t	2
Toomer	51	747	14.6	48	0
I. Hilliard	49	437	8.9	43	0
Finn	15	112	7.5	15	0
Carter	12	182	15.2	38t	1
Tyree	10	155	15.5	49	1
Taylor	6	146	24.3	52	0
Rivers	5	36	7.2	13	1
Shiancoe	5	25	5.0	9	1
Dayne	1	7	7.0	7	0
Cloud	1	3	3.0	3	0
Ponder	1	3	3.0	3	0
Giants	269	3,097	11.5	62t	12
Opponents	292	3,280	11.2	53	28

INTERCEPTIONS

	No.	Yds	Avg	LG	TD
Wilson	3	39	13.0	39	0
Alexander	3	3	1.0	2	0
F. Walker	2	20	10.0	10	0
Peterson	2	9	4.5	9	0
Robbins	1	13	13.0	13	0
Burns	1	12	12.0	12	0
W. Allen	1	11	11.0	11	0
Cousin	1	6	6.0	6	0
Giants	14	113	8.1	39	0
Opponents	13	134	10.3	41	0

PUNTING

	No.	Yds.	Avg.	In 20	LG
Feagles	74	3,069	41.5	23	55
Christie	1	19	19.0	1	19
Giants	77	3,088	40.1	24	55
Opponents	77	2,997	38.9	19	58

PUNT RETURNS

	Ret	FC	Yds	Avg	LG	TD
Jones	34	11	227	6.7	29	0
I. Hilliard	4	0	26	6.5	15	0
Giants	38	11	253	6.7	29	0
Opponents	38	15	356	9.4	42	0

KICKOFF RETURNS

	No.	Yds	Avg	LG	TD
Ponder	36	967	26.9	91t	1
Ward	16	436	27.3	92t	1
Cloud	8	175	21.9	38	0
Jones	2	37	18.5	20	0
Dayne	1	11	11.0	11	0
Finn	1	16	16.0	16	0
Rivers	1	8	8.0	8	0
Shiancoe	1	8	8.0	8	0
Giants	66	1,658	25.1	92t	2
Opponents	66	1,278	19.4	49	0

FIELD GOALS

	1-19	20-29	30-39	40-49	50+
Christie	1/1	8/8	6/8	4/7	3/4
Giants	1/1	8/8	6/8	4/7	3/4
Opponents	0/0	6/6	2/3	12/14	0/2

SACKS

	No.
Umenyiora	7.0
Robbins	5.0
Strahan	4.0
Torbor	3.0
Wilson	3.0
Alexander	2.0
Greisen	2.0
Joseph	2.0
Legree	2.0
K. Allen	1.0
W. Allen	1.0
Duckett	1.0
Emmons	1.0
Hand	1.0
Lewis	1.0
Maxwell	1.0
Washington	1.0
Wiley	0.5
D. Williams	0.5
Giants	40.0
Opponents	52.0

RECORD HOLDERS
INDIVIDUAL RECORDS—CAREER

Category	Name	Performance
Rushing (Yds.)	Tiki Barber, 1997-2004	6,927
Passing (Yds.)	Phil Simms, 1979-1993	33,462
Passing (TDs)	Phil Simms, 1979-1993	199
Receiving (No.)	Tiki Barber, 1997-2004	474
Receiving (Yds.)	Amani Toomer, 1996-2004	7,113
Interceptions	Emlen Tunnell, 1948-1958	74
Punting (Avg.)	Don Chandler, 1956-1964	43.8
Punt Return (Avg.)	Ward Cuff, 1941-45	12.1
Kickoff Return (Avg.)	Rocky Thompson, 1971-73	27.2
Field Goals	Pete Gogolak, 1966-1974	126
Touchdowns (Tot.)	Frank Gifford, 1952-1964	78
Points	Pete Gogolak, 1966-1974	646

INDIVIDUAL RECORDS—SINGLE SEASON

Category	Name	Performance
Rushing (Yds.)	Tiki Barber, 2004	1,518
Passing (Yds.)	Kerry Collins, 2002	4,073
Passing (TDs)	Y.A. Tittle, 1963	36
Receiving (No.)	Amani Toomer, 2002	82
Receiving (Yds.)	Amani Toomer, 2002	1,343
Interceptions	Otto Schnellbacher, 1951	11
	Jim Patton, 1958	11
Punting (Avg.)	Don Chandler, 1959	46.6
Punt Return (Avg.)	Merle Hapes, 1942	15.5
Kickoff Return (Avg.)	John Salscheider, 1949	31.6
Field Goals	Ali Haji-Sheikh, 1983	35
Touchdowns (Tot.)	Joe Morris, 1985	21
Points	Ali Haji-Sheikh, 1983	127

INDIVIDUAL RECORDS—SINGLE GAME

Category	Name	Performance
Rushing (Yds.)	Gene Roberts, 11-12-50	218
Passing (Yds.)	Phil Simms, 10-13-85	513
Passing (TDs)	Y.A. Tittle, 10-28-62	*7
Receiving (No.)	Tiki Barber, 1-2-00	13
Receiving (Yds.)	Del Shofner, 10-28-62	269
Interceptions	Many times	3
	Last time by Terry Kinard, 9-20-87	
Field Goals	Joe Danelo, 10-18-81	6
Touchdowns (Tot.)	Ron Johnson, 10-2-72	4
	Earnest Gray, 9-7-80	4
	Rodney Hampton, 9-24-95	4
Points	Ron Johnson, 10-2-72	24
	Earnest Gray, 9-7-80	24
	Rodney Hampton, 9-24-95	24

*NFL Record

2005 VETERAN ROSTER

No.	Name	Pos.	Ht.	Wt.	Birthdate	NFL Exp.	College	Hometown	How Acq.	'04 Games/ Starts
26	Alexander, Brent	S	5-11	200	7/10/71	12	Tennessee State	Gallatin, Tenn.	FA-'04	16/16
97	Allen, Kenderick	DT	6-6	315	9/14/78	3	Lousiana State	Bogalusa, La.	W(NO)-'04	5/2
25	Allen, Will	CB	5-10	196	8/5/78	5	Syracuse	Syracuse, N.Y.	D1-'01	16/16
21	Barber, Tiki	RB	5-10	200	4/7/75	9	Virginia	Roanoke, Va.	D2-'97	16/14
22	Brewer, Jack	S	6-0	194	1/8/79	4	Minnesota	Grapevine, Texas	W(Minn)'04	13/0
29	Burns, Curry	S	6-0	203	2/12/81	2	Louisville	Miami, Fla.	FA-'04	8/2
17	Burress, Plaxico	WR	6-5	226	8/12/77	6	Michigan State	Virginia Beach, Va.	UFA(Pitt)-'05	11/11*
84	Carter, Tim	WR	6-0	200	9/21/79	4	Auburn	Lakewood, Fla.	D2-'02	5/0
70	Clancy, Kendrick	DT	6-1	305	9/17/78	6	Mississippi	Tuscaloosa, Ala.	UFA(Pitt)-'05	9/0*
30	Cloud, Michael	RB	5-10	205	7/1/75	7	Boston College	Portsmouth, R.I.	FA-'04	10/0
39	DeLoatch, Curtis	CB	6-2	217	10/4/81	2	North Carolina A&T	Murfreesboro, N.C.	FA-'04	16/0
66	Diehl, David	T	6-5	315	9/15/80	3	Illinois	Oak Lawn, Ill.	D5-'03	16/16
99	Duckett, Damane	DT	6-6	300	1/21/81	2	East Carolina	Lexington, N.C.	FA-'04	4/1
51	Emmons, Carlos	LB	6-5	250	9/3/73	10	Arkansas State	Greenwood, Miss.	UFA(Phil)-'04	15/15
18	Feagles, Jeff	P	6-1	215	3/7/66	18	Miami	Phoenix, Ariz.	UFA(Sea)-'03	16/0
2	Feely, Jay	K	5-10	206	5/23/76	4	Michigan	Odessa, Fla.	UFA(Atl)-'05	16/0*
20	Finn, Jim	FB	6-0	245	12/9/76	6	Pennsylvania	Fair Lawn, N.J.	UFA(Ind)-'03	16/9
52	Green, Barrett	LB	6-0	225	10/29/77	6	West Virginia	West Palm Beach, Fla.	UFA(Det)-'04	10/9
54	Greisen, Nick	LB	6-1	245	8/10/79	4	Wisconsin	Sturgeon Bay, Wis.	D5-'02	15/7
55	Hollowell, T.J.	LB	6-0	235	4/8/81	2	Nebraska	Copperas Cove, Texas	FA-'04	4/0
89	Jones, Mark	WR-DB	5-9	185	11/3/80	2	Tennessee	Wallingford, Pa.	W(TB)-'04	14/0
94	Joseph, William	DT	6-5	315	9/3/79	3	Miami	Miami, Fla.	D1-'03	15/4
61	Kelly, Lewis	G/T	6-4	306	4/21/77	5	South Carolina State	Lithonia, Ga.	FA-'05	0*
90	Kuehl, Ryan	LS	6-5	280	1/18/72	9	Virginia	Potomac, Md.	UFA(Cle) -'03	16/0
59	Lewis, Kevin	LB	6-1	235	10/6/78	6	Duke	Orlando, Fla.	FA-'01	16/0
62	Lucier, Wayne	C/G	6-3	300	12/5/79	3	Colorado	Salem, N.H.	D7b-'03	15/9
88	Luzar, Chris	TE	6-7	265	2/12/79	3	Virginia	Newport News, Va.	FA-'05	0*
10	Manning, Eli	QB	6-4	218	1/3/81	2	Mississippi	New Orleans, La.	T(SD)-'04	9/7
57	Maxwell, Jim	LB	6-4	242	8/8/81	2	Gardner Webb	Johnsonville, S.C.	FA-'04	14/0
67	McKenzie, Kareem	T	6-6	327	5/24/79	5	Penn State	Willingboro, N.J.	UFA(NYJ)-'05	16/16*
15	Miller, Jim	QB	6-2	225	2/9/71	11	Michigan State	Waterford, Mich.	UFA(NE)-'05	0*
60	O'Hara, Shaun	C/G	6-3	306	6/23/77	6	Rutgers	Hillsborough, N.J.	UFA(Cle)-'04	12/12
3	Palmer, Jesse	QB	6-2	225	10/5/78	5	Florida	Toronto, Ontario, Canada	D4b-'01	0*
24	Peterson, Will	CB	6-0	200	6/15/79	5	Western Illinois	Uniontown, Pa.	D3-'01	16/15
77	Petitgout, Luke	T	6-6	310	6/16/76	7	Notre Dame	Georgetown, Del.	D1-'99	16/16
53	Pierce, Antonio	LB	6-1	240	10/26/78	5	Arizona	Ontario, Calif.	UFA(Wash)-'05	16/16*
87	Ponder, Willie	WR	6-0	205	2/14/80	3	Southeast Missouri State	Tulsa, Okla.	D6a-'03	11/0
98	Robbins, Fred	DT	6-4	325	3/25/77	6	Wake Forest	Pensacola, Fla.	UFA(Minn)-'04	15/15
69	Seubert, Rich	G	6-3	305	3/30/79	5	Western Illinois	Rozellville, Wis.	FA-'01	0*
82	Shiancoe, Visanthe	TE	6-4	250	6/18/80	3	Morgan State	Laurel, Md.	D3-'03	16/7
80	Shockey, Jeremy	TE	6-5	253	8/18/80	4	Miami	Ada, Okla.	D1-'02	15/15
76	Snee, Chris	G	6-3	314	1/8/82	2	Boston College	Montrose, Pa.	D2-'04	11/11
92	Strahan, Michael	DE	6-5	275	11/21/71	13	Texas Southern	Westbury, Texas	D2-'93	8/8
86	Taylor, Jamaar	WR	6-0	197	2/25/81	2	Texas A&M	Mission, Texas	D6-'04	8/0
81	Toomer, Amani	WR	6-3	208	9/8/74	10	Michigan	Berkeley, Calif.	D2-'96	15/14
58	Torbor, Reggie	LB	6-2	254	1/25/81	2	Auburn	Baton Rouge, La.	D4-'04	16/1
85	Tyree, David	WR	6-0	205	1/3/80	3	Syracuse	Montclair, N.J.	D6c-'03	16/1
72	Umenyiora, Osi	DE	6-3	280	11/16/80	3	Troy State	Auburn, Ala.	D2-'03	16/7
41	Walker, Frank	CB	5-10	198	8/6/81	3	Tuskegee	Tuskegee, Ala.	D6b-'03	13/1
73	Walker, Greg	T/G	6-5	341	10/1/81	2	Clemson	Sumter, S.C.	FA-'04	7/0
34	Ward, Derrick	RB	5-11	233	8/30/80	2	Ottawa	Moreno Valley, Calif.	FA-'04	5/0
71	Whitfield, Bob	T	6-5	310	10/18/71	14	Stanford	Carson, Calif.	UFA(Jax)-'05	10/0*
65	Whittle, Jason	G	6-4	305	3/7/75	8	Southwest Missouri State	Camdenton, Mo.	T(TB)-'04	16/16
96	Williams, Davern	DT	6-3	305	2/13/83	2	Troy State	Montgomery, Ala.	FA-'04	2/1
36	Williams, Shaun	S	6-2	218	10/10/76	8	UCLA	Encino, Calif.	D1-'98	2/2
28	Wilson, Gibril	S	6-0	197	11/12/81	2	Tennessee	San Jose, Calif.	D5-'04	8/7
68	Winey, Brandon	T	6-6	311	1/27/78	3	Louisiana State	Lake Charles, La.	FA-'04	13/0

* Burress played 11 games with Pittsburgh in '04; Clancy played 9 games with Pittsburgh; Feely played 16 games with Atlanta; Kelly last active with Minnesota in '03; Luzar last active with Jacksonville in '03; McKenzie played 16 games with N.Y. Jets; Miller inactive for 16 games with New England; Palmer did not play in 1 game; Pierce played 16 games with Washington; Seubert missed the '04 season because of injury; Whitfield played 10 games with Jacksonville.

Players lost through free agency (3): RB Ron Dayne (Den; 14 games in '04), DT Lance Legree (NYJ; 15); QB Kurt Warner (Ariz; 10).

Also played with Giants in '04—DE Lorenzo Bromell (2 games), K Steve Christie (16), CB Terry Cousin (16), DT Norman Hand (11), WR Ike Hilliard (16), LB Wesly Mallard (4), TE Marcellus Rivers (16), S Omar Stoutmire (1), DE Regan Upshaw (3), DE Keith Washington (8), DE Chuck Wiley (3).

2005 FIRST-YEAR ROSTER

Name	Pos.	Ht.	Wt.	Birthdate	College	Hometown	How Acq.
Awasom, Adrian	DE	6-5	275	10/25/83	North Texas	Fort Bend, Texas	FA
Bragg, Michael	CB	6-1	183	12/31/81	Texas A&M-Kingsville	Lakewood, Calif.	FA
Butler, James	S	6-3	210	9/7/82	Georgia Tech	Climax, Ga.	FA
Cash, Ataveus (1)	WR	6-1	205	5/2/79	Hampton	Washington, D.C.	FA
Childress, Ahmad (1)	DT	6-5	331	6/15/81	Alabama	Nashville, Tenn.	FA-'04
Eddins, Brett	DE	6-5	273	4/20/82	Aubrun	Montgomery, Ala.	FA
Ferri, Diamond	S	5-10	223	8/6/81	Syracuse	Everett, Mass.	FA
Frederick, Charles	WR	5-10	194	2/2/82	Washington	Boca Raton, Fla.	FA
Grant, Ryan	RB	6-1	218	12/9/82	Notre Dame	Ramsey, N.J.	FA
Hilliard, Jason (1)	T/G	6-6	328	6/29/81	Louisville	Jeffersonville, Ind.	FA-'04
Jacobs, Brandon	RB	6-4	256	7/6/82	Southern Illinois	Napoleanville, La.	D4
Jemison, Mike	RB	6-1	225	6/3/83	Indiana (PA)	Greencastle, Pa.	FA
Jennings, Michael (1)	WR	5-11	175	9/7/79	Florida State	Jacksonville, Fla.	FA-04
Kimball, David (1)	K	6-1	209	1/13/82	Penn State	State College, Pa.	FA
Lawton, Luke (1)	FB	5-11	237	8/26/80	McNeese State	Lafayette, La.	W(Atl)
Lorenzen, Jared (1)	QB	6-4	275	2/14/81	Kentucky	Ft. Thomas, Ky.	FA-'04
Moore, Eric	DE	6-4	268	2/28/81	Florida State	Pahokee, Fla.	D6
Orr, Raheem (1)	DE	6-3	258	11/8/80	Rutgers	Elizabeth, N.J.	FA-'04
Pears, Morgan (1)	T/G	6-6	325	5/4/80	Colorado State	Denver, Colo.	FA-'04
Scott, Joseph	LB	6-1	237	12/17/81	Jackson State	Hattiesburgh, Miss.	FA
Seawright, Jonas	DT	6-6	312	4/12/82	North Carolina	Orangeburg, S.C.	FA
Smith, Brandon	WR	5-11	193	11/20/83	Vanderbilt	New Orleans, La.	FA
Thomas, Art (1)	CB/S	6-2	205	9/24/79	Virginia	Mechanicsburg, Pa.	FA-'04
Tidwell-Neal, Andy	C	6-5	310	10/4/82	Georgia Tech	Plymouth, Minn.	FA
Treaudo, Ahmad	CB	5-10	181	4/15/82	Southern	New Orleans, La.	FA
Tuck, Justin	DE	6-5	268	3/29/83	Notre Dame	Kellyton, Ala.	D3
Wake, Derek	LB	6-3	241	1/30/82	Penn State	Beltsville, Md.	FA
Wallace, Kyle	T	6-6	295	3/3/83	Georgia Tech	Lawrenceville, Ga.	FA
Webster, Corey	CB	6-0	204	3/2/82	Louisiana State	Vacherie, La.	D2
Williams, Darius	TE	6-6	270	3/16/82	Georgia Tech	Clarkson, Ga.	FA
Williams, Davern (1)	DT	6-3	305	2/13/83	Troy State	Montgomery, Ala.	FA-'04

The term NFL Rookie is defined as a player who is in his first season of professional football and has not been on the roster of another professional football team for any regular-season or postseason games. A Rookie is designated by an "R" on NFL rosters. Players who have been active in another professional football league or players who have NFL experience, including either preseason training camp or being on an Active List or Inactive List, or on Reserve/Injured or Reserve/Physically Unable to Perform for fewer than six regular-season games, are termed NFL First-Year Players. An NFL First-Year Player is designated by a "1" on NFL rosters. Thereafter, a player is credited with an additional year of experience for each season in which he accumulates six games on the Active List or Inactive List, or on Reserve/Injured or Reserve/Physically Unable to Perform.

Log on to www.giants.com for an up-to-date roster.

COACHING STAFF

Head Coach,
Tom Coughlin
Pro Career: Was named the sixteenth head coach in Giants history on January 6, 2004. Coughlin previously spent eight years (1995-2002) with the Jacksonville Jaguars. Under Coughlin, the Jaguars had the most victories of any NFL expansion team in its first seven seasons. They were also the only expansion team in NFL history to advance to the playoffs four times in their first five seasons. Coughlin's team went 9-7 in 1996 on the way to the AFC Championship Game, and earned playoff berths in both 1997 and 1998. In 1999, Coughlin posted an NFL-best 14-2 mark in the regular season and a second AFC Championship Game appearance. Became the first head coach of the Jaguars on February 21, 1994. Coughlin previously coached wide receivers for the Philadelphia Eagles (1984-85), Green Bay Packers (1986-87), and New York Giants (1988-1990). He was a member of the Giants' Super Bowl XXV champion coaching staff. Career record: 78-74.
Background: Served as head coach at Boston College (1991-93), where he posted a 21-13-1 record, and coached at Syracuse (1969, 1974-1980), Rochester Institute of Technology 1970-73 (head coach), and Boston College (1981-83). Played wingback for Syracuse (1965-67), with teammates Larry Csonka and Floyd Little. Received Syracuse 1967 Orange Key Award as outstanding scholar athlete, and graduated with bachelor's and master's degree from Syracuse.
Personal: Born August 31, 1947, Waterloo, N.Y. Tom and his wife, Judy, have two daughters, Keli and Katie, two sons, Brian and Tim, a daughter-in-law, Andrea (Tim's wife), and two grandchildren, Emma Rose and Dylan.

ASSISTANT COACHES

Andy Barnett, asst. strength and conditioning; born January 12, 1960, Des Moines, Iowa. Attended Wyoming, Calgary. No college or pro playing experience. College coach: Wyoming 1988-1991, Calgary 1993-95, Olympic Training Center, Calgary 1995-2000, International Performance Institute 2000-2003. Pro coach: Joined Giants in 2004.
John DeFilippo, offensive quality control; born April 12, 1978, Youngstown, Ohio. Quarterback James Madison 1996-99. No pro playing experience. College coach: Fordham 2000, Notre Dame 2001-02, Columbia 2003-04. Pro coach: Joined Giants in 2005.
Dave DeGuglielmo, asst. offensive line; born July 15, 1968, Cambridge, Mass. Attended Boston University. No college or pro playing experience. College coach: Boston College 1991-92, Boston University 1993-96, Connecticut 1997-98, South Carolina 1999-2003. Pro

coach: Joined Giants in 2004.
Pat Flaherty, offensive line; born April 27, 1956, Hanover, Pa. Center East Stroudsburg 1974-77. No pro playing experience. College coach: East Stroudsburg 1980-81, Penn State 1982-83, Rutgers 1984-1991, East Carolina 1992, Wake Forest 1993-98, Iowa 1999. Pro coach: Washington Redskins 2000, Chicago Bears 2001-03, joined Giants in 2004.
Kevin Gilbride, quarterbacks, born August 27, 1951, New Haven, Conn. Quarterback/tight end Southern Connecticut State 1971-73. No pro playing experience. College coach: Idaho State 1974-75, Tufts 1976-77, American International 1978-79. Southern Connecticut State 1980-84, East Carolina 1987-88. Pro coach: Ottawa Rough Riders (CFL) 1985-86, Houston Oilers 1989-1994, Jacksonville Jaguars 1995-96, San Diego Chargers 1997-98 (head coach), Pittsburgh Steelers 1999-2000, Buffalo Bills 2002-2003, joined Giants 2004.
John Hufnagel, offensive coordinator; born September 13, 1951, Pittsburgh. Quarterback Penn State 1969-1972. Pro quarterback Denver Broncos 1973-75, Calgary Stampeders (CFL) 1976-79, Saskatchewan Roughriders (CFL) 1980-83, 1987, Winnipeg Blue Bombers (CFL) 1984-86. Pro coach: Saskatchewan Roughriders (CFL) 1988, Calgary Stampeders (CFL) 1990-96, New Jersey Red Dogs (AFL) 1997-98, Cleveland Browns 1999-2000, Indianapolis Colts 2001, Jacksonville Jaguars 2002, New England Patriots 2003, joined Giants in 2004.
Jerald Ingram, running backs; born December 24, 1960, Dayton, Ohio. Fullback Michigan 1979-1983. College coach: Michigan 1984, Ball State 1985-1990, Boston College, 1991-93. Pro coach: Jacksonville Jaguars 1994-2002, joined Giants in 2004.
Tim Lewis, defensive coordinator; born December 18, 1961, Quakertown, Pa. Defensive back Pittsburgh 1979-1982. Pro cornerback Green Bay Packers 1983-86. College coach: Texas A&M 1987-88, Southern Methodist 1989-1992, Pittsburgh 1993-94. Pro coach: Pittsburgh Steelers 1995-2003, joined Giants in 2004.
David Merritt Sr., defensive assistant; born September 8, 1971, Raleigh, N.C. Linebacker North Carolina State 1989-1992. Pro linebacker Miami Dolphins 1993, Arizona Cardinals 1993-94, Rhein Fire (NFLE) 1997. College coach: Chattanooga 1997, Virginia Military Institute 1998-2000. Pro coach: New York Jets 2001-2003, joined Giants in 2004.
Ron Milus, defensive secondary; born November 25, 1963, Tacoma, Wash. Cornerback-punt returner Washington 1982-1985. No pro playing experience. College coach: Washington 1991-98, Texas A&M 1999. Pro coach: Denver Broncos 2000-02, Arizona Cardinals

2003, joined Giants in 2004.
Jerry Palmieri, strength and conditioning; born October 30, 1958, Englewood, N.J. Attended Montclair State. No college or pro playing experience. College coach: North Carolina 1982-83, Oklahoma State 1984-86, Kansas State 1987-1992, Boston College 1993-94. Pro coach: Jacksonville Jaguars 1995-2002, New Orleans Saints 2003, joined Giants in 2004.
Michael Pope, tight ends; born March 15, 1942, Monroe, N.C. Quarterback Lenoir-Rhyne 1962-64. No pro playing experience. College coach: Florida State 1970-74, Texas Tech 1975-77, Mississippi 1978-1982. Pro coach: New York Giants 1983-1991, Cincinnati Bengals 1992-93, New England Patriots 1994-96, Washington Redskins 1997-99, rejoined Giants in 2000.
Mike Priefer, asst. special teams; born August 21, 1966, Cleveland. Attended U.S. Naval Academy. No college or pro playing experience. College coach: U.S. Naval Academy 1994-96, Youngstown State 1997-98, Virginia Military Institute 1999, Northern Illinois 2000-01. Pro coach: Jacksonville Jaguars 2002, joined Giants in 2003.
Bill Sheridan, linebackers; born January 27, 1959, Detroit. Linebacker Grand Valley State 1979-1982. No pro playing experience. College coach: Michigan 1985-86, Maine 1987-88, Cincinnati 1989-1991, Army 1992-97, Michigan State 1998-2000, Notre Dame 2001, Michigan 2002-04. Pro coach: Joined Giants in 2005.
Mike Sullivan, wide receivers; born January 28, 1967, Santa Maria, Calif. Defensive back Army 1987-88. No pro playing experience. College coach: Mt. San Jacinto (Calif.) J.C. 1993, Humboldt State 1993-94, Army 1995-96, 1999-2000, Youngstown State 1997-98, Ohio 2001. Pro coach: Jacksonville Jaguars 2002-03, joined Giants 2004.
Mike Sweatman, special teams coordinator; born October 23, 1946, Kansas City, Mo. Linebacker Kansas 1964-67. Linebacker Quantico Marines 1969. College coach: Okinawa Devil Dogs 1970, Quantico Marines 1971-72, Kansas 1973-74, 1979-1982, Coffeyville (Kan.) C.C. 1975-76, Tulsa 1977-78, Tennessee 1983. Pro coach: Minnesota Vikings 1984, New York Giants 1985-1992, New England Patriots 1993-96, New York Jets 1997-2000, Chicago Bears 2001-2003, rejoined Giants in 2004.
Mike Waufle, defensive line; born June 27, 1954, Hornell, N.Y. U.S. Marines 1972-75. Defensive lineman Bakersfield (Calif.) J.C. 1975-76, Utah State 1977-78. No pro playing experience. College coach: Alfred 1979, Utah State 1980-84, Fresno State 1985-88, UCLA 1989, Oregon State 1990-91, California 1992-97. Pro coach: Oakland Raiders 1998-2003, joined Giants in 2004.

National Football Conference
East Division
Team Colors: Midnight Green, Silver, Black,
and White
NovaCare Complex
One NovaCare Way
Philadelphia, Pennsylvania 19145
Telephone: (215) 463-2500

2005 SCHEDULE
PRESEASON
Aug. 15 at Pittsburgh..........................8:00
Aug. 20 at Baltimore..........................8:00
Aug. 26 **Cincinnati** 7:30
Sept. 1 **New York Jets** 7:30

REGULAR SEASON
Sept. 12 at Atlanta (Mon.) 9:00
Sept. 18 **San Francisco**....................1:00
Sept. 25 **Oakland** 1:00
Oct. 2   at Kansas City 12:00
Oct. 9   at Dallas..............................3:15
Oct. 16 Open Date
Oct. 23 **San Diego**............................1:00
Oct. 30 at Denver............................2:15
Nov. 6   at Washington 8:30
Nov. 14 **Dallas** (Mon.)......................9:00
Nov. 20 at New York Giants 1:00
Nov. 27 **Green Bay**...........................4:15
Dec. 5   **Seattle** (Mon.) 9:00
Dec. 11 **New York Giants** 4:05
Dec. 18 at St. Louis..........................3:15
Dec. 24 at Arizona (Sat.) 2:05
Jan. 1   **Washington** 4:15

Stadium: Lincoln Financial Field
(opened in 2003)
• **Capacity:** 68,400
One Lincoln Financial Field Way
Philadelphia, Pennsylvania 19148
Playing Surface: Natural Grass
Training Camp: Lehigh University
Bethlehem, Pennsylvania
18015

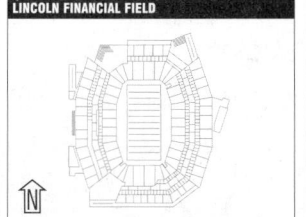

LINCOLN FINANCIAL FIELD

CLUB OFFICIALS
Chairman/Chief Executive Officer:
Jeffrey Lurie
President: Joe Banner
Head Coach/Executive Vice President of
Football Operations: Andy Reid
Vice President of Player Personnel:
Tom Heckert
Senior Vice President of Business
Operations: Mark Donovan
Senior Vice President/Chief Financial
Officer: Don Smolenski
Vice President of Sales and Service:
Bill Manning
Vice President of Stadium Operations and
Facility Management: Scott Jenkins
Executive Director of Eagles Youth
Partnership: Sarah Martinez-Helfman
Director of Pro Personnel: Scott Cohen
Assistant Director of Player Personnel:
Jason Licht
Director of Football Administration:
Howie Roseman
Director of Football Media Relations:
Derek Boyko
Assistant Director of Football Media
Services: Rich Burg, Bob Lange
Senior Director of Marketing:
Tim McDermott
Manager of Community Relations:
Julie Dubin
Director of Human Resources:
Eric Newman
Director of Stadium Operations:
Dave Duernberger
Director, Broadcasting: Rob Alberino
Director of Events: Leonard Bonacci
Director of Ticket Operations:
Laini Delawter
Director of Ticket Client Relations:
Leo Carlin
Director of Merchandise:
Steve Strawbridge
Travel Manager: Tracey Detweiler
Director of Team Security:
Anthony (Butch) Buchanico
Director of Facility and Stadium Security:
Victor Cooper
Head Athletic Trainer: Rick Burkholder
Asst. Athletic Trainers: Eric Sugarman,
Chris Peduzzi
Video Director: Mike Dougherty
Head Equipment Manager: John Hatfield

COACHING HISTORY
(471-516-25)
Records include postseason games

1933-35	Lud Wray	9-21-1
1936-1940	Bert Bell	10-44-2
1941-1950	Earle (Greasy) Neale*	66-44-5
1951	Alvin (Bo) McMillin**	2-0-0
1951	Wayne Millner	2-8-0
1952-55	Jim Trimble	25-20-3
1956-57	Hugh Devore	7-16-1
1958-1960	Lawrence (Buck) Shaw	20-16-1
1961-63	Nick Skorich	15-24-3
1964-68	Joe Kuharich	28-41-1
1969-1971	Jerry Williams***	7-22-2
1971-72	Ed Khayat	8-15-2
1973-75	Mike McCormack	16-25-1
1976-1982	Dick Vermeil	57-51-0
1983-85	Marion Campbell****	17-29-1
1985	Fred Bruney	1-0-0
1986-1990	Buddy Ryan	43-38-1
1991-94	Rich Kotite	37-29-0
1995-98	Ray Rhodes	30-36-1
1999-2004	Andy Reid	71-37-0

*Co-coach with Walt Kiesling in Philadelphia-
Pittsburgh merger in 1943
**Retired after two games in 1951
***Released after three games in 1971
****Released after 15 games in 1985

ATTENDANCE
Home 530,365   Away 552,687
Total 1,083,052
Single-game home record,
72,111 (11/1/81)
Single-season home record,
557,325 (1980)

2005 DRAFT CHOICES

Round	Name	Pos.	College
1	Mike Patterson	DT	Southern California
2	Reggie Brown	WR	Georgia
	Matt McCoy	LB	San Diego State
3	Ryan Moats	RB	Louisiana Tech
4	Sean Considine	DB	Iowa
	Todd Herremans	T	Saginaw Valley St.
5	Trent Cole	LB	Cincinnati
	Scott Young	G	Brigham Young
6	Calvin Armstrong	T	Washington State
7	Keyonta Marshall	DT	Grand Valley St.
	David Bergeron	LB	Stanford

2004 TEAM RECORD

PRESEASON (1-3)

Date	Result	Opponent
8/13	L 6-24	at New England
8/20	W 26-17	Baltimore
8/26	L 21-27	Pittsburgh
9/3	L 27-28	at N.Y. Jets

REGULAR SEASON (13-3)

Date	Result	Opponent	Att.
9/12	W 31-17	N.Y. Giants	67,532
9/20	W 27-16	Minnesota	67,676
9/26	W 30-13	at Detroit	62,472
10/3	W 19-9	at Chicago	61,894
10/17	W 30-8	Carolina	67,707
10/24	W 34-31	at Cleveland (OT)	73,394
10/31	W 15-10	Baltimore	67,715
11/7	L 3-27	at Pittsburgh	64,975
11/15	W 49-21	at Dallas	64,190
11/21	W 28-6	Washington	67,720
11/28	W 27-6	at N.Y. Giants	78,830
12/5	W 47-17	Green Bay	67,723
12/12	W 17-14	at Washington	90,089
12/19	W 12-7	Dallas	67,723
12/27	L 7-20	at St. Louis	66,129
1/2	L 10-38	Cincinnati	67,074

(OT) Overtime

POSTSEASON (2-1)

1/16	W 27-14	Minnesota	67,722
1/23	W 27-10	Atlanta	67,717
2/6	L 21-24	vs. New England at Jacksonville	78,125

SCORE BY PERIODS

Eagles	100	121	79	83	3	—	386
Opponents	54	83	41	82	0	—	260

2004 TEAM STATISTICS

	Eagles	Opp.
Total First Downs	301	299
Rushing	87	101
Passing	188	165
Penalty	26	33
3rd Down: Made/Att	72/195	82/229
3rd Down Pct.	36.9	35.8
4th Down: Made/Att	0/4	9/19
4th Down Pct.	0.0	47.4
Possession Avg.	28:26	31:34
Total Net Yards	5618	5115
Avg. Per Game	351.1	319.7
Total Plays	960	1039
Avg. Per Play	5.9	4.9
Net Yards Rushing	1639	1903
Avg. Per Game	102.4	118.9
Total Rushes	376	442
Net Yards Passing	3979	3212
Avg. Per Game	248.7	200.8
Sacked/Yards Lost	37/229	47/263
Gross Yards	4208	3475
Att./Completions	547/336	550/334
Completion Pct.	61.4	60.7
Had Intercepted	11	17
Punts/Average	73/42.0	89/42.5
Net Punting Avg.	73/37.1	89/35.4
Penalties/Yards	124/952	119/1001
Fumbles/Ball Lost	17/11	29/11
Touchdowns	44	30
Rushing	10	13
Passing	32	16
Returns	2	1

2004 INDIVIDUAL STATISTICS

PASSING

	Att.	Comp.	Yds.	Pct.	TD	Int.	Tkld.	Rate
McNabb	469	300	3,875	64.0	31	8	32/192	104.7
Detmer	40	18	207	45.0	0	2	2/16	40.3
Blake	37	18	126	48.6	1	1	2/17	54.6
Bartrum	1	0	0	0.0	0	0	0/0	39.6
Westbrook	0	0	0	—	0	0	1/4	—
Eagles	547	336	4,208	61.4	32	11	37/229	96.4
Opponents	550	334	3,475	60.7	16	17	47/263	75.8

SCORING

	TD R	TD P	TD Rt	PAT	FG	Saf	PTS
Akers	0	0	0	41/42	27/32	0	122
Owens	0	14	0	0/0	0/0	0	84
Westbrook	3	6	0	0/0	0/0	0	54
Smith	0	5	0	0/0	0/0	0	30
Levens	4	0	0	0/0	0/0	0	24
C. Lewis	0	3	0	0/0	0/0	0	18
McNabb	3	0	0	0/0	0/0	0	18
Mitchell	0	2	0	0/0	0/0	0	12
Sheppard	0	0	2	0/0	0/0	0	12
Bartrum	0	1	0	0/0	0/0	0	6
Pinkston	0	1	0	0/0	0/0	0	6
Eagles	10	32	2	41/42	27/32	0	386
Opponents	13	16	1	27/27	17/24	0	260

2-Pt. Conversions: None.
Eagles 0-2, Opponents 1-3.

RUSHING

	No.	Yds	Avg	LG	TD
Westbrook	177	812	4.6	50	3
Levens	94	410	4.4	45	4
McNabb	41	220	5.4	28	3
Mahe	23	91	4.0	22	0
McCoo	9	54	6.0	12	0
Tapeh	12	42	3.5	10	0
G. Lewis	4	16	4.0	11	0
Blake	3	6	2.0	8	0
Owens	3	-5	-1.7	6	0
Detmer	10	-7	-0.7	2	0
Eagles	376	1,639	4.4	50	10
Opponents	442	1,903	4.3	72t	13

RECEIVING

	No.	Yds	Avg	LG	TD
Owens	77	1,200	15.6	59t	14
Westbrook	73	703	9.6	50	6
Pinkston	36	676	18.8	80	1
Smith	34	377	11.1	31	5
C. Lewis	29	267	9.2	21	3
Mitchell	22	377	17.1	60	2
G. Lewis	17	183	10.8	25	0
Mahe	14	123	8.8	30	0
Levens	9	92	10.2	23	0
Parry	9	75	8.3	22	0
Bartrum	5	45	9.0	17	1
Ritchie	4	36	9.0	11	0
McMullen	3	24	8.0	15	0
McCoo	2	15	7.5	8	0
Tapeh	2	15	7.5	13	0
Eagles	336	4,208	12.5	80	32
Opponents	334	3,475	10.4	52	16

INTERCEPTIONS

	No.	Yds	Avg	LG	TD
Sheppard	5	172	34.4	101t	2
Dawkins	4	40	10.0	32	0
Brown	2	33	16.5	33	0
Reese	2	22	11.0	15	0
Hood	1	20	20.0	20	0
Jones	1	0	0.0	0	0
M. Lewis	1	0	0.0	0	0
Mikell	1	0	0.0	0	0
Eagles	17	287	16.9	101t	2
Opponents	11	140	12.7	41	1

PUNTING

	No.	Yds.	Avg.	In 20	LG
Johnson	72	3,032	42.1	20	62
Akers	1	36	36.0	0	36
Eagles	73	3,068	42.0	20	62
Opponents	89	3,785	42.5	29	68

PUNT RETURNS

	Ret	FC	Yds	Avg	LG	TD
Mahe	19	8	109	5.7	25	0
Wynn	18	7	194	10.8	40	0
Sheppard	2	5	42	21.0	39	0
Westbrook	2	0	14	7.0	14	0
Reed	0	0	18	—	18	0
Eagles	41	20	377	9.2	40	0
Opponents	34	13	221	6.5	25	0

KICKOFF RETURNS

	No.	Yds	Avg	LG	TD
Reed	33	761	23.1	66	0
Hood	15	336	22.4	45	0
Mahe	3	44	14.7	22	0
G. Lewis	2	28	14.0	15	0
Parry	2	24	12.0	14	0
Wynn	1	21	21.0	21	0
Eagles	56	1,214	21.7	66	0
Opponents	73	1,693	23.2	73	0

FIELD GOALS

	1-19	20-29	30-39	40-49	50+
Akers	0/0	4/4	6/7	15/18	2/3
Eagles	0/0	4/4	6/7	15/18	2/3
Opponents	1/1	5/5	5/7	4/9	2/2

SACKS

	No.
Kearse	7.5
Rayburn	6.0
Simon	5.5
Walker	4.5
Brown	3.0
Dawkins	3.0
Douglas	3.0
Burgess	2.5
McDougle	2.0
Simoneau	1.5
Green	1.0
Reese	1.0
Sheppard	1.0
Trotter	1.0
Wayne	1.0
Wynn	1.0
Jones	0.5
Eagles	47.0
Opponents	37.0

RECORD HOLDERS
INDIVIDUAL RECORDS—CAREER

Category	Name	Performance
Rushing (Yds.)	Wilbert Montgomery, 1977-1984	6,538
Passing (Yds.)	Ron Jaworski, 1977-1986	26,963
Passing (TDs)	Ron Jaworski, 1977-1986	175
Receiving (No.)	Harold Carmichael, 1971-1983	589
Receiving (Yds.)	Harold Carmichael, 1971-1983	8,978
Interceptions	Bill Bradley, 1969-1976	34
	Eric Allen, 1988-1994	34
Punting (Avg.)	Joe Muha, 1946-1950	42.9
Punt Return (Avg.)	Brian Westbrook, 2002-04	14.5
Kickoff Return (Avg.)	Steve Van Buren, 1944-1951	26.7
Field Goals	David Akers, 1999-2004	139
Touchdowns (Tot.)	Harold Carmichael, 1971-1983	79
Points	Bobby Walston, 1951-1962	881

INDIVIDUAL RECORDS—SINGLE SEASON

Category	Name	Performance
Rushing (Yds.)	Wilbert Montgomery, 1979	1,512
Passing (Yds.)	Donovan McNabb, 2004	3,875
Passing (TDs)	Sonny Jurgensen, 1961	32
Receiving (No.)	Irving Fryar, 1996	88
Receiving (Yds.)	Mike Quick, 1983	1,409
Interceptions	Bill Bradley, 1971	11
Punting (Avg.)	Joe Muha, 1948	47.2
Punt Return (Avg.)	Steve Van Buren, 1944	15.3
Kickoff Return (Avg.)	Al Nelson, 1972	29.1
Field Goals	Paul McFadden, 1984	30
	David Akers, 2002	30
Touchdowns (Tot.)	Steve Van Buren, 1945	18
Points	David Akers, 2002	133

INDIVIDUAL RECORDS—SINGLE GAME

Category	Name	Performance
Rushing (Yds.)	Steve Van Buren, 11-27-49	205
Passing (Yds.)	Donovan McNabb, 12-5-04	464
Passing (TDs)	Adrian Burk, 10-17-54	*7
Receiving (No.)	Don Looney, 12-1-40	14
Receiving (Yds.)	Tommy McDonald, 12-10-60	237
Interceptions	Russ Craft, 9-24-50	*4
Field Goals	Tom Dempsey, 11-12-72	6
Touchdowns (Tot.)	Many times	4
	Last time by Irving Fryar, 10-20-96	
Points	Bobby Walston, 10-17-54	25

*NFL Record

2005 VETERAN ROSTER

No.	Name	Pos.	Ht.	Wt.	Birthdate	NFL Exp.	College	Hometown	How Acq.	'04 Games/Starts
57	Adams, Keith	LB	5-11	223	11/22/79	5	Clemson	Atlanta, Ga.	W(Dall)-'02	16/2
2	Akers, David	K	5-10	200	12/9/74	7	Louisville	Lexington, Ky.	FA-'99	16/0
73	Andrews, Shawn	T/G	6-4	340	12/25/82	2	Arkansas	Camden, Ark.	D1-'04	1/1
88	Bartrum, Mike	TE/LS	6-4	245	6/23/70	12	Marshall	Pomeroy, Ohio	FA-'00	16/0
24	Brown, Sheldon	CB	5-10	200	3/19/79	4	South Carolina	Ft. Lawn, S.C.	D2b-'02	16/16
28	Buckhalter, Correll	RB	6-0	222	10/6/78	5	Nebraska	Collins, Miss.	D4-'01	0*
61	Clarke, Adrien	G	6-5	330	3/26/81	2	Ohio State	Shaker Heights, Ohio	D7a-'04	0*
66	Darilek, Trey	T/G	6-5	310	4/23/81	2	Texas-El Paso	San Antonio, Texas	D4b-'04	3/0
20	Dawkins, Brian	S	6-0	210	10/13/73	10	Clemson	Jacksonville, Fla.	D2b-'96	15/15
10	Detmer, Koy	QB	6-1	195	7/5/73	9	Colorado	San Antonio, Texas	D7a-'97	16/1
53	Douglas, Hugh	LB/DE	6-2	281	8/23/71	11	Central State (OH)	Mansfield, Ohio	FA-'04	16/3
63	Fraley, Hank	C/G	6-2	300	9/21/77	6	Robert Morris	Gaithersburg, Md.	W(Pitt)-'00	16/16
75	Furio, Dominic	C	6-3	305	6/4/81	2	Nevada-Las Vegas	San Pedro, Calif.	D7c-'04	0*
96	Grasmanis, Paul	DT	6-3	298	8/2/74	10	Notre Dame	Jenison, Mich.	UFA(Den)-'00	4/0
65	Green, Jamaal	DE	6-2	272	6/5/80	3	Miami	Camden, N.J.	D4-'03	8/0
77	Hicks, Artis	T/G	6-4	320	11/28/78	4	Memphis	Jackson, Tenn.	FA-'02	14/13
29	Hood, Roderick	CB	5-11	196	10/3/81	3	Auburn	Columbus, Ga.	FA-'03	16/2
67	Jackson, Jamaal	G/C	6-4	330	5/8/80	2	Delaware State	Miami, Fla.	FA-'03	0*
8	Johnson, Dirk	P	6-0	205	6/1/75	3	Northern Colorado	Montrose, Colo.	FA-'03	16/0
55	Jones, Dhani	LB	6-1	240	2/22/78	6	Michigan	Potomac, Md.	UFA(NYG)-'04	16/15
94	Kalu, N.D.	DE	6-3	265	8/3/75	9	Rice	San Antonio, Texas	UFA(Wash)-'01	0*
93	Kearse, Jevon	DE	6-4	265	9/3/76	7	Florida	Ft. Myers, Fla.	UFA(Tenn)-'04	14/14
59	Labinjo, Mike	LB	6-1	255	7/8/80	2	Michigan State	Toronto, Ontario, Canada	FA-'04	3/0
89	#Lewis, Chad	TE	6-6	252	10/5/71	9	Brigham Young	Orem, Utah	W(StL)-'99	15/9
83	Lewis, Greg	WR	6-0	180	2/12/80	3	Illinois	Matteson, Ill.	FA-'03	16/3
32	Lewis, Michael	S	6-1	211	4/29/80	4	Colorado	Richmond, Texas	D2a-'02	16/16
34	Mahe, Reno	RB	5-10	212	6/3/80	3	Brigham Young	Salt Lake City, Utah	FA-'03	11/0
95	McDougle, Jerome	DE	6-2	264	12/15/78	3	Miami	Pompano Beach, Fla.	D1-'03	11/0
4	McMahon, Mike	QB	6-2	215	2/8/79	5	Rutgers	North Allegheny, Pa.	UFA(Det)-'05	1/0*
80	McMullen, Billy	WR	6-4	210	3/8/80	3	Virginia	Richmond, Va.	D3-'03	8/0
5	McNabb, Donovan	QB	6-2	240	11/25/76	7	Syracuse	Chicago, Ill.	D1-'99	15/15
27	Mikell, Quintin	S	5-10	206	9/16/80	3	Boise State	Eugene, Ore.	FA-'03	14/0
81	Owens, Terrell	WR	6-3	226	12/7/73	10	Tennessee-Chattanooga	Alexander City, Ala.	T(Balt)-'04	14/14
49	Parry, Josh	FB	6-2	250	4/5/78	2	San Jose State	Sonora, Calif.	FA-'04	13/4
35	Perry, Bruce	RB	5-10	200	3/22/81	2	Maryland	Philadelphia, Pa.	D7b-'04	0*
87	Pinkston, Todd	WR	6-3	180	4/23/77	6	Southern Mississippi	Forest, Miss.	D2a-'00	16/16
91	Rayburn, Sam	DT	6-3	303	10/20/80	3	Tulsa	Chickasha, Okla.	FA-'03	16/2
30	Reed, J.R.	S	5-11	202	2/11/82	2	South Florida	Tampa, Fla.	D4a-'04	14/1
48	Ritchie, Jon	FB	6-2	250	9/4/74	8	Stanford	Mechanicsburg, Pa.	UFA(Oak)-'03	3/0
69	Runyan, Jon	T	6-7	330	11/27/73	10	Michigan	Flint, Mich.	UFA(Tenn)-'00	16/16
68	Sciullo, Steve	G	6-5	325	8/27/80	3	Marshall	Pittsburgh, Pa.	W(Ind)-'04	15/5
26	Sheppard, Lito	CB	5-10	194	4/8/81	4	Florida	Jacksonville, Fla.	D1-'02	15/15
52	Short, Jason	LB	6-4	254	7/15/78	2	Eastern Michigan	Painesville, Ohio	FA-'03	11/0
90	†Simon, Corey	DT	6-2	293	3/2/77	6	Florida State	Pompano Beach, Fla.	D1-'00	16/16
50	Simoneau, Mark	LB	6-0	245	1/16/77	6	Kansas State	Smith Center, Kan.	T(Atl)-'03	14/13
82	Smith, L.J.	TE	6-3	258	5/13/80	3	Rutgers	Highland Park, N.J.	D2-'03	16/8
41	Tapeh, Thomas	FB	6-1	243	3/28/80	2	Minnesota	St. Paul, Minn.	D5-'04	7/0
78	Thomas, Hollis	DT	6-0	306	1/10/74	10	Northern Illinois	St. Louis, Mo.	FA-'96	13/2
72	Thomas, Tra	T	6-7	349	11/20/74	8	Florida State	Deland, Fla.	D1-'98	15/15
54	Trotter, Jeremiah	LB	6-1	262	1/20/77	8	Stephen F. Austin	Hooks, Texas	FA-'04	16/9
97	Walker, Darwin	DT	6-3	294	6/15/77	6	Tennessee	Walterboro, S.C.	W(Ariz)-'00	16/16
21	Ware, Matt	CB	6-2	210	12/2/82	2	UCLA	Los Angeles, Calif.	D3-'04	12/0
36	Westbrook, Brian	RB	5-10	205	9/2/79	4	Villanova	Ft. Washington, Md.	D3-'02	13/12
85	Whalen, James	TE	6-2	244	12/11/77	5	Kentucky	Portland, Ore.	FA-'05	0*
31	Wynn, Dexter	CB	5-9	177	2/25/81	2	Colorado State	Colorado Springs, Colo.	D6b-'04	12/0

* Buckhalter missed '04 season because of injury; Clarke missed '04 season because of injury; Furio missed '04 season because of injury; Jackson missed '04 season due to injury; Kalu missed '04 season because of injury; McMahon played 1 game with Detroit in '04; Perry missed '04 season because of injury; Whalen last active with Dallas in '03.

† franchise player; subject to developments.

Unrestricted free agents; subject to developments.

Players lost through free agency (3): DE Derrick Burgess (Oak; 12 games in '04), G Jermane Mayberry (NO; 12), LB Ike Reese (Atl; 16).

Also played with Eagles in '04—T Ian Allen (4 games), QB Jeff Blake (3), C/G Alonzo Ephraim (14), RB Dorsey Levens (15), WR Freddie Mitchell (16), LB Nate Wayne (9).

2005 FIRST-YEAR ROSTER

Name	Pos.	Ht.	Wt.	Birthdate	College	Hometown	How Acq.
Adams, Grant	WR	6-1	201	5/8/82	Boston College	Glen Rock, N.J.	FA
Armstrong, Calvin	T	6-7	325	3/31/82	Washington State	Centralia, Wash.	D6
Bergeron, David	LB	6-3	245	12/4/81	Stanford	Lake Oswego, Ore.	D7b
Brown, Reggie	WR	6-1	197	1/13/81	Georgia	Carrollton, Ga.	D2a
Cole, Trent	DE	6-3	240	10/5/82	Cincinnati	Xenia, Ohio	D5a
Considine, Sean	S	6-0	212	10/28/81	Iowa	Byron, Ill.	D4a
Hall, Andy (1)	QB	6-3	218	11/26/80	Delaware	Cheraw, S.C.	D6a-'04
Hall, Branden (1)	G	6-3	330	2/19/82	Troy State	Auburn, Ala.	FA-'04
Herremans, Todd	T	6-6	321	10/13/82	Saginaw Valley State	Ravenna, Mich.	D4b
Heuer, Norm (1)	DT	6-5	288	12/6/80	Michigan	Peoria, Ariz.	FA
Jenkins, Justin (1)	WR	6-0	207	12/10/80	Mississippi State	Pearl, Miss.	FA-'04
Jones, Jared	WR	6-0	205	5/22/82	Syracuse	Hillsborough, N.J.	FA
Marshall, Keyonta	DT	6-1	325	8/13/81	Grand Valley State	Saginaw, Mich.	D7a
Mariscal, Mark (1)	P	6-2	200	9/10/79	Colorado	Tallahassee, Fla.	FA
McCoo, Eric (1)	RB	5-10	210	9/6/80	Penn State	Red Bank, N.J.	FA-'03
McCoy, Matt	LB	6-0	234	10/14/82	San Diego State	Tustin, Calif.	D2b
Moats, Ryan	RB	5-8	210	12/17/82	Louisiana Tech	Dallas, Texas	D3
Patterson, Martin	LB	6-1	243	2/18/83	Texas Christian	DeSoto, Texas	FA
Patterson, Mike	DT	6-0	292	9/1/83	Southern California	Los Alamitos, Calif.	D1
Peebler, Jason	WR	6-1	202	3/19/83	Massachusetts	Modesto, Calif.	FA
Perez, Carlos (1)	WR	6-0	210	9/15/80	Florida	Hoboken, N.J.	FA-'04
Redd, Robert (1)	WR	5-10	200	9/1/80	Bowling Green	Dayton, Ohio	FA
Richmond, Greg (1)	LB	6-1	235	7/15/81	Oklahoma State	Oklahoma City, Okla.	FA-'04
Shell, Linj	CB	5-11	175	10/22/81	Jacksonville	Orlando, Fla.	FA
Spach, Stephen	TE	6-4	250	7/18/82	Fresno State	Clovis, Calif.	FA
Stovall, Chauncey	WR	6-1	221	8/22/81	Florida State	Vero Beach, Fla.	FA
Strojny, Drew (1)	T	6-7	327	6/30/81	Duke	Wrentham, Mass.	FA-'04
Thorn, Andy	TE	6-5	250	2/4/82	Northern Iowa	Warren, Mich.	FA
Thornburg, Jeremy	FS	6-0	190	5/7/82	Northern Arizona	Cathedral City, Calif.	FA
West, Isaac	WR	6-0	186	4/5/82	Furman	Augusta, Ga.	FA
Williams, Aric	CB	5-11	172	3/21/82	Oregon State	Los Angeles, Calif.	FA
Young, Scott	G	6-4	312	7/15/81	Brigham Young	Salt Lake City, Utah	D5b

The term NFL Rookie is defined as a player who is in his first season of professional football and has not been on the roster of another professional football team for any regular-season or postseason games. A Rookie is designated by an "R" on NFL rosters. Players who have been active in another professional football league or players who have NFL experience, including either preseason training camp or being on an Active List or Inactive List, or on Reserve/Injured or Reserve/Physically Unable to Perform for fewer than six regular-season games, are termed NFL First-Year Players. An NFL First-Year Player is designated by a "1" on NFL rosters. Thereafter, a player is credited with an additional year of experience for each season in which he accumulates six games on the Active List or Inactive List, or on Reserve/Injured or Reserve/Physically Unable to Perform.

Log on to www.philadelphiaeagles.com for an up-to-date roster.

COACHING STAFF

Head Coach/Executive Vice President of Football Operations, Andy Reid

Pro Career: The winningest coach in team history, Reid has led the Eagles to four consecutive NFC East division titles, four consecutive trips to the NFC Championship Game, and their first Super Bowl appearance since 1980. Reid's .657 overall winning percentage (71-37) ranks second behind Joe Gibbs among all active NFL coaches and his playoff win total (7) is the most in club history. In his 13-year pro coaching career, Reid's teams have made the playoffs 11 times. He has coached in the Super Bowl three times and the NFC Championship Game seven times. Reid became the twentieth head coach in franchise history on January 11, 1999, and was promoted to head coach/executive vice president of football operations in 2001. He was named NFL coach of the year in 2000 and 2002. He joined the Eagles after a seven-year stint as an assistant coach with Green Bay (1992-98) under Mike Holmgren. With Green Bay, Reid helped the Packers earn a Super Bowl XXXI victory over New England. Career record: 71-37.

Background: Coached at Brigham Young (1982), San Francisco State (1983-85), Northern Arizona (1986), Texas-El Paso (1987-88), and Missouri (1989-1991). Reid first met Holmgren, who was a member of BYU's coaching staff, when Reid was an offensive tackle and guard on three Cougar Holiday Bowl teams. Reid graduated with a bachelor's degree in physical education. He also received a master's degree in professional leadership in physical education and athletics.

Personal: Born in Los Angeles on March 19, 1958, Reid and his wife Tammy have five children—Garrett, Britt, Crosby, Drew Ann, and Spencer.

ASSISTANT COACHES

Tommy Brasher, defensive line; born Dec. 30, 1940, El Dorado, Ark.. Linebacker Arkansas 1962-63. No pro playing experience. College coach: Arkansas 1970, Virginia Tech 1971, Northeast Louisiana 1974, 1976, Southern Methodist 1977-1981. Pro coach: Shreveport Steamer (WFL) 1975, New England Patriots 1982-84, Philadelphia Eagles 1985, Atlanta Falcons 1986-89, Tampa Bay Buccaneers 1990, Seattle Seahawks 1992-98, rejoined Eagles in 1999.

Juan Castillo, offensive line; born October 8, 1959, Port Isabel, Texas. Linebacker Texas A&I (now Texas A&M-Kingsville) 1978-1980. Pro linebacker San Antonio Gunslingers (USFL) 1984-85. College coach: Texas A&I/Texas A&M-Kingsville 1982-85, 1990-94. Pro coach: Joined Eagles in 1995.

Brad Childress, offensive coordinator; born June 27, 1956, Aurora, Ill. Eastern Illinois 1975-78. No pro playing experience. College coach: Illinois 1978-1984, Northern Arizona 1986-89, Utah 1990, Wisconsin 1991-98. Pro coach: Indianapolis Colts 1985, joined Eagles in 1999.

David Culley, wide receivers; born September 17, 1955, Sparta, Tenn. Quarterback Vanderbilt 1973-77. No pro playing experience. College coach: Austin Peay 1978, Vanderbilt 1979-1981, Middle Tennessee State 1982, Tennessee-Chattanooga 1983, Western Kentucky 1984, Southwestern Louisiana 1985-88, Texas-El Paso 1989-1990, Texas A&M 1991-93. Pro coach: Tampa Bay Buccaneers 1994-95, Pittsburgh Steelers 1996-1998, joined Eagles in 1999.

Ted Daisher, special teams quality control; born February 2, 1955, Taylor, Mich. Wide receiver/defensive back Western Michigan 1975-77. No pro playing experience. College coach: Illinois 1979, Northern Illinois 1980-84, Eastern Michigan 1985-88, Cincinnati 1989-1992, Army 1995-97, Indiana 1998-2000, East Carolina 2001-2002. Pro coach: Joined Eagles in 2004.

John Harbaugh, special teams; born September 23, 1962, Perrysburg, Ohio. Defensive back Miami (Ohio) 1980-83. No pro playing experience. College coach: Western Michigan 1984-86, Pittsburgh 1987, Morehead State 1988, Cincinnati 1989-1996, Indiana 1997. Pro coach: Joined Eagles in 1998.

Jim Johnson, defensive coordinator; born May 26, 1941, Maywood, Ill. Quarterback Missouri 1959-1962. Pro tight end Buffalo Bills 1963-64. College coach: Missouri Southern 1967-68 (head coach), Drake 1969-1972, Indiana 1973-76, Notre Dame 1977-1980. Pro coach: Oklahoma Outlaws (USFL) 1984, Jacksonville Bulls (USFL) 1985, Phoenix Cardinals 1986-1993, Indianapolis Colts 1994-97, Seattle Seahawks 1998, joined Eagles in 1999.

Sean McDermott, secondary/safeties; born March 21, 1974, Omaha, Neb. Safety William & Mary 1994-97. No pro playing experience. College coach: William & Mary 1998. Pro coach: Joined Eagles in 1998.

Tom Melvin, tight ends; born October 1, 1961, Redwood City, Calif. Offensive lineman San Francisco State 1982-83. No pro playing experience. College coach: San Francisco State 1984-85, Northern Arizona 1986-87, California-Santa Barbara 1988-1990, Occidental College 1991-98. Pro coach: Joined Eagles in 1999.

Marty Mornhinweg, asst. head coach; born March 29, 1962, Edmond, Okla.. Quarterback Montana 1981-84. Pro quarterback Denver Dynamite (AFL) 1987. College coach: Montana 1985, Texas-El Paso 1986-87, Northern Arizona 1994, Southeast Missouri State 1989-1990, Missouri 1991-93. Pro coach: Green Bay Packers 1995-96, San Francisco 49ers 1997-2000, Detroit Lions 2001-02 (head coach), joined Eagles in 2003.

Mike Reed, defensive assistant/quality control; born August 16, 1972, Wilmington, Del. Defensive back Boston College 1991-94. Pro defensive back Carolina Panthers 1995-96, Frankfurt Galaxy (NFL Europe) 1998-99. College coach: Richmond 2000-02. Pro coach: Joined Eagles in 2003.

Bill Shuey, offensive assistant/quality control; born October 5, 1974, Bethlehem, Pa. Attended Slippery Rock. No college or pro playing experience. Pro coach: Joined Eagles in 2003.

Pat Shurmur, quarterbacks; born April 14, 1965, Dearborn Heights, Mich. Center Michigan State 1983-87. No pro playing experience. College coach: Michigan State 1988-1997, Stanford 1998. Pro coach: Joined Eagles in 1999.

Steve Spagnuolo, linebackers; born December 21, 1959, Witinsville, Mass. Wide receiver Springfield College 1979-1981. No pro playing experience. College coach: Massachusetts 1982-83, Lafayette 1984-86, Connecticut 1987-1991, Maine 1993, Rutgers 1994-95, Bowling Green 1996-97. Pro coach: Barcelona Dragons (World League) 1992, Frankfurt Galaxy (NFLE) 1998, joined Eagles in 1999.

Trent Walters, secondary; born November 20. 1943, Knoxville, Tenn. Defensive back Indiana 1963-65. Pro defensive back Edmonton Eskimos (CFL) 1966-67. College coach: Indiana 1968-1971, Louisville 1972, 1986-1990, Indiana 1973-1980, Washington 1981-83, Pittsburgh 1985, Texas A&M 1991-93, Notre Dame 2002-03. Pro coach: Cincinnati Bengals 1984, Minnesota Vikings 1994-2001, joined Eagles in 2004.

Ted Williams, running backs; born November 17, 1943, Lyons, Texas. Attended Cal Poly-Pomona. No college or pro playing experience. College coach: UCLA 1980-89, Washington State 1991-93, Arizona 1994. Pro coach: Joined Eagles in 1995.

Mike Wolf, strength and conditioning; born May 15, 1965, Allentown, Pa. Center Penn State 1983-87. No pro playing experience. College coach: Vanderbilt 1988-89, Lehigh 1990, Penn State 1991. Pro coach: Minnesota Vikings 1992-94, joined Eagles in 1995.

National Football Conference
West Division
Team Colors: New Century Gold,
　　　　　　Millennium Blue, and White
One Rams Way
St. Louis, Missouri 63045
Telephone: (314) 982-7267

2005 SCHEDULE
PRESEASON
Aug. 12 **Chicago** 7:00
Aug. 21 at San Diego.......................1:00
Aug. 29 at Detroit 8:00
Sept. 2 **Kansas City** 7:00

REGULAR SEASON
Sept. 11 at San Francisco.................1:15
Sept. 18 at Arizona...........................1:05
Sept. 25 **Tennessee** 12:00
Oct. 2 　at New York Giants 1:00
Oct. 9 　**Seattle** 12:00
Oct. 17 at Indianapolis (Mon.).........8:00
Oct. 23 **New Orleans** 12:00
Oct. 30 **Jacksonville** 12:00
Nov. 6 　Open Date
Nov. 13 at Seattle 1:15
Nov. 20 **Arizona** 12:00
Nov. 27 at Houston 12:00
Dec. 4 　**Washington** 3:05
Dec. 11 at Minnesota 12:00
Dec. 18 **Philadelphia** 3:15
Dec. 24 **San Francisco** (Sat.)........12:00
Jan. 1 　at Dallas............................7:30

Stadium: Edward Jones Dome
　　　　　(opened in 1995)
　　　　　•**Capacity:** 66,000
　　　　　701 Convention Plaza
　　　　　St. Louis, Missouri 63101
Playing Surface: FieldTurf
Training Camp: Rams Park
　　　　　　　　Training Facility
　　　　　　　　St. Louis, Missouri 63045

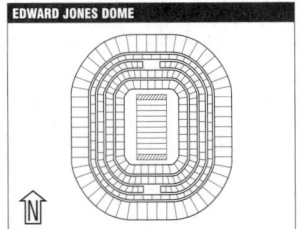

CLUB OFFICIALS
Owner/Chairman: Georgia Frontiere
Owner/Vice Chairman: Stan Kroenke
President: John Shaw
President-Football Operations:
　Jay Zygmunt
Executive Vice President: Bob Wallace
Treasurer: Jeff Brewer
Vice President-Finance: Adrian Bracy
General Manager: Charley Armey
Vice President-Sales and Marketing:
　Phil Thomas
Director-Player Personnel:
　Lawrence McCutcheon
Vice President-Ticket Operations:
　Michael T. Naughton
Vice President-Operations:
　John Oswald
Director-Football Administration:
　Samir Suleiman
Director-Football Media: Duane Lewis
Head Trainer: Jim Anderson
Assistant Trainers: Dake Walden,
　Ron DuBuque, James Lomax
Equipment Manager: Todd Hewitt
Scouts: Dick Daniels, Mel Foels,
　Tom Marino, John Mancini,
　David Razzano, Luke Driscoll,
　Dave Boller

COACHING HISTORY
Cleveland 1937-1945,
Los Angeles 1946-1994
(503-447-20)
Records include postseason games
1937-38	Hugo Bezdek*	1-13-0
1938	Art Lewis	4-4-0
1939-1942	Earl (Dutch) Clark	..16-26-2
1944	Aldo (Buff) Donelli	4-6-0
1945-46	Adam Walsh	16-5-1
1947	Bob Snyder	6-6-0
1948-49	Clark Shaughnessy	..14-8-3
1950-52	Joe Stydahar**	19-9-0
1952-54	Hamp Pool	23-11-2
1955-59	Sid Gillman	28-32-1
1960-62	Bob Waterfield***	..9-24-1
1962-65	Harland Svare	14-31-3
1966-1970	George Allen	49-19-4
1971-72	Tommy Prothro	14-12-2
1973-77	Chuck Knox	57-20-1
1978-1982	Ray Malavasi	43-36-0
1983-1991	John Robinson	79-74-0
1992-94	Chuck Knox	15-33-0
1995-96	Rich Brooks	13-19-0
1997-99	Dick Vermeil	25-26-0
2000-04	Mike Martz	54-33-0

　*Released after three games in 1938
　**Resigned after one game in 1952
　***Resigned after eight games in 1962

ATTENDANCE
Home 514,692　　　　Away 524,553
Total 1,039,245
Single-game home record,
　66,273 (12/10/00)
Single-season home record,
　520,926 (1999)

2005 DRAFT CHOICES
Round	Name	Pos.	College
1	Alex Barron	T	Florida State
2	Ronald Bartell	DB	Howard
3	Oshiomogho Atogwe	DB	Stanford
	Richie Incognito	G	Nebraska
4	Jerome Carter	DB	Florida State
	Claude Terrell	G	New Mexico
5	Jerome Collins	TE	Notre Dame
6	Dante Ridgeway	WR	Ball State
	Reggie Hodges	P	Ball State
7	Ryan Fitzpatrick	QB	Harvard
	Madison Hedgecock	RB	North Carolina

2004 TEAM RECORD

PRESEASON (1-3)

Date	Result	Opponent
8/12	L 10-13	Chicago
8/23	L 7-24	at Kansas City
8/27	W 28-3	Washington
9/2	L 24-28	at Oakland

REGULAR SEASON (8-8)

Date	Result	Opponent	Att.
9/12	W 17-10	Arizona	65,538
9/19	L 17-34	at Atlanta	70,882
9/26	L 25-28	New Orleans (OT)	65,856
10/3	W 24-14	at San Francisco	66,696
10/10	W 33-27	at Seattle (OT)	66,940
10/18	W 28-21	Tampa Bay	66,040
10/24	L 14-31	at Miami	72,945
11/7	L 22-40	New England	66,107
11/14	W 23-12	Seattle	66,044
11/21	L 17-37	at Buffalo	72,393
11/29	L 17-45	at Green Bay	70,385
12/5	W 16-6	San Francisco	65,793
12/12	L 7-20	at Carolina	73,306
12/19	L 7-31	at Arizona	40,070
12/27	W 20-7	Philadelphia	66,129
1/2	W 32-29	N.Y. Jets (OT)	65,877

(OT) Overtime

POSTSEASON (1-1)

Date	Result	Opponent	
1/8	W 27-20	at Seattle	65,397
1/15	L 17-47	at Atlanta	70,709

SCORE BY PERIODS

Rams	69	115	40	86	9	—	319
Opponents	78	127	90	94	3	—	392

2004 TEAM STATISTICS

	Rams	Opp.
Total First Downs	321	311
Rushing	96	118
Passing	203	172
Penalty	22	21
3rd Down: Made/Att	89/211	76/209
3rd Down Pct.	42.2	36.4
4th Down: Made/Att	13/19	12/17
4th Down Pct.	68.4	70.6
Possession Avg.	31:05	28:55
Total Net Yards	5877	5353
Avg. Per Game	367.3	334.6
Total Plays	1011	1006
Avg. Per Play	5.8	5.3
Net Yards Rushing	1624	2179
Avg. Per Game	101.5	136.2
Total Rushes	381	480
Net Yards Passing	4253	3174
Avg. Per Game	265.8	198.4
Sacked/Yards Lost	50/362	34/241
Gross Yards	4615	3415
Att./Completions	580/372	492/292
Completion Pct.	64.1	59.3
Had Intercepted	22	6
Punts/Average	68/41.9	71/42.5
Net Punting Avg.	68/34.0	71/37.6
Penalties/Yards	127/993	109/827
Fumbles/Ball Lost	27/17	18/9
Touchdowns	37	43
Rushing	11	13
Passing	23	24
Returns	3	6

2004 INDIVIDUAL STATISTICS

PASSING

	Att.	Comp.	Yds.	Pct.	TD	Int.	Tkld.	Rate
Bulger	485	321	3,964	66.2	21	14	41/302	93.7
C. Chandler	62	35	463	56.5	2	8	7/54	51.4
Martin	30	16	188	53.3	0	0	2/6	72.6
Bruce	2	0	0	0.0	0	0	0/0	39.6
Wilkins	1	0	0	0.0	0	0	0/0	39.6
Rams	580	372	4,615	64.1	23	22	50/362	86.1
Opponents	492	292	3,415	59.3	24	6	34/241	91.6

SCORING

	TD R	TD P	TD Rt	PAT	FG	Saf	PTS
Wilkins	0	0	0	32/32	19/24	0	89
Holt	0	10	0	0/0	0/0	0	60
Bruce	0	6	0	0/0	0/0	0	36
M. Faulk	3	1	0	0/0	0/0	0	28
S. Jackson	4	0	0	0/0	0/0	0	26
Bulger	3	0	0	0/0	0/0	0	18
McDonald	0	3	0	0/0	0/0	0	18
Curtis	0	2	0	0/0	0/0	0	14
Little	0	0	2	0/0	0/0	0	12
Archuleta	0	0	1	0/0	0/0	0	6
Goodspeed	1	0	0	0/0	0/0	0	6
Manumaleuna	0	1	0	0/0	0/0	0	6
Rams	11	23	3	32/32	19/24	0	319
Opponents	13	24	6	39/39	31/36	0	392

2-Pt. Conversions: M. Faulk 2, Curtis, S. Jackson.
Rams 4-4, Opponents 1-4

RUSHING

	No.	Yds	Avg	LG	TD
M. Faulk	195	774	4.0	40	3
S. Jackson	134	673	5.0	48	4
Bulger	19	89	4.7	19t	3
Harris	20	63	3.2	14	0
Curtis	3	24	8.0	15	0
Goodspeed	3	6	2.0	2t	1
C. Chandler	1	2	2.0	2	0
McDonald	4	0	0.0	7	0
Cleeland	1	-2	-2.0	-2	0
Wilkins	1	-5	-5.0	-5	0
Rams	381	1,624	4.3	48	11
Opponents	480	2,179	4.5	42t	13

RECEIVING

	No.	Yds	Avg	LG	TD
Holt	94	1,372	14.6	75t	10
Bruce	89	1,292	14.5	56	6
M. Faulk	50	310	6.2	25	1
McDonald	37	494	13.4	52t	3
Curtis	32	421	13.2	41t	2
S. Jackson	19	189	9.9	28	0
Manumaleuna	15	174	11.6	48	1
Looker	13	183	14.1	29	0
Goodspeed	11	71	6.5	13	0
Cleeland	7	57	8.1	15	0
Harris	4	44	11.0	21	0
Furrey	1	8	8.0	8	0
Rams	372	4,615	12.4	75t	23
Opponents	292	3,415	11.7	71t	24

INTERCEPTIONS

	No.	Yds	Avg	LG	TD
Butler	5	15	3.0	10	0
T. Fisher	1	30	30.0	30	0
Rams	6	45	7.5	30	0
Opponents	22	191	8.7	38t	1

PUNTING

	No.	Yds.	Avg.	In 20	LG
Landeta	40	1,733	43.3	9	63
Stemke	28	1,115	39.8	12	56
Rams	68	2,848	41.9	21	63
Opponents	71	3,014	42.5	17	65

PUNT RETURNS

	Ret	FC	Yds	Avg	LG	TD
McDonald	30	18	143	4.8	39	0
Rams	30	18	143	4.8	39	0
Opponents	35	17	416	11.9	86t	1

KICKOFF RETURNS

	No.	Yds	Avg	LG	TD
Harris	47	951	20.2	29	0
Cason	14	310	22.1	31	0
Furrey	8	157	19.6	23	0
Anderson	4	71	17.8	25	0
S. Jackson	4	79	19.8	23	0
Manumaleuna	2	13	6.5	13	0
Coady	1	-1	-1.0	-1	0
M. Faulk	1	0	0.0	0	0
Flowers	1	0	0.0	0	0
Goodspeed	1	9	9.0	9	0
Groce	1	15	15.0	15	0
Rams	84	1,604	19.1	31	0
Opponents	66	1,680	25.5	94t	1

FIELD GOALS

	1-19	20-29	30-39	40-49	50+
Wilkins	0/0	7/7	5/6	3/6	4/5
Rams	0/0	7/7	5/6	3/6	4/5
Opponents	0/0	8/8	11/12	9/11	3/5

SACKS

	No.
B. Fisher	8.5
Little	7.0
Lewis	5.0
T. Jackson	4.0
Archuleta	2.0
Pickett	2.0
Polley	2.0
Tinoisamoa	1.5
Flowers	1.0
Hargrove	1.0
Rams	34.0
Opponents	50.0

RECORD HOLDERS
INDIVIDUAL RECORDS—CAREER

Category	Name	Performance
Rushing (Yds.)	Eric Dickerson, 1983-87	7,245
Passing (Yds.)	Jim Everett, 1986-1993	23,758
Passing (TDs)	Roman Gabriel, 1962-1972	154
Receiving (No.)	Isaac Bruce, 1994-2004	777
Receiving (Yds.)	Isaac Bruce, 1994-2004	11,753
Interceptions	Ed Meador, 1959-1970	46
Punting (Avg.)	Danny Villanueva, 1960-64	44.3
Punt Return (Avg.)	Az-Zahir Hakim, 1998-2001	11.4
Kickoff Return (Avg.)	Ron Brown, 1984-89, 1991	26.3
Field Goals	Jeff Wilkins, 1997-2004	182
Touchdowns (Tot.)	Marshall Faulk, 1999-2004	84
Points	Jeff Wilkins, 1997-2004	878

INDIVIDUAL RECORDS—SINGLE SEASON

Category	Name	Performance
Rushing (Yds.)	Eric Dickerson, 1984	*2,105
Passing (Yds.)	Kurt Warner, 2001	4,830
Passing (TDs)	Kurt Warner, 1999	41
Receiving (No.)	Isaac Bruce, 1995	119
Receiving (Yds.)	Isaac Bruce, 1995	1,781
Interceptions	Dick (Night Train) Lane, 1952	*14
Punting (Avg.)	Danny Villanueva, 1962	45.5
Punt Return (Avg.)	Woodley Lewis, 1952	18.5
Kickoff Return (Avg.)	Verda (Vitamin T) Smith, 1950	33.7
Field Goals	Jeff Wilkins, 2003	39
Touchdowns (Tot.)	Marshall Faulk, 2000	26
Points	Jeff Wilkins, 2003	163

INDIVIDUAL RECORDS—SINGLE GAME

Category	Name	Performance
Rushing (Yds.)	Willie Ellison, 12-5-71	247
Passing (Yds.)	Norm Van Brocklin, 9-28-51	*554
Passing (TDs)	Many times	5
	Last time by Kurt Warner, 10-10-99	
Receiving (No.)	Tom Fears, 12-3-50	18
Receiving (Yds.)	Willie Anderson, 11-26-89	*336
Interceptions	Many times	3
	Last time by Keith Lyle, 12-15-96	
Field Goals	Bob Waterfield, 12-9-51	5
	Jeff Wilkins, 10-1-00	5
Touchdowns (Tot.)	Many times	4
	Last time by Marshall Faulk, 10-20-02	
Points	Many times	24
	Last time by Marshall Faulk, 10-20-02	

*NFL Record

2005 VETERAN ROSTER

No.	Name	Pos.	Ht.	Wt.	Birthdate	NFL Exp.	College	Hometown	How Acq.	'04 Games/ Starts
72	Alford, Darnell	G	6-4	334	6/11/77	4	Boston College	Fredericksburg, Va.	FA-'04	0*
20	Anderson, Dwight	CB	5-10	172	7/5/81	2	South Dakota	Bloomfield, Conn.	FA-'04	12/0
31	Archuleta, Adam	S	6-0	223	11/27/77	5	Arizona State	Chandler, Ariz.	D1b-'01	16/14
80	Bruce, Isaac	WR	6-0	188	11/10/72	12	Memphis State	Fort Lauderdale, Fla.	D2a-'94	16/16
10	Bulger, Marc	QB	6-3	215	4/5/77	5	West Virginia	Pittsburgh, Pa.	FA-'01	14/14
23	Butler, Jerametrius	CB	5-10	181	11/28/78	5	Kansas State	Dallas, Texas	D5-'01	16/16
27	Cason, Aveion	RB	5-10	204	7/12/79	5	Illinois State	St. Petersburg, Fla.	FA-'04	3/0
54	Chillar, Brandon	LB	6-3	253	10/21/82	2	UCLA	Carlsbad, Calif.	D4-'04	16/5
59	Claiborne, Chris	LB	6-3	255	7/26/78	7	Southern California	Riverdale, Calif.	UFA(Minn)-'05	12/12*
52	Coakley, Dexter	LB	5-10	236	10/20/72	9	Appalachian State	Mt. Pleasant, S.C.	FA-'05	16/16
83	Curtis, Kevin	WR	5-11	186	7/17/78	3	Utah State	South Jordan, Utah	D3-'03	15/0
30	Fair, Terry	CB	5-10	191	7/20/76	8	Tennessee	Phoenix, Ariz.	FA-'05	0*
28	Faulk, Marshall	RB	5-10	211	2/26/73	12	San Diego State	New Orleans, La.	T(Ind)-'99	14/14
57	Faulk, Trev	LB	6-3	254	8/6/81	4	Louisiana State	Lafayette, La.	FA-'03	13/2
22	Fisher, Travis	CB	5-10	189	9/12/79	4	Central Florida	Tallahassee, Fla.	D2-'02	10/10
25	Furrey, Mike	S	6-0	185	5/12/77	3	Northern Iowa	Hilliard, Ohio	FA-'03	8/0
21	Garrett, Kevin	CB	5-10	194	7/29/80	3	Southern Methodist	Brazoria, Texas	D5c-'03	14/1
44	Goodspeed, Joey	FB	6-1	247	2/22/78	4	Notre Dame	Oswego, Ill.	FA-'03	16/5
93	Green, Brandon	DE	6-3	264	9/5/80	3	Rice	Vanderbilt, Texas	FA-'05	3/0*
24	Groce, DeJuan	CB	5-10	192	2/17/80	3	Nebraska	Garfield Heights, Ohio	D4b-'03	11/4
95	Hargrove, Anthony	DE	6-3	269	7/20/83	2	Georgia Tech	Punta Gorda, Fla.	D3-'03	15/2
33	Harris, Arlen	RB	5-10	212	4/22/80	3	Virginia	Downingtown, Pa.	FA-'03	14/1
26	Hawthorne, Michael	CB/S	6-3	204	1/26/77	6	Purdue	Sarasota, Fla.	FA-'05	16/5*
81	Holt, Torry	WR	6-0	190	6/5/76	7	North Carolina State	Greensboro, N.C.	D1-'99	16/16
98	Howard, Brian	DT	6-4	278	9/9/81	2	Idaho	Kent, Wash.	FA-'04	15/1
35	Ivy, Corey	CB	5-9	188	3/29/77	4	Oklahoma	Moore, Okla.	FA-'05	16/0*
39	Jackson, Steven	RB	6-2	231	7/22/83	2	Oregon State	Las Vegas, Nev.	D1-'04	14/3
97	Jackson, Tyoka	DT	6-2	280	11/22/71	11	Penn State	Forrestville, Md.	UFA(TB)-'01	14/0
49	Jensen, Erik	TE	6-2	253	10/11/80	2	Iowa	Appleton, Wis.	D7a-'04	0*
73	Kennedy, Jimmy	DT	6-4	320	11/15/79	3	Penn State	Yonkers, N.Y.	D1-'03	9/5
92	Lewis, Damione	DT	6-2	301	3/1/78	5	Miami	Sulphur Springs, Texas	D1a-'01	16/10
91	Little, Leonard	DE	6-3	261	10/19/74	8	Tennessee	Asheville, N.C.	D3-'98	16/16
89	Looker, Dane	WR	6-0	194	5/5/76	5	Washington	Puyallup, Wash.	FA-'02	14/0
56	Loyd, Jeremy	LB	6-2	235	7/30/80	3	Iowa State	Pittsburg, Texas	FA-'03	0*
86	Manumaleuna, Brandon	TE	6-2	288	1/4/80	5	Arizona	Lomita, Calif.	D4b-'01	16/16
11	Martin, Jamie	QB	6-2	205	2/8/70	11	Weber State	Arroyo Grande, Calif.	FA-'04	1/0
45	Massey, Chris	FB	6-0	245	8/21/79	4	Marshall	Chesapeake, W. Va.	D7-'02	16/0
67	McCollum, Andy	C	6-4	300	6/2/70	12	Toledo	Richfield, Ohio	UFA(NO)-'99	16/16
84	McDonald, Shaun	WR	5-10	183	6/13/81	3	Arizona State	Phoenix, Ariz.	D4a-'03	16/0
76	Pace, Orlando	T	6-7	325	11/4/75	8	Ohio State	Sandusky, Ohio	D1-'97	16/16
79	Pickett, Ryan	DT	6-2	310	10/8/79	5	Ohio State	Zephyrhills, Fla.	D1c-'01	16/16
60	Saipaia, Blaine	T	6-3	310	8/25/78	2	Colorado State	Oxnard, Calif.	FA-'04	8/5
9	Smoker, Jeff	QB	6-3	223	6/13/81	2	Michigan State	Manheim, Pa.	D6-'04	0*
34	Stone, Michael	S	6-0	201	2/13/78	5	Memphis	Southfield, Mich.	UFA(Ariz)-'05	14/0*
63	Tercero, Scott	T	6-4	303	10/28/81	3	California	Pico Rivera, Calif.	FA-'03	8/4
55	Thomas, Robert	LB	6-1	237	7/17/80	4	UCLA	Imperial, Calif.	D1-'02	14/11
62	Timmerman, Adam	G	6-4	310	8/14/71	11	South Dakota State	Cherokee, Iowa	UFA(GB)-'99	16/16
50	Tinoisamoa, Pisa	LB	6-1	235	7/15/81	3	Hawaii	Vista, Calif.	D2-'03	16/16
66	Tucker, Rex	G	6-5	315	12/20/76	7	Texas A&M	Midland, Texas	FA-'05	6/5*
68	Turley, Kyle	T	6-5	309	9/24/75	8	San Diego State	Moreno Valley, Calif.	T(NO)-'03	0*
64	Turner, Larry	C	6-2	290	3/8/82	2	Eastern Kentucky	Huber Heights, Ohio	D7b-'04	14/1
58	Wahlroos, Drew	LB	6-3	235	6/7/80	2	Colorado	Poway, Calif.	FA-'04	6/0
14	Wilkins, Jeff	K	6-2	205	4/19/72	12	Youngstown State	Austintown, Ohio	RFA(SF)-'97	16/0
77	Williams, Grant	T	6-7	320	5/10/74	10	Louisiana Tech	Clinton, Miss.	T(NE)-'02	16/11
96	Williams, Jay	DE	6-3	270	10/13/71	11	Wake Forest	Washington, D.C.	FA-'05	16/1*
88	Williams, Roland	TE	6-5	265	4/27/75	8	Syracuse	Rochester, N.Y.	FA-'05	12/3*

* Alford did not play in 2 games; Claiborne played 12 games with Chicago in '04; Fair last active with Carolina in '02; Green played 3 games with Jacksonville; Hawthorne played 16 games with Green Bay; Ivy played 16 games with Tampa Bay; Jensen missed '04 season because of injury; Loyd missed '04 season because of injury; Smoker did not play in 1 game; Stone played 14 games with Arizona; Tucker played 6 games with Chicago; Turley missed '04 season because of injury; J. Williams played 16 games with Miami; R. Williams played 12 games with Oakland.

Players lost through free agency (4): S Rich Coady (Atl; 16 games in '04), DE Bryce Fisher (Sea; 16), G Matt Lehr (Atl; 0), LB Tommy Polley (Balt; 15).

Also played with Rams in '04—QB Chris Chandler (5 games), TE Cameron Cleeland (16), G Chris Dishman (7), S Antuan Edwards (6), DE Erik Flowers (9), P Sean Landeta (10), S Kwamie Lassiter (4), S Justin Lucas (7), S Tod McBride (2), G Tom Nütten (8), RB Stephen Trejo (2), S Aeneas Williams (13).

2005 FIRST-YEAR ROSTER

Name	Pos.	Ht.	Wt.	Birthdate	College	Hometown	How Acq.
Atogwe, Oshiomogho	S	5-11	203	6/23/81	Stanford	Windsor, Ontario, Canada	D3a
Barron, Alex	T	6-7	320	9/28/82	Florida State	Orangeburg, S.C.	D1
Bartell, Ron	CB	6-1	208	2/22/82	Howard	Detroit, Mich.	D2
Bray, Zach	G	6-3	303	10/8/81	Texas Christian	Montgomery, Texas	FA
Burley, Nick	FB	6-3	243	3/31/80	Fresno State	Mountain View, Calif.	FA
Calahan, Jeremy	DT	6-2	298	7/7/83	Rice	Pflugerville, Texas	FA
Carter, Jeremy	WR	5-11	194	11/20/79	Western Carolina	Raleigh, N.C.	FA
Carter, Jerome	S	5-11	219	10/25/82	Florida State	Lake City, Fla.	D4a
Cecil, Toby	C	6-4	290	12/26/80	Texas Tech	Richardson, Texas	FA
Coleman, Michael	WR	6-0	190	9/7/80	Widener	Wilmington, Del.	FA
Collins, Jerome	TE	6-4	267	4/18/82	Notre Dame	Warrenville, Ill.	D5
Dukes, Clifford	LB	6-3	270	6/26/81	Michigan State	Lexington Park, Md.	FA
Fitzpatrick, Ryan	QB	6-2	221	11/24/82	Harvard	Gilbert, Ariz.	D7a
Hedgecock, Madison	FB	6-3	266	8/27/81	North Carolina	Wallburg, N.C.	D7b
Hodges, Reggie	P	6-0	226	1/26/82	Ball State	Champaign, Ill.	D6b
Incognito, Richie	G	6-3	305	7/5/83	Nebraska	Glendale, Ariz.	D3b
Jamison, Vontrell	DE	6-6	277	7/26/82	Clemson	Holly Hill, S.C.	FA
McChesney, Matt	DT	6-4	292	11/6/81	Colorado	Longmont, Colo.	FA
McGrorty, Dusty	RB	5-10	218	5/9/81	Southern Oregon	Warrenton, Ore.	FA
Middleton, Brandon	WR	5-10	190	1/2/81	Houston	Houston, Texas	FA
Morgan, Matt	T	6-6	304	12/3/80	Pittsburgh	Pittsburgh, Pa.	FA
Newson, Tony	LB	6-1	247	9/11/79	Utah State	Las Vegas, Nev.	FA
Ridgeway, Dante	WR	5-11	212	4/18/84	Ball State	Decatur, Ill.	D6a
Robinson, Dominic	WR	6-0	210	6/21/81	Florida State	Diamond Bar, Calif.	FA
Terrell, Claude	G	6-2	343	4/20/82	New Mexico	LaMarque, Texas	D4b
Thompson, Dominique	WR	5-11	197	12/28/82	William & Mary	Durham, N.C.	FA
Thompson, Duvol	CB	5-9	183	1/28/83	Pennsylvania	Calumet City, Ill.	FA

The term NFL Rookie is defined as a player who is in his first season of professional football and has not been on the roster of another professional football team for any regular-season or postseason games. A Rookie is designated by an "R" on NFL rosters. Players who have been active in another professional football league or players who have NFL experience, including either preseason training camp or being on an Active List or Inactive List, or on Reserve/Injured or Reserve/Physically Unable to Perform for fewer than six regular-season games, are termed NFL First-Year Players. An NFL First-Year Player is designated by a "1" on NFL rosters. Thereafter, a player is credited with an additional year of experience for each season in which he accumulates six games on the Active List or Inactive List, or on Reserve/Injured or Reserve/Physically Unable to Perform.

Log on to www.stlouisrams.com for an up-to-date roster.

COACHING STAFF

Head Coach,
Mike Martz

Pro Career: Named twenty-first head coach of the Rams on February 2, 2000. Led Rams to two division titles and four playoff berths in his five seasons as head coach, including berth in Super Bowl XXXVI. Martz became the third-winningest coach in franchise history in 2004, passing George Allen (49) and finishing the season with 54 wins. In 2004, the Rams also became the first 8-8 team in NFL history to win a playoff game, and Martz was just the sixth head coach since the NFL instituted the 16-game schedule in 1978 to lead his team to victories over two 10-plus win teams in the final two weeks of the season. In 2003, he led the Rams to their second division title in three years. In 2002, he became only second coach in NFL history to lead team to five consecutive wins after an 0-5 start. Offensive mastermind behind one of the most explosive offenses in NFL history, as Rams are the only franchise in league history to score at least 500 points in three different seasons (526 in 1999, 540 in 2000, 503 in 2001). Since he rejoined the Rams as offensive coordinator in 1999, the Rams have scored more points (2,651), gained more total yards (37,070), and accumulated more passing yards (26,616) than any club during a six-year span in NFL history. The Rams also produced three consecutive NFL most valuable players (quarterback Kurt Warner 1999 and 2001, running back Marshall Faulk 2000). Martz re-joined the Rams in 1999 after two seasons as quarterbacks coach of Washington Redskins. He began his NFL career with the Rams, where he coached tight ends, receivers, and quarterbacks (1992-96). Career record: 54-33.

Background: Played tight end at Fresno State (1972) after transferring from the University of California-Santa Barbara. Began coaching career in 1973 at Bullard High in Fresno, California, before coaching collegiately at San Diego Mesa C.C. (1974, 1976-77), San Jose State (1975), Santa Ana College (1978), Fresno State (1979), Pacific (1980-81), Minnesota (1982), and Arizona State (1983-1991), where he served as the Sun Devils' offensive coordinator the final five seasons.

Personal: Born May 13, 1951, Sioux Falls, S.D. Graduated summa cum laude from Fresno State (1973). Lives with wife Julie and has three sons and one daughter.

ASSISTANT COACHES

Charles Bankins, asst. special teams; born August 4, 1972, Baltimore. Running back James Madison 1990-92. College coach: Eastern Kentucky 1997, James Madison 1998, Indiana (Pa.) 1999, Hampton 2000-04. Pro coach: Joined Rams in 2005.

John Benton, offensive line; born December 13, 1963, Los Angeles. Offensive lineman Colorado State 1986-1990. No pro playing experience. College coach: California (Pa.) University 1990-94, Colorado State 1996-2003. Pro coach: Joined Rams in 2004.

Gill Byrd, secondary assistant; born February 20, 1961, San Francisco. Cornerback San Jose State 1979-1982. Pro cornerback San Diego Chargers 1983-1992. Pro coach: Joined Rams in 2003.

Pat Carter, offensive assistant; born August 1, 1966, Saratota, Fla. Tight end Florida State 1984-87. Pro tight end Detroit Lions 1988, Los Angeles Rams 1989-1994, Houston Oilers 1995-96, Arizona Cardinals 1997. Pro coach: Joined Rams in 2005.

Chris Clausen, strength and conditioning coordinator; born February 21, 1958, Evergreen Park, Ill. Cornerback Indiana 1976-79. No pro playing experience. College coach: San Diego State 1987-88. Pro coach: San Diego Chargers 1989-1991, joined Rams in 1992.

Henry Ellard, wide receivers; born July 21, 1961, Fresno, Calif. Wide receiver Fresno State 1979-1982. Pro wide receiver/punt returner Los Angeles Rams 1983-1993, Washington Redskins 1994-97, New England Patriots 1998, Washington Redskins 1999. College coach: Fresno State 2000. Pro coach: Joined Rams in 2001.

Steve Fairchild, offensive coordinator; born June 21, 1958, Decatur, Ill. Quarterback Colorado State 1980-81. No pro playing experience. College coach: Mesa (Colo.) C.C. 1982-83, Ferris State 1984-85, San Diego State 1991-92, Colorado State 1997-2000. Pro coach: Buffalo Bills 2001-02, joined Rams in 2003.

Frank Falks, tight ends; born March 9, 1943, Tampa. Linebacker Joplin (Mo.) J.C. 1963-64, Parsons College 1965-66. No pro playing experience. College coach: Parsons College 1967-69, Kansas State 1970-72, Arkansas 1973-77, Wyoming 1978-79, San Diego State 1980, Oklahoma State 1981-82, Southern California 1983-86, Arizona State 1987-1991, Ohio State 1992-93. Pro coach: San Diego Chargers 1994-96, Detroit Lions 1997-2000, joined Rams in 2003.

Bill Kollar, defensive line; born November 27, 1952, Warren, Ohio. Defensive end Montana State 1971-74. Pro defensive end Cincinnati Bengals 1974-76, Tampa Bay Buccaneers 1977-1981. College coach: Illinois 1985-87, Purdue 1988-89. Pro coach: Tampa Bay Buccaneers 1984, Atlanta Falcons 1990-2000, joined Rams in 2001.

Dana LeDuc, strength and conditioning; born March 22, 1953, Tacoma, Wash. Attended Texas. No college or no playing experience. College coach: Texas 1977-1992, Miami 1993-94. Pro coach: Seattle Seahawks 1995-98, joined Rams in 1999.

Bob Ligashesky, special teams; born June 2, 1962, Pittsburgh. Linebacker Indiana (Pa.) 1983-84. No pro playing experience. College coach: Wake Forest 1985, Arizona State 1986-89, Kent State 1990, Bowling Green 1991-99, Pittsburgh 2000-03. Pro coach: Jacksonville Jaguars 2004, joined Rams in 2005.

Larry Marmie, defensive coordinator; born October 17, 1942, Barnesville, Ohio. Quarterback Eastern Kentucky 1962-65. No pro playing experience. College coach: Eastern Kentucky 1967-68, 1972-76, Morehead State 1968-1971, Tulsa 1977-78, North Carolina 1979-1982, Tennessee 1983-84, 1992-94, Arizona State 1988-91 (head coach), UCLA 1995. Pro coach: Arizona Cardinals 1996-2003, joined Rams in 2004.

John Matsko, associate head coach/offensive line; born February 2, 1951, Cleveland. Fullback Kent State 1970-73. No pro playing experience. College coach Kent State 1973, Miami (Ohio) 1974-75, 1977, North Carolina 1978-1984, Navy 1985, Arizona 1986, Southern California 1987-1991. Pro coach: Phoenix Cardinals 1992-93, New Orleans Saints 1994-96, New York Giants 1997-98, joined Rams in 1999.

Wilbert Montgomery, running backs; born September 16, 1954, Greenville, Miss. Running back Abilene Christian 1973-76. Pro running back Philadelphia Eagles 1977-1984, Detroit Lions 1985-86. Pro coach: Joined Rams in 1997.

John Ramsdell, quarterbacks; born August 16, 1954, Lafayette, Ind. Running back Springfield (Mass.) College 1972-75. No pro playing experience. College coach: San Francisco State 1976-77, Long Beach State 1978, Pacific 1979-1982, Oregon 1983-1994. Pro coach: Joined Rams in 1995.

Kurt Schottenheimer, secondary; born October 1, 1949, McDonald, Pa. Quarterback Coffeyville (Kan.) J.C. 1967-1968, defensive back Miami 1969-1970. No pro playing experience. College coach: William Patterson 1974, Michigan State 1978-1982, Tulane 1983, Louisiana State 1984-85, Notre Dame 1986. Pro coach: Cleveland Browns 1987-88, Kansas City Chiefs 1989-2000, Washington Redskins 2001, Detroit Lions 2002-03, Green Bay Packers 2004, joined Rams in 2005.

Matt Sheldon, special assistant; born February 26, 1969, Berwyn, Ill. Cornerback Minnesota 1987-1991. No pro playing experience. College coach: Wisconsin 1997-99. Pro coach: Joined Rams in 2001.

Joe Vitt, asst. head coach/linebackers; born August 23, 1954, Syracuse, N.Y. Linebacker Towson State 1973-75. No pro playing experience. Pro coach: Baltimore Colts 1979, Seattle Seahawks 1982-1991, L.A. Rams 1992-94, Philadelphia Eagles 1995-98, Green Bay Packers 1999, Kansas City Chiefs 2000-2003, joined Rams in 2004.

National Football Conference
West Division
Team Colors: Metalllic Gold,
  Cardinal Red, and Beige
4949 Centennial Boulevard
Santa Clara, California 95054
Telephone: (408) 562-4949

2005 SCHEDULE
PRESEASON
Aug. 13	**Oakland**	7:00
Aug. 20	at Denver	7:00
Aug. 26	**Tennessee**	7:00
Sept. 1	at San Diego	7:00

REGULAR SEASON
Sept. 11	**St. Louis**	1:15
Sept. 18	at Philadelphia	1:00
Sept. 25	**Dallas**	1:05
Oct. 2	at Arizona (Mexico)	7:30
Oct. 9	**Indianapolis**	1:05
Oct. 16	Open Date	
Oct. 23	at Washington	1:00
Oct. 30	**Tampa Bay**	1:15
Nov. 6	**New York Giants**	1:05
Nov. 13	at Chicago	12:00
Nov. 20	**Seattle**	1:05
Nov. 27	at Tennessee	12:00
Dec. 4	**Arizona**	1:05
Dec. 11	at Seattle	1:05
Dec. 18	at Jacksonville	1:00
Dec. 24	at St. Louis (Sat.)	12:00
Jan. 1	**Houston**	1:05

Stadium: Monster Park (opened in 1958)
  • **Capacity:** 69,732
  San Francisco, California
  94124
Playing Surface: Natural Grass
Training Camp: Marie P. DeBartolo
  Sports Center
  4949 Centennial Boulevard
  Santa Clara, CA 95054

MONSTER PARK

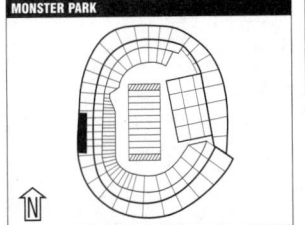

CLUB OFFICIALS
Owner: Denise DeBartolo York
Owner: John York
Owner: The DeBartolo Corporation
Vice President, CFO: Larry MacNeil
Vice President of Business Affairs,
  General Counsel: Ed Goines
Vice President, Operations: Murlan Fowell
Vice President, Player Personnel:
  Scot McCloughan
Vice President, Sales and Marketing:
  David Peart
Director, Football Operations:
  Paraag Marathe
Director, Football Administration:
  Terry Tumey
Director, Ticket Sales: Lynn Carrozzi
Director, Security: Fred Formosa
Director, Information Technology:
  Alexander Ignacio
Director, Stadium Operations:
  Jim Mercurio
Director, Public Relations:
  Kirk Reynolds
Equipment Manager: Steve Urbaniak
Manager, Video Operations: Keith Yanagi

COACHING HISTORY
(459-364-13)
Records include postseason games
1950-54	Lawrence (Buck) Shaw	33-25-2
1955	Norman (Red) Strader	4-8-0
1956-58	Frankie Albert	19-17-1
1959-1963	Howard (Red) Hickey*	27-27-1
1963-67	Jack Christiansen	26-38-3
1968-1975	Dick Nolan	56-56-5
1976	Monte Clark	8-6-0
1977	Ken Meyer	5-9-0
1978	Pete McCulley**	1-8-0
1978	Fred O'Connor	1-6-0
1979-1988	Bill Walsh	102-63-1
1989-1996	George Seifert	108-35-0
1997-2002	Steve Mariucci	60-43-0
2003-04	Dennis Erickson	9-23-0

  *Resigned after three games in 1963
  **Released after nine games in 1978

ATTENDANCE
Home 518,271   Away 500,236
Total 1,018,507
Single-game home record,
  69,014 (11/13/94)
Single-season home record,
  544,228 (1999)

2005 DRAFT CHOICES
Round	Name	Pos.	College
1	Alex Smith	QB	Utah
2	David Baas	G	Michigan
3	Frank Gore	RB	Miami
	Adam Snyder	T	Oregon
5	Ronald Fields	DT	Mississippi St.
	Rasheed Marshall	WR	West Virginia
6	Derrick Johnson	DB	Washington
7	Daven Holly	DB	Cincinnati
	Marcus Maxwell	WR	Oregon
	Patrick Estes	TE	Virginia
	Billy Bajema	TE	Oklahoma St.

2004 TEAM RECORD
PRESEASON (0-4)

Date	Result	Opponent
8/14	L	30-33 Oakland
8/21	L	13-20 at Chicago
8/27	L	10-23 at Minnesota
9/2	L	15-31 San Diego

REGULAR SEASON (2-14)

Date	Result	Opponent	Att.
9/12	L	19-21 Atlanta	65,584
9/19	L	27-30 at New Orleans	64,900
9/26	L	0-34 at Seattle	66,709
10/3	L	14-24 St. Louis	66,696
10/10	W	31-28 Arizona (OT)	62,836
10/17	L	14-22 at N.Y. Jets	78,189
10/31	L	13-23 at Chicago	62,054
11/7	L	27-42 Seattle	64,423
11/14	L	27-37 Carolina	63,618
11/21	L	3-35 at Tampa Bay	65,234
11/28	L	17-24 Miami	66,156
12/5	L	6-16 at St. Louis	65,793
12/12	W	31-28 at Arizona (OT)	35,069
12/18	L	16-26 Washington	65,710
12/26	L	7-41 Buffalo	63,248
1/2	L	7-21 at New England	68,756

(OT) Overtime

SCORE BY PERIODS

49ers	68	62	35	88	6	—	259
Opponents	86	141	84	141	0	—	452

2004 TEAM STATISTICS

	49ers	Opp.
Total First Downs	280	322
Rushing	83	121
Passing	172	179
Penalty	25	22
3rd Down: Made/Att	72/222	83/206
3rd Down Pct.	32.4	40.3
4th Down: Made/Att	14/19	6/9
4th Down Pct.	73.7	66.7
Possession Avg.	29:00	31:00
Total Net Yards	4585	5481
Avg. Per Game	286.6	342.6
Total Plays	1026	1014
Avg. Per Play	4.5	5.4
Net Yards Rushing	1449	1995
Avg. Per Game	90.6	124.7
Total Rushes	413	495
Net Yards Passing	3136	3486
Avg. Per Game	196.0	217.9
Sacked/Yards Lost	52/319	29/194
Gross Yards	3455	3680
Att./Completions	561/325	490/308
Completion Pct.	57.9	62.9
Had Intercepted	21	9
Punts/Average	96/41.6	80/40.9
Net Punting Avg.	96/35.3	80/35.8
Penalties/Yards	103/859	107/867
Fumbles/Ball Lost	33/19	24/12
Touchdowns	29	54
Rushing	10	22
Passing	16	27
Returns	3	5

2004 INDIVIDUAL STATISTICS

PASSING

	Att.	Comp.	Yds.	Pct.	TD	Int.	Tkld.	Rate
Rattay	325	198	2,169	60.9	10	10	37/211	78.1
Dorsey	226	123	1,231	54.4	6	9	13/94	62.4
Pickett	10	4	55	40.0	0	2	2/14	18.8
49ers	561	325	3,455	57.9	16	21	52/319	69.9
Opponents	490	308	3,680	62.9	27	9	29/194	96.5

SCORING

	TD R	TD P	TD Rt	PAT	FG	Saf	PTS
T. Peterson	0	0	0	23/23	18/22	0	77
Barlow	7	0	0	0/0	0/0	0	42
Lloyd	0	6	0	0/0	0/0	0	38
Conway	0	3	0	0/0	0/0	0	20
Wilson	0	3	0	0/0	0/0	0	18
Hicks	2	0	0	0/0	0/0	0	12
E. Johnson	0	2	0	0/0	0/0	0	12
Battle	0	0	1	0/0	0/0	0	6
Bush	0	1	0	0/0	0/0	0	6
Carpenter	0	0	1	0/0	0/0	0	6
Robertson	1	0	0	0/0	0/0	0	6
D. Smith	0	0	1	0/0	0/0	0	6
Woods	0	1	0	0/0	0/0	0	6
Rattay	0	0	0	0/0	0/0	0	0
49ers	10	16	3	23/23	18/22	1	259
Opponents	22	27	5	51/51	25/29	0	452

2-Pt. Conversions: Conway, Lloyd, Rattay.
49ers 3-6, Opponents 1-3.

RUSHING

	No.	Yds	Avg	LG	TD
Barlow	244	822	3.4	60	7
Hicks	96	362	3.8	35	2
Jackson	26	101	3.9	13	0
Robertson	16	71	4.4	16	1
Rattay	12	55	4.6	15	0
Beasley	9	15	1.7	4	0
Dorsey	5	7	1.4	3	0
Wilson	1	6	6.0	6	0
Battle	2	5	2.5	7	0
Pickett	1	5	5.0	5	0
Isom	1	0	0.0	0	0
49ers	413	1,449	3.5	60	10
Opponents	495	1,995	4.0	29	22

RECEIVING

	No.	Yds	Avg	LG	TD
E. Johnson	82	825	10.1	25	2
Wilson	47	641	13.6	39	3
Lloyd	43	565	13.1	52	6
Conway	38	403	10.6	37	3
Barlow	35	212	6.1	15	0
Jackson	21	139	6.6	22	0
Hicks	16	154	9.6	19	0
Walker	10	115	11.5	30	0
Beasley	10	44	4.4	9	0
Battle	8	143	17.9	65	0
Woods	7	160	22.9	59	1
Robertson	4	34	8.5	14	0
Bush	2	10	5.0	6	1
Ware	1	9	9.0	9	0
Isom	1	1	1.0	1	0
49ers	325	3,455	10.6	65	16
Opponents	308	3,680	11.9	60	27

INTERCEPTIONS

	No.	Yds	Avg	LG	TD
Parrish	4	64	16.0	26	0
Carpenter	1	31	31.0	31	0
Ulbrich	1	19	19.0	19	0
Heard	1	14	14.0	14	0
Winborn	1	1	1.0	1	0
M. Adams	1	0	0.0	0	0
49ers	9	129	14.3	31	0
Opponents	21	479	22.8	85	4

PUNTING

	No.	Yds.	Avg.	In 20	LG
Lee	96	3,990	41.6	25	81
49ers	96	3,990	41.6	25	81
Opponents	80	3,268	40.9	28	61

PUNT RETURNS

	Ret	FC	Yds	Avg	LG	TD
Battle	31	20	266	8.6	71t	1
Wilson	2	1	21	10.5	13	0
Fleck	1	0	10	10.0	10	0
J. Peterson	1	0	6	6.0	6	0
49ers	35	21	303	8.7	71t	1
Opponents	51	17	445	8.7	35	0

KICKOFF RETURNS

	No.	Yds	Avg	LG	TD
Hicks	31	623	20.1	35	0
Robertson	25	560	22.4	37	0
Battle	13	257	19.8	40	0
Wilson	10	196	19.6	36	0
J. Williams	3	58	19.3	23	0
Jackson	2	22	11.0	14	0
49ers	84	1,716	20.4	40	0
Opponents	56	1,119	20.0	73	0

FIELD GOALS

	1-19	20-29	30-39	40-49	50+
T. Peterson	1/1	3/3	7/8	5/6	2/4
49ers	1/1	3/3	7/8	5/6	2/4
Opponents	0/0	10/11	7/9	4/4	4/5

SACKS

	No.
Engelberger	6.0
Winborn	4.5
Young	3.0
J. Peterson	2.5
Carpenter	2.0
Carter	2.0
D. Smith	1.5
Brown	1.0
C. Cooper	1.0
Hanson	1.0
Leverette	1.0
Moore	1.0
Ulbrich	1.0
J. Williams	1.0
Parrish	0.5
49ers	29.0
Opponents	52.0

RECORD HOLDERS
INDIVIDUAL RECORDS—CAREER

Category	Name	Performance
Rushing (Yds.)	Joe Perry, 1950-1960, 1963	7,344
Passing (Yds.)	Joe Montana, 1979-1992	35,124
Passing (TDs)	Joe Montana, 1979-1992	244
Receiving (No.)	Jerry Rice, 1985-2000	1,281
Receiving (Yds.)	Jerry Rice, 1985-2000	19,247
Interceptions	Ronnie Lott, 1981-1990	51
Punting (Avg.)	Tommy Davis, 1959-1969	44.7
Punt Return (Avg.)	Dana McLemore, 1982-87	10.8
Kickoff Return (Avg.)	Abe Woodson, 1958-1964	29.4
Field Goals	Ray Wersching, 1977-1987	190
Touchdowns (Tot.)	Jerry Rice, 1985-2000	187
Points	Jerry Rice, 1985-2000	1,130

INDIVIDUAL RECORDS—SINGLE SEASON

Category	Name	Performance
Rushing (Yds.)	Garrison Hearst, 1998	1,570
Passing (Yds.)	Jeff Garcia, 2000	4,278
Passing (TDs)	Steve Young, 1998	36
Receiving (No.)	Jerry Rice, 1995	122
Receiving (Yds.)	Jerry Rice, 1995	*1,848
Interceptions	Dave Baker, 1960	10
	Ronnie Lott, 1986	10
Punting (Avg.)	Tommy Davis, 1965	45.8
Punt Return (Avg.)	Dana McLemore, 1982	22.3
Kickoff Return (Avg.)	Joe Arenas, 1953	34.4
Field Goals	Jeff Wilkins, 1996	30
Touchdowns (Tot.)	Jerry Rice, 1987	23
Points	Jerry Rice, 1987	138

INDIVIDUAL RECORDS—SINGLE GAME

Category	Name	Performance
Rushing (Yds.)	Charlie Garner, 9-24-00	201
Passing (Yds.)	Joe Montana, 10-14-90	476
Passing (TDs)	Joe Montana, 10-14-90	6
Receiving (No.)	Terrell Owens, 12-17-00	*20
Receiving (Yds.)	Jerry Rice, 12-18-95	289
Interceptions	Dave Baker, 12-4-60	*4
Field Goals	Ray Wersching, 10-16-83	6
	Jeff Wilkins, 9-29-96	6
Touchdowns (Tot.)	Jerry Rice, 10-14-90	5
Points	Jerry Rice, 10-14-90	30

*NFL Record

2005 VETERAN ROSTER

No.	Name	Pos.	Ht.	Wt.	Birthdate	NFL Exp.	College	Hometown	How Acq.	'04 Games/ Starts
91	Adams, Anthony	DT	6-0	300	6/18/80	3	Penn State	Detroit, Mich.	D2-'03	14/12
20	Adams, Mike	S	5-11	193	3/24/81	2	Delaware	Paterson, N.J.	FA-'04	8/0
32	Barlow, Kevan	RB	6-1	238	1/7/79	4	Pittsburgh	Pittsburgh, Pa.	D3-'01	15/14
83	Battle, Arnaz	WR	6-1	217	2/22/80	3	Notre Dame	Shreveport, La.	D6-'03	14/0
40	Beasley, Fred	FB	6-0	246	9/18/74	8	Auburn	Montgomery, Ala.	D6-'98	14/10
92	Brown, Tony	DT	6-1	280	9/29/80	2	Memphis	Chattanooga, Tenn.	FA-'04	16/4
44	Bush, Steve	TE	6-3	267	7/4/74	9	Arizona State	Paradise Valley, Ariz.	FA-'04	5/2
35	Carpenter, Dwaine	S	6-1	203	11/4/76	3	North Carolina A&T	Troy, N.C.	FA-'03	15/6
96	Carter, Andre	DE	6-4	265	5/12/79	5	California	San Jose, Calif.	D1-'01	7/6
93	Cooper, Chris	DT	6-5	290	12/27/77	5	Nebraska-Omaha	Lincoln, Neb.	FA-'04	8/2
7	Dorsey, Ken	QB	6-4	218	4/22/81	3	Miami	Orinda, Calif.	D7-'03	8/7
94	Douglas, Marques	DT	6-2	280	3/15/77	6	Howard	Greensboro, N.C.	UFA(Balt)-'05	16/15*
95	Engelberger, John	DE	6-4	268	10/18/76	6	VirginiaTech	Blacksburg, Va.	D2a-'00	16/15
78	Gragg, Scott	T	6-8	315	2/28/72	11	Montana	Silverton, Ore.	UFA(NYG)-'00	16/16
88	Hamilton, Derrick	WR	6-4	203	11/30/81	2	Clemson	Dillon, S.C.	D3-'04	2/0
27	Hanson, Joselio	CB	5-9	175	8/13/81	2	Texas Tech	Los Angeles, Calif.	FA-'03	13/3
77	Harris, Kwame	T	6-7	310	3/15/82	3	Stanford	Newark, Del.	D1-'03	14/7
66	Heitmann, Eric	G	6-3	305	2/24/80	4	Stanford	Katy, Texas	D7a-'02	16/16
43	Hicks, Maurice	RB	5-11	200	7/22/78	2	North Carolina A&T	Emporia, Va.	FA-'04	9/2
22	Jackson, Terry	FB	6-0	232	1/10/76	7	Florida	Gainesville, Fla.	D5-'99	16/0
86	Jennings, Brian	TE/LS	6-5	245	10/14/76	6	Arizona State	Mesa, Ariz.	D7b-'00	16/0
75	Jennings, Jonas	T	6-3	325	11/21/77	5	Georgia	College Park, Ga.	FA-'04	14/14*
82	Johnson, Eric	TE	6-3	256	9/15/79	5	Yale	Needham, Mass.	D7b-'01	16/14
4	Lee, Andy	P	6-0	206	8/11/82	2	Pittsburgh	Westminster, N.C.	D6a-'04	16/0
28	Lewis, Keith	S	6-0	210	10/20/81	2	Oregon	Sacramento, Calif.	D6b-'04	16/0
85	Lloyd, Brandon	WR	6-0	192	7/5/81	3	Illinois	Blue Springs, Mo.	D4-'03	13/13
56	Moore, Brandon	LB	6-1	242	1/16/79	4	Oklahoma	Baldwin, N.Y.	FA-'02	12/1
68	Murphy, Rob	C/G	6-5	310	1/18/77	4	Ohio State	Cincinnati, Ohio	FA-'03	15/0
6	Nedney, Joe	K	6-5	225	3/22/73	9	San Jose State	San Jose, Calif.	FA-'05	0*
62	Newberry, Jeremy	C	6-5	310	3/23/76	8	California	Antioch, Calif.	D2-'98	1/1
33	Parrish, Tony	S	6-0	210	11/23/75	8	Washington	Huntington Beach, Calif.	UFA(Chi)-'02	16/16
67	Peters, Scott	C/G	6-3	300	11/23/78	3	Arizona State	Pleasanton, Calif.	FA-'04	0*
98	Peterson, Julian	LB	6-3	235	7/28/78	6	MichiganState	Hillcrest Heights, Md.	D1a-'00	5/5
3	Pickett, Cody	QB	6-3	227	6/30/80	2	Washington	Caldwell, Idaho	D7a-'04	1/0
29	Plummer, Ahmed	CB	6-0	191	3/26/76	6	Ohio State	Wyoming, Ohio	D1b-'00	6/6
51	Rasheed, Saleem	LB	6-2	229	6/15/81	4	Alabama	Birmingham, Ala.	D3-'02	14/2
13	Rattay, Tim	QB	6-0	200	3/15/77	6	Louisiana Tech	Elyria, Ohio	D7a-'00	9/9
31	Reed, Rayshun	CB	5-10	185	4/10/81	2	Troy State	Columbus, Ga.	FA-'04	7/1
24	Rumph, Mike	CB	6-2	205	11/8/79	4	Miami	Boynton Beach, Fla.	D1-'02	2/2
54	Seigler, Richard	LB	6-2	238	10/19/80	2	Oregon State	Las Vegas, Nev.	D4b-'04	7/0
65	Smiley, Justin	G	6-3	301	11/11/81	2	Alabama	Ellabel, Ga.	D2a-'04	16/9
71	Smith, Corey	DE	6-2	250	10/2/79	3	North Carolina State	Richmond, Va.	FA-'04	1/0
50	Smith, Derek	LB	6-2	245	1/18/75	9	Arizona State	American Fork, Utah	UFA(Wash)-'01	14/14
90	Sopoaga, Isaac	DT	6-2	321	9/4/81	2	Hawaii	Pago Pago, American Samoa	D4a-'04	0*
36	Spencer, Shawntae	CB	6-1	181	2/22/82	2	Pittsburgh	Rankin, Pa.	D2b-'04	16/12
53	Ulbrich, Jeff	LB	6-0	249	2/17/77	6	Hawaii	San Jose, Calif.	D3b-'00	16/14
49	Walker, Aaron	TE	6-6	252	3/14/80	3	Florida	Mims, Fla.	D5-'03	16/4
59	Wells, Ray	LB	6-1	234	8/20/80	2	Arizona	Oakland, Calif.	FA-'04	6/0
99	Williams, Andrew	DE	6-2	263	4/18/79	3	Miami	Tampa, Fla.	D3-'03	7/3
55	Winborn, Jamie	LB	5-11	242	5/14/79	5	Vanderbilt	Wetumpka, Ala.	D2-'01	14/10
81	Woods, Rashaun	WR	6-2	202	10/17/80	2	Oklahoma State	Oklahoma City, Okla.	D1-'04	13/0
97	Young, Bryant	DT	6-3	291	1/27/72	12	Notre Dame	Chicago Heights, Ill.	D1-'94	16/16

* Douglas played 16 games with Baltimore in '04; Jennings played 14 games with Buffalo; Nedney missed '04 season with Tennessee because of injury; Peters inactive for 3 games; Sopoaga missed '04 season because of injury.

Players lost through free agency (5): S Ronnie Heard (Atl; 16 games in '04), T Kyle Kosier (Det; 16), K Todd Peterson (Atl; 16), CB Jimmy Williams (NO; 12), WR Cedrick Wilson (Pitt; 15).

Also played with 49ers in '04—WR Curtis Conway (16 games), T Jerome Davis (2), C Brock Gutierrez (16), FB Jasen Isom (5), DT Daleroy Stewart (9), DE Brandon Whiting (5).

2005 FIRST-YEAR ROSTER

Name	Pos.	Ht.	Wt.	Birthdate	College	Hometown	How Acq.
Amey, Fred	WR	5-10	197	12/4/81	Sacramento State	Union City, Calif.	FA
Amundson, Allan (1)	CB	5-9	186	9/9/80	Oregon	Kentfield, Calif.	FA
Baas, David	G	6-4	319	9/28/81	Michigan	Sarasota, Fla.	D2
Bajema, Billy	TE	6-4	261	10/31/82	Oklahoma State	Oklahoma City, Okla.	D7d
Cooper, Josh (1)	DE	6-3	261	12/5/80	Mississippi	Marietta, Ga.	FA-'04
Darby, Brendan	T	6-7	295	6/25/81	San Diego State	Larkspur, Calif.	FA
Downey, Khiawatha (1)	T	6-3	336	9/20/79	Indiana (PA)	Pittsburgh, Pa.	FA
Drew, Randee (1)	CB	5-9	192	1/22/81	Northern Illinois	Milwaukee, Wis.	FA
Estes, Patrick	TE	6-7	280	2/4/83	Virginia	Richmond, Va.	D7c
Farden, Cole	P	5-10	200	2/1/80	Nebraska	Grapevine, Texas	FA
Ficklin, Tony	RB	6-1	258	10/21/81	San Jose State	Shreveport, La.	FA
Fields, Ronnie	DT	6-2	315	9/13/81	Mississippi State	Bogalusa, La.	D5a
Fleck, P.J. (1)	WR	5-10	191	11/29/80	Northern Illinois	Sugar Grove, Ill.	FA-'04
Gore, Frank	RB	5-9	217	5/14/83	Miami	Coral Gables, Fla.	D3a
Herrion, Thomas (1)	G	6-3	310	12/15/81	Utah	Fort Worth, Texas	FA-'04
Holly, Daven	CB	5-10	192	8/8/82	Cincinnati	Clairton, Pa.	D7a
Johnson, Brian (1)	FB	6-3	260	4/6/79	New Mexico	Highlands Ranch, Colo.	FA
Johnson, Derrick	CB	5-10	188	2/9/82	Washington	Riverside, Calif.	D6
Katnik, Norm (1)	C	6-4	298	7/2/81	Southern California	Santa Ana, Calif.	FA-'04
Long, Chace (1)	K	6-0	205	4/8/78	Nebraska	Wahoo, Neb.	FA
Marshall, Rasheed	QB	6-1	190	7/11/81	West Virginia	Pittsburgh, Pa.	D5b
Maxwell, Marcus	WR	6-4	205	7/8/83	Oregon	Berkeley, Calif.	D7b
Parker, Arnold (1)	S	6-2	201	7/1/81	Utah	Las Vegas, Nev.	FA
Provost, Tim (1)	T	6-5	300	8/24/80	San Jose State	Downey, Calif.	FA-'04
Purfiy, Bobby	RB	6-1	201	11/19/81	Colorado	Long Beach, Calif.	FA
Scharff, Scott	DE	6-3	277	2/7/82	Stanford	Wisconsin Rapids, Wis.	FA
Smith, Alex	QB	6-4	212	5/7/84	Utah	San Diego, Calif.	D1
Snyder, Adam	T	6-6	325	1/30/82	Oregon	Fullerton, Calif.	D3b
Yates, Max (1)	LB	6-3	238	10/30/79	Marshall	Newport News, Va.	FA-'04
Yliniemi, Kirk (1)	K	6-1	207	1/31/79	Oregon State	Independence, Ore.	FA
Zeigler, Doug (1)	TE	6-3	254	10/25/79	Mississippi	Marietta, Ga.	FA-'04

The term NFL Rookie is defined as a player who is in his first season of professional football and has not been on the roster of another professional football team for any regular-season or postseason games. A Rookie is designated by an "R" on NFL rosters. Players who have been active in another professional football league or players who have NFL experience, including either preseason training camp or being on an Active List or Inactive List, or on Reserve/Injured or Reserve/Physically Unable to Perform for fewer than six regular-season games, are termed NFL First-Year Players. An NFL First-Year Player is designated by a "1" on NFL rosters. Thereafter, a player is credited with an additional year of experience for each season in which he accumulates six games on the Active List or Inactive List, or on Reserve/Injured or Reserve/Physically Unable to Perform.

Log on to www.sf49ers.com for an up-to-date roster.

COACHING STAFF

Head Coach,
Mike Nolan

Pro Career: Named the fifteenth head coach in 49ers history on January 19, 2005, Mike Nolan will begin his first season as head coach of the San Francisco 49ers. Nolan is in his eigteenth year in the NFL and twenty-fourth year in coaching. Nolan joins San Francisco after an impressive stint as defensive coordinator of the Baltimore Ravens, a position he has held with three other teams: New York Jets (2000), Washington Redskins (1997-99), and New York Giants (1993-96). In Baltimore, Nolan's defense was among the NFL's best, finishing third overall. Baltimore ranked first in the AFC with 17 fumble recoveries and led the NFL in sacks (47) and tied for first in the AFC and second in the NFL with 41 takeaways. Nolan joined the Ravens after a one-year stay as the New York Jets defensive coordinator in 2000. Under Nolan's tutelage, the Jets defense rebounded to tenth overall (tied with Philadelphia) in the league—an improvement of 11 spots from the previous year. From 1997-99 Nolan was the defensive coordinator of the Washington Redskins. In 1997, the Redskins allowed the eighth-fewest points in NFL and finished third overall in pass defense. He also spent four seasons as defensive coordinator under then-head coach Dan Reeves for the New York Giants (1993-96). In his first season, the Giants' defense allowed the fewest points in the NFL (205). Nolan also worked on Reeves' staff from 1987-1992 with the Denver Broncos as linebackers coach and as special teams coach/defensive assistant. Career record: 0-0.

Background: Nolan participated in the Broncos' 1981 training camp as a defensive back under Dan Reeves. He joined the Broncos after earning three letters at free safety for the Oregon Ducks (1978-1980). Nolan graduated from Woodside (Calif.) high school. He is the son of former NFL head coach Dick Nolan (San Francisco and New Orleans).

Personal: Born March 7, 1959, Baltimore. He and wife Kathy, have four children: sons, Michael and Christopher, and daughters, Laura and Jennifer.

ASSISTANT COACHES

Duane Carlisle, asst. strength and conditioning; born Nov. 13, 1965, Haverhill, Mass. Attended Maryland. No college or pro playing experience. Pro coach: Speed development consultant for Philadelphia Eagles 2000-04, joined 49ers in 2005.

A.J. Christoff, secondary; born November 18, 1948, Ritzville, Wash. Linebacker/defensive end Idaho 1968-1971. College coach: Oregon State 1972, New Mexico 1973-74, Idaho 1975-76, Oregon 1977-1982, Stanford 1983, Notre Dame 1984-85, Georgia Tech 1986, Alabama 1987-89, UCLA 1990-94, Colorado 1995-98,

Southern California 2000, Cincinnati 2001-02, Stanford 2003-04. Pro coach: Joined 49ers in 2005.

Billy Davis, defensive coordinator; born November 5, 1965, Youngstown, Ohio. Quarterback Cincinnati 1984-88. College coach: Michigan State 1990-91. Pro coach: Pittsburgh Steelers 1992-94, Carolina Panthers 1995-98, Cleveland Browns 1999, Green Bay Packers 2000, Atlanta Falcons 2001-03, New York Giants 2004, joined 49ers in 2005.

Gary Emanuel, defensive line; born October 30, 1958, Philadelphia. Offensive lineman West Chester (Pa.) C.C. 1976-78, Plymouth State 1979-1980. College coach: Plymouth State 1981-84, West Chester C.C. 1985, Massachusetts 1986-87, Dartmouth 1988-90, Syracuse 1991-93, Washington State 1994-96, Purdue 1997-2004. Pro coach: Joined 49ers in 2005.

Bishop Harris, running backs; born November 23, 1941, Phenix City, Ala. Running back/defensive back North Carolina College 1960-63. College coach: Duke 1972-75, North Carolina State 1977-79, Louisiana State 1980-83, Notre Dame 1984-85, Minnesota 1986-1990, North Carolina Central 1991-92 (head coach). Pro coach: Denver Broncos 1993-94, Oakland Raiders 1995-97, Buffalo Bills 1998-99, New York Jets 2001-04, joined 49ers in 2005.

Pete Hoener, tight ends; born June 14, 1954, Peoria, Ill. Tight end/defensive end Bradley 1969-1970. College coach: Missouri 1975-76, Illinois State 1977, Indiana State 1978-1984, Illinois 1986-88, Purdue 1989-1990, Texas Christian 1991-97, Iowa State 1998-99, Texas A&M 2000. Pro coach: St. Louis Cardinals 1985-86, Arizona Cardinals 2003, Chicago Bears 2004, joined 49ers in 2005.

Jim Hostler, quarterbacks; born November 11, 1966, Pittsburgh. Defensive back Indiana (Pa.) 1986-89. College coach: Indiana (Pa.) 1990-92, 1994-99, Juanita (Pa.) 1993. Pro coach: Kansas City Chiefs 2000, New Orleans Saints 2001-02, New York Jets 2003-04, joined 49ers in 2005.

Vance Joseph, secondary assistant; born September 20, 1972, Marrero, La. Defensive back Colorado 1990-94. Pro defensive back New York Jets 1995, Indianapolis Colts 1996. College coach: Colorado 1999-2001, 2002-03, Wyoming 2002, Bowling Green State 2004. Pro coach: Joined 49ers in 2005.

Larry Mac Duff, special teams coordinator; born June 22, 1948, Clinton, Iowa. Defensive end Fullerton (Calif.) J.C. 1966-67, Oklahoma 1968-69. No pro playing experience. College coach: Stanford 1980-83, Hawaii 1984-86, Arizona 1987-96, 2001-02. Pro coach: New York Giants 1997-2000, joined 49ers in 2003.

Ben McAdoo, asst. offensive line/quality control; born July 7, 1977, Homer City,

Pa. Attended Indiana University (Pa.). No college or pro playing experience. College coach: Michigan State 2001-02, Fairfield 2002, Akron 2003, Pittsburgh 2003. Pro coach: New Orleans Saints 2004, joined 49ers in 2005.

Mike McCarthy, offensive coordinator; born November 10, 1963, Pittsburgh. Tight end Baker 1985-86. College coach: Fort Hays State 1987-88, Pittsburgh 1989-1992. Pro coach: Kansas City Chiefs 1993-98, Green Bay Packers 1999, New Orleans 2000-04, joined 49ers in 2005.

Johnny Parker, strength & conditioning; born February 1, 1947, Greenville, S.C. Attended Mississippi. No college or pro playing experience. College coach: South Carolina, 1974-76, Indiana 1977-79, Louisiana State 1980, Mississippi 1981-83. Pro coach: New York Giants 1984-92, New England Patriots 1993-99, Tampa Bay Buccaneers 2002, joined 49ers in 2005.

Jeff Rodgers, special teams assistant; born January 12, 1978, St. Paul, Minn. Linebacker North Texas 1997-2000. No pro playing experience. College coach: Arizona 2001-02. Pro coach: Joined 49ers in 2003.

Mike Singletary, asst. head coach/linebackers; born October 9, 1958, Houston. Linebacker Baylor 1977-1980. Pro linebacker Chicago Bears 1981-1992. Inducted into Pro Football Hall of Fame 1998. Pro coach: Baltimore Ravens 2003-04, joined 49ers in 2005.

Jerry Sullivan, wide receivers; born July 13, 1944, Miami, Fla. Quarterback Florida State 1963-64. No pro playing experience. College coach: Kansas State 1971-72, Texas Tech 1973-75, South Carolina 1976-1982, Indiana 1983, Louisiana State 1984-1990, Ohio State 1991. Pro coach: San Diego Chargers 1992-96, Detroit Lions 1997-2000, Arizona Cardinals 2001-03, Miami Dolphins 2004, joined 49ers in 2005.

Robert Talley, special asst. to the head coach; born December 14, 1968, New York City. Defensive back Boston University 1987-1990. No pro playing experience. College coach: Massachusetts 1991-95, Colby College 1996, Dartmouth 1997-2004. Pro coach: Joined 49ers in 2005.

Jason Tarver, defensive quality control/defensive assistant; born August 28, 1974, Stanford, Calif. Defensive back West Valley College 1994-95. No pro playing experience. College coach: West Valley College 1996-97, UCLA 1998-2000. Pro coach: Joined 49ers in 2001.

George Warhop, offensive line; born September 19, 1961, Riverside, Ca. Guard/center Mt. San Jacinto (Calif.) J.C. 1979-1980, Cincinnati 1981-82. College coach: Cincinnati 1983, Kansas 1984-86, Vanderbilt 1987-89, New Mexico 1990, Southern Methodist 1993, Boston College 1994-95. Pro coach: London Monarchs (WL) 1991-92, St. Louis Rams 1996-97, Arizona Cardinals 1998-2002, Dallas Cowboys 2003-04, joined 49ers in 2005.

National Football Conference
West Division
Team Colors: Seahawks Blue, Seahawks Navy, Seahawks Bright Green
11220 N.E. 53ᴿᴰ Street
Kirkland, Washington, 98033
Telephone: (425) 827-9777

2005 SCHEDULE
PRESEASON
Aug. 12 at New Orleans 7:00
Aug. 22 **Dallas** 5:00
Aug. 27 at Kansas City 7:30
Sept. 2 **Minnesota** 6:00

REGULAR SEASON
Sept. 11 at Jacksonville....................1:00
Sept. 18 **Atlanta** 1:05
Sept. 25 **Arizona** 1:05
Oct. 2   at Washington 1:00
Oct. 9   at St. Louis......................12:00
Oct. 16 **Houston** 5:30
Oct. 23 **Dallas** 1:05
Oct. 30 Open Date
Nov. 6   at Arizona...........................2:05
Nov. 13 **St. Louis** 1:15
Nov. 20 at San Francisco.................1:05
Nov. 27 **New York Giants** 1:15
Dec. 5   at Philadelphia (Mon.).........9:00
Dec. 11 **San Francisco** 1:05
Dec. 18 at Tennessee 12:00
Dec. 24 **Indianapolis** (Sat.) 1:15
Jan. 1   at Green Bay 3:15

Stadium: Qwest Field
(opened in 2002)
•**Capacity:** 67,000
Playing Surface: FieldTurf
Training Camp: Eastern Washington Univ.
Cheney, Washington 99004

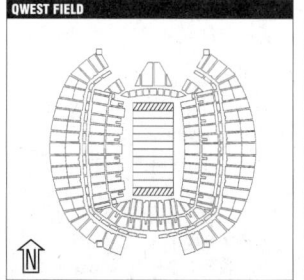
QWEST FIELD

CLUB OFFICIALS
Chairman: Paul Allen
CEO: Tod Leiweke
President of Football Operations:
Tim Ruskell
Executive VP of Football Operations/
Head Coach: Mike Holmgren
VP/Community Outreach: Mike Flood
VP/Corporate Partnership/Legal Affairs:
Lance Lopes
VP/Corporate Sales: Scott Patrick
VP/Administration: Gary Wright
Director of Marketing, Suite Sales and
Service: Ron Jenkins
Director of Pro Personnel: Will Lewis
Director of Communications and
Broadcasting: Dave Pearson
Asst. Director of Communications:
Lane Gammel
Director of Community Outreach:
Sandy Gregory
Director of Ticket Sales/Operations:
Chuck Arnold
Gameday Presentation: Rick Crawford
Football Operations Coordinator/Team
Travel: Bill Nayes
Video Director Football: Thom Fermstad
Head Athletic Trainer: Sam Ramsden
Equipment Manager: Erik Kennedy

COACHING HISTORY
(217-245-0)
Records include postseason games
1976-1982 Jack Patera* 35-59-0
1982   Mike McCormack 4-3-0
1983-1991 Chuck Knox.................83-67-0
1992-94   Tom Flores...................14-34-0
1995-98   Dennis Erickson...........31-33-0
1999-2004 Mike Holmgren 50-49-0
*Released after two games in 1982

ATTENDANCE
Home 520,435   Away 494,502
Total 1,014,937
Single-game home record,
68,681 (12/16/00)
Single-season home record,
522,656 (1999)

2005 DRAFT CHOICES
Round	Name	Pos.	College
1	Chris Spencer	C	Mississippi
2	Lofa Tatupu	LB	Southern California
3	David Greene	QB	Georgia
	LeRoy Hill	LB	Clemson
4	Ray Willis	T	Florida State
5	Jeb Huckeba	DE	Arkansas
6	Tony Jackson	RB	Iowa
7	Cornelius Wortham	LB	Alabama
	Doug Nienhuis	G	Oregon State

2004 TEAM RECORD

PRESEASON (3-1)

Date	Result		Opponent
8/16	W	21-3	at Green Bay
8/21	L	3-19	Denver
8/27	W	26-20	at San Diego
9/2	W	23-21	Minnesota

REGULAR SEASON (9-7)

Date	Result		Opponent	Att.
9/12	W	21-7	at New Orleans	64,900
9/19	W	10-6	at Tampa Bay	65,089
9/26	W	34-0	San Francisco	66,709
10/10	L	27-33	St. Louis (OT)	66,940
10/17	L	20-30	at New England	68,756
10/24	L	17-25	at Arizona	35,695
10/31	W	23-17	Carolina	66,214
11/7	W	42-27	at San Francisco	64,423
11/14	L	12-23	at St. Louis	66,044
11/21	W	24-17	Miami	66,644
11/28	L	9-38	Buffalo	66,271
12/6	L	39-43	Dallas	68,093
12/12	W	27-23	at Minnesota	64,110
12/19	L	14-37	at N.Y. Jets	77,894
12/26	W	24-21	Arizona	65,825
1/2	W	28-26	Atlanta	66,740
(OT) Overtime				

POSTSEASON (0-1)

Date	Result		Opponent	
1/4	L	20-27	St. Louis	65,397

SCORE BY PERIODS

Seahawks	86	129	70	86	0	—	371
Opponents	89	113	52	113	6	—	373

2004 TEAM STATISTICS

	Seahawks	Opp.
Total First Downs	320	311
Rushing	110	102
Passing	189	191
Penalty	21	18
3rd Down: Made/Att	76/210	97/229
3rd Down Pct.	36.2	42.4
4th Down: Made/Att	6/11	6/9
4th Down Pct.	54.5	66.7
Possession Avg.	29:00	31:00
Total Net Yards	5634	5621
Avg. Per Game	352.1	351.3
Total Plays	1034	1047
Avg. Per Play	5.4	5.4
Net Yards Rushing	2095	2031
Avg. Per Game	130.9	126.9
Total Rushes	468	452
Net Yards Passing	3539	3590
Avg. Per Game	221.2	224.4
Sacked/Yards Lost	34/218	36/218
Gross Yards	3715	3808
Att./Completions	532/304	559/340
Completion Pct.	57.1	60.8
Had Intercepted	18	23
Punts/Average	79/38.4	74/41.8
Net Punting Avg.	79/34.3	74/37.3
Penalties/Yards	79/669	91/748
Fumbles/Ball Lost	19/9	25/12
Touchdowns	43	42
Rushing	17	17
Passing	23	24
Returns	3	1

2004 INDIVIDUAL STATISTICS

PASSING	Att.	Comp.	Yds.	Pct.	TD	Int.	Tkld.	Rate
Hasselbeck	474	279	3,382	58.9	22	15	30/155	83.1
Dilfer	58	25	333	43.1	1	3	4/21	46.1
Seahawks	532	304	3,715	57.1	23	18	34/176	79.1
Opponents	559	340	3,808	60.8	24	23	36/218	78.3

SCORING	TD R	TD P	TD Rt	PAT	FG	Saf	PTS
Alexander	16	4	0	0/0	0/0	0	120
J. Brown	0	0	0	40/40	23/25	0	109
Jackson	0	7	0	0/0	0/0	0	44
Stevens	0	3	0	0/0	0/0	0	20
Rice	0	3	0	0/0	0/0	0	18
Engram	0	2	0	0/0	0/0	0	12
K. Robinson	0	2	0	0/0	0/0	0	12
Boulware	0	0	1	0/0	0/0	0	6
Hasselbeck	1	0	0	0/0	0/0	0	6
Lucas	0	0	1	0/0	0/0	0	6
Mili	0	1	0	0/0	0/0	0	6
Simmons	0	0	1	0/0	0/0	0	6
Urban	0	1	0	0/0	0/0	0	6
Seahawks	17	23	3	40/40	23/25	0	371
Opponents	17	24	1	38/39	27/32	1	373

2-Pt. Conversions: Jackson, Stevens.
Seahawks 2-3, Opponents 0-2.

RUSHING	No.	Yds	Avg	LG	TD
Alexander	353	1,696	4.8	44	16
Strong	36	131	3.6	11	0
Morris	30	126	4.2	12	0
Hasselbeck	27	90	3.3	19	1
Evans	7	20	2.9	7	0
Carter	4	15	3.8	6	0
Dilfer	10	14	1.4	11	0
K. Robinson	1	3	3.0	3	0
Seahawks	468	2,095	4.5	44	17
Opponents	452	2,031	4.5	53	17

RECEIVING	No.	Yds	Avg	LG	TD
Jackson	87	1,199	13.8	56t	7
Engram	36	499	13.9	60	2
K. Robinson	31	495	16.0	33	2
Stevens	31	349	11.3	32	3
Rice	25	362	14.5	56	3
Mili	23	240	10.4	20	1
Alexander	23	170	7.4	24	4
Strong	21	99	4.7	13	0
Morris	9	53	5.9	12	0
Hannam	8	110	13.8	36	0
Urban	6	117	19.5	33	1
Evans	2	12	6.0	9	0
Bannister	2	10	5.0	8	0
Seahawks	304	3,715	12.2	60	23
Opponents	340	3,808	11.2	63	24

INTERCEPTIONS	No.	Yds	Avg	LG	TD
Lucas	6	46	7.7	25	1
Trufant	5	141	28.2	58	0
Boulware	5	69	13.8	63t	1
Hamlin	4	48	12.0	24	0
Simmons	1	23	23.0	23t	1
Bierria	1	10	10.0	10	0
Cochran	1	0	0.0	0	0
Seahawks	23	337	14.7	63t	3
Opponents	18	158	8.8	48t	1

PUNTING	No.	Yds.	Avg.	In 20	LG
D. Jones	26	988	38.0	6	51
Rouen	26	1,093	42.0	10	60
Walter	24	920	38.3	4	50
J. Brown	1	35	35.0	0	35
Seahawks	79	3,036	38.4	20	60
Opponents	74	3,091	41.8	31	60

PUNT RETURNS	Ret	FC	Yds	Avg	LG	TD
Morris	15	4	75	5.0	22	0
Engram	10	19	118	11.8	48	0
Richard	4	3	31	7.8	14	0
Hannam	1	0	6	6.0	6	0
Seahawks	30	26	230	7.7	48	0
Opponents	33	21	244	7.4	39	0

KICKOFF RETURNS	No.	Yds	Avg	LG	TD
Morris	47	994	21.1	34	0
Carter	21	448	21.3	36	0
Evans	3	51	17.0	21	0
Locklear	1	12	12.0	12	0
Mili	1	12	12.0	12	0
Stevens	1	12	12.0	12	0
Seahawks	74	1,529	20.7	36	0
Opponents	77	1,677	21.8	51	0

FIELD GOALS	1-19	20-29	30-39	40-49	50+
J. Brown	1/1	7/7	8/9	6/7	1/1
Seahawks	1/1	7/7	8/9	6/7	1/1
Opponents	0/0	6/6	12/15	6/7	3/4

SACKS	No.
Okeafor	8.5
Cochran	6.5
Bernard	3.5
Wistrom	3.5
Hamlin	2.0
Moore	2.0
Boulware	1.0
C. Brown	1.0
Huff	1.0
Kacyvenski	1.0
Koutouvides	1.0
Mitchell	1.0
Trufant	1.0
Tubbs	1.0
White	1.0
Woodard	1.0
Seahawks	36.0
Opponents	34.0

RECORD HOLDERS
INDIVIDUAL RECORDS—CAREER

Category	Name	Performance
Rushing (Yds.)	Chris Warren, 1990-97	6,706
Passing (Yds.)	Dave Krieg, 1980-1991	26,132
Passing (TDs)	Dave Krieg, 1980-1991	195
Receiving (No.)	Steve Largent, 1976-1989	819
Receiving (Yds.)	Steve Largent, 1976-1989	13,089
Interceptions	Dave Brown, 1976-1986	50
Punting (Avg.)	Rick Tuten, 1991-97	43.8
Punt Return (Avg.)	Charlie Rogers, 1999-2001	12.7
Kickoff Return (Avg.)	Steve Broussard, 1995-98	23.2
Field Goals	Norm Johnson, 1982-1990	159
Touchdowns (Tot.)	Steve Largent, 1976-1989	101
Points	Norm Johnson, 1982-1990	810

INDIVIDUAL RECORDS—SINGLE SEASON

Category	Name	Performance
Rushing (Yds.)	Shaun Alexander, 2004	1,696
Passing (Yds.)	Matt Hasselbeck, 2003	3,841
Passing (TDs)	Dave Krieg, 1984	32
Receiving (No.)	Darrell Jackson, 2004	87
Receiving (Yds.)	Steve Largent, 1985	1,287
Interceptions	John Harris, 1981	10
	Kenny Easley, 1984	10
Punting (Avg.)	Rick Tuten, 1995	45.0
Punt Return (Avg.)	Charlie Rogers, 1999	14.5
Kickoff Return (Avg.)	Charlie Rogers, 2000	24.9
Field Goals	Todd Peterson, 1999	34
Touchdowns (Tot.)	Shaun Alexander, 2004	20
Points	Todd Peterson, 1999	134

INDIVIDUAL RECORDS—SINGLE GAME

Category	Name	Performance
Rushing (Yds.)	Shaun Alexander, 11-11-01	266
Passing (Yds.)	Matt Hasselbeck, 12-29-02	449
Passing (TDs)	Dave Krieg, 12-2-84, 9-15-85, 11-28-88	5
	Warren Moon, 10-26-97	5
	Matt Hasselbeck, 11-23-03	5
Receiving (No.)	Steve Largent, 10-18-87	15
Receiving (Yds.)	Steve Largent, 10-18-87	261
Interceptions	Kenny Easley, 9-3-84	3
	Eugene Robinson, 12-6-92	3
	Darryl Williams, 9-21-97	3
Field Goals	Norm Johnson, 9-20-87, 12-18-88	5
Touchdowns (Tot.)	Shaun Alexander, 9-29-02	5
Points	Shaun Alexander, 9-29-02	30

2005 VETERAN ROSTER

No.	Name	Pos.	Ht.	Wt.	Birthdate	NFL Exp.	College	Hometown	How Acq.	'04 Games/ Starts
37	Alexander, Shaun	RB	5-11	225	8/30/77	6	Alabama	Florence, Ky.	D1a-'00	16/16
2	Araguz, Leo	P	5-11	190	1/18/70	6	Stephen F. Austin	Pharr, Texas	FA-'05	0*
27	Babineaux, Jordan	CB	6-0	200	8/31/82	2	Southern Arkansas	Port Arthur, Texas	FA-'04	6/0
85	Bannister, Alex	WR	6-5	207	4/23/79	5	Eastern Kentucky	Cincinnati, Ohio	D5-'01	7/1
50	Bates, Solomon	LB	6-1	243	4/18/82	3	Arizona State	Moreno Valley, Calif.	D4b-'03	10/3
57	Bentley, Kevin	LB	6-0	245	12/29/79	4	Northwestern	Montclair, Calif.	UFA(Cle)-'05	16/3*
99	Bernard, Rocky	DT	6-3	293	4/19/79	4	Texas A&M	Baytown, Texas	D5a-'02	14/1
34	Bierria, Terreal	S	6-3	211	10/11/80	4	Georgia	Slidell, La.	D4-'02	16/12
28	Boulware, Michael	S	6-3	223	9/17/81	2	Florida State	Columbia, S.C.	D2-'04	16/4
3	Brown, Josh	K	6-0	202	4/29/79	3	Nebraska	Foyil, Okla.	D7a-'03	16/0
32	Carter, Kerry	RB	6-1	238	12/19/80	3	Stanford	Vaughn, Ontario	FA-'03	16/0
78	Cochran, Antonio	DE	6-4	299	6/21/76	7	Georgia	Montezuma, Ga.	D4-'99	16/7
92	Darby, Chuck	DT	6-0	270	10/22/75	5	South Carolina State	North, S.C.	UFA(TB)-'05	16/16*
52	Darche, Jean-Philippe	LS	6-0	246	2/28/75	6	McGill	Montreal, Quebec, Canada	FA-'00	16/0
22	Dyson, Andre	CB	5-10	183	5/25/79	5	Utah	Clearfield, Utah	UFA(Tenn)-'05	16/16*
84	Engram, Bobby	WR	5-10	188	1/7/73	10	Penn State	Camden, S.C.	UFA(Chi)-'01	13/7
91	Fisher, Bryce	DE	6-3	268	5/12/77	5	Air Force	Renton, Wash.	UFA(StL)-'05	16/14*
62	Gray, Chris	G	6-4	308	6/19/70	13	Auburn	Birmingham, Ala.	UFA(Chi)-'98	16/16
18	Hackett, D.J.	WR	6-2	199	7/31/81	2	Colorado	Ontario, Calif.	D5-'04	0*
26	Hamlin, Ken	S	6-2	209	1/20/81	3	Arkansas	Memphis, Tenn.	D2-'03	16/16
83	Hannam, Ryan	TE	6-2	248	2/24/80	4	Northern Iowa	St. Ansgar, Iowa	D5b-'02	16/0
8	Hasselbeck, Matt	QB	6-4	223	9/25/75	7	Boston College	Westwood, Mass.	T(GB)-'01	14/14
31	Herndon, Kelly	CB	5-10	180	11/3/76	4	Toledo	Twinsburg, Ohio	RFA(Den)-'05	16/16*
	House, Kevin	CB	6-0	185	1/9/79	4	South Carolina	Tampa, Fla.	FA-'05	0*
73	Hunter, Wayne	T	6-5	303	7/2/81	3	Hawaii	Honolulu, Hawaii	D3-'03	1/0
76	Hutchinson, Steve	G	6-5	313	11/1/77	5	Michigan	Ft. Lauderdale, Fla.	D1b-'01	16/16
82	Jackson, Darrell	WR	6-0	201	12/6/78	6	Florida	Tampa, Fla.	D3-'00	16/16
9	Jones, Donnie	P	6-2	222	7/5/80	4	Louisiana State	Baton Rouge, La.	D7-'04	6/0
71	Jones, Walter	T	6-5	315	1/19/74	9	Florida State	Aliceville, Ala.	D1b-'97	16/16
19	Jurevicius, Joe	WR	6-5	230	12/23/74	8	Penn State	Cleveland, Ohio	UFA(TB)-'05	10/4*
58	Kacyvenski, Isaiah	LB	6-1	252	10/3/77	6	Harvard	Endicott, N.Y.	D4b-'00	16/13
53	Koutouvides, Niko	LB	6-2	238	3/25/81	2	Purdue	Plainville, Conn.	D4-'04	16/2
67	Leverette, Otis	DE	6-7	278	5/31/78	4	Alabama-Birmingham	Americus, Ga.	FA-'04	5/1*
54	Lewis, D.D.	LB	6-1	241	1/8/79	4	Texas	Houston, Texas	FA-'02	0*
75	Locklear, Sean	T	6-4	301	5/29/81	2	North Carolina State	Lumberton, N.C.	D3-'04	16/0
41	Lowe, Omare	CB	6-1	195	4/20/78	4	Washington	Seattle, Wash.	FA-'05	3/0*
33	Manuel, Marquand	S	6-0	209	7/11/79	4	Florida	Miami, Fla.	W(Cin)-'04	15/0
88	Mili, Itula	TE	6-4	260	4/20/73	9	Brigham Young	Laie, Hawaii	D6-'97	15/4
95	Moore, Rashad	DT	6-3	324	3/16/79	3	Tennessee	Huntsville, Ala.	D6-'03	16/12
20	Morris, Maurice	RB	5-11	202	12/1/79	4	Oregon	Chester, S.C.	D2a-'02	15/0
16	Pathon, Jerome	WR	6-0	195	12/16/75	8	Washington	Vancouver, B.C.	UFA(NO)-'05	15/11*
42	Richard, Kris	CB	5-11	190	10/28/78	4	Southern California	Carson, Calif.	D3-'02	16/0
81	Robinson, Koren	WR	6-1	205	3/19/80	5	North Carolina State	Belmont, N.C.	D1a-'01	10/8
55	Sharper, Jamie	LB	6-3	239	11/23/74	9	Virginia	Richmond, Va.	UFA(Hou)-'05	16/16*
64	Smith, Ron	DT	6-3	310	8/18/78	2	Lane College	St. Louis, Mo.	FA-'05	0*
86	Stevens, Jerramy	TE	6-7	260	11/13/79	4	Washington	Olympia, Wash.	D1-'02	16/5
38	Strong, Mack	FB	6-0	245	9/11/71	13	Georgia	Columbus, Ga.	FA-'93	16/14
69	Tafoya, Joe	DE	6-4	265	9/6/78	5	Arizona	Pittsburgh, Calif.	W(TB)-'05	0*
24	Taylor, Bobby	CB	6-3	216	12/28/73	11	Notre Dame	Houston, Texas	UFA(Phil)-'04	9/0
93	Terrill, Craig	DT	6-2	294	6/27/80	2	Purdue	Lebanon, Ind.	D6-'04	4/0
61	Tobeck, Robbie	C	6-4	297	3/6/70	12	Washington State	Tarpon Springs, Fla.	UFA(Atl)-'00	16/16
23	Trufant, Marcus	CB	5-11	199	12/25/80	3	Washington State	Tacoma, Wash.	D1-'03	16/16
90	Tubbs, Marcus	DT	6-3	324	5/16/81	2	Texas	DeSoto, Texas	D1-'04	11/3
89	Urban, Jerheme	WR	6-3	212	11/26/80	3	Trinity	Victoria, Texas	FA-'03	7/1
15	Wallace, Seneca	QB	5-11	196	8/6/80	3	Iowa State	Sacramento, Calif.	D4a-'03	0*
87	Wallace, Taco	WR	6-1	190	4/14/81	3	Kansas State	Los Angeles, Calif.	D7-'03	3/0
59	White, Tracy	LB	6-0	230	4/14/81	3	Howard	St. Stephens, S.C.	FA-'03	10/2
14	Willis, Jason	WR	6-1	196	7/26/80	3	Oregon	Los Angeles, Calif.	FA-'03	1/0
96	Wistrom, Grant	DE	6-4	272	7/3/76	8	Nebraska	Webb City, Mo.	UFA(StL)-'04	9/9
77	Womack, Floyd	T/G	6-4	333	11/15/78	5	Mississippi State	Cleveland, Miss.	D4c-'01	16/8
98	Woodard, Cedric	DT	6-2	310	9/5/77	6	Texas	Sweeny, Texas	W(Balt)-'00	16/16
70	Wunsch, Jerry	T/G	6-6	339	1/21/74	9	Wisconsin	Eau Claire, Wis.	UFA(TB)-'02	5/0

* Araguz last active with Minnesota in '03; Bentley played 16 games with Cleveland in '04; Darby played 16 games with Tampa Bay; Dyson played 16 games with Tennessee; Fisher played 16 games with St. Louis; Hackett inactive for 7 games; Herndon played 16 games with Denver; House last active with San Diego in '03; Jurevicius played 10 games with Tampa Bay; Leverette played 5 games with San Francisco; Lewis last active with Seattle in '03; Lowe played 3 games with New England; Pathon played 15 games with New Orleans; Sharper played 16 games with Houston; Smith last active with Cincinnati in '02; Tafoya last active with Chicago in '03; S. Wallace did not play in 1 game.

Traded—QB Trent Dilfer (6 games in '04) to Cleveland.

Players lost through free agency (6): FB Heath Evans (Mia; 15 games in '04), LB Orlando Huff (Ariz; 16), CB Ken Lucas (Car; 16), DE Brandon Mitchell (Atl; 15), DE Chike Okeafor (Ariz; 16), P Tom Rouen (Car; 4).

Also played with Seahawks in '04—LB Chad Brown (7), DE Anton Palepoi (1), LB Curtis Randall (4), WR Jerry Rice (11), LB Anthony Simmons (7), T Chris Terry (8), P Ken Walter (7).

2005 FIRST-YEAR ROSTER

Name	Pos.	Ht.	Wt.	Birthdate	College	Hometown	How Acq.
Brimmer, Jamaal	S	6-1	216	6/29/82	Nevada-Las Vegas	Las Vegas, Nev.	FA
Davis, Marque (1)	WR	5-11	190	1/15/81	Fresno State	Dos Palos, Calif.	FA-'04
Donald, Tony (1)	TE	6-3	248	6/4/79	Western State	Jacksonville, Fla.	FA-'04
Dutton, Ryan	P	6-4	213	12/27/77	Minnesota State	Oshkosh, Wis.	FA
Emanuel, Kevin (1)	DE	6-4	259	12/6/79	Florida State	Waco, Texas	FA-'04
Galloway, Tim	LS	6-2	238	9/4/81	Washington	Auburn, Wash.	FA
Gibbs, Steven	G	6-3	339	9/27/83	Arkansas State	Bartlett, Tenn.	FA
Hamdan, Gibran	QB	6-6	240	2/8/81	Indiana	San Diego, Calif.	FA
Harden, Michael (1)	CB	5-11	190	10/20/81	Missouri	Kansas City, Mo.	FA-'04
Hollenbeck, Joey (1)	C	6-4	281	2/26/80	Washington State	Enumclaw, Wash.	FA-'04
Holley, Terry	S	6-1	211	3/17/82	Rice	Oklahoma City, Okla.	FA
Kluwe, Chris	P	6-4	215	12/24/81	UCLA	Seal Beach, Calif.	FA
Luke, R.J. (1)	FB	6-3	256	5/25/79	Western Illinois	Bloomington, Ill.	FA-'04
Lumsden, Jesse	RB	6-2	224	8/3/82	McMaster	Burlington, Ontario, Canada	FA
Miller, Kevin	K	6-0	212	1/16/80	East Carolina	Virginia Beach, Va.	FA
Mohr, Christian (1)	DE	6-5	237	4/5/80	Sporthochschule, Köln	Aachen, Germany	FA-'04
Powell, Calen	TE	6-5	256	2/16/81	Duke	Bellevue, Wash.	FA
Robinson, Terrence	LB	6-0	240	3/12/80	Oklahoma State	Tyler, Texas	FA
Rosegreen, Junior	S	5-11	193	2/23/80	Auburn	Fort Lauderdale, Fla.	FA
Tucker, B.J. (1)	CB	5-10	188	10/12/80	Wisconsin	Sierra Leone	FA
Weaver, Leonard	FB	6-0	251	9/23/82	Carson-Newman	Melbourne, Fla.	FA
Weeks, Marquis	RB	5-10	216	10/2/80	Virginia	Norristown, Pa.	FA
Wrobel, Brian	QB	6-2	191	4/4/82	Winona State	Stoddard, Wis.	FA

The term NFL Rookie is defined as a player who is in his first season of professional football and has not been on the roster of another professional football team for any regular-season or postseason games. A Rookie is designated by an "R" on NFL rosters. Players who have been active in another professional football league or players who have NFL experience, including either preseason training camp or being on an Active List or Inactive List, or on Reserve/Injured or Reserve/Physically Unable to Perform for fewer than six regular-season games, are termed NFL First-Year Players. An NFL First-Year Player is designated by a "1" on NFL rosters. Thereafter, a player is credited with an additional year of experience for each season in which he accumulates six games on the Active List or Inactive List, or on Reserve/Injured or Reserve/Physically Unable to Perform.

Log on to www.seahawks.com for an up-to-date roster.

COACHING STAFF

Executive Vice President of Football Operations/Head Coach,
Mike Holmgren

Pro Career: Named as the Seahawks' sixth head coach on January 8, 1999. In 2004, the Seahawks won their first NFC West crown and third-ever division title. Under Holmgren's tutelage in 2003, the Seahawks posted their first double-digit victory total since 1986. In his first season, 1999, Holmgren guided the Seahawks to their first postseason appearance since 1988. Holmgren joined Seattle after serving as the head coach of the Green Bay Packers (1992-98). By winning at least one game in five consecutive postseasons (1993-97) Holmgren joined John Madden (1973-77) as the only coaches in league history to accomplish that feat. In 18 NFL seasons (1999-2004 head coach Seattle, 1992-98 head coach Green Bay, 1986-1991 assistant coach San Francisco) Holmgren's teams have a 196-108-1 (.644) record, posted double-digit win totals 11 times, made the postseason 14 times, won three Super Bowls (XXIII, XXIV, and XXXI), and reached another (XXXII). Career record: 134-91.
Background: Quarterback at Southern California (1966-69) and was drafted by the St. Louis Cardinals in the eighth round of the 1970 NFL Draft. He served as an assistant coach at San Francisco State (1981) and Brigham Young (1982-85). Earned his bachelor degree in business finance at Southern California.
Personal: Born June 15, 1948, in San Francisco. He and his wife, Kathy, have four daughters—Calla, Jenny, Emily, and Gretchen.

ASSISTANT COACHES

Teryl Austin, defensive backs; born March 3, 1965, Sharon, Pa. Defensive back Pittsburgh 1984-87. Pro defensive back Montreal Machine (WLAF) 1991. College coach: Penn State 1991-92, Wake Forest 1993-95, Syracuse 1996-98, Michigan 1999-2002. Pro coach: Joined Seahawks in 2003.
Dwaine Board, defensive line; born November 29, 1956, Rocky Mount, Va. Defensive lineman North Carolina A&T 1974-77. Pro defensive lineman San Francisco 49ers 1979-1987, New Orleans Saints 1988. Pro coach: San Francisco 49ers 1990-2002, joined Seahawks in 2003.
Bob Casullo, special teams; born March 21, 1951, Little Falls, N.Y. Running back Brockport (N.Y.) State College 1970-73. No pro playing experience. College coach: Syracuse 1985-1994, Georgia Tech 1995-98, Michigan State 1999. Pro coach: Oakland Raiders 2000-03, New York Jets 2004, joined Seahawks in 2005.
Mike Clark, strength and conditioning; born August 22, 1954, Wichita, Kan. Linebacker Ottawa College 1973-76. No

pro playing experience. College coach: Kansas 1977-78, 1982, Wyoming 1981, Oregon 1983-87, Southern California 1988-89, Texas A&M 2000-2003, joined Seahawks in 2004.
Nolan Cromwell, wide receivers; born January 30, 1955, Smith Center, Kan. Quarterback/safety Kansas 1973-76. Pro defensive back Los Angeles Rams 1977-1987. Pro coach: Los Angeles Rams 1991, Green Bay Packers 1992-98, joined Seahawks in 1999.
Gil Haskell, offensive coordinator; born September 24, 1943, San Francisco. Defensive back San Francisco State 1961, 1963-65. No pro playing experience. College coach: Southern California 1978-1982. Pro coach: Los Angeles Rams 1983-1991, Green Bay Packers 1992-97, Carolina Panthers 1998-99, joined Seahawks in 2000.
Darren Krein, asst. strength & conditioning; born July 7, 1971, Aurora, Colo. Linebacker/defensive end Miami 1989-1993. Pro linebacker San Diego Chargers 1994, Barcelona Dragons (NFLE) 1996. Pro coach: Seattle 1997-98, re-joined Seahawks in 2002.
Bill Laveroni, offensive line; born July 20, 1948, San Francisco. Center California 1967-69. No pro playing experience. College coach: California 1970, 1978, 1983-89, San Francisco 1971, Utah State 1979-1982, San Jose State 1990-94, Rutgers 1996-2000, Vanderbilt 2001. Pro coach: San Jose Sabercats (AFL) 1995, joined Seahawks in 2002.
Jim Lind, tight ends; born Novemeber 11, 1947, Isle, Minn. Linebacker Bethel College 1965-66, defensive back Bemidji State 1971-72. No pro playing experience. College coach: St. Cloud State 1977-78, St. John's (Minn.) 1979-1980, Brigham Young 1981-82, Minnesota-Morris 1983-86 (head coach), Wisconsin-Eau Claire 1987-1991 (head coach). Pro coach: Green Bay Packers 1992-98, joined Seahawks in 1999.
John Marshall, linebackers; born October 2, 1945, Arroyo Grande, Calif. Linebacker Washington State 1964. No pro playing experience. College coach: Oregon 1970-76, Southern California 1977-79. Pro coach: Green Bay Packers 1980-82, Indianapolis Colts 1986-88, San Francisco 49ers 1989-1998, Carolina Panthers 1999-2001, Detroit Lions 2002, joined Seahawks in 2003.
Stump Mitchell, running backs; born March 15, 1959, St. Mary's, Ga. Tailback The Citadel 1977-1980. Running back St. Louis/Phoenix Cardinals 1981-89. College coach: Morgan State 1995-98 (head coach 1996-98). Pro coach: San Antonio Rough Riders (WLAF) 1991, joined Seahawks in 1999.
Gary Reynolds, offensive assistant/quality control; born October 15, 1966, Boston. Attended Texas A&M. No college or pro playing experience. College coach:

Texas A&M 1991, Tennessee 1992. Pro coach: Green Bay Packers 1996-98, joined Seahawks in 1999.
Ray Rhodes, defensive coordinator; born October 20, 1950, Mexia, Texas. Running back Texas Christian 1969-1970, wide receiver/defensive back/kick returner Tulsa 1972-73. Pro wide receiver/defensive back New York Giants 1974-79, San Francisco 49ers 1980. Pro coach: San Francisco 49ers 1981-1991, 1994, Green Bay Packers 1992-93, 1999 (head coach 1999), Philadelphia Eagles 1995-98 (head coach), Washington Redskins 2000, Denver Broncos 2001-02, joined Seahawks in 2003.
Zerick Rollins, defensive assistant; born June 20, 1975, Houston. Defensive end Texas A&M 1995-97. No pro playing experience. Graduate assistant Texas A&M 1997-2000. Pro coach: Joined Seahawks in 2001.
Jim Zorn, quarterbacks; born May 10, 1953, Whittier, Calif. Quarterback Cal Poly-Pomona 1973-75. Pro quarterback Seattle Seahawks 1975-1984, Green Bay Packers 1985, Winnipeg Blue Bombers (CFL) 1986, Tampa Bay Buccaneers 1987. College coach: Boise State 1989-1991, Utah State 1992-94, Minnesota 1995-96. Pro coach: Seattle Seahawks 1997, Detroit Lions 1998-2000, re-joined Seahawks in 2001.

National Football Conference
South Division
Team Colors: Buccaneer Red, Pewter,
Black, and Orange
One Buccaneer Place
Tampa, Florida 33607
Telephone: (813) 870-2700

2005 SCHEDULE
PRESEASON
Aug. 12 at Tennessee 7:00
Aug. 20 **Jacksonville** 7:30
Aug. 27 at Miami...........................7:30
Sept. 1 **Houston**...........................7:30

REGULAR SEASON
Sept. 11 at Minnesota 12:00
Sept. 18 **Buffalo**...............................1:00
Sept. 25 at Green Bay 12:00
Oct. 2 **Detroit**..............................1:00
Oct. 9 at New York Jets 1:00
Oct. 16 **Miami**................................1:00
Oct. 23 Open Date
Oct. 30 at San Francisco.................1:15
Nov. 6 **Carolina**............................1:00
Nov. 13 **Washington** 1:00
Nov. 20 at Atlanta.............................1:00
Nov. 27 **Chicago** 1:00
Dec. 4 at New Orleans.................12:00
Dec. 11 at Carolina............................1:00
Dec. 17 at New England (Sat.).........1:30
Dec. 24 **Atlanta** (Sat.) 1:00
Jan. 1 **New Orleans**......................1:00

Stadium: Raymond James Stadium
(opened in 1998)
•**Capacity:** 65,657
Tampa, Florida 33607
Playing Surface: Grass
Training Camp: Disney's Wide World of
Sports
Lake Buena Vista, Florida
92830

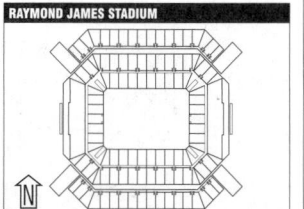

RAYMOND JAMES STADIUM

CLUB OFFICIALS
Owner/President: Malcolm Glazer
Executive Vice President: Bryan Glazer
Executive Vice President: Joel Glazer
Executive Vice President: Edward Glazer
General Manager: Bruce Allen
Senior Director of Business
Administration: Mike Newquist
Director of Football Operations:
Mark Arteaga
Director of Player Personnel:
Ruston Webster
Director of College Scouting:
Dennis Hickey
Director of Pro Personnel: Mark Dominik
Personnel Executive: Doug Williams
General Counsel: Roxanne Kosarzycki
Director of Player Development:
Cedric Saunders
College Scouts: Jim, Abrams,
Frank Dorazio, Brian Gardner,
Seth Turner
National Combine Scout: Mike Martin
Director of Marketing: Jeff Ajluni
Director of Public Relations: Jeff Kamis
Director of Security/Facilities:
Andre Trescastro
Director of Team Services: Tom Szubka
Director of Ticketing and Luxury Suite
Relations: Jeff Leinen
Director of Information Technology:
Scott Burgin
Director of Game Day and Video
Production: Chris Kartzmark
Director of Accounting: Nick Reader
Broadcasting Operations Manager:
Jeff Ryan
Internet Manager: Scott Smith
Public Relations Manager: Jason Wahlers
Trainer: Todd Toriscelli
Director of Rehabilitation:
Shannon Merrick
Equipment Manager: Tim Sain
Assistant Equipment Manager:
Mark Meschede
Video Director: Dave Levy
Assistant Video Director: Pat Brazil

COACHING HISTORY
(178-286-1)
Records include postseason games
1976-1984 John McKay.................45-91-1
1985-86 Leeman Bennett.............4-28-0
1987-1990 Ray Perkins*...............19-41-0
1990-91 Richard Williamson 4-15-0
1992-95 Sam Wyche 23-41-0
1996-2001 Tony Dungy................56-46-0
2002-04 Jon Gruden 27-24-0
*Released after 13 games in 1990

ATTENDANCE
Home 509,082   Away 516,702
Total 1,025,784
Single-game home record,
73,523 (12/7/97)
Single-season home record,
545,980 (1979)

2005 DRAFT CHOICES
Round	Name	Pos.	College
1	Carnell Williams	RB	Auburn
2	Barrett Ruud	LB	Nebraska
3	Alex Smith	TE	Stanford
	Chris Colmer	T	North Carolina St.
4	Dan Buenning	G	Wisconsin
5	Donte Nicholson	DB	Oklahoma
	Larry Brackins	WR	Pearl River JC
6	Anthony Bryant	DT	Alabama
7	Rick Razzano	RB	Mississippi
	Paris Warren	WR	Utah
	Hamza Abdullah	DB	Washington St.
	J.R. Russell	WR	Louisville

2004 TEAM RECORD

PRESEASON (3-1)

Date	Result	Opponent
8/14	W 20-6	Cincinnati
8/20	L 6-14	at Jacksonville
8/28	W 17-10	Miami
9/2	W 17-9	at Houston

REGULAR SEASON (5-11)

Date	Result	Opponent	Att.
9/12	L 10-16	at Washington	90,098
9/19	L 6-10	Seattle	65,089
9/26	L 20-30	at Oakland	60,874
10/3	L 13-16	Denver	65,341
10/10	W 20-17	at New Orleans	64,900
10/18	L 21-28	at St. Louis	66,040
10/24	W 19-7	Chicago	65,550
11/7	W 34-31	Kansas City	65,495
11/14	L 14-24	at Atlanta	70,810
11/21	W 35-3	San Francisco	65,234
11/28	L 14-21	at Carolina	73,124
12/5	W 27-0	Atlanta	65,556
12/12	L 24-31	at San Diego	65,858
12/19	L 17-21	New Orleans	65,075
12/26	L 20-37	Carolina	65,380
1/2	L 7-12	at Arizona	31,650

SCORE BY PERIODS

Buccaneers	48	101	83	69	0 —	301
Opponents	68	91	69	76	0 —	304

2004 TEAM STATISTICS

	Buccaneers	Opp.
Total First Downs	271	258
Rushing	74	101
Passing	175	131
Penalty	22	26
3rd Down: Made/Att	75/199	77/218
3rd Down Pct.	37.7	35.3
4th Down: Made/Att	4/6	3/8
4th Down Pct.	66.7	37.5
Possession Avg.	29:43	30:17
Total Net Yards	4963	4552
Avg. Per Game	310.2	284.5
Total Plays	949	961
Avg. Per Play	5.2	4.7
Net Yards Rushing	1489	1973
Avg. Per Game	93.1	123.3
Total Rushes	393	480
Net Yards Passing	3474	2579
Avg. Per Game	217.1	161.2
Sacked/Yards Lost	44/299	45/264
Gross Yards	3773	2843
Att./Completions	512/340	436/247
Completion Pct.	66.4	56.7
Had Intercepted	18	16
Punts/Average	83/41.8	87/44.4
Net Punting Avg.	83/36.8	87/40.2
Penalties/Yards	117/916	112/897
Fumbles/Ball Lost	32/18	21/11
Touchdowns	37	35
Rushing	9	8
Passing	24	21
Returns	4	6

2004 INDIVIDUAL STATISTICS

PASSING

	Att.	Comp.	Yds.	Pct.	TD	Int.	Tkld.	Rate
Griese	336	233	2,632	69.3	20	12	26/169	97.5
Johnson	103	65	674	63.1	3	3	8/55	79.5
Simms	73	42	467	57.5	1	3	10/75	64.1
Buccaneers	512	340	3,773	66.4	24	18	44/299	89.1
Opponents	436	247	2,843	56.7	21	16	45/264	77.2

SCORING

	TD R	TD P	TD Rt	PAT	FG	Saf	PTS
Pittman	7	3	0	0/0	0/0	0	60
Gramatica	0	0	0	21/22	11/19	0	54
Clayton	0	7	0	0/0	0/0	0	42
Galloway	0	5	1	0/0	0/0	0	36
Jay Taylor	0	0	0	11/11	4/5	0	23
Dilger	0	3	0	0/0	0/0	0	20
Alstott	2	0	0	0/0	0/0	0	12
Barber	0	0	2	0/0	0/0	0	12
Jurevicius	0	2	0	0/0	0/0	0	12
T. Brown	0	1	0	0/0	0/0	0	6
Cook	0	1	0	0/0	0/0	0	6
Cox	0	0	1	0/0	0/0	0	6
Heller	0	1	0	0/0	0/0	0	6
Schroeder	0	1	0	0/0	0/0	0	6
Buccaneers	9	24	4	32/33	15/24	0	301
Opponents	8	21	6	34/35	20/31	0	304

2-Pt. Conversions: Dilger.
Buccaneers 1-4, Opponents 0-0.

RUSHING

	No.	Yds	Avg	LG	TD
Pittman	219	926	4.2	78t	7
Alstott	67	230	3.4	32	2
Garner	30	111	3.7	25	0
Graham	13	73	5.6	13	0
Clayton	5	30	6.0	15	0
Smart	2	26	13.0	25	0
Johnson	5	23	4.6	7	0
J. White	13	20	1.5	10	0
Galloway	2	19	9.5	14	0
Griese	30	17	0.6	7	0
Simms	7	14	2.0	12	0
Buccaneers	393	1,489	3.8	78t	9
Opponents	480	1,973	4.1	64t	8

RECEIVING

	No.	Yds	Avg	LG	TD
Clayton	80	1,193	14.9	75t	7
Pittman	41	391	9.5	68	3
Dilger	39	345	8.8	45t	3
Galloway	33	416	12.6	36t	5
Alstott	29	202	7.0	20	0
Jurevicius	27	333	12.3	42t	2
T. Brown	24	200	8.3	21	1
Lee	15	207	13.8	35	0
Heller	12	98	8.2	22	1
Garner	9	62	6.9	31	0
Schroeder	7	156	22.3	54	1
Cook	7	44	6.3	9	1
J. White	4	17	4.3	12	0
Dudley	3	48	16.0	24	0
Moore	3	17	5.7	10	0
Smart	2	10	5.0	5	0
Lawrie	1	15	15.0	15	0
Comella	1	12	12.0	12	0
Baber	1	7	7.0	7	0
Coleman	1	4	4.0	4	0
Griese	1	-4	-4.0	-4	0
Buccaneers	340	3,773	11.1	75t	24
Opponents	247	2,843	11.5	79t	21

INTERCEPTIONS

	No.	Yds	Avg	LG	TD
Kelly	4	101	25.3	75	0
Barber	3	23	7.7	23	0
D. Smith	3	13	4.3	13	0
Cox	1	55	55.0	55t	1
Gold	1	31	31.0	31	0
Brooks	1	3	3.0	3	0
Nece	1	2	2.0	2	0
Allen	1	0	0.0	0	0
Phillips	1	0	0.0	0	0
Ivy	0	11	—	11	0
Buccaneers	16	239	14.9	75	1
Opponents	18	328	18.2	46t	4

PUNTING

	No.	Yds.	Avg.	In 20	LG
Bidwell	82	3,472	42.3	23	60
Buccaneers	83	3,472	41.8	23	60
Opponents	87	3,867	44.4	34	81

PUNT RETURNS

	Ret	FC	Yds	Avg	LG	TD
Galloway	20	8	142	7.1	59t	1
T. Brown	6	12	48	8.0	14	0
Schroeder	6	1	21	3.5	12	0
Clayton	1	1	2	2.0	2	0
Buccaneers	33	22	213	6.5	59t	1
Opponents	31	24	279	9.0	53	0

KICKOFF RETURNS

	No.	Yds	Avg	LG	TD
Cox	33	866	26.2	59	0
Murphy	8	208	26.0	54	0
Smart	8	167	20.9	27	0
J. White	4	99	24.8	44	0
Graham	3	52	17.3	18	0
Schroeder	2	29	14.5	16	0
Comella	1	20	20.0	20	0
D. White	1	9	9.0	9	0
Buccaneers	60	1,450	24.2	59	0
Opponents	58	1,315	22.7	98t	1

FIELD GOALS

	1-19	20-29	30-39	40-49	50+
Gramatica	0/0	6/7	3/6	1/5	1/1
Jay Taylor	0/0	0/0	2/3	1/1	1/1
Buccaneers	0/0	6/7	5/9	2/6	2/2
Opponents	0/0	4/4	7/11	8/11	1/5

SACKS

	No.
Rice	12.0
Spires	8.0
D. White	6.0
Ahanotu	3.5
Quarles	3.5
Barber	3.0
Brooks	3.0
McFarland	3.0
Bradley	1.0
Phillips	1.0
Gold	0.5
Gooch	0.5
Buccaneers	45.0
Opponents	44.0

RECORD HOLDERS
INDIVIDUAL RECORDS—CAREER

Category	Name	Performance
Rushing (Yds.)	James Wilder, 1981-89	5,957
Passing (Yds.)	Vinny Testaverde, 1987-1992	14,820
Passing (TDs)	Vinny Testaverde, 1987-1992	77
Receiving (No.)	James Wilder, 1981-89	430
Receiving (Yds.)	Mark Carrier, 1987-1992	5,018
Interceptions	Donnie Abraham, 1996-2001	31
Punting (Avg.)	Tom Tupa, 2002-03	43.0
Punt Return (Avg.)	Jacquez Green, 1998-2001	12.0
Kickoff Return (Avg.)	Aaron Stecker, 2000-03	23.8
Field Goals	Martín Gramatica, 1999-2004	137
Touchdowns (Tot.)	Mike Alstott, 1996-2004	61
Points	Martín Gramatica, 1999-2004	592

INDIVIDUAL RECORDS—SINGLE SEASON

Category	Name	Performance
Rushing (Yds.)	James Wilder, 1984	1,544
Passing (Yds.)	Brad Johnson, 2003	3,811
Passing (TDs)	Brad Johnson, 2003	26
Receiving (No.)	Keyshawn Johnson, 2001	106
Receiving (Yds.)	Mark Carrier, 1989	1,422
Interceptions	Ronde Barber, 2001	10
Punting (Avg.)	Tom Tupa, 2003	43.3
Punt Return (Avg.)	Karl Williams, 1996	21.1
Kickoff Return (Avg.)	Karl Williams, 1996	27.4
Field Goals	Martín Gramatica, 2002	32
Touchdowns (Tot.)	James Wilder, 1984	13
Points	Martín Gramatica, 2002	128

INDIVIDUAL RECORDS—SINGLE GAME

Category	Name	Performance
Rushing (Yds.)	James Wilder, 11-6-83	219
Passing (Yds.)	Doug Williams, 11-16-80	486
Passing (TDs)	Steve DeBerg, 9-13-87	5
	Brad Johnson, 11-3-02	5
Receiving (No.)	James Wilder, 9-15-85	13
Receiving (Yds.)	Mark Carrier, 12-6-87	212
Interceptions	Ronde Barber, 12-23-01	3
Field Goals	Martín Gramatica, 12-29-02	5
Touchdowns (Tot.)	Jimmie Giles, 10-20-85	4
Points	Jimmie Giles, 10-20-85	24

2005 VETERAN ROSTER

No.	Name	Pos.	Ht.	Wt.	Birthdate	NFL Exp.	College	Hometown	How Acq.	'04 Games/ Starts
	Adams, Blue	CB	5-9	182	10/15/79	2	Cincinnati	Miami, Fla.	FA-'05	0*
26	Allen, Will	S	6-1	193	6/17/82	2	Ohio State	Dayton, Ohio	D4-'04	16/0
40	Alstott, Mike	FB	6-1	248	12/21/73	10	Purdue	Joliet, Ill.	D2-'96	14/11
20	Barber, Ronde	CB	5-10	184	4/7/75	9	Virginia	Roanoke, Va.	D3b-'97	16/16
88	Becht, Anthony	TE	6-5	272	8/8/77	6	West Virginia	Drexel Hill, Pa.	UFA(NYJ)-'05	16/16*
9	Bidwell, Josh	P	6-3	220	3/13/76	6	Oregon	Winston, Ore.	UFA(GB)-'04	16/0
21	Bolden, Juran	CB	6-2	207	6/27/74	8	Mississippi Delta	Tampa, Fla.	FA-'05	13/0*
73	Bradley, Jon	DT	6-0	301	1/13/81	2	Arkansas State	West Helena, Ark.	FA-'04	6/0
55	Brooks, Derrick	LB	6-0	235	4/18/73	11	Florida State	Pensacola, Fla.	D1b-'95	16/16
3	Bryant, Matt	K	5-9	200	5/29/75	5	Baylor	Orange, Texas	FA-'05	4/0*
80	Clayton, Michael	WR	6-4	197	10/13/82	2	Louisiana State	Baton Rouge, La.	D1-'04	16/13
43	Cook, Jameel	FB	5-10	237	2/8/79	5	Illinois	Miami, Fla.	D6a-'01	12/5
58	Cooper, Marquis	LB	6-3	213	3/11/82	2	Washington	Gilbert, Ariz.	D3-'04	14/0
	Cowsette, Delbert	DT	6-1	296	9/3/77	3	Maryland	Cleveland, Ohio	FA-'05	0*
27	Cox, Torrie	CB	5-10	181	10/29/80	3	Pittsburgh	Miami, Fla.	D6-'03	10/0
69	Davis, Anthony	T	6-4	322	3/27/80	2	Virginia Tech	Victoria, Va.	FA-'03	2/0
70	Deese, Derrick	T	6-3	289	5/17/70	14	Southern California	Culver City, Calif.	FA-'04	16/16
84	Galloway, Joey	WR	5-11	197	11/20/71	11	Ohio State	Bellaire, Ohio	T(Dall)-'04	10/7
30	Garner, Charlie	RB	5-10	190	2/13/72	12	Tennessee	Fairfax, Va.	UFA(Oak)-'04	3/3
50	Gooch, Jeff	LB	5-11	226	10/31/74	10	Austin Peay	Nashville, Tenn.	UFA (Det)-'04	16/1
33	Graham, Earnest	RB	5-9	225	1/15/80	2	Florida	Ft. Myers, Fla.	FA-'03	9/0
66	Gregory, Damian	DT	6-2	305	1/21/77	5	Illinois State	Lansing, Mich.	FA-'04	6/0
8	Griese, Brian	QB	6-3	214	3/18/75	8	Michigan	Miami, Fla.	FA-'04	11/10
89	Heller, Will	TE	6-6	250	2/28/81	3	Georgia Tech	Dunwoody, Ga.	FA-'03	10/2
19	Hilliard, Ike	WR	5-11	210	4/5/76	9	Florida	Patterson, La.	FA-'05	16/15*
95	Hovan, Chris	DT	6-2	298	5/12/78	6	Boston College	Rocky River, Ohio	UFA(Minn)-'05	13/9*
34	Jackson, Dexter	S	6-1	203	7/28/77	7	Florida State	Quincy, Fla.	FA-'04	6/1
41	Johnson, Robert	TE	6-6	270	5/20/80	2	Auburn	Montgomery, Ala.	FA-'04	0*
25	Kelly, Brian	CB	5-11	193	1/14/76	8	Southern California	Aurora, Colo.	D2b-'98	16/16
10	Lewis, Derrick	WR	6-2	185	10/30/75	2	San Diego State	New Orleans, La.	FA-'05	0*
17	Madise, Adrian	WR	5-11	215	3/23/80	2	Texas Christian	Lancaster, Texas	FA-'05	0*
79	Mahan, Sean	G	6-3	301	5/28/80	3	Notre Dame	Jenks, Okla.	D5-'03	16/8
71	Martin, Matt	T	6-6	300	10/12/79	3	Kansas State	Edison, Calif.	FA-'05	0*
12 t-	McCown, Luke	QB	6-3	212	7/12/81	2	Louisiana Tech	Jacksonville, Texas	T(Cle)-'05	5/4*
92	McFarland, Anthony	DT	6-0	300	12/18/77	7	Louisiana State	Winnsboro, La.	D1-'99	8/8
98	McNeal, Bryant	DE	6-4	248	7/13/79	2	Clemson	Swansea, S.C.	FA-'04	0*
83	Moore, Dave	TE	6-2	250	11/11/69	14	Pittsburgh	Succasunna, N.J.	FA-'04	15/0
56	Nece, Ryan	LB	6-3	224	2/24/79	4	UCLA	San Bernardino, Calif.	FA-'02	16/0
23	Phillips, Jermaine	S	6-1	214	3/27/79	4	Georgia	Roswell, Ga.	D5-'02	9/9
32	Pittman, Michael	RB	6-0	218	8/14/75	8	Fresno State	San Diego, Calif.	UFA(Ariz)-'02	13/13
53	Quarles, Shelton	LB	6-1	225	9/11/71	9	Vanderbilt	Whites Creek, Tenn.	FA-'97	15/15
97	Rice, Simeon	DE	6-5	268	2/24/74	10	Illinois	Chicago, Ill.	UFA(Ariz)-'01	16/16
93	Savage, Josh	DE	6-4	276	9/28/80	2	Utah	Salt Lake City, Utah	FA-'04	6/0
86	Shepherd, Edell	WR	6-1	175	5/18/80	3	San Jose State	Los Angeles, Calif.	FA-'03	0*
2	Simms, Chris	QB	6-4	220	8/29/80	3	Texas	Ramapo, N.J.	D3-'03	5/2
36	Smart, Ian	RB	5-8	192	2/28/80	2	C.W. Post	Babylon, N.Y.	FA-'04	0*
1	Smith, Akili	QB	6-3	220	8/21/75	5	Oregon	San Diego, Calif.	FA-'05	0*
94	Spires, Greg	DE	6-1	265	8/12/74	8	Florida State	Cape Coral, Fla.	UFA(Cle)-'02	16/16
75	Steussie, Todd	T	6-6	320	12/1/70	12	California	Agoura, Calif.	FA-'04	16/5
78	Stinchcomb, Matt	G/T	6-6	310	6/3/77	7	Georgia	Lilburn, Ga.	UFA(Oak)-'04	16/16
77	Terry, Jeb	G	6-5	311	4/10/81	2	North Carolina	Dallas, Texas	D5-'04	4/0
76	Wade, John	C	6-5	299	1/25/75	8	Marshall	Harrisonburg, Va.	UFA(Jax)-'03	8/8
67	Walker, Kenyatta	T	6-5	302	2/1/79	5	Florida	Meridian, Miss.	D1-'01	13/11
90	White, Dewayne	DE	6-2	273	10/19/79	3	Louisville	Marbury, Ala.	D2-'03	16/3
	White, Mitch	T	6-4	311	3/25/78	2	Oregon State	San Diego, Calif.	FA-'05	0*
96	Wyms, Ellis	DT	6-3	279	4/12/79	5	Mississippi State	Indianola, Miss.	D6b-'01	6/0

* Adams last active with Jacksonville in '03; Becht played 16 games with N.Y. Jets; Bolden played 13 games with Jacksonville; Bryant played 3 games with Miami and 1 game with Indianapolis; Cowsette last active with Washington in '02; Hilliard played 16 games with N.Y. Giants; Hovan played 13 games with Minnesota; Johnson last active with Chicago in '03; Lewis inactive for 1 game; Madise inactive for 1 game; Martin last active with Tennessee in '03; McCown played 5 games with Cleveland; McNeal inactive for 2 games; Shepherd missed '04 season because of injury; Smith last active with Cincinnati in '02; M. White last active with Washington in '03.

t-Buccaneers traded for McCown (Cle).

Players lost through free agency (5)—LB Keith Burns (Den; 16 games in '03), G Cosey Coleman (Cle; 16), DT Chartric Darby (Sea; 16), G Matt O'Dwyer (GB; 4), S Dwight Smith (NO; 16).

Also played with Buccaneers in '04—DE Chidi Ahanotu (8 games), WR Tim Brown (15), FB Greg Comella (7), TE Ken Dilger (16), TE Rickey Dudley (3), CB Mario Edwards (15), LB Ian Gold (16), K Martin Gramatica (11), S John Howell (16), CB Corey Ivy (16), S Dexter Jackson (6), QB Brad Johnson (4), WR Joe Jurevicius (10), WR Charles Lee (7), WR Frank Murphy (3), WR Bill Schroeder (7), DE Corey Smith (4), RB Jamel White (7).

2005 FIRST-YEAR ROSTER

Name	Pos.	Ht.	Wt.	Birthdate	College	Hometown	How Acq.
Abdullah, Hamza	S	6-2	213	8/20/83	Washington State	Pomona, Calif.	D7c
Allen, Jared	QB	6-3	215	8/26/81	Florida Atlantic	Edmond, Okla.	FA
Arbet, Kevin	CB	5-10	187	3/26/81	Southern California	Stockton, Calif.	FA
Brackins, Larry	WR	6-4	205	11/5/82	Pearl River (MS) J.C.	Dothan, Ala.	D5b
Bryant, Anthony	DT	6-3	336	11/6/81	Alabama	Newbern, Ala.	D6
Buckles, Doug	G	6-5	311	6/18/82	Mississippi	Madison, Miss.	FA
Buenning, Dan	G	6-4	320	10/26/81	Wisconsin	Green Bay, Wis.	D4
Buhl, Josh (1)	LB	6-0	210	5/4/81	Kansas State	Mesquite, Texas	FA
Campbell, Carlos	CB	5-11	178	11/18/82	Notre Dame	Hampton, Va.	FA
Clinkscale, Jonathan	G/C	6-2	315	4/17/82	Wisconsin	Altadena, Calif.	FA
Colmer, Chris	T	6-5	310	11/21/80	North Carolina State	Port Jefferson, N.Y.	D3b
Davis, Chris (1)	WR	6-2	200	10/9/81	Southern	New Orleans, La.	FA
Dozier, Ukee	CB	6-1	190	3/10/82	Minnesota	Bradenton, Fla.	FA
Fischer, Kevin	G	6-4	260	12/17/82	Florida Atlantic	Boca Raton, Fla.	FA
France, Todd (1)	K	6-2	185	2/13/80	Toledo	Maumee, Ohio	FA
Grootegoed, Matt	LB	5-10	218	5/6/82	Southern California	Santa Ana, Calif.	FA
Hardmon, Byron (1)	LB	6-1	230	1/7/81	Florida	Jacksonville, Fla.	FA
Jackson, Scott (1)	C	6-4	300	1/19/79	Brigham Young	Ranch Palos Verdes, Calif.	FA
Lawrie, Nate (1)	TE	6-7	256	10/14/81	Yale	Indianapolis, Ind.	FA
McCoy, Derek (1)	WR	6-3	210	11/13/80	Colorado	Thornton, Colo.	FA
McGruder, Lynn	DT	6-2	302	2/13/82	Oklahoma	Las Vegas, Nev.	FA
Metcalf, Terrance (1)	WR	6-3	200	5/20/80	South Carolina State	Seattle, Wash.	FA
Morris, Dominique	CB	6-0	195	4/12/83	Vanderbilt	Nashville, Tenn.	FA
Nicholson, Donte	S	6-1	216	12/18/81	Oklahoma	Diamond Bay, Calif.	D5a
Patrick, James	CB	5-11	175	6/7/82	Stillman	Tuskegee, Ala.	FA
Pearson, Kalvin (1)	CB/S	5-10	190	10/22/78	Grambling State	Town Creek, Ala.	FA-'04
Razzano, Rick	FB	5-11	240	1/28/81	Mississippi	Milford, Ohio	D7a
Reese, Johnathan (1)	RB	6-1	220	4/15/80	Columbia	St. Louis, Mo.	FA
Reid, Fred	RB	5-9	184	3/16/82	Mississippi State	Tampa, Fla.	FA
Robinson, Leon	G/T	6-4	314	7/31/80	Georgia Tech	Garden City, Ga.	FA
Rubin, DeAndrew (1)	WR	5-11	175	10/9/78	South Florida	St. Petersburg, Fla.	FA
Russell, J.R.	WR	6-3	206	12/5/81	Louisville	Tampa, Fla.	D7d
Ruud, Barrett	LB	6-1	242	5/20/83	Nebraska	Lincoln, Neb.	D2
Save, Bryan (1)	DT	6-4	313	12/16/81	Colorado State	Santa Ana, Calif.	FA
Sawyer, Brian (1)	LS	6-2	250	5/7/81	Florida State	Cordele, Ga.	FA
Simnjanovski, Brian (1)	P	6-3	205	5/29/81	San Diego State	Escondido, Calif.	FA
Smith, Alex	TE	6-4	258	5/22/82	Stanford	Denver, Colo.	D3a
Taylor, Jermaine (1)	LB	6-0	215	11/29/81	Bridgewater	Miramar, Fla.	FA
Ward, Eli (1)	S	5-11	204	12/6/80	Minnesota	Akron, Ohio	FA
Warren, Paris	WR	6-0	213	9/6/82	Utah	Sacramento, Calif.	D7b
Watson, Derek (1)	RB	6-0	212	5/1/81	South Carolina State	Williamson, S.C.	FA
Whitaker, Ronyell (1)	CB	5-11	196	3/19/79	Virginia Tech	Norfolk, Va.	FA-'03
Williams, Carnell	RB	5-11	217	4/21/82	Auburn	Attalla, Ala.	D1
Wright, Keith (1)	DT	6-2	275	6/8/80	Missouri	Santa Clara, Calif.	FA
Youngblood, Kevin (1)	WR	6-5	215	11/22/80	Clemson	Jacksonville, Fla.	FA

The term NFL Rookie is defined as a player who is in his first season of professional football and has not been on the roster of another professional football team for any regular-season or postseason games. A Rookie is designated by an "R" on NFL rosters. Players who have been active in another professional football league or players who have NFL experience, including either preseason training camp or being on an Active List or Inactive List, or on Reserve/Injured or Reserve/Physically Unable to Perform for fewer than six regular-season games, are termed NFL First-Year Players. An NFL First-Year Player is designated by a "1" on NFL rosters. Thereafter, a player is credited with an additional year of experience for each season in which he accumulates six games on the Active List or Inactive List, or on Reserve/Injured or Reserve/Physically Unable to Perform.

Log on to www.buccaneers.com for an up-to-date roster.

COACHING STAFF

Head Coach,
Jon Gruden

Pro Career: Gruden was named the seventh head coach in Buccaneers history on February 18, 2002, when he signed a five-year contract. Gruden, the NFL's youngest head coach (42), led Tampa Bay to its first Super Bowl title in his first season as head coach in 2002. Gruden set two NFL records—he became the youngest head coach in four sea-sons as head coach in 2002. Gruden set was the first veteran head coach to lead his team to the Super Bowl in his first season with a new team. Prior to joining the Buccaneers, Gruden guided the Oakland Raiders to division titles in each of his final two seasons. He steered the Raiders to a 40-28 mark in four seasons (1998-2001), with postseason appearances in 2000 and 2001. Under Gruden, the Raiders advanced to the AFC title game in 2000 and in 2001 lost a divisional playoff game to eventual Super Bowl champion New England. Prior to his four seasons in Oakland, Gruden spent 1995-97 as offensive coordinator for the Philadelphia Eagles and three years (1992-94) as wide receivers coach for Green Bay Packers. He worked as offensive assistant for the San Francisco 49ers in 1990. Career record: 67-52.

Background: Quarterback at Dayton (1982-84), graduating with a degree in communications. The Flyers had a 24-7 record in Gruden's three varsity seasons. Coach collegiately at Tennessee (1986-87), Southeast Missouri State (1988), Pacific (1989), and Pittsburgh (1991).

Personal: Born August 17, 1963 in Sandusky, Ohio. Jon and his wife Cindy, have three sons, Jon II, Michael, and Jayson.

ASSISTANT COACHES

Joe Barry, linebackers; born July 5, 1970, Boulder, Colo. Linebacker Southern California 1991-93. No pro playing experi-ence. College coach: Southern California 1994-95, Northern Arizona 1996-98, Nevada-Las Vegas 1999. Pro coach: San Francisco 49ers 2000, joined Buccaneers in 2001.

Richard Bisaccia, special teams; born June 3, 1960, Yonkers, N.Y. Defensive back Yankton College 1979-1982, Philadelphia Stars (USFL) 1983. College coach: Wayne State College 1983-87, South Carolina 1988-1993, Clemson 1994-98, Mississippi 1999-2001. Pro coach: Joined Buccaneers in 2002.

Garrett Giemont, strength and condition-ing coordinator; born August 31, 1957, Fullerton, Calif. Attended Fullerton College. No college or pro playing experi-ence. Pro coach: Los Angeles Rams 1978-1991, Oakland Raiders 1995-2002, joined Buccaneers in 2003.

Jay Gruden, offensive assistant; born March 4, 1967. Quarterback Louisville 1985-88. Pro quarterback Tampa Bay Storm (AFL) 1991-96, Orlando Predators (AFL) 2002-03. Pro coach: Nashville Kats (AFL) 1997, Orlando Predators (AFL) 1998-2001, joined Buccaneers in 2002.

Paul Hackett, quarterbacks; born July 5, 1947, Burlington, Vt. Quarterback Cal-Davis 1965-68. No pro playing experi-ence. College coach: Cal-Davis 1969-1971, California 1972-75, Southern California 1976-1980, 1998-2000 (head coach 1998-2000), Pittsburgh 1989-1992 (head coach 1990-92). Pro coach: Cleveland Browns 1981-82, San Francisco 49ers 1983-85, Dallas Cowboys 1986-88, Kansas City Chiefs 1993-97, New York Jets 2001-04, joined Jaguars in 2005.

Monte Kiffin, defensive coordinator; born February 29, 1940, Lexington, Neb. Offensive/defensive tackle Nebraska 1959-1963. Pro defensive end Winnipeg Blue Bombers (CFL) 1965. College coach: Nebraska 1966-1976, Arkansas 1977-79, North Carolina State 1980-82 (head coach). Pro coach: Green Bay Packers 1983, Buffalo Bills 1984-85, Minnesota Vikings 1986-89, 1991-94, New York Jets 1990, New Orleans Saints 1995, joined Buccaneers in 1996.

Aaron Kromer, senior assistant; born April 30, 1967, Sandusky, Ohio. Offensive tackle Miami (Ohio) 1986-89. No pro playing experience. College coach: Miami (Ohio) 1990-98, Northwestern 1999-2000. Pro coach: Oakland Raiders 2001-04, joined Jaguars in 2005.

Richard Mann, wide receivers; born April 20, 1947, Aliquippa, Pa. Wide receiver Arizona State 1966-68. No pro playing experience. College coach: Arizona State 1974-79, Louisville 1980-81. Pro coach: Baltimore/Indianapolis Colts 1982-84, Cleveland Browns 1985-1993, New York Jets 1994-96, Baltimore Ravens 1997-98, Kansas City Chiefs 1999-2000, Washington Redskins 2001, joined Buccaneers in 2002.

Rod Marinelli, asst. head coach/defen-sive line; born July 13, 1949, Rosemead, Calif. Offensive/defensive tackle Utah 1968, offensive tackle California Lutheran 1970-72 (military service 1969-1970). No pro playing experience. College coach: Utah State 1976-1982, California 1983-1991, Arizona State 1992-94, Southern California 1995. Pro coach: Joined Buccaneers in 1996.

Ron Middleton, tight ends/asst. special teams; born July 17, 1965, Atmore, Ala. Tight end Auburn 1982-85. Pro tight end Atlanta Falcons 1986-87, Washington Redskins 1988, 1990-93, Cleveland Browns 1989, Los Angeles Rams 1994, San Diego Chargers 1995. College coach: Troy State 1997-98, Mississippi 1999-2003. Pro coach: Joined Buccaneers in 2004.

Mike Morris, asst. strength and condi-tioning; born May 7, 1964, Ayer, Mass. Wide receiver Syracuse 1981-85. No pro playing experience. Pro coach: New England Patriots 1997-99, joined Buccaneers in 2002.

Raheem Morris, asst. defensive backs; born September 3, 1976, Irvington, N.J. Safety Hofstra 1994-97. No pro playing experience. College coach: Hofstra 1998, 2000-2001, Cornell 1999. Pro coach: New York Jets 2001, joined Buccaneers in 2002.

Bill Muir, offensive coordinator/offensive line; born October 26, 1942, Pittsburgh. Tackle Susquehanna 1962-64. No pro playing experience. College coach: Susquehanna 1965, Delaware Valley 1966-67, Rhode Island 1970-71, Idaho State 1972-73, Southern Methodist 1976-77. Pro coach: Orlando (Continental Football League) 1968-69, Houston Shreveport Steamer (WFL) 1975, New England Patriots 1982-88, Indianapolis Colts 1989-1991, Philadelphia Eagles 1992-94, New York Jets 1995-2001, joined Buccaneers in 2002.

Kyle Shanahan, offensive quality control; born December 14, 1979, Minneapolis. Wide receiver Duke 1998-99, Texas 2000-02. No pro playing experience. College coach: UCLA 2003. Pro coach: Joined Buccaneers in 2004.

Mike Tomlin, defensive backs; born March 15, 1972, Hampton, Va. Wide receiver William & Mary 1991-94. No pro playing experience. College coach: Virginia Military Institute 1995, Memphis 1996, Tennessee-Martin 1997, Arkansas State 1997-98, Cincinnati 1999-2000. Pro coach: Joined Buccaneers in 2001.

Art Valero, running backs; born May 12, 1958, Whittier, Calif. Offensive lineman Boise State 1979-1980. No pro playing experience. College coach: Boise State 1981-82, Iowa State 1983, Long Beach State 1984-86, New Mexico 1987-89, Idaho 1990-94, Louisville 1998-2001. Pro coach: Kansas City Chiefs 1994, Buffalo Bills 1996, joined Buccaneers in 2002.

Chris Wiesehan, offensive assistant; born August 29, 1971, St. Louis, Mo. Wide receiver Wabash 1990-93. College coach: Ft. Hays State 1994-95, Purdue 1996-97, Notre Dame 1997-98, Buffalo 1999-2000, Northern Arizona 2001-04. Pro coach: Joined Buccaneers in 2005.

Joe Woods, defensive quality control; born June 25, 1970, Natrona Heights, Pa.. Safety Illinois State 1988-1991. No pro playing experience. College coach: Muskingum 1992, Eastern Michigan 1993-94, Northwestern (La.) State 1994, Grand Valley State 1994-97, Kent State 1997, Hofstra 1998-2000, Western Michigan 2001-03. Pro coach: Joined Buccaneers in 2004.

**National Football Conference
East Division**
Team Colors: Burgundy and Gold
Redskin Park
21300 Redskin Park Drive
Ashburn, Virginia 20147
Telephone: (703) 726-7000

2005 SCHEDULE
PRESEASON
Aug. 13	at Carolina	8:00
Aug. 19	Cincinnati	8:00
Aug. 26	Pittsburgh	8:00
Sept. 1	at Baltimore	8:00

REGULAR SEASON
Sept. 11	Chicago	1:00
Sept. 19	at Dallas (Mon.)	8:00
Sept. 25	Open Date	
Oct. 2	Seattle	1:00
Oct. 9	at Denver	2:15
Oct. 16	at Kansas City	12:00
Oct. 23	San Francisco	1:00
Oct. 30	at New York Giants	1:00
Nov. 6	Philadelphia	8:30
Nov. 13	at Tampa Bay	1:00
Nov. 20	Oakland	1:00
Nov. 27	San Diego	1:00
Dec. 4	at St. Louis	3:05
Dec. 11	at Arizona	2:05
Dec. 18	Dallas	1:00
Dec. 24	New York Giants (Sat.)	1:00
Jan. 1	at Philadelphia	4:15

Stadium: FedExField (opened in 1997)
• **Capacity:** 91,665
1600 FedEx Way
Landover, Maryland 20785
Playing Surface: Natural Grass
Training Camp: Redskins Park
Ashburn, Virginia 20147

FEDEXFIELD

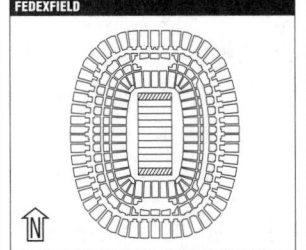

CLUB OFFICIALS
Owner: Daniel M. Snyder
Chief Operating Officer: David Pauken
Chief Financial Officer: Jay Sloan
General Counsel: Norm Chirite
Senior Vice President: Karl Swanson
Senior Vice President, Marketing:
Mike Stevens
Senior Vice President, Stadium
Operations: Michael Dillow
Director of Ticket Operations: Jeff Ritter
Vice President, Football Operations:
Vinny Cerrato
Director of Pro Personnel: Louis Riddick
Director of College Scouting:
Scott Campbell
College Scouts: Tim Gribble,
Shemy Schembechler
National Scout: Joel Patten
Contracts Manager: Eric Schaffer
Director of Player Development:
John "JJ" Jefferson
Director of Public Relations:
Patrick Wixted
Leadership Council/Community Affairs:
Charlene Lefkowitz, Alex Hahn
Director of Team Administration:
Derrick Crawford
Video Director: Mike Bracken
Video Department: Steve Pratti,
Matt Shea
Director of Sports Medicine: Bubba Tyer
Head Athletic Trainer: John Burrell
Assistant Athletic Trainers: Eric Steward,
Larry Hess
Equipment Manager: Brad Berlin
Assistant Equipment Manager:
Anders Beutel

COACHING HISTORY
Boston 1932-36
(527-477-27)
Records include postseason games
1932	Lud Wray	4-4-2
1933-34	William (Lone Star) Dietz	11-11-2
1935	Eddie Casey	2-8-1
1936-1942	Ray Flaherty	56-23-3
1943	Arthur (Dutch) Bergman	7-4-1
1944-45	Dudley DeGroot	14-6-1
1946-48	Glen (Turk) Edwards	16-18-1
1949	John Whelchel*	3-3-1
1949-1951	Herman Ball**	4-16-0
1951	Dick Todd	5-4-0
1952-53	Earl (Curly) Lambeau	10-13-1
1954-58	Joe Kuharich	26-32-2
1959-1960	Mike Nixon	4-18-2
1961-65	Bill McPeak	21-46-3
1966-68	Otto Graham	17-22-3
1969	Vince Lombardi	7-5-2
1970	Bill Austin	6-8-0
1971-77	George Allen	69-35-1
1978-1980	Jack Pardee	24-24-0
1981-1992	Joe Gibbs	140-65-0
1993	Richie Petitbon	4-12-0
1994-2000	Norv Turner***	50-60-1
2000	Terry Robiskie	1-2-0
2001	Marty Schottenheimer	8-8-0
2002-03	Steve Spurrier	12-20-0
2004	Joe Gibbs	6-10-0

*Released after seven games in 1949
**Released after three games in 1951
***Released after 13 games in 2000

ATTENDANCE
Home 707,920   Away 530,893
Total 1,238,813
Single-game home record,
88,678 (9/27/04)
Single-season home record,
707,920 (2004)

2005 DRAFT CHOICES
Round	Name	Pos.	College
1	Carlos Rogers	DB	Auburn
	Jason Campbell	QB	Auburn
4	Manuel White	RB	UCLA
5	Robert McCune	LB	Louisville
6	Jared Newberry	LB	Stanford
7	Nehemiah Broughton	RB	Citadel

2004 TEAM RECORD

PRESEASON (3-2)

Date	Result	Opponent
8/9	W 20-17	vs. Denver
		at Canton, OH
8/14	L 20-23	Carolina
8/21	W 17-0	Miami
8/27	L 3-28	at St. Louis
9/3	W 27-0	Atlanta

REGULAR SEASON (6-10)

Date	Result	Opponent	Att.
9/12	W 16-10	Tampa Bay	90,098
9/19	L 14-20	at N.Y. Giants	78,767
9/27	L 18-21	Dallas	90,367
10/3	L 13-17	at Cleveland	73,348
10/10	L 10-17	Baltimore	90,287
10/17	W 13-10	at Chicago	61,945
10/31	L 14-28	Green Bay	89,295
11/7	W 17-10	at Detroit	62,657
11/14	L 10-17	Cincinnati	87,786
11/21	L 6-28	at Philadelphia	67,720
11/28	L 7-16	at Pittsburgh	63,707
12/5	W 31-7	N.Y. Giants	87,872
12/12	L 14-17	Philadelphia	90,089
12/18	W 26-16	at San Francisco	65,710
12/26	L 10-13	at Dallas	63,705
1/2	W 21-18	Minnesota	76,876

SCORE BY PERIODS

Redskins	54	80	34	72	0	—	240
Opponents	44	78	69	74	0	—	265

2004 TEAM STATISTICS

	Redskins	Opp.
Total First Downs	269	251
Rushing	91	67
Passing	156	153
Penalty	22	31
3rd Down: Made/Att	70/221	70/226
3rd Down Pct.	31.7	31.0
4th Down: Made/Att	4/11	7/17
4th Down Pct.	36.4	41.2
Possession Avg.	31:19	28:41
Total Net Yards	4397	4281
Avg. Per Game	274.8	267.6
Total Plays	1023	974
Avg. Per Play	4.3	4.4
Net Yards Rushing	1765	1304
Avg. Per Game	110.3	81.5
Total Rushes	471	419
Net Yards Passing	2632	2977
Avg. Per Game	164.5	186.1
Sacked/Yards Lost	38/242	40/245
Gross Yards	2874	3222
Att./Completions	514/288	515/294
Completion Pct.	56.0	57.1
Had Intercepted	17	18
Punts/Average	104/43.7	104/40.2
Net Punting Avg.	104/35.2	104/35.9
Penalties/Yards	115/1047	97/797
Fumbles/Ball Lost	20/10	17/8
Touchdowns	26	30
Rushing	6	7
Passing	18	17
Returns	2	6

2004 INDIVIDUAL STATISTICS

PASSING	Att.	Comp.	Yds.	Pct.	TD	Int.	Tkld.	Rate
Ramsey	272	169	1,665	62.1	10	11	23/137	74.8
Brunell	237	118	1,194	49.8	7	6	15/105	63.9
Gardner	3	0	0	0.0	0	0	0/0	39.6
Portis	2	1	15	50.0	1	0	0/0	114.6
Redskins	514	288	2,874	56.0	18	17	38/242	70.0
Opponents	515	294	3,222	57.1	17	18	40/245	72.2

SCORING	TD R	TD P	TD Rt	PAT	FG	Saf	PTS
Portis	5	2	0	0/0	0/0	0	42
Hall	0	0	0	13/13	8/11	0	37
Cooley	0	6	0	0/0	0/0	0	36
Gardner	0	5	0	0/0	0/0	0	30
Kimrin	0	0	0	6/6	6/10	0	24
Royal	0	4	0	0/0	0/0	0	24
Chandler	0	0	0	6/6	5/6	0	21
Betts	1	0	0	0/0	0/0	0	6
Coles	0	1	0	0/0	0/0	0	6
Harris	0	0	1	0/0	0/0	0	6
Pierce	0	0	1	0/0	0/0	0	6
Jacobs	0	0	0	0/0	0/0	0	6
Redskins	6	18	2	25/25	19/27	0	240
Opponents	7	17	6	28/28	17/20	1	265

2-Pt. Conversions: Jacobs.
Redskins 1-1, Opponents 2-2.

RUSHING	No.	Yds	Avg	LG	TD
Portis	343	1,315	3.8	64t	5
Betts	90	371	4.1	27	1
Brunell	19	62	3.3	21	0
Ramsey	10	19	1.9	17	0
Gardner	3	7	2.3	11	0
Cartwright	2	0	0.0	2	0
Coles	3	-3	-1.0	7	0
Jacobs	1	-6	-6.0	-6	0
Redskins	471	1,765	3.7	64t	6
Opponents	419	1,304	3.1	26	7

RECEIVING	No.	Yds	Avg	LG	TD
Coles	90	950	10.6	45	1
Gardner	51	650	12.7	51	5
Portis	40	235	5.9	18	2
Cooley	37	314	8.5	31	6
Thrash	17	203	11.9	31	0
Jacobs	16	178	11.1	45	0
Betts	15	108	7.2	20	0
Royal	8	70	8.8	23	4
McCants	5	71	14.2	27	0
Rasby	5	52	10.4	13	0
Kozlowski	3	29	9.7	13	0
Sellers	1	14	14.0	14	0
Redskins	288	2,874	10.0	51	18
Opponents	294	3,222	11.0	80	17

INTERCEPTIONS	No.	Yds	Avg	LG	TD
Springs	5	117	23.4	38	0
Taylor	4	85	21.3	45	0
Smoot	3	17	5.7	17	0
Pierce	2	94	47.0	78t	1
Harris	2	31	15.5	31	0
Warner	1	39	39.0	39	0
Franz	1	22	22.0	22	0
Redskins	18	405	22.5	78t	1
Opponents	17	201	11.8	70t	1

PUNTING	No.	Yds.	Avg.	In 20	LG
Tupa	103	4,544	44.1	30	61
Redskins	104	4,544	43.7	30	61
Opponents	104	4,180	40.2	26	58

PUNT RETURNS	Ret	FC	Yds	Avg	LG	TD
Thrash	19	8	162	8.5	43	0
Morton	13	12	80	6.2	14	0
A. Brown	10	2	89	8.9	39	0
Marshall	0	1	0	—	—	0
Redskins	42	23	331	7.9	43	0
Opponents	65	11	727	11.2	78t	1

KICKOFF RETURNS	No.	Yds	Avg	LG	TD
Betts	23	528	23.0	70	0
Morton	16	358	22.4	49	0
Thrash	9	186	20.7	36	0
Sellers	4	56	14.0	17	0
A. Brown	1	66	66.0	66	0
Kozlowski	1	4	4.0	4	0
Molinaro	1	5	5.0	5	0
Redskins	55	1,203	21.9	70	0
Opponents	57	1,223	21.5	92t	1

FIELD GOALS	1-19	20-29	30-39	40-49	50+
Hall	1/1	3/3	3/3	1/3	0/1
Kimrin	0/0	3/3	2/3	1/3	0/1
Chandler	0/0	4/4	0/0	1/1	0/1
Redskins	1/1	10/10	5/6	3/7	0/3
Opponents	0/0	4/4	9/9	4/6	0/1

SACKS	No.
Griffin	6.0
Springs	6.0
Washington	4.5
Warner	3.5
Clemons	3.0
Wynn	3.0
Evans	2.5
Bowen	2.0
Salave'a	2.0
Marshall	1.5
Arrington	1.0
Daniels	1.0
Haley	1.0
Noble	1.0
Pierce	1.0
Taylor	1.0
Redskins	40.0
Opponents	38.0

RECORD HOLDERS
INDIVIDUAL RECORDS—CAREER

Category	Name	Performance
Rushing (Yds.)	John Riggins, 1976-79, 1981-85	7,472
Passing (Yds.)	Joe Theismann, 1974-1985	25,206
Passing (TDs)	Sammy Baugh, 1937-1952	187
Receiving (No.)	Art Monk, 1980-1993	888
Receiving (Yds.)	Art Monk, 1980-1993	12,028
Interceptions	Darrell Green, 1983-2001	54
Punting (Avg.)	Sammy Baugh, 1937-1952	*45.1
Punt Return (Avg.)	Johnny Williams, 1952-53	12.8
Kickoff Return (Avg.)	Bobby Mitchell, 1962-68	28.5
Field Goals	Mark Moseley, 1974-1986	263
Touchdowns (Tot.)	Charley Taylor, 1964-1977	90
Points	Mark Moseley, 1974-1986	1,206

INDIVIDUAL RECORDS—SINGLE SEASON

Category	Name	Performance
Rushing (Yds.)	Stephen Davis, 2001	1,432
Passing (Yds.)	Jay Schroeder, 1986	4,109
Passing (TDs)	Sonny Jurgensen, 1967	31
Receiving (No.)	Art Monk, 1984	106
Receiving (Yds.)	Bobby Mitchell, 1963	1,436
Interceptions	Dan Sandifer, 1948	13
Punting (Avg.)	Sammy Baugh, 1940	*51.4
Punt Return (Avg.)	Johnny Williams, 1952	15.3
Kickoff Return (Avg.)	Mike Nelms, 1981	29.7
Field Goals	Mark Moseley, 1983	33
Touchdowns (Tot.)	John Riggins, 1983	24
Points	Mark Moseley, 1983	161

INDIVIDUAL RECORDS—SINGLE GAME

Category	Name	Performance
Rushing (Yds.)	Gerald Riggs, 9-17-89	221
Passing (Yds.)	Sammy Baugh, 10-31-43	446
Passing (TDs)	Sammy Baugh, 10-31-43, 11-23-47	6
	Mark Rypien, 11-10-91	6
Receiving (No.)	Art Monk, 12-15-85, 11-4-90	13
	Kelvin Bryant, 12-7-86	13
Receiving (Yds.)	Anthony Allen, 10-4-87	255
Interceptions	Sammy Baugh, 11-14-43	*4
	Dan Sandifer, 10-31-48	*4
Field Goals	Many times	5
	Last time by Chip Lohmiller, 10-25-92	
Touchdowns (Tot.)	Dick James, 12-17-61	4
	Larry Brown, 12-16-73	4
Points	Dick James, 12-17-61	24
	Larry Brown, 12-16-73	24

*NFL Record

2005 VETERAN ROSTER

No.	Name	Pos.	Ht.	Wt.	Birthdate	NFL Exp.	College	Hometown	How Acq.	'04 Games/ Starts
71	Albright, Ethan	LS	6-5	260	5/1/71	11	North Carolina	Greensboro, N.C.	UFA(Buff)-'01	16/0
55	Allen, Brian	LB	6-0	232	4/1/78	5	Florida State	Lake City, Fla.	UFA(Car)-'05	14/0*
56	Arrington, LaVar	LB	6-3	255	6/20/78	6	Penn State	Pittsburgh, Pa.	D1-'00	4/2
43	Baber, Billy	HB	6-4	260	1/17/79	3	Virginia	Crozet, Va.	FA-'05	1/0*
51	Barnes, Brandon	LB	6-0	235	6/12/81	2	Missouri	Sikeston, Mo.	FA-'04	12/0
58	Barrow, Mike	LB	6-2	242	4/19/70	12	Miami	Homestead, Fla.	UFA(NYG)-'04	0*
46	Betts, Ladell	RB	5-10	216	8/27/79	4	Iowa	Blue Springs, Mo.	D2-'02	16/1
15	Black, Nathan	WR	6-0	193	6/20/78	2	Northwestern State	Monroe, La.	FA-'05	0*
73	Boschetti, Ryan	DE/DT	6-4	295	10/7/81	2	UCLA	Belmont, Calif.	FA-'04	3/1
41	Bowen, Matt	S	6-1	201	11/12/76	6	Iowa	Glen Ellyn, Ill.	RFA(GB)-'03	5/5
86	Brown, Antonio	WR	5-10	175	3/3/78	3	West Virginia	Miami, Fla.	FA-'04	3/0
67	Brown, Ray	T/G	6-5	318	12/12/62	20	Arkansas State	Marion, Ark.	UFA(Det)-'04	16/14
8	Brunell, Mark	QB	6-1	217	9/17/70	13	Washington	Santa Maria, Calif.	T(Jax)-'04	9/9
50	Campbell, Khary	LB	6-3	235	4/4/79	4	Bowling Green	Toledo, Ohio	FA-'04	9/0
31	Cartwright, Rock	RB	5-7	212	12/3/79	4	Kansas State	Conroe, Texas	D7-'02	13/0
5	Chandler, Jeff	K	6-2	218	6/18/79	3	Florida	Jacksonville, Fla.	FA-'04	5/0*
25	Clark, Ryan	CB/S	5-11	200	10/12/79	4	Louisiana State	Merraro, La.	FA-'04	15/11
57	Clemons, Chris	LB	6-3	234	10/30/81	2	Georgia	Griffin, Ga.	UFA-'03	6/0
47	Cooley, Chris	HB	6-3	254	7/11/82	2	Utah State	Powell, Utah	D3-'04	16/9
93	Daniels, Phillip	DE/DT	6-3	285	3/4/73	10	Georgia	Donaldson, Ga.	UFA(Chi)-'04	5/5
66	Dockery, Derrick	T/G	6-6	332	9/7/80	3	Texas	Lakeview, Texas	D3-'03	16/16
92	Evans, Demetric	DE/DT	6-3	283	3/3/79	4	Georgia	Haynesville, Ga.	FA-'04	12/8
16	Farris, Jimmy	WR	6-0	200	4/13/78	3	Montana	Lewiston, Idaho	FA-'05	14/0*
39	Forsey, Brock	RB	5-11	208	2/11/80	3	Boise State	Meridian, Idaho	FA-;05	6/0*
64	Friedman, Lennie	T/G	6-3	285	8/13/76	6	Duke	Livingston, N.J.	UFA(Den)-'03	5/2
87	Gardner, Rod	WR	6-2	215	10/26/77	5	Clemson	Jacksonville, Fla.	D1-'01	16/14
96	Griffin, Cornelius	DT	6-3	300	12/3/76	6	Alabama	Brundidge, Ala.	UFA(NYG)-'04	15/15
10	Hall, John	K	6-3	230	3/17/74	9	Wisconsin	Port Charlotte, Fla.	UFA(NYJ)-'03	8/0
27	Harris, Walt	CB	5-11	191	8/10/74	10	Mississippi State	LaGrange, Ga.	UFA(Ind)-'04	16/2
48	Holdman, Warrick	LB	6-1	235	11/22/75	7	Texas A&M	Alief, Texas	UFA(Cle)-'05	16/14*
82	Holloway, Jabari	TE	6-2	262	12/18/78	3	Notre Dame	Riverdale, Ga.	FA-'05	0*
84	Jacobs, Taylor	WR	6-0	200	5/30/81	3	Florida	Tallahassee, Fla.	D2-'03	15/4
76	Jansen, Jon	T	6-6	305	1/28/76	6	Michigan	Clawson, Mich.	D2-'99	0*
23	Jimoh, Ade	CB/S	6-1	186	4/18/80	3	Utah State	Woodland Hills, Calif.	FA-'03	15/0
91	Killings, Cedric	DE/DT	6-2	290	12/14/77	3	Carson-Newman	Miami, Fla.	FA-'04	0*
34	Lott, Andre	CB/S	5-10	193	5/31/79	4	Tennessee	Memphis, Tenn.	D5-'02	4/3
98	Marshall, Lemar	LB	6-2	229	12/17/76	4	Michigan State	Cincinnati, Ohio	FA-'01	16/14
85	McCants, Darnerien	WR	6-3	211	8/1/78	4	Delaware State	Odenton, Md.	D5-'01	5/0
69	Molinaro, Jim	T/G	6-6	300	4/27/81	2	Notre Dame	Bethlehem, Pa.	D6-'04	11/0
20	Morton, Chad	RB-KR	5-8	195	4/4/77	6	Southern California	Torrance, Calif.	RFA(NYJ)-'03	6/0
89 t-	Moss, Santana	WR	5-10	185	6/1/79	5	Miami	Miami, Fla.	T(NYJ)-'05	15/14*
75	Noble, Brandon	DT	6-2	299	4/10/74	6	Penn State	Virginia Beach, Va.	UFA(Dall)-'03	16/7
80	Patten, David	WR	5-10	190	8/19/74	9	Western Carolina	Columbia, S.C.	UFA(NE)-'05	16/11*
26	Portis, Clinton	RB	5-11	210	9/1/81	4	Miami	Gainesville, Fla.	T(Den)-'04	15/15
29	Prioleau, Pierson	CB/S	5-11	188	8/6/77	7	Virginia Tech	Alvin, S.C.	UFA(Buff)-'05	16/2*
61	Rabach, Casey	T/G	6-4	301	9/24/77	4	Wisconsin	Sturgeon Bay, Wis.	UFA(Balt)-'05	16/16*
11	Ramsey, Patrick	QB	6-2	223	2/14/79	4	Tulane	Ruston, La.	D1-'02	9/7
52	Raymer, Cory	C	6-3	298	3/3/73	10	Wisconsin	Fond du Lac, Wis.	UFA(SD)-'04	15/14
88	Royal, Robert	TE	6-4	252	5/15/79	3	Louisiana State	New Orleans, La.	D5-'02	14/9
95	Salave'a, Joe	DE/DT	6-3	308	3/25/75	7	Arizona	Leone, American Samoa	FA-'04	15/9
60	Samuels, Chris	T	6-5	302	7/28/77	6	Alabama	Mobile, Ala.	D1-'00	16/16
45	Sellers, Mike	HB	6-3	278	7/21/75	6	Walla Walla (WA) C.C.	North Thurston, Wash.	FA-'04	16/1
24	Springs, Shawn	CB	6-0	200	3/11/75	9	Ohio State	Silver Spring, Md.	UFA(Sea)-'04	13/13
21	Taylor, Sean	S	6-2	230	4/1/83	2	Miami	Miami, Fla.	D1-'04	15/13
77	Thomas, Randy	G	6-5	306	1/19/76	7	Mississippi State	East Point, Ga.	UFA(NYJ)-'03	15/15
83	Thrash, James	WR	6-0	200	4/28/75	9	Missouri Southern	Wewoka, Okla.	T(Phil)-'04	16/4
	Tuipala, Joe	LB	6-0	237	9/13/76	3	San Diego State	Honolulu, Hawaii	FA-'05	15/0*
19	Tupa, Tom	P	6-4	220	2/6/66	17	Ohio State	Cleveland, Ohio	UFA(TB)-'04	16/0
74	Warner, Josh	T/G	6-5	318	5/15/79	2	SUNY-Brockport	Cato, N.Y.	FA-'05	0*
94	Warner, Ron	DE	6-3	270	9/26/75	4	Kansas	Independence, Kan.	FA-'03	14/2
53	Washington, Marcus	LB	6-3	243	10/17/76	6	Auburn	Auburn, Ala.	UFA(Ind)-'04	16/16
72	Williams, Melvin	DE/DT	6-2	269	2/2/79	3	Kansas State	St. Louis, Mo.	FA-'05	3/0*
22	Williams, Roosevelt	CB/S	6-1	210	9/10/78	3	Tuskegee	Jacksonville, Fla.	FA-'05	0*
63	Wilson, Mark	T/G	6-6	318	11/11/80	2	California	San Jose, Calif.	D5-'04	2/1
97	Wynn, Renaldo	DE/DT	6-3	286	9/3/74	9	Notre Dame	Chicago, Ill.	UFA(Jax)-'02	16/16

* Allen played 14 games with Carolina in '04; Baber played 1 game with Tampa Bay; Barrow missed '04 season because of injury; Black missed '03 season with Carolina because of injury; Chandler played 2 games with Carolina and 3 with Washington; Farris played 14 games with Atlanta; Forsey played 6 games with Miami; Holdman played 16 games with Cleveland; Holloway last active with Houston in '03; Jansen missed '04 season because of injury; Killings inactive for 4 games; Moss played 15 games for N.Y. Jets; Patten played 16 games with New England; Prioleau played 16 games with Buffalo; Rabach played 16 games with Baltimore; Tuipala missed '03 season with Jacksonville because of injury; J. Warner last active with Chicago in '03; M. Williams played 3 games with San Francisco; R. Williams last active with Cleveland in '03.

t — Redskins traded for Moss (NYJ).

Traded—WR Laveranues Coles (16 games in '04) to N.Y. Jets.

Players lost through free agency (2): LB Antonio Pierce (NYG; 16 games in '04), CB Fred Smoot (Minn; 16).

Also played with Redskins in '04—S Pat Dennis (11 games), S Jason Doering (6), S Todd Franz (16), DT Jermaine Haley (13), K Ola Kimrin (5), TE Brian Kozlowski (11), LB Devin Lemons (1), T Vaughn Parker (1), TE Walter Rasby (6), LB Dominique Stevenson (1), LB Billy Strother (2).

2005 FIRST-YEAR ROSTER

Name	Pos.	Ht.	Wt.	Birthdate	College	Hometown	How Acq.
Alston, Jon	G/T	6-5	306	9/4/82	South Carolina	Goose Creek, S.C.	FA
Bethea, James (1)	CB	5-10	190	9/24/82	California	Waikiki Beach, Calif.	FA-'04
Broughton, Nehemiah	RB	5-11	245	11/4/81	Citadel	North Charleston, S.C.	D7
Brown, Rufus (1)	CB	5-9	190	7/18/80	Florida State	El Paso, Texas	FA-'04
Campbell, Jason	QB	6-4	230	12/31/81	Auburn	Taylorsville, Miss.	D1b
Clemons, Nic (1)	DE/DT	6-6	278	2/3/80	Georgia	Griffin, Ga.	FA-'03
Diedrick, Dahrran (1)	RB	6-0	225	1/11/79	Nebraska	Scarborough, Canada	FA-'04
Gonzalez, Adrian	G/T	6-5	328	12/3/82	Louisiana Tech	Dallas, Texas	FA
Groom, Andy	P	6-0	196	9/10/79	Ohio State	Columbus, Ohio	FA
Harris, Steven	WR	5-10	183	11/10/81	Arkansas	Miami, Fla.	FA
Holiday, Pedro	WR	6-1	179	3/1/82	Middle Tennessee State	Rome, Ga.	FA
Howard, Charles	DE/DT	6-2	259	7/15/81	Florida State	Lake Butler, Fla.	FA
Jones, Aki	DE/DT	6-4	276	5/21/82	Fordham	Jamaica, N.Y.	FA
Keasey, Zak	LB	6-0	236	3/19/82	Princeton	Clarkston, Mich.	FA
Luebke, Tyler	DE/DT	6-0	284	8/20/81	Iowa	Iowa City, Iowa	FA
McCune, Robert	LB	6-0	244	3/9/79	Louisville	Mobile, Ala.	D5
Newberry, Jared	LB	6-1	232	4/11/81	Stanford	Minneapolis, Minn.	FA
Nichols, Jerome	DE/DT	6-2	285	4/4/82	Wake Forest	Glenndale, Md.	FA
Nowland, Ben (1)	G/T	6-2	298	5/27/80	Auburn	Jacksonville, Fla.	FA-'04
Palmer, William	TE	6-3	260	1/27/81	Notre Dame	Wyntree Heathrow, Fla.	FA
Parson, Rich	WR	5-9	186	5/16/80	Maryland	Newark, Del.	FA
Richardson, Dominique	G/T	6-4	301	6/23/82	Howard	Dayton, Ohio	FA
Rogers, Carlos	CB	6-0	200	7/2/81	Auburn	Augusta, Ga.	D1a
Smith, Clifton (1)	LB	6-3	255	7/21/80	Syracuse	Freeport, N.Y.	FA-'03
Spinner, Bryson	QB	6-3	235	11/7/80	Richmond	Alexandria, Va.	FA
White, Manuel	HB	6-2	235	7/2/82	UCLA	Canyon Country, Calif.	D4
Wilds, Garnell (1)	CB	5-11	189	6/8/81	Virginia Tech	Tampa, Fla.	FA-'04

The term NFL Rookie is defined as a player who is in his first season of professional football and has not been on the roster of another professional football team for any regular-season or postseason games. A Rookie is designated by an "R" on NFL rosters. Players who have been active in another professional football league or players who have NFL experience, including either preseason training camp or being on an Active List or Inactive List, or on Reserve/Injured or Reserve/Physically Unable to Perform for fewer than six regular-season games, are termed NFL First-Year Players. An NFL First-Year Player is designated by a "1" on NFL rosters. Thereafter, a player is credited with an additional year of experience for each season in which he accumulates six games on the Active List or Inactive List, or on Reserve/Injured or Reserve/Physically Unable to Perform.

Log on to www.redskins.com for an up-to-date roster.

COACHING STAFF

Head Coach,
Joe Gibbs

Pro Career: On January 7, 2004 Joe Gibbs made his return to the Washington Redskins as head coach and team president. The most successful coach in Redskins history, Gibbs, who coached the team from 1981-1992, led the Redskins to four Super Bowls (XVI, XVII, XXII, and XXVI). He is the only coach to win three Super Bowls with three different quarterbacks. His 146 wins ranks 14th in NFL history, and his .661 win percentage is third among all NFL coaches with more than 125 wins. Gibbs coached with the St. Louis Cardinals (1973-1977), Tampa Bay Buccaneers (1978), and San Diego Chargers (1979-1980), before joining the Redskins in 1981. Career record: 146-75.
Background: Played tight end, offensive guard and linebacker at San Diego State. Coached at San Diego State (1964-66), Florida State (1967-1968), USC (1969-1970), and Arkansas (1971-1972).
Personal: Born November 25, 1940 in Mocksville, N.C,. lives in Charlotte, with wife Pat. They have two sons: J.D. and Coy.

ASSISTANT COACHES

Greg Blache, defensive coordinator-defensive line; born March 9, 1949, New Orleans. Attended Notre Dame. No college or pro playing experience. College coach: Notre Dame 1972-75, 1981-83, Tulane 1976-1980, Southern 1986, Kansas 1987. Pro coach: Jacksonville Bulls (USFL) 1984-85, Green Bay Packers 1988-1993, Indianapolis Colts 1994-98, Chicago Bears 1999-2003, joined Redskins in 2004.
Don Breaux, offensive coordinator; born August 3, 1940, Jennings, La. Quarterback McNeese State 1958-1961. Pro quarterback Denver Broncos 1963, San Diego Chargers 1964-65. College coach: Florida State 1966-67, Arkansas 1968-1971, 1977-1980, Florida 1973-74, Texas 1975-76. Pro coach: Houston Oilers 1972, Washington Redskins 1981-1993, New York Jets 1994, Carolina Panthers 1995-2001, re-joined Redskins in 2004.
Joe Bugel, asst. head coach-offense; born March 10, 1940, Pittsburgh. Guard/linebacker Western Kentucky 1960-63. No pro playing experience. College coach: Western Kentucky 1964-1968, Navy 1969-1972, Iowa State 1973, Ohio State 1974. Pro coach: Detroit Lions 1975-76, Houston Oilers 1977-1980, Washington Redskins 1981-89, Phoenix Cardinals 1990-1993 (head coach), Oakland Raiders 1995-97 (head coach 1997), San Diego Chargers 1998-2001, re-joined Redskins in 2004.
Jack Burns, offensive assistant; born January 3, 1949, Tampa. Safety Florida 1967-1970. No pro playing experience.

College coach: Florida 1971-73, 1975, Louisville 1974, 1985-88, Texas 1976, Vanderbilt 1977-78, Auburn 1979-1980. Pro coach: Tampa Bay Bandits (USFL) 1983, Washington Redskins 1989-1991, Minnesota Vikings 1992-93, Atlanta Falcons 1997-2003, re-joined Redskins in 2004.
Earnest Byner, running backs; born September 15, 1962, Milledgeville, Ga. Running back East Carolina 1980-83. Pro running back Cleveland Browns 1984-88, 1994-95, Washington Redskins 1989-1993, Baltimore Ravens 1996-97. Pro coach: Joined Redskins in 2004.
Bobby Crumpler, strength and conditioning; born April 23, 1965, Newton Grove, N.C. Running back North Carolina State 1983-87. No pro playing experience. College coach: North Carolina State 1989, 1992-96, 2000-01, Kansas 2002. Pro coach: Joined Redskins in 2003.
John Dunn, head strength and conditioning; born July 22, 1956, Wayne, N.J. Guard Penn State 1974-77. No pro playing experience. College coach: Penn State 1978. Pro coach: Washington Redskins 1984-86, Los Angeles Raiders 1987-89, San Diego Chargers 1990-96, New York Giants 1997-2003, re-joined Redskins in 2004.
Coy Gibbs, quality control-offense; born December 9, 1972, Little Rock, Ark. Linebacker Stanford 1991-94. No pro playing experience. Pro coach: Joined Redskins in 2004.
John Hastings, strength and conditioning; born July 5, 1964, Newport News, Va.. Attended Ohio University. No college or pro playing experience. Pro coach: San Diego Chargers 1990-2001, joined Redskins in 2002.
Stan Hixon, wide receivers; born July 24, 1957, Lakeland, Fla. Wide receiver Iowa State 1975-78. No pro playing experience. College coach: Morehead State 1980-82, Appalachian State 1983-88, South Carolina 1989-1992, Wake Forest 1993-94, Georgia Tech 1995-99, Louisiana State 2000-03. Pro coach: Joined Redskins in 2004.
Steve Jackson, third down-safeties; born April 8, 1969, Houston. Defensive back Purdue 1987-1990. Pro defensive back Houston Oilers/Tennessee Titans 1991-1999. Pro coach: Buffalo Bills 2001-03, joined Redskins in 2004.
Bill Lazor, offensive assistant; born June 14, 1972, Scranton, Pa. Quarterback Cornell 1991-93. No pro playing experience. College coach: Cornell 1994-2000, Buffalo 2001-02. Pro coach: Atlanta Falcons 2003, joined Redskins in 2004.
Dale Lindsey, linebackers; born January 18, 1943, Bedford, Ind. Linebacker Western Kentucky 1961-64. Pro linebacker Cleveland Browns 1965-1973. College coach: Southern Methodist 1988-89. Pro coach: Green Bay Packers 1986-87, New England Patriots 1990, Tampa

Bay Buccaneers 1991, San Diego Chargers 1992-96, 2002-03, Washington Redskins 1997-98, Chicago Bears 1999-2001, re-joined Redskins in 2004.
Bill Musgrave, quarterbacks; born November 11, 1967, Grand Junction, Colo. Quarterback Oregon 1987-1990. Pro quarterback San Francisco 49ers 1991-94, Denver Broncos 1995-96. College coach: Virginia 2001-02. Pro coach: Oakland Raiders 1997, Philadelphia Eagles 1998, Carolina Panthers 1999-2000, Jacksonville Jaguars 2003-04, joined Redskins in 2005.
Kirk Olivadotti, asst. defensive backs; born January 1, 1974, Wilmington, Del. Wide receiver Purdue 1992-1996. No pro playing experience. College coach: Maine Maritime Academy 1997, Indiana State 1998-99. Pro coach: Joined Redskins in 2000.
Warren (Rennie) Simmons, tight end; born February 25, 1942, Poughkeepsie, N.Y. Center San Diego State 1961-65. No pro playing experience. College coach: Cal State-Fullerton 1974-78, Cerritos (Calif.) J.C. 1978-1980, Vanderbilt 1995. Pro coach: Washington Redskins 1981-1993, Los Angeles Rams 1994, Houston Oilers 1996, Atlanta Falcons 1997-2003, re-joined Redskins in 2004.
Danny Smith, special teams; born September 7, 1953, Pittsburgh. Defensive back Edinboro State 1972-75. No pro playing experience. College coach: Edinboro State 1976, Clemson 1979, William & Mary 1980-83, The Citadel 1984-86, Georgia Tech 1987-1994. Pro coach: Philadelphia Eagles 1995-98, Detroit Lions 1999-2000, Buffalo Bills 2001-03, joined Redskins in 2004.
DeWayne Walker, secondary-cornerbacks; born December 3, 1960. Cornerback Pasadena (Calif.) C.C. 1978-79, Minnesota 1980-81. Pro cornerback Edmonton Eskimos (CFL) 1982, Oakland Invaders (USFL) 1985. College coach: Mt. San Antonio (Calif.) C.C. 1988-1992, Utah State 1993, Brigham Young 1994, Oklahoma State 1995, California 1996-97, Southern California 2001. Pro coach: New England Patriots 1998-2000, New York Giants 2002-03, joined Redskins in 2004.
Gregg Williams, asst. head coach-defense; born July 15, 1958, Excelsior Springs, Mo. Quarterback Northeast Missouri State 1976-79. No pro playing experience. College coach: Houston 1988-89. Pro coach: Houston Oilers/Tennessee Titans 1990-2000, Buffalo Bills 2001-03 (head coach), joined Redskins in 2004.

2004 Season in Review

2004 TRADES

Quarterback **A.J. Feeley** from Philadelphia to Miami for the Dolphins' second-round selection in 2005 (WR **Reggie Brown**). (3/3)

Quarterback **Mark Brunell** from Jacksonville to Washington for the Redskins' third-round selection in 2004 (#72). (3/3)

Running back **Clinton Portis** from Denver to Washington for cornerback **Champ Bailey** and the Redskins' second-round selection in 2004 (RB **Tatum Bell**). (3/4)

Wide receiver **Terrell Owens** from San Francisco to Baltimore for the Ravens' second-round selection in 2004 (#51). (3/4)

Wide receiver **Justin McCareins** from Tennessee to New York Jets for the Jets' second-round selection in 2004 (DE **Travis LaBoy**). (3/8)

Wide receiver **Terrell Owens** from Baltimore to Philadelphia. Defensive tackle **Brandon Whiting** from Philadelphia to San Francisco. Baltimore's second-round selection (#51) from San Francisco to Baltimore. Philadelphia's fifth-round selection (#160) from Philadelphia to Baltimore. (3/16)

Defensive back **Jamar Fletcher** and the Dolphins' sixth-round selection in 2005 (G **Wes Sims**) from Miami to San Diego for wide receiver **David Boston**. (3/16)

Quarterback **Drew Henson** from Houston to Dallas for the Cowboys' third-round selection in 2005 (RB **Vernand Morency**). (3/19)

Wide receiver **Joey Galloway** from Dallas to Tampa Bay for wide receiver **Keyshawn Johnson**. (3/22)

Running back **Bryan Johnson** from Washington to Chicago for the Bears' sixth-round selection in 2004 (#180). (3/29)

Wide receiver **James Thrash** from Philadelphia to Washington for the Redskins' fifth-round selection in 2005 (LB **Trent Cole**). (3/31)

Defensive back **Jason Craft** from Jacksonville to New Orleans for the Saints' fifth-round selection in 2004 (DB **Chris Thompson**). (4/8)

Defensive back **Deltha O'Neal** and the Broncos' first-round selection in 2004 (#17) and fourth-round selection (DE **Robert Geathers**) from Denver to Cincinnati for the Bengals' first-round selection in 2004 (LB **D.J. Williams**). (4/9)

Running back **Corey Dillon** from Cincinnati to New England for the Dolphins' second-round selection in 2004 (DB **Madieu Williams**). (4/20)

Quarterback **Eli Manning** from San Diego to New York Giants for quarterback **Philip Rivers** and the Giants' third-round selection in 2004 (K **Nate Kaeding**) and first-round (LB **Shawne Merriman**) and fifth-round selection (#144) in 2005. (4/24)

Cleveland's first-round selection in 2004 (WR **Roy Williams**) and second-round selection in 2004 (LB **Teddy Lehman**) from Cleveland to Detroit for the Lions' first-round selection in 2004 (TE **Kellen Winslow**). (4/24)

Philadelphia's first-round selection in 2004 (#28) and second-round selection in 2004 (DB **Shawntae Spencer**) from Philadelphia to San Francisco for the 49ers' first-round selection in 2004 (T **Shawn Andrews**). (4/24)

Miami's first-round selection in 2004 (DE **Kenechi Udeze**) and fourth-round selection in 2004 (RB **Mewelde Moore**) from Miami to Minnesota for the Vikings' first-round selection in 2004 (T **Vernon Carey**). (4/24)

Buffalo's second-round selection in 2004 (RB **Julius Jones**), fifth-round selection in 2004 (TE **Sean Ryan**), and first-round selection in 2005 (DE **Marcus Spears**) from Buffalo to Dallas for the Cowboys' first-round selection in 2004 (QB **J.P. Losman**). (4/24)

Denver's first-round selection in 2004 (RB **Steven Jackson**) from Cincinnati to St. Louis for the Rams' first-round selection in 2004 (RB **Chris Perry**) and fourth-round selection in 2004 (T **Stacy Andrews**). (4/24)

Houston's second-round selection in 2004 (TE **Ben Troupe**), third-round selection in 2004 (DT **Randy Starks**), fourth-round selection in 2004 (DE **Bo Schobel**) and fifth-round selection in 2004 (T **Jacob Bell**) from Houston to Tennessee for the Titans' first-round selection in 2004 (LB **Jason Babin**) and fifth-round selection in 2004 (#159). (4/24)

Carolina's first-round selection in 2004 (WR **Rashaun Woods**) and second-round selection in 2004 (LB **Richard Seigler**) from Carolina to San Francisco for the Eagles' first-round selection in 2004 (DB **Chris Gamble**). (4/24)

Atlanta's second-round selection in 2004 (#38), third-round selection in 2004 (LB **Gilbert Gardner**), and the Eagles' fourth-round selection in 2004 (DB **Jason David**) from Atlanta to Indianapolis for the Colts' first-round selection in 2004 (WR **Michael Jenkins**) and third-round selection in 2004 (QB **Matt Schaub**). (4/24)

Detroit's second-round selection in 2004 (DT **Junior Siavii**), fourth-round selection in 2004 (WR **Samie Parker**), and fifth-round selection in 2005 (DB **Alphonso Hodge**) from Detroit to Kansas City for the Chiefs' first-round selection in 2004 (RB **Kevin Jones**). (4/24)

Atlanta's second-round selection in 2004 (DB **Ricardo Colclough**) from Indianapolis to Pittsburgh for the Steelers' second-round selection in 2004 (DB **Bob Sanders**) and fourth-round selection in 2004 (LB **Kendyll Pope**). (4/24)

Minnesota's second-round selection in 2004 (WR **Devery Henderson**) and fifth-round selection in 2004 (#151) from Minnesota to New Orleans for the Saints' second-round selection in 2004 (LB **Dontarrious Thomas**). (4/24)

Green Bay's second-round selection in 2004 (RB **Greg Jones**) from Green Bay to Jacksonville for the Jaguars' third-round selection in 2004 (DB **Joey Thomas**) and fourth-round selection in 2004 (#102). (4/24)

Cleveland's third-round selection in 2004 (TE **Ben Hartsock**), fifth-round selection in 2004 (T **Jake Scott**), and sixth-round selection in 2004 (DB **Von Hutchins**) from Cleveland to Indianapolis for the Colts' second-round selection in 2004 (DB **Sean Jones**) and fifth-round selection in 2004 (DT **Amon Gordon**). (4/24)

Green Bay's third-round selection in 2004 (LB **Jorge Cordova**) and fourth-round selection in 2004 (DT **Anthony Maddox**) from Green Bay to Jacksonville for the Redskins' third-round selection in 2004 (DT **Donnell Washington**). (4/24)

New Orleans' third-round selection in 2004 (TE **Chris Cooley**) and the Vikings' fifth-round selection in 2004 (T **Mark Wilson**) from New Orleans to Washington for the Redskins' fifth-round selection in 2004 (DT **Rodney Leisle**) and second-round selection in 2005 (DB **Josh Bullocks**). (4/24)

Baltimore's third-round selection in 2004 (DE **Darrion Scott**) and fifth-round selection in 2004 (LB **Rod Davis**) from Baltimore to Minnesota for the Vikings' third-round selection in 2004 (WR **Devard Darling**). (4/24)

Jacksonville's fourth-round selection in 2004 (DB **Will Poole**) and fifth-round selection in 2004 (#153) from Green Bay to Miami for the Dolphins' third-round selection in 2004 (P **B.J. Sander**). (4/24)

Washington's fourth-round selection in 2004 (DT **Isaac Sopoaga**) from Chicago to San Francisco for the 49ers' fourth-round selection in 2004 (LB **Leon Joe**) and fifth-round selection in 2004 (DE **Claude Harriet**). (4/25)

Wide receiver **Kevin Johnson** from Jacksonville to Baltimore for the Ravens' fourth-round selection in 2004 (WR **Ernest Wilford**). (4/25)

Philadelphia's fifth-round selection in 2004 (LB **Tony Bua**) and seventh-round selection (LB **Derrick Pope**) from Baltimore to Miami for the Packers' fifth-round selection in 2004 (LB **Roderick Green**). (4/25)

Dallas' fifth-round selection in 2004 (RB **Mike Karney**) from Dallas to New Orleans for the Saints' sixth-round selection in 2004 (#182) and the Redskins' seventh-round selection in 2004 (#206). (4/25)

Guard **John Welbourn** from Philadelphia to Kansas City for the Chiefs' fifth-round selection in 2004 (RB **Thomas Tapeh**) and third-round selection in 2005 (RB **Ryan Moats**). (4/25)

Tennessee's fifth-round selection in 2004 (T **Sean Bubin**) from Houston to Jacksonville for the Jaguars' sixth-round selection in 2004 (DB **Jammal Lord**) and seventh-round selection in 2004 (LB **Raheem Orr**). (4/25)

Atlanta's sixth-round selection in 2004 (G **Rex Hadnot**) from Atlanta to Miami for the Dolphins' sixth-round selection in 2004 (DB **Etric Pruitt**) and the Saints' seventh-round selection in 2004 (RB **Quincy Wilson**). (4/25).

Dallas' sixth-round selection in 2004 (P **Andy Lee**) and seventh-round selection in 2004 (DT **Christian Ferrara**) from Green Bay to San Francisco for the 49ers' sixth-round selection in 2004 (DT **Corey Williams**). (4/25)

Dallas' sixth-round selection in 2004 via New Orleans (LB **Cody Spencer**) from Dallas to Oakland for the Raiders' sixth-round selection in 2004 (DB **Nathan Jones**) and the Cowboys' seventh-round selection in 2004 (DB **Jacques Reeves**). (4/25)

Running back **Darian Barnes** and the Buccaneers' seventh-round selection in 2004 (WR **Patrick Clayton**) from Tampa Bay to Dallas for the Cowboys' seventh-round selection in 2004 (WR **Mark

Jones). (4/25)

Tackle **Roman Oben** from Tampa Bay to San Diego for an unannounced future selection choice. (6/9)

Defensive end **Jamal Reynolds** from Green Bay to Indianapolis for an unannounced future selection choice. (7/8)

Defensive end **Quinn Dorsey** from New England to Chicago for an unannounced future selection choice. (8/17)

Defensive end **Adewale Ogunleye** from Miami to Chicago for wide receiver **Marty Booker** and the Bears' third-round selection in 2005 (LB **Channing Crowder**). (8/24)

Tackle **Javiar Collins** from Dallas to Carolina for an unannounced future selection choice. (8/25)

Defensive end **Shurron Pierson** from Oakland to Chicago for an unannounced future selection choice. (8/30)

Running back **Troy Hambrick** and defensive end **Peppi Zellner** from Oakland to Arizona for an unannounced future selection choice. (8/31)

Tackle **Jason Whittle** from Tampa Bay to the New York Giants for an unannounced future selection choice. (8/31)

Punter **Steve Cheek** from Houston to Kansas City for an unannounced future selection choice. (9/1)

Defensive back **Marques Anderson** from Green Bay to Oakland for the Raiders' fifth-round selection in 2005 (C **Junius Coston**). (9/3)

Tackle **Todd Fordham** from Pittsburgh to Carolina for an unannounced future selection choice. (9/4)

Defensive end **R-Kal Truluck** from Kansas City to Green Bay for the Packers' fifth-round selection in 2005 (#162) and sixth-round selection in 2005 (DE **Khari Long**). (9/5)

Tackle **Brad Bedell** from Miami to Green Bay for an unannounced future selection choice. (9/5)

Running back **Lamar Gordon** from St. Louis to Miami for the Dolphins' third-round selection in 2005 (DB **Oshiomogho Atogwe**). (9/9)

Defensive tackle **Chris Cooper** from Oakland to Dallas for an unannounced future selection choice. (9/11)

Defensive tackle **Ellis Johnson** from Atlanta to Denver for an unannounced future selection choice. (9/24)

Defensive back **Mike McKenzie** and an unannounced future selection choice from the Packers to New Orleans for quarterback **J.T. O'Sullivan** and the Saints' second-round selection (DB **Nick Collins**). (10/4)

Wide receiver **Quincy Morgan** from Cleveland to Dallas for wide receiver **Antonio Bryant**. (10/19)

Wide receiver **Jerry Rice** from Oakland to Seattle for an unannounced future selection choice. (10/19)

Wide receiver **Keenan McCardell** from Tampa Bay to San Diego for the Chargers' third-round selection in 2005 (T **Chris Colmer**) and sixth-round selection in 2005 (#203). (10/19)

2005 TRADES

Defensive tackle **Gerard Warren** from Cleveland to Denver for a fourth-round selection in 2005 (#126). (3/3)

Wide receiver **Randy Moss** from Minnesota to Oakland for linebacker Napoleon Harris and the Raiders' first-round selec-

tion in 2005 (WR **Troy Williamson**) and seventh-round selection in 2005 (DB **Adrian Ward**). (3/3)

Cornerback **Duane Starks** and the Cardinals' fifth-round selection in 2005 (#145) from Arizona to New England for the Patriots' third-round selection in 2005 (LB **Darryl Blackstock**) and fifth-round selection in 2005 (LB **Lance Mitchell**). (3/4)

Quarterback **Trent Dilfer** from Seattle to Cleveland for the Broncos' fourth-round selection in 2005 (#126). (3/7)

Wide receiver **Santana Moss** from New York Jets to Washington for wide receiver **Laveranues Coles**. (3/7)

Linebacker **Sam Cowart** from New York Jets to Minnesota for the Vikings' seventh-round selection in 2005 (#230). (3/18)

Defensive end **Ebenezer Ekuban** and defensive tackle **Michael Myers** from Cleveland to Denver for running back **Rueben Droughns** (#230). (3/18)

Defensive end and **Carlos Hall** from Tennessee to Minnesota for the Vikings' seventh-round selection in 2005 (#230). (3/18)

Denver's first-round selection in 2005 (QB **Jason Campbell**) from Denver to Washington for the Redskins' first-round selection in 2005 (DB **Karl Paymah**) and unannounced future selection choice. (4/20)

Defensive back **Phillip Buchanon** from Oakland to Houston for the Texans' second-round selection in 2005 (#47) and third-round selection in 2005 (LB **Kirk Morrison**). (4/21)

Tight end **Doug Jolley** and the Texans' second-round selection in 2005 (K **Mike Nugent**), the Cardinals' sixth-round selection in 2005 (RB **Cedric Houston**) and the Cowboys' sixth-round selection in 2005 #185) from Oakland to New York Jets for the Jets' first-round selection in 2005 (#26) and the Vikings' sixth-round selection in 2005 (#230). (4/21)

Defensive back **Patrick Surtain** and the Dolphins' fifth-round selection in 2005 (LB **Boomer Grigsby**) from Miami to Kansas City for the Chiefs' second-round selection in 2005 (#46) and the Packers' fifth-round selection in 2005 (T **Anthony Alabi**). (4/23)

Houston's first-round selection in 2005 (T **Jammal Brown**) from Houston to New Orleans for the Saints' first-round selection in 2005 (DE **Travis Johnson**) and third-round selection in 2006. (4/23)

New York Jets' first-round selection in 2005 (C **Chris Spencer**) and fourth-round selection in 2005 (T **Ray Willis**) from Oakland to Seattle for the Seahawks' first-round selection in 2005 (DB **Fabian Washington**). (4/21)

Detroit's second-round selection in 2005 (T **Michael Roos**) and fourth-round selection in 2005 (T **David Stewart**) from Detroit to Tennessee for the Titans' second-round selection in 2005 (DT **Shaun Cody**). (4/23)

Carolina's second-round selection in 2005 (LB **Lofa Tatupu**) from Carolina to Seattle for the Seahawks' second-round selection in 2005 (RB **Eric Shelton**), Seahawks' fourth-round selection (QB **Stefan LeFors**) and Broncos' fourth-round selection in 2005 (#126). (4/23)

Baltimore's third-round selection in 2005 (DB **Ellis Hobbs**), the Ravens' sixth-

round selection in 2005 (#195), and the Ravens' third-round selection in 2006 from Baltimore to New England for the Patriots' second-round selection in 2005 (T **Adam Terry**). (4/23)

Carolina's fourth-round selection in 2005 (DB **Marviel Underwood**) and the Broncos' fourth-round selection in 2005 (#126) from Carolina to Green Bay for the Packers' third-round selection in 2005 (DT **Atiyyah Ellison**). (4/23)

Philadelphia's third-round selection in 2005 (T **Adam Snyder**) from Philadelphia to San Francisco for the 49ers' fourth-round selection in 2005 (DB **Sean Considine**) and sixth-round selection in 2005 (#175). (4/23)

Minnesota's fourth-round selection in 2005 (RB **Manuel White**) and fifth-round selection in 2005 (LB **Robert McCune**) from Minnesota to Washington for the Redskins' fourth-round selection in 2005 (RB **Ciatrick Fason**). (4/23)

Quarterback **Luke McCown** from Cleveland to Tampa Bay for the Chargers' sixth-round selection in 2005 (DE **Andrew Hoffman**). (4/24)

Jacksonville's fourth-round selection in 2005 (DB **Kerry Rhodes**) from Jacksonville to New York Jets for the Jets' fourth-round selection in 2005 (RB **Alvin Pearman**) and the Cowboys' sixth-round selection in 2005 (KR **Chad Owens**). (4/24)

Denver's fourth-round selection in 2005 (T **Todd Herremans**) from Green Bay to Philadelphia for the Eagles' fifth-round selection in 2005 (DB **Michael Hawkins**), the 49ers' sixth-round selection in 2005 (#175) and seventh-round selection in 2005 (DB **Kurt Campbell**). (4/24)

Dallas' fifth-round selection in 2005 (#148) and fourth-round selection in 2006 from Dallas to Philadelphia for the Eagles' fourth-round selection in 2005 (DE **Chris Canty**) and sixth-round selection in 2006. (4/24)

St. Louis' fifth-round selection in 2005 (WR **Larry Brackins**) and the Rams' seventh-round selection in 2005 (DB **Hamza Abdullah**) from St. Louis to Tampa Bay for the Giants' fifth-round selection in 2005 (TE **Jerome Collins**). (4/24)

Detroit's fourth-round selection in 2006 from Detroit to New England for the Cardinals' fifth-round selection in 2005 (QB **Dan Orlovsky**) and sixth-round selection in 2005 (LB **Johnathan Goddard**). (4/24)

Indianapolis' fourth-round seleciton in 2006 from Indianapolis to Philadelphia for the Cowboys' fifth-round selection in 2005 (DB **Jonathan Welsh**). (4/24)

San Francisco's sixth-round selection in 2005 (#175) from Green Bay to New England for the Ravens' sixth-round selection in 2005 (WR **Craig Bragg**) and the Patriots' seventh-round selection in 2005 (G **William Whittcker**). (4/24)

San Francisco's sixth-round selection in 2005 (DT **Anttaj Hawthorne**) from New England to Oakland for the Vikings' seventh-round selection in 2005 (QB **Matt Cassel**) and Raiders' fifth-round selection in 2006. (4/24)

Punter **Todd Sauerbrun** from Carolina to Denver for punter **Jason Baker** and an unannounced future selection choice. (5/19)

* Draft choice number is listed if club later traded the pick.

PRESEASON STANDINGS
AMERICAN FOOTBALL CONFERENCE

East Division

	W	L	T	Pct.	Pts.	OP
N.Y. Jets	3	1	0	.750	89	67
Miami	2	2	0	.500	46	58
Buffalo	1	3	0	.250	65	72
New England	1	3	0	.250	44	88

North Division

	W	L	T	Pct.	Pts.	OP
Baltimore	3	1	0	.750	85	49
Cleveland	3	1	0	.750	65	63
Cincinnati	2	2	0	.500	63	73
Pittsburgh	2	2	0	.500	99	67

South Division

	W	L	T	Pct.	Pts.	OP
Jacksonville	3	1	0	.750	59	29
Tennessee	3	1	0	.750	84	45
Indianapolis	2	2	0	.500	71	81
Houston	1	3	0	.250	47	86

West Division

	W	L	T	Pct.	Pts.	OP
Oakland	3	1	0	.750	98	91
San Diego	2	2	0	.500	106	75
Denver	2	3	0	.400	94	89
Kansas City	1	3	0	.250	87	86

AFC PRESEASON RECORDS—TEAM BY TEAM

East Division

BUFFALO (1-3)

16	Denver	6
15	Tennessee	16
17	at Indianapolis	30
17	at Detroit	20
65		72

MIAMI (2-2)

16	Jacksonville	5
0	Washington	17
10	at Tampa Bay	17
20	at New Orleans	19
46		58

NEW ENGLAND (1-3)

24	Philadelphia	6
3	at Cincinnati	31
17	at Carolina	20
0	Jacksonville	31
44		88

N.Y. JETS (3-1)

13	at New Orleans	23
31	at Indianapolis	7
17	N.Y. Giants	10
28	Philadelphia	27
89		67

North Division

BALTIMORE (3-1)

24	Atlanta	0
17	at Philadelphia	26
17	Detroit	6
27	at N.Y. Giants	17
85		49

CINCINNATI (2-2)

6	at Tampa Bay	20
31	New England	3
10	at Atlanta	37
16	Indianapolis	13
63		73

CLEVELAND (3-1)

3	at Tennessee	24
17	Detroit	10
21	at Kansas City	19
24	Chicago	10
65		63

PITTSBURGH (2-2)

21	at Detroit	27
38	Houston	3
27	at Philadelphia	21
13	Carolina	16
99		67

South Division

HOUSTON (1-3)

18	Dallas	0
3	at Pittsburgh	38
17	at Denver	31
9	Tampa Bay	17
47		86

INDIANAPOLIS (2-2)

21	at San Diego	17
7	N.Y. Jets	31
30	Buffalo	17
13	at Cincinnati	16
71		81

JACKSONVILLE (3-1)

5	at Miami	16
14	Tampa Bay	6
9	Green Bay	7
31	at New England	0
59		29

TENNESSEE (3-1)

24	Cleveland	3
16	at Buffalo	15
17	at Dallas	20
27	Green Bay	7
84		45

West Division

DENVER (2-3)

17	vs. Washington (a)	20
6	at Buffalo	16
19	at Seattle	3
31	Houston	17
21	Arizona	33
94		89

KANSAS CITY (1-3)

24	at N.Y. Giants	34
24	St. Louis	7
19	Cleveland	21
20	at Dallas	24
87		86

OAKLAND (3-1)

33	at San Francisco	30
20	Dallas	21
17	at Arizona	16
28	St. Louis	24
98		91

SAN DIEGO (2-2)

17	Indianapolis	21
38	at Arizona	13
20	Seattle	26
31	at San Francisco	15
106		75

(a) Pro Football Hall of Fame Game at Canton, Ohio

NFC PRESEASON RECORDS—TEAM BY TEAM

East Division

DALLAS (3-1)

0	at Houston	18
21	at Oakland	20
20	Tennessee	17
24	Kansas City	20
65		**75**

N.Y. GIANTS (1-3)

34	Kansas City	24
20	at Carolina	27
10	at N.Y. Jets	17
17	Baltimore	27
81		**95**

PHILADELPHIA (1-3)

6	at New England	24
26	Baltimore	17
21	Pittsburgh	27
27	at N.Y. Jets	28
80		**96**

WASHINGTON (3-2)

20	vs. Denver (a)	17
20	Carolina	23
17	at Miami	0
3	at St. Louis	28
27	Atlanta	0
87		**68**

North Division

CHICAGO (2-2)

13	at St. Louis	10
20	San Francisco	13
13	New Orleans	17
10	at Cleveland	24
56		**64**

DETROIT (2-2)

27	Pittsburgh	21
10	at Cleveland	17
6	at Baltimore	17
20	Buffalo	17
63		**72**

GREEN BAY (1-3)

3	Seattle	21
19	New Orleans	14
7	at Jacksonville	9
7	at Tennessee	27
36		**71**

MINNESOTA (2-2)

23	Arizona	6
24	at Atlanta	27
23	San Francisco	10
21	at Seattle	23
91		**66**

South Division

ATLANTA (2-2)

0	at Baltimore	24
27	Minnesota	24
37	Cincinnati	10
0	at Washington	27
64		**85**

CAROLINA (4-0)

23	at Washington	20
27	N.Y. Giants	20
20	New England	17
16	at Pittsburgh	13
86		**70**

NEW ORLEANS (2-2)

23	N.Y. Jets	13
14	at Green Bay	19
17	at Miami	13
19	Chicago	20
73		**65**

TAMPA BAY (3-1)

20	Cincinnati	6
6	at Jacksonville	14
17	Miami	10
17	at Houston	9
60		**39**

West Division

ARIZONA (1-3)

6	at Minnesota	23
13	San Diego	38
16	Oakland	17
33	at Denver	21
68		**99**

ST. LOUIS (1-3)

10	Chicago	13
7	at Kansas City	24
28	Washington	3
24	at Oakland	28
69		**68**

SAN FRANCISCO (0-4)

30	Oakland	33
13	at Chicago	20
10	at Minnesota	23
15	San Diego	31
68		**107**

SEATTLE (3-1)

21	at Green Bay	3
3	Denver	19
26	at San Diego	20
23	Minnesota	21
73		**63**

PRESEASON STANDINGS
NATIONAL FOOTBALL CONFERENCE

East Division

	W	L	T	Pct.	Pts.	OP
Dallas	3	1	0	.750	65	75
Washington	3	2	0	.600	87	68
N.Y. Giants	1	3	0	.250	81	95
Philadelphia	1	3	0	.250	80	96

North Division

	W	L	T	Pct.	Pts.	OP
Chicago	2	2	0	.500	56	64
Detroit	2	2	0	.500	63	72
Minnesota	2	2	0	.500	91	66
Green Bay	1	3	0	.250	36	71

South Division

	W	L	T	Pct.	Pts.	OP
Carolina	4	0	0	1.000	86	70
Tampa Bay	3	1	0	.750	60	39
Atlanta	2	2	0	.500	64	85
New Orleans	2	2	0	.500	73	65

West Division

	W	L	T	Pct.	Pts.	OP
Seattle	3	1	0	.750	73	63
Arizona	1	3	0	.250	68	99
St. Louis	1	3	0	.250	69	68
San Francisco	0	4	0	.000	68	107

(a) Pro Football Hall of Fame Game at Canton, Ohio

AMERICAN FOOTBALL CONFERENCE

BALTIMORE (9-7)

3	at Cleveland	20
30	PITTSBURGH	13
23	at Cincinnati	9
24	KANSAS CITY	27
17	at Washington	10
20	BUFFALO	6
10	at Philadelphia	15
27	CLEVELAND	13
20	at N.Y. Jets (OT)	17
30	DALLAS	10
3	at New England	24
26	CINCINNATI	27
37	N.Y. GIANTS	14
10	at Indianapolis	20
7	at Pittsburgh	20
30	MIAMI	23
317		**268**

BUFFALO (9-7)

10	JACKSONVILLE	13
10	at Oakland	13
17	NEW ENGLAND	31
14	at N. Y. Jets	16
20	MIAMI	13
6	at Baltimore	20
38	ARIZONA	14
22	N.Y. JETS	17
6	at New England	29
37	ST. LOUIS	17
42	at Miami	32
37	CLEVELAND	7
33	at Cincinnati	17
41	at San Francisco	7
24	PITTSBURGH	29
395		**284**

CINCINNATI (8-8)

24	at N.Y. Jets	31
16	MIAMI	13
9	BALTIMORE	23
17	at Pittsburgh	28
17	at Cleveland	34
23	DENVER	10
20	at Tennessee	27
26	DALLAS	3
17	at Washington	10
14	PITTSBURGH	19
58	CLEVELAND	48
27	at Baltimore	26
28	at New England	35
17	BUFFALO	33
23	N.Y. GIANTS	22
38	at Philadelphia	10
374		**372**

CLEVELAND (4-12)

20	BALTIMORE	3
12	at Dallas	19
10	at N.Y. Giants	27
17	WASHINGTON	13
23	at Pittsburgh	34
34	CINCINNATI	17
31	PHILADELPHIA (OT)	34
13	at Baltimore	27
10	PITTSBURGH	24
7	N.Y. JETS	10
48	at Cincinnati	58
15	NEW ENGLAND	42
7	at Buffalo	37
0	SAN DIEGO	21
7	at Miami	10
22	at Houston	14
276		**390**

DENVER (10-6)

34	KANSAS CITY	24
6	at Jacksonville	7
23	SAN DIEGO	13
16	at Tampa Bay	13
20	CAROLINA	17
31	at Oakland	3
10	at Cincinnati	23
28	ATLANTA	41
31	HOUSTON	13
34	at New Orleans	13
24	OAKLAND	25
17	at San Diego	20
20	MIAMI	17
17	at Kansas City	45
37	at Tennessee	16
33	INDIANAPOLIS	14
381		**304**

HOUSTON (7-9)

20	SAN DIEGO	27
16	at Detroit	28
24	at Kansas City	21
30	OAKLAND	17
28	MINNESOTA (OT)	34
20	at Tennessee	10
20	JACKSONVILLE	6
13	at Denver	31
14	at Indianapolis	49
13	GREEN BAY	16
31	TENNESSEE	21
7	at N.Y. Jets	29
14	INDIANAPOLIS	23
24	at Chicago	5
21	at Jacksonville	0
14	CLEVELAND	22
309		**339**

INDIANAPOLIS (12-4)

24	at New England	27
31	at Tennessee	17
45	GREEN BAY	31
24	at Jacksonville	17
35	OAKLAND	14
24	JACKSONVILLE	27
35	at Kansas City	45
31	MINNESOTA	28
49	HOUSTON	14
41	at Chicago	10
41	at Detroit	9
51	TENNESSEE	24
23	at Houston	14
20	BALTIMORE	10
34	SAN DIEGO (OT)	31
14	at Denver	33
522		**351**

JACKSONVILLE (9-7)

13	at Buffalo	10
7	DENVER	6
15	at Tennessee	12
17	INDIANAPOLIS	24
21	at San Diego	34
22	KANSAS CITY	16
27	at Indianapolis	24
6	at Houston	20
23	DETROIT (OT)	17
15	TENNESSEE	18
16	at Minnesota	27
16	PITTSBURGH	17
22	CHICAGO	3
28	at Green Bay	25
0	HOUSTON	21
13	at Oakland	6
261		**280**

KANSAS CITY (7-9)

24	at Denver	34
17	CAROLINA	28
21	HOUSTON	24
27	at Baltimore	24
16	at Jacksonville	22
56	ATLANTA	10
45	INDIANAPOLIS	35
31	at Tampa Bay	34
20	at New Orleans	27
19	NEW ENGLAND	27
31	SAN DIEGO	34
34	at Oakland	27
49	at Tennessee	38
45	DENVER	17
31	OAKLAND	30
17	at San Diego	24
483		**435**

MIAMI (4-12)

7	TENNESSEE	17
13	at Cincinnati	16
3	PITTSBURGH	13
9	N.Y. JETS	17
10	at New England	24
13	at Buffalo	20
31	ST. LOUIS	14
14	at N.Y. Jets	41
23	ARIZONA	24
17	at Seattle	24
24	at San Francisco	17
32	BUFFALO	42
17	at Denver	20
29	NEW ENGLAND	28
10	CLEVELAND	7
23	at Baltimore	30
275		**354**

NEW ENGLAND (14-2)

27	INDIANAPOLIS	24
23	at Cardinals	12
31	at Buffalo	17
24	MIAMI	10
30	SEATTLE	20
13	N.Y. JETS	7
20	at Pittsburgh	34
40	at St. Louis	22
29	BUFFALO	6
27	at Kansas City	19
24	BALTIMORE	3
42	at Cleveland	15
35	CINCINNATI	28
28	at Miami	29
23	at N.Y. Jets	7
21	SAN FRANCISCO	7
437		**260**

N.Y. JETS (10-6)

31	CINCINNATI	24
34	at San Diego	28
17	at Miami	9
16	BUFFALO	14
22	SAN FRANCISCO	14
7	at New England	13
41	MIAMI	14
17	at Buffalo	22
17	BALTIMORE (OT)	20
10	at Cleveland	7
13	at Arizona	3
29	HOUSTON	7
6	at Pittsburgh	17
37	SEATTLE	14
7	NEW ENGLAND	23
29	at St. Louis (OT)	32
333		**261**

OAKLAND (5-11)

21	at Pittsburgh	24
13	BUFFALO	10
30	TAMPA BAY	20
17	at Houston	30
14	at Indianapolis	35
3	DENVER	31
26	NEW ORLEANS	31
14	SAN DIEGO	42
27	at Carolina	24
17	at San Diego	23
25	at Denver	24
27	KANSAS CITY	34
10	at Atlanta	35
40	TENNESSEE	35
30	at Kansas City	31
6	JACKSONVILLE	13
320		**442**

PITTSBURGH (15-1)

24	OAKLAND	21
13	at Baltimore	30
13	at Miami	3
28	CINCINNATI	17
34	CLEVELAND	23
24	at Dallas	20
34	NEW ENGLAND	20
27	PHILADELPHIA	3
24	at Cleveland	10
19	at Cincinnati	14
16	WASHINGTON	7
17	at Jacksonville	16
17	N.Y. JETS	6
33	at N.Y. Giants	30
20	BALTIMORE	7
29	at Buffalo	24
372		**251**

SAN DIEGO (12-4)

27	at Houston	20
28	N.Y. JETS	34
13	at Denver	23
38	TENNESSEE	17
34	JACKSONVILLE	21
20	at Atlanta	21
17	at Carolina	6
42	OAKLAND	14
43	NEW ORLEANS	17
23	at Oakland	17
34	at Kansas City	31
20	DENVER	17
31	TAMPA BAY	24
21	at Cleveland	0
31	at Indianapolis (OT)	34
24	KANSAS CITY	17
446		**313**

TENNESSEE (5-11)

17	at Miami	7
17	INDIANAPOLIS	31
12	JACKSONVILLE	15
17	at San Diego	38
48	at Green Bay	27
10	HOUSTON	20
3	at Minnesota	20
27	CINCINNATI	20
17	CHICAGO (OT)	19
18	at Jacksonville	15
21	at Houston	31
24	at Indianapolis	51
38	KANSAS CITY	49
35	at Oakland	40
16	DENVER	37
24	DETROIT	19
344		**439**

NATIONAL FOOTBALL CONFERENCE

ARIZONA (6-10)

10	at St. Louis	17
12	NEW ENGLAND	23
3	at Atlanta	6
34	NEW ORLEANS	10
28	at San Francisco (OT)	31
25	SEATTLE	17
14	at Buffalo	38
24	at Miami	23
17	N.Y. GIANTS	14
10	at Carolina	35
3	N.Y. JETS	13
12	at Detroit	26
28	SAN FRANCISCO (OT)	31
31	ST. LOUIS	7
21	at Seattle	24
12	TAMPA BAY	7
284		**322**

ATLANTA (11-5)

21	at San Francisco	19
34	ST. LOUIS	17
6	ARIZONA	3
27	at Carolina	10
10	DETROIT	17
21	SAN DIEGO	20
10	at Kansas City	56
41	at Denver	28
24	TAMPA BAY	14
14	at N.Y. Giants	10
24	NEW ORLEANS	21
0	at Tampa Bay	27
35	OAKLAND	10
34	CAROLINA (OT)	31
13	at New Orleans	26
26	at Seattle	28
340		**337**

CAROLINA (7-9)

14	GREEN BAY	24
28	at Kansas City	17
10	ATLANTA	27
17	at Denver	20
8	at Philadelphia	30
6	SAN DIEGO	17
17	at Seattle	23
24	OAKLAND	27
37	at San Francisco	27
35	ARIZONA	10
21	TAMPA BAY	14
32	at New Orleans	21
20	ST. LOUIS	7
31	at Atlanta (OT)	34
37	at Tampa Bay	20
18	NEW ORLEANS	21
355		**339**

CHICAGO (5-11)

16	DETROIT	20
21	at Green Bay	10
22	at Minnesota	27
9	PHILADELPHIA	19
10	WASHINGTON	13
7	at Tampa Bay	19
23	SAN FRANCISCO	13
28	at N.Y. Giants	21
19	at Tennessee (OT)	17
10	INDIANAPOLIS	41
7	at Dallas	21
24	MINNESOTA	14
3	at Jacksonville	22
5	HOUSTON	24
13	at Detroit	19
14	GREEN BAY	31
231		**331**

DALLAS (6-10)

17	at Minnesota	35
19	CLEVELAND	12
21	at Washington	18
10	N.Y. GIANTS	26
20	PITTSBURGH	24
20	at Green Bay	41
31	DETROIT	21
3	at Cincinnati	26
21	PHILADELPHIA	49
10	at Baltimore	30
21	CHICAGO	7
43	at Seattle	39
13	NEW ORLEANS	27
7	at Philadelphia	12
13	WASHINGTON	10
24	at N.Y. Giants	28
293		**405**

DETROIT (6-10)

20	at Chicago	16
28	HOUSTON	16
13	PHILADELPHIA	30
17	at Atlanta	10
10	GREEN BAY	38
28	at N.Y. Giants	13
21	at Dallas	31
10	WASHINGTON	17
17	at Jacksonville (OT)	23
19	at Minnesota	22
9	INDIANAPOLIS	41
26	ARIZONA	12
13	at Green Bay	16
27	MINNESOTA	28
19	CHICAGO	13
19	at Tennessee	24
296		**350**

GREEN BAY (10-6)

24	at Carolina	14
10	CHICAGO	21
31	at Indianapolis	45
7	N.Y. GIANTS	14
27	TENNESSEE	48
38	at Detroit	10
41	DALLAS	20
28	at Washington	14
34	MINNESOTA	31
16	at Houston	13
45	ST. LOUIS	17
17	at Philadelphia	47
16	DETROIT	13
25	JACKSONVILLE	28
34	at Minnesota	31
31	at Chicago	14
424		**380**

MINNESOTA (8-8)

35	DALLAS	17
16	at Philadelphia	27
27	CHICAGO	22
34	at Houston (OT)	28
38	at New Orleans	31
20	TENNESSEE	3
13	N.Y. GIANTS	34
28	at Indianapolis	31
31	at Green Bay	34
22	DETROIT	19
27	JACKSONVILLE	16
14	at Chicago	24
23	SEATTLE	27
28	at Detroit	27
31	GREEN BAY	34
18	at Washington	21
405		**395**

NEW ORLEANS (8-8)

7	SEATTLE	21
30	SAN FRANCISCO	27
28	at St. Louis (OT)	25
10	at Arizona	34
17	TAMPA BAY	20
31	MINNESOTA	38
31	at Oakland	26
17	at San Diego	43
27	KANSAS CITY	20
13	DENVER	34
21	at Atlanta	24
21	CAROLINA	32
27	at Dallas	13
21	at Tampa Bay	17
26	ATLANTA	13
21	at Carolina	18
348		**405**

N.Y. GIANTS (6-10)

17	at Philadelphia	31
20	WASHINGTON	14
27	CLEVELAND	10
14	at Green Bay	7
26	at Dallas	10
13	DETROIT	28
34	at Minnesota	13
21	CHICAGO	28
14	at Arizona	17
10	ATLANTA	14
6	PHILADELPHIA	27
7	at Washington	31
14	at Baltimore	37
30	PITTSBURGH	33
22	at Cincinnati	33
28	DALLAS	24
303		**347**

PHILADELPHIA (13-3)

31	N.Y. GIANTS	17
27	MINNESOTA	16
30	at Detroit	13
19	at Chicago	9
30	CAROLINA	8
34	at Cleveland (OT)	31
15	BALTIMORE	10
3	at Pittsburgh	27
49	at Dallas	21
28	WASHINGTON	6
27	at N.Y. Giants	6
47	GREEN BAY	17
17	at Washington	14
12	DALLAS	7
7	at St. Louis	20
10	CINCINNATI	38
386		**260**

ST. LOUIS (8-8)

17	ARIZONA	10
17	at Atlanta	34
25	NEW ORLEANS (OT)	28
24	at San Francisco	14
33	at Seattle (OT)	27
28	TAMPA BAY	21
14	at Miami	31
22	NEW ENGLAND	40
23	SEATTLE	12
17	at Buffalo	37
17	at Green Bay	45
16	SAN FRANCISCO	6
7	at Carolina	20
7	at Arizona	31
20	PHILADELPHIA	7
32	N.Y. JETS	29
319		**392**

SAN FRANCISCO (2-14)

19	ATLANTA	21
27	at New Orleans	30
0	at Seattle	34
14	ST. LOUIS	24
31	ARIZONA (OT)	28
14	at N.Y. Jets	22
13	at Chicago	23
27	SEATTLE	42
27	CAROLINA	37
3	at Tampa Bay	35
17	MIAMI	24
6	at St. Louis	16
31	at Arizona (OT)	28
16	WASHINGTON	26
7	BUFFALO	41
7	at New England	21
259		**452**

SEATTLE (9-7)

21	at New Orleans	7
10	at Tampa Bay	6
34	SAN FRANCISCO	0
27	ST. LOUIS (OT)	33
20	at New England	30
17	at Arizona	25
23	CAROLINA	17
42	at San Francisco	27
12	at St. Louis	23
24	MIAMI	17
9	BUFFALO	38
39	DALLAS	43
27	at Minnesota	23
14	at N.Y. Jets	37
24	ARIZONA	21
28	ATLANTA	26
371		**373**

TAMPA BAY (5-11)

10	at Washington	16
6	SEATTLE	10
20	at Oakland	30
13	DENVER	16
20	at New Orleans	17
21	at St. Louis	28
19	CHICAGO	7
34	KANSAS CITY	31
14	at Atlanta	24
35	SAN FRANCISCO	3
14	at Carolina	21
27	ATLANTA	0
24	at San Diego	31
17	NEW ORLEANS	21
20	CAROLINA	37
7	at Arizona	12
301		**304**

WASHINGTON (6-10)

16	TAMPA BAY	10
14	at N.Y. Giants	20
18	DALLAS	21
13	at Cleveland	17
10	BALTIMORE	17
13	at Chicago	10
14	GREEN BAY	28
17	at Detroit	10
17	CINCINNATI	17
6	at Philadelphia	28
7	at Pittsburgh	16
31	N.Y. GIANTS	7
14	PHILADELPHIA	17
26	at San Francisco	16
10	at Dallas	13
21	MINNESOTA	18
240		**265**

FINAL STANDINGS

AMERICAN FOOTBALL CONFERENCE

East Division	W	L	T	Pct.	Pts.	OP
New England	14	2	0	.875	437	260
N.Y. Jets*	10	6	0	.625	333	261
Buffalo	9	7	0	.563	395	284
Miami	4	12	0	.250	275	354
North Division						
Pittsburgh#	15	1	0	.938	372	251
Baltimore	9	7	0	.563	317	268
Cincinnati	8	8	0	.500	374	372
Cleveland	4	12	0	.250	276	390
South Division						
Indianapolis	12	4	0	.750	522	351
Jacksonville	9	7	0	.563	261	280
Houston	7	9	0	.438	309	339
Tennessee	5	11	0	.313	344	439
West Division						
San Diego	12	4	0	.750	446	313
Denver*	10	6	0	.625	381	304
Kansas City	7	9	0	.438	483	435
Oakland	5	11	0	.313	320	442

NATIONAL FOOTBALL CONFERENCE

East Division	W	L	T	Pct.	Pts.	OP
Philadelphia#	13	3	0	.813	386	260
N.Y. Giants	6	10	0	.375	303	347
Dallas	6	10	0	.375	293	405
Washington	6	10	0	.375	240	265
North Division						
Green Bay	10	6	0	.625	424	380
Minnesota*	8	8	0	.500	405	395
Detroit	6	10	0	.375	296	350
Chicago	5	11	0	.313	231	331
South Division						
Atlanta	11	5	0	.688	340	337
New Orleans	8	8	0	.500	348	405
Carolina	7	9	0	.438	355	339
Tampa Bay	5	11	0	.313	301	304
West Division						
Seattle	9	7	0	.563	371	373
St. Louis*	8	8	0	.500	319	392
Arizona	6	10	0	.375	284	322
San Francisco	2	14	0	.125	259	452

* Wild-Card qualifier for playoffs
# Top playoff seed in conference

Indianapolis finished ahead of San Diego based on head-to-head victory. N.Y. Jets finished ahead of Denver based on better record vs. common opponents (5-0 to 3-2). St. Louis finished ahead of Minnesota and New Orleans based on best conference record (STL, 7-5; NO, 6-6; MINN, 5-7), and Minnesota finished ahead of New Orleans based on head-to-head victory. N.Y. Giants finished ahead of Dallas and Washington based on better head-to-head record (NYG, 3-1; DALL, 2-2; WASH, 1-3), and Dallas finished ahead of Washington based on head-to-head sweep (2-0).

WILD-CARD PLAYOFFS

AFC
N.Y. Jets 20, SAN DIEGO 17 (OT)
INDIANAPOLIS 49, Denver 24
NFC
St. Louis 27, SEATTLE 20
Minnesota 31, GREEN BAY 17

DIVISIONAL PLAYOFFS

AFC
PITTSBURGH 20, N.Y. Jets 17 (OT)
NEW ENGLAND 20, Indianapolis 3
NFC
ATLANTA 47, St. Louis 17
PHILADELPHIA 27, Minnesota 14

CHAMPIONSHIP GAMES

AFC
New England 41, PITTSBURGH 27
NFC
PHILADELPHIA 27, Atlanta 10

SUPER BOWL XXXIX

New England (AFC) 24, Philadelphia (NFC) 21
at ALLTEL Stadium, Jacksonville, Florida

AFC-NFC PRO BOWL

AFC 38, NFC 27
at Aloha Stadium, Honolulu, Hawaii

Home teams in playoff games are indicated in CAPS.

FIRST WEEK SUMMARIES
American Football Conference

East Division	W	L	T	Pct.	Pts.	OP
New England	1	0	0	1.000	27	24
N.Y. Jets	1	0	0	1.000	31	24
Buffalo	0	1	0	.000	10	13
Miami	0	1	0	.000	7	17

North Division	W	L	T	Pct.	Pts.	OP
Cleveland	1	0	0	1.000	20	3
Pittsburgh	1	0	0	1.000	24	21
Baltimore	0	1	0	.000	3	20
Cincinnati	0	1	0	.000	24	31

South Division	W	L	T	Pct.	Pts.	OP
Jacksonville	1	0	0	1.000	13	10
Tennessee	1	0	0	1.000	17	7
Houston	0	1	0	.000	20	27
Indianapolis	0	1	0	.000	24	27

West Division	W	L	T	Pct.	Pts.	OP
Denver	1	0	0	1.000	34	24
San Diego	1	0	0	1.000	27	20
Kansas City	0	1	0	.000	24	34
Oakland	0	1	0	.000	21	24

National Football Conference

East Division	W	L	T	Pct.	Pts.	OP
Philadelphia	1	0	0	1.000	31	17
Washington	1	0	0	1.000	16	10
Dallas	0	1	0	.000	17	35
N.Y. Giants	0	1	0	.000	17	31

North Division	W	L	T	Pct.	Pts.	OP
Detroit	1	0	0	1.000	20	16
Green Bay	1	0	0	1.000	24	14
Minnesota	1	0	0	1.000	35	17
Chicago	0	1	0	.000	16	20

South Division	W	L	T	Pct.	Pts.	OP
Atlanta	1	0	0	1.000	21	19
Carolina	0	1	0	.000	14	24
New Orleans	0	1	0	.000	7	21
Tampa Bay	0	1	0	.000	10	16

West Division	W	L	T	Pct.	Pts.	OP
St. Louis	1	0	0	1.000	17	10
Seattle	1	0	0	1.000	21	7
Arizona	0	1	0	.000	10	17
San Francisco	0	1	0	.000	19	21

THURSDAY NIGHT, SEPTEMBER 9

NEW ENGLAND 27, INDIANAPOLIS 24—at Gillette Stadium, attendance 68,756. Tom Brady passed for 3 touchdowns and the defending Super Bowl champions needed a big sack by Willie McGinest to defeat the Colts. The Colts drove into the Patriots' red zone in each of their first-half possessions to take a 17-10 lead. The Patriots responded with a field goal as the half expired, forced a three-and-out punt to begin the second half, and then drove 69 yards, capped by Brady's 25-yard pass to David Patten, for a 20-17 lead. The Colts drove to the Patriots' 22, but Edgerrin James fumbled and Eugene Wilson recovered. Seven plays later Brady hit Daniel Graham with an 8-yard touchdown pass for a 27-17 lead. The Colts cut the deficit to three points when Manning's 7-yard scoring pass to Brandon Stokley capped an 11-play, 74-yard drive. The Colts reached the Patriots' 1, but James fumbled again, forced by Wilson, and Vince Wilfork recovered. The Colts got the ball back with 1:43 left, and Manning's 45-yard pass to Stokley to the Patriots' 19 set up a chance to tie the game. On third-and-8 from the 17, McGinest sacked Manning for an 11-yard loss, forcing Mike Vanderjagt to attempt a 48-yard field goal, which sailed wide right. Brady was 26 of 38 for 335 yards and 3 touchdowns, with 1 interception. Manning was 16 of 29 for 256 yards and 2 touchdowns, with 1 interception. James rushed 30 times for 142 yards.

Indianapolis	0	17	7	0 — 24
New England	3	10	14	0 — 27

NE	—	FG Vinatieri 32
Ind	—	FG Vanderjagt 32
Ind	—	Rhodes 3 run (Vanderjagt kick)
NE	—	Branch 16 pass from Brady (Vinatieri kick)
Ind	—	Harrison 3 pass from Manning (Vanderjagt kick)

NE	—	FG Vinatieri 43
NE	—	Patten 25 pass from Brady (Vinatieri kick)
NE	—	Graham 8 pass from Brady (Vinatieri kick)
Ind	—	Stokley 7 pass from Manning (Vanderjagt kick)

SATURDAY, SEPTEMBER 11

TENNESSEE 17, MIAMI 7—at Pro Player Stadium, attendance 69,987. Chris Brown rushed for 100 yards and the Titans' defense forced 3 turnovers to defeat the Dolphins. The game, which was played in partly cloudy, 87 degree weather, was moved up one day to avoid oncoming Hurricane Ivan. The Dolphins only got first downs on one of their first-half possessions, and Samari Rolle's interception in the end zone for a touchback thwarted that drive. Andre Dyson's interception later in the second quarter, followed by Brown's 52-yard run to the Dolphins' 1 set up Steve McNair's 1-yard touchdown pass to Erron Kinney. Lamont Thompson intercepted a pass and returned it 37 yards for a touchdown and 14-0 lead. A.J. Feeley's 15-yard touchdown pass to Randy McMichael cut the deficit to 17-7 with 3:22 left, and Steve Greenwood recovered the ensuing onside kick, but Will Poole was offside and the ensuing kickoff went out of bounds. McNair was 9 of 14 for 73 yards and 1 touchdown. Brown rushed 16 times for 100 yards. Jay Fiedler started and was 5 of 13 for 42 yards, with 2 interceptions. Feeley came in the second half and was 21 of 31 for 168 yards and 1 touchdown, with 1 interception.

Tennessee	0	7	7	3 — 17
Miami	0	0	0	7 — 7

Tenn	—	Kinney 1 pass from McNair (Elling kick)
Tenn	—	Thompson 37 interception return (Elling kick)
Tenn	—	FG Elling 22
Mia	—	McMichael 15 pass from Feeley (Mare kick)

SUNDAY, SEPTEMBER 12

JACKSONVILLE 13, BUFFALO 10—at Ralph Wilson Stadium, attendance 72,389. Rookie Ernest Wilford caught a 7-yard touchdown pass amidst three Bills' defenders as time expired to lift the Jaguars to victory. Nate Clements intercepted a pass in the first quarter, and two plays later Drew Bledsoe completed an 18-yard touchdown pass to Eric Moulds for a 7-0 lead. Trailing 7-3 in the third quarter, Bledsoe fumbled and Donovin Darius recovered to set up Josh Scobee's second field goal. Early in the fourth quarter Izell Reese intercepted a pass to set up a field goal for a 10-6 lead with 10:15 to play. The Jaguars got the ball at their own 20 with 2:07 left, and Byron Leftwich completed 5 of his first 6 passes on the drive to reach the Bills' 16 with 52 seconds left. On fourth-and-2, Troy Edwards caught a pass for first-and-goal at the Bills' 7 with 14 seconds left. Three incomplete passes set up fourth-and-goal from the 7-yard line with four seconds left. Leftwich lofted the pass to the right side and Wilford outleaped a host of Bills in the back of the end zone for the winning catch. Leftwich was 18 of 36 for 147 yards and 1 touchdown, with 2 interceptions. Bledsoe was 17 of 26 for 153 yards and 1 touchdown.

Jacksonville	0	3	3	7 — 13
Buffalo	7	0	3	0 — 10

Buff	—	Moulds 17 pass from Bledsoe (Lindell kick)
Jax	—	FG Scobee 25
Jax	—	FG Scobee 27
Buff	—	FG Lindell 25
Jax	—	Wilford 7 pass from Leftwich (Scobee kick)

DETROIT 20, CHICAGO 16—at Soldier Field, attendance 61,535. Bracy Walker returned a blocked field goal for a touchdown and intercepted a pass in the end zone in the final minute to defeat the Bears. The Bears led 7-3 at halftime and lined up for a field goal early in the third quarter. But Shaun Rogers blocked Paul Edinger's 27-yard attempt and Bracy Walker scooped up the ball and raced 92 yards for a touchdown. Rogers recovered a fumble by Rex Grossman later in the third quarter to set up Jason Hanson's 21-yard field goal for a 13-7 lead. The Bears regained the lead early in the fourth quarter when Thomas Jones' second touchdown capped a 64-yard drive. Eddie Drummond returned the ensuing kickoff 41 yards and five plays later Harrington found Az-Zahir Hakim open for a 4-yard touchdown and 20-14 lead with 9:54 left. Faced with fourth-and-11 from their own 7 Lions' punter, Nick Harris, purposely ran out of the end zone for a safety with 1:53 left. The Bears gained possession at the Lions' 47 after the free kick and reached the Lions' 9. On third down, Grossman's pass intended for David Terrell was intercepted in the end zone by Walker with 18 seconds left. Harrington was 14 of 26 for 187 yards and 1 touchdown, with 1 interception. Grossman was 16 of 35 for 227 yards, with 2 interceptions. Terrell had 5 receptions for 126 yards.

Detroit	0	3	10	7 — 20
Chicago	7	0	0	9 — 16

Chi	—	T. Jones 2 run (Edinger kick)
Det	—	FG Hanson 27
Det	—	Walker 92 blocked field goal return (Hanson kick)
Det	—	FG Hanson 21
Chi	—	T. Jones 2 run (Edinger kick)
Det	—	Hakim 4 pass from Harrington (Hanson kick)
Chi	—	Safety, Harris ran out of end zone

CLEVELAND 20, BALTIMORE 3—at Cleveland Browns Stadium, attendance 73,068. In his first game for the Browns Jeff Garcia passed for 180 yards and 1 touchdown, and ran for another score, to defeat the Ravens. With the game tied 3-3 late in the third quarter, Garcia completed a 46-yard touchdown pass to Quincy Morgan. Anthony Henry intercepted Kyle Boller four plays later to set up Phil Dawson's 25-yard field goal for a 13-3 lead. Three plays later, Kenard Lang sacked Boller and forced him to fumble. Michael Myers recovered the ball at the Ravens' 6 and three plays later Garcia scored on third-and-goal from the Ravens' 3 for a 20-3 lead with 4:20 to play. Garcia was 15 of 24 for 180 yards and 1 touchdown. Lang had 3 sacks and a forced fumble. Boller was 22 of 38 for 191 yards, with 2 interceptions.

Baltimore	0	0	3	0 — 3
Cleveland	0	3	7	10 — 20

Cle	—	FG Dawson 37
Balt	—	FG Stover 42
Cle	—	Morgan 46 pass from Garcia (Dawson kick)
Cle	—	FG Dawson 25
Cle	—	Garcia 3 run (Dawson kick)

SAN DIEGO 27, HOUSTON 20—at Reliant Stadium, attendance 70,255. Drew Brees passed for 209 yards and 2 touchdowns and the Chargers' defense forced 4 turnovers to defeat the Texans. The Texans had nearly twice as many first-half turnovers, yet led just 13-10 because Terrence Kiel recovered a fumble by Domanick Davis at the Texans' 45 to set up LaDainian Tomlinson's touchdown run. Steve Foley intercepted a David Carr pass early in the second half, and Brees completed a 36-yard touchdown pass to Reche Caldwell to give the Chargers a 17-13 lead. J.J. Moses returned the ensuing kickoff 49 yards to set up Davis' 1-yard touchdown run for a 20-17 lead. With the score tied 20-20, Brees completed a 13-yard pass to Antonio Gates on third down, followed by a 29-yard pass to the Texans' 15. On third-and-14, Eric Parker caught Brees' pass in the back of the end zone for a 27-20 lead with 8:34 left. The Texans reached the Chargers' 17, but Randall Godfrey forced Davis to fumble and Foley recovered with

3:48 left. The Chargers converted 2 third-down situations, the last an 8-yard run by Tomlinson on third-and-4, to run out the clock. Brees was 17 of 24 for 209 yards and 2 touchdowns. Gates had 8 receptions for 123 yards, and Tomlinson rushed 26 times for 121 yards. Carr was 19 of 25 for 229 yards, with 2 interceptions.

San Diego	3	7	10	7	—	27
Houston	3	10	7	0	—	20

Hou	—	FG K. Brown 37
SD	—	FG Kaeding 48
Hou	—	FG K. Brown 20
SD	—	Tomlinson 1 run (Kaeding kick)
Hou	—	Davis 2 run (K. Brown kick)
SD	—	Caldwell 36 pass from Brees (Kaeding kick)
Hou	—	Davis 1 run (K. Brown kick)
SD	—	FG Kaeding 29
SD	—	Parker 19 pass from Brees (Kaeding kick)

MINNESOTA 35, DALLAS 17—at Metrodome, attendance 64,105. Daunte Culpepper passed for 5 touchdowns, including 2 to Randy Moss, as the Vikings defeated the Cowboys. Dallas led 3-0 and drove 85 yards in 20 plays to the Vikings' 6 to try a field goal, but holder Mat McBriar could not handle the snap and his pass fell incomplete. The Vikings responded by scoring touchdowns with their next four possessions to take a 28-17 lead with 6:01 left in the third quarter. After an exchange of punts, the Cowboys drove to the Vikings' 19 but Richie Anderson fumbled and Antonie Winfield recovered. Four plays later Culpepper completed a 43-yard touchdown pass to Kelly Campbell for a 35-17 lead with 6:56 left. Culpepper was 17 of 23 for 242 yards and 5 touchdowns. Testaverde was 29 of 50 for 355 yards and 1 touchdown. Keyshawn Johnson had 9 receptions for 11 yards, and Antonio Bryant had 8 catches for 112 yards.

Dallas	3	7	7	0	—	17
Minnesota	0	14	14	7	—	35

Dall	—	FG Cundiff 27
Minn	—	O. Smith 63 pass from Culpepper (Andersen kick)
Minn	—	Robinson 3 pass from Culpepper (Andersen kick)
Dall	—	Glenn 32 pass from Testaverde (Cundiff kick)
Minn	—	Moss 3 pass from Culpepper (Andersen kick)
Dall	—	Lee 7 run (Cundiff kick)
Minn	—	Moss 1 pass from Culpepper (Andersen kick)
Minn	—	Campbell 43 pass from Culpepper (Andersen kick)

SEATTLE 21, NEW ORLEANS 7—at Louisiana Superdome, attendance 64,900. Shaun Alexander rushed for 135 yards and scored 3 touchdowns to defeat the Saints. Late in the first quarter, Boo Williams fumbled at the Seahawks' 21 and Ken Lucas recovered to set up Alexander's scoring catch. In the third quarter, with Seattle leading 14-7, Michael Boulware intercepted Aaron Brooks' pass at the Saints' 26, and Alexander scored two plays later for a 21-7 lead. The Saints drove to the Seahawks' 19, but Brooks' fourth-down pass fell incomplete with 9:27 left, and the Saints did not threaten again. Hasselbeck was 19 of 29 for 246 yards and 1 touchdown, with 1 interception. Brooks was 18 of 37 for 223 yards and 1 touchdown, with 1 interception. Joe Horn had 6 receptions for 110 yards.

Seattle	0	14	7	0	—	21
New Orleans	0	7	0	0	—	7

Sea	—	Alexander 14 pass from Hasselbeck (J. Brown kick)
Sea	—	Alexander 6 run (J. Brown kick)
NO	—	Conwell 6 pass from Brooks (Carney kick)
Sea	—	Alexander 9 run (J. Brown kick)

N.Y. JETS 31, CINCINNATI 24—at Meadowlands, attendance 77,230. Curtis Martin rushed for 196 yards and scored 2 touchdowns as the Jets held off the Bengals. The Jets fumbled the opening kickoff and Rudi Johnson scored four plays later for a 7-0 lead. The Jets answered with touchdown drives of 68 and 86 yards for a 14-10 halftime lead. Sam Cowart forced Johnson to fumble early in the second half, and Donnie Abraham recovered and ran 41 yards for a touchdown. The Bengals answered with a touchdown, but Doug Brien kicked a field goal to extend the Jets lead to 24-17. The Jets' defense forced a three-and-out punt and Martin scored on a 24-yard run nine plays later for a 31-17 lead. Carson Palmer's 53-yard touchdown pass to Chad Johnson cut the deficit to 31-24 lead with 6:28 to play. The Bengals forced a punt and drove to the Bengals' 49, but Erik Coleman intercepted Palmer's pass with 1:51 left, and Martin ran for 2 first downs to run out the clock. Chad Pennington was 20 of 27 for 224 yards and 2 touchdowns. Martin rushed 29 times for 196 yards. Palmer, making his first NFL appearance, was 18 of 27 for 248 yards and 2 touchdowns, with 1 interception.

Cincinnati	7	3	7	7	—	24
N.Y. Jets	14	0	10	7	—	31

Cin	—	R. Johnson 9 run (Graham kick)
NYJ	—	Martin 3 pass from Pennington (Brien kick)
NYJ	—	J. Carter 46 pass from Pennington (Brien kick)
Cin	—	FG Graham 22
NYJ	—	Abraham 41 fumble return (Brien kick)
Cin	—	Watson 6 pass from Palmer (Graham kick)
NYJ	—	FG Brien 21
NYJ	—	Martin 24 run (Brien kick)
Cin	—	C. Johnson 53 pass from Palmer (Graham kick)

PHILADELPHIA 31, N.Y. GIANTS 17—at Lincoln Financial Field, attendance 67,532. Donovan McNabb passed for 330 yards and 4 touchdowns, 3 to Terrell Owens, to defeat the Giants. The Eagles trailed 7-0 before scoring on four consecutive possessions, with the Giants gaining just 2 first downs on their three possessions, to take a 24-7 lead. McNabb's third touchdown pass to Owens capped a 71-yard drive to extend the lead to 31-10. The Giants responded by driving to the Eagles' 1, but Kurt Warner mishandled the snap and Jevon Kearse recovered the fumble. On their next possession, the Giants drove to the Eagles' 5, but Warner's fourth-down pass fell incomplete with 6:25 left. Tiki Barber scored on a 72-yard touchdown run, and following an Eagles' punt, rookie Eli Manning completed 3 of 9 passes for 66 yards on his one possession before time expired. McNabb was 26 of 36 for 330 yards and 4 touchdowns. Brian Westbrook rushed 17 times for 119 yards. Warner was 16 of 28 for 203 yards. Barber rushed 9 times for 125 yards.

N.Y. Giants	7	3	0	7	—	17
Philadelphia	14	10	7	0	—	31

NYG	—	Dayne 3 run (Christie kick)
Phil	—	Owens 20 pass from McNabb (Akers kick)
Phil	—	Owens 3 pass from McNabb (Akers kick)
Phil	—	L. Smith 14 pass from McNabb (Akers kick)
Phil	—	FG Akers 45
NYG	—	FG Christie 53
Phil	—	Owens 12 pass from McNabb (Akers kick)
NYG	—	Barber 72 run (Christie kick)

PITTSBURGH 24, OAKLAND 21—at Heinz Field, attendance 60,147. Jerome Bettis had 5 carries for 1 yard, but scored 3 touchdowns, and Jeff Reed kicked a 42-yard field goal with seven seconds left to lift the Steelers to victory. Bettis scored 2 touchdowns in the first half, the second culminating a 20-yard drive set up by Aaron Smith's fumble recovery, to take a 14-0 lead. Leading 14-10 in the third quarter, Tommy Maddox completed a 39-yard pass to Hines Ward to set up Bettis' third touchdown run. Maddox fumbled three plays later and Travian Smith recovered the ball. Eight plays later Sebastian Janikowski's 38-yard field goal trimmed the deficit to 21-13, and following a three-and-out, the Raiders drove into Steelers' territory but faced fourth-and-12 from the 38-yard line. Rich Gannon completed a 38-yard touchdown pass to Alvis Whitted and 2-point conversion pass, also to Whitted, to tie the score with 4:51 to play. Maddox engineered a 10-play, 54-yard drive, highlighted by Ward's 15-yard catch to the Raiders' 24, and capped by Reed's 42-yard field goal with seven seconds left. Maddox was 13 of 22 for 142 yards. Gannon was 20 of 37 for 305 yards and 2 touchdowns, with 2 interceptions.

Oakland	0	7	3	11	—	21
Pittsburgh	7	7	7	3	—	24

Pitt	—	Bettis 1 run (Reed kick)
Pitt	—	Bettis 1 run (Reed kick)
Oak	—	Gabriel 58 pass from Gannon (Janikowski kick)
Oak	—	FG Janikowski 28
Pitt	—	Bettis 1 run (Reed kick)
Oak	—	FG Janikowski 38
Oak	—	Whitted 38 pass from Gannon (Whitted pass from Gannon)
Pitt	—	FG Reed 42

ST. LOUIS 17, ARIZONA 10—at Edward Jones Dome, attendance 65,538. Marc Bulger passed for 272 yards and the go-ahead touchdown early in the fourth quarter as the Rams held off the Cardinals. The Rams led 6-3 halftime lead, and held the ball for 9:10 to begin the second half but settled for a field goal for a 9-3 lead. Arizona responded by driving for an 8-yard touchdown by Emmitt Smith's 11-yard touchdown run to give the Cardinals a 10-9 lead. The Rams answered by driving to the Cardinals' 13. On the next play, Adrian Wilson intercepted Bulger's pass and returned it 95 yards for a touchdown, but defensive holding nullified the play. Two plays later Bulger completed an 8-yard touchdown pass to Isaac Bruce, and Marshall Faulk ran in the 2-point conversion for a 17-10 lead. The Cardinals had the ball four times in the final 14:27 but failed to cross midfield. The Rams outgained the Cardinals 448-260 yards. Bulger was 23 of 34 for 272 yards and 1 touchdown, with 1 interception. Bruce had 9 catches for 112 yards, and Faulk rushed 22 times for 128 yards. Josh McCown was 18 of 29 for 181 yards.

Arizona	0	3	7	0	—	10
St. Louis	0	6	3	8	—	17

StL	—	FG Wilkins 50
Ariz	—	FG Rackers 22
StL	—	FG Wilkins 28
StL	—	FG Wilkins 22
Ariz	—	Smith 11 run (Rackers kick)
StL	—	Bruce 8 pass from Bulger (Faulk kick)

ATLANTA 21, SAN FRANCISCO 19—at 3Com Park, attendance 65,584. Rod Coleman batted down Tim Rattay's 2-point conversion pass attempt with 40 seconds left as the Falcons withstood a late rally to defeat the 49ers. Early in the fourth quarter, the 49ers trailed 14-6 but drove to the Falcons' 3. Aaron Beasley intercepted Rattay's pass and returned it 85 yards to the 49ers' 14, setting up Warrick Dunn's 9-yard touchdown run for a 21-6 lead with 8:57 to play. The 49ers drove 74 yards for a touchdown, forced a three-and-out punt, and drove another 62 yards, capped by Eric Johnson's 16-yard touchdown catch with 40 seconds left. Michael Vick was 13 of 22 for 163 yards and 1 touchdown, with 1 interception. Rattay was 18 of 31 for 175 yards and 2 touchdowns, with 1 interception, but sat the second and third quarter with a sore shoulder. Ken Dorsey replaced him during those two quarters and was 9 of 15 for 111 yards.

| Atlanta | 7 | 7 | 0 | 7 | — | 21 |
| San Francisco | 0 | 3 | 3 | 13 | — | 19 |

Atl	—	Crumpler 15 pass from Vick (Feely kick)
Atl	—	Dunn 2 run (Feely kick)
SF	—	FG Peterson 23
SF	—	FG Peterson 32
Atl	—	Dunn 9 run (Feely kick)
SF	—	Wilson 8 pass from Rattay (Peterson kick)
SF	—	Jonson 16 pass from Rattay (pass failed)

WASHINGTON 16, TAMPA BAY 10—at FedExField, attendance 90,098. Clinton Portis scored on a 64-yard touchdown run the first time he touched the ball as a Redskins' player to lead his new team to victory. The Redskins led 10-3 in the third quarter when Mark Brunell fumbled the snap and Ronde Barber recovered and returned the ball 9 yards for a touchdown to tie the game. Antonio Pierce intercepted Brad Johnson's pass early in the fourth quarter to set up a 27-yard drive capped by John Hall's go-ahead 30-yard field goal with 8:55 to play. The Redskins forced a punt 5:03 left and ran off all but the final 16 seconds, adding Hall's third field goal, and LaVar Arrington sacked Johnson to end the game. The Redskins' defense allowed just 169 yards. Brunell was 13 of 24 for 125 yards. Portis rushed 29 times for 148 yards. Johnson was 24 of 37 for 169 yards, with 1 interception.

| Tampa Bay | 0 | 3 | 7 | 0 | — | 10 |
| Washington | 7 | 3 | 0 | 6 | — | 16 |

Wash	—	Portis 62 run (Hall kick)
Wash	—	FG Hall 20
TB	—	FG Gramatica 47
TB	—	R. Barber 9 fumble return (Gramatica kick)
Wash	—	FG Hall 30
Wash	—	FG Hall 34

SUNDAY NIGHT, SEPTEMBER 12
DENVER 34, KANSAS CITY 24—at INVESCO Field at Mile High, attendance 75,939. Quentin Griffin rushed for 156 yards and 2 touchdowns as the Broncos pulled away from the Chiefs. Trailing 7-0, the Broncos scored on their first three possessions to take a 17-7 lead. A pair of third-quarter interceptions set up 10 points in the span of 1:30 to tie the game 17-17. Griffin scored on a 47-yard run on the ensuing possession to give Denver the lead, but the Chiefs scored seven plays later on Priest Holmes' 33-yard run to tie the game 24-24 with 5:50 left in the third quarter. Jason Elam's 45-yard field goal early in the fourth quarter gave Denver the lead, and following a punt, the Broncos drove 13 plays, 87 yards, and took 7:10 off the clock capped by Jake Plummer's 2-yard touchdown pass to Patrick Hape with 2:12 remaining. Plummer was 18 of 29 for 230 yards and 2 touchdowns, with 2 interceptions. Griffin rushed 23 times for 156 yards. Green was 16 of 32 for 174 yards, with 1 interception. Kennison had 6 catches for 101 yards, and Holmes rushed 26 times for 151 yards.

| Kansas City | 7 | 0 | 17 | 0 | — | 24 |
| Denver | 3 | 14 | 7 | 10 | — | 34 |

KC	—	Holmes 2 run (Tynes kick)
Den	—	FG Elam 43
Den	—	Griffith 1 pass from Plummer (Tynes kick)
Den	—	Griffin 25 run (Elam kick)
KC	—	FG Tynes 50
KC	—	Holmes 4 run (Tynes kick)
Den	—	Griffin 47 run (Elam kick)
KC	—	Holmes 33 run (Tynes kick)
Den	—	FG Elam 45
Den	—	Hape 2 pass from Plummer (Elam kick)

MONDAY NIGHT, SEPTEMBER 13
GREEN BAY 24, CAROLINA 14—at Bank of Ameri-

ca Stadium, attendance 73,656. Ahman Green rushed for 119 yards and scored 3 touchdowns as the Packers defeated the defending NFC champions. The Packers led 10-7 at halftime, and Aaron Kampman recovered a mishandled snap two plays into the second half. Brett Favre completed 2 third-down conversion passes to Donald Driver, and Green's 3-yard run increased the lead to 17-7. Six plays later, Nick Barnett intercepted Jake Delhomme and Favre capped the ensuing drive with a 3-yard touchdown pass to Green. Muhsin Muhammad caught a 30-yard touchdown pass with 4:46 remaining, but Darren Sharper recovered the onside kick. Favre was 15 of 22 for 143 yards and 1 touchdown. Green rushed 33 times for 119 yards. Nick Barnett had 1 sack and 1 interception. Delhomme was 23 of 39 for 284 yards and 2 touchdowns, with 1 interception.

| Green Bay | 3 | 7 | 14 | 0 | — | 24 |
| Carolina | 0 | 7 | 0 | 7 | — | 14 |

GB	—	FG Longwell 41
Car	—	Hoover 1 pass from Delhomme (Kasay kick)
GB	—	Green 6 run (Longwell kick)
GB	—	Green 3 run (Longwell kick)
GB	—	Green 3 pass from Favre (Longwell kick)
Car	—	Muhammad 30 pass from Delhomme (Kasay kick)

SECOND WEEK SUMMARIES
American Football Conference

East Division	W	L	T	Pct.	Pts.	OP
New England	2	0	0	1.000	50	36
N.Y. Jets	2	0	0	1.000	65	52
Buffalo	0	2	0	.000	20	26
Miami	0	2	0	.000	20	33

North Division	W	L	T	Pct.	Pts.	OP
Baltimore	1	1	0	.500	33	33
Cincinnati	1	1	0	.500	40	44
Cleveland	1	1	0	.500	32	22
Pittsburgh	1	1	0	.500	37	51

South Division	W	L	T	Pct.	Pts.	OP
Jacksonville	2	0	0	1.000	20	16
Indianapolis	1	1	0	.500	55	44
Tennessee	1	1	0	.500	34	38
Houston	0	2	0	.000	36	55

West Division	W	L	T	Pct.	Pts.	OP
Denver	1	1	0	.500	40	31
Oakland	1	1	0	.500	34	34
San Diego	1	1	0	.500	55	54
Kansas City	0	2	0	.000	41	62

National Football Conference

East Division	W	L	T	Pct.	Pts.	OP
Philadelphia	2	0	0	1.000	58	33
Dallas	1	1	0	.500	36	47
N.Y. Giants	1	1	0	.500	37	45
Washington	1	1	0	.500	30	30

North Division	W	L	T	Pct.	Pts.	OP
Detroit	2	0	0	1.000	48	32
Chicago	1	1	0	.500	37	30
Green Bay	1	1	0	.500	34	35
Minnesota	1	1	0	.500	51	44

South Division	W	L	T	Pct.	Pts.	OP
Atlanta	2	0	0	1.000	55	36
Carolina	1	1	0	.500	42	41
New Orleans	1	1	0	.500	37	48
Tampa Bay	0	2	0	.000	16	26

West Division	W	L	T	Pct.	Pts.	OP
Seattle	2	0	0	1.000	31	13
St. Louis	1	1	0	.500	34	44
Arizona	0	2	0	.000	22	40
San Francisco	0	2	0	.000	46	51

SUNDAY, SEPTEMBER 19
NEW ENGLAND 23, ARIZONA 12—at Sun Devil Stadium, attendance 51,557. Tom Brady passed for 2 touchdowns, and the Patriots' defense allowed just 167 yards to win their fourteenth consecutive game. The Patriots led 14-0, but a fumble and interception in their own territory in the second quarter led to 2 field goals by Neil Rackers. The Patriots began the second half with a field goal, but the Car-

dinals responded with a 11-play, 80-yard drive capped by Emmitt Smith's 1-yard run to cut the deficit to 17-12 with 1:33 left in the third quarter. The Patriots answered as Brady completed passes of 20, 19, and 12 yards to David Givens to set up Adam Vinatieri's 28-yard field goal with 12:02 to play. Eugene Wilson intercepted Josh McCown three plays later to set up Vinatieri's third field goal with 6:22 remaining, and the Cardinals failed to threaten thereafter. Brady was 15 of 26 for 217 yards and 2 touchdowns, with 2 interceptions. Givens had 6 receptions for 118 yards, and Corey Dillon rushed 32 times for 158 yards. Rodney Harrison had 2 sacks and forced a fumble. McCown was 13 of 29 for 160 yards, with 2 interceptions.

| New England | 7 | 7 | 3 | 6 | — | 23 |
| Arizona | 0 | 6 | 6 | 0 | — | 12 |

NE	—	Graham 2 pass from Brady (Vinatieri kick)
NE	—	Graham 19 pass from Brady (Vinatieri kick)
Ariz	—	FG Rackers 51
Ariz	—	FG Rackers 52
NE	—	FG Vinatieri 29
Ariz	—	Smith 1 run (pass failed)
NE	—	FG Vinatieri 28
NE	—	FG Vinatieri 24

ATLANTA 34, ST. LOUIS 17—at Georgia Dome, attendance 70,822. Warrick Dunn scored 2 touchdowns, and Michael Vick rushed for 109 yards as the Falcons defeated the Rams. The Rams trailed 17-7 at halftime, but scored on successive third-quarter possessions to tie the game 17-17. Vick completed a 33-yard pass to Alge Crumpler to set up Dunn's second touchdown. Starting from their own 10, Patrick Kerney sacked Marc Bulger for a 9-yard loss, and on the next play Brady Smith sacked Bulger and forced him to fumble. Smith recovered the ball and the Falcons had 14 points in a span of 48 seconds for a 31-17 lead with 11:48 to play. Three plays later Aaron Beasley intercepted a pass to set up Jay Feely's final field goal. Vick was 14 of 19 for 179 yards and 1 touchdown, and rushed 12 times for 109 yards. Bulger was 24 of 31 for 285 yards and 1 touchdown, with 1 interception. Torry Holt had 9 receptions for 121 yards, and Isaac Bruce added 8 catches for 102 yards.

| St. Louis | 0 | 7 | 10 | 0 | — | 17 |
| Atlanta | 7 | 10 | 0 | 17 | — | 34 |

Atl	—	Griffith 3 pass from Vick (Feely kick)
Atl	—	Dunn 2 run (Feely kick)
StL	—	Faulk 1 run (Wilkins kick)
Atl	—	FG Feely 35
StL	—	Holt 33 pass from Bulger (Wilkins kick)
StL	—	FG Wilkins 46
Atl	—	Dunn 2 run (Feely kick)
Atl	—	Smith fumble recovery in end zone (Feely kick)
Atl	—	FG Feely 25

BALTIMORE 30, PITTSBURGH 13—at M&T Bank Stadium, attendance 69,859. Jamal Lewis rushed for 2 touchdowns as the Ravens defeated the Steelers. The Ravens led 13-0 at halftime. The Ravens got the ball to begin the second half, and Gary Baxter sacked Tommy Maddox and forced him to fumble. Terrell Suggs recovered and returned the ball 24 yards to the Steelers' 1. On the next play, Lewis scored to give the Ravens a 20-0 lead. Ben Roethlisberger replaced an injured Maddox and passed for 2 fourth quarter touchdowns, the second ending with his 2-point conversion pass falling incomplete, to pull within 23-13 with 6:10 remaining. The Steelers' defense forced a punt, but Chris McAlister intercepted Roethlisberger's pass and returned it 51 yards for a touchdown with 2:56 to play. Kyle Boller was 10 of 18 for 98 yards. Tommy Maddox was 4 of 13 for 67 yards. Roethlisberger was 12 of 20 for

176 yards and 2 touchdowns, with 2 interceptions. Hines Ward had 6 receptions for 151 yards.

| Pittsburgh | 0 | 0 | 0 | 13 | — | 13 |
| Baltimore | 7 | 6 | 7 | 10 | — | 30 |

Balt	—	J. Lewis 3 run (Stover kick)
Balt	—	FG Stover 35
Balt	—	FG Stover 27
Balt	—	J. Lewis 1 run (Stover kick)
Pitt	—	Randle El 3 pass from Roethlisberger (Reed kick)
Balt	—	FG Stover 34
Pitt	—	McAlister 51 interception return (Stover kick)

DALLAS 19, CLEVELAND 12—at Texas Stadium, attendance 63,119. Vinny Testaverde passed for 322 yards and 1 touchdown, and the Cowboys' defense permitted just 202 yards, as Dallas held off the Browns. Testaverde became just the second Cowboys' quarterback, the other being Don Meredith, to post consecutive 300-yard passing games. The Cowboys led 10-9 at halftime. In the third quarter, Dat Nguyen intercepted Jeff Garcia's pass at the Cowboys' 27, and Testaverde's 37-yard pass to Antonio Bryant set up Eddie George's 3-yard run late for a 17-9 lead. Phil Dawson kicked a fourth field goal early in the fourth quarter, and the teams then traded interceptions, 2 each, on the ensuing four possessions. The Browns forced a punt and started the drive on their own 1 with nine seconds left. Joquain Gonzalez committed holding in the end zone for a safety to allow Dawson to attempt an onside kick. Anthony Henry recovered the kick at the Browns' 43. Strong-armed Luke McCown entered the game, and his Hail Mary pass was knocked down by Keyshawn Johnson near the end zone as time expired. Testaverde was 23 of 35 for 322 yards and 1 touchdown, with 3 interceptions. Jeff Garcia was 8 of 27 for 71 yards, with 3 interceptions.

| Cleveland | 0 | 9 | 0 | 3 | — | 12 |
| Dallas | 7 | 3 | 7 | 2 | — | 19 |

Dall	—	Robinson 1 pass from Testaverde (Cundiff kick)
Cle	—	FG Dawson 45
Cle	—	FG Dawson 23
Dall	—	FG Cundiff 30
Cle	—	FG Dawson 49
Dall	—	George 3 run (Cundiff kick)
Cle	—	FG Dawson 22
Dall	—	Safety, Gonzalez penalized for holding in end zone

DETROIT 28, HOUSTON 16—at Ford Field, attendance 61,465. Joey Harrington passed for 3 touchdowns, 2 to Roy Williams, as the Lions improved to 2-0. Aaron Glenn's interception early in the second half gave the Texans a chance to take the lead. But Domanick Davis fumbled two plays later, and Bracy Walker recovered the ball at the Lions' 21. The Lions responded with a 79-yard touchdown drive to give Detroit a 14-3 lead. David Carr completed a 54-yard touchdown pss to Andre Johnson, but Eddie Drummond returned the ensuing kickoff 99 yards for a touchdown and 21-10 lead. The Texans drove 81 yards for a touchdown to cut the deficit to 21-16, but Carr's 2-point conversion pass fell incomplete. The Lions took the ensuing kickoff and marched 12 plays for 80 yards, capped by Williams' 14-yard touchdown pass with 4:41 to play. Houston drove to the Lions' 5, but Carr's fourth-and-goal scramble ended up 4 yards shy of the end zone with 36 seconds left. Harrington was 18 of 25 for 176 yards and 3 touchdowns, with 1 interception. Carr was 23 of 34 for 313 yards and 2 touchdowns, with 1 interception. Davis had 11 receptions for 95 yards.

| Houston | 0 | 3 | 7 | 6 | — | 16 |
| Detroit | 0 | 7 | 14 | 7 | — | 28 |

Det	—	Schlesinger 1 pass from Harrington (Hanson kick)
Hous	—	FG K. Brown 34
Det	—	Williams 31 pass from Harrington (Hanson kick)

Hous	—	Johnson 54 pass from Carr (K. Brown kick)
Det	—	Drummond 99 kickoff return (Hanson kick)
Hous	—	Bradford 27 pass from Carr (pass failed)
Det	—	Williams 14 pass from Harrington (Hanson kick)

CHICAGO 21, GREEN BAY 10—at Lambeau Field, attendance 70,688. Thomas Jones rushed 23 times for 152 yards and Mike Brown returned a fumble 95 yards for a touchdown for Lovie Smith's first victory. The Bears led 7-3, but the Packers drove to the Bears' 2. Brian Urlacher stripped Ahman Green of the ball, and Brown picked it up and ran 95 yards for a touchdown and a 14-3 lead, instead of a 10-7 deficit, with 1:44 left in the half. The Bears drove 79 yards with the second half's opening kickoff, capped by Jones' 1-yard run, for a 21-3 lead. The Packers answered with a 19-play, 89-yard touchdown drive, but the Packers added just 1 first down on their next three possessions before driving to the Bears' 11 and being stopped on downs with 1:12 to play. Rex Grossman was 10 of 18 for 132 yards and 1 touchdown, with 1 interception. Jones rushed 23 times for 152 yards. Brett Favre was 24 of 42 for 252 yards and 1 touchdown, with 2 interceptions. Javon Walker had 7 receptions for 102 yards, and Green rushed 24 times for 128 yards.

| Chicago | 0 | 14 | 7 | 0 | — | 21 |
| Green Bay | 3 | 0 | 7 | 0 | — | 10 |

GB	—	FG Longwell 25
Chi	—	Johnson 11 pass from Grossman (Edinger kick)
Chi	—	Brown 95 fumble return (Edinger kick)
Chi	—	Jones 1 run (Edinger kick)
GB	—	Ferguson 18 pass from Favre (Longwell kick)

JACKSONVILLE 7, DENVER 6—at ALLTEL Stadium, attendance 69,127. Akin Ayodele recovered Quentin Griffin's fumble at the Jaguars' 21 with 37 seconds remaining as Jacksonville improved to 2-0. The Broncos had advantages in first downs (20-8), yards (356-176), and time of possession (37:08-22:52). Jermaine Lewis returned a punt 50 yards late in the first quarter to set up Byron Leftwich's 12-yard touchdown pass to Ernest Wilford. Jason Elam added 2 field goals, including a 22-yard boot as the half expired, to pull within 7-6 at halftime. Late in the third quarter, Elam attempted a 51-yard field goal that fell just short. Denver's final possession began at its own 11 with 2:20 to play. The Broncos converted 2 third downs, including a roughing the passer penalty, to drive to the Jaguars' 24. On third-and-9 with 27 seconds left, Griffin dropped the handoff from Jake Plummer and Ayodele recovered. Leftwich was 8 of 16 for 120 yards and 1 touchdown. Plummer was 23 of 39 for 250 yards.

| Denver | 0 | 6 | 0 | 0 | — | 6 |
| Jacksonville | 0 | 7 | 0 | 0 | — | 7 |

Jax	—	Wilford 12 pass from Leftwich (Scobee kick)
Den	—	FG Elam 44
Den	—	FG Elam 22

CAROLINA 28, KANSAS CITY 17—at Arrowhead Stadium, attendance 78,136. Jake Delhomme passed for 3 touchdowns and DeShaun Foster rushed for 174 yards and a score, as the Panthers rallied to defeat the Chiefs. Carolina took a 14-10 lead on a 16-play, 80-yard drive to begin the second half, but Eric Warfield intercepted Delhomme's pass and returned it 43 yards for a touchdown with 3:34 left in the third quarter to give the Chiefs a 17-14 lead. The Panthers responded with touchdown drives of 56 and 74 yards on their next two possessions, the latter set up by Foster's 71-yard run, for a 28-17 lead with 10:35 left. Chris Gamble thwarted one possession with an interception, and Derrick

Blaylock was stopped 1-yard shy of a first down on fourth-and-3 near midfield with 4:18 left. Delhomme was 16 of 29 for 180 yards and 3 touchdowns, with 2 interceptions. Foster rushed 32 times for 174 yards. Trent Green was 17 of 34 for 187 yards, with 1 interception.

| Carolina | 7 | 0 | 7 | 14 | — | 28 |
| Kansas City | 3 | 7 | 7 | 0 | — | 17 |

KC	—	FG Tynes 33
Car	—	Mangum 3 pass from Delhomme (Kasay kick)
KC	—	Holmes 1 run (Tynes kick)
Car	—	Colbert 9 pass from Delhomme (Kasay kick)
KC	—	Warfield 43 interception return (Tynes kick)
Car	—	Seidman 1 pass from Delhomme (Kasay kick)
Car	—	Foster 3 run (Kasay kick)

NEW ORLEANS 30, SAN FRANCISCO 27—at Louisiana Superdome, attendance 64,900. Aaron Brooks completed a 16-yard touchdown pass to Donte' Stallworth with 1:01 remaining as the Saints defeated the 49ers. Kevan Barlow capped a 78-yard drive with a touchdown just before halftime to pull within 20-17. The Saints extended their lead with a field goal to begin the second half, and Todd Peterson responded with a field goal, and Jamal Robertson's 1-yard run capped a 94-yard drive to give the 49ers a 27-23 lead with 7:07 to play. Jay Bellamy recovered Robertson's fumble with 3:42 to play, and Brooks completed 4 of 6 passes to drive to the 49ers' 16. On second-and-10, Stallworth caught a 16-yard touchdown pass with 1:01 left. Ashley Ambrose intercepted Ken Dorsey's pass at the Saints' 34 with four seconds left to clinch the victory. Brooks was 25 of 34 for 279 yards and 3 touchdowns. Stallworth had 9 receptions for 113 yards. Dorsey was 18 of 32 for 205 yards, with 1 interception. Barlow rushed 20 times for 114 yards, and Curtis Conway had 8 catches for 112 yards.

| San Francisco | 3 | 14 | 3 | 7 | — | 27 |
| New Orleans | 10 | 10 | 3 | 7 | — | 30 |

SF	—	FG Peterson 30
NO	—	Horn 8 pass from Brooks (Carney kick)
NO	—	FG Carney 32
SF	—	Barlow 10 run (Peterson kick)
NO	—	Pathon 37 pass from Brooks (Carney kick)
NO	—	FG Carney 36
SF	—	Barlow 1 run (Peterson kick)
NO	—	FG Carney 37
SF	—	FG Peterson 33
SF	—	Robertson 1 run (Peterson kick)
NO	—	Stallworth 16 pass from Brooks (Carney kick)

N.Y. GIANTS 20, WASHINGTON 14—at Giants Stadium, attendance 78,767. Kurt Warner passed for 232 yards and 1 touchdown, and the Giants' defense forced 7 turnovers as the Giants defeated the Redskins. With the score 7-7 in the second quarter, Shaun Williams forced Clinton Portis to fumble. Barrett Green recovered the ball and returned it 16 yards for a touchdown and 14-7 lead. Two plays later, Fred Robbins intercepted Mark Brunell's pass to set up Steve Christie's first field goal. Following a three-and-out, Christie added a second field goal with 37 seconds left in the half for a 20-7 halftime lead. Portis caught a 13-yard touchdown pass from Patrick Ramsey early in the fourth quarter, and Todd Franz recovered Willie Ponder's fumble near midfield on the ensuing kickoff. But five plays later Gibril Wilson intercepted Ramsey's pass at the Giants' 10. The Giants' defense failed to allow a first down in the Redskins' own territory with 1:24 left to ensure the victory. Warner was 22 of 33 for 232 yards and 1 touchdown. Coles had 6 receptions for 100 yards. Mark Brunell was 10 of 18 for 92 yards and 1 touchdown, with 1 interception. Ramsey was 9 of 18 for

142 yards and 1 touchdown, with 3 interceptions.

| Washington | 7 | 0 | 0 | 7 | — | 14 |
| N.Y. Giants | 0 | 20 | 0 | 0 | — | 20 |

Wash	—	Cooley 2 pass from Brunell (Hall kick)
NYG	—	Carter 38 pass from Warner (Christie kick)
NYG	—	Green 16 fumble return (Christie kick)
NYG	—	FG Christie 38
NYG	—	FG Christie 22
Wash	—	Portis 13 pass from Ramsey (Hall kick)

OAKLAND 13, BUFFALO 10—at Network Associates Coliseum, attendance 53,610. Rich Gannon passed for 1 touchdown and Sebastian Janikowski added 2 field goals for the Raiders. Rich Gannon's 43-yard touchdown pass to Ronald Curry gave the Raiders a 7-0 lead. Leading 7-3 at halftime, Ray Buchanan intercepted Drew Bledsoe's pass to set up Janikowski's first field goal. The Bills had a chance to tie the game on the first play of the fourth quarter, but Travis Henry was stopped by Charles Woodson and Terdell Sands. Janikowski added a 33-yard field goal with 2:27 remaining. A 65-yard pass from Drew Bledsoe to Lee Evans set up Eric Moulds' 5-yard touchdown catch with 1:20 left, but Jerry Porter recovered Rian Lindell's onside kick with 1:20 remaining. Gannon was 19 of 27 for 209 yards and 1 touchdown. Bledsoe was 13 of 24 for 198 yards and 1 touchdown, with 1 interception.

| Buffalo | 0 | 3 | 0 | 7 | — | 10 |
| Oakland | 0 | 7 | 3 | 3 | — | 13 |

Oak	—	Curry 43 pass from Gannon (Janikowski kick)
Buff	—	FG Lindell 32
Oak	—	FG Janikowski 21
Oak	—	FG Janikowski 33
Buff	—	Moulds 5 pass from Bledsoe (Lindell kick)

N.Y. JETS 34, SAN DIEGO 28—at Qualcomm Stadium, attendance 57,310. Curtis Martin rushed for 119 yards and 2 touchdowns as the Jets held onto a 20-point lead to defeat the Chargers. The Jets' defense forced 4 turnovers, which resulted into 17 points. The Jets drove 80 yards for a touchdown with their first possession, and an interception by Erik Coleman set up a 44-yard drive for a 14-0 lead. A fumble recovery by Eric Barton led to Doug Brien's field goal and a 17-0 lead, but Tim Dwight returned the ensuing kickoff 87 yards for a touchdown. The Jets scored on their first two possessions of the second half, the latter set up by Jon McGraw's interception, to take a 27-7 lead with 3:31 left in the third quarter. The Chargers scored twice to cut the deficit to 27-21 with 7:38 to play. Chad Pennington completed a 48-yard pass to Santana Moss to the Chargers' 3, and Pennington's 1-yard touchdown pass to Chris Baker increased the lead to 34-21 with 3:56 remaining. Doug Flutie entered the game and engineered an 18-play, 81-yard touchdown drive, capped by Flutie's 6-yard run with 30 seconds left, but Shayne Chrebet recovered the ensuing onside kick. Pennington was 22 of 29 for 258 yards and 2 touchdowns. Martin rushed 32 times for 119 yards. Drew Brees was 8 of 19 for 146 yards. Flutie was 7 of 16 for 77 yards.

| N.Y. Jets | 14 | 3 | 10 | 7 | — | 34 |
| San Diego | 0 | 7 | 14 | 7 | — | 28 |

NYJ	—	Martin 1 run (Brien kick)
NYJ	—	Martin 2 run (Brien kick)
NYJ	—	FG Brien 28
SD	—	Dwight 87 kickoff return (Kaeding kick)
NYJ	—	FG Brien 23
NYJ	—	Sowell 4 pass from Pennington (Brien kick)
SD	—	Tomlinson 4 run (Kaeding kick)
SD	—	Caldwell 33 pass from Brees (Kaeding kick)

NYJ	—	Baker 1 pass from Pennington (Brien kick)
SD	—	Flutie 6 run (Kaeding kick)

SEATTLE 10, TAMPA BAY 6—at Raymond James Stadium, attendance 65,089. Matt Hasselbeck passed for the game's lone touchdown in the second quarter as the Seahawks held off the Buccaneers. The Buccaneers' defense allowed just 9 first downs, but the Seahawks drove just 24 yards for a Josh Brown field goal, and Marcus Trufant's interceptions and return to the Buccaneers' 29 set up Koren Robinson's 27-yard touchdown catch for a 10-0 lead early in the second quarter. The Buccaneers, trailing 10-3, drove to the Seahawks' 6 with 6:10 remaining, but an incompletion, sack, and 2-yard pass set up fourth-and-goal from the Seahawks' 9. Martin Gramatica kicked a 27-yard field goal with 4:35 left, and the defense forced another punt. The Buccaneers' offense reached the Seahawks' 26 with 1:11 left, but Michael Boulware intercepted Chris Simms' pass. Hasselbeck was 12 of 26 for 147 yards and 1 touchdown, with 1 interception. Brad Johnson was 4 of 7 for 34 yards, with 1 interception, before being removed following Trufant's interception. Chris Simms replaced him and was 21 of 32 for 175 yards, with 1 interception.

| Seattle | 0 | 3 | 7 | 0 | — | 10 |
| Tampa Bay | 0 | 3 | 0 | 3 | — | 6 |

Sea	—	FG J. Brown 44
Sea	—	Robinson 27 pass from Hasselbeck (J. Brown kick)
TB	—	FG Gramatica 24
TB	—	FG Gramatica 27

INDIANAPOLIS 31, TENNESSEE 17—at The Coliseum, attendance 68,932. Edgerrin James rushed for 124 yards and 2 fourth-quarter touchdowns as the Colts rallied to defeat the Titans. The Titans led 10-3 at halftime, but could have led by more except Chris Brown was stopped on fourth-and-1 at the Colts' 4 in the second quarter to thwart a scoring opportunity. The Colts took the second half's opening kickoff and drove 75 yards, capped by Peyton Manning's 5-yard touchdown pass to Reggie Wayne. The Titans needed just six plays to retake the lead on Steve McNair's 1-yard dive, but the Colts tied the game on the first play of the fourth quarter. The Titans drove to the Colts' 27, but McNair's fourth-and-2 pass was intercepted by Nick Harper. Manning's 34-yard pass to Marvin Harrison highlighted the ensuing 11-play, 80-yard drive, capped by James' 4-yard touchdown with 7:31 to play. Following a punt, James scored on a 30-yard run with 2:22 to play. The Titans drove to the Colts' 19, but Brad Scioli forced McNair to fumble and Robert Mathis recovered to clinch the victory. Manning was 24 of 33 for 254 yards and 2 touchdowns. Harrison had 10 catches for 98 yards, and Wayne had 7 receptions for 119 yards. McNair was 25 of 39 for 273 yards, with 1 interception. Derrick Mason had 8 catches for 104 yards, and Brown added 26 carries for 152 yards.

| Indianapolis | 3 | 0 | 7 | 21 | — | 31 |
| Tennessee | 7 | 3 | 7 | 0 | — | 17 |

Tenn	—	C. Brown 20 run (Anderson kick)
Ind	—	FG Vanderjagt 28
Tenn	—	FG Anderson 39
Ind	—	Wayne 5 pass from Manning (Vanderjagt kick)
Tenn	—	McNair 1 run (Anderson kick)
Ind	—	Pollard 1 pass from Manning (Vanderjagt kick)
Ind	—	James 4 run (Vanderjagt kick)
Ind	—	James 30 run (Vanderjagt kick)

SUNDAY NIGHT, SEPTEMBER 19
CINCINNATI 16, MIAMI 13—at Paul Brown Stadium, attendance 65,705. The Dolphins led 3-0 early in the third quarter when Brian Simmons intercepted a pass and returned it 50 yards for a touchdown. Shayne Graham added 2 field goals, as the Bengals'

defense forced 5 consecutive punts, to take a 13-3 lead with less than six minutes remaining in the game. A.J. Feeley's 4-yard scoring pass to Chris Chambers cut the deficit to 13-10 with 3:39 left. The Dolphins' defense forced a three-and-out, and Lamont Brightful returned the punt 36 yards to set up Olindo Mare's game-tying 47-yard field goal with 1:53 left. Carson Palmer, in just his second NFL start, completed 6 consecutive passes, highlighted by a 13-yard pass to T.J. Houshmandzadeh, that led to Shayne Graham's 39-yard field goal with two seconds left. Palmer was 21 of 38 for 147 yards, with 1 interception. Feeley was 21 of 39 for 218 yards and 1 touchdown, with 2 interceptions.

| Miami | 0 | 3 | 0 | 10 | — | 13 |
| Cincinnati | 0 | 0 | 13 | 3 | — | 16 |

Mia	—	FG Mare 43
Cin	—	Simmons 50 interception return (Graham kick)
Cin	—	FG Graham 48
Cin	—	FG Graham 36
Mia	—	Chambers 4 pass from Feeley (Mare kick)
Mia	—	FG Mare 47
Cin	—	FG Graham 39

MONDAY NIGHT, SEPTEMBER 20
PHILADELPHIA 27, MINNESOTA 16—at Lincoln Financial Field, attendance 67,676. Donovan McNabb passed for 2 touchdowns and ran for another as the Eagles defeated the Vikings. Both teams scored on their first two possessions to give the Eagles a 10-6 lead. The Vikings drove to the Eagles' 2, but Nate Wayne forced Culpepper to fumble and Brian Dawkins recovered the ball with 48 seconds left. McNabb outran three defenders on his early fourth-quarter scramble to take a 17-6 lead. The Vikings tried to comeback, but Morten Andersen's 44-yard field goal with 9:14 left fell short, and McNabb fired a 45-yard touchdown pass to Terrell Owens with 7:40 remaining. Culpepper's 4-yard touchdown pass to Randy Moss pulled the Vikings within 24-16 with 3:32 left. The Vikings kicked deep, but J.R. Reed returned the kick 43 yards to set up David Akers' 47-yard field goal with 1:11 to play. McNabb was 18 of 28 for 245 yards and 2 touchdowns. Culpepper was 37 of 47 for 343 yards and 1 touchdown, with 1 interception.

| Minnesota | 3 | 3 | 3 | 7 | — | 16 |
| Philadelphia | 7 | 3 | 7 | 10 | — | 27 |

Minn	—	FG Andersen 42
Phil	—	Smith 11 pass from McNabb (Akers kick)
Minn	—	FG Andersen 19
Phil	—	FG Akers 37
Phil	—	McNabb 20 run (Akers kick)
Minn	—	FG Andersen 19
Phil	—	Owens 45 pass from McNabb (Akers kick)
Minn	—	Moss 4 pass from Culpepper (Andersen kick)
Phil	—	FG Akers 47

THIRD WEEK SUMMARIES
American Football Conference

East Division	W	L	T	Pct.	Pts.	OP
New England	2	0	0	1.000	50	36
N.Y. Jets	2	0	0	1.000	65	52
Buffalo	0	2	0	.000	20	26
Miami	0	3	0	.000	23	46

North Division	W	L	T	Pct.	Pts.	OP
Baltimore	2	1	0	.667	56	42
Pittsburgh	2	1	0	.667	50	54
Cincinnati	1	2	0	.333	49	67
Cleveland	1	2	0	.333	42	49

South Division	W	L	T	Pct.	Pts.	OP
Jacksonville	3	0	0	1.000	35	28
Indianapolis	2	1	0	.667	100	75
Houston	1	2	0	.333	60	76
Tennessee	1	2	0	.333	46	53

West Division	W	L	T	Pct.	Pts.	OP
Denver	2	1	0	.667	63	44

2004 WEEK BY WEEK

	W	L	T	Pct.	Pts.	OP
Oakland	2	1	0	.667	64	54
San Diego	1	2	0	.333	68	77
Kansas City	0	3	0	.000	62	86

National Football Conference

East Division	W	L	T	Pct.	Pts.	OP
Philadelphia	3	0	0	1.000	88	46
Dallas	2	1	0	.667	57	65
N.Y. Giants	2	1	0	.667	64	55
Washington	1	2	0	.333	48	51
North Division	**W**	**L**	**T**	**Pct.**	**Pts.**	**OP**
Detroit	2	1	0	.667	61	62
Minnesota	2	1	0	.667	78	66
Chicago	1	2	0	.333	59	57
Green Bay	1	2	0	.333	65	80
South Division	**W**	**L**	**T**	**Pct.**	**Pts.**	**OP**
Atlanta	3	0	0	1.000	61	39
New Orleans	2	1	0	.667	65	73
Carolina	1	1	0	.500	42	41
Tampa Bay	0	3	0	.000	36	56
West Division	**W**	**L**	**T**	**Pct.**	**Pts.**	**OP**
Seattle	3	0	0	1.000	65	13
St. Louis	1	2	0	.333	59	72
Arizona	0	3	0	.000	25	46
San Francisco	0	3	0	.000	46	85

SUNDAY, SEPTEMBER 26

ATLANTA 6, ARIZONA 3—at Georgia Dome, attendance 70,534. The Falcons' defense forced 4 turnovers, including 3 inside the Red Zone in the second half, but had to overcome 4 turnovers of their own to remain undefeated. Jay Feely's field goals capped two of Atlanta's first three possessions, but Karlos Dansby recovered Michael Vick's fumble at the Cardinals' 4 just before halftime to limit the Falcons to a 6-0 lead. In the third quarter, on third-and-four from the Falcons' 8, Rod Coleman forced Josh McCown to fumble and Ed Jasper recovered. Facing second-and-goal from the Falcons' 6 early in the fourth quarter, Brady Smith forced McCown to fumble. Travis Hall recovered, but Adrian Wilson intercepted Vick's pass two plays later to set up Neil Rackers' 30-yard field goal with 9:24 left. Duane Starks recovered Warrick Dunn's fumble at the Cardinals' 19 with 3:19 remaining, but Karl Williams fumbled two plays later and Bryan Scott recovered at 2:26 left. Vick was 10 of 20 for 115 yards, with 1 interception. Dunn rushed 20 times for 117 yards. Patrick Kerney had 3 of the Falcons' 6 sacks. McCown was 20 of 26 for 198 yards, and Shaun King was 5 of 6 for 40 yards.

Arizona	0	0	0	3	—	3
Atlanta	3	3	0	0	—	6

Atl	—	FG Feely 25
Atl	—	FG Feely 23
Ariz	—	FG Rackers 30

BALTIMORE 23, CINCINNATI 9—at Paul Brown Stadium, attendance 65,575. Jamal Lewis rushed for 186 yards and 1 touchdown, and the Ravens' defense forced 4 turnovers to hold off the Bengals. A 63-yard punt return by B.J. Sams led to Kyle Boller's 10-yard scoring pass, and the first of Ed Reed's 2 interceptions set up Boller's 38-yard touchdown pass to Randy Hymes just before halftime for a 17-3 lead. The Bengals added field goals on consecutive possessions, and Nate Webster's sack and fumble recovery set up Shayne Graham's third field goal to cut the deficit to 17-9 with 9:03 remaining. On the next play from scrimmage, Lewis found a seam on the left side of the line and raced 75 yards for a touchdown. Kyle Boller was 11 of 18 for 126 yards and 1 touchdown, and Lewis rushed 18 times for 186 yards. Palmer was 25 of 52 for 316 yards, with 3 interceptions. T.J. Houshmandzadeh had 7 receptions for 116 yards.

Baltimore	10	7	0	6	—	23
Cincinnati	0	3	3	3	—	9

Balt	—	FG Stover 21
Balt	—	Boller 7 run (Stover kick)
Balt	—	Hymes 38 pass from Boller (Stover kick)
Cin	—	FG Graham 29
Cin	—	FG Graham 47
Cin	—	FG Graham 26
Balt	—	J. Lewis 75 run (pass failed)

DENVER 23, SAN DIEGO 13—at INVESCO Field at Mile High, attendance 75,533. Jake Plummer passed for 2 touchdowns and the Broncos' defense allowed just 214 yards to defeat the Chargers. The Broncos led 13-3 in the third quarter when Randall Godfrey's fumble recovery at the broncos' 36 led to Drew Brees' 1-yard touchdown run. The Broncos drove to the Chargers' 33 with their next possession but were faced with fourth-and-9. Denver went for it and Plummer completed a 33-yard touchdown pass to Ashley Lelie. The Chargers answered with a field goal, but Reuben Droughns' 48-yard kickoff return set up Jason Elam's 43-yard field goal with 11:12 to play. Plummer was 25 of 36 for 294 yards and 2 touchdowns. Brees was 14 of 29 for 121 yards.

San Diego	3	0	7	3	—	13
Denver	7	6	7	3	—	23

Den	—	Smith 16 pass from Plummer (Elam kick)
SD	—	FG Kaeding 23
Den	—	FG Elam 22
Den	—	FG Elam 23
SD	—	Brees 1 run (Kaeding kick)
Den	—	Lelie 33 pass from Plummer (Elam kick)
SD	—	FG Kaeding 51
Den	—	FG Elam 43

PHILADELPHIA 30, DETROIT 13—at Ford Field, attendance 62,472. Donovan McNabb passed for 356 yards and 2 touchdowns as the Eagles downed the Lions. The Eagles scored on three consecutive first-half possessions, with drive of 88 and 87 yards sandwiched around a 29-yard, 1-play drive set up by Rodrick Hood's fumble recovery, to stake the Eagles to a 21-0 lead. Three second-half David Akers field goals increased the lead to 30-7 with 10:22 to play. McNabb was 29 of 42 for 356 yards and 2 touchdowns. Terrell Owens had 6 receptions for 107 yards. Joey Harrington was 21 of 38 for 199 yards and 2 touchdowns. Roy Williams had 9 receptions for 135 yards.

Philadelphia	14	7	6	3	—	30
Detroit	0	7	0	6	—	13

Phil	—	McNabb 1 run (Akers kick)
Phil	—	Owens 29 pass from McNabb (Akers kick)
Phil	—	Bartrum 1 pass from McNabb (Akers kick)
Det	—	R. Williams 12 pass from Harrington (Hanson kick)
Phil	—	FG Akers 26
Phil	—	FG Akers 47
Phil	—	FG Akers 39
Det	—	R. Williams 29 pass from Harrington (pass failed)

INDIANAPOLIS 45, GREEN BAY 31—at RCA Dome, attendance 57,280. Peyton Manning passed for 5 touchdowns, all in the first half, as the Colts outlasted the Packers. The teams combined for 910 yards. The Colts scored on their first four possessions, on drives of 66, 60, 72, and 94 yards to take a 28-14 lead with 13:43 left in the first half. Ryan Longwell made a 38-yard field goal, but missed a 52-yard kick and the Colts responded with a 57-yard drive capped by Manning's 1-yard scoring pass to James Mungro with 57 seconds left in the half. Brett Favre began the second half with a 65-yard drive that culminated in a Javon Walker's 12-yard touchdown catch. Following Mike Vanderjagt's 45-yard field goal early in the fourth quarter, Robert Ferguson's ensuing 71-yard kickoff return led to Donald Driver's 20-yard scoring catch to pull the Packers within 38-31 with 13:12 to play. With 6:07 left, Walker fumbled near midfield and Nick Harper recovered. Nine plays later Edgerrin James scored with 1:49 remaining to ice the game. Manning was 28 of 40 for 393 yards and 5 touchdowns. Reggie Wayne had 11 receptions for 184 yards, and Brandon Stokley had 8 catches for 110 yards. Favre was 30 of 44 for 358 yards and 4 touchdowns. Walker had 11 receptions for 198 yards.

Green Bay	14	3	7	7	—	31
Indianapolis	21	14	0	10	—	45

Ind	—	Wayne 36 pass from Manning (Vanderjagt kick)
GB	—	Walker 36 pass from Favre (Longwell kick)
Ind	—	Harrison 28 pass from Manning (Vanderjagt kick)
GB	—	Walker 79 pass from Favre (Longwell kick)
Ind	—	Stokley 34 pass from Manning (Vanderjagt kick)
Ind	—	Stokley 37 pass from Manning (Vanderjagt kick)
GB	—	FG Longwell 38
Ind	—	Mungro 1 pass from Manning (Vanderjagt kick)
GB	—	Walker 12 pass from Favre (Longwell kick)
Ind	—	FG Vanderjagt 45
GB	—	Driver 27 pass from Favre (Longwell kick)
Ind	—	James 1 run (Vanderjagt kick)

HOUSTON 24, KANSAS CITY 21—at Arrowhead Superdome, attendance 77,433. Kris Brown kicked a 49-yard field goal with two seconds remaining as the Texans kept the Chiefs winless. The Chiefs led at halftime and scored on the opening drive of the second half for a 14-6 lead, and then drove to the Texans' 2 on their next possession. But on second-and-goal Trent Green's pass intended for Tony Gonzalez was intercepted by Marcus Coleman, who raced 102 yards for a touchdown. Jonathan Wells' 2-point conversion run tied the game. Early in the fourth quarter, Jason Dunn's 5-yard scoing catch gave the Chiefs the lead, but the Texans answered with a 68-yard drive, highlighted by David Carr's 20-yard pass to Derick Armstrong on third-and-17, and capped by Jabar Gaffney's 9-yard catch to tie the game. The Texans forced a punt, and Armstrong's 35-yard catch to the Chiefs' 30 set up Brown's winning kick. Carr was 13 of 25 for 233 yards and 1 touchdown, with 1 interception. Green was 20 of 31 for 224 yards and 3 touchdowns, with 1 interception. Gonzalez had 8 catches for 106 yards. Priest Holmes carried 32 times for 134 yards.

Houston	0	6	8	10	—	24
Kansas City	7	0	7	7	—	21

KC	—	Gonzalez 14 pass from T. Green (Tynes kick)
Hous	—	FG K. Brown 28
Hous	—	FG K. Brown 49
KC	—	Horn 6 pass from T. Green (Tynes kick)
Hous	—	Coleman 102 interception return (Wells run)
KC	—	Dunn 5 pass from T. Green (Tynes kick)
Hous	—	Gaffney 9 pass from Carr (K. Brown kick)
Hous	—	FG K. Brown 49

MINNESOTA 27, CHICAGO 22—at Metrodome, attendance 64,163. Daunte Culpepper passed for 360 yards and 2 touchdowns as the Vikings held off the Bears. The Bears drove inside the Vikings' red zone with each of their first three possessions, but settled for 2 field goals and lost a fumble to lead just 6-0. The Vikings responded by driving inside the Bears' red zone with six of their next seven possessions, scoring five times, capped by Culpepper's 2-yard touchdown pass to Randy Moss for a 27-15 lead with 5:39 to play. The Bears drove 61 yards with the ensuing kickoff, culminated by Rex Grossman's 6-yard touchdown run with 2:00 left. However, Grossman suffered a season-ending knee injury on the play, so when the Bears forced a punt with 1:36 left, Jonathan Quinn came in and threw 3 incompletions and was sacked on fourth down. Moss had 7 receptions for 119 yards, and Onterrio Smith had 6 catches for 104 yards and rushed for 94 yards. Grossman was 21 of 31 for 248 yards, and Thomas Jones rushed 22 times for 110 yards.

Chicago	3	3	0	16	—	22
Minnesota	0	10	7	10	—	27

Chi	—	FG Edinger 34
Chi	—	FG Edinger 23
Minn	—	Moss 3 pass from Culpepper (Andersen kick)
Minn	—	FG Andersen 42
Minn	—	Culpepper 1 run (Andersen kick)
Chi	—	FG Edinger 32
Minn	—	FG Andersen 24
Chi	—	T. Jones 1 run (pass failed)
Minn	—	Moss 2 pass from Culpepper (Andersen kick)
Chi	—	Grossman 6 run (Edinger kick)

N.Y. GIANTS 27, CLEVELAND 10—at Giants Stadium, attendance 78,521. Tiki Barber rushed for 106 yards and 1 touchdown as the Giants downed the Browns. The Browns trailed 10-0 in the third quarter and drove to the Giants' 5, but Jeff Garcia fumbled and Michael Strahan recovered the ball. Eleven plays later Kurt Warner scored on a 1-yard run to take a 17-0 lead. Following an exchange of field goals, Garcia completed a 3-yard pass to Quincy Morgan with 3:36 to play, but Jack Brewer recovered the ensuing onside kick for the Giants and five plays later Mike Cloud scored on a 5-yard run to cap the scoring. Warner was 19 of 27 for 286 yards. Amani Toomer had 5 receptions for 126 yards, and Barber rushed 23 times for 106 yards. Garcia was 21 of 31 for 180 yards and 1 touchdown, with 1 interception.

Cleveland	0	0	0	10	—	10
N.Y. Giants	3	7	10	7	—	27

NYG	—	Barber 8 run (Christie kick)
NYG	—	FG Christie 43
NYG	—	Warner 1 run (Christie kick)
Cle	—	FG Dawson 49
NYG	—	FG Christie 25
Cle	—	Morgan 3 pass from Garcia (Dawson kick)
NYG	—	Cloud 5 run (Christie kick)

NEW ORLEANS 28, ST. LOUIS 25 (OT)—at Edward Jones Dome, attendance 65,956. John Carney kicked 5 field goals, including a 38-yard field goal at the end of regulation and capped by a 31-yard boot in overtime. The Saints scored on five consecutive possessions spanning the second into the fourth quarter, to take a 22-17 lead with 8:23 to play. The Saints had a chance to increase the lead to eight points, but Carney's 51-yard field-goal attempt with 1:53 left was wide left. Marc Bulger completed 2 key third-down passes, to Dane Looker and Isaac Bruce, to set up Bulger's 19-yard scramble with 28 seconds left. Bulger's 2-point conversion pass to Kevin Curtis was successful, giving the Rams a 25-22 lead. Will Smith fielded the short kickoff and returned it 17 yards to the Saints' 42. Aaron Brooks completed a 25-yard pass to Michael Lewis and a 13-yard pass to Boo Williams, and Carney's 38-yard field goal tied the game. The Saints' defense forced a punt in overtime, and Brooks completed 2 passes to Donte' Stallworth and scrambled 12 yards to set up Carney's winning boot. Brooks was 24 of 41 for 316 yards and 1 touchdown. Aaron Stecker, playing for the injured Deuce McAllister, rushed 18 times for 106 yards. Bulger was 32 of 49 for 358 yards and 1 touchdown. Bruce had 8 receptions for 134 yards.

New Orleans	0	13	3	9	3	— 28
St. Louis	7	3	0	15	0	— 25

StL	—	Holt 32 pass from Bulger (Wilkins kick)
NO	—	FG Carney 52
StL	—	FG Wilkins 53
NO	—	Stecker 42 run (Carney kick)

NO	—	FG Carney 53
NO	—	FG Carney 39
StL	—	Faulk 3 run (Wilkins kick)
NO	—	Horn 9 pass from Brooks (pass failed)
StL	—	Bulger 19 run (Curtis pass from Bulger)
NO	—	FG Carney 38
NO	—	FG Carney 31

SEATTLE 34, SAN FRANCISCO 0—at Qwest Field, attendance 66,709. Shaun Alexander scored 3 touchdowns and the Seahawks' defense allowed just 175 yards and 9 first down to defeat the 49ers. Ken Lucas' interception and return to the Seahawks' 26 set up Josh Brown's 35-yard field goal. Following a punt and 60-yard pass from Matt Hasselbeck to Bobby Engram, Alexander scored on a 1-yard run, and two plays later Chris Woodard recovered a fumble to set up Alexander caught a 3-yard touchdown pass for a 17-0 lead with 2:28 left in the first quarter. Alexander scored again with 1:02 left in the first half, and Itula Mili's 1-yard touchdown catch capped the opening drive of the second half to give Seattle a 31-0 lead. Hasselbeck was 21 of 30 for 254 yards and 2 touchdowns. Ken Lucas had 1 interception and 3 passes defensed. Ken Dorsey was 19 of 32 for 153 yards, with 2 interceptions.

San Francisco	0	0	0	0	—	0
Seattle	17	7	10	0	—	34

Sea	—	FG J. Brown 35
Sea	—	Alexander 1 run (J. Brown kick)
Sea	—	Alexander 3 pass from Hasselbeck (J. Brown kick)
Sea	—	Alexander 1 run (J. Brown kick)
Sea	—	Mili 1 pass from Hasselbeck (J. Brown kick)
Sea	—	FG J. Brown 28

JACKSONVILLE 15, TENNESSEE 12—at The Coliseum, attendance 68,932. Fred Taylor scored on a 1-yard touchdown run with nine seconds left as the Jaguars started 3-0 for the first time since 1998. The Jaguars were forced to punt on their first six possessions, but trailed just 6-0. Taylor's 25-yard run highlighted a 73-yard third-quarter drive, capped by Byron Leftwich's 7-yard touchdown pass to George Wrighster to give Jacksonville a 7-6 lead. Following an exchange of punts, the Titans drove 74 yards, keyed by 3 third-down conversions, including 2 scrambles by Steve McNair, to set up Chris Brown's 26-yard run for a 12-7 lead with 5:37 to play. The Jaguars completed 2 third downs and Greg Jones ran 3 yards on fourth-and-1 as the Jaguars reached the Titans' 17 with 46 seconds left. A pass interference penalty put the ball at the Titans' 1. Taylor was stopped for no gain on first down, but scored on a run to the right side with nine seconds left. Leftwich was 14 of 20 for 124 yards and 1 touchdown. Rashean Mathis had 1 interception, 1 forced fumble, and 2 passes defensed. McNair was 16 of 26 for 143 yards, with 1 interception. Brown rushed 23 times for 101 yards.

Jacksonville	0	0	7	8	—	15
Tennessee	0	6	0	6	—	12

Tenn	—	FG Anderson 26
Tenn	—	FG Anderson 40
Jax	—	Wrighster 7 pass from Leftwich (Scobee kick)
Tenn	—	Brown 26 run (pass failed)
Jax	—	Taylor 1 run (R. Williams pass from Leftwich)

SUNDAY NIGHT, SEPTEMBER 26
OAKLAND 30, TAMPA BAY 20—at Network Associates Coliseum, attendance 60,874. Reserve Kerry Collins passed for 228 yards and 1 touchdown as the Raiders jumped to a 30-6 lead en route to victory. Collins, playing in place of Rich Gannon, who suffered a season-ending neck injury in the first quarter, took over on the second possession and guided the Raiders 53 yards to set up Sebastian

Janikowski's 40-yard field goal to take a 6-3 lead. With the score tied 6-6, Collins was 7 for 7 on a 10-play, 84-yard drive, capped by his 19-yard pass to Ronald Curry with 1:16 left in the half. Janikowski kicked a field goal to culminate the opening drive of the second half, and three plays later Phillip Buchanon intercepted a pass and returned it 32 yards for a touchdown and 23-6 lead. Tyrone Wheatley's touchdown on the next possession increased the lead to 30-6. Collins was 16 of 27 for 228 yards and 1 touchdown, with 1 interception. Wheatley rushed 18 times for 102 yards. Brad Johnson was 22 of 36 for 309 yards and 2 touchdowns, with 1 interception. Bill Schroeder had 4 catches for 126 yards.

Tampa Bay	3	3	0	14	—	20
Oakland	3	10	17	0	—	30

TB	—	FG Gramatica 36
Oak	—	FG Janikowski 23
Oak	—	FG Janikowski 40
TB	—	FG Gramatica 30
Oak	—	Curry 19 pass from Collins (Janikowski kick)
Oak	—	FG Janikowski 39
Oak	—	Buchanon 32 interception return (Janikowski kick)
Oak	—	Wheatley 2 run (Janikowski kick)
TB	—	Brown 16 pass from B. Johnson (pass failed)
TB	—	Schroeder 41 pass from B. Johnson (Dilger pass from B. Johnson)

PITTSBURGH 13, MIAMI 3—at Pro Player Stadium, attendance 72,225. Ben Roethlisberger, making his first NFL start, passed for 1 touchdown as the Steelers defeated the Dolphins. The game was played in a downpour, and the start was moved back 7 1/2 hours to miss the eye of Hurricane Jeanne. The Steelers' defense allowed just 169 yards and forced 4 turnovers. Roethlisberger's first pass was intercepted, but Ike Taylor intercepted A.J. Feeley moments later to set up Jeff Reed's 40-yard field goal. Reed missed 44- and 45-yard field goals in the treacherous footing, but connected from 51 yards in the third quarter. The Dolphins did not run a play inside the Steelers' 40 until the fourth quarter, and settled for Olindo Mare's 34-yard field goal with 13:25 to play to pull within 6-3. After an exchange of punts, the Steelers drove 61 yards, keyed by Roethlisberger's 18-yard pass to Plaxico Burress on third-and-12 and his 20-yard pass to Hines Ward on third-and-4, and capped by Ward's 7-yard touchdown catch with 6:16 to play. The Dolphins drove to the Steelers' 29, but Joey Porter forced Feeley to fumble, and James Farrior recovered to clinch the victory. Roethlisberger was 12 of 22 for 163 yards and 1 touchdown, with 1 interception. Staley rushed 22 times for 101 yards. Feeley was 13 of 27 for 137 yards, with 2 interceptions.

Pittsburgh	3	0	3	7	—	13
Miami	0	0	0	3	—	3

Pitt	—	FG Reed 40
Pitt	—	FG Reed 51
Mia	—	FG Mare 34
Pitt	—	Ward 7 pass from Roethlisberger (Reed kick)

MONDAY NIGHT, SEPTEMBER 27
DALLAS 21, WASHINGTON 18—at FedExField, attendance 90,367. Richie Anderson halfback-option 26-yard touchdown pass to Terry Glenn, and the Cowboys' defense recorded 5 sacks, to help the Cowboys defeat the Redskins. In the third quarter, Vinny Testaverde's 48-yard pass to Antonio Bryant set up his 10-yard scoring pass to Jason Witten for a 14-3 lead. The Redskins answered with a 14-play, 62-yard drive capped by Rod Gardner's 1-yard touchdown catch. After an exchange of punts, on first-and-10 from the Redskins' 38, Anderson took a handoff and rolled right and completed a touchdown pass to Glenn. Gardner's second scoring catch with

4:30 remaining cut the deficit to 21-18, but did not get the ball back until their were just 21 seconds left and no time outs. Mark Brunell completed a 46-yard Hail Mary pass to Gardner, who caught the ball in bounds at the Cowboys' 21, but time expired. Testaverde was 14 of 29 for 214 yards and 1 touchdown. Brunell was 25 of 43 for 325 yards and 2 touchdowns. Gardner had 10 catches for 167 yards.

Dallas	7	0	7	7	— 21
Washington	0	3	7	8	— 18

Dall	—	George 1 run (Cundiff kick)
Wash	—	FG Hall 19
Dall	—	Witten 10 pass from Testaverde (Cundiff kick)
Wash	—	Gardner 1 pass from Brunell (Hall kick)
Dall	—	Glenn 26 pass from Anderson (Cundiff kick)
Wash	—	Gardner 15 pass from Brunell (Jacobs pass from Brunell)

FOURTH WEEK SUMMARIES
American Football Conference

East Division	W	L	T	Pct.	Pts.	OP
New England	3	0	0	1.000	81	53
N.Y. Jets	3	0	0	1.000	82	61
Buffalo	0	3	0	.000	37	57
Miami	0	4	0	.000	32	63
North Division	W	L	T	Pct.	Pts.	OP
Pittsburgh	3	1	0	.750	78	71
Baltimore	2	2	0	.500	80	69
Cleveland	2	2	0	.500	59	62
Cincinnati	1	3	0	.250	66	95
South Division	W	L	T	Pct.	Pts.	OP
Indianapolis	3	1	0	.750	124	92
Jacksonville	3	1	0	.750	52	52
Houston	2	2	0	.500	90	93
Tennessee	1	3	0	.250	63	91
West Division	W	L	T	Pct.	Pts.	OP
Denver	3	1	0	.750	79	57
Oakland	2	2	0	.500	81	84
San Diego	2	2	0	.500	106	94
Kansas City	1	3	0	.333	89	110

National Football Conference

East Division	W	L	T	Pct.	Pts.	OP
Philadelphia	4	0	0	1.000	107	55
N.Y. Giants	3	1	0	.750	78	62
Dallas	2	1	0	.667	57	65
Washington	1	3	0	.250	61	68
North Division	W	L	T	Pct.	Pts.	OP
Detroit	2	1	0	.667	61	62
Minnesota	2	1	0	.667	78	66
Chicago	1	3	0	.250	68	76
Green Bay	1	3	0	.250	72	94
South Division	W	L	T	Pct.	Pts.	OP
Atlanta	4	0	0	1.000	88	49
New Orleans	2	2	0	.500	75	107
Carolina	1	2	0	.500	52	68
Tampa Bay	0	4	0	.000	49	72
West Division	W	L	T	Pct.	Pts.	OP
Seattle	3	0	0	1.000	65	13
St. Louis	2	2	0	.500	83	86
Arizona	1	3	0	.250	59	56
San Francisco	0	4	0	.000	60	109

SUNDAY, OCTOBER 3

ARIZONA 34, NEW ORLEANS 10—at Sun Devil Stadium, attendance 28,109. Emmitt Smith rushed for 127 yards and one touchdown, and threw his first career touchdown pass, as the Cardinals wore down the Saints in 93 degree weather. Smith rushed 21 times for 127 yards and set an NFL record with his seventy-seventh 100-yard rushing game. The Saints drove to the Cardinals' 1 on the opening drive, but Brooks fumbled and Gerald Hayes recovered for a touchback. Later in the first quarter, Aaron Stecker fumbled and Adrian Wilson recovered the ball and raced 35 yards for a touchdown. With Arizona leading 7-3, Smith took a handoff and completed a 21-yard touchdown pass to Obafemi Ayanbadejo with 1:12 left in the half for a 14-3 lead. The Saints pulled within 14-10 early in the third quarter when Steve

Gleason blocked Scott Player's punt and Mel Mitchell recovered the ball in the end zone, the Saints' first blocked punt for a touchdown in 27 years. Arizona led 20-10 with 5:10, and on third-and-3, Smith ran 29 yards up the middle for a touchdown and 27-10 lead. Josh McCown was 12 of 18 for 157 yards. Smith rushed 21 times for 127 yards. Brooks was 24 of 40 for 242 yards.

New Orleans	0	3	7	0	— 10
Arizona	7	7	3	17	— 34

Ariz	—	Wilson 35 fumble return (Rackers kick)
NO	—	FG Carney 20
Ariz	—	Ayanbadejo 21 pass from E. Smith (Rackers kick)
NO	—	Mitchell blocked punt recovery in end zone (Carney kick)
Ariz	—	FG Rackers 26
Ariz	—	FG Rackers 33
Ariz	—	E. Smith 29 run (Rackers kick)
Ariz	—	Hambrick 11 run (Rackers kick)

NEW ENGLAND 31, BUFFALO 17—at Ralph Wilson Stadium, attendance 72,698. Tom Brady passed for 2 touchdowns and Richard Seymour returned a fumble 68 yards for a touchdown as the Patriots won their fifteenth consecutive game. In the second quarter, with the score tied 10-10, Chris Kelsay recovered Corey Dillon's fumble at the Bills' 4. Six plays later, Drew Bledsoe completed a 41-yard touchdown pass to Eric Moulds. With 2:43 left in the half, the 14-point swing gave the Bills a 17-10 lead. The Patriots need just six plays to tie the game on Brady's 30-yard touchdown pass to David Patten. Early in the fourth quarter, Adam Vinatieri made a 31-yard field goal, but the Bills were flagged for offsides. New England took the field goal off the board, and Brady's touchdown pass to Daniel Graham two plays later gave the Patriots a 24-17 lead with 11:17 left. With 2:59 remaining, the Bills faced fourth-and-3 on the Patriots' 17. Bledsoe was sacked by Tedy Bruschi and fumbled. Seymour picked up the ball and ran 68 yards for a touchdown. Brady was 17 of 30 for 298 yards and 2 touchdowns. Patten had 4 receptions for 113 yards. Bruschi had 2 sacks and 1 forced fumble. Bledsoe was 18 of 30 for 247 yards and 1 touchdown, with 1 interception. Moulds had 10 catches for 126 yards.

New England	10	7	14	— 31
Buffalo	10	7	0	0	— 17

NE	—	Dillon 15 run (Vinatieri kick)
Buff	—	FG Lindell 33
NE	—	FG Vinatieri 42
Buff	—	McGee 98 kickoff return (Lindell kick)
Buff	—	Moulds 41 pass from Bledsoe (Lindell kick)
NE	—	Patton 30 pass from Brady (Vinatieri kick)
NE	—	Graham 2 pass from Brady (Vinatieri kick)
NE	—	Seymour 68 fumble return (Vinatieri kick)

ATLANTA 27, CAROLINA 10—at Bank of America Stadium, attendance 73,461. Kevin Mathis' 35-yard interception return for a touchdown helped the 4-0 Falcons match their best start in franchise history. The Falcons scored on their first three drives to take a 13-7 lead. John Kasay kicked a 26-yard field goal just before halftime, and the Panthers had the ball early in the fourth quarter when Mathis intercepted Jake Delhomme's pass and returned it 35 yards for a touchdown and 20-10 lead. Allen Rossum's 25-yard punt return later in the quarter set up T.J. Duckett's 4-yard scoring run with 4:13 to play. Michael Vick was 10 of 18 for 148 yards. Delhomme was 23 of 38 for 308 yards, with 2 interceptions. Muhsin Muhammad had 7 receptions for 114 yards.

Atlanta	10	3	0	14	— 27
Carolina	7	3	0	0	— 10

Atl	—	Dunn 38 run (Feely kick)

Car	—	Foster 1 run (Kasay kick)
Atl	—	FG Feely 47
Atl	—	FG Feely 30
Car	—	FG Kasay 26
Atl	—	Mathis 35 interception return (Feely kick)
Atl	—	Duckett 4 run (Feely kick)

PHILADELPHIA 19, CHICAGO 9—at Soldier Field, attendance 61,894. David Akers kicked 4 field goals as the Eagles improved to 4-0 for the first time since 1993. The Eagles held the ball for 37:21. The Eagles scored on four of their last five possessions of the first half to take a 16-0 lead. Trailing 19-3, the Bears drove 70 yards for a touchdown with 3:57 left, but Thomas Jones was stopped on the two-point conversion try. Donovan McNabb was 24 of 38 for 237 yards and 1 touchdown, with 1 interception. Terrell Owens had 8 catches for 110 yards. Brian Westbrook rushed 23 times for 115 yards. Jonathan Quinn, making his first start after the season-ending injury to Rex Grossman the previous week, was 26 of 43 for 215 yards and 1 touchdown. David Terrell had 9 catches for 116 yards.

Philadelphia	3	13	3	0	— 19
Chicago	0	3	0	6	— 9

Phil	—	FG Akers 51
Phil	—	FG Akers 42
Phil	—	Owens 11 pass from McNabb (Akers kick)
Phil	—	FG Akers 42
Chi	—	FG Edinger 25
Phil	—	FG Akers 40
Chi	—	B. Johnson 2 pass from Quinn (run failed)

CLEVELAND 17, WASHINGTON 13—at Cleveland Browns Stadium, attendance 73,348. Lee Suggs scored on a 3-yard run in the fourth quarter as the Browns rallied to hand the Redskins their third consecutive loss. The Redskins led 10-3 at halftime, but Clinton Portis fumbled on the first play of the second half and Michael Myers recovered. Four plays later, Jeff Garcia completed a third-and-6 15-yard touchdown pass to Aaron Shea to tie the game. John Hall's 26-yard field goal two plays in the fourth quarter capped an 80-yard drive and gave the Redskins a 13-10 lead. After and exchange of punts, the Browns drove 80 yards, highlighted by Garcia's 13-yard touchdown pass to Quincy Morgan on third-and-8, and capped by Suggs' scoring run. The Browns attempted a fake field goal from the Redskins' 28 with 2:15 left, but holder Derrick Frost was stopped shy of the first down. Two plays later, Laveranues Coles fumbled and Earl Little recovered to seal the victory. Garcia was 14 of 21 for 195 yards and 1 touchdown. Mark Brunell was 17 of 32 for 192 yards. Coles had 7 catches for 122 yards.

Washington	3	7	0	3	— 13
Cleveland	3	0	7	7	— 17

Wash	—	FG Hall 31
Cle	—	FG Dawson 30
Wash	—	Portis 1 run (Hall kick)
Cle	—	Shea 15 pass from Garcia (Dawson kick)
Wash	—	FG Hall 26
Cle	—	Suggs 3 run (Dawson kick)

N.Y. GIANTS 14, GREEN BAY 7—at Lambeau Field, attendance 70,623. Kurt Warner's fourth-quarter touchdown pass to Jeremy Shockey dropped the Packers to their first 1-3 start since 1993. Brett Favre suffered a slight concussion early in the second half, but two plays later came back onto the field and completed a 28-yard touchdown pass to Javon Walker on fourth-and-5 to give the Packers a 7-0 lead. Favre left the game following the pass and did not return. Two plays later, Tiki Barber beat the blitz and ran for a 52-yard touchdown to tie the game. Barber's 38-yard run early in the fourth quarter set up Shockey's touchdown catch on third-and-goal from the Packers' 4 with 12:07 remaining. Third-string quarterback Craig Nall entered the game for an injured Doug Pederson with 15 seconds left and completed a 24-yard pass to Robert Ferguson at the Giants' 32, but was unable to spike the ball in time for a final play. Warner was 20 of 26 for 187 yards and 1 touchdown, with 1 interception. Favre was 12 of 18 for 110 yards and 1 touchdown, with 1 interception. Doug Pederson was 7 of 17 for 86 yards, with 1 interception.

		1	2	3	4		
N.Y. Giants		0	0	7	7	—	14
Green Bay		0	0	7	0	—	7
GB	—	Walker 28 pass from Favre (Longwell kick)					
NYG	—	Barber 52 run (Christie kick)					
NYG	—	Shockey 4 pass from Warner (Christie kick)					

HOUSTON 30, OAKLAND 17—at Reliant Stadium, attendance 70,741. The Texans' defense forced turnovers on the Raiders' final four possessions, including 2 interceptions by Dunta Robinson, as the Texans won consecutive games for the first time in franchise's three-year history. Tied 3-3 in the second quarter, Jamie Sharper sacked Kerry Collins and forced him to fumble. Sharper picked up the ball and ran 16 yards for a touchdown. Amos Zereoue scored twice later in the quarter to tie the game. Robinson intercepted Collins' pass at the Raiders' 44 in the middle of the third quarter to set up Kris Brown's 21-yard field goal. Collins fumbled a snap on the next drive. Jay Foreman recovered at the Raiders' 30, and David Carr completed a 15-yard scoring pass to Andre Johnson for a 27-17 lead. The Raiders drove to the Texans' 24, and Demarcus Faggins intercepted Collins' pass at the Texans' 1. The Texans responded with a 14-play, 73-yard drive capped by Brown's 44-yard field goal with 3:19 to play. Carr was 14 of 23 for 228 yards and 1 touchdown. Jonathan Wells rushed 26 times for 105 yards, and Johnson had 6 catches for 115 yards. Collins was 21 of 38 for 237 yards, with 3 interceptions. Zereoue rushed 14 times for 117 yards.

		1	2	3	4		
Oakland		3	14	0	0	—	17
Houston		3	14	3	10	—	30
Hous	—	FG K. Brown 46					
Oak	—	FG Janikowski 50					
Hous	—	Sharper 16 fumble return (K. Brown kick)					
Oak	—	Zereoue 55 run (Janikowski kick)					
Hous	—	Wells 1 run (K. Brown kick)					
Oak	—	Zereoue 3 run (Janikowski kick)					
Hous	—	FG K. Brown 21					
Hous	—	Johnson 15 pass from Carr (K. Brown kick)					
Hous	—	FG K. Brown 44					

INDIANAPOLIS 24, JACKSONVILLE 17—at ALLTEL Stadium, attendance 73,114. Peyton Manning passed for 220 yards and 2 touchdowns, and Edgerrin James scored the deciding touchdown with 3:33 left as the Colts snapped the Jaguars' three-game winning streak. The Colts led 10-0 with 40 seconds left in the first half. Byron Leftwich responded by completing 5 consecutive passes to set up Josh Scobee's 48-yard field goal to end the half. The Jaguars scored on their first three possessions of the second half, the last of which was set up by Daryl Smith's interception and capped by Leftwich's 40-yard touchdown pass to Jimmy Smith and 2-point conversion toss to Brian Jones, to tie the game with 10:37 to play. The Colts answered with a 13-play, 74-yard drive capped by Edgerrin James' 3-yard touchdown run, which was preceded one play earlier by Manning's 8-yard pass to Brandon Stokley on third-and-6, to take a 24-17 lead with 3:33 to play. The Jaguars drove to the Colts' 45, but Fred Taylor was stopped for no gain on fourth-and-1 with 1:52 left. Manning was 20 of 29 for 220 yards and 2 touchdowns, with 1 interception. Leftwich was 29 of 41 for 318 yards and 1 touchdown.

		1	2	3	4		
Indianapolis		7	3	7	7	—	24
Jacksonville		0	3	3	11	—	17

Ind	—	Harrison 15 pass from Manning (Vanderjagt kick)
Ind	—	FG Vanderjagt 46
Jax	—	FG Scobee 48
Jax	—	FG Scobee 42
Ind	—	Pollard 16 pass from Manning (Vanderjagt kick)
Jax	—	FG Scobee 22
Jax	—	J. Smith 40 pass from Leftwich (B. Jones pass from Leftwich)
Ind	—	James 3 run (Vanderjagt kick)

N.Y. JETS 17, MIAMI 9—at Pro Player Stadium, attendance 73,157. Curtis Martin rushed for 110 yards and 1 touchdown and Donnie Abraham returned an interception 66 yards for a touchdown as the Jets improved to 3-0 for just the third time in franchise history. The Jets led 10-9 at halftime and increased that thanks to Abraham's 66-yard interception return early in the third quarter. The Jets' offense gained just 5 first downs in the second half, but the defense, which forced 4 turnovers and recorded 4 sacks, did not allow Miami to run a play inside the Jets' 35 in the second half. Jason Ferguson sacked Jay Fiedler and forced him to fumble. John Abraham recovered at the Dolphins' 21 with 1:47 left to seal the victory. Chad Pennington was 14 of 24 for 143 yards, with 1 interception. Martin rushed 24 times for 110 yards. Fiedler was 18 of 33 for 206 yards, with 2 interceptions.

		1	2	3	4		
N.Y. Jets		7	3	7	0	—	17
Miami		0	9	0	0	—	9
NYJ	—	Martin 1 run (Brien kick)					
Mia	—	FG Mare 36					
Mia	—	FG Mare 37					
NYJ	—	FG Brien 53					
Mia	—	FG Mare 23					
NYJ	—	Abraham 66 interception return (Brien kick)					

PITTSBURGH 28, CINCINNATI 17—at Heinz Field, attendance 62,402. Duce Staley rushed for 124 yards and Jerome Bettis scored 2 touchdowns and Troy Polamalu returned an interception with just over two minutes remaining as the Steelers rallied and then held off the Bengals. Trailing 14-10 at halftime, the Bengals engineered a 14-play, 71-yard drive to begin the second half, capped by Rudi Johnson's 2-yard run for a 17-14 lead. The Steelers took the lead with 9:03 left as Bettis' 1-yard run culminated a 13-play, 89-yard drive that featured a 16-yard run by Staley on third-and-1. The Bengals, trailing 21-17, regained possessions with 2:19 left, but on the first play Polamalu intercepted Carson Palmer's pass, and bowled over Palmer at the goal line to score the game's final points. Ben Roethlisberger was 17 of 25 for 174 yards and 1 touchdown. Staley rushed 25 times for 123 yards. Palmer was 20 of 37 for 164 yards and 1 touchdown, with 2 interceptions. Johnson rushed 24 times for 123 yards.

		1	2	3	4		
Cincinnati		7	3	7	0	—	17
Pittsburgh		7	7	0	14	—	28
Cin	—	J. Johnson 2 pass from Palmer (Graham kick)					
Pitt	—	Bettis 2 run (Reed kick)					
Pitt	—	Haynes 11 pass from Roethlisberger (Reed kick)					
Cin	—	FG Graham 34					
Cin	—	R. Johnson 2 run (Graham kick)					
Pitt	—	Bettis 1 run (Reed kick)					
Pitt	—	Polamalu 26 interception return (Reed kick)					

SAN DIEGO 38, TENNESSEE 17—at Qualcomm Stadium, attendance 54,006. Drew Brees passed for 3 touchdowns as the Chargers snapped a two-game losing streak. With the score 7-7, the Chargers capped a 59-yard drive with Brees' 11-yard touchdown pass to Antonio Gates with 5:16 left in the half. Following a three-and-out, the Chargers drove 51 yards and took a 21-7 lead on Brees' 10-yard scoring pass to Justin Peelle with 38 seconds left in the

half. A 42-yard run by LaDainian Tomlinson set up Nate Kaeding's third-quarter field goal, but the Titans scored on their next two possessions, with Donnie Nickey's onside kick recovery allowing the Titans to consecutively maintain possession for 12:14, to pull within 24-17 with 7:04 to play. The Chargers needed just two plays to respond, with Brees' 58-yard touchdown pass to Reche Caldwell for a 31-17 lead with 6:42 left. Brees was 16 of 20 for 206 yards and 3 touchdowns. Tomlinson rushed 17 times for 147 yards. Caldwell had 3 receptions for 110 yards. Billy Volek, playing for an injured Steve McNair, was 39 of 58 for 278 yards and 2 touchdowns. Derrick Mason had 12 catches for 94 yards, and Drew Bennett added 9 receptions for 109 yards.

		1	2	3	4		
Tennessee		0	7	0	10	—	17
San Diego		7	14	3	14	—	38
SD	—	Tomlinson 15 run (Kaeding kick)					
Tenn	—	Mason 4 pass from Volek (Anderson kick)					
SD	—	Gates 11 pass from Brees (Kaeding kick)					
SD	—	Peelle 10 pass from Brees (Kaeding kick)					
SD	—	FG Kaeding 31					
Tenn	—	FG Anderson 42					
Tenn	—	Meier 3 pass from Volek (Anderson kick)					
SD	—	Caldwell 58 pass from Brees (Kaeding kick)					
SD	—	Chatman 21 run (Kaeding kick)					

DENVER 16, TAMPA BAY 13—at Raymond James Stadium, attendance 65,341. Jason Elam kicked 3 field goals as the Buccaneers dropped their sixth consecutive game. Trailing 13-7, Martin Gramatica kicked a 28-yard field goal as the half expired and a 30-yard field goal with the Buccaneers' opening possession of the second half to tie the game 13-13. Beginning from their own 11, the Broncos drove 84 yards in 14 plays, capped by Elam's 23-yard field goal with 9:03 left. The Broncos forced a three-and-out, and then held onto the ball for more than seven minutes to run out all but the final three seconds. Jake Plummer was 13 of 31 for 138 yards and 1 touchdown. Brad Johnson was 15 of 23 for 162 yards and 1 touchdown.

		1	2	3	4		
Denver		7	6	0	3	—	16
Tampa Bay		0	10	3	0	—	13
Den	—	Hape 5 pass from Plummer (Elam kick)					
Den	—	FG Elam 49					
TB	—	Clayton 51 pass from B. Johnson (Gramatica kick)					
Den	—	FG Elam 50					
TB	—	FG Gramatica 28					
TB	—	FG Gramatica 30					
Den	—	FG Elam 23					

SUNDAY NIGHT, OCTOBER 3
ST. LOUIS 24, SAN FRANCISCO 14—at Monster Park, attendance 66,696. Marc Bulger passed for 186 yards and 1 touchdown as the Rams jumped to a 24-0 lead and beat the 49ers. The Rams scored on their first four possessions, on drives of 80, 11, 79, and 91 yards, to take a 24-0 lead with 29 seconds left in the half. Trailing 24-6, the 49ers drove to the Rams' 4 with 4:21 left, but Tim Rattay threw 3 incompletions and Terry Jackson's catch on fourth down gained just 2 yards. Rashaun Woods' 18-yard scoring catch came with just 16 seconds left. Bulger was 17 of 25 for 186 yards and 1 touchdown. Isaac Bruce had 7 catches for 100 yards. Marshall Faulk rushed 23 times for 121 yards. Rattay was 31 of 47 for 299 yards and 2 touchdowns, with 1 interception. Eric Johnson had 10 catches for 113 yards.

		1	2	3	4		
St. Louis		14	10	0	0	—	24
San Francisco		0	0	0	14	—	14
StL	—	Goodspeed 2 run (Wilkins kick)					
StL	—	McDonald 6 pass from Bulger (Wilkins kick)					
StL	—	FG Wilkins 20					

StL — S. Jackson 2 run (Wilkins kick)
SF — Conway 9 pass from Rattay (pass failed)
SF — Woods 18 pass from Rattay (Conway pass from Rattay)

MONDAY NIGHT, OCTOBER 4
KANSAS CITY 27, BALTIMORE 24—at M & T Bank Stadium, attendance 69,827. Priest Holmes rushed for 125 yards and 2 touchdowns as the Chiefs snapped a three-game losing streak. The Chiefs' defense allowed just 207 yards, and Kansas City maintained possession for 39:43. Randy Hymes caught a 57-yard touchdown pass from Kyle Boller to tie the game 10-10 early in the second quarter. The Chiefs took the ensuing kickoff and marched 79 yards in 14 plays, capped by Holmes' 4-yard run. With 1:30 left in the half, B.J. Sams returned a punt 58 yards for a touchdown to tie the game. The Chiefs responded by engineering 12- and 13-play drives, covering 60 and 80 yards, with their first two drives of the second half to take a 27-17 lead with 14:57 to play. Jamal Lewis' 1-yard run cut the deficit to 27-24 with 9:14 left. The Ravens' final drive began at their own 27 with 2:33 remaining. The Ravens gained just 13 yards before Boller's fourth-and-13 pass fell incomplete with 1:23 to play. Trent Green was 21 of 31 for 223 yards and 1 touchdown. Holmes rushed 33 times for 125 yards. Boller was 10 of 17 for 154 yards and 1 touchdown.

| Kansas City | 10 | 7 | 3 | 7 | — | 27 |
| Baltimore | 3 | 14 | 0 | 7 | — | 24 |

Balt — FG Stover 50
KC — Dunn 3 pass from T. Green (Tynes kick)
KC — FG Tynes 42
Balt — Hymes 57 pass from Boller (Stover kick)
KC — Holmes 4 run (Tynes kick)
Balt — Sams 58 punt return (Stover kick)
KC — FG Tynes 38
KC — Holmes 1 run (Tynes kick)
Balt — J. Lewis 1 run (Stover kick)

FIFTH WEEK SUMMARIES
American Football Conference

East Division	W	L	T	Pct.	Pts.	OP
New England	4	0	0	1.000	105	63
N.Y. Jets	4	0	0	1.000	98	75
Buffalo	0	4	0	.000	51	73
Miami	0	5	0	.000	42	87
North Division	W	L	T	Pct.	Pts.	OP
Pittsburgh	4	1	0	.800	112	94
Baltimore	3	2	0	.600	97	79
Cleveland	2	3	0	.400	82	96
Cincinnati	1	3	0	.250	66	95
South Division	W	L	T	Pct.	Pts.	OP
Indianapolis	4	1	0	.800	159	106
Jacksonville	3	2	0	.600	73	86
Houston	2	3	0	.400	118	127
Tennessee	1	4	0	.200	111	118
West Division	W	L	T	Pct.	Pts.	OP
Denver	4	1	0	.800	99	74
San Diego	3	2	0	.600	140	115
Oakland	2	3	0	.400	95	119
Kansas City	1	3	0	.250	89	110

National Football Conference

East Division	W	L	T	Pct.	Pts.	OP
Philadelphia	4	0	0	1.000	107	55
N.Y. Giants	4	1	0	.800	104	72
Dallas	2	2	0	.500	67	91
Washington	1	4	0	.200	71	85
North Division	W	L	T	Pct.	Pts.	OP
Detroit	3	1	0	.750	78	72
Minnesota	3	1	0	.750	112	94
Chicago	1	3	0	.250	68	76
Green Bay	1	4	0	.200	99	142
South Division	W	L	T	Pct.	Pts.	OP
Atlanta	4	1	0	.800	98	66
New Orleans	2	3	0	.400	92	127
Carolina	1	3	0	.250	69	88

Tampa Bay	1	4	0	.200	69	89
West Division	W	L	T	Pct.	Pts.	OP
Seattle	3	1	0	.750	92	46
St. Louis	3	2	0	.600	116	113
Arizona	1	4	0	.200	87	87
San Francisco	1	4	0	.200	91	137

SUNDAY, OCTOBER 10
DETROIT 17, ATLANTA 10—at Georgia Dome, attendance 70,434. The Lions' defense forced 4 turnovers and recorded 6 sacks as Detroit snapped the Falcons' four-game winning streak. Following Joey Harrington's 39-yard touchdown pass to Az-Zahir Hakim, Alex Lewis intercepted Michael Vick's pass on the next play from scrimmage. Artose Pinner scored three plays later to give Detroit 14 points in 1:23 and a 14-7 lead. The Falcons had a chance to score just before halftime, but instead of a 29-yard field-goal attempt, the Falcons faked it and Jay Feely caught a pass from Chris Mohr, but Terrence Holt dropped Feely for a 2-yard loss. Late in the third quarter, Eddie Drummond recovered Allen Rossum's muffed punt to set up Jason Hanson's 23-yard field goal for a 17-7 lead. The Falcons responded with a field goal, and after an exchange of punts started at their own 29 with 2:07 remaining. Three completions by Vick drove the Falcons to the Lions' 21 with 1:16 left. A spiked pass and sack by Shaun Rogers set up third-and-15. Vick was sacked by Jared DeVries and fumbled, and James Hall recovered at the Lions' 32 with 45 seconds remaining. Harrington was 16 of 24 for 146 yards and 1 touchdown. Hall had 1 sack, a forced fumble, and the game-clinching fumble recovery. Vick was 18 of 29 for 196 yards, with 1 interception.

| Detroit | 0 | 14 | 3 | 0 | — | 17 |
| Atlanta | 0 | 7 | 0 | 3 | — | 10 |

Atl — Dunn 2 run (Feely kick)
Det — Hakim 39 pass from Harrington (Hanson kick)
Det — Pinner 1 run (Hanson kick)
Det — FG Hanson 23
Atl — FG Feely 27

N.Y. GIANTS 26, DALLAS 10—at Texas Stadium, attendance 64,018. Tiki Barber rushed for 122 yards and 1 touchdown as the Giants won their fourth consecutive game. The Cowboys moved the ball at will in the first half, but were stopped on downs at the Giants' 5 and took just 10-3 with 45 seconds left in the half when Jason Witten fumbled and Barrett Green recovered at the Giants' 47. Five plays later Steve Christie kicked a field goal as the half expired. The Cowboys' defense forced a punt early in the second half, but Keith Davis was called for running into punter Jeff Feagles. Barber's 58-yard run on the next play set up Kurt Warner's 1-yard touchdown pass for a 13-10 lead with 4:58 left in the third quarter. Billy Cundiff missed a 47-yard field goal on the next drive, and the Giants answered by scoring with their next three possessions en route to a 26-10 lead with 2:14 to play. Warner was 18 of 33 for 217 yards and 1 touchdown. Testaverde was 15 of 24 for 126 yards and 1 touchdown, with 1 interception.

| N.Y. Giants | 3 | 3 | 7 | 13 | — | 26 |
| Dallas | 0 | 10 | 0 | 0 | — | 10 |

NYG — FG Christie 31
Dall — K. Johnson 7 pass from Testaverde (Cundiff kick)
Dall — FG Cundiff 41
NYG — FG Christie 51
NYG — Shockey 1 pass from Warner (Christie kick)
NYG — FG Christie 47
NYG — FG Christie 26
NYG — Barber 3 run (Christie kick)

DENVER 20, CAROLINA 17—at INVESCO Field at Mile High, attendance 75,072. Jake Plummer passed for 2 touchdowns and Reuben Droughns rushed for 193 yards as the Broncos rallied to remain in first place. The Broncos outgained the

Panthers (434-227), but led just 13-10 at halftime. In the third quarter, Julius Peppers intercepted Plummer's pass in the end zone and returned 101 yards to the Broncos' 3. Jake Delhomme scored on a quarterback sneak to take a 17-13 third-quarter lead. Plummer's 39-yard touchdown pass to Ashley Lelie on third-and-7 with 9:42 remaining gave the Broncos a 20-17 lead. The Broncos' defense forced a punt with 6:42 left, and the offense generated 4 first downs, capped by Droughns' 6-yard run on third-and-2 just after the two-minute warning to clinch the victory. Plummer was 17 of 29 for 226 yards and 2 touchdowns, with 2 interceptions. Droughns rushed 30 times for 193 yards. Delhomme was 13 of 20 for 173 yards and 1 touchdown. Keary Colbert had 4 catches for 115 yards.

| Carolina | 0 | 10 | 7 | 0 | — | 17 |
| Denver | 6 | 7 | 0 | 7 | — | 20 |

Den — FG Elam 32
Den — FG Elam 33
Car — Colbert 26 pass from Delhomme (Kasay kick)
Car — FG Kasay 53
Den — Droughns 5 pass from Plummer (Elam kick)
Car — Delhomme 1 run (Kasay kick)
Den — Lelie 39 pass from Plummer (Elam kick)

MINNESOTA 34, HOUSTON 28 (OT)—at Reliant Stadium, attendance 70,718. Daunte Culpepper passed for 396 yards and 5 touchdowns, including a 50-yard scoring pass to Marcus Robinson in overtime, as the Vikings held off a late rally. Robinson's 10-yard scoring catch with 11:50 left in the third quarter staked the Vikings to a 21-0 lead. The Texans had touchdown drives of 94 and 58 yards to pull within 21-14, but Culpepper's 50-yard touchdown pass to Randy Moss increased the lead to 28-14 with 6:49 to play. David Carr's 11-yard touchdown pass to Derick Armstrong had an 11-yard touchdown catch with 3:11 left. The Vikings were forced to punt, and J.J. Moses' 15-yard return gave Houston the ball with 2:21 to play. Three plays later, Andre Johnson caught a 22-yard scoring pass to tie the game. In overtime, the Vikings won the toss and, following an exchange of punts, Culpepper's 50-yard touchdown pass to Robinson on third-and-12 with 7:05 left, with Robinson splitting the defense and running the final 15 yards, won the game. Culpepper was 36 of 50 for 396 yards and 5 touchdowns. Mewelde Moore had 12 receptions for 90 yards, and Robinson had 9 catches for 150 yards. Carr was 27 of 43 for 372 yards and 3 touchdowns, and Johnson had 12 catches for 170 yards.

| Minnesota | 0 | 14 | 7 | 7 | 6 | — | 34 |
| Houston | 0 | 0 | 7 | 21 | 0 | — | 28 |

Minn — Moss 1 pass from Culpepper (Andersen kick)
Minn — Burleson 5 pass from Culpepper (Andersen kick)
Minn — Robinson 10 pass from Culpepper (Andersen kick)
Hous — Johnson 2 pass from Carr (K. Brown kick)
Hous — Davis 1 run (K. Brown kick)
Minn — Moss 50 pass from Culpepper (Andersen kick)
Hous — Armstrong 11 pass from Carr (K. Brown kick)
Hous — Johnson 22 pass from Carr (K. Brown kick)
Minn — Robinson 50 pass from Culpepper

INDIANAPOLIS 35, OAKLAND 14—at RCA Dome, attendance 57,230. Peyton Manning passed for 3 touchdowns as the Colts won their fourth consecutive game. Courtney Anderson's 4-yard touchdown catch cut the deficit to 28-14 with 6:14 left. After three punts, the Raiders got the ball starting from their own 8-yard-line. Jason David intercepted

Kerry Collins' pass and returned it 34 yards for a touchdown with 1:48 remaining to clinch the victory. Manning was 16 of 26 for 198 yards and 3 touchdowns, with 1 interception. James rushed 32 times for 136 yards and 1 touchdown. Collins was 28 of 44 for 245 yards and 1 touchdown, with 3 interceptions. Ronald Curry had 10 catches for 72 yards.

| Oakland | 0 | 7 | 0 | 7 | — | 14 |
| Indianapolis | 7 | 14 | 0 | 14 | — | 35 |

Ind	—	Mungro 1 pass from Manning (Bryant kick)
Ind	—	Wayne 35 pass from Manning (Bryant kick)
Oak	—	Fargas 1 run (Janikowski kick)
Ind	—	Clark 4 pass from Manning (Bryant kick)
Ind	—	James 1 run (Bryant kick)
Oak	—	Anderson 21 pass from Collins (Janikowski kick)
Ind	—	David 34 interception return (Bryant kick)

NEW ENGLAND 24, MIAMI 10—at Gillette Stadium, attendance 68,756. Tom Brady passed for 2 touchdowns as the Patriots won their seventeenth consecutive game. The Dolphins' defense allowed just 204 yards, but the offense and special teams committed mistakes that led to 3 short touchdown drives. The Patriots' led 10-7 with 3:15 left in the half when they forced a punt. A poor snap forced Matt Turk to run with the ball, and he was stopped at the Dolphins' 46. Brady's 5-yard touchdown pass to David Givens five plays later staked New England to a 17-7 lead. Dexter Reid recovered Jay Fiedler's fumble at the Dolphins' 48 on the opening drive of the second half, setting up Rahib Abdullah's 1-yard run. The Dolphins cut the deficit to 24-10 and drove inside the Patriots' red zone three times in the fourth quarter, but fourth down passes from the Patriots' 21-, 16-, and 7-yard lines all fell incomplete. Brady was 7 of 19 for 76 yards and 2 touchdowns, with 1 interception. Fiedler was 20 of 41 for 251 yards and 1 touchdown, with 1 interception. Marty Booker had 7 catches for 123 yards.

| Miami | 0 | 7 | 3 | 0 | — | 10 |
| New England | 7 | 10 | 7 | 0 | — | 24 |

NE	—	Graham 1 pass from Brady (Vinatieri kick)
NE	—	FG Vinatieri 40
Mia	—	Chambers 10 pass from Fiedler (Welker kick)
NE	—	Givens 5 pass from Brady (Vinatieri kick)
NE	—	Abdullah 1 run (Vinatieri kick)
Mia	—	FG Welker 29

TAMPA BAY 20, NEW ORLEANS 17—at Louisiana Superdome, attendance 64,900. Reserve Brian Griese passed for 194 yards and 1 touchdown as the Buccaneers won their first game. The Buccaneers began the second half with a 71-yard drive, capped by Griese's 45-yard scoring pass to Ken Dilger for a 20-7 lead. Martin Gramatica missed a 41-yard field-goal attempt later in the third quarter and the Saints responded with Joe Horn's 3-yard touchdown catch. Horn's catch came two plays after the Saints had kicked a field goal, but then took it off the board to accept a leverage penalty on the Buccaneers. John Carney's 47-yard field goal with 3:43 to play cut the deficit to 20-17, but the Buccaneers gained 2 first downs, including a 10-yard run by Michael Pittman on third-and-5, to clinch the victory. Griese was 16 of 19 for 194 yards and 1 touchdown after replacing Chris Simms, who was 5 of 8 for 68 yards in his first NFL start before injuring his shoulder. Aaron Brooks was 11 of 23 for 106 yards and 2 touchdowns, with 1 interception. McAllister rushed 21 times for 102 yards.

| Tampa Bay | 3 | 10 | 7 | 0 | — | 20 |
| New Orleans | 0 | 7 | 7 | 3 | — | 17 |

TB	—	FG Gramatica 23
NO	—	Williams 17 pass from Brooks (Carney kick)
TB	—	FG Gramatica 53
TB	—	Barber 18 fumble return (Gramatica kick)
TB	—	Dilger 45 pass from Griese (Gramatica kick)
NO	—	Horn 3 pass from Brooks (Carney kick)
NO	—	FG Carney 47

N.Y. JETS 16, BUFFALO 14—at Meadowlands, attendance 77,976. Doug Brien kicked a 38-yard field goal with 58 seconds remaining as the Jets remained undefeated. The Bills were forced to punt following their first seven possessions, and trailed 13-0 when Jeff Posey intercepted Chad Pennington's pass at the Bills' 31 with 12:21 to play. A 21-yard run by Willis McGahee on third-and-9 set up Mark Campbell's 16-yard scoring catch with 8:57 left. The Bills forced a punt, and Bledsoe connected with Lee Evans on a 46-yard touchdown two plays later to take a 14-13 lead with 5:58 to play. Pennington completed 6 consecutive passes to set up Brien's go-ahead field goal. Terrell Buckley intercepted Bledsoe's long pass at the Jets' 6 as time expired. Pennington was 31 of 42 for 304 yards and 1 touchdown, with 1 interception. John Abraham had 3 sacks. Bledsoe was 16 of 29 for 197 yards and 2 touchdowns, with 1 interception.

| Buffalo | 0 | 0 | 0 | 14 | — | 14 |
| N.Y. Jets | 0 | 10 | 3 | 3 | — | 16 |

NYJ	—	Baker 1 pass from Pennington (Brien kick)
NYJ	—	FG Brien 37
NYJ	—	FG Brien 36
Buff	—	Campbell 16 pass from Bledsoe (Lindell kick)
Buff	—	Evans 46 pass from Bledsoe (Lindell kick)
NYJ	—	FG Brien 38

PITTSBURGH 34, CLEVELAND 23—at Heinz Field, attendance 63,609. Ben Roethlisberger passed for 1 touchdown and ran for another as the Steelers outlasted the Browns. The Steelers scored on six of their first eight possessions, capped by Jerome Bettis' 1-yard run to begin the second half and take a 34-13 lead. Jeff Garcia's 7-yard touchdown pass to Andre' Davis trimmed the deficit to 34-23 with 8:44 remaining, and the Browns' defense forced a three-and-out, but Garcia fumbled and Clark Haggans recovered near midfield with 4:26 to play. Roethlisberger was 16 of 21 for 231 yards and 1 touchdown, with 1 interception. Burress had 6 receptions for 136 yards, and Duce Staley had 21 rushes for 117 yards. Garcia was 16 of 34 for 210 yards and 1 touchdown, and Davis had 5 catches for 107 yards.

| Cleveland | 10 | 3 | 3 | 7 | — | 23 |
| Pittsburgh | 14 | 13 | 7 | 0 | — | 34 |

Pitt	—	Staley 25 run (Reed kick)
Cle	—	Crocker 20 interception return (Dawson kick)
Pitt	—	Roethlisberger 6 run (Reed kick)
Cle	—	FG Dawson 24
Pitt	—	FG Reed 47
Pitt	—	Burress 37 pass from Roethlisberger (Reed kick)
Cle	—	FG Dawson 34
Pitt	—	FG Reed 26
Pitt	—	Bettis 3 run (Reed kick)
Cle	—	FG Dawson 46
Cle	—	Andre' Davis 7 pass from Garcia (Dawson kick)

SAN DIEGO 34, JACKSONVILLE 21—at Qualcomm Stadium, attendance 52,101. Drew Brees passed for 2 touchdowns, both caught by Antonio Gates, as the Chargers won their second consecutive game. The Chargers scored touchdowns on drives of 66 and 76 yards with their first 2 possessions, and Drayton Florence's second-quarter interception set up Gates'

11-yard touchdown catch for a 21-0 lead with 9:23 left in the first half. Byron Leftwich capped a 14-play, 77-yard drive with a 2-yard run to pull within 27-14 with 10:42 to play, but Jesse Chatman had a 31-yard run followed on the next play by a 41-yard run with 9:54 to play. The Jaguars trailed 34-21 and drove to the Chargers' 1, but Leftwich's fourth-and-goal fell incomplete with 14 seconds left. Brees was 17 of 26 for 211 yards and 2 touchdowns. Chatman rushed 11 times for 103 yards. Leftwich was 36 of 54 for 357 yards and 1 touchdown, with 2 interceptions. Jimmy Smith had 8 receptions for 113 yards.

| Jacksonville | 0 | 7 | 0 | 14 | — | 21 |
| San Diego | 14 | 7 | 6 | 7 | — | 34 |

SD	—	Gates 1 pass from Brees (Kaeding kick)
SD	—	Tomlinson 1 run (Kaeding kick)
SD	—	Gates 11 pass from Brees (Kaeding kick)
Jax	—	Fuamatu-Ma'afala 1 run (Scobee kick)
SD	—	FG Kaeding 21
SD	—	FG Kaeding 28
Jax	—	Leftwich 2 run (Scobee kick)
SD	—	Chatman 41 run (Kaeding kick)
Jax	—	Hankton 7 pass from Leftwich (Scobee kick)

SAN FRANCISCO 31, ARIZONA 28 (OT)—at Monster Park, attendance 62,836. Tim Rattay passed for 417 yards and 2 touchdowns, and Todd Peterson kicked a 32-yard field goal in overtime, as the 49ers overcame a 16-point deficit in the final five minutes for their first victory. The 49ers trailed 14-12 late in the third quarter but drove to the Cardinals' 15. Jamal Robertson fumbled, and Bertrand Berry recovered to set up an 86-yard drive capped by Emmitt Smith's 10-yard run for a 21-12 lead with 11:47 to play. The Cardinals' defense forced a punt and Josh McCown connected on a 24-yard touchdown pass to Larry Fitzgerald three plays later for a 28-12 lead with 8:19 remaining. Rattay completed 2 third-down passes to keep alive a 15-play, 80-yard drive that culminated with eric Johnson's 6-yard touchdown catch and Rattay ran in the 2-point conversion with 4:35 to play. The 49ers forced another punt and Brandon Lloyd caught a 23-yard scoring catch with 1:07 to play. Rattay's 2-point conversion pass to Lloyd tied the game. In overtime, the 49ers won the toss and drove 47 yards, with a roughing the passer penalty by Darnell Dockett sustaining the drive, and capped by Todd Peterson's 32-yard field goal with 11:37 left. Rattay was 38 of 57 for 417 yards and 2 touchdowns. Eric Johnson had 13 receptions for 162 yards. McCown was 19 of 34 for 231 yards and 3 touchdowns, with 1 interception.

| Arizona | 0 | 14 | 0 | 14 | 0 | — | 28 |
| San Francisco | 0 | 6 | 6 | 16 | 3 | — | 31 |

Ariz	—	Jones 16 pass from McCown (Rackers kick)
SF	—	FG Peterson 37
Ariz	—	Hambrick 2 pass from McCown (Rackers kick)
SF	—	FG Peterson 42
SF	—	Battle 71 punt return (pass failed)
Ariz	—	Smith 10 run (Rackers kick)
Ariz	—	Fitzgerald 24 pass from McCown (Rackers kick)
SF	—	Johnson 6 pass from Rattay (Rattay run)
SF	—	Lloyd 23 pass from Rattay (Lloyd pass from Rattay)
SF	—	FG Peterson 32

ST. LOUIS 33, SEATTLE 27 (OT)—at Qwest Field, attendance 66,940. Shaun McDonald caught a 52-yard touchdown pass from Marc Bulger in overtime as the Rams overcame a 17-point deficit in the final six minutes of regulation to hand the Seahawks their first loss. The Seahawks outgained the Rams 306-122 in the first half, capped by Matt Hasselbeck's 56-yard touchdown pass to Darrell Jackson, to take a 24-7 halftime lead. Leading 24-10, Marcus Trufant intercepted a pass early in the fourth quarter en route to a 34-yard field goal by Josh Brown for a 17-point lead with 8:42 to play. The Rams responded with a 66-yard drive, including key third-down conversions by Bulger to Isaac Bruce and McDonald, to set up Brandon Manumaleuna's 8-yard scoring catch with 5:34 remaining. The Rams forced a three-and-out, and McDonald returned the punt 39 yards. On the next play, Bulger found Kevin Curtis with a 41-yard touchdown pass with 3:30 to play. The Rams forced another punt, getting the ball on their own 36 with 1:14 left. Bulger completed a 27-yard pass to Bruce and 16-yard pass to Dane Looker to set up Jeff Wilkins' 36-yard field goal with eight seconds remaining in regulation. In overtime, the Rams won the toss and Bulger completed a 13-yard pass to Torry Holt on third-and-6 before hitting McDonald with a 52-yard catch-and-run touchdown with 11:58 left on the overtime clock. Bulger was 24 of 42 for 325 yards and 3 touchdowns, with 3 interceptions. Hasselbeck was 20 of 35 for 216 yards and 2 touchdowns. Alexander rushed 23 times for 150 yards.

St. Louis	0	7	3	17	6	—	33
Seattle	7	17	0	3	0	—	27

Sea	—	Alexander 1 run (J. Brown kick)
Sea	—	FG J. Brown 48
StL	—	Bulger 9 run (Wilkins kick)
Sea	—	Stevens 24 pass from Hasselbeck (J. Brown kick)
Sea	—	D. Jackson 56 pass from Hasselbeck (J. Brown kick)
StL	—	FG Wilkins 39
Sea	—	FG J. Brown 34
StL	—	Manumaleuna 8 pass from Bulger (Wilkins kick)
StL	—	Curtis 41 pass from Bulger (Wilkins kick)
StL	—	FG Wilkins 36
StL	—	McDonald 52 pass from Bulger

SUNDAY NIGHT, OCTOBER 10
BALTIMORE 17, WASHINGTON 10—at FedExField, attendance 90,287. The Ravens' defense permitted just 107 total yards and stifled the Redskins without the benefit of an offensive touchdown. The Redskins' defense intercepted 3 passes in the second quarter, the first of which led to a field goal. The third interception, by Todd Franz returned 22 yards to the Ravens' 8 with 1:03 left in the half, set up Mark Brunell's 7-yard touchdown pass to Chris Cooley for a 10-0 lead. In the third quarter, Ed Reed sacked Brunell, forced him to fumble, picked up the ball and returned it 22 yards for a touchdown. Just over two minutes later, the Ravens forced a punt and B.J. Sams returned it 78 yards for a touchdown and 14-10 lead. Deion Sanders intercepted a pass on the next possession to set up Matt Stover's 33-yard field goal with 11:49 to play. The Redskins failed to drive inside the Redskins' 45, and Baltimore's offense ran off the final 4:42. Kyle Boller was 9 of 18 for 81 yards, with 3 interceptions. Jamal Lewis rushed 28 times for 116 yards. Brunell was 13 of 29 for 83 yards and 1 touchdown, with 1 interception.

Baltimore	0	0	14	3	— 17
Washington	0	10	0	0	— 10

Wash	—	FG Hall 26
Wash	—	Cooley 7 pass from Brunell (Hall kick)
Balt	—	Reed 22 fumble return (Stover kick)
Balt	—	Sams 78 punt return (Stover kick)
Balt	—	FG Stover 33

MONDAY NIGHT, OCTOBER 11
TENNESSEE 48, GREEN BAY 27—at Lambeau Field, attendance 70,420. Chris Brown rushed for 148 yards and 2 touchdowns and the Titans' defense forced 6 turnovers en route to victory. The

Titans scored on five of their first six possessions to jump out to a 27-10 lead. Ryan Longwell kicked a 53-yard field goal just before the half, and had the ball to begin the second half. Brett Favre was intercepted on the Packers' first two possessions of the half, with the latter interception by Lamont Thompson set up Steve McNair's 11-yard touchdown catch by Eddie Berlin for a 34-13 lead. The Packers responded by driving to the Titans 3, but Favre's third-and fourth-down passes fell incomplete. The Titans were forced to punt moments later, but Antonio Chatman muffed the punt and Darrell Hill recovered. Two plays later, wide receiver Drew Bennett caught a lateral and then completed a 26-yard touchdown pass to Derrick Mason for a 41-13 lead with 13:42 to play. McNair was 15 of 26 for 206 yards and 2 touchdowns. Brown rushed 27 times for 148 yards. Favre was 24 of 44 for 338 yards and 2 touchdowns, with 3 interceptions. Craig Nall was 7 of 8 for 64 yards and 1 touchdown. Donald Driver had 10 catches for 150 yards, and Javon Walker had 8 receptions for 159 yards.

Tennessee	17	10	7	14	— 48
Green Bay	3	10	0	14	— 27

Tenn	—	Brown 37 run (Anderson kick)
Tenn	—	Brown 29 run (Anderson kick)
Tenn	—	FG Anderson 36
GB	—	FG Longwell 39
Tenn	—	Fleming 14 pass from McNair (Anderson kick)
GB	—	Franks 1 pass from Favre (Longwell kick)
Tenn	—	FG Anderson 38
GB	—	FG Longwell 53
Tenn	—	Berlin 11 pass from McNair (Anderson kick)
Tenn	—	Mason 26 pass from Bennett (Anderson kick)
GB	—	Franks 11 pass from Favre (Longwell kick)
Tenn	—	Smith 15 run (Anderson kick)
GB	—	Walker 1 pass from Nall (Longwell kick)

SIXTH WEEK SUMMARIES
American Football Conference

East Division	W	L	T	Pct.	Pts.	OP
New England	5	0	0	1.000	135	83
N.Y. Jets	5	0	0	1.000	120	89
Buffalo	1	4	0	.200	71	86
Miami	0	6	0	.000	55	107
North Division	**W**	**L**	**T**	**Pct.**	**Pts.**	**OP**
Pittsburgh	5	1	0	.833	136	114
Baltimore	3	2	0	.600	97	79
Cleveland	3	3	0	.500	116	113
Cincinnati	1	4	0	.200	83	129
South Division	**W**	**L**	**T**	**Pct.**	**Pts.**	**OP**
Indianapolis	4	1	0	.800	159	106
Jacksonville	4	2	0	.667	95	102
Houston	3	3	0	.500	138	137
Tennessee	2	4	0	.333	121	138
West Division	**W**	**L**	**T**	**Pct.**	**Pts.**	**OP**
Denver	5	1	0	.833	130	77
San Diego	3	3	0	.500	160	136
Oakland	2	4	0	.333	98	150
Kansas City	1	4	0	.200	105	132

National Football Conference

East Division	W	L	T	Pct.	Pts.	OP
Philadelphia	5	0	0	1.000	137	63
N.Y. Giants	4	1	0	.800	104	72
Dallas	2	3	0	.400	87	115
Washington	2	4	0	.333	84	95
North Division	**W**	**L**	**T**	**Pct.**	**Pts.**	**OP**
Minnesota	4	1	0	.800	150	125
Detroit	3	2	0	.600	88	110
Green Bay	2	4	0	.333	137	152
Chicago	1	4	0	.200	78	89
South Division	**W**	**L**	**T**	**Pct.**	**Pts.**	**OP**
Atlanta	5	1	0	.833	119	86
New Orleans	2	4	0	.333	123	165
Carolina	1	4	0	.200	77	118
Tampa Bay	1	5	0	.167	90	117

West Division	W	L	T	Pct.	Pts.	OP
St. Louis	4	2	0	.667	144	134
Seattle	3	2	0	.600	112	76
Arizona	1	4	0	.200	87	87
San Francisco	1	5	0	.167	105	159

SUNDAY, OCTOBER 17
ATLANTA 21, SAN DIEGO 20—at Georgia Dome, attendance 70,187. Michael Vick passed for 218 yards and 2 touchdowns, and ran for another score, as the Falcons rallied to defeat the Chargers. Trailing 7-0, the Chargers tied the game on LaDainian Tomlinson's 1-yard run on fourth-and-goal. Drayton Florence intercepted Vick's pass five plays later to set up Drew Brees' 17-yard touchdown pass to Eric Parker with 18 seconds left in the half for 14 points in one minute. The Falcons trailed 17-7 when Peerless Price caught a 50-yard pass and Vick scored from 14 yards with 13:09 left. Following a three-and-out, Vick completed a 32-yard touchdown pass to Dez White for a 21-17 lead with 10:12 to play. The Chargers answered with Nate Kaeding's 28-yard field goal with 6:01 left, but the Falcons ran out the remainder of the clock, capped by Vick's 24-yard pass to Justin Griffith on second-and-10 with 2:00 left. Vick was 12 of 21 for 218 yards and 2 touchdowns, with 1 interception. Brees was 23 of 31 for 227 yards and 1 touchdown, with 1 interception.

San Diego	0	14	3	0	— 20
Atlanta	0	7	0	14	— 21

Atl	—	Crumpler 19 pass from Vick (Feely kick)
SD	—	Tomlinson 1 run (Kaeding kick)
SD	—	Parker 17 pass from Brees (Kaeding kick)
SD	—	FG Kaeding 53
Atl	—	Vick 14 run (Feely kick)
Atl	—	White 32 pass from Vick (Feely kick)
SD	—	FG Kaeding 28

BUFFALO 20, MIAMI 13—at Ralph Wilson Stadium, attendance 72,714. Takeo Spikes returned an interception for a touchdown and the Bills' defense recorded 5 sacks and allowed just 212 yards to defeat the Dolphins. The Bills opened the second half with a field goal, forced a three-and-out, and then needed just four plays, keyed by Drew Bledsoe's 30-yard pass to Eric Moulds and capped by Mark Campbell's 5-yard scoring catch for a 17-10 lead. The Dolphins reached the Bills' 1 with their next possession, but Sammy Morris lost a yard and Aaron Schobel and Pat Williams combined to sack Jay Fiedler on second down, and Schobel sacked Fielder again on third down to force a field goal. The Bills responded with a seven-minute drive to the Dolphins' 1, but were stopped three consecutive plays and forced to settle for a field goal, too, in a 20-13 lead with 7:57 to play. The Bills' defense forced a three-and-out, thanks to another sack by Schobel, and the offense ran out the final 6:22. Bledsoe was 15 of 28 for 212 yards and 1 touchdown. Willis McGahee rushed 26 times for 111 yards. Fiedler was 12 of 23 for 136 yards and 1 touchdown, with 1 interception.

Miami	0	10	0	3	— 13
Buffalo	7	0	10	3	— 20

Buff	—	Spikes 11 interception return (Lindell kick)
Mia	—	FG Bryant 47
Mia	—	Thompson 24 pass from Fiedler (Bryant kick)
Buff	—	FG Lindell 43
Buff	—	Campbell 5 pass from Bledsoe (Lindell kick)
Mia	—	FG Bryant 28
Buff	—	FG Lindell 20

WASHINGTON 13, CHICAGO 10—at Soldier Field, attendance 61,945. Clinton Portis rushed for 171 yards as the Redskins snapped a four-game losing streak. The Redskins' defense allowed just 160 yards for the game, and permitted only 2 first downs in the Bears' initial nine possessions. The Redskins had two drives of more than 40 yards, resulting in Rod Gardner's 18-yard touchdown catch and Ola Kimrin's 26-yard field goal with 11:13 to play for a 13-7 lead. The Bears responded with Paul Edinger's 46-yard field goal with 5:10 to play. The Bears' final possession began a their own 35 with 1:28 left, but Cornelius Griffin sacked Jonathan Quinn twice, and Sean Taylor intercepted Quinn's pass with 13 seconds left to clinch the victory. Mark Brunell was 8 of 22 for 95 yards and 1 touchdown, with 1 interception. Portis rushed 36 times for 171 yards. Quinn was 10 of 22 for 65 yards, with 1 interception.

Washington	3	7	0	3	—	13
Chicago	0	7	0	3	—	10

Wash	—	FG Kimrin 41
Wash	—	Gardner 18 pass from Brunell (Kimrin kick)
Chi	—	Azumah 70 interception return (Edinger kick)
Wash	—	FG Kimrin 26
Chi	—	FG Edinger 46

CLEVELAND 34, CINCINNATI 17—at Cleveland Browns Stadium, attendance 73,263. Jeff Garcia passed for 310 yards and 4 touchdowns as the Browns improved to 3-0 at home. The Browns outgained the Bengals 449-189, but the Bengals forced 4 turnovers to keep the game close. The Browns began their second possession at their own 1-yard line following Kyle Larson's punt downed by Landon Johnson. On the first play after the punt, Garcia completed a pass to Andre' Davis near the Browns' 40, and Davis outran the single coverage for a 99-yard touchdown. Trailing 14-0 with 13:30 left in the half, Kevin Kaesviharn recovered Lee Suggs' fumble and returned it 3 yards for a touchdown, Tory James intercepted Garcia's pass to set up Matt Schobel's touchdown catch to tie the game, and Johnson recovered Garcia's fumble that led to Shayne Graham's 32-yard field goal and the Bengals led 17-14 with 6:10 remaining in the half. The Browns drove to the Bengals' 5, and Garcia completed a 5-yard scoring pass to Aaron Shea with no time remaining for a 21-17 halftime lead. Suggs caught a 59-yard touchdown pass for a 31-17 lead with 10:15 to play to pull away. Garcia was 16 of 23 for 310 yards and 4 touchdowns, with 2 interceptions. Suggs had 5 catches for 100 yards, and William Green rushed 25 times for 115 yards. Carson Palmer was 20 of 36 for 148 yards and 1 touchdown, with 1 interception.

Cincinnati	0	17	0	0	—	17
Cleveland	7	14	3	10	—	34

Cle	—	Andre' Davis 99 pass from Garcia (Dawson kick)
Cle	—	Morgan 10 pass from Garcia (Dawson kick)
Cin	—	Kaesviharn 3 fumble return (Graham kick)
Cin	—	Schobel 6 pass from Palmer (Graham kick)
Cin	—	FG Graham 32
Cle	—	Shea 5 pass from Garcia (Dawson kick)
Cle	—	FG Dawson 23
Cle	—	Suggs 59 pass from Garcia (Dawson kick)
Cle	—	FG Dawson 33

PITTSBURGH 24, DALLAS 20—at Texas Stadium, attendance 64,162. Jerome Bettis scored on a 2-yard touchdown run with 30 seconds remaining to give the Steelers their fourth consecutive victory. The Cowboys scored on three consecutive possessions spanning the second and third quarters, capped by Vinny Testaverde's 22-yard touchdown pass to Keyshawn Johnson for a 20-10 lead. The Steelers responded with an 11-play, 74-yard drive in which Ben Roethlisberger completed all 7 of his pass attempts and scrambled for a first down, and capped by Jerame Tuman's 7-yard touchdown

catch with 11:48 to play. With 2:36 to play, on third-and-13 from the Steelers' 47, James Farrior sacked Testaverde and forced him to fumble. Kimo von Oelhoffen recovered and returned it 21 yards to the Cowboys' 24. Five plays later, Bettis scored on a 2-yard run with 30 seconds left. Dallas reached the Steelers' 30 with one second left and had a chance for the win, but Russell Stuvaints knocked down Testaverde's pass, intended for Johnson, in the end zone as time expired. Roethlisberger was 21 of 25 for 193 yards and 2 touchdowns. James Farrior had 2 sacks and forced 3 fumbles. Testaverde was 23 of 36 for 284 yards and 1 touchdown. Terry Glenn had 7 catches for 140 yards.

Pittsburgh	7	3	0	14	—	24
Dallas	7	3	10	0	—	20

Dall	—	Anderson 21 run (Cundiff kick)
Pitt	—	Burress 5 pass from Roethlisberger (Reed kick)
Pitt	—	FG Reed 51
Dall	—	FG Cundiff 47
Dall	—	FG Cundiff 39
Dall	—	K. Johnson 22 pass from Testaverde (Cundiff kick)
Pitt	—	Tuman 7 pass from Roethlisberger (Reed kick)
Pitt	—	Bettis 2 run (Reed kick)

GREEN BAY 38, DETROIT 10—at Ford Field, attendance 62,938. The Packers' defense permitted just 5 first downs as Green Bay snapped a 2-game losing streak. The Packers had advantages in yards (434-125) and time of possession (39:41-20:19), but led just 14-10 last in the second quarter before Favre engineered an 8-play, 50-yard drive in the final 1:47 of the first half, capped by Ryan Longwell's 50-yard field goal. Darren Sharper's 36-yard interception return for a touchdown early in the third quarter increased the lead, and following a three-and-out, the Packers drove 63 yards in 11 plays that culminated with Najeh Davenport's 13-yard run with 3:28 left in the third quarter for a 31-10 lead. Ahman Green's 20-yard halfback-option pass to Donald Driver on the Packers' next drive capped a 77-yard drive to complete the scoring. Favre was 25 of 38 for 257 yards and 2 touchdowns. Driver had 9 receptions for 110 yards. Joey Harrington was 12 of 23 for 101 yards and a touchdown, with 1 interception.

Green Bay	7	10	14	7	—	38
Detroit	7	3	0	0	—	10

GB	—	Driver 7 pass from Favre (Longwell kick)
Det	—	Hakim 28 pass from Harrington (Hanson kick)
GB	—	Fisher 13 pass from Favre (Longwell kick)
Det	—	FG Hanson 48
GB	—	FG Longwell 50
GB	—	Sharper 36 interception return (Longwell kick)
GB	—	Davenport 13 run (Longwell kick)
GB	—	Driver 20 pass from Green (Longwell kick)

JACKSONVILLE 22, KANSAS CITY 16—at ALLTEL Stadium, attendance 66,413. Carl Hankton caught a 14-yard touchdown pass with 45 seconds left as the Jaguars improved to 4-0 in games decided by six points or less. Byron Leftwich's 64-yard touchdown pass to Fred Taylor gave Jacksonville a 14-3 lead early in the second quarter. In the fourth quarter, Green twice completed passes to Gonzalez on third down to set up Priest Holmes' 28-yard scoring catch with 4:45 left, but Lawrence Tynes hit the upright with the extra-point attempt for a 16-14 lead. On the ensuing possession, Leftwich's fourth-and-1 pass from his own 33-yard line fell incomplete. The Chiefs missed a 42-yard field-goal attempt wide right with 2:16 left. Leftwich responded by completing 7 of 8 passes to drive 67 yards in eight plays, capped by

Hankton's 67-yard run with 45 seconds left. Deke Cooper intercepted Green's long pass towards the end zone as time expired. Leftwich was 24 of 36 for 298 yards and 2 touchdowns. Green was 23 of 33 for 315 yards and 2 touchdowns, with 1 interception. Johnnie Morton had 7 catches for 111 yards.

Kansas City	3	0	7	6	—	16
Jacksonville	7	7	0	8	—	22

Jax	—	Leftwich 7 run (Scobee kick)
KC	—	FG Tynes 31
Jax	—	Taylor 64 pass from Leftwich (Scobee kick)
KC	—	Gonzalez 24 pass from Green (Tynes kick)
KC	—	Holmes 28 pass from Green (kick failed)
Jax	—	Hankton 14 pass from Leftwich (Williams pass from Leftwich)

NEW ENGLAND 30, SEATTLE 20—at Gillette Stadium, attendance 68,756. Corey Dillon rushed for 105 yards and the game-clinching touchdown with 1:55 remaining as the Patriots equalled the 1933-34 Chicago Bears' NFL record of 17 consecutive victories. The Patriots scored on their first four possessions, the first two set up by interceptions by Willie McGinest and Ty Law, to take a 20-3 lead. Josh Brown added 2 more field goals to trim the deficit to 20-9, and Michael Boulware intercepted Tom Brady's pass at the Patriots' 45 to set up Shaun Alexander's 9-yard run, and Jerramy Stevens' 2-point conversion catch, to pull within 20-17 with 11:05 left. After an exchange of field goals, Bethel Johnson caught a 48-yard pass on third-and-7 that led to Dillon's 9-yard run with 1:55 left. The Seahawks drove to the Patriots' 4 with 12 seconds left, but did not score on their final three plays. Brady was 19 of 30 for 231 yards and 1 touchdown, with 1 interception. Matt Hasselbeck was 27 of 50 for 349 yards, with 2 interceptions. Koren Robinson had 9 catches for 150 yards.

Seattle	0	6	3	11	—	20
New England	10	10	0	10	—	30

NE	—	Dillon 1 run (Vinatieri kick)
NE	—	FG Vinatieri 40
NE	—	Patten 6 pass from Brady (Vinatieri kick)
Sea	—	FG J. Brown 33
NE	—	FG Vinatieri 39
Sea	—	FG J. Brown 40
Sea	—	FG J. Brown 28
Sea	—	Alexander 9 run (Stevens pass from Hasselbeck)
NE	—	FG Vinatieri 30
Sea	—	FG J. Brown 31
NE	—	Dillon 9 run (Vinatieri kick)

N.Y. JETS 22, SAN FRANCISCO 14—at Meadowlands, attendance 78,189. Curtis Martin rushed for 111 yards and 2 touchdowns as the Jets rallied for the first 5-0 start in franchise history. The 49ers scored on touchdown drives of 78 and 88 yards in the first half to take a 14-3 lead. The 49ers failed to cross the Jets' 35 with their six second-half possessions, and the Jets drove 91 and 70 yards with their first two drives after intermission to take a 15-14 lead with 11:41 to play. Jonathan Vilma's interception and 14-yard return to the 49ers' 20 set up Martin's 9-yard run on third-and-goal with 25 seconds left. Shaun Ellis sacked Tim Rattay to thwart any final threat by the 49ers. Pennington was 20 of 30 for 222 yards. Martin rushed 25 times for 111 yards. Rattay was 18 of 28 for 286 yards and 1 touchdown, with 1 interception.

San Francisco	7	7	0	0	—	14
N.Y. Jets	0	3	6	13	—	22

SF	—	Lloyd 33 pass from Rattay (Peterson kick)
SF	—	Barlow 2 run (Peterson kick)
NYJ	—	FG Brien 43
NYJ	—	Jordan 17 run (run failed)
NYJ	—	Martin 1 run (pass failed)

NYJ — Martin 9 run (Brien kick)

DENVER 31, OAKLAND 3—at Network Associates Coliseum, attendance 57,293. Jake Plummer passed for 3 touchdowns and Reuben Droughns rushed for 176 yards as the Broncos improved their record to 5-1. The Broncos outgained the Raiders 444-145. An interception by Marques Anderson set up Sebastian Janikowski's 35-yard field goal in the first quarter. The Broncos drove 71, 80, and 58 yards with their next three possessions, capped by Ashley Lelie's 31-yard scoring catch for a 21-3 lead. The Raiders last scoring threat came in the first half, but John Lynch forced Jerry Porter to fumble and Kenoy Kennedy recovered at the Broncos' 7. Plummer was 11 of 20 for 190 yards and 3 touchdowns, with 1 interception. Droughns had 38 carries for 176 yards. Kerry Collins was 15 of 31 for 136 yards, with 1 interception.

Denver	7	14	10	0	—	31
Oakland	3	0	0	0	—	3

Oak — FG Janikowski 35
Den — Putzier 12 pass from Plummer (Elam kick)
Den — Carswell 10 pass from Plummer (Elam kick)
Den — Lelie 31 pass from Plummer (Elam kick)
Den — FG Elam 33
Den — Droughns 4 run (Elam kick)

PHILADELPHIA 30, CAROLINA 8—at Lincoln Financial Field, attendance 67,707. The Eagles' defense intercepted 4 passes, including Lito Sheppard's 64-yard interception return for a touchdown, en route to their first 5-0 start since 1981. The Eagles, who held the ball for 38:30, scored on three of their first four possessions for a 13-0 halftime lead. Roderick Hood's third-quarter interception led to David Akers' 43-yard field goal, and Sheppard extended the lead to 23-0 with his 64-yard interception return for a touchdown when 4:32 left in the third quarter. The Panthers' lone drive inside the Eagles' 30 resulted in a touchdown with 2:48 to play, but Brian Westbrook had a 42-yard touchdown run for a 30-8 lead with 2:08 left. McNabb was 14 of 26 for 209 yards, with 1 interception. Terrell Owens had 4 catches for 123 yards. Sheppard had 2 interceptions and 3 passes defensed. Delhomme was 24 of 42 for 205 yards and 1 touchdown, with 4 interceptions.

Carolina	0	0	0	8	—	8
Philadelphia	10	3	10	7	—	30

Phil — FG Akers 48
Phil — Levens 1 run (Akers kick)
Phil — FG Akers 34
Phil — FG Akers 43
Phil — Sheppard 64 interception return (Akers kick)
Car — Muhammad 2 pass from Delhomme (Colbert pass from Delhomme)
Phil — Westbrook 42 run (Akers kick)

HOUSTON 20, TENNESSEE 10—at The Coliseum, attendance 68,932. The Texans' defense intercepted 4 passes and David Carr passed for 266 yards and 1 touchdown as the Texans moved to .500 at the latest point of the season in club history. In the second quarter, Tank Williams sacked Carr, and forced him to fumble. Carlos Hall recovered the fumble and Drew Bennett scored three plays later for a 7-3 Tennessee lead. The Texans marched 74 yards on their ensuing drive for Jabar Gaffney's touchdown catch for a 10-7 advantage. Jonathan Wells scored on a 4-yard run with 4:42 left to cap a 65-yard drive for a 20-10 lead. Carr was 16 of 26 for 266 yards and 1 touchdown, with 1 interception. Steve McNair was 19 of 41 for 210 yards and 1 touchdown, with 4 interceptions.

Houston	3	10	0	7	—	20
Tennessee	0	10	0	0	—	10

Hous — FG K. Brown 21

Tenn — Bennett 10 pass from McNair (Anderson kick)
Hous — Gaffney 20 pass from Carr (K. Brown kick)
Tenn — FG Anderson 40
Hous — FG K. Brown 50
Hous — Wells 4 run (K. Brown kick)

SUNDAY NIGHT, OCTOBER 17
MINNESOTA 38, NEW ORLEANS 31—at Louisiana Superdome, attendance 64,900. Daunte Culpepper passed for 425 yards and 5 touchdowns as the Vikings rolled up 605 yards to outlast the Saints. Culpepper's 16-yard touchdown pass to Marcus Robinson increased the lead to 21-7 with 1:53 left in the first half. Aaron Brooks responded by completing all 4 pass attempts on a 73-yard drive, capped by Joe Horn's 7-yard touchdown catch with 21 seconds left, to pull within 21-14. The Vikings forced a three-and-out to begin the second half, and both teams then scored with their next three possessions, beginning with Culpepper's scoring pass to Jermaine Wiggins for a 28-14 lead. The Saints never got closer than seven points, with Brooks' 5-yard run with 2:51 left cutting the deficit to 38-31. On third-and-4, Culpepper completed an 11-yard pass to Nate Burleson for one first down, and Moe Williams' 49-yard run with 1:56 left clinched the victory. Culpepper was 26 of 37 for 425 yards and 5 touchdowns, with 2 interceptions. Mewelde Moore had 15 carries for 109 yards. Burleson had 6 catches for 134 yards. Brooks was 22 of 38 for 249 yards and 1 touchdown, with 1 interceptions.

Minnesota	7	14	10	7	—	38
New Orleans	0	14	7	10	—	31

Minn — Wiggins 1 pass from Culpepper (Andersen kick)
Minn — Moss 43 pass from Culpepper (Andersen kick)
NO — McAllister 2 run (Carney kick)
Minn — Robinson 16 pass from Culpepper (Andersen kick)
NO — Horn 7 pass from Brooks (Carney kick)
Minn — Wiggins 9 pass from Culpepper (Andersen kick)
NO — McAllister 1 run (Carney kick)
Minn — FG Andersen 39
NO — FG Carney 45
Minn — Robinson 1 pass from Culpepper (Andersen kick)
NO — Brooks 5 run (Carney kick)

MONDAY NIGHT, OCTOBER 18
ST. LOUIS 28, TAMPA BAY 21—at Edward Jones Dome, attendance 66,040. Torry Holt caught 2 long touchdown passes and Adam Archuleta returned an interception 93 yards for a score as the Rams posted their third consecutive victory. The Rams' defense forced 4 turnovers, which led to 14 points. The Buccaneers led 14-7 late in the second quarter when Brian Griese fumbled the snap and Leonard Little recovered at the Buccaneers' 5 to set up Marshall Faulk's fourth-down touchdown to tie the game. In the third quarter, Michael Pittman fumbled at the Rams' 7 and Adam Archuleta alertly picked up the ball and returned it 93 yards for a touchdown and 21-14 lead. Anthony McFarland recovered Bulger's fumble late in the third quarter to set up Will Heller's touchdown catch. The Rams responded with a 36-yard touchdown pass to Torry Holt for a 28-21 lead with 10:46 left. Jerametrius Butler intercepted a pass in the end zone for a touchback to end one threat, and Aeneas Williams recovered Tim Brown's fumble at the Rams' 12 with 26 seconds left to clinch the victory. Bulger was 18 of 30 for 264 yards and 2 touchdowns, with 1 interception. Holt had 4 catches for 124 yards. Griese was 27 of 40 for 286 yards and 2 touchdowns, with 1 interception. Michael Clayton had 8 receptions for 142 yards.

Tampa Bay	7	7	7	0	—	21
St. Louis	7	7	7	7	—	28

StL — Holt 52 pass from Bulger (Wilkins kick)
TB — Alstott 1 run (Gramatica kick)
TB — Pittman 5 pass from Griese (Gramatica kick)
StL — Faulk 1 run (Wilkins kick)
StL — Archuleta 93 fumble return (Wilkins kick)
TB — Heller 1 pass from Griese (Gramatica kick)
StL — Holt 36 pass from Bulger (Wilkins kick)

SEVENTH WEEK SUMMARIES
American Football Conference

East Division	W	L	T	Pct.	Pts.	OP
New England	6	0	0	1.000	148	90
N.Y. Jets	5	1	0	.833	127	102
Buffalo	1	5	0	.167	77	106
Miami	1	6	0	.143	86	121

North Division	W	L	T	Pct.	Pts.	OP
Pittsburgh	5	1	0	.833	136	114
Baltimore	4	2	0	.667	117	85
Cleveland	3	4	0	.429	147	147
Cincinnati	2	4	0	.333	106	139

South Division	W	L	T	Pct.	Pts.	OP
Jacksonville	5	2	0	.714	122	126
Indianapolis	4	2	0	.667	183	133
Houston	3	3	0	.500	138	137
Tennessee	2	5	0	.286	124	158

West Division	W	L	T	Pct.	Pts.	OP
Denver	5	2	0	.714	140	100
San Diego	4	3	0	.571	177	142
Kansas City	2	4	0	.333	161	142
Oakland	2	5	0	.286	124	181

National Football Conference

East Division	W	L	T	Pct.	Pts.	OP
Philadelphia	6	0	0	1.000	171	94
N.Y. Giants	4	2	0	.667	117	100
Dallas	2	4	0	.333	107	156
Washington	2	4	0	.333	84	95

North Division	W	L	T	Pct.	Pts.	OP
Minnesota	5	1	0	.833	170	128
Detroit	4	2	0	.667	176	123
Green Bay	3	4	0	.429	178	172
Chicago	1	5	0	.167	85	108

South Division	W	L	T	Pct.	Pts.	OP
Atlanta	5	2	0	.714	129	142
New Orleans	3	4	0	.429	154	191
Tampa Bay	2	5	0	.286	109	124
Carolina	1	5	0	.167	83	135

West Division	W	L	T	Pct.	Pts.	OP
St. Louis	4	3	0	.571	158	165
Seattle	3	3	0	.500	129	101
Arizona	2	4	0	.333	112	104
San Francisco	1	5	0	.167	105	159

SUNDAY, OCTOBER 24
ARIZONA 25, SEATTLE 17—at Sun Devil Stadium, attendance 35,695. Neil Rackers tied an NFL record with 3 field goals in excess of 50 yards as the Cardinals rallied against the Seahawks. The Cardinals' defense intercepted 4 passes, which led to 17 points, beginning with Renaldo Hill's interception on the Seahawks' first possession that led to Josh McCown's 11-yard touchdown pass to Larry Fitzgerald. In the second quarter, Rackers kicked a 55-yard field goal with 3:01 left in the half. Karlos Dansby intercepted Matt Hasselbeck's pass on the next play, and Rackers made another 55-yard kick with 1:01 left in the half for a 13-3 lead. Hasselbeck's 1-yard touchdown pass to Darrell Jackson culminated a 72-yard drive to pull within 13-10, and Ken Lucas intercepted McCown's pass three plays later and returned it 21 yards for a touchdown and 17-16 lead. Gerald Hayes blocked Donnie Jones' punt for a safety to give Arizona an 18-17 lead with 8:50 left, and Duane Starks' interception set up Emmitt Smith's 23-yard touchdown run on third-and-9 with 1:53 remaining. The Seahawks drove to their own 45 only to have David Macklin intercept Hasselbeck's final pass. Rackers' 50-yard field goal

in the third quarter capped a 6:48 drive and staked the Cardinals to 16-3 lead. McCown was 22 of 36 for 212 yards and 1 touchdown, with 1 interception. Smith rushed 26 times for 106 yards. Hasselbeck was 14 of 41 for 195 yards and 1 touchdown, with 4 interceptions. Jackson had 8 receptions for 117 yards for the Seahawks.

Seattle	0	3	7	7 —	17
Arizona	7	6	3	9 —	25

Ariz	—	Fitzgerald 25 pass from McCown (Rackers kick)
Sea	—	FG J. Brown 54
Ariz	—	FG Rackers 55
Ariz	—	FG Rackers 55
Ariz	—	FG Rackers 50
Sea	—	D. Jackson 1 pass from Hasselbeck (J. Brown kick)
Sea	—	Lucas 21 interception return (J. Brown kick)
Ariz	—	Safety, Hayes blocked punt out of end zone
Ariz	—	E. Smith 23 run (Rackers kick)

BALTIMORE 20, BUFFALO 6—at M & T Bank Stadium, attendance 69,809. The Ravens' defense forced 5 turnovers, highlighted by Deion Sanders' interception return, and 4 sacks to outlast the Bills. The Bills' defense allowed just 160 yards, including just 17 yards in 23 plays and 1 first down in the second half, but were unable to catch the Ravens. Trailing 3-0, the Ravens drove 54 yards for a field goal, Sanders returned an interception for a touchdown, and the Ravens forced a punt and drove 83 yards for B.J. Sams' 5-yard touchdown run for a 17-3 lead with 10:13 left in the half. The Bills added a field goal in the third quarter before committing 4 consecutive turnovers. Sanders intercepted a pass at the Ravens' 19 to stop one drive, and Chad Williams intercepted a pass at the Ravens' 1 to stop another. Williams returned his interception 93 yards to set up Matt Stover's 19-yard field goal with 4:42 left. Kyle Boller was 10 of 19 for 86 yards. Sanders had 2 interceptions and 2 passes defensed. Drew Bledsoe was 20 of 36 for 203 yards, with 4 interceptions.

Buffalo	3	0	3	0 —	6
Baltimore	10	7	0	3 —	20

Balt	—	FG Lindell 24
Buff	—	FG Stover 24
Balt	—	Sanders 48 interception return (Stover kick)
Balt	—	Sams 5 run (Stover kick)
Buff	—	FG Lindell 21
Balt	—	FG Stover 19

SAN DIEGO 17, CAROLINA 6—at Bank of America Stadium, attendance 73,096. Jesse Chatman's 5-yard touchdown run with 1:42 remaining helped the Chargers hold off the Panthers. The Panthers kicked field goals with their first two possessions, then failed to reach the Chargers' red zone the remainder of the game. Nate Kaeding missed a 29-yard field-goal attempt just before halftime, but John Kasay missed from 46 yards early in the second half. The Chargers answered with a 64-yard drive, capped by LaDainian Tomlinson's 8-yard run for a 7-6 lead. Following a three-and-out, Kaeding made a 44-yard kick. The Panthers drove to the Chargers' 24 with 3:19 left, but Jake Delhomme's fourth-down pass fell incomplete. Drew Brees then completed a 16-yard jump pass to Eric Parker on third-and-10 to keep alive the drive, and Chatman followed with a 52-yard run. On third-and-goal from the Panthers' 5, needing a touchdown to clinch the victory, Chatman powered over right guard for a touchdown and 17-6 lead. Brees was 21 of 32 for 196 yards. Delhomme was 17 of 36 for 155 yards, with 1 interception.

San Diego	0	0	10	7 —	17
Carolina	6	0	0	0 —	6

Car	—	FG Kasay 28
Car	—	FG Kasay 21
SD	—	Tomlinson 8 run (Kaeding kick)
SD	—	FG Kaeding 44

SD — Chatman 5 run (Kaeding kick)

PHILADELPHIA 34, CLEVELAND 31 (OT)—at Cleveland Browns Stadium, attendance 73,394. David Akers kicked a 50-yard field goal 9:58 into overtime as the Eagles improved to 6-0. Steve Heiden's 21-yard touchdown catch with 7:31 left in the third quarter gave the Browns a 24-21 advantage. After an exchange of punts, Donovan McNabb tossed a 2-yard touchdown pass to L.J. Smith on third-and-goal with 14:06 left. Frisman Jackson fumbled the ensuing kickoff, and Quintin Mikell recovered the ball to set up David Akers' 38-yard field goal for a 31-24 lead with 10:47 to play. Jeff Garcia tied the game by scrambling and diving into the end zone from 4 yards with 30 seconds left to cap a 54-yard drive that benefited from Brian Dawkins' roughing-the-passer penalty on fourth down from the Eagles' 32. The Eagles won the overtime toss, and after an exchange of punts, McNabb scrambled 28 yards, and his 12-yard pass to Reno Mahe led to Akers' game-winning kick. McNabb was 28 of 43 for 376 yards and 4 touchdowns, with 1 interception. Todd Pinkston had 6 catches for 100 yards, and Terrell Owens had 4 receptions for 109 yards. Garcia was 21 of 32 for 236 yards and 1 touchdown, with 1 interception.

Philadelphia	14	7	0	10	3 —	34
Cleveland	7	10	7	7	0 —	31

Phil	—	Lewis 10 pass from McNabb (Akers kick)
Cle	—	Green 11 run (Dawson kick)
Phil	—	Owens 39 pass from McNabb (Akers kick)
Cle	—	FG Dawson 38
Phil	—	Owens 40 pass from McNabb (Akers kick)
Cle	—	Suggs 13 run (Dawson kick)
Cle	—	Heiden 21 pass from Garcia (Dawson kick)
Phil	—	L. Smith 2 pass from McNabb (Akers kick)
Phil	—	FG Akers 38
Cle	—	Garcia 4 run (Dawson kick)
Phil	—	FG Akers 50

GREEN BAY 41, DALLAS 20—at Lambeau Field, attendance 70,679. Ahman Green rushed for 163 yards and 2 touchdowns as the Packers avoided what would have been their first 0-4 start at home since 1986. The Packers had 480 yards and scored on their first seven possessions. Six of the Packers' drives were at least 50 yards, capped by Green's 90-yard touchdown run with 1:25 left in the third quarter to take a 41-13 lead. Brett Favre was 23 of 29 for 258 yards and 2 touchdowns. Javon Walker had 8 catches for 129 yards, and Green rushed 15 times for 163 yards. Vinny Testaverde was 23 of 35 for 308 yards and 1 touchdown. Jason Witten had 8 catches for 112 yards.

Dallas	6	0	7	7 —	20
Green Bay	3	17	21	0 —	41

Dall	—	FG Cundiff 46
GB	—	FG Longwell 26
Dall	—	FG Cundiff 24
GB	—	Green 1 run (Longwell kick)
GB	—	Walker 5 pass from Favre (Longwell kick)
GB	—	FG Longwell 40
GB	—	Franks 8 pass from Fisher (Longwell kick)
Dall	—	Witten 42 pass from Testaverde (Cundiff kick)
GB	—	Driver 33 pass from Favre (Longwell kick)
GB	—	Green 90 run (Longwell kick)
Dall	—	George 5 run (Cundiff kick)

JACKSONVILLE 27, INDIANAPOLIS 24—at RCA Dome, attendance 56,615. Josh Scobee made a 53-yard field goal with 38 seconds remaining as the Jaguars snapped the Colts' four-game winning

streak. The Colts strung together consecutive drives of 92 and 80 yards, capped by Dallas Clark's touchdown catch with 12 seconds left in the half, to take a 14-10 lead. Jason David intercepted Byron Leftwich's pass to begin the second half, and Josh Williams recovered Leftwich's fumbled snap at the Colts' 2 to thwart another drive. The Jaguars' defense forced 2 punts, the second of which led to Scobee's 32-yard field goal to pull within 14-13. Donovin Darius recovered Clark's fumble on the next play, and Scobee kicked another field goal for a 16-14 Jacksonville lead. Mike Vanderjagt kicked a field goal with 9:32 to play, but the Jaguars answered five plays later, on Jimmy Smith's 25-yard touchdown catch. Peyton Manning's 39-yard scoring pass with 3:52 left tied the game, but Leftwich completed a 9-yard pass on third-and-7 to the Colts' 30. Ron Mathis sacked Leftwich for a six-yard loss on third down, but Scobee came out and made a 53-yard kick. Leftwich was 23 of 30 for 300 yards and 2 touchdowns, with 1 interception. Fred Taylor had 20 carries for 107 yards. Smith had 5 catches for 113 yards. Manning was 27 of 39 for 368 yards and 3 touchdowns. Brandon Stokley had 7 catches for 112 yards.

Jacksonville	0	10	3	14 —	27
Indianapolis	0	14	0	10 —	24

Jax	—	Brady 4 pass from Leftwich (Scobee kick)
Ind	—	Harrison 7 pass from Manning (Vanderjagt kick)
Jax	—	FG Scobee 26
Ind	—	Clark 17 pass from Manning (Vanderjagt kick)
Jax	—	FG Scobee 32
Jax	—	FG Scobee 26
Ind	—	FG Vanderjagt 34
Jax	—	J. Smith 25 pass from Leftwich (Scobee kick)
Ind	—	Harrison 39 pass from Manning (Vanderjagt kick)
Jax	—	FG Scobee 53

KANSAS CITY 56, ATLANTA 10—at Arrowhead Stadium, attendance 78,260. Priest Holmes and Derrick Blaylock became the first pair of teammates to each score 4 touchdowns in an NFL game as the Chiefs rolled past the Falcons. The Chiefs outgained the Falcons 540-222 and had an advantage in time of possession (38:54-21:06). Trailing 3-0, the Chiefs scored touchdowns on four of their next five possessions for a 28-3 lead, and Eric Warfield intercepted Michael Vick's pass and returned it 6 yards to the Falcons' 16. Allen Rossum returned a punt early in the third quarter, but Blaylock, who was playing in place of an injured Holmes, who left in the third quarter, scored 3 more times. Trent Green was 20 of 27 for 269 yards. Vick was 7 of 21 for 119 yards, with 2 interceptions.

Atlanta	3	0	7	0 —	10
Kansas City	14	21	7	14 —	56

Atl	—	FG Feely 19
KC	—	Holmes 15 run (Tynes kick)
KC	—	Blaylock 7 run (Tynes kick)
KC	—	Holmes 2 run (Tynes kick)
KC	—	Holmes 2 run (Tynes kick)
KC	—	Holmes 1 run (Tynes kick)
Atl	—	Rossum 75 punt return (Feely kick)
KC	—	Blaylock 1 run (Tynes kick)
KC	—	Blaylock 3 run (Tynes kick)
KC	—	Blaylock 2 run (Tynes kick)

MIAMI 31, ST. LOUIS 14—at Pro Player Stadium, attendance 72,945. Jay Fiedler passed for 2 touchdowns as the Dolphins won their first game. With the score 7-7, Fiedler's third-and-18 pass from the Rams' 32 fell incomplete. A holding penalty was called, and the Rams accepted the penalty. Faced with third-and-28, Fiedler completed a 42-yard touchdown pass to Randy McMichael with 22 seconds left in the half. The Rams drove into the Dolphins red zone to begin the second half, but Sammy

Knight intercepted Marc Bulger's pass for a touchback. Travis Minor scored three plays into the fourth quarter for a 21-7 lead, and following a three-and-out, Matt Bryant kicked a 43-yard field goal with 8:47 remaining. The Rams cut the deficit to 24-14 and forced the Dolphins into third-and-7 on their next possession, but Fiedler completed a 71-yard touchdown pass to Chris Chambers. Fiedler was 13 of 17 for 203 yards and 2 touchdowns. Chambers had 3 catches for 128 yards. Bulger was 23 of 39 for 295 yards and 1 touchdown, with 1 interception.

St. Louis	0	7	0	7	—	14
Miami	7	7	0	17	—	31
Mia	—	Morris 8 run (Bryant kick)				
StL	—	Bulger 15 run (Wilkins kick)				
Mia	—	McMichael 42 pass from Fiedler (Bryant kick)				
Mia	—	Minor 13 run (Bryant kick)				
Mia	—	FG Bryant 43				
StL	—	McDonald 15 pass from Bulger (Wilkins kick)				
Mia	—	Chambers 71 pass from Fiedler (Bryant kick)				

MINNESOTA 20, TENNESSEE 3—at Metrodome, attendance 64,108. Daunte Culpepper passed for 183 yards and 1 touchdown and Minnesota's defense forced 4 turnovers as the Vikings won their fourth consecutive game. The Titans drove for a field goal on their opening possession, but Steve McNair injured his sternum on the first play of the second quarter with the score 3-3. Moe Williams' 1-yard run on the next possession gave the Vikings a 10-3 lead. Antoine Winfield's interception and return to midfield, along with Culpepper's 14-yard pass to Nate Burleson on fourth-and-6, set up Culpepper's 2-yard touchdown pass to Marcus Robinson with 23 seconds left in the half for a 17-3 lead. The Titans drove to the Vikings' 5 to begin the second half, but Raonall Smith intercepted Billy Volek's pass to end the Titans' final scoring threat. Culpepper was 24 of 30 for 183 yards and 1 touchdown. Mewelde Moore had 20 carries for 138 yards. McNair was 2 of 5 for 2 yards before being replaced by Volek, who was 17 of 36 for 190 yards, with 3 interceptions.

Tennessee	3	0	0	0	—	3
Minnesota	3	14	0	3	—	20
Tenn	—	FG Anderson 40				
Minn	—	FG Andersen 29				
Minn	—	Williams 1 run (Andersen kick)				
Minn	—	Robinson 2 pass from Culpepper (Andersen kick)				
Minn	—	FG Andersen 29				

NEW ENGLAND 13, N.Y. JETS 7—at Gillette Stadium, attendance 68,756. Tom Brady's 7-yard touchdown pass to David Patten with five seconds left in the half propelled the Patriots to victory in a game of undefeated teams. The Patriots kicked 2 field goals with their first two possessions to take a 6-0 lead. The Jets answered with a 13-play, 78-yard drive, capped by Chad Pennington's 1-yard run, for a 7-6 lead with 1:55 left in the half. Brady engineered a 62-yard drive with just one timeout at his disposal, capped by his 7-yard pass to Patten with five seconds left in the half. The Jets final possession of the game produced the only scoring threat of the second half. On third-and-5 from the Jets' 27, Curtis Martin was dropped for a 3-yard loss, and Pennington's fourth-and-8 pass fell incomplete with 2:14 left. On third-and-2, Corey Dillon gained 4 yards off left tackle to clinch the victory. Brady was 20 of 29 for 230 yards and 1 touchdown. David Givens had 5 catches for 107 yards. Dillon rushed 22 times for 115 yards. Pennington was 19 of 30 for 162 yards.

N.Y. Jets	0	7	0	0	—	7
New England	3	10	0	0	—	13
NE	—	FG Vinatieri 41				
NE	—	FG Vinatieri 27				
NYJ	—	Pennington 1 run (Brien kick)				
NE	—	Patten 7 pass from Brady (Vinatieri kick)				

DETROIT 28, N.Y. GIANTS 13—at Giants Stadium, attendance 78,841. Joey Harrington passed for 2 touchdowns and the Lions' defense recorded 6 sacks as Detroit pulled away. The Giants' led 10-7 late in the second quarter and drove to the Lions' 11 with 52 seconds left in the half, but Kurt Warner's pass into the end zone was intercepted by Chris Cash for a touchdown. The Lions' defense forced a punt to begin the second half, and Kevin Jones scored on a 2-yard run to cap a 68-yard drive for a 14-10 lead. Steve Christie pulled the Giants within 14-13 with 8:18 left in the third quarter. The Lions responded with a 70-yard drive, highlighted by Harrington's 20-yard pass to Reggie Swinton on third-and-7, and the pair hooked up for a 2-yard touchdown on third-and-goal with 2:52 left in the game. Warner's fourth-down pass was incomplete from the Giants' 22, and Artose Pinner scored four plays later to clinch the victory. Harrington was 18 of 22 for 230 yards and 2 touchdowns. Shaun Rogers had 5 tackles and 1 sack. Warner was 23 of 34 for 270 yards and 1 touchdown, with 1 interception. Tiki Barber had 7 catches for 102 yards.

Detroit	7	0	7	14	—	28
N.Y. Giants	7	3	0	3	—	13
Det	—	R. Williams 18 pass from Harrington (Hanson kick)				
NYG	—	Barber 62 pass from Warner (Christie kick)				
NYG	—	FG Christie 19				
Det	—	K. Jones 2 run (Hanson kick)				
NYG	—	FG Christie 25				
Det	—	Swinton 2 pass from Harrington (Hanson kick)				
Det	—	Pinner 8 run (Hanson kick)				

NEW ORLEANS 31, OAKLAND 26—at Network Associates Coliseum, attendance 45,337. A fumbled kickoff allowed the Saints to score 10 points in 11 seconds to snap a three-game losing streak. The Raiders scored on their next two drives to cut the deficit to 21-19 with 9:51 to play. On the ensuing possession, Aaron Brooks twice completed passes to Joe Horn on third down to set up John Carney's 41-yard field goal with 4:31 remaining. Carlos Francis fumbled on the ensuing kick return. Colby Bockwoldt recovered the ball and returned it 6 yards for a touchdown and a 31-19 lead. The Raiders cut the lead to five points with 2:34 remaining, but Brooks completed a third-and-7 pass to Horn and then had a 2-yard quarterback sneak on third-and-1 moments later to clinch the victory. Brooks was 23 of 39 for 282 yards and 1 touchdown. Horn had 9 receptions for 123 yards. Kerry Collins was 26 of 45 for 350 yards and 2 touchdowns, with 1 interception. Jerry Porter had 6 catches for 113 yards.

New Orleans	0	7	14	10	—	31
Oakland	6	3	0	17	—	26
Oak	—	FG Janikowski 28				
Oak	—	FG Janikowski 42				
Oak	—	FG Janikowski 44				
NO	—	Hall 4 pass from Brooks (Carney kick)				
NO	—	McAllister 3 run (Carney kick)				
NO	—	McAllister 1 run (Carney kick)				
Oak	—	Jolley 34 pass from Collins (Janikowski kick)				
Oak	—	FG Janikowski 40				
NO	—	FG Carney 41				
NO	—	Bockwoldt 6 fumble return (Carney kick)				
Oak	—	Porter 13 pass from Collins (Janikowski kick)				

TAMPA BAY 19, CHICAGO 7—at Raymond James Stadium, attendance 65,550. The Buccaneers' defense allowed just 167 yards, had 4 sacks and forced 2 turnovers. Leading 3-0, the Buccaneers engineered a 16-play, 93-yard drive, capped by Brian Griese's 6-yard touchdown pass to Michael Clayton with 48 seconds left in the half for a 10-0 lead. The Bears trailed 13-0 in the third quarter when

Todd Johnson recovered Michael Pittman's fumble at the Bears' 31. Six plays later, Jones scored from 1-yard out to pull within 13-7. Mike Green recovered Mike Alstott's fumble at the Buccaneers' 39 two plays later, but Shelton Quarles sacked Craig Krenzel at the Buccaneers' 39 on third down forcing a punt. Ronde Barber intercepted Krenzel's pass early in the fourth quarter to place the ball on the Bears' 11, and Pittman scored three plays later. Griese was 15 of 23 for 163 yards and 1 touchdown. Pittman rushed 23 times for 109 yards. Jonathan Quinn was 5 of 9 for 47 yards before replaced by Krenzel, who was 9 of 19 for 69 yards, with 1 interception.

Chicago	0	0	7	0	—	7
Tampa Bay	0	10	3	6	—	19
TB	—	FG Gramatica 22				
TB	—	Clayton 6 pass from Griese (Gramatica kick)				
TB	—	FG Gramatica 22				
Chi	—	T. Jones 1 run (Edinger kick)				
TB	—	Pittman 3 run (pass failed)				

MONDAY NIGHT, OCTOBER 25
CINCINNATI 23, DENVER 10—at Paul Brown Stadium, attendance 65,806. Rudi Johnson's 36-yard touchdown run late in the third quarter helped the Bengals pull away from the Broncos. Carson Palmer's 50-yard touchdown pass to Chad Johnson staked the Bengals to an early 7-0 lead. The Bengals twice drove inside the Broncos' 10 in the first half, but Rudi Johnson was stopped on downs and Champ Bailey intercepted Palmer's pass to thwart the other drive. Deltha O'Neal's interception led to Shayne Graham's 53-yard field goal for a 10-0 lead, and after the Broncos scored Graham added a 34-yard field goal to end the half. Leading 13-10 late in the third quarter, Palmer completed a 23-yard pass to Chad Johnson on third-and-3, and two plays later Rudi Johnson rumbled 36 yards for a touchdown and 20-10 lead. Tory James' interception at the Broncos' 20 led to Graham's third field goal, and Justin Smith sacked Jake Plummer on fourth-and-17 at the Broncos' 39 with 4:05 left. Palmer was 12 of 21 for 198 yards and 1 touchdown, with 1 interception. Chad Johnson had 7 receptions for 149 yards, and Rudi Johnson had 24 carries for 119 yards. Plummer was 23 of 40 for 221 yards and 1 touchdown, with 2 interceptions. Reuben Droughns rushed 24 times for 110 yards.

Denver	0	7	3	0	—	10
Cincinnati	7	6	7	3	—	23
Cin	—	C. Johnson 50 pass from Palmer (Graham kick)				
Cin	—	FG Graham 53				
Den	—	R. Smith 3 pass from Plummer (Elam kick)				
Cin	—	FG Graham 34				
Den	—	FG Elam 29				
Cin	—	R. Johnson 36 run (Graham kick)				
Cin	—	FG Graham 35				

EIGHTH WEEK SUMMARIES
American Football Conference

East Division	W	L	T	Pct.	Pts.	OP
New England	6	1	0	.857	168	124
N.Y. Jets	6	1	0	.857	168	116
Buffalo	2	5	0	.286	115	120
Miami	1	7	0	.125	100	162
North Division	**W**	**L**	**T**	**Pct.**	**Pts.**	**OP**
Pittsburgh	6	1	0	.857	170	134
Baltimore	4	3	0	.571	127	100
Cleveland	3	4	0	.429	147	147
Cincinnati	2	5	0	.286	126	166
South Division	**W**	**L**	**T**	**Pct.**	**Pts.**	**OP**
Jacksonville	4	3	0	.625	128	146
Houston	4	3	0	.571	158	143
Indianapolis	4	3	0	.571	218	178
Tennessee	3	5	0	.375	151	178
West Division	**W**	**L**	**T**	**Pct.**	**Pts.**	**OP**
Denver	5	3	0	.625	168	141
San Diego	5	3	0	.625	219	156

	W	L	T	Pct.	Pts.	OP
Kansas City	3	4	0	.429	206	177
Oakland	2	6	0	.250	138	223

National Football Conference

East Division	W	L	T	Pct.	Pts.	OP
Philadelphia	7	0	0	1.000	186	104
N.Y. Giants	5	2	0	.714	151	113
Dallas	3	4	0	.429	138	177
Washington	2	5	0	.286	98	123
North Division	**W**	**L**	**T**	**Pct.**	**Pts.**	**OP**
Minnesota	5	2	0	.714	183	162
Detroit	4	3	0	.571	137	154
Green Bay	4	4	0	.500	206	186
Chicago	2	5	0	.286	108	121
South Division	**W**	**L**	**T**	**Pct.**	**Pts.**	**OP**
Atlanta	6	2	0	.750	170	170
New Orleans	3	4	0	.429	154	191
Tampa Bay	2	5	0	.286	109	124
Carolina	1	6	0	.143	100	158
West Division	**W**	**L**	**T**	**Pct.**	**Pts.**	**OP**
St. Louis	4	3	0	.571	158	165
Seattle	4	3	0	.571	152	118
Arizona	2	5	0	.286	126	142
San Francisco	1	6	0	.143	118	182

SUNDAY, OCTOBER 31

BUFFALO 38, ARIZONA 14—at Ralph Wilson Stadium, attendance 65,887. Willis McGahee rushed for 102 yards and 2 touchdowns as the Bills won a game played in 20-to-30-mile-per-hour winds and the rain. The Bills gained just 209 yards, but returned one kickoff for a touchdown, and their other scoring drives were 19, 55, 19, 11, and 30 yards. The Cardinals drove 58 yards for a touchdown to pull within 10-7, but Terrence McGee returned the ensuing kickoff 87 yards for a touchdown and 17-7 lead. Nate Clements returned a punt 34 yards late in the third quarter to set up Drew Bledsoe's 8-yard touchdown pass to Eric Moulds. The Bills forced a three-and-out, and Clements returned the punt 40 yards. Three plays later, Bledsoe completed a 12-yard touchdown pass to Tim Euhus for a 31-7 lead. McGahee scored following another three-and-out to cap the Bills' scoring. Bledsoe was 8 of 17 for 81 yards and 2 touchdowns. McGahee had 30 carries for 102 yards. Josh McCown was 9 of 24 for 101 yards and 1 touchdown.

Arizona	0	7	0	7	—	14
Buffalo	10	7	0	21	—	38

Buff	—	FG Lindell 25
Buff	—	McGahee 5 run (Lindell kick)
Ariz	—	Ayanbadejo 4 run (Rackers kick)
Buff	—	McGee 87 kickoff return (Lindell kick)
Buff	—	Moulds 8 pass from Bledsoe (Lindell kick)
Buff	—	Euhus 12 pass from Bledsoe (Lindell kick)
Buff	—	McGahee 1 run (Lindell kick)
Ariz	—	B. Johnson 28 pass from McCown (Rackers kick)

DALLAS 31, DETROIT 21—at Texas Stadium, attendance 63,616. Vinny Testaverde passed for 3 touchdowns as the Cowboys snapped a three-game losing streak. Dre' Bly intercepted Testaverde's pass and returned it 55 yards for a touchdown to take a 14-7 lead in the second quarter. The Cowboys responded with an 11-play, 80-yard drive to tie the game. ReShard Lee returned the second half's opening kickoff 52 yards, and a 43-yard pass interference penalty led Testaverde's 3-yard touchdown run, his first rushing touchdown since 1998. Trailing 21-14, the Lions went for it on fourth-and-1 at the Cowboys' 37 early in the fourth quarter, but Nathan Jones sacked Joey Harrington. Billy Cundiff capitalized with a 40-yard field goal with 6:59 to play, but the Lions needed just three plays to pull within 24-21 on Harrington's 50-yard touchdown pass to David Kircus with 5:29 remaining. Faced with third-and-8, Testaverde completed a 30-yard pass to two-way player Terrence Newman. Three plays later, on another third-and-8, Testaverde hit Keyshawn John-

son with a 38-yard touchdown pass on a deep post for a 31-21 lead with 1:54 to play. Testaverde was 19 of 24 for 235 yards and 3 touchdowns, with 3 interceptions. Harrington was 19 of 32 for 255 yards and 2 touchdowns, with 1 interception.

Detroit	7	7	0	7	—	21
Dallas	7	7	7	10	—	31

Det	—	K. Jones 1 pass from Harrington (Hanson kick)
Dall	—	Witten 17 pass from Testaverde (Cundiff kick)
Det	—	Bly 55 interception return (Hanson kick)
Dall	—	K. Johnson 26 pass from Testaverde (Cundiff kick)
Dall	—	Testaverde 3 run (Cundiff kick)
Dall	—	FG Cundiff 40
Det	—	Kircus 50 pass from Harrington (Hanson kick)
Dall	—	K. Johnson 38 pass from Testaverde (Cundiff kick)

ATLANTA 41, DENVER 28—at INVESCO Field at Mile High, attendance 75,083. Michael Vick passed for 2 touchdowns and rushed for 115 yards as the Falcons won despite allowing a Broncos-record 567 total yards. The Falcons scored on four of their first five possessions to take a 20-14 halftime lead. And added the first two touchdowns of the second half, capped by Peerless Price's 25-yard scoring catch with 14:17 left, for a 34-14 lead. Five of the Falcons' scoring drive were at least 60 yards. The Broncos pulled within 34-21, forced a punt, and drove to the Falcons' 7 before Jake Plummer's fourth-down pass fell incomplete with 3:53 left. Two plays after another punt, Kevin Mathis intercepted Plummer's pass and returned it 66 yards for a touchdown with 2:20 remaining. Vick was 18 of 24 for 252 yards and 2 touchdowns, and rushed 12 times for 115 yards. Plummer was 31 of 55 for a franchise-best 499 yards and 4 touchdowns, with 3 interceptions. Rod Smith had 9 catches for 208 yards.

Atlanta	3	17	7	14	—	41
Denver	14	0	0	14	—	28

Den	—	Hape 1 pass from Plummer (Elam kick)
Den	—	FG Feely 24
Den	—	R. Smith 80 pass from Plummer (Elam kick)
Atl	—	Duckett 21 run (Feely kick)
Atl	—	Price 34 pass from Vick (Feely kick)
Atl	—	FG Feely 43
Atl	—	Dunn 5 run (Feely kick)
Atl	—	Price 25 pass from Vick (Feely kick)
Den	—	Watts 7 pass from Plummer (Elam kick)
Atl	—	Mathis 66 interception return (Feely kick)
Den	—	Lelie 35 pass from Plummer (Elam kick)

HOUSTON 20, JACKSONVILLE 6—at Reliant Stadium, attendance 70,502. Demarcus Faggins returned an interception 43 yards for a touchdown with 42 seconds remaining to thwart a possible-game-tying drive as the Texans won for the fourth time in five games. Trailing 7-3, Josh Scobee missed a 49-yard field-goal attempt with 16 seconds left in the half. David Carr completed a 26-yard pass to Andre Johnson and Kris Brown missed a 53-yard attempt with one second remaining, but the Jaguars were penalized 15 yards for leverage. Brown proceeded to drill the 38-yard attempt as the half expired for a 10-3 lead. Kailee Wong's interception at the Texans' 44 early in the fourth quarter led to Brown's 21-yard field goal with 6:45 to play. The Jaguars drove 65 yards for a field goal, and forced a punt to begin at their own 33 with 56 seconds left. On second down, Faggins intercepted Byron Leftwich's pass and returned it 43 yards to clinch the victory. Carr was

26 of 34 for 276 yards and 1 touchdown. Leftwich was 25 of 40 for 227 yards, with 2 interceptions. Jimmy Smith had 9 receptions for 117 yards.

Jacksonville	0	3	0	3	—	6
Houston	7	3	0	10	—	20

Hous	—	Bradford 15 pass from Carr (K. Brown kick)
Jax	—	FG Scobee 44
Hous	—	FG K. Brown 38
Hous	—	FG K. Brown 21
Jax	—	FG Scobee 36
Hous	—	Faggins 43 interception return (K. Brown kick)

KANSAS CITY 45, INDIANAPOLIS 35—at Arrowhead Stadium, attendance 78,312. Priest Holmes rushed for 143 yards and 3 touchdowns, and Trent Green passed for 389 yards and 3 scores, as the Chiefs posted consecutive victories. The teams combined for 1,095 yards, third-most in NFL history (Chiefs 590-505), but the Chiefs controlled the ball for 37:33. The Chiefs fumbled at the Colts' 4 on the opening drive, and then scored 4 consecutive touchdowns and added a field goal in the final minutes for a 31-14 lead. Four of the five drives exceeded 60 yards. Undaunted, the Colts scored on their first two possessions of the second half, driving 92 and 76 yards, both in three plays, to pull within 31-28 with 4:16 left in the third quarter. Green's 12-yard pass to Dante Hall on third-and-8 highlighted an 11-play drive capped by Holmes' 1-yard scoring run with 12:58 to play. After an exchange of punts, Peyton Manning connected on a 6-yard touchdown pass to Reggie Wayne with 5:27 remaining to cut the deficit to 38-35. Faced with third-and-6, Green completed a 25-yard pass to Eddie Kennison and three plays later, on third-and-5, found Tony Gonzalez for a 14-yard touchdown with 2:17 left. Greg Wesley intercepted Manning's pass in the end zone three plays later to clinch the victory. Green was 27 of 34 for 389 yards and 3 touchdowns. Holmes rushed 32 times for 143 yards and Gonzalez added 8 catches for 125 yards. Manning was 25 of 44 for 472 yards and 5 touchdowns, with 1 interception. Wayne had 6 catches for 119 yards, and Marvin Harrison added 5 receptions, also for 119 yards.

Indianapolis	7	7	14	7	—	35
Kansas City	7	24	0	14	—	45

Ind	—	Harrison 52 pass from Manning (Vanderjagt kick)
KC	—	Gonzalez 21 pass from Green (Tynes kick)
KC	—	Morton 7 pass from Green (Tynes kick)
KC	—	Holmes 21 run (Tynes kick)
Ind	—	Pollard 5 pass from Manning (Vanderjagt kick)
KC	—	Holmes 11 run (Tynes kick)
KC	—	FG Tynes 32
Ind	—	Harrison 22 pass from Manning (Vanderjagt kick)
Ind	—	Wayne 41 pass from Manning (Vanderjagt kick)
KC	—	Holmes 1 run (Tynes kick)
Ind	—	Wayne 6 pass from Manning (Vanderjagt kick)
KC	—	Gonzalez 14 pass from Green (Tynes kick)

N.Y. GIANTS 34, MINNESOTA 13—at Metrodome, attendance 64,012. Tiki Barber rushed for 101 yards and 2 touchdowns as the Giants jumped to a 34-0 lead on the road en route to victory. The Giants' defense forced 3 turnovers, which led to 17 points. Leading 10-0 in the second quarter, Gibril Wilson intercepted Daunte Culpepper's pass and returned it 39 yards to the Vikings' 36. Five plays later Barber scored his second touchdown for a 17-0 lead. Moments later Morten Andersen's 38-yard field-goal attempt hit the left upright, and Steve Christie's 30-yard field goal with five seconds left increased the lead to 20-0. Will Allen's third-quarter interception led to the first of Mike Cloud's 2 touchdown runs, the last of which gave the Giants a 34-0 lead with 12:08 remaining. Kurt Warner was 13 of 21 for 144 yards. Barber rushed 24 times for 101 yards. Culpepper was 24 of 42 for 231 yards and 1 touchdown, with 2 interceptions.

| N.Y. Giants | 10 | 10 | 7 | 7 | — | 34 |
| Minnesota | 0 | 0 | 13 | 0 | — | 13 |

NYG	—	FG Christie 50
NYG	—	Barber 2 run (Christie kick)
NYG	—	Barber 5 run (Christie kick)
NYG	—	FG Christie 30
NYG	—	Cloud 1 run (Christie kick)
NYG	—	Cloud 2 run (Christie kick)
Minn	—	Bennett 10 run (Andersen kick)
Minn	—	Burleson 1 pass from Culpepper (pass failed)

PHILADELPHIA 15, BALTIMORE 10—at Lincoln Financial Field, attendance 67,715. David Akers kicked 3 field goals and Donovan McNabb completed an 11-yard scoring pass to Terrell Owens as the Eagles improved to 7-0 for the first time in club history. The Eagles led 9-3 in the fourth quarter when Brian Dawkins forced Chester Taylor to fumble. Hollis Thomas recovered the ball to spark a 65-yard drive, capped by McNabb's scoring pass to Owens with 9:12 to play. The Ravens used a 52-yard pass from Kyle Boller to Clarence Moore to set up Daniel Wilcox's 7-yard touchdown reception on third-and-5 with 5:52 remaining to pull within 15-10. The Ravens' defense forced a three-and-out, but gained just 1 first down and punted. Following another three-and-out, the Ravens' began at their own 29 with 1:34 left. Boller completed a 23-yard pass to Travis Taylor, but then threw 4 consecutive incompletions as the Eagles held on. McNabb was 18 of 33 for 219 yards and 1 touchdown. Owens had 8 catches for 101 yards. Boller was 24 of 38 for 223 yards and 1 touchdown, with 1 interception.

| Baltimore | 3 | 0 | 0 | 7 | — | 10 |
| Philadelphia | 3 | 3 | 0 | 9 | — | 15 |

Phil	—	FG Akers 20
Balt	—	FG Stover 44
Phil	—	FG Akers 41
Phil	—	FG Akers 43
Phil	—	Owens 11 pass from McNabb (pass failed)
Balt	—	Wilcox 7 pass from Boller (Stover kick)

PITTSBURGH 34, NEW ENGLAND 20—at Heinz Field, attendance 64,737. Joey Porter had 3 sacks and forced 2 fumbles as the Steelers forced 4 turnovers to snap the Patriots' NFL-record 18-game winning streak. The Steelers took a 24-3 lead in the second quarter, forcing the Patriots to play come-from-behind football. Playing without injured running back Corey Dillon, the Patriots rushed just 6 times for 5 yards, and the Steelers had a 42:58-17:02 advantage in time of possession. Following Ben Roethlisberger's first touchdown pass, Tom Brady was sacked by Joey Porter and fumbled on the next play. Kimo von Oelhoffen recovered the ball to set up Plaxico Burress' second touchdown catch of the quarter. On the next play, Deshea Townsend intercepted Brady's pass and returned it 39 yards for a touchdown. The Steelers had scored 21 points in 3:33 for a 21-3 lead. The Patriots cut the deficit to 24-10 at halftime and began the second half with the ball. But Kevin Faulk fumbled on the first play from scrimmage, and Aaron Smith recovered at the Patriots' 17 to set up Jerome Bettis' 2-yard run for a 31-10 lead. Brady's 23-yard touchdown pass to David Givens cut the deficit to 34-20 with 6:33 remaining, but the Steelers gained three first downs on the final drive to run out the clock and clinch the victory. Roethlisberger was 18 of 24 for 196 yards and 2 touchdowns. Duce Staley rushed 25 times for 125 yards. Brady was 25 of 43 for 271 yards and 2 touchdowns, with 2 interceptions. Givens had 8 catches for 101 yards.

| New England | 3 | 7 | 3 | 7 | — | 20 |
| Pittsburgh | 21 | 3 | 10 | 0 | — | 34 |

NE	—	FG Vinatieri 43
Pitt	—	Burress 47 pass from Roethlisberger (Reed kick)
Pitt	—	Burress 4 pass from Roethlisberger (Reed kick)
Pitt	—	Townsend 39 interception return (Reed kick)
Pitt	—	FG Reed 19
NE	—	Givens 2 pass from Brady (Vinatieri kick)
Pitt	—	Bettis 2 run (Reed kick)
NE	—	FG Vinatieri 25
Pitt	—	FG Reed 29
NE	—	Givens 23 pass from Brady (Vinatieri kick)

SAN DIEGO 42, OAKLAND 14—at Qualcomm Stadium, attendance 66,210. Drew Brees passed for 5 touchdowns as the Chargers scored on six of their first seven possessions to down the Raiders. The Chargers led 21-7 before Clinton Hart intercepted Kerry Collins' pass at the Chargers' 34 to stop a rally and set up Tim Dwight's 23-yard touchdown catch with 36 seconds left in the half for a 28-7 halftime lead. Dwight returned the second half's opening kickoff 50 yards to spark a five-play scoring drive, capped by Antonio Gates' touchdown catch. After a three-and-out, Brees engineered a 12-play, 90-yard drive, that culminated with Gates' second touchdown for a 42-7 lead with 3:08 left in the third quarter. Brees was 22 of 25 for 281 yards and 5 touchdowns. Collins was 24 of 39 for 263 yards and 1 touchdown, with 2 interceptions.

| Oakland | 0 | 7 | 0 | 7 | — | 14 |
| San Diego | 14 | 14 | 14 | 0 | — | 42 |

SD	—	Peelle 17 pass from Brees (Kaeding kick)
SD	—	Tomlinson 1 run (Kaeding kick)
Oak	—	Wheatley 5 run (Janikowski kick)
SD	—	McCardell 13 pass from Brees (Kaeding kick)
SD	—	Dwight 23 pass from Brees (Kaeding kick)
SD	—	Gates 5 pass from Brees (Kaeding kick)
SD	—	Gates 1 pass from Brees (Kaeding kick)
Oak	—	Jolley 13 pass from Collins (Janikowski kick)

SEATTLE 23, CAROLINA 17—at Qwest Field, attendance 66,214. Shaun Alexander scored twice and Josh Brown kicked 3 field goals as the Seahawks snapped their three-game losing streak. The Panthers kicked a field goal to begin the second half to pull within 14-10, but 3 Josh Brown field goals increased Seattle's lead to 23-10 with 5:42 left. Marcus Trufant's interception stopped one drive, but a mishandled snap on a field-goal attempt kept the score 23-10 with 2:04 left. Jake Delhomme completed a 63-yard pass to Keary Colbert to set up Muhsin Muhammad's scoring catch with 1:39 left. Trufant recovered the onside kick and the Seahawks ran out the clock. Hasselbeck was 21 of 30 for 201 yards and 1 touchdown, with 1 interception. Shaun Alexander had 32 carries for 195 yards. Delhomme was 19 of 36 for 248 yards, with 1 interception.

| Carolina | 0 | 7 | 3 | 7 | — | 17 |
| Seattle | 7 | 7 | 3 | 6 | — | 23 |

Sea	—	Alexander 3 pass from Hasselbeck (J. Brown kick)
Sea	—	Alexander 4 run (J. Brown kick)
Car	—	Muhammad 15 pass from Delhomme (Kasay kick)
Car	—	FG Kasay 30
Sea	—	FG J. Brown 27
Sea	—	FG J. Brown 45
Sea	—	FG J. Brown 22
Car	—	Muhammad 7 pass from Delhomme (Kasay kick)

TENNESSEE 27, CINCINNATI 20—at The Coliseum, attendance 68,932. Chris Brown rushed for 147 yards and 1 touchdown and Albert Haynesworth forced a fumble in the final minute as the Titans held off the Bengals. The Titans scored on their first three possessions to take a 13-3 lead, and had the ball to begin the second half. But Madieu Williams intercepted Billy Volek's pass and returned it 51 yards for a touchdown to cut the deficit to 13-10. The Titans needed just five plays to drive 70 yards to retake the lead on Troy Fleming's 13-yard touchdown catch on a third-and-4 pass with 2:10 left in the third quarter. Andre Dyson intercepted Carson Palmer's pass on the next play from scrimmage, and Brown scored three plays later for a 27-13 lead. T.J. Houshmandzadeh's 62-yard catch moments later set up Rudi Johnson's 6-yard run to pull the Bengals within 27-20 and cap a wild run of 24 points in six minutes and two seconds. The Bengals' final drive began at their own 33-yard line with 2:07 to play. Palmer completed 5 of 7 passes to reach the Bengals' 9 with 35 seconds left. On second-and-goal, Albert Haynesworth sacked Palmer and forced him to fumble. Juqua Thomas recovered the ball to clinch the victory. Volek, playing for the injured Steve McNair, was 21 of 32 or 210 yards and 2 touchdowns, with 1 interception. Brown rushed 32 times for 147 yards. Palmer was 20 of 36 for 247 yards, with 1 interception.

| Cincinnati | 3 | 0 | 10 | 7 | — | 20 |
| Tennessee | 0 | 13 | 14 | 0 | — | 27 |

Cin	—	FG Graham 28
Tenn	—	FG Anderson 23
Tenn	—	FG Anderson 45
Tenn	—	Meier 1 pass from Volek (Anderson kick)
Cin	—	M. Williams 51 interception return (Graham kick)
Cin	—	FG Graham 50
Tenn	—	Fleming 13 pass from Volek (Anderson kick)
Tenn	—	Brown 1 run (Anderson kick)
Cin	—	R. Johnson 6 run (Graham kick)

GREEN BAY 28, WASHINGTON 14—at FedExField, attendance 89,295. Ahman Green rushed for 2 touchdowns as the Packers won their third consecutive game. The Packers scored on their first three possessions, driving 69, 75, and 76 yards to take a 17-0 lead. Shawn Springs' interception and 28-yard return late in the first half set up Mark Brunell's first touchdown pass to Rod Gardner. Trailing 20-7, Ola Kimrin missed a 35-yard field-goal attempt with 11:50 left, but Springs' second interception and 29-yard return led to Gardner's 12-yard scoring catch to pull the Redskins within 20-14 with 4:46 remaining. Fred Smoot intercepted Brett Favre's pass two plays later, and Clinton Portis scored on a 43-yard touchdown pass. However, an illegal motion penalty nullified the touchdown, and Al Harris intercepted Brunell's pass on the next play with 2:25 left. Green scored four plays later with 1:44 left to cap the scoring. Favre was 20 of 33 for 289 yards and 1 touchdown, with 3 interceptions. Brunell was 25 of 44 for 218 yards and 2 touchdowns, with 2 interceptions.

| Green Bay | 3 | 14 | 3 | 8 | — | 28 |
| Washington | 0 | 7 | 0 | 7 | — | 14 |

GB	—	FG Longwell 37
GB	—	Green 1 run (Longwell kick)
GB	—	Walker 9 pass from Favre (Longwell kick)
Wash	—	Gardner 12 pass from Brunell (Kimrin kick)
GB	—	FG Longwell 39
Wash	—	Gardner 12 pass from Brunell (Kimrin kick)
GB	—	Green 11 run (Ferguson pass from Favre)

SUNDAY NIGHT, OCTOBER 31

CHICAGO 23, SAN FRANCISCO 13—at Soldier Field, attendance 62,054. Nathan Vasher's 71-yard interception return with 3:52 remaining propelled the Bears to victory. The Bears' defense allowed just 162 yards, and the offense scored on their second play on Bernard Berrian's 49-yard touchdown for a quick 7-0 lead. The Bears' drove to the 49ers' 12 on their next possession, but Brandon Moore sacked Krenzel and forced him to fumble. Dwaine Carpenter recovered the ball and returned it 80 yards for a touchdown. Paul Edinger's 27-yard field goal gave the Bears a 16-13 lead with 13:59 remaining. Todd Peterson missed a 50-yard field-goal attempt on the ensuing possession, and following a punt, the 49ers drove to the Bears' 36. On second-and-10, Vasher stepped in front of Ken Dorsey's pass and returned it 71 yards for a 23-13 lead. Craig Krenzel was 13 of 25 for 168 yards and 1 touchdown, with 1 interceptions. Brian Urlacher had 2 sacks. Dorsey was 16 of 36 for 122 yards, with 1 interception.

San Francisco	10	3	0	0 —	13
Chicago	7	6	0	10 —	23

Chi	—	Berrian 49 pass from Krenzel (Edinger kick)
SF	—	Carpenter 80 fumble return (Peterson kick)
SF	—	FG Peterson 48
Chi	—	FG Edinger 52
SF	—	FG Peterson 51
Chi	—	FG Edinger 45
Chi	—	FG Edinger 27
Chi	—	Vasher 71 interception return (Edinger kick)

MONDAY NIGHT, NOVEMBER 1

N.Y. JETS 41, MIAMI 14—at Meadowlands, attendance 78,216. Chad Pennington passed for 3 touchdowns and Curtis Martin and LaMont Jordan each rushed for 115 yards for the Jets. The Jets' defense forced 3 turnovers and recorded 4 sacks. Jay Fiedler's 21-yard touchdown pass to Randy McMichael capped a 91-yard drive to tie the game 7-7 with 4:35 left in the first half. The Jets answered by scoring on their next six possessions in the span of 19 minutes, 53 seconds, while the defense permitted just 1 first down during the stretch, to take a 41-7 lead on Jordan's 15-yard run with 11:14 left. Pennington was 11 of 19 for 189 yards and 3 touchdowns. Martin rushed 19 times, and Jordan had 14 carries, each for 115 yards, marking the first time since 1975 that the Jets had two 100-yard rushers in the same game. Fiedler was 20 of 41 for 218 yards and 2 touchdowns, with 2 interceptions.

Miami	0	7	0	7 —	14
N.Y. Jets	7	10	14	10 —	41

NYJ	—	Chrebet 35 pass from Pennington (Brien kick)
Mia	—	McMichael 21 pass from Fiedler (Bryant kick)
NYJ	—	McCareins 27 pass from Pennington (Brien kick)
NYJ	—	FG Brien 49
NYJ	—	Martin 25 run (Brien kick)
NYJ	—	Baker 1 pass from Pennington (Brien kick)
NYJ	—	FG Brien 43
NYJ	—	Jordan 25 run (Brien kick)
Mia	—	Thompson 29 pass from Fiedler (Bryant kick)

NINTH WEEK SUMMARIES
American Football Conference

East Division	W	L	T	Pct.	Pts.	OP
New England	7	1	0	.778	208	146
N.Y. Jets	6	2	0	.750	185	138
Buffalo	3	5	0	.375	137	137
Miami	1	8	0	.111	123	186
North Division	**W**	**L**	**T**	**Pct.**	**Pts.**	**OP**
Pittsburgh	7	1	0	.875	197	137
Baltimore	5	3	0	.625	154	113
Cincinnati	3	5	0	.375	152	169
Cleveland	3	5	0	.375	160	174
South Division	**W**	**L**	**T**	**Pct.**	**Pts.**	**OP**
Indianapolis	5	3	0	.625	259	206

Jacksonville	5	3	0	.625	128	146
Houston	4	4	0	.500	171	174
Tennessee	3	5	0	.375	151	178
West Division	**W**	**L**	**T**	**Pct.**	**Pts.**	**OP**
Denver	6	3	0	.667	199	154
San Diego	6	3	0	.667	262	173
Kansas City	3	5	0	.375	237	211
Oakland	3	6	0	.333	165	247

National Football Conference

East Division	W	L	T	Pct.	Pts.	OP
Philadelphia	7	1	0	.875	189	131
N.Y. Giants	5	3	0	.625	172	141
Dallas	3	5	0	.375	141	203
Washington	3	5	0	.375	115	133
North Division	**W**	**L**	**T**	**Pct.**	**Pts.**	**OP**
Minnesota	5	3	0	.625	211	193
Detroit	4	4	0	.500	147	171
Green Bay	4	4	0	.500	206	186
Chicago	3	5	0	.375	136	142
South Division	**W**	**L**	**T**	**Pct.**	**Pts.**	**OP**
Atlanta	6	2	0	.750	170	170
New Orleans	3	5	0	.375	171	234
Tampa Bay	3	5	0	.375	143	155
Carolina	1	7	0	.125	124	185
West Division	**W**	**L**	**T**	**Pct.**	**Pts.**	**OP**
Seattle	5	3	0	.625	194	145
St. Louis	4	4	0	.500	180	205
Arizona	3	5	0	.375	150	165
San Francisco	1	7	0	.125	145	224

SUNDAY, NOVEMBER 7

BUFFALO 22, N.Y. JETS 17—at Ralph Wilson Stadium, attendance 72,574. Willis McGahee rushed for 132 yards and 1 touchdown as the Bills won their third consecutive home game. Rian Lindell tied the game with a 20-yard field goal as the half expired. Buffalo took the second half's opening kickoff and marched 77 yards to take a 17-10 lead on Lee Evans' 4-yard scoring catch. Lawyer Milloy's interception early in the fourth quarter set up Lindell's second field goal for a 20-10 lead. Brian Moorman's 39-yard punt went out of bounds at the 1-yard line with 6:11 remaining, and on the next play Pat Williams tackled Curtis Martin for a safety with 6:04 left. Quincy Carter replaced an injured Chad Pennington and completed a 51-yard touchdown pass to Santana Moss with 4:06 left, but the Bills ran out the clock. Buffalo controlled the ball for 37 minutes, 28 seconds. Drew Bledsoe was 18 of 30 for 184 yards and 1 touchdown. Pennington was 7 of 15 for 141 yards and 1 touchdown, with 1 interception.

N.Y. Jets	0	10	0	7 —	17
Buffalo	7	3	7	5 —	22

Buff	—	McGahee 12 run (Lindell kick)
NYJ	—	FG Brien 41
NYJ	—	McCareins 6 pass from Pennington (Brien kick)
Buff	—	FG Lindell 20
Buff	—	Evans 4 pass from Bledsoe (Lindell kick)
Buff	—	FG Lindell 30
Buff	—	Safety, Martin tackled in end zone
NYJ	—	Moss 51 pass from Carter (Brien kick)

OAKLAND 27, CAROLINA 24—at Bank of America Stadium, attendance 73,518. Sebastian Janikowski kicked a 19-yard field goal with six seconds remaining to snap the Raiders' 13-game road losing streak. The Raiders led 17-14 late in the third quarter before having an 11-play, 77-yard drive capped by Amos Zereoue's 7-yard touchdown run with 9:16 to play. Carolina responded with John Kasay's 38-yard field goal to cut the deficit to 24-17, and then forced a punt. From Carolina's own 25 with 3:16 left, Jake Delhomme completed four consecutive passes, 2 each to Ricky Proehl and Nick Goings, capped by the latter's 3-yard touchdown catch with 2:25 left. A 38-yard pass interference penalty on David Wesley while guarding Doug Gabriel put the ball on the Panthers' 3 with 1:18 left, and Janikowski made the

winning kick three plays later. Kerry Collins was 20 of 32 for 231 yards, with 1 interception. Delhomme was 25 of 45 for 299 yards and 3 touchdowns.

Oakland	3	14	0	10 —	27
Carolina	0	7	7	10 —	24

Oak	—	FG Janikowski 26
Oak	—	Wheatley 1 run (Janikowski kick)
Car	—	Mangum 1 pass from Delhomme (Kasay kick)
Oak	—	Wheatley 1 run (Janikowski kick)
Car	—	Hoover 16 pass from Delhomme (Kasay kick)
Oak	—	Zereoue 7 run (Janikowski kick)
Car	—	FG Kasay 38
Car	—	Goings 3 pass from Delhomme (Kasay kick)
Oak	—	FG Janikowski 19

CINCINNATI 26, DALLAS 3—at Paul Brown Stadium, attendance 65,721. Carson Palmer passed for 212 yards and 1 touchdown and the Bengals' defense forced 5 turnovers to defeat the Cowboys. First-half fumbles by Vinny Testaverde and Keyshawn Johnson set up 2 of Shayne Graham's 3 field goals for a 9-3 halftime lead. In the third quarter, Palmer completed a 76-yard touchdown pass to Mike Schobel. Palmer's 2-yard run with 2:20 remaining capped a 14-play, 66-yard drive to take a 26-3 lead. Palmer was 21 of 32 for 212 yards and 1 touchdown. Vinny Testaverde was 18 of 30 for 207 yards, with 3 interceptions.

Dallas	0	3	0	0 —	3
Cincinnati	3	6	7	10 —	26

Cin	—	FG Graham 35
Cin	—	FG Graham 47
Cin	—	FG Graham 45
Dall	—	FG Cundiff 24
Cin	—	Schobel 76 pass from Palmer (Graham kick)
Cin	—	FG Graham 30
Cin	—	Palmer 2 run (Graham kick)

DENVER 31, HOUSTON 13—at INVESCO Field at Mile High, attendance 74,292. Jake Plummer passed for 234 yards and 4 touchdowns for the Broncos. The Broncos scored on five of six possessions during one stretch of the game. The lone non-scoring drive ended in a blocked punt by Antwan Peek which set up Domanick Davis' first touchdown to cut the deficit to 10-7. Denver responded with touchdown drives of 60 and 53 yards in the final 5:12 of the half, and then drove 80 yards with the opening kickoff of the second half to take a 31-7 lead with 11:07 remaining in the third quarter. Rod Smith's 13-yard touchdown reception with 32 seconds left in the half allowed him to supplant Shannon Sharpe as the club leader in career scoring catches. Earlier in the game, he had surpassed Sharpe on the club's career reception list. Plummer was 16 of 24 for 234 yards and 4 touchdowns. Reuben Droughns rushed 29 times for 120 yards.

Houston	0	7	0	6 —	13
Denver	7	17	7	0 —	31

Den	—	Putzier 34 pass from Plummer (Elam kick)
Den	—	FG Elam 52
Hous	—	Davis 1 run (Brown kick)
Den	—	Lelie 40 pass from Plummer (Elam kick)
Den	—	Smith 13 pass from Plummer (Elam kick)
Den	—	K. Johnson 23 pass from Plummer (Elam kick)
Hous	—	Davis 1 run (Brown kick)

WASHINGTON 17, DETROIT 10—at Ford Field, attendance 62,657. The Redskins used a halfback option pass and a blocked punt to score two touchdowns to defeat the Lions. With the game tied 3-3 at halftime, the Redskins drove 66 yards to open the second half, capped by Clinton Portis' first-ever NFL pass, a 15-yard touchdown to Laveranues Coles.

Later in the quarter, Taylor Jacobs blocked Nate Harris' punt and Walt Harris returned it 13 yards for a touchdown and 17-3 lead. Joey Harrington completed five consecutive passes, capped by Cory Schlesinger's 1-yard scoring catch with 2:08 left, and got the ball back on their own 2 with 1:36 left but failed to cross midfield. Mark Brunell was 6 of 17 for 58 yards. Harrington was 26 of 52 for 269 yards and 1 touchdown, with 1 interception. Az-Zahir Hakim had 7 receptions for 120 yards.

Washington	0	3	14	0	—	17
Detroit	0	3	0	7	—	10

Wash	—	FG Kimrin 24
Det	—	FG Hanson 40
Wash	—	Coles 15 pass from Portis (Kimrin kick)
Wash	—	Harris 13 blocked punt return (Kimrin kick)
Det	—	Schlesinger 1 pass from Harrington (Hanson kick)

ARIZONA 24, MIAMI 23—at Pro Player Stadium, attendance 72,612. Josh McCown's 2-yard touchdown pass to Larry Fitzgerald with 19 seconds remaining as the Cardinals snapped a 17-game road losing streak. Duane Starks intercepted a pass by A.J. Feeley and returned it 41 yards for a touchdown late in the third quarter. Following a Dolphins' punt, the Cardinals drove 80 yards in eight plays, capped by Emmitt Smith's 5-yard touchdown run with 9:44 left to give Arizona a 17-12 lead. Bill Gramatica's 28-yard field goal cut the deficit to 17-15, and Feeley's 35-yard pass to Marty Booker to the Cardinals' 1 set up Sammy Morris' 1-yard run. The 2-point conversion pass from Feeley to Randy McMichael gave Miami a 23-17 lead with 1:56 left, but McCown hit Fitzgerald with a 48-yard pass to the Dolphins' 3 with 41 seconds left. A defensive holding penalty three plays later negated a sack which would have forced the Cardinals to score on fourth down from the 15-yard line. Instead, McCown tossed a 2-yard scoring pass to Fitzgerald and Neil Rackers made the extra point. McCown was 18 of 31 for 162 yards and 1 touchdown. Jay Fiedler was 12 of 21 for 129 yards and 1 touchdown before being injured and replaced in the third quarter by Feeley, who was 6 of 15 for 129 yards, with 1 interception.

Arizona	3	0	7	14	—	24
Miami	9	3	0	11	—	23

Mia	—	FG B. Gramatica 30
Ariz	—	FG Rackers 29
Mia	—	Konrad 20 pass from Fiedler (kick failed)
Mia	—	FG B. Gramatica 29
Ariz	—	Starks 41 interception return (Rackers kick)
Ariz	—	E. Smith 5 run (Rackers kick)
Mia	—	FG B. Gramatica 28
Mia	—	Morris 1 run (McMichael pass from Feeley)
Ariz	—	Fitzpatrick 2 pass from McCown (Rackers kick)

CHICAGO 28, N.Y. GIANTS 21—at Giants Stadium, attendance 78,786. The Bears' defense forced 5 turnovers and recorded 3 sacks, including 4 by Alex Brown, as the Bears scored 28 consecutive points to win their second consecutive game. Trailing 14-7 in the second quarter, the Bears forced 3 turnovers in three successive plays. Mike Green recovered Ike Hilliard's fumble at the Giants' 29. Two plays later, Anthony Thomas scored on a 4-yard run with 2:35 left in the half to tie the game. Nathan Vasher intercepted Kurt Warner's pass on the next play and returned it to the Giants' 9 to set up Paul Edinger's first field goal. Jerry Azumah intercepted Warner on the next play and kicked a 21-yard field goal as the half expired for a 20-14 lead. Thomas' second touchdown increased the lead to 28-14, and Jeremy Shockey's 1-yard scoring catch cut the deficit to 28-21 with 1:56 left and Jack Brewer recovered the onside kick, but Warner was sacked twice and his fourth-down pass fell incomplete. Craig Krenzel was 8 of 21 for 144 yards and 1 touchdown. Thomas carried 28 times for 110 yards and 2 touchdowns. Warner was 18 of 36 for 195 yards and 1 touchdown, with 2 interceptions.

Chicago	0	20	0	8	—	28
N.Y. Giants	14	0	0	7	—	21

NYG	—	Barber 3 run (Christie kick)
NYG	—	Barber 1 run (Christie kick)
Chi	—	Berrian 35 pass from Krenzel (Edinger kick)
Chi	—	Thomas 4 run (Edinger kick)
Chi	—	FG Edinger 22
Chi	—	FG Edinger 21
Chi	—	Thomas 41 run (Krenzel run)
NYG	—	Shockey 1 pass from Warner (Christie kick)

PITTSBURGH 27, PHILADELPHIA 3—at Heinz Field, attendance 64,975. Jerome Bettis rushed for 149 yards and Hines Ward scored 2 touchdowns and the Steelers' defense allowed just 113 total yards to snap the Eagles' perfect record. Pittsburgh scored on its first three drives, covering 75, 64, and 57 yards, 2 of which were capped by Ben Roethlisberger touchdown passes, for a 21-0 lead with 10:51 left in the first half. The Eagles responded with a field goal, but drove inside the Steelers' 40 only once the remainder of the day. The Steelers had more yards (420-113) and time of possession (41:49-18:11). Roethlisberger was 11 of 18 for 183 yards and 2 touchdowns, with 1 interception. Bettis rushed 33 times for 149 yards. Donovan McNabb was 15 of 24 for 109 yards, with 1 interception.

Philadelphia	0	3	0	0	—	3
Pittsburgh	14	7	3	3	—	27

Pitt	—	Ward 16 run (Reed kick)
Pitt	—	Ward 20 pass from Roethlisberger (Reed kick)
Pitt	—	Riemersma 2 pass from Roethlisberger (Reed kick)
Phil	—	FG Akers 33
Pitt	—	FG Reed 42
Pitt	—	FG Reed 31

NEW ENGLAND 40, ST. LOUIS 22—at Edward Jones Dome, attendance 66,107. Adam Vinatieri kicked 4 field goals and passed for a touchdown as the Patriots bounced back from their first loss. Vinatieri kicked 2 field goals in the final 3:03 of the second quarter to give New England a 19-14 lead. The Patriots drove to the Rams' 4 with their first possession of the second half. On fourth down New England set up for a field-goal attempt. Troy Brown lined up wide and Vinatieri took a direct snap and completed a 4-yard touchdown pass to Brown. Roman Phifer's interception four plays later set up Corey Dillon's 5-yard touchdown run for a 33-14 lead. The Patriots played without both starting cornerbacks, and a first-quarter injury to Asante Samuel forced Brown to play both wide receiver and defensive back. Brady was 18 of 31 for 234 yards and 2 touchdowns. David Givens had 5 catches for 100 yards, and Dillon rushed 25 times for 112 yards. Marc Bulger was 23 of 33 for 285 yards and 2 touchdowns, with 1 interception, and Torry Holt had 6 receptions for 111 yards for the Rams.

New England	6	13	14	7	—	40
St. Louis	0	14	0	8	—	22

NE	—	FG Vinatieri 43
NE	—	FG Vinatieri 31
StL	—	Little fumble recovery in end zone (Wilkins kick)
NE	—	Vrabel 2 pass from Brady (Vinatieri kick)
StL	—	Bruce 11 pass from Bulger (Wilkins kick)
NE	—	FG Vinatieri 45
NE	—	FG Vinatieri 36
NE	—	T. Brown 4 pass from Vinatieri (Vinatieri kick)
NE	—	Dillon 5 run (Vinatieri kick)
StL	—	Holt 16 pass from Bulger (Faulk run)
NE	—	B. Johnson 4 pass from Brady (Vinatieri kick)

SAN DIEGO 43, NEW ORLEANS 17—at Qualcomm Stadium, attendance 59,662. Drew Brees passed for 257 yards and 4 touchdowns as the Chargers posted their highest point total since 1993. The Chargers scored on their first four possessions, on drives of 61, 70, 41, and 59 yards en route to a 20-7 halftime lead. Leading 22-7, the Chargers scored twice in a span of 1:11 late in the third quarter, the latter score set up by Aaron Brooks' fumble forced by Steve Foley and recovered by Stephen Cooper, to take a 36-7 lead. San Diego maintained possession for 36:50 and outgained the Saints 402-243. Philip Rivers made his NFL debut with 4:04 left, but did not attempt a pass. Brees was 22 of 36 for 257 yards and 4 touchdowns. Aaron Brooks was 16 of 29 for 173 yards and 1 touchdown, with 1 interception.

New Orleans	0	7	10	0	—	17
San Diego	14	6	16	7	—	43

SD	—	Gates 12 pass from Brees (Kaeding kick)
SD	—	Tomlinson 1 run (Kaeding kick)
SD	—	FG Kaeding 40
NO	—	McAllister 2 run (Carney kick)
SD	—	FG Kaeding 27
SD	—	Safety, Gandy penalized for offensive holding in end zone
SD	—	Gates 7 pass from Brees (Kaeding kick)
SD	—	Gates 2 pass from Brees (Kaeding kick)
NO	—	FG Carney 37
SD	—	Osgood 12 pass from Brees (Kaeding kick)
NO	—	Williams 6 pass from Brooks (Carney kick)

SEATTLE 42, SAN FRANCISCO 27—at Monster Park, attendance 64,423. Matt Hasselbeck passed for 285 yards and 3 touchdowns as the Seahawks moved into first place. The Seahawks took a 21-14 lead with 1:57 left in the first half, but the 49ers got a field goal from Todd Peterson just before halftime and Brandon Lloyd caught a 39-yard touchdown pass from Tim Rattay to cap the opening drive of the second half to give the 49ers a 24-21 lead. But the Seahawks needed just three plays, all passes by Hasselbeck, to take a 28-24 lead. Midway through the fourth quarter, Anthony Simmons intercepted a pass and returned it 23 yards for a touchdown to finish the scoring. Alexander rushed 26 times for 160 yards and 2 touchdowns, Darrell Jackson added 5 receptions for 114 yards. Rattay was 23 of 35 for 259 yards and 2 touchdowns, with 1 interception.

Seattle	7	14	14	7	—	42
San Francisco	14	3	7	3	—	27

SF	—	Barlow 3 run (Peterson kick)
Sea	—	Jackson 33 pass from Hasselbeck (J. Brown kick)
SF	—	Conway 28 pass from Rattay (Peterson kick)
Sea	—	Alexander 1 run (J. Brown kick)
Sea	—	Alexander 4 run (J. Brown kick)
SF	—	FG Peterson 27
SF	—	Lloyd 39 pass from Rattay (Peterson kick)
Sea	—	Robinson 25 pass from Hasselbeck (J. Brown kick)
Sea	—	Jackson 39 pass from Hasselbeck (J. Brown kick)
SF	—	FG Peterson 30
Sea	—	Simmons 23 interception return (J. Brown kick)

TAMPA BAY 34, KANSAS CITY 31—at Raymond James Stadium, attendance 65,495. Michael Pittman rushed for 128 yards and 3 touchdowns as the Buccaneers posted consecutive victories. The Chiefs scored on four of their five first-half possessions, but Tampa Bay trailed just 24-21. Pittman gave the Buccaneers the lead with a 78-yard run on the second play of the third quarter. Jason Dunn caught a 1-yard touchdown pass from Trent Green to give Kansas City a 31-28 lead late in the third quarter, but Tampa Bay responded with a 9-play, 73-yard drive capped by Pittman's third touchdown with 11:50 left. Jermaine Phillips intercepted Green's pass in the end zone to thwart a drive with 5:48 left. On their final possession, the Chiefs reached the Buccaneers' 43 with 1:50 left but sacks by Ronde Barber and, on fourth down, Dewayne White, clinched the victory. Brian Griese was 22 of 34 for 296 yards and 2 touchdowns. Tim Brown saw his 179 consecutive game streak with at least 1 reception come to an end. Green was 32 of 42 for 369 yards and 3 touchdowns, with 2 interceptions.

Kansas City	7	17	7	0	—	31
Tampa Bay	7	14	7	6	—	34

KC	—	Morton 25 pass from Green (Tynes kick)
TB	—	Cook 8 pass from Griese (Gramatica kick)
TB	—	Pittman 1 run (Gramatica kick)
KC	—	Holmes 2 run (Tynes kick)
KC	—	FG Tynes 31
TB	—	Dilger 3 pass from Griese (Gramatica kick)
KC	—	Gonzalez 23 pass from Green (Tynes kick)
TB	—	Pittman 78 run (Gramatica kick)
KC	—	Dunn 1 pass from Green (Tynes kick)
TB	—	Pittman 3 run (kick failed)

SUNDAY NIGHT, NOVEMBER 7
BALTIMORE 27, CLEVELAND 13—at M&T Bank Stadium, attendance 69,781. Ed Reed returned an interception an NFL record 106 yards with 26 seconds remaining to stop the Browns' game-tying threat and lift the Ravens to victory. The defenses dominated, as the teams combined for 457 yards. Richard Alston, in his second NFL game, returned the opening kickoff 93 yards for a touchdown. The Browns led 13-12 in the fourth quarter when B.J. Sams and Chad Williams combined to down Dave Zastudil's punt at the Browns' 1. Three plays netted 1 yard and Derrick Frost shanked his punt 7 yards. Jamal Lewis scored three plays later, and Kyle Boller completed a 2-point conversion pass to Clarence Moore to give the Ravens a 20-13 lead with 7:03 to play. Jeff Garcia drove to the Ravens' 5, but his second-down pass bounced off Aaron Shea and was intercepted and returned down the right sideline for a touchdown by Reed. Boller was 17 of 30 for 142 yards. Garcia was 15 of 26 for 146 yards, with 1 interception.

Cleveland	10	0	0	3	—	13
Baltimore	3	9	0	15	—	27

Cle	—	Alston 93 kick return (Dawson kick)
Balt	—	FG Stover 44
Cle	—	FG Dawson 50
Balt	—	FG Stover 39
Balt	—	FG Stover 43
Balt	—	FG Stover 36
Cle	—	FG Dawson 29
Balt	—	J. Lewis 2 run (Moore pass from Boller)
Balt	—	Reed 106 interception return (Stover kick)

MONDAY NIGHT, NOVEMBER 8
INDIANAPOLIS 31, MINNESOTA 28—at RCA Dome, attendance 57,307. Mike Vanderjagt kicked a 35-yard field goal with two seconds left to defeat the Vikings. The Colts led 14-6 in the third quarter when Nate Burleson returned a punt 91 yards for a touchdown and Daunte Culpepper ran in the 2-point conversion to tie the game. Each team scored touch-

downs on successive possessions, the last of which was a 24-yard run by Onterrio Smith to tie the game 28-28 with 2:54 left. Peyton Manning scrambled 15 yards for a first down, and a 15-yard unnecessary roughness penalty on Lance Johnstone at the end of the play placed the ball on the Vikings' 26 with 2:04 remaining. A 6-yard pass from Manning to Edgerrin James on third-and-5 enabled the Colts to run the clock down to Vanderjagt's field goal with two seconds left. Manning passed for 268 yards and 4 touchdowns. James had 26 carries for 123 yards. Culpepper was 16 of 19 for 169 yards and 1 touchdown.

Minnesota	0	6	8	14	—	28
Indianapolis	7	7	7	10	—	31

Ind	—	Wayne 5 pass from Manning (Vanderjagt kick)
Ind	—	Pollard 10 pass from Manning (Vanderjagt kick)
Minn	—	FG Andersen 42
Minn	—	FG Andersen 23
Minn	—	Burleson 91 punt return (Culpepper run)
Ind	—	Clark 4 pass from Manning (Vanderjagt kick)
Minn	—	Burleson 8 pass from Culpepper (Andersen kick)
Ind	—	Pollard 19 pass from Manning (Vanderjagt kick)
Minn	—	O. Smith 24 run (Andersen kick)
Ind	—	FG Vanderjagt 35

TENTH WEEK SUMMARIES
American Football Conference

East Division	W	L	T	Pct.	Pts.	OP
New England	8	1	0	.889	237	152
N.Y. Jets	6	3	0	.667	202	158
Buffalo	3	6	0	.333	143	166
Miami	1	8	0	.111	123	186
North Division	**W**	**L**	**T**	**Pct.**	**Pts.**	**OP**
Pittsburgh	8	1	0	.889	221	147
Baltimore	6	3	0	.667	174	130
Cincinnati	4	5	0	.444	169	179
Cleveland	3	6	0	.333	170	198
South Division	**W**	**L**	**T**	**Pct.**	**Pts.**	**OP**
Indianapolis	6	3	0	.667	298	220
Jacksonville	6	3	0	.667	151	163
Houston	4	5	0	.444	185	223
Tennessee	3	6	0	.333	168	197
West Division	**W**	**L**	**T**	**Pct.**	**Pts.**	**OP**
Denver	6	3	0	.667	199	154
San Diego	6	3	0	.667	262	173
Kansas City	3	5	0	.333	257	238
Oakland	3	6	0	.333	165	247

National Football Conference

East Division	W	L	T	Pct.	Pts.	OP
Philadelphia	8	1	0	.889	238	152
N.Y. Giants	5	4	0	.556	186	158
Dallas	3	6	0	.333	162	252
Washington	3	6	0	.333	125	150
North Division	**W**	**L**	**T**	**Pct.**	**Pts.**	**OP**
Green Bay	5	4	0	.556	240	217
Minnesota	5	4	0	.556	242	227
Chicago	4	5	0	.444	155	159
Detroit	4	5	0	.444	164	194
South Division	**W**	**L**	**T**	**Pct.**	**Pts.**	**OP**
Atlanta	7	2	0	.778	194	184
New Orleans	4	5	0	.444	198	254
Tampa Bay	3	6	0	.333	157	179
Carolina	2	7	0	.222	161	212
West Division	**W**	**L**	**T**	**Pct.**	**Pts.**	**OP**
St. Louis	5	4	0	.556	203	217
Seattle	5	4	0	.556	206	168
Arizona	4	5	0	.444	167	179
San Francisco	1	8	0	.111	172	261

SUNDAY, NOVEMBER 14
ARIZONA 17, N.Y. GIANTS 14—at Sun Devil Stadium, attendance 42,297. Emmitt Smith rushed for 2 touchdowns as the Cardinals moved within one game of first place in the NFC West. The Giants scored touchdowns on their first two possessions,

but Smith capped a 68-yard drive with a 2-yard run just 39 seconds before halftime to trim the deficit to 14-10. The Giants took seven minutes off the clock to begin the second half, but Ronald McKinnon blocked Steve Christie's 44-yard field-goal attempt. Later in the quarter, Karl Williams returned a punt 38 yards to set up Smith's second touchdown and give Arizona a 17-14 lead. The Cardinals' defense did not allow the Giants to run a play inside their 48 in their final five possessions. Josh McCown was 12 of 24 for 90 yards. Bertrand Berry had 4 sacks. Kurt Warner was 19 of 30 for 193 yards and 1 touchdown. Amani Toomer had 8 catches for 100 yards, and Tiki Barber rushed 21 times for 108 yards.

N.Y. Giants	7	7	0	0	—	14
Arizona	0	10	7	0	—	17

NYG	—	Shockey 2 pass from Warner (Christie kick)
Ariz	—	FG Rackers 41
NYG	—	Barber 2 run (Christie kick)
Ariz	—	Smith 2 run (Rackers kick)
Ariz	—	Smith 3 run (Rackers kick)

ATLANTA 24, TAMPA BAY 14—at Georgia Dome, attendance 70,810. The Falcons' defense allowed just 193 total yards and recorded 3 sacks to defeat the Buccaneers. The Falcons drove 65, 62, and 79 yards on their first three possessions to take a 17-0 lead. In the third quarter, Ronde Barber intercepted Michael Vick's pass, and four plays later Brian Griese completed a 22-yard touchdown pass to Ken Dilger to cut the lead to 17-14. Early in the fourth quarter at the Falcons' 28, Michael Pittman was stopped twice on third- and fourth-and-1 and three plays later Vick hit Crumpler with a 49-yard touchdown with 9:49 left. Vick was 8 of 16 for 147 yards and 1 touchdown, with 1 interception. Crumpler had 4 receptions for 148 yards. Griese was 19 of 26 for 174 yards and 2 touchdowns, with 1 interception.

Tampa Bay	0	7	0	7	—	14
Atlanta	10	0	7	7	—	24

Atl	—	FG Feely 33
Atl	—	Duckett 2 run (Feely kick)
Atl	—	Duckett 1 run (Feely kick)
TB	—	Clayton 25 pass from Griese (Gramatica kick)
TB	—	Dilger 22 pass from Griese (Gramatica kick)
Atl	—	Crumpler 49 pass from Vick (Feely kick)

PITTSBURGH 24, CLEVELAND 10—at Cleveland Browns Stadium, attendance 73,703. Jerome Bettis rushed for 103 yards and 2 touchdowns as Ben Roethlisberger became the first rookie quarterback since 1970 to win his first seven career starts. The Steelers' defense allowed just 228 yards and forced 4 turnovers and recorded 4 sacks. In the fourth quarter, Deshea Townsend recovered Lee Suggs' fumble to set up Jeff Reed's 20-yard field goal, and four plays later Aaron Smith sacked Jeff Garcia and forced him to fumble. Russell Stuvaints recovered the ball and returned it 24 yards for a touchdown and 24-3 lead. Roethlisberger was 10 of 16 for 134 yards, with 1 interception. Bettis rushed 29 times for 103 yards. Troy Polamalu had 2 interceptions. Garcia was 7 of 16 for 110 yards, with 1 interception. Kelly Holcomb replaced him and was 5 of 9 for 64 yards and 1 touchdown, with 1 interception.

Pittsburgh	7	7	0	10	—	24
Cleveland	3	0	0	7	—	10

Cle	—	FG Dawson 31
Pitt	—	Bettis 5 run (Reed kick)
Pitt	—	Bettis 1 run (Reed kick)
Pitt	—	FG Reed 20
Pitt	—	Stuvaints 24 fumble return (Reed kick)
Cle	—	Shea 7 pass from Holcomb (Dawson kick)

GREEN BAY 34, MINNESOTA 31—at Lambeau Field, attendance 70,671. Ryan Longwell kicked a

33-yard field goal as time expired as the Packers overcame a late rally to move into first place in the NFC North. Both quarterbacks passed for 4 touchdowns. The Packers had touchdown drives of 73, 65, and 69 yards in the first half en route to a 24-10 lead. Brett Favre's fourth touchdown pass, a 6-yard toss to William Henderson, gave the Packers a 31-17 lead with 13:24 remaining. After an exchange of punts, the Vikings drove 86 yards in 16 plays, capped by Daunte Culpepper's 2-yard touchdown pass to Onterrio Smith with 2:53 to play. The Vikings' defense forced a punt, and Culpepper's 40-yard pass to Nate Burleson set up his 17-yard scoring pass to Moe Williams with 1:20 left to tie the game. Robert Ferguson returned the ensuing kickoff 37 yards, and Ben Steele recovered his fumble to allow the Packers to maintain possession. Two plays later, Favre lofted a 25-yard pass to Tony Fisher to set up Longwell's winning kick. Favre was 20 for 29 for 236 yards and 4 touchdowns. Ahman Green rushed 21 times for 145 yards. Culpepper was 27 of 44 for 363 yards and 4 touchdowns.

Minnesota	7	3	7	14	—	31
Green Bay	7	17	0	10	—	34

GB	—	Walker 50 pass from Favre (Longwell kick)
Minn	—	Wiggins 13 pass from Culpepper (Andersen kick)
GB	—	Fisher 2 pass from Favre (Longwell kick)
Minn	—	FG Andersen 21
GB	—	Franks 17 pass from Favre (Longwell kick)
GB	—	FG Longwell 43
Minn	—	Burleson 8 pass from Culpepper (Andersen kick)
GB	—	Henderson 6 pass from Favre (Longwell kick)
Minn	—	Smith 2 pass from Culpepper (Andersen kick)
Minn	—	Williams 17 pass from Culpepper (Andersen kick)
GB	—	FG Longwell 33

INDIANAPOLIS 49, HOUSTON 14—at RCA Dome, attendance 56,511. Peyton Manning passed for 5 touchdowns as the Colts posted their biggest margin of victory since 1997. Manning's 69-yard touchdown pass to Brandon Stokley two plays into the second half gave Indianapolis a 28-0 lead. The Colts' defense recorded 5 sacks and forced 4 turnovers, including a 37-yard fumble return for touchdown by Bob Sanders and a 77-yard interception return by Von Hutchins to finish the scoring. Manning was 18 of 27 for 320 yards and 5 touchdowns, with 2 interceptions. Stokley had 5 receptions for 132 yards and Dallas Clark had 3 catches for 102 yards. David Carr was 22 of 41 for 215 yards, with 3 interceptions.

Houston	0	0	7	7	—	14
Indianapolis	7	14	21	7	—	49

Ind	—	Stokley 4 pass from Manning (Vanderjagt kick)
Ind	—	Wayne 5 pass from Manning (Vanderjagt kick)
Ind	—	Clark 1 pass from Manning (Vanderjagt kick)
Ind	—	Stokley 69 pass from Manning (Vanderjagt kick)
Ind	—	Sanders 37 fumble return (Vanderjagt kick)
Hous	—	Davis 1 run (Brown kick)
Ind	—	Clark 80 pass from Manning (Vanderjagt kick)
Hous	—	Davis 1 run (Brown kick)
Ind	—	Hutchins 77 interception return (Vanderjagt kick)

JACKSONVILLE 23, DETROIT 17 (OT)—at ALLTEL Stadium, attendance 66,431. David Garrard completed a 36-yard touchdown pass to Jimmy Smith in overtime as the Jaguars overcame 2 fourth-quarter

punt returns for touchdowns by Eddie Drummond. Playing without injured Byron Leftwich, Jacksonville took a 17-0 lead into the fourth quarter. Drummond returned a punt 55 yards for a touchdown with 13:07 remaining. Jason Hanson kicked a 21-yard field goal on the Lions' next possession to pull within seven points, and Drummond's 83-yard punt return with 46 seconds left tied the game. The Jaguars won the overtime coin toss, and Garrard completed passes to Kyle Brady and Smith on separate third downs to keep the drive alive. Facing third-and-8 from the Lions' 36, Garrard threw the winning pass to Smith to cap the 11-play, 76-yard drive. Making his first start in more than two years, Garrard was 19 of 36 for 198 yards and 2 touchdowns. Smith had 7 receptions for 109 yards. Fred Taylor had 23 carries for 144 yards. Joey Harrington was 11 of 33.for 121 yards, with 1 interception.

Detroit	0	0	0	17	0	— 17
Jacksonville	7	3	7	0	6	— 23

Jax	—	Toefield 12 pass from Garrard (Scobee kick)
Jax	—	FG Scobee 31
Jax	—	Jones 1 run (Scobee kick)
Det	—	Drummond 55 punt return (Hanson kick)
Det	—	FG Hanson 21
Det	—	Drummond 83 punt return (Hanson kick)
Jax	—	Smith 36 pass from Garrard

NEW ORLEANS 27, KANSAS CITY 20—at Louisiana Superdome, attendance 64,900. Joe Horn caught a 42-yard touchdown pass from Aaron Brooks as the Saints rallied to defeat the Chiefs. The Chiefs gained 497 yards of offense, and jumped to a 10-0 lead. But the Saints responded with consecutive touchdown drives for a 14-10 lead. Derrick Blaylock scored on a 3-yard touchdown run to cap a 78-yard drive and tie the game 20-20 with 8:07 remaining. The Saints needed just five plays to retake the lead on Horn's 42-yard touchdown catch with 5:28 remaining. The Chiefs drove to the Saints' 17, but Blaylock could not hold onto Trent Green's pass and Orlando Ruff intercepted the pass at the Saints' 4 with 1:16 remaining to ice the game. The Saints' forced 4 turnovers. Brooks was 15 of 27 for 259 yards and 1 touchdown, with 1 interception. Horn had 5 receptions for 167 yards, and Deuce McAllister had 16 carries for 127 yards. Green was 22 of 32 for 311 yards and 1 touchdown, with 2 interceptions. Blaylock had 33 carries for 186 yards, and Eddie Kennison had 7 receptions for 121 yards.

Kansas City	10	3	0	7	—	20
New Orleans	0	14	3	10	—	27

KC	—	Kennison 21 pass from Green (Tynes kick)
KC	—	FG Tynes 24
NO	—	Brooks 1 run (Carney kick)
NO	—	McAllister 13 run (Carney kick)
KC	—	FG Tynes 44
NO	—	FG Carney 39
NO	—	FG Carney 38
KC	—	Blaylock 3 run (Tynes kick)
NO	—	Horn 42 pass from Brooks (Carney kick)

BALTIMORE 20, N.Y. JETS 17 (OT)—at Meadowlands, attendance 77,826. Matt Stover kicked a 42-yard field goal in overtime as the Ravens rallied to victory. The Jets drove to the Ravens' 17 with 1:33 left in the first half and a chance to improve on a 14-0 lead. LaMont Jordan attempted a halfback option pass and Ed Reed intercepted the pass and returned it 104 yards for an apparent touchdown, but a holding penalty placed the ball on the Jets' 36. Six plays later Kyle Boller completed a 6-yard scoring pass to Clarence Moore to cut the deficit to 14-7 at halftime. In the fourth quarter, Moore's 16-yard touchdown pass gave the Ravens the lead with 4:13 left. The Jets drove to the Ravens' 4 with 18 seconds left, but Jordan gained 1 yard and Quin-

cy Carter threw an incomplete pass. With eight seconds left, the Jets opted to kick the tying field goal. Boller was 19 of 33 for 213 yards and 2 touchdowns. Carter, making his first start in place of injured Chad Pennington, was 13 of 22 for 175 yards. Martin had 28 carries for 119 yards.

Baltimore	0	7	3	7	3	— 20
N.Y. Jets	0	14	0	3	0	— 17

NYJ	—	Martin 1 run (Brien kick)
NYJ	—	Martin 9 run (Brien kick)
Balt	—	Moore 6 pass from Boller (Stover kick)
Balt	—	FG Stover 24
Balt	—	Moore 16 pass from Boller (Stover kick)
NYJ	—	FG Brien 20
Balt	—	FG Stover 42

ST. LOUIS 23, SEATTLE 12—at Edward Jones Dome, attendance 66,044. Marshall Faulk rushed for 139 yards and Jeff Wilkins kicked 3 field goals as the Rams swept the season series from Seattle. The Rams drove 71 and 73 yards for touchdowns on their first two possessions, and then had an 81-yard drive capped by Wilkins' first field goal, for a 17-0 lead with 12:18 left in the first half. Josh Brown's fourth field goal cut the deficit to 20-12 with 3:54 left in the third quarter, but Rich Coady recovered Shaun Alexander's fumble near midfield on the Seahawks' next possession. A 5:36 drive later in the quarter led to Wilkins' game-clinching 23-yard field goal with 26 seconds left. Marc Bulger was 23 of 34 for 262 yards and 1 touchdown, with 10 different Rams catching a pass. Isaac Bruce had 7 receptions for 104 yards, and Faulk had 18 carries for 139 yards. Matt Hasselbeck was 15 of 36 for 172 yards, with 1 interception. Alexander had 22 carries for 176 yards.

Seattle	0	6	6	0	—	12
St. Louis	14	3	3	3	—	23

StL	—	Curtis 15 pass from Bulger (Wilkins kick)
StL	—	Jackson 4 run (Wilkins kick)
StL	—	FG Wilkins 36
Sea	—	FG J. Brown 28
Sea	—	FG J. Brown 30
StL	—	FG Wilkins 47
Sea	—	FG J. Brown 45
Sea	—	FG J. Brown 41
StL	—	FG Wilkins 23

CAROLINA 37, SAN FRANCISCO 27—at Monster Park, attendance 63,618. Jake Delhomme passed for 3 touchdowns, all to Muhsin Muhammad including 2 in the fourth quarter, as the Panthers rallied to defeat the 49ers. The 49ers jumped to a 17-0 lead, but the Panthers scored on three consecutive possessions to begin the second half, highlighted by Mark Fields' interception return to the 49ers' 1, to take a 20-17 lead. The 49ers tied the game with Todd Peterson's field goal and took a 27-20 edge on Tim Rattay's 30-yard touchdown pass to Brandon Lloyd with 10:41 to play. The Panthers responded with a 69-yard touchdown drive capped by Muhammad's second touchdown catch. Following Mike Rucker's fumble recovery, punter Todd Sauerbrun, kicking because of John Kasay's leg injury suffered during the second quarter, kicked a 34-yard field goal, the first of his career, with 4:25 left for a 30-27 lead. Two plays later, Brentson Buckner intercepted Rattay's pass and Delhomme hit Muhammad for the game-clinching 26-yard pass. Delhomme was 19 of 34 for 303 yards and 3 touchdowns. Muhammad had 6 catches for 123 yards. Rattay was 22 of 37 for 284 yards and 1 touchdown, with 4 interceptions. Cedrick Wilson had 5 catches for 101 yards.

Carolina	0	3	17	17	—	37
San Francisco	10	7	3	7	—	27

SF	—	Barlow 1 run (Peterson kick)
SF	—	FG Peterson 28
SF	—	Barlow 3 run (Peterson kick)
Car	—	FG Kasay 37
Car	—	FG Kasay 25

Car — Bennett 1 run (Sauerbrun kick)
Car — Muhammad 40 pass from Delhomme (Sauerbrun kick)
SF — FG Peterson 46
SF — Lloyd 30 pass from Rattay (Peterson kick)
Car — Muhammad 4 pass from Delhomme (Sauerbrun kick)
Car — FG Sauerbrun 34
Car — Muhammad 26 pass from Delhomme (Sauerbrun kick)

CHICAGO 19, TENNESSEE 17 (OT)—at The Coliseum, attendance 68,932. Adewale Ogunleye tackled Fred Miller in the end zone for a safety in overtime as the Bears won despite just 176 total yards. The game marked just the second time in NFL history (Vikings-Rams 1989) that an overtime game ended with a safety. The Bears had just 3 first downs but led 14-7 after three quarters thanks to Michael Haynes' 45-yard interception return with just 18 seconds left in the first half, and R.W. McQuarters' 75-yard punt return. Trailing 14-10, Andre Dyson's interception set up Billy Volek's 47-yard touchdown pass to Drew Bennett for a 17-14 lead. Later in the quarter the Bears mounted their longest drive, 69 yards, and tied the game on Paul Edinger's 29-yard field goal. Tennessee had a chance to win in regulation, but Marc Columbo blocked Craig Hentrich's 52-yard field-goal attempt. The Bears won the overtime toss, but were forced to punt. Faced with third-and-14 from its own 5, Alex Brown sacked Volek in the end zone and forced him to fumble. Miller fell on the ball in the end zone and Ogunleye fell on Miller for the game-ending safety. Craig Krenzel was 10 of 28 for 116 yards, with 2 interceptions. Volek was 27 of 44 for 334 yards and 2 touchdowns, with 1 interception. Bennett had 6 receptions for 148 yards.

	1	2	3	4		
Chicago	0	7	3	2	—	19
Tennessee	7	0	0	10	—	17

Tenn — Mason 29 pass from Volek (Anderson kick)
Chi — Haynes 45 interception return (Edinger kick)
Chi — McQuarters 75 punt return (Edinger kick)
Tenn — FG Anderson 33
Tenn — Bennett 47 pass from Volek (Anderson kick)
Chi — FG Edinger 29
Chi — Safety, Miller tackled in end zone

CINCINNATI 17, WASHINGTON 10—at FedExField, attendance 87,786. The Bengals jumped to a 17-0 lead and withstood a late rally to snap a six-game road losing streak. The Redskins did not string together 2 first downs in a drive until the fourth quarter. Reserve quarterback Patrick Ramsey, who entered late in the second quarter, guided the Redskins to three consecutive scoring chances in the fourth quarter. Ola Kimrin missed a 47-yard field-goal attempt, connected from 33 yards, and Ramsey hit Chris Cooley with a touchdown pass with 2:22 left to pull within 17-10. The Redskins' defense forced a three-and-out, but Kim Herring's interception of a desperation pass with two seconds left iced the game. Palmer was 24 of 39 for 217 yards and 1 touchdown, with 2 interceptions. Rudi Johnson rushed 31 times for 102 yards. Starter Mark Brunell was 1 of 8 for 6 yards. Ramsey was 18 of 37 for 210 yards and 1 touchdown, with 2 interceptions.

	1	2	3	4		
Cincinnati	7	10	0	0	—	17
Washington	0	0	0	10	—	10

Cin — R. Johnson 1 run (Graham kick)
Cin — Stewart 1 pass from Palmer (Graham kick)
Cin — FG Graham 41
Wash — FG Kimrin 33
Wash — Cooley 9 pass from Ramsey (Kimrin kick)

SUNDAY NIGHT, NOVEMBER 14
NEW ENGLAND 29, BUFFALO 6—at Gillette Stadium, attendance 68,756. Tom Brady passed for 2 touchdowns, Adam Vinatieri kicked 5 field goals, and the Patriots' defense allowed 125 total yards to defeat the Bills. The Patriots had advantages in first downs (25-8), total yards (428-125), and time of possession (41:22-18:38). The Patriots scored on five of their first six possessions to take a 23-0 lead. Jonathan Smith's 70-yard punt return was Buffalo's lone touchdown. Wide receiver Troy Brown, playing in Nickel situations for the Patriots' injury-riddled secondary, early in the fourth quarter grabbed his first career interception. Brady was 19 of 35 for 233 yards and 2 touchdowns, with 1 interception. Corey Dillon rushed 26 times for 151 yards. Drew Bledsoe was 8 of 19 for 76 yards, with 3 interceptions.

	1	2	3	4		
Buffalo	0	0	6	0	—	6
New England	3	17	3	6	—	29

NE — FG Vinatieri 27
NE — FG Vinatieri 24
NE — Patten 13 pass from Brady (Vinatieri kick)
NE — Fauria 5 pass from Brady (Vinatieri kick)
NE — FG Vinatieri 20
Buff — J. Smith 70 punt return (run failed)
NE — FG Vinatieri 45
NE — FG Vinatieri 37

MONDAY NIGHT, NOVEMBER 15
PHILADELPHIA 49, DALLAS 21—at Texas Stadium, attendance 64,190. Donovan McNabb passed for 345 yards and 4 touchdowns, including 3 to Terrell Owens, as the Eagles pulled away from the Cowboys. The Eagles gained 485 yards, including 343 in the first half. Leading 7-0 late in the first quarter, Roderick Hood recovered Lance Frazier's muffed punt at the Cowboys' 14 to set up Dorsey Levens' 4-yard touchdown run. The Eagles proceeded to score touchdowns on their next four possessions, with drives of 77, 68, 75, and 83 yards, capped by Brian Westbrook's 1-yard run with 6:04 left in the third quarter, for a 42-14 lead. McNabb was 15 of 28 for 345 yards and 4 touchdowns, and Owens had 6 catches for 134 yards. Testaverde was 21 of 30 for 254 yards and 2 touchdowns, with 1 interception. Jason Witten had 9 catches for 133 yards.

	1	2	3	4		
Philadelphia	28	7	7	7	—	49
Dallas	0	14	7	0	—	21

Phil — Owens 59 pass from McNabb (Akers kick)
Phil — Levens 4 run (Akers kick)
Dall — Witten 29 pass from Testaverde (Cundiff kick)
Phil — Owens 27 pass from McNabb (Akers kick)
Phil — Pinkston 59 pass from McNabb (Akers kick)
Dall — Witten 24 pass from Testaverde (Cundiff kick)
Phil — Westbrook 1 run (Akers kick)
Dall — George 15 run (Cundiff kick)
Phil — Owens 16 pass from McNabb (Akers kick)
Phil — Sheppard 101 interception return (Akers kick)

ELEVENTH WEEK SUMMARIES
American Football Conference

East Division	W	L	T	Pct.	Pts.	OP
New England	9	1	0	.900	264	171
N.Y. Jets	7	3	0	.700	212	165
Buffalo	4	6	0	.400	180	183
Miami	1	9	0	.100	140	210
North Division	W	L	T	Pct.	Pts.	OP
Pittsburgh	9	1	0	.900	240	161
Baltimore	7	3	0	.700	204	140
Cincinnati	4	6	0	.400	183	198
Cleveland	3	7	0	.300	177	208
South Division	W	L	T	Pct.	Pts.	OP
Indianapolis	7	3	0	.700	339	230
Jacksonville	6	4	0	.600	166	181
Houston	4	6	0	.400	198	239
Tennessee	4	6	0	.400	186	212
West Division	W	L	T	Pct.	Pts.	OP
Denver	7	3	0	.700	233	167
San Diego	7	3	0	.700	285	190
Kansas City	3	7	0	.300	276	265
Oakland	3	7	0	.300	182	270

National Football Conference

East Division	W	L	T	Pct.	Pts.	OP
Philadelphia	9	1	0	.900	266	158
N.Y. Giants	5	5	0	.500	196	172
Dallas	3	7	0	.300	172	282
Washington	3	7	0	.300	131	178
North Division	W	L	T	Pct.	Pts.	OP
Green Bay	6	4	0	.600	256	230
Minnesota	6	4	0	.600	264	246
Chicago	4	6	0	.400	165	200
Detroit	4	6	0	.400	183	216
South Division	W	L	T	Pct.	Pts.	OP
Atlanta	8	2	0	.800	208	194
New Orleans	4	6	0	.400	211	288
Tampa Bay	4	6	0	.400	192	182
Carolina	3	7	0	.300	196	222
West Division	W	L	T	Pct.	Pts.	OP
Seattle	6	4	0	.600	230	185
St. Louis	5	5	0	.500	220	254
Arizona	4	6	0	.400	177	214
San Francisco	1	9	0	.100	175	296

SUNDAY, NOVEMBER 21
BALTIMORE 30, DALLAS 10—at M&T Bank Stadium, attendance 69,924. Kyle Boller passed for 2 touchdowns as the Ravens scored 30 unanswered points in the second half. With Jamal Lewis having left the game with a first-quarter injury, Boller was 6 of 7 on a third-quarter 79-yard drive, capped by a 17-yard touchdown pass to Darnell Dinkins for a 7-3 lead. On the next play, Ed Reed intercepted a pass to set up Boller's 31-yard scoring pass to Kevin Johnson. In the fourth quarter, the Ravens used an interception and fumble recovery to score 16 points in a span of 1 minute and 36 seconds to take a 30-3 lead with 9:46 left. Drew Henson made his NFL debut late in the game, replacing an injured Vinny Testaverde, and completed a 1-yard touchdown pass to Jeff Robinson. Boller was 23 of 34 for 232 yards and 2 touchdowns. Testaverde was 9 of 22 for 109 yards, with 2 interceptions. Henson was 6 of 6 for 47 yards and 1 touchdown.

	1	2	3	4		
Dallas	3	0	0	7	—	10
Baltimore	0	0	14	16	—	30

Dall — FG Cundiff 19
Balt — Dinkins 17 pass from Boller (Stover kick)
Balt — K. Johnson 31 pass from Boller (Stover kick)
Balt — FG Stover 50
Balt — Williams 44 interception return (Stover kick)
Dall — C. Taylor 1 run (bobbled snap)
Balt — Robinson 1 pass from Henson (Cundiff kick)

BUFFALO 37, ST. LOUIS 17—at Ralph Wilson Stadium, attendance 72,393. Drew Bledsoe completed 3 touchdown passes, all to Mark Campbell, as the Bills won their fourth consecutive home game. The Bills fell behind 10-0 before scoring on their next five possessions. With the score tied 17-17, Jonathan Smith returned an interception 53 yards to set up Bledsoe's third touchdown pass to Campbell. Less than three minutes later, the Bills forced another punt and Nate Clements returned the ball 86 yards for a 31-17 lead. The Rams then muffed the ensuing kickoff and Jason Peters recovered to set up Rian Lindell's field goal for a 34-17 lead with 8:03 left in the third quarter. Bledsoe was 15 of 24 for 185 yards and 3 touchdowns, with 1 interception. Willis McGahee rushed 20 times for 100 yards. Lawyer Milloy had 3 sacks. Bulger was 27 of 45 for 287 yards and 2 touchdowns, with 3 interceptions.

	1	2	3	4		T
St. Louis	10	7	0	0	—	17
Buffalo	0	17	20	0	—	37

StL	—	FG Wilkins 41
StL	—	Bruce 18 pass from Bulger (Wilkins kick)
Buff	—	Campbell 10 pass from Bledsoe (Lindell kick)
Buff	—	Campbell 19 pass from Bledsoe (Lindell kick)
StL	—	Holt 11 pass from Bulger (Wilkins kick)
Buff	—	FG Lindell 21
Buff	—	Campbell 5 pass from Bledsoe (Lindell kick)
Buff	—	Clements 86 punt return (Lindell kick)
Buff	—	FG Lindell 35
Buff	—	FG Lindell 33

CAROLINA 35, ARIZONA 10—at Bank of America Stadium, attendance 72,796. Nick Goings rushed for 121 yards and 3 first-half touchdowns as the reigning NFC champions posted back-to-back victories for the first time. Plagued by injuries, Goings received the start, entering the game with 130 rushing yards. Goings' third touchdown, a 1-yard run with 4:31 left in the first half, was set up by Colin Branch's 76-yard interception return to give Carolina a 21-0 lead. Jake Delhomme completed 2 touchdown passes to Muhsin Muhammad, including a 28-yard pass with two seconds left in the first half for a 28-0 lead. Muhammad had 6 catches for 118 yards. Delhomme was 12 of 25 for 157 yards and 2 touchdowns, with 1 interception. Shaun King made his first start of the season and was 28 of 52 for 343 yards and 1 touchdown, with 3 interceptions.

	1	2	3	4		T
Arizona	0	0	10	0	—	10
Carolina	14	14	0	7	—	35

Car	—	Goings 2 run (Chandler kick)
Car	—	Goings 57 run (Chandler kick)
Car	—	Goings 1 run (Chandler kick)
Car	—	Muhammad 28 pass from Delhomme (Chandler kick)
Ariz	—	Fitzgerald 21 pass from King (Rackers kick)
Ariz	—	FG Rackers 28
Car	—	Muhammad 17 pass from Delhomme (Chandler kick)

INDIANAPOLIS 41, CHICAGO 10—at Soldier Field, attendance 61,908. Edgerrin James rushed for 204 yards and Peyton Manning passed for 4 touchdowns, and neither played in the fourth quarter, as the Colts forced 5 turnovers. The Colts scored on five of their seven first-half possessions to take a 27-3 lead, with the last 13 points following Bears' turnovers. Manning's 35-yard touchdown pass to Reggie Wayne early in the second quarter marked the 200th scoring pass of his career, with only Dan Marino having reached the milestone in fewer games (106 Manning, 89 Marino). The Colts outgained the Bears 486-224 total yards. Manning was 17 of 28 for 211 yards and 4 touchdowns, with 1 interception. James rushed 23 times for 204 yards, and Wayne had 6 receptions for 106 yards. Craig Krenzel was 14 of 24 for 175 yards and 1 touchdown, with 2 interceptions.

	1	2	3	4		T
Indianapolis	7	20	14	0	—	41
Chicago	3	0	0	7	—	10

Ind	—	Pollard 14 run from Manning (Vanderjagt kick)
Chi	—	FG Edinger 51
Ind	—	Wayne 35 pass from Manning (Vanderjagt kick)
Ind	—	FG Vanderjagt 34
Ind	—	Harrison 10 pass from Manning (Vanderjagt kick)
Ind	—	FG Vanderjagt 20
Ind	—	Wayne 27 pass from Manning (Vanderjagt kick)

Ind	—	James 11 run (Vanderjagt kick)
Chi	—	Lyman 2 pass from Krenzel (Edinger kick)

PITTSBURGH 19, CINCINNATI 14—at Paul Brown Stadium, attendance 65,780. Jerome Bettis rushed for 129 yards and the Steelers' defense allowed just 42 yards in the second half as Pittsburgh improved to 9-1 for the first time since 1978. In the first half, Carson Palmer engineered touchdown drives of 67 and 73 yards. He also threw an interception that was returned for a touchdown by James Farrior, but the Bengals led 14-10 at halftime. Ben Roethlisberger completed a 8-yard touchdown pass to Dan Kreider to finish a 53-yard drive, with a 26-yard pass to Jerame Tuman serving as the key play, to take a 17-14 lead late in the third quarter. In six second-half possessions, the Steelers' defense did not allow the Bengals to cross midfield, and an intentional grounding penalty on Palmer in the end zone resulted in a safety with 2:38 remaining. On third-and-3, Roethlisberger scampered around right end for 4 yards to get the game-clinching first down. Roethlisberger was 15 of 21 for 138 yards and 1 touchdown, and became the first quarterback since 1970 to win his first eight career starts. Bettis carried 29 times for 129 yards. Palmer was 13 of 25 for 165 yards and 2 touchdowns, with 1 interception. Duane Clemons had 2 1/2 of Cincinnati's 7 sacks.

	1	2	3	4		T
Pittsburgh	3	7	7	2	—	19
Cincinnati	7	7	0	0	—	14

Pitt	—	FG Reed 32
Cin	—	C. Johnson 36 pass from Palmer (Graham kick)
Pitt	—	Farrior 14 interception return (Reed kick)
Cin	—	Washington 19 pass from Palmer (Graham kick)
Pitt	—	Kreider 8 pass from Roethlisberger (Reed kick)
Pitt	—	Safety, Palmer penalized for intentional grounding in end zone

N.Y. JETS 10, CLEVELAND 7—at Cleveland Browns Stadium, attendance 72,547. The Jets rallied from a halftime deficit and then needed 2 missed field goals by Phil Dawson to defeat the Browns. Curtis Martin rushed for 88 yards and became just the second player, joining Barry Sanders, to rush for at least 1,000 yards in each of his first 10 seasons. The Jets punted on seven consecutive first-half possessions, but trailed just 7-0 at halftime. Doug Brien's 41-yard field goal to open the Jets' third quarter cut the deficit to 7-3. Phil Dawson, who had made 27 consecutive field goals, missed a 34-yard attempt wide right with 11:27 remaining. The Jets responded with a 10-play, 75-yard drive, highlighted by Quincy Carter's pass to Justin McCareins on third-and-11 for a first down and capped by the duo's 11-yard touchdown connection with 5:32 to play. The Jets forced a punt and LaMont Jordan rushed for 3 first downs in the final 3:55 to run out the clock. Carter was 11 of 20 for 116 yards and 1 touchdown, with 1 interception. Jeff Garcia was 10 of 17 for 88 yards and 1 touchdown before leaving with a shoulder injury. Kelly Holcomb was 4 of 10 for 32 yards.

	1	2	3	4		T
N.Y. Jets	0	0	3	7	—	10
Cleveland	0	7	0	0	—	7

Cle	—	Shea 3 pass from Garcia (Dawson kick)
NYJ	—	FG Brien 41
NYJ	—	McCareins 11 pass from Carter (Brien kick)

TENNESSEE 18, JACKSONVILLE 15—at ALLTEL Stadium, attendance 65,780. After missing the previous two games with an injured chest, Steve McNair engineered a game-winning 57-yard drive, capped by Antowain Smith's 2-yard run and McNair's 2-point conversion run, to give the Titans just their second win in seven games. David Garrard, playing for the injured Byron Leftwich, passed

for 24 yards and rushed for 16 yards, including a 5-yard touchdown run, to give the Jaguars a 13-10 lead late in the third quarter. In the fourth quarter, Chris Hanson's punt, downed by Juran Bolden, pinned the Titans to their own 4-yard line, and Greg Favors sacked McNair in the end zone for a safety and 15-10 lead with 9:12 left. With 4:08 left starting from their own 41, McNair completed 3 of 5 passes, including a 21-yard pass to Erron Kinney, to set up Smith's go-ahead touchdown with 3:31 left. Rich Gardner's interception with 17 seconds remaining iced the game. McNair was 18 of 30 for 209 yards and 1 touchdown, with 2 interceptions. Garrard was 13 of 27 for 129 yards, with 1 interception.

	1	2	3	4		T
Tennessee	3	7	0	8	—	18
Jacksonville	0	6	7	2	—	15

Tenn	—	FG Anderson 41
Jax	—	FG Scobee 35
Tenn	—	Mason 37 pass from McNair (Anderson kick)
Jax	—	FG Scobee 48
Jax	—	Garrard 5 run (Scobee kick)
Jax	—	Safety, McNair sacked in end zone by Favors
Tenn	—	A. Smith 2 run (McNair run)

MINNESOTA 22, DETROIT 19—at Metrodome, attendance 64,156. Daunte Culpepper passed for 2 touchdowns as the Vikings put together two long drives in the second half to end a three-game losing streak. Eddie Drummond returned the opening kickoff 92 yards for a touchdown en route to the Lions 17-7 halftime lead. Early in the third quarter, Nick Harris' 47-yard punt was downed by Wali Rainer at the Vikings' 1 and Cory Redding tackled Onterrio Smith for a safety and 19-7 lead. Following a Lions' punt, Culpepper engineered a 17-play, 78-yard drive, capped by his 6-yard touchdown pass to Nate Burleson. The duo combined for a two-point conversion to cut the deficit to 19-15. The Vikings' defense forced a three-and-out, and the offense responded wit ha 13-play, 62-yard drive, keyed by Culpepper's 14-yard pass to Moe Williams on third-and-12 to the Lions' 1 to set up Williams' scoring plunge with 5:27 left for a 22-19 lead. Antoine Winfield's interception with 1:18 remaining secured the victory. Culpepper was 22 of 32 for 233 yards and 2 touchdowns, with 1 interception. Joey Harrington was 12 of 19 for 91 yards and 1 touchdown, with 1 interception.

	1	2	3	4		T
Detroit	14	3	2	0	—	19
Minnesota	7	0	15	0	—	22

Det	—	Drummond 92 kickoff return (Hanson kick)
Minn	—	Wiggins 8 pass from Culpepper (Andersen kick)
Det	—	Alexander 1 pass from Harrington (Hanson kick)
Det	—	FG Hanson 48
Det	—	Safety, O. Smith tackled in end zone by Redding
Minn	—	Burleson 6 pass from Culpepper (Burleson pass from Culpepper)
Minn	—	M. Williams 1 run (Andersen kick)

DENVER 34, NEW ORLEANS 13—at Louisiana Superdome, attendance 64,900. Reuben Droughns rushed for 166 yards and Jake Plummer passed for 2 touchdowns as the Broncos jumped to a 20-0 first quarter lead en route to victory. Droughns' 51-yard touchdown run on the Broncos' first play from scrimmage set the tone. On the third play of their next possession, Plummer hit Ashley Lelie with a 37-yard touchdown. Leading 20-3, Al Wilson intercepted an ill-advised underhanded throw by Aaron Brooks and returned it 7 yards for a touchdown and 27-3 lead midway through the second quarter. Plummer was 19 of 29 for 224 yards and 2 touchdowns. Droughns rushed 28 times for 166 yards and 1 touchdown. Brooks set Saints' club records with 34 completions and 60 attempts. He passed for 377 yards and 1 touchdown, with 3 interceptions. Deuce McAllister had 11 receptions for 87 yards and Donte' Stallworth added 10 catches for 122 yards.

Denver	20	7	0	7	—	34
New Orleans	0	13	0	0	—	13

Den	—	Droughns 51 run (Elam kick)
Den	—	Lelie 37 pass from Plummer (Elam kick)
Den	—	FG Elam 48
Den	—	FG Elam 34
NO	—	FG Carney 24
Den	—	Wilson 7 interception return (Elam kick)
NO	—	Stallworth 30 pass from Brooks (Carney kick)
NO	—	FG Carney 36
Den	—	K. Johnson 19 pass from Plummer (Elam kick)

ATLANTA 14, N.Y. GIANTS 10—at Giants Stadium, attendance 78,793. Michael Vick passed for 115 yards and 2 touchdowns, and rushed for 104 yards, as the Falcons spoiled the starting debut of Eli Manning. The Falcons scored on two of their first three possessions, driving 84 and 89 yards, both capped by touchdown catches by Alge Crumpler for a 14-0 lead. The Giants drove 16 plays on their first drive of the second half, culminated by Manning's 6-yard touchdown pass to Jeremy Shockey with 4:37 left in the third quarter. On the Giants' next possession, Brady Smith intercepted a pass at the Falcons' 20 to thwart a drive, but Manning rallied back and drove 65 yards to set up Steve Christie's 24-yard field goal to pull within 14-10 with 6:28 to play. The Giants got the ball back on their own 26 with 1:52 left following a punt, and Manning's fourth-and-3 pass from the Falcons' 42 with 49 seconds left was knocked down. Vick was 12 of 20 for 115 yards and 2 touchdowns, and rushed 15 times for 104 yards to become the first quarterback with five career 100-yard rushing games. Manning was 17 of 37 for 162 yards and 1 touchdown, with 2 interceptions.

Atlanta	7	7	0	0	—	14
N.Y. Giants	0	0	7	3	—	10

Atl	—	Crumpler 6 pass from Vick (Feely kick)
Atl	—	Crumpler 2 pass from Vick (Feely kick)
NYG	—	Shockey 6 pass from Manning (Christie kick)
NYG	—	FG Christie 24

SAN DIEGO 23, OAKLAND 17—at Network Associates Coliseum, attendance 46,905. LaDainian Tomlinson rushed for 164 yards and 1 touchdown as the Chargers won their fourth consecutive game. The Chargers drove inside the Raiders' 11 on three of their first four possessions, but a fumble near the goal line by Lorenzo Neal ended one scoring threat and Nate Kaeding had an extra-point attempt blocked by Langston Walker. The Raiders capitalized with Ronald Curry's 22-yard touchdown catch to trim the deficit to 13-7 at halftime. Kaeding missed a field goal early in the third quarter, and later in the quarter the Chargers settled for a 19-yard field goal when stopped at the 1-yard line. On the ensuing drive, Teyo Johnson's 8-yard touchdown cut the deficit to 16-14, but the Chargers answered with a 12-play drive capped by Tomlinson's 1-yard run. Trailing 23-17, Oakland punted on fourth-and-5 from their own 43 with 3:57 left, and Drew Brees completed a 20-yard jump pass to Keenan McCardell on third down to help San Diego run out the clock. Brees was 18 of 34 for 226 yards and 1 touchdown. Antonio Gates had 8 catches for 101 yards. Tomlinson had 37 carries for 164 yards. Collins was 18 of 30 for 227 yards and 2 touchdowns.

San Diego	6	7	3	7	—	23
Oakland	0	7	3	7	—	17

SD	—	Gates 11 pass from Brees (kick blocked)

SD	—	Brees 6 run (Kaeding kick)
Oak	—	Curry 22 pass from Collins (Janikowski kick)
SD	—	FG Kaeding 19
Oak	—	Te. Johnson 8 pass from Collins (Janikowski kick)
SD	—	Tomlinson 6 run (Kaeding kick)
Oak	—	FG Janikowski 31

PHILADELPHIA 28, WASHINGTON 6—at Lincoln Financial Field, attendance 67,720. Donovan McNabb passed for 222 yards and 4 touchdowns as the Eagles improved to 9-1 for the first time since 1980. Philadelphia led 7-6 at halftime, and McNabb's 10-yard touchdown pass to Terrell Owens with 3:06 left in the third quarter capped an 80-yard drive and stretched the lead to 14-6. Washington drove to the Eagles' 11 early in the fourth quarter, but three penalties pushed the Redskins back to the 30-yard line and Ola Kimrin missed a 48-yard field goal attempt. With a 21-6 lead, the Eagles stopped Patrick Ramsey on fourth-and-1 on the Redskins' 32, and McNabb found Brian Westbrook with a 14-yard touchdown pass with 6:54 left to complete the scoring. The Eagles' defense limited the Redskins to 213 yards, while the offense converted 9 of 15 third-down conversions. McNabb was 18 of 26 for 222 yards and 4 touchdowns, with 1 interception. Todd Pinkston had 5 catches for 106 yards. Patrick Ramsey was 21 of 34 for 162 yards, with 1 interception.

Washington	3	3	0	0	—	6
Philadelphia	7	0	7	14	—	28

Wash	—	FG Kimrin 35
Phil	—	Lewis 2 pass from McNabb (Akers kick)
Wash	—	FG Kimrin 24
Phil	—	Owens 10 pass from McNabb (Akers kick)
Phil	—	Westbrook 1 pass from McNabb (Akers kick)
Phil	—	Westbrook 14 pass from McNabb (Akers kick)

SEATTLE 24, MIAMI 17—at Qwest Field, attendance 66,644. Michael Boulware returned an interception 63 yards for a touchdown with 56 seconds remaining as the Seahawks spoiled the debut of coach Jim Bates. Seattle jumped to a 17-7 halftime lead, including Jerry Rice's first touchdown catch with the Seahawks. Miami trailed 17-14 early in the fourth quarter. Olindo Mare missed a 34-yard field goal with 8:06 left, but made a 39-yard attempt with 2:20 remaining to tie the game. Miami forced a punt and drove to the Seahawks' 41. Boulware intercepted A.J. Feeley's short pass and returned it 63 yards for a touchdown. On the next play from scrimmage, Antonio Cochran sacked Feeley and forced him to fumble. Chad Brown recovered the ball to clinch the victory. Dilfer, making his first start since October 27, 2002 and playing in place of injured Matt Hasselbeck, was 14 of 28 for 196 yards and 1 touchdown, with 2 interceptions. Feeley was 22 of 45 for 229 yards and 1 touchdown, with 2 interceptions. Chambers had 9 receptions for 103 yards.

Miami	7	0	3	7	—	17
Seattle	10	7	0	7	—	24

Sea	—	Rice 21 pass from Dilfer (J. Brown kick)
Mia	—	Feeley 7 run (Mare kick)
Sea	—	FG J. Brown 33
Sea	—	Alexander 4 run (J. Brown kick)
Mia	—	Chambers 16 pass from Feeley (Mare kick)
Mia	—	FG Mare 39
Sea	—	Boulware 63 interception return (J. Brown kick)

TAMPA BAY 35, SAN FRANCISCO 3—at Raymond James Stadium, attendance 65,234. Brian Griese passed for 210 yards and 2 touchdowns, both to Joe Jurevicius, and Tampa Bay's defense recorded 5 sacks and allowed just 197 yards to hand the

49ers' their fifth consecutive defeat. Tampa Bay led 21-0 at halftime, and the defense had allowed just 2 first downs. The Buccaneers drove 62 yards for a touchdown to begin the second half, and Torrie Cox ended the scoring with a 55-yard interception return with 8:13 remaining. Griese was 15 of 21 for 210 yards and 2 touchdowns, with 2 interceptions. Michael Pittman rushed 21 times for 106 yards and 2 touchdowns. Tim Rattay was 15 of 31 for 147 yards, with 1 interception.

San Francisco	0	0	3	0	—	3
Tampa Bay	7	14	7	7	—	35

TB	—	Pittman 14 run (Gramatica kick)
TB	—	Jurevicius 9 pass from Griese (Gramatica kick)
TB	—	Jurevicius 42 pass from Griese (Gramatica kick)
TB	—	Pittman 6 run (Gramatica kick)
SF	—	FG Peterson 47
TB	—	Cox 55 interception return (Gramatica kick)

SUNDAY NIGHT, NOVEMBER 21
GREEN BAY 16, HOUSTON 13—at Reliant Stadium, attendance 70,769. Ryan Longwell made a 46-yard field goal as time expired to give the Packers' their best fourth-quarter road comeback in Brett Favre's career. The victory marked the first time since 1990 the Packers had comeback from a 10-point fourth-quarter deficit on the road to win. Houston scored on three successive possessions of the second quarter to take a 13-3 halftime lead. Trailing by that same score, the Packers' started on their own 19 with 14:53 remaining. Favre completed 4 of 6 passes on a 7-play, 81-yard drive, capped by his 24-yard scoring pass to Donald Driver. Following a Houston punt, Favre's 15-yard pass to Driver on third-and-16 set up Longwell's game-tying 39-yard field goal with 7:55 remaining. The Packers got the ball at their own 31-yard line with 2:00 remaining, and Favre completed 6 of 7 passes, with the incompletion being a spike to stop the clock. Driver's 12-yard reception at the Texans' 28 with four seconds left set up Longwell's winning field goal. Favre was 33 of 50 for 383 yards and 1 touchdown, with 2 interceptions. Driver had 10 receptions for 148 yards. Carr was 13 of 26 for 164 yards and 1 touchdown, and Andre Johnson had 6 catches for 107 yards.

Green Bay	0	3	0	13	—	16
Houston	0	13	0	0	—	13

GB	—	FG Longwell 23
Hous	—	Davis 6 pass from Carr (K. Brown kick)
Hous	—	FG K. Brown 46
Hous	—	FG K. Brown 40
GB	—	Driver 24 pass from Favre (Longwell kick)
GB	—	FG Longwell 39
GB	—	FG Longwell 46

MONDAY NIGHT, NOVEMBER 22
NEW ENGLAND 27, KANSAS CITY 19—at Arrowhead Stadium, attendance 78,431. Tom Brady passed for 315 yards and 1 touchdown as the Patriots held off the Chiefs. The Patriots trailed 10-7 in the second quarter before scoring twice before halftime. To begin the second half the Chiefs had to settle for Lawrence Tynes' 24-yard field goal when Derrick Blaylock was stopped on third-and-1 from the Patriots' 4. Three plays later, Brady connected on a 46-yard pass to David Patten and, on the next play, found Deion Branch open for a 26-yard touchdown. Eddie Kennison caught a 26-yard touchdown with 6:13 to play, but Trent Green's 2-point conversion pass to Kennison was incomplete, allowing the Patriots to maintain a 24-19 lead. New England took the ensuing kickoff and marched 11 plays, capped by Adam Vinatieri's 28-yard field goal with 1:46 left. Willie McGinest sacked Green on fourth down with 53 seconds left to seal the victory. Brady was 17 of 26 for 315 yards and 1 touchdown, and Branch had 6 receptions for 105 yards. Green was 27 of 42 for

381 yards and 2 touchdowns, with 1 interception. Johnnie Morton had 5 catches for 107 yards.

New England	7	10	7	3	—	27
Kansas City	10	0	3	6	—	19

NE	—	Dillon 5 run (Vinatieri kick)
KC	—	FG Tynes 44
KC	—	Kennison 65 pas from Green (Tynes kick)
NE	—	Dillon 1 run (Vinatieri kick)
NE	—	FG Vinatieri 37
KC	—	FG Tynes 24
NE	—	Branch 26 pass from Brady (Vinatieri kick)
KC	—	Kennison 26 pass from Green (pass failed)
NE	—	FG Vinatieri 28

TWELFTH WEEK SUMMARIES
American Football Conference

East Division	W	L	T	Pct.	Pts.	OP
New England	10	1	0	.909	288	174
N.Y. Jets	8	3	0	.727	225	168
Buffalo	5	6	0	.455	218	192
Miami	2	9	0	.182	164	227
North Division	W	L	T	Pct.	Pts.	OP
Pittsburgh	10	1	0	.909	256	168
Baltimore	7	4	0	.636	207	164
Cincinnati	5	6	0	.455	241	246
Cleveland	3	8	0	.273	225	266
South Division	W	L	T	Pct.	Pts.	OP
Indianapolis	8	3	0	.727	380	239
Jacksonville	6	5	0	.545	182	208
Houston	5	6	0	.455	229	260
Tennessee	4	7	0	.364	207	243
West Division	W	L	T	Pct.	Pts.	OP
San Diego	8	3	0	.727	319	221
Denver	7	4	0	.636	257	192
Oakland	4	7	0	.364	207	294
Kansas City	3	8	0	.273	307	299

National Football Conference

East Division	W	L	T	Pct.	Pts.	OP
Philadelphia*	10	1	0	.909	293	164
N.Y. Giants	5	6	0	.455	202	199
Dallas	4	7	0	.364	193	289
Washington	3	8	0	.273	138	194
North Division	W	L	T	Pct.	Pts.	OP
Green Bay	7	4	0	.636	301	247
Minnesota	7	4	0	.636	291	262
Chicago	4	7	0	.364	172	221
Detroit	4	7	0	.364	192	257
South Division	W	L	T	Pct.	Pts.	OP
Atlanta	9	2	0	.818	232	215
Carolina	4	7	0	.364	217	236
New Orleans	4	7	0	.364	232	312
Tampa Bay	4	7	0	.364	206	203
West Division	W	L	T	Pct.	Pts.	OP
Seattle	6	5	0	.545	239	223
St. Louis	5	6	0	.455	237	299
Arizona	4	7	0	.364	180	227
San Francisco	1	10	0	.091	192	320

*Clinched division title

THURSDAY, NOVEMBER 25
INDIANAPOLIS 41, DETROIT 9—at Ford Field, attendance 63,107. Peyton Manning passed for 6 touchdowns, becoming the first quarterback to have four games in a season with at least 5 touchdown passes, as the Colts won their fourth consecutive game. The Lions outgained the Colts 385-356, and reached the red zone three times. Detroit settled for field goals by Jason Hanson each time. The Colts reached the red zone five times, and scored a touchdown on all five possessions. Leading 13-6 with 4:19 left in the half, Rob Morris sacked Joey Harrington and forced him to fumble. Montae Reagor recovered the ball at the Lions' 47, and Manning completed a 25-yard touchdown pass to Brandon Stokley five plays later for a 20-6 lead. Two plays later, David Thornton forced Shawn Bryson to fumble. Robert Mathis recovered at the Lions' 31, and Manning's 13-yard touchdown pass to Marvin Harrison three plays later gave the Colts 14 points in the

span of 1:30 and a 27-6 lead with 50 seconds left in the half. Manning was 23 of 28 for 236 yards and 6 touchdowns. Harrison had 12 receptions for 127 yards. Edgerrin James rushed 23 times for 105 yards. Harrington was 14 of 23 for 156 yards, and was replaced in the third quarter by Mike McMahon, who was 11 of 15 for 77 yards, with 1 interception.

Indianapolis	13	14	14	0	—	41
Detroit	6	3	0	0	—	9

Ind	—	Stokley 4 pass from Manning (Vanderjagt kick)
Det	—	FG Hanson 20
Ind	—	Stokley 12 pass from Manning (kick blocked)
Det	—	FG Hanson 34
Ind	—	Stokley 25 pass from Manning (Vanderjagt kick)
Ind	—	Harrison 13 pass from Manning (Vanderjagt kick)
Det	—	FG Hanson 32
Ind	—	Harrison 10 pass from Manning (Vanderjagt kick)
Ind	—	Harrison 5 pass from Manning (Vanderjagt kick)

DALLAS 21, CHICAGO 7—at Texas Stadium, attendance 64,026. Julius Jones rushed for a career high 150 yards and 2 touchdowns as the Cowboys kept their playoff hopes alive. Jones' 33-yard run capped the opening drive, but R.W. McQuarters tied the game with a 45-yard interception return of Drew Henson's pass with 5:57 left in the half. Vinny Testaverde replaced Henson at halftime, but McQuarters intercepted his pass early in the third quarter and returned it to 40 yards to the Cowboys' 29 but fumbled and Flozell Adams recovered. Later in the third quarter, Paul Edinger missed a 48-yard field-goal attempt wide right. Testaverde capped a 61-yard drive early in the fourth quarter with a 5-yard touchdown pass to Darian Barnes. Not only was it Barnes' first career touchdown, Testaverde tied an NFL record, shared with Steve DeBerg, by completing a touchdown pass to his sixty-second different receiver. On the next play from Scrimmage Terence Newman intercepted Jonathan Quinn's pass and Jones scored seven plays later. The Cowboys' defense allowed just 140 yards. Henson made his first NFL start and was 4 of 12 for 31 yards, with 1 interception, before replaced at halftime by Vinny Testaverde, who was 9 of 14 for 92 yards and 1 touchdown, with 1 interception. Craig Krenzel was 5 of 10 for 46 yards before leaving in the second quarter with an injury. His replacement, Quinn, was 10 of 21 for 86 yards, with 2 interceptions.

Chicago	0	7	0	0	—	7
Dallas	7	0	14	0	—	21

Dall	—	J. Jones 33 run (Cundiff kick)
Chi	—	McQuarters 45 interception return (Edinger kick)
Dall	—	Barnes 5 pass from Testaverde (Cundiff kick)
Dall	—	J. Jones 4 run (Cundiff kick)

SUNDAY, NOVEMBER 28
N.Y. JETS 13, ARIZONA 3—at Sun Devil Stadium, attendance 35,820. Curtis Martin rushed for 99 yards and Quincy Carter completed a long touchdown pass to Santana Moss as the Jets fought off the Cardinals. Carter started the game, left with an injury in the first quarter, but returned midway through the second quarter and guided the Jets on three consecutive scoring drives, capped by Moss' 69-yard touchdown catch. The Cardinals responded by driving to the Jets' 21, but Jonathan Vilma intercepted Shaun King's pass to quell the threat. Josh McCown replaced King and drove the Cardinals to the Jets' 29, but David Barrett intercepted his pass at the Jets' 2 with 1:50 left to end the final threat. Carter was 8 of 12 for 133 yards and 1 touchdown. Brooks Bollinger was 5 of 9 for 60 yards, and Moss had 5 receptions for 109 yards. King was 14 of 26 for 119 yards, with 1 interception, and McCown was

5 of 10 for 62 yards, with 2 interceptions.

N.Y. Jets	0	3	10	0	—	13
Arizona	0	3	0	0	—	3

NYJ	—	FG Brien 28
Ariz	—	FG Rackers 20
NYJ	—	FG Brien 46
NYJ	—	S. Moss 69 pass from Carter (Brien kick)

ATLANTA 24, NEW ORLEANS 21—at Georgia Dome, attendance 70,521. Michael Vick completed a 20-yard touchdown pass to Alge Crumpler with 1:22 remaining as the Falcons expanded their lead in the NFC South to five games with five to play. The Saints cut the lead to 14-6 and had the ball on their own 22 with 38 seconds left in the half. Aaron Brooks attempted a pass, and Allen Rossum intercepted it to set up Jay Feely's 31-yard field goal as the half expired. Ed Jasper blocked John Carney's 37-yard field-goal attempt early in the third quarter, but the Saints responded with consecutive touchdowns drives, the latter set up by Charles Grant's interception and 8-yard return to the Falcons' 30, to take a 21-17 lead. The Falcons drove to the Saints' 6, but Warrick Dunn fumbled and James Allen recovered with 3:03 remaining. Atlanta's defense forced a punt, and Vick completed a 27-yard pass to Crumpler followed by the 20-yard touchdown with 1:22 left. DeAngelo Hall intercepted Brooks' desperation pass at the Falcons' 21 as time expired. Vick was 16 of 29 for 212 yards and 2 touchdowns, with 1 interception. Crumpler had 4 receptions for 103 yards. Brooks was 19 of 34 for 189 yards and 1 touchdown, with 2 interceptions. Joe Horn had 9 receptions for 101 yards, and Deuce McAllister had 23 carries for 100 yards.

New Orleans	0	6	8	7	—	21
Atlanta	7	10	0	7	—	24

Atl	—	Vick 16 run (Feely kick)
Atl	—	Pritchett 1 pass from Vick (Feely kick)
NO	—	FG Carney 48
NO	—	FG Carney 38
Atl	—	FG Feely 31
NO	—	Brooks 1 run (Horn pass from Brooks)
NO	—	Horn 7 pass from Brooks (Carney kick)
Atl	—	Crumpler 20 pass from Vick (Feely kick)

CAROLINA 21, TAMPA BAY 14—at Bank of America Stadium, attendance 73,124. Keary Colbert caught a 40-yard touchdown pass from Jake Delhomme with 20 seconds remaining to give the Panthers their third consecutive victory. Jeff Chandler missed one field-goal attempt and had the second blocked by Dewayne White on the Panthers' first two second-half possessions. Two plays after the block, Julius Peppers intercepted Brian Griese's pass and returned it 46 yards for a touchdown. Tampa Bay made three more ventures into the Panthers' red zone, but scored just once as Michael Pittman fumbled and Gramatica missed a third field goal with 1:53 left. Delhomme completed all 4 pass attempts on the final drive, capped by his 40-yard pass to Colbert. Griese's last desperation pass from midfield was incomplete. Delhomme was 14 of 21 for 213 yards and 2 touchdowns, with 1 interception. Nick Goings had 23 carries for 106 yards. Griese was 27 of 39 for 347 yards and 2 touchdowns, with 1 interception. Pittman had 8 receptions for 134 yards.

Tampa Bay	0	7	0	7	—	14
Carolina	7	0	7	7	—	21

Car	—	Colbert 24 pass from Delhomme (Chandler kick)
TB	—	Pittman 6 pass from Griese (Gramatica kick)
Car	—	Peppers 46 interception return (Chandler kick)
TB	—	Pittman 8 pass from Griese (Gramatica kick)

Car — Colbert 40 pass from Delhomme
(Chandler kick)

CINCINNATI 58, CLEVELAND 48—at Paul Brown Stadium, attendance 65,677. Carson Palmer passed for 4 touchdowns and Rudi Johnson rushed for 202 yards and 2 scores as the Bengals and Browns combined for 106 points in the second-highest scoring game in NFL history. Cincinnati led 14-13 in the second quarter before scoring on their next six possessions, but led just 44-34 with 14:15 remaining. Cleveland, which had scored touchdowns on its previous three possessions, needed just six plays to drive 80 yards and cut the deficit to 44-41 on William Green's 1-yard touchdown. On the next play, Barry Gardner intercepted Palmer's pass and returned it to the Bengals' 1. Steve Heiden caught Kelly Holcomb's fifth touchdown for a 48-44 Cleveland lead with 10:22 left. Seven plays later, Rudi Johnson scored on a 7-yard run for a 51-48 lead with 6:29 left. The Browns had the ball with 1:52 left, but Deltha O'Neal intercepted Holcomb's pass in the flat and returned it untouched 31 yards for the game-clinching touchdown. The clubs combined for 966 yards (504 for the Bengals), including 346 yards for Cleveland in the second half. The Bengals had seven drives in excess of 57 yards. Palmer was 22 of 29 for 251 yards and 4 touchdowns, with 3 interceptions. Chad Johnson had 10 receptions for 117 yards, and Rudi Johnson rushed 26 times for 202 yards. Holcomb was 30 of 39 for 413 yards and 5 touchdowns, with 2 interceptions. Bryant had 8 receptions for 131 yards.

Cleveland	10	3	21	14	—	48
Cincinnati	14	13	14	17	—	58

Cle — Heiden 7 pass from Holcomb (Dawson kick)
Cin — Washington 18 pass from Palmer (Graham kick)
Cin — C. Johnson 46 pass from Palmer (Graham kick)
Cin — FG Dawson 23
Cin — FG Dawson 29
Cin — Houshmandzadeh 3 pass from Palmer (Graham kick)
Cin — FG Graham 21
Cin — FG Graham 32
Cin — Heiden 20 pass from Holcomb (Dawson kick)
Cin — Houshmandzadeh 53 pass from Palmer (Graham kick)
Cle — Bryant 9 pass from Holcomb (Dawson kick)
Cle — R. Johnson 7 run (Graham kick)
Cle — Bryant 55 pass from Holcomb (Dawson kick)
Cin — FG Graham 36
Cle — Green 1 run (Dawson kick)
Cle — Heiden 1 pass from Holcomb (Dawson kick)
Cin — R. Johnson 7 run (Graham kick)
Cin — O'Neal 31 interception return (Graham kick)

HOUSTON 31, TENNESSEE 21—at Reliant Stadium, attendance 70,721. David Carr passed for 2 touchdowns and Domanick Davis rushed for 129 yards as the Texans scored the game's final 28 points. Late in the third quarter, Gary Walker forced Steve McNair to fumble and DaShon Polk recovered to set up Carr's 11-yard touchdown pass to Andre Johnson and a 24-21 lead. Moments later, on third-and-10 from the Texans' 13, Antwan Peek sacked McNair and forced him to fumble again. Kailee Wong recovered to quell the drive, and an interception by Marlon McCree stopped Tennessee's next drive with 1:47 left. Two plays later, Davis scored on a 41-yard run with 1:34 left to ice the game. Carr was 21 of 30 for 201 yards and 2 touchdowns, with 1 interception. Davis had 16 carries for 129 yards. McNair was 25 of 34 for 227 yards and 3 touchdowns, with 1 interception.

Tennessee	14	7	0	0	—	21
Houston	3	7	14	7	—	31

Tenn — Kinney 12 pass from McNair (Anderson kick)
Tenn — Kinney 11 pass from McNair (Anderson kick)
Hous — FG K. Brown 29
Tenn — Mason 4 pass from McNair (Anderson kick)
Hous — Wells 7 run (K. Brown kick)
Hous — Miller 14 pass from Carr (K. Brown kick)
Hous — A. Johnson 11 pass from Carr (K. Brown kick)
Hous — Davis 41 run (K. Brown kick)

SAN DIEGO 34, KANSAS CITY 31—at Arrowhead Stadium, attendance 77,447. Nate Kaeding's 43-yard field goal with 2:24 remaining capped a fourth-quarter comeback and gave the Chargers their first victory in Kansas City since 1996. With Denver's loss to Oakland Sunday night, the Chargers moved into first place in the AFC West. Kaeding missed 2 field goals in the first half as the Chiefs took a 17-14 lead. Dante Hall opened the second half with a 77-yard kickoff return, but Kassim Osgood forced Hall to fumble and Jerrell Pippens recovered at the Chargers' 5. The Chiefs took a 23-17 on Derrick Blaylock's 22-yard scoring run early in the fourth quarter, but the Chargers responded with a 6-play, 71-yard drive, capped by Drew Brees' 18-yard scoring pass to Antonio Gates. Hall redeemed himself by returning the ensuing kickoff 96 yards for a touchdown and 31-24 lead with 10:00 left. Brees completed a 65-yard pass to Osgood to set up Gates' 11-yard touchdown pass and Dillon's 6:28 left to tie the game. Three plays later, Donnie Edwards intercepted Trent Green's pass to set up Kaeding's field goal. Brees was 28 of 37 for 378 yards and 2 touchdowns. Tomlinson had 10 receptions for 57 yards. Green was 21 of 34 for 208 yards, with 1 interception. Tony Gonzalez had 8 receptions for 105 yards.

San Diego	7	7	3	17	—	34
Kansas City	7	10	0	14	—	31

SD — Tomlinson 1 run (Kaeding kick)
KC — Blaylock 5 run (Tynes kick)
KC — L. Johnson 6 run (Tynes kick)
SD — Tomlinson 3 run (Kaeding kick)
KC — FG Tynes 28
SD — FG Kaeding 25
KC — Blaylock 22 run (kick failed)
SD — Gates 18 pass from Brees (Kaeding kick)
KC — Hall 96 kickoff return (Kennison pass from Green)
SD — Gates 11 pass from Brees (Kaeding kick)
SD — FG Kaeding 43

MINNESOTA 27, JACKSONVILLE 16—at Metrodome, attendance 64,004. Kenechi Udeze forced a fumble and Kevin Williams returned it 77 yards for a touchdown with 1:59 remaining as the Vikings held off the Jaguars. Daunte Culpepper's 2-yard touchdown pass to Randy Moss capped a 16-play, 80-yard drive to begin the second half. Minnesota led 20-16 in the fourth quarter and reached the Jaguars' 18, but Bobby McCray forced Culpepper to fumble and Marcus Stroud recovered the ball. Eleven plays later, the Jaguars faced third-and-6 at the Vikings' 19. Byron Leftwich scrambled but was hit from behind by Udeze. Williams picked up the loose ball and rumbled 77 yards for the game-clinching touchdown. Culpepper was 19 of 27 for 235 yards and 1 touchdown, with 1 interception. Leftwich was 19 of 34 for 235 yards and 1 touchdown. Fred Taylor rushed 22 times for 147 yards.

Jacksonville	0	13	0	3	—	16
Minnesota	3	10	7	7	—	27

Minn — FG Andersen 25
Jax — B. Jones 26 pass from Leftwich (Scobee kick)
Jax — FG Scobee 33
Minn — Culpepper 1 run (Andersen kick)
Jax — FG Scobee 32
Minn — FG Andersen 33
Minn — Moss 2 pass from Culpepper (Andersen kick)
Jax — FG Scobee 42
Minn — K. Williams 77 fumble return (Andersen kick)

NEW ENGLAND 24, BALTIMORE 3—at Gillette Stadium, attendance 68,756. Corey Dillon rushed for 123 yards and 1 touchdown, and the Patriots' defense allowed just 124 yards, as New England won in a downpour. Matt Stover's 22-yard field goal with two seconds left in the first half tied the game 3-3. The Patriots started the first three drives of the second half at the Patriots' 41, 48, and the Ravens' 48 and converted 18 each into 3 field goals and Dillon's touchdown for a 17-3 lead with 14:57 remaining. Two plays later, Tedy Bruschi sacked Kyle Boller and forced him to fumble. Jarvis Green recovered the ball in the end zone for a 24-3 lead. The Patriots' defense permitted just 29 yards in the second half. Tom Brady was 15 of 30 for 172 yards. Dillon carried 30 times for 123 yards. Boller was 15 of 35 for 93 yards, with 1 interception.

Baltimore	0	3	0	0	—	3
New England	0	3	6	15	—	24

NE — FG Vinatieri 28
Balt — FG Stover 22
NE — FG Vinatieri 40
NE — FG Vinatieri 48
NE — Dillon 1 run (Dillon run)
NE — J. Green fumble recovery in end zone (Vinatieri kick)

PHILADELPHIA 27, N.Y. GIANTS 6—at Giants Stadium, attendance 78,830. Brian Westbrook scored 2 touchdowns as the Eagles won the NFC East. Trailing 7-3, the Giants drove to the Eagles' 3 but Quintin Mikill intercepted Eli Manning's pass in the end zone. The Eagles scored on their first four possessions of the second half, the second set up by Brian Dawkins' interception and the third followed by Jevon Kearse's blocked punt. McNabb was 18 of 27 for 244 yards and 1 touchdown. Manning was 6 of 21 for 148 yards, with 2 interceptions and was sacked 5 times. Jamaar Taylor had 2 catches for 102 yards.

Philadelphia	0	7	13	7	—	27
N.Y. Giants	3	3	0	0	—	6

NYG — FG Christie 22
Phil — McNabb 4 run (Akers kick)
NYG — FG Christie 31
Phil — FG Akers 47
Phil — FG Akers 42
Phil — Westbrook 1 run (Akers kick)
Phil — Westbrook 34 pass from McNabb (Akers kick)

PITTSBURGH 16, WASHINGTON 7—at Heinz Field, attendance 63,707. Jerome Bettis rushed for 100 yards and 1 touchdown, and the Steelers' defense allowed just 156 yards, as Pittsburgh won its ninth consecutive game. The Redskins' defense allowed just 207 yards, but allowed Antwaan Randle El to return punts 60 and 43 yards to set up Pittsburgh's first two scores. The Redskins drove 13 plays, 81 yards for a third-quarter touchdown, capped by Chris Cooley's 2-yard scoring catch, to cut the deficit to 13-7. Pittsburgh answered with a 71-yard drive later in the half, and Jeff Reed's 32-yard field goal gave Pittsburgh a nine-point lead with 9:54 to play. Deshea Townsend's interception at the Steelers' 13 with 4:39 left ended the Redskins' final scoring threat. Ben Roethlisberger was 9 of 20 for 131 yards. Bettis carried 31 times for 100 yards. Patrick Ramsey was 19 of 34 for 138 yards and 1 touchdown, with 1 interception.

Washington	0	0	7	0	—	7
Pittsburgh	3	10	0	3	—	16

Pitt — FG Reed 33

Pitt	—	Bettis 4 run (Reed kick)
Pitt	—	FG Reed 36
Wash	—	Cooley 2 pass from Ramsey (Hall kick)
Pitt	—	FG Reed 32

SAN FRANCISCO 24, MIAMI 17—at Monster Park, attendance 66,156. A.J. Feeley passed for 2 touchdowns and the Dolphins' defense recorded 8 sacks and forced 3 fourth-quarter turnovers to give Jim Bates his first victory. Early in the fourth quarter, Derek Smith recovered Feeley's fumble and returned it 46 yards for a 10-7 lead. Patrick Surtain recovered a fumble at the 49ers' 21 moments later and Feeley's 15-yard scoring pass to Randy McMichael allowed Miami to regain the lead. Jay Williams forced Tim Rattay to fumble on the next possession, and Surtain again recovered to set up Olindo Mare's 50-yard field goal and a 17-10 lead. With 3:10 left, Jason Taylor sacked Rattay in the end zone and forced him to fumble. Derrick Pope picked up the ball on the 1-yard line and walked into the end zone. Maurice Hicks scored with 37 seconds left, but Surtain recovered the onside kick. Feeley was 17 of 33 for 159 yards and 2 touchdowns, with 1 interception. Taylor had 3 of the Dolphins' 8 sacks. Rattay was 23 of 38 for 181 yards.

Miami	7 0 0 17 —	24
San Francisco	0 3 0 14 —	17
Mia	—	Chambers 25 pass from Feeley (Mare kick)
SF	—	FG Peterson 19
SF	—	O. Smith 46 fumble return (Peterson kick)
Mia	—	McMichael 15 pass from Feeley (Mare kick)
Mia	—	FG Mare 50
Mia	—	Pope 1 fumble return (Mare kick)
SF	—	Hicks 1 run (Peterson kick)

BUFFALO 38, SEATTLE 9—at Qwest Field, attendance 66,271. Willis McGahee rushed for 116 yards and a career-high 4 touchdowns as the Bills won their first road game. The Bills had advantages in yards (434-230) and time of possession (36:24-23:36). The Bills led just 10-7 late in the first half, but Lee Evans' 3-yard touchdown catch with six seconds remaining increased the lead to 10 points. Terrence McGee's interception early in the second half led to McGahee's second touchdown, and Pat Williams' recovery of Matt Hasselbeck's fumble, set up by Ryan Denney's sack, led to McGahee's final touchdown with 7:14 left. Bledsoe was 25 of 37 for 275 yards and 1 touchdown, with 3 interceptions. Hasselbeck was 19 of 38 for 185 yards and 1 touchdown, with 1 interception.

Buffalo	7 10 7 14 —	38
Seattle	0 3 0 6 —	9
Buff	—	McGahee 2 run (Lindell kick)
Buff	—	FG Lindell 25
Sea	—	FG J. Brown 19
Buff	—	Evans 3 pass from Bledsoe (Lindell kick)
Buff	—	McGahee 2 run (Lindell kick)
Buff	—	McGahee 30 run (Lindell kick)
Buff	—	McGahee 1 run (Lindell kick)
Sea	—	Engram 8 pass from Hasselbeck (pass failed)

SUNDAY NIGHT, NOVEMBER 28
OAKLAND 25, DENVER 24—at INVESCO Field at Mile High, attendance 75,936. Kerry Collins passed for 4 touchdowns and Langston Walker blocked Jason Elam's potential game-winning field goal as the Raiders won in the snow. Collins' 42-yard touchdown pass to Jerry Porter with 16 seconds left in the half cut the deficit to 10-7, and the pair hooked up for a 14-yard touchdown 2:10 into the second half, following a Reuben Droughns fumble, to give Oakland a 13-10 lead. Plummer's 57-yard pass to Ashley Lelie on the first play of the fourth quarter set up Droughns' 3-yard touchdown run, and two plays

later Ellis Johnson intercepted Collins' tipped pass and returned it 32 yards for a touchdown and 24-13 Denver lead. John Lynch intercepted a pass in the end zone to thwart an Oakland drive, but the Raiders forced a punt and four plays later Ronald Curry made a one-handed catch in the back of the end zone to cut the deficit to 24-19 with 6:11 left. The Raiders forced another three-and-out, and Collins connected with Curry for a 63-yard pass to set up Porter's 5-yard scoring grab on fourth-and-goal with 1:49 left. Denver drove to the Raiders' 24, but Walker blocked Elam's 43-yard field-goal attempt. Collins was 26 of 45 for 339 yards and 4 touchdowns, with 2 interceptions. Porter had 6 receptions for 135 yards and Curry had 6 catches for 110 yards. Plummer was 14 of 23 for 245 yards and 1 touchdown, with 1 interception. Droughns rushed 28 times for 102 yards.

Oakland	0 7 6 12 —	25
Denver	0 10 0 14 —	24
Den	—	FG Elam 32
Den	—	R. Smith 85 pass from Plummer (Elam kick)
Oak	—	Porter 42 pass from Collins (Janikowski kick)
Oak	—	Porter 14 pass from Collins (kick failed)
Den	—	Droughns 3 run (Elam kick)
Den	—	E. Johnson 32 interception return (Elam kick)
Oak	—	Curry 6 pass from Collins (pass failed)
Oak	—	Porter 5 pass from Collins (pass failed)

MONDAY NIGHT, NOVEMBER 29
GREEN BAY 45, ST. LOUIS 17—at Lambeau Field, attendance 70,385. Brett Favre made his 200th consecutive start and passed for 3 touchdowns to guide the Packers to their sixth consecutive victory. Ahmad Carroll returned Isaac Bruce's fumble 40 yards for a touchdown less than three minutes into the game, and Michael Hawthorne returned a fumble by Bruce 34 yards for the game's final points with just 46 seconds remaining. Favre guided the Packers on scoring drives of 75, 83, 71, 65, and 84 yards. With his first touchdown pass, a 7-yard toss to Bubba Franks with 7:25 left in the half, Favre passed Dan Marino to become the only quarterback with 11 consecutive seasons with at least 20 touchdown passes. Trailing 21-10 early in the second half, the Rams attempted a fake field goal. Instead of kicking a 42-yard attempt, Jeff Wilkins attempted to run but lost 5 yards on fourth-and-7. The Packers scored on their next three possessions. Favre was 18 of 27 for 215 yards and 3 touchdowns. Najeh Davenport, making his first NFL start in place of injured Ahman Green, carried 19 times for 178 yards and 1 touchdown. Marc Bulger was 35 of 53 for 448 yards, the most ever allowed by the Packers, and 2 touchdowns, with 1 interception. Bruce had 9 receptions for 170 yards and 1 touchdown.

St. Louis	0 10 0 7 —	17
Green Bay	7 14 7 17 —	45
GB	—	Carroll 40 fumble return (Longwell kick)
StL	—	FG Wilkins 34
GB	—	Franks 7 pass from Favre (Longwell kick)
GB	—	Walker 10 pass from Favre (Longwell kick)
StL	—	Bruce 4 pass from Bulger (Wilkins kick)
GB	—	Driver 16 pass from Favre (Longwell kick)
StL	—	Faulk 8 pass from Bulger (Wilkins kick)
GB	—	FG Longwell 27
GB	—	Davenport 40 run (Longwell kick)
GB	—	Hawthorne 34 fumble return (Longwell kick)

THIRTEENTH WEEK SUMMARIES
American Football Conference

East Division	W	L	T	Pct.	Pts.	OP
New England	11	1	0	.917	330	189
N.Y. Jets	9	3	0	.750	251	175
Buffalo	6	6	0	.500	260	224
Miami	2	10	0	.167	196	269
North Division	W	L	T	Pct.	Pts.	OP
Pittsburgh	11	1	0	.917	273	184
Baltimore	7	5	0	.583	233	191
Cincinnati	6	6	0	.500	268	272
Cleveland	3	9	0	.250	240	308
South Division	W	L	T	Pct.	Pts.	OP
Indianapolis	9	3	0	.750	431	263
Jacksonville	6	6	0	.500	198	225
Houston	5	7	0	.417	236	289
Tennessee	4	8	0	.333	231	294
West Division	W	L	T	Pct.	Pts.	OP
San Diego	9	3	0	.750	339	238
Denver	7	5	0	.583	274	212
Kansas City	4	8	0	.333	341	326
Oakland	4	8	0	.333	234	328

National Football Conference

East Division	W	L	T	Pct.	Pts.	OP
Philadelphia*	11	1	0	.917	340	181
N.Y. Giants	5	7	0	.417	209	230
Dallas	5	7	0	.417	236	328
Washington	4	8	0	.333	169	201
North Division	W	L	T	Pct.	Pts.	OP
Green Bay	7	5	0	.583	318	294
Minnesota	7	5	0	.583	305	286
Chicago	5	7	0	.417	196	235
Detroit	5	7	0	.417	218	269
South Division	W	L	T	Pct.	Pts.	OP
Atlanta	9	3	0	.750	232	242
Carolina	5	7	0	.417	249	257
Tampa Bay	5	7	0	.417	233	203
New Orleans	4	8	0	.333	253	344
West Division	W	L	T	Pct.	Pts.	OP
St. Louis	6	6	0	.500	253	305
Seattle	6	6	0	.500	278	266
Arizona	4	8	0	.333	192	253
San Francisco	1	11	0	.083	195	336

Clinched division title

SUNDAY, DECEMBER 5
CINCINNATI 27, BALTIMORE 26—at M&T Bank Stadium, attendance 69,695. Carson Palmer passed for 3 fourth-quarter touchdowns and Shayne Graham kicked the winning 24-yard field goal as time expired. The Bengals broke a 42-game losing streak in road games against teams with a winning record, dating back to 1990. The Ravens led 13-3 in the third quarter when Ed Reed intercepted a pass and returned it to the Ravens' 36, where he fumbled. Chris McAlister scooped up the ball and raced the remaining 64 yards for a touchdown and 20-3 lead with 2:29 left in the third quarter. Moments later, B.J. Sams muffed a punt and Marcus Wilkins recovered at the Ravens' 19. Chad Johnson caught 2 touchdown passes within the next five minutes to cut the Bengals' deficit to 20-17. Chester Taylor's 47-yard run set up a field goal with 8:34 left, but T.J. Houshmandzadeh caught passes of 24 and 34 yards and capped the drive with a 9-yard scoring catch to take a 24-23 lead. Matt Stover's 45-yard field goal with 1:42 left gave the Ravens the lead, but Palmer hit Houshmandzadeh with a 32-yard pass to set up Graham's game winner. Palmer was 29 of 36 for 382 yards and 3 touchdowns, with 1 interception. Houshmandzadeh grabbed 10 receptions for 171 yards. Johnson added 10 catches for 161 yards. Kyle Boller was 19 of 33 for 172 yards, with 1 interception. Taylor had 23 carries for 139 yards.

Cincinnati	0 3 0 24 —	27
Baltimore	3 3 14 6 —	26
Balt	—	FG Stover 20
Cin	—	FG Graham 41
Balt	—	FG Stover 22
Balt	—	C. Taylor 1 run (Stover kick)
Balt	—	McAlister 64 fumble return (Stover kick)

Cin — C. Johnson 13 pass from Palmer (Graham kick)
Cin — C. Johnson 12 pass from Palmer (Graham kick)
Balt — FG Stover 38
Cin — Houshmandzadeh 9 pass from Palmer (Graham kick)
Balt — FG Stover 45
Cin — FG Graham 24

CHICAGO 24, MINNESOTA 14—at Soldier Field, attendance 62,051. Making his first start of the season, Chad Hutchinson passed for 3 touchdowns as the Bears pulled within two games of the NFC North. The Bears' defense forced 4 turnovers and recorded 5 sacks. The Vikings trailed 10-7 in the second quarter and drove to the Bears' 3, but Brian Urlacher intercepted Daunte Culpepper's pass. Culpepper's 40-yard touchdown pass to Marcus Robinson gave the Vikings a 14-10 lead, but Hutchinson answered with a 15-yard scoring pass to David Terrell with just 22 seconds left in the half for a 17-14 Chicago lead. Following a missed field goal, the Bears drove 72 yards in 13 plays, capped by Jason McKie's 5-yard touchdown catch with 10:23 to play. Jerry Azumah intercepted a pass at the Bears' 12 with 2:01 left to end the Vikings' final threat. Hutchinson was 18 of 30 for 213 yards and 3 touchdowns. Culpepper was 23 of 33 for 279 yards and 2 touchdowns, with 3 interceptions.

	1	2	3	4		
Minnesota	7	7	0	0	—	14
Chicago	7	10	0	7	—	24

Chi — Clark 6 pass from Hutchinson (Edinger kick)
Minn — Burleson 4 pass from Culpepper (Andersen kick)
Chi — FG Edinger 53
Minn — Robinson 40 pass from Culpepper (Andersen kick)
Chi — Terrell 15 pass from Hutchinson (Edinger kick)
Chi — McKie 5 pass from Hutchinson (Edinger kick)

NEW ENGLAND 42, CLEVELAND 15—at Cleveland Browns Stadium, attendance 73,028. Corey Dillon rushed for 2 touchdowns and the Patriots' defense forced 4 turnovers to win their fifth consecutive game. Bethel Johnson returned the opening kickoff for a touchdown, and Randall Gay returned a fumble three plays into the second half 41 yards for a touchdown and a 28-7 lead. The Patriots scored on their first two offensive possessions of the second half, with a fumble recovery by Eugene Wilson setting up the latter score, a 44-yard touchdown pass to David Patten, for a 42-7 lead with 6:00 left in the third quarter. Tom Brady was 11 of 20 for 157 yards and 1 touchdown, with 1 interception. Dillon had 18 carries for 100 yards. Luke McCown, making his first NFL start, was 20 of 34 for 277 yards and 2 touchdowns, with 2 interceptions. Antonio Bryant had 7 receptions for 115 yards.

	1	2	3	4		
New England	14	7	21	0	—	42
Cleveland	0	7	0	8	—	15

NE — B. Johnson 93 kickoff return (Vinatieri kick)
NE — Dillon 4 run (Vinatieri kick)
NE — Dillon 1 run (Vinatieri kick)
Cle — Bryant 16 pass from McCown (Dawson kick)
NE — Gay 41 fumble return (Vinatieri kick)
NE — Faulk 42 run (Vinatieri kick)
NE — Patten 44 pass from Brady (Vinatieri kick)
Cle — Bryant 40 pass from McCown (Heiden pass from McCown)

DETROIT 26, ARIZONA 12—at Ford Field, attendance 62,262. Kevin Jones rushed for 196 yards and Jason Hanson kicked 4 field goals as the Lions stayed in the playoff hunt. The Lions led 14-12 late in the first half and were driving for more points when David Macklin intercepted Joey Harrington's pass at the Cardinals' 2 and returned it to the Cardinals' 18. John Navarre, making his first NFL start, guided the Cardinals to the Lions' 35, but Dre' Bly intercepted his pass with seven seconds left in the half. In the second half, the Lions' defense allowed just 3 first downs, and 2 of Hanson's 4 field goals were set up by interceptions. Harrington was 15 of 27 for 196 yards and 1 touchdown, with 1 interception. Navarre was 18 of 40 for 168 yards and 1 touchdown, with 4 interceptions.

	1	2	3	4		
Arizona	3	9	0	0	—	12
Detroit	7	7	6	6	—	26

Ariz — FG Rackers 42
Det — Streets 17 pass from Harrington (Hanson kick)
Ariz — FG Rackers 33
Det — K. Jones 2 run (Hanson kick)
Ariz — F. Jones 33 pass from Navarre (pass failed)
Det — FG Hanson 45
Det — FG Hanson 22
Det — FG Hanson 31
Det — FG Hanson 36

INDIANAPOLIS 51, TENNESSEE 24—at RCA Dome, attendance 57,278. Peyton Manning passed for 425 yards and 3 touchdowns as the Colts tied an NFL record by scoring at least 40 points in four consecutive games. Tennessee had six possessions in the first quarter, compared to just three for the Colts, thanks to successfully recovering 2 of its 3 onside kicks. Billy Volek completed 3 touchdown passes to Drew Bennett, the last one, from 48 yards, to end the quarter, giving the Titans a 24-17 lead. The 41-point first quarter was the second-best in NFL history. With the score tied 24-24 in the second quarter, Gary Anderson's 43-yard field-goal attempt was blocked by Montae Reagor and recovered by Rob Morris, who returned it 68 yards for a touchdown. The Colts drove inside the Titans' 25 in each of their first five second-half possessions, while the Titans failed to reach the red zone until their final drive. The Colts tallied 567 yards, including 338 in the first half, while their defense allowed just 72 yards in the second half. Manning was 25 of 33 for 425 yards and 3 touchdowns, with 2 interceptions. Brandon Stokley had 8 receptions for 153 yards, and Marvin Harrison added 4 catches for 106 yards. Volek was 21 of 35 for 269 yards and 3 touchdowns, with 2 interceptions. Bennett had 3 catches for 124 yards. Chris Brown had 19 rushes for 104 yards.

	1	2	3	4		
Tennessee	24	0	0	0	—	24
Indianapolis	17	14	10	10	—	51

Ind — FG Vanderjagt 47
Tenn — Bennett 48 pass from Volek (Anderson kick)
Tenn — FG Anderson 45
Ind — Harrison 24 pass from Manning (Vanderjagt kick)
Tenn — Bennett 28 pass from Volek (Anderson kick)
Ind — James 4 run (Vanderjagt kick)
Tenn — Bennett 48 pass from Volek (Anderson kick)
Ind — Stokley 28 pass from Manning (Vanderjagt kick)
Ind — Morris 68 blocked field goal return (Vanderjagt kick)
Ind — FG Vanderjagt 20
Ind — James 12 run (Vanderjagt kick)
Ind — Wayne 10 pass from Manning (Vanderjagt kick)
Ind — FG Vanderjagt 37

BUFFALO 42, MIAMI 32—at Pro Player Stadium, attendance 73,084. Drew Bledsoe passed for 4 touchdowns and the Bills forced 7 turnovers, capped by Pat Williams' 20-yard interception return with 1:55 left, as the Bills won their third consecu-tive game. A.J. Feeley completed 3 touchdown passes in the first 12:25, as Miami overcame Terrence McGee's 104-yard kickoff return to begin the game and take a 21-14 lead. Bledsoe's 69-yard touchdown pass to Lee Evans on the final play of the third quarter gave Buffalo a 28-25 lead. Rashad Baker's interception four plays later led to Eric Moulds' 30-yard scoring catch. The Dolphins responded with a 15-play, 76-yard drive, capped by Travis Minor's 3-yard touchdown run with 7:14 left to cut the deficit to 35-32. The Dolphins' defense forced a punt, but Brian Moorman's 33-yard punt was downed by Kevin Thomas at the Dolphins' 2. Three plays later, Williams intercepted Feeley's pass at the line of scrimmage and rumbled into the end zone with the game's final points. Bledsoe was 19 of 30 for 277 yards and 4 touchdowns. Evans had 4 receptions for 110 yards. Feeley was 25 of 51 for 303 yards and 3 touchdowns, with 5 interceptions.

	1	2	3	4		
Buffalo	14	7	14	7	—	42
Miami	21	3	0	8	—	32

Buff — McGee 104 kickoff return (Lindell kick)
Mia — Gilmore 27 pass from Feeley (Mare kick)
Buff — Euhus 15 pass from Bledsoe (Lindell kick)
Mia — Chambers 2 pass from Feeley (Mare kick)
Mia — Lee 15 pass from Feeley (Mare kick)
Mia — FG Mare 47
Buff — Evans 21 pass from Bledsoe (Lindell kick)
Buff — Evans 69 pass from Bledsoe (Lindell kick)
Buff — Moulds 30 pass from Bledsoe (Lindell kick)
Mia — Minor 3 run (Chambers pass from Feeley)
Buff — P. Williams 20 interception return (Lindell kick)

CAROLINA 32, NEW ORLEANS 21—at Louisiana Superdome, attendance 58,878. The Panthers jumped to a 23-0 lead and controlled the ball for 41:51 to win their fourth consecutive game. Carolina led 13-0 late in the first quarter and drove 75, 50, and 60 yards with their next three possessions to score as well to take a 26-7 lead. An interception by Artell Hawkins at the Panthers' 4 stopped one second-half drive, and an interception by Will Witherspoon in the fourth quarter set up the fifth of John Kasay's 6 field goals. Delhomme was 22 of 29 for 294 yards and 1 touchdown. Muhammad had 10 carries for 179 yards, and Nick Goings had 36 carries for 122 yards. Aaron Brooks was 20 of 40 for 251 yards and 3 touchdowns, with 2 interceptions. Joe Horn had 8 catches for 160 yards.

	1	2	3	4		
Carolina	13	13	0	6	—	32
New Orleans	0	7	7	7	—	21

Car — FG Kasay 30
Car — FG Kasay 50
Car — Muhammad 10 pass from Delhomme (Kasay kick)
Car — Goings 6 run (Kasay kick)
Car — FG Kasay 46
NO — Horn 13 pass from Brooks (Carney kick)
Car — FG Kasay 25
NO — Horn 24 pass from Brooks (Carney kick)
Car — FG Kasay 21
Car — FG Kasay 21
NO — Stallworth 25 pass from Brooks (Carney kick)

N.Y. JETS 29, HOUSTON 7—at Meadowlands, attendance 77,875. Curtis Martin rushed for 134 yards and scored twice and Chad Pennington returned from a two-game absence because of injury and passed for 2 touchdowns for the Jets.

Trailing 7-6 in the third quarter, Santana Moss returned a punt 46 yards to the Texans' 4 to set up Martin's touchdown run. The Jets scored on their next two drives, as well, to take a 26-7 lead with 9:05 to play. The Jets' defense allowed just 76 yards in the second half. Pennington was 20 of 27 for 155 yards and 2 touchdowns, with 1 interception. Martin rushed 23 times for 134 yards. David Carr was 12 of 25 for 157 yards, with 2 interceptions.

Houston	0	7	0	0	—	7
N.Y. Jets	3	3	7	16	—	29

NYJ	—	FG Brien 41
NYJ	—	FG Brien 26
Hous	—	Davis 2 run (K. Brown kick)
NYJ	—	Martin 4 run (Brien kick)
NYJ	—	Martin 5 pass from Pennington (pass failed)
NYJ	—	Becht 2 pass from Pennington (Brien kick)
NYJ	—	FG Brien 25

KANSAS CITY 34, OAKLAND 27—at Network Associates Coliseum, attendance 51,292. Trent Green completed a 70-yard touchdown pass to Eddie Kennison with 2:04 left as the Chiefs rallied for victory on the road. The Chiefs gained 500 yards, but fell behind 20-7 when the Raiders scored on four of their first five possessions. The Chiefs responded by driving 70 yards for a field goal just before halftime, and then drove 86, 80, 74, and 88 yards with their first four drives of the second half, resulting in three touchdowns and a field goal. With the score tied, Green completed a pass to Kennison at the Raiders' 30. Kennison broke a tackle and raced the final 30 yards for a touchdown. A sack by Gary Stills put the Raiders in third-and fourth-and-19, and Kerry Collins' final 2 passes fell incomplete. Green was 23 of 35 for 340 yards, with 1 interception. Kennison had 8 catches for 149 yards. Larry Johnson rushed 20 times for 118 yards. Collins was 27 of 41 for 343 yards and 3 touchdowns. Ronald Curry had 9 catches for 141 yards.

Kansas City	7	3	14	10	—	34
Oakland	6	14	0	7	—	27

Oak	—	FG Janikowski 27
KC	—	Blaylock 20 pass from Green (Tynes kick)
Oak	—	FG Janikowski 36
Oak	—	Curry 34 pass from Collins (Janikowski kick)
Oak	—	Porter 51 pass from Collins (Janikowski kick)
KC	—	FG Tynes 28
KC	—	Johnson 5 run (Tynes kick)
KC	—	Johnson 10 pass from Green (Tynes kick)
Oak	—	Curry 26 pass from Collins (Janikowski kick)
KC	—	FG Tynes 22
KC	—	Kennison 70 pass from Collins (Tynes kick)

PHILADELPHIA 47, GREEN BAY 17—at Lincoln Financial Field, attendance 67,723. Donovan McNabb passed for a club-record 464 yards and career-high 5 touchdowns, all in the first half, as the Eagles jumped to a 35-0 lead en route to victory. By completing his first 10 pass attempts of the game, along with completing the last 14 passes the previous week, McNabb set an NFL record with 24 consecutive completions. The Eagles outgained the Packers 542-249 total yards. Sheldon Brown intercepted a pass from Brett Favre at the Eagles' 7 early in the second quarter, and Philadelphia responded with 4 touchdowns in the final 10:27 of the half. The Packers gained just 1 first down in their three possessions amidst the touchdowns, and Brian Westbrook's third touchdown catch of the half, with 1:48 left, gave Philadelphia a 35-0 lead. The Eagles added field goals on their first four possessions of the second half. Favre's streak of 36 consecutive games with a touchdown pass, second longest in

NFL history trailing Johnny Unitas' 47, was snapped. McNabb was 32 of 43 for 464 yards and 5 touchdowns. Westbrook had 11 catches for 156 yards, and Terrell Owens added 8 receptions for 161 yards. Favre was 14 of 29 for 131 yards, with 2 interceptions, and Craig Nall played the fourth quarter and was 8 of 11 for 95 yards and 2 touchdowns.

Green Bay	0	3	0	14	—	17
Philadelphia	7	28	9	3	—	47

Phil	—	Owens 41 pass from McNabb (Akers kick)
Phil	—	Westbrook 9 pass from McNabb (Akers kick)
Phil	—	Westbrook 41 pass from McNabb (Akers kick)
Phil	—	Smith 6 pass from McNabb (Akers kick)
Phil	—	Westbrook 12 pass from McNabb (Akers kick)
GB	—	FG Longwell 40
Phil	—	FG Akers 22
Phil	—	FG Akers 45
Phil	—	FG Akers 47
Phil	—	FG Akers 22
GB	—	Henderson 1 pass from Nall (Longwell kick)
GB	—	Walker 17 pass from Nall (Longwell kick)

ST. LOUIS 16, SAN FRANCISCO 6—at Edward Jones Dome, attendance 65,793. Chris Chandler passed for 216 yards and Steven Jackson posted his first career 100-yard rushing game. The Rams had outgained the 49ers (350-160) despite playing most of the game without Marc Bulger, who was injured in the first quarter. Early in the fourth quarter the 49ers trailed just 13-6 and had the ball at the Rams' 19 when Jerametrius Butler intercepted Tim Rattay's pass. Chandler engineered a 10-play, 60-yard drive, capped by Jeff Wilkins' 52-yard field goal with 6:44 to play. Bulger was 3 of 4 for 22 yards before being replaced by Chandler, who was 18 of 27 for 216 yards and 1 touchdown, with 1 interception. Holt had 10 receptions for 160 yards, and Jackson carried 26 times for 119 yards while filling in for injured Marshall Faulk. Rattay was 10 of 21 for 121 yards, with 1 interception.

San Francisco	3	0	3	0	—	6
St. Louis	3	10	0	3	—	16

StL	—	FG Wilkins 29
SF	—	FG Peterson 51
StL	—	Holt 22 pass from Chandler (Wilkins kick)
StL	—	FG Wilkins 52
SF	—	FG Peterson 40
StL	—	FG Wilkins 52

SAN DIEGO 20, DENVER 17—at Qualcomm Stadium, attendance 65,395. LaDainian Tomlinson rushed for 2 touchdowns and the defense intercepted 4 passes as the Chargers clinched their first winning season since 1995. The first interception, by Drayton Florence less than two minutes into the game, set up Tomlinson's first touchdown. Marco Coleman recovered Eric Parker's fumble late in the first quarter, and Tatum Bell scored five plays later to tie the game. Shaun Phillips' interception at the Broncos' 17 with 1:30 left in the half led to Nate Kaeding's 23-yard field goal for a 17-7 lead. A 45-yard pass from Jake Plummer to Rod Smith led to Reuben Droughns' touchdown early in the fourth quarter to cut the deficit to 20-14, and Jason Elam's field goal on the next possession made it 20-17 with 9:26 to play. The Broncos forced another three-and-out, and the offense drove to the Chargers' 7, but Plummer's fade pass for Smith into the end zone was tipped by Florence and intercepted by Jerry Wilson. With eight seconds left from the Chargers' 46 on fourth-and-10, Plummer's short pass to Darius Watts netted a first down but Watts could not get out of bounds and the time expired. Brees was 14 of 27 for 106 yards, with 1 interception. Tomlinson rushed

30 times for 113 yards. Plummer was 16 of 40 for 278 yards, with 4 interceptions. Ashley Lelie had 4 receptions for 105 yards.

Denver	0	7	0	10	—	17
San Diego	7	10	3	0	—	20

SD	—	Tomlinson 5 run (Kaeding kick)
Den	—	Bell 16 run (Elam kick)
SD	—	Tomlinson 1 run (Kaeding kick)
SD	—	FG Kaeding 23
SD	—	FG Kaeding 23
Den	—	Droughns 4 run (Elam kick)
Den	—	FG Elam 31

TAMPA BAY 27, ATLANTA 0—at Raymond James Stadium, attendance 65,556. The Buccaneers' defense forced 5 turnovers, which led to 20 points, and recorded 5 sacks to shutout the Falcons. Michael Pittman capped the Buccaneers' first drive with a touchdown. In the second quarter, from the Buccaneers' 1, Derrick Brooks tipped Michael Vick's pass and Dwight Smith intercepted for a touchback. Jay Taylor, in his first NFL game, kicked a 50-yard field goal, and added a 30-yard field goal following Greg Spires' fumble recovery. In the third quarter, Simeon Rice forced Vick to fumble. Rice recovered, and Brian Griese fired a 36-yard touchdown pass to Joey Galloway on the next play for a 20-0 lead. Brian Kelly's end-zone interception and 75-yard return in the fourth quarter led to Mike Alstott's 5-yard scoring run. Griese was 13 of 21 for 131 yards and 1 touchdown, with 1 interception. Brooks had 2 sacks, 2 passes defensed, and 1 forced fumble. Vick was 13 of 27 for 115 yards, with 2 interceptions.

Atlanta	0	0	0	0	—	0
Tampa Bay	7	6	7	7	—	27

TB	—	Pittman 4 run (Taylor kick)
TB	—	FG Taylor 50
TB	—	FG Taylor 30
TB	—	Galloway 36 pass from Griese (Taylor kick)
TB	—	Alstott 5 run (Taylor kick)

WASHINGTON 31, N.Y. GIANTS 7—at FedExField, attendance 87,872. Clinton Portis scored twice, the Redskins scored more than 20 points for the first time this season, and the defense allowed just 7 first downs to defeat the Giants. The Redskins owned advantages in yards (379-145) and time of possession (40:29-19:31). Of the Giants' 10 possessions, the Redskins only allowed first downs three times, and never allowed New York to reach the red zone. The Redskins scored touchdowns on three of their first four drives, including drives of 93 and 91 yards. Patrick Ramsey was 19 of 22 for 174 yards and 3 touchdowns. Portis rushed 31 times for 148 yards. Eli Manning was 12 of 25 for 113 yards.

N.Y. Giants	0	0	0	7	—	7
Washington	7	14	3	7	—	31

Wash	—	Portis 1 run (Hall kick)
Wash	—	Portis 4 pass from Ramsey (Hall kick)
Wash	—	Royal 9 pass from Ramsey (Hall kick)
Wash	—	FG Hall 46
NYG	—	Ward 92 kickoff return (Christie kick)
Wash	—	Cooley 6 pass from Ramsey (Hall kick)

SUNDAY NIGHT, DECEMBER 5
PITTSBURGH 17, JACKSONVILLE 16—at ALLTEL Stadium, attendance 76,877. Jeff Reed kicked a 37-yard field goal with 18 seconds remaining as the Steelers won their tenth consecutive game. Ben Roethlisberger guided the Steelers on touchdown drives of 77 and 72 yards on their first two possessions en route to a 14-7 lead. The Jaguars' defense stiffened and did not allow the Steelers to drive inside their 40 with their next six possessions. The Jaguars' offense drove inside the red zone four times. Josh Scobee missed a 32-yard field goal in the first half, but connected three times in the sec-

ond half, the last a 36-yard field goal with 1:55 remaining to cap a 12-play, 62-yard drive and give the Jaguars a 16-14 lead. Roethlisberger completed 3 passes, 2 to Lee Mays, to set up Reed's kick. Byron Leftwich completed a 19-yard pass to Jimmy Smith to the Steelers' 42 with four seconds left, and Scobee attempted a 60-yard field goal to win the game, but the kick fell wide right. Roethlisberger was 14 of 17 for 221 yards and 2 touchdowns. Leftwich was 16 of 27 for 268 yards and 1 touchdown.

Pittsburgh	7	7	0	3	—	17
Jacksonville	7	0	6	3	—	16

Pitt	—	Ward 37 pass from Roethlisberger (Reed kick)
Jax	—	Edwards 22 pass from Leftwich (Scobee kick)
Pitt	—	Riemersma 26 pass from Roethlisberger (Reed kick)
Jax	—	FG Scobee 20
Jax	—	FG Scobee 29
Jax	—	FG Scobee 36
Pitt	—	FG Reed 37

MONDAY NIGHT, DECEMBER 6

DALLAS 43, SEATTLE 39—at Qwest Field, attendance 68,093. Julius Jones scored on a 17-yard run with 32 seconds left as the Cowboys became the first team to overcome a 10-point deficit in the final two minutes in the 35-year history of NFL Monday Night Football. The Seahawks tallied 507 yards, but allowed 405, including 121 yards in the final 2:46. Trailing 14-3, the Cowboys scored 3 touchdowns and 2 field goals in a stretch of five consecutive possessions, two set up by fumbles, to take a 29-14 lead with 10:10 left in the third quarter. Seattle responded by scoring on its next four possessions, on drives of 77, 72, 72, and 41 yards, the last set up by Ken Hamlin's interception near midfield, to score 25 unanswered points and take a 39-29 lead with 2:46 to play. Vinny Testaverde completed 4 consecutive passes on the Cowboys' next drive, capped by his 34-yard touchdown pass to Keyshawn Johnson in the back of the end zone with 1:45 left. Jason Witten then recovered the onside kick, and the Cowboys reached the Seahawks' 33 and faced third-and-9 with 51 seconds left. Jones took a handoff and raced 16 yards for a first down, and needing a field goal to tie, two plays later Jones broke free up the middle for a 17-yard touchdown with 32 seconds left. Jerry Rice caught a 28-yard pass, but Matt Hasselbeck's Hail Mary pass was batted down in the end zone. With his 2 scoring runs, Shaun Alexander became the first player to post four consecutive seasons with at least 15 touchdowns. Testaverde was 18 of 34 for 225 yards and 2 touchdowns, with 2 interceptions. Johnson had 6 catches for 116 yards. Jones had 30 carries for 198 yards. Hasselbeck was 28 of 40 for 414 yards and 3 touchdowns. Darrell Jackson had 9 catches for 113 yards, and Rice had 8 for 145 yards.

Dallas	3	16	10	14	—	43
Seattle	14	0	3	22	—	39

Sea	—	Rice 27 pass from Hasselbeck (J. Brown kick)
Dall	—	FG Cundiff 39
Sea	—	Jackson 2 pass from Hasselbeck (J. Brown kick)
Dall	—	FG Cundiff 49
Dall	—	Copper 9 pass from Testaverde (run failed)
Dall	—	J. Jones 8 run (Cundiff kick)
Dall	—	J. Jones 10 run (Cundiff kick)
Dall	—	FG Cundiff 47
Dall	—	FG J. Brown 21
Sea	—	Alexander 1 run (J. Brown kick)
Sea	—	Urban 19 pass from Hasselbeck (Jackson pass from Hasselbeck)
Sea	—	Alexander 32 run (J. Brown kick)
Sea	—	K. Johnson 34 pass from Testaverde (Cundiff kick)
Dall	—	J. Jones 17 run (Cundiff kick)

FOURTEENTH WEEK SUMMARIES
American Football Conference

East Division	W	L	T	Pct.	Pts.	OP
New England*	12	1	0	.923	365	217
N.Y. Jets	9	4	0	.692	260	192
Buffalo	7	6	0	.538	297	231
Miami	2	11	0	.154	213	289
North Division	**W**	**L**	**T**	**Pct.**	**Pts.**	**OP**
Pittsburgh*	12	1	0	.923	290	190
Baltimore	8	5	0	.615	270	205
Cincinnati	6	7	0	.462	296	307
Cleveland	3	10	0	.231	247	345
South Division	**W**	**L**	**T**	**Pct.**	**Pts.**	**OP**
Indianapolis*	10	3	0	.769	454	277
Jacksonville	7	6	0	.538	220	228
Houston	5	8	0	.385	250	312
Tennessee	4	9	0	.308	269	343
West Division	**W**	**L**	**T**	**Pct.**	**Pts.**	**OP**
San Diego	10	3	0	.769	370	262
Denver	8	5	0	.615	294	229
Kansas City	5	8	0	.385	390	364
Oakland	4	9	0	.308	244	363

National Football Conference

East Division	W	L	T	Pct.	Pts.	OP
Philadelphia*	12	1	0	.923	357	195
N.Y. Giants	5	8	0	.385	223	267
Dallas	5	8	0	.385	249	355
Washington	4	9	0	.308	183	218
North Division	**W**	**L**	**T**	**Pct.**	**Pts.**	**OP**
Green Bay	8	5	0	.615	334	307
Minnesota	7	6	0	.538	328	313
Chicago	5	8	0	.385	199	257
Detroit	5	8	0	.385	231	285
South Division	**W**	**L**	**T**	**Pct.**	**Pts.**	**OP**
Atlanta*	10	3	0	.769	267	252
Carolina	6	7	0	.462	269	264
New Orleans	5	8	0	.385	280	357
Tampa Bay	5	8	0	.385	257	234
West Division	**W**	**L**	**T**	**Pct.**	**Pts.**	**OP**
Seattle	7	6	0	.538	305	289
St. Louis	6	7	0	.462	260	325
Arizona	4	9	0	.308	220	284
San Francisco	2	11	0	.154	229	364

*Clinched division title

SUNDAY, DECEMBER 12

SAN FRANCISCO 31, ARIZONA 28 (OT)—at Sun Devil Stadium, attendance 35,069. Todd Peterson kicked a 31-yard field goal in overtime as the 49ers overcame blowing a 25-point lead to sweep the season series from the Cardinals. Ken Dorsey passed for 3 touchdowns, and his second to Cedrick Wilson with 9:57 left in the third quarter gave the 49ers a 28-3 lead. Following an exchange of punts, the Cardinals put together drives of 87 and 53 yards, both capped by touchdown runs by Obafemi Ayanbadejo, to pull within 28-17 with 11:53 left in the game. The Cardinals started at their own 44 with 4:18 left and Josh McCown completed 4 of 5 passes to reach the 49ers' 8. Emmitt Smith broke three tackles to score on the next play, followed by McCown's 2-point conversion run, to cut the deficit to 28-25 with 2:40 remaining. David Macklin recovered a fumble three plays later at the 49ers' 20, and the Cardinals had a chance to take the lead, but McCown's third-and-goal pass to Freddie Jones in the end zone was knocked down by Joselio Hanson. On the next play, Neil Rackers kicked a 24-yard field goal with 59 seconds left to tie the game. The 49ers won the overtime toss, and both teams punted before the 49ers started at the Cardinals' 49. Dorsey completed a 19-yard pass to Wilson on third-and-17, and Maurice Hicks ran 17 yards to set up Peterson's winning kick. Dorsey was 18 of 34 for 191 yards and 3 touchdowns. Hicks rushed 34 times for 139 yards. McCown was 26 of 44 for 307 yards, with 1 interception. Anquan Boldin had 9 receptions for 109 yards.

San Francisco	7	14	7	0	3	—	31
Arizona	0	3	7	18	0	—	28

SF	—	Lloyd 5 pass from Dorsey (Peterson kick)
SF	—	Wilson 19 pas from Dorsey (Peterson kick)
SF	—	Hicks 1 run (Peterson kick)
Ariz	—	FG Rackers 44
SF	—	Wilson 27 pass from Dorsey (Peterson kick)
Ariz	—	Ayanbadejo 4 run (Rackers kick)
Ariz	—	Ayanbadejo 1 run (Rackers kick)
Ariz	—	Smith 8 run (Rackers kick)
Ariz	—	FG Rackers 22
SF	—	FG Peterson 31

ATLANTA 35, OAKLAND 10—at Georgia Dome, attendance 70,616. T.J. Duckett rushed for 4 touchdowns as the Falcons clinched the third division title in franchise history. The Falcons' defense forced 3 turnovers, which the offense turned into 14 points. Brady Smith recovered J.R. Redmond's fumble in the second quarter, and Duckett scored his second touchdown with 2:11 left in the half. With 1:25 remaining in the half, Rod Coleman intercepted Kerry Collins' pass and returned it 39 yards for a touchdown and 21-3 lead. Duckett's third touchdown capped a 9:29 drive to begin the second half, and on their next possession drove 7:40 capped by Duckett's fourth touchdown with 9:00 to play. The Falcons controlled the time of possession (36:33-23:27). Vick was 13 of 28 for 166 yards, with 1 interception. Collins was 14 of 28 for 166 yards, with 1 interception.

Oakland	3	0	0	7	—	10
Atlanta	0	21	7	7	—	35

Oak	—	FG Janikowski 52
Atl	—	Duckett 28 run (Feely kick)
Atl	—	Duckett 2 run (Feely kick)
Atl	—	Coleman 39 interception return (Feely kick)
Atl	—	Duckett 4 run (Feely kick)
Atl	—	Duckett 4 run (Feely kick)
Oak	—	Crockett 1 run (Janikowski kick)

BALTIMORE 37, N.Y. GIANTS 14—at M&T Bank Stadium, attendance 69,856. Kyle Boller passed for 4 touchdowns and the Ravens' defense forced 6 turnovers and yielded just 196 yards to hand the Giants their sixth consecutive loss. The Ravens led 17-0 when Osi Umenyiora picked up Kyle Boller's fumble and ran 50 yards for a touchdown with 2:43 left in the half. The Ravens responded with a 73-yard drive, capped by Boller's 8-yard touchdown pass to Clarence Moore with 21 seconds left. Ed Reed intercepted Eli Manning's pass on the next play, lateralled to Deion Sanders who returned it 16 yards to set up Matt Stover's 44-yard field goal as the half expired. Kelly Gregg recovered Manning's third-quarter fumble to set up Todd Heap's second scoring catch for a 37-7 lead with 1:42 left in the third quarter. Boller was 18 of 34 for 219 yards and 4 touchdowns. Chester Taylor rushed 25 times for 104 yards. Manning was 4 of 18 for 27 yards, with 2 interceptions, before being replaced in the fourth quarter by Kurt Warner, who was 6 of 9 for 127 yards.

N.Y. Giants	0	7	0	7	—	14
Baltimore	10	17	10	0	—	37

Balt	—	Moore 12 pass from Boller (Stover kick)
Balt	—	FG Stover 46
Balt	—	Heap 6 pass from Boller (Stover kick)
NYG	—	Umenyiora 50 fumble return (Christie kick)
Balt	—	Moore 8 pass from Boller (Stover kick)
Balt	—	FG Stover 44
Balt	—	FG Stover 27
Balt	—	Heap 1 pass from Boller (Stover kick)
NYG	—	Barber 1 run (Christie kick)

BUFFALO 37, CLEVELAND 7—at Ralph Wilson Stadium, attendance 72,330. The Bills' defense allowed just 17 total yards, forced 5 turnovers, and recorded 8 sacks to win their fourth consecutive game. In the second quarter, Clements recovered William Green's fumble to set up Bledsoe's 7-yard scoring pass to Lee Evans. Following a three-and-out, the Bills drove 10 plays, 52 yards capped by Willis McGahee's 13-yard touchdown run for a 17-7 lead. Jeff Garcia came in at the end of the third quarter, and fumbled three plays later to set up McGahee's second touchdown for a 27-7 lead with 14:49 to play. The Bills had more yards (321-17) and first downs (22-6). Bledsoe was 12 of 27 for 100 yards and 1 touchdown, with 1 interception. McGahee rushed for 105 yards. McCown was 8 of 20 for 62 yards and 1 touchdown, with 2 interceptions.

	1	2	3	4		T
Cleveland	7	0	0	0	—	7
Buffalo	3	14	3	17	—	37

Buff	—	FG Lindell 23
Cle	—	Northcutt 3 pass from McCown (Dawson kick)
Buff	—	Evans 7 pass from Bledsoe (Lindell kick)
Buff	—	McGahee 13 run (Lindell kick)
Buff	—	FG Lindell 21
Buff	—	McGahee 6 run (Lindell kick)
Buff	—	FG Lindell 37
Buff	—	S. Williams 4 run (Lindell kick)

CAROLINA 20, ST. LOUIS 7—at Bank of America Stadium, attendance 73,306. The Panthers' defense forced 7 turnovers, including 6 interceptions, as Carolina won its fifth consecutive game and the Rams fell out of first place in the NFC West. The Panthers took an early 14-0 lead. The Rams responded with Chris Chandler's 75-yard scoring pass to Torry Holt. John Kasay added 2 field goals, including a 20-yard kick with 39 seconds left in the half that was set up by Will Witherspoon's interception, for a 20-7 lead. The Rams failed to score a play inside the Panthers' red zone the entire game. Delhomme was 16 of 30 for 206 yards and 1 touchdown, with 1 interception. Nick Goings rushed 31 times for 108 yards. Dan Morgan had 2 interceptions, 2 passes defensed, and 1 forced fumble. Chandler was 14 of 29 for 243 yards and 1 touchdown, with 6 interceptions.

	1	2	3	4		T
St. Louis	7	0	0	0	—	7
Carolina	14	6	0	0	—	20

Car	—	Muhammad 14 pass from Delhomme (Kasay kick)
Car	—	Goings 1 run (Kasay kick)
StL	—	Holt 75 pass from Chandler (Wilkins kick)
Car	—	FG Kasay 27
Car	—	FG Kasay 20

NEW ORLEANS 27, DALLAS 13—at Texas Stadium, attendance 64,056. Deuce McAllister rushed for 2 touchdowns as the Saints rallied to defeat the Cowboys. The Cowboys led 10-0 in the second quarter when Mike McKenzie intercepted Vinny Testaverde's pass at the Cowboys' 26 to set up McAllister's first touchdown. The score was tied 13-13 in the fourth quarter when the Saints drove to the Cowboys' 20. On third-and-10, Aaron Brooks threw a 14-yard pass to Joe Horn and McAllister scored his second touchdown two plays later with 5:21 left. The Saints forced a punt, and Michael Lewis returned it 43 yards. Two plays later, on third-and-6, Brooks lofted a 31-yard touchdown pass to Horn with 2:47 left. Brooks was 18 of 31 for 252 yards and 1 touchdown, with 2 interceptions. Donte' Stallworth had 5 receptions for 113 yards. Testaverde was 14 of 35 for 160 yards, with 1 interception.

	1	2	3	4		T
New Orleans	0	10	3	14	—	27
Dallas	10	0	3	0	—	13

Dall	—	FG Cundiff 34
Dall	—	J. Jones 1 run (Cundiff kick)
NO	—	McAllister 5 run (Carney kick)
Dall	—	FG Carney 39
Dall	—	FG Cundiff 41
NO	—	FG Carney 44
NO	—	McAllister 4 run (Carney kick)
NO	—	Horn 31 pass from Brooks (Carney kick)

DENVER 20, MIAMI 17—at INVESCO Field at Mile High, attendance 75,027. Tatum Bell rushed for 123 yards and 2 touchdowns as the Broncos held off the Dolphins. The Broncos gained nearly twice as many yards (415-214), but the Dolphins' defense forced 3 turnovers, 2 in the red zone, to keep the game close. Jake Plummer's 32-yard pass to Ashley Lelie set up Bell's 11-yard touchdown run just before halftime to tie the game. Al Wilson intercepted A.J. Feeley's pass on the first play of the second half to set up Jason Elam's 20-yard field goal. The Dolphins tied the game late in the third quarter, and Sammy Knight's interception at the Dolphins' 3 in the middle of the fourth quarter maintained the 17-17 tie. The Broncos forced a three-and-out, and starting at their own 45, a 21-yard run by Reuben Droughns led to Elam's 50-yard field goal with 2:50 to play. The Dolphins failed to gain a first down with their final possessions. Plummer was 16 of 30 for 219 yards, with 2 interceptions. Feeley was 17 of 35 for 170 yards and 1 touchdown, with 1 interception.

	1	2	3	4		T
Miami	7	7	3	0	—	17
Denver	0	14	3	3	—	20

Mia	—	Booker 8 pass from Feeley (Mare kick)
Den	—	Bell 7 run (Elam kick)
Mia	—	Morris 11 run (Mare kick)
Den	—	Bell 11 run (Elam kick)
Den	—	FG Elam 20
Mia	—	FG Mare 32
Den	—	FG Elam 50

GREEN BAY 16, DETROIT 13—at Lambeau Field, attendance 70,497. Ryan Longwell kicked 3 field goals, including the game-winner with two seconds remaining, as the Packers rallied from a 13-0 half-time deficit to maintain first place in the NFC North. The Packers, who did not cross the Lions' 48 in the first half and trailed 13-0, drove 63 yards for a field goal to begin the second half. The Lions then punted, and the Packers drove 90 yards in 10 plays, capped by Donald Driver's 23-yard scoring catch. Favre's 39-yard pass to Driver set up Longwell's tying field goal with 10:46 to play. Following the Lions' fifth punt, in five possessions, the Packers took over at the Lions' 42 with 3:27 to play. Brett Favre completed a 10-yard pass to Javon Walker on third-and-8, and Ahman Green ran for a first down to help run the clock down. Longwell's 23-yard field goal with two seconds left won the game. Favre was 19 of 36 for 188 yards and 1 touchdown. Joey Harrington was 5 of 22 for 47 yards.

	1	2	3	4		T
Detroit	3	10	0	0	—	13
Green Bay	0	0	10	6	—	16

Det	—	FG Hanson 31
Det	—	K. Jones 24 run (Hanson kick)
Det	—	FG Hanson 36
GB	—	FG Longwell 36
GB	—	Driver 23 pass from Favre (Longwell kick)
GB	—	FG Longwell 28
GB	—	FG Longwell 23

INDIANAPOLIS 23, HOUSTON 14—at Reliant Stadium, attendance 70,762. Peyton Manning passed for 298 yards and 2 touchdowns as the Colts won the AFC South. The Colts' defense forced 2 turnovers and recorded 5 sacks, including 3 by Dwight Freeney. The Colts scored touchdowns on their first two possessions, giving Manning 46 touchdown passes. Domanick Davis scored on a 15-yard run in the third quarter to pull within 17-14. After an exchange of punts, Manning engineered a 10-play, 64-yard drive, capped by Mike Vanderjagt's 43-yard field goal with 7:38 to play. The Colts' defense forced a three-and-out, and the Colts held the ball for 11 plays, with Vanderjagt's 44-yard field goal with 1:56 left giving the Colts a 23-14 lead. Manning was 26 of 33 for 298 yards and 2 touchdowns. Edgerrin James rushed 28 times for 104 yards. David Carr was 16 of 21 for 167 yards and 1 touchdown, with

1 interception. Davis rushed 23 times for 128 yards.

	1	2	3	4		T
Indianapolis	14	0	3	6	—	23
Houston	0	7	7	0	—	14

Ind	—	Harrison 3 pass from Manning (Vanderjagt kick)
Ind	—	Wayne 13 pass from Manning (Vanderjagt kick)
Hous	—	Wells 3 pass from Carr (K. Brown kick)
Ind	—	FG Vanderjagt 30
Hous	—	D. Davis 15 run (K. Brown kick)
Ind	—	FG Vanderjagt 43
Ind	—	FG Vanderjagt 44

JACKSONVILLE 22, CHICAGO 3—at ALLTEL Stadium, attendance 67,572. Byron Leftwich passed for 2 touchdowns and the Jaguars' defense allowed just 210 yards to stay in the playoff hunt. The Jaguars led 13-3 in the third quarter when Daryl Smith sacked Chad Hutchinson for a safety. The Jaguars drove 61 yards with the ensuing free kick, capped by Leftwich's 31-yard touchdown pass to Jimmy Smith, for a 22-3 lead with 9:26 to play. The Bears were stopped by an interception, fumble, and on downs with their final three possessions. Leftwich was 25 of 45 for 242 yards and 2 touchdowns, with 1 interception. Hutchinson was 17 of 33 for 212 yards, with 1 interception.

	1	2	3	4		T
Chicago	0	3	0	0	—	3
Jacksonville	7	3	3	9	—	22

Jax	—	R. Williams 6 pass from Leftwich (Scobee kick)
Chi	—	FG Edinger 42
Jax	—	FG Scobee 30
Jax	—	FG Scobee 25
Jax	—	Safety, D. Smith sacked Hutchinson in end zone
Jax	—	J. Smith 31 pass from Leftwich (Scobee kick)

SEATTLE 27, MINNESOTA 23—at Metrodome, attendance 64,110. Matt Hasselbeck passed for 334 yards and 3 touchdowns as the Seahawks held on to defeat the Vikings. The Seahawks led 24-23 in the fourth quarter when Rashad Moore recovered Culpepper's fumbled snap at the Vikings' 26. Six plays later Josh Brown booted a 28-yard field goal for a 27-23 lead with 3:40 to play. The Vikings drove to the Seahawks' 20, and Randy Moss took a handoff on a reverse. Running to his right, he attempted a pass for Marcus Robinson, thrown into double coverage in the end zone, which was intercepted by Michael Boulware for a touchback with 2:09 remaining. The Vikings drove to the Seahawks' 23 with four seconds left. Daunte Culpepper rolled right and appeared to be sacked by Antonio Cochran. Culpepper's knee never hit the ground and he popped up and fired a pass into the end zone. Thinking the game was over, Jermaine Wiggins did not attempt to catch the pass, and the ball bounced harmlessly off his hands to end the game. Hasselbeck was 23 of 34 for 334 yards and 3 touchdowns, with 2 interceptions. Darrell Jackson had 10 catches for 135 yards. Shaun Alexander rushed 27 times for 112 yards. Culpepper was 21 of 33 for 270 yards and 1 touchdown. Moss had 4 receptions for 104 yards.

	1	2	3	4		T
Seattle	7	14	3	3	—	27
Minnesota	10	10	3	0	—	23

Minn	—	FG Andersen 48
Minn	—	O. Smith 5 run (Andersen kick)
Sea	—	Engram 35 pass from Hasselbeck (J. Brown kick)
Sea	—	Alexander 12 pass from Hasselbeck (J. Brown kick)
Minn	—	FG Andersen 32
Minn	—	Moss 3 pass from Culpepper (Andersen kick)
Sea	—	D. Jackson 19 pass from Hasselbeck (J. Brown kick)
Minn	—	FG Andersen 31
Sea	—	FG J. Brown 33
Sea	—	FG J. Brown 28

NEW ENGLAND 35, CINCINNATI 28—at Gillette Stadium, attendance 68,756. Tom Brady passed for 2 touchdowns and the defense forced 3 turnovers as the Patriots won their sixth consecutive game. The Patriots scored on three of their four first-half possessions, on drives of 84, 70, and 53 yards, and buoyed by Asante Samuel's 34-yard interception return for a touchdown, to take a 28-14 halftime lead. The Patriots then drove 11 plays, 75 yards with the opening kickoff of the second half, capped by Christian Fauria's 17-yard touchdown catch for a 35-14 lead with 9:14 left in the third quarter. The Bengals drove to the Patriots' 11, and on fourth-and-5 the Bengals lined up for a field goal. Holder Kyle Larson took the snap and ran through a hole on the left side for an 11-yard touchdown. The Bengals forced a punt, and, with Jon Kitna having replaced an injured Carson Palmer, drove to the Patriots' 10. On third-and-goal, Troy Brown intercepted Kitna's pass in the end zone. The Bengals rallied later in the quarter, with Kitna completing all 4 pass attempts on a 61-yard drive capped by Kelley Washington's 27-yard touchdown catch to pull within 35-28 with 3:50 to play. The Patriots gained 3 first downs on their final possession, highlighted by Brady's 20-yard pass to Brown with 1:58 to play, to run out the clock. Brady was 18 of 26 for 260 yards and 2 touchdowns. Palmer had 5 receptions for 107 yards. Palmer was 18 of 24 for 202 yards and 2 touchdowns, with 1 interception. Kitna was 9 of 13 for 126 yards and 1 touchdown, with 1 interception. T.J. Houshmandzadeh had 12 receptions for 145 yards.

Cincinnati	0	14	7	7	—	28
New England	7	21	7	0	—	35

NE	—	Dillon 1 run (Vinatieri kick)
Cin	—	Schobel 2 pass from Palmer (Graham kick)
NE	—	Patten 48 pass from Brady (Vinatieri kick)
NE	—	Samuel 34 interception return (Vinatieri kick)
Cin	—	C. Johnson 5 pass from Palmer (Graham kick)
NE	—	Faulk 4 run (Vinatieri kick)
NE	—	Fauria 17 pass from Brady (Vinatieri kick)
Cin	—	Larson 11 run (Graham kick)
Cin	—	Washington 27 pass from Kitna (Graham kick)

PITTSBURGH 17, N.Y. JETS 6—at Heinz Field, attendance 63,581. Jerome Bettis rushed for a touchdown and passed for another score as the Steelers converted 5 of 7 third-down situations in the second half to break a tie and clinch the AFC North title. Troy Polamalu's interception and 22-yard return set up Jeff Reed's first-quarter field goal. James Farrior's interception at the Steelers' 26 just before halftime allowed Pittsburgh to maintain a 3-0 halftime lead. Tied 3-3 early in the fourth quarter, and on third-and-3 from the Jets' 10, Bettis rolled right and lofted a 10-yard touchdown pass to Jerame Tuman. The Jets responded with a 14-play drive for a field goal, but on the next drive Ben Roethlisberger completed a 46-yard pass to Lee Mays on third-and-4, and Bettis rumbled 12 yards for a touchdown on third-and-5 with 3:00 left to end the scoring. Roethlisberger was 8 of 19 for 144 yards, with 2 interceptions. Chad Pennington was 17 of 31 for 189 yards, with 3 interceptions. Curtis Martin and Bettis, both surpassed the 13,000-yard barrier during the game, becoming just the fifth and sixth players, respectively, to reach the mark.

N.Y. Jets	0	0	3	3	—	6
Pittsburgh	3	0	0	14	—	17

Pitt	—	FG Reed 34
NYJ	—	FG Brien 43
Pitt	—	Tuman 10 pass from Bettis (Reed kick)
NYJ	—	FG Brien 41
Pitt	—	Bettis 12 run (Reed kick)

SAN DIEGO 31, TAMPA BAY 24—at Qualcomm Stadium, attendance 65,585. Donnie Edwards intercepted 2 passes, including a 30-yard return for a touchdown with 4:09 remaining to break a tie and lift the Chargers to their seventh consecutive victory. The Chargers led 21-14 in the fourth quarter when Dwight Smith forced LaDainian Tomlinson to fumble. Dewayne White recovered at the Chargers' 37, and three plays later Brian Griese completed a 20-yard touchdown pass to Michael Clayton to tie the game with 6:53 left. The Buccaneers then forced a three-and-out, but three plays later Edwards intercepted Griese's short pass and returned it 30 yards for a 28-21 lead. Three plays later, Steve Foley forced Griese to fumble, and Shaun Phillips recovered to set up Nate Kaeding's 40-yard field goal with 2:06 left. Jay Taylor's 41-yard field goal with 16 seconds left cut the deficit to seven points. Edwards recovered the ensuing onside kick to clinch the victory. Drew Brees was 17 of 23 for 220 yards, with 2 touchdowns, with 2 interceptions. Eric Parker had 6 receptions for 118 yards, and Tomlinson rushed 25 times for 131 yards. Griese was 36 of 50 for 392 yards and 3 touchdowns, with 3 interceptions. Clayton had 9 receptions for 145 yards.

Tampa Bay	0	7	7	10	—	24
San Diego	0	14	7	10	—	31

SD	—	Parker 79 pass from Brees (Kaeding kick)
TB	—	Galloway 36 pass from Griese (Taylor kick)
SD	—	Osgood 19 pass from Brees (Kaeding kick)
TB	—	Galloway 4 pass from Griese (Taylor kick)
SD	—	Tomlinson 7 run (Kaeding kick)
TB	—	Clayton 20 pass from Griese (Taylor kick)
SD	—	Edwards 30 interception return (Kaeding kick)
SD	—	FG Kaeding 40
TB	—	FG Taylor 41

SUNDAY NIGHT, DECEMBER 12

PHILADELPHIA 17, WASHINGTON 14—at FedExField, attendance 90,089. Donovan McNabb passed for 260 yards and 1 touchdown as the Eagles held off the Redskins. Ladell Betts returned the opening kickoff 70 yards to set up Clinton Portis' 5-yard touchdown run just 46 seconds into the game. The Eagles responded with a 66-yard scoring drive to tie the game. Terrell Owens fumbled at the Redskins' 4-yard line early in the second quarter and Washington recovered to thwart a drive. David Akers kicked a 38-yard field goal to begin the second half, and a 20-yard run by Brian Westbrook later in the quarter led to Dorsey Levens' 1-yard run for a 17-7 lead. Shawn Springs' interception near midfield set up Portis' second touchdown run to pull the Redskins within 17-14 with 12:04 to play. The Redskins drove to the Eagles' 27 with 1:54 left, but Patrick Ramsey's pass intended for Chris Cooley was intercepted by Brian Dawkins in the end zone. McNabb was 21 of 38 for 260 yards and 1 touchdown, with 1 interception. Ramsey was 29 of 45 for 251 yards, with 1 interception. Laveranues Coles had 12 receptions for 100 yards.

Philadelphia	7	0	10	0	—	17
Washington	7	0	0	7	—	14

Wash	—	Portis 5 run (Hall kick)
Phil	—	Smith 2 pass from McNabb (Akers kick)
Phil	—	FG Akers 38
Phil	—	Levens 1 run (Akers kick)
Wash	—	Portis 2 run (Hall kick)

MONDAY NIGHT, DECEMBER 13

KANSAS CITY 49, TENNESSEE 38—at The Coliseum, attendance 68,932. Eddie Kennison caught 2 touchdown passes, including the go-ahead score with 32 seconds left, as the Chiefs rallied to keep their playoff hopes alive. The Titans outgained the

Chiefs (542-383) and led in time of possession (37:59-22:01), but the Chiefs' defense recorded 5 sacks and forced 4 turnovers. The Titans led 21-14 at halftime, and scored on their first possession of the second half. However, that touchdown was sandwiched around two touchdown drives by the Chiefs to tie the score 28-28 midway through the third quarter. Larry Johnson's 41-yard touchdown run capped an 81-yard drive to give the Chiefs their first lead, 35-28, with 4:49 remaining. Billy Volek completed a 31-yard pass to Antowain Smith on the ensuing drive to set up Derrick Mason's 4-yard touchdown catch with 2:26 to play. Two plays later, Trent Green fumbled and Randy Starks recovered at the Chiefs' 17. Randy Holcombe was stopped for no gain on third-and-2, and the Titans settled for Gary Anderson's 27-yard field goal with 1:39 to play. Dante Hall's 33-yard kickoff return sparked a 64-yard drive, capped by Green's 9-yard touchdown pass to Kennison with 32 seconds left. Two plays later, the Titans tried the hook-and-ladder play, but Shad Meier's pitch was an errant toss. Kawika Mitchell picked up the ball and ran 39 yards for a touchdown with eight seconds left. Green was 18 of 32 for 244 yards and 3 touchdowns, with 1 interception. Johnson had 7 carries for 104 yards. Volek was 29 of 43 for 426 yards and 4 touchdowns. Drew Bennett had 12 catches for 233 yards.

Kansas City	0	14	14	21	—	49
Tennessee	7	14	7	10	—	38

Tenn	—	C. Brown 1 run (Anderson kick)
Tenn	—	Bennett 42 pass from Volek (Anderson kick)
KC	—	Kennison 58 pass from Green (Tynes kick)
KC	—	Morton 30 pass from Green (Tynes kick)
Tenn	—	Bennett 22 pass from Volek (Anderson kick)
KC	—	Blaylock 1 run (Tynes kick)
Tenn	—	Bennett 7 pass from Volek (Anderson kick)
KC	—	Johnson 46 run (Tynes kick)
KC	—	Johnson 41 run (Tynes kick)
Tenn	—	Mason 4 pass from Volek (Anderson kick)
Tenn	—	FG Anderson 27
KC	—	Kennison 9 pass from Green (Tynes kick)
KC	—	Mitchell 39 fumble return (Tynes kick)

FIFTEENTH WEEK SUMMARIES
American Football Conference

East Division	W	L	T	Pct.	Pts.	OP
New England*	12	2	0	.857	393	246
N.Y. Jets	10	4	0	.714	297	206
Buffalo	8	6	0	.571	330	248
Miami	3	11	0	.214	242	317
North Division	**W**	**L**	**T**	**Pct.**	**Pts.**	**OP**
Pittsburgh*	13	1	0	.929	323	220
Baltimore	8	6	0	.571	280	225
Cincinnati	6	8	0	.429	313	340
Cleveland	3	11	0	.214	247	366
South Division	**W**	**L**	**T**	**Pct.**	**Pts.**	**OP**
Indianapolis*	11	3	0	.786	474	287
Jacksonville	8	6	0	.571	248	253
Houston	6	8	0	.429	274	317
Tennessee	4	10	0	.286	304	383
West Division	**W**	**L**	**T**	**Pct.**	**Pts.**	**OP**
San Diego*	11	3	0	.786	391	262
Denver	8	6	0	.571	311	274
Kansas City	6	8	0	.429	435	381
Oakland	5	9	0	.357	284	398

National Football Conference

East Division	W	L	T	Pct.	Pts.	OP
Philadelphia*	13	1	0	.929	369	202
Dallas	5	9	0	.357	256	367
N.Y. Giants	5	9	0	.357	253	300
Washington	5	9	0	.357	209	234
North Division	**W**	**L**	**T**	**Pct.**	**Pts.**	**OP**
Green Bay#	8	6	0	.571	359	335

	W	L	T	Pct.	Pts.	OP
Minnesota	8	6	0	.571	356	340
Chicago	5	9	0	.357	204	281
Detroit	5	9	0	.357	258	313
South Division	**W**	**L**	**T**	**Pct.**	**Pts.**	**OP**
Atlanta*	11	3	0	.786	301	283
Carolina	6	8	0	.429	300	298
New Orleans	6	8	0	.429	301	374
Tampa Bay	5	9	0	.357	274	255
West Division	**W**	**L**	**T**	**Pct.**	**Pts.**	**OP**
Seattle	7	7	0	.500	319	326
St. Louis	6	8	0	.429	267	356
Arizona	5	9	0	.357	251	291
San Francisco	2	12	0	.143	245	390

*Clinched division title
#Clinched playoff berth

SATURDAY, DECEMBER 18

PITTSBURGH 33, N.Y. GIANTS 30—at Giants Stadium, attendance 78,836. Jerome Bettis rushed for 140 yards and 1 touchdown, and Ben Roethlisberger passed for 316 yards and a score, as the Steelers won their twelfth consecutive game. Willie Ponder returned the opening kickoff 91 yards for a touchdown, becoming the first-ever Giants' player to return the opening kickoff for a touchdown in a home game. The Steelers scored on four consecutive first-half possessions, keyed by a shovel pass for a touchdown from Antwaan Randle El to Vernon Haynes, and capped by Jeff Reed's 21-yard field goal just before halftime for a 20-14 lead. Brent Alexander intercepted a pass three plays into the second half to set up Steve Christie's 22-yard field goal. The Steelers responded with a field goal, but Eli Manning answered with a 49-yard pass to David Tyree to set up his 1-yard touchdown pass to Marcellus Rivers for a 24-23 lead. The Steelers settled for a fourth field goal, but Ponder returned the ensuing kickoff 31 yards and Tiki Barber scored seven plays later on a 30-26 Giants lead with 8:15 to play. Roethlisberger completed 4 consecutive passes, highlighted by a 36-yard pass to Randle El, to set up Bettis' 1-yard run with 4:57 to play. Three plays later, Willie Williams intercepted Manning's pass, and the Steelers gained two first downs to run out the clock. Roethlisberger was 18 of 28 for 316 yards and 1 touchdown, with 2 interceptions. Ward had 9 receptions for 134 yards, and Randle El added 5 catches for 149 yards. Bettis rushed 36 times for 140 yards. Manning was 16 of 23 for 182 yards and 2 touchdowns, with 1 interception.

Pittsburgh	10	10	3	10	—	33
N.Y. Giants	14	0	10	6	—	30

NYG	—	Ponder 91 kickoff return (Christie kick)
Pitt	—	Haynes 10 pass from Randle El (Reed kick)
NYG	—	Shockey 2 pass from Manning (Christie kick)
Pitt	—	FG Reed 33
Pitt	—	Randle El 35 pass from Roethlisberger (Reed kick)
Pitt	—	FG Reed 21
NYG	—	FG Christie 22
Pitt	—	FG Reed 36
NYG	—	Rivers 1 pass from Manning (Christie kick)
Pitt	—	FG Reed 28
NYG	—	Barber 1 run (pass failed)
Pitt	—	Bettis 1 run (Reed kick)

WASHINGTON 26, SAN FRANCISCO 16—at Monster Park, attendance 65,710. Clinton Portis rushed for 110 yards as the Redskins remained in the playoff chase. Keith Lewis blocked Tom Tupa's punt out of the end zone for a safety to cut the deficit to 16-9, and the 49ers took the free kick and drove to the Redskins' 23. On third-and-8, Antonio Pierce intercepted Ken Dorsey's pass and returned it 78 yards for a touchdown and 23-9 lead with 48 seconds left in the half. Dorsey's 11-yard touchdown pass to Curtis Conway pulled the 49ers to 26-16 with 4:26 to play. The 49ers then forced a punt with 3:09 left,

but four plays later Walt Harris intercepted Dorsey's pass with 2:34 remaining to clinch the victory. Patrick Ramsey was 18 of 27 for 214 yards and 1 touchdown. Rod Gardner had 6 receptions for 111 yards, and Portis rushed 35 times for 110 yards. Dorsey was 20 of 38 for 206 yards and 2 touchdowns, with 4 interceptions.

Washington	7	16	3	0	—	26
San Francisco	7	2	0	7	—	16

Wash	—	Royal 12 pass from Ramsey (Chandler kick)
SF	—	Lloyd 17 pass from Dorsey (Peterson kick)
Wash	—	FG Chandler 49
Wash	—	FG Chandler 25
Wash	—	FG Chandler 20
SF	—	Safety, Tupa's punt blocked out of end zone
Wash	—	Pierce 78 interception return (Chandler kick)
Wash	—	FG Chandler 26
SF	—	Conway 11 pass from Dorsey (Peterson kick)

SATURDAY NIGHT, DECEMBER 18

ATLANTA 34, CAROLINA 31 (OT)—at Georgia Dome, attendance 70,845. Michael Vick passed for 2 touchdowns and rushed for another as the Falcons rallied, capped by Jay Feely's 38-yard field goal in overtime, to snap the Panthers' five-game winning streak. Both defenses forced 4 turnovers and recorded 4 sacks. John Kasay kicked a 21-yard field goal with 21 seconds left in the half to tie the game. The Falcons drove 71 and 49 yards with their first two possessions of the second half to score two touchdowns and take a 24-10 lead. Carolina changed the momentum when Chris Gamble intercepted Vick's long pass at the Panthers' 3. Nine plays later Delhomme completed an 11-yard touchdown pass to Ken Mangum. The Panthers forced a punt, but Jamall Broussard muffed the punt and Kevin McCadam recovered the ball. The Falcons again had a chance to pull away, but Brentson Buckner sacked Vick and forced him to fumble. Julius Peppers recovered the ball and returned it 60 yards for a touchdown to tie the game with 10:09 remaining. Six plays later, Dan Morgan recovered Alge Crumpler's fumble and Nick Goings scored with 3:37 to play to culminate a 78-yard drive and take a 31-24 lead. Vick completed a 54-yard pass to Dez White in scoring position. Faced with fourth-and-goal from the Panthers' 12, Vick scrambled up the middle for the tying touchdown with 1:37 remaining. The Panthers won the overtime coin toss, but Aaron Beasley intercepted Delhomme's third-and-9 pass and returned the ball 30 yards to the Panthers' 23. Three plays later, Feely kicked a 38-yard field goal to win the game. Vick was 11 of 28 for 154 yards and 2 touchdowns, with 2 interceptions. Warrick Dunn rushed 28 times for 134 yards. Delhomme was 24 of 35 for 340 yards and 2 touchdowns, with 1 interception. Muhsin Muhammad had 10 receptions for 135 yards.

Carolina	0	10	0	21	0	—	31
Atlanta	7	3	14	7	3	—	34

Atl	—	Finneran 3 pass from Vick (Feely kick)
Atl	—	FG Feely 37
Car	—	Muhammad 6 pass from Delhomme (Kasay kick)
Car	—	FG Kasay 21
Atl	—	Dunn 6 run (Feely kick)
Atl	—	White 12 pass from Vick (Feely kick)
Car	—	Mangum 11 pass from Delhomme (Kasay kick)
Car	—	Peppers 60 fumble return (Kasay kick)
Car	—	Goings 5 run (Kasay kick)
Atl	—	Vick 12 run (Feely kick)
Atl	—	FG Feely 38

SUNDAY, DECEMBER 19

ARIZONA 31, ST. LOUIS 7—at Sun Devil Stadium, attendance 40,070. Josh McCown passed for 287 yards and 2 touchdowns, both to Larry Fitzgerald, and ran for another score as the Cardinals kept their playoff hopes alive. The Cardinals held advantages in first downs (26-12), total yards (402-185), and time of possession (37:29-22:31). Leading 17-0, the Cardinals drove to the Rams' 29 just before halftime, but Anthony Hargrove forced McCown to fumble, and Leonard Little picked up the ball and ran 60 yards for a touchdown to trim the deficit to 17-7. After an exchange of punts to begin the second half, McCown capped a 10-play drive with a 4-yard touchdown pass to Fitzgerald. The Rams threatened late in the third quarter, but Torry Holt fumbled at the Cardinals' 1 and Ifeanyi Ohalete recovered the ball for a touchback. Ten plays later McCown scored on a 9-yard run. McCown was 22 of 34 for 287 yards and 2 touchdowns. Chris Chandler was 1 for 6 for 1 yard, with 1 interception, before being replaced by Jamie Martin, who was 16 of 31 for 188 yards.

St. Louis	0	7	0	0	—	7
Arizona	10	7	7	7	—	31

Ariz	—	McCown 1 run (Rackers kick)
Ariz	—	FG Rackers 48
Ariz	—	Fitzgerald 8 pass from McCown (Rackers kick)
StL	—	Little 61 fumble recovery (Wilkins kick)
Ariz	—	Fitzgerald 4 pass from McCown (Rackers kick)
Ariz	—	McCown 9 run (Rackers kick)

HOUSTON 24, CHICAGO 5—at Soldier Field, attendance 62,122. David Carr passed for 1 touchdown as the Texans survived the minus-8 wind chill to defeat the Bears. Carr's 37-yard touchdown pass to Corey Bradford with 21 seconds left in the half gave Houston a 7-0 lead. Backed up to his own 5-yard-line late in the third quarter, Carr was penalized for intentional grounding in the end zone, which is a safety. Following an exchange of punts, Paul Edinger made a 43-yard field goal to cut the deficit to 7-5 with 14:09 left. The Texans answered with a 76-yard drive capped by Kris Brown's field goal, and following a punt Domanick Davis culminated a 14-play drive with an 11-yard scoring run with 4:34 to play. Six plays later, Dunta Robinson forced Chad Hutchinson to fumble, and Charlie Anderson returned the ball 60 yards for the final points. Carr was 13 of 28 for 220 yards and 1 touchdown. Jabar Gaffney had 4 catches for 109 yards, and Davis had 25 carries for 95 yards. Hutchinson was 17 of 34 for 168 yards, with 1 interception.

Houston	0	7	0	17	—	24
Chicago	0	0	2	3	—	5

Hous	—	Bradford 37 pass from Carr (K. Brown kick)
Chi	—	Safety, Carr penalized for intentional grounding in end zone
Chi	—	FG Edinger 43
Hous	—	FG K. Brown 20
Hous	—	Davis 11 run (K. Brown kick)
Hous	—	Anderson 60 fumble recovery (K. Brown kick)

BUFFALO 33, CINCINNATI 17—at Paul Brown Stadium, attendance 65,378. In a game played in a four-degree wind chill, Rian Lindell kicked 4 field goals and the Bills scored on defense and special teams to post their fifth consecutive victory. The Bengals defense permitted just 212 yards, but the Bills' defense forced 4 turnovers. With the score tied 7-7, Jason Peters blocked Kyle Larson's punt and recovered it in the end zone for a touchdown. The Bengals then drove to the Bills' 30, but Takeo Spikes intercepted Jon Kitna's attempted screen pass and returned it 62 yards for a touchdown. Lindell kicked a 23-yard field goal for a 24-10 lead with 1:13 left in the half. Chris Kelsay intercepted Kitna on the next play from scrimmage, and Lindell added a 39-yard field goal as the half expired for a commanding 27-10 lead. Drew Bledsoe was 15 of 30 for 183 yards and 1 touchdown. Lee Evans had 5 catches for 101 yards. Kitna, staring for the injured Carson Palmer, was 16 of 32 for 151 yards and 1 touchdown, with 2 interceptions. Rudi Johnson had 23 carries for 130 yards.

Buffalo	14	13	0	6	—	33
Cincinnati	7	3	0	7	—	17

Cin — R. Johnson 3 run (Graham kick)
Buff — Evans 5 pass from Bledsoe (Lindell kick)
Buff — Peters blocked punt recovery in end zone (Lindell kick)
Buff — Spikes 62 interception return (Lindell kick)
Cin — FG Graham 24
Buff — FG Lindell 23
Buff — FG Lindell 39
Buff — FG Lindell 21
Buff — FG Lindell 33
Cin — Schobel 4 pass from Kitna (Graham kick)

SAN DIEGO 21, CLEVELAND 0—at Cleveland Browns Stadium, attendance 72,489. LaDainian Tomlinson rushed for 111 yards and 2 touchdowns as the Chargers won the AFC West while posting their first shutout in 11 years. In a game played in minus-10 wind chill and snow, a muffed punt recovered at the Chargers' 5 gave the Browns their best scoring chance, but Donnie Edwards intercepted a pass for a touchdown. Fourteen plays later Tomlinson scored on a 1-yard run. The Chargers led 14-0 at halftime, and Drayton Florence recovered the Browns' surprise onside kick attempt. Tomlinson scored 11 plays later for a 21-0 lead. Brees was 4 of 6 for 85 yards and 1 touchdown. Tomlinson rushed 26 times for 111 yards. Luke McCown was 11 of 27 for 108 yards, with 1 interception. Lee Suggs carried 21 times for 105 yards.

San Diego	7	7	7	0	—	21
Cleveland	0	0	0	0	—	0

SD — Tomlinson 1 run (Kaeding kick)
SD — Gates 72 pass from Brees (Kaeding kick)
SD — Tomlinson 1 run (Kaeding kick)

MINNESOTA 28, DETROIT 27—at Ford Field, attendance 62,337. A poor snap foiled Jason Hanson's extra-point attempt with eight seconds left, allowing the Vikings to escape with a hard-fought victory. The Packers loss later in the afternoon moved the Vikings into a tie for first place in the NFC North. Both teams gained over 460 yards (463-461 in favor of Detroit). The Vikings led 14-13 at halftime, and Brian Williams' interception early in the fourth quarter sparked a 68-yard drive, capped by Daunte Culpepper's 37-yard touchdown pass to Nate Burleson for a 21-13 lead. Joey Harrington completed a 9-yard touchdown pass to Roy Williams, and 2-point conversion pass to Tai Streets, to tie the game 21-21 with 6:11 to play. The Vikings reached the Lions' 13 with 1:52 remaining, when Michael Bennett fumbled the ball. Bennett recovered his own fumble, but on the next play Moe Williams bowled his way over defenders into the end zone for a 28-21 lead with 1:37 remaining. With no time outs, the Lions drove to the Vikings' 15. A pass interference penalty on a pass intended for Roy Williams placed the ball on the 1-yard line, and Harrington lobbed a touchdown pass to Williams on the next play with eight seconds left. As the Lions attempted the extra point, long snapper Don Muhlbach's snap bounced to holder Nick Harris, who was unable to spot the ball and was tackled by Terrance Shaw. Randy Moss recovered the ensuing onside kick to clinch the victory for Minnesota. Culpepper was 25 of 35 for 404 yards and 3 touchdowns, with 1 interception. Burleson had 5 receptions for 134 yards, and Moss added 4 catches for 102 yards. Harrington was 25 of 44 for 361 yards and 2 touchdowns, with 2 interceptions.

Roy Williams had 7 catches for 104 yards, and Az-Zahir Hakim added 4 receptions for 108 yards.

Minnesota	7	7	0	14	—	28
Detroit	3	10	0	14	—	27

Det — FG Hanson 32
Minn — Burleson 36 pass from Culpepper (Anderson kick)
Minn — Moss 82 pass from Culpepper (Anderson kick)
Det — Jones 16 run (Hanson kick)
Det — FG Hanson 23
Minn — Burleson 37 pass from Culpepper (Anderson kick)
Det — R. Williams 9 pass from Harrington (Streets pass from Harrington)
Minn — M. Williams 11 run (Anderson kick)
Det — R. Williams 1 pass from Harrington (snap failed)

JACKSONVILLE 28, GREEN BAY 25—at Lambeau Field, attendance 70,437. Fred Taylor rushed for 165 yards and a touchdown, and Byron Leftwich added 2 passing scores as the Jaguars withstood the minus-3 wind chill to keep pace for the final AFC playoff berth. The Packers gained 444 yards, but the Jaguars' defense forced 5 turnovers. Green Bay took the opening kickoff of the second half and drove 76 yards for a touchdown and 17-14 lead. The Jaguars scored four plays later, capped by Taylor's 37-yard run, to retake the lead. The Packers drove to the Jaguars' 3, but Brett Favre's pass into the end zone was intercepted by Rashean Mathis. Early in the fourth quarter, the Jaguars drove to the Packers' 1 and, on fourth-and-goal, Greg Jones scored to give Jacksonville a 28-17 lead with 9:49 to play. Mathis and Deon Grant intercepted Favre on the next two possessions. Favre did engineer a 67-yard drive, culminated with his 6-yard touchdown pass to Antonio Chatman with 1:08 left, but Nick Sorensen recovered the onside kick to ensure the victory. Leftwich was 9 of 20 for 121 yards and 2 touchdowns. Favre was 30 of 44 for 367 yards and 2 touchdowns, with 3 interceptions. Javon Walker had 11 catches for 152 yards.

Jacksonville	7	7	7	7	—	28
Green Bay	0	10	7	8	—	25

Jax — J. Smith 31 pass from Leftwich (Scobee kick)
GB — FG Longwell 35
GB — Sharper 15 fumble return (Longwell kick)
Jax — J. Smith 16 pass from Leftwich (Scobee kick)
GB — Driver 32 pass from Favre (Longwell kick)
Jax — Taylor 37 run (Scobee kick)
Jax — G. Jones 1 run (Scobee kick)
GB — Chatman 7 pass from Favre (Driver pass from Favre)

KANSAS CITY 45, DENVER 17—at Arrowhead Stadium, attendance 77,702. Trent Green passed for 3 touchdowns and Larry Johnson rushed for 151 yards and 2 scores as the Chiefs were unaffected by the minus-1 wind chill and defeated the Broncos. Dante Hall returned the opening kickoff 97 yards for a touchdown. Kansas City also scored on three of its next four possessions, the middle touchdown set up by Dexter McCleon's interception, to take a 28-7 lead. The Chiefs put together drives of 9 plays, 90 yards and 10 plays, 99 yards with their first two possessions of the second half en route to a 42-10 lead with 14:13 left. Green was 16 of 19 for 224 yards and 3 touchdowns. Eddie Kennison had 7 catches for 101 yards. Jake Plummer was 23 of 41 for 292 yards and 1 touchdown, with 2 interceptions.

Denver	7	3	0	7	—	17
Kansas City	14	14	7	10	—	45

KC — Hall 97 kickoff return (Tynes kick)
KC — L. Johnson 5 run (Tynes kick)

Den — Smith 22 pass from Plummer (Elam kick)
KC — Kennison 7 pass from Green (Tynes kick)
KC — L. Johnson 32 run (Tynes kick)
Den — FG Elam 27
KC — Parker 48 pass from Green (Tynes kick)
KC — Kennison 18 pass from Green (Tynes kick)
KC — FG Tynes 39
Den — Hearst 4 run (Elam kick)

N.Y. JETS 37, SEATTLE 14—at Meadowlands, attendance 77,894. Chad Pennington passed for 253 yards and 3 touchdowns, and Curtis Martin rushed for 134 yards and 2 scores, as the Jets improved their wild-card chances. The Jets outgained the Seahawks 482-275 and forced 3 turnovers. The Jets had eight possessions in the game, and drove into the red zone all but one time. The Jets scored on all four first-half possessions, but Jerramy Stevens' 6-yard touchdown catch with three seconds left cut the deficit to 24-14 at halftime. Seattle got the ball to begin the second half, but went three-and-out, and the Jets drove 82 yards, capped by Pennington's 7-yard touchdown pass to Santana Moss for a 31-14 lead. The Seahawks responded with a 68-yard drive, but on fourth-and-goal from the Jets' 1, Shaun Alexander fumbled as he was going into the end zone, forced by Eric Barton, and Shaun Ellis recovered. Barton recovered a fumble on the Seahawks' next possession, and Justin McCareins' 5-yard scoring reception with 8:14 remaining clinched the win. Pennington was 18 of 24 for 253 yards and 3 touchdowns. Martin rushed 24 times for 134 yards. Barton had 1 sack, 1 interception, 1 forced fumble, and 1 fumble recovery. Matt Hasselbeck was 22 of 30 for 201 yards and 2 touchdowns, with 1 interception.

Seattle	7	7	0	0	—	14
N.Y. Jets	3	21	6	7	—	37

NYJ — FG Brien 21
Sea — Rice 12 pass from Hasselbeck (J. Brown kick)
NYJ — Martin 1 run (Brien kick)
NYJ — Martin 3 run (Brien kick)
NYJ — Moss 32 pass from Pennington (Brien kick)
Sea — Stevens 6 pass from Hasselbeck (J. Brown kick)
NYJ — Moss 7 pass from Pennington (kick failed)
NYJ — McCareins 5 pass from Pennington (Brien kick)

OAKLAND 40, TENNESSEE 35—at Network Associates Coliseum, attendance 44,299. Kerry Collins passed for 371 yards and 5 touchdowns, 3 to Jerry Porter, as the Raiders outscored the Titans. The Titans held the advantage in total yards (527-415), but were stopped on downs in the end zone and missed a field goal. The Raiders led 28-21 in the third quarter when Tommy Kelly sacked Billy Volek and forced him to fumble. Warren Sapp recovered at the Titans' 21 and Porter caught his third touchdown four plays later to give the Raiders a 35-21 lead. Keith Bulluck's interception sparked a 12-play, 66-yard drive capped by Volek's 3-yard touchdown pass to Derrick Mason on fourth-and-goal with 11:53 left. The Titans forced a punt and drove to the Raiders' 18. Trailing by seven, on fourth-and-1 the Titans lined up for a field goal, but holder Craig Hentrich's pass into the end zone for Shad Meier fell incomplete. Collins' 57-yard pass to Alvis Whitted led to Sebastian Janikowski's 42-yard field goal with 3:39 left. Volek scored with 1:21 left to pull within 38-35, but Teyo Johnson recovered the onside kick. The Titans forced a punt but, starting at their own 12, Volek was penalized for intentional grounding in the end zone, which resulted in a safety. Gabriel recovered the ensuing onside kick with eight seconds left to preserve the victory. Collins was 21 of 37 for 371 yards and 5 touchdowns, with 1 interception. Porter had 8 catches for 148 yards. Volek was 40 of 60 for 492 yards, the tenth highest total in NFL history, and 4 touchdowns, with 1 interception. Drew Bennett had 13 receptions for 160 yards.

Tennessee	7	14	0	14 —	35
Oakland	14	7	14	5 —	40

Oak	—	T. Johnson 18 pass from Collins (Janikowski kick)
Tenn	—	Bennett 17 pass from Volek (Anderson kick)
Oak	—	Porter 32 pass from Collins (Janikowski kick)
Tenn	—	Bennett 23 pass from Volek (Anderson kick)
Oak	—	Porter 18 pass from Collins (Janikowski kick)
Tenn	—	Troupe 7 pass from Volek (Anderson kick)
Oak	—	Gabriel 45 pass from Collins (Janikowski kick)
Oak	—	Porter 3 pass from Collins (Janikowski kick)
Tenn	—	Mason 3 pass from Volek (Anderson kick)
Oak	—	FG Janikowski 42
Tenn	—	Volek 1 run (Anderson kick)
Oak	—	Safety, Volek penalized for intentional grounding in end zone

PHILADELPHIA 12, DALLAS 7—at Lincoln Financial Field, attendance 67,723. Donovan McNabb had 2 big scrambles in the final minutes to set up the winning touchdown as the Eagles won the game but lost Terrell Owens for the season. Owens injured his knee late in the third quarter when tackled from behind by Roy Williams. The Eagles drove 70 yards for a touchdown in the second quarter, but Kurt Vollers blocked the extra point. On the Eagles' next possession, Greg Ellis forced McNabb to fumble and Eric Ogbogu recovered to set up Keyshawn Johnson's 7-yard touchdown catch. Terance Newman and Williams had third-quarter interceptions in Cowboys' territory to stop scoring threats. Billy Cundiff's 46-yard field goal with 6:03 left sailed wide left. McNabb then had runs of 12 and 19 yards to set up Dorsey Levens' 2-yard scoring run with 1:57 left. Lito Sheppard intercepted Vinny Testaverde's pass three plays later to clinch the victory. McNabb was 20 of 35 for 223 yards and 1 touchdown, with 2 interceptions. Testaverde was 16 of 28 for 176 yards and 1 touchdown, with 2 interceptions.

Dallas	0	7	0	0 —	7
Philadelphia	0	6	0	6 —	12

Phil	—	C. Lewis 2 pass from McNabb (kick blocked)
Dall	—	K. Johnson 7 pass from Testaverde (Cundiff kick)
Phil	—	Levens 2 run (pass failed)

NEW ORLEANS 21, TAMPA BAY 17—at Raymond James Stadium, attendance 65,075. Donte' Stallworth caught a 7-yard touchdown pass from Aaron Brooks with 32 seconds remaining kept the Saints' playoff hopes alive. Aaron Stecker bobbled the opening kickoff, but then avoided a host of Buccaneers inside his own 5 and then flew down the right sideline 98 yards for a touchdown. Joey Galloway returned a punt 59 yards for a touchdown in the middle of third quarter, and Mario Edwards recovered Jerome Pathon's fumble late in the third quarter to set up Jay Taylor's field goal for a 17-7 lead with 11:17 remaining. John Carney missed a 38-yard field goal, but the Saints then forced a punt and Michael Lewis returned it 53 yards to the Buccaneer's 4. Brooks' 4-yard touchdown pass to Joe Horn cut the deficit to 17-14 with 3:33 left. Michael Pittman fumbled on the next play, and Fakhir Brown recovered at the Buccaneers' 41. Brooks completed a 22-yard pass to Boo Williams to set up Stallworth's catch at the goal line with 32 seconds left.

Darren Howard sacked Brian Griese near midfield as time expired. Brooks was 14 of 21 for 169 yards and 2 touchdowns. Griese was 13 of 22 for 118 yards and 1 touchdown, with 1 interception. Pittman had 24 times for 131 yards.

New Orleans	7	0	0	14 —	21
Tampa Bay	7	0	7	3 —	17

NO	—	Stecker 98 kickoff return (Carney kick)
TB	—	Galloway 3 pass from Griese (Taylor kick)
TB	—	Galloway 59 punt return (Taylor kick)
TB	—	FG Taylor 37
NO	—	Horn 4 pass from Brooks (Carney kick)
NO	—	Stallworth 7 pass from Brooks (Carney kick)

SUNDAY NIGHT, DECEMBER 19
INDIANAPOLIS 20, BALTIMORE 10—at RCA Dome, attendance 57,240. Peyton Manning completed his 47th touchdown pass of the season as the Colts dealt a blow to the Ravens' postseason chances. With just 1 touchdown pass, Manning's NFL record streak of 13 consecutive games with multiple touchdown passes was snapped. The Colts kicked a field goal to begin the game, but the Ravens' defense forced five consecutive punts. With 13 seconds left in the half, Mike Doss intercepted Kyle Boller's pass and returned it 32 yards to the Ravens' 4. Manning's 31-yard pass to Marcus Pollard set up Mike Vanderjagt's 33-yard field goal as the half expired for a 6-3 Colts lead. The Colts scored on their first two possessions of the second half, the latter a 31-yard drive following Larry Triplett's blocked field-goal attempt and Von Hutchins' 24-yard return. The Colts scored on their next possession, Cato June intercepted Boller with 59 seconds left to clinch the victory. Manning was 20 of 33 for 249 yards and 1 touchdown. Boller was 19 of 40 for 210 yards and 1 touchdown, with 2 interceptions. Jamal Lewis rushed 20 times for 130 yards.

Baltimore	0	3	0	7 —	10
Indianapolis	3	3	14	0 —	20

Ind	—	FG Vanderjagt 24
Balt	—	FG Stover 42
Ind	—	FG Vanderjagt 33
Ind	—	Harrison 29 pass from Manning (Vanderjagt kick)
Ind	—	James 3 run (Vanderjagt kick)
Balt	—	Heap 13 pass from Boller (Stover kick)

MONDAY NIGHT, DECEMBER 20
MIAMI 29, NEW ENGLAND 28—at Pro Player Stadium, attendance 73,629. A.J. Feeley completed a 21-yard touchdown pass to Derrius Thompson with 1:23 left as the Dolphins' defense intercepted 2 passes in the final two minutes to snap the Patriots' six-game winning streak. The Patriots led 14-10 at halftime, but Sammy Knight intercepted Brady early in the second half and Travis Minor scored ten plays later to give Miami a 17-14 lead. Brady completed a pair of 2-yard touchdown passes to stake the Patriots to a 28-17 lead with 3:59 left. The Dolphins drove 68 yards in 1:52 to pull within 28-23 with 2:07 remaining. Three plays later, on third-and-9, Jason Taylor pressured Brady. As Brady was spinning to the ground he heaved the ball downfield. Brendon Ayanbadejo intercepted the pass at the Patriots' 21. On fourth-and-10, Feeley beat the blitz and threw the ball to Thompson, who beat two-way player Troy Brown's one-on-one coverage for the touchdown. Arturo Freeman intercepted Brady's pass two plays later to clinch the victory. Feeley was 22 of 35 for 198 yards and 1 touchdown. Brady was 18 of 29 for 171 yards and 3 touchdowns, with 4 interceptions. Dillon rushed 26 times for 121 yards.

New England	7	7	7	7 —	28
Miami	7	3	7	12 —	29

NE	—	Faulk 31 pass from Brady (Vinatieri kick)
Mia	—	Morris 2 run (Mare kick)
NE	—	Dillon 3 run (Vinatieri kick)
Mia	—	FG Mare 30
Mia	—	Minor 1 run (Mare kick)
NE	—	Dillon 2 pass from Brady (Vinatieri kick)
NE	—	Graham 2 pass from Brady (Vinatieri kick)
Mia	—	Morris 1 run (pass failed)
Mia	—	Thompson 21 pass from Feeley (pass failed)

SIXTEENTH WEEK SUMMARIES
American Football Conference

East Division	W	L	T	Pct.	Pts.	OP
New England*	13	2	0	.867	416	253
N.Y. Jets	10	5	0	.667	304	229
Buffalo	9	6	0	.600	371	255
Miami	4	11	0	.267	252	324

North Division	W	L	T	Pct.	Pts.	OP
Pittsburgh*	14	1	0	.933	343	227
Baltimore	8	7	0	.533	287	245
Cincinnati	7	8	0	.467	336	362
Cleveland	3	12	0	.200	254	376

South Division	W	L	T	Pct.	Pts.	OP
Indianapolis*	12	3	0	.786	474	287
Jacksonville	8	7	0	.533	248	274
Houston	7	8	0	.467	295	317
Tennessee	4	11	0	.267	320	420

West Division	W	L	T	Pct.	Pts.	OP
San Diego*	11	4	0	.733	422	296
Denver	9	6	0	.600	348	290
Kansas City	7	8	0	.467	466	411
Oakland	5	10	0	.333	314	429

National Football Conference

East Division	W	L	T	Pct.	Pts.	OP
Philadelphia*	13	2	0	.867	376	222
Dallas	6	9	0	.400	269	377
N.Y. Giants	5	10	0	.333	275	323
Washington	5	10	0	.333	219	247

North Division	W	L	T	Pct.	Pts.	OP
Green Bay*	9	6	0	.600	393	366
Minnesota	8	7	0	.533	387	374
Detroit	6	9	0	.400	277	326
Chicago	5	10	0	.333	217	300

South Division	W	L	T	Pct.	Pts.	OP
Atlanta*	11	4	0	.733	314	309
Carolina	7	8	0	.467	337	318
New Orleans	7	8	0	.467	327	387
Tampa Bay	5	10	0	.333	294	292

West Division	W	L	T	Pct.	Pts.	OP
Seattle#	8	7	0	.533	343	347
St. Louis	7	8	0	.467	287	363
Arizona	5	10	0	.333	272	315
San Francisco	2	13	0	.133	252	431

*Clinched division title
#Clinched playoff berth

FRIDAY, DECEMBER 24
GREEN BAY 34, MINNESOTA 31—at Metrodome, attendance 64,311. Ryan Longwell kicked a 29-yard field goal as time expired as the Packers won their third consecutive NFC North title. In their earlier matchup on November 14, the Packers also won that game 34-31 on Longwell's field goal as time expired. In the second quarter, the Vikings attempted four plays from scrimmage, and scored three touchdowns. The Packers had the ball for the remaining 14:08 of the quarter and scored 2 touchdowns and a field goal as the half expired to pull within 21-17. With the score 24-24, Chris Claiborne made a leaping interception of a Brett Favre pass and returned it 15 yards for a touchdown with 8:18 remaining. Favre engineered a 13-play, 80-yard drive on the next possession, capped by Donald Driver's 3-yard touchdown catch on fourth-and-goal, to tie the game 31-31 with 3:34 to play. Beginning from their own 13 with 1:35 remaining, Favre completed 5 of 7 pass attempts, highlighted by a 31-yard pass to Javon Walker to the Vikings' 7, to set up Long-

well's winning kick. Favre was 30 of 43 for 365 yards and 3 touchdowns, with 1 interception. Driver had 11 catches for 162 yards. Culpepper was 16 of 23 for 285 yards and 3 touchdowns. Nate Burleson had 2 receptions for 110 yards.

Green Bay	0	17	7	10	—	34
Minnesota	0	21	0	10	—	31

Minn	—	Moss 12 pass from Culpepper (Andersen kick)
GB	—	Green 1 run (Longwell kick)
Minn	—	Burleson 68 pass from Culpepper (Andersen kick)
GB	—	Franks 22 pass from Favre (Longwell kick)
Minn	—	Bennett 38 pass from Culpepper (Andersen kick)
GB	—	FG Longwell 42
GB	—	Walker 9 pass from Favre (Longwell kick)
Minn	—	FG Andersen 29
Minn	—	Claiborne 15 interception return (Andersen kick)
GB	—	Driver 3 pass from Favre (Longwell kick)
GB	—	FG Longwell 29

SATURDAY, DECEMBER 25
KANSAS CITY 31, OAKLAND 30—at Arrowhead Stadium, attendance 77,289. Lawrence Tynes kicked a 38-yard field goal with 22 seconds remaining to temporarily keep the Chiefs' playoff hopes alive. The Broncos' victory in Tennessee three hours later knocked the Chiefs out of postseason contention. The Chiefs scored touchdowns on three successive possessions to take a 21-14 lead. Alvis Whitted's 32-yard touchdown catch tied the game with 24 seconds left in the half. Tynes attempted a 50-yard field goal as the half expired, but the ball hit the crossbar and bounced back onto the field. Larry Johnson's 1-yard touchdown run capped a 65-yard drive and gave the Chiefs a 28-24 lead with 6:11 remaining. Janikowski kicked a 45-yard field goal with 3:49 left in the game. With 1:48 left, Ted Washington sacked Trent Green and forced him to fumble. Warren Sapp recovered at the Raiders' 43, and Janikowski's 46-yard field goal with 1:03 left gave the Raiders a 30-28 lead. The Raiders squib the ball on the kickoff, but Dante Hall still returned the ball 49 yards to the Raiders' 36. Six plays later, Tynes drilled a 38-yard field goal with 22 seconds left. Benny Sapp intercepted Kerry Collins' Hail Mary pass at the Raiders' 23 as time expired. Green was 32 of 45 for 358 yards and 2 touchdowns, with 1 interception. Tony Gonzalez had 11 receptions for 124 yards. Collins was 18 of 37 for 217 yards and 2 touchdowns, with 1 interception.

Oakland	7	14	3	6	—	30
Kansas City	7	14	0	10	—	31

Oak	—	Porter 5 pass from Collins (Janikowski kick)
KC	—	L. Johnson 6 run (Tynes kick)
Oak	—	Crockett 3 run (Janikowski kick)
KC	—	Gonzalez 2 pass from Green (Tynes kick)
KC	—	Gonzalez 26 pass from Green (Tynes kick)
Oak	—	Whitted 32 pass from Collins (Janikowski kick)
Oak	—	FG Janikowski 40
KC	—	L. Johnson 4 run (Tynes kick)
Oak	—	FG Janikowski 45
Oak	—	FG Janikowski 46
KC	—	FG Tynes 38

SATURDAY NIGHT, DECEMBER 25
DENVER 37, TENNESSEE 16—at The Coliseum, attendance 68,809. Jake Plummer passed for 303 yards and 2 touchdowns as the Broncos kept their wild-card hopes alive. The Broncos outgained the Titans 496-153 in total yards and maintained possession for 39:24. The Broncos scored on their first three possessions to take a 17-3 lead. Leading 24-

10, Gay Anderson kicked a 43-yard field goal with 43 seconds left in the half. Keith Bulluck intercepted Jake Plummer's pass three plays later and Craig Hentrich made a 50-yard field goal as the half expired to pull within 24-16. The Broncos' defense allowed just 1 first down on the Titans' first four possessions of the second half, and the offense added 2 field goals, for a 30-16 lead. Plummer connected on a 45-yard pass to Ashley Lelie to set up Reuben Droughns' 23-yard touchdown run with 6:55 to play. Plummer was 21 of 26 for 303 yards and 2 touchdowns, with 1 interception. D.J. Williams had an interception and 3 passes defensed. Billy Volek was 8 of 20 for 111 yards, with 2 interceptions, before suffering a knee injury in the third quarter. Doug Johnson replaced Volek and was 4 of 7 for 26 yards.

Denver	17	7	3	10	—	37
Tennessee	10	6	0	0	—	16

Den	—	Droughns 23 pass from Plummer (Elam kick)
Den	—	FG Elam 22
Tenn	—	FG Anderson 44
Den	—	Droughns 8 run (Elam kick)
Tenn	—	A. Smith 13 run (Anderson kick)
Den	—	R. Smith 7 pass from Plummer (Elam kick)
Tenn	—	FG Anderson 43
Tenn	—	FG Hentrich 50
Den	—	FG Elam 22
Den	—	FG Elam 30
Den	—	Droughns 23 run (Elam kick)

SUNDAY, DECEMBER 26
CINCINNATI 23, N.Y. GIANTS 22—at Paul Brown Stadium, attendance 64,606. Chad Johnson caught a 4-yard touchdown pass from Jon Kitna with 44 seconds left as the Bengals handed the Giants their eighth consecutive loss. The Giants' defense allowed just 233 yards, and the offense scored on six consecutive possessions but settled for field goals on four of their five red zone possessions. Steve Christie's fifth field goal provided the Giants a 22-17 lead with 5:15 to play, and the Giants' defense forced a three-and-out. After one first down, the Giants punted and Keiwan Ratliff returned the ball 42 yards to the Giants' 24 with 2:05 to play. On fourth-and-10, Kitna completed a 19-yard pass to T.J. Houshmandzadeh, and Johnson caught Kitna's pass along the left sideline two plays later for the lead. Kitna's 2-point conversion pass fell incomplete, and Willie Ponder returned the ensuing kickoff 35 yards to the Giants' 48. On the first play, Eli Manning's pass was tipped by Robert Geathers and intercepted by Carl Powell. Kitna, playing for the injured Carson Palmer, was 20 of 32 for 186 yards and 2 touchdowns, with 1 interception. Manning was 19 of 37 for 201 yards, with 1 interception. Tiki Barber rushed 22 times for 109 yards.

N.Y. Giants	0	13	3	6	—	22
Cincinnati	7	3	7	6	—	23

Cin	—	C. Johnson 5 pass from Kitna (Graham kick)
NYG	—	Barber 1 run (Christie kick)
Cin	—	FG Graham 42
NYG	—	FG Christie 31
NYG	—	FG Christie 36
NYG	—	FG Christie 44
Cin	—	R. Johnson 1 run (Graham kick)
NYG	—	FG Christie 41
NYG	—	FG Christie 28
Cin	—	C. Johnson 4 pass from Kitna (pass failed)

DALLAS 13, WASHINGTON 10—at Texas Stadium, attendance 63,705. Patrick Crayton caught a 39-yard touchdown pass from Vinny Testaverde with 30 seconds left as the Cowboys defeated the Redskins in Texas Stadium for the ninth consecutive time. Lynn Scott intercepted a pass at the Cowboys' 3 in the first half to thwart a rally and help Dallas to 6-3 lead. Late in the third quarter, Shawn Springs intercepted a pass in the end zone to stop the Cow-

boys. Patrick Ramsey's 5-yard touchdown pass to Robert Royal capped a 13-play, 80-yard drive and gave the Redskins a 10-6 lead with 6:44 to play. Marcus Washington tackled Julius Jones for no gain on fourth-and-1 at the Redskins' 33 with 1:46 left. The Cowboys forced a punt and began at their own 25 with 1:25 to play. On fourth-and-10, Testaverde hit Crayton with a 15-yard pass. Five plays later, on third-and-3 with 37 seconds left, Testaverde threw deep down the right sideline to Crayton for his first NFL touchdown. Ramsey completed a 32-yard pass to Laveranues Coles, but Jeff Chandler's 57-yard field-goal attempt fell short as time expired. Testaverde was 23 of 39 for 234 yards and 1 touchdown, with 1 interception. Ramsey was 9 of 29 for 158 yards and 1 touchdown, with 2 interceptions.

Washington	3	0	0	7	—	10
Dallas	0	6	0	7	—	13

Wash	—	FG Chandler 25
Dall	—	FG Cundiff 26
Dall	—	FG Cundiff 23
Wash	—	Royal 5 pass from Ramsey (Chandler kick)
Dall	—	Crayton 39 pass from Testaverde (Cundiff kick)

DETROIT 19, CHICAGO 13—at Ford Field, attendance 61,924. Jason Hanson kicked four field goals as the Lions defeated a team twice in the same season for the first time since 1998. The Lions jumped to a 16-0 lead, and led 19-7 with the Bears' lone score coming on Lance Briggs' 38-yard interception return. The Bears did not drive inside the Lions' 48 until the fourth quarter, and Jason McKie's 15-yard touchdown reception cut the deficit to 19-13 with 7:04 remaining. The Bears forced a punt and drove to the Lions' 43. A near-touchdown pass to Bernard Berrain was ruled incomplete, and Chad Hutchinson tossed three more incompletions to turn the ball over with 1:11 remaining. Joey Harrington was 15 of 30 for 166 yards, with 1 interception. Kevin Jones rushed 25 times for 123 yards. Hutchinson was 20 of 35 for 114 yards and 1 touchdown. Thomas Jones rushed 22 times for 109 yards.

Chicago	0	0	6	7	—	13
Detroit	3	13	0	3	—	19

Det	—	FG Hanson 31
Det	—	K. Jones 1 run (Hanson kick)
Det	—	FG Hanson 39
Det	—	FG Hanson 34
Chi	—	Briggs 38 interception return (pass failed)
Det	—	FG Hanson 40
Chi	—	McKie 15 pass from Hutchinson (Edinger kick)

INDIANAPOLIS 34, SAN DIEGO 31 (OT)—at RCA Dome, attendance 57,330. Mike Vanderjagt's 30-yard field goal in overtime allowed the Colts' to clinch the third seed in the playoffs. Peyton Manning broke Dan Marino's single-season record of 48 touchdowns by throwing 2 touchdown passes, setting the mark on a 21-yard pass to Brandon Stokley with 56 seconds left to force overtime. The Colts drove into the red zone four times in the first half, but Donnie Edwards intercepted a pass on the first possession and the Colts settled for three field goals. Following Edwards' interception, the Chargers scored on five of six possessions, excluding a one-play kneeldown at the end of the half. The drives were 92, 37, 61, 79, and 71 yards, capped by LaDainian Tomlinson's 16-yard touchdown run with 14:55 to play for a 31-16 lead. Dominic Rhodes returned the ensuing kickoff 88 yards for a touchdown, and the Colts' defense forced a punt. Vanderjagt missed a 47-yard field goal with 4:47 left, but the Colts' defense forced a three-and-out. From their own 20 with 3:42 left, the Colts drove 80 yards in 9 plays, highlighted by Manning's 19-yard pass to Reggie Wayne on fourth-and-4, and capped by Stokley's 21-yard touchdown catch on a post pattern with 56 seconds left. Rob Morris intercepted

Drew Brees' pass at the Colts' 27 with three seconds left to force overtime. The Colts won the toss and needed just five plays, including a 35-yard catch-and-run by Wayne, to set up Vanderjagt's winning kick. Manning was 27 of 44 for 383 yards and 2 touchdowns, with 1 interception. Stokley had 7 receptions for 123 yards and Marvin Harrison had 6 catches for 111 yards. Brees was 21 of 31 for 290 yards and 3 touchdowns, with 1 interception. Eric Parker had 7 catches for 103 yards. Antonio Gates caught a 4-yard touchdown shovel pass, giving him 13 touchdown catches, a single-season NFL record for a tight end.

San Diego	7	10	7	7	0	—	31
Indianapolis	0	9	7	15	3	—	34

SD	—	Tomlinson 74 pass from Brees (Kaeding kick)
Ind	—	FG Vanderjagt 36
SD	—	FG Kaeding 50
SD	—	Parker 19 pass from Brees (Kaeding kick)
Ind	—	FG Vanderjagt 26
Ind	—	FG Vanderjagt 23
SD	—	Gates 4 pass from Brees (Kaeding kick)
Ind	—	Mungro 3 pass from Manning (Vanderjagt kick)
SD	—	Tomlinson 16 run (Kaeding kick)
Ind	—	Rhodes 88 kickoff return (Vanderjagt kick)
Ind	—	Stokley 21 pass from Manning (James run)
Ind	—	FG Vanderjagt 30

HOUSTON 21, JACKSONVILLE 0—at ALLTEL Stadium, attendance 66,227. Domanick Davis rushed for 150 yards and 1 touchdown as the Texans posted the first shutout in franchise history. The Texans' defense allowed just 126 yards and forced 3 turnovers as the Jaguars played without injured Fred Taylor. The Texans drove 65 yards for a touchdown with their opening possession. The Jaguars only drove inside the Texans' 30 one time, and Josh Scobee missed a 31-yard field-goal attempt in the third quarter. Houston led 14-0 in the fourth quarter, and Dunta Robinson forced Troy Edwards to fumble. Antwan Peek recovered the ball and rumbled 66 yards for a touchdown and 21-0 lead with 3:11 to play. David Carr was 14 of 20 for 139 yards and 1 touchdown, with 2 interceptions. Davis rushed 30 yards, with 1 touchdown. Byron Leftwich was 6 of 14 for 35 yards, with 1 interception. David Garrard replaced an injured Leftwich in the fourth quarter and was 4 of 7 for 19 yards.

Houston	7	7	0	7	—	21
Jacksonville	0	0	0	0	—	0

Hous	—	Davis 1 run (K. Brown kick)
Hous	—	A. Johnson 10 pass from Carr (K. Brown kick)
Hous	—	Peek 66 fumble return (K. Brown kick)

NEW ORLEANS 26, ATLANTA 13—at Louisiana Superdome, attendance 64,900. Aaron Brooks passed for 227 yards and Michael Lewis returned a kickoff 96 yards for a touchdown as the Saints won their third consecutive game and kept their playoff hopes alive. The Falcons, who had clinched the second seed in the NFC, played without Michael Vick. The Saints led 12-6 at halftime, and opened the second half with a five-play, 70-yard drive capped by Donte' Stallworth's 39-yard touchdown catch. The Falcons answered with a 12-play, 70-yard drive drive culminated with Warrick Dunn's 16-yard run cut the deficit to 19-13, but Lewis returned the ensuing kickoff 96 yards. Mike McKenzie grabbed interceptions on the Falcons' final two drives to clinch the victory for the Saints. Brooks was 12 of 24 for 227 yards and 1 touchdown, with 2 interceptions. Deuce McAllister rushed 29 times for 128 yards. Matt Schaub was 17 of 41 for 188 yards, with 2 interceptions.

Atlanta	0	6	7	0	—	13
New Orleans	5	7	14	0	—	26

NO	—	Safety, Bryant tackled Schaub in end zone
NO	—	FG Carney 22
Atl	—	FG Feely 25
Atl	—	FG Feely 20
NO	—	Brooks 1 run (Carney kick)
NO	—	Stallworth 39 pass from Brooks (Carney kick)
Atl	—	Dunn 16 run (Feely kick)
NO	—	Lewis 96 kickoff return (Carney kick)

NEW ENGLAND 23, N.Y. JETS 7—at Meadowlands, attendance 77,975. Tom Brady passed for 2 touchdowns as the Patriots clinched the AFC's second seed. The Patriots scored on three consecutive second-quarter possessions to take a 13-0 lead. Trailing 16-0, Chad Pennington was intercepted by Eugene Wilson, and his 15-yard return to the Jets' 15 set up Deion Branch's 6-yard touchdown catch for a 23-0 lead with 12:36 to play. Santana Moss caught a 15-yard touchdown pass on the Jets' next possession, and the Jets had the ball two more times, but Justin McCareins was stopped 1 yard shy of a first down at the Patriots' 31 with 4:07 left and Jarvis Green recovered Pennington's fumble, forced by Roosevelt Colvin, with 2:17 remaining to clinch the victory. Brady was 21 of 32 for 264 yards and 2 touchdowns. Pennington was 22 of 36 for 252 yards and 1 touchdown, with 2 interceptions.

New England	0	13	3	7	—	23
N.Y. Jets	0	0	0	7	—	7

NE	—	FG Vinatieri 28
NE	—	Graham 16 pass from Brady (Vinatieri kick)
NE	—	FG Vinatieri 29
NE	—	FG Vinatieri 26
NE	—	Branch 6 pass from Brady (Vinatieri kick)
NYJ	—	Moss 15 pass from Pennington (Brien kick)

PITTSBURGH 20, BALTIMORE 7—at Heinz Field, attendance 64,227. Ben Roethlisberger passed for 2 touchdowns as the Steelers won their thirteenth consecutive game and clinched the AFC's first seed. Joey Porter intercepted Kyle Boller's pass at the Steelers' 32 to set up Jeff Reed's 23-yard field goal in the second quarter to give Pittsburgh a 10-7 halftime lead. The Steelers drove 14 plays, 71 yards to begin the second half, capped by Roethlisberger's 2-yard scoring pass to Jerame Tuman. On the play, Roethlisberger was hit by Terrell Suggs, who was flagged for roughing, and left the game with bruised ribs. The Ravens had just two possessions in the second half, for a combined 9:14, finishing with a missed field goal and incomplete pass from the Steelers' 34. The Steelers ran the ball 7:41 off the clock. Roethlisberger was 14 of 19 for 221 yards and 2 touchdowns, with 1 interception. Jerome Bettis rushed 27 times for 117 yards. Kyle Boller was 18 of 32 for 177 yards, with 1 interception.

Baltimore	7	0	0	0	—	7
Pittsburgh	3	7	3	7	—	20

Pitt	—	Burress 36 pass from Roethlisberger (Reed kick)
Balt	—	J. Lewis 5 run (Stover kick)
Pitt	—	FG Reed 23
Pitt	—	Tuman 2 pass from Roethlisberger (Reed kick)
Pitt	—	FG Reed 40

BUFFALO 41, SAN FRANCISCO 7—at Monster Park, attendance 63,248. Willis McGahee and Lee Evans each scored twice as the Bills won their sixth consecutive game. The Bills outgained the 49ers 441-189 total yards, and the Bills' defense forced 4 turnovers. The Bills led 17-0 at halftime, and reserve Shane Matthews' 33-yard touchdown pass to Evans gave Buffalo a 34-0 lead with 13:26 to play. Josh

Stamer's interception on the next play set up Shaud Williams' first NFL touchdown, on a 27-yard run, for a 41-0 lead with 12:39 left. The 49ers drove inside the Bills' 47 just once, scoring on Kevan Barlow's 1-yard run with 6:19 remaining. Drew Bledsoe was 21 of 32 for 172 yards and 1 touchdown. McGahee rushed 15 times for 102 yards. Ken Dorsey was 5 of 10 for 54 yards, with 1 interception, and Cody Pickett was 4 of 10 for 55 yards, with 2 interceptions.

Buffalo	0	17	10	14	—	41
San Francisco	0	0	0	7	—	7

Buff	—	McGahee 3 run (Lindell kick)
Buff	—	FG Lindell 23
Buff	—	Evans 8 pass from Bledsoe (Lindell kick)
Buff	—	FG Lindell 31
Buff	—	McGahee 1 run (Lindell kick)
Buff	—	Evans 33 pass from Matthews (Lindell kick)
Buff	—	S. Williams 27 run (Lindell kick)
SF	—	Barlow 1 run (Peterson kick)

SEATTLE 24, ARIZONA 21—at Qwest Field, attendance 67,723. Shaun Alexander scored 3 touchdowns as the Seahawks reached the postseason in successive years for the first time since 1983-84. Seattle scored 24 consecutive points in a span of 19:54, capped by Marcus Trufant's interception that set up Alexander's 23-yard run with 14:50 to play, to take a 24-7 lead. On the next possession, Josh McCown completed a 29-yard touchdown pass to Larry Fitzgerald. Four plays later, Duane Starks intercepted Trent Dilfer's pass at the Cardinals' 46, but Neil Rackers missed a 52-yard field-goal attempt. Following a punt, Fitzgerald's second 29-yard touchdown catch of the quarter cut the deficit to 24-21 with 2:30 left. The Cardinals kicked off deep, and on third-and-6 Dilfer scrambled for a first down to allow the Seahawks to run out the clock. Dilfer, playing for the injured Matt Hasselbeck, was 10 of 26 for 128 yards, with 1 interception. Darrell Jackson had 6 receptions for 101 yards and Alexander rushed 30 times for 154 yards. McCown was 21 of 33 for 248 yards and 3 touchdowns, with 2 interceptions, and Anquan Boldin had 7 receptions for 107 yards.

Arizona	7	0	0	14	—	21
Seattle	0	10	7	7	—	24

Ariz	—	Boldin 31 pass from McCown (Rackers kick)
Sea	—	Alexander 1 run (J. Brown kick)
Sea	—	FG J. Brown 34
Sea	—	Alexander 17 run (J. Brown kick)
Sea	—	Alexander 23 run (J. Brown kick)
Ariz	—	Fitzgerald 29 pass from McCown (Rackers kick)
Ariz	—	Fitzgerald 29 pass from McCown (Rackers kick)

CAROLINA 37, TAMPA BAY 20—at Raymond James Stadium, attendance 65,075. Jake Delhomme passed for 4 touchdowns as the Panthers kept their playoff hopes alive. Karl Hankton blocked Josh Bidwell's punt with 20 seconds remaining in the half. Three plays later John Kasay kicked a 26-yard field goal for a 17-14 lead. Late in the third quarter, Tampa Bay trailed 24-14 and Brian Griese fumbled the snap. Al Wallace recovered near midfield, and Mike Seidman caught a 2-yard touchdown pass with 12:14 remaining for a 30-14 lead. The Buccaneers cut the deficit to 30-20 and had the ball with 5:06 left, but Kindal Moorehead intercepted Griese's pass at the line of scrimmage and returned it 17 yards for a touchdown. Delhomme was 19 of 24 for 214 yards and 4 touchdowns. Muhsin Muhammad had 8 receptions for 115 yards, and Nick Goings rushed 33 times for 127 yards. Griese was 30 of 41 for 321 yards and 3 touchdowns, with 2 interceptions.

Carolina	7	10	7	13	—	37
Tampa Bay	7	0	7	6	—	20

Car	—	Muhammad 15 pass from Delhomme (Kasay kick)

TB	—	Clayton 22 pass from Griese (Taylor kick)
Car	—	Muhammad 6 pass from Delhomme (Kasay kick)
Car	—	FG Kasay 26
Car	—	Colbert 4 pass from Delhomme (Kasay kick)
TB	—	Clayton 6 pass from Griese (Taylor kick)
Car	—	Seidman 2 pass from Delhomme (kick failed)
TB	—	Galloway 14 pass from Griese (pass failed)
Car	—	Moorehead 17 interception return (Kasay kick)

SUNDAY NIGHT, DECEMBER 26
MIAMI 10, CLEVELAND 7—at Pro Player Stadium, attendance 73,169. Olindo Mare kicked a 51-yard field goal with seven seconds left to give Miami seven consecutive victories for the first time this season. With the score 7-7 in the third quarter, Phil Dawson missed a 43-yard field-goal attempt. Starting from their own 28 with 1:49 left in the game, the Dolphins drove 8 plays, 40 yards, highlighted by Sammy Morris' 13-yard run, to set up Mare's winning kick. A.J. Feeley was 25 of 43 for 176 yards and 1 touchdown. Luke McCown was 9 of 16 for 161 yards and 1 touchdown, with 2 interceptions. Dennis Northcutt had 4 receptions for 114 yards.

Cleveland	7	0	0	0	—	7
Miami	7	0	0	3	—	10

Mia	—	D. Thompson 18 pass from Feeley (Mare kick)
Cle	—	Northcutt 58 pass from McCown (Dawson kick)
Mia	—	FG Mare 51

MONDAY NIGHT, DECEMBER 27
ST. LOUIS 20, PHILADELPHIA 7—at Edward Jones Dome, attendance 66,129. Steven Jackson rushed for 148 yards and 1 touchdown and the Rams' defense allowed just 155 yards to maintain an opportunity for a postseason berth. The Eagles, which had clinched the NFC's first seed, tied the game 7-7 on Donovan McNabb's 7-yard touchdown pass to Freddie Mitchell to complete their opening drive. McNabb did not play the rest of the game, and the Eagles gained just 92 yards on their final nine possessions. The Rams led 10-7 at halftime and extended the lead to 17-7 as Isaac Bruce caught a 7-yard touchdown reception with 7:38 left in the third quarter. Marc Bulger was 20 of 27 for 225 yards and 1 touchdown. Jackson rushed 24 times for 148 yards. Bryce Fisher had 1 sack and forced fumble. Marshall Faulk's streak of 158 consecutive games with a reception, the NFL's longest active streak, was snapped. McNabb was 3 for 3 for 36 yards and 1 touchdown. Koy Detmer was 1 of 6 for 5 yards and Jeff Blake was 4 of 14 for 41 yards.

Philadelphia	7	0	0	0	—	7
St. Louis	7	3	7	3	—	20

StL	—	Jackson 5 run (Wilkins kick)
Phil	—	Mitchell 7 pass from McNabb (Akers kick)
StL	—	FG Wilkins 28
StL	—	Bruce 7 pass from Bulger (Wilkins kick)
StL	—	FG Wilkins 29

SEVENTEENTH WEEK SUMMARIES
American Football Conference

East Division	W	L	T	Pct.	Pts.	OP
New England*	14	2	0	.875	437	260
N.Y. Jets#	10	6	0	.625	333	261
Buffalo	9	7	0	.563	395	284
Miami	4	12	0	.250	275	354
North Division	W	L	T	Pct.	Pts.	OP
Pittsburgh*	15	1	0	.938	372	251
Baltimore	9	7	0	.563	317	268
Cincinnati	8	8	0	.500	374	372
Cleveland	4	12	0	.250	276	390

South Division	W	L	T	Pct.	Pts.	OP
Indianapolis*	12	4	0	.750	522	351
Jacksonville	9	7	0	.563	261	280
Houston	7	9	0	.438	309	339
Tennessee	5	11	0	.313	344	439
West Division	W	L	T	Pct.	Pts.	OP
San Diego*	12	4	0	.750	466	313
Denver#	10	6	0	.625	381	304
Kansas City	7	9	0	.438	483	435
Oakland	5	11	0	.313	320	442

National Football Conference

East Division	W	L	T	Pct.	Pts.	OP
Philadelphia*	13	3	0	.813	386	260
N.Y. Giants	6	10	0	.375	303	347
Dallas	6	10	0	.375	293	405
Washington	6	10	0	.375	240	265
North Division	W	L	T	Pct.	Pts.	OP
Green Bay*	10	6	0	.625	424	380
Minnesota#	8	8	0	.500	405	395
Detroit	6	10	0	.375	296	350
Chicago	5	11	0	.313	231	331
South Division	W	L	T	Pct.	Pts.	OP
Atlanta*	11	5	0	.688	340	337
New Orleans	8	8	0	.500	348	405
Carolina	7	9	0	.438	355	339
Tampa Bay	5	11	0	.313	301	304
West Division	W	L	T	Pct.	Pts.	OP
Seattle*	9	7	0	.563	371	373
St. Louis#	8	8	0	.500	319	392
Arizona	6	10	0	.375	284	322
San Francisco	2	14	0	.125	259	452

Clinched division title
#Clinched playoff berth

SUNDAY, JANUARY 2
ARIZONA 12, TAMPA BAY 7—at Sun Devil Stadium, attendance 31,650. Neil Rackers kicked 4 field goals and the Cardinals' defense forced 4 turnovers and had 4 sacks to defeat the Buccaneers. Tampa Bay trailed 3-0 and drove to the Cardinals' 24 when Darnell Dockett intercepted Chris Simms' pass with 43 seconds left in the half. Rackers kicked a 45-yard field goal just before halftime for a 6-0 lead. In the third quarter, Michael Clayton took a short pass and ran across field for a 75-yard touchdown and 7-6 lead. But the Cardinals answered with a field goal, and the Buccaneers' failed to cross midfield in the fourth quarter. Josh McCown was 16 of 36 for 115 yards, with 1 interception. Simms was 16 of 32 for 224 yard and 1 touchdown, with 2 interceptions.

Tampa Bay	0	0	7	0	—	7
Arizona	3	3	0	6	—	12

Ariz	—	FG Rackers 40
Ariz	—	FG Rackers 45
TB	—	Clayton 75 pass from Simms (Taylor kick)
Ariz	—	FG Rackers 39
Ariz	—	FG Rackers 31

BALTIMORE 30, MIAMI 23—at M&T Bank Stadium, attendance 77,289. Jamal Lewis rushed for 167 yards and 1 touchdown as the Ravens kept themselves in the playoff hunt. However, the Ravens were eliminated from a wild-card berth later in the afternoon when the Jaguars defeated the Raiders. Making his first NFL start, Sage Rosenfels completed a 76-yard touchdown pass to Chris Chambers on the first play from scrimmage. The Ravens responded by scoring the next 27 points, with Jarret Johnson's 6-yard interception return for a touchdown and Ed Reed's 41-yard interception return to the Dolphins' 2 setting up Lewis' touchdown for a 27-7 lead with 11:24 left in the third quarter. Wes Welker returned the ensuing kickoff 95 yards for a touchdown, and after a punt Sammy Morris raced 35 yards for a touchdown to pull within 27-21 with 5:10 remaining in the third quarter. The Ravens answered with Matt Stover's third field goal. The Dolphins drove to the Ravens' 1, and on third-and-goal Anthony Weaver intercepted Rosenfels' pass. On the next play, David Bowens forced Lewis to fumble and Kyle Boller fell on the ball in the end zone for a safety with 10:13 to

play. The Dolphins drove to the Ravens' 28 with 4:09 left, but Terrell Suggs sacked Rosenfels for a 14-yard loss on third-and-2, forcing a punt. The Dolphins failed to cross midfield with their final possession. Boller was 14 of 27 for 142 yards and 1 touchdown. Lewis rushed 34 times for 167 yards. Rosenfels was 16 of 38 for 264 yards and 1 touchdown, with 3 interceptions. Chambers had 4 receptions for 146 yards.

Miami	7	0	14	2	—	23
Baltimore	7	13	10	0	—	30

Mia	—	Chambers 76 pass from Rosenfels (Mare kick)
Balt	—	Jones 1 pass from Boller (Stover kick)
Balt	—	FG Stover 25
Balt	—	J. Johnson 6 interception return (Stover kick)
Balt	—	FG Stover 19
Balt	—	J. Lewis 2 run (Stover kick)
Mia	—	Welker 95 kickoff return (Mare kick)
Mia	—	Morris 35 run (Mare kick)
Balt	—	FG Stover 33
Mia	—	Safety, B. Robinson tackled Boller in end zone

PITTSBURGH 29, BUFFALO 24—at Ralph Wilson Stadium, attendance 73,414. Jeff Reed kicked 5 field goals and James Harrison returned a fumble for a touchdown as the Steelers finished the season with fourteen consecutive victories. With home-field advantage secured, the Steelers did not play most of their starters. Larry Foote recovered a fumble to set up Reed's first field goal, and Foote intercepted a pass that led to Tommy Maddox's 16-yard touchdown pass to Antwaan Randle El for a 10-7 lead. Nate Clements' 30-yard interception return early in the third quarter gave Buffalo a 17-16 lead. The Bills then forced a punt and drove to the Steelers' 11, but Rian Lindell's 28-yard field-goal attempt sailed wide right. Willie Parker ran 58 yards on the next play to set up Reed's fourth field goal, and three plays later Ricardo Colclough sacked Drew Bledsoe and forced him to fumble. Harrison caught the ball in midair and ran 18 yards for a touchdown and 26-17 lead with 13:24 to play. The Steelers forced a punt and ran 8:53 off the clock for Reed's fifth field goal with 2:23 remaining. Willis McGahee scored with 1:18 to play, but Ike Taylor recovered the onside kick. Maddox, starting for the first time since week 2 in place of the injured Ben Roethlisberger, was 12 of 24 for 120 yards and 1 touchdown, with 2 interceptions. Parker rushed 19 times for 102 yards. Bledsoe was 16 of 30 for 189 yards, with 1 interception.

Pittsburgh	10	6	0	13	—	29
Buffalo	7	3	7	7	—	24

Pitt	—	FG Reed 22
Buff	—	McGahee 3 run (Lindell kick)
Pitt	—	Randle El 16 pass from Maddox (Reed kick)
Pitt	—	FG Reed 21
Pitt	—	FG Reed 31
Buff	—	FG Lindell 37
Buff	—	Clements 30 interception return (Lindell kick)
Pitt	—	FG Reed 37
Pitt	—	Harrison 18 fumble return (Reed kick)
Pitt	—	FG Reed 33
Buff	—	McGahee 1 run (Lindell kick)

NEW ORLEANS 21, CAROLINA 18—at Bank of America Stadium, attendance 73,302. Deuce McAllister rushed for 140 yards and 1 touchdown as the Saints won their fourth consecutive game and eliminated the Panthers' postseason chances. The Saints' wild-card hopes were dashed 15 minutes after the game's conclusion when the Rams defeated the Jets. McAllister's 71-yard run set up Aaron Stecker's 7-yard touchdown run late in the first quarter. The Panthers drove to the Saints' 12, but on third down Charles Grant forced Jake Delhomme to fumble. Will Smith recovered, and the Saints drove 83 yards, capped by McAllister's 1-yard run. Delhomme's 9-yard touchdown pass to Muhsin Muhammad pulled the Panthers within 14-10, but Aaron Brooks answered three plays later with a 44-yard touchdown pass to Joe Horn for a 21-10 lead with 3:10 left in the third quarter. Smith forced Delhomme to fumble in the middle of the fourth quarter, and Darren Howard recovered the ball at the Panthers' 28. The Panthers stopped the Saints, John Carney missed a 38-yard field goal, and Carolina drove 72 yards for Muhammad's second touchdown catch to cut the deficit to 21-18 with 5:08 remaining. The Panthers final possession began at their own 2 with 50 seconds left. A 20-yard pass to Muhammad put the ball at the Panthers' 42, and a fake spike and quick pass to Muhammad netted 16 yards to the Saints' 42. John Kasay attempted a 60-yard field-goal with four seconds left, and Tony Bryant blocked the kick. Brooks was 14 of 24 for 216 yards and 1 touchdown. McAllister rushed 28 times for 140 yards. Delhomme was 24 of 50 for 307 yards and 2 touchdowns.

New Orleans	7	7	7	0	—	21
Carolina	3	0	7	8	—	18

Car	—	FG Kasay 54
NO	—	Stecker 7 run (Carney kick)
NO	—	McAllister 1 run (Carney kick)
Car	—	Muhammad 9 pass from Delhomme (Kasay kick)
NO	—	Horn 44 pass from Brooks (Carney kick)
Car	—	Muhammad 9 pass from Delhomme (Seidman pass from Delhomme)

GREEN BAY 31, CHICAGO 14—at Soldier Field, attendance 62,197. Brett Favre passed for 2 touchdowns as the Packers won at Soldier Field for the eleventh consecutive time. Favre finished the season with 31 touchdown passes, marking an NFL record eight 30-plus touchdown seasons. With the score tied 7-7, the Packers scored 21 points in a span of 7:02 of the second quarter, the middle touchdown scored by Darren Sharper on a 43-yard interception return, and capped by Craig Nall's 25-yard touchdown pass to Javon Walker with 6:14 left in the half for a 28-7 lead. Thomas Jones' second touchdown, in the middle of the third quarter, cut the deficit to 28-14, but the Packers answered with a 70-yard drive capped by Ryan Longwell's 20-yard field goal. Favre was 9 of 13 for 196 yards and 2 touchdowns, and Nall replaced him late in the second quarter and was 7 of 13 for 131 yards and 1 touchdown. Chad Hutchinson was 20 of 29 for 196 yards, with 1 interception. Jones rushed 26 times for 108 yards.

Green Bay	7	21	3	0	—	31
Chicago	7	0	7	0	—	14

Chi	—	T. Jones 2 run (Edinger kick)
GB	—	Franks 17 pass from Favre (Longwell kick)
GB	—	Henderson 38 pass from Favre (Longwell kick)
GB	—	Sharper 43 interception return (Longwell kick)
GB	—	Walker 25 pass from Nall (Longwell kick)
Chi	—	T. Jones 1 run (Edinger kick)
GB	—	FG Longwell 20

DENVER 33, INDIANAPOLIS 14—at INVESCO Field at Mile High, attendance 75,149. Jake Plummer passed for 2 touchdowns and ran for another as the Broncos reached the playoffs. The Colts had already clinched the third seed, and were outgained 453-200 yards. Trailing 7-0, the Broncos drove 75, 57, and 77 yards on their next three possessions to take a 17-7 lead. Reggie Wayne's 71-yard touchdown catch three plays later cut the deficit to 17-14, but Kelly Herndon recovered Dominic Rhodes' fumble at the Colts' 3 just before halftime. Jason Elam kicked

his second field goal to give the Broncos a 20-14 halftime lead. Plummer's 5-yard scoring run capped a 68-yard drive in the third quarter, and Charlie Adams' 39-yard punt return set up Elam's third goal. The Colts failed to cross midfield with their final three possessions. Plummer was 17 of 30 for 246 yards, and finished the season by taking every snap. Peyton Manning was 1 of 2 for 6 yards and played just the first series. Jim Sorgi was 16 of 25 for 168 yards and 2 touchdowns.

Indianapolis	7	7	0	0	—	14
Denver	7	13	10	3	—	33

Ind	—	Harrison 7 pass from Sorgi (Vanderjagt kick)
Den	—	Lelie 38 pass from Plummer (Elam kick)
Den	—	FG Elam 45
Den	—	Hape 2 pass from Plummer (Elam kick)
Ind	—	Wayne 71 pass from Sorgi (Vanderjagt kick)
Den	—	FG Elam 23
Den	—	Plummer 5 run (Elam kick)
Den	—	FG Elam 40
Den	—	FG Elam 40

CLEVELAND 22, HOUSTON 14—at Reliant Stadium, attendance 70,724. Phil Dawson kicked 5 field goals and Lee Suggs rushed for 131 yards as the Browns snapped a nine-game losing streak. Making only his second start, Kelly Holcomb guided the Browns to field goals on three of their first four possessions. Early in the third quarter, the Browns drove 11 plays, 80 yards and capped by Steve Heiden's 9-yard touchdown catch with 5:24 remaining in the third quarter. Domanick Davis scored on a 1-yard run with 1:23 left, but Andre King recovered the onside kick and the Browns ran out the clock. Holcomb was 20 of 29 for 228 yards and 1 touchdown, with 2 interceptions. Suggs rushed 26 times for 131 yards and became the first Browns player with three consecutive 100-yard rushing games since Greg Pruitt in 1978. David Carr was 15 of 25 for 114 yards and 1 touchdown. Davis rushed 17 times for 103 yards.

Cleveland	3	6	7	6	—	22
Houston	7	0	0	7	—	14

Cle	—	FG Dawson 45
Hous	—	Wells 6 pass from Carr (K. Brown kick)
Cle	—	FG Dawson 22
Cle	—	FG Dawson 29
Cle	—	Heiden 9 pass from Holcomb (Dawson kick)
Cle	—	FG Dawson 45
Cle	—	FG Dawson 22
Hous	—	D. Davis 1 run (K. Brown kick)

NEW ENGLAND 21, SAN FRANCISCO 7—at Gillette Stadium, attendance 68,756. Ken Dorsey's 4-yard touchdown pass to Steve Bush with 2:48 left in the first quarter, set up by Dwaine Carpenter's 31-yard interception return to the Patriots' 2, snapped the Patriots' NFL record 23-game streak of having scored first. The 49ers then forced a punt and drove to the Patriots' 21, but Todd Peterson's 39-yard field goal hit the right upright. The Patriots responded with an 8-play, 71-yard drive capped by Tom Brady's 1-yard toss to linebacker-turned-eligible receiver Mike Vrabel. In the third quarter, Corey Dillon's 29-yard run set up Brady's touchdown pass to Deion Branch for a 14-7 lead. Tully Banta-Cain recovered Maurice Hicks' fumble late in the third quarter to set up Dillon's 6-yard scoring run with 14:24 to play. On fourth-and-1 from the Patriots' 8 with 8:36 remaining, Kevan Barlow was stopped by Banta-Cain and Roman Phifer to thwart the 49ers' last scoring threat. Dorsey was 18 of 29 for 189 yards and 1touchdown. Barlow had 25 carries for 103 yards. Brady was 22 of 30 for 226 yards and 2 touchdowns, with 1 interception. Dillon rushed 14 times for 116 yards.

San Francisco	7	0	0	0	—	7
New England	0	7	7	7	—	21

SF	—	Bush 4 pass from Dorsey (Peterson kick) I
NE	—	Vrabel 1 pass from Brady (Vinatieri kick)
NE	—	Branch 8 pass from Brady (Vinatieri kick)
NE	—	Dillon 6 run (Vinatieri kick)

JACKSONVILLE 13, OAKLAND 6—at Network Associates Coliseum, attendance 41,112. Ernest Wilford's one-handed 46-yard catch in the rain set up the game's lone touchdown as the Jaguars finished with their best record since 1999. The Jaguars were eliminated from playoff contention when the Broncos won moments after their victory. With the score 3-3 late in the second quarter, both teams benefited from fumbles in their own territory to set up field goals to tie the game 6-6. Faced with third-and-9 in the middle of the third quarter, Byron Leftwich lofted a long pass downfield. Wilford leaped and caught the ball with one hand at the Raiders' 6. Two plays later, Greg Jones scored on a 1-yard run to take a 13-6 lead. The Raiders drove to the Jaguars' 1 late in the third quarter, and Zack Crockett scored on a 1-yard run only to have it nullified by Roland Williams' 15-yard tripping penalty. After a 10-yard pass to Alvis Whitted, Kerry Collins' fourth-and-goal pass from the 6-yard line was intercepted by Donovin Darius. The Raiders forced a punt and drove to the Jaguars' 2, but Collins fumbled on fourth-and-goal and Bobby McCray tackled him to clinch the victory. Leftwich was 15 of 28 for 149 yards, with 1 interception. Collins was 15 of 39 for 142 yards, with 3 interceptions. Crockett rushed 22 times for 134 yards.

Jacksonville	0	3	10	0	—	13
Oakland	3	3	0	0	—	6

Oak	—	FG Janikowski 35
Jax	—	FG Scobee 26
Oak	—	FG Janikowski 27
Jax	—	FG Scobee 22
Jax	—	G. Jones 1 run (Scobee kick)

CINCINNATI 38, PHILADELPHIA 10—at Lincoln Financial Field, attendance 67,074. Rudi Johnson scored 3 touchdowns and the Bengals' defense forced 5 turnovers to hand the Eagles their second consecutive loss. The Eagles had clinched home field in the NFC two weeks earlier, thus did not use Donovan McNabb, Brian Westbrook, and others. In 15 possessions, the Bengals gained more than 10 yards just 5 times, but four of those resulted in touchdowns. The Bengals led 17-3 in the third quarter when Robert Geathers intercepted Jeff Blake's pass and returned it 36 yards for a touchdown. Rodrick Hood then fumbled the kickoff return, and Marcus Wilkins recovered. Three plays later Johnson scored on a 6-yard run to give the Bengals a 31-3 lead. Jon Kitna was 16 of 27 for 160 yards and 1 touchdown. Koy Detmer was 17 of 31 for 202 yards, with 2 interceptions, and Blake was 14 of 23 for 85 yards and 1 touchdown, with 1 interception.

Cincinnati	0	17	14	7	—	38
Philadelphia	0	3	0	7	—	10

Cin	—	R. Johnson 5 run (Graham kick)
Cin	—	Houshmandzadeh 20 pass from Kitna (Graham kick)
Cin	—	FG Graham 50
Phil	—	FG Akers 46
Cin	—	Geathers 36 interception return (Graham kick)
Cin	—	R. Johnson 6 run (Graham kick)
Cin	—	R. Johnson 3 run (Graham kick)
Phil	—	Mitchell 3 pass from Blake (Akers kick)

SAN DIEGO 24, KANSAS CITY 17—at Qualcomm Stadium, attendance 64,920. Doug Flutie and Philip Rivers each passed for a score, and Flutie added a running touchdown, as the Chargers snapped the

Chiefs' four-game winning streak. Locked into the fourth seed, the Chargers did not play many of their skill players, but with Flutie at the helm San Diego outgained the Chiefs 284-169 in the first half. Terrence Kiel's interception at the Chargers' 36 with 52 seconds left in the half set up Flutie's 10-yard touchdown pass to Ryan Krause with 12 seconds left in the half for a 17-3 lead. Rivers played in the second half and tossed his first touchdown pass, 13 yards to Malcolm Floyd, for a 24-3 lead with 7:11 to play. The Chiefs responded with a 78-yard touchdown drive, capped by Larry Johnson's 2-yard run, and Scott Fujita recovered the onside kick to set up Johnson's touchdown catch with 2:10 to play. Clinton Hart recovered the ensuing onside kick, but the Chiefs forced a punt. From his own 30 with time winding down, Drayton Florence intercepted Trent Green's pass to clinch the victory. Flutie was 13 of 22 for 199 yards and 1 touchdown, and Rivers was 5 of 8 for 33 yards and 1 touchdown. Green was 33 of 53 for 373 yards and 1 touchdown, with 4 interceptions for the Chiefs.

| Kansas City | 0 | 3 | 0 | 14 | — | 17 |
| San Diego | 3 | 14 | 0 | 7 | — | 24 |

SD	—	FG Kaeding 34
KC	—	FG Tynes 50
SD	—	Flutie 1 run (Kaeding kick)
SD	—	Krause 10 pass from Flutie (Kaeding kick)
SD	—	Floyd 13 pass from Rivers (Kaeding kick)
KC	—	L. Johnson 2 run (Tynes kick)
KC	—	L. Johnson 14 pass from Green (Tynes kick)

ST. LOUIS 32, N.Y. JETS 29 (OT)—at Edward Jones Dome, attendance 65,877. Jeff Wilkins kicked a 31-yard field goal in overtime to put the Rams into the playoffs for the fifth time in six seasons. The Jets earned a postseason berth when the Bills lost to Pittsburgh just prior to the Jets' game-tying field goal at the end of regulation. The Rams outgained the Jets 479-324, but committed 3 turnovers and allowed Jerricho Cotchery to return a kickoff 94 yards for a touchdown to trim an 11-point deficit to 21-17 early in the third quarter. Jonathan Vilma's 38-yard interception return for a touchdown with 1:12 left in the third quarter gave the Jets a 26-21 lead. Marc Bulger's 19-yard touchdown pass to Torry Holt, and Steven Jackson's 2-point conversion run gave the Rams a 29-26 lead with 5:06 left. The Jets drove to the Rams' 9 in the final minute, and Adam Archuleta dropped a potential interception on third-and-goal, and the Jets settled for Doug Brien's tying field goal with three seconds left. The Rams won the coin toss, and after three punts, the Jets drove to the Rams' 35, but Brien's 53-yard field-goal attempt sailed wide right. The Rams needed just six plays, highlighted by Jackson's 22-yard catch, to set up Wilkins' game-winning kick 3:02 left. Chad Pennington was 21 of 36 for 181 yards and 1 touchdown. Curtis Martin rushed 28 times for 153 yards to earn his first NFL rushing title. Bulger was 29 of 39 for 450 yards and 3 touchdowns, with 2 interceptions. Holt had 7 receptions for 116 yards.

| N.Y. Jets | 3 | 7 | 16 | 3 | 0 | — | 29 |
| St. Louis | 0 | 14 | 7 | 8 | 3 | — | 32 |

NYJ	—	FG Brien 47
StL	—	Bruce 27 pass from Bulger (Wilkins kick)
NYJ	—	Baker 8 pass from Pennington (Brien kick)
StL	—	Holt 44 pass from Bulger (Wilkins kick)
StL	—	Jackson 20 run (Wilkins kick)
NYJ	—	Cotchery 94 kickoff return (Brien kick)
NYJ	—	FG Brien 33
NYJ	—	Vilma 38 interception return (pass failed)
StL	—	Holt 19 pass from Bulger (Jackson run)

| NYJ | — | FG Brien 27 |
| StL | — | FG Wilkins 31 |

SEATTLE 28, ATLANTA 26—at Qwest Field, attendance 66,740. Isaiah Kacyvenski tackled Warrick Dunn just shy of the goal line to deny the Falcons' 2-point conversion attempt with no time remaining to give the Seahawks their third division title in franchise history. The Falcons, who had clinched the second seed after week 15, took out Michael Vick in the second quarter with a 17-14 lead. Marcus Trufant intercepted Matt Schaub's pass early in the third quarter to set up Matt Hasselbeck's 3-yard touchdown pass to Jerramy Stevens for a 21-17 Seattle lead. Jay Feely missed a 39-yard field goal in the third quarter, but converted from 40 yard with 10:12 to play to pull within 21-20. The Seahawks answered with a 60-yard drive, capped by Hasselbeck's 1-yard sneak with 4:28 to play, for a 28-20 lead. The Falcons responded with a 15-play, 69-yard drive, which featured 2 third-down conversions, a 9-yard completion to Fred McCrary on fourth-and-1, and capped by Brian Finneran's 3-yard touchdown catch in the back of the end zone as time expired. On the 2-point conversion, Dunn took a misdirection handoff and tried to cut up the middle but Kacyvenski stopped Dunn before receiving help from a host of defenders. Hasselbeck was 21 of 27 for 191 yards and 2 touchdowns, with 1 interception. Vick was 6 of 7 for 35 yards and 1 touchdown. Schaub was 14 of 22 for 132 yards and 1 touchdown, with 1 interception. Dunn rushed 25 times for 132 yards.

| Atlanta | 7 | 10 | 0 | 9 | — | 26 |
| Seattle | 7 | 7 | 7 | 7 | — | 28 |

Atl	—	Price 2 pass from Vick (Feely kick)
Sea	—	Alexander 1 run (J. Brown kick)
Atl	—	FG Feely 33
Atl	—	Hall 48 interception return (Feely kick)
Sea	—	Jackson 3 pass from Hasselbeck (J. Brown kick)
Sea	—	Stevens 3 pass from Hasselbeck (J. Brown kick)
Atl	—	FG Feely 40
Sea	—	Hasselbeck 1 run (J. Brown kick)
Atl	—	Finnernan 3 pass from Schaub (run failed)

TENNESSEE 24, DETROIT 19—at The Coliseum, attendance 68,809. Antowain Smith rushed for 89 yards and 1 touchdown as the Titans snapped a five-game losing streak. The Titans answered Jason Hanson's third-quarter field goal with an 80-yard drive, highlighted by Smith's 43-yard run, and capped by his 2-yard plunge with 1:00 left in the third quarter for a 21-13 lead. Trailing 24-13, Shaun Rogers blocked Gary Anderson's 27-yard field-goal attempt with 7:45 to play, and the Lions responded with an 82-yard drive culminated with Roy Williams' 17-yard touchdown catch with 4:06 remaining. Joey Harrington's 2-point conversion pass to Williams was incomplete, with the score remaining 24-19. The Lions forced a punt and drove to the Titans' 16, but Harrington threw 3 consecutive incompletions, the fourth-down pass knocked down by Donnie Nickey, to turn the ball over on downs. Billy Volek was 16 of 28 for 175 yards and 1 touchdown. Harrington was 33 of 49 for 346 yards and 2 touchdowns, with 1 interception.

| Detroit | 3 | 7 | 3 | 6 | — | 19 |
| Tennessee | 7 | 7 | 3 | 7 | — | 24 |

Tenn	—	Bulluck 39 fumble return (Anderson kick)
Det	—	FG Hanson 26
Det	—	Schlesinger 21 pass from Harrington (Hanson kick)
Tenn	—	Bennett 32 pass from Volek (Anderson kick)
Det	—	FG Hanson 26
Tenn	—	A. Smith 2 run (Anderson kick)

| Tenn | — | FG Anderson 40 |
| Det | — | R. Williams 17 pass from Harrington (pass failed) |

WASHINGTON 21, MINNESOTA 18—at FedExField, attendance 76,876. Patrick Ramsey passed for 2 touchdowns and Ladell Betts rushed for 118 yards and a score for the Redskins. The Vikings moved into the playoffs when the Panthers lost to the Saints moments after their game had concluded. Antonio Brown's 66-yard kickoff return to begin the game set up Chris Cooley's touchdown catch for a quick 7-0 lead. An 11-play, 64-yard drive in the second quarter led to Ramsey's second touchdown, a 4-yard catch by Robert Royal, to take a 14-3 lead. Leading 14-10, Taylor Jacobs caught a 45-yard pass to the Vikings' 1 to set up Betts' 1-yard run with 10:41 to play. Marcus Robinson caught a 38-yard long pass with two seconds left, but Mike Sellers recovered the ensuing onside kick. Ramsey was 17 of 26 for 216 yards and 2 touchdowns, with 1 interception. Daunte Culpepper was 27 of 44 for 299 yards and 2 touchdowns.

| Minnesota | 0 | 3 | 7 | 8 | — | 18 |
| Washington | 7 | 7 | 0 | 7 | — | 21 |

Wash	—	Cooley 6 pass from Ramsey (Chandler kick)
Minn	—	FG Andersen 23
Wash	—	Royal 4 pass from Ramsey (Chandler kick)
Minn	—	Moss 26 pass from Culpepper (Andersen kick)
Wash	—	Betts 1 run (Chandler kick)
Minn	—	Robinson 38 pass from Culpepper (O. Smith pass from Culpepper)

SUNDAY NIGHT, JANUARY 2
N.Y. GIANTS 28, DALLAS 24—at Giants Stadium, attendance 78,500. Tiki Barber scored the game-winning touchdown with 11 seconds left as the Giants snapped an eight-game losing streak. The Cowboys drove inside the Giants' 30 on five consecutive possessions, but settled for 3 field goals and were intercepted to lead just 16-7 with 45 seconds left in the third quarter. A 43-yard pass interference penalty set up Eli Manning's 15-yard touchdown pass to David Tyree with 14:55 to play. Osi Umenyiora sacked Vinny Testaverde on the next play from scrimmage and forced a fumble. Reggie Torbor recovered the ball at the Cowboys' 20, and Barber caught a 3-yard touchdown pass six plays later for a 21-16 lead with 11:51 remaining. After an exchange of punts, Julius Jones capped an 80-yard drive by scoring on fourth-and-goal from the Giants' 1 with 1:49 to play. Jason Witten's 2-point conversion catch staked the Cowboys to a 24-21 lead, but Barber caught a 23-yard pass to get the Cowboys' in field-goal range. On first-and-goal from the Cowboys' 3 with 16 seconds and no timeouts, Manning handed the ball to Barber, who went up the middle for the touchdown. Manning was 18 of 27 for 144 yards and 3 touchdowns, with 1 interception. Testaverde was 23 of 30 for 231 yards and 1 touchdown. Jones rushed 29 times for 149 yards.

| Dallas | 3 | 6 | 7 | 8 | — | 24 |
| N.Y. Giants | 0 | 7 | 0 | 21 | — | 28 |

Dall	—	FG Cundiff 40
NYG	—	Shiancoe 2 pass from Manning (Christie kick)
Dall	—	FG Cundiff 24
Dall	—	FG Cundiff 45
Dall	—	Witten 7 pass from Testaverde (Cundiff kick)
NYG	—	Tyree 15 pass from Manning (Christie kick)
NYG	—	Barber 3 pass from Manning (Christie kick)
Dall	—	J. Jones 1 run (Witten pass from Testaverde)
NYG	—	Barber 3 run (Christie kick)

2004 PRO FOOTBALL AWARDS

ASSOCIATED PRESS

Most Valuable Player	Peyton Manning
Offensive Player of the Year	Peyton Manning
Defensive Player of the Year	Ed Reed
Offensive Rookie of the Year	Ben Roethlisberger
Defensive Rookie of the Year	Jonathan Vilma
Coach of the Year	Marty Schottenheimer
Comeback Player of the Year	Drew Brees

THE SPORTING NEWS

Player of the Year	Peyton Manning
Rookie of the Year	Ben Roethlisberger
Coach of the Year	Bill Cowher

PRO FOOTBALL WEEKLY/PFWA

Executive of the Year	A.J. Smith
Most Valuable Player	Peyton Manning
Defensive Most Valuable Player	Ed Reed
Offensive Rookie of the Year	Ben Roethlisberger
Defensive Rookie of the Year	Dunta Robinson
Coach of the Year	Marty Schottenheimer
Assistant Coach of the Year	Dick LeBeau
Golden Toe	Adam Vinatieri
Comeback Player of the Year	Willis McGahee
Most Improved Player of the Year	Drew Brees

FOOTBALL DIGEST

Offensive Player of the Year	Peyton Manning
Defensive Player of the Year	Ed Reed
Offensive Rookie of the Year	Ben Roethlisberger
Defensive Rookie of the Year	Jonathan Vilma
Coach of the Year	Bill Cowher

SPORTS ILLUSTRATED

Player of the Year	Peyton Manning
Rookie of the Year	Ben Roethlisberger
Coach of the Year	Bill Belichick

MAXWELL CLUB PLAYER OF THE YEAR

(Bert Bell Trophy)	Peyton Manning

MAXWELL CLUB COACH OF THE YEAR

(Earle "Greasy" Neale Trophy)	Marty Schottenheimer

PEPSI ROOKIE OF THE YEAR

Rookie of the Year	Ben Roethlisberger

WALTER PAYTON/ NFL MAN OF THE YEAR

Man of the Year	Warrick Dunn

SUPER BOWL MOST VALUABLE PLAYER

Pete Rozelle Trophy	Deion Branch

AFC-NFC PRO BOWL PLAYER OF THE GAME

Dan McGuire Award	Peyton Manning

2004 ALL-PRO TEAMS

2004 PFW/PFWA ALL-PRO TEAM

Selected by *Pro Football Weekly* and the Professional Football Writers of America

Offense:

Peyton Manning, Indianapolis	Quarterback
Shaun Alexander, Seattle	Running Back
Curtis Martin, New York Jets	Running Back
Terrell Owens, Philadelphia	Wide Receiver
Muhsin Muhammad, Carolina	Wide Receiver
Antonio Gates, San Diego	Tight End
Walter Jones, Seattle	Tackle
Willie Roaf, Kansas City	Tackle
Alan Faneca, Pittsburgh	Guard
Brian Waters, Kansas City	Guard
Kevin Mawae, New York Jets	Center

Defense:

Dwight Freeney, Indianapolis	End
Julius Peppers, Carolina	End
Richard Seymour, New England	Tackle
Kevin Williams, Minnesota	Tackle
Derrick Brooks, Tampa Bay	Outside Linebacker
Takeo Spikes, Buffalo	Outside Linebacker
James Farrior, Pittsburgh	Inside Linebacker
Champ Bailey, Denver	Cornerback
Lito Sheppard, Philadelphia	Cornerback
Brian Dawkins, Philadelphia	Safety
Ed Reed, Baltimore	Safety

Special Teams:

Adam Vinatieri, New England	Kicker
Shane Lechler, Oakland	Punter
Terrence McGee, Buffalo	Kick Returner
Eddie Drummond, Detroit	Punt Returner
Larry Izzo, New England	Special Teams Player

2004 ASSOCIATED PRESS ALL-PRO TEAM

Selected by the *Associated Press*

Offense:

Peyton Manning, Indianapolis	Quarterback
Curtis Martin, New York Jets	Running Back
LaDainian Tomlinson, San Diego	Running Back
William Henderson, Green Bay	Fullback
Terrell Owens, Philadelphia	Wide Receiver
Muhsin Muhammad, Carolina	Wide Receiver
Antonio Gates, San Diego	Tight End
Willie Anderson, Cincinnati	Tackle
Walter Jones, Seattle	Tackle
Willie Roaf, Kansas City	Tackle
Alan Faneca, Pittsburgh	Guard
Brian Waters, Kansas City	Guard
Jeff Hartings, Pittsburgh	Center

Defense:

Dwight Freeney, Indianapolis	End
Julius Peppers, Carolina	End
Richard Seymour, New England	Tackle
Kevin Williams, Minnesota	Tackle
Derrick Brooks, Tampa Bay	Linebacker
James Farrior, Pittsburgh	Linebacker
Ray Lewis, Baltimore	Linebacker
Takeo Spikes, Buffalo	Linebacker
Ronde Barber, Tampa Bay	Cornerback
Champ Bailey, Denver	Cornerback
Lito Sheppard, Philadelphia	Cornerback
Brian Dawkins, Philadelphia	Safety
Ed Reed, Baltimore	Safety

Specialists:

Adam Vinatieri, New England	Kicker
Eddie Drummond, Detroit	Kick Returner
Shane Lechler, Oakland	Punter

2004 ALL-NFL TEAM

Selected by the *Associated Press, Pro Football Weekly,* and the Professional Football Writers of America

Offense:

Peyton Manning, Indianapolis (AP, PFW)	Quarterback
Curtis Martin, New York Jets (AP, PFW)	Running Back
LaDainian Tomlinson, San Diego (AP)	Running Back
Shaun Alexander, Seattle (PFW)	Running Back
William Henderson, Green Bay (AP)	Fullback
Terrell Owens, Philadelphia (AP, PFW)	Wide Receiver
Muhsin Muhammad, Carolina (AP, PFW)	Wide Receiver
Antonio Gates, San Diego (AP, PFW)	Tight End
Willie Anderson, Cincinnati (AP)	Tackle
Walter Jones, Seattle (AP, PFW)	Tackle
Willie Roaf, Kansas City (AP, PFW)	Tackle
Alan Faneca, Pittsburgh (AP, PFW)	Guard
Brian Waters, Kansas City (AP, PFW)	Guard
Jeff Hartings, Pittsburgh (AP)	Center
Kevin Mawae, New York Jets (PFW)	Center

Defense:

Dwight Freeney, Indianapolis (AP, PFW)	End
Julius Peppers, Carolina (AP, PFW)	End
Richard Seymour, New England (AP, PFW)	Tackle
Kevin Williams, Minnesota (AP, PFW)	Tackle
Derrick Brooks, Tampa Bay (AP, PFW)	Linebacker
James Farrior, Pittsburgh (AP, PFW)	Linebacker
Ray Lewis, Baltimore (AP)	Linebacker
Takeo Spikes, Buffalo (AP, PFW)	Linebacker
Ronde Barber, Tampa Bay (AP)	Cornerback
Champ Bailey, Denver (AP, PFW)	Cornerback
Lito Sheppard, Philadelphia (AP, PFW)	Cornerback
Brian Dawkins, Philadelphia (AP, PFW)	Safety
Ed Reed, Baltimore (AP, PFW)	Safety

Special Teams:

Adam Vinatieri, New England (AP, PFW)	Kicker
Shane Lechler, Oakland (AP, PFW)	Punter
Terrence McGee, Buffalo (PFW)	Kick Returner
Eddie Drummond, Detroit (AP, PFW)	Punt Returner
Larry Izzo, New England (PFW)	Special Teams Player

2004 PFW/PFWA ALL-ROOKIE TEAM

Selected by *Pro Football Weekly* and the Professional Football Writers of America

Offense:

Ben Roethlisberger, Pittsburgh	Quarterback
Kevin Jones, Detroit	Running Back
Julius Jones, Dallas	Running Back
Michael Clayton, Tampa Bay	Wide Receiver
Roy Williams, Detroit	Wide Receiver
Chris Cooley, Washington	Tight End
Robert Gallery, Oakland	Tackle
Shane Olivea, San Diego	Tackle
Chris Snee, New York Giants	Guard
Jacob Bell, Tennessee	Guard
Alex Stepanovich, Arizona	Center

Defense:

Jared Allen, Kansas City	End
Will Smith, New Orleans	End
Darnell Dockett, Arizona	Tackle
Tommie Harris, Chicago	Tackle
D.J. Williams, Denver	Outside Linebacker
Karlos Dansby, Arizona	Outside Linebacker
Jonathan Vilma, New York Jets	Inside Linebacker
Dunta Robinson, Houston	Cornerback
Chris Gamble, Carolina	Cornerback
Michael Boulware, Seattle	Safety
Sean Taylor, Washington	Safety

Special Teams:

Nate Kaeding, San Diego	Kicker
Kyle Larson, Cincinnati	Punter
Wes Welker, Miami	Kick Returner
B.J. Sams, Baltimore	Punt Returner
Keith Lewis, San Francisco	Special Teams Player

2004 AFC PLAYERS OF THE WEEK

	Offense		Defense		Special Teams	
Week 1	RB	Curtis Martin, New York Jets	DE	Kenard Lang, Cleveland	P-K	Micah Knorr, Denver
Week 2	RB	Edgerrin James, Indianapolis	S	Rodney Harrison, New England	P	Shane Lechler, Oakland
Week 3	QB	Peyton Manning, Indianapolis	CB	Rashean Mathis, Jacksonville	K	Kris Brown, Houston
Week 4	RB	Priest Holmes, Kansas City	LB	Tedy Bruschi, New England	K	Jason Elam, Denver
Week 5	RB	Chris Brown, Tennessee	DE	John Abraham, New York Jets	KR-PR-K	Wes Welker, Miami
Week 6	QB	Ben Roethlisberger, Pittsburgh	LB	James Farrior, Pittsburgh	P	Brian Moorman, Buffalo
Week 7	G	Brian Waters, Kansas City	CB	Deion Sanders, Baltimore	K	Josh Scobee, Jacksonville
Week 8	QB	Drew Brees, San Diego	LB	Joey Porter, Pittsburgh	KR-CB	Terrence McGee, Buffalo
Week 9	RB	Jerome Bettis, Pittsburgh	S	Ed Reed, Baltimore	K	Adam Vinatieri, New England
Week 10	QB	Peyton Manning, Indianapolis	S	Troy Polamalu, Pittsburgh	QB-P	Kordell Stewart, Baltimore
Week 11	RB	Edgerrin James, Indianapolis	S	Lawyer Milloy, Buffalo	P	Chris Gardocki, Pittsburgh
Week 12	QB	Peyton Manning, Indianapolis	DE	Jason Taylor, Miami	T	Langston Walker, Oakland
Week 13	QB	Carson Palmer, Cincinnati	CB	Drayton Florence, San Diego	KR-CB	Terrence McGee, Buffalo
Week 14	QB	Kyle Boller, Baltimore	LB	Donnie Edwards, San Diego	P	Chris Gardocki, Pittsburgh
Week 15	RB	Fred Taylor, Jacksonville	LB	Eric Barton, New York Jets	KR-PR	Dante Hall, Kansas City
Week 16	QB	Peyton Manning, Indianapolis	LB	D.J. Williams, Denver	KR-PR	Dante Hall, Kansas City
Week 17	QB	Jake Plummer, Denver	LB	Tedy Bruschi, New England	K	Jeff Reed, Pittsburgh

2004 AFC PLAYERS OF THE MONTH

	Offense		Defense		Special Teams	
September	WR	Hines Ward, Pittsburgh	S	Eugene Wilson, New England	KR	Reuben Droughns, Denver
October	RB	Priest Holmes, Kansas City	DE	John Abraham, N.Y. Jets	KR-PR	B.J. Sams, Baltimore
November	QB	Peyton Manning, Indianapolis	S	Ed Reed, Baltimore	K	Adam Vinatieri, New England
December	RB	Corey Dillon, New England	DE	Dwight Freeney, Indianapolis	K	Jeff Reed, Pittsburgh

2004 NFC PLAYERS OF THE WEEK

	Offense		Defense		Special Teams	
Week 1	QB	Daunte Culpepper, Minnesota	LB	Nick Barnett, Green Bay	S	Bracy Walker, Detroit
Week 2	QB	Michael Vick, Atlanta	LB	Brian Urlacher, Chicago	P	Tom Rouen, Seattle
Week 3	QB	Daunte Culpepper, Minnesota	CB	Ken Lucas, Seattle	K	John Carney, New Orleans
Week 4	RB	Tiki Barber, N.Y. Giants	S	Adrian Wilson, Arizona	K	David Akers, Philadelphia
Week 5	QB	Tim Rattay, San Francisco	DE	James Hall, Detroit	K	Steve Christie, N.Y. Giants
Week 6	QB	Daunte Culpepper, Minnesota	CB	Lito Sheppard, Philadelphia	P	Sean Landeta. St. Louis
Week 7	RB	Ahman Green, Green Bay	DT	Shaun Rogers, Detroit	K	Neil Rackers, Arizona
Week 8	QB	Michael Vick, Atlanta	LB	Brian Urlacher, Chicago	WR	David Tyree, N.Y. Giants
Week 9	RB	Michael Pittman, Tampa Bay	DE	Alex Brown, Chicago	WR	James Thrash, Washington
Week 10	QB	Brett Favre, Green Bay	DE	Bertrand Berry, Arizona	PR	Eddie Drummond, Detroit
Week 11	RB	Nick Goings, Carolina	S	Michael Boulware, Seattle	K	Ryan Longwell, Green Bay
Week 12	TE	Alge Crumpler, Atlanta	DT	Kevin Williams, Minnesota	DE	Jevon Kearse, Philadelphia
Week 13	QB	Donovan McNabb, Philadelphia	LB	Derrick Brooks, Tampa Bay	K	John Kasay, Carolina
Week 14	WR	Darrell Jackson, Seattle	LB	Dan Morgan, Carolina	P	Mitch Berger, New Orleans
Week 15	QB	Daunte Culpepper, Minnesota	CB	Sheldon Brown, Philadelphia	KR	Aaron Stecker, New Orleans
Week 16	QB	Shaun Alexander, Seattle	DE	Bryce Fisher, St. Louis	KR	Michael Lewis, New Orleans
Week 17	QB	Marc Bulger, St. Louis	DE	Kabeer Gbaja-Biamila, Green Bay	DE	Tony Bryant, New Orleans

2004 NFC PLAYERS OF THE MONTH

	Offense		Defense		Special Teams	
September	QB	Donovan McNabb, Philadelphia	DE	Patrick Kerney, Atlanta	KR	Eddie Drummond, Detroit
October	QB	Daunte Culpepper, Minnesota	CB	Lito Sheppard, Philadelphia	K	Ryan Longwell, Green Bay
November	QB	Brett Favre, Green Bay	DE	Julius Peppers, Carolina	KR	Eddie Drummond, Detroit
December	QB	Matt Hasselbeck, Seattle	DE	Bryce Fisher, St. Louis	K	Ryan Longwell, Green Bay

2004 NFL PLAYOFF PLAYERS OF THE WEEK

	Offense		Defense		Special Teams	
Wild Card	WR	Reggie Wayne, Indianapolis	CB	Antoine Winfield, Minnesota	K	Doug Brien, N.Y. Jets
Divisional	QB	Donovan McNabb, Philadelphia	LB	Tedy Bruschi, New England	PR	Allen Rossum, Atlanta
Championship	WR	Deion Branch, New England	DE	Derrick Burgess, Philadelphia	K	Adam Vinatieri, New England

2004 NFL ROOKIES OF THE MONTH

	Offense (College)		Defense (College)	
September	WR	Roy Williams, Detroit (Texas)	S	Erik Coleman, N.Y. Jets (Washington State)
October	QB	Ben Roethlisberger, Pittsburgh (Miami, OH)	S	Gibril Wilson, N.Y. Giants (Tennessee)
November	RB	Julius Jones, Dallas (Notre Dame)	LB	Jonathan Vilma, N.Y. Jets (Miami)
December	RB	Kevin Jones, Detroit (Virginia Tech)	DE	D.J. Williams, Denver (Miami)

TEN BEST RUSHING PERFORMANCES, 2004

	Att.	Yards	TD
1. Edgerrin James	23	204	1
Indianapolis vs. Chicago, Nov. 21			
2. Rudi Johnson	26	202	2
Cincinnati vs. Cleveland, Nov. 28			
3. Julius Jones	30	198	3
Dallas vs. Seattle, Dec. 6			
4. Kevin Jones	26	196	1
Detroit vs. Arizona, Dec. 5			
Curtis Martin	29	196	1
New York Jets vs. Cincinnati, Sept. 12			
6. Shaun Alexander	32	195	1
Seattle vs. Carolina, Oct. 31			
7. Reuben Droughns	30	193	0
Denver vs. Carolina, Oct. 10			
8. Derrick Blaylock	33	186	1
Kansas City vs. Atlanta, Nov. 14			
Jamal Lewis	18	186	1
Baltimore vs. Cincinnati, Sept. 26			
10. Tiki Barber	23	182	1
New York Giants vs. Green Bay, Oct. 3			

100-YARD RUSHING PERFORMANCES, 2004

First Week

Curtis Martin, New York Jets	196 yards vs. Cincinnati
Quentin Griffin, Denver	156 yards vs. Kansas City
Priest Holmes, Kansas City	151 yards vs. Denver
Clinton Portis, Washington	148 yards vs. Tampa Bay
Edgerrin James, Indianapolis	142 yards vs. New England
Shaun Alexander, Seattle	135 yards vs. New Orleans
Marshall Faulk, St. Louis	128 yards vs. Arizona
Tiki Barber, New York Giants	125 yards vs. Philadelphia
LaDainian Tomlinson, San Diego	121 yards vs. Houston
Ahman Green, Green Bay	119 yards vs. Carolina
Brian Westbrook, Philadelphia	119 yards vs. New York Giants
Chris Brown, Tennessee	100 yards vs. Miami

Second Week

DeShaun Foster, Carolina	174 yards vs. Kansas City
Corey Dillon, New England	158 yards vs. Arizona
Chris Brown, Tennessee	152 yards vs. Indianapolis
Thomas Jones, Chicago	152 yards vs. Green Bay
Ahman Green, Green Bay	128 yards vs. Chicago
Edgerrin James, Indianapolis	124 yards vs. Tennessee
Curtis Martin, New York Jets	119 yards vs. San Diego
Kevan Barlow, San Francisco	114 yards vs. New Orleans
Michael Vick, Atlanta	109 yards vs. St. Louis

Third Week

Jamal Lewis, Baltimore	186 yards vs. Cincinnati
Priest Holmes, Kansas City	134 yards vs. Houston
Warrick Dunn, Atlanta	117 yards vs. Arizona
Thomas Jones, Chicago	110 yards vs. Minnesota
Tiki Barber, New York Giants	106 yards vs. Cleveland
Aaron Stecker, New Orleans	106 yards vs. St. Louis
Tyrone Wheatley, Oakland	102 yards vs. Tampa Bay
Chris Brown, Tennessee	101 yards vs. Jacksonville
Duce Staley, Pittsburgh	101 yards vs. Miami

Fourth Week

Tiki Barber, New York Giants	182 yards vs. Green Bay
LaDainian Tomlinson, San Diego	147 yards vs. Tennessee
Emmitt Smith, Arizona	127 yards vs. New Orleans
Priest Holmes, Kansas City	125 yards vs. Baltimore
Rudi Johnson, Cincinnati	123 yards vs. Pittsburgh
Duce Staley, Pittsburgh	123 yards vs. Cincinnati
Marshall Faulk, St. Louis	121 yards vs. San Francisco
Brian Westbrook, Philadelphia	119 yards vs. Chicago
Amos Zereoue, Oakland	117 yards vs. Houston
Curtis Martin, New York Jets	110 yards vs. Miami
Jonathan Wells, Houston	105 yards vs. Oakland

Fifth Week

Reuben Droughns, Denver	193 yards vs. Carolina
Shaun Alexander, Seattle	150 yards vs. St. Louis
Chris Brown, Tennessee	148 yards vs. Green Bay
Edgerrin James, Indianapolis	136 yards vs. Oakland
Tiki Barber, New York Giants	122 yards vs. Dallas
Duce Staley, Pittsburgh	117 yards vs. Cleveland
Jamal Lewis, Baltimore	116 yards vs. Washington
Jesse Chatman, San Diego	103 yards vs. Jacksonville
Deuce McAllister, New Orleans	102 yards vs. Tampa Bay

Sixth Week

Reuben Droughns, Denver	176 yards vs. Oakland
Clinton Portis, Washington	171 yards vs. Chicago
William Green, Cleveland	115 yards vs. Cincinnati
Curtis Martin, New York Jets	111 yards vs. San Francisco
Willis McGahee, Buffalo	111 yards vs. Miami
Mewelde Moore, Minnesota	109 yards vs. New Orleans
Corey Dillon, New England	105 yards vs. Seattle

Seventh Week

Ahman Green, Green Bay	163 yards vs. Dallas
Priest Holmes, Kansas City	139 yards vs. Atlanta
Mewelde Moore, Minnesota	138 yards vs. Tennessee
Rudi Johnson, Cincinnati	119 yards vs. Denver
Corey Dillon, New England	115 yards vs. New York Jets
Reuben Droughns, Denver	110 yards vs. Cincinnati
Michael Pittman, Tampa Bay	109 yards vs. Chicago
Fred Taylor, Jacksonville	107 yards vs. Indianapolis
Emmitt Smith, Arizona	106 yards vs. Seattle

Eighth Week

Shaun Alexander, Seattle	195 yards vs. Carolina
Chris Brown, Tennessee	147 yards vs. Cincinnati
Priest Holmes, Kansas City	143 yards vs. Indianapolis
Duce Staley, Pittsburgh	125 yards vs. New England
LaMont Jordan, New York Jets	115 yards vs. Miami
Curtis Martin, New York Jets	115 yards vs. Miami
Michael Vick, Atlanta	115 yards vs. Denver
Willis McGahee, Buffalo	102 yards vs. Arizona
Tiki Barber, New York Giants	101 yards vs. Minnesota

Ninth Week

Shaun Alexander, Seattle	160 yards vs. San Francisco
Jerome Bettis, Pittsburgh	149 yards vs. Philadelphia
Clinton Portis, Washington	147 yards vs. Detroit
Willis McGahee, Buffalo	132 yards vs. New York Jets
Michael Pittman, Tampa Bay	128 yards vs. Kansas City
Edgerrin James, Indianapolis	123 yards vs. Minnesota
Reuben Droughns, Denver	120 yards vs. Houston
Corey Dillon, New England	112 yards vs. St. Louis
Anthony Thomas, Chicago	110 yards vs. New York Giants

Tenth Week

Derrick Blaylock, Kansas City	186 yards vs. New Orleans
Shaun Alexander, Seattle	176 yards vs. St. Louis
Corey Dillon, New England	151 yards vs. Buffalo
Ahman Green, Green Bay	145 yards vs. Minnesota
Fred Taylor, Jacksonville	144 yards vs. Detroit
Marshall Faulk, St. Louis	139 yards vs. Seattle
Deuce McAllister, New Orleans	127 yards vs. Kansas City
Curtis Martin, New York Jets	119 yards vs. Baltimore
Tiki Barber, New York Giants	108 yards vs. Arizona
Jerome Bettis, Pittsburgh	103 yards vs. Cleveland
Rudi Johnson, Cincinnati	102 yards vs. Washington

Eleventh Week

Edgerrin James, Indianapolis	204 yards vs. Chicago
Reuben Droughns, Denver	166 yards vs. New Orleans
LaDainian Tomlinson, San Diego	164 yards vs. Oakland
Jerome Bettis, Pittsburgh	129 yards vs. Cincinnati
Nick Goings, Carolina	121 yards vs. Arizona
Tiki Barber, New York Giants	107 yards vs. Atlanta
Michael Pittman, Tampa Bay	106 yards vs. San Francisco
Michael Vick, Atlanta	104 yards vs. New York Giants
Fred Taylor, Jacksonville	103 yards vs. Tennessee

Kevin Jones, Detroit	100 yards vs. Minnesota	Julius Jones, Dallas	149 yards vs. New York Giants
Willis McGahee, Buffalo	100 yards vs. St. Louis	Deuce McAllister, New Orleans	140 yards vs. Carolina

Twelfth Week — Zack Crockett, Oakland — 134 yards vs. Jacksonville

Rudi Johnson, Cincinnati	202 yards vs. Cleveland	Warrick Dunn, Atlanta	132 yards vs. Seattle
Najeh Davenport, Green Bay	178 yards vs. St. Louis	Lee Suggs, Cleveland	131 yards vs. Houston
Julius Jones, Dallas	150 yards vs. Chicago	Ladell Betts, Washington	118 yards vs. Minnesota
Fred Taylor, Jacksonville	147 yards vs. Minnesota	Corey Dillon, New England	116 yards vs. San Francisco
Domanick Davis, Houston	129 yards vs. Tennessee	Thomas Jones, Chicago	108 yards vs. Green Bay
Corey Dillon, New England	123 yards vs. Baltimore	Kevan Barlow, San Francisco	103 yards vs. New England
Willis McGahee, Buffalo	116 yards vs. Seattle	Domanick Davis, Houston	103 yards vs. Cleveland
Tiki Barber, New York Giants	110 yards vs. Philadelphia	Willie Parker, Pittsburgh	102 yards vs. Buffalo
Nick Goings, Carolina	106 yards vs. Tampa Bay		
Edgerrin James, Indianapolis	105 yards vs. Detroit		
Reuben Droughns, Denver	102 yards vs. Oakland		
Jerome Bettis, Pittsburgh	100 yards vs. Washington		
Deuce McAllister, New Orleans	100 yards vs. Atlanta		

Times 100 or More (179)

Barber, Dillon, Martin, 9; James, 8; Alexander, McGahee, 7; Bettis, Brown, Droughns, Tomlinson, 6; Goings, Holmes, R. Johnson, McAllister, Portis, F. Taylor, 5; Davis, Dunn, A. Green, K. Jones, T. Jones, Lewis, Pittman, Staley, 4; Faulk, L. Johnson, J. Jones, Suggs, Vick, 3; Barlow, Jackson, Moore, Smith, C. Taylor, Westbrook, 2.

Thirteenth Week

Julius Jones, Dallas	198 yards vs. Seattle
Kevin Jones, Detroit	196 yards vs. Arizona
Clinton Portis, Washington	148 yards vs. New York Giants
Chester Taylor, Baltimore	139 yards vs. Cincinnati
Curtis Martin, New York Jets	134 yards vs. Houston
Nick Goings, Carolina	122 yards vs. New Orleans
Steven Jackson, St. Louis	119 yards vs. San Francisco
Larry Johnson, Kansas City	118 yards vs. Oakland
LaDainian Tomlinson, San Diego	113 yards vs. Denver
Edgerrin James, Indianapolis	105 yards vs. Tennessee
Chris Brown, Tennessee	104 yards vs. Indianapolis
Corey Dillon, New England	100 yards vs. Cleveland

Fourteenth Week

Kevin Jones, Detroit	156 yards vs. Green Bay
Maurice Hicks, San Francisco	139 yards vs. Arizona
LaDainian Tomlinson, San Diego	131 yards vs. Tampa Bay
Domanick Davis, Houston	128 yards vs. Indianapolis
Tatum Bell, Denver	123 yards vs. Miami
Shaun Alexander, Seattle	112 yards vs. Minnesota
Nick Goings, Carolina	108 yards vs. St. Louis
Willis McGahee, Buffalo	105 yards vs. Cleveland
Edgerrin James, Indianapolis	104 yards vs. Houston
Larry Johnson, Kansas City	104 yards vs. Tennessee
Chester Taylor, Baltimore	104 yards vs. New York Giants
Warrick Dunn, Atlanta	103 yards vs. Oakland

Fifteenth Week

Fred Taylor, Jacksonville	165 yards vs. Green Bay
Larry Johnson, Kansas City	151 yards vs. Denver
Jerome Bettis, Pittsburgh	140 yards vs. New York Giants
Warrick Dunn, Atlanta	134 yards vs. Carolina
Curtis Martin, New York Jets	134 yards vs. Seattle
Michael Pittman, Tampa Bay	131 yards vs. New Orleans
Rudi Johnson, Cincinnati	130 yards vs. Buffalo
Jamal Lewis, Baltimore	130 yards vs. Indianapolis
Corey Dillon, New England	121 yards vs. Miami
LaDainian Tomlinson, San Diego	111 yards vs. Cleveland
Clinton Portis, Washington	110 yards vs. San Francisco
Lee Suggs, Cleveland	105 yards vs. San Diego

Sixteenth Week

Domanick Davis, Houston	158 yards vs. Jacksonville
Shaun Alexander, Seattle	154 yards vs. Arizona
Steven Jackson, St. Louis	148 yards vs. Philadelphia
Lee Suggs, Cleveland	143 yards vs. Miami
Deuce McAllister, New Orleans	128 yards vs. Atlanta
Nick Goings, Carolina	127 yards vs. Tampa Bay
Kevin Jones, Detroit	123 yards vs. Chicago
Jerome Bettis, Pittsburgh	117 yards vs. Baltimore
Tiki Barber, New York Giants	109 yards vs. Cincinnati
Thomas Jones, Chicago	109 yards vs. Detroit
Willis McGahee, Buffalo	102 yards vs. San Francisco

Seventeenth Week

Jamal Lewis, Baltimore	167 yards vs. Miami
Curtis Martin, New York Jets	153 yards vs. St. Louis

TEN BEST PASSING PERFORMANCES, 2004

	Att.	Comp.	Yards	TD
1. Jake Plummer	55	31	499	4
Denver vs. Atlanta, Oct. 31				
2. Billy Volek	60	40	492	4
Tennessee vs. Oakland, Dec. 19				
3. Peyton Manning	44	25	472	5
Indianapolis vs. Kansas City, Oct. 31				
4. Donovan McNabb	43	32	464	5
Philadelphia vs. Green Bay, Dec. 5				
5. Marc Bulger	39	29	450	3
St. Louis vs. New York Jets, Jan. 2				
6. Marc Bulger	53	35	448	2
St. Louis vs. Green Bay, Nov. 29				
7. Billy Volek	43	29	426	4
Tennessee vs. Kansas City, Dec. 13				
8. Daunte Culpepper	37	26	425	5
Minnesota vs. New Orleans, Oct. 17				
Peyton Manning	33	25	425	3
Indianapolis vs. Tennessee, Dec. 5				
10. Tim Rattay	57	38	417	2
San Francisco vs. Arizona, Oct. 10				

300-YARD PASSING PERFORMANCES, 2004

First Week

Vinny Testaverde, Dallas	355 yards vs. Minnesota
Tom Brady, New England	335 yards vs. Indianapolis
Donovan McNabb, Philadelphia	330 yards vs. New York Giants
Rich Gannon, Oakland	305 yards vs. Pittsburgh

Second Week

Daunte Culpepper, Minnesota	343 yards vs. Philadelphia
Vinny Testaverde, Dallas	322 yards vs. Cleveland
David Carr, Houston	313 yards vs. Detroit

Third Week

Peyton Manning, Indianapolis	393 yards vs. Green Bay
Daunte Culpepper, Minnesota	360 yards vs. Chicago
Brett Favre, Green Bay	360 yards vs. Indianapolis
Marc Bulger, St. Louis	358 yards vs. New Orleans
Donovan McNabb, Philadelphia	356 yards vs. Detroit
Mark Brunell, Washington	325 yards vs. Dallas
Aaron Brooks, New Orleans	316 yards vs. St. Louis
Carson Palmer, Cincinnati	316 yards vs. Baltimore
Brad Johnson, Tampa Bay	309 yards vs. Oakland

Fourth Week

Byron Leftwich, Jacksonville	318 yards vs. Indianapolis
Jake Delhomme, Carolina	308 yards vs. Atlanta

Fifth Week

Tim Rattay, San Francisco	417 yards vs. Arizona
Daunte Culpepper, Minnesota	396 yards vs. Houston
David Carr, Houston	372 yards vs. Minnesota
Byron Leftwich, Jacksonville	357 yards vs. San Diego
Brett Favre, Green Bay	338 yards vs. Tennessee
Marc Bulger, St. Louis	325 yards vs. Seattle
Chad Pennington, New York Jets	304 yards vs. Buffalo

Sixth Week

Daunte Culpepper, Minnesota	425 yards vs. New Orleans
Matt Hasselbeck, Seattle	349 yards vs. New England
Trent Green, Kansas City	315 yards vs. Jacksonville
Jeff Garcia, Cleveland	310 yards vs. Cincinnati

Seventh Week

Donovan McNabb, Philadelphia	376 yards vs. Cleveland
Peyton Manning, Indianapolis	368 yards vs. Jacksonville
Kerry Collins, Oakland	350 yards vs. New Orleans
Vinny Testaverde, Dallas	308 yards vs. Green Bay
Byron Leftwich, Jacksonville	300 yards vs. Indianapolis

Eighth Week

Jake Plummer, Denver	499 yards vs. Atlanta
Peyton Manning, Indianapolis	472 yards vs. Kansas City
Trent Green, Kansas City	389 yards vs. Indianapolis

Ninth Week

Trent Green, Kansas City	369 yards vs. Tampa Bay

Tenth Week

Daunte Culpepper, Minnesota	363 yards vs. Green Bay
Donovan McNabb, Philadelphia	345 yards vs. Dallas
Billy Volek, Tennessee	334 yards vs. Chicago
Peyton Manning, Indianapolis	320 yards vs. Houston
Trent Green, Kansas City	311 yards vs. New Orleans
Jake Delhomme, Carolina	303 yards vs. San Francisco

Eleventh Week

Brett Favre, Green Bay	383 yards vs. Houston
Trent Green, Kansas City	381 yards vs. New England
Aaron Brooks, New Orleans	377 yards vs. Denver
Shaun King, Arizona	343 yards vs. Carolina
Tom Brady, New England	315 yards vs. Kansas City

Twelfth Week

Marc Bulger, St. Louis	448 yards vs. Green Bay
Kelly Holcomb, Cleveland	413 yards vs. Cincinnati
Drew Brees, San Diego	378 yards vs. Kansas City
Brian Griese, Tampa Bay	347 yards vs. Carolina
Kerry Collins, Oakland	339 yards vs. Denver

Thirteenth Week

Donovan McNabb, Philadelphia	464 yards vs. Green Bay
Peyton Manning, Indianapolis	425 yards vs. Tennessee
Matt Hasselbeck, Seattle	414 yards vs. Dallas
Carson Palmer, Cincinnati	382 yards vs. Baltimore
Kerry Collins, Oakland	343 yards vs. Kansas City
Trent Green, Kansas City	340 yards vs. Oakland
A.J. Feeley, Miami	303 yards vs. Buffalo

Fourteenth Week

Billy Volek, Tennessee	426 yards vs. Kansas City
Brian Griese, Tampa Bay	392 yards vs. San Diego
Matt Hasselbeck, Seattle	334 yards vs. Minnesota
Josh McCown, Arizona	307 yards vs. San Francisco

Fifteenth Week

Billy Volek, Tennessee	492 yards vs. Oakland
Daunte Culpepper, Minnesota	404 yards vs. Detroit
Kerry Collins, Oakland	371 yards vs. Tennessee
Brett Favre, Green Bay	367 yards vs. Jacksonville
Joey Harrington, Detroit	361 yards vs. Minnesota
Jake Delhomme, Carolina	340 yards vs. Atlanta
Ben Roethlisberger, Pittsburgh	316 yards vs. New York Giants

Sixteenth Week

Peyton Manning, Indianapolis	383 yards vs. San Diego
Brett Favre, Green Bay	365 yards vs. Minnesota
Trent Green, Kansas City	358 yards vs. Oakland
Brian Griese, Tampa Bay	321 yards vs. Carolina

Jake Plummer, Denver	303 yards vs. Tennessee

Seventeenth Week

Marc Bulger, St. Louis	450 yards vs. New York Jets
Trent Green, Kansas City	373 yards vs. San Diego
Joey Harrington, Detroit	346 yards vs. Tennessee
Jake Delhomme, Carolina	307 yards vs. New Orleans

Times 300 or more (81)

Green, 8; Culpepper, Manning, 6; Favre, McNabb, 5; Bulger, Collins, Delhomme, 4; Griese, Hasselbeck, Leftwich, Testaverde, Volek, 3; Brady, Brooks, Carr, Harrington, Palmer, Plummer, 2.

TEN BEST RECEIVING PERFORMANCES, 2004

	No.	Yards	TD
1. Drew Bennett	12	233	3
Tennessee vs. Kansas City, Dec. 13			
2. Rod Smith	9	208	1
Denver vs. Atlanta, Oct. 31			
3. Javon Walker	11	200	3
Green Bay vs. Indianapolis, Sept. 26			
4. Reggie Wayne	11	184	1
Indianapolis vs. Green Bay, Sept. 26			
5. Muhsin Muhammad	10	179	1
Carolina vs. New Orleans, Dec. 5			
6. T.J. Houshmandzadeh	10	171	1
Cincinnati vs. Baltimore, Dec. 5			
7. Isaac Bruce	9	170	1
St. Louis vs. Green Bay, Nov. 29			
Andre Johnson	12	170	2
Houston vs. Minnesota, Oct. 10			
9. Rod Gardner	10	167	2
Washington vs. Dallas, Sept. 27			
Joe Horn	5	167	1
New Orleans vs. Kansas City, Nov. 14			

100-YARD RECEIVING PERFORMANCES, 2004

First Week

David Terrell, Chicago	126 yards vs. Detroit
Antonio Gates, San Diego	123 yards vs. Houston
Isaac Bruce, St. Louis	112 yards vs. Arizona
Antonio Bryant, Dallas	112 yards vs. Minnesota
Keyshawn Johnson, Dallas	111 yards vs. Minnesota
Joe Horn, New Orleans	110 yards vs. Seattle
Eddie Kennison, Kansas City	101 yards vs. Denver

Second Week

Hines Ward, Pittsburgh	151 yards vs. Baltimore
Torry Holt, St. Louis	121 yards vs. Atlanta
David Givens, New England	120 yards vs. Arizona
Reggie Wayne Indianapolis	119 yards vs. Tennessee
Donte' Stallworth, New Orleans	113 yards vs. San Francisco
Curtis Conway, San Francisco	112 yards vs. New Orleans
Derrick Mason, Tennessee	104 yards vs. Indianapolis
Isaac Bruce, St. Louis	102 yards vs. Atlanta
Javon Walker, Green Bay	102 yards vs. Chicago
Laveranues Coles, Washington	100 yards vs. New York Giants

Third Week

Javon Walker, Green Bay	200 yards vs. Indianapolis
Reggie Wayne, Indianapolis	184 yards vs. Green Bay
Rod Gardner, Washington	167 yards vs. Dallas
Roy Williams, Detroit	135 yards vs. Philadelphia
Isaac Bruce, St. Louis	134 yards vs. New Orleans
Bill Schroeder, Tampa Bay	126 yards vs. Oakland
Amani Toomer, New York Giants	126 yards vs. Cleveland
Randy Moss, Minnesota	119 yards vs. Chicago

T.J. Houshmandzadeh, Cincinnati 116 yards vs. Baltimore
Brandon Stokley, Indianapolis 110 yards vs. Green Bay
Terrell Owens, Philadelphia 107 yards vs. Detroit
Tony Gonzalez, Kansas City 106 yards vs. Houston
Onterrio Smith, Minnesota 104 yards vs. Chicago
Fourth Week
Eric Moulds, Buffalo 126 yards vs. New England
Laveranues Coles, Washington 122 yards vs. Cleveland
David Terrell, Chicago 116 yards vs. Philadelphia
Andre Johnson, Houston 115 yards vs. Oakland
Muhsin Muhammad, Carolina 114 yards vs. Atlanta
Eric Johnson, San Francisco 113 yards vs. St. Louis
David Patten, New England 113 yards vs. Buffalo
Reche Caldwell, San Diego 110 yards vs. Tennessee
Terrell Owens, Philadelphia 110 yards vs. Chicago
Drew Bennett, Tennessee 109 yards vs. San Diego
Isaac Bruce, St. Louis 100 yards vs. San Francisco
Fifth Week
Andre Johnson, Houston 170 yards vs. Minnesota
Eric Johnson, San Francisco 162 yards vs. Arizona
Javon Walker, Green Bay 159 yards vs. Tennessee
Donald Driver, Green Bay 150 yards vs. Tennessee
Marcus Robinson, Minnesota 150 yards vs. Houston
Plaxico Burress, Pittsburgh 136 yards vs. Cleveland
Marty Booker, Miami 123 yards vs. New England
Keary Colbert, Carolina 115 yards vs. Denver
Jimmy Smith, Jacksonville 113 yards vs. San Diego
Derick Armstrong, Houston 101 yards vs. Minnesota
Andre Davis, Cleveland 101 yards vs. Pittsburgh
Sixth Week
Koren Robinson, Seattle 150 yards vs. New England
Michael Clayton, Tampa Bay 142 yards vs. St. Louis
Terry Glenn, Dallas 140 yards vs. Pittsburgh
Nate Burleson, Minnesota 134 yards vs. New Orleans
Torry Holt, St. Louis 124 yards vs. Tampa Bay
Terrell Owens, Philadelphia 123 yards vs. Carolina
Johnnie Morton, Kansas City 111 yards vs. Jacksonville
Donald Driver, Green Bay 110 yards vs. Detroit
Lee Suggs, Cleveland 100 yards vs. Cincinnati
Seventh Week
Chad Johnson, Cincinnati 149 yards vs. Denver
Javon Walker, Green Bay 129 yards vs. Dallas
Chris Chambers, Miami 128 yards vs. St. Louis
Joe Horn, New Orleans 123 yards vs. Oakland
Jerry Porter, Oakland 113 yards vs. New Orleans
Jimmy Smith, Jacksonville 113 yards vs. Indianapolis
Brandon Stokley, Indianapolis 112 yards vs. Jacksonville
Jason Witten, Dallas 112 yards vs. Green Bay
Darrell Jackson, Seattle 109 yards vs. Arizona
Terrell Owens, Philadelphia 109 yards vs. Cleveland
David Givens, New England 107 yards vs. New York Jets
Tiki Barber, New York Giants 102 yards vs. Detroit
Todd Pinkston, Philadelphia 100 yards vs. Cleveland
Eighth Week
Rod Smith, Denver 208 yards vs. Atlanta
Tony Gonzalez, Kansas City 125 yards vs. Indianapolis
Marvin Harrison, Indianapolis 119 yards vs. Kansas City
Reggie Wayne, Indianapolis 119 yards vs. Kansas City
Jimmy Smith, Jacksonville 117 yards vs. Houston
Muhsin Muhammad, Carolina 106 yards vs. Seattle
David Givens, New England 101 yards vs. Pittsburgh
Terrell Owens, Philadelphia 101 yards vs. Baltimore
Keary Colbert, Carolina 100 yards vs. Seattle
Ninth Week
Santana Moss, New York Jets 157 yards vs. Buffalo
Tony Gonzalez, Kansas City 123 yards vs. Tampa Bay
Az-Zahir Hakim, Detroit 120 yards vs. Washington
Darrell Jackson, Seattle 114 yards vs. San Francisco
Torry Holt, St. Louis 111 yards vs. New England
Chris Chambers, Miami 104 yards vs. Arizona

Eddie Kennison, Kansas City 104 yards vs. Tampa Bay
David Givens, New England 100 yards vs. St. Louis
Tenth Week
Joe Horn, New Orleans 167 yards vs. Kansas City
Drew Bennett, Tennessee 148 yards vs. Chicago
Nate Burleson, Minnesota 141 yards vs. Green Bay
Terrell Owens, Philadelphia 134 yards vs. Dallas
Jason Witten, Dallas 133 yards vs. Philadelphia
Brandon Stokley, Indianapolis 132 yards vs. Houston
Muhsin Muhammad, Carolina 123 yards vs. San Francisco
Eddie Kennison, Kansas City 121 yards vs. New Orleans
Alge Crumpler, Atlanta 118 yards vs. Tampa Bay
Jimmy Smith, Jacksonville 109 yards vs. Detroit
Isaac Bruce, St. Louis 104 yards vs. Seattle
Dallas Clark, Indianapolis 102 yards vs. Houston
Cedrick Wilson, San Francisco 101 yards vs. Carolina
Amani Toomer, New York Giants 100 yards vs. Arizona
Eleventh Week
Donald Driver, Green Bay 148 yards vs. Houston
Donte' Stallworth, New Orleans 122 yards vs. Denver
Muhsin Muhammad, Carolina 118 yards vs. Arizona
Andre Johnson, Houston 107 yards vs. Green Bay
Johnnie Morton, Kansas City 107 yards vs. New England
Todd Pinkston, Philadelphia 106 yards vs. Washington
Reggie Wayne, Indianapolis 106 yards vs. Chicago
Deion Branch, New England 105 yards vs. Kansas City
Chris Chambers, Miami 103 yards vs. Seattle
Antonio Gates, San Diego 101 yards vs. Oakland
Twelfth Week
Isaac Bruce, St. Louis 170 yards vs. Green Bay
Jerry Porter, Oakland 135 yards vs. Denver
Michael Pittman, Tampa Bay 134 yards vs. Carolina
Antonio Bryant, Cleveland 131 yards vs. Cincinnati
Marvin Harrison, Indianapolis 127 yards vs. Detroit
Chad Johnson, Cincinnati 117 yards vs. Cleveland
Ronald Curry, Oakland 110 yards vs. Denver
Santana Moss, New York Jets 109 yards vs. Arizona
Tony Gonzalez, Kansas City 105 yards vs. San Diego
Alge Crumpler, Atlanta 103 yards vs. New Orleans
Jamaar Taylor, New York Giants 102 yards vs. Philadelphia
Joe Horn, New Orleans 101 yards vs. Atlanta
Thirteenth Week
Muhsin Muhammad, Carolina 179 yards vs. New Orleans
T.J. Houshmandzadeh, Cincinnati 171 yards vs. Baltimore
Chad Johnson, Cincinnati 161 yards vs. Baltimore
Terrell Owens, Philadelphia 161 yards vs. Green Bay
Torry Holt, St. Louis 160 yards vs. San Francisco
Joe Horn, New Orleans 160 yards vs. Carolina
Brian Westbrook, Philadelphia 156 yards vs. Green Bay
Brandon Stokley, Indianapolis 153 yards vs. Tennessee
Eddie Kennison, Kansas City 149 yards vs. Oakland
Jerry Rice, Seattle 145 yards vs. Dallas
Ronald Curry, Oakland 141 yards vs. Kansas City
Andre Johnson, Houston 125 yards vs. New York Jets
Drew Bennett, Tennessee 124 yards vs. Indianapolis
Keyshawn Johnson, Dallas 116 yards vs. Seattle
Antonio Bryant, Cleveland 115 yards vs. New England
Darrell Jackson, Seattle 113 yards vs. Dallas
Lee Evans, Buffalo 110 yards vs. Miami
Marvin Harrison, Indianapolis 106 yards vs. Tennessee
Ashley Lelie, Denver 105 yards vs. San Diego
Fourteenth Week
Drew Bennett, Tennessee 233 yards vs. Kansas City
Torry Holt, St. Louis 151 yards vs. Carolina
Michael Clayton, Tampa Bay 145 yards vs. San Diego
T.J. Houshmandzadeh, Cincinnati 145 yards vs. New England
Darrell Jackson, Seattle 135 yards vs. Minnesota
Eric Parker, San Diego 118 yards vs. Tampa Bay
Donte' Stallworth, New Orleans 113 yards vs. Dallas
Anquan Boldin, Arizona 109 yards vs. San Francisco

David Patten, New England — 107 yards vs. Cincinnati
Randy Moss, Minnesota — 104 yards vs. Seattle
Laveranues Coles, Washington — 100 yards vs. Philadelphia

Fifteenth Week
Drew Bennett, Tennessee — 160 yards vs. Oakland
Javon Walker, Green Bay — 152 yards vs. Jacksonville
Antwaan Randle El, Pittsburgh — 149 yards vs. New York Giants
Jerry Porter, Oakland — 148 yards vs. Tennessee
Muhsin Muhammad, Carolina — 135 yards vs. Atlanta
Nate Burleson, Minnesota — 134 yards vs. Detroit
Hines Ward, Pittsburgh — 134 yards vs. New York Giants
Derrick Mason, Tennessee — 121 yards vs. Oakland
Rod Gardner, Washington — 111 yards vs. San Francisco
Jabar Gaffney, Houston — 109 yards vs. Chicago
Az-Zahir Hakim, Detroit — 108 yards vs. Minnesota
Roy Williams, Detroit — 104 yards vs. Minnesota
Randy Moss, Minnesota — 102 yards vs. Detroit
Lee Evans, Buffalo — 101 yards vs. Cincinnati
Eddie Kennison, Kansas City — 101 yards vs. Denver

Sixteenth Week
Donald Driver, Green Bay — 162 yards vs. Minnesota
Tony Gonzalez, Kansas City — 124 yards vs. Oakland
Brandon Stokley, Indianapolis — 123 yards vs. San Diego
Muhsin Muhammad, Carolina — 115 yards vs. Tampa Bay
Dennis Northcutt, Cleveland — 114 yards vs. Miami
Marvin Harrison, Indianapolis — 111 yards vs. San Diego
Nate Burleson, Minnesota — 110 yards vs. Green Bay
Anquan Boldin, Arizona — 107 yards vs. Seattle
Eric Parker, San Diego — 103 yards vs. Indianapolis
Darrell Jackson, Seattle — 101 yards vs. Arizona

Seventeenth Week
Chris Chambers, Miami — 146 yards vs. Baltimore
Tony Gonzalez, Kansas City — 144 yards vs. San Diego
Torry Holt, St. Louis — 116 yards vs. New York Jets
Larry Johnson, Kansas City — 115 yards vs. San Diego

Times 100 or more (186)
Muhammad, Owens, 7; Bruce, Gonzalez, Holt, 6; Bennett, Horn, Jackson, Kennison, Stokley, Walker, 5; Burleson, Chambers, Driver, Givens, Harrison, A. Johnson, Smith, Wayne, 4; Bryant, Coles, Houshmandzadeh, C. Johnson, R. Moss, Porter, Stallworth, 3; Boldin, Clayton, Colbert, Crumpler, Curry, Evans, Gardner, Gates, Hakim, E. Johnson, K. Johnson, Mason, Morton, S. Moss, Parker, Patten, Pinkston, Terrell, Toomer, Ward, Witten, R. Williams, 2.

TOP QUARTERBACK SACK PERFORMANCES, 2004
(3.0 or More Sacks Per Game Needed to Qualify)

First Week
Kenard Lang, Cleveland — 3.0 vs. Baltimore
Second Week
None
Third Week
Charles Grant, New Orleans — 3.0 vs. St. Louis
Jevon Kearse, Philadelphia — 3.0 vs. Detroit
Patrick Kerney, Atlanta — 3.0 vs. Arizona
Fourth Week
None
Fifth Week
John Abraham, New York Jets — 3.0 vs. Buffalo
Sixth Week
None
Seventh Week
None
Eighth Week
Joey Porter, Pittsburgh — 3.0 vs. New England
Ninth Week
Alex Brown, Chicago — 4.0 vs. New York Giants
Tenth Week
Bertrand Berry, Arizona — 4.0 vs. New York Giants
Kevin Carter, Tennessee — 3.0 vs. Chicago
Robert Mathis, Indianapolis — 3.0 vs. Houston
Eleventh Week
Lance Johnstone, Minnesota — 3.0 vs. Detroit
Lawyer Milloy, Buffalo — 3.0 vs. St. Louis
Twelfth Week
Eric Ogbogu, Dallas — 3.5 vs. Chicago
Jason Taylor, Miami — 3.0 vs. San Francisco
Thirteenth Week
Dwight Freeney, Indianapolis — 3.0 vs. Tennessee
Fourteenth Week
Dwight Freeney, Indianapolis — 3.0 vs. Houston
Fifteenth Week
Simeon Rice, Tampa Bay — 3.0 vs. New Orleans
Sixteenth Week
Steve Foley, San Diego — 3.0 vs. Indianapolis
Reggie Hayward, Denver — 3.0 vs. Tennessee
Seventeenth Week
Kabeer Gbaja-Biamila, Green Bay — 4.0 vs. Chicago
Shaun Ellis, New York Jets — 3.0 vs. St. Louis

2005 PLAYER RANKINGS AND PROJECTIONS

The *NFL.com 2005 Fantasy Football Preview*, available at newsstands now, contians 196 pages of fantasy football facts, tips, and projections for the upcoming season. The following eight pages display the projections for the running backs, wide receivers, quarterbacks, tight ends, and kickers for the 2005 season, as devised by the magzazine's experts. Page 299 provides the statistical average for each team's defense over the past three seasons, allowing you a comprehensive look at which team defense can consistently help lead your fantasy team to the title. Pick up a copy of the *NFL.com 2005 Fantasy Football Preview* today.

RUNNING BACKS	Rushing Yards	Rushing Touchdowns	Receiving	Receiving Yards	Receiving Touchdowns	Total Touchdowns
1. LaDainian Tomlinson, San Diego	1300	19	40	350	3	22
2. Priest Holmes, Kansas City	1350	15	35	375	5	20
3. Edgerrin James, Indianapolis	1400	12	40	400	3	15
4. Shaun Alexander, Seattle	1425	13	20	150	1	14
5. Jamal Lewis, Baltimore	1275	14	15	175	2	16
6. Corey Dillon, New England	1400	12	20	100	2	14
7. Domanick Davis, Houston	1250	11	55	450	1	12
8. Clinton Portis, Washington	1375	11	25	175	1	12
9. Julius Jones, Dallas	1375	10	20	225	0	10
10. Rudi Johnson, Cincinnati	1225	11	20	150	1	12
11. Ahman Green, Green Bay	1200	10	30	200	1	11
12. Deuce McAllister, New Orleans	1150	10	30	250	1	11
13. Willis McGahee, Buffalo	1200	9	20	125	1	10
14. Tiki Barber, N.Y. Giants	1075	8	40	375	1	9
15. Chris Brown, Tennessee	1225	7	30	250	1	8
16. Brian Westbrook, Philadelphia	950	6	50	525	2	8
17. Steven Jackson, St. Louis	1300	9	15	125	0	9
18. Kevin Jones, Detroit	1250	8	20	175	0	8
19. Curtis Martin, N.Y. Jets	1250	7	25	150	1	8
20. Tatum Bell, Denver	1300	8	15	125	0	8
21. LaMont Jordan, Oakland	975	10	25	225	1	11
22. Thomas Jones, Chicago	600	4	40	350	3	7
23. Kevan Barlow, San Francisco	925	8	40	325	1	9
24. DeShaun Foster, Carolina	1075	8	15	125	0	8
25. Fred Taylor, Jacksonville	1175	8	25	200	1	9
26. Michael Pittman, Tampa Bay	750	4	40	425	3	7
27. Duce Staley, Pittsburgh	1075	6	20	175	0	6
28. Warrick Dunn, Atlanta	875	6	20	200	2	8
29. Larry Johnson, Kansas City	325	3	10	125	1	4
30. Onterrio Smith, Minnesota	425	3	40	400	3	6
31. Michael Bennett, Minnesota	625	4	15	175	0	4
32. T.J. Duckett, Atlanta	450	6	10	75	0	6
33. Derrick Blaylock, N.Y. Jets	450	4	15	125	1	5
34. Travis Henry, Buffalo	375	3	15	175	1	4
35. Reuben Droughns, Cleveland	525	4	30	175	0	4
36. Jerome Bettis, Pittsburgh	400	6	5	50	0	6
37. Marcel Shipp, Arizona	400	2	20	225	1	3
38. Stephen Davis, Carolina	375	4	10	125	0	4
39. Lee Suggs, Cleveland	475	4	10	100	0	4
40. Marshall Faulk, St. Louis	300	1	35	300	3	4
41. Dominic Rhodes, Indianapolis	300	2	15	100	0	2
42. Correll Buckhalter, Philadelphia	325	4	15	100	0	4
43. Chester Taylor, Baltimore	275	2	20	150	1	3
44. Ladell Betts, Washington	275	3	10	100	0	3
45. Troy Hambrick, Arizona	275	3	5	50	0	3
46. Mewelde Moore, Minnesota	250	1	10	150	1	2
47. Sammy Morris, Miami	325	3	10	50	0	3
48. Nick Goings, Carolina	250	2	15	125	0	2
49. J.J. Arrington, Arizona	*1125*	*13*	*35*	*245*	*1*	*14*
50. Ronnie Brown, Miami	*975*	*7*	*45*	*380*	*1*	*8*
51. Carnell Williams, Tampa Bay	*650*	*5*	*20*	*240*	*0*	*5*
52. Cedric Benson, Chicago	*450*	*7*	*15*	*135*	*0*	*7*
53. Greg Jones, Jacksonville	235	4	6	45	0	4
54. Maurice Hicks, San Francisco	240	2	12	135	0	2
55. Najeh Davenport, Green Bay	235	3	2	15	0	3
56. Eric Shelton, Carolina	*220*	*4*	*5*	*40*	*0*	*4*
57. Verron Haynes, Pittsburgh	235	0	25	240	1	1
58. William Henderson, Green Bay	2	0	30	255	2	2

	Rushing Yards	Rushing Touchdowns	Receiving	Receiving Yards	Receiving Touchdowns	Total Touchdowns
59. Jonathan Wells, Houston	185	2	7	60	1	3
60. Tony Fisher, Green Bay	150	0	30	245	1	1
61. Shawn Bryson, Detroit	110	1	38	450	1	2
62. Quentin Griffin, Denver	225	1	9	210	0	1
63. Kevin Faulk, New England	225	2	30	310	0	2
64. Mike Alstott, Tampa Bay	180	3	20	190	0	3
65. Eddie George	165	2	5	40	0	2
66. Anthony Thomas, Dallas	200	2	8	90	0	2
67. Antowain Smith, New Orleans	190	3	10	110	0	3
68. Mike Cloud, N.Y. Giants	140	1	2	15	0	1
69. Jesse Chatman, San Diego	140	2	4	20	0	2
70. Zack Crockett, Oakland	120	2	8	75	0	2
71. Chris Perry, Cincinnati	160	1	9	85	0	1
72. LaBrandon Toefield, Jacksonville	125	1	20	175	1	2
73. Lamar Gordon, Miami	125	1	5	40	0	1
74. Tyrone Wheatley	140	2	10	85	0	2
75. Maurice Morris, Seattle	210	1	8	55	0	1
76. Arlen Harris, St. Louis	145	2	10	110	0	2
77. Obafemi Ayanbadejo, Arizona	100	1	15	145	0	1
78. Justin Griffith, Atlanta	45	1	25	210	1	2
79. Brad Hoover, Carolina	125	0	20	140	1	0
80. Moe Williams, Minnesota	120	3	25	320	2	5
81. Cory Schlesinger, Detroit	10	0	8	65	2	2
82. Charlie Garner	125	1	20	180	0	1
83. Frank Gore, San Francisco	*120*	*1*	*5*	*45*	*0*	*1*
84. Cedric Houston, N.Y. Jets	*150*	*1*	*5*	*45*	*0*	*1*
85. Marion Barber III, Dallas	*65*	*2*	*10*	*75*	*0*	*2*
86. Anthony Davis, Indianapolis	*120*	*0*	*4*	*40*	*0*	*0*
87. Patrick Pass, New England	140	1	20	165	0	1
88. Maurice Clarett, Denver	*85*	*1*	*3*	*15*	*0*	*1*
89. Chris Fuamatu-Ma'afala, Jacksonville	110	1	2	11	0	1
90. Dan Kreider, Pittsburgh	15	1	13	110	0	1
91. Mack Strong, Seattle	125	1	20	145	0	1
92. J.R. Redmond, Oakland	25	0	20	185	1	1
93. Amos Zereoue	85	0	35	280	1	1
94. Dorsey Levens	150	2	5	45	0	2
95. Justin Fargas, Oakland	100	0	8	75	0	0
96. William Green, Cleveland	125	2	10	65	0	2
97. Fred Beasley, San Francisco	25	0	12	85	1	1
98. Jeremi Johnson, Cincinnati	10	0	15	65	1	0
99. Ron Dayne, Denver	110	1	3	10	0	1
100. Tony Richardson, Kansas City	45	0	15	110	0	0

Players in bold/italics are rookies who could have significantly higher value.

For more in-depth analysis, pick up a copy of the NFL.com 2005 Fantasy Football Preview, *available at newsstands today.*

WIDE RECEIVERS	Receiving	Yards	Touchdowns
1. Terrell Owens, Philadelphia	86	1250	15
2. Marvin Harrison, Indianapolis	102	1350	13
3. Randy Moss, Oakland	82	1100	14
4. Chad Johnson, Cincinnati	101	1450	12
5. Torry Holt, St. Louis	85	1100	12
6. Hines Ward, Pittsburgh	90	1275	11
7. Andre Johnson, Houston	83	1125	10
8. Javon Walker, Green Bay	76	1075	10
9. Joe Horn, New Orleans	86	1200	10
10. Anquan Boldin, Arizona	85	1300	6
11. Nate Burleson, Minnesota	81	1275	8
12. Roy Williams, Detroit	74	1100	8
13. Reggie Wayne, Indianapolis	70	1100	8
14. Darrell Jackson, Seattle	82	1050	10
15. Jerry Porter, Oakland	70	1075	8
16. Ashley Lelie, Denver	65	950	8
17. Laveranues Coles, N.Y. Jets	80	1000	7
18. Drew Bennett, Tennessee	72	1100	6
19. Deion Branch, New England	67	875	8
20. Derrick Mason, Baltimore	75	950	6
21. Michael Clayton, Tampa Bay	86	1075	5
22. Steve Smith, Carolina	75	1050	5
23. Jimmy Smith, Jacksonville	63	900	6
24. Muhsin Muhammad, Chicago	72	850	7
25. Chris Chambers, Miami	77	1025	6
26. Marcus Robinson, Minnesota	60	900	7
27. Joey Galloway, Tampa Bay	65	900	7
28. Plaxico Burress, N.Y. Giants	76	950	6
29. Lee Evans, Buffalo	70	950	6
30. Keyshawn Johnson, Dallas	84	1100	4
31. Donald Driver, Green Bay	72	975	5
32. Eddie Kennison, Kansas City	68	925	6
33. Larry Fitzgerald, Arizona	63	950	5
34. Brandon Stokley, Indianapolis	55	875	6
35. Tyrone Calico, Tennessee	65	850	7
36. Antonio Bryant, Cleveland	61	850	6
37. T.J. Houshmandzadeh, Cincinnati	64	925	5
38. Eric Moulds, Buffalo	70	975	4
39. Brandon Lloyd, San Francisco	64	825	6
40. Peerless Price, Atlanta	62	800	6
41. Isaac Bruce, St. Louis	65	900	4
42. Rod Smith, Denver	64	900	4
43. Donte' Stallworth, New Orleans	55	875	5
44. Keenan McCardell, San Diego	77	900	4
45. Travis Taylor, Minnesota	48	625	5
46. Kelley Washington, Cincinnati	44	600	5
47. Charles Rogers, Detroit	54	675	4
48. Keary Colbert, Carolina	50	725	3
49. Reggie Williams, Jacksonville	57	600	6
50. David Givens, New England	50	625	5
51. Antwaan Randle El, Pittsburgh	55	725	4
52. Andre Davis, Cleveland	44	675	3
53. Marc Boerigter, Kansas City	47	650	4
54. Santana Moss, Washington	60	650	4
55. Amani Toomer, N.Y. Giants	45	700	3
56. Koren Robinson, Seattle	42	625	4
57. Todd Pinkston, Philadelphia	40	675	3
58. Justin McCareins, N.Y. Jets	45	575	5
59. Rod Gardner, Washington	75	825	2
60. Jabar Gaffney, Houston	50	625	4
61. Michael Jenkins, Atlanta	41	550	4
62. Clarence Moore, Baltimore	42	475	3
63. Darius Watts, Denver	40	550	2
64. David Terrell, New England	37	450	3
65. Ronald Curry, Oakland	30	360	5
66. Braylon Edwards, Cleveland	*65*	*820*	*8*
67. Mike Williams, Detroit	*55*	*650*	*7*
68. Rashaun Woods, San Francisco	30	360	6
69. Kevin Curtis, St. Louis	45	480	2

#	Player			
70.	Johnnie Morton, Kansas City	35	450	4
71.	Quincy Morgan, Dallas	40	600	3
72.	David Boston	40	525	3
73.	*Mark Clayton, Baltimore*	*45*	*585*	*2*
74.	*Mark Bradley, Chicago*	*35*	*520*	*2*
75.	*Troy Williamson, Minnesota*	*30*	*420*	*2*
76.	Shaun McDonald, St. Louis	48	480	3
77.	Eric Parker, San Diego	40	470	2
78.	*Roddy White, Atlanta*	*35*	*450*	*3*
79.	Dennis Northcutt, Cleveland	50	450	1
80.	Justin Gage, Chicago	25	420	2
81.	Bill Schroeder, Tampa Bay	30	420	2
82.	Marty Booker, Miami	31	415	2
83.	Terry Glenn, Dallas	30	410	2
84.	Troy Edwards, Jacksonville	25	400	2
85.	Ricky Proehl, Carolina	30	380	2
86.	Joe Jurevicius, Seattle	25	350	3
87.	Dane Looker, St. Louis	28	440	1
88.	Derrius Thompson, Miami	24	350	2
89.	Ike Hilliard	38	400	1
90.	Bryant Johnson, Arizona	30	320	3
91.	Reche Caldwell, San Diego	32	360	1
92.	Troy Brown	32	340	2
93.	Darnerian McCants, Washington	20	320	2
94.	Bobby Wade, Chicago	45	385	1
95.	Ernest Wilford, Jacksonville	25	320	2
96.	David Patten, Washington	25	310	2
97.	Cedrick Wilson, Pittsburgh	30	350	1
98.	Tim Carter, N.Y. Giants	25	340	1
99.	Dez White, Atlanta	30	310	1
100.	Bobby Engram, Seattle	30	350	1
101.	Curtis Conway	30	350	1
102.	Randy Hymes, Baltimore	25	305	2
103.	Greg Lewis, Philadelphia	25	320	1
104.	Jerome Pathon, Seattle	30	300	1
105.	Taylor Jacobs, Washington	25	300	1
106.	Peter Warrick, Cincinnati	20	305	1
107.	Jerricho Cotchery, N.Y. Jets	20	300	1
108.	Corey Bradford, Houston	15	270	2
109.	Derick Armstrong, Houston	27	300	0
110.	*Reggie Brown, Philadelphia*	*25*	*290*	*1*
111.	Robert Ferguson, Green Bay	25	280	1
112.	Samie Parker, Kansas City	20	250	2
113.	Jerry Rice	20	250	2
114.	Kassim Osgood, San Diego	20	220	2
115.	Dante Hall, Kansas City	25	300	1
116.	Brian Finneran, Atlanta	24	280	1
117.	*Roscoe Parrish, Buffalo*	*22*	*260*	*1*
118.	Doug Gabriel, Oakland	20	250	1
119.	*Jerome Mathis, Houston*	*16*	*240*	*1*
120.	Az-Zahir Hakim	17	255	1
121.	Bernard Berrian, Chicago	18	250	1
122.	*Courtney Roby, Tennessee*	*18*	*230*	*1*
123.	Bethel Johnson, New England	18	220	1
124.	*Matt Jones, Jacksonville*	*18*	*215*	*1*
125.	*Chris Henry, Cincinnati*	*12*	*200*	*1*
126.	Kelly Campbell, Minnesota	15	210	1
127.	Tai Streets	15	205	1
128.	Jason McAddley, Tennessee	15	200	1
129.	*Larry Brackins, Tampa Bay*	*18*	*200*	*1*
130.	Patrick Crayton, Dallas	16	190	1
131.	Devery Henderson, New Orleans	15	180	1
132.	Josh Reed, Buffalo	20	210	0
133.	Wayne Chrebet, N.Y. Jets	25	180	0
134.	Kevin Johnson, Detroit	20	170	0
135.	Freddie Mitchell	11	115	0
136.	Triandos Luke, Denver	10	110	0
137.	*Vincent Jackson, San Diego*	*10*	*95*	*0*

Players in bold/italics are rookies who could have significantly higher value.

For more in-depth analysis, pick up a copy of the NFL.com 2005 Fantasy Football Preview, available at newsstands today.

QUARTERBACKS	Passing Yards	Passing Touchdowns	Rushing Yards	Rushing Touchdowns
1. Peyton Manning, Indianapolis	4200	38	50	1
2. Daunte Culpepper, Minnesota	3850	30	295	7
3. Donovan McNabb, Philadelphia	3600	26	200	2
4. Trent Green, Kansas City	4125	29	100	1
5. Kerry Collins, Oakland	4000	33	50	0
6. Michael Vick, Atlanta	3100	21	575	6
7. Marc Bulger, St. Louis	3650	24	75	1
8. Matt Hasselbeck, Seattle	3900	26	100	0
9. Aaron Brooks, New Orleans	3525	22	225	3
10. Carson Palmer, Cincinnati	3475	25	75	1
11. Brett Favre, Green Bay	3425	23	40	1
12. Tom Brady, New England	3300	24	100	2
13. Jake Plummer, Denver	3225	20	225	3
14. David Carr, Houston	3725	19	125	2
15. Jake Delhomme, Carolina	3350	20	75	0
16. Chad Pennington, N.Y. Jets	3200	21	75	1
17. Steve McNair, Tennessee	2850	18	100	5
18. Byron Leftwich, Jacksonville	3100	18	100	2
19. Brian Griese, Tampa Bay	2850	21	50	0
20. Joey Harrington, Detroit	2900	18	125	1
21. Drew Brees, San Diego	2650	18	75	1
22. Patrick Ramsey, Washington	3000	17	30	0
23. Eli Manning, N.Y. Giants	2850	17	75	0
24. Ben Roethlisberger, Pittsburgh	2650	18	100	0
25. Kurt Warner, Arizona	2600	19	50	0
26. Drew Bledsoe, Dallas	2500	16	25	0
27. Rex Grossman, Chicago	2475	16	125	1
28. Trent Dilfer, Cleveland	2150	15	75	0
29. J.P. Losman, Buffalo	1975	13	100	3
30. Kyle Boller, Baltimore	2200	15	150	0
31. Tim Rattay, San Francisco	1700	14	25	0
32. Gus Frerotte, Miami	1600	12	25	0
33. Billy Volek, Tennessee	900	7	50	1
34. Jeff Garcia, Detroit	825	6	75	0
35. Kelly Holcomb, Buffalo	1050	4	25	0
36. A.J. Feeley, Miami	1400	8	25	0
37. Jay Fiedler, N.Y. Jets	500	3	75	1
38. Brad Johnson, Minnesota	250	2	10	0
39. Jim Sorgi, Indianapolis	325	3	10	0
40. Mike McMahon, Philadelphia	250	1	50	1
41. Alex Smith, San Francisco	*1100*	*7*	*60*	*2*
42. Matt Schaub, Atlanta	275	2	15	0
43. Josh McCown, Arizona	275	4	20	0
44. Chad Hutchinson, Chicago	250	2	10	0
45. Drew Henson, Dallas	250	2	10	0
46. David Garrard, Jacksonville	250	2	110	2
47. Philip Rivers, San Diego	225	2	10	0
48. Jon Kitna, Cincinnati	200	2	15	0
49. Luke McCown, Tampa Bay	180	2	20	0
50. Tommy Maddox, Pittsburgh	170	1	5	0
51. Aaron Rodgers, Green Bay	*150*	*1*	*10*	*0*
52. Kordell Stewart, Baltimore	140	2	35	1
53. Jason Campbell, Washington	*175*	*2*	*20*	*0*
54. Jeff Blake, Philadelphia	175	1	10	0
55. Mark Brunell, Washington	150	1	10	0
56. Tony Banks, Houston	125	1	5	0
57. Jamie Martin, St. Louis	135	0	5	0
58. Todd Collins, Kansas City	140	0	10	0
59. Chris Simms, Tampa Bay	90	1	20	0
60. Doug Flutie, New England	125	1	45	1

Players in bold/italics are rookies who could have significantly higher value.

TIGHT ENDS	Receiving	Yards	Touchdowns
1. Tony Gonzalez, Kansas City	84	1000	10
2. Antonio Gates, San Diego	76	950	9
3. Alge Crumpler, Atlanta	56	850	6
4. Todd Heap, Baltimore	68	800	8
5. Jeremy Shockey, N.Y. Giants	70	750	7
6. Randy McMichael, Miami	62	700	7
7. Jason Witten, Dallas	76	825	5
8. Dallas Clark, Indianapolis	47	725	6
9. Chris Cooley, Washington	64	650	7
10. Bubba Franks, Green Bay	29	275	6
11. Eric Johnson, San Francisco	68	800	4
12. Daniel Graham, New England	41	425	4
13. Ben Troupe, Tennessee	44	475	5
14. Jermaine Wiggins, Minnesota	49	450	2
15. Kellen Winslow, Cleveland	38	395	4
16. Jeb Putzier, Denver	32	425	3
17. L. J. Smith, Philadelphia	35	325	2
18. Marcus Pollard, Detroit	33	340	2
19. Jerramy Stevens, Seattle	28	320	3
20. Boo Williams, New Orleans	30	330	3
21. Mark Campbell, Buffalo	32	280	2
22. Anthony Becht, Tampa Bay	30	275	2
23. Kris Mangum, Carolina	29	280	1
24. Teyo Johnson, Oakland	23	265	3
25. Doug Jolley, N.Y. Jets	23	260	2
26. Brandon Manumaleuna, St. Louis	22	200	3
27. Freddie Jones, Carolina	23	300	2
28. Itula Mili, Seattle	22	175	2
29. Heath Miller, Pittsburgh	*21*	*205*	*3*
30. Christian Fauria, New England	20	175	2
31. Eric Edwards, Arizona	22	175	2
32. Mike Seidman, Carolina	20	165	2
33. Billy Miller, Houston	20	180	1
34. Reggie Kelly, Cincinnati	21	200	1
35. Mark Bruener, Houston	20	205	2
36. Ken Dilger, Tampa Bay	20	175	0
37. Desmond Clark, Chicago	18	190	1
38. Kyle Brady, Jacksonville	17	125	2
39. Stephen Alexander, Denver	16	140	1
40. Robert Royal, Washington	10	85	3
41. George Wrighster, Jacksonville	15	125	1
42. Aaron Shea, Cleveland	17	135	1
43. Casey FitzSimmons, Detroit	15	120	1
44. Chris Baker, NY Jets	13	100	2
45. Erron Kinney, Tennessee	17	125	1
46. Terry Jones, Baltimore	14	130	1
47. Alex Smith, Tampa Bay	*13*	*105*	*1*
48. Tim Euhus, Buffalo	9	65	2
49. Chad Lewis	11	90	1
50. Ben Watson, New England	10	80	0

For more in-depth analysis, pick up a copy of the NFL.com 2005 Fantasy Football Preview, available at newsstands today.

KICKERS	PTS	XP/XPA	FG/FGA
1. David Akers, Philadelphia	140	44/44	32/38
2. Mike Vanderjagt, Indianapolis	139	49/49	30/36
3. Adam Vinatieri, New England	114	36/36	26/30
4. Sebastian Janikowski, Oakland	116	44/44	24/30
5. Jason Elam, Denver	111	36/36	25/32
6. Shayne Graham, Cincinnati	114	45/46	23/26
7. Josh Brown, Seattle	111	36/37	25/32
8. Matt Stover, Baltimore	110	32/32	26/30
9. John Kasay, Carolina	111	30/30	27/32
10. Jason Hanson, Detroit	112	37/37	25/27
11. Ryan Longwell, Green Bay	105	39/40	22/30
12. Jeff Reed, Pittsburgh	105	33/34	24/29
13. John Carney, New Orleans	103	43/43	20/28
14. Lawrence Tynes, Kansas City	106	46/47	20/28
15. Neil Rackers, Arizona	104	35/36	23/26
16. Paul Edinger, Chicago	102	33/34	23/27
17. Nate Kaeding, San Diego	101	38/40	21/28
18. Jeff Wilkins, St. Louis	101	35/35	22/26
19. Kris Brown, Houston	99	39/39	20/25
20. Aaron Elling, Minnesota	100	43/44	19/28
21. Olindo Mare, Miami	96	30/30	22/27
22. Matt Bryant, Tampa Bay	95	32/33	21/25
23. Billy Cundiff, Dallas	98	35/36	21/28
24. Todd Peterson, Atlanta	97	34/35	21/27
25. Mike Nugent, N.Y. Jets	*99*	*30/31*	*23/31*
26. Phil Dawson, Cleveland	94	34/34	20/26
27. Joe Nedney, San Francisco	88	28/28	20/27
28. Rian Lindell, Buffalo	84	30/30	18/27
29. Gary Anderson	87	24/24	21/25
30. Ola Kimrin, Tennessee	84	24/24	20/25
31. Jay Feely, N.Y. Giants	82	28/28	18/28
32. Josh Scobee, Jacksonville	81	33/33	16/21
33. Morten Andersen	77	23/23	18/21
34. Seth Marler	75	24/24	17/28
35. Doug Brien, Chicago	69	21/21	16/24
36. John Hall, Washington	50	17/17	11/16
37. Jeff Chandler, Washington	47	17/17	10/16
38. Jay Taylor	39	12/12	9/12
39. Steve Christie	30	9/9	7/8
40. Martin Gramatica	20	11/11	3/5

Players in bold/italics are rookies who could have significantly higher value.

DEFENSE/ SPECIAL TEAMS*	Yards Per Game	Points Per Game	Takeaways	Sacks	Safeties	Touchdowns DEF/RET
1. Ravens	302.0	18.8	35.3	39.7	0.0	7.7
2. Eagles	316.2	16.4	30.7	47.0	0.3	3.0
3. Steelers	286.5	19.2	31.0	42.0	0.3	3.7
4. Buccaneers	272.1	15.9	32.7	41.3	1.0	4.7
5. Patriots	312.8	17.6	35.3	40.0	0.3	6.0
6. Falcons	346.9	22.4	34.0	43.7	0.0	4.3
7. Redskins	301.7	20.9	27.3	35.7	0.7	2.0
8. Jets	326.2	18.7	25.3	34.0	0.3	3.0
9. Bears	332.2	22.0	25.7	29.3	1.0	4.0
10. Jaguars	315.1	19.3	27.3	32.3	1.3	0.7
11. Cowboys	304.3	20.7	25.7	29.7	1.0	2.7
12. Bengals	338.6	25.2	26.7	30.3	0.7	3.7
13. Bills	286.0	20.0	25.3	38.0	1.3	5.3
14. Panthers	307.4	19.7	32.6	42.0	0.7	4.0
15. Colts	325.6	20.8	31.0	37.3	0.0	3.0
16. Giants	322.0	21.1	25.0	40.7	0.0	3.3
17. Texans	349.4	22.4	24.3	26.0	1.0	3.7
18. Broncos	285.8	19.8	20.7	38.0	0.7	2.7
19. Dolphins	298.7	19.1	30.3	42.3	0.7	2.7
20. Cardinals	347.2	24.9	26.0	26.7	0.3	2.3
21. Chiefs	374.8	24.3	29.7	37.0	0.0	5.0
22. Vikings	354.8	24.8	26.7	34.3	1.0	2.7
23. Lions	351.6	24.6	25.3	33.0	0.3	6.3
24. 49ers	324.3	23.7	28.3	34.3	0.7	2.7
25. Rams	321.5	22.7	29.0	38.0	0.3	3.3
26. Seahawks	348.2	22.3	31.0	34.7	0.3	4.0
27. Chargers	353.9	23.4	26.7	32.7	0.7	2.3
28. Browns	323.4	21.5	26.3	31.7	0.0	2.3
29. Saints	357.7	23.4	32.7	36.0	0.7	4.3
30. Packers	325.6	21.2	30.7	39.0	0.0	4.0
31. Titans	324.8	22.7	31.0	36.7	0.3	4.3
32. Raiders	350.4	23.4	24.7	31.0	0.7	4.0

*Defense/Special Team stats reflect an average of the past three seasons (2002-04); they are not projections.

For more in-depth analysis, pick up a copy of the NFL.com 2005 Fantasy Football Preview, available at newsstands today.

AMERICAN FOOTBALL CONFERENCE OFFENSE

	Balt.	Buff.	Cin.	Cle.	Den.	Hou.	Ind.	Jax.	KC	Mia.	NE	NYJ	Oak.	Pitt.	SD	Tenn.
First Downs	260	271	286	245	351	300	379	279	398	267	344	313	275	310	328	308
Rushing	103	102	93	94	127	103	94	88	138	71	120	135	75	134	131	85
Passing	135	149	172	125	184	174	238	161	228	165	193	163	176	147	160	200
Penalty	22	20	21	26	40	23	47	30	32	31	31	15	24	29	37	23
Rushes	491	483	437	441	534	481	427	446	496	384	524	527	327	618	525	420
Net Yds. Gained	2063	1874	1839	1657	2333	1882	1852	1850	2289	1339	2134	2388	1295	2464	2185	1871
Avg. Gain	4.2	3.9	4.2	3.8	4.4	3.9	4.3	4.1	4.6	3.5	4.1	4.5	4.0	4.0	4.2	4.5
Avg. Yds. per Game	128.9	117.1	114.9	103.6	145.8	117.6	115.8	115.6	143.1	83.7	133.4	149.3	80.9	154.0	136.6	116.9
Passes Attempted	465	461	536	439	521	471	527	513	561	586	485	438	582	358	450	589
Completed	258	262	324	251	303	286	353	305	370	309	293	282	330	228	288	356
% Completed	55.5	56.8	60.4	57.2	58.2	60.7	67.0	59.5	66.0	52.7	60.4	64.4	56.7	63.7	64.0	60.4
Total Yds. Gained	2559	3032	3520	3076	4089	3547	4732	3315	4633	3391	3750	3231	4019	2970	3506	3933
Times Sacked	35	38	31	41	15	49	14	32	32	52	26	31	30	36	21	44
Yds. Lost	247	215	219	252	90	301	109	156	227	326	162	181	161	250	149	317
Net Yds. Gained	2312	2817	3301	2824	3999	3246	4623	3159	4406	3065	3588	3050	3858	2720	3357	3616
Avg. Yds. per Game	144.5	176.1	206.3	176.5	249.9	202.9	288.9	197.4	275.4	191.6	224.3	190.6	241.1	170.0	209.8	226.0
Net Yds. per Pass Play	4.62	5.65	5.82	5.88	7.46	6.24	8.55	5.80	7.43	4.80	7.02	6.50	6.30	6.90	7.13	5.71
Yds. Gained per Comp.	9.92	11.57	10.86	12.25	13.50	12.40	13.41	10.87	12.52	10.97	12.80	11.46	12.18	13.03	12.17	11.05
Combined Net																
Yds. Gained	4375	4691	5140	4481	6332	5128	6475	5009	6695	4404	5722	5438	5153	5184	5542	5487
% Total Yds. Rushing	47.2	39.9	35.8	37.0	36.8	36.7	28.6	36.9	34.2	30.4	37.3	43.9	25.1	47.5	39.4	34.1
% Total Yds. Passing	52.8	60.1	64.2	63.0	63.2	63.3	71.4	63.1	65.8	69.6	62.7	56.1	74.9	52.5	60.6	65.9
Avg. Yds. per Game	273.4	293.2	321.3	280.1	395.8	320.5	404.7	313.1	418.4	275.3	357.6	339.9	322.1	324.0	346.4	342.9
Ball Control Plays	991	982	1004	921	1070	1001	968	991	1089	1022	1035	996	939	1012	996	1053
Avg. Yds. per Play	4.4	4.8	5.1	4.9	5.9	5.1	6.7	5.1	6.1	4.3	5.5	5.5	5.5	5.1	5.6	5.2
Avg. Time of Poss.	29:36	30:21	29:20	28:03	32:38	29:59	28:40	30:28	32:14	28:20	31:22	31:51	26:47	34:00	31:30	31:40
Third Down Efficiency	35.1	35.8	40.2	29.1	37.9	38.4	42.7	36.9	47.2	34.5	45.1	42.5	35.5	42.9	46.6	34.1
Had Intercepted	11	17	22	21	20	14	10	11	17	26	14	11	22	13	8	19
Yds. Opp Returned	172	357	446	232	344	157	191	163	244	464	242	332	356	190	66	306
Ret. by Opp. for TD	0	1	4	2	1	1	0	1	1	8	1	0	3	3	0	2
Punts	97	78	84	85	70	73	54	84	55	99	56	80	73	67	69	79
Yds. Punted	3935	3362	3499	3404	2834	3009	2443	3592	2172	4107	2350	3057	3409	2879	2974	3389
Avg. Yds. per Punt	40.6	43.1	41.7	40.0	40.5	41.2	45.2	42.8	39.5	41.5	42.0	38.2	46.7	43.0	43.1	42.9
Punt Returns	60	46	35	36	43	40	24	42	24	52	40	41	24	44	29	40
Yds. Returned	616	491	328	432	400	329	171	405	232	564	230	313	132	365	243	173
Avg. Yds. per Return	10.3	10.7	9.4	12.0	9.3	8.2	7.1	9.6	9.7	10.8	5.8	7.6	5.5	8.3	8.4	4.3
Returned for TD	2	2	0	0	0	0	0	0	0	0	0	0	0	0	0	0
Kickoff Returns	61	63	68	75	53	69	66	57	75	70	56	46	83	62	62	79
Yds. Returned	1264	1542	1403	1504	1122	1450	1545	1087	1820	1660	1302	1038	1700	1335	1478	1558
Avg. Yds. per Return	20.7	24.5	20.6	20.1	21.2	21.0	23.4	19.1	24.3	23.7	23.3	22.6	20.5	21.5	23.8	19.7
Returned for TD	0	3	0	1	0	0	1	0	2	1	1	0	0	0	1	0
Fumbles	26	26	17	32	23	22	19	23	20	42	24	19	23	20	27	33
Lost	12	12	10	19	9	11	7	11	10	16	13	5	13	8	10	12
Out of Bounds	1	1	1	3	4	2	2	3	0	3	2	0	1	4	2	2
Own Rec. for TD	1	0	0	0	0	0	0	0	0	0	0	0	0	0	0	0
Opp. Rec. by	13	15	16	13	8	8	17	11	7	10	16	14	9	13	10	12
Opp. Rec. for TD	1	0	1	0	0	3	1	0	1	1	3	1	0	2	0	1
Penalties	94	121	103	115	93	106	106	109	117	112	101	91	134	99	108	110
Yds. Penalized	894	1047	810	854	880	928	801	940	963	852	822	693	1013	837	875	923
Total Points Scored	317	395	374	276	381	309	522	261	483	275	437	333	320	372	446	344
Total TDs	33	46	42	29	42	37	66	26	62	31	49	38	35	41	55	41
TDs Rushing	11	15	14	6	13	16	10	9	31	10	15	15	10	16	24	12
TDs Passing	13	21	23	21	27	16	51	17	27	19	29	19	24	20	29	27
TDs on Ret. and Rec.	9	10	5	2	2	5	5	0	4	2	5	4	1	5	2	2
Extra Point Kicks	30	45	41	28	42	34	64	21	58	26	48	33	31	40	54	39
Extra Point Kicks Att.	30	45	41	28	42	34	65	21	60	27	48	34	32	40	55	39
2Pt Conversions	1	0	0	1	0	1	1	4	1	2	1	0	1	0	0	1
2Pt Conversions Att.	3	1	1	1	0	3	1	4	2	4	1	4	3	1	0	2
Safeties	0	1	0	0	0	0	0	2	0	1	0	0	1	1	1	0
Field Goals Made	29	24	27	24	29	17	20	24	17	19	31	24	25	28	20	19
Field Goals Attempted	32	28	31	29	34	24	26	31	23	23	33	29	28	33	25	27
% Successful	90.6	85.7	87.1	82.8	85.3	70.8	76.9	77.4	73.9	82.6	93.9	82.8	89.3	84.8	80.0	70.4

AMERICAN FOOTBALL CONFERENCE DEFENSE

	Balt.	Buff.	Cin.	Cle.	Den.	Hou.	Ind.	Jax.	KC	Mia.	NE	NYJ	Oak.	Pitt.	SD	Tenn.
First Downs	273	258	303	307	235	304	331	290	327	281	290	282	367	248	320	318
Rushing	88	79	123	141	83	89	103	83	97	107	83	87	115	79	79	99
Passing	158	150	158	144	130	194	209	181	190	139	177	169	210	146	200	189
Penalty	27	29	22	22	22	21	19	26	40	35	30	26	42	23	41	30
Rushes	469	447	474	532	396	417	440	438	397	539	405	432	537	357	355	421
Net Yds. Gained	1681	1604	2062	2314	1512	1843	2037	1777	1834	2302	1572	1566	2012	1299	1307	1917
Avg. Gain	3.6	3.6	4.4	4.3	3.8	4.4	4.6	4.1	4.6	4.3	3.9	3.6	3.7	3.6	3.7	4.6
Avg. Yds. per Game	105.1	100.3	128.9	144.6	94.5	115.2	127.3	111.1	114.6	143.9	98.3	97.9	125.8	81.2	81.7	119.8
Passes Attempted	501	486	520	460	484	530	557	497	522	434	538	497	510	484	607	524
Completed	276	261	313	277	272	344	364	306	312	244	315	289	315	269	372	333
% Completed	55.1	53.7	60.2	60.2	56.2	64.9	65.4	61.6	59.8	56.2	58.6	58.1	61.8	55.6	61.3	63.5
Total Yds. Gained	3386	2943	3560	3091	3213	3776	4232	3574	4453	2815	3711	3532	4106	3060	4195	4027
Times Sacked	39	45	37	32	38	24	45	37	41	36	45	37	25	41	29	32
Yds. Lost	264	319	257	190	266	161	340	217	250	223	311	220	182	225	142	220
Net Yds. Gained	3122	2624	3303	2901	2947	3615	3892	3357	4203	2592	3400	3312	3924	2835	4053	3807
Avg. per Game	195.1	164.0	206.4	181.3	184.2	225.9	243.3	209.8	262.7	162.0	212.5	207.0	245.3	177.2	253.3	237.9
Net Yds. per Pass Play	5.78	4.94	5.93	5.90	5.65	6.53	6.47	6.29	7.47	5.51	5.83	6.20	7.33	5.40	6.37	6.85
Yds. Gained per Comp.	12.27	11.28	11.37	11.16	11.81	10.98	11.63	11.68	14.27	11.54	11.78	12.22	13.03	11.38	11.28	12.09
Combined Net Yds. Gained	4803	4228	5365	5215	4459	5458	5929	5134	6037	4894	4972	4878	5936	4134	5360	5724
% Total Yds. Rushing	35.0	37.9	38.4	44.4	33.9	33.8	34.4	34.6	30.4	47.0	31.6	32.1	33.9	31.4	24.4	33.5
% Total Yds. Passing	65.0	62.1	61.6	55.6	66.1	66.2	65.6	65.4	69.6	53.0	68.4	67.9	66.1	68.6	75.6	66.5
Avg. Yds. per Game	300.2	264.3	335.3	325.9	278.7	341.1	370.6	320.9	377.3	305.9	310.8	304.9	371.0	258.4	335.0	357.8
Ball Control Plays	1009	978	1031	1024	918	971	1042	972	960	1009	988	966	1072	882	991	977
Avg. Yds. per Play	4.8	4.3	5.2	5.1	4.9	5.6	5.7	5.3	6.3	4.9	5.0	5.0	5.5	4.7	5.4	5.9
Avg. Time of Poss.	30:24	29:39	30:40	31:57	27:23	30:01	31:20	29:32	27:46	31:40	28:38	28:09	33:13	26:01	28:30	28:20
Third Down Efficiency	34.4	36.0	36.7	36.1	31.1	43.4	41.9	41.0	38.4	32.3	38.8	38.0	47.4	32.6	35.2	33.3
Intercepted By	21	24	20	15	12	22	19	16	13	15	20	19	9	19	23	18
Yds. Returned By	700	333	272	250	175	393	252	126	173	92	290	243	221	293	180	285
Returned for TD	5	4	4	1	2	2	2	0	1	0	1	2	1	3	1	1
Punts	94	79	79	85	95	69	52	74	64	102	69	89	68	79	64	74
Yds. Punted	3767	3218	3309	3537	4250	2880	2220	3265	2703	4177	2866	3571	2808	3375	2713	3223
Avg. Yds. per Punt	40.1	40.7	41.9	41.6	44.7	41.7	42.7	44.1	42.2	41.0	41.5	40.1	41.3	42.7	42.4	43.6
Punt Returns	36	37	51	48	32	30	29	38	24	45	31	34	35	34	23	31
Yds. Returned	281	315	378	313	295	265	395	429	301	258	365	221	413	252	164	195
Avg. Yds. per Return	7.8	8.5	7.4	6.5	9.2	8.8	13.6	11.3	12.5	5.7	11.8	6.5	11.8	7.4	7.1	6.3
Returned for TD	0	0	0	0	0	0	1	2	2	0	1	0	0	0	0	1
Kickoff Returns	65	77	80	59	68	60	92	50	85	51	86	72	62	74	83	69
Yds. Returned	1509	1406	1573	1336	1635	1386	1960	995	1908	1114	2003	1557	1458	1595	1846	1389
Avg. Yds. per Return	23.2	18.3	19.7	22.6	24.0	23.1	21.3	19.9	22.4	21.8	23.3	21.6	23.5	21.6	22.2	20.1
Returned for TD	2	0	0	1	1	1	0	0	0	1	1	1	0	1	2	0
Fumbles	23	31	40	20	24	22	36	30	23	22	31	29	14	28	19	22
Lost	13	15	16	13	8	8	17	12	8	10	16	14	9	13	10	12
Out of Bounds	0	4	2	1	0	1	0	2	6	3	3	2	0	3	0	1
Own Rec. for TD	0	0	1	0	0	0	0	0	0	0	0	0	0	0	0	0
Opp. Rec. by	12	12	10	19	8	10	7	11	10	10	16	13	5	13	10	12
Opp. Rec. for TD	2	2	1	3	0	0	0	3	0	1	1	0	2	0	0	1
Penalties	101	120	106	109	120	123	116	118	117	107	118	86	102	104	109	95
Yds. Penalized	798	865	887	890	1062	979	877	966	957	852	1014	720	837	875	940	774
Total Points Scored	268	284	372	390	304	339	351	280	435	354	260	261	442	251	313	439
Total TDs	27	29	41	45	35	39	39	31	53	42	31	30	56	26	36	52
TDs Rushing	9	6	11	22	16	4	12	7	18	12	9	8	21	8	15	18
TDs Passing	14	20	23	17	17	32	26	18	32	20	18	21	30	14	19	29
TDs on Ret. and Rec.	4	3	7	6	2	3	1	6	3	10	4	1	5	4	2	5
Extra Point Kicks	24	27	40	44	31	37	36	27	50	42	23	29	53	24	33	50
Extra Point Kicks Att.	24	27	40	44	32	37	36	28	51	42	23	29	54	24	34	50
2Pt Conversions	1	1	0	1	0	0	3	2	2	0	3	1	1	1	2	1
2Pt Conversions Att.	3	2	1	1	3	1	3	3	2	0	8	1	2	2	2	1
Safeties	1	0	1	1	0	1	0	0	0	0	1	0	0	0	0	3
Field Goals Made	26	27	28	24	21	22	25	21	21	20	15	16	17	23	20	23
Field Goals Attempted	31	32	31	28	26	29	31	28	27	28	18	19	25	27	27	28
% Successful	83.9	84.4	90.3	85.7	80.8	75.9	80.6	75.0	77.8	71.4	83.3	84.2	68.0	85.2	74.1	82.1

NATIONAL FOOTBALL CONFERENCE OFFENSE

	Ariz.	Atl.	Car.	Chi.	Dall.	Det.	GB	Minn.	NO	NYG	Phil.	StL	SF	Sea.	TB	Wash.
First Downs	280	284	308	230	296	263	354	351	291	281	301	321	280	320	271	269
Rushing	86	133	85	84	101	92	98	98	82	105	87	96	83	110	74	91
Passing	152	120	192	121	171	142	228	225	177	143	188	203	172	189	175	156
Penalty	42	31	31	25	24	29	28	28	32	33	26	22	25	21	22	22
Rushes	475	524	422	430	449	407	441	387	406	424	376	381	413	468	393	471
Net Yds. Gained	1668	2672	1582	1624	1769	1777	1908	1823	1606	1904	1639	1624	1449	2095	1489	1765
Avg. Gain	3.5	5.1	3.7	3.8	3.9	4.4	4.3	4.7	4.0	4.5	4.4	4.3	3.5	4.5	3.8	3.7
Avg. Yds. per Game	104.3	167.0	98.9	101.5	110.6	111.1	119.3	113.9	100.4	119.0	102.4	101.5	90.6	130.9	93.1	110.3
Passes Attempted	533	395	536	471	519	505	598	552	542	475	547	580	561	532	512	514
Completed	299	217	311	249	308	285	382	380	309	269	336	372	325	304	340	288
% Completed	56.1	54.9	58.0	52.9	59.3	56.4	63.9	68.8	57.0	56.6	61.4	64.1	57.9	57.1	66.4	56.0
Total Yds. Gained	3202	2692	3889	2641	3636	3124	4550	4754	3810	3097	4208	4615	3455	3715	3773	2874
Times Sacked	39	50	33	66	36	37	14	46	41	52	37	50	52	34	44	38
Yds. Lost	320	280	246	449	208	208	101	238	223	279	229	362	319	176	299	242
Net Yds. Gained	2882	2412	3643	2192	3428	2916	4449	4516	3587	2818	3979	4253	3136	3539	3474	2632
Avg. Yds. per Game	180.1	150.8	227.7	137.0	214.3	182.3	278.1	282.3	224.2	176.1	248.7	265.8	196.0	221.2	217.1	164.5
Net Yds. per Pass Play	5.04	5.42	6.40	4.08	6.18	5.38	7.27	7.55	6.15	5.35	6.81	6.75	5.12	6.25	6.25	4.77
Yds. Gained per Comp.	10.71	12.41	12.50	10.61	11.81	10.96	11.91	12.51	12.33	11.51	12.52	12.41	10.63	12.22	11.10	9.98
Combined Net																
Yds. Gained	4550	5084	5225	3816	5197	4693	6357	6339	5193	4722	5618	5877	4585	5634	4963	4397
% Total Yds. Rushing	36.7	52.6	30.3	42.6	34.0	37.9	30.0	28.8	30.9	40.3	29.2	27.6	31.6	37.2	30.0	40.1
% Total Yds. Passing	63.3	47.4	69.7	57.4	66.0	62.1	70.0	71.2	69.1	59.7	70.8	72.4	68.4	62.8	70.0	59.9
Avg. Yds. per Game	284.4	317.8	326.6	238.5	324.8	293.3	397.3	396.2	324.6	295.1	351.1	367.3	286.6	352.1	310.2	274.8
Ball Control Plays	1047	969	991	967	1004	949	1053	985	989	951	960	1011	1026	1034	949	1023
Avg. Yds. per Play	4.3	5.2	5.3	3.9	5.2	4.9	6.0	6.4	5.3	5.0	5.9	5.8	4.5	5.4	5.2	4.3
Avg. Time of Poss.	30:53	29:10	29:56	28:20	30:37	28:03	30:28	30:02	28:18	28:52	28:26	31:05	29:00	29:00	29:43	31:19
Third Down Efficiency	34.9	36.3	40.3	25.1	36.4	31.4	47.3	52.3	33.3	29.5	36.9	42.2	32.4	36.2	37.7	31.7
Had Intercepted	18	16	15	16	23	13	19	12	16	13	11	22	21	18	18	17
Yds. Opp Returned	263	201	321	222	526	194	166	207	260	134	140	191	479	158	328	201
Ret. by Opp. for TD	1	0	3	1	4	2	1	0	1	0	1	1	4	1	4	1
Punts	99	76	79	110	76	93	66	57	85	77	73	68	96	79	83	104
Yds. Punted	4230	3082	3402	4691	3216	3765	2644	2240	3704	3088	3068	2848	3990	3036	3472	4544
Avg. Yds. per Punt	42.7	40.6	43.1	42.6	42.3	40.5	40.1	39.3	43.6	40.1	42.0	41.9	41.6	38.4	41.8	43.7
Punt Returns	49	37	28	46	44	40	33	31	40	38	41	30	35	30	33	42
Yds. Returned	329	457	165	510	390	420	254	275	388	253	377	143	303	230	213	331
Avg. Yds. per Return	6.7	12.4	5.9	11.1	8.9	10.5	7.7	8.9	9.7	6.7	9.2	4.8	8.7	7.7	6.5	7.9
Returned for TD	0	1	0	1	0	2	0	1	0	0	0	0	1	0	1	0
Kickoff Returns	65	61	61	74	78	66	70	73	83	66	56	84	84	74	60	55
Yds. Returned	1293	1331	1307	1607	1603	1568	1522	1448	1879	1658	1214	1604	1716	1529	1450	1203
Avg. Yds. per Return	19.9	21.8	21.4	21.7	20.6	23.8	21.7	19.8	22.6	25.1	21.7	19.1	20.4	20.7	24.2	21.9
Returned for TD	0	0	0	0	0	2	0	0	2	2	0	0	0	0	0	0
Fumbles	34	26	23	35	26	12	22	20	23	29	17	27	33	19	32	20
Lost	11	14	11	21	14	7	10	9	10	11	11	17	19	9	18	10
Out of Bounds	5	1	1	1	1	0	2	1	0	1	1	2	0	2	3	0
Own Rec. for TD	0	0	0	0	0	0	0	0	0	0	0	0	0	0	0	0
Opp. Rec. by	15	13	12	12	9	10	7	11	20	14	11	9	12	12	11	8
Opp. Rec. for TD	1	1	1	1	0	0	3	1	1	2	0	3	2	0	2	0
Penalties	124	109	123	124	105	121	116	117	129	118	124	127	103	79	117	115
Yds. Penalized	948	1005	1020	956	867	1000	950	884	1141	977	952	993	859	669	916	1047
Total Points Scored	284	340	355	231	293	296	424	405	348	303	386	319	259	371	301	240
Total TDs	31	41	42	26	33	32	50	50	40	34	44	37	29	43	37	26
TDs Rushing	15	20	10	10	14	7	9	8	15	18	10	11	10	17	9	6
TDs Passing	14	15	29	9	19	19	36	39	21	12	32	23	16	23	24	18
TDs on Ret. and Rec.	2	6	3	7	0	6	5	3	4	4	2	3	3	3	4	2
Extra Point Kicks	28	40	39	22	31	28	48	45	38	33	41	32	23	40	32	25
Extra Point Kicks Att.	28	40	40	22	31	28	48	45	38	33	42	32	23	40	33	25
2Pt Conversions	1	0	2	1	1	1	2	3	1	0	0	4	3	2	1	1
2Pt Conversions Att.	3	1	2	4	2	4	2	4	2	1	2	4	6	3	4	1
Safeties	1	0	0	3	1	1	0	0	1	0	0	1	0	0	0	0
Field Goals Made	22	18	20	15	20	24	24	18	22	22	27	19	18	23	15	19
Field Goals Attempted	29	23	25	24	26	28	28	22	27	28	32	24	22	25	24	27
% Successful	75.9	78.3	80.0	62.5	76.9	85.7	85.7	81.8	81.5	78.6	84.4	79.2	81.8	92.0	62.5	70.4

NATIONAL FOOTBALL CONFERENCE DEFENSE

	Ariz.	Atl.	Car.	Chi.	Dall.	Det.	GB	Minn.	NO	NYG	Phil.	StL	SF	Sea.	TB	Wash.
First Downs	282	310	307	302	297	320	307	350	343	310	299	311	322	311	258	251
Rushing	101	107	98	109	88	118	92	110	118	112	101	118	121	102	101	67
Passing	153	183	177	165	180	167	181	220	193	170	165	172	179	191	131	153
Penalty	28	20	32	28	29	35	34	20	32	28	33	21	22	18	26	31
Rushes	450	434	474	496	425	498	409	435	485	498	442	480	495	452	480	419
Net Yds. Gained	2105	1681	1904	2050	1764	1887	1878	2006	2253	2157	1903	2179	1995	2031	1973	1304
Avg. Gain	4.7	3.9	4.0	4.1	4.2	3.8	4.6	4.6	4.6	4.3	4.3	4.5	4.0	4.5	4.1	3.1
Avg. Yds. per Game	131.6	105.1	119.0	128.1	110.3	117.9	117.4	125.4	140.8	134.8	118.9	136.2	124.7	126.9	123.3	81.5
Passes Attempted	505	517	513	515	502	535	518	544	545	467	550	492	490	559	436	515
Completed	271	328	303	287	310	328	314	338	324	292	334	292	308	340	247	294
% Completed	53.7	63.4	59.1	55.7	61.8	61.3	60.6	62.1	59.4	62.5	60.7	59.3	62.9	60.8	56.7	57.1
Total Yds. Gained	3265	3838	3703	3513	3718	3736	3943	4130	4095	3280	3475	3415	3680	3808	2843	3222
Times Sacked	38	48	34	35	33	38	40	39	37	40	47	34	29	36	45	40
Yds. Lost	229	312	225	173	197	222	280	234	207	250	263	241	194	218	264	245
Net Yds. Gained	3036	3526	3478	3340	3521	3514	3663	3896	3888	3030	3212	3174	3486	3590	2579	2977
Avg. Yds. per Game	189.8	220.4	217.4	208.8	220.1	219.6	228.9	243.5	243.0	189.4	200.8	198.4	217.9	224.4	161.2	186.1
Net Yds. per Pass Play	5.59	6.24	6.36	6.07	6.58	6.13	6.56	6.68	6.68	5.98	5.38	6.03	6.72	6.03	5.36	5.36
Yds. Gained per Comp.	12.05	11.70	12.22	12.24	11.99	11.39	12.56	12.22	12.64	11.23	10.40	11.70	11.95	11.20	11.51	10.96
Combined Net																
Yds. Gained	5141	5207	5382	5390	5285	5401	5541	5902	6141	5187	5115	5353	5481	5621	4552	4281
% Total Yds. Rushing	40.9	32.3	35.4	38.0	33.4	34.9	33.9	34.0	36.7	41.6	37.2	40.7	36.4	36.1	43.3	30.5
% Total Yds. Passing	59.1	67.7	64.6	62.0	66.6	65.1	66.1	66.0	63.3	58.4	62.8	59.3	63.6	63.9	56.7	69.5
Avg. Yds. per Game	321.3	325.4	336.4	336.9	330.3	337.6	346.3	368.9	383.8	324.2	319.7	334.6	342.6	351.3	284.5	267.6
Ball Control Plays	993	999	1021	1046	960	1071	967	1018	1067	1005	1039	1006	1014	1047	961	974
Avg. Yds. per Play	5.2	5.2	5.3	5.2	5.5	5.0	5.7	5.8	5.8	5.2	4.9	5.3	5.4	5.4	4.7	4.4
Avg. Time of Poss.	29:07	30:50	30:04	31:40	29:23	31:57	29:32	29:58	31:42	31:08	31:34	28:55	31:00	31:00	30:17	28:41
Third Down Efficiency	31.6	36.0	46.0	30.5	39.1	42.4	35.0	45.9	38.1	41.8	35.8	36.4	40.3	42.4	35.3	31.0
Intercepted By	15	19	26	17	13	14	8	11	13	14	17	6	9	23	16	18
Yds. Returned By	214	442	420	546	109	216	165	207	101	113	287	45	129	337	239	405
Returned for TD	1	4	2	5	0	1	2	1	0	0	2	0	0	3	1	1
Punts	97	80	64	92	78	84	81	59	71	77	89	71	80	74	87	104
Yds. Punted	4064	3466	2630	3713	3260	3658	3176	2488	2896	2997	3785	3014	3268	3091	3867	4180
Avg. Yds. per Punt	41.9	43.3	41.1	40.4	41.8	43.5	39.2	42.2	40.8	38.9	42.5	42.5	40.9	41.8	44.4	40.2
Punt Returns	56	33	38	57	39	46	34	26	43	38	34	35	51	33	31	65
Yds. Returned	486	134	303	380	410	441	301	169	310	356	221	416	445	244	279	727
Avg. Yds. per Return	8.7	4.1	8.0	6.7	10.5	9.6	8.9	6.5	7.2	9.4	6.5	11.9	8.7	7.4	9.0	11.2
Returned for TD	1	0	0	0	0	0	0	0	1	0	0	1	0	0	0	1
Kickoff Returns	46	56	69	54	62	54	79	75	74	66	73	66	56	77	58	57
Yds. Returned	1017	1117	1477	1160	1083	1058	1594	1869	1710	1278	1693	1680	1119	1677	1315	1223
Avg. Yds. per Return	22.1	19.9	21.4	21.5	17.5	19.6	20.2	24.9	23.1	19.4	23.2	25.5	20.0	21.8	22.7	21.5
Returned for TD	1	1	0	0	0	0	0	1	0	0	0	1	0	0	1	1
Fumbles	32	24	29	21	20	20	17	25	31	27	29	18	24	25	21	17
Lost	15	13	12	12	9	10	7	11	20	14	11	9	12	12	11	8
Out of Bounds	2	1	3	2	1	1	1	1	2	4	0	3	1	0	1	1
Own Rec. for TD	0	0	0	0	0	0	0	0	0	0	0	0	0	0	0	0
Opp. Rec. by	11	14	11	21	14	7	10	9	10	11	11	17	19	9	18	10
Opp. Rec. for TD	1	1	0	2	0	1	1	0	2	0	0	3	1	0	1	3
Penalties	139	129	117	120	104	114	112	110	119	120	119	109	107	91	112	97
Yds. Penalized	1121	930	1078	914	879	976	942	974	965	1007	1001	827	867	748	897	797
Total Points Scored	322	337	339	331	405	350	380	395	405	347	260	392	452	373	304	265
Total TDs	35	41	40	36	49	43	47	46	44	41	30	43	54	42	35	30
TDs Rushing	12	20	19	9	14	10	12	15	16	13	13	22	17	8	8	7
TDs Passing	18	19	18	23	31	29	33	30	24	28	16	24	27	24	21	17
TDs on Ret. and Rec.	5	2	3	4	4	4	2	1	4	0	1	6	5	1	6	6
Extra Point Kicks	29	39	39	35	44	37	47	43	42	37	27	39	51	38	34	28
Extra Point Kicks Att.	30	39	39	35	45	38	47	43	42	37	27	39	51	39	35	28
2Pt Conversions	4	1	0	0	2	1	0	1	2	2	1	1	1	0	0	2
2Pt Conversions Att.	5	2	1	1	4	4	0	3	2	4	3	4	3	2	0	2
Safeties	0	1	0	1	0	1	0	1	1	0	0	0	0	1	0	1
Field Goals Made	25	16	20	26	21	17	17	24	31	20	17	31	25	27	20	17
Field Goals Attempted	26	18	28	36	23	20	25	27	35	25	24	36	29	32	31	20
% Successful	96.2	88.9	71.4	72.2	91.3	85.0	68.0	88.9	88.6	80.0	70.8	86.1	86.2	84.4	64.5	85.0

AFC, NFC, AND NFL SUMMARY

	AFC Offense Total	AFC Offense Average	AFC Defense Total	AFC Defense Average	NFC Offense Total	NFC Offense Average	NFC Defense Total	NFC Defense Average	NFL Total	NFL Average
First Downs	4914	307.1	4734	295.9	4700	293.8	4880	305.0	9614	300.4
Rushing	1693	105.8	1535	95.9	1505	94.1	1663	103.9	3198	99.9
Passing	2770	173.1	2744	171.5	2754	172.1	2780	173.8	5524	172.6
Penalty	451	28.2	455	28.4	441	27.6	437	27.3	892	27.9
Rushes	7561	472.6	7056	441.0	6867	429.2	7372	460.8	14428	450.9
Net Yds. Gained	31315	1957.2	28639	1789.9	28394	1774.6	31070	1941.9	59709	1865.9
Avg. Gain	—	4.1	—	4.1	—	4.1	—	4.2	—	4.1
Avg. Yds. per Game	—	122.3	—	111.9	—	110.9	—	121.4	—	116.6
Passes Attempted	7982	498.9	8151	509.4	8372	523.3	8203	512.7	16354	511.1
Completed	4798	299.9	4862	303.9	4974	310.9	4910	306.9	9772	305.4
% Completed	—	60.1	—	59.6	—	59.4	—	59.9	—	59.8
Total Yds. Gained	57303	3581.4	57674	3604.6	58035	3627.2	57664	3604.0	115338	3604.3
Times Sacked	527	32.9	583	36.4	669	41.8	613	38.3	1196	37.4
Yds. Lost	3362	210.1	3787	236.7	4179	261.2	3754	234.6	7541	235.7
Net Yds. Gained	53941	3371.3	53887	3367.9	53856	3366.0	53910	3369.4	107797	3368.7
Avg. Yds. per Game	—	210.7	—	210.5	—	210.4	—	210.6	—	210.5
Net Yds. per Pass Play	—	6.34	—	6.17	—	5.96	—	6.12	—	6.14
Yds. Gained per Comp.	—	11.94	—	11.86	—	11.67	—	11.74	—	11.80
Combined Net										
Yds. Gained	85256	5328.5	82526	5157.9	82250	5140.6	84980	5311.3	167506	5234.6
% Total Yds. Rushing	—	36.7	—	34.7	—	34.5	—	36.6	—	35.6
% Total Yds. Passing	—	63.3	—	65.3	—	65.5	—	63.4	—	64.4
Avg. Yds. per Game	—	333.0	—	322.4	—	321.3	—	332.0	—	327.2
Ball Control Plays	16070	1004.4	15790	986.9	15908	994.3	16188	1011.8	31978	999.3
Avg. Yds. per Play	—	5.3	—	5.2	—	5.2	—	5.2	—	5.2
Third Down Efficiency	—	38.9	—	37.3	—	36.4	—	37.9	—	37.6
Interceptions	256	16.0	285	17.8	268	16.8	239	14.9	524	16.4
Yds. Returned	4262	266.4	4278	267.4	3991	249.4	3975	248.4	8253	257.9
Returned for TD	28	1.8	30	1.9	25	1.6	23	1.4	53	1.7
Punts	1203	75.2	1236	77.3	1321	82.6	1288	80.5	2524	78.9
Yds. Punted	50415	3150.9	51882	3242.6	55020	3438.8	53553	3347.1	105435	3294.8
Avg. Yds. per Punt	—	41.9	—	42.0	—	41.7	—	41.6	—	41.8
Punt Returns	620	38.8	558	34.9	597	37.3	659	41.2	1217	38.0
Yds. Returned	5424	339.0	4840	302.5	5038	314.9	5622	351.4	10462	326.9
Avg. Yds. per Return	—	8.7	—	8.7	—	8.4	—	8.5	—	8.6
Returned for TD	4	0.3	7	0.4	7	0.4	4	0.3	11	0.3
Kickoff Returns	1045	65.3	1133	70.8	1110	69.4	1022	63.9	2155	67.3
Yds. Returned	22808	1425.5	24670	1541.9	23932	1495.8	22070	1379.4	46740	1460.6
Avg. Yds. per Return	—	21.8	—	21.8	—	21.6	—	21.6	—	21.7
Returned for TD	11	0.7	11	0.7	6	0.4	6	0.4	17	0.5
Fumbles	396	24.8	414	25.9	398	24.9	380	23.8	794	24.8
Lost	178	11.1	194	12.1	202	12.6	186	11.6	380	11.9
Out of Bounds	31	1.9	28	1.8	21	1.3	24	1.5	52	1.6
Own Rec. for TD	1	0.1	1	0.1	0	0.0	0	0.0	1	0.0
Opp. Rec.	192	12.0	176	11.0	186	11.6	202	12.6	378	11.8
Opp. Rec. for TD	15	0.9	17	1.1	18	1.1	16	1.0	33	1.0
Penalties	1719	107.4	1751	109.4	1851	115.7	1819	113.7	3570	111.6
Yds. Penalized	14132	883.3	14293	893.3	15084	942.8	14923	932.7	29216	913.0
Total Points Scored	5845	365.3	5343	333.9	5155	322.2	5657	353.6	11000	343.8
Total TDs	673	42.1	612	38.3	595	37.2	656	41.0	1268	39.6
TDs Rushing	227	14.2	196	12.3	189	11.8	220	13.8	416	13.0
TDs Passing	383	23.9	350	21.9	349	21.8	382	23.9	732	22.9
TDs on Ret. and Rec.	63	3.9	66	4.1	57	3.6	54	3.4	120	3.8
Extra Point Kicks	634	39.6	570	35.6	545	34.1	609	38.1	1179	36.8
Extra Point Kicks Att.	641	40.1	575	35.9	548	34.3	614	38.4	1189	37.2
2Pt Conversions	14	0.9	19	1.2	23	1.4	18	1.1	37	1.2
2Pt Conversions Att.	31	1.9	36	2.3	45	2.8	40	2.5	76	2.4
Safeties	7	0.4	8	0.5	8	0.5	7	0.4	15	0.5
Field Goals Made	377	23.6	349	21.8	326	20.4	354	22.1	703	22.0
Field Goals Attempted	456	28.5	435	27.2	414	25.9	435	27.2	870	27.2
% Successful	—	82.7	—	80.2	—	78.7	—	81.4	—	80.8

CLUB LEADERS

	Offense	Defense
First Downs	Kansas City 398	Denver 235
Rushing	Kansas City 138	Washington 67
Passing	Indianapolis 238	Denver 130
Penalty	Indianapolis 47	Seattle 18
Rushes	Pittsburgh 618	San Diego 355
Net Yds. Gained	Atlanta 2672	Pittsburgh 1299
Avg. Gain	Atlanta 5.1	Washington 3.1
Passes Attempted	Green Bay 598	Miami 434
Completed	Green Bay 382	Miami 244
% Completed	Minnesota 68.8	Arizona 53.7
Total Yds. Gained	Minnesota 4754	Miami 2815
Times Sacked	Green Bay &	Atlanta 48
	Indianapolis 14	
Yds. Lost	Denver 90	Indianapolis 340
Net Yds. Gained	Indianapolis 4623	Tampa Bay 2579
Net Yds. per Pass Play	Indianapolis 8.5	Buffalo 4.9
Yds. Gained per Comp.	Denver 13.5	Philadelphia 10.4
Combined Net Yds. Gained	Kansas City 6695	Pittsburgh 4134
% Total Yds. Rushing	Atlanta 52.6	San Diego 24.4
% Total Yds. Passing	Oakland 74.9	Miami 53.0
Ball Control Plays	Kansas City 1089	Pittsburgh 882
Avg. Yds. per Play	Indianapolis 6.7	Buffalo 4.3
Avg. Time of Poss.	Pittsburgh 33:59	—
Third Down Efficiency	Minnesota 52.3	Chicago 30.5
Interceptions	—	Carolina 26
Yds. Returned	—	Baltimore 700
Returned for TD	—	Baltimore &
		Chicago 5
Punts	Chicago 110	—
Yds. Punted	Chicago 4691	—
Avg. Yds. per Punt	Oakland 46.7	—
Punt Returns	Baltimore 60	San Diego 23
Yds. Returned	Baltimore 616	Atlanta 134
Avg. Yds. per Return	Atlanta 12.4	Atlanta 4.1
Returned for TD	Baltimore &	—
	Buffalo & Detroit 2	
Kickoff Returns	St. Louis &	Arizona 46
	San Francisco 84	
Yds. Returned	New Orleans 1879	Jacksonville 995
Avg. Yds. per Return	New York Giants 25.1	Dallas 17.5
Returned for TD	Buffalo 3	—
Total Points Scored	Indianapolis 522	Pittsburgh 251
Total TDs	Indianapolis 66	Pittsburgh 26
TDs Rushing	Kansas City 31	Houston 4
TDs Passing	Indianapolis 51	Baltimore &
		Pittsburgh 14
TDs on Ret. and Rec.	Buffalo 10	New York Giants 0
Extra Point Kicks	Indianapolis 64	New England 23
2-Point Conversions	Jacksonville &	—
	St. Louis 4	
Safeties	Chicago 3	
Field Goals Made	New England 31	New England 15
Field Goals Attempted	Denver 34	Atlanta &
		New England 18
% Successful	New England 93.9	Tampa Bay 64.5

NFL CLUB RANKINGS BY YARDS

	Offense			Defense		
	Total	Rush	Pass	Total	Rush	Pass
Arizona	27	22	24	12	27	9
Atlanta	20	*1	30	14	8T	22
Baltimore	31	9	31	6	8T	10
Buffalo	25	13	27	2	7	3
Carolina	13	28	9	20	17	18
Chicago	32	25T	32	21	25	15
Cincinnati	18	17	17	19	26	13
Cleveland	28	23	25	15	32	5
Dallas	14	20	15	16	10	21
Denver	5	4	6	4	4	6
Detroit	24	19	23	22	15	20
Green Bay	3	10	3	25	14	25
Houston	19	12	18	23	13	24
Indianapolis	2	15	*1	29	24	28
Jacksonville	21	16	19	11	11	16
Kansas City	*1	5	4	31	12	32
Miami	29	31	21	8	31	2
Minnesota	4	18	2	28	21	29
New England	7	7	11	9	6	17
New Orleans	15	27	12	32	30	27
N.Y. Giants	23	11	26	13	28	8
N.Y. Jets	12	3	22	7	5	14
Oakland	17	32	8	30	22	30
Philadelphia	9	24	7	10	16	12
Pittsburgh	16	2	28	*1	*1	4
St. Louis	6	25T	5	17	29	11
San Diego	10	6	16	18	3	31
San Francisco	26	30	20	24	20	19
Seattle	8	8	13	26	23	23
Tampa Bay	22	29	14	5	19	*1
Tennessee	11	14	10	27	18	26
Washington	30	21	29	3	2	7

T = Tied for position   * = League Leader

AFC TAKEAWAYS/GIVEAWAYS

	Takeaways			Giveaways			Net
	Int	Fum	Total	Int	Fum	Total	Diff.
Indianapolis	19	17	36	10	7	17	+19
N.Y. Jets	19	14	33	11	5	16	+17
San Diego	23	10	33	8	10	18	+15
Baltimore	21	13	34	11	12	23	+11
Pittsburgh	19	13	32	13	8	21	+11
Buffalo	24	15	39	17	12	29	+10
New England	20	16	36	14	13	27	+9
Jacksonville	16	12	28	11	11	22	+6
Houston	22	8	30	14	11	25	+5
Cincinnati	20	16	36	22	10	32	+4
Tennessee	18	12	30	19	12	31	-1
Kansas City	13	8	21	17	10	27	-6
Denver	12	8	20	20	9	29	-9
Cleveland	15	13	28	21	19	40	-12
Miami	15	10	25	26	16	42	-17
Oakland	9	9	18	22	13	35	-17
AFC Totals	285	194	479	256	178	434	+45

NFC TAKEAWAYS/GIVEAWAYS

	Takeaways			Giveaways			Net
	Int	Fum	Total	Int	Fum	Total	Diff.
Carolina	26	12	38	15	11	26	+12
Seattle	23	12	35	18	9	27	+8
New Orleans	13	20	33	16	10	26	+7
Philadelphia	17	11	28	11	11	22	+6
Detroit	14	10	24	13	7	20	+4
N.Y. Giants	14	14	28	13	11	24	+4
Atlanta	19	13	32	16	14	30	+2
Arizona	15	15	30	18	11	29	+1
Minnesota	11	11	22	12	9	21	+1
Washington	18	8	26	17	10	27	-1
Chicago	17	12	29	16	21	37	-8
Tampa Bay	16	11	27	18	18	36	-9
Green Bay	8	7	15	19	10	29	-14
Dallas	13	9	22	23	14	37	-15
San Francisco	9	12	21	21	19	40	-19
St. Louis	6	9	15	22	17	39	-24
NFC Totals	239	186	425	268	202	470	-45

SCORING

POINTS

AFC:	141	Adam Vinatieri, New England
NFC:	122	David Akers, Philadelphia

TOUCHDOWNS

NFC:	20	Shaun Alexander, Seattle
AFC:	18	LaDainian Tomlinson, San Diego

EXTRA POINT KICKS

AFC:	59	Mike Vanderjagt, Indianapolis
NFC:	48	Ryan Longwell, Green Bay

TWO-POINT EXTRA POINT PLAYS

AFC:	2	* Reggie Williams, Jacksonville
NFC:	2	Marshall Faulk, St. Louis

FIELD GOALS

AFC:	31	Adam Vinatieri, New England
NFC:	27	David Akers, Philadelphia

FIELD GOAL ATTEMPTS

AFC:	34	Jason Elam, Denver
NFC:	32	David Akers, Philadelphia

LONGEST FIELD GOAL

NFC:	55	Neil Rackers, Arizona vs. Seattle, October 24
	55	Neil Rackers, Arizona vs. Seattle, October 24
AFC:	53	Doug Brien, New York Jets at Miami, October 3
	53	* Nate Kaeding, San Diego at Atlanta, October 17
	53	* Josh Scobee, Jacksonville at Indianapolis, October 24
	53	Shayne Graham, Cincinnati vs. Denver, October 25

MOST POINTS, GAME

AFC:	24	Derrick Blaylock, Kansas City vs. Atlanta, October 24 (4 TD)
	24	Priest Holmes, Kansas City vs. Atlanta, October 24 (4 TD)
	24	Willis McGahee, Buffalo at Seattle, November 28 (4 TD)
NFC:	24	T.J. Duckett, Atlanta vs. Oakland, December 12 (4 TD)

TEAM LEADERS, POINTS

AFC: BALTIMORE, 117, Matt Stover; BUFFALO, 117, Rian Lindell; CINCINNATI, 122, Shayne Graham; CLEVELAND, 100, Phil Dawson; DENVER, 129, Jason Elam; HOUSTON, 85, Kris Brown; INDIANAPOLIS, 119, Mike Vanderjagt; JACKSONVILLE, 93, *Josh Scobee; KANSAS CITY, 109, Lawrence Tynes; MIAMI, 54, Olindo Mare; NEW ENGLAND, 141, Adam Vinatieri; N.Y. JETS, 105, Doug Brien; OAKLAND, 106, Sebastian Janikowski; PITTSBURGH, 124, Jeff Reed; SAN DIEGO, 114, *Nate Kaeding; TENNESSEE, 88, Gary Anderson

NFC: ARIZONA, 94, Neil Rackers; ATLANTA, 94, Jay Feely; CAROLINA, 96, Muhsin Muhammad; CHICAGO, 67, Paul Edinger; DALLAS, 91, Billy Cundiff; DETROIT, 100, Jason Hanson; GREEN BAY, 120, Ryan Longwell; MINNESOTA, 99, Morten Andersen; NEW ORLEANS, 104, John Carney; N.Y. GIANTS, 99, Steve Christie; PHILADELPHIA, 122, David Akers; ST. LOUIS, 89, Jeff Wilkins; SAN FRANCISCO, 77, Todd Peterson; SEATTLE, 120, Shaun Alexander; TAMPA BAY, 60, Michael Pittman; WASHINGTON, 42, Clinton Portis

TEAM CHAMPION

AFC:	522	Indianapolis
NFC:	424	Green Bay

NFL TOP TEN SCORERS—KICKERS

	XP	XPA	FG	FGA	PTS
Vinatieri, Adam, N.E.	48	48	31	33	141
Elam, Jason, Den.	42	42	29	34	129
Reed, Jeff, Pit.	40	40	28	33	124
Akers, David, Phi.	41	42	27	32	122
Graham, Shayne, Cin.	41	41	27	31	122
Longwell, Ryan, G.B.	48	48	24	28	120
Vanderjagt, Mike, Ind.	59	60	20	25	119
Lindell, Rian, Buf.	45	45	24	28	117
Stover, Matt, Bal.	30	30	29	32	117
* Kaeding, Nate, S.D.	54	55	20	25	114

NFL TOP TEN SCORERS—NONKICKERS

	TD	TDR	TDP	TDM	2-PT.	PTS
Alexander, Shaun, Sea.	20	16	4	0	0	120
Tomlinson, LaDainian, S.D.	18	17	1	0	0	108
Muhammad, Muhsin, Car.	16	0	16	0	0	96
Barber, Tiki, NY-G	15	13	2	0	0	90
Harrison, Marvin, Ind.	15	0	15	0	0	90
Holmes, Priest, K.C.	15	14	1	0	0	90
Davis, Domanick, Hou.	14	13	1	0	0	84
Martin, Curtis, NYJ	14	12	2	0	0	84
Owens, Terrell, Phi.	14	0	14	0	0	84
Dillon, Corey, N.E.	13	12	1	0	1	80

AFC—INDIVIDUAL SCORERS

KICKERS

	XP	XPA	FG	FGA	PTS
Vinatieri, Adam, N.E.	48	48	31	33	141
Elam, Jason, Den.	42	42	29	34	129
Reed, Jeff, Pit.	40	40	28	33	124
Graham, Shayne, Cin.	41	41	27	31	122
Vanderjagt, Mike, Ind.	59	60	20	25	119
Lindell, Rian, Buf.	45	45	24	28	117
Stover, Matt, Bal.	30	30	29	32	117
* Kaeding, Nate, S.D.	54	55	20	25	114
Tynes, Lawrence, K.C.	58	60	17	23	109
Janikowski, Sebastian, Oak.	31	32	25	28	106
Brien, Doug, NYJ	33	34	24	29	105
Dawson, Phil, Cle.	28	28	24	29	100
* Scobee, Josh, Jac.	21	21	24	31	93
Anderson, Gary, Ten.	37	37	17	22	88
Brown, Kris, Hou.	34	34	17	24	85
Mare, Olindo, Mia.	18	18	12	16	54
Bryant, Matt, Ind.-Mia.	12	12	3	4	21
* Welker, Wes, S.D.-Mia.	1	1	1	1 #	10
Gramatica, Bill, Mia.	0	1	3	3	9
Elling, Aaron, Ten.	2	2	1	2	5
Hentrich, Craig, Ten.	0	0	1	3	3

NONKICKERS

	TD	TDR	TDP	TDM	2-PT.	PTS
Tomlinson, LaDainian, S.D.	18	17	1	0	0	108
Harrison, Marvin, Ind.	15	0	15	0	0	90
Holmes, Priest, K.C.	15	14	1	0	0	90
Davis, Domanick, Hou.	14	13	1	0	0	84
Martin, Curtis, NYJ	14	12	2	0	0	84
Dillon, Corey, N.E.	13	12	1	0	1	80
Bettis, Jerome, Pit.	13	13	0	0	0	78
Gates, Antonio, S.D.	13	0	13	0	0	78
McGahee, Willis, Buf.	13	13	0	0	0	78
Johnson, Rudi, Cin.	12	12	0	0	0	72
Wayne, Reggie, Ind.	12	0	12	0	0	72

* Player that was a rookie in 2004
# Appears in "Kickers" and "Nonkickers"

	TD	TDR	TDP	TDM	2-PT	PTS
Bennett, Drew, Ten.	11	0	11	0	0	66
Johnson, Larry, K.C.	11	9	2	0	0	66
Stokley, Brandon, Ind.	10	0	10	0	0	60
James, Edgerrin, Ind.	9	9	0	0	1	56
Blaylock, Derrick, K.C.	9	8	1	0	0	54
* Evans, Lee, Buf.	9	0	9	0	0	54
Johnson, Chad, Cin.	9	0	9	0	0	54
Porter, Jerry, Oak.	9	0	9	0	0	54
Kennison, Eddie, K.C.	8	0	8	0	1	50
Droughns, Reuben, Den.	8	6	2	0	0	48
Chambers, Chris, Mia.	7	0	7	0	1	44
Gonzalez, Tony, K.C.	7	0	7	0	0	42
Graham, Daniel, N.E.	7	0	7	0	0	42
Lelie, Ashley, Den.	7	0	7	0	0	42
Lewis, Jamal, Bal.	7	7	0	0	0	42
Mason, Derrick, Ten.	7	0	7	0	0	42
Patten, David, N.E.	7	0	7	0	0	42
Smith, Rod, Den.	7	0	7	0	0	42
Brown, Chris, Ten.	6	6	0	0	0	36
Curry, Ronald, Oak.	6	0	6	0	0	36
Johnson, Andre, Hou.	6	0	6	0	0	36
Morris, Sammy, Mia.	6	6	0	0	0	36
Pollard, Marcus, Ind.	6	0	6	0	0	36
Smith, Jimmy, Jac.	6	0	6	0	0	36
Heiden, Steve, Cle.	5	0	5	0	1	32
Wells, Jonathan, Hou.	5	3	2	0	1	32
Burress, Plaxico, Pit.	5	0	5	0	0	30
Campbell, Mark, Buf.	5	0	5	0	0	30
Clark, Dallas, Ind.	5	0	5	0	0	30
Moss, Santana, NYJ	5	0	5	0	0	30
Moulds, Eric, Buf.	5	0	5	0	0	30
Ward, Hines, Pit.	5	1	4	0	0	30
McMichael, Randy, Mia.	4	0	4	0	1	26
* Moore, Clarence, Bal.	4	0	4	0	1	26
Baker, Chris, NYJ	4	0	4	0	0	24
Branch, Deion, N.E.	4	0	4	0	0	24
Bryant, Antonio, Cle.	4	0	4	0	0	24
Hape, Patrick, Den.	4	0	4	0	0	24
Houshmandzadeh, T.J., Cin.	4	0	4	0	0	24
McCareins, Justin, NYJ	4	0	4	0	0	24
Parker, Eric, S.D.	4	0	4	0	0	24
Schobel, Matt, Cin.	4	0	4	0	0	24
Shea, Aaron, Cle.	4	0	4	0	0	24
Smith, Antowain, Ten.	4	4	0	0	0	24
Thompson, Derrius, Mia.	4	0	4	0	0	24
Wheatley, Tyrone, Oak.	4	4	0	0	0	24
* Bell, Tatum, Den.	3	3	0	0	0	18
Bradford, Corey, Hou.	3	0	3	0	0	18
Caldwell, Reche, S.D.	3	0	3	0	0	18
Chatman, Jesse, S.D.	3	3	0	0	0	18
Dunn, Jason, K.C.	3	0	3	0	0	18
Faulk, Kevin, N.E.	3	2	1	0	0	18
Givens, David, N.E.	3	0	3	0	0	18
Griffin, Quentin, Den.	3	2	1	0	0	18
Heap, Todd, Bal.	3	0	3	0	0	18
* Jones, Greg, Jac.	3	3	0	0	0	18
Kinney, Erron, Ten.	3	0	3	0	0	18
McGee, Terrence, Buf.	3	0	0	3	0	18
Minor, Travis, Mia.	3	3	0	0	0	18
Morgan, Quincy, Cle.	3	0	3	0	0	18
Morton, Johnnie, K.C.	3	0	3	0	0	18
Mungro, James, Ind.	3	0	3	0	0	18
Randle El, Antwaan, Pit.	3	0	3	0	0	18
* Sams, B.J., Bal.	3	1	0	2	0	18
Suggs, Lee, Cle.	3	2	1	0	0	18
Taylor, Fred, Jac.	3	2	1	0	0	18
Tuman, Jerame, Pit.	3	0	3	0	0	18
Washington, Kelley, Cin.	3	0	3	0	0	18
Zereoue, Amos, Oak.	3	3	0	0	0	18

	TD	TDR	TDP	TDM	2-PT	PTS
Whitted, Alvis, Oak.	2	0	2	0	1	14
* Wilford, Ernest, Jac.	2	0	2	0	1	14
Abraham, Donnie, NYJ	2	0	0	2	0	12
Brees, Drew, S.D.	2	2	0	0	0	12
Clements, Nate, Buf.	2	0	0	2	0	12
Crockett, Zack, Oak.	2	2	0	0	0	12
Davis, Andre, Cle.	2	0	2	0	0	12
Dwight, Tim, S.D.	2	0	1	1	0	12
* Euhus, Tim, Buf.	2	0	2	0	0	12
Fauria, Christian, N.E.	2	0	2	0	0	12
* Fleming, Troy, Ten.	2	0	2	0	0	12
Flutie, Doug, S.D.	2	2	0	0	0	12
Gabriel, Doug, Oak.	2	0	2	0	0	12
Gaffney, Jabar, Hou.	2	0	2	0	0	12
Garcia, Jeff, Cle.	2	2	0	0	0	12
Green, William, Cle.	2	2	0	0	0	12
Hall, Dante, K.C.	2	0	0	2	0	12
Hankton, Cortez, Jac.	2	0	2	0	0	12
Haynes, Verron, Pit.	2	0	2	0	0	12
Hymes, Randy, Bal.	2	0	2	0	0	12
Johnson, Kyle, Den.	2	0	2	0	0	12
Johnson, Bethel, N.E.	2	0	1	1	0	12
Johnson, Teyo, Oak.	2	0	2	0	0	12
Jolley, Doug, Oak.	2	0	2	0	0	12
Jordan, LaMont, NYJ	2	2	0	0	0	12
Leftwich, Byron, Jac.	2	2	0	0	0	12
McAlister, Chris, Bal.	2	0	0	2	0	12
Meier, Shad, Ten.	2	0	2	0	0	12
Northcutt, Dennis, Cle.	2	0	2	0	0	12
Osgood, Kassim, S.D.	2	0	2	0	0	12
Peelle, Justin, S.D.	2	0	2	0	0	12
Putzier, Jeb, Den.	2	0	2	0	0	12
Reed, Ed, Bal.	2	0	0	2	0	12
Rhodes, Dominic, Ind.	2	1	0	1	0	12
Riemersma, Jay, Pit.	2	0	2	0	0	12
Spikes, Takeo, Buf.	2	0	0	2	0	12
Taylor, Chester, Bal.	2	2	0	0	0	12
Vrabel, Mike, N.E.	2	0	2	0	0	12
* Williams, Shaud, Buf.	2	2	0	0	0	12
* Welker, Wes, Mia.	1	0	0	1	0	#10
* Williams, Reggie, Jac.	1	0	1	0	2	10
* Jones, Brian, Jac.	1	0	1	0	1	8
McNair, Steve, Ten.	1	1	0	0	1	8
Williams, Pat, Buf.	1	0	0	1	0	^8
Abdullah, Rabih, N.E.	1	1	0	0	0	6
Alston, Richard, Cle.	1	0	0	1	0	6
* Anderson, Charlie, Hou.	1	0	0	1	0	6
* Anderson, Courtney, Oak.	1	0	1	0	0	6
Armstrong, Derick, Hou.	1	0	1	0	0	6
Becht, Anthony, NYJ	1	0	1	0	0	6
Berlin, Eddie, Ten.	1	0	1	0	0	6
Boller, Kyle, Bal.	1	1	0	0	0	6
Booker, Marty, Mia.	1	0	1	0	0	6
Brady, Kyle, Jac.	1	0	1	0	0	6
Brown, Troy, N.E.	1	0	1	0	0	6
Buchanon, Phillip, Oak.	1	0	0	1	0	6
Bulluck, Keith, Ten.	1	0	0	1	0	6
Carswell, Dwayne, Den.	1	0	1	0	0	6
Carter, Jonathan, NYJ	1	0	1	0	0	6
Chrebet, Wayne, NYJ	1	0	1	0	0	6
Coleman, Marcus, Hou.	1	0	0	1	0	6
* Cotchery, Jerricho, NYJ	1	0	0	1	0	6
Crocker, Chris, Cle.	1	0	0	1	0	6
* David, Jason, Ind.	1	0	0	1	0	6
Dinkins, Darnell, Bal.	1	0	1	0	0	6
Edwards, Donnie, S.D.	1	0	0	1	0	6
Edwards, Troy, Jac.	1	0	1	0	0	6
Faggins, Demarcus, Hou.	1	0	0	1	0	6
Fargas, Justin, Oak.	1	1	0	0	0	6

	TD	TDR	TDP	TDM	2-PT	PTS
Farrior, James, Pit.	1	0	0	1	0	6
Feeley, A.J., Mia.	1	1	0	0	0	6
* Floyd, Malcom, S.D.	1	0	1	0	0	6
Fuamatu-Ma'afala, Chris, Jac.	1	0	0	0	0	6
Garrard, David, Jac.	1	1	0	0	0	6
* Gay, Randall, N.E.	1	0	0	1	0	6
* Geathers, Robert, Cin.	1	0	0	1	0	6
Gilmore, Bryan, Mia.	1	0	1	0	0	6
Green, Jarvis, N.E.	1	0	0	1	0	6
Harrison, James, Pit.	1	0	0	1	0	6
Hearst, Garrison, Den.	1	1	0	0	0	6
Horn, Chris, K.C.	1	0	1	0	0	6
* Hutchins, Von, Ind.	1	0	0	1	0	6
Johnson, Ellis, Den.	1	0	0	1	0	6
Johnson, Jarret, Bal.	1	0	0	1	0	6
Johnson, Jeremi, Cin.	1	0	1	0	0	6
Johnson, Kevin, Bal.	1	0	1	0	0	6
Jones, Terry, Bal.	1	0	1	0	0	6
Kaesviharn, Kevin, Cin.	1	0	0	1	0	6
Konrad, Rob, Mia.	1	0	1	0	0	6
* Krause, Ryan, S.D.	1	0	1	0	0	6
Kreider, Dan, Pit.	1	0	1	0	0	6
* Larson, Kyle, Cin.	1	1	0	0	0	6
Lee, Donald, Mia.	1	0	1	0	0	6
McCardell, Keenan, S.D.	1	0	1	0	0	6
Miller, Billy, Hou.	1	0	1	0	0	6
Mitchell, Kawika, K.C.	1	0	0	1	0	6
Morris, Rob, Ind.	1	0	0	1	0	6
O'Neal, Deltha, Cin.	1	0	0	1	0	6
Palmer, Carson, Cin.	1	1	0	0	0	6
* Parker, Samie, K.C.	1	0	1	0	0	6
Peek, Antwan, Hou.	1	0	0	1	0	6
Pennington, Chad, NYJ	1	1	0	0	0	6
* Peters, Jason, Buf.	1	0	0	1	0	6
Plummer, Jake, Den.	1	1	0	0	0	6
Polamalu, Troy, Pit.	1	0	0	1	0	6
* Pope, Derrick, Mia.	1	0	0	1	0	6
* Roethlisberger, Ben, Pit.	1	1	0	0	0	6
Samuel, Asante, N.E.	1	0	0	1	0	6
Sanders, Deion, Bal.	1	0	0	1	0	6
* Sanders, Bob, Ind.	1	0	0	1	0	6
Seymour, Richard, N.E.	1	0	0	1	0	6
Sharper, Jamie, Hou.	1	0	0	1	0	6
Simmons, Brian, Cin.	1	0	0	1	0	6
* Smith, Jonathan, Buf.	1	0	0	1	0	6
Sowell, Jerald, NYJ	1	0	1	0	0	6
Staley, Duce, Pit.	1	1	0	0	0	6
Stewart, Tony, Cin.	1	0	1	0	0	6
Stuvaints, Russell, Pit.	1	0	0	1	0	6
Thompson, Lamont, Ten.	1	0	0	1	0	6
Toefield, LaBrandon, Jac.	1	0	1	0	0	6
Townsend, Deshea, Pit.	1	0	0	1	0	6
* Troupe, Ben, Ten.	1	0	1	0	0	6
* Vilma, Jonathan, NYJ	1	0	0	1	0	6
Volek, Billy, Ten.	1	1	0	0	0	6
Warfield, Eric, K.C.	1	0	0	1	0	6
Watson, Kenny, Cin.	1	0	1	0	0	6
* Watts, Darius, Den.	1	0	1	0	0	6
Wilcox, Daniel, Bal.	1	0	1	0	0	6
Williams, Chad, Bal.	1	0	0	1	0	6
* Williams, Madieu, Cin.	1	0	0	1	0	6
Wilson, Al, Den.	1	0	0	1	0	6
Wrighster, George, Jac.	1	0	1	0	0	6
Hentrich, Craig, Ten.	0	0	0	0	0	3
Favors, Greg, Jac.	0	0	0	0	0	^ 2
Knight, Sammy, Mia.	0	0	0	0	0	^ 2
* Smith, Daryl, Jac.	0	0	0	0	0	^ 2

^ Safety; Team safety credited to Oakland, Pittsburgh, San Diego
* Player that was a rookie in 2004
\# Appears in "Kickers" and "Nonkickers"

NFC—INDIVIDUAL SCORERS

KICKERS

	XP	XPA	FG	FGA	PTS
Akers, David, Phi.	41	42	27	32	122
Longwell, Ryan, G.B.	48	48	24	28	120
Brown, Josh, Sea.	40	40	23	25	109
Carney, John, N.O.	38	38	22	27	104
Hanson, Jason, Det.	28	28	24	28	100
Andersen, Morten, Min.	45	45	18	22	99
Christie, Steve, NY-G	33	33	22	28	99
Feely, Jay, Atl.	40	40	18	23	94
Rackers, Neil, Ariz	28	28	22	29	94
Cundiff, Billy, Dal.	31	31	20	26	91
Wilkins, Jeff, St.L	32	32	19	24	89
Kasay, John, Car.	27	28	19	22	84
Peterson, Todd, S.F.	23	23	18	22	77
Edinger, Paul, Chi.	22	22	15	24	67
Gramatica, Martín, T.B.	21	22	11	19	54
Hall, John, Was.	13	13	8	11	37
Chandler, Jeff, Car.-Was.	14	14	5	8	29
* Kimrin, Ola, Was.	6	6	6	10	24
* Taylor, Jay, T.B.	11	11	4	5	23
Sauerbrun, Todd, Car.	4	4	1	1	7

NONKICKERS

	TD	TDR	TDP	TDM	2-PT.	PTS
Alexander, Shaun, Sea.	20	16	4	0	0	120
Muhammad, Muhsin, Car.	16	0	16	0	0	96
Barber, Tiki, NY-G	15	13	2	0	0	90
Owens, Terrell, Phi.	14	0	14	0	0	84
Moss, Randy, Min.	13	0	13	0	0	78
Walker, Javon, G.B.	12	0	12	0	0	72
Horn, Joe, N.O.	11	0	11	0	1	68
Burleson, Nate, Min.	10	0	9	1	1	62
Holt, Torry, St.L	10	0	10	0	0	60
Pittman, Michael, T.B.	10	7	3	0	0	60
Driver, Donald, G.B.	9	0	9	0	1	56
Dunn, Warrick, Atl.	9	9	0	0	0	54
McAllister, Deuce, N.O.	9	9	0	0	0	54
Smith, Emmitt, Ariz	9	9	0	0	0	54
Westbrook, Brian, Phi.	9	3	6	0	0	54
Duckett, T.J., Atl.	8	8	0	0	0	48
* Fitzgerald, Larry, Ariz	8	0	8	0	0	48
Green, Ahman, G.B.	8	7	1	0	0	48
Robinson, Marcus, Min.	8	0	8	0	0	48
* Williams, Roy, Det.	8	0	8	0	0	48
Jackson, Darrell, Sea.	7	0	7	0	1	44
Barlow, Kevan, S.F.	7	7	0	0	0	42
* Clayton, Michael, T.B.	7	0	7	0	0	42
Franks, Bubba, G.B.	7	0	7	0	0	42
Goings, Nick, Car.	7	6	1	0	0	42
* Jones, Julius, Dal.	7	7	0	0	0	42
Jones, Thomas, Chi.	7	7	0	0	0	42
Portis, Clinton, Was.	7	5	2	0	0	42
Lloyd, Brandon, S.F.	6	0	6	0	1	38
Witten, Jason, Dal.	6	0	6	0	1	38
Bruce, Isaac, St.L	6	0	6	0	0	36
* Cooley, Chris, Was.	6	0	6	0	0	36
Crumpler, Alge, Atl.	6	0	6	0	0	36
Galloway, Joey, T.B.	6	0	5	1	0	36
Johnson, Keyshawn, Dal.	6	0	6	0	0	36
* Jones, Kevin, Det.	6	5	1	0	0	36
Shockey, Jeremy, NY-G	6	0	6	0	0	36
* Colbert, Keary, Car.	5	0	5	0	1	32
Gardner, Rod, Was.	5	0	5	0	0	30
Smith, L.J., Phi.	5	0	5	0	0	30
Stallworth, Donte', N.O.	5	0	5	0	0	30
Faulk, Marshall, St.L	4	3	1	0	2	28
* Jackson, Steven, St.L	4	4	0	0	1	26
Smith, Onterrio, Min.	4	2	2	0	1	26

Player	TD	TDR	TDP	TDM	2-PT	PTS
Ayanbadejo, Obafemi, Ariz	4	3	1	0	0	24
Brooks, Aaron, N.O.	4	4	0	0	0	24
Drummond, Eddie, Det.	4	0	0	4	0	24
George, Eddie, Dal.	4	4	0	0	0	24
Levens, Dorsey, Phi.	4	4	0	0	0	24
Royal, Robert, Was.	4	0	4	0	0	24
Wiggins, Jermaine, Min.	4	0	4	0	0	24
Williams, Moe, Min.	4	3	1	0	0	24
Conway, Curtis, S.F.	3	0	3	0	1	20
Dilger, Ken, T.B.	3	0	3	0	1	20
Stevens, Jerramy, Sea.	3	0	3	0	1	20
Bulger, Marc, St.L	3	3	0	0	0	18
Cloud, Mike, NY-G	3	3	0	0	0	18
Hakim, Az-Zahir, Det.	3	0	3	0	0	18
Henderson, William, G.B.	3	0	3	0	0	18
Lewis, Chad, Phi.	3	0	3	0	0	18
Mangum, Kris, Car.	3	0	3	0	0	18
McDonald, Shaun, St.L	3	0	3	0	0	18
McNabb, Donovan, Phi.	3	3	0	0	0	18
Price, Peerless, Atl.	3	0	3	0	0	18
Rice, Jerry, Sea.	3	0	3	0	0	18
Schlesinger, Cory, Det.	3	0	3	0	0	18
Sharper, Darren, G.B.	3	0	0	3	0	18
Stecker, Aaron, N.O.	3	2	0	1	0	18
Vick, Michael, Atl.	3	3	0	0	0	18
Wilson, Cedrick, S.F.	3	0	3	0	0	18
Culpepper, Daunte, Min.	2	2	0	0	1	14
Curtis, Kevin, St.L	2	0	2	0	1	14
McCown, Josh, Ariz	2	2	0	0	1	14
Seidman, Mike, Car.	2	0	2	0	1	14
Alstott, Mike, T.B.	2	2	0	0	0	12
Barber, Ronde, T.B.	2	0	0	2	0	12
Bennett, Michael, Min.	2	1	1	0	0	12
* Berrian, Bernard, Chi.	2	0	2	0	0	12
Davenport, Najeh, G.B.	2	2	0	0	0	12
Engram, Bobby, Sea.	2	0	2	0	0	12
Finneran, Brian, Atl.	2	0	2	0	0	12
Fisher, Tony, G.B.	2	0	2	0	0	12
Foster, DeShaun, Car.	2	2	0	0	0	12
Glenn, Terry, Dal.	2	0	2	0	0	12
Hambrick, Troy, Ariz	2	1	1	0	0	12
Hicks, Maurice, S.F.	2	2	0	0	0	12
Hoover, Brad, Car.	2	0	2	0	0	12
Johnson, Bryan, Chi.	2	0	2	0	0	12
Johnson, Eric, S.F.	2	0	2	0	0	12
Jones, Freddie, Ariz	2	0	2	0	0	12
Jurevicius, Joe, T.B.	2	0	2	0	0	12
Little, Leonard, St.L	2	0	0	2	0	12
Mathis, Kevin, Atl.	2	0	0	2	0	12
McKie, Jason, Chi.	2	0	2	0	0	12
McQuarters, R.W., Chi.	2	0	0	2	0	12
Mitchell, Freddie, Phi.	2	0	2	0	0	12
Peppers, Julius, Car.	2	0	0	2	0	12
Pinner, Artose, Det.	2	2	0	0	0	12
Robinson, Jeff, Dal.	2	0	2	0	0	12
Robinson, Koren, Sea.	2	0	2	0	0	12
Sheppard, Lito, Phi.	2	0	0	2	0	12
Thomas, Anthony, Chi.	2	2	0	0	0	12
White, Dez, Atl.	2	0	2	0	0	12
Williams, Boo, N.O.	2	0	2	0	0	12
Ferguson, Robert, G.B.	1	0	1	0	1	8
Streets, Tai, Det.	1	0	1	0	1	8
Alexander, Stephen, Det.	1	0	1	0	0	6
Anderson, Richie, Dal.	1	1	0	0	0	6
Archuleta, Adam, St.L	1	0	0	1	0	6
Azumah, Jerry, Chi.	1	0	0	1	0	6
Barnes, Darian, Dal.	1	0	1	0	0	6
Bartrum, Mike, Phi.	1	0	1	0	0	6
Battle, Arnaz, S.F.	1	0	0	1	0	6
Bennett, Brandon, Car.	1	1	0	0	0	6
Betts, Ladell, Was.	1	1	0	0	0	6
Bly, Dre', Det.	1	0	0	1	0	6
* Bockwoldt, Colby, N.O.	1	0	0	1	0	6
Boldin, Anquan, Ariz	1	0	1	0	0	6
* Boulware, Michael, Sea.	1	0	0	1	0	6
Briggs, Lance, Chi.	1	0	0	1	0	6
Brown, Mike, Chi.	1	0	0	1	0	6
Brown, Tim, T.B.	1	0	1	0	0	6
Bush, Steve, S.F.	1	0	1	0	0	6
Campbell, Kelly, Min.	1	0	1	0	0	6
Carpenter, Dwaine, S.F.	1	0	0	1	0	6
* Carroll, Ahmad, G.B.	1	0	0	1	0	6
Carter, Tim, NY-G	1	0	1	0	0	6
Chatman, Antonio, G.B.	1	0	1	0	0	6
Claiborne, Chris, Min.	1	0	0	1	0	6
Clark, Desmond, Chi.	1	0	1	0	0	6
Coleman, Rod, Atl.	1	0	0	1	0	6
Coles, Laveranues, Was.	1	0	1	0	0	6
Conwell, Ernie, N.O.	1	0	1	0	0	6
Cook, Jameel, T.B.	1	0	1	0	0	6
* Copper, Terrance, Dal.	1	0	1	0	0	6
Cox, Torrie, T.B.	1	0	0	1	0	6
* Crayton, Patrick, Dal.	1	0	1	0	0	6
Dayne, Ron, NY-G	1	1	0	0	0	6
Delhomme, Jake, Car.	1	1	0	0	0	6
Goodspeed, Joey, St.L	1	1	0	0	0	6
Green, Barrett, NY-G	1	0	0	1	0	6
Griffith, Justin, Atl.	1	0	1	0	0	6
Grossman, Rex, Chi.	1	1	0	0	0	6
* Hall, DeAngelo, Atl.	1	0	0	1	0	6
Hall, Lamont, N.O.	1	0	1	0	0	6
Harris, Walt, Was.	1	1	0	0	0	6
Hasselbeck, Matt, Sea.	1	1	0	0	0	6
Hawthorne, Michael, G.B.	1	0	0	1	0	6
Haynes, Michael, Chi.	1	0	0	1	0	6
Heller, Will, T.B.	1	0	1	0	0	6
Johnson, Bryant, Ariz	1	0	1	0	0	6
Kircus, David, Det.	1	0	1	0	0	6
Lee, ReShard, Dal.	1	1	0	0	0	6
Lewis, Michael, N.O.	1	0	0	1	0	6
Lucas, Ken, Sea.	1	0	0	1	0	6
Lyman, Dustin, Chi.	1	0	1	0	0	6
Manumaleuna, Brandon, St.L	1	0	1	0	0	6
Mili, Itula, Sea.	1	0	1	0	0	6
Mitchell, Mel, N.O.	1	0	0	1	0	6
Moorehead, Kindal, Car.	1	0	0	1	0	6
Pathon, Jerome, N.O.	1	0	1	0	0	6
Pierce, Antonio, Was.	1	0	0	1	0	6
Pinkston, Todd, Phi.	1	0	1	0	0	6
Ponder, Willie, NY-G	1	0	0	1	0	6
Pritchett, Stanley, Atl.	1	0	1	0	0	6
Rivers, Marcellus, NY-G	1	0	1	0	0	6
Robertson, Jamal, S.F.	1	1	0	0	0	6
Rossum, Allen, Atl.	1	0	0	1	0	6
Schroeder, Bill, T.B.	1	0	1	0	0	6
Shiancoe, Visanthe, NY-G	1	0	1	0	0	6
Simmons, Anthony, Sea.	1	0	0	1	0	6
Smith, Brady, Atl.	1	0	0	1	0	6
Smith, Derek M., S.F.	1	0	0	1	0	6
Starks, Duane, Ariz	1	0	0	1	0	6
Swinton, Reggie, Det.	1	0	1	0	0	6
Terrell, David, Chi.	1	0	1	0	0	6
Testaverde, Vinny, Dal.	1	1	0	0	0	6
Tyree, David, NY-G	1	0	1	0	0	6
Umenyiora, Osi, NY-G	1	0	0	1	0	6
Urban, Jerheme, Sea.	1	0	1	0	0	6
* Vasher, Nathan, Chi.	1	0	0	1	0	6
Walker, Bracy, Det.	1	0	0	1	0	6

	TD	TDR	TDP	TDM	2-PT.	PTS.
* Ward, Derrick, NY-G	1	0	0	1	0	6
Warner, Kurt, NY-G	1	1	0	0	0	6
Williams, Kevin, Min.	1	0	0	1	0	6
Wilson, Adrian, Ariz	1	0	0	1	0	6
* Woods, Rashaun, S.F.	1	0	1	0	0	6
Bryant, Tony, N.O.	0	0	0	0	0	^2
Jacobs, Taylor, Was.	0	0	0	0	1	2
* Krenzel, Craig, Chi.	0	0	0	0	1	2
Ogunleye, Adewale, Chi.	0	0	0	0	0	^2

	TD	TDR	TDP	TDM	2-PT.	PTS.
Rattay, Tim, S.F.	0	0	0	0	1	2
Redding, Cory, Det.	0	0	0	0	0	^2

^ Safety; Team safety credited to Arizona, Chicago, Dallas, and San Francisco
* Player that was a rookie in 2004

AMERICAN FOOTBALL CONFERENCE—SCORING

	TD	TDR	TDP	TDM	XKG	XKAtt	X2G	X2Att	FG	FGA	SAF	POINTS
Indianapolis	66	10	51	5	64	65	1	1	20	26	0	522
Kansas City	62	31	27	4	58	60	1	2	17	23	0	483
San Diego	55	24	29	2	54	55	0	0	20	25	1	446
New England	49	15	29	5	48	48	1	1	31	33	0	437
Buffalo	46	15	21	10	45	45	0	1	24	28	1	395
Denver	42	13	27	2	42	42	0	0	29	34	0	381
Cincinnati	42	14	23	5	41	41	0	1	27	31	0	374
Pittsburgh	41	16	20	5	40	40	0	1	28	33	1	372
Tennessee	41	12	27	2	39	39	1	2	19	27	0	344
N.Y. Jets	38	15	19	4	33	34	0	4	24	29	0	333
Oakland	35	10	24	1	31	32	1	3	25	28	1	320
Baltimore	33	11	13	9	30	30	1	3	29	32	0	317
Houston	37	16	16	5	34	34	1	3	17	24	0	309
Cleveland	29	6	21	2	28	28	1	1	24	29	0	276
Miami	31	10	19	2	26	27	2	4	19	23	1	275
Jacksonville	26	9	17	0	21	21	4	4	24	31	2	261
AFC Total	673	227	383	63	634	641	14	31	377	456	7	5845
AFC Average	42.1	14.2	23.9	3.9	39.6	40.1	0.9	1.9	23.6	28.5	0.4	365.3

NATIONAL FOOTBALL CONFERENCE—SCORING

	TD	TDR	TDP	TDM	XKG	XKAtt	X2G	X2Att	FG	FGA	SAF	POINTS
Green Bay	50	9	36	5	48	48	2	2	24	28	0	424
Minnesota	50	8	39	3	45	45	3	4	18	22	0	405
Philadelphia	44	10	32	2	41	42	0	2	27	32	0	386
Seattle	43	17	23	3	40	40	2	3	23	25	0	371
Carolina	42	10	29	3	39	40	2	2	20	25	0	355
New Orleans	40	15	21	4	38	38	1	2	22	27	1	348
Atlanta	41	20	15	6	40	40	0	1	18	23	0	340
St. Louis	37	11	23	3	32	32	4	4	19	24	0	319
N.Y. Giants	34	18	12	4	33	33	0	1	22	28	0	303
Tampa Bay	37	9	24	4	32	33	1	4	15	24	0	301
Detroit	32	7	19	6	28	28	1	4	24	28	1	296
Dallas	33	14	19	0	31	31	1	2	20	26	0	293
Arizona	31	15	14	2	28	28	1	3	22	29	0	284
San Francisco	29	10	16	3	23	23	3	6	18	22	1	259
Washington	26	6	18	2	25	25	1	1	19	27	0	240
Chicago	26	10	9	7	22	22	1	4	15	24	3	231
NFC Total	595	189	349	57	545	548	23	45	326	414	8	5155
NFC Average	37.2	11.8	21.8	3.6	34.1	34.3	1.4	2.8	20.4	25.9	0.5	322.2
NFL Total	1268	416	732	120	1179	1189	37	76	703	870	15	11000
NFL Average	39.6	13.0	22.9	3.8	36.8	37.2	1.2	2.4	22.0	27.2	0.5	343.8

FIELD GOALS

FIELD GOAL PERCENTAGE
AFC: .939 Adam Vinatieri, New England
NFC: .920 Josh Brown, Seattle

FIELD GOALS
AFC: 31 Adam Vinatieri, New England
NFC: 27 David Akers, Philadelphia

FIELD GOAL ATTEMPTS
AFC: 34 Jason Elam, Denver
NFC: 32 David Akers, Philadelphia

FIELD GOALS, GAME
NFC: 6 John Kasay, Carolina at New Orleans, December 5 (6 attempts)
AFC: 5 Adam Vinatieri, New England vs. Buffalo, November 14 (5 attempts)
5 Jeff Reed, Pittsburgh at Buffalo, January 2 (5 attempts)
5 Phil Dawson, Cleveland at Houston, January 2 (5 attempts)

LONGEST FIELD GOAL
NFC: 55 Neil Rackers, Arizona vs. Seattle, October 24
55 Neil Rackers, Arizona vs. Seattle, October 24
AFC: 53 Doug Brien, New York Jets at Miami, October 3
53 * Nate Kaeding, San Diego at Atlanta, October 17
53 * Josh Scobee, Jacksonville at Indianapolis, October 24
53 Shayne Graham, Cincinnati vs. Denver, October 25

AVERAGE YARDS MADE
NFC: 39.8 David Akers, Philadelphia
AFC: 39.1 Olindo Mare, Miami

* Player that was a rookie in 2004

AMERICAN FOOTBALL CONFERENCE—FIELD GOALS

	FG	FGA	Pct	Long
New England	31	33	.939	48
Baltimore	29	32	.906	50
Oakland	25	28	.893	52
Cincinnati	27	31	.871	53
Buffalo	24	28	.857	43
Denver	29	34	.853	52
Pittsburgh	28	33	.848	51
Cleveland	24	29	.828	50
N.Y. Jets	24	29	.828	53
Miami	19	23	.826	51
San Diego	20	25	.800	53
Jacksonville	24	31	.774	53
Indianapolis	20	26	.769	47
Kansas City	17	23	.739	50
Houston	17	24	.708	50
Tennessee	19	27	.704	50
AFC Total	377	456	—	53
AFC Average	23.6	28.5	.827	—

NATIONAL FOOTBALL CONFERENCE—FIELD GOALS

	FG	FGA	Pct	Long
Seattle	23	25	.920	54
Detroit	24	28	.857	48
Green Bay	24	28	.857	53
Philadelphia	27	32	.844	51
Minnesota	18	22	.818	48
San Francisco	18	22	.818	51
New Orleans	22	27	.815	53
Carolina	20	25	.800	54
St. Louis	19	24	.792	53
N.Y. Giants	22	28	.786	53
Atlanta	18	23	.783	47
Dallas	20	26	.769	49
Arizona	22	29	.759	55
Washington	19	27	.704	49
Chicago	15	24	.625	53
Tampa Bay	15	24	.625	53
NFC Total	326	414	—	55
NFC Average	20.4	25.9	.787	—
League Total	703	870	—	55
League Average	22.0	27.2	.808	—

AFC—INDIVIDUAL FIELD GOALS

	1-19 Yards	20-29 Yards	30-39 Yards	40-49 Yards	50 or Longer	Totals	Avg Yds Att	Avg Yds Made	Avg Yds Miss	Long
Vinatieri, Adam, N.E.	0-0 —	13-13 1.000	7-7 1.000	11-12 .917	0-1 .000	31-33 .939	34.9	34.0	48.5	48
Stover, Matt, Bal.	2-2 1.000	9-9 1.000	7-8 .875	9-10 .900	2-3 .667	29-32 .906	34.8	34.1	41.7	50
Janikowski, Sebastian, Oak.	1-1 1.000	7-7 1.000	7-8 .875	8-10 .800	2-2 1.000	25-28 .893	36.3	35.5	43.0	52
Graham, Shayne, Cin.	0-0 —	7-7 1.000	10-12 .833	7-8 .875	3-4 .750	27-31 .871	37.2	36.3	43.0	53
Lindell, Rian, Buf.	0-0 —	13-14 .929	10-11 .909	1-3 .333	0-0 —	24-28 .857	29.5	28.1	37.8	43
Elam, Jason, Den.	0-0 —	10-10 1.000	7-8 .875	9-12 .750	3-4 .750	29-34 .853	36.1	34.7	44.0	52
Reed, Jeff, Pit.	1-1 1.000	8-9 .889	12-13 .923	5-8 .625	2-2 1.000	28-33 .848	34.0	33.1	38.8	51
Brien, Doug, NYJ	0-0 —	9-10 .900	4-6 .667	10-11 .909	1-2 .500	24-29 .828	35.9	35.5	38.2	53
Dawson, Phil, Cle.	0-0 —	11-11 1.000	6-8 .750	6-9 .667	1-1 1.000	24-29 .828	34.7	33.5	40.6	50
* Kaeding, Nate, S.D.	1-1 1.000	9-11 .818	2-2 1.000	5-6 .833	3-5 .600	20-25 .800	35.3	34.0	40.6	53
Vanderjagt, Mike, Ind.	0-0 —	6-6 1.000	9-11 .818	5-7 .714	0-1 .000	20-25 .800	35.5	33.4	44.2	47
* Scobee, Josh, Jac.	0-0 —	10-10 1.000	8-11 .727	5-7 .714	1-3 .333	24-31 .774	35.2	32.9	43.1	53
Anderson, Gary, Ten.	0-0 —	4-5 .800	4-4 1.000	9-12 .750	0-1 .000	17-22 .773	37.6	36.7	40.6	45
Mare, Olindo, Mia.	0-0 —	1-2 .500	6-7 .857	3-4 .750	2-3 .667	12-16 .750	39.0	39.1	38.8	51
Tynes, Lawrence, K.C.	0-0 —	5-5 1.000	7-8 .875	3-6 .500	2-4 .500	17-23 .739	37.9	35.2	45.5	50
Brown, Kris, Hou.	0-0 —	7-7 1.000	3-5 .600	6-9 .667	1-3 .333	17-24 .708	37.5	34.9	43.7	50
(Nonqualifiers)										
Bryant, Matt, Ind.-Mia.	0-0 —	1-1 1.000	0-0 —	2-3 .667	0-0 —	3-4 .750	40.5	39.3	44.0	47
Gramatica, Bill, Mia.	0-0 —	2-2 1.000	1-1 1.000	0-0 —	0-0 —	3-3 1.000	29.0	29.0	—	30
Hentrich, Craig, Ten.	0-0 —	0-0 —	0-0 —	0-0 —	1-3 .333	1-3 .333	53.3	50.0	55.0	50
Elling, Aaron, Ten.	0-0 —	1-1 1.000	0-1 .000	0-0 —	0-0 —	1-2 .500	27.5	22.0	33.0	22
* Welker, Wes, Mia.	0-0 —	1-1 1.000	0-0 —	0-0 —	0-0 —	1-1 1.000	29.0	29.0	—	29
AFC Totals	5-5 1.000	134-141 .950	110-131 .840	104-137 .759	24-42 .571	377-456 .827	35.6	34.2	42.2	53
NFL Totals	12-12 1.000	243-252 .964	210-258 .814	185-257 .720	53-91 .582	703-870 .808	36.1	34.4	43.2	55

*Player that was a rookie in 2004
Leader based on overall percentage, minimum 16 field goals

NFC—INDIVIDUAL FIELD GOALS

	1-19 Yards	20-29 Yards	30-39 Yards	40-49 Yards	50 or Longer	Totals	Avg Yds Att	Avg Yds Made	Avg Yds Miss	Long
Brown, Josh, Sea.	1-1 1.000	7-7 1.000	8-9 .889	6-7 .857	1-1 1.000	23-25 .920	34.5	34.0	40.5	54
Kasay, John, Car.	0-0 —	11-11 1.000	4-4 1.000	1-2 .500	3-5 .600	19-22 .864	34.4	31.5	52.7	54
Hanson, Jason, Det.	0-0 —	9-9 1.000	10-11 .909	5-8 .625	0-0 —	24-28 .857	33.6	31.9	43.8	48
Longwell, Ryan, G.B.	0-0 —	8-8 1.000	8-9 .889	6-8 .750	2-3 .667	24-28 .857	36.8	35.5	44.3	53
Akers, David, Phi.	0-0 —	4-4 1.000	6-7 .857	15-18 .833	2-3 .667	27-32 .844	40.8	39.8	46.0	51
Andersen, Morten, Min.	1-1 1.000	8-8 1.000	5-7 .714	4-6 .667	0-0 —	18-22 .818	33.5	31.7	41.5	48
Peterson, Todd, S.F.	1-1 1.000	3-3 1.000	7-8 .875	5-6 .833	2-4 .500	18-22 .818	37.8	35.9	46.3	51
Carney, John, N.O.	0-0 —	3-3 1.000	12-15 .800	5-6 .833	2-3 .667	22-27 .815	38.7	38.0	42.0	53
Wilkins, Jeff, St.L	0-0 —	7-7 1.000	5-6 .833	3-6 .500	4-5 .800	19-24 .792	38.1	36.6	43.8	53
Christie, Steve, NY-G	1-1 1.000	8-8 1.000	6-8 .750	4-7 .571	3-4 .750	22-28 .786	35.5	33.6	42.3	53
Feely, Jay, Atl.	1-1 1.000	7-7 1.000	7-9 .778	3-6 .500	0-0 —	18-23 .783	33.5	30.8	43.2	47
Cundiff, Billy, Dal.	1-1 1.000	6-6 1.000	4-4 1.000	9-13 .692	0-2 .000	20-26 .769	38.0	35.3	47.0	49
Rackers, Neil, Ariz	0-0 —	6-6 1.000	5-7 .714	6-7 .857	5-9 .556	22-29 .759	40.6	38.0	48.6	55
Edinger, Paul, Chi.	0-0 —	6-7 .857	2-5 .400	4-7 .571	3-5 .600	15-24 .625	38.9	36.3	43.2	53
Gramatica, Martín, T.B.	0-0 —	6-7 .857	3-6 .500	1-5 .200	1-1 1.000	11-19 .579	34.6	31.1	39.5	53
(Nonqualifiers)										
Hall, John, Was.	1-1 1.000	3-3 1.000	3-3 1.000	1-3 .333	0-1 .000	8-11 .727	33.3	29.0	44.7	46
* Kimrin, Ola, Was.	0-0 —	3-3 1.000	2-3 .667	1-3 .333	0-1 .000	6-10 .600	36.4	30.5	45.3	41
Chandler, Jeff, Car.-Was.	0-0 —	4-4 1.000	0-2 .000	1-1 1.000	0-1 .000	5-8 .625	34.8	29.0	44.3	49
* Taylor, Jay, T.B.	0-0 —	0-0 —	2-3 .667	1-1 1.000	1-1 1.000	4-5 .800	37.6	39.5	30.0	50
Sauerbrun, Todd, Car.	0-0 —	0-0 —	1-1 1.000	0-0 —	0-0 —	1-1 1.000	34.0	34.0	—	34
NFC Totals	7-7 1.000	109-111 .982	100-127 .787	81-120 .675	29-49 .592	326-414 .787	36.6	34.7	44.0	55
NFL Totals	12-12 1.000	243-252 .964	210-258 .814	185-257 .720	53-91 .582	703-870 .808	36.1	34.4	43.2	55

*Player that was a rookie in 2004
Leader based on overall percentage, minimum 16 field goals

RUSHING

YARDS
AFC: 1697 Curtis Martin, New York Jets
NFC: 1696 Shaun Alexander, Seattle

YARDS, GAME
AFC: 204 Edgerrin James, Indianapolis at Chicago, November 21 (23 attempts, 1 TD)
NFC: 198 * Julius Jones, Dallas at Seattle, December 6 (30 attempts, 3 TD)

LONGEST
NFC: 90 Ahman Green, Green Bay vs. Dallas, October 24 - TD
AFC: 75 Jamal Lewis, Baltimore at Cincinnati, September 26 - TD

ATTEMPTS
AFC: 371 Curtis Martin, New York Jets
NFC: 353 Shaun Alexander, Seattle

ATTEMPTS, GAME
AFC: 38 Reuben Droughns, Denver at Oakland, October 17 (176 yards, 1 TD)
38 Lee Suggs, Cleveland at Miami, December 26 (143 yards, 0 TD)
NFC: 36 Clinton Portis, Washington at Chicago, October 17 (171 yards, 0 TD)
36 Nick Goings, Carolina at New Orleans, December 5 (122 yards, 1 TD)

YARDS PER ATTEMPT
NFC: 7.5 Michael Vick, Atlanta
AFC: 4.9 Chris Brown, Tennessee

TOUCHDOWNS
AFC: 17 LaDainian Tomlinson, San Diego
NFC: 16 Shaun Alexander, Seattle

TEAM LEADERS, YARDS
AFC: BALTIMORE, 1006, Jamal Lewis; BUFFALO, 1128, Willis McGahee; CINCINNATI, 1454, Rudi Johnson; CLEVELAND, 744, Lee Suggs; DENVER, 1240, Reuben Droughns; HOUSTON, 1188, Domanick Davis; INDIANAPOLIS, 1548, Edgerrin James; JACKSONVILLE, 1224, Fred Taylor; KANSAS CITY, 892, Priest Holmes; MIAMI, 523, Sammy Morris; NEW ENGLAND, 1635, Corey Dillon; N.Y. JETS, 1697, Curtis Martin; OAKLAND, 425, Amos Zereoue; PITTSBURGH, 941, Jerome Bettis; SAN DIEGO, 1335, LaDainian Tomlinson; TENNESSEE, 1067, Chris Brown

NFC: ARIZONA, 937, Emmitt Smith; ATLANTA, 1106, Warrick Dunn; CAROLINA, 821, Nick Goings; CHICAGO, 948, Thomas Jones; DALLAS, 819, *Julius Jones; DETROIT, 1133, *Kevin Jones; GREEN BAY, 1163, Ahman Green; MINNESOTA, 544, Onterrio Smith; NEW ORLEANS, 1074, Deuce McAllister; N.Y. GIANTS, 1518, Tiki Barber; PHILADELPHIA, 812, Brian Westbrook; ST. LOUIS, 774, Marshall Faulk; SAN FRANCISCO, 822, Kevan Barlow; SEATTLE, 1696, Shaun Alexander; TAMPA BAY, 926, Michael Pittman; WASHINGTON, 1315, Clinton Portis

TEAM CHAMPION
NFC: 2672 Atlanta
AFC: 2464 Pittsburgh

Player that was a rookie in 2004

NFL TOP TEN RUSHERS

	Att	Yards	Avg	Long	TD
Martin, Curtis, NYJ	371	1697	4.6	25t	12
Alexander, Shaun, Sea.	353	1696	4.8	44	16
Dillon, Corey, N.E.	345	1635	4.7	44	12
James, Edgerrin, Ind.	334	1548	4.6	40	9
Barber, Tiki, NY-G	322	1518	4.7	72t	13
Johnson, Rudi, Cin.	361	1454	4.0	52	12
Tomlinson, LaDainian, S.D.	339	1335	3.9	42	17
Portis, Clinton, Was.	343	1315	3.8	64t	5
Droughns, Reuben, Den.	275	1240	4.5	51t	6
Taylor, Fred, Jac.	260	1224	4.7	46	2

AFC—INDIVIDUAL RUSHERS

	Att	Yards	Avg	Long	TD
Martin, Curtis, NYJ	371	1697	4.6	25t	12
Dillon, Corey, N.E.	345	1635	4.7	44	12
James, Edgerrin, Ind.	334	1548	4.6	40	9
Johnson, Rudi, Cin.	361	1454	4.0	52	12
Tomlinson, LaDainian, S.D.	339	1335	3.9	42	17
Droughns, Reuben, Den.	275	1240	4.5	51t	6
Taylor, Fred, Jac.	260	1224	4.7	46	2
Davis, Domanick, Hou.	302	1188	3.9	44	13
McGahee, Willis, Buf.	284	1128	4.0	41	13
Brown, Chris, Ten.	220	1067	4.9	52	6
Lewis, Jamal, Bal.	235	1006	4.3	75t	7
Bettis, Jerome, Pit.	250	941	3.8	29	13
Holmes, Priest, K.C.	196	892	4.6	33t	14
Staley, Duce, Pit.	192	830	4.3	38	1
Suggs, Lee, Cle.	199	744	3.7	39	2
Taylor, Chester, Bal.	160	714	4.5	47	2
Green, William, Cle.	163	585	3.6	46	2
Johnson, Larry, K.C.	120	581	4.8	46t	9
Blaylock, Derrick, K.C.	118	539	4.6	24	8
Morris, Sammy, Mia.	132	523	4.0	35t	6
Smith, Antowain, Ten.	137	509	3.7	43	4
Jordan, LaMont, NYJ	93	479	5.2	33	2
Zereoue, Amos, Oak.	112	425	3.8	55t	3
* Bell, Tatum, Den.	75	396	5.3	29	3
Chatman, Jesse, S.D.	65	392	6.0	52	3
Minor, Travis, Mia.	109	388	3.6	34	1
Wheatley, Tyrone, Oak.	85	327	3.8	60	4
Henry, Travis, Buf.	94	326	3.5	19	0
Griffin, Quentin, Den.	85	311	3.7	47t	2
Carr, David, Hou.	73	299	4.1	24	0
Wells, Jonathan, Hou.	82	299	3.6	14	3
Haynes, Verron, Pit.	55	272	4.9	18	0
Faulk, Kevin, N.E.	54	255	4.7	20	1
Rhodes, Dominic, Ind.	53	254	4.8	55	1
Crockett, Zack, Oak.	48	232	4.8	47	2
Plummer, Jake, Den.	62	202	3.3	22	1
Boller, Kyle, Bal.	53	189	3.6	19	1
* Parker, Willie, Pit.	32	186	5.8	58	0
Garcia, Jeff, Cle.	35	169	4.8	21	2
Toefield, LaBrandon, Jac.	51	169	3.3	16	0
* Williams, Shaud, Buf.	42	167	4.0	27t	2
* Jones, Greg, Jac.	62	162	2.6	12	3
Watson, Kenny, Cin.	26	161	6.2	25	0
Leftwich, Byron, Jac.	39	148	3.8	17	2
* Roethlisberger, Ben, Pit.	56	144	2.6	20	1
Henry, Leonard, Mia.	46	141	3.1	53	0
Pass, Patrick, N.E.	39	141	3.6	19	0
McNair, Steve, Ten.	23	128	5.6	23	1
Fargas, Justin, Oak.	35	126	3.6	15	1
Pennington, Chad, NYJ	34	126	3.7	16	1
Redmond, J.R., Oak.	21	119	5.7	18	0
* Turner, Michael, S.D.	20	104	5.2	30	0
Brees, Drew, S.D.	53	85	1.6	22	2
* Evans, Lee, Buf.	5	85	17.0	48	0
Green, Trent, K.C.	25	85	3.4	13	0

	Att	Yards	Avg	Long	TD
White, Jamel, T.B.-Bal.	27	82	3.0	16	0
Hearst, Garrison, Den.	20	81	4.1	11	1
Jackson, James, Cle.	12	81	6.8	38	0
Chambers, Chris, Mia.	9	76	8.4	24	0
Garrard, David, Jac.	12	76	6.3	12	1
Burns, Joe, Buf.	20	73	3.7	21	0
Fuamatu-Ma'afala, Chris, Jac.	20	69	3.5	10	1
Gordon, Lamar, Mia.	35	64	1.8	11	0
Holcombe, Robert, Ten.	17	62	3.6	20	0
Fiedler, Jay, Mia.	12	59	4.9	26	0
Hall, Dante, K.C.	8	56	7.0	17	0
Richardson, Tony, K.C.	12	56	4.7	13	0
Dwight, Tim, S.D.	4	54	13.5	48	0
Forsey, Brock, Mia.	19	53	2.8	15	0
Neal, Lorenzo, S.D.	16	53	3.3	8	0
Parker, Eric, S.D.	4	53	13.3	38	0
Houshmandzadeh, T.J., Cin.	6	51	8.5	16	0
* Cobbs, Cedric, N.E.	22	50	2.3	13	0
Volek, Billy, Ten.	11	50	4.5	14	1
Smith, Musa, Bal.	12	48	4.0	13	0
Hollings, Tony, Hou.	11	47	4.3	13	0
Palmer, Carson, Cin.	18	47	2.6	14	1
Caldwell, Reche, S.D.	4	45	11.3	20	0
Morton, Johnnie, K.C.	7	43	6.1	14	0
Kitna, Jon, Cin.	10	42	4.2	15	0
* Fleming, Troy, Ten.	7	40	5.7	13	0
Flutie, Doug, S.D.	5	39	7.8	20	2
Johnson, Chad, Cin.	4	39	9.8	18	0
Manning, Peyton, Ind.	25	38	1.5	19	0
Bledsoe, Drew, Buf.	22	37	1.7	17	0
Collins, Kerry, Oak.	16	36	2.3	8	0
Ricard, Alan, Bal.	10	36	3.6	14	0
Randle El, Antwaan, Pit.	8	34	4.3	12	0
Smith, Rod, Den.	5	33	6.6	14	0
* Watts, Darius, Den.	5	33	6.6	10	0
Sapp, Cecil, Den.	4	32	8.0	18	0
Gaffney, Jabar, Hou.	4	30	7.5	10	0
Brady, Tom, N.E.	43	28	0.7	10	0
Sowell, Jerald, NYJ	2	28	14.0	19	0
Gannon, Rich, Oak.	5	26	5.2	20	0
Pinnock, Andrew, S.D.	9	26	2.9	11	0
* Echemandu, Adimchinobe, Cle.	8	25	3.1	6	0
* McCown, Luke, Cle.	6	25	4.2	11	0
Ward, Hines, Pit.	7	25	3.6	16t	1
Askew, B.J., NYJ	6	23	3.8	14	0
Moorman, Brian, Buf.	2	23	11.5	34	0
Carter, Quincy, NYJ	12	20	1.7	9	0
Moulds, Eric, Buf.	5	19	3.8	12	0
Mungro, James, Ind.	5	19	3.8	8	0
Northcutt, Dennis, Cle.	8	19	2.4	8	0
* Sams, B.J., Bal.	4	19	4.8	8	1
Konrad, Rob, Mia.	2	18	9.0	15	0
Kreider, Dan, Pit.	4	18	4.5	6	0
Moss, Santana, NYJ	6	18	3.0	12	0
Kennison, Eddie, K.C.	2	15	7.5	15	0
* Losman, J.P., Buf.	2	15	7.5	10	0
Maddox, Tommy, Pit.	9	15	1.7	10	0
Russell, Cliff, Cin.	3	15	5.0	13	0
Warrick, Peter, Cin.	2	14	7.0	8	0
Abdullah, Rabih, N.E.	13	13	1.0	5	1
Feeley, A.J., Mia.	14	13	0.9	7t	1
Bennett, Drew, Ten.	1	12	12.0	12	0
Horn, Chris, K.C.	1	12	12.0	12	0
Johnson, Andre, Hou.	4	12	3.0	14	0
* Larson, Kyle, Cin.	1	11	11.0	11t	1
* Smith, Jonathan, Buf.	2	11	5.5	8	0
* King, Vick, Mia.	4	9	2.3	3	0
Smith, Terrelle, Cle.	4	9	2.3	4	0

	Att	Yards	Avg	Long	TD
Hentrich, Craig, Ten.	1	8	8.0	8	0
Johnson, Bethel, N.E.	2	8	4.0	11	0
Gabriel, Doug, Oak.	2	7	3.5	4	0
Gonzalez, Tony, K.C.	1	5	5.0	5	0
Johnson, Jeremi, Cin.	3	5	1.7	4	0
Lelie, Ashley, Den.	3	5	1.7	8	0
Patten, David, N.E.	1	5	5.0	5	0
Stanley, Chad, Hou.	1	5	5.0	5	0
Collins, Todd, K.C.	1	4	4.0	4	0
Hetherington, Chris, Oak.	1	4	4.0	4	0
Jackson, Frisman, Cle.	1	4	4.0	4	0
McCardell, Keenan, S.D.	1	3	3.0	3	0
Turk, Matt, Mia.	1	3	3.0	3	0
Bollinger, Brooks, NYJ	1	2	2.0	2	0
Brown, Dante, Pit.	1	2	2.0	2	0
Edwards, Troy, Jac.	2	2	1.0	2	0
Smith, Hunter, Ind.	1	2	2.0	2	0
Baxter, Jarrod, Hou.	2	1	0.5	1	0
Easy, Omar, K.C.	4	1	0.3	4	0
Frost, Derrick, Cle.	1	1	1.0	1	0
* Perry, Chris, Cin.	2	1	0.5	1	0
Shaw, Bobby, S.D.	1	1	1.0	1	0
Simmons, Jason, Hou.	1	1	1.0	1	0
Cheek, Steve, K.C.	1	0	0.0	0	0
Izzo, Larry, N.E.	1	0	0.0	0	0
Johnson, Kevin, Bal.	1	0	0.0	0	0
Norris, Moran, Hou.	1	0	0.0	0	0
Davey, Rohan, N.E.	4	-1	-0.2	3	0
Reed, Josh, Buf.	2	-1	-0.5	6	0
Stewart, Kordell, Bal.	1	-1	-1.0	-1	0
Washington, Kelley, Cin.	1	-1	-1.0	-1	0
Holcomb, Kelly, Cle.	3	-2	-0.7	0	0
Johnson, Doug, Ten.	2	-2	-1.0	-1	0
Curry, Ronald, Oak.	1	-3	-3.0	-3	0
Davis, Andre, Cle.	1	-3	-3.0	-3	0
Mason, Derrick, Ten.	1	-3	-3.0	-3	0
Matthews, Shane, Buf.	2	-3	-1.5	-1	0
St. Pierre, Brian, Pit.	4	-3	-0.7	2	0
Porter, Jerry, Oak.	1	-4	-4.0	-4	0
Wayne, Reggie, Ind.	1	-4	-4.0	-4	0
McCareins, Justin, NYJ	2	-5	-2.5	-2	0
* Rivers, Philip, S.D.	4	-5	-1.2	-1	0
* Sorgi, Jim, Ind.	8	-5	-0.6	2	0
* Greer, Jabari, Buf.	1	-6	-6.0	-6	0
Booker, Marty, Mia.	1	-8	-8.0	-8	0
Sanders, Deion, Bal.	1	-10	-10.0	-10	0

t = Touchdown; *Player that was a rookie in 2004
Leader based on most yards gained

NFC—INDIVIDUAL RUSHERS

	Att	Yards	Avg	Long	TD
Alexander, Shaun, Sea.	353	1696	4.8	44	16
Barber, Tiki, NY-G	322	1518	4.7	72t	13
Portis, Clinton, Was.	343	1315	3.8	64t	5
Green, Ahman, G.B.	259	1163	4.5	90t	7
* Jones, Kevin, Det.	241	1133	4.7	74	5
Dunn, Warrick, Atl.	265	1106	4.2	60	9
McAllister, Deuce, N.O.	269	1074	4.0	71	9
Jones, Thomas, Chi.	240	948	4.0	54	7
Smith, Emmitt, Ariz	267	937	3.5	29t	9
Pittman, Michael, T.B.	219	926	4.2	78t	7
Vick, Michael, Atl.	120	902	7.5	58	3
Barlow, Kevan, S.F.	244	822	3.4	60	7
Goings, Nick, Car.	217	821	3.8	57t	6
* Jones, Julius, Dal.	197	819	4.2	53	7
Westbrook, Brian, Phi.	177	812	4.6	50	3
Faulk, Marshall, St.L	195	774	4.0	40	3

2004 INDIVIDUAL STATISTICS—RUSHING

Player	Att	Yards	Avg	Long	TD
* Jackson, Steven, St.L	134	673	5.0	48	4
Smith, Onterrio, Min.	124	544	4.4	38	2
Duckett, T.J., Atl.	104	509	4.9	35	8
George, Eddie, Dal.	132	432	3.3	24	4
Levens, Dorsey, Phi.	94	410	4.4	45	4
Culpepper, Daunte, Min.	88	406	4.6	16	2
Thomas, Anthony, Chi.	122	404	3.3	41t	2
* Moore, Mewelde, Min.	65	379	5.8	33	0
Betts, Ladell, Was.	90	371	4.1	27	1
Hicks, Maurice, S.F.	96	362	3.8	35	2
Davenport, Najeh, G.B.	71	359	5.1	40t	2
Hambrick, Troy, Ariz	63	283	4.5	62	1
Bennett, Michael, Min.	70	276	3.9	25	1
Bryson, Shawn, Det.	50	264	5.3	28	0
Foster, DeShaun, Car.	59	255	4.3	71	2
Anderson, Richie, Dal.	57	246	4.3	27	1
Hoover, Brad, Car.	68	246	3.6	16	0
Stecker, Aaron, N.O.	58	244	4.2	42t	2
Alstott, Mike, T.B.	67	230	3.4	32	2
Fisher, Tony, G.B.	65	224	3.4	24	0
McNabb, Donovan, Phi.	41	220	5.4	28	3
Dayne, Ron, NY-G	52	179	3.4	15	1
Harrington, Joey, Det.	48	175	3.6	17	0
Pinner, Artose, Det.	57	174	3.1	14	2
Brooks, Aaron, N.O.	58	173	3.0	15	4
Williams, Moe, Min.	30	161	5.4	49	3
Strong, Mack, Sea.	36	131	3.6	11	0
Lee, ReShard, Dal.	27	128	4.7	14	1
Morris, Maurice, Sea.	30	126	4.2	12	0
Ayanbadejo, Obafemi, Ariz	30	122	4.1	23	3
McCown, Josh, Ariz	36	112	3.1	12	2
Garner, Charlie, T.B.	30	111	3.7	25	0
Jackson, Terry, S.F.	26	101	3.9	13	0
Davis, Stephen, Car.	24	92	3.8	12	0
Mahe, Reno, Phi.	23	91	4.0	22	0
Cloud, Mike, NY-G	21	90	4.3	26	3
Hasselbeck, Matt, Sea.	27	90	3.3	19	1
Bulger, Marc, St.L	19	89	4.7	19t	3
Scobey, Josh, Ariz	27	89	3.3	10	0
* Croom, Larry, Ariz	29	76	2.6	20	0
Wade, Bobby, Chi.	12	76	6.3	14	0
* Graham, Earnest, T.B.	13	73	5.6	13	0
Delhomme, Jake, Car.	25	71	2.8	13	1
Robertson, Jamal, S.F.	16	71	4.4	16	1
Harris, Arlen, St.L	20	63	3.2	14	0
Brunell, Mark, Was.	19	62	3.3	21	0
Rattay, Tim, S.F.	12	55	4.6	15	0
McAfee, Fred, N.O.	2	54	27.0	53	0
* McCoo, Eric, Phi.	9	54	6.0	12	0
* Harris, Joey, Car.	15	53	3.5	19	0
Burleson, Nate, Min.	6	49	8.2	11	0
Grossman, Rex, Chi.	11	48	4.4	8	1
* Tapeh, Thomas, Phi.	12	42	3.5	10	0
Williams, Walter, G.B.	6	42	7.0	28	0
* Krenzel, Craig, Chi.	18	41	2.3	12	0
Griffith, Justin, Atl.	9	39	4.3	10	0
Testaverde, Vinny, Dal.	21	38	1.8	10	1
Stallworth, Donte', N.O.	6	37	6.2	26	0
Chatman, Antonio, G.B.	4	36	9.0	17	0
Favre, Brett, G.B.	16	36	2.3	17	0
* Manning, Eli, NY-G	6	35	5.8	15	0
Quinn, Jonathan, Chi.	3	35	11.7	23	0
Hilliard, Ike, NY-G	3	34	11.3	17	0
Price, Peerless, Atl.	3	34	11.3	16	0
Coakley, Dexter, Dal.	1	33	33.0	33	0
* Clayton, Michael, T.B.	5	30	6.0	15	0
King, Shaun, Ariz	9	30	3.3	16	0
Warner, Kurt, NY-G	13	30	2.3	13	1

Player	Att	Yards	Avg	Long	TD
* Berrian, Bernard, Chi.	8	28	3.5	25	0
* Schaub, Matt, Atl.	8	26	3.3	11	0
* Smart, Ian, T.B.	2	26	13.0	25	0
Curtis, Kevin, St.L	3	24	8.0	15	0
Luchey, Nicolas, G.B.	10	24	2.4	4	0
Carter, Tim, NY-G	2	23	11.5	15	0
Johnson, Brad, T.B.	5	23	4.6	7	0
Morgan, Quincy, Dal.	2	23	11.5	24	0
Evans, Heath, Sea.	7	20	2.9	7	0
Galloway, Joey, T.B.	2	19	9.5	14	0
Peterson, Adrian, Chi.	6	19	3.2	13	0
Ramsey, Patrick, Was.	10	19	1.9	17	0
McMahon, Mike, Det.	2	18	9.0	14	0
Pritchett, Stanley, Atl.	6	18	3.0	8	0
Bennett, Brandon, Car.	6	17	2.8	11	1
Carter, Ki-Jana, N.O.	10	17	1.7	8	0
Griese, Brian, T.B.	30	17	0.6	7	0
Lewis, Greg, Phi.	4	16	4.0	11	0
Beasley, Fred, S.F.	9	15	1.7	4	0
Carter, Kerry, Sea.	4	15	3.8	6	0
Muhammad, Muhsin, Car.	3	15	5.0	13	0
Pederson, Doug, G.B.	2	15	7.5	9	0
Dilfer, Trent, Sea.	10	14	1.4	11	0
* Fitzgerald, Larry, Ariz	8	14	1.8	10	0
Hutchinson, Chad, Chi.	6	14	2.3	11	0
Simms, Chris, T.B.	7	14	2.0	12	0
White, Dez, Atl.	3	14	4.7	26	0
Johnson, Keyshawn, Dal.	2	13	6.5	13	0
Williams, Randal, Dal.	1	13	13.0	13	0
Layne, George, Atl.	1	12	12.0	12	0
Ward, Dedric, Dal.	1	11	11.0	11	0
Barnes, Darian, Dal.	5	10	2.0	8	0
Terrell, David, Chi.	3	10	3.3	20	0
* Wright, Jason, Atl.	3	10	3.3	8	0
Drummond, Eddie, Det.	1	9	9.0	9	0
Proehl, Ricky, Car.	1	9	9.0	9	0
Dorsey, Ken, S.F.	5	7	1.4	3	0
Finn, Jim, NY-G	3	7	2.3	5	0
Gardner, Rod, Was.	3	7	2.3	11	0
* Henson, Drew, Dal.	1	7	7.0	7	0
* Karney, Mike, N.O.	3	7	2.3	4	0
Nall, Craig, G.B.	3	7	2.3	9	0
Schlesinger, Cory, Det.	4	7	1.8	2	0
Blake, Jeff, Phi.	3	6	2.0	8	0
Goodspeed, Joey, St.L	3	6	2.0	2t	1
Williams, Karl, Ariz	2	6	3.0	3	0
Wilson, Cedrick, S.F.	1	6	6.0	6	0
Battle, Arnaz, S.F.	2	5	2.5	7	0
* Pickett, Cody, S.F.	1	5	5.0	5	0
Campbell, Kelly, Min.	3	4	1.3	16	0
Driver, Donald, G.B.	3	4	1.3	14	0
Russell, Brian, Min.	1	4	4.0	4	0
Smart, Rod, Car.	3	4	1.3	3	0
Boldin, Anquan, Ariz	1	3	3.0	3	0
Robinson, Koren, Sea.	1	3	3.0	3	0
Swinton, Reggie, Det.	1	3	3.0	3	0
Anderson, Damien, Ariz	1	2	2.0	2	0
Chandler, Chris, St.L	1	2	2.0	2	0
* Jenkins, Michael, Atl.	1	2	2.0	2	0
McKie, Jason, Chi.	1	1	1.0	1	0
* Williams, Roy, Det.	1	1	1.0	1	0
Cartwright, Rock, Was.	2	0	0.0	2	0
Hakim, Az-Zahir, Det.	1	0	0.0	0	0
Isom, Jasen, S.F.	1	0	0.0	0	0
McDonald, Shaun, St.L	4	0	0.0	7	0
Rossum, Allen, Atl.	1	0	0.0	0	0
* Copper, Terrance, Dal.	1	-1	-1.0	-1	0
Peete, Rodney, Car.	1	-1	-1.0	-1	0

	Att	Yards	Avg	Long	TD
Cleeland, Cameron, St.L	1	-2	-2.0	-2	0
O'Sullivan, J.T., G.B.	2	-2	-1.0	-1	0
Coles, Laveranues, Was.	3	-3	-1.0	7	0
Glenn, Terry, Dal.	1	-3	-3.0	-3	0
Ponder, Willie, NY-G	1	-4	-4.0	-4	0
Owens, Terrell, Phi.	3	-5	-1.7	6	0
Wilkins, Jeff, St.L	1	-5	-5.0	-5	0
Jacobs, Taylor, Was.	1	-6	-6.0	-6	0
Johnson, Bryant, Ariz	2	-6	-3.0	1	0
Detmer, Koy, Phi.	10	-7	-0.7	2	0
Harris, Nick, Det.	1	-7	-7.0	-7	0
* Taylor, Jamaar, NY-G	1	-8	-8.0	-8	0

t = Touchdown; *Player that was a rookie in 2004
Leader based on most yards gained

AMERICAN FOOTBALL CONFERENCE—RUSHING

	Att	Yards	Avg	Long	TD
Pittsburgh	618	2464	4.0	58	16
N.Y. Jets	527	2388	4.5	33	15
Denver	534	2333	4.4	51t	13
Kansas City	496	2289	4.6	46t	31
San Diego	525	2185	4.2	52	24
New England	524	2134	4.1	44	15
Baltimore	491	2063	4.2	75t	11
Houston	481	1882	3.9	44	16
Buffalo	483	1874	3.9	48	15
Tennessee	420	1871	4.5	52	12
Indianapolis	427	1852	4.3	55	10
Jacksonville	446	1850	4.1	46	9
Cincinnati	437	1839	4.2	52	14
Cleveland	441	1657	3.8	46	6
Miami	384	1339	3.5	53	10
Oakland	327	1295	4.0	60	10
AFC Total	7561	31315	4.1	75t	227
AFC Average	472.6	1957.2	4.1	—	14.2

NATIONAL FOOTBALL CONFERENCE—RUSHING

	Att	Yards	Avg	Long	TD
Atlanta	524	2672	5.1	60	20
Seattle	468	2095	4.5	44	17
Green Bay	441	1908	4.3	90t	9
N.Y. Giants	424	1904	4.5	72t	18
Minnesota	387	1823	4.7	49	8
Detroit	407	1777	4.4	74	7
Dallas	449	1769	3.9	53	14
Washington	471	1765	3.7	64t	6
Arizona	475	1668	3.5	62	15
Philadelphia	376	1639	4.4	50	10
Chicago	430	1624	3.8	54	10
St. Louis	381	1624	4.3	48	11
New Orleans	406	1606	4.0	71	15
Carolina	422	1582	3.7	71	10
Tampa Bay	393	1489	3.8	78t	9
San Francisco	413	1449	3.5	60	10
NFC Total	6867	28394	4.1	90t	189
NFC Average	429.2	1774.6	4.1	—	11.8
League Total	14428	59709	—	90t	416
League Average	450.9	1865.9	4.1	—	13.0

PASSING

HIGHEST RATING
AFC: 121.1 Peyton Manning, Indianapolis
NFC: 110.9 Daunte Culpepper, Minnesota

COMPLETION PERCENTAGE
NFC: 69.3 Brian Griese, Tampa Bay
AFC: 67.6 Peyton Manning, Indianapolis

ATTEMPTS
AFC: 556 Trent Green, Kansas City
NFC: 548 Daunte Culpepper, Minnesota

COMPLETIONS
NFC: 379 Daunte Culpepper, Minnesota
AFC: 369 Trent Green, Kansas City

YARDS
NFC: 4717 Daunte Culpepper, Minnesota
AFC: 4591 Trent Green, Kansas City

YARDS, GAME
AFC: 499 Jake Plummer, Denver vs. Atlanta,
October 31 (31-55, 4 TD)
NFC: 464 Donovan McNabb, Philadelphia vs. Green
Bay, December 5 (32-43, 5 TD)

LONGEST
AFC: 99 Jeff Garcia (to Andre Davis) Cleveland vs.
Cincinnati, October 17 - TD
NFC: 82 Daunte Culpepper (to Randy Moss)
Minnesota at Detroit, December 19 - TD

YARDS PER ATTEMPT
AFC: 9.17 Peyton Manning, Indianapolis
NFC: 8.61 Daunte Culpepper, Minnesota

TOUCHDOWN PASSES
AFC: 49 Peyton Manning, Indianapolis
NFC: 39 Daunte Culpepper, Minnesota

TOUCHDOWN PASSES, GAME
AFC: 6 Peyton Manning, Indianapolis at Detroit,
November 25 (23-28, 236 yards)
NFC: 5 Daunte Culpepper, Minnesota vs. Dallas,
September 12 (17-23, 242 yards)
5 Daunte Culpepper, Minnesota at Houston,
October 10 (36-50, 396 yards) - (OT)
5 Daunte Culpepper, Minnesota at New
Orleans, October 17 (26-37, 425 yards)
5 Donovan McNabb, Philadelphia vs. Green
Bay, December 5 (32-43, 464 yards)

LOWEST INTERCEPTION PERCENTAGE
AFC: 1.8 Drew Brees, San Diego
NFC: 1.4 Kurt Warner, New York Giants

TEAM CHAMPION (MOST NET YARDS)
AFC: 4623 Indianapolis
NFC: 4516 Minnesota

NFL TOP TEN PASSERS

	Att	Comp	Pct Comp	Yds	Avg Gain	TD	Pct TD	Long	Int	Pct Int	Sack	Yds Lost	Rating Points
Manning, Peyton, Ind.	497	336	67.6	4557	9.17	49	9.9	80t	10	2.0	13	101	121.1
Culpepper, Daunte, Min.	548	379	69.2	4717	8.61	39	7.1	82t	11	2.0	46	238	110.9
Brees, Drew, S.D.	400	262	65.5	3159	7.90	27	6.8	79t	7	1.8	18	131	104.8
McNabb, Donovan, Phi.	469	300	64.0	3875	8.26	31	6.6	80	8	1.7	32	192	104.7
* Roethlisberger, Ben, Pit.	295	196	66.4	2621	8.88	17	5.8	58	11	3.7	30	213	98.1
Griese, Brian, T.B.	336	233	69.3	2632	7.83	20	6.0	68	12	3.6	26	169	97.5
Green, Trent, K.C.	556	369	66.4	4591	8.26	27	4.9	70t	17	3.1	32	227	95.2
Bulger, Marc, St.L	485	321	66.2	3964	8.17	21	4.3	56	14	2.9	41	302	93.7
Brady, Tom, N.E.	474	288	60.8	3692	7.79	28	5.9	50	14	3.0	26	162	92.6
Favre, Brett, G.B.	540	346	64.1	4088	7.57	30	5.6	79t	17	3.1	12	93	92.4

*Player that was a rookie in 2004

AMERICAN FOOTBALL CONFERENCE—PASSING

	Att	Comp	Pct Comp	Gross Yards	Sacked	Yds Lost	Net Yards	Yds/ Att	Yards/ Comp	TD	Pct TD	Long	Int	Pct Int
Indianapolis	527	353	67.0	4732	14	109	4623	8.98	13.41	51	9.68	80t	10	1.9
Kansas City	561	370	66.0	4633	32	227	4406	8.26	12.52	27	4.81	70t	17	3.0
Denver	521	303	58.2	4089	15	90	3999	7.85	13.50	27	5.18	85t	20	3.8
Oakland	582	330	56.7	4019	30	161	3858	6.91	12.18	24	4.12	63	22	3.8
Tennessee	589	356	60.4	3933	44	317	3616	6.68	11.05	27	4.58	48t	19	3.2
New England	485	293	60.4	3750	26	162	3588	7.73	12.80	29	5.98	50	14	2.9
Houston	471	286	60.7	3547	49	301	3246	7.53	12.40	16	3.40	69	14	3.0
Cincinnati	536	324	60.4	3520	31	219	3301	6.57	10.86	23	4.29	76t	22	4.1
San Diego	450	288	64.0	3506	21	149	3357	7.79	12.17	29	6.44	79t	8	1.8
Miami	586	309	52.7	3391	52	326	3065	5.79	10.97	19	3.24	76t	26	4.4
Jacksonville	513	305	59.5	3315	32	156	3159	6.46	10.87	17	3.31	65	11	2.1
N.Y. Jets	438	282	64.4	3231	31	181	3050	7.38	11.46	19	4.34	69t	11	2.5
Cleveland	439	251	57.2	3076	41	252	2824	7.01	12.25	21	4.78	99t	21	4.8
Buffalo	461	262	56.8	3032	38	215	2817	6.58	11.57	21	4.56	69t	17	3.7
Pittsburgh	358	228	63.7	2970	36	250	2720	8.30	13.03	20	5.59	58	13	3.6
Baltimore	465	258	55.5	2559	35	247	2312	5.50	9.92	13	2.80	57t	11	2.4
AFC Total	7982	4798	—	57303	527	3362	53941	—	—	383	—	99t	256	—
AFC Average	498.9	299.9	60.1	3581.4	32.9	210.1	3371.3	7.18	11.94	23.9	4.8	—	16.0	3.2

NATIONAL FOOTBALL CONFERENCE—PASSING

	Att	Comp	Pct Comp	Gross Yards	Sacked	Yds Lost	Net Yards	Yds/ Att	Yards/ Comp	TD	Pct TD	Long	Int	Pct Int
Minnesota	552	380	68.8	4754	46	238	4516	8.61	12.51	39	7.07	82t	12	2.2
St. Louis	580	372	64.1	4615	50	362	4253	7.96	12.41	23	3.97	75t	22	3.8
Green Bay	598	382	63.9	4550	14	101	4449	7.61	11.91	36	6.02	79t	19	3.2
Philadelphia	547	336	61.4	4208	37	229	3979	7.69	12.52	32	5.85	80	11	2.0
Carolina	536	311	58.0	3889	33	246	3643	7.26	12.50	29	5.41	63	15	2.8
New Orleans	542	309	57.0	3810	41	223	3587	7.03	12.33	21	3.87	57	16	3.0
Tampa Bay	512	340	66.4	3773	44	299	3474	7.37	11.10	24	4.69	75t	18	3.5
Seattle	532	304	57.1	3715	34	176	3539	6.98	12.22	23	4.32	60	18	3.4
Dallas	519	308	59.3	3636	36	208	3428	7.01	11.81	19	3.66	53	23	4.4
San Francisco	561	325	57.9	3455	52	319	3136	6.16	10.63	16	2.85	65	21	3.7
Arizona	533	299	56.1	3202	39	320	2882	6.01	10.71	14	2.63	48	18	3.4
Detroit	505	285	56.4	3124	37	208	2916	6.19	10.96	19	3.76	62	13	2.6
N.Y. Giants	475	269	56.6	3097	52	279	2818	6.52	11.51	12	2.53	62t	13	2.7
Washington	514	288	56.0	2874	38	242	2632	5.59	9.98	18	3.50	51	17	3.3
Atlanta	395	217	54.9	2692	50	280	2412	6.82	12.41	15	3.80	62	16	4.1
Chicago	471	249	52.9	2641	66	449	2192	5.61	10.61	9	1.91	63	16	3.4
NFC Total	8372	4974	—	58035	669	4179	53856	—	—	349	—	82t	268	—
NFC Average	523.3	310.9	59.4	3627.2	41.8	261.2	3366.0	6.93	11.67	21.8	4.2	—	16.8	3.2
League Total	16354	9772	—	115338	1196	7541	107797	—	—	732	—	99t	524	—
League Average	511.1	305.4	59.8	3604.3	37.4	235.7	3368.7	7.05	11.80	22.9	4.5	—	16.4	3.2

AFC—INDIVIDUAL PASSERS

	Att	Comp	Pct Comp	Yds	Avg Gain	TD	Pct TD	Long	Int	Pct Int	Sack	Yds Lost	Rating Points
Manning, Peyton, Ind.	497	336	67.6	4557	9.17	49	9.9	80t	10	2.0	13	101	121.1
Brees, Drew, S.D.	400	262	65.5	3159	7.90	27	6.8	79t	7	1.8	18	131	104.8
* Roethlisberger, Ben, Pit.	295	196	66.4	2621	8.88	17	5.8	58	11	3.7	30	213	98.1
Green, Trent, K.C.	556	369	66.4	4591	8.26	27	4.9	70t	17	3.1	32	227	95.2
Brady, Tom, N.E.	474	288	60.8	3692	7.79	28	5.9	50	14	3.0	26	162	92.6
Pennington, Chad, NYJ	370	242	65.4	2673	7.22	16	4.3	48	9	2.4	18	103	91.0
Volek, Billy, Ten.	357	218	61.1	2486	6.96	18	5.0	48t	10	2.8	30	216	87.1
Plummer, Jake, Den.	521	303	58.2	4089	7.85	27	5.2	85t	20	3.8	15	90	84.5
Carr, David, Hou.	466	285	61.2	3531	7.58	16	3.4	69	14	3.0	49	301	83.5
Leftwich, Byron, Jac.	441	267	60.5	2941	6.67	15	3.4	65	10	2.3	25	114	82.2
Palmer, Carson, Cin.	432	263	60.9	2897	6.71	18	4.2	76t	18	4.2	25	178	77.3
Garcia, Jeff, Cle.	252	144	57.1	1731	6.87	10	4.0	99t	9	3.6	24	99	76.7
Bledsoe, Drew, Buf.	450	256	56.9	2932	6.52	20	4.4	69t	16	3.6	37	215	76.6
Collins, Kerry, Oak.	513	289	56.3	3495	6.81	21	4.1	63	20	3.9	25	144	74.8
Boller, Kyle, Bal.	464	258	55.6	2559	5.52	13	2.8	57t	11	2.4	35	247	70.9
Feeley, A.J., Mia.	356	191	53.7	1893	5.32	11	3.1	38	15	4.2	23	136	61.7
(Nonqualifiers)													
* Sorgi, Jim, Ind.	29	17	58.6	175	6.03	2	6.9	71t	0	0.0	1	8	99.1
Carter, Quincy, NYJ	58	35	60.3	498	8.59	3	5.2	69t	1	1.7	12	70	98.2
Holcomb, Kelly, Cle.	87	59	67.8	737	8.47	7	8.0	55t	5	5.7	5	31	96.8
Gannon, Rich, Oak.	68	41	60.3	524	7.71	3	4.4	58t	2	2.9	5	17	86.9
Flutie, Doug, S.D.	38	20	52.6	276	7.26	1	2.6	29	0	0.0	1	7	85.0
Kitna, Jon, Cin.	104	61	58.7	623	5.99	5	4.8	30	4	3.8	6	41	75.9
McNair, Steve, Ten.	215	129	60.0	1343	6.25	8	3.7	37t	9	4.2	13	95	73.1
Garrard, David, Jac.	72	38	52.8	374	5.19	2	2.8	36t	1	1.4	6	35	71.2
Johnson, Doug, Ten.	12	6	50.0	68	5.67	0	0.0	33	0	0.0	1	6	67.4
Fiedler, Jay, Mia.	190	101	53.2	1186	6.24	7	3.7	71t	8	4.2	25	165	67.1
Maddox, Tommy, Pit.	60	30	50.0	329	5.48	1	1.7	39	2	3.3	6	37	58.3
Davey, Rohan, N.E.	10	4	40.0	54	5.40	0	0.0	20	0	0.0	0	0	57.9
* McCown, Luke, Cle.	98	48	49.0	608	6.20	4	4.1	58t	7	7.1	12	122	52.6
Rosenfels, Sage, Mia.	39	16	41.0	264	6.77	1	2.6	76t	3	7.7	3	16	41.0
(Fewer than 10 attempts)													
Banks, Tony, Hou.	2	1	50.0	16	8.00	0	0.0	16	0	0.0	0	0	77.1
Bennett, Drew, Ten.	1	1	100.0	26	26.00	1	100.0	26t	0	0.0	0	0	158.3
Bettis, Jerome, Pit.	1	1	100.0	10	10.00	1	100.0	10t	0	0.0	0	0	147.9
Bollinger, Brooks, NYJ	9	5	55.6	60	6.67	0	0.0	26	0	0.0	1	8	76.2
Booker, Marty, Mia.	1	1	100.0	48	48.00	0	0.0	48	0	0.0	0	0	118.8
Collins, Todd, K.C.	5	1	20.0	42	8.40	0	0.0	42	0	0.0	0	0	62.1
Curry, Ronald, Oak.	1	0	0.0	0	0.00	0	0.0	0	0	0.0	0	0	39.6
* Echemandu, Adimchinobe, Cle.	1	0	0.0	0	0.00	0	0.0	0	0	0.0	0	0	39.6
Gaffney, Jabar, Hou.	3	0	0.0	0	0.00	0	0.0	0	0	0.0	0	0	39.6
Hentrich, Craig, Ten.	4	2	50.0	10	2.50	0	0.0	6	0	0.0	0	0	56.3
Hymes, Randy, Bal.	1	0	0.0	0	0.00	0	0.0	0	0	0.0	0	0	39.6
Jackson, Frisman, Cle.	1	0	0.0	0	0.00	0	0.0	0	0	0.0	0	0	39.6
Jordan, LaMont, NYJ	1	0	0.0	0	0.00	0	0.0	0	1	100.0	0	0	0.0
* Losman, J.P., Buf.	5	3	60.0	32	6.40	0	0.0	17	1	20.0	1	0	39.2
Matthews, Shane, Buf.	3	2	66.7	44	14.67	1	33.3	33t	0	0.0	0	0	149.3
McCardell, Keenan, S.D.	1	0	0.0	0	0.00	0	0.0	0	0	0.0	0	0	39.6
Moorman, Brian, Buf.	3	1	33.3	24	8.00	0	0.0	24	0	0.0	0	0	63.2
Morris, Sammy, Mia.	0	0	—	0	—	0	—	—	0	—	1	9	—
Randle El, Antwaan, Pit.	1	1	100.0	10	10.00	1	100.0	10t	0	0.0	0	0	147.9
* Rivers, Philip, S.D.	8	5	62.5	33	4.13	1	12.5	13t	0	0.0	1	10	110.9
Saturday, Jeff, Ind.	1	0	0.0	0	0.00	0	0.0	0	0	0.0	0	0	39.6
Scifres, Mike, S.D.	1	0	0.0	0	0.00	0	0.0	0	1	100.0	0	0	0.0
St. Pierre, Brian, Pit.	1	0	0.0	0	0.00	0	0.0	0	0	0.0	0	0	39.6
Toefield, LaBrandon, Jac.	0	0	—	0	—	0	—	—	0	—	1	7	—
Tomlinson, LaDainian, S.D.	2	1	50.0	38	19.00	0	0.0	38	0	0.0	1	1	95.8
Vinatieri, Adam, N.E.	1	1	100.0	4	4.00	1	100.0	4t	0	0.0	0	0	122.9

*t = Touchdown; *Player that was a rookie in 2004*
Leader based on rating points, minimum 224 attempts

NFC—INDIVIDUAL PASSERS

	Att	Comp	Pct Comp	Yds	Avg Gain	TD	Pct TD	Long	Int	Pct Int	Sack	Yds Lost	Rating Points
Culpepper, Daunte, Min.	548	379	69.2	4717	8.61	39	7.1	82t	11	2.0	46	238	110.9
McNabb, Donovan, Phi.	469	300	64.0	3875	8.26	31	6.6	80	8	1.7	32	192	104.7
Griese, Brian, T.B.	336	233	69.3	2632	7.83	20	6.0	68	12	3.6	26	169	97.5
Bulger, Marc, St.L	485	321	66.2	3964	8.17	21	4.3	56	14	2.9	41	302	93.7
Favre, Brett, G.B.	540	346	64.1	4088	7.57	30	5.6	79t	17	3.1	12	93	92.4
Delhomme, Jake, Car.	533	310	58.2	3886	7.29	29	5.4	63	15	2.8	33	246	87.3
Warner, Kurt, NY-G	277	174	62.8	2054	7.42	6	2.2	62t	4	1.4	39	196	86.5
Hasselbeck, Matt, Sea.	474	279	58.9	3382	7.14	22	4.6	60	15	3.2	30	155	83.1
Brooks, Aaron, N.O.	542	309	57.0	3810	7.03	21	3.9	57	16	3.0	41	223	79.5
Rattay, Tim, S.F.	325	198	60.9	2169	6.67	10	3.1	65	10	3.1	37	211	78.1
Vick, Michael, Atl.	321	181	56.4	2313	7.21	14	4.4	62	12	3.7	46	266	78.1
Harrington, Joey, Det.	489	274	56.0	3047	6.23	19	3.9	62	12	2.5	36	196	77.5
Testaverde, Vinny, Dal.	495	297	60.0	3532	7.14	17	3.4	53	20	4.0	34	182	76.4
Ramsey, Patrick, Was.	272	169	62.1	1665	6.12	10	3.7	51	11	4.0	23	137	74.8
McCown, Josh, Ariz	408	233	57.1	2511	6.15	11	2.7	48	10	2.5	31	263	74.1
Brunell, Mark, Was.	237	118	49.8	1194	5.04	7	3.0	49	6	2.5	15	105	63.9
Dorsey, Ken, S.F.	226	123	54.4	1231	5.45	6	2.7	59	9	4.0	13	94	62.4
(Nonqualifiers)													
Nall, Craig, G.B.	33	23	69.7	314	9.52	4	12.1	43	0	0.0	2	8	139.4
Johnson, Brad, T.B.	103	65	63.1	674	6.54	3	2.9	54	3	2.9	8	55	79.5
Hutchinson, Chad, Chi.	161	92	57.1	903	5.61	4	2.5	63	3	1.9	23	160	73.6
Martin, Jamie, St.L	30	16	53.3	188	6.27	0	0.0	26	0	0.0	2	6	72.6
Grossman, Rex, Chi.	84	47	56.0	607	7.23	1	1.2	40	3	3.6	5	22	67.9
Simms, Chris, T.B.	73	42	57.5	467	6.40	1	1.4	75t	3	4.1	10	75	64.1
* Henson, Drew, Dal.	18	10	55.6	78	4.33	1	5.6	16	1	5.6	2	26	61.8
King, Shaun, Ariz	84	47	56.0	502	5.98	1	1.2	40	4	4.8	6	42	57.7
McMahon, Mike, Det.	15	11	73.3	77	5.13	0	0.0	19	1	6.7	1	12	56.8
* Manning, Eli, NY-G	197	95	48.2	1043	5.29	6	3.0	52	9	4.6	13	83	55.4
Blake, Jeff, Phi.	37	18	48.6	126	3.41	1	2.7	21	1	2.7	2	17	54.6
Quinn, Jonathan, Chi.	98	51	52.0	413	4.21	1	1.0	32	3	3.1	15	109	53.7
* Krenzel, Craig, Chi.	127	59	46.5	718	5.65	3	2.4	49t	6	4.7	23	158	52.5
Chandler, Chris, St.L	62	35	56.5	463	7.47	2	3.2	75t	8	12.9	7	54	51.4
Dilfer, Trent, Sea.	58	25	43.1	333	5.74	1	1.7	56	3	5.2	4	21	46.1
* Schaub, Matt, Atl.	70	33	47.1	330	4.71	1	1.4	59	4	5.7	4	14	42.0
Detmer, Koy, Phi.	40	18	45.0	207	5.18	0	0.0	31	2	5.0	2	16	40.3
Pederson, Doug, G.B.	23	11	47.8	120	5.22	0	0.0	24	2	8.7	0	0	27.4
* Navarre, John, Ariz	40	18	45.0	168	4.20	1	2.5	33t	4	10.0	1	8	25.8
* Pickett, Cody, S.F.	10	4	40.0	55	5.50	0	0.0	18	2	20.0	2	14	18.8
(Fewer than 10 attempts)													
Anderson, Richie, Dal.	1	1	100.0	26	26.00	1	100.0	26t	0	0.0	0	0	158.3
Bartrum, Mike, Phi.	1	0	0.0	0	0.00	0	0.0	0	0	0.0	0	0	39.6
Bruce, Isaac, St.L	2	0	0.0	0	0.00	0	0.0	0	0	0.0	0	0	39.6
* Crayton, Patrick, Dal.	1	0	0.0	0	0.00	0	0.0	0	1	100.0	0	0	0.0
Edinger, Paul, Chi.	1	0	0.0	0	0.00	0	0.0	0	1	100.0	0	0	0.0
Feagles, Jeff, NY-G	1	0	0.0	0	0.00	0	0.0	0	0	0.0	0	0	39.6
Fisher, Tony, G.B.	1	1	100.0	8	8.00	1	100.0	8t	0	0.0	0	0	139.6
* Fitzgerald, Larry, Ariz	0	0	—	0	—	0	—	0	0	—	1	7	—
Frerotte, Gus, Min.	1	0	0.0	0	0.00	0	0.0	0	0	0.0	0	0	39.6
Gardner, Rod, Was.	3	0	0.0	0	0.00	0	0.0	0	0	0.0	0	0	39.6
Glenn, Terry, Dal.	1	0	0.0	0	0.00	0	0.0	0	0	0.0	0	0	39.6
Green, Ahman, G.B.	1	1	100.0	20	20.00	1	100.0	20t	0	0.0	0	0	158.3
Johnson, Keyshawn, Dal.	2	0	0.0	0	0.00	0	0.0	0	1	50.0	0	0	0.0
McBriar, Mat, Dal.	1	0	0.0	0	0.00	0	0.0	0	0	0.0	0	0	39.6
Mohr, Chris, Atl.	3	2	66.7	24	8.00	0	0.0	26	0	0.0	0	0	91.0
* Moore, Mewelde, Min.	1	0	0.0	0	0.00	0	0.0	0	0	0.0	0	0	39.6
Moss, Randy, Min.	2	1	50.0	37	18.50	0	0.0	37	1	50.0	0	0	56.3
Peete, Rodney, Car.	1	1	100.0	3	3.00	0	0.0	3	0	0.0	0	0	79.2
Portis, Clinton, Was.	2	1	50.0	15	7.50	1	50.0	15t	0	0.0	0	0	114.6
Price, Peerless, Atl.	1	1	100.0	25	25.00	0	0.0	25	0	0.0	0	0	118.8
Proehl, Ricky, Car.	1	0	0.0	0	0.00	0	0.0	0	0	0.0	0	0	39.6
Smith, Emmitt, Ariz	1	1	100.0	21	21.00	1	100.0	21t	0	0.0	0	0	158.3
Smith, Steve, Car.	1	0	0.0	0	0.00	0	0.0	0	0	0.0	0	0	39.6
Westbrook, Brian, Phi.	0	0	—	0	—	0	—	0	0	—	1	4	—
Wilkins, Jeff, St.L	1	0	0.0	0	0.00	0	0.0	0	0	0.0	0	0	39.6
* Williams, Roy, Det.	1	0	0.0	0	0.00	0	0.0	0	0	0.0	0	0	39.6

t = Touchdown; *Player that was a rookie in 2004
Leader based on rating points, minimum 224 attempts

PASS RECEIVING

RECEPTIONS

AFC:	102	Tony Gonzalez, Kansas City
NFC:	94	Torry Holt, St. Louis
	94	Joe Horn, New Orleans

RECEPTIONS, GAME

AFC:	14	Tony Gonzalez, Kansas City at San Diego, January 2 (144 yards, 0 TD)
NFC:	13	Eric Johnson, San Francisco vs. Arizona, October 10 (162 yards, 1 TD) - (OT)

YARDS

NFC:	1405	Muhsin Muhammad, Carolina
AFC:	1274	Chad Johnson, Cincinnati

YARDS, GAME

AFC:	233	Drew Bennett, Tennessee vs. Kansas City, December 13 (12 receptions, 3 TD)
NFC:	200	Javon Walker, Green Bay at Indianapolis, September 26 (11 receptions, 3 TD)

LONGEST

AFC:	99	Andre Davis (from Jeff Garcia) Cleveland vs. Cincinnati, October 17 - TD
NFC:	82	Randy Moss (from Daunte Culpepper) Minnesota at Detroit, December 19 - TD

YARDS PER RECEPTION

AFC:	20.1	Ashley Lelie, Denver
NFC:	18.8	Todd Pinkston, Philadelphia

TOUCHDOWNS

NFC:	16	Muhsin Muhammad, Carolina
AFC:	15	Marvin Harrison, Indianapolis

TEAM LEADERS, RECEPTIONS

AFC: BALTIMORE, 35, Kevin Johnson; BUFFALO, 88, Eric Moulds; CINCINNATI, 95, Chad Johnson; CLEVELAND, 55, Dennis Northcutt; DENVER, 79, Rod Smith; HOUSTON, 79, Andre Johnson; INDIANAPOLIS, 86, Marvin Harrison; JACKSONVILLE, 74, Jimmy Smith; KANSAS CITY, 102, Tony Gonzalez; MIAMI, 73, Randy McMichael; NEW ENGLAND, 56, David Givens; N.Y. JETS, 56, Justin McCareins; OAKLAND, 64, Jerry Porter; PITTSBURGH, 80, Hines Ward; SAN DIEGO, 81, Antonio Gates; TENNESSEE, 96, Derrick Mason

NFC: ARIZONA, 58, *Larry Fitzgerald; ATLANTA, 48, Alge Crumpler; CAROLINA, 93, Muhsin Muhammad; CHICAGO, 56, Thomas Jones; DALLAS, 87, Jason Witten; DETROIT, 54, *Roy Williams; GREEN BAY, 89, Javon Walker; MINNESOTA, 71, Jermaine Wiggins; NEW ORLEANS, 94, Joe Horn; N.Y. GIANTS, 61, Jeremy Shockey; PHILADELPHIA, 77, Terrell Owens; ST. LOUIS, 94, Torry Holt; SAN FRANCISCO, 82, Eric Johnson; SEATTLE, 87, Darrell Jackson; TAMPA BAY, 80, *Michael Clayton; WASHINGTON, 90, Laveranues Coles

Player that was a rookie in 2004

NFL TOP TEN PASS RECEIVERS

	No	Yards	Avg	Long	TD
Gonzalez, Tony, K.C.	102	1258	12.3	32	7
Mason, Derrick, Ten.	96	1168	12.2	37t	7
Johnson, Chad, Cin.	95	1274	13.4	53t	9
Holt, Torry, St.L	94	1372	14.6	75t	10
Horn, Joe, N.O.	94	1399	14.9	57	11
Muhammad, Muhsin, Car.	93	1405	15.1	51	16
Coles, Laveranues, Was.	90	950	10.6	45	1
Bruce, Isaac, St.L	89	1292	14.5	56	6
Walker, Javon, G.B.	89	1382	15.5	79t	12
Moulds, Eric, Buf.	88	1043	11.9	49	5

NFL TOP TEN RECEIVERS BY YARDS

	Yards	No	Avg	Long	TD
Muhammad, Muhsin, Car.	1405	93	15.1	51	16
Horn, Joe, N.O.	1399	94	14.9	57	11
Walker, Javon, G.B.	1382	89	15.5	79t	12
Holt, Torry, St.L	1372	94	14.6	75t	10
Bruce, Isaac, St.L	1292	89	14.5	56	6
Johnson, Chad, Cin.	1274	95	13.4	53t	9
Gonzalez, Tony, K.C.	1258	102	12.3	32	7
Bennett, Drew, Ten.	1247	80	15.6	48t	11
Wayne, Reggie, Ind.	1210	77	15.7	71t	12
Driver, Donald, G.B.	1208	84	14.4	50	9

AFC—INDIVIDUAL RECEIVERS

	No	Yards	Avg	Long	TD
Gonzalez, Tony, K.C.	102	1258	12.3	32	7
Mason, Derrick, Ten.	96	1168	12.2	37t	7
Johnson, Chad, Cin.	95	1274	13.4	53t	9
Moulds, Eric, Buf.	88	1043	11.9	49	5
Harrison, Marvin, Ind.	86	1113	12.9	59	15
Gates, Antonio, S.D.	81	964	11.9	72t	13
Bennett, Drew, Ten.	80	1247	15.6	48t	11
Ward, Hines, Pit.	80	1004	12.6	58	4
Smith, Rod, Den.	79	1144	14.5	85t	7
Johnson, Andre, Hou.	79	1142	14.5	54t	6
Wayne, Reggie, Ind.	77	1210	15.7	71t	12
Smith, Jimmy, Jac.	74	1172	15.8	65	6
Houshmandzadeh, T.J., Cin.	73	978	13.4	62	4
McMichael, Randy, Mia.	73	791	10.8	42t	4
Chambers, Chris, Mia.	69	898	13.0	76t	7
Stokley, Brandon, Ind.	68	1077	15.8	69t	10
Davis, Domanick, Hou.	68	588	8.6	38	1
Porter, Jerry, Oak.	64	998	15.6	52	9
Kennison, Eddie, K.C.	62	1086	17.5	70t	8
Bryant, Antonio, Dal.-Cle.	58	812	14.0	55t	4
Givens, David, N.E.	56	874	15.6	50	3
McCareins, Justin, NYJ	56	770	13.8	43	4
Northcutt, Dennis, Cle.	55	806	14.7	58t	2
Morton, Johnnie, K.C.	55	795	14.5	52	3
Lelie, Ashley, Den.	54	1084	20.1	58	7
Tomlinson, LaDainian, S.D.	53	441	8.3	74t	1
James, Edgerrin, Ind.	51	483	9.5	56	0
Curry, Ronald, Oak.	50	679	13.6	63	6
Booker, Marty, Mia.	50	638	12.8	45	1
Edwards, Troy, Jac.	50	533	10.7	36	1
* Evans, Lee, Buf.	48	843	17.6	69t	9
Parker, Eric, S.D.	47	690	14.7	79t	4
Moss, Santana, NYJ	45	838	18.6	69t	5
Sowell, Jerald, NYJ	45	342	7.6	34	1
Patten, David, N.E.	44	800	18.2	48t	7
Randle El, Antwaan, Pit.	43	601	14.0	39	3
Gaffney, Jabar, Hou.	41	632	15.4	69	2
Martin, Curtis, NYJ	41	245	6.0	22	2
Zereoue, Amos, Oak.	39	284	7.3	13	0
Putzier, Jeb, Den.	36	572	15.9	39	2
Taylor, Fred, Jac.	36	345	9.6	64t	1
Burress, Plaxico, Pit.	35	698	19.9	48	5

Player	No	Yards	Avg	Long	TD	Player	No	Yards	Avg	Long	TD
Branch, Deion, N.E.	35	454	13.0	26t	4	Wheatley, Tyrone, Oak.	15	78	5.2	20	0
Johnson, Kevin, Bal.	35	373	10.7	35	1	Yoder, Todd, Jac.	14	157	11.2	56	0
Taylor, Travis, Bal.	34	421	12.4	47	0	Brady, Kyle, Jac.	14	103	7.4	21	1
Gabriel, Doug, Oak.	33	551	16.7	58t	2	Green, William, Cle.	14	84	6.0	17	0
* Troupe, Ben, Ten.	33	329	10.0	33	1	* Anderson, Courtney, Oak.	13	175	13.5	28	1
Droughns, Reuben, Den.	32	241	7.5	23t	2	Jackson, Frisman, Cle.	13	168	12.9	24	0
Redmond, J.R., Oak.	32	233	7.3	22	0	Lee, Donald, Mia.	13	110	8.5	15t	1
Chrebet, Wayne, NYJ	31	397	12.8	35t	1	Becht, Anthony, NYJ	13	100	7.7	19	1
McCardell, Keenan, S.D.	31	393	12.7	31	1	Minor, Travis, Mia.	13	75	5.8	20	0
* Watts, Darius, Den.	31	385	12.4	28	1	Gordon, Lamar, Mia.	13	74	5.7	20	0
Washington, Kelley, Cin.	31	378	12.2	28	3	Neal, Lorenzo, S.D.	13	66	5.1	12	0
Graham, Daniel, N.E.	30	364	12.1	48	7	Aiken, Sam, Buf.	11	148	13.5	54	0
Taylor, Chester, Bal.	30	184	6.1	23	0	Warrick, Peter, Cin.	11	127	11.5	30	0
Armstrong, Derick, Hou.	29	415	14.3	44	1	* Euhus, Tim, Buf.	11	98	8.9	17	2
Pollard, Marcus, Ind.	29	309	10.7	31	6	Wells, Jonathan, Hou.	11	79	7.2	28	2
Heiden, Steve, Cle.	28	287	10.3	30	5	Fargas, Justin, Oak.	11	68	6.2	21	0
Pass, Patrick, N.E.	28	215	7.7	22	0	Holcombe, Robert, Ten.	11	60	5.5	9	0
Toefield, LaBrandon, Jac.	28	151	5.4	16	1	Ricard, Alan, Bal.	11	39	3.5	8	0
Bradford, Corey, Hou.	27	399	14.8	47	3	Johnson, Bethel, N.E.	10	174	17.4	48	1
Jolley, Doug, Oak.	27	313	11.6	34t	2	Carter, Jonathan, NYJ	10	173	17.3	46t	1
Heap, Todd, Bal.	27	303	11.2	37	3	Lewis, Jamal, Bal.	10	116	11.6	46	0
* Williams, Reggie, Jac.	27	268	9.9	26	1	Peelle, Justin, S.D.	10	84	8.4	17t	2
Hymes, Randy, Bal.	26	323	12.4	57t	2	Kreider, Dan, Pit.	10	75	7.5	13	1
Shea, Aaron, Cle.	26	252	9.7	35	4	Wrighster, George, Jac.	10	69	6.9	12	1
Faulk, Kevin, N.E.	26	248	9.5	31t	1	Griffin, Quentin, Den.	10	68	6.8	22	1
Clark, Dallas, Ind.	25	423	16.9	80t	5	Stewart, Tony, Cin.	10	48	4.8	9	1
Blaylock, Derrick, K.C.	25	246	9.8	30	1	Henry, Travis, Buf.	10	45	4.5	10	0
Hall, Dante, K.C.	25	230	9.2	22	0	Whitted, Alvis, Oak.	9	227	25.2	57	2
Wilcox, Daniel, Bal.	25	219	8.8	20	1	Mays, Lee, Pit.	9	137	15.2	46	0
Kinney, Erron, Ten.	25	193	7.7	21	3	* Parker, Samie, K.C.	9	137	15.2	48t	1
Watson, Kenny, Cin.	25	171	6.8	21	1	Johnson, Teyo, Oak.	9	131	14.6	25	2
Meier, Shad, Ten.	25	127	5.1	29	2	Johnson, Kyle, Den.	9	126	14.0	31	2
* Moore, Clarence, Bal.	24	293	12.2	52	4	Dinkins, Darnell, Bal.	9	94	10.4	18	1
Thompson, Derrius, Mia.	23	359	15.6	36	4	Tuman, Jerame, Pit.	9	89	9.9	26	3
Johnson, Larry, K.C.	22	278	12.6	40	2	Hankton, Cortez, Jac.	9	81	9.0	14t	2
Carswell, Dwayne, Den.	22	198	9.0	20	1	Weaver, Jed, N.E.	8	93	11.6	25	0
McGahee, Willis, Buf.	22	169	7.7	16	0	Jackson, Nate, Den.	8	73	9.1	20	0
Smith, Antowain, Ten.	22	169	7.7	31	0	Konrad, Rob, Mia.	8	69	8.6	20t	1
Morris, Sammy, Mia.	22	124	5.6	24	0	Walter, Kevin, Cin.	8	67	8.4	18	0
Schobel, Matt, Cin.	21	201	9.6	76t	4	Hape, Patrick, Den.	8	35	4.4	11	4
Berlin, Eddie, Ten.	20	278	13.9	31	1	Riemersma, Jay, Pit.	7	82	11.7	26t	2
Suggs, Lee, Cle.	20	178	8.9	59t	1	Edwards, Marc, Jac.	7	41	5.9	15	0
Jones, Terry, Bal.	20	152	7.6	19	1	Smith, Terrelle, Cle.	7	39	5.6	16	0
Brown, Chris, Ten.	20	147	7.4	21	0	Mungro, James, Ind.	7	36	5.1	16	3
* Wilford, Ernest, Jac.	19	271	14.3	46	2	* Jones, Brian, Jac.	6	87	14.5	26t	1
Holmes, Priest, K.C.	19	187	9.8	52	1	Neufeld, Ryan, Buf.	6	61	10.2	29	0
* Fleming, Troy, Ten.	19	164	8.6	37	2	* Cotchery, Jerricho, NYJ	6	60	10.0	18	0
Richardson, Tony, K.C.	19	118	6.2	22	0	Staley, Duce, Pit.	6	55	9.2	21	0
Caldwell, Reche, S.D.	18	310	17.2	58t	3	* Luke, Triandos, Den.	6	52	8.7	12	0
Baker, Chris, NYJ	18	182	10.1	23	4	Bettis, Jerome, Pit.	6	46	7.7	20	0
Haynes, Verron, Pit.	18	142	7.9	26	2	Jackson, James, Cle.	6	22	3.7	13	0
Campbell, Mark, Buf.	17	203	11.9	27	5	White, Jamel, T.B.-Bal.	6	21	3.5	12	0
Brown, Troy, N.E.	17	184	10.8	22	1	* Krause, Ryan, S.D.	5	81	16.2	29	1
Miller, Billy, Hou.	17	178	10.5	27	1	* Bell, Tatum, Den.	5	80	16.0	58	0
Dunn, Jason, K.C.	17	120	7.1	17	3	Shaw, Bobby, Buf.	5	59	11.8	20	0
Shelton, Daimon, Buf.	17	114	6.7	24	0	* Winslow, Kellen, Cle.	5	50	10.0	21	0
Davis, Andre, Cle.	16	416	26.0	99t	4	King, Andre, Cle.	5	49	9.8	16	0
Fauria, Christian, N.E.	16	195	12.2	25	2	Hollings, Tony, Hou.	5	46	9.2	27	0
Reed, Josh, Buf.	16	153	9.6	20	0	Bruener, Mark, Hou.	4	52	13.0	27	0
Crockett, Zack, Oak.	16	87	5.4	11	0	* Hartsock, Ben, Ind.	4	33	8.3	17	0
Johnson, Jeremi, Cin.	16	53	3.3	9	1	Fuamatu-Ma'afala, Chris, Jac.	4	19	4.8	8	0
Osgood, Kassim, S.D.	15	308	20.5	65	2	Martin, Jamar, Mia.	4	15	3.8	7	0
Gilmore, Bryan, Mia.	15	206	13.7	37	1	Norris, Moran, Hou.	4	13	3.3	7	0
Horn, Chris, K.C.	15	178	11.9	30	1	* Turner, Michael, S.D.	4	8	2.0	7	0
Jordan, LaMont, NYJ	15	112	7.5	25	0	Stone, John, Oak.	3	80	26.7	55	0
Dillon, Corey, N.E.	15	103	6.9	20	1	* Floyd, Malcom, S.D.	3	49	16.3	27	1
Kelly, Reggie, Cin.	15	85	5.7	14	0	* Perry, Chris, Cin.	3	33	11.0	13	0
Johnson, Rudi, Cin.	15	84	5.6	30	0	Hetherington, Chris, Oak.	3	28	9.3	14	0

	No	Yards	Avg	Long	TD		No	Yards	Avg	Long	TD
Pinnock, Andrew, S.D.	3	26	8.7	14	0	Jones, Thomas, Chi.	56	427	7.6	45	0
* Echemandu, Adimchinobe, Cle.	3	25	8.3	19	0	* Williams, Roy, Det.	54	817	15.1	46	8
* Trafford, Rod, Buf.	3	25	8.3	10	0	Barber, Tiki, NY-G	52	578	11.1	62t	2
* Smith, Jonathan, Buf.	3	21	7.0	11	0	Toomer, Amani, NY-G	51	747	14.6	48	0
* Williams, Shaud, Buf.	3	19	6.3	10	0	Gardner, Rod, Was.	51	650	12.7	51	5
Klecko, Dan, N.E.	3	18	6.0	11	0	Faulk, Marshall, St.L	50	310	6.2	25	1
* Parker, Willie, Pit.	3	16	5.3	12	0	Moss, Randy, Min.	49	767	15.7	82t	13
* Jones, Greg, Jac.	3	13	4.3	9	0	Johnson, Bryant, Ariz	49	537	11.0	40	1
Henry, Leonard, Mia.	3	12	4.0	7	0	Hilliard, Ike, NY-G	49	437	8.9	43	0
McAddley, Jason, Ten.	2	38	19.0	36	0	Crumpler, Alge, Atl.	48	774	16.1	49t	6
Dwight, Tim, S.D.	2	31	15.5	23t	1	* Colbert, Keary, Car.	47	754	16.0	63	5
Smith, Musa, Bal.	2	31	15.5	25	0	Robinson, Marcus, Min.	47	657	14.0	50t	8
Rhodes, Dominic, Ind.	2	24	12.0	20	0	Wilson, Cedrick, S.F.	47	641	13.6	39	3
Hearst, Garrison, Den.	2	20	10.0	15	0	Price, Peerless, Atl.	45	575	12.8	50	3
Chatman, Jesse, S.D.	2	17	8.5	17	0	Jones, Freddie, Ariz	45	426	9.5	40	2
* Watson, Ben, N.E.	2	16	8.0	14	0	Goings, Nick, Car.	45	394	8.8	37	1
Calico, Tyrone, Ten.	2	13	6.5	9	0	Bryson, Shawn, Det.	44	322	7.3	30	0
Askew, B.J., NYJ	2	12	6.0	11	0	Lloyd, Brandon, S.F.	43	565	13.1	52	6
Pyatt, Brad, Ind.	2	12	6.0	7	0	Terrell, David, Chi.	42	699	16.6	63	1
Allen, David, Jac.	2	8	4.0	5	0	Wade, Bobby, Chi.	42	481	11.5	40	0
* Darling, Devard, Bal.	2	5	2.5	4	0	Pittman, Michael, T.B.	41	391	9.5	68	3
Vrabel, Mike, N.E.	2	3	1.5	2t	2	Alexander, Stephen, Det.	41	377	9.2	30	1
Brees, Drew, S.D.	1	38	38.0	38	0	Green, Ahman, G.B.	40	275	6.9	48	1
Thomas, Kevin, Buf.	1	24	24.0	24	0	Portis, Clinton, Was.	40	235	5.9	18	2
Russell, Cliff, Cin.	1	21	21.0	21	0	Dilger, Ken, T.B.	39	345	8.8	45t	3
* Morant, Johnnie, Oak.	1	20	20.0	20	0	Conway, Curtis, S.F.	38	403	10.6	37	3
Cushing, Matt, Pit.	1	17	17.0	17	0	Fisher, Tony, G.B.	38	277	7.3	25	2
Bailey, Champ, Den.	1	11	11.0	11	0	McDonald, Shaun, St.L	37	494	13.4	52t	3
Abdullah, Rabih, N.E.	1	9	9.0	9	0	* Cooley, Chris, Was.	37	314	8.5	31	6
Mustard, Chad, Cle.	1	9	9.0	9	0	Pinkston, Todd, Phi.	36	676	18.8	80	1
* Bellamy, Ronald, Mia.	1	8	8.0	8	0	Engram, Bobby, Sea.	36	499	13.9	60	2
* King, Vick, Mia.	1	8	8.0	8	0	Smith, Onterrio, Min.	36	394	10.9	63t	2
Morey, Sean, Pit.	1	8	8.0	8	0	Barlow, Kevan, S.F.	35	212	6.1	15	0
Burns, Joe, Buf.	1	7	7.0	7	0	Pathon, Jerome, N.O.	34	581	17.1	38	1
Moorehead, Aaron, Ind.	1	7	7.0	7	0	Proehl, Ricky, Car.	34	497	14.6	34	0
Walters, Troy, Ind.	1	5	5.0	5	0	Smith, L.J., Phi.	34	377	11.1	31	5
* Easlick, Doug, Mia.	1	4	4.0	4	0	Franks, Bubba, G.B.	34	361	10.6	29	7
Lewis, Jermaine, Jac.	1	4	4.0	4	0	Mangum, Kris, Car.	34	323	9.5	26	3
Baxter, Jarrod, Hou.	1	3	3.0	3	0	Henderson, William, G.B.	34	239	7.0	38t	3
* Sams, B.J., Bal.	1	2	2.0	2	0	McAllister, Deuce, N.O.	34	228	6.7	20	0
Heinrich, Keith, Cle.	1	1	1.0	1	0	Galloway, Joey, T.B.	33	416	12.6	36t	5
Volek, Billy, Ten.	1	0	0.0	0	0	Williams, Boo, N.O.	33	362	11.0	22	2
Leftwich, Byron, Jac.	1	-7	-7.0	-7	0	Curtis, Kevin, St.L	32	421	13.2	41t	2
						Hakim, Az-Zahir, Det.	31	533	17.2	39t	3
						Robinson, Koren, Sea.	31	495	16.0	33	2
						Morgan, Quincy, Cle.-Dal.	31	404	13.0	53	3
						Stevens, Jerramy, Sea.	31	349	11.3	32	3
						Rice, Jerry, Oak.-Sea.	30	429	14.3	56	3

t = Touchdown; *Player that was a rookie in 2004
Leader based on receptions

NFC—INDIVIDUAL RECEIVERS

	No	Yards	Avg	Long	TD		No	Yards	Avg	Long	TD
Horn, Joe, N.O.	94	1399	14.9	57	11	White, Dez, Atl.	30	370	12.3	54	2
Holt, Torry, St.L	94	1372	14.6	75t	10	Dunn, Warrick, Atl.	29	294	10.1	59	0
Muhammad, Muhsin, Car.	93	1405	15.1	51	16	Lewis, Chad, Phi.	29	267	9.2	21	3
Coles, Laveranues, Was.	90	950	10.6	45	1	Alstott, Mike, T.B.	29	202	7.0	20	0
Walker, Javon, G.B.	89	1382	15.5	79t	12	Stecker, Aaron, N.O.	29	174	6.0	26	0
Bruce, Isaac, St.L	89	1292	14.5	56	6	Streets, Tai, Det.	28	260	9.3	22	1
Jackson, Darrell, Sea.	87	1199	13.8	56t	7	* Jones, Kevin, Det.	28	180	6.4	34	1
Witten, Jason, Dal.	87	980	11.3	42t	6	Jurevicius, Joe, T.B.	27	333	12.3	42t	2
Driver, Donald, G.B.	84	1208	14.4	50	9	* Moore, Mewelde, Min.	27	238	8.8	26	0
Johnson, Eric, S.F.	82	825	10.1	25	2	Anderson, Richie, Dal.	26	207	8.0	28	0
* Clayton, Michael, T.B.	80	1193	14.9	75t	7	Glenn, Terry, Dal.	24	400	16.7	48	2
Owens, Terrell, Phi.	77	1200	15.6	59t	14	Ferguson, Robert, G.B.	24	367	15.3	48	1
Westbrook, Brian, Phi.	73	703	9.6	50	6	Clark, Desmond, Chi.	24	282	11.8	31	1
Wiggins, Jermaine, Min.	71	705	9.9	39	4	Brown, Tim, T.B.	24	200	8.3	21	1
Johnson, Keyshawn, Dal.	70	981	14.0	39	6	Finneran, Brian, Atl.	23	258	11.2	26	2
Burleson, Nate, Min.	68	1006	14.8	68t	9	Mili, Itula, Sea.	23	240	10.4	20	1
Shockey, Jeremy, NY-G	61	666	10.9	38	6	Alexander, Shaun, Sea.	23	170	7.4	24	4
* Fitzgerald, Larry, Ariz	58	780	13.4	48	8	Mitchell, Freddie, Phi.	22	377	17.1	60	2
Stallworth, Donte', N.O.	58	767	13.2	45	5	Chatman, Antonio, G.B.	22	246	11.2	21	1
Boldin, Anquan, Ariz	56	623	11.1	31t	1	Griffith, Justin, Atl.	22	220	10.0	62	1
						Williams, Moe, Min.	21	233	11.1	28	1

	No	Yards	Avg	Long	TD
Bennett, Michael, Min.	21	207	9.9	38t	1
Hoover, Brad, Car.	21	161	7.7	34	2
Jackson, Terry, S.F.	21	139	6.6	22	0
Strong, Mack, Sea.	21	99	4.7	13	0
Campbell, Kelly, Min.	19	364	19.2	61	1
* Jackson, Steven, St.L	19	189	9.9	28	0
Ayanbadejo, Obafemi, Ariz	19	171	9.0	21t	1
Swinton, Reggie, Det.	18	213	11.8	28	1
Williams, Karl, Ariz	18	197	10.9	33	0
Scobey, Josh, Ariz	18	191	10.6	42	0
Thrash, James, Was.	17	203	11.9	31	0
Lewis, Greg, Phi.	17	183	10.8	25	0
Thomas, Anthony, Chi.	17	132	7.8	30	0
* Jones, Julius, Dal.	17	109	6.4	37	0
Jacobs, Taylor, Was.	16	178	11.1	45	0
Hicks, Maurice, S.F.	16	154	9.6	19	0
* Berrian, Bernard, Chi.	15	225	15.0	49t	2
Lee, Charles, T.B.	15	207	13.8	35	0
Manumaleuna, Brandon, St.L	15	174	11.6	48	1
Finn, Jim, NY-G	15	112	7.5	15	0
Betts, Ladell, Was.	15	108	7.2	20	0
Smith, Emmitt, Ariz	15	105	7.0	18	0
Mahe, Reno, Phi.	14	123	8.8	30	0
Johnson, Bryan, Chi.	14	55	3.9	14	2
Looker, Dane, St.L	13	183	14.1	29	0
Seidman, Mike, Car.	13	123	9.5	27	2
McKie, Jason, Chi.	13	70	5.4	15t	2
Carter, Tim, NY-G	12	182	15.2	38t	1
* Crayton, Patrick, Dal.	12	162	13.5	39t	1
Gage, Justin, Chi.	12	156	13.0	32	0
Heller, Will, T.B.	12	98	8.2	22	1
Lyman, Dustin, Chi.	11	73	6.6	13	1
Pinner, Artose, Det.	11	72	6.5	26	0
Goodspeed, Joey, St.L	11	71	6.5	13	0
Tyree, David, NY-G	10	155	15.5	49	1
Walker, Aaron, S.F.	10	115	11.5	30	0
Fitzsimmons, Casey, Det.	10	103	10.3	27	0
Conwell, Ernie, N.O.	10	102	10.2	28	1
Schlesinger, Cory, Det.	10	91	9.1	30	3
Barnes, Darian, Dal.	10	59	5.9	14	1
Beasley, Fred, S.F.	10	44	4.4	9	0
Levens, Dorsey, Phi.	9	92	10.2	23	0
George, Eddie, Dal.	9	83	9.2	28	0
Berton, Sean, Min.	9	78	8.7	14	0
Foster, DeShaun, Car.	9	76	8.4	42	0
Parry, Josh, Phi.	9	75	8.3	22	0
Garner, Charlie, T.B.	9	62	6.9	31	0
Morris, Maurice, Sea.	9	53	5.9	12	0
Battle, Arnaz, S.F.	8	143	17.9	65	0
Lewis, Michael, N.O.	8	127	15.9	30	0
Hannam, Ryan, Sea.	8	110	13.8	36	0
Royal, Robert, Was.	8	70	8.8	23	4
* Owens, Richard, Min.	8	69	8.6	18	0
* Woods, Rashaun, S.F.	7	160	22.9	59	1
Schroeder, Bill, T.B.	7	156	22.3	54	1
* Jenkins, Michael, Atl.	7	119	17.0	46	0
* Copper, Terrance, Dal.	7	84	12.0	22	1
Cleeland, Cameron, St.L	7	57	8.1	15	0
Cook, Jameel, T.B.	7	44	6.3	9	1
* Taylor, Jamaar, NY-G	6	146	24.3	52	0
Urban, Jerheme, Sea.	6	117	19.5	33	1
Smith, Steve, Car.	6	60	10.0	15	0
* Karney, Mike, N.O.	6	42	7.0	17	0
Martin, David, G.B.	5	88	17.6	35	0
McCants, Darnerien, Was.	5	71	14.2	27	0
Poole, Nate, Ariz	5	70	14.0	24	0
Rasby, Walter, Was.	5	52	10.4	13	0
* Edwards, Eric, Ariz	5	51	10.2	19	0
Bartrum, Mike, Phi.	5	45	9.0	17	1

	No	Yards	Avg	Long	TD
Rivers, Marcellus, NY-G	5	36	7.2	13	1
Shiancoe, Visanthe, NY-G	5	25	5.0	9	1
Harris, Arlen, St.L	4	44	11.0	21	0
* Steele, Ben, G.B.	4	42	10.5	27	0
Trejo, Stephen, Det.	4	37	9.3	18	0
Ritchie, Jon, Phi.	4	36	9.0	11	0
Blakley, Dwayne, Atl.	4	35	8.8	13	0
* Gaines, Michael, Car.	4	34	8.5	14	0
Robertson, Jamal, S.F.	4	34	8.5	14	0
Davenport, Najeh, G.B.	4	33	8.3	12	0
Hambrick, Troy, Ariz	4	16	4.0	9	1
Kircus, David, Det.	3	68	22.7	50t	1
* Vines, Scott, Det.	3	51	17.0	26	0
Dudley, Rickey, T.B.	3	48	16.0	24	0
Kozlowski, Brian, Was.	3	29	9.7	13	0
McMullen, Billy, Phi.	3	24	8.0	15	0
Diamond, Lorenzo, Ariz	3	19	6.3	8	0
Moore, Dave, T.B.	3	17	5.7	10	0
Duckett, T.J., Atl.	3	15	5.0	11	0
Davis, Stephen, Car.	2	32	16.0	22	0
Peterson, Adrian, Chi.	2	30	15.0	30	0
Hankton, Karl, Car.	2	25	12.5	20	0
Kleinsasser, Jimmy, Min.	2	24	12.0	18	0
McCrary, Fred, Atl.	2	23	11.5	14	0
Luchey, Nicolas, G.B.	2	20	10.0	11	0
Campbell, Dan, Dal.	2	16	8.0	9	0
* Croom, Larry, Ariz	2	16	8.0	8	0
* McCoo, Eric, Phi.	2	15	7.5	8	0
* Tapeh, Thomas, Phi.	2	15	7.5	13	0
Evans, Heath, Sea.	2	12	6.0	9	0
* Thurman, Andrae, G.B.	2	12	6.0	9	0
Bannister, Alex, Sea.	2	10	5.0	8	0
Bush, Steve, S.F.	2	10	5.0	6	1
* Smart, Ian, T.B.	2	10	5.0	5	0
Pritchett, Stanley, Atl.	2	5	2.5	4	1
Robinson, Jeff, Dal.	2	2	1.0	1t	2
Gardner, Talman, N.O.	1	23	23.0	23	0
Lawrie, Nate, T.B.	1	15	15.0	15	0
Sellers, Mike, Was.	1	14	14.0	14	0
Williams, Randal, Dal.	1	14	14.0	14	0
Comella, Greg, T.B.	1	12	12.0	12	0
Gilmore, John, Chi.	1	11	11.0	11	0
Ned, Larry, Min.	1	9	9.0	9	0
Ware, Kevin, S.F.	1	9	9.0	9	0
Furrey, Mike, St.L	1	8	8.0	8	0
Baber, Billy, T.B.	1	7	7.0	7	0
Dayne, Ron, NY-G	1	7	7.0	7	0
Layne, George, Atl.	1	6	6.0	6	0
Newhouse, Reggie, Ariz	1	5	5.0	5	0
Smart, Rod, Car.	1	5	5.0	5	0
Ward, Dedric, Dal.	1	5	5.0	5	0
Coleman, Cosey, T.B.	1	4	4.0	4	0
Hall, Lamont, N.O.	1	4	4.0	4t	1
Lee, ReShard, Dal.	1	4	4.0	4	0
* Polite, Lousaka, Dal.	1	4	4.0	4	0
Cloud, Mike, NY-G	1	3	3.0	3	0
Howry, Keenan, Min.	1	3	3.0	3	0
Ponder, Willie, NY-G	1	3	3.0	3	0
Brooks, Aaron, N.O.	1	1	1.0	1	0
Isom, Jasen, S.F.	1	1	1.0	1	0
Feely, Jay, Atl.	1	-2	-2.0	-2	0
Griese, Brian, T.B.	1	-4	-4.0	-4	0
McCown, Josh, Ariz	1	-5	-5.0	-5	0

t = Touchdown; *Player that was a rookie in 2004
Leader based on receptions

INTERCEPTIONS

INTERCEPTIONS

AFC:	9	Edward Reed, Baltimore
NFC:	6	* Chris Gamble, Carolina
	6	Ken Lucas, Seattle

INTERCEPTIONS, GAME

AFC:
- 2   Eric Warfield, Kansas City vs. Carolina, September 19 (43 yards, 1 TD)
- 2   Eugene Wilson, New England at Arizona, September 19 (27 yards, 0 TD)
- 2   Edward Reed, Baltimore at Cincinnati, September 26 (90 yards, 0 TD)
- 2 * Dunta Robinson, Houston vs. Oakland, October 3 (86 yards, 0 TD)
- 2   Lamont Thompson, Tennessee at Green Bay, October 11 (31 yards, 0 TD)
- 2   Tory James, Cincinnati at Cleveland, October 17 (23 yards, 0 TD)
- 2   Deion Sanders, Baltimore vs. Buffalo, October 24 (48 yards, 1 TD)
- 2   Troy Polamalu, Pittsburgh at Cleveland, November 14 (0 yards, 0 TD)
- 2   Andre Dyson, Tennessee vs. Chicago, November 14 (21 yards, 0 TD) - (OT)
- 2   Donnie Edwards, San Diego vs. Tampa Bay, December 12 (34 yards, 1 TD)
- 2   Rashean Mathis, Jacksonville at Green Bay, December 19 (0 yards, 0 TD)
- 2   Dexter McCleon, Kansas City vs. Denver, December 19 (23 yards, 0 TD)
- 2   Sammy Knight, Miami vs. New England, December 20 (32 yards, 0 TD)
- 2   Donovin Darius, Jacksonville at Oakland, January 2 (37 yards, 0 TD)

NFC:
- 2   Brent Alexander, New York Giants vs. Washington, September 19 (1 yard, 0 TD)
- 2   Ken Lucas, Seattle vs. St. Louis, October 10 (0 yards, 0 TD) - (OT)
- 2   Lito Sheppard, Philadelphia vs. Carolina, October 17 (64 yards, 1 TD)
- 2   Dre' Bly, Detroit at Dallas, October 31 (85 yards, 1 TD)
- 2   Shawn Springs, Washington vs. Green Bay, October 31 (57 yards, 0 TD)
- 2   Colin Branch, Carolina vs. Arizona, November 21 (79 yards, 0 TD)
- 2   Tony Parrish, San Francisco at Tampa Bay, November 21 (39 yards, 0 TD)
- 2   R.W. McQuarters, Chicago at Dallas, November 25 (85 yards, 1 TD)
- 2   Ken Hamlin, Seattle vs. Buffalo, November 28 (36 yards, 0 TD)
- 2   Jerry Azumah, Chicago vs. Minnesota, December 5 (53 yards, 0 TD)
- 2   Dre' Bly, Detroit vs. Arizona, December 5 (22 yards, 0 TD)
- 2   Ricky Manning, Carolina vs. St. Louis, December 12 (46 yards, 0 TD)
- 2   Dan Morgan, Carolina vs. St. Louis, December 12 (20 yards, 0 TD)
- 2 * Chris Gamble, Carolina at Atlanta, December 18 (2 yards, 0 TD) - (OT)
- 2   Mike McKenzie, New Orleans vs. Atlanta, December 26 (0 yards, 0 TD)

Player that was a rookie in 2004

YARDS

AFC:	358	Ed Reed, Baltimore
NFC:	177	* Nathan Vasher, Chicago

LONGEST

AFC:	106	Ed Reed, Baltimore vs. Cleveland, November 7 - TD
NFC:	101	Lito Sheppard, Philadelphia at Dallas, November 15 - TD

TOUCHDOWNS

AFC:	2	Takeo Spikes, Buffalo
NFC:	2	Kevin Mathis, Atlanta
	2	Darren Sharper, Green Bay
	2	Lito Sheppard, Philadelphia

TEAM LEADERS, INTERCEPTIONS;

AFC: BALTIMORE, 9, Ed Reed; BUFFALO, 6, Nate Clements; CINCINNATI, 8, Tory James; CLEVELAND, 4, Anthony Henry; DENVER, 3, Champ Bailey; HOUSTON, 6, *Dunta Robinson; INDIANAPOLIS, 4, *Jason David; JACKSONVILLE, 5, Donovin Darius, Rashean Mathis; KANSAS CITY, 4, Eric Warfield, Greg Wesley; MIAMI, 4, Arturo Freeman, Sammy Knight, Patrick Surtain; NEW ENGLAND, 4, Eugene Wilson; N.Y. JETS, 4, *Erik Coleman; OAKLAND, 3, Phillip Buchanon; PITTSBURGH, 5, Troy Polamalu; SAN DIEGO, 5, Donnie Edwards; TENNESSEE, 6, Andre Dyson

NFC: ARIZONA, 4, David Macklin; ATLANTA, 4, Aaron Beasley; CAROLINA, 6, *Chris Gamble; CHICAGO, 5, *Nathan Vasher; DALLAS, 4, Terence Newman; DETROIT, 4, Dre' Bly; GREEN BAY, 4, Darren Sharper; MINNESOTA, 3, Antoine Winfield; NEW ORLEANS, 5, Mike McKenzie; N.Y. GIANTS, 4, *Gibril Wilson, Brent Alexander; PHILADELPHIA, 5, Lito Sheppard; ST. LOUIS, 5, Jerametrius Butler; SAN FRANCISCO, 4, Tony Parrish; SEATTLE, 6, Ken Lucas; TAMPA BAY, 4, Brian Kelly; WASHINGTON, 5, Shawn Springs

TEAM CHAMPION

NFC:	26	Carolina
AFC:	24	Buffalo

NFL TOP TEN INTERCEPTORS

	No	Yards	Avg	Long	TD
Reed, Ed, Bal.	9	358	39.8	106t	1
James, Tory, Cin.	8	66	8.3	23	0
Clements, Nate, Buf.	6	77	12.8	35	1
Dyson, Andre, Ten.	6	135	22.5	44	0
* Gamble, Chris, Car.	6	15	2.5	13	0
Lucas, Ken, Sea.	6	46	7.7	25	1
* Robinson, Dunta, Hou.	6	146	24.3	61	0
Boulware, Michael, Sea.	5	69	13.8	63t	1
Butler, Jerametrius, St.L	5	15	3.0	10	0
Darius, Donovin, Jac.	5	80	16.0	37	0
Edwards, Donnie, S.D.	5	49	9.8	30t	1
Glenn, Aaron, Hou.	5	40	8.0	23	0
Mathis, Rashean, Jac.	5	42	8.4	21	0
McKenzie, Mike, N.O.	5	19	3.8	14	0
Polamalu, Troy, Pit.	5	58	11.6	26t	1
Sheppard, Lito, Phi.	5	172	34.4	101t	2
Spikes, Takeo, Buf.	5	122	24.4	62t	2
Springs, Shawn, Was.	5	117	23.4	38	0
Trufant, Marcus, Sea.	5	141	28.2	58	0
* Vasher, Nathan, Chi.	5	177	35.4	71t	1

AFC—INDIVIDUAL INTERCEPTORS

	No	Yards	Avg	Long	TD
Reed, Ed, Bal.	9	358	39.8	106t	1
James, Tory, Cin.	8	66	8.3	23	0
* Robinson, Dunta, Hou.	6	146	24.3	61	0
Dyson, Andre, Ten.	6	135	22.5	44	0
Clements, Nate, Buf.	6	77	12.8	35	1
Spikes, Takeo, Buf.	5	122	24.4	62t	2
Darius, Donovin, Jac.	5	80	16.0	37	0
Polamalu, Troy, Pit.	5	58	11.6	26t	1
Edwards, Donnie, S.D.	5	49	9.8	30t	1
Mathis, Rashean, Jac.	5	42	8.4	21	0
Glenn, Aaron, Hou.	5	40	8.0	23	0
Farrior, James, Pit.	4	113	28.3	41	1
Wesley, Greg, K.C.	4	92	23.0	65	0
Henry, Anthony, Cle.	4	83	20.8	51	0
Thompson, Lamont, Ten.	4	77	19.3	37t	1
O'Neal, Deltha, Cin.	4	60	15.0	31t	1
Freeman, Arturo, Mia.	4	59	14.8	47	0
Florence, Drayton, S.D.	4	54	13.5	40	0
Townsend, Deshea, Pit.	4	54	13.5	39t	1
Wilson, Eugene, N.E.	4	51	12.8	24	0
Warfield, Eric, K.C.	4	49	12.3	43t	1
* Coleman, Erik, NYJ	4	43	10.8	37	0
* David, Jason, Ind.	4	36	9.0	34t	1
Knight, Sammy, Mia.	4	32	8.0	32	0
Surtain, Patrick, Mia.	4	2	0.5	2	0
Williams, Chad, Bal.	3	156	52.0	94	1
Sanders, Deion, Bal.	3	87	29.0	48t	1
Bruschi, Tedy, N.E.	3	70	23.3	36	0
Buchanan, Phillip, Oak.	3	69	23.0	37	1
* Vilma, Jonathan, NYJ	3	58	19.3	38t	1
* Williams, Madieu, Cin.	3	51	17.0	51t	1
Faggins, Demarcus, Hou.	3	47	15.7	43t	1
Davis, Andra, Cle.	3	35	11.7	30	0
Buckley, Terrell, NYJ	3	30	10.0	18	0
Brown, Troy, N.E.	3	22	7.3	17	0
McGee, Terrence, Buf.	3	21	7.0	21	0
Harper, Nick, Ind.	3	12	4.0	12	0
Wilson, Jerry, S.D.	3	12	4.0	12	0
Bailey, Champ, Den.	3	0	0.0	0	0
Wong, Kailee, Hou.	3	0	0.0	0	0
Coleman, Marcus, Hou.	2	116	58.0	102t	1
June, Cato, Ind.	2	71	35.5	71	0
Abraham, Donnie, NYJ	2	66	33.0	66t	1
Simmons, Brian, Cin.	2	61	30.5	50t	1
Sanders, Lewis, Cle.	2	36	18.0	24	0
Doss, Mike, Ind.	2	32	16.0	32	0
Kiel, Terrence, S.D.	2	31	15.5	31	0
Bulluck, Keith, Ten.	2	25	12.5	25	0
* Gay, Randall, N.E.	2	23	11.5	13	0
McCleon, Dexter, K.C.	2	23	11.5	23	0
Milloy, Lawyer, Buf.	2	20	10.0	11	0
Herndon, Kelly, Den.	2	17	8.5	15	0
Wilson, Al, Den.	2	17	8.5	10	1
Barrett, David, NYJ	2	14	7.0	14	0
Harrison, Rodney, N.E.	2	12	6.0	12	0
Foley, Steve, S.D.	2	4	2.0	4	0
Grant, Deon, Jac.	2	4	2.0	4	0
Brackett, Gary, Ind.	2	2	1.0	2	0
McCutcheon, Daylon, Cle.	2	0	0.0	2	0
McGraw, Jon, NYJ	2	0	0.0	0	0
Washington, Dewayne, Jac.	2	0	0.0	0	0
* Hutchins, Von, Ind.	1	77	77.0	77t	1
Hayward, Reggie, Den.	1	76	76.0	76	0
McAlister, Chris, Bal.	1	51	51.0	51t	1
Walker, Denard, Oak.	1	45	45.0	45	0
Hope, Chris, Pit.	1	41	41.0	41	0
* Geathers, Robert, Cin.	1	36	36.0	36t	1
Samuel, Asante, N.E.	1	34	34.0	34t	1
Baxter, Gary, Bal.	1	33	33.0	33	0
Reese, Izell, Buf.	1	33	33.0	33	0
Johnson, Ellis, Den.	1	32	32.0	32t	1
Gardner, Barry, Cle.	1	30	30.0	30	0
Little, Earl, Cle.	1	28	28.0	28	0
Buchanan, Ray, Oak.	1	27	27.0	27	0
McGinest, Willie, N.E.	1	27	27.0	27	0
* Baker, Rashad, Buf.	1	26	26.0	26	0
Phifer, Roman, N.E.	1	26	26.0	26	0
Woodson, Charles, Oak.	1	25	25.0	25	0
Woolfolk, Andre, Ten.	1	25	25.0	25	0
Brayton, Tyler, Oak.	1	24	24.0	24	0
McCree, Marlon, Hou.	1	24	24.0	24	0
Anderson, Marques, Oak.	1	23	23.0	23	0
Scott, Chad, Pit.	1	23	23.0	23	0
Tongue, Reggie, NYJ	1	23	23.0	23	0
Kennedy, Kenoy, Den.	1	21	21.0	21	0
Poole, Tyrone, N.E.	1	21	21.0	21	0
Crocker, Chris, Cle.	1	20	20.0	20t	1
Peek, Antwan, Hou.	1	20	20.0	20	0
Williams, Pat, Buf.	1	20	20.0	20t	1
Griffith, Robert, Cle.	1	18	18.0	18	0
Morris, Rob, Ind.	1	17	17.0	17	0
Hart, Clinton, S.D.	1	13	13.0	13	0
Williams, Tank, Ten.	1	13	13.0	13	0
Jammer, Quentin, S.D.	1	12	12.0	12	0
McGarrahan, Scott, Ten.	1	11	11.0	11	0
Barber, Shawn, K.C.	1	10	10.0	10	0
* Williams, D.J., Den.	1	10	10.0	10	0
Johnson, Tim, Oak.	1	8	8.0	8	0
Thomas, Adalius, Bal.	1	8	8.0	8	0
Vincent, Troy, Buf.	1	8	8.0	8	0
Barton, Eric, NYJ	1	7	7.0	7	0
Johnson, Jarret, Bal.	1	6	6.0	6t	1
Thornton, David, Ind.	1	5	5.0	5	0
Banta-Cain, Tully, N.E.	1	4	4.0	4	0
Davis, Sammy, S.D.	1	4	4.0	4	0
Kelsay, Chris, Buf.	1	3	3.0	3	0
Porter, Joey, Pit.	1	3	3.0	3	0
Posey, Jeff, Buf.	1	3	3.0	3	0
Ayanbadejo, Brendon, Mia.	1	2	2.0	2	0
Hobson, Victor, NYJ	1	2	2.0	2	0
Lynch, John, Den.	1	2	2.0	2	0
Dingle, Adrian, S.D.	1	1	1.0	1	0
Foote, Larry, Pit.	1	1	1.0	1	0
Weaver, Tony, Bal.	1	1	1.0	1	0

Name	No	Yards	Avg	Long	TD
Adams, Sam, Buf.	1	0	0.0	0	0
* Bacon, Waine, Ind.	1	0	0.0	0	0
Cooper, Deke, Jac.	1	0	0.0	0	0
Demps, Will, Bal.	1	0	0.0	0	0
Fletcher, Jamar, S.D.	1	0	0.0	0	0
Herring, Kim, Cin.	1	0	0.0	0	0
Jefferson, Joseph, Ind.	1	0	0.0	0	0
Law, Ty, N.E.	1	0	0.0	0	0
Nelson, Jim, Ind.	1	0	0.0	0	0
* Phillips, Shaun, S.D.	1	0	0.0	0	0
Rolle, Samari, Ten.	1	0	0.0	0	0
* Sapp, Benny, K.C.	1	0	0.0	0	0
Simmons, Jason, Hou.	1	0	0.0	0	0
* Smith, Daryl, Jac.	1	0	0.0	0	0
Stamer, Josh, Buf.	1	0	0.0	0	0
Taylor, Ike, Pit.	1	0	0.0	0	0
* Waddell, Michael, Ten.	1	0	0.0	0	0
Wilhelm, Matt, S.D.	1	0	0.0	0	0
Williams, Jay, Mia.	1	0	0.0	0	0
Williams, Willie, Pit.	1	0	0.0	0	0
Beisel, Monty, K.C.	1	-1	-1.0	-1	0
* Gardner, Rich, Ten.	1	-1	-1.0	-1	0
Powell, Carl, Cin.	1	-2	-2.0	-2	0
Taylor, Jason, Mia.	1	-3	-3.0	-3	0

t = Touchdown; *Player that was a rookie in 2004
Leader based on interceptions

NFC—INDIVIDUAL INTERCEPTORS

Name	No	Yards	Avg	Long	TD
Lucas, Ken, Sea.	6	46	7.7	25	1
* Gamble, Chris, Car.	6	15	2.5	13	0
* Vasher, Nathan, Chi.	5	177	35.4	71t	1
Sheppard, Lito, Phi.	5	172	34.4	101t	2
Trufant, Marcus, Sea.	5	141	28.2	58	0
Springs, Shawn, Was.	5	117	23.4	38	0
* Boulware, Michael, Sea.	5	69	13.8	63t	1
McKenzie, Mike, N.O.	5	19	3.8	14	0
Butler, Jerametrius, St.L	5	15	3.0	10	0
Azumah, Jerry, Chi.	4	128	32.0	70t	1
Beasley, Aaron, Atl.	4	115	28.8	85	0
Bly, Dre', Det.	4	107	26.8	55t	1
Kelly, Brian, T.B.	4	101	25.3	75	0
Sharper, Darren, G.B.	4	97	24.3	43t	2
* Taylor, Sean, Was.	4	85	21.3	45	0
Parrish, Tony, S.F.	4	64	16.0	26	0
Hamlin, Ken, Sea.	4	48	12.0	24	0
Witherspoon, Will, Car.	4	48	12.0	25	0
Manning, Ricky, Car.	4	46	11.5	30	0
Dawkins, Brian, Phi.	4	40	10.0	32	0
Newman, Terence, Dal.	4	31	7.8	21	0
Macklin, David, Ariz	4	18	4.5	16	0
Winfield, Antoine, Min.	3	89	29.7	56	0
Branch, Colin, Car.	3	79	26.3	76	0
Wilson, Adrian, Ariz	3	62	20.7	27	0
Starks, Duane, Ariz	3	46	15.3	41t	1
Marion, Brock, Det.	3	43	14.3	24	0
Brooking, Keith, Atl.	3	41	13.7	27	0
* Wilson, Gibril, NY-G	3	39	13.0	39	0
Barber, Ronde, T.B.	3	23	7.7	23	0
Ambrose, Ashley, N.O.	3	19	6.3	19	0
Nguyen, Dat, Dal.	3	19	6.3	19	0
Smoot, Fred, Was.	3	17	5.7	17	0
Smith, Dwight, T.B.	3	13	4.3	13	0
Alexander, Brent, NY-G	3	3	1.0	2	0
Peppers, Julius, Car.	2	143	71.5	97	1
Mathis, Kevin, Atl.	2	101	50.5	66t	1
Pierce, Antonio, Was.	2	94	47.0	78t	1
McQuarters, R.W., Chi.	2	85	42.5	45t	1

Name	No	Yards	Avg	Long	TD
Williams, Roy, Dal.	2	53	26.5	33	0
* Hall, DeAngelo, Atl.	2	50	25.0	48t	1
Brown, Sheldon, Phi.	2	33	16.5	33	0
Harris, Walt, Was.	2	31	15.5	31	0
Reese, Ike, Phi.	2	22	11.0	15	0
Rossum, Allen, Atl.	2	22	11.0	14	0
Morgan, Dan, Car.	2	20	10.0	11	0
Walker, Frank, NY-G	2	20	10.0	10	0
Williams, Brian, Min.	2	14	7.0	14	0
Peterson, Will, NY-G	2	9	4.5	9	0
* Frazier, Lance, Dal.	2	2	1.0	2	0
Brown, Fakhir, N.O.	2	0	0.0	0	0
Green, Michael, Chi.	2	0	0.0	0	0
Darling, James, Ariz	1	65	65.0	65	0
Cox, Torrie, T.B.	1	55	55.0	55t	1
Jones, Tebucky, N.O.	1	55	55.0	55	0
Haynes, Michael, Chi.	1	45	45.0	45t	1
Urlacher, Brian, Chi.	1	42	42.0	42	0
Russell, Brian, Min.	1	41	41.0	41	0
Coleman, Rod, Atl.	1	39	39.0	39t	1
Warner, Ron, Was.	1	39	39.0	39	0
Briggs, Lance, Chi.	1	38	38.0	38t	1
Draft, Chris, Atl.	1	33	33.0	33	0
* Lewis, Alex, Det.	1	33	33.0	33	0
Carpenter, Dwaine, S.F.	1	31	31.0	31	0
Gold, Ian, T.B.	1	31	31.0	31	0
Gray, Bobby, Chi.	1	31	31.0	31	0
Fisher, Travis, St.L	1	30	30.0	30	0
Hall, James, Det.	1	30	30.0	30	0
Harris, Al, G.B.	1	29	29.0	29	0
Jue, Bhawoh, G.B.	1	23	23.0	23	0
Simmons, Anthony, Sea.	1	23	23.0	23t	1
Franz, Todd, Was.	1	22	22.0	22	0
Scott, Bryan, Atl.	1	22	22.0	22	0
Shaw, Terrance, Min.	1	22	22.0	22	0
Allen, Brian, Car.	1	21	21.0	21	0
* Dockett, Darnell, Ariz	1	20	20.0	20	0
Hood, Roderick, Phi.	1	20	20.0	20	0
Smith, Raonall, Min.	1	19	19.0	19	0
Ulbrich, Jeff, S.F.	1	19	19.0	19	0
Webster, Jason, Atl.	1	18	18.0	18	0
Moorehead, Kindal, Car.	1	17	17.0	17t	1
Barnett, Nick, G.B.	1	16	16.0	16	0
Claiborne, Chris, Min.	1	15	15.0	15t	1
Fields, Mark, Car.	1	14	14.0	14	0
Heard, Ronnie, S.F.	1	14	14.0	14	0
Robbins, Fred, NY-G	1	13	13.0	13	0
Burns, Curry, NY-G	1	12	12.0	12	0
Allen, Will, NY-G	1	11	11.0	11	0
Bierria, Terreal, Sea.	1	10	10.0	10	0
Hawkins, Artrell, Car.	1	9	9.0	9	0
Buckner, Brentson, Car.	1	8	8.0	8	0
Grant, Charles, N.O.	1	8	8.0	8	0
Williams, Kevin, Min.	1	7	7.0	7	0
Cousin, Terry, NY-G	1	6	6.0	6	0
Brooks, Derrick, T.B.	1	3	3.0	3	0
* Dansby, Karlos, Ariz	1	2	2.0	2	0
Hill, Renaldo, Ariz	1	2	2.0	2	0
Hunter, Pete, Dal.	1	2	2.0	2	0
Nece, Ryan, T.B.	1	2	2.0	2	0
Scott, Lynn, Dal.	1	2	2.0	2	0
* Smith, Keith, Det.	1	2	2.0	2	0
* Lehman, Teddy, Det.	1	1	1.0	1	0
Smith, Brady, Atl.	1	1	1.0	1	0
Winborn, Jamie, S.F.	1	1	1.0	1	0
* Adams, Mike, S.F.	1	0	0.0	0	0
* Allen, Will, T.B.	1	0	0.0	0	0
* Carroll, Ahmad, G.B.	1	0	0.0	0	0
Cash, Chris, Det.	1	0	0.0	0	0

	No	Yards	Avg	Long	TD
Chavous, Corey, Min.	1	0	0.0	0	0
Cochran, Antonio, Sea.	1	0	0.0	0	0
Goodman, Andre', Det.	1	0	0.0	0	0
Jones, Dhani, Phi.	1	0	0.0	0	0
Kerney, Patrick, Atl.	1	0	0.0	0	0
Lewis, Michael, Phi.	1	0	0.0	0	0
Mikell, Quintin, Phi.	1	0	0.0	0	0
Phillips, Jermaine, T.B.	1	0	0.0	0	0
Ruff, Orlando, N.O.	1	0	0.0	0	0
Walker, Bracy, Det.	1	0	0.0	0	0
Harris, Quentin, Ariz	1	-1	-1.0	-1	0
Ivy, Corey, T.B.	0	11	—	11	0

t = Touchdown; *Player that was a rookie in2004
Leader based on interceptions

AMERICAN FOOTBALL CONFERENCE—INTERCEPTIONS

	No	Yards	Avg	Long	TD
Buffalo	24	333	13.9	62t	4
San Diego	23	180	7.8	40	1
Houston	22	393	17.9	102t	2
Baltimore	21	700	33.3	106t	5
Cincinnati	20	272	13.6	51t	4
New England	20	290	14.5	36	1
Indianapolis	19	252	13.3	77t	2
N.Y. Jets	19	243	12.8	66t	2
Pittsburgh	19	293	15.4	41	3
Tennessee	18	285	15.8	44	1
Jacksonville	16	126	7.9	37	0
Cleveland	15	250	16.7	51	1
Miami	15	92	6.1	47	0
Kansas City	13	173	13.3	65	1
Denver	12	175	14.6	76	2
Oakland	9	221	24.6	45	1
AFC Total	285	4278	15.0	106t	30
AFC Average	17.8	267.4	15.0	—	1.9

NATIONAL FOOTBALL CONFERENCE—INTERCEPTIONS

	No	Yards	Avg	Long	TD
Carolina	26	420	16.2	97	2
Seattle	23	337	14.7	63t	3
Atlanta	19	442	23.3	85	4
Washington	18	405	22.5	78t	1
Chicago	17	546	32.1	71t	5
Philadelphia	17	287	16.9	101t	2
Tampa Bay	16	239	14.9	75	1
Arizona	15	214	14.3	65	1
Detroit	14	216	15.4	55t	1
N.Y. Giants	14	113	8.1	39	0
Dallas	13	109	8.4	33	0
New Orleans	13	101	7.8	55	0
Minnesota	11	207	18.8	56	1
San Francisco	9	129	14.3	31	0
Green Bay	8	165	20.6	43t	2
St. Louis	6	45	7.5	30	0
NFC Total	239	3975	16.6	101t	23
NFC Average	14.9	248.4	16.6	—	1.4
League Total	524	8253	—	106t	53
League Average	16.4	257.9	15.8	—	1.7

KICKOFF RETURNS

YARDS PER RETURN

NFC:	26.9	Willie Ponder, New York Giants
AFC:	26.3	Terrence McGee, Buffalo

YARDS

AFC:	1718	Dante Hall, Kansas City
NFC:	1250	Allen Rossum, Atlanta

YARDS, GAME

NFC:	259	Willie Ponder, New York Giants vs. Pittsburgh, December 18 (8 returns, 1 TD)
AFC:	236	Dominic Rhodes, Indianapolis vs. San Diego, December 26 (6 returns, 1 TD) - (OT)

LONGEST

AFC:	104	Terrence McGee, Buffalo at Miami, December 5 - TD
NFC:	99	Eddie Drummond, Detroit vs. Houston, September 19 - TD

RETURNS

AFC:	68	Dante Hall, Kansas City
NFC:	58	Allen Rossum, Atlanta

RETURNS, GAME

AFC:	10	Richard Alston, Cleveland at Cincinnati, November 28 (212 yards, 0 TD)
NFC:	8	Antonio Chatman, Green Bay vs. Tennessee, October 11 (163 yards, 0 TD)
	8	Aaron Stecker, New Orleans vs. Carolina, December 5 (214 yards, 0 TD)
	8	Willie Ponder, New York Giants vs. Pittsburgh, December 18 (259 yards, 1 TD)

TOUCHDOWNS

AFC:	3	Terrence McGee, Buffalo
NFC:	2	Eddie Drummond, Detroit

TEAM CHAMPION

NFC:	25.1	New York Giants
AFC:	24.5	Buffalo

NFL TOP TEN KICKOFF RETURNERS

	No	Yards	Avg	Long	TD
Ponder, Willie, NY-G	36	967	26.9	91t	1
Drummond, Eddie, Det.	41	1092	26.6	99t	2
McGee, Terrence, Buf.	52	1370	26.3	104t	3
Cox, Torrie, T.B.	33	866	26.2	59	0
Hall, Dante, K.C.	68	1718	25.3	97t	2
Randle El, Antwaan, Pit.	21	527	25.1	41	0
Ferguson, Robert, G.B.	21	526	25.0	71	0
Johnson, Bethel, N.E.	41	1016	24.8	93t	1
Rhodes, Dominic, Ind.	48	1188	24.8	88t	1
Dwight, Tim, S.D.	50	1222	24.4	87t	1

AFC—INDIVIDUAL KICKOFF RETURNERS

	No	Yards	Avg	Long	TD
McGee, Terrence, Buf.	52	1370	26.3	104t	3
Hall, Dante, K.C.	68	1718	25.3	97t	2
Randle El, Antwaan, Pit.	21	527	25.1	41	0
Johnson, Bethel, N.E.	41	1016	24.8	93t	1
Rhodes, Dominic, Ind.	48	1188	24.8	88t	1
Dwight, Tim, S.D.	50	1222	24.4	87t	1
* Welker, Wes, S.D.-Mia.	61	1415	23.2	95t	1
Russell, Cliff, Cin.	39	872	22.4	40	0
McAddley, Jason, Ten.	38	849	22.3	45	0
Alston, Richard, Cle.	46	1016	22.1	93t	1
Moses, J.J., Hou.	59	1303	22.1	49	0
* Colclough, Ricardo, Pit.	26	566	21.8	48	0

	No	Yards	Avg	Long	TD
Gabriel, Doug, Oak.	53	1140	21.5	64	0
* Sams, B.J., Bal.	59	1251	21.2	64	0
Lewis, Jermaine, Jac.	21	386	18.4	26	0
(Nonqualifiers)					
* Alexander, Roc, Den.	19	386	20.3	32	0
* Fleming, Troy, Ten.	18	316	17.6	30	0
Carter, Jonathan, NYJ	17	374	22.0	40	0
* Waddell, Michael, Ten.	17	342	20.1	33	0
Edwards, Troy, Jac.	15	335	22.3	45	0
* Luke, Triandos, Den.	15	306	20.4	32	0
Droughns, Reuben, Den.	14	344	24.6	48	0
Jordan, LaMont, NYJ	14	284	20.3	40	0
* Francis, Carlos, Oak.	14	259	18.5	33	0
* Cotchery, Jerricho, NYJ	13	362	27.8	94t	1
Brown, Dee, Cle.	13	243	18.7	30	0
Watson, Kenny, Cin.	13	240	18.5	32	0
Allen, David, Jac.	11	210	19.1	25	0
Taylor, Ike, Pit.	11	184	16.7	22	0
Pyatt, Brad, Ind.	10	230	23.0	32	0
Houshmandzadeh, T.J., Cin.	10	227	22.7	32	0
Redmond, J.R., Oak.	8	153	19.1	31	0
Mungro, James, Ind.	7	111	15.9	24	0
Pass, Patrick, N.E.	6	115	19.2	24	0
Brightful, Lamont, Mia.	5	126	25.2	32	0
Gilmore, Bryan, Mia.	5	114	22.8	53	0
King, Andre, Cle.	5	95	19.0	24	0
* Jones, Greg, Jac.	5	90	18.0	23	0
Chatman, Jesse, S.D.	4	89	22.3	35	0
Fletcher, London, Buf.	4	86	21.5	23	0
Faulk, Kevin, N.E.	4	73	18.3	24	0
Jackson, Frisman, Cle.	4	70	17.5	22	0
Curry, Ronald, Oak.	4	63	15.8	25	0
Griffin, Quentin, Den.	4	52	13.0	21	0
Horn, Chris, K.C.	4	44	11.0	17	0
Kasper, Kevin, N.E.	3	61	20.3	21	0
Cushing, Matt, Pit.	3	45	15.0	20	0
Toefield, LaBrandon, Jac.	3	43	14.3	19	0
Holcombe, Robert, Ten.	3	26	8.7	14	0
Stewart, Tony, Cin.	3	20	6.7	10	0
Jackson, James, Cle.	2	39	19.5	23	0
* Butler, Robb, S.D.	2	35	17.5	24	0
Gaffney, Jabar, Hou.	2	31	15.5	27	0
Washington, Todd, Hou.	2	27	13.5	16	0
Wells, Jonathan, Hou.	2	27	13.5	18	0
Norris, Moran, Hou.	2	25	12.5	15	0
Shelton, Daimon, Buf.	2	25	12.5	15	0
Shea, Aaron, Cle.	2	19	9.5	13	0
Askew, B.J., NYJ	2	18	9.0	13	0
Mustard, Chad, Cle.	2	13	6.5	9	0
Wyrick, Jimmy, Mia.	1	58	58.0	58	0
Kennison, Eddie, K.C.	1	36	36.0	36	0
Whitted, Alvis, Oak.	1	36	36.0	36	0
Sapp, Cecil, Den.	1	34	34.0	34	0
* Smith, Jonathan, Buf.	1	28	28.0	28	0
Morris, Sammy, Mia.	1	27	27.0	27	0
Hetherington, Chris, Oak.	1	23	23.0	23	0
Hollings, Tony, Hou.	1	23	23.0	23	0
Blaylock, Derrick, K.C.	1	22	22.0	22	0
* Poole, Will, Mia.	1	22	22.0	22	0
Banta-Cain, Tully, N.E.	1	21	21.0	21	0
Kinney, Erron, Ten.	1	21	21.0	21	0
Stone, John, Oak.	1	20	20.0	20	0
* Turner, Michael, S.D.	1	18	18.0	18	0
Patten, David, N.E.	1	16	16.0	16	0
Walters, Troy, Ind.	1	16	16.0	16	0
Brady, Kyle, Jac.	1	15	15.0	15	0
Moore, Langston, Cin.	1	15	15.0	15	0
O'Neal, Deltha, Cin.	1	15	15.0	15	0
Clements, Nate, Buf.	1	14	14.0	14	0

	No	Yards	Avg	Long	TD
Kelly, Reggie, Cin.	1	14	14.0	14	0
Kelsay, Chris, Buf.	1	14	14.0	14	0
* Starling, Kendrick, Hou.	1	14	14.0	14	0
Kirschke, Travis, Pit.	1	13	13.0	13	0
Neal, Lorenzo, S.D.	1	12	12.0	12	0
* Schobel, Bo, Ten.	1	12	12.0	12	0
Sanders, Lewis, Cle.	1	9	9.0	10	0
Edwards, Marc, Jac.	1	8	8.0	8	0
Dinkins, Darnell, Bal.	1	7	7.0	7	0
Johnson, Jarret, Bal.	1	6	6.0	6	0
Porter, Jerry, Oak.	1	6	6.0	6	0
Neufeld, Ryan, Buf.	1	3	3.0	3	0
Moulds, Eric, Buf.	1	2	2.0	2	0
Stills, Gary, K.C.	1	0	0.0	0	0
Bennett, Drew, Ten.	1	-8	-8.0	-8	0
Edwards, Donnie, S.D.	0	0	—	—	0
Klecko, Dan, N.E.	0f	0	—	—	0
Peko, Tupe, Ind.	0f	0	—	—	0

t = Touchdown; *Player that was a rookie in 2004
f = Fair Catch
Leader based on average return, minimum 20 returns

NFC—INDIVIDUAL KICKOFF RETURNERS

	No	Yards	Avg	Long	TD
Ponder, Willie, NY-G	36	967	26.9	91t	1
Drummond, Eddie, Det.	41	1092	26.6	99t	2
Cox, Torrie, T.B.	33	866	26.2	59	0
Ferguson, Robert, G.B.	21	526	25.0	71	0
Robertson, Jamal, S.F.-Car.	31	740	23.9	49	0
Lewis, Michael, N.O.	51	1215	23.8	96t	1
Lee, ReShard, Dal.	41	964	23.5	62	0
* Broussard, Jamall, Car.	24	555	23.1	49	0
* Reed, J.R., Phi.	33	761	23.1	66	0
Betts, Ladell, Was.	23	528	23.0	70	0
Chatman, Antonio, G.B.	25	565	22.6	59	0
Scobey, Josh, Ariz	32	723	22.6	71	0
Azumah, Jerry, Chi.	42	924	22.0	73	0
Campbell, Kelly, Min.	35	760	21.7	55	0
Rossum, Allen, Atl.	58	1250	21.6	49	0
Carter, Kerry, Sea.	21	448	21.3	36	0
Morris, Maurice, Sea.	47	994	21.1	34	0
Harris, Arlen, St.L	47	951	20.2	29	0
Hicks, Maurice, S.F.	31	623	20.1	35	0
* Moore, Mewelde, Min.	20	386	19.3	33	0
(Nonqualifiers)					
Stecker, Aaron, N.O.	18	469	26.1	98t	1
Swinton, Reggie, Det.	18	410	22.8	43	0
* Berrian, Bernard, Chi.	17	385	22.6	41	0
* Ward, Derrick, NY-G	16	436	27.3	92t	1
Morton, Chad, Was.	16	358	22.4	49	0
* Croom, Larry, Ariz	16	314	19.6	35	0
* Copper, Terrance, Dal.	16	307	19.2	39	0
Hood, Roderick, Phi.	15	336	22.4	45	0
Cason, Aveion, St.L	14	310	22.1	31	0
Davenport, Najeh, G.B.	14	286	20.4	27	0
Battle, Arnaz, S.F.	13	257	19.8	40	0
* Reeves, Jacques, Dal.	13	199	15.3	27	0
Wilson, Cedrick, S.F.	10	196	19.6	36	0
Thrash, James, Was.	9	186	20.7	36	0
Smith, Onterrio, Min.	9	155	17.2	24	0
Murphy, Frank, T.B.	8	208	26.0	54	0
Bennett, Brandon, Car.	8	177	22.1	43	0
Cloud, Mike, NY-G	8	175	21.9	38	0
Smart, Rod, Car.	8	169	21.1	33	0
* Smart, Ian, T.B.	8	167	20.9	27	0
Furrey, Mike, St.L	8	157	19.6	23	0
McAfee, Fred, N.O.	8	137	17.1	26	0
Johnson, Bryant, Ariz	6	135	22.5	47	0

	No	Yards	Avg	Long	TD
Jones, Daryl, Chi.	6	112	18.7	23	0
White, Jamel, T.B.	4	99	24.8	44	0
* Jackson, Steven, St.L	4	79	19.8	23	0
* Anderson, Dwight, St.L	4	71	17.8	25	0
Sellers, Mike, Was.	4	56	14.0	17	0
McKie, Jason, Chi.	3	65	21.7	25	0
Proehl, Ricky, Car.	3	64	21.3	27	0
* Thurman, Andrae, G.B.	3	59	19.7	28	0
Williams, Jimmy, S.F.	3	58	19.3	23	0
Peterson, Adrian, Chi.	3	57	19.0	22	0
* Graham, Earnest, T.B.	3	52	17.3	18	0
Evans, Heath, Sea.	3	51	17.0	21	0
Ayanbadejo, Obafemi, Ariz	3	50	16.7	21	0
Mahe, Reno, Phi.	3	44	14.7	22	0
* Edwards, Eric, Ariz	3	40	13.3	14	0
Hall, Lamont, N.O.	3	20	6.7	8	0
Hayes, Gerald, Ariz	3	6	2.0	6	0
Burleson, Nate, Min.	2	51	25.5	29	0
McQuarters, R.W., Chi.	2	46	23.0	37	0
Howry, Keenan, Min.	2	45	22.5	24	0
* Jones, Nate, Dal.	2	43	21.5	25	0
* Thornton, Bruce, Dal.	2	43	21.5	24	0
Baker, Eugene, Car.	2	39	19.5	23	0
* Jones, Mark, NY-G	2	37	18.5	20	0
Ross, Derek, Min.	2	33	16.5	19	0
Whitley, James, G.B.	2	33	16.5	20	0
* Carroll, Ahmad, G.B.	2	31	15.5	16	0
* Colbert, Keary, Car.	2	30	15.0	19	0
Hoover, Brad, Car.	2	30	15.0	16	0
Schroeder, Bill, T.B.	2	29	14.5	16	0
Lewis, Greg, Phi.	2	28	14.0	15	0
Bryson, Shawn, Det.	2	27	13.5	14	0
Morgan, Quincy, Dal.	2	25	12.5	19	0
Parry, Josh, Phi.	2	24	12.0	14	0
Jackson, Terry, S.F.	2	22	11.0	14	0
Seidman, Mike, Car.	2f	20	10.0	12	0
Foster, DeShaun, Car.	2	16	8.0	14	0
Henderson, William, G.B.	2	16	8.0	10	0
Manumaleuna, Brandon, St.L	2	13	6.5	13	0
Trejo, Stephen, Det.	2	12	6.0	10	0
Brown, Antonio, Was.	1	66	66.0	66	0
* Hall, DeAngelo, Atl.	1	48	48.0	48	0
Griffith, Justin, Atl.	1	31	31.0	31	0
Schlesinger, Cory, Det.	1	23	23.0	23	0
* Wynn, Dexter, Phi.	1	21	21.0	21	0
Cornella, Greg, T.B.	1	20	20.0	20	0
Johnson, Bryan, Chi.	1	18	18.0	18	0
Williams, Karl, Ariz	1	18	18.0	18	0
* Smith, Will, N.O.	1	17	17.0	17	0
Finn, Jim, NY-G	1	16	16.0	16	0
* Davis, Rod, Min.	1	15	15.0	15	0
Groce, DeJuan, St.L	1	15	15.0	15	0
Wesley, Dante, Car.	1	15	15.0	15	0
* Pierce, Brett, Dal.	1	13	13.0	13	0
* Locklear, Sean, Sea.	1	12	12.0	12	0
Mili, Itula, Sea.	1	12	12.0	12	0
Rasmussen, Kemp, Car.	1	12	12.0	12	0
Stevens, Jerramy, Sea.	1	12	12.0	12	0
Whitehead, Willie, N.O.	1	12	12.0	12	0
Dayne, Ron, NY-G	1	11	11.0	11	0
Goodspeed, Joey, St.L	1	9	9.0	9	0
Lehr, Matt, Dal.	1	9	9.0	9	0
Ruff, Orlando, N.O.	1	9	9.0	9	0
White, Dewayne, T.B.	1	9	9.0	9	0
Rivers, Marcellus, NY-G	1	8	8.0	8	0
Shiancoe, Visanthe, NY-G	1	8	8.0	8	0
Vanden Bosch, Kyle, Ariz	1	7	7.0	7	0
Peterson, Kenny, G.B.	1	6	6.0	6	0
DeVries, Jared, Det.	1	5	5.0	5	0

	No	Yards	Avg	Long	TD
* Molinaro, Jim, Was.	1	5	5.0	5	0
Kozlowski, Brian, Was.	1	4	4.0	4	0
Berton, Sean, Min.	1	3	3.0	3	0
Pritchett, Stanley, Atl.	1	2	2.0	2	0
Faulk, Marshall, St.L	1	0	0.0	0	0
Flowers, Erik, St.L	1	0	0.0	0	0
* Johnson, Spencer, Min.	1	0	0.0	0	0
Coady, Rich, St.L	1	-1	-1.0	-1	0
Curry, Donte, Det.	1	-1	-1.0	-1	0

t = Touchdown; *Player that was a rookie in 2004
f = Fair Catch
Leader based on average return, minimum 20 returns

AMERICAN FOOTBALL CONFERENCE—KICKOFF RETURNS

	No	Yards	Avg	Long	TD
Buffalo	63	1542	24.5	104t	3
Kansas City	75	1820	24.3	97t	2
San Diego	62	1478	23.8	87t	1
Miami	70	1660	23.7	95t	1
Indianapolis	66	1545	23.4	88t	1
New England	56	1302	23.3	93t	1
N.Y. Jets	46	1038	22.6	94t	1
Pittsburgh	62	1335	21.5	48	0
Denver	53	1122	21.2	48	0
Houston	69	1450	21.0	49	0
Baltimore	61	1264	20.7	64	0
Cincinnati	68	1403	20.6	40	0
Oakland	83	1700	20.5	64	0
Cleveland	75	1504	20.1	93t	1
Tennessee	79	1558	19.7	45	0
Jacksonville	57	1087	19.1	45	0
AFC Total	1045	22808	21.8	104t	11
AFC Average	65.3	1425.5	21.8	—	0.7

NATIONAL FOOTBALL CONFERENCE—KICKOFF RETURNS

	No	Yards	Avg	Long	TD
N.Y. Giants	66	1658	25.1	92t	2
Tampa Bay	60	1450	24.2	59	0
Detroit	66	1568	23.8	99t	2
New Orleans	83	1879	22.6	98t	2
Washington	55	1203	21.9	70	0
Atlanta	61	1331	21.8	49	0
Green Bay	70	1522	21.7	71	0
Chicago	74	1607	21.7	73	0
Philadelphia	56	1214	21.7	66	0
Carolina	61	1307	21.4	49	0
Seattle	74	1529	20.7	36	0
Dallas	78	1603	20.6	62	0
San Francisco	84	1716	20.4	40	0
Arizona	65	1293	19.9	71	0
Minnesota	73	1448	19.8	55	0
St. Louis	84	1604	19.1	31	0
NFC Total	1110	23932	21.6	99t	6
NFC Average	69.4	1495.8	21.6	—	0.4
League Total	2155	46740	—	104t	17
League Average	67.3	1460.6	21.7	—	0.5

PUNTING

AVERAGE YARDS PER PUNT
AFC: 46.7   Shane Lechler, Oakland
NFC: 44.1   Tom Tupa, Washington

NET AVERAGE YARDS PER PUNT
NFC: 39.0   Mitch Berger, New Orleans
AFC: 38.4   Mike Scifres, San Diego

LONGEST
NFC: 81   * Andy Lee, San Francisco at Tampa Bay,
                November 21
AFC: 80   Brian Moorman, Buffalo vs. Jacksonville,
                September 12

Player that was a rookie in 2004

PUNTS

NFC: 108   Brad Maynard, Chicago
AFC: 98   Matt Turk, Miami

PUNTS, GAME
NFC: 11   Brad Maynard, Chicago at Tennessee,
                November 14 (509 yards) - (OT)
AFC: 10   * Kyle Larson, Cincinnati vs. Miami,
                September 19 (418 yards)
         10   Matt Turk, Miami at Cincinnati, September 19
                (400 yards)
         10   * Nick Murphy, Baltimore at New England,
                November 28 (444 yards)

TEAM CHAMPION
AFC: 46.7   Oakland
NFC: 43.7   Washington

AMERICAN FOOTBALL CONFERENCE—PUNTING

	Total Punts	Yards	Long	Avg	TB	Blk	Opp Ret	Return Yards	In 20	Net Avg
Oakland	73	3409	67	46.7	14	0	35	413	22	37.2
Indianapolis	54	2443	62	45.2	3	0	29	395	21	36.8
Buffalo	78	3362	80	43.1	10	0	37	315	17	36.5
San Diego	69	2974	60	43.1	8	0	23	164	29	38.4
Pittsburgh	67	2879	61	43.0	6	0	34	252	24	37.4
Tennessee	79	3389	64	42.9	9	0	31	195	21	38.2
Jacksonville	84	3592	69	42.8	9	0	38	429	28	35.5
New England	56	2350	69	42.0	5	0	31	365	19	33.7
Cincinnati	84	3499	66	41.7	7	1	51	378	21	35.5
Miami	99	4107	67	41.5	10	0	45	258	29	36.9
Houston	73	3009	57	41.2	7	0	30	265	19	35.7
Baltimore	97	3935	61	40.6	15	0	36	281	34	34.6
Denver	70	2834	66	40.5	7	1	32	295	19	34.3
Cleveland	85	3404	54	40.0	4	0	48	313	24	35.4
Kansas City	55	2172	58	39.5	7	0	24	301	12	31.5
N.Y. Jets	80	3057	58	38.2	8	0	34	221	22	33.5
AFC Total	1203	50415	80	—	129	2	558	4840	361	—
AFC Average	75.2	3150.9	—	41.9	8.1	0.1	34.9	302.5	22.6	35.7

NATIONAL FOOTBALL CONFERENCE—PUNTING

	Total Punts	Yards	Long	Avg	TB	Blk	Opp Ret	Return Yards	In 20	Net Avg
Washington	104	4544	61	43.7	8	1	65	727	30	35.2
New Orleans	85	3704	63	43.6	4	0	43	310	28	39.0
Carolina	79	3402	65	43.1	9	1	38	303	25	36.9
Arizona	99	4230	57	42.7	7	1	56	486	32	36.4
Chicago	110	4691	58	42.6	5	0	57	380	35	38.3
Dallas	76	3216	68	42.3	7	0	39	410	23	35.1
Philadelphia	73	3068	62	42.0	7	0	34	221	20	37.1
St. Louis	68	2848	63	41.9	6	0	35	416	21	34.0
Tampa Bay	83	3472	60	41.8	7	1	31	279	23	36.8
San Francisco	96	3990	81	41.6	8	0	51	445	25	35.3
Atlanta	76	3082	56	40.6	7	0	33	134	19	36.9
Detroit	93	3765	60	40.5	7	1	46	441	32	34.2
N.Y. Giants	77	3088	55	40.1	4	2	38	356	24	34.4
Green Bay	66	2644	64	40.1	7	0	34	301	16	33.4
Minnesota	57	2240	61	39.3	3	0	26	169	18	35.3
Seattle	79	3036	60	38.4	4	2	33	244	20	34.3
NFC Total	1321	55020	81	—	100	9	659	5622	391	—
NFC Average	82.6	3438.8	—	41.7	6.3	0.6	41.2	351.4	24.4	35.9
NFL Total	2524	105435	81	—	229	11	1217	10462	752	—
NFL Average	78.9	3294.8	—	41.8	7.2	0.3	38.0	326.9	23.5	35.8

NFL TOP TEN PUNTERS

	No	Yards	Long	Avg	Total Punts	TB	Blk	Opp Ret	Return Yards	In 20	Net Avg
Lechler, Shane, Oak.	73	3409	67	46.7	73	14	0	35	413	22	37.2
Smith, Hunter, Ind.	54	2443	62	45.2	54	3	0	29	395	21	36.8
Tupa, Tom, Was.	103	4544	61	44.1	104	8	1	65	727	30	35.2
Sauerbrun, Todd, Car.	76	3351	65	44.1	77	8	1	38	303	25	37.5
Berger, Mitch, N.O.	85	3704	63	43.6	85	4	0	43	310	28	39.0
Landeta, Sean, St.L	40	1733	63	43.3	40	3	0	24	372	9	32.5
Moorman, Brian, Buf.	77	3325	80	43.2	77	9	0	37	315	17	36.8
Player, Scott, Ariz	98	4230	57	43.2	99	7	1	56	486	32	36.4
Scifres, Mike, S.D.	69	2974	60	43.1	69	8	0	23	164	29	38.4
Gardocki, Chris, Pit.	67	2879	61	43.0	67	6	0	34	252	24	37.4

AFC—INDIVIDUAL PUNTERS

	No	Yards	Long	Avg	Total Punts	TB	Blk	Opp Ret	Return Yards	In 20	Net Avg
Lechler, Shane, Oak.	73	3409	67	46.7	73	14	0	35	413	22	37.2
Smith, Hunter, Ind.	54	2443	62	45.2	54	3	0	29	395	21	36.8
Moorman, Brian, Buf.	77	3325	80	43.2	77	9	0	37	315	17	36.8
Scifres, Mike, S.D.	69	2974	60	43.1	69	8	0	23	164	29	38.4
Gardocki, Chris, Pit.	67	2879	61	43.0	67	6	0	34	252	24	37.4
Hanson, Chris, Jac.	84	3592	69	42.8	84	9	0	38	429	28	35.5
Hentrich, Craig, Ten.	73	3117	64	42.7	73	8	0	29	184	20	38.0
* Larson, Kyle, Cin.	83	3499	66	42.2	84	7	1	51	378	21	35.5
Miller, Josh, N.E.	56	2350	69	42.0	56	5	0	31	365	19	33.7
Turk, Matt, Mia.	98	4088	67	41.7	98	10	0	44	241	29	37.2
Knorr, Micah, Den.	54	2243	66	41.5	55	6	1	26	240	12	34.2
Stanley, Chad, Hou.	73	3009	57	41.2	73	7	0	30	265	19	35.7
Zastudil, Dave, Bal.	73	2948	61	40.4	73	12	0	24	181	26	34.6
Frost, Derrick, Cle.	85	3404	54	40.0	85	4	0	48	313	24	35.4
Cheek, Steve, K.C.	42	1643	55	39.1	42	6	0	18	197	8	31.6
Gowin, Toby, NYJ	80	3057	58	38.2	80	8	0	34	221	22	33.5
(Nonqualifiers)											
Baker, Jason, K.C.-Den.	24	931	52	38.8	24	1	0	10	153	10	31.6
* Murphy, Nick, Bal.-K.C.	22	966	58	43.9	22	3	0	11	85	7	37.3
Elling, Aaron, Ten.	6	272	58	45.3	6	1	0	2	11	1	40.2
Stewart, Kordell, Bal.	5	177	42	35.4	5	0	0	3	21	2	31.2
Lindell, Rian, Buf.	1	37	37	37.0	1	1	0	0	0	0	17.0
Stover, Matt, Bal.	1	33	33	33.0	1	1	0	0	0	0	13.0
Mare, Olindo, Mia.	1	19	19	19.0	1	0	0	1	17	0	2.0

NFC—INDIVIDUAL PUNTERS

	No	Yards	Long	Avg	Total Punts	TB	Blk	Opp Ret	Return Yards	In 20	Net Avg
Tupa, Tom, Was.	103	4544	61	44.1	104	8	1	65	727	30	35.2
Sauerbrun, Todd, Car.	76	3351	65	44.1	77	8	1	38	303	25	37.5
Berger, Mitch, N.O.	85	3704	63	43.6	85	4	0	43	310	28	39.0
Landeta, Sean, St.L	40	1733	63	43.3	40	3	0	24	372	9	32.5
Player, Scott, Ariz	98	4230	57	43.2	99	7	1	56	486	32	36.4
Maynard, Brad, Chi.	108	4638	58	42.9	108	5	0	55	363	34	38.7
McBriar, Mat, Dal.	75	3182	68	42.4	75	7	0	39	410	22	35.1
Bidwell, Josh, T.B.	82	3472	60	42.3	83	7	1	31	279	23	36.8
Johnson, Dirk, Phi.	72	3032	62	42.1	72	6	0	34	221	20	37.4
* Lee, Andy, S.F.	96	3990	81	41.6	96	8	0	51	445	25	35.3
Feagles, Jeff, NY-G	74	3069	55	41.5	76	4	2	38	356	23	34.6
Harris, Nick, Det.	92	3765	60	40.9	93	7	1	46	441	32	34.2
Mohr, Chris, Atl.	76	3082	56	40.6	76	7	0	33	134	19	36.9
Barker, Bryan, G.B.	66	2644	64	40.1	66	7	0	34	301	16	33.4
Bennett, Darren, Min.	57	2240	61	39.3	57	3	0	26	169	18	35.3
(Nonqualifiers)											
* Stemke, Kevin, St.L	28	1115	56	39.8	28	3	0	11	44	12	36.1
Rouen, Tom, Sea.	26	1093	60	42.0	26	1	0	10	91	10	37.8
* Jones, Donnie, Sea.	26	988	51	38.0	27	2	1	11	79	6	32.2
Walter, Ken, Sea.	24	920	50	38.3	25	1	1	11	74	4	33.0
Edinger, Paul, Chi.	2	53	30	26.5	2	0	0	2	17	1	18.0
Kasay, John, Car.	2	51	34	25.5	2	1	0	0	0	0	15.5
Akers, David, Phi.	1	36	36	36.0	1	0	0	0	0	0	16.0
Brown, Josh, Sea.	1	35	35	35.0	1	0	0	1	0	0	35.0
Cundiff, Billy, Dal.	1	34	34	34.0	1	0	0	0	0	1	34.0
Christie, Steve, NY-G	1	19	19	19.0	1	0	0	0	0	1	19.0

*Player that was a rookie in 2004
Leader based on average, minimum 40 punts

PUNT RETURNS

YARDS PER RETURN
NFC:	13.2	Eddie Drummond, Detroit
AFC:	12.0	Dennis Northcutt, Cleveland

YARDS
AFC:	575	* B.J. Sams, Baltimore
NFC:	457	Allen Rossum, Atlanta

YARDS, GAME
NFC:	199	Eddie Drummond, Detroit at Jacksonville, November 14 (6 returns, 2 TD) - (OT)
AFC:	111	Antwaan Randle El, Pittsburgh vs. Washington, November 28 (6 returns, 0 TD)

LONGEST
NFC:	91	Nate Burleson, Minnesota at Indianapolis, November 8 - TD
AFC:	86	Nate Clements, Buffalo vs. St. Louis, November 21 - TD

RETURNS
AFC:	55	* B.J. Sams, Baltimore
NFC:	44	R.W. McQuarters, Chicago

RETURNS, GAME
NFC:	8	Dedric Ward, Dallas at Washington, September 27 (67 yards, 0 TD)
AFC:	7	Lamont Brightful, Miami at Cincinnati, September 19 (78 yards, 0 TD)
	7	* B.J. Sams, Baltimore at New York Jets, November 14 (45 yards, 0 TD) - (OT)
	7	Antwaan Randle El, Pittsburgh at Cincinnati, November 21 (83 yards, 0 TD)

FAIR CATCHES
NFC:	27	Antonio Chatman, Green Bay
AFC:	17	Dante Hall, Kansas City

TOUCHDOWNS
AFC:	2	* B.J. Sams, Baltimore
NFC:	2	Eddie Drummond, Detroit

TEAM CHAMPION
NFC:	12.4	Atlanta
AFC:	12.0	Cleveland

NFL TOP TEN PUNT RETURNERS

	No	FC	Yards	Avg	Long	TD
Drummond, Eddie, Det.	24	8	316	13.2	83t	2
Rossum, Allen, Atl.	37	14	457	12.4	75t	1
Northcutt, Dennis, Cle.	36	12	432	12.0	44	0
Lewis, Michael, N.O.	34	11	382	11.2	53	0
* Welker, Wes, Mia.	43	12	464	10.8	71	0
* Sams, B.J., Bal.	55	12	575	10.5	78t	2
Smith, Rod, Den.	22	8	223	10.1	30	0
Hall, Dante, K.C.	23	17	232	10.1	46	0
McQuarters, R.W., Chi.	44	13	435	9.9	75t	1
Lewis, Jermaine, Jac.	23	7	227	9.9	50	0

AFC—INDIVIDUAL PUNT RETURNERS

	No	FC	Yards	Avg	Long	TD
Northcutt, Dennis, Cle.	36	12	432	12.0	44	0
* Welker, Wes, Mia.	43	12	464	10.8	71	0
* Sams, B.J., Bal.	55	12	575	10.5	78t	2
Smith, Rod, Den.	22,	8	223	10.1	30	0
Hall, Dante, K.C.	23	17	232	10.1	46	0
Lewis, Jermaine, Jac.	23	7	227	9.9	50	0
Clements, Nate, Buf.	35	10	327	9.3	86t	1
Parker, Eric, S.D.	27	10	237	8.8	32	0
Moses, J.J., Hou.	36	13	309	8.6	27	0
Moss, Santana, NYJ	27	7	225	8.3	46	0
Randle El, Antwaan, Pit.	42	13	347	8.3	60	0
Faulk, Kevin, N.E.	20	11	133	6.7	16	0
Buchanon, Phillip, Oak.	21	7	121	5.8	18	0
Mason, Derrick, Ten.	24	12	93	3.9	13	0
(Nonqualifiers)						
* Luke, Triandos, Den.	19	8	135	7.1	21	0
* Ratliff, Keiwan, Cin.	17	5	207	12.2	49	0
Allen, David, Jac.	15	2	144	9.6	32	0
McCareins, Justin, NYJ	14	6	88	6.3	26	0
Brown, Troy, N.E.	12	3	83	6.9	23	0
Houshmandzadeh, T.J., Cin.	11	7	88	8.0	28	0
* Smith, Jonathan, Buf.	9	0	157	17.4	70t	1
Brightful, Lamont, Mia.	9	2	89	9.9	36	0
* Waddell, Michael, Ten.	9	3	54	6.0	18	0
* David, Jason, Ind.	8	4	50	6.3	13	0
Pyatt, Brad, Ind.	8	5	47	5.9	13	0
Walters, Troy, Ind.	7	6	40	5.7	14	0
O'Neal, Deltha, Cin.	7	6	33	4.7	17	0
Berlin, Eddie, Ten.	7	1	26	3.7	13	0
Sanders, Deion, Bal.	5	0	41	8.2	23	0
Glenn, Aaron, Hou.	4	0	22	5.5	18	0
Johnson, Bethel, N.E.	4	1	8	2.0	6	0
Edwards, Troy, Jac.	3	1	26	8.7	14	0
Adams, Charlie, Den.	2	1	42	21.0	39	0
Gabriel, Doug, Oak.	2	2	7	3.5	7	0
Poole, Tyrone, N.E.	2	0	6	3.0	6	0
Moorehead, Aaron, Ind.	1	0	34	34.0	34	0
* Colclough, Ricardo, Pit.	1	0	13	13.0	13	0
Mathis, Rashean, Jac.	1	0	8	8.0	8	0
Reed, Josh, Buf.	1	0	7	7.0	7	0
Dwight, Tim, S.D.	1	5	6	6.0	6	0
Haynes, Verron, Pit.	1	0	5	5.0	5	0
Woodson, Charles, Oak.	1	0	4	4.0	4	0
Branch, Deion, N.E.	1	0	0	0.0	0	0
Florence, Drayton, S.D.	1	0	0	0.0	0	0
* Gay, Randall, N.E.	1	0	0	0.0	0	0
Harts, Shaunard, K.C.	1	0	0	0.0	0	0
* Williams, Shaud, Buf.	1	0	0	0.0	0	0
Gilmore, Bryan, Mia.	0	0	11	—	11	0
* Robinson, Dunta, Hou.	0	0	-2	—	-2	0

t = Touchdown; *Player that was a rookie in 2004
Leader based on average return, minimum 20 returns

NFC—INDIVIDUAL PUNT RETURNERS

	No	FC	Yards	Avg	Long	TD
Drummond, Eddie, Det.	24	8	316	13.2	83t	2
Rossum, Allen, Atl.	37	14	457	12.4	75t	1
Lewis, Michael, N.O.	34	11	382	11.2	53	0
McQuarters, R.W., Chi.	44	13	435	9.9	75t	1
* Frazier, Lance, Dal.	24	9	229	9.5	55	0
Battle, Arnaz, S.F.	31	20	266	8.6	71t	1
Burleson, Nate, Min.	25	9	214	8.6	91t	1
Chatman, Antonio, G.B.	32	27	245	7.7	28	0
Galloway, Joey, T.B.	20	8	142	7.1	59t	1
Williams, Karl, Ariz	42	12	286	6.8	38	0
* Jones, Mark, NY-G	34	11	227	6.7	29	0
McDonald, Shaun, St.L	30	18	143	4.8	39	0
(Nonqualifiers)						
Thrash, James, Was.	19	8	162	8.5	43	0
Mahe, Reno, Phi.	19	8	109	5.7	25	0
* Wynn, Dexter, Phi.	18	7	194	10.8	40	0
Swinton, Reggie, Det.	16	9	104	6.5	18	0
Morris, Maurice, Sea.	15	4	75	5.0	22	0
Ward, Dedric, Dal.	14	6	114	8.1	13	0
Morton, Chad, Was.	13	12	80	6.2	14	0
Engram, Bobby, Sea.	10	19	118	11.8	48	0
Brown, Antonio, Was.	10	2	89	8.9	39	0
* Broussard, Jamall, Car.	10	8	43	4.3	13	0
* Gamble, Chris, Car.	9	2	69	7.7	16	0
Baker, Eugene, Car.	8	3	49	6.1	18	0
Starks, Duane, Ariz	7	1	43	6.1	15	0
Brown, Tim, T.B.	6	12	48	8.0	14	0
Schroeder, Bill, T.B.	6	1	21	3.5	12	0
Stallworth, Donte', N.O.	6	1	6	1.0	4	0
* Crayton, Patrick, Dal.	4	1	34	8.5	17	0
Richard, Kris, Sea.	4	3	31	7.8	14	0
* Moore, Mewelde, Min.	4	1	28	7.0	17	0
Hilliard, Ike, NY-G	4	0	26	6.5	15	0
Sheppard, Lito, Phi.	2	5	42	21.0	39	0
Howry, Keenan, Min.	2	3	33	16.5	21	0
Wilson, Cedrick, S.F.	2	1	21	10.5	13	0
Westbrook, Brian, Phi.	2	0	14	7.0	14	0
Newman, Terence, Dal.	2	0	13	6.5	7	0
* Berrian, Bernard, Chi.	2	2	10	5.0	12	0
* Fleck, P.J., S.F.	1	0	10	10.0	10	0
Sharper, Darren, G.B.	1	0	9	9.0	9	0
Hannam, Ryan, Sea.	1	0	6	6.0	6	0
Peterson, Julian, S.F.	1	0	6	6.0	6	0
Hawkins, Artrell, Car.	1	0	4	4.0	4	0
* Clayton, Michael, T.B.	1	1	2	2.0	2	0
Gage, Justin, Chi.	0	0	56	—	56	0
* Reed, J.R., Phi.	0	0	18	—	18	0
Gray, Bobby, Chi.	0	0	9	—	9	0
Boldin, Anquan, Ariz	0	1	0	—	—	0
Finneran, Brian, Atl.	0	3	0	—	—	0
Marshall, Lemar, Was.	0	1	0	—	—	0
Moss, Randy, Min.	0	1	0	—	—	0
Smith, Steve, Car.	0	1	0	—	—	0

t = Touchdown; *Player that was a rookie in 2004
Leader based on average return, minimum 20 returns

AMERICAN FOOTBALL CONFERENCE—PUNT RETURNS

	No	FC	Yards	Avg	Long	TD
Cleveland	36	12	432	12.0	44	0
Miami	52	14	564	10.8	71	0
Buffalo	46	10	491	10.7	86t	2
Baltimore	60	12	616	10.3	78t	2
Kansas City	24	17	232	9.7	46	0
Jacksonville	42	10	405	9.6	50	0
Cincinnati	35	18	328	9.4	49	0
Denver	43	17	400	9.3	39	0
San Diego	29	15	243	8.4	32	0
Pittsburgh	44	13	365	8.3	60	0
Houston	40	13	329	8.2	27	0
N.Y. Jets	41	13	313	7.6	46	0
Indianapolis	24	15	171	7.1	34	0
New England	40	15	230	5.8	23	0
Oakland	24	9	132	5.5	18	0
Tennessee	40	16	173	4.3	20	0
AFC Total	620	219	5424	8.7	86t	4
AFC Average	38.8	13.7	339.0	8.7	—	0.3

NATIONAL FOOTBALL CONFERENCE—PUNT RETURNS

	No	FC	Yards	Avg	Long	TD
Atlanta	37	17	457	12.4	75t	1
Chicago	46	15	510	11.1	75t	1
Detroit	40	17	420	10.5	83t	2
New Orleans	40	12	388	9.7	53	0
Philadelphia	41	20	377	9.2	40	0
Minnesota	31	14	275	8.9	91t	1
Dallas	44	16	390	8.9	55	0
San Francisco	35	21	303	8.7	71t	1
Washington	42	23	331	7.9	43	0
Green Bay	33	27	254	7.7	28	0
Seattle	30	26	230	7.7	48	0
Arizona	49	14	329	6.7	38	0
N.Y. Giants	38	11	253	6.7	29	0
Tampa Bay	33	22	213	6.5	59t	1
Carolina	28	14	165	5.9	18	0
St. Louis	30	18	143	4.8	39	0
NFC Total	597	287	5038	8.4	91t	7
NFC Average	37.3	17.9	314.9	8.4	—	0.4
League Total	1217	506	10462	—	91t	11
League Average	38.0	15.8	326.9	8.6	—	0.3

FUMBLES

MOST FUMBLES

NFC:	16	Michael Vick, Atlanta
AFC:	11	Kyle Boller, Baltimore
	11	Trent Green, Kansas City

MOST FUMBLES, GAME

NFC:	4	Shaun King, Arizona at Carolina, November 21
	4	Jake Delhomme, Carolina at Atlanta, December 18 - (OT)
	4	Chad Hutchinson, Chicago vs. Houston, December 19
AFC:	3	Rich Gannon, Oakland at Pittsburgh, September 12
	3	Lamont Brightful, Miami at Cincinnati, September 19
	3	A.J. Feeley, Miami vs. Pittsburgh, September 26
	3	Trent Green, Kansas City at Jacksonville, October 17
	3	David Carr, Houston at Indianapolis, November 14
	3	Kerry Collins, Oakland vs. Jacksonville, January 2

OWN FUMBLES RECOVERED

AFC:	6	Jake Plummer, Denver
NFC:	6	Aaron Brooks, New Orleans

OWN FUMBLES RECOVERED, GAME

AFC:	3	Lamont Brightful, Miami at Cincinnati, September 19 (11 yards, 0 TD)
NFC:	2	Michael Vick, Atlanta at San Francisco, September 12 (0 yards, 0 TD)
	2	Aaron Brooks, New Orleans vs. San Francisco, September 19 (0 yards, 0 TD)
	2	Clinton Portis, Washington vs. Dallas, September 27 (0 yards, 0 TD)
	2	Jake Delhomme, Carolina at Atlanta, December 18 (0 yards, 0 TD) - (OT)
	2	Chad Hutchinson, Chicago vs. Houston, December 19 (0 yards, 0 TD)
	2	Torry Holt, St. Louis vs. Philadelphia, December 27 (0 yards, 0 TD)

OPPONENTS' FUMBLES RECOVERED

AFC:	4	Eric Barton, New York Jets
	4	Donovin Darius, Jacksonville
NFC:	4	Michael Green, Chicago
	4	Leonard Little, St. Louis
	4	Osi Umenyiora, New York Giants

OPPONENTS' FUMBLES RECOVERED, GAME

AFC:	2	Donovin Darius, Jacksonville at Buffalo, September 12 (0 yards, 0 TD)
	2	James Farrior, Pittsburgh at Miami, September 26 (0 yards, 0 TD)
	2	Kawika Mitchell, Kansas City at Tennessee, December 13 (39 yards, 1 TD)
	2	Gary Stills, Kansas City at Tennessee, December 13 (0 yards, 0 TD)
NFC:	2	Michael Strahan, New York Giants vs. Cleveland, September 26 (0 yards, 0 TD)
	2	Greg Spires, Tampa Bay vs. Atlanta, December 5 (0 yards, 0 TD)

*Player that was a rookie in 2004

YARDS

NFC:	95	Mike Brown, Chicago
AFC:	68	Richard Seymour, New England

LONGEST

NFC:	95	Mike Brown, Chicago at Green Bay, September 19 - TD
AFC:	68	Richard Seymour, New England at Buffalo, October 3 - TD

AFC—TOUCHDOWNS ON FUMBLE RECOVERIES

Abraham, Donnie, NYJ	1
* Anderson, Charlie, Hou.	1
Bulluck, Keith, Ten.	1
* Gay, Randall, N.E.	1
Green, Jarvis, N.E.	1
Harrison, James, Pit.	1
Kaesviharn, Kevin, Cin.	1
McAlister, Chris, Bal.	1
Mitchell, Kawika, K.C.	1
Peek, Antwan, Hou.	1
* Pope, Derrick, Mia.	1
Reed, Ed, Bal.	1
* Sanders, Bob, Ind.	1
Seymour, Richard, N.E.	1
Sharper, Jamie, Hou.	1
Stuvaints, Russell, Pit.	1

NFC—TOUCHDOWNS ON FUMBLE RECOVERIES

Barber, Ronde, T.B.	2
Little, Leonard, St.L	2
Archuleta, Adam, St.L	1
* Bockwoldt, Colby, N.O.	1
Brown, Mike, Chi.	1
Carpenter, Dwaine, S.F.	1
* Carroll, Ahmad, G.B.	1
Green, Barrett, NY-G	1
Hawthorne, Michael, G.B.	1
Peppers, Julius, Car.	1
Sharper, Darren, G.B.	1
Smith, Brady, Atl.	1
Smith, Derek M., S.F.	1
Umenyiora, Osi, NY-G	1
Williams, Kevin, Min.	1
Wilson, Adrian, Ariz	1

AFC FUMBLES—INDIVIDUAL

	Fum	Own Rec	Opp Rec	Yards	Tot Rec
Abraham, John, NYJ	0	0	1	0	1
Abraham, Donnie, NYJ	0	0	2	39	2
* Alexander, Roc, Den.	0	0	1	0	1
Allen, David, Jac.	2	0	0	0	0
Alston, Richard, Cle.	2	0	0	0	0
* Anderson, Charlie, Hou.	0	0	1	60	1
Anderson, Marques, Oak.	0	0	2	0	2
Askew, B.J., NYJ	0	0	1	0	1
Ayodele, Akin, Jac.	0	0	1	0	1
* Babin, Jason, Hou.	0	0	2	22	2
Badger, Brad, Oak.	0	1	0	0	1
Baker, Chris, NYJ	1	1	0	0	1
Banta-Cain, Tully, N.E.	0	0	1	0	1
Barton, Eric, NYJ	0	0	4	2	4
Bashir, Idrees, Ind.	0	0	1	0	1
Baxter, Gary, Bal.	1	0	0	0	0
Beisel, Monty, K.C.	0	0	1	9	1
* Bell, Tatum, Den.	1	0	0	0	0
Bennett, Drew, Ten.	3	2	0	0	2
Bettis, Jerome, Pit.	1	1	0	0	1
Bledsoe, Drew, Buf.	9	2	0	-56	2

	Fum	Own Rec	Opp Rec	Yards	Tot Rec
Boller, Kyle, Bal.	11	4	0	-5	4
Brady, Tom, N.E.	7	1	0	-17	1
Branch, Deion, N.E.	1	1	0	-1	1
Brees, Drew, S.D.	7	3	0	-9	3
Brightful, Lamont, Mia.	3	3	0	11	3
Brock, Raheem, Ind.	0	0	2	0	2
Brown, Chris, Ten.	6	0	0	0	0
Brown, Orlando, Bal.	0	1	0	0	1
Brown, Troy, N.E.	1	2	0	0	2
Buchanon, Phillip, Oak.	2	1	1	0	2
Bulluck, Keith, Ten.	0	0	1	39	1
Burress, Plaxico, Pit.	1	1	0	0	1
Caldwell, Reche, S.D.	1	0	0	0	0
Calmus, Rocky, Ten.	0	0	1	0	1
Campbell, Mark, Buf.	1	0	0	0	0
* Carey, Vernon, Mia.	0	1	0	0	1
Carr, David, Hou.	10	4	0	-8	4
Carswell, Dwayne, Den.	0	1	0	0	1
Carter, Dyshod, Cle.	0	0	1	0	1
Carter, Jonathan, NYJ	2	0	0	0	0
Carter, Kevin, Ten.	0	0	1	0	1
Carter, Quincy, NYJ	2	0	0	0	0
* Celestin, Oliver, NYJ	0	1	0	0	1
Chambers, Chris, Mia.	1	0	0	-5	0
Chatman, Jesse, S.D.	1	0	0	0	0
Cheek, Steve, K.C.	1	0	0	-7	0
Clark, Dallas, Ind.	2	1	0	0	1
Clements, Nate, Buf.	3	1	1	0	2
* Cobbs, Cedric, N.E.	1	0	0	0	0
* Colclough, Ricardo, Pit.	3	0	0	0	0
* Coleman, Erik, NYJ	0	0	1	0	1
Coleman, Marco, Den.	0	0	1	-2	1
Collins, Kerry, Oak.	7	3	0	-21	3
Cooper, Jarrod, Oak.	0	1	0	0	1
Cooper, Stephen, S.D.	0	0	1	0	1
Curry, Ronald, Oak.	1	1	0	0	1
Dalton, Lional, K.C.	0	0	1	0	1
Darius, Donovin, Jac.	0	0	4	0	4
* Darling, Devard, Bal.	1	0	0	0	0
Davis, Andra, Cle.	0	0	1	0	1
Davis, Domanick, Hou.	4	0	0	0	0
Demps, Will, Bal.	0	0	2	2	2
DeMulling, Rick, Ind.	1	0	0	-2	0
Dillon, Corey, N.E.	5	1	0	0	1
Droughns, Reuben, Den.	5	0	0	0	0
* Echemandu, Adimchinobe, Cle.	1	0	0	0	0
Edwards, Troy, Jac.	3	0	0	-24	0
Ekuban, Ebenezer, Cle.	0	0	2	4	2
Ellis, Shaun, NYJ	0	0	1	0	1
* Evans, Lee, Buf.	1	1	0	0	1
Faine, Jeff, Cle.	2	1	0	-47	1
Fargas, Justin, Oak.	1	0	0	0	0
Farrior, James, Pit.	0	0	3	0	3
Fatafehi, Mario, Den.	0	0	1	8	1
Faulk, Kevin, N.E.	2	1	0	0	1
Fauria, Christian, N.E.	0	1	0	0	1
Feeley, A.J., Mia.	10	1	0	-4	1
Fiedler, Jay, Mia.	9	1	0	0	1
* Fleming, Troy, Ten.	0	1	0	0	1
Fletcher, Jamar, S.D.	0	0	1	7	1
Fletcher, London, Buf.	0	0	1	0	1
Florence, Drayton, S.D.	1	0	0	0	0
Foley, Steve, S.D.	0	0	2	0	2
Foote, Larry, Pit.	0	0	1	0	1
Foreman, Jay, Hou.	0	0	1	3	1
Forsey, Brock, Mia.	1	0	0	0	0
Fowler, Melvin, Cle.	0	0	1	0	1
* Francis, Carlos, Oak.	1	0	0	0	0

	Fum	Own Rec	Opp Rec	Yards	Tot Rec
Freeman, Arturo, Mia.	1	0	0	0	0
Gabriel, Doug, Oak.	2	0	0	0	0
Gaffney, Jabar, Hou.	1	0	0	0	0
* Gallery, Robert, Oak.	0	1	0	0	1
Gannon, Rich, Oak.	3	1	0	0	1
Garcia, Jeff, Cle.	9	0	0	-9	0
Gardner, Barry, Cle.	0	0	1	0	1
* Gardner, Rich, Ten.	2	0	0	0	0
* Gay, Randall, N.E.	1	0	2	41	2
Gilmore, Bryan, Mia.	1	0	0	0	0
Glenn, Aaron, Hou.	2	1	0	0	1
Glenn, Jason, NYJ	0	1	1	2	2
Godfrey, Randall, S.D.	0	0	1	0	1
Goff, Mike, S.D.	0	2	0	11	2
Gonzalez, Tony, K.C.	0	1	0	0	1
Gonzalez, Joaquin, Cle.	0	1	0	0	1
Gordon, Lamar, Mia.	1	1	0	0	1
Grant, Deon, Jac.	0	0	1	0	1
Green, Jarvis, N.E.	0	0	3	0	3
Green, Trent, K.C.	11	3	0	-6	3
Green, William, Cle.	3	0	0	0	0
Gregg, Kelly, Bal.	0	0	1	0	1
Griffin, Quentin, Den.	3	0	0	0	0
* Hadnot, Rex, Mia.	0	1	0	0	1
Haggan, Mario, Buf.	0	2	0	0	2
Haggans, Clark, Pit.	0	0	1	0	1
Hall, Carlos, Ten.	0	0	1	0	1
Hall, Dante, K.C.	1	0	0	0	0
Hamilton, Ben, Den.	0	1	0	0	1
* Hardwick, Nick, S.D.	0	1	0	0	1
Harper, Nick, Ind.	0	0	1	15	1
Harrison, James, Pit.	0	0	1	18	1
Harrison, Marvin, Ind.	1	0	0	0	0
Hartwell, Edgerton, Bal.	0	0	1	-1	1
Hartwig, Justin, Ten.	0	1	0	0	1
Haynes, Verron, Pit.	0	0	1	2	1
Hayward, Reggie, Den.	0	0	1	0	1
Heiden, Steve, Cle.	1	2	0	0	2
Henderson, John, Jac.	0	0	1	0	1
Henry, Leonard, Mia.	1	0	0	0	0
Herndon, Kelly, Den.	0	0	1	0	1
Hetherington, Chris, Oak.	1	0	0	0	0
Hill, Darrell, Ten.	0	0	1	0	1
Holcomb, Kelly, Cle.	1	2	0	-5	2
Hollings, Tony, Hou.	0	1	0	0	1
Holmes, Priest, K.C.	4	0	0	0	0
Howard, Reggie, Mia.	0	0	1	0	1
Jackson, Frisman, Cle.	1	0	0	0	0
Jackson, James, Cle.	1	0	0	0	0
James, Edgerrin, Ind.	6	1	0	0	1
James, Jeno, Mia.	0	3	0	0	3
James, Tory, Cin.	0	0	1	0	1
Jameson, Michael, Cle.	0	0	1	0	1
Johnson, Andre, Hou.	1	1	0	0	1
Johnson, Bethel, N.E.	2	1	0	0	1
Johnson, Chad, Cin.	1	0	0	0	0
Johnson, Jarret, Bal.	0	0	1	0	1
Johnson, Jeremi, Cin.	1	0	0	0	0
Johnson, Kevin, Bal.	1	2	0	0	2
* Johnson, Landon, Cin.	0	0	1	0	1
Johnson, Rudi, Cin.	4	0	0	0	0
* Jones, Greg, Jac.	1	0	0	0	0
Jordan, LaMont, NYJ	1	0	0	0	0
June, Cato, Ind.	0	0	2	-1	2
Kaesviharn, Kevin, Cin.	0	0	1	3	1
Kassell, Brad, Ten.	0	1	0	0	1
* Kelly, Tommy, Oak.	0	0	1	0	1
Kelsay, Chris, Buf.	0	0	2	0	2

	Fum	Own Rec	Opp Rec	Yards	Tot Rec
Kennedy, Kenoy, Den.	0	0	1	5	1
Kennison, Eddie, K.C.	1	0	0	0	0
Kiel, Terrence, S.D.	0	0	1	0	1
Kitna, Jon, Cin.	2	1	0	-1	1
Klecko, Dan, N.E.	1	0	0	0	0
Knight, Sammy, Mia.	1	0	1	0	1
Koppen, Dan, N.E.	1	1	0	-6	1
Kramer, Jordan, Ten.	0	0	1	0	1
Kreider, Dan, Pit.	0	2	0	0	2
* LaBoy, Travis, Ten.	0	0	1	0	1
Leber, Ben, S.D.	0	0	1	25	1
Lee, Donald, Mia.	2	1	0	8	1
Leftwich, Byron, Jac.	5	3	0	0	3
Lewis, Jamal, Bal.	2	1	0	-2	1
Lewis, Jermaine, Jac.	1	1	0	0	1
Lewis, Ray, Bal.	0	0	2	0	2
Little, Earl, Cle.	0	0	1	14	1
* Losman, J.P., Buf.	1	0	0	0	0
* Luke, Triandos, Den.	2	0	0	0	0
Maddox, Tommy, Pit.	3	0	0	0	0
Madison, Sam, Mia.	1	0	0	4	0
Manning, Peyton, Ind.	5	3	0	-3	3
Manuwai, Vince, Jac.	1	2	0	-3	2
Martin, Curtis, NYJ	2	2	0	-9	2
Martin, Jamar, Mia.	1	0	0	0	0
Mason, Derrick, Ten.	2	2	0	0	2
Mathis, Robert, Ind.	0	0	3	26	3
Mays, Lee, Pit.	0	0	1	0	1
McAddley, Jason, Ten.	1	0	0	0	0
McAlister, Chris, Bal.	0	1	1	65	2
McCareins, Justin, NYJ	3	4	0	0	4
McCleon, Dexter, K.C.	0	0	1	0	1
* McCown, Luke, Cle.	2	1	0	-12	1
McGahee, Willis, Buf.	4	0	0	0	0
McGee, Terrence, Buf.	2	0	1	38	1
McGinest, Willie, N.E.	0	0	1	0	1
McIntosh, Damion, Mia.	0	2	0	0	2
McKenzie, Kareem, NYJ	0	2	0	0	2
McKinley, Alvin, Cle.	0	0	2	0	2
McKinney, Seth, Mia.	0	2	0	0	2
McKinney, Steve, Hou.	1	0	0	-7	0
McMichael, Randy, Mia.	2	2	0	0	2
McNair, Steve, Ten.	5	1	0	0	1
Meester, Brad, Jac.	1	1	0	-14	1
Meier, Shad, Ten.	1	1	0	0	1
Middlebrooks, Willie, Den.	0	0	1	0	1
Miller, Billy, Hou.	1	0	0	0	0
* Miller, Caleb, Cin.	0	0	1	0	1
Miller, Fred, Ten.	0	1	0	0	1
Minor, Travis, Mia.	0	1	0	0	1
Mitchell, Anthony, Cin.	0	0	1	0	1
Mitchell, Kawika, K.C.	0	0	2	39	2
Moore, Eddie, Mia.	0	0	2	0	2
Moorman, Brian, Buf.	2	2	0	0	2
Moreland, Earthwind, N.E.	0	0	1	0	1
Morgan, Quincy, Cle.	1	0	0	0	0
Morris, Sammy, Mia.	1	0	0	0	0
Morton, Johnnie, K.C.	2	1	0	0	1
Moses, J.J., Hou.	1	0	0	0	0
Moss, Santana, NYJ	2	2	0	0	2
Moulds, Eric, Buf.	1	0	0	0	0
Myers, Michael, Cle.	0	0	1	0	1
Myles, Reggie, Cin.	0	0	1	0	1
Naeole, Chris, Jac.	1	1	0	0	1
Nalen, Tom, Den.	1	0	0	0	0
Neal, Lorenzo, S.D.	1	0	0	0	0
Nelson, Jim, Ind.	0	0	2	0	2
Northcutt, Dennis, Cle.	2	1	0	0	1
Ogden, Jonathan, Bal.	0	1	0	0	1
* Olivea, Shane, S.D.	0	1	0	0	1
Orr, Shantee, Hou.	0	1	0	3	1
Palmer, Carson, Cin.	2	0	0	0	0
Parker, Eric, S.D.	5	4	0	-14	4
Pass, Patrick, N.E.	1	0	0	0	0
Patterson, Elton, Jac.	0	0	1	0	1
Paxton, Lonie, N.E.	0	0	1	0	1
Peek, Antwan, Hou.	0	0	1	66	1
Peelle, Justin, S.D.	1	0	0	0	0
Pennington, Chad, NYJ	5	1	0	-3	1
* Peters, Jason, Buf.	0	0	1	0	1
Peterson, Mike, Jac.	0	0	1	0	1
Phifer, Roman, N.E.	0	0	1	0	1
* Phillips, Shaun, S.D.	0	0	2	0	2
Pinnock, Andrew, S.D.	1	0	0	0	0
* Pippens, Jerrell, S.D.	0	0	1	0	1
Plummer, Jake, Den.	6	6	0	-8	6
Polk, DaShon, Hou.	0	0	1	0	1
Poole, Tyrone, N.E.	1	0	0	0	0
* Pope, Derrick, Mia.	0	0	1	1	1
Porter, Jerry, Oak.	2	0	0	0	0
Posey, Jeff, Buf.	0	0	1	0	1
Prioleau, Pierson, Buf.	0	0	1	12	1
Rabach, Casey, Bal.	1	0	0	0	0
Randle El, Antwaan, Pit.	5	2	0	0	2
* Ratliff, Keiwan, Cin.	2	2	1	0	3
Reagor, Montae, Ind.	0	0	1	0	1
Redmond, J.R., Oak.	2	0	0	0	0
Reed, Ed, Bal.	1	0	2	44	2
* Reid, Dexter, N.E.	0	0	1	0	1
Rhodes, Dominic, Ind.	2	0	0	0	0
Richardson, Tony, K.C.	0	2	0	0	2
* Rivers, Philip, S.D.	1	1	0	0	1
Roaf, Willie, K.C.	0	1	0	0	1
* Roethlisberger, Ben, Pit.	2	0	0	-6	0
Rolle, Samari, Ten.	0	1	1	5	2
Rosenfels, Sage, Mia.	2	0	0	0	0
Russell, Cliff, Cin.	2	1	0	0	1
* Sams, B.J., Bal.	5	1	0	0	1
* Sanders, Bob, Ind.	0	0	2	37	2
Sapp, Warren, Oak.	0	0	2	0	2
Saturday, Jeff, Ind.	0	1	0	0	1
Schobel, Aaron, Buf.	0	0	3	0	3
Schobel, Matt, Cin.	1	0	1	0	1
Scifres, Mike, S.D.	1	1	0	0	1
Scott, Bart, Bal.	0	0	1	0	1
* Scott, Jake, Ind.	0	1	0	0	1
Seau, Junior, Mia.	0	0	1	0	1
Seymour, Richard, N.E.	0	0	1	68	1
Sharper, Jamie, Hou.	0	0	1	16	1
Shields, Will, K.C.	0	1	0	0	1
Simmons, Brian, Cin.	0	0	1	18	1
Smith, Aaron, Pit.	0	0	2	54	2
Smith, Antowain, Ten.	2	1	0	0	1
* Smith, Daryl, Jac.	0	0	1	0	1
Smith, Hunter, Ind.	0	0	1	0	1
Smith, Jimmy, Jac.	2	0	0	0	0
Smith, Justin, Cin.	0	0	2	0	2
Smith, Rod, Den.	4	3	0	0	3
Smith, Travian, Oak.	0	0	1	0	1
* Sorgi, Jim, Ind.	1	1	0	-5	1
Sowell, Jerald, NYJ	1	0	0	0	0
Spears, Marcus, Hou.	0	1	0	0	1
* Spencer, Cody, Ten.	0	1	0	0	1
Spikes, Takeo, Buf.	0	0	1	0	1
Spragan, Donnie, Den.	0	0	1	0	1
Staley, Duce, Pit.	3	1	0	0	1

	Fum	Own Rec	Opp Rec	Yards	Tot Rec
* Starks, Randy, Ten.	0	0	2	0	2
St. Clair, John, Mia.	0	1	0	0	1
* Stevens, Larry, Cin.	0	1	0	0	1
Stills, Gary, K.C.	0	0	2	0	2
Stokley, Brandon, Ind.	1	2	0	0	2
Stroud, Marcus, Jac.	0	0	1	0	1
Stuvaints, Russell, Pit.	0	0	1	24	1
Suggs, Lee, Cle.	6	1	0	0	1
Suggs, Terrell, Bal.	0	0	2	24	2
Surtain, Patrick, Mia.	0	1	1	8	2
Taylor, Chester, Bal.	1	0	0	0	0
Taylor, Fred, Jac.	3	0	0	0	0
Taylor, Ike, Pit.	1	0	0	0	0
Taylor, Jason, Mia.	0	0	3	1	3
Taylor, Travis, Bal.	1	0	0	0	0
Teague, Trey, Buf.	0	1	0	0	1
Thomas, Juqua, Ten.	0	0	1	0	1
Thompson, Chaun, Cle.	0	0	1	0	1
Toefield, LaBrandon, Jac.	1	0	0	0	0
Tomlinson, LaDainian, S.D.	6	2	0	0	2
Tongue, Reggie, NYJ	0	0	1	0	1
Townsend, Deshea, Pit.	0	0	1	0	1
* Trafford, Rod, Buf.	0	1	0	0	1
* Troupe, Ben, Ten.	2	1	0	0	1
Tucker, Ross, Buf.	1	0	0	-5	0
Tucker, Ryan, Cle.	0	1	0	0	1
Turner, Michael, S.D.	1	0	0	0	0
Villarrial, Chris, Buf.	0	1	0	0	1
* Vilma, Jonathan, NYJ	0	0	1	0	1
Vincent, Troy, Buf.	0	0	1	0	1
Volek, Billy, Ten.	6	3	0	0	3
von Oelhoffen, Kimo, Pit.	0	0	2	21	2
* Waddell, Michael, Ten.	3	2	0	33	2
Walker, Denard, Oak.	0	0	1	28	1
Walls, Raymond, Bal.	0	1	0	0	1
Wand, Seth, Hou.	0	1	0	0	1
Ward, Hines, Pit.	1	0	0	0	0
Watson, Kenny, Cin.	2	1	0	0	1
* Watts, Darius, Den.	1	0	0	0	0
Weaver, Tony, Bal.	0	0	1	0	1
Webster, Nate, Cin.	0	0	1	0	1
* Welker, Wes, Mia.	4	1	0	0	1
Wells, Jonathan, Hou.	1	0	0	0	0
Westmoreland, Eric, Cle.	0	0	1	0	1
Whitley, Taylor, Mia.	0	1	0	0	1
Wiegmann, Casey, K.C.	0	1	0	0	1
Wilcox, Daniel, Bal.	1	0	0	0	0
* Wilfork, Vince, N.E.	0	0	2	0	2
Wilkins, Marcus, Cin.	0	0	2	0	2
Williams, Tank, Ten.	0	0	1	28	1
Williams, Josh, Ind.	0	0	2	0	2
* Williams, Madieu, Cin.	0	0	2	-3	2
Williams, Maurice, Jac.	0	1	0	0	1
Williams, Pat, Buf.	0	0	1	0	1
* Williams, Reggie, Jac.	1	0	0	0	0
* Williams, Shaud, Buf.	1	2	0	0	2
Wilson, Eugene, N.E.	0	0	2	0	2
Wire, Coy, Buf.	0	0	1	0	1
Wong, Kailee, Hou.	0	0	1	0	1
Woodson, Charles, Oak.	0	0	1	0	1
Wrighster, George, Jac.	1	0	0	0	0
Wright, Kenyatta, NYJ	0	0	1	0	1
Zereoue, Amos, Oak.	1	0	0	0	0

*Player that was a rookie in 2004
Yards includes aborted plays, own recoveries, and opponents' recoveries.

NFC FUMBLES—INDIVIDUAL

	Fum	Own Rec	Opp Rec	Yards	Tot Rec
Adams, Flozell, Dal.	0	0	1	0	1
* Adams, Mike, S.F.	0	0	1	0	1
Alexander, Brent, NY-G	0	0	2	29	2
Alexander, Shaun, Sea.	5	2	0	0	2
Allen, James, N.O.	0	0	2	1	2
Alstott, Mike, T.B.	2	0	0	0	0
Ambrose, Ashley, N.O.	0	0	1	40	1
Anderson, Richie, Dal.	1	0	0	0	0
Archuleta, Adam, St.L	0	0	1	93	1
Ayanbadejo, Obafemi, Ariz	1	0	0	0	0
Azumah, Jerry, Chi.	1	0	0	0	0
Backus, Jeff, Det.	0	1	0	0	1
Barber, Tiki, NY-G	5	2	0	0	2
Barber, Ronde, T.B.	0	0	2	27	2
Barlow, Kevan, S.F.	2	0	0	0	0
Barnes, Darian, Dal.	1	1	0	0	1
Barnett, Nick, G.B.	0	0	1	7	1
Bartrum, Mike, Phi.	1	1	0	0	1
Battle, Arnaz, S.F.	2	3	0	0	3
Bellamy, Jay, N.O.	0	0	3	12	3
Bennett, Michael, Min.	1	1	0	0	1
Bernard, Rocky, Sea.	0	0	1	0	1
Berry, Bertrand, Ariz	0	0	2	9	2
Bidwell, Josh, T.B.	1	1	0	0	1
Birk, Matt, Min.	2	0	0	-31	0
Blake, Jeff, Phi.	1	0	0	0	0
* Bockwoldt, Colby, N.O.	0	0	1	6	1
Boldin, Anquan, Ariz	1	0	0	0	0
Briggs, Lance, Chi.	0	0	0	11	0
Brooking, Keith, Atl.	0	0	1	4	1
Brooks, Aaron, N.O.	13	6	0	-12	6
* Broussard, Jamall, Car.	2	0	0	0	0
Brown, Alex, Chi.	0	0	1	0	1
Brown, Antonio, Was.	1	0	0	0	0
Brown, Chad, Sea.	0	0	1	15	1
Brown, Fakhir, N.O.	0	0	3	2	3
Brown, Mike, Chi.	0	0	1	95	1
Brown, Tim, T.B.	2	0	0	0	0
Bruce, Isaac, St.L	5	0	1	0	1
Brunell, Mark, Was.	6	2	0	-6	2
Bryant, Antonio, Was.	1	0	0	0	0
Bryson, Shawn, Det.	1	0	0	0	0
Bulger, Marc, St.L	5	0	0	0	0
Burleson, Nate, Min.	1	1	0	0	1
Butler, Jerametrius, St.L	0	0	1	2	1
Campbell, Kelly, Min.	1	0	0	0	0
Carpenter, Dwaine, S.F.	0	0	1	80	1
* Carroll, Ahmad, G.B.	0	0	1	40	1
Carson, Leonardo, Dal.	0	0	1	0	1
* Carstens, Jordan, Car.	0	0	1	1	1
Chandler, Chris, St.L	1	0	0	0	0
Chatman, Antonio, G.B.	3	0	0	0	0
Claiborne, Chris, Min.	0	0	1	0	1
Clark, Desmond, Chi.	1	0	0	0	0
* Clayton, Michael, T.B.	1	1	0	0	1
Clement, Anthony, Ariz	0	1	0	0	1
Cloud, Mike, NY-G	0	1	0	0	1
Coady, Rich, St.L	0	0	1	0	1
Coakley, Dexter, Dal.	0	0	1	0	1
Cochran, Antonio, Sea.	0	0	1	0	1
* Colbert, Keary, Car.	1	0	0	0	0
Coleman, Rod, Atl.	0	0	1	0	1
Coles, Laveranues, Was.	1	0	0	0	0
Colombo, Marc, Chi.	0	1	0	0	1
Conwell, Ernie, N.O.	0	1	0	0	1
Cox, Torrie, T.B.	0	0	1	0	1
* Croom, Larry, Ariz	2	1	0	0	1

	Fum	Own Rec	Opp Rec	Yards	Tot Rec		Fum	Own Rec	Opp Rec	Yards	Tot Rec
Crumpler, Alge, Atl.	1	0	0	0	0	Heard, Ronnie, S.F.	0	0	1	0	1
Culpepper, Daunte, Min.	9	0	0	-11	0	Heitmann, Eric, S.F.	0	1	0	0	1
Curry, Donte, Det.	0	0	1	0	1	Heller, Will, T.B.	1	1	0	0	1
Curtis, Kevin, St.L	1	1	0	1	1	* Henson, Drew, Dal.	1	0	0	0	0
Daniels, Phillip, Was.	0	0	1	0	1	Hicks, Maurice, S.F.	3	2	0	0	2
* Dansby, Karlos, Ariz	0	0	3	0	3	Hillenmeyer, Hunter, Chi.	0	0	1	13	1
Darby, Chartric, T.B.	0	0	1	0	1	Hilliard, Ike, NY-G	3	1	0	0	1
Darling, James, Ariz	1	0	0	0	0	Holt, Torry, St.L	3	3	0	0	3
Davenport, Najeh, G.B.	1	0	0	0	0	Hood, Roderick, Phi.	1	0	3	1	3
Davis, James, Det.	0	0	1	0	1	Hoover, Brad, Car.	0	1	1	0	2
Davis, Leonard, Ariz	0	2	0	0	2	Hovan, Chris, Min.	0	0	1	0	1
Dawkins, Brian, Phi.	0	0	1	0	1	Howard, Darren, N.O.	0	0	3	0	3
Dayne, Ron, NY-G	0	1	0	0	1	Huff, Orlando, Sea.	0	0	2	0	2
Delhomme, Jake, Car.	12	5	0	-13	5	Hutchinson, Chad, Chi.	8	2	0	-11	2
Detmer, Koy, Phi.	1	0	0	0	0	Hutchinson, Steve, Sea.	1	2	0	0	2
Diehl, David, NY-G	0	2	0	0	2	Ivy, Corey, T.B.	0	1	0	0	1
Dilfer, Trent, Sea.	1	0	0	0	0	Jackson, Darrell, Sea.	2	0	0	0	0
* Dockett, Darnell, Ariz	0	0	1	-4	1	* Jackson, Steven, St.L	1	0	0	0	0
Dorsey, Ken, S.F.	5	1	0	-3	1	Jackson, Terry, S.F.	3	1	0	0	1
Driver, Donald, G.B.	2	1	0	0	1	Jasper, Ed, Atl.	0	0	2	0	2
Drummond, Eddie, Det.	0	0	1	0	1	Jenkins, Cullen, G.B.	0	0	1	0	1
Duckett, T.J., Atl.	2	0	0	0	0	* Jenkins, Michael, Atl.	0	1	0	0	1
Dunn, Warrick, Atl.	3	1	0	0	1	Johnson, Al, Dal.	1	0	0	-8	0
Edwards, Kalimba, Det.	0	0	1	0	1	Johnson, Bryant, Ariz	1	0	0	0	0
Edwards, Mario, T.B.	0	0	1	0	1	Johnson, Eric, S.F.	1	1	0	0	1
Edwards, Steve, Chi.	0	2	0	0	2	Johnson, Brad, T.B.	2	0	0	0	0
Engelberger, John, S.F.	0	0	1	0	1	Johnson, Keyshawn, Dal.	1	1	0	0	1
Engram, Bobby, Sea.	1	0	0	0	0	* Johnson, Spencer, Min.	1	0	0	0	0
Evans, Heath, Sea.	1	1	0	0	1	Johnson, Todd, Chi.	0	0	1	0	1
Faulk, Marshall, St.L	2	0	0	0	0	Jones, Dhani, Phi.	0	0	1	0	1
Favre, Brett, G.B.	4	1	0	-8	1	Jones, Freddie, Ariz	0	0	1	0	1
Ferguson, Robert, G.B.	1	1	0	16	1	* Jones, Julius, Dal.	3	0	0	0	0
Fields, Mark, Car.	0	0	1	0	1	Jones, Kevin, Det.	2	1	0	0	1
Finneran, Brian, Atl.	1	0	0	0	0	* Jones, Mark, NY-G	1	1	0	0	1
Fisher, Tony, G.B.	1	1	0	0	1	Jones, Tebucky, N.O.	0	0	1	0	1
* Fitzgerald, Larry, Ariz	1	1	0	0	1	Jones, Thomas, Chi.	2	0	0	0	0
Flowers, Erik, St.L	1	0	0	0	0	Kampman, Aaron, G.B.	0	0	1	3	1
Franz, Todd, Was.	0	0	1	0	1	Kearse, Jevon, Phi.	0	0	1	0	1
* Frazier, Lance, Dal.	2	1	1	0	2	Kelly, Brian, T.B.	0	0	1	32	1
Friedman, Lennie, Was.	1	1	0	-11	1	Kerney, Patrick, Atl.	0	0	1	0	1
Galloway, Joey, T.B.	3	2	0	0	2	King, Shaun, Ariz	4	1	0	-3	1
* Gamble, Chris, Car.	1	1	0	0	1	* Krenzel, Craig, Chi.	8	1	0	-11	1
Garza, Roberto, Atl.	0	1	0	0	1	Kreutz, Olin, Chi.	1	1	0	0	1
George, Eddie, Dal.	3	1	0	0	1	* Lavalais, Chad, Atl.	0	0	2	0	2
Goings, Nick, Car.	1	1	0	0	1	Lee, Charles, T.B.	1	0	0	0	0
Goodspeed, Joey, St.L	1	0	0	0	0	* Lewis, Keith, S.F.	0	0	1	0	1
Grant, Charles, N.O.	0	0	1	0	1	Lewis, Kevin, NY-G	0	0	1	16	1
Green, Ahman, G.B.	7	2	0	0	2	Lewis, Michael, N.O.	1	0	0	0	0
Green, Barrett, NY-G	0	0	2	16	2	Lewis, Michael, Phi.	0	0	1	0	1
Green, Michael, Chi.	0	0	4	3	4	Little, Leonard, St.L	0	0	4	66	4
Greisen, Nick, NY-G	0	0	1	0	1	Liwienski, Chris, Min.	0	1	0	0	1
Griese, Brian, T.B.	6	2	0	-7	2	Looker, Dane, St.L	1	0	0	0	0
Griffin, Cornelius, Was.	0	0	1	0	1	Lucas, Ken, Sea.	0	0	2	3	2
Grossman, Rex, Chi.	2	0	0	0	0	Lucier, Wayne, NY-G	0	1	0	0	1
Gutierrez, Brock, S.F.	1	1	0	-7	1	Macklin, David, Ariz	0	0	1	1	1
Haayer, Adam, Min.	0	1	0	0	1	Mahan, Sean, T.B.	1	0	0	0	0
Haley, Jermaine, Was.	0	0	1	0	1	Mahe, Reno, Phi.	1	1	0	0	1
Hall, Cory, Atl.	0	0	1	0	1	* Manning, Eli, NY-G	3	0	0	-9	0
Hall, James, Det.	0	0	1	0	1	Manning, Ricky, Car.	1	0	0	0	0
Hall, Travis, Atl.	0	0	1	0	1	Marshall, Torrance, G.B.	0	1	0	0	1
Harper, Deveron, N.O.	0	0	1	0	1	Martin, Jamie, St.L	1	0	0	0	0
Harrington, Joey, Det.	6	0	0	-6	0	McAllister, Deuce, N.O.	5	2	0	0	2
Harris, Arlen, St.L	1	0	0	0	0	McBriar, Mat, Dal.	1	1	0	0	1
Harris, Quentin, Ariz	0	0	1	0	1	McCadam, Kevin, Atl.	0	0	1	0	1
Hasselbeck, Matt, Sea.	5	2	0	-8	2	McClure, Todd, Atl.	0	1	0	0	1
Hawkins, Artrell, Car.	1	0	0	0	0	McCollum, Andy, St.L	0	1	0	0	1
Hawthorne, Michael, G.B.	0	0	2	34	2	McCown, Josh, Ariz	12	2	0	0	2
Hayes, Gerald, Ariz	1	0	1	0	1	McDonald, Shaun, St.L	4	1	0	0	1

	Fum	Own Rec	Opp Rec	Yards	Tot Rec
McFarland, Anthony, T.B.	0	0	1	0	1
McKie, Jason, Chi.	1	0	0	0	0
McKinnie, Bryant, Min.	0	1	0	0	1
McMahon, Mike, Det.	1	1	0	0	1
McMillon, Todd, Chi.	0	2	0	0	2
McNabb, Donovan, Phi.	8	1	0	-6	1
McQuarters, R.W., Chi.	5	1	1	3	2
Mikell, Quintin, Phi.	0	0	1	0	1
Minter, Mike, Car.	0	0	2	0	2
Mitchell, Qasim, Chi.	0	1	0	0	1
Moore, Rashad, Sea.	0	0	3	0	3
* Moore, Mewelde, Min.	0	1	0	0	1
Moorehead, Kindal, Car.	0	0	1	0	1
Morgan, Dan, Car.	0	0	2	0	2
Morton, Chad, Was.	0	1	0	0	1
Moss, Randy, Min.	1	0	0	0	0
Muhammad, Muhsin, Car.	3	1	0	0	1
Nall, Craig, G.B.	1	0	0	0	0
Nece, Ryan, T.B.	0	0	1	0	1
Nesbit, Jamar, N.O.	0	1	0	0	1
Nguyen, Dat, Dal.	0	0	1	9	1
Nutten, Tom, St.L	0	1	0	0	1
Ogbogu, Eric, Dal.	0	0	1	0	1
Ogunleye, Adewale, Chi.	0	0	1	7	1
Ohalete, Ifeanyi, Ariz	0	1	1	0	2
O'Neil, Keith, Dal.	0	0	1	0	1
Owens, Terrell, Phi.	2	0	0	0	0
Parrish, Tony, S.F.	0	0	1	8	1
Pathon, Jerome, N.O.	1	0	0	0	0
Peppers, Julius, Car.	0	0	1	60	1
Peterson, Julian, S.F.	1	0	0	0	0
Petitgout, Luke, NY-G	0	1	0	0	1
* Pickett, Cody, S.F.	1	0	0	0	0
Pierce, Antonio, Was.	0	0	2	2	2
Pinner, Artose, Det.	0	1	0	0	1
Pittman, Michael, T.B.	6	0	0	0	0
Player, Scott, Ariz	1	1	0	0	1
Ponder, Willie, NY-G	1	0	0	0	0
Portis, Clinton, Was.	5	2	0	0	2
Quinn, Jonathan, Chi.	2	0	0	0	0
Raiola, Dominic, Det.	0	1	0	0	1
Ramsey, Patrick, Was.	6	1	0	-5	1
Rasheed, Saleem, S.F.	0	0	1	0	1
Rattay, Tim, S.F.	11	2	0	-8	2
Redding, Cory, Det.	0	0	2	0	2
* Reeves, Jacques, Dal.	0	0	1	0	1
Riley, Victor, N.O.	0	1	0	0	1
Rivers, Marcellus, NY-G	1	2	0	0	2
Robertson, Jamal, S.F.	3	0	0	0	0
Robinson, Marcus, Min.	1	0	0	0	0
Rogers, Shaun, Det.	0	0	1	0	1
Rossum, Allen, Atl.	2	1	0	0	1
Royal, Robert, Was.	0	1	0	0	1
Rucker, Mike, Car.	0	0	1	0	1
Runyan, Jon, Phi.	0	1	0	0	1
Russell, Brian, Min.	0	0	1	0	1
* Ryan, Sean, Dal.	0	1	0	1	1
Saipaia, Blaine, St.L	0	1	0	0	1
Samuels, Chris, Was.	0	2	0	0	2
* Schaub, Matt, Atl.	1	0	0	0	0
Schroeder, Bill, T.B.	2	1	0	0	1
Scobey, Josh, Ariz	1	1	0	0	1
Scott, Bryan, Atl.	0	0	1	1	1
* Scott, Darrion, Min.	0	0	2	0	2
Scott, Ian, Chi.	0	0	1	9	1
Scott, Lynn, Dal.	0	0	1	26	1
Shaffer, Kevin, Atl.	0	1	0	0	1
Sharper, Darren, G.B.	0	0	1	15	1
Shiancoe, Visanthe, NY-G	0	1	0	0	1
Shockey, Jeremy, NY-G	1	0	0	0	0
Short, Brandon, Car.	0	1	0	0	1
Simms, Chris, T.B.	3	1	0	0	1
Simoneau, Mark, Phi.	0	0	1	7	1
Smart, Rod, Car.	1	0	0	0	0
Smith, Brady, Atl.	0	0	2	0	2
Smith, Derek M., S.F.	0	0	2	46	2
Smith, Emmitt, Ariz	4	2	0	4	2
Smith, Onterrio, Min.	2	1	0	0	1
* Smith, Will, N.O.	0	0	1	-1	1
Smoot, Fred, Was.	0	0	1	0	1
* Snee, Chris, NY-G	0	3	0	0	3
Spires, Greg, T.B.	0	0	2	0	2
Stallworth, Donte', N.O.	0	1	0	0	1
Starks, Duane, Ariz	0	0	2	2	2
Stecker, Aaron, N.O.	1	0	0	-14	0
* Steele, Ben, G.B.	0	1	0	0	1
* Stepanovich, Alex, Ariz	0	2	0	-4	2
Steussie, Todd, T.B.	0	1	0	0	1
Strahan, Michael, NY-G	0	0	3	0	3
Strong, Mack, Sea.	2	0	0	0	0
Swinton, Reggie, Det.	1	0	0	0	0
Terrell, David, Chi.	1	0	0	0	0
Testaverde, Vinny, Dal.	8	4	0	-3	4
Thomas, Anthony, Chi.	1	1	0	0	1
* Thomas, Dontarrious, Min.	0	0	1	2	1
Thomas, Fred, N.O.	0	0	2	0	2
Thomas, Hollis, Phi.	0	0	1	0	1
Tillman, Charles, Chi.	0	1	0	4	1
Tinoisamoa, Pisa, St.L	0	0	1	10	1
Tobeck, Robbie, Sea.	0	1	0	0	1
Toomer, Amani, NY-G	1	0	0	0	0
* Torbor, Reggie, NY-G	0	0	1	0	1
* Udeze, Kenechi, Min.	0	0	1	-2	1
Umenyiora, Osi, NY-G	0	0	4	88	4
Urban, Jerheme, Sea.	1	0	0	0	0
* Vasher, Nathan, Chi.	0	0	1	12	1
Vick, Michael, Atl.	16	4	0	-5	4
Wade, John, T.B.	1	0	0	-2	0
Wade, Bobby, Chi.	2	0	0	0	0
Wahle, Mike, G.B.	0	1	0	0	1
Walker, Bracy, Det.	0	0	2	2	2
Walker, Javon, G.B.	2	1	0	11	1
Wallace, Al, Car.	0	0	1	0	1
Ward, Dedric, Dal.	1	1	0	0	1
* Ward, Derrick, NY-G	1	0	0	0	0
Ware, Kevin, S.F.	0	1	0	0	1
* Ware, Matt, Phi.	0	0	1	9	1
Warner, Kurt, NY-G	12	1	0	-3	1
Washington, Marcus, Was.	0	0	1	-4	1
Weiner, Todd, Atl.	0	1	0	0	1
Westbrook, Brian, Phi.	1	0	0	0	0
White, Dewayne, T.B.	0	0	1	0	1
Wiggins, Jermaine, Min.	1	1	0	0	1
Williams, Boo, N.O.	2	1	0	0	1
Williams, Jimmy, S.F.	0	0	1	0	1
Williams, Karl, Ariz	4	1	0	0	1
Williams, Kevin, Min.	0	0	3	77	3
Williams, Moe, Min.	0	1	0	0	1
* Williams, Roy, Det.	1	0	0	0	0
Willig, Matt, Car.	0	1	0	0	1
Wilson, Adrian, Ariz	0	0	2	35	2
Winborn, Jamie, S.F.	0	1	1	10	2
Winfield, Antoine, Min.	0	0	1	0	1
Wistrom, Grant, Sea.	0	0	1	0	1
Witherspoon, Will, Car.	0	0	1	0	1
Withrow, Cory, Min.	0	1	0	0	1

	Fum	Own Rec	Opp Rec	Yards	Tot Rec
Witten, Jason, Dal.	2	0	0	0	0
Woodard, Cedric, Sea.	0	0	1	0	1
Woods, LeVar, Ariz	0	1	0	0	1
* Wynn, Dexter, Phi.	1	1	0	0	1
Young, Bryant, S.F.	0	0	1	4	1
Young, Brian, N.O.	0	0	1	0	1
Zellner, Peppi, Ariz	0	0	1	0	1

*Player that was a rookie in 2004
Yards includes aborted plays, own recoveries, and opponents' recoveries.

AMERICAN FOOTBALL CONFERENCE—FUMBLES

	Fum	Own Rec	Fum OB	TD	Opp Rec	TD	Fum Yards	Tot Rec
Cincinnati	17	6	1	0	16	1	17	22
Indianapolis	19	10	2	0	17	1	67	27
N.Y. Jets	19	14	0	0	14	1	31	28
Kansas City	20	10	0	0	7	1	35	17
Pittsburgh	20	8	4	0	13	2	113	21
Houston	22	10	2	0	8	3	155	18
Denver	23	11	4	0	8	0	3	19
Jacksonville	23	9	3	0	11	0	-41	20
Oakland	23	9	1	0	9	0	7	18
New England	24	9	2	0	16	3	85	25
Baltimore	26	13	1	1	13	1	127	26
Buffalo	26	13	1	0	15	0	-11	28
San Diego	27	15	2	0	10	0	20	25
Cleveland	32	10	3	0	13	0	-55	23
Tennessee	33	19	2	0	12	1	105	31
Miami	42	23	3	0	10	1	24	33
AFC Total	396	189	31	1	192	15	682	381
AFC Average	24.8	11.8	1.9	0.1	12.0	0.9	42.6	23.8

NATIONAL FOOTBALL CONFERENCE—FUMBLES

	Fum	Own Rec	Fum OB	TD	Opp Rec	TD	Fum Yards	Tot Rec
Detroit	12	5	0	0	10	0	-4	15
Philadelphia	17	5	1	0	11	0	11	16
Seattle	19	8	2	0	12	0	10	20
Minnesota	20	10	1	0	11	1	35	21
Washington	20	10	0	0	8	0	-24	18
Green Bay	22	10	2	0	7	3	118	17
Carolina	23	11	1	0	12	1	48	23
New Orleans	23	13	0	0	20	1	34	33
Atlanta	26	11	1	0	13	1	0	24
Dallas	26	11	1	0	9	0	25	20
St. Louis	27	8	2	0	9	3	172	17
N.Y. Giants	29	17	1	0	14	2	137	31
Tampa Bay	32	11	3	0	11	2	50	22
San Francisco	33	14	0	0	12	2	130	26
Arizona	34	18	5	0	15	1	40	33
Chicago	35	13	1	0	12	1	135	25
NFC Total	398	175	21	0	186	18	917	361
NFC Average	24.9	10.9	1.3	0.0	11.6	1.1	57.3	22.6
NFL Total	794	364	52	1	378	33	1599	742
NFL Average	24.8	11.4	1.6	0.0	11.8	1.0	50.0	23.2

SACKS

MOST SACKS

AFC: 16.0 Dwight Freeney, Indianapolis
NFC: 14.5 Bertrand Berry, Arizona

MOST SACKS, GAME

NFC: 4.0 Alex Brown, Chicago at New York Giants, November 7
4.0 Bertrand Berry, Arizona vs. New York Giants, November 14
4.0 Kabeer Gbaja-Biamila, Green Bay at Chicago, January 2
AFC: 3.0 Kenard Lang, Cleveland vs. Baltimore, September 12
3.0 John Abraham, New York Jets vs. Buffalo, October 10
3.0 Joey Porter, Pittsburgh vs. New England, October 31
3.0 Robert Mathis, Indianapolis vs. Houston, November 14
3.0 Kevin Carter, Tennessee vs. Chicago, November 14 - (OT)
3.0 Lawyer Milloy, Buffalo vs. St. Louis, November 21
3.0 Jason Taylor, Miami at San Francisco, November 28
3.0 Dwight Freeney, Indianapolis vs. Tennessee, December 5
3.0 Dwight Freeney, Indianapolis at Houston, December 12
3.0 Reggie Hayward, Denver at Tennessee, December 25
3.0 Steve Foley, San Diego at Indianapolis, December 26 - (OT)
3.0 Shaun Ellis, New York Jets at St. Louis, January 2 - (OT)

AFC: BALTIMORE, 10.5, Terrell Suggs; BUFFALO, 8.0, Aaron Schobel; CINCINNATI, 8.0, Justin Smith; CLEVELAND, 8.0, Ebenezer Ekuban; DENVER, 10.5, Reggie Hayward; HOUSTON, 5.5, Kailee Wong; INDIANAPOLIS, 16.0, Dwight Freeney; JACKSONVILLE, 5.5, Greg Favors, John Henderson; KANSAS CITY, 9.0, *Jared Allen; MIAMI, 9.5, Jason Taylor; NEW ENGLAND, 9.5, Willie McGinest; N.Y. JETS, 11.0, Shaun Ellis; OAKLAND, 4.0, *Tommy Kelly; PITTSBURGH, 8.0, Aaron Smith; SAN DIEGO, 10.0, Steve Foley; TENNESSEE, 6.0, Kevin Carter

NFC: ARIZONA, 14.5, Bertrand Berry; ATLANTA, 13.0, Patrick Kerney; CAROLINA, 11.0, Julius Peppers; CHICAGO, 6.0, Alex Brown; DALLAS, 9.0, Greg Ellis; DETROIT, 11.5, James Hall; GREEN BAY, 13.5, Kabeer Gbaja-Biamila; MINNESOTA, 11.5, Kevin Williams; NEW ORLEANS, 11.0, Darren Howard; N.Y. GIANTS, 7.0, Osi Umenyiora; PHILADELPHIA, 7.5, Jevon Kearse; ST. LOUIS, 8.5, Bryce Fisher; SAN FRANCISCO, 6.0, John Engelberger; SEATTLE, 8.5, Chike Okeafor; TAMPA BAY, 12.0, Simeon Rice; WASHINGTON, 6.0, Cornelius Griffin, Shawn Springs

TEAM CHAMPION

NFC:	48	Atlanta
AFC:	45	Buffalo
	45	Indianapolis
	45	New England

NFL TOP TEN LEADERS—SACKS

	Sacks
Freeney, Dwight, Ind.	16.0
Berry, Bertrand, Ariz	14.5
Gbaja-Biamila, Kabeer, G.B.	13.5
Kerney, Patrick, Atl.	13.0
Rice, Simeon, T.B.	12.0
Coleman, Rod, Atl.	11.5
Hall, James, Det.	11.5
Williams, Kevin, Min.	11.5
Ellis, Shaun, NYJ	11.0
Howard, Darren, N.O.	11.0
Johnstone, Lance, Min.	11.0
Peppers, Julius, Car.	11.0

AMERICAN FOOTBALL CONFERENCE—SACKS

	Sacks	Yards
Buffalo	45	319
Indianapolis	45	340
New England	45	311
Kansas City	41	250
Pittsburgh	41	225
Baltimore	39	264
Denver	38	266
Cincinnati	37	257
Jacksonville	37	217
N.Y. Jets	37	220
Miami	36	223
Cleveland	32	190
Tennessee	32	220
San Diego	29	142
Oakland	25	182
Houston	24	161
AFC Total	583	3787
AFC Average	36.4	236.7

NATIONAL FOOTBALL CONFERENCE—SACKS

	Sacks	Yards
Atlanta	48	312
Philadelphia	47	263
Tampa Bay	45	264
Green Bay	40	280
N.Y. Giants	40	250
Washington	40	245
Minnesota	39	234
Arizona	38	229
Detroit	38	222
New Orleans	37	207
Seattle	36	218
Chicago	35	173
Carolina	34	225
St. Louis	34	241
Dallas	33	197
San Francisco	29	194
NFC Total	613	3754
NFC Average	38.3	234.6
League Total	1196	7541
League Average	37.4	235.7

AFC—INDIVIDUAL SACKS

	Sacks
Freeney, Dwight, Ind.	16.0
Ellis, Shaun, NYJ	11.0
Hayward, Reggie, Den.	10.5
Mathis, Robert, Ind.	10.5
Suggs, Terrell, Bal.	10.5
Foley, Steve, S.D.	10.0
Abraham, John, NYJ	9.5
McGinest, Willie, N.E.	9.5
Taylor, Jason, Mia.	9.5
* Allen, Jared, K.C.	9.0
Ekuban, Ebenezer, Cle.	8.0
Schobel, Aaron, Buf.	8.0
Smith, Aaron, Pit.	8.0
Smith, Justin, Cin.	8.0
Thomas, Adalius, Bal.	8.0
Bowens, David, Mia.	7.0
Lang, Kenard, Cle.	7.0
Porter, Joey, Pit.	7.0
Brock, Raheem, Ind.	6.5
Clemons, Duane, Cin.	6.5
Carter, Kevin, Ten.	6.0
Haggans, Clark, Pit.	6.0
Douglas, Marques, Bal.	5.5
Favors, Greg, Jac.	5.5
Henderson, John, Jac.	5.5
Vrabel, Mike, N.E.	5.5
Wong, Kailee, Hou.	5.5
Adams, Sam, Buf.	5.0
Bulluck, Keith, Ten.	5.0
Colvin, Rosevelt, N.E.	5.0
Hicks, Eric, K.C.	5.0
Long, Rien, Ten.	5.0
Peterson, Mike, Jac.	5.0
Reagor, Montae, Ind.	5.0
Seymour, Richard, N.E.	5.0
Zgonina, Jeff, Mia.	5.0
Browning, John, K.C.	4.5
Fujita, Scott, K.C.	4.5
Kelsay, Chris, Buf.	4.5
* Starks, Randy, Ten.	4.5
Stroud, Marcus, Jac.	4.5
* Babin, Jason, Hou.	4.0
Dalton, Lional, K.C.	4.0
Edwards, Ron, Buf.	4.0
Green, Jarvis, N.E.	4.0
Hardy, Kevin, Cin.	4.0
* Kelly, Tommy, Oak.	4.0
Milloy, Lawyer, Buf.	4.0
* Phillips, Shaun, S.D.	4.0
Townsend, Deshea, Pit.	4.0
Warren, Gerard, Cle.	4.0
Weaver, Tony, Bal.	4.0
Williams, Jamal, S.D.	4.0
Bruschi, Tedy, N.E.	3.5
Ferguson, Jason, NYJ	3.5
Fletcher, London, Buf.	3.5
* Geathers, Robert, Cin.	3.5
* LaBoy, Travis, Ten.	3.5
* McCray, Bobby, Jac.	3.5
Romero, Dario, Mia.	3.5
Warren, Ty, N.E.	3.5
Denney, Ryan, Buf.	3.0
Farrior, James, Pit.	3.0
Foote, Larry, Pit.	3.0
Gildon, Jason, Jac.	3.0
Harrison, Rodney, N.E.	3.0
Johnson, Ellis, Den.	3.0
McKinley, Alvin, Cle.	3.0

	Sacks
Morris, Rob, Ind.	3.0
Palepoi, Anton, Den.	3.0
Robertson, Dewayne, NYJ	3.0
* Robinson, Dunta, Hou.	3.0
Spikes, Takeo, Buf.	3.0
Thornton, John, Cin.	3.0
Washington, Ted, Oak.	3.0
Barton, Eric, NYJ	2.5
Beisel, Monty, K.C.	2.5
Brayton, Tyler, Oak.	2.5
Coleman, Marco, Den.	2.5
Demps, Will, Bal.	2.5
Fatafehi, Mario, Den.	2.5
Hall, Carlos, Ten.	2.5
Sapp, Warren, Oak.	2.5
Stills, Gary, K.C.	2.5
Thompson, Chaun, Cle.	2.5
Williams, Pat, Buf.	2.5
Wilson, Al, Den.	2.5
Woodson, Charles, Oak.	2.5
Ayodele, Akin, Jac.	2.0
Baxter, Gary, Bal.	2.0
Clark, Danny, Oak.	2.0
* Coleman, Erik, NYJ	2.0
Crocker, Chris, Cle.	2.0
Elliss, Luther, Den.	2.0
Godfrey, Randall, S.D.	2.0
Grant, DeLawrence, Oak.	2.0
* Johnson, Landon, Cin.	2.0
Kennedy, Kenoy, Den.	2.0
Leber, Ben, S.D.	2.0
Lynch, John, Den.	2.0
McGee, Terrence, Buf.	2.0
* Odom, Antwan, Ten.	2.0
Payne, Seth, Hou.	2.0
Peek, Antwan, Hou.	2.0
* Pope, Derrick, Mia.	2.0
Powell, Carl, Cin.	2.0
Reed, Ed, Bal.	2.0
Reed, James, NYJ	2.0
Scioli, Brad, Ind.	2.0
Sharper, Jamie, Hou.	2.0
Sims, Ryan, K.C.	2.0
* Smith, Daryl, Jac.	2.0
Smith, Robaire, Hou.	2.0
Thomas, Zach, Mia.	2.0
* Vilma, Jonathan, NYJ	2.0
* Wilfork, Vince, N.E.	2.0
Williams, Chad, Bal.	2.0
* Williams, D.J., Den.	2.0
Williams, Jay, Mia.	2.0
* Williams, Madieu, Cin.	2.0
Banta-Cain, Tully, N.E.	1.5
Bartee, William, K.C.	1.5
* Colclough, Ricardo, Pit.	1.5
Gregg, Kelly, Bal.	1.5
Phifer, Roman, N.E.	1.5
Rogers, Tyrone, Cle.	1.5
Scott, DeQuincy, S.D.	1.5
Thomas, Bryan, NYJ	1.5
Asomugha, Nnamdi, Oak.	1.0
Barber, Shawn, K.C.	1.0
Barnes, Lionel, Jac.	1.0
Chukwurah, Patrick, Den.	1.0
Cooper, Jarrod, Oak.	1.0
Cooper, Deke, Jac.	1.0
Dingle, Adrian, S.D.	1.0
Doss, Mike, Ind.	1.0
Edwards, Antuan, Mia.	1.0

AFC

Player	Sacks
Edwards, Donnie, S.D.	1.0
Fisk, Jason, S.D.	1.0
Gbaja-Biamila, Akbar, Oak.	1.0
Grant, Deon, Jac.	1.0
* Greer, Jabari, Buf.	1.0
Griffith, Robert, Cle.	1.0
Hamilton, Bobby, Oak.	1.0
Harrison, James, Pit.	1.0
Haynesworth, Albert, Ten.	1.0
Herndon, Kelly, Den.	1.0
Hoke, Chris, Pit.	1.0
Irons, Grant, Oak.	1.0
Johnson, Raylee, Den.	1.0
Johnson, Ted, N.E.	1.0
Kiel, Terrence, S.D.	1.0
Kirschke, Travis, Pit.	1.0
Lewis, Ray, Bal.	1.0
Middlebrooks, Willie, Den.	1.0
Mitchell, Kawika, K.C.	1.0
Moore, Langston, Cin.	1.0
Myers, Michael, Cle.	1.0
* Olshansky, Igor, S.D.	1.0
O'Neal, Deltha, Cin.	1.0
Patterson, Elton, Jac.	1.0
Polamalu, Troy, Pit.	1.0
Polk, DaShon, Hou.	1.0
* Poole, Will, Mia.	1.0
Pope, Monsanto, Den.	1.0
Posey, Jeff, Buf.	1.0
Roye, Orpheus, Cle.	1.0
Schulters, Lance, Ten.	1.0
Seau, Junior, Mia.	1.0
* Siavii, Junior, K.C.	1.0
Simmons, Brian, Cin.	1.0
Spragan, Donnie, Den.	1.0
Surtain, Patrick, Mia.	1.0
* Thomas, Josh, Ind.	1.0
Thomas, Kevin, Buf.	1.0
Vincent, Troy, Buf.	1.0
von Oelhoffen, Kimo, Pit.	1.0
Webster, Nate, Cin.	1.0
Williams, Tank, Ten.	1.0
Williams, Willie, Pit.	1.0
Wire, Coy, Buf.	1.0
Woods, Jerome, K.C.	1.0
Wright, Kenny, Hou.	1.0
Cesaire, Jacques, S.D.	0.5
Clements, Nate, Buf.	0.5
Davis, Andra, Cle.	0.5
Holdman, Warrick, Cle.	0.5
Johnson, Tim, Oak.	0.5
Kriewaldt, Clint, Pit.	0.5
McGarrahan, Scott, Ten.	0.5
Meier, Rob, Jac.	0.5
Ransom, Derrick, Jac.	0.5
Walker, Gary, Hou.	0.5
Wilkerson, Jimmy, K.C.	0.5

*Player that was a rookie in 2004

NFC—INDIVIDUAL SACKS

Player	Sacks
Berry, Bertrand, Ariz	14.5
Gbaja-Biamila, Kabeer, G.B.	13.5
Kerney, Patrick, Atl.	13.0
Rice, Simeon, T.B.	12.0
Coleman, Rod, Atl.	11.5
Hall, James, Det.	11.5
Williams, Kevin, Min.	11.5
Howard, Darren, N.O.	11.0
Johnstone, Lance, Min.	11.0
Peppers, Julius, Car.	11.0
Grant, Charles, N.O.	10.5
Ellis, Greg, Dal.	9.0
Fisher, Bryce, St.L	8.5
Okeafor, Chike, Sea.	8.5
Spires, Greg, T.B.	8.0
Kearse, Jevon, Phi.	7.5
* Smith, Will, N.O.	7.5
Glover, La'Roi, Dal.	7.0
Little, Leonard, St.L	7.0
Umenyiora, Osi, NY-G	7.0
Cochran, Antonio, Sea.	6.5
Brown, Alex, Chi.	6.0
Engelberger, John, S.F.	6.0
Griffin, Cornelius, Was.	6.0
Rayburn, Sam, Phi.	6.0
Smith, Brady, Atl.	6.0
Springs, Shawn, Was.	6.0
White, Dewayne, T.B.	6.0
Simon, Corey, Phi.	5.5
Urlacher, Brian, Chi.	5.5
* Dansby, Karlos, Ariz	5.0
Lewis, Damione, St.L	5.0
Ogunleye, Adewale, Chi.	5.0
Robbins, Fred, NY-G	5.0
* Udeze, Kenechi, Min.	5.0
Ahanotu, Chidi, Mia.-T.B.	4.5
Edwards, Kalimba, Det.	4.5
Jenkins, Cullen, G.B.	4.5
Kampman, Aaron, G.B.	4.5
Ogbogu, Eric, Dal.	4.5
Pace, Calvin, Ariz	4.5
Walker, Darwin, Phi.	4.5
Washington, Marcus, Was.	4.5
Winborn, Jamie, S.F.	4.5
Fields, Mark, Car.	4.0
Jackson, Tyoka, St.L	4.0
Rogers, Shaun, Det.	4.0
Strahan, Michael, NY-G	4.0
Bernard, Rocky, Sea.	3.5
Buckner, Brentson, Car.	3.5
Davis, James, Det.	3.5
* Dockett, Darnell, Ariz	3.5
* Harris, Tommie, Chi.	3.5
Newman, Keith, Min.	3.5
Quarles, Shelton, T.B.	3.5
Roman, Mark, G.B.	3.5
Rucker, Mike, Car.	3.5
Warner, Ron, Was.	3.5
Wistrom, Grant, Sea.	3.5
Barber, Ronde, T.B.	3.0
Barnett, Nick, G.B.	3.0
Brooks, Derrick, T.B.	3.0
Brown, Sheldon, Phi.	3.0
Clemons, Chris, Was.	3.0
Dawkins, Brian, Phi.	3.0
DeVries, Jared, Det.	3.0
Dixon, Tony, Dal.	3.0
Douglas, Hugh, Phi.	3.0
Hall, Travis, Atl.	3.0
McFarland, Anthony, T.B.	3.0
Redding, Cory, Det.	3.0
* Torbor, Reggie, NY-G	3.0
Wiley, Marcellus, Dal.	3.0
* Wilson, Gibril, NY-G	3.0
Witherspoon, Will, Car.	3.0
Wynn, Renaldo, Was.	3.0
Young, Bryant, S.F.	3.0
Boone, Alfonso, Chi.	2.5
Brooking, Keith, Atl.	2.5
Burgess, Derrick, Phi.	2.5
Evans, Demetric, Was.	2.5
Hillenmeyer, Hunter, Chi.	2.5
Mixon, Kenny, Min.	2.5
Peterson, Julian, S.F.	2.5
Scott, Bryan, Atl.	2.5
Truluck, R-Kal, G.B.	2.5
* Williams, Demorrio, Atl.	2.5
Young, Brian, N.O.	2.5
Alexander, Brent, NY-G	2.0
Archuleta, Adam, St.L	2.0
Bell, Marcus, Det.	2.0
Bowen, Matt, Was.	2.0
Bryant, Tony, N.O.	2.0
Carpenter, Dwaine, S.F.	2.0
* Carroll, Ahmad, G.B.	2.0
Carter, Andre, S.F.	2.0
Greisen, Nick, NY-G	2.0
Hamlin, Ken, Sea.	2.0
Haynes, Michael, Chi.	2.0
Hunt, Cletidus, G.B.	2.0
Jasper, Ed, Atl.	2.0
Joseph, William, NY-G	2.0
Legree, Lance, NY-G	2.0
* Lewis, Alex, Det.	2.0
McDougle, Jerome, Phi.	2.0
Minter, Mike, Car.	2.0
Moore, Rashad, Sea.	2.0
Moorehead, Kindal, Car.	2.0
Morgan, Dan, Car.	2.0
Pickett, Ryan, St.L	2.0
Polley, Tommy, St.L	2.0
Salave'a, Joe, Was.	2.0
Scott, Ian, Chi.	2.0
* Watson, Courtney, N.O.	2.0
Zellner, Peppi, Ariz	2.0
Azumah, Jerry, Chi.	1.5
Green, Michael, Chi.	1.5
Hovan, Chris, Min.	1.5
Marshall, Lemar, Was.	1.5
Simoneau, Mark, Phi.	1.5
Smith, Derek M., S.F.	1.5
Stewart, Matt, Atl.	1.5
Tinoisamoa, Pisa, St.L	1.5
Wilkinson, Dan, Det.	1.5
Allen, Kenderick, NY-G	1.0
Allen, Will, NY-G	1.0
Arrington, LaVar, Was.	1.0
Beasley, Aaron, Atl.	1.0
* Bockwoldt, Colby, N.O.	1.0
* Boulware, Michael, Sea.	1.0
* Bradley, Jon, T.B.	1.0
Brown, Tony, S.F.	1.0
Brown, Chad, Sea.	1.0
Claiborne, Chris, Min.	1.0
Coleman, Kenyon, Dal.	1.0
Cooper, Chris, S.F.	1.0
Daniels, Phillip, Was.	1.0

	Sacks
Darling, James, Ariz	1.0
Davis, Russell, Ariz	1.0
Diggs, Na'il, G.B.	1.0
* Duckett, Damane, NY-G	1.0
Emmons, Carlos, NY-G	1.0
Flowers, Erik, St.L	1.0
* Glymph, Junior, Atl.	1.0
Green, Jamaal, Phi.	1.0
Haley, Jermaine, Was.	1.0
Hand, Norman, NY-G	1.0
Hanson, Joselio, S.F.	1.0
* Hargrove, Anthony, St.L	1.0
Harris, Quentin, Ariz	1.0
Henderson, E.J., Min.	1.0
Hill, Renaldo, Ariz	1.0
Huff, Orlando, Sea.	1.0
Hunter, Pete, Dal.	1.0
Idonije, Israel, Chi.	1.0
Jackson, Grady, G.B.	1.0
Jenkins, Kris, Car.	1.0
* Johnson, Spencer, Min.	1.0
* Jones, Nate, Dal.	1.0
Jordan, Omari, Car.	1.0
Kacyvenski, Isaiah, Sea.	1.0
Kolodziej, Ross, Ariz	1.0
* Koutouvides, Niko, Sea.	1.0
Lee, James, G.B.	1.0
* Lehman, Teddy, Det.	1.0
Leverette, Otis, S.F.	1.0
Lewis, Kevin, NY-G	1.0
* Maxwell, Jim, NY-G	1.0
Mitchell, Brandon, Sea.	1.0
Moore, Brandon, S.F.	1.0
Nguyen, Dat, Dal.	1.0
Noble, Brandon, Was.	1.0
Phillips, Jermaine, T.B.	1.0
Pierce, Antonio, Was.	1.0
Pritchett, Kelvin, Det.	1.0
Reese, Ike, Phi.	1.0
Rossum, Allen, Atl.	1.0
Scott, Lynn, Dal.	1.0
Sheppard, Lito, Phi.	1.0
Starks, Duane, Ariz	1.0
* Taylor, Sean, Was.	1.0
Thompson, Raynoch, Ariz	1.0
Trotter, Jeremiah, Phi.	1.0
Trufant, Marcus, Sea.	1.0
* Tubbs, Marcus, Sea.	1.0
Ulbrich, Jeff, S.F.	1.0
Walker, Bracy, Det.	1.0
Wallace, Al, Car.	1.0
Washington, Keith, NY-G	1.0
Wayne, Nate, Phi.	1.0
White, Tracy, Sea.	1.0
* Williams, Corey, G.B.	1.0
Williams, Jimmy, S.F.	1.0
Williams, Tyrone, Dal.	1.0
Wilson, Adrian, Ariz	1.0
Woodard, Cedric, Sea.	1.0
Worrell, Cameron, Chi.	1.0
* Wynn, Dexter, Phi.	1.0
Briggs, Lance, Chi.	0.5
Carson, Leonardo, Dal.	0.5
Gold, Ian, T.B.	0.5
Gooch, Jeff, T.B.	0.5
* Hall, DeAngelo, Atl.	0.5
* Johnson, Tank, Chi.	0.5
Jones, Dhani, Phi.	0.5
Macklin, David, Ariz	0.5

	Sacks
Martin, Steve, Min.	0.5
Navies, Hannibal, G.B.	0.5
Parrish, Tony, S.F.	0.5
Sullivan, Johnathan, N.O.	0.5
* Thomas, Dontarrious, Min.	0.5
Wiley, Chuck, NY-G	0.5
Williams, Davern, NY-G	0.5

*Player that was a rookie in 2004

2004 NFL PAID ATTENDANCE BREAKDOWN

	Games	Attendance	Average
NFL Preseason Total	65	3,918,848	60,290
NFL Regular-Season Total	256	17,000,811	66,409
NFL Postseason Total	12	788,965	65,747
NFL All Games	333	21,708,624	65,191

1.1-MILLION CLUB

During the 2004 season, 12 teams drew more than 1.1 million paid attendance home and away during the regular season. The Washington Redskins led the league for the fifth consecutive season by drawing 1,238,813 fans in 2004, and set an NFL home attendance record for the fifth year in a row with 707,920 fans.

Team	Total Paid Home Attendance	Total Paid Visiting Attendance	Total Paid Attendance
Washington	707,920	530,893	1,238,813
New York Giants	629,874	522,143	1,152,017
Kansas City	623,264	515,419	1,138,683
Miami	580,808	556,787	1,137,595
New York Jets	622,985	505,467	1,128,452
Cleveland	567,060	549,592	1,116,652
Denver	589,534	525,858	1,115,392
Carolina	577,019	536,514	1,113,533
New England	558,532	550,025	1,108,557
Baltimore	550,783	557,431	1,108,214
Atlanta	547,131	560,049	1,107,180
Green Bay	564,344	538,984	1,103,328

For complete year-by-year attendance records, see pages 615-616.

Inside the Numbers

GREATEST COMEBACKS IN NFL HISTORY
(Most Points Overcome To Win Game)

REGULAR SEASON GAMES

FROM 28 POINTS BEHIND TO WIN:
December 7, 1980, at San Francisco

New Orleans	14	21	0	0	0	— 35
San Francisco	0	7	14	14	3	— 38

- NO — Harris 33 pass from Manning (Ricardo kick)
- NO — Childs 21 pass from Manning (Ricardo kick)
- NO — Holmes 1 run (Ricardo kick)
- SF — Solomon 57 punt return (Wersching kick)
- NO — Holmes 1 run (Ricardo kick)
- NO — Harris 41 pass from Manning (Ricardo kick)
- SF — Montana 1 run (Wersching kick)
- SF — Clark 71 pass from Montana (Wersching kick)
- SF — Solomon 14 pass from Montana (Wersching kick)
- SF — Elliott 7 run (Wersching kick)
- SF — FG Wersching 36

FROM 26 POINTS BEHIND TO WIN:
September 21, 1997, at Buffalo

Indianapolis	14	12	0	9	— 35
Buffalo	0	10	6	21	— 37

- Ind — Bailey 10 pass from Harbaugh (Blanchard kick)
- Ind — Faulk 10 run (Blanchard kick)
- Ind — FG Blanchard 39
- Ind — FG Blanchard 36
- Ind — FG Blanchard 49
- Ind — FG Blanchard 22
- Buff — Johnson 16 pass from Collins (Christie kick)
- Buff — FG Christie 27
- Buff — A. Smith 15 run (2-pt attempt failed)
- Ind — FG Blanchard 25
- Buff — Early 4 pass from Collins (Christie kick)
- Buff — A. Smith 1 run (Christie kick)
- Buff — A. Smith 54 run (Christie kick)
- Ind — Harrison 2 pass from Justin (2-pt attempt failed)

FROM 25 POINTS BEHIND TO WIN:
November 8, 1987, at St. Louis

Tampa Bay	7	7	14	0	— 28
St. Louis	0	3	0	28	— 31

- TB — Carrier 5 pass from DeBerg (Igwebuike kick)
- TB — Carter 3 pass from DeBerg (Igwebuike kick)
- StL — FG Gallery 31
- TB — Smith 34 pass from DeBerg (Igwebuike kick)
- TB — Smith 3 run (Igwebuike kick)

- StL — Awalt 4 pass from Lomax (Gallery kick)
- StL — Noga 23 fumble recovery (Gallery kick)
- StL — J. Smith 11 pass from Lomax (Gallery kick)
- StL — J. Smith 17 pass from Lomax (Gallery kick)

FROM 24 POINTS BEHIND TO WIN:
October 27, 1946, at Washington

Philadelphia	0	0	14	14	— 28
Washington	10	14	0	0	— 24

- Wash — Rosato 2 run (Poillon kick)
- Wash — FG Poillon 28
- Wash — Rosato 4 run (Poillon kick)
- Wash — Lapka recovered fumble in end zone (Poillon kick)
- Phil — Steele 1 run (Lio kick)
- Phil — Pritchard 45 pass from Thompson (Lio kick)
- Phil — Steinke 7 pass from Thompson (Lio kick)
- Phil — Ferrante 30 pass from Thompson (Lio kick)

FROM 24 POINTS BEHIND TO WIN:
October 20, 1957, at Detroit

Baltimore	7	14	6	0	— 27
Detroit	0	3	7	21	— 31

- Balt — Mutscheller 15 pass from Unitas (Rechichar kick)
- Det — FG Martin 47
- Balt — Moore 72 pass from Unitas (Rechichar kick)
- Balt — Mutscheller 52 pass from Unitas (Rechichar kick)
- Balt — Moore 4 pass from Unitas (kick failed)
- Det — Junker 14 pass from Rote (Layne kick)
- Det — Cassady 26 pass from Layne (Layne kick)
- Det — Johnson 1 run (Layne kick)
- Det — Cassady 29 pass from Layne (Layne kick)

FROM 24 POINTS BEHIND TO WIN:
October 25, 1959, at Minneapolis

Philadelphia	0	0	21	7	— 28
Chicago Cardinals	7	10	7	0	— 24

- Cardinals — Crow 10 pass from Roach (Conrad kick)
- Cardinals — J. Hill 77 blocked field goal return (Conrad kick)
- Cardinals — FG Conrad 15
- Cardinals — Lane 37 interception return (Conrad kick)
- Phil — Barnes 1 run (Walston kick)
- Phil — McDonald 29 pass from Van Brocklin (Walston kick)
- Phil — Barnes 2 run (Walston kick)
- Phil — McDonald 22 pass from Van Brocklin (Walston kick)

FROM 24 POINTS BEHIND TO WIN:
October 23, 1960, at Denver

Boston	10	7	7	0	— 24
Denver	0	0	14	17	— 31

- Bos — FG Cappelletti 12

- Bos — Colclough 10 pass from Songin (Cappelletti kick)
- Bos — Wells 6 pass from Songin (Cappelletti kick)
- Bos — Miller 47 pass from Songin (Cappelletti kick)
- Den — Carmichael 21 pass from Tripucka (Mingo kick)
- Den — Jessup 19 pass from Tripucka (Mingo kick)
- Den — Carmichael 35 lateral from Taylor, pass from Tripucka (Mingo kick)
- Den — Taylor 8 pass from Tripucka (Mingo kick)
- Den — FG Mingo 9

FROM 24 POINTS BEHIND TO WIN:
December 15, 1974, at Miami

New England	21	3	0	3	— 27
Miami	0	17	7	10	— 34

- NE — Hannah recovered fumble in end zone (J. Smith kick)
- NE — Sanders 23 interception return (J. Smith kick)
- NE — Herron 4 pass from Plunkett (J. Smith kick)
- NE — FG J. Smith 46
- Mia — Nottingham 1 run (Yepremian kick)
- Mia — Baker 37 pass from Morrall (Yepremian kick)
- Mia — FG Yepremian 28
- Mia — Baker 46 pass from Morrall (Yepremian kick)
- NE — FG J. Smith 34
- Mia — Nottingham 2 run (Yepremian kick)
- Mia — FG Yepremian 40

FROM 24 POINTS BEHIND TO WIN:
December 4, 1977, at Minnesota

San Francisco	0	10	14	3	— 27
Minnesota	0	0	7	21	— 28

- SF — Delvin Williams 2 run (Wersching kick)
- SF — FG Wersching 31
- SF — Dave Williams 80 kickoff return (Wersching kick)
- SF — Delvin Williams 5 run (Wersching kick)
- Minn — McClanahan 15 pass from Lee (Cox kick)
- Minn — Rashad 8 pass from Kramer (Cox kick)
- Minn — Tucker 9 pass from Kramer (Cox kick)
- SF — FG Wersching 31
- Minn — S. White 69 pass from Kramer (Cox kick)

FROM 24 POINTS BEHIND TO WIN:
September 23, 1979, at Denver

Seattle	10	10	14	0	— 34
Denver	0	10	21	6	— 37

- Sea — FG Herrera 28
- Sea — Doornink 5 run (Herrera kick)
- Den — FG Turner 27

Sea — Doornink 5 run
(Herrera kick)
Den — Armstrong 2 run
(Turner kick)
Sea — FG Herrera 22
Sea — McCullum 13 pass from
Zorn (Herrera kick)
Sea — Smith 1 run (Herrera kick)
Den — Studdard 2 pass from Morton (Turner kick)
Den — Moses 11 pass from Morton (Turner kick)
Den — Upchurch 35 pass from
Morton (Turner kick)
Den — Lytle 1 run (kick failed)

FROM 24 POINTS BEHIND TO WIN:
September 23, 1979, at Cincinnati

Houston	0	10	17	0	3	—	30
Cincinnati	14	10	0	3	0	—	27

Cin — Johnson 1 run (Bahr kick)
Cin — Alexander 2 run (Bahr kick)
Cin — Johnson 1 run (Bahr kick)
Cin — FG Bahr 52
Hou — Burrough 35 pass from
Pastorini (Fritsch kick)
Hou — FG Fritsch 33
Hou — Campbell 8 run
(Fritsch kick)
Hou — Caster 22 pass from
Pastorini (Fritsch kick)
Hou — FG Fritsch 47
Cin — FG Bahr 55
Hou — FG Fritsch 29

FROM 24 POINTS BEHIND TO WIN:
November 22, 1982, at Los Angeles

San Diego	10	14	0	0	— 24
L.A. Raiders	0	7	14	7	— 28

SD — Benirschke 19
SD — Scales 29 pass from Fouts
(Benirschke kick)
SD — Muncie 2 run
(Benirschke kick)
SD — Muncie 1 run
(Benirschke kick)
Raiders — Christensen 1 pass from
Plunkett (Bahr kick)
Raiders — Allen 3 run (Bahr kick)
Raiders — Allen 6 run (Bahr kick)
Raiders — Hawkins 1 run (Bahr kick)

FROM 24 POINTS BEHIND TO WIN:
September 26, 1988, at Denver

L.A. Raiders	0	0	14	13	3	— 30
Denver	7	17	0	3	0	— 27

Den — Dorsett 1 run (Karlis kick)
Den — Dorsett 1 run (Karlis kick)
Den — Sewell 7 pass from Elway
(Karlis kick)
Den — FG Karlis 39
Raiders — Smith 40 pass from
Schroeder (Bahr kick)
Raiders — Smith 42 pass from
Schroeder (Bahr kick)
Raiders — FG Bahr 28
Raiders — Allen 4 run (Bahr kick)
Den — FG Karlis 25
Raiders — FG Bahr 44
Raiders — FG Bahr 35

FROM 24 POINTS BEHIND TO WIN:
December 6, 1992, at Tampa

L.A. Rams	0	3	21	7	— 31
Tampa Bay	6	21	0	0	— 27

TB — FG Murray 34
TB — FG Murray 47
TB — Armstrong 81 pass from
Testaverde (Murray kick)
TB — Jones 26 fumble recovery
(Murray kick)
Rams — FG Zendejas 18
TB — Carrier 10 pass from Testaverde (Murray kick)
Rams — Anderson 40 pass from
Everett (Zendejas kick)
Rams — Chadwick 27 pass from
Everett (Zendejas kick)
Rams— Lang 1 run (Zendejas kick)
Rams— Carter 8 pass from Everett
(Zendejas kick)

POSTSEASON GAMES

FROM 32 POINTS BEHIND TO WIN:
AFC First-Round Playoff Game
January 3, 1993, at Buffalo

Houston	7	21	7	3	0	— 38
Buffalo	3	0	28	7	3	— 41

Hou — Jeffires 3 pass from Moon
(Del Greco kick)
Buff — FG Christie 36
Hou — Slaughter 7 pass from Moon
(Del Greco kick)
Hou — Duncan 26 pass from Moon
(Del Greco kick)
Hou — Jeffires 27 pass from Moon
(Del Greco kick)
Hou — McDowell 58 interception
return (Del Greco kick)
Buff — Davis 1 run (Christie kick)
Buff — Beebe 38 pass from Reich
(Christie kick)
Buff — Reed 26 pass from Reich
(Christie kick)
Buff — Reed 18 pass from Reich
(Christie kick)
Buff — Reed 17 pass from Reich
(Christie kick)
Hou — FG Del Greco 26
Buff — FG Christie 32

FROM 24 POINTS BEHIND TO WIN:
NFC First-Round Playoff Game
January 5, 2003, at San Francisco

N.Y. Giants	7	21	10	0	— 38
San Francisco	7	7	8	17	— 39

SF — Owens 76 pass from Garcia
(Chandler kick)
NYG — Toomer 12 pass from
Collins (Bryant kick)
NYG — Shockey 2 pass from
Collins (Bryant kick)
SF — Barlow 1 run (Chandler
kick)
NYG — Toomer 8 pass from Collins
(Bryant kick)
NYG — Toomer 24 pass from
Collins (Bryant kick)
NYG — Barber 6 run (Bryant kick)
NYG — FG Bryant 21

SF — Owens 26 pass from Garcia
(Owens from Garcia)
SF — Garcia 14 run
(Owens from Garcia)
SF — Garcia 14 run
(Owens from Garcia)
SF — FG Chandler 25
SF — Streets 13 pass from Garcia
(2-pt attempt failed)

FROM 20 POINTS BEHIND TO WIN:
Western Conference Playoff Game
December 22, 1957, at San Francisco

Detroit	0	7	14	10	— 31
San Francisco	14	10	3	0	— 27

SF — Owens 34 pass from Tittle
(Soltau kick)
SF — McElhenny 47 pass from
Tittle (Soltau kick)
Det — Junker 4 pass from Rote
(Martin kick)
SF — Wilson 12 pass from Tittle
(Soltau kick)
SF — FG Soltau 25
SF — FG Soltau 10
Det — Tracy 2 run (Martin kick)
Det — Tracy 58 run (Martin kick)
Det — Gedman 3 run (Martin kick)
Det — FG Martin 14

FROM 18 POINTS BEHIND TO WIN:
NFC Divisional Playoff Game
December 23, 1972, at San Francisco

Dallas	3	10	0	17	— 30
San Francisco	7	14	7	0	— 28

SF — Washington 97 kickoff
return (Gossett kick)
Dall — FG Fritsch 37
SF — Schreiber 1 run
(Gossett kick)
SF — Schreiber 1 run
(Gossett kick)
Dall — FG Fritsch 45
Dall — Alworth 28 pass from
Morton (Fritsch kick)
SF — Schreiber 1 run
(Gossett kick)
Dall — FG Fritsch 27
Dall — Parks 20 pass from
Staubach (Fritsch kick)
Dall — Sellers 10 pass from
Staubach (Fritsch kick)

FROM 18 POINTS BEHIND TO WIN:
AFC Divisional Playoff Game
January 4, 1986, at Miami

Cleveland	7	7	7	0	— 21
Miami	3	0	14	7	— 24

Mia — FG Reveiz 51
Cle — Newsome 16 pass from
Kosar (Bahr kick)
Cle — Byner 21 run (Bahr kick)
Cle — Byner 66 run (Bahr kick)
Mia — Moore 6 pass from Marino
(Reveiz kick)
Mia — Davenport 31 run
(Reveiz kick)
Mia — Davenport 1 run
(Reveiz kick)

RECORDS FOR NFL TEAMS FOR MOST POINTS IN A GAME (REGULAR SEASON ONLY)

Note: When the record has been achieved more than once, only the most recent game is shown; summaries are listed in alphabetical order by conference. Bold face indicates team holding record.

BALTIMORE RAVENS
November 30, 2003, at Baltimore

San Francisco	3	3	0	0	— 6
Baltimore	7	17	0	20	— 44

TD: Balt—Terry Jones, Jamal Lewis, Ray Lewis, Marcus Robinson, Musa Smith. TD Passes: Balt—Anthony Wright 2. FG: Balt—Matt Stover 3; SF—Todd Peterson 2.

BUFFALO BILLS
September 18, 1966, at Buffalo

Miami	3	7	0	14	— 24
Buffalo	21	27	3	7	— 58

TD: Buff—Bobby Burnett 2, Butch Byrd 2, Jack Spikes 2, Bobby Crockett, Jack Kemp; Mia—Dave Kocourek, Bo Roberson, John Roderick. TD Passes: Buff—Jack Kemp, Daryle Lamonica; Mia—George Wilson 3. FG: Buff—Booth Lusteg; Mia—Gene Mingo.

CINCINNATI BENGALS
December 17, 1989, at Cincinnati

Houston	0	0	0	7	— 7
Cincinnati	21	10	21	9	— 61

TD: Cin—Eddie Brown 2, Eric Ball, James Brooks, Ira Hillary, Rodney Holman, Tim McGee, Craig Taylor; Hou—Lorenzo White. TD Passes: Cin—Boomer Esiason 4, Erik Wilhelm. FG: Cin—Jim Breech 2.

CLEVELAND BROWNS
November 7, 1954, at Cleveland

Washington	0	3	0	0	— 3
Cleveland	13	14	21	14	— 62

TD: Cle—Darrell Brewster 2, Mo Bassett, Ken Gorgal, Otto Graham, Dub Jones, Dante Lavelli, Curley Morrison. TD Passes: Cle—George Ratterman 3, Otto Graham; Wash—Vic Janowicz.

DENVER BRONCOS
October 6, 1963, at Denver

San Diego	13	7	0	14	— 34
Denver	3	14	9	24	— 50

TD: Den—Lionel Taylor 2, Goose Gonsoulin, Gene Prebola, Donnie Stone; SD—Keith Lincoln 2, Lance Alworth, Paul Lowe, Jacque MacKinnon. TD Passes: Den—John McCormick 3, John Hadl 2. FG: Den—Gene Mingo 5.

HOUSTON TEXANS
November 28, 2004 at Houston

Tennessee	14	7	0	0	— 21
Houston	3	7	14	7	— 31

TD: Tenn—Erron Kinney 2, Derrick Mason; Hou—Domanick Davis, Andre Johnson, Billy Miller, Jonathan Wells. TD Passes: Tenn—Steve McNair 3; Hou—David Carr 2. FG: Hou—Kris Brown.

INDIANAPOLIS COLTS
December 12, 1976, at Baltimore

Buffalo	3	3	7	7	— 20
Baltimore Colts	7	13	28	10	— 58

TD: Balt—Roger Carr, Raymond Chester, Glenn Doughty, Roosevelt Leaks, Derrel Luce, Lydell Mitchell, Howard Stevens; Buff—Bob Chandler, O.J. Simpson. TD Passes: Balt—Bert Jones 3; Buff—Gary Marangi. FG: Balt—Toni Linhart 3; Buff—George Jakowenko 2.

JACKSONVILLE JAGUARS
December 3, 2000, at Jacksonville

Cleveland	0	0	0	0	— 0
Jacksonville	3	17	21	7	— 48

TD: Jax—Fred Taylor 3, Keenan McCardell, Mark Brunell, Shyrone Stith. TD Passes: Jax—Mark Brunell. FG: Jax—Mike Hollis 2.

KANSAS CITY CHIEFS
September 7, 1963, at Denver

Kansas City	14	14	21	10	— 59
Denver	0	7	0	0	— 7

TD: KC—Chris Burford 2, Frank Jackson 2, Dave Grayson, Abner Haynes, Sherrill Headrick, Curtis McClinton; Den—Lionel Taylor. TD Passes: KC—Len Dawson 4, Curtis McClinton; Den—Mickey Slaughter. FG: KC—Tommy Brooker.

MIAMI DOLPHINS
November 24, 1977, at St. Louis

Miami	14	14	20	7	— 55
St. Louis Cardinals	7	0	0	7	— 14

TD: Mia—Nat Moore 3, Gary Davis, Duriel Harris, Leroy Harris, Benny Malone, Andre Tillman; StL—Ike Harris, Terry Metcalf. TD Passes: Mia—Bob Griese 6; StL—Jim Hart.

NEW ENGLAND PATRIOTS
September 9, 1979, at New England

New York Jets	3	0	0	0	— 3
New England	14	21	7	14	— 56

TD: NE—Harold Jackson 3, Stanley Morgan 2, Allan Clark, Andy Johnson, Don Westbrook. TD Passes: NE—Steve Grogan 5, Tom Owen. FG: NYJ—Pat Leahy.

NEW YORK JETS
November 17, 1985, at New York

Tampa Bay	14	7	7	0	— 28
New York Jets	17	24	14	7	— 62

TD: NYJ—Mickey Shuler 3, Johnny Hector 2, Tony Paige, Al Toon, Wesley Walker; TB—James Wilder 2, Kevin House, Calvin Magee. TD Passes: NYJ—Ken O'Brien 5; TB—Steve DeBerg 2. FG: NYJ—Pat Leahy 2.

OAKLAND RAIDERS
September 29, 2002 at Oakland

Tennessee	7	0	12	6	— 25
Oakland	21	10	7	14	— 52

TD: Oak—Tim Brown, Phillip Buchanon, Charlie Garner, Terry Kirby, Jerry Porter, Jim Rice, Rod Woodson; Tenn—Drew Bennett, Eddie George, Justin McCareins, John Simon. TD Passes: Oak—Rich Gannon 4; Tenn—Steve McNair 2. FG: Oak—Sebastian Janikowski.

PITTSBURGH STEELERS
November 30, 1952, at Pittsburgh

New York Giants	0	0	7	0	— 7
Pittsburgh	14	14	7	28	— 63

TD: Pitt—Lynn Chandnois 2, Dick Hensley 2, Jack Butler, George Hays, Ray Mathews, Ed Modzelewski, Elbie Nickel; NYG—Bill Stribling. TD Passes: Pitt—Jim Finks 4, Gary Kerkorian; NYG—Tom Landry.

SAN DIEGO CHARGERS
December 22, 1963, at San Diego

Denver	7	10	3	0	— 20
San Diego	10	16	10	22	— 58

TD: SD—Paul Lowe 2, Chuck Allen, Bobby Jackson, Dave Kocourek, Keith Lincoln, Jacque MacKinnon; Den—Billy Joe, Donnie Stone. TD Passes: SD—John Hadl, Tobin Rote; Den—Don Breaux. FG: SD—George Blair 3; Den—Gene Mingo 2.

TENNESSEE TITANS
December 9, 1990, at Houston

Cleveland	0	7	7	0	— 14
Houston Oilers	14	31	7	6	— 58

TD: Hou—Lorenzo White 4, Ernest Givins, Leonard Harris, Tony Jones, Terry Kinard; Cle—Eric Metcalf 2. TD Passes: Hou—Warren Moon 2, Cody Carlson; Cle—Bernie Kosar. FG: Hou—Teddy Garcia.

ARIZONA CARDINALS
November 13, 1949, at New York

Chicago Cardinals	7	31	14	13 —	65
New York Bulldogs	7	0	6	7 —	20

TD: Chi—Red Cochran 2, Pat Harder 2, Bill Dewell, Mel Kutner, Bob Ravensburg, Vic Schwall, Charlie Trippi; NY—Joe Golding, Frank Muehlheuser, Johnny Rauch. TD Passes: Chi—Paul Christman 3, Jim Hardy 3; NY—Bobby Layne. FG: Chi—Pat Harder.

ATLANTA FALCONS
September 16, 1973, at New Orleans

Atlanta	0	24	21	17 —	62
New Orleans	0	0	7	0 —	7

TD: Atl—Ken Burrow 2, Eddie Ray 2, Wes Chesson, Tom Hayes, Art Malone, Joe Profit; NO—Bill Butler. TD Passes: Atl—Dick Shiner 3, Bob Lee; NO—Archie Manning. FG: Atl—Nick Mike-Mayer 2.

CAROLINA PANTHERS
December 8, 2002, at Carolina

Cincinnati	7	10	14	0 —	31
Carolina	9	7	21	15 —	52

TD: Car—Steve Smith 3, Dee Brown, Muhsin Muhammad, Al Wallace, Wesley Walls; Cin—Peter Warrick 2, Jon Kitna, Takeo Spikes. TD Passes: Car—Rodney Peete 3; Cin—Jon Kitna 2. FG: Cin—Neil Rackers.

CHICAGO BEARS
December 7, 1980, at Chicago

Green Bay	0	7	0	0 —	7
Chicago	0	28	13	20 —	61

TD: Chi—Walter Payton 2, Brian Baschnagel, Robin Earl, Roland Harper, Willie McClendon, Len Walterscheid, Rickey Watts; GB—James Lofton. TD Passes: Chi—Vince Evans 3; GB—Lynn Dickey.

DALLAS COWBOYS
October 12, 1980, at Dallas

San Francisco	0	7	0	7 —	14
Dallas	14	24	14	7 —	59

TD: Dall—Drew Pearson 3, Ron Springs 2, Tony Dorsett, Billy Joe DuPree, Robert Newhouse; SF—Dwight Clark 2. TD Passes: Dall—Danny White 4; SF—Steve DeBerg 2. FG: Dall—Rafael Septien.

DETROIT LIONS
November 27, 1997, at Detroit

Chicago	14	6	0	0 —	20
Detroit	3	14	17	21 —	55

TD: Det—Herman Moore, Johnnie Morton, Ron Rivers, Barry Sanders 3, Tracy Scroggins; Chi—Raymont Harris, Ricky Proehl. TD Passes: Det—Scott Mitchell 2; Chi—Erik Kramer. FG: Det—Jason Hanson 2; Chi—Jeff Jaeger 2.

GREEN BAY PACKERS
October 7, 1945, at Milwaukee

Detroit	0	7	7	7 —	21
Green Bay	0	41	9	7 —	57

TD: GB—Don Hutson 4, Charley Brock, Irv Comp, Ted Fritsch, Clyde Goodnight; Det—Chuck Fenenbock, John Greene, Bob Westfall. TD Passes: GB—Tex McKay 4, Lou Brock, Irv Comp; Det—Dave Ryan.

MINNESOTA VIKINGS
October 18, 1970, at Minnesota

Dallas	3	3	0	7 —	13
Minnesota	14	20	17	3 —	54

TD: Minn—Clint Jones 2, Ed Sharockman 2, John Beasley, Dave Osborn; Dall—Calvin Hill. TD Pass: Minn—Gary Cuozzo. FG: Minn—Fred Cox 4; Dall—Mike Clark 2.

NEW ORLEANS SAINTS
November 21, 1976, at Seattle

New Orleans	3	17	28	3 —	51
Seattle	6	0	7	14 —	27

TD: NO—Bobby Douglass 2, Tony Galbreath, Chuck Muncie, Tom Myers, Elex Price; Sea—Sherman Smith 2, Steve Largent, Jim Zorn. TD Pass: Sea—Bill Munson. FG: NO—Rich Szaro 3.

NEW YORK GIANTS
November 26, 1972, at New York

Philadelphia	3	7	0	0 —	10
New York Giants	14	24	10	14 —	62

TD: NYG—Don Herrmann 2, Ron Johnson 2, Bob Tucker 2, Randy Johnson; Phil—Harold Jackson. TD Passes: NYG—Norm Snead 3, Randy Johnson 2; Phil—John Reaves. FG: NYG—Pete Gogolak 2; Phil—Tom Dempsey.

PHILADELPHIA EAGLES
November 6, 1934, at Philadelphia

Cincinnati Reds	0	0	0	0 —	0
Philadelphia	26	6	12	20 —	64

TD: Phil—Joe Carter 3, Swede Hanson 3, Marvin Ellstrom, Roger Kirkman, Ed Matesic, Ed Storm. TD Passes: Phil—Ed Matesic 2, Albert Weiner 2, Marvin Elstrom.

ST. LOUIS RAMS
October 22, 1950, at Los Angeles

Baltimore	13	0	7	7 —	27
Los Angeles Rams	21	14	14	21 —	70

TD: LA—Bob Boyd 2, Vitamin T. Smith 2, Tom Fears, Elroy (Crazylegs) Hirsch, Dick Hoerner, Ralph Pasquariello, Dan Towler, Bob Waterfield; Balt—Chet Mutryn 2, Adrian Burk, Billy Stone. TD Passes: LA—Norm Van Brocklin 2, Bob Waterfield 2, Glenn Davis; Balt—Adrian Burk 3.

SAN FRANCISCO 49ERS
October 18, 1992, at San Francisco

Atlanta	7	3	0	7 —	17
San Francisco	21	21	14	0 —	56

TD: SF—Jerry Rice 3, Ricky Watters 3, Brent Jones, Tom Rathman; Atl—Michael Haynes, Jason Phillips. TD Passes: SF—Steve Young 3; Atl—Chris Miller, Wade Wilson. FG: Atl—Norm Johnson.

SEATTLE SEAHAWKS
October 30, 1977, at Seattle

Buffalo	3	0	7	7 —	17
Seattle	14	28	7	7 —	56

TD: Sea—Steve Largent 2, Duke Fergerson, Al Hunter, David Sims, Sherman Smith, Don Testerman, Jim Zorn; Buff—Joe Ferguson, John Kimbrough. TD Passes: Sea—Jim Zorn 4; Buff—Joe Ferguson. FG: Buff—Carson Long.

TAMPA BAY BUCCANEERS
December 23, 2001, at Tampa Bay

New Orleans	0	0	7	14 —	21
Tampa Bay	17	13	3	15 —	48

TD: TB—Mike Alstott, Ronde Barber, Warrick Dunn, Dave Moore, Karl Williams; NO—Joe Horn 2, Eddie Williams. TD Passes: TB—Brad Johnson 3; NO—Aaron Brooks 3. FG: TB—Martin Gramatica 4.

WASHINGTON REDSKINS
November 27, 1966, at Washington

New York Giants	0	14	14	13 —	41
Washington	13	21	14	24 —	72

TD: Wash—A.D. Whitfield 3, Brig Owens 2, Charley Taylor 2, Rickie Harris, Joe Don Looney, Bobby Mitchell; NYG—Allen Jacobs, Homer Jones, Dan Lewis, Joe Morrison, Aaron Thomas, Gary Wood. TD Passes: Wash—Sonny Jurgensen 3; NYG—Gary Wood 2, Tom Kennedy. FG: Wash—Charlie Gogolak.

RECORDS OF NFL TEAMS SINCE 1970 AFL-NFL MERGER

AFC	W	L	T	Pct.	Division Titles	Playoff Berths	Postseason Record	Super Bowl Record
Miami	338	196	2	.633	12	21	20-19	2-3
Pittsburgh	322	212	2	.603	17	21	24-17	4-1
Oakland	313	217	6	.590	12	18	22-15	3-1
Denver	310	220	6	.584	9	16	16-14	2-4
Jacksonville**	82	78	0	.513	2	4	4-4	0-0
Kansas City	269	260	7	.508	5	10	3-10	0-0
Baltimore***	72	71	1	.503	1	3	5-2	1-0
New England	265	271	0	.494	7	12	15-9	3-2
Tennessee	258	276	2	.483	4	14	12-14	0-1
Buffalo	257	277	2	.481	7	13	12-13	0-4
Cleveland+	224	261	3	.462	6	11	4-11	0-0
Indianapolis	243	291	2	.455	8	13	9-12	1-0
San Diego	234	297	5	.441	6	8	6-8	0-1
N.Y. Jets	235	299	2	.440	2	9	6-9	0-0
Cincinnati	235	301	0	.438	5	7	5-7	0-2
Houston****	16	32	0	.333	0	0	0-0	0-0

NFC	W	L	T	Pct.	Division Titles	Playoff Berths	Postseason Record	Super Bowl Record
Dallas	316	220	0	.590	15	23	31-18	5-3
San Francisco	314	219	3	.589	17	21	25-16	5-0
Minnesota	310	224	2	.580	14	22	16-22	0-3
Washington	301	233	2	.564	6	14	19-11	3-2
St. Louis	293	239	4	.551	11	19	16-18	1-2
Philadelphia	271	258	7	.512	6	15	12-15	0-2
Green Bay	268	260	8	.507	7	12	12-11	1-1
Chicago	259	276	1	.484	7	11	7-10	1-0
N.Y. Giants	253	280	3	.475	5	10	12-8	2-1
Seattle*	214	238	0	.473	3	7	3-7	0-0
Carolina**	71	89	0	.444	2	2	4-2	0-1
Detroit	231	301	4	.435	3	9	1-9	0-0
Atlanta	225	306	5	.424	3	8	6-8	0-1
New Orleans	222	310	4	.417	2	5	1-5	0-0
Arizona	214	316	6	.404	2	4	1-4	0-0
Tampa Bay*	172	279	1	.382	4	8	6-7	1-0

*Entered NFL in 1976.
**Entered NFL in 1995.
***Entered NFL in 1996.
****Entered NFL in 2002.
+Did not play 1996-98.
Oakland totals include L.A. Raiders, 1982-1994.
Tennessee totals include Houston, 1970-1996.
Indianapolis totals include Baltimore, 1970-1983.
St. Louis totals include L.A. Rams, 1970-1994.
Arizona totals include St. Louis, 1970-1987, and Phoenix, 1988-1993.
Tie games before 1972 are not calculated in won-lost percentage.

HOME RECORDS OF NFL TEAMS SINCE 1970 AFL-NFL MERGER

AFC	W	L	T	Pct.
Miami	194	72	1	.728
Pittsburgh	193	74	1	.722
Denver	190	75	4	.715
Oakland	174	92	2	.654
Baltimore***	44	27	1	.618
Kansas City	163	101	3	.617
Jacksonville**	49	31	0	.613
New England	155	113	0	.578
Buffalo	151	117	1	.563
Tennessee	148	119	1	.554
Cincinnati	146	122	0	.545
Cleveland+	123	118	2	.510
San Diego	135	130	2	.509
Indianapolis	129	137	2	.485
N.Y. Jets	125	141	1	.470
Houston****	8	16	0	.333

NFC	W	L	T	Pct.
Dallas	183	85	0	.683
Minnesota	182	86	1	.678
Washington	171	94	2	.645
San Francisco	168	98	2	.631
Green Bay	162	101	5	.614
St. Louis	163	103	2	.613
Chicago	154	113	1	.576
Philadelphia	152	114	3	.571
Detroit	150	117	1	.562
Seattle*	127	100	0	.559
N.Y. Giants	141	127	1	.526
Atlanta	136	132	1	.507
Carolina**	40	40	0	.500
Arizona	127	137	3	.481
Tampa Bay*	107	118	2	.476
New Orleans	120	147	1	.449

*Entered NFL in 1976.
**Entered NFL in 1995.
***Entered NFL in 1996.
****Entered NFL in 2002.
+Did not play 1996-98.
Oakland totals include L.A. Raiders, 1982-1994.
Tennessee totals include Houston, 1970-1996.
Indianapolis totals include Baltimore, 1970-1983.
St. Louis totals include L.A. Rams, 1970-1994.
Arizona totals include St. Louis, 1970-1987, and Phoenix, 1988-1993.
Tie games before 1972 are not calculated in won-lost percentage.

ROAD RECORDS OF NFL TEAMS SINCE 1970 AFL-NFL MERGER

AFC	W	L	T	Pct.
Miami	144	124	1	.537
Oakland	139	125	4	.526
Pittsburgh	129	138	1	.483
Denver	120	145	2	.453
Indianapolis	114	154	0	.425
Cleveland+	101	143	1	.414
Jacksonville**	33	47	0	.413
Tennessee	110	157	1	.412
N.Y. Jets	110	158	1	.411
New England	110	158	0	.410
Kansas City	106	159	4	.401
Buffalo	106	160	1	.398
Baltimore***	28	44	0	.389
San Diego	99	167	3	.373
Houston****	8	16	0	.333
Cincinnati	89	179	0	.332

NFC	W	L	T	Pct.
San Francisco	146	121	1	.547
Dallas	133	135	0	.496
St. Louis	130	136	2	.489
Washington	130	139	0	.483
Minnesota	128	138	1	.481
Philadelphia	119	144	4	.453
N.Y. Giants	112	153	2	.423
Green Bay	106	159	3	.401
Chicago	105	163	0	.392
Carolina**	31	49	0	.388
Seattle*	87	138	0	.387
New Orleans	102	163	3	.385
Atlanta	89	174	4	.339
Arizona	87	179	3	.328
Detroit	81	184	3	.307
Tampa Bay*	65	161	0	.288

*Entered NFL in 1976.
**Entered NFL in 1995.
***Entered NFL in 1996.
****Entered NFL in 2002.
+Did not play 1996-98.
Oakland totals include L.A. Raiders, 1982-1994.
Tennessee totals include Houston, 1970-1996.
Indianapolis totals include Baltimore, 1970-1983.
St. Louis totals include L.A. Rams, 1970-1994.
Arizona totals include St. Louis, 1970-1987, and Phoenix, 1988-1993.
Tie games before 1972 are not calculated in won-lost percentage.

RECORDS OF TEAMS ON OPENING DAY, 1933-2004

AFC	W	L	T	Pct.	Longest W Strk.	Longest L Strk.	Current Streak
Jacksonville	7	3	0	.700	6	2	W-1
Houston	2	1	0	.667	2	1	L-1
Denver	29	15	1	.659	4	4	W-4
Miami	22	16	1	.579	11	5	L-2
San Diego	26	19	0	.578	6	6	W-1
Kansas City	25	20	0	.556	7	4	L-1
Oakland	24	21	0	.533	5	5	L-2
Tennessee	24	21	0	.533	4	3	W-3
Cleveland	27	25	0	.519	5	6	W-1
Pittsburgh	34	32	4	.515	4	3	W-2
Indianapolis	30	30	1	.500	8	8	L-1
New England	21	24	0	.467	6	3	W-1
Cincinnati	16	21	0	.432	4	4	L-3
N.Y. Jets	19	26	0	.422	3	5	W-1
Buffalo	18	27	0	.400	6	5	L-1
Baltimore	3	6	0	.333	2	3	L-3

NFC	W	L	T	Pct.	Longest W Strk.	Longest L Strk.	Current Streak
Dallas	30	14	1	.682	17	5	L-5
N.Y. Giants	40	28	4	.588	4	3	L-1
Minnesota	25	18	1	.581	5	3	W-2
Chicago	40	31	1	.563	9	6	L-2
St. Louis	37	30	0	.552	5	6	W-1
Green Bay	38	31	3	.551	5	6	W-1
Detroit	37	33	2	.529	7	4	W-2
San Francisco	28	26	1	.519	5	3	L-1
Washington	35	33	4	.515	6	5	W-3
Atlanta	20	19	0	.513	5	3	W-2
Tampa Bay	12	17	0	.414	3	5	L-1
Carolina	4	6	0	.400	3	4	L-1
Philadelphia	28	42	1	.400	5	9	W-1
Arizona	27	43	1	.386	6	7	L-5
Seattle	9	20	0	.310	3	8	W-2
New Orleans	11	27	0	.289	2	6	L-2

Kansas City totals include Dallas Texans, 1960-62.
Oakland totals include L.A. Raiders, 1982-1994.
San Diego totals include L.A. Chargers, 1960.
Indianapolis totals include Baltimore, 1953-1983.
Tennessee totals include Houston, 1960-1996.
New England totals include Boston, 1960-1970.
St. Louis totals include Cleveland, 1937-1942 and 1944-45, and L.A. Rams, 1946-1994.
Detroit totals include Portsmouth, 1933.
Arizona totals include Chi. Cardinals, 1933-1959, St. Louis, 1960-1987, and Phoenix, 1988-1993.
NOTE: All tied games occurred prior to 1972, when calculation of ties in percentages as half-win, half-loss was begun.

RECORDS OF NFL TEAMS, 1995-2004

AFC	W	L	T	Pct.	Division Titles	Playoff Berths	Postseason Record	Super Bowl Record
Denver	101	59	0	.631	2	6	7-4	2-0
Pittsburgh	98	61	1	.616	6	6	7-6	0-1
New England	97	63	0	.606	5	6	12-3	3-1
Kansas City	92	68	0	.575	3	3	0-3	0-0
Tennessee	92	68	0	.575	2	4	5-4	0-1
Miami	90	70	0	.563	1	6	3-6	0-0
Indianapolis	87	73	0	.544	3	7	5-7	0-0
Jacksonville	82	78	0	.513	2	4	4-4	0-0
Buffalo	81	79	0	.506	1	4	1-4	0-0
Baltimore	72	71	1	.503	1	3	5-2	1-0
N.Y. Jets	77	83	0	.481	2	4	3-4	0-0
Oakland	77	83	0	.481	3	3	4-3	0-1
San Diego	64	96	0	.400	1	2	0-2	0-0
Cincinnati	57	103	0	.356	0	0	0-0	0-0
Houston	16	32	0	.333	0	0	0-0	0-0
Cleveland	35	77	0	.313	0	1	0-1	0-0

Baltimore entered the NFL in 1996.
Cleveland did not play from 1996-98.
Houston entered the NFL in 2002.
Tennessee totals include Houston, 1995-96.

NFC	W	L	T	Pct.	Division Titles	Playoff Berths	Postseason Record	Super Bowl Record
Green Bay	109	51	0	.681	6	8	9-7	1-1
Philadelphia	93	66	1	.584	4	7	8-7	0-1
Minnesota	90	70	0	.563	2	6	5-6	0-0
San Francisco	89	71	0	.556	3	6	4-6	0-0
St. Louis	86	74	0	.538	3	5	6-4	1-1
Tampa Bay	85	75	0	.531	2	5	5-4	1-0
Seattle	81	79	0	.506	2	3	0-3	0-0
Dallas	77	83	0	.481	3	5	4-4	1-0
N.Y. Giants	75	84	1	.472	2	3	2-3	0-1
Atlanta	74	85	1	.466	2	4	4-4	0-1
Washington	73	86	1	.459	1	1	1-1	0-0
Carolina	71	89	0	.444	2	2	4-2	0-1
New Orleans	67	93	0	.419	1	1	1-1	0-0
Chicago	64	96	0	.400	1	1	0-1	0-0
Detroit	62	98	0	.388	0	3	0-3	0-0
Arizona	55	105	0	.344	0	1	1-1	0-0

Seattle was in the AFC from 1995-2001

HOME RECORDS, 1995-2004

AFC	W-L-T	Pct.
Denver	62-18-0	.775
Kansas City	58-22-0	.725
New England	56-24-0	.700
Pittsburgh	55-24-1	.694
Miami	53-27-0	.663
Baltimore	44-27-1	.618
Buffalo	49-31-0	.613
Indianapolis	49-31-0	.613
Jacksonville	49-31-0	.613
Tennessee	47-33-0	.588
Oakland	44-36-0	.550
N.Y. Jets	41-39-0	.513
San Diego	39-41-0	.488
Cincinnati	36-44-0	.450
Houston	8-16-0	.333
Cleveland	17-39-0	.304

NFC	W-L-T	Pct.
Green Bay	65-15-0	.813
Minnesota	57-23-0	.713
San Francisco	54-26-0	.675
Philadelphia	52-28-0	.650
Tampa Bay	52-28-0	.650
Dallas	51-29-0	.638
St. Louis	51-29-0	.638
Seattle	49-31-0	.613
Atlanta	44-36-0	.550
Detroit	44-36-0	.550
Washington	43-36-1	.544
Carolina	40-40-0	.500
Chicago	40-40-0	.500
N.Y. Giants	40-40-0	.500
Arizona	38-42-0	.475
New Orleans	34-46-0	.425

Baltimore entered the NFL in 1996.
Cleveland did not play from 1996-98.
Houston entered the NFL in 2002.
Tennessee totals include Houston, 1995-96.
Seattle was in the AFC from 1995-2001.

ROAD RECORDS, 1995-2004

AFC	W-L-T	Pct.
Tennessee	45-35-0	.563
Pittsburgh	43-37-0	.538
New England	41-39-0	.513
Denver	39-41-0	.488
Indianapolis	38-42-0	.475
Miami	37-43-0	.463
N.Y. Jets	36-44-0	.450
Kansas City	34-46-0	.425
Jacksonville	33-47-0	.413
Oakland	33-47-0	.413
Buffalo	32-48-0	.400
Baltimore	28-44-0	.389
Houston	8-16-0	.333
Cleveland	18-38-0	.321
San Diego	25-55-0	.313
Cincinnati	21-59-0	.263

NFC	W-L-T	Pct.
Green Bay	44-36-0	.550
Philadelphia	41-38-1	.519
N.Y. Giants	35-44-1	.444
St. Louis	35-45-0	.438
San Francisco	35-45-0	.438
Minnesota	33-47-0	.413
New Orleans	33-47-0	.413
Tampa Bay	33-47-0	.413
Seattle	32-48-0	.400
Carolina	31-49-0	.388
Atlanta	30-49-1	.381
Washington	30-50-0	.375
Dallas	26-54-0	.325
Chicago	24-56-0	.300
Detroit	18-62-0	.225
Arizona	17-63-0	.213

Baltimore entered the NFL in 1996.
Cleveland did not play from 1996-98.
Houston entered the NFL in 2002.
Tennessee totals include Houston, 1995-96.
Seattle was in the AFC from 1995-2001.

RECORDS BY MONTHS, 1995-2004

AFC	Sept. W-L-T	Oct. W-L-T	Nov. W-L-T	Dec. W-L-T	Total W-L-T	Pct.
Denver	28-11-0	23-16-0	28-11-0	22-21-0	101- 59-0	.631
Pittsburgh	18-16-0	29-10-0	25-17-1	26-18-0	98- 61-1	.616
New England	20-14-0	22-20-0	28-14-0	27-15-0	97- 63-0	.606
Kansas City	25-14-0	23-14-0	19-23-0	25-17-0	92- 68-0	.575
Tennessee	16-19-0	26-14-0	23-17-0	27-18-0	92- 68-0	.575
Miami	23-10-0	23-17-0	23-20-0	21-23-0	90- 70-0	.563
Indianapolis	19-15-0	20-19-0	21-22-0	27-17-0	87- 73-0	.544
Jacksonville	20-17-0	16-24-0	22-17-0	24-20-0	82- 78-0	.513
Buffalo	15-18-0	24-19-0	22-19-0	20-23-0	81- 79-0	.506
Baltimore	18-15-0	13-21-0	20-18-1	21-17-0	72- 71-1	.503
N.Y. Jets	13-23-0	19-20-0	25-15-0	20-25-0	77- 83-0	.481
Oakland	22-16-0	20-17-0	19-22-0	16-28-0	77- 83-0	.481
San Diego	20-18-0	16-22-0	12-29-0	16-27-0	64- 96-0	.400
Cincinnati	9-27-0	11-28-0	17-25-0	20-23-0	57-103-0	.356
Houston	4-7-0	4-6-0	5-8-0	3-11-0	16- 32-0	.333
Cleveland	11-14-0	10-19-0	7-20-0	7-24-0	35- 77-0	.313

Baltimore entered the NFL in 1996.
Cleveland did not play from 1996-98.
Houston entered the NFL in 2002.
Tennessee totals include Houston, 1995-96.
September totals include August; December totals include January

NFC	Sept. W-L-T	Oct. W-L-T	Nov. W-L-T	Dec. W-L-T	Total W-L-T	Pct.
Green Bay	27-12-0	20-14-0	26-16-0	36-9-0	109- 51-0	.681
Philadelphia	16-21-0	26-12-0	27-16-1	24-17-0	93- 66-1	.584
Minnesota	24-14-0	24-13-0	22-19-0	20-24-0	90- 70-0	.563
San Francisco	20-15-0	22-18-0	23-18-0	24-20-0	89- 71-0	.556
St. Louis	20-17-0	21-16-0	18-24-0	27-17-0	86- 74-0	.538
Tampa Bay	19-18-0	17-21-0	25-16-0	24-20-0	85- 75-0	.531
Seattle	19-18-0	15-21-0	23-20-0	24-20-0	81- 79-0	.506
Dallas	20-16-0	20-18-0	21-23-0	16-26-0	77- 83-0	.481
N.Y. Giants	19-19-0	21-17-0	13-28-1	22-20-0	75- 84-1	.472
Atlanta	14-22-0	16-24-0	23-17-1	21-22-0	74- 85-1	.466
Washington	17-20-0	8-21-0	16-25-1	22-20-0	73- 86-1	.459
Carolina	15-18-0	13-29-0	19-23-0	24-19-0	71- 89-0	.444
New Orleans	13-23-0	19-21-0	17-23-0	18-26-0	67- 93-0	.419
Chicago	9-28-0	19-19-0	17-25-0	19-24-0	64- 96-0	.400
Detroit	17-21-0	13-22-0	19-27-0	13-28-0	62- 98-0	.388
Arizona	11-25-0	13-24-0	18-26-0	13-30-0	55-105-0	.344

Seattle was in the AFC from 1995-2001.
September totals include August; December totals include January

TAKEAWAYS/GIVEAWAYS, 1995-2004

| | Takeaways | | | Giveaways | | | |
AFC	Int.	Fum.	Total	Int.	Fum.	Total	Net.Diff.
Kansas City	176	140	316	148	92	240	76
New England	196	125	321	155	115	270	51
Pittsburgh	180	141	321	171	113	284	37
Jacksonville	141	135	276	33	107	240	36
Tennessee	162	140	302	145	125	270	32
N.Y. Jets	177	123	300	171	101	272	28
Denver	162	121	283	163	100	263	20
Miami	194	123	317	176	32	308	9
Baltimore	179	108	287	154	128	282	5
Oakland	161	123	284	155	131	286	-2
Houston	46	27	73	47	34	81	-8
Indianapolis	129	127	256	161	110	271	-15
Cincinnati	149	118	267	172	122	294	-27
Cleveland	117	73	190	136	91	227	-37
Buffalo	147	107	254	172	30	302	-48
San Diego	177	99	276	209	126	335	-59

Baltimore entered the NFL in 1996.
Cleveland did not play from 1996-98.
Houston entered the NFL in 2002.
Tennessee totals include Houston, 1995-96.

| | Takeaways | | | Giveaways | | | |
NFC	Int.	Fum.	Total	Int.	Fum.	Total	Net.Diff.
San Francisco	193	109	302	145	109	254	48
Tampa Bay	197	123	320	161	130	291	29
Philadelphia	167	147	314	151	135	286	28
N.Y. Giants	171	123	294	157	122	279	15
Washington	179	123	302	168	119	287	15
Green Bay	193	117	310	177	119	296	14
Seattle	186	127	313	178	125	303	10
Atlanta	164	136	300	173	122	295	5
Detroit	158	114	272	182	92	274	-2
Carolina	188	142	330	187	154	341	-11
Minnesota	161	121	282	177	119	296	-14
Dallas	153	110	263	158	128	286	-23
New Orleans	167	144	311	189	145	334	-23
Chicago	146	136	282	171	148	319	-37
St. Louis	200	119	319	211	168	379	-60
Arizona	154	121	275	217	150	367	-92

Seattle was in the AFC from 1995-2001.

BEST TAKEAWAY/GIVEAWAY DIFFERENTIAL, SEASON
+43 Washington, 1983
+26 Kansas City, 1990
+25 N.Y. Giants, 1997

HIGH AND LOW SINGLE-GAME YARDAGE TOTALS, 1995-2004
Most Total Yards, Game
645 Pittsburgh vs. Atlanta, Nov. 10, 2002 (OT)
615 Arizona at Washington, Nov. 10, 1996 (OT)
614 St. Louis vs. San Diego, Oct. 1, 2000
605 Minnesota at New Orleans, Oct. 17, 2004
591 Seattle at San Diego, Dec. 29, 2002 (OT)
Fewest Total Yards, Game
26 Cleveland at Buffalo, Dec. 12, 2004
40 Cleveland vs. Pittsburgh, Sept. 12, 1999
47 Houston at Pittsburgh, Dec. 8, 2002
53 Cleveland at Jacksonville, Dec. 3, 2000
89 Seattle at Kansas City, Dec. 24, 1995
Most Yards Rushing, Game
407 Cincinnati vs. Denver, Oct. 22, 2000
343 Baltimore vs. Cleveland, Sept. 14, 2003
337 St. Louis vs. Carolina, Nov. 11, 2001
328 San Francisco vs. Detroit, Dec. 14, 1998
319 Seattle vs. Oakland, Nov. 11, 2001
Fewest Yards Rushing, Game
4 Buffalo at Tennessee, Nov. 23, 1997
Cincinnati at Baltimore, Sept. 24, 2000
5 New England at Pittsburgh, Oct. 31, 2004
8 Oakland vs. Kansas City, Dec. 3, 1995
Dallas at New Orleans, Dec. 6, 1998
Most Yards Passing, Game
507 Arizona at Washington, Nov. 10, 1996 (OT)
499 Denver vs. Atlanta, Oct. 31, 2004
474 Kansas City at Oakland, Nov. 5, 2000
473 N.Y. Jets at Baltimore, Dec. 24, 2000
472 Indianapolis at Kansas City, Oct. 31, 2004
Fewest Yards Passing, Game
-19 San Diego at Kansas City, Sept. 20, 1998
-9 Cleveland at Jacksonville, Dec. 3, 2000
-3 Cleveland at Buffalo, Dec. 12, 2004
0 Oakland at San Diego, Dec. 28, 2003
9 Dallas at Tennessee, Dec. 25, 2000

NFL INDIVIDUAL LEADERS, 1995-2004

Points		Passing Yards	
Jason Elam	1,204	Brett Favre	39,322
Matt Stover	1,114	Drew Bledsoe	32,759
Gary Anderson	1,091	Kerry Collins	29,878
Jeff Wilkins	1,071	Peyton Manning	29,442
Adam Vinatieri	1,058	Mark Brunell	26,892

Touchdowns		TD Passes	
Marshall Faulk	123	Brett Favre	306
Emmitt Smith	100	Peyton Manning	216
Marvin Harrison	98	Drew Bledsoe	181
Terrell Owens	97	Vinny Testaverde	161
Curtis Martin	95	Kerry Collins	153

Field Goals		Receptions	
Matt Stover	271	Marvin Harrison	845
Jason Elam	261	Jimmy Smith	792
Adam Vinatieri	243	Tim Brown	778
Jason Hanson	235	Isaac Bruce	756
John Carney	234	Keenan McCardell	731

Rushes		Reception Yards	
Curtis Martin	3,298	Isaac Bruce	11,481
Eddie George	2,865	Jimmy Smith	11,264
Emmitt Smith	2,779	Marvin Harrison	11,185
Jerome Bettis	2,756	Tim Brown	10,200
Marshall Faulk	2,457	Two tied	9,772

Rushing Yards		Receiving TDs	
Curtis Martin	13,366	Marvin Harrison	98
Emmitt Smith	11,172	Terrell Owens	95
Jerome Bettis	10,840	Randy Moss	90
Marshall Faulk	10,705	Cris Carter	81
Eddie George	10,441	Isaac Bruce	71

Rushing TDs		Interceptions	
Emmitt Smith	93	Ashley Ambrose	40
Marshall Faulk	89	Terrell Buckley	40
Curtis Martin	85	Rod Woodson	39
Priest Holmes	80	Donnie Abraham	38
Jerome Bettis	72	Two tied	36

Pass Attempts		Sacks	
Brett Favre	5,424	Michael Strahan	112.5
Drew Bledsoe	4,929	Simeon Rice	105.0
Kerry Collins	4,517	John Randle	89.5
Peyton Manning	3,880	Kevin Carter	86.0
Mark Brunell	3,853	Bruce Smith	84.0

Completions	
Brett Favre	3,323
Drew Bledsoe	2,835
Kerry Collins	2,524
Peyton Manning	2,464
Mark Brunell	2,302

NFL GAMES IN WHICH A TEAM HAS SCORED 60 OR MORE POINTS

(Home team in capitals)

Regular Season

WASHINGTON 72, New York Giants 41	November 27, 1966
LOS ANGELES RAMS 70, Baltimore 27	October 22, 1950
Chicago Cardinals 65, NEW YORK BULLDOGS 20	November 13, 1949
LOS ANGELES RAMS 65, Detroit 24	October 29, 1950
PHILADELPHIA 64, Cincinnati 0	November 6, 1934
CHICAGO CARDINALS 63, New York Giants 35	October 17, 1948
AKRON 62, Oorang 0	October 29, 1922
PITTSBURGH 62, New York Giants 7	November 30, 1952
CLEVELAND 62, New York Giants 14	December 6, 1953
CLEVELAND 62, Washington 3	November 7, 1954
NEW YORK GIANTS 62, Philadelphia 10	November 26, 1972
Atlanta 62, NEW ORLEANS 7	September 16, 1973
NEW YORK JETS 62, Tampa Bay 28	November 17, 1985
CHICAGO 61, San Francisco 20	December 12, 1965
Cincinnati 61, HOUSTON 17	December 17, 1972
CHICAGO 61, Green Bay 7	December 7, 1980
CINCINNATI 61, Houston 7	December 17, 1989
ROCK ISLAND 60, Evansville 0	October 15, 1922
CHICAGO CARDINALS 60, Rochester 0	October 7, 1923

Postseason

Chicago Bears 73, WASHINGTON 0	December 8, 1940
JACKSONVILLE 62, Miami 7	January 15, 2000

YOUNGEST AND OLDEST PLAYERS IN NFL IN 2004

10 Youngest Players

	Birthdate	Games	Starts	Position
Randy Starks, Tennessee	12/14/1983	14	8	DT
DeAngelo Hall, Atlanta	11/19/1983	10	9	CB
Nat Dorsey, Minnesota	9/9/1983	13	7	T
Larry Fitzgerald, Arizona	8/31/1983	16	16	WR
Robert Geathers, Cincinnati	8/11/1983	14	1	DE
Ahmad Carroll, Green Bay	8/4/1983	14	11	CB
Steven Jackson, St. Louis	7/22/1983	14	3	RB
Kellen Winslow, Cleveland	7/21/1983	2	2	TE
Anthony Hargrove, St. Louis	7/20/1983	15	2	DE
Reggie Williams, Jacksonville	5/17/1983	16	15	WR

10 Oldest Players

	Birthdate	Games	Starts	Position
Gary Anderson, Tennessee	7/16/1959	15	0	K
Morten Andersen, Minnesota	8/19/1960	16	0	K
Sean Landeta, St. Louis	1/6/1962	10	0	P
Jerry Rice, Oakland-Seattle	10/13/1962	17	14	WR
Doug Flutie, San Diego	10/23/1962	2	1	QB
Ray Brown, Washington	12/12/1962	16	14	T
Vinny Testaverde, Dallas	11/13/1963	16	15	QB
John Carney, New Orleans	4/20/1964	16	0	K
Bryan Barker, Green Bay	6/28/1964	16	0	P
Darren Bennett, Minnesota	1/9/1965	15	0	P

YOUNGEST AND OLDEST REGULAR STARTERS BY POSITION IN 2004

Minimum: 8 Games Started

	Youngest		Oldest	
QB	3/2/1982	Ben Roethlisberger, Pit.	11/13/1963	Vinny Testaverde, Dal.
RB	8/21/1982	Kevin Jones, Det.	5/15/1969	Emmitt Smith, Ariz
WR	8/31/1983	Larry Fitzgerald, Ariz	10/13/1962	Jerry Rice, Oak.-Sea.
TE	7/11/1982	Chris Cooley, Was.	2/2/1971	Ken Dilger, TB
T	10/7/1982	Shane Olivea, SD	12/12/1962	Ray Brown, Was.
G	1/8/1982	Chris Snee, NYG	1/5/1969	David Dixon, Min.
C	9/25/1981	Alex Stepanovich, Ariz	3/6/1970	Robbie Tobeck, Sea.
DE	3/5/1983	Kenechi Udeze, Min.	12/18/1969	Marco Coleman, Den.
DT	12/14/1983	Randy Starks, Ten.	4/13/1968	Ted Washington, Oak.
LB	10/11/1982	Terrell Suggs, Bal.	1/19/1969	Junior Seau, Mia.
CB	11/19/1983	DeAngelo Hall, Atl.	12/26/1970	Willie Williams, Pit.
S	4/1/1983	Sean Taylor, Was.	1/29/1968	Aeneas Williams, St.L

OLDEST INDIVIDUAL SINGLE-SEASON OR SINGLE-GAME RECORDS IN NFL RECORD & FACT BOOK

Most Points, Game—40, Ernie Nevers, Chi. Cardinals vs. Chi. Bears, Nov. 28, 1929 (6-td, 4-pat)

Most Touchdowns Rushing, Game—6, Ernie Nevers, Chi. Cardinals vs. Chi. Bears, Nov. 28, 1929

Highest Rushing Average Gain, Season (Qualifiers)—8.44, Beattie Feathers, Chi. Bears, 1934 (119-1,004)

Highest Punting Average, Season (Qualifiers)—51.40, Sammy Baugh, Washington, 1940 (35-1,799)

Highest Punting Average, Rookie, Season (Qualifiers)—45.92, Frank Sinkwich, Detroit, 1943 (12-551)

Highest Punting Average, Game (minimum: 4 punts)—61.75, Bob Cifers, Detroit vs. Chi. Bears, Nov. 24, 1946 (4-247)

Highest Average Gain, Pass Receptions, Season (minimum: 24 receptions)—32.58, Don Currivan, Boston, 1947 (24-782)

Highest Average Gain, Passing, Game (minimum: 20 passes)—18.58, Sammy Baugh, Washington vs. Boston, Oct. 31, 1948 (24-446)

Most Touchdowns, Fumble Recoveries, Game—2, Fred (Dippy) Evans, Chi. Bears vs. Washington, Nov. 28, 1948

Most Yards Gained, Intercepted Passes, Rookie, Season—301, Don Doll, Detroit, 1949

Most Passes Had Intercepted, Game—8, Jim Hardy, Chi. Cardinals vs. Philadelphia, Sept. 24, 1950

Highest Kickoff Return Average, Game (minimum: 3 returns)—73.50, Wally Triplett, Detroit vs. Los Angeles, Oct. 29, 1950 (4-294)

Highest Punt Return Average, Season (Qualifiers)—23.00, Herb Rich, Baltimore, 1950 (12-276)

Highest Punt Return Average, Rookie, Season (Qualifiers)—23.00, Herb Rich, Baltimore, 1950 (12-276)

Most Yards Passing, Game—554, Norm Van Brocklin, Los Angeles vs. N.Y. Yanks, Sept. 28, 1951

Most Touchdowns, Punt Returns, Rookie, Season—4, Jack Christiansen, Detroit, 1951

Most Interceptions By, Season—14, Dick (Night Train) Lane, Los Angeles, 1952

Most Interceptions By, Rookie, Season—14, Dick (Night Train) Lane, Los Angeles, 1952

Highest Average Gain, Passing, Season (Qualifiers)—11.17, Tommy O'Connell, Cleveland, 1957 (110-1,229)

Most Points, Season—176, Paul Hornung, Green Bay, 1960 (15-td, 41-pat,15-fg)

Most Yards Gained, Pass Receptions, Rookie, Season—1,473, Bill Groman, Houston, 1960

NFL INDIVIDUAL LEADERS OVER RECENT SEASONS

Points

Last 2 Seasons		Last 3 Seasons		Last 4 Seasons	
276	Mike Vanderjagt	396	Priest Holmes	504	Mike Vanderjagt
253	Adam Vinatieri	379	Mike Vanderjagt	493	Jason Elam
252	Priest Holmes	370	Adam Vinatieri	484	David Akers
252	Jeff Wilkins	369	David Akers	483	Adam Vinatieri
251	Matt Stover	369	Jason Elam	473	Jeff Wilkins

Touchdowns

42	Priest Holmes	66	Priest Holmes	76	Priest Holmes
36	Shaun Alexander	54	Shaun Alexander	70	Shaun Alexander
35	LaDainian Tomlinson	50	LaDainian Tomlinson	60	LaDainian Tomlinson
30	Randy Moss	38	Clinton Portis	53	Terrell Owens
28	Ahman Green	37	Three tied	52	Marvin Harrison

Field Goals

62	Matt Stover	83	Matt Stover	113	Jason Elam
58	Jeff Wilkins	83	Adam Vinatieri	113	Matt Stover
57	Mike Vanderjagt	82	Jason Elam	108	Mike Vanderjagt
56	Jason Elam	81	David Akers	107	David Akers
56	Adam Vinatieri	80	Mike Vanderjagt	107	Adam Vinatieri

Rushes

694	Curtis Martin	1,024	LaDainian Tomlinson	1,363	LaDainian Tomlinson
679	Shaun Alexander	974	Shaun Alexander	1,288	Curtis Martin
652	LaDainian Tomlinson	955	Curtis Martin	1,283	Shaun Alexander
644	Edgerrin James	945	Deuce McAllister	1,204	Ahman Green
633	Clinton Portis	930	Jamal Lewis	1,156	Priest Holmes

Rushing Yards

3,131	Shaun Alexander	4,663	LaDainian Tomlinson	5,899	LaDainian Tomlinson
3,072	Jamal Lewis	4,414	Clinton Portis	5,673	Ahman Green
3,046	Ahman Green	4,399	Jamal Lewis	5,624	Shaun Alexander
3,005	Curtis Martin	4,306	Shaun Alexander	5,612	Curtis Martin
2,980	LaDainian Tomlinson	4,286	Ahman Green	5,482	Priest Holmes

Rushing Touchdowns

41	Priest Holmes	62	Priest Holmes	70	Priest Holmes
30	Shaun Alexander	46	Shaun Alexander	60	Shaun Alexander
30	LaDainian Tomlinson	44	LaDainian Tomlinson	54	LaDainian Tomlinson
22	Ahman Green	34	Clinton Portis	38	Ahman Green
21	Three tied	30	Deuce McAllister	34	Clinton Portis

Passes

1,079	Trent Green	1,654	Peyton Manning	2,201	Peyton Manning
1,063	Peyton Manning	1,602	Tom Brady	2,146	Aaron Brooks
1,060	Aaron Brooks	1,588	Aaron Brooks	2,126	Kerry Collins
1,043	Joey Harrington	1,562	Brett Favre	2,072	Brett Favre
1,017	Marc Bulger	1,558	Kerry Collins	2,072	Trent Green

Completions

715	Peyton Manning	1,107	Peyton Manning	1,450	Peyton Manning
699	Trent Green	1,007	Daunte Culpepper	1,309	Brett Favre
674	Daunte Culpepper	995	Brett Favre	1,282	Trent Green
657	Marc Bulger	986	Trent Green	1,242	Tom Brady
654	Brett Favre	978	Tom Brady	1,242	Daunte Culpepper

Passing Yards

8,824	Peyton Manning	13,024	Peyton Manning	17,155	Peyton Manning
8,630	Trent Green	12,320	Trent Green	16,103	Trent Green
8,196	Daunte Culpepper	12,049	Daunte Culpepper	15,028	Brett Favre
7,809	Marc Bulger	11,107	Brett Favre	14,760	Aaron Brooks
7,449	Brett Favre	11,076	Tom Brady	14,661	Daunte Culpepper

Last 2 Seasons	Last 3 Seasons	Last 4 Seasons

Touchdown Passes

Last 2 Seasons	Last 3 Seasons	Last 4 Seasons
78 Peyton Manning	105 Peyton Manning	131 Peyton Manning
64 Daunte Culpepper	89 Brett Favre	121 Brett Favre
62 Brett Favre	82 Daunte Culpepper	98 Aaron Brooks
51 Tom Brady	79 Tom Brady	97 Tom Brady
51 Trent Green	77 Trent Green	96 Daunte Culpepper

Receptions

Last 2 Seasons	Last 3 Seasons	Last 4 Seasons
211 Torry Holt	323 Marvin Harrison	432 Marvin Harrison
191 Derrick Mason	302 Torry Holt	383 Torry Holt
185 Chad Johnson	287 Hines Ward	381 Hines Ward
180 Marvin Harrison	270 Derrick Mason	355 Rod Smith
175 Hines Ward	266 Randy Moss	350 Terrell Owens

Reception Yards

Last 2 Seasons	Last 3 Seasons	Last 4 Seasons
3,068 Torry Holt	4,370 Torry Holt	5,733 Torry Holt
2,629 Chad Johnson	4,107 Marvin Harrison	5,631 Marvin Harrison
2,471 Derrick Mason	3,795 Chad Johnson	5,014 Terrell Owens
2,399 Randy Moss	3,746 Randy Moss	4,979 Randy Moss
2,385 Marvin Harrison	3,684 Joe Horn	4,949 Joe Horn

Receiving Touchdowns

Last 2 Seasons	Last 3 Seasons	Last 4 Seasons
30 Randy Moss	37 Randy Moss	52 Terrell Owens
25 Marvin Harrison	36 Marvin Harrison	51 Marvin Harrison
23 Terrell Owens	36 Terrell Owens	47 Randy Moss
22 Torry Holt	28 Joe Horn	37 Joe Horn
21 Two tied	26 Two tied	33 Torry Holt

Interceptions

Last 2 Seasons	Last 3 Seasons	Last 4 Seasons
16 Ed Reed	21 Ed Reed	23 Tony Parrish
13 Tony Parrish	20 Tony Parrish	22 Darren Sharper
12 Tory James	17 Patrick Surtain	21 Tory James
11 Patrick Surtain	16 Three tied	21 Ed Reed
10 Four tied		20 Patrick Surtain

Sacks

Last 2 Seasons	Last 3 Seasons	Last 4 Seasons
27.0 Dwight Freeney	42.5 Simeon Rice	56.0 Michael Strahan
27.0 Simeon Rice	41.0 Jason Taylor	53.5 Simeon Rice
26.0 Bertrand Berry	40.0 Dwight Freeney	49.5 Jason Taylor
23.5 Kabeer Gbaja-Biamila	35.5 Kabeer Gbaja-Biamila	49.0 Kabeer Gbaja-Biamila
23.5 Shaun Ellis	33.5 Michael Strahan	46.0 Leonard Little

NFL TEAM LEADERS OVER RECENT SEASONS

Highest Won-Lost Percentage

Last 2 Seasons	Last 3 Seasons	Last 4 Seasons
.875 New England	.771 New England	.750 New England
.781 Philadelphia	.771 Philadelphia	.750 Philadelphia
.750 Indianapolis	.708 Indianapolis	.695 Pittsburgh
.656 Pittsburgh	.667 Green Bay	.688 Green Bay
.625 Four tied	.656 Pittsburgh	.641 St. Louis

Most Points

Last 2 Seasons	Last 3 Seasons	Last 4 Seasons
969 Indianapolis	1,434 Kansas City	1,754 Kansas City
967 Kansas City	1,318 Indianapolis	1,731 Indianapolis
866 Green Bay	1,264 Green Bay	1,654 Green Bay
821 Minnesota	1,211 Minnesota	1,585 St. Louis
785 New England	1,175 Philadelphia	1,537 New England

Most Total Yards

Last 2 Seasons	Last 3 Seasons	Last 4 Seasons
12,633 Minnesota	18,825 Minnesota	24,278 Kansas City
12,605 Kansas City	18,605 Kansas City	24,010 Minnesota
12,349 Indianapolis	18,020 Denver	23,920 Indianapolis
12,155 Green Bay	17,965 Indianapolis	23,583 St. Louis
11,930 Denver	17,715 Green Bay	23,178 Green Bay

Last 2 Seasons	Last 3 Seasons	Last 4 Seasons

Most Rushing Yards

Last 2 Seasons	Last 3 Seasons	Last 4 Seasons
4,962 Denver	7,228 Denver	9,105 Denver
4,737 Baltimore	6,989 Atlanta	8,846 Pittsburgh
4,621 Atlanta	6,673 Minnesota	8,751 Atlanta
4,466 Green Bay	6,596 Kansas City	8,604 Kansas City
4,331 San Diego	6,529 Baltimore	8,339 Baltimore

Most Passing Yards

Last 2 Seasons	Last 3 Seasons	Last 4 Seasons
8,802 Indianapolis	12,857 Indianapolis	17,031 St. Louis
8,467 Minnesota	12,368 St. Louis	16,846 Indianapolis
8,387 Kansas City	12,152 Minnesota	15,728 Minnesota
8,214 St. Louis	12,009 Kansas City	15,674 Kansas City
7,689 Green Bay	11,316 Green Bay	15,086 Green Bay

*Fewest Turnovers

Last 2 Seasons	Last 3 Seasons	Last 4 Seasons
36 N.Y. Jets	55 N.Y. Jets	76 N.Y. Jets
37 Indianapolis	60 Kansas City	92 Philadelphia
44 Philadelphia	68 San Francisco	93 Kansas City
45 Kansas City	68 Philadelphia	95 Jacksonville
45 Minnesota	69 Oakland	101 San Francisco

*Fewest Points Allowed

Last 2 Seasons	Last 3 Seasons	Last 4 Seasons
498 New England	764 Tampa Bay	996 Philadelphia
547 Philadelphia	788 Philadelphia	1,044 Tampa Bay
549 Baltimore	844 New England	1,116 New England
560 N.Y. Jets	896 N.Y. Jets	1,135 Pittsburgh
563 Buffalo	903 Baltimore	1,168 Baltimore

*Fewest Total Yards Allowed

Last 2 Seasons	Last 3 Seasons	Last 4 Seasons
8,541 Buffalo	13,062 Tampa Bay	17,715 Tampa Bay
8,892 Denver	13,718 Denver	17,889 Pittsburgh
8,917 Pittsburgh	13,730 Buffalo	18,492 Denver
9,018 Tampa Bay	13,752 Pittsburgh	18,943 Baltimore
9,144 Baltimore	14,337 Miami	18,945 Miami

*Fewest Rushing Yards Allowed

Last 2 Seasons	Last 3 Seasons	Last 4 Seasons
3,006 New England	4,415 Pittsburgh	5,610 Pittsburgh
3,040 Pittsburgh	4,606 Denver	6,067 Tennessee
3,117 Denver	4,636 Tennessee	6,098 Denver
3,183 Jacksonville	4,979 Baltimore	6,390 Baltimore
3,189 Dallas	5,007 Dallas	6,717 Dallas

*Fewest Passing Yards Allowed

Last 2 Seasons	Last 3 Seasons	Last 4 Seasons
5,289 Tampa Bay	7,779 Tampa Bay	10,730 Tampa Bay
5,331 Buffalo	8,398 Buffalo	11,557 Buffalo
5,747 Cleveland	9,016 Cleveland	11,858 Miami
5,775 Denver	9,029 Miami	12,105 Cleveland
5,877 Pittsburgh	9,112 Denver	12,182 Washington

Most Opponents' Turnovers

Last 2 Seasons	Last 3 Seasons	Last 4 Seasons
77 New England	106 Baltimore	141 New England
75 Baltimore	106 New England	137 Tampa Bay
66 Indianapolis	102 Atlanta	134 Baltimore
64 Carolina	98 New Orleans	133 Carolina
64 Tennessee	98 Tampa Bay	132 Atlanta

Houston excluded from "Last 4 Seasons" list.

CURTIS MARTIN'S CAREER RUSHING VS. EACH OPPONENT

Opponent	Games	Rushes	Yards	Yards Per Rush	Yards Per Game	TD
Arizona	3	89	322	3.6	107.3	1
Atlanta	2	39	145	3.7	72.5	2
Baltimore	4	89	276	3.1	69.0	2
Buffalo	20	437	1,631	3.7	81.6	9
Carolina	3	72	354	4.9	118.0	4
Chicago	3	52	235	4.5	78.3	1
Cincinnati	2	53	274	5.2	137.0	1
Cleveland	3	54	255	4.7	85.0	1
Dallas	3	67	268	4.0	89.3	0
Denver	6	91	310	3.4	51.7	4
Detroit	2	38	164	4.3	82.0	1
Green Bay	3	66	258	3.9	86.0	2
Houston	2	40	222	5.6	111.0	1
Indianapolis	15	345	1,645	4.8	109.7	7
Jacksonville	4	70	254	3.6	63.5	1
Kansas City	4	84	305	3.6	76.3	4
Miami	19	378	1,435	3.8	75.5	13
Minnesota	2	42	174	4.1	87.0	1
New England	14	296	1,189	4.0	84.9	5
New Orleans	2	52	178	3.4	89.0	2
N.Y. Giants	3	42	121	2.9	40.3	0
N.Y. Jets	6	163	737	4.5	122.8	7
Oakland	5	89	271	3.0	54.2	0
Philadelphia	1	20	110	5.5	110.0	0
Pittsburgh	5	107	483	4.5	96.6	0
St. Louis	2	42	216	5.1	108.0	0
San Diego	4	86	294	3.4	73.5	3
San Francisco	4	91	308	3.4	77.0	4
Seattle	3	75	329	4.4	109.7	4
Tampa Bay	2	26	116	4.5	58.0	0
Tennessee	2	51	190	3.7	95.0	2
Washington	3	52	297	5.7	99.0	3
Totals	156	3,298	13,366	4.1	85.7	85

Arizona totals include eight games vs. Phoenix
Oakland totals include one game vs. L.A. Raiders
St. Louis totals include two games vs. L.A. Rams
Tennessee totals include two games vs. Houston

JEROME BETTIS' CAREER RUSHING VS. EACH OPPONENT

Opponent	Games	Rushes	Yards	Yards Per Rush	Yards Per Game	TD
Arizona	4	91	363	4.0	90.8	4
Atlanta	9	160	686	4.3	76.2	2
Baltimore	14	253	947	3.7	67.6	2
Buffalo	4	56	274	4.9	68.5	3
Carolina	5	99	378	3.8	75.6	5
Chicago	4	90	358	4.0	89.5	2
Cincinnati	18	401	1,725	4.3	95.8	16
Cleveland	11	230	907	3.9	82.5	7
Dallas	2	20	71	3.6	35.5	1
Denver	3	71	250	3.5	83.3	2
Detroit	2	49	180	3.7	90.0	0
Green Bay	4	68	193	2.8	48.3	0
Houston	1	14	30	2.1	30.0	0
Indianapolis	3	52	228	4.4	76.0	3
Jacksonville	14	264	957	3.6	68.4	3
Kansas City	7	154	639	4.1	91.3	1
Miami	4	53	200	3.8	50.0	0
Minnesota	1	19	81	4.3	81.0	1
New England	4	63	228	3.6	57.0	1
New Orleans	6	122	597	4.9	99.5	2
N.Y. Giants	4	92	300	3.3	75.0	1
N.Y. Jets	4	59	244	4.1	61.0	2
Oakland	5	76	289	3.8	57.8	4
Philadelphia	4	93	390	4.2	97.5	1
Pittsburgh	1	16	76	4.8	76.0	1
St. Louis	2	31	171	5.5	85.5	2

Opponent	Games	Rushes	Yards	Yards Per Rush	Yards Per Game	TD
San Diego	4	84	275	3.3	68.8	1
San Francisco	9	129	493	3.8	54.8	6
Seattle	3	56	227	4.1	75.7	0
Tampa Bay	4	73	295	4.0	73.8	1
Tennessee	14	209	749	3.6	53.5	5
Washington	6	122	493	4.0	82.2	3
Totals	180	3,369	13,294	3.9	73.9	82

Arizona totals include one game vs. Phoenix
Oakland totals include one game vs. L.A. Raiders
Tennessee totals include three games vs. Houston

MARSHALL FAULK'S CAREER RUSHING VS. EACH OPPONENT

Opponent	Games	Rushes	Yards	Yards Per Rush	Yards Per Game	TD
Arizona	6	104	513	4.9	85.5	2
Atlanta	8	143	906	6.3	113.3	5
Baltimore	4	75	338	4.5	84.5	4
Buffalo	11	207	696	3.4	63.3	5
Carolina	7	136	795	5.8	113.6	5
Chicago	2	30	157	5.2	78.5	0
Cincinnati	7	125	471	3.8	67.3	4
Cleveland	3	62	296	4.8	98.7	2
Dallas	1	18	73	4.1	73.0	0
Denver	2	24	97	4.0	48.5	2
Detroit	4	49	159	3.2	39.8	2
Green Bay	2	24	123	5.1	61.5	0
Indianapolis	1	25	118	4.7	118.0	3
Jacksonville	1	22	54	2.5	54.0	1
Kansas City	3	47	151	3.2	50.3	1
Miami	11	193	737	3.8	67.0	4
Minnesota	3	65	345	5.3	115.0	9
New England	11	166	603	3.6	54.8	1
New Orleans	8	165	760	4.6	95.0	7
N.Y. Giants	4	47	208	4.4	52.0	2
N.Y. Jets	11	193	725	3.8	65.9	5
Oakland	2	40	199	5.0	99.5	2
Philadelphia	5	68	335	4.9	67.0	4
Pittsburgh	2	35	116	3.3	58.0	0
St. Louis	1	19	177	9.3	177.0	3
San Diego	6	82	237	2.9	39.5	1
San Francisco	12	222	1,000	4.5	83.3	8
Seattle	11	215	866	4.0	78.7	8
Tampa Bay	6	87	327	3.8	54.5	6
Tennessee	2	39	233	6.0	116.5	3
Washington	3	44	172	3.9	57.3	1
Totals	160	2,771	11,987	4.3	74.9	100

Tennessee totals include one game vs. Houston

COREY DILLON'S CAREER RUSHING VS. EACH OPPONENT

Opponent	Games	Rushes	Yards	Yards Per Rush	Yards Per Game	TD
Arizona	4	74	379	5.1	94.8	1
Atlanta	1	18	66	3.7	66.0	0
Baltimore	15	260	907	3.5	60.5	3
Buffalo	4	69	326	4.7	81.5	2
Carolina	2	38	168	4.4	84.0	0
Chicago	1	16	30	1.9	30.0	0
Cincinnati	1	22	88	4.0	88.0	1
Cleveland	11	217	1,111	5.1	101.0	7
Dallas	2	46	221	4.8	110.5	1
Denver	4	76	480	6.3	120.0	2
Detroit	2	44	261	5.9	130.5	3
Green Bay	1	16	28	1.8	28.0	0
Houston	1	22	92	4.2	92.0	0
Indianapolis	5	75	383	5.1	76.6	3
Jacksonville	10	175	625	3.6	62.5	3
Kansas City	2	32	119	3.7	59.5	2
Miami	3	66	325	4.9	108.3	1

Opponent	Games	Rushes	Yards	Yards Per Rush	Yards Per Game	TD
Minnesota	1	21	66	3.1	66.0	0
New England	2	52	183	3.5	91.5	1
New Orleans	1	18	126	7.0	126.0	0
N.Y. Giants	1	5	8	1.6	8.0	1
N.Y. Jets	4	82	337	4.1	84.3	2
Oakland	2	32	143	4.5	71.5	1
Philadelphia	2	35	153	4.4	76.5	0
Pittsburgh	13	217	893	4.1	68.7	5
St. Louis	3	47	188	4.0	62.7	1
San Diego	5	73	324	4.4	64.8	1
San Francisco	3	48	273	5.7	91.0	2
Seattle	2	39	186	4.8	93.0	2
Tampa Bay	3	58	208	3.6	69.3	0
Tennessee	11	217	999	4.6	90.8	12
Totals	122	2,210	9,696	4.4	79.5	57

JERRY RICE'S CAREER RECEIVING VS. EACH OPPONENT

Opponent	Games	Rec.	Yards	Yards/ Rec.	Yards/ Game	TD
Arizona	11	50	776	15.5	70.5	9
Atlanta	30	175	2,731	15.6	91.0	25
Baltimore	2	9	106	11.8	53.0	2
Buffalo	7	20	259	13.0	37.0	2
Carolina	11	59	789	13.4	71.7	4
Chicago	7	34	551	16.2	78.7	7
Cincinnati	6	36	548	15.2	91.3	4
Cleveland	4	21	294	14.0	73.5	4
Dallas	10	62	940	15.2	94.0	8
Denver	12	55	738	13.4	61.5	4
Detroit	10	50	630	12.6	63.0	2
Green Bay	9	57	875	15.4	97.2	7
Houston	1	1	18	18.0	18.0	0
Indianapolis	6	26	458	17.6	76.3	5
Jacksonville	1	2	17	8.5	17.0	0
Kansas City	10	44	541	12.3	54.1	4
Miami	6	25	427	17.1	71.2	6
Minnesota	12	61	991	16.2	82.6	10
New England	6	30	474	15.8	79.0	6
New Orleans	30	147	2,025	13.8	67.5	14
N.Y. Giants	9	40	615	15.4	68.3	5
N.Y. Jets	8	35	541	15.5	67.6	5
Oakland	5	23	408	17.7	81.6	3
Philadelphia	7	33	524	15.9	74.9	5
Pittsburgh	8	44	423	9.6	52.9	4
St. Louis	32	166	2,551	15.4	79.7	20
San Diego	10	69	1,069	15.5	106.9	11
San Francisco	2	7	79	11.3	39.5	0
Seattle	6	27	473	17.5	78.8	6
Tampa Bay	9	49	737	15.0	81.9	10
Tennessee	8	51	601	11.8	75.1	3
Washington	8	41	686	16.7	85.8	2
Totals	303	1,549	22,895	14.8	75.6	197

Arizona totals include one game vs. St. Louis, four games vs. Phoenix
Oakland totals include four games vs. L.A. Raiders
St. Louis totals include 20 games vs. L.A. Rams
Tennessee totals include four games vs. Houston

TIM BROWN'S CAREER RECEIVING VS. EACH OPPONENT

Opponent	Games	Rec.	Yards	Yards/ Rec.	Yards/ Game	TD
Arizona	4	11	108	9.8	27.0	2
Atlanta	6	24	393	16.4	65.5	3
Baltimore	3	13	140	10.8	46.7	2
Buffalo	8	28	591	21.1	73.9	5
Carolina	4	14	189	13.5	47.3	1
Chicago	6	21	248	11.8	41.3	2
Cincinnati	8	25	441	17.6	55.1	6

Opponent	Games	Rec.	Yards	Yards/ Rec.	Yards/ Game	TD
Cleveland	4	7	97	13.9	24.3	0
Dallas	4	25	338	13.5	84.5	1
Denver	31	143	1,826	12.8	58.9	13
Detroit	3	12	97	8.1	32.3	1
Green Bay	4	17	191	11.2	47.8	0
Indianapolis	4	20	329	16.5	82.3	0
Jacksonville	2	19	224	11.8	112.0	1
Kansas City	30	148	2,021	13.7	67.4	6
Miami	10	49	613	12.5	61.3	5
Minnesota	5	17	200	11.8	40.0	1
New England	2	7	117	16.7	58.5	0
New Orleans	7	22	291	13.2	41.6	3
N.Y. Giants	4	17	371	21.8	92.8	4
N.Y. Jets	9	59	831	14.1	92.3	5
Oakland	1	4	41	10.3	41.0	0
Philadelphia	3	12	158	13.2	52.7	1
Pittsburgh	6	26	264	10.2	44.0	0
St. Louis	6	16	269	16.8	44.8	1
San Diego	32	133	1,711	12.9	53.5	9
San Francisco	6	18	294	16.3	49.0	3
Seattle	28	114	1,686	14.8	60.2	14
Tampa Bay	3	13	180	13.8	60.0	1
Tennessee	8	37	476	12.9	59.5	7
Washington	4	23	199	8.7	49.8	2
Totals	255	1,094	14,934	13.7	58.6	100

St. Louis totals include three games vs. L.A. Rams
Tennessee totals include three games vs. Houston

MARVIN HARRISON'S CAREER RECEIVING VS. EACH OPPONENT

Opponent	Games	Rec.	Yards	Yards/ Rec.	Yards/ Game	TD
Arizona	1	6	85	14.2	85.0	1
Atlanta	2	12	183	15.3	91.5	2
Baltimore	5	25	367	14.7	73.4	2
Buffalo	13	59	810	13.7	62.3	9
Carolina	1	8	119	14.9	119.0	1
Chicago	2	10	91	9.1	45.5	1
Cincinnati	4	31	469	15.1	117.3	3
Cleveland	3	32	354	11.1	118.0	2
Dallas	3	23	239	10.4	79.7	3
Denver	4	31	353	11.4	88.3	3
Detroit	3	24	266	11.1	88.7	5
Green Bay	3	15	191	12.7	63.7	2
Houston	6	32	393	12.3	65.5	1
Jacksonville	7	26	341	13.1	48.7	6
Kansas City	5	35	528	15.1	105.6	6
Miami	14	79	1,059	13.4	75.6	8
Minnesota	3	25	255	10.2	85.0	4
New England	14	85	1,185	13.9	84.6	10
New Orleans	3	19	308	16.2	102.7	3
N.Y. Giants	2	16	237	14.8	118.5	3
N.Y. Jets	12	66	747	11.3	62.3	5
Oakland	3	21	245	11.7	81.7	3
Philadelphia	3	17	303	17.8	101.0	4
Pittsburgh	2	11	128	11.6	64.0	1
St. Louis	1	5	96	19.2	96.0	0
San Diego	5	29	428	14.8	85.6	2
San Francisco	2	14	226	16.1	113.0	4
Seattle	2	11	172	15.6	86.0	0
Tampa Bay	2	14	233	16.6	116.5	2
Tennessee	6	47	562	12.0	93.7	3
Washington	3	17	212	12.5	70.7	0
Totals	139	845	11,205	13.2	80.5	98

ISAAC BRUCE'S CAREER RECEIVING VS. EACH OPPONENT

Opponent	Games	Rec.	Yards	Yards/ Rec.	Yards/ Game	TD
Arizona	8	133	483	14.6	60.4	4

Opponent	Games	Rec.	Yards	Yards/Rec.	Yards/Game	TD
Atlanta	16	71	1,283	18.1	80.2	10
Baltimore	3	21	334	15.9	111.3	2
Buffalo	2	12	194	16.2	97.0	1
Carolina	13	61	790	13.0	60.8	4
Chicago	6	34	456	13.4	76.0	1
Cincinnati	2	10	192	19.2	96.0	0
Cleveland	2	7	75	10.7	37.5	2
Dallas	1	3	52	17.3	52.0	1
Denver	4	11	140	12.7	35.0	0
Detroit	3	8	100	12.5	33.3	0
Green Bay	6	33	462	14.0	77.0	3
Indianapolis	2	13	256	19.7	128.0	2
Jacksonville	1	2	30	15.0	30.0	0
Kansas City	4	19	282	14.8	70.5	4
Miami	4	29	416	14.3	104.0	1
Minnesota	3	21	315	15.0	105.0	2
New England	2	11	189	17.2	94.5	1
New Orleans	14	79	1,397	17.7	99.8	11
N.Y. Giants	6	27	381	14.1	63.5	2
N.Y. Jets	4	18	254	14.1	63.5	3
Oakland	2	9	118	13.1	59.0	1
Philadelphia	5	26	366	14.1	73.2	2
Pittsburgh	2	10	181	18.1	90.5	0
San Diego	3	20	343	17.2	114.3	5
San Francisco	20	95	1,452	15.3	72.6	9
Seattle	8	40	571	14.3	71.4	2
Tampa Bay	4	11	163	14.8	40.8	0
Tennessee	1	6	53	8.8	53.0	1
Washington	5	37	425	11.5	85.0	0
Totals	156	777	11,753	15.1	75.3	74

Oakland totals include one game vs. L.A. Raiders

GARY ANDERSON'S CAREER KICKING VS. EACH OPPONENT

Opponent	Games	FG	FGA	FG%	Long FG	XP	XPA	Pts.
Arizona	8	14	19	73.7	44	22	22	64
Atlanta	9	10	14	71.4	39	34	34	64
Baltimore	2	7	7	100.0	46	2	2	23
Buffalo	11	19	23	82.6	49	23	23	80
Carolina	7	10	12	83.3	48	20	21	50
Chicago	14	23	27	85.2	50	29	29	98
Cincinnati	27	41	50	82.0	52	63	63	186
Cleveland	26	35	52	67.3	49	47	47	152
Dallas	13	22	28	78.6	49	27	27	93
Denver	12	21	25	84.0	44	25	25	88
Detroit	16	22	31	71.0	44	47	47	113
Green Bay	15	24	30	80.0	48	38	40	110
Houston	4	4	4	100.0	41	12	12	24
Indianapolis	12	15	18	83.3	53	29	29	74
Jacksonville	6	11	12	91.7	53	10	10	43
Kansas City	11	24	31	77.4	49	29	29	101
Miami	12	19	24	79.2	53	30	30	87
Minnesota	6	4	8	50.0	44	10	10	22
New England	10	15	18	83.3	49	23	23	68
New Orleans	11	23	25	92.0	51	25	25	94
N.Y. Giants	10	12	14	85.7	46	24	24	60
N.Y. Jets	10	14	20	70.0	45	27	27	69
Oakland	6	5	13	38.5	37	13	13	28
Philadelphia	5	6	8	75.0	52	11	11	29
Pittsburgh	2	1	2	50.0	25	5	5	8
St. Louis	8	9	11	81.8	46	22	22	49
San Diego	15	26	28	92.9	55	43	44	121
San Francisco	5	8	11	72.7	50	12	12	36
Seattle	11	14	17	82.4	43	12	12	54
Tampa Bay	14	21	25	84.0	44	30	30	93
Tennessee	27	47	52	90.4	54	56	58	197
Washington	8	12	13	92.3	49	20	21	56
Totals	353	538	672	80.1	55	820	827	2,434

Arizona totals include one game vs. St. Louis, one game vs. Phoenix
Indianapolis totals include one game vs. Baltimore
Oakland totals include three games vs. L.A. Raiders
Tennessee totals include 25 games vs. Houston
St. Louis totals include three games vs. L.A. Rams

MORTEN ANDERSEN'S CAREER KICKING VS. EACH OPPONENT

Opponent	Games	FG	FGA	FG%	Long FG	XP	XPA	Pts.
Arizona	15	23	25	92.0	52	43	44	112
Atlanta	25	40	51	78.4	49	56	58	176
Baltimore	2	3	4	75.0	46	3	3	12
Buffalo	6	9	14	64.3	50	14	14	41
Carolina	12	22	28	78.6	51	23	23	89
Chicago	9	8	13	61.5	60	23	23	47
Cincinnati	6	7	11	63.6	49	18	18	39
Cleveland	6	11	12	91.7	53	16	16	49
Dallas	14	22	30	73.3	54	27	27	93
Denver	10	8	14	57.1	55	31	33	55
Detroit	13	12	19	63.2	50	31	31	67
Green Bay	10	15	17	88.2	52	29	29	74
Houston	2	0	0	—	0	10	10	10
Indianapolis	4	5	7	71.4	46	13	13	28
Jacksonville	4	6	7	85.7	46	7	7	25
Kansas City	6	11	12	91.7	50	10	10	43
Miami	6	7	9	77.8	50	21	21	42
Minnesota	12	18	23	78.3	51	20	20	74
New England	7	11	13	84.6	54	21	21	54
New Orleans	14	23	29	79.3	55	36	36	105
N.Y. Giants	10	17	21	81.0	45	16	16	67
N.Y. Jets	7	13	14	92.9	53	14	14	53
Oakland	10	13	16	81.3	51	21	21	60
Philadelphia	14	27	33	81.8	56	22	22	103
Pittsburgh	7	7	10	70.0	50	15	16	36
St. Louis	37	53	62	85.5	51	94	96	253
San Diego	7	7	11	63.6	46	20	20	41
San Francisco	38	62	74	83.8	59	60	62	246
Seattle	8	13	14	92.9	48	17	17	56
Tampa Bay	16	24	32	75.0	50	35	35	107
Tennessee	7	11	15	73.3	47	15	15	48
Washington	10	12	18	66.7	50	17	17	53
Totals	354	520	658	79.0	60	798	808	2,358

Arizona totals include five games vs. St. Louis, four games vs. Phoenix
Oakland totals include four games vs. L.A. Raiders
St. Louis totals include 23 games vs. L.A. Rams
Tennessee totals include five games vs. Houston

BRETT FAVRE'S CAREER PASSING VS. EACH OPPONENT

Opponent	Games	Att.	Cmp.	Pct.	Yards	Avg. Gain	TD	Int.	Sacked
Arizona	3	98	61	62.2	833	8.50	4	2	3/21
Atlanta	4	152	103	67.8	1,143	7.52	7	5	8/56
Baltimore	2	75	49	65.3	597	7.96	5	2	3/14
Buffalo	4	126	74	58.7	753	5.98	8	3	7/54
Carolina	7	261	160	61.3	1,864	7.14	16	11	16/121
Chicago	26	824	521	63.2	6,136	7.45	51	25	38/245

Opponent	Games	Att.	Cmp.	Pct.	Yards	Avg. Gain	TD	Int.	Sacked
Cincinnati	3	117	76	65.0	902	7.71	6	2	9/68
Cleveland	3	89	61	68.5	572	6.43	6	0	4/22
Dallas	7	269	161	59.9	1,641	6.10	13	4	13/97
Denver	4	114	59	51.8	751	6.59	6	9	4/26
Detroit	26	927	576	62.1	6,889	7.43	46	31	47/297
Houston	1	50	33	66.0	383	7.66	1	2	0/0
Indianapolis	3	105	71	67.6	1,024	9.75	9	3	6/52
Jacksonville	3	116	74	63.8	931	8.03	7	4	5/36
Kansas City	3	119	72	60.5	799	6.71	5	5	11/65
Miami	4	147	92	62.6	996	6.78	5	3	9/42
Minnesota	25	822	503	61.2	5,510	6.70	43	29	46/305
New England	3	108	65	60.2	680	6.30	7	2	6/46
New Orleans	3	106	68	64.2	728	6.87	7	1	9/48
N.Y. Giants	5	150	89	59.3	1,112	7.41	7	4	7/44
N.Y. Jets	3	95	50	52.6	507	5.34	4	2	3/21
Oakland	3	105	64	61.0	922	8.78	9	3	6/31
Philadelphia	9	291	161	55.3	1,956	6.72	11	15	23/153
Pittsburgh	3	90	59	65.6	745	8.28	4	1	7/44
St. Louis	9	278	171	61.5	1,954	7.03	15	11	16/136
San Diego	4	111	70	63.1	828	7.46	10	4	5/56
San Francisco	6	199	122	61.3	1,515	7.61	10	8	9/54
Seattle	3	94	53	56.4	574	6.11	7	4	6/36
Tampa Bay	22	750	460	61.3	4,930	6.57	35	20	42/235
Tennessee	4	134	77	57.5	945	7.05	8	5	7/18
Washington	4	81	51	63.0	614	7.58	4	6	4/49
Totals	209	7,003	4,306	61.5	49,734	7.10	376	226	379/2,491

Oakland totals include one game vs. L.A. Raiders
St. Louis totals include four games vs. L.A. Rams
Tennessee totals include one game vs. Houston

DREW BLEDSOE'S CAREER PASSING VS. EACH OPPONENT

Opponent	Games	Att.	Cmp.	Pct.	Yards	Avg. Gain	TD	Int.	Sacked
Arizona	4	91	51	56.0	663	7.29	10	0	9/55
Atlanta	1	34	19	55.9	229	6.74	1	1	5/48
Baltimore	3	101	60	59.4	621	6.15	5	5	6/24
Buffalo	16	504	280	55.6	3,327	6.60	22	10	37/261
Carolina	1	44	22	50.0	228	5.18	0	0	0/0
Chicago	4	157	100	63.7	1,131	7.20	9	2	9/72
Cincinnati	7	242	142	58.7	1,595	6.59	7	3	13/77
Cleveland	6	242	131	54.1	1,383	5.71	4	7	12/78
Dallas	3	99	51	51.5	458	4.63	0	5	4/19
Denver	7	260	144	55.4	1,751	6.73	9	3	21/152
Detroit	4	150	87	58.0	940	6.27	3	3	9/52
Green Bay	3	125	67	53.6	781	6.25	3	6	10/72
Houston	2	59	34	57.6	438	7.42	2	0	7/55
Indianapolis	16	518	315	60.8	3,622	6.99	25	11	25/185
Jacksonville	4	130	89	68.5	956	7.35	6	1	7/38
Kansas City	6	236	145	61.4	1,457	6.17	10	7	14/107
Miami	22	765	412	53.9	5,397	7.05	30	29	50/324
Minnesota	4	196	128	65.3	1,392	7.10	9	2	9/72
New England	6	202	115	56.9	1,266	6.27	5	11	19/127
New Orleans	2	66	39	59.1	514	7.79	1	5	5/32
N.Y. Giants	3	104	70	67.3	786	7.56	4	2	6/45
N.Y. Jets	22	734	409	55.7	4,544	6.19	21	29	56/404
Oakland	3	132	68	51.5	936	7.09	5	7	15/80
Philadelphia	2	92	50	54.3	627	.82	1	4	8/52
Pittsburgh	5	208	115	55.3	1,359	6.53	8	12	7/55
St. Louis	2	59	26	44.1	361	6.12	4	2	5/40
San Diego	4	137	77	56.2	903	6.59	9	2	5/16
San Francisco	2	83	42	50.6	413	4.98	1	3	5/23
Seattle	2	81	45	55.6	513	6.33	2	5	3/21
Tampa Bay	2	64	39	60.9	333	5.20	1	2	11/84
Tennessee	2	60	35	58.3	418	6.97	3	0	7/38
Washington	2	74	42	56.8	466	6.30	1	2	3/25
Totals	172	6,049	3,449	57.0	39,808	6.58	221	181	402/2,733

Arizona totals include one game vs. Phoenix
Oakland totals include one game vs. L.A. Raiders

PEYTON MANNING'S CAREER PASSING VS. EACH OPPONENT

Opponent	Games	Att.	Cmp.	Pct.	Yards	Avg. Gain	TD	Int.	Sacked
Atlanta	3	92	67	72.8	774	8.41	10	3	1/9
Baltimore	4	163	104	63.8	1,200	7.36	7	3	10/87
Buffalo	9	281	168	59.8	2,014	7.17	12	9	9/66
Carolina	2	68	40	58.8	518	7.62	2	3	5/18
Chicago	2	67	43	64.2	513	7.66	6	2	2/21
Cincinnati	3	93	55	59.1	718	7.72	7	2	1/6
Cleveland	3	120	74	61.7	764	6.37	2	3	2/10
Dallas	2	72	51	70.8	565	7.85	3	1	1/13
Denver	4	99	56	56.6	572	5.78	2	2	5/30
Detroit	2	61	45	73.8	524	8.59	9	2	1/7
Green Bay	2	84	53	63.1	687	8.18	8	1	4/27
Houston	6	184	128	69.6	1,569	8.53	14	7	7/55
Jacksonville	7	241	158	65.6	1,948	8.08	17	4	2/17
Kansas City	4	139	87	62.6	1,236	8.89	9	3	7/62
Miami	10	341	208	61.0	2,372	6.96	14	18	17/126
Minnesota	2	65	48	73.8	551	8.48	8	1	1/4
New England	10	361	218	60.4	2,542	7.04	20	15	14/88
New Orleans	3	85	57	67.1	885	10.41	8	4	5/26
N.Y. Giants	2	81	50	61.7	602	7.43	5	3	2/16
N.Y. Jets	9	343	212	61.8	2,286	6.66	12	11	11/60
Oakland	3	115	75	65.2	806	7.01	8	5	4/33
Philadelphia	2	49	34	69.4	554	11.31	6	0	1/8
Pittsburgh	1	48	32	66.7	304	6.33	1	3	2/9
St. Louis	1	28	15	53.6	195	6.96	0	1	2/17
San Diego	3	121	68	56.2	924	7.64	5	3	4/23
San Francisco	2	81	49	60.5	601	7.42	4	4	2/6
Seattle	2	69	43	62.3	616	8.93	2	1	3/6
Tampa Bay	1	47	34	72.3	186	8.21	2	1	1/5
Tennessee	6	213	148	69.5	1,704	8.00	9	6	9/60
Washington	2	69	44	63.8	512	7.42	4	3	4/26
Totals	112	3,880	2,464	63.5	29,442	7.59	216	120	139/941

STEVE McNAIR'S CAREER PASSING VS. EACH OPPONENT

Opponent	Games	Att.	Cmp.	Pct.	Yards	Avg. Gain	TD	Int.	Sacked
Arizona	1	17	9	52.9	146	8.59	2	0	2/13
Atlanta	3	50	29	58.0	369	7.38	3	0	3/18
Baltimore	12	401	229	57.1	2,404	6.00	6	11	25/151
Buffalo	3	81	44	54.3	487	6.01	2	1	7/45
Carolina	2	39	22	56.4	281	7.21	1	1	4/31
Chicago	1	29	18	62.1	187	6.45	1	1	4/11
Cincinnati	12	291	173	59.5	2,292	7.88	20	3	17/115
Cleveland	7	144	86	59.7	1,087	7.55	7	5	8/52
Dallas	3	78	46	59.0	495	6.35	3	3	3/24
Detroit	2	62	31	50.0	419	6.76	2	3	3/25
Green Bay	3	110	69	62.7	752	6.84	7	1	5/28
Houston	6	181	97	53.6	1,383	7.64	11	8	5/23
Indianapolis	5	143	95	66.4	965	6.75	5	1	9/68
Jacksonville	15	427	266	62.3	3,151	7.38	18	12	26/150
Kansas City	1	18	11	61.1	93	5.17	0	2	2/5
Miami	5	112	62	55.4	706	6.30	4	5	7/36
Minnesota	3	71	43	60.6	565	7.96	2	0	6/52
New England	3	107	62	57.9	698	6.52	1	4	6/36
New Orleans	1	33	22	66.7	252	7.64	2	0	2/1
N.Y. Giants	3	101	67	66.3	810	8.02	6	1	4/19
N.Y. Jets	4	103	53	51.5	749	7.27	5	2	7/52
Oakland	5	156	97	62.2	1,141	7.31	6	9	11/70
Philadelphia	2	71	47	66.2	479	6.75	2	1	3/13
Pittsburgh	12	301	180	59.8	2,234	7.42	16	10	20/118
St. Louis	1	29	13	44.8	186	6.41	2	0	1/8
San Diego	1	34	20	58.8	193	5.68	1	0	3/19
San Francisco	1	9	5	55.6	45	5.00	0	1	1/10
Seattle	3	80	42	52.5	525	6.56	2	3	5/24
Tampa Bay	2	39	24	61.5	353	9.05	1	1	3/22
Washington	3	78	51	65.4	533	6.83	2	3	7/25
Totals	125	3,395	2,013	59.3	23,980	7.06	140	92	209/1,264

The NFL rates its passers for statistical purposes against a fixed performance standard based on statistical achievements of all qualified pro passers since 1960. The current system replaced one that rated passers in relation to their position in a total group based on various criteria. The current system, which was adopted in 1973, removes inequities that existed in the former method and, at the same time, provides a means of comparing passing performances from one season to the next.

It is important to remember that the system is used to rate passers, not quarterbacks. Statistics do not reflect leadership, play-calling, and other intangible factors that go into making a successful professional quarterback. Four categories are used as a basis for compiling a rating:

—Percentage of completions per attempt
—Average yards gained per attempt
—Percentage of touchdown passes per attempt
—Percentage of interceptions per attempt

The average standard is 1.000. The bottom is .000. To earn a 2.000 rating, a passer must perform at exceptional levels, i.e., 70 percent in completions, 10 percent in touchdowns, 1.5 percent in interceptions, and 11 yards average gain per pass attempt. The maximum a passer can receive in any category is 2.375.

For example, to gain a 2.375 in completion percentage, a passer would have to complete 77.5 percent of his passes. The NFL record is 70.55 by Ken Anderson (Cincinnati, 1982). To earn a 2.375 in percentage of touchdowns, a passer would have to achieve a percentage of 11.9. The record is 13.9 by Sid Luckman (Chicago, 1943). To gain 2.375 in percentage of interceptions, a passer would have to go the entire season without an interception. The 2.375 figure in average yards is 12.50, compared with the NFL record of 11.17 by Tommy O'Connell (Cleveland, 1957).

In order to make the rating more understandable, the point rating is then converted into a scale of 100, with 158.3 being the highest rating a passer can achieve. In cases where statistical

performance has been superior, it is possible for a passer to surpass a 100 rating. For example, take Steve Young's record-setting season in 1994 when he completed 324 of 461 passes for 3,969 yards, 35 touchdowns, and 10 interceptions. The four calculations would be:

—Percentage of Completions—324 of 461 is 70.28 percent. Subtract 30 from the completion percentage (40.28) and multiply the result by 0.05. The result is a point rating of 2.014.
Note: If the result is less than zero (Comp. Pct. less than 30.0), award zero points. If the results are greater than 2.375 (Comp. Pct. greater than 77.5), award 2.375.

—Average Yards Gained Per Attempt—3,969 yards divided by 461 attempts is 8.61. Subtract three yards from yards-per-attempt (5.61) and multiply the result by 0.25. The result is 1.403.
Note: If the result is less than zero (yards per attempt less than 3.0), award zero points. If the result is greater than 2.375 (yards per attempt greater than 12.5), award 2.375 points.

—Percentage of Touchdown Passes—35 touchdowns in 461 attempts is 7.59 percent. Multiply the touchdown percentage by 0.2. The result is 1.518.
Note: If the result is greater than 2.375 (touchdown percentage greater than 11.875), award 2.375.

—Percentage of Interceptions—10 interceptions in 461 attempts is 2.17 percent. Multiply the interception percentage by 0.25 (0.542) and subtract the number from 2.375. The result is 1.833.
Note: If the result is less than zero (interception percentage greater than 9.5), award zero points.

The sum of the four steps is (2.014 + 1.403 + 1.518 + 1.833) 6.768. The sum is then divided by six (1.128) and multiplied by 100. In this case, the result is 112.8. This same formula can be used to determine a passer rating for any player who attempts at least one pass.

The following is a list of the 36 qualifying passers who had a single-season passer rating of 100 or higher:

Player, Team	Season	Rating	Att.	Comp.	Pct.	Yds.	Avg.	TD	TD Pct.	Int.	Int. Pct.
Peyton Manning, Indianapolis	2004	121.1	497	336	67.6	4,557	9.17	49	9.9	10	2.0
Steve Young, San Francisco	1994	112.8	461	324	70.2	3,969	8.61	35	7.6	10	2.2
Joe Montana, San Francisco	1989	112.4	386	271	70.2	3,521	9.12	26	6.7	8	2.1
Daunte Culpepper, Minnesota	2004	110.9	548	379	69.2	4,717	8.61	39	7.1	11	2.0
Milt Plum, Cleveland	1960	110.4	250	151	60.4	2,297	9.19	21	8.4	5	2.0
Sammy Baugh, Washington	1945	109.9	182	128	70.3	1,669	9.17	11	6.0	4	2.2
Kurt Warner, St. Louis	1999	109.2	499	325	65.1	4,353	8.72	41	8.2	13	2.6
Dan Marino, Miami	1984	108.9	564	362	64.2	5,084	9.01	48	8.5	17	3.0
Sid Luckman, Chicago Bears	1943	107.5	202	110	54.5	2,194	10.86	28	13.9	12	5.9
Steve Young, San Francisco	1992	107.0	402	268	66.7	3,465	8.62	25	6.2	7	1.7
Randall Cunningham, Minnesota	1998	106.0	425	259	60.9	3,704	8.72	34	8.0	10	2.4
Bart Starr, Green Bay	1966	105.0	251	156	62.2	2,257	8.99	14	5.6	3	1.2
Drew Brees, San Diego	2004	104.8	400	262	65.5	3,159	7.90	27	6.8	7	1.8
Roger Staubach, Dallas	1971	104.8	211	126	59.7	1,882	8.92	15	7.1	4	1.9
Y.A. Tittle, N.Y. Giants	1963	104.8	367	221	60.2	3,145	8.57	36	9.8	14	3.8
Donovan McNabb, Philadelphia	2004	104.7	469	300	64.0	3,875	8.06	31	6.6	8	1.7
Steve Young, San Francisco	1997	104.7	356	241	67.7	3,029	8.51	19	5.3	6	1.7
Bart Starr, Green Bay	1968	104.3	171	109	63.7	1,617	9.46	15	8.8	8	4.7
Chad Pennington, N.Y. Jets	2002	104.2	399	275	68.9	3,120	7.82	22	5.5	6	1.5
Ken Stabler, Oakland	1976	103.4	291	194	66.7	2,737	9.41	27	9.3	17	5.8
Brian Griese, Denver	2000	102.9	336	216	64.3	2,688	8.00	19	5.7	4	1.2
Joe Montana, San Francisco	1984	102.9	432	279	64.6	3,630	8.40	28	6.5	10	2.3
Charlie Conerly, N.Y. Giants	1959	102.7	194	113	58.2	1,706	8.79	14	7.2	4	2.1
Bert Jones, Baltimore	1976	102.5	343	207	60.3	3,104	9.05	24	7.0	9	2.6
Joe Montana, San Francisco	1987	102.1	398	266	66.8	3,054	7.67	31	7.8	13	3.3
Trent Green, St. Louis	2000	101.8	240	145	60.4	2,063	8.60	16	6.7	5	2.1
Steve Young, San Francisco	1991	101.8	279	180	64.5	2,517	9.02	17	6.1	8	2.9
Len Dawson, Kansas City	1966	101.7	284	159	56.0	2,527	8.90	26	9.2	10	3.5
Vinny Testaverde, N.Y. Jets	1998	101.6	421	259	61.5	3,256	7.73	29	6.9	7	1.7
Steve Young, San Francisco	1993	101.5	462	314	68.0	4,023	8.71	29	6.3	16	3.5
Kurt Warner, St. Louis	2001	101.4	546	375	68.7	4,830	8.85	36	6.6	22	4.0
Jim Kelly, Buffalo	1990	101.2	346	219	63.3	2,829	8.18	24	6.9	9	2.6
Steve Young, San Francisco	1998	101.1	517	322	62.3	4,170	8.07	36	7.0	12	2.3
Chris Chandler, Atlanta	1998	100.9	327	190	58.1	3,154	9.65	25	7.6	12	3.7
Jim Harbaugh, Indianapolis	1995	100.7	314	200	63.7	2,575	8.20	17	5.4	5	1.6
Steve McNair, Tennessee	2003	100.4	400	250	62.5	3,215	8.04	24	6.0	7	1.8

HIGHEST NFL POSTSEASON PASSER RATINGS (MINIMUM: 150 ATTEMPTS)

Player	Games	Att.	Cmp.	Pct.	Yards	Avg. Gain	TD	Int.	Rating
Bart Starr	10	213	130	61.0	1,753	8.23	15	3	104.8
Joe Montana	23	734	460	62.7	5,772	7.86	45	21	95.6
Ken Anderson	6	166	110	66.3	1,321	7.96	9	6	93.5
Kurt Warner	7	268	169	63.1	2,221	8.29	15	10	92.3
Joe Theismann	10	211	128	60.7	1,782	8.45	11	7	91.4
Peyton Manning	8	283	171	60.4	2,172	7.67	14	8	89.1
Tom Brady	9	304	190	62.5	1,951	6.42	11	3	88.9
Troy Aikman	16	502	320	63.7	3,849	7.67	23	17	88.3
Steve Young	22	471	292	62.0	3,326	7.06	20	13	85.8
Warren Moon	10	403	259	64.3	2,870	7.12	17	14	84.9

HIGHEST NFL POSTSEASON PASSER RATINGS, ACTIVE PLAYERS (MINIMUM: 150 ATTEMPTS)

Player	Games	Att.	Cmp.	Pct.	Yards	Avg. Gain	TD	Int.	Rating
Kurt Warner	7	268	169	63.1	2,221	8.29	15	10	92.3
Peyton Manning	8	283	171	60.4	2,172	7.67	14	8	89.1
Tom Brady	9	304	190	62.5	1,951	6.42	11	3	88.9
Rich Gannon	10	240	154	64.2	1,691	7.05	11	9	84.6
Brett Favre	20	663	401	60.5	4,902	7.39	34	26	84.0
Vinny Testaverde	5	189	114	60.3	1,320	6.98	6	5	81.0
Donovan McNabb	12	419	249	59.4	2,630	6.28	18	12	80.1
Kerry Collins	6	199	115	57.8	1,275	6.41	12	10	76.1
Steve McNair	9	282	166	58.9	1,591	5.64	6	9	68.4
Mark Brunell	9	255	127	49.8	1,550	6.08	10	10	65.6

ALL-TIME RANKINGS OF PLAYERS IN FOUR CATEGORIES THAT DETERMINE NFL PASSER RATING
Minimum: 1,500 Attempts

COMPLETION PERCENTAGE	Pct.	Att.	Comp.
Kurt Warner	65.90	1,965	1,295
Daunte Culpepper	64.37	2,391	1.539
Steve Young	64.28	4,149	2,667
Peyton Manning	63.51	3,880	2,464
Joe Montana	63.24	5,391	3,409
Brian Griese	63.01	2,144	1,351
Brad Johnson	61.82	3,504	2,166
Tom Brady	61.60	2,018	1,243
Brett Favre	61.49	7,003	4,306
Troy Aikman	61.46	4,715	2,898

TOUCHDOWN PERCENTAGE	Pct.	Att.	TD
Sid Luckman	7.86	1,744	137
Frank Ryan	6.99	2,133	149
Len Dawson	6.39	3,741	239
Daryle Lamonica	6.31	2,601	164
Sammy Baugh	6.24	2,995	187
Charley Conerly	6.11	2,833	173
Bob Waterfield	6.00	1,617	97
Earl Morrall	5.99	2,689	161
Sonny Jurgensen	5.98	4,262	255
Norm Van Brocklin	5.98	2,895	173

AVERAGE YARDS PER PASS	Avg.	Att.	Yards
Otto Graham	8.63	1,565	13,499
Sid Luckman	8.42	1,744	14,686
Kurt Waner	8.40	1,965	16,501
Norm Van Brocklin	8.16	2,895	23,611
Steve Young	7.98	4,149	33,124
Ed Brown	7.85	1,987	15,600
Bart Starr	7.85	3,149	24,718
Daunte Culpepper	7.78	2,391	18,598
Johnny Unitas	7.76	5,186	40,239
Earl Morrall	7.74	2,689	20,809

INTERCEPTION PERCENTAGE	Pct.	Att.	Int.
Neil O'Donnell	2.11	3,229	68
Donovan McNabb	2.20	2,586	57
Mark Brunell	2.37	3,880	92
Steve Bono	2.47	1,701	42
Rich Gannon	2.47	4,206	104
Jeff Garcia	2.49	2,612	65
Tom Brady	2.58	2,018	52
Joe Montana	2.58	5,391	139
Steve Young	2.58	4,149	107
Bernie Kosar	2.59	3,365	87

STARTING RECORDS OF ACTIVE NFL QUARTERBACKS
Minimum: 10 starts

	W - L - T	Pct.
Ben Roethlisberger	13-0-0	1.000
Tom Brady	48-14-0	.774
Marc Bulger	26-10-0	.722
Donovan McNabb	56-23-0	.709
Kurt Warner	40-19-0	.678
Brett Favre	135-70-0	.659
Michael Vick	23-12-1	.653
Jay Fiedler	37-23-0	.617
Steve McNair	72-45-0	.615
Peyton Manning	66-46-0	.589
Chad Pennington	20-14-0	.588
Brad Johnson	58-41-0	.586
Kordell Stewart	48-34-0	.585
Shaun King	14-10-0	.583
Doug Flutie	38-28-0	.576
Rich Gannon	76-56-0	.576
Kyle Boller	14-11-0	.560
Jim Miller	15-12-0	.556
Trent Dilfer	53-43-0	.552
Jake Delhomme	18-15-0	.545
A.J. Feeley	7-6-0	.538
Quincy Carter	18-16-0	.529
Mark Brunell	66-60-0	.524
Matt Hasselbeck	27-25-0	.519
Rodney Peete	45-42-0	.517
Brian Griese	34-32-0	.515
Aaron Brooks	35-34-0	.507
Trent Green	42-41-0	.506
Drew Bledsoe	86-85-0	.503
Drew Brees	21-21-0	.500
Shane Matthews	11-11-0	.500
Anthony Wright	6-6-0	.500
Daunte Culpepper	36-37-0	.493
Byron Leftwich	13-14-0	.481
Kerry Collins	62-68-0	.477
Jeff Garcia	38-43-0	.469
Carson Palmer	6-7-0	.462
Tommy Maddox	15-18-1	.456
Jon Kitna	36-43-0	.456
Jake Plummer	49-60-0	.450
Tony Banks	35-43-0	.449
Chris Chandler	67-85-0	.441
Ty Detmer	11-14-0	.440
Danny Kanell	10-13-1	.438
Josh McCown	7-9-0	.438
Gus Frerotte	27-36-1	.430
Vinny Testaverde	87-116-1	.429
Charlie Batch	19-27-0	.413
Todd Collins	7-10-0	.412
Patrick Ramsey	9-14-0	.391
Jeff Blake	39-61-0	.390
Jeff George	46-78-0	.371
Rick Mirer	24-44-0	.353
David Carr	14-29-0	.326
Joey Harrington	14-30-0	.318
Kelly Holcomb	4-9-0	.308
Tim Rattay	3-9-0	.250
Chad Hutchinson	3-11-0	.214
Doug Johnson	2-9-0	.182
Doug Pederson	3-14-0	.176
Chris Weinke	1-15-0	.063

TEAMS THAT FINISHED IN FIRST PLACE IN THEIR DIVISION THE SEASON AFTER FINISHING IN LAST PLACE

Season	Team	Record	Prior Season
1967	Houston	9-4-1	*3-11-0
1968	Minnesota	8-6-0	3- 8-3
1970	Cincinnati	8-6-0	4- 9-1
1970	San Francisco	10-3-1	4- 8-2

1972	Green Bay	10-4-0	4- 8-2
1975	Baltimore	10-4-0	2-12-0
1979	Tampa Bay	10-6-0	5-11-0
1981	Cincinnati	12-4-0	6-10-0
1987	Indianapolis	9-6-0	3-13-0
1988	Cincinnati	12-4-0	4-11-0
1990	Cincinnati	9-7-0	8- 8-0
1991	Denver	12-4-0	5-11-0
1992	San Diego	11-5-0	4-12-0
1993	Detroit	10-6-0	5-11-0
1997	N.Y. Giants	10-5-1	6-10-0
1999	Indianapolis	13-3-0	3-13-0
1999	St. Louis	13-3-0	4-12-0
2000	New Orleans	10-6-0	3-13-0
2001	Chicago	13-3-0	5-11-0
2001	New England	11-5-0	5-11-0
2003	Carolina	11-5-0	7- 9-0
2003	Kansas City	13-3-0	*8- 8-0
2004	Atlanta	11-5-0	5-11-0
2004	San Diego	12-4-0	*4-12-0

*tied for last place

LONGEST WINNING STREAKS SINCE 1970

18	New England, 2003-04	(12 in 2003, 6 in 2004)
16	Miami, 1971-73	(1 in 1971, 14 in 1972, 1 in 1973)
16	Miami, 1983-84	(5 in 1983, 11 in 1984)
15	San Francisco, 1989-90	(5 in 1989, 10 in 1990)
14	Oakland, 1976-77	(10 in 1976, 4 in 1977)
14	Denver, 1997-98	(1 in 1997, 13 in 1998)
14	Pittsburgh, 2004	
13	Minnesota, 1974-75	(3 in 1974, 10 in 1975)
13	Chicago, 1984-85	(1 in 1984, 12 in 1985)
13	N.Y. Giants, 1989-90	(3 in 1989, 10 in 1990)
12	Washington, 1990-91	(1 in 1990, 11 in 1991)
11	Pittsburgh, 1975	
11	Baltimore, 1975-76	(9 in 1975, 2 in 1976)
11	Chicago, 1986-87	(7 in 1986, 4 in 1987)
11	Houston, 1993	
11	San Francisco, 1997	
11	Jacksonville, 1999	
11	Indianapolis, 1999	
10	Miami, 1973	
10	Pittsburgh, 1976-77	(9 in 1976, 1 in 1977)
10	Denver, 1984	
10	San Francisco, 1994	
10	Minnesota, 1999-00	(3 in 1999, 7 in 2000)

NFL PLAYOFF APPEARANCES BY SEASONS

Team	Number of Seasons in Playoffs
Dallas	27
St. Louis	27
N.Y. Giants	26
Cleveland	24
Minnesota	24
Green Bay	23
Chicago	22
Pittsburgh	22
San Francisco	22
Miami	21
Oakland	21
Washington	20
Philadelphia	19
Tennessee	19
Indianapolis	18
Buffalo	17
Denver	16
Detroit	14
Kansas City	14
New England	13
San Diego	13
N.Y. Jets	11
Atlanta	8

Tampa Bay	8
Cincinnati	7
Seattle	7
Arizona	6
New Orleans	5
Jacksonville	4
Baltimore	3
Carolina	2

1998	89	151	0	.371
1999	100	148	0	.403
2000	110	138	0	.444
2001	112	136	0	.452
2002	107	148	1	.420
2003	99	157	0	.387
2004	111	145	0	.434

TEAMS IN SUPER BOWL CONTENTION (1978-2004)

	With 3 Weeks to Play	With 2 Weeks to Play	With 1 Week to Play
2004	*27	*26	17
2003	22	17	14
2002	21	21	*19
2001	23	16	13
2000	19	17	16
1999	23	20	16
1998	22	19	14
1997	22	18	14
1996	23	21	13
1995	*27	21	18
1994	25	22	15
1993	20	18	16
1992	20	16	14
1991	20	18	13
1990	23	20	15
1989	21	18	17
1988	21	18	15
1987	19	19	15
1986	19	17	14
1985	21	18	13
1984	18	14	13
1983	24	19	15
1982	20	17	16
1981	21	20	16
1980	20	14	12
1979	19	15	13
1978	20	17	12

RECORD OF TEAMS ON THE ROAD (1970-2004)

Year	W	L	T	Pct
1970	72	101	9	.420
1971	74	100	8	.429
1972	87	90	5	.492
1973	66	109	7	.382
1974	82	99	1	.453
1975	81	101	0	.445
1976	83	112	1	.426
1977	83	113	0	.423
1978	93	130	1	.417
1979	92	132	0	.411
1980	101	122	1	.453
1981	84	139	1	.377
1982	57	68	1	.456
1983	104	119	1	.467
1984	94	129	1	.422
1985	80	144	0	.357
1986	104	118	2	.469
1987	95	114	1	.455
1988	92	131	1	.413
1989	95	128	1	.426
1990	93	131	0	.415
1991	92	132	0	.411
1992	88	136	0	.393
1993	101	123	0	.451
1994	96	128	0	.429
1995	96	144	0	.400
1996	91	149	0	.379
1997	93	145	2	.392

GAMES DECIDED BY 7 POINTS OR LESS AND 3 POINTS OR LESS (1970-2004)

	Games Decided by 7 Points or Less	Games Decided by 3 Points or Less
1970	59 of 182 (32.4%)	34 of 182 (18.7%)
1971	76 of 182 (41.8%)	35 of 182 (19.2%)
1972	71 of 182 (39.0%)	38 of 182 (20.9%)
1973	60 of 182 (32.9%)	28 of 182 (15.4%)
1974	91 of 182 (50.0%)	37 of 182 (20.3%)
1975	62 of 182 (34.1%)	35 of 182 (19.2%)
1976	73 of 196 (37.2%)	38 of 196 (19.4%)
1977	85 of 196 (43.4%)	36 of 196 (18.4%)
1978	108 of 224 (48.2%)	49 of 224 (21.9%)
1979	104 of 224 (46.4%)	51 of 224 (22.8%)
1980	108 of 224 (48.2%)	58 of 224 (25.9%)
1981	91 of 224 (40.6%)	60 of 224 (26.8%)
1982	61 of 126 (48.4%)	33 of 126 (26.2%)
1983	106 of 224 (47.3%)	54 of 224 (24.1%)
1984	95 of 224 (42.4%)	58 of 224 (25.9%)
1985	87 of 224 (38.8%)	38 of 224 (17.0%)
1986	106 of 224 (47.3%)	48 of 224 (21.4%)
1987	99 of 210 (47.1%)	40 of 210 (19.0%)
1988	113 of 224 (50.4%)	62 of 224 (27.7%)
1989	107 of 224 (47.8%)	55 of 224 (24.6%)
1990	97 of 224 (43.3%)	54 of 224 (24.1%)
1991	112 of 224 (50.0%)	57 of 224 (25.4%)
1992	88 of 224 (39.3%)	48 of 224 (21.4%)
1993	*105 of 224 (46.9%)	53 of 224 (23.7%)
1994	115 of 224 (51.3%)	60 of 224 (26.8%)
1995	115 of 240 (47.9%)	61 of 240 (25.4%)
1996	109 of 240 (45.4%)	47 of 240 (19.6%)
1997	111 of 240 (46.3%)	67 of 240 (27.9%)
1998	113 of 240 (47.1%)	50 of 240 (20.8%)
1999	115 of 248 (46.4%)	**64 of 248 (25.8%)
2000	109 of 248 (44.0%)	61 of 248 (24.6%)
2001	121 of 248 (48.8%)	62 of 248 (25.0%)
2002	126 of 256 (49.2%)	63 of 256 (24.6%)
2003	124 of 256 (48.4%)	60 of 256 (23.4%)
2004	116 of 256 (45.3%)	61 of 256 (23.8%)

*Week record: Dec. 11-13, 1993 (Week 15), 12 of 14 games (86%) decided by 7 points or less.
**Week record: Oct. 10-11, 1999 (Week 5), 10 of 14 games (71%) decided by 3 points or less.

GAMES DECIDED BY 8 PTS. OR LESS (1994-2004)

1994	121 of 224 (54.0%)	2000	119 of 248 (48.0%)
1995	123 of 240 (51.3%)	2001	128 of 248 (51.6%)
1996	115 of 240 (47.9%)	2002	137 of 256 (53.5%)
1997	120 of 240 (50.0%)	2003	132 of 256 (51.6%)
1998	120 of 240 (50.0%)	2004	121 of 256 (47.3%)
1999	124 of 248 (50.0%)		

TWO-POINT CONVERSION RESULTS (1994-2004)

1994	59 of 116 (50.9%)	2000	35 of 85 (41.2%)
1995	40 of 104 (38.5%)	2001	40 of 90 (44.4%)
1996	44 of 92 (47.8%)	2002	47 of 98 (48.0%)
1997	47 of 109 (43.1%)	2003	29 of 66 (43.9%)
1998	41 of 105 (39.1%)	2004	37 of 76 (48.7%)
1999	31 of 84 (36.9%)		

RECORDS AFTER BYE WEEKS (1990-2004)

AFC		NFC	
Baltimore	5-4	Arizona	8-8
Buffalo	10-6	Atlanta	8-8
Cincinnati	4-12	Carolina	3-7
Cleveland	3-8	Chicago	10-6
Denver	12-4	Dallas	11-5
Houston	1-2	Detroit	7-9
Indianapolis	7-9	Green Bay	9-7
Jacksonville	6-4	Minnesota	13-3
Kansas City	10-6	New Orleans	8-8
Miami	10-6	N.Y. Giants	3-13
New England	7-9	Philadelphia	12-4
N.Y. Jets	8-8	St. Louis	9-7
Oakland	9-7	San Francisco	8-8
Pittsburgh	9-7	Seattle	3-13
San Diego	7-8	Tampa Bay	6-10
Tennessee	9-7	Washington	8-8

2004 RECORDS OF TEAMS IN CLOSE GAMES

AFC	Overall Record	Decided by 8 Pts. or Less	Decided By 3 Pts. or Less
Baltimore	9-7	3-3	1-2
Buffalo	9-7	2-4	0-3
Cincinnati	8-8	84-4	3-0
Cleveland	4-12	2-4	0-3
Denver	10-6	3-3	3-3
Houston	7-9	1-4	1-1
Indianapolis	12-4	3-2	2-2
Jacksonville	9-7	8-3	5-2
Kansas City	7-9	3-7	2-3
Miami	4-12	3-7	2-3
New England	14-2	4-1	1-1
N.Y. Jets	10-6	6-4	2-2
Oakland	5-11	4-6	3-2
Pittsburgh	15-1	6-0	3-0
San Diego	12-4	6-3	2-2
Tennessee	5-11	3-3	1-2

NFC	Overall Record	Decided by 8 Pts. or Less	Decided By 3 Pts. or Less
Arizona	6-10	4-5	2-4
Atlanta	11-5	6-2	5-1
Carolina	7-9	1-5	0-4
Chicago	5-11	2-4	1-1
Dallas	6-10	4-3	2-0
Detroit	6-10	3-6	0-3
Green Bay	10-6	4-2	4-1
Minnesota	8-8	5-5	2-4
New Orleans	8-8	6-3	3-2
N.Y. Giants	6-10	3-5	0-3
Philadelphia	13-3	4-0	2-0
St. Louis	8-8	4-1	1-1
San Francisco	2-14	2-4	2-2
Seattle	9-7	6-3	2-0
Tampa Bay	5-11	2-8	2-1
Washington	6-10	4-7	2-3

SUPER BOWL CHAMPIONS THAT DID NOT MAKE PLAYOFFS THE FOLLOWING YEAR

Tampa Bay—Super Bowl XXXVII champions did not make playoffs in 2003 season.

New England—Super Bowl XXXVI champions did not make playoffs in the 2002 season.

Denver—Super Bowl XXXIII champions did not make playoffs in the 1999 season.

N.Y. Giants—Super Bowl XXV champions did not make playoffs in the 1991 season.

Washington—Super Bowl XXII champions did not make play-offs in the 1988 season.

N.Y. Giants—Super Bowl XXI champions did not make playoffs in the 1987 season.

San Francisco—Super Bowl XVI champions did not make playoffs in the 1982 season.

Oakland—Super Bowl XV champions did not make playoffs in the 1981 season.

Pittsburgh—Super Bowl XIV champions did not make playoffs in the 1980 season.

Kansas City—Super Bowl IV champions did not make playoffs in the 1970 season.

Green Bay—Super Bowl II champions did not make playoffs in the 1968 season.

NON-DIVISION WINNERS THAT PLAYED IN SUPER BOWL

2000	Baltimore Ravens	Super Bowl XXXV
	(Defeated N.Y. Giants, 34-7)	
1999	Tennessee Titans	Super Bowl XXXIV
	(Lost to St. Louis, 23-16)	
1997	Denver Broncos	Super Bowl XXXII
	(Defeated Green Bay, 31-24)	
1992	Buffalo Bills	Super Bowl XXVII
	(Lost to Dallas, 52-17)	
1985	New England Patriots	Super Bowl XX
	(Lost to Chicago, 46-10)	
1980	Oakland Raiders	Super Bowl XV
	(Defeated Philadelphia, 27-10)	
1975	Dallas Cowboys	Super Bowl X
	(Lost to Pittsburgh, 21-17)	
1969	Kansas City Chiefs	Super Bowl IV
	(Defeated Minnesota, 23-7)	

TEAMS AT OR UNDER .500 IN POSTSEASON PLAY

2004	Minnesota Vikings	8-8
2004	St. Louis Rams	8-8
1999	Dallas Cowboys	8-8
1999	Detroit Lions	8-8
1991	New York Jets	8-8
1990	New Orleans Saints	8-8
1985	Cleveland Browns	8-8
1982	Cleveland Browns	4-5
1982	Detroit Lions	4-5
1969	Houston Oilers	6-6-2

COLDEST NFL GAMES ON RECORD

-13 degrees (-48 degree wind chill)—December 31, 1967, Lambeau Field, Green Bay, Wisconsin, NFL Championship (Green Bay 21, Dallas 17)

-9 degrees (-59 degree wind chill)—January 10, 1982, Riverfront Stadium, Cincinnati, Ohio, AFC Championship (Cincinnati 27, San Diego 7)

0 degrees (-32 degree wind chill)—January 15, 1994, Rich Stadium, Orchard Park, New York, AFC Divisional Playoff (Buffalo 29, Los Angeles Raiders 23)

TEAM LEADERS

Offense	Most Scored		Fewest Scored	
1st Quarter	123	Pittsburgh	29	New Orleans
2nd Quarter	159	New England	59	Miami
3rd Quarter	118	Indianapolis	34	Miami/Wash.
4th Quarter	140	Kansas City	69	Tampa Bay

Defense	Most Allowed		Fewest Allowed	
1st Quarter	117	New Orleans	34	N.Y. Jets
2nd Quarter	155	Oakland	42	Pittsburgh
3rd Quarter	99	Tennessee	12	Buffalo
4th Quarter	155	Dallas	48	Denver

2004 NFL SCORE BY QUARTERS

AFC Offense	1	2	3	4	OT	PTS
Indianapolis	120	157	118	124	3	522
Kansas City	113	137	93	140	0	483
San Diego	92	138	106	110	0	446
New England	87	159	102	89	0	437
Buffalo	89	101	80	125	0	395
Denver	102	138	50	91	0	381
Cincinnati	69	108	96	101	0	374
Pittsburgh	123	90	47	112	0	372
Tennessee	106	111	49	78	0	344
N.Y. Jets	51	94	95	93	0	333
Oakland	51	121	60	88	0	320
Baltimore	63	89	75	87	3	317
Houston	33	101	60	115	0	309
Cleveland	67	62	55	92	0	276
Miami	79	59	34	103	0	275
Jacksonville	35	75	56	89	6	261

NFC Offense	1	2	3	4	OT	PTS
Green Bay	57	146	107	114	0	424
Minnesota	54	136	73	136	6	405
Philadelphia	100	121	79	83	3	386
Seattle	86	129	70	86	0	371
Carolina	78	90	62	125	0	355
New Orleans	9	132	83	101	3	348
Atlanta	71	118	42	106	3	340
St. Louis	69	115	40	86	9	319
N.Y. Giants	72	79	55	97	0	303
Tampa Bay	48	101	83	69	0	301
Detroit	60	97	45	94	0	296
Dallas	63	82	72	76	0	293
Arizona	40	78	57	109	0	284
San Francisco	68	62	35	88	6	259
Washington	54	80	34	72	0	240
Chicago	34	80	36	79	2	231

AFC Defense	1	2	3	4	OT	PTS
Pittsburgh	79	42	66	64	0	251
New England	55	94	45	66	0	260
N.Y. Jets	34	104	34	83	6	261
Baltimore	46	59	57	106	0	268
Jacksonville	61	86	34	99	0	280
Buffalo	78	100	12	94	0	284
Denver	68	121	67	48	0	304
San Diego	37	97	52	124	3	313
Houston	61	105	85	82	6	339
Indianapolis	78	102	73	98	0	351
Miami	79	88	95	92	0	354
Cincinnati	75	117	82	98	0	372
Cleveland	107	107	72	101	3	390
Kansas City	81	152	73	129	0	435
Tennessee	76	117	99	145	2	439
Oakland	68	155	89	130	0	442

NFC Defense	1	2	3	4	OT	PTS
Philadelphia	54	83	41	82	0	260
Washington	44	78	69	74	0	265
Tampa Bay	68	91	69	76	0	304
Arizona	64	100	63	89	6	322
Chicago	78	117	50	86	0	331
Atlanta	57	105	76	99	0	337
Carolina	80	79	92	85	3	339
N.Y. Giants	72	114	71	90	0	347
Detroit	86	80	92	86	6	350
Seattle	89	113	52	113	6	373
Green Bay	82	147	58	93	0	380
St. Louis	78	127	90	94	3	392
Minnesota	78	135	54	128	0	395
Dallas	47	120	83	155	0	405
New Orleans	117	110	70	108	0	405
San Francisco	86	141	84	141	0	452
NFL Totals	**2,263**	**3,386**	**2,149**	**3,158**	**44**	**11,000**

LARGEST TRADES IN NFL HISTORY
(Based on number of players or draft choices involved)

18—October 13, 1989—RB Herschel Walker from the Dallas Cowboys to Minnesota. Dallas also traded its third-round choice in 1990, its tenth-round choice in 1990, and its third-round choice in 1991 to Minnesota. Minnesota traded LB Jesse Solomon, LB David Howard, CB Issiac Holt, and DE Alex Stewart along with its first-round choice in 1990, its second-round choice in 1990, its sixth-round choice in 1990, its first-round choice in 1991, its second-round choice in 1991, its first-round choice in 1992, its second-round choice in 1992, and its third-round choice in 1992 to Dallas. Minnesota traded RB Darrin Nelson to Dallas, which traded Nelson to San Diego for the Chargers' fifth-round choice in 1990, which Dallas then sent to Minnesota.

15—March 26, 1953—T Mike McCormack, DT Don Colo, LB Tom Catlin, DB John Petitbon, and G Herschell Forester from Baltimore to Cleveland for DB Don Shula, DB Bert Rechichar, DB Carl Taseff, LB Ed Sharkey, E Gern Nagler, QB Harry Agganis, T Dick Batten, T Stu Sheets, G Art Spinney, and G Elmer Willhoite.

15—January 28, 1971—LB Marlin McKeever, first- and third-round choices in 1971, and third-, fourth-, fifth-, sixth-, and seventh-round choices in 1972 from Washington to the Los Angeles Rams for LB Maxie Baughan, LB Jack Pardee, LB Myron Pottios, RB Jeff Jordan, G John Wilbur, DT Diron Talbert, and a fifth-round choice in 1971.

12—June 13, 1952—Selection rights to Les Richter from the Dallas Texans to the Los Angeles Rams for RB Dick Hoerner, DB Tom Keane, DB George Sims, C Joe Reid, HB Billy Baggett, T Jack Halliday, FB Dick McKissack, LB Vic Vasicek, E Richard Wilkins, C Aubrey Phillips, and RB Dave Anderson.

10—March 23, 1959—HB Ollie Matson from the Chicago Cardinals to the Los Angeles Rams for T Frank Fuller, DE Glenn Holtzman, T Ken Panfil, DT Art Hauser, E John Tracey, FB Larry Hickman, HB Don Brown, the Rams second-round choice in 1960, and a player to be delivered during the 1959 training camp.

10—October 31, 1987—RB Eric Dickerson from the Los Angeles Rams to Indianapolis. The rights to LB Cornelius Bennett from Indianapolis to Buffalo. Indianapolis running back Owen Gill and the Colts' first- and second-round choices in 1988 and second-round choice in 1989, plus Bills running back Greg Bell and Buffalo's first-round choice in 1988 and first- and second-round choices in 1989 to the Rams.

2005 TOP 100 TELEVISION MARKETS
(NFL TEAM MARKETS IN BOLD)

RANK	MARKET	TOTAL HOUSEHOLDS	TV HOUSEHOLDS	% of U.S.
1	**New York**	**7,528,700**	**7,355,710**	**6.712**
2	Los Angeles	5,554,300	5,431,140	4.956
3	**Chicago**	**3,467,700**	**3,417,330**	**3.118**
4	**Philadelphia**	**2,952,000**	**2,919,410**	**2.664**
5	**Boston (Manchester)**	**2,430,600**	**2,391,840**	**2.183**
6	**San Francisco-Oakland-San Jose**	**2,454,400**	**2,359,870**	**2.153**
7	**Dallas-Ft. Worth**	**2,323,800**	**2,292,760**	**2.092**
8	**Washington, DC (Hagerstown)**	**2,279,200**	**2,241,610**	**2.045**
9	**Atlanta**	**2,092,000**	**2,059,450**	**1.879**
10	**Detroit**	**1,962,400**	**1,943,930**	**1.774**
11	**Houston**	**1,936,800**	**1,902,810**	**1.736**
12	**Seattle-Tacoma**	**1,755,100**	**1,690,640**	**1.543**
13	**Tampa-St. Petersburg (Sarasota)**	**1,694,300**	**1,671,040**	**1.525**
14	**Minneapolis-St. Paul**	**1,686,000**	**1,665,540**	**1.520**
15	**Phoenix**	**1,635,000**	**1,596,950**	**1.457**
16	**Cleveland**	**1,575,500**	**1,556,670**	**1.420**
17	**Miami-Ft. Lauderdale**	**1,527,700**	**1,496,810**	**1.366**
18	**Denver**	**1,439,800**	**1,401,760**	**1.279**
19	Sacramento-Stockton-Modesto	1,345,900	1,315,030	1.200
20	Orlando-Daytona Beach-Melbourne	1,320,300	1,303,150	1.189
21	**St. Louis**	**1,231,900**	**1,216,700**	**1.110**
22	**Pittsburgh**	**1,199,000**	**1,186,010**	**1.082**
23	**Baltimore**	**1,101,100**	**1,087,730**	**0.993**
24	Portland, OR	1,125,600	1,086,900	0.992
25	**Indianapolis**	**1,066,200**	**1,053,020**	**0.961**
26	**San Diego**	**1,054,300**	**1,025,730**	**0.936**
27	Hartford & New Haven	1,031,000	1,017,530	0.928
28	**Charlotte**	**1,017,200**	**1,004,440**	**0.917**
29	Raleigh-Durham (Fayeteville)	980,200	966,720	0.882
30	**Nashville**	**930,500**	**916,170**	**0.836**
31	**Kansas City**	**905,100**	**894,580**	**0.816**
32	Milwaukee	892,900	886,770	0.809
33	**Cincinnati**	**892,900**	**883,230**	**0.806**
34	Columbus, OH	876,600	867,490	0.792
35	Greenville-Spartanburg-Asheville-Anderson	827,700	813,210	0.742
36	Salt Lake City	816,400	800,000	0.730
37	San Antonio	765,000	748,950	0.683
38	Grand Rapids-Kalamazoo-Battle Creek	741,600	732,600	0.668
39	West Palm Beach-Ft. Pierce	742,300	729,010	0.665
40	Birmingham (Anniston,Tuscaloosa)	726,700	717,300	0.655
41	Norfolk-Portsmouth-Newport News	716,800	707,750	0.646
42	Harrisburg-Lancaster-Lebanon-York	721,700	702,590	0.641
43	**New Orleans**	**685,800**	**675,760**	**0.617**
44	Memphis	669,500	658,250	0.601
45	Oklahoma City	663,500	655,250	0.598
46	**Buffalo**	**658,700**	**651,970**	**0.595**
47	Albuquerque-Santa Fe	679,600	649,680	0.593
48	Greensboro-High Point-Winston Salem	655,900	648,860	0.592
49	Providence-New Bedford	650,800	644,980	0.589
50	Louisville	645,100	637,680	0.582

2005 TOP 100 TELEVISION MARKETS
(NFL TEAM MARKETS IN BOLD)

RANK	MARKET	TOTAL HOUSEHOLDS	TV HOUSEHOLDS	% of U.S.
51	Las Vegas	624,600	614,150	0.560
52	**Jacksonville, Brunswick**	**623,500**	**613,000**	**0.559**
53	Wilkes Barre-Scranton	601,200	592,560	0.541
54	Austin	580,300	567,870	0.518
55	Albany-Schenectady-Troy	563,500	555,640	0.507
56	Dayton	542,800	537,710	0.491
57	Little Rock-Pine Bluff	540,600	531,770	0.485
58	Fresno-Visalia	538,200	527,770	0.482
59	Knoxville	521,600	513,630	0.469
60	Tulsa	518,500	510,960	0.466
61	Richmond-Petersburg	516,600	509,860	0.465
62	Charleston-Huntington	517,000	508,750	0.464
63	Mobile-Pensacola (Ft. Walton Beach)	499,700	492,070	0.449
64	Lexington	491,200	481,120	0.439
65	Flint-Saginaw-Bay City	483,500	479,520	0.438
66	Wichita-Hutchinson Plus	453,300	445,690	0.407
67	Roanoke-Lynchburg	454,000	445,670	0.407
68	Ft. Myers-Naples	450,300	444,130	0.405
69	**Green Bay-Appleton**	**436,300**	**433,640**	**0.396**
70	Toledo	435,800	432,430	0.395
71	Honolulu	434,600	417,120	0.381
72	Tucson (Sierra Vista)	428,100	417,070	0.381
73	Des Moines-Ames	416,000	412,230	0.376
74	Portland-Auburn	416,200	409,060	0.373
75	Rochester, NY	400,100	396,880	0.362
76	Omaha	400,300	396,460	0.362
77	Syracuse	402,000	395,400	0.361
78	Springfield, MO	396,300	388,530	0.355
79	Paducah-Cape Girardeau-Harrisburg-Mount Vernon	390,200	384,860	0.351
80	Spokane	399,200	384,060	0.350
81	Shreveport	389,500	382,700	0.349
82	Champaign & Springfield-Decatur	387,500	382,460	0.349
83	Columbia, SC	380,200	374,680	0.342
84	Huntsville-Decatur (Florence)	374,700	370,160	0.338
85	Madison	369,900	364,000	0.332
86	Chattanooga	358,300	353,210	0.322
87	South Bend-Elkhart	337,400	332,860	0.304
88	Cedar Rapids-Waterloo & Dubuque	335,800	331,610	0.303
89	Tri-Cities, TN-VA	335,300	329,910	0.301
90	Burlington-Plattsburgh	338,300	329,200	0.300
91	Jackson, MS	334,400	327,670	0.299
92	Colorado Springs-Pueblo	319,000	313,170	0.286
93	Harlingen-Weslaco-Brownsville-McAllen	319,700	312,300	0.285
94	Davenport-Rock Island-Moline	312,500	309,900	0.283
95	Waco-Temple-Bryan	314,100	308,970	0.282
96	Baton Rouge	311,200	306,910	0.280
97	Johnstown-Altoona	305,900	300,850	0.275
98	Savannah	298,400	293,170	0.268
99	Evansville	292,700	289,840	0.264
100	El Paso	292,400	288,440	0.263
	TOTAL NFL MARKETS	**52,543,500**	**51,606,110**	**47.090**
	TOTAL TOP 100 MARKETS	**95,815,800**	**94,121,930**	**85.885**
	TOTAL	**111,597,300**	**109,590,170**	**100.000**

RETIRED UNIFORM NUMBERS IN NFL

AFC

Baltimore	None	
Buffalo	Jim Kelly	12
Cincinnati	Bob Johnson	54
Cleveland	Otto Graham	14
	Jim Brown	32
	Ernie Davis	45
	Don Fleming	46
	Lou Groza	76
Denver	John Elway	7
	Frank Tripucka	18
	Floyd Little	44
Houston	None	
Indianapolis	Johnny Unitas	19
	Buddy Young	22
	Lenny Moore	24
	Art Donovan	70
	Jim Parker	77
	Raymond Berry	82
	Gino Marchetti	89
Jacksonville	None	
Kansas City	Jan Stenerud	3
	Len Dawson	16
	Abner Haynes	28
	Stone Johnson	33
	Mack Lee Hill	36
	Willie Lanier	63
	Bobby Bell	78
	Buck Buchanan	86
Miami	Bob Griese	12
	Dan Marino	13
	Larry Csonka	39
New England	Bruce Armstrong	78
	Gino Cappelletti	20
	Mike Haynes	40
	Steve Nelson	57
	John Hannah	73
	Jim Lee Hunt	79
	Bob Dee	89
New York Jets	Joe Namath	12
	Don Maynard	13
	Joe Klecko	73
Oakland	None	
Pittsburgh	Ernie Stautner	70
San Diego	Dan Fouts	14
Tennessee	Earl Campbell	34
	Jim Norton	43
	Mike Munchak	63
	Elvin Bethea	65
	Bruce Matthews	74

NFC

Arizona	Larry Wilson	8
	Pat Tillman	40
	Stan Mauldin	77
	J.V. Cain	88
	Marshall Goldberg	99
Atlanta	Steve Bartkowski	10
	William Andrews	31
	Jeff Van Note	57
	Tommy Nobis	60
Carolina	None	
Chicago	Bronko Nagurski	3
	George McAfee	5
	George Halas	7
	Willie Galimore	28
	Walter Payton	34
	Gale Sayers	40
	Brian Piccolo	41
	Sid Luckman	42
	Dick Butkus	51
	Bill Hewitt	56
	Bill George	61
	Bulldog Turner	66
	Red Grange	77
Dallas	None	
Detroit	Dutch Clark	7
	Bobby Layne	22
	Doak Walker	37
	Joe Schmidt	56
	Chuck Hughes	85
Green Bay	Tony Canadeo	3
	Don Hutson	14
	Bart Starr	15
	Ray Nitschke	66
Minnesota	Fran Tarkenton	10
	Mick Tingelhoff	53
	Jim Marshall	70
	Korey Stringer	77
	Cris Carter	80
	Alan Page	88
New Orleans	Jim Taylor	31
	Doug Atkins	81
New York Giants	Ray Flaherty	1
	Tuffy Leemans	4
	Mel Hein	7
	Phil Simms	11
	Y.A. Tittle	14
	Frank Gifford	16
	Al Blozis	32
	Joe Morrison	40
	Charlie Conerly	42
	Ken Strong	50
	Lawrence Taylor	56
Philadelphia	Steve Van Buren	15
	Tom Brookshier	40
	Pete Retzlaff	44
	Chuck Bednarik	60
	Al Wistert	70
	Reggie White	92
	Jerome Brown	99
St. Louis	Bob Waterfield	7
	Eric Dickerson	29
	Merlin Olsen	74
	Jackie Slater	78
	Jack Youngblood	85
San Francisco	John Brodie	12
	Joe Montana	16
	Joe Perry	34
	Jimmy Johnson	37
	Hugh McElhenny	39
	Ronnie Lott	42
	Charlie Krueger	70
	Leo Nomellini	73
	Bob St. Clair	79
	Dwight Clark	87
Seattle	"Fans/the twelfth man"	12
	Steve Largent	80
Tampa Bay	Lee Roy Selmon	63
Washington	Sammy Baugh	33

ALL-TIME REGULAR-SEASON RECORDS OF CURRENT NFL TEAMS

AFC
BALTIMORE RAVENS

	All Games			Home Games			Road Games		
Season	W	L	T	W	L	T	W	L	T
1996	4	12		4	4		0	8	
1997	6	9	1	3	4	1	3	5	
1998	6	10		4	4		2	6	
1999	8	8		4	4		4	4	
2000	12	4		6	2		6	2	
2001	10	6		6	2		4	4	
2002	7	9		4	4		3	5	
2003	10	6		7	1		3	5	
2004	9	7		6	2		3	5	
	72	71	1	44	27	1	28	44	

BUFFALO BILLS

	All Games			Home Games			Road Games		
Season	W	L	T	W	L	T	W	L	T
1960	5	8	1	3	4		2	4	1
1961	6	8		2	5		4	3	
1962	7	6	1	3	3	1	4	3	
1963	7	6	1	4	2	1	3	4	
1964	12	2		6	1		6	1	
1965	10	3	1	5	2		5	1	1
1966	9	4	1	4	2	1	5	2	
1967	4	10		2	5		2	5	
1968	1	12	1	1	6		0	6	1
1969	4	10		4	3		0	7	
1970	3	10	1	1	6		2	4	1
1971	1	13		1	6		0	7	
1972	4	9	1	2	4	1	2	5	
1973	9	5		5	2		4	3	
1974	9	5		5	2		4	3	
1975	8	6		3	4		5	2	
1976	2	12		1	6		1	6	
1977	3	11		1	6		2	5	
1978	5	11		4	4		1	7	
1979	7	9		3	5		4	4	
1980	11	5		6	2		5	3	
1981	10	6		7	1		3	5	
1982	4	5		4	1		0	4	
1983	8	8		3	5		5	3	
1984	2	14		2	6		0	8	
1985	2	14		2	6		0	8	
1986	4	12		3	5		1	7	
1987	7	8		4	4		3	4	
1988	12	4		8	0		4	4	
1989	9	7		6	2		3	5	
1990	13	3		8	0		5	3	
1991	13	3		7	1		6	2	
1992	11	5		6	2		5	3	
1993	12	4		6	2		6	2	
1994	7	9		4	4		3	5	
1995	10	6		6	2		4	4	
1996	10	6		7	1		3	5	
1997	6	10		4	4		2	6	
1998	10	6		6	2		4	4	
1999	11	5		6	2		5	3	
2000	8	8		5	3		3	5	
2001	3	13		1	7		2	6	
2002	8	8		5	3		3	5	
2003	6	10		4	4		2	6	
2004	9	7		5	3		4	4	
	322	346	8	185	150	4	137	196	4

CINCINNATI BENGALS

	All Games			Home Games			Road Games		
Season	W	L	T	W	L	T	W	L	T
1968	3	11		2	5		1	6	
1969	4	9	1	4	3		0	6	1
1970	8	6		5	2		3	4	
1971	4	10		3	4		1	6	
1972	8	6		4	3		4	3	
1973	10	4		7	0		3	4	
1974	7	7		4	3		3	4	
1975	11	3		6	1		5	2	
1976	10	4		6	1		4	3	
1977	8	6		5	2		3	4	
1978	4	12		3	5		1	7	
1979	4	12		4	4		0	8	
1980	6	10		3	5		3	5	
1981	12	4		6	2		6	2	
1982	7	2		4	0		3	2	
1983	7	9		4	4		3	5	
1984	8	8		5	3		3	5	
1985	7	9		5	3		2	6	
1986	10	6		6	2		4	4	
1987	4	11		1	7		3	4	
1988	12	4		8	0		4	4	
1989	8	8		5	3		3	5	
1990	9	7		5	3		4	4	
1991	3	13		3	5		0	8	
1992	5	11		3	5		2	6	
1993	3	13		3	5		0	8	
1994	3	13		2	6		1	7	
1995	7	9		3	5		4	4	
1996	8	8		6	2		2	6	
1997	7	9		6	2		1	7	
1998	3	13		1	7		2	6	
1999	4	12		2	6		2	6	
2000	4	12		3	5		1	7	
2001	6	10		4	4		2	6	
2002	2	14		1	7		1	7	
2003	8	8		5	3		3	5	
2004	8	8		5	3		3	5	
	242	321	1	152	130		90	191	1

CLEVELAND BROWNS*

	All Games			Home Games			Road Games		
Season	W	L	T	W	L	T	W	L	T
1950	10	2		5	1		5	1	
1951	11	1		6	0		5	1	
1952	8	4		4	2		4	2	
1953	11	1		6	0		5	1	
1954	9	3		5	1		4	2	
1955	9	2	1	5	1		4	1	1
1956	5	7		1	5		4	2	
1957	9	2	1	6	0		3	2	1
1958	9	3		4	2		5	1	
1959	7	5		3	3		4	2	
1960	8	3	1	4	2		4	1	1
1961	8	5	1	4	3		4	2	1
1962	7	6	1	4	2	1	3	4	
1963	10	4		5	2		5	2	
1964	10	3	1	5	1	1	5	2	
1965	11	3		5	2		6	1	
1966	9	5		5	2		4	3	
1967	9	5		6	1		3	4	
1968	10	4		5	2		5	2	
1969	10	3	1	5	1	1	5	2	
1970	7	7		4	3		3	4	
1971	9	5		4	3		5	2	
1972	10	4		4	3		6	1	
1973	7	5	2	5	1	1	2	4	1
1974	4	10		3	4		1	6	

Season	All Games W L T	Home Games W L T	Road Games W L T
1975	3 11	3 4	0 7
1976	9 5	6 1	3 4
1977	6 8	2 5	4 3
1978	8 8	5 3	3 5
1979	9 7	5 3	4 4
1980	11 5	6 2	5 3
1981	5 11	3 5	2 6
1982	4 5	2 2	2 3
1983	9 7	6 2	3 5
1984	5 11	2 6	3 5
1985	8 8	5 3	3 5
1986	12 4	6 2	6 2
1987	10 5	5 2	5 3
1988	10 6	6 2	4 4
1989	9 6 1	5 2 1	4 4
1990	3 13	2 6	1 7
1991	6 10	3 5	3 5
1992	7 9	4 4	3 5
1993	7 9	4 4	3 5
1994	11 5	6 2	5 3
1995	5 11	3 5	2 6
1999	2 14	0 8	2 6
2000	3 13	2 6	1 7
2001	7 9	4 4	3 5
2002	9 7	3 5	6 2
2003	5 11	2 6	3 5
2004	4 12	3 5	1 7
	404 332 10	216 151 5	188 181 5

Did not play from 1996-98.

DENVER BRONCOS

Season	All Games W L T	Home Games W L T	Road Games W L T
1960	4 9 1	2 4 1	2 5
1961	3 11	2 5	1 6
1962	7 7	3 4	4 3
1963	2 11 1	2 5	0 6 1
1964	2 11 1	2 4 1	0 7
1965	4 10	2 5	2 5
1966	4 10	3 4	1 6
1967	3 11	1 6	2 5
1968	5 9	3 4	2 5
1969	5 8 1	4 2 1	1 6
1970	5 8 1	3 3 1	2 5
1971	4 9 1	2 4 1	2 5
1972	5 9	3 4	2 5
1973	7 5 2	3 3 1	4 2 1
1974	7 6 1	3 3 1	4 3
1975	6 8	5 2	1 6
1976	9 5	6 1	3 4
1977	12 2	6 1	6 1
1978	10 6	6 2	4 4
1979	10 6	6 2	4 4
1980	8 8	4 4	4 4
1981	10 6	8 0	2 6
1982	2 7	1 4	1 3
1983	9 7	6 2	3 5
1984	13 3	7 1	6 2
1985	11 5	6 2	5 3
1986	11 5	7 1	4 4
1987	10 4 1	7 1	3 3 1
1988	8 8	6 2	2 6
1989	11 5	6 2	5 3
1990	5 11	4 4	1 7
1991	12 4	7 1	5 3
1992	8 8	7 1	1 7
1993	9 7	5 3	4 4
1994	7 9	4 4	3 5

Season	All Games W L T	Home Games W L T	Road Games W L T
1995	8 8	6 2	2 6
1996	13 3	8 0	5 3
1997	12 4	8 0	4 4
1998	14 2	8 0	6 2
1999	6 10	3 5	3 5
2000	11 5	6 2	5 3
2001	8 8	6 2	2 6
2002	9 7	5 3	4 4
2003	10 6	6 2	4 4
2004	10 6	6 2	4 4
	349 317 10	214 118 7	135 199 3

HOUSTON TEXANS

Season	All Games W L T	Home Games W L T	Road Games W L T
2002	4 12	2 6	2 6
2003	5 11	3 5	2 6
2004	7 9	3 5	4 4
	16 32	8 16	8 16

INDIANAPOLIS COLTS*

Season	All Games W L T	Home Games W L T	Road Games W L T
1953	3 9	2 4	1 5
1954	3 9	2 4	1 5
1955	5 6 1	4 1 1	1 5
1956	5 7	4 2	1 5
1957	7 5	4 2	3 3
1958	9 3	6 0	3 3
1959	9 3	4 2	5 1
1960	6 6	4 2	2 4
1961	8 6	5 2	3 4
1962	7 7	3 4	4 3
1963	8 6	4 3	4 3
1964	12 2	7 1	5 1
1965	10 3 1	5 2	5 1 1
1966	9 5	5 2	4 3
1967	11 1 2	6 0 1	5 1 1
1968	13 1	6 1	7 0
1969	8 5 1	4 2 1	4 3
1970	11 2 1	5 1 1	6 1
1971	10 4	5 2	5 2
1972	5 9	2 5	3 4
1973	4 10	3 4	1 6
1974	2 12	0 7	2 5
1975	10 4	5 2	5 2
1976	11 3	6 1	5 2
1977	10 4	6 1	4 3
1978	5 11	2 6	3 5
1979	5 11	3 5	2 6
1980	7 9	2 6	5 3
1981	2 14	1 7	1 7
1982	0 8 1	0 3 1	0 5
1983	7 9	3 5	4 4
1984	4 12	2 6	2 6
1985	5 11	4 4	1 7
1986	3 13	1 7	2 6
1987	9 6	4 4	5 2
1988	9 7	6 2	3 5
1989	8 8	6 2	2 6
1990	7 9	3 5	4 4
1991	1 15	0 8	1 7
1992	9 7	4 4	5 3
1993	4 12	2 6	2 6
1994	8 8	5 3	3 5
1995	9 7	5 3	4 4
1996	9 7	6 2	3 5
1997	3 13	2 6	1 7

Season	All Games W	L	T	Home Games W	L	T	Road Games W	L	T
1998	3	13		3	5		0	8	
1999	13	3		7	1		6	2	
2000	10	6		6	2		4	4	
2001	6	10		3	5		3	5	
2002	10	6		5	3		5	3	
2003	12	4		5	3		7	1	
2004	12	4		7	1		5	3	
	376	375	7	204	171	5	172	204	2

*includes Baltimore Colts (1953-1983).

Season	All Games W	L	T	Home Games W	L	T	Road Games W	L	T
2000	7	9		5	3		2	6	
2001	6	10		3	5		3	5	
2002	8	8		6	2		2	6	
2003	13	3		8	0		5	3	
2004	7	9		4	4		3	5	
	356	308	12	211	122	4	145	186	8

*includes Dallas Texans (1960-62).

JACKSONVILLE JAGUARS

Season	All Games W	L	T	Home Games W	L	T	Road Games W	L	T
1995	4	12		2	6		2	6	
1996	9	7		7	1		2	6	
1997	11	5		7	1		4	4	
1998	11	5		7	1		4	4	
1999	14	2		7	1		7	1	
2000	7	9		4	4		3	5	
2001	6	10		3	5		3	5	
2002	6	10		3	5		3	5	
2003	5	11		5	3		0	8	
2004	9	7		4	4		5	3	
	82	78		49	31		33	47	

KANSAS CITY CHIEFS*

Season	All Games W	L	T	Home Games W	L	T	Road Games W	L	T
1960	8	6		5	2		3	4	
1961	6	8		4	3		2	5	
1962	11	3		6	1		5	2	
1963	5	7	2	4	3		1	4	2
1964	7	7		4	3		3	4	
1965	7	5	2	5	2		2	3	2
1966	11	2	1	4	2	1	7	0	
1967	9	5		4	3		5	2	
1968	12	2		6	1		6	1	
1969	11	3		6	1		5	2	
1970	7	5	2	4	1	2	3	4	
1971	10	3	1	7	0		3	3	1
1972	8	6		3	4		5	2	
1973	7	5	2	5	1	1	2	4	1
1974	5	9		1	6		4	3	
1975	5	9		3	4		2	5	
1976	5	9		1	6		4	3	
1977	2	12		1	6		1	6	
1978	4	12		3	5		1	7	
1979	7	9		3	5		4	4	
1980	8	8		3	5		5	3	
1981	9	7		5	3		4	4	
1982	3	6		2	2		1	4	
1983	6	10		5	3		1	7	
1984	8	8		5	3		3	5	
1985	6	10		5	3		1	7	
1986	10	6		6	2		4	4	
1987	4	11		3	4		1	7	
1988	4	11	1	4	4		0	7	1
1989	8	7	1	5	3		3	4	1
1990	11	5		6	2		5	3	
1991	10	6		6	2		4	4	
1992	10	6		7	1		3	5	
1993	11	5		7	1		4	4	
1994	9	7		5	3		4	4	
1995	13	3		8	0		5	3	
1996	9	7		5	3		4	4	
1997	13	3		8	0		5	3	
1998	7	9		5	3		2	6	
1999	9	7		6	2		3	5	

MIAMI DOLPHINS

Season	All Games W	L	T	Home Games W	L	T	Road Games W	L	T
1966	3	11		2	5		1	6	
1967	4	10		4	3		0	7	
1968	5	8	1	1	5	1	4	3	
1969	3	10	1	2	4	1	1	6	
1970	10	4		6	1		4	3	
1971	10	3	1	6	1		4	2	1
1972	14	0		7	0		7	0	
1973	12	2		7	0		5	2	
1974	11	3		7	0		4	3	
1975	10	4		5	2		5	2	
1976	6	8		3	4		3	4	
1977	10	4		6	1		4	3	
1978	11	5		7	1		4	4	
1979	10	6		6	2		4	4	
1980	8	8		5	3		3	5	
1981	11	4	1	6	1	1	5	3	
1982	7	2		4	0		3	2	
1983	12	4		7	1		5	3	
1984	14	2		7	1		7	1	
1985	12	4		8	0		4	4	
1986	8	8		4	4		4	4	
1987	8	7		4	3		4	4	
1988	6	10		4	4		2	6	
1989	8	8		4	4		4	4	
1990	12	4		7	1		5	3	
1991	8	8		5	3		3	5	
1992	11	5		6	2		5	3	
1993	9	7		4	4		5	3	
1994	10	6		6	2		4	4	
1995	9	7		5	3		4	4	
1996	8	8		4	4		4	4	
1997	9	7		6	2		3	5	
1998	10	6		7	1		3	5	
1999	9	7		5	3		4	4	
2000	11	5		5	3		6	2	
2001	11	5		7	1		4	4	
2002	9	7		7	1		2	6	
2003	10	6		4	4		6	2	
2004	4	12		3	5		1	7	
	353	235	4	203	89	3	150	146	1

NEW ENGLAND PATRIOTS*

Season	All Games W	L	T	Home Games W	L	T	Road Games W	L	T
1960	5	9		3	4		2	5	
1961	9	4	1	4	2	1	5	2	
1962	9	4	1	6	1		3	3	1
1963	7	6	1	5	1	1	2	5	
1964	10	3	1	4	2	1	6	1	
1965	4	8	2	1	4	2	3	4	
1966	8	4	2	4	2	1	4	2	1
1967	3	10	1	2	4		1	6	1
1968	4	10		2	5		2	5	
1969	4	10		2	5		2	5	
1970	2	12		1	6		1	6	
1971	6	8		5	2		1	6	
1972	3	11		2	5		1	6	

Season	All Games W	L	T	Home Games W	L	T	Road Games W	L	T
1973	5	9		3	4		2	5	
1974	7	7		3	4		4	3	
1975	3	11		2	5		1	6	
1976	11	3		6	1		5	2	
1977	9	5		6	1		3	4	
1978	11	5		5	3		6	2	
1979	9	7		6	2		3	5	
1980	10	6		6	2		4	4	
1981	2	14		2	6		0	8	
1982	5	4		3	1		2	3	
1983	8	8		5	3		3	5	
1984	9	7		5	3		4	4	
1985	11	5		7	1		4	4	
1986	11	5		4	4		7	1	
1987	8	7		5	3		3	4	
1988	9	7		7	1		2	6	
1989	5	11		3	5		2	6	
1990	1	15		0	8		1	7	
1991	6	10		4	4		2	6	
1992	2	14		1	7		1	7	
1993	5	11		3	5		2	6	
1994	10	6		5	3		5	3	
1995	6	10		3	5		3	5	
1996	11	5		6	2		5	3	
1997	10	6		6	2		4	4	
1998	9	7		6	2		3	5	
1999	8	8		5	3		3	5	
2000	5	11		3	5		2	6	
2001	11	5		6	2		5	3	
2002	9	7		5	3		4	4	
2003	14	2		8	0		6	2	
2004	14	2		8	0		6	2	
	328	339	9	188	143	6	140	196	3

*includes Boston Patriots (1960-1970).

NEW YORK JETS*

Season	All Games W	L	T	Home Games W	L	T	Road Games W	L	T
1960	7	7		3	4		4	3	
1961	7	7		5	2		2	5	
1962	5	9		2	5		3	4	
1963	5	8	1	4	2	1	1	6	
1964	5	8	1	5	1	1	0	7	
1965	5	8	1	3	3	1	2	5	
1966	6	6	2	4	3		2	3	2
1967	8	5	1	4	2	1	4	3	
1968	11	3		6	1		5	2	
1969	10	4		5	2		5	2	
1970	4	10		2	5		2	5	
1971	6	8		4	3		2	5	
1972	7	7		4	3		3	4	
1973	4	10		2	4		2	6	
1974	7	7		3	4		4	3	
1975	3	11		1	6		2	5	
1976	3	11		2	5		1	6	
1977	3	11		1	6		2	5	
1978	8	8		4	4		4	4	
1979	8	8		6	2		2	6	
1980	4	12		2	6		2	6	
1981	10	5	1	6	2		4	3	1
1982	6	3		3	1		3	2	
1983	7	9		2	6		5	3	
1984	7	9		3	5		4	4	
1985	11	5		7	1		4	4	
1986	10	6		5	3		5	3	
1987	6	9		4	4		2	5	
1988	8	7	1	5	2	1	3	5	
1989	4	12		1	7		3	5	
1990	6	10		3	5		3	5	
1991	8	8		4	4		4	4	
1992	4	12		3	5		1	7	
1993	8	8		3	5		5	3	
1994	6	10		4	4		2	6	
1995	3	13		2	6		1	7	
1996	1	15		0	8		1	7	
1997	9	7		5	3		4	4	
1998	12	4		7	1		5	3	
1999	8	8		4	4		4	4	
2000	9	7		5	3		4	4	
2001	10	6		3	5		7	1	
2002	9	7		5	3		4	4	
2003	6	10		4	4		2	6	
2004	10	6		6	2		4	4	
	304	364	8	166	166	5	138	198	3

*includes New York Titans (1960-62).

OAKLAND RAIDERS*

Season	All Games W	L	T	Home Games W	L	T	Road Games W	L	T
1960	6	8		3	4		3	4	
1961	2	12		1	6		1	6	
1962	1	13		1	6		0	7	
1963	10	4		6	1		4	3	
1964	5	7	2	5	2		0	5	2
1965	8	5	1	5	2		3	3	1
1966	8	5	1	3	3	1	5	2	
1967	13	1		7	0		6	1	
1968	12	2		6	1		6	1	
1969	12	1	1	7	0		5	1	1
1970	8	4	2	6	1		2	3	2
1971	8	4	2	5	1	1	3	3	1
1972	10	3	1	5	1	1	5	2	
1973	9	4	1	5	2		4	2	1
1974	12	2		6	1		6	1	
1975	11	3		6	1		5	2	
1976	13	1		7	0		6	1	
1977	11	3		6	1		5	2	
1978	9	7		4	4		5	3	
1979	9	7		6	2		3	5	
1980	11	5		6	2		5	3	
1981	7	9		4	4		3	5	
1982	8	1		4	0		4	1	
1983	12	4		6	2		6	2	
1984	11	5		6	2		5	3	
1985	12	4		7	1		5	3	
1986	8	8		3	5		5	3	
1987	5	10		3	5		2	5	
1988	7	9		3	5		4	4	
1989	8	8		7	1		1	7	
1990	12	4		6	2		6	2	
1991	9	7		5	3		4	4	
1992	7	9		5	3		2	6	
1993	10	6		5	3		5	3	
1994	9	7		4	4		5	3	
1995	8	8		4	4		4	4	
1996	7	9		4	4		3	5	
1997	4	12		2	6		2	6	
1998	8	8		4	4		4	4	
1999	8	8		5	3		3	5	
2000	12	4		7	1		5	3	
2001	10	6		5	3		5	3	
2002	11	5		6	2		5	3	
2003	4	12		4	4		0	8	
2004	5	11		3	5		2	6	
	390	275	11	218	117	3	172	158	8

*includes Los Angeles Raiders (1982-1994).

PITTSBURGH STEELERS*

Season	All Games W	L	T	Home Games W	L	T	Road Games W	L	T
1933	3	6	2	2	3		1	3	2
1934	2	10		1	5		1	5	
1935	4	8		2	5		2	3	
1936	6	6		4	1		2	5	
1937	4	7		2	4		2	3	
1938	2	9		0	5		2	4	
1939	1	9	1	1	4		0	5	1
1940	2	7	2	1	2	2	1	5	
1941	1	9	1	1	4		0	5	1
1942	7	4		3	2		4	2	
1945	2	8		1	4		1	4	
1946	5	5	1	4	1		1	4	1
1947	8	4		5	1		3	3	
1948	4	8		4	2		0	6	
1949	6	5	1	3	2	1	3	3	
1950	6	6		2	4		4	2	
1951	4	7	1	1	4	1	3	3	
1952	5	7		2	4		3	3	
1953	6	6		3	3		3	3	
1954	5	7		4	2		1	5	
1955	4	8		3	2		1	6	
1956	5	7		3	3		2	4	
1957	6	6		4	2		2	4	
1958	7	4	1	5	1		2	3	1
1959	6	5	1	3	2	1	3	3	
1960	5	6	1	4	2		1	4	1
1961	6	8		4	3		2	5	
1962	9	5		4	3		5	2	
1963	7	4	3	5	0	2	2	4	1
1964	5	9		2	5		3	4	
1965	2	12		1	6		1	6	
1966	5	8	1	3	3	1	2	5	
1967	4	9	1	1	6		3	3	1
1968	2	11	1	1	6		1	5	1
1969	1	13		1	6		0	7	
1970	5	9		4	3		1	6	
1971	6	8		5	2		1	6	
1972	11	3		7	0		4	3	
1973	10	4		7	1		3	3	
1974	10	3	1	5	2		5	1	1
1975	12	2		6	1		6	1	
1976	10	4		6	1		4	3	
1977	9	5		6	1		3	4	
1978	14	2		7	1		7	1	
1979	12	4		8	0		4	4	
1980	9	7		6	2		3	5	
1981	8	8		5	3		3	5	
1982	6	3		4	0		2	3	
1983	10	6		4	4		6	2	
1984	9	7		6	2		3	5	
1985	7	9		5	3		2	6	
1986	6	10		4	4		2	6	
1987	8	7		4	3		4	4	
1988	5	11		4	4		1	7	
1989	9	7		4	4		5	3	
1990	9	7		6	2		3	5	
1991	7	9		5	3		2	6	
1992	11	5		7	1		4	4	
1993	9	7		6	2		3	5	
1994	12	4		7	1		5	3	
1995	11	5		6	2		5	3	
1996	10	6		7	1		3	5	
1997	11	5		7	1		4	4	
1998	7	9		5	3		2	6	
1999	6	10		2	6		4	4	
2000	9	7		4	4		5	3	
2001	13	3		7	1		6	2	
2002	10	5	1	5	2	1	5	3	
2003	6	10		4	4		2	6	
2004	15	1		8	0		7	1	
	479	465	20	283	186	9	196	279	11

*includes Pittsburgh Pirates (1933-1940).

SAN DIEGO CHARGERS*

Season	All Games W	L	T	Home Games W	L	T	Road Games W	L	T
1960	10	4		5	2		5	2	
1961	12	2		6	1		6	1	
1962	4	10		3	4		1	6	
1963	11	3		6	1		5	2	
1964	8	5	1	4	3		4	2	1
1965	9	2	3	4	1	2	5	1	1
1966	7	6	1	5	2		2	4	1
1967	8	5	1	5	2	1	3	3	
1968	9	5		4	3		5	2	
1969	8	6		5	2		3	4	
1970	5	6	3	2	3	2	3	3	1
1971	6	8		6	1		0	7	
1972	4	9	1	2	5		2	4	1
1973	2	11	1	2	5		0	6	1
1974	5	9		3	4		2	5	
1975	2	12		1	6		1	6	
1976	6	8		3	4		3	4	
1977	7	7		3	4		4	3	
1978	9	7		5	3		4	4	
1979	12	4		7	1		5	3	
1980	11	5		6	2		5	3	
1981	10	6		5	3		5	3	
1982	6	3		3	1		3	2	
1983	6	10		4	4		2	6	
1984	7	9		4	4		3	5	
1985	8	8		6	2		2	6	
1986	4	12		2	6		2	6	
1987	8	7		4	3		4	4	
1988	6	10		3	5		3	5	
1989	6	10		4	4		2	6	
1990	6	10		3	5		3	5	
1991	4	12		3	5		1	7	
1992	11	5		6	2		5	3	
1993	8	8		4	4		4	4	
1994	11	5		5	3		6	2	
1995	9	7		5	3		4	4	
1996	8	8		5	3		3	5	
1997	4	12		2	6		2	6	
1998	5	11		4	4		1	7	
1999	8	8		4	4		4	4	
2000	1	15		1	7		0	8	
2001	5	11		4	4		1	7	
2002	8	8		5	3		3	5	
2003	4	12		2	6		2	6	
2004	12	4		7	1		5	3	
	320	345	11	182	151	5	138	194	6

*includes Los Angeles Chargers (1960).

TENNESSEE TITANS*

Season	All Games W	L	T	Home Games W	L	T	Road Games W	L	T
1960	10	4		6	1		4	3	
1961	10	3	1	6	1		4	2	1
1962	11	3		6	1		5	2	
1963	6	8		4	3		2	5	
1964	4	10		3	4		1	6	
1965	4	10		3	4		1	6	
1966	3	11		3	4		0	7	
1967	9	4	1	5	2		4	2	1

Season	All Games W	L	T	Home Games W	L	T	Road Games W	L	T
1968	7	7		3	4		4	3	
1969	6	6	2	4	2	1	2	4	1
1970	3	10	1	1	6		2	4	1
1971	4	9	1	3	3	1	1	6	
1972	1	13		1	6		0	7	
1973	1	13		0	7		1	6	
1974	7	7		3	4		4	3	
1975	10	4		5	2		5	2	
1976	5	9		3	4		2	5	
1977	8	6		5	2		3	4	
1978	10	6		5	3		5	3	
1979	11	5		6	2		5	3	
1980	11	5		6	2		5	3	
1981	7	9		5	3		2	6	
1982	1	8		1	4		0	4	
1983	2	14		2	6		0	8	
1984	3	13		2	6		1	7	
1985	5	11		4	4		1	7	
1986	5	11		4	4		1	7	
1987	9	6		5	2		4	4	
1988	10	6		7	1		3	5	
1989	9	7		6	2		3	5	
1990	9	7		6	2		3	5	
1991	11	5		7	1		4	4	
1992	10	6		5	3		5	3	
1993	12	4		7	1		5	3	
1994	2	14		2	6		0	8	
1995	7	9		3	5		4	4	
1996	8	8		2	6		6	2	
1997	8	8		6	2		2	6	
1998	8	8		3	5		5	3	
1999	13	3		8	0		5	3	
2000	13	3		7	1		6	2	
2001	7	9		3	5		4	4	
2002	11	5		6	2		5	3	
2003	12	4		7	1		5	3	
2004	5	11		2	6		3	5	
	328	342	6	191	145	2	137	197	4

*includes Houston Oilers (1960-1996) and Tennessee Oilers (1997-98).

NFC
ARIZONA CARDINALS*

Season	All Games W	L	T	Home Games W	L	T	Road Games W	L	T
1920	6	2	2	5	1	1	1	1	1
1921	3	3	2	3	3	1	0	0	1
1922	8	3		8	3		0	0	
1923	8	4		8	3		0	1	
1924	5	4	1	5	3	1	0	1	
1925	11	2	1	11	2		0	0	1
1926	5	6	1	3	3		2	3	1
1927	3	7	1	2	3	1	1	4	
1928	1	5		1	1		0	4	
1929	6	6	1	3	2		3	4	1
1930	5	6	2	3	2		2	4	2
1931	5	4		3	0		2	4	
1932	2	6	2	1	2	1	1	4	1
1933	1	9	1	0	4	1	1	5	
1934	5	6		2	2		3	4	
1935	6	4	2	2	2		4	2	2
1936	3	8	1	3	1	1	0	7	
1937	5	5	1	1	3		4	2	1
1938	2	9		1	4		1	5	
1939	1	10		0	4		1	6	
1940	2	7	2	2	1	1	0	6	1
1941	3	7	1	0	3	1	3	4	
1942	3	8		2	2		1	6	
1943	0	10		0	3		0	7	
1945	1	9		0	3		1	6	
1946	6	5		2	2		4	3	
1947	9	3		5	0		4	3	
1948	11	1		5	1		6	0	
1949	6	5	1	2	3	1	4	2	
1950	5	7		3	3		2	4	
1951	3	9		1	5		2	4	
1952	4	8		2	4		2	4	
1953	1	10	1	0	5	1	1	5	
1954	2	10		2	4		0	6	
1955	4	7	1	3	2	1	1	5	
1956	7	5		4	2		3	3	
1957	3	9		0	6		3	3	
1958	2	9	1	1	4	1	1	5	
1959	2	10		2	4		0	6	
1960	6	5	1	3	2	1	3	3	
1961	7	7		3	4		4	3	
1962	4	9	1	2	4	1	2	5	
1963	9	5		3	4		6	1	
1964	9	3	2	4	1	1	5	2	1
1965	5	9		2	5		3	4	
1966	8	5	1	5	1	1	3	4	
1967	6	7	1	3	3	1	3	4	
1968	9	4	1	4	2	1	5	2	
1969	4	9	1	3	4		1	5	1
1970	8	5	1	6	1		2	4	1
1971	4	9	1	1	5	1	3	4	
1972	4	9	1	2	5		2	4	1
1973	4	9	1	2	4	1	2	5	
1974	10	4		5	2		5	2	
1975	11	3		6	1		5	2	
1976	10	4		6	1		4	3	
1977	7	7		4	3		3	4	
1978	6	10		3	5		3	5	
1979	5	11		3	5		2	6	
1980	5	11		2	6		3	5	
1981	7	9		5	3		2	6	
1982	5	4		1	3		4	1	
1983	8	7	1	4	3	1	4	4	
1984	9	7		5	3		4	4	
1985	5	11		4	4		1	7	
1986	4	11	1	3	5		1	6	1
1987	7	8		4	3		3	5	
1988	7	9		4	4		3	5	
1989	5	11		2	6		3	5	
1990	5	11		3	5		2	6	
1991	4	12		2	6		2	6	
1992	4	12		3	5		1	7	
1993	7	9		4	4		3	5	
1994	8	8		5	3		3	5	
1995	4	12		3	5		1	7	
1996	7	9		5	3		2	6	
1997	4	12		3	5		1	7	
1998	9	7		5	3		4	4	
1999	6	10		4	4		2	6	
2000	3	13		3	5		0	8	
2001	7	9		3	5		4	4	
2002	5	11		3	5		2	6	
2003	4	12		4	4		0	8	
2004	6	10		5	3		1	7	
	446	627	39	260	272	22	186	355	17

*includes Chicago Cardinals (1920-1959), St. Louis Cardinals (1960-1987), and Phoenix Cardinals (1988-1993).

ATLANTA FALCONS

Season	All Games W	L	T	Home Games W	L	T	Road Games W	L	T
1966	3	11		1	6		2	5	
1967	1	12	1	1	5	1	0	7	
1968	2	12		1	6		1	6	
1969	6	8		4	3		2	5	
1970	4	8	2	3	4		1	4	2
1971	7	6	1	4	3		3	3	1
1972	7	7		4	3		3	4	
1973	9	5		4	3		5	2	
1974	3	11		2	5		1	6	
1975	4	10		3	4		1	6	
1976	4	10		3	4		1	6	
1977	7	7		4	3		3	4	
1978	9	7		7	1		2	6	
1979	6	10		3	5		3	5	
1980	12	4		6	2		6	2	
1981	7	9		4	4		3	5	
1982	5	4		2	3		3	1	
1983	7	9		4	4		3	5	
1984	4	12		2	6		2	6	
1985	4	12		3	5		1	7	
1986	7	8	1	2	5	1	5	3	
1987	3	12		2	6		1	6	
1988	5	11		2	6		3	5	
1989	3	13		3	5		0	8	
1990	5	11		5	3		0	8	
1991	10	6		6	2		4	4	
1992	6	10		5	3		1	7	
1993	6	10		4	4		2	6	
1994	7	9		5	3		2	6	
1995	9	7		7	1		2	6	
1996	3	13		2	6		1	7	
1997	7	9		3	5		4	4	
1998	14	2		8	0		6	2	
1999	5	11		4	4		1	7	
2000	4	12		3	5		1	7	
2001	7	9		3	5		4	4	
2002	9	6	1	5	3		4	3	1
2003	5	11		2	6		3	5	
2004	11	5		7	1		4	4	
	237	349	6	143	152	2	94	197	4

CAROLINA PANTHERS

Season	All Games W	L	T	Home Games W	L	T	Road Games W	L	T
1995	7	9		5	3		2	6	
1996	12	4		8	0		4	4	
1997	7	9		2	6		5	3	
1998	4	12		2	6		2	6	
1999	8	8		5	3		3	5	
2000	7	9		5	3		2	6	
2001	1	15		0	8		1	7	
2002	7	9		4	4		3	5	
2003	11	5		6	2		5	3	
2004	7	9		3	5		4	4	
	71	89		40	40		31	49	

CHICAGO BEARS*

Season	All Games W	L	T	Home Games W	L	T	Road Games W	L	T
1920	10	1	2	6	0	1	4	1	1
1921	9	1	1	9	1	1	0	0	
1922	9	3		7	1		2	2	
1923	9	2	1	7	1	1	2	1	
1924	6	1	4	5	0	3	1	1	1
1925	9	5	3	7	1	1	2	4	2
1926	12	1	3	10	0	2	2	1	1
1927	9	3	2	7	1	1	2	2	1
1928	7	5	1	6	3		1	2	1
1929	4	9	2	1	5	2	3	4	
1930	9	4	1	5	2	1	4	2	
1931	8	5		6	3		2	2	
1932	7	1	6	6	1	1	1	0	5
1933	10	2	1	6	0		4	2	1
1934	13	0		5	0		8	0	
1935	6	4	2	1	2	2	5	2	
1936	9	3		3	1		6	2	
1937	9	1	1	4	1		5	0	1
1938	6	5		2	3		4	2	
1939	8	3		4	1		4	2	
1940	8	3		5	0		3	3	
1941	10	1		5	1		5	0	
1942	11	0		6	0		5	0	
1943	8	1	1	5	0		3	1	1
1944	6	3	1	4	0	1	2	3	
1945	3	7		2	3		1	4	
1946	8	2	1	4	1	1	4	1	
1947	8	4		4	2		4	2	
1948	10	2		5	1		5	1	
1949	9	3		5	1		4	2	
1950	9	3		6	0		3	3	
1951	7	5		3	3		4	2	
1952	5	7		3	3		2	4	
1953	3	8	1	1	4	1	2	4	
1954	8	4		4	2		4	2	
1955	8	4		5	1		3	3	
1956	9	2	1	6	0		3	2	1
1957	5	7		2	4		3	3	
1958	8	4		5	1		3	3	
1959	8	4		4	2		4	2	
1960	5	6	1	4	2		1	4	1
1961	8	6		5	2		3	4	
1962	9	5		4	3		5	2	
1963	11	1	2	6	0	1	5	1	1
1964	5	9		2	5		3	4	
1965	9	5		5	2		4	3	
1966	5	7	2	4	1	2	1	6	
1967	7	6	1	3	3	1	4	3	
1968	7	7		2	5		5	2	
1969	1	13		1	6		0	7	
1970	6	8		3	4		3	4	
1971	6	8		4	3		2	5	
1972	4	9	1	1	5	1	3	4	
1973	3	11		1	6		2	5	
1974	4	10		4	3		0	7	
1975	4	10		3	4		1	6	
1976	7	7		4	3		3	4	
1977	9	5		5	2		4	3	
1978	7	9		4	4		3	5	
1979	10	6		6	2		4	4	
1980	7	9		5	3		2	6	
1981	6	10		4	4		2	6	
1982	3	6		2	2		1	4	
1983	8	8		5	3		3	5	
1984	10	6		6	2		4	4	
1985	15	1		8	0		7	1	
1986	14	2		7	1		7	1	
1987	11	4		6	2		5	2	
1988	12	4		7	1		5	3	
1989	6	10		4	4		2	6	
1990	11	5		7	1		4	4	
1991	11	5		6	2		5	3	
1992	5	11		4	4		1	7	
1993	7	9		3	5		4	4	
1994	9	7		5	3		4	4	
1995	9	7		5	3		4	4	

Season	All Games W	L	T	Home Games W	L	T	Road Games W	L	T
1996	7	9		6	2		1	7	
1997	4	12		2	6		2	6	
1998	4	12		3	5		1	7	
1999	6	10		3	5		3	5	
2000	5	11		3	5		2	6	
2001	13	3		7	1		6	2	
2002	4	12		3	5		1	7	
2003	7	9		6	2		1	7	
2004	5	11		2	6		3	5	
	646	474	42	381	198	24	265	276	18

*includes Decatur Staleys (1920) and Chicago Staleys (1921).

DALLAS COWBOYS

Season	All Games W	L	T	Home Games W	L	T	Road Games W	L	T
1960	0	11	1	0	6		0	5	1
1961	4	9	1	2	4	1	2	5	
1962	5	8	1	2	4	1	3	4	
1963	4	10		3	4		1	6	
1964	5	8	1	2	4	1	3	4	
1965	7	7		5	2		2	5	
1966	10	3	1	6	1		4	2	1
1967	9	5		5	2		4	3	
1968	12	2		5	2		7	0	
1969	11	2	1	6	0	1	5	2	
1970	10	4		6	1		4	3	
1971	11	3		6	1		5	2	
1972	10	4		5	2		5	2	
1973	10	4		6	1		4	3	
1974	8	6		5	2		3	4	
1975	10	4		5	2		5	2	
1976	11	3		6	1		5	2	
1977	12	2		6	1		6	1	
1978	12	4		7	1		5	3	
1979	11	5		6	2		5	3	
1980	12	4		8	0		4	4	
1981	12	4		8	0		4	4	
1982	6	3		3	2		3	1	
1983	12	4		6	2		6	2	
1984	9	7		5	3		4	4	
1985	10	6		7	1		3	5	
1986	7	9		3	5		4	4	
1987	7	8		3	4		4	4	
1988	3	13		1	7		2	6	
1989	1	15		0	8		1	7	
1990	7	9		5	3		2	6	
1991	11	5		6	2		5	3	
1992	13	3		7	1		6	2	
1993	12	4		6	2		6	2	
1994	12	4		6	2		6	2	
1995	12	4		6	2		6	2	
1996	10	6		6	2		4	4	
1997	6	10		5	3		1	7	
1998	10	6		6	2		4	4	
1999	8	8		7	1		1	7	
2000	5	11		3	5		2	6	
2001	5	11		4	4		1	7	
2002	5	11		4	4		1	7	
2003	10	6		6	2		4	4	
2004	6	10		4	4		2	6	
	383	285	6	219	114	4	164	171	2

DETROIT LIONS*

Season	All Games W	L	T	Home Games W	L	T	Road Games W	L	T
1930	5	6	3	5	1	2	0	5	1
1931	11	3		8	0		3	3	
1932	6	2	4	3	0	2	3	2	2

Season	All Games W	L	T	Home Games W	L	T	Road Games W	L	T
1933	6	5		4	1		2	4	
1934	10	3		6	2		4	1	
1935	7	3	2	5	0	1	2	3	1
1936	8	4		5	1		3	3	
1937	7	4		4	2		3	2	
1938	7	4		4	3		3	1	
1939	6	5		4	2		2	3	
1940	5	5	1	3	3		2	2	1
1941	4	6	1	3	2		1	4	1
1942	0	11		0	7		0	4	
1943	3	6	1	2	2	1	1	4	
1944	6	3	1	4	2		2	1	1
1945	7	3		4	1		3	2	
1946	1	10		1	5		0	5	
1947	3	9		2	4		1	5	
1948	2	10		2	4		0	6	
1949	4	8		2	4		2	4	
1950	6	6		4	2		2	4	
1951	7	4	1	3	3	1	4	1	
1952	9	3		6	1		3	2	
1953	10	2		5	1		5	1	
1954	9	2	1	5	0	1	4	2	
1955	3	9		3	4		0	5	
1956	9	3		5	1		4	2	
1957	8	4		5	1		3	3	
1958	4	7	1	2	4		2	3	1
1959	3	8	1	2	4		1	4	1
1960	7	5		5	1		2	4	
1961	8	5	1	2	5		6	0	1
1962	11	3		7	0		4	3	
1963	5	8	1	3	3	1	2	5	
1964	7	5	2	3	3	1	4	2	1
1965	6	7	1	2	4	1	4	3	
1966	4	9	1	3	4		1	5	1
1967	5	7	2	3	4		2	3	2
1968	4	8	2	1	4	2	3	4	
1969	9	4	1	5	2		4	2	1
1970	10	4		6	1		4	3	
1971	7	6	1	3	4		4	2	1
1972	8	5	1	5	2		3	3	1
1973	6	7	1	4	3		2	4	1
1974	7	7		5	2		2	5	
1975	7	7		4	3		3	4	
1976	6	8		5	2		1	6	
1977	6	8		5	2		1	6	
1978	7	9		5	3		2	6	
1979	2	14		2	6		0	8	
1980	9	7		6	2		3	5	
1981	8	8		7	1		1	7	
1982	4	5		2	3		2	2	
1983	9	7		6	2		3	5	
1984	4	11	1	2	5	1	2	6	
1985	7	9		6	2		1	7	
1986	5	11		1	7		4	4	
1987	4	11		1	6		3	5	
1988	4	12		2	6		2	6	
1989	7	9		4	4		3	5	
1990	6	10		3	5		3	5	
1991	12	4		8	0		4	4	
1992	5	11		3	5		2	6	
1993	10	6		5	3		5	3	
1994	9	7		6	2		3	5	
1995	10	6		7	1		3	5	
1996	5	11		4	4		1	7	
1997	9	7		6	2		3	5	
1998	5	11		4	4		1	7	
1999	8	8		6	2		2	6	
2000	9	7		4	4		5	3	

Season	All Games W	L	T	Home Games W	L	T	Road Games W	L	T
2001	2	14		2	6		0	8	
2002	3	13		3	5		0	8	
2003	5	11		5	3		0	8	
2004	6	10		3	5		3	5	
	473	520	32	295	214	14	178	306	18

includes Portsmouth Spartans (1930-33).

GREEN BAY PACKERS

Season	All Games W	L	T	Home Games W	L	T	Road Games W	L	T
1921	3	2	1	2	1		1	1	1
1922	4	3	3	4	1	1	0	2	2
1923	7	2	1	4	2	1	3	0	
1924	7	4		5	0		2	4	
1925	8	5		6	0		2	5	
1926	7	3	3	4	1	2	3	2	1
1927	7	2	1	6	1		1	1	1
1928	6	4	3	2	2	2	4	2	1
1929	12	0	1	5	0		7	0	1
1930	10	3	1	6	0		4	3	1
1931	12	2		8	0		4	2	
1932	10	3	1	5	0	1	5	3	
1933	5	7	1	3	2	1	2	5	
1934	7	6		4	2		3	4	
1935	8	4		5	2		3	2	
1936	10	1	1	5	1		5	0	1
1937	7	4		3	2		4	2	
1938	8	3		4	2		4	1	
1939	9	2		4	1		5	1	
1940	6	4	1	4	2		2	2	1
1941	10	1		4	1		6	0	
1942	8	2	1	4	1		4	1	1
1943	7	2	1	2	1	1	5	1	
1944	8	2		5	0		3	2	
1945	6	4		4	1		2	3	
1946	6	5		2	3		4	2	
1947	6	5	1	4	2		2	3	1
1948	3	9		2	4		1	5	
1949	2	10		1	5		1	5	
1950	3	9		3	3		0	6	
1951	3	9		2	4		1	5	
1952	6	6		3	3		3	3	
1953	2	9	1	1	5		1	4	1
1954	4	8		2	4		2	4	
1955	6	6		5	1		1	5	
1956	4	8		2	4		2	4	
1957	3	9		1	5		2	4	
1958	1	10	1	1	4	1	0	6	
1959	7	5		4	2		3	3	
1960	8	4		4	2		4	2	
1961	11	3		6	1		5	2	
1962	13	1		7	0		6	1	
1963	11	2	1	6	1		5	1	1
1964	8	5	1	4	3		4	2	1
1965	10	3	1	6	1		4	2	1
1966	12	2		6	1		6	1	
1967	9	4	1	4	2	1	5	2	
1968	6	7	1	2	5		4	2	1
1969	8	6		5	2		3	4	
1970	6	8		4	3		2	5	
1971	4	8	2	3	3	1	1	5	1
1972	10	4		4	3		6	1	
1973	5	7	2	3	2	2	2	5	
1974	6	8		4	3		2	5	
1975	4	10		3	4		1	6	
1976	5	9		4	3		1	6	
1977	4	10		2	5		2	5	
1978	8	7	1	5	2	1	3	5	
1979	5	11		4	4		1	7	
1980	5	10	1	4	4		1	6	1
1981	8	8		4	4		4	4	
1982	5	3	1	3	1		2	2	1
1983	8	8		5	3		3	5	
1984	8	8		5	3		3	5	
1985	8	8		5	3		3	5	
1986	4	12		1	7		3	5	
1987	5	9	1	2	5	1	3	4	
1988	4	12		2	6		2	6	
1989	10	6		6	2		4	4	
1990	6	10		3	5		3	5	
1991	4	12		2	6		2	6	
1992	9	7		6	2		3	5	
1993	9	7		6	2		3	5	
1994	9	7		7	1		2	6	
1995	11	5		7	1		4	4	
1996	13	3		8	0		5	3	
1997	13	3		8	0		5	3	
1998	11	5		7	1		4	4	
1999	8	8		5	3		3	5	
2000	9	7		6	2		3	5	
2001	12	4		7	1		5	3	
2002	12	4		8	0		4	4	
2003	10	6		5	3		5	3	
2004	10	6		4	4		6	2	
	612	480	36	353	194	16	259	286	20

MINNESOTA VIKINGS

Season	All Games W	L	T	Home Games W	L	T	Road Games W	L	T
1961	3	11		3	4		0	7	
1962	2	11	1	1	5	1	1	6	
1963	5	8	1	3	4		2	4	1
1964	8	5	1	4	3		4	2	1
1965	7	7		2	5		5	2	
1966	4	9	1	2	5		2	4	1
1967	3	8	3	1	4	2	2	4	1
1968	8	6		4	3		4	3	
1969	12	2		7	0		5	2	
1970	12	2		7	0		5	2	
1971	11	3		5	2		6	1	
1972	7	7		3	4		4	3	
1973	12	2		7	0		5	2	
1974	10	4		4	3		6	1	
1975	12	2		7	0		5	2	
1976	11	2	1	6	0	1	5	2	
1977	9	5		5	2		4	3	
1978	8	7	1	5	3		3	4	1
1979	7	9		5	3		2	6	
1980	9	7		5	3		4	4	
1981	7	9		5	3		2	6	
1982	5	4		4	1		1	3	
1983	8	8		3	5		5	3	
1984	3	13		2	6		1	7	
1985	7	9		4	4		3	5	
1986	9	7		5	3		4	4	
1987	8	7		5	3		3	4	
1988	11	5		7	1		4	4	
1989	10	6		8	0		2	6	
1990	6	10		4	4		2	6	
1991	8	8		4	4		4	4	
1992	11	5		5	3		6	2	
1993	9	7		4	4		5	3	
1994	10	6		6	2		4	4	
1995	8	8		6	2		2	6	
1996	9	7		5	3		4	4	
1997	9	7		5	3		4	4	

Season	All Games W	L	T	Home Games W	L	T	Road Games W	L	T
1998	15	1		8	0		7	1	
1999	10	6		6	2		4	4	
2000	11	5		7	1		4	4	
2001	5	11		5	3		0	8	
2002	6	10		4	4		2	6	
2003	9	7		6	2		3	5	
2004	8	8		5	3		3	5	
	362	291	9	209	119	4	153	172	5

NEW ORLEANS SAINTS

Season	All Games W	L	T	Home Games W	L	T	Road Games W	L	T
1967	3	11		2	5		1	6	
1968	4	9	1	3	4		1	5	1
1969	5	9		3	4		2	5	
1970	2	11	1	2	5		0	6	1
1971	4	8	2	2	4	1	2	4	1
1972	2	11	1	2	5		0	6	1
1973	5	9		5	2		0	7	
1974	5	9		4	3		1	6	
1975	2	12		2	5		0	7	
1976	4	10		2	5		2	5	
1977	3	11		2	5		1	6	
1978	7	9		3	5		4	4	
1979	8	8		3	5		5	3	
1980	1	15		0	8		1	7	
1981	4	12		2	6		2	6	
1982	4	5		2	3		2	2	
1983	8	8		5	3		3	5	
1984	7	9		3	5		4	4	
1985	5	11		3	5		2	6	
1986	7	9		4	4		3	5	
1987	12	3		6	1		6	2	
1988	10	6		5	3		5	3	
1989	9	7		5	3		4	4	
1990	8	8		5	3		3	5	
1991	11	5		6	2		5	3	
1992	12	4		6	2		6	2	
1993	8	8		4	4		4	4	
1994	7	9		3	5		4	4	
1995	7	9		4	4		3	5	
1996	3	13		2	6		1	7	
1997	6	10		3	5		3	5	
1998	6	10		4	4		2	6	
1999	3	13		3	5		0	8	
2000	10	6		3	5		7	1	
2001	7	9		3	5		4	4	
2002	9	7		4	4		5	3	
2003	8	8		5	3		3	5	
2004	8	8		3	5		5	3	
	234	339	5	128	160	1	106	179	4

NEW YORK GIANTS

Season	All Games W	L	T	Home Games W	L	T	Road Games W	L	T
1925	8	4		7	2		1	2	
1926	8	4	1	5	2	1	3	2	
1927	11	1	1	7	1		4	0	1
1928	4	7	2	1	2	2	3	5	
1929	13	1	1	7	1		6	0	1
1930	13	4		6	2		7	2	
1931	7	6	1	4	2	1	3	4	
1932	4	6	2	3	2	1	1	4	1
1933	11	3		7	0		3	4	
1934	8	5		5	1		3	4	
1935	9	3		4	2		5	1	
1936	5	6	1	3	3	1	2	3	
1937	6	3	2	4	2	1	2	1	1

Season	All Games W	L	T	Home Games W	L	T	Road Games W	L	T
1938	8	2	1	6	1		2	1	1
1939	9	1	1	6	0		3	1	1
1940	6	4	1	4	3		2	1	1
1941	8	3		5	2		3	1	
1942	5	5	1	3	2	1	2	3	
1943	6	3	1	4	2		2	1	1
1944	8	1	1	5	1		3	0	1
1945	3	6	1	2	4		1	2	1
1946	7	3	1	5	1	1	2	2	
1947	2	8	2	2	3	1	0	5	1
1948	4	8		2	4		2	4	
1949	6	6		2	4		4	2	
1950	10	2		5	1		5	1	
1951	9	2	1	5	1		4	1	1
1952	7	5		2	4		5	1	
1953	3	9		2	4		1	5	
1954	7	5		4	2		3	3	
1955	6	5	1	4	1	1	2	4	
1956	8	3	1	4	1	1	4	2	
1957	7	5		3	3		4	2	
1958	9	3		5	1		4	2	
1959	10	2		5	1		5	1	
1960	6	4	2	1	3	2	5	1	
1961	10	3	1	4	2	1	6	1	
1962	12	2		6	1		6	1	
1963	11	3		5	2		6	1	
1964	2	10	2	2	5		0	5	2
1965	7	7		3	4		4	3	
1966	1	12	1	1	6		0	6	1
1967	7	7		5	2		2	5	
1968	7	7		3	4		4	3	
1969	6	8		5	2		1	6	
1970	9	5		5	2		4	3	
1971	4	10		1	6		3	4	
1972	8	6		4	3		4	3	
1973	2	11	1	2	4	1	0	7	
1974	2	12		0	7		2	5	
1975	5	9		2	5		3	4	
1976	3	11		3	4		0	7	
1977	5	9		3	4		2	5	
1978	6	10		5	3		1	7	
1979	6	10		4	4		2	6	
1980	4	12		2	6		2	6	
1981	9	7		4	4		5	3	
1982	4	5		2	3		2	2	
1983	3	12	1	1	7		2	5	1
1984	9	7		6	2		3	5	
1985	10	6		6	2		4	4	
1986	14	2		8	0		6	2	
1987	6	9		5	3		1	6	
1988	10	6		5	3		5	3	
1989	12	4		7	1		5	3	
1990	13	3		7	1		6	2	
1991	8	8		5	3		3	5	
1992	6	10		4	4		2	6	
1993	11	5		6	2		5	3	
1994	9	7		4	4		5	3	
1995	5	11		3	5		2	6	
1996	6	10		3	5		3	5	
1997	10	5	1	6	2		4	3	1
1998	8	8		5	3		3	5	
1999	7	9		4	4		3	5	
2000	12	4		5	3		7	1	
2001	7	9		5	3		2	6	
2002	10	6		5	3		5	3	
2003	4	12		1	7		3	5	
2004	6	10		3	5		3	5	
	577	487	33	324	226	16	253	261	17

2005 NFL Record & Fact Book

PHILADELPHIA EAGLES

Season	All Games W	L	T	Home Games W	L	T	Road Games W	L	T
1933	3	5	1	2	3	1	1	1	2
1934	4	7		2	4		2	3	
1935	2	9		0	5		2	4	
1936	1	11		1	6		0	5	
1937	2	8	1	0	5	1	2	3	
1938	5	6		2	3		3	3	
1939	1	9	1	1	3	1	0	6	
1940	1	10		1	4		0	6	
1941	2	8	1	1	4	1	1	4	
1942	2	9		0	5		2	4	
1944	7	1	2	3	1	2	4	0	
1945	7	3		6	0		1	3	
1946	6	5		3	2		3	3	
1947	8	4		6	1		2	3	
1948	9	2	1	6	0		3	2	1
1949	11	1		6	0		5	1	
1950	6	6		2	4		4	2	
1951	4	8		1	5		3	3	
1952	7	5		4	2		3	3	
1953	7	4	1	5	0	1	2	4	
1954	7	4	1	5	1		2	3	1
1955	4	7	1	4	2		0	5	1
1956	3	8	1	2	3	1	1	5	
1957	4	8		3	3		1	5	
1958	2	9	1	2	4		0	5	1
1959	7	5		5	1		2	4	
1960	10	2		5	1		5	1	
1961	10	4		5	2		5	2	
1962	3	10	1	2	5		1	5	1
1963	2	10	2	1	5	1	1	5	1
1964	6	8		3	4		3	4	
1965	5	9		2	5		3	4	
1966	9	5		5	2		4	3	
1967	6	7	1	5	2		1	5	1
1968	2	12		1	6		1	6	
1969	4	9	1	2	5		2	4	1
1970	3	10	1	3	3	1	0	7	
1971	6	7	1	3	4		3	3	1
1972	2	11	1	0	6	1	2	5	
1973	5	8	1	4	3		1	5	1
1974	7	7		5	2		2	5	
1975	4	10		2	5		2	5	
1976	4	10		2	5		2	5	
1977	5	9		4	3		1	6	
1978	9	7		5	3		4	4	
1979	11	5		5	3		6	2	
1980	12	4		7	1		5	3	
1981	10	6		6	2		4	4	
1982	3	6		1	4		2	2	
1983	5	11		1	7		4	4	
1984	6	9	1	5	3		1	6	1
1985	7	9		4	4		3	5	
1986	5	10	1	2	5	1	3	5	
1987	7	8		4	4		3	4	
1988	10	6		5	3		5	3	
1989	11	5		6	2		5	3	
1990	10	6		6	2		4	4	
1991	10	6		4	4		6	2	
1992	11	5		8	0		3	5	
1993	8	8		3	5		5	3	
1994	7	9		5	3		2	6	
1995	10	6		6	2		4	4	
1996	10	6		5	3		5	3	
1997	6	9	1	6	2		0	7	1
1998	3	13		3	5		0	8	
1999	5	11		4	4		1	7	
2000	11	5		5	3		6	2	
2001	11	5		4	4		7	1	
2002	12	4		7	1		5	3	
2003	12	4		5	3		7	1	
2004	13	3		7	1		6	2	
	450	496	24	256	222	12	194	274	12

ST. LOUIS RAMS*

Season	All Games W	L	T	Home Games W	L	T	Road Games W	L	T
1937	1	10		0	5		1	5	
1938	4	7		2	2		2	5	
1939	5	5	1	3	2	1	2	3	
1940	4	6	1	3	1	1	1	5	
1941	2	9		1	4		1	5	
1942	5	6		3	2		2	4	
1944	4	6		1	2		3	4	
1945	9	1		4	0		5	1	
1946	6	4	1	3	2		3	2	1
1947	6	6		3	3		3	3	
1948	6	5	1	3	2	1	3	3	
1949	8	2	2	5	1		3	1	2
1950	9	3		5	1		4	2	
1951	8	4		5	2		3	2	
1952	9	3		5	1		4	2	
1953	8	3	1	5	1		3	2	1
1954	6	5	1	3	2	1	3	3	
1955	8	3	1	5	1		3	2	1
1956	4	8		4	2		0	6	
1957	6	6		5	1		1	5	
1958	8	4		4	2		4	2	
1959	2	10		0	6		2	4	
1960	4	7	1	2	3	1	2	4	
1961	4	10		4	3		0	7	
1962	1	12	1	0	7		1	5	1
1963	5	9		3	4		2	5	
1964	5	7	2	3	2	2	2	5	
1965	4	10		3	4		1	6	
1966	8	6		5	2		3	4	
1967	11	1	2	5	1	1	6	0	1
1968	10	3	1	5	2		5	1	1
1969	11	3		5	2		6	1	
1970	9	4	1	3	3	1	6	1	
1971	8	5	1	4	2	1	4	3	
1972	6	7	1	4	3		2	4	1
1973	12	2		7	0		5	2	
1974	10	4		6	1		4	3	
1975	12	2		6	1		6	1	
1976	10	3	1	5	2		5	1	1
1977	10	4		7	0		3	4	
1978	12	4		6	2		6	2	
1979	9	7		4	4		5	3	
1980	11	5		6	2		5	3	
1981	6	10		4	4		2	6	
1982	2	7		1	4		1	3	
1983	9	7		5	3		4	4	
1984	10	6		5	3		5	3	
1985	11	5		6	2		5	3	
1986	10	6		6	2		4	4	
1987	6	9		3	4		3	5	
1988	10	6		4	4		6	2	
1989	11	5		6	2		5	3	
1990	5	11		2	6		3	5	
1991	3	13		2	6		1	7	
1992	6	10		4	4		2	6	
1993	5	11		3	5		2	6	
1994	4	12		3	5		1	7	
1995	7	9		4	4		3	5	
1996	6	10		4	4		2	6	

Season	All Games W	L	T	Home Games W	L	T	Road Games W	L	T
1997	5	11		2	6		3	5	
1998	4	12		2	6		2	6	
1999	13	3		8	0		5	3	
2000	10	6		5	3		5	3	
2001	14	2		6	2		8	0	
2002	7	9		6	2		1	7	
2003	12	4		8	0		4	4	
2004	8	8		6	2		2	6	
	484	423	20	270	178	10	214	245	10

*includes Cleveland Rams (1937-1942, 1944-45) and Los Angeles Rams (1946-1994).

SAN FRANCISCO 49ERS

Season	All Games W	L	T	Home Games W	L	T	Road Games W	L	T
1950	3	9		3	3		0	6	
1951	7	4	1	5	1		2	3	1
1952	7	5		3	3		4	2	
1953	9	3		5	1		4	2	
1954	7	4	1	4	2		3	2	1
1955	4	8		2	4		2	4	
1956	5	6	1	3	3		2	3	1
1957	8	4		5	1		3	3	
1958	6	6		4	2		2	4	
1959	7	5		4	2		3	3	
1960	7	5		3	3		4	2	
1961	7	6	1	5	1	1	2	5	
1962	6	8		1	6		5	2	
1963	2	12		2	5		0	7	
1964	4	10		3	4		1	6	
1965	7	6	1	4	2	1	3	4	
1966	6	6	2	4	2	1	2	4	1
1967	7	7		3	4		4	3	
1968	7	6	1	3	3	1	4	3	
1969	4	8	2	3	3	1	1	5	1
1970	10	3	1	5	1	1	5	2	
1971	9	5		4	3		5	2	
1972	8	5	1	4	2	1	4	3	
1973	5	9		3	4		2	5	
1974	6	8		3	4		3	4	
1975	5	9		2	5		3	4	
1976	8	6		4	3		4	3	
1977	5	9		3	4		2	5	
1978	2	14		2	6		0	8	
1979	2	14		2	6		0	8	
1980	6	10		4	4		2	6	
1981	13	3		7	1		6	2	
1982	3	6		0	5		3	1	
1983	10	6		4	4		6	2	
1984	15	1		7	1		8	0	
1985	10	6		5	3		5	3	
1986	10	5	1	6	2		4	3	1
1987	13	2		6	1		7	1	
1988	10	6		4	4		6	2	
1989	14	2		6	2		8	0	
1990	14	2		6	2		8	0	
1991	10	6		7	1		3	5	
1992	14	2		7	1		7	1	
1993	10	6		6	2		4	4	
1994	13	3		7	1		6	2	
1995	11	5		6	2		5	3	
1996	12	4		6	2		6	2	
1997	13	3		8	0		5	3	
1998	12	4		8	0		4	4	
1999	4	12		3	5		1	7	
2000	6	10		4	4		2	6	
2001	12	4		7	1		5	3	
2002	10	6		5	3		5	3	

Season	All Games W	L	T	Home Games W	L	T	Road Games W	L	T
2003	7	9		6	2		1	7	
2004	2	14		1	7		1	7	
	434	347	13	237	153	7	197	194	6

SEATTLE SEAHAWKS

Season	All Games W	L	T	Home Games W	L	T	Road Games W	L	T
1976	2	12		1	6		1	6	
1977	5	9		3	4		2	5	
1978	9	7		5	3		4	4	
1979	9	7		5	3		4	4	
1980	4	12		0	8		4	4	
1981	6	10		5	3		1	7	
1982	4	5		3	2		1	3	
1983	9	7		5	3		4	4	
1984	12	4		7	1		5	3	
1985	8	8		5	3		3	5	
1986	10	6		7	1		3	5	
1987	9	6		6	2		3	4	
1988	9	7		5	3		4	4	
1989	7	9		3	5		4	4	
1990	9	7		5	3		4	4	
1991	7	9		5	3		2	6	
1992	2	14		1	7		1	7	
1993	6	10		4	4		2	6	
1994	6	10		3	5		3	5	
1995	8	8		5	3		3	5	
1996	7	9		4	4		3	5	
1997	8	8		4	4		4	4	
1998	8	8		6	2		2	6	
1999	9	7		5	3		4	4	
2000	6	10		3	5		3	5	
2001	9	7		6	2		3	5	
2002	7	9		3	5		4	4	
2003	10	6		8	0		2	6	
2004	9	7		5	3		4	4	
	214	238		127	100		87	138	

TAMPA BAY BUCCANEERS

Season	All Games W	L	T	Home Games W	L	T	Road Games W	L	T
1976	0	14		0	7		0	7	
1977	2	12		1	6		1	6	
1978	5	11		3	5		2	6	
1979	10	6		5	3		5	3	
1980	5	10	1	2	5	1	3	5	
1981	9	7		6	2		3	5	
1982	5	4		4	1		1	3	
1983	2	14		1	7		1	7	
1984	6	10		6	2		0	8	
1985	2	14		2	6		0	8	
1986	2	14		1	7		1	7	
1987	4	11		2	5		2	6	
1988	5	11		3	5		2	6	
1989	5	11		2	6		3	5	
1990	6	10		4	4		2	6	
1991	3	13		3	5		0	8	
1992	5	11		3	5		2	6	
1993	5	11		3	5		2	6	
1994	6	10		4	4		2	6	
1995	7	9		5	3		2	6	
1996	6	10		5	3		1	7	
1997	10	6		5	3		5	3	
1998	8	8		6	2		2	6	
1999	11	5		7	1		4	4	
2000	10	6		6	2		4	4	
2001	9	7		5	3		4	4	
2002	12	4		6	2		6	2	

Season	All Games W	L	T	Home Games W	L	T	Road Games W	L	T
2003	7	9		3	5		4	4	
2004	5	11		4	4		1	7	
	172	279	1	107	118	1	65	161	

WASHINGTON REDSKINS*

Season	All Games W	L	T	Home Games W	L	T	Road Games W	L	T
1932	4	4	2	2	3	1	2	1	1
1933	5	5	2	4	2		1	3	2
1934	6	6		4	3		2	3	
1935	2	8	1	2	5		0	3	1
1936	7	5		4	3		3	2	
1937	8	3		4	2		4	1	
1938	6	3	2	3	1	1	3	2	1
1939	8	2	1	5	0	1	3	2	
1940	9	2		6	0		3	2	
1941	6	5		4	2		2	3	
1942	10	1		5	1		5	0	
1943	6	3	1	4	2		2	1	1
1944	6	3	1	4	2		2	1	1
1945	8	2		6	0		2	2	
1946	5	5	1	3	2	1	2	3	
1947	4	8		4	2		0	6	
1948	7	5		4	2		3	3	
1949	4	7	1	3	3		1	4	1
1950	3	9		1	5		2	4	
1951	5	7		2	4		3	3	
1952	4	8		1	5		3	3	
1953	6	5	1	3	3		3	2	1
1954	3	9		3	3		0	6	
1955	8	4		3	3		5	1	
1956	6	6		4	2		2	4	
1957	5	6	1	2	3	1	3	3	
1958	4	7	1	3	2	1	1	5	
1959	3	9		2	4		1	5	
1960	1	9	2	1	4	1	0	5	1
1961	1	12	1	1	6		0	6	1
1962	5	7	2	3	4		2	3	2
1963	3	11		1	6		2	5	
1964	6	8		4	3		2	5	
1965	6	8		3	4		3	4	
1966	7	7		4	3		3	4	
1967	5	6	3	2	4	1	3	2	2
1968	5	9		3	4		2	5	
1969	7	5	2	4	2	1	3	3	1
1970	6	8		4	3		2	5	
1971	9	4	1	4	2	1	5	2	
1972	11	3		6	1		5	2	
1973	10	4		7	0		3	4	
1974	10	4		6	1		4	3	
1975	8	6		5	2		3	4	
1976	10	4		5	2		5	2	
1977	9	5		5	2		4	3	
1978	8	8		5	3		3	5	
1979	10	6		6	2		4	4	
1980	6	10		4	4		2	6	
1981	8	8		5	3		3	5	
1982	8	1		3	1		5	0	
1983	14	2		7	1		7	1	
1984	11	5		7	1		4	4	
1985	10	6		5	3		5	3	
1986	12	4		7	1		5	3	
1987	11	4		6	1		5	3	
1988	7	9		4	4		3	5	
1989	10	6		4	4		6	2	
1990	10	6		7	1		3	5	
1991	14	2		7	1		7	1	
1992	9	7		6	2		3	5	
1993	4	12		3	5		1	7	
1994	3	13		0	8		3	5	
1995	6	10		4	4		2	6	
1996	9	7		5	3		4	4	
1997	8	7	1	5	2	1	3	5	
1998	6	10		4	4		2	6	
1999	10	6		6	2		4	4	
2000	8	8		4	4		4	4	
2001	8	8		4	4		4	4	
2002	7	9		5	3		2	6	
2003	5	11		3	5		2	6	
2004	6	10		3	5		3	5	
	505	462	27	292	203	11	213	259	16

*includes Boston Braves (1932) and Boston Redskins (1933-36).

ALL-TIME RECORDS OF NFL TEAMS

AFC	W	L	T	Pct.
Miami	353	235	4	.600
Oakland	390	275	11	.586
Cleveland	404	332	10	.549
Kansas City	356	308	12	.536
Denver	349	317	10	.524
Jacksonville	82	78	0	.513
Pittsburgh	479	465	20	.507
Baltimore	72	71	1	.503
Indianapolis	376	375	7	.501
New England	328	339	9	.492
Tennessee	328	342	6	.490
Buffalo	322	346	8	.482
San Diego	320	345	11	.481
N.Y. Jets	304	364	8	.455
Cincinnati	242	321	1	.430
Houston	16	32	0	.333

NFC	W	L	T	Pct.
Chicago	646	474	42	.577
Dallas	383	285	6	.573
Green Bay	612	480	36	.560
San Francisco	434	347	13	.556
Minnesota	362	291	9	.554
N.Y. Giants	577	487	33	.542
St. Louis	484	423	20	.534
Washington	505	462	27	.522
Detroit	473	520	32	.476
Philadelphia	450	496	24	.476
Seattle	214	238	0	.473
Carolina	71	89	0	.444
Arizona	446	627	39	.416
New Orleans	234	339	5	.409
Atlanta	237	349	6	.405
Tampa Bay	172	279	1	.382

History

The Professional Football Hall of Fame is located in Canton, Ohio, site of the organizational meeting on September 17, 1920, from which the National Football League evolved. The NFL recognized Canton as the Hall of Fame site on April 27, 1961. Canton area individuals, foundations, and companies donated almost $400,000 in cash and services to provide funds for the construction of the original two-building complex, which was dedicated on September 7, 1963. Since that time, the Hall added three buildings with major expansion projects in 1971, 1978, and 1995. The Hall's largest-ever expansion, a $9.2 million project, was completed in early fall 1995. With the new fifth building, the Hall's size is now 82,307 square feet, more than four times its original size.

The expanded Hall represents the sport of pro football in many ways—through (1) GameDay Stadium, a dynamic two-part turntable theater featuring NFL action in Cinemascope for the first time, (2) a standard theater showing NFL films hourly, (3) six large exhibition areas where the history of pro football is detailed in memento, picture, and story form, (4) an extensive archive and information center, and (5) a new and enlarged museum store.

Throughout the years, the Pro Football Hall of Fame has become an extremely popular tourist attraction. At the end of 2004, a total of 7,593,502 fans had visited the Hall of Fame.

New members of the Pro Football Hall of Fame are elected annually by a 39-member National Board of Selectors, made up of media representatives from every league city, six at-large representatives, and a representative of the Pro Football Writers of America. Between three and six new members are elected each year. An affirmative vote of approximately 80 percent is needed for election.

Any fan may nominate any eligible player or contributor simply by writing to the Pro Football Hall of Fame. Players must be retired five years to be eligible, while a coach needs only to be retired with no time limit specified. Contributors (administrators, owners, *et al.*) may be elected while they are still active.

The charter class of 17 enshrinees was elected in 1963 and the honor roll now stands at 229 (146 living as of June 1, 2005) with the election of a four-man class in 2005. That class consists of Benny Friedman, Dan Marino, Fritz Pollard, and Steve Young.

ROSTER OF MEMBERS

HERB ADDERLEY
Cornerback. 6-0, 205. Born in Philadelphia, Pennsylvania, June 8, 1939. Michigan State. Inducted in 1980. 1961-69 Green Bay Packers, 1970-72 Dallas Cowboys. **Highlights:** 48 interceptions, 7 touchdowns. Played in four Super Bowls, five Pro Bowls.

GEORGE ALLEN
Coach. Born in Detroit, Michigan, April 29, 1918. Died December 31, 1990. Alma College, Eastern Michigan, Marquette, Michigan. Inducted in 2002. 1966-1970 Los Angeles Rams, 1971-77 Washington Redskins. **Highlights:** 118-54-5 overall record. Never suffered a losing season, and ranked tenth in coaching victories at time of retirement.

MARCUS ALLEN
Running back. 6-2, 210. Born in San Diego, California, March 26, 1960. Southern California. Inducted in 2003. 1982-1992 Los Angeles Raiders, 1993-1997 Kansas City Chiefs. **Highlights:** First player in NFL history to tally 10,000 rushing yards and 5,000 receiving yards. MVP, Super Bowl XVIII.

LANCE ALWORTH
Wide receiver. 6-0, 184. Born in Houston, Texas, August 3, 1940. Arkansas. Inducted in 1978. 1962-1970 San Diego Chargers, 1971-72 Dallas Cowboys. **Highlights:** 542 receptions for 10,266 yards, 85 touchdowns. All-AFL seven times, seven All-Star games.

DOUG ATKINS
Defensive end. 6-8, 275. Born in Humboldt, Tennessee, May 8, 1930. Tennessee. Inducted in 1982. 1953-54 Cleveland Browns, 1955-1966 Chicago Bears, 1967-69 New Orleans Saints. **Highlights:** Eight Pro Bowls, All-NFL four times. Played for 17 years, 205 games.

MORRIS (RED) BADGRO
End. 6-0, 190. Born in Orillia, Washington, December 1, 1902. Died July 13, 1998. Southern California. Inducted in 1981. 1927-28 New York Yankees, 1930-35 New York Giants, 1936 Brooklyn Dodgers. **Highlights:** First- or second-team All-NFL four times. Scored first touchdown in NFL Championship Game series.

LEM BARNEY
Cornerback. 6-0, 190. Born in Gulfport, Mississippi, September 8, 1945. Jackson State. Inducted in 1992. 1967-1977 Detroit Lions. **Highlights:** 56 interceptions for 1,077 yards, 11 touchdowns (7 defensive, 4 special teams). Seven Pro Bowls, All-NFL/NFC four times.

CLIFF BATTLES
Halfback. 6-1, 195. Born in Akron, Ohio, May 1, 1910. Died April 28, 1981. West Virginia Wesleyan. Inducted in 1968. 1932 Boston Braves, 1933-36 Boston Redskins, 1937 Washington Redskins. **Highlights:** NFL rushing champion 1932, 1937. First to gain more than 200 yards in a game, 1933.

SAMMY BAUGH
Quarterback. 6-2, 180. Born in Temple, Texas, March 17, 1914. Texas Christian. Inducted in 1963. 1937-1952 Washington Redskins. **Highlights:** Charter enshrinee. Six-time NFL passing leader. NFL passing, punting, interception champ, 1943.

CHUCK BEDNARIK
Center-linebacker. 6-3, 230. Born in Bethlehem, Pennsylvania, May 1, 1925. Pennsylvania. Inducted in 1967. 1949-1962 Philadelphia Eagles. **Highlights:** Eight Pro Bowls. Missed three games in 14 years. Named NFL all-time center, 1969.

BERT BELL
Team owner. Commissioner. Born in Philadelphia, Pennsylvania, February 25, 1895. Died October 11, 1959. Pennsylvania. Inducted in 1963. 1933-1940 Philadelphia Eagles, 1941-42 Pittsburgh Steelers, 1943 Phil-Pitt, 1944 Card-Pitt, 1945-46 Pittsburgh Steelers. Commissioner, 1946-1959. **Highlights:** Charter enshrinee. Built NFL image as commissioner, 1946-1959. Set up long-term television policies.

BOBBY BELL
Linebacker. 6-4, 225. Born in Shelby, North Carolina, June 17, 1940. Minnesota. Inducted in 1983. 1963-1974 Kansas City Chiefs. **Highlights:** 26 interceptions. All-AFL/AFC eight times. Nine career touchdowns, 1 on onside kick return.

RAYMOND BERRY
End. 6-2, 187. Born in Corpus Christi, Texas, February 27, 1933. Southern Methodist. Inducted in 1973. 1955-1967 Baltimore Colts. **Highlights:** 631 receptions for 9,275 yards, 68 touchdowns. Set NFL title game mark with 12 catches for 178 yards, 1958.

ELVIN BETHEA
Defensive end. 6-2, 260. Born in Trenton, New Jersey, March 1, 1946. North Carolina A&T. Inducted in 2003. 1968-1983 Houston Oilers. **Highlights:** Led team in sacks six times. Elected to eight Pro Bowls. Played for 16 years, 210 games.

CHARLES W. BIDWILL SR.
Team owner. Born in Chicago, Illinois, September 16, 1895. Died April 19, 1947. Loyola of Chicago. Inducted in 1967. 1933-1943 Chicago Cardinals, 1944 Card-Pitt, 1945-47 Chicago Cardinals. **Highlights:** Guiding light for NFL during depression years. Built famous "Dream Backfield."

FRED BILETNIKOFF
Wide receiver. 6-1, 190. Born in Erie, Pennsylvania, February 23, 1943. Florida State. Inducted in 1988. 1965-1978 Oakland Raiders. **Highlights:** 589 receptions for 8,974 yards, 76 touchdowns. 40 catches 10 straight years. MVP, Super Bowl XI.

GEORGE BLANDA
Quarterback-kicker. 6-2, 215. Born in Youngwood, Pennsylvania, September 17, 1927. Kentucky. Inducted in 1981. 1949-1958 Chicago Bears, 1950 Baltimore Colts, 1960-66 Houston Oilers, 1967-1975 Oakland Raiders. **Highlights:** 2,002 career points. 26-season, 340-game career longest in NFL history.

MEL BLOUNT
Cornerback. 6-3, 205. Born in Vidalia, Georgia, April 10, 1948. Southern University. Inducted in 1989. 1970-1983 Pittsburgh Steelers. **Highlights:** 57 interceptions for 736 yards. NFL defensive MVP, 1975. Played in five Pro Bowls.

TERRY BRADSHAW
Quarterback. 6-3, 210. Born in Shreveport, Louisiana, September 2, 1948. Louisiana Tech. Inducted in 1989. 1970-1983 Pittsburgh Steelers. **Highlights:** 27,989 yards passing, 212 touchdowns. MVP in Super Bowls XIII, XIV.

BOB (BOOMER) BROWN
Tackle. 6-4, 280. Born in Cleveland, Ohio, December 8, 1941. Nebraska. Inducted in 2004. 1964-68 Philadelphia Eagles, 1969-1970 Los Angeles Rams, 1971-73 Oakland Raiders. **Highlights:** All-NFL seven of 10 seasons, six Pro Bowls. Named to 1960s All-Decade Team.

JIM BROWN
Fullback. 6-2, 228. Born in St. Simons, Georgia, February 17, 1936. Syracuse. Inducted in 1971. 1957-1965 Cleveland Browns. **Highlights:** 12,312 yards rushing, 756 points. Led NFL rushers eight years. Nine consecutive Pro Bowls.

PAUL BROWN
Coach. Born in Norwalk, Ohio, September 7, 1908. Died August 5, 1991. Miami (Ohio). Inducted in 1967. 1946-49 Cleveland Browns (AAFC), 1950-1962 Cleveland Browns. **Highlights:** Built Cleveland dynasty with 167-53-8 record, four AAFC titles, three NFL crowns. Returned to coaching with Cincinnati Bengals after induction, 1968-1975.

ROOSEVELT BROWN
Tackle. 6-3, 255. Born in Charlottesville, Virginia, October 20, 1932. Died June 9, 2004. Morgan State. Inducted in 1975. 1953-1965 New York Giants. **Highlights:** All-NFL eight consecutive years, nine Pro Bowls. NFL's lineman of year, 1956.

WILLIE BROWN
Cornerback. 6-1, 210. Born in Yazoo City, Mississippi, December 2, 1940. Grambling. Inducted in 1984. 1963-66 Denver Broncos, 1967-1978 Oakland Raiders. **Highlights:** 54 interceptions for 472 yards. Scored on 75-yard interception in Super Bowl XI.

BUCK BUCHANAN
Defensive tackle. 6-7, 274. Born in Gainesville, Alabama, September 10, 1940. Died July 16, 1992. Grambling. Inducted in 1990. 1963-1975 Kansas City Chiefs. **Highlights:** Led Chiefs defensive efforts in Super Bowl I, IV. Did not miss a game in 13 years.

NICK BUONICONTI
Linebacker. 5-11, 220. Born in Springfield, Massachusetts, December 15, 1940. Notre Dame. Inducted in 2001. 1962-68 Boston Patriots, 1969-1974, 1976 Miami Dolphins. **Highlights:** All-AFL/AFC eight times. Named to AFL's All-Time Team.

DICK BUTKUS
Linebacker. 6-3, 245. Born in Chicago, Illinois, December 9, 1942. Illinois. Inducted in 1979. 1965-1973 Chicago Bears. **Highlights:** All-NFL six years, eight consecutive Pro Bowls. 27 fumble recoveries.

EARL CAMPBELL
Running back. 5-11, 233. Born in Tyler, Texas, March 29, 1955. Texas. Inducted in 1991. 1978-1984 Houston Oilers, 1984-85 New Orleans Saints. **Highlights:** 9,407 yards rushing, 74 touchdowns. 1,934 yards rushing in 1980, including four games with at least 200 yards.

TONY CANADEO
Halfback. 5-11, 195. Born in Chicago, Illinois, May 5, 1919. Died November 29, 2003. Gonzaga. Inducted in 1974. 1941-44, 1946-1952 Green Bay Packers. **Highlights:** Two-way player. Third player to rush for 1,000 yards in single season, 1949.

JOE CARR
NFL president. Born in Columbus, Ohio, October 22, 1880. Died May 20, 1939. Did not attend college. Inducted in 1963. President, 1921-1939 National Football League. **Highlights:** Charter enshrinee. NFL co-organizer, 1920. Introduced standard player contract.

DAVE CASPER
Tight end. 6-4, 240. Born in Bemidji, Minnesota, February 2, 1952. Notre Dame. Inducted in 2002. 1974-1980 Oakland Raiders, 1980-83 Houston Oilers, 1983 Minnesota Vikings, 1984 Los Angeles Raiders. **Highlights:** 378 receptions for 5,216 yards, 52 touchdowns. Five consecutive Pro Bowls.

GUY CHAMBERLIN
End. Coach. 6-2, 196. Born in Blue Springs, Nebraska, January 16, 1894. Died April 4, 1967. Nebraska. Inducted in 1965. 1919 Canton Bulldogs, 1920 Decatur Staleys, 1921 Chicago Staleys, player-coach 1922-23 Canton Bulldogs, 1924 Cleveland Bulldogs, 1925-26 Frankford Yellowjackets, 1927-28 Chicago Cardinals. **Highlights:** Player-coach of four NFL championship teams. Six-year coaching record of 58-16-7.

JACK CHRISTIANSEN
Safety. 6-1, 185. Born in Sublette, Kansas, December 20, 1928. Died June 29, 1986. Colorado State. Inducted in 1970. 1951-58 Detroit Lions. **Highlights:** 46 interceptions. NFL interception leader, 1953, 1957. Eight punt returns for touchdowns.

EARL (DUTCH) CLARK
Quarterback. 6-0, 185. Born in Fowler, Colorado, October 11, 1906. Died August 5, 1978. Colorado College. Inducted in 1963. 1931-32 Portsmouth Spartans, 1934-38 Detroit Lions. **Highlights:** Charter enshrinee. NFL scoring champion three years. Led Lions to 1935 NFL title.

GEORGE CONNOR
Tackle-linebacker. 6-3, 240. Born in Chicago, Illinois, January 21, 1925. Died March 31, 2003. Holy Cross, Notre Dame. Inducted in 1975. 1948-1955 Chicago Bears. **Highlights:** All-NFL at three positions—T, DT, LB. All-NFL five years. Played in first four Pro Bowls.

JIMMY CONZELMAN
Quarterback. Coach. Team owner. 6-0, 180. Born in St. Louis, Missouri, March 6, 1898. Died July 31, 1970. Washington of St. Louis. Inducted in 1964. 1920 Decatur Staleys, 1921-22 Rock Island Independents, 1922-24 Milwaukee Badgers; owner-coach 1925-26 Detroit Panthers; player-coach 1927-29, coach 1930 Providence Steam Roller; coach 1940-42, 1946-48 Chicago Cardinals. **Highlights:** Player-coach of four NFL teams in 1920's. Coached Cardinals to 1947 NFL crown.

LOU CREEKMUR
Tackle-guard. 6-4, 255. Born in Hopelawn, New Jersey. January 22, 1927. William & Mary. Inducted in 1996. 1950-59 Detroit Lions. **Highlights:** All-NFL six times, twice at guard and four times at tackle. Selected to eight Pro Bowls and played on three NFL championship teams.

LARRY CSONKA
Running back. 6-3, 235. Born in Stow, Ohio, December 25, 1946. Syracuse. Inducted in 1987. 1968-1974, 1979 Miami Dolphins, 1976-78 New York Giants. **Highlights:** 8,081 yards rushing, 68 touchdowns. MVP Super Bowl VIII. Only 21 fumbles in 1,891 carries and 106 receptions.

AL DAVIS
Team, League Administrator. Born in Brockton, Massachusetts, July 4, 1929. Wittenberg, Syracuse. Inducted in 1992. 1963-1981, 1995-present Oakland Raiders, 1982-1994 Los Angeles Raiders, 1966 American Football League. **Highlights:** Only person to serve in pros as personnel assistant, scout, assistant coach, head coach, general manager, commissioner, team owner/CEO.

WILLIE DAVIS
Defensive end. 6-3, 245. Born in Lisbon, Louisiana, July 24, 1934. Grambling. Inducted in 1981. 1958-59 Cleveland Browns, 1960-69 Green Bay Packers. **Highlights:** All-NFL five seasons, five Pro Bowls. Did not miss game in 12-year career.

LEN DAWSON
Quarterback. 6-0, 190. Born in Alliance, Ohio, June 20, 1935. Purdue. Inducted in 1987. 1957-59 Pittsburgh Steelers, 1960-61 Cleveland Browns, 1962 Dallas Texans, 1963-1975 Kansas City Chiefs. **Highlights:** 28,711 yards passing, 239 touchdowns. Four AFL passing crowns. MVP, Super Bowl IV.

JOE DeLAMIELLEURE
Guard. 6-3, 254. Born in Detroit, Michigan, March 16, 1951. Michigan State. Inducted in 2003. 1973-1979, 1985 Buffalo Bills, 1980-1984 Cleveland Browns. **Highlights:** Selected All-Pro and All-AFC six consecutive times, 1975-1980. Named to six Pro Bowls. Played 13 years, 185 games.

ERIC DICKERSON
Running back. 6-3, 220. Born in Sealy, Texas, September 2, 1960. Southern Methodist. Inducted in 1999. 1983-87 Los Angeles Rams, 1987-1991 Indianapolis Colts, 1992 Los Angeles Raiders, 1993 Atlanta Falcons. **Highlights:** Rushed for 13,259 career yards, including an NFL record 2,105 yards in 1984. All-Pro five times, six Pro Bowls.

DAN DIERDORF
Tackle. 6-3, 290. Born in Canton, Ohio, June 29, 1949. Michigan. Inducted in 1996. 1971-1983 St. Louis Cardinals. **Highlights:** All-Pro five times, played in six Pro Bowls, named NFL's best blocker three times.

MIKE DITKA
Tight end. 6-3, 225. Born in Carnegie, Pennsylvania, October 18, 1939. Pittsburgh. Inducted in 1988. 1961-66 Chicago Bears, 1967-68 Philadelphia Eagles, 1969-1972 Dallas Cowboys. **Highlights:** 427 receptions for 5,812 yards, 43 touchdowns. First tight end selected to Hall of Fame. Five consecutive Pro Bowls.

ART DONOVAN
Defensive tackle. 6-3, 265. Born in Bronx, New York, June 5, 1925. Boston College. Inducted in 1968. 1950 Baltimore Colts, 1951 New York Yanks, 1952 Dallas Texans, 1953-1961 Baltimore Colts. **Highlights:** Five Pro Bowls. Vital part of Baltimore's climb to powerhouse status in 1950s.

TONY DORSETT
Running back. 5-11, 184. Born in Rochester, Pennsylvania, April 7, 1954. Pittsburgh. Inducted in 1994. 1977-1987 Dallas Cowboys, 1988 Denver Broncos. **Highlights:** 12,739 yards rushing, 398 receptions, 91 touchdowns. Ran record 99 yards for touchdown vs. Minnesota, January, 1983.

JOHN (PADDY) DRISCOLL
Quarterback. 5-11, 160. Born in Evanston, Illinois, January 11, 1896. Died June 29, 1968. Northwestern. Inducted in 1965. 1919 Hammond Pros, 1920 Decatur Staleys, 1920-25 Chicago Cardinals, 1926-29 Chicago Bears. **Highlights:** All-NFL seven times. Dropkicked record 4 field goals in one game, 1925.

BILL DUDLEY
Halfback. 5-10, 182. Born in Bluefield, Virginia, December 24, 1921. Virginia. Inducted in 1966. 1942, 1945-46 Pittsburgh Steelers, 1947-49 Detroit Lions, 1950-51, 1953 Washington Redskins. **Highlights:** Won NFL rushing, interception, punt return titles, 1946. All-NFL 1942, 1946, and 1947.

ALBERT GLEN (TURK) EDWARDS
Tackle. 6-2, 260. Born in Mold, Washington, September 28, 1907. Died January 12, 1973. Washington State. Inducted in 1969. 1932 Boston Braves, 1933-36 Boston Redskins, 1937-1940 Washington Redskins. **Highlights:** All-NFL 1932-34, 1936, 1937. Steamrolling blocker, smothering tackler.

CARL ELLER
Defensive end. 6-6, 247. Born in Winston-Salem, North Carolina, January 25, 1942. Minnesota. Inducted in 2004. 1964-1978 Minnesota Vikings, 1979 Seattle Seahawks. **Highlights:** Fixture on Vikings' "Purple People Eaters" defensive line, All-Pro five time, elected to six Pro Bowls.

JOHN ELWAY
Quarterback. 6-3, 215. Born in Port Angeles, Washington, June 28, 1960. Stanford. Inducted in 2004. 1983-1998 Denver Broncos. **Highlights:** Passed for 51,475 yards, 300 touchdowns. Named to nine Pro Bowls. NFL MVP, 1987; MVP, Super Bowl XXXIII.

WEEB EWBANK
Coach. Born in Richmond, Indiana, May 6, 1907. Died November 17, 1998. Miami (Ohio). Inducted in 1978. 1954-1962 Baltimore Colts, 1963-1973 New York Jets. **Highlights:** Only coach to win championships in both NFL, AFL. Led both Colts (1958 and 1959) and Jets (1968) to championships.

TOM FEARS
End. 6-2, 215. Born in Guadalajara, Mexico, December 3, 1923. Died January 4, 2000. Santa Clara, UCLA. Inducted in 1970. 1948-1956 Los Angeles Rams. **Highlights:** 400 receptions for 5,397 yards, 38 touchdowns. Led NFL receivers first three seasons. Had then-record 18 receptions in single game.

JIM FINKS
Administrator. Born in St. Louis, Missouri, August 31, 1927. Died May 8, 1994. Tulsa. Inducted 1995. 1964-1973 Minnesota Vikings, 1974-1982 Chicago Bears, 1986-1993 New Orleans Saints. **Highlights:** Developed Vikings, Bears, Saints—all teams with losing records—into winners.

RAY FLAHERTY

Coach. Born in Spokane, Washington, September 1, 1903. Died July 19, 1994. Gonzaga. Inducted in 1976. 1936-1942 Boston/Washington Redskins, 1946-48 New York Yankees (AAFC), 1949 Chicago Hornets (AAFC). **Highlights:** 82-41-5 coaching record. Introduced screen pass in 1937 title game and platoon system.

LEN FORD

Defensive end. 6-4, 260. Born in Washington, D.C., February 18, 1926. Died March 14, 1972. Morgan State, Michigan. Inducted in 1976. 1948-49 Los Angeles Dons (AAFC), 1950-57 Cleveland Browns, 1958 Green Bay Packers. **Highlights:** All-NFL five times, four Pro Bowls. Recovered 20 opponents' fumbles.

DAN FORTMANN

Guard. 6-0, 210. Born in Pearl River, New York, April 11, 1916. Died May 23, 1995. Colgate. Inducted in 1965. 1936-1943 Chicago Bears. **Highlights:** At 20, became youngest starter in NFL. First- or second-team All-NFL every season of career.

DAN FOUTS

Quarterback. 6-3, 210. Born in San Francisco, California, June 10, 1951. Oregon. Inducted in 1993. 1973-1987 San Diego Chargers. **Highlights:** 43,040 passing yards, 254 touchdowns. Six Pro Bowls, NFL MVP, 1982.

BENNY FRIEDMAN

Quarterback. 5-10, 183. Born in Cleveland, Ohio, March 18, 1905. Died November 23, 1982. Michigan. Inducted in 2005. 1927 Cleveland Bulldogs, 1928 Detroit Wolverines, 1929-1931 New York Giants, 1932-34 Brooklyn Dodgers. **Highlights:** NFL's first great passer. Set league mark for touchdowns with 20 in 1929. Led NFL in touchdown passes each of his first four seasons.

FRANK GATSKI

Center. 6-3, 240. Born in Farmington, West Virginia, March 18, 1922. Marshall, Auburn. Inducted in 1985. 1946-49 Cleveland Browns (AAFC), 1950-56 Cleveland Browns, 1957 Detroit Lions. **Highlights:** Never missed game in high school, college, or pro football. Played 11 championship games, winning eight.

BILL GEORGE

Linebacker. 6-2, 230. Born in Waynesburg, Pennsylvania, October 27, 1930. Died September 30, 1982. Wake Forest. Inducted in 1974. 1952-1965 Chicago Bears, 1966 Los Angeles Rams. **Highlights:** All-NFL eight years, eight consecutive Pro Bowls. 14 years of service, longest of any Bears player.

JOE GIBBS

Coach. Born in Mocksville, North Carolina, November 25, 1940. Cerritos (Calif.) J.C., San Diego State. Inducted in 1996. 1981-1992 Washington Redskins. **Highlights:** 124-60-0 record in regular season, 16-5 in postseason, including four Super Bowl appearances—winning three. Won 10 or more games eight times.

FRANK GIFFORD

Halfback. 6-1, 195. Born in Santa Monica, California, August 16, 1930. Southern California. Inducted in 1977. 1952-1960, 1962-64 New York Giants. **Highlights:** Starred on both offense and defense. Seven Pro Bowls, 1956 NFL player of the year.

SID GILLMAN

Coach. Born in Minneapolis, Minnesota, October 26, 1911. Died January 3, 2003. Ohio State. Inducted in 1983. 1955-59 Los Angeles Rams, 1960-69, 1971 Los Angeles/San Diego Chargers, 1973-74 Houston Oilers. **Highlights:** 123-104-7 coaching record. First to win division titles in both NFL, AFL.

OTTO GRAHAM

Quarterback. 6-1, 195. Born in Waukegan, Illinois, December 6, 1921. Died December 17, 2003. Northwestern. Inducted in 1965. 1946-49 Cleveland Browns (AAFC), 1950-55 Cleveland Browns. **Highlights:** 23,584 passing yards, 174 touchdowns. Guided Browns to 10 division or league crowns in 10 years.

HAROLD (RED) GRANGE

Halfback. 6-0, 185. Born in Forksville, Pennsylvania, June 13, 1903. Died January 28, 1991. Illinois. Inducted in 1963. 1925 Chicago Bears, 1926 New York Yankees (AFL), 1927 New York Yankees, 1929-1934 Chicago Bears. **Highlights:** Charter enshrinee. Nicknamed "Galloping Ghost." Name produced first huge pro football crowds.

BUD GRANT

Coach. Born in Superior, Wisconsin, May 20, 1927. Minnesota. Inducted in 1994. 1967-1983, 1985 Minnesota Vikings. **Highlights:** 168-108-5 coaching record. Led Vikings to 11 division championships, four Super Bowls.

JOE GREENE

Defensive tackle. 6-4, 260. Born in Temple, Texas, September 24, 1946. North Texas State. Inducted in 1987. 1969-1981 Pittsburgh Steelers. **Highlights:** NFL defensive player of the year, 1972, 1974. Four-time Super Bowl champion, 10 Pro Bowls.

FORREST GREGG

Tackle. 6-4, 250. Born in Birthright, Texas, October 18, 1933. Southern Methodist. Inducted in 1977. 1956, 1958-1970 Green Bay Packers, 1971 Dallas Cowboys. **Highlights:** Played 188 consecutive games. Nine Pro Bowls. Played on six NFL championship teams, three Super Bowl winners.

BOB GRIESE

Quarterback. 6-1, 190. Born in Evansville, Indiana, February 3, 1945. Purdue. Inducted in 1990. 1967-1980 Miami Dolphins. **Highlights:** 25,092 passing yards, 192 touchdowns. Led Miami to three AFC titles, Super Bowl VII, VIII wins.

LOU GROZA

Tackle-kicker. 6-3, 250. Born in Martins Ferry, Ohio, January 25, 1924. Died November 29, 2000. Ohio State. Inducted in 1974. 1946-49 Cleveland Browns (AAFC), 1950-59, 1961-67 Cleveland Browns. **Highlights:** 1,608 points in 21 years. Nine Pro Bowls, All-NFL six years. NFL player of the year, 1954.

JOE GUYON

Halfback. 6-1, 180. Born on White Earth Indian Reservation, Minnesota, November 26, 1892. Died November 27, 1971. Carlisle, Georgia Tech. Inducted in 1966. 1919-1920 Canton Bulldogs, 1921 Cleveland Indians, 1922-23 Oorang Indians, 1924 Rock Island Independents, 1924-25 Kansas City Cowboys, 1927 New York Giants. **Highlights:** Touchdown pass gave Giants victory over Bears to win 1927 championship.

GEORGE HALAS

End. Coach. Team owner. Born in Chicago, Illinois, February 2, 1895. Died October 31, 1983. Illinois. Inducted in 1963. Player-coach 1920 Decatur Staleys, 1922-29 Chicago Bears; coach 1933-1942, 1946-1955, 1958-1967 Chicago Bears. **Highlights:** Charter enshrinee. 324 coaching wins. Only person associated with NFL throughout first 50 years. Coached Bears 40 seasons, won six NFL titles.

JACK HAM

Linebacker. 6-1, 225. Born in Johnstown, Pennsylvania, December 23, 1948. Penn State. Inducted in 1988. 1971-1982 Pittsburgh Steelers. **Highlights:** Won four Super Bowls, 21 opponents' fumbles recovered, 32 interceptions. Eight consecutive Pro Bowls.

DAN HAMPTON

Defensive tackle-defensive end. 6-5, 264. Born in Oklahoma City, Oklahoma, September 19, 1957. Arkansas. Inducted in 2002. 1979-1990 Chicago Bears. **Highlights:** A versatile player, he earned all-pro honors at both defensive tackle and defensive end. Named to four Pro Bowls.

JOHN HANNAH
Guard. 6-3, 265. Born in Canton, Georgia, April 4, 1951. Alabama. Inducted in 1991. 1973-1985 New England Patriots. **Highlights:** Renowned as premier guard of era. All-Pro 10 years, nine Pro Bowls.

FRANCO HARRIS
Running back. 6-2, 225. Born in Fort Dix, New Jersey, March 7, 1950. Penn State. Inducted in 1990. 1972-1983 Pittsburgh Steelers, 1984 Seattle Seahawks. **Highlights:** 12,120 rushing yards, 100 total touchdowns. 1,556 rushing yards in 19 postseason games. MVP in Super Bowl IX.

MIKE HAYNES
Cornerback. 6-2, 195. Born in Denison, Texas, July 1, 1953. Arizona State. Inducted in 1997. 1976-1982 New England Patriots, 1983-89 Los Angeles Raiders. **Highlights:** Defensive rookie of the year. Selected to nine Pro Bowls and intercepted 46 passes, plus one pick in Super Bowl XVIII.

ED HEALEY
Tackle. 6-3, 220. Born in Indian Orchard, Massachusetts, December 28, 1894. Died December 9, 1978. Dartmouth. Inducted in 1964. 1920-22 Rock Island Independents, 1922-27 Chicago Bears. **Highlights:** Two-way star. Perennial all-pro with Bears.

MEL HEIN
Center. 6-2, 225. Born in Redding, California, August 22, 1909. Died January 31, 1992. Washington State. Inducted in 1963. 1931-1945 New York Giants. **Highlights:** Charter enshrinee. 60-minute regular for 15 years. All-NFL eight consecutive years.

TED HENDRICKS
Linebacker. 6-7, 235. Born in Guatemala City, Guatemala, November 1, 1947. Miami. Inducted in 1990. 1969-1973 Baltimore Colts, 1974 Green Bay Packers, 1975-1981 Oakland Raiders, 1982-83 Los Angeles Raiders. **Highlights:** 25 blocked field goals, extra points, and punts, 26 interceptions. Played in 215 consecutive games.

WILBUR (PETE) HENRY
Tackle. 6-0, 250. Born in Mansfield, Ohio, October 31, 1897. Died February 7, 1952. Washington & Jefferson. Inducted in 1963. 1920-23, 1925-26 Canton Bulldogs, 1927 New York Giants, 1927-28 Pottsville Maroons. **Highlights:** Charter enshrinee. Largest player of his time at 250 pounds. Bulwark of Canton's championship lines.

ARNIE HERBER
Quarterback. 6-0, 200. Born in Green Bay, Wisconsin, April 2, 1910. Died October 14, 1969. Wisconsin, Regis College. Inducted in 1966. 1930-1940 Green Bay Packers, 1944-45 New York Giants. **Highlights:** NFL passing leader 1932, 1934, 1936. Came out of retirement to lead 1944 Giants to NFL Eastern crown.

BILL HEWITT
End. 5-11, 191. Born in Bay City, Michigan, October 8, 1909. Died January 14, 1947. Michigan. Inducted in 1971. 1932-36 Chicago Bears, 1937-39 Philadelphia Eagles, 1943 Phil-Pitt. **Highlights:** First to be named all-NFL with two teams—1933, 1934, 1936 Bears; 1937 Eagles.

CLARKE HINKLE
Fullback. 5-11, 201. Born in Toronto, Ohio, April 10, 1909. Died November 9, 1988. Bucknell. Inducted in 1964. 1932-1941 Green Bay Packers. **Highlights:** 3,860 yards rushing, 379 points. Fullback on offense, linebacker on defense.

ELROY (CRAZYLEGS) HIRSCH
Halfback-end. 6-2, 190. Born in Wausau, Wisconsin, June 17, 1923. Died January 28, 2004. Wisconsin, Michigan. Inducted in 1968. 1946-48 Chicago Rockets (AAFC), 1949-1957 Los Angeles Rams. **Highlights:** 387 receptions for 7,029 yards, 60 touchdowns. Key part of Rams' revolutionary "three end" offense, 1949.

PAUL HORNUNG
Halfback. 6-2, 220. Born in Louisville, Kentucky, December 23, 1935. Notre Dame. Inducted in 1986. 1957-1962, 1964-66 Green Bay Packers. **Highlights:** 760 points. Led NFL scorers three years, including record 176 points, 1960. Record 19 points scored in 1961 NFL title game.

KEN HOUSTON
Safety. 6-3, 198. Born in Lufkin, Texas. Prairie View A&M. Inducted in 1986. 1967-1972 Houston Oilers, 1973-1980 Washington Redskins. **Highlights:** 49 interceptions, 898 yards, 9 touchdowns. NFL's premier strong safety of 1970s. 12 Pro Bowls.

ROBERT (CAL) HUBBARD
Tackle. 6-5, 250. Born in Keytesville, Missouri, October 31, 1900. Died October 17, 1977. Centenary, Geneva. Inducted in 1963. 1927-28 New York Giants, 1929-1933, 1935 Green Bay Packers, 1936 New York Giants, 1936 Pittsburgh Pirates. **Highlights:** Charter enshrinee. Most feared lineman of his time. All-NFL six years, 1927-29, 1931-33.

SAM HUFF
Linebacker. 6-1, 230. Born in Morgantown, West Virginia, October 4, 1934. West Virginia. Inducted in 1982. 1956-1963 New York Giants, 1964-67, 1969 Washington Redskins. **Highlights:** 30 interceptions. Played in six NFL title games, five Pro Bowls. Redskins player-coach, 1969.

LAMAR HUNT
Team owner. Born in El Dorado, Arkansas, August 2, 1932. Southern Methodist. Inducted in 1972. 1959-present Dallas Texans/Kansas City Chiefs. **Highlights:** Driving force behind organization of AFL. Spearheaded merger negotiations with NFL, 1966.

DON HUTSON
End. 6-1, 180. Born in Pine Bluff, Arkansas, January 31, 1913. Died June 26, 1997. Alabama. Inducted in 1963. 1935-1945 Green Bay Packers. **Highlights:** Charter enshrinee. 488 receptions for 7,991 yards, 99 touchdowns. NFL receiving champion eight years. NFL MVP, 1941, 1942.

JIMMY JOHNSON
Cornerback. 6-2, 187. Born in Dallas, Texas, March 31, 1938. UCLA. Inducted in 1994. 1961-1976 San Francisco 49ers. **Highlights:** 47 interceptions for 615 yards. Five Pro Bowls. Opposing passers avoided throwing in his area.

JOHN HENRY JOHNSON
Fullback. 6-2, 225. Born in Waterproof, Louisiana, November 24, 1929. St. Mary's, Arizona State. Inducted in 1987. 1954-56 San Francisco 49ers, 1957-59 Detroit Lions, 1960-65 Pittsburgh Steelers, 1966 Houston Oilers. **Highlights:** 6,803 yards rushing, 55 total touchdowns. Member of San Francisco's "Million-Dollar" backfield.

CHARLIE JOINER
Wide receiver. 5-11, 180. Born in Many, Louisiana, October 14, 1947. Grambling. Inducted in 1996. 1969-1972 Houston Oilers, 1972-75 Cincinnati Bengals, 1976-1986 San Diego Chargers. **Highlights:** 750 receptions for 12,146 yards and 65 touchdowns. Played 18 seasons, 239 games, most ever for wide receiver at time of retirement.

DAVID (DEACON) JONES
Defensive end. 6-5, 260. Born in Eatonville, Florida, December 9, 1938. South Carolina State, Mississippi Vocational. Inducted in 1980. 1961-1971 Los Angeles Rams, 1972-73 San Diego Chargers, 1974 Washington Redskins. **Highlights:** Specialized in quarterback "sacks," a term he invented. Unanimous all-league five consecutive years.

STAN JONES
Guard-defensive tackle. 6-1, 250. Born in Altoona, Pennsylvania, November 24, 1931. Maryland. Inducted in 1991. 1954-1965 Chicago Bears, 1966 Washington Redskins. **Highlights:** Seven consecutive Pro Bowls. First to rely on weightlifting for football preparation.

HENRY JORDAN
Defensive tackle, 6-3, 240. Born in Emporia, Virginia, January 26, 1935. Died February 21, 1977. Virginia. Inducted in 1995. 1957-58 Cleveland Browns, 1959-1969 Green Bay Packers. **Highlights:** Fixture at DT during Packers' dynasty. Played in four Pro Bowls, seven NFL title games, Super Bowls I, II.

SONNY JURGENSEN
Quarterback. 6-0, 203. Born in Wilmington, North Carolina, August 23, 1934. Duke. Inducted in 1983. 1957-1963 Philadelphia Eagles, 1964-1974 Washington Redskins. **Highlights:** 32,224 yards passing, 255 touchdowns, 82.63 passer rating. Surpassed 3,000 yards passing in five seasons.

JIM KELLY
Quarterback. 6-3, 225. Born in Pittsburgh, Pennsylvania, February 14, 1960. Miami. Inducted in 2002. 1986-1996 Buffalo Bills. **Highlights:** Passed for more than 3,000 yards eight times. Mastered the no-huddle offense that propelled Bills to four consecutive Super Bowls.

LEROY KELLY
Running back. 6-0, 205. Born in Philadelphia, Pennsylvania, May 20, 1942. Morgan State. Inducted in 1994. 1964-1973 Cleveland Browns. **Highlights:** 7,274 yards rushing, 90 total touchdowns, 1,000-yard rusher first three years as starter. Punt return champion, 1965.

WALT KIESLING
Guard. Coach. 6-2, 245. Born in St. Paul, Minnesota, March 27, 1903. Died March 2, 1962. St. Thomas (Minnesota). Inducted in 1966. 1926-27 Duluth Eskimos, 1928 Pottsville Maroons, 1929-1933 Chicago Cardinals, 1934 Chicago Bears, 1935-36 Green Bay Packers, 1937-38 Pittsburgh Pirates; coach, 1939 Pittsburgh Pirates, 1940-42 Pittsburgh Steelers; co-coach, 1943 Phil-Pitt; 1944 Card-Pitt; coach, 1954-56 Pittsburgh Steelers. **Highlights:** 34-year career as pro player, assistant coach, head coach. Led Steelers to first winning season, 1942.

FRANK (BRUISER) KINARD
Tackle. 6-1, 210. Born in Pelahatchie, Mississippi, October 23, 1914. Died September 7, 1985. Mississippi. Inducted in 1971. 1938-1943 Brooklyn Dodgers, 1944 Brooklyn Tigers, 1946-47 New York Yankees (AAFC). **Highlights:** First man to earn both All-NFL, All-AAFC honors. Out because of injury only once.

PAUL KRAUSE
Safety. 6-3, 200. Born in Flint, Michigan, February 19, 1942. Iowa. Inducted in 1998. 1964-67 Washington Redskins, 1968-1979 Minnesota Vikings. **Highlights:** NFL all-time leader with 81 interceptions. Played in eight Pro Bowls. Starting safety in four Super Bowls.

EARL (CURLY) LAMBEAU
Coach. Born in Green Bay, Wisconsin, April 9, 1898. Died June 1, 1965. Notre Dame. Inducted in 1963. 1919-1949 Green Bay Packers, 1950-51 Chicago Cardinals, 1952-53 Washington Redskins. **Highlights:** Charter enshrinee. 229-134-22 coaching record with six NFL championships. Founded pre-NFL Packers, 1919.

JACK LAMBERT
Linebacker. 6-4, 220. Born in Mantua, Ohio, July 8, 1952. Kent State. Inducted in 1990. 1974-1984 Pittsburgh Steelers. **Highlights:** Leader of 'Steel Curtain.' NFL defensive player of year in 1976, nine Pro Bowls.

TOM LANDRY
Coach. Born in Mission, Texas, September 11, 1924. Died February 12, 2000. Texas. Inducted in 1990. 1960-1988 Dallas Cowboys. **Highlights:** 270-178-6 coaching record. 20 consecutive winning seasons. Innovator on offense and defense.

DICK (NIGHT TRAIN) LANE
Cornerback. 6-2, 210. Born in Austin, Texas, April 16, 1928. Died January 29, 2002. Scottsbluff Junior College. Inducted in 1974. 1952-53 Los Angeles Rams, 1954-59 Chicago Cardinals, 1960-65 Detroit Lions. **Highlights:** 68 interceptions for 1,207 yards, 5 touchdowns. Record 14 interceptions as rookie. Seven Pro Bowls.

JIM LANGER
Center. 6-2, 255. Born in Little Falls, Minnesota, May 16, 1948. South Dakota State. Inducted in 1987. 1970-79 Miami Dolphins, 1980-81 Minnesota Vikings. **Highlights:** Played every offensive down in Dolphins' perfect 1972 season. Six Pro Bowls.

WILLIE LANIER
Linebacker. 6-1, 245. Born in Clover, Virginia, August 21, 1945. Morgan State. Inducted in 1986. 1967-1977 Kansas City Chiefs. **Highlights:** 27 interceptions. Defensive star in Super Bowl IV upset. Nicknamed 'Contact' for ferocious tackling.

STEVE LARGENT
Wide receiver. 5-11, 191. Born in Tulsa, Oklahoma, September 28, 1954. Tulsa. Inducted in 1995. 1976-1989 Seattle Seahawks. **Highlights:** 819 receptions for 13,089 yards, 100 touchdowns. Receptions in 177 consecutive games.

YALE LARY
Defensive back-punter. 5-11, 189. Born in Fort Worth, Texas, November 24, 1930. Texas A&M. Inducted in 1979. 1952-53, 1956-1964 Detroit Lions. **Highlights:** 50 interceptions. Three NFL punting crowns, three touchdowns on punt returns. Nine Pro Bowls.

DANTE LAVELLI
End. 6-0, 199. Born in Hudson, Ohio, February 23, 1923. Ohio State. Inducted in 1975. 1946-49 Cleveland Browns (AAFC), 1950-56 Cleveland Browns. **Highlights:** 386 receptions for 6,488 yards, 62 touchdowns. 24 catches in six NFL title games.

BOBBY LAYNE
Quarterback. 6-2, 190. Born in Santa Anna, Texas, December 19, 1926. Died December 1, 1986. Texas. Inducted in 1967. 1948 Chicago Bears, 1949 New York Bulldogs, 1950-58 Detroit Lions, 1958-1962 Pittsburgh Steelers. **Highlights:** 26,768 yards passing, 196 touchdowns, 2,451 yards rushing. Late touchdown pass won 1953 NFL title game.

ALPHONSE (TUFFY) LEEMANS
Fullback. 6-0, 200. Born in Superior, Wisconsin, November 12, 1912. Died January 19, 1979. Oregon, George Washington. Inducted in 1978. 1936-1943 New York Giants. **Highlights:** 3,132 yards rushing, 2,318 yards passing, 422 yards receiving. Led NFL rushers as rookie, 1936.

MARV LEVY
Coach. Born in Chicago, Illinois, August 3, 1925. Wyoming, Coe College, Harvard. Inducted in 2001. 1978-1982 Kansas City Chiefs, 1986-1997 Buffalo Bills. **Highlights:** Led Bills to unprecedented four consecutive Super Bowls. Had 154-120 record. Coaching victories ranked 10th when retired.

BOB LILLY
Defensive tackle. 6-5, 260. Born in Olney, Texas, July 26, 1939. Texas Christian. Inducted in 1980. 1961-1974 Dallas Cowboys. **Highlights:** Eleven Pro Bowls. Played 196 consecutive games. Foundation of great Dallas defensive units.

LARRY LITTLE
Guard. 6-1, 265. Born in Groveland, Georgia, November 2, 1945. Bethune-Cookman. Inducted in 1993. 1967-68 San Diego Chargers, 1969-1980 Miami Dolphins. **Highlights:** Five Pro Bowls, started in three Super Bowls. Epitome of powerful Dolphins rushing game of 1970s.

JAMES LOFTON
Wide receiver. 6-3, 192. Born in Fort Ord, California, July 5, 1956. Stanford. Inducted in 2003. 1978-1986 Green Bay Packers, 1987-88 Los Angeles Raiders, 1989-1992 Buffalo Bills, 1993 Los Angeles Rams, 1993 Philadelphia Eagles. **Highlights:** Played 16 seasons, 233 games. Caught 764 passes for 75 touchdowns and a then-record 14,004 yards. All-Pro four times, eight Pro Bowls.

VINCE LOMBARDI
Coach. Born in Brooklyn, New York, June 11, 1913. Died September 3, 1970. Fordham. Inducted in 1971. 1959-1967 Green Bay Packers, 1969 Washington Redskins. **Highlights:** 105-35-6 coaching record in 10 years, including five NFL titles and victories in Super Bowls I and II.

HOWIE LONG
Defensive end. 6-5, 268. Born in Somerville, Massachusetts, January 6, 1960. Villanova. Inducted in 2000. 1981-1993 Oakland/Los Angeles Raiders. **Highlights:** All-Pro 1983, 1984, 1985. Named All-AFC four times, 1983-1986. Eight Pro Bowls.

RONNIE LOTT
Cornerback-safety. 6-0, 203. Born in Albuquerque, New Mexico, May 8, 1959. Southern California. Inducted in 2000. 1981-1990 San Francisco 49ers, 1991-92 Los Angeles Raiders, 1993-94 New York Jets. **Highlights:** Ten Pro Bowls, 63 career interceptions, and was named to the NFL's 75th Anniversary Team.

SID LUCKMAN
Quarterback. 6-0, 195. Born in Brooklyn, New York, November 21, 1916. Died July 5, 1998. Columbia. Inducted in 1965. 1939-1950 Chicago Bears. **Highlights:** 137 touchdown passes. All-NFL five times. League MVP in 1943.

WILLIAM ROY (LINK) LYMAN
Tackle. 6-2, 252. Born in Table Rock, Nebraska, November 30, 1898. Died December 28, 1972. Nebraska. Inducted in 1964. 1922-23, 1925 Canton Bulldogs, 1924 Cleveland Bulldogs, 1925 Frankford Yellowjackets, 1926-28, 1930-31, 1933-34 Chicago Bears. **Highlights:** Played for four NFL champions. In 16 seasons of college and pro football, played on one losing team.

TOM MACK
Guard. 6-3, 250. Born in Cleveland, Ohio, November 1, 1943. Michigan. Inducted in 1999. 1966-1978 Los Angeles Rams. **Highlights:** Never missed a game in entire 184-game career. Elected to 11 Pro Bowls.

JOHN MACKEY
Tight end. 6-2, 224. Born in New York, New York, September 24, 1941. Syracuse. Inducted in 1992. 1963-1971 Baltimore Colts, 1972 San Diego Chargers. **Highlights:** 331 receptions for 5,236 yards, 38 touchdowns. Second tight end to enter Hall of Fame.

TIM MARA
Team owner. Born in New York, New York, July 29, 1887. Died February 16, 1959. Did not attend college. Inducted in 1963. 1925-1959 New York Giants. **Highlights:** Charter enshrinee. Founder of New York Giants. Built team into powerhouse winning four NFL titles, 10 division titles.

WELLINGTON MARA
Team owner. Born in New York, New York, August 14, 1916. Fordham. Inducted in 1997. 1937-present New York Giants. **Highlights:** Lifetime contributor to NFL and New York Giants. Worked as Giants' ballboy, secretary, vice-president, president and co-CEO. NFC president 1984-present.

GINO MARCHETTI
Defensive end. 6-4, 245. Born in Smithers, West Virginia, January 2, 1927. San Francisco. Inducted in 1972. 1952 Dallas Texans, 1953-1964, 1966 Baltimore Colts. **Highlights:** Named top defensive end of NFL's first 50 years. 10 consecutive Pro Bowls. All-NFL seven times.

DAN MARINO
Quarterback. 6-4, 218. Born in Pittsburgh, Pennsylvania, September 15, 1961. Pittsburgh. Inducted in 2005. 1983-1999 Miami Dolphins. **Highlights:** Holds NFL records for career passing yardage (61,361), completions (4,967), attempts (8,358), and touchdowns (420). Voted to nine Pro Bowls.

GEORGE PRESTON MARSHALL
Team owner. Born in Grafton, West Virginia, October 11, 1896. Died August 9, 1969. Randolph-Macon. Inducted in 1963. 1932 Boston Braves, 1933-36 Boston Redskins, 1937-1969 Washington Redskins. **Highlights:** Charter enshrinee. Sponsored progressive rules changes. Organized first team band, pioneered halftime shows.

OLLIE MATSON
Halfback. 6-2, 220. Born in Trinity, Texas, May 1, 1930. San Francisco. Inducted in 1972. 1952, 1954-58 Chicago Cardinals, 1959-1962 Los Angeles Rams, 1963 Detroit Lions, 1964-66 Philadelphia Eagles. **Highlights:** Nine touchdowns on kickoff, punt returns. Traded for nine players in 1959.

DON MAYNARD
Wide receiver. 6-1, 185. Born in Crosbyton, Texas, January 25, 1935. Texas Western. Inducted in 1987. 1958 New York Giants, 1960-62 New York Titans, 1963-1972 New York Jets, 1973 St. Louis Cardinals. **Highlights:** 633 receptions for 11,834 yards, 88 touchdowns. At least 50 catches and 1,000 yards in five different seasons.

GEORGE McAFEE
Halfback. 6-0, 177. Born in Corbin, Kentucky, March 13, 1918. Duke. Inducted in 1966. 1940-41, 1945-1950 Chicago Bears. **Highlights:** Two-way star. 25 interceptions, 234 points. Career punt-return average of 12.78 yards per return.

MIKE McCORMACK
Tackle. 6-4, 250. Born in Chicago, Illinois, June 21, 1930. Kansas. Inducted in 1984. 1951 New York Yanks, 1954-1962 Cleveland Browns. **Highlights:** Excelled as offensive right tackle for eight years. Six Pro Bowls.

TOMMY McDONALD
Wide receiver. 5-9, 175. Born in Roy, New Mexico, July 26, 1934. Oklahoma. Inducted in 1998. 1957-1963 Philadelphia Eagles, 1964 Dallas Cowboys, 1965-66 Los Angeles Rams, 1967 Atlanta Falcons, 1968 Cleveland Browns. **Highlights:** Recorded 495 receptions for 8,410 yards, 84 touchdowns.

HUGH McELHENNY
Halfback. 6-1, 198. Born in Los Angeles, California, December 31, 1928. Washington. Inducted in 1970. 1952-1960 San Francisco 49ers, 1961-62 Minnesota Vikings, 1963 New York Giants, 1964 Detroit Lions. **Highlights:** 5,281 rushing yards, 360 points. Totaled 11,369 yards rushing, receiving, and returning kicks.

JOHNNY (BLOOD) McNALLY
Halfback. 6-0, 185. Born in New Richmond, Wisconsin, November 27, 1903. Died November 28, 1985. Notre Dame, St. John's (Minnesota). Inducted in 1963. 1925-26 Milwaukee Badgers, 1926-27 Duluth Eskimos, 1928 Pottsville Maroons, 1929-1933, 1935-36 Green Bay Packers, 1934 Pittsburgh Pirates; player-coach, 1937-38 Pittsburgh Pirates. **Highlights:** Charter enshrinee. 49 touchdowns, 297 points in 14 seasons with five teams.

MIKE MICHALSKE
Guard. 6-0, 209. Born in Cleveland, Ohio, April 24, 1903. Died October 26, 1983. Penn State. Inducted in 1964. 1926 New York Yankees (AFL), 1927-28 New York Yankees, 1929-1935, 1937 Green Bay Packers. **Highlights:** Anchored Packers' championship lines, 1929-1931. First guard enshrined in Canton.

WAYNE MILLNER
End. 6-0, 191. Born in Roxbury, Massachusetts, January 31, 1913. Died November 19, 1976. Notre Dame. Inducted in 1968. 1936 Boston Redskins, 1937-1941, 1945 Washington Redskins. **Highlights:** Redskins' all-time leader with 124 catches when retired. 55- and 78-yard touchdown receptions in 1937 NFL Championship Game.

BOBBY MITCHELL
Running back-wide receiver. 6-0, 195. Born in Hot Springs, Arkansas, June 6, 1935. Illinois. Inducted in 1983. 1958-1961 Cleveland Browns, 1962-68 Washington Redskins. **Highlights:** 91 touchdowns, including 8 on kickoff and punt returns. 14,078 combined yards.

RON MIX
Tackle. 6-4, 255. Born in Los Angeles, California, March 10, 1938. Southern California. Inducted in 1979. 1960 Los Angeles Chargers, 1961-69 San Diego Chargers, 1971 Oakland Raiders. **Highlights:** All-AFL nine times. Only two holding penalties in 10 years with the Chargers.

JOE MONTANA
Quarterback. 6-2, 200. Born in New Eagle, Pennsylvania, June, 11, 1956. Notre Dame. Inducted in 2000. 1979-1992 San Francisco 49ers, 1993-94 Kansas City Chiefs. **Highlights:** MVP in Super Bowl's XVI, XIX, and XXIV. Eight Pro Bowls and All-NFL three times.

LENNY MOORE
Flanker-running back. 6-1, 198. Born in Reading, Pennsylvania, November 25, 1933. Penn State. Inducted in 1975. 1956-1967 Baltimore Colts. **Highlights:** From 1963-65, scored touchdowns in record 18 consecutive games. 113 career touchdowns, 12,451 combined net yards.

MARION MOTLEY
Fullback. 6-1, 238. Born in Leesburg, Georgia, June 5, 1920. Died June 27, 1999. South Carolina State, Nevada. Inducted in 1968. 1946-49 Cleveland Browns (AAFC), 1950-53 Cleveland Browns, 1955 Pittsburgh Steelers. **Highlights:** AAFC's all-time rushing champion. Led league in rushing in first NFL season.

MIKE MUNCHAK
Guard. 6-3, 281. Born in Scranton, Pennsylvania, March 5, 1960. Penn State. Inducted in 2001. 1982-1993 Houston Oilers. **Highlights:** Devastating blocker, All-AFC seven times, elected to nine Pro Bowls.

ANTHONY MUÑOZ
Tackle. 6-6, 278. Born in Ontario, California, August 19, 1958. Southern California. Inducted in 1998. 1980-1992 Cincinnati Bengals. **Highlights:** All-Pro choice 11 consecutive years, 1981-1991. Selected to 11 straight Pro Bowls.

GEORGE MUSSO
Guard-tackle. 6-2, 270. Born in Collinsville, Illinois. April 8, 1910. Died September 5, 2000. Millikin. Inducted in 1982. 1933-1944 Chicago Bears. **Highlights:** First player to achieve All-NFL status at two positions—tackle in 1935 and guard in 1937.

BRONKO NAGURSKI
Fullback. 6-2, 225. Born in Rainy River, Ontario, Canada, November 3, 1908. Died January 7, 1990. Minnesota. Inducted in 1963. 1930-37, 1943 Chicago Bears. **Highlights:** Charter enshrinee. 2,778 rushing yards in nine seasons. All-NFL five times.

JOE NAMATH
Quarterback. 6-2, 200. Born in Beaver Falls, Pennsylvania, May 31, 1943. Alabama. Inducted in 1985. 1965-1976 New York Jets, 1977 Los Angeles Rams. **Highlights:** First quarterback to pass for more than 4,000 yards in a season, 1967. Guaranteed, delivered victory over Colts in Super Bowl III.

EARLE (GREASY) NEALE
Coach. Born in Parkersburg, West Virginia, November 5, 1891. Died November 2, 1973. West Virginia Wesleyan. Inducted in 1969. 1941-42, 1944-1950 Philadelphia Eagles; co-coach, 1943 Phil-Pitt. **Highlights:** Turned Eagles into winners with three consecutive division crowns, NFL championships in 1948 and 1949.

ERNIE NEVERS
Fullback. 6-1, 205. Born in Willow River, Minnesota, June 11, 1903. Died May 3, 1976. Stanford. Inducted in 1963. 1926-27 Duluth Eskimos, 1929-1931 Chicago Cardinals. **Highlights:** Charter enshrinee. Holds NFL's longest-standing record, 40 points in one game in 1929.

OZZIE NEWSOME
Tight end. 6-2, 232. Born in Muscle Shoals, Alabama, March 16, 1956. Alabama. Inducted in 1999. 1978-1990 Cleveland Browns. **Highlights:** Finished career as all-time leader among tight ends with 662 receptions for 7,980 yards.

RAY NITSCHKE
Linebacker. 6-3, 235. Born in Elmwood Park, Illinois, December 29, 1936. Died March 8, 1998. Illinois. Inducted in 1978. 1958-1972 Green Bay Packers. **Highlights:** MVP of 1962 title game. Named NFL's all-time linebacker in 1969.

CHUCK NOLL
Coach. Born in Cleveland, Ohio, January 5, 1932. Dayton. Inducted in 1993. 1969-1991 Pittsburgh Steelers. **Highlights:** Coached for 23 years. Only coach to win four Super Bowl titles (IX, X, XIII, XIV).

LEO NOMELLINI
Defensive tackle. 6-3, 264. Born in Lucca, Italy, June 19, 1924. Died October 17, 2000. Minnesota. Inducted in 1969. 1950-1963 San Francisco 49ers. **Highlights:** Played every 49ers game for 14 seasons. 10 Pro Bowls.

MERLIN OLSEN
Defensive tackle. 6-5, 270. Born in Logan, Utah, September 15, 1940. Utah State. Inducted in 1982. 1962-1976 Los Angeles Rams. **Highlights:** Member of the Fearsome "Foursome. Named" to 14 consecutive Pro Bowls, Rams' all-time team.

JIM OTTO
Center. 6-2, 255. Born in Wausau, Wisconsin, January 5, 1938. Miami. Inducted in 1980. 1960-1974 Oakland Raiders. **Highlights:** Named AFL's all-time center. Played in 210 games, 12 AFL All-Star Games or Pro Bowls, six AFL/AFC title games.

STEVE OWEN
Tackle. Coach. 6-2, 235. Born in Cleo Springs, Oklahoma, April 21, 1898. Died May 17, 1964. Phillips. Inducted in 1966. 1924-25 Kansas City Cowboys, 1925 Cleveland Bulldogs, 1926-1931, 1933 New York Giants; coach, 1930-1953 New York Giants. **Highlights:** Both player and coach. Coached Giants to record of 155-108-17, eight divisional titles, two NFL championships.

ALAN PAGE
Defensive tackle. 6-4, 225. Born in Canton, Ohio, August 7, 1945. Notre Dame. Inducted in 1988. 1967-1978 Minnesota Vikings, 1978-1981 Chicago Bears. **Highlights:** Dominating defensive tackle played in 218 consecutive games, four Super Bowls. Won league MVP honors in 1971.

CLARENCE (ACE) PARKER
Quarterback. 5-11, 168. Born in Portsmouth, Virginia, May 17, 1912. Duke. Inducted in 1972. 1937-1941 Brooklyn Dodgers, 1945 Boston Yanks, 1946 New York Yankees (AAFC). **Highlights:** Two-way threat. Two-time All-NFL performer, league MVP in 1940.

JIM PARKER
Guard-tackle. 6-3, 273. Born in Macon, Georgia, April 3, 1934. Ohio State. Inducted in 1973. 1957-1967 Baltimore Colts. **Highlights:** First full-time offensive lineman elected to Hall of Fame. All-NFL eight consecutive years, eight Pro Bowls.

WALTER PAYTON
Running back. 5-10, 202. Born in Columbia, Mississippi, July 25, 1954. Died November 1, 1999. Jackson State. Inducted in 1993. 1975-1987 Chicago Bears. **Highlights:** NFL's all-time leading rusher with 16,726 yards and combined net yardage with 21,803 at time of retirement.

JOE PERRY
Fullback. 6-0, 200. Born in Stevens, Arkansas, January 22, 1927. Compton Junior College. Inducted in 1969. 1948-49 San Francisco 49ers (AAFC), 1950-1960, 1963 San Francisco 49ers, 1961-62 Baltimore Colts. **Highlights:** First player in NFL history to gain 1,000 yards two consecutive seasons. 12,532 combined yards.

PETE PIHOS
End. 6-1, 210. Born in Orlando, Florida, October 22, 1923. Indiana. Inducted in 1970. 1947-1955 Philadelphia Eagles. **Highlights:** Three-time NFL receiving champion. Caught winning touchdown in 1949 NFL Championship Game.

FRITZ POLLARD
Halfback-Coach. 5-9, 165. Born in Chicago, Illinois, January 27, 1894. Died May 11, 1986. Bates, Brown. Inducted in 2005. 1919-1921, 1925-26 Akron Pros/Indians, 1922 Milwaukee Badgers, 1923, 1925 Hammond Pros, 1925 Providence Steam Roller. **Highlights:** True pioneer as one of two African American players in the NFL in 1920 and helped lead Akron to league title that season. In 1921, became the league's first black head coach.

HUGH (SHORTY) RAY
Supervisor of officials 1938-1952. Born in Highland Park, Illinois, September 21, 1884. Died September 16, 1956. Illinois. Inducted in 1966. **Highlights:** Supervisor of Officials, 1938-1952. Streamlined rules to improve game tempo, player safety.

DAN REEVES
Team owner. Born in New York, New York, June 30, 1912. Died April 15, 1971. Georgetown. Inducted in 1967. 1941-45 Cleveland Rams, 1946-1971 Los Angeles Rams. **Highlights:** Moved Rams to Los Angeles in 1946 and opened up West Coast to pro football. First postwar owner to sign African-American player.

MEL RENFRO
Cornerback-safety. 6-0, 192. Born in Houston, Texas, December 30, 1941. Oregon. Inducted in 1996. 1964-1977 Dallas Cowboys. **Highlights:** 52 interceptions for 626 yards and 3 touchdowns. Also added 842 yards on punt returns, 2,246 yards on kickoff returns. Elected to Pro Bowl first 10 seasons.

JOHN RIGGINS
Running back. 6-2, 240. Born in Seneca, Kansas, August 4, 1949. Kansas. Inducted in 1992. 1971-75 New York Jets, 1976-79, 1981-85 Washington Redskins. **Highlights:** 11,352 rushing yards, 116 total touchdowns. MVP of Super Bowl XVII with 166 rushing yards including game-winning 43-yard touchdown.

JIM RINGO
Center. 6-2, 230. Born in Orange, New Jersey, November 21, 1931. Syracuse. Inducted in 1981. 1953-1963 Green Bay Packers, 1964-67 Philadelphia Eagles. **Highlights:** Ten-time Pro Bowl selection, seven-time All-NFL selection. Started in then-record 182 consecutive games.

ANDY ROBUSTELLI
Defensive end. 6-0, 230. Born in Stamford, Connecticut, December 6, 1925. Arnold College. Inducted in 1971. 1951-55 Los Angeles Rams, 1956-1964 New York Giants. **Highlights:** Anchored defense in eight championship games. Named NFL's top player in 1962.

ART ROONEY
Team owner. Born in Coulterville, Pennsylvania, January 27, 1901. Died August 25, 1988. Georgetown, Duquesne. Inducted in 1964. 1933-39 Pittsburgh Pirates, 1940-42, 1945-1988 Pittsburgh Steelers, 1943 Phil-Pitt, 1944 Card-Pitt. **Highlights:** Founded Pittsburgh Pirates in 1933 and renamed them Steelers in 1940. Team won four Super Bowls in 1970s.

DAN ROONEY
Team owner. Born in Pittsburgh, Pennsylvania, July, 20, 1932. Duquesne. Inducted in 2000. 1955-present Pittsburgh Steelers. **Highlights:** Has been on the board of directors for the NFL Trust Fund, NFL Films, and Scheduling Committee. Played a key role in the labor agreement reached in 1993 between the NFL owners and players.

PETE ROZELLE
Commissioner. Born in South Gate, California, March 1, 1926. Died December 6, 1996. Compton Junior College, San Francisco. Inducted in 1985. Commissioner, 1960-1989. **Highlights:** Negotiated first league-wide television contract in 1962. Generally recognized as premiere commissioner in all of sports. Credited with making NFL the nation's most popular sport.

BOB ST. CLAIR
Tackle. 6-9, 265. Born in San Francisco, California, February 18, 1931. San Francisco, Tulsa. Inducted in 1990. 1953-1963 San Francisco 49ers. **Highlights:** Exceptional offensive lineman. Also played goal-line defense and had 10 blocked field goals, 1956.

BARRY SANDERS
Running back. 5-8, 203. Born in Wichita, Kansas, July 16, 1968. Oklahoma State. Inducted in 2004. 1989-1998 Detroit Lions. **Highlights:** 15,269 rushing yards, 99 touchdowns. Rushed for 1,000 yards in each of 10 seasons. NFL co-MVP, 1997. Selected to 10 Pro Bowls.

GALE SAYERS
Running back. 6-0, 200. Born in Wichita, Kansas, May 30, 1943. Kansas. Inducted in 1977. 1965-1971 Chicago Bears. **Highlights:** Broke into league by scoring rookie-record 22 touchdowns. Led league in rushing in 1966, 1969. MVP of three Pro Bowls.

JOE SCHMIDT
Linebacker. 6-0, 222. Born in Pittsburgh, Pennsylvania, January 18, 1932. Pittsburgh. Inducted in 1973. 1953-1965 Detroit Lions. **Highlights:** 24 interceptions. Lions' team captain for nine years. Mastered middle linebacker position that evolved in 1950s.

TEX SCHRAMM
Team president-general manager. Born in San Gabriel, California, June 2, 1920. Died July 15, 2003. Texas. Inducted in 1991. 1947-1956 Los Angeles Rams. 1960-1989 Dallas Cowboys. **Highlights:** Played prominent role in AFL-NFL merger. Chairman of Competition Committee from 1966-1988.

LEE ROY SELMON
Defensive end. 6-3, 250. Born in Eufaula, Oklahoma, October 20, 1954. Oklahoma. Inducted in 1995. 1976-1984 Tampa Bay Buccaneers. **Highlights:** 78½ sacks, 380 quarterback pressures, forced 28 fumbles. Six consecutive Pro Bowl selections.

BILLY SHAW

Guard. 6-2, 258. Born in Natchez, Mississippi, December 15, 1938. Georgia Tech. Inducted in 1999. 1961-69 Buffalo Bills. **Highlights:** First player who played entire career in AFL to be elected to Hall of Fame. Named to AFL's all-time team.

ART SHELL

Tackle. 6-5, 285. Born in Charleston, South Carolina, November 26, 1946. Maryland State-Eastern Shore. Inducted in 1989. 1968-82 Oakland/Los Angeles Raiders. **Highlights:** Cornerstone of Raiders' offensive line in 1970s. 207 regular-season games, 23 postseason games, eight Pro Bowls.

DON SHULA

Coach. Born in Grand River, Ohio, January 4, 1930. John Carroll. Inducted in 1997. 1963-69 Baltimore Colts, 1970-1995 Miami Dolphins. **Highlights:** Won more games (347) than any coach in NFL history. Won two Super Bowl titles, including Super Bowl VII when Dolphins recorded NFL's only perfect season (17-0).

O.J. SIMPSON

Running back. 6-1, 212. Born in San Francisco, California, July 9, 1947. City College (San Francisco), Southern California. Inducted in 1985. 1969-1977 Buffalo Bills, 1978-79 San Francisco 49ers. **Highlights:** In 1973, became first player to rush for 2,000 yards in season. Finished career with four rushing titles, 11,236 yards.

MIKE SINGLETARY

Linebacker. 6-0, 230. Born in Houston, Texas, October 9, 1958. Baylor. Inducted in 1998. 1981-1992 Chicago Bears. **Highlights:** All-Pro choice eight times and All-NFC nine consecutive seasons. Selected to 10 Pro Bowls.

JACKIE SLATER

Tackle. 6-4, 277. Born in Jackson, Mississippi, May 27, 1954. Jackson State. Inducted in 2001. 1976-1995 Los Angeles/St. Louis Rams. **Highlights:** Played 20 seasons, 259 games. Blocked for seven different 1,000-yard rushers. Seven Pro Bowls.

JACKIE SMITH

Tight end. 6-4, 232. Born in Columbia, Mississippi, February 23, 1940. Northwestern State (Louisiana). Inducted in 1994. 1963-1977 St. Louis Cardinals, 1978 Dallas Cowboys. **Highlights:** 480 receptions for 7,918 yards, 40 touchdowns. Third tight end to be elected to Hall of Fame.

JOHN STALLWORTH

Wide receiver. 6-2, 191. Born in Tuscaloosa, Alabama, July 15, 1952. Alabama A&M. Inducted in 2002. 1974-1987 Pittsburgh Steelers. **Highlights:** 537 receptions for 8,723 yards, 63 touchdowns. Scored go-ahead touchdown in Super Bowl XIV on 73-yard reception.

BART STARR

Quarterback. 6-1, 200. Born in Montgomery, Alabama, January 9, 1934. Alabama. Inducted in 1977. 1956-1971 Green Bay Packers. **Highlights:** Quarterbacked Packers to six division titles, five NFL titles, and first two Super Bowls in which he was MVP.

ROGER STAUBACH

Quarterback. 6-3, 202. Born in Cincinnati, Ohio, February 5, 1942. New Mexico Military Institute, Navy. Inducted in 1985. 1969-1979 Dallas Cowboys. **Highlights:** Led Cowboys to four NFC titles and victories in Super Bowls VI, XII. When retired, 83.4 career passer rating was best of all time.

ERNIE STAUTNER

Defensive tackle. 6-2, 235. Born in Prinzing-by-Cham, Bavaria, April 20, 1925. Boston College. Inducted in 1969. 1950-1963 Pittsburgh Steelers. **Highlights:** Played in nine Pro Bowls and won the best lineman award in 1957. Recorded 3 safeties.

JAN STENERUD

Kicker. 6-2, 190. Born in Fetsund, Norway, November 26, 1942. Montana State. Inducted in 1991. 1967-1979 Kansas City Chiefs, 1980-83 Green Bay Packers, 1984-85 Minnesota Vikings. **Highlights:** 1,699 points on 580 extra points, 373 field goals. First pure placekicker to enter Hall of Fame.

DWIGHT STEPHENSON

Center. 6-2, 255. Born in Murfreesboro, North Carolina, November 20, 1957. Alabama. Inducted in 1998. 1980-87 Miami Dolphins. **Highlights:** Recognized as premier center of his time. All-Pro, All-AFC five straight years. Selected to five Pro Bowls.

HANK STRAM

Coach. Born in Chicago, Illinois, January 3, 1923. Purdue. Inducted in 2003. 1960-1974 Dallas Texans/Kansas City Chiefs, 1976-1977 New Orleans Saints. **Highlights:** Overall record of 136-100-10. Recorded most wins in AFL history. Guided teams to titles in 1962, 1966, and 1969. Led Chiefs to AFL win in Super Bowl IV.

KEN STRONG

Halfback. 5-11, 210. Born in West Haven, Connecticut, April 21, 1906. Died October 5, 1979. New York University. Inducted in 1967. 1929-1932 Staten Island Stapletons, 1933-35, 1939, 1944-47 New York Giants, 1936-37 New York Yanks (AFL). **Highlights:** Scored 17 points to lead Giants to victory in 1934 'Sneakers' game, led NFL with 64 points, 1933.

JOE STYDAHAR

Tackle. 6-4, 230. Born in Kaylor, Pennsylvania, March 17, 1912. Died March 23, 1977. West Virginia. Inducted in 1967. 1936-1942, 1945-46 Chicago Bears. **Highlights:** One of stalwarts of Bears' 'Monsters of the Midway.' Played on five divisional, three NFL championship teams.

LYNN SWANN

Wide receiver. 5-11, 180. Born in Alcoa, Tennessee, March 7, 1952. Southern California. Inducted in 2001. 1974-1982 Pittsburgh Steelers. **Highlights:** All-AFC three times. Selected to three Pro Bowls. MVP, Super Bowl X.

FRAN TARKENTON

Quarterback. 6-0, 185. Born in Richmond, Virginia, February 3, 1940. Georgia. Inducted in 1986. 1961-66, 1972-78 Minnesota Vikings, 1967-1971 New York Giants. **Highlights:** At retirement, held NFL records for attempts (6,467), completions (3,686), yards (47,003), and touchdowns (342). Four touchdowns passes in first NFL game.

CHARLEY TAYLOR

Running back-wide receiver. 6-3, 210. Born in Grand Prairie, Texas, September 28, 1941. Arizona State. Inducted in 1984. 1964-1975, 1977 Washington Redskins. **Highlights:** Won rookie of year honors as running back. Switched to wide receiver and won receiving titles in 1966, 1967.

JIM TAYLOR

Fullback. 6-0, 216. Born in Baton Rouge, Louisiana, September 20, 1935. Louisiana State. Inducted in 1976. 1958-1966 Green Bay Packers, 1967 New Orleans Saints. **Highlights:** 8,597 rushing yards, 558 points. In 1962, led league in rushing and scoring with 19 touchdowns.

LAWRENCE TAYLOR

Linebacker. 6-3, 237. Born in Williamsburg, Virginia, February 4, 1959. North Carolina. Inducted in 1999. 1981-1993 New York Giants. **Highlights:** Redefined the position of outside linebacker. All-Pro nine times, 10 Pro Bowls. NFL MVP in 1986.

JIM THORPE
Halfback. 6-1, 190. Born in Prague, Oklahoma, May 28, 1888. Died March 28, 1953. Carlisle. Inducted in 1963. 1915-17, 1919-1920, 1926 Canton Bulldogs, 1921 Cleveland Indians, 1922-23 Oorang Indians, 1924 Rock Island Independents, 1925 New York Giants, 1928 Chicago Cardinals. **Highlights:** Charter enshrinee. First president of American Professional Football Association, 1920. Played for 12 seasons.

Y.A. TITTLE
Quarterback. 6-0, 200. Born in Marshall, Texas, October 24, 1926. Louisiana State. Inducted in 1971. 1948-49 Baltimore Colts (AAFC), 1950 Baltimore Colts, 1951-1960 San Francisco 49ers, 1961-64 New York Giants. **Highlights:** 33,070 yards, 242 touchdowns. 33 touchdown passes in 1962 and 36 in 1963. Two-time league MVP.

GEORGE TRAFTON
Center. 6-2, 235. Born in Chicago, Illinois, December 6, 1896. Died September 5, 1971. Notre Dame. Inducted in 1964. 1920-1932 Decatur Staleys/Chicago Staleys/Chicago Bears. **Highlights:** First center to snap with one hand. Named top NFL center of 1920s.

CHARLEY TRIPPI
Halfback-quarterback. 6-0, 185. Born in Pittston, Pennsylvania, December 14, 1922. Georgia. Inducted in 1968. 1947-1955 Chicago Cardinals. **Highlights:** One of football's most versatile performers. Played halfback five years, quarterback for two, defense for two.

EMLEN TUNNELL
Safety. 6-1, 200. Born in Bryn Mawr, Pennsylvania, March 29, 1925. Died July 22, 1975. Toledo, Iowa. Inducted in 1967. 1948-1958 New York Giants, 1959-1961 Green Bay Packers. **Highlights:** 79 interceptions. Gained more yards on kickoff, punt, and interception returns (924) in 1952 than that season's NFL rushing leader.

CLYDE (BULLDOG) TURNER
Center. 6-2, 235. Born in Plains, Texas, March 10, 1919. Died October 30, 1998. Hardin-Simmons. Inducted in 1966. 1940-1952 Chicago Bears. **Highlights:** Anchored defense for four NFL championship teams, including 4 interceptions in five title games.

JOHNNY UNITAS
Quarterback. 6-1, 195. Born in Pittsburgh, Pennsylvania, May 7, 1933. Died September 11, 2002. Louisville. Inducted in 1979. 1956-1972 Baltimore Colts, 1973 San Diego Chargers. **Highlights:** 40,239 passing yards, 290 touchdowns. Led Colts to two NFL championships. Passed for at least one touchdown in 47 consecutive games.

GENE UPSHAW
Guard. 6-5, 255. Born in Robstown, Texas, August 15, 1945. Texas A & I. Inducted in 1987. 1967-1981 Oakland Raiders. **Highlights:** Premier guard of his era played in 10 AFL/AFC Championship Games, three Super Bowls, seven Pro Bowls.

NORM VAN BROCKLIN
Quarterback. 6-1, 190. Born in Eagle Butte, South Dakota, March 15, 1926. Died May 2, 1983. Oregon. Inducted in 1971. 1949-1957 Los Angeles Rams, 1958-1960 Philadelphia Eagles. **Highlights:** NFL-record 554 yards passing in 1951 season opener. Guided Eagles to NFL crown as league MVP in 1960.

STEVE VAN BUREN
Halfback. 6-1, 200. Born in La Ceiba, Honduras, December 28, 1920. Louisiana State. Inducted in 1965. 1944-1951 Philadelphia Eagles. **Highlights:** Four-time rushing champion. Won 1944 punt-return title and was 1945 kickoff-return champion.

DOAK WALKER
Halfback. 5-11, 173. Born in Dallas, Texas, January 1, 1927. Died September 27, 1998. Southern Methodist. Inducted in 1986. 1950-55 Detroit Lions. **Highlights:** 534 points. Won two NFL scoring titles. Had winning 67-yard scoring run in 1952 title game.

BILL WALSH
Coach. Born in Los Angeles, California, November 30, 1931. San Jose State. Inducted in 1993. 1979-1988 San Francisco 49ers. **Highlights:** 102-63-1 coaching record. Guided 49ers to three Super Bowl titles (XVI, XIX, XXIII) in 10 years.

PAUL WARFIELD
Wide receiver. 6-0, 188. Born in Warren, Ohio, November 28, 1942. Ohio State. Inducted in 1983. 1964-69, 1976-77 Cleveland Browns, 1970-74 Miami Dolphins. **Highlights:** 8,565 yards receiving, 85 touchdowns. Eight-time Pro Bowl player. Key to both Cleveland and Miami offenses.

BOB WATERFIELD
Quarterback. 6-2, 200. Born in Elmira, New York, July 26, 1920. Died March 25, 1983. UCLA. Inducted in 1965. 1945 Cleveland Rams, 1946-1952 Los Angeles Rams. **Highlights:** NFL MVP as rookie in 1945 and led Rams to NFL title. Grabbed 20 interceptions in limited defensive duties.

MIKE WEBSTER
Center. 6-2, 260. Born in Tomahawk, Wisconsin, March 18, 1952. Died September 24, 2002. Wisconsin. Inducted in 1997. 1974-1988 Pittsburgh Steelers, 1989-1990 Kansas City Chiefs. **Highlights:** Played in 245 games, nine Pro Bowls, and won four Super Bowls during 17-year career.

ARNIE WEINMEISTER
Defensive tackle. 6-4, 235. Born in Rhein, Saskatchewan, Canada, March 23, 1923. Died June 29, 2000. Washington. Inducted in 1984. 1948-49 New York Yankees (AAFC), 1950-53 New York Giants. **Highlights:** Dominant defensive tackle of his time. Four-time All-NFL selection, four Pro Bowls.

RANDY WHITE
Defensive tackle. 6-4, 265. Born in Pittsburgh, Pennsylvania, January 15, 1953. Maryland. Inducted in 1994. 1975-1988 Dallas Cowboys. **Highlights:** Missed only one game in 14 seasons. Co-MVP of Super Bowl XII. Nine-time Pro Bowl selection.

DAVE WILCOX
Linebacker. 6-3, 241. Born in Ontario, Oregon, September, 29, 1942. Boise State, Oregon. Inducted in 2000. 1964-1974 San Francisco 49ers. **Highlights:** Seven Pro Bowls, All-NFL five times. Missed only one game because of injury.

BILL WILLIS
Guard. 6-2, 215. Born in Columbus, Ohio, October 5, 1921. Ohio State. Inducted in 1977. 1946-1953 Cleveland Browns (AAFC/NFL). **Highlights:** Two-way player who excelled on defense. Four-time All-NFL player, played in three Pro Bowls.

LARRY WILSON
Safety. 6-0, 190. Born in Rigby, Idaho, March 24, 1938. Utah. Inducted in 1978. 1960-1972 St. Louis Cardinals. **Highlights:** 52 interceptions. Had interception in seven consecutive games in 1966. Made "safety blitz" famous.

KELLEN WINSLOW
Tight end. 6-5, 250. Born in St. Louis, Missouri, November 5, 1957. Missouri. Inducted in 1995. 1979-1987 San Diego Chargers. **Highlights:** 541 receptions for 6,741 yards, 45 touchdowns. 13 catches, blocked field goal in 1981 playoff win over Miami.

ALEX WOJCIECHOWICZ
Center. 6-0, 235. Born in South River, New Jersey, August 12, 1915. Died July 13, 1992. Fordham. Inducted in 1968. 1938-1946 Detroit Lions, 1946-1950 Philadelphia Eagles. **Highlights:** One of league's first iron men. Played both ways for eight years with Lions.

WILLIE WOOD
Safety. 5-10, 190. Born in Washington, D.C., December 23, 1936. Southern California. Inducted in 1989. 1960-1971 Green Bay Packers. **Highlights:** 48 interceptions. Competed in six NFL Championship Games and Super Bowls I and II.

RON YARY
Tackle. 6-5, 255. Born in Chicago, Illinois, July 16, 1946. Cerritos (Calif.) J.C., Southern California. Inducted in 2001. 1968-1981 Minnesota Vikings, 1982 Los Angeles Rams. **Highlights:** All-Pro six consecutive seasons, All-NFC eight consecutive years. Named to seven Pro Bowls. Started in four Super Bowls and five NFL/NFC Championship Games.

STEVE YOUNG
Quarterback. 6-2, 205. Born in Salt Lake City, Utah, October 11, 1961. Brigham Young. Inducted in 2005. 1985-86 Tampa Bay Buccaneers, 1987-1999 San Francisco 49ers. **Highlights:** Led the NFL in passing a record-tying six times. Passed for more than 33,000 yards and 232 touchdowns in career. MVP of Super Bowl XXIX. Elected to seven Pro Bowls.

JACK YOUNGBLOOD
Defensive end. 6-4, 247. Born in Jacksonville, Florida, January 26, 1950. Florida. Inducted in 2001. 1971-1984 Los Angeles Rams. **Highlights:** Played in club-record 201 consecutive games. Played in five NFC Championship Games, one Super Bowl. Named All-Pro five times, All-NFC seven times. Elected to seven consecutive Pro Bowls.

ENSHRINEES BY YEAR OF INDUCTION
*Deceased
(Date of enshrinement in parentheses)*

1963 CHARTER CLASS
(September 7, 1963)
Sammy Baugh
Bert Bell*
Joe Carr*
Earl (Dutch) Clark*
Harold (Red) Grange*
George Halas*
Mel Hein*
Wilbur (Pete) Henry*
Robert (Cal) Hubbard*
Don Hutson*
Earl (Curly) Lambeau*
Tim Mara*
George Preston Marshall*
John (Blood) McNally*
Bronko Nagurski*
Ernie Nevers*
Jim Thorpe*

CLASS OF 1964
(September 6, 1964)
Jimmy Conzelman*
Ed Healey*
Clarke Hinkle*
William Roy (Link) Lyman*
Mike Michalske*
Art Rooney*
George Trafton*

CLASS OF 1965
(September 12, 1965)
Guy Chamberlin*
John (Paddy) Driscoll*
Dan Fortmann*
Otto Graham*
Sid Luckman*
Steve Van Buren*
Bob Waterfield*

CLASS OF 1966
(September 17, 1966)
Bill Dudley
Joe Guyon*
Arnie Herber*
Walt Kiesling*
George McAfee*
Steve Owen*
Hugh (Shorty) Ray*
Clyde (Bulldog) Turner*

CLASS OF 1967
(August 5, 1967)
Chuck Bednarik
Charles W. Bidwill Sr.*
Paul Brown*
Bobby Layne*
Dan Reeves*
Ken Strong*
Joe Stydahar*
Emlen Tunnell*

CLASS OF 1968
(August 3, 1968)
Cliff Battles*
Art Donovan
Elroy (Crazylegs) Hirsch*
Wayne Millner*
Marion Motley*
Charley Trippi
Alex Wojciechowicz*

CLASS OF 1969
(September 13, 1969)
Albert Glen (Turk) Edwards*
Earle (Greasy) Neale*
Leo Nomellini*
Joe Perry
Ernie Stautner

CLASS OF 1970
(August 8, 1970)
Jack Christiansen*
Tom Fears*
Hugh McElhenny
Pete Pihos

CLASS OF 1971
(July 31, 1971)
Jim Brown
Bill Hewitt*
Frank (Bruiser) Kinard*
Vince Lombardi*
Andy Robustelli
Y. A. Tittle
Norm Van Brocklin*

CLASS OF 1972
(July 29, 1972)
Lamar Hunt
Gino Marchetti
Ollie Matson
Clarence (Ace) Parker

CLASS OF 1973
(July 28, 1973)
Raymond Berry
Jim Parker
Joe Schmidt

CLASS OF 1974
(July 27, 1974)
Tony Canadeo*
Bill George*
Lou Groza*
Dick (Night Train) Lane*

CLASS OF 1975
(August 2, 1975)
Roosevelt Brown*
George Connor*
Dante Lavelli
Lenny Moore

CLASS OF 1976
(July 24, 1976)
Ray Flaherty*
Len Ford*
Jim Taylor

CLASS OF 1977
(July 30, 1977)
Frank Gifford
Forrest Gregg
Gale Sayers
Bart Starr
Bill Willis

CLASS OF 1978
(July 29, 1978)
Lance Alworth
Weeb Ewbank*
Alphonse (Tuffy) Leemans*
Ray Nitschke*
Larry Wilson

CLASS OF 1979
(July 28, 1979)
Dick Butkus
Yale Lary
Ron Mix
Johnny Unitas*

CLASS OF 1980
(August 2, 1980)
Herb Adderley
David (Deacon) Jones
Bob Lilly
Jim Otto

CLASS OF 1981
(August 1, 1981)
Morris (Red) Badgro*
George Blanda
Willie Davis
Jim Ringo

CLASS OF 1982
(August 7, 1982)
Doug Atkins
Sam Huff
George Musso*
Merlin Olsen

CLASS OF 1983
(July 30, 1983)
Bobby Bell
Sid Gillman*
Sonny Jurgensen
Bobby Mitchell
Paul Warfield

CLASS OF 1984
(July 28, 1984)
Willie Brown
Mike McCormack
Charley Taylor
Arnie Weinmeister*

CLASS OF 1985
(August 3, 1985)
Frank Gatski
Joe Namath
Pete Rozelle*
O. J. Simpson
Roger Staubach

CLASS OF 1986
(August 2, 1986)
Paul Hornung
Ken Houston
Willie Lanier
Fran Tarkenton
Doak Walker*

CLASS OF 1987
(August 8, 1987)
Larry Csonka
Len Dawson
Joe Greene
John Henry Johnson
Jim Langer
Don Maynard
Gene Upshaw

CLASS OF 1988
(July 30, 1988)
Fred Biletnikoff
Mike Ditka
Jack Ham
Alan Page

CLASS OF 1989
(August 5, 1989)
Mel Blount
Terry Bradshaw
Art Shell
Willie Wood

CLASS OF 1990
(August 4, 1990)
Buck Buchanan*
Bob Griese
Franco Harris
Ted Hendricks
Jack Lambert
Tom Landry*
Bob St. Clair

CLASS OF 1991
(July 27, 1991)
Earl Campbell
John Hannah
Stan Jones
Tex Schramm*
Jan Stenerud

CLASS OF 1992
(August 1, 1992)
Lem Barney
Al Davis
John Mackey
John Riggins

CLASS OF 1993
(July 31, 1993)
Dan Fouts
Larry Little
Chuck Noll
Walter Payton*
Bill Walsh

CLASS OF 1994
(July 30, 1994)
Tony Dorsett
Bud Grant
Jimmy Johnson
Leroy Kelly
Jackie Smith
Randy White

CLASS OF 1995
(July 29, 1995)
Jim Finks*
Henry Jordan*
Steve Largent
Lee Roy Selmon
Kellen Winslow

CLASS OF 1996
(July 27, 1996)
Lou Creekmur
Dan Dierdorf
Joe Gibbs
Charlie Joiner
Mel Renfro

CLASS OF 1997
(July 26, 1997)
Mike Haynes
Wellington Mara
Don Shula
Mike Webster*

CLASS OF 1998
(August 1, 1998)
Paul Krause
Tommy McDonald
Anthony Muñoz
Mike Singletary
Dwight Stephenson

CLASS OF 1999
(August 7, 1999)
Eric Dickerson
Tom Mack
Ozzie Newsome
Billy Shaw
Lawrence Taylor

CLASS OF 2000
(July 29, 2000)
Howie Long
Ronnie Lott
Joe Montana
Dan Rooney
Dave Wilcox

CLASS OF 2001
(August 4, 2001)
Nick Buoniconti
Marv Levy
Mike Munchak
Jackie Slater
Lynn Swann
Ron Yary
Jack Youngblood

CLASS OF 2002
(August 3, 2002)
George Allen*
Dave Casper
Dan Hampton
Jim Kelly
John Stallworth

CLASS OF 2003
(August 3, 2003)
Marcus Allen
Elvin Bethea
Joe DeLamielleure
James Lofton
Hank Stram

CLASS OF 2004
(August 8, 2004)
Bob (Boomer) Brown
Carl Eller
John Elway
Barry Sanders

CLASS OF 2005
(August 7, 2005)
Benny Friedman*
Dan Marino
Fritz Pollard*
Steve Young

1869
Rutgers and Princeton played a college soccer football game, the first ever, November 6. The game used modified London Football Association rules. During the next seven years, rugby gained favor with the major eastern schools over soccer, and modern football began to develop from rugby.

1876
At the Massasoit convention, the first rules for American football were written. Walter Camp, who would become known as the father of American football, first became involved with the game.

1892
In an era in which football was a major attraction of local athletic clubs, an intense competition between two Pittsburgh-area clubs, the Allegheny Athletic Association (AAA) and the Pittsburgh Athletic Club (PAC), led to the making of the first professional football player. Former Yale All-America guard William (Pudge) Heffelfinger was paid $500 by the AAA to play in a game against the PAC, becoming the first person to be paid to play football, November 12. The AAA won the game 4-0 when Heffelfinger picked up a PAC fumble and ran 35 yards for a touchdown.

1893
The Pittsburgh Athletic Club signed one of its players, probably halfback Grant Dibert, to the first known pro football contract, which covered all of the PAC's games for the year.

1895
John Brallier became the first football player to openly turn pro, accepting $10 and expenses to play for the Latrobe YMCA against the Jeannette Athletic Club.

1896
The Allegheny Athletic Association team fielded the first completely professional team for its abbreviated two-game season.

1897
The Latrobe Athletic Association football team went entirely professional, becoming the first team to play a full season with only professionals.

1898
A touchdown was changed from four points to five.

1899
Chris O'Brien formed a neighborhood team, which played under the name the Morgan Athletic Club, on the south side of Chicago. The team later became known as the Normals, then the Racine (for a street in Chicago) Cardinals, the Chicago Cardinals, the St. Louis Cardinals, the Phoenix Cardinals, and, in 1994, the Arizona Cardinals. The team remains the oldest continuing operation in pro football.

1900
William C. Temple took over the team payments for the Duquesne Country and Athletic Club, becoming the first known individual club owner.

1902
Baseball's Philadelphia Athletics, managed by Connie Mack, and the Philadelphia Phillies formed professional football teams, joining the Pittsburgh Stars in the first attempt at a pro football league, named the National Football League. The Athletics won the first night football game ever played, 39-0 over Kanaweola AC at Elmira, New York, November 21.

All three teams claimed the pro championship for the year, but the league president, Dave Berry, named the Stars as champions. Pitcher Rube Waddell was with the Athletics, and pitcher Christy Mathewson a fullback for Pittsburgh.

The first World Series of pro football, actually a five-team tournament, was played among a team made up of players from both the Athletics and the Phillies, but simply named New York; the New York Knickerbockers; the Syracuse AC; the Warlow AC; and the Orange (New Jersey) AC at New York's original Madison Square Garden. New York and Syracuse played the first indoor football game before 3,000, December 28. Syracuse, with Glen (Pop) Warner at guard, won 6-0 and

went on to win the tournament.

1903
The Franklin (Pa.) Athletic Club won the second and last World Series of pro football over the Oreos AC of Asbury Park, New Jersey; the Watertown Red and Blacks; and the Orange AC.

Pro football was popularized in Ohio when the Massillon Tigers, a strong amateur team, hired four Pittsburgh pros to play in the season-ending game against Akron. At the same time, pro football declined in the Pittsburgh area, and the emphasis on the pro game moved west from Pennsylvania to Ohio.

1904
A field goal was changed from five points to four.

Ohio had at least seven pro teams, with Massillon winning the Ohio Independent Championship, that is, the pro title. Talk surfaced about forming a state-wide league to end spiraling salaries brought about by constant bidding for players and to write universal rules for the game. The feeble attempt to start the league failed.

Halfback Charles Follis signed a contract with the Shelby (Ohio) AC, making him the first known black pro football player.

1905
The Canton AC, later to become known as the Bulldogs, became a professional team. Massillon again won the Ohio League championship.

1906
The forward pass was legalized. The first authenticated pass completion in a pro game came on October 27, when George (Peggy) Parratt of Massillon threw a completion to Dan (Bullet) Riley in a victory over a combined Benwood-Moundsville team.

Arch-rivals Canton and Massillon, the two best pro teams in America, played twice, with Canton winning the first game but Massillon winning the second and the Ohio League championship. A betting scandal and the financial disaster wrought upon the two clubs by paying huge salaries

caused a temporary decline in interest in pro football in the two cities and, somewhat, throughout Ohio.

1909
A field goal dropped from four points to three.

1912
A touchdown was increased from five points to six.

Jack Cusack revived a strong pro team in Canton.

1913
Jim Thorpe, a former football and track star at the Carlisle Indian School (Pa.) and a double gold medal winner at the 1912 Olympics in Stockholm, played for the Pine Village Pros in Indiana.

1915
Massillon again fielded a major team, reviving the old rivalry with Canton. Cusack signed Thorpe to play for Canton for $250 a game.

1916
With Thorpe and former Carlisle teammate Pete Calac starring, Canton went 9-0-1, won the Ohio League championship, and was acclaimed the pro football champion.

1917
Despite an upset by Massillon, Canton again won the Ohio League championship.

1919
Canton again won the Ohio League championship, despite the team having been turned over from Cusack to Ralph Hay. Thorpe and Calac were joined in the backfield by Joe Guyon.

Earl (Curly) Lambeau and George Calhoun organized the Green Bay Packers. Lambeau's employer at the Indian Packing Company provided $500 for equipment and allowed the team to use the company field for practices. The Packers went 10-1.

1920
Pro football was in a state of confusion due to three major problems: dramatically rising salaries; players continually jumping from one team to another following the highest offer; and the use of college players still enrolled in school.

A league in which all the members would follow the same rules seemed the answer. An organizational meeting, at which the Akron Pros, Canton Bulldogs, Cleveland Indians, and Dayton Triangles were represented, was held at the Jordan and Hupmobile auto showroom in Canton, Ohio, August 20. This meeting resulted in the formation of the American Professional Football Conference.

A second organizational meeting was held in Canton, September 17. The teams were from four states—Akron, Canton, Cleveland, and Dayton from Ohio; the Hammond Pros and Muncie Flyers from Indiana; the Rochester Jeffersons from New York; and the Rock Island Independents, Decatur Staleys, and Racine Cardinals from Illinois. The name of the league was changed to the American Professional Football Association. Hoping to capitalize on his fame, the members elected Thorpe president; Stanley Cofall of Cleveland was elected vice president. A membership fee of $100 per team was charged to give an appearance of respectability, but no team ever paid it. Scheduling was left up to the teams, and there were wide variations, both in the overall number of games played and in the number played against APFA member teams.

Four other teams—the Buffalo All-Americans, Chicago Tigers, Columbus Panhandles, and Detroit Heralds—joined the league sometime during the year. On September 26, the first game featuring an APFA team was played at Rock Island's Douglas Park. A crowd of 800 watched the Independents defeat the St. Paul Ideals 48-0. A week later, October 3, the first game matching two APFA teams was held. At Triangle Park, Dayton defeated Columbus 14-0, with Lou Partlow of Dayton scoring the first touchdown in a game between Association teams. The same day, Rock Island defeated Muncie 45-0.

By the beginning of December, most of the teams in the APFA had abandoned their hopes for a championship, and some of them, including the Chicago Tigers and the Detroit Heralds, had finished their seasons, disbanded, and had their franchises canceled by the Association. Four teams—Akron, Buffalo, Canton, and Decatur—still had championship as-pirations, but a series of late-season games among them left Akron as the only undefeated team in the Association. At one of these games, Akron sold tackle Bob Nash to Buffalo for $300 and five percent of the gate receipts—the first APFA player deal.

1921

At the league meeting in Akron, April 30, the championship of the 1920 season was awarded to the Akron Pros. The APFA was reorganized, with Joe Carr of the Columbus Panhandles named president and Carl Storck of Dayton secretary-treasurer. Carr moved the Association's headquarters to Columbus, drafted a league constitution and by-laws, gave teams territorial rights, restricted player movements, developed membership criteria for the franchises, and issued standings for the first time, so that the APFA would have a clear champion.

The Association's membership increased to 22 teams, including the Green Bay Packers, who were awarded to John Clair of the Acme Packing Company.

Thorpe moved from Canton to the Cleveland Indians, but he was hurt early in the season and played very little.

A.E. Staley turned the Decatur Staleys over to player-coach George Halas, who moved the team to Cubs Park in Chicago. Staley paid Halas $5,000 to keep the name Staleys for one more year. Halas made halfback Ed (Dutch) Sternaman his partner.

Player-coach Fritz Pollard of the Akron Pros became the first black head coach.

The Staleys claimed the APFA championship with a 9-1-1 record, as did Buffalo at 9-1-2. Carr ruled in favor of the Staleys, giving Halas his first championship.

1922

After admitting the use of players who had college eligibility remaining during the 1921 season, Clair and the Green Bay management withdrew from the APFA, January 28. Curly Lambeau promised to obey league rules and then used $50 of his own money to buy back the franchise. Bad weather and low attendance plagued the Packers, and Lambeau went broke, but local merchants arranged a $2,500 loan for the club. A public non-profit corporation was set up to operate the team, with Lambeau as head coach and manager.

The American Professional Football Association changed its name to the National Football League, June 24. The Chicago Staleys became the Chicago Bears.

The NFL fielded 18 teams, including the new Oorang Indians of Marion, Ohio, an all-Indian team featuring Thorpe, Joe Guyon, and Pete Calac, and sponsored by the Oorang dog kennels.

Canton, led by player-coach Guy Chamberlin and tackles Link Lyman and Wilbur (Pete) Henry, emerged as the league's first true powerhouse, going 10-0-2.

1923

For the first time, all of the franchises considered to be part of the NFL fielded teams. Thorpe played his second and final season for the Oorang Indians. Against the Bears, Thorpe fumbled, and Halas picked up the ball and returned it 98 yards for a touchdown, a record that would last until 1972.

Canton had its second consecutive undefeated season, going 11-0-1 for the NFL title.

1924

The league had 18 franchises, including new ones in Kansas City, Kenosha, and Frankford, a section of Philadelphia. League champion Canton, successful on the field but not at the box office, was purchased by the owner of the Cleveland franchise, who kept the Canton franchise inactive, while using the best players for his Cleveland team, which he renamed the Bulldogs. Cleveland won the title with a 7-1-1 record.

1925

Five new franchises were admitted to the NFL—the New York Giants, who were awarded to Tim Mara and Billy Gibson for $500; the Detroit Panthers, featuring Jimmy Conzelman as owner, coach, and tailback; the Providence Steam Roller; a new Canton Bulldogs team; and the Pottsville Maroons, who had been perhaps the most successful independent pro team. The NFL established its first player limit, at 16 players.

Late in the season, the NFL made its greatest coup in gaining national recognition. Shortly after the University of Illinois season ended in November, All-America halfback Harold (Red) Grange signed a contract to play with the Chicago Bears. On Thanksgiving Day, a crowd of 36,000—the largest in pro football history—watched Grange and the Bears play the Chicago Cardinals to a scoreless tie at Wrigley Field. At the beginning of December, the Bears left on a barnstorming tour that saw them play eight games in 12 days, in St. Louis, Philadelphia, New York City, Washington, Boston, Pittsburgh, Detroit, and Chicago. A crowd of 73,000 watched the game against the Giants at the Polo Grounds, helping assure the future of the troubled NFL franchise in New York. The Bears then played nine more games in the South and West, including a game in Los Angeles, in which 75,000 fans watched them defeat the Los Angeles Tigers in the Los Angeles Memorial Coliseum.

Pottsville and the Chicago Cardinals were the top contenders for the league title, with Pottsville winning a late-season meeting 21-7. Pottsville scheduled a game against a team of former Notre Dame players for Shibe Park in Philadelphia. Frankford lodged a protest not only because the game was in Frankford's protected territory, but because it was being played the same day as a Yellow Jackets home game. Carr gave three different notices forbidding Pottsville to play the game, but Pottsville played anyway, December 12. That day, Carr fined the club, suspended it from all rights and privileges (including the right to play for the NFL championship), and re-turned its franchise to the league. The Cardinals, who ended the season with the best record in the league, were named the 1925 champions.

1926

Grange's manager, C.C. Pyle, told the Bears that Grange wouldn't play for them unless he was paid a five-figure salary and given one-third ownership of the team. The Bears refused. Pyle leased Yankee Stadium in New York City, then petitioned for an NFL franchise. After he was refused, he started the first American Football League. It lasted one season and included Grange's New York Yankees and eight other teams. The AFL champion Philadelphia Quakers played a December game against the New York Giants, seventh in the NFL, and the Giants won 31-0. At the end of the season, the AFL folded.

Halas pushed through a rule that prohibited any team from signing a player whose college class had not graduated.

The NFL grew to 22 teams, including the Duluth Eskimos, who signed All-America fullback Ernie Nevers of Stanford, giving the league a gate attraction to rival Grange. The 15-member Eskimos, dubbed the Iron Men of the North, played 29 exhibition and league games, 28 on the road, and Nevers played in all but 29 minutes of them.

Frankford edged the Bears for the championship, despite Halas having obtained John (Paddy) Driscoll from the Cardinals. On December 4, the Yellow Jackets scored in the final two minutes to defeat the Bears 7-6 and move ahead of them in the standings.

1927

At a special meeting in Cleveland, April 23, Carr decided to secure the NFL's future by eliminating the financially weaker teams and consolidating the quality players onto a limited number of more successful teams. The new-look NFL dropped to 12 teams, and the center of gravity of the league left the Midwest, where

the NFL had started, and began to emerge in the large cities of the East. One of the new teams was Grange's New York Yankees, but Grange suffered a knee injury and the Yankees finished in the middle of the pack. The NFL championship was won by the crosstown rival New York Giants, who posted 10 shutouts in 13 games.

1928

Grange and Nevers both retired from pro football, and Duluth disbanded, as the NFL was reduced to only 10 teams. The Providence Steam Roller of Jimmy Conzelman and Pearce Johnson won the championship, playing in the Cycledrome, a 10,000-seat oval that had been built for bicycle races.

1929

Chris O'Brien sold the Chicago Cardinals to David Jones, July 27.

The NFL added a fourth official, the field judge, July 28.

Grange and Nevers returned to the NFL. Nevers scored six rushing touchdowns and four extra points as the Cardinals beat Grange's Bears 40-6, November 28. The 40 points set a record that remains the NFL's oldest.

Providence became the first NFL team to host a game at night under floodlights, against the Cardinals, November 6.

The Packers added back Johnny Blood (McNally), tackle Cal Hubbard, and guard Mike Michalske, and won their first NFL championship, edging the Giants, who featured quarterback Benny Friedman.

1930

Dayton, the last of the NFL's original franchises, was purchased by William B. Dwyer and John C. Depler, moved to Brooklyn, and renamed the Dodgers. The Portsmouth, Ohio, Spartans entered the league.

The Packers edged the Giants for the title, but the most improved team was the Bears. Halas retired as a player and replaced himself as coach of the Bears with Ralph Jones, who refined the T-formation by introducing wide

ends and a halfback in motion. Jones also introduced rookie All-America fullback-tackle Bronko Nagurski.

The Giants defeated a team of former Notre Dame players coached by Knute Rockne 22-0 before 55,000 at the Polo Grounds, December 14. The proceeds went to the New York Unemployment Fund to help those suffering because of the Great Depression, and the easy victory helped give the NFL credibility with the press and the public.

1931

The NFL decreased to 10 teams, and halfway through the season the Frankford franchise folded. Carr fined the Bears, Packers, and Portsmouth $1,000 each for using players whose college classes had not graduated.

The Packers won an unprecedented third consecutive title, beating out the Spartans, who were led by rookie backs Earl (Dutch) Clark and Glenn Presnell.

1932

George Preston Marshall, Vincent Bendix, Jay O'Brien, and M. Dorland Doyle were awarded a franchise for Boston, July 9. Despite the presence of two rookies—halfback Cliff Battles and tackle Glen (Turk) Edwards—the new team, named the Braves, lost money and Marshall was left as the sole owner at the end of the year.

NFL membership dropped to eight teams, the lowest in history. Official statistics were kept for the first time. The Bears and the Spartans finished the season in the first-ever tie for first place. After the season finale, the league office arranged for an additional regular-season game to determine the league champion. The game was moved indoors to Chicago Stadium because of bitter cold and heavy snow. The arena allowed only an 80-yard field that came right to the walls. The goal posts were moved from the end lines to the goal lines and, for safety, inbounds lines or hashmarks where the ball would be put in play were drawn 10 yards from the walls that butted against the sidelines. The Bears won 9-0, December 18, scoring the

winning touchdown on a two-yard pass from Nagurski to Grange. The Spartans claimed Nagurski's pass was thrown from less than five yards behind the line of scrimmage, violating the existing passing rule, but the play stood.

1933

The NFL, which long had followed the rules of college football, made a number of significant changes from the college game for the first time and began to develop rules serving its needs and the style of play it preferred. The innovations from the 1932 championship game—inbounds line or hashmarks and goal posts on the goal lines—were adopted. Also the forward pass was legalized from anywhere behind the line of scrimmage, February 25.

Marshall and Halas pushed through a proposal that divided the NFL into two divisions, with the winners to meet in an annual championship game, July 8.

Three new franchises joined the league—the Pittsburgh Pirates of Art Rooney, the Philadelphia Eagles of Bert Bell and Lud Wray, and the Cincinnati Reds. The Staten Island Stapletons suspended operations for a year, but never returned to the league.

Halas bought out Sternaman, became sole owner of the Bears, and reinstated himself as head coach. Marshall changed the name of the Boston Braves to the Redskins. David Jones sold the Chicago Cardinals to Charles W. Bidwill.

In the first NFL Championship Game scheduled before the season, the Western Division champion Bears defeated the Eastern Division champion Giants 23-21 at Wrigley Field, December 17.

1934

G.A. (Dick) Richards purchased the Portsmouth Spartans, moved them to Detroit, and renamed them the Lions.

Professional football gained new prestige when the Bears were matched against the best college football players in the first Chicago College All-Star Game, August 31. The game ended in a scoreless tie before 79,432 at Soldier Field.

The Cincinnati Reds lost their first eight games, then were suspended from the league for defaulting on payments. The St. Louis Gunners, an independent team, joined the NFL by buying the Cincinnati franchise and went 1-2 the last three weeks.

Rookie Beattie Feathers of the Bears became the NFL's first 1,000-yard rusher, gaining 1,004 on 101 carries. The Thanksgiving Day game between the Bears and the Lions became the first NFL game broadcast nationally, with Graham McNamee the announcer for NBC radio.

In the championship game, on an extremely cold and icy day at the Polo Grounds, the Giants trailed the Bears 13-3 in the third quarter before changing to basketball shoes for better footing. The Giants won 30-13 in what has come to be known as the Sneakers Game, December 9.

The player waiver rule was adopted, December 10.

1935
The NFL adopted Bert Bell's proposal to hold an annual draft of college players, to begin in 1936, with teams selecting in an inverse order of finish, May 19. The inbounds line or hashmarks were moved nearer the center of the field, 15 yards from the sidelines.

All-America end Don Hutson of Alabama joined Green Bay. The Lions defeated the Giants 26-7 in the NFL Championship Game, December 15.

1936
There were no franchise transactions for the first year since the formation of the NFL. It also was the first year in which all member teams played the same number of games.

The Eagles made University of Chicago halfback and Heisman Trophy winner Jay Berwanger the first player ever selected in the NFL draft, February 8. The Eagles traded his rights to the Bears, but Berwanger never played pro football. The first player selected to actually sign was the number-two pick, Riley Smith of Alabama, who was selected by Boston.

A rival league was formed, and it became the second to

call itself the American Football League. The Boston Shamrocks were its champions.

Because of poor attendance, Marshall, the owner of the host team, moved the Championship Game from Boston to the Polo Grounds in New York. Green Bay defeated the Redskins 21-6, December 13.

1937
Homer Marshman was granted a Cleveland franchise, named the Rams, February 12. Marshall moved the Redskins to Washington, D.C., February 13. The Redskins signed TCU All-America tailback Sammy Baugh, who led them to a 28-21 victory over the Bears in the NFL Championship Game, December 12.

The Los Angeles Bulldogs had an 8-0 record to win the AFL title, but then the 2-year-old league folded.

1938
At the suggestion of Halas, Hugh (Shorty) Ray became a technical advisor on rules and officiating to the NFL. A new rule called for a 15-yard penalty for roughing the passer.

Rookie Byron (Whizzer) White of the Pittsburgh Pirates led the NFL in rushing. The Giants defeated the Packers 23-17 for the NFL title, December 11.

Marshall, *Los Angeles Times* sports editor Bill Henry, and promoter Tom Gallery established the Pro Bowl game between the NFL champion and a team of pro all-stars.

1939
The New York Giants defeated the Pro All-Stars 13-10 in the first Pro Bowl, at Wrigley Field, Los Angeles, January 15.

Carr, NFL president since 1921, died in Columbus, May 20. Carl Storck was named acting president, May 25.

An NFL game was televised for the first time when NBC broadcast the Brooklyn Dodgers-Philadelphia Eagles game from Ebbets Field to the approximately 1,000 sets then in New York, October 22.

Green Bay defeated New York 27-0 in the NFL Championship Game, December 10 at Milwaukee. NFL attendance

exceeded 1 million in a season for the first time, reaching 1,071,200.

1940
A six-team rival league, the third to call itself the American Football League, was formed, and the Columbus Bullies won its championship.

Halas' Bears, with additional coaching by Clark Shaughnessy of Stanford, defeated the Redskins 73-0 in the NFL Championship Game, December 8. The game, which was the most decisive victory in NFL history, popularized the Bears' T-formation with a man-in-motion. It was the first championship carried on network radio, broadcast by Red Barber to 120 stations of the Mutual Broadcasting System, which paid $2,500 for the rights.

Art Rooney sold the Pittsburgh franchise to Alexis Thompson, December 9, then bought part interest in the Philadelphia Eagles.

1941
Elmer Layden was named the first Commissioner of the NFL, March 1; Storck, the acting president, resigned, April 5. NFL headquarters were moved to Chicago.

Bell and Rooney traded the Eagles to Thompson for the Pirates, then re-named their new team the Steelers. Homer Marshman sold the Rams to Daniel F. Reeves and Fred Levy, Jr.

The league by-laws were revised to provide for playoffs in case there were ties in division races, and sudden-death overtimes in case a playoff game was tied after four quarters. An official *NFL Record Manual* was published for the first time.

Columbus again won the championship of the AFL, but the two-year-old league then folded.

The Bears and the Packers finished in a tie for the Western Division championship, setting up the first divisional playoff game in league history. The Bears won 33-14, then defeated the Giants 37-9 for the NFL championship, December 21.

1942
Players departing for service

in World War II depleted the rosters of NFL teams. Halas left the Bears in midseason to join the Navy, and Luke Johnsos and Heartley (Hunk) Anderson served as co-coaches as the Bears went 11-0 in the regular season. The Redskins defeated the Bears 14-6 in the NFL Championship Game, December 13.

1943
The Cleveland Rams, with co-owners Reeves and Levy in the service, were granted permission to suspend operations for one season, April 6. Levy transferred his stock in the team to Reeves, April 16.

The NFL adopted free substitution, April 7. The league also made the wearing of helmets mandatory and approved a 10-game schedule for all teams.

Philadelphia and Pittsburgh were granted permission to merge for one season, June 19. The team, known as Phil-Pitt (and called the Steagles by fans), divided home games between the two cities, and Earle (Greasy) Neale of Philadelphia and Walt Kiesling of Pittsburgh served as co-coaches. The merger automatically dissolved the last day of the season, December 5.

Ted Collins was granted a franchise for Boston, to become active in 1944.

Sammy Baugh led the league in passing, punting, and interceptions. He led the Redskins to a tie with the Giants for the Eastern Division title, and then to a 28-0 victory in a divisional playoff game. The Bears beat the Redskins 41-21 in the NFL Championship Game, December 26.

1944
Collins, who had wanted a franchise in Yankee Stadium in New York, named his new team in Boston the Yanks. Cleveland resumed operations. The Brooklyn Dodgers changed their name to the Tigers.

Coaching from the bench was legalized, April 20.

The Cardinals and the Steelers were granted permission to merge for one year under the name Card-Pitt, April 21. Phil Handler of the Cardinals and Walt Kiesling of the Steelers served as co-coaches. The merger automatically dissolved the last day of the season, December 3.

In the NFL Championship Game, Green Bay defeated the New York Giants 14-7, December 17.

1945

The inbounds lines or hashmarks were moved from 15 yards away from the sidelines to nearer the center of the field—20 yards from the sidelines.

Brooklyn and Boston merged into a team that played home games in both cities and was known simply as The Yanks. The team was coached by former Boston head coach Herb Kopf. In December, the Brooklyn franchise withdrew from the NFL to join the new All-America Football Conference; all the players on its active and reserve lists were assigned to The Yanks, who once again became the Boston Yanks.

Halas rejoined the Bears late in the season after service with the U.S. Navy. Although Halas took over much of the coaching duties, Anderson and Johnsos remained the coaches of record throughout the season.

Steve Van Buren of Philadelphia led the NFL in rushing, kickoff returns, and scoring.

After the Japanese surrendered ending World War II, a count showed that the NFL service roster, limited to men who had played in league games, totaled 638, 21 of whom had died in action.

Rookie quarterback Bob Waterfield led Cleveland to a 15-14 victory over Washington in the NFL Championship Game, December 16.

1946

The contract of Commissioner Layden was not renewed, and Bert Bell, the co-owner of the Steelers, replaced him, January 11. Bell moved the league headquarters from Chicago to the Philadelphia suburb of Bala-Cynwyd.

Free substitution was withdrawn and substitutions were limited to no more than three men at a time. Forward passes were made automatically incomplete upon striking the goal posts, January 11.

The NFL took on a truly national appearance for the first time when Reeves was granted permission by the league to move his NFL champion Rams to Los Angeles.

Halfback Kenny Washington (March 21) and end Woody Strode (May 7) signed with the Los Angeles Rams to become the first African-Americans to play in the NFL in the modern era. Guard Bill Willis (August 6) and running back Marion Motley (August 9) joined the AAFC with the Cleveland Browns.

The rival All-America Football Conference began play with eight teams. The Cleveland Browns, coached by Paul Brown, won the AAFC's first championship, defeating the New York Yankees 14-9.

Bill Dudley of the Steelers led the NFL in rushing, interceptions, and punt returns, and won the league's most valuable player award.

Backs Frank Filchock and Merle Hapes of the Giants were questioned about an attempt by a New York man to fix the championship game with the Bears. Bell suspended Hapes but allowed Filchock to play; he played well, but Chicago won 24-14, December 15.

1947

The NFL added a fifth official, the back judge.

A bonus choice was made for the first time in the NFL draft. One team each year would select the special choice before the first round began. The Chicago Bears won a lottery and the rights to the first choice and drafted back Bob Fenimore of Oklahoma A&M.

The Cleveland Browns again won the AAFC title, defeating the New York Yankees 14-3.

Charles Bidwill, Sr., owner of the Cardinals, died April 19, but his wife and sons retained ownership of the team. On December 28, the Cardinals won the NFL Championship Game 28-21 over the Philadelphia Eagles, who had beaten Pittsburgh 21-0 in a playoff.

1948

Plastic helmets were prohibited. A flexible artificial tee was permitted at the kickoff. Officials other than the referee

were equipped with whistles, not horns, January 14.

Fred Mandel sold the Detroit Lions to a syndicate headed by D. Lyle Fife, January 15.

Halfback Fred Gehrke of the Los Angeles Rams painted horns on the Rams' helmets, the first modern helmet emblems in pro football.

The Cleveland Browns won their third straight championship in the AAFC, going 14-0 and then defeating the Buffalo Bills 49-7.

In a blizzard, the Eagles defeated the Cardinals 7-0 in the NFL Championship Game, December 19.

1949

Alexis Thompson sold the champion Eagles to a syndicate headed by James P. Clark, January 15. The Boston Yanks became the New York Bulldogs, sharing the Polo Grounds with the Giants.

Free substitution was adopted for one year, January 20.

The NFL had two 1,000-yard rushers in the same season for the first time—Steve Van Buren of Philadelphia and Tony Canadeo of Green Bay.

The AAFC played its season with a one-division, seven-team format. On December 9, Bell announced a merger agreement in which three AAFC franchises—Cleveland, San Francisco, and Baltimore—would join the NFL in 1950. The Browns won their fourth consecutive AAFC title, defeating the 49ers 21-7, December 11.

In a heavy rain, the Eagles defeated the Rams 14-0 in the NFL Championship Game, December 18.

1950

Unlimited free substitution was restored, opening the way for the era of two platoons and specialization in pro football, January 20.

Curly Lambeau, founder of the franchise and Green Bay's head coach since 1921, resigned under fire, February 1.

The name National Football League was restored after about three months and the National-American Football League. The American and National conferences were created to replace the Eastern

and Western divisions, March 3.

The New York Bulldogs became the Yanks and divided the players of the former AAFC Yankees with the Giants. A special allocation draft was held in which the 13 teams drafted the remaining AAFC players, with special consideration for Baltimore, which received 15 choices compared to 10 for other teams.

The Los Angeles Rams became the first NFL team to have all of its games—both home and away—televised. The Washington Redskins followed the Rams in arranging to televise their games; other teams made deals to put selected games on television.

In the first game of the season, former AAFC champion Cleveland defeated NFL champion Philadelphia 35-10. For the first time, deadlocks occurred in both conferences and playoffs were necessary. The Browns defeated the Giants in the American and the Rams defeated the Bears in the National. Cleveland defeated Los Angeles 30-28 in the NFL Championship Game, December 24.

1951

The Pro Bowl game, dormant since 1942, was revived under a new format matching the all-stars of each conference at the Los Angeles Memorial Coliseum. The American Conference defeated the National Conference 28-27, January 14.

Abraham Watner returned the Baltimore franchise and its player contracts back to the NFL for $50,000. Baltimore's former players were made available for drafting at the same time as college players, January 18.

A rule was passed that no tackle, guard, or center would be eligible to catch a forward pass, January 18.

The Rams reversed their television policy and televised only road games.

The NFL Championship Game was televised coast-to-coast for the first time, December 23. The DuMont Network paid $75,000 for the rights to the game, in which the Rams defeated the Browns 24-17.

1952

Ted Collins sold the New York Yanks' franchise back to the NFL, January 19. A new franchise was awarded to a group in Dallas after it purchased the assets of the Yanks, January 24. The new Texans went 1-11, with the owners turning the franchise back to the league in midseason. For the last five games of the season, the commissioner's office operated the Texans as a road team, using Hershey, Pennsylvania, as a home base. At the end of the season the franchise was canceled, the last time an NFL team failed.

The Pittsburgh Steelers abandoned the Single-Wing for the T-formation, the last pro team to do so.

The Detroit Lions won their first NFL championship in 17 years, defeating the Browns 17-7 in the title game, December 28.

1953

A Baltimore group headed by Carroll Rosenbloom was granted a franchise and was awarded the holdings of the defunct Dallas organization, January 23. The team, named the Colts, put together the largest trade in league history, acquiring 10 players from Cleveland in exchange for five.

The names of the American and National conferences were changed to the Eastern and Western conferences, January 24.

Jim Thorpe died, March 28. Mickey McBride, founder of the Cleveland Browns, sold the franchise to a syndicate headed by Dave R. Jones, June 10.

The NFL policy of blacking out home games was upheld by Judge Allan K. Grim of the U.S. District Court in Philadelphia, November 12.

The Lions again defeated the Browns in the NFL Championship Game, winning 17-16, December 27.

1954

The Canadian Football League began a series of raids on NFL teams, signing quarterback Eddie LeBaron and defensive end Gene Brito of Washington and defensive tackle Arnie Weinmeister of the Giants, among others.

Fullback Joe Perry of the 49ers became the first player in league history to gain 1,000 yards rushing in consecutive seasons.

Cleveland defeated Detroit 56-10 in the NFL Championship Game, December 26.

1955

The sudden-death overtime rule was used for the first time in a preseason game between the Rams and Giants at Portland, Oregon, August 28. The Rams won 23-17 three minutes into overtime.

A rule change declared the ball dead immediately if the ball carrier touched the ground with any part of his body except his hands or feet while in the grasp of an opponent.

The Baltimore Colts made an 80-cent phone call to Johnny Unitas and signed him as a free agent. Another quarterback, Otto Graham, played his last game as the Browns defeated the Rams 38-14 in the NFL Championship Game, December 26. Graham had quarterbacked the Browns to 10 championship-game appearances in 10 years.

NBC replaced DuMont as the network for the title game, paying a rights fee of $100,000.

1956

The NFL Players Association was founded.

Grabbing an opponent's facemask (other than the ball carrier) was made illegal. Using radio receivers to communicate with players on the field was prohibited. A natural leather ball with white end stripes replaced the white ball with black stripes for night games.

The Giants moved from the Polo Grounds to Yankee Stadium.

Halas retired as coach of the Bears, and was replaced by Paddy Driscoll.

CBS became the first network to broadcast some NFL regular-season games to selected television markets across the nation.

The Giants routed the Bears 47-7 in the NFL Championship Game, December 30.

1957

Pete Rozelle was named general manager of the Rams. Anthony J. Morabito, founder and co-owner of the 49ers, died of a heart attack during a game against the Bears at Kezar Stadium, October 28. An NFL-record crowd of 102,368 saw the 49ers-Rams game at the Los Angeles Memorial Coliseum, November 10.

The Lions came from 20 points down to post a 31-27 playoff victory over the 49ers, December 22. Detroit defeated Cleveland 59-14 in the NFL Championship Game, December 29.

1958

The bonus selection in the draft was eliminated, January 29. The last selection was quarterback King Hill of Rice by the Chicago Cardinals.

Halas reinstated himself as coach of the Bears.

Jim Brown of Cleveland gained an NFL-record 1,527 yards rushing. In a divisional playoff game, the Giants held Brown to eight yards and defeated Cleveland 10-0.

Baltimore, coached by Weeb Ewbank, defeated the Giants 23-17 in the first sudden-death overtime in an NFL Championship Game, December 28. The game ended when Colts fullback Alan Ameche scored on a one-yard touchdown run after 8:15 of overtime.

1959

Vince Lombardi was named head coach of the Green Bay Packers, January 28. Tim Mara, the co-founder of the Giants, died, February 17.

Lamar Hunt of Dallas announced his intentions to form a second pro football league. The first meeting was held in Chicago, August 14, and consisted of Hunt representing Dallas; Bob Howsam, Denver; K.S. (Bud) Adams, Houston; Barron Hilton, Los Angeles; Max Winter and Bill Boyer, Minneapolis; and Harry Wismer, New York City. They made plans to begin play in 1960.

The new league was named the American Football League, August 22. Buffalo, owned by Ralph Wilson, became the seventh franchise, October 28. Boston, owned by William H. Sullivan, became the eighth team, November 22. The first AFL draft, lasting 33 rounds, was held, November 22. Joe Foss was named AFL Commissioner, November 30. An additional draft of 20 rounds was held by the AFL, December 2.

NFL Commissioner Bert Bell died of a heart attack suffered at Franklin Field, Philadelphia, during the last two minutes of a game between the Eagles and the Steelers, October 11. Treasurer Austin Gunsel was named president in the office of the commissioner, October 14.

The Colts again defeated the Giants in the NFL Championship Game, 31-16, December 27.

1960

Pete Rozelle was elected NFL Commissioner as a compromise choice on the twenty-third ballot, January 26. Rozelle moved the league offices to New York City.

Hunt was elected AFL president for 1960, January 26. Minneapolis withdrew from the AFL, January 27, and the same ownership was given an NFL franchise for Minnesota (to start in 1961), January 28. Dallas received an NFL franchise for 1960, January 28. Oakland received an AFL franchise, January 30.

The AFL adopted the two-point option on points after touchdown, January 28. A no-tampering verbal pact, relative to players' contracts, was agreed to between the NFL and AFL, February 9.

The NFL owners voted to allow the transfer of the Chicago Cardinals to St. Louis, March 13.

The AFL signed a five-year television contract with ABC, June 9.

The Boston Patriots defeated the Buffalo Bills 28-7 before 16,000 at Buffalo in the first AFL preseason game, July 30. The Denver Broncos defeated the Patriots 13-10 before 21,597 at Boston in the first AFL regular-season game, September 9.

Philadelphia defeated Green Bay 17-13 in the NFL Championship Game, December 26.

1961

The Houston Oilers defeated the Los Angeles Chargers 24-16 before 32,183 in the first AFL Championship Game,

January 1.
Detroit defeated Cleveland 17-16 in the first Playoff Bowl, or Bert Bell Benefit Bowl, between second-place teams in each conference in Miami, January 7.

End Willard Dewveall of the Bears played out his option and joined the Oilers, becoming the first player to play out his contract and jump from the NFL to the AFL, January 14.

Ed McGah, Wayne Valley, and Robert Osborne bought out their partners in the ownership of the Raiders, January 17. The Chargers were transferred to San Diego, February 10. Dave R. Jones sold the Browns to a group headed by Arthur B. Modell, March 22. The Howsam brothers sold the Broncos to a group headed by Calvin Kunz and Gerry Phipps, May 26.

NBC was awarded a two-year contract for radio and television rights to the NFL Championship Game for $615,000 annually, $300,000 of which was to go directly into the NFL Player Benefit Plan, April 5.

Canton, Ohio, where the league that became the NFL was formed in 1920, was chosen as the site of the Pro Football Hall of Fame, April 27. Dick McCann, a former Redskins executive, was named executive director.

A bill legalizing single-network television contracts by professional sports leagues was introduced in Congress by Representative Emanuel Celler. It passed the House and Senate and was signed into law by President John F. Kennedy, September 30.

Houston defeated San Diego 10-3 for the AFL championship, December 24. Green Bay won its first NFL championship since 1944, defeating the New York Giants 37-0, December 31.

1962
The Western Division defeated the Eastern Division 47-27 in the first AFL All-Star Game, played before 20,973 in San Diego, January 7.

Both leagues prohibited grabbing any player's facemask. The AFL voted to make the scoreboard clock the official timer of the game.

The NFL entered into a single-network agreement with CBS for telecasting all regular-season games for $4.65 million annually, January 10.

Judge Roszel Thompson of the U.S. District Court in Baltimore ruled against the AFL in its antitrust suit against the NFL, May 21. The AFL had charged the NFL with monopoly and conspiracy in areas of expansion, television, and player signings. The case lasted two and a half years, the trial two months.

McGah and Valley acquired controlling interest in the Raiders, May 24. The AFL assumed financial responsibility for the New York Titans, November 8. With Commissioner Rozelle as referee, Daniel F. Reeves regained the ownership of the Rams, outbidding his partners in sealed-envelope bidding for the team, November 27.

The Dallas Texans defeated the Oilers 20-17 for the AFL championship at Houston after 17 minutes, 54 seconds of overtime on a 25-yard field goal by Tommy Brooker, December 23. The game lasted a record 77 minutes, 54 seconds.

Judge Edward Weinfeld of the U.S. District Court in New York City upheld the legality of the NFL's television blackout within a 75-mile radius of home games and denied an injunction that would have forced the championship game between the Giants and the Packers to be televised in the New York City area, December 28. The Packers beat the Giants 16-7 for the NFL title, December 30.

1963
The Dallas Texans transferred to Kansas City, becoming the Chiefs, February 8. The New York Titans were sold to a five-man syndicate headed by David (Sonny) Werblin, March 28. Weeb Ewbank became the Titans' new head coach and the team's name was changed to the Jets, April 15. They began play in Shea Stadium.

NFL Properties, Inc., was founded to serve as the licensing arm of the NFL.

Rozelle indefinitely suspended Green Bay halfback Paul Hornung and Detroit defensive tackle Alex Karras for placing bets on their own teams and on other NFL games; he also fined five other Detroit players $2,000 each for betting on one game in which they did not participate, and the Detroit Lions Football Company $2,000 on each of two counts for failure to report information promptly and for lack of sideline supervision.

Paul Brown, head coach of the Browns since their inception, was fired and replaced by Blanton Collier. Don Shula replaced Weeb Ewbank as head coach of the Colts.

The AFL allowed the Jets and Raiders to select players from other franchises in hopes of giving the league more competitive balance, May 11.

NBC was awarded exclusive network broadcasting rights for the 1963 AFL Championship Game for $926,000, May 23.

The Pro Football Hall of Fame was dedicated at Canton, Ohio, September 7.

The U.S. Fourth Circuit Court of Appeals reaffirmed the lower court's finding for the NFL in the $10-million suit brought by the AFL, ending three and a half years of litigation, November 21.

Jim Brown of Cleveland rushed for an NFL single-season record 1,863 yards.

Boston defeated Buffalo 26-8 in the first divisional playoff game in AFL history, December 28.

The Bears defeated the Giants 14-10 in the NFL Championship Game, a record sixth and last title for Halas in his thirty-sixth season as the Bears' coach, December 29.

1964
The Chargers defeated the Patriots 51-10 in the AFL Championship Game, January 5.

William Clay Ford, the Lions' president since 1961, purchased the team, January 10. A group representing the late James P. Clark sold the Eagles to a group headed by Jerry Wolman, January 21. Carroll Rosenbloom, the majority owner of the Colts since 1953, acquired complete ownership of the team, January 23.

The AFL signed a five-year, $36-million television contract with NBC to begin with the 1965 season, January 29.

Hornung and Karras were reinstated by Rozelle, March 16.

CBS submitted the winning bid of $14.1 million per year for the NFL regular-season television rights for 1964 and 1965, January 24. CBS acquired the rights to the championship games for 1964 and 1965 for $1.8 million per game, April 17.

Pete Gogolak of Cornell signed a contract with Buffalo, becoming the first soccer-style kicker in pro football.

Buffalo defeated San Diego 20-7 in the AFL Championship Game, December 26. Cleveland defeated Baltimore 27-0 in the NFL Championship Game, December 27.

1965
The NFL teams pledged not to sign college seniors until completion of all their games, including bowl games, and empowered the Commissioner to discipline the clubs up to as much as the loss of an entire draft list for a violation of the pledge, February 15.

The NFL added a sixth official, the line judge, February 19. The color of the officials' penalty flags was changed from white to bright gold, April 5.

Commissioner Rozelle negotiated an agreement on behalf of the NFL clubs to purchase Ed Sabol's Blair Motion Pictures, which was renamed NFL Films, April.

Atlanta was awarded an NFL franchise for 1966, with Rankin Smith, Sr., as owner, June 30. Miami was awarded an AFL franchise for 1966, with Joe Robbie and Danny Thomas as owners, August 16.

Field Judge Burl Toler became the first black official in NFL history, September 19.

According to a Harris survey, sports fans chose professional football (41 percent) as their favorite sport, overtaking baseball (38 percent) for the first time, October.

Green Bay defeated Baltimore 13-10 in sudden-death overtime in a Western Conference playoff game. Don Chandler kicked a 25-yard field goal for the Packers after 13 minutes, 39 seconds of overtime, December 26. The Packers then defeated the Browns 23-12 in the NFL Championship Game, January 2.

In the AFL Championship Game, the Bills again defeated the Chargers, 23-0, December 26.

CBS acquired the rights to the NFL regular-season games in 1966 and 1967, with an option for 1968, for $18.8 million per year, December 29.

1966

The AFL-NFL war reached its peak, as the leagues spent a combined $7 million to sign their 1966 draft choices. The NFL signed 75 percent of its 232 draftees, the AFL 46 percent of its 181. Of the 111 common draft choices, 79 signed with the NFL, 28 with the AFL, and 4 went unsigned.

Buddy Young became the first African-American to work in the league office when Commissioner Rozelle named him director of player relations, February 1.

The rights to the 1966 and 1967 NFL Championship Games were sold to CBS for $2 million per game, February 14.

Foss resigned as AFL Commissioner, April 7. Al Davis, the head coach and general manager of the Raiders, was named to replace him, April 8.

Goal posts offset from the goal line, painted bright yellow, and with uprights 20 feet above the cross-bar were made standard in the NFL, May 16.

A series of secret meetings regarding a possible AFL-NFL merger were held in the spring between Hunt of Kansas City and Tex Schramm of Dallas. Rozelle announced the merger, June 8. Under the agreement, the two leagues would combine to form an expanded league with 24 teams, to be increased to 26 in 1968 and to 28 by 1970 or soon thereafter. All existing franchises would be retained, and no franchises would be transferred outside their metropolitan areas. While maintaining separate schedules through 1969, the leagues agreed to play an annual AFL-NFL World Championship Game beginning in January, 1967, and to hold a combined draft, also beginning in 1967. Preseason games would be held between teams of each league starting in 1967. Official regular-sea-

son play would start in 1970 when the two leagues would officially merge to form one league with two conferences. Rozelle was named Commissioner of the expanded league setup.

Davis rejoined the Raiders, and Milt Woodard was named president of the AFL, July 25.

The St. Louis Cardinals moved into newly constructed Busch Memorial Stadium.

Barron Hilton sold the Chargers to a group headed by Eugene Klein and Sam Schulman, August 25.

Congress approved the AFL-NFL merger, passing legislation exempting the agreement itself from antitrust action, October 21.

New Orleans was awarded an NFL franchise to begin play in 1967, November 1. John Mecom, Jr., of Houston was designated majority stockholder and president of the franchise, December 15.

The NFL was realigned for the 1967-69 seasons into the Capitol and Century Divisions in the Eastern Conference and the Central and Coastal Divisions in the Western Conference, December 2. New Orleans and the New York Giants agreed to switch divisions in 1968 and return to the 1967 alignment in 1969.

The rights to the Super Bowl for four years were sold to CBS and NBC for $9.5 million, December 13.

1967

Green Bay earned the right to represent the NFL in the first AFL-NFL World Championship Game by defeating Dallas 34-27, January 1. The same day, Kansas City defeated Buffalo 31-7 to represent the AFL. The Packers defeated the Chiefs 35-10 before 61,946 fans at the Los Angeles Memorial Coliseum in the first game between AFL and NFL teams, January 15. The winning players' share for the Packers was $15,000 each, and the losing players' share for the Chiefs was $7,500 each. The game was televised by both CBS and NBC.

The "sling-shot" goal post and a six-foot-wide border around the field were made standard in the NFL, February 22.

Baltimore made Bubba

Smith, a Michigan State defensive lineman, the first choice in the first combined AFL-NFL draft, March 14.

The AFL awarded a franchise to begin play in 1968 to Cincinnati, May 24. A group with Paul Brown as part owner, general manager, and head coach, was awarded the Cincinnati franchise, September 27.

Arthur B. Modell, the president of the Cleveland Browns, was elected president of the NFL, May 28.

Defensive back Emlen Tunnell of the New York Giants became the first black player to enter the Pro Football Hall of Fame, August 5.

An AFL team defeated an NFL team for the first time, when Denver beat Detroit 13-7 in a preseason game, August 5.

Green Bay defeated Dallas 21-17 for the NFL championship on a last-minute 1-yard quarterback sneak by Bart Starr in 13-below-zero temperature at Green Bay, December 31. The same day, Oakland defeated Houston 40-7 for the AFL championship.

1968

Green Bay defeated Oakland 33-14 in Super Bowl II at Miami, January 14. The game had the first $3-million gate in pro football history.

Vince Lombardi resigned as head coach of the Packers, but remained as general manager, January 28.

Art McNally, a nine-year NFL game official, was named Supervisor of Officials, April 8.

Werblin sold his shares in the Jets to his partners Don Lillis, Leon Hess, Townsend Martin, and Phil Iselin, May 21. Lillis assumed the presidency of the club, but then died July 23. Iselin was appointed president, August 6.

Halas retired for the fourth and last time as head coach of the Bears, May 27.

The Oilers left Rice Stadium for the Astrodome and became the first NFL team to play its home games in a domed stadium.

The movie *Heidi* became a footnote in sports history when NBC didn't show the last 50 seconds of the Jets-Raiders game in order to permit the children's special to

begin on time. The Raiders scored two touchdowns in the last 42 seconds to win 43-32, November 17.

Ewbank became the first coach to win titles in both the NFL and AFL when his Jets defeated the Raiders 27-23 for the AFL championship, December 29. The same day, Baltimore defeated Cleveland 34-0.

1969

The AFL established a playoff format for the 1969 season, with the winner in one division playing the runner-up in the other, January 11.

An AFL team won the Super Bowl for the first time, as the Jets defeated the Colts 16-7 in Miami, January 12 in Super Bowl III. The title Super Bowl was recognized by the NFL for the first time.

Vince Lombardi became part owner, executive vice-president, and head coach of the Washington Redskins, February 7.

Wolman sold the Eagles to Leonard Tose, May 1.

Baltimore, Cleveland, and Pittsburgh agreed to join the AFL teams to form the 13-team American Football Conference of the NFL in 1970, May 17. The NFL also agreed on a playoff format that would include one "wild-card" team per conference—the second-place team with the best record.

The NFL announced a three-year agreement with ABC to televise *Monday Night Football*. The new series makes the NFL the first league with a regular series of national telecasts in prime time, May 26.

George Preston Marshall, president emeritus of the Redskins, died at 72, August 9.

The NFL marked its fiftieth year by the wearing of a special patch by each of the 16 teams.

1970

Kansas City defeated Minnesota 23-7 in Super Bowl IV at New Orleans, January 11. The gross receipts of approximately $3.8 million were the largest ever for a one-day sports event.

Four-year television contracts, under which CBS would televise all NFC games and NBC all AFC games (except Monday night games) and the two would divide televising the Super Bowl and AFC-NFC Pro Bowl games, were announced, January 26.

Art Modell resigned as president of the NFL, March 12. Milt Woodard resigned as president of the AFL, March 13. Lamar Hunt was elected president of the AFC and George Halas was elected president of the NFC, March 19.

The merged 26-team league adopted rules changes putting names on the backs of players' jerseys, making a point after touchdown worth only one point, and making the scoreboard clock the official timing device of the game, March 18.

The Players Negotiating Committee and the NFL Players Association announced a four-year agreement guaranteeing approximately $4,535,000 annually to player pension and insurance benefits, August 3. The owners also agreed to contribute $250,000 annually to improve or implement items such as disability payments, widows' benefits, maternity benefits, and dental benefits. The agreement also provided for increased preseason game and per diem payments, averaging approximately $2.6 million annually.

The Pittsburgh Steelers moved into Three Rivers Stadium. The Cincinnati Bengals moved to Riverfront Stadium.

Vince Lombardi died of cancer at 57, September 3.

The Super Bowl trophy was renamed the Vince Lombardi trophy, September 10.

Tom Dempsey of New Orleans kicked a game-winning NFL-record 63-yard field goal against Detroit, November 8.

1971
Baltimore defeated Dallas 16-13 on Jim O'Brien's 32-yard field goal with five seconds to go in Super Bowl V at Miami, January 17. The NBC telecast was viewed in an estimated 23,980,000 homes, the largest audience ever for a one-day sports event.

The NFC defeated the AFC 27-6 in the first AFC-NFC Pro Bowl at Los Angeles, January 24.

The Boston Patriots changed their name to the New England Patriots, March 25. Their new stadium, Schaefer Stadium, was dedicated in a 20-14 preseason victory over the Giants.

The Philadelphia Eagles left Franklin Field and played their games at the new Veterans Stadium.

The San Francisco 49ers left Kezar Stadium and moved their games to Candlestick Park.

Daniel F. Reeves, the president and general manager of the Rams, died at 58, April 15.

The Dallas Cowboys moved from the Cotton Bowl into their new home, Texas Stadium, October 24.

Miami defeated Kansas City 27-24 in sudden-death overtime in an AFC Divisional Playoff Game, December 25. Garo Yepremian kicked a 37-yard field goal for the Dolphins after 22 minutes, 40 seconds of overtime, as the game lasted 82 minutes, 40 seconds overall, making it the longest game in history.

1972
Dallas defeated Miami 24-3 in Super Bowl VI at New Orleans, January 16. The CBS telecast was viewed in an estimated 27,450,000 homes, the top-rated one-day telecast ever.

The inbounds lines or hashmarks were moved nearer the center of the field, 23 yards, 1 foot, 9 inches from the sidelines, March 23. The method of determining won-lost percentage in standings changed. Tie games, previously not counted in the standings, were made equal to a half-game won and a half-game lost, May 24.

Robert Irsay purchased the Los Angeles Rams and transferred ownership of the club to Carroll Rosenbloom in exchange for the Baltimore Colts, July 13.

William V. Bidwill purchased the stock of his brother Charles (Stormy) Bidwill to become the sole owner of the St. Louis Cardinals, September 2.

The National District Attorneys Association endorsed the position of professional leagues in opposing proposed legalization of gambling on professional team sports,

September 28.

Franco Harris' "Immaculate Reception" gave the Steelers their first postseason win ever, 13-7 over the Raiders, December 23.

1973
Rozelle announced that all Super Bowl VII tickets were sold and that the game would be telecast in Los Angeles, the site of the game, on an experimental basis, January 3.

Miami defeated Washington 14-7 in Super Bowl VII at Los Angeles, completing a 17-0 season, the first perfect-record regular-season and postseason mark in NFL history, January 14. The NBC telecast was viewed by approximately 75 million people.

The AFC defeated the NFC 33-28 in the Pro Bowl in Dallas, the first time since 1942 that the game was played outside Los Angeles, January 21.

A jersey numbering system was adopted, April 5: 1-19 for quarterbacks and specialists, 20-49 for running backs and defensive backs, 50-59 for centers and linebackers, 60-79 for defensive linemen and interior offensive linemen other than centers, and 80-89 for wide receivers and tight ends. Players who had been in the NFL in 1972 could continue to use old numbers.

NFL Charities, a nonprofit organization, was created to derive an income from monies generated from NFL Properties' licensing of NFL trademarks and team names, June 26. NFL Charities was set up to support education and charitable activities and to supply economic support to persons formerly associated with professional football who were no longer able to support themselves.

Congress adopted experimental legislation (for three years) requiring any NFL game that had been declared a sellout 72 hours prior to kickoff to be made available for local televising, September 14. The legislation provided for an annual review to be made by the Federal Communications Commission.

The Buffalo Bills moved their home games from War Memorial Stadium to Rich Stadium in nearby Orchard Park. The Giants tied the Eagles

23-23 in the final game in Yankee Stadium, September 23. The Giants played the rest of their home games at the Yale Bowl in New Haven, Connecticut.

A rival league, the World Football League, was formed and was reported in operation, October 2. It had plans to start play in 1974.

O.J. Simpson of Buffalo became the first player to rush for more than 2,000 yards in a season, gaining 2,003.

1974
Miami defeated Minnesota 24-7 in Super Bowl VIII at Houston, the second consecutive Super Bowl championship for the Dolphins, January 13. The CBS telecast was viewed by approximately 75 million people.

Rozelle was given a 10-year contract effective January 1, 1973, February 27.

Tampa Bay was awarded a franchise to begin operation in 1976, April 24.

Sweeping rules changes were adopted to add action and tempo to games: one sudden-death overtime period was added for preseason and regular-season games; the goal posts were moved from the goal line to the end lines; kickoffs were moved from the 40- to the 35-yard line; after missed field goals from beyond the 20, the ball was to be returned to the line of scrimmage; restrictions were placed on members of the punting team to open up return possibilities; roll-blocking and cutting of wide receivers was eliminated; the extent of downfield contact a defender could have with an eligible receiver was restricted; the penalties for offensive holding, illegal use of the hands, and tripping were reduced from 15 to 10 yards; wide receivers blocking back toward the ball within three yards of the line of scrimmage were prevented from blocking below the waist, April 25.

Seattle was awarded an NFL franchise to begin play in 1976, June 4. Lloyd W. Nordstrom, president of the Seattle Seahawks, and Hugh Culverhouse, president of the Tampa Bay Buccaneers, signed franchise agreements, December 5.

The Birmingham Americans defeated the Florida Blazers 22-21 in the WFL World Bowl, winning the league championship, December 5.

1975

Pittsburgh defeated Minnesota 16-6 in Super Bowl IX at New Orleans, the Steelers' first championship since entering the NFL in 1933. The NBC telecast was viewed by approximately 78 million people.

The Memphis Southmen of the WFL signed Larry Csonka, Jim Kiick, and Paul Warfield of Miami, March 31.

The divisional winners with the highest won-loss percentage were made the home team for the divisional playoffs, and the surviving winners with the highest percentage made home teams for the championship games, June 26.

Referees were equipped with wireless microphones for all preseason, regular-season, and playoff games.

The Lions moved to the new Pontiac Silverdome. The Giants played their home games in Shea Stadium. The Saints moved into the Louisiana Superdome.

The World Football League folded, October 22.

1976

Pittsburgh defeated Dallas 21-17 in Super Bowl X in Miami. The Steelers joined Green Bay and Miami as the only teams to win two Super Bowls; the Cowboys became the first wild-card team to play in the Super Bowl. The CBS telecast was viewed by an estimated 80 million people, the largest television audience in history.

Lloyd Nordstrom, the president of the Seahawks, died at 66, January 20. His brother Elmer succeeded him as majority representative of the team.

The owners awarded Super Bowl XII, to be played on January 15, 1978, to New Orleans. They also adopted the use of two 30-second clocks for all games, visible to both players and fans to note the official time between the ready-for-play signal and snap of the ball, March 16.

A veteran player allocation was held to stock the Seattle and Tampa Bay franchises with 39 players each, March 30-31. In the college draft, Seattle and Tampa Bay each received eight extra choices, April 8-9.

The Giants moved into new Giants Stadium in East Rutherford, New Jersey.

The Steelers defeated the College All-Stars in a storm-shortened Chicago College All-Star Game, the last of the series, July 23. St. Louis defeated San Diego 20-10 in a preseason game before 38,000 in Korakuen Stadium, Tokyo, in the first NFL game outside of North America, August 16.

1977

Oakland defeated Minnesota 32-14 in Super Bowl XI at Pasadena, January 9. The paid attendance was a pro record 103,438. The NBC telecast was viewed by 81.9 million people, the largest ever to view a sports event. The victory was the fifth consecutive for the AFC in the Super Bowl.

The NFL Players Association and the NFL Management Council ratified a collective bargaining agreement extending until 1982, covering five football seasons while continuing the pension plan—including years 1974, 1975, and 1976—with contributions totaling more than $55 million. The total cost of the agreement was estimated at $107 million. The agreement called for a college draft at least through 1986; contained a no-strike, no-suit clause; established a 43-man active player limit; reduced pension vesting to four years; provided for increases in minimum salaries and preseason and postseason pay; improved insurance, medical, and dental benefits; modified previous practices in player movement and control; and reaffirmed the NFL Commissioner's disciplinary authority. Additionally, the agreement called for the NFL member clubs to make payments totaling $16 million the next 10 years to settle various legal disputes, February 25.

The San Francisco 49ers were sold to Edward J. DeBartolo, Jr., March 28.

A 16-game regular season, 4-game preseason was adopted to begin in 1978, March 29. A second wild-card team was adopted for the playoffs beginning in 1978, with the wild-card teams to play each other and the winners advancing to a round of eight postseason series.

The Seahawks were permanently aligned in the AFC Western Division and the Buccaneers in the NFC Central Division, March 31.

The owners awarded Super Bowl XIII, to be played on January 21, 1979, to Miami, to be played in the Orange Bowl; Super Bowl XIV, to be played January 20, 1980, was awarded to Pasadena, to be played in the Rose Bowl, June 14.

Rules changes were adopted to open up the passing game and to cut down on injuries. Defenders were permitted to make contact with eligible receivers only once; the head slap was outlawed; offensive linemen were prohibited from thrusting their hands to an opponent's neck, face, or head; and wide receivers were prohibited from clipping, even in the legal clipping zone.

Rozelle negotiated contracts with the three television networks to televise all NFL regular-season and postseason games, plus selected preseason games, for four years beginning with the 1978 season. ABC was awarded yearly rights to 16 Monday night games, four prime-time games, the AFC-NFC Pro Bowl, and the Hall of Fame games. CBS received the rights to all NFC regular-season and postseason games (except those in the ABC package) and to Super Bowls XIV and XVI. NBC received the rights to all AFC regular-season and postseason games (except those in the ABC package) and to Super Bowls XIII and XV. Industry sources considered it the largest single television package ever negotiated, October 12.

Chicago's Walter Payton set a single-game rushing record with 275 yards (40 carries) against Minnesota, November 20.

1978

Dallas defeated Denver 27-10 in Super Bowl XII, held indoors for the first time, at the Louisiana Superdome in New Orleans, January 15. The CBS telecast was viewed by more than 102 million people, meaning the game was watched by more viewers than any other show of any kind in the history of television. Dallas' victory was the first for the NFC in six years.

According to a Louis Harris Sports Survey, 70 percent of the nation's sports fans said they followed football, compared to 54 percent who followed baseball. Football increased its lead as the country's favorite, 26 percent to 16 percent for baseball, January 19.

A seventh official, the side judge, was added to the officiating crew, March 14.

The NFL continued a trend toward opening up the game. Rules changes permitted a defender to maintain contact with a receiver within five yards of the line of scrimmage, but restricted contact beyond that point. The pass-blocking rule was interpreted to permit the extending of arms and open hands, March 17.

A study on the use of instant replay as an officiating aid was made during seven nationally televised preseason games.

The NFL played for the first time in Mexico City, with the Saints defeating the Eagles 14-7 in a preseason game, August 5.

Bolstered by the expansion of the regular-season schedule from 14 to 16 weeks, NFL paid attendance exceeded 12 million (12,771,800) for the first time. The per-game average of 57,017 was the third-highest in league history and the most since 1973.

1979

Pittsburgh defeated Dallas 35-31 in Super Bowl XIII at Miami to become the first team ever to win three Super Bowls, January 21. The NBC telecast was viewed in 35,090,000 homes, by an estimated 96.6 million fans.

The owners awarded three future Super Bowl sites: Super Bowl XV to the Louisiana Superdome in New Orleans, to be played on January 25, 1981; Super Bowl XVI to the

Pontiac Silverdome in Pontiac, Michigan, to be played on January 24, 1982; and Super Bowl XVII to Pasadena's Rose Bowl, to be played on January 30, 1983, March 13.

NFL rules changes emphasized additional player safety. The changes prohibited players on the receiving team from blocking below the waist during kickoffs, punts, and field-goal attempts; prohibited the wearing of torn or altered equipment and exposed pads that could be hazardous; extended the zone in which there could be no crackback blocks; and instructed officials to quickly whistle a play dead when a quarterback was clearly in the grasp of a tackler, March 16.

Carroll Rosenbloom, the president of the Rams, drowned at 72, April 2. His widow, Georgia, assumed control of the club.

1980

Pittsburgh defeated the Los Angeles Rams 31-19 in Super Bowl XIV at Pasadena to become the first team to win four Super Bowls, January 20. The game was viewed in a record 35,330,000 homes.

The AFC-NFC Pro Bowl, won 37-27 by the NFC, was played before 48,060 fans at Aloha Stadium in Honolulu, Hawaii. It was the first time in the 30-year history of the Pro Bowl that the game was played in a non-NFL city.

Rules changes placed greater restrictions on contact in the area of the head, neck, and face. Under the heading of "personal foul," players were prohibited from directly striking, swinging, or clubbing on the head, neck, or face. Starting in 1980, a penalty could be called for such contact whether or not the initial contact was made below the neck area.

CBS, with a record bid of $12 million, won the national radio rights to 26 NFL regular-season games, including Monday Night Football, and all 10 postseason games for the 1980-83 seasons.

The Los Angeles Rams moved their home games to Anaheim Stadium in nearby Orange County, California.

The Oakland Raiders joined the Los Angeles Coliseum Commission's antitrust suit against the NFL. The suit contended the league violated antitrust laws in declining to approve a proposed move by the Raiders from Oakland to Los Angeles.

NFL regular-season attendance of nearly 13.4 million set a record for the third year in a row. The average paid attendance for the 224-game 1980 regular season was 59,787, the highest in the league's 61-year history. NFL games in 1980 were played before 92.4 percent of total stadium capacity.

Television ratings in 1980 were the second-best in NFL history, trailing only the combined ratings of the 1976 season. All three networks posted gains, and NBC's 15.0 rating was its best ever. CBS and ABC had their best ratings since 1977, with 15.3 and 20.8 ratings, respectively. CBS Radio reported a record audience of 7 million for Monday night and special games.

1981

Oakland defeated Philadelphia 27-10 in Super Bowl XV at the Louisiana Superdome in New Orleans, to become the first wild-card team to win a Super Bowl, January 25.

Edgar F. Kaiser, Jr., purchased the Denver Broncos from Gerald and Allan Phipps, February 26.

The owners adopted a disaster plan for re-stocking a team should the club be involved in a fatal accident, March 20.

The owners awarded Super Bowl XVIII to Tampa, to be played in Tampa Stadium on January 22, 1984, June 3.

A CBS-New York Times poll showed that 48 percent of sports fans preferred football to 31 percent for baseball.

The NFL teams hosted 167 representatives from 44 predominantly black colleges during training camps for a total of 289 days. The program was adopted for renewal during each training camp period.

NFL regular-season attendance—13.6 million for an average of 60,745—set a record for the fourth year in a row. It also was the first time the per-game average exceeded 60,000. NFL games in 1981 were played before 93.8 percent of total stadium capacity.

ABC and CBS set all-time rating highs. ABC finished with a 21.7 rating and CBS with a 17.5 rating. NBC was down slightly to 13.9.

1982

San Francisco defeated Cincinnati 26-21 in Super Bowl XVI at the Pontiac Silverdome, in the first Super Bowl held in the North, January 24. The CBS telecast achieved the highest rating of any televised sports event ever, 49.1 with a 73.0 share. The game was viewed by a record 110.2 million fans. CBS Radio reported a record 14 million listeners for the game.

The NFL signed a five-year contract with the three television networks (ABC, CBS, and NBC) to televise all NFL regular-season and postseason games starting with the 1982 season.

The owners awarded the 1983, 1984, and 1985 AFC-NFC Pro Bowls to Honolulu's Aloha Stadium.

A jury ruled against the NFL in the antitrust trial brought by the Los Angeles Coliseum Commission and the Oakland Raiders, May 7. The verdict cleared the way for the Raiders to move to Los Angeles, where they defeated Green Bay 24-3 in their first preseason game, August 29.

The 1982 season was reduced from a 16-game schedule to nine as the result of a 57-day players' strike. The strike was called by the NFLPA at midnight on Monday, September 20, following the Green Bay at New York Giants game. Play resumed November 21-22 following ratification of the Collective Bargaining Agreement by NFL owners, November 17 in New York.

Under the Collective Bargaining Agreement, which was to run through the 1986 season, the NFL draft was extended through 1992 and the veteran free-agent system was left basically unchanged. A minimum salary schedule for years of experience was established; training camp and postseason pay were increased; players' medical, insurance, and retirement benefits were increased; and a severance-pay system was introduced to aid in career transition, a first in professional sports.

Despite the players' strike, the average paid attendance in 1982 was 58,472, the fifth-highest in league history.

The owners awarded the sites of two Super Bowls, December 14: Super Bowl XIX, to be played on January 20, 1985, to Stanford University Stadium in Stanford, California, with San Francisco as host team; and Super Bowl XX, to be played on January 26, 1986, to the Louisiana Superdome in New Orleans.

1983

Because of the shortened season, the NFL adopted a format of 16 teams competing in a Super Bowl Tournament for the 1982 playoffs. The NFC's number-one seed, Washington, defeated the AFC's number-two seed, Miami, 27-17 in Super Bowl XVII at the Rose Bowl in Pasadena, January 30.

Super Bowl XVII was the second-highest rated live television program of all time, giving the NFL a sweep of the top 10 live programs in television history. The game was viewed in more than 40 million homes, the largest ever for a live telecast.

George Halas, the owner of the Bears and the last surviving member of the NFL's second organizational meeting, died at 88, October 31.

1984

The Los Angeles Raiders defeated Washington 38-9 in Super Bowl XVIII at Tampa Stadium, January 22. The game achieved a 46.4 rating and 71.0 share.

An 11-man group headed by H.R. (Bum) Bright purchased the Dallas Cowboys from Clint Murchison, Jr., March 20. Club president Tex Schramm was designated as managing general partner.

Wellington Mara was named president of the NFC, March 20.

Patrick Bowlen purchased a majority interest in the Denver Broncos from Edgar Kaiser, Jr., March 21.

The Colts relocated to Indianapolis, March 28. Their new home became the Hoosier Dome.

The owners awarded two Super Bowl sites at their May 23-25 meetings: Super Bowl XXI, to be played on January 25, 1987, to the Rose Bowl in Pasadena; and Super Bowl XXII, to be played on January 31, 1988, to San Diego Jack Murphy Stadium.

The New York Jets moved their home games to Giants Stadium in East Rutherford, New Jersey.

Alex G. Spanos purchased a majority interest in the San Diego Chargers from Eugene V. Klein, August 28.

Houston defeated Pittsburgh 23-20 to mark the one-hundredth overtime game in regular-season play since overtime was adopted in 1974, December 2.

On the field, many all-time records were set: Dan Marino of Miami passed for 5,084 yards and 48 touchdowns; Eric Dickerson of the Los Angeles Rams rushed for 2,105 yards; Art Monk of Washington caught 106 passes; and Walter Payton of Chicago broke Jim Brown's career rushing mark, finishing the season with 13,309 yards.

According to a CBS Sports/*New York Times* survey, 53 percent of the nation's sports fans said they most enjoyed watching football, compared to 18 percent for baseball, December 2-4.

NFL paid attendance exceeded 13 million for the fifth consecutive complete regular season when 13,398,112, an average of 59,813, attended games. The figure was the second-highest in league history. Teams averaged 42.4 points per game, the second-highest total since the 1970 merger.

1985
San Francisco defeated Miami 38-16 in Super Bowl XIX at Stanford Stadium in Stanford, California, January 20. The game was viewed on television by more people than any other live event in history. President Ronald Reagan, who took his second oath of office before tossing the coin for the game, was one of 115,936,000 viewers. The game drew a 46.4 rating and a 63.0 share. In addition, 6 million people watched the Super Bowl in the United Kingdom and a similar number in Italy. Super Bowl XIX had a direct economic impact of $113.5 million on the San Francisco Bay area.

NBC Radio and the NFL entered into a two-year agreement granting NBC the radio rights to a 37-game package in each of the 1985-86 seasons, March 6. The package included 27 regular-season games and 10 postseason games.

The owners awarded two Super Bowl sites at their annual meeting, March 10-15: Super Bowl XXIII, to be played on January 22, 1989, to the proposed Dolphins Stadium in Miami; and Super Bowl XXIV, to be played on January 28, 1990, to the Louisiana Superdome in New Orleans.

Norman Braman, in partnership with Edward Leibowitz, bought the Philadelphia Eagles from Leonard Tose, April 29.

A group headed by Tom Benson, Jr., was approved to purchase the New Orleans Saints from John W. Mecom, Jr., June 3.

The NFL owners adopted a resolution calling for a series of overseas preseason games, beginning in 1986, with one game to be played in England/Europe and/or one game in Japan each year. The game would be a fifth preseason game for the clubs involved and all arrangements and selection of the clubs would be under the control of the Commissioner, May 23.

The league-wide conversion to videotape from movie film for coaching study was approved.

Commissioner Rozelle was authorized to extend the commitment to Honolulu's Aloha Stadium for the AFC-NFC Pro Bowl for 1988, 1989, and 1990, October 15.

The NFL set a single-weekend paid attendance record when 902,657 tickets were sold for the weekend of October 27-28.

A Louis Harris poll in December revealed that pro football remained the sport most followed by Americans. Fifty-nine percent of those surveyed followed pro football, compared with 54 percent who followed baseball.

The Chicago-Miami Monday game had the highest rating, 29.6, and share, 46.0, of any prime-time game in NFL history, December 2. The game was viewed in more than 25 million homes.

The NFL showed a ratings increase on all three networks for the season, gaining 4 percent on NBC, 10 on CBS, and 16 on ABC.

1986
Chicago defeated New England 46-10 in Super Bowl XX at the Louisiana Superdome, January 26. The Patriots had earned the right to play the Bears by becoming the first wild-card team to win three consecutive games on the road. The NBC telecast replaced the final episode of *M*A*S*H* as the most-viewed television program in history, with an audience of 127 million viewers, according to A.C. Nielsen figures. In addition to drawing a 48.3 rating and a 70 percent share in the United States, Super Bowl XX was televised to 59 foreign countries and beamed via satellite to the QE II. An estimated 300 million Chinese viewed a tape delay of the game in March. CBS Radio figures indicated an audience of 10 million for the game.

The owners adopted limited use of instant replay as an officiating aid, prohibited players from wearing or otherwise displaying equipment, apparel, or other items that carry commercial names, names of organizations, or personal messages of any type, March 11.

After an 11-week trial, a jury in U.S. District Court in New York awarded the United States Football League one dollar in its $1.7 billion antitrust suit against the NFL. The jury rejected all of the USFL's television-related claims, which were the self-proclaimed heart of the USFL's case. The jury deliberated five days, July 29.

Chicago defeated Dallas 17-6 at Wembley Stadium in London in the first American Bowl. The game drew a sellout crowd of 82,699 and the NBC national telecast in this country produced a 12.4 rating and 36 percent share, making it the highest daytime preseason television audience ever with 10.65-million viewers, August 3.

ABC's *NFL Monday Night Football*, in its seventeenth season, became the longest-running prime-time series in the history of the network.

1987
The New York Giants defeated Denver 39-20 in Super Bowl XXI and captured their first NFL title since 1956. The game, played in Pasadena's Rose Bowl, drew a sellout crowd of 101,063. According to A.C. Nielsen figures, the CBS broadcast of the game was viewed in the U.S. on television by 122.64-million people, making the telecast the second most-watched television show of all-time behind Super Bowl XX. The game was watched live or on tape in 55 foreign countries and NBC Radio's broadcast of the game was heard by a record 10.1 million people.

New three-year TV contracts with ABC, CBS, and NBC were announced for 1987-89 at the NFL annual meeting in Maui, Hawaii, March 15. Commissioner Rozelle and Broadcast Committee Chairman Art Modell also announced a three-year contract with ESPN to televise 13 prime-time games each season. The ESPN contract was the first with a cable network. However, NFL games on ESPN also were scheduled for regular television in the city of the visiting team and in the home city if the game was sold out 72 hours in advance.

A special payment program was adopted to benefit nearly 1,000 former NFL players who participated in the League before the current Bert Bell NFL Pension Plan was created and made retroactive to the 1959 season. Players covered by the new program spent at least five years in the League and played all or part of their career prior to 1959. Each vested player would receive $60 per month for each year of service in the League for life.

NFL and CBS Radio jointly announced agreement granting CBS the radio rights to a 40-game package in each of the next three NFL seasons, 1987-89, April 7.

NFL owners awarded Super

Bowl XXV, to be played on January 27, 1991, to Tampa Stadium, May 20.

Over 400 former NFL players from the pre-1959 era received first payments from NFL owners, July 1.

The NFL's debut on ESPN produced the two highest-rated and most-watched sports programs in basic cable history. The Chicago at Miami game on August 16 drew an 8.9 rating in 3.81 million homes. Those records fell two weeks later when the Los Angeles Raiders at Dallas game achieved a 10.2 cable rating in 4.36 million homes.

The 1987 season was reduced from a 16-game season to 15 as the result of a 24-day players' strike. The strike was called by the NFLPA on Tuesday, September 22, following the New England at New York Jets game. Games scheduled for the third weekend were canceled but the games of weeks four, five, and six were played with replacement teams. Striking players returned for the seventh week of the season, October 25.

In a three-team deal involving 10 players and/or draft choices, the Los Angeles Rams traded running back Eric Dickerson to the Indianapolis Colts for six draft choices and two players. Buffalo obtained the rights to linebacker Cornelius Bennett from Indianapolis, sending Greg Bell and three draft choices to the Rams. The Colts added Owen Gill and three draft choices of their own to complete the deal with the Rams, October 31.

The Chicago at Minnesota game became the highest-rated and most-watched sports program in basic cable history when it drew a 14.4 cable rating in 6.5 million homes, December 6.

1988
Washington defeated Denver 42-10 in Super Bowl XXII to earn its second victory this decade in the NFL Championship Game. The game, played for the first time in San Diego Jack Murphy Stadium, drew a sellout crowd of 73,302. According to A.C. Nielsen figures, the ABC broadcast of the game was viewed in the U.S. on televi-

sion by 115,000,000 people. The game was seen live or on tape in 60 foreign countries, including the People's Republic of China, and CBS's radio broadcast of the game was heard by 13.7 million people.

In a unanimous 3-0 decision, the 2nd Circuit Court of Appeals in New York upheld the verdict of the jury that in July, 1986, had awarded the United States Football League one dollar in its $1.7 billion antitrust suit against the NFL. In a 91-page opinion, Judge Ralph K. Winter said the USFL sought through court decree the success it failed to gain among football fans, March 10.

By a 23-5 margin, owners voted to continue the instant replay system for the third consecutive season with the Instant Replay Official to be assigned to a regular seven-man, on-the-field crew. At the NFL annual meeting in Phoenix, Arizona, a 45-second clock was also approved to replace the 30-second clock. For a normal sequence of plays, the interval between plays was changed to 45 seconds from the time the ball is signaled dead until it is snapped on the succeeding play.

NFL owners approved the transfer of the Cardinals' franchise from St. Louis to Phoenix; approved two supplemental drafts each year—one prior to training camp and one prior to the regular season; and voted to initiate an annual series of games in Japan/Asia as early as the 1989 preseason, March 14-18.

The NFL Annual Selection Meeting returned to a separate two-day format and for the first time originated on a Sunday. ESPN drew a 3.6 rating during their seven-hour coverage of the draft, which was viewed in 1.6 million homes, April 24-25.

Art Rooney, founder and owner of the Steelers, died at 87, August 25.

Johnny Grier became the first African-American referee in NFL history, September 4.

Commissioner Rozelle announced that two teams would play a preseason game as part of the American Bowl series on August 6, 1989, in

the Korakuen Tokyo Dome in Japan, December 16.

1989
San Francisco defeated Cincinnati 20-16 in Super Bowl XXIII. The game, played for the first time at Joe Robbie Stadium in Miami, was attended by a sellout crowd of 75,129. NBC's telecast of the game was watched by an estimated 110,780,000 viewers, according to A.C. Nielsen, making it the sixth most-watched program in television history. The game was seen live or on tape in 60 foreign countries, including an estimated 300 million in China. The CBS Radio broadcast of the game was heard by 11.2 million people.

Commissioner Rozelle announced his retirement, pending the naming of a successor, March 22 at the NFL annual meeting in Palm Desert, California.

Following the announcement, AFC president Lamar Hunt and NFC president Wellington Mara announced the formation of a six-man search committee composed of Art Modell, Robert Parins, Dan Rooney, and Ralph Wilson. Hunt and Mara served as co-chairmen.

By a 24-4 margin, owners voted to continue the instant replay system for the fourth straight season. A strengthened policy regarding anabolic steroids and masking agents was announced by Commissioner Rozelle. NFL clubs called for strong disciplinary measures in cases of feigned injuries and adopted a joint proposal by the Long-Range Planning and Finance committees regarding player personnel rules, March 19-23.

Two hundred twenty-nine unconditional free agents signed with new teams under management's Plan B system, April 1.

Jerry Jones purchased a majority interest in the Dallas Cowboys from H.R. (Bum) Bright, April 18.

Tex Schramm was named president of the new World League of American Football to work with a six-man committee of Dan Rooney, chairman; Norman Braman, Lamar Hunt, Victor Kiam, Mike Lynn, and Bill Walsh, April 18.

NFL and CBS Radio jointly

announced agreement extending CBS's radio rights to an annual 40-game package through the 1994 season, April 18.

NFL owners awarded Super Bowl XXVI, to be played on January 26, 1992, to Minneapolis, May 24.

As of opening day, September 10, of the 229 Plan B free agents, 111 were active and 23 others were on teams' reserve lists. Ninety-two others were waived and three retired.

Art Shell was named head coach of the Los Angeles Raiders making him the NFL's first black head coach since Fritz Pollard coached the Akron Pros in 1921, October 3.

The site of the New England Patriots at San Francisco 49ers game scheduled for Candlestick Park on October 22 was switched to Stanford Stadium in the aftermath of the Bay Area Earthquake of October 17. The change was announced on October 19.

Paul Tagliabue became the seventh chief executive of the NFL on October 26 when he was chosen to succeed Commissioner Pete Rozelle on the sixth ballot of a three-day meeting in Cleveland, Ohio.

In all, 12 ballots were required to select Tagliabue. Two were conducted at a meeting in Chicago on July 6, and four at a meeting in Dallas on October 10-11. On the twelfth ballot, with Seattle absent, Tagliabue received more than the 19 affirmative votes required for election from among the 27 clubs present.

The transfer from Commissioner Rozelle to Commissioner Tagliabue took place at 12:01 A.M. on Sunday, November 5.

NFL Charities donated $1 million through United Way to benefit Bay Area earthquake victims, November 6.

NFL paid attendance of 17,399,538 was the highest total in league history. This included a total of 13,625,662 for an average of 60,829— both NFL records—for the 224-game regular season.

1990
San Francisco defeated Denver 55-10 in Super Bowl XXIV

at the Louisiana Superdome, January 28. San Francisco joined Pittsburgh as the NFL's only teams to win four Super Bowls.

The NFL announced revisions in its 1990 draft eligibility rules. College juniors became eligible but must renounce their collegiate football eligibility before applying for the NFL Draft, February 16.

Commissioner Tagliabue announced NFL teams will play their 16-game schedule over 17 weeks in 1990 and 1991 and 16 games over 18 weeks in 1992 and 1993, February 27.

The NFL revised its playoff format to include two additional wild-card teams (one per conference), which raised the total to six wild-card teams.

Commissioner Tagliabue and Broadcast Committee Chairman Art Modell announced a four-year contract with Turner Broadcasting to televise nine Sunday-night games.

New four-year TV agreements were ratified for 1990-93 for ABC, CBS, NBC, ESPN, and TNT at the NFL annual meeting in Orlando, Florida, March 12. The contracts totaled $3.6 billion, the largest in TV history.

The NFL announced plans to expand its American Bowl series of preseason games. In addition to games in London and Tokyo, American Bowl games were scheduled for Berlin, Germany, and Montreal, Canada, in 1990.

For the fifth straight year, NFL owners voted to continue a limited system of Instant Replay. Beginning in 1990, the replay official will have a two-minute time limit to make a decision. The vote was 21-7, March 12.

Commissioner Tagliabue announced the formation of a Committee on Expansion and Realignment, March 13. He also named a Player Advisory Council, comprised of 12 former NFL players, March 14.

One-hundred eighty-four Plan B unconditional free agents signed with new teams, April 2.

Commissioner Tagliabue appointed Dr. John Lombardo as the League's Drug Advisor for Anabolic Steroids, April 25 and named Dr. Lawrence

Brown as the League's Advisor for Drugs of Abuse, May 17.

NFL owners awarded Super Bowl XXVIII, to be played in 1994, to the proposed Georgia Dome, May 23.

Commissioner Tagliabue named NFL referee Jerry Seeman as NFL Director of Officiating, replacing Art McNally, who announced his retirement after 31 years on the field and at the league office, July 12.

NFL International Week was celebrated with four preseason games in seven days in Tokyo, London, Berlin, and Montreal. More than 200,000 fans on three continents attended the four games, August 4-11.

Commissioner Tagliabue announced the NFL Teacher of the Month program in which the League furnishes grants and scholarships in recognition of teachers who provided a positive influence upon NFL players in elementary and secondary schools, September 20.

For the first time since 1957, every NFL club won at least one of its first four games, October 1.

The Super Bowl Most Valuable Player trophy was renamed the Pete Rozelle trophy, October 8.

NFL total paid attendance of 17,665,671 was the highest total in League history. The regular-season total paid attendance of 13,959,896 and average of 62,321 for 224 games were the highest ever, surpassing the previous records set in the 1989 season.

1991

The New York Giants defeated Buffalo 20-19 in Super Bowl XXV to capture their second title in five years. The game was played before a sellout crowd of 73,813 at Tampa Stadium and became the first Super Bowl decided by one point, January 26. The ABC broadcast of the game was seen by more than 112-million people in the United States and was seen live or taped in 60 other countries.

NFL playoff games earned the top television rating spot of the week for each week of the month-long playoffs, January 29.

New York businessman Robert Tisch purchased a 50 percent interest in the New York Giants from Mrs. Helen Mara Nugent and her children, Tim Mara and Maura Mara Concannon, February 2.

NFL owners awarded Super Bowl XXVII, to be played on January 31, 1993, to Pasadena, March 19.

NFL clubs voted to continue a limited system of Instant Replay for the sixth consecutive year. The vote was 21-7, March 19.

The NFL launched the World League of American Football, the first sports league to operate on a weekly basis on two separate continents, March 23.

NFL Charities presented a $250,000 donation to the United Service Organization. The donation was the second largest single grant ever by NFL Charities, April 5.

Commissioner Tagliabue named Harold Henderson as Executive Vice President for Labor Relations and Chairman of the NFL Management Council Executive Committee, April 8.

NFL clubs approved a recommendation by the Expansion and Realignment Committee to add two teams for the 1994 season, resulting in six divisions of five teams each, May 22.

NFL clubs awarded Super Bowl XXIX, to be played on January 29, 1995, to Miami, May 23.

"NFL International Week" featured six 1990 playoff teams playing nationally televised games in London, Berlin, and Tokyo on July 28 and August 3-4. The games drew more than 150,000 fans.

Paul Brown, founder of the Cleveland Browns and Cincinnati Bengals, died at age 82, August 5.

NFL clubs approved a resolution establishing an international division. A three-year financial plan for the World League was approved by NFL clubs at a meeting in Dallas, October 23.

1992

The NFL agreed to provide a minimum of $2.5 million in financial support to the NFL Alumni Association and assistance to NFL Alumni-related

programs. The agreement included contributions from NFL Charities to the Pre-59ers and Dire Need Programs for former players, January 25.

The Washington Redskins defeated the Buffalo Bills 37-24 in Super Bowl XXVI to capture their third world championship in 10 years, January 26. The game was played before a sellout crowd of 63,130 at the Hubert H. Humphrey Metrodome in Minneapolis and attracted the second largest television audience in Super Bowl history. The CBS broadcast was seen by more than 123 million people nationally, second only to the 127 million who viewed Super Bowl XX.

The use in officiating of a limited system of Instant Replay was not approved. The vote was 17-11 in favor of approval (21 votes were required). Instant Replay had been used for six consecutive years (1986-1991), March 18.

St. Louis businessman James Orthwein purchased controlling interest in the New England Patriots from Victor Kiam, May 11.

In a Harris Poll taken during the NFL offseason, professional football again was declared the nation's most popular sport. Professional football finished atop similar surveys conducted by Harris in 1985 and 1989, May 23.

NFL clubs accepted the report of the Expansion Committee at a league meeting in Pasadena. The report names five cities as finalists for the two expansion teams—Baltimore, Charlotte, Jacksonville, Memphis, and St. Louis, May 19.

At a league meeting in Dallas, NFL clubs approved a proposal by the World League Board of Directors to restructure the World League and place future emphasis on its international success, September 17.

NFL teams played their 16-game regular-season schedule over 18 weeks for the only time in league history.

1993

The NFL and lawyers for the players announced a settlement of various lawsuits and an agreement on the terms of a seven-year deal that included a new player system to be in place through the 1999 season, January 6.

Commissioner Tagliabue announced the establishment of the "NFL World Partnership Program" to develop amateur football internationally through a series of clinics conducted by former NFL players and coaches, January 14.

As part of Super Bowl XXVII, the NFL announced the creation of the first NFL Youth Education Town, a facility located in south central Los Angeles for inner city youth. January 25.

The Dallas Cowboys defeated the Buffalo Bills 52-17 in Super Bowl XXVII to capture their first NFL title since 1978. The game was played before a crowd of 98,374 at the Rose Bowl in Pasadena, California. The NBC broadcast of the game was the most watched program in television history and was seen by 133,400,000 people in the United States. The rating for the game was 45.1, the tenth highest for any televised sports event. The game also was seen live or taped in 101 other countries, January 31.

NFL clubs awarded Super Bowl XXX to the city of Phoenix, to be played on January 28, 1996, at Sun Devil Stadium, March 23.

The NFL and the NFL Players Association officially signed a 7-year Collective Bargaining Agreement in Washington, D.C., which guarantees more than $1 billion in pension, health, and post-career benefits for current and retired players—the most extensive benefits plan in pro sports. It was the NFL's first CBA since the 1982 agreement expired in 1987, June 29.

NFL Enterprises, a newly formed division of the NFL responsible for NFL Films, home video, and special domestic and international television programming was announced, August 19.

NFL announced plans to allow fans, for the first time ever, to join players and coaches in selecting the annual AFC and NFC Pro Bowl teams, October 12.

NFL clubs unanimously awarded the league's twenty-

ninth franchise to the Carolina Panthers and owner Jerry Richardson at a meeting in Chicago. NFL clubs also awarded Super Bowl XXXI to New Orleans and Super Bowl XXXII to San Diego, October 26.

At the same meeting in Chicago, NFL clubs approved a plan to form a European league with joint venture partners, October 27.

Don Shula became the winningest coach in NFL history when Miami beat Philadelphia to give Shula his 325th victory, one more than George Halas, November 14.

NFL clubs awarded the league's thirtieth franchise to the Jacksonville Jaguars and owner Wayne Weaver at a meeting in Chicago, November 30.

The NFL announced new 4-year television agreements with NBC, ABC, ESPN, TNT, and NFL newcomer FOX, which took over the NFC package from CBS, December 18.

The NFL completed its new TV agreements by announcing that NBC would retain the rights to the AFC package, December 20.

1994
The Dallas Cowboys defeated the Buffalo Bills 30-13 in Super Bowl XXVIII to become the fifth team to win back-to-back Super Bowl titles. The game was viewed by the largest U.S. audience in television history—134.8 million people. The game's 45.5 rating was the highest for a Super Bowl since 1987 and the tenth highest-rated Super Bowl ever, January 30.

NFL clubs unanimously approved the transfer of the New England Patriots from James Orthwein to Robert Kraft at a meeting in Orlando, February 22.

In a move to increase offensive production, NFL clubs at the league's annual meeting in Orlando adopted a package of changes, including modifications in line play, chucking rules, and the roughing-the-passer rule, plus the adoption of the two-point conversion and moving the spot of the kickoff back to the 30-yard line, March 22.

NFL clubs approved the transfer of the majority interest

in the Miami Dolphins from the Robbie family to H. Wayne Huizenga, March 23.

The NFL and FOX announced the formation of a joint venture to create a six-team World League to begin play in Europe in April, 1995, March 23.

The Carolina Panthers earned the right to select first in the 1995 NFL draft by winning a coin toss with the Jacksonville Jaguars. The Jaguars received the second selection in the 1995 draft, April 24.

NFL clubs approved the transfer of the Philadelphia Eagles from Norman Braman to Jeffrey Lurie, May 6.

The NFL launched "NFL Sunday Ticket," a new season subscription service for satellite television dish owners, June 1.

An all-time NFL record crowd of 112,376 attended the American Bowl game between Dallas and Houston in Mexico City. It concluded the biggest American Bowl series in NFL history with four games attracting a record 256,666 fans, August 15.

The NFL reached agreement on a new seven-year contract with its game officials, September 22.

The NFL Management Council and the NFL Players Association announced an agreement on the formulation and implementation of the most comprehensive drug and alcohol policy in sports, October 28.

At an NFL meeting in Chicago, Commissioner Tagliabue slotted the two new expansion teams into the AFC Central (Jacksonville Jaguars) and NFC West (Carolina Panthers) for the 1995 season only. He also appointed a special committee on realignment to make recommendations on the 1996 season and beyond, November 2.

1995
The San Francisco 49ers became the first team to win five Super Bowls when they defeated the San Diego Chargers 49-26 in Super Bowl XXIX at Joe Robbie Stadium in Miami, January 29.

Carolina and Jacksonville stocked their expansion rosters with a total of 66 players from other NFL teams in a

veteran player allocation draft in New York, February 16.

CBS Radio and the NFL agreed to a new four-year contract for an annual 53-game package of games, continuing a relationship that spanned 15 of the past 17 years, February 22.

NFL clubs approved the transfer of the Tampa Bay Buccaneers from the estate of the late Hugh Culverhouse to South Florida businessman Malcolm Glazer, March 13.

A series of safety-related rules changes were adopted at a league meeting in Phoenix, primarily related to the use of the helmet against defenseless players, March 14.

After a two-year hiatus, the World League of American Football returned to action with six teams in Europe, April 8.

The NFL became the first major sports league to establish a site on the Internet system of on-line computer communication, April 10.

The transfer of the Rams from Los Angeles to St. Louis was approved by a vote of NFL clubs at a meeting in Dallas, April 12.

ABC's *NFL Monday Night Football* finished the 1994-95 television season as the fifth highest-rated show out of 146 with a 17.8 average rating, the highest finish in the 25-year history of the series, April 18.

In an ABC News Poll taken during the NFL offseason, America's sports fans chose football as their favorite spectator sport by more than a 2-to-1 margin over basketball and baseball (35%-16%-12%), April 26.

The Frankfurt Galaxy defeated the Amsterdam Admirals 26-22 to win the 1995 World Bowl before a crowd of 23,847 in Amsterdam's Olympic Stadium, June 23.

Former NFL quarterback and Rhein Fire general manager Oliver Luck was named President of the World League, July 13.

The transfer of the Raiders from Los Angeles to Oakland was approved by a vote of the NFL clubs at a meeting in Chicago, July 22.

Jacksonville Municipal Stadium opened in Jacksonville, Florida before a sold-out crowd of more than 70,000 as the St. Louis Rams defeated the Jacksonville Jaguars

27-10 in their first preseason game, August 18.

NFL Charities and 50 NFL players donated $1 million to the United Negro College Fund in honor of the fiftieth anniversity of the UNCF and the integration of the modern NFL, September 15.

The Pro Football Hall of Fame in Canton, Ohio, completed an $8.9 million expansion including a $4 million contribution by the NFL clubs, October 14.

The Trans World Dome opened in St. Louis with a sold-out crowd of 65,598 as the Rams defeated the Carolina Panthers 28-17, November 12.

NFL paid attendance totaled 963,521 for 15 games in Week 12, the highest weekend total in the league's 76-year history, November 19-20.

On the field, many significant records and milestones were achieved: Miami's Dan Marino surpassed Pro Football Hall of Famer Fran Tarkenton in four major passing categories—attempts, completions, yards, and touchdowns—to become the NFL's all-time career leader. San Francisco's Jerry Rice became the all-time reception and receiving-yardage leader with career totals of 942 catches and 15,123 yards. Dallas' Emmitt Smith scored 25 touchdowns, breaking the season record of 24 set by Washington's John Riggins in 1983.

1996

The Dallas Cowboys won their third Super Bowl title in four years when they defeated the Pittsburgh Steelers 27-17 in Super Bowl XXX at Sun Devil Stadium in Tempe, Arizona. The game was viewed by the largest audience in U.S. television history—138.5 million people, January 28.

An agreement between the NFL and the city of Cleveland regarding the Cleveland Browns' relocation was approved by a vote of the NFL clubs, February 9. According to the agreement, the city of Cleveland retained the Browns' heritage and records, including the name, logo, colors, history, playing records, trophies, and memorabilia, and committed to building a

new 72,000-seat stadium for a reactivated Browns' franchise to begin play there no later than 1999. Art Modell received approval to move his franchise to Baltimore and rename it.

NFL total paid attendance for all 1995 games reached a record level for the seventh consecutive year, exceeding 19 million for the first time (19,202,757), March 7.

The transfer of the Oilers from Houston to Nashville for the 1998 season was approved by a vote of the NFL clubs at a meeting in Atlanta, April 30.

The Scottish Claymores defeated the Frankfurt Galaxy 32-27 to win the 1996 World Bowl in front of 38,982 at Murrayfield Stadium in Edinburgh, Scotland, June 23.

The NFL returned to Baltimore when the new Baltimore Ravens defeated the Philadelphia Eagles 17-9 in a preseason game before a crowd of 63,804 at Memorial Stadium, August 3.

Ericsson Stadium opened in Charlotte, North Carolina with a crowd of 65,350 as the Carolina Panthers defeated the Chicago Bears 30-12 in a preseason game, August 3.

NFL owners awarded Super Bowl XXXIII, to be played on January 31, 1999, to South Florida; Super Bowl XXXIV, to be played on January, 30, 2000, to Atlanta; and Super Bowl XXXV, to be played on January 28, 2001, to Tampa, October 31.

Points scored totaled 762 and NFL paid attendance totaled 964,079 for 15 games in Week 11, the highest weekend totals in either category in the league's 77-year history, November 10-11.

Former NFL Commissioner Pete Rozelle died at his home in Rancho Santa Fe, California. Rozelle, regarded as the premiere commissioner in sports history, led the NFL for 29 years, from 1960-1989, December 6.

1997

Indianapolis Colts owner Robert Irsay died from complications related to a stroke he suffered in 1995. Irsay acquired the club in 1972 when he traded his Los Angeles Rams to Carrol Rosenbloom

for the Colts. He later moved the Colts from Baltimore to Indianapolis in 1984, January 14.

The Green Bay Packers won their first NFL title in 29 years by defeating the New England Patriots 35-21 in Super Bowl XXXI at the Louisiana Superdome in New Orleans. The game was viewed by the fourth-largest audience in U.S. television history—128 million people, January 26.

The rules governing cross-ownership were modified, permitting NFL club owners to also own teams in other sports in their home market or markets without NFL teams. The vote was 24-5 (one abstention) in favor of approval, March 11.

Washington Redskins owner Jack Kent Cooke died at his home in Washington, D.C. Cooke became majority owner in 1974 and the Redskins won three Super Bowls under his leadership, April 6.

The Barcelona Dragons defeated the Rhein Fire 38-24 to win the 1997 World Bowl in front of 31,100 fans at Estadi Olimpic de Montjuic in Barcelona, Spain, June 22.

NFL clubs approved the transfer of the Seattle Seahawks from Ken Behring to Paul Allen, August 5.

Jack Kent Cooke Stadium opened in Raljon, Maryland with a crowd of 78,270 as the Washington Redskins defeated the Arizona Cardinals 19-13 in overtime, September 14.

The 10,000th regular-season game in NFL history was played when the Seattle Seahawks defeated the Tennessee Oilers 16-13 at the Kingdome in Seattle, October 5.

Atlanta Falcons owner Rankin Smith died of heart failure three days prior to his seventy-sixth birthday. Smith was the founder of the Falcons and was instrumental in bringing Super Bowls XXVIII and XXXIV to Atlanta, October 26.

NFL paid attendance totaled 999,778 for 15 games in Week 12, the highest weekend total in league history, November 16-17.

1998

The NFL reached agreement on record eight-year television contracts with four networks. ABC (*NFL Monday Night Football*) and FOX (NFC) retained

their previous rights, CBS took over the AFC package from NBC, and ESPN won the right to broadcast the entire Sunday night cable package, January 13.

The World League was renamed the NFL Europe League, January 22.

The Denver Broncos won their first Super Bowl by defeating the defending champion Green Bay Packers 31-24 in Super Bowl XXXII at Qualcomm Stadium in San Diego. The game tied Super Bowl XXVII for the third-largest audience in U.S. television history with 133.4 million viewers, January 25.

The NFL clubs approved an extension of the Collective Bargaining Agreement through 2003. The extended CBA also created a $100 million fund for youth football, March 22.

The NFL clubs unanimously approved an expansion team for Cleveland to fulfill the commitment to return the Browns to the field in 1999, March 23.

A total of $25.1 million, in largest NFL postseason pool ever, was divided among 737 players who participated in the 1997 playoffs, March 24.

The Rhein Fire defeated the Frankfurt Galaxy 34-10 to win the 1998 World Bowl in front of 47,846 fans in Frankfurt's Waldstadion—the biggest crowd to witness a World Bowl since 1991, June 14.

NFL clubs approved the transfer of the Minnesota Vikings from a 10-man ownership group to Red McCombs, July 28.

The NFL Stadium at Camden Yards opened in Baltimore, Maryland before a crowd of 65,938 as the Baltimore Ravens defeated the Chicago Bears 19-14 in a preseason game, August 8.

NFL paid attendance totaled 997,835 for 15 games in Week 1, the highest opening weekend total in league history and the second-highest total ever. In 1997, paid attendance totaled 999,778 for 15 games in Week 12, September 6-7.

Raymond James Stadium opened in Tampa, Florida before a crowd of 62,410 as the Tampa Bay Buccaneers defeated the Chicago Bears 27-15, September 20.

A Harris Poll says 55 percent of adults follow professional football, up 4 percent from 1997 and 6 percent from 1992, October 15.

NFL owners awarded Super Bowl XXXVI, to be played on January 27, 2002, to New Orleans, October 28.

Tennessee Oilers owner Bud Adams announced the team will change its name to the Tennessee Titans following the 1998 season. The NFL announced that the name Oilers will be retired—a first in league history, November 14.

1999

The Denver Broncos won their second consecutive Super Bowl title by defeating the NFC champion Atlanta Falcons 34-19 in Super Bowl XXXIII at Pro Player Stadium in Miami. The game was viewed by 127.5 million viewers, the sixth most-watched program in U.S. television history, January 31.

Jim Pyne, a center allocated by the Detroit Lions, was the first selection of the Cleveland Browns in the 1999 NFL Expansion Draft. The Browns eventually selected 37 players, February 9.

CBS Radio/Westwood One agreed to a 3-year extension of their exclusive national radio rights to NFL games, March 11.

NFL paid attendance of 19,741,493 for all games played during the 1998 season was the highest in league history, topping the 19,202,757 fans who paid to attend games in 1995. The 1998 regular-season total paid attendance of 15,364,873 for an average of 64,020 were also records, March 15.

By a vote of 28-3, the owners adopted an instant replay system as an officiating aid for the 1999 season, March 17.

New York Jets owner Leon Hess died from complications of a blood disease. Hess had been involved in the ownership of the Jets since 1963 and was sole owner of the club since 1984, May 9.

A group led by Washington area businessman Daniel Snyder is approved by NFL clubs as the new owner of the Washington Redskins at a league meeting in Atlanta, May 25.

NFL owners awarded Super Bowl XXXVII, to be played on January 26, 2003, to San Diego, May 26.

The Frankfurt Galaxy became the first team in NFL Europe League history to win a second World Bowl by defeating the Barcelona Dragons 38-24 at Rheinstadion, in Düsseldorf, Germany, June 27.

The Cleveland Browns returned to the field for the first time since 1995 and defeated the Dallas Cowboys 20-17 in overtime in the annual Hall of Fame Game at Canton, Ohio, August 9.

Cleveland Browns Stadium opened in Cleveland, Ohio before a crowd of 71,398 as the Minnesota Vikings defeated the Browns in a preseason game, 24-17, August 21.

Adelphia Coliseum opened in Nashville, Tennessee before a crowd of 65,729 with the Tennessee Titans defeating the Atlanta Falcons 17-3 in a preseason game, August 26.

Houston, Texas and owner Robert McNair were awarded the NFL's thirty-second franchise in a vote of the NFL clubs at a league meeting in Atlanta. The team will begin play in 2002. The NFL clubs also voted to realign into eight divisions of four teams each for the 2002 season, October 6.

Walter Payton, the NFL's all-time leading rusher, died of liver cancer at the age of 45. Payton played for the Chicago Bears from 1975-1987 and rushed for an NFL-record 16,726 yards, November 1.

Former NFL Commissioner Pete Rozelle, who guided a still-developing league to its position today as America's most popular sport, was named by The Sporting News as the most powerful person in sports in the 20th Century, December 15.

2000

New York businessman Robert Wood Johnson IV was approved by NFL clubs as the new owner of the New York Jets at a league meeting, January 18.

The St. Louis Rams won their first Super Bowl by defeating the AFC champion Tennessee Titans 23-16 in Super Bowl XXXIV at the Georgia Dome in Atlanta. The game was viewed by 130.7 million viewers, the fifth most-watched program in U.S. television history, January 30.

For the first time in league history, paid attendance topped 16 million for the regular season and more than 65,000 per game, an increase of 1,300 per game over 1998. Paid attendance for all NFL games increased in 1999 for the third year in a row and was the highest ever in the 80-year history of the league. It marked the first time in league history that the 20-million paid attendance mark was reached for all games in a season, March 27.

The Rhein Fire won their second World Bowl in three years, defeating the Scottish Claymores 13-10 to win World Bowl 2000 in front of 35,680 at Frankfurt's Waldstadion, June 25.

More than 100 of the 136 living members of the Pro Football Hall of Fame gathered to celebrate Pro Football's Greatest Reunion in Canton, Ohio, July 28-31.

Paul Brown Stadium opened in Cincinnati, Ohio with a crowd of 56,180 as the Cincinnati Bengals defeated the Chicago Bears 24-20 in a preseason game, August 19.

Cincinnati's Corey Dillon set a single-game rushing record with 278 yards (22 carries) against Denver, breaking the previous record of 275 yards by Chicago's Walter Payton in 1977, October 22.

Minnesota's Gary Anderson converted a 21-yard field goal against Buffalo to pass George Blanda as the NFL's all-time scoring leader with 2,004 points, October 22.

NFL owners awarded Super Bowl XXXVIII, to be played on February 1, 2004, to Houston; Super Bowl XXXIX, to be played on February 6, 2005, to Jacksonville; and Super Bowl XL, to be played on February 5, 2006, to Detroit, November 1.

The NFL named Mike Pereira as Director of Officiating and Larry Upson as Director of Officiating Operations to replace retiring Senior Director of Officiating Jerry Seeman, December 1.

San Francisco's Terrell Owens set a single-game receiving record with 20 receptions (283 yards) against Chicago, surpassing the previous mark of 18 by Tom Fears of the Los Angeles Rams in 1950, December 17.

2001

NFL clubs approved additional league-wide revenue sharing at a special league meeting in Dallas. The teams agreed to pool the visiting team share of gate receipts for all preseason and regular-season games and divide the pool equally starting in 2002, January 17.

The Baltimore Ravens won their first Super Bowl by defeating the NFC champion New York Giants 34-7 in Super Bowl XXXV at Raymond James Stadium in Tampa. The game was witnessed by 131.2 million viewers, the fifth most-watched program in U.S. television history, January 28.

The Sports Business Daily named NFL Commissioner Paul Tagliabue the 2000 Sports Industrialist of the Year, February 28.

The NFL set an all-time paid attendance record in 2000 for the third consecutive year, reaching the 20-million paid attendance mark for only the second time in league history. Regular-season paid attendance of 16,387,289 for an average of 66,078 per game also was an all-time record for the third consecutive season. The Washington Redskins set an all-time NFL regular-season home paid attendance record with a total of 656,599 for eight games, breaking the record of 634,204 held by the 1980 Detroit Lions, March 26.

NFL owners unanimously approved a realignment plan for the league starting in 2002. With the addition of the Houston Texans, the league's 32 teams will be divided into eight four-team divisions. Seven clubs change divisions, and the Seattle Seahawks change conferences, moving from the AFC to the NFC. A new scheduling format ensures that every team meets every other team in the league at least once every four years, May 22.

The Berlin Thunder won their first World Bowl, defeating the Barcelona Dragons 24-17 to win World Bowl IX in front of 32,116 at Amsterdam ArenA, June 30.

Heinz Field opened in Pittsburgh, Pennsylvania before a crowd of 57,829 with the Pittsburgh Steelers defeating the Detroit Lions 20-7 in a preseason game; and INVESCO Field at Mile High opened in Denver, Colorado before a crowd of 74,063 with the Denver Broncos defeating the New Orleans Saints 31-24 in a preseason game, August 25.

President George W. Bush became the first United States President to be involved in an NFL regular-season pregame coin toss as he helped kick off the 2001 season from the White House. Via satellite, President Bush tossed the coin for the 10 regular-season games that started at 1:00 P.M. ET, September 9.

In the wake of the September 11 terrorist attacks, Commissioner Paul Tagliabue postponed the games scheduled for September 16-17, September 13.

The league's 16-game regular season was retained when the postponed Week 2 games were rescheduled for the weekend of January 6-7, September 18.

The NFL and its game officials agreed to a new six-year Collective Bargaining Agreement, ending a two-week lockout of the regular officials, who returned to work on September 23, September 19.

The NFL announced that the league's prohibition of anabolic steroids and related substances had been strengthened to include supplements containing ephedrine and other high-risk supplements, September 27.

The NFL announced that the Super Bowl would be rescheduled from January 27 to February 3 in order to retain the full playoff format for the 2002 season. It will be the first Super Bowl played in February, October 3.

President Bush designated Super Bowl XXXVI as a "National Special Security Event," allowing all security for the game to be coordinated by the Secret Service, November 26.

George Young, the NFL's senior vice president of football operations and former general manager of the New York Giants, died at the age of 71, December 8.

2002
The NFL and the NFL Players Association agreed to a fourth extension of the 1993 Collective Bargaining Agreement through 2007, January 7.

In an AFC Wild Card matchup, the Oakland Raiders defeated the New York Jets 38-24 in the NFL's first-ever prime-time playoff game, January 12.

In a special meeting in New Orleans, NFL owners voted unanimously to approve the purchase of the Atlanta Falcons to Home Depot co-founder Arthur Blank, February 2.

The New England Patriots won their first Super Bowl by defeating the NFC champion St. Louis Rams 20-17 in Super Bowl XXXVI at the Louisiana Superdome in New Orleans. The game marked the first time in Super Bowl history that the winning points came on the final play, a 48-yard field goal by Patriots kicker Adam Vinatieri. Super Bowl XXXVI was viewed by 131.7 million viewers, the fifth-most watched program in U.S. television history, February 3.

Tennessee Titans head coach Jeff Fisher was named co-chairman of the NFL Competition Committee, February 6.

Tony Boselli, a five-time Pro Bowl tackle allocated by the Jacksonville Jaguars, was the first selection of the Houston Texans in the 2002 NFL Expansion Draft. The Texans selected 19 players, February 18.

The NFL and Westwood One/CBS Radio Sports announced the renewal of a multiyear agreement for Westwood One/CBS Radio Sports to continue as the exclusive network radio home of the NFL, April 9.

NFL Europe kicked off its tenth season with a record 254 players allocated by NFL clubs, April 13-14.

The Berlin Thunder became the first team to win consecutive World Bowls, defeating the Rhein Fire 26-20 to win World Bowl X in front of 53,109 fans at Rheinstadion, June 22.

Seahawks Stadium opened in Seattle, Washington with an attendance of 52,902 fans as the Indianapolis Colts defeated

the Seattle Seahawks 28-10 in a preseason game, August 10.

Gillette Stadium opened in Foxboro, Massachusetts with a crowd of 68,436 fans as the New England Patriots defeated the Philadelphia Eagles 16-15 in a preseason game, August 17.

Reliant Stadium opened in Houston, Texas with 69,432 fans in attendance, the largest non-Super Bowl crowd to ever watch an NFL game in Houston as the Miami Dolphins defeated the Houston Texans 24-3 in a preseason game, August 24.

For the first time, the NFL season kicked off on a Thursday night in prime time as the San Francisco 49ers defeated the New York Giants 16-13 at Giants Stadium. The game was preceded by "NFL Kickoff Live From Times Square," presented by New York City and the NFL, a football and music festival honoring the resilient spirit of New York and America, September 5.

Week 1 of the 2002 season produced the highest-scoring and most competitive Kickoff Weekend in NFL history. The 16 games averaged 49.3 points per game. A total of 788 points and 89 touchdowns were scored, the most in league history for an opening weekend. Eleven of the 16 games were decided by one score (eight points or less), a Kickoff Weekend record, September 5-9.

Johnny Unitas, the legendary quarterback for the Baltimore Colts and a Pro Football Hall of Fame member, died of a heart attack at the age of 69, September 11.

Oakland Raiders wide receiver Jerry Rice became the all-time leader in yards from scrimmage, surpassing Pro Football Hall of Fame running back Walter Payton (21,281 yards), September 29.

Baltimore Ravens cornerback Chris McAlister set an NFL record for the longest scoring play with a 107-yard touchdown return of an errant 57-yard field goal attempt by Denver Broncos kicker Jason Elam, September 30.

Cleveland Browns owner Al Lerner, the NFL Finance Committee Chairman and Chairman and CEO of MBNA Cor-

poration, died at the age of 69, October 23.

Dallas Cowboys running back Emmitt Smith became the NFL's all-time rushing leader, surpassing Pro Football Hall of Fame running back Walter Payton (16,726 yards), October 27.

The NFL and NFLPA announced the creation of USA Football, the first national advocacy organization representing all levels of amateur football, December 5.

Indianapolis Colts wide receiver Marvin Harrison set the NFL single-season record for pass receptions with 143, surpassing Herman Moore (123), December 29.

The 2002 season concluded with 25 overtime games, the most in NFL history, December 30.

2003
The NFL announced the appointment of Steve Bornstein as executive vice president-media and president and chief executive officer of the NFL Network, to be launched in 2003. The NFL Network will be the first television programming service fully dedicated to the NFL and the sport of football, January 16.

The Tampa Bay Buccaneers won their first Super Bowl by defeating the AFC champion Oakland Raiders 48-21 in Super Bowl XXXVII at Qualcomm Stadium in San Diego. The game was witnessed by 138.9 million viewers, making Super Bowl XXXVII the most-watched program in U.S. television history, January 26.

The NFL set an all-time paid attendance record in 2002 with 21,505,138, the first time paid attendance topped 21-million. Regular-season paid attendance of 16,833,310 was also an all-time record, March 26.

Chicago Bears chairman emeritus Edward W. McCaskey died at the age of 83, April 8.

The Frankfurt Galaxy became the first team to win three World Bowls, defeating the Rhein Fire 35-16 to win World Bowl XI in front of 28,138 fans at Hampden Park, June 14.

Tex Schramm, the legendary team president and general manager of the Dallas

Cowboys and a member of the Pro Football Hall of Fame, died at the age of 83, July 15.

Lincoln Financial Field opened in Philadelphia, Pennsylvania with an attendance of 66,279 fans as the New England Patriots defeated the Philadelphia Eagles 24-12 in a preseason game, August 22.

A renovated Lambeau Field opened in Green Bay, Wisconsin with a crowd of 69,831 fans as the Carolina Panthers defeated the Green Bay Packers 20-7 in a preseason game, August 23.

NFL owners awarded Super Bowl XLI, to be played on February 4, 2007 to Miami, September 17.

A renovated Soldier Field opened in Chicago, Illinois with an attendance of 61,500 fans as the Green Bay Packers defeated the Chicago Bears 38-23 in a regular season game on ABC's *NFL Monday Night Football*, September 29.

NFL owners awarded Super Bowl XLII, to be played on February 3, 2008 to Glendale, Arizona, October 30.

NFL Network, the first 24-hour, year-round television channel dedicated to the NFL and the sport of football, launched on DirecTV, November 4.

Otto Graham, the legendary quarterback of the Cleveland Browns and a member of the Pro Football Hall of Fame, died at the age of 82, December 17.

NFL paid attendance totaled 1,106,818 for 16 games in Week 17, the highest weekend total in league history, December 27-28.

2004

The New England Patriots won their second Super Bowl in three years by defeating the NFC champion Carolina Panthers 32-29 in Super Bowl XXXVIII at Reliant Stadium in Houston. The game was witnessed by 144.4 million viewers, making Super Bowl XXXVIII the most-watched program in U.S. television history, February 1.

The NFL set an all-time paid attendance record in 2003 for the second consecutive year with a mark of 21,639,040. Regular-season paid attendance of 16,913,584 for an average of 66,328 per game

were both all-time records, March 29.

By a vote of 29-3, NFL owners extended the instant replay system for another five seasons through 2008, March 30.

Steve Bisciotti took over as the controlling owner of the Baltimore Ravens, succeeding Art Modell, who operated the franchise for 43 years, April 8.

Former Arizona Cardinals safety Pat Tillman was killed in a firefight while on combat patrol with the U.S. Army Rangers in Afghanistan, April 22.

A federal appeals court formally ruled in favor of the NFL's draft eligibility rule in Maurice Clarett's lawsuit, citing federal labor policy in permitting the NFL and the Players Association to set rules for when players can enter the league, May 24.

The Berlin Thunder defeated the Frankfurt Galaxy 30-24 to win World Bowl XII in front of 35,413 fans at Arena Auf-Schalke, June 12.

The New England Patriots defeated the New York Jets 13-7 for their NFL-record 18th consecutive regular-season victory, October 24.

The NFL reached an agreement on six-year contract extensions with two of its network television partners—CBS and FOX—to run through the 2011 season, November 8.

The NFL and DirecTV announced a five-year extension on the NFL Sunday Ticket subscription television package to run through the 2010 season, November 8.

NFL Europe named the Hamburg Sea Devils as the league's newest team, November 24.

2005

Indianapolis Colts quarterback Peyton Manning set the NFL single-season record with 49 touchdown passes, January 2.

The New England Patriots became the second team in NFL history to win three Super Bowls in four seasons by defeating the Philadelphia Eagles 24-21 in Super Bowl XXXIX at ALLTEL Stadium in Jacksonville. The game was witnessed by 133.7 million viewers, making Super Bowl

XXXIX the fifth-most watched program in U.S. television history, February 6.

The NFL announced that, for the first time in its 86-year history, the league would play a regular-season game outside the United States on October 2 in Mexico City between the Arizona Cardinals and the San Francisco 49ers, March 21.

The NFL set an all-time paid attendance record in 2004 for the third consecutive year with a mark of 21,708,624. Regular-season paid attendance increased to 17,000,811, the first time the NFL reached the 17-million mark. Average paid attendance of 66,409 was also an all-time high, March 21.

The Pat Tillman USO Center opened in Afghanistan. The NFL donated $250,000 to the USO to honor the memory of the former Arizona Cardinals player who died in Afghanistan while serving in the U.S. Army, April 1.

The NFL reached long-term agreements for its Sunday and Monday primetime TV packages. NBC returned to the NFL by acquiring the Sunday night package for six years (2006-2011). ESPN agreed on an eight-year deal to televise *Monday Night Football* from 2006-2013, April 18.

The NFL strengthened its steroids program by adopting the Olympic testosterone testing standard, tripling the number of times a player can be randomly tested during the offseason from two to six, adding substances to the list of banned substances, and putting new language in the policy to allow for testing of designer drugs and other substances that may have evaded detection, April 27.

NFL owners voted unanimously to approve the purchase of the Minnesota Vikings to real-estate developer Zygmunt Wilf, May 25.

NFL owners awarded Super Bowl XLIII, to be played on February 1, 2009 to Tampa, May 25.

NFL COMMISSIONERS AND PRESIDENTS*

1920	Jim Thorpe, President
1921-39	Joe Carr, President
1939-41	Carl Storck, President
1941-46	Elmer Layden, Commissioner
1946-1959	Bert Bell, Commissioner
1960-1989	Pete Rozelle, Commissioner
1989-present	Paul Tagliabue, Commissioner

NFL treasurer Austin Gunsel served as president in the office of the commissioner following the death of Bert Bell (Oct. 11, 1959) until the election of Pete Rozelle (Jan. 26, 1960).

2004

AMERICAN CONFERENCE

East Division

	W	L	T	Pct.	Pts.	OP
New England	14	2	0	.875	437	260
N.Y. Jets*	10	6	0	.625	333	261
Buffalo	9	7	0	.563	395	284
Miami	4	12	0	.250	275	354

North Division

	W	L	T	Pct.	Pts.	OP
Pittsburgh#	15	1	0	.938	372	251
Baltimore	9	7	0	.563	317	268
Cincinnati	8	8	0	.500	374	372
Cleveland	4	12	0	.250	276	390

South Division

	W	L	T	Pct.	Pts.	OP
Indianapolis	12	4	0	.750	522	351
Jacksonville	9	7	0	.563	261	280
Houston	7	9	0	.438	309	339
Tennessee	5	11	0	.313	344	439

West Division

	W	L	T	Pct.	Pts.	OP
San Diego	12	4	0	.750	446	313
Denver*	10	6	0	.625	381	304
Kansas City	7	9	0	.438	483	435
Oakland	5	11	0	.313	320	442

NATIONAL CONFERENCE

East Division

	W	L	T	Pct.	Pts.	OP
Philadelphia#	13	3	0	.813	386	260
N.Y. Giants	6	10	0	.375	303	347
Dallas	6	10	0	.375	293	405
Washington	6	10	0	.375	240	265

North Division

	W	L	T	Pct.	Pts.	OP
Green Bay	10	6	0	.625	424	380
Minnesota*	8	8	0	.500	405	395
Detroit	6	10	0	.375	296	350
Chicago	5	11	0	.313	231	331

South Division

	W	L	T	Pct.	Pts.	OP
Atlanta	11	5	0	.688	340	337
New Orleans	8	8	0	.500	348	405
Carolina	7	9	0	.438	355	339
Tampa Bay	5	11	0	.313	301	304

West Division

	W	L	T	Pct.	Pts.	OP
Seattle	9	7	0	.563	371	373
St. Louis*	8	8	0	.500	319	392
Arizona	6	10	0	.375	284	322
San Francisco	2	14	0	.125	259	452

*Wild Card qualifier for playoffs; #Top playoff seed in conference

Indianapolis finished ahead of San Diego based on head-to-head victory. N.Y. Jets finished ahead of Denver based on better record vs. common opponents (5-0 to 3-2). St. Louis finished ahead of New Orleans and Minnesota based on best conference record (7-5 to Saints' 6-6 to Vikings' 5-7), and Minnesota finished ahead of New Orleans based on head-to-head victory. N.Y. Giants finished ahead of Dallas and Washington based on better head-to-head record (3-1 to Cowboys' 2-2 to Redskins' 1-3), and Dallas finished ahead of Washington based on head-to-head sweep (2-0).

Wild Card playoffs: N.Y. Jets 20, SAN DIEGO 17 (OT)
  INDIANAPOLIS 49, Denver 24
Divisional playoffs: PITTSBURGH 20, N.Y. Jets 17 (OT)
  NEW ENGLAND 20, Indianapolis 3
AFC Championship: New England 41, PITTSBURGH 27
Wild Card playoffs: St. Louis 27, SEATTLE 20
  Minnesota 31, GREEN BAY 17
Divisional playoffs: ATLANTA 47, St. Louis 17
  PHILADELPHIA 27, Minnesota 14
NFC Championship: PHILADELPHIA 27, Atlanta 10
Super Bowl XXXIX: New England (AFC) 24, Philadelphia (NFC) 21
  at ALLTEL Stadium, Jacksonville, Florida

In Past Standings section, home teams in playoff games are indicated by capital letters.

Playoff Seeds

AFC	NFC
1. Pittsburgh	**1. Philadelphia**
2. New England	2. Atlanta
3. Indianapolis	3. Green Bay
4. San Diego	4. Seattle
5. N.Y. Jets	5. St. Louis
6. Denver	6. Minnesota

2003

AMERICAN CONFERENCE

East Division

	W	L	T	Pct.	Pts.	OP
New England#	14	2	0	.875	348	238
Miami	10	6	0	.625	311	261
Buffalo	6	10	0	.375	243	279
N.Y. Jets	6	10	0	.375	283	299

North Division

	W	L	T	Pct.	Pts.	OP
Baltimore	10	6	0	.625	391	281
Cincinnati	8	8	0	.500	346	384
Pittsburgh	6	10	0	.375	300	327
Cleveland	5	11	0	.313	254	322

South Division

	W	L	T	Pct.	Pts.	OP
Indianapolis	12	4	0	.750	447	336
Tennessee*	12	4	0	.750	435	324
Houston	5	11	0	.313	255	380
Jacksonville	5	11	0	.313	276	331

West Division

	W	L	T	Pct.	Pts.	OP
Kansas City	13	3	0	.813	484	332
Denver*	10	6	0	.625	381	301
Oakland	4	12	0	.250	270	379
San Diego	4	12	0	.250	313	441

NATIONAL CONFERENCE

East Division

	W	L	T	Pct.	Pts.	OP
Philadelphia#	12	4	0	.750	374	287
Dallas*	10	6	0	.625	289	260
Washington	5	11	0	.313	287	372
N.Y. Giants	4	12	0	.250	243	387

North Division

	W	L	T	Pct.	Pts.	OP
Green Bay	10	6	0	.625	442	307
Minnesota	9	7	0	.563	416	353
Chicago	7	9	0	.438	283	346
Detroit	5	11	0	.313	270	379

South Division

	W	L	T	Pct.	Pts.	OP
Carolina	11	5	0	.688	325	304
New Orleans	8	8	0	.500	340	326
Tampa Bay	7	9	0	.438	301	264
Atlanta	5	11	0	.313	299	422

West Division

	W	L	T	Pct.	Pts.	OP
St. Louis	12	4	0	.750	447	328
Seattle*	10	6	0	.625	404	327
San Francisco	7	9	0	.438	384	337
Arizona	4	12	0	.250	225	452

*Wild Card qualifier for playoffs; #Top playoff seed in conference

Buffalo finished ahead of N.Y. Jets based on better division record (2-4 to Jets' 1-5). Indianapolis finished ahead of Tennessee based on head-to-head sweep (2-0). Jacksonville finished ahead of Houston based on better division record (2-4 to Texans' 1-5). Denver finished ahead of Miami based on better conference record (9-3 to Dolphins' 7-5). Oakland finished ahead of San Diego based on better conference record (3-9 to Chargers' 2-10). Philadelphia finished ahead of St. Louis based on better conference record (9-3 to Rams' 8-4). Seattle finished ahead of Dallas based on better strength of victory (65-95 to Cowboys' 62-98).

Wild Card playoffs: Tennessee 20, BALTIMORE 17;
  INDIANAPOLIS 41, Denver 10
Divisional playoffs: NEW ENGLAND 17, Tennessee 14;
  Indianapolis 38, KANSAS CITY 31
AFC Championship: NEW ENGLAND 24, Indianapolis 14
Wild Card playoffs: CAROLINA 29, Dallas 10;
  GREEN BAY 33, Seattle 27 (OT)
Divisional playoffs: Carolina 29, ST. LOUIS 23 (2OT);
  PHILADELPHIA 20, Green Bay 17 (OT)
NFC Championship: Carolina 14, PHILADELPHIA 3
Super Bowl XXXVIII: New England (AFC) 32, Carolina (NFC) 29
  at Reliant Stadium, Houston, Texas

Playoff Seeds

AFC	NFC
1. New England	1. Philadelphia
2. Kansas City	2. St. Louis
3. Indianapolis	**3. Carolina**
4. Baltimore	4. Green Bay
5. Tennessee	5. Seattle
6. Denver	6. Dallas

2002

AMERICAN CONFERENCE

East Division

	W	L	T	Pct.	Pts.	OP
N.Y. Jets	9	7	0	.563	359	336
New England	9	7	0	.563	381	346
Miami	9	7	0	.563	378	301
Buffalo	8	8	0	.500	379	397

North Division

	W	L	T	Pct.	Pts.	OP
Pittsburgh	10	5	1	.656	390	345
Cleveland*	9	7	0	.563	344	320
Baltimore	7	9	0	.438	316	354
Cincinnati	2	14	0	.125	279	456

South Division

	W	L	T	Pct.	Pts.	OP
Tennessee	11	5	0	.688	367	324
Indianapolis*	10	6	0	.625	349	313
Jacksonville	6	10	0	.375	328	315
Houston	4	12	0	.250	213	356

West Division

	W	L	T	Pct.	Pts.	OP
Oakland#	11	5	0	.688	450	304
Denver	9	7	0	.563	392	344
San Diego	8	8	0	.500	333	367
Kansas City	8	8	0	.500	467	399

NATIONAL CONFERENCE

East Division

	W	L	T	Pct.	Pts.	OP
Philadelphia#	12	4	0	.750	415	241
N.Y. Giants*	10	6	0	.625	320	279
Washington	7	9	0	.438	307	365
Dallas	5	11	0	.313	217	329

North Division

	W	L	T	Pct.	Pts.	OP
Green Bay	12	4	0	.750	398	328
Minnesota	6	10	0	.375	390	442
Chicago	4	12	0	.250	281	379
Detroit	3	13	0	.188	306	451

South Division

	W	L	T	Pct.	Pts.	OP
Tampa Bay	12	4	0	.750	346	196
Atlanta*	9	6	1	.594	402	314
New Orleans	9	7	0	.563	432	388
Carolina	7	9	0	.438	258	302

West Division

	W	L	T	Pct.	Pts.	OP
San Francisco	10	6	0	.625	367	351
St. Louis	7	9	0	.438	316	369
Seattle	7	9	0	.438	355	369
Arizona	5	11	0	.313	262	417

*Wild Card qualifier for playoffs; #Top playoff seed in conference
New York Jets finished ahead of New England based on better record in common games (8-4 to Patriots' 7-5) and Miami based on better division record (4-2 to Dolphins' 2-4). New England finished ahead of Miami based on better division record (4-2 to Dolphins' 2-4). Cleveland finished ahead of Denver and New England based on better conference record (7-5 to Broncos' 5-7 and Patriots' 6-6). Oakland finished ahead of Tennessee based on better head-to-head record (1-0). San Diego finished ahead of Kansas City based on better division record (3-3 to Chiefs' 2-4). Philadelphia finished ahead of Green Bay and Tampa Bay based on better conference record (11-1 to Packers' 9-3 and Buccaneers' 9-3). Tampa Bay finished ahead of Green Bay based on better head-to-head record (1-0). St. Louis finished ahead of Seattle based on better division record (4-2 to Seahawks' 2-4).
Wild Card playoffs: N.Y. JETS 41, Indianapolis 0;
  PITTSBURGH 36, Cleveland 33
Divisional playoffs: TENNESSEE 34, Pittsburgh 31 (OT);
  OAKLAND 30, N.Y. Jets 10
AFC Championship: OAKLAND 41, Tennessee 24
Wild Card playoffs: Atlanta 27, GREEN BAY 7;
  SAN FRANCISCO 39, N.Y. Giants 38
Divisional playoffs: PHILADELPHIA 20, Atlanta 6;
  TAMPA BAY 31, San Francisco 6
NFC Championship: Tampa Bay 27, PHILADELPHIA 10
Super Bowl XXXVII: Tampa Bay (NFC) 48, Oakland (AFC) 21
  at Qualcomm Stadium, San Diego, California

Playoff Seeds

AFC	NFC
1. **Oakland**	1. Philadelphia
2. Tennessee	2. **Tampa Bay**
3. Pittsburgh	3. Green Bay
4. N.Y. Jets	4. San Francisco
5. Indianapolis	5. N.Y. Giants
6. Cleveland	6. Atlanta

2001

AMERICAN CONFERENCE

Eastern Division

	W	L	T	Pct.	Pts.	OP
New England	11	5	0	.688	371	272
Miami*	11	5	0	.688	344	290
N.Y. Jets*	10	6	0	.625	308	295
Indianapolis	6	10	0	.375	413	486
Buffalo	3	13	0	.188	265	420

Central Division

	W	L	T	Pct.	Pts.	OP
Pittsburgh#	13	3	0	.813	352	212
Baltimore*	10	6	0	.625	303	265
Cleveland	7	9	0	.438	285	319
Tennessee	7	9	0	.438	336	388
Jacksonville	6	10	0	.375	294	286
Cincinnati	6	10	0	.375	226	309

Western Division

	W	L	T	Pct.	Pts.	OP
Oakland	10	6	0	.625	399	327
Seattle	9	7	0	.563	301	324
Denver	8	8	0	.500	340	339
Kansas City	6	10	0	.375	320	344
San Diego	5	11	0	.313	332	321

NATIONAL CONFERENCE

Eastern Division

	W	L	T	Pct.	Pts.	OP
Philadelphia	11	5	0	.688	343	208
Washington	8	8	0	.500	256	303
N.Y. Giants	7	9	0	.438	294	321
Arizona	7	9	0	.438	295	343
Dallas	5	11	0	.313	246	338

Central Division

	W	L	T	Pct.	Pts.	OP
Chicago	13	3	0	.813	338	203
Green Bay*	12	4	0	.750	390	266
Tampa Bay*	9	7	0	.563	324	280
Minnesota	5	11	0	.313	290	390
Detroit	2	14	0	.125	270	424

Western Division

	W	L	T	Pct.	Pts.	OP
St. Louis#	14	2	0	.875	503	273
San Francisco*	12	4	0	.750	409	282
New Orleans	7	9	0	.438	333	409
Atlanta	7	9	0	.438	291	377
Carolina	1	15	0	.063	253	410

*Wild Card qualifier for playoffs; #Top playoff seed in conference
New England finished ahead of Miami based on better division record (6-2 to Dolphins' 5-3). Baltimore was second Wild Card ahead of N.Y. Jets based on better record against common opponents (3-2 to Jets' 2-2). Cleveland finished ahead of Tennessee based on better division record (5-5 to Titans' 3-7). Jacksonville finished ahead of Cincinnati based on head-to-head record (2-0). N.Y. Giants finished ahead of Arizona based on head-to-head record (2-0). Green Bay was first Wild Card ahead of San Francisco based on better conference record (9-3 to 49ers' 8-4). New Orleans finished ahead of Atlanta based on better division record (4-4 to Falcons' 3-5).
Wild Card playoffs: OAKLAND 38, N.Y. Jets 24;
  Baltimore 20, MIAMI 3
Divisional playoffs: NEW ENGLAND 16, Oakland 13 (OT);
  PITTSBURGH 27, Baltimore 10
AFC Championship: New England 24, PITTSBURGH 17
Wild Card playoffs: PHILADELPHIA 31, Tampa Bay 9;
  GREEN BAY 25, San Francisco 15
Divisional playoffs: Philadelphia 33, CHICAGO 19;
  ST. LOUIS 45, Green Bay 17
NFC Championship: ST. LOUIS 29, Philadelphia 24
Super Bowl XXXVI: New England (AFC) 20, St. Louis (NFC) 17
  at Louisiana Superdome, New Orleans, Louisiana

Playoff Seeds

AFC	NFC
1. Pittsburgh	1. **St. Louis**
2. **New England**	2. Chicago
3. Oakland	3. Philadelphia
4. Miami	4. Green Bay
5. Baltimore	5. San Francisco
6. N.Y. Jets	6. Tampa Bay

2000

AMERICAN CONFERENCE

Eastern Division

	W	L	T	Pct.	Pts.	OP
Miami	11	5	0	.688	323	226
Indianapolis*	10	6	0	.625	429	326
N.Y. Jets	9	7	0	.563	321	321
Buffalo	8	8	0	.500	315	350
New England	5	11	0	.313	276	338

Central Division

	W	L	T	Pct.	Pts.	OP
Tennessee#	13	3	0	.813	346	191
Baltimore*	12	4	0	.750	333	165
Pittsburgh	9	7	0	.563	321	255
Jacksonville	7	9	0	.438	367	327
Cincinnati	4	12	0	.250	185	359
Cleveland	3	13	0	.188	161	419

Western Division

	W	L	T	Pct.	Pts.	OP
Oakland	12	4	0	.750	479	299
Denver*	11	5	0	.688	485	369
Kansas City	7	9	0	.438	355	354
Seattle	6	10	0	.375	320	405
San Diego	1	15	0	.063	269	440

NATIONAL CONFERENCE

Eastern Division

	W	L	T	Pct.	Pts.	OP
N.Y. Giants#	12	4	0	.750	328	246
Philadelphia*	11	5	0	.688	351	245
Washington	8	8	0	.500	281	269
Dallas	5	11	0	.313	294	361
Arizona	3	13	0	.188	210	443

Central Division

	W	L	T	Pct.	Pts.	OP
Minnesota	11	5	0	.688	397	371
Tampa Bay*	10	6	0	.625	388	269
Green Bay	9	7	0	.563	353	323
Detroit	9	7	0	.563	307	307
Chicago	5	11	0	.313	216	355

Western Division

	W	L	T	Pct.	Pts.	OP
New Orleans	10	6	0	.625	354	305
St. Louis*	10	6	0	.625	540	471
Carolina	7	9	0	.438	310	310
San Francisco	6	10	0	.375	388	422
Atlanta	4	12	0	.250	252	413

*Wild Card qualifier for playoffs; #Top playoff seed in conference
Green Bay finished ahead of Detroit based on better division record (5-3 to Lions' 3-5). New Orleans finished ahead of St. Louis based on better division record (7-1 to Rams' 5-3). Tampa Bay was second Wild Card based on head-to-head victory over St. Louis (1-0).
Wild Card playoffs: MIAMI 23, Indianapolis 17 (OT); BALTIMORE 21, Denver 3
Divisional playoffs: OAKLAND 27, Miami 0; Baltimore 24, TENNESSEE 10
AFC Championship: Baltimore 16, OAKLAND 3
Wild Card playoffs: NEW ORLEANS 31, St. Louis 28; PHILADELPHIA 21, Tampa Bay 3
Divisional playoffs: MINNESOTA 34, New Orleans 16; N.Y. GIANTS 20, Philadelphia 10
NFC Championship: N.Y. GIANTS 41, Minnesota 0
Super Bowl XXXV: Baltimore (AFC) 34, N.Y. Giants (NFC) 7 at Raymond James Stadium, Tampa, Florida

Playoff Seeds

AFC	NFC
1. Tennessee	1. N.Y. Giants
2. Oakland	2. Minnesota
3. Miami	3. New Orleans
4. Baltimore	4. Philadelphia
5. Denver	5. Tampa Bay
6. Indianapolis	6. St. Louis

1999

AMERICAN CONFERENCE

Eastern Division

	W	L	T	Pct.	Pts.	OP
Indianapolis	13	3	0	.813	423	333
Buffalo*	11	5	0	.688	320	229
Miami*	9	7	0	.563	326	336
N.Y. Jets	8	8	0	.500	308	309
New England	8	8	0	.500	299	284

Central Division

	W	L	T	Pct.	Pts.	OP
Jacksonville#	14	2	0	.875	396	217
Tennessee*	13	3	0	.813	392	324
Baltimore	8	8	0	.500	324	277
Pittsburgh	6	10	0	.375	317	320
Cincinnati	4	12	0	.250	283	460
Cleveland	2	14	0	.125	217	437

Western Division

	W	L	T	Pct.	Pts.	OP
Seattle	9	7	0	.563	338	298
Kansas City	9	7	0	.563	390	322
San Diego	8	8	0	.500	269	316
Oakland	8	8	0	.500	390	329
Denver	6	10	0	.375	314	318

NATIONAL CONFERENCE

Eastern Division

	W	L	T	Pct.	Pts.	OP
Washington	10	6	0	.625	443	377
Dallas*	8	8	0	.500	352	276
N.Y. Giants	7	9	0	.438	299	358
Arizona	6	10	0	.375	245	382
Philadelphia	5	11	0	.313	272	357

Central Division

	W	L	T	Pct.	Pts.	OP
Tampa Bay	11	5	0	.688	270	235
Minnesota*	10	6	0	.625	399	335
Detroit*	8	8	0	.500	322	323
Green Bay	8	8	0	.500	357	341
Chicago	6	10	0	.375	272	341

Western Division

	W	L	T	Pct.	Pts.	OP
St. Louis#	13	3	0	.813	526	242
Carolina	8	8	0	.500	421	381
Atlanta	5	11	0	.313	285	380
San Francisco	4	12	0	.250	295	453
New Orleans	3	13	0	.188	260	434

*Wild Card qualifier for playoffs; #Top playoff seed in conference
Miami was third Wild Card ahead of Kansas City based on better record against common opponents (6-1 to Chiefs' 5-3). N.Y. Jets finished ahead of New England based on better division record (4-4 to Patriots' 2-6). Seattle finished ahead of Kansas City based on head-to-head sweep (2-0). San Diego finished ahead of Oakland based on better division record (5-3 to Raiders' 3-5). Dallas was second Wild Card based on better record against common opponents (3-2 to Lions' 3-3) and better conference record than Carolina (7-5 to Panthers' 6-6). Detroit was third Wild Card based on better conference record than Green Bay (7-5 to Packers' 6-6) and better conference record than Carolina (7-5 to Panthers' 6-6).
Wild Card playoffs: TENNESSEE 22, Buffalo 16; Miami 20, SEATTLE 17
Divisional playoffs: JACKSONVILLE 62, Miami 7; Tennessee 19, INDIANAPOLIS 16
AFC Championship: Tennessee 33, JACKSONVILLE 14
Wild Card playoffs: WASHINGTON 27, Detroit 13; MINNESOTA 27, Dallas 10
Divisional playoffs: TAMPA BAY 14, Washington 13; ST. LOUIS 49, Minnesota 37
NFC Championship: ST. LOUIS 11, Tampa Bay 6
Super Bowl XXXIV: St. Louis (NFC) 23, Tennessee (AFC) 16 at Georgia Dome, Atlanta, Georgia

Playoff Seeds

AFC	NFC
1. Jacksonville	1. St. Louis
2. Indianapolis	2. Tampa Bay
3. Seattle	3. Washington
4. Tennessee	4. Minnesota
5. Buffalo	5. Dallas
6. Miami	6. Detroit

1998

AMERICAN CONFERENCE

Eastern Division

	W	L	T	Pct.	Pts.	OP
N.Y. Jets	12	4	0	.750	416	266
Miami*	10	6	0	.625	321	265
Buffalo*	10	6	0	.625	400	333
New England*	9	7	0	.563	337	329
Indianapolis	3	13	0	.188	310	444

Central Division

	W	L	T	Pct.	Pts.	OP
Jacksonville	11	5	0	.688	392	338
Tennessee	8	8	0	.500	330	320
Pittsburgh	7	9	0	.438	263	303
Baltimore	6	10	0	.375	269	335
Cincinnati	3	13	0	.188	268	452

Western Division

	W	L	T	Pct.	Pts.	OP
Denver#	14	2	0	.875	501	309
Oakland	8	8	0	.500	288	356
Seattle	8	8	0	.500	372	310
Kansas City	7	9	0	.438	327	363
San Diego	5	11	0	.313	241	342

NATIONAL CONFERENCE

Eastern Division

	W	L	T	Pct.	Pts.	OP
Dallas	10	6	0	.625	381	275
Arizona*	9	7	0	.563	325	378
N.Y. Giants	8	8	0	.500	287	309
Washington	6	10	0	.375	319	421
Philadelphia	3	13	0	.188	161	344

Central Division

	W	L	T	Pct.	Pts.	OP
Minnesota#	15	1	0	.938	556	296
Green Bay*	11	5	0	.688	408	319
Tampa Bay	8	8	0	.500	314	295
Detroit	5	11	0	.313	306	378
Chicago	4	12	0	.250	276	368

Western Division

	W	L	T	Pct.	Pts.	OP
Atlanta	14	2	0	.875	442	289
San Francisco*	12	4	0	.750	479	328
New Orleans	6	10	0	.375	305	359
Carolina	4	12	0	.250	336	413
St. Louis	4	12	0	.250	285	378

*Wild Card qualifier for playoffs; #Top playoff seed in conference
Miami finished ahead of Buffalo based on better net division points
(6 to Bills' 0). Oakland finished ahead of Seattle based on head-to-head sweep (2-0). Carolina finished ahead of St. Louis based on head-to-head sweep (2-0).
Wild Card playoffs: MIAMI 24, Buffalo 17;
   JACKSONVILLE 25, New England 10
Divisional playoffs: DENVER 38, Miami 3;
   N.Y. JETS 34, Jacksonville 24
AFC Championship: DENVER 23, N.Y. Jets 10
Wild Card playoffs: Arizona 20, DALLAS 7;
   SAN FRANCISCO 30, Green Bay 27
Divisional playoffs: ATLANTA 20, San Francisco 18;
   MINNESOTA 41, Arizona 21
NFC Championship: Atlanta 30, MINNESOTA 27 (OT)
Super Bowl XXXIII: Denver (AFC) 34, Atlanta (NFC) 19,
   at Pro Player Stadium, Miami, Florida

Playoff Seeds

AFC	NFC
1. Denver	1. Minnesota
2. N.Y. Jets	**2. Atlanta**
3. Jacksonville	3. Dallas
4. Miami	4. San Francisco
5. Buffalo	5. Green Bay
6. New England	6. Arizona

1997

AMERICAN CONFERENCE

Eastern Division

	W	L	T	Pct.	Pts.	OP
New England	10	6	0	.625	369	289
Miami*	9	7	0	.563	339	327
N.Y. Jets	9	7	0	.563	348	287
Buffalo	6	10	0	.375	255	367
Indianapolis	3	13	0	.188	313	401

Central Division

	W	L	T	Pct.	Pts.	OP
Pittsburgh	11	5	0	.688	372	307
Jacksonville*	11	5	0	.688	394	318
Tennessee	8	8	0	.500	333	310
Cincinnati	7	9	0	.438	355	405
Baltimore	6	9	1	.406	326	345

Western Division

	W	L	T	Pct.	Pts.	OP
Kansas City#	13	3	0	.813	375	232
Denver*	12	4	0	.750	472	287
Seattle	8	8	0	.500	365	362
Oakland	4	12	0	.250	324	419
San Diego	4	12	0	.250	266	425

NATIONAL CONFERENCE

Eastern Division

	W	L	T	Pct.	Pts.	OP
N.Y. Giants	10	5	1	.656	307	265
Washington	8	7	1	.531	327	289
Philadelphia	6	9	1	.406	317	372
Dallas	6	10	0	.375	304	314
Arizona	4	12	0	.250	283	379

Central Division

	W	L	T	Pct.	Pts.	OP
Green Bay	13	3	0	.813	422	282
Tampa Bay*	10	6	0	.625	299	263
Detroit*	9	7	0	.563	379	306
Minnesota*	9	7	0	.563	354	359
Chicago	4	12	0	.250	263	421

Western Division

	W	L	T	Pct.	Pts.	OP
San Francisco#	13	3	0	.813	375	265
Carolina	7	9	0	.438	265	314
Atlanta	7	9	0	.438	320	361
New Orleans	6	10	0	.375	237	327
St. Louis	5	11	0	.313	299	359

*Wild Card qualifier for playoffs; #Top playoff seed in conference
Miami finished ahead of N.Y. Jets based on head-to-head sweep (2-0). Pittsburgh finished ahead of Jacksonville based on better net division points (78 to Jaguars' 23). Oakland finished ahead of San Diego based on better division record (2-6 to Chargers' 1-7). San Francisco was top playoff seed based on better conference record than Green Bay (11-1 to Packers' 10-2). Detroit finished ahead of Minnesota based on head-to-head sweep (2-0). Carolina finished ahead of Atlanta based on head-to-head sweep (2-0).
Wild Card playoffs: DENVER 42, Jacksonville 17;
   NEW ENGLAND 17, Miami 3
Divisional playoffs: PITTSBURGH 7, New England 6;
   Denver 14, KANSAS CITY 10
AFC Championship: Denver 24, PITTSBURGH 21
Wild Card playoffs: Minnesota 23, N.Y. GIANTS 22;
   TAMPA BAY 20, Detroit 10
Divisional playoffs: SAN FRANCISCO 38, Minnesota 22;
   GREEN BAY 21, Tampa Bay 7
NFC Championship: Green Bay 23, SAN FRANCISCO 10
Super Bowl XXXII: Denver (AFC) 31, Green Bay (NFC) 24,
   at Qualcomm Stadium, San Diego, California

Playoff Seeds

AFC	NFC
1. Kansas City	1. San Francisco
2. Pittsburgh	**2. Green Bay**
3. New England	3. N.Y. Giants
4. Denver	4. Tampa Bay
5. Jacksonville	5. Detroit
6. Miami	6. Minnesota

1996

AMERICAN CONFERENCE
Eastern Division

	W	L	T	Pct.	Pts.	OP
New England	11	5	0	.688	418	313
Buffalo*	10	6	0	.625	319	266
Indianapolis*	9	7	0	.563	317	334
Miami	8	8	0	.500	339	325
N.Y. Jets	1	15	0	.063	279	454

Central Division

	W	L	T	Pct.	Pts.	OP
Pittsburgh	10	6	0	.625	344	257
Jacksonville*	9	7	0	.563	325	335
Cincinnati	8	8	0	.500	372	369
Houston	8	8	0	.500	345	319
Baltimore	4	12	0	.250	371	441

Western Division

	W	L	T	Pct.	Pts.	OP
Denver#	13	3	0	.813	391	275
Kansas City	9	7	0	.563	297	300
San Diego	8	8	0	.500	310	376
Oakland	7	9	0	.438	340	293
Seattle	7	9	0	.438	317	376

NATIONAL CONFERENCE
Eastern Division

	W	L	T	Pct.	Pts.	OP
Dallas	10	6	0	.625	286	250
Philadelphia*	10	6	0	.625	363	341
Washington	9	7	0	.563	364	312
Arizona	7	9	0	.438	300	397
N.Y. Giants	6	10	0	.375	242	297

Central Division

	W	L	T	Pct.	Pts.	OP
Green Bay#	13	3	0	.813	456	210
Minnesota*	9	7	0	.563	298	315
Chicago	7	9	0	.438	283	305
Tampa Bay	6	10	0	.375	221	293
Detroit	5	11	0	.313	302	368

Western Division

	W	L	T	Pct.	Pts.	OP
Carolina	12	4	0	.750	367	218
San Francisco*	12	4	0	.750	398	257
St. Louis	6	10	0	.375	303	409
Atlanta	3	13	0	.188	309	461
New Orleans	3	13	0	.188	229	339

*Wild Card qualifier for playoffs; #Top playoff seed in conference
Jacksonville was second Wild Card ahead of Indianapolis and
   Kansas City based on better conference record (7-5 to Colts' 6-6
   and Chiefs' 5-7). Indianapolis was third Wild Card based on
   head-to-head victory over Kansas City (1-0). Cincinnati finished
   ahead of Houston based on better net division points (19 to
   Oilers' 11). Oakland finished ahead of Seattle based on better
   division record (3-5 to Seahawks' 2-6). Dallas finished ahead of
   Philadelphia based on better record against common opponents
   (8-5 to Eagles' 7-6). Minnesota was third Wild Card based on
   better conference record than Washington (8-4 to Redskins'
   6-6). Carolina finished ahead of San Francisco based on head-to-
   head sweep (2-0). Atlanta finished ahead of New Orleans based
   on head-to-head sweep (2-0).
Wild Card playoffs: Jacksonville 30, BUFFALO 27;
   PITTSBURGH 42, Indianapolis 14
Divisional playoffs: Jacksonville 30, DENVER 27;
   NEW ENGLAND 28, Pittsburgh 3
AFC Championship: NEW ENGLAND 20, Jacksonville 6
Wild Card playoffs: DALLAS 40, Minnesota 15;
   SAN FRANCISCO 14, Philadelphia 0
Divisional playoffs: GREEN BAY 35, San Francisco 14;
   CAROLINA 26, Dallas 17
NFC Championship: GREEN BAY 30, Carolina 13
Super Bowl XXXI: Green Bay (NFC) 35, New England (AFC) 21,
   at Louisiana Superdome, New Orleans, Louisiana

Playoff Seeds

AFC	NFC
1. Denver	1. Green Bay
2. New England	2. Carolina
3. Pittsburgh	3. Dallas
4. Buffalo	4. San Francisco
5. Jacksonville	5. Philadelphia
6. Indianapolis	6. Minnesota

1995

AMERICAN CONFERENCE
Eastern Division

	W	L	T	Pct.	Pts.	OP
Buffalo	10	6	0	.625	350	335
Indianapolis*	9	7	0	.563	331	316
Miami*	9	7	0	.563	398	332
New England	6	10	0	.375	294	377
N.Y. Jets	3	13	0	.188	233	384

Central Division

	W	L	T	Pct.	Pts.	OP
Pittsburgh	11	5	0	.688	407	327
Cincinnati	7	9	0	.438	349	374
Houston	7	9	0	.438	348	324
Cleveland	5	11	0	.313	289	356
Jacksonville	4	12	0	.250	275	404

Western Division

	W	L	T	Pct.	Pts.	OP
Kansas City#	13	3	0	.813	358	241
San Diego*	9	7	0	.563	321	323
Seattle	8	8	0	.500	363	366
Denver	8	8	0	.500	388	345
Oakland	8	8	0	.500	348	332

NATIONAL CONFERENCE
Eastern Division

	W	L	T	Pct.	Pts.	OP
Dallas#	12	4	0	.750	435	291
Philadelphia*	10	6	0	.625	318	338
Washington	6	10	0	.375	326	359
N.Y. Giants	5	11	0	.313	290	340
Arizona	4	12	0	.250	275	422

Central Division

	W	L	T	Pct.	Pts.	OP
Green Bay	11	5	0	.688	404	314
Detroit*	10	6	0	.625	436	336
Chicago	9	7	0	.563	392	360
Minnesota	8	8	0	.500	412	385
Tampa Bay	7	9	0	.438	238	335

Western Division

	W	L	T	Pct.	Pts.	OP
San Francisco	11	5	0	.688	457	258
Atlanta*	9	7	0	.563	362	349
St. Louis	7	9	0	.438	309	418
Carolina	7	9	0	.438	289	325
New Orleans	7	9	0	.438	319	348

*Wild Card qualifier for playoffs; #Top playoff seed in conference
Indianapolis finished ahead of Miami based on head-to-head sweep
   (2-0). San Diego was first Wild Card based on head-to-head victory over Indianapolis (1-0). Cincinnati finished ahead of Houston
   based on better division record (4-4 to Oilers' 3-5). Seattle finished ahead of Denver and Oakland based on best head-to-head
   record (3-1 to Broncos' 2-2 and Raiders' 1-3). Denver finished
   ahead of Oakland based on head-to-head sweep (2-0). Philadelphia was first Wild Card ahead of Detroit based on better conference record (9-3 to Lions' 7-5). San Francisco was second playoff seed ahead of Green Bay based on better conference record
   (8-4 to Packers' 7-5). Atlanta was third Wild Card ahead of
   Chicago based on better record against common opponents
   (4-2 to Bears' 3-3). St. Louis finished ahead of Carolina and
   New Orleans based on best head-to-head record (3-1 to
   Panthers' 1-3 and Saints' 2-2). Carolina finished ahead of
   New Orleans based on better conference record (4-8 to 3-9).
Wild Card playoffs: BUFFALO 37, Miami 22;
   Indianapolis 35, SAN DIEGO 20
Divisional playoffs: PITTSBURGH 40, Buffalo 21;
   Indianapolis 10, KANSAS CITY 7
AFC Championship: PITTSBURGH 20, Indianapolis 16
Wild Card playoffs: PHILADELPHIA 58, Detroit 37;
   GREEN BAY 37, Atlanta 20
Divisional playoffs: Green Bay 27, SAN FRANCISCO 17;
   DALLAS 30, Philadelphia 11
NFC Championship: DALLAS 38, Green Bay 27
Super Bowl XXX: Dallas (NFC) 27, Pittsburgh (AFC)17,
   at Sun Devil Stadium, Tempe, Arizona

Playoff Seeds

AFC	NFC
1. Kansas City	1. Dallas
2. Pittsburgh	2. San Francisco
3. Buffalo	3. Green Bay
4. San Diego	4. Philadelphia
5. Indianapolis	5. Detroit
6. Miami	6. Atlanta

1994

AMERICAN CONFERENCE

Eastern Division

	W	L	T	Pct.	Pts.	OP
Miami	10	6	0	.625	389	327
New England*	10	6	0	.625	351	312
Indianapolis	8	8	0	.500	307	320
Buffalo	7	9	0	.438	340	356
N.Y. Jets	6	10	0	.375	264	320

Central Division

	W	L	T	Pct.	Pts.	OP
Pittsburgh#	12	4	0	.750	316	234
Cleveland*	11	5	0	.688	340	204
Cincinnati	3	13	0	.188	276	406
Houston	2	14	0	.125	226	352

Western Division

	W	L	T	Pct.	Pts.	OP
San Diego	11	5	0	.688	381	306
Kansas City*	9	7	0	.563	319	298
L.A. Raiders	9	7	0	.563	303	327
Denver	7	9	0	.438	347	396
Seattle	6	10	0	.375	287	323

NATIONAL CONFERENCE

Eastern Division

	W	L	T	Pct.	Pts.	OP
Dallas	12	4	0	.750	414	248
N.Y. Giants	9	7	0	.563	279	305
Arizona	8	8	0	.500	235	267
Philadelphia	7	9	0	.438	308	308
Washington	3	13	0	.188	320	412

Central Division

	W	L	T	Pct.	Pts.	OP
Minnesota	10	6	0	.625	356	314
Green Bay*	9	7	0	.563	382	287
Detroit*	9	7	0	.563	357	342
Chicago*	9	7	0	.563	271	307
Tampa Bay	6	10	0	.375	251	351

Western Division

	W	L	T	Pct.	Pts.	OP
San Francisco#	13	3	0	.813	505	296
New Orleans	7	9	0	.438	348	407
Atlanta	7	9	0	.438	317	385
L.A. Rams	4	12	0	.250	286	365

*Wild Card qualifier for playoffs; #Top playoff seed in conference
Miami finished ahead of New England based on head-to-head sweep (2-0). Kansas City finished ahead of L.A. Raiders based on head-to-head sweep (2-0). Green Bay was first Wild Card based on best head-to-head record (3-1) vs. Detroit (2-2) and Chicago (1-3) and better conference record (8-4) than N.Y. Giants (6-6). Detroit was second Wild Card based on better division record (4-4) than Chicago (3-5) and head-to-head victory over N.Y. Giants (1-0). Chicago was third Wild Card based on better record against common opponents (4-4) than N.Y. Giants (3-5). New Orleans finished ahead of Atlanta based on head-to-head sweep (2-0).
Wild Card playoffs: MIAMI 27, Kansas City 17; CLEVELAND 20, New England 13
Divisional playoffs: PITTSBURGH 29, Cleveland 9; SAN DIEGO 22, Miami 21
AFC Championship: San Diego 17, PITTSBURGH 13
Wild Card playoffs: GREEN BAY 16, Detroit 12; Chicago 35, MINNESOTA 18
Divisional playoffs: SAN FRANCISCO 44, Chicago 15; DALLAS 35, Green Bay 9
NFC Championship: SAN FRANCISCO 38, Dallas 28
Super Bowl XXIX: San Francisco (NFC) 49, San Diego (AFC) 26, at Joe Robbie Stadium, Miami, Florida

Playoff Seeds

AFC	NFC
1. Pittsburgh	1. San Francisco
2. San Diego	2. Dallas
3. Miami	3. Minnesota
4. Cleveland	4. Green Bay
5. New England	5. Detroit
6. Kansas City	6. Chicago

1993

AMERICAN CONFERENCE

Eastern Division

	W	L	T	Pct.	Pts.	OP
Buffalo#	12	4	0	.750	329	242
Miami	9	7	0	.563	349	351
N.Y. Jets	8	8	0	.500	270	247
New England	5	11	0	.313	238	286
Indianapolis	4	12	0	.250	189	378

Central Division

	W	L	T	Pct.	Pts.	OP
Houston	12	4	0	.750	368	238
Pittsburgh*	9	7	0	.563	308	281
Cleveland	7	9	0	.438	304	307
Cincinnati	3	13	0	.188	187	319

Western Division

	W	L	T	Pct.	Pts.	OP
Kansas City	11	5	0	.688	328	291
L.A. Raiders*	10	6	0	.625	306	326
Denver*	9	7	0	.563	373	284
San Diego	8	8	0	.500	322	290
Seattle	6	10	0	.375	280	314

NATIONAL CONFERENCE

Eastern Division

	W	L	T	Pct.	Pts.	OP
Dallas#	12	4	0	.750	376	229
N.Y. Giants*	11	5	0	.688	288	205
Philadelphia	8	8	0	.500	293	315
Phoenix	7	9	0	.438	326	269
Washington	4	12	0	.250	230	345

Central Division

	W	L	T	Pct.	Pts.	OP
Detroit	10	6	0	.625	298	292
Minnesota*	9	7	0	.563	277	290
Green Bay*	9	7	0	.563	340	282
Chicago	7	9	0	.438	234	230
Tampa Bay	5	11	0	.313	237	376

Western Division

	W	L	T	Pct.	Pts.	OP
San Francisco	10	6	0	.625	473	295
New Orleans	8	8	0	.500	317	343
Atlanta	6	10	0	.375	316	385
L.A. Rams	5	11	0	.313	221	367

*Wild Card qualifier for playoffs; #Top playoff seed in conference
Buffalo was top playoff seed based on head-to-head victory over Houston (1-0). Denver was second Wild Card, and Pittsburgh was third Wild Card ahead of Miami, based on better conference record (8-4 to Steelers' 7-5 to Dolphins' 6-6). San Francisco was second playoff seed based on head-to-head victory over Detroit (1-0). Minnesota finished ahead of Green Bay based on head-to-head sweep (2-0).
Wild Card playoffs: KANSAS CITY 27, Pittsburgh 24 (OT); L.A. RAIDERS 42, Denver 24
Divisional playoffs: BUFFALO 29, L.A. Raiders 23; Kansas City 28, HOUSTON 20
AFC Championship: BUFFALO 30, Kansas City 13
Wild Card playoffs: Green Bay 28, DETROIT 24; N.Y. GIANTS 17, Minnesota 10
Divisional playoffs: SAN FRANCISCO 44, N.Y. Giants 3; DALLAS 27, Green Bay 17
NFC Championship: DALLAS 38, San Francisco 21
Super Bowl XXVIII: Dallas (NFC) 30, Buffalo (AFC) 13, at Georgia Dome, Atlanta, Georgia

Playoff Seeds

AFC	NFC
1. Buffalo	1. Dallas
2. Houston	2. San Francisco
3. Kansas City	3. Detroit
4. L.A. Raiders	4. N.Y. Giants
5. Denver	5. Minnesota
6. Pittsburgh	6. Green Bay

1992

AMERICAN CONFERENCE

Eastern Division

	W	L	T	Pct.	Pts.	OP
Miami	11	5	0	.688	340	281
Buffalo*	11	5	0	.688	381	283
Indianapolis	9	7	0	.563	216	302
N.Y. Jets	4	12	0	.250	220	315
New England	2	14	0	.125	205	363

Central Division

	W	L	T	Pct.	Pts.	OP
Pittsburgh#	11	5	0	.688	299	225
Houston*	10	6	0	.625	352	258
Cleveland	7	9	0	.438	272	275
Cincinnati	5	11	0	.313	274	364

Western Division

	W	L	T	Pct.	Pts.	OP
San Diego	11	5	0	.688	335	241
Kansas City*	10	6	0	.625	348	282
Denver	8	8	0	.500	262	329
L.A. Raiders	7	9	0	.438	249	281
Seattle	2	14	0	.125	140	312

NATIONAL CONFERENCE

Eastern Division

	W	L	T	Pct.	Pts.	OP
Dallas	13	3	0	.813	409	243
Philadelphia*	11	5	0	.688	354	245
Washington*	9	7	0	.563	300	255
N.Y. Giants	6	10	0	.375	306	367
Phoenix	4	12	0	.250	243	332

Central Division

	W	L	T	Pct.	Pts.	OP
Minnesota	11	5	0	.688	374	249
Green Bay	9	7	0	.563	276	296
Tampa Bay	5	11	0	.313	267	365
Chicago	5	11	0	.313	295	361
Detroit	5	11	0	.313	273	332

Western Division

	W	L	T	Pct.	Pts.	OP
San Francisco#	14	2	0	.875	431	236
New Orleans*	12	4	0	.750	330	202
Atlanta	6	10	0	.375	327	414
L.A. Rams	6	10	0	.375	313	383

*Wild Card qualifier for playoffs; #Top playoff seed in conference
Pittsburgh was top playoff seed, and Miami was second playoff seed ahead of San Diego, based on conference record (10-2 to Dolphins' 9-3 to Chargers' 9-5). Miami finished ahead of Buffalo based on better conference record (9-3 to Bills' 7-5). Houston was second Wild Card based on head-to-head victory over Kansas City (1-0). Washington was third Wild Card based on better conference record than Green Bay (7-5 to Packers' 6-6). Tampa Bay finished ahead of Chicago and Detroit based on better conference record (5-9 to Bears' 4-8 and Lions' 3-9). Atlanta finished ahead of L.A. Rams based on better record against common opponents (5-7 to Rams' 4-8).
Wild Card playoffs: SAN DIEGO 17, Kansas City 0; BUFFALO 41, Houston 38 (OT).
Divisional playoffs: Buffalo 24, PITTSBURGH 3; MIAMI 31, San Diego 0.
AFC Championship: Buffalo 29, MIAMI 10.
Wild Card playoffs: Washington 24, MINNESOTA 7; Philadelphia 36, NEW ORLEANS 20.
Divisional playoffs: SAN FRANCISCO 20, Washington 13; DALLAS 34, Philadelphia 10.
NFC Championship: Dallas 30, SAN FRANCISCO 20.
Super Bowl XXVII: Dallas (NFC) 52, Buffalo (AFC) 17, at Rose Bowl, Pasadena, California

Playoff Seeds

AFC	NFC
1. Pittsburgh	1. San Francisco
2. Miami	**2. Dallas**
3. San Diego	3. Minnesota
4. Buffalo	4. New Orleans
5. Houston	5. Philadelphia
6. Kansas City	6. Washington

1991

AMERICAN CONFERENCE

Eastern Division

	W	L	T	Pct.	Pts.	OP
Buffalo#	13	3	0	.813	458	318
N.Y. Jets*	8	8	0	.500	314	293
Miami	8	8	0	.500	343	349
New England	6	10	0	.375	211	305
Indianapolis	1	15	0	.063	143	381

Central Division

	W	L	T	Pct.	Pts.	OP
Houston	11	5	0	.688	386	251
Pittsburgh	7	9	0	.438	292	344
Cleveland	6	10	0	.375	293	298
Cincinnati	3	13	0	.188	263	435

Western Division

	W	L	T	Pct.	Pts.	OP
Denver	12	4	0	.750	304	235
Kansas City*	10	6	0	.625	322	252
L.A. Raiders*	9	7	0	.563	298	297
Seattle	7	9	0	.438	276	261
San Diego	4	12	0	.250	274	342

NATIONAL CONFERENCE

Eastern Division

	W	L	T	Pct.	Pts.	OP
Washington#	14	2	0	.875	485	224
Dallas*	11	5	0	.688	342	310
Philadelphia	10	6	0	.625	285	244
N.Y. Giants	8	8	0	.500	281	297
Phoenix	4	12	0	.250	196	344

Central Division

	W	L	T	Pct.	Pts.	OP
Detroit	12	4	0	.750	339	295
Chicago*	11	5	0	.688	299	269
Minnesota	8	8	0	.500	301	306
Green Bay	4	12	0	.250	273	313
Tampa Bay	3	13	0	.188	199	365

Western Division

	W	L	T	Pct.	Pts.	OP
New Orleans	11	5	0	.688	341	211
Atlanta*	10	6	0	.625	361	338
San Francisco	10	6	0	.625	393	239
L.A. Rams	3	13	0	.188	234	390

*Wild Card qualifier for playoffs; #Top playoff seed in conference
N.Y. Jets finished ahead of Miami based on head-to-head sweep (2-0). Chicago was first Wild Card based on better conference record than Dallas (9-3 to Cowboys' 8-4). Atlanta finished ahead of San Francisco based on head-to-head sweep (2-0), and was third Wild Card ahead of Philadelphia based on better conference record (7-5 to Eagles' 6-6).
Wild Card playoffs: KANSAS CITY 10, L.A. Raiders 6; HOUSTON 17, N.Y. Jets 10.
Divisional playoffs: DENVER 26, Houston 24; BUFFALO 37, Kansas City 14.
AFC Championship: BUFFALO 10, Denver 7.
Wild Card playoffs: Atlanta 27, NEW ORLEANS 20; Dallas 17, CHICAGO 13.
Divisional playoffs: WASHINGTON 24, Atlanta 7; DETROIT 38, Dallas 6.
NFC Championship: WASHINGTON 41, Detroit 10.
Super Bowl XXVI: Washington (NFC) 37, Buffalo (AFC) 24, at Hubert H. Humphrey Metrodome, Minneapolis, Minnesota

Playoff Seeds

AFC	NFC
1. Buffalo	**1. Washington**
2. Denver	2. Detroit
3. Houston	3. New Orleans
4. Kansas City	4. Chicago
5. L.A. Raiders	5. Dallas
6. N.Y. Jets	6. Atlanta

1990

AMERICAN CONFERENCE

Eastern Division

	W	L	T	Pct.	Pts.	OP
Buffalo#	13	3	0	.813	428	263
Miami*	12	4	0	.750	336	242
Indianapolis	7	9	0	.438	281	353
N.Y. Jets	6	10	0	.375	295	345
New England	1	15	0	.063	181	446

Central Division

	W	L	T	Pct.	Pts.	OP
Cincinnati	9	7	0	.563	360	352
Houston*	9	7	0	.563	405	307
Pittsburgh	9	7	0	.563	292	240
Cleveland	3	13	0	.188	228	462

Western Division

	W	L	T	Pct.	Pts.	OP
L.A. Raiders	12	4	0	.750	337	268
Kansas City*	11	5	0	.688	369	257
Seattle	9	7	0	.563	306	286
San Diego	6	10	0	.375	315	281
Denver	5	11	0	.313	331	374

NATIONAL CONFERENCE

Eastern Division

	W	L	T	Pct.	Pts.	OP
N.Y. Giants	13	3	0	.813	335	211
Philadelphia*	10	6	0	.625	396	299
Washington*	10	6	0	.625	381	301
Dallas	7	9	0	.438	244	308
Phoenix	5	11	0	.313	268	396

Central Division

	W	L	T	Pct.	Pts.	OP
Chicago	11	5	0	.688	348	280
Tampa Bay	6	10	0	.375	264	367
Detroit	6	10	0	.375	373	413
Green Bay	6	10	0	.375	271	347
Minnesota	6	10	0	.375	351	326

Western Division

	W	L	T	Pct.	Pts.	OP
San Francisco#	14	2	0	.875	353	239
New Orleans*	8	8	0	.500	274	275
L.A. Rams	5	11	0	.313	345	412
Atlanta	5	11	0	.313	348	365

*Wild Card qualifier for playoffs; #Top playoff seed in conference
Cincinnati finished ahead of Houston and Pittsburgh based on best head-to-head record (3-1 to Oilers' 2-2 to Steelers' 1-3). Houston was Wild Card based on better conference record (8-4) than Seattle (7-5) and Pittsburgh (6-6). Philadelphia finished ahead of Washington based on better division record (5-3 to Redskins' 4-4). Tampa Bay was second in NFC Central based on best head-to-head record (5-1) against Detroit (2-4), Green Bay (3-3), and Minnesota (2-4). Detroit finished third based on best net division points (minus 8) against Green Bay (minus 40). Green Bay finished ahead of Minnesota based on better conference record (5-7 to Vikings' 4-8). The L.A. Rams finished ahead of Atlanta based on net points in division (plus 1 to Falcons' minus 31).
Wild Card playoffs: MIAMI 17, Kansas City 16;
   CINCINNATI 41, Houston 14
Divisional playoffs: BUFFALO 44, Miami 34;
   L.A. RAIDERS 20, Cincinnati 10
AFC Championship: BUFFALO 51, L.A. Raiders 3
Wild Card playoffs: Washington 20, PHILADELPHIA 6;
   CHICAGO 16, New Orleans 6
Divisional playoffs: SAN FRANCISCO 28, Washington 10;
   N.Y. GIANTS 31, Chicago 3
NFC Championship: N.Y. Giants 15, SAN FRANCISCO 13
Super Bowl XXV: N.Y. Giants (NFC) 20, Buffalo (AFC) 19,
   at Tampa Stadium, Tampa, Florida

Playoff Seeds

AFC	NFC
1. Buffalo	1. San Francisco
2. L.A. Raiders	**2. N.Y. Giants**
3. Cincinnati	3. Chicago
4. Miami	4. Philadelphia
5. Kansas City	5. Washington
6. Houston	6. New Orleans

1989

AMERICAN CONFERENCE

Eastern Division

	W	L	T	Pct.	Pts.	OP
Buffalo	9	7	0	.563	409	317
Indianapolis	8	8	0	.500	298	301
Miami	8	8	0	.500	331	379
New England	5	11	0	.313	297	391
N.Y. Jets	4	12	0	.250	253	411

Central Division

	W	L	T	Pct.	Pts.	OP
Cleveland	9	6	1	.594	334	254
Houston*	9	7	0	.563	365	412
Pittsburgh*	9	7	0	.563	265	326
Cincinnati	8	8	0	.500	404	285

Western Division

	W	L	T	Pct.	Pts.	OP
Denver#	11	5	0	.688	362	226
Kansas City	8	7	1	.531	318	286
L.A. Raiders	8	8	0	.500	315	297
Seattle	7	9	0	.438	241	327
San Diego	6	10	0	.375	266	290

NATIONAL CONFERENCE

Eastern Division

	W	L	T	Pct.	Pts.	OP
N.Y. Giants	12	4	0	.750	348	252
Philadelphia*	11	5	0	.688	342	274
Washington	10	6	0	.625	386	308
Phoenix	5	11	0	.313	258	377
Dallas	1	15	0	.063	204	393

Central Division

	W	L	T	Pct.	Pts.	OP
Minnesota	10	6	0	.625	351	275
Green Bay	10	6	0	.625	362	356
Detroit	7	9	0	.438	312	364
Chicago	6	10	0	.375	358	377
Tampa Bay	5	11	0	.313	320	419

Western Division

	W	L	T	Pct.	Pts.	OP
San Francisco#	14	2	0	.875	442	253
L.A. Rams*	11	5	0	.688	426	344
New Orleans	9	7	0	.563	386	301
Atlanta	3	13	0	.188	279	437

*Wild Card qualifier for playoffs; #Top playoff seed in conference
Indianapolis finished ahead of Miami based on better conference record (7-5 vs. Dolphins' 6-8). Houston finished ahead of Pittsburgh based on head-to-head sweep (2-0). The L.A. Rams did not play San Francisco in the divisional playoffs because, from 1970-1989, two teams from the same division could not meet prior to the conference championship game. Philadelphia was first Wild Card ahead of L.A. Rams based on better record against common opponents (6-3 to Rams' 5-4). Minnesota finished ahead of Green Bay based on better division record (6-2 vs. Packers' 5-3).
Wild Card playoff: Pittsburgh 26, HOUSTON 23 (OT)
Divisional playoffs: CLEVELAND 34, Buffalo 30;
   DENVER 24, Pittsburgh 23
AFC Championship: DENVER 37, Cleveland 21
Wild Card playoff: L.A. Rams 21, PHILADELPHIA 7
Divisional playoffs: L.A. Rams 19, N.Y. GIANTS 13 (OT);
   SAN FRANCISCO 41, Minnesota 13
NFC Championship: SAN FRANCISCO 30, L.A. Rams 3
Super Bowl XXIV: San Francisco (NFC) 55, Denver (AFC) 10,
   at Louisiana Superdome, New Orleans, Louisiana

1988

AMERICAN CONFERENCE
Eastern Division

	W	L	T	Pct.	Pts.	OP
Buffalo	12	4	0	.750	329	237
Indianapolis	9	7	0	.563	354	315
New England	9	7	0	.563	250	284
N.Y. Jets	8	7	1	.531	372	354
Miami	6	10	0	.375	319	380

Central Division

	W	L	T	Pct.	Pts.	OP
Cincinnati#	12	4	0	.750	448	329
Cleveland*	10	6	0	.625	304	288
Houston*	10	6	0	.625	424	365
Pittsburgh	5	11	0	.313	336	421

Western Division

	W	L	T	Pct.	Pts.	OP
Seattle	9	7	0	.563	339	329
Denver	8	8	0	.500	327	352
L.A. Raiders	7	9	0	.438	325	369
San Diego	6	10	0	.375	231	332
Kansas City	4	11	1	.281	254	320

NATIONAL CONFERENCE
Eastern Division

	W	L	T	Pct.	Pts.	OP
Philadelphia	10	6	0	.625	379	319
N.Y. Giants	10	6	0	.625	359	304
Washington	7	9	0	.438	345	387
Phoenix	7	9	0	.438	344	398
Dallas	3	13	0	.188	265	381

Central Division

	W	L	T	Pct.	Pts.	OP
Chicago#	12	4	0	.750	312	215
Minnesota*	11	5	0	.688	406	233
Tampa Bay	5	11	0	.313	261	350
Detroit	4	12	0	.250	220	313
Green Bay	4	12	0	.250	240	315

Western Division

	W	L	T	Pct.	Pts.	OP
San Francisco	10	6	0	.625	369	294
L.A. Rams*	10	6	0	.625	407	293
New Orleans	10	6	0	.625	312	283
Atlanta	5	11	0	.313	244	315

*Wild Card qualifier for playoffs; #Top playoff seed in conference
Cincinnati was top playoff seed ahead of Buffalo based on head-to-head victory (1-0). Indianapolis finished ahead of New England based on better record against common opponents (7-5 to Patriots' 6-6). Cleveland finished ahead of Houston based on better division record (4-2 to Oilers' 3-3). Houston did not play Cincinnati, and Minnesota did not play Chicago in the divisional playoffs because, from 1970-1989, two teams from the same division could not meet prior to the conference championship game. Philadelphia finished first in NFC East based on head-to-head sweep of N.Y. Giants (2-0). Washington finished third in NFC East based on better division record (4-4) than Phoenix (3-5). Detroit finished fourth in NFC Central based on head-to-head sweep of Green Bay (2-0). San Francisco finished first in NFC West based on better head-to-head record (3-1) against L.A. Rams (2-2) and New Orleans (1-3). L.A. Rams finished second in NFC West based on better division record (4-2) than New Orleans (3-3) and earned Wild-Card position based on better conference record (8-4) than N.Y. Giants (9-5) and New Orleans (6-6).
Wild Card playoff: Houston 24, CLEVELAND 23
Divisional playoffs: CINCINNATI 21, Seattle 13;
    BUFFALO 17, Houston 10
AFC Championship: CINCINNATI 21, Buffalo 10
Wild Card playoff: MINNESOTA 28, L.A. Rams 17
Divisional playoffs: CHICAGO 20, Philadelphia 12;
    SAN FRANCISCO 34, Minnesota 9
NFC Championship: San Francisco 28, CHICAGO 3
Super Bowl XXIII: San Francisco (NFC) 20, Cincinnati (AFC) 16,
    at Joe Robbie Stadium, Miami, Florida

1987

AMERICAN CONFERENCE
Eastern Division

	W	L	T	Pct.	Pts.	OP
Indianapolis	9	6	0	.600	300	238
New England	8	7	0	.533	320	293
Miami	8	7	0	.533	362	335
Buffalo	7	8	0	.467	270	305
N.Y. Jets	6	9	0	.400	334	360

Central Division

	W	L	T	Pct.	Pts.	OP
Cleveland	10	5	0	.667	390	239
Houston*	9	6	0	.600	345	349
Pittsburgh	8	7	0	.533	285	299
Cincinnati	4	11	0	.267	285	370

Western Division

	W	L	T	Pct.	Pts.	OP
Denver#	10	4	1	.700	379	288
Seattle*	9	6	0	.600	371	314
San Diego	8	7	0	.533	253	317
L.A. Raiders	5	10	0	.333	301	289
Kansas City	4	11	0	.267	273	388

NATIONAL CONFERENCE
Eastern Division

	W	L	T	Pct.	Pts.	OP
Washington	11	4	0	.733	379	285
Dallas	7	8	0	.467	340	348
St. Louis	7	8	0	.467	362	368
Philadelphia	7	8	0	.467	337	380
N.Y. Giants	6	9	0	.400	280	312

Central Division

	W	L	T	Pct.	Pts.	OP
Chicago	11	4	0	.733	356	282
Minnesota*	8	7	0	.533	336	335
Green Bay	5	9	1	.367	255	300
Tampa Bay	4	11	0	.267	286	360
Detroit	4	11	0	.267	269	384

Western Division

	W	L	T	Pct.	Pts.	OP
San Francisco#	13	2	0	.867	459	253
New Orleans*	12	3	0	.800	422	283
L.A. Rams	6	9	0	.400	317	361
Atlanta	3	12	0	.200	205	436

*Wild Card qualifier for playoffs; #Top playoff seed in conference
New England finished ahead of Miami based on head-to-head sweep (2-0). Houston was first Wild Card ahead of Seattle based on better conference record (7-4 to Seahawks' 5-6). Chicago was second playoff seed ahead of Washington based on better conference record (9-2 to Redskins' 9-3). Dallas finished ahead of St. Louis and Philadelphia based on better division record (4-4 to Cardinals' 3-5 and Eagles' 3-5). St. Louis finished ahead of Philadelphia based on better conference record (7-7 to Eagles' 4-7). Tampa Bay finished ahead of Detroit based on better division record (3-4 to Lions' 2-5).
Wild Card playoff: HOUSTON 23, Seattle 20 (OT)
Divisional playoffs: CLEVELAND 38, Indianapolis 21;
    DENVER 34, Houston 10
AFC Championship: DENVER 38, Cleveland 33
Wild Card playoff: Minnesota 44, NEW ORLEANS 10
Divisional playoffs: Minnesota 36, SAN FRANCISCO 24;
    Washington 21, CHICAGO 17
NFC Championship: WASHINGTON 17, Minnesota 10
Super Bowl XXII: Washington (NFC) 42, Denver (AFC) 10,
    at San Diego Jack Murphy Stadium, San Diego, California
Note: 1987 regular season was reduced from 16 to 15 games for
    each team due to players' strike.

1986

AMERICAN CONFERENCE

Eastern Division

	W	L	T	Pct.	Pts.	OP
New England	11	5	0	.688	412	307
N.Y. Jets*	10	6	0	.625	364	386
Miami	8	8	0	.500	430	405
Buffalo	4	12	0	.250	287	348
Indianapolis	3	13	0	.188	229	400

Central Division

	W	L	T	Pct.	Pts.	OP
Cleveland#	12	4	0	.750	391	310
Cincinnati	10	6	0	.625	409	394
Pittsburgh	6	10	0	.375	307	336
Houston	5	11	0	.313	274	329

Western Division

	W	L	T	Pct.	Pts.	OP
Denver	11	5	0	.688	378	327
Kansas City*	10	6	0	.625	358	326
Seattle	10	6	0	.625	366	293
L.A. Raiders	8	8	0	.500	323	346
San Diego	4	12	0	.250	335	396

NATIONAL CONFERENCE

Eastern Division

	W	L	T	Pct.	Pts.	OP
N.Y. Giants#	14	2	0	.875	371	236
Washington*	12	4	0	.750	368	296
Dallas	7	9	0	.438	346	337
Philadelphia	5	10	1	.344	256	312
St. Louis	4	11	1	.281	218	351

Central Division

	W	L	T	Pct.	Pts.	OP
Chicago	14	2	0	.875	352	187
Minnesota	9	7	0	.563	398	273
Detroit	5	11	0	.313	277	326
Green Bay	4	12	0	.250	254	418
Tampa Bay	2	14	0	.125	239	473

Western Division

	W	L	T	Pct.	Pts.	OP
San Francisco	10	5	1	.656	374	247
L.A. Rams*	10	6	0	.625	309	267
Atlanta	7	8	1	.469	280	280
New Orleans	7	9	0	.438	288	287

*Wild Card qualifier for playoffs; #Top playoff seed in conference

Denver was second playoff seed ahead of New England based on head-to-head victory (1-0). N.Y. Jets were first Wild Card based on better conference record (8-4) than Kansas City (9-5), Seattle (7-5), and Cincinnati (7-5). Kansas City was second Wild Card based on better conference record (9-5) than Seattle (7-5) and Cincinnati (7-5). N.Y. Giants were top playoff seed based on better conference record than Chicago (11-1 to Bears' 10-2). Washington did not play the N.Y. Giants in the divisional playoffs because, from 1970-1989, two teams from the same division could not meet prior to the conference championship game.

Wild Card playoff: N.Y. JETS 35, Kansas City 15

Divisional playoffs: CLEVELAND 23, N.Y. Jets 20 (OT); DENVER 22, New England 17

AFC Championship: Denver 23, CLEVELAND 20 (OT)

Wild Card playoff: WASHINGTON 19, L.A. Rams 7

Divisional playoffs: Washington 27, CHICAGO 13 N.Y. GIANTS 49, San Francisco 3

NFC Championship: N.Y. GIANTS 17, Washington 0

Super Bowl XXI: N.Y. Giants (NFC) 39, Denver (AFC) 20, at Rose Bowl, Pasadena, California

1985

AMERICAN CONFERENCE

Eastern Division

	W	L	T	Pct.	Pts.	OP
Miami	12	4	0	.750	428	320
N.Y. Jets*	11	5	0	.688	393	264
New England*	11	5	0	.688	362	290
Indianapolis	5	11	0	.313	320	386
Buffalo	2	14	0	.125	200	381

Central Division

	W	L	T	Pct.	Pts.	OP
Cleveland	8	8	0	.500	287	294
Cincinnati	7	9	0	.438	441	437
Pittsburgh	7	9	0	.438	379	355
Houston	5	11	0	.313	284	412

Western Division

	W	L	T	Pct.	Pts.	OP
L.A. Raiders#	12	4	0	.750	354	308
Denver	11	5	0	.688	380	329
Seattle	8	8	0	.500	349	303
San Diego	8	8	0	.500	467	435
Kansas City	6	10	0	.375	317	360

NATIONAL CONFERENCE

Eastern Division

	W	L	T	Pct.	Pts.	OP
Dallas	10	6	0	.625	357	333
N.Y. Giants*	10	6	0	.625	399	283
Washington	10	6	0	.625	297	312
Philadelphia	7	9	0	.438	286	310
St. Louis	5	11	0	.313	278	414

Central Division

	W	L	T	Pct.	Pts.	OP
Chicago#	15	1	0	.938	456	198
Green Bay	8	8	0	.500	337	355
Minnesota	7	9	0	.438	346	359
Detroit	7	9	0	.438	307	366
Tampa Bay	2	14	0	.125	294	448

Western Division

	W	L	T	Pct.	Pts.	OP
L.A. Rams	11	5	0	.688	340	277
San Francisco*	10	6	0	.625	411	263
New Orleans	5	11	0	.313	294	401
Atlanta	4	12	0	.250	282	452

*Wild Card qualifier for playoffs; #Top playoff seed in conference

L.A. Raiders were top playoff seed ahead of Miami based on better record against common opponents (5-1 to 4-2). N.Y. Jets were first Wild Card based on better conference record (9-3) than New England (8-4) and Denver (8-4). New England was second Wild Card ahead of Denver based on better record against common opponents (4-2 to Broncos' 3-3). Cincinnati finished ahead of Pittsburgh based on head-to-head sweep (2-0). Seattle finished ahead of San Diego based on head-to-head sweep (2-0). Dallas finished ahead of N.Y. Giants and Washington based on better head-to-head record (4-0 to Giants' 1-3 and Redskins' 1-3). N.Y. Giants were first Wild Card based on better conference record (8-4) than San Francisco (7-5) and Washington (6-6). San Francisco was second Wild Card based on head-to-head victory over Washington (1-0). Minnesota finished ahead of Detroit based on better division record (3-5 to Lions' 2-6).

Wild Card playoff: New England 26, N.Y. JETS 14

Divisional playoffs: MIAMI 24, Cleveland 21; New England 27, L.A. RAIDERS 20

AFC Championship: New England 31, MIAMI 14

Wild Card playoff: N.Y. GIANTS 17, San Francisco 3

Divisional playoffs: L.A. RAMS 20, Dallas 0; CHICAGO 21, N.Y. Giants 0

NFC Championship: CHICAGO 24, L.A. Rams 0

Super Bowl XX: Chicago (NFC) 46, New England (AFC) 10, at Louisiana Superdome, New Orleans, Louisiana

1984

AMERICAN CONFERENCE

Eastern Division

	W	L	T	Pct.	Pts.	OP
Miami#	14	2	0	.875	513	298
New England	9	7	0	.563	362	352
N.Y. Jets	7	9	0	.438	332	364
Indianapolis	4	12	0	.250	239	414
Buffalo	2	14	0	.125	250	454

Central Division

	W	L	T	Pct.	Pts.	OP
Pittsburgh	9	7	0	.563	387	310
Cincinnati	8	8	0	.500	339	339
Cleveland	5	11	0	.313	250	297
Houston	3	13	0	.188	240	437

Western Division

	W	L	T	Pct.	Pts.	OP
Denver	13	3	0	.813	353	241
Seattle*	12	4	0	.750	418	282
L.A. Raiders*	11	5	0	.688	368	278
Kansas City	8	8	0	.500	314	324
San Diego	7	9	0	.438	394	413

NATIONAL CONFERENCE

Eastern Division

	W	L	T	Pct.	Pts.	OP
Washington	11	5	0	.688	426	310
N.Y. Giants*	9	7	0	.563	299	301
St. Louis	9	7	0	.563	423	345
Dallas	9	7	0	.563	308	308
Philadelphia	6	9	1	.406	278	320

Central Division

	W	L	T	Pct.	Pts.	OP
Chicago	10	6	0	.625	325	248
Green Bay	8	8	0	.500	390	309
Tampa Bay	6	10	0	.375	335	380
Detroit	4	11	1	.281	283	408
Minnesota	3	13	0	.188	276	484

Western Division

	W	L	T	Pct.	Pts.	OP
San Francisco#	15	1	0	.938	475	227
L.A. Rams*	10	6	0	.625	346	316
New Orleans	7	9	0	.438	298	361
Atlanta	4	12	0	.250	281	382

*Wild Card qualifier for playoffs; #Top playoff seed in conference
N.Y. Giants finished ahead of St. Louis and Dallas based on best head-to-head record (3-1 to Cardinals' 2-2 and Cowboys' 1-3). St. Louis finished ahead of Dallas based on better division record (5-3 to Cowboys' 3-5).
Wild Card playoff: SEATTLE 13, L.A. Raiders 7
Divisional playoffs: MIAMI 31, Seattle 10;
   Pittsburgh 24, DENVER 17
AFC Championship: MIAMI 45, Pittsburgh 28
Wild Card playoff: N.Y. Giants 16, L.A. RAMS 13
Divisional playoffs: SAN FRANCISCO 21, N.Y. Giants 10;
   Chicago 23, WASHINGTON 19
NFC Championship: SAN FRANCISCO 23, Chicago 0
Super Bowl XIX: San Francisco (NFC) 38, Miami (AFC) 16,
   at Stanford Stadium, Stanford, California

1983

AMERICAN CONFERENCE

Eastern Division

	W	L	T	Pct.	Pts.	OP
Miami	12	4	0	.750	389	250
New England	8	8	0	.500	274	289
Buffalo	8	8	0	.500	283	351
Baltimore	7	9	0	.438	264	354
N.Y. Jets	7	9	0	.438	313	331

Central Division

	W	L	T	Pct.	Pts.	OP
Pittsburgh	10	6	0	.625	355	303
Cleveland	9	7	0	.563	356	342
Cincinnati	7	9	0	.438	346	302
Houston	2	14	0	.125	288	460

Western Division

	W	L	T	Pct.	Pts.	OP
L.A. Raiders#	12	4	0	.750	442	338
Seattle*	9	7	0	.563	403	397
Denver*	9	7	0	.563	302	327
San Diego	6	10	0	.375	358	462
Kansas City	6	10	0	.375	386	367

NATIONAL CONFERENCE

Eastern Division

	W	L	T	Pct.	Pts.	OP
Washington#	14	2	0	.875	541	332
Dallas*	12	4	0	.750	479	360
St. Louis	8	7	1	.531	374	428
Philadelphia	5	11	0	.313	233	322
N.Y. Giants	3	12	1	.219	267	347

Central Division

	W	L	T	Pct.	Pts.	OP
Detroit	9	7	0	.563	347	286
Green Bay	8	8	0	.500	429	439
Chicago	8	8	0	.500	311	301
Minnesota	8	8	0	.500	316	348
Tampa Bay	2	14	0	.125	241	380

Western Division

	W	L	T	Pct.	Pts.	OP
San Francisco	10	6	0	.625	432	293
L.A. Rams*	9	7	0	.563	361	344
New Orleans	8	8	0	.500	319	337
Atlanta	7	9	0	.438	370	389

*Wild Card qualifier for playoffs; #Top playoff seed in conference
L.A. Raiders were top playoff seed ahead of Miami based on head-to-head victory (1-0). Seattle was second Wild Card ahead of Denver based on better division record (5-3 to Broncos' 3-5) after Cleveland was eliminated from three-way tie based on head-to-head record (Seattle and Denver 2-1 to Browns' 0-2). Seattle did not play the L.A. Raiders in the divisional playoffs because, from 1970-1989, two teams from the same division could not meet prior to the conference championship game. New England finished ahead of Buffalo based on head-to-head sweep (2-0). Baltimore finished ahead of N.Y. Jets based on better conference record (5-9 to Jets' 4-8). San Diego finished ahead of Kansas City based on head-to-head sweep (2-0). Green Bay finished ahead of Chicago based on better record against common opponents (5-5 to Bears' 4-6) after Minnesota was eliminated from three-way tie based on conference record (Chicago 7-7 and Green Bay 6-6 to Vikings' 4-8).
Wild Card playoff: SEATTLE 31, Denver 7
Divisional playoffs: Seattle 27, MIAMI 20;
   L.A. RAIDERS 38, Pittsburgh 10
AFC Championship: L.A. RAIDERS 30, Seattle 14
Wild Card playoff: L.A. Rams 24, DALLAS 17
Divisional playoffs: SAN FRANCISCO 24, Detroit 23;
   WASHINGTON 51, L.A. Rams 7
NFC Championship: WASHINGTON 24, San Francisco 21
Super Bowl XVIII: L.A. Raiders (AFC) 38, Washington (NFC) 9,
   at Tampa Stadium, Tampa, Florida

1982

AMERICAN CONFERENCE

	W	L	T	Pct.	Pts.	OP
L.A. Raiders#	8	1	0	.889	260	200
Miami	7	2	0	.778	198	131
Cincinnati	7	2	0	.778	232	177
Pittsburgh	6	3	0	.667	204	146
San Diego	6	3	0	.667	288	221
N.Y. Jets	6	3	0	.667	245	166
New England	5	4	0	.556	143	157
Cleveland	4	5	0	.444	140	182
Buffalo	4	5	0	.444	150	154
Seattle	4	5	0	.444	127	147
Kansas City	3	6	0	.333	176	184
Denver	2	7	0	.222	148	226
Houston	1	8	0	.111	136	245
Baltimore	0	8	1	.056	113	236

NATIONAL CONFERENCE

	W	L	T	Pct.	Pts.	OP
Washington#	8	1	0	.889	190	128
Dallas	6	3	0	.667	226	145
Green Bay	5	3	1	.611	226	169
Minnesota	5	4	0	.556	187	198
Atlanta	5	4	0	.556	183	199
St. Louis	5	4	0	.556	135	170
Tampa Bay	5	4	0	.556	158	178
Detroit	4	5	0	.444	181	176
New Orleans	4	5	0	.444	129	160
N.Y. Giants	4	5	0	.444	164	160
San Francisco	3	6	0	.333	209	206
Chicago	3	6	0	.333	141	174
Philadelphia	3	6	0	.333	191	195
L.A. Rams	2	7	0	.222	200	250

As the result of a 57-day players' strike, the 1982 NFL regular season schedule was reduced from 16 weeks to 9. At the conclusion of the regular season, the NFL conducted a 16-team postseason Super Bowl Tournament. Eight teams from each conference were seeded 1-8 based on their records during the season.

#Top playoff seed in conference

Miami finished ahead of Cincinnati based on better conference record (6-1 to Bengals' 6-2). Pittsburgh finished ahead of San Diego based on better record against common opponents (3-1 to Chargers' 2-1) after N.Y. Jets were eliminated from three-way tie based on conference record (Pittsburgh and San Diego 5-3 to Jets' 2-3). Cleveland finished ahead of Buffalo and Seattle based on better conference record (4-3 to Bills' 3-3 to Seahawks' 3-5). Buffalo finished ahead of Seattle based on better conference record (3-3 to Seahawks' 3-5). Minnesota (4-1), Atlanta (4-3), St. Louis (5-4), Tampa Bay (3-3) seeds were determined by best won-lost record in conference games. Detroit finished ahead of New Orleans and the N.Y. Giants based on best conference record (4-4 to Saints' 3-5 to Giants' 3-5). San Francisco finished ahead of Chicago, and Chicago finished ahead of Philadelphia, based on conference record (49ers' 2-3 to Bears' 2-5 to Eagles' 1-5).

First round playoff: MIAMI 28, New England 13;
  L.A. RAIDERS 27, Cleveland 10;
  N.Y. Jets 44, CINCINNATI 17;
  San Diego 31, PITTSBURGH 28
Second round playoff: N.Y. Jets 17, L.A. RAIDERS 14;
  MIAMI 34, San Diego 13
AFC Championship: MIAMI 14, N.Y. Jets 0
First round playoff: WASHINGTON 31, Detroit 7;
  GREEN BAY 41, St. Louis 16;
  MINNESOTA 30, Atlanta 24;
  DALLAS 30, Tampa Bay 17
Second round playoff: WASHINGTON 21, Minnesota 7;
  DALLAS 37, Green Bay 26
NFC Championship: WASHINGTON 31, Dallas 17
Super Bowl XVII: Washington (NFC) 27, Miami (AFC) 17,
  at Rose Bowl, Pasadena, California

1981

AMERICAN CONFERENCE

Eastern Division

	W	L	T	Pct.	Pts.	OP
Miami	11	4	1	.719	345	275
N.Y. Jets*	10	5	1	.656	355	287
Buffalo*	10	6	0	.625	311	276
Baltimore	2	14	0	.125	259	533
New England	2	14	0	.125	322	370

Central Division

	W	L	T	Pct.	Pts.	OP
Cincinnati#	12	4	0	.750	421	304
Pittsburgh	8	8	0	.500	356	297
Houston	7	9	0	.438	281	355
Cleveland	5	11	0	.313	276	375

Western Division

	W	L	T	Pct.	Pts.	OP
San Diego	10	6	0	.625	478	390
Denver	10	6	0	.625	321	289
Kansas City	9	7	0	.563	343	290
Oakland	7	9	0	.438	273	343
Seattle	6	10	0	.375	322	388

NATIONAL CONFERENCE

Eastern Division

	W	L	T	Pct.	Pts.	OP
Dallas	12	4	0	.750	367	277
Philadelphia*	10	6	0	.625	368	221
N.Y. Giants*	9	7	0	.563	295	257
Washington	8	8	0	.500	347	349
St. Louis	7	9	0	.438	315	408

Central Division

	W	L	T	Pct.	Pts.	OP
Tampa Bay	9	7	0	.563	315	268
Detroit	8	8	0	.500	397	322
Green Bay	8	8	0	.500	324	361
Minnesota	7	9	0	.438	325	369
Chicago	6	10	0	.375	253	324

Western Division

	W	L	T	Pct.	Pts.	OP
San Francisco#	13	3	0	.813	357	250
Atlanta	7	9	0	.438	426	355
Los Angeles	6	10	0	.375	303	351
New Orleans	4	12	0	.250	207	378

*Wild Card qualifier for playoffs; #Top playoff seed in conference

Baltimore finished ahead of New England based on head-to-head sweep (2-0). San Diego finished ahead of Denver based on better division record (6-2 to Broncos' 5-3). Buffalo was second Wild Card based on head-to-head victory over Denver (1-0). Detroit finished ahead of Green Bay based on better record against common opponents (5-5 to Packers' 4-6).

Wild Card playoff: Buffalo 31, N.Y. JETS 27
Divisional playoffs: San Diego 41, MIAMI 38 (OT);
  CINCINNATI 28, Buffalo 21
AFC Championship: CINCINNATI 27, San Diego 7
Wild Card playoff: N.Y. Giants 27, PHILADELPHIA 21
Divisional playoffs: DALLAS 38, Tampa Bay 0;
  SAN FRANCISCO 38, N.Y. Giants 24
NFC Championship: SAN FRANCISCO 28, Dallas 27
Super Bowl XVI: San Francisco (NFC) 26, Cincinnati (AFC) 21,
  at Silverdome, Pontiac, Michigan

1980

AMERICAN CONFERENCE

Eastern Division

	W	L	T	Pct.	Pts.	OP
Buffalo	11	5	0	.688	320	260
New England	10	6	0	.625	441	325
Miami	8	8	0	.500	266	305
Baltimore	7	9	0	.438	355	387
N.Y. Jets	4	12	0	.250	302	395

Central Division

	W	L	T	Pct.	Pts.	OP
Cleveland	11	5	0	.688	357	310
Houston*	11	5	0	.688	295	251
Pittsburgh	9	7	0	.563	352	313
Cincinnati	6	10	0	.375	244	312

Western Division

	W	L	T	Pct.	Pts.	OP
San Diego#	11	5	0	.688	418	327
Oakland*	11	5	0	.688	364	306
Kansas City	8	8	0	.500	319	336
Denver	8	8	0	.500	310	323
Seattle	4	12	0	.250	291	408

NATIONAL CONFERENCE

Eastern Division

	W	L	T	Pct.	Pts.	OP
Philadelphia	12	4	0	.750	384	222
Dallas*	12	4	0	.750	454	311
Washington	6	10	0	.375	261	293
St. Louis	5	11	0	.313	299	350
N.Y. Giants	4	12	0	.250	249	425

Central Division

	W	L	T	Pct.	Pts.	OP
Minnesota	9	7	0	.563	317	308
Detroit	9	7	0	.563	334	272
Chicago	7	9	0	.438	304	264
Tampa Bay	5	10	1	.344	271	341
Green Bay	5	10	1	.344	231	371

Western Division

	W	L	T	Pct.	Pts.	OP
Atlanta#	12	4	0	.750	405	272
Los Angeles*	11	5	0	.688	424	289
San Francisco	6	10	0	.375	320	415
New Orleans	1	15	0	.063	291	487

*Wild Card qualifier for playoffs; #Top playoff seed in conference
San Diego was top playoff seed based on better conference record than Cleveland and Buffalo (9-3 to Browns' 8-4 and Bills' 8-4). Cleveland was second playoff seed based on better record against common opponents (5-2 to Bills' 5-3). Cleveland finished ahead of Houston based on better conference record (8-4 to Oilers' 7-5). Oakland was first Wild Card based on better conference record than Houston (9-3 to Oilers' 7-5). San Diego finished ahead of Oakland based on better net points in division games (plus 60 net points to Raiders' plus 37). Oakland did not play San Diego in the divisional playoffs because, from 1970-1989, two teams from the same division could not meet prior to the conference championship game. Kansas City finished ahead of Denver based on head-to-head sweep (2-0). Atlanta was top playoff seed based on head-to-head victory over Philadelphia (1-0). Philadelphia finished ahead of Dallas based on better net points in division games (plus 84 net points to Cowboys' plus 50). Minnesota finished ahead of Detroit based on better conference record (8-4 to Lions' 9-5). Tampa Bay finished ahead of Green Bay based on better head-to-head record (1-0-1 to Packers' 0-1-1).
Wild Card playoff: OAKLAND 27, Houston 7
Divisional playoffs: SAN DIEGO 20, Buffalo 14; Oakland 14, CLEVELAND 12
AFC Championship: Oakland 34, SAN DIEGO 27
Wild Card playoff: DALLAS 34, Los Angeles 13
Divisional playoffs: PHILADELPHIA 31, Minnesota 16; Dallas 30, ATLANTA 27
NFC Championship: PHILADELPHIA 20, Dallas 7
Super Bowl XV: Oakland (AFC) 27, Philadelphia (NFC) 10, at Louisiana Superdome, New Orleans, Louisiana

1979

AMERICAN CONFERENCE

Eastern Division

	W	L	T	Pct.	Pts.	OP
Miami	10	6	0	.625	341	257
New England	9	7	0	.563	411	326
N.Y. Jets	8	8	0	.500	337	383
Buffalo	7	9	0	.438	268	279
Baltimore	5	11	0	.313	271	351

Central Division

	W	L	T	Pct.	Pts.	OP
Pittsburgh	12	4	0	.750	416	262
Houston*	11	5	0	.688	362	331
Cleveland	9	7	0	.563	359	352
Cincinnati	4	12	0	.250	337	421

Western Division

	W	L	T	Pct.	Pts.	OP
San Diego#	12	4	0	.750	411	246
Denver*	10	6	0	.625	289	262
Seattle	9	7	0	.563	378	372
Oakland	9	7	0	.563	365	337
Kansas City	7	9	0	.438	238	262

NATIONAL CONFERENCE

Eastern Division

	W	L	T	Pct.	Pts.	OP
Dallas#	11	5	0	.688	371	313
Philadelphia*	11	5	0	.688	339	282
Washington	10	6	0	.625	348	295
N.Y. Giants	6	10	0	.375	237	323
St. Louis	5	11	0	.313	307	358

Central Division

	W	L	T	Pct.	Pts.	OP
Tampa Bay	10	6	0	.625	273	237
Chicago*	10	6	0	.625	306	249
Minnesota	7	9	0	.438	259	337
Green Bay	5	11	0	.313	246	316
Detroit	2	14	0	.125	219	365

Western Division

	W	L	T	Pct.	Pts.	OP
Los Angeles	9	7	0	.563	323	309
New Orleans	8	8	0	.500	370	360
Atlanta	6	10	0	.375	300	388
San Francisco	2	14	0	.125	308	416

*Wild Card qualifier for playoffs; #Top playoff seed in conference
San Diego was top playoff seed based on head-to-head victory over Pittsburgh (1-0). Seattle finished ahead of Oakland based on head-to-head sweep (2-0). Dallas finished ahead of Philadelphia based on better conference record (10-2 to Eagles' 9-3). Philadelphia did not play Dallas in the divisional playoffs because, from 1970-1989, two teams from the same division could not meet prior to the conference championship game. Tampa Bay finished ahead of Chicago based on a better division record (6-2 to Bears' 5-3). Chicago was second Wild Card ahead of Washington based on better net points in all games (57 to Redskins' 53).
Wild Card playoff: HOUSTON 13, Denver 7
Divisional playoffs: Houston 17, SAN DIEGO 14; PITTSBURGH 34, Miami 14
AFC Championship: PITTSBURGH 27, Houston 13
Wild Card playoff: PHILADELPHIA 27, Chicago 17
Divisional playoffs: TAMPA BAY 24, Philadelphia 17; Los Angeles 21, DALLAS 19
NFC Championship: Los Angeles 9, TAMPA BAY 0
Super Bowl XIV: Pittsburgh (AFC) 31, Los Angeles (NFC) 19, at Rose Bowl, Pasadena, California

1978

AMERICAN CONFERENCE
Eastern Division

	W	L	T	Pct.	Pts.	OP
New England	11	5	0	.688	358	286
Miami*	11	5	0	.688	372	254
N.Y. Jets	8	8	0	.500	359	364
Buffalo	5	11	0	.313	302	354
Baltimore	5	11	0	.313	239	421

Central Division

	W	L	T	Pct.	Pts.	OP
Pittsburgh#	14	2	0	.875	356	195
Houston*	10	6	0	.625	283	298
Cleveland	8	8	0	.500	334	356
Cincinnati	4	12	0	.250	252	284

Western Division

	W	L	T	Pct.	Pts.	OP
Denver	10	6	0	.625	282	198
Oakland	9	7	0	.563	311	283
Seattle	9	7	0	.563	345	358
San Diego	9	7	0	.563	355	309
Kansas City	4	12	0	.250	243	327

NATIONAL CONFERENCE
Eastern Division

	W	L	T	Pct.	Pts.	OP
Dallas	12	4	0	.750	384	208
Philadelphia*	9	7	0	.563	270	250
Washington	8	8	0	.500	273	283
St. Louis	6	10	0	.375	248	296
N.Y. Giants	6	10	0	.375	264	298

Central Division

	W	L	T	Pct.	Pts.	OP
Minnesota	8	7	1	.531	294	306
Green Bay	8	7	1	.531	249	269
Detroit	7	9	0	.438	290	300
Chicago	7	9	0	.438	253	274
Tampa Bay	5	11	0	.313	241	259

Western Division

	W	L	T	Pct.	Pts.	OP
Los Angeles#	12	4	0	.750	316	245
Atlanta*	9	7	0	.563	240	290
New Orleans	7	9	0	.438	281	298
San Francisco	2	14	0	.125	219	350

*Wild Card qualifier for playoffs; #Top playoff seed in conference
New England finished ahead of Miami based on better division record (6-2 to Dolphins' 5-3). Buffalo finished ahead of Baltimore based on head-to-head sweep (2-0). Oakland finished ahead of Seattle and San Diego based on better record against common opponents (6-2 to Seahawks' 5-3 and Chargers' 4-4). Atlanta was first Wild Card based on better conference record than Philadelphia (8-4 to Eagles' 6-6). Houston did not play Pittsburgh, and Atlanta did not play Los Angeles in the divisional playoffs because, from 1970-1989, two teams from the same division could not meet prior to the conference championship game. St. Louis finished ahead of N.Y. Giants based on better division record (3-5 to Giants' 2-6). Minnesota finished ahead of Green Bay based on better head-to-head record (1-0-1). Detroit finished ahead of Chicago based on better division record (4-4 to Bears' 3-5).
Wild Card playoff: Houston 17, MIAMI 9
Divisional playoffs: Houston 31, NEW ENGLAND 14;
   PITTSBURGH 33, Denver 10
AFC Championship: PITTSBURGH 34, Houston 5
Wild Card playoff: ATLANTA 14, Philadelphia 13
Divisional playoffs: DALLAS 27, Atlanta 20;
   LOS ANGELES 34, Minnesota 10
NFC Championship: Dallas 28, LOS ANGELES 0
Super Bowl XIII: Pittsburgh (AFC) 35, Dallas (NFC) 31,
   at Orange Bowl, Miami, Florida

1977

AMERICAN CONFERENCE
Eastern Division

	W	L	T	Pct.	Pts.	OP
Baltimore	10	4	0	.714	295	221
Miami	10	4	0	.714	313	197
New England	9	5	0	.643	278	217
Buffalo	3	11	0	.214	160	313
N.Y. Jets	3	11	0	.214	191	300

Central Division

	W	L	T	Pct.	Pts.	OP
Pittsburgh	9	5	0	.643	283	243
Cincinnati	8	6	0	.571	238	235
Houston	8	6	0	.571	299	230
Cleveland	6	8	0	.429	269	267

Western Division

	W	L	T	Pct.	Pts.	OP
Denver#	12	2	0	.857	274	148
Oakland*	11	3	0	.786	351	230
San Diego	7	7	0	.500	222	205
Seattle	5	9	0	.357	282	373
Kansas City	2	12	0	.143	225	349

NATIONAL CONFERENCE
Eastern Division

	W	L	T	Pct.	Pts.	OP
Dallas#	12	2	0	.857	345	212
Washington	9	5	0	.643	196	189
St. Louis	7	7	0	.500	272	287
Philadelphia	5	9	0	.357	220	207
N.Y. Giants	5	9	0	.357	181	265

Central Division

	W	L	T	Pct.	Pts.	OP
Minnesota	9	5	0	.643	231	227
Chicago*	9	5	0	.643	255	253
Detroit	6	8	0	.429	183	252
Green Bay	4	10	0	.286	134	219
Tampa Bay	2	12	0	.143	103	223

Western Division

	W	L	T	Pct.	Pts.	OP
Los Angeles	10	4	0	.714	302	146
Atlanta	7	7	0	.500	179	129
San Francisco	5	9	0	.357	220	260
New Orleans	3	11	0	.214	232	336

*Wild Card qualifier for playoffs; #Top playoff seed in conference
Baltimore finished ahead of Miami based on better conference record (9-3 to Dolphins' 8-4). Buffalo finished ahead of N.Y. Jets based on better strength of schedule (.582 to Jets' .536). Cincinnati finished ahead of Houston based on better division record (6-3 to Oilers' 5-4). Oakland did not play Denver in the divisional playoffs because, from 1970-1989, two teams from the same division could not meet prior to the conference championship game. Minnesota finished ahead of Chicago based on fewer losses by common opponents (11 losses to 14 losses by the Bears' opponents). Chicago won Wild Card ahead of Washington based on better net points in conference games (48 to Redskins' 4). Philadelphia finished ahead of N.Y. Giants based on head-to-head sweep (2-0).
Divisional playoffs: DENVER 34, Pittsburgh 21;
   Oakland 37, BALTIMORE 31 (OT)
AFC Championship: DENVER 20, Oakland 17
Divisional playoffs: DALLAS 37, Chicago 7;
   Minnesota 14, LOS ANGELES 7
NFC Championship: DALLAS 23, Minnesota 6
Super Bowl XII: Dallas (NFC) 27, Denver (AFC) 10,
   at Louisiana Superdome, New Orleans, Louisiana

1976

AMERICAN CONFERENCE

Eastern Division

	W	L	T	Pct.	Pts.	OP
Baltimore	11	3	0	.786	417	246
New England*	11	3	0	.786	376	236
Miami	6	8	0	.429	263	264
N.Y. Jets	3	11	0	.214	169	383
Buffalo	2	12	0	.143	245	363

Central Division

	W	L	T	Pct.	Pts.	OP
Pittsburgh	10	4	0	.714	342	138
Cincinnati	10	4	0	.714	335	210
Cleveland	9	5	0	.643	267	287
Houston	5	9	0	.357	222	273

Western Division

	W	L	T	Pct.	Pts.	OP
Oakland#	13	1	0	.929	350	237
Denver	9	5	0	.643	315	206
San Diego	6	8	0	.429	248	285
Kansas City	5	9	0	.357	290	376
Tampa Bay	0	14	0	.000	125	412

NATIONAL CONFERENCE

Eastern Division

	W	L	T	Pct.	Pts.	OP
Dallas	11	3	0	.786	296	194
Washington*	10	4	0	.714	291	217
St. Louis	10	4	0	.714	309	267
Philadelphia	4	10	0	.286	165	286
N.Y. Giants	3	11	0	.214	170	250

Central Division

	W	L	T	Pct.	Pts.	OP
Minnesota#	11	2	1	.821	305	176
Chicago	7	7	0	.500	253	216
Detroit	6	8	0	.429	262	220
Green Bay	5	9	0	.357	218	299

Western Division

	W	L	T	Pct.	Pts.	OP
Los Angeles	10	3	1	.750	351	190
San Francisco	8	6	0	.571	270	190
New Orleans	4	10	0	.286	253	346
Seattle	2	12	0	.143	229	429

*Wild Card qualifier for playoffs; #Top playoff seed in conference
Baltimore finished ahead of New England based on better division record (7-1 to Patriots' 6-2). Pittsburgh finished ahead of Cincinnati based on head-to-head sweep (2-0). Washington finished ahead of St. Louis based on head-to-head sweep (2-0). Atlanta finished ahead of New Orleans based on better division record (2-4 to Saints' 1-5).

Divisional playoffs: OAKLAND 24, New England 21; Pittsburgh 40, BALTIMORE 14

AFC Championship: OAKLAND 24, Pittsburgh 7

Divisional playoffs: MINNESOTA 35, Washington 20; Los Angeles 14, DALLAS 12

NFC Championship: MINNESOTA 24, Los Angeles 13

Super Bowl XI: Oakland (AFC) 32, Minnesota (NFC) 14, at Rose Bowl, Pasadena, California

1975

AMERICAN CONFERENCE

Eastern Division

	W	L	T	Pct.	Pts.	OP
Baltimore	10	4	0	.714	395	269
Miami	10	4	0	.714	357	222
Buffalo	8	6	0	.571	420	355
N.Y. Jets	3	11	0	.214	258	433
New England	3	11	0	.214	258	358

Central Division

	W	L	T	Pct.	Pts.	OP
Pittsburgh#	12	2	0	.857	373	162
Cincinnati*	11	3	0	.786	340	246
Houston	10	4	0	.714	293	226
Cleveland	3	11	0	.214	218	372

Western Division

	W	L	T	Pct.	Pts.	OP
Oakland	11	3	0	.786	375	255
Denver	6	8	0	.429	254	307
Kansas City	5	9	0	.357	282	341
San Diego	2	12	0	.143	189	345

NATIONAL CONFERENCE

Eastern Division

	W	L	T	Pct.	Pts.	OP
St. Louis	11	3	0	.786	356	276
Dallas*	10	4	0	.714	350	268
Washington	8	6	0	.571	325	276
N.Y. Giants	5	9	0	.357	216	306
Philadelphia	4	10	0	.286	225	302

Central Division

	W	L	T	Pct.	Pts.	OP
Minnesota#	12	2	0	.857	377	180
Detroit	7	7	0	.500	245	262
Chicago	4	10	0	.286	191	379
Green Bay	4	10	0	.286	226	285

Western Division

	W	L	T	Pct.	Pts.	OP
Los Angeles	12	2	0	.857	312	135
San Francisco	5	9	0	.357	255	286
Atlanta	4	10	0	.286	240	289
New Orleans	2	12	0	.143	165	360

*Wild Card qualifier for playoffs; #Top playoff seed in conference
Baltimore finished ahead of Miami based on head-to-head sweep (2-0). Cincinnati did not play Pittsburgh in the divisional playoffs because, from 1970-1989, two teams from the same division could not meet prior to the conference championship game. N.Y. Jets finished ahead of New England based on head-to-head sweep (2-0). Minnesota was top playoff seed based on better Point Rating system than Los Angeles (3 to 6). Chicago finished ahead of Green Bay based on better division record (2-4 to Bears' 1-5).

Divisional playoffs: PITTSBURGH 28, Baltimore 10; OAKLAND 31, Cincinnati 28

AFC Championship: PITTSBURGH 16, Oakland 10

Divisional playoffs: LOS ANGELES 35, St. Louis 23; Dallas 17, MINNESOTA 14

NFC Championship: Dallas 37, LOS ANGELES 7

Super Bowl X: Pittsburgh (AFC) 21, Dallas (NFC) 17, at Orange Bowl, Miami, Florida

1974

AMERICAN CONFERENCE

Eastern Division

	W	L	T	Pct.	Pts.	OP
Miami	11	3	0	.786	327	216
Buffalo*	9	5	0	.643	264	244
New England	7	7	0	.500	348	289
N.Y. Jets	7	7	0	.500	279	300
Baltimore	2	12	0	.143	190	329

Central Division

	W	L	T	Pct.	Pts.	OP
Pittsburgh	10	3	1	.750	305	189
Houston	7	7	0	.500	236	282
Cincinnati	7	7	0	.500	283	259
Cleveland	4	10	0	.286	251	344

Western Division

	W	L	T	Pct.	Pts.	OP
Oakland	12	2	0	.857	355	228
Denver	7	6	1	.536	302	294
Kansas City	5	9	0	.357	233	293
San Diego	5	9	0	.357	212	285

NATIONAL CONFERENCE

Eastern Division

	W	L	T	Pct.	Pts.	OP
St. Louis	10	4	0	.714	285	218
Washington*	10	4	0	.714	320	196
Dallas	8	6	0	.571	297	235
Philadelphia	7	7	0	.500	242	217
N.Y. Giants	2	12	0	.143	195	299

Central Division

	W	L	T	Pct.	Pts.	OP
Minnesota	10	4	0	.714	310	195
Detroit	7	7	0	.500	256	270
Green Bay	6	8	0	.429	210	206
Chicago	4	10	0	.286	152	279

Western Division

	W	L	T	Pct.	Pts.	OP
Los Angeles	10	4	0	.714	263	181
San Francisco	6	8	0	.429	226	236
New Orleans	5	9	0	.357	166	263
Atlanta	3	11	0	.214	111	271

Wild Card qualifier for playoffs

New England finished ahead of N.Y. Jets based on better record against common opponents (5-4 to Jets' 4-5). Houston finished ahead of Cincinnati based on head-to-head sweep (2-0). Kansas City finished ahead of San Diego based on better record against common opponents (4-6 to Chargers' 3-7). St. Louis finished ahead of Washington based on head-to-head sweep (2-0).

Divisional playoffs: OAKLAND 28, Miami 26;
   PITTSBURGH 32, Buffalo 14
AFC Championship: Pittsburgh 24, OAKLAND 13
Divisional playoffs: MINNESOTA 30, St. Louis 14;
   LOS ANGELES 19, Washington 10
NFC Championship: MINNESOTA 14, Los Angeles 10
Super Bowl IX: Pittsburgh (AFC) 16, Minnesota (NFC) 6,
   at Tulane Stadium, New Orleans, Louisiana

From 1933-1974, sites for league/conference championship games alternated by division.

1973

AMERICAN CONFERENCE

Eastern Division

	W	L	T	Pct.	Pts.	OP
Miami	12	2	0	.857	343	150
Buffalo	9	5	0	.643	259	230
New England	5	9	0	.357	258	300
N.Y. Jets	4	10	0	.286	240	306
Baltimore	4	10	0	.286	226	341

Central Division

	W	L	T	Pct.	Pts.	OP
Cincinnati	10	4	0	.714	286	231
Pittsburgh*	10	4	0	.714	347	210
Cleveland	7	5	2	.571	234	255
Houston	1	13	0	.071	199	447

Western Division

	W	L	T	Pct.	Pts.	OP
Oakland	9	4	1	.679	292	175
Kansas City	7	5	2	.571	231	192
Denver	7	5	2	.571	354	296
San Diego	2	11	1	.179	188	386

NATIONAL CONFERENCE

Eastern Division

	W	L	T	Pct.	Pts.	OP
Dallas	10	4	0	.714	382	203
Washington*	10	4	0	.714	325	198
Philadelphia	5	8	1	.393	310	393
St. Louis	4	9	1	.321	286	365
N.Y. Giants	2	11	1	.179	226	362

Central Division

	W	L	T	Pct.	Pts.	OP
Minnesota	12	2	0	.857	296	168
Detroit	6	7	1	.464	271	247
Green Bay	5	7	2	.429	202	259
Chicago	3	11	0	.214	195	334

Western Division

	W	L	T	Pct.	Pts.	OP
Los Angeles	12	2	0	.857	388	178
Atlanta	9	5	0	.643	318	224
San Francisco	5	9	0	.357	262	319
New Orleans	5	9	0	.357	163	312

Wild Card qualifier for playoffs

Cincinnati finished ahead of Pittsburgh based on better conference record (8-3 to Steelers' 7-4). N.Y. Jets finished ahead of Baltimore based on head-to-head sweep (2-0). Kansas City finished ahead of Denver based on better division record (4-2 to Broncos' 3-2-1). Dallas finished ahead of Washington based on better point differential in head-to-head games (13 points). San Francisco finished ahead of New Orleans based on better division record (2-4 to Saints' 1-5).

Divisional playoffs: OAKLAND 33, Pittsburgh 14;
   MIAMI 34, Cincinnati 16
AFC Championship: MIAMI 27, Oakland 10
Divisional playoffs: MINNESOTA 27, Washington 20;
   DALLAS 27, Los Angeles 16
NFC Championship: Minnesota 27, DALLAS 10
Super Bowl VIII: Miami (AFC) 24, Minnesota (NFC) 7,
   at Rice Stadium, Houston, Texas

1972

AMERICAN CONFERENCE

Eastern Division

	W	L	T	Pct.	Pts.	OP
Miami	14	0	0	1.000	385	171
N.Y. Jets	7	7	0	.500	367	324
Baltimore	5	9	0	.357	235	252
Buffalo	4	9	1	.321	257	377
New England	3	11	0	.214	192	446

Central Division

	W	L	T	Pct.	Pts.	OP
Pittsburgh	11	3	0	.786	343	175
Cleveland*	10	4	0	.714	268	249
Cincinnati	8	6	0	.571	299	229
Houston	1	13	0	.071	164	380

Western Division

	W	L	T	Pct.	Pts.	OP
Oakland	10	3	1	.750	365	248
Kansas City	8	6	0	.571	287	254
Denver	5	9	0	.357	325	350
San Diego	4	9	1	.321	264	344

NATIONAL CONFERENCE

Eastern Division

	W	L	T	Pct.	Pts.	OP
Washington	11	3	0	.786	336	218
Dallas*	10	4	0	.714	319	240
N.Y. Giants	8	6	0	.571	331	247
St. Louis	4	9	1	.321	193	303
Philadelphia	2	11	1	.179	145	352

Central Division

	W	L	T	Pct.	Pts.	OP
Green Bay	10	4	0	.714	304	226
Detroit	8	5	1	.607	339	290
Minnesota	7	7	0	.500	301	252
Chicago	4	9	1	.321	225	275

Western Division

	W	L	T	Pct.	Pts.	OP
San Francisco	8	5	1	.607	353	249
Atlanta	7	7	0	.500	269	274
Los Angeles	6	7	1	.464	291	286
New Orleans	2	11	1	.179	215	361

*Wild Card qualifier for playoffs
Dallas did not play Washington in the divisional playoffs because, from 1970-1989, two teams from the same division could not meet prior to the conference championship game.
Divisional playoffs: PITTSBURGH 13, Oakland 7; MIAMI 20, Cleveland 14
AFC Championship: Miami 21, PITTSBURGH 17
Divisional playoffs: Dallas 30, SAN FRANCISCO 28; WASHINGTON 16, Green Bay 3
NFC Championship: WASHINGTON 26, Dallas 3
Super Bowl VII: Miami (AFC) 14, Washington (NFC) 7, at Memorial Coliseum, Los Angeles, California

1971

AMERICAN CONFERENCE

Eastern Division

	W	L	T	Pct.	Pts.	OP
Miami	10	3	1	.769	315	174
Baltimore*	10	4	0	.714	313	140
New England	6	8	0	.429	238	325
N.Y. Jets	6	8	0	.429	212	299
Buffalo	1	13	0	.071	184	394

Central Division

	W	L	T	Pct.	Pts.	OP
Cleveland	9	5	0	.643	285	273
Pittsburgh	6	8	0	.429	246	292
Houston	4	9	1	.308	251	330
Cincinnati	4	10	0	.286	284	265

Western Division

	W	L	T	Pct.	Pts.	OP
Kansas City	10	3	1	.769	302	208
Oakland	8	4	2	.667	344	278
San Diego	6	8	0	.429	311	341
Denver	4	9	1	.308	203	275

NATIONAL CONFERENCE

Eastern Division

	W	L	T	Pct.	Pts.	OP
Dallas	11	3	0	.786	406	222
Washington*	9	4	1	.692	276	190
Philadelphia	6	7	1	.462	221	302
St. Louis	4	9	1	.308	231	279
N.Y. Giants	4	10	0	.286	228	362

Central Division

	W	L	T	Pct.	Pts.	OP
Minnesota	11	3	0	.786	245	139
Detroit	7	6	1	.538	341	286
Chicago	6	8	0	.429	185	276
Green Bay	4	8	2	.333	274	298

Western Division

	W	L	T	Pct.	Pts.	OP
San Francisco	9	5	0	.643	300	216
Los Angeles	8	5	1	.615	313	260
Atlanta	7	6	1	.538	274	277
New Orleans	4	8	2	.333	266	347

*Wild Card qualifier for playoffs
New England finished ahead of N.Y. Jets based on better strength of schedule (.537 to Jets' .510).
Divisional playoffs: Miami 27, KANSAS CITY 24 (OT); Baltimore 20, CLEVELAND 3
AFC Championship: MIAMI 21, Baltimore 0
Divisional playoffs: Dallas 20, MINNESOTA 12; SAN FRANCISCO 24, Washington 20
NFC Championship: DALLAS 14, San Francisco 3
Super Bowl VI: Dallas (NFC) 24, Miami (AFC) 3, at Tulane Stadium, New Orleans, Louisiana

From 1920-1971, tie games were not included in winning percentage.

1970

AMERICAN CONFERENCE
Eastern Division

	W	L	T	Pct.	Pts.	OP
Baltimore	11	2	1	.846	321	234
Miami*	10	4	0	.714	297	228
N.Y. Jets	4	10	0	.286	255	286
Buffalo	3	10	1	.231	204	337
Boston Patriots	2	12	0	.143	149	361

Central Division

	W	L	T	Pct.	Pts.	OP
Cincinnati	8	6	0	.571	312	255
Cleveland	7	7	0	.500	286	265
Pittsburgh	5	9	0	.357	210	272
Houston	3	10	1	.231	217	352

Western Division

	W	L	T	Pct.	Pts.	OP
Oakland	8	4	2	.667	300	293
Kansas City	7	5	2	.583	272	244
San Diego	5	6	3	.455	282	278
Denver	5	8	1	.385	253	264

NATIONAL CONFERENCE
Eastern Division

	W	L	T	Pct.	Pts.	OP
Dallas	10	4	0	.714	299	221
N.Y. Giants	9	5	0	.643	301	270
St. Louis	8	5	1	.615	325	228
Washington	6	8	0	.429	297	314
Philadelphia	3	10	1	.231	241	332

Central Division

	W	L	T	Pct.	Pts.	OP
Minnesota	12	2	0	.857	335	143
Detroit*	10	4	0	.714	347	202
Green Bay	6	8	0	.429	196	293
Chicago	6	8	0	.429	256	261

Western Division

	W	L	T	Pct.	Pts.	OP
San Francisco	10	3	1	.769	352	267
Los Angeles	9	4	1	.692	325	202
Atlanta	4	8	2	.333	206	261
New Orleans	2	11	1	.154	172	347

Wild Card qualifier for playoffs
Miami did not play Baltimore, and Detroit did not play Minnesota, in the divisional playoffs because, from 1970-1989, two teams from the same division could not meet prior to the conference championship game. Green Bay finished ahead of Chicago based on better division record (2-4 to Bears' 1-5).
Divisional playoffs: BALTIMORE 17, Cincinnati 0;
  OAKLAND 21, Miami 14
AFC Championship: BALTIMORE 27, Oakland 17
Divisional playoffs: DALLAS 5, Detroit 0;
  San Francisco 17, MINNESOTA 14
NFC Championship: Dallas 17, SAN FRANCISCO 10
Super Bowl V: Baltimore (AFC) 16, Dallas (NFC) 13,
  at Orange Bowl, Miami, Florida

1969 NFL

EASTERN CONFERENCE
Capitol Division

	W	L	T	Pct.	Pts.	OP
Dallas	11	2	1	.846	369	223
Washington	7	5	2	.583	307	319
New Orleans	5	9	0	.357	311	393
Philadelphia	4	9	1	.308	279	377

Century Division

	W	L	T	Pct.	Pts.	OP
Cleveland	10	3	1	.769	351	300
N.Y. Giants	6	8	0	.429	264	298
St. Louis	4	9	1	.308	314	389
Pittsburgh	1	13	0	.071	218	404

WESTERN CONFERENCE
Coastal Division

	W	L	T	Pct.	Pts.	OP
Los Angeles	11	3	0	.786	320	243
Baltimore	8	5	1	.615	279	268
Atlanta	6	8	0	.429	276	268
San Francisco	4	8	2	.333	277	319

Central Division

	W	L	T	Pct.	Pts.	OP
Minnesota	12	2	0	.857	379	133
Detroit	9	4	1	.692	259	188
Green Bay	8	6	0	.571	269	221
Chicago	1	13	0	.071	210	339

Conference championships: Cleveland 38, DALLAS 14;
  MINNESOTA 23, Los Angeles 20
NFL championship: MINNESOTA 27, Cleveland 7
Super Bowl IV: Kansas City (AFL) 23, Minnesota (NFL) 7,
  at Tulane Stadium, New Orleans, Louisiana

1969 AFL

EASTERN DIVISION

	W	L	T	Pct.	Pts.	OP
N.Y. Jets	10	4	0	.714	353	269
Houston	6	6	2	.500	278	279
Boston Patriots	4	10	0	.286	266	316
Buffalo	4	10	0	.286	230	359
Miami	3	10	1	.231	233	332

WESTERN DIVISION

	W	L	T	Pct.	Pts.	OP
Oakland	12	1	1	.923	377	242
Kansas City	11	3	0	.786	359	177
San Diego	8	6	0	.571	288	276
Denver	5	8	1	.385	297	344
Cincinnati	4	9	1	.308	280	367

Divisional playoffs: Kansas City 13, N.Y. JETS 6;
  OAKLAND 56, Houston 7
AFL championship: Kansas City 17, OAKLAND 7

1968 NFL

EASTERN CONFERENCE
Capitol Division

	W	L	T	Pct.	Pts.	OP
Dallas	12	2	0	.857	431	186
N.Y. Giants	7	7	0	.500	294	325
Washington	5	9	0	.357	249	358
Philadelphia	2	12	0	.143	202	351

Century Division

	W	L	T	Pct.	Pts.	OP
Cleveland	10	4	0	.714	394	273
St. Louis	9	4	1	.692	325	289
New Orleans	4	9	1	.308	246	327
Pittsburgh	2	11	1	.154	244	397

WESTERN CONFERENCE
Coastal Division

	W	L	T	Pct.	Pts.	OP
Baltimore	13	1	0	.929	402	144
Los Angeles	10	3	1	.769	312	200
San Francisco	7	6	1	.538	303	310
Atlanta	2	12	0	.143	170	389

Central Division

	W	L	T	Pct.	Pts.	OP
Minnesota	8	6	0	.571	282	242
Chicago	7	7	0	.500	250	333
Green Bay	6	7	1	.462	281	227
Detroit	4	8	2	.333	207	241

Conference championships: CLEVELAND 31, Dallas 20;
  BALTIMORE 24, Minnesota 14
NFL championship: Baltimore 34, CLEVELAND 0
Super Bowl III: N.Y. Jets (AFL) 16, Baltimore (NFL) 7,
  at Orange Bowl, Miami, Florida

1968 AFL

EASTERN DIVISION

	W	L	T	Pct.	Pts.	OP
N.Y. Jets	11	3	0	.786	419	280
Houston	7	7	0	.500	303	248
Miami	5	8	1	.385	276	355
Boston Patriots	4	10	0	.286	229	406
Buffalo	1	12	1	.077	199	367

WESTERN DIVISION

	W	L	T	Pct.	Pts.	OP
Oakland	12	2	0	.857	453	233
Kansas City	12	2	0	.857	371	170
San Diego	9	5	0	.643	382	310
Denver	5	9	0	.357	255	404
Cincinnati	3	11	0	.214	215	329

Western Division playoff: OAKLAND 41, Kansas City 6
AFL championship: N.Y. JETS 27, Oakland 23

1967 NFL

EASTERN CONFERENCE
Capitol Division

	W	L	T	Pct.	Pts.	OP
Dallas	9	5	0	.643	342	268
Philadelphia	6	7	1	.462	351	409
Washington	5	6	3	.455	347	353
New Orleans	3	11	0	.214	233	379

Century Division

	W	L	T	Pct.	Pts.	OP
Cleveland	9	5	0	.643	334	297
N.Y. Giants	7	7	0	.500	369	379
St. Louis	6	7	1	.462	333	356
Pittsburgh	4	9	1	.308	281	320

WESTERN CONFERENCE
Coastal Division

	W	L	T	Pct.	Pts.	OP
Los Angeles	11	1	2	.917	398	196
Baltimore	11	1	2	.917	394	198
San Francisco	7	7	0	.500	273	337
Atlanta	1	12	1	.077	175	422

Central Division

	W	L	T	Pct.	Pts.	OP
Green Bay	9	4	1	.692	332	209
Chicago	7	6	1	.538	239	218
Detroit	5	7	2	.417	260	259
Minnesota	3	8	3	.273	233	294

Los Angeles finished ahead of Baltimore based on better point differential in head-to-head games (net 24 points).
Conference championships: DALLAS 52, Cleveland 14; GREEN BAY 28, Los Angeles 7
NFL championship: GREEN BAY 21, Dallas 17
Super Bowl II: Green Bay (NFL) 33, Oakland (AFL) 14, at Orange Bowl, Miami, Florida

1967 AFL

EASTERN DIVISION

	W	L	T	Pct.	Pts.	OP
Houston	9	4	1	.692	258	199
N.Y. Jets	8	5	1	.615	371	329
Buffalo	4	10	0	.286	237	285
Miami	4	10	0	.286	219	407
Boston Patriots	3	10	1	.231	280	389

WESTERN DIVISION

	W	L	T	Pct.	Pts.	OP
Oakland	13	1	0	.929	468	233
Kansas City	9	5	0	.643	408	254
San Diego	8	5	1	.615	360	352
Denver	3	11	0	.214	256	409

AFL championship: OAKLAND 40, Houston 7

1966 NFL

EASTERN CONFERENCE

	W	L	T	Pct.	Pts.	OP
Dallas	10	3	1	.769	445	239
Cleveland	9	5	0	.643	403	259
Philadelphia	9	5	0	.643	326	340
St. Louis	8	5	1	.615	264	265
Washington	7	7	0	.500	351	355
Pittsburgh	5	8	1	.385	316	347
Atlanta	3	11	0	.214	204	437
N.Y. Giants	1	12	1	.077	263	501

WESTERN CONFERENCE

	W	L	T	Pct.	Pts.	OP
Green Bay	12	2	0	.857	335	163
Baltimore	9	5	0	.643	314	226
Los Angeles	8	6	0	.571	289	212
San Francisco	6	6	2	.500	320	325
Chicago	5	7	2	.417	234	272
Detroit	4	9	1	.308	206	317
Minnesota	4	9	1	.308	292	304

NFL championship: Green Bay 34, DALLAS 27
Super Bowl I: Green Bay (NFL) 35, Kansas City (AFL) 10, at Memorial Coliseum, Los Angeles, California

1966 AFL

EASTERN DIVISION

	W	L	T	Pct.	Pts.	OP
Buffalo	9	4	1	.692	358	255
Boston Patriots	8	4	2	.677	315	283
N.Y. Jets	6	6	2	.500	322	312
Houston	3	11	0	.214	335	396
Miami	3	11	0	.214	213	362

WESTERN DIVISION

	W	L	T	Pct.	Pts.	OP
Kansas City	11	2	1	.846	448	276
Oakland	8	5	1	.615	315	288
San Diego	7	6	1	.538	335	284
Denver	4	10	0	.286	196	381

AFL championship: Kansas City 31, BUFFALO 7

1965 NFL

EASTERN CONFERENCE

	W	L	T	Pct.	Pts.	OP
Cleveland	11	3	0	.786	363	325
Dallas	7	7	0	.500	325	280
N.Y. Giants	7	7	0	.500	270	338
Washington	6	8	0	.429	257	301
Philadelphia	5	9	0	.357	363	359
St. Louis	5	9	0	.357	296	309
Pittsburgh	2	12	0	.143	202	397

WESTERN CONFERENCE

	W	L	T	Pct.	Pts.	OP
Green Bay	10	3	1	.769	316	224
Baltimore	10	3	1	.769	389	284
Chicago	9	5	0	.643	409	275
San Francisco	7	6	1	.538	421	402
Minnesota	7	7	0	.500	383	403
Detroit	6	7	1	.462	257	295
Los Angeles	4	10	0	.286	269	328

Western Conference playoff: GREEN BAY 13, Baltimore 10 (OT)
NFL championship: GREEN BAY 23, Cleveland 12

1965 AFL

EASTERN DIVISION

	W	L	T	Pct.	Pts.	OP
Buffalo	10	3	1	.769	313	226
N.Y. Jets	5	8	1	.385	285	303
Boston Patriots	4	8	2	.333	244	302
Houston	4	10	0	.286	298	429

WESTERN DIVISION

	W	L	T	Pct.	Pts.	OP
San Diego	9	2	3	.818	340	227
Oakland	8	5	1	.615	298	239
Kansas City	7	5	2	.583	322	285
Denver	4	10	0	.286	303	392

AFL championship: Buffalo 23, SAN DIEGO 0

1964 NFL

EASTERN CONFERENCE

	W	L	T	Pct.	Pts.	OP
Cleveland	10	3	1	.769	415	293
St. Louis	9	3	2	.750	357	331
Philadelphia	6	8	0	.429	312	313
Washington	6	8	0	.429	307	305
Dallas	5	8	1	.385	250	289
Pittsburgh	5	9	0	.357	253	315
N.Y. Giants	2	10	2	.167	241	399

WESTERN CONFERENCE

	W	L	T	Pct.	Pts.	OP
Baltimore	12	2	0	.857	428	225
Green Bay	8	5	1	.615	342	245
Minnesota	8	5	1	.615	355	296
Detroit	7	5	2	.583	280	260
Los Angeles	5	7	2	.417	283	339
Chicago	5	9	0	.357	260	379
San Francisco	4	10	0	.286	236	330

NFL championship: CLEVELAND 27, Baltimore 0

1964 AFL

EASTERN DIVISION

	W	L	T	Pct.	Pts.	OP
Buffalo	12	2	0	.857	400	242
Boston Patriots	10	3	1	.769	365	297
N.Y. Jets	5	8	1	.385	278	315
Houston	4	10	0	.286	310	355

WESTERN DIVISION

	W	L	T	Pct.	Pts.	OP
San Diego	8	5	1	.615	341	300
Kansas City	7	7	0	.500	366	306
Oakland	5	7	2	.417	303	350
Denver	2	11	1	.154	240	438

AFL championship: BUFFALO 20, San Diego 7

1963 NFL

EASTERN CONFERENCE

	W	L	T	Pct.	Pts.	OP
N.Y. Giants	11	3	0	.786	448	280
Cleveland	10	4	0	.714	343	262
St. Louis	9	5	0	.643	341	283
Pittsburgh	7	4	3	.636	321	295
Dallas	4	10	0	.286	305	378
Washington	3	11	0	.214	279	398
Philadelphia	2	10	2	.167	242	381

WESTERN CONFERENCE

	W	L	T	Pct.	Pts.	OP
Chicago	11	1	2	.917	301	144
Green Bay	11	2	1	.846	369	206
Baltimore	8	6	0	.571	316	285
Detroit	5	8	1	.385	326	265
Minnesota	5	8	1	.385	309	390
Los Angeles	5	9	0	.357	210	350
San Francisco	2	12	0	.143	198	391

NFL championship: CHICAGO 14, N.Y. Giants 10

1963 AFL

EASTERN DIVISION

	W	L	T	Pct.	Pts.	OP
Boston Patriots	7	6	1	.538	327	257
Buffalo	7	6	1	.538	304	291
Houston	6	8	0	.429	302	372
N.Y. Jets	5	8	1	.385	249	399

WESTERN DIVISION

	W	L	T	Pct.	Pts.	OP
San Diego	11	3	0	.786	399	255
Oakland	10	4	0	.714	363	282
Kansas City	5	7	2	.417	347	263
Denver	2	11	1	.154	301	473

Eastern Division playoff: Boston 26, BUFFALO 8
AFL championship: SAN DIEGO 51, Boston 10

1962 NFL

EASTERN CONFERENCE	W	L	T	Pct.	Pts.	OP	WESTERN CONFERENCE	W	L	T	Pct.	Pts.	OP
N.Y. Giants	12	2	0	.857	398	283	Green Bay	13	1	0	.929	415	148
Pittsburgh	9	5	0	.643	312	363	Detroit	11	3	0	.786	315	177
Cleveland	7	6	1	.538	291	257	Chicago	9	5	0	.643	321	287
Washington	5	7	2	.417	305	376	Baltimore	7	7	0	.500	293	288
Dallas Cowboys	5	8	1	.385	398	402	San Francisco	6	8	0	.429	282	331
St. Louis	4	9	1	.308	287	361	Minnesota	2	11	1	.154	254	410
Philadelphia	3	10	1	.231	282	356	Los Angeles	1	12	1	.077	220	334

NFL championship: Green Bay 16, N.Y. GIANTS 7

1962 AFL

EASTERN DIVISION	W	L	T	Pct.	Pts.	OP	WESTERN DIVISION	W	L	T	Pct.	Pts.	OP
Houston	11	3	0	.786	387	270	Dallas Texans	11	3	0	.786	389	233
Boston Patriots	9	4	1	.692	346	295	Denver	7	7	0	.500	353	334
Buffalo	7	6	1	.538	309	272	San Diego	4	10	0	.286	314	392
N.Y. Titans	5	9	0	.357	278	423	Oakland	1	13	0	.071	213	370

AFL championship: Dallas Texans 20, HOUSTON 17 (OT)

1961 NFL

EASTERN CONFERENCE	W	L	T	Pct.	Pts.	OP	WESTERN CONFERENCE	W	L	T	Pct.	Pts.	OP
N.Y. Giants	10	3	1	.769	368	220	Green Bay	11	3	0	.786	391	223
Philadelphia	10	4	0	.714	361	297	Detroit	8	5	1	.615	270	258
Cleveland	8	5	1	.615	319	270	Baltimore	8	6	0	.571	302	307
St. Louis	7	7	0	.500	279	267	Chicago	8	6	0	.571	326	302
Pittsburgh	6	8	0	.429	295	287	San Francisco	7	6	1	.538	346	272
Dallas Cowboys	4	9	1	.308	236	380	Los Angeles	4	10	0	.286	263	333
Washington	1	12	1	.077	174	392	Minnesota	3	11	0	.214	285	407

NFL championship: GREEN BAY 37, N.Y. Giants 0

1961 AFL

EASTERN DIVISION	W	L	T	Pct.	Pts.	OP	WESTERN DIVISION	W	L	T	Pct.	Pts.	OP
Houston	10	3	1	.769	513	242	San Diego	12	2	0	.857	396	219
Boston Patriots	9	4	1	.692	413	313	Dallas Texans	6	8	0	.429	334	343
N.Y. Titans	7	7	0	.500	301	390	Denver	3	11	0	.214	251	432
Buffalo	6	8	0	.429	294	342	Oakland	2	12	0	.143	237	458

AFL championship: Houston 10, SAN DIEGO 3

1960 NFL

EASTERN CONFERENCE	W	L	T	Pct.	Pts.	OP	WESTERN CONFERENCE	W	L	T	Pct.	Pts.	OP
Philadelphia	10	2	0	.833	321	246	Green Bay	8	4	0	.667	332	209
Cleveland	8	3	1	.727	362	217	Detroit	7	5	0	.583	239	212
N.Y. Giants	6	4	2	.600	271	261	San Francisco	7	5	0	.583	208	205
St. Louis	6	5	1	.545	288	230	Baltimore	6	6	0	.500	288	234
Pittsburgh	5	6	1	.455	240	275	Chicago	5	6	1	.455	194	299
Washington	1	9	2	.100	178	309	L.A. Rams	4	7	1	.364	265	297
							Dallas Cowboys	0	11	1	.000	177	369

NFL championship: PHILADELPHIA 17, Green Bay 13

1960 AFL

EASTERN CONFERENCE	W	L	T	Pct.	Pts.	OP	WESTERN CONFERENCE	W	L	T	Pct.	Pts.	OP
Houston	10	4	0	.714	379	285	L.A. Chargers	10	4	0	.714	373	336
N.Y. Titans	7	7	0	.500	382	399	Dallas Texans	8	6	0	.571	362	253
Buffalo	5	8	1	.385	296	303	Oakland	6	8	0	.429	319	388
Boston	5	9	0	.357	286	349	Denver	4	9	1	.308	309	393

AFL championship: HOUSTON 24, L.A. Chargers 16

1959

EASTERN CONFERENCE	W	L	T	Pct.	Pts.	OP	WESTERN CONFERENCE	W	L	T	Pct.	Pts.	OP
N.Y. Giants	10	2	0	.833	284	170	Baltimore	9	3	0	.750	374	251
Cleveland	7	5	0	.583	270	214	Chi. Bears	8	4	0	.667	252	196
Philadelphia	7	5	0	.583	268	278	Green Bay	7	5	0	.583	248	246
Pittsburgh	6	5	1	.545	257	216	San Francisco	7	5	0	.583	255	237
Washington	3	9	0	.250	185	350	Detroit	3	8	1	.273	203	275
Chi. Cardinals	2	10	0	.167	234	324	Los Angeles	2	10	0	.167	242	315

NFL championship: BALTIMORE 31, N.Y. Giants 16

1958

EASTERN CONFERENCE	W	L	T	Pct.	Pts.	OP	WESTERN CONFERENCE	W	L	T	Pct.	Pts.	OP
N.Y. Giants	9	3	0	.750	246	183	Baltimore	9	3	0	.750	381	203
Cleveland	9	3	0	.750	302	217	Chi. Bears	8	4	0	.667	298	230
Pittsburgh	7	4	1	.636	261	230	Los Angeles	8	4	0	.667	344	278
Washington	4	7	1	.364	214	268	San Francisco	6	6	0	.500	257	324
Chi. Cardinals	2	9	1	.182	261	356	Detroit	4	7	1	.364	261	276
Philadelphia	2	9	1	.182	235	306	Green Bay	1	10	1	.091	193	382

Eastern Conference playoff: N.Y. GIANTS 10, Cleveland 0
NFL championship: Baltimore 23, N.Y. GIANTS 17 (OT)

1957

EASTERN CONFERENCE	W	L	T	Pct.	Pts.	OP	WESTERN CONFERENCE	W	L	T	Pct.	Pts.	OP
Cleveland	9	2	1	.818	269	172	Detroit	8	4	0	.667	251	231
N.Y. Giants	7	5	0	.583	254	211	San Francisco	8	4	0	.667	260	264
Pittsburgh	6	6	0	.500	161	178	Baltimore	7	5	0	.583	303	235
Washington	5	6	1	.455	251	230	Los Angeles	6	6	0	.500	307	278
Philadelphia	4	8	0	.333	173	230	Chi. Bears	5	7	0	.417	203	211
Chi. Cardinals	3	9	0	.250	200	299	Green Bay	3	9	0	.250	218	311

Western Conference playoff: Detroit 31, SAN FRANCISCO 27
NFL championship: DETROIT 59, Cleveland 14

1956

EASTERN CONFERENCE	W	L	T	Pct.	Pts.	OP	WESTERN CONFERENCE	W	L	T	Pct.	Pts.	OP
N.Y. Giants	8	3	1	.727	264	197	Chi. Bears	9	2	1	.818	363	246
Chi. Cardinals	7	5	0	.583	240	182	Detroit	9	3	0	.750	300	188
Washington	6	6	0	.500	183	225	San Francisco	5	6	1	.455	233	284
Cleveland	5	7	0	.417	167	177	Baltimore	5	7	0	.417	270	322
Pittsburgh	5	7	0	.417	217	250	Green Bay	4	8	0	.333	264	342
Philadelphia	3	8	1	.273	143	215	Los Angeles	4	8	0	.333	291	307

NFL championship: N.Y. GIANTS 47, Chi. Bears 7

1955

EASTERN CONFERENCE	W	L	T	Pct.	Pts.	OP	WESTERN CONFERENCE	W	L	T	Pct.	Pts.	OP
Cleveland	9	2	1	.818	349	218	Los Angeles	8	3	1	.727	260	231
Washington	8	4	0	.667	246	222	Chi. Bears	8	4	0	.667	294	251
N.Y. Giants	6	5	1	.545	267	223	Green Bay	6	6	0	.500	258	276
Chi. Cardinals	4	7	1	.364	224	252	Baltimore	5	6	1	.455	214	239
Philadelphia	4	7	1	.364	248	231	San Francisco	4	8	0	.333	216	298
Pittsburgh	4	8	0	.333	195	285	Detroit	3	9	0	.250	230	275

NFL championship: Cleveland 38, LOS ANGELES 14

1954

EASTERN CONFERENCE

	W	L	T	Pct.	Pts.	OP
Cleveland	9	3	0	.750	336	162
Philadelphia	7	4	1	.636	284	230
N.Y. Giants	7	5	0	.583	293	184
Pittsburgh	5	7	0	.417	219	263
Washington	3	9	0	.250	207	432
Chi. Cardinals	2	10	0	.167	183	347

WESTERN CONFERENCE

	W	L	T	Pct.	Pts.	OP
Detroit	9	2	1	.818	337	189
Chi. Bears	8	4	0	.667	301	279
San Francisco	7	4	1	.636	313	251
Los Angeles	6	5	1	.545	314	285
Green Bay	4	8	0	.333	234	251
Baltimore	3	9	0	.250	131	279

NFL championship: CLEVELAND 56, Detroit 10

1953

EASTERN CONFERENCE

	W	L	T	Pct.	Pts.	OP
Cleveland	11	1	0	.917	348	162
Philadelphia	7	4	1	.636	352	215
Washington	6	5	1	.545	208	215
Pittsburgh	6	6	0	.500	211	263
N.Y. Giants	3	9	0	.250	179	277
Chi. Cardinals	1	10	1	.091	190	337

WESTERN CONFERENCE

	W	L	T	Pct.	Pts.	OP
Detroit	10	2	0	.833	271	205
San Francisco	9	3	0	.750	372	237
Los Angeles	8	3	1	.727	366	236
Chi. Bears	3	8	1	.273	218	262
Baltimore	3	9	0	.250	182	350
Green Bay	2	9	1	.182	200	338

NFL championship: DETROIT 17, Cleveland 16

1952

AMERICAN CONFERENCE

	W	L	T	Pct.	Pts.	OP
Cleveland	8	4	0	.667	310	213
N.Y. Giants	7	5	0	.583	234	231
Philadelphia	7	5	0	.583	252	271
Pittsburgh	5	7	0	.417	300	273
Chi. Cardinals	4	8	0	.333	172	221
Washington	4	8	0	.333	240	287

NATIONAL CONFERENCE

	W	L	T	Pct.	Pts.	OP
Detroit	9	3	0	.750	344	192
Los Angeles	9	3	0	.750	349	234
San Francisco	7	5	0	.583	285	221
Green Bay	6	6	0	.500	295	312
Chi. Bears	5	7	0	.417	245	326
Dallas Texans	1	11	0	.083	182	427

National Conference playoff: DETROIT 31, Los Angeles 21
NFL championship: Detroit 17, CLEVELAND 7

1951

AMERICAN CONFERENCE

	W	L	T	Pct.	Pts.	OP
Cleveland	11	1	0	.917	331	152
N.Y. Giants	9	2	1	.818	254	161
Washington	5	7	0	.417	183	296
Pittsburgh	4	7	1	.364	183	235
Philadelphia	4	8	0	.333	234	264
Chi. Cardinals	3	9	0	.250	210	287

NATIONAL CONFERENCE

	W	L	T	Pct.	Pts.	OP
Los Angeles	8	4	0	.667	392	261
Detroit	7	4	1	.636	336	259
San Francisco	7	4	1	.636	255	205
Chi. Bears	7	5	0	.583	286	282
Green Bay	3	9	0	.250	254	375
N.Y. Yanks	1	9	2	.100	241	382

NFL championship: LOS ANGELES 24, Cleveland 17

1950

AMERICAN CONFERENCE

	W	L	T	Pct.	Pts.	OP
Cleveland	10	2	0	.833	310	144
N.Y. Giants	10	2	0	.833	268	150
Philadelphia	6	6	0	.500	254	141
Pittsburgh	6	6	0	.500	180	195
Chi. Cardinals	5	7	0	.417	233	287
Washington	3	9	0	.250	232	326

NATIONAL CONFERENCE

	W	L	T	Pct.	Pts.	OP
Los Angeles	9	3	0	.750	466	309
Chi. Bears	9	3	0	.750	279	207
N.Y. Yanks	7	5	0	.583	366	367
Detroit	6	6	0	.500	321	285
Green Bay	3	9	0	.250	244	406
San Francisco	3	9	0	.250	213	300
Baltimore	1	11	0	.083	213	462

American Conference playoff: CLEVELAND 8, N.Y. Giants 3
National Conference playoff: LOS ANGELES 24, Chi. Bears 14
NFL championship: CLEVELAND 30, Los Angeles 28

1949

EASTERN DIVISION

	W	L	T	Pct.	Pts.	OP
Philadelphia	11	1	0	.917	364	134
Pittsburgh	6	5	1	.545	224	214
N.Y. Giants	6	6	0	.500	287	298
Washington	4	7	1	.364	268	339
N.Y. Bulldogs	1	10	1	.091	153	368

WESTERN DIVISION

	W	L	T	Pct.	Pts.	OP
Los Angeles	8	2	2	.800	360	239
Chi. Bears	9	3	0	.750	332	218
Chi. Cardinals	6	5	1	.545	360	301
Detroit	4	8	0	.333	237	259
Green Bay	2	10	0	.167	114	329

NFL championship: Philadelphia 14, LOS ANGELES 0

1948

EASTERN DIVISION

	W	L	T	Pct.	Pts.	OP
Philadelphia	9	2	1	.818	376	156
Washington	7	5	0	.583	291	287
N.Y. Giants	4	8	0	.333	297	388
Pittsburgh	4	8	0	.333	200	243
Boston	3	9	0	.250	174	372

WESTERN DIVISION

	W	L	T	Pct.	Pts.	OP
Chi. Cardinals	11	1	0	.917	395	226
Chi. Bears	10	2	0	.833	375	151
Los Angeles	6	5	1	.545	327	269
Green Bay	3	9	0	.250	154	290
Detroit	2	10	0	.167	200	407

NFL championship: PHILADELPHIA 7, Chi. Cardinals 0

1947

EASTERN DIVISION

	W	L	T	Pct.	Pts.	OP
Philadelphia	8	4	0	.667	308	242
Pittsburgh	8	4	0	.667	240	259
Boston	4	7	1	.364	168	256
Washington	4	8	0	.333	295	367
N.Y. Giants	2	8	2	.200	190	309

WESTERN DIVISION

	W	L	T	Pct.	Pts.	OP
Chi. Cardinals	9	3	0	.750	306	231
Chi. Bears	8	4	0	.667	363	241
Green Bay	6	5	1	.545	274	210
Los Angeles	6	6	0	.500	259	214
Detroit	3	9	0	.250	231	305

Eastern Division playoff: Philadelphia 21, PITTSBURGH 0
NFL championship: CHI. CARDINALS 28, Philadelphia 21

1946

EASTERN DIVISION

	W	L	T	Pct.	Pts.	OP
N.Y. Giants	7	3	1	.700	236	162
Philadelphia	6	5	0	.545	231	220
Washington	5	5	1	.500	171	191
Pittsburgh	5	5	1	.500	136	117
Boston	2	8	1	.200	189	273

WESTERN DIVISION

	W	L	T	Pct.	Pts.	OP
Chi. Bears	8	2	1	.800	289	193
Los Angeles	6	4	1	.600	277	257
Green Bay	6	5	0	.545	148	158
Chi. Cardinals	6	5	0	.545	260	198
Detroit	1	10	0	.091	142	310

NFL championship: Chi. Bears 24, N.Y. GIANTS 14

1945

EASTERN DIVISION

	W	L	T	Pct.	Pts.	OP
Washington	8	2	0	.800	209	121
Philadelphia	7	3	0	.700	272	133
N.Y. Giants	3	6	1	.333	179	198
Boston	3	6	1	.333	123	211
Pittsburgh	2	8	0	.200	79	220

WESTERN DIVISION

	W	L	T	Pct.	Pts.	OP
Cleveland	9	1	0	.900	244	136
Detroit	7	3	0	.700	195	194
Green Bay	6	4	0	.600	258	173
Chi. Bears	3	7	0	.300	192	235
Chi. Cardinals	1	9	0	.100	98	228

NFL championship: CLEVELAND 15, Washington 14

1944

EASTERN DIVISION

	W	L	T	Pct.	Pts.	OP
N.Y. Giants	8	1	1	.889	206	75
Philadelphia	7	1	2	.875	267	131
Washington	6	3	1	.667	169	180
Boston	2	8	0	.200	82	233
Brooklyn	0	10	0	.000	69	166

WESTERN DIVISION

	W	L	T	Pct.	Pts.	OP
Green Bay	8	2	0	.800	238	141
Chi. Bears	6	3	1	.667	258	172
Detroit	6	3	1	.667	216	151
Cleveland	4	6	0	.400	188	224
Card-Pitt	0	10	0	.000	108	328

NFL championship: Green Bay 14, N.Y. GIANTS 7

1943

EASTERN DIVISION	W	L	T	Pct.	Pts.	OP	WESTERN DIVISION	W	L	T	Pct.	Pts.	OP
Washington	6	3	1	.667	229	137	Chi. Bears	8	1	1	.889	303	157
N.Y. Giants	6	3	1	.667	197	170	Green Bay	7	2	1	.778	264	172
Phil-Pitt	5	4	1	.556	225	230	Detroit	3	6	1	.333	178	218
Brooklyn	2	8	0	.200	65	234	Chi. Cardinals	0	10	0	.000	95	238

Eastern Division playoff: Washington 28, N.Y. GIANTS 0
NFL championship: CHI. BEARS 41, Washington 21

1942

EASTERN DIVISION	W	L	T	Pct.	Pts.	OP	WESTERN DIVISION	W	L	T	Pct.	Pts.	OP
Washington	10	1	0	.909	227	102	Chi. Bears	11	0	0	1.000	376	84
Pittsburgh	7	4	0	.636	167	119	Green Bay	8	2	1	.800	300	215
N.Y. Giants	5	5	1	.500	155	139	Cleveland	5	6	0	.455	150	207
Brooklyn	3	8	0	.273	100	168	Chi. Cardinals	3	8	0	.273	98	209
Philadelphia	2	9	0	.182	134	239	Detroit	0	11	0	.000	38	263

NFL championship: WASHINGTON 14, Chi. Bears 6

1941

EASTERN DIVISION	W	L	T	Pct.	Pts.	OP	WESTERN DIVISION	W	L	T	Pct.	Pts.	OP
N.Y. Giants	8	3	0	.727	238	114	Chi. Bears	10	1	0	.909	396	147
Brooklyn	7	4	0	.636	158	127	Green Bay	10	1	0	.909	258	120
Washington	6	5	0	.545	176	174	Detroit	4	6	1	.400	121	195
Philadelphia	2	8	1	.200	119	218	Chi. Cardinals	3	7	1	.300	127	197
Pittsburgh	1	9	1	.100	103	276	Cleveland	2	9	0	.182	116	244

Western Division playoff: CHI. BEARS 33, Green Bay 14
NFL championship: CHI. BEARS 37, N.Y. Giants 9

1940

EASTERN DIVISION	W	L	T	Pct.	Pts.	OP	WESTERN DIVISION	W	L	T	Pct.	Pts.	OP
Washington	9	2	0	.818	245	142	Chi. Bears	8	3	0	.727	238	152
Brooklyn	8	3	0	.727	186	120	Green Bay	6	4	1	.600	238	155
N.Y. Giants	6	4	1	.600	131	133	Detroit	5	5	1	.500	138	153
Pittsburgh	2	7	2	.222	60	178	Cleveland	4	6	1	.400	171	191
Philadelphia	1	10	0	.091	111	211	Chi. Cardinals	2	7	2	.222	139	222

NFL championship: Chi. Bears 73, WASHINGTON 0

1939

EASTERN DIVISION	W	L	T	Pct.	Pts.	OP	WESTERN DIVISION	W	L	T	Pct.	Pts.	OP
N.Y. Giants	9	1	1	.900	168	85	Green Bay	9	2	0	.818	233	153
Washington	8	2	1	.800	242	94	Chi. Bears	8	3	0	.727	298	157
Brooklyn	4	6	1	.400	108	219	Detroit	6	5	0	.545	145	150
Philadelphia	1	9	1	.100	105	200	Cleveland	5	5	1	.500	195	164
Pittsburgh	1	9	1	.100	114	216	Chi. Cardinals	1	10	0	.091	84	254

NFL championship: GREEN BAY 27, N.Y. Giants 0

1938

EASTERN DIVISION	W	L	T	Pct.	Pts.	OP	WESTERN DIVISION	W	L	T	Pct.	Pts.	OP
N.Y. Giants	8	2	1	.800	194	79	Green Bay	8	3	0	.727	223	118
Washington	6	3	2	.667	148	154	Detroit	7	4	0	.636	119	108
Brooklyn	4	4	3	.500	131	161	Chi. Bears	6	5	0	.545	194	148
Philadelphia	5	6	0	.455	154	164	Cleveland	4	7	0	.364	131	215
Pittsburgh	2	9	0	.182	79	169	Chi. Cardinals	2	9	0	.182	111	168

NFL championship: N.Y. GIANTS 23, Green Bay 17

1937

EASTERN DIVISION	W	L	T	Pct.	Pts.	OP	WESTERN DIVISION	W	L	T	Pct.	Pts.	OP
Washington	8	3	0	.727	195	120	Chi. Bears	9	1	1	.900	201	100
N.Y. Giants	6	3	2	.667	128	109	Green Bay	7	4	0	.636	220	122
Pittsburgh	4	7	0	.364	122	145	Detroit	7	4	0	.636	180	105
Brooklyn	3	7	1	.300	82	174	Chi. Cardinals	5	5	1	.500	135	165
Philadelphia	2	8	1	.200	86	177	Cleveland	1	10	0	.091	75	207

NFL championship: Washington 28, CHI. BEARS 21

1936

EASTERN DIVISION	W	L	T	Pct.	Pts.	OP	WESTERN DIVISION	W	L	T	Pct.	Pts.	OP
Boston	7	5	0	.583	149	110	Green Bay	10	1	1	.909	248	118
Pittsburgh	6	6	0	.500	98	187	Chi. Bears	9	3	0	.750	222	94
N.Y. Giants	5	6	1	.455	115	163	Detroit	8	4	0	.667	235	102
Brooklyn	3	8	1	.273	92	161	Chi. Cardinals	3	8	1	.273	74	143
Philadelphia	1	11	0	.083	51	206							

NFL championship: Green Bay 21, Boston 6, at Polo Grounds, N.Y.

1935

EASTERN DIVISION	W	L	T	Pct.	Pts.	OP	WESTERN DIVISION	W	L	T	Pct.	Pts.	OP
N.Y. Giants	9	3	0	.750	180	96	Detroit	7	3	2	.700	191	111
Brooklyn	5	6	1	.455	90	141	Green Bay	8	4	0	.667	181	96
Pittsburgh	4	8	0	.333	100	209	Chi. Bears	6	4	2	.600	192	106
Boston	2	8	1	.200	65	123	Chi. Cardinals	6	4	2	.600	99	97
Philadelphia	2	9	0	.182	60	179							

NFL championship: DETROIT 26, N.Y. Giants 7
One game between Boston and Philadelphia was canceled.

1934

EASTERN DIVISION	W	L	T	Pct.	Pts.	OP	WESTERN DIVISION	W	L	T	Pct.	Pts.	OP
N.Y. Giants	8	5	0	.615	147	107	Chi. Bears	13	0	0	1.000	286	86
Boston	6	6	0	.500	107	94	Detroit	10	3	0	.769	238	59
Brooklyn	4	7	0	.364	61	153	Green Bay	7	6	0	.538	156	112
Philadelphia	4	7	0	.364	127	85	Chi. Cardinals	5	6	0	.455	80	84
Pittsburgh	2	10	0	.167	51	206	St. Louis	1	2	0	.333	27	61
							Cincinnati	0	8	0	.000	10	243

NFL championship: N.Y. GIANTS 30, Chi. Bears 13

1933

EASTERN DIVISION	W	L	T	Pct.	Pts.	OP	WESTERN DIVISION	W	L	T	Pct.	Pts.	OP
N.Y. Giants	11	3	0	.786	244	101	Chi. Bears	10	2	1	.833	133	82
Brooklyn	5	4	1	.556	93	54	Portsmouth	6	5	0	.545	128	87
Boston	5	5	2	.500	103	97	Green Bay	5	7	1	.417	170	107
Philadelphia	3	5	1	.375	77	158	Cincinnati	3	6	1	.333	38	110
Pittsburgh	3	6	2	.333	67	208	Chi. Cardinals	1	9	1	.100	52	101

NFL championship: CHI. BEARS 23, N.Y. Giants 21

1932

	W	L	T	Pct.
Chicago Bears	7	1	6	.875
Green Bay Packers	10	3	1	.769
Portsmouth Spartans	6	2	4	.750
Boston Braves	4	4	2	.500
New York Giants	4	6	2	.400
Brooklyn Dodgers	3	9	0	.250
Chicago Cardinals	2	6	2	.250
Staten Island Stapletons	2	7	3	.222

Chicago Bears and Portsmouth finished regularly scheduled games tied for first place. Bears won playoff game, which counted in standings, 9-0.

1931

	W	L	T	Pct.
Green Bay Packers	12	2	0	.857
Portsmouth Spartans	11	3	0	.786
Chicago Bears	8	5	0	.615
Chicago Cardinals	5	4	0	.556
New York Giants	7	6	1	.538
Providence Steam Roller	4	4	3	.500
Staten Island Stapletons	4	6	1	.400
Cleveland Indians	2	8	0	.200
Brooklyn Dodgers	2	12	0	.143
Frankford Yellow Jackets	1	6	1	.143

1930

	W	L	T	Pct.
Green Bay Packers	10	3	1	.769
New York Giants	13	4	0	.765
Chicago Bears	9	4	1	.692
Brooklyn Dodgers	7	4	1	.636
Providence Steam Roller	6	4	1	.600
Staten Island Stapletons	5	5	2	.500
Chicago Cardinals	5	6	2	.455
Portsmouth Spartans	5	6	3	.455
Frankford Yellow Jackets	4	13	1	.222
Minneapolis Red Jackets	1	7	1	.125
Newark Tornadoes	1	10	1	.091

1929

	W	L	T	Pct.
Green Bay Packers	12	0	1	1.000
New York Giants	13	1	1	.929
Frankford Yellow Jackets	10	4	5	.714
Chicago Cardinals	6	6	1	.500
Boston Bulldogs	4	4	0	.500
Staten Island Stapletons	3	4	3	.429
Providence Steam Roller	4	6	2	.400
Orange Tornadoes	3	5	4	.375
Chicago Bears	4	9	2	.308
Buffalo Bisons	1	7	1	.125
Minneapolis Red Jackets	1	9	0	.100
Dayton Triangles	0	6	0	.000

1928

	W	L	T	Pct.
Providence Steam Roller	8	1	2	.889
Frankford Yellow Jackets	11	3	2	.786
Detroit Wolverines	7	2	1	.778
Green Bay Packers	6	4	3	.600
Chicago Bears	7	5	1	.583
New York Giants	4	7	2	.364
New York Yankees	4	8	1	.333
Pottsville Maroons	2	8	0	.200
Chicago Cardinals	1	5	0	.167
Dayton Triangles	0	7	0	.000

1927

	W	L	T	Pct.
New York Giants	11	1	1	.917
Green Bay Packers	7	2	1	.778
Chicago Bears	9	3	2	.750
Cleveland Bulldogs	8	4	1	.667
Providence Steam Roller	8	5	1	.615
New York Yankees	7	8	1	.467
Frankford Yellow Jackets	6	9	3	.400
Pottsville Maroons	5	8	0	.385
Chicago Cardinals	3	7	1	.300
Dayton Triangles	1	6	1	.143
Duluth Eskimos	1	8	0	.111
Buffalo Bisons	0	5	0	.000

1926

	W	L	T	Pct.
Frankford Yellow Jackets	14	1	2	.933
Chicago Bears	12	1	3	.923
Pottsville Maroons	10	2	2	.833
Kansas City Cowboys	8	3	0	.727
Green Bay Packers	7	3	3	.700
Los Angeles Buccaneers	6	3	1	.667
New York Giants	8	4	1	.667
Duluth Eskimos	6	5	3	.545
Buffalo Rangers	4	4	2	.500
Chicago Cardinals	5	6	1	.455
Providence Steam Roller	5	7	1	.417
Detroit Panthers	4	6	2	.400
Hartford Blues	3	7	0	.300
Brooklyn Lions	3	8	0	.273
Milwaukee Badgers	2	7	0	.222
Akron Indians	1	4	3	.200
Dayton Triangles	1	4	1	.200
Racine Tornadoes	1	4	0	.200
Columbus Tigers	1	6	0	.143
Canton Bulldogs	1	9	3	.100
Hammond Pros	0	4	0	.000
Louisville Colonels	0	4	0	.000

1925

	W	L	T	Pct.
Chicago Cardinals	11	2	1	.846
Pottsville Maroons	10	2	0	.833
Detroit Panthers	8	2	2	.800
New York Giants	8	4	0	.667
Akron Indians	4	2	2	.667
Frankford Yellow Jackets	13	7	0	.650
Chicago Bears	9	5	3	.643
Rock Island Independents	5	3	3	.625
Green Bay Packers	8	5	0	.615
Providence Steam Roller	6	5	1	.545
Canton Bulldogs	4	4	0	.500
Cleveland Bulldogs	5	8	1	.385
Kansas City Cowboys	2	5	1	.286
Hammond Pros	1	4	0	.200
Buffalo Bisons	1	6	2	.143
Duluth Kelleys	0	3	0	.000
Rochester Jeffersons	0	6	1	.000
Milwaukee Badgers	0	6	0	.000
Dayton Triangles	0	7	1	.000
Columbus Tigers	0	9	0	.000

1924

	W	L	T	Pct.
Cleveland Bulldogs	7	1	1	.875
Chicago Bears	6	1	4	.857
Frankford Yellow Jackets	11	2	1	.846
Duluth Kelleys	5	1	0	.833
Rock Island Independents	5	2	2	.714
Green Bay Packers	7	4	0	.636
Racine Legion	4	3	3	.571
Chicago Cardinals	5	4	1	.556
Buffalo Bisons	6	5	0	.545
Columbus Tigers	4	4	0	.500
Hammond Pros	2	2	1	.500
Milwaukee Badgers	5	8	0	.385
Akron Indians	2	6	0	.250
Dayton Triangles	2	6	0	.250
Kansas City Blues	2	7	0	.222
Kenosha Maroons	0	4	1	.000
Minneapolis Marines	0	6	0	.000
Rochester Jeffersons	0	7	0	.000

1923

	W	L	T	Pct.
Canton Bulldogs	11	0	1	1.000
Chicago Bears	9	2	1	.818
Green Bay Packers	7	2	1	.778
Milwaukee Badgers	7	2	3	.778
Cleveland Indians	3	1	3	.750
Chicago Cardinals	8	4	0	.667
Duluth Kelleys	4	3	0	.571
Buffalo All-Americans	5	4	3	.556
Columbus Tigers	5	4	1	.556
Racine Legion	4	4	2	.500
Toledo Maroons	3	3	2	.500
Rock Island Independents	2	3	3	.400
Minneapolis Marines	2	5	2	.286
St. Louis All-Stars	1	4	2	.200
Hammond Pros	1	5	1	.167
Dayton Triangles	1	6	1	.143
Akron Indians	1	6	0	.143
Oorang Indians	1	10	0	.091
Louisville Brecks	0	3	0	.000
Rochester Jeffersons	0	4	0	.000

1922

	W	L	T	Pct.
Canton Bulldogs	10	0	2	1.000
Chicago Bears	9	3	0	.750
Chicago Cardinals	8	3	0	.727
Toledo Maroons	5	2	2	.714
Rock Island Independents	4	2	1	.667
Racine Legion	6	4	1	.600
Dayton Triangles	4	3	1	.571
Green Bay Packers	4	3	3	.571
Buffalo All-Americans	5	4	1	.556
Akron Pros	3	5	2	.375
Milwaukee Badgers	2	4	3	.333
Oorang Indians	3	6	0	.333
Minneapolis Marines	1	3	0	.250
Louisville Brecks	1	3	0	.250
Evansville Crimson Giants	0	3	0	.000
Rochester Jeffersons	0	4	1	.000
Hammond Pros	0	5	1	.000
Columbus Panhandles	0	8	0	.000

1921

	W	L	T	Pct.
Chicago Staleys	9	1	1	.900
Buffalo All-Americans	9	1	2	.900
Akron Pros	8	3	1	.727
Canton Bulldogs	5	2	3	.714
Rock Island Independents	4	2	1	.667
Evansville Crimson Giants	3	2	0	.600
Green Bay Packers	3	2	1	.600
Dayton Triangles	4	4	1	.500
Chicago Cardinals	3	3	2	.500
Rochester Jeffersons	2	3	0	.400
Cleveland Indians	3	5	0	.375
Washington Senators	1	2	0	.333
Cincinnati Celts	1	3	0	.250
Hammond Pros	1	3	1	.250
Minneapolis Marines	1	3	0	.250
Detroit Heralds	1	5	1	.167
Columbus Panhandles	1	8	0	.111
Tonawanda Kardex	0	1	0	.000
Muncie Flyers	0	2	0	.000
Louisville Brecks	0	2	0	.000
New York Giants	0	2	0	.000

1920*

	W	L	T	Pct.
Akron Pros	8	0	3	1.000
Decatur Staleys	10	1	2	.909
Buffalo All-Americans	9	1	1	.900
Chicago Cardinals	6	2	2	.750
Rock Island Independents	6	2	2	.750
Dayton Triangles	5	2	2	.714
Rochester Jeffersons	6	3	2	.667
Canton Bulldogs	7	4	2	.636
Detroit Heralds	2	3	3	.400
Cleveland Tigers	2	4	2	.333
Chicago Tigers	2	5	1	.286
Hammond Pros	2	5	0	.286
Columbus Panhandles	2	6	2	.250
Muncie Flyers	0	1	0	.000

No official standings were maintained for the 1920 season, and the championship was awarded to the Akron Pros in a League meeting on April 30, 1921. Clubs played schedules that included games against nonleague opponents.

RS=REGULAR SEASON
PS=POSTSEASON

*ARIZONA vs. ATLANTA
RS: Cardinals lead series, 13-9
1966—Falcons, 16-10 (A)
1968—Cardinals, 17-12 (StL)
1971—Cardinals, 26-9 (A)
1973—Cardinals, 32-10 (A)
1975—Cardinals, 23-20 (StL)
1978—Cardinals, 42-21 (StL)
1980—Falcons, 33-27 (StL) OT
1981—Falcons, 41-20 (A)
1982—Cardinals, 23-20 (A)
1986—Falcons, 33-13 (A)
1987—Cardinals, 34-21 (A)
1989—Cardinals, 34-20 (P)
1990—Cardinals, 24-13 (A)
1991—Cardinals, 16-10 (P)
1992—Falcons, 20-17 (A)
1993—Cardinals, 27-10 (A)
1994—Falcons, 10-6 (Atl)
1995—Cardinals, 40-37 (Ariz) OT
1997—Cardinals, 29-26 (Ariz)
1999—Falcons, 37-14 (Atl)
2001—Falcons, 34-14 (Ariz)
2004—Falcons, 6-3 (Atl)
(RS Pts.—Cardinals 491, Falcons 459)
*Franchise known as Phoenix prior to
1994 and in St. Louis prior to 1988*

*ARIZONA vs. BALTIMORE
RS: Ravens lead series, 2-1
1997—Cardinals, 16-13 (B)
2000—Ravens, 13-7 (A)
2003—Ravens, 26-18 (A)
(RS Pts.—Ravens 52, Cardinals 41)

*ARIZONA vs. BUFFALO
RS: Bills lead series, 5-3
1971—Cardinals, 28-23 (B)
1975—Bills, 32-14 (StL)
1981—Cardinals, 24-0 (StL)
1984—Cardinals, 37-7 (StL)
1986—Bills, 17-10 (B)
1990—Bills, 45-14 (B)
1999—Bills, 31-21 (A)
2004—Bills, 38-14 (B)
(RS Pts.—Bills 193, Cardinals 162)
*Franchise known as Phoenix prior to
1994 and in St. Louis prior to 1988*

ARIZONA vs. CAROLINA
RS: Panthers lead series, 3-2
1995—Panthers, 27-7 (C)
2001—Cardinals, 30-7 (C)
2002—Cardinals, 16-13 (C)
2003—Panthers, 20-17 (A)
2004—Panthers, 35-10 (C)
(RS Pts.—Panthers 102, Cardinals 80)

*ARIZONA vs. **CHICAGO
RS: Bears lead series, 54-26-6
(NP denotes Normal Park;
Wr denotes Wrigley Field;
Co denotes Comiskey Park;
So denotes Soldier Field;
all Chicago)
1920—Cardinals, 7-6 (NP)
　　　　Staleys, 10-0 (Wr)
1921—Tie, 0-0 (Wr)
1922—Cardinals, 6-0 (Co)
　　　　Cardinals, 9-0 (Co)
1923—Bears, 3-0 (Wr)
1924—Bears, 6-0 (Wr)

Bears, 21-0 (Co)
1925—Cardinals, 9-0 (Co)
　　　　Tie, 0-0 (Wr)
1926—Bears, 16-0 (Wr)
　　　　Bears, 10-0 (So)
　　　　Tie, 0-0 (Wr)
1927—Bears, 9-0 (NP)
　　　　Cardinals, 3-0 (Wr)
1928—Bears, 15-0 (NP)
　　　　Bears, 34-0 (Wr)
1929—Tie, 0-0 (Wr)
　　　　Cardinals, 40-6 (Co)
1930—Bears, 32-6 (Co)
　　　　Bears, 6-0 (Wr)
1931—Bears, 26-13 (Wr)
　　　　Bears, 18-7 (Wr)
1932—Tie, 0-0 (Wr)
　　　　Bears, 34-0 (Wr)
1933—Bears, 12-9 (Wr)
　　　　Bears, 22-6 (Wr)
1934—Bears, 20-0 (Wr)
　　　　Bears, 17-6 (Wr)
1935—Tie, 7-7 (Wr)
　　　　Bears, 13-0 (Wr)
1936—Bears, 7-3 (Wr)
　　　　Cardinals, 14-7 (Wr)
1937—Bears, 16-7 (Wr)
　　　　Bears, 42-28 (Wr)
1938—Bears, 16-13 (So)
　　　　Bears, 34-28 (Wr)
1939—Bears, 44-7 (Wr)
　　　　Bears, 48-7 (Co)
1940—Cardinals, 21-7 (Co)
　　　　Bears, 31-23 (Wr)
1941—Bears, 53-7 (Wr)
　　　　Bears, 34-24 (Co)
1942—Bears, 41-14 (Wr)
　　　　Bears, 21-7 (Co)
1943—Bears, 20-0 (Wr)
　　　　Bears, 35-24 (Co)
1945—Cardinals, 16-7 (Wr)
　　　　Bears, 28-20 (Co)
1946—Bears, 34-17 (Co)
　　　　Cardinals, 35-28 (Wr)
1947—Cardinals, 31-7 (Co)
　　　　Cardinals, 30-21 (Wr)
1948—Bears, 28-17 (Co)
　　　　Cardinals, 24-21 (Wr)
1949—Bears, 17-7 (Co)
　　　　Bears, 52-21 (Wr)
1950—Bears, 27-6 (Wr)
　　　　Cardinals, 20-10 (Co)
1951—Cardinals, 28-14 (Co)
　　　　Cardinals, 24-14 (Wr)
1952—Cardinals, 21-10 (Co)
　　　　Bears, 10-7 (Wr)
1953—Cardinals, 24-17 (Wr)
1954—Bears, 29-7 (Co)
1955—Cardinals, 53-14 (Co)
1956—Bears, 10-3 (Wr)
1957—Bears, 14-6 (Co)
1958—Bears, 30-14 (Wr)
1959—Bears, 31-7 (So)
1965—Bears, 34-13 (Wr)
1966—Cardinals, 24-17 (StL)
1967—Bears, 30-3 (Wr)
1969—Cardinals, 20-17 (StL)
1972—Bears, 27-10 (StL)
1975—Cardinals, 34-20 (So)
1977—Cardinals, 16-13 (StL)

1978—Bears, 17-10 (So)
1979—Bears, 42-6 (So)
1982—Cardinals, 10-7 (So)
1984—Cardinals, 38-21 (StL)
1990—Bears, 31-21 (P)
1994—Bears, 19-16 (A) OT
1998—Cardinals, 20-7 (A)
2001—Bears, 20-13 (C)
2003—Bears, 28-3 (C)
(RS Pts.—Bears 1,622, Cardinals 1,050)
*Franchise known as Phoenix prior to
1994, in St. Louis prior to 1988, and in
Chicago prior to 1960
**Franchise in Decatur prior to 1921 and
known as Staleys prior to 1922*

*ARIZONA vs. CINCINNATI
RS: Bengals lead series, 5-3
1973—Bengals, 42-24 (C)
1979—Bengals, 34-28 (C)
1985—Cardinals, 41-27 (StL)
1988—Bengals, 21-14 (C)
1994—Cardinals, 28-7 (A)
1997—Bengals, 24-21 (C)
2000—Bengals, 24-13 (A)
2003—Cardinals, 17-14 (A)
(RS Pts.—Bengals 193, Cardinals 186)
*Franchise known as Phoenix prior to
1994 and in St. Louis prior to 1988*

*ARIZONA vs. CLEVELAND
RS: Browns lead series, 33-11-3
1950—Browns, 34-24 (Cle)
　　　　Browns, 10-7 (Chi)
1951—Browns, 34-17 (Chi)
　　　　Browns, 49-28 (Cle)
1952—Browns, 28-13 (Cle)
　　　　Browns, 10-0 (Chi)
1953—Browns, 27-7 (Chi)
　　　　Browns, 27-16 (Cle)
1954—Browns, 31-7 (Cle)
　　　　Browns, 35-3 (Chi)
1955—Browns, 26-20 (Chi)
　　　　Browns, 35-24 (Cle)
1956—Cardinals, 9-7 (Chi)
　　　　Cardinals, 24-7 (Cle)
1957—Browns, 17-7 (Chi)
　　　　Browns, 31-0 (Cle)
1958—Browns, 35-28 (Cle)
　　　　Browns, 38-24 (Chi)
1959—Browns, 34-7 (Chi)
　　　　Browns, 17-7 (Cle)
1960—Browns, 28-27 (Cle)
　　　　Tie, 17-17 (StL)
1961—Browns, 20-17 (Cle)
　　　　Browns, 21-10 (StL)
1962—Browns, 34-7 (StL)
　　　　Browns, 38-14 (Cle)
1963—Cardinals, 20-14 (Cle)
　　　　Browns, 24-10 (StL)
1964—Tie, 33-33 (Cle)
　　　　Cardinals, 28-19 (StL)
1965—Cardinals, 49-13 (Cle)
　　　　Browns, 27-24 (StL)
1966—Cardinals, 34-28 (Cle)
　　　　Browns, 38-10 (StL)
1967—Browns, 20-16 (Cle)
　　　　Browns, 20-16 (StL)
1968—Cardinals, 27-21 (Cle)
　　　　Cardinals, 27-16 (StL)
1969—Tie, 21-21 (Cle)
　　　　Browns, 27-21 (StL)

1974—Cardinals, 29-7 (StL)
1979—Browns, 38-20 (StL)
1985—Cardinals, 27-24 (Cle) OT
1988—Browns, 29-21 (P)
1994—Browns, 32-0 (Cle)
2000—Cardinals, 29-21 (A)
2003—Browns, 44-6 (Cle)
(RS Pts.—Browns 1,206, Cardinals 832)
*Franchise known as Phoenix prior to
1994, in St. Louis prior to 1988,
and in Chicago prior to 1960
*ARIZONA vs. DALLAS
RS: Cowboys lead series, 53-27-1
PS: Cardinals lead series, 1-0
1960—Cardinals, 12-10 (StL)
1961—Cardinals, 31-17 (D)
    Cardinals, 31-13 (StL)
1962—Cardinals, 28-24 (D)
    Cardinals, 52-20 (StL)
1963—Cardinals, 34-7 (D)
    Cowboys, 28-24 (StL)
1964—Cardinals, 16-6 (D)
    Cowboys, 31-13 (StL)
1965—Cardinals, 20-13 (StL)
    Cowboys, 27-13 (D)
1966—Tie, 10-10 (StL)
    Cowboys, 31-17 (D)
1967—Cowboys, 46-21 (D)
1968—Cowboys, 27-10 (StL)
1969—Cowboys, 24-3 (D)
1970—Cardinals, 20-7 (StL)
    Cardinals, 38-0 (D)
1971—Cowboys, 16-13 (StL)
    Cowboys, 31-12 (D)
1972—Cowboys, 33-24 (D)
    Cowboys, 27-6 (StL)
1973—Cowboys, 45-10 (D)
    Cowboys, 30-3 (StL)
1974—Cardinals, 31-28 (StL)
    Cowboys, 17-14 (D)
1975—Cowboys, 37-31 (D) OT
    Cardinals, 31-17 (StL)
1976—Cardinals, 21-17 (StL)
    Cowboys, 19-14 (D)
1977—Cowboys, 30-24 (StL)
    Cardinals, 24-17 (D)
1978—Cowboys, 21-12 (D)
    Cowboys, 24-21 (StL) OT
1979—Cowboys, 22-21 (StL)
    Cowboys, 22-13 (D)
1980—Cowboys, 27-24 (StL)
    Cowboys, 31-21 (D)
1981—Cowboys, 30-17 (D)
    Cardinals, 20-17 (StL)
1982—Cowboys, 24-7 (StL)
1983—Cowboys, 34-17 (StL)
    Cowboys, 35-17 (D)
1984—Cardinals, 31-20 (D)
    Cowboys, 24-17 (StL)
1985—Cardinals, 21-10 (StL)
    Cowboys, 35-17 (D)
1986—Cowboys, 31-7 (StL)
    Cowboys, 37-6 (D)
1987—Cardinals, 24-13 (StL)
    Cowboys, 21-16 (D)
1988—Cowboys, 17-14 (P)
    Cardinals, 16-10 (D)
1989—Cardinals, 19-10 (D)
    Cardinals, 24-20 (P)
1990—Cardinals, 20-3 (P)

    Cowboys, 41-10 (D)
1991—Cowboys, 17-9 (P)
    Cowboys, 27-7 (D)
1992—Cowboys, 31-20 (D)
    Cowboys, 16-10 (P)
1993—Cowboys, 17-10 (P)
    Cowboys, 20-15 (D)
1994—Cowboys, 38-3 (D)
    Cowboys, 28-21 (A)
1995—Cowboys, 34-20 (D)
    Cowboys, 37-13 (A)
1996—Cowboys, 17-3 (D)
    Cowboys, 10-6 (A)
1997—Cardinals, 25-22 (A) OT
    Cowboys, 24-6 (D)
1998—Cowboys, 38-10 (D)
    Cowboys, 35-28 (A)
    **Cardinals, 20-7 (D)
1999—Cowboys, 35-7 (D)
    Cardinals, 13-9 (A)
2000—Cardinals, 32-31 (A)
    Cowboys, 48-7 (D)
2001—Cowboys, 17-3 (D)
    Cardinals, 17-10 (A)
2002—Cardinals, 9-6 (A) OT
2003—Cowboys, 24-7 (D)
(RS Pts.—Cowboys 1,875, Cardinals 1,384)
(PS Pts.—Cardinals 20, Cowboys 7)
*Franchise known as Phoenix prior to
1994 and in St. Louis prior to 1988
**NFC First-Round Playoff
*ARIZONA vs. DENVER
RS: Broncos lead series, 6-0-1
1973—Tie, 17-17 (StL)
1977—Broncos, 7-0 (D)
1989—Broncos, 37-0 (P)
1991—Broncos, 24-19 (D)
1995—Broncos, 38-6 (D)
2001—Broncos, 38-17 (A)
2002—Broncos, 37-7 (D)
(RS Pts.—Broncos 198, Cardinals 66)
*Franchise known as Phoenix prior to
1994 and in St. Louis prior to 1988
*ARIZONA vs. **DETROIT
RS: Lions lead series, 30-21-5
1930—Tie, 0-0 (Port)
    Cardinals, 23-0 (C)
1931—Spartans, 13-3 (Port)
    Cardinals, 20-19 (C)
1932—Tie, 7-7 (Port)
1933—Spartans, 7-6 (Port)
1934—Lions, 6-0 (D)
    Lions, 17-13 (C)
1935—Tie, 10-10 (D)
    Lions, 7-6 (C)
1936—Lions, 39-0 (D)
    Lions, 14-7 (C)
1937—Lions, 16-7 (C)
    Lions, 16-7 (D)
1938—Lions, 10-0 (D)
    Lions, 7-3 (C)
1939—Lions, 21-3 (D)
    Lions, 17-3 (C)
1940—Tie, 0-0 (Buffalo)
    Lions, 43-14 (C)
1941—Tie, 14-14 (C)
    Lions, 21-3 (D)
1942—Cardinals, 13-0 (C)
    Cardinals, 7-0 (D)
1943—Lions, 35-17 (D)

    Lions, 7-0 (Buffalo)
1945—Lions, 10-0 (Milwaukee)
    Lions, 26-0 (D)
1946—Cardinals, 34-14 (C)
    Cardinals, 36-14 (D)
1947—Cardinals, 45-21 (C)
    Cardinals, 17-7 (D)
1948—Cardinals, 56-20 (C)
    Cardinals, 28-14 (D)
1949—Lions, 24-7 (C)
    Cardinals, 42-19 (D)
1959—Lions, 45-21 (D)
1961—Lions, 45-14 (StL)
1967—Cardinals, 38-28 (StL)
1969—Lions, 20-0 (D)
1970—Lions, 16-3 (D)
1973—Lions, 20-16 (StL)
1975—Cardinals, 24-13 (D)
1978—Cardinals, 21-14 (StL)
1980—Lions, 20-7 (D)
    Cardinals, 24-23 (StL)
1989—Cardinals, 16-13 (D)
1993—Lions, 26-20 (D)
    Lions, 21-14 (Phx)
1995—Cardinals, 20-17 (D)
1998—Cardinals, 17-15 (D)
1999—Cardinals, 23-19 (A)
2001—Cardinals, 45-38 (A)
2002—Cardinals, 23-20 (A) OT
2003—Lions, 42-24 (D)
2004—Lions, 26-12 (D)
(RS Pts.—Lions 996, Cardinals 843)
*Franchise known as Phoenix prior to
1994, in St. Louis prior to 1988,
and in Chicago prior to 1960
**Franchise in Portsmouth prior to 1934
and known as the Spartans
*ARIZONA vs. GREEN BAY
RS: Packers lead series, 41-22-4
PS: Packers lead series, 1-0
1921—Tie, 3-3 (C)
1922—Cardinals, 16-3 (C)
1924—Cardinals, 3-0 (C)
1925—Cardinals, 9-6 (C)
1926—Cardinals, 13-7 (GB)
    Packers, 3-0 (C)
1927—Packers, 13-0 (GB)
    Tie, 6-6 (C)
1928—Packers, 20-0 (GB)
1929—Packers, 9-2 (GB)
    Packers, 7-6 (C)
    Packers, 12-0 (C)
1930—Packers, 14-0 (GB)
    Cardinals, 13-6 (C)
1931—Packers, 26-7 (GB)
    Cardinals, 21-13 (C)
1932—Packers, 15-7 (GB)
    Packers, 19-9 (C)
1933—Packers, 14-6 (C)
1934—Packers, 15-0 (GB)
    Cardinals, 9-0 (Mil)
    Cardinals, 6-0 (C)
1935—Cardinals, 7-6 (GB)
    Cardinals, 3-0 (Mil)
    Cardinals, 9-7 (C)
1936—Packers, 10-7 (GB)
    Packers, 24-0 (Mil)
    Tie, 0-0 (C)
1937—Cardinals, 14-7 (GB)
    Packers, 34-13 (Mil)

1938—Packers, 28-7 (Mil)
    Packers, 24-22 (Buffalo)
1939—Packers, 14-10 (GB)
    Packers, 27-20 (Mil)
1940—Packers, 31-6 (Mil)
    Packers, 28-7 (C)
1941—Packers, 14-13 (Mil)
    Packers, 17-9 (GB)
1942—Packers, 17-13 (C)
    Packers, 55-24 (GB)
1943—Packers, 28-7 (C)
    Packers, 35-14 (Mil)
1945—Packers, 33-14 (GB)
1946—Packers, 19-7 (C)
    Cardinals, 24-6 (GB)
1947—Packers, 14-10 (GB)
    Cardinals, 21-20 (C)
1948—Cardinals, 17-7 (Mil)
    Cardinals, 42-7 (C)
1949—Cardinals, 39-17 (Mil)
    Cardinals, 41-21 (C)
1955—Packers, 31-14 (GB)
1956—Packers, 24-21 (C)
1962—Packers, 17-0 (Mil)
1963—Packers, 30-7 (StL)
1967—Packers, 31-23 (StL)
1969—Packers, 45-28 (GB)
1971—Tie, 16-16 (StL)
1973—Packers, 25-21 (GB)
1976—Cardinals, 29-0 (StL)
1982—**Packers, 41-16 (GB)
1984—Packers, 24-23 (GB)
1985—Cardinals, 43-28 (StL)
1988—Packers, 26-17 (P)
1990—Packers, 24-21 (P)
1999—Packers, 49-24 (GB)
2000—Packers, 29-3 (A)
2003—Cardinals, 20-13 (A)
(RS Pts.—Packers 1,169, Cardinals 870)
(PS Pts.—Packers 41, Cardinals 16)
*Franchise known as Phoenix prior to
1994, in St. Louis prior to 1988,
and in Chicago prior to 1960
**NFC First-Round Playoff
ARIZONA vs. **INDIANAPOLIS
RS: Series tied, 6-6
1961—Colts, 16-0 (B)
1964—Colts, 47-27 (B)
1968—Colts, 27-0 (B)
1972—Cardinals, 10-3 (B)
1976—Cardinals, 24-17 (StL)
1978—Colts, 30-17 (StL)
1980—Cardinals, 17-10 (B)
1981—Cardinals, 35-24 (B)
1984—Cardinals, 34-33 (I)
1990—Cardinals, 20-17 (P)
1992—Colts, 16-13 (I)
1996—Colts, 20-13 (I)
(RS Pts.—Colts 260, Cardinals 210)
*Franchise known as Phoenix prior to
1994 and in St. Louis prior to 1988
**Franchise in Baltimore prior to 1984
ARIZONA vs. JACKSONVILLE
RS: Jaguars lead series, 1-0
2000—Jaguars, 44-10 (J)
(RS Pts.—Jaguars 44, Cardinals 10)
ARIZONA vs. KANSAS CITY
RS: Chiefs lead series, 6-2-1
1970—Tie, 6-6 (KC)
1974—Chiefs, 17-13 (StL)

1980—Chiefs, 21-13 (StL)
1983—Chiefs, 38-14 (KC)
1986—Cardinals, 23-14 (StL)
1995—Chiefs, 24-3 (A)
1998—Chiefs, 34-24 (KC)
2001—Cardinals, 24-16 (A)
2002—Chiefs, 49-0 (KC)
(RS Pts.—Chiefs 219, Cardinals 120)
*Franchise known as Phoenix prior to
1994 and in St. Louis prior to 1988
ARIZONA vs. MIAMI
RS: Dolphins lead series, 8-1
1972—Dolphins, 31-10 (M)
1977—Dolphins, 55-14 (StL)
1978—Dolphins, 24-10 (M)
1981—Dolphins, 20-7 (StL)
1984—Dolphins, 36-28 (StL)
1990—Dolphins, 23-3 (M)
1996—Dolphins, 38-10 (A)
1999—Dolphins, 19-16 (M)
2004—Cardinals, 24-23 (M)
(RS Pts.—Dolphins 269, Cardinals 122)
*Franchise known as Phoenix prior to
1994 and in St. Louis prior to 1988
ARIZONA vs. MINNESOTA
RS: Cardinals lead series, 9-8
PS: Vikings lead series, 2-0
1963—Cardinals, 56-14 (M)
1967—Cardinals, 34-24 (M)
1969—Vikings, 27-10 (StL)
1972—Cardinals, 19-17 (M)
1974—Vikings, 28-24 (StL)
    **Vikings, 30-14 (M)
1977—Cardinals, 27-7 (M)
1979—Cardinals, 37-7 (StL)
1981—Cardinals, 30-17 (StL)
1983—Cardinals, 41-31 (StL)
1991—Vikings, 34-7 (M)
    Vikings, 28-0 (P)
1994—Cardinals, 17-7 (A)
1995—Vikings, 30-24 (A) OT
1996—Vikings, 41-17 (M)
1997—Vikings, 20-19 (A)
1998—**Vikings, 41-21 (M)
2000—Vikings, 31-14 (M)
2003—Cardinals, 18-17 (A)
(RS Pts.—Cardinals 394, Vikings 380)
(PS Pts.—Vikings 71, Cardinals 35)
*Franchise known as Phoenix prior to
1994 and in St. Louis prior to 1988
**NFC Divisional Playoff
ARIZONA vs. **NEW ENGLAND
RS: Cardinals lead series, 6-5
1970—Cardinals, 31-0 (StL)
1975—Cardinals, 24-17 (StL)
1978—Patriots, 16-6 (StL)
1981—Cardinals, 27-20 (NE)
1984—Cardinals, 33-10 (NE)
1990—Cardinals, 34-14 (P)
1991—Cardinals, 24-10 (P)
1993—Patriots, 23-21 (P)
1996—Patriots, 31-0 (NE)
1999—Patriots, 27-3 (A)
2004—Patriots, 23-12 (A)
(RS Pts.—Cardinals 215, Patriots 191)
*Franchise known as Phoenix prior to
1994 and in St. Louis prior to 1988
**Franchise in Boston prior to 1971
ARIZONA vs. NEW ORLEANS
RS: Cardinals lead series, 13-11

1967—Cardinals, 31-20 (StL)
1968—Cardinals, 21-20 (NO)
    Cardinals, 31-17 (StL)
1969—Saints, 51-42 (StL)
1970—Cardinals, 24-17 (StL)
1974—Saints, 14-0 (NO)
1977—Cardinals, 49-31 (StL)
1980—Cardinals, 40-7 (NO)
1981—Cardinals, 30-3 (StL)
1982—Cardinals, 21-7 (NO)
1983—Saints, 28-17 (NO)
1984—Saints, 34-24 (NO)
1985—Cardinals, 28-16 (StL)
1986—Saints, 16-7 (StL)
1987—Cardinals, 24-19 (StL)
1990—Saints, 28-7 (NO)
1991—Saints, 27-3 (P)
1992—Saints, 30-21 (P)
1993—Saints, 20-17 (P)
1996—Cardinals, 28-14 (NO)
1997—Saints, 27-10 (NO)
1998—Cardinals, 19-17 (A)
2000—Saints, 21-10 (A)
2004—Cardinals, 34-10 (A)
(RS Pts.—Cardinals 538, Saints 494)
*Franchise known as Phoenix prior to
1994 and in St. Louis prior to 1988
ARIZONA vs. N.Y. GIANTS
RS: Giants lead series, 77-41-2
1926—Giants, 20-0 (NY)
1927—Giants, 28-7 (NY)
1929—Giants, 24-21 (NY)
1930—Giants, 25-12 (NY)
    Giants, 13-7 (C)
1935—Cardinals, 14-13 (NY)
1936—Giants, 14-6 (NY)
1938—Giants, 6-0 (NY)
1939—Giants, 17-7 (NY)
1941—Cardinals, 10-7 (NY)
1942—Giants, 21-7 (NY)
1943—Giants, 24-13 (NY)
1946—Giants, 28-24 (NY)
1947—Giants, 35-31 (NY)
1948—Cardinals, 63-35 (NY)
1949—Giants, 41-38 (C)
1950—Cardinals, 17-3 (C)
    Giants, 51-21 (NY)
1951—Giants, 28-17 (NY)
    Giants, 10-0 (C)
1952—Cardinals, 24-23 (NY)
    Giants, 28-6 (C)
1953—Giants, 21-7 (NY)
    Giants, 23-20 (C)
1954—Giants, 41-10 (C)
    Giants, 31-17 (NY)
1955—Cardinals, 28-17 (C)
    Giants, 10-0 (NY)
1956—Cardinals, 35-27 (C)
    Giants, 23-10 (NY)
1957—Giants, 27-14 (NY)
    Giants, 28-21 (C)
1958—Giants, 37-7 (Buffalo)
    Cardinals, 23-6 (NY)
1959—Giants, 9-3 (NY)
    Giants, 30-20 (Minn)
1960—Giants, 35-14 (StL)
    Cardinals, 20-13 (NY)
1961—Cardinals, 21-10 (NY)
    Giants, 24-9 (StL)
1962—Giants, 31-14 (StL)

Giants, 31-28 (NY)
1963—Giants, 38-21 (StL)
Cardinals, 24-17 (NY)
1964—Giants, 34-17 (NY)
Tie, 10-10 (StL)
1965—Giants, 14-10 (NY)
Giants, 28-15 (StL)
1966—Cardinals, 24-19 (StL)
Cardinals, 20-17 (NY)
1967—Giants, 37-20 (StL)
Giants, 37-14 (NY)
1968—Cardinals, 28-21 (NY)
1969—Cardinals, 42-17 (StL)
Giants, 49-6 (NY)
1970—Giants, 35-17 (NY)
Giants, 34-17 (StL)
1971—Giants, 21-20 (StL)
Cardinals, 24-7 (NY)
1972—Giants, 27-21 (NY)
Giants, 13-7 (StL)
1973—Cardinals, 35-27 (StL)
Giants, 24-13 (New Haven)
1974—Cardinals, 23-21 (New Haven)
Cardinals, 26-14 (StL)
1975—Cardinals, 26-14 (StL)
Cardinals, 20-13 (NY)
1976—Cardinals, 27-21 (StL)
Cardinals, 17-14 (NY)
1977—Cardinals, 28-0 (StL)
Giants, 27-7 (NY)
1978—Cardinals, 20-10 (StL)
Giants, 17-0 (NY)
1979—Cardinals, 27-14 (NY)
Cardinals, 29-20 (StL)
1980—Giants, 41-35 (StL)
Cardinals, 23-7 (NY)
1981—Giants, 34-14 (NY)
Giants, 20-10 (StL)
1982—Cardinals, 24-21 (StL)
1983—Tie, 20-20 (StL) OT
Cardinals, 10-6 (NY)
1984—Giants, 16-10 (NY)
Cardinals, 31-21 (StL)
1985—Giants, 27-17 (NY)
Giants, 34-3 (StL)
1986—Giants, 13-6 (StL)
Giants, 27-7 (NY)
1987—Giants, 30-7 (NY)
Cardinals, 27-24 (StL)
1988—Cardinals, 24-17 (P)
Giants, 44-7 (NY)
1989—Giants, 35-7 (NY)
Giants, 20-13 (P)
1990—Giants, 20-19 (NY)
Giants, 24-21 (P)
1991—Giants, 20-9 (NY)
Giants, 21-14 (P)
1992—Giants, 31-21 (NY)
Cardinals, 19-0 (P)
1993—Giants, 19-17 (NY)
Cardinals, 17-6 (P)
1994—Giants, 20-17 (A)
Cardinals, 10-9 (NY)
1995—Giants, 27-21 (NY) OT
Giants, 10-6 (A)
1996—Giants, 16-8 (NY)
Cardinals, 31-23 (A)
1997—Giants, 27-13 (A)
Giants, 19-10 (NY)
1998—Giants, 34-7 (NY)

Giants, 23-19 (A)
1999—Cardinals, 14-3 (A)
Cardinals, 34-24 (NY)
2000—Giants, 21-16 (NY)
Giants, 31-7 (A)
2001—Giants, 17-10 (A)
Giants, 17-13 (NY)
2002—Cardinals, 21-7 (A)
2004—Cardinals, 17-14 (A)
(RS Pts.—Giants 2,619, Cardinals 2,027)
*Franchise known as Phoenix prior to
1994, in St. Louis prior to 1988,
and in Chicago prior to 1960

*ARIZONA vs. N.Y. JETS
RS: Jets lead series, 4-2
1971—Cardinals, 17-10 (StL)
1975—Cardinals, 37-6 (NY)
1978—Jets, 23-10 (NY)
1996—Jets, 31-21 (A)
1999—Jets, 12-7 (NY)
2004—Jets, 13-3 (A)
(RS Pts.—Cardinals 95, Jets 95)
*Franchise known as Phoenix prior to
1994 and in St. Louis prior to 1988

*ARIZONA vs. **OAKLAND
RS: Raiders lead series, 4-2
1973—Raiders, 17-10 (StL)
1983—Cardinals, 34-24 (LA)
1989—Raiders, 16-14 (LA)
1998—Raiders, 23-20 (A)
2001—Cardinals, 34-31 (O) OT
2002—Raiders, 41-20 (A)
(RS Pts.— Raiders 152, Cardinals 132)
*Franchise known as Phoenix prior to
1994 and in St. Louis prior to 1988
**Franchise in Los Angeles from
1982-1994

*ARIZONA vs. PHILADELPHIA
RS: Series tied, 52-52-5
PS: Series tied, 1-1
1935—Cardinals, 12-3 (C)
1936—Cardinals, 13-0 (C)
1937—Tie, 6-6 (P)
1938—Eagles, 7-0 (Erie, Pa.)
1941—Eagles, 21-14 (P)
1945—Eagles, 21-6 (P)
1947—Cardinals, 45-21 (P)
**Cardinals, 28-21 (C)
1948—Cardinals, 21-14 (C)
**Eagles, 7-0 (P)
1949—Eagles, 28-3 (P)
1950—Eagles, 45-7 (C)
Cardinals, 14-10 (P)
1951—Eagles, 17-14 (C)
1952—Eagles, 10-7 (P)
Cardinals, 28-22 (C)
1953—Eagles, 56-17 (C)
Eagles, 38-0 (P)
1954—Eagles, 35-16 (C)
Eagles, 30-14 (P)
1955—Tie, 24-24 (C)
Eagles, 27-3 (P)
1956—Cardinals, 20-6 (P)
Cardinals, 28-17 (C)
1957—Eagles, 38-21 (C)
Cardinals, 31-27 (P)
1958—Tie, 21-21 (C)
Eagles, 49-21 (P)
1959—Eagles, 28-24 (Minn)
Eagles, 27-17 (P)

1960—Eagles, 31-27 (P)
Eagles, 20-6 (StL)
1961—Cardinals, 30-27 (P)
Eagles, 20-7 (StL)
1962—Cardinals, 27-21 (P)
Cardinals, 45-35 (StL)
1963—Cardinals, 28-24 (P)
Cardinals, 38-14 (StL)
1964—Cardinals, 38-13 (P)
Cardinals, 36-34 (StL)
1965—Eagles, 34-27 (P)
Eagles, 28-24 (StL)
1966—Cardinals, 16-13 (StL)
Cardinals, 41-10 (P)
1967—Cardinals, 48-14 (StL)
1968—Cardinals, 45-17 (P)
1969—Eagles, 34-30 (StL)
1970—Cardinals, 35-20 (P)
Cardinals, 23-14 (StL)
1971—Cardinals, 37-20 (StL)
Eagles, 19-7 (P)
1972—Tie, 6-6 (P)
Cardinals, 24-23 (StL)
1973—Cardinals, 34-23 (P)
Eagles, 27-24 (StL)
1974—Cardinals, 7-3 (StL)
Cardinals, 13-3 (P)
1975—Cardinals, 31-20 (StL)
Cardinals, 24-23 (P)
1976—Cardinals, 33-14 (StL)
Cardinals, 17-14 (P)
1977—Cardinals, 21-17 (P)
Cardinals, 21-16 (StL)
1978—Cardinals, 16-10 (P)
Eagles, 14-10 (StL)
1979—Eagles, 24-20 (StL)
Eagles, 16-13 (P)
1980—Cardinals, 24-14 (StL)
Eagles, 17-3 (P)
1981—Eagles, 52-10 (StL)
Eagles, 38-0 (P)
1982—Cardinals, 23-20 (P)
1983—Cardinals, 14-11 (P)
Cardinals, 31-7 (StL)
1984—Cardinals, 34-14 (P)
Cardinals, 17-16 (StL)
1985—Eagles, 30-7 (P)
Eagles, 24-14 (StL)
1986—Cardinals, 13-10 (StL)
Tie, 10-10 (P) OT
1987—Eagles, 28-23 (StL)
Cardinals, 31-19 (P)
1988—Eagles, 31-21 (P)
Eagles, 23-17 (Phx)
1989—Eagles, 17-5 (Phx)
Eagles, 31-14 (P)
1990—Cardinals, 23-21 (P)
Eagles, 23-21 (Phx)
1991—Cardinals, 26-10 (P)
Eagles, 34-14 (Phx)
1992—Eagles, 31-14 (Phx)
Eagles, 7-3 (P)
1993—Eagles, 23-17 (P)
Cardinals, 16-3 (Phx)
1994—Eagles, 17-7 (P)
Cardinals, 12-6 (A)
1995—Eagles, 31-19 (A)
Eagles, 21-20 (P)
1996—Cardinals, 36-30 (A)
Eagles, 29-19 (P)

1997—Eagles, 13-10 (P) OT
  Cardinals, 31-21 (A)
1998—Cardinals, 17-3 (A)
  Cardinals, 20-17 (P) OT
1999—Cardinals, 25-24 (P)
  Cardinals, 21-17 (A)
2000—Eagles, 33-14 (A)
  Eagles, 34-9 (P)
2001—Cardinals, 21-20 (P)
  Eagles, 21-7 (A)
2002—Eagles, 38-14 (P)
(RS Pts.—Eagles 2,319, Cardinals 2,106)
(PS Pts.—Eagles 28, Cardinals 28)
*Franchise known as Phoenix prior to
1994, in St. Louis prior to 1988,
and in Chicago prior to 1960
**NFL Championship
ARIZONA vs. **PITTSBURGH
RS: Steelers lead series, 31-22-3
1933—Pirates, 14-13 (C)
1935—Pirates, 17-13 (P)
1936—Cardinals, 14-6 (C)
1937—Cardinals, 13-7 (P)
1939—Cardinals, 10-0 (P)
1940—Tie, 7-7 (P)
1942—Steelers, 19-3 (P)
1945—Steelers, 23-0 (P)
1946—Steelers, 14-7 (P)
1948—Cardinals, 24-7 (P)
1950—Steelers, 28-17 (C)
  Steelers, 28-7 (P)
1951—Steelers, 28-14 (C)
1952—Steelers, 34-28 (C)
  Steelers, 17-14 (P)
1953—Steelers, 31-28 (P)
  Steelers, 21-17 (C)
1954—Cardinals, 17-14 (C)
  Steelers, 20-17 (P)
1955—Steelers, 14-7 (P)
  Cardinals, 27-13 (C)
1956—Steelers, 14-7 (P)
  Cardinals, 38-27 (C)
1957—Steelers, 29-20 (P)
  Steelers, 27-2 (C)
1958—Steelers, 27-20 (C)
  Steelers, 38-21 (P)
1959—Cardinals, 45-24 (C)
  Steelers, 35-20 (P)
1960—Steelers, 27-14 (P)
  Cardinals, 38-7 (StL)
1961—Steelers, 30-27 (P)
  Cardinals, 20-0 (StL)
1962—Steelers, 26-17 (StL)
  Steelers, 19-7 (P)
1963—Steelers, 23-10 (P)
  Cardinals, 24-23 (StL)
1964—Cardinals, 34-30 (StL)
  Cardinals, 21-20 (P)
1965—Cardinals, 20-7 (P)
  Cardinals, 21-17 (StL)
1966—Steelers, 30-9 (P)
  Cardinals, 6-3 (StL)
1967—Cardinals, 28-14 (P)
  Tie, 14-14 (StL)
1968—Tie, 28-28 (StL)
  Cardinals, 20-10 (P)
1969—Cardinals, 27-14 (P)
  Cardinals, 47-10 (StL)
1972—Steelers, 25-19 (StL)
1979—Cardinals, 24-21 (StL)

1985—Steelers, 23-10 (P)
1988—Cardinals, 31-14 (Phx)
1994—Cardinals, 20-17 (A) OT
1997—Steelers, 26-20 (A) OT
2003—Steelers, 28-15 (P)
(RS Pts.—Steelers 1,092, Cardinals 1,038)
*Franchise known as Phoenix prior to
1994, in St. Louis prior to 1988,
and in Chicago prior to 1960
**Steelers known as Pirates prior to 1941
ARIZONA vs. **ST. LOUIS
RS: Rams lead series, 28-22-2
PS: Rams lead series, 1-0
1937—Cardinals, 6-0 (Clev)
  Cardinals, 13-7 (Chi)
1938—Cardinals, 7-6 (Clev)
  Cardinals, 31-17 (Chi)
1939—Rams, 24-0 (Chi)
  Rams, 14-0 (Clev)
1940—Rams, 26-14 (Clev)
  Cardinals, 17-7 (Chi)
1941—Rams, 10-6 (Clev)
  Cardinals, 7-0 (Chi)
1942—Cardinals, 7-0 (Buffalo)
  Rams, 7-3 (Clev)
1945—Rams, 21-0 (Chi)
  Rams, 35-21 (Chi)
1946—Cardinals, 34-10 (Chi)
  Rams, 17-14 (LA)
1947—Rams, 27-7 (LA)
  Cardinals, 17-10 (Chi)
1948—Cardinals, 27-22 (LA)
  Cardinals, 27-24 (Chi)
1949—Tie, 28-28 (Chi)
  Cardinals, 31-27 (LA)
1951—Rams, 45-21 (LA)
1953—Tie, 24-24 (Chi)
1954—Rams, 28-17 (LA)
1958—Rams, 20-14 (Chi)
1960—Cardinals, 43-21 (LA)
1965—Rams, 27-3 (StL)
1968—Rams, 24-13 (StL)
1970—Rams, 34-13 (LA)
1972—Cardinals, 24-14 (StL)
1975—***Rams, 35-23 (LA)
1976—Cardinals, 30-28 (LA)
1979—Rams, 21-0 (LA)
1980—Rams, 21-13 (StL)
1984—Rams, 16-13 (StL)
1985—Rams, 46-14 (LA)
1986—Rams, 16-10 (StL)
1987—Rams, 27-24 (StL)
1988—Cardinals, 41-27 (LA)
1989—Rams, 37-14 (LA)
1991—Cardinals, 24-14 (LA)
1992—Cardinals, 20-14 (LA)
1993—Cardinals, 38-10 (P)
1994—Rams, 14-12 (LA)
1996—Cardinals, 31-28 (A) OT
1998—Cardinals, 20-17 (StL)
2002—Rams, 27-14 (A)
  Rams, 30-28 (StL)
2003—Rams, 37-13 (StL)
  Rams, 30-27 (A) OT
2004—Rams, 17-10 (StL)
  Cardinals, 31-7 (A)
(RS Pts.—Rams 1,060, Cardinals 916)
(PS Pts.—Rams 35, Cardinals 23)
*Franchise known as Phoenix prior to
1994, in St. Louis prior to 1988,

and in Chicago prior to 1960
**Franchise in Los Angeles prior to 1995
and in Cleveland prior to 1946
***NFC Divisional Playoff
ARIZONA vs. SAN DIEGO
RS: Chargers lead series, 7-3
1971—Chargers, 20-17 (SD)
1976—Chargers, 43-24 (SD)
1983—Cardinals, 44-14 (StL)
1987—Chargers, 28-24 (SD)
1989—Chargers, 24-13 (P)
1992—Chargers, 27-21 (P)
1995—Chargers, 28-25 (SD)
1998—Cardinals, 16-13 (A)
2001—Cardinals, 20-17 (SD)
2002—Chargers, 23-15 (A)
(RS Pts.—Chargers 237, Cardinals 219)
*Franchise known as Phoenix prior to
1994, in St. Louis prior to 1988,
ARIZONA vs. SAN FRANCISCO
RS: 49ers lead series, 17-10
1951—Cardinals, 27-21 (SF)
1957—Cardinals, 20-10 (SF)
1962—49ers, 24-17 (StL)
1964—Cardinals, 23-13 (SF)
1968—49ers, 35-17 (SF)
1971—49ers, 26-14 (StL)
1974—Cardinals, 34-9 (SF)
1976—Cardinals, 23-20 (StL) OT
1978—Cardinals, 16-10 (SF)
1979—Cardinals, 13-10 (StL)
1980—49ers, 24-21 (SF) OT
1982—49ers, 31-20 (StL)
1983—49ers, 42-27 (StL)
1986—49ers, 43-17 (SF)
1987—49ers, 34-28 (SF)
1988—Cardinals, 24-23 (P)
1991—49ers, 14-10 (SF)
1992—Cardinals, 24-14 (P)
1993—49ers, 28-14 (SF)
1999—49ers, 24-10 (A)
2000—49ers, 27-20 (SF)
2002—49ers, 38-28 (SF)
  49ers, 17-14 (A)
2003—Cardinals, 16-13 (A) OT
  49ers, 50-14 (SF)
2004—49ers, 31-28 (SF) OT
  49ers, 31-28 (A) OT
(RS Pts.—49ers 662, Cardinals 547)
*Franchise known as Phoenix prior to
1994, in St. Louis prior to 1988,
and in Chicago prior to 1960
ARIZONA vs. SEATTLE
RS: Cardinals lead series, 7-5
1976—Cardinals, 30-24 (S)
1983—Cardinals, 33-28 (StL)
1989—Cardinals, 34-24 (S)
1993—Cardinals, 30-27 (S) OT
1995—Cardinals, 20-14 (A) OT
1998—Seahawks, 33-14 (S)
2002—Cardinals, 24-13 (S)
  Seahawks, 27-6 (A)
2003—Seahawks, 38-0 (A)
  Seahawks, 28-10 (S)
2004—Cardinals, 25-17 (A)
  Seahawks, 24-21 (S)
(RS Pts.—Seahawks 297, Cardinals 247)
*Franchise known as Phoenix prior to
1994 and in St. Louis prior to 1988

*ARIZONA vs. TAMPA BAY
RS: Cardinals lead series, 8-7
1977—Buccaneers, 17-7 (TB)
1981—Buccaneers, 20-10 (TB)
1983—Cardinals, 34-27 (TB)
1985—Buccaneers, 16-0 (TB)
1986—Cardinals, 30-19 (TB)
 Cardinals, 21-17 (StL)
1987—Cardinals, 31-28 (StL)
 Cardinals, 31-14 (TB)
1988—Cardinals, 30-24 (TB)
1989—Buccaneers, 14-13 (P)
1992—Buccaneers, 23-7 (TB)
 Buccaneers, 7-3 (P)
1996—Cardinals, 13-9 (A)
1997—Buccaneers, 19-18 (TB)
2004—Cardinals, 12-7 (A)
(RS Pts.—Buccaneers 261, Cardinals 260)
*Franchise known as Phoenix prior to
1994 and in St. Louis prior to 1988
*ARIZONA vs. **TENNESSEE
RS: Cardinals lead series, 4-3
1970—Cardinals, 44-0 (StL)
1974—Cardinals, 31-27 (H)
1979—Cardinals, 24-17 (H)
1985—Oilers, 20-10 (StL)
1988—Oilers, 38-20 (H)
1994—Cardinals, 30-12 (H)
1997—Oilers, 41-14 (A)
(RS Pts.—Cardinals 173, Titans 155)
*Franchise known as Phoenix prior to
1994 and in St. Louis prior to 1988
**Franchise in Houston prior to 1997;
known as Oilers prior to 1999
*ARIZONA vs. **WASHINGTON
RS: Redskins lead series, 70-44-2
1932—Cardinals, 9-0 (B)
 Braves, 8-6 (C)
1933—Redskins, 10-0 (C)
 Tie, 0-0 (B)
1934—Redskins, 9-0 (B)
1935—Cardinals, 6-0 (B)
1936—Redskins, 13-10 (B)
1937—Cardinals, 21-14 (W)
1939—Redskins, 28-7 (W)
1940—Redskins, 28-21 (W)
1942—Redskins, 28-0 (W)
1943—Redskins, 13-7 (W)
1945—Redskins, 24-21 (W)
1947—Redskins, 45-21 (W)
1949—Cardinals, 38-7 (C)
1950—Redskins, 38-28 (W)
1951—Redskins, 7-3 (C)
 Redskins, 20-17 (W)
1952—Redskins, 23-7 (C)
 Cardinals, 17-6 (W)
1953—Redskins, 24-13 (C)
 Redskins, 28-17 (W)
1954—Cardinals, 38-16 (C)
 Redskins, 37-20 (W)
1955—Cardinals, 24-10 (W)
 Redskins, 31-0 (C)
1956—Cardinals, 31-3 (W)
 Redskins, 17-14 (C)
1957—Redskins, 37-14 (C)
 Cardinals, 44-14 (W)
1958—Cardinals, 37-10 (C)
 Redskins, 45-31 (W)
1959—Cardinals, 49-21 (C)
 Redskins, 23-14 (W)

1960—Cardinals, 44-7 (StL)
 Cardinals, 26-14 (W)
1961—Cardinals, 24-0 (W)
 Cardinals, 38-24 (StL)
1962—Redskins, 24-14 (W)
 Tie, 17-17 (StL)
1963—Cardinals, 21-7 (W)
 Cardinals, 24-20 (StL)
1964—Cardinals, 23-17 (W)
 Cardinals, 38-24 (StL)
1965—Cardinals, 37-16 (W)
 Redskins, 24-20 (StL)
1966—Cardinals, 23-7 (StL)
 Redskins, 26-20 (W)
1967—Cardinals, 27-21 (W)
1968—Cardinals, 41-14 (StL)
1969—Redskins, 33-17 (W)
1970—Cardinals, 27-17 (StL)
 Redskins, 28-27 (W)
1971—Redskins, 24-17 (StL)
 Redskins, 20-0 (W)
1972—Redskins, 24-10 (W)
 Redskins, 33-3 (StL)
1973—Cardinals, 34-27 (StL)
 Redskins, 31-13 (W)
1974—Cardinals, 17-10 (W)
 Cardinals, 23-20 (StL)
1975—Redskins, 27-17 (W)
 Cardinals, 20-17 (StL) OT
1976—Redskins, 20-10 (W)
 Redskins, 16-10 (StL)
1977—Redskins, 24-14 (W)
 Redskins, 26-20 (StL)
1978—Redskins, 28-10 (StL)
 Cardinals, 27-17 (W)
1979—Redskins, 17-7 (StL)
 Redskins, 30-28 (W)
1980—Redskins, 23-0 (W)
 Redskins, 31-7 (StL)
1981—Cardinals, 40-30 (StL)
 Redskins, 42-21 (W)
1982—Redskins, 12-7 (StL)
 Redskins, 28-0 (W)
1983—Redskins, 38-14 (StL)
 Redskins, 45-7 (W)
1984—Cardinals, 26-24 (StL)
 Redskins, 29-27 (W)
1985—Redskins, 27-10 (W)
 Redskins, 27-16 (StL)
1986—Redskins, 28-21 (W)
 Redskins, 20-17 (StL)
1987—Redskins, 28-21 (W)
 Redskins, 34-17 (StL)
1988—Cardinals, 30-21 (P)
 Redskins, 33-17 (W)
1989—Redskins, 30-28 (W)
 Redskins, 29-10 (P)
1990—Redskins, 31-0 (W)
 Redskins, 38-10 (P)
1991—Redskins, 34-0 (W)
 Redskins, 20-14 (P)
1992—Cardinals, 27-24 (P)
 Redskins, 41-3 (W)
1993—Cardinals, 17-10 (W)
 Cardinals, 36-6 (P)
1994—Cardinals, 19-16 (W) OT
 Cardinals, 17-15 (A)
1995—Redskins, 27-7 (W)
 Cardinals, 24-20 (A)
1996—Cardinals, 37-34 (W) OT

 Cardinals, 27-26 (A)
1997—Redskins, 19-13 (W) OT
 Redskins, 38-28 (A)
1998—Cardinals, 29-27 (A)
 Cardinals, 45-42 (W)
1999—Redskins, 24-10 (A)
 Redskins, 28-3 (W)
2000—Cardinals, 16-15 (A)
 Redskins, 20-3 (W)
2001—Redskins, 20-10 (A)
 Redskins, 20-17 (W)
2002—Redskins, 31-23 (W)
(RS Pts.—Redskins 2,583, Cardinals 2,154)
*Franchise known as Phoenix prior to
1994, in St. Louis prior to 1988,
and in Chicago prior to 1960
**Franchise in Boston prior to 1937 and
known as Braves prior to 1933

ATLANTA vs. ARIZONA
RS: Cardinals lead series, 13-9;
See Arizona vs. Atlanta
ATLANTA vs. BALTIMORE
RS: Series tied, 1-1
1999—Ravens, 19-13 (A) OT
2002—Falcons, 20-17 (A)
(RS Pts.—Ravens 36, Falcons 33)
ATLANTA vs. BUFFALO
RS: Series tied, 4-4
1973—Bills, 17-6 (A)
1977—Bills, 3-0 (B)
1980—Falcons, 30-14 (B)
1983—Falcons, 31-14 (A)
1989—Falcons, 30-28 (A)
1992—Bills, 41-14 (B)
1995—Bills, 23-17 (B)
2001—Falcons, 33-30 (A)
(RS Pts.—Bills 170, Falcons 161)
ATLANTA vs. CAROLINA
RS: Falcons lead series, 14-6
1995—Falcons, 23-20 (A) OT
 Panthers, 21-17 (C)
1996—Panthers, 29-6 (C)
 Falcons, 20-17 (A)
1997—Panthers, 9-6 (A)
 Panthers, 21-12 (C)
1998—Falcons, 19-14 (C)
 Falcons, 51-23 (A)
1999—Falcons, 27-20 (A)
 Panthers, 34-28 (C)
2000—Falcons, 15-10 (C)
 Falcons, 13-12 (A)
2001—Falcons, 24-16 (A)
 Falcons, 10-7 (C)
2002—Falcons, 30-0 (A)
 Falcons, 41-0 (C)
2003—Panthers, 23-3 (C)
 Falcons, 20-14 (A) OT
2004—Falcons, 27-10 (C)
 Falcons, 34-31 (A) OT
(RS Pts.—Falcons 426, Panthers 331)
ATLANTA vs. CHICAGO
RS: Bears lead series, 11-10
1966—Bears, 23-6 (C)
1967—Bears, 23-14 (A)
1968—Falcons, 16-13 (C)
1969—Falcons, 48-31 (A)
1970—Bears, 23-14 (A)
1972—Falcons, 37-21 (C)
1973—Falcons, 46-6 (A)

1974—Falcons, 13-10 (A)
1976—Falcons, 10-0 (C)
1977—Falcons, 16-10 (C)
1978—Bears, 13-7 (C)
1980—Falcons, 28-17 (A)
1983—Falcons, 20-17 (C)
1985—Bears, 36-0 (C)
1986—Bears, 13-10 (A)
1990—Bears, 30-24 (C)
1992—Bears, 41-31 (C)
1993—Bears, 6-0 (C)
1998—Falcons, 20-13 (A)
2001—Bears, 31-3 (A)
2002—Bears, 14-13 (A)
(RS Pts.—Bears 391, Falcons 376)

ATLANTA vs. CINCINNATI
RS: Bengals lead series, 7-3
1971—Falcons, 9-6 (C)
1975—Bengals, 21-14 (A)
1978—Bengals, 37-7 (C)
1981—Bengals, 30-28 (A)
1984—Bengals, 35-14 (C)
1987—Bengals, 16-10 (A)
1990—Falcons, 38-17 (A)
1993—Bengals, 21-17 (C)
1996—Bengals, 41-31 (C)
2002—Falcons, 30-3 (A)
(RS Pts.—Bengals 227, Falcons 198)

ATLANTA vs. CLEVELAND
RS: Browns lead series, 9-2
1966—Browns, 49-17 (A)
1968—Browns, 30-7 (C)
1971—Falcons, 31-14 (C)
1976—Browns, 20-17 (A)
1978—Browns, 24-16 (A)
1981—Browns, 28-17 (C)
1984—Browns, 23-7 (A)
1987—Browns, 38-3 (C)
1990—Browns, 13-10 (C)
1993—Falcons, 17-14 (A)
2002—Browns, 24-16 (C)
(RS Pts.—Browns 277, Falcons 158)

ATLANTA vs. DALLAS
RS: Cowboys lead series, 12-8
PS: Cowboys lead series, 2-0
1966—Cowboys, 47-14 (A)
1967—Cowboys, 37-7 (D)
1969—Cowboys, 24-17 (A)
1970—Cowboys, 13-0 (A)
1974—Cowboys, 24-0 (A)
1976—Falcons, 17-10 (A)
1978—*Cowboys, 27-20 (D)
1980—*Cowboys, 30-27 (A)
1985—Cowboys, 24-10 (D)
1986—Falcons, 37-35 (D)
1987—Falcons, 21-10 (D)
1988—Cowboys, 26-20 (D)
1989—Falcons 27-21 (A)
1990—Falcons, 26-7 (A)
1991—Cowboys, 31-27 (D)
1992—Cowboys, 41-17 (A)
1993—Falcons, 27-14 (A)
1995—Cowboys, 28-13 (A)
1996—Cowboys, 32-28 (D)
1999—Cowboys, 24-7 (D)
2001—Falcons, 20-13 (A)
2003—Falcons, 27-13 (D)
(RS Pts.—Cowboys 474, Falcons 362)
(PS Pts.—Cowboys 57, Falcons 47)
*NFC Divisional Playoff

ATLANTA vs. DENVER
RS: Broncos lead series, 7-4
PS: Broncos lead series, 1-0
1970—Broncos, 24-10 (D)
1972—Falcons, 23-20 (A)
1975—Falcons, 35-21 (A)
1979—Broncos, 20-17 (A) OT
1982—Falcons, 34-27 (D)
1985—Broncos, 44-28 (A)
1988—Broncos, 30-14 (D)
1994—Broncos, 32-28 (D)
1997—Broncos, 29-21 (A)
1998—*Broncos, 34-19 (Miami)
2000—Broncos, 42-14 (D)
2004—Falcons, 41-28 (D)
(RS Pts.—Broncos 317, Falcons 265)
(PS Pts.—Broncos 34, Falcons 19)
*Super Bowl XXXIII

ATLANTA vs. DETROIT
RS: Lions lead series, 22-8
1966—Lions, 28-10 (D)
1967—Lions, 24-3 (D)
1968—Lions, 24-7 (A)
1969—Lions, 27-21 (D)
1971—Lions, 41-38 (D)
1972—Lions, 26-23 (A)
1973—Lions, 31-6 (D)
1975—Lions, 17-14 (A)
1976—Lions, 24-10 (D)
1977—Falcons, 17-6 (A)
1978—Falcons, 14-0 (A)
1979—Lions, 24-23 (D)
1980—Falcons, 43-28 (A)
1983—Falcons, 30-14 (D)
1984—Lions, 27-24 (A) OT
1985—Lions, 28-27 (A)
1986—Falcons, 20-6 (D)
1987—Lions, 30-13 (A)
1988—Lions, 31-17 (D)
1989—Lions, 31-24 (A)
1990—Lions, 21-14 (D)
1993—Lions, 30-13 (D)
1994—Lions, 31-28 (D) OT
1995—Falcons, 34-22 (A)
1996—Lions, 28-24 (D)
1997—Lions, 28-17 (D)
1998—Falcons, 24-17 (D)
2000—Lions, 13-10 (D)
2002—Falcons, 36-15 (A)
2004—Lions, 17-10 (A)
(RS Pts.—Lions 689, Falcons 594)

ATLANTA vs. GREEN BAY
RS: Packers lead series, 11-10
PS: Series tied, 1-1
1966—Packers, 56-3 (Mil)
1967—Packers, 23-0 (Mil)
1968—Packers, 38-7 (A)
1969—Packers, 28-10 (GB)
1970—Packers, 27-24 (GB)
1971—Falcons, 28-21 (A)
1972—Falcons, 10-9 (Mil)
1974—Falcons, 10-3 (A)
1975—Packers, 22-13 (GB)
1976—Packers, 24-20 (A)
1979—Falcons, 25-7 (A)
1981—Falcons, 31-17 (GB)
1982—Packers, 38-7 (A)
1983—Falcons, 47-41 (A) OT
1988—Falcons, 20-0 (A)
1989—Packers, 23-21 (Mil)

1991—Falcons, 35-31 (A)
1992—Falcons, 24-10 (A)
1994—Packers, 21-17 (Mil)
1995—*Packers, 37-20 (GB)
2001—Falcons, 23-20 (GB)
2002—Packers, 37-34 (GB) OT
        *Falcons, 27-7 (GB)
(RS Pts.—Packers 496, Falcons 409)
(PS Pts.—Falcons 47, Packers 44)
*NFC First-Round Playoff

ATLANTA vs. HOUSTON
RS: Texans lead series, 1-0
2003—Texans, 17-13 (H)
(RS Pts.—Texans 17, Falcons 13)

ATLANTA vs. *INDIANAPOLIS
RS: Colts lead series, 12-1
1966—Colts, 19-7 (A)
1967—Colts, 38-31 (B)
        Colts, 49-7 (A)
1968—Colts, 28-20 (A)
        Colts, 44-0 (B)
1969—Colts, 21-14 (A)
        Colts, 13-6 (B)
1974—Colts, 17-7 (A)
1986—Colts, 28-23 (A)
1989—Colts, 13-9 (I)
1998—Falcons, 28-21 (A)
2001—Colts, 41-27 (I)
2003—Colts, 38-7 (I)
(RS Pts.—Colts 370, Falcons 186)
*Franchise in Baltimore prior to 1984

ATLANTA vs. JACKSONVILLE
RS: Jaguars lead series, 2-1
1996—Jaguars, 19-17 (J)
1999—Jaguars, 30-7 (A)
2003—Falcons, 21-14 (A)
(RS Pts.—Jaguars 63, Falcons 45)

ATLANTA vs. KANSAS CITY
RS: Chiefs lead series, 5-1
1972—Chiefs, 17-14 (A)
1985—Chiefs, 38-10 (KC)
1991—Chiefs, 14-3 (KC)
1994—Falcons, 30-10 (A)
2000—Falcons, 29-13 (A)
2004—Chiefs, 56-10 (KC)
(RS Pts.—Chiefs 168, Falcons 76)

ATLANTA vs. MIAMI
RS: Dolphins lead series, 7-2
1970—Dolphins, 20-7 (A)
1974—Dolphins, 42-7 (M)
1980—Dolphins, 20-17 (A)
1983—Dolphins, 31-24 (M)
1986—Falcons, 20-14 (M)
1992—Dolphins, 21-17 (M)
1995—Dolphins, 21-20 (M)
1998—Falcons, 38-16 (A)
2001—Dolphins, 21-14 (M)
(RS Pts.—Dolphins 206, Falcons 164)

ATLANTA vs. MINNESOTA
RS: Vikings lead series, 14-7
PS: Series tied, 1-1
1966—Falcons, 20-13 (M)
1967—Falcons, 21-20 (A)
1968—Vikings, 47-7 (M)
1969—Falcons, 10-3 (A)
1970—Vikings, 37-7 (A)
1971—Vikings, 24-7 (M)
1973—Falcons, 20-14 (A)
1974—Vikings, 23-10 (M)
1975—Vikings, 38-0 (M)

1977—Vikings, 14-7 (A)
1980—Vikings, 24-23 (M)
1981—Falcons, 31-30 (A)
1982—*Vikings, 30-24 (M)
1984—Vikings, 27-20 (M)
1985—Falcons, 14-13 (A)
1987—Vikings, 24-13 (M)
1989—Vikings, 43-17 (M)
1991—Vikings, 20-19 (A)
1996—Vikings, 23-17 (A)
1998—**Falcons, 30-27 (M) OT
1999—Vikings, 17-14 (A)
2002—Falcons, 30-24 (M) OT
2003—Vikings, 39-26 (A)
(RS Pts.—Vikings 517, Falcons 333)
(PS Pts.—Vikings 57, Falcons 54)
*NFC First-Round Playoff
**NFC Championship

ATLANTA vs. NEW ENGLAND
RS: Falcons lead series, 6-4
1972—Patriots, 21-20 (NE)
1977—Patriots, 16-10 (A)
1980—Falcons, 37-21 (NE)
1983—Falcons, 24-13 (A)
1986—Patriots, 25-17 (NE)
1989—Falcons, 16-15 (A)
1992—Falcons, 34-0 (A)
1995—Falcons, 30-17 (A)
1998—Falcons, 41-10 (NE)
2001—Patriots, 24-10 (A)
(RS Pts.—Falcons 239, Patriots 162)

ATLANTA vs. NEW ORLEANS
RS: Falcons lead series, 41-30
PS: Falcons lead series, 1-0
1967—Saints, 27-24 (NO)
1969—Falcons, 45-17 (A)
1970—Falcons, 14-3 (NO)
　　　Falcons, 32-14 (A)
1971—Falcons, 28-6 (A)
　　　Falcons, 24-20 (NO)
1972—Falcons, 21-14 (A)
　　　Falcons, 36-20 (A)
1973—Falcons, 62-7 (NO)
　　　Falcons, 14-10 (A)
1974—Saints, 14-13 (NO)
　　　Saints, 13-3 (A)
1975—Falcons, 14-7 (A)
　　　Saints, 23-7 (NO)
1976—Saints, 30-0 (NO)
　　　Falcons, 23-20 (A)
1977—Saints, 21-20 (NO)
　　　Falcons, 35-7 (A)
1978—Falcons, 20-17 (NO)
　　　Falcons, 20-17 (A)
1979—Falcons, 40-34 (NO) OT
　　　Saints, 37-6 (A)
1980—Falcons, 41-14 (NO)
　　　Falcons, 31-13 (A)
1981—Falcons, 27-0 (A)
　　　Falcons, 41-10 (NO)
1982—Falcons, 35-0 (A)
　　　Saints, 35-6 (NO)
1983—Saints, 19-17 (A)
　　　Saints, 27-10 (NO)
1984—Falcons, 36-28 (NO)
　　　Saints, 17-13 (A)
1985—Falcons, 31-24 (A)
　　　Falcons, 16-10 (NO)
1986—Falcons, 31-10 (NO)
　　　Saints, 14-9 (A)

1987—Saints, 38-0 (A)
1988—Saints, 29-21 (A)
　　　Saints, 10-9 (NO)
1989—Saints, 20-13 (NO)
　　　Saints, 26-17 (A)
1990—Falcons, 28-27 (A)
　　　Saints, 10-7 (NO)
1991—Saints, 27-6 (A)
　　　Falcons, 23-20 (NO) OT
　　　*Falcons, 27-20 (NO)
1992—Saints, 10-7 (A)
　　　Saints, 22-14 (NO)
1993—Saints, 34-31 (A)
　　　Falcons, 26-15 (NO)
1994—Saints, 33-32 (NO)
　　　Saints, 29-20 (A)
1995—Falcons, 27-24 (NO) OT
　　　Falcons, 19-14 (A)
1996—Falcons, 17-15 (A)
　　　Falcons, 31-15 (NO)
1997—Falcons, 23-17 (NO)
　　　Falcons, 20-3 (A)
1998—Falcons, 31-23 (A)
　　　Falcons, 27-17 (NO)
1999—Falcons, 20-17 (NO)
　　　Falcons, 35-12 (A)
2000—Saints, 21-19 (A)
　　　Saints, 23-7 (NO)
2001—Falcons, 20-13 (NO)
　　　Saints, 28-10 (A)
2002—Falcons, 37-35 (NO)
　　　Falcons, 24-17 (A)
2003—Saints, 45-17 (A)
　　　Saints, 23-20 (NO)
2004—Falcons, 24-21 (A)
　　　Saints, 26-13 (NO)
(RS Pts.—Falcons 1,540, Saints 1,358)
(PS Pts.—Falcons 27, Saints 20)
*NFC First-Round Playoff

ATLANTA vs. N.Y. GIANTS
RS: Falcons lead series, 10-7
1966—Falcons, 27-16 (NY)
1968—Falcons, 24-21 (A)
1971—Giants, 21-17 (A)
1974—Falcons, 14-7 (New Haven)
1977—Falcons, 17-3 (A)
1978—Falcons, 23-20 (A)
1979—Giants, 24-3 (NY)
1981—Falcons, 27-24 (A) OT
1982—Falcons, 16-14 (NY)
1983—Giants, 16-13 (A) OT
1984—Giants, 19-7 (A)
1988—Falcons, 23-16 (A)
1998—Falcons, 34-20 (NY)
2000—Giants, 13-6 (A)
2002—Falcons, 17-10 (NY)
2003—Falcons, 27-7 (NY)
2004—Falcons, 14-10 (NY)
(RS Pts.—Falcons 299, Giants 271)

ATLANTA vs. N.Y. JETS
RS: Series tied, 4-4
1973—Falcons, 28-20 (NY)
1980—Jets, 14-7 (A)
1983—Falcons, 27-21 (NY)
1986—Jets, 28-14 (A)
1989—Jets, 27-7 (NY)
1992—Falcons, 20-17 (A)
1995—Falcons, 13-3 (A)
1998—Jets, 28-3 (NY)
(RS Pts.—Jets 158, Falcons 119)

ATLANTA vs. *OAKLAND
RS: Raiders lead series, 7-4
1971—Falcons, 24-13 (A)
1975—Raiders, 37-34 (O) OT
1979—Raiders, 50-19 (O)
1982—Raiders, 38-14 (A)
1985—Raiders, 34-24 (A)
1988—Falcons, 12-6 (LA)
1991—Falcons, 21-17 (A)
1994—Raiders, 30-17 (LA)
1997—Raiders, 36-31 (A)
2000—Raiders, 41-14 (O)
2004—Falcons, 35-10 (A)
(RS Pts.—Raiders 312, Falcons 245)
*Franchise in Los Angeles from 1982-1994

ATLANTA vs. PHILADELPHIA
RS: Eagles lead series, 11-9-1
PS: Eagles lead series, 2-1
1966—Eagles, 23-10 (P)
1967—Eagles, 38-7 (A)
1969—Falcons, 27-3 (P)
1970—Tie, 13-13 (P)
1973—Falcons, 44-27 (P)
1976—Eagles, 14-13 (A)
1978—*Falcons, 14-13 (A)
1979—Falcons, 14-10 (P)
1980—Falcons, 20-17 (P)
1981—Eagles, 16-13 (P)
1983—Eagles, 28-24 (A)
1984—Falcons, 26-10 (A)
1985—Eagles, 23-17 (P) OT
1986—Eagles, 16-0 (A)
1988—Falcons, 27-24 (P)
1990—Eagles, 24-23 (A)
1994—Falcons, 28-21 (A)
1996—Eagles, 33-18 (A)
1997—Falcons, 20-17 (A)
1998—Falcons, 17-12 (A)
2000—Eagles, 38-10 (P)
2002—**Eagles, 20-6 (P)
2003—Eagles, 23-16 (A)
2004—***Eagles, 27-10 (P)
(RS Pts.—Eagles 430, Falcons 387)
(PS Pts.—Eagles 60, Falcons 30)
*NFC First-Round Playoff
**NFC Divisional Playoff
***NFC Championship

ATLANTA vs. PITTSBURGH
RS: Steelers lead series, 11-1-1
1966—Steelers, 57-33 (A)
1968—Steelers, 41-21 (A)
1970—Falcons, 27-16 (A)
1974—Steelers, 24-17 (P)
1978—Steelers, 31-7 (P)
1981—Steelers, 34-20 (A)
1984—Steelers, 35-10 (P)
1987—Steelers, 28-12 (A)
1990—Steelers, 21-9 (P)
1993—Steelers, 45-17 (A)
1996—Steelers, 20-17 (A)
1999—Steelers, 13-9 (P)
2002—Tie, 34-34 (P) OT
(RS Pts.—Steelers 399, Falcons 233)

ATLANTA vs. *ST. LOUIS
RS: Rams lead series, 46-24-2
PS: Falcons lead series, 1-0
1966—Rams, 19-14 (A)
1967—Rams, 31-3 (A)
　　　Rams, 20-3 (LA)
1968—Rams, 27-14 (LA)

Rams, 17-10 (A)
1969—Rams, 17-7 (LA)
Rams, 38-6 (A)
1970—Tie, 10-10 (LA)
Rams, 17-7 (A)
1971—Tie, 20-20 (LA)
Rams, 24-16 (A)
1972—Falcons, 31-3 (A)
Rams, 20-7 (LA)
1973—Rams, 31-0 (LA)
Falcons, 15-13 (A)
1974—Rams, 21-0 (LA)
Rams, 30-7 (A)
1975—Rams, 22-7 (LA)
Rams, 16-7 (A)
1976—Rams, 30-14 (A)
Rams, 59-0 (LA)
1977—Falcons, 17-6 (A)
Rams, 23-7 (LA)
1978—Rams, 10-0 (LA)
Falcons, 15-7 (A)
1979—Rams, 20-14 (LA)
Rams, 34-13 (A)
1980—Falcons, 13-10 (A)
Rams, 20-17 (LA) OT
1981—Rams, 37-35 (A)
Rams, 21-16 (LA)
1982—Rams, 34-17 (A)
1983—Rams, 27-21 (LA)
Rams, 36-13 (A)
1984—Falcons, 30-28 (LA)
Rams, 24-10 (A)
1985—Rams, 17-6 (LA)
Falcons, 30-14 (A)
1986—Falcons, 26-14 (A)
Rams, 14-7 (LA)
1987—Falcons, 24-20 (A)
Rams, 33-0 (LA)
1988—Rams, 33-0 (A)
Rams, 22-7 (LA)
1989—Rams, 31-21 (A)
Rams, 26-14 (LA)
1990—Rams, 44-24 (LA)
Falcons, 20-13 (A)
1991—Falcons, 31-14 (A)
Falcons, 31-14 (LA)
1992—Falcons, 30-28 (A)
Rams, 38-27 (LA)
1993—Falcons, 30-24 (A)
Falcons, 13-0 (LA)
1994—Falcons, 31-13 (A)
Falcons, 8-5 (LA)
1995—Rams, 21-19 (StL)
Falcons, 31-6 (A)
1996—Rams, 59-16 (StL)
Rams, 34-27 (A)
1997—Falcons, 34-31 (A)
Falcons, 27-21 (StL)
1998—Falcons, 37-15 (A)
Falcons, 21-10 (StL)
1999—Rams, 35-7 (StL)
Rams, 41-13 (A)
2000—Rams, 41-20 (A)
Rams, 45-29 (StL)
2001—Rams, 35-6 (A)
Rams, 31-13 (StL)
2003—Rams, 36-0 (StL)
2004—Falcons, 34-17 (A)
    **Falcons, 47-17 (A)
(RS Pts.—Rams 1,700, Falcons 1,167)

(PS Pts.—Falcons 47, Rams 17)
Franchise in Los Angeles prior to 1995
***NFC Divisional Playoff*
ATLANTA vs. SAN DIEGO
RS: Falcons lead series, 6-1
1973—Falcons, 41-0 (SD)
1979—Falcons, 28-26 (SD)
1988—Chargers, 10-7 (A)
1991—Falcons, 13-10 (SD)
1994—Falcons, 10-9 (A)
1997—Falcons, 14-3 (SD)
2004—Falcons, 21-20 (A)
(RS Pts.—Falcons 134, Chargers 78)
ATLANTA vs. SAN FRANCISCO
RS: 49ers lead series, 44-26-1
PS: Falcons lead series, 1-0
1966—49ers, 44-7 (A)
1967—49ers, 38-7 (SF)
49ers, 34-28 (A)
1968—49ers, 28-13 (SF)
49ers, 14-12 (A)
1969—Falcons, 24-12 (A)
Falcons, 21-7 (SF)
1970—Falcons, 21-20 (A)
49ers, 24-20 (SF)
1971—Falcons, 20-17 (A)
49ers, 24-3 (SF)
1972—49ers, 49-14 (A)
49ers, 20-0 (SF)
1973—49ers, 13-9 (A)
Falcons, 17-3 (SF)
1974—49ers, 16-10 (A)
49ers, 27-0 (SF)
1975—Falcons, 17-3 (SF)
Falcons, 31-9 (A)
1976—49ers, 15-0 (SF)
Falcons, 21-16 (A)
1977—Falcons, 7-0 (SF)
49ers, 10-3 (A)
1978—Falcons, 20-17 (SF)
Falcons, 21-10 (A)
1979—49ers, 20-15 (SF)
Falcons, 31-21 (A)
1980—Falcons, 20-17 (SF)
Falcons, 35-10 (A)
1981—Falcons, 34-17 (A)
49ers, 17-14 (SF)
1982—Falcons, 17-7 (SF)
1983—49ers, 24-20 (SF)
Falcons, 28-24 (A)
1984—49ers, 14-5 (SF)
49ers, 35-17 (A)
1985—49ers, 35-16 (SF)
49ers, 38-17 (A)
1986—Tie, 10-10 (A) OT
49ers, 20-0 (SF)
1987—49ers, 25-17 (A)
49ers, 35-7 (SF)
1988—Falcons, 34-17 (SF)
49ers, 13-3 (A)
1989—49ers, 45-3 (SF)
49ers, 23-10 (A)
1990—49ers, 19-13 (SF)
49ers, 45-35 (A)
1991—49ers, 39-34 (SF)
Falcons, 17-14 (A)
1992—49ers, 56-17 (SF)
49ers, 41-3 (A)
1993—49ers, 37-30 (SF)
Falcons, 27-24 (A)

1994—49ers, 42-3 (A)
49ers, 50-14 (SF)
1995—49ers, 41-10 (SF)
Falcons, 28-27 (A)
1996—49ers, 39-17 (SF)
49ers, 34-10 (A)
1997—49ers, 34-7 (SF)
49ers, 35-28 (A)
1998—49ers, 31-20 (SF)
Falcons, 31-19 (A)
    *Falcons, 20-18 (A)
1999—49ers, 26-7 (SF)
Falcons, 34-29 (A)
2000—Falcons, 36-28 (A)
49ers, 16-6 (SF)
2001—49ers, 16-13 (SF) OT
49ers, 37-31 (A) OT
2004—Falcons, 21-19 (SF)
(RS Pts.—49ers 1,730, Falcons 1,196)
(PS Pts.—Falcons 20, 49ers 18)
NFC Divisional Playoff
ATLANTA vs. SEATTLE
RS: Seahawks lead series, 7-2
1976—Seahawks, 30-13 (S)
1979—Seahawks, 31-28 (A)
1985—Seahawks, 30-26 (S)
1988—Seahawks, 31-20 (A)
1991—Falcons, 26-13 (A)
1997—Falcons, 24-17 (S)
2000—Seahawks, 30-10 (A)
2002—Seahawks, 30-24 (A) OT
2004—Seahawks, 28-26 (S)
(RS Pts.—Seahawks 240, Falcons 197)
ATLANTA vs. TAMPA BAY
RS: Buccaneers lead series, 13-10
1977—Falcons, 17-0 (TB)
1978—Buccaneers, 14-9 (TB)
1979—Falcons, 17-14 (A)
1981—Buccaneers, 24-23 (TB)
1984—Buccaneers, 23-6 (TB)
1986—Falcons, 23-20 (TB) OT
1987—Buccaneers, 48-10 (TB)
1988—Falcons, 17-10 (A)
1990—Buccaneers, 23-17 (TB)
1991—Falcons, 43-7 (A)
1992—Falcons, 35-7 (TB)
1993—Buccaneers, 31-24 (A)
1994—Falcons, 34-13 (A)
1995—Falcons, 24-21 (TB)
1997—Buccaneers, 31-10 (A)
1999—Buccaneers, 19-10 (TB)
2000—Buccaneers, 27-14 (A)
2002—Buccaneers, 20-6 (A)
Buccaneers, 34-10 (TB)
2003—Buccaneers, 31-10 (A)
Falcons, 30-28 (TB)
2004—Falcons, 24-14 (A)
Buccaneers, 27-0 (TB)
(RS Pts.—Buccaneers 486, Falcons 413)
ATLANTA vs. *TENNESSEE
RS: Titans lead series, 6-5
1972—Falcons, 20-10 (A)
1976—Oilers, 20-14 (H)
1978—Falcons, 20-14 (A)
1981—Falcons, 31-27 (H)
1984—Falcons, 42-10 (A)
1987—Oilers, 37-33 (H)
1990—Falcons, 47-27 (A)
1993—Oilers, 33-17 (H)
1996—Oilers, 23-13 (A)

1999—Titans, 30-17 (T)
2003—Titans, 38-31 (A)
(RS Pts.—Falcons 285, Titans 269)
*Franchise in Houston prior to 1997;
known as Oilers prior to 1999*
ATLANTA vs. WASHINGTON
RS: Redskins lead series, 14-4-1
PS: Redskins lead series, 1-0
1966—Redskins, 33-20 (W)
1967—Tie, 20-20 (A)
1969—Redskins, 27-20 (W)
1972—Redskins, 24-13 (W)
1975—Redskins, 30-27 (A)
1977—Redskins, 10-6 (W)
1978—Falcons, 20-17 (A)
1979—Redskins, 16-7 (A)
1980—Falcons, 10-6 (A)
1983—Redskins, 37-21 (W)
1984—Redskins, 27-14 (W)
1985—Redskins, 44-10 (A)
1987—Falcons, 21-20 (A)
1989—Redskins, 31-30 (A)
1991—Redskins, 56-17 (W)
    *Redskins, 24-7 (W)
1992—Redskins, 24-17 (W)
1993—Redskins, 30-17 (W)
1994—Falcons, 27-20 (W)
2003—Redskins, 33-31 (A)
(RS Pts.—Redskins 505, Falcons 348)
(PS Pts.—Redskins 24, Falcons 7)
NFC Divisional Playoff

BALTIMORE vs. ARIZONA
RS: Ravens lead series, 2-1;
See Arizona vs. Baltimore
BALTIMORE vs. ATLANTA
RS: Series tied, 1-1;
See Atlanta vs. Baltimore
BALTIMORE vs. BUFFALO
RS: Series tied, 1-1
1999—Bills, 13-10 (Balt)
2004—Ravens, 20-6 (Balt)
(RS Pts.—Ravens 30, Bills 19)
BALTIMORE vs. CAROLINA
RS: Panthers lead series, 2-0
1996—Panthers, 27-16 (C)
2002—Panthers, 10-7 (C)
(RS Pts.—Panthers 37, Ravens 23)
BALTIMORE vs. CHICAGO
RS: Series tied, 1-1
1998—Bears, 24-3 (C)
2001—Ravens, 17-6 (B)
(RS Pts.—Bears 30, Ravens 20)
BALTIMORE vs. CINCINNATI
RS: Ravens lead series, 12-6
1996—Bengals, 24-21 (B)
    Bengals, 21-14 (C)
1997—Ravens, 23-10 (B)
    Bengals, 16-14 (C)
1998—Ravens, 31-24 (B)
    Ravens, 20-13 (C)
1999—Ravens, 34-31 (C)
    Ravens, 22-0 (B)
2000—Ravens, 37-0 (B)
    Ravens, 27-7 (C)
2001—Bengals, 21-10 (C)
    Ravens, 16-0 (B)
2002—Ravens, 38-27 (B)
    Ravens, 27-23 (C)
2003—Bengals, 34-26 (C)

    Ravens, 31-13 (B)
2004—Ravens, 23-9 (C)
    Bengals, 27-26 (B)
(RS Pts.—Ravens 440, Bengals 300)
BALTIMORE vs. CLEVELAND
RS: Ravens lead series, 8-4
1999—Ravens, 17-10 (B)
    Ravens, 41-9 (C)
2000—Ravens, 12-0 (C)
    Ravens, 44-7 (B)
2001—Browns, 24-14 (C)
    Browns, 27-17 (B)
2002—Ravens, 26-21 (C)
    Browns, 14-13 (B)
2003—Ravens, 33-13 (B)
    Ravens, 35-0 (C)
2004—Browns, 20-3 (C)
    Ravens, 27-13 (B)
(RS Pts.—Ravens 282, Browns 158)
BALTIMORE vs. DALLAS
RS: Ravens lead series, 2-0
2000—Ravens, 27-0 (B)
2004—Ravens, 30-10 (B)
(RS Pts.—Ravens 57, Cowboys 10)
BALTIMORE vs. DENVER
RS: Ravens lead series, 3-1
PS: Ravens lead series, 1-0
1996—Broncos, 45-34 (B)
2000—*Ravens, 21-3 (B)
2001—Ravens, 20-13 (D)
2002—Ravens, 34-23 (B)
2003—Ravens, 26-6 (B)
(RS Pts.—Ravens 114, Broncos 87)
(PS Pts.—Ravens 21, Broncos 3)
AFC First-Round Playoff
BALTIMORE vs. DETROIT
RS: Ravens lead series, 1-0
1998—Ravens, 19-10 (B)
(RS Pts.—Ravens 19, Lions 10)
BALTIMORE vs. GREEN BAY
RS: Packers lead series, 2-0
1998—Packers, 28-10 (GB)
2001—Packers, 31-23 (GB)
(RS Pts.—Packers 59, Ravens 33)
BALTIMORE vs. HOUSTON
RS: Ravens lead series, 1-0
2002—Ravens, 23-19 (H)
(RS Pts.—Ravens 23, Texans 19)
BALTIMORE vs. INDIANAPOLIS
RS: Colts lead series, 3-2
1996—Colts, 26-21 (I)
1998—Ravens, 38-31 (B)
2001—Ravens, 39-27 (B)
2002—Colts, 22-20 (I)
2004—Colts, 20-10 (I)
(RS Pts.—Ravens 128, Colts 126)
BALTIMORE vs. JACKSONVILLE
RS: Jaguars lead series, 8-6
1996—Jaguars, 30-27 (J)
    Jaguars, 28-25 (B) OT
1997—Jaguars, 28-27 (B)
    Jaguars, 29-27 (J)
1998—Jaguars, 24-10 (J)
    Jaguars, 45-19 (B)
1999—Jaguars, 6-3 (J)
    Jaguars, 30-23 (B)
2000—Ravens, 39-36 (B)
    Ravens, 15-10 (J)
2001—Ravens, 18-17 (B)
    Ravens, 24-21 (J)

2002—Ravens, 17-10 (B)
2003—Ravens, 24-17 (B)
(RS Pts.—Jaguars 331, Ravens 298)
BALTIMORE vs. KANSAS CITY
RS: Chiefs lead series, 3-0
1999—Chiefs, 35-8 (B)
2003—Chiefs, 17-10 (B)
2004—Chiefs, 27-24 (B)
(RS Pts.—Chiefs 79, Ravens 42)
BALTIMORE vs. MIAMI
RS: Dolphins lead series, 4-1
PS: Ravens lead series, 1-0
1997—Dolphins, 24-13 (B)
2000—Dolphins, 19-6 (M)
2001—*Ravens, 20-3 (M)
2002—Dolphins, 26-7 (M)
2003—Dolphins, 9-6 (M) OT
2004—Ravens, 30-23 (B)
(RS Pts.—Dolphins 101, Ravens 62)
(PS Pts.—Ravens 20, Dolphins 3)
AFC First-Round Playoff
BALTIMORE vs. MINNESOTA
RS: Series tied, 1-1
1998—Vikings, 38-28 (B)
2001—Ravens, 19-3 (B)
(RS Pts.—Ravens 47, Vikings 41)
BALTIMORE vs. NEW ENGLAND
RS: Patriots lead series, 3-0
1996—Patriots, 46-38 (B)
1999—Patriots, 20-3 (NE)
2004—Patriots, 24-3 (NE)
(RS Pts.—Patriots 90, Ravens 44)
BALTIMORE vs. NEW ORLEANS
RS: Ravens lead series, 2-1
1996—Ravens, 17-10 (B)
1999—Ravens, 31-8 (B)
2002—Saints, 37-25 (B)
(RS Pts.—Ravens 73, Saints 55)
BALTIMORE vs. N.Y. GIANTS
RS: Ravens lead series, 2-0
PS: Ravens lead series, 1-0
1997—Ravens, 24-23 (NY)
2000—*Ravens, 34-7 (Tampa)
2004—Ravens, 37-14 (B)
(RS Pts.—Ravens 61, Giants 37)
(PS Pts.—Ravens 34, Giants 7)
Super Bowl XXXV
BALTIMORE vs. N.Y. JETS
RS: Ravens lead series, 3-1
1997—Jets, 19-16 (NY) OT
1998—Ravens, 24-10 (NY)
2000—Ravens, 34-20 (B)
2004—Ravens, 20-17 (NY) OT
(RS Pts.—Ravens 94, Jets 66)
BALTIMORE vs. OAKLAND
RS: Ravens lead series, 2-1
PS: Ravens lead series, 1-0
1996—Ravens, 19-14 (B)
1998—Ravens, 13-10 (B)
2000—*Ravens, 16-3 (O)
2003—Raiders, 20-12 (O)
(RS Pts.—Ravens 44, Raiders 44)
(PS Pts.—Ravens 16, Raiders 3)
AFC Championship
BALTIMORE vs. PHILADELPHIA
RS: Eagles lead series, 1-0-1
1997—Tie, 10-10 (B) OT
2004—Eagles, 15-10 (P)
(RS Pts.—Eagles 25, Ravens 20)

BALTIMORE vs. PITTSBURGH
RS: Steelers lead series, 12-6
PS: Steelers lead series, 1-0
1996—Steelers, 31-17 (P)
 Ravens, 31-17 (B)
1997—Steelers, 42-34 (B)
 Steelers, 37-0 (P)
1998—Steelers, 20-13 (B)
 Steelers, 16-6 (P)
1999—Steelers, 23-20 (B)
 Ravens, 31-24 (P)
2000—Ravens, 16-0 (P)
 Steelers, 9-6 (B)
2001—Ravens, 13-10 (P)
 Steelers, 26-21 (B)
 *Steelers, 27-10 (P)
2002—Steelers, 31-18 (B)
 Steelers, 34-31 (P)
2003—Steelers, 34-15 (P)
 Ravens, 13-10 (B) OT
2004—Ravens, 30-13 (B)
 Steelers, 20-7 (P)
(RS Pts.—Steelers 397, Ravens 322)
(PS Pts.—Steelers 27, Ravens 10)
*AFC Divisional Playoff
BALTIMORE vs. ST. LOUIS
RS: Rams lead series, 2-1
1996—Ravens, 37-31 (B) OT
1999—Rams, 27-10 (StL)
2003—Rams, 33-22 (StL)
(RS Pts.—Rams 91, Ravens 69)
BALTIMORE vs. SAN DIEGO
RS: Series tied, 2-2
1997—Chargers, 21-17 (SD)
1998—Chargers, 14-13 (SD)
2000—Ravens, 24-3 (B)
2003—Ravens, 24-10 (SD)
(RS Pts.—Ravens 78, Chargers 48)
BALTIMORE vs. SAN FRANCISCO
RS: Series tied, 1-1
1996—49ers, 38-20 (SF)
2003—Ravens, 44-6 (B)
(RS Pts.—Ravens 64, 49ers 44)
BALTIMORE vs. SEATTLE
RS: Ravens lead series, 2-0
1997—Ravens, 31-24 (B)
2003—Ravens, 44-41 (B) OT
(RS Pts.—Ravens 75, Seahawks 65)
BALTIMORE vs. TAMPA BAY
RS: Buccaneers lead series, 2-0
2001—Buccaneers, 22-10 (TB)
2002—Buccaneers, 25-0 (B)
(RS Pts.—Buccaneers 47, Ravens 10)
BALTIMORE vs. *TENNESSEE
RS: Ravens lead series, 7-6
PS: Series tied, 1-1
1996—Oilers, 29-13 (H)
 Oilers, 24-21 (B)
1997—Ravens, 36-10 (T)
 Ravens, 21-19 (B)
1998—Oilers, 12-8 (B)
 Oilers, 16-14 (T)
1999—Titans, 14-11 (T)
 Ravens, 41-14 (B)
2000—Titans, 14-6 (B)
 Ravens, 24-23 (T)
 **Ravens, 24-10 (T)
2001—Ravens, 26-7 (B)
 Ravens, 16-10 (T)
2002—Ravens, 13-12 (B)

2003—***Titans, 20-17 (B)
(RS Pts.—Ravens 250, Titans 204)
(PS Pts.—Ravens 41, Titans 30)
*Franchise in Houston prior to 1997;
known as Oilers prior to 1999
**AFC Divisional Playoff
***AFC First-Round Playoff
BALTIMORE vs. WASHINGTON
RS: Ravens lead series, 2-1
1997—Ravens, 20-17 (W)
2000—Redskins, 10-3 (W)
2004—Ravens, 17-10 (W)
(RS Pts.—Ravens 40, Redskins 37)

BUFFALO vs. ARIZONA
RS: Bills lead series, 5-3;
See Arizona vs. Buffalo
BUFFALO vs. ATLANTA
RS: Series tied, 4-4;
See Atlanta vs. Buffalo
BUFFALO vs. BALTIMORE
RS: Series tied, 1-1;
See Baltimore vs. Buffalo
BUFFALO vs. CAROLINA
RS: Bills lead series, 3-0
1995—Bills, 31-9 (B)
1998—Bills, 30-14 (C)
2001—Bills, 25-24 (B)
(RS Pts.—Bills 86, Panthers 47)
BUFFALO vs. CHICAGO
RS: Bears lead series, 5-4
1970—Bears, 31-13 (C)
1974—Bills, 16-6 (B)
1979—Bears, 7-0 (B)
1988—Bears, 24-3 (C)
1991—Bills, 35-20 (B)
1994—Bears, 20-13 (C)
1997—Bears, 20-3 (C)
2000—Bills, 20-3 (B)
2002—Bills, 33-27 (B) OT
(RS Pts.—Bears 158, Bills 136)
BUFFALO vs. CINCINNATI
RS: Bills lead series, 12-9
PS: Bengals lead series, 2-0
1968—Bengals, 34-23 (C)
1969—Bills, 16-13 (B)
1970—Bengals, 43-14 (B)
1973—Bengals, 16-13 (C)
1975—Bengals, 33-24 (C)
1978—Bills, 5-0 (B)
1979—Bills, 51-24 (B)
1980—Bills, 14-0 (C)
1981—Bengals, 27-24 (C) OT
 *Bengals, 28-21 (C)
1983—Bills, 10-6 (C)
1984—Bengals, 52-21 (C)
1985—Bengals, 23-17 (B)
1986—Bengals, 36-33 (C) OT
1988—Bengals, 35-21 (C)
 **Bengals, 21-10 (C)
1989—Bills, 24-7 (B)
1991—Bills, 35-16 (B)
1996—Bills, 31-17 (B)
1998—Bills, 33-20 (C)
2002—Bills, 27-9 (B)
2003—Bills, 22-16 (B) OT
2004—Bills, 33-17 (C)
(RS Pts.—Bills 491, Bengals 444)
(PS Pts.—Bengals 49, Bills 31)
*AFC Divisional Playoff

**AFC Championship
BUFFALO vs. CLEVELAND
RS: Browns lead series, 7-5
PS: Browns lead series, 1-0
1972—Browns, 27-10 (C)
1974—Bills, 15-10 (C)
1977—Browns, 27-16 (B)
1978—Browns, 41-20 (C)
1981—Bills, 22-13 (B)
1984—Browns, 13-10 (B)
1985—Browns, 17-7 (C)
1986—Browns, 21-17 (B)
1987—Browns, 27-21 (C)
1989—*Browns, 34-30 (C)
1990—Bills, 42-0 (C)
1995—Bills, 22-19 (C)
2004—Bills, 37-7 (B)
(RS Pts.—Bills 239, Browns 222)
(PS Pts.—Browns 34, Bills 30)
*AFC Divisional Playoff
BUFFALO vs. DALLAS
RS: Cowboys lead series, 4-3
PS: Cowboys lead series, 2-0
1971—Cowboys, 49-37 (B)
1976—Cowboys, 17-10 (D)
1981—Cowboys, 27-14 (D)
1984—Bills, 14-3 (B)
1992—*Cowboys, 52-17 (Pasadena)
1993—Bills, 13-10 (D)
 **Cowboys, 30-13 (Atlanta)
1996—Bills, 10-7 (B)
2003—Cowboys, 10-6 (D)
(RS Pts.—Cowboys 123, Bills 104)
(PS Pts.—Cowboys 82, Bills 30)
*Super Bowl XXVII
**Super Bowl XXVIII
BUFFALO vs. DENVER
RS: Bills lead series, 17-13-1
PS: Bills lead series, 1-0
1960—Broncos, 27-21 (B)
 Tie, 38-38 (B)
1961—Broncos, 22-10 (B)
 Bills, 23-10 (D)
1962—Broncos, 23-20 (B)
 Bills, 45-38 (D)
1963—Bills, 30-28 (B)
 Bills, 27-17 (B)
1964—Bills, 30-13 (B)
 Bills, 30-19 (D)
1965—Bills, 30-15 (D)
 Bills, 31-13 (B)
1966—Bills, 38-21 (B)
1967—Bills, 17-16 (D)
 Broncos, 21-20 (B)
1968—Broncos, 34-32 (D)
1969—Bills, 41-28 (B)
1970—Bills, 25-10 (B)
1975—Bills, 38-14 (B)
1977—Broncos, 26-6 (D)
1979—Broncos, 19-16 (B)
1981—Bills, 9-7 (B)
1984—Broncos, 37-7 (B)
1987—Bills, 21-14 (B)
1989—Broncos, 28-14 (B)
1990—Bills, 29-28 (B)
1991—*Bills, 10-7 (B)
1992—Bills, 27-17 (B)
1994—Bills, 27-20 (B)
1995—Broncos, 22-7 (D)
1997—Broncos, 23-20 (B) OT

2002—Broncos, 28-23 (D)
(RS Pts.—Bills 737, Broncos 691)
(PS Pts.—Bills 10, Broncos 7)
*AFC Championship
BUFFALO vs. DETROIT
RS: Series tied, 3-3-1
1972—Tie, 21-21 (B)
1976—Lions, 27-14 (D)
1979—Bills, 20-17 (D)
1991—Lions, 17-14 (B) OT
1994—Lions, 35-21 (D)
1997—Bills, 22-13 (B)
2002—Bills, 24-17 (B)
(RS Pts.—Lions 147, Bills 136)
BUFFALO vs. GREEN BAY
RS: Bills lead series, 6-3
1974—Bills, 27-7 (GB)
1979—Bills, 19-12 (B)
1982—Packers, 33-21 (Mil)
1988—Bills, 28-0 (B)
1991—Bills, 34-24 (Mil)
1994—Bills 29-20 (B)
1997—Packers, 31-21 (GB)
2000—Bills 27-18 (B)
2002—Packers, 10-0 (GB)
(RS Pts.—Bills 206, Packers 155)
BUFFALO vs. HOUSTON
RS: Series tied, 1-1
2002—Bills, 31-24 (H)
2003—Texans, 12-10 (B)
(RS Pts.—Bills 41, Texans 36)
BUFFALO vs. *INDIANAPOLIS
RS: Bills lead series, 34-29-1
1970—Tie, 17-17 (Balt)
    Colts, 20-14 (Buff)
1971—Colts, 43-0 (Buff)
    Colts, 24-0 (Balt)
1972—Colts, 17-0 (Buff)
    Colts, 35-7 (Balt)
1973—Bills, 31-13 (Buff)
    Bills, 24-17 (Balt)
1974—Bills, 27-14 (Balt)
    Bills, 6-0 (Buff)
1975—Bills, 38-31 (Balt)
    Colts, 42-35 (Buff)
1976—Colts, 31-13 (Buff)
    Colts, 58-20 (Balt)
1977—Colts, 17-14 (Balt)
    Colts, 31-13 (Buff)
1978—Bills, 24-17 (Buff)
    Bills, 21-14 (Balt)
1979—Bills, 31-13 (Balt)
    Colts, 14-13 (Buff)
1980—Colts, 17-12 (Buff)
    Colts, 28-24 (Balt)
1981—Bills, 35-3 (Balt)
    Bills, 23-17 (Buff)
1982—Bills, 20-0 (Buff)
1983—Bills, 28-23 (Buff)
    Bills, 30-7 (Balt)
1984—Colts, 31-17 (I)
    Bills, 21-15 (Buff)
1985—Colts, 49-17 (I)
    Bills, 21-9 (Buff)
1986—Bills, 24-13 (Buff)
    Colts, 24-14 (I)
1987—Colts, 47-6 (Buff)
    Bills, 27-3 (I)
1988—Bills, 34-23 (Buff)
    Colts, 17-14 (I)

1989—Colts, 37-14 (I)
    Bills, 30-7 (Buff)
1990—Bills, 26-10 (Buff)
    Bills, 31-7 (I)
1991—Bills, 42-6 (Buff)
    Bills, 35-7 (I)
1992—Bills, 38-0 (Buff)
    Colts, 16-13 (I) OT
1993—Bills, 23-9 (Buff)
    Bills, 30-10 (I)
1994—Colts, 27-17 (Buff)
    Colts, 10-9 (I)
1995—Bills, 20-14 (Buff)
    Bills, 16-10 (I)
1996—Bills, 16-13 (Buff) OT
    Colts, 13-10 (I) OT
1997—Bills, 37-35 (B)
    Bills, 9-6 (I)
1998—Bills, 31-24 (I)
    Bills, 34-11 (B)
1999—Colts, 31-14 (I)
    Bills, 31-6 (B)
2000—Colts, 18-16 (B)
    Colts, 44-20 (I)
2001—Colts, 42-26 (I)
    Colts, 30-14 (B)
2003—Colts, 17-14 (B)
(RS Pts.—Bills 1,331, Colts 1,254)
*Franchise in Baltimore prior to 1984
BUFFALO vs. JACKSONVILLE
RS: Bills lead series, 3-2
PS: Jaguars lead series, 1-0
1996—*Jaguars, 30-27 (B)
1997—Jaguars, 20-14 (B)
1998—Bills, 17-16 (B)
2001—Bills, 13-10 (J)
2003—Bills, 38-17 (J)
2004—Jaguars, 13-10 (B)
(RS Pts.—Bills 92, Jaguars 76)
(PS Pts.—Jaguars 30, Bills 27)
*AFC First-Round Playoff
BUFFALO vs. *KANSAS CITY
RS: Bills lead series, 18-16-1
PS: Bills lead series, 2-1
1960—Texans, 45-28 (B)
    Texans, 24-7 (D)
1961—Bills, 27-24 (B)
    Bills, 30-20 (D)
1962—Texans, 41-21 (D)
    Bills, 23-14 (B)
1963—Tie, 27-27 (B)
    Bills, 35-26 (KC)
1964—Bills, 34-17 (B)
    Bills, 35-22 (KC)
1965—Bills, 23-7 (KC)
    Bills, 34-25 (B)
1966—Chiefs, 42-20 (B)
    Bills, 29-14 (KC)
    **Chiefs, 31-7 (B)
1967—Chiefs, 23-13 (KC)
1968—Chiefs, 18-7 (B)
1969—Chiefs, 29-7 (B)
    Chiefs, 22-19 (KC)
1971—Chiefs, 22-9 (KC)
1973—Bills, 23-14 (B)
1976—Bills, 50-17 (B)
1978—Bills, 28-13 (B)
    Chiefs, 14-10 (KC)
1982—Bills, 14-9 (B)
1983—Bills, 14-9 (KC)

1986—Chiefs, 20-17 (B)
    Bills, 17-14 (KC)
1991—Chiefs, 33-6 (KC)
    ***Bills, 37-14 (B)
1993—Chiefs, 23-7 (KC)
    ****Bills, 30-13 (B)
1994—Bills, 44-10 (B)
1996—Bills, 20-9 (B)
1997—Chiefs, 22-16 (KC)
2000—Bills, 21-17 (KC)
2002—Chiefs, 17-16 (KC)
2003—Chiefs, 38-5 (KC)
(RS Pts.—Chiefs 741, Bills 736)
(PS Pts.—Bills 74, Chiefs 58)
*Franchise in Dallas prior to 1963 and
known as Texans
**AFL Championship
***AFC Divisional Playoff
****AFC Championship
BUFFALO vs. MIAMI
RS: Dolphins lead series, 48-29-1
PS: Bills lead series, 3-1
1966—Bills, 58-24 (B)
    Bills, 29-0 (M)
1967—Bills, 35-13 (B)
    Dolphins, 17-14 (M)
1968—Tie, 14-14 (M)
    Dolphins, 21-17 (B)
1969—Dolphins, 24-6 (M)
    Bills, 28-3 (B)
1970—Dolphins, 33-14 (B)
    Dolphins, 45-7 (M)
1971—Dolphins, 29-14 (B)
    Dolphins, 34-0 (M)
1972—Dolphins, 24-23 (M)
    Dolphins, 30-16 (B)
1973—Dolphins, 27-6 (M)
    Dolphins, 17-0 (B)
1974—Dolphins, 24-16 (B)
    Dolphins, 35-28 (M)
1975—Dolphins, 35-30 (B)
    Dolphins, 31-21 (M)
1976—Dolphins, 30-21 (B)
    Dolphins, 45-27 (M)
1977—Dolphins, 13-0 (B)
    Dolphins, 31-14 (M)
1978—Dolphins, 31-24 (M)
    Dolphins, 25-24 (B)
1979—Dolphins, 9-7 (B)
    Dolphins, 17-7 (M)
1980—Bills, 17-7 (B)
    Dolphins, 17-14 (M)
1981—Bills, 31-21 (B)
    Dolphins, 16-6 (M)
1982—Dolphins, 9-7 (B)
    Dolphins, 27-10 (M)
1983—Dolphins, 12-0 (B)
    Bills, 38-35 (M) OT
1984—Dolphins, 21-17 (B)
    Dolphins, 38-7 (M)
1985—Dolphins, 23-14 (B)
    Dolphins, 28-0 (M)
1986—Dolphins, 27-14 (M)
    Dolphins, 34-24 (B)
1987—Bills, 34-31 (M) OT
    Bills, 27-0 (B)
1988—Bills, 9-6 (B)
    Bills, 31-6 (M)
1989—Bills, 27-24 (M)
    Bills, 31-17 (B)

1990—Dolphins, 30-7 (M)
　　　Bills, 24-14 (B)
　　　*Bills, 44-34 (B)
1991—Bills, 35-31 (B)
　　　Bills, 41-27 (M)
1992—Dolphins, 37-10 (B)
　　　Bills, 26-20 (M)
　　　**Bills, 29-10 (M)
1993—Dolphins, 22-13 (M)
　　　Bills, 47-34 (M)
1994—Bills, 21-11 (B)
　　　Bills, 42-31 (M)
1995—Dolphins, 23-6 (M)
　　　Bills, 23-20 (B)
　　　***Bills, 37-22 (B)
1996—Dolphins, 21-7 (B)
　　　Dolphins, 16-14 (M)
1997—Bills, 9-6 (B)
　　　Dolphins, 30-13 (M)
1998—Dolphins, 13-7 (M)
　　　Bills, 30-24 (B)
　　　***Dolphins, 24-17 (M)
1999—Bills, 23-18 (M)
　　　Bills, 23-3 (B)
2000—Dolphins, 22-13 (M)
　　　Dolphins, 33-6 (B)
2001—Dolphins, 34-27 (B)
　　　Dolphins, 34-7 (M)
2002—Bills, 23-10 (M)
　　　Bills, 38-21 (B)
2003—Dolphins, 17-7 (M)
　　　Dolphins, 20-3 (B)
2004—Bills, 20-13 (B)
　　　Bills, 42-32 (M)
(RS Pts.—Dolphins 1,747, Bills 1,465)
(PS Pts.—Bills 127, Dolphins 90)
*AFC Divisional Playoff
**AFC Championship
***AFC First-Round Playoff
BUFFALO vs. MINNESOTA
RS: Vikings lead series, 7-3
1971—Vikings, 19-0 (M)
1975—Vikings, 35-13 (B)
1979—Vikings, 10-3 (M)
1982—Bills, 23-22 (B)
1985—Vikings, 27-20 (B)
1988—Bills, 13-10 (B)
1994—Vikings, 21-17 (B)
1997—Vikings, 34-13 (B)
2000—Vikings, 31-27 (M)
2002—Bills, 45-39 (M) OT
(RS Pts.—Vikings 248, Bills 174)
BUFFALO vs. *NEW ENGLAND
RS: Patriots lead series, 48-40-1
PS: Patriots lead series, 1-0
1960—Bills, 13-0 (Bos)
　　　Bills, 38-14 (Buff)
1961—Patriots, 23-21 (Buff)
　　　Patriots, 52-21 (Bos)
1962—Tie, 28-28 (Buff)
　　　Patriots, 21-10 (Bos)
1963—Bills, 28-21 (Buff)
　　　Patriots, 17-7 (Bos)
　　　**Patriots, 26-8 (Buff)
1964—Patriots, 36-28 (Buff)
　　　Bills, 24-14 (Bos)
1965—Bills, 24-7 (Buff)
　　　Bills, 23-7 (Bos)
1966—Patriots, 20-10 (Buff)
　　　Patriots, 14-3 (Bos)

1967—Patriots, 23-0 (Buff)
　　　Bills, 44-16 (Bos)
1968—Patriots, 16-7 (Buff)
　　　Patriots, 23-6 (Bos)
1969—Bills, 23-16 (Buff)
　　　Patriots, 35-21 (Bos)
1970—Bills, 45-10 (Bos)
　　　Patriots, 14-10 (Buff)
1971—Patriots, 38-33 (NE)
　　　Bills, 27-20 (Buff)
1972—Bills, 38-14 (Buff)
　　　Bills, 27-24 (NE)
1973—Bills, 31-13 (NE)
　　　Bills, 37-13 (Buff)
1974—Bills, 30-28 (Buff)
　　　Bills, 29-28 (NE)
1975—Bills, 45-31 (Buff)
　　　Bills, 34-14 (NE)
1976—Patriots, 26-22 (Buff)
　　　Patriots, 20-10 (NE)
1977—Bills, 24-14 (NE)
　　　Patriots, 20-7 (Buff)
1978—Patriots, 14-10 (Buff)
　　　Patriots, 26-24 (NE)
1979—Patriots, 26-6 (Buff)
　　　Bills, 16-13 (NE) OT
1980—Bills, 31-13 (Buff)
　　　Patriots, 24-2 (NE)
1981—Bills, 20-17 (Buff)
　　　Bills, 19-10 (NE)
1982—Patriots, 30-19 (NE)
1983—Patriots, 31-0 (Buff)
　　　Patriots, 21-7 (NE)
1984—Patriots, 21-17 (Buff)
　　　Patriots, 38-10 (NE)
1985—Patriots, 17-14 (Buff)
　　　Patriots, 14-3 (NE)
1986—Patriots, 23-3 (Buff)
　　　Patriots, 22-19 (NE)
1987—Patriots, 14-7 (NE)
　　　Patriots, 13-7 (Buff)
1988—Patriots, 16-14 (NE)
　　　Bills, 23-20 (Buff)
1989—Bills, 31-10 (Buff)
　　　Patriots, 33-24 (NE)
1990—Bills, 27-10 (NE)
　　　Bills, 14-0 (Buff)
1991—Bills, 22-17 (Buff)
　　　Patriots, 16-13 (NE)
1992—Bills, 41-7 (NE)
　　　Bills, 16-7 (Buff)
1993—Bills, 38-14 (Buff)
　　　Bills, 13-10 (NE) OT
1994—Bills, 38-35 (NE)
　　　Patriots, 41-17 (Buff)
1995—Patriots, 27-14 (NE)
　　　Patriots, 35-25 (Buff)
1996—Bills, 17-10 (Buff)
　　　Patriots, 28-25 (NE)
1997—Patriots, 33-6 (NE)
　　　Patriots, 31-10 (Buff)
1998—Bills, 13-10 (Buff)
　　　Patriots, 25-21 (NE)
1999—Bills, 17-7 (Buff)
　　　Bills, 13-10 (NE) OT
2000—Bills, 16-13 (NE) OT
　　　Patriots, 13-10 (Buff) OT
2001—Patriots, 21-11 (NE)
　　　Patriots, 12-9 (Buff) OT
2002—Patriots, 38-7 (Buff)

　　　Patriots, 27-17 (NE)
2003—Bills, 31-0 (B)
　　　Patriots, 31-0 (NE)
2004—Patriots, 31-17 (B)
　　　Patriots, 29-6 (NE)
(RS Pts.—Patriots 1,782, Bills 1,680)
(PS Pts.—Patriots 26, Bills 8)
*Franchise in Boston prior to 1971
**Division Playoff
BUFFALO vs. NEW ORLEANS
RS: Bills lead series, 4-3
1973—Saints, 13-0 (NO)
1980—Bills, 35-26 (NO)
1983—Bills, 27-21 (B)
1989—Saints, 22-19 (B)
1992—Bills, 20-16 (NO)
1998—Bills, 45-33 (NO)
2001—Saints, 24-6 (B)
(RS Pts.—Saints 155, Bills 152)
BUFFALO vs. N.Y. GIANTS
RS: Bills lead series, 6-3
PS: Giants lead series, 1-0
1970—Giants, 20-6 (NY)
1975—Giants, 17-14 (B)
1978—Bills, 41-17 (B)
1987—Bills, 6-3 (B) OT
1990—Bills, 17-13 (NY)
　　　*Giants, 20-19 (Tampa)
1993—Bills, 17-14 (B)
1996—Bills, 23-20 (NY) OT
1999—Giants, 19-17 (B)
2003—Bills, 24-7 (NY)
(RS Pts.—Bills 165, Giants 130)
(PS Pts.—Giants 20, Bills 19)
*Super Bowl XXV
BUFFALO vs. *N.Y. JETS
RS: Bills lead series, 48-40
PS: Bills lead series, 1-0
1960—Titans, 27-3 (NY)
　　　Titans, 17-13 (B)
1961—Bills, 41-31 (B)
　　　Titans, 21-14 (NY)
1962—Titans, 17-6 (B)
　　　Bills, 20-3 (NY)
1963—Bills, 45-14 (B)
　　　Bills, 19-10 (NY)
1964—Bills, 34-24 (B)
　　　Bills, 20-7 (NY)
1965—Bills, 33-21 (B)
　　　Jets, 14-12 (NY)
1966—Bills, 33-23 (NY)
　　　Bills, 14-3 (B)
1967—Bills, 20-17 (B)
　　　Jets, 20-10 (NY)
1968—Bills, 37-35 (B)
　　　Jets, 25-21 (NY)
1969—Jets, 33-19 (B)
　　　Jets, 16-6 (NY)
1970—Bills, 34-31 (B)
　　　Bills, 10-6 (NY)
1971—Jets, 28-17 (NY)
　　　Jets, 20-7 (B)
1972—Jets, 41-24 (B)
　　　Jets, 41-3 (NY)
1973—Bills, 9-7 (B)
　　　Bills, 34-14 (NY)
1974—Bills, 16-12 (B)
　　　Jets, 20-10 (NY)
1975—Bills, 42-14 (B)
　　　Bills, 24-23 (NY)

1976—Jets, 17-14 (NY)
Jets, 19-14 (B)
1977—Jets, 24-19 (B)
Bills, 14-10 (NY)
1978—Jets, 21-20 (B)
Jets, 45-14 (NY)
1979—Bills, 46-31 (B)
Bills, 14-12 (NY)
1980—Bills, 20-10 (B)
Bills, 31-24 (NY)
1981—Bills, 31-0 (B)
Jets, 33-14 (NY)
**Bills, 31-27 (NY)
1983—Jets, 34-10 (B)
Bills, 24-17 (NY)
1984—Jets, 28-26 (B)
Jets, 21-17 (NY)
1985—Jets, 42-3 (NY)
Jets, 27-7 (B)
1986—Jets, 28-24 (B)
Jets, 14-13 (NY)
1987—Jets, 31-28 (NY)
Bills, 17-14 (NY)
1988—Bills, 37-14 (NY)
Bills, 9-6 (B) OT
1989—Bills, 34-3 (B)
Bills, 37-0 (NY)
1990—Bills, 30-7 (NY)
Bills, 30-27 (B)
1991—Bills, 23-20 (NY)
Bills, 24-13 (B)
1992—Bills, 24-20 (NY)
Jets, 24-17 (B)
1993—Bills, 19-10 (NY)
Bills, 16-14 (B)
1994—Jets, 23-3 (B)
Jets, 22-17 (NY)
1995—Bills, 29-10 (B)
Bills, 28-26 (NY)
1996—Bills, 25-22 (NY)
Bills, 35-10 (B)
1997—Bills, 28-22 (NY)
Bills, 20-10 (B)
1998—Jets, 34-12 (NY)
Jets, 17-10 (B)
1999—Bills, 17-3 (B)
Jets, 17-7 (NY)
2000—Jets, 27-14 (NY)
Bills, 23-20 (B)
2001—Bills, 42-36 (B)
Bills, 14-9 (NY)
2002—Jets, 37-31 (B) OT
Jets, 31-13 (NY)
2003—Jets, 30-3 (NY)
Bills, 17-6 (B)
2004—Jets, 16-14 (NY)
Bills, 22-17 (B)
(RS Pts.—Bills 1,788, Jets 1,746)
(PS Pts.—Bills 31, Jets 27)
*Jets known as Titans prior to 1963
**AFC First-Round Playoff
BUFFALO vs. *OAKLAND
RS: Raiders lead series, 18-15
PS: Bills lead series, 2-0
1960—Bills, 38-9 (B)
Raiders, 20-7 (O)
1961—Raiders, 31-22 (B)
Bills, 26-21 (O)
1962—Bills, 14-6 (B)
Bills, 10-6 (O)

1963—Raiders, 35-17 (O)
Bills, 12-0 (B)
1964—Bills, 23-20 (B)
Raiders, 16-13 (O)
1965—Bills, 17-12 (B)
Bills, 17-14 (O)
1966—Bills, 31-10 (O)
1967—Raiders, 24-20 (B)
Raiders, 28-21 (O)
1968—Raiders, 48-6 (B)
Raiders, 13-10 (O)
1969—Raiders, 50-21 (O)
1972—Raiders, 28-16 (O)
1974—Bills, 21-20 (B)
1977—Raiders, 34-13 (O)
1980—Bills, 24-7 (B)
1983—Raiders, 27-24 (B)
1987—Raiders, 34-21 (LA)
1988—Bills, 37-21 (B)
1990—Bills, 38-24 (B)
**Bills, 51-3 (B)
1991—Bills, 30-27 (LA) OT
1992—Raiders, 20-3 (LA)
1993—Raiders, 25-24 (B)
***Bills, 29-23 (B)
1998—Bills, 44-21 (B)
1999—Raiders, 20-14 (B)
2002—Raiders, 49-31 (B)
2004—Raiders, 13-10 (O)
(RS Pts.—Raiders 733, Bills 675)
(PS Pts.—Bills 80, Raiders 26)
*Franchise in Los Angeles from 1982-1994
**AFC Championship
***AFC Divisional Playoff
BUFFALO vs. PHILADELPHIA
RS: Bills lead series, 5-5
1973—Bills, 27-26 (B)
1981—Eagles, 20-14 (B)
1984—Eagles, 27-17 (B)
1985—Eagles, 21-17 (P)
1987—Eagles, 17-7 (P)
1990—Bills, 30-23 (B)
1993—Bills, 10-7 (P)
1996—Bills, 24-17 (P)
1999—Bills, 26-0 (B)
2003—Eagles, 23-13 (B)
(RS Pts.—Bills 185, Eagles 181)
BUFFALO vs. PITTSBURGH
RS: Steelers lead series, 10-8
PS: Steelers lead series, 2-1
1970—Steelers, 23-10 (P)
1972—Steelers, 38-21 (B)
1974—*Steelers, 32-14 (P)
1975—Bills, 30-21 (P)
1978—Steelers, 28-17 (B)
1979—Steelers, 28-0 (P)
1980—Bills, 28-13 (B)
1982—Bills, 13-0 (B)
1985—Steelers, 30-24 (P)
1986—Bills, 16-12 (B)
1988—Bills, 36-28 (B)
1991—Bills, 52-34 (B)
1992—Bills, 28-20 (B)
*Bills, 24-3 (P)
1993—Steelers, 23-0 (P)
1994—Steelers, 23-10 (P)
1995—*Steelers, 40-21 (P)
1996—Steelers, 24-6 (P)
1999—Bills, 24-21 (B)
2001—Steelers, 20-3 (B)

2004—Steelers, 29-24 (B)
(RS Pts.—Steelers 415, Bills 342)
(PS Pts.—Steelers 75, Bills 59)
*AFC Divisional Playoff
BUFFALO vs. *ST. LOUIS
RS: Bills lead series, 5-4
1970—Rams, 19-0 (B)
1974—Rams, 19-14 (LA)
1980—Bills, 10-7 (B) OT
1983—Rams, 41-17 (LA)
1989—Bills, 23-20 (B)
1992—Bills, 40-7 (B)
1995—Bills, 45-27 (StL)
1998—Rams, 34-33 (B)
2004—Bills, 37-17 (B)
(RS Pts.—Bills 219, Rams 191)
*Franchise in Los Angeles prior to 1995
BUFFALO vs. *SAN DIEGO
RS: Chargers lead series, 18-9-2
PS: Bills lead series, 2-1
1960—Chargers, 24-10 (B)
Bills, 32-3 (LA)
1961—Chargers, 19-11 (B)
Chargers, 28-10 (SD)
1962—Bills, 35-10 (B)
Bills, 40-20 (SD)
1963—Chargers, 14-10 (SD)
Chargers, 23-13 (B)
1964—Bills, 30-3 (B)
Bills, 27-24 (SD)
**Bills, 20-7 (B)
1965—Chargers, 34-3 (B)
Tie, 20-20 (SD)
**Bills, 23-0 (SD)
1966—Chargers, 27-7 (SD)
Tie, 17-17 (B)
1967—Chargers, 37-17 (B)
1968—Chargers, 21-6 (B)
1969—Chargers, 45-6 (SD)
1971—Chargers, 20-3 (SD)
1973—Chargers, 34-7 (SD)
1976—Chargers, 34-13 (B)
1979—Chargers, 27-19 (SD)
1980—Bills, 26-24 (SD)
***Chargers, 20-14 (SD)
1981—Bills, 28-27 (SD)
1985—Chargers, 14-9 (B)
Chargers, 40-7 (SD)
1998—Chargers, 16-14 (SD)
2000—Bills, 27-24 (B) OT
2001—Chargers, 27-24 (SD)
2002—Bills, 20-13 (B)
(RS Pts.—Chargers 669, Bills 491)
(PS Pts.—Bills 57, Chargers 27)
*Franchise in Los Angeles prior to 1961
**AFL Championship
***AFC Divisional Playoff
BUFFALO vs. SAN FRANCISCO
RS: Bills lead series, 5-4
1972—Bills, 27-20 (B)
1980—Bills, 18-13 (B)
1983—49ers, 23-10 (B)
1989—49ers, 21-10 (SF)
1992—Bills, 34-31 (SF)
1995—49ers, 27-17 (SF)
1998—Bills, 26-21 (B)
2001—49ers, 35-0 (SF)
2004—Bills, 41-7 (SF)
(RS Pts.—49ers 198, Bills 183)

BUFFALO vs. SEATTLE
RS: Seahawks lead series, 6-4
1977—Seahawks, 56-17 (S)
1984—Seahawks, 31-28 (S)
1988—Bills, 13-3 (S)
1989—Seahawks, 17-16 (S)
1995—Bills, 27-21 (B)
1996—Seahawks, 26-18 (S)
1999—Seahawks, 26-16 (S)
2000—Bills, 42-23 (S)
2001—Seahawks, 23-20 (B)
2004—Bills, 38-9 (S)
(RS Pts.—Bills 235, Seahawks 235)
BUFFALO vs. TAMPA BAY
RS: Buccaneers lead series, 5-2
1976—Bills, 14-9 (TB)
1978—Buccaneers, 31-10 (TB)
1982—Buccaneers, 24-23 (TB)
1986—Buccaneers, 34-28 (TB)
1988—Buccaneers, 10-5 (TB)
1991—Bills, 17-10 (TB)
2000—Buccaneers, 31-17 (TB)
(RS Pts.—Buccaneers 149, Bills 114)
BUFFALO vs. *TENNESSEE
RS: Titans lead series, 23-14
PS: Bills lead series, 2-1
1960—Bills, 25-24 (B)
      Oilers, 31-23 (H)
1961—Bills, 22-12 (H)
      Oilers, 28-16 (B)
1962—Oilers, 28-23 (B)
      Oilers, 17-14 (H)
1963—Bills, 31-20 (B)
      Oilers, 28-14 (H)
1964—Bills, 48-17 (H)
      Bills, 24-10 (B)
1965—Bills, 19-17 (B)
      Bills, 29-18 (H)
1966—Bills, 27-20 (B)
      Bills, 42-20 (H)
1967—Bills, 20-3 (B)
      Oilers, 10-3 (H)
1968—Oilers, 30-7 (B)
      Oilers, 35-6 (H)
1969—Oilers, 17-3 (B)
      Oilers, 28-14 (H)
1971—Oilers, 20-14 (B)
1974—Oilers, 21-9 (B)
1976—Oilers, 13-3 (B)
1978—Oilers, 17-10 (H)
1983—Bills, 30-13 (B)
1985—Bills, 20-0 (B)
1986—Oilers, 16-7 (H)
1987—Bills, 34-30 (B)
1988—**Bills, 17-10 (B)
1989—Bills, 47-41 (H) OT
1990—Oilers, 27-24 (H)
1992—Oilers, 27-3 (H)
      ***Bills, 41-38 (B) OT
1993—Bills, 35-7 (B)
1994—Bills, 15-7 (H)
1995—Oilers, 28-17 (B)
1997—Oilers, 31-14 (T)
1999—***Titans, 22-16 (T)
2000—Bills, 16-13 (B)
2003—Titans, 28-26 (T)
(RS Pts.—Titans 782, Bills 704)
(PS Pts.—Bills 74, Titans 70)
*Franchise in Houston prior to 1997;
known as Oilers prior to 1999

**AFC Divisional Playoff
***AFC First-Round Playoff
BUFFALO vs. WASHINGTON
RS: Bills lead series, 6-4
PS: Redskins lead series, 1-0
1972—Bills, 24-17 (W)
1977—Redskins, 10-0 (B)
1981—Bills, 21-14 (B)
1984—Redskins, 41-14 (W)
1987—Redskins, 27-7 (B)
1990—Redskins, 29-14 (W)
1991—*Redskins, 37-24 (Minneapolis)
1993—Bills, 24-10 (B)
1996—Bills, 38-13 (B)
1999—Bills, 34-17 (W)
2003—Bills, 24-7 (B)
(RS Pts.—Bills 200, Redskins 185)
(PS Pts.—Redskins 37, Bills 24)
*Super Bowl XXVI

CAROLINA vs. ARIZONA
RS: Panthers lead series, 3-2;
See Arizona vs. Carolina
CAROLINA vs. ATLANTA
RS: Falcons lead series, 14-6;
See Atlanta vs. Carolina
CAROLINA vs. BALTIMORE
RS: Panthers lead series, 2-0;
See Baltimore vs. Carolina
CAROLINA vs. BUFFALO
RS: Bills lead series, 3-0;
See Buffalo vs. Carolina
CAROLINA vs. CHICAGO
RS: Series tied, 1-1
1995—Bears, 31-27 (Chi)
2002—Panthers, 24-14 (Car)
(RS Pts.—Panthers 51, Bears 45)
CAROLINA vs. CINCINNATI
RS: Panthers lead series, 2-0
1999—Panthers, 27-3 (Car)
2002—Panthers, 52-31 (Car)
(RS Pts.—Panthers 79, Bengals 34)
CAROLINA vs. CLEVELAND
RS: Panthers lead series, 2-0
1999—Panthers, 31-17 (Cle)
2002—Panthers, 13-6 (Cle)
(RS Pts.—Panthers 44, Browns 23)
CAROLINA vs. DALLAS
RS: Cowboys lead series, 4-1
PS: Panthers lead series, 2-0
1996—*Panthers, 26-17 (C)
1997—Panthers, 23-13 (D)
1998—Cowboys, 27-20 (D)
2000—Cowboys, 16-13 (C) OT
2002—Cowboys, 14-13 (D)
2003—Cowboys, 24-20 (D)
      **Panthers, 29-10 (C)
(RS Pts.—Cowboys 94, Panthers 89)
(PS Pts.—Panthers 55, Cowboys 27)
*NFC Divisional Playoff
*NFC First-Round Playoff
CAROLINA vs. DENVER
RS: Broncos lead series, 2-0
1997—Broncos, 34-0 (D)
2004—Broncos, 20-17 (D)
(RS Pts.—Broncos 54, Panthers 17)
CAROLINA vs. DETROIT
RS: Panthers lead series, 2-1
1999—Lions, 24-9 (C)
2002—Panthers, 31-7 (C)

2003—Panthers, 20-14 (C)
(RS Pts.—Panthers 60, Lions 45)
CAROLINA vs. GREEN BAY
RS: Packers lead series, 5-2
PS: Packers lead series, 1-0
1996—*Packers, 30-13 (GB)
1997—Packers, 31-10 (C)
1998—Packers, 37-30 (C)
1999—Panthers, 33-31 (GB)
2000—Panthers, 31-14 (C)
2001—Packers, 28-7 (C)
2002—Packers, 17-14 (GB)
2004—Packers, 24-14 (C)
(RS Pts.—Packers 182, Panthers 139)
(PS Pts.—Packers 30, Panthers 13)
*NFC Championship
CAROLINA vs. HOUSTON
RS: Texans lead series, 1-0
2003—Texans, 14-10 (H)
(RS Pts.—Texans 14, Panthers 10)
CAROLINA vs. INDIANAPOLIS
RS: Panthers lead series, 3-0
1995—Panthers, 13-10 (C)
1998—Panthers, 27-19 (I)
2003—Panthers, 23-20 (I) OT
(RS Pts.—Panthers 63, Colts 49)
CAROLINA vs. JACKSONVILLE
RS: Jaguars lead series, 2-1
1996—Jaguars, 24-14 (J)
1999—Jaguars, 22-20 (J)
2003—Panthers, 24-23 (C)
(RS Pts.—Jaguars 69, Panthers 58)
CAROLINA vs. KANSAS CITY
RS: Chiefs lead series, 2-1
1997—Chiefs, 35-14 (C)
2000—Chiefs, 15-14 (KC)
2004—Panthers, 28-17 (KC)
(RS Pts.—Chiefs 67, Panthers 56)
CAROLINA vs. MIAMI
RS: Dolphins lead series, 2-0
1998—Dolphins, 13-9 (C)
2001—Dolphins, 23-6 (M)
(RS Pts.—Dolphins 36, Panthers 15)
CAROLINA vs. MINNESOTA
RS: Vikings lead series, 3-2
1996—Vikings, 14-12 (M)
1997—Vikings, 21-14 (M)
2000—Vikings, 31-17 (M)
2001—Panthers, 24-13 (M)
2002—Panthers, 21-14 (M)
(RS Pts.—Vikings 93, Panthers 88)
CAROLINA vs. NEW ENGLAND
RS: Series tied, 1-1
PS: Patriots lead series, 1-0
1995—Panthers, 20-17 (NE) OT
2001—Patriots, 38-6 (C)
2003—*Patriots, 32-29 (Houston)
(RS Pts.—Patriots 55, Panthers 26)
(PS Pts.—Patriots 32, Panthers 29)
*Super Bowl XXXVIII
CAROLINA vs. NEW ORLEANS
RS: Series tied, 10-10
1995—Panthers, 20-3 (C)
      Saints, 34-26 (NO)
1996—Panthers, 22-20 (NO)
      Panthers, 19-7 (C)
1997—Panthers, 13-0 (NO)
      Saints, 16-13 (C)
1998—Saints, 19-14 (NO)
      Panthers, 31-17 (C)

1999—Saints, 19-10 (NO)
    Panthers, 45-13 (C)
2000—Saints, 24-6 (NO)
    Saints, 20-10 (C)
2001—Saints, 27-25 (C)
    Saints, 27-23 (NO)
2002—Saints, 34-24 (C)
    Panthers, 10-6 (NO)
2003—Panthers, 19-13 (C)
    Panthers, 23-20 (NO) OT
2004—Panthers, 32-21 (NO)
    Saints, 21-18 (C)
(RS Pts.—Panthers 403, Saints 361)

CAROLINA vs. N.Y. GIANTS
RS: Panthers lead series, 2-0
1996—Panthers, 27-17 (C)
2003—Panthers, 37-24 (NY)
(RS Pts.—Panthers 64, Giants 41)

CAROLINA vs. N.Y. JETS
RS: Jets lead series, 2-1
1995—Panthers, 26-15 (C)
1998—Jets, 48-21 (NY)
2001—Jets, 13-12 (C)
(RS Pts.—Jets 76, Panthers 59)

CAROLINA vs. OAKLAND
RS: Raiders lead series, 2-1
1997—Panthers, 38-14 (C)
2000—Raiders, 52-9 (O)
2004—Raiders, 27-24 (C)
(RS Pts.— Raiders 93, Panthers 71)

CAROLINA vs. PHILADELPHIA
RS: Eagles lead series, 3-1
PS: Panthers lead series, 1-0
1996—Eagles, 20-9 (P)
1999—Panthers, 33-7 (C)
2003—Eagles, 25-16 (C)
    *Panthers, 14-3 (P)
2004—Eagles, 30-8 (P)
(RS Pts.—Eagles 82, Panthers 66)
(PS Pts.—Panthers 14, Eagles 3)
NFC Championship

CAROLINA vs. PITTSBURGH
RS: Steelers lead series, 2-1
1996—Panthers, 18-14 (C)
1999—Steelers, 30-20 (P)
2002—Steelers, 30-14 (P)
(RS Pts.—Steelers 74, Panthers 52)

CAROLINA vs. ST. LOUIS
RS: Panthers lead series, 8-7
PS: Panthers lead series, 1-0
1995—Rams, 31-10 (C)
    Rams, 28-17 (StL)
1996—Panthers, 45-13 (C)
    Panthers, 20-10 (StL)
1997—Panthers, 16-10 (StL)
    Rams, 30-18 (C)
1998—Panthers, 24-20 (StL)
    Panthers, 20-13 (C)
1999—Rams, 35-10 (StL)
    Rams, 34-21 (C)
2000—Panthers, 27-24 (StL)
    Panthers, 16-3 (C)
2001—Rams, 48-14 (StL)
    Rams, 38-32 (C)
2003—*Panthers, 29-23 (StL) 2OT
2004—Panthers, 20-7 (C)
(RS Pts.—Rams 344, Panthers 310)
(PS Pts.—Panthers 29, Rams 23)
NFC Divisional Playoff

CAROLINA vs. SAN DIEGO
RS: Panthers lead series, 2-1
1997—Panthers, 26-7 (SD)
2000—Panthers, 30-22 (C)
2004—Chargers, 17-6 (C)
(RS Pts.—Panthers 62, Chargers 46)

CAROLINA vs. SAN FRANCISCO
RS: Panthers lead series, 8-7
1995—Panthers, 13-7 (SF)
    49ers, 31-10 (C)
1996—Panthers, 23-7 (C)
    Panthers, 30-24 (SF)
1997—49ers, 34-21 (C)
    49ers, 27-19 (SF)
1998—49ers, 25-23 (SF)
    49ers, 31-28 (C) OT
1999—Panthers, 31-29 (SF)
    Panthers, 41-24 (C)
2000—Panthers, 38-22 (SF)
    Panthers, 34-16 (C)
2001—49ers, 24-14 (SF)
    49ers, 25-22 (C) OT
2004—Panthers, 37-27 (SF)
(RS Pts.—Panthers 384, 49ers 353)

CAROLINA vs. SEATTLE
RS: Series tied, 1-1
2000—Panthers, 26-3 (C)
2004—Seahawks, 23-17 (S)
(RS Pts.—Panthers 43, Seahawks 26)

CAROLINA vs. TAMPA BAY
RS: Panthers lead series, 5-4
1995—Buccaneers, 20-13 (C)
1996—Panthers, 24-0 (C)
1998—Buccaneers, 16-13 (TB)
2002—Buccaneers, 12-9 (C)
    Buccaneers, 23-10 (TB)
2003—Panthers, 12-9 (TB) OT
    Panthers, 27-24 (C)
2004—Panthers, 21-14 (C)
    Panthers, 37-20 (TB)
(RS Pts.—Panthers 166, Buccaneers 138)

CAROLINA vs. *TENNESSEE
RS: Series tied, 1-1
1996—Panthers, 31-6 (H)
2003—Titans, 37-17 (C)
(RS Pts.—Panthers 48, Titans 43)
Franchise in Houston prior to 1997;
known as Oilers prior to 1999

CAROLINA vs. WASHINGTON
RS: Redskins lead series, 6-1
1995—Redskins, 20-17 (W)
1997—Redskins, 24-10 (C)
1998—Redskins, 28-25 (C)
1999—Redskins, 38-36 (W)
2000—Redskins, 20-17 (W)
2001—Redskins, 17-14 (W) OT
2003—Panthers, 20-17 (C)
(RS Pts.—Redskins 164, Panthers 139)

CHICAGO vs. ARIZONA
RS: Bears lead series, 54-26-6;
See Arizona vs. Chicago

CHICAGO vs. ATLANTA
RS: Bears lead series, 11-10;
See Atlanta vs. Chicago

CHICAGO vs. BALTIMORE
RS: Series tied, 1-1;
See Baltimore vs. Chicago

CHICAGO vs. BUFFALO
RS: Bears lead series, 5-4;

See Buffalo vs. Chicago
CHICAGO vs. CAROLINA
RS: Series tied, 1-1;
See Carolina vs. Chicago

CHICAGO vs. CINCINNATI
RS: Bengals lead series, 4-3
1972—Bengals, 13-3 (Chi)
1980—Bengals, 17-14 (Chi) OT
1986—Bears, 44-7 (Cin)
1989—Bears, 17-14 (Chi)
1992—Bengals, 31-28 (Chi) OT
1995—Bengals, 16-10 (Cin)
2001—Bears, 24-0 (Cin)
(RS Pts.—Bears 140, Bengals 98)

CHICAGO vs. CLEVELAND
RS: Browns lead series, 8-4
1951—Browns, 42-21 (Cle)
1954—Browns, 39-10 (Chi)
1960—Browns, 42-0 (Cle)
1961—Bears, 17-14 (Chi)
1967—Browns, 24-0 (Chi)
1969—Browns, 28-24 (Chi)
1972—Bears, 17-0 (Cle)
1980—Browns, 27-21 (Cle)
1986—Bears, 41-31 (Chi)
1989—Browns, 27-7 (Cle)
1992—Browns, 27-14 (Cle)
2001—Bears, 27-21 (Chi) OT
(RS Pts.—Browns 322, Bears 199)

CHICAGO vs. DALLAS
RS: Cowboys lead series, 10-8
PS: Cowboys lead series, 2-0
1960—Bears, 17-7 (C)
1962—Bears, 34-33 (D)
1964—Cowboys, 24-10 (C)
1968—Cowboys, 34-3 (C)
1971—Bears, 23-19 (C)
1973—Cowboys, 20-17 (C)
1976—Cowboys, 31-21 (D)
1977—*Cowboys, 37-7 (D)
1979—Cowboys, 24-20 (D)
1981—Cowboys, 10-9 (D)
1984—Cowboys, 23-14 (C)
1985—Bears, 44-0 (D)
1986—Bears, 24-10 (D)
1988—Bears, 17-7 (C)
1991—**Cowboys, 17-13 (C)
1992—Cowboys, 27-14 (D)
1996—Bears, 22-6 (C)
1997—Cowboys, 27-3 (D)
1998—Bears, 13-12 (C)
2004—Cowboys, 21-7 (D)
(RS Pts.—Cowboys 335, Bears 312)
(PS Pts.—Cowboys 54, Bears 20)
NFC Divisional Playoff
**NFC First-Round Playoff*

CHICAGO vs. DENVER
RS: Series tied, 6-6
1971—Broncos, 6-3 (D)
1973—Bears, 33-14 (D)
1976—Broncos, 28-14 (C)
1978—Broncos, 16-7 (D)
1981—Bears, 35-24 (C)
1983—Bears, 31-14 (C)
1984—Bears, 27-0 (C)
1987—Broncos, 31-29 (D)
1990—Bears, 16-13 (D) OT
1993—Broncos, 13-3 (C)
1996—Broncos, 17-12 (D)
2003—Bears, 19-10 (D)

(RS Pts.—Bears 229, Broncos 186)
CHICAGO vs. *DETROIT
RS: Bears lead series, 83-62-5
1930—Spartans, 7-6 (P)
    Bears, 14-6 (C)
1931—Bears, 9-6 (C)
    Spartans, 3-0 (P)
1932—Tie, 13-13 (C)
    Tie, 7-7 (P)
    Bears, 9-0 (C)
1933—Bears, 17-14 (C)
    Bears, 17-7 (P)
1934—Bears, 19-16 (D)
    Bears, 10-7 (C)
1935—Tie, 20-20 (C)
    Lions, 14-2 (C)
1936—Bears, 12-10 (C)
    Lions, 13-7 (D)
1937—Bears, 28-20 (C)
    Bears, 13-0 (D)
1938—Lions, 13-7 (C)
    Lions, 14-7 (D)
1939—Lions, 10-0 (C)
    Bears, 23-13 (D)
1940—Bears, 7-0 (C)
    Lions, 17-14 (D)
1941—Bears, 49-0 (C)
    Bears, 24-7 (D)
1942—Bears, 16-0 (C)
    Bears, 42-0 (D)
1943—Bears, 27-21 (D)
    Bears, 35-14 (C)
1944—Tie, 21-21 (C)
    Lions, 41-21 (D)
1945—Lions, 16-10 (D)
    Lions, 35-28 (C)
1946—Bears, 42-6 (C)
    Bears, 45-24 (D)
1947—Bears, 33-24 (C)
    Bears, 34-14 (D)
1948—Bears, 28-0 (C)
    Bears, 42-14 (D)
1949—Bears, 27-24 (C)
    Bears, 28-7 (D)
1950—Bears, 35-21 (D)
    Bears, 6-3 (C)
1951—Bears, 28-23 (D)
    Lions, 41-28 (C)
1952—Bears, 24-23 (C)
    Lions, 45-21 (D)
1953—Lions, 20-16 (C)
    Lions, 13-7 (D)
1954—Lions, 48-23 (D)
    Bears, 28-24 (C)
1955—Bears, 24-14 (D)
    Bears, 21-20 (C)
1956—Lions, 42-10 (D)
    Bears, 38-21 (C)
1957—Bears, 27-7 (D)
    Lions, 21-13 (C)
1958—Bears, 20-7 (D)
    Bears, 21-16 (C)
1959—Bears, 24-14 (D)
    Bears, 25-14 (C)
1960—Bears, 28-7 (C)
    Lions, 36-0 (D)
1961—Bears, 31-17 (D)
    Lions, 16-15 (C)
1962—Lions, 11-3 (D)
    Bears, 3-0 (C)

1963—Bears, 37-21 (D)
    Bears, 24-14 (C)
1964—Lions, 10-0 (C)
    Bears, 27-24 (D)
1965—Bears, 38-10 (C)
    Bears, 17-10 (D)
1966—Lions, 14-3 (D)
    Tie, 10-10 (C)
1967—Bears, 14-3 (C)
    Bears, 27-13 (D)
1968—Lions, 42-0 (D)
    Bears, 28-10 (C)
1969—Lions, 13-7 (D)
    Lions, 20-3 (C)
1970—Lions, 28-14 (D)
    Lions, 16-10 (C)
1971—Bears, 28-23 (D)
    Bears, 28-3 (C)
1972—Lions, 38-24 (C)
    Lions, 14-0 (D)
1973—Lions, 30-7 (C)
    Lions, 40-7 (D)
1974—Bears, 17-9 (C)
    Lions, 34-17 (D)
1975—Lions, 27-7 (D)
    Bears, 25-21 (C)
1976—Bears, 10-3 (C)
    Lions, 14-10 (D)
1977—Bears, 30-20 (C)
    Bears, 31-14 (D)
1978—Bears, 19-0 (D)
    Lions, 21-17 (C)
1979—Bears, 35-7 (C)
    Lions, 20-0 (D)
1980—Bears, 24-7 (C)
    Bears, 23-17 (D) OT
1981—Lions, 48-17 (D)
    Lions, 23-7 (C)
1982—Lions, 17-10 (D)
    Bears, 20-17 (C)
1983—Lions, 31-17 (D)
    Lions, 38-17 (C)
1984—Bears, 16-14 (C)
    Bears, 30-13 (D)
1985—Bears, 24-3 (C)
    Bears, 37-17 (D)
1986—Bears, 13-7 (C)
    Bears, 16-13 (D)
1987—Bears, 30-10 (C)
    Bears, 24-7 (D)
1988—Bears, 24-7 (D)
    Bears, 13-12 (C)
1989—Bears, 47-27 (D)
    Lions, 27-17 (C)
1990—Bears, 23-17 (C) OT
    Lions, 38-21 (D)
1991—Bears, 20-10 (C)
    Lions, 16-6 (D)
1992—Bears, 27-24 (C)
    Lions, 16-3 (D)
1993—Bears, 10-6 (D)
    Lions, 20-14 (C)
1994—Lions, 21-16 (D)
    Bears, 20-10 (C)
1995—Lions, 24-17 (C)
    Lions, 27-7 (D)
1996—Lions, 35-16 (D)
    Bears, 31-14 (C)
1997—Lions, 32-7 (C)
    Lions, 55-20 (D)
1998—Bears, 31-27 (C)

    Lions, 26-3 (D)
1999—Lions, 21-17 (D)
    Bears, 28-10 (C)
2000—Lions, 21-14 (C)
    Bears, 23-20 (D)
2001—Bears, 13-10 (C)
    Bears, 24-0 (D)
2002—Lions, 23-20 (D) OT
    Bears, 20-17 (C) OT
2003—Bears, 24-16 (C)
    Lions, 12-10 (D)
2004—Lions, 20-16 (C)
    Lions, 19-13 (D)
(RS Pts.—Bears 2,776, Lions 2,616)
*Franchise in Portsmouth prior to 1934
and known as the Spartans*
CHICAGO vs. GREEN BAY
RS: Bears lead series, 84-78-6
PS: Bears lead series, 1-0
1921—Staleys, 20-0 (C)
1923—Bears, 3-0 (GB)
1924—Bears, 3-0 (C)
1925—Packers, 14-10 (GB)
    Bears, 21-0 (C)
1926—Tie, 6-6 (GB)
    Bears, 19-13 (C)
    Tie, 3-3 (C)
1927—Bears, 7-6 (GB)
    Bears, 14-6 (C)
1928—Tie, 12-12 (GB)
    Packers, 16-6 (C)
    Packers, 6-0 (C)
1929—Packers, 23-0 (GB)
    Packers, 14-0 (C)
    Packers, 25-0 (C)
1930—Packers, 7-0 (GB)
    Packers, 13-12 (C)
    Bears, 21-0 (C)
1931—Packers, 7-0 (GB)
    Packers, 6-2 (C)
    Bears, 7-6 (C)
1932—Tie, 0-0 (GB)
    Packers, 2-0 (C)
    Bears, 9-0 (C)
1933—Bears, 14-7 (GB)
    Bears, 10-7 (C)
    Bears, 7-6 (C)
1934—Bears, 24-10 (GB)
    Bears, 27-14 (C)
1935—Packers, 7-0 (GB)
    Packers, 17-14 (C)
1936—Bears, 30-3 (GB)
    Packers, 21-10 (C)
1937—Bears, 14-2 (GB)
    Packers, 24-14 (C)
1938—Bears, 2-0 (GB)
    Packers, 24-17 (C)
1939—Packers, 21-16 (GB)
    Bears, 30-27 (C)
1940—Bears, 41-10 (GB)
    Bears, 14-7 (C)
1941—Bears, 25-17 (GB)
    Packers, 16-14 (C)
    **Bears, 33-14 (C)
1942—Bears, 44-28 (GB)
    Bears, 38-7 (C)
1943—Tie, 21-21 (GB)
    Bears, 21-7 (C)
1944—Packers, 42-28 (GB)
    Bears, 21-0 (C)

1945—Packers, 31-21 (GB)
    Bears, 28-24 (C)
1946—Bears, 30-7 (GB)
    Bears, 10-7 (C)
1947—Packers, 29-20 (GB)
    Bears, 20-17 (C)
1948—Packers, 45-7 (GB)
    Bears, 7-6 (C)
1949—Bears, 17-0 (GB)
    Bears, 24-3 (C)
1950—Packers, 31-21 (GB)
    Bears, 28-14 (C)
1951—Bears, 31-20 (GB)
    Bears, 24-13 (C)
1952—Bears, 24-14 (GB)
    Packers, 41-28 (C)
1953—Bears, 17-13 (GB)
    Tie, 21-21 (C)
1954—Bears, 10-3 (GB)
    Bears, 28-23 (C)
1955—Packers, 24-3 (GB)
    Bears, 52-31 (C)
1956—Bears, 37-21 (GB)
    Bears, 38-14 (C)
1957—Packers, 21-17 (GB)
    Bears, 21-14 (C)
1958—Bears, 34-20 (GB)
    Bears, 24-10 (C)
1959—Packers, 9-6 (GB)
    Bears, 28-17 (C)
1960—Bears, 17-14 (GB)
    Packers, 41-13 (C)
1961—Packers, 24-0 (GB)
    Packers, 31-28 (C)
1962—Packers, 49-0 (GB)
    Packers, 38-7 (C)
1963—Bears, 10-3 (GB)
    Bears, 26-7 (C)
1964—Packers, 23-12 (GB)
    Packers, 17-3 (C)
1965—Packers, 23-14 (GB)
    Bears, 31-10 (C)
1966—Packers, 17-0 (C)
    Packers, 13-6 (GB)
1967—Packers, 13-10 (GB)
    Packers, 17-13 (C)
1968—Bears, 13-10 (GB)
    Packers, 28-27 (C)
1969—Packers, 17-0 (GB)
    Packers, 21-3 (C)
1970—Packers, 20-19 (GB)
    Bears, 35-17 (C)
1971—Packers, 17-14 (C)
    Packers, 31-10 (GB)
1972—Packers, 20-17 (GB)
    Packers, 23-17 (C)
1973—Bears, 31-17 (GB)
    Packers, 21-0 (C)
1974—Bears, 10-9 (C)
    Packers, 20-3 (Mil)
1975—Bears, 27-14 (C)
    Packers, 28-7 (GB)
1976—Bears, 24-13 (C)
    Bears, 16-10 (GB)
1977—Bears, 26-0 (GB)
    Bears, 21-10 (C)
1978—Packers, 24-14 (GB)
    Bears, 14-0 (C)
1979—Bears, 6-3 (C)
    Bears, 15-14 (GB)

1980—Packers, 12-6 (GB) OT
    Bears, 61-7 (C)
1981—Packers, 16-9 (C)
    Packers, 21-17 (GB)
1983—Packers, 31-28 (GB)
    Bears, 23-21 (C)
1984—Bears, 9-7 (GB)
    Packers, 20-14 (C)
1985—Bears, 23-7 (C)
    Bears, 16-10 (GB)
1986—Bears, 25-12 (GB)
    Bears, 12-10 (C)
1987—Bears, 26-24 (GB)
    Bears, 23-10 (C)
1988—Bears, 24-6 (GB)
    Bears, 16-0 (C)
1989—Packers, 14-13 (GB)
    Packers, 40-28 (C)
1990—Bears, 31-13 (GB)
    Bears, 27-13 (C)
1991—Bears, 10-0 (GB)
    Bears, 27-13 (C)
1992—Bears, 30-10 (GB)
    Packers, 17-3 (C)
1993—Packers, 17-3 (GB)
    Bears, 30-17 (C)
1994—Packers, 33-6 (C)
    Packers, 40-3 (GB)
1995—Packers, 27-24 (C)
    Packers, 35-28 (GB)
1996—Packers, 37-6 (C)
    Packers, 28-17 (GB)
1997—Packers, 38-24 (C)
    Packers, 24-23 (C)
1998—Packers, 26-20 (GB)
    Packers, 16-13 (C)
1999—Bears, 14-13 (GB)
    Packers, 35-19 (C)
2000—Bears, 27-24 (GB)
    Packers, 28-6 (C)
2001—Packers, 20-12 (C)
    Packers, 17-7 (GB)
2002—Packers, 34-21 (C)
    Packers, 30-20 (GB)
2003—Packers, 38-23 (C)
    Packers, 34-21 (GB)
2004—Bears, 21-10 (GB)
    Packers, 31-14 (C)
(RS Pts.—Bears 2,847, Packers 2,748)
(PS Pts.—Bears 33, Packers 14)
*Bears known as Staleys prior to 1922
**Division Playoff

CHICAGO vs. HOUSTON
RS: Texans lead series, 1-0
2004—Texans, 24-5 (C)
(RS Pts.—Texans 24, Bears 5)

CHICAGO vs. *INDIANAPOLIS
RS: Colts lead series, 22-17
1953—Colts, 13-9 (B)
    Colts, 16-14 (C)
1954—Bears, 28-9 (C)
    Bears, 28-13 (B)
1955—Colts, 23-17 (B)
    Bears, 38-10 (C)
1956—Colts, 28-21 (B)
    Bears, 58-27 (C)
1957—Colts, 21-10 (B)
    Colts, 29-14 (C)
1958—Colts, 51-38 (B)
    Colts, 17-0 (C)

1959—Bears, 26-21 (B)
    Colts, 21-7 (C)
1960—Colts, 42-7 (B)
    Colts, 24-20 (C)
1961—Bears, 24-10 (C)
    Bears, 21-20 (B)
1962—Bears, 35-15 (C)
    Bears, 57-0 (B)
1963—Bears, 10-3 (C)
    Bears, 17-7 (B)
1964—Colts, 52-0 (B)
    Colts, 40-24 (C)
1965—Colts, 26-21 (C)
    Bears, 13-0 (B)
1966—Colts, 27-17 (C)
    Colts, 21-16 (B)
1967—Colts, 24-3 (C)
1968—Colts, 28-7 (B)
1969—Colts, 24-21 (C)
1970—Colts, 21-20 (B)
1975—Colts, 35-7 (C)
1983—Colts, 22-19 (B) OT
1985—Bears, 17-10 (C)
1988—Bears, 17-13 (I)
1991—Bears, 31-17 (I)
2000—Bears, 27-24 (C)
2004—Colts, 41-10 (C)
(RS Pts.—Colts 835, Bears 779)
*Franchise in Baltimore prior to 1984

CHICAGO vs. JACKSONVILLE
RS: Series tied, 2-2
1995—Bears, 30-27 (J)
1998—Jaguars, 24-23 (C)
2001—Bears, 33-13 (C)
2004—Jaguars, 22-3 (J)
(RS Pts.—Bears 89, Jaguars 86)

CHICAGO vs. KANSAS CITY
RS: Bears lead series, 5-4
1973—Chiefs, 19-7 (KC)
1977—Bears, 28-27 (C)
1981—Bears, 16-13 (KC) OT
1987—Bears, 31-28 (C)
1990—Chiefs, 21-10 (C)
1993—Bears, 19-17 (KC)
1996—Chiefs, 14-10 (KC)
1999—Bears, 20-17 (C)
2003—Chiefs, 31-3 (KC)
(RS Pts.—Chiefs 187, Bears 144)

CHICAGO vs. MIAMI
RS: Dolphins lead series, 6-3
1971—Dolphins, 34-3 (M)
1975—Dolphins, 46-13 (C)
1979—Dolphins, 31-16 (M)
1985—Dolphins, 38-24 (M)
1988—Bears, 34-7 (C)
1991—Dolphins, 16-13 (C) OT
1994—Bears, 17-14 (M)
1997—Bears, 36-33 (M) OT
2002—Dolphins, 27-9 (M)
(RS Pts.—Dolphins 246, Bears 165)

CHICAGO vs. MINNESOTA
RS: Vikings lead series, 47-38-2
PS: Bears lead series, 1-0
1961—Vikings, 37-13 (M)
    Bears, 52-35 (C)
1962—Bears, 13-0 (M)
    Bears, 31-30 (C)
1963—Bears, 28-7 (M)
    Tie, 17-17 (C)
1964—Bears, 34-28 (M)

Vikings, 41-14 (C)
1965—Bears, 45-37 (M)
Vikings, 24-17 (C)
1966—Bears, 13-10 (M)
Bears, 41-28 (C)
1967—Bears, 17-7 (M)
Tie, 10-10 (C)
1968—Bears, 27-17 (M)
Bears, 26-24 (C)
1969—Vikings, 31-0 (C)
Vikings, 31-14 (M)
1970—Vikings, 24-0 (C)
Vikings, 16-13 (M)
1971—Bears, 20-17 (M)
Vikings, 27-10 (C)
1972—Bears, 13-10 (C)
Vikings, 23-10 (M)
1973—Vikings, 22-13 (C)
Vikings, 31-13 (M)
1974—Vikings, 11-7 (M)
Vikings, 17-0 (C)
1975—Vikings, 28-3 (M)
Vikings, 13-9 (C)
1976—Vikings, 20-19 (M)
Bears, 14-13 (C)
1977—Vikings, 22-16 (M) OT
Bears, 10-7 (C)
1978—Vikings, 24-20 (C)
Vikings, 17-14 (M)
1979—Bears, 26-7 (C)
Vikings, 30-27 (M)
1980—Vikings, 34-14 (C)
Vikings, 13-7 (M)
1981—Vikings, 24-21 (M)
Bears, 10-9 (C)
1982—Vikings, 35-7 (M)
1983—Vikings, 23-14 (C)
Bears, 19-13 (M)
1984—Bears, 16-7 (C)
Bears, 34-3 (M)
1985—Bears, 33-24 (M)
Bears, 27-9 (C)
1986—Bears, 23-0 (C)
Vikings, 23-7 (M)
1987—Bears, 27-7 (C)
Bears, 30-24 (M)
1988—Vikings, 31-7 (C)
Vikings, 28-27 (M)
1989—Bears, 38-7 (C)
Vikings, 27-16 (M)
1990—Bears, 19-16 (C)
Vikings, 41-13 (M)
1991—Bears, 10-6 (C)
Bears, 34-17 (M)
1992—Vikings, 21-20 (M)
Vikings, 38-10 (C)
1993—Vikings, 10-7 (M)
Vikings, 19-12 (C)
1994—Vikings, 42-14 (C)
Vikings, 33-27 (M) OT
*Bears, 35-18 (M)
1995—Bears, 31-14 (C)
Bears, 14-6 (M)
1996—Vikings, 20-14 (C)
Bears, 15-13 (M)
1997—Vikings, 27-24 (C)
Vikings, 29-22 (M)
1998—Vikings, 31-28 (M)
Vikings, 48-22 (M)
1999—Bears, 24-22 (M)

Vikings, 27-24 (C) OT
2000—Vikings, 30-27 (M)
Vikings, 28-16 (C)
2001—Bears, 17-10 (C)
Bears, 13-6 (M)
2002—Bears, 27-23 (C)
Vikings, 25-7 (M)
2003—Vikings, 24-13 (M)
Bears, 13-10 (C)
2004—Vikings, 27-22 (M)
Bears, 24-14 (C)
RS Pts.—Vikings 1,811, Bears 1,609)
(PS Pts.—Bears 35, Vikings 18)
*NFC First-Round Playoff

CHICAGO vs. NEW ENGLAND
RS: Patriots lead series, 6-3
PS: Bears lead series, 1-0
1973—Patriots, 13-10 (C)
1979—Patriots, 27-7 (C)
1982—Bears, 26-13 (C)
1985—Bears, 20-7 (C)
       *Bears, 46-10 (New Orleans)
1988—Patriots, 30-7 (NE)
1994—Patriots, 13-3 (C)
1997—Patriots, 31-3 (NE)
2000—Bears, 24-17 (C)
2002—Patriots, 33-30 (C)
(RS Pts.—Patriots 184, Bears 130)
(PS Pts.—Bears 46, Patriots 10)
*Super Bowl XX

CHICAGO vs. NEW ORLEANS
RS: Saints lead series, 11-10
PS: Bears lead series, 1-0
1968—Bears, 23-17 (NO)
1970—Bears, 24-3 (NO)
1971—Bears, 35-14 (C)
1973—Saints, 21-16 (NO)
1974—Bears, 24-10 (C)
1975—Bears, 42-17 (NO)
1977—Saints, 42-24 (C)
1980—Bears, 22-3 (C)
1982—Saints, 10-0 (C)
1983—Saints, 34-31 (NO) OT
1984—Bears, 20-7 (C)
1987—Saints, 19-17 (C)
1990—*Bears, 16-6 (C)
1991—Bears, 20-17 (NO)
1992—Saints, 28-6 (NO)
1994—Bears, 17-7 (C)
1996—Saints, 27-24 (NO)
1997—Saints, 20-17 (C)
1999—Bears, 14-10 (C)
2000—Saints, 31-10 (C)
2002—Saints, 29-23 (C)
2003—Saints, 20-13 (NO)
(RS Pts.—Bears 422, Saints 386)
(PS Pts.—Bears 16, Saints 6)
*NFC First-Round Playoff

CHICAGO vs. N.Y. GIANTS
RS: Bears lead series, 26-17-2
PS: Bears lead series, 5-3
1925—Bears, 19-7 (NY)
       Giants, 9-0 (C)
1926—Bears, 7-0 (C)
1927—Giants, 13-7 (NY)
1928—Bears, 13-0 (C)
1929—Giants, 26-14 (C)
       Giants, 34-0 (NY)
       Giants, 14-9 (C)
1930—Giants, 12-0 (C)

Bears, 12-0 (NY)
1931—Bears, 6-0 (C)
       Bears, 12-6 (NY)
       Giants, 25-6 (C)
1932—Bears, 28-8 (NY)
       Bears, 6-0 (C)
1933—Bears, 14-10 (C)
       Giants, 3-0 (NY)
       *Bears, 23-21 (C)
1934—Bears, 27-7 (C)
       Bears, 10-9 (NY)
       *Giants, 30-13 (NY)
1935—Bears, 20-3 (NY)
       Giants, 3-0 (C)
1936—Bears, 25-7 (NY)
1937—Tie, 3-3 (NY)
1939—Giants, 16-13 (NY)
1940—Bears, 37-21 (NY)
1941—*Bears, 37-9 (C)
1942—Bears, 26-7 (NY)
1943—Bears, 56-7 (NY)
1946—Giants, 14-0 (NY)
       *Bears, 24-14 (NY)
1948—Bears, 35-14 (C)
1949—Giants, 35-28 (NY)
1956—Tie, 17-17 (NY)
       *Giants, 47-7 (NY)
1962—Giants, 26-24 (C)
1963—*Bears, 14-10 (C)
1965—Bears, 35-14 (NY)
1967—Bears, 34-7 (C)
1969—Giants, 28-24 (NY)
1970—Bears, 24-16 (NY)
1974—Bears, 16-13 (C)
1977—Bears, 12-9 (NY) OT
1985—**Bears, 21-0 (C)
1987—Bears, 34-19 (C)
1990—**Giants, 31-3 (NY)
1991—Bears, 20-17 (C)
1992—Giants, 27-14 (C)
1993—Giants, 26-20 (C)
1995—Bears, 27-24 (C)
2000—Giants, 14-7 (C)
2004—Bears, 28-21 (NY)
(RS Pts.—Bears 769, Giants 591)
(PS Pts.—Giants 162, Bears 142)
*NFL Championship
**NFC Divisional Playoff

CHICAGO vs. N.Y. JETS
RS: Bears lead series, 5-3
1974—Jets, 23-21 (C)
1979—Bears, 23-13 (C)
1985—Bears, 19-6 (NY)
1991—Bears, 19-13 (C) OT
1994—Bears, 19-7 (NY)
1997—Jets, 23-15 (C)
2000—Jets, 17-10 (NY)
2002—Bears, 20-13 (C)
(RS Pts.—Bears 146, Jets 115)

CHICAGO vs. *OAKLAND
RS: Raiders lead series, 6-5
1972—Raiders, 28-21 (O)
1976—Raiders, 28-27 (C)
1978—Raiders, 25-19 (C) OT
1981—Bears, 23-6 (O)
1984—Bears, 17-6 (C)
1987—Bears, 6-3 (LA)
1990—Raiders, 24-10 (LA)
1993—Raiders, 16-14 (C)
1996—Bears, 19-17 (C)

1999—Raiders, 24-17 (O)
2003—Bears, 24-21 (C)
(RS Pts.—Raiders 198, Bears 197)
Franchise in Los Angeles from 1982-1994
CHICAGO vs. PHILADELPHIA
RS: Bears lead series, 24-8-1
PS: Eagles lead series, 2-1
1933—Tie, 3-3 (P)
1935—Bears, 39-0 (P)
1936—Bears, 17-0 (P)
    Bears, 28-7 (P)
1938—Bears, 28-6 (P)
1939—Bears, 27-14 (C)
1941—Bears, 49-14 (P)
1942—Bears, 45-14 (C)
1944—Bears, 28-7 (P)
1946—Bears, 21-14 (C)
1947—Bears, 40-7 (C)
1948—Eagles, 12-7 (P)
1949—Bears, 38-21 (C)
1955—Bears, 17-10 (C)
1961—Eagles, 16-14 (P)
1963—Bears, 16-7 (C)
1968—Bears, 29-16 (P)
1970—Bears, 20-16 (C)
1972—Bears, 21-12 (P)
1975—Bears, 15-13 (C)
1979—*Eagles, 27-17 (P)
1980—Eagles, 17-14 (P)
1983—Bears, 7-6 (P)
    Bears, 17-14 (C)
1986—Bears, 13-10 (C) OT
1987—Bears, 35-3 (P)
1988—**Bears, 20-12 (C)
1989—Bears, 27-13 (C)
1993—Bears, 17-6 (P)
1994—Eagles, 30-22 (P)
1995—Bears, 20-14 (C)
1999—Eagles, 20-16 (C)
2000—Eagles, 13-9 (P)
2001—**Eagles, 33-19 (C)
2002—Eagles, 19-13 (C)
2004—Eagles, 19-9 (C)
(RS Pts.—Bears 721, Eagles 393)
(PS Pts.—Eagles 72, Bears 56)
NFC First-Round Playoff
**NFC Divisional Playoff*
CHICAGO vs. *PITTSBURGH
RS: Bears lead series, 16-6-1
1934—Bears, 28-0 (P)
1935—Bears, 23-7 (P)
1936—Bears, 27-9 (P)
    Bears, 26-6 (C)
1937—Bears, 7-0 (P)
1939—Bears, 32-0 (P)
1941—Bears, 34-7 (C)
1945—Bears, 28-7 (C)
1947—Bears, 49-7 (C)
1949—Bears, 30-21 (C)
1958—Steelers, 24-10 (P)
1959—Bears, 27-21 (C)
1963—Tie, 17-17 (P)
1967—Steelers, 41-13 (P)
1969—Bears, 38-7 (C)
1971—Bears, 17-15 (C)
1975—Steelers, 34-3 (P)
1980—Steelers, 38-3 (P)
1986—Bears, 13-10 (C) OT
1989—Bears, 20-0 (P)
1992—Bears, 30-6 (C)

1995—Steelers, 37-34 (C) OT
1998—Steelers, 17-12 (P)
(RS Pts.—Bears 521, Steelers 331)
Steelers known as Pirates prior to 1941
CHICAGO vs. *ST. LOUIS
RS: Bears lead series, 47-34-3
PS: Series tied, 1-1
1937—Bears, 20-2 (Clev)
    Bears, 15-7 (C)
1938—Rams, 14-7 (C)
    Rams, 23-21 (Clev)
1939—Bears, 30-21 (Clev)
    Bears, 35-21 (C)
1940—Bears, 21-14 (Clev)
    Bears, 47-25 (C)
1941—Bears, 48-21 (Clev)
    Bears, 31-13 (C)
1942—Bears, 21-7 (Clev)
    Bears, 47-0 (C)
1944—Rams, 19-7 (Clev)
    Bears, 28-21 (C)
1945—Rams, 17-0 (Clev)
    Rams, 41-21 (C)
1946—Tie, 28-28 (C)
    Bears, 27-21 (LA)
1947—Bears, 41-21 (LA)
    Rams, 17-14 (C)
1948—Bears, 42-21 (C)
    Bears, 21-6 (LA)
1949—Rams, 31-16 (C)
    Rams, 27-24 (LA)
1950—Bears, 24-20 (LA)
    Bears, 24-14 (C)
    **Rams, 24-14 (LA)
1951—Rams, 42-17 (C)
1952—Rams, 31-7 (LA)
    Rams, 40-24 (C)
1953—Bears, 38-24 (LA)
    Bears, 24-21 (C)
1954—Rams, 42-38 (LA)
    Bears, 24-13 (C)
1955—Bears, 31-20 (LA)
    Bears, 24-3 (C)
1956—Bears, 35-24 (LA)
    Bears, 30-21 (C)
1957—Bears, 34-26 (C)
    Bears, 16-10 (LA)
1958—Bears, 31-10 (C)
    Rams, 41-35 (LA)
1959—Rams, 28-21 (C)
    Bears, 26-21 (LA)
1960—Bears, 34-27 (C)
    Tie, 24-24 (LA)
1961—Bears, 21-17 (LA)
    Bears, 28-24 (C)
1962—Bears, 27-23 (LA)
    Bears, 30-14 (C)
1963—Bears, 52-14 (LA)
    Bears, 6-0 (C)
1964—Bears, 38-17 (C)
    Bears, 34-24 (LA)
1965—Rams, 30-28 (LA)
    Bears, 31-6 (C)
1966—Rams, 31-17 (LA)
    Bears, 17-10 (C)
1967—Bears, 28-17 (C)
1968—Bears, 17-16 (LA)
1969—Rams, 9-7 (C)
1971—Rams, 17-3 (LA)
1972—Tie, 13-13 (C)

1973—Rams, 26-0 (C)
1975—Rams, 38-10 (LA)
1976—Rams, 20-12 (LA)
1977—Bears, 24-23 (C)
1979—Bears, 27-23 (C)
1981—Bears, 24-7 (C)
1982—Bears, 34-26 (LA)
1983—Rams, 21-14 (LA)
1984—Rams, 29-13 (LA)
1985—***Bears, 24-0 (C)
1986—Rams, 20-17 (C)
1988—Rams, 23-3 (LA)
1989—Bears, 20-10 (C)
1990—Bears, 38-9 (C)
1993—Bears, 20-6 (LA)
1994—Bears, 27-13 (C)
1995—Rams, 34-28 (StL)
1996—Bears, 35-9 (C)
1997—Bears, 13-10 (StL)
1998—Rams, 20-12 (C)
1999—Rams, 34-12 (StL)
2002—Rams, 21-16 (StL)
2003—Rams, 23-21 (C)
(RS Pts.—Bears 1,934, Rams 1,723)
(PS Pts.—Bears 38, Rams 24)
*Franchise in Los Angeles prior to 1995
and in Cleveland prior to 1946*
**Conference Playoff*
***NFC Championship*
CHICAGO vs. SAN DIEGO
RS: Bears lead series, 5-4
1970—Chargers, 20-7 (C)
1974—Chargers, 28-21 (SD)
1978—Chargers, 40-7 (SD)
1981—Bears, 20-17 (C) OT
1984—Chargers, 20-7 (SD)
1993—Bears, 16-13 (SD)
1996—Bears, 27-14 (C)
1999—Bears, 23-20 (SD) OT
2003—Bears, 20-7 (C)
(RS Pts.—Chargers 179, Bears 148)
CHICAGO vs. SAN FRANCISCO
RS: Series tied, 27-27-1
PS: 49ers lead series, 3-0
1950—Bears, 32-20 (SF)
    Bears, 17-0 (C)
1951—Bears, 13-7 (C)
1952—49ers, 40-16 (C)
    Bears, 20-17 (SF)
1953—49ers, 35-28 (C)
    49ers, 24-14 (SF)
1954—49ers, 31-24 (C)
    Bears, 31-27 (SF)
1955—49ers, 20-19 (C)
    Bears, 34-23 (SF)
1956—Bears, 31-7 (C)
    Bears, 38-21 (SF)
1957—49ers, 21-17 (C)
    49ers, 21-17 (SF)
1958—Bears, 28-6 (C)
    Bears, 27-14 (SF)
1959—49ers, 20-17 (SF)
    Bears, 14-3 (C)
1960—Bears, 27-10 (C)
    49ers, 25-7 (SF)
1961—Bears, 31-0 (C)
    49ers, 41-31 (SF)
1962—Bears, 30-14 (SF)
    49ers, 34-27 (C)
1963—49ers, 20-14 (SF)

Bears, 27-7 (C)
1964—49ers, 31-21 (SF)
Bears, 23-21 (C)
1965—49ers, 52-24 (SF)
Bears, 61-20 (C)
1966—Tie, 30-30 (C)
49ers, 41-14 (SF)
1967—Bears, 28-14 (SF)
1968—Bears, 27-19 (C)
1969—49ers, 42-21 (SF)
1970—49ers, 37-16 (C)
1971—49ers, 13-0 (SF)
1972—Bears, 34-21 (C)
1974—49ers, 34-0 (C)
1975—49ers, 31-3 (SF)
1976—Bears, 19-12 (SF)
1978—Bears, 16-13 (SF)
1979—Bears, 28-27 (SF)
1981—49ers, 28-17 (SF)
1983—Bears, 13-3 (C)
1984—*49ers, 23-0 (SF)
1985—Bears, 26-10 (SF)
1987—49ers, 41-0 (SF)
1988—Bears, 10-9 (C)
*49ers, 28-3 (C)
1989—49ers, 26-0 (SF)
1991—49ers, 52-14 (SF)
1994—**49ers, 44-15 (SF)
2000—49ers, 17-0 (SF)
2001—Bears, 37-31 (C) OT
2003—49ers, 49-7 (SF)
2004—Bears, 23-13 (C)
(RS Pts.—49ers 1,258, Bears 1,130)
(PS Pts.—49ers 95, Bears 18)
*NFC Championship
**NFC Divisional Playoff
CHICAGO vs. SEATTLE
RS: Seahawks lead series, 6-2
1976—Bears, 34-7 (S)
1978—Seahawks, 31-29 (C)
1982—Seahawks, 20-14 (S)
1984—Seahawks, 38-9 (S)
1987—Seahawks, 34-21 (C)
1990—Bears, 17-0 (C)
1999—Seahawks, 14-13 (C)
2003—Seahawks, 24-17 (S)
(RS Pts.—Seahawks 168, Bears 154)
CHICAGO vs. TAMPA BAY
RS: Bears lead series, 33-17
1977—Bears, 10-0 (TB)
1978—Buccaneers, 33-19 (TB)
Bears, 14-3 (C)
1979—Buccaneers, 17-13 (C)
Bears, 14-0 (TB)
1980—Bears, 23-0 (C)
Bears, 14-13 (TB)
1981—Bears, 28-17 (C)
Buccaneers, 20-10 (TB)
1982—Buccaneers, 26-23 (TB) OT
1983—Bears, 17-10 (C)
Bears, 27-0 (TB)
1984—Bears, 34-14 (C)
Bears, 44-9 (TB)
1985—Bears, 38-28 (C)
Bears, 27-19 (TB)
1986—Bears, 23-3 (TB)
Bears, 48-14 (C)
1987—Bears, 20-3 (C)
Bears, 27-26 (TB)
1988—Bears, 28-10 (C)

Bears, 27-15 (TB)
1989—Buccaneers, 42-35 (TB)
Buccaneers, 32-31 (C)
1990—Bears, 26-6 (TB)
Bears, 27-14 (C)
1991—Bears, 21-20 (TB)
Bears, 27-0 (C)
1992—Bears, 31-14 (C)
Buccaneers, 20-17 (TB)
1993—Bears, 47-17 (C)
Buccaneers, 13-10 (TB)
1994—Bears, 21-9 (C)
Bears, 20-6 (TB)
1995—Bears, 25-6 (TB)
Bears, 31-10 (C)
1996—Bears, 13-10 (C)
Buccaneers, 34-19 (TB)
1997—Bears, 13-7 (C)
Buccaneers, 31-15 (TB)
1998—Buccaneers, 27-15 (TB)
Buccaneers, 31-17 (C)
1999—Buccaneers, 6-3 (TB)
Buccaneers, 20-6 (C)
2000—Buccaneers, 41-0 (TB)
Bears, 13-10 (C)
2001—Bears, 27-24 (TB)
Bears, 27-3 (C)
2002—Buccaneers, 15-0 (C)
2004—Buccaneers, 19-7 (TB)
(RS Pts.—Bears 1,072, Buccaneers 767)
CHICAGO vs. *TENNESSEE
RS: Series tied, 5-4
1973—Bears, 35-14 (C)
1977—Oilers, 47-0 (H)
1980—Oilers, 10-6 (C)
1986—Bears, 20-7 (H)
1989—Oilers, 33-28 (C)
1992—Oilers, 24-7 (H)
1995—Bears, 35-32 (C)
1998—Bears, 23-20 (T)
2004—Bears, 19-17 (T) OT
(RS Pts.—Titans 204, Bears 173)
*Franchise in Houston prior to 1997;
known as Oilers prior to 1999
CHICAGO vs. *WASHINGTON
RS: Bears lead series, 20-16-1
PS: Redskins lead series, 4-3
1932—Tie, 7-7 (B)
1933—Bears, 7-0 (C)
Redskins, 10-0 (B)
1934—Bears, 21-0 (B)
1935—Bears, 30-14 (B)
1936—Bears, 26-0 (B)
1937—**Redskins, 28-21 (C)
1938—Bears, 31-7 (C)
1940—Redskins, 7-3 (W)
**Bears, 73-0 (W)
1941—Bears, 35-21 (C)
1942—**Redskins, 14-6 (W)
1943—Redskins, 21-7 (W)
**Bears, 41-21 (C)
1945—Redskins, 28-21 (W)
1946—Bears, 24-20 (C)
1947—Bears, 56-20 (W)
1948—Bears, 48-13 (C)
1949—Bears, 31-21 (W)
1951—Bears, 27-0 (W)
1953—Bears, 27-24 (W)
1957—Redskins, 14-3 (C)
1964—Redskins, 27-20 (W)

1968—Redskins, 38-28 (C)
1971—Bears, 16-15 (C)
1974—Redskins, 42-0 (W)
1976—Bears, 33-7 (C)
1978—Bears, 14-10 (W)
1980—Bears, 35-21 (C)
1981—Redskins, 24-7 (C)
1984—***Bears, 23-19 (W)
1985—Bears, 45-10 (C)
1986—***Redskins, 27-13 (C)
1987—***Redskins, 21-17 (C)
1988—Bears, 34-14 (W)
1989—Redskins, 38-14 (W)
1990—Redskins, 10-9 (W)
1991—Bears, 20-7 (C)
1996—Redskins, 10-3 (W)
1997—Redskins, 31-8 (C)
1999—Redskins, 48-22 (W)
2001—Bears, 20-15 (W)
2003—Bears, 27-24 (C)
2004—Redskins, 13-10 (C)
(RS Pts.—Bears 756, Redskins 644)
(PS Pts.—Bears 194, Redskins 130)
*Franchise in Boston prior to 1937 and
known as Braves prior to 1933
**NFL Championship
***NFC Divisional Playoff

CINCINNATI vs. ARIZONA
RS: Bengals lead series, 5-3;
See Arizona vs. Cincinnati
CINCINNATI vs. ATLANTA
RS: Bengals lead series, 7-3;
See Atlanta vs. Cincinnati
CINCINNATI vs. BALTIMORE
RS: Ravens lead series, 12-6;
See Baltimore vs. Cincinnati
CINCINNATI vs. BUFFALO
RS: Bills lead series, 12-9
PS: Bengals lead series, 2-0;
See Buffalo vs. Cincinnati
CINCINNATI vs. CAROLINA
RS: Panthers lead series, 2-0;
See Carolina vs. Cincinnati
CINCINNATI vs. CHICAGO
RS: Bengals lead series, 4-3;
See Chicago vs. Cincinnati
CINCINNATI vs. CLEVELAND
RS: Browns lead series, 33-30
1970—Browns, 30-27 (Cle)
Bengals, 14-10 (Cin)
1971—Browns, 27-24 (Cin)
Browns, 31-27 (Cle)
1972—Browns, 27-6 (Cle)
Browns, 27-24 (Cin)
1973—Browns, 17-10 (Cle)
Bengals, 34-17 (Cin)
1974—Bengals, 33-7 (Cin)
Bengals, 34-24 (Cle)
1975—Bengals, 24-17 (Cin)
Browns, 35-23 (Cle)
1976—Bengals, 45-24 (Cle)
Bengals, 21-6 (Cin)
1977—Browns, 13-3 (Cin)
Bengals, 10-7 (Cle)
1978—Browns, 13-10 (Cle) OT
Bengals, 48-16 (Cin)
1979—Browns, 28-27 (Cle)
Bengals, 16-12 (Cin)
1980—Browns, 31-7 (Cle)

Browns, 27-24 (Cin)
1981—Browns, 20-17 (Cin)
Bengals, 41-21 (Cle)
1982—Bengals, 23-10 (Cin)
1983—Browns, 17-7 (Cle)
Bengals, 28-21 (Cin)
1984—Bengals, 12-9 (Cin)
Bengals, 20-17 (Cle) OT
1985—Bengals, 27-10 (Cin)
Browns, 24-6 (Cle)
1986—Bengals, 30-13 (Cle)
Browns, 34-3 (Cin)
1987—Browns, 34-0 (Cin)
Browns, 38-24 (Cle)
1988—Bengals, 24-17 (Cin)
Browns, 23-16 (Cle)
1989—Bengals, 21-14 (Cin)
Bengals, 21-0 (Cle)
1990—Bengals, 34-13 (Cle)
Bengals, 21-14 (Cin)
1991—Browns, 14-13 (Cle)
Bengals, 23-21 (Cin)
1992—Bengals, 30-10 (Cin)
Browns, 37-21 (Cle)
1993—Browns, 27-14 (Cle)
Bengals, 28-17 (Cin)
1994—Browns, 28-20 (Cin)
Browns, 37-13 (Cle)
1995—Browns, 29-26 (Cin) OT
Browns, 26-10 (Cle)
1999—Bengals, 18-17 (Cle)
Bengals, 44-28 (Cin)
2000—Browns, 24-7 (Cin)
Bengals, 12-3 (Cle)
2001—Bengals, 24-14 (Cin)
Browns, 18-0 (Cle)
2002—Browns, 20-7 (Cle)
Browns, 27-20 (Cin)
2003—Bengals, 21-14 (Cle)
Browns, 22-14 (Cin)
2004—Browns, 34-17 (Cle)
Bengals, 58-48 (Cin)
(RS Pts.—Browns 1,321, Bengals 1,295)
CINCINNATI vs. DALLAS
RS: Cowboys lead series, 5-4
1973—Cowboys, 38-10 (D)
1979—Cowboys, 38-13 (D)
1985—Bengals, 50-24 (C)
1988—Bengals, 38-24 (D)
1991—Cowboys, 35-23 (D)
1994—Bengals, 23-20 (C)
1997—Bengals, 31-24 (C)
2000—Cowboys, 23-6 (D)
2004—Bengals, 26-3 (C)
(RS Pts.—Cowboys 232, Bengals 217)
CINCINNATI vs. DENVER
RS: Broncos lead series, 15-8
1968—Bengals, 24-10 (C)
Broncos, 10-7 (D)
1969—Broncos, 30-23 (C)
Broncos, 27-16 (D)
1971—Bengals, 24-10 (D)
1972—Bengals, 21-10 (C)
1973—Broncos, 28-10 (D)
1975—Bengals, 17-16 (D)
1976—Bengals, 17-7 (C)
1977—Broncos, 24-13 (C)
1979—Broncos, 10-0 (D)
1981—Bengals, 38-21 (C)
1983—Broncos, 24-17 (D)

1984—Broncos, 20-17 (D)
1986—Broncos, 34-28 (D)
1991—Broncos, 45-14 (D)
1994—Broncos, 15-13 (D)
1996—Broncos, 14-10 (C)
1997—Broncos, 38-20 (D)
1998—Broncos, 33-26 (C)
2000—Bengals, 31-21 (C)
2003—Broncos, 30-10 (C)
2004—Bengals, 23-10 (C)
(RS Pts.—Broncos 487, Bengals 419)
CINCINNATI vs. DETROIT
RS: Bengals lead series, 5-3
1970—Lions, 38-3 (D)
1974—Lions, 23-19 (C)
1983—Bengals, 17-9 (C)
1986—Bengals, 24-17 (D)
1989—Bengals, 42-7 (C)
1992—Lions, 19-13 (C)
1998—Bengals, 34-28 (D) OT
2001—Bengals, 31-27 (D)
(RS Pts.—Bengals 183, Lions 168)
CINCINNATI vs. GREEN BAY
RS: Packers lead series, 5-4
1971—Packers, 20-17 (GB)
1976—Bengals, 28-7 (C)
1977—Bengals, 17-7 (Mil)
1980—Packers, 14-9 (GB)
1983—Bengals, 34-14 (C)
1986—Bengals, 34-28 (Mil)
1992—Packers, 24-23 (GB)
1995—Packers, 24-10 (GB)
1998—Packers, 13-6 (C)
(RS Pts.—Bengals 178, Packers 151)
CINCINNATI vs. HOUSTON
RS: Bengals lead series, 2-0
2002—Bengals, 38-3 (H)
2003—Bengals, 34-27 (C)
(RS Pts.—Bengals 72, Texans 30)
CINCINNATI vs. *INDIANAPOLIS
RS: Colts lead series, 12-8
PS: Colts lead series, 1-0
1970—**Colts, 17-0 (B)
1972—Colts, 20-19 (C)
1974—Bengals, 24-14 (B)
1976—Colts, 28-27 (B)
1979—Colts, 38-28 (B)
1980—Bengals, 34-33 (C)
1981—Bengals, 41-19 (B)
1982—Bengals, 20-17 (B)
1983—Colts, 34-31 (C)
1987—Bengals, 23-21 (I)
1989—Colts, 23-12 (C)
1990—Colts, 34-20 (C)
1992—Colts, 21-17 (C)
1993—Colts, 9-6 (C)
1994—Colts, 17-13 (C)
1995—Bengals, 24-21 (I) OT
1996—Bengals, 31-24 (C)
1997—Bengals, 28-13 (I)
1998—Colts, 39-26 (I)
1999—Colts, 31-10 (I)
2002—Colts, 28-21 (I)
(RS Pts.—Colts 484, Bengals 455)
(PS Pts.—Colts 17, Bengals 0)
*Franchise in Baltimore prior to 1984
**AFC Divisional Playoff
CINCINNATI vs. JACKSONVILLE
RS: Jaguars lead series, 10-5
1995—Bengals, 24-17 (C)

Bengals, 17-13 (J)
1996—Bengals, 28-21 (C)
Jaguars, 30-27 (J)
1997—Jaguars, 21-13 (J)
Bengals, 31-26 (C)
1998—Jaguars, 24-11 (J)
Jaguars, 34-17 (C)
1999—Jaguars, 41-10 (C)
Jaguars, 24-7 (J)
2000—Jaguars, 13-0 (J)
Bengals, 17-14 (C)
2001—Jaguars, 30-13 (J)
Jaguars, 14-10 (C)
2002—Jaguars, 29-15 (C)
(RS Pts.—Jaguars 351, Bengals 240)
CINCINNATI vs. KANSAS CITY
RS: Chiefs lead series, 11-10
1968—Chiefs, 13-3 (KC)
Chiefs, 16-9 (C)
1969—Bengals, 24-19 (C)
Chiefs, 42-22 (KC)
1970—Chiefs, 27-19 (C)
1972—Bengals, 23-16 (KC)
1973—Bengals, 14-6 (C)
1974—Bengals, 33-6 (C)
1976—Bengals, 27-24 (KC)
1977—Bengals, 27-7 (KC)
1978—Chiefs, 24-23 (C)
1979—Chiefs, 10-7 (C)
1980—Bengals, 20-6 (KC)
1983—Chiefs, 20-15 (KC)
1984—Chiefs, 27-22 (C)
1986—Chiefs, 24-14 (KC)
1987—Bengals, 30-27 (C) OT
1988—Chiefs, 31-28 (KC)
1989—Bengals, 21-17 (KC)
1993—Chiefs, 17-15 (KC)
2003—Bengals, 24-19 (C)
(RS Pts.—Bengals 420, Chiefs 398)
CINCINNATI vs. MIAMI
RS: Dolphins lead series, 12-4
PS: Dolphins lead series, 1-0
1968—Dolphins, 24-22 (C)
Bengals, 38-21 (M)
1969—Bengals, 27-21 (C)
1971—Dolphins, 23-13 (C)
1973—*Dolphins, 34-16 (M)
1974—Dolphins, 24-3 (M)
1977—Bengals, 23-17 (C)
1978—Bengals, 21-0 (M)
1980—Dolphins, 17-16 (M)
1983—Dolphins, 38-14 (M)
1987—Dolphins, 20-14 (C)
1989—Dolphins, 20-13 (C)
1991—Dolphins, 37-13 (M)
1994—Dolphins, 23-7 (C)
1995—Dolphins, 26-23 (C)
2000—Dolphins, 31-16 (C)
2004—Bengals, 16-13 (C)
(RS Pts.—Dolphins 376, Bengals 258)
(PS Pts.—Dolphins 34, Bengals 16)
*AFC Divisional Playoff
CINCINNATI vs. MINNESOTA
RS: Vikings lead series, 5-4
1973—Bengals, 27-0 (C)
1977—Vikings, 42-10 (M)
1980—Bengals, 14-0 (C)
1983—Vikings, 20-14 (M)
1986—Bengals, 24-20 (C)
1989—Vikings, 29-21 (M)

1992—Vikings, 42-7 (C)
1995—Bengals, 27-24 (C)
1998—Vikings, 24-3 (M)
(RS Pts.—Vikings 201, Bengals 147)
CINCINNATI vs. *NEW ENGLAND
RS: Patriots lead series, 11-8
1968—Patriots, 33-14 (B)
1969—Patriots, 25-14 (C)
1970—Bengals, 45-7 (C)
1972—Bengals, 31-7 (NE)
1975—Bengals, 27-10 (C)
1978—Patriots, 10-3 (C)
1979—Patriots, 20-14 (C)
1984—Patriots, 20-14 (NE)
1985—Patriots, 34-23 (NE)
1986—Bengals, 31-7 (NE)
1988—Patriots, 27-21 (NE)
1990—Bengals, 41-7 (C)
1991—Bengals, 29-7 (C)
1992—Bengals, 20-10 (C)
1993—Patriots, 7-2 (NE)
1994—Patriots, 31-28 (C)
2000—Patriots, 16-13 (NE)
2001—Bengals, 23-17 (C)
2004—Patriots, 35-28 (NE)
(RS Pts.—Bengals 421, Patriots 330)
Franchise in Boston prior to 1971
CINCINNATI vs. NEW ORLEANS
RS: Series tied, 5-5
1970—Bengals, 26-6 (C)
1975—Bengals, 21-0 (NO)
1978—Saints, 20-18 (C)
1981—Saints, 17-7 (NO)
1984—Bengals, 24-21 (NO)
1987—Saints, 41-24 (C)
1990—Saints, 21-7 (C)
1993—Saints, 20-13 (NO)
1996—Bengals, 30-15 (C)
2002—Bengals, 20-13 (C)
(RS Pts.—Bengals 190, Saints 174)
CINCINNATI vs. N.Y. GIANTS
RS: Bengals lead series, 5-2
1972—Bengals, 13-10 (C)
1977—Bengals, 30-13 (C)
1985—Bengals, 35-30 (C)
1991—Bengals, 27-24 (C)
1994—Giants, 27-20 (NY)
1997—Giants, 29-27 (NY)
2004—Benglas, 23-22 (NY)
(RS Pts.—Bengals 175, Giants 155)
CINCINNATI vs. N.Y. JETS
RS: Jets lead series, 12-6
PS: Jets lead series, 1-0
1968—Jets, 27-14 (NY)
1969—Jets, 21-7 (C)
Jets, 40-7 (NY)
1971—Jets, 35-21 (NY)
1973—Bengals, 20-14 (C)
1976—Bengals, 42-3 (NY)
1981—Bengals, 31-30 (NY)
1982—*Jets, 44-17 (C)
1984—Jets, 43-23 (NY)
1985—Jets, 29-20 (C)
1986—Bengals, 52-21 (C)
1987—Jets, 27-20 (NY)
1988—Bengals, 36-19 (C)
1990—Bengals, 25-20 (C)
1992—Jets, 17-14 (NY)
1993—Jets, 17-12 (NY)
1997—Jets, 31-14 (C)

2001—Jets, 15-14 (NY)
2004—Jets, 31-24 (NY)
(RS Pts.—Jets 440, Bengals 396)
(PS Pts.—Jets 44, Bengals 17)
AFC First-Round Playoff
CINCINNATI vs. *OAKLAND
RS: Raiders lead series, 17-7
PS: Raiders lead series, 2-0
1968—Raiders, 31-10 (O)
Raiders, 34-0 (C)
1969—Bengals, 31-17 (C)
Raiders, 37-17 (O)
1970—Bengals, 31-21 (C)
1971—Bengals, 31-27 (C)
1972—Raiders, 20-14 (C)
1974—Raiders, 30-27 (O)
1975—Bengals, 14-10 (C)
**Raiders, 31-28 (O)
1976—Raiders, 35-20 (O)
1978—Raiders, 34-21 (C)
1980—Raiders, 28-17 (O)
1982—Bengals, 31-17 (C)
1983—Raiders, 20-10 (C)
1985—Raiders, 13-6 (LA)
1988—Bengals, 45-21 (LA)
1989—Raiders, 28-7 (LA)
1990—Raiders, 24-7 (LA)
**Raiders, 20-10 (LA)
1991—Raiders, 38-14 (C)
1992—Bengals, 24-21 (C) OT
1993—Bengals, 16-10 (C)
1995—Raiders, 20-17 (C)
1998—Raiders, 27-10 (C)
2003—Raiders, 23-20 (O)
(RS Pts.—Raiders 590, Bengals 436)
(PS Pts.—Raiders 51, Bengals 38)
Franchise in Los Angeles from 1982-1994
**AFC Divisional Playoff
CINCINNATI vs. PHILADELPHIA
RS: Bengals lead series, 7-3
1971—Bengals, 37-14 (C)
1975—Bengals, 31-0 (P)
1979—Bengals, 37-13 (C)
1982—Bengals, 18-14 (P)
1988—Bengals, 28-24 (P)
1991—Eagles, 17-10 (P)
1994—Bengals, 33-30 (C)
1997—Eagles, 44-42 (P)
2000—Eagles, 16-7 (P)
2004—Bengals, 38-10 (P)
(RS Pts.—Bengals 281, Eagles 182)
CINCINNATI vs. PITTSBURGH
RS: Steelers lead series, 41-28
1970—Steelers, 21-10 (P)
Bengals, 34-7 (C)
1971—Steelers, 21-10 (P)
Steelers, 21-13 (C)
1972—Bengals, 15-10 (C)
Steelers, 40-17 (P)
1973—Bengals, 19-7 (C)
Steelers, 20-13 (P)
1974—Steelers, 17-10 (C)
Steelers, 27-3 (P)
1975—Steelers, 30-24 (C)
Steelers, 35-14 (P)
1976—Steelers, 23-6 (P)
Steelers, 7-3 (C)
1977—Steelers, 20-14 (P)
Bengals, 17-10 (C)
1978—Steelers, 28-3 (C)

Steelers, 7-6 (P)
1979—Bengals, 34-10 (C)
Steelers, 37-17 (P)
1980—Bengals, 30-28 (C)
Bengals, 17-16 (P)
1981—Bengals, 34-7 (C)
Bengals, 17-10 (P)
1982—Steelers, 26-20 (P) OT
1983—Steelers, 24-14 (C)
Bengals, 23-10 (P)
1984—Steelers, 38-17 (P)
Bengals, 22-20 (C)
1985—Bengals, 37-24 (P)
Bengals, 26-21 (C)
1986—Bengals, 24-22 (C)
Steelers, 30-9 (P)
1987—Steelers, 23-20 (P)
Steelers, 30-16 (C)
1988—Bengals, 17-12 (P)
Bengals, 42-7 (C)
1989—Bengals, 41-10 (C)
Bengals, 26-16 (P)
1990—Bengals, 27-3 (C)
Bengals, 16-12 (P)
1991—Steelers, 33-27 (C) OT
Steelers, 17-10 (P)
1992—Steelers, 20-0 (P)
Steelers, 21-9 (C)
1993—Steelers, 34-7 (P)
Steelers, 24-16 (C)
1994—Steelers, 14-10 (P)
Steelers, 38-15 (C)
1995—Bengals, 27-9 (C)
Steelers, 49-31 (C)
1996—Steelers, 20-10 (P)
Bengals, 34-24 (C)
1997—Steelers, 26-10 (C)
Steelers, 20-3 (P)
1998—Bengals, 25-20 (C)
Bengals, 25-24 (P)
1999—Steelers, 17-3 (C)
Bengals, 27-20 (P)
2000—Steelers, 15-0 (P)
Steelers, 48-28 (C)
2001—Steelers, 16-7 (P)
Bengals, 26-23 (C) OT
2002—Steelers, 34-7 (C)
Steelers, 29-21 (P)
2003—Steelers, 17-10 (C)
Bengals, 24-20 (P)
2004—Steelers, 28-17 (P)
Steelers, 19-14 (C)
(RS Pts.—Steelers 1,459, Bengals 1,227)
CINCINNATI vs. *ST. LOUIS
RS: Series tied, 5-5
1972—Rams, 15-12 (LA)
1976—Bengals, 20-12 (C)
1978—Bengals, 20-19 (LA)
1981—Bengals, 24-10 (C)
1984—Rams, 24-14 (C)
1990—Bengals, 34-31 (LA) OT
1993—Bengals, 15-3 (C)
1996—Rams, 26-16 (StL)
1999—Rams, 38-10 (C)
2003—Rams, 27-10 (StL)
(RS Pts.—Rams 205, Bengals 175)
Franchise in Los Angeles prior to 1995
CINCINNATI vs. SAN DIEGO
RS: Chargers lead series, 17-10
PS: Bengals lead series, 1-0

1968—Chargers, 29-13 (SD)
    Chargers, 31-10 (C)
1969—Bengals, 34-20 (C)
    Chargers, 21-14 (SD)
1970—Bengals, 17-14 (SD)
1971—Bengals, 31-0 (C)
1973—Bengals, 20-13 (SD)
1974—Chargers, 20-17 (C)
1975—Bengals, 47-17 (C)
1977—Chargers, 24-3 (SD)
1978—Chargers, 22-13 (SD)
1979—Chargers, 26-24 (C)
1980—Chargers, 31-14 (C)
1981—Bengals, 40-17 (SD)
    *Bengals, 27-7 (C)
1982—Chargers, 50-34 (SD)
1985—Chargers, 44-41 (C)
1987—Chargers, 10-9 (C)
1988—Bengals, 27-10 (C)
1990—Bengals, 21-16 (SD)
1992—Chargers, 27-10 (SD)
1994—Chargers, 27-10 (SD)
1996—Chargers, 27-14 (SD)
1997—Bengals, 38-31 (C)
1999—Chargers, 34-7 (C)
2001—Chargers, 28-14 (SD)
2002—Chargers, 34-6 (C)
2003—Bengals, 34-27 (SD)
(RS Pts.—Chargers 650, Bengals 562)
(PS Pts.—Bengals 27, Chargers 7)
*AFC Championship
CINCINNATI vs. SAN FRANCISCO
RS: 49ers lead series, 7-3
PS: 49ers lead series, 2-0
1974—Bengals, 21-3 (SF)
1978—49ers, 28-12 (SF)
1981—Bengals, 21-3 (C)
    *49ers, 26-21 (Detroit)
1984—49ers, 23-17 (SF)
1987—49ers, 27-26 (C)
1988—**49ers, 20-16 (Miami)
1990—49ers, 20-17 (C) OT
1993—49ers, 21-8 (SF)
1996—49ers, 28-21 (SF)
1999—Bengals, 44-30 (C)
2003—Bengals, 41-38 (C)
(RS Pts.—49ers 239, Bengals 210)
(PS Pts.—49ers 46, Bengals 37)
*Super Bowl XVI
**Super Bowl XXIII
CINCINNATI vs. SEATTLE
RS: Series tied, 8-8
PS: Bengals lead series, 1-0
1977—Bengals, 42-20 (C)
1981—Bengals, 27-21 (C)
1982—Bengals, 24-10 (C)
1984—Seahawks, 26-6 (C)
1985—Seahawks, 28-24 (C)
1986—Bengals, 34-7 (C)
1987—Bengals, 17-10 (S)
1988—*Bengals, 21-13 (C)
1989—Seahawks, 24-17 (C)
1990—Seahawks, 31-16 (S)
1991—Seahawks, 13-7 (C)
1992—Bengals, 21-3 (S)
1993—Seahawks, 19-10 (C)
1994—Bengals, 20-17 (S) OT
1995—Seahawks, 24-21 (S)
1999—Seahawks, 37-20 (S)
2003—Bengals, 27-24 (C)

(RS Pts.—Bengals 333, Seahawks 314)
(PS Pts.—Bengals 21, Seahawks 13)
*AFC Divisional Playoff
CINCINNATI vs. TAMPA BAY
RS: Buccaneers lead series, 5-3
1976—Bengals, 21-0 (C)
1980—Buccaneers, 17-12 (C)
1983—Bengals, 23-17 (TB)
1989—Bengals, 56-23 (C)
1995—Buccaneers, 19-16 (TB)
1998—Buccaneers, 35-0 (C)
2001—Buccaneers, 16-13 (C) OT
2002—Buccaneers, 35-7 (C)
(RS Pts.— Buccaneers 162, Bengals 148)
CINCINNATI vs. *TENNESSEE
RS: Titans lead series, 38-29-1
PS: Bengals lead series, 1-0
1968—Oilers, 27-17 (C)
1969—Tie, 31-31 (H)
1970—Oilers, 20-13 (C)
    Bengals, 30-20 (H)
1971—Oilers, 10-6 (H)
    Bengals, 28-13 (C)
1972—Bengals, 30-7 (C)
    Bengals, 61-17 (H)
1973—Bengals, 24-10 (C)
    Bengals, 27-24 (H)
1974—Oilers, 34-21 (C)
    Oilers, 20-3 (H)
1975—Bengals, 21-19 (H)
    Bengals, 23-19 (C)
1976—Bengals, 27-7 (H)
    Bengals, 31-27 (C)
1977—Bengals, 13-10 (C) OT
    Oilers, 21-16 (H)
1978—Bengals, 28-13 (C)
    Oilers, 17-10 (H)
1979—Oilers, 30-27 (C) OT
    Oilers, 42-21 (H)
1980—Oilers, 13-10 (C)
    Oilers, 23-3 (H)
1981—Oilers, 17-10 (H)
    Bengals, 34-21 (C)
1982—Bengals, 27-6 (C)
    Bengals, 35-27 (H)
1983—Bengals, 55-14 (H)
    Bengals, 38-10 (C)
1984—Bengals, 13-3 (C)
    Bengals, 31-13 (H)
1985—Oilers, 44-27 (H)
    Bengals, 45-27 (C)
1986—Bengals, 31-28 (C)
    Oilers, 32-28 (H)
1987—Bengals, 31-29 (C)
    Oilers, 21-17 (H)
1988—Bengals, 44-21 (H)
    Oilers, 41-6 (H)
1989—Oilers, 26-24 (H)
    Bengals, 61-7 (C)
1990—Oilers, 48-17 (H)
    Bengals, 40-20 (C)
    **Bengals, 41-14 (C)
1991—Oilers, 30-7 (C)
    Oilers, 35-3 (H)
1992—Oilers, 38-24 (C)
    Oilers, 26-10 (H)
1993—Oilers, 28-12 (H)
    Oilers, 38-3 (C)
1994—Oilers, 20-13 (H)
    Bengals, 34-31 (C)

1995—Oilers, 38-28 (C)
    Bengals, 32-25 (H)
1996—Oilers, 30-27 (C) OT
    Bengals, 21-13 (H)
1997—Oilers, 30-7 (T)
    Bengals, 41-14 (C)
1998—Oilers, 23-14 (C)
    Oilers, 44-14 (T)
1999—Titans, 36-35 (T)
    Titans, 24-14 (C)
2000—Titans, 23-14 (C)
    Titans, 35-3 (T)
2001—Titans, 20-7 (C)
    Bengals, 23-21 (T)
2002—Titans, 30-24 (C)
2004—Titans, 27-20 (T)
(RS Pts.—Titans 1,610, Bengals 1,563)
(PS Pts.—Bengals 41, Titans 14)
*Franchise in Houston prior to 1997;
known as Oilers prior to 1999
**AFC First-Round Playoff
CINCINNATI vs. WASHINGTON
RS: Redskins lead series, 4-3
1970—Redskins, 20-0 (W)
1974—Bengals, 28-17 (C)
1979—Redskins, 28-14 (W)
1985—Redskins, 27-24 (W)
1988—Bengals, 20-17 (C) OT
1991—Redskins, 34-27 (C)
2004—Bengals, 17-10 (W)
(RS Pts.—Redskins 153, Bengals 130)

CLEVELAND vs. ARIZONA
RS: Browns lead series, 33-11-3;
See Arizona vs. Cleveland
CLEVELAND vs. ATLANTA
RS: Browns lead series, 9-2;
See Atlanta vs. Cleveland
CLEVELAND vs. BALTIMORE
RS: Ravens lead series, 8-4;
See Baltimore vs. Cleveland
CLEVELAND vs. BUFFALO
RS: Browns lead series, 7-5
PS: Browns lead series, 1-0;
See Buffalo vs. Cleveland
CLEVELAND vs. CAROLINA
RS: Panthers lead series, 2-0;
See Carolina vs. Cleveland
CLEVELAND vs. CHICAGO
RS: Browns lead series, 8-4;
See Chicago vs. Cleveland
CLEVELAND vs. CINCINNATI
RS: Browns lead series, 33-30;
See Cincinnati vs. Cleveland
CLEVELAND vs. DALLAS
RS: Browns lead series, 15-10
PS: Browns lead series, 2-1
1960—Browns, 48-7 (D)
1961—Browns, 25-7 (C)
    Browns, 38-17 (D)
1962—Browns, 19-10 (C)
    Cowboys, 45-21 (D)
1963—Browns, 41-24 (D)
    Browns, 27-17 (C)
1964—Browns, 27-6 (C)
    Browns, 20-16 (D)
1965—Browns, 23-17 (C)
    Browns, 24-17 (D)
1966—Browns, 30-21 (C)
    Cowboys, 26-14 (D)

1967—Cowboys, 21-14 (C)
   *Cowboys, 52-14 (D)
1968—Cowboys, 28-7 (C)
   *Browns, 31-20 (C)
1969—Browns, 42-10 (C)
   *Browns, 38-14 (D)
1970—Cowboys, 6-2 (C)
1974—Cowboys, 41-17 (D)
1979—Browns, 26-7 (C)
1982—Cowboys, 31-14 (D)
1985—Cowboys, 20-7 (D)
1988—Browns, 24-21 (C)
1991—Cowboys, 26-14 (C)
1994—Browns, 19-14 (D)
2004—Cowboys, 19-12 (D)
(RS Pts.—Browns 555, Cowboys 474)
(PS Pts.—Cowboys 86, Browns 83)
*Conference Championship
CLEVELAND vs. DENVER
RS: Broncos lead series, 15-5
PS: Broncos lead series, 3-0
1970—Browns, 27-13 (D)
1971—Broncos, 27-0 (C)
1972—Broncos, 27-20 (D)
1974—Browns, 23-21 (C)
1975—Broncos, 16-15 (D)
1976—Broncos, 44-13 (D)
1978—Broncos, 19-7 (C)
1980—Broncos, 19-16 (C)
1981—Broncos, 23-20 (D) OT
1983—Broncos, 27-6 (D)
1984—Broncos, 24-14 (C)
1986—*Broncos, 23-20 (C) OT
1987—*Broncos, 38-33 (D)
1988—Broncos, 30-7 (D)
1989—Browns, 16-13 (C)
   *Broncos, 37-21 (D)
1990—Browns, 30-29 (D)
1991—Broncos, 17-7 (C)
1992—Broncos, 12-0 (C)
1993—Broncos, 29-14 (C)
1994—Broncos, 26-14 (C)
2000—Broncos, 44-10 (D)
2003—Broncos, 23-20 (D) OT
(RS Pts.—Broncos 476, Browns 286)
(PS Pts.—Broncos 98, Browns 74)
*AFC Championship
CLEVELAND vs. DETROIT
RS: Lions lead series, 12-4
PS: Lions lead series, 3-1
1952—Lions, 17-6 (D)
   *Lions, 17-7 (C)
1953—*Lions, 17-16 (D)
1954—Lions, 14-10 (C)
   *Browns, 56-10 (C)
1957—Lions, 20-7 (D)
   *Lions, 59-14 (D)
1958—Lions, 30-10 (C)
1963—Lions, 38-10 (C)
1964—Browns, 37-21 (C)
1967—Lions, 31-14 (D)
1969—Lions, 28-21 (C)
1970—Lions, 41-24 (C)
1975—Lions, 21-10 (D)
1983—Browns, 31-26 (D)
1986—Browns, 24-21 (C)
1989—Lions, 13-10 (D)
1992—Lions, 24-14 (D)
1995—Lions, 38-20 (D)
2001—Browns, 24-14 (C)

(RS Pts.—Lions 397, Browns 272)
(PS Pts.—Lions 103, Browns 93)
*NFL Championship
CLEVELAND vs. GREEN BAY
RS: Packers lead series, 9-6
PS: Packers lead series, 1-0
1953—Browns, 27-0 (Mil)
1955—Browns, 41-10 (C)
1956—Browns, 24-7 (Mil)
1961—Packers, 49-17 (C)
1964—Packers, 28-21 (Mil)
1965—*Packers, 23-12 (GB)
1966—Packers, 21-20 (C)
1967—Packers, 55-7 (Mil)
1969—Browns, 20-7 (C)
1972—Packers, 26-10 (C)
1980—Browns, 26-21 (C)
1983—Packers, 35-21 (Mil)
1986—Packers, 17-14 (C)
1992—Browns, 17-6 (C)
1995—Packers, 31-20 (C)
2001—Packers, 30-7 (GB)
(RS Pts.—Packers 343, Browns 292)
(PS Pts.—Packers 23, Browns 12)
*NFL Championship
CLEVELAND vs. HOUSTON
RS: Browns lead series, 2-0
2002—Browns, 34-17 (C)
2004—Browns, 22-14 (H)
(RS Pts.—Browns 56, Texans 31)
CLEVELAND vs. *INDIANAPOLIS
RS: Browns lead series, 13-10
PS: Series tied, 2-2
1956—Colts, 21-7 (C)
1959—Browns, 38-31 (B)
1962—Colts, 36-14 (C)
1964—**Browns, 27-0 (C)
1968—Browns, 30-20 (B)
   **Colts, 34-0 (C)
1971—Browns, 14-13 (B)
   ***Colts, 20-3 (C)
1973—Browns, 24-14 (C)
1975—Colts, 21-7 (B)
1978—Browns, 45-24 (B)
1979—Browns, 13-10 (C)
1980—Browns, 28-27 (B)
1981—Browns, 42-28 (C)
1983—Browns, 41-23 (C)
1986—Browns, 24-9 (I)
1987—Colts, 9-7 (C)
   ***Browns, 38-21 (C)
1988—Browns, 23-17 (C)
1989—Colts, 23-17 (I) OT
1991—Browns, 31-0 (I)
1992—Colts, 14-3 (I)
1993—Colts, 23-10 (I)
1994—Browns, 21-14 (I)
1999—Colts, 29-28 (C)
2002—Colts, 28-23 (C)
2003—Colts, 9-6 (C)
(RS Pts.—Browns 496, Colts 443)
(PS Pts.—Colts 75, Browns 68)
*Franchise in Baltimore prior to 1984
**NFL Championship
***AFC Divisional Playoff
CLEVELAND vs. JACKSONVILLE
RS: Jaguars lead series, 7-2
1995—Jaguars, 23-15 (C)
   Jaguars, 24-21 (J)
1999—Jaguars, 24-7 (J)

Jaguars, 24-14 (C)
2000—Jaguars, 27-7 (C)
   Jaguars, 48-0 (J)
2001—Browns, 23-14 (J)
   Jaguars, 15-10 (C)
2002—Browns, 21-20 (J)
(RS Pts.—Jaguars 219, Browns 118)
CLEVELAND vs. KANSAS CITY
RS: Chiefs lead series, 9-8-2
1971—Chiefs, 13-7 (KC)
1972—Chiefs, 31-7 (C)
1973—Tie, 20-20 (KC)
1975—Browns, 40-14 (C)
1976—Chiefs, 39-14 (KC)
1977—Browns, 44-7 (C)
1978—Chiefs, 17-3 (KC)
1979—Browns, 27-24 (KC)
1980—Browns, 20-13 (C)
1984—Chiefs, 10-6 (KC)
1986—Browns, 20-7 (C)
1988—Browns, 6-3 (KC)
1989—Tie, 10-10 (C) OT
1990—Chiefs, 34-0 (KC)
1991—Browns, 20-15 (C)
1994—Browns, 20-13 (KC)
1995—Browns, 35-17 (C)
2002—Chiefs, 40-39 (C)
2003—Chiefs, 41-20 (KC)
(RS Pts.—Chiefs 375, Browns 351)
CLEVELAND vs. MIAMI
RS: Dolphins lead series, 7-4
PS: Dolphins lead series, 2-0
1970—Browns, 28-0 (M)
1972—*Dolphins, 20-14 (M)
1973—Dolphins, 17-9 (C)
1976—Browns, 17-13 (C)
1979—Browns, 30-24 (C) OT
1985—*Dolphins, 24-21 (M)
1986—Browns, 26-16 (C)
1988—Dolphins, 38-31 (M)
1989—Dolphins, 13-10 (M) OT
1990—Dolphins, 30-13 (C)
1992—Dolphins, 27-23 (C)
1993—Dolphins, 24-14 (C)
2004—Dolphins, 10-7 (M)
(RS Pts.—Dolphins 212, Browns 208)
(PS Pts.—Dolphins 44, Browns 35)
*AFC Divisional Playoff
CLEVELAND vs. MINNESOTA
RS: Vikings lead series, 8-3
PS: Vikings lead series, 1-0
1965—Vikings, 27-17 (C)
1967—Browns, 14-10 (C)
1969—Vikings, 51-3 (M)
   *Vikings, 27-7 (M)
1973—Vikings, 26-3 (M)
1975—Vikings, 42-10 (C)
1980—Vikings, 28-23 (M)
1983—Vikings, 27-21 (C)
1986—Browns, 23-20 (M)
1989—Browns, 23-17 (C) OT
1992—Vikings, 17-13 (C)
1995—Vikings, 27-11 (M)
(RS Pts.—Vikings 292, Browns 161)
(PS Pts.—Vikings 27, Browns 7)
*NFL Championship
CLEVELAND vs. NEW ENGLAND
RS: Browns lead series, 11-8
PS: Browns lead series, 1-0
1971—Browns, 27-7 (C)

1974—Browns, 21-14 (NE)
1977—Browns, 30-27 (C) OT
1980—Patriots, 34-17 (NE)
1982—Browns, 10-7 (C)
1983—Browns, 30-0 (NE)
1984—Patriots, 17-16 (C)
1985—Browns, 24-20 (C)
1987—Browns, 20-10 (NE)
1991—Browns, 20-0 (NE)
1992—Browns, 19-17 (NE)
1993—Patriots, 20-17 (C)
1994—Browns, 13-6 (C)
    *Browns, 20-13 (C)
1995—Patriots, 17-14 (NE)
1999—Patriots, 19-7 (C)
2000—Browns, 19-11 (NE)
2001—Patriots, 27-16 (NE)
2003—Patriots, 9-3 (NE)
2004—Patriots, 42-15 (C)
(RS Pts.—Browns 338, Patriots 304)
(PS Pts.—Browns 20, Patriots 13)
*AFC First-Round Playoff
CLEVELAND vs. NEW ORLEANS
RS: Browns lead series, 11-3
1967—Browns, 42-7 (NO)
1968—Browns, 24-10 (NO)
    Browns, 35-17 (C)
1969—Browns, 27-17 (NO)
1971—Browns, 21-17 (NO)
1975—Browns, 17-16 (C)
1978—Browns, 24-16 (NO)
1981—Browns, 20-17 (C)
1984—Saints, 16-14 (C)
1987—Saints, 28-21 (NO)
1990—Saints, 25-20 (NO)
1993—Browns, 17-13 (C)
1999—Browns, 21-16 (NO)
2002—Browns, 24-15 (NO)
(RS Pts.—Browns 327, Saints 230)
CLEVELAND vs. N.Y. GIANTS
RS: Browns lead series, 25-19-2
PS: Series tied, 1-1
1950—Giants, 6-0 (C)
    Giants, 17-13 (NY)
    *Browns, 8-3 (C)
1951—Browns, 14-13 (C)
    Browns, 10-0 (NY)
1952—Giants, 17-9 (C)
    Giants, 37-34 (NY)
1953—Browns, 7-0 (C)
    Browns, 62-14 (C)
1954—Browns, 24-14 (C)
    Browns, 16-7 (NY)
1955—Browns, 24-14 (C)
    Tie, 35-35 (NY)
1956—Giants, 21-9 (C)
    Browns, 24-7 (NY)
1957—Browns, 6-3 (C)
    Browns, 34-28 (NY)
1958—Giants, 21-17 (C)
    Giants, 13-10 (NY)
    *Giants, 10-0 (NY)
1959—Giants, 10-6 (C)
    Giants, 48-7 (NY)
1960—Giants, 17-13 (C)
    Browns, 48-34 (NY)
1961—Giants, 37-21 (C)
    Tie, 7-7 (NY)
1962—Browns, 17-7 (C)
    Giants, 17-13 (NY)

1963—Browns, 35-24 (NY)
    Giants, 33-6 (C)
1964—Browns, 42-20 (C)
    Browns, 52-20 (NY)
1965—Browns, 38-14 (NY)
    Browns, 34-21 (C)
1966—Browns, 28-7 (NY)
    Browns, 49-40 (C)
1967—Giants, 38-34 (NY)
    Browns, 24-14 (C)
1968—Browns, 45-10 (C)
1969—Browns, 28-17 (C)
    Giants, 27-14 (NY)
1973—Browns, 12-10 (C)
1977—Browns, 21-7 (NY)
1985—Browns, 35-33 (NY)
1991—Giants, 13-10 (NY)
1994—Giants, 16-13 (C)
2000—Giants, 24-3 (C)
2004—Browns, 27-10 (NY)
(RS Pts.—Browns 1,013, Giants 859)
(PS Pts.—Giants 13, Browns 8)
*Conference Playoff
CLEVELAND vs. N.Y. JETS
RS: Browns lead series, 10-7
PS: Browns lead series, 1-0
1970—Browns, 31-21 (C)
1972—Browns, 26-10 (NY)
1976—Browns, 38-17 (C)
1978—Browns, 37-34 (C) OT
1979—Browns, 25-22 (NY) OT
1980—Browns, 17-14 (C)
1981—Jets, 14-13 (C)
1983—Browns, 10-7 (C)
1984—Jets, 24-20 (C)
1985—Jets, 37-10 (NY)
1986—*Browns, 23-20 (C) OT
1988—Jets, 23-3 (C)
1989—Browns, 38-24 (C)
1990—Jets, 24-21 (NY)
1991—Jets, 17-14 (C)
1994—Browns, 27-7 (C)
2002—Browns, 24-21 (NY)
2004—Jets, 10-7 (C)
(RS Pts.—Browns 361, Jets 326)
(PS Pts.—Browns 23, Jets 20)
*AFC Divisional Playoff
CLEVELAND vs. *OAKLAND
RS: Raiders lead series, 9-5
PS: Raiders lead series, 2-0
1970—Raiders, 23-20 (O)
1971—Raiders, 34-20 (C)
1973—Browns, 7-3 (O)
1974—Raiders, 40-24 (C)
1975—Raiders, 38-17 (C)
1977—Raiders, 26-10 (C)
1979—Raiders, 19-14 (O)
1980—**Raiders, 14-12 (C)
1982—***Raiders, 27-10 (LA)
1985—Raiders, 21-20 (C)
1986—Raiders, 27-14 (LA)
1987—Browns, 24-17 (LA)
1992—Browns, 28-16 (LA)
1993—Browns, 19-16 (LA)
2000—Raiders, 36-10 (O)
2003—Browns, 13-7 (C)
(RS Pts.—Raiders 323, Browns 240)
(PS Pts.—Raiders 41, Browns 22)
*Franchise in Los Angeles from 1982-1994
**AFC Divisional Playoff

***AFC First-Round Playoff
CLEVELAND vs. PHILADELPHIA
RS: Browns lead series, 31-14-1
1950—Browns, 35-10 (P)
    Browns, 13-7 (C)
1951—Browns, 20-17 (C)
    Browns, 24-9 (P)
1952—Browns, 49-7 (P)
    Eagles, 28-20 (C)
1953—Browns, 37-13 (C)
    Eagles, 42-27 (P)
1954—Eagles, 28-10 (P)
    Browns, 6-0 (C)
1955—Browns, 21-17 (C)
    Eagles, 33-17 (P)
1956—Browns, 16-0 (P)
    Browns, 17-14 (C)
1957—Browns, 24-7 (C)
    Eagles, 17-7 (P)
1958—Browns, 28-14 (C)
    Browns, 21-14 (P)
1959—Browns, 28-7 (C)
    Browns, 28-21 (P)
1960—Browns, 41-24 (P)
    Eagles, 31-29 (C)
1961—Eagles, 27-20 (P)
    Browns, 45-24 (C)
1962—Eagles, 35-7 (P)
    Tie, 14-14 (C)
1963—Browns, 37-7 (C)
    Browns, 23-17 (P)
1964—Browns, 28-20 (P)
    Browns, 38-24 (C)
1965—Browns, 35-17 (P)
    Browns, 38-34 (C)
1966—Browns, 27-7 (C)
    Eagles, 33-21 (P)
1967—Eagles, 28-24 (P)
1968—Browns, 47-13 (C)
1969—Browns, 27-20 (P)
1972—Browns, 27-17 (P)
1976—Browns, 24-3 (C)
1979—Browns, 24-19 (P)
1982—Eagles, 24-21 (C)
1988—Browns, 19-3 (C)
1991—Eagles, 32-30 (C)
1994—Browns, 26-7 (P)
2000—Eagles, 35-24 (C)
2004—Eagles, 34-31 (C) OT
(RS Pts.—Browns 1,175, Eagles 854)
CLEVELAND vs. PITTSBURGH
RS: Browns lead series, 55-49
PS: Steelers lead series, 2-0
1950—Browns, 30-17 (P)
    Browns, 45-7 (C)
1951—Browns, 17-0 (C)
    Browns, 28-0 (P)
1952—Browns, 21-20 (P)
    Browns, 29-28 (C)
1953—Browns, 34-16 (C)
    Browns, 20-16 (P)
1954—Steelers, 55-27 (P)
    Browns, 42-7 (C)
1955—Browns, 41-14 (C)
    Browns, 30-7 (P)
1956—Browns, 14-10 (P)
    Steelers, 24-16 (C)
1957—Browns, 23-12 (P)
    Browns, 24-0 (C)
1958—Browns, 45-12 (P)

Browns, 27-10 (C)
1959—Steelers, 17-7 (P)
Steelers, 21-20 (C)
1960—Browns, 28-20 (C)
Steelers, 14-10 (P)
1961—Browns, 30-28 (P)
Steelers, 17-13 (C)
1962—Browns, 41-14 (P)
Browns, 35-14 (C)
1963—Browns, 35-23 (C)
Steelers, 9-7 (P)
1964—Steelers, 23-7 (C)
Browns, 30-17 (P)
1965—Browns, 24-19 (C)
Browns, 42-21 (P)
1966—Browns, 41-10 (C)
Steelers, 16-6 (P)
1967—Browns, 21-10 (C)
Browns, 34-14 (P)
1968—Browns, 31-24 (C)
Browns, 45-24 (P)
1969—Browns, 42-31 (C)
Browns, 24-3 (P)
1970—Browns, 15-7 (C)
Steelers, 28-9 (P)
1971—Browns, 27-17 (C)
Steelers, 26-9 (P)
1972—Browns, 26-24 (C)
Steelers, 30-0 (P)
1973—Steelers, 33-6 (P)
Browns, 21-16 (C)
1974—Steelers, 20-16 (P)
Steelers, 26-16 (C)
1975—Steelers, 42-6 (C)
Steelers, 31-17 (P)
1976—Steelers, 31-14 (P)
Browns, 18-16 (C)
1977—Steelers, 28-14 (C)
Steelers, 35-31 (P)
1978—Steelers, 15-9 (P) OT
Steelers, 34-14 (C)
1979—Steelers, 51-35 (C)
Steelers, 33-30 (P) OT
1980—Browns, 27-26 (C)
Steelers, 16-13 (P)
1981—Steelers, 13-7 (P)
Steelers, 32-10 (C)
1982—Browns, 10-9 (C)
Steelers, 37-21 (P)
1983—Steelers, 44-17 (P)
Browns, 30-17 (C)
1984—Browns, 20-10 (C)
Steelers, 23-20 (P)
1985—Steelers, 17-7 (C)
Steelers, 10-9 (P)
1986—Browns, 27-24 (P)
Browns, 37-31 (C) OT
1987—Browns, 34-10 (C)
Browns, 19-13 (P)
1988—Browns, 23-9 (P)
Browns, 27-7 (C)
1989—Browns, 51-0 (P)
Steelers, 17-7 (C)
1990—Browns, 13-3 (C)
Steelers, 35-0 (P)
1991—Browns, 17-14 (C)
Steelers, 17-10 (P)
1992—Browns, 17-9 (C)
Steelers, 23-13 (P)
1993—Browns, 28-23 (C)

Steelers, 16-9 (P)
1994—Steelers, 17-10 (C)
Steelers, 17-7 (P)
*Steelers, 29-9 (P)
1995—Steelers, 20-3 (P)
Steelers, 20-17 (C)
1999—Steelers, 43-0 (C)
Browns, 16-15 (P)
2000—Browns, 23-20 (C)
Steelers, 22-0 (P)
2001—Steelers, 15-12 (C) OT
Steelers, 28-7 (P)
2002—Steelers, 16-13 (P) OT
Steelers, 23-20 (C)
**Steelers, 36-33 (P)
2003—Browns, 33-13 (P)
Steelers, 13-6 (C)
2004—Steelers, 34-23 (P)
Steelers, 24-10 (C)
(RS Pts.—Browns 2,152, Steelers 2,022)
(PS Pts.—Steelers 65, Browns 42)
*AFC Divisional Playoff
**AFC First-Round Playoff
CLEVELAND vs. *ST. LOUIS
RS: Rams lead series, 9-8
PS: Browns lead series, 2-1
1950—**Browns, 30-28 (C)
1951—Browns, 38-23 (LA)
**Rams, 24-17 (LA)
1952—Browns, 37-7 (C)
1955—**Browns, 38-14 (LA)
1957—Browns, 45-31 (C)
1958—Browns, 30-27 (LA)
1963—Browns, 20-6 (C)
1965—Rams, 42-7 (LA)
1968—Rams, 24-6 (C)
1973—Rams, 30-17 (LA)
1977—Rams, 9-0 (C)
1978—Browns, 30-19 (C)
1981—Rams, 27-16 (LA)
1984—Rams, 20-17 (LA)
1987—Browns, 30-17 (C)
1990—Rams, 38-23 (C)
1993—Browns, 42-14 (LA)
1999—Rams, 34-3 (StL)
2003—Rams, 26-20 (C)
(RS Pts.—Rams 394, Browns 381)
(PS Pts.—Browns 85, Rams 66)
*Franchise in Los Angeles prior to 1995
**NFL Championship
CLEVELAND vs. SAN DIEGO
RS: Chargers lead series, 12-7-1
1970—Chargers, 27-10 (C)
1972—Browns, 21-17 (SD)
1973—Tie, 16-16 (C)
1974—Chargers, 36-35 (SD)
1976—Browns, 21-17 (C)
1977—Chargers, 37-14 (SD)
1981—Chargers, 44-14 (C)
1982—Chargers, 30-13 (C)
1983—Browns, 30-24 (SD) OT
1985—Browns, 21-7 (SD)
1986—Browns, 47-17 (C)
1987—Chargers, 27-24 (SD) OT
1990—Chargers, 24-14 (C)
1991—Browns, 30-24 (SD) OT
1992—Chargers, 14-13 (C)
1995—Chargers, 31-13 (SD)
1999—Chargers, 23-10 (SD)
2001—Browns, 20-16 (C)

2003—Chargers, 26-20 (C)
2004—Chargers, 21-0 (C)
(RS Pts.—Chargers 478, Browns 386)
CLEVELAND vs. SAN FRANCISCO
RS: Browns lead series, 10-6
1950—Browns, 34-14 (C)
1951—49ers, 24-10 (SF)
1953—Browns, 23-21 (C)
1955—Browns, 38-3 (SF)
1959—49ers, 21-20 (C)
1962—Browns, 13-10 (SF)
1968—Browns, 33-21 (SF)
1970—49ers, 34-31 (SF)
1974—Browns, 7-0 (C)
1978—Browns, 24-7 (C)
1981—49ers, 15-12 (SF)
1984—49ers, 41-7 (C)
1987—49ers, 38-24 (SF)
1990—49ers, 20-17 (SF)
1993—49ers, 23-13 (C)
2003—Browns, 13-12 (SF)
(RS Pts.—Browns 332, 49ers 291)
CLEVELAND vs. SEATTLE
RS: Seahawks lead series, 11-4
1977—Seahawks, 20-19 (S)
1978—Seahawks, 47-24 (S)
1979—Seahawks, 29-24 (C)
1980—Browns, 27-3 (S)
1981—Seahawks, 42-21 (S)
1982—Browns, 21-7 (S)
1983—Seahawks, 24-9 (C)
1984—Seahawks, 33-0 (S)
1985—Seahawks, 31-13 (S)
1988—Seahawks, 16-10 (C)
1989—Browns, 17-7 (S)
1993—Seahawks, 22-5 (S)
1994—Browns, 35-9 (C)
2001—Seahawks, 9-6 (C)
2003—Seahawks, 34-7 (S)
(RS Pts.—Seahawks 333, Browns 238)
CLEVELAND vs. TAMPA BAY
RS: Browns lead series, 5-1
1976—Browns, 24-7 (TB)
1980—Browns, 34-27 (TB)
1983—Browns, 20-0 (C)
1989—Browns, 42-31 (TB)
1995—Browns, 22-6 (C)
2002—Buccaneers 17-3 (TB)
(RS Pts.—Browns 145, Buccaneers 88)
CLEVELAND vs. *TENNESSEE
RS: Browns lead series, 32-26
PS: Titans lead series, 1-0
1970—Browns, 28-14 (C)
Browns, 21-10 (H)
1971—Browns, 31-0 (C)
Browns, 37-24 (H)
1972—Browns, 23-17 (H)
Browns, 20-0 (C)
1973—Browns, 42-13 (C)
Browns, 23-13 (H)
1974—Browns, 20-7 (C)
Oilers, 28-24 (H)
1975—Oilers, 40-10 (C)
Oilers, 21-10 (H)
1976—Browns, 21-7 (H)
Browns, 13-10 (C)
1977—Browns, 24-23 (H)
Oilers, 19-15 (C)
1978—Oilers, 16-13 (C)
Oilers, 14-10 (H)

1979—Oilers, 31-10 (H)
Browns, 14-7 (C)
1980—Oilers, 16-7 (C)
Browns, 17-14 (H)
1981—Oilers, 9-3 (C)
Oilers, 17-13 (H)
1982—Browns, 20-14 (H)
1983—Browns, 25-19 (C) OT
Oilers, 34-27 (H)
1984—Browns, 27-10 (C)
Browns, 27-20 (H)
1985—Browns, 21-6 (H)
Browns, 28-21 (C)
1986—Browns, 23-20 (H)
Browns, 13-10 (C) OT
1987—Oilers, 15-10 (C)
Browns, 40-7 (H)
1988—Oilers, 24-17 (H)
Browns, 28-23 (C)
**Oilers, 24-23 (C)
1989—Browns, 28-17 (C)
Browns, 24-20 (H)
1990—Oilers, 35-23 (C)
Oilers, 58-14 (H)
1991—Oilers, 28-24 (H)
Oilers, 17-14 (C)
1992—Browns, 24-14 (H)
Oilers, 17-14 (C)
1993—Oilers, 27-20 (C)
Oilers, 19-17 (H)
1994—Browns, 11-8 (H)
Browns, 34-10 (C)
1995—Browns, 14-7 (H)
Oilers, 37-10 (C)
1999—Titans, 26-9 (T)
Titans, 33-21 (C)
2000—Titans, 24-10 (T)
Titans, 24-0 (C)
2001—Titans, 31-15 (C)
Browns, 41-38 (T)
2002—Browns, 31-28 (T) OT
(RS Pts.—Browns 1,153, Titans 1,111)
(PS Pts.—Titans 24, Browns 23)
*Franchise in Houston prior to 1997;
known as Oilers prior to 1999
**AFC First-Round Playoff
CLEVELAND vs. WASHINGTON
RS: Browns lead series, 33-9-1
1950—Browns, 20-14 (C)
Browns, 45-21 (W)
1951—Browns, 45-0 (C)
1952—Browns, 19-15 (C)
Browns, 48-24 (W)
1953—Browns, 30-14 (W)
Browns, 27-3 (C)
1954—Browns, 62-3 (C)
Browns, 34-14 (W)
1955—Redskins, 27-17 (C)
Browns, 24-14 (W)
1956—Redskins, 20-9 (W)
Redskins, 20-17 (C)
1957—Browns, 21-17 (C)
Tie, 30-30 (W)
1958—Browns, 20-10 (W)
Browns, 21-14 (C)
1959—Browns, 34-7 (C)
Browns, 31-17 (W)
1960—Browns, 31-10 (W)
Browns, 27-16 (C)
1961—Browns, 31-7 (C)

Browns, 17-6 (W)
1962—Redskins, 17-16 (C)
Redskins, 17-9 (W)
1963—Browns, 37-14 (C)
Browns, 27-20 (W)
1964—Browns, 27-13 (W)
Browns, 34-24 (C)
1965—Browns, 17-7 (W)
Browns, 24-16 (C)
1966—Browns, 38-14 (W)
Browns, 14-3 (C)
1967—Browns, 42-37 (C)
1968—Browns, 24-21 (W)
1969—Browns, 27-23 (C)
1971—Browns, 20-13 (W)
1975—Redskins, 23-7 (C)
1979—Redskins, 13-9 (C)
1985—Redskins, 14-7 (C)
1988—Browns, 17-13 (W)
1991—Redskins, 42-17 (W)
2004—Browns, 17-13 (C)
(RS Pts.—Browns 1,090, Redskins 680)

DALLAS vs. ARIZONA
RS: Cowboys lead series, 53-27-1
PS: Cardinals lead series, 1-0;
See Arizona vs. Dallas
DALLAS vs. ATLANTA
RS: Cowboys lead series, 12-8
PS: Cowboys lead series, 2-0;
See Atlanta vs. Dallas
DALLAS vs. BALTIMORE
RS: Ravens lead series, 2-0;
See Baltimore vs. Dallas
DALLAS vs. BUFFALO
RS: Cowboys lead series, 4-3
PS: Cowboys lead series, 2-0;
See Buffalo vs. Dallas
DALLAS vs. CAROLINA
RS: Cowboys lead series, 4-1
PS: Panthers lead series, 2-0;
See Carolina vs. Dallas
DALLAS vs. CHICAGO
RS: Cowboys lead series, 10-8
PS: Cowboys lead series, 2-0;
See Chicago vs. Dallas
DALLAS vs. CINCINNATI
RS: Cowboys lead series, 5-4;
See Cincinnati vs. Dallas
DALLAS vs. CLEVELAND
RS: Browns lead series, 15-10
PS: Browns lead series, 2-1;
See Cleveland vs. Dallas
DALLAS vs. DENVER
RS: Series tied, 4-4
PS: Cowboys lead series, 1-0
1973—Cowboys, 22-10 (Den)
1977—Cowboys, 14-6 (Dall)
*Cowboys, 27-10 (New Orleans)
1980—Broncos, 41-20 (Den)
1986—Broncos, 29-14 (Den)
1992—Cowboys, 31-27 (Den)
1995—Cowboys, 31-21 (Dall)
1998—Broncos, 42-23 (Den)
2001—Broncos, 26-24 (Dall)
(RS Pts.—Broncos 202, Cowboys 179)
(PS Pts.—Cowboys 27, Broncos 10)
*Super Bowl XII
DALLAS vs. DETROIT
RS: Cowboys lead series, 9-8

PS: Series tied, 1-1
1960—Lions, 23-14 (Det)
1963—Cowboys, 17-14 (Dal)
1968—Cowboys, 59-13 (Dal)
1970—*Cowboys, 5-0 (Dal)
1972—Cowboys, 28-24 (Dal)
1975—Cowboys, 36-10 (Det)
1977—Cowboys, 37-0 (Dal)
1981—Lions, 27-24 (Det)
1985—Lions, 26-21 (Det)
1986—Cowboys, 31-7 (Det)
1987—Lions, 27-17 (Det)
1991—Lions, 34-10 (Det)
*Lions, 38-6 (Det)
1992—Cowboys, 37-3 (Det)
1994—Lions, 20-17 (Dal) OT
2001—Lions, 15-10 (Det)
2002—Lions, 9-7 (Det)
2003—Cowboys, 38-7 (Det)
2004—Cowboys, 31-21 (Dall)
(RS Pts.—Cowboys 434, Lions 280)
(PS Pts.—Lions 38, Cowboys 11)
*NFC Divisional Playoff
DALLAS vs. GREEN BAY
RS: Series tied, 10-10
PS: Cowboys lead series, 4-2
1960—Packers, 41-7 (GB)
1964—Packers, 45-21 (D)
1965—Packers, 13-3 (Mil)
1966—*Packers, 34-27 (D)
1967—*Packers, 21-17 (GB)
1968—Packers, 28-17 (D)
1970—Cowboys, 16-3 (D)
1972—Packers, 16-13 (Mil)
1975—Packers, 19-17 (D)
1978—Cowboys, 42-14 (Mil)
1980—Cowboys, 28-7 (Mil)
1982—**Cowboys, 37-26 (D)
1984—Cowboys, 20-6 (D)
1989—Packers, 31-13 (GB)
Packers, 20-10 (D)
1991—Cowboys, 20-17 (Mil)
1993—Cowboys, 36-14 (D)
***Cowboys, 27-17 (D)
1994—Cowboys, 42-31 (D)
***Cowboys, 35-9 (D)
1995—Cowboys, 34-24 (D)
****Cowboys, 38-27 (D)
1996—Cowboys, 21-6 (D)
1997—Packers, 45-17 (GB)
1999—Cowboys, 27-13 (D)
2004—Packers, 41-20 (GB)
(RS Pts.—Cowboys 434, Packers 424)
(PS Pts.—Cowboys 181, Packers 134)
*NFL Championship
**NFC Second-Round Playoff
***NFC Divisional Playoff
****NFC Championship
DALLAS vs. HOUSTON
RS: Texans lead series, 1-0
2002—Texans, 19-10 (H)
(RS Pts.—Texans 19, Cowboys 10)
DALLAS vs. *INDIANAPOLIS
RS: Cowboys lead series, 7-5
PS: Colts lead series, 1-0
1960—Colts, 45-7 (D)
1967—Colts, 23-17 (B)
1969—Cowboys, 27-10 (D)
1970—**Colts, 16-13 (Miami)
1972—Cowboys, 21-0 (B)

1976—Cowboys, 30-27 (D)
1978—Cowboys, 38-0 (D)
1981—Cowboys, 37-13 (B)
1984—Cowboys, 22-3 (D)
1993—Cowboys, 27-3 (I)
1996—Colts, 25-24 (D)
1999—Colts, 34-24 (I)
2002—Colts, 20-3 (I)
(RS Pts.—Cowboys 277, Colts 203)
(PS Pts.—Colts 16, Cowboys 13)
*Franchise in Baltimore prior to 1984
**Super Bowl V

DALLAS VS. JACKSONVILLE
RS: Cowboys lead series, 2-1
1997—Cowboys, 26-22 (D)
2000—Jaguars, 23-17 (D) OT
2002—Cowboys, 21-19 (D)
(RS Pts.—Cowboys 64, Jaguars 64)

DALLAS vs. KANSAS CITY
RS: Cowboys lead series, 4-3
1970—Cowboys, 27-16 (KC)
1975—Chiefs, 34-31 (D)
1983—Cowboys, 41-21 (D)
1989—Chiefs, 36-28 (KC)
1992—Cowboys, 17-10 (D)
1995—Cowboys, 24-12 (D)
1998—Chiefs, 20-17 (KC)
(RS Pts.—Cowboys 185, Chiefs 149)

DALLAS vs. MIAMI
RS: Dolphins lead series, 7-3
PS: Cowboys lead series, 1-0
1971—*Cowboys, 24-3 (New Orleans)
1973—Dolphins, 14-7 (D)
1978—Dolphins, 23-16 (M)
1981—Cowboys, 28-27 (D)
1984—Dolphins, 28-21 (M)
1987—Dolphins, 20-14 (D)
1989—Dolphins, 17-14 (D)
1993—Dolphins, 16-14 (D)
1996—Cowboys, 29-10 (M)
1999—Cowboys, 20-0 (D)
2003—Dolphins, 40-21 (D)
(RS Pts.—Dolphins 195, Cowboys 184)
(PS Pts.—Cowboys 24, Dolphins 3)
*Super Bowl VI

DALLAS vs. MINNESOTA
RS: Vikings lead series, 10-9
PS: Cowboys lead series, 4-2
1961—Cowboys, 21-7 (D)
        Cowboys, 28-0 (M)
1966—Cowboys, 28-17 (D)
1968—Cowboys, 20-7 (M)
1970—Vikings, 54-13 (M)
1971—*Cowboys, 20-12 (M)
1973—**Vikings, 27-10 (D)
1974—Vikings, 23-21 (D)
1975—*Cowboys, 17-14 (M)
1977—Cowboys, 16-10 (M) OT
        **Cowboys, 23-6 (D)
1978—Vikings, 21-10 (D)
1979—Cowboys, 36-20 (M)
1982—Vikings, 31-27 (M)
1983—Cowboys, 37-24 (M)
1987—Vikings, 44-38 (D) OT
1988—Vikings, 43-3 (D)
1993—Cowboys, 37-20 (M)
1995—Cowboys, 23-17 (M) OT
1996—***Cowboys, 40-15 (D)
1998—Vikings, 46-36 (M)
1999—Vikings, 27-17 (M)

***Vikings, 27-10 (M)
2000—Vikings, 27-15 (D)
2004—Vikings, 35-17 (M)
(RS Pts.—Vikings 473, Cowboys 443)
(PS Pts.—Cowboys 120, Vikings 101)
*NFC Divisional Playoff
**NFC Championship
***NFC First-Round Playoff

DALLAS vs. NEW ENGLAND
RS: Cowboys lead series, 7-2
1971—Cowboys, 44-21 (D)
1975—Cowboys, 34-31 (NE)
1978—Cowboys, 17-10 (D)
1981—Cowboys, 35-21 (NE)
1984—Cowboys, 20-17 (D)
1987—Cowboys, 23-17 (NE) OT
1996—Cowboys, 12-6 (D)
1999—Patriots, 13-6 (NE)
2003—Patriots, 12-0 (NE)
(RS Pts.—Cowboys 191, Patriots 148)

DALLAS vs. NEW ORLEANS
RS: Cowboys lead series, 14-7
1967—Cowboys, 14-10 (D)
        Cowboys, 27-10 (NO)
1968—Cowboys, 17-3 (NO)
1969—Cowboys, 21-17 (NO)
        Cowboys, 33-17 (D)
1971—Saints, 24-14 (NO)
1973—Cowboys, 40-3 (D)
1976—Cowboys, 24-6 (NO)
1978—Cowboys, 27-7 (D)
1982—Cowboys, 21-7 (D)
1983—Cowboys, 21-20 (D)
1984—Cowboys, 30-27 (D) OT
1988—Saints, 20-17 (NO)
1989—Saints, 28-0 (NO)
1990—Cowboys, 17-13 (D)
1991—Cowboys, 23-14 (D)
1994—Cowboys, 24-16 (NO)
1998—Saints, 22-3 (NO)
1999—Saints, 31-24 (NO)
2003—Saints, 13-7 (NO)
2004—Saints, 27-13 (D)
(RS Pts.—Cowboys 417, Saints 335)

DALLAS vs. N.Y. GIANTS
RS: Cowboys lead series, 50-33-2
1960—Tie, 31-31 (NY)
1961—Giants, 31-10 (D)
        Cowboys, 17-16 (NY)
1962—Cowboys, 41-10 (D)
        Giants, 41-31 (NY)
1963—Giants, 37-21 (NY)
        Giants, 34-27 (D)
1964—Tie, 13-13 (D)
        Cowboys, 31-21 (NY)
1965—Cowboys, 31-2 (D)
        Cowboys, 38-20 (NY)
1966—Cowboys, 52-7 (D)
        Cowboys, 17-7 (NY)
1967—Cowboys, 38-24 (D)
1968—Giants, 27-21 (D)
        Cowboys, 28-10 (NY)
1969—Cowboys, 25-3 (D)
1970—Cowboys, 28-10 (D)
        Giants, 23-20 (NY)
1971—Cowboys, 20-13 (D)
        Cowboys, 42-14 (NY)
1972—Cowboys, 23-14 (NY)
        Giants, 23-3 (D)
1973—Cowboys, 45-28 (D)

Cowboys, 23-10 (New Haven)
1974—Giants, 14-6 (D)
        Cowboys, 21-7 (New Haven)
1975—Cowboys, 13-7 (NY)
        Cowboys, 14-3 (D)
1976—Cowboys, 24-14 (NY)
        Cowboys, 9-3 (D)
1977—Cowboys, 41-21 (D)
        Cowboys, 24-10 (NY)
1978—Cowboys, 34-24 (NY)
        Cowboys, 24-3 (D)
1979—Cowboys, 16-14 (NY)
        Cowboys, 28-7 (D)
1980—Cowboys, 24-3 (D)
        Giants, 38-35 (NY)
1981—Cowboys, 18-10 (D)
        Giants, 13-10 (NY) OT
1983—Cowboys, 28-13 (D)
        Cowboys, 38-20 (NY)
1984—Giants, 28-7 (NY)
        Giants, 19-7 (D)
1985—Cowboys, 30-29 (NY)
        Cowboys, 28-21 (D)
1986—Cowboys, 31-28 (D)
        Giants, 17-14 (NY)
1987—Cowboys, 16-14 (NY)
        Cowboys, 33-24 (D)
1988—Giants, 12-10 (D)
        Giants, 29-21 (NY)
1989—Giants, 30-13 (D)
        Giants, 15-0 (NY)
1990—Giants, 28-7 (D)
        Giants, 31-17 (NY)
1991—Cowboys, 21-16 (D)
        Giants, 22-9 (NY)
1992—Cowboys, 34-28 (NY)
        Cowboys, 30-3 (D)
1993—Cowboys, 31-9 (D)
        Cowboys, 16-13 (NY) OT
1994—Cowboys, 38-10 (D)
        Giants, 15-10 (NY)
1995—Cowboys, 35-0 (NY)
        Cowboys, 21-20 (D)
1996—Cowboys, 27-0 (D)
        Giants, 20-6 (NY)
1997—Cowboys, 20-17 (NY)
        Giants, 20-7 (D)
1998—Cowboys, 31-7 (NY)
        Cowboys, 16-6 (D)
1999—Giants, 13-10 (NY)
        Cowboys, 26-18 (D)
2000—Giants, 19-14 (NY)
        Giants, 17-13 (D)
2001—Giants, 27-24 (NY) OT
        Cowboys, 20-13 (D)
2002—Giants, 21-17 (D)
        Giants, 37-7 (NY)
2003—Cowboys, 35-32 (NY) OT
        Cowboys, 19-3 (D)
2004—Giants, 26-10 (D)
        Giants, 28-24 (NY)
(RS Pts.—Cowboys 1,854, Giants 1,512)

DALLAS vs. N.Y. JETS
RS: Cowboys lead series, 6-2
1971—Cowboys, 52-10 (D)
1975—Cowboys, 31-21 (NY)
1978—Cowboys, 30-7 (NY)
1987—Cowboys, 38-24 (NY)
1990—Jets, 24-9 (NY)
1993—Cowboys, 28-7 (NY)

1999—Jets, 22-21 (D)
2003—Cowboys, 17-6 (NY)
(RS Pts.—Cowboys 226, Jets 121)
DALLAS vs. *OAKLAND
RS: Raiders lead series, 5-3
1974—Raiders, 27-23 (O)
1980—Cowboys, 19-13 (O)
1983—Raiders, 40-38 (D)
1986—Raiders, 17-13 (D)
1992—Cowboys, 28-13 (LA)
1995—Cowboys, 34-21 (O)
1998—Raiders, 13-12 (D)
2001—Raiders, 28-21 (O)
(RS Pts.—Cowboys 188, Raiders 172)
Franchise in Los Angeles from 1982-1994
DALLAS vs. PHILADELPHIA
RS: Cowboys lead series, 49-39
PS: Cowboys lead series, 2-1
1960—Eagles, 27-25 (D)
1961—Eagles, 43-7 (D)
       Eagles, 35-13 (P)
1962—Cowboys, 41-19 (D)
       Eagles, 28-14 (P)
1963—Eagles, 24-21 (P)
       Cowboys, 27-20 (D)
1964—Eagles, 17-14 (D)
       Eagles, 24-14 (P)
1965—Eagles, 35-24 (D)
       Cowboys, 21-19 (P)
1966—Cowboys, 56-7 (D)
       Eagles, 24-23 (P)
1967—Eagles, 21-14 (P)
       Cowboys, 38-17 (D)
1968—Cowboys, 45-13 (P)
       Cowboys, 34-14 (D)
1969—Cowboys, 38-7 (P)
       Cowboys, 49-14 (D)
1970—Cowboys, 17-7 (P)
       Cowboys, 21-17 (D)
1971—Cowboys, 42-7 (P)
       Cowboys, 20-7 (D)
1972—Cowboys, 28-6 (D)
       Cowboys, 28-7 (P)
1973—Eagles, 30-16 (P)
       Cowboys, 31-10 (D)
1974—Eagles, 13-10 (P)
       Cowboys, 31-24 (D)
1975—Cowboys, 20-17 (P)
       Cowboys, 27-17 (D)
1976—Cowboys, 27-7 (D)
       Cowboys, 26-7 (P)
1977—Cowboys, 16-10 (P)
       Cowboys, 24-14 (D)
1978—Cowboys, 14-7 (D)
       Cowboys, 31-13 (P)
1979—Eagles, 31-21 (D)
       Cowboys, 24-17 (P)
1980—Eagles, 17-10 (P)
       Cowboys, 35-27 (D)
       *Eagles, 20-7 (P)
1981—Cowboys, 17-14 (P)
       Cowboys, 21-10 (D)
1982—Eagles, 24-20 (D)
1983—Cowboys, 37-7 (D)
       Cowboys, 27-20 (P)
1984—Cowboys, 23-17 (D)
       Cowboys, 26-10 (P)
1985—Eagles, 16-14 (P)
       Cowboys, 34-17 (D)
1986—Cowboys, 17-14 (P)

Eagles, 23-21 (D)
1987—Cowboys, 41-22 (D)
       Eagles, 37-20 (P)
1988—Eagles, 24-23 (P)
       Eagles, 23-7 (D)
1989—Eagles, 27-0 (D)
       Eagles, 20-10 (P)
1990—Eagles, 21-20 (D)
       Eagles, 17-3 (P)
1991—Eagles, 24-0 (D)
       Cowboys, 25-13 (P)
1992—Eagles, 31-7 (P)
       Cowboys, 20-10 (D)
       **Cowboys, 34-10 (D)
1993—Cowboys, 23-10 (P)
       Cowboys, 23-17 (D)
1994—Cowboys, 24-13 (D)
       Cowboys, 31-19 (P)
1995—Cowboys, 34-12 (D)
       Eagles, 20-17 (P)
       **Cowboys, 30-11 (D)
1996—Cowboys, 23-19 (P)
       Eagles, 31-21 (D)
1997—Cowboys, 21-20 (P)
       Eagles, 13-12 (P)
1998—Cowboys, 34-0 (P)
       Cowboys, 13-9 (D)
1999—Eagles, 13-10 (P)
       Cowboys, 20-10 (D)
2000—Eagles, 41-14 (D)
       Eagles, 16-13 (P) OT
2001—Eagles, 40-18 (P)
       Eagles, 36-3 (D)
2002—Eagles, 44-13 (P)
       Eagles, 27-3 (D)
2003—Cowboys, 23-21 (D)
       Eagles, 36-10 (P)
2004—Eagles, 49-21 (D)
       Eagles, 12-7 (P)
(RS Pts.—Cowboys 1,901, Eagles 1,689)
(PS Pts.—Cowboys 71, Eagles 41)
NFC Championship
**NFC Divisional Playoff*
DALLAS vs. PITTSBURGH
RS: Cowboys lead series, 14-12
PS: Steelers lead series, 2-1
1960—Steelers, 35-28 (D)
1961—Cowboys, 27-24 (D)
       Steelers, 37-7 (P)
1962—Steelers, 30-28 (D)
       Cowboys, 42-27 (P)
1963—Steelers, 27-21 (P)
       Steelers, 24-19 (D)
1964—Steelers, 23-17 (P)
       Cowboys, 17-14 (D)
1965—Steelers, 22-13 (P)
       Cowboys, 24-17 (D)
1966—Cowboys, 52-21 (D)
       Cowboys, 20-7 (P)
1967—Cowboys, 24-21 (P)
1968—Cowboys, 28-7 (D)
1969—Cowboys, 10-7 (P)
1972—Cowboys, 17-13 (D)
1975—*Steelers, 21-17 (Miami)
1977—Steelers, 28-13 (P)
1978—**Steelers, 35-31 (Miami)
1979—Steelers, 14-3 (P)
1982—Steelers, 36-28 (D)
1985—Cowboys, 27-13 (D)
1988—Steelers, 24-21 (P)

1991—Cowboys, 20-10 (D)
1994—Cowboys, 26-9 (P)
1995—***Cowboys, 27-17 (Tempe)
1997—Cowboys, 37-7 (P)
2004—Steelers, 24-20 (D)
(RS Pts.—Cowboys 589, Steelers 521)
(PS Pts.—Cowboys 75, Steelers 73)
Super Bowl X
**Super Bowl XIII*
***Super Bowl XXX*
DALLAS vs. *ST. LOUIS
RS: Series tied, 9-9
PS: Series tied, 4-4
1960—Rams, 38-13 (D)
1962—Cowboys, 27-17 (LA)
1967—Rams, 35-13 (D)
1969—Rams, 24-23 (LA)
1971—Cowboys, 28-21 (D)
1973—Rams, 37-31 (LA)
       **Cowboys, 27-16 (D)
1975—Cowboys, 18-7 (D)
       ***Cowboys, 37-7 (LA)
1976—**Rams, 14-12 (D)
1978—Rams, 27-14 (LA)
       ***Cowboys, 28-0 (LA)
1979—Cowboys, 30-6 (D)
       **Rams, 21-19 (D)
1980—Rams, 38-14 (LA)
       ****Cowboys, 34-13 (D)
1981—Cowboys, 29-17 (D)
1983—****Rams, 24-17 (D)
1984—Cowboys, 20-13 (LA)
1985—**Rams, 20-0 (LA)
1986—Rams, 29-10 (LA)
1987—Rams, 29-21 (LA)
1989—Rams, 35-31 (D)
1990—Cowboys, 24-21 (LA)
1992—Rams, 27-23 (D)
2002—Cowboys, 13-10 (StL)
(RS Pts.—Rams 423, Cowboys 390)
(PS Pts.—Cowboys 174, Rams 115)
Franchise in Los Angeles prior to 1995
**NFC Divisional Playoff*
***NFC Championship*
****NFC First-Round Playoff*
DALLAS vs. SAN DIEGO
RS: Cowboys lead series, 5-2
1972—Cowboys, 34-28 (SD)
1980—Cowboys, 42-31 (D)
1983—Chargers, 24-23 (SD)
1986—Cowboys, 24-21 (SD)
1990—Cowboys, 17-14 (D)
1995—Cowboys, 23-9 (SD)
2001—Chargers, 32-21 (D)
(RS Pts.—Cowboys 184, Chargers 159)
DALLAS vs. SAN FRANCISCO
RS: 49ers lead series, 14-8-1
PS: Cowboys lead series, 5-2
1960—49ers, 26-14 (D)
1963—49ers, 31-24 (SF)
1965—Cowboys, 39-31 (D)
1967—49ers, 24-16 (SF)
1969—Tie, 24-24 (D)
1970—*Cowboys, 17-10 (SF)
1971—*Cowboys, 14-3 (D)
1972—49ers, 31-10 (D)
       **Cowboys, 30-28 (SF)
1974—Cowboys, 20-14 (D)
1977—Cowboys, 42-35 (SF)
1979—Cowboys, 21-13 (SF)

1980—Cowboys, 59-14 (D)
1981—49ers, 45-14 (SF)
    *49ers, 28-27 (SF)
1983—49ers, 42-17 (SF)
1985—49ers, 31-16 (SF)
1989—49ers, 31-14 (D)
1990—49ers, 24-6 (D)
1992—*Cowboys, 30-20 (SF)
1993—Cowboys, 26-17 (D)
    *Cowboys, 38-21 (D)
1994—49ers, 21-14 (SF)
    *49ers, 38-28 (SF)
1995—49ers, 38-20 (D)
1996—Cowboys, 20-17 (SF) OT
1997—49ers, 17-10 (SF)
2000—49ers, 41-24 (D)
2001—Cowboys, 27-21 (D)
2002—49ers, 31-27 (D)
(RS Pts.—49ers 619, Cowboys 504)
(PS Pts.—Cowboys 184, 49ers 148)
*NFC Championship
**NFC Divisional Playoff
DALLAS vs. SEATTLE
RS: Cowboys lead series, 6-3
1976—Cowboys, 28-13 (S)
1980—Cowboys, 51-7 (D)
1983—Cowboys, 35-10 (S)
1986—Seahawks, 31-14 (D)
1992—Cowboys, 27-0 (D)
1998—Cowboys, 30-22 (D)
2001—Seahawks, 29-3 (S)
2002—Seahawks, 17-14 (D)
2004—Cowboys, 43-39 (S)
(RS Pts.—Cowboys 245, Seahawks 168)
DALLAS vs. TAMPA BAY
RS: Cowboys lead series, 6-3
PS: Cowboys lead series, 2-0
1977—Cowboys, 23-7 (D)
1980—Cowboys, 28-17 (D)
1981—*Cowboys, 38-0 (D)
1982—Cowboys, 14-9 (D)
    **Cowboys, 30-17 (D)
1983—Cowboys, 27-24 (D) OT
1990—Cowboys, 14-10 (D)
    Cowboys, 17-13 (TB)
2000—Buccaneers, 27-7 (TB)
2001—Buccaneers, 10-6 (D)
2003—Buccaneers, 16-0 (TB)
(RS Pts.—Cowboys 136, Buccaneers 133)
(PS Pts.—Cowboys 68, Buccaneers 17)
*NFC Divisional Playoff
**NFC First-Round Playoff
DALLAS vs. *TENNESSEE
RS: Cowboys lead series, 6-5
1970—Cowboys, 52-10 (D)
1974—Cowboys, 10-0 (H)
1979—Oilers, 30-24 (D)
1982—Cowboys, 37-7 (H)
1985—Cowboys, 17-10 (H)
1988—Oilers, 25-17 (D)
1991—Oilers, 26-23 (H) OT
1994—Cowboys, 20-17 (D)
1997—Oilers, 27-14 (D)
2000—Titans, 31-0 (T)
2002—Cowboys, 21-13 (D)
(RS Pts.—Cowboys 235, Titans 196)
*Franchise in Houston prior to 1997;
known as Oilers prior to 1999
DALLAS vs. WASHINGTON
RS: Cowboys lead series, 54-32-2

PS: Redskins lead series, 2-0
1960—Redskins, 26-14 (W)
1961—Tie, 28-28 (D)
    Redskins, 34-24 (W)
1962—Tie, 35-35 (D)
    Cowboys, 38-10 (W)
1963—Redskins, 21-17 (W)
    Cowboys, 35-20 (D)
1964—Cowboys, 24-18 (D)
    Redskins, 28-16 (W)
1965—Cowboys, 27-7 (D)
    Redskins, 34-31 (W)
1966—Cowboys, 31-30 (W)
    Redskins, 34-31 (D)
1967—Cowboys, 17-14 (W)
    Redskins, 27-20 (D)
1968—Cowboys, 44-24 (W)
    Cowboys, 29-20 (D)
1969—Cowboys, 41-28 (W)
    Cowboys, 20-10 (D)
1970—Cowboys, 45-21 (W)
    Cowboys, 34-0 (D)
1971—Redskins, 20-16 (D)
    Cowboys, 13-0 (W)
1972—Redskins, 24-20 (W)
    Cowboys, 34-24 (D)
    *Redskins, 26-3 (W)
1973—Redskins, 14-7 (W)
    Cowboys, 27-7 (D)
1974—Redskins, 28-21 (W)
    Cowboys, 24-23 (D)
1975—Redskins, 30-24 (W) OT
    Cowboys, 31-10 (D)
1976—Cowboys, 20-7 (W)
    Redskins, 27-14 (D)
1977—Cowboys, 34-16 (D)
    Cowboys, 14-7 (W)
1978—Redskins, 9-5 (W)
    Cowboys, 37-10 (D)
1979—Redskins, 34-20 (W)
    Cowboys, 35-34 (D)
1980—Cowboys, 17-3 (W)
    Cowboys, 14-10 (D)
1981—Cowboys, 26-10 (W)
    Cowboys, 24-10 (D)
1982—Cowboys, 24-10 (W)
    *Redskins, 31-17 (W)
1983—Cowboys, 31-30 (W)
    Redskins, 31-10 (D)
1984—Redskins, 34-14 (D)
    Redskins, 30-28 (D)
1985—Cowboys, 44-14 (D)
    Cowboys, 13-7 (W)
1986—Cowboys, 30-6 (D)
    Redskins, 41-14 (W)
1987—Redskins, 13-7 (D)
    Redskins, 24-20 (W)
1988—Redskins, 35-17 (D)
    Cowboys, 24-17 (W)
1989—Redskins, 30-7 (D)
    Cowboys, 13-3 (W)
1990—Redskins, 19-15 (W)
    Cowboys, 27-17 (D)
1991—Redskins, 33-31 (D)
    Cowboys, 24-21 (W)
1992—Cowboys, 23-10 (D)
    Redskins, 20-17 (W)
1993—Redskins, 35-16 (W)
    Cowboys, 38-3 (D)
1994—Cowboys, 34-7 (W)

    Cowboys, 31-7 (D)
1995—Redskins, 27-23 (W)
    Redskins, 24-17 (D)
1996—Cowboys, 21-10 (D)
    Redskins, 37-10 (W)
1997—Redskins, 21-16 (W)
    Cowboys, 17-14 (D)
1998—Cowboys, 31-10 (W)
    Cowboys, 23-7 (D)
1999—Cowboys, 41-35 (W) OT
    Cowboys, 38-20 (D)
2000—Cowboys, 27-21 (W)
    Cowboys, 32-13 (D)
2001—Cowboys, 9-7 (D)
    Cowboys, 20-14 (W)
2002—Cowboys, 27-20 (D)
    Redskins, 20-14 (W)
2003—Cowboys, 21-14 (D)
    Cowboys, 27-0 (W)
2004—Cowboys, 21-18 (W)
    Cowboys, 13-10 (D)
(RS Pts.—Cowboys 2,078, Redskins 1,665)
(PS Pts.—Redskins 57, Cowboys 20)
*NFC Championship

DENVER vs. ARIZONA
RS: Broncos lead series, 6-0-1;
See Arizona vs. Denver
DENVER vs. ATLANTA
RS: Broncos lead series, 7-4
PS: Broncos lead series, 1-0;
See Atlanta vs. Denver
DENVER vs. BALTIMORE
RS: Ravens lead series, 3-1
PS: Ravens lead series, 1-0;
See Baltimore vs. Denver
DENVER vs. BUFFALO
RS: Bills lead series, 17-13-1
PS: Bills lead series, 1-0;
See Buffalo vs. Denver
DENVER vs. CAROLINA
RS: Broncos lead series, 2-0;
See Carolina vs. Denver
DENVER vs. CHICAGO
RS: Series tied, 6-6;
See Chicago vs. Denver
DENVER vs. CINCINNATI
RS: Broncos lead series, 15-8;
See Cincinnati vs. Denver
DENVER vs. CLEVELAND
RS: Broncos lead series, 15-5
PS: Broncos lead series, 3-0;
See Cleveland vs. Denver
DENVER vs. DALLAS
RS: Series tied, 4-4
PS: Cowboys lead series, 1-0;
See Dallas vs. Denver
DENVER vs. DETROIT
RS: Broncos lead series, 6-3
1971—Lions, 24-20 (Den)
1974—Broncos, 31-27 (Den)
1978—Lions, 17-14 (Det)
1981—Broncos, 27-21 (Den)
1984—Broncos, 28-7 (Det)
1987—Broncos, 34-0 (Det)
1990—Lions, 40-27 (Det)
1999—Broncos, 17-7 (Det)
2003—Broncos, 20-16 (Den)
(RS Pts.—Broncos 218, Lions 159)

DENVER vs. GREEN BAY
RS: Broncos lead series, 5-4-1
PS: Broncos lead series, 1-0
1971—Packers, 34-13 (Mil)
1975—Broncos, 23-13 (D)
1978—Broncos, 16-3 (D)
1984—Broncos, 17-14 (D)
1987—Tie, 17-17 (Mil) OT
1990—Broncos, 22-13 (D)
1993—Packers, 30-27 (GB)
1996—Packers, 41-6 (GB)
1997—*Broncos, 31-24 (San Diego)
1999—Broncos, 31-10 (D)
2003—Packers, 31-3 (GB)
(RS Pts.—Packers 206, Broncos 175)
(PS Pts.—Broncos 31, Packers 24)
*Super Bowl XXXII

DENVER vs. HOUSTON
RS: Broncos lead series, 1-0
2004—Broncos, 31-13 (D)
(RS Pts.—Broncos 31, Texans 13)

DENVER vs. *INDIANAPOLIS
RS: Broncos lead series, 11-4
PS: Colts lead series, 2-0
1974—Broncos, 17-6 (B)
1977—Broncos, 27-13 (D)
1978—Colts, 7-6 (B)
1981—Broncos, 28-10 (D)
1983—Broncos, 17-10 (B)
      Broncos, 21-19 (D)
1985—Broncos, 15-10 (I)
1988—Colts, 55-23 (I)
1989—Broncos, 14-3 (D)
1990—Broncos, 27-17 (I)
1993—Broncos, 35-13 (D)
2001—Colts, 29-10 (I)
2002—Colts, 23-20 (D) OT
2003—Broncos, 31-17 (I)
      **Colts, 41-10 (I)
2004—Broncos, 33-14 (D)
      **Colts, 49-24 (I)
(RS Pts.—Broncos 324, Colts 246)
(PS Pts.—Colts 90, Broncos 34)
*Franchise in Baltimore prior to 1984
**AFC First-Round Playoff

DENVER vs. JACKSONVILLE
RS: Series tied, 2-2
PS: Series tied, 1-1
1995—Broncos, 31-23 (D)
1996—*Jaguars, 30-27 (D)
1997—**Broncos, 42-17 (D)
1998—Broncos, 37-24 (D)
1999—Jaguars, 27-24 (J)
2004—Jaguars, 7-6 (J)
(RS Pts.—Broncos 98, Jaguars 81)
(PS Pts.—Broncos 69, Jaguars 47)
*AFC Divisional Playoff
**AFC First-Round Playoff

DENVER vs. *KANSAS CITY
RS: Chiefs lead series, 50-39
PS: Broncos lead series, 1-0
1960—Texans, 17-14 (D)
      Texans, 34-7 (Dal)
1961—Texans, 19-12 (D)
      Texans, 49-21 (Dal)
1962—Texans, 24-3 (D)
      Texans, 17-10 (Dal)
1963—Chiefs, 59-7 (D)
      Chiefs, 52-21 (KC)
1964—Broncos, 33-27 (D)

Chiefs, 49-39 (KC)
1965—Chiefs, 31-23 (D)
      Chiefs, 45-35 (KC)
1966—Chiefs, 37-10 (KC)
      Chiefs, 56-10 (D)
1967—Chiefs, 52-9 (KC)
      Chiefs, 38-24 (D)
1968—Chiefs, 34-2 (KC)
      Chiefs, 30-7 (D)
1969—Chiefs, 26-13 (D)
      Chiefs, 31-17 (KC)
1970—Broncos, 26-13 (D)
      Chiefs, 16-0 (KC)
1971—Chiefs, 16-3 (D)
      Chiefs, 28-10 (KC)
1972—Chiefs, 45-24 (D)
      Chiefs, 24-21 (KC)
1973—Chiefs, 16-14 (KC)
      Broncos, 14-10 (D)
1974—Broncos, 17-14 (KC)
      Chiefs, 42-34 (D)
1975—Broncos, 37-33 (D)
      Chiefs, 26-13 (KC)
1976—Broncos, 35-26 (KC)
      Broncos, 17-16 (D)
1977—Broncos, 23-7 (D)
      Broncos, 14-7 (KC)
1978—Broncos, 23-17 (KC) OT
      Broncos, 24-3 (D)
1979—Broncos, 24-10 (KC)
      Broncos, 20-3 (D)
1980—Chiefs, 23-17 (D)
      Chiefs, 31-14 (KC)
1981—Chiefs, 28-14 (KC)
      Broncos, 16-13 (D)
1982—Chiefs, 37-16 (D)
1983—Broncos, 27-24 (D)
      Chiefs, 48-17 (KC)
1984—Broncos, 21-0 (D)
      Chiefs, 16-13 (KC)
1985—Broncos, 30-10 (KC)
      Broncos, 14-13 (D)
1986—Broncos, 38-17 (D)
      Chiefs, 37-10 (KC)
1987—Broncos, 26-17 (KC)
      Broncos, 20-17 (D)
1988—Chiefs, 20-13 (KC)
      Broncos, 17-11 (D)
1989—Broncos, 34-20 (D)
      Broncos, 16-13 (KC)
1990—Broncos, 24-23 (D)
      Chiefs, 31-20 (KC)
1991—Chiefs, 19-16 (D)
      Broncos, 24-20 (KC)
1992—Broncos, 20-19 (D)
      Chiefs, 42-20 (KC)
1993—Chiefs, 15-7 (KC)
      Broncos, 27-21 (D)
1994—Chiefs, 31-28 (D)
      Broncos, 20-17 (KC) OT
1995—Chiefs, 21-7 (D)
      Chiefs, 20-17 (KC)
1996—Chiefs, 17-14 (KC)
      Broncos, 34-7 (D)
1997—Broncos, 19-3 (D)
      Chiefs, 24-22 (KC)
      **Broncos, 14-10 (KC)
1998—Broncos, 30-7 (KC)
      Broncos, 35-31 (D)
1999—Chiefs, 26-10 (KC)

Chiefs, 16-10 (D)
2000—Chiefs, 23-22 (D)
      Chiefs, 20-7 (KC)
2001—Broncos, 20-6 (D)
      Chiefs, 26-23 (KC) OT
2002—Broncos, 37-34 (KC) OT
      Broncos, 31-24 (D)
2003—Chiefs, 24-23 (KC)
      Broncos, 45-27 (D)
2004—Broncos, 34-24 (D)
      Chiefs, 45-17 (KC)
(RS Pts.—Chiefs 2,154, Broncos 1,749)
(PS Pts.—Broncos 14, Chiefs 10)
*Franchise in Dallas prior to 1963 and
known as Texans
**AFC Divisional Playoff

DENVER vs. MIAMI
RS: Dolphins lead series, 9-3-1
PS: Broncos lead series, 1-0
1966—Dolphins, 24-7 (M)
      Broncos, 17-7 (D)
1967—Dolphins, 35-21 (M)
1968—Broncos, 21-14 (D)
1969—Dolphins, 27-24 (M)
1971—Tie, 10-10 (D)
1975—Dolphins, 14-13 (M)
1985—Dolphins, 30-26 (D)
1998—Dolphins, 31-21 (M)
      *Broncos, 38-3 (D)
1999—Dolphins, 38-21 (D)
2001—Dolphins, 21-10 (M)
2002—Dolphins, 24-22 (D)
2004—Broncos, 20-17 (D)
(RS Pts.—Dolphins 292, Broncos 233)
(PS Pts.—Broncos 38, Dolphins 3)
*AFC Divisional Playoff

DENVER vs. MINNESOTA
RS: Vikings lead series, 7-4
1972—Vikings, 23-20 (D)
1978—Vikings, 12-9 (M) OT
1981—Broncos, 19-17 (D)
1984—Broncos, 42-21 (D)
1987—Vikings, 34-27 (M)
1990—Vikings, 27-22 (M)
1991—Broncos, 13-6 (M)
1993—Vikings, 26-23 (D)
1996—Broncos, 21-17 (M)
1999—Vikings, 23-20 (D)
2003—Vikings, 28-20 (M)
(RS Pts.—Broncos 236, Vikings 234)

DENVER vs. *NEW ENGLAND
RS: Broncos lead series, 22-15
PS: Broncos lead series, 1-0
1960—Broncos, 13-10 (B)
      Broncos, 31-24 (D)
1961—Patriots, 45-17 (B)
      Patriots, 28-24 (D)
1962—Patriots, 41-16 (B)
      Patriots, 33-29 (D)
1963—Broncos, 14-10 (D)
      Patriots, 40-21 (B)
1964—Patriots, 39-10 (D)
      Patriots, 12-7 (B)
1965—Broncos, 27-10 (B)
      Patriots, 28-20 (D)
1966—Patriots, 24-10 (D)
      Broncos, 17-10 (B)
1967—Broncos, 26-21 (D)
1968—Patriots, 20-17 (D)
      Broncos, 35-14 (B)

1969—Broncos, 35-7 (D)
1972—Broncos, 45-21 (D)
1976—Patriots, 38-14 (NE)
1979—Broncos, 45-10 (D)
1980—Patriots, 23-14 (NE)
1984—Broncos, 26-19 (D)
1986—Broncos, 27-20 (D)
    **Broncos, 22-17 (D)
1987—Broncos, 31-20 (D)
1988—Broncos, 21-10 (D)
1991—Broncos, 9-6 (NE)
    Broncos, 20-3 (D)
1995—Broncos, 37-3 (NE)
1996—Broncos, 34-8 (NE)
1997—Broncos, 34-13 (D)
1998—Broncos, 27-21 (D)
1999—Patriots, 24-23 (NE)
2000—Patriots, 28-19 (D)
2001—Broncos, 31-20 (D)
2002—Broncos, 24-16 (NE)
2003—Patriots, 30-26 (D)
(RS Pts.—Broncos 876, Patriots 749)
(PS Pts.—Broncos 22, Patriots 17)
Franchise in Boston prior to 1971
**AFC Divisional Playoff*

DENVER vs. NEW ORLEANS
RS: Broncos lead series, 6-2
1970—Broncos, 31-6 (NO)
1974—Broncos, 33-17 (D)
1979—Broncos, 10-3 (D)
1985—Broncos, 34-23 (D)
1988—Saints, 42-0 (NO)
1994—Saints, 30-28 (D)
2000—Broncos, 38-23 (NO)
2004—Broncos, 34-13 (NO)
(RS Pts.—Broncos 208, Saints 157)

DENVER vs. N.Y. GIANTS
RS: Series tied, 4-4
PS: Giants lead series, 1-0
1972—Giants, 29-17 (NY)
1976—Broncos, 14-13 (D)
1980—Broncos, 14-9 (NY)
1986—Giants, 19-16 (NY)
    *Giants, 39-20 (Pasadena)
1989—Giants, 14-7 (D)
1992—Broncos, 27-13 (D)
1998—Giants, 20-16 (NY)
2001—Broncos, 31-20 (D)
(RS Pts.—Broncos 142, Giants 137)
(PS Pts.—Giants 39, Broncos 20)
Super Bowl XXI

DENVER vs. *N.Y. JETS
RS: Series tied, 14-14-1
PS: Broncos lead series, 1-0
1960—Titans, 28-24 (NY)
    Titans, 30-27 (D)
1961—Titans, 35-28 (NY)
    Broncos, 27-10 (D)
1962—Broncos, 32-10 (NY)
    Titans, 46-45 (D)
1963—Tie, 35-35 (NY)
    Jets, 14-9 (D)
1964—Jets, 30-6 (NY)
    Broncos, 20-16 (D)
1965—Broncos, 16-13 (D)
    Jets, 45-10 (NY)
1966—Jets, 16-7 (D)
1967—Jets, 38-24 (D)
    Broncos, 33-24 (NY)
1968—Broncos, 21-13 (NY)

1969—Broncos, 21-19 (D)
1973—Broncos, 40-28 (NY)
1976—Broncos, 46-3 (D)
1978—Jets, 31-28 (D)
1980—Broncos, 31-24 (D)
1986—Jets, 22-10 (NY)
1992—Broncos, 27-16 (D)
1993—Broncos, 26-20 (NY)
1994—Jets, 25-22 (NY) OT
1996—Broncos, 31-6 (D)
1998—**Broncos, 23-10 (D)
1999—Jets, 21-13 (D)
2000—Broncos, 30-23 (NY)
2002—Jets, 19-13 (NY)
(RS Pts.—Broncos 702, Jets 660)
(PS Pts.—Broncos 23, Jets 10)
Jets known as Titans prior to 1963
**AFC Championship*

DENVER vs. *OAKLAND
RS: Raiders lead series, 53-34-2
PS: Series tied, 1-1
1960—Broncos, 31-14 (D)
    Raiders, 48-10 (O)
1961—Raiders, 33-19 (O)
    Broncos, 27-24 (D)
1962—Broncos, 44-7 (D)
    Broncos, 23-6 (O)
1963—Raiders, 26-10 (O)
    Raiders, 35-31 (O)
1964—Raiders, 40-7 (O)
    Tie, 20-20 (D)
1965—Raiders, 28-20 (D)
    Raiders, 24-13 (O)
1966—Raiders, 17-3 (D)
    Raiders, 28-10 (O)
1967—Raiders, 51-0 (O)
    Raiders, 21-17 (D)
1968—Raiders, 43-7 (D)
    Raiders, 33-27 (O)
1969—Raiders, 24-14 (D)
    Raiders, 41-10 (O)
1970—Raiders, 35-23 (O)
    Raiders, 24-19 (D)
1971—Raiders, 27-16 (O)
    Raiders, 21-13 (D)
1972—Broncos, 30-23 (D)
    Raiders, 37-20 (D)
1973—Tie, 23-23 (D)
    Raiders, 21-17 (O)
1974—Raiders, 28-17 (D)
    Broncos, 20-17 (O)
1975—Raiders, 42-17 (D)
    Raiders, 17-10 (O)
1976—Raiders, 17-10 (D)
    Raiders, 19-6 (O)
1977—Broncos, 30-7 (O)
    Raiders, 24-14 (D)
    **Broncos, 20-17 (D)
1978—Broncos, 14-6 (D)
    Broncos, 21-6 (O)
1979—Raiders, 27-3 (O)
    Raiders, 14-10 (D)
1980—Raiders, 9-3 (O)
    Raiders, 24-21 (D)
1981—Broncos, 9-7 (D)
    Broncos, 17-0 (O)
1982—Raiders, 27-10 (LA)
1983—Raiders, 22-7 (D)
    Raiders, 22-20 (LA)
1984—Broncos, 16-13 (D)

    Broncos, 22-19 (LA) OT
1985—Raiders, 31-28 (LA) OT
    Raiders, 17-14 (D) OT
1986—Broncos, 38-36 (D)
    Broncos, 21-10 (LA)
1987—Broncos, 30-14 (D)
    Broncos, 23-17 (LA)
1988—Raiders, 30-27 (D) OT
    Raiders, 21-20 (LA)
1989—Broncos, 31-21 (D)
    Raiders, 16-13 (LA) OT
1990—Raiders, 14-9 (LA)
    Raiders, 23-20 (D)
1991—Raiders, 16-13 (LA)
    Raiders, 17-16 (D)
1992—Broncos, 17-13 (D)
    Raiders, 24-0 (LA)
1993—Raiders, 23-20 (D)
    Raiders, 33-30 (LA) OT
    ***Raiders, 42-24 (LA)
1994—Raiders, 48-16 (D)
    Raiders, 23-13 (LA)
1995—Broncos, 27-0 (D)
    Broncos, 31-28 (O)
1996—Broncos, 22-21 (D)
    Broncos, 24-19 (D)
1997—Raiders, 28-25 (O)
    Broncos, 31-3 (D)
1998—Broncos, 34-17 (O)
    Broncos, 40-14 (D)
1999—Broncos, 16-13 (O)
    Broncos, 27-21 (D) OT
2000—Broncos, 33-24 (O)
    Broncos, 27-24 (D)
2001—Raiders, 38-28 (O)
    Broncos, 23-17 (D)
2002—Raiders, 34-10 (D)
    Raiders, 28-16 (O)
2003—Broncos, 31-10 (D)
    Broncos, 22-8 (O)
2004—Broncos, 31-3 (O)
    Raiders, 25-24 (D)
(RS Pts.—Raiders 1,963, Broncos 1,722)
(PS Pts.—Raiders 59, Broncos 44)
Franchise in Los Angeles from 1982-1994
**AFC Championship*
***AFC First-Round Playoff*

DENVER vs. PHILADELPHIA
RS: Eagles lead series, 6-3
1971—Eagles, 17-16 (P)
1975—Broncos, 25-10 (D)
1980—Eagles, 27-6 (P)
1983—Eagles, 13-10 (D)
1986—Broncos, 33-7 (P)
1989—Eagles, 28-24 (D)
1992—Eagles, 30-0 (P)
1995—Eagles, 31-13 (P)
1998—Broncos, 41-16 (D)
(RS Pts.—Eagles 179, Broncos 168)

DENVER vs. PITTSBURGH
RS: Broncos lead series, 11-6-1
PS: Broncos lead series, 3-2
1970—Broncos, 16-13 (D)
1971—Broncos, 22-10 (P)
1973—Broncos, 23-13 (P)
1974—Tie, 35-35 (D) OT
1975—Steelers, 20-9 (P)
1977—Broncos, 21-7 (D)
    *Broncos, 34-21 (D)
1978—Steelers, 21-17 (D)

*Steelers, 33-10 (P)
1979—Steelers, 42-7 (P)
1983—Broncos, 14-10 (P)
1984—*Steelers, 24-17 (D)
1985—Broncos, 31-23 (P)
1986—Broncos, 21-10 (P)
1988—Steelers, 39-21 (P)
1989—Broncos, 34-7 (D)
*Broncos, 24-23 (D)
1990—Steelers, 34-17 (D)
1991—Broncos, 20-13 (D)
1993—Broncos, 37-13 (D)
1997—Steelers, 35-24 (P)
**Broncos, 24-21 (P)
2003—Broncos, 17-14 (D)
(RS Pts.—Broncos 386, Steelers 359)
(PS Pts.—Steelers 122, Broncos 109)
*AFC Divisional Playoff
**AFC Championship

DENVER vs. *ST. LOUIS
RS: Series tied, 5-5
1972—Broncos, 16-10 (LA)
1974—Rams, 17-10 (D)
1979—Rams, 13-9 (D)
1982—Broncos, 27-24 (LA)
1985—Rams, 20-16 (LA)
1988—Broncos, 35-24 (D)
1994—Rams, 27-21 (LA)
1997—Broncos, 35-14 (D)
2000—Rams, 41-36 (StL)
2002—Broncos, 23-16 (D)
(RS Pts.—Broncos 228, Rams 206)
*Franchise in Los Angeles prior to 1995

DENVER vs. *SAN DIEGO
RS: Broncos lead series, 50-39-1
1960—Chargers, 23-19 (D)
Chargers, 41-33 (LA)
1961—Chargers, 37-0 (SD)
Chargers, 19-16 (D)
1962—Broncos, 30-21 (D)
Chargers, 23-20 (SD)
1963—Broncos, 50-34 (D)
Chargers, 58-20 (SD)
1964—Chargers, 42-14 (SD)
Chargers, 31-20 (D)
1965—Chargers, 34-31 (SD)
Chargers, 33-21 (D)
1966—Chargers, 24-17 (SD)
Broncos, 20-17 (D)
1967—Chargers, 38-21 (D)
Chargers, 24-20 (SD)
1968—Chargers, 55-24 (SD)
Chargers, 47-23 (D)
1969—Broncos, 13-0 (D)
Chargers, 45-24 (SD)
1970—Chargers, 24-21 (SD)
Tie, 17-17 (D)
1971—Broncos, 20-16 (D)
Chargers, 45-17 (SD)
1972—Chargers, 37-14 (SD)
Broncos, 38-13 (D)
1973—Broncos, 30-19 (D)
Broncos, 42-28 (SD)
1974—Broncos, 27-7 (D)
Chargers, 17-0 (SD)
1975—Broncos, 27-17 (SD)
Broncos, 13-10 (D) OT
1976—Broncos, 26-0 (D)
Broncos, 17-0 (SD)
1977—Broncos, 17-14 (SD)

Broncos, 17-9 (D)
1978—Broncos, 27-14 (D)
Chargers, 23-0 (SD)
1979—Broncos, 7-0 (D)
Chargers, 17-7 (SD)
1980—Chargers, 30-13 (D)
Broncos, 20-13 (SD)
1981—Broncos, 42-24 (D)
Chargers, 34-17 (SD)
1982—Chargers, 23-3 (D)
Chargers, 30-20 (SD)
1983—Broncos, 14-6 (D)
Chargers, 31-7 (SD)
1984—Broncos, 16-13 (SD)
Broncos, 16-13 (D)
1985—Chargers, 30-10 (SD)
Broncos, 30-24 (D) OT
1986—Broncos, 31-14 (SD)
Chargers, 9-3 (D)
1987—Broncos, 31-17 (SD)
Broncos, 24-0 (D)
1988—Broncos, 34-3 (D)
Broncos, 12-0 (SD)
1989—Broncos, 16-10 (D)
Chargers, 19-16 (SD)
1990—Chargers, 19-7 (SD)
Broncos, 20-10 (D)
1991—Broncos, 27-19 (D)
Broncos, 17-14 (SD)
1992—Broncos, 21-13 (D)
Chargers, 24-21 (SD)
1993—Broncos, 34-17 (D)
Chargers, 13-10 (SD)
1994—Chargers, 37-34 (D)
Broncos, 20-15 (SD)
1995—Chargers, 17-6 (SD)
Broncos, 30-27 (D)
1996—Broncos, 28-17 (D)
Chargers, 16-10 (SD)
1997—Broncos, 38-28 (SD)
Broncos, 38-3 (D)
1998—Broncos, 27-10 (D)
Broncos, 31-16 (SD)
1999—Broncos, 33-17 (SD)
Chargers, 12-6 (D)
2000—Broncos, 21-7 (SD)
Broncos, 38-37 (D)
2001—Chargers, 27-10 (SD)
Broncos, 26-16 (D)
2002—Broncos, 26-9 (D)
Chargers, 30-27 (SD) OT
2003—Broncos, 37-13 (SD)
Broncos, 37-8 (D)
2004—Broncos, 23-13 (D)
Chargers, 20-17 (SD)
(RS Pts.—Broncos 1,918, Chargers 1,839)
*Franchise in Los Angeles prior to 1961

DENVER vs. SAN FRANCISCO
RS: Broncos lead series, 6-4
PS: 49ers lead series, 1-0
1970—49ers, 19-14 (SF)
1973—49ers, 36-34 (D)
1979—Broncos, 38-28 (SF)
1982—Broncos, 24-21 (D)
1985—Broncos, 17-16 (D)
1988—Broncos, 16-13 (SF) OT
1989—*49ers, 55-10 (New Orleans)
1994—49ers, 42-19 (SF)
1997—49ers, 34-17 (SF)
2000—Broncos, 38-9 (D)

2002—Broncos, 24-14 (SF)
(RS Pts.—Broncos 241, 49ers 232)
(PS Pts.—49ers 55, Broncos 10)
*Super Bowl XXIV

DENVER vs. SEATTLE
RS: Broncos lead series, 33-17
PS: Seahawks lead series, 1-0
1977—Broncos, 24-13 (S)
1978—Broncos, 28-7 (D)
Broncos, 20-17 (S) OT
1979—Broncos, 37-34 (D)
Seahawks, 28-23 (S)
1980—Broncos, 36-20 (D)
Broncos, 25-17 (S)
1981—Seahawks, 13-10 (S)
Broncos, 23-13 (D)
1982—Seahawks, 17-10 (S)
Seahawks, 13-11 (S)
1983—Seahawks, 27-19 (S)
Broncos, 38-27 (D)
*Seahawks, 31-7 (S)
1984—Seahawks, 27-24 (D)
Broncos, 31-14 (S)
1985—Broncos, 13-10 (D) OT
Broncos, 27-24 (S)
1986—Broncos, 20-13 (D)
Seahawks, 41-16 (S)
1987—Broncos, 40-17 (D)
Seahawks, 28-21 (S)
1988—Seahawks, 21-14 (D)
Seahawks, 42-14 (S)
1989—Broncos, 24-21 (S) OT
Broncos, 41-14 (D)
1990—Broncos, 34-31 (D) OT
Seahawks, 17-12 (S)
1991—Broncos, 16-10 (D)
Seahawks, 13-10 (S)
1992—Seahawks, 16-13 (S) OT
Broncos, 10-6 (D)
1993—Broncos, 28-17 (D)
Broncos, 17-9 (S)
1994—Broncos, 16-9 (S)
Broncos, 17-10 (D)
1995—Seahawks, 27-10 (S)
Seahawks, 31-27 (D)
1996—Broncos, 30-20 (S)
Broncos, 34-7 (D)
1997—Broncos, 35-14 (S)
Broncos, 30-27 (D)
1998—Broncos, 21-16 (S)
Broncos, 28-21 (D)
1999—Seahawks, 20-17 (S)
Broncos, 36-30 (D) OT
2000—Broncos, 38-31 (S)
Broncos, 31-24 (D)
2001—Seahawks, 34-21 (S)
Broncos, 20-7 (D)
2002—Broncos, 31-9 (S)
(RS Pts.—Broncos 1,171, Seahawks 974)
(PS Pts.—Seahawks 31, Broncos 7)
*AFC First-Round Playoff

DENVER vs. TAMPA BAY
RS: Broncos lead series, 4-2
1976—Broncos, 48-13 (D)
1981—Broncos, 24-7 (TB)
1993—Buccaneers, 17-10 (D)
1996—Broncos, 27-23 (D)
1999—Buccaneers, 13-10 (TB)
2004—Broncos, 16-13 (TB)
(RS Pts.—Broncos 135, Buccaneers 86)

DENVER vs. *TENNESSEE
RS: Titans lead series, 20-12-1
PS: Broncos lead series, 2-1
1960—Oilers, 45-25 (D)
　　　Oilers, 20-10 (H)
1961—Oilers, 55-14 (D)
　　　Oilers, 45-14 (H)
1962—Broncos, 20-10 (D)
　　　Oilers, 34-17 (H)
1963—Oilers, 20-14 (H)
　　　Oilers, 33-24 (D)
1964—Oilers, 38-17 (D)
　　　Oilers, 34-15 (H)
1965—Broncos, 28-17 (D)
　　　Broncos, 31-21 (H)
1966—Oilers, 45-7 (H)
　　　Broncos, 40-38 (D)
1967—Oilers, 10-6 (H)
　　　Oilers, 20-18 (D)
1968—Oilers, 38-17 (H)
1969—Oilers, 24-21 (H)
　　　Tie, 20-20 (D)
1970—Oilers, 31-21 (H)
1972—Broncos, 30-17 (D)
1973—Broncos, 48-20 (H)
1974—Broncos, 37-14 (D)
1976—Oilers, 17-3 (H)
1977—Broncos, 24-14 (H)
1979—**Oilers, 13-7 (H)
1980—Oilers, 20-16 (D)
1983—Broncos, 26-14 (H)
1985—Broncos, 31-20 (D)
1987—Oilers, 40-10 (D)
　　　***Broncos, 34-10 (D)
1991—Oilers, 42-14 (H)
　　　***Broncos, 26-24 (D)
1992—Broncos, 27-21 (D)
1995—Oilers, 42-33 (H)
2004—Broncos, 37-16 (T)
(RS Pts.—Titans 895, Broncos 715)
(PS Pts.—Broncos 67, Titans 47)
*Franchise in Houston prior to 1997;
known as the Oilers prior to 1999
**AFC First-Round Playoff
***AFC Divisional Playoff

DENVER vs. WASHINGTON
RS: Broncos lead series, 5-4
PS: Redskins lead series, 1-0
1970—Redskins, 19-3 (D)
1974—Redskins, 30-3 (W)
1980—Broncos, 20-17 (D)
1986—Broncos, 31-30 (D)
1987—*Redskins, 42-10 (San Diego)
1989—Broncos, 14-10 (W)
1992—Redskins, 34-3 (W)
1995—Broncos, 38-31 (D)
1998—Broncos, 38-16 (W)
2001—Redskins, 17-10 (D)
(RS Pts.—Redskins 204, Broncos 160)
(PS Pts.—Redskins 42, Broncos 10)
*Super Bowl XXII

DETROIT vs. ARIZONA
RS: Lions lead series, 30-21-5;
See Arizona vs. Detroit
DETROIT vs. ATLANTA
RS: Lions lead series, 22-8;
See Atlanta vs. Detroit
DETROIT vs. BALTIMORE
RS: Ravens lead series, 1-0;

See Baltimore vs. Detroit
DETROIT vs. BUFFALO
RS: Series tied, 3-3-1;
See Buffalo vs. Detroit
DETROIT vs. CAROLINA
RS: Panthers lead series, 2-1;
See Carolina vs. Detroit
DETROIT vs. CHICAGO
RS: Bears lead series, 83-62-5;
See Chicago vs. Detroit
DETROIT vs. CINCINNATI
RS: Bengals lead series, 5-3;
See Cincinnati vs. Detroit
DETROIT vs. CLEVELAND
RS: Lions lead series, 12-4
PS: Lions lead series, 3-1;
See Cleveland vs. Detroit
DETROIT vs. DALLAS
RS: Cowboys lead series, 9-8
PS: Series tied, 1-1;
See Dallas vs. Detroit
DETROIT vs. DENVER
RS: Broncos lead series, 6-3;
See Denver vs. Detroit
***DETROIT vs. GREEN BAY**
RS: Packers lead series, 79-63-7
PS: Packers lead series, 2-0
1930—Packers, 47-13 (GB)
　　　Tie, 6-6 (P)
1932—Packers, 15-10 (GB)
　　　Spartans, 19-0 (P)
1933—Packers, 17-0 (GB)
　　　Spartans, 7-0 (P)
1934—Lions, 3-0 (GB)
　　　Packers, 3-0 (D)
1935—Packers, 13-9 (Mil)
　　　Packers, 31-7 (GB)
　　　Lions, 20-10 (D)
1936—Packers, 20-18 (GB)
　　　Packers, 26-17 (D)
1937—Packers, 26-6 (GB)
　　　Packers, 14-13 (D)
1938—Lions, 17-7 (GB)
　　　Packers, 28-7 (D)
1939—Packers, 26-7 (GB)
　　　Packers, 12-7 (D)
1940—Lions, 23-14 (GB)
　　　Packers, 50-7 (D)
1941—Packers, 23-0 (GB)
　　　Packers, 24-7 (D)
1942—Packers, 38-7 (Mil)
　　　Packers, 28-7 (D)
1943—Packers, 35-14 (GB)
　　　Packers, 27-6 (D)
1944—Packers, 27-6 (Mil)
　　　Packers, 14-0 (D)
1945—Packers, 57-21 (Mil)
　　　Lions, 14-3 (D)
1946—Packers, 10-7 (Mil)
　　　Packers, 9-0 (D)
1947—Packers, 34-17 (GB)
　　　Packers, 35-14 (D)
1948—Packers, 33-21 (GB)
　　　Lions, 24-20 (D)
1949—Packers, 16-14 (Mil)
　　　Lions, 21-7 (D)
1950—Lions, 45-7 (GB)
　　　Lions, 24-21 (D)
1951—Lions, 24-17 (GB)
　　　Lions, 52-35 (D)

1952—Lions, 52-17 (GB)
　　　Lions, 48-24 (D)
1953—Lions, 14-7 (GB)
　　　Lions, 34-15 (D)
1954—Lions, 21-17 (GB)
　　　Lions, 28-24 (D)
1955—Packers, 20-17 (GB)
　　　Lions, 24-10 (D)
1956—Lions, 20-16 (GB)
　　　Packers, 24-20 (D)
1957—Packers, 24-14 (GB)
　　　Lions, 18-6 (D)
1958—Tie, 13-13 (GB)
　　　Lions, 24-14 (D)
1959—Packers, 28-10 (GB)
　　　Packers, 24-17 (D)
1960—Packers, 28-9 (GB)
　　　Lions, 23-10 (D)
1961—Lions, 17-13 (Mil)
　　　Packers, 17-9 (D)
1962—Packers, 9-7 (GB)
　　　Lions, 26-14 (D)
1963—Packers, 31-10 (Mil)
　　　Tie, 13-13 (D)
1964—Packers, 14-10 (D)
　　　Packers, 30-7 (GB)
1965—Packers, 31-21 (D)
　　　Lions, 12-7 (GB)
1966—Packers, 23-14 (GB)
　　　Packers, 31-7 (D)
1967—Tie, 17-17 (GB)
　　　Packers, 27-17 (D)
1968—Lions, 23-17 (GB)
　　　Tie, 14-14 (D)
1969—Packers, 28-17 (D)
　　　Lions, 16-10 (GB)
1970—Lions, 40-0 (GB)
　　　Lions, 20-0 (D)
1971—Lions, 31-28 (D)
　　　Tie, 14-14 (Mil)
1972—Packers, 24-23 (D)
　　　Packers, 33-7 (GB)
1973—Tie, 13-13 (GB)
　　　Lions, 34-0 (D)
1974—Packers, 21-19 (Mil)
　　　Lions, 19-17 (D)
1975—Lions, 30-16 (Mil)
　　　Lions, 13-10 (D)
1976—Packers, 24-14 (GB)
　　　Lions, 27-6 (D)
1977—Lions, 10-6 (D)
　　　Packers, 10-9 (GB)
1978—Packers, 13-7 (D)
　　　Packers, 35-14 (Mil)
1979—Packers, 24-16 (Mil)
　　　Packers, 18-13 (D)
1980—Lions, 29-7 (Mil)
　　　Lions, 24-3 (D)
1981—Lions, 31-27 (D)
　　　Packers, 31-17 (GB)
1982—Lions, 30-10 (D)
　　　Lions, 27-24 (D)
1983—Lions, 38-14 (D)
　　　Lions, 23-20 (Mil) OT
1984—Packers, 41-9 (GB)
　　　Lions, 31-28 (D)
1985—Packers, 43-10 (GB)
　　　Packers, 26-23 (D)
1986—Lions, 21-14 (GB)
　　　Packers, 44-40 (D)

1987—Lions, 19-16 (GB) OT
Packers, 34-33 (D)
1988—Lions, 19-9 (Mil)
Lions, 30-14 (D)
1989—Packers, 23-20 (Mil) OT
Lions, 31-22 (D)
1990—Packers, 24-21 (D)
Lions, 24-17 (GB)
1991—Lions, 23-14 (D)
Lions, 21-17 (GB)
1992—Packers, 27-13 (D)
Packers, 38-10 (Mil)
1993—Packers, 26-17 (Mil)
Lions, 30-20 (D)
**Packers, 28-24 (D)
1994—Packers, 38-30 (Mil)
Lions, 34-31 (D)
**Packers, 16-12 (GB)
1995—Packers, 30-21 (GB)
Lions, 24-16 (D)
1996—Packers, 28-18 (GB)
Packers, 31-3 (D)
1997—Lions, 26-15 (D)
Packers, 20-10 (GB)
1998—Packers, 38-19 (GB)
Lions, 27-20 (D)
1999—Lions, 23-15 (D)
Packers, 26-17 (GB)
2000—Lions, 31-24 (D)
Packers, 26-13 (GB)
2001—Packers, 28-6 (GB)
Packers, 29-27 (D)
2002—Packers, 37-31 (D)
Packers, 40-14 (GB)
2003—Packers, 31-6 (GB)
Lions, 22-14 (D)
2004—Packers, 38-10 (D)
Packers, 16-13 (GB)
(RS Pts.—Packers 3,078, Lions 2,696)
(PS Pts.—Packers 44, Lions 36)
*Franchise in Portsmouth prior to 1934
and known as the Spartans
**NFC First-Round Playoff
DETROIT vs. HOUSTON
RS: Lions lead series, 1-0
2004—Lions, 28-16 (D)
(RS Pts.—Lions 28, Texans 16)
DETROIT vs. *INDIANAPOLIS
RS: Colts lead series, 19-18-2
1953—Lions, 27-17 (B)
Lions, 17-7 (D)
1954—Lions, 35-0 (D)
Lions, 27-3 (B)
1955—Colts, 28-13 (B)
Lions, 24-14 (D)
1956—Lions, 31-14 (B)
Lions, 27-3 (D)
1957—Colts, 34-14 (B)
Lions, 31-27 (D)
1958—Colts, 28-15 (B)
Colts, 40-14 (D)
1959—Colts, 21-9 (B)
Colts, 31-24 (D)
1960—Lions, 30-17 (D)
Lions, 20-15 (B)
1961—Lions, 16-15 (B)
Colts, 17-14 (D)
1962—Lions, 29-20 (B)
Lions, 21-14 (D)
1963—Colts, 25-21 (D)

Colts, 24-21 (B)
1964—Colts, 34-0 (D)
Lions, 31-14 (B)
1965—Colts, 31-7 (B)
Tie, 24-24 (D)
1966—Colts, 45-14 (B)
Lions, 20-14 (D)
1967—Colts, 41-7 (B)
1968—Colts, 27-10 (D)
1969—Tie, 17-17 (B)
1973—Colts, 29-27 (D)
1977—Lions, 13-10 (B)
1980—Colts, 10-9 (D)
1985—Colts, 14-6 (I)
1991—Lions, 33-24 (I)
1997—Lions, 32-10 (D)
2000—Colts, 30-18 (I)
2004—Colts, 41-9 (D)
(RS Pts.—Colts 829, Lions 757)
*Franchise in Baltimore prior to 1984
DETROIT vs. JACKSONVILLE
RS: Jaguars lead series, 2-1
1995—Lions, 44-0 (D)
1998—Jaguars, 37-22 (J)
2004—Jaguars, 23-17 (J) OT
(RS Pts.—Lions 83, Jaguars 60)
DETROIT vs. KANSAS CITY
RS: Chiefs lead series, 7-3
1971—Lions, 32-21 (D)
1975—Chiefs, 24-21 (KC) OT
1980—Chiefs, 20-17 (KC)
1981—Lions, 27-10 (D)
1987—Chiefs, 27-20 (D)
1988—Lions, 7-6 (KC)
1990—Chiefs, 43-24 (KC)
1996—Chiefs, 28-24 (D)
1999—Chiefs, 31-21 (KC)
2003—Chiefs, 45-17 (KC)
(RS Pts.—Chiefs 255, Lions 210)
DETROIT vs. MIAMI
RS: Dolphins lead series, 6-2
1973—Dolphins, 34-7 (M)
1979—Dolphins, 28-10 (D)
1985—Lions, 31-21 (D)
1991—Lions, 17-13 (D)
1994—Dolphins, 27-20 (M)
1997—Dolphins, 33-30 (M)
2000—Dolphins, 23-8 (D)
2002—Dolphins, 49-21 (M)
(RS Pts.—Dolphins 228, Lions 144)
DETROIT vs. MINNESOTA
RS: Vikings lead series, 56-29-2
1961—Lions, 37-10 (M)
Lions, 13-7 (D)
1962—Lions, 17-6 (M)
Lions, 37-23 (D)
1963—Lions, 28-10 (D)
Vikings, 34-31 (M)
1964—Lions, 24-20 (M)
Tie, 23-23 (D)
1965—Lions, 31-29 (M)
Vikings, 29-7 (D)
1966—Lions, 32-31 (M)
Vikings, 28-16 (D)
1967—Tie, 10-10 (M)
Lions, 14-3 (D)
1968—Vikings, 24-10 (M)
Vikings, 13-6 (D)
1969—Vikings, 24-10 (M)
Vikings, 27-0 (D)

1970—Vikings, 30-17 (D)
Vikings, 24-20 (M)
1971—Vikings, 16-13 (D)
Vikings, 29-10 (M)
1972—Vikings, 34-10 (D)
Vikings, 16-14 (M)
1973—Vikings, 23-9 (D)
Vikings, 28-7 (M)
1974—Vikings, 7-6 (D)
Lions, 20-16 (M)
1975—Vikings, 25-19 (M)
Lions, 17-10 (D)
1976—Vikings, 10-9 (D)
Vikings, 31-23 (M)
1977—Vikings, 14-7 (M)
Vikings, 30-21 (D)
1978—Vikings, 17-7 (M)
Lions, 45-14 (D)
1979—Vikings, 13-10 (D)
Vikings, 14-7 (M)
1980—Lions, 27-7 (D)
Vikings, 34-0 (M)
1981—Vikings, 26-24 (M)
Lions, 45-7 (D)
1982—Vikings, 34-31 (D)
1983—Vikings, 20-17 (M)
Lions, 13-2 (D)
1984—Vikings, 29-28 (D)
Lions, 16-14 (M)
1985—Vikings, 16-13 (M)
Lions, 41-21 (D)
1986—Lions, 13-10 (M)
Vikings, 24-10 (D)
1987—Vikings, 34-19 (M)
Vikings, 17-14 (D)
1988—Vikings, 44-17 (M)
Vikings, 23-0 (D)
1989—Vikings, 24-17 (M)
Vikings, 20-7 (D)
1990—Lions, 34-27 (M)
Vikings, 17-7 (D)
1991—Lions, 24-20 (D)
Lions, 34-14 (M)
1992—Lions, 31-17 (D)
Vikings, 31-14 (M)
1993—Lions, 30-27 (M)
Vikings, 13-0 (D)
1994—Vikings, 10-3 (M)
Lions, 41-19 (D)
1995—Vikings, 20-10 (M)
Lions, 44-38 (D)
1996—Vikings, 17-13 (M)
Vikings, 24-22 (D)
1997—Lions, 38-15 (D)
Lions, 14-13 (M)
1998—Vikings, 29-6 (M)
Vikings, 34-13 (D)
1999—Lions, 25-23 (D)
Vikings, 24-17 (M)
2000—Vikings, 31-24 (D)
Vikings, 24-17 (M)
2001—Vikings, 31-26 (M)
Lions, 27-24 (D)
2002—Vikings, 31-24 (M)
Vikings, 38-36 (D)
2003—Vikings, 23-13 (D)
Vikings, 24-14 (M)
2004—Vikings, 22-19 (M)
Vikings, 28-27 (D)
(RS Pts.—Vikings 1,866, Lions 1,636)

DETROIT vs. NEW ENGLAND
RS: Series tied, 4-4
1971—Lions, 34-7 (NE)
1976—Lions, 30-10 (D)
1979—Patriots, 24-17 (NE)
1985—Patriots, 23-6 (NE)
1993—Lions, 19-16 (NE) OT
1994—Patriots, 23-17 (D)
2000—Lions, 34-9 (D)
2002—Patriots, 20-12 (D)
(RS Pts.—Lions 169, Patriots 132)

DETROIT vs. NEW ORLEANS
RS: Series tied, 8-8-1
1968—Tie, 20-20 (D)
1970—Saints, 19-17 (NO)
1972—Lions, 27-14 (D)
1973—Saints, 20-13 (NO)
1974—Lions, 19-14 (D)
1976—Saints, 17-16 (NO)
1977—Lions, 23-19 (D)
1979—Saints, 17-7 (NO)
1980—Lions, 24-13 (D)
1988—Saints, 22-14 (D)
1989—Lions, 21-14 (D)
1990—Lions, 27-10 (NO)
1992—Saints, 13-7 (D)
1993—Saints, 14-3 (NO)
1997—Saints, 35-17 (NO)
2000—Lions, 14-10 (NO)
2002—Lions, 26-21 (D)
(RS Pts.—Lions 295, Saints 292)

*DETROIT vs. N.Y. GIANTS
RS: Lions lead series, 20-17-1
PS: Lions lead series, 1-0
1930—Giants, 19-6 (P)
1931—Spartans, 14-6 (P)
    Giants, 14-0 (NY)
1932—Spartans, 7-0 (P)
    Spartans, 6-0 (NY)
1933—Spartans, 17-7 (P)
    Giants, 13-10 (NY)
1934—Lions, 9-0 (D)
1935—**Lions, 26-7 (D)
1936—Giants, 14-7 (NY)
    Lions, 38-0 (D)
1937—Lions, 17-0 (NY)
1939—Lions, 18-14 (D)
1941—Giants, 20-13 (NY)
1943—Tie, 0-0 (D)
1945—Giants, 35-14 (NY)
1947—Lions, 35-7 (D)
1949—Lions, 45-21 (NY)
1953—Lions, 27-16 (NY)
1955—Giants, 24-19 (D)
1958—Giants, 19-17 (D)
1962—Lions, 17-14 (NY)
1964—Lions, 26-3 (D)
1967—Lions, 30-7 (NY)
1969—Lions, 24-0 (D)
1972—Lions, 30-16 (D)
1974—Lions, 20-19 (D)
1976—Giants, 24-10 (NY)
1982—Giants, 13-6 (D)
1983—Lions, 15-9 (D)
1988—Giants, 30-10 (NY)
    Giants, 13-10 (D) OT
1989—Giants, 24-14 (NY)
1990—Giants, 20-0 (NY)
1994—Lions, 28-25 (NY) OT
1996—Giants, 35-7 (D)

1997—Giants, 26-20 (D) OT
2000—Lions, 31-21 (NY)
2004—Lions, 28-13 (NY)
(RS Pts.—Lions 642, Giants 544)
(PS Pts.—Lions 26, Giants 7)
*Franchise in Portsmouth prior to 1934
and known as the Spartans
**NFL Championship

DETROIT vs. N.Y. JETS
RS: Lions lead series, 6-4
1972—Lions, 37-20 (D)
1979—Jets, 31-10 (NY)
1982—Jets, 28-13 (D)
1985—Lions, 31-20 (D)
1988—Jets, 17-10 (D)
1991—Lions, 34-20 (D)
1994—Lions, 18-7 (NY)
1997—Lions, 13-10 (D)
2000—Lions, 10-7 (NY)
2002—Jets, 31-14 (D)
(RS Pts.—Jets 191, Lions 190)

DETROIT vs. *OAKLAND
RS: Raiders lead series, 6-3
1970—Lions, 28-14 (D)
1974—Raiders, 35-13 (O)
1978—Raiders, 29-17 (O)
1981—Lions, 16-0 (D)
1984—Raiders, 24-3 (D)
1987—Raiders, 27-7 (LA)
1990—Raiders, 38-31 (D)
1996—Raiders, 37-21 (O)
2003—Lions, 23-13 (D)
(RS Pts.—Raiders 217, Lions 159)
*Franchise in Los Angeles from 1982-1994

*DETROIT vs. PHILADELPHIA
RS: Series tied, 12-12-2
PS: Eagles lead series, 1-0
1933—Spartans, 25-0 (P)
1934—Lions, 10-0 (P)
1935—Lions, 35-0 (D)
1936—Lions, 23-0 (P)
1938—Eagles, 21-7 (D)
1940—Lions, 21-0 (P)
1941—Lions, 21-17 (D)
1945—Lions, 28-24 (D)
1948—Eagles, 45-21 (P)
1949—Eagles, 22-14 (D)
1951—Lions, 28-10 (P)
1954—Tie, 13-13 (D)
1957—Lions, 27-16 (P)
1960—Eagles, 28-10 (P)
1961—Eagles, 27-24 (D)
1965—Lions, 35-28 (P)
1968—Eagles, 12-0 (D)
1971—Eagles, 23-20 (D)
1974—Eagles, 28-17 (P)
1977—Lions, 17-13 (D)
1979—Eagles, 44-7 (P)
1984—Tie, 23-23 (D) OT
1986—Lions, 13-11 (P)
1995—**Eagles, 58-37 (P)
1996—Eagles, 24-17 (D)
1998—Eagles, 10-9 (P)
2004—Eagles, 30-13 (D)
(RS Pts.—Lions 478, Eagles 469)
(PS Pts.—Eagles 58, Lions 37)
*Franchise in Portsmouth prior to 1934
and known as the Spartans
**NFC First-Round Playoff

DETROIT vs. *PITTSBURGH
RS: Lions lead series, 14-13-1
1934—Lions, 40-7 (D)
1936—Lions, 28-3 (D)
1937—Lions, 7-3 (D)
1938—Lions, 16-7 (D)
1940—Pirates, 10-7 (D)
1942—Steelers, 35-7 (D)
1946—Lions, 17-7 (D)
1947—Steelers, 17-10 (P)
1948—Lions, 17-14 (D)
1949—Steelers, 14-7 (P)
1950—Lions, 10-7 (D)
1952—Lions, 31-6 (P)
1953—Lions, 38-21 (D)
1955—Lions, 31-28 (D)
1956—Lions, 45-7 (D)
1959—Tie, 10-10 (P)
1962—Lions, 45-7 (D)
1966—Steelers, 17-3 (P)
1967—Steelers, 24-14 (D)
1969—Steelers, 16-13 (P)
1973—Steelers, 24-10 (P)
1983—Lions, 45-3 (D)
1986—Steelers, 27-17 (P)
1989—Steelers, 23-3 (D)
1992—Steelers, 17-14 (P)
1995—Steelers, 23-20 (P)
1998—Lions, 19-16 (D) OT
2001—Steelers, 47-14 (P)
(RS Pts.—Lions 538, Steelers 440)
*Steelers known as Pirates prior to 1941

DETROIT vs. *ST. LOUIS
RS: Rams lead series, 40-37-1
PS: Lions lead series, 1-0
1937—Lions, 28-0 (C)
    Lions, 27-7 (D)
1938—Rams, 21-17 (C)
    Lions, 6-0 (D)
1939—Lions, 15-7 (D)
    Rams, 14-3 (C)
1940—Lions, 6-0 (D)
    Rams, 24-0 (C)
1941—Lions, 17-7 (D)
    Lions, 14-0 (C)
1942—Rams, 14-0 (D)
    Rams, 27-7 (C)
1944—Rams, 20-17 (D)
    Lions, 26-14 (C)
1945—Rams, 28-21 (D)
1946—Rams, 35-14 (LA)
    Rams, 41-20 (D)
1947—Rams, 27-13 (D)
    Rams, 28-17 (LA)
1948—Rams, 44-7 (LA)
    Rams, 34-27 (D)
1949—Rams, 27-24 (LA)
    Rams, 21-10 (D)
1950—Rams, 30-28 (D)
    Rams, 65-24 (LA)
1951—Rams, 27-21 (D)
    Lions, 24-22 (LA)
1952—Lions, 17-14 (LA)
    Lions, 24-16 (D)
    **Lions, 31-21 (D)
1953—Rams, 31-19 (D)
    Rams, 37-24 (LA)
1954—Lions, 21-3 (D)
    Lions, 27-24 (LA)
1955—Rams, 17-10 (D)

Rams, 24-13 (LA)
1956—Lions, 24-21 (D)
Lions, 16-7 (D)
1957—Lions, 10-7 (D)
Rams, 35-17 (LA)
1958—Rams, 42-28 (D)
Lions, 41-24 (LA)
1959—Lions, 17-7 (LA)
Lions, 23-17 (D)
1960—Rams, 48-35 (LA)
Lions, 12-10 (D)
1961—Lions, 14-13 (D)
Lions, 28-10 (LA)
1962—Lions, 13-10 (D)
Lions, 12-3 (LA)
1963—Lions, 23-2 (LA)
Rams, 28-21 (D)
1964—Tie, 17-17 (LA)
Lions, 37-17 (D)
1965—Lions, 20-0 (D)
Lions, 31-7 (LA)
1966—Rams, 14-7 (D)
Rams, 23-3 (LA)
1967—Rams, 31-7 (D)
1968—Rams, 10-7 (LA)
1969—Lions, 28-0 (D)
1970—Lions, 28-23 (LA)
1971—Rams, 21-13 (D)
1972—Lions, 34-17 (LA)
1974—Rams, 16-13 (LA)
1975—Rams, 20-0 (D)
1976—Rams, 20-17 (D)
1980—Lions, 41-20 (LA)
1981—Rams, 20-13 (LA)
1982—Lions, 19-14 (LA)
1983—Rams, 21-10 (LA)
1986—Rams, 14-10 (LA)
1987—Rams, 37-16 (D)
1988—Rams, 17-10 (LA)
1991—Lions, 21-10 (D)
1993—Lions, 16-13 (LA)
1999—Lions, 31-27 (D)
2001—Rams, 35-0 (D)
2003—Lions, 30-20 (D)
(RS Pts.—Rams 1,518, Lions 1,401)
(PS Pts.—Lions 31, Rams 21)
*Franchise in Los Angeles prior to 1995
and in Cleveland prior to 1946
**Conference Playoff
DETROIT vs. SAN DIEGO
RS: Chargers lead series, 5-3
1972—Lions, 34-20 (D)
1977—Lions, 20-0 (D)
1978—Lions, 31-14 (D)
1981—Chargers, 28-23 (SD)
1984—Chargers, 27-24 (SD)
1996—Chargers, 27-21 (SD)
1999—Chargers, 20-10 (D)
2003—Chargers, 14-7 (D)
(RS Pts.—Lions 170, Chargers 150)
DETROIT vs. SAN FRANCISCO
RS: 49ers lead series, 31-26-1
PS: Series tied, 1-1
1950—Lions, 24-7 (D)
49ers, 28-27 (SF)
1951—49ers, 20-10 (D)
49ers, 21-17 (SF)
1952—49ers, 17-3 (SF)
49ers, 28-0 (D)
1953—Lions, 24-21 (D)

Lions, 14-10 (SF)
1954—49ers, 37-31 (SF)
Lions, 48-7 (D)
1955—49ers, 27-24 (D)
49ers, 38-21 (SF)
1956—Lions, 20-17 (D)
Lions, 17-13 (SF)
1957—49ers, 35-31 (SF)
Lions, 31-10 (D)
*Lions, 31-27 (SF)
1958—49ers, 24-21 (SF)
Lions, 35-21 (D)
1959—49ers, 34-13 (D)
49ers, 33-7 (SF)
1960—49ers, 14-10 (D)
Lions, 24-0 (SF)
1961—49ers, 49-0 (D)
Tie, 20-20 (SF)
1962—Lions, 45-24 (D)
Lions, 38-24 (SF)
1963—Lions, 26-3 (D)
Lions, 45-7 (SF)
1964—Lions, 26-17 (SF)
Lions, 24-7 (D)
1965—49ers, 27-21 (D)
49ers, 17-14 (SF)
1966—49ers, 27-24 (SF)
49ers, 41-14 (D)
1967—Lions, 45-3 (SF)
1968—49ers, 14-7 (D)
1969—Lions, 26-14 (SF)
1970—Lions, 28-7 (D)
1971—49ers, 31-27 (SF)
1973—Lions, 30-20 (D)
1974—Lions, 17-13 (D)
1975—Lions, 28-17 (D)
1977—49ers, 28-7 (SF)
1978—Lions, 33-14 (D)
1980—Lions, 17-13 (D)
1981—Lions, 24-17 (D)
1983—**49ers, 24-23 (SF)
1984—49ers, 30-27 (D)
1985—Lions, 23-21 (D)
1988—49ers, 20-13 (SF)
1991—49ers, 35-3 (SF)
1992—49ers, 24-6 (SF)
1993—49ers, 55-17 (D)
1994—49ers, 27-21 (D)
1995—Lions, 27-24 (D)
1996—49ers, 24-14 (SF)
1998—49ers, 35-13 (SF)
2001—49ers, 21-13 (SF)
2003—49ers, 24-17 (SF)
(RS Pts.—49ers 1,256, Lions 1,232)
(PS Pts.—Lions 54, 49ers 51)
*Conference Playoff
**NFC Divisional Playoff
DETROIT vs. SEATTLE
RS: Seahawks lead series, 5-4
1976—Lions, 41-14 (S)
1978—Seahawks, 28-16 (S)
1984—Seahawks, 38-17 (S)
1987—Seahawks, 37-14 (D)
1990—Seahawks, 30-10 (S)
1993—Lions, 30-10 (D)
1996—Lions, 17-16 (D)
1999—Lions, 28-20 (S)
2003—Seahawks, 35-14 (S)
(RS Pts.—Seahawks 228, Lions 187)

DETROIT vs. TAMPA BAY
RS: Lions lead series, 26-23
PS: Buccaneers lead series, 1-0
1977—Lions, 16-7 (D)
1978—Lions, 15-7 (TB)
Lions, 34-23 (D)
1979—Buccaneers, 31-16 (TB)
Buccaneers, 16-14 (D)
1980—Lions, 24-10 (TB)
Lions, 27-14 (D)
1981—Buccaneers, 28-10 (TB)
Buccaneers, 20-17 (D)
1982—Buccaneers, 23-21 (TB)
1983—Lions, 11-0 (TB)
Lions, 23-20 (D)
1984—Buccaneers, 21-17 (TB)
Lions, 13-7 (D) OT
1985—Lions, 30-9 (D)
Buccaneers, 19-16 (TB) OT
1986—Buccaneers, 24-20 (D)
Lions, 38-17 (TB)
1987—Buccaneers, 31-27 (D)
Lions, 20-10 (TB)
1988—Buccaneers, 23-20 (D)
Buccaneers, 21-10 (TB)
1989—Lions, 17-16 (TB)
Lions, 33-7 (D)
1990—Buccaneers, 38-21 (D)
Buccaneers, 23-20 (TB)
1991—Lions, 31-3 (D)
Buccaneers, 30-21 (TB)
1992—Buccaneers, 27-23 (D)
Lions, 38-7 (TB)
1993—Buccaneers, 27-10 (TB)
Lions, 23-0 (D)
1994—Buccaneers, 24-14 (TB)
Lions, 14-9 (D)
1995—Lions, 27-24 (D)
Lions, 37-10 (TB)
1996—Lions, 21-6 (D)
Lions, 27-0 (TB)
1997—Buccaneers, 24-17 (D)
Lions, 27-9 (TB)
*Buccaneers, 20-10 (TB)
1998—Lions, 27-6 (D)
Lions, 28-25 (TB)
1999—Lions, 20-3 (D)
Buccaneers, 23-16 (TB)
2000—Buccaneers, 31-10 (D)
Lions, 28-14 (TB)
2001—Buccaneers, 20-17 (D)
Buccaneers, 15-12 (TB)
2002—Buccaneers, 23-20 (D)
(RS Pts—Lions 1,038, Buccaneers 825)
(PS Pts.—Buccaneers 20, Lions 10)
*NFC First-Round Playoff
DETROIT vs. TENNESSEE
RS: Titans lead series, 6-3
1971—Lions, 31-7 (H)
1975—Oilers, 24-8 (H)
1983—Oilers, 27-17 (H)
1986—Lions, 24-13 (D)
1989—Oilers, 35-31 (H)
1992—Oilers, 24-21 (D)
1995—Lions, 24-17 (D)
2001—Titans, 27-24 (D)
2004—Titans, 24-19 (T)
(RS Pts.—Lions 199, Titans 198)
*Franchise in Houston prior to 1997;
known as Oilers prior to 1999

*DETROIT vs. **WASHINGTON
RS: Redskins lead series, 25-10
PS: Redskins lead series, 3-0
1932—Spartans, 10-0 (P)
1933—Spartans, 13-0 (B)
1934—Lions, 24-0 (D)
1935—Lions, 17-7 (B)
　　　Lions, 14-0 (D)
1938—Redskins, 7-5 (D)
1939—Redskins, 31-7 (W)
1940—Redskins, 20-14 (D)
1942—Redskins, 15-3 (D)
1943—Redskins, 42-20 (W)
1946—Redskins, 17-16 (W)
1947—Lions, 38-21 (D)
1948—Redskins, 46-21 (W)
1951—Lions, 35-17 (D)
1956—Redskins, 18-17 (W)
1965—Lions, 14-10 (D)
1968—Redskins, 14-3 (W)
1970—Redskins, 31-10 (W)
1973—Redskins, 20-0 (D)
1976—Redskins, 20-7 (W)
1978—Redskins, 21-19 (D)
1979—Redskins, 27-24 (D)
1981—Redskins, 33-31 (W)
1982—***Redskins, 31-7 (W)
1983—Redskins, 38-17 (W)
1984—Redskins, 28-14 (W)
1985—Redskins, 24-3 (W)
1987—Redskins, 20-13 (W)
1990—Redskins, 41-38 (D) OT
1991—Redskins, 45-0 (W)
　　　****Redskins, 41-10 (W)
1992—Redskins, 13-10 (W)
1995—Redskins, 36-30 (W) OT
1997—Redskins, 30-7 (W)
1999—Lions, 33-17 (D)
　　　***Redskins, 27-13 (W)
2000—Lions, 15-10 (D)
2004—Redskins, 17-10 (D)
(RS Pts.—Redskins 736, Lions 552)
(PS Pts.—Redskins 99, Lions 30)
**Franchise in Portsmouth prior to 1934
and known as the Spartans.*
**Franchise in Boston prior to 1937
***NFC First-Round Playoff
****NFC Championship

GREEN BAY vs. ARIZONA
RS: Packers lead series, 41-22-4
PS: Packers lead series, 1-0;
See Arizona vs. Green Bay
GREEN BAY vs. ATLANTA
RS: Packers lead series, 11-10
PS: Series tied, 1-1;
See Atlanta vs. Green Bay
GREEN BAY vs. BALTIMORE
RS: Packers lead series, 2-0;
See Baltimore vs. Green Bay
GREEN BAY vs. BUFFALO
RS: Bills lead series, 6-3;
See Buffalo vs. Green Bay
GREEN BAY vs. CAROLINA
RS: Packers lead series, 5-2
PS: Packers lead series, 1-0;
See Carolina vs. Green Bay
GREEN BAY vs. CHICAGO
RS: Bears lead series, 84-78-6
PS: Bears lead series, 1-0;

See Chicago vs. Green Bay
GREEN BAY vs. CINCINNATI
RS: Packers lead series, 5-4;
See Cincinnati vs. Green Bay
GREEN BAY vs. CLEVELAND
RS: Packers lead series, 9-6
PS: Packers lead series, 1-0;
See Cleveland vs. Green Bay
GREEN BAY vs. DALLAS
RS: Series tied, 10-10
PS: Cowboys lead series, 4-2;
See Dallas vs. Green Bay
GREEN BAY vs. DENVER
RS: Broncos lead series, 5-4-1
PS: Broncos lead series, 1-0;
See Denver vs. Green Bay
GREEN BAY vs. DETROIT
RS: Packers lead series, 79-63-7
PS: Packers lead series, 2-0;
See Detroit vs. Green Bay
GREEN BAY vs. HOUSTON
RS: Packers lead series, 1-0
2004—Packers, 16-13 (H)
(RS Pts.—Packers 16, Texans 13)
GREEN BAY vs. *INDIANAPOLIS
RS: Colts lead series, 20-19-1
PS: Packers lead series, 1-0
1953—Packers, 37-14 (GB)
　　　Packers, 35-24 (B)
1954—Packers, 7-6 (B)
　　　Packers, 24-13 (Mil)
1955—Colts, 24-20 (Mil)
　　　Colts, 14-10 (B)
1956—Packers, 38-33 (Mil)
　　　Colts, 28-21 (B)
1957—Colts, 45-17 (Mil)
　　　Packers, 24-21 (B)
1958—Colts, 24-17 (Mil)
　　　Colts, 56-0 (B)
1959—Colts, 38-21 (B)
　　　Colts, 28-24 (Mil)
1960—Packers, 35-21 (GB)
　　　Colts, 38-24 (B)
1961—Packers, 45-7 (GB)
　　　Colts, 45-21 (B)
1962—Packers, 17-6 (B)
　　　Packers, 17-13 (GB)
1963—Packers, 31-20 (GB)
　　　Packers, 34-20 (B)
1964—Colts, 21-20 (GB)
　　　Colts, 24-21 (B)
1965—Packers, 20-17 (Mil)
　　　Packers, 42-27 (B)
　　　**Packers, 13-10 (GB) OT
1966—Packers, 24-3 (Mil)
　　　Packers, 14-10 (B)
1967—Colts, 13-10 (B)
1968—Colts, 16-3 (GB)
1969—Colts, 14-6 (B)
1970—Colts, 13-10 (Mil)
1974—Packers, 20-13 (B)
1982—Tie, 20-20 (B) OT
1985—Colts, 37-10 (I)
1988—Colts, 20-13 (GB)
1991—Packers, 14-10 (Mil)
1997—Colts, 41-38 (I)
2000—Packers, 26-24 (GB)
2004—Colts, 45-31 (I)
(RS Pts.—Colts 906, Packers 861)
(PS Pts.—Packers 13, Colts 10)

*Franchise in Baltimore prior to 1984
**Conference Playoff
GREEN BAY vs. JACKSONVILLE
RS: Packers lead series, 2-1
1995—Packers, 24-14 (J)
2001—Packers, 28-21 (J)
2004—Jaguars, 28-25 (GB)
(RS Pts.—Packers 77, Jaguars 63)
GREEN BAY vs. KANSAS CITY
RS: Chiefs lead series, 6-1-1
PS: Packers lead series, 1-0
1966—*Packers, 35-10 (Los Angeles)
1973—Tie, 10-10 (Mil)
1977—Chiefs, 20-10 (KC)
1987—Packers, 23-3 (KC)
1989—Chiefs, 21-3 (GB)
1990—Chiefs, 17-3 (GB)
1993—Chiefs, 23-16 (KC)
1996—Chiefs, 27-20 (KC)
2003—Chiefs, 40-34 (GB) OT
(RS Pts.—Chiefs 161, Packers 119)
(PS Pts.—Packers 35, Chiefs 10)
*Super Bowl I
GREEN BAY vs. MIAMI
RS: Dolphins lead series, 9-2
1971—Dolphins, 27-6 (Mia)
1975—Dolphins, 31-7 (GB)
1979—Dolphins, 27-7 (Mia)
1985—Dolphins, 34-24 (GB)
1988—Dolphins, 24-17 (Mia)
1989—Dolphins, 23-20 (Mia)
1991—Dolphins, 16-13 (Mia)
1994—Dolphins, 24-14 (Mil)
1997—Packers, 23-18 (GB)
2000—Dolphins, 28-20 (Mia)
2002—Packers, 24-10 (GB)
(RS Pts.—Dolphins 262, Packers 175)
GREEN BAY vs. MINNESOTA
RS: Packers lead series, 44-42-1
PS: Vikings lead series, 1-0
1961—Packers, 33-7 (Minn)
　　　Packers, 28-10 (Mil)
1962—Packers, 34-7 (GB)
　　　Packers, 48-21 (Minn)
1963—Packers, 37-28 (Minn)
　　　Packers, 28-7 (GB)
1964—Vikings, 24-23 (GB)
　　　Packers, 42-13 (Minn)
1965—Packers, 38-13 (Minn)
　　　Packers, 24-19 (GB)
1966—Vikings, 20-17 (GB)
　　　Packers, 28-16 (Minn)
1967—Vikings, 10-7 (Mil)
　　　Packers, 30-27 (Minn)
1968—Packers, 26-13 (Mil)
　　　Vikings, 14-10 (Minn)
1969—Vikings, 19-7 (Minn)
　　　Vikings, 9-7 (Mil)
1970—Packers, 13-10 (Mil)
　　　Vikings, 10-3 (Minn)
1971—Vikings, 24-13 (GB)
　　　Vikings, 3-0 (Minn)
1972—Vikings, 27-13 (GB)
　　　Packers, 23-7 (Minn)
1973—Vikings, 11-3 (Minn)
　　　Vikings, 31-7 (GB)
1974—Vikings, 32-17 (GB)
　　　Packers, 19-7 (Minn)
1975—Vikings, 28-17 (GB)
　　　Vikings, 24-3 (Minn)

1976—Vikings, 17-10 (Mil)
Vikings, 20-9 (Minn)
1977—Vikings, 19-7 (Minn)
Vikings, 13-6 (GB)
1978—Vikings, 21-7 (Minn)
Tie, 10-10 (GB) OT
1979—Vikings, 27-21 (Minn) OT
Packers, 19-7 (Mil)
1980—Packers, 16-3 (GB)
Packers, 25-13 (Minn)
1981—Vikings, 30-13 (Mil)
Packers, 35-23 (Minn)
1982—Packers, 26-7 (Mil)
1983—Vikings, 20-17 (GB) OT
Packers, 29-21 (Minn)
1984—Packers, 45-17 (Mil)
Packers, 38-14 (Minn)
1985—Packers, 20-17 (Mil)
Packers, 27-17 (Minn)
1986—Vikings, 42-7 (Minn)
Vikings, 32-6 (GB)
1987—Packers, 23-16 (Minn)
Packers, 16-10 (Mil)
1988—Packers, 34-14 (Minn)
Packers, 18-6 (GB)
1989—Vikings, 26-14 (Minn)
Packers, 20-19 (Mil)
1990—Packers, 24-10 (Mil)
Vikings, 23-7 (Minn)
1991—Vikings, 35-21 (GB)
Packers, 27-7 (Minn)
1992—Vikings, 23-20 (GB) OT
Vikings, 27-7 (Minn)
1993—Vikings, 15-13 (Minn)
Vikings, 21-17 (Mil)
1994—Packers, 16-10 (GB)
Vikings, 13-10 (Minn) OT
1995—Packers, 38-21 (GB)
Vikings, 27-24 (Minn)
1996—Vikings, 30-21 (Minn)
Packers, 38-10 (GB)
1997—Packers, 38-32 (GB)
Packers, 27-11 (Minn)
1998—Vikings, 37-24 (GB)
Vikings, 28-14 (Minn)
1999—Packers, 23-20 (GB)
Vikings, 24-20 (Minn)
2000—Packers, 26-20 (GB) OT
Packers, 33-28 (Minn)
2001—Vikings, 35-13 (Minn)
Packers, 24-13 (GB)
2002—Vikings, 31-21 (Minn)
Packers, 26-22 (GB)
2003—Vikings, 30-25 (GB)
Packers, 30-27 (M)
2004—Packers, 34-31 (GB)
Packers, 34-31 (M)
*Vikings, 31-17 (GB)
(RS Pts.—Packers 1,798, Vikings 1,677)
(PS Pts.—Vikings 31, Packers 17)
*NFC First-Round Playoff
GREEN BAY vs. NEW ENGLAND
RS: Packers lead series, 4-3
PS: Packers lead series, 1-0
1973—Patriots, 33-24 (NE)
1979—Packers, 27-14 (GB)
1985—Patriots, 26-20 (NE)
1988—Packers, 45-3 (Mil)
1994—Patriots, 17-16 (NE)
1996—*Packers, 35-21 (New Orleans)

1997—Packers, 28-10 (NE)
2002—Packers, 28-10 (NE)
(RS Pts.—Packers 188, Patriots 113)
(PS Pts.—Packers 35, Patriots 21)
*Super Bowl XXXI
GREEN BAY vs. NEW ORLEANS
RS: Packers lead series, 13-5
1968—Packers, 29-7 (Mil)
1971—Saints, 29-21 (Mil)
1972—Packers, 30-20 (NO)
1973—Packers, 30-10 (Mil)
1975—Saints, 20-19 (NO)
1976—Packers, 32-27 (Mil)
1977—Packers, 24-20 (NO)
1978—Packers, 28-17 (Mil)
1979—Packers, 28-19 (Mil)
1981—Packers, 35-7 (NO)
1984—Packers, 23-13 (NO)
1985—Packers, 38-14 (Mil)
1986—Saints, 24-10 (NO)
1987—Saints, 33-24 (NO)
1989—Packers, 35-34 (GB)
1993—Packers, 19-17 (NO)
1995—Packers, 34-23 (NO)
2002—Saints, 35-20 (NO)
(RS Pts.—Packers 479, Saints 369)
GREEN BAY vs. N.Y. GIANTS
RS: Packers lead series, 24-21-2
PS: Packers lead series, 4-1
1928—Giants, 6-0 (GB)
Packers, 7-0 (NY)
1929—Packers, 20-6 (NY)
1930—Packers, 14-7 (GB)
Giants, 13-6 (NY)
1931—Packers, 27-7 (GB)
Packers, 14-10 (NY)
1932—Packers, 13-0 (GB)
Giants, 6-0 (NY)
1933—Giants, 10-7 (Mil)
Giants, 17-6 (NY)
1934—Packers, 20-6 (Mil)
Giants, 17-3 (NY)
1935—Packers, 16-7 (GB)
1936—Packers, 26-14 (NY)
1937—Giants, 10-0 (NY)
1938—Giants, 15-3 (NY)
*Giants, 23-17 (NY)
1939—*Packers, 27-0 (Mil)
1940—Packers, 7-3 (NY)
1942—Tie, 21-21 (NY)
1943—Packers, 35-21 (NY)
1944—Giants, 24-0 (NY)
*Packers, 14-7 (NY)
1945—Packers, 23-14 (NY)
1947—Tie, 24-24 (NY)
1948—Giants, 49-3 (Mil)
1949—Giants, 30-10 (GB)
1952—Packers, 17-3 (NY)
1957—Giants, 31-17 (GB)
1959—Giants, 20-3 (NY)
1961—Packers, 20-17 (Mil)
*Packers, 37-0 (GB)
1962—*Packers, 16-7 (NY)
1967—Packers, 48-21 (NY)
1969—Packers, 20-10 (Mil)
1971—Giants, 42-40 (GB)
1973—Packers, 16-14 (New Haven)
1975—Packers, 40-14 (Mil)
1980—Giants, 27-21 (NY)
1981—Packers, 27-14 (NY)

Packers, 26-24 (Mil)
1982—Packers, 27-19 (NY)
1983—Giants, 27-3 (NY)
1985—Packers, 23-20 (GB)
1986—Giants, 55-24 (NY)
1987—Giants, 20-10 (NY)
1992—Giants, 27-7 (NY)
1995—Packers, 14-6 (GB)
1998—Packers, 37-3 (NY)
2001—Packers, 34-25 (NY)
2004—Giants, 14-7 (GB)
(RS Pts.—Giants 794, Packers 782)
(PS Pts.—Packers 111, Giants 37)
*NFL Championship
GREEN BAY vs. N.Y. JETS
RS: Jets lead series, 7-2
1973—Packers, 23-7 (Mil)
1979—Jets, 27-22 (GB)
1981—Jets, 28-3 (NY)
1982—Jets, 15-13 (NY)
1985—Jets, 24-3 (Mil)
1991—Jets, 19-16 (NY) OT
1994—Packers, 17-10 (GB)
2000—Jets, 20-16 (GB)
2002—Jets, 42-17 (NY)
(RS Pts.—Jets 192, Packers 130)
GREEN BAY vs. *OAKLAND
RS: Raiders lead series, 5-4
PS: Packers lead series, 1-0
1967—**Packers, 33-14 (Miami)
1972—Raiders, 20-14 (GB)
1976—Raiders, 18-14 (O)
1978—Raiders, 28-3 (GB)
1984—Raiders, 28-7 (LA)
1987—Raiders, 20-0 (GB)
1990—Packers, 29-16 (LA)
1993—Packers, 28-0 (GB)
1999—Packers, 28-24 (GB)
2003—Packers, 41-7 (O)
(RS Pts.—Packers 164, Raiders 161)
(PS Pts.—Packers 33, Raiders 14)
*Franchise in Los Angeles from 1982-1994
**Super Bowl II
GREEN BAY vs. PHILADELPHIA
RS: Packers lead series, 22-11
PS: Eagles lead series, 2-0
1933—Packers, 35-9 (GB)
Packers, 10-0 (P)
1934—Packers, 19-6 (GB)
1935—Packers, 13-6 (P)
1937—Packers, 37-7 (Mil)
1939—Packers, 23-16 (P)
1940—Packers, 27-20 (GB)
1942—Packers, 7-0 (P)
1946—Packers, 19-7 (P)
1947—Eagles, 28-14 (P)
1951—Packers, 37-24 (GB)
1952—Packers, 12-10 (Mil)
1954—Packers, 37-14 (P)
1958—Packers, 38-35 (GB)
1960—*Eagles, 17-13 (P)
1962—Packers, 49-0 (P)
1968—Packers, 30-13 (GB)
1970—Packers, 30-17 (Mil)
1974—Eagles, 36-14 (P)
1976—Packers, 28-13 (GB)
1978—Eagles, 10-3 (P)
1979—Eagles, 21-10 (GB)
1987—Packers, 16-10 (GB) OT
1990—Eagles, 31-0 (P)

1991—Eagles, 20-3 (GB)
1992—Packers, 27-24 (Mil)
1993—Eagles, 20-17 (GB)
1994—Eagles, 13-7 (P)
1996—Packers, 39-13 (GB)
1997—Eagles, 10-9 (P)
1998—Packers, 24-16 (GB)
2000—Packers, 6-3 (GB)
2003—Eagles, 17-14 (GB)
 **Eagles, 20-17 (P) OT
2004—Eagles, 47-17 (P)
(RS Pts.—Packers 671, Eagles 516)
(PS Pts.—Eagles 37, Packers 30)
*NFL Championship
**NFC Divisional Playoff
GREEN BAY vs. *PITTSBURGH
RS: Packers lead series, 18-12
1933—Packers, 47-0 (GB)
1935—Packers, 27-0 (GB)
 Packers, 34-14 (P)
1936—Packers, 42-10 (Mil)
1938—Packers, 20-0 (GB)
1940—Packers, 24-3 (Mil)
1941—Packers, 54-7 (P)
1942—Packers, 24-21 (Mil)
1946—Packers, 17-7 (GB)
1947—Steelers, 18-17 (Mil)
1948—Steelers, 38-7 (P)
1949—Steelers, 30-7 (Mil)
1951—Packers, 35-33 (Mil)
 Steelers, 28-7 (P)
1953—Steelers, 31-14 (P)
1954—Steelers, 21-20 (GB)
1957—Packers, 27-10 (P)
1960—Packers, 19-13 (P)
1963—Packers, 33-14 (Mil)
1965—Packers, 41-9 (P)
1967—Steelers, 24-17 (GB)
1969—Packers, 38-34 (P)
1970—Packers, 20-12 (P)
1975—Steelers, 16-13 (Mil)
1980—Steelers, 22-20 (P)
1983—Steelers, 25-21 (GB)
1986—Steelers, 27-3 (P)
1992—Packers, 17-3 (GB)
1995—Packers, 24-19 (GB)
1998—Steelers, 27-20 (P)
(RS Pts.—Packers 709, Steelers 516)
*Steelers known as Pirates prior to 1941
GREEN BAY vs. *ST. LOUIS
RS: Rams lead series, 44-40-2
PS: Series tied, 1-1
1937—Packers, 35-10 (C)
 Packers, 35-7 (GB)
1938—Packers, 26-17 (GB)
 Packers, 28-7 (C)
1939—Rams, 27-24 (GB)
 Packers, 7-6 (C)
1940—Packers, 31-14 (GB)
 Tie, 13-13 (C)
1941—Packers, 24-7 (Mil)
 Packers, 17-14 (C)
1942—Packers, 45-28 (GB)
 Packers, 30-12 (C)
1944—Packers, 30-21 (GB)
 Packers, 42-7 (C)
1945—Rams, 27-14 (GB)
 Rams, 20-7 (C)
1946—Rams, 21-17 (Mil)
 Rams, 38-17 (LA)

1947—Packers, 17-14 (Mil)
 Packers, 30-10 (LA)
1948—Packers, 16-0 (GB)
 Rams, 24-10 (LA)
1949—Rams, 48-7 (GB)
 Rams, 35-7 (LA)
1950—Rams, 45-14 (GB)
 Rams, 51-14 (LA)
1951—Rams, 28-0 (Mil)
 Rams, 42-14 (LA)
1952—Rams, 30-28 (Mil)
 Rams, 45-27 (LA)
1953—Rams, 38-20 (Mil)
 Rams, 33-17 (LA)
1954—Packers, 35-17 (Mil)
 Rams, 35-27 (LA)
1955—Packers, 30-28 (Mil)
 Rams, 31-17 (LA)
1956—Packers, 42-17 (Mil)
 Rams, 49-21 (LA)
1957—Rams, 31-27 (Mil)
 Rams, 42-17 (LA)
1958—Rams, 20-7 (GB)
 Rams, 34-20 (LA)
1959—Rams, 45-6 (Mil)
 Packers, 38-20 (LA)
1960—Rams, 33-31 (Mil)
 Packers, 35-21 (LA)
1961—Packers, 35-17 (GB)
 Packers, 24-17 (LA)
1962—Packers, 41-10 (Mil)
 Packers, 20-17 (LA)
1963—Packers, 42-10 (GB)
 Packers, 31-14 (LA)
1964—Rams, 27-17 (Mil)
 Tie, 24-24 (LA)
1965—Packers, 6-3 (Mil)
 Rams, 21-10 (LA)
1966—Packers, 24-13 (GB)
 Packers, 27-23 (LA)
1967—Rams, 27-24 (LA)
 **Packers, 28-7 (Mil)
1968—Rams, 16-14 (Mil)
1969—Rams, 34-21 (LA)
1970—Rams, 31-21 (GB)
1971—Rams, 30-13 (LA)
1973—Rams, 24-7 (LA)
1974—Packers, 17-6 (Mil)
1975—Rams, 22-5 (LA)
1977—Rams, 24-6 (Mil)
1978—Rams, 31-14 (LA)
1980—Rams, 51-21 (LA)
1981—Rams, 35-23 (LA)
1982—Packers, 35-23 (Mil)
1983—Packers, 27-24 (Mil)
1984—Packers, 31-6 (Mil)
1985—Rams, 34-17 (LA)
1988—Rams, 34-7 (GB)
1989—Rams, 41-38 (LA)
1990—Packers, 36-24 (GB)
1991—Rams, 23-21 (LA)
1992—Packers, 28-13 (GB)
1993—Packers, 36-6 (Mil)
1994—Packers, 24-17 (GB)
1995—Rams, 17-14 (GB)
1996—Packers, 24-9 (StL)
1997—Packers, 17-7 (GB)
2001—***Rams, 45-17 (StL)
2003—Rams, 34-24 (StL)
2004—Packers, 45-17 (GB)

(RS Pts.—Rams 2,018, Packers 1,927)
(PS Pts.—Rams 52, Packers 45)
*Franchise in Los Angeles prior to 1995
and in Cleveland prior to 1946
**Conference Championship
***NFC Divisional Playoff
GREEN BAY vs. SAN DIEGO
RS: Packers lead series, 7-1
1970—Packers, 22-20 (SD)
1974—Packers, 34-0 (GB)
1978—Packers, 24-3 (SD)
1984—Chargers, 34-28 (GB)
1993—Packers, 20-13 (SD)
1996—Packers, 42-10 (GB)
1999—Packers, 31-3 (SD)
2003—Packers, 38-21 (SD)
(RS Pts.—Packers 239, Chargers 104)
GREEN BAY vs. SAN FRANCISCO
RS: Packers lead series, 27-25-1
PS: Packers lead series, 4-1
1950—Packers, 25-21 (GB)
 49ers, 30-14 (SF)
1951—49ers, 31-19 (SF)
1952—49ers, 24-14 (SF)
1953—49ers, 37-7 (Mil)
 49ers, 48-14 (SF)
1954—49ers, 23-17 (Mil)
 49ers, 35-0 (SF)
1955—Packers, 27-21 (GB)
 Packers, 28-7 (SF)
1956—49ers, 17-16 (GB)
 49ers, 38-20 (SF)
1957—49ers, 24-14 (Mil)
 49ers, 27-20 (SF)
1958—49ers, 33-12 (Mil)
 49ers, 48-21 (SF)
1959—Packers, 21-20 (GB)
 Packers, 36-14 (SF)
1960—Packers, 41-14 (Mil)
 Packers, 13-0 (SF)
1961—Packers, 30-10 (GB)
 49ers, 22-21 (SF)
1962—Packers, 31-13 (Mil)
 Packers, 31-21 (SF)
1963—Packers, 28-10 (Mil)
 Packers, 21-17 (SF)
1964—Packers, 24-14 (Mil)
 49ers, 24-14 (SF)
1965—Packers, 27-10 (GB)
 Tie, 24-24 (SF)
1966—49ers, 21-20 (SF)
 Packers, 20-7 (Mil)
1967—Packers, 13-0 (GB)
1968—49ers, 27-20 (SF)
1969—Packers, 14-7 (Mil)
1970—49ers, 26-10 (SF)
1972—49ers, 34-24 (Mil)
1973—49ers, 20-6 (SF)
1974—49ers, 7-6 (SF)
1976—49ers, 26-14 (GB)
1977—49ers, 16-14 (Mil)
1980—Packers, 23-16 (Mil)
1981—Packers, 13-3 (Mil)
1986—49ers, 31-17 (Mil)
1987—49ers, 23-12 (GB)
1989—Packers, 21-17 (SF)
1990—49ers, 24-20 (GB)
1995—*Packers, 27-17 (SF)
1996—Packers, 23-20 (GB) OT
 *Packers, 35-14 (GB)

1997—**Packers, 23-10 (SF)
1998—Packers, 36-22 (GB)
    ***49ers, 30-27 (SF)
1999—Packers, 20-3 (SF)
2000—Packers, 31-28 (GB)
2001—***Packers, 25-15 (GB)
2002—Packers, 20-14 (SF)
2003—Packers, 20-10 (GB)
(RS Pts.—49ers 1,077, Packers 1,049)
(PS Pts.—Packers 137, 49ers 86)
NFC Divisional Playoff
**NFC Championship*
***NFC First-Round Playoff*
GREEN BAY vs. SEATTLE
RS: Packers lead series, 5-4
PS: Packers lead series, 1-0
1976—Packers, 27-20 (Mil)
1978—Packers, 45-28 (Mil)
1981—Packers, 34-24 (GB)
1984—Seahawks, 30-24 (Mil)
1987—Seahawks, 24-13 (S)
1990—Seahawks, 20-14 (Mil)
1996—Packers, 31-10 (S)
1999—Seahawks, 27-7 (GB)
2003—Packers, 35-13 (GB)
    *Packers, 33-27 (GB) OT
(RS Pts.—Packers 230, Seahawks 196)
(PS Pts.—Packers 33, Seahawks 27)
NFC First-Round Playoff
GREEN BAY vs. TAMPA BAY
RS: Packers lead series, 29-18-1
PS: Packers lead series, 1-0
1977—Packers, 13-0 (TB)
1978—Packers, 9-7 (GB)
    Packers, 17-7 (TB)
1979—Buccaneers, 21-10 (GB)
    Packers, 21-3 (TB)
1980—Tie, 14-14 (TB) OT
    Buccaneers, 20-17 (Mil)
1981—Packers, 21-10 (GB)
    Buccaneers, 37-3 (TB)
1983—Packers, 55-14 (GB)
    Packers, 12-9 (TB) OT
1984—Buccaneers, 30-27 (TB) OT
    Packers, 27-14 (GB)
1985—Packers, 21-0 (GB)
    Packers, 20-17 (TB)
1986—Packers, 31-7 (Mil)
    Packers, 21-7 (TB)
1987—Buccaneers, 23-17 (Mil)
1988—Buccaneers, 13-10 (GB)
    Buccaneers, 27-24 (TB)
1989—Buccaneers, 23-21 (GB)
    Packers, 17-16 (TB)
1990—Buccaneers, 26-14 (TB)
    Packers, 20-10 (Mil)
1991—Packers, 15-13 (GB)
    Packers, 27-0 (TB)
1992—Buccaneers, 31-3 (TB)
    Packers, 19-14 (Mil)
1993—Packers, 37-14 (TB)
    Packers, 13-10 (GB)
1994—Packers, 30-3 (GB)
    Packers, 34-19 (TB)
1995—Packers, 35-13 (GB)
    Buccaneers, 13-10 (TB) OT
1996—Packers, 34-3 (TB)
    Packers, 13-7 (GB)
1997—Packers, 21-16 (GB)
    Packers, 17-6 (TB)

    *Packers, 21-7 (GB)
1998—Packers, 23-15 (GB)
    Buccaneers, 24-22 (TB)
1999—Packers, 26-23 (GB)
    Buccaneers, 29-10 (TB)
2000—Buccaneers, 20-15 (TB)
    Packers, 17-14 (GB) OT
2001—Buccaneers, 14-10 (TB)
    Packers, 21-20 (GB)
2002—Buccaneers, 21-7 (TB)
2003—Packers, 20-13 (TB)
(RS Pts.—Packers 912, Buccaneers 739)
(PS Pts.—Packers 21, Buccaneers 7)
NFC Divisional Playoff
GREEN BAY vs. *TENNESSEE
RS: Titans lead series, 5-4
1972—Packers, 23-10 (H)
1977—Oilers, 16-10 (GB)
1980—Oilers, 22-3 (GB)
1983—Packers, 41-38 (H) OT
1986—Oilers, 31-3 (GB)
1992—Packers, 16-14 (H)
1998—Packers, 30-22 (GB)
2001—Titans, 26-20 (T)
2004—Titans, 48-27 (GB)
(RS Pts.—Titans 227, Packers 173)
Franchise in Houston prior to 1997; known as Oilers prior to 1999
GREEN BAY vs. *WASHINGTON
RS: Packers lead series, 16-12-1
PS: Series tied, 1-1
1932—Packers, 21-0 (B)
1933—Tie, 7-7 (GB)
    Redskins, 20-7 (B)
1934—Packers, 10-0 (B)
1936—Redskins, 31-2 (GB)
    Packers, 7-3 (B)
    **Packers, 21-6 (New York)
1937—Redskins, 14-6 (W)
1939—Packers, 24-14 (Mil)
1941—Packers, 22-17 (W)
1943—Redskins, 33-7 (Mil)
1946—Packers, 20-7 (W)
1947—Packers, 27-10 (Mil)
1948—Packers, 23-7 (Mil)
1949—Redskins, 30-0 (W)
1950—Packers, 35-21 (Mil)
1952—Packers, 35-20 (Mil)
1958—Redskins, 37-21 (W)
1959—Packers, 21-0 (GB)
1968—Packers, 27-7 (W)
1972—Redskins, 21-16 (W)
    ***Redskins, 16-3 (W)
1974—Redskins, 17-6 (GB)
1977—Redskins, 10-9 (W)
1979—Redskins, 38-21 (W)
1983—Packers, 48-47 (GB)
1986—Redskins, 16-7 (GB)
1988—Redskins, 20-17 (Mil)
2001—Packers, 37-0 (GB)
2002—Packers, 30-9 (GB)
2004—Packers, 28-14 (W)
(RS Pts.—Packers 554, Redskins 457)
(PS Pts.—Packers 24, Redskins 22)
Franchise in Boston prior to 1937 and known as Braves prior to 1933
**NFL Championship*
***NFC Divisional Playoff*

HOUSTON vs. ATLANTA
RS: Texans lead series, 1-0;
See Atlanta vs. Houston
HOUSTON vs. BALTIMORE
RS: Ravens lead series, 1-0;
See Baltimore vs. Houston
HOUSTON vs. BUFFALO
RS: Series tied, 1-1;
See Buffalo vs. Houston
HOUSTON vs. CAROLINA
RS: Texans lead series, 1-0;
See Carolina vs. Houston
HOUSTON vs. CHICAGO
RS: Texans lead series, 1-0;
See Chicago vs. Houston
HOUSTON vs. CINCINNATI
RS: Bengals lead series, 2-0;
See Cincinnati vs. Houston
HOUSTON vs. CLEVELAND
RS: Browns lead series, 2-0;
See Cleveland vs. Houston
HOUSTON vs. DALLAS
RS: Texans lead series, 1-0;
See Dallas vs. Houston
HOUSTON vs. DENVER
RS: Broncos lead series, 1-0;
See Denver vs. Houston
HOUSTON vs. DETROIT
RS: Lions lead series, 1-0;
See Detroit vs. Houston
HOUSTON vs. GREEN BAY
RS: Packers lead series, 1-0;
See Green Bay vs. Houston
HOUSTON vs. INDIANAPOLIS
RS: Colts lead series, 6-0
2002—Colts, 23-3 (H)
    Colts, 19-3 (I)
2003—Colts, 30-21 (I)
    Colts, 20-17 (H)
2004—Colts, 49-14 (I)
    Colts, 23-14 (H)
(RS Pts.—Colts 164, Texans 72)
HOUSTON vs. JACKSONVILLE
RS: Texans lead series, 4-2
2002—Texans, 21-19 (J)
    Jaguars, 24-21 (H)
2003—Texans, 24-20 (H)
    Jaguars, 27-0 (J)
2004—Texans, 20-6 (H)
    Texans, 21-0 (J)
(RS Pts.—Texans 107, Jaguars 96)
HOUSTON vs. KANSAS CITY
RS: Series tied, 1-1
2003—Chiefs, 42-14 (H)
2004—Texans, 24-21 (KC)
(RS Pts.—Chiefs 63, Texans 38)
HOUSTON vs. MIAMI
RS: Texans lead series, 1-0
2003—Texans, 21-20 (M)
(RS Pts.—Texans 21, Dolphins 20)
HOUSTON vs. MINNESOTA
RS: Vikings lead series, 1-0
2004—Vikings, 34-28 (H) OT
(RS Pts.—Vikings 34, Texans 28)
HOUSTON vs. NEW ENGLAND
RS: Patriots lead series, 1-0
2003—Patriots, 23-20 (H) OT
(RS Pts.—Patriots 23, Texans 20)
HOUSTON vs. NEW ORLEANS
RS: Saints lead series, 1-0

2003—Saints, 31-10 (NO)
(RS Pts.—Saints 31, Texans 10)
HOUSTON vs. N.Y. GIANTS
RS: Texans lead series, 1-0
2002—Texans, 16-14 (H)
(RS Pts.—Texans 16, Giants 14)
HOUSTON vs. N.Y. JETS
RS: Jets lead series, 2-0
2003—Jets, 19-14 (H)
2004—Jets, 29-7 (NY)
(RS Pts.—Jets 48, Texans 21)
HOUSTON vs. OAKLAND
RS: Texans lead series, 1-0
2004—Texans, 30-17 (H)
(RS Pts.—Texans 30, Raiders 17)
HOUSTON vs. PHILADELPHIA
RS: Eagles lead series, 1-0
2002—Eagles, 35-17 (P)
(RS Pts.—Eagles 35, Texans 17)
HOUSTON vs. PITTSBURGH
RS: Texans lead series, 1-0
2002—Texans, 24-6 (P)
(RS Pts.—Texans 24, Steelers 6)
HOUSTON vs. SAN DIEGO
RS: Chargers lead series, 2-0
2002—Chargers, 24-3 (SD)
2004—Chargers, 27-20 (H)
(RS Pts.—Chargers 51, Texans 23)
HOUSTON vs. TAMPA BAY
RS: Buccaneers lead series, 1-0
2003—Buccaneers, 16-3 (TB)
(RS Pts.—Buccaneers 16, Texans 3)
HOUSTON vs. TENNESSEE
RS: Titans lead series, 4-2
2002—Titans, 17-10 (T)
  Titans, 13-3 (H)
2003—Titans, 38-17 (T)
  Titans, 27-24 (H)
2004—Texans, 20-10 (T)
  Texans, 31-21 (H)
(RS Pts.—Titans 126, Texans 105)
HOUSTON vs. WASHINGTON
RS: Redskins lead series, 1-0
2002—Redskins, 26-10 (W)
(RS Pts.—Redskins 26, Texans 10)

INDIANAPOLIS vs. ARIZONA
RS: Series tied, 6-6;
See Arizona vs. Indianapolis
INDIANAPOLIS vs. ATLANTA
RS: Colts lead series, 12-1;
See Atlanta vs. Indianapolis
INDIANAPOLIS vs. BALTIMORE
RS: Colts lead series, 3-2;
See Baltimore vs. Indianapolis
INDIANAPOLIS vs. BUFFALO
RS: Bills lead series, 34-29-1;
See Buffalo vs. Indianapolis
INDIANAPOLIS vs. CAROLINA
RS: Panthers lead series, 3-0;
See Carolina vs. Indianapolis
INDIANAPOLIS vs. CHICAGO
RS: Colts lead series, 22-17;
See Chicago vs. Indianapolis
INDIANAPOLIS vs. CINCINNATI
RS: Colts lead series, 12-8
PS: Colts lead series, 1-0;
See Cincinnati vs. Indianapolis
INDIANAPOLIS vs. CLEVELAND
RS: Browns lead series, 13-10

PS: Series tied, 2-2;
See Cleveland vs. Indianapolis
INDIANAPOLIS vs. DALLAS
RS: Cowboys lead series, 7-5
PS: Colts lead series, 1-0;
See Dallas vs. Indianapolis
INDIANAPOLIS vs. DENVER
RS: Broncos lead series, 11-4
PS: Colts lead series, 2-0;
See Denver vs. Indianapolis
INDIANAPOLIS vs. DETROIT
RS: Colts lead series, 19-18-2;
See Detroit vs. Indianapolis
INDIANAPOLIS vs. GREEN BAY
RS: Colts lead series, 20-19-1
PS: Packers lead series, 1-0;
See Green Bay vs. Indianapolis
INDIANAPOLIS vs. HOUSTON
RS: Colts lead series, 6-0;
See Houston vs. Indianapolis
INDIANAPOLIS vs. JACKSONVILLE
RS: Colts lead series, 6-2
1995—Colts, 41-31 (J)
2000—Colts, 43-14 (I)
2002—Colts, 28-25 (J)
  Colts, 20-13 (I)
2003—Colts, 23-13 (I)
  Jaguars, 28-23 (J)
2004—Colts, 24-17 (J)
  Jaguars, 27-24 (I)
(RS Pts.—Colts 226, Jaguars 168)
*****INDIANAPOLIS vs. KANSAS CITY**
RS: Colts lead series, 8-7
PS: Colts lead series, 2-0
1970—Chiefs, 44-24 (B)
1972—Chiefs, 24-10 (KC)
1975—Colts, 28-14 (B)
1977—Colts, 17-6 (KC)
1979—Chiefs, 14-0 (KC)
  Chiefs, 10-7 (B)
1980—Colts, 31-24 (KC)
  Chiefs, 38-28 (B)
1985—Colts, 20-7 (KC)
1990—Colts, 23-19 (I)
1995—**Colts, 10-7 (KC)
1996—Colts, 24-19 (KC)
1999—Colts, 25-17 (I)
2000—Colts, 27-14 (KC)
2001—Colts, 35-28 (KC)
2003—**Colts, 38-31 (KC)
2004—Chiefs, 45-35 (KC)
(RS Pts.—Chiefs 336, Colts 321)
(PS Pts.—Colts 48, Chiefs 38)
Franchise in Baltimore prior to 1984
**AFC Divisional Playoff*
*****INDIANAPOLIS vs. MIAMI**
RS: Dolphins lead series, 44-22
PS: Dolphins lead series, 2-0
1970—Colts, 35-0 (B)
  Dolphins, 34-17 (M)
1971—Dolphins, 17-14 (M)
  Colts, 14-3 (B)
  **Dolphins, 21-0 (M)
1972—Dolphins, 23-0 (B)
  Dolphins, 16-0 (M)
1973—Dolphins, 44-0 (M)
  Colts, 16-3 (B)
1974—Dolphins, 17-7 (M)
  Dolphins, 17-16 (B)
1975—Colts, 33-17 (M)

  Colts, 10-7 (B) OT
1976—Colts, 28-14 (B)
  Colts, 17-16 (M)
1977—Colts, 45-28 (B)
  Dolphins, 17-6 (M)
1978—Dolphins, 42-0 (B)
  Dolphins, 26-8 (M)
1979—Dolphins, 19-0 (M)
  Dolphins, 28-24 (B)
1980—Colts, 30-17 (M)
  Dolphins, 24-14 (B)
1981—Dolphins, 31-28 (B)
  Dolphins, 27-10 (M)
1982—Dolphins, 24-20 (M)
  Dolphins, 34-7 (B)
1983—Dolphins, 21-7 (B)
  Dolphins, 37-0 (M)
1984—Dolphins, 44-7 (M)
  Dolphins, 35-17 (I)
1985—Dolphins, 30-13 (M)
  Dolphins, 34-20 (I)
1986—Dolphins, 30-10 (M)
  Dolphins, 17-13 (I)
1987—Dolphins, 23-10 (I)
  Colts, 40-21 (M)
1988—Colts, 15-13 (I)
  Colts, 31-28 (M)
1989—Dolphins, 19-13 (M)
  Colts, 42-13 (I)
1990—Dolphins, 27-7 (I)
  Dolphins, 23-17 (M)
1991—Dolphins, 17-6 (M)
  Dolphins, 10-6 (I)
1992—Colts, 31-20 (M)
  Dolphins, 28-0 (I)
1993—Dolphins, 24-20 (I)
  Dolphins, 41-27 (M)
1994—Dolphins, 22-21 (M)
  Colts, 10-6 (I)
1995—Colts, 27-24 (M) OT
  Colts, 36-28 (I)
1996—Colts, 10-6 (I)
  Dolphins, 37-13 (M)
1997—Dolphins, 16-10 (M)
  Colts, 41-0 (I)
1998—Dolphins, 24-15 (I)
  Dolphins, 27-14 (M)
1999—Dolphins, 34-31 (I)
  Colts, 37-34 (M)
2000—Dolphins, 17-14 (I)
  Colts, 20-13 (M)
  ***Dolphins 23-17 (M) OT
2001—Dolphins, 27-24 (I)
  Dolphins, 41-6 (M)
2002—Dolphins, 21-13 (I)
2003—Colts, 23-17 (M)
(RS Pts.—Dolphins 1,494, Colts 1,116)
(PS Pts.—Dolphins 44, Colts 17)
Franchise in Baltimore prior to 1984
**AFC Championship*
***AFC First-Round Playoff*
*****INDIANAPOLIS vs. MINNESOTA**
RS: Colts lead series, 13-7-1
PS: Colts lead series, 1-0
1961—Colts, 34-33 (B)
  Vikings, 28-20 (M)
1962—Colts, 34-7 (M)
  Colts, 42-17 (B)
1963—Colts, 37-34 (M)
  Colts, 41-10 (B)

1964—Vikings, 34-24 (M)
Colts, 17-14 (B)
1965—Colts, 35-16 (B)
Colts, 41-21 (M)
1966—Colts, 38-23 (M)
Colts, 20-17 (B)
1967—Tie, 20-20 (M)
1968—Colts, 21-9 (B)
**Colts, 24-14 (B)
1969—Vikings, 52-14 (M)
1971—Vikings, 10-3 (M)
1982—Vikings, 13-10 (M)
1988—Vikings, 12-3 (M)
1997—Vikings, 39-28 (M)
2000—Colts, 31-10 (I)
2004—Colts, 31-28 (I)
(RS Pts.—Colts 544, Vikings 447)
(PS Pts.—Colts 24, Vikings 14)
*Franchise in Baltimore prior to 1984
**Conference Championship
**INDIANAPOLIS vs. **NEW ENGLAND
RS: Patriots lead series, 41-24
PS: Patriots lead series, 2-0
1970—Colts, 14-6 (Bos)
Colts, 27-3 (Balt)
1971—Colts, 23-3 (NE)
Patriots, 21-17 (Balt)
1972—Colts, 24-17 (NE)
Colts, 31-0 (Balt)
1973—Patriots, 24-16 (NE)
Colts, 18-13 (Balt)
1974—Patriots, 42-3 (NE)
Patriots, 27-17 (Balt)
1975—Patriots, 21-10 (NE)
Colts, 34-21 (Balt)
1976—Colts, 27-13 (NE)
Patriots, 21-14 (Balt)
1977—Patriots, 17-3 (NE)
Colts, 30-24 (Balt)
1978—Colts, 34-27 (NE)
Patriots, 35-14 (Balt)
1979—Colts, 31-26 (Balt)
Patriots, 50-21 (NE)
1980—Patriots, 37-21 (Balt)
Patriots, 47-21 (NE)
1981—Colts, 29-28 (NE)
Colts, 23-21 (Balt)
1982—Patriots, 24-13 (Balt)
1983—Colts, 29-23 (NE) OT
Colts, 12-7 (Balt)
1984—Patriots, 50-17 (I)
Patriots, 16-10 (NE)
1985—Patriots, 34-15 (NE)
Patriots, 38-31 (I)
1986—Patriots, 33-3 (NE)
Patriots, 30-21 (I)
1987—Colts, 30-16 (I)
Patriots, 24-0 (NE)
1988—Patriots, 21-17 (NE)
Colts, 24-21 (I)
1989—Patriots, 23-20 (I) OT
Patriots, 22-16 (NE)
1990—Patriots, 16-14 (I)
Colts, 13-10 (NE)
1991—Patriots, 16-7 (I)
Patriots, 23-17 (NE) OT
1992—Patriots, 37-34 (I) OT
Colts, 6-0 (NE)
1993—Colts, 9-6 (I)
Patriots, 38-0 (NE)

1994—Patriots, 12-10 (I)
Patriots, 28-13 (NE)
1995—Colts, 24-10 (NE)
Colts, 10-7 (I)
1996—Patriots, 27-9 (I)
Patriots, 27-13 (NE)
1997—Patriots, 31-6 (I)
Patriots, 20-17 (NE)
1998—Patriots, 29-6 (NE)
Patriots, 21-16 (I)
1999—Patriots, 31-28 (NE)
Colts, 20-15 (I)
2000—Patriots, 24-16 (NE)
Colts, 30-23 (I)
2001—Patriots, 44-13 (NE)
Patriots, 38-17 (I)
2003—Patriots, 38-34 (I)
***Patriots, 24-14 (NE)
2004—Patriots, 27-24 (NE)
****Patriots, 20-3 (NE)
(RS Pts.—Patriots 1,524, Colts 1,166)
(PS Pts.—Patriots 44, Colts 17)
*Franchise in Baltimore prior to 1984
**Franchise in Boston prior to 1971
***AFC Championship
****AFC Divisional Playoff
*INDIANAPOLIS vs. NEW ORLEANS
RS: Saints lead series, 5-4
1967—Colts, 30-10 (B)
1969—Colts, 30-10 (NO)
1973—Colts, 14-10 (B)
1986—Saints, 17-14 (I)
1989—Saints, 41-6 (NO)
1995—Saints, 17-14 (NO)
1998—Saints, 19-13 (I) OT
2001—Saints, 34-20 (NO)
2003—Colts, 55-21 (NO)
(RS Pts.—Colts 196, Saints 179)
*Franchise in Baltimore prior to 1984
*INDIANAPOLIS vs. N.Y. GIANTS
RS: Series tied, 6-6
PS: Colts lead series, 2-0
1954—Colts, 20-14 (B)
1955—Giants, 17-7 (NY)
1958—Giants, 24-21 (NY)
**Colts, 23-17 (NY) OT
1959—**Colts, 31-16 (B)
1963—Giants, 37-28 (B)
1968—Colts, 26-0 (NY)
1971—Colts, 31-7 (NY)
1975—Colts, 21-0 (NY)
1979—Colts, 31-7 (NY)
1990—Giants, 24-7 (I)
1993—Giants, 20-6 (NY)
1999—Colts, 27-19 (NY)
2002—Giants, 44-27 (I)
(RS Pts.—Colts 252, Giants 213)
(PS Pts.—Colts 54, Giants 33)
*Franchise in Baltimore prior to 1984
**NFL Championship
*INDIANAPOLIS vs. N.Y. JETS
RS: Colts lead series, 39-25
PS: Jets lead series, 2-0
1968—**Jets 16-7 (Miami)
1970—Colts, 29-22 (NY)
Colts, 35-20 (B)
1971—Colts, 22-0 (B)
Colts, 14-13 (NY)
1972—Jets, 44-34 (B)
Jets, 24-20 (NY)

1973—Jets, 34-10 (B)
Jets, 20-17 (NY)
1974—Colts, 35-20 (NY)
Jets, 45-38 (B)
1975—Colts, 45-28 (NY)
Colts, 52-19 (B)
1976—Colts, 20-0 (NY)
Colts, 33-16 (B)
1977—Colts, 20-12 (NY)
Colts, 33-12 (B)
1978—Jets, 33-10 (B)
Jets, 24-16 (NY)
1979—Colts, 10-8 (B)
Jets, 30-17 (NY)
1980—Colts, 17-14 (NY)
Colts, 35-21 (B)
1981—Jets, 41-14 (B)
Jets, 25-0 (NY)
1982—Jets, 37-0 (NY)
1983—Colts, 17-14 (NY)
Jets, 10-6 (B)
1984—Jets, 23-14 (I)
Colts, 9-5 (NY)
1985—Jets, 25-20 (NY)
Jets, 35-17 (I)
1986—Jets, 26-7 (I)
Jets, 31-16 (NY)
1987—Colts, 6-0 (I)
Colts, 19-14 (NY)
1988—Colts, 38-14 (I)
Jets, 34-16 (NY)
1989—Colts, 17-10 (NY)
Colts, 27-10 (I)
1990—Colts, 17-14 (I)
Colts, 29-21 (NY)
1991—Jets, 17-6 (I)
Colts, 28-27 (NY)
1992—Colts, 6-3 (I) OT
Colts, 10-6 (NY)
1993—Jets, 17-10 (I)
Colts, 9-6 (NY)
1994—Jets, 16-6 (NY)
Colts, 28-25 (I)
1995—Colts, 27-24 (NY) OT
Colts, 17-10 (I)
1996—Colts, 21-7 (NY)
Colts, 34-29 (I)
1997—Jets, 16-12 (I)
Colts, 22-14 (NY)
1998—Jets, 44-6 (NY)
Colts, 24-23 (I)
1999—Colts, 16-13 (NY)
Colts, 13-6 (I)
2000—Colts, 23-15 (I)
Jets, 27-17 (NY)
2001—Colts, 45-24 (NY)
Jets, 29-28 (I)
2002—***Jets, 41-0 (NY)
2003—Colts, 38-31 (I)
(RS Pts.—Colts 1,304, Jets 1,291)
(PS Pts.—Jets 57, Colts 7)
*Franchise in Baltimore prior to 1984
**Super Bowl III
***AFC First-Round Playoff
*INDIANAPOLIS vs **OAKLAND
RS: Raiders lead series, 7-3
PS: Series tied, 1-1
1970—***Colts, 27-17 (B)
1971—Colts, 37-14 (O)
1973—Raiders, 34-21 (B)

1975—Raiders, 31-20 (B)
1977—****Raiders, 37-31 (B) OT
1984—Raiders, 21-7 (LA)
1986—Colts, 30-24 (LA)
1991—Raiders, 16-0 (LA)
1995—Raiders, 30-17 (O)
2000—Raiders, 38-31 (I)
2001—Raiders, 23-18 (I)
2004—Colts, 35-14 (I)
(RS Pts.—Raiders 245, Colts 216)
(PS Pts.—Colts 58, Raiders 54)
*Franchise in Baltimore prior to 1984
**Franchise in Los Angeles from
1982-1994
***AFC Championship
****AFC Divisional Playoff
*INDIANAPOLIS vs. PHILADELPHIA
RS: Colts lead series, 9-6
1953—Eagles, 45-14 (P)
1965—Colts, 34-24 (B)
1967—Colts, 38-6 (P)
1969—Colts, 24-20 (B)
1970—Colts, 29-10 (B)
1974—Eagles, 30-10 (P)
1978—Eagles, 17-14 (B)
1981—Eagles, 38-13 (P)
1983—Colts, 22-21 (P)
1984—Eagles, 16-7 (P)
1990—Colts, 24-23 (P)
1993—Eagles, 20-10 (I)
1996—Colts, 37-10 (I)
1999—Colts, 44-17 (P)
2002—Colts, 35-13 (P)
(RS Pts.—Colts 355, Eagles 310)
*Franchise in Baltimore prior to 1984
*INDIANAPOLIS vs. PITTSBURGH
RS: Steelers lead series, 13-4
PS: Steelers lead series, 4-0
1957—Steelers, 19-13 (B)
1968—Colts, 41-7 (P)
1971—Colts, 34-21 (B)
1974—Steelers, 30-0 (P)
1975—**Steelers, 28-10 (P)
1976—**Steelers, 40-14 (B)
1977—Colts, 31-21 (B)
1978—Steelers, 35-13 (P)
1979—Steelers, 17-13 (P)
1980—Steelers, 20-17 (B)
1983—Steelers, 24-13 (B)
1984—Colts, 17-16 (I)
1985—Steelers, 45-3 (P)
1987—Steelers, 21-7 (P)
1991—Steelers, 21-3 (I)
1992—Steelers, 30-14 (P)
1994—Steelers, 31-21 (P)
1995—***Steelers, 20-16 (P)
1996—****Steelers, 42-14 (P)
1997—Steelers, 24-22 (P)
2002—Steelers, 28-10 (P)
(RS Pts.—Steelers 410, Colts 272)
(PS Pts.—Steelers 130, Colts 54)
*Franchise in Baltimore prior to 1984
**AFC Divisional Playoff
***AFC Championship
****AFC First-Round Playoff
*INDIANAPOLIS vs. **ST. LOUIS
RS: Colts lead series, 21-17-2
1953—Rams, 21-13 (B)
　　　Rams, 45-2 (LA)
1954—Rams, 48-0 (B)

Colts, 22-21 (LA)
1955—Tie, 17-17 (B)
　　　Rams, 20-14 (LA)
1956—Colts, 56-21 (B)
　　　Rams, 31-7 (LA)
1957—Colts, 31-14 (B)
　　　Rams, 37-21 (LA)
1958—Colts, 34-7 (B)
　　　Rams, 30-28 (LA)
1959—Colts, 35-21 (B)
　　　Colts, 45-26 (LA)
1960—Colts, 31-17 (B)
　　　Rams, 10-3 (LA)
1961—Colts, 27-24 (B)
　　　Rams, 34-17 (LA)
1962—Colts, 30-27 (B)
　　　Colts, 14-2 (LA)
1963—Rams, 17-16 (LA)
　　　Colts, 19-16 (B)
1964—Colts, 35-20 (B)
　　　Colts, 24-7 (LA)
1965—Colts, 35-20 (B)
　　　Colts, 20-17 (LA)
1966—Colts, 17-3 (LA)
　　　Rams, 23-7 (B)
1967—Tie, 24-24 (B)
　　　Rams, 34-10 (LA)
1968—Colts, 27-10 (B)
　　　Colts, 28-24 (LA)
1969—Rams, 27-20 (B)
　　　Colts, 13-7 (LA)
1971—Colts, 24-17 (B)
1975—Rams, 24-13 (LA)
1986—Rams, 24-7 (I)
1989—Rams, 31-17 (LA)
1995—Colts, 21-18 (I)
2001—Rams, 42-17 (StL)
(RS Pts.—Rams 878, Colts 841)
*Franchise in Baltimore prior to 1984
**Franchise in Los Angeles prior to 1995
*INDIANAPOLIS vs. SAN DIEGO
RS: Chargers lead series, 12-8
PS: Colts lead series, 1-0
1970—Colts, 16-14 (SD)
1972—Chargers, 23-20 (B)
1976—Colts, 37-21 (SD)
1981—Chargers, 43-14 (B)
1982—Chargers, 44-26 (SD)
1984—Chargers, 38-10 (I)
1986—Chargers, 17-3 (I)
1987—Chargers, 16-13 (I)
　　　Colts, 20-7 (SD)
1988—Colts, 16-0 (I)
1989—Colts, 10-6 (I)
1992—Chargers, 34-14 (I)
　　　Chargers, 26-0 (SD)
1993—Chargers, 31-0 (I)
1995—Chargers, 27-24 (I)
　　　**Colts, 35-20 (SD)
1996—Chargers, 26-19 (I)
1997—Chargers, 35-19 (SD)
1998—Colts, 17-12 (I)
1999—Colts, 27-19 (SD)
2004—Colts, 34-31 (I) OT
(RS Pts.—Chargers 470, Colts 339)
(PS Pts.—Colts 35, Chargers 20)
*Franchise in Baltimore prior to 1984
**AFC First-Round Playoff
*INDIANAPOLIS vs. SAN FRANCISCO
RS: Colts lead series, 22-18

1953—49ers, 38-21 (B)
　　　49ers, 45-14 (SF)
1954—Colts, 17-13 (B)
　　　49ers, 10-7 (SF)
1955—Colts, 26-14 (B)
　　　49ers, 35-24 (SF)
1956—49ers, 20-17 (B)
　　　49ers, 30-17 (SF)
1957—Colts, 27-21 (B)
　　　49ers, 17-13 (SF)
1958—Colts, 35-27 (B)
　　　49ers, 21-12 (SF)
1959—Colts, 45-14 (B)
　　　Colts, 34-14 (SF)
1960—49ers, 30-22 (B)
　　　49ers, 34-10 (SF)
1961—Colts, 20-17 (B)
　　　Colts, 27-24 (SF)
1962—49ers, 21-13 (B)
　　　Colts, 22-3 (SF)
1963—Colts, 20-14 (SF)
　　　Colts, 20-3 (B)
1964—Colts, 37-7 (B)
　　　Colts, 14-3 (SF)
1965—Colts, 27-24 (B)
　　　Colts, 34-28 (SF)
1966—Colts, 36-14 (B)
　　　Colts, 30-14 (SF)
1967—Colts, 41-7 (B)
　　　Colts, 26-9 (SF)
1968—Colts, 27-10 (B)
　　　Colts, 42-14 (SF)
1969—49ers, 24-21 (B)
　　　49ers, 20-17 (SF)
1972—49ers, 24-21 (SF)
1986—49ers, 35-14 (SF)
1989—49ers, 30-24 (I)
1995—Colts, 18-17 (I)
1998—49ers, 34-31 (SF)
2001—49ers, 40-21 (I)
(RS Pts.—Colts 944, 49ers 819)
*Franchise in Baltimore prior to 1984
*INDIANAPOLIS vs. SEATTLE
RS: Colts lead series, 5-3
1977—Colts, 29-14 (S)
1978—Colts, 17-14 (S)
1991—Seahawks, 31-3 (S)
1994—Colts, 17-15 (I)
　　　Colts, 31-19 (S)
1997—Seahawks, 31-3 (I)
1998—Seahawks, 27-23 (S)
2000—Colts, 37-24 (S)
(RS Pts.—Seahawks 175, Colts 160)
*Franchise in Baltimore prior to 1984
*INDIANAPOLIS vs. TAMPA BAY
RS: Colts lead series, 6-4
1976—Colts, 42-17 (B)
1979—Buccaneers, 29-26 (B) OT
1985—Colts, 31-23 (TB)
1987—Colts, 24-6 (I)
1988—Colts, 35-31 (I)
1991—Buccaneers, 17-3 (TB)
1992—Colts, 24-14 (TB)
1994—Buccaneers, 24-10 (TB)
1997—Buccaneers, 31-28 (I)
2003—Colts, 38-35 (TB) OT
(RS Pts.—Colts 261, Buccaneers 227)
*Franchise in Baltimore prior to 1984
*INDIANAPOLIS vs. **TENNESSEE
RS: Colts lead series, 11-9

PS: Titans lead series, 1-0
1970—Colts, 24-20 (H)
1973—Oilers, 31-27 (B)
1976—Colts, 38-14 (B)
1979—Oilers, 28-16 (B)
1980—Oilers, 21-16 (H)
1983—Colts, 20-10 (B)
1984—Colts, 35-21 (H)
1985—Colts, 34-16 (I)
1986—Oilers, 31-17 (H)
1987—Colts, 51-27 (I)
1988—Oilers, 17-14 (I) OT
1990—Oilers, 24-10 (H)
1992—Oilers, 20-10 (I)
1994—Colts, 45-21 (I)
1999—***Titans, 19-16 (I)
2002—Titans, 23-15 (I)
Titans, 27-17 (T)
2003—Colts, 33-7 (I)
Colts, 29-27 (T)
2004—Colts, 31-17 (T)
Colts, 51-24 (I)
(RS Pts.—Colts 533, Titans 426)
(PS Pts.—Titans 19, Colts 16)
*Franchise in Baltimore prior to 1984
**Franchise in Houston prior to 1997;
known as Oilers prior to 1999
***AFC Divisional Playoff
INDIANAPOLIS vs. WASHINGTON
RS: Colts lead series, 17-10
1953—Colts, 27-17 (B)
1954—Redskins, 24-21 (W)
1955—Redskins, 14-13 (B)
1956—Colts, 19-17 (B)
1957—Colts, 21-17 (W)
1958—Colts, 35-10 (B)
1959—Redskins, 27-24 (W)
1960—Colts, 20-0 (B)
1961—Colts, 27-6 (W)
1962—Colts, 34-21 (B)
1963—Colts, 36-20 (W)
1964—Colts, 45-17 (B)
1965—Colts, 38-7 (W)
1966—Colts, 37-10 (B)
1967—Colts, 17-13 (W)
1969—Colts, 41-17 (B)
1973—Redskins, 22-14 (W)
1977—Colts, 10-3 (B)
1978—Colts, 21-17 (B)
1981—Redskins, 38-14 (W)
1984—Redskins, 35-7 (I)
1990—Colts, 35-28 (I)
1993—Redskins, 30-24 (W)
1994—Redskins, 41-27 (I)
1996—Redskins, 31-16 (W)
1999—Colts, 24-21 (I)
2002—Redskins, 26-21 (W)
(RS Pts.—Colts 668, Redskins 529)
*Franchise in Baltimore prior to 1984

JACKSONVILLE vs. ARIZONA
RS: Jaguars lead series, 1-0;
See Arizona vs. Jacksonville
JACKSONVILLE vs. ATLANTA
RS: Jaguars lead series, 2-1;
See Atlanta vs. Jacksonville
JACKSONVILLE vs. BALTIMORE
RS: Jaguars lead series, 8-6;
See Baltimore vs. Jacksonville
JACKSONVILLE vs. BUFFALO

RS: Bills lead series, 3-2
PS: Jaguars lead series, 1-0;
See Buffalo vs. Jacksonville
JACKSONVILLE vs. CAROLINA
RS: Jaguars lead series, 2-1;
See Carolina vs. Jacksonville
JACKSONVILLE vs. CHICAGO
RS: Series tied, 2-2;
See Chicago vs. Jacksonville
JACKSONVILLE vs. CINCINNATI
RS: Jaguars lead series, 10-5;
See Cincinnati vs. Jacksonville
JACKSONVILLE vs. CLEVELAND
RS: Jaguars lead series, 7-2;
See Cleveland vs. Jacksonville
JACKSONVILLE vs. DALLAS
RS: Cowboys lead series, 2-1;
See Dallas vs. Jacksonville
JACKSONVILLE vs. DENVER
RS: Series tied, 2-2
PS: Series tied, 1-1;
See Denver vs. Jacksonville
JACKSONVILLE vs. DETROIT
RS: Jaguars lead series, 2-1;
See Detroit vs. Jacksonville
JACKSONVILLE vs. GREEN BAY
RS: Packers lead series, 2-1;
See Green Bay vs. Jacksonville
JACKSONVILLE vs. HOUSTON
RS: Texans lead series, 4-2;
See Houston vs. Jacksonville
JACKSONVILLE vs. INDIANAPOLIS
RS: Colts lead series, 6-2;
See Indianapolis vs. Jacksonville
JACKSONVILLE vs. KANSAS CITY
RS: Jaguars lead series, 4-1
1997—Jaguars, 24-10 (J)
1998—Jaguars, 21-16 (J)
2001—Chiefs, 30-26 (J)
2002—Jaguars, 23-16 (KC)
2004—Jaguars, 22-16 (J)
(RS Pts.—Jaguars 116, Chiefs 88)
JACKSONVILLE vs. MIAMI
RS: Series tied, 1-1
PS: Jaguars lead series, 1-0
1998—Jaguars, 28-21 (J)
1999—*Jaguars, 62-7 (J)
2003—Dolphins, 24-10 (J)
(RS Pts.—Dolphins 45, Jaguars 38)
(PS Pts.—Jaguars 62, Dolphins 7)
*AFC Divisional Playoff
JACKSONVILLE vs. MINNESOTA
RS: Vikings lead series, 2-1
1998—Vikings, 50-10 (M)
2001—Jaguars, 33-3 (M)
2004—Vikings, 27-16 (M)
(RS Pts.—Vikings 80, Jaguars 59)
JACKSONVILLE vs. NEW ENGLAND
RS: Patriots lead series, 3-0
PS: Series tied, 1-1
1996—Patriots, 28-25 (NE) OT
*Patriots, 20-6 (NE)
1997—Patriots, 26-20 (J)
1998—**Jaguars, 25-10 (J)
2003—Patriots, 27-13 (NE)
(RS Pts.—Patriots 81, Jaguars 58)
(PS Pts.—Jaguars 31, Patriots 30)
*AFC Championship
**AFC First-Round Playoff

JACKSONVILLE vs. NEW ORLEANS
RS: Jaguars lead series, 2-1
1996—Saints, 17-13 (NO)
1999—Jaguars, 41-23 (J)
2003—Jaguars, 20-19 (J)
(RS Pts.—Jaguars 74, Saints 59)
JACKSONVILLE vs. N.Y. GIANTS
RS: Giants lead series, 2-1
1997—Jaguars, 40-13 (J)
2000—Giants, 28-25 (NY)
2002—Giants, 24-17 (NY)
(RS Pts.—Jaguars 82, Giants 65)
JACKSONVILLE vs. N.Y. JETS
RS: Jaguars lead series, 3-2
PS: Jets lead series, 1-0
1995—Jets, 27-10 (NY)
1996—Jaguars, 21-17 (J)
1998—*Jets, 34-24 (NY)
1999—Jaguars, 16-6 (NY)
2002—Jaguars, 28-3 (J)
2003—Jets, 13-10 (NY)
(RS Pts.—Jaguars 85, Jets 66)
(PS Pts.—Jets 34, Jaguars 24
*AFC Divisional Playoff
JACKSONVILLE vs. OAKLAND
RS: Jaguars lead series, 2-1
1996—Raiders, 17-3 (O)
1997—Jaguars, 20-9 (O)
2004—Jaguars, 13-6 (O)
(RS Pts.—Jaguars 36, Raiders 32)
JACKSONVILLE vs. PHILADELPHIA
RS: Jaguars lead series, 2-0
1997—Jaguars, 38-21 (J)
2002—Jaguars, 28-25 (J)
(RS Pts.—Jaguars 66, Eagles 46)
JACKSONVILLE vs. PITTSBURGH
RS: Series tied, 8-8
1995—Jaguars, 20-16 (J)
Steelers, 24-7 (P)
1996—Jaguars, 24-9 (J)
Steelers, 28-3 (P)
1997—Jaguars, 30-21 (J)
Steelers, 23-17 (P) OT
1998—Steelers, 30-15 (P)
Jaguars, 21-3 (J)
1999—Jaguars, 17-3 (P)
Jaguars, 20-6 (J)
2000—Steelers, 24-13 (J)
Jaguars, 34-24 (P)
2001—Jaguars, 21-3 (J)
Steelers, 20-7 (P)
2002—Steelers, 25-23 (J)
2004—Steelers, 17-16 (J)
(RS Pts.—Jaguars 288, Steelers 276)
JACKSONVILLE vs. ST. LOUIS
RS: Rams lead series, 1-0
1996—Rams, 17-14 (StL)
(RS Pts.—Rams 17, Jaguars 14)
JACKSONVILLE vs. SAN DIEGO
RS: Series tied, 1-1
2003—Jaguars, 27-21 (J)
2004—Chargers, 34-21 (SD)
(RS Pts.—Chargers 55, Jaguars 48)
JACKSONVILLE vs. SAN FRANCISCO
RS: Jaguars lead series, 1-0
1999—Jaguars, 41-3 (J)
(RS Pts.—Jaguars 41, 49ers 3)
JACKSONVILLE vs. SEATTLE
RS: Seahawks lead series, 3-1
1995—Seahawks, 47-30 (J)

1996—Jaguars, 20-13 (J)
2000—Seahawks, 28-21 (J)
2001—Seahawks, 24-15 (S)
(RS Pts.—Seahawks 112, Jaguars 86)
JACKSONVILLE vs. TAMPA BAY
RS: Jaguars lead series, 2-1
1995—Buccaneers, 17-16 (TB)
1998—Jaguars, 29-24 (J)
2003—Jaguars, 17-10 (J)
(RS Pts.—Jaguars 62, Buccaneers 51)
JACKSONVILLE vs. *TENNESSEE
RS: Titans lead series, 12-8
PS: Titans lead, 1-0
1995—Oilers, 10-3 (J)
Jaguars, 17-16 (H)
1996—Oilers, 34-27 (J)
Jaguars, 23-17 (H)
1997—Jaguars, 30-24 (T)
Jaguars, 17-9 (J)
1998—Jaguars, 27-22 (T)
Oilers, 16-13 (J)
1999—Titans, 20-19 (J)
Titans, 41-14 (T)
**Titans, 33-14 (J)
2000—Titans, 27-13 (T)
Jaguars, 16-13 (J)
2001—Jaguars, 13-6 (J)
Titans, 28-24 (T)
2002—Titans, 23-14 (T)
Titans, 28-10 (J)
2003—Titans, 30-17 (J)
Titans, 10-3 (T)
2004—Jaguars, 15-12 (T)
Titans, 18-15 (J)
(RS Pts.—Titans 404, Jaguars 330)
(PS Pts.—Titans 33, Jaguars 14)
*Franchise in Houston prior to 1997;
known as Oilers prior to 1999
**AFC Championship
JACKSONVILLE vs. WASHINGTON
RS: Redskins lead series, 2-1
1997—Redskins, 24-12 (W)
2000—Redskins, 35-16 (J)
2002—Jaguars, 26-7 (J)
(RS Pts.—Redskins 66, Jaguars 54)

KANSAS CITY vs. ARIZONA
RS: Chiefs lead series, 6-2-1;
See Arizona vs. Kansas City
KANSAS CITY vs. ATLANTA
RS: Chiefs lead series, 5-1;
See Atlanta vs. Kansas City
KANSAS CITY vs. BALTIMORE
RS: Chiefs lead series, 3-0;
See Baltimore vs. Kansas City
KANSAS CITY vs. BUFFALO
RS: Bills lead series, 18-16-1
PS: Bills lead series, 2-1;
See Buffalo vs. Kansas City
KANSAS CITY vs. CAROLINA
RS: Chiefs lead series, 2-1;
See Carolina vs. Kansas City
KANSAS CITY vs. CHICAGO
RS: Bears lead series, 5-4;
See Chicago vs. Kansas City
KANSAS CITY vs. CINCINNATI
RS: Chiefs lead series, 11-10;
See Cincinnati vs. Kansas City
KANSAS CITY vs. CLEVELAND
RS: Chiefs lead series, 9-8-2;

See Cleveland vs. Kansas City
KANSAS CITY vs. DALLAS
RS: Cowboys lead series, 4-3;
See Dallas vs. Kansas City
KANSAS CITY vs. DENVER
RS: Chiefs lead series, 50-39
PS: Broncos lead series, 1-0;
See Denver vs. Kansas City
KANSAS CITY vs. DETROIT
RS: Chiefs lead series, 7-3;
See Detroit vs. Kansas City
KANSAS CITY vs. GREEN BAY
RS: Chiefs lead series, 6-1-1
PS: Packers lead series, 1-0;
See Green Bay vs. Kansas City
KANSAS CITY vs. HOUSTON
RS: Series tied, 1-1;
See Houston vs. Kansas City
KANSAS CITY vs. INDIANAPOLIS
RS: Colts lead series, 8-7
PS: Colts lead series, 2-0;
See Indianapolis vs. Kansas City
KANSAS CITY vs. JACKSONVILLE
RS: Jaguars lead series, 4-1;
See Jacksonville vs. Kansas City
KANSAS CITY vs. MIAMI
RS: Chiefs lead series, 11-10
PS: Dolphins lead series, 3-0
1966—Chiefs, 34-16 (KC)
Chiefs, 19-18 (M)
1967—Chiefs, 24-0 (M)
Chiefs, 41-0 (KC)
1968—Chiefs, 48-3 (M)
1969—Chiefs, 17-10 (KC)
1971—*Dolphins, 27-24 (KC) OT
1972—Dolphins, 20-10 (KC)
1974—Dolphins, 9-3 (M)
1976—Chiefs, 20-17 (M) OT
1981—Dolphins, 17-7 (KC)
1983—Dolphins, 14-6 (M)
1985—Dolphins, 31-0 (M)
1987—Dolphins, 42-0 (M)
1989—Chiefs, 26-21 (KC)
Chiefs, 27-24 (M)
1990—**Dolphins, 17-16 (M)
1991—Chiefs, 42-7 (KC)
1993—Dolphins, 30-10 (M)
1994—Dolphins, 45-28 (M)
**Dolphins, 27-17 (M)
1995—Dolphins, 13-6 (M)
1997—Dolphins, 17-14 (M)
2002—Chiefs, 48-30 (KC)
(RS Pts.—Chiefs 430, Dolphins 384)
(PS Pts.—Dolphins 71, Chiefs 57)
*AFC Divisional Playoff
**AFC First-Round Playoff
KANSAS CITY vs. MINNESOTA
RS: Series tied, 4-4
PS: Chiefs lead series, 1-0
1969—*Chiefs, 23-7 (New Orleans)
1970—Vikings, 27-10 (M)
1974—Vikings, 35-15 (KC)
1981—Chiefs, 10-6 (M)
1990—Chiefs, 24-21 (KC)
1993—Vikings, 30-10 (M)
1996—Chiefs, 21-6 (M)
1999—Chiefs, 31-28 (KC)
2003—Vikings, 45-20 (M)
(RS Pts.—Vikings 198, Chiefs 141)
(PS Pts.—Chiefs 23, Vikings 7)

*Super Bowl IV
KANSAS CITY vs. **NEW ENGLAND
RS: Chiefs lead series, 15-11-3
1960—Patriots, 42-14 (B)
Texans, 34-0 (D)
1961—Patriots, 18-17 (D)
Patriots, 28-21 (B)
1962—Texans, 42-28 (D)
Texans, 27-7 (B)
1963—Tie, 24-24 (B)
Chiefs, 35-3 (KC)
1964—Patriots, 24-7 (B)
Patriots, 31-24 (KC)
1965—Chiefs, 27-17 (KC)
Tie, 10-10 (B)
1966—Chiefs, 43-24 (B)
Tie, 27-27 (KC)
1967—Chiefs, 33-10 (B)
1968—Chiefs, 31-17 (KC)
1969—Chiefs, 31-0 (B)
1970—Chiefs, 23-10 (KC)
1973—Chiefs, 10-7 (NE)
1977—Patriots, 21-17 (NE)
1981—Patriots, 33-17 (NE)
1990—Chiefs, 37-7 (NE)
1992—Chiefs, 27-20 (KC)
1995—Chiefs, 31-26 (KC)
1998—Patriots, 40-10 (NE)
1999—Chiefs, 16-14 (KC)
2000—Patriots, 30-24 (NE)
2002—Patriots, 41-38 (NE) OT
2004—Patriots, 27-19 (KC)
(RS Pts.—Chiefs 716, Patriots 586)
*Franchise located in Dallas prior to 1963
and known as Texans
**Franchise in Boston prior to 1971
KANSAS CITY vs. NEW ORLEANS
RS: Series tied, 4-4
1972—Chiefs, 20-17 (NO)
1976—Saints, 27-17 (KC)
1982—Saints, 27-17 (NO)
1985—Saints, 47-27 (NO)
1991—Saints, 17-10 (KC)
1994—Chiefs, 30-17 (NO)
1997—Chiefs, 25-13 (KC)
2004—Saints, 27-20 (NO)
(RS Pts.—Chiefs 186, Saints 172)
KANSAS CITY vs. N.Y. GIANTS
RS: Giants lead series, 8-2
1974—Giants, 33-27 (KC)
1978—Giants, 26-10 (KC)
1979—Giants, 21-17 (KC)
1983—Chiefs, 38-17 (KC)
1984—Giants, 28-27 (KC)
1988—Giants, 28-12 (NY)
1992—Giants, 35-21 (NY)
1995—Chiefs, 20-17 (KC) OT
1998—Giants, 28-7 (NY)
2001—Giants, 13-3 (KC)
(RS Pts.—Giants 246, Chiefs 182)
KANSAS CITY vs. **N.Y. JETS
RS: Chiefs lead series, 15-14-1
PS: Series tied, 1-1
1960—Titans, 37-35 (D)
Titans, 41-35 (NY)
1961—Titans, 28-7 (NY)
Texans, 35-24 (D)
1962—Texans, 20-17 (D)
Texans, 52-31 (NY)
1963—Jets, 17-0 (NY)

Chiefs, 48-0 (KC)
1964—Jets, 27-14 (NY)
Chiefs, 24-7 (KC)
1965—Chiefs, 14-10 (NY)
Jets, 13-10 (KC)
1966—Chiefs, 32-24 (NY)
1967—Chiefs, 42-18 (KC)
Chiefs, 21-7 (NY)
1968—Jets, 20-19 (KC)
1969—Chiefs, 34-16 (NY)
***Chiefs, 13-6 (NY)
1971—Jets, 13-10 (NY)
1974—Chiefs, 24-16 (KC)
1975—Jets, 30-24 (KC)
1982—Chiefs, 37-13 (KC)
1984—Jets, 17-16 (KC)
Jets, 28-7 (NY)
1986—****Jets, 35-15 (NY)
1987—Jets, 16-9 (KC)
1988—Tie, 17-17 (NY)
Chiefs, 38-34 (KC)
1992—Chiefs, 23-7 (NY)
1998—Jets, 20-17 (KC)
2001—Jets, 27-7 (NY)
2002—Chiefs, 29-25 (NY)
(RS Pts.—Chiefs 700, Jets 600)
(PS Pts.—Jets 41, Chiefs 28)
*Franchise in Dallas prior to 1963 and
known as Texans
**Jets known as Titans prior to 1963
***Inter-Divisional Playoff
****AFC First-Round Playoff
KANSAS CITY vs. **OAKLAND
RS: Chiefs lead series, 45-42-2
PS: Chiefs lead series, 2-1
1960—Texans, 34-16 (O)
Raiders, 20-19 (D)
1961—Texans, 42-35 (O)
Texans, 43-11 (D)
1962—Texans, 26-16 (O)
Texans, 35-7 (D)
1963—Raiders, 10-7 (O)
Raiders, 22-7 (KC)
1964—Chiefs, 21-9 (O)
Chiefs, 42-7 (KC)
1965—Raiders, 37-10 (O)
Chiefs, 14-7 (KC)
1966—Chiefs, 32-10 (O)
Raiders, 34-13 (KC)
1967—Raiders, 23-21 (O)
Raiders, 44-22 (KC)
1968—Chiefs, 24-10 (KC)
Raiders, 38-21 (O)
***Raiders, 41-6 (O)
1969—Raiders, 27-24 (KC)
Raiders, 10-6 (O)
****Chiefs, 17-7 (O)
1970—Tie, 17-17 (KC)
Raiders, 20-6 (O)
1971—Tie, 20-20 (O)
Chiefs, 16-14 (KC)
1972—Chiefs, 27-14 (KC)
Raiders, 26-3 (O)
1973—Chiefs, 16-3 (KC)
Raiders, 37-7 (O)
1974—Raiders, 27-7 (O)
Raiders, 7-6 (KC)
1975—Chiefs, 42-10 (KC)
Raiders, 28-20 (O)
1976—Raiders, 24-21 (KC)

Raiders, 21-10 (O)
1977—Raiders, 37-28 (KC)
Raiders, 21-20 (O)
1978—Raiders, 28-6 (O)
Raiders, 20-10 (KC)
1979—Chiefs, 35-7 (KC)
Chiefs, 24-21 (O)
1980—Raiders, 27-14 (KC)
Chiefs, 31-17 (O)
1981—Chiefs, 27-0 (KC)
Chiefs, 28-17 (O)
1982—Chiefs, 21-16 (KC)
1983—Raiders, 21-20 (LA)
Raiders, 28-20 (KC)
1984—Raiders, 22-20 (KC)
Raiders, 17-7 (LA)
1985—Chiefs, 36-20 (KC)
Raiders, 19-10 (LA)
1986—Raiders, 24-17 (KC)
Chiefs, 20-17 (LA)
1987—Raiders, 35-17 (LA)
Chiefs, 16-10 (KC)
1988—Raiders, 27-17 (KC)
Raiders, 17-10 (LA)
1989—Chiefs, 24-19 (KC)
Raiders, 20-14 (LA)
1990—Chiefs, 9-7 (KC)
Chiefs, 27-24 (LA)
1991—Chiefs, 24-21 (KC)
Chiefs, 27-21 (LA)
*****Chiefs, 10-6 (KC)
1992—Chiefs, 27-7 (KC)
Raiders, 28-7 (LA)
1993—Chiefs, 24-9 (KC)
Chiefs, 31-20 (LA)
1994—Chiefs, 13-3 (KC)
Chiefs, 19-9 (LA)
1995—Chiefs, 23-17 (KC) OT
Chiefs, 29-23 (O)
1996—Chiefs, 19-3 (KC)
Raiders, 26-7 (O)
1997—Chiefs, 28-27 (O)
Chiefs, 30-0 (KC)
1998—Chiefs, 28-8 (KC)
Chiefs, 31-24 (O)
1999—Chiefs, 37-34 (O)
Raiders, 41-38 (KC) OT
2000—Raiders, 20-17 (KC)
Raiders, 49-31 (O)
2001—Raiders, 27-24 (KC)
Raiders, 28-26 (O)
2002—Chiefs, 20-10 (KC)
Raiders, 24-0 (O)
2003—Chiefs, 17-10 (O)
Chiefs, 27-24 (KC)
2004—Chiefs, 34-27 (O)
Chiefs, 31-30 (KC)
(RS Pts.—Chiefs 1,873, Raiders 1,774)
(PS Pts.—Raiders 54, Chiefs 33)
*Franchise in Dallas prior to 1963 and
known as Texans
**Franchise in Los Angeles from
1982-1994
***Division Playoff
****AFL Championship
*****AFC First-Round Playoff
KANSAS CITY vs. PHILADELPHIA
RS: Series tied, 2-2
1972—Eagles, 21-20 (KC)
1992—Chiefs, 24-17 (KC)

1998—Chiefs, 24-21 (P)
2001—Eagles, 23-10 (KC)
(RS Pts.—Eagles 82, Chiefs 78)
KANSAS CITY vs. PITTSBURGH
RS: Steelers lead series, 16-8
PS: Chiefs lead series, 1-0
1970—Chiefs, 31-14 (P)
1971—Chiefs, 38-16 (KC)
1972—Steelers, 16-7 (P)
1974—Steelers, 34-24 (KC)
1975—Steelers, 28-3 (P)
1976—Steelers, 45-0 (KC)
1978—Steelers, 27-24 (P)
1979—Steelers, 30-3 (KC)
1980—Steelers, 21-16 (P)
1981—Chiefs, 37-33 (P)
1982—Steelers, 35-14 (P)
1984—Steelers, 37-27 (P)
1985—Steelers, 36-28 (KC)
1986—Chiefs, 24-19 (P)
1987—Steelers, 17-16 (KC)
1988—Steelers, 16-10 (P)
1989—Steelers, 23-17 (P)
1992—Steelers, 27-3 (KC)
1993—*Chiefs, 27-24 (KC) OT
1996—Steelers, 17-7 (KC)
1997—Chiefs, 13-10 (KC)
1998—Steelers, 20-13 (KC)
1999—Chiefs, 35-19 (KC)
2001—Steelers, 20-17 (KC)
2003—Chiefs, 41-20 (KC)
(RS Pts.—Steelers 570, Chiefs 458)
(PS Pts.—Chiefs 27, Steelers 24)
*AFC First-Round Playoff
KANSAS CITY vs. *ST. LOUIS
RS: Series tied, 4-4
1973—Rams, 23-13 (KC)
1982—Rams, 20-14 (LA)
1985—Rams, 16-0 (KC)
1991—Chiefs, 27-20 (LA)
1994—Rams, 16-0 (KC)
1997—Chiefs, 28-20 (StL)
2000—Chiefs, 54-34 (KC)
2002—Chiefs, 49-10 (KC)
(RS Pts.—Chiefs 185, Rams 159)
*Franchise in Los Angeles prior to 1995
KANSAS CITY vs. **SAN DIEGO
RS: Chiefs lead series, 47-41-1
PS: Chargers lead series, 1-0
1960—Chargers, 21-20 (LA)
Texans, 17-0 (D)
1961—Chargers, 26-10 (D)
Chargers, 24-14 (SD)
1962—Chargers, 32-28 (SD)
Texans, 26-17 (D)
1963—Chargers, 24-10 (SD)
Chargers, 38-17 (KC)
1964—Chargers, 28-14 (KC)
Chiefs, 49-6 (SD)
1965—Tie, 10-10 (SD)
Chiefs, 31-7 (KC)
1966—Chiefs, 24-14 (KC)
Chiefs, 27-17 (SD)
1967—Chargers, 45-31 (SD)
Chargers, 17-16 (KC)
1968—Chiefs, 27-20 (KC)
Chiefs, 40-3 (SD)
1969—Chiefs, 27-9 (SD)
Chiefs, 27-3 (KC)
1970—Chiefs, 26-14 (KC)

Chargers, 31-13 (SD)
1971—Chargers, 21-14 (SD)
Chiefs, 31-10 (KC)
1972—Chiefs, 26-14 (SD)
Chargers, 27-17 (KC)
1973—Chiefs, 19-0 (SD)
Chiefs, 33-6 (KC)
1974—Chiefs, 24-14 (SD)
Chargers, 14-7 (KC)
1975—Chiefs, 12-10 (SD)
Chargers, 28-20 (KC)
1976—Chargers, 30-16 (KC)
Chiefs, 23-20 (SD)
1977—Chargers, 23-7 (KC)
Chiefs, 21-16 (SD)
1978—Chargers, 29-23 (SD) OT
Chiefs, 23-0 (KC)
1979—Chargers, 20-14 (KC)
Chargers, 28-7 (SD)
1980—Chargers, 24-7 (SD)
Chargers, 20-7 (KC)
1981—Chargers, 42-31 (KC)
Chargers, 22-20 (SD)
1982—Chiefs, 19-12 (KC)
1983—Chargers, 17-14 (KC)
Chargers, 41-38 (SD)
1984—Chiefs, 31-13 (KC)
Chiefs, 42-21 (SD)
1985—Chargers, 31-20 (SD)
Chiefs, 38-34 (KC)
1986—Chiefs, 42-41 (KC)
Chiefs, 24-23 (SD)
1987—Chiefs, 20-13 (KC)
Chargers, 42-21 (SD)
1988—Chargers, 24-23 (KC)
Chargers, 24-13 (SD)
1989—Chargers, 21-6 (SD)
Chargers, 20-13 (KC)
1990—Chiefs, 27-10 (KC)
Chiefs, 24-21 (SD)
1991—Chiefs, 14-13 (SD)
Chiefs, 20-17 (KC) OT
1992—Chiefs, 24-10 (SD)
Chiefs, 16-14 (KC)
***Chargers, 17-0 (SD)
1993—Chiefs, 17-14 (SD)
Chiefs, 28-24 (KC)
1994—Chargers, 20-6 (SD)
Chargers, 14-13 (KC)
1995—Chargers, 29-23 (KC) OT
Chiefs, 22-7 (SD)
1996—Chargers, 22-19 (SD)
Chargers, 28-14 (KC)
1997—Chiefs, 31-3 (SD)
Chiefs, 29-7 (SD)
1998—Chiefs, 23-7 (KC)
Chargers, 38-37 (SD)
1999—Chargers, 21-14 (SD)
Chiefs, 34-0 (KC)
2000—Chiefs, 42-10 (KC)
Chargers, 17-16 (SD)
2001—Chiefs, 25-20 (SD)
Chiefs, 20-17 (KC)
2002—Chargers, 35-34 (SD)
Chiefs, 24-22 (KC)
2003—Chiefs, 27-14 (KC)
Chiefs, 28-24 (SD)
2004—Chargers, 34-31 (KC)
Chargers, 24-17 (SD)
(RS Pts.—Chiefs 1,975, Chargers 1,731)

(PS Pts.—Chargers 17, Chiefs 0)
*Franchise in Dallas prior to 1963 and
known as Texans
**Franchise in Los Angeles prior to 1961
***AFC First-Round Playoff
KANSAS CITY vs. SAN FRANCISCO
RS: 49ers lead series, 6-3
1971—Chiefs, 26-17 (SF)
1975—49ers, 20-3 (KC)
1982—49ers, 26-13 (KC)
1985—49ers, 31-3 (SF)
1991—49ers, 28-14 (SF)
1994—Chiefs, 24-17 (KC)
1997—Chiefs, 44-9 (KC)
2000—49ers, 21-7 (SF)
2002—49ers, 17-13 (SF)
(PS Pts.—49ers 186, Chiefs 147)
KANSAS CITY vs. SEATTLE
RS: Chiefs lead series, 30-18
1977—Seahawks, 34-31 (KC)
1978—Seahawks, 13-10 (KC)
Seahawks, 23-19 (S)
1979—Chiefs, 24-6 (S)
Chiefs, 37-21 (KC)
1980—Chiefs, 17-16 (KC)
Chiefs, 31-30 (S)
1981—Chiefs, 20-14 (S)
Chiefs, 40-13 (KC)
1983—Chiefs, 17-13 (KC)
Seahawks, 51-48 (S) OT
1984—Seahawks, 45-0 (S)
Chiefs, 34-7 (KC)
1985—Chiefs, 28-7 (KC)
Seahawks, 24-6 (S)
1986—Seahawks, 23-17 (S)
Chiefs, 27-7 (KC)
1987—Seahawks, 43-14 (S)
Chiefs, 41-20 (KC)
1988—Seahawks, 31-10 (S)
Chiefs, 27-24 (KC)
1989—Chiefs, 20-16 (S)
Chiefs, 20-10 (KC)
1990—Seahawks, 19-7 (S)
Seahawks, 17-16 (KC)
1991—Chiefs, 20-13 (KC)
Chiefs, 19-6 (S)
1992—Chiefs, 26-7 (KC)
Chiefs, 24-14 (S)
1993—Chiefs, 31-16 (S)
Chiefs, 34-24 (KC)
1994—Chiefs, 38-23 (KC)
Seahawks, 10-9 (S)
1995—Chiefs, 34-10 (S)
Chiefs, 26-3 (KC)
1996—Chiefs, 35-17 (S)
Chiefs, 34-16 (KC)
1997—Chiefs, 20-17 (KC) OT
Chiefs, 19-14 (S)
1998—Chiefs, 17-6 (KC)
Seahawks, 24-12 (S)
1999—Seahawks, 31-19 (KC)
Seahawks, 23-14 (S)
2000—Chiefs, 24-17 (KC)
Chiefs, 24-19 (S)
2001—Chiefs, 19-7 (KC)
Seahawks, 21-18 (S)
2002—Seahawks, 39-32 (S)
(RS Pts.—Chiefs 1,108, Seahawks 905)
KANSAS CITY vs. TAMPA BAY
RS: Chiefs lead series, 5-4

1976—Chiefs, 28-19 (TB)
1978—Buccaneers, 30-13 (KC)
1979—Buccaneers, 3-0 (TB)
1981—Chiefs, 19-10 (KC)
1984—Chiefs, 24-20 (KC)
1986—Chiefs, 27-20 (KC)
1993—Chiefs, 27-3 (TB)
1999—Buccaneers, 17-10 (TB)
2004—Buccaneers, 34-31 (TB)
(RS Pts.—Chiefs 179, Buccaneers 156)
*KANSAS CITY vs. **TENNESSEE
RS: Chiefs lead series, 25-18
PS: Chiefs lead series, 2-0
1960—Oilers, 20-10 (H)
Texans, 24-0 (D)
1961—Texans, 26-21 (D)
Oilers, 38-7 (H)
1962—Texans, 31-7 (H)
Oilers, 14-6 (D)
***Texans, 20-17 (H) OT
1963—Chiefs, 28-7 (KC)
Oilers, 28-7 (H)
1964—Chiefs, 28-7 (KC)
Chiefs, 28-19 (H)
1965—Chiefs, 52-21 (KC)
Oilers, 38-36 (H)
1966—Chiefs, 48-23 (KC)
1967—Chiefs, 25-20 (H)
Oilers, 24-19 (KC)
1968—Chiefs, 26-21 (H)
Chiefs, 24-10 (KC)
1969—Chiefs, 24-0 (KC)
1970—Chiefs, 24-9 (KC)
1971—Chiefs, 20-16 (H)
1973—Chiefs, 38-14 (KC)
1974—Chiefs, 17-7 (H)
1975—Chiefs, 17-13 (KC)
1977—Oilers, 34-20 (H)
1978—Oilers, 20-17 (KC)
1979—Oilers, 20-6 (H)
1980—Chiefs, 21-20 (KC)
1981—Chiefs, 23-10 (KC)
1983—Chiefs, 13-10 (H) OT
1984—Oilers, 17-16 (KC)
1985—Oilers, 23-20 (H)
1986—Chiefs, 27-13 (KC)
1988—Oilers, 7-6 (H)
1989—Chiefs, 34-0 (KC)
1990—Oilers, 27-10 (KC)
1991—Oilers, 17-7 (H)
1992—Oilers, 23-20 (H) OT
1993—Oilers, 30-0 (H)
****Chiefs, 28-20 (H)
1994—Chiefs, 31-9 (KC)
1995—Chiefs, 20-13 (KC)
1996—Chiefs, 20-19 (H)
2000—Titans, 17-14 (T) OT
2004—Chiefs, 49-38 (T)
(RS Pts.—Chiefs 935, Titans 748)
(PS Pts.—Chiefs 48, Titans 37)
*Franchise in Dallas prior to 1963 and
known as Texans
**Franchise in Houston prior to 1997;
known as Oilers prior to 1999
***AFL Championship
****AFC Divisional Playoff
KANSAS CITY vs. WASHINGTON
RS: Chiefs lead series, 5-1
1971—Chiefs, 27-20 (KC)
1976—Chiefs, 33-30 (W)

1983—Redskins, 27-12 (W)
1992—Chiefs, 35-16 (KC)
1995—Chiefs, 24-3 (KC)
2001—Chiefs, 45-13 (W)
(RS Pts.—Chiefs 176, Redskins 109)

MIAMI vs. ARIZONA
RS: Dolphins lead series, 8-1;
See Arizona vs. Miami
MIAMI vs. ATLANTA
RS: Dolphins lead series, 7-2;
See Atlanta vs. Miami
MIAMI vs. BALTIMORE
RS: Dolphins lead series, 4-1
PS: Ravens lead series, 1-0;
See Baltimore vs. Miami
MIAMI vs. BUFFALO
RS: Dolphins lead series, 48-29-1
PS: Bills lead series, 3-1;
See Buffalo vs. Miami
MIAMI vs. CAROLINA
RS: Dolphins lead series, 2-0;
See Carolina vs. Miami
MIAMI vs. CHICAGO
RS: Dolphins lead series, 6-3;
See Chicago vs. Miami
MIAMI vs. CINCINNATI
RS: Dolphins lead series, 12-4
PS: Dolphins lead series, 1-0;
See Cincinnati vs. Miami
MIAMI vs. CLEVELAND
RS: Dolphins lead series, 7-4
PS: Dolphins lead series, 2-0;
See Cleveland vs. Miami
MIAMI vs. DALLAS
RS: Dolphins lead series, 7-3
PS: Cowboys lead series, 1-0;
See Dallas vs. Miami
MIAMI vs. DENVER
RS: Dolphins lead series, 9-3-1
PS: Broncos lead series, 1-0;
See Denver vs. Miami
MIAMI vs. DETROIT
RS: Dolphins lead series, 6-2;
See Detroit vs. Miami
MIAMI vs. GREEN BAY
RS: Dolphins lead series, 9-2;
See Green Bay vs. Miami
MIAMI vs. HOUSTON
RS: Texans lead series, 1-0;
See Houston vs. Miami
MIAMI vs. INDIANAPOLIS
RS: Dolphins lead series, 44-22
PS: Dolphins lead series, 2-0;
See Indianapolis vs. Miami
MIAMI vs. JACKSONVILLE
RS: Series tied, 1-1
PS: Jaguars lead series, 1-0;
See Jacksonville vs. Miami
MIAMI vs. KANSAS CITY
RS: Chiefs lead series, 11-10
PS: Dolphins lead series, 3-0;
See Kansas City vs. Miami
MIAMI vs. MINNESOTA
RS: Series tied, 4-4
PS: Dolphins lead series, 1-0
1972—Dolphins, 16-14 (Minn)
1973—*Dolphins, 24-7 (Houston)
1976—Vikings, 29-7 (Mia)
1979—Dolphins, 27-12 (Minn)

1982—Dolphins, 22-14 (Mia)
1988—Dolphins, 24-7 (Mia)
1994—Vikings, 38-35 (Minn)
2000—Vikings, 13-7 (Minn)
2002—Vikings, 20-17 (Minn)
(RS Pts.—Dolphins 155, Vikings 147)
(PS Pts.—Dolphins 24, Vikings 7)
*Super Bowl VIII
MIAMI vs. *NEW ENGLAND
RS: Dolphins lead series, 45-31
PS: Patriots lead series, 2-1
1966—Patriots, 20-14 (M)
1967—Patriots, 41-10 (B)
        Dolphins, 41-32 (M)
1968—Patriots, 34-10 (B)
        Dolphins, 38-7 (M)
1969—Dolphins, 17-16 (B)
        Patriots, 38-23 (Tampa)
1970—Patriots, 27-14 (B)
        Dolphins, 37-20 (M)
1971—Dolphins, 41-3 (M)
        Patriots, 34-13 (NE)
1972—Dolphins, 52-0 (M)
        Dolphins, 37-21 (NE)
1973—Dolphins, 44-23 (M)
        Dolphins, 30-14 (NE)
1974—Patriots, 34-24 (NE)
        Dolphins, 34-27 (M)
1975—Dolphins, 22-14 (NE)
        Dolphins, 20-7 (M)
1976—Patriots, 30-14 (NE)
        Dolphins, 10-3 (M)
1977—Dolphins, 17-5 (M)
        Patriots, 14-10 (NE)
1978—Patriots, 33-24 (NE)
        Dolphins, 23-3 (M)
1979—Patriots, 28-13 (NE)
        Dolphins, 39-24 (M)
1980—Patriots, 34-0 (NE)
        Dolphins, 16-13 (M) OT
1981—Dolphins, 30-27 (NE) OT
        Dolphins, 24-14 (M)
1982—Patriots, 3-0 (NE)
        **Dolphins, 28-13 (M)
1983—Dolphins, 34-24 (M)
        Patriots, 17-6 (NE)
1984—Dolphins, 28-7 (M)
        Dolphins, 44-24 (NE)
1985—Patriots, 17-13 (NE)
        Dolphins, 30-27 (M)
        ***Patriots, 31-14 (M)
1986—Patriots, 34-7 (NE)
        Patriots, 34-27 (M)
1987—Patriots, 28-21 (NE)
        Patriots, 24-10 (M)
1988—Patriots, 21-10 (NE)
        Patriots, 6-3 (M)
1989—Dolphins, 24-10 (NE)
        Dolphins, 31-10 (M)
1990—Dolphins, 27-24 (NE)
        Dolphins, 17-10 (M)
1991—Dolphins, 20-10 (NE)
        Dolphins, 30-20 (M)
1992—Dolphins, 38-17 (M)
        Dolphins, 16-13 (NE) OT
1993—Dolphins, 17-13 (M)
        Patriots, 33-27 (NE) OT
1994—Dolphins, 39-35 (M)
        Dolphins, 23-3 (NE)
1995—Dolphins, 20-3 (NE)

        Patriots, 34-17 (M)
1996—Dolphins, 24-10 (M)
        Patriots, 42-23 (NE)
1997—Patriots, 27-24 (NE)
        Patriots, 14-12 (M)
        **Patriots, 17-3 (NE)
1998—Dolphins, 12-9 (M) OT
        Patriots, 26-23 (NE)
1999—Dolphins, 31-30 (NE)
        Dolphins, 27-17 (M)
2000—Dolphins, 10-3 (M)
        Dolphins, 27-24 (NE)
2001—Dolphins, 30-10 (M)
        Patriots, 20-13 (NE)
2002—Dolphins, 26-13 (M)
        Patriots, 27-24 (NE) OT
2003—Patriots, 19-13 (M) OT
        Patriots, 12-0 (NE)
2004—Patriots, 24-10 (NE)
        Dolphins, 29-28 (M)
(RS Pts.—Dolphins 1,702, Patriots 1,472)
(PS Pts.—Patriots 61, Dolphins 45)
*Franchise in Boston prior to 1971
**AFC First-Round Playoff
***AFC Championship
MIAMI vs. NEW ORLEANS
RS: Dolphins lead series, 5-3
1970—Dolphins, 21-10 (M)
1974—Dolphins, 21-0 (NO)
1980—Dolphins, 21-16 (M)
1983—Saints, 17-7 (NO)
1986—Dolphins, 31-27 (NO)
1992—Saints, 24-13 (NO)
1995—Saints, 33-30 (NO)
1998—Dolphins, 30-10 (M)
(RS Pts.—Dolphins 174, Saints 137)
MIAMI vs. N.Y. GIANTS
RS: Giants lead series, 3-2
1972—Dolphins, 23-13 (NY)
1990—Giants, 20-3 (NY)
1993—Giants, 19-14 (M)
1996—Giants, 17-7 (M)
2003—Dolphins, 23-10 (NY)
(RS Pts.—Giants 79, Dolphins 70)
MIAMI vs. N.Y. JETS
RS: Jets lead series, 40-37-1
PS: Dolphins lead series, 1-0
1966—Jets, 19-14 (M)
        Jets, 30-13 (NY)
1967—Jets, 29-7 (NY)
        Jets, 33-14 (M)
1968—Jets, 35-17 (NY)
        Jets, 31-7 (M)
1969—Jets, 34-31 (NY)
        Jets, 27-9 (M)
1970—Dolphins, 20-6 (NY)
        Dolphins, 16-10 (M)
1971—Jets, 14-10 (M)
        Dolphins, 30-14 (NY)
1972—Dolphins, 27-17 (NY)
        Dolphins, 28-24 (M)
1973—Dolphins, 31-3 (M)
        Dolphins, 24-14 (NY)
1974—Dolphins, 21-17 (M)
        Jets, 17-14 (NY)
1975—Dolphins, 43-0 (NY)
        Dolphins, 27-7 (M)
1976—Dolphins, 16-0 (M)
        Dolphins, 27-7 (NY)
1977—Dolphins, 21-17 (M)

Dolphins, 14-10 (NY)
1978—Jets, 33-20 (NY)
Jets, 24-13 (M)
1979—Jets, 33-27 (NY)
Jets, 27-24 (M)
1980—Jets, 17-14 (NY)
Jets, 24-17 (M)
1981—Tie, 28-28 (M) OT
Jets, 16-15 (NY)
1982—Dolphins, 45-28 (NY)
Dolphins, 20-19 (M)
*Dolphins, 14-0 (M)
1983—Dolphins, 32-14 (NY)
Dolphins, 34-14 (M)
1984—Dolphins, 31-17 (NY)
Dolphins, 28-17 (M)
1985—Jets, 23-7 (NY)
Dolphins, 21-17 (M)
1986—Jets, 51-45 (NY) OT
Dolphins, 45-3 (M)
1987—Jets, 37-31 (NY) OT
Dolphins, 37-28 (M)
1988—Jets, 44-30 (M)
Jets, 38-34 (NY)
1989—Jets, 40-33 (M)
Dolphins, 31-23 (NY)
1990—Dolphins, 20-16 (M)
Dolphins, 17-3 (NY)
1991—Jets, 41-23 (NY)
Jets, 23-20 (M) OT
1992—Jets, 26-14 (NY)
Dolphins, 19-17 (M)
1993—Jets, 24-14 (M)
Jets, 27-10 (NY)
1994—Dolphins, 28-14 (M)
Dolphins, 28-24 (NY)
1995—Dolphins, 52-14 (M)
Jets, 17-16 (NY)
1996—Dolphins, 36-27 (M)
Dolphins, 31-28 (NY)
1997—Dolphins, 31-20 (NY)
Dolphins, 24-17 (M)
1998—Jets, 20-9 (NY)
Jets, 21-16 (M)
1999—Jets, 28-20 (NY)
Jets, 38-31 (M)
2000—Jets, 40-37 (NY) OT
Jets, 20-3 (M)
2001—Jets, 21-17 (NY)
Jets, 24-0 (M)
2002—Dolphins, 30-3 (M)
Jets, 13-10 (NY)
2003—Dolphins, 21-10 (NY)
Dolphins, 23-21 (M)
2004—Jets, 17-9 (M)
Jets, 41-14 (NY)
(RS Pts.—Dolphins 1,766, Jets 1,685)
(PS Pts.—Dolphins 14, Jets 0)
*AFC Championship
MIAMI vs. *OAKLAND
RS: Raiders lead series, 15-10-1
PS: Raiders lead series, 3-1
1966—Raiders, 23-14 (M)
Raiders, 21-10 (O)
1967—Raiders, 31-17 (O)
1968—Raiders, 47-21 (M)
1969—Raiders, 20-17 (O)
Tie, 20-20 (M)
1970—Dolphins, 20-13 (M)
**Raiders, 21-14 (O)

1973—Raiders, 12-7 (O)
***Dolphins, 27-10 (M)
1974—**Raiders, 28-26 (O)
1975—Raiders, 31-21 (M)
1978—Dolphins, 23-6 (M)
1979—Raiders, 13-3 (O)
1980—Raiders, 16-10 (O)
1981—Raiders, 33-17 (M)
1983—Raiders, 27-14 (LA)
1984—Raiders, 45-34 (M)
1986—Raiders, 30-28 (M)
1988—Dolphins, 24-14 (LA)
1990—Raiders, 13-10 (M)
1992—Dolphins, 20-7 (M)
1994—Dolphins, 20-17 (M) OT
1996—Raiders, 17-7 (O)
1997—Dolphins, 34-16 (O)
1998—Dolphins, 27-17 (O)
1999—Dolphins, 16-9 (O)
2000—**Raiders, 27-0 (O)
2001—Dolphins, 18-15 (M)
2002—Dolphins, 23-17 (M)
(RS Pts.—Raiders 530, Dolphins 475)
(PS Pts.—Raiders 86, Dolphins 67)
*Franchise in Los Angeles from 1982-1994
**AFC Divisional Playoff
***AFC Championship
MIAMI vs. PHILADELPHIA
RS: Dolphins lead series, 7-4
1970—Eagles, 24-17 (P)
1975—Dolphins, 24-16 (M)
1978—Eagles, 17-3 (P)
1981—Dolphins, 13-10 (M)
1984—Dolphins, 24-23 (M)
1987—Dolphins, 28-10 (P)
1990—Dolphins, 23-20 (M) OT
1993—Dolphins, 19-14 (P)
1996—Eagles, 35-28 (P)
1999—Dolphins, 16-13 (M)
2003—Eagles, 34-27 (M)
(RS Pts.—Dolphins 222, Eagles 216)
MIAMI vs. PITTSBURGH
RS: Dolphins lead series, 9-8
PS: Dolphins lead series, 2-1
1971—Dolphins, 24-21 (M)
1972—*Dolphins, 21-17 (P)
1973—Dolphins, 30-26 (M)
1976—Steelers, 14-3 (P)
1979—**Steelers, 34-14 (P)
1980—Steelers, 23-10 (P)
1981—Dolphins, 30-10 (M)
1984—Dolphins, 31-7 (P)
*Dolphins, 45-28 (M)
1985—Dolphins, 24-20 (M)
1987—Dolphins, 35-24 (M)
1988—Steelers, 40-24 (P)
1989—Steelers, 34-14 (M)
1990—Dolphins, 28-6 (P)
1993—Steelers, 21-20 (M)
1994—Steelers, 16-13 (P) OT
1995—Dolphins, 23-10 (M)
1996—Steelers, 24-17 (M)
1998—Dolphins, 21-0 (M)
2004—Steelers, 13-3 (M)
(RS Pts.—Dolphins 350, Steelers 309)
(PS Pts.—Dolphins 80, Steelers 79)
*AFC Championship
**AFC Divisional Playoff
MIAMI vs. *ST. LOUIS
RS: Dolphins lead series, 8-2

1971—Dolphins, 20-14 (LA)
1976—Rams, 31-28 (M)
1980—Dolphins, 35-14 (LA)
1983—Dolphins, 30-14 (M)
1986—Dolphins, 37-31 (LA) OT
1992—Dolphins, 26-10 (M)
1995—Dolphins, 41-22 (StL)
1998—Dolphins, 14-0 (M)
2001—Rams, 42-10 (StL)
2004—Dolphins, 31-14 (M)
(RS Pts.—Dolphins 272, Rams 192)
*Franchise in Los Angeles prior to 1995
MIAMI vs. SAN DIEGO
RS: Series tied, 10-10
PS: Series tied, 2-2
1966—Chargers, 44-10 (SD)
1967—Chargers, 24-0 (SD)
Dolphins, 41-24 (M)
1968—Chargers, 34-28 (SD)
1969—Chargers, 21-14 (M)
1972—Dolphins, 24-10 (M)
1974—Dolphins, 28-21 (SD)
1977—Chargers, 14-13 (M)
1978—Dolphins, 28-21 (SD)
1980—Chargers, 27-24 (M) OT
1981—*Chargers, 41-38 (M) OT
1982—**Dolphins, 34-13 (M)
1984—Chargers, 34-28 (SD) OT
1986—Chargers, 50-28 (SD)
1988—Dolphins, 31-28 (SD)
1991—Chargers, 38-30 (SD)
1992—*Dolphins, 31-0 (M)
1993—Chargers, 45-20 (SD)
1994—*Chargers, 22-21 (SD)
1995—Dolphins, 24-14 (SD)
1999—Dolphins, 12-9 (M)
2000—Dolphins, 17-7 (SD)
2002—Dolphins, 30-3 (M)
2003—Dolphins, 26-10 (Ariz)
(RS Pts.—Chargers 478, Dolphins 456)
(PS Pts.—Dolphins 124, Chargers 76)
*AFC Divisional Playoff
**AFC Second-Round Playoff
MIAMI vs. SAN FRANCISCO
RS: Dolphins lead series, 5-4
PS: 49ers lead series, 1-0
1973—Dolphins, 21-13 (M)
1977—Dolphins, 19-15 (SF)
1980—Dolphins, 17-13 (M)
1983—Dolphins, 20-17 (SF)
1984—*49ers, 38-16 (Stanford)
1986—49ers, 31-16 (M)
1992—49ers, 27-3 (SF)
1995—49ers, 44-20 (M)
2001—49ers, 21-0 (SF)
2004—Dolphins, 24-17 (SF)
(RS Pts.—49ers 198, Dolphins 140)
(PS Pts.—49ers 38, Dolphins 16)
*Super Bowl XIX
MIAMI vs. SEATTLE
RS: Dolphins lead series, 6-3
PS: Dolphins lead series, 2-1
1977—Dolphins, 31-13 (M)
1979—Dolphins, 19-10 (M)
1983—*Seahawks, 27-20 (M)
1984—*Dolphins, 31-10 (M)
1987—Seahawks, 24-20 (S)
1990—Dolphins, 24-17 (M)
1992—Dolphins, 19-17 (S)
1996—Seahawks, 22-15 (M)

1999—**Dolphins, 20-17 (S)
2000—Dolphins, 23-0 (M)
2001—Dolphins, 24-20 (S)
2004—Seahawks, 24-17 (S)
(RS Pts.—Dolphins 192, Seahawks 147)
(PS Pts.—Dolphins 71, Seahawks 54)
*AFC Divisional Playoff
**AFC First-Round Playoff
MIAMI vs. TAMPA BAY
RS: Dolphins lead series, 4-3
1976—Dolphins, 23-20 (TB)
1982—Buccaneers, 23-17 (TB)
1985—Dolphins, 41-38 (M)
1988—Dolphins, 17-14 (TB)
1991—Dolphins, 33-14 (M)
1997—Buccaneers, 31-21 (TB)
2000—Buccaneers, 16-13 (M)
(RS Pts.—Dolphins 165, Buccaneers 156)
MIAMI vs. *TENNESSEE
RS: Dolphins lead series, 15-13
PS: Titans lead series, 1-0
1966—Dolphins, 20-13 (H)
       Dolphins, 29-28 (M)
1967—Oilers, 17-14 (H)
       Oilers, 41-10 (M)
1968—Oilers, 24-10 (M)
       Dolphins, 24-7 (H)
1969—Oilers, 22-10 (H)
       Oilers, 32-7 (M)
1970—Dolphins, 20-10 (H)
1972—Dolphins, 34-13 (M)
1975—Oilers, 20-19 (H)
1977—Dolphins, 27-7 (M)
1978—Oilers, 35-30 (H)
       **Oilers, 17-9 (M)
1979—Oilers, 9-6 (M)
1981—Dolphins, 16-10 (H)
1983—Dolphins, 24-17 (H)
1984—Dolphins, 28-10 (M)
1985—Oilers, 26-23 (H)
1986—Dolphins, 28-7 (M)
1989—Oilers, 39-7 (H)
1991—Oilers, 17-13 (M)
1992—Dolphins, 19-16 (M)
1996—Dolphins, 23-20 (H)
1997—Dolphins, 16-13 (M) OT
1999—Dolphins, 17-0 (M)
2001—Dolphins, 31-23 (T)
2003—Titans, 31-7 (T)
2004—Titans, 17-7 (M)
(RS Pts.—Titans 524, Dolphins 519)
(PS Pts.—Titans 17, Dolphins 9)
*Franchise in Houston prior to 1997;
known as Oilers prior to 1999
**AFC First-Round Playoff
MIAMI vs. WASHINGTON
RS: Dolphins lead series, 6-3
PS: Series tied, 1-1
1972—*Dolphins, 14-7 (Los Angeles)
1974—Redskins, 20-17 (W)
1978—Dolphins, 16-0 (W)
1981—Dolphins, 13-10 (M)
1982—**Redskins, 27-17 (Pasadena)
1984—Dolphins, 35-17 (W)
1987—Dolphins, 23-21 (M)
1990—Redskins, 42-20 (W)
1993—Dolphins, 17-10 (M)
1999—Redskins, 21-10 (W)
2003—Dolphins, 24-23 (M)
(RS Pts.—Dolphins 175, Redskins 164)

(PS Pts.—Redskins 34, Dolphins 31)
*Super Bowl VII
**Super Bowl XVII

MINNESOTA vs. ARIZONA
RS: Cardinals lead series, 9-8
PS: Vikings lead series, 2-0;
See Arizona vs. Minnesota
MINNESOTA vs. ATLANTA
RS: Vikings lead series, 14-7
PS: Series tied, 1-1;
See Atlanta vs. Minnesota
MINNESOTA vs. BALTIMORE
RS: Series tied, 1-1;
See Baltimore vs. Minnesota
MINNESOTA vs. BUFFALO
RS: Vikings lead series, 7-3;
See Buffalo vs. Minnesota
MINNESOTA vs. CAROLINA
RS: Vikings lead series, 3-2;
See Carolina vs. Minnesota
MINNESOTA vs. CHICAGO
RS: Vikings lead series, 47-38-2
PS: Bears lead series, 1-0;
See Chicago vs. Minnesota
MINNESOTA vs. CINCINNATI
RS: Vikings lead series, 5-4;
See Cincinnati vs. Minnesota
MINNESOTA vs. CLEVELAND
RS: Vikings lead series, 8-3
PS: Vikings lead series, 1-0;
See Cleveland vs. Minnesota
MINNESOTA vs. DALLAS
RS: Vikings lead series, 10-9
PS: Cowboys lead series, 4-2;
See Dallas vs. Minnesota
MINNESOTA vs. DENVER
RS: Vikings lead series, 7-4;
See Denver vs. Minnesota
MINNESOTA vs. DETROIT
RS: Vikings lead series, 56-29-2;
See Detroit vs. Minnesota
MINNESOTA vs. GREEN BAY
RS: Packers lead series, 44-42-1
PS: Vikings lead series, 1-0;
See Green Bay vs. Minnesota
MINNESOTA vs. HOUSTON
RS: Vikings lead series, 1-0;
See Houston vs. Minnesota
MINNESOTA vs. INDIANAPOLIS
RS: Colts lead series, 13-7-1
PS: Colts lead series, 1-0;
See Indianapolis vs. Minnesota
MINNESOTA vs. JACKSONVILLE
RS: Vikings lead series, 2-1;
See Jacksonville vs. Minnesota
MINNESOTA vs. KANSAS CITY
RS: Series tied, 4-4
PS: Chiefs lead series, 1-0;
See Kansas City vs. Minnesota
MINNESOTA vs. MIAMI
RS: Series tied, 4-4
PS: Dolphins lead series, 1-0;
See Miami vs. Minnesota
MINNESOTA vs. *NEW ENGLAND
RS: Patriots lead series, 5-4
1970—Vikings, 35-14 (B)
1974—Patriots, 17-14 (M)
1979—Patriots, 27-23 (NE)
1988—Vikings, 36-6 (M)

1991—Patriots, 26-23 (NE) OT
1994—Patriots, 26-20 (NE) OT
1997—Vikings, 23-18 (M)
2000—Vikings, 21-13 (NE)
2002—Patriots, 24-17 (NE)
(RS Pts.—Vikings 212, Patriots 171)
*Franchise in Boston prior to 1971
MINNESOTA vs. NEW ORLEANS
RS: Vikings lead series, 16-7
PS: Vikings lead series, 2-0
1968—Saints, 20-17 (NO)
1970—Vikings, 26-0 (M)
1971—Vikings, 23-10 (NO)
1972—Vikings, 37-6 (M)
1974—Vikings, 29-9 (M)
1975—Vikings, 20-7 (NO)
1976—Vikings, 40-9 (NO)
1978—Saints, 31-24 (NO)
1980—Vikings, 23-20 (NO)
1981—Vikings, 20-10 (M)
1983—Saints, 17-16 (NO)
1985—Saints, 30-23 (M)
1986—Vikings, 33-17 (M)
1987—*Vikings, 44-10 (NO)
1988—Vikings, 45-3 (M)
1990—Vikings, 32-3 (M)
1991—Saints, 26-0 (NO)
1993—Saints, 17-14 (M)
1994—Vikings, 21-20 (M)
1995—Vikings, 43-24 (M)
1998—Vikings, 31-24 (M)
2000—**Vikings, 34-16 (M)
2001—Saints, 28-15 (NO)
2002—Vikings, 32-31 (M)
2004—Vikings, 38-31 (NO)
(RS Pts.—Vikings 602, Saints 393)
(PS Pts.—Vikings 78, Saints 26)
*NFC First-Round Playoff
**NFC Divisional Playoff
MINNESOTA vs. N.Y. GIANTS
RS: Vikings lead series, 9-8
PS: Giants lead series, 2-1
1964—Vikings, 30-21 (NY)
1965—Vikings, 40-14 (M)
1967—Vikings, 27-24 (M)
1969—Giants, 24-23 (NY)
1971—Vikings, 17-10 (M)
1973—Vikings, 31-7 (New Haven)
1976—Vikings, 24-7 (M)
1986—Giants, 22-20 (M)
1989—Giants, 24-14 (NY)
1990—Giants, 23-15 (NY)
1993—*Giants, 17-10 (NY)
1994—Vikings, 27-10 (NY)
1996—Giants, 15-10 (NY)
1997—*Vikings, 23-22 (NY)
1999—Vikings, 34-17 (NY)
2000—**Giants, 41-0 (NY)
2001—Vikings, 28-16 (M)
2002—Giants, 27-20 (M)
2003—Giants, 29-17 (M)
2004—Giants, 34-13 (M)
(RS Pts.—Vikings 390, Giants 324)
(PS Pts.—Giants 80, Vikings 33)
*NFC First-Round Playoff
**NFC Championship
MINNESOTA vs. N.Y. JETS
RS: Jets lead series, 6-1
1970—Jets, 20-10 (NY)
1975—Vikings, 29-21 (M)

1979—Jets, 14-7 (NY)
1982—Jets, 42-14 (M)
1994—Jets, 31-21 (M)
1997—Jets, 23-21 (NY)
2002—Jets, 20-7 (NY)
(RS Pts.—Jets 171, Vikings 109)
MINNESOTA vs. *OAKLAND
RS: Raiders lead series, 8-3
PS: Raiders lead series, 1-0
1973—Vikings, 24-16 (M)
1976—**Raiders, 32-14 (Pasadena)
1977—Raiders, 35-13 (O)
1978—Raiders, 27-20 (O)
1981—Raiders, 36-10 (M)
1984—Raiders, 23-20 (LA)
1987—Vikings, 31-20 (M)
1990—Raiders, 28-24 (M)
1993—Raiders, 24-7 (LA)
1996—Vikings, 16-13 (O) OT
1999—Raiders, 22-17 (M)
2003—Raiders, 28-18 (O)
(RS Pts.—Raiders 272, Vikings 200)
(PS Pts.—Raiders 32, Vikings 14)
Franchise in Los Angeles from 1982-1994
**Super Bowl XI*
MINNESOTA vs. PHILADELPHIA
RS: Vikings lead series, 11-8
PS: Eagles lead series, 2-0
1962—Vikings, 31-21 (M)
1963—Vikings, 34-13 (P)
1968—Vikings, 24-17 (P)
1971—Vikings, 13-0 (P)
1973—Vikings, 28-21 (M)
1976—Vikings, 31-12 (M)
1978—Vikings, 28-27 (M)
1980—Eagles, 42-7 (M)
    *Eagles, 31-16 (P)
1981—Vikings, 35-23 (M)
1984—Eagles, 19-17 (P)
1985—Vikings, 28-23 (P)
    Eagles, 37-35 (M)
1988—Vikings, 23-21 (M)
1989—Eagles, 10-9 (P)
1990—Eagles, 32-24 (P)
1992—Eagles, 28-17 (P)
1997—Vikings, 28-19 (M)
2001—Eagles, 48-17 (P)
2004—Eagles, 27-16 (P)
    *Eagles, 27-14 (P)
(RS Pts.—Vikings 445, Eagles 440)
(PS Pts.—Eagles 58, Vikings 30)
NFC Divisional Playoff
MINNESOTA vs. PITTSBURGH
RS: Vikings lead series, 8-5
PS: Steelers lead series, 1-0
1962—Steelers, 39-31 (P)
1964—Vikings, 30-10 (M)
1967—Vikings, 41-27 (P)
1969—Vikings, 52-14 (M)
1972—Steelers, 23-10 (P)
1974—*Steelers, 16-6 (New Orleans)
1976—Vikings, 17-6 (M)
1980—Steelers, 23-17 (M)
1983—Vikings, 17-14 (P)
1986—Vikings, 31-7 (M)
1989—Steelers, 27-14 (P)
1992—Vikings, 6-3 (M)
1995—Vikings, 44-24 (P)
2001—Steelers, 21-16 (P)
(RS Pts.—Vikings 326, Steelers 238)

(PS Pts.—Steelers 16, Vikings 6)
Super Bowl IX
MINNESOTA vs. *ST. LOUIS
RS: Vikings lead series, 16-13-2
PS: Vikings lead series, 5-2
1961—Rams, 31-17 (LA)
    Vikings, 42-21 (M)
1962—Vikings, 38-14 (LA)
    Tie, 24-24 (M)
1963—Rams, 27-24 (LA)
    Vikings, 21-13 (M)
1964—Rams, 22-13 (LA)
    Vikings, 34-13 (M)
1965—Vikings, 38-35 (LA)
    Vikings, 24-13 (M)
1966—Vikings, 35-7 (M)
    Rams, 21-6 (LA)
1967—Rams, 39-3 (LA)
1968—Rams, 31-3 (M)
1969—Vikings, 20-13 (LA)
    **Vikings, 23-20 (M)
1970—Vikings, 13-3 (M)
1972—Vikings, 45-41 (LA)
1973—Vikings, 10-9 (M)
1974—Rams, 20-17 (LA)
    ***Vikings, 14-10 (M)
1976—Tie, 10-10 (M) OT
    ***Vikings, 24-13 (M)
1977—Rams, 35-3 (LA)
    ****Vikings, 14-7 (LA)
1978—Rams, 34-17 (M)
    ****Rams, 34-10 (LA)
1979—Rams, 27-21 (LA) OT
1985—Rams, 13-10 (LA)
1987—Vikings, 21-16 (LA)
1988—*****Vikings, 28-17 (M)
1989—Vikings, 23-21 (M) OT
1991—Vikings, 20-14 (M)
1992—Vikings, 31-17 (LA)
1998—Vikings, 38-31 (StL)
1999—*****Rams, 49-37 (StL)
2000—Rams, 40-29 (StL)
2003—Rams, 48-17 (StL)
(RS Pts.—Rams 703, Vikings 667)
(PS Pts.—Rams 150, Vikings 150)
Franchise in Los Angeles prior to 1995
**Conference Championship*
***NFC Championship*
****NFC Divisional Playoff*
*****NFC First-Round Playoff*
MINNESOTA vs. SAN DIEGO
RS: Chargers lead series, 5-4
1971—Chargers, 30-14 (SD)
1975—Vikings, 28-13 (M)
1978—Chargers, 13-7 (M)
1981—Vikings, 33-31 (SD)
1984—Chargers, 42-13 (M)
1985—Vikings, 21-17 (M)
1993—Chargers, 30-17 (M)
1999—Vikings, 35-27 (M)
2003—Chargers, 42-28 (SD)
(RS Pts.—Chargers 245, Vikings 196)
MINNESOTA vs. SAN FRANCISCO
RS: Vikings lead series, 18-17-1
PS: 49ers lead series, 4-1
1961—49ers, 38-24 (M)
    49ers, 38-28 (SF)
1962—49ers, 21-7 (SF)
    49ers, 35-12 (M)
1963—Vikings, 24-20 (SF)

    Vikings, 45-14 (M)
1964—Vikings, 27-22 (SF)
    Vikings, 24-7 (M)
1965—Vikings, 42-41 (SF)
    49ers, 45-24 (M)
1966—Tie, 20-20 (SF)
    Vikings, 28-3 (SF)
1967—49ers, 27-21 (M)
1968—Vikings, 30-20 (SF)
1969—Vikings, 10-7 (M)
1970—*49ers, 17-14 (M)
1971—49ers, 13-9 (M)
1972—49ers, 20-17 (SF)
1973—Vikings, 17-13 (SF)
1975—Vikings, 27-17 (M)
1976—49ers, 20-16 (SF)
1977—Vikings, 28-27 (M)
1979—Vikings, 28-22 (M)
1983—49ers, 48-17 (M)
1984—49ers, 51-7 (M)
1985—Vikings, 28-21 (M)
1986—Vikings, 27-24 (SF) OT
1987—*Vikings, 36-24 (SF)
1988—49ers, 24-21 (SF)
    *49ers, 34-9 (SF)
1989—*49ers, 41-13 (SF)
1990—49ers, 20-17 (M)
1991—Vikings, 17-14 (M)
1992—49ers, 20-17 (M)
1993—Vikings, 38-19 (SF)
1994—Vikings, 21-14 (M)
1995—49ers, 37-30 (SF)
1997—49ers, 28-17 (SF)
    *49ers, 38-22 (SF)
1999—Vikings, 40-16 (M)
2003—Vikings, 35-7 (M)
(RS Pts.—49ers 852, Vikings 821)
(PS Pts.—49ers 154, Vikings 94)
NFC Divisional Playoff
MINNESOTA vs. SEATTLE
RS: Seahawks lead series, 6-3
1976—Vikings, 27-21 (M)
1978—Seahawks, 29-28 (S)
1984—Seahawks, 20-12 (M)
1987—Seahawks, 28-17 (S)
1990—Vikings, 24-21 (S)
1996—Seahawks, 42-23 (S)
2002—Seahawks, 48-23 (S)
2003—Vikings, 34-7 (M)
2004—Seahawks, 27-23 (M)
(RS Pts.—Seahawks 243, Vikings 211)
MINNESOTA vs. TAMPA BAY
RS: Vikings lead series, 31-18
1977—Vikings, 9-3 (TB)
1978—Buccaneers, 16-10 (M)
    Vikings, 24-7 (TB)
1979—Buccaneers, 12-10 (M)
    Vikings, 23-22 (TB)
1980—Vikings, 38-30 (M)
    Vikings, 21-10 (TB)
1981—Buccaneers, 21-13 (TB)
    Vikings, 25-10 (M)
1982—Vikings, 17-10 (M)
1983—Vikings, 19-16 (TB) OT
    Buccaneers, 17-12 (M)
1984—Buccaneers, 35-31 (TB)
    Vikings, 27-24 (M)
1985—Vikings, 31-16 (TB)
    Vikings, 26-7 (M)
1986—Vikings, 23-10 (TB)

Vikings, 45-13 (M)
1987—Buccaneers, 20-10 (TB)
Vikings, 23-17 (M)
1988—Vikings, 14-13 (M)
Vikings, 49-20 (TB)
1989—Vikings, 17-3 (M)
Vikings, 24-10 (TB)
1990—Buccaneers, 23-20 (M) OT
Buccaneers, 26-13 (TB)
1991—Vikings, 28-13 (M)
Vikings, 26-24 (TB)
1992—Vikings, 26-20 (M)
Vikings, 35-7 (TB)
1993—Vikings, 15-0 (M)
Buccaneers, 23-10 (TB)
1994—Vikings, 36-13 (TB)
Buccaneers, 20-17 (M) OT
1995—Buccaneers, 20-17 (TB) OT
Vikings, 31-17 (M)
1996—Buccaneers, 24-13 (TB)
Vikings, 21-10 (M)
1997—Buccaneers, 28-14 (M)
Vikings, 10-6 (TB)
1998—Vikings, 31-7 (M)
Buccaneers, 27-24 (TB)
1999—Vikings, 21-14 (M)
Buccaneers, 24-17 (TB)
2000—Vikings, 30-23 (M)
Buccaneers, 41-13 (TB)
2001—Vikings, 20-16 (M)
Buccaneers, 41-14 (TB)
2002—Buccaneers, 38-24 (TB)
(RS Pts.—Vikings 1,067, Buccaneers 867)
MINNESOTA vs. *TENNESSEE
RS: Vikings lead series, 7-3
1974—Vikings, 51-10 (M)
1980—Oilers, 20-16 (H)
1983—Vikings, 34-14 (M)
1986—Oilers, 23-10 (H)
1989—Vikings, 38-7 (M)
1992—Oilers, 17-13 (M)
1995—Vikings, 23-17 (M) OT
1998—Vikings, 26-16 (T)
2001—Vikings, 42-24 (M)
2004—Vikings, 20-3 (M)
(RS Pts.—Vikings 273, Titans 151)
*Franchise in Houston prior to 1997;
known as Oilers prior to 1999
MINNESOTA vs. WASHINGTON
RS: Redskins lead series, 7-5
PS: Redskins lead series, 3-2
1968—Vikings, 27-14 (M)
1970—Vikings, 19-10 (M)
1972—Redskins, 24-21 (M)
1973—*Vikings, 27-20 (M)
1975—Redskins, 31-30 (W)
1976—*Vikings, 35-20 (M)
1980—Vikings, 39-14 (W)
1982—**Redskins, 21-7 (W)
1984—Redskins, 31-17 (M)
1986—Redskins, 44-38 (W) OT
1987—Redskins, 27-24 (M) OT
***Redskins, 17-10 (W)
1992—Redskins, 15-13 (M)
****Redskins, 24-7 (M)
1993—Vikings, 14-9 (W)
1998—Vikings, 41-7 (M)
2004—Redskins, 21-18 (W)
(RS Pts.—Vikings 301, Redskins 247)
(PS Pts.—Redskins 102, Vikings 86)

*NFC Divisional Playoff
**NFC Second-Round Playoff
***NFC Championship
****NFC First-Round Playoff

NEW ENGLAND vs. ARIZONA
RS: Cardinals lead series, 6-5;
See Arizona vs. New England
NEW ENGLAND vs. ATLANTA
RS: Falcons lead series, 6-4;
See Atlanta vs. New England
NEW ENGLAND vs. BALTIMORE
RS: Patriots lead series, 3-0;
See Baltimore vs. New England
NEW ENGLAND vs. BUFFALO
RS: Patriots lead series, 48-40-1
PS: Patriots lead series, 1-0;
See Buffalo vs. New England
NEW ENGLAND vs. CAROLINA
RS: Series tied, 1-1
PS: Patriots lead series, 1-0;
See Carolina vs. New England
NEW ENGLAND vs. CHICAGO
RS: Patriots lead series, 6-3
PS: Bears lead series, 1-0;
See Chicago vs. New England
NEW ENGLAND vs. CINCINNATI
RS: Patriots lead series, 11-8;
See Cincinnati vs. New England
NEW ENGLAND vs. CLEVELAND
RS: Browns lead series, 11-8
PS: Browns lead series, 1-0;
See Cleveland vs. New England
NEW ENGLAND vs. DALLAS
RS: Cowboys lead series, 7-2;
See Dallas vs. New England
NEW ENGLAND vs. DENVER
RS: Broncos lead series, 22-15
PS: Broncos lead series, 1-0;
See Denver vs. New England
NEW ENGLAND vs. DETROIT
RS: Series tied, 4-4;
See Detroit vs. New England
NEW ENGLAND vs. GREEN BAY
RS: Packers lead series, 4-3
PS: Packers lead series, 1-0;
See Green Bay vs. New England
NEW ENGLAND vs. HOUSTON
RS: Patriots lead series, 1-0;
See Houston vs. New England
NEW ENGLAND vs. INDIANAPOLIS
RS: Patriots lead series, 41-24
PS: Patriots lead series, 2-0;
See Indianapolis vs. New England
NEW ENGLAND vs. JACKSONVILLE
RS: Patriots lead series, 3-0
PS: Series tied, 1-1;
See Jacksonville vs. New England
NEW ENGLAND vs. KANSAS CITY
RS: Chiefs lead series, 15-11-3;
See Kansas City vs. New England
NEW ENGLAND vs. MIAMI
RS: Dolphins lead series, 45-31
PS: Patriots lead series, 2-1;
See Miami vs. New England
NEW ENGLAND vs. MINNESOTA
RS: Patriots lead series, 5-4;
See Minnesota vs. New England
NEW ENGLAND vs. NEW ORLEANS
RS: Patriots lead series, 7-3

1972—Patriots, 17-10 (NO)
1976—Patriots, 27-6 (NE)
1980—Patriots, 38-27 (NO)
1983—Patriots, 7-0 (NE)
1986—Patriots, 21-20 (NO)
1989—Saints, 28-24 (NE)
1992—Saints, 31-14 (NE)
1995—Saints, 31-17 (NE)
1998—Patriots, 30-27 (NO)
2001—Patriots, 34-17 (NE)
(RS Pts.—Patriots 229, Saints 197)
*NEW ENGLAND vs. N.Y. GIANTS
RS: Patriots lead series, 4-3
1970—Giants, 16-0 (B)
1974—Patriots, 28-20 (New Haven)
1987—Giants, 17-10 (NY)
1990—Giants, 13-10 (NY)
1996—Patriots, 23-22 (NY)
1999—Patriots, 16-14 (NE)
2003—Patriots, 17-6 (NE)
(RS Pts.—Giants 108, Patriots 104)
*Franchise in Boston prior to 1971
*NEW ENGLAND vs. **N.Y. JETS
RS: Jets lead series, 47-41-1
PS: Patriots lead series, 1-0
1960—Patriots, 28-24 (NY)
Patriots, 38-21 (B)
1961—Titans, 21-20 (B)
Titans, 37-30 (NY)
1962—Patriots, 43-14 (NY)
Patriots, 24-17 (B)
1963—Patriots, 38-14 (B)
Jets, 31-24 (NY)
1964—Patriots, 26-10 (B)
Jets, 35-14 (NY)
1965—Jets, 30-20 (B)
Patriots, 27-23 (NY)
1966—Tie, 24-24 (B)
Jets, 38-28 (NY)
1967—Jets, 30-23 (NY)
Jets, 29-24 (B)
1968—Jets, 47-31 (Birmingham)
Jets, 48-14 (NY)
1969—Jets, 23-14 (B)
Jets, 23-17 (NY)
1970—Jets, 31-21 (B)
Jets, 17-3 (NY)
1971—Patriots, 20-0 (NE)
Jets, 13-6 (NY)
1972—Jets, 41-13 (NE)
Jets, 34-10 (NY)
1973—Jets, 9-7 (NE)
Jets, 33-13 (NY)
1974—Patriots, 24-0 (NY)
Jets, 21-16 (NE)
1975—Jets, 36-7 (NY)
Jets, 30-28 (NE)
1976—Patriots, 41-7 (NE)
Patriots, 38-24 (NY)
1977—Jets, 30-27 (NY)
Patriots, 24-13 (NE)
1978—Patriots, 55-21 (NE)
Patriots, 19-17 (NY)
1979—Patriots, 56-3 (NE)
Jets, 27-26 (NY)
1980—Patriots, 21-11 (NY)
Patriots, 34-21 (NE)
1981—Jets, 28-24 (NY)
Jets, 17-6 (NE)
1982—Jets, 31-7 (NE)

1983—Patriots, 23-13 (NE)
    Jets, 26-3 (NY)
1984—Patriots, 28-21 (NY)
    Patriots, 30-20 (NE)
1985—Patriots, 20-13 (NE)
    Jets, 16-13 (NY) OT
    ***Patriots, 26-14 (NY)
1986—Patriots, 20-6 (NY)
    Jets, 31-24 (NE)
1987—Jets, 43-24 (NY)
    Patriots, 42-20 (NE)
1988—Patriots, 28-3 (NE)
    Patriots, 14-13 (NY)
1989—Patriots, 27-24 (NY)
    Jets, 27-26 (NE)
1990—Jets, 37-13 (NE)
    Jets, 42-7 (NY)
1991—Jets, 28-21 (NE)
    Patriots, 6-3 (NY)
1992—Jets, 30-21 (NY)
    Patriots, 24-3 (NE)
1993—Jets, 45-7 (NY)
    Jets, 6-0 (NE)
1994—Jets, 24-17 (NY)
    Patriots, 24-13 (NE)
1995—Patriots, 20-7 (NY)
    Patriots, 31-28 (NE)
1996—Patriots, 31-27 (NY)
    Patriots, 34-10 (NE)
1997—Patriots, 27-24 (NE) OT
    Jets, 24-19 (NY)
1998—Jets, 24-14 (NE)
    Jets, 31-10 (NY)
1999—Patriots, 30-28 (NY)
    Jets, 24-17 (NE)
2000—Jets, 20-19 (NY)
    Jets, 34-17 (NE)
2001—Jets, 10-3 (NE)
    Patriots, 17-16 (NY)
2002—Patriots, 44-7 (NY)
    Jets, 30-17 (NE)
2003—Patriots, 23-16 (NE)
    Patriots, 21-16 (NY)
2004—Patriots, 13-7 (NE)
    Patriots, 23-7 (NY)
(RS Pts.—Jets 1,951, Patriots 1,945)
(PS Pts.—Patriots 26, Jets 14)
*Franchise in Boston prior to 1971
**Jets known as Titans prior to 1963
***AFC First-Round Playoff
NEW ENGLAND vs. **OAKLAND
RS: Raiders lead series, 14-12-1
PS: Patriots lead series, 2-1
1960—Raiders, 27-14 (O)
    Patriots, 34-28 (B)
1961—Patriots, 20-17 (B)
    Patriots, 35-21 (O)
1962—Patriots, 26-16 (B)
    Raiders, 20-0 (O)
1963—Patriots, 20-14 (O)
    Patriots, 20-14 (B)
1964—Patriots, 17-14 (O)
    Tie, 43-43 (B)
1965—Raiders, 24-10 (B)
    Raiders, 30-21 (O)
1966—Patriots, 24-21 (B)
1967—Raiders, 35-7 (O)
    Raiders, 48-14 (B)
1968—Raiders, 41-10 (O)
1969—Raiders, 38-23 (B)

1971—Patriots, 20-6 (NE)
1974—Raiders, 41-26 (O)
1976—Patriots, 48-17 (NE)
    ***Raiders, 24-21 (O)
1978—Patriots, 21-14 (O)
1981—Raiders, 27-17 (O)
1985—Raiders, 35-20 (NE)
    ***Patriots, 27-20 (LA)
1987—Patriots, 26-23 (NE)
1989—Raiders, 24-21 (LA)
1994—Patriots, 21-17 (NE)
2001—***Patriots, 16-13 (NE) OT
2002—Raiders, 27-20 (O)
(RS Pts.—Raiders 686, Patriots 574)
(PS Pts.—Patriots 64, Raiders 57)
*Franchise in Boston prior to 1971
**Franchise in Los Angeles from
1982-1994
***AFC Divisional Playoff
NEW ENGLAND vs. PHILADELPHIA
RS: Eagles lead series, 6-3
PS: Patriots lead series, 1-0
1973—Eagles, 24-23 (P)
1977—Patriots, 14-6 (NE)
1978—Patriots, 24-14 (NE)
1981—Eagles, 13-3 (P)
1984—Eagles, 27-17 (P)
1987—Eagles, 34-31 (NE) OT
1990—Eagles, 48-20 (P)
1999—Eagles, 24-9 (P)
2003—Patriots, 31-10 (P)
2004—*Patriots, 24-21 (Jacksonvillle)
(RS Pts.—Eagles 200, Patriots 172)
(PS Pts.—Patriots 24, Eagles 21)
*Super Bowl XXXIX
NEW ENGLAND vs. PITTSBURGH
RS: Steelers lead series, 12-5
PS: Patriots lead series, 3-1
1972—Steelers, 33-3 (P)
1974—Steelers, 21-17 (NE)
1976—Patriots, 30-27 (P)
1979—Steelers, 16-13 (NE) OT
1981—Steelers, 27-21 (P) OT
1982—Steelers, 37-14 (P)
1983—Steelers, 28-23 (P)
1986—Patriots, 34-0 (P)
1989—Steelers, 28-10 (P)
1990—Steelers, 24-3 (P)
1991—Steelers, 20-6 (P)
1993—Steelers, 17-14 (P)
1995—Steelers, 41-27 (P)
1996—*Patriots, 28-3 (NE)
1997—Steelers, 24-21 (NE) OT
    *Steelers, 7-6 (P)
1998—Patriots, 23-9 (P)
2001—**Patriots, 24-17 (P)
2002—Patriots, 30-14 (NE)
2004—Steelers, 34-20 (P)
    **Patriots, 41-27 (P)
(RS Pts.—Steelers 395, Patriots 314)
(PS Pts.—Patriots 99, Steelers 54)
*AFC Divisional Playoff
**AFC Championship
NEW ENGLAND vs. *ST. LOUIS
RS: Rams lead series, 5-4
PS: Patriots lead series, 1-0
1974—Patriots, 20-14 (NE)
1980—Rams, 17-14 (NE)
1983—Patriots, 21-7 (LA)
1986—Patriots, 30-28 (LA)

1989—Rams, 24-20 (NE)
1992—Rams, 14-0 (LA)
1998—Rams, 32-18 (StL)
2001—Rams, 24-17 (NE)
    **Patriots, 20-17 (New Orleans)
2004—Patriots, 40-22 (StL)
(RS Pts.—Rams 182, Patriots 180)
(PS Pts.—Patriots 20, Rams 17)
*Franchise in Los Angeles prior to 1995
**Super Bowl XXXVI
NEW ENGLAND vs. **SAN DIEGO
RS: Patriots lead series, 17-12-2
PS: Chargers lead series, 1-0
1960—Patriots, 35-0 (LA)
    Chargers, 45-16 (B)
1961—Chargers, 38-27 (B)
    Patriots, 41-0 (SD)
1962—Patriots, 24-20 (B)
    Patriots, 20-14 (SD)
1963—Chargers, 17-13 (SD)
    Chargers, 7-6 (B)
    ***Chargers, 51-10 (SD)
1964—Patriots, 33-28 (SD)
    Chargers, 26-17 (B)
1965—Tie, 10-10 (B)
    Patriots, 22-6 (SD)
1966—Chargers, 24-0 (SD)
    Patriots, 35-17 (B)
1967—Chargers, 28-14 (SD)
    Tie, 31-31 (SD)
1968—Chargers, 27-17 (B)
1969—Chargers, 13-10 (B)
    Chargers, 28-18 (SD)
1970—Chargers, 16-14 (B)
1973—Patriots, 30-14 (NE)
1975—Patriots, 33-19 (SD)
1977—Patriots, 24-20 (SD)
1978—Patriots, 28-23 (NE)
1979—Patriots, 27-21 (NE)
1983—Patriots, 37-21 (NE)
1994—Patriots, 23-17 (NE)
1996—Patriots, 45-7 (SD)
1997—Patriots, 41-7 (NE)
2001—Patriots, 29-26 (NE) OT
2002—Chargers, 21-14 (SD)
(RS Pts.—Patriots 734, Chargers 591)
(PS Pts.—Chargers 51, Patriots 10)
*Franchise in Boston prior to 1971
**Franchise in Los Angeles prior to 1961
***AFL Championship
NEW ENGLAND vs. SAN FRANCISCO
RS: 49ers lead series, 7-3
1971—49ers, 27-10 (SF)
1975—Patriots, 24-16 (NE)
1980—49ers, 21-17 (SF)
1983—49ers, 33-13 (NE)
1986—49ers, 29-24 (NE)
1989—49ers, 37-20 (SF)
1992—49ers, 24-12 (NE)
1995—49ers, 28-3 (SF)
1998—Patriots, 24-21 (NE)
2004—Patriots, 21-7 (NE)
(RS Pts.—49ers 243, Patriots 168)
NEW ENGLAND vs. SEATTLE
RS: Series tied, 7-7
1977—Patriots, 31-0 (NE)
1980—Patriots, 37-31 (S)
1982—Patriots, 16-0 (S)
1983—Seahawks, 24-6 (S)
1984—Patriots, 38-23 (NE)

1985—Patriots, 20-13 (S)
1986—Seahawks, 38-31 (NE)
1988—Patriots, 13-7 (NE)
1989—Seahawks, 24-3 (NE)
1990—Seahawks, 33-20 (NE)
1992—Seahawks, 10-6 (NE)
1993—Seahawks, 17-14 (NE)
　　　Seahawks, 10-9 (S)
2004—Patriots, 30-20 (NE)
(RS Pts.—Patriots 274, Seahawks 250)
NEW ENGLAND vs. TAMPA BAY
RS: Patriots lead series, 3-2
1976—Patriots, 31-14 (TB)
1985—Patriots, 32-14 (TB)
1988—Patriots, 10-7 (NE) OT
1997—Buccaneers, 27-7 (TB)
2000—Buccaneers, 21-16 (NE)
(RS Pts.—Patriots 96, Buccaneers 83)
***NEW ENGLAND vs. **TENNESSEE**
RS: Patriots lead series, 19-15-1
PS: Series tied, 1-1
1960—Oilers, 24-10 (B)
　　　Oilers, 37-21 (H)
1961—Tie, 31-31 (B)
　　　Oilers, 27-15 (H)
1962—Patriots, 34-21 (B)
　　　Oilers, 21-17 (H)
1963—Patriots, 45-3 (B)
　　　Patriots, 46-28 (H)
1964—Patriots, 25-24 (B)
　　　Patriots, 34-17 (H)
1965—Oilers, 31-10 (H)
　　　Patriots, 42-14 (B)
1966—Patriots, 27-21 (B)
　　　Patriots, 38-14 (H)
1967—Patriots, 18-7 (B)
　　　Oilers, 27-6 (H)
1968—Oilers, 16-0 (B)
　　　Oilers, 45-17 (H)
1969—Patriots, 24-0 (B)
　　　Oilers, 27-23 (H)
1971—Patriots, 28-20 (NE)
1973—Patriots, 32-0 (H)
1975—Oilers, 7-0 (NE)
1978—Patriots, 26-23 (NE)
　　　***Oilers, 31-14 (NE)
1980—Oilers, 38-34 (H)
1981—Patriots, 38-10 (NE)
1982—Patriots, 29-21 (NE)
1987—Patriots, 21-7 (H)
1988—Oilers, 31-6 (H)
1989—Patriots, 23-13 (NE)
1991—Patriots, 24-20 (NE)
1993—Oilers, 28-14 (NE)
1998—Patriots, 27-16 (NE)
2002—Titans, 24-7 (T)
2003—Patriots, 38-30 (NE)
　　　***Patriots, 17-14 (NE)
(RS Pts.—Patriots 827, Titans 726)
(PS Pts.—Titans 45, Patriots 31)
Franchise in Boston prior to 1971
**Franchise in Houston prior to 1997;*
known as Oilers prior to 1999
****AFC Divisional Playoff*
NEW ENGLAND vs. WASHINGTON
RS: Redskins lead series, 6-1
1972—Patriots, 24-23 (NE)
1978—Redskins, 16-14 (NE)
1981—Redskins, 24-22 (W)
1984—Redskins, 26-10 (NE)

1990—Redskins, 25-10 (NE)
1996—Redskins, 27-22 (NE)
2003—Redskins, 20-17 (W)
(RS Pts.—Redskins 161, Patriots 119)

NEW ORLEANS vs. ARIZONA
RS: Cardinals lead series, 13-11;
See Arizona vs. New Orleans
NEW ORLEANS vs. ATLANTA
RS: Falcons lead series, 41-30
PS: Falcons lead series, 1-0;
See Atlanta vs. New Orleans
NEW ORLEANS vs. BALTIMORE
RS: Ravens lead series, 2-1;
See Baltimore vs. New Orleans
NEW ORLEANS vs. BUFFALO
RS: Bills lead series, 4-3;
See Buffalo vs. New Orleans
NEW ORLEANS vs. CAROLINA
RS: Series tied, 10-10;
See Carolina vs. New Orleans
NEW ORLEANS vs. CHICAGO
RS: Saints lead series, 11-10
PS: Bears lead series, 1-0;
See Chicago vs. New Orleans
NEW ORLEANS vs. CINCINNATI
RS: Series tied, 5-5;
See Cincinnati vs. New Orleans
NEW ORLEANS vs. CLEVELAND
RS: Browns lead series, 11-3;
See Cleveland vs. New Orleans
NEW ORLEANS vs. DALLAS
RS: Cowboys lead series, 14-7;
See Dallas vs. New Orleans
NEW ORLEANS vs. DENVER
RS: Broncos lead series, 6-2;
See Denver vs. New Orleans
NEW ORLEANS vs. DETROIT
RS: Series tied, 8-8-1;
See Detroit vs. New Orleans
NEW ORLEANS vs. GREEN BAY
RS: Packers lead series, 13-5;
See Green Bay vs. New Orleans
NEW ORLEANS vs. HOUSTON
RS: Saints lead series, 1-0;
See Houston vs. New Orleans
NEW ORLEANS vs. INDIANAPOLIS
RS: Saints lead series, 5-4;
See Indianapolis vs. New Orleans
NEW ORLEANS vs. JACKSONVILLE
RS: Jaguars lead series, 2-1;
See Jacksonville vs. New Orleans
NEW ORLEANS vs. KANSAS CITY
RS: Series tied, 4-4;
See Kansas City vs. New Orleans
NEW ORLEANS vs. MIAMI
RS: Dolphins lead series, 5-3;
See Miami vs. New Orleans
NEW ORLEANS vs. MINNESOTA
RS: Vikings lead series, 16-7
PS: Vikings lead series, 2-0;
See Minnesota vs. New Orleans
NEW ORLEANS vs. NEW ENGLAND
RS: Patriots lead series, 7-3;
See New England vs. New Orleans
NEW ORLEANS vs. N.Y. GIANTS
RS: Giants lead series, 13-9
1967—Giants, 27-21 (NY)
1968—Giants, 38-21 (NY)
1969—Saints, 25-24 (NY)

1970—Saints, 14-10 (NO)
1972—Giants, 45-21 (NY)
1975—Giants, 28-14 (NY)
1978—Giants, 28-17 (NO)
1979—Saints, 24-14 (NO)
1981—Giants, 20-7 (NY)
1984—Saints, 10-3 (NY)
1985—Giants, 21-13 (NO)
1986—Giants, 20-17 (NY)
1987—Saints, 23-14 (NO)
1988—Giants, 13-12 (NY)
1993—Giants, 24-14 (NO)
1994—Saints, 27-22 (NO)
1995—Giants, 45-29 (NY)
1996—Saints 17-3 (NY)
1997—Giants, 14-9 (NY)
1999—Giants, 31-3 (NY)
2001—Giants, 21-13 (NY)
2003—Saints, 45-7 (NO)
(RS Pts.—Giants 461, Saints 407)
NEW ORLEANS vs. N.Y. JETS
RS: Jets lead series, 5-4
1972—Jets, 18-17 (NY)
1977—Jets, 16-13 (NO)
1980—Saints, 21-20 (NY)
1983—Jets, 31-28 (NO)
1986—Jets, 28-23 (NY)
1989—Saints, 29-14 (NO)
1992—Saints, 20-0 (NY)
1995—Saints, 12-0 (NY)
2001—Jets, 16-9 (NO)
(RS Pts.—Saints 172, Jets 143)
NEW ORLEANS vs. *OAKLAND
RS: Raiders lead series, 5-4-1
1971—Tie, 21-21 (NO)
1975—Raiders, 48-10 (O)
1979—Raiders, 42-35 (NO)
1985—Raiders, 23-13 (LA)
1988—Saints, 20-6 (NO)
1991—Saints, 27-0 (NO)
1994—Raiders, 24-19 (LA)
1997—Saints, 13-10 (O)
2000—Raiders, 31-22 (NO)
2004—Saints, 31-26 (O)
(RS Pts.—Raiders 231, Saints 211)
Franchise in Los Angeles from 1982-1994
NEW ORLEANS vs. PHILADELPHIA
RS: Eagles lead series, 14-8
PS: Eagles lead series, 1-0
1967—Saints, 31-24 (NO)
　　　Eagles, 48-21 (P)
1968—Eagles, 29-17 (P)
1969—Eagles, 13-10 (P)
　　　Saints, 26-17 (NO)
1972—Saints, 21-3 (NO)
1974—Saints, 14-10 (NO)
1977—Eagles, 28-7 (P)
1978—Saints, 24-17 (NO)
1979—Eagles, 26-14 (NO)
1980—Saints, 34-21 (NO)
1981—Saints, 31-14 (NO)
1983—Saints, 20-17 (P) OT
1985—Saints, 23-21 (NO)
1987—Eagles, 27-17 (P)
1989—Saints, 30-20 (NO)
1991—Saints, 13-6 (P)
1992—Eagles, 15-13 (P)
　　　*Eagles, 36-20 (NO)
1993—Eagles, 37-26 (P)
1995—Eagles, 15-10 (NO)

2000—Eagles, 21-7 (NO)
2003—Eagles, 33-20 (P)
(RS Pts.—Eagles 499, Saints 392)
(PS Pts.—Eagles 36, Saints 20)
*NFC First-Round Playoff
NEW ORLEANS vs. PITTSBURGH
RS: Series tied, 6-6
1967—Steelers, 14-10 (NO)
1968—Saints, 16-12 (P)
Saints, 24-14 (NO)
1969—Saints, 27-24 (NO)
1974—Steelers, 28-7 (NO)
1978—Steelers, 20-14 (P)
1981—Steelers, 20-6 (NO)
1984—Saints, 27-24 (NO)
1987—Saints, 20-16 (P)
1990—Steelers, 9-6 (NO)
1993—Steelers, 37-14 (P)
2002—Saints, 32-29 (NO)
(RS Pts.—Steelers 247, Saints 203)
NEW ORLEANS vs. *ST. LOUIS
RS: Rams lead series, 36-29
PS: Saints lead series, 1-0
1967—Rams, 27-13 (NO)
1969—Rams, 36-17 (LA)
1970—Rams, 30-17 (NO)
Rams, 34-16 (LA)
1971—Saints, 24-20 (NO)
Rams, 45-28 (LA)
1972—Rams, 34-14 (LA)
Saints, 19-16 (NO)
1973—Rams, 29-7 (LA)
Rams, 24-13 (NO)
1974—Rams, 24-0 (LA)
Saints, 20-7 (NO)
1975—Rams, 38-14 (LA)
Rams, 14-7 (NO)
1976—Rams, 16-10 (NO)
Rams, 33-14 (LA)
1977—Rams, 14-7 (LA)
Saints, 27-26 (NO)
1978—Rams, 26-20 (NO)
Saints, 10-3 (LA)
1979—Rams, 35-17 (NO)
Saints, 29-14 (LA)
1980—Rams, 45-31 (LA)
Rams, 27-7 (NO)
1981—Saints, 23-17 (NO)
Saints, 21-13 (LA)
1983—Rams, 30-27 (LA)
Rams, 26-24 (NO)
1984—Rams, 28-10 (NO)
Rams, 34-21 (LA)
1985—Rams, 28-10 (LA)
Saints, 29-3 (NO)
1986—Saints, 6-0 (NO)
Rams, 26-13 (LA)
1987—Rams, 37-10 (NO)
Saints, 31-14 (LA)
1988—Rams, 12-10 (NO)
Saints, 14-10 (LA)
1989—Saints, 40-21 (LA)
Rams, 20-17 (NO) OT
1990—Saints, 24-20 (LA)
Saints, 20-17 (NO)
1991—Saints, 24-7 (NO)
Saints, 24-17 (LA)
1992—Saints, 13-10 (NO)
Saints, 37-14 (LA)
1993—Saints, 37-6 (LA)

Rams, 23-20 (NO)
1994—Saints, 37-34 (NO)
Saints, 31-15 (LA)
1995—Rams, 17-13 (StL)
Saints, 19-10 (NO)
1996—Rams, 26-10 (NO)
Rams, 14-13 (StL)
1997—Rams, 38-24 (NO)
Rams, 34-27 (NO)
1998—Saints, 24-17 (StL)
Saints, 24-3 (NO)
1999—Rams, 43-12 (StL)
Rams, 30-14 (NO)
2000—Saints, 31-24 (StL)
Rams, 26-21 (NO)
**Saints, 31-28 (NO)
2001—Rams, 34-31 (StL)
Rams, 34-21 (NO)
2004—Saints, 28-25 (StL) OT
(RS Pts.—Rams 1,444, Saints 1,296)
(PS Pts.—Saints 31, Rams 28)
*Franchise in Los Angeles prior to 1995
**NFC First-Round Playoff
NEW ORLEANS vs. SAN DIEGO
RS: Chargers lead series, 7-2
1973—Chargers, 17-14 (SD)
1977—Chargers, 14-0 (NO)
1979—Chargers, 35-0 (NO)
1988—Saints, 23-17 (SD)
1991—Chargers, 24-21 (SD)
1994—Chargers, 36-22 (NO)
1997—Chargers, 20-6 (NO)
2000—Saints, 28-27 (SD)
2004—Chargers, 43-17 (SD)
(RS Pts.—Chargers 233, Saints 131)
NEW ORLEANS vs. SAN FRANCISCO
RS: 49ers lead series, 45-20-2
1967—49ers, 27-13 (NO)
1969—Saints, 43-38 (NO)
1970—Tie, 20-20 (SF)
49ers, 38-27 (NO)
1971—49ers, 38-20 (NO)
Saints, 26-20 (SF)
1972—49ers, 37-2 (NO)
Tie, 20-20 (SF)
1973—49ers, 40-0 (SF)
Saints, 16-10 (NO)
1974—49ers, 17-13 (NO)
49ers, 35-21 (SF)
1975—49ers, 35-21 (SF)
49ers, 16-6 (NO)
1976—49ers, 33-3 (SF)
49ers, 27-7 (NO)
1977—49ers, 10-7 (NO) OT
49ers, 20-17 (SF)
1978—Saints, 14-7 (SF)
Saints, 24-13 (NO)
1979—Saints, 30-21 (SF)
Saints, 31-20 (NO)
1980—49ers, 26-23 (NO)
49ers, 38-35 (SF) OT
1981—49ers, 21-14 (SF)
49ers, 21-17 (NO)
1982—Saints, 23-20 (SF)
1983—49ers, 32-13 (NO)
49ers, 27-0 (SF)
1984—49ers, 30-20 (SF)
49ers, 35-3 (NO)
1985—Saints, 20-17 (SF)
49ers, 31-19 (NO)

1986—49ers, 26-17 (SF)
Saints, 23-10 (NO)
1987—49ers, 24-22 (NO)
Saints, 26-24 (SF)
1988—49ers, 34-33 (NO)
49ers, 30-17 (SF)
1989—49ers, 24-20 (NO)
49ers, 31-13 (SF)
1990—49ers, 13-12 (NO)
Saints, 13-10 (SF)
1991—Saints, 10-3 (NO)
49ers, 38-24 (SF)
1992—49ers, 16-10 (NO)
49ers, 21-20 (SF)
1993—Saints, 16-13 (NO)
49ers, 42-7 (SF)
1994—49ers, 24-13 (SF)
49ers, 35-14 (NO)
1995—49ers, 24-22 (NO)
Saints, 11-7 (SF)
1996—49ers, 27-11 (SF)
49ers, 24-17 (NO)
1997—49ers, 33-7 (SF)
49ers, 23-0 (NO)
1998—49ers, 31-0 (NO)
49ers, 31-20 (SF)
1999—49ers, 28-21 (SF)
Saints, 24-6 (NO)
2000—Saints, 31-15 (NO)
Saints, 31-27 (SF)
2001—49ers, 28-27 (SF)
49ers, 38-0 (NO)
2002—Saints, 35-27 (NO)
2004—Saints, 30-27 (NO)
(RS Pts.—49ers 1,654, Saints 1,165)
NEW ORLEANS vs. SEATTLE
RS: Seahawks lead series, 5-4
1976—Saints, 51-27 (S)
1979—Seahawks, 38-24 (S)
1985—Seahawks, 27-3 (NO)
1988—Saints, 20-19 (S)
1991—Saints, 27-24 (NO)
1997—Saints, 20-17 (NO) OT
2000—Seahawks, 20-10 (S)
2003—Seahawks, 27-10 (S)
2004—Seahawks, 21-7 (NO)
(RS Pts.—Seahawks 220, Saints 172)
NEW ORLEANS vs. TAMPA BAY
RS: Saints lead series, 17-9
1977—Buccaneers, 33-14 (NO)
1978—Saints, 17-10 (TB)
1979—Saints, 42-14 (TB)
1981—Buccaneers, 31-14 (NO)
1982—Buccaneers, 13-10 (NO)
1983—Saints, 24-21 (NO)
1984—Saints, 17-13 (NO)
1985—Saints, 20-13 (NO)
1986—Saints, 38-7 (NO)
1987—Saints, 44-34 (NO)
1988—Saints, 13-9 (NO)
1989—Buccaneers, 20-10 (TB)
1990—Saints, 35-7 (NO)
1991—Saints, 23-7 (NO)
1992—Saints, 23-21 (NO)
1994—Saints, 9-7 (TB)
1996—Buccaneers, 13-7 (TB)
1998—Saints, 9-3 (NO)
1999—Buccaneers, 31-16 (NO)
2001—Buccaneers, 48-21 (TB)
2002—Saints, 26-20 (TB) OT

Saints, 23-20 (NO)
2003—Saints, 17-14 (TB)
    Buccaneers, 14-7 (NO)
2004—Buccaneers, 20-17 (NO)
    Saints, 21-17 (TB)
(RS Pts.—Saints 517, Buccaneers 460)

NEW ORLEANS vs. *TENNESSEE
RS: Titans lead series, 6-4-1
1971—Tie, 13-13 (H)
1976—Oilers, 31-26 (NO)
1978—Oilers, 17-12 (NO)
1981—Saints, 27-24 (H)
1984—Saints, 27-10 (H)
1987—Saints, 24-10 (NO)
1990—Oilers, 23-10 (H)
1993—Saints, 33-21 (NO)
1996—Oilers, 31-14 (NO)
1999—Titans, 24-21 (NO)
2003—Titans, 27-12 (T)
(RS Pts.—Titans 231, Saints 219)
*Franchise in Houston prior to 1997;
known as Oilers prior to 1999*

NEW ORLEANS vs. WASHINGTON
RS: Redskins lead series, 13-7
1967—Redskins, 30-10 (NO)
    Saints, 30-14 (W)
1968—Saints, 37-17 (NO)
1969—Redskins, 26-20 (NO)
    Redskins, 17-14 (W)
1971—Redskins, 24-14 (W)
1973—Saints, 19-3 (NO)
1975—Redskins, 41-3 (W)
1979—Saints, 14-10 (W)
1980—Redskins, 22-14 (W)
1982—Redskins, 27-10 (NO)
1986—Redskins, 14-6 (NO)
1988—Redskins, 27-24 (W)
1989—Redskins, 16-14 (NO)
1990—Redskins, 31-17 (W)
1992—Saints, 20-3 (NO)
1994—Redskins, 38-24 (NO)
2001—Redskins, 40-10 (NO)
2002—Saints, 43-27 (W)
2003—Saints, 24-20 (W)
(RS Pts.—Redskins 447, Saints 367)

N.Y. GIANTS vs. ARIZONA
RS: Giants lead series, 77-41-2;
See Arizona vs. N.Y. Giants
N.Y. GIANTS vs. ATLANTA
RS: Falcons lead series, 10-7;
See Atlanta vs. N.Y. Giants
N.Y. GIANTS vs. BALTIMORE
RS: Ravens lead series, 2-0
PS: Ravens lead series, 1-0;
See Baltimore vs. N.Y. Giants
N.Y. GIANTS vs. BUFFALO
RS: Bills lead series, 6-3
PS: Giants lead series, 1-0;
See Buffalo vs. N.Y. Giants
N.Y. GIANTS vs. CAROLINA
RS: Panthers lead series, 2-0;
See Carolina vs. N.Y. Giants
N.Y. GIANTS vs. CHICAGO
RS: Bears lead series, 26-17-2
PS: Bears lead series, 5-3;
See Chicago vs. N.Y. Giants
N.Y. GIANTS vs. CINCINNATI
RS: Bengals lead series, 5-2;
See Cincinnati vs. N.Y. Giants

N.Y. GIANTS vs. CLEVELAND
RS: Browns lead series, 25-19-2
PS: Series tied, 1-1;
See Cleveland vs. N.Y. Giants
N.Y. GIANTS vs. DALLAS
RS: Cowboys lead series, 50-33-2;
See Dallas vs. N.Y. Giants
N.Y. GIANTS vs. DENVER
RS: Series tied, 4-4
PS: Giants lead series, 1-0;
See Denver vs. N.Y. Giants
N.Y. GIANTS vs. DETROIT
RS: Lions lead series, 20-17-1
PS: Lions lead series, 1-0;
See Detroit vs. N.Y. Giants
N.Y. GIANTS vs. GREEN BAY
RS: Packers lead series, 24-21-2
PS: Packers lead series, 4-1;
See Green Bay vs. N.Y. Giants
N.Y. GIANTS vs. HOUSTON
RS: Texans lead series, 1-0;
See Houston vs. N.Y. Giants
N.Y. GIANTS vs. INDIANAPOLIS
RS: Series tied, 6-6
PS: Colts lead series, 2-0;
See Indianapolis vs. N.Y. Giants
N.Y. GIANTS vs. JACKSONVILLE
RS: Giants lead series, 2-1;
See Jacksonville vs. N.Y. Giants
N.Y. GIANTS vs. KANSAS CITY
RS: Giants lead series, 8-2;
See Kansas City vs. N.Y. Giants
N.Y. GIANTS vs. MIAMI
RS: Giants lead series, 3-2;
See Miami vs. N.Y. Giants
N.Y. GIANTS vs. MINNESOTA
RS: Vikings lead series, 9-8
PS: Giants lead series, 2-1;
See Minnesota vs. N.Y. Giants
N.Y. GIANTS vs. NEW ENGLAND
RS: Patriots lead series, 4-3;
See New England vs. N.Y. Giants
N.Y. GIANTS vs. NEW ORLEANS
RS: Giants lead series, 13-9;
See New Orleans vs. N.Y. Giants
N.Y. GIANTS vs. N.Y. JETS
RS: Giants lead series, 6-4
1970—Giants, 22-10 (NYJ)
1974—Jets, 26-20 (New Haven) OT
1981—Jets, 26-7 (NYG)
1984—Giants, 20-10 (NYJ)
1987—Giants, 20-7 (NYG)
1988—Jets, 27-21 (NYJ)
1993—Jets, 10-6 (NYG)
1996—Giants, 13-6 (NYJ)
1999—Giants, 41-28 (NYG)
2003—Giants, 31-28 (NYJ) OT
(RS Pts.—Giants 201, Jets 178)
N.Y. GIANTS vs. *OAKLAND
RS: Raiders lead series, 7-2
1973—Raiders, 42-0 (O)
1980—Raiders, 33-17 (NY)
1983—Raiders, 27-12 (LA)
1986—Giants, 14-9 (LA)
1989—Giants, 34-17 (NY)
1992—Raiders, 13-10 (LA)
1995—Raiders, 17-13 (NY)
1998—Raiders, 20-17 (O)
2001—Raiders, 28-10 (NY)
(RS Pts.—Raiders 206, Giants 127)

Franchise in Los Angeles from 1982-1994
N.Y. GIANTS vs. PHILADELPHIA
RS: Giants lead series, 73-65-2
PS: Giants lead series, 2-0
1933—Giants, 56-0 (NY)
    Giants, 20-14 (P)
1934—Giants, 17-0 (NY)
    Eagles, 6-0 (P)
1935—Giants, 10-0 (NY)
    Giants, 21-14 (P)
1936—Eagles, 10-7 (P)
    Giants, 21-17 (NY)
1937—Giants, 16-7 (P)
    Giants, 21-0 (NY)
1938—Eagles, 14-10 (P)
    Giants, 17-7 (NY)
1939—Giants, 13-3 (P)
    Giants, 27-10 (NY)
1940—Giants, 20-14 (P)
    Giants, 17-7 (NY)
1941—Giants, 24-0 (P)
    Giants, 16-0 (NY)
1942—Giants, 35-17 (NY)
    Giants, 14-0 (P)
1944—Eagles, 24-17 (NY)
    Tie, 21-21 (P)
1945—Eagles, 38-17 (P)
    Giants, 28-21 (NY)
1946—Giants, 24-14 (P)
    Giants, 45-17 (NY)
1947—Eagles, 23-0 (P)
    Eagles, 41-24 (NY)
1948—Giants, 45-0 (P)
    Eagles, 35-14 (NY)
1949—Eagles, 24-3 (NY)
    Eagles, 17-3 (P)
1950—Giants, 7-3 (NY)
    Giants, 9-7 (P)
1951—Giants, 26-24 (NY)
    Giants, 23-7 (P)
1952—Giants, 31-7 (P)
    Eagles, 14-10 (NY)
1953—Eagles, 30-7 (P)
    Giants, 37-28 (NY)
1954—Giants, 27-14 (NY)
    Eagles, 29-14 (P)
1955—Eagles, 27-17 (P)
    Giants, 31-7 (NY)
1956—Giants, 20-3 (NY)
    Giants, 21-7 (P)
1957—Giants, 24-20 (P)
    Giants, 13-0 (NY)
1958—Eagles, 27-24 (P)
    Giants, 24-10 (NY)
1959—Eagles, 49-21 (P)
    Giants, 24-7 (NY)
1960—Eagles, 17-10 (NY)
    Eagles, 31-23 (P)
1961—Giants, 38-21 (NY)
    Giants, 28-24 (P)
1962—Giants, 29-13 (P)
    Giants, 19-14 (NY)
1963—Giants, 37-14 (P)
    Giants, 42-14 (NY)
1964—Eagles, 38-7 (P)
    Eagles, 23-17 (NY)
1965—Eagles, 16-14 (P)
    Giants, 35-27 (NY)
1966—Eagles, 35-17 (P)
    Eagles, 31-3 (NY)

1967—Giants, 44-7 (NY)
1968—Giants, 34-25 (P)
Giants, 7-6 (NY)
1969—Eagles, 23-20 (NY)
1970—Giants, 30-23 (NY)
Eagles, 23-20 (P)
1971—Eagles, 23-7 (P)
Eagles, 41-28 (NY)
1972—Giants, 27-12 (P)
Giants, 62-10 (NY)
1973—Tie, 23-23 (NY)
Eagles, 20-16 (P)
1974—Eagles, 35-7 (P)
Eagles, 20-7 (New Haven)
1975—Giants, 23-14 (P)
Eagles, 13-10 (NY)
1976—Eagles, 20-7 (P)
Eagles, 10-0 (NY)
1977—Eagles, 28-10 (NY)
Eagles, 17-14 (P)
1978—Eagles, 19-17 (NY)
Eagles, 20-3 (P)
1979—Eagles, 23-17 (P)
Eagles, 17-13 (NY)
1980—Eagles, 35-3 (P)
Eagles, 31-16 (NY)
1981—Eagles, 24-10 (NY)
Giants, 20-10 (P)
*Giants, 27-21 (P)
1982—Giants, 23-7 (NY)
Giants, 26-24 (P)
1983—Eagles, 17-13 (NY)
Giants, 23-0 (P)
1984—Giants, 28-27 (NY)
Eagles, 24-10 (P)
1985—Giants, 21-0 (NY)
Giants, 16-10 (P) OT
1986—Giants, 35-3 (NY)
Giants, 17-14 (P)
1987—Giants, 20-17 (P)
Giants, 23-20 (NY) OT
1988—Eagles, 24-13 (P)
Eagles, 23-17 (NY) OT
1989—Eagles, 21-19 (P)
Eagles, 24-17 (NY)
1990—Giants, 27-20 (NY)
Eagles, 31-13 (P)
1991—Eagles, 30-7 (P)
Eagles, 19-14 (NY)
1992—Eagles, 47-34 (NY)
Eagles, 20-10 (P)
1993—Giants, 21-10 (NY)
Giants, 7-3 (P)
1994—Giants, 28-23 (NY)
Giants, 16-13 (P)
1995—Eagles, 17-14 (NY)
Eagles, 28-19 (P)
1996—Giants, 19-10 (NY)
Eagles, 24-0 (P)
1997—Giants, 31-17 (NY)
Giants, 31-21 (P)
1998—Giants, 20-0 (NY)
Giants, 20-10 (P)
1999—Giants, 16-15 (NY)
Giants, 23-17 (P) OT
2000—Giants, 33-18 (P)
Giants, 24-7 (NY)
**Giants, 20-10 (NY)
2001—Eagles, 10-9 (NY)
Eagles, 24-21 (P)

2002—Eagles, 17-3 (P)
Giants, 10-7 (NY) OT
2003—Eagles, 14-10 (NY)
Eagles, 28-10 (P)
2004—Eagles, 31-17 (P)
Eagles, 27-6 (NY)
(RS Pts.—Giants 2,619, Eagles 2,500)
(PS Pts.—Giants 47, Eagles 31)
*NFC First-Round Playoff
**NFC Divisional Playoff
N.Y. GIANTS vs. *PITTSBURGH
RS: Giants lead series, 43-28-3
1933—Giants, 23-2 (P)
Giants, 27-3 (NY)
1934—Giants, 14-12 (P)
Giants, 17-7 (NY)
1935—Giants, 42-7 (P)
Giants, 13-0 (NY)
1936—Pirates, 10-7 (P)
1937—Giants, 10-7 (P)
Giants, 17-0 (NY)
1938—Giants, 27-14 (P)
Pirates, 13-10 (NY)
1939—Giants, 14-7 (P)
Giants, 23-7 (NY)
1940—Tie, 10-10 (P)
Giants, 12-0 (NY)
1941—Giants, 37-10 (P)
Giants, 28-7 (NY)
1942—Steelers, 13-10 (P)
Steelers, 17-9 (NY)
1945—Giants, 34-6 (P)
Steelers, 21-7 (NY)
1946—Giants, 17-14 (P)
Giants, 7-0 (NY)
1947—Steelers, 38-21 (NY)
Steelers, 24-7 (P)
1948—Giants, 34-27 (NY)
Steelers, 38-28 (P)
1949—Steelers, 28-7 (P)
Steelers, 21-17 (NY)
1950—Giants, 18-7 (P)
Steelers, 17-6 (NY)
1951—Tie, 13-13 (P)
Giants, 14-0 (NY)
1952—Steelers, 63-7 (P)
1953—Steelers, 24-14 (P)
Steelers, 14-10 (NY)
1954—Giants, 30-6 (P)
Giants, 24-3 (NY)
1955—Steelers, 30-23 (P)
Steelers, 19-17 (NY)
1956—Giants, 38-10 (NY)
Giants, 17-14 (P)
1957—Giants, 35-0 (NY)
Steelers, 21-10 (P)
1958—Giants, 17-6 (NY)
Steelers, 31-10 (P)
1959—Giants, 21-16 (P)
Steelers, 14-9 (NY)
1960—Giants, 19-17 (P)
Giants, 27-24 (NY)
1961—Giants, 17-14 (P)
Giants, 42-21 (NY)
1962—Giants, 31-27 (P)
Steelers, 20-17 (NY)
1963—Steelers, 31-0 (P)
Giants, 33-17 (NY)
1964—Steelers, 27-24 (P)
Steelers, 44-17 (NY)

1965—Giants, 23-13 (P)
Giants, 35-10 (NY)
1966—Tie, 34-34 (P)
Steelers, 47-28 (NY)
1967—Giants, 27-24 (P)
Giants, 28-20 (NY)
1968—Giants, 34-20 (P)
1969—Giants, 10-7 (NY)
Giants, 21-17 (P)
1971—Steelers, 17-13 (P)
1976—Steelers, 27-0 (NY)
1985—Giants, 28-10 (NY)
1991—Giants, 23-20 (P)
1994—Steelers, 10-6 (NY)
2000—Giants, 30-10 (NY)
2004—Steelers, 33-30 (NY)
(RS Pts.—Giants 1,459, Steelers 1,232)
*Steelers known as Pirates prior to 1941
N.Y. GIANTS vs. *ST. LOUIS
RS: Rams lead series, 25-11
PS: Series tied, 1-1
1938—Giants, 28-0 (NY)
1940—Rams, 13-0 (NY)
1941—Giants, 49-14 (NY)
1945—Rams, 21-17 (NY)
1946—Rams, 31-21 (NY)
1947—Rams, 34-10 (LA)
1948—Rams, 52-37 (NY)
1953—Rams, 21-7 (LA)
1954—Rams, 17-16 (NY)
1959—Giants, 23-21 (LA)
1961—Giants, 24-14 (NY)
1966—Rams, 55-14 (LA)
1968—Rams, 24-21 (LA)
1970—Rams, 31-3 (NY)
1973—Rams, 40-6 (LA)
1976—Rams, 24-10 (LA)
1978—Rams, 20-17 (LA)
1979—Giants, 20-14 (LA)
1980—Rams, 28-7 (NY)
1981—Rams, 10-7 (NY)
1983—Rams, 16-6 (NY)
1984—Rams, 33-12 (LA)
**Giants, 16-13 (LA)
1985—Rams, 24-19 (NY)
1988—Rams, 45-31 (NY)
1989—Rams, 31-10 (LA)
***Rams, 19-13 (NY) OT
1990—Giants, 31-7 (LA)
1991—Rams, 19-13 (NY)
1992—Rams, 38-17 (LA)
1993—Giants, 20-10 (NY)
1994—Rams, 17-10 (LA)
1997—Rams, 13-3 (StL)
1999—Rams, 31-10 (StL)
2000—Rams, 38-24 (NY)
2001—Rams, 15-14 (StL)
2002—Giants, 26-21 (StL)
2003—Giants, 23-13 (NY)
(RS Pts.—Rams 847, Giants 614)
(PS Pts.—Rams 32, Giants 29)
*Franchise in Los Angeles prior to 1995 and in Cleveland prior to 1946
**NFC First-Round Playoff
***NFC Divisional Playoff
N.Y. GIANTS vs. SAN DIEGO
RS: Giants lead series, 5-3
1971—Giants, 35-17 (NY)
1975—Giants, 35-24 (NY)
1980—Chargers, 44-7 (SD)

1983—Chargers, 41-34 (NY)
1986—Giants, 20-7 (NY)
1989—Giants, 20-13 (SD)
1995—Chargers, 27-17 (NY)
1998—Giants, 34-16 (SD)
(RS Pts.—Giants 202, Chargers 189)

N.Y. GIANTS vs. SAN FRANCISCO
RS: 49ers lead series, 13-11
PS: 49ers lead series, 4-3
1952—Giants, 23-14 (NY)
1956—Giants, 38-21 (SF)
1957—49ers, 27-17 (NY)
1960—Giants, 21-19 (SF)
1963—Giants, 48-14 (NY)
1968—49ers, 26-10 (NY)
1972—Giants, 23-17 (SF)
1975—Giants, 26-23 (SF)
1977—Giants, 20-17 (NY)
1978—Giants, 27-10 (NY)
1979—Giants, 32-16 (NY)
1980—49ers, 12-0 (SF)
1981—49ers, 17-10 (SF)
      *49ers, 38-24 (SF)
1984—49ers, 31-10 (NY)
      *49ers, 21-10 (SF)
1985—**Giants, 17-3 (NY)
1986—Giants, 21-17 (SF)
      *Giants, 49-3 (NY)
1987—49ers, 41-21 (NY)
1988—49ers, 20-17 (NY)
1989—49ers, 34-24 (SF)
1990—49ers, 7-3 (SF)
      ***Giants, 15-13 (SF)
1991—Giants, 16-14 (NY)
1992—49ers, 31-14 (NY)
1993—*49ers, 44-3 (SF)
1995—49ers, 20-6 (SF)
1998—49ers, 31-7 (SF)
2002—49ers, 16-13 (NY)
      **49ers, 39-38 (SF)
(RS Pts.—49ers 495, Giants 447)
(PS Pts.—49ers 161, Giants 156)
*NFC Divisional Playoff
**NFC First-Round Playoff
***NFC Championship

N.Y. GIANTS vs. SEATTLE
RS: Giants lead series, 7-3
1976—Giants, 28-16 (NY)
1980—Giants, 27-21 (S)
1981—Giants, 32-0 (S)
1983—Seahawks, 17-12 (NY)
1986—Seahawks, 17-12 (S)
1989—Giants, 15-3 (NY)
1992—Giants, 23-10 (NY)
1995—Seahawks, 30-28 (S)
2001—Giants, 27-24 (NY)
2002—Giants, 9-6 (NY)
(RS Pts.—Giants 213, Seahawks 144)

N.Y. GIANTS vs. TAMPA BAY
RS: Giants lead series, 9-6
1977—Giants, 10-0 (TB)
1978—Giants, 19-13 (TB)
      Giants, 17-14 (NY)
1979—Giants, 17-14 (NY)
      Buccaneers, 31-3 (TB)
1980—Buccaneers, 30-13 (TB)
1984—Giants, 17-14 (NY)
      Buccaneers, 20-17 (TB)
1985—Giants, 22-20 (NY)
1991—Giants, 21-14 (TB)

1993—Giants, 23-7 (NY)
1997—Buccaneers, 20-8 (NY)
1998—Buccaneers, 20-3 (TB)
1999—Giants, 17-13 (TB)
2003—Buccaneers, 19-13 (TB)
(RS Pts.—Buccaneers 249, Giants 220)

N.Y. GIANTS vs. *TENNESSEE
RS: Giants lead series, 5-3
1973—Giants, 34-14 (NY)
1982—Giants, 17-14 (NY)
1985—Giants, 35-14 (H)
1991—Giants, 24-20 (NY)
1994—Giants, 13-10 (H)
1997—Oilers, 10-6 (T)
2000—Titans, 28-14 (T)
2002—Titans, 32-29 (NY) OT
(RS Pts.—Giants 172, Titans 142)
*Franchise in Houston prior to 1997;
known as Oilers prior to 1999

N.Y. GIANTS vs. *WASHINGTON
RS: Giants lead series, 81-59-4
PS: Series tied, 1-1
1932—Braves, 14-6 (B)
      Tie, 0-0 (NY)
1933—Redskins, 21-20 (B)
      Giants, 7-0 (NY)
1934—Giants, 16-13 (B)
      Giants, 3-0 (NY)
1935—Giants, 20-12 (B)
      Giants, 17-6 (NY)
1936—Giants, 7-0 (B)
      Redskins, 14-0 (NY)
1937—Redskins, 13-3 (W)
      Redskins, 49-14 (NY)
1938—Giants, 10-7 (W)
      Giants, 36-0 (NY)
1939—Tie, 0-0 (W)
      Giants, 9-7 (NY)
1940—Redskins, 21-7 (W)
      Giants, 21-7 (NY)
1941—Giants, 17-10 (W)
      Giants, 20-13 (NY)
1942—Giants, 14-7 (W)
      Redskins, 14-7 (NY)
1943—Giants, 14-10 (NY)
      Giants, 31-7 (W)
      **Redskins, 28-0 (NY)
1944—Giants, 16-13 (NY)
      Giants, 31-0 (W)
1945—Redskins, 24-14 (NY)
      Redskins, 17-0 (W)
1946—Redskins, 24-14 (W)
      Giants, 31-0 (NY)
1947—Redskins, 28-20 (W)
      Giants, 35-10 (NY)
1948—Redskins, 41-10 (W)
      Redskins, 28-21 (NY)
1949—Giants, 45-35 (W)
      Giants, 23-7 (NY)
1950—Giants, 21-17 (W)
      Giants, 24-21 (NY)
1951—Giants, 35-14 (W)
      Giants, 28-14 (NY)
1952—Giants, 14-10 (W)
      Redskins, 27-17 (NY)
1953—Redskins, 13-9 (W)
      Redskins, 24-21 (NY)
1954—Giants, 51-21 (W)
      Giants, 24-7 (NY)
1955—Giants, 35-7 (NY)

      Giants, 27-20 (W)
1956—Redskins, 33-7 (W)
      Giants, 28-14 (NY)
1957—Giants, 24-20 (W)
      Redskins, 31-14 (NY)
1958—Giants, 21-14 (W)
      Giants, 30-0 (NY)
1959—Giants, 45-14 (W)
      Giants, 24-10 (W)
1960—Tie, 24-24 (NY)
      Giants, 17-3 (W)
1961—Giants, 24-21 (W)
      Giants, 53-0 (W)
1962—Giants, 49-34 (NY)
      Giants, 42-24 (W)
1963—Giants, 24-14 (NY)
      Giants, 44-14 (NY)
1964—Giants, 13-10 (NY)
      Redskins, 36-21 (W)
1965—Redskins, 23-7 (NY)
      Giants, 27-10 (W)
1966—Giants, 13-10 (NY)
      Redskins, 72-41 (W)
1967—Redskins, 38-34 (W)
1968—Giants, 48-21 (W)
      Giants, 13-10 (W)
1969—Redskins, 20-14 (W)
1970—Giants, 35-33 (NY)
      Giants, 27-24 (W)
1971—Redskins, 30-3 (NY)
      Redskins, 23-7 (W)
1972—Redskins, 23-16 (NY)
      Redskins, 27-13 (W)
1973—Redskins, 21-3 (New Haven)
      Redskins, 27-24 (W)
1974—Redskins, 13-10 (New Haven)
      Redskins, 24-3 (W)
1975—Redskins, 49-13 (W)
      Redskins, 21-13 (NY)
1976—Redskins, 19-17 (W)
      Giants, 12-9 (NY)
1977—Giants, 20-17 (NY)
      Giants, 17-6 (W)
1978—Giants, 17-6 (NY)
      Redskins, 16-13 (W) OT
1979—Redskins, 27-0 (W)
      Giants, 14-6 (NY)
1980—Redskins, 23-21 (NY)
      Redskins, 16-13 (W)
1981—Giants, 17-7 (W)
      Redskins, 30-27 (NY) OT
1982—Redskins, 27-17 (NY)
      Redskins, 15-14 (W)
1983—Redskins, 33-17 (NY)
      Redskins, 31-22 (W)
1984—Redskins, 30-14 (W)
      Giants, 37-13 (NY)
1985—Giants, 17-3 (NY)
      Redskins, 23-21 (W)
1986—Giants, 27-20 (NY)
      Giants, 24-14 (W)
      ***Giants, 17-0 (NY)
1987—Redskins, 38-12 (NY)
      Redskins, 23-19 (W)
1988—Giants, 27-20 (NY)
      Giants, 24-23 (W)
1989—Giants, 27-24 (NY)
      Giants, 20-17 (NY)
1990—Giants, 24-20 (W)
      Giants, 21-10 (NY)

1991—Redskins, 17-13 (NY)
    Redskins, 34-17 (W)
1992—Giants, 24-7 (W)
    Redskins, 28-10 (NY)
1993—Giants, 41-7 (W)
    Giants, 20-6 (NY)
1994—Giants, 31-23 (NY)
    Giants, 21-19 (W)
1995—Giants, 24-15 (W)
    Giants, 20-13 (NY)
1996—Redskins, 31-10 (NY)
    Redskins, 31-21 (W)
1997—Tie, 7-7 (W) OT
    Giants, 30-10 (NY)
1998—Giants, 31-24 (NY)
    Redskins, 21-14 (W)
1999—Redskins, 50-21 (NY)
    Redskins, 23-13 (W)
2000—Redskins, 16-6 (NY)
    Giants, 9-7 (W)
2001—Giants, 23-9 (NY)
    Redskins, 35-21 (W)
2002—Giants, 19-17 (NY)
    Giants, 27-21 (W)
2003—Giants, 24-21 (NY) OT
    Redskins, 20-7 (NY)
2004—Giants, 20-14 (W)
    Redskins, 31-7 (W)
(RS Pts.—Giants 2,836, Redskins 2,625)
(PS Pts.—Redskins 28, Giants 17)
*Franchise in Boston prior to 1937 and known as Braves prior to 1933
**Division Playoff
***NFC Championship

N.Y. JETS vs. ARIZONA
RS: Jets lead series, 4-2;
See Arizona vs. N.Y. Jets
N.Y. JETS vs. ATLANTA
RS: Series tied, 4-4;
See Atlanta vs. N.Y. Jets
N.Y. JETS vs BALTIMORE
RS: Ravens lead series, 3-1;
See Baltimore vs. N.Y. Jets
N.Y. JETS vs. BUFFALO
RS: Bills lead series, 48-40
PS: Bills lead series, 1-0;
See Buffalo vs. N.Y. Jets
N.Y. JETS vs. CAROLINA
RS: Jets lead series, 2-1;
See Carolina vs. N.Y. Jets
N.Y. JETS vs. CHICAGO
RS: Bears lead series, 5-3;
See Chicago vs. N.Y. Jets
N.Y. JETS vs. CINCINNATI
RS: Jets lead series, 12-6
PS: Jets lead series, 1-0;
See Cincinnati vs. N.Y. Jets
N.Y. JETS vs. CLEVELAND
RS: Browns lead series, 10-7
PS: Browns lead series, 1-0;
See Cleveland vs. N.Y. Jets
N.Y. JETS vs. DALLAS
RS: Cowboys lead series, 6-2;
See Dallas vs. N.Y. Jets
N.Y. JETS vs. DENVER
RS: Series tied, 14-14-1
PS: Broncos lead series, 1-0;
See Denver vs. N.Y. Jets

N.Y. JETS vs. DETROIT
RS: Lions lead series, 6-4;
See Detroit vs. N.Y. Jets
N.Y. JETS vs. GREEN BAY
RS: Jets lead series, 7-2;
See Green Bay vs. N.Y. Jets
N.Y. JETS vs. HOUSTON
RS: Jets lead series, 2-0;
See Houston vs. N.Y. Jets
N.Y. JETS vs. INDIANAPOLIS
RS: Colts lead series, 39-25
PS: Jets lead series, 2-0;
See Indianapolis vs. N.Y. Jets
N.Y. JETS vs. JACKSONVILLE
RS: Jaguars lead series, 3-2
PS: Jets lead series, 1-0;
See Jacksonville vs. N.Y. Jets
N.Y. JETS vs. KANSAS CITY
RS: Chiefs lead series, 15-14-1
PS: Series tied, 1-1;
See Kansas City vs. N.Y. Jets
N.Y. JETS vs. MIAMI
RS: Jets lead series, 40-37-1
PS: Dolphins lead series, 1-0;
See Miami vs. N.Y. Jets
N.Y. JETS vs. MINNESOTA
RS: Jets lead series, 6-1;
See Minnesota vs. N.Y. Jets
N.Y. JETS vs. NEW ENGLAND
RS: Jets lead series, 47-41-1
PS: Patriots lead series, 1-0;
See New England vs. N.Y. Jets
N.Y. JETS vs. NEW ORLEANS
RS: Jets lead series, 5-4;
See New Orleans vs. N.Y. Jets
N.Y. JETS vs. N.Y. GIANTS
RS: Giants lead series, 6-4;
See N.Y. Giants vs. N.Y. Jets
***N.Y. JETS vs. **OAKLAND**
RS: Raiders lead series, 19-12-2
PS: Series tied, 2-2
1960—Raiders, 28-27 (NY)
    Titans, 31-28 (O)
1961—Titans, 14-6 (O)
    Titans, 23-12 (NY)
1962—Titans, 28-17 (O)
    Titans, 31-21 (NY)
1963—Jets, 10-7 (NY)
    Raiders, 49-26 (O)
1964—Jets, 35-13 (NY)
    Raiders, 35-26 (O)
1965—Tie, 24-24 (NY)
    Raiders, 24-14 (O)
1966—Raiders, 24-21 (NY)
    Tie, 28-28 (O)
1967—Jets, 27-14 (NY)
    Raiders, 38-29 (O)
1968—Raiders, 43-32 (O)
    ***Jets, 27-23 (NY)
1969—Raiders, 27-14 (NY)
1970—Raiders, 14-13 (NY)
1972—Raiders, 24-16 (O)
1977—Raiders, 28-27 (NY)
1979—Jets, 28-19 (NY)
1982—****Jets, 17-14 (LA)
1985—Raiders, 31-0 (LA)
1989—Raiders, 14-7 (NY)
1993—Raiders, 24-20 (LA)
1995—Raiders, 47-10 (NY)
1996—Raiders, 34-13 (NY)

1997—Jets 23-22 (NY)
1999—Raiders, 24-23 (O)
2000—Raiders, 31-7 (O)
2001—Jets, 24-22 (O)
    *****Raiders, 38-24 (O)
2002—Raiders, 26-20 (O)
    ****Raiders, 30-10 (O)
2003—Jets, 27-24 (O) OT
(RS Pts.—Raiders 822, Jets 698)
(PS Pts.—Raiders 105, Jets 78)
*Jets known as Titans prior to 1963
**Franchise in Los Angeles from 1982-1994
***AFL Championship
****AFC Second-Round Playoff
*****AFC First-Round Playoff
N.Y. JETS vs. PHILADELPHIA
RS: Eagles lead series, 7-0
1973—Eagles, 24-23 (P)
1977—Eagles, 27-0 (P)
1978—Eagles, 17-9 (P)
1987—Eagles, 38-27 (NY)
1993—Eagles, 35-30 (NY)
1996—Eagles, 21-20 (NY)
2003—Eagles, 24-17 (P)
(RS Pts.—Eagles 186, Jets 126)
N.Y. JETS vs. PITTSBURGH
RS: Steelers lead series, 15-2
PS: Steelers lead series, 1-0
1970—Steelers, 21-17 (P)
1973—Steelers, 26-14 (P)
1975—Steelers, 20-7 (NY)
1977—Steelers, 23-20 (NY)
1978—Steelers, 28-17 (NY)
1981—Steelers, 38-10 (P)
1983—Steelers, 34-7 (NY)
1984—Steelers, 23-17 (NY)
1986—Steelers, 45-24 (NY)
1988—Jets, 24-20 (NY)
1989—Steelers, 13-0 (NY)
1990—Steelers, 24-7 (NY)
1992—Steelers, 27-10 (P)
2000—Steelers, 20-3 (NY)
2001—Steelers, 18-7 (P)
2003—Jets, 6-0 (NY)
2004—Steelers, 17-6 (P)
    *Steelers, 20-17 (P) OT
(RS Pts.—Steelers 397, Jets 196)
(PS Pts.—Steelers 20, Jets 17)
*AFC Divisional Playoff
N.Y. JETS vs. *ST. LOUIS
RS: Rams lead series, 9-2
1970—Jets, 31-20 (LA)
1974—Rams, 20-13 (NY)
1980—Rams, 38-13 (LA)
1983—Jets, 27-24 (NY) OT
1986—Rams, 17-3 (NY)
1989—Rams, 38-14 (LA)
1992—Rams, 18-10 (LA)
1995—Rams, 23-20 (NY)
1998—Rams, 30-10 (StL)
2001—Rams, 34-14 (NY)
2004—Rams, 32-29 (StL) OT
(RS Pts.—Rams 294, Jets 184)
*Franchise in Los Angeles prior to 1995
***N.Y. JETS vs. **SAN DIEGO**
RS: Chargers lead series, 17-11-1
PS: Jets lead series, 1-0
1960—Chargers, 21-7 (NY)
    Chargers, 50-43 (LA)

1961—Chargers, 25-10 (NY)
    Chargers, 48-13 (SD)
1962—Chargers, 40-14 (SD)
    Titans, 23-3 (NY)
1963—Chargers, 24-20 (SD)
    Chargers, 53-7 (NY)
1964—Tie, 17-17 (NY)
    Chargers, 38-3 (SD)
1965—Chargers, 34-9 (NY)
    Chargers, 38-7 (SD)
1966—Jets, 17-16 (NY)
    Chargers, 42-27 (SD)
1967—Jets, 42-31 (NY)
1968—Jets, 23-20 (NY)
    Jets, 37-15 (SD)
1969—Chargers, 34-27 (SD)
1971—Chargers, 49-21 (SD)
1974—Jets, 27-14 (NY)
1975—Chargers, 24-16 (SD)
1983—Jets, 41-29 (SD)
1989—Jets, 20-17 (SD)
1990—Chargers, 39-3 (NY)
    Chargers, 38-17 (SD)
1991—Jets, 24-3 (NY)
1994—Chargers, 21-6 (NY)
2002—Jets, 44-13 (SD)
2004—Jets, 34-28 (SD)
    ***Jets, 20-17 (SD) OT
(RS Pts.—Chargers 824, Jets 599)
(PS Pts.—Jets 20, Chargers 17)
*Jets known as Titans prior to 1963
**Franchise in Los Angeles prior to 1961
***AFC First-Round Playoff
N.Y. JETS vs. SAN FRANCISCO
RS: 49ers lead series, 8-2
1971—49ers, 24-21 (NY)
1976—49ers, 17-6 (SF)
1980—49ers, 37-27 (NY)
1983—Jets, 27-13 (SF)
1986—49ers, 24-10 (SF)
1989—49ers, 23-10 (NY)
1992—49ers, 31-14 (NY)
1998—49ers, 36-30 (SF) OT
2001—49ers, 19-17 (NY)
2004—Jets, 22-14 (NY)
(RS Pts.—49ers 238, Jets 184)
N.Y. JETS vs. SEATTLE
RS: Series tied, 8-8
1977—Seahawks, 17-0 (NY)
1978—Seahawks, 24-17 (NY)
1979—Seahawks, 30-7 (S)
1980—Seahawks, 27-17 (NY)
1981—Seahawks, 19-3 (NY)
    Seahawks, 27-23 (S)
1983—Seahawks, 17-10 (NY)
1985—Jets, 17-14 (NY)
1986—Jets, 38-7 (S)
1987—Jets, 30-14 (NY)
1991—Seahawks, 20-13 (S)
1995—Jets, 16-10 (S)
1997—Jets, 41-3 (S)
1998—Jets, 32-31 (NY)
1999—Jets, 19-9 (NY)
2004—Jets, 37-14 (NY)
(RS Pts.—Jets 320, Seahawks 283)
N.Y. JETS vs. TAMPA BAY
RS: Jets lead series, 7-1
1976—Jets, 34-0 (NY)
1982—Jets, 32-17 (NY)
1984—Buccaneers, 41-21 (TB)

1985—Jets, 62-28 (NY)
1990—Jets, 16-14 (TB)
1991—Jets, 16-13 (NY)
1997—Jets, 31-0 (NY)
2000—Jets, 21-17 (TB)
(RS Pts.—Jets 233, Buccaneers 130)
***N.Y. JETS vs. **TENNESSEE**
RS: Titans lead series, 20-14-1
PS: Titans lead series, 1-0
1960—Oilers, 27-21 (H)
    Oilers, 42-28 (NY)
1961—Oilers, 49-13 (H)
    Oilers, 48-21 (NY)
1962—Oilers, 56-17 (H)
    Oilers, 44-10 (NY)
1963—Jets, 24-17 (NY)
    Oilers, 31-27 (H)
1964—Jets, 24-21 (NY)
    Oilers, 33-17 (H)
1965—Oilers, 27-21 (H)
    Jets, 41-14 (NY)
1966—Jets, 52-13 (NY)
    Oilers, 24-0 (H)
1967—Tie, 28-28 (NY)
1968—Jets, 20-14 (H)
    Jets, 26-7 (NY)
1969—Jets, 26-17 (NY)
    Jets, 34-26 (H)
1972—Oilers, 26-20 (H)
1974—Oilers, 27-22 (NY)
1977—Oilers, 20-0 (H)
1979—Oilers, 27-24 (H) OT
1980—Jets, 31-28 (NY) OT
1981—Jets, 33-17 (NY)
1984—Oilers, 31-20 (H)
1988—Jets, 45-3 (NY)
1990—Jets, 17-12 (H)
1991—Oilers, 23-20 (NY)
    ***Oilers, 17-10 (H)
1993—Oilers, 24-0 (H)
1994—Oilers, 24-10 (NY)
1995—Oilers, 23-6 (H)
1996—Oilers, 35-10 (NY)
1998—Jets, 24-3 (T)
2003—Jets, 24-17 (NY)
(RS Pts.—Titans 878, Jets 756)
(PS Pts.—Titans 17, Jets 10)
*Jets known as Titans prior to 1963
**Franchise in Houston prior to 1997;
known as Oilers prior to 1999
***AFC First-Round Playoff
N.Y. JETS vs. WASHINGTON
RS: Redskins lead series, 7-1
1972—Redskins, 35-17 (NY)
1976—Redskins, 37-16 (NY)
1978—Redskins, 23-3 (W)
1987—Redskins, 17-16 (W)
1993—Jets, 3-0 (W)
1996—Redskins, 31-16 (W)
1999—Redskins, 27-20 (W)
2003—Redskins, 16-13 (W)
(RS Pts.—Redskins 186, Jets 104)

OAKLAND vs. ARIZONA
RS: Raiders lead series, 4-2;
See Arizona vs. Oakland
OAKLAND vs. ATLANTA
RS: Raiders lead series, 7-4;
See Atlanta vs. Oakland

OAKLAND vs. BALTIMORE
RS: Ravens lead series, 2-1
PS: Ravens lead series, 1-0;
See Baltimore vs. Oakland
OAKLAND vs. BUFFALO
RS: Raiders lead series, 18-15
PS: Bills lead series, 2-0;
See Buffalo vs. Oakland
OAKLAND vs CAROLINA
RS: Raiders lead series, 2-1;
See Carolina vs Oakland
OAKLAND vs. CHICAGO
RS: Raiders lead series, 6-5;
See Chicago vs. Oakland
OAKLAND vs. CINCINNATI
RS: Raiders lead series, 17-7
PS: Raiders lead series, 2-0;
See Cincinnati vs. Oakland
OAKLAND vs. CLEVELAND
RS: Raiders lead series, 9-5
PS: Raiders lead series, 2-0;
See Cleveland vs. Oakland
OAKLAND vs. DALLAS
RS: Raiders lead series, 5-3;
See Dallas vs. Oakland
OAKLAND vs. DENVER
RS: Raiders lead series, 53-34-2
PS: Series tied, 1-1;
See Denver vs. Oakland
OAKLAND vs. DETROIT
RS: Raiders lead series, 6-3;
See Detroit vs. Oakland
OAKLAND vs. GREEN BAY
RS: Raiders lead series, 5-4
PS: Packers lead series, 1-0;
See Green Bay vs. Oakland
OAKLAND vs. HOUSTON
RS: Texans lead series, 1-0
See Houston vs. Oakland
OAKLAND vs. INDIANAPOLIS
RS: Raiders lead series, 7-3
PS: Series tied, 1-1;
See Indianapolis vs. Oakland
OAKLAND vs. JACKSONVILLE
RS: Jaguars lead series, 2-1;
See Jacksonville vs. Oakland
OAKLAND vs. KANSAS CITY
RS: Chiefs lead series, 45-42-2
PS: Chiefs lead series, 2-1;
See Kansas City vs. Oakland
OAKLAND vs. MIAMI
RS: Raiders lead series, 15-10-1
PS: Raiders lead series, 3-1;
See Miami vs. Oakland
OAKLAND vs. MINNESOTA
RS: Raiders lead series, 8-3
PS: Raiders lead series, 1-0;
See Minnesota vs. Oakland
OAKLAND vs. NEW ENGLAND
RS: Raiders lead series, 14-12-1
PS: Patriots lead series, 2-1;
See New England vs. Oakland
OAKLAND vs. NEW ORLEANS
RS: Raiders lead series, 5-4-1;
See New Orleans vs. Oakland
OAKLAND vs. N.Y. GIANTS
RS: Raiders lead series, 7-2;
See N.Y. Giants vs. Oakland
OAKLAND vs. N.Y. JETS
RS: Raiders lead series, 19-12-2

PS: Series tied, 2-2;
See N.Y. Jets vs. Oakland
*OAKLAND vs. PHILADELPHIA
RS: Series tied, 4-4
PS: Raiders lead series, 1-0
1971—Raiders, 34-10 (O)
1976—Raiders, 26-7 (P)
1980—Eagles, 10-7 (P)
    **Raiders, 27-10 (New Orleans)
1986—Eagles, 33-27 (LA) OT
1989—Eagles, 10-7 (P)
1992—Eagles, 31-10 (P)
1995—Raiders, 48-17 (O)
2001—Raiders, 20-10 (P)
(RS Pts.—Raiders 179, Eagles 128)
(PS Pts.—Raiders 27, Eagles 10)
*Franchise in Los Angeles from 1982-1994
**Super Bowl XV
*OAKLAND vs. PITTSBURGH
RS: Series tied, 8-8
PS: Series tied, 3-3
1970—Raiders, 31-14 (O)
1972—Steelers, 34-28 (P)
    **Steelers, 13-7 (P)
1973—Steelers, 17-9 (O)
    **Raiders, 33-14 (O)
1974—Raiders, 17-0 (P)
    ***Steelers, 24-13 (O)
1975—***Steelers, 16-10 (P)
1976—Raiders, 31-28 (O)
    ***Raiders, 24-7 (O)
1977—Raiders, 16-7 (P)
1980—Raiders, 45-34 (P)
1981—Raiders, 30-27 (O)
1983—**Raiders, 38-10 (LA)
1984—Steelers, 13-7 (LA)
1990—Raiders, 20-3 (LA)
1994—Steelers, 21-3 (LA)
1995—Steelers, 29-10 (O)
2000—Steelers, 21-20 (P)
2002—Raiders, 30-17 (O)
2003—Steelers, 27-7 (P)
2004—Steelers, 24-21 (P)
(RS Pts.—Raiders 325, Steelers 316)
(PS Pts.—Raiders 125, Steelers 84)
*Franchise in Los Angeles from 1982-1994
**AFC Divisional Playoff
***AFC Championship
*OAKLAND vs. **ST. LOUIS
RS: Raiders lead series, 7-3
1972—Raiders, 45-17 (O)
1977—Rams, 20-14 (LA)
1979—Raiders, 24-17 (LA)
1982—Raiders, 37-31 (LA Raiders)
1985—Raiders, 16-6 (LA Rams)
1988—Rams, 22-17 (LA Raiders)
1991—Raiders, 20-17 (LA Raiders)
1994—Raiders, 20-17 (LA Rams)
1997—Raiders, 35-17 (O)
2002—Rams, 28-13 (StL)
(RS Pts.—Raiders 241, Rams 192)
*Franchise in Los Angeles from 1982-1994
**Franchise in Los Angeles prior to 1995
*OAKLAND vs. **SAN DIEGO
RS: Raiders lead series, 54-34-2
PS: Raiders lead series, 1-0
1960—Chargers, 52-28 (LA)
    Chargers, 41-17 (O)
1961—Chargers, 44-0 (SD)
    Chargers, 41-10 (O)

1962—Chargers, 42-33 (O)
    Chargers, 31-21 (SD)
1963—Raiders, 34-33 (SD)
    Raiders, 41-27 (O)
1964—Chargers, 31-17 (SD)
    Raiders, 21-20 (O)
1965—Chargers, 17-6 (O)
    Chargers, 24-14 (SD)
1966—Chargers, 29-20 (O)
    Raiders, 41-19 (SD)
1967—Raiders, 51-10 (O)
    Raiders, 41-21 (SD)
1968—Raiders, 23-14 (O)
    Raiders, 34-27 (SD)
1969—Raiders, 24-12 (SD)
    Raiders, 21-16 (O)
1970—Tie, 27-27 (SD)
    Raiders, 20-17 (O)
1971—Raiders, 34-0 (O)
    Raiders, 34-33 (O)
1972—Tie, 17-17 (O)
    Raiders, 21-19 (SD)
1973—Raiders, 27-17 (SD)
    Raiders, 31-3 (O)
1974—Raiders, 14-10 (SD)
    Raiders, 17-10 (O)
1975—Raiders, 6-0 (SD)
    Raiders, 25-0 (O)
1976—Raiders, 27-17 (SD)
    Raiders, 24-0 (O)
1977—Raiders, 24-0 (O)
    Chargers, 12-7 (SD)
1978—Raiders, 21-20 (SD)
    Chargers, 27-23 (O)
1979—Chargers, 30-10 (SD)
    Raiders, 45-22 (O)
1980—Chargers, 30-24 (SD) OT
    Raiders, 38-24 (O)
    ***Raiders, 34-27 (SD)
1981—Raiders, 55-21 (O)
    Chargers, 23-10 (SD)
1982—Raiders, 28-24 (LA)
    Raiders, 41-34 (SD)
1983—Raiders, 42-10 (SD)
    Raiders, 30-14 (LA)
1984—Raiders, 33-30 (LA)
    Raiders, 44-37 (SD)
1985—Raiders, 34-21 (LA)
    Chargers, 40-34 (SD) OT
1986—Raiders, 17-13 (LA)
    Raiders, 37-31 (SD) OT
1987—Chargers, 23-17 (LA)
    Chargers, 16-14 (SD)
1988—Raiders, 24-13 (LA)
    Raiders, 13-3 (SD)
1989—Raiders, 40-14 (LA)
    Chargers, 14-12 (SD)
1990—Raiders, 24-9 (SD)
    Raiders, 17-12 (LA)
1991—Chargers, 21-13 (LA)
    Raiders, 9-7 (SD)
1992—Chargers, 27-3 (SD)
    Chargers, 36-14 (LA)
1993—Chargers, 30-23 (LA)
    Raiders, 12-7 (SD)
1994—Chargers, 26-24 (LA)
    Raiders, 24-17 (SD)
1995—Raiders, 17-7 (O)
    Chargers, 12-6 (SD)
1996—Chargers, 40-34 (O)

    Raiders, 23-14 (SD)
1997—Chargers, 25-10 (O)
    Raiders, 38-13 (SD)
1998—Raiders, 7-6 (O)
    Raiders, 17-10 (SD)
1999—Raiders, 28-9 (O)
    Chargers, 23-20 (SD)
2000—Raiders, 9-6 (O)
    Raiders, 15-13 (SD)
2001—Raiders, 34-24 (O)
    Raiders, 13-6 (SD)
2002—Chargers, 27-21 (O) OT
    Raiders, 27-7 (SD)
2003—Raiders, 34-31 (O) OT
    Chargers, 21-14 (SD)
2004—Chargers, 42-14 (SD)
    Chargers, 23-17 (O)
(RS Pts.—Raiders 2,056, Chargers 1,861)
(PS Pts.—Raiders 34, Chargers 27)
*Franchise in Los Angeles from 1982-1994
**Franchise in Los Angeles prior to 1961
***AFC Championship
*OAKLAND vs. SAN FRANCISCO
RS: Raiders lead series, 6-4
1970—49ers, 38-7 (O)
1974—Raiders, 35-24 (SF)
1979—Raiders, 23-10 (O)
1982—Raiders, 23-17 (SF)
1985—49ers, 34-10 (LA)
1988—Raiders, 9-3 (SF)
1991—Raiders, 12-6 (LA)
1994—49ers, 44-14 (SF)
2000—Raiders, 34-28 (SF) OT
2002—49ers, 23-20 (O) OT
(RS Pts.—49ers 227, Raiders 187)
*Franchise in Los Angeles from 1982-1994
*OAKLAND vs. SEATTLE
RS: Raiders lead series, 27-22
PS: Series tied, 1-1
1977—Raiders, 44-7 (O)
1978—Seahawks, 27-7 (S)
    Seahawks, 17-16 (O)
1979—Seahawks, 27-10 (S)
    Seahawks, 29-24 (O)
1980—Raiders, 33-14 (O)
    Raiders, 19-17 (S)
1981—Raiders, 20-10 (O)
    Raiders, 32-31 (S)
1982—Raiders, 28-23 (LA)
1983—Seahawks, 38-36 (S)
    Seahawks, 34-21 (LA)
    **Raiders, 30-14 (LA)
1984—Raiders, 28-14 (LA)
    Seahawks, 17-14 (S)
    ***Seahawks, 13-7 (S)
1985—Seahawks, 33-3 (S)
    Raiders, 13-3 (LA)
1986—Raiders, 14-10 (LA)
    Seahawks, 37-0 (S)
1987—Seahawks, 35-13 (LA)
    Raiders, 37-14 (S)
1988—Seahawks, 35-27 (LA)
    Seahawks, 43-37 (LA)
1989—Seahawks, 24-20 (LA)
    Seahawks, 23-17 (S)
1990—Raiders, 17-13 (S)
    Raiders, 24-17 (LA)
1991—Raiders, 23-20 (S) OT
    Raiders, 31-7 (LA)
1992—Raiders, 19-0 (S)

Raiders, 20-3 (LA)
1993—Raiders, 17-13 (S)
Raiders, 27-23 (LA)
1994—Seahawks, 38-9 (LA)
Raiders, 17-16 (S)
1995—Raiders, 34-14 (O)
Seahawks, 44-10 (S)
1996—Raiders, 27-21 (S)
Seahawks, 28-21 (O)
1997—Seahawks, 45-34 (S)
Seahawks, 22-21 (O)
1998—Raiders, 31-18 (S)
Raiders, 20-17 (O)
1999—Seahawks, 22-21 (S)
Raiders, 30-21 (O)
2000—Raiders, 31-3 (O)
Seahawks, 27-24 (S)
2001—Raiders, 38-14 (O)
Seahawks, 34-27 (S)
2002—Raiders, 31-17 (O)
(RS Pts.—Raiders 1,117, Seahawks 1,059)
(PS Pts.—Raiders 37, Seahawks 27)
*Franchise in Los Angeles from 1982-1994
**AFC Championship
***AFC First-Round Playoff
OAKLAND vs. TAMPA BAY
RS: Raiders lead series, 5-1
PS: Buccaneers lead series, 1-0
1976—Raiders, 49-16 (O)
1981—Raiders, 18-16 (O)
1993—Raiders, 27-20 (LA)
1996—Buccaneers, 20-17 (TB) OT
1999—Raiders, 45-0 (O)
2002—**Buccaneers, 48-21 (San Diego)
2004—Raiders, 30-20 (O)
(RS Pts.—Raiders 186, Buccaneers 92)
(PS Pts.—Buccaneers 48, Raiders 21)
*Franchise in Los Angeles from 1982-1994
**Super Bowl XXXVII
OAKLAND vs. **TENNESSEE
RS: Raiders lead series, 22-17
PS: Raiders lead series, 4-0
1960—Oilers, 37-22 (O)
Raiders, 14-13 (H)
1961—Oilers, 55-0 (H)
Oilers, 47-16 (O)
1962—Oilers, 28-20 (O)
Oilers, 32-17 (H)
1963—Raiders, 24-13 (H)
Raiders, 52-49 (O)
1964—Oilers, 42-28 (H)
Raiders, 20-10 (O)
1965—Raiders, 21-17 (O)
Raiders, 33-21 (H)
1966—Oilers, 31-0 (H)
Raiders, 38-23 (O)
1967—Raiders, 19-7 (H)
***Raiders, 40-7 (O)
1968—Raiders, 24-15 (H)
1969—Raiders, 21-17 (O)
****Raiders, 56-7 (O)
1971—Raiders, 41-21 (O)
1972—Raiders, 34-0 (H)
1973—Raiders, 17-6 (H)
1975—Oilers, 27-26 (O)
1976—Raiders, 14-13 (H)
1977—Raiders, 34-29 (O)
1978—Raiders, 21-17 (O)
1979—Oilers, 31-17 (H)
1980—*****Raiders, 27-7 (O)

1981—Oilers, 17-16 (H)
1983—Raiders, 20-6 (LA)
1984—Raiders, 24-14 (H)
1986—Raiders, 28-17 (H)
1988—Oilers, 38-35 (H)
1989—Oilers, 23-7 (H)
1991—Oilers, 47-17 (H)
1994—Raiders, 17-14 (LA)
1997—Oilers, 24-21 (T) OT
1999—Titans, 21-14 (T)
2001—Titans, 13-10 (O)
2002—Raiders, 52-25 (O)
******Raiders, 41-24 (O)
2003—Titans, 25-20 (T)
2004—Raiders, 40-35 (O)
(RS Pts.—Titans 920, Raiders 894)
(PS Pts.—Raiders 164, Titans 45)
*Franchise in Los Angeles from 1982-1994
**Franchise in Houston prior to 1997;
known as Oilers prior to 1999
***AFL Championship
****Inter-Divisional Playoff
*****AFC First-Round Playoff
******AFC Championship
OAKLAND vs. WASHINGTON
RS: Raiders lead series, 6-3
PS: Raiders lead series, 1-0
1970—Raiders, 34-20 (O)
1975—Raiders, 26-23 (W) OT
1980—Raiders, 24-21 (O)
1983—Redskins, 37-35 (W)
**Raiders, 38-9 (Tampa)
1986—Redskins, 10-6 (W)
1989—Raiders, 37-24 (LA)
1992—Raiders, 21-20 (W)
1995—Raiders, 20-8 (W)
1998—Redskins, 29-19 (O)
(RS Pts.—Raiders 222, Redskins 192)
(PS Pts.—Raiders 38, Redskins 9)
*Franchise in Los Angeles from
1982-1994
**Super Bowl XVIII

PHILADELPHIA vs. ARIZONA
RS: Series tied, 52-52-5
PS: Series tied, 1-1;
See Arizona vs. Philadelphia
PHILADELPHIA vs. ATLANTA
RS: Eagles lead series, 11-9-1
PS: Eagles lead series, 2-1;
See Atlanta vs. Philadelphia
PHILADELPHIA vs. BALTIMORE
RS: Eagles lead series, 1-0-1;
See Baltimore vs. Philadelphia
PHILADELPHIA vs. BUFFALO
RS: Series tied, 5-5;
See Buffalo vs. Philadelphia
PHILADELPHIA vs. CAROLINA
RS: Eagles lead series, 3-1
PS: Panthers lead series, 1-0;
See Carolina vs. Philadelphia
PHILADELPHIA vs. CHICAGO
RS: Bears lead series, 24-8-1
PS: Eagles lead series, 2-1;
See Chicago vs. Philadelphia
PHILADELPHIA vs. CINCINNATI
RS: Bengals lead series, 7-3;
See Cincinnati vs. Philadelphia
PHILADELPHIA vs. CLEVELAND
RS: Browns lead series, 31-14-1;

See Cleveland vs. Philadelphia
PHILADELPHIA vs. DALLAS
RS: Cowboys lead series, 49-39
PS: Cowboys lead series, 2-1;
See Dallas vs. Philadelphia
PHILADELPHIA vs. DENVER
RS: Eagles lead series, 6-3;
See Denver vs. Philadelphia
PHILADELPHIA vs. DETROIT
RS: Series tied, 12-12-2
PS: Eagles lead series, 1-0;
See Detroit vs. Philadelphia
PHILADELPHIA vs. GREEN BAY
RS: Packers lead series, 22-11
PS: Eagles lead series, 2-0;
See Green Bay vs. Philadelphia
PHILADELPHIA vs. HOUSTON
RS: Eagles lead series, 1-0;
See Houston vs. Philadelphia
PHILADELPHIA vs. INDIANAPOLIS
RS: Colts lead series, 9-6;
See Indianapolis vs. Philadelphia
PHILADELPHIA vs. JACKSONVILLE
RS: Jaguars lead series, 2-0;
See Jacksonville vs. Philadelphia
PHILADELPHIA vs. KANSAS CITY
RS: Series tied, 2-2;
See Kansas City vs. Philadelphia
PHILADELPHIA vs. MIAMI
RS: Dolphins lead series, 7-4;
See Miami vs. Philadelphia
PHILADELPHIA vs. MINNESOTA
RS: Vikings lead series, 11-8
PS: Eagles lead series, 2-0;
See Minnesota vs. Philadelphia
PHILADELPHIA vs. NEW ENGLAND
RS: Eagles lead series, 6-3
PS: Patriots lead series, 1-0;
See New England vs. Philadelphia
PHILADELPHIA vs. NEW ORLEANS
RS: Eagles lead series, 14-8
PS: Eagles lead series, 1-0;
See New Orleans vs. Philadelphia
PHILADELPHIA vs. N.Y. GIANTS
RS: Giants lead series, 73-65-2
PS: Giants lead series, 2-0;
See N.Y. Giants vs. Philadelphia
PHILADELPHIA vs. N.Y. JETS
RS: Eagles lead series, 7-0;
See N.Y. Jets vs. Philadelphia
PHILADELPHIA vs. OAKLAND
RS: Series tied, 4-4
PS: Raiders lead series, 1-0;
See Oakland vs. Philadelphia
PHILADELPHIA vs. *PITTSBURGH
RS: Eagles lead series, 45-27-3
PS: Eagles lead series, 1-0
1933—Eagles, 25-6 (Phila)
1934—Eagles, 17-0 (Pitt)
Pirates, 9-7 (Phila)
1935—Pirates, 17-7 (Phila)
Eagles, 17-6 (Pitt)
1936—Pirates, 17-0 (Pitt)
Pirates, 6-0 (Johnstown, Pa.)
1937—Pirates, 27-14 (Pitt)
Pirates, 16-7 (Pitt)
1938—Eagles, 27-7 (Buffalo)
Eagles, 14-7 (Charleston, W. Va.)
1939—Eagles, 17-14 (Phila)
Pirates, 24-12 (Pitt)

1940—Pirates, 7-3 (Pitt)
Eagles, 7-0 (Phila)
1941—Eagles, 10-7 (Pitt)
Tie, 7-7 (Phila)
1942—Eagles, 24-14 (Pitt)
Steelers, 14-0 (Phila)
1945—Eagles, 45-3 (Pitt)
Eagles, 30-6 (Phila)
1946—Steelers, 10-7 (Pitt)
Eagles, 10-7 (Phila)
1947—Steelers, 35-24 (Pitt)
Eagles, 21-0 (Phila)
**Eagles, 21-0 (Pitt)
1948—Eagles, 34-7 (Pitt)
Eagles, 17-0 (Phila)
1949—Eagles, 38-7 (Pitt)
Eagles, 34-17 (Phila)
1950—Eagles, 17-10 (Pitt)
Steelers, 9-7 (Phila)
1951—Eagles, 34-13 (Pitt)
Steelers, 17-13 (Phila)
1952—Eagles, 31-25 (Pitt)
Eagles, 26-21 (Phila)
1953—Eagles, 23-17 (Phila)
Eagles, 35-7 (Pitt)
1954—Eagles, 24-22 (Phila)
Steelers, 17-7 (Pitt)
1955—Steelers, 13-7 (Pitt)
Eagles, 24-0 (Phila)
1956—Eagles, 35-21 (Pitt)
Eagles, 14-7 (Phila)
1957—Steelers, 6-0 (Pitt)
Eagles, 7-6 (Phila)
1958—Steelers, 24-3 (Pitt)
Steelers, 31-24 (Phila)
1959—Eagles, 28-24 (Phila)
Steelers, 31-0 (Pitt)
1960—Eagles, 34-7 (Phila)
Steelers, 27-21 (Pitt)
1961—Eagles, 21-16 (Phila)
Eagles, 35-24 (Pitt)
1962—Steelers, 13-7 (Pitt)
Steelers, 26-17 (Phila)
1963—Tie, 21-21 (Phila)
Tie, 20-20 (Pitt)
1964—Eagles, 21-7 (Phila)
Eagles, 34-10 (Pitt)
1965—Steelers, 20-14 (Phila)
Eagles, 47-13 (Pitt)
1966—Eagles, 31-14 (Pitt)
Eagles, 27-23 (Phila)
1967—Eagles, 34-24 (Phila)
1968—Steelers, 6-3 (Pitt)
1969—Eagles, 41-27 (Phila)
1970—Eagles, 30-20 (Phila)
1974—Steelers, 27-0 (Pitt)
1979—Eagles, 17-14 (Phila)
1988—Eagles, 27-26 (Pitt)
1991—Eagles, 23-14 (Phila)
1994—Steelers, 14-3 (Pitt)
1997—Eagles, 23-20 (Phila)
2000—Eagles, 26-23 (Pitt) OT
2004—Steelers, 27-3 (Pitt)
(RS Pts.—Eagles 1,414, Steelers 1,091)
(PS Pts.—Eagles 21, Steelers 0)
*Steelers known as Pirates prior to 1941
**Division Playoff
PHILADELPHIA vs. *ST. LOUIS
RS: Rams lead series, 17-15-1
PS: Rams lead series, 2-1

1937—Rams, 21-3 (P)
1939—Rams, 35-13 (Colorado Springs)
1940—Rams, 21-13 (C)
1942—Rams, 24-14 (Akron)
1944—Eagles, 26-13 (P)
1945—Eagles, 28-14 (P)
1946—Eagles, 25-14 (LA)
1947—Eagles, 14-7 (P)
1948—Tie, 28-28 (LA)
1949—Eagles, 38-14 (P)
**Eagles, 14-0 (LA)
1950—Eagles, 56-20 (P)
1955—Rams, 23-21 (P)
1956—Rams, 27-7 (LA)
1957—Rams, 17-13 (LA)
1959—Eagles, 23-20 (P)
1964—Rams, 20-10 (A)
1967—Rams, 33-17 (LA)
1969—Rams, 23-17 (P)
1972—Rams, 34-3 (P)
1975—Rams, 42-3 (P)
1977—Rams, 20-0 (LA)
1978—Rams, 16-14 (P)
1983—Eagles, 13-9 (P)
1985—Rams, 17-6 (P)
1986—Eagles, 34-20 (P)
1988—Eagles, 30-24 (P)
1989—***Rams, 21-7 (P)
1990—Eagles, 27-21 (LA)
1995—Eagles, 20-9 (P)
1998—Eagles, 17-14 (P)
1999—Eagles, 38-31 (P)
2001—Rams, 20-17 (P) OT
****Rams, 29-24 (StL)
2002—Rams, 10-3 (P)
2004—Rams, 20-7 (StL)
(RS Pts.—Rams 674, Eagles 605)
(PS Pts.—Rams 50, Eagles 45)
*Franchise in Los Angeles prior to 1995
and in Cleveland prior to 1946
**NFL Championship
***NFC First-Round Playoff
****NFC Championship
PHILADELPHIA vs. SAN DIEGO
RS: Chargers lead series, 5-3
1974—Eagles, 13-7 (SD)
1980—Chargers, 22-21 (SD)
1985—Chargers, 20-14 (SD)
1986—Eagles, 23-7 (P)
1989—Chargers, 20-17 (SD)
1995—Chargers, 27-21 (P)
1998—Chargers, 13-10 (SD)
2001—Eagles, 24-14 (P)
(RS Pts.—Eagles 143, Chargers 130)
PHILADELPHIA vs. SAN FRANCISCO
RS: 49ers lead series, 16-7-1
PS: 49ers lead series, 1-0
1951—Eagles, 21-14 (P)
1953—49ers, 31-21 (SF)
1956—Tie, 10-10 (P)
1958—49ers, 30-24 (P)
1959—49ers, 24-14 (SF)
1964—49ers, 28-24 (P)
1966—Eagles, 35-34 (SF)
1967—49ers, 28-27 (P)
1969—49ers, 14-13 (SF)
1971—49ers, 31-3 (P)
1973—49ers, 38-28 (SF)
1975—Eagles, 27-17 (P)
1983—Eagles, 22-17 (SF)

1984—49ers, 21-9 (P)
1985—49ers, 24-13 (SF)
1989—49ers, 38-28 (P)
1991—49ers, 23-7 (P)
1992—49ers, 20-14 (SF)
1993—Eagles, 37-34 (SF) OT
1994—Eagles, 40-8 (SF)
1996—*49ers, 14-0 (SF)
1997—49ers, 24-12 (P)
2001—49ers, 13-3 (SF)
2002—Eagles, 38-17 (SF)
2003—49ers, 31-28 (P) OT
(RS Pts.—49ers 569, Eagles 498)
(PS Pts.—49ers 14, Eagles 0)
*NFC First-Round Playoff
PHILADELPHIA vs. SEATTLE
RS: Eagles lead series, 6-3
1976—Eagles, 27-10 (P)
1980—Eagles, 27-20 (S)
1986—Seahawks, 24-20 (S)
1989—Eagles, 31-7 (P)
1992—Eagles, 20-17 (S) OT
1995—Seahawks, 26-14 (S)
1998—Seahawks, 38-0 (P)
2001—Eagles, 27-3 (S)
2002—Eagles, 27-20 (S)
(RS Pts.—Eagles 193, Seahawks 165)
PHILADELPHIA vs. TAMPA BAY
RS: Eagles lead series, 5-4
PS: Series tied, 2-2
1977—Eagles, 13-3 (P)
1979—*Buccaneers, 24-17 (TB)
1981—Eagles, 20-10 (P)
1988—Eagles, 41-14 (TB)
1991—Buccaneers, 14-13 (TB)
1995—Buccaneers, 21-6 (P)
1999—Buccaneers, 19-5 (P)
2000—**Eagles, 21-3 (P)
2001—Eagles, 17-13 (TB)
**Eagles, 31-9 (P)
2002—Eagles, 20-10 (P)
***Buccaneers, 27-10 (P)
2003—Buccaneers, 17-0 (P)
(RS Pts.—Eagles 135, Buccaneers 121)
(PS Pts.—Eagles 79, Buccaneers 63)
*NFC Divisional Playoff
**NFC First-Round Playoff
***NFC Championship
PHILADELPHIA vs. *TENNESSEE
RS: Eagles lead series, 6-2
1972—Eagles, 18-17 (H)
1979—Eagles, 26-20 (H)
1982—Eagles, 35-14 (P)
1988—Eagles, 32-23 (P)
1991—Eagles, 13-6 (H)
1994—Eagles, 21-6 (P)
2000—Titans, 15-13 (P)
2002—Titans, 27-24 (T)
(RS Pts.—Eagles 182, Titans 128)
*Franchise in Houston prior to 1997;
known as Oilers prior to 1999
PHILADELPHIA vs. *WASHINGTON
RS: Redskins lead series, 72-62-5
PS: Redskins lead series, 1-0
1934—Redskins, 6-0 (B)
Redskins, 14-7 (P)
1935—Eagles, 7-6 (B)
1936—Redskins, 26-3 (P)
Redskins, 17-7 (B)
1937—Eagles, 14-0 (W)

Redskins, 10-7 (P)
1938—Redskins, 26-23 (P)
Redskins, 20-14 (W)
1939—Redskins, 7-0 (P)
Redskins, 7-6 (W)
1940—Redskins, 34-17 (P)
Redskins, 13-6 (W)
1941—Redskins, 21-17 (P)
Redskins, 20-14 (W)
1942—Redskins, 14-10 (P)
Redskins, 30-27 (W)
1944—Tie, 31-31 (P)
Eagles, 37-7 (W)
1945—Redskins, 24-14 (W)
Eagles, 16-0 (P)
1946—Eagles, 28-24 (W)
Redskins, 27-10 (P)
1947—Eagles, 45-42 (P)
Eagles, 38-14 (W)
1948—Eagles, 45-0 (W)
Eagles, 42-21 (P)
1949—Eagles, 49-14 (P)
Eagles, 44-21 (W)
1950—Eagles, 35-3 (P)
Eagles, 33-0 (W)
1951—Redskins, 27-23 (P)
Eagles, 35-21 (W)
1952—Eagles, 38-20 (P)
Redskins, 27-21 (W)
1953—Tie, 21-21 (P)
Redskins, 10-0 (W)
1954—Eagles, 49-21 (W)
Eagles, 41-33 (P)
1955—Redskins, 31-30 (P)
Redskins, 34-21 (W)
1956—Eagles, 13-9 (P)
Redskins, 19-17 (W)
1957—Eagles, 21-12 (P)
Redskins, 42-7 (W)
1958—Redskins, 24-14 (P)
Redskins, 20-0 (W)
1959—Eagles, 30-23 (P)
Eagles, 34-14 (W)
1960—Eagles, 19-13 (P)
Eagles, 38-28 (W)
1961—Eagles, 14-7 (P)
Eagles, 27-24 (W)
1962—Redskins, 27-21 (P)
Eagles, 37-14 (W)
1963—Eagles, 37-24 (W)
Redskins, 13-10 (P)
1964—Redskins, 35-20 (W)
Redskins, 21-10 (P)
1965—Redskins, 23-21 (W)
Eagles, 21-14 (P)
1966—Redskins, 27-13 (P)
Eagles, 37-28 (W)
1967—Eagles, 35-24 (P)
Tie, 35-35 (W)
1968—Redskins, 17-14 (W)
Redskins, 16-10 (P)
1969—Tie, 28-28 (W)
Redskins, 34-29 (P)
1970—Redskins, 33-21 (P)
Redskins, 24-6 (W)
1971—Tie, 7-7 (W)
Redskins, 20-13 (P)
1972—Redskins, 14-0 (W)
Redskins, 23-7 (P)
1973—Redskins, 28-7 (P)

Redskins, 38-20 (W)
1974—Redskins, 27-20 (P)
Redskins, 26-7 (W)
1975—Eagles, 26-10 (P)
Eagles, 26-3 (W)
1976—Redskins, 20-17 (P) OT
Redskins, 24-0 (W)
1977—Redskins, 23-17 (W)
Redskins, 17-14 (P)
1978—Redskins, 35-30 (W)
Eagles, 17-10 (P)
1979—Eagles, 28-17 (P)
Redskins, 17-7 (W)
1980—Eagles, 24-14 (P)
Eagles, 24-0 (W)
1981—Eagles, 36-13 (P)
Redskins, 15-13 (W)
1982—Redskins, 37-34 (P) OT
Redskins, 13-9 (W)
1983—Redskins, 23-13 (P)
Redskins, 28-24 (W)
1984—Redskins, 20-0 (W)
Eagles, 16-10 (P)
1985—Eagles, 19-6 (W)
Redskins, 17-12 (P)
1986—Redskins, 41-14 (W)
Redskins, 21-14 (P)
1987—Redskins, 34-24 (W)
Eagles, 31-27 (P)
1988—Redskins, 17-10 (W)
Redskins, 20-19 (P)
1989—Eagles, 42-37 (W)
Redskins, 10-3 (P)
1990—Redskins, 13-7 (W)
Eagles, 28-14 (P)
**Redskins, 20-6 (P)
1991—Redskins, 23-0 (W)
Eagles, 24-22 (P)
1992—Redskins, 16-12 (W)
Eagles, 17-13 (P)
1993—Eagles, 34-31 (P)
Eagles, 17-14 (W)
1994—Eagles, 21-17 (P)
Eagles, 31-29 (W)
1995—Eagles, 37-34 (P) (OT)
Eagles, 14-7 (W)
1996—Eagles, 17-14 (W)
Redskins, 26-21 (P)
1997—Eagles, 24-10 (P)
Redskins, 35-32 (W)
1998—Eagles, 17-12 (P)
Redskins, 28-3 (W)
1999—Eagles, 35-28 (P)
Redskins, 20-17 (W) OT
2000—Redskins, 17-14 (P)
Eagles, 23-20 (W)
2001—Redskins, 13-3 (P)
Eagles, 20-6 (W)
2002—Eagles, 37-7 (W)
Eagles, 34-21 (P)
2003—Eagles, 27-25 (P)
Eagles, 31-7 (W)
2004—Eagles, 28-6 (P)
Eagles, 17-14 (W)
(RS Pts.—Eagles 2,850, Redskins 2,720)
(PS Pts.—Redskins 20, Eagles 6)
*Franchise in Boston prior to 1937
**NFC First-Round Playoff

PITTSBURGH vs. ARIZONA
RS: Steelers lead series, 31-22-3;
See Arizona vs. Pittsburgh
PITTSBURGH vs. ATLANTA
RS: Steelers lead series, 11-1-1;
See Atlanta vs. Pittsburgh
PITTSBURGH vs. BALTIMORE
RS: Steelers lead series, 12-6
PS: Steelers lead series, 1-0;
See Baltimore vs. Pittsburgh
PITTSBURGH vs. BUFFALO
RS: Steelers lead series, 10-8
PS: Steelers lead series, 2-1;
See Buffalo vs. Pittsburgh
PITTSBURGH vs. CAROLINA
RS: Steelers lead series, 2-1;
See Carolina vs. Pittsburgh
PITTSBURGH vs. CHICAGO
RS: Bears lead series, 16-6-1;
See Chicago vs. Pittsburgh
PITTSBURGH vs. CINCINNATI
RS: Steelers lead series, 41-28;
See Cincinnati vs. Pittsburgh
PITTSBURGH vs. CLEVELAND
RS: Browns lead series, 55-49
PS: Steelers lead series, 2-0;
See Cleveland vs. Pittsburgh
PITTSBURGH vs. DALLAS
RS: Cowboys lead series, 14-12
PS: Steelers lead series, 2-1;
See Dallas vs. Pittsburgh
PITTSBURGH vs. DENVER
RS: Broncos lead series, 11-6-1
PS: Broncos lead series, 3-2;
See Denver vs. Pittsburgh
PITTSBURGH vs. DETROIT
RS: Lions lead series, 14-13-1;
See Detroit vs. Pittsburgh
PITTSBURGH vs. GREEN BAY
RS: Packers lead series, 18-12;
See Green Bay vs. Pittsburgh
PITTSBURGH vs. HOUSTON
RS: Texans lead series, 1-0;
See Houston vs. Pittsburgh
PITTSBURGH vs. INDIANAPOLIS
RS: Steelers lead series, 13-4
PS: Steelers lead series, 4-0;
See Indianapolis vs. Pittsburgh
PITTSBURGH vs. JACKSONVILLE
RS: Series tied, 8-8;
See Jacksonville vs. Pittsburgh
PITTSBURGH vs. KANSAS CITY
RS: Steelers lead series, 16-8
PS: Chiefs lead series, 1-0;
See Kansas City vs. Pittsburgh
PITTSBURGH vs. MIAMI
RS: Dolphins lead series, 9-8
PS: Dolphins lead series, 2-1;
See Miami vs. Pittsburgh
PITTSBURGH vs. MINNESOTA
RS: Vikings lead series, 8-5
PS: Steelers lead series, 1-0;
See Minnesota vs. Pittsburgh
PITTSBURGH vs. NEW ENGLAND
RS: Steelers lead series, 12-5
PS: Patriots lead series, 3-1;
See New England vs. Pittsburgh
PITTSBURGH vs. NEW ORLEANS
RS: Series tied, 6-6;
See New Orleans vs. Pittsburgh

PITTSBURGH vs. N.Y. GIANTS
RS: Giants lead series, 43-28-3;
See N.Y. Giants vs. Pittsburgh
PITTSBURGH vs. N.Y. JETS
RS: Steelers lead series, 15-2
PS: Steelers lead series, 1-0;
See N.Y. Jets vs. Pittsburgh
PITTSBURGH vs. OAKLAND
RS: Series tied, 8-8
PS: Series tied, 3-3;
See Oakland vs. Pittsburgh
PITTSBURGH vs. PHILADELPHIA
RS: Eagles lead series, 45-27-3
PS: Eagles lead series, 1-0;
See Philadelphia vs. Pittsburgh
*PITTSBURGH vs. **ST. LOUIS
RS: Rams lead series, 15-5-2
PS: Steelers lead series, 1-0
1938—Rams, 13-7 (New Orleans)
1939—Tie, 14-14 (C)
1941—Rams, 17-14 (Akron)
1947—Rams, 48-7 (P)
1948—Rams, 31-14 (LA)
1949—Tie, 7-7 (P)
1952—Rams, 28-14 (LA)
1955—Rams, 27-26 (LA)
1956—Steelers, 30-13 (P)
1961—Rams, 24-14 (LA)
1964—Rams, 26-14 (P)
1968—Rams, 45-10 (LA)
1971—Rams, 23-14 (P)
1975—Rams, 10-3 (LA)
1978—Rams, 10-7 (LA)
1979—***Steelers, 31-19 (Pasadena)
1981—Steelers, 24-0 (P)
1984—Steelers, 24-14 (P)
1987—Rams, 31-21 (LA)
1990—Steelers, 41-10 (P)
1993—Rams, 27-0 (LA)
1996—Steelers, 42-6 (P)
2003—Rams, 33-21 (P)
(RS Pts.—Rams 457, Steelers 368)
(PS Pts.—Steelers 31, Rams 19)
*Steelers known as Pirates prior to 1941
**Franchise in Los Angeles prior to 1995
and in Cleveland prior to 1946
***Super Bowl XIV
PITTSBURGH vs. SAN DIEGO
RS: Steelers lead series, 18-5
PS: Chargers lead series, 2-0
1971—Steelers, 21-17 (P)
1972—Steelers, 24-2 (SD)
1973—Steelers, 38-21 (P)
1975—Steelers, 37-0 (SD)
1976—Steelers, 23-0 (P)
1977—Steelers, 10-9 (SD)
1979—Chargers, 35-7 (SD)
1980—Chargers, 26-17 (SD)
1982—*Chargers, 31-28 (P)
1983—Steelers, 26-3 (P)
1984—Steelers, 52-24 (P)
1985—Chargers, 54-44 (SD)
1987—Steelers, 20-16 (SD)
1988—Chargers, 20-14 (SD)
1989—Steelers, 20-17 (P)
1990—Steelers, 36-14 (P)
1991—Steelers, 26-20 (P)
1992—Steelers, 23-6 (SD)
1993—Steelers,.16-3 (P)
1994—Chargers, 37-34 (SD)

**Chargers, 17-13 (P)
1995—Steelers, 31-16 (P)
1996—Steelers, 16-3 (P)
2000—Steelers, 34-21 (SD)
2003—Steelers, 40-24 (P)
(RS Pts.—Steelers 609, Chargers 388)
(PS Pts.—Chargers 48, Steelers 41)
*AFC First-Round Playoff
**AFC Championship
PITTSBURGH vs. SAN FRANCISCO
RS: 49ers lead series, 10-8
1951—49ers, 28-24 (P)
1952—Steelers, 24-7 (SF)
1954—49ers, 31-3 (SF)
1958—49ers, 23-20 (SF)
1961—Steelers, 20-10 (P)
1965—49ers, 27-17 (SF)
1968—49ers, 45-28 (P)
1973—Steelers, 37-14 (SF)
1977—Steelers, 27-0 (P)
1978—Steelers, 24-7 (SF)
1981—49ers, 17-14 (P)
1984—Steelers, 20-17 (SF)
1987—Steelers, 30-17 (P)
1990—49ers, 27-7 (SF)
1993—49ers, 24-13 (P)
1996—49ers, 25-15 (P)
1999—Steelers, 27-6 (SF)
2003—49ers, 30-14 (SF)
(RS Pts.—Steelers 364, 49ers 355)
PITTSBURGH vs. SEATTLE
RS: Seahawks lead series, 8-6
1977—Steelers, 30-20 (P)
1978—Steelers, 21-10 (P)
1981—Seahawks, 24-21 (S)
1982—Seahawks, 16-0 (S)
1983—Steelers, 27-21 (S)
1986—Steelers, 30-0 (S)
1987—Steelers, 13-9 (P)
1991—Seahawks, 27-7 (P)
1992—Steelers, 20-14 (P)
1993—Seahawks, 16-6 (S)
1994—Seahawks, 30-13 (S)
1998—Steelers, 13-10 (P)
1999—Seahawks, 29-10 (P)
2003—Seahawks, 23-16 (S)
(RS Pts.—Seahawks 279, Steelers 197)
PITTSBURGH vs. TAMPA BAY
RS: Steelers lead series, 6-1
1976—Steelers, 42-0 (P)
1980—Steelers, 24-21 (TB)
1983—Steelers, 17-12 (P)
1989—Steelers, 31-22 (TB)
1998—Buccaneers, 16-3 (TB)
2001—Steelers, 17-10 (TB)
2002—Steelers, 17-7 (TB)
(RS Pts.—Steelers 151, Buccaneers 88)
PITTSBURGH vs. *TENNESSEE
RS: Steelers lead series, 37-28
PS: Steelers lead series, 3-1
1970—Oilers, 19-7 (P)
Steelers, 7-3 (H)
1971—Steelers, 23-16 (P)
Oilers, 29-3 (H)
1972—Steelers, 24-7 (P)
Steelers, 9-3 (H)
1973—Steelers, 36-7 (H)
Steelers, 33-7 (P)
1974—Steelers, 13-7 (H)
Oilers, 13-10 (P)

1975—Steelers, 24-17 (P)
Steelers, 32-9 (H)
1976—Steelers, 32-16 (P)
Steelers, 21-0 (H)
1977—Oilers, 27-10 (H)
Steelers, 27-10 (P)
1978—Oilers, 24-17 (P)
Steelers, 13-3 (H)
**Steelers, 34-5 (P)
1979—Steelers, 38-7 (P)
Oilers, 20-17 (H)
**Steelers, 27-13 (P)
1980—Steelers, 31-17 (P)
Oilers, 6-0 (H)
1981—Steelers, 26-13 (P)
Oilers, 21-20 (H)
1982—Steelers, 24-10 (H)
1983—Steelers, 40-28 (H)
Steelers, 17-10 (P)
1984—Steelers, 35-7 (P)
Oilers, 23-20 (H) OT
1985—Steelers, 20-0 (P)
Steelers, 30-7 (H)
1986—Steelers, 22-16 (H) OT
Steelers, 21-10 (P)
1987—Oilers, 23-3 (P)
Oilers, 24-16 (H)
1988—Oilers, 34-14 (P)
Steelers, 37-34 (H)
1989—Oilers, 27-0 (H)
Oilers, 23-16 (P)
***Steelers, 26-23 (H) OT
1990—Steelers, 20-9 (P)
Oilers, 34-14 (H)
1991—Steelers, 26-14 (P)
Oilers, 31-6 (H)
1992—Steelers, 29-24 (P)
Steelers, 21-20 (P)
1993—Oilers, 23-3 (H)
Oilers, 26-17 (P)
1994—Steelers, 30-14 (P)
Steelers, 12-9 (H) OT
1995—Steelers, 34-17 (H)
Steelers, 21-7 (P)
1996—Steelers, 30-16 (P)
Oilers, 23-13 (H)
1997—Steelers, 37-24 (P)
Oilers, 16-6 (T)
1998—Steelers, 41-31 (P)
Oilers, 23-14 (T)
1999—Titans, 16-10 (T)
Titans, 47-36 (P)
2000—Titans, 23-20 (P)
Titans, 9-7 (T)
2001—Steelers, 34-7 (P)
Steelers, 34-24 (T)
2002—Titans, 31-23 (T)
****Titans, 34-31 (T) OT
2003—Titans, 30-13 (P)
(RS Pts.—Steelers 1,329, Titans 1,135)
(PS Pts.—Steelers 118, Titans 75)
*Franchise in Houston prior to 1997;
known as Oilers prior to 1999
**AFC Championship
***AFC First-Round Playoff
****AFC Divisional Playoff
*PITTSBURGH vs. **WASHINGTON
RS: Redskins lead series, 42-30-3
1933—Redskins, 21-6 (P)
Pirates, 16-14 (B)

1934—Redskins, 7-0 (P)
    Redskins, 39-0 (B)
1935—Pirates, 6-0 (P)
    Redskins, 13-3 (B)
1936—Pirates, 10-0 (P)
    Redskins, 30-0 (B)
1937—Redskins, 34-20 (W)
    Pirates, 21-13 (P)
1938—Redskins, 7-0 (P)
    Redskins, 15-0 (W)
1939—Redskins, 44-14 (W)
    Redskins, 21-14 (P)
1940—Redskins, 40-10 (P)
    Redskins, 37-10 (W)
1941—Redskins, 24-20 (P)
    Redskins, 23-3 (W)
1942—Redskins, 28-14 (W)
    Redskins, 14-0 (P)
1945—Redskins, 14-0 (P)
    Redskins, 24-0 (W)
1946—Tie, 14-14 (W)
    Steelers, 14-7 (P)
1947—Redskins, 27-26 (W)
    Steelers, 21-14 (P)
1948—Redskins, 17-14 (W)
    Steelers, 10-7 (P)
1949—Redskins, 27-14 (P)
    Redskins, 27-14 (W)
1950—Steelers, 26-7 (W)
    Redskins, 24-7 (P)
1951—Redskins, 22-7 (P)
    Steelers, 20-10 (W)
1952—Redskins, 28-24 (P)
    Steelers, 24-23 (W)
1953—Redskins, 17-9 (P)
    Steelers, 14-13 (W)
1954—Steelers, 37-7 (P)
    Redskins, 17-14 (W)
1955—Redskins, 23-14 (P)
    Redskins, 28-17 (W)
1956—Redskins, 30-13 (P)
    Steelers, 23-0 (W)
1957—Steelers, 28-7 (P)
    Redskins, 10-3 (W)
1958—Steelers, 24-16 (P)
    Tie, 14-14 (W)
1959—Redskins, 23-17 (P)
    Steelers, 27-6 (W)
1960—Tie, 27-27 (W)
    Steelers, 22-10 (P)
1961—Steelers, 20-0 (P)
    Steelers, 30-14 (W)
1962—Steelers, 23-21 (P)
    Steelers, 27-24 (W)
1963—Steelers, 38-27 (P)
    Steelers, 34-28 (W)
1964—Redskins, 30-0 (P)
    Steelers, 14-7 (W)
1965—Redskins, 31-3 (P)
    Redskins, 35-14 (W)
1966—Redskins, 33-27 (P)
    Redskins, 24-10 (W)
1967—Redskins, 15-10 (P)
1968—Redskins, 16-13 (W)
1969—Redskins, 14-7 (P)
1973—Steelers, 21-16 (P)
1979—Steelers, 38-7 (P)
1985—Redskins, 30-23 (P)
1988—Redskins, 30-29 (W)
1991—Redskins, 41-14 (P)

1997—Steelers, 14-13 (P)
2000—Steelers, 24-3 (P)
2004—Steelers, 16-7 (P)
(RS Pts.—Redskins 1,413, Steelers 1,171)
*Steelers known as Pirates prior to 1941
**Franchise in Boston prior to 1937

ST. LOUIS vs. ARIZONA
RS: Rams lead series, 28-22-2
PS: Rams lead series, 1-0;
See Arizona vs. St. Louis
ST. LOUIS vs. ATLANTA
RS: Rams lead series, 46-24-2
PS: Falcons lead series, 1-0;
See Atlanta vs. St. Louis
ST. LOUIS vs. BALTIMORE
RS: Rams lead series, 2-1;
See Baltimore vs. St. Louis
ST. LOUIS vs. BUFFALO
RS: Bills lead series, 5-4;
See Buffalo vs. St. Louis
ST. LOUIS vs. CAROLINA
RS: Panthers lead series, 8-7
PS: Panthers lead series, 1-0;
See Carolina vs. St. Louis
ST. LOUIS vs. CHICAGO
RS: Bears lead series, 47-34-3
PS: Series tied, 1-1;
See Chicago vs. St. Louis
ST. LOUIS vs. CINCINNATI
RS: Series tied, 5-5;
See Cincinnati vs. St. Louis
ST. LOUIS vs. CLEVELAND
RS: Rams lead series, 9-8
PS: Browns lead series, 2-1;
See Cleveland vs. St. Louis
ST. LOUIS vs. DALLAS
RS: Series tied, 9-9
PS: Series tied, 4-4;
See Dallas vs. St. Louis
ST. LOUIS vs. DENVER
RS: Series tied, 5-5;
See Denver vs. St. Louis
ST. LOUIS vs. DETROIT
RS: Rams lead series, 40-37-1
PS: Lions lead series, 1-0;
See Detroit vs. St. Louis
ST. LOUIS vs. GREEN BAY
RS: Rams lead series, 44-40-2
PS: Series tied, 1-1;
See Green Bay vs. St. Louis
ST. LOUIS vs. INDIANAPOLIS
RS: Colts lead series, 21-17-2;
See Indianapolis vs. St. Louis
ST. LOUIS vs. JACKSONVILLE
RS: Rams lead series, 1-0;
See Jacksonville vs. St. Louis
ST. LOUIS vs. KANSAS CITY
RS: Series tied, 4-4;
See Kansas City vs. St. Louis
ST. LOUIS vs. MIAMI
RS: Dolphins lead series, 8-2;
See Miami vs. St. Louis
ST. LOUIS vs. MINNESOTA
RS: Vikings lead series, 16-13-2
PS: Vikings lead series, 5-2;
See Minnesota vs. St. Louis
ST. LOUIS vs. NEW ENGLAND
RS: Rams lead series, 5-4
PS: Patriots lead series, 1-0;

See New England vs. St. Louis
ST. LOUIS vs. NEW ORLEANS
RS: Rams lead series, 36-29
PS: Saints lead series, 1-0;
See New Orleans vs. St. Louis
ST. LOUIS vs. N.Y. GIANTS
RS: Rams lead series, 25-11
PS: Series tied, 1-1;
See N.Y. Giants vs. St. Louis
ST. LOUIS vs. N.Y. JETS
RS: Rams lead series, 9-2;
See N.Y. Jets vs. St. Louis
ST. LOUIS vs. OAKLAND
RS: Raiders lead series, 7-3;
See Oakland vs. St. Louis
ST. LOUIS vs. PHILADELPHIA
RS: Rams lead series, 17-15-1
PS: Rams lead series, 2-1;
See Philadelphia vs. St. Louis
ST. LOUIS vs. PITTSBURGH
RS: Rams lead series, 15-5-2
PS: Steelers lead series, 1-0;
See Pittsburgh vs. St. Louis
***ST. LOUIS vs. SAN DIEGO**
RS: Rams lead series, 5-3
1970—Rams, 37-10 (LA)
1975—Rams, 13-10 (SD) OT
1979—Chargers, 40-16 (LA)
1988—Chargers, 38-24 (LA)
1991—Rams, 30-24 (LA)
1994—Chargers, 31-17 (SD)
2000—Rams, 57-31 (StL)
2002—Rams, 28-24 (StL)
(RS Pts.—Rams 222, Chargers 208)
*Franchise in Los Angeles prior to 1995
***ST. LOUIS vs. SAN FRANCISCO**
RS: Rams lead series, 58-50-2
PS: 49ers lead series, 1-0
1950—Rams, 35-14 (SF)
    Rams, 28-21 (LA)
1951—49ers, 44-17 (SF)
    Rams, 23-16 (LA)
1952—Rams, 35-9 (LA)
    Rams, 34-21 (SF)
1953—49ers, 31-30 (SF)
    49ers, 31-27 (LA)
1954—Tie, 24-24 (LA)
    Rams, 42-34 (SF)
1955—Rams, 23-14 (SF)
    Rams, 27-14 (LA)
1956—49ers, 33-30 (SF)
    Rams, 30-6 (LA)
1957—49ers, 23-20 (SF)
    Rams, 37-24 (LA)
1958—Rams, 33-3 (SF)
    Rams, 56-7 (LA)
1959—49ers, 34-0 (SF)
    49ers, 24-16 (LA)
1960—49ers, 13-9 (SF)
    49ers, 23-7 (LA)
1961—49ers, 35-0 (SF)
    Rams, 17-7 (LA)
1962—Rams, 28-14 (SF)
    49ers, 24-17 (LA)
1963—Rams, 28-21 (SF)
    Rams, 21-17 (SF)
1964—Rams, 42-14 (LA)
    49ers, 28-7 (SF)
1965—49ers, 45-21 (LA)
    49ers, 30-27 (SF)

1966—Rams, 34-3 (LA)
    49ers, 21-13 (SF)
1967—49ers, 27-24 (LA)
    Rams, 17-7 (SF)
1968—Rams, 24-10 (LA)
    Tie, 20-20 (SF)
1969—Rams, 27-21 (SF)
    Rams, 41-30 (LA)
1970—49ers, 20-6 (LA)
    Rams, 30-13 (SF)
1971—Rams, 20-13 (SF)
    Rams, 17-6 (LA)
1972—Rams, 31-7 (LA)
    Rams, 26-16 (SF)
1973—Rams, 40-20 (LA)
    Rams, 31-13 (LA)
1974—Rams, 37-14 (LA)
    Rams, 15-13 (SF)
1975—Rams, 23-14 (SF)
    49ers, 24-23 (LA)
1976—49ers, 16-0 (LA)
    Rams, 23-3 (SF)
1977—Rams, 34-14 (LA)
    Rams, 23-10 (SF)
1978—Rams, 27-10 (LA)
    Rams, 31-28 (SF)
1979—Rams, 27-24 (LA)
    Rams, 26-20 (SF)
1980—Rams, 48-26 (LA)
    Rams, 31-17 (SF)
1981—49ers, 20-17 (SF)
    49ers, 33-31 (LA)
1982—49ers, 30-24 (LA)
    Rams, 21-20 (SF)
1983—Rams, 10-7 (SF)
    49ers, 45-35 (LA)
1984—49ers, 33-0 (LA)
    49ers, 19-16 (SF)
1985—49ers, 28-14 (LA)
    Rams, 27-20 (SF)
1986—Rams, 16-13 (LA)
    49ers, 24-14 (SF)
1987—49ers, 31-10 (LA)
    49ers, 48-0 (SF)
1988—49ers, 24-21 (LA)
    Rams, 38-16 (SF)
1989—Rams, 13-12 (SF)
    49ers, 30-27 (LA)
    **49ers, 30-3 (SF)
1990—49ers, 28-17 (SF)
    49ers, 26-10 (LA)
1991—49ers, 27-10 (SF)
    49ers, 33-10 (LA)
1992—49ers, 27-24 (SF)
    49ers, 27-10 (LA)
1993—49ers, 40-17 (SF)
    49ers, 35-10 (LA)
1994—49ers, 34-19 (LA)
    49ers, 31-27 (SF)
1995—49ers, 44-10 (StL)
    49ers, 41-13 (SF)
1996—49ers, 34-0 (SF)
    49ers, 28-11 (StL)
1997—49ers, 15-12 (StL)
    49ers, 30-10 (SF)
1998—49ers, 28-10 (StL)
    49ers, 38-19 (SF)
1999—Rams, 42-20 (StL)
    Rams, 23-7 (SF)
2000—Rams, 41-24 (StL)

Rams, 34-24 (SF)
2001—Rams, 30-26 (SF)
    Rams, 27-14 (StL)
2002—49ers, 37-13 (SF)
    Rams, 31-20 (StL)
2003—Rams, 27-24 (StL) OT
    49ers, 30-10 (SF)
2004—Rams, 24-14 (SF)
    Rams, 16-6 (StL)
(RS Pts.—Rams 2,462, 49ers 2,432)
(PS Pts.—49ers 30, Rams 3)
*Franchise in Los Angeles prior to 1995
**NFC Championship

*ST. LOUIS vs. SEATTLE
RS: Rams lead series, 9-4
PS: Rams lead series, 1-0
1976—Rams, 45-6 (LA)
1979—Rams, 24-0 (S)
1985—Rams, 35-24 (S)
1988—Rams, 31-10 (LA)
1991—Seahawks, 23-9 (S)
1997—Seahawks, 17-9 (StL)
2000—Rams, 37-34 (Sea)
2002—Rams, 37-20 (StL)
    Seahawks, 30-10 (Sea)
2003—Seahawks, 24-23 (Sea)
    Rams, 27-22 (StL)
2004—Rams, 33-27 (Sea) OT
    Rams, 23-12 (StL)
    **Rams, 27-20 (Sea)
(RS Pts.—Rams 343, Seahawks 249)
(PS Pts.—Rams 27, Seahawks 20)
*Franchise in Los Angeles prior to 1995
**NFC First-Round Playoff

*ST. LOUIS vs. TAMPA BAY
RS: Rams lead series, 9-6
PS: Rams lead series, 2-0
1977—Rams, 31-0 (LA)
1978—Rams, 26-23 (LA)
1979—Buccaneers, 21-6 (TB)
    **Rams, 9-0 (TB)
1980—Buccaneers, 10-9 (TB)
1984—Rams, 34-33 (TB)
1985—Rams, 31-27 (TB)
1986—Rams, 26-20 (LA) OT
1987—Rams, 35-3 (LA)
1990—Rams, 35-14 (TB)
1992—Rams, 31-27 (TB)
1994—Buccaneers, 24-14 (TB)
1999—**Rams, 11-6 (StL)
2000—Buccaneers, 38-35 (TB)
2001—Buccaneers, 24-17 (StL)
2002—Buccaneers, 26-14 (TB)
2004—Rams, 28-21 (StL)
(RS Pts.—Rams 372, Buccaneers 311)
(PS Pts.—Rams 20, Buccaneers 6)
*Franchise in Los Angeles prior to 1995
**NFC Championship

*ST. LOUIS vs. **TENNESSEE
RS: Rams lead series, 5-3
PS: Rams lead series, 1-0
1973—Rams, 31-26 (H)
1978—Rams, 10-6 (H)
1981—Oilers, 27-20 (LA)
1984—Rams, 27-16 (LA)
1987—Oilers, 20-16 (H)
1990—Rams, 17-13 (LA)
1993—Rams, 28-13 (H)
1999—Titans, 24-21 (T)
    ***Rams, 23-16 (Atlanta)

(RS Pts.—Rams 170, Titans 145)
(PS Pts.—Rams 23, Titans 16)
*Franchise in Los Angeles prior to 1995
**Franchise in Houston prior to 1997;
known as Oilers prior to 1999
***Super Bowl XXXIV

*ST. LOUIS vs. WASHINGTON
RS: Redskins lead series, 19-6-1
PS: Series tied, 2-2
1937—Redskins, 16-7 (C)
1938—Redskins, 37-13 (W)
1941—Redskins, 17-13 (W)
1942—Redskins, 33-14 (W)
1944—Redskins, 14-10 (W)
1945—**Redskins, 15-14 (C)
1948—Rams, 41-13 (W)
1949—Rams, 53-27 (LA)
1951—Redskins, 31-21 (W)
1962—Redskins, 20-14 (W)
1963—Redskins, 37-14 (LA)
1967—Tie, 28-28 (LA)
1969—Rams, 24-13 (W)
1971—Redskins, 38-24 (LA)
1974—Redskins, 23-17 (LA)
    ***Rams, 19-10 (LA)
1977—Redskins, 17-14 (W)
1981—Redskins, 30-7 (LA)
1983—Redskins, 42-20 (LA)
    ***Redskins, 51-7 (W)
1986—****Redskins, 19-7 (W)
1987—Rams, 30-26 (W)
1991—Redskins, 27-6 (LA)
1993—Rams, 10-6 (LA)
1994—Redskins, 24-21 (LA)
1995—Redskins, 35-23 (StL)
1996—Redskins, 17-10 (StL)
1997—Rams, 23-20 (W)
2000—Redskins, 33-20 (StL)
2002—Redskins, 20-17 (W)
(RS Pts.—Redskins 644, Rams 494)
(PS Pts.—Redskins 94, Rams 48)
*Franchise in Los Angeles prior to 1995
and in Cleveland prior to 1946
**NFL Championship
***NFC Divisional Playoff
****NFC First-Round Playoff

SAN DIEGO vs. ARIZONA
RS: Chargers lead series, 7-3;
See Arizona vs. San Diego
SAN DIEGO vs. ATLANTA
RS: Falcons lead series, 6-1;
See Atlanta vs. San Diego
SAN DIEGO vs BALTIMORE
RS: Series tied, 2-2;
See Baltimore vs. San Diego
SAN DIEGO vs. BUFFALO
RS: Chargers lead series, 18-9-2
PS: Bills lead series, 2-1;
See Buffalo vs. San Diego
SAN DIEGO vs. CAROLINA
RS: Panthers lead series, 2-1;
See Carolina vs. San Diego
SAN DIEGO vs. CHICAGO
RS: Bears lead series, 5-4;
See Chicago vs. San Diego
SAN DIEGO vs. CINCINNATI
RS: Chargers lead series, 17-10
PS: Bengals lead series, 1-0;
See Cincinnati vs. San Diego

SAN DIEGO vs. CLEVELAND
RS: Chargers lead series, 12-7-1;
See Cleveland vs. San Diego
SAN DIEGO vs. DALLAS
RS: Cowboys lead series, 5-2;
See Dallas vs. San Diego
SAN DIEGO vs. DENVER
RS: Broncos lead series, 50-39-1;
See Denver vs. San Diego
SAN DIEGO vs. DETROIT
RS: Chargers lead series, 5-3;
See Detroit vs. San Diego
SAN DIEGO vs. GREEN BAY
RS: Packers lead series, 7-1;
See Green Bay vs. San Diego
SAN DIEGO vs. HOUSTON
RS: Chargers lead series, 2-0;
See Houston vs. San Diego
SAN DIEGO vs. INDIANAPOLIS
RS: Chargers lead series, 12-8
PS: Colts lead series, 1-0;
See Indianapolis vs. San Diego
SAN DIEGO vs. JACKSONVILLE
RS: Series tied, 1-1;
See Jacksonville vs. San Diego
SAN DIEGO vs. KANSAS CITY
RS: Chiefs lead series, 47-41-1
PS: Chargers lead series, 1-0;
See Kansas City vs. San Diego
SAN DIEGO vs. MIAMI
RS: Series tied, 10-10
PS: Series tied, 2-2;
See Miami vs. San Diego
SAN DIEGO vs. MINNESOTA
RS: Chargers lead series, 5-4;
See Minnesota vs. San Diego
SAN DIEGO vs. NEW ENGLAND
RS: Patriots lead series, 17-12-2
PS: Chargers lead series, 1-0;
See New England vs. San Diego
SAN DIEGO vs. NEW ORLEANS
RS: Chargers lead series, 7-2;
See New Orleans vs. San Diego
SAN DIEGO vs. N.Y. GIANTS
RS: Giants lead series, 5-3;
See N.Y. Giants vs. San Diego
SAN DIEGO vs. N.Y. JETS
RS: Chargers lead series, 17-11-1
PS: Jets lead series, 1-0;
See N.Y. Jets vs. San Diego
SAN DIEGO vs. OAKLAND
RS: Raiders lead series, 54-34-2
PS: Raiders lead series, 1-0;
See Oakland vs. San Diego
SAN DIEGO vs. PHILADELPHIA
RS: Chargers lead series, 5-3;
See Philadelphia vs. San Diego
SAN DIEGO vs. PITTSBURGH
RS: Steelers lead series, 18-5
PS: Chargers lead series, 2-0;
See Pittsburgh vs. San Diego
SAN DIEGO vs. ST. LOUIS
RS: Rams lead series, 5-3;
See St. Louis vs. San Diego
SAN DIEGO vs. SAN FRANCISCO
RS: 49ers lead series, 6-4
PS: 49ers lead series, 1-0
1972—49ers, 34-3 (SF)
1976—Chargers, 13-7 (SD) OT
1979—Chargers, 31-9 (SD)

1982—Chargers, 41-37 (SF)
1988—49ers, 48-10 (SD)
1991—49ers, 34-14 (SF)
1994—49ers, 38-15 (SD)
     *49ers, 49-26 (Miami)
1997—49ers, 17-10 (SF)
2000—49ers, 45-17 (SD)
2002—Chargers, 20-17 (SD) OT
(RS Pts.—49ers 286, Chargers 174)
(PS Pts.—49ers 49, Chargers 26)
*Super Bowl XXIX
SAN DIEGO vs. SEATTLE
RS: Seahawks lead series, 25-22
1977—Chargers, 30-28 (S)
1978—Chargers, 24-20 (S)
     Chargers, 37-10 (SD)
1979—Chargers, 33-16 (S)
     Chargers, 20-10 (SD)
1980—Chargers, 34-13 (S)
     Chargers, 21-14 (SD)
1981—Chargers, 24-10 (SD)
     Seahawks, 44-23 (S)
1983—Seahawks, 34-31 (S)
     Chargers, 28-21 (SD)
1984—Seahawks, 31-17 (S)
     Seahawks, 24-0 (SD)
1985—Seahawks, 49-35 (SD)
     Seahawks, 26-21 (S)
1986—Seahawks, 33-7 (S)
     Seahawks, 34-24 (SD)
1987—Seahawks, 34-3 (S)
1988—Chargers, 17-6 (SD)
     Seahawks, 17-14 (S)
1989—Seahawks, 17-16 (SD)
     Seahawks, 10-7 (S)
1990—Chargers, 31-14 (S)
     Seahawks, 13-10 (SD) OT
1991—Seahawks, 20-9 (S)
     Chargers, 17-14 (SD)
1992—Chargers, 17-6 (SD)
     Chargers, 31-14 (S)
1993—Chargers, 18-12 (SD)
     Seahawks, 31-14 (S)
1994—Chargers, 24-10 (S)
     Chargers, 35-15 (SD)
1995—Chargers, 14-10 (SD)
     Chargers, 35-25 (S)
1996—Chargers, 29-7 (SD)
     Seahawks, 32-13 (S)
1997—Seahawks, 26-22 (S)
     Seahawks, 37-31 (SD)
1998—Seahawks, 27-20 (SD)
     Seahawks, 38-17 (S)
1999—Chargers, 13-10 (S)
     Chargers, 19-16 (S)
2000—Seahawks, 20-12 (SD)
     Seahawks, 17-15 (S)
2001—Seahawks, 13-10 (S) OT
     Seahawks, 25-22 (SD)
2002—Seahawks, 31-28 (SD) OT
(RS Pts.—Seahawks 984, Chargers 972)
SAN DIEGO vs. TAMPA BAY
RS: Chargers lead series, 7-1
1976—Chargers, 23-0 (TB)
1981—Chargers, 24-23 (TB)
1987—Chargers, 17-13 (TB)
1990—Chargers, 41-10 (SD)
1992—Chargers, 29-14 (SD)
1993—Chargers, 32-17 (TB)
1996—Buccaneers, 25-17 (SD)

2004—Chargers, 31-24 (SD)
(RS Pts.—Chargers 214, Buccaneers 126)
*SAN DIEGO vs. **TENNESSEE
RS: Chargers lead series, 20-13-1
PS: Titans lead series, 3-0
1960—Oilers, 38-28 (H)
     Chargers, 24-21 (LA)
     ***Oilers, 24-16 (H)
1961—Chargers, 34-24 (SD)
     Oilers, 33-13 (H)
     ***Oilers, 10-3 (SD)
1962—Oilers, 42-17 (SD)
     Oilers, 33-27 (H)
1963—Chargers, 27-0 (SD)
     Chargers 20-14 (H)
1964—Chargers, 27-21 (SD)
     Chargers, 20-17 (H)
1965—Chargers, 31-14 (SD)
     Chargers, 37-26 (H)
1966—Chargers, 28-22 (H)
1967—Chargers, 13-3 (SD)
     Oilers, 24-17 (H)
1968—Chargers, 30-14 (SD)
1969—Chargers, 21-17 (H)
1970—Tie, 31-31 (SD)
1971—Oilers, 49-33 (H)
1972—Chargers, 34-20 (SD)
1974—Oilers, 21-14 (H)
1975—Oilers, 33-17 (H)
1976—Chargers, 30-27 (SD)
1978—Chargers, 45-24 (H)
1979—****Oilers, 17-14 (SD)
1984—Chargers, 31-14 (SD)
1985—Oilers, 37-35 (H)
1986—Chargers, 27-0 (SD)
1987—Oilers, 33-18 (H)
1989—Oilers, 34-27 (SD)
1990—Oilers, 17-7 (SD)
1992—Oilers, 27-0 (H)
1993—Chargers, 18-17 (SD)
1998—Chargers, 13-7 (T)
2004—Chargers, 38-17 (SD)
(RS Pts.—Chargers 832, Titans 771)
(PS Pts.—Titans 51, Chargers 33)
*Franchise in Los Angeles prior to 1961
**Franchise in Houston prior to 1997;
known as Oilers prior to 1999
***AFL Championship
****AFC Divisional Playoff
SAN DIEGO vs. WASHINGTON
RS: Redskins lead series, 6-1
1973—Redskins, 38-0 (W)
1980—Redskins, 40-17 (W)
1983—Redskins, 27-24 (SD)
1986—Redskins, 30-27 (SD)
1989—Redskins, 26-21 (W)
1998—Redskins, 24-20 (W)
2001—Chargers, 30-3 (SD)
(RS Pts.—Redskins 188, Chargers 139)

SAN FRANCISCO vs. ARIZONA
RS: 49ers lead series, 17-10;
See Arizona vs. San Francisco
SAN FRANCISCO vs. ATLANTA
RS: 49ers lead series, 44-26-1
PS: Falcons lead series, 1-0;
See Atlanta vs. San Francisco
SAN FRANCISCO vs. BALTIMORE
RS: Series tied, 1-1;
See Baltimore vs. San Francisco

SAN FRANCISCO vs. BUFFALO
RS: Bills lead series, 5-4;
See Buffalo vs. San Francisco
SAN FRANCISCO vs. CAROLINA
RS: Panthers lead series, 8-7;
See Carolina vs. San Francisco
SAN FRANCISCO vs. CHICAGO
RS: Series tied, 27-27-1
PS: 49ers lead series, 3-0;
See Chicago vs. San Francisco
SAN FRANCISCO vs. CINCINNATI
RS: 49ers lead series, 7-3
PS: 49ers lead series, 2-0;
See Cincinnati vs. San Francisco
SAN FRANCISCO vs. CLEVELAND
RS: Browns lead series, 10-6;
See Cleveland vs. San Francisco
SAN FRANCISCO vs. DALLAS
RS: 49ers lead series, 14-8-1
PS: Cowboys lead series, 5-2;
See Dallas vs. San Francisco
SAN FRANCISCO vs. DENVER
RS: Broncos lead series, 6-4
PS: 49ers lead series, 1-0;
See Denver vs. San Francisco
SAN FRANCISCO vs. DETROIT
RS: 49ers lead series, 31-26-1
PS: Series tied, 1-1;
See Detroit vs. San Francisco
SAN FRANCISCO vs. GREEN BAY
RS: Packers lead series, 27-25-1
PS: Packers lead series, 4-1;
See Green Bay vs. San Francisco
SAN FRANCISCO vs. INDIANAPOLIS
RS: Colts lead series, 22-18;
See Indianapolis vs. San Francisco
SAN FRANCISCO vs. JACKSONVILLE
RS: Jaguars lead series, 1-0;
See Jacksonville vs. San Francisco
SAN FRANCISCO vs. KANSAS CITY
RS: 49ers lead series, 6-3;
See Kansas City vs. San Francisco
SAN FRANCISCO vs. MIAMI
RS: Dolphins lead series, 5-4
PS: 49ers lead series, 1-0;
See Miami vs. San Francisco
SAN FRANCISCO vs. MINNESOTA
RS: Vikings lead series, 18-17-1
PS: 49ers lead series, 4-1;
See Minnesota vs. San Francisco
SAN FRANCISCO vs. NEW ENGLAND
RS: 49ers lead series, 7-3;
See New England vs. San Francisco
SAN FRANCISCO vs. NEW ORLEANS
RS: 49ers lead series, 45-20-2;
See New Orleans vs. San Francisco
SAN FRANCISCO vs. N.Y. GIANTS
RS: 49ers lead series, 13-11
PS: 49ers lead series, 4-3;
See N.Y. Giants vs. San Francisco
SAN FRANCISCO vs. N.Y. JETS
RS: 49ers lead series, 8-2;
See N.Y. Jets vs. San Francisco
SAN FRANCISCO vs. OAKLAND
RS: Raiders lead series, 6-4;
See Oakland vs. San Francisco
SAN FRANCISCO vs. PHILADELPHIA
RS: 49ers lead series, 16-7-1
PS: 49ers lead series, 1-0;
See Philadelphia vs. San Francisco

SAN FRANCISCO vs. PITTSBURGH
RS: 49ers lead series, 10-8;
See Pittsburgh vs. San Francisco
SAN FRANCISCO vs. ST. LOUIS
RS: Rams lead series, 58-50-2
PS: 49ers lead series, 1-0;
See St. Louis vs. San Francisco
SAN FRANCISCO vs. SAN DIEGO
RS: 49ers lead series, 6-4
PS: 49ers lead series, 1-0;
See San Diego vs. San Francisco
SAN FRANCISCO vs. SEATTLE
RS: Series tied, 6-6
1976—49ers, 37-21 (Sea)
1979—Seahawks, 35-24 (SF)
1985—49ers, 19-6 (SF)
1988—49ers, 38-7 (Sea)
1991—49ers, 24-22 (Sea)
1997—Seahawks, 38-9 (Sea)
2002—49ers, 28-21 (Sea)
　　　49ers, 31-24 (SF)
2003—Seahawks, 20-19 (Sea)
　　　Seahawks, 24-17 (SF)
2004—Seahawks, 34-0 (Sea)
　　　Seahawks, 42-27 (SF)
(RS Pts.—Seahawks 294, 49ers 273)
SAN FRANCISCO vs. TAMPA BAY
RS: 49ers lead series, 13-3
PS: Buccaneers lead series, 1-0
1977—49ers, 20-10 (SF)
1978—49ers, 6-3 (SF)
1979—49ers, 23-7 (SF)
1980—Buccaneers, 24-23 (SF)
1983—49ers, 35-21 (SF)
1984—49ers, 24-17 (SF)
1986—49ers, 31-7 (TB)
1987—49ers, 24-10 (TB)
1989—49ers, 20-16 (TB)
1990—49ers, 31-7 (SF)
1992—49ers, 21-14 (SF)
1993—49ers, 45-21 (TB)
1994—49ers, 41-16 (SF)
1997—Buccaneers, 13-6 (TB)
2002—*Buccaneers, 31-6 (TB)
2003—49ers, 24-7 (SF)
2004—Buccaneers, 35-3 (TB)
(RS Pts.—49ers 377, Buccaneers 228)
(PS Pts.—Buccaneers 31, 49ers 6)
*NFC Divisional Playoff
SAN FRANCISCO vs. *TENNESSEE
RS: 49ers lead series, 7-3
1970—49ers, 30-20 (H)
1975—Oilers, 27-13 (SF)
1978—Oilers, 20-19 (H)
1981—49ers, 28-6 (SF)
1984—49ers, 34-21 (H)
1987—49ers, 27-20 (SF)
1990—49ers, 24-21 (H)
1993—Oilers, 10-7 (SF)
1996—49ers, 10-9 (H)
1999—49ers, 24-22 (SF)
(RS Pts.—49ers 216, Titans 176)
*Franchise in Houston prior to 1997;
known as Oilers prior to 1999
SAN FRANCISCO vs. WASHINGTON
RS: 49ers lead series, 13-8-1
PS: 49ers lead series, 3-1
1952—49ers, 23-17 (W)
1954—49ers, 41-7 (SF)
1955—Redskins, 7-0 (W)

1961—49ers, 35-3 (SF)
1967—Redskins, 31-28 (W)
1969—Tie, 17-17 (SF)
1970—49ers, 26-17 (SF)
1971—*49ers, 24-20 (SF)
1973—Redskins, 33-9 (W)
1976—Redskins, 24-21 (SF)
1978—Redskins, 38-20 (W)
1981—49ers, 30-17 (W)
1983—**Redskins, 24-21 (W)
1984—49ers, 37-31 (SF)
1985—49ers, 35-8 (W)
1986—Redskins, 14-6 (W)
1988—49ers, 37-21 (SF)
1990—49ers, 26-13 (SF)
　　　*49ers, 28-10 (SF)
1992—*49ers, 20-13 (SF)
1994—49ers, 37-22 (W)
1996—49ers, 19-16 (W) OT
1998—49ers, 45-10 (W)
1999—Redskins, 26-20 (SF) OT
2002—49ers, 20-10 (SF)
2004—Redskins, 26-16 (SF)
(RS Pts.—49ers 548, Redskins 408)
(PS Pts.—49ers 93, Redskins 67)
*NFC Divisional Playoff
**NFC Championship

SEATTLE vs. ARIZONA
RS: Cardinals lead series, 7-5;
See Arizona vs. Seattle
SEATTLE vs. ATLANTA
RS: Seahawks lead series, 7-2;
See Atlanta vs. Seattle
SEATTLE vs. BALTIMORE
RS: Ravens lead series, 2-0;
See Baltimore vs. Seattle
SEATTLE vs. BUFFALO
RS: Seahawks lead series, 6-4;
See Buffalo vs. Seattle
SEATTLE vs. CAROLINA
RS: Series tied, 1-1;
See Carolina vs. Seattle
SEATTLE vs. CHICAGO
RS: Seahawks lead series, 6-2;
See Chicago vs. Seattle
SEATTLE vs. CINCINNATI
RS: Series tied, 8-8
PS: Bengals lead series, 1-0;
See Cincinnati vs. Seattle
SEATTLE vs. CLEVELAND
RS: Seahawks lead series, 11-4;
See Cleveland vs. Seattle
SEATTLE vs. DALLAS
RS: Cowboys lead series, 6-3;
See Dallas vs. Seattle
SEATTLE vs. DENVER
RS: Broncos lead series, 33-17
PS: Seahawks lead series, 1-0;
See Denver vs. Seattle
SEATTLE vs. DETROIT
RS: Seahawks lead series, 5-4;
See Detroit vs. Seattle
SEATTLE vs. GREEN BAY
RS: Packers lead series, 5-4
PS: Packers lead series, 1-0;
See Green Bay vs. Seattle
SEATTLE vs. INDIANAPOLIS
RS: Colts lead series, 5-3;
See Indianapolis vs. Seattle

SEATTLE vs. JACKSONVILLE
RS: Seahawks lead series, 3-1;
See Jacksonville vs. Seattle
SEATTLE vs. KANSAS CITY
RS: Chiefs lead series, 30-18;
See Kansas City vs. Seattle
SEATTLE vs. MIAMI
RS: Dolphins lead series, 6-3
PS: Dolphins lead series, 2-1;
See Miami vs. Seattle
SEATTLE vs. MINNESOTA
RS: Seahawks lead series, 6-3;
See Minnesota vs. Seattle
SEATTLE vs. NEW ENGLAND
RS: Series tied, 7-7;
See New England vs. Seattle
SEATTLE vs. NEW ORLEANS
RS: Seahawks lead series, 5-4;
See New Orleans vs. Seattle
SEATTLE vs. N.Y. GIANTS
RS: Giants lead series, 7-3;
See N.Y. Giants vs. Seattle
SEATTLE vs. N.Y. JETS
RS: Series tied, 8-8;
See N.Y. Jets vs. Seattle
SEATTLE vs. OAKLAND
RS: Raiders lead series, 27-22
PS: Series tied, 1-1;
See Oakland vs. Seattle
SEATTLE vs. PHILADELPHIA
RS: Eagles lead series, 6-3;
See Philadelphia vs. Seattle
SEATTLE vs. PITTSBURGH
RS: Seahawks lead series, 8-6;
See Pittsburgh vs. Seattle
SEATTLE vs. ST. LOUIS
RS: Rams lead series, 9-4
PS: Rams lead series, 1-0;
See St. Louis vs. Seattle
SEATTLE vs. SAN DIEGO
RS: Seahawks lead series, 25-22;
See San Diego vs. Seattle
SEATTLE vs. SAN FRANCISCO
RS: Series tied, 6-6;
See San Francisco vs. Seattle
SEATTLE vs. TAMPA BAY
RS: Seahawks lead series, 5-1
1976—Seahawks, 13-10 (TB)
1977—Seahawks, 30-23 (S)
1994—Seahawks, 22-21 (S)
1996—Seahawks, 17-13 (TB)
1999—Buccaneers, 16-3 (S)
2004—Seahawks, 10-6 (TB)
(RS Pts.—Seahawks 95, Buccaneers 89)
SEATTLE vs. *TENNESSEE
RS: Seahawks lead series, 8-4
PS: Titans lead series, 1-0
1977—Oilers, 22-10 (S)
1979—Seahawks, 34-14 (S)
1980—Seahawks, 26-7 (H)
1981—Oilers, 35-17 (H)
1982—Oilers, 23-21 (H)
1987—**Oilers, 23-20 (H) OT
1988—Seahawks, 27-24 (S)
1990—Seahawks, 13-10 (S) OT
1993—Oilers, 24-14 (H)
1994—Seahawks, 16-14 (H)
1996—Seahawks, 23-16 (S)
1997—Seahawks, 16-13 (S)
1998—Seahawks, 20-18 (S)

(RS Pts.—Seahawks 237, Titans 220)
(PS Pts.—Titans 23, Seahawks 20)
*Franchise in Houston prior to 1997;
known as Oilers prior to 1999
**AFC First-Round Playoff
SEATTLE vs. WASHINGTON
RS: Redskins lead series, 8-4
1976—Redskins, 31-7 (W)
1980—Seahawks, 14-0 (W)
1983—Redskins, 27-17 (S)
1986—Redskins, 19-14 (W)
1989—Redskins, 29-0 (S)
1992—Redskins, 16-3 (S)
1994—Seahawks, 28-7 (W)
1995—Seahawks, 27-20 (W)
1998—Seahawks, 24-14 (S)
2001—Redskins, 27-14 (W)
2002—Redskins, 14-3 (S)
2003—Redskins, 27-20 (W)
(RS Pts.—Redskins 231, Seahawks 171)

TAMPA BAY vs. ARIZONA
RS: Cardinals lead series, 8-7;
See Arizona vs. Tampa Bay
TAMPA BAY vs. ATLANTA
RS: Buccaneers lead series, 13-10;
See Atlanta vs. Tampa Bay
TAMPA BAY vs. BALTIMORE
RS: Buccaneers lead series, 2-0;
See Baltimore vs. Tampa Bay
TAMPA BAY vs. BUFFALO
RS: Buccaneers lead series, 5-2;
See Buffalo vs. Tampa Bay
TAMPA BAY vs. CAROLINA
RS: Panthers lead series, 5-4;
See Carolina vs. Tampa Bay
TAMPA BAY vs. CHICAGO
RS: Bears lead series, 33-17;
See Chicago vs. Tampa Bay
TAMPA BAY vs. CINCINNATI
RS: Buccaneers lead series, 5-3;
See Cincinnati vs. Tampa Bay
TAMPA BAY vs. CLEVELAND
RS: Browns lead series, 5-1;
See Cleveland vs. Tampa Bay
TAMPA BAY vs. DALLAS
RS: Cowboys lead series, 6-3
PS: Cowboys lead series, 2-0;
See Dallas vs. Tampa Bay
TAMPA BAY vs. DENVER
RS: Broncos lead series, 4-2;
See Denver vs. Tampa Bay
TAMPA BAY vs. DETROIT
RS: Lions lead series, 26-23
PS: Buccaneers lead series, 1-0;
See Detroit vs. Tampa Bay
TAMPA BAY vs. GREEN BAY
RS: Packers lead series, 29-18-1
PS: Packers lead series, 1-0;
See Green Bay vs. Tampa Bay
TAMPA BAY vs. HOUSTON
RS: Buccaneers lead series, 1-0;
See Houston vs. Tampa Bay
TAMPA BAY vs. INDIANAPOLIS
RS: Colts lead series, 6-4;
See Indianapolis vs. Tampa Bay
TAMPA BAY vs. JACKSONVILLE
RS: Jaguars lead series, 2-1;
See Jacksonville vs. Tampa Bay

TAMPA BAY vs. KANSAS CITY
RS: Chiefs lead series, 5-4;
See Kansas City vs. Tampa Bay
TAMPA BAY vs. MIAMI
RS: Dolphins lead series, 4-3;
See Miami vs. Tampa Bay
TAMPA BAY vs. MINNESOTA
RS: Vikings lead series, 31-18;
See Minnesota vs. Tampa Bay
TAMPA BAY vs. NEW ENGLAND
RS: Patriots lead series, 3-2;
See New England vs. Tampa Bay
TAMPA BAY vs. NEW ORLEANS
RS: Saints lead series, 17-9;
See New Orleans vs. Tampa Bay
TAMPA BAY vs. N.Y. GIANTS
RS: Giants lead series, 9-6;
See N.Y. Giants vs. Tampa Bay
TAMPA BAY vs. N.Y. JETS
RS: Jets lead series, 7-1;
See N.Y. Jets vs. Tampa Bay
TAMPA BAY vs. OAKLAND
RS: Raiders lead series, 5-1
PS: Buccaneers lead series, 1-0;
See Oakland vs. Tampa Bay
TAMPA BAY vs. PHILADELPHIA
RS: Eagles lead series, 5-4
PS: Series tied, 2-2;
See Philadelphia vs. Tampa Bay
TAMPA BAY vs. PITTSBURGH
RS: Steelers lead series, 6-1;
See Pittsburgh vs. Tampa Bay
TAMPA BAY vs. ST. LOUIS
RS: Rams lead series, 9-6
PS: Rams lead series, 2-0;
See St. Louis vs. Tampa Bay
TAMPA BAY vs. SAN DIEGO
RS: Chargers lead series, 7-1;
See San Diego vs. Tampa Bay
TAMPA BAY vs. SAN FRANCISCO
RS: 49ers lead series, 13-3
PS: Buccaneers lead series, 1-0;
See San Francisco vs. Tampa Bay
TAMPA BAY vs. SEATTLE
RS: Seahawks lead series, 5-1;
See Seattle vs. Tampa Bay
TAMPA BAY vs. *TENNESSEE
RS: Titans lead series, 7-1
1976—Oilers, 20-0 (H)
1980—Oilers, 20-14 (H)
1983—Buccaneers, 33-24 (TB)
1989—Oilers, 20-17 (H)
1995—Oilers, 19-7 (H)
1998—Oilers, 31-22 (TB)
2001—Titans, 31-28 (Tenn) OT
2003—Titans, 33-13 (T)
(RS Pts.—Titans 198, Buccaneers 134)
*Franchise in Houston prior to 1997;
known as Oilers prior to 1999
TAMPA BAY vs. WASHINGTON
RS: Redskins lead series, 7-5
PS: Buccaneers lead series, 1-0;
1977—Redskins, 10-0 (TB)
1982—Redskins, 21-13 (TB)
1989—Redskins, 32-28 (W)
1993—Redskins, 23-17 (TB)
1994—Buccaneers, 26-21 (TB)
      Buccaneers, 17-14 (W)
1995—Buccaneers, 14-6 (TB)
1996—Buccaneers, 24-10 (TB)

1998—Redskins, 20-16 (W)
1999—*Buccaneers, 14-13 (TB)
2000—Redskins, 20-17 (W) OT
2003—Buccaneers, 35-13 (W)
2004—Redskins, 16-10 (W)
(RS Pts.—Buccaneers 217, Redskins 206)
(PS Pts.—Buccaneers 14, Redskins 13)
*NFC Divisional Playoff

TENNESSEE VS. ARIZONA
RS: Cardinals lead series, 4-3;
See Arizona vs. Tennessee
TENNESSEE vs. ATLANTA
RS: Titans lead series, 6-5;
See Atlanta vs. Tennessee
TENNESSEE vs. BALTIMORE
RS: Ravens lead series, 7-6
PS: Series tied, 1-1;
See Baltimore vs. Tennessee
TENNESSEE vs. BUFFALO
RS: Titans lead series, 23-14
PS: Bills lead series, 2-1;
See Buffalo vs. Tennessee
TENNESSEE vs. CAROLINA
RS: Series tied, 1-1;
See Carolina vs. Tennessee
TENNESSEE vs. CHICAGO
RS: Bears lead series, 5-4;
See Chicago vs. Tennessee
TENNESSEE vs. CINCINNATI
RS: Titans lead series, 38-29-1
PS: Bengals lead series, 1-0;
See Cincinnati vs. Tennessee
TENNESSEE vs. CLEVELAND
RS: Browns lead series, 32-26
PS: Titans lead series, 1-0;
See Cleveland vs. Tennessee
TENNESSEE vs. DALLAS
RS: Cowboys lead series, 6-5;
See Dallas vs. Tennessee
TENNESSEE vs. DENVER
RS: Titans lead series, 20-12-1
PS: Broncos lead series, 2-1;
See Denver vs. Tennessee
TENNESSEE vs. DETROIT
RS: Titans lead series, 6-3;
See Detroit vs. Tennessee
TENNESSEE vs. GREEN BAY
RS: Titans lead series, 5-4;
See Green Bay vs. Tennessee
TENNESSEE vs. HOUSTON
RS: Titans lead series, 4-2;
See Houston vs. Tennessee
TENNESSEE vs. INDIANAPOLIS
RS: Colts lead series, 11-9
PS: Titans lead series, 1-0;
See Indianapolis vs. Tennessee
TENNESSEE vs. JACKSONVILLE
RS: Titans lead series, 12-8
PS: Titans lead series, 1-0;
See Jacksonville vs. Tennessee
TENNESSEE vs. KANSAS CITY
RS: Chiefs lead series, 25-18
PS: Chiefs lead series, 2-0;
See Kansas City vs. Tennessee
TENNESSEE vs. MIAMI
RS: Dolphins lead series, 15-13
PS: Titans lead series, 1-0;
See Miami vs. Tennessee

TENNESSEE vs. MINNESOTA
RS: Vikings lead series, 7-3;
See Minnesota vs. Tennessee
TENNESSEE vs. NEW ENGLAND
RS: Patriots lead series, 19-15-1
PS: Series tied, 1-1;
See New England vs. Tennessee
TENNESSEE vs. NEW ORLEANS
RS: Titans lead series, 6-4-1;
See New Orleans vs. Tennessee
TENNESSEE vs. N.Y. GIANTS
RS: Giants lead series, 5-3;
See N.Y. Giants vs. Tennessee
TENNESSEE vs. N.Y. JETS
RS: Titans lead series, 20-14-1
PS: Titans lead series, 1-0;
See N.Y. Jets vs. Tennessee
TENNESSEE vs. OAKLAND
RS: Raiders lead series, 22-17
PS: Raiders lead series, 4-0;
See Oakland vs. Tennessee
TENNESSEE vs. PHILADELPHIA
RS: Eagles lead series, 6-2;
See Philadelphia vs. Tennessee
TENNESSEE vs. PITTSBURGH
RS: Steelers lead series, 37-28
PS: Steelers lead series, 3-1;
See Pittsburgh vs. Tennessee
TENNESSEE vs. ST. LOUIS
RS: Rams lead series, 5-3
PS: Rams lead series, 1-0;
See St. Louis vs. Tennessee
TENNESSEE vs. SAN DIEGO
RS: Chargers lead series, 20-13-1
PS: Titans lead series, 3-0;
See San Diego vs. Tennessee
TENNESSEE vs. SAN FRANCISCO
RS: 49ers lead series, 7-3;
See San Francisco vs. Tennessee
TENNESSEE vs. SEATTLE
RS: Seahawks lead series, 8-4
PS: Titans lead series, 1-0;
See Seattle vs. Tennessee
TENNESSEE vs. TAMPA BAY
RS: Titans lead series, 7-1;
See Tampa Bay vs. Tennessee
*TENNESSEE vs. WASHINGTON
RS: Titans lead series, 5-4
1971—Redskins, 22-13 (W)
1975—Oilers, 13-10 (H)
1979—Oilers, 29-27 (W)
1985—Redskins, 16-13 (W)
1988—Oilers, 41-17 (H)
1991—Redskins, 16-13 (W) OT
1997—Oilers, 28-14 (T)
2000—Titans, 27-21 (W)
2002—Redskins, 31-14 (T)
(RS—Titans 191, Redskins 174)
*Franchise in Houston prior to 1997;
known as Oilers prior to 1999

WASHINGTON vs. ARIZONA
RS: Redskins lead series, 70-44-2;
See Arizona vs. Washington
WASHINGTON vs. ATLANTA
RS: Redskins lead series, 14-4-1
PS: Redskins lead series, 1-0;
See Atlanta vs. Washington
WASHINGTON vs BALTIMORE
RS: Ravens lead series, 2-1;

See Baltimore vs. Washington
WASHINGTON vs. BUFFALO
RS: Bills lead series, 6-4
PS: Redskins lead series, 1-0;
See Buffalo vs. Washington
WASHINGTON vs. CAROLINA
RS: Redskins lead series, 6-1;
See Carolina vs. Washington
WASHINGTON vs. CHICAGO
RS: Bears lead series, 20-16-1
PS: Redskins lead series, 4-3;
See Chicago vs. Washington
WASHINGTON vs. CINCINNATI
RS: Redskins lead series, 4-3;
See Cincinnati vs. Washington
WASHINGTON vs. CLEVELAND
RS: Browns lead series, 33-9-1;
See Cleveland vs. Washington
WASHINGTON vs. DALLAS
RS: Cowboys lead series, 54-32-2
PS: Redskins lead series, 2-0;
See Dallas vs. Washington
WASHINGTON vs. DENVER
RS: Broncos lead series, 5-4
PS: Redskins lead series, 1-0;
See Denver vs. Washington
WASHINGTON vs. DETROIT
RS: Redskins lead series, 25-10
PS: Redskins lead series, 3-0;
See Detroit vs. Washington
WASHINGTON vs. GREEN BAY
RS: Packers lead series, 16-12-1
PS: Series tied, 1-1;
See Green Bay vs. Washington
WASHINGTON vs. HOUSTON
RS: Redskins lead series, 1-0;
See Houston vs. Washington
WASHINGTON vs. INDIANAPOLIS
RS: Colts lead series, 17-10;
See Indianapolis vs. Washington
WASHINGTON vs. JACKSONVILLE
RS: Redskins lead series, 2-1;
See Jacksonville vs. Washington
WASHINGTON vs. KANSAS CITY
RS: Chiefs lead series, 5-1;
See Kansas City vs. Washington
WASHINGTON vs. MIAMI
RS: Dolphins lead series, 6-3
PS: Series tied, 1-1;
See Miami vs. Washington
WASHINGTON vs. MINNESOTA
RS: Redskins lead series, 7-5
PS: Redskins lead series, 3-2;
See Minnesota vs. Washington
WASHINGTON vs. NEW ENGLAND
RS: Redskins lead series, 6-1;
See New England vs. Washington
WASHINGTON vs. NEW ORLEANS
RS: Redskins lead series, 13-7;
See New Orleans vs. Washington
WASHINGTON vs. N.Y. GIANTS
RS: Giants lead series, 81-59-4
PS: Series tied, 1-1;
See N.Y. Giants vs. Washington
WASHINGTON vs. N.Y. JETS
RS: Redskins lead series, 7-1;
See N.Y. Jets vs. Washington
WASHINGTON vs. OAKLAND
RS: Raiders lead series, 6-3
PS: Raiders lead series, 1-0;

See Oakland vs. Washington

WASHINGTON vs. PHILADELPHIA
RS: Redskins lead series, 72-62-5
PS: Redskins lead series, 1-0;
See Philadelphia vs. Washington

WASHINGTON vs. PITTSBURGH
RS: Redskins lead series, 42-30-3;
See Pittsburgh vs. Washington

WASHINGTON vs. ST. LOUIS
RS: Redskins lead series, 19-6-1
PS: Series tied, 2-2;
See St. Louis vs. Washington

WASHINGTON vs. SAN DIEGO
RS: Redskins lead series, 6-1;
See San Diego vs. Washington

WASHINGTON vs. SAN FRANCISCO
RS: 49ers lead series, 13-8-1
PS: 49ers lead series, 3-1;
See San Francisco vs. Washington

WASHINGTON vs. SEATTLE
RS: Redskins lead series, 8-4;
See Seattle vs. Washington

WASHINGTON vs. TAMPA BAY
RS: Redskins lead series, 7-5
PS: Buccaneers lead series, 1-0;
See Tampa Bay vs. Washington

WASHINGTON vs. TENNESSEE
RS: Titans lead series, 5-4;
See Tennessee vs. Washington

SUPER BOWL COMPOSITE STANDINGS

	W	L	Pct.	Pts.	OP
San Francisco 49ers	5	0	1.000	188	89
Baltimore Ravens	1	0	1.000	34	7
Chicago Bears	1	0	1.000	46	10
New York Jets	1	0	1.000	16	7
Tampa Bay Buccaneers	1	0	1.000	48	21
Pittsburgh Steelers	4	1	.800	120	100
Green Bay Packers	3	1	.750	127	76
New York Giants	2	1	.667	66	73
Dallas Cowboys	5	3	.625	221	132
New England Patriots	3	2	.600	107	148
Oakland/L.A. Raiders	3	2	.600	132	114
Washington Redskins	3	2	.600	122	103
Baltimore Colts	1	1	.500	23	29
Kansas City Chiefs	1	1	.500	33	42
Miami Dolphins	2	3	.400	74	103
Denver Broncos	2	4	.333	115	206
St. Louis/L.A. Rams	1	2	.333	59	67
Atlanta Falcons	0	1	.000	19	34
Carolina Panthers	0	1	.000	29	32
San Diego Chargers	0	1	.000	26	49
Tennessee Titans	0	1	.000	16	23
Cincinnati Bengals	0	2	.000	37	46
Philadelphia Eagles	0	2	.000	31	51
Buffalo Bills	0	4	.000	73	139
Minnesota Vikings	0	4	.000	34	95

SUPER BOWL HOST CITIES

New Orleans	9	
Miami	8	
Los Angeles	7	(LA Coliseum 2, Rose Bowl 5)
San Diego	3	
Tampa	3	
Atlanta	2	
Houston	2	
Detroit	1	
Jacksonville	1	
Minneapolis	1	
Stanford	1	
Tempe	1	

FUTURE SUPER BOWL SITES

Super Bowl XL	Feb. 5, 2006	Ford Field, Detroit, Michigan
Super Bowl XLI	Feb. 4, 2007	Dolphins Stadium, Miami, Florida
Super Bowl XLII	Feb. 3, 2008	Cardinals Stadium, Glendale, Arizona
Super Bowl XLIII	Feb. 1, 2009*	Raymond James Stadium, Tampa, Florida

*Tentative Date

PETE ROZELLE TROPHY/SUPER BOWL MVPs*

Super Bowl I	— QB Bart Starr, Green Bay
Super Bowl II	— QB Bart Starr, Green Bay
Super Bowl III	— QB Joe Namath, N.Y. Jets
Super Bowl IV	— QB Len Dawson, Kansas City
Super Bowl V	— LB Chuck Howley, Dallas
Super Bowl VI	— QB Roger Staubach, Dallas
Super Bowl VII	— S Jake Scott, Miami
Super Bowl VIII	— RB Larry Csonka, Miami
Super Bowl IX	— RB Franco Harris, Pittsburgh
Super Bowl X	— WR Lynn Swann, Pittsburgh
Super Bowl XI	— WR Fred Biletnikoff, Oakland
Super Bowl XII	— DT Randy White and DE Harvey Martin, Dallas
Super Bowl XIII	— QB Terry Bradshaw, Pittsburgh
Super Bowl XIV	— QB Terry Bradshaw, Pittsburgh
Super Bowl XV	— QB Jim Plunkett, Oakland
Super Bowl XVI	— QB Joe Montana, San Francisco
Super Bowl XVII	— RB John Riggins, Washington
Super Bowl XVIII	— RB Marcus Allen, L.A. Raiders
Super Bowl XIX	— QB Joe Montana, San Francisco
Super Bowl XX	— DE Richard Dent, Chicago
Super Bowl XXI	— QB Phil Simms, N.Y. Giants
Super Bowl XXII	— QB Doug Williams, Washington
Super Bowl XXIII	— WR Jerry Rice, San Francisco
Super Bowl XXIV	— QB Joe Montana, San Francisco
Super Bowl XXV	— RB Ottis Anderson, N.Y. Giants
Super Bowl XXVI	— QB Mark Rypien, Washington
Super Bowl XXVII	— QB Troy Aikman, Dallas
Super Bowl XXVIII	— RB Emmitt Smith, Dallas
Super Bowl XXIX	— QB Steve Young, San Francisco
Super Bowl XXX	— CB Larry Brown, Dallas
Super Bowl XXXI	— KR-PR Desmond Howard, Green Bay
Super Bowl XXXII	— RB Terrell Davis, Denver
Super Bowl XXXIII	— QB John Elway, Denver
Super Bowl XXXIV	— QB Kurt Warner, St. Louis
Super Bowl XXXV	— LB Ray Lewis, Baltimore
Super Bowl XXXVI	— QB Tom Brady, New England
Super Bowl XXXVII	— S Dexter Jackson, Tampa Bay
Super Bowl XXXVIII	— QB Tom Brady, New England
Super Bowl XXXIX	— WR Deion Branch, New England

* Award named Pete Rozelle Trophy since Super Bowl XXV.

SUPER BOWL MVP BY POSITION

Quarterback	20
Running Back	7
Wide Receiver	4
Defensive End	2
Linebacker	2
Safety	2
Cornerback	1
Defensive Tackle	1
Kick Returner-Punt Returner	1

A defensive end and defensive tackle shared the Super Bowl XII MVP award.

SUPER BOWL SUMMARIES

RESULTS

NFC leads AFC, 21-18

Super Bowl	Date	Winner (Share)	Loser (Share)	Score	Site	Attendance
XXXIX	2-6-05	New England ($68,000)	Philadelphia ($36,500)	24-21	Jacksonville	78,125
XXXVIII	2-1-04	New England ($68,000)	Carolina ($36,500)	32-29	Houston	71,525
* XXXVII	1-26-03	Tampa Bay ($63,000)	Oakland ($35,000)	48-21	San Diego	67,603
* XXXVI	2-3-02	New England ($63,000)	St. Louis ($34,500)	20-17	New Orleans	72,922
XXXV	1-28-01	Baltimore ($58,000)	N.Y. Giants ($34,500)	34-7	Tampa	71,921
* XXXIV	1-30-00	St. Louis ($58,000)	Tennessee ($33,000)	23-16	Atlanta	72,625
XXXIII	1-31-99	Denver ($53,000)	Atlanta ($32,500)	34-19	Miami	74,803
XXXII	1-25-98	Denver ($48,000)	Green Bay ($29,000)	31-24	San Diego	68,912
XXXI	1-26-97	Green Bay ($48,000)	New England ($29,000)	35-21	New Orleans	72,301
XXX	1-28-96	Dallas ($42,000)	Pittsburgh ($27,000)	27-17	Tempe	76,347
XXIX	1-29-95	San Francisco ($42,000)	San Diego ($26,000)	49-26	Miami	74,107
* XXVIII	1-30-94	Dallas ($38,000)	Buffalo ($23,500)	30-13	Atlanta	72,817
XXVII	1-31-93	Dallas ($36,000)	Buffalo ($18,000)	52-17	Pasadena	98,374
XXVI	1-26-92	Washington ($36,000)	Buffalo ($18,000)	37-24	Minneapolis	63,130
* XXV	1-27-91	N.Y. Giants ($36,000)	Buffalo ($18,000)	20-19	Tampa	73,813
XXIV	1-28-90	San Francisco ($36,000)	Denver ($18,000)	55-10	New Orleans	72,919
XXIII	1-22-89	San Francisco ($36,000)	Cincinnati ($18,000)	20-16	Miami	75,129
XXII	1-31-88	Washington ($36,000)	Denver ($18,000)	42-10	San Diego	73,302
XXI	1-25-87	N.Y. Giants ($36,000)	Denver ($18,000)	39-20	Pasadena	101,063
XX	1-26-86	Chicago ($36,000)	New England ($18,000)	46-10	New Orleans	73,818
XIX	1-20-85	San Francisco ($36,000)	Miami ($18,000)	38-16	Stanford	84,059
XVIII	1-22-84	L.A. Raiders ($36,000)	Washington ($18,000)	38-9	Tampa	72,920
* XVII	1-30-83	Washington ($36,000)	Miami ($18,000)	27-17	Pasadena	103,667
XVI	1-24-82	San Francisco ($18,000)	Cincinnati ($9,000)	26-21	Pontiac	81,270
XV	1-25-81	Oakland ($18,000)	Philadelphia ($9,000)	27-10	New Orleans	76,135
XIV	1-20-80	Pittsburgh ($18,000)	Los Angeles ($9,000)	31-19	Pasadena	103,985
XIII	1-21-79	Pittsburgh ($18,000)	Dallas ($9,000)	35-31	Miami	79,484
XII	1-15-78	Dallas ($18,000)	Denver ($9,000)	27-10	New Orleans	75,583
XI	1-9-77	Oakland ($15,000)	Minnesota ($7,500)	32-14	Pasadena	103,438
X	1-18-76	Pittsburgh ($15,000)	Dallas ($7,500)	21-17	Miami	80,187
IX	1-12-75	Pittsburgh ($15,000)	Minnesota ($7,500)	16-6	New Orleans	80,997
VIII	1-13-74	Miami ($15,000)	Minnesota ($7,500)	24-7	Houston	71,882
VII	1-14-73	Miami ($15,000)	Washington ($7,500)	14-7	Los Angeles	90,182
VI	1-16-72	Dallas ($15,000)	Miami ($7,500)	24-3	New Orleans	81,023
V	1-17-71	Baltimore ($15,000)	Dallas ($7,500)	16-13	Miami	79,204
* IV	1-11-70	Kansas City ($15,000)	Minnesota ($7,500)	23-7	New Orleans	80,562
III	1-12-69	N.Y. Jets ($15,000)	Baltimore ($7,500)	16-7	Miami	75,389
II	1-14-68	Green Bay ($15,000)	Oakland ($7,500)	33-14	Miami	75,546
I	1-15-67	Green Bay ($15,000)	Kansas City ($7,500)	35-10	Los Angeles	61,946

* One week between conference championship games and Super Bowl; all others had two weeks between conference championship games and Super Bowl.

SUPER BOWL XXXIX

ALLTEL Stadium, Jacksonville, Florida
February 6, 2005, Attendance: 78,125
NEW ENGLAND 24, PHILADELPHIA 21—Deion Branch had 11 receptions for 133 yards and the Patriots' defense forced 4 turnovers en route to becoming the eighth team to post consecutive Super Bowl titles. The Patriots matched the Dallas Cowboys (XXVII, XXVIII, and XXX) as the only team with three Super Bowl victories in the span of four seasons. The Eagles threatened first, driving to the Patriots' 8 late in the first quarter. On first down, Mike Vrabel sacked Donovan McNabb for a 16-yard loss and, after a penalty overturned an interception, Rodney Harrison stepped in front of a pass for an interception at the Eagles' 4. Early in the second quarter the Eagles drove 81 yards, keyed by Todd Pinkston's 40-yard catch, and capped by McNabb's 6-yard touchdown pass to L.J. Smith on third-and-goal for a 7-0 lead. The Patriots responded by driving to the Eagles' 4, but Tom Brady fumbled on a fake handoff attempt and Darwin Walker recovered. Later in the quarter, a 29-yard punt by Dirk Johnson allowed the Patriots to drive just 37 yards, keyed by Branch's 7-yard catch on third-and-3, and capped by Brady's pass to David Givens on the right side of the end zone to tie the game with 1:10 left in the half. New England began the second half with a 9-play, 69-yard drive, including 4 receptions, 2 on third down, by Branch, and capped by Vrabel's 2-yard catch. The Eagles put together a 10-play, 74-yard drive later in the third quarter, keyed by Brian Westbrook's 4-yard catch on third-and-3, and followed on the next play by his 10-yard touchdown catch to tie the game. On the ensuing drive, Kevin Faulk caught screen passes of 13 and 14 yards, and had a 12-yard run, and Corey Dillon capped the possession with a 2-yard run with 13:44 remaining for a 21-14 lead. The Patriots' defense forced a three-and-out, and Branch's 19-yard catch set up Adam Vinatieri's 22-yard field goal with 8:40 to play. Tedy Bruschi intercepted McNabb's pass at the Patriots' 24 with 7:20 remaining. The Eagles forced a punt and, beginning at their own 21 with 5:40 to play, needed 13 plays to drive 79 yards, capped by McNabb's 30-yard touchdown pass on a post-pattern to Greg Lewis with 1:48 to play. Christian Fauria recovered the onside kick, but the Eagles' defense forced a punt. Dexter Reid downed Josh Miller's 32-yard punt at the Eagles' 4 with 46 seconds left, and Harrison intercepted McNabb's pass three plays later to clinch the title. Brady was 23 of 33 for 236 yards and 2 touchdowns. Branch earned MVP honors with his Super Bowl-record-tying

520

2005 NFL Record & Fact Book

11 catches. McNabb was 30 of 51 for 357 yards and 3 touchdowns, with 3 interceptions. Terrell Owens had 9 receptions for 122 yards.

New England (24) Offense Philadelphia (21)

New England (24)		Philadelphia (21)
David Givens	WR	Todd Pinkston
Matt Light	LT	Tra Thomas
Joe Andruzzi	LG	Artis Hicks
Dan Koppen	C	Hank Fraley
Stephen Neal	RG	Jermane Mayberry
Brandon Gorin	RT	Jon Runyan
Daniel Graham	TE	L.J. Smith
Deion Branch	WR	Terrell Owens
Tom Brady	QB	Donovan McNabb
Patrick Pass	FB	Josh Parry
Corey Dillon	RB	Brian Westbrook
Defense		
Rosevelt Colvin	OLB-LE	Derrick Burgess
Vince Wilfork	NT-LT	Corey Simon
Jarvis Green	RE-RT	Darwin Walker
Mike Vrabel	OLB-RE	Jevon Kearse
Tedy Bruschi	ILB-WLB	Keith Adams
Roman Phifer	ILB-MLB	Jeremiah Trotter
Willie McGinest	OLB-SLB	Dhani Jones
Randall Gay	LCB	Lito Sheppard
Asante Samuel	RCB	Sheldon Brown
Eugene Wilson	FS	Brian Dawkins
Rodney Harrison	SS	Michael Lewis

SUBSTITUTIONS

NEW ENGLAND—Specialists: K—Adam Vinatieri. P—Josh Miller. LS—Lonie Paxton. Offense: RB—Rabih Abdullah, Kevin Faulk. WR—Troy Brown, Bethel Johnson, David Patten. TE—Christian Fauria. G—Russ Hochstein. G-C—Gene Mruczkowski. Defense: DT—Keith Traylor, DE-DT—Richard Seymour, Ty Warren. LB—Tully Banta-Cain, Matt Chatham, Don Davis, Larry Izzo, Ted Johnson. CB—Hank Poteat. CB-S—Je'Rod Cherry. S—Dexter Reid. DNP: QB—Rohan Davey. Inactive: QB—Jim Miller. RB—Cedric Cobbs. WR—Kevin Kasper. TE—Jed Weaver. G—Billy Yates. DT—Ethan Kelley. DE—Marquise Hill. CB—Earthwind Moreland.
PHILADELPHIA—Specialists: K—David Akers. P—Dirk Johnson. LS-TE—Mike Bartrum. Offense: QB—Koy Detmer. RB—Dorsey Levens, Reno Mahe. WR—Greg Lewis, Freddie Mitchell. TE—Jeff Thomason. G—Steve Sciullo. Defense: DE—Jerome McDougle. DT—Sam Rayburn, Hollis Thomas. LB—Mike Labinjo, Ike Reese, Mark Simoneau, Nate Wayne. CB—Roderick Hood, Matt Ware. S—Quintin Mikell, J.R. Reed. DNP: C—Alonzo Ephraim. LB-DE—Hugh Douglas. Inactive: QB—Jeff Blake. RB—Eric McCoo. WR—Billy McMullen. T—Ian Allen. T-G—Trey Darilek. DT—Paul Grasmanis. DE—Jamall Green. CB—Dexter Wynn.

OFFICIALS

Referee—Terry McAulay. Umpire—Carl Paganelli. Line Judge—Mark Steinkerchner. Side Judge—Rick Patterson. Head Linesman—Gary Slaughter. Back Judge—Tony Steratore. Field Judge—Tom Sifferman. Replay Official—Al Hynes. Video Operator—xxxxxx.

SCORING

	NE	PHIL
New England (AFC)	0 7 7 10	— 24
Philadelphia (NFC)	0 7 7 7	— 21

Phil— Smith 6 pass from McNabb (Akers kick) (9:55)
NE— Givens 4 pass from Brady (Vinatieri kick) (1:10)
NE— Vrabel 2 pass from Brady (Vinatieri kick) (11:04)
Phil— Westbrook 10 pass from McNabb (Akers kick) (3:35)
NE— Dillon 2 run (Vinatieri kick) (13:44)
NE— FG Vinatieri 22 (8:40)
Phil— G. Lewis 30 pass from McNabb (Akers kick) (1:48)

TEAM STATISTICS

	NE	PHIL
Total First Downs	21	24
Rushing	6	4
Passing	14	18
Penalty	1	2
Total Net Yardage	331	369
Total Offensive Plays	63	72
Avg. Gain Per Offensive Play	5.3	5.1
Rushes	28	17
Yards Gained Rushing (Net)	112	45
Avg. Yards per Rush	4.0	2.6
Passes Attempted	33	51
Passes Completed	23	30
Had Intercepted	0	3
Tackled Attempting to Pass	2	4
Yards Lost Attempting to Pass	17	33
Yards Gained Passing (Net)	219	324
Punts	7	5
Avg. Distance	45.1	42.8
Punt Returns	4	3
Punt Return Yardage	26	19
Kickoff Returns	4	5
Kickoff Return Yardage	63	114
Interception Return Yardage	5	0
Total Return Yardage	94	133
Fumbles	1	2
Fumbles Lost	1	1
Own Fumbles Recovered	0	1
Opponent Fumbles Recovered	1	1
Penalties	7	3
Yards Penalized	47	35
Field Goals	1	0
Field Goals Attempted	1	0
Third-Down Efficiency	4/12	9/16
Fourth-Down Efficiency	0/0	0/0
Time of Possession	31:37	28:23

INDIVIDUAL STATISTICS

RUSHING: NE: Dillon 18-75-1, Faulk 8-38-0, Pass 1-0-0, Brady 1-(-1)-0. PHIL: Westbrook 15-44-0, Levens 1-1-0, McNabb 1-0-0.
PASSING: NE: Brady 33-23-236-2-0. PHIL: McNabb 51-30-357-3-3.
RECEIVING: NE: Branch 11-133-0, Dillon 3-31-0, Givens 3-19-1, Faulk 2-27-0, Brown 2-17-0, Graham 1-7-0, Vrabel 1-2-1. PHIL: Owens 9-122-0, Westbrook 7-60-1, Pinkston 4-82-0, G. Lewis 4-53-1, Smith 4-27-1, Mitchell 1-11-0, Parry 1-2-0.
KICKOFF RETURNS: NE: B. Johnson 2-44-0, Pass 1-17-0, Fauria 1-2-0. PHIL:

Reed 4-82-0, Hood 1-32-0.
PUNT RETURNS: NE: T. Brown 3-12-0, B. Johnson 1-14-0. PHIL: Westbrook 3-19-0, Sheppard 0-0-0.
PUNTING: NE: Miller 7-316-45.1. PHIL: D. Johnson 5-214-42.8.
INTERCEPTIONS: NE: Harrison 2-5-0, Bruschi 1-0-0. PHIL: None.
SACKS: NE: Bruschi, Harrison, Seymour, Vrabel. PHIL: Burgess, Team.

SUPER BOWL XXXVIII

Reliant Stadium, Houston, Texas
February 1, 2004, Attendance: 71,525
NEW ENGLAND 32, CAROLINA 29—Adam Vinatieri kicked a 41-yard field goal with four seconds remaining as the Patriots won their second Super Bowl in three seasons. While it took a Super Bowl-record 26 minutes and 55 seconds for the first points to be scored, the teams combined for 868 yards (481 by New England) and the game also featured the highest scoring quarter (combined 37 points in the fourth). Vinatieri missed a 31-yard field goal on the Patriots' first possession, and had a 36-yard attempt blocked by Shane Burton with 6:00 left in the second quarter. But three plays later, Mike Vrabel sacked Jake Delhomme and forced him to fumble. Richard Seymour recovered at the Panthers' 20, and a 12-yard scramble by Tom Brady on third-and-7 set up his 5-yard touchdown pass to Deion Branch with 3:05 left in the first half. The Panthers responded with an 8-play, 95-yard drive capped by Delhomme's 39-yard perfectly placed touchdown pass to Steve Smith with 1:07 left in the half. Delhomme beat the blitz by lofting the pass deep down the left sideline. Brady's 52-yard pass to Branch with 37 seconds left in the half set up David Givens' 5-yard touchdown catch with 18 seconds left. New England squibbed the ensuing kickoff and Kris Mangum returned it 12 yards to the Panthers' 47. A 21-yard run by Stephen Davis set up John Kasay's 50-yard field goal as the half expired for a 14-10 New England lead. Neither team scored in the third quarter, but Antowain Smith's 2-yard touchdown run two plays into the final quarter capped a 71-yard drive and gave the Patriots a 21-10 lead. Undaunted, Carolina scored on its next two possessions. First, Delhomme completed passes of 18 and 22 yards to Smith to set up DeShaun Foster's 33-yard touchdown run to cut the deficit to 21-16 with 12:39 to play. Carolina went for the 2-point conversion, but Delhomme's pass was incomplete. New England marched to the Panthers' 9 with the ensuing kickoff, but Reggie Howard intercepted Brady's third-and-goal pass in the end zone. Two plays later, Delhomme rolled left and fired a Super Bowl-record 85-yard touchdown pass to Muhammad for a 22-21 lead with 6:53 left. Once again, the Panthers went for 2 points and Delhomme's pass was incomplete. New

England drove 68 yards on its next possession, with Givens catching a 25-yard pass and 18-yard pass on third-and-9, to set up Brady's 1-yard touchdown pass to Vrabel, who was lined up as a tight end. A direct snap to Kevin Faulk resulted in a 2-point conversion for a 29-22 lead with 2:51 left. Delhomme completed passes of 19 yards to Muhammad and 31 yards to Ricky Proehl before finding Proehl from 12 yards with the tying touchdown with 1:08 remaining. Kasay's ensuing kickoff went out of bounds, giving New England the ball at their own 40. Five plays later, faced with third-and-3 from the Panthers' 40 with 14 seconds left, Brady fired a 17-yard pass to Branch to set up Vinatieri's Super Bowl-winning 41-yard field goal. Brady, who was named the Super Bowl most valuable player for the second time in his career, was 32 of 48 for 354 yards and 3 touchdowns, with 1 interception. Branch had 10 receptions for 143 yards. Delhomme was 16 of 33 for 323 yards and 3 touchdowns, and Muhammad had 4 catches for 140 yards.

Carolina (NFC)	0 10 0 19	— 29
New England (AFC)	0 14 0 18	— 32

NE	Branch 5 pass from Brady (Vinatieri kick) (3:05)	
Car—	Smith 39 pass from Delhomme (Kasay kick) (1:07)	
NE	Givens 5 pass from Brady (Vinatieri kick) (0:18)	
Car—	FG Kasay 50 (0:00)	
NE	Smith 2 run (Vinatieri kick) (14:49)	
Car—	Foster 33 run (pass failed) (12:39)	
Car—	Muhammad 85 pass from Delhomme (pass failed) (6:53)	
NE	Vrabel 1 pass from Brady (Faulk run) (2:51)	
Car—	Proehl 12 pass from Delhomme (Kasay kick) (1:08)	
NE	FG Vinatieri 41 (0:04)	

SUPER BOWL XXXVII
Qualcomm Stadium, San Diego, CA
January 26, 2003, Attendance: 67,603
TAMPA BAY 48, OAKLAND 21—The Buccaneers' defense intercepted 5 passes, 3 of which were returned for touchdowns, and recorded 5 sacks as Tampa Bay scored 34 unanswered points en route to its first Super Bowl victory. Charles Woodson intercepted Brad Johnson three plays into the game to give Oakland the ball at the Buccaneers' 36. But Simeon Rice sacked Rich Gannon on third down to force the Raiders to settle for Sebastian Janikowski's 40-yard field goal. On their next nine possessions, the Raiders registered just 2 first downs and did not run a play inside the Buccaneers' 40 as Tampa Bay scored the next 34 points. The Buccaneers answered Janikowski's field goal with Martin Gramatica's 31-yard boot to tie the game. An interception by Dexter Jackson set up Gramatica's go-ahead

field goal early in the second quarter. Midway through the second quarter, a 25-yard punt return by Karl Williams and a 19-yard run by Michael Pittman led to Mike Alstott's 2-yard touchdown run. Late in the half, the Buccaneers drove 77 yards, aided by 3 defensive penalties and pass receptions of 16 and 12 yards by Alstott, to set up Brad Johnson's 5-yard touchdown pass to Keenan McCardell with 30 seconds left in the half, which gave Tampa Bay a 20-3 lead. With their first possession of the second half, the Buccaneers put together a 14-play, 89-yard drive that consumed 7:52 and was culminated by Johnson's 8-yard scoring toss to McCardell. Two plays later, Dwight Smith intercepted Gannon's pass and returned it 44 yards for a touchdown and a 34-3 lead with 4:47 left in the third quarter. Tampa Bay scored 4 touchdowns in a span of 16:37. Jerry Porter's 39-yard touchdown catch in the back of the end zone made it 34-9. Less than three minutes later, Tim Johnson blocked Tom Tupa's punt. Eric Johnson caught the ball and dove into the end zone for a touchdown to cut the deficit to 34-15 with 14:16 remaining. The Buccaneers drove deep downfield again, but Tupa mishandled the snap for a field-goal attempt, allowing the Raiders to regain possession. Gannon hit Jerry Rice with a 48-yard touchdown pass with 6:06 left to trim the lead to 34-21. A 9-yard pass by Johnson to Alstott on third-and-7 allowed Tampa Bay to take another two minutes off the clock before Tupa punted with 2:44 remaining. On third-and-18 from the Raiders' 29, Derrick Brooks intercepted Gannon's pass and raced 44 yards down the left sideline for a touchdown with 1:18 remaining to give Tampa Bay a commanding 41-21 lead. Smith intercepted a tipped pass and returned it 50 yards for a touchdown with ten seconds left to finish the scoring. Johnson was 18 of 34 for 215 yards and 2 touchdowns, with 1 interception. Pittman had 29 carries for 124 yards. Gannon was 24 of 44 for 272 yards and 2 touchdowns, with a Super Bowl record 5 interceptions. Jackson, who had the first 2 interceptions, 1 of which led to the go-ahead field goal, was named the game's most valuable player.

Oakland (AFC)	3 0	6 12	— 21
Tampa Bay (NFC)	3 17	14 14	— 48

Oak —	FG Janikowski 40 (10:40)
TB —	FG Gramatica 31 (7:51)
TB —	FG Gramatica 43 (11:16)
TB —	Alstott 2 run (Gramatica kick) (6:24)
TB —	McCardell 5 pass from B. Johnson (Gramatica kick) (0:30)
TB —	McCardell 8 pass from B. Johnson (Gramatica kick) (5:30)
TB —	D. Smith 44 interception return (Gramatica kick) (4:47)

Oak —	Porter 39 pass from Gannon (pass failed) (2:14)
Oak —	E. Johnson 13 return of blocked punt (pass failed) (14:16)
Oak —	Rice 48 pass from Gannon (pass failed) (6:06)
TB —	Brooks 44 interception return (Gramatica kick) (1:18)
TB —	D. Smith 50 interception return (Gramatica kick) (0:02)

SUPER BOWL XXXVI
Louisiana Superdome, New Orleans, LA
February 3, 2002, Attendance: 72,922
NEW ENGLAND 20, ST. LOUIS 17—Adam Vinatieri's 48-yard field goal as time expired gave the New England Patriots their first Super Bowl title. The Rams outgained the Patriots 427-267 in total yards, but the Patriots forced 3 turnovers, which resulted in 17 points, while committing no turnovers. Jeff Wilkins' 50-yard field goal capped a 10-play, 48-yard drive midway through the first quarter to give the Rams a 3-0 lead. The first turnover came with 8:49 left in the second quarter, when Ty Law stepped in front of an out-pattern pass intended for Isaac Bruce and raced 47 yards untouched down the left sideline into the end zone. Late in the first half, Kurt Warner completed a 15-yard pass to Ricky Proehl to the Patriots' 40, but Antwan Harris forced Proehl to fumble and Terrell Buckley recovered. Five plays later, Tom Brady's 8-yard touchdown pass to David Patten with 31 seconds left in the quarter gave New England a 14-3 halftime lead. Late in the third quarter, Torry Holt slipped coming off the line of scrimmage, and Otis Smith intercepted Warner's pass and returned it 30 yards to the Rams' 33 to set up Vinatieri's 37-yard field goal and a 17-3 lead. The Rams responded by driving to the Patriots' 3. On fourth-and-goal, Warner scrambled, was tackled by Roman Phifer, and fumbled. Tebucky Jones picked up the ball and raced the length of the field for an apparent touchdown, but the play was negated by Willie McGinest's holding penalty. Warner scored two plays later to trim the deficit to 17-10 with 9:31 left. The Patriots went three and out on their next two possessions, giving the Rams the ball on their 45-yard-line with 1:51 left. Warner completed an 18-yard pass to Az-Zahir Hakim and an 11-yard pass to Yo Murphy before connecting on a 26-yard touchdown pass to Proehl with 1:30 left to tie the game. Operating without any time outs, Brady completed 3 short passes to J.R. Redmond to reach the Patriots' 41 with 33 seconds left. After an incompletion, Brady completed 23- and 16-yard passes to Troy Brown and Jermaine Wiggins, respectively, to reach the Rams' 30, and then spiked the ball with 7 seconds remaining. Vinatieri drilled the 48-yard field-goal attempt, marking the first time in Super Bowl history the game had been won on the final

play. Brady, who earned most valuable player honors, was 16 of 27 for 145 yards and 1 touchdown. Warner was 28 of 44 for 365 yards and 1 touchdown, with 2 interceptions.

St. Louis (NFC)	3 0 0 14	— 17
New England (AFC)	0 14 3 3	— 20

StL — FG Wilkins 50 (3:10)
NE — Law 47 interception return (Vinatieri kick) (8:49)
NE — Patten 8 pass from Brady (Vinatieri kick) (0:31)
NE — FG Vinatieri 37 (1:18)
StL — Warner 2 run (Wilkins kick) (9:31)
StL — Proehl 26 pass from Warner (Wilkins kick) (1:30)
NE — FG Vinatieri 48 (0:00)

SUPER BOWL XXXV
Raymond James Stadium, Tampa, Florida
January 28, 2001, Attendance: 71,921
BALTIMORE 34, N.Y. GIANTS 7—The Ravens' defense completed a dominating season by permitting just 152 yards, forcing 5 turnovers, recording 4 sacks, and not allowing an offensive touchdown en route to the franchise's first Super Bowl victory. Jermaine Lewis' punt return into Giants' territory midway through the first quarter was followed two plays later by Trent Dilfer's 38-yard touchdown pass to Brandon Stokley, which gave the Ravens a 7-0 lead. Early in the second quarter, Jessie Armstead intercepted a short pass by Dilfer and returned it 43 yards for a touchdown, but the play was nullified by a penalty. Dilfer's 36-yard pass to Qadry Ismail in the second quarter set up Matt Stover's 47-yard field goal with 1:48 left in the half. Tiki Barber's 27-yard run gave the Giants their deepest penetration of the game, to the Ravens' 29, but Chris McAlister intercepted Kerry Collins' pass on the next play to preserve a 10-0 lead. In the third quarter, Duane Starks stepped in front of Amani Toomer and intercepted Collins' pass. Starks returned it 49 yards untouched for a 17-0 lead. The Giants immediately cut the lead to 10 points when Ron Dixon returned the ensuing kickoff 97 yards for a touchdown. However, Jermaine Lewis then matched Dixon's kickoff return as he cut across the field and raced 84 yards for a 24-7 lead with 3:13 left in the third quarter. The 3 touchdowns in 36 seconds were a Super Bowl record. The Giants gained just 1 first down on their final four possessions. Jamal Lewis' 3-yard touchdown run midway through the fourth quarter gave Baltimore a 31-7 lead, and Robert Bailey recovered Dixon's fumble on the ensuing kickoff return to set up Stover's 34-yard field goal with 5:27 remaining to finish the scoring. Dilfer completed 12 of 25 passes for 153 yards and 1 touchdown. Jamal Lewis had 27 carries for 102 yards. Collins was 15 of 39 for 112 yards, with 4 interceptions. Ray Lewis was named

Super Bowl most valuable player.

Baltimore (AFC)	7 3 14 10	— 34
N.Y. Giants (NFC)	0 0 7 0	— 7

Balt — Stokley 38 pass from Dilfer (Stover kick) (6:50)
Balt — FG Stover 47 (1:41)
Balt — Starks 49 interception return (Stover kick) (3:49)
NYG — Dixon 97 kickoff return (Daluiso kick) (3:31)
Balt — Je. Lewis 84 kickoff return (Stover kick) (3:13)
Balt — Ja. Lewis 3 run (Stover kick) (8:45)
Balt — FG Stover 34 (5:27)

SUPER BOWL XXXIV
Georgia Dome, Atlanta, Georgia
January 30, 2000, Attendance: 72,625
ST. LOUIS 23, TENNESSEE 16—Mike Jones tackled Kevin Dyson at the 1-yard line as time expired, preserving the Rams' first-ever Super Bowl title. The Rams drove inside the Titans' 20 with each of their first six possessions, but compiled just 3 field goals and 1 touchdown to take a 16-0 lead. Holder Mike Horan's bobbled snap averted a 35-yard field-goal attempt to conclude the Rams' first drive. The Titans responded with a 42-yard drive, their longest of the half, but Al Del Greco missed a 47-yard attempt. Jeff Wilkins added 3 field goals and missed a 34-yard attempt while the Titans did not threaten the rest of the half, giving the Rams a 9-0 lead at intermission despite outgaining the Titans in total yards (294-89). Tennessee drove 43 yards with the second half's opening kickoff, but Todd Lyght blocked Del Greco's 47-yard attempt to keep the Titans off the board. Kurt Warner's 31-yard pass to Isaac Bruce keyed the ensuing drive that was capped by Warner's 9-yard touchdown pass to Torry Holt with 7:20 left in the third quarter to give the Rams a 16-0 lead. The Titans responded with touchdown drives in excess of seven minutes on each of their next two possessions. Steve McNair's 23-yard scramble set up Eddie George's 1-yard run in the final minute of the third quarter. McNair's 2-point conversion pass to Frank Wycheck was incomplete, but the Titans' defense forced a punt and the offense drove 79 yards in 13 plays, highlighted by 21-yard passes from McNair to Isaac Byrd and Jackie Harris, and capped by George's 2-yard run to cut the deficit to 16-13 with 7:21 remaining. The Rams once again failed to get a first down, and following a punt, the Titans needed just 28 yards to set up Del Greco's game-tying 43-yard kick with 2:12 left. On the next play from scrimmage, Warner fired a deep pass down the right sideline to Bruce, who caught the ball at the Titans' 38, cut toward the inside, and outran the defense to the end zone to give the Rams a 23-16 lead with 1:54 left. The Titans drove downfield, and McNair avoided a sack and

completed a 16-yard pass to Kevin Dyson at the Rams' 10 with six seconds remaining. With no timeouts, McNair attempted a quick pass to a slanting Dyson, who caught the ball in stride at the Rams' 3. However, Jones reacted quickly and stepped up to tackle Dyson at the 1-yard line as time expired. Warner, who was named the game's most valuable player, was 24 of 45 for a Super Bowl-record 414 yards and 2 touchdowns. Bruce had 6 catches for 162 yards, and Holt had 7 for 109 yards. McNair was 22 of 36 for 214 yards. The Titans were the first team in Super Bowl history to come back from a 16-point deficit.

St. Louis (NFC)	3 6 7 7	— 23
Tennessee (AFC)	0 0 6 10	— 16

StL — FG Wilkins 27 (3:00)
StL — FG Wilkins 29 (4:16)
StL — FG Wilkins 28 (0:15)
StL — Holt 9 pass from Warner (Wilkins kick) (3:59)
Tenn — George 1 run (pass failed) (0:14)
Tenn — George 2 run (Del Greco kick) (7:21)
Tenn — FG Del Greco 43 (2:12)
StL — Bruce 73 pass from Warner (Wilkins kick) (1:54)

SUPER BOWL XXXIII
Pro Player Stadium, Miami, Florida
January 31, 1999, Attendance: 74,803
DENVER 34, ATLANTA 19—John Elway, in his last game, passed for 336 yards and ran for a touchdown to earn most valuable player honors as the Broncos became the first AFC team to win consecutive Super Bowls since the Steelers won XIII and XIV. A 25-yard pass interference penalty on Ray Crockett assisted the Falcons' nine-play, 48-yard game-opening drive that was capped by Morten Andersen's 32-yard field goal. Elway's 41-yard pass to Rod Smith kept alive Denver's ensuing drive and led to Howard Griffith's 1-yard touchdown run. Ronnie Bradford's interception and return to the Broncos' 35 late in the first quarter gave Atlanta excellent field position. However, Jamal Anderson was stopped for no gain on third-and-1 and thrown for a 2-yard loss on fourth down. Denver capitalized on its defensive effort with Jason Elam's 26-yard field goal. The Falcons responded by driving to the Broncos' 8, but Andersen's 26-yard field-goal attempt sailed wide right and on the next play, Elway fired an 80-yard touchdown pass to Smith to turn a possible 10-6 game into a 17-3 Broncos lead. Andersen's 28-yard field goal and 2 misses by Elam on the Broncos' first two second-half possessions gave Atlanta an opportunity to climb back into the game. However, Darrien Gordon dashed the Falcons' hopes with interceptions on consecutive possessions inside the Broncos' 20 to stop drives and set up Broncos touchdowns. Gordon returned the first

interception, on a tipped pass, 58 yards to the Falcons' 24 to set up Griffith's second touchdown five plays later, and picked the second pass off at the Broncos' 2 and returned it 50 yards. Terrell Davis turned a short pass into a 39-yard gain, and Elway scored two plays later to give Denver a 31-6 lead. Tim Dwight returned the ensuing kickoff for a touchdown, and, after a field goal by Elam, the Falcons' offense scored with 2:04 remaining on Chandler's 3-yard pass to Terance Mathis. Byron Chamberlain recovered the ensuing onside kick, but Tyrone Braxton recovered Anderson's fumble at the Falcons' 33 with 1:30 remaining to ice the game. The Falcons drove inside the Broncos' 30 seven times, but tallied just 1 touchdown and 2 field goals, throwing 2 interceptions, missing 1 field goal, and turning the ball over 1 time on downs during the other possessions. Elway was 18 of 29 for 336 yards and 1 touchdown, with 1 interception. Davis had 25 carries for 102 yards. Smith had 5 receptions for 152 yards. Chandler was 19 of 35 for 219 yards and 1 touchdown, with 3 interceptions.

Denver (AFC)	7	10	0	17 —	34
Atlanta (NFC)	3	3	0	13 —	19

Atl	—	FG Andersen 32 (9:35)
Den	—	Griffith 1 run (Elam kick) (3:55)
Den	—	FG Elam 26 (9:17)
Den	—	R. Smith 80 pass from Elway (Elam kick) (4:54)
Atl	—	FG Andersen 28 (2:25)
Den	—	Griffith 1 run (Elam kick) (14:56)
Den	—	Elway 3 run (Elam kick) (11:20)
Atl	—	Dwight 94 kickoff return (Andersen kick) (11:01)
Den	—	FG Elam 37 (7:08)
Atl	—	Mathis 3 pass from Chandler (pass failed) (2:04)

SUPER BOWL XXXII
Qualcomm Stadium, San Diego, California
January 25, 1998, Attendance: 68,912
DENVER 31, GREEN BAY 24—Terrell Davis rushed for 157 yards and a Super Bowl-record 3 touchdowns to lead the Broncos to their first NFL championship and break the NFC's streak of Super Bowl victories at 13. The defending Super Bowl champion Packers took the opening kickoff and marched 76 yards in just over four minutes, scoring the first points on Brett Favre's 22-yard touchdown pass to Antonio Freeman. The Broncos responded with a 10-play, 58-yard drive capped by Davis' 1-yard run to tie the game. Tyrone Braxton intercepted Favre two plays later, and John Elway scored on a third-and-goal play to begin the second quarter. Steve Atwater forced Favre to fumble three plays later, and Neil Smith recovered at the Packers' 33. Jason Elam converted a 51-yard field goal, the second longest in Super Bowl history, to give the Broncos a

17-7 lead with 12:21 left in the half. After an exchange of punts, the Packers produced a 17-play, 95-yard drive that consumed 7:26 and finished with Favre's 6-yard touchdown pass to Mark Chmura on third-and-5 with 12 seconds left in the half. Tyrone Williams forced and recovered Davis' fumble at the Broncos' 26 on the first play from scrimmage in the second half. However, the Broncos' defense kept the Packers out of the end zone as Ryan Longwell's 27-yard field goal tied the game with 11:59 left in the third quarter. After another exchange of punts, Elway's 36-yard pass to Ed McCaffrey keyed a 13-play, 92-yard drive capped by Davis' 1-yard touchdown run with 34 seconds left in the third quarter. Tim McKyer recovered Freeman's fumble at the Packers' 22 on the ensuing kickoff return, giving the Broncos a golden opportunity, but Eugene Robinson intercepted Elway's pass in the end zone on the next play. Sparked by Robinson's play, the Packers took just four plays, three on passes to Freeman, to score the tying touchdown with 13:32 remaining. Each defense stiffened, forcing two punts, but the Broncos got great field position following Craig Hentrich's 39-yard punt to the Packers' 49 with 3:27 left and the score tied 24-24. Davis rushed for 2 yards on the first play, but Darrius Holland's 15-yard facemask penalty moved the ball to the Packers' 32. Elway threw a 23-yard pass to Howard Griffith two plays later, and after a holding penalty, Davis rushed 17 yards to the Packers' 1 with 1:47 left. After a timeout, Davis waltzed into the end zone to give Denver a 31-24 lead with 1:45 remaining. Freeman returned the kickoff 22 yards to the Broncos' 30, and Favre completed 22- and 13-yard screen passes to Dorsey Levens to reach the Broncos' 35 with 1:04 left. But after a 4-yard pass to Levens and incompletions to Freeman and Brooks, John Mobley knocked away Favre's pass to Chmura with 32 seconds left to give the Broncos the Vince Lombardi Trophy. Elway was 12 of 22 for 123 yards, with 1 interception. Davis was 25 of 42 for 256 yards and 1 touchdown, with 1 interception. Freeman had 9 receptions for 126 yards. Davis was named the game's most valuable player.

Green Bay (NFC)	7	7	3	7 — 24
Denver (AFC)	7	10	7	7 — 31

GB	—	Freeman 22 pass from Favre (Longwell kick) (10:58)
Den	—	Davis 1 run (Elam kick) (5:39)
Den	—	Elway 1 run (Elam kick) (14:55)
Den	—	FG Elam 51 (12:21)
GB	—	Chmura 6 pass from Favre (Longwell kick) (0:12)
GB	—	FG Longwell 27 (11:59)
Den	—	Davis 1 run (Elam kick) (0:34)
GB	—	Freeman 13 pass from Favre (Longwell kick) (13:32)
Den	—	Davis 1 run (Elam kick) (1:45)

SUPER BOWL XXXI
Louisiana Superdome, New Orleans, LA
January 26, 1997, Attendance: 72,301
GREEN BAY 35, NEW ENGLAND 21— Desmond Howard returned a kickoff 99 yards for a touchdown and Brett Favre passed for 2 touchdowns and ran for a score as the Packers won their first Super Bowl in twenty-nine years. Howard, en route to garnering the MVP trophy, equaled a Super Bowl record with 244 total return yards. It was Favre's arm that struck first, as he hit Andre Rison on a 54-yard touchdown pass on the Packers' second play from scrimmage to take a 7-0 lead. Two plays later Doug Evans made a diving interception of Drew Bledsoe's pass at the 28-yard line, setting up Chris Jacke's field goal and giving the Packers a 10-0 lead just 6:18 into the Super Bowl. The Patriots answered with touchdowns on their next two possessions. Craig Newsome's pass interference penalty set up the first touchdown and a 44-yard completion from Bledsoe to Terry Glenn preceeding Ben Coates' touchdown gave New England its first and only lead. The 24 combined first quarter points were the most in Super Bowl history. Green Bay struck again 56 seconds into the second quarter as Favre hit Antonio Freeman with a Super Bowl-record 81-yard touchdown bomb. Jacke booted his second field goal on Green Bay's next possession. After a Mike Prior interception, Favre orchestrated a 74-yard, nearly 6-minute drive that concluded with a diving Favre touching the ball against the pylon to give Green Bay a 27-14 halftime lead. Curtis Martin brought the Patriots to within a score by running in from 18 yards out with 3:27 left in the third quarter. But Howard broke the Patriots' spirit by returning the ensuing kickoff a Super Bowl-record 99 yards. Favre found Mark Chmura for the 2-point conversion to finish the scoring. Bledsoe was intercepted twice in the fourth quarter as the Patriots never crossed midfield in 4 fourth-quarter possessions. Reggie White set a Super Bowl record with 3 sacks. Favre completed 14 of 27 passes for 246 yards, with no interceptions. Bledsoe completed 11 more passes than Favre, but for just 7 more yards, and threw 4 interceptions.

New England (AFC)	14	0	7	0 — 21
Green Bay (NFC)	10	17	8	0 — 35

GB	—	Rison 54 pass from Favre (Jacke kick) (11:28)
GB	—	FG Jacke 37 (8:42)
NE	—	Byars 1 pass from Bledsoe (Vinatieri kick) (6:35)
NE	—	Coates 4 pass from Bledsoe (Vinatieri kick) (2:33)
GB	—	Freeman 81 pass from Favre (Jacke kick) (14:04)
GB	—	FG Jacke 31 (8:15)
GB	—	Favre 2 run (Jacke kick) (1:11)

NE — Martin 18 run (Vinatieri kick) (3:27)

GB — Howard 99 kickoff return (Chmura pass from Favre) (3:10)

SUPER BOWL XXX

Sun Devil Stadium, Tempe, Arizona
January 28, 1996, Attendance: 76,347
DALLAS 27, PITTSBURGH 17—Corner-back Larry Brown's 2 interceptions led to 14 second-half points and helped lift the Cowboys to their third Super Bowl victory in the last four seasons and their record-tying fifth title overall. Brown's intercep-tions foiled the comeback efforts of the Steelers, and earned him the Pete Rozelle Trophy as the game's most valuable play-er. Dallas scored on each of its first three possessions, taking a 13-0 lead on Troy Aikman's 3-yard touchdown pass to Jay Novacek and a pair of field goals by Chris Boniol. Neil O'Donnell's 6-yard touch-down pass to Yancey Thigpen 13 seconds before halftime pulled Pittsburgh within 6 points, and the Steelers had the ball near midfield midway through the third quarter. But O'Donnell's third-down pass was intercepted by Brown at the Cowboys' 38-yard line and his 44-yard return carried to Pittsburgh's 18. After Aikman's 17-yard completion to Michael Irvin, Emmitt Smith ran 1 yard for the touchdown that put Dal-las ahead again by 13 points. The Steelers rallied, though, behind Norm Johnson's 46-yard field goal, a successful surprise onside kick, and Byron (Bam) Morris' 1-yard touchdown run with 6:36 to play in the game. And when they forced a punt and took possession at their own 32-yard line trailing only 20-17 with 4:15 remain-ing, it appeared they might have a chance to break the NFC's recent domination in the Super Bowl. But on second down, Brown struck again, intercepting O'Don-nell's pass at the 39 and returning it 33 yards to the 6. Two plays later, Smith bar-reled over from 4 yards out for the clinch-ing touchdown with 3:43 to go. Pittsburgh limited the Cowboys' powerful running game to only 56 yards and enjoyed a whopping 201-61 advantage in total yards in the second half, but could not over-come the 3 interceptions (another came on the game's final play) thrown by O'Donnell, the NFL's career leader for fewest interceptions per pass attempt. In all, O'Donnell completed 28 of 49 passes for 239 yards. Morris rushed for a game-high 73 yards on 19 carries. For Dallas, Aikman completed 15 of 23 pass attempts for 209 yards. The Cowboys' victory was the twelfth in a row for NFC teams over AFC teams in the Super Bowl.

Dallas (NFC)	10	3	7	7 — 27
Pittsburgh (AFC)	0	7	0	10 — 17

Dall — FG Boniol 42 (12:05)
Dall — Novacek 3 pass from Aikman (Boniol kick) (5:23)
Dall — FG Boniol 35 (6:03)

Pitt — Thigpen 6 pass from O'Donnell (N. Johnson kick) (0:13)
Dall — E. Smith 1 run (Boniol kick) (6:42)
Pitt — FG N. Johnson 46 (11:20)
Pitt — Morris 1 run (N. Johnson kick) (6:36)
Dall — E. Smith 4 run (Boniol kick) (3:43)

SUPER BOWL XXIX

Joe Robbie Stadium, Miami, Florida
January 29, 1995, Attendance: 74,107
SAN FRANCISCO 49, SAN DIEGO 26—Steve Young passed for a record 6 touch-downs, and the 49ers became the first team to win five Super Bowls when they routed the Chargers. Young, the game's most valuable player, directed an explo-sive offense that generated 7 touch-downs, 28 first downs, and 455 total yards. He completed 24 of 36 passes for 325 yards, and broke the record of 5 touchdown passes set by fromer 49ers quarterback Joe Montana in Super Bowl XXIV. San Francisco wasted little time scoring, taking the lead for good on Young's 44-yard touchdown pass to Jerry Rice only three plays and 1:24 into the game. The next time they had the ball, the 49ers marched 79 yards in four plays, taking a 14-0 lead when Young teamed with running back Ricky Watters on a 51-yard touchdown pass with 10:05 still to play in the opening period. San Diego then put together its most impressive posses-sion of the game, a 13-play, 78-yard drive that consumed more than 7 minutes and was capped by Natrone Means' 1-yard touchdown run, to cut its deficit to 14-7 late in the quarter. But San Francis-co countered with a 70-yard drive of its own, and Young's 5-yard touchdown pass to fullback William Floyd made it 21-7. Young's fourth touchdown pass of the half, 8 yards to Watters 4:44 before halftime, increased the advantage to 28-7, and the Chargers could get no closer than 18 points after that. Watters, who ran 9 yards for a touchdown in the third quarter, equaled the Super Bowl record with 3 touchdowns. Rice also scored 3 touch-downs (the second time in his career he'd done that in a Super Bowl) while catching 10 passes for 149 yards. He established career records for receptions, yards, and touchdowns in a Super Bowl. Young, who scrambled 21 yards and 15 yards to set up touchdowns in the first half, was the game's leading rusher with 49 yards on 5 carries. San Diego's Means, who rushed for 1,350 yards during the regular season, was limited to 33 yards on 13 attempts. Chargers quarterback Stan Humphries completed 24 of 49 passes for 275 yards. Rookie Andre Coleman became only the third player in Super Bowl history to return a kickoff for a touchdown, going 98 yards in the third quarter. The 75 points scored

by the two teams established another record, breaking the previous mark of 69 set in Dallas' 52-17 victory over Buffalo in XXVII. The 49ers' victory was the eleventh straight for NFC teams over AFC teams in the Super Bowl.

San Diego (AFC)	7	3	8	8 — 26
San Francisco (NFC)	14	14	14	7 — 49

SF — Rice 44 pass from S. Young (Brien kick) (13:36)
SF — Watters 51 pass from S. Young (Brien kick) (10:05)
SD — Means 1 run (Carney kick) (2:44)
SF — Floyd 5 pass from S. Young (Brien kick) (13:02)
SF — Watters 8 pass from S. Young (Brien kick) (4:44)
SD — FG Carney 31 (1:44)
SF — Watters 9 run (Brien kick) (9:35)
SF — Rice 15 pass from S. Young (Brien kick) (3:18)
SD — Coleman 98 kickoff return (Seay pass from Humphries) (3:01)
SF — Rice 7 pass from S. Young (Brien kick) (13:49)
SD — Martin 30 pass from Humphries (Pupunu pass from Humphries) (2:25)

SUPER BOWL XXVIII

Georgia Dome, Atlanta, Georgia
January 30, 1994, Attendance: 72,817
DALLAS 30, BUFFALO 13—Emmitt Smith rushed for 132 yards and 2 second-half touchdowns to power the Cowboys to their second consecutive NFL title. By winning, Dallas joined San Francisco and Pittsburgh as the only franchises with four Super Bowl victories. The Bills, mean-while, extended a dubious string by losing in the Super Bowl for the fourth consecu-tive year. To win, the Cowboys had to rally from a 13-6 halftime deficit. Buffalo had forged its lead on Thurman Thomas' 4-yard touchdown run and a pair of field goals by Steve Christie, including a 54-yard kick, the longest in Super Bowl histo-ry. But just 55 seconds into the second half, Thomas was stripped of the ball by Dallas defensive tackle Leon Lett. Safety James Washington recovered and weaved his way 46 yards for a touchdown to tie the game at 13-13. After forcing the Bills to punt, the Cowboys began their next possession on their 36-yard line and Smith, the game's most valuable player, took over. He carried 7 times for 61 yards on the ensuing 8-play, 64-yard drive, cap-ping the march with a 15-yard touchdown run to give Dallas the lead for good with 8:42 remaining in the third quarter. Early in the fourth quarter, Washington inter-cepted Jim Kelly's pass and returned it 12 yards to Buffalo's 34. A penalty moved the ball back to the 39, but Smith carried twice for 10 yards and caught a screen pass for 9, and quarterback Troy Aikman

completed a 16-yard pass to Alvin Harper to give the Cowboys a first-and-goal at the 6. Smith took it from there, cracking the end zone on fourth-and-goal from the 1 to put Dallas ahead 27-13 with 9:50 remaining. Eddie Murray's third field goal, from 20 yards with 2:50 left, ended any doubt about the game's outcome. Smith had 30 carries in all, with 19 of his attempts and 92 yards coming after intermission. Washington, normally a reserve who played most of the game because the Cowboys used five defensive backs to combat the Bills' No-Huddle offense, had 11 tackles and forced another fumble by Thomas in the first quarter. Aikman completed 19 of 27 passes for 207 yards. Buffalo's Kelly completed a Super Bowl-record 31 passes in 50 attempts for 260 yards. Dallas, the first team in NFL history to begin the regular season 0-2 and go on to win the Super Bowl, also became the fifth to win back-to-back titles, following Green Bay, Miami, Pittsburgh (the Steelers did it twice), and San Francisco. Buffalo became the third team, along with Minnesota and Denver, to lose four Super Bowls. The Cowboys' victory was the tenth in succession for the NFC over the AFC.

| Dallas (NFC) | 6 | 0 | 14 | 10 | — | 30 |
| Buffalo (AFC) | 3 | 10 | 0 | 0 | — | 13 |

Dall — FG Murray 41 (12:41)
Buff — FG Christie 54 (10:19)
Dall — FG Murray 24 (3:55)
Buff — Thomas 4 run (Christie kick) (12:26)
Buff — FG Christie 28 (0:00)
Dall — Washington 46 fumble return (Murray kick) (14:05)
Dall — E. Smith 15 run (Murray kick) (8:42)
Dall — E. Smith 1 run (Murray kick) (9:50)
Dall — FG Murray 20 (2:50)

SUPER BOWL XXVII

Rose Bowl, Pasadena, California
January 31, 1993, Attendance: 98,374
DALLAS 52, BUFFALO 17—Troy Aikman passed for 4 touchdowns, Emmitt Smith rushed for 108 yards, and the Cowboys converted 9 turnovers into 35 points while coasting to the victory. Dallas' win was its third in its record sixth Super Bowl appearance; the Bills became the first team to drop three in succession. Buffalo led 7-0 until the last 2 of its record number of turnovers helped the Cowboys take the lead for good late in the opening quarter. First, Dallas safety James Washington intercepted Jim Kelly's pass and returned it 13 yards to the Bills' 47, setting up Aikman's 23-yard touchdown pass to tight end Jay Novacek with 1:36 remaining in the period. On the next play from scrimmage, Kelly was sacked by Charles Haley and fumbled at the Bills' 2-yard line where the Cowboys' Jimmie Jones picked up the loose ball and ran 2 yards for a touch-

down. Dallas, which recovered 5 fumbles and intercepted 4 passes, struck just as quickly late in the first half, when Aikman tossed 19- and 18-yard touchdown passes to Michael Irvin 18 seconds apart to give the Cowboys a 28-10 lead at intermission. The second score was set up when Bills running back Thurman Thomas lost a fumble at his 19-yard line. Buffalo scored for the last time when backup quarterback Frank Reich, playing because Kelly was injured while attempting to pass midway through the second quarter, threw a 40-yard touchdown pass to Don Beebe on the final play of the third period to trim the deficit to 31-17. But Dallas put the game out of reach by scoring three times in a span of 2:33 of the fourth quarter. Aikman, the game's most valuable player, completed 22 of 30 passes for 273 yards. The victory was the ninth in succession for the NFC over the AFC.

| Buffalo (AFC) | 7 | 3 | 7 | 0 | — | 17 |
| Dallas (NFC) | 14 | 14 | 3 | 21 | — | 52 |

Buff — Thomas 2 run (Christie kick) (10:00)
Dall — Novacek 23 pass from Aikman (Elliott kick) (1:36)
Dall — J. Jones 2 fumble recovery return (Elliott kick) (1:21)
Buff — FG Christie 21 (3:24)
Dall — Irvin 19 pass from Aikman (Elliott kick) (1:54)
Dall — Irvin 18 pass from Aikman (Elliott kick) (1:36)
Dall — FG Elliott 20 (8:21)
Buff — Beebe 40 pass from Reich (Christie kick) (0:00)
Dall — Harper 45 pass from Aikman (Elliott kick) (10:04)
Dall — E. Smith 10 run (Elliott kick) (8:12)
Dall — Norton 9 fumble recovery return (Elliott kick) (7:31)

SUPER BOWL XXVI

Metrodome, Minneapolis, Minnesota
January 26, 1992, Attendance: 63,130
WASHINGTON 37, BUFFALO 24—Mark Rypien passed for 292 yards and 2 touchdowns as the Redskins overwhelmed the Bills to win their third Super Bowl in the past 10 years. Rypien, the game's most valuable player, completed 18 of 33 passes, including a 10-yard scoring strike to Earnest Byner and a 30-yard touchdown to Gary Clark. The latter came late in the third quarter after Buffalo had trimmed a 24-0 deficit to 24-10, and effectively put the game out of reach. Washington went on to lead by as much as 37-10 before the Bills made it close wih a pair of touchdowns in the final six minutes. Though the Redskins struggled early, converting their first three drives inside the Bills' 20-yard line into only 3 points, they built a 17-0 halftime lead. And they made it 24-0 just 16 seconds into the second half, after Kurt Gouveia intercepted Buffalo quarterback Jim Kelly's pass on the first play of

the third quarter and returned it 23 yards to the Bills' 2. One play later, Gerald Riggs scored his second touchdown of the game to make it 24-0. Kelly, forced to make a comeback, completed 28 of a Super Bowl-record 58 passes for 275 yards and 2 touchdowns, but was intercepted 4 times. Bills running back Thurman Thomas, who had an AFC-high 1,407 yards rushing and an NFL-best 2,038 total yards from scrimmage during the regular season, ran for only 13 yards on 10 carries and was limited to 27 yards on 4 receptions. Clark had 7 catches for 114 yards and Art Monk added 7 for 113 for the Redskins, who amassed 417 yards of total offense while limiting the explosive Bills to 283. Washington's Joe Gibbs became only the third head coach to win three Super Bowls.

| Washington (NFC) | 0 | 17 | 14 | 6 | — | 37 |
| Buffalo (AFC) | 0 | 0 | 10 | 14 | — | 24 |

Wash — FG Lohmiller 34 (13:02)
Wash — Byner 10 pass from Rypien (Lohmiller kick) (9:54)
Wash — Riggs 1 run (Lohmiller kick) (7:17)
Wash — Riggs 2 run (Lohmiller kick) (14:44)
Buff — FG Norwood 21 (11:59)
Buff — Thomas 1 run (Norwood kick) (5:58)
Wash — Clark 30 pass from Rypien (Lohmiller kick) (1:24)
Wash — FG Lohmiller 25 (14:54)
Wash — FG Lohmiller 39 (11:36)
Buff — Metzelaars 2 pass from Kelly (Norwood kick) (5:59)
Buff — Beebe 4 pass from Kelly (Norwood kick) (3:55)

SUPER BOWL XXV

Tampa Stadium, Tampa, Florida
January 27, 1991, Attendance: 73,813
NEW YORK GIANTS 20, BUFFALO 19—The NFC champion New York Giants won their second Super Bowl in five years with a 20-19 victory over AFC titlist Buffalo. New York, employing its ball-control offense, had possession for 40 minutes, 33 seconds, a Super Bowl record. The Bills, who scored 95 points in their previous two playoff games leading to Super Bowl XXV, had the ball for less than eight minutes in the second half and just 19:27 for the game. Fourteen of New York's 73 plays came on its initial drive of the third quarter, which covered 75 yards and consumed a Super Bowl-record 9:29 before running back Ottis Anderson ran 1 yard for a touchdown. Giants quarterback Jeff Hostetler kept the long drive going by converting three third-down plays—an 11-yard pass to running back David Meggett on third-and-eight, a 14-yard toss to wide receiver Mark Ingram on third-and-13, and a 9-yard pass to Howard Cross on third-and-four—to give New York a 17-12 lead in the third quarter. Buffalo jumped to a 12-3 lead midway through the second

quarter before Hostetler completed a 14-yard scoring strike to wide receiver Stephen Baker to close the score to 12-10 at halftime. Buffalo's Thurman Thomas ran 31 yards for a touchdown on the opening play of the fourth quarter to help Buffalo recapture the lead 19-17. Matt Bahr's 21-yard field goal gave the Giants a 20-19 lead, but Buffalo's Scott Norwood had a chance to win the game with seconds remaining before his 47-yard field-goal attempt sailed wide right. Hostetler completed 20 of 32 passes for 222 yards and 1 touchdown. Anderson rushed 21 times for 102 yards and 1 touchdown to capture most-valuable-player honors. Thomas totaled 190 scrimmage yards, rushing 15 times for 135 yards and catching 5 passes for 55 yards.

Buffalo (AFC)	3 9 0 7	—	19
N.Y. Giants (NFC)	3 7 7 3	—	20

NYG — FG Bahr 28 (7:14)
Buff — FG Norwood 23 (5:51)
Buff — D. Smith 1 run (Norwood kick) (12:30)
Buff — Safety, B. Smith tackled Hostetler in end zone (8:27)
NYG — Baker 14 pass from Hostetler (Bahr kick) (0:25)
NYG — Anderson 1 run (Bahr kick) (5:31)
Buff — Thomas 31 run (Norwood kick) (14:52)
NYG — FG Bahr 21 (7:20)

SUPER BOWL XXIV
Louisiana Superdome, New Orleans, LA
January 28, 1990, Attendance: 72,919
SAN FRANCISCO 55, DENVER 10—NFC titlist San Francisco won its fourth Super Bowl championship with a 55-10 victory over AFC champion Denver. The 49ers, who also won Super Bowls XVI, XIX, and XXIII, tied the Pittsburgh Steelers for most Super Bowl victories. The Steelers captured Super Bowls IX, X, XIII, and XIV. San Francisco's 55 points broke the previous Super Bowl scoring mark of 46 points by Chicago in Super Bowl XX. San Francisco scored touchdowns on four of its six first-half possessions to hold a 27-3 lead at halftime. Interceptions by Michael Walter and Chet Brooks ended the Broncos' first two possessions of the second half. San Francisco quarterback Joe Montana was named the Super Bowl most valuable player for a record third time. Montana completed 22 of 29 passes for 297 yards and a Super Bowl-record 5 touchdowns. Jerry Rice, Super Bowl XXIII most valuable player, caught 7 passes for 148 yards and 3 touchdowns. The 49ers' domination included first downs (28 to 12), net yards (461 to 167), and time of possession (39:31 to 20:29).

San Francisco (NFC)	13 14 14 14	— 55
Denver (AFC)	3 0 7 0	— 10

SF — Rice 20 pass from Montana (Cofer kick) (10:06)
Den — FG Treadwell 42 (6:47)

SF — Jones 7 pass from Montana (kick failed) (0:03)
SF — Rathman 1 run (Cofer kick) (7:15)
SF — Rice 38 pass from Montana (Cofer kick) (0:34)
SF — Rice 28 pass from Montana (Cofer kick) (12:48)
SF — Taylor 35 pass from Montana (Cofer kick) (9:44)
Den — Elway 3 run (Treadwell kick) (6:53)
SF — Rathman 3 run (Cofer kick) (14:57)
SF — Craig 1 run (Cofer kick) (13:47)

SUPER BOWL XXIII
Joe Robbie Stadium, Miami, Florida
January 22, 1989, Attendance: 75,129
SAN FRANCISCO 20, CINCINNATI 16—NFC champion San Francisco captured its third Super Bowl of the 1980s by defeating AFC champion Cincinnati 20-16. The 49ers, who also won Super Bowls XVI and XIX, became the first NFC team to win three Super Bowls. Pittsburgh, with four Super Bowl titles (IX, X, XIII, and XIV), and the Oakland/Los Angeles Raiders, with three (XI, XV, and XVIII), lead AFC franchises. Even though San Francisco held an advantage in total net yards (453 to 229), the 49ers found themselves trailing the Bengals late in the game. With the score 13-13, Cincinnati took a 16-13 lead on Jim Breech's 40-yard field goal with 3:20 remaining. It was Breech's third field goal of the day, following earlier successes from 34 and 43 yards. The 49ers started their winning drive at their 8-yard line. Over the next 11 plays, San Francisco covered 92 yards with the decisive score coming on a 10-yard pass from quarterback Joe Montana to wide receiver John Taylor with 34 seconds remaining. At halftime, the score was 3-3, the first time in Super Bowl history the game was tied at intermission. After the teams traded third-period field goals, the Bengals jumped ahead 13-6 on Stanford Jennings' 93-yard kickoff return for a touchdown with 34 seconds remaining in the quarter. The 49ers didn't waste any time coming back as they covered 85 yards in four plays, concluding with Montana's 14-yard scoring pass to Jerry Rice 57 seconds into the final stanza. Rice was named the game's most valuable player after compiling 11 catches for a Super Bowl-record 215 yards. Montana completed 23 of 36 passes for a Super Bowl-record 357 yards and 2 touchdowns.

Cincinnati (AFC)	0 3 10 3	— 16
San Francisco (NFC)	3 0 3 14	— 20

SF — FG Cofer 41 (3:14)
Cin — FG Breech 34 (1:15)
Cin — FG Breech 43 (5:39)
SF — FG Cofer 32 (0:50)
Cin — Jennings 93 kickoff return (Breech kick) (0:34)

SF — Rice 14 pass from Montana (Cofer kick) (14:03)
Cin — FG Breech 40 (3:20)
SF — Taylor 10 pass from Montana (Cofer kick) (0:34)

SUPER BOWL XXII
San Diego Jack Murphy Stadium, San Diego, CA
January 31, 1988, Attendance: 73,302
WASHINGTON 42, DENVER 10—NFC champion Washington won Super Bowl XXII and its second NFL championship of the 1980s with a 42-10 decision over AFC champion Denver. The Redskins, who also won Super Bowl XVII, enjoyed a record-setting second quarter en route to the victory. The Broncos broke in front 10-0 when quarterback John Elway threw a 56-yard touchdown pass to wide receiver Ricky Nattiel on the Broncos' first play from scrimmage. Following a Washington punt, Denver's Rich Karlis kicked a 24-yard field goal to cap a seven-play, 61-yard scoring drive. The Redskins then erupted for 35 points on five straight possessions in the second period and coasted thereafter. The 35 points established an NFL postseason mark for most points in a period. Redskins quarterback Doug Williams led the second-period explosion by passing for a Super Bowl record-tying 4 touchdowns, including 80- and 50-yard passes to wide receiver Ricky Sanders, a 27-yard toss to wide receiver Gary Clark, and an 8-yard pass to tight end Clint Didier. Washington scored 5 touchdowns in 18 plays with total time of possession of only 5:47. Overall, Williams completed 18 of 29 passes for 340 yards and was named the game's most valuable player. His pass-yardage total eclipsed the Super Bowl record of 331 yards by Joe Montana of San Francisco in Super Bowl XIX. Sanders ended with 193 yards on 8 catches, breaking the previous Super Bowl yardage record of 161 yards by Lynn Swann of Pittsburgh in Game X. Rookie running back Timmy Smith was the game's leading rusher with 22 carries for a Super Bowl-record 204 yards, breaking the previous mark of 191 yards by Marcus Allen of the Raiders in Game XVIII. Smith also scored twice on runs of 58 and 4 yards. Washington's 6 touchdowns and 602 total yards gained also set Super Bowl records. Redskins cornerback Barry Wilburn had 2 of the team's 3 interceptions, and strong safety Alvin Walton had 2 of Washington's 5 sacks.

Washington (NFC)	0 35 0 7	— 42
Denver (AFC)	10 0 0 0	— 10

Den — Nattiel 56 pass from Elway (Karlis kick) (13:03)
Den — FG Karlis 24 (9:09)
Wash — Sanders 80 pass from Williams (Haji-Sheikh kick) (14:07)
Wash — Clark 27 pass from Williams (Haji-Sheikh kick) (10:15)

Wash — Smith 58 run (Haji-Sheikh kick) (6:27)
Wash — Sanders 50 pass from Williams (Haji-Sheikh kick) (3:42)
Wash — Didier 8 pass from Williams (Haji-Sheikh kick) (1:04)
Wash — Smith 4 run (Haji-Sheikh kick) (13:09)

SUPER BOWL XXI

Rose Bowl, Pasadena, California
January 25, 1987, Attendance: 101,063
NEW YORK GIANTS 39, DENVER 20—
The NFC champion New York Giants captured their first NFL title since 1956 when they downed the AFC champion Denver Broncos 39-20 in Super Bowl XXI. The victory marked the NFC's fifth NFL title in the past six seasons. The Broncos, behind the passing of quarterback John Elway, who was 13 of 20 for 187 yards in the first half, held a 10-9 lead at intermission, the narrowest halftime margin in Super Bowl history. Denver's Rich Karlis opened the scoring with a Super Bowl record-tying 48-yard field goal. New York drove 78 yards in nine plays on the next series to take a 7-3 lead on quarterback Phil Simms' 6-yard touchdown pass to tight end Zeke Mowatt. The Broncos came right back with a 58-yard scoring drive on six plays capped by Elway's 4-yard touchdown run. The only scoring in the second period was the sack of Elway in the end zone by defensive end George Martin for a New York safety. The Giants produced a key defensive stand early in the second quarter when the Broncos had a first down at the New York 1-yard line, but failed to score on three running plays and Karlis' 23-yard missed field-goal attempt. The Giants took command of the game in the third period en route to a 30-point second half, the most ever scored in one half of Super Bowl play. New York took the lead for good on tight end Mark Bavaro's 13-yard touchdown catch 4:52 into the third period. The nine-play, 63-yard scoring drive included the successful conversion of a fourth-and-1 play on the New York 46-yard line. Denver was limited to only 2 net yards on 10 offensive plays in the third period. Simms set Super Bowl records for most consecutive completions (10) and highest completion percentage (88 percent on 22 completions in 25 attempts). He also passed for 268 yards and 3 touchdowns and was named the game's most valuable player. New York running back Joe Morris was the game's leading rusher with 20 carries for 67 yards. Denver wide receiver Vance Johnson led all receivers with 5 catches for 121 yards.

Denver (AFC)   10   0   0 10 — 20
N.Y. Giants (NFC)   7   2 17 13 — 39
Den — FG Karlis 48 (10:51)
NYG — Mowatt 6 pass from Simms (Allegre kick) (5:27)

Den — Elway 4 run (Karlis kick) (2:06)
NYG — Safety, Martin tackled Elway in end zone (2:46)
NYG — Bavaro 13 pass from Simms (Allegre kick) (10:08)
NYG — FG Allegre 21 (3:54)
NYG — Morris 1 run (Allegre kick) (0:24)
NYG — McConkey 6 pass from Simms (Allegre kick) (10:56)
Den — FG Karlis 28 (6:01)
NYG — Anderson 2 run (kick failed) (4:18)
Den — V. Johnson 47 pass from Elway (Karlis kick) (2:06)

SUPER BOWL XX

Louisiana Superdome, New Orleans, LA
January 26, 1986, Attendance: 73,818
CHICAGO 46, NEW ENGLAND 10—The NFC champion Chicago Bears, seeking their first NFL title since 1963, scored a Super Bowl-record 46 points in downing AFC champion New England 46-10 in Super Bowl XX. The previous record for most points in a Super Bowl was 38, shared by San Francisco in XIX and the Los Angeles Raiders in XVIII. The Bears' league-leading defense tied the Super Bowl record for sacks (7) and limited the Patriots to a record-low 7 rushing yards. New England took the quickest lead in Super Bowl history when Tony Franklin kicked a 36-yard field goal with 1:19 elapsed in the first period. The score came about because of Larry McGrew's fumble recovery at the Chicago 19-yard line. However, the Bears rebounded for a 23-3 first-half lead, while building a yardage advantage of 236 total yards to New England's minus 19. Running back Matt Suhey rushed 8 times for 37 yards, including an 11-yard touchdown run, and caught 1 pass for 24 yards in the first half. After the Patriot's first drive of the second half ended with a punt to the Bears' 4-yard line, Chicago marched 96 yards in nine plays with quarterback Jim McMahon's 1-yard scoring run capping the drive. McMahon became the first quarterback in Super Bowl history to rush for a pair of touchdowns. The Bears completed their scoring via a 28-yard interception return by reserve cornerback Reggie Phillips, 1-yard run by defensive tackle/fullback William Perry, and a safety when defensive end Henry Waechter tackled Patriots quarterback Steve Grogan in the end zone. Bears defensive end Richard Dent became the fourth defender to be named the game's most valuable player after contributing 1 1/2 sacks. The Bears' victory margin of 36 points was the largest in Super Bowl history, bettering the previous mark of 29 by the Los Angeles Raiders when they topped Washington 38-9 in Game XVIII. McMahon completed 12 of 20 passes for 256 yards before leaving the game in the fourth period with a wrist

injury. The NFL's all-time leading rusher, Bears running back Walter Payton, carried 22 times for 61 yards. Wide receiver Willie Gault caught 4 passes for 129 yards, the fourth-most receiving yards in a Super Bowl. Chicago coach Mike Ditka became the second man (Tom Flores of Raiders was the other) to win a Super Bowl ring as a player and as a coach.

Chicago (NFC)   13 10 21   2 — 46
New England (AFC)   3   0   0   7 — 10
NE — FG Franklin 36 (13:41)
Chi — FG Butler 28 (9:20)
Chi — FG Butler 24 (1:26)
Chi — Suhey 11 run (Butler kick) (0:23)
Chi — McMahon 2 run (Butler kick) (7:24)
Chi — FG Butler 24 (0:00)
Chi — McMahon 1 run (Butler kick) (7:22)
Chi — Phillips 28 interception return (Butler kick) (6:16)
Chi — Perry 1 run (Butler kick) (3:22)
NE — Fryar 8 pass from Grogan (Franklin kick) (13:14)
Chi — Safety, Waechter tackled Grogan in end zone (5:36)

SUPER BOWL XIX

Stanford Stadium, Stanford, California
January 20, 1985, Attendance: 84,059
SAN FRANCISCO 38, MIAMI 16—The San Francisco 49ers captured their second Super Bowl title with a dominating offense and a defense that tamed Miami's explosive passing attack. The Dolphins held a 10-7 lead at the end of the first period, which represented the most points scored by two teams in an opening quarter of a Super Bowl. However, the 49ers used excellent field position in the second period to build a 28-16 halftime lead. Running back Roger Craig set a Super Bowl record by scoring 3 touchdowns on pass receptions of 8 and 16 yards and a run of 2 yards. San Francisco's Joe Montana was voted the game's most valuable player. He joined Green Bay's Bart Starr and Pittsburgh's Terry Bradshaw as the only two-time Super Bowl most valuable players. Montana completed 24 of 35 passes for a Super Bowl-record 331 yards and 3 touchdowns, and rushed 5 times for 59 yards, including a 6-yard touchdown. Craig had 58 yards on 15 carries and caught 7 passes for 77 yards. Wendell Tyler rushed 13 times for 65 yards and had 4 catches for 70 yards. Dwight Clark had 6 receptions for 77 yards, while Russ Francis had 5 for 60. San Francisco's 537 total net yards bettered the previous Super Bowl record of 429 yards by Oakland in Super Bowl XI. The 49ers also held a time of possession advantage over the Dolphins of 37:11 to 22:49.

Miami (AFC)   10   6   0   0 — 16
San Francisco (NFC)   7 21 10   0 — 38
Mia — FG von Schamann 37 (7:24)

SF — Monroe 33 pass from Montana (Wersching kick) (3:12)
Mia — D. Johnson 2 pass from Marino (von Schamann kick) (0:45)
SF — Craig 8 pass from Montana (Wersching kick) (11:34)
SF — Montana 6 run (Wersching kick) (6:58)
SF — Craig 2 run (Wersching kick) (2:05)
Mia — FG von Schamann 31 (0:12)
Mia — FG von Schamann 30 (0:00)
SF — FG Wersching 27 (10:12)
SF — Craig 16 pass from Montana (Wersching kick) (6:18)

SUPER BOWL XVIII
Tampa Stadium, Tampa, Florida
January 22, 1984, Attendance: 72,920
LOS ANGELES RAIDERS 38, WASHINGTON 9—The Los Angeles Raiders dominated the Washington Redskins from the beginning in Super Bowl XVIII and achieved the most lopsided victory in Super Bowl history, surpassing Green Bay's 35-10 win over Kansas City in Super Bowl I. The Raiders took a 7-0 lead 4:52 into the game when Derrick Jensen blocked Jeff Hayes' punt and recovered it in the end zone for a touchdown. With 9:14 remaining in the first half, Raiders quarterback Jim Plunkett fired a 12-yard touchdown pass to wide receiver Cliff Branch to complete a three-play, 65-yard drive. Washington cut the Raiders' lead to 14-3 on a 24-yard field goal by Mark Moseley. With seven seconds left in the first half, Raiders linebacker Jack Squirek intercepted Joe Theismann's pass at the Redskins' 5-yard line and ran it in for a touchdown to give Los Angeles a 21-3 halftime lead. In the third period, running back Marcus Allen, who rushed for a Super Bowl-record 191 yards on 20 carries, increased the Raiders' lead to 35-9 on touchdown runs of 5 and 74 yards, the latter erasing the Super Bowl record of 58 yards set by Baltimore's Tom Matte in Game III. Allen was named the game's most valuable player. The victory over Washington raised Raiders coach Tom Flores' playoff record to 8-1, including a 27-10 win over Philadelphia in Super Bowl XV. The 38 points scored by the Raiders were the highest total by a Super Bowl team. The previous high was 35 points by Green Bay in Game I.

Washington (NFC)	0 3 6	—	9
L.A. Raiders (AFC)	7 14 14 3	—	38

Raiders — Jensen recovered blocked punt in end zone (Bahr kick) (10:08)
Raiders — Branch 12 pass from Plunkett (Bahr kick) (9:14)
Wash — FG Moseley 24 (3:05)
Raiders — Squirek 5 interception return (Bahr kick) (0:07)

Wash — Riggins 1 run (kick blocked) (10:52)
Raiders — Allen 5 run (Bahr kick) (7:06)
Raiders — Allen 74 run (Bahr kick) (0:00)
Raiders — FG Bahr 21 (2:24)

SUPER BOWL XVII
Rose Bowl, Pasadena, California
January 30, 1983, Attendance: 103,667
WASHINGTON 27, MIAMI 17—Fullback John Riggins ran for a Super Bowl-record 166 yards on 38 carries to spark Washington to a 27-17 victory over AFC champion Miami. It was Riggins' fourth straight 100-yard rushing game during the playoffs, also a record. The win marked Washington's first NFL title since 1942, and was only the second time in Super Bowl history NFL/NFC teams scored consecutive victories (Green Bay did it in Super Bowls I and II and San Francisco won Super Bowl XVI). The Redskins, under second-year head coach Joe Gibbs, used a balanced offense that accounted for 400 total yards (a Super Bowl-record 276 yards rushing and 124 passing), second in Super Bowl history to 429 yards by Oakland in Super Bowl XI. The Dolphins built a 17-10 halftime lead on a 76-yard touchdown pass from quarterback David Woodley to wide receiver Jimmy Cefalo 6:49 into the first period, a 20-yard field goal by Uwe von Schamann with 6:00 left in the half, and a Super Bowl-record 98-yard kickoff return by Fulton Walker with 1:38 remaining. Washington had tied the score at 10-10 with 1:51 left on a 4-yard touchdown pass from Joe Theismann to wide receiver Alvin Garrett. Mark Moseley started the Redskins' scoring with a 31-yard field goal late in the first period, and added a 20-yard kick midway through the third period to cut the Dolphins' lead to 17-13. Riggins, who was voted the game's most valuable player, gave Washington its first lead of the game with 10:01 left when he ran 43 yards off left tackle for a touchdown on a fourth-and-1 situation. Wide receiver Charlie Brown caught a 6-yard scoring pass from Theismann with 1:55 left to complete the scoring. The Dolphins managed only 176 yards (142 in first half). Theismann completed 15 of 23 passes for 143 yards, with 2 touchdowns and 2 interceptions. For Miami, Woodley was 4 of 14 for 97 yards, with 1 touchdown, and 1 interception. Don Strock was 0 for 3 in relief.

Miami (AFC)	7 10 0 0	—	17
Washington (NFC)	0 10 3 14	—	27

Mia — Cefalo 76 pass from Woodley (von Schamann kick) (8:11)
Wash — FG Moseley 31 (0:39)
Mia — FG von Schamann 20 (6:00)
Wash — Garrett 4 pass from Theismann (Moseley kick) (1:51)
Mia — Walker 98 kickoff return (von Schamann kick) (1:38)

Wash — FG Moseley 20 (8:09)
Wash — Riggins 43 run (Moseley kick) (10:01)
Wash — Brown 6 pass from Theismann (Moseley kick) (1:55)

SUPER BOWL XVI
Pontiac Silverdome, Pontiac, Michigan
January 24, 1982, Attendance: 81,270
SAN FRANCISCO 26, CINCINNATI 21—Ray Wersching's Super Bowl record-tying 4 field goals and Joe Montana's controlled passing helped lift the San Francisco 49ers to their first NFL championship with a 26-21 victory over Cincinnati. The 49ers built a game-record 20-0 halftime lead via Montana's 1-yard touchdown run, which capped an 11-play, 68-yard drive; fullback Earl Cooper's 11-yard scoring pass from Montana, which climaxed a Super Bowl record 92-yard drive on 12 plays; and Wersching's 22- and 26-yard field goals. The Bengals rebounded in the second half, closing the gap to 20-14 on quarterback Ken Anderson's 5-yard run and Dan Ross' 4-yard reception from Anderson, who established Super Bowl passing records for completions (25) and completion percentage (73.5 percent on 25 of 34). Wersching added early fourth-period field goals of 40 and 23 yards to increase the 49ers' lead to 26-14. The Bengals managed to score on an Anderson-to-Ross 3-yard pass with only 16 seconds remaining. Ross set a Super Bowl record with 11 receptions for 104 yards. Montana, the game's most valuable player, completed 14 of 22 passes for 157 yards. Cincinnati compiled 356 yards to San Francisco's 275, which marked the first time in Super Bowl history that the team that gained the most yards from scrimmage lost the game.

San Francisco (NFC)	7 13 0 6	—	26
Cincinnati (AFC)	0 0 7 14	—	21

SF — Montana 1 run (Wersching kick) (5:52)
SF — Cooper 11 pass from Montana (Wersching kick) (6:53)
SF — FG Wersching 22 (0:15)
SF — FG Wersching 26 (0:02)
Cin — Anderson 5 run (Breech kick) (11:25)
Cin — Ross 4 pass from Anderson (Breech kick) (10:06)
SF — FG Wersching 40 (5:25)
SF — FG Wersching 23 (1:57)
Cin — Ross 3 pass from Anderson (Breech kick) (0:16)

SUPER BOWL XV
Louisiana Superdome, New Orleans, LA
January 25, 1981, Attendance: 76,135
OAKLAND 27, PHILADELPHIA 10—Jim Plunkett passed for 3 touchdowns, including an 80-yard strike to Kenny King, as the Raiders became the first wild-card team to win the Super Bowl. Plunkett's touchdown bomb to King—the longest play in

Super Bowl history—gave Oakland a decisive 14-0 lead with nine seconds left in the first period. Linebacker Rod Martin had set up Oakland's first touchdown, a 2-yard reception by Cliff Branch, with a 17-yard interception return to the Eagles' 30-yard line. The Eagles never recovered from that early deficit, managing only Tony Franklin's field goal (30 yards) and an 8-yard touchdown pass from Ron Jaworski to Keith Krepfle. Plunkett, who became a starter in the sixth game of the season, completed 13 of 21 for 261 yards and was named the game's most valuable player. Oakland won 9 of 11 games with Plunkett starting, but that was good enough only for second place in the AFC West, although they tied division winner San Diego with an 11-5 record. The Raiders, who had previously won Super Bowl XI over Minnesota, had to win three playoff games to get to the championship game. Oakland defeated Houston 27-7 at home followed by road victories over Cleveland (14-12) and San Diego (34-27). Oakland's Mark van Eeghen was the game's leading rusher with 75 yards on 18 carries. Philadelphia's Wilbert Montgomery led all receivers with 6 receptions for 91 yards. Branch had 5 for 67 and Harold Carmichael of Philadelphia 5 for 83. Martin finished the game with 3 interceptions, a Super Bowl record.

Oakland (AFC)	14	0	10	3 — 27
Philadelphia (NFC)	0	3	0	7 — 10

Oak — Branch 2 pass from Plunkett (Bahr kick) (8:56)
Oak — King 80 pass from Plunkett (Bahr kick) (0:09)
Phil — FG Franklin 30 (10:28)
Oak — Branch 29 pass from Plunkett (Bahr kick) (12:24)
Oak — FG Bahr 46 (4:35)
Phil — Krepfle 8 pass from Jaworski (Franklin kick) (13:59)
Oak — FG Bahr 35 (8:29)

SUPER BOWL XIV
Rose Bowl, Pasadena, California
January 20, 1980, Attendance: 103,985
PITTSBURGH 31, LOS ANGELES 19—Terry Bradshaw completed 14 of 21 passes for 309 yards and set two passing records as the Steelers became the first team to win four Super Bowls. Despite 3 interceptions by the Rams, Bradshaw kept his poise and brought the Steelers from behind twice in the second half. Trailing 13-10 at halftime, Pittsburgh went ahead 17-13 when Bradshaw hit Lynn Swann with a 47-yard touchdown pass after 2:48 of the third quarter. On the Rams' next possession Vince Ferragamo, who was 15 of 25 for 212 yards, responded with a 50-yard pass to Billy Waddy that moved Los Angeles from its 26 to the Steelers' 24. On the following play, Lawrence McCutcheon connected with Ron Smith on a halfback option pass that gave the Rams a 19-17 lead. On Pittsburgh's initial

possession of the final period, Bradshaw lofted a 73-yard scoring pass to John Stallworth to put the Steelers in front to stay 24-19. Franco Harris scored on a 1-yard run later in the quarter to seal the verdict. A 45-yard pass from Bradshaw to Stallworth was the key play in the drive to Harris' score. Bradshaw, the game's most valuable player for the second straight year, set career Super Bowl records for most touchdown passes (9) and most passing yards (932). Larry Anderson gave the Steelers excellent field position throughout the game with 5 kickoff returns for a record 162 yards.

Los Angeles (NFC)	7	6	6	0 — 19
Pittsburgh (AFC)	3	7	7	14 — 31

Pitt — FG Bahr 41 (7:31)
LA — Bryant 1 run (Corral kick) (2:44)
Pitt — Harris 1 run (Bahr kick) (12:52)
LA — FG Corral 31 (7:21)
LA — FG Corral 45 (0:14)
Pitt — Swann 47 pass from Bradshaw (Bahr kick) (12:12)
LA — Smith 24 pass from McCutcheon (kick failed) (10:15)
Pitt — Stallworth 73 pass from Bradshaw (Bahr kick) (12:04)
Pitt — Harris 1 run (Bahr kick) (1:49)

SUPER BOWL XIII
Orange Bowl, Miami, Florida
January 21, 1979, Attendance: 79,484
PITTSBURGH 35, DALLAS 31—Terry Bradshaw passed for a record 4 touchdowns to lead the Steelers to victory. The Steelers became the first team to win three Super Bowls, mostly because of Bradshaw's accurate arm. Bradshaw, voted the game's most valuable player, completed 17 of 30 passes for 318 yards, a personal high. Four of those passes went for touchdowns—2 to John Stallworth and the third, with 26 seconds remaining in the second period, to Rocky Bleier for a 21-14 halftime lead. The Cowboys scored twice before intermission on Roger Staubach's 39-yard pass to Tony Hill and a 37-yard fumble return by linebacker Mike Hegman, who stole the ball from Bradshaw. The Steelers broke open the contest with 2 touchdowns in a span of 19 seconds midway through the final period. Franco Harris rambled 22 yards up the middle to give the Steelers a 28-17 lead with 7:10 left. Pittsburgh got the ball right back when Randy White fumbled the kickoff and Dennis Winston recovered for the Steelers. On first down, Bradshaw fired his fourth touchdown pass, an 18-yard pass to Lynn Swann to boost the Steelers' lead to 35-17 with 6:51 to play. The Cowboys refused to let the Steelers run away with the contest. Staubach connected with Billy Joe DuPree on a 7-yard scoring pass with 2:23 left. Then the Cowboys recovered an onside kick and

Staubach took them in for another score, passing 4 yards to Butch Johnson with 22 seconds remaining. Bleier recovered another onside kick with 17 seconds left to seal the victory for the Steelers.

Pittsburgh (AFC)	7	14	0	14 — 35
Dallas (NFC)	7	7	3	14 — 31

Pitt — Stallworth 28 pass from Bradshaw (Gerela kick) (9:47)
Dall — Hill 39 pass from Staubach (Septien kick) (0:00)
Dall — Hegman 37 fumble recovery return (Septien kick) (12:08)
Pitt — Stallworth 75 pass from Bradshaw (Gerela kick) (10:25)
Pitt — Bleier 7 pass from Bradshaw (Gerela kick) (0:26)
Dall — FG Septien 27 (2:36)
Pitt — Harris 22 run (Gerela kick) (7:10)
Pitt — Swann 18 pass from Bradshaw (Gerela kick) (6:51)
Dall — DuPree 7 pass from Staubach (Septien kick) (2:23)
Dall — B. Johnson 4 pass from Staubach (Septien kick) (0:22)

SUPER BOWL XII
Louisiana Superdome, New Orleans, LA
January 15, 1978, Attendance: 75,583
DALLAS 27, DENVER 10—The Cowboys evened their Super Bowl record to 2-2 by defeating Denver before a sellout crowd plus 102,010,000 television viewers, the largest audience ever to watch a sporting event. Dallas converted 2 interceptions into 10 points and Efren Herrera added a 35-yard field goal for a 13-0 halftime advantage. In the third period Craig Morton engineered a drive to the Cowboys' 30 and Jim Turner's 47-yard field goal made the score 13-3. After an exchange of punts, Butch Johnson made a spectacular diving catch in the end zone to complete a 45-yard pass from Roger Staubach and put the Cowboys ahead 20-3. Following Rick Upchurch's 67-yard kickoff return, Norris Weese guided the Broncos to a touchdown to cut the deficit to 20-10. Dallas clinched the victory when running back Robert Newhouse tossed a 29-yard touchdown pass to Golden Richards with 7:04 left in the game. It was the first pass thrown by Newhouse since 1975. Harvey Martin and Randy White, who were named co-most valuable players, led the Cowboys' defense, which recovered 4 fumbles and intercepted 4 passes.

Dallas (NFC)	10	3	7	7 — 27
Denver (AFC)	0	0	10	0 — 10

Dall — Dorsett 3 run (Herrera kick) (4:29)
Dall — FG Herrera 35 (1:31)
Dall — FG Herrera 43 (11:16)
Den — FG Turner 47 (12:32)
Dall — Johnson 45 pass from Staubach (Herrera kick) (6:59)
Den — Lytle 1 run (Turner kick) (5:39)

Dall — Richards 29 pass from Newhouse (Herrera kick) (7:04)

SUPER BOWL XI

Rose Bowl, Pasadena, California
January 9, 1977, Attendance: 103,438
OAKLAND 32, MINNESOTA 14—The Raiders won their first NFL championship before a record Super Bowl crowd plus 81 million television viewers, the largest audience ever to watch a sporting event. The Raiders gained a record-breaking 429 yards, including running back Clarence Davis' 137 rushing yards. Wide receiver Fred Biletnikoff made 4 key receptions, which earned him the game's most valuable player trophy. Oakland scored on three successive possessions in the second quarter to build a 16-0 halftime lead. Errol Mann's 24-yard field goal opened the scoring, then the AFC champions put together drives of 64 and 35 yards, scoring on a 1-yard pass from Ken Stabler to Dave Casper and a 1-yard run by Pete Banaszak. The Raiders increased their lead to 19-0 on a 40-yard field goal in the third quarter, but Minnesota responded with a 12-play, 58-yard drive late in the period, with Fran Tarkenton passing 8 yards to wide receiver Sammy White to cut the deficit to 19-7. Two fourth-quarter interceptions clinched the title for the Raiders. One set up Banaszak's second touchdown run, the other resulted in cornerback Willie Brown's Super Bowl-record 75-yard interception return.

Oakland (AFC)	0	16	3	13 — 32
Minnesota (NFC)	0	0	7	7 — 14

Oak — FG Mann 24 (14:12)
Oak — Casper 1 pass from Stabler (Mann kick) (7:10)
Oak — Banaszak 1 run (kick failed) (3:33)
Oak — FG Mann 40 (5:16)
Minn — S. White 8 pass from Tarkenton (Cox kick) (0:47)
Oak — Banaszak 2 run (Mann kick) (7:39)
Oak — Brown 75 interception return (kick failed) (5:43)
Minn — Voigt 13 pass from Lee (Cox kick) (0:25)

SUPER BOWL X

Orange Bowl, Miami, Florida
January 18, 1976, Attendance: 80,187
PITTSBURGH 21, DALLAS 17—The Steelers won the Super Bowl for the second year in a row on Terry Bradshaw's 64-yard touchdown pass to Lynn Swann and an aggressive defense that snuffed out a late rally by the Cowboys with an end-zone interception on the final play of the game. In the fourth quarter, Pittsburgh ran on fourth down and gave up the ball on the Cowboys' 39 with 1:22 to play. Roger Staubach ran and passed for 2 first downs but his last desperation pass was picked off by Glen Edwards. Dallas' scor-

ing was the result of 2 touchdown passes by Staubach, one to Drew Pearson for 29 yards and the other to Percy Howard for 34 yards. Howard's reception was the only catch of his NFL career. Toni Fritsch had a 36-yard field goal. The Steelers scored on 2 touchdown passes by Bradshaw, 1 to Randy Grossman for 7 yards and the long bomb to Swann. Roy Gerela had 36- and 18-yard field goals. Reggie Harrison blocked a punt through the end zone for a safety. Swann set a Super Bowl record by gaining 161 yards on his 4 receptions.

Dallas (NFC)	7	3	0	7 — 17
Pittsburgh (AFC)	7	0	0	14 — 21

Dall — D. Pearson 29 pass from Staubach (Fritsch kick) (10:24)
Pitt — Grossman 7 pass from Bradshaw (Gerela kick) (5:57)
Dall — FG Fritsch 36 (14:45)
Pitt — Safety, Harrison blocked Hoopes' punt through end zone (11:28)
Pitt — FG Gerela 36 (8:41)
Pitt — FG Gerela 18 (6:37)
Pitt — Swann 64 pass from Bradshaw (kick failed) (3:02)
Dall — P. Howard 34 pass from Staubach (Fritsch kick) (1:48)

SUPER BOWL IX

Tulane Stadium, New Orleans, Louisiana
January 12, 1975, Attendance: 80,997
PITTSBURGH 16, MINNESOTA 6—AFC champion Pittsburgh, in its initial Super Bowl appearance, and NFC champion Minnesota, making a third bid for its first Super Bowl title, struggled through a first half in which the only score was produced by the Steelers' defense when Dwight White downed Vikings' quarterback Fran Tarkenton in the end zone for a safety 7:49 into the second period. The Steelers forced another break and took advantage on the second-half kickoff when Minnesota's Bill Brown fumbled and Marv Kellum recovered for Pittsburgh on the Vikings' 30. After Rocky Bleier failed to gain on first down, Franco Harris carried 3 consecutive times for 24 yards, a loss of 3, and a 9-yard touchdown and a 9-6 lead. Though its offense was completely stymied by Pittsburgh's defense, Minnesota managed to move into a threatening position after 4:27 of the final period when Matt Blair blocked Bobby Walden's punt and Terry Brown recovered the ball in the end zone for a touchdown. Fred Cox's kick failed and the Steelers led 9-6. Pittsburgh wasted no time putting the victory away. The Steelers took the ensuing kickoff and marched 66 yards in 11 plays, climaxed by Terry Bradshaw's 4-yard scoring pass to Larry Brown with 3:31 left. Pittsburgh's defense permitted Minnesota only 119 yards total offense, including a Super Bowl low of 17 rushing yards. The Steelers, meanwhile, gained 333 yards,

including Harris' record 158 yards on 34 carries.

Pittsburgh (AFC)	0	2	7	7 — 16
Minnesota (NFC)	0	0	0	6 — 6

Pitt — Safety, White downed Tarkenton in end zone (7:11)
Pitt — Harris 9 run (Gerela kick) (13:25)
Minn — T. Brown recovered blocked punt in end zone (kick failed) (10:33)
Pitt — L. Brown 4 pass from Bradshaw (Gerela kick) (3:31)

SUPER BOWL VIII

Rice Stadium, Houston, Texas
January 13, 1974, Attendance: 71,882
MIAMI 24, MINNESOTA 7—The defending NFL champion Dolphins, representing the AFC for the third straight year, scored the first two times they had possession on marches of 62 and 56 yards while the Miami defense limited the Vikings to only seven plays in the first period. Larry Csonka climaxed the initial 10-play drive with a 5-yard touchdown bolt through right guard after 5:27 had elapsed. Four plays later, Miami began another 10-play scoring drive, which ended with Jim Kiick bursting 1 yard through the middle for another touchdown after 13:38 of the period. Garo Yepremian added a 28-yard field goal midway in the second period for a 17-0 Miami lead. Minnesota then drove from its 20 to a second-and-2 situation on the Miami 7 yard line with 1:18 left in the half. But on two plays, Miami limited Oscar Reed to 1 yard. On fourth-and-1 from the 6, Reed went over right tackle, but Dolphins middle linebacker Nick Buoniconti jarred the ball loose and Jake Scott recovered for Miami to halt the Minnesota threat. The Vikings were unable to muster enough offense in the second half to threaten the Dolphins. Csonka rushed 33 times for a Super Bowl-record 145 yards. Bob Griese of Miami completed 6 of 7 passes for 73 yards.

Minnesota (NFC)	0	0	7	0 — 7
Miami (AFC)	14	3	7	0 — 24

Mia — Csonka 5 run (Yepremian kick) (5:27)
Mia — Kiick 1 run (Yepremian kick) (1:22)
Mia — FG Yepremian 28 (6:02)
Mia — Csonka 2 run (Yepremian kick) (8:44)
Minn — Tarkenton 4 run (Cox kick) (13:25)

SUPER BOWL VII

Memorial Coliseum, Los Angeles, CA
January 14, 1973, Attendance: 90,182
MIAMI 14, WASHINGTON 7—The Dolphins played virtually perfect football in the first half as their defense permitted the Redskins to cross midfield only once and their offense turned good field position into 2 touchdowns. On its third possession, Miami opened its first scoring drive

from the Dolphins' 37 yard line. An 18-yard pass from Bob Griese to Paul Warfield preceded by three plays Griese's 28-yard touchdown pass to Howard Twilley. After Washington moved from its 17 to the Miami 48 with two minutes remaining in the first half, Dolphins linebacker Nick Buoniconti intercepted Billy Kilmer's pass at the Miami 41 and returned it to the Washington 27. Jim Kiick ran for 3 yards, Larry Csonka for 3, Griese passed to Jim Mandich for 19, and Kiick gained 1 to the 1-yard line. With 18 seconds left until intermission, Kiick scored from the 1. Washington's only touchdown came with 2:07 left in the game and resulted from a misplayed field-goal attempt and fumble by Garo Yepremian, with the Redskins' Mike Bass picking the ball out of the air and running 49 yards for the score. Dolphins safety Jake Scott, who had 2 interceptions, including 1 in the end zone to kill a Redskins' drive, was voted the game's most valuable player.

Miami (AFC)	7	7	0	0	—	14
Washington (NFC)	0	0	0	7	—	7

Mia — Twilley 28 pass from Griese (Yepremian kick) (0:01)
Mia — Kiick 1 run (Yepremian kick) (0:18)
Wash — Bass 49 fumble recovery return (Knight kick) (2:07)

SUPER BOWL VI
Tulane Stadium, New Orleans, Louisiana
January 16, 1972, Attendance: 81,023
DALLAS 24, MIAMI 3—The Cowboys rushed for a record 252 yards and their defense limited the Dolphins to a low of 185 yards while not permitting a touchdown for the first time in Super Bowl history. Dallas converted Chuck Howley's recovery of Larry Csonka's first fumble of the season into a 3-0 advantage and led at halftime 10-3. After Dallas received the second-half kickoff, Duane Thomas led a 71-yard march in eight plays for a 17-3 margin. Howley intercepted Bob Griese's pass at the 50 and returned it to the Miami 9 early in the fourth period, and three plays later Roger Staubach passed 7 yards to Mike Ditka for the final touchdown. Thomas rushed for 95 yards and Walt Garrison gained 74. Staubach, voted the game's most valuable player, completed 12 of 19 passes for 119 yards and 2 touchdowns.

Dallas (NFC)	3	7	7	7	—	24
Miami (AFC)	0	3	0	0	—	3

Dall — FG Clark 9 (1:23)
Dall — Alworth 7 pass from Staubach (Clark kick) (1:15)
Mia — FG Yepremian 31 (0:04)
Dall — D. Thomas 3 run (Clark kick) (9:43)
Dall — Ditka 7 pass from Staubach (Clark kick) (11:42)

SUPER BOWL V
Orange Bowl, Miami, Florida
January 17, 1971, Attendance: 79,204
BALTIMORE 16, DALLAS 13—A 32-yard field goal by rookie kicker Jim O'Brien brought the Baltimore Colts a victory over the Dallas Cowboys in the final five seconds of Super Bowl V. The game between the champions of the AFC and NFC was played on artificial turf for the first time. Dallas led 13-6 at the half but interceptions by Rick Volk and Mike Curtis set up a Baltimore touchdown and O'Brien's decisive kick in the fourth period. Earl Morrall relieved an injured Johnny Unitas late in the first half, although Unitas completed the Colts' only scoring pass. It caromed off receiver Eddie Hinton's fingertips, off Dallas defensive back Mel Renfro, and finally settled into the grasp of John Mackey, who went 45 yards to score on a 75-yard play.

Baltimore (AFC)	0	6	0	10	—	16
Dallas (NFC)	3	10	0	0	—	13

Dall — FG Clark 14 (5:32)
Dall — FG Clark 30 (14:52)
Balt — Mackey 75 pass from Unitas (kick blocked) (14:55)
Dall — Thomas 7 pass from Morton (Clark kick) (7:53)
Balt — Nowatzke 2 run (O'Brien kick) (7:35)
Balt — FG O'Brien 32 (0:05)

SUPER BOWL IV
Tulane Stadium, New Orleans, Louisiana
January 11, 1970, Attendance: 80,562
KANSAS CITY 23, MINNESOTA 7—The AFL squared the Super Bowl at two games apiece with the NFL, building a 16-0 halftime lead behind Len Dawson's superb quarterbacking and a powerful defense. Dawson, the fourth consecutive quarterback to be chosen the Super Bowl's top player, called an almost flawless game, completing 12 of 17 passes and hitting Otis Taylor on a 46-yard play for the final Chiefs touchdown. The Kansas City defense limited Minnesota's strong rushing game to 67 yards and had 3 interceptions and 2 fumble recoveries. The crowd of 80,562 set a Super Bowl record, as did the gross receipts of $3,817,872.69.

Minnesota (NFL)	0	0	7	0	—	7
Kansas City (AFL)	3	13	7	0	—	23

KC — FG Stenerud 48 (6:52)
KC — FG Stenerud 32 (13:20)
KC — FG Stenerud 25 (7:52)
KC — Garrett 5 run (Stenerud kick) (5:34)
Minn — Osborn 4 run (Cox kick) (4:32)
KC — Taylor 46 pass from Dawson (Stenerud kick) (1:22)

SUPER BOWL III
Orange Bowl, Miami, Florida
January 12, 1969, Attendance: 75,389
NEW YORK JETS 16, BALTIMORE 7—Jets quarterback Joe Namath "guaranteed" victory on the Thursday before the game, then went out and led the AFL to its first Super Bowl victory over a Baltimore team that had lost only once in 16 games all season. Namath, chosen the outstanding player, completed 17 of 28 passes for 206 yards and directed a steady attack that dominated the NFL champions after the Jets' defense had intercepted Colts quarterback Earl Morrall 3 times in the first half. The Jets had 337 total yards, including 121 rushing yards by Matt Snell. Johnny Unitas, who had missed most of the season with a sore elbow, came off the bench and led Baltimore to its only touchdown late in the fourth quarter after New York led 16-0.

New York Jets (AFL)	0	7	6	3	—	16
Baltimore (NFL)	0	0	0	7	—	7

NYJ — Snell 4 run (Turner kick) (9:03)
NYJ — FG Turner 32 (10:08)
NYJ — FG Turner 30 (3:58)
NYJ — FG Turner 9 (13:26)
Balt — Hill 1 run (Michaels kick) (3:19)

SUPER BOWL II
Orange Bowl, Miami, Florida
January 14, 1968, Attendance: 75,546
GREEN BAY 33, OAKLAND 14—Green Bay, after winning its third consecutive NFL championship, won the Super Bowl title for the second straight year, defeating the AFL champion Raiders in a game that drew the first $3-million gate in football history. Bart Starr again was chosen the game's most valuable player as he completed 13 of 24 passes for 202 yards and 1 touchdown and directed a Packers' attack that was in control all the way after building a 16-7 halftime lead. Don Chandler kicked 4 field goals and all-pro cornerback Herb Adderley capped the Green Bay scoring with a 60-yard interception return. The game marked the last for Vince Lombardi as Packers coach, ending nine years at Green Bay in which he won six Western Conference championships, five NFL championships, and two Super Bowls.

Green Bay (NFL)	3	13	10	7	—	33
Oakland (AFL)	0	7	0	7	—	14

GB — FG Chandler 39 (9:53)
GB — FG Chandler 20 (11:52)
GB — Dowler 62 pass from Starr (Chandler kick) (10:50)
Oak — Miller 23 pass from Lamonica (Blanda kick) (6:15)
GB — FG Chandler 43 (0:01)
GB — Anderson 2 run (Chandler kick) (5:54)
GB — FG Chandler 31 (0:02)
GB — Adderley 60 interception return (Chandler kick) (11:03)

Oak — Miller 23 pass from Lamonica (Blanda kick) (9:13)

SUPER BOWL I
Memorial Coliseum, Los Angeles, CA
January 15, 1967, Attendance: 61,946
GREEN BAY 35, KANSAS CITY 10—The Green Bay Packers opened the Super Bowl series by defeating the AFL champion Chiefs behind the passing of Bart Starr, the receiving of Max McGee, and a key interception by all-pro safety Willie Wood. Green Bay broke open the game with 3 second-half touchdowns, the first of which was set up by Wood's 50-yard return of an interception. McGee, filling in for ailing Boyd Dowler after having caught only 4 passes all season, caught 7 from Starr for 138 yards and 2 touchdowns. Elijah Pitts ran for 2 other scores. The Chiefs' 10 points came in the second quarter, the only touchdown on a 7-yard pass from Len Dawson to Curtis McClinton. Starr completed 16 of 23 passes for 250 yards and 2 touchdowns and was chosen the most valuable player. The Packers collected $15,000 per man and the Chiefs $7,500—the largest single-game shares in the history of team sports.

Kansas City (AFL)	0	10	0	0	— 10
Green Bay (NFL)	7	7	14	7	— 35

GB — McGee 37 pass from Starr (Chandler kick) (6:04)
KC — McClinton 7 pass from Dawson (Mercer kick) (10:40)
GB — Taylor 14 run (Chandler kick) (4:37)
KC — FG Mercer 31 (0:54)
GB — Pitts 5 run (Chandler kick) (12:33)
GB — McGee 13 pass from Starr (Chandler kick) (0:51)
GB — Pitts 1 run (Chandler kick) (6:35)

AFC CHAMPIONSHIP GAME RESULTS
Includes AFL Championship Games (1960-69)

Season	Date	Winner (Share)	Loser (Share)	Score	Site	Attendance
2004	Jan. 23	New England ($36,500)	Pittsburgh ($36,500)	41-27	Pittsburgh	65,242
2003	Jan. 18	New England ($36,500)	Indianapolis ($36,500)	24-14	Foxborough	68,436
2002	Jan. 19	Oakland ($35,000)	Tennessee ($35,000)	41-24	Oakland	62,544
2001	Jan. 27	New England ($34,500)	Pittsburgh ($34,500)	24-17	Pittsburgh	64,704
2000	Jan. 14	Baltimore ($34,500)	Oakland ($34,500)	16-3	Oakland	62,784
1999	Jan. 23	Tennessee ($33,000)	Jacksonville ($33,000)	33-14	Jacksonville	75,206
1998	Jan. 17	Denver ($32,500)	N.Y. Jets ($32,500)	23-10	Denver	75,482
1997	Jan. 11	Denver ($30,000)	Pittsburgh ($30,000)	24-21	Pittsburgh	61,382
1996	Jan. 12	New England ($29,000)	Jacksonville ($29,000)	20-6	Foxborough	60,190
1995	Jan. 14	Pittsburgh ($27,000)	Indianapolis ($27,000)	20-16	Pittsburgh	61,062
1994	Jan. 15	San Diego ($26,000)	Pittsburgh ($26,000)	17-13	Pittsburgh	61,545
1993	Jan. 23	Buffalo ($23,500)	Kansas City ($23,500)	30-13	Buffalo	76,642
1992	Jan. 17	Buffalo ($18,000)	Miami ($18,000)	29-10	Miami	72,703
1991	Jan. 12	Buffalo ($18,000)	Denver ($18,000)	10-7	Buffalo	80,272
1990	Jan. 20	Buffalo ($18,000)	L.A. Raiders ($18,000)	51-3	Buffalo	80,325
1989	Jan. 14	Denver ($18,000)	Cleveland ($18,000)	37-21	Denver	76,046
1988	Jan. 8	Cincinnati ($18,000)	Buffalo ($18,000)	21-10	Cincinnati	59,747
1987	Jan. 17	Denver ($18,000)	Cleveland ($18,000)	38-33	Denver	76,197
1986	Jan. 11	Denver ($18,000)	Cleveland ($18,000)	23-20*	Cleveland	79,973
1985	Jan. 12	New England ($18,000)	Miami ($18,000)	31-14	Miami	75,662
1984	Jan. 6	Miami ($18,000)	Pittsburgh ($18,000)	45-28	Miami	76,029
1983	Jan. 8	L.A. Raiders ($18,000)	Seattle ($18,000)	30-14	Los Angeles	91,445
1982	Jan. 23	Miami ($18,000)	N.Y. Jets ($18,000)	14-0	Miami	67,396
1981	Jan. 10	Cincinnati ($9,000)	San Diego ($9,000)	27-7	Cincinnati	46,302
1980	Jan. 11	Oakland ($9,000)	San Diego ($9,000)	34-27	San Diego	52,675
1979	Jan. 6	Pittsburgh ($9,000)	Houston ($9,000)	27-13	Pittsburgh	50,475
1978	Jan. 7	Pittsburgh ($9,000)	Houston ($9,000)	34-5	Pittsburgh	50,725
1977	Jan. 1	Denver ($9,000)	Oakland ($9,000)	20-17	Denver	75,044
1976	Dec. 26	Oakland ($8,500)	Pittsburgh ($5,500)	24-7	Oakland	53,821
1975	Jan. 4	Pittsburgh ($8,500)	Oakland ($5,500)	16-10	Pittsburgh	50,609
1974	Dec. 29	Pittsburgh ($8,500)	Oakland ($5,500)	24-13	Oakland	53,800
1973	Dec. 30	Miami ($8,500)	Oakland ($5,500)	27-10	Miami	79,325
1972	Dec. 31	Miami ($8,500)	Pittsburgh ($5,500)	21-17	Pittsburgh	50,845
1971	Jan. 2	Miami ($8,500)	Baltimore ($5,500)	21-0	Miami	76,622
1970	Jan. 3	Baltimore ($8,500)	Oakland ($5,500)	27-17	Baltimore	54,799
1969	Jan. 4	Kansas City ($7,755)	Oakland ($6,252)	17-7	Oakland	53,564
1968	Dec. 29	N.Y. Jets ($7,007)	Oakland ($5,349)	27-23	New York	62,627
1967	Dec. 31	Oakland ($6,321)	Houston ($4,996)	40-7	Oakland	53,330
1966	Jan. 1	Kansas City ($5,309)	Buffalo ($3,799)	31-7	Buffalo	42,080
1965	Dec. 26	Buffalo ($5,189)	San Diego ($3,447)	23-0	San Diego	30,361
1964	Dec. 26	Buffalo ($2,668)	San Diego ($1,738)	20-7	Buffalo	40,242
1963	Jan. 5	San Diego ($2,498)	Boston ($1,596)	51-10	San Diego	30,127
1962	Dec. 23	Dallas ($2,206)	Houston ($1,471)	20-17*	Houston	37,981
1961	Dec. 24	Houston ($1,792)	San Diego ($1,111)	10-3	San Diego	29,556
1960	Jan. 1	Houston ($1,025)	L.A. Chargers ($718)	24-16	Houston	32,183

Sudden death overtime

AFC CHAMPIONSHIP GAME COMPOSITE STANDINGS

	W	L	Pct.	Pts.	OP
Cincinnati Bengals	2	0	1.000	48	17
Baltimore Ravens	1	0	1.000	16	3
Denver Broncos	6	1	.857	172	132
New England Patriots**	5	1	.833	150	129
Buffalo Bills	6	2	.750	180	92
Kansas City Chiefs*	3	1	.750	81	61
Miami Dolphins	5	2	.714	152	115
Pittsburgh Steelers	5	7	.417	251	253
Tennessee Titans##	3	5	.375	133	195
Oakland Raiders###	5	9	.357	272	304
New York Jets	1	2	.333	37	60
San Diego Chargers***	2	6	.250	128	161
Indianapolis Colts#	1	3	.250	57	82
Seattle Seahawks	0	1	.000	14	30
Jacksonville Jaguars	0	2	.000	20	53
Cleveland Browns	0	3	.000	74	98

* One game played when franchise was in Dallas (Texans) (Won 20-17)

** One game played when franchise was in Boston (Lost 51-10)

*** One game played when franchise was in Los Angeles (Lost 24-16)

\# Two games played when franchise was in Baltimore (Won 27-17, lost 21-0)

\#\# Six games played when franchise was in Houston and known as Oilers (Won 2, lost 4)

\#\#\# Two games played when franchise was in Los Angeles (Won 30-14, lost 51-3)

2004 AFC CHAMPIONSHIP GAME
Heinz Field, Pittsburgh, Pennsylvania
January 23, 2005, Attendance: 65,242
NEW ENGLAND 41, PITTSBURGH 27—Tom Brady passed for 2 touchdowns and the Patriots' defense forced 4 turnovers, which resulted in 24 points, as New England advanced to its third Super

Bowl in four seasons. Eugene Wilson intercepted Ben Roethlisberger's first pass to set up Adam Vinatieri's 48-yard field goal just 3:40 into the game. On Pittsburgh's next possession, Jerome Bettis fumbled on fourth-and-1 and Mike Vrabel recovered. Brady completed a 60-yard touchdown pass to Deion Branch on the next play for a 10-0 lead. Leading 10-3 in the second quarter, Brady's 45-yard pass to Branch set up David Givens' 9-yard scoring catch with 7:08 left in the second quarter. The Steelers responded by driving to the Patriots' 19, but on second-and-6 Rodney Harrison intercepted a pass and returned it 87 yards for a touchdown and 24-3 lead with 2:14 left in the half. Trailing 31-10 and faced with fourth-and-5, Roethlisberger completed a pass to Hines Ward, who caught the ball at the 15-yard line and got a block to walk into the end zone for a 30-yard touchdown. The Steelers' defense then forced a three-and-out and the offense drove to the Patriots' 4. Bettis gained one yard on first down, and Plaxico Burress was unable to come down with an alley-oop pass on second down. Bettis gained 1 yard on third down, and faced with fourth-and-goal from the Patriots' 2, the Steelers settled for Jeff Reed's field goal to cut the deficit to 31-20. The Patriots responded with a field goal and Wilson's second interception two plays later led to Branch's 23-yard touchdown run on a reverse with 2:23 remaining for a 41-20 lead. Brady was 14 of 21 for 207 yards and 2 touchdowns. Branch had 4 receptions for 116 yards. Roethlisberger was 14 of 24 for 226 yards and 2 touchdowns, with 3 interceptions. Ward had 5 catches for 109 yards.

New England (41)	Offense	Pittsburgh (27)
Christian Fauria	TE-WR	Plaxico Burress
Matt Light	LT	Marvel Smith
Joe Andruzzi	LG	Alan Faneca
Dan Koppen	C	Jeff Hartings
Stephen Neal	RG	Keydrick Vincent
Brandon Gorin	RT	Oliver Ross
Daniel Graham	TE	Jerame Tuman
Deion Branch	WR	Hines Ward
Tom Brady	QB	Ben Roethlisberger
Corey Dillon	RB	Jerome Bettis
Russ Hochstein	TE-FB	Dan Kreider
	Defense	
Ty Warren	LE	Aaron Smith
Keith Traylor	LT-NT	Chris Hoke
Jarvis Green	RT-RE	Kimo von Oelhoffen
Mike Vrabel	RE-OLB	Clark Haggans
Tedy Bruschi	LLB-ILB	James Farrior
Ted Johnson	MLB-ILB	Larry Foote
Willie McGinest	RLB-OLB	Joey Porter
Randall Gay	LCB	Willie Williams
Asante Samuel	RCB	Deshea Townsend
Rodney Harrison	SS	Troy Polamalu
Eugene Wilson	FS	Chris Hope

SUBSTITUTIONS
New England—Specialists: K—Adam Vinatieri. P—Josh Miller. LS—Lonie Paxton. Offense: FB—Patrick Pass. RB—Rahib Abdullah, Kevin Faulk. WR—Troy Brown, David Givens, Bethel Johnson, David Patten. G-C—Gene Mruzkowski. Defense: DT-DE—Vince Wilfork. LB—Tully Banta-Cain, Matt Chatham, Rosevelt Colvin, Don Davis, Larry Izzo, Roman Phifer. CB—Hank Poteat. S—Je'Rod Cherry, Dexter Reid. DNP: QB—Rohan Davey. DT—Ethan Kelley.
Pittsburgh—Specialists: K—Jeff Reed. P—Chris Gardocki. LS—Mike Schneck. Defense: RB—Verron Haynes, Duce Staley. WR—Lee Mays, Sean Morey, Antwaan Randle El. TE—Mike Cushing, Walter Rasby. T—Max Starks. C-G—Chukky Okobi. Defense: DT—Travis Kirschke. DE—Brett Keisel. NT—Kendrick Clancy. LB—James Harrison, Clint Kriewaldt. CB—Ricardo Colclough, Chad Scott, Ike Taylor. S—Tyrone Carter, Russell Stuvaints. DNP: QB—Tommy Maddox.

OFFICIALS
Referee—Walt Anderson. Umpire—Butch Hannah. Line Judge—Gary Arthur. Side Judge—Carl Cheffers. Head Linesman—Ron Marinucci. Back Judge—Billy Smith. Field Judge—Bill Lovett.

SCORING

New England	10	14	7	10	—	41
Pittsburgh	3	0	14	10	—	27

NE — FG Vinatieri 48
NE — Branch 60 pass from Brady (Vinatieri kick)
Pitt — FG Reed 43
NE — Givens 9 pass from Brady (Vinatieri kick)
NE — Harrison 87 interception return (Vinatieri kick)
Pitt — Bettis 5 run (Reed kick)
NE — Dillon 25 run (Vinatieri kick)
Pitt — Ward 30 pass from Roethlisberger (Reed kick)
Pitt — FG Reed 20
NE — FG Vinatieri 31
NE — Branch 23 run (Vinatieri kick)
Pitt — Burress 7 pass from Roethlisberger (Reed kick)

TEAM STATISTICS	NE	PITT
Total First Downs	18	19
Rushing	7	8
Passing	9	11
Penalty	2	0
Total Net Yardage	322	388
Total Offensive Plays	55	62
Average Gain Per Offensive Play	5.9	6.3
Rushes	32	37
Yards Gained Rushing (Net)	126	163
Average Yards per Rush	3.9	4.4
Passes Attempted	21	24
Passes Completed	14	14
Had Intercepted	0	3
Tackled Attempting to Pass	2	1
Yards Lost Attempting to Pass	11	1
Yards Gained Passing (Net)	196	225
Punts	4	3
Average Distance	40.3	43.0
Punt Returns	2	3
Punt Return Yardage	6	40
Kickoff Returns	5	8
Kickoff Return Yardage	107	115
Interception Return Yardage	87	0
Total Return Yardage	200	155
Fumbles	1	2
Fumbles Lost	0	1
Own Fumbles Recovered	1	1
Opponent Fumbles Recovered	1	0
Penalties	1	2
Yards Penalized	5	20
Field Goals	2	2
Field Goals Attempted	2	2
Third-Down Efficiency	5/12	4/12
Fourth-Down Efficiency	1/1	1/2
Time of Possession	28:29	31:31

INDIVIDUAL STATISTICS
RUSHING: NE: Dillon 24-73-1, Branch 2-37-1, Faulk 3-20-0, Brady 2-(-2)-0, Givens 1-(-2)-0. PITT: Bettis 17-64-1, Roethlisberger 5-45-0, Haynes 5-28-0, Staley 10-26-0.
PASSING: NE: Brady 21-14-207-2-0. PITT: Roethlisberger 24-14-226-2-3.
RECEIVING: NE: Givens 5-59-1, Branch 4-116-1, Brown 1-11-0, Fauria 1-9-0, Patten 1-8-0, Dillon 1-5-0, Graham 1-(-1)-0. PITT: Ward 5-109-1, Randle El 3-52-0, Burress 3-37-1, Haynes 1-14-0, Tuman 1-8-0, Rasby 1-6-0.
KICKOFF RETURNS: NE: B. Johnson 4-90-0, Pass 1-17-0. PITT: Randle El 4-75-0, Taylor 3-29-0, Cushing 1-11-0.
PUNT RETURNS: NE: Brown 2-6-0. PITT: Randle El 3-40-0.
PUNTING: NE: Miller 4-161-40.3. PITT: Gardocki 3-129-43.0.
INTERCEPTIONS: NE: Wilson 2-0-0, Harrison 1-87-1. PITT: None.
SACKS: NE: Green. PITT: Haggans, Porter.

NFC CHAMPIONSHIP GAME RESULTS
Includes NFL Championship Games (1933-1969)

Season	Date	Winner (Share)	Loser (Share)	Score	Site	Attendance
2004	Jan. 23	Philadelphia ($36,500)	Atlanta ($36,500)	27-10	Philadelphia	67,717
2003	Jan. 18	Carolina ($36,500)	Philadelphia ($36,500)	14-3	Philadelphia	67,862
2002	Jan. 19	Tampa Bay ($35,000)	Philadelphia ($35,000)	27-10	Philadelphia	66,713
2001	Jan. 27	St. Louis ($34,500)	Philadelphia ($34,500)	29-24	St. Louis	66,502
2000	Jan. 14	N.Y. Giants ($34,500)	Minnesota ($34,500)	41-0	East Rutherford	79,310
1999	Jan. 23	St. Louis ($33,000)	Tampa Bay ($33,000)	11-6	St. Louis	66,396
1998	Jan. 17	Atlanta ($32,500)	Minnesota ($32,500)	30-27*	Minneapolis	64,060
1997	Jan. 11	Green Bay ($30,000)	San Francisco ($30,000)	23-10	San Francisco	68,987
1996	Jan. 12	Green Bay ($29,000)	Carolina ($29,000)	30-13	Green Bay	60,216
1995	Jan. 14	Dallas ($27,000)	Green Bay ($27,000)	38-27	Dallas	65,135
1994	Jan. 15	San Francisco ($26,000)	Dallas ($26,000)	38-28	San Francisco	69,125
1993	Jan. 23	Dallas ($23,500)	San Francisco ($23,500)	38-21	Dallas	64,902
1992	Jan. 17	Dallas ($18,000)	San Francisco ($18,000)	30-20	San Francisco	64,920
1991	Jan. 12	Washington ($18,000)	Detroit ($18,000)	41-10	Washington	55,585
1990	Jan. 20	N.Y. Giants ($18,000)	San Francisco ($18,000)	15-13	San Francisco	65,750
1989	Jan. 14	San Francisco ($18,000)	L.A. Rams ($18,000)	30-3	San Francisco	65,634
1988	Jan. 8	San Francisco ($18,000)	Chicago ($18,000)	28-3	Chicago	66,946
1987	Jan. 17	Washington ($18,000)	Minnesota ($18,000)	17-10	Washington	55,212
1986	Jan. 11	New York Giants ($18,000)	Washington ($18,000)	17-0	East Rutherford	76,891
1985	Jan. 12	Chicago ($18,000)	L.A. Rams ($18,000)	24-0	Chicago	66,030
1984	Jan. 6	San Francisco ($18,000)	Chicago ($18,000)	23-0	San Francisco	61,336
1983	Jan. 8	Washington ($18,000)	San Francisco ($18,000)	24-21	Washington	55,363
1982	Jan. 22	Washington ($18,000)	Dallas ($18,000)	31-17	Washington	55,045
1981	Jan. 10	San Francisco ($9,000)	Dallas ($9,000)	28-27	San Francisco	60,525
1980	Jan. 11	Philadelphia ($9,000)	Dallas ($9,000)	20-7	Philadelphia	71,522
1979	Jan. 6	Los Angeles ($9,000)	Tampa Bay ($9,000)	9-0	Tampa	72,033
1978	Jan. 7	Dallas ($9,000)	Los Angeles ($9,000)	28-0	Los Angeles	71,086
1977	Jan. 1	Dallas ($9,000)	Minnesota ($9,000)	23-6	Dallas	64,293
1976	Dec. 26	Minnesota ($8,500)	Los Angeles ($5,500)	24-13	Minneapolis	48,379
1975	Jan. 4	Dallas ($8,500)	Los Angeles ($5,500)	37-7	Los Angeles	88,919
1974	Dec. 29	Minnesota ($8,500)	Los Angeles ($5,500)	14-10	Minneapolis	48,444
1973	Dec. 30	Minnesota ($8,500)	Dallas ($5,500)	27-10	Dallas	64,422
1972	Dec. 31	Washington ($8,500)	Dallas ($5,500)	26-3	Washington	53,129
1971	Jan. 2	Dallas ($8,500)	San Francisco ($5,500)	14-3	Dallas	63,409
1970	Jan. 3	Dallas ($8,500)	San Francisco ($5,500)	17-10	San Francisco	59,364
1969	Jan. 4	Minnesota ($7,930)	Cleveland ($5,118)	27-7	Minneapolis	46,503
1968	Dec. 29	Baltimore ($9,306)	Cleveland ($5,963)	34-0	Cleveland	78,410
1967	Dec. 31	Green Bay ($7,950)	Dallas ($5,299)	21-17	Green Bay	50,861
1966	Jan. 1	Green Bay ($9,813)	Dallas ($6,527)	34-27	Dallas	74,152
1965	Jan. 2	Green Bay ($7,819)	Cleveland ($5,288)	23-12	Green Bay	50,777
1964	Dec. 27	Cleveland ($8,052)	Baltimore ($5,571)	27-0	Cleveland	79,544
1963	Dec. 29	Chicago ($5,899)	New York ($4,218)	14-10	Chicago	45,801
1962	Dec. 30	Green Bay ($5,888)	New York ($4,166)	16-7	New York	64,892
1961	Dec. 31	Green Bay ($5,195)	New York ($3,339)	37-0	Green Bay	39,029
1960	Dec. 26	Philadelphia ($5,116)	Green Bay ($3,105)	17-13	Philadelphia	67,325
1959	Dec. 27	Baltimore ($4,674)	New York ($3,083)	31-16	Baltimore	57,545
1958	Dec. 28	Baltimore ($4,718)	New York ($3,111)	23-17*	New York	64,185
1957	Dec. 29	Detroit ($4,295)	Cleveland ($2,750)	59-14	Detroit	55,263
1956	Dec. 30	New York ($3,779)	Chi. Bears ($2,485)	47-7	New York	56,836
1955	Dec. 26	Cleveland ($3,508)	Los Angeles ($2,316)	38-14	Los Angeles	85,693
1954	Dec. 26	Cleveland ($2,478)	Detroit ($1,585)	56-10	Cleveland	43,827
1953	Dec. 27	Detroit ($2,424)	Cleveland ($1,654)	17-16	Detroit	54,577
1952	Dec. 28	Detroit ($2,274)	Cleveland ($1,712)	17-7	Cleveland	50,934
1951	Dec. 23	Los Angeles ($2,108)	Cleveland ($1,483)	24-17	Los Angeles	57,522
1950	Dec. 24	Cleveland ($1,113)	Los Angeles ($686)	30-28	Cleveland	29,751
1949	Dec. 18	Philadelphia ($1,094)	Los Angeles ($739)	14-0	Los Angeles	27,980
1948	Dec. 19	Philadelphia ($1,540)	Chi. Cardinals ($874)	7-0	Philadelphia	36,309
1947	Dec. 28	Chi. Cardinals ($1,132)	Philadelphia ($754)	28-21	Chicago	30,759
1946	Dec. 15	Chi. Bears ($1,975)	New York ($1,295)	24-14	New York	58,346
1945	Dec. 16	Cleveland ($1,469)	Washington ($902)	15-14	Cleveland	32,178
1944	Dec. 17	Green Bay ($1,449)	New York ($814)	14-7	New York	46,016
1943	Dec. 26	Chi. Bears ($1,146)	Washington ($765)	41-21	Chicago	34,320
1942	Dec. 13	Washington ($965)	Chi. Bears ($637)	14-6	Washington	36,006
1941	Dec. 21	Chi. Bears ($430)	New York ($288)	37-9	Chicago	13,341
1940	Dec. 8	Chi. Bears ($873)	Washington ($606)	73-0	Washington	36,034

Season	Date	Winner (Share)	Loser (Share)	Score	Site	Attendance
1939	Dec. 10	Green Bay ($703.97)	New York ($455.57)	27-0	Milwaukee	32,279
1938	Dec. 11	New York ($504.45)	Green Bay ($368.81)	23-17	New York	48,120
1937	Dec. 12	Washington ($225.90)	Chi. Bears ($127.78)	28-21	Chicago	15,870
1936	Dec. 13	Green Bay ($250)	Boston ($180)	21-6	New York	29,545
1935	Dec. 15	Detroit ($313.35)	New York ($200.20)	26-7	Detroit	15,000
1934	Dec. 9	New York ($621)	Chi. Bears ($414.02)	30-13	New York	35,059
1933	Dec. 17	Chi. Bears ($210.34)	New York ($140.22)	23-21	Chicago	26,000

*Sudden death overtime

NFC CHAMPIONSHIP GAME COMPOSITE STANDINGS

	W	L	Pct.	Pts.	OP
Green Bay Packers	10	3	.769	303	177
Baltimore Colts	3	1	.750	88	60
Detroit Lions	4	2	.667	139	141
Washington Redskins*	7	5	.583	222	255
Philadelphia Eagles	5	4	.556	143	128
Chicago Bears	7	6	.538	286	245
Dallas Cowboys	8	8	.500	361	319
Minnesota Vikings	4	4	.500	135	151
Arizona Cardinals**	1	1	.500	28	28
Atlanta Falcons	1	1	.500	40	54
Carolina Panthers	1	1	.500	27	33
San Francisco 49ers	5	7	.417	245	222
Cleveland Browns	4	7	.364	224	253
St. Louis Rams***	5	9	.357	163	300
New York Giants	6	11	.353	281	322
Tampa Bay Buccaneers	1	2	.333	33	30

*One game played when franchise was in Boston (Lost 21-6)
**Both games played when franchise was in Chicago (Won 28-21, lost 7-0)
***One game played when franchise was in Cleveland (Won 15-14), and 11 games when franchise was in Los Angeles (Won 2, lost 9, scored 108 points, allowed 256 points).

2004 NFC CHAMPIONSHIP GAME

Lincoln Financial Field, Philadelphia, Pennsylvania
January 23, 2005, Attendance: 67,717

PHILADELPHIA 27, ATLANTA 10—Donovan McNabb completed 2 touchdown passes as the Eagles reached their first Super Bowl since Super Bowl XV after the 1980 season. The Eagles, who had lost the previous three NFC Championship Games, allowed just 202 yards in a game played in a wind chill between 0 and -5 degrees. The Eagles had the wind in the first quarter, but used a 36-yard run by Brian Westbrook to set up Dorsey Levens' touchdown run. The Falcons responded with a 17-play drive, but after reaching the 2-yard line, the Falcons had to settle for a field goal after Hollis Thomas sacked Michael Vick on third-and-goal from the Eagles' 3. The Eagles drove into the 35-mile-per-hour wind and drove 72 yards, keyed by Freddie Mitchell's 13-yard reception on third-and-11 near midfield, and Greg Lewis' 45-yard catch that led to Chad Lewis' 3-yard scoring grab. Atlanta needed just five plays late in the half to pull within 14-10 on Warrick Dunn's 10-yard run. The Eagles added a field goal to begin the second half, and Brian Dawkins' interception and 19-yard return to the Falcons' 11 led to David Akers' second field goal and a 20-10 lead. The Falcons were unable to take advantage of the wind in the fourth quarter, failing to drive beyond the Eagles' 37 in three possessions. Philadelphia extended the lead on an 11-play, 65-yard drive that culminated with Chad Lewis' 2-yard catch with 3:21 remaining. McNabb was 17 of 26 for 180 yards and 2 touchdowns. Vick was 11 of 24 for 136 yards, with 1 interception.

Atlanta (10)	Offense	Philadelphia (27)
Dez White	WR	Todd Pinkston
Kevin Shaffer	LT	Tra Thomas
Roberto Garza	LG	Artis Hicks
Todd McClure	C	Hank Fraley
Kynan Forney	RG	Jermane Mayberry
Todd Weiner	RT	Jon Runyan
Alge Crumpler	TE	Chad Lewis
Peerless Price	WR	Freddie Mitchell
Michael Vick	QB	Donovan McNabb
Eric Beverly	TE-FB	Josh Parry
Warrick Dunn	RB	Brian Westbrook
Defense		
Brady Smith	LE	Jevon Kearse
Ed Jasper	LT	Corey Simon
Rod Coleman	RT	Darwin Walker
Patrick Kerney	RE	Derrick Burgess
Keith Brooking	OLB-WLB	Keith Adams
Chris Draft	MLB	Jeremiah Trotter
Matt Stewart	OLB-SLB	Dhani Jones
Jason Webster	LCB	Lito Sheppard
DeAngelo Hall	RCB	Sheldon Brown
Bryan Scott	SS	Michael Lewis
Cory Hall	FS	Brian Dawkins

SUBSTITUTIONS

Atlanta—Specialists: K—Jay Feely. P—Chris Mohr. Offense: QB—Matt Schaub. FB—Carey Davis, Fred McCrary. RB—T.J. Duckett. WR—Brian Finneran, Michael Jenkins. TE—Dwayne Blakley, Derek Rackley. G—Steve Herndon. C—Austin King. Defense: DT—Chad Lavalais. DE—Antwan Lake, Khaleed Vaughn. LB—Eric Johnson, Artie Ulmer, Demorrio Williams. CB—Aaron Beasley, Christian Morton, Allen Rossum. S—Kevin McCadam, Siddeeq Shabazz.

Philadelphia—Specialists: K—David Akers. P—Dirk Johnson. Offense: QB—Koy Detmer. RB—Dorsey Levens, Reno Mahe. WR—Greg Lewis, Billy McMullen. TE—Mike Bartrum, L.J. Smith. C—Alonzo Ephraim, G—Steve Sciullo. Defense: DT—Sam Rayburn, Hollis Thomas. DE—Jerome McDougle. LB—Hugh Douglas, Mike Labinjo, Ike Reese, Nate Wayne. CB—Roderick Hood, Matt Ware, Dexter Wynn. S—Quintin Mikell, J.R. Reed.

OFFICIALS

Referee—Bill Carollo. Umpire—Jim Quirk. Line Judge—Byron Boston. Side Judge—John Parry. Head Linesman—Tony Veteri. Back Judge—Steve Freeman. Field Judge—Doug Rosenbaum.

SCORING

Atlanta	0	10	0	0	—	10
Philadelphia	7	7	6	7	—	27

Phil — Levens 4 run (Akers kick)
Atl — FG Feely 23
Phil — C. Lewis 3 pass from McNabb (Akers kick)
Atl — Dunn 10 run (Feely kick)
Phil — FG Akers 31
Phil — FG Akers 34
Phil — C. Lewis 2 pass from McNabb (Akers kick)

TEAM STATISTICS	ATL	PHIL
Total First Downs	14	22
Rushing	7	9
Passing	4	9
Penalty	3	4
Total Net Yardage	202	326
Total Offensive Plays	54	62
Average Gain Per Offensive Play	3.7	5.3
Rushes	26	33
Yards Gained Rushing (Net)	99	156
Average Yards per Rush	3.8	4.7
Passes Attempted	24	27
Passes Completed	11	18
Had Intercepted	1	0
Tackled Attempting to Pass	4	2
Yards Lost Attempting to Pass	33	13
Yards Gained Passing (Net)	103	170
Punts	5	3
Average Distance	26.0	38.3
Punt Returns	2	1
Punt Return Yardage	20	(-4)
Kickoff Returns	5	3
Kickoff Return Yardage	117	54
Interception Return Yardage	0	19
Total Return Yardage	137	69
Fumbles	1	2
Fumbles Lost	0	0
Own Fumbles Recovered	1	2
Opponent Fumbles Recovered	0	0
Penalties	5	6
Yards Penalized	24	59
Field Goals	1	2
Field Goals Attempted	1	2
Third-Down Efficiency	2/11	7/14
Fourth-Down Efficiency	2/3	0/1
Time of Possession	26:45	33:15

INDIVIDUAL STATISTICS

RUSHING: ATL: Dunn 15-59-1, Vick 4-26-0, Duckett 7-14-0. PHIL: Westbrook 16-96-0, McNabb 10-32-0, Levens 6-18-1, G. Lewis 1-10-0.

PASSING: ATL: Vick 24-11-136-0-1. PHIL: McNabb 26-17-180-2-0, Detmer 1-1-3-0-0.

RECEIVING: ATL: Crumpler 4-49-0, Price 2-37-0, Finneran 1-29-0, Jenkins 1-7-0, White 1-7-0, Dunn 1-4-0, McCrary 1-3-0. PHIL: Westbrook 5-39-0, C. Lewis 4-20-2, G. Lewis 2-65-0, Mitchell 2-20-0, Levens 2-2-0, Smith 1-21-0, Pinkston 1-13-0, Parry 1-3-0.

KICKOFF RETURNS: ATL: Rossum 4-102-0, Hall 1-15-0. PHIL: Hood 2-33-0, Reed 1-21-0.

PUNT RETURNS: ATL: Rossum 2-20-0. PHIL: Mahe 1-(-4)-0.

PUNTING: ATL: Mohr 5-130-26.0. PHIL: Johnson 3-115-38.3.

INTERCEPTIONS: ATL: None. PHIL: Dawkins 1-19-0.

SACKS: ATL: Kerney, B. Smith. PHIL: Burgess 2.0, Kearse, Thomas.

AFC DIVISIONAL PLAYOFFS RESULTS

Includes Second-Round Playoff Games (1982), AFC Inter-Divisional Games (1969), and special playoff games to break ties for AFL Division Championships (1963, 1968)

Season	Date	Winner (Share)	Loser (Share)	Score	Site	Attendance
2004	Jan. 16	New England ($18,000)	Indianapolis ($18,000)	20-3	Foxborough	68,756
	Jan. 15	Pittsburgh ($18,000)	N.Y. Jets ($18,000)	20-17*	Pittsburgh	64,915
2003	Jan. 11	Indianapolis ($18,000)	Kansas City ($18,000)	38-31	Kansas City	79,159
	Jan. 10	New England ($18,000)	Tennessee ($18,000)	17-14	Foxborough	68,436
2002	Jan. 12	Oakland ($17,000)	N.Y. Jets ($17,000)	30-10	Oakland	62,207
	Jan. 11	Tennessee ($17,000)	Pittsburgh ($17,000)	34-31*	Nashville	68,809
2001	Jan. 20	Pittsburgh ($17,000)	Baltimore ($17,000)	27-10	Pittsburgh	63,976
	Jan. 19	New England ($17,000)	Oakland ($17,000)	16-13*	Foxborough	60,292
2000	Jan. 7	Baltimore ($16,000)	Tennessee ($16,000)	24-10	Nashville	68,527
	Jan. 6	Oakland ($16,000)	Miami ($16,000)	27-0	Oakland	61,998
1999	Jan. 16	Tennessee ($16,000)	Indianapolis ($16,000)	19-16	Indianapolis	57,097
	Jan. 15	Jacksonville ($16,000)	Miami ($16,000)	62-7	Jacksonville	75,173
1998	Jan. 10	N.Y. Jets ($15,000)	Jacksonville ($15,000)	34-24	East Rutherford	78,817
	Jan. 9	Denver ($15,000)	Miami ($15,000)	38-3	Denver	75,729
1997	Jan. 4	Denver ($15,000)	Kansas City ($15,000)	14-10	Kansas City	76,965
	Jan. 3	Pittsburgh ($15,000)	New England ($15,000)	7-6	Pittsburgh	61,228
1996	Jan. 5	New England ($14,000)	Pittsburgh ($14,000)	28-3	Foxborough	60,188
	Jan. 4	Jacksonville ($14,000)	Denver ($14,000)	30-27	Denver	75,678
1995	Jan. 7	Indianapolis ($13,000)	Kansas City ($13,000)	10-7	Kansas City	77,594
	Jan. 6	Pittsburgh ($13,000)	Buffalo ($13,000)	40-21	Pittsburgh	59,072
1994	Jan. 8	San Diego ($12,000)	Miami ($12,000)	22-21	San Diego	63,381
	Jan. 7	Pittsburgh ($12,000)	Cleveland ($12,000)	29-9	Pittsburgh	58,185
1993	Jan. 16	Kansas City ($12,000)	Houston ($12,000)	28-20	Houston	64,011
	Jan. 15	Buffalo ($12,000)	L.A. Raiders ($12,000)	29-23	Buffalo	61,923
1992	Jan. 10	Miami ($10,000)	San Diego ($10,000)	31-0	Miami	71,224
	Jan. 9	Buffalo ($10,000)	Pittsburgh ($10,000)	24-3	Pittsburgh	60,407
1991	Jan. 5	Buffalo ($10,000)	Kansas City ($10,000)	37-14	Buffalo	80,182
	Jan. 4	Denver ($10,000)	Houston ($10,000)	26-24	Denver	75,301
1990	Jan. 13	L.A. Raiders ($10,000)	Cincinnati ($10,000)	20-10	Los Angeles	92,045
	Jan. 12	Buffalo ($10,000)	Miami ($10,000)	44-34	Buffalo	77,087
1989	Jan. 7	Denver ($10,000)	Pittsburgh ($10,000)	24-23	Denver	75,477
	Jan. 6	Cleveland ($10,000)	Buffalo ($10,000)	34-30	Cleveland	78,921
1988	Jan. 1	Buffalo ($10,000)	Houston ($10,000)	17-10	Buffalo	79,532
	Dec. 31	Cincinnati ($10,000)	Seattle ($10,000)	21-13	Cincinnati	58,560

Season	Date	Winner (Share)	Loser (Share)	Score	Site	Attendance
1987	Jan. 10	Denver ($10,000)	Houston ($10,000)	34-10	Denver	75,440
	Jan. 9	Cleveland ($10,000)	Indianapolis ($10,000)	38-21	Cleveland	79,372
1986	Jan. 4	Denver ($10,000)	New England ($10,000)	22-17	Denver	75,262
	Jan. 3	Cleveland ($10,000)	N.Y. Jets ($10,000)	23-20*	Cleveland	79,720
1985	Jan. 5	New England ($10,000)	L.A. Raiders ($10,000)	27-20	Los Angeles	87,163
	Jan. 4	Miami ($10,000)	Cleveland ($10,000)	24-21	Miami	74,667
1984	Dec. 30	Pittsburgh ($10,000)	Denver ($10,000)	24-17	Denver	74,981
	Dec. 29	Miami ($10,000)	Seattle ($10,000)	31-10	Miami	73,469
1983	Jan. 1	L.A. Raiders ($10,000)	Pittsburgh ($10,000)	38-10	Los Angeles	90,380
	Dec. 31	Seattle ($10,000)	Miami ($10,000)	27-20	Miami	74,136
1982	Jan. 16	Miami ($10,000)	San Diego ($10,000)	34-13	Miami	71,383
	Jan. 15	N.Y. Jets ($10,000)	L.A. Raiders ($10,000)	17-14	Los Angeles	90,038
1981	Jan. 3	Cincinnati ($5,000)	Buffalo ($5,000)	28-21	Cincinnati	55,420
	Jan. 2	San Diego ($5,000)	Miami ($5,000)	41-38*	Miami	73,735
1980	Jan. 4	Oakland ($5,000)	Cleveland ($5,000)	14-12	Cleveland	78,245
	Jan. 3	San Diego ($5,000)	Buffalo ($5,000)	20-14	San Diego	52,253
1979	Dec. 30	Pittsburgh ($5,000)	Miami ($5,000)	34-14	Pittsburgh	50,214
	Dec. 29	Houston ($5,000)	San Diego ($5,000)	17-14	San Diego	51,192
1978	Dec. 31	Houston ($5,000)	New England ($5,000)	31-14	Foxborough	60,735
	Dec. 30	Pittsburgh ($5,000)	Denver ($5,000)	33-10	Pittsburgh	50,230
1977	Dec. 24	Oakland ($5,000)	Baltimore ($5,000)	37-31*	Baltimore	59,925
	Dec. 24	Denver ($5,000)	Pittsburgh ($5,000)	34-21	Denver	75,059
1976	Dec. 19	Pittsburgh [$]	Baltimore [$]	40-14	Baltimore	59,296
	Dec. 18	Oakland [$]	New England [$]	24-21	Oakland	53,050
1975	Dec. 28	Oakland [$]	Cincinnati [$]	31-28	Oakland	53,030
	Dec. 27	Pittsburgh [$]	Baltimore [$]	28-10	Pittsburgh	49,557
1974	Dec. 22	Pittsburgh [$]	Buffalo [$]	32-14	Pittsburgh	49,841
	Dec. 21	Oakland [$]	Miami [$]	28-26	Oakland	53,023
1973	Dec. 23	Miami [$]	Cincinnati [$]	34-16	Miami	78,928
	Dec. 22	Oakland [$]	Pittsburgh [$]	33-14	Oakland	52,646
1972	Dec. 24	Miami [$]	Cleveland [$]	20-14	Miami	78,916
	Dec. 23	Pittsburgh [$]	Oakland [$]	13-7	Pittsburgh	50,327
1971	Dec. 26	Baltimore [$]	Cleveland [$]	20-3	Cleveland	70,734
	Dec. 25	Miami [$]	Kansas City [$]	27-24*	Kansas City	50,374
1970	Dec. 27	Oakland [$]	Miami [$]	21-14	Oakland	52,594
	Dec. 26	Baltimore [$]	Cincinnati [$]	17-0	Baltimore	49,694
1969	Dec. 21	Oakland [$]	Houston [$]	56-7	Oakland	53,539
	Dec. 20	Kansas City [$]	N.Y. Jets [$]	13-6	New York	62,977
1968	Dec. 22	Oakland [$]	Kansas City [$]	41-6	Oakland	53,605
1963	Dec. 28	Boston [$]	Buffalo [$]	26-8	Buffalo	33,044

*Sudden death overtime
$ Players received 1/14 of annual salary for playoff appearances.

2004 AFC DIVISIONAL PLAYOFF GAMES

Gillette Stadium, Foxborough, Massachusetts
January 16, 2005, Attendance: 68,756
NEW ENGLAND 20, INDIANAPOLIS 3—The Patriots' defense permitted just 276 yards and forced 3 turnovers as New England held the NFL's highest-scoring offense without a touchdown in a game played in sleet and a 16-degree wind chill. The Patriots held possession for 37:43, including 21:26 in the second half. The Colts had just 2 first downs when Adam Vinatieri's second second-quarter field goal gave the Patriots a 6-0 lead. The Colts drove 67 yards in the final 1:52 of the half. With two seconds remaining, Eugene Wilson knocked down Peyton Manning's pass in the end zone for an incompletion, forcing the Colts to settle for Mike Vanderjagt's 23-yard field goal. After an exchange of punts to begin the second half, the Patriots used 8:16 to drive 87 yards in 15 plays, on the ground, and capped by David Givens' 5-yard touchdown catch for a 13-3 lead with 1:30 left in the third quarter. Five plays later, the Colts punted and the Patriots drove 94 yards in 14 plays, with 7:50 elapsing off the clock. Corey Dillon's 27-yard run to the Patriots' 1 set up Tom Brady's 1-yard sneak for a 20-3 lead with 7:10 to play. Rodney Harrison intercepted Manning's pass in the end zone with four seconds left to preserve the 17-point margin of victory. Brady was 18 of 27 for 144 yards and 1 touchdown. Dillon rushed 23 times for 144 yards. Manning was 27 of 42 for 238 yards, with 1 interception.

Indianapolis	0	3	0	0	—	3
New England	0	6	7	7	—	20

NE — FG Vinatieri 24
NE — FG Vinatieri 31
Ind — FG Vanderjagt 23
NE — Givens 5 pass from Brady (Vinatieri kick)
NE — Brady 1 run (Vinatieri kick)

Heinz Field, Pittsburgh, Pennsylvania
January 15, 2005, Attendance: 64,915
PITTSBURGH 20, N.Y. JETS 17 (OT)—Jeff Reed kicked a 33-yard field goal in overtime as the Steelers survived two missed field goals by the Jets in regulation to advance to the fifth AFC Championship Game in Bill Cowher's thirteen-year tenure. Two plays after Reed's 45-yard first-quarter field goal, Troy Polamalu intercepted Chad Pennington's pass and returned it 14 yards to the Jets' 25. Jerome Bettis scored five plays later for a 10-0 lead. Trailing 10-3, Santana Moss fielded a punt and returned it 75 yards down the left sideline for a touchdown with 3:00 left in the half to tie the game. The Steelers drove to the Jets' 33 late in the third quarter when Reggie Tongue intercepted Ben Roethlisberg-

er's pass and returned it 86 yards for a touchdown and 17-10 lead. The Steelers drove to the Jets' 22, but Bettis fumbled and Erik Coleman recovered. The Steelers forced a three-and-out, and the offense converted 3 third-down situations, including 2 passes by Roethlisberger, to set up his 4-yard touchdown pass to Hines Ward to tie the game with 6:00 left. The Jets drove to the Steelers' 28 with 1:58 left, but Doug Brien's 47-yard field goal hit the upright. On the next play, David Barrett intercepted Roethlisberger's pass at the Steelers' 37, but Brien's 43-yard field-goal attempt went wide left as time expired. In overtime, the Jets won the toss but were forced to punt. Roethlisberger completed a 17-yard pass to Ward on third-and-6, and Verron Haynes gained 8 yards on third-and-4 to keep the drive alive and set up Reed's winning kick 11:04 into overtime. Roethlisberger was 17 of 30

for 181 yards and 1 touchdown, with 2 interceptions, and became just the fourth rookie since 1970 to win his first post-season start. Bettis rushed 27 times for 101 yards, and Ward added 10 catches for 105 yards. Pennington was 21 of 33 for 182 yards, with 1 interception.

N.Y. Jets	0	10	7	0	0	—	17
Pittsburgh	10	0	0	7	3	—	20

Pitt — FG Reed 45
Pitt — Bettis 3 run (Reed kick)
NYJ — FG Brien 42
NYJ — Moss 75 punt return (Brien kick)
NYJ — Tongue 86 interception return (Brien kick)
Pitt — Ward 4 pass from Roethlisberger (Reed kick)
Pitt — FG Reed 33

NFC DIVISIONAL PLAYOFFS RESULTS

Includes Second-Round Playoff Games (1982), NFL Conference Championship Games (1967-69), and special playoff games to break ties for NFL Division or Conference Championships (1941, 1943, 1947, 1950, 1952, 1957, 1958, 1965).

Season	Date	Winner (Share)	Loser (Share)	Score	Site	Attendance
2004	Jan. 16	Philadelphia ($18,000)	Minnesota ($18,000)	27-14	Philadelphia	67,722
	Jan. 15	Atlanta ($18,000)	St. Louis ($18,000)	47-17	Atlanta	70,709
2003	Jan. 11	Philadelphia ($18,000)	Green Bay ($18,000)	20-17*	Philadelphia	67,707
	Jan. 10	Carolina ($18,000)	St. Louis ($18,000)	29-23*	St. Louis	66,165
2002	Jan. 12	Tampa Bay ($17,000)	San Francisco ($17,000)	31-6	Tampa	65,599
	Jan. 11	Philadelphia ($17,000)	Atlanta ($17,000)	20-6	Philadelphia	66,452
2001	Jan. 20	St. Louis ($17,000)	Green Bay ($17,000)	45-17	St. Louis	66,338
	Jan. 19	Philadelphia ($17,000)	Chicago ($17,000)	33-19	Chicago	66,944
2000	Jan. 7	N.Y. Giants ($16,000)	Philadelphia ($16,000)	20-10	East Rutherford	78,765
	Jan. 6	Minnesota ($16,000)	New Orleans ($16,000)	34-16	Minneapolis	63,881
1999	Jan. 16	St. Louis ($16,000)	Minnesota ($16,000)	49-37	St. Louis	66,194
	Jan. 15	Tampa Bay ($16,000)	Washington ($16,000)	14-13	Tampa	65,835
1998	Jan. 10	Minnesota ($15,000)	Arizona ($15,000)	41-21	Minneapolis	63,760
	Jan. 9	Atlanta ($15,000)	San Francisco ($15,000)	20-18	Atlanta	70,262
1997	Jan. 4	Green Bay ($15,000)	Tampa Bay ($15,000)	21-7	Green Bay	60,327
	Jan. 3	San Francisco ($15,000)	Minnesota ($15,000)	38-22	San Francisco	65,018
1996	Jan. 5	Carolina ($14,000)	Dallas ($14,000)	26-17	Charlotte	72,808
	Jan. 4	Green Bay ($14,000)	San Francisco ($14,000)	35-14	Green Bay	60,787
1995	Jan. 7	Dallas ($13,000)	Philadelphia ($13,000)	30-11	Dallas	64,371
	Jan. 6	Green Bay ($13,000)	San Francisco ($13,000)	27-17	San Francisco	69,311
1994	Jan. 8	Dallas ($12,000)	Green Bay ($12,000)	35-9	Dallas	64,745
	Jan. 7	San Francisco ($12,000)	Chicago ($12,000)	44-15	San Francisco	64,644
1993	Jan. 16	Dallas ($12,000)	Green Bay ($12,000)	27-17	Dallas	64,790
	Jan. 15	San Francisco ($12,000)	N.Y. Giants ($12,000)	44-3	San Francisco	67,143
1992	Jan. 10	Dallas ($10,000)	Philadelphia ($10,000)	34-10	Dallas	63,721
	Jan. 9	San Francisco ($10,000)	Washington ($10,000)	20-13	San Francisco	64,991
1991	Jan. 5	Detroit ($10,000)	Dallas ($10,000)	38-6	Detroit	78,290
	Jan. 4	Washington ($10,000)	Atlanta ($10,000)	24-7	Washington	55,181
1990	Jan. 13	N.Y. Giants ($10,000)	Chicago ($10,000)	31-3	East Rutherford	77,025
	Jan. 12	San Francisco ($10,000)	Washington ($10,000)	28-10	San Francisco	65,292
1989	Jan. 7	L.A. Rams ($10,000)	N.Y. Giants ($10,000)	19-13*	East Rutherford	76,526
	Jan. 6	San Francisco ($10,000)	Minnesota ($10,000)	41-13	San Francisco	64,918
1988	Jan. 1	San Francisco ($10,000)	Minnesota ($10,000)	34-9	San Francisco	61,848
	Dec. 31	Chicago ($10,000)	Philadelphia ($10,000)	20-12	Chicago	65,534
1987	Jan. 10	Washington ($10,000)	Chicago ($10,000)	21-17	Chicago	65,268
	Jan. 9	Minnesota ($10,000)	San Francisco ($10,000)	36-24	San Francisco	63,008
1986	Jan. 4	N.Y. Giants ($10,000)	San Francisco ($10,000)	49-3	East Rutherford	75,691
	Jan. 3	Washington ($10,000)	Chicago ($10,000)	27-13	Chicago	65,524
1985	Jan. 5	Chicago ($10,000)	N.Y. Giants ($10,000)	21-0	Chicago	65,670
	Jan. 4	L.A. Rams ($10,000)	Dallas ($10,000)	20-0	Anaheim	66,581
1984	Dec. 30	Chicago ($10,000)	Washington ($10,000)	23-19	Washington	55,431
	Dec. 29	San Francisco ($10,000)	N.Y. Giants ($10,000)	21-10	San Francisco	60,303
1983	Jan. 1	Washington ($10,000)	L.A. Rams ($10,000)	51-7	Washington	54,440
	Dec. 31	San Francisco ($10,000)	Detroit ($10,000)	24-23	San Francisco	59,979
1982	Jan. 16	Dallas ($10,000)	Green Bay ($10,000)	37-26	Dallas	63,972
	Jan. 15	Washington ($10,000)	Minnesota ($10,000)	21-7	Washington	54,593
1981	Jan. 3	San Francisco ($5,000)	N.Y. Giants ($5,000)	38-24	San Francisco	58,360
	Jan. 2	Dallas ($5,000)	Tampa Bay ($5,000)	38-0	Dallas	64,848

Season	Date	Winner (Share)	Loser (Share)	Score	Site	Attendance
1980	Jan. 4	Dallas ($5,000)	Atlanta ($5,000)	30-27	Atlanta	59,793
	Jan. 3	Philadelphia ($5,000)	Minnesota ($5,000)	31-16	Philadelphia	70,178
1979	Dec. 30	Los Angeles ($5,000)	Dallas ($5,000)	21-19	Dallas	64,792
	Dec. 29	Tampa Bay ($5,000)	Philadelphia ($5,000)	24-17	Tampa	71,402
1978	Dec. 31	Los Angeles ($5,000)	Minnesota ($5,000)	34-10	Los Angeles	70,436
	Dec. 30	Dallas ($5,000)	Atlanta ($5,000)	27-20	Dallas	63,406
1977	Dec. 26	Dallas ($5,000)	Chicago ($5,000)	37-7	Dallas	63,260
	Dec. 26	Minnesota ($5,000)	Los Angeles ($5,000)	14-7	Los Angeles	70,203
1976	Dec. 19	Los Angeles [$]	Dallas [$]	14-12	Dallas	63,283
	Dec. 18	Minnesota [$]	Washington [$]	35-20	Minneapolis	47,466
1975	Dec. 28	Dallas [$]	Minnesota [$]	17-14	Minneapolis	48,050
	Dec. 27	Los Angeles [$]	St. Louis [$]	35-23	Los Angeles	73,459
1974	Dec. 22	Los Angeles [$]	Washington [$]	19-10	Los Angeles	77,925
	Dec. 21	Minnesota [$]	St. Louis [$]	30-14	Minneapolis	48,150
1973	Dec. 23	Dallas [$]	Los Angeles [$]	27-16	Dallas	63,272
	Dec. 22	Minnesota [$]	Washington [$]	27-20	Minneapolis	48,040
1972	Dec. 24	Washington [$]	Green Bay [$]	16-3	Washington	52,321
	Dec. 23	Dallas [$]	San Francisco [$]	30-28	San Francisco	59,746
1971	Dec. 26	San Francisco [$]	Washington [$]	24-20	San Francisco	45,327
	Dec. 25	Dallas [$]	Minnesota [$]	20-12	Minneapolis	47,307
1970	Dec. 27	San Francisco [$]	Minnesota [$]	17-14	Minneapolis	45,103
	Dec. 26	Dallas [$]	Detroit [$]	5-0	Dallas	69,613
1969	Dec. 28	Cleveland [$]	Dallas [$]	38-14	Dallas	69,321
	Dec. 27	Minnesota [$]	Los Angeles [$]	23-20	Minneapolis	47,900
1968	Dec. 22	Baltimore [$]	Minnesota [$]	24-14	Baltimore	60,238
	Dec. 21	Cleveland [$]	Dallas [$]	31-20	Cleveland	81,497
1967	Dec. 24	Dallas [$]	Cleveland [$]	52-14	Dallas	70,786
	Dec. 23	Green Bay [$]	Los Angeles [$]	28-7	Milwaukee	49,861
1965	Dec. 26	Green Bay [$]	Baltimore [$]	13-10*	Green Bay	50,484
1958	Dec. 21	N.Y. Giants (#)	Cleveland (#)	10-0	New York	61,274
1957	Dec. 22	Detroit (#)	San Francisco (#)	31-27	San Francisco	60,118
1952	Dec. 21	Detroit (#)	Los Angeles (#)	31-21	Detroit	47,645
1950	Dec. 17	Los Angeles (#)	Chicago Bears (#)	24-14	Los Angeles	83,501
	Dec. 17	Cleveland (#)	N.Y. Giants (#)	8-3	Cleveland	33,054
1947	Dec. 21	Philadelphia (#)	Pittsburgh (#)	21-0	Pittsburgh	35,729
1943	Dec. 19	Washington (¢)	N.Y. Giants (¢)	28-0	New York	42,800
1941	Dec. 14	Chicago Bears (¢)	Green Bay (¢)	33-14	Chicago	43,425

*Sudden death overtime   # Players received 1/12 of annual salary for playoff appearances.
$ Players received 1/14 of annual salary for playoff appearances.   ¢ Players received 1/10 of annual salary for playoff appearances.

2004 NFC DIVISIONAL PLAYOFF GAMES

Lincoln Financial Field, Philadelphia, Pennsylvania
January 16, 2005, Attendance: 67,722
PHILADELPHIA 27, MINNESOTA 14—Freddie Mitchell scored 2 touchdowns as the Eagles earned a berth in their fourth consecutive NFC Championship Game. The Eagles drove 53 and 92 yards for touchdowns to jump to a 14-0 lead. Following Daunte Culpepper's 7-yard scoring scramble, the Eagles drove to the Vikings' 14. Donovan McNabb completed a pass to L.J. Smith, who was hit by Antoine Winfield at the 4-yard line and fumbled. The ball popped into the air and Mitchell caught it on the fly in the end zone for a touchdown and 21-7 lead with 10:08 left in the half. Both teams failed on two scoring chances. The Vikings failed fake-field-goal attempt from the Eagles' 3 ended a drive before halftime, and Ike Reese intercepted a tipped pass at the Eagles' 28 in the third quarter. Dorsey Levens was tackled at the Vikings' 5 as time expired in the first half, and, while reaching for the pylon in the third quarter, Mitchell fumbled the ball out of the end zone for a touchback. At the end of the third quarter, Culpepper's fourth-and-22 pass into the end zone, intended for Randy Moss, fell incomplete, and the Eagles made 2 fourth-quarter field goals to pull away. McNabb was 21 of 33 for 286 yards and 2 touchdowns. Culpepper was 24 of 46 for 316 yards and 1 touchdown, with 2 interceptions. Marcus Robinson had 5 receptions for 119 yards.

Minnesota	0	7	0	7	—	14
Philadelphia	7	14	0	6	—	27

Phil — Mitchell 2 pass from McNabb (Akers kick)
Phil — Westbrook 7 pass from McNabb (Akers kick)
Minn — Culpepper 7 run (Andersen kick)
Phil — Mitchell fumble recovery in end zone (Akers kick)
Phil — FG Akers 21
Phil — FG Akers 23
Minn — Robinson 32 pass from Culpepper (Andersen kick)

Georgia Dome, Atlanta, Georgia
January 15, 2005, Attendance: 70,709
ATLANTA 47, ST. LOUIS 17—The Falcons rushed for 327 yards and Allen Rossum set a postseason record with 152 punt-return yards as the Falcons advanced to their second NFC Championship Game appearance. The Falcons had a 35:35-24:25 advantage in time of possession, and scored on five of their first six possessions to jump to a 38-17 lead with 5:54 left in the third quarter. On the first possession, faced with third-and-3, Michael Vick scrambled around right end and ran 47 yards to set up Alge Crumpler's 18-yard touchdown pass just three minutes into the game. The Rams tied the game five plays later with Kevin Curtis' 57-yard touchdown catch, but the Falcons needed just four plays to retake the lead on Warrick Dunn's 62-yard scoring run. Leading 21-14, Rossum returned a punt 68 yards for a touchdown with 59 seconds left in the half for a 28-14 lead, and

PLAYOFF GAME SUMMARIES

Rossum's 39-yard return early in the third quarter led to Peerless Price's 6-yard catch for a 35-17 lead. Rossum's 45-yard punt return to the Rams' 13 moments later led to Jay Feely's 38-yard field goal for a 38-17 lead. Vick was 12 of 16 of 82 yards and 2 touchdowns, and rushed 8 times for 119 yards. Dunn rushed 17 times for 142 yards. Marc Bulger was 23 of 35 for 299 yards and 2 touchdowns, with 1 interception. Curtis had 7 catches for 128 yards.

St. Louis	7	10	0	0	—	17
Atlanta	14	14	10	9	—	47

Atl — Crumpler 18 pass from Vick (Feely kick)
StL— Curtis 57 pass from Bulger (Wilkins kick)
Atl— Dunn 62 run (Feely kick)
Atl — Dunn 19 run (Feely kick)
StL— Holt 28 pass from Bulger (Wilkins kick)
Atl — Rossum 68 punt return (Feely kick)
StL— FG Wilkins 55
Atl— Price 6 pass from Vick (Feely kick)
Atl— FG Feely 38
Atl — Safety, B. Smith sacked Bulger in end zone
Atl — Duckett 4 run (Feely kick)

AFC WILD CARD PLAYOFF GAMES RESULTS

Season	Date	Winner (Share)	Loser (Share)	Score	Site	Attendance
2004	Jan. 9	Indianapolis ($18,000)	Denver ($15,000)	49-24	Indianapolis	56,609
	Jan. 8	N.Y. Jets ($15,000)	San Diego ($18,000)	20-17*	San Diego	67,536
2003	Jan. 4	Indianapolis ($18,000)	Denver ($15,000)	41-10	Indianapolis	56,586
	Jan. 3	Tennessee ($15,000)	Baltimore ($18,000)	20-17	Baltimore	69,452
2002	Jan. 5	Pittsburgh ($17,000)	Cleveland ($12,500)	36-33	Pittsburgh	62,595
	Jan. 4	N.Y. Jets ($17,000)	Indianapolis ($12,500)	41-0	East Rutherford	78,524
2001	Jan. 13	Baltimore ($12,500)	Miami ($12,500)	20-3	Miami	72,251
	Jan. 12	Oakland ($17,000)	N.Y. Jets ($12,500)	38-24	Oakland	61,503
2000	Dec. 31	Baltimore (12,500)	Denver ($12,500)	21-3	Baltimore	69,638
	Dec. 30	Miami ($16,000)	Indianapolis ($12,500)	23-17*	Miami	73,193
1999	Jan. 9	Miami ($10,000)	Seattle ($16,000)	20-17	Seattle	66,170
	Jan. 8	Tennessee ($10,000)	Buffalo ($10,000)	22-16	Nashville	66,672
1998	Jan. 3	Jacksonville ($15,000)	New England ($10,000)	25-10	Jacksonville	71,139
	Jan. 2	Miami ($10,000)	Buffalo ($10,000)	24-17	Miami	72,698
1997	Dec. 28	New England ($15,000)	Miami ($10,000)	17-3	Foxborough	60,041
	Dec. 27	Denver ($10,000)	Jacksonville ($10,000)	42-17	Denver	74,481
1996	Dec. 29	Pittsburgh ($14,000)	Indianapolis ($10,000)	42-14	Pittsburgh	58,078
	Dec. 28	Jacksonville ($10,000)	Buffalo ($10,000)	30-27	Buffalo	70,213
1995	Dec. 31	Indianapolis ($7,500)	San Diego ($7,500)	35-20	San Diego	61,182
	Dec. 30	Buffalo ($13,000)	Miami ($7,500)	37-22	Buffalo	73,103
1994	Jan. 1	Cleveland ($7,500)	New England ($7,500)	20-13	Cleveland	77,452
	Dec. 31	Miami ($12,000)	Kansas City ($7,500)	27-17	Miami	67,487
1993	Jan. 9	L.A. Raiders ($7,500)	Denver ($7,500)	42-24	Los Angeles	65,314
	Jan. 8	Kansas City ($12,000)	Pittsburgh ($7,500)	27-24*	Kansas City	74,515
1992	Jan. 3	Buffalo ($6,000)	Houston ($6,000)	41-38*	Buffalo	75,141
	Jan. 2	San Diego ($10,000)	Kansas City ($6,000)	17-0	San Diego	58,278
1991	Dec. 29	Houston ($10,000)	N.Y. Jets ($6,000)	17-10	Houston	61,485
	Dec. 28	Kansas City ($6,000)	L.A. Raiders ($6,000)	10-6	Kansas City	75,827
1990	Jan. 6	Cincinnati ($10,000)	Houston ($6,000)	41-14	Cincinnati	60,012
	Jan. 5	Miami ($6,000)	Kansas City ($6,000)	17-16	Miami	67,276
1989	Dec. 31	Pittsburgh ($6,000)	Houston ($6,000)	26-23*	Houston	59,406
1988	Dec. 26	Houston ($6,000)	Cleveland ($6,000)	24-23	Cleveland	75,896
1987	Jan. 3	Houston ($6,000)	Seattle ($6,000)	23-20*	Houston	50,519
1986	Dec. 28	N.Y. Jets ($6,000)	Kansas City ($6,000)	35-15	East Rutherford	75,210
1985	Dec. 28	New England ($6,000)	N.Y. Jets ($6,000)	26-14	East Rutherford	75,945
1984	Dec. 22	Seattle ($6,000)	L.A. Raiders ($6,000)	13-7	Seattle	62,049
1983	Dec. 24	Seattle ($6,000)	Denver ($6,000)	31-7	Seattle	64,275
1982	Jan. 9	N.Y. Jets ($6,000)	Cincinnati ($6,000)	44-17	Cincinnati	57,560
	Jan. 9	San Diego ($6,000)	Pittsburgh ($6,000)	31-28	Pittsburgh	53,546
	Jan. 8	L.A. Raiders ($6,000)	Cleveland ($6,000)	27-10	Los Angeles	56,555
	Jan. 8	Miami ($6,000)	New England ($6,000)	28-13	Miami	68,842
1981	Dec. 27	Buffalo ($3,000)	N.Y. Jets ($3,000)	31-27	New York	57,050
1980	Dec. 28	Oakland ($3,000)	Houston ($3,000)	27-7	Oakland	53,333
1979	Dec. 23	Houston ($3,000)	Denver ($3,000)	13-7	Houston	48,776
1978	Dec. 24	Houston ($3,000)	Miami ($3,000)	17-9	Miami	72,445

*Sudden death overtime

2004 AFC WILD CARD PLAYOFF GAMES

RCA Dome, Indianapolis, Indiana
January 9, 2005, Attendance: 56,609

INDIANAPOLIS 49, DENVER 24—Peyton Manning passed for 457 yards, the second-most in postseason history. Reggie Wayne had 221 receiving yards, the third-highest mark in post-season annals, on 10 receptions for the Colts. Manning passed for 360 yards and 3 touchdowns in the first half, and the Colts outgained the Broncos 529-338 for the game, and 395-103 in the first half. The Colts scored 7 touchdowns in 10 possessions, punting twice, and driving at least 75 yards four times. Manning's 1-yard sneak with 38 seconds left in the half capped a 75-yard drive and gave the Colts a 35-3 halftime lead. The Broncos scored on their first three possessions of the second half, but got no closer than 18 points. The Broncos pulled within 42-24 on Tatum Bell's 1-yard run with 7:45 to play, but Manning completed a 22-yard pass to Dallas Clark on third-and-4 to set up Dominic Rhodes' 2-yard run with 2:02 remaining. Manning was 27 of 33 for 457 yards and 4 touchdowns, with 1 interception. Wayne had 10 catches for 221 yards, and Clark added 6 catches for 112 yards. Jake Plummer was 24 of 34 for 284 yards and 2 touchdowns, with 1 interception.

Denver	0	3	14	7	—	24
Indianapolis	14	21	0	14	—	49

Ind— Mungro 2 pass from Manning (Vanderjagt kick)
Ind— James 1 run (Vanderjagt kick)
Ind— Clark 19 pass from Manning (Vanderjagt kick)
Den— FG Elam 33
Ind— Wayne 35 pass from Manning (Vanderjagt kick)
Ind— Manning 1 run (Vanderjagt kick)
Den— R. Smith 9 pass from Plummer (Elam kick)
Den— Putzier 35 pass from Plummer (Elam kick)
Ind— Wayne 43 pass from Manning (Vanderjagt kick)
Den— Bell 1 run (Elam kick)
Ind— Rhodes 2 run (Vanderjagt kick)

Qualcomm Stadium, San Diego, California
January 8, 2005, Attendance: 67,536

N.Y. JETS 20, SAN DIEGO 17 (OT)—Doug Brien kicked a 28-yard field goal in overtime as the Jets overcame a game-tying Chargers' touchdown in the final minute of regulation and a missed Chargers' field-goal attempt in overtime to give the Jets their first road postseason victory since 1982. With the game played in a steady rain on a soaked field, Brien missed a 33-yard field-goal attempt in the first quarter as the teams went into locker room tied 7-7. The Jets scored on their first possession of the second half when Chad Pennington completed a 47-yard perfectly placed touchdown pass to Santana Moss, just over the outstretched arms of Quentin Jammer and Jerry Wilson, and Brien added a 42-yard field goal, that bounced off the upright and crossbar before going through, on their next possession for a 17-7 lead. Nate Kaeding capped the ensuing possession with a 35-yard field goal with 10:43 to play to pull within 17-10, and the Chargers forced a punt and started from their own 20 with 4:46 left. Antonio Gates had catches of 21 and 44 yards as the Chargers reached the Jets' 1. On third-and-goal, LaDainian Tomlinson was dropped for a 1-yard loss. On fourth-and-goal with 24 seconds left, Brees was chased 20 yards behind the line of scrimmage and lofted a pass into the end zone that fell incomplete. Roughing the passer was called on Eric Barton, placing the ball at the Jets' 1, and Brees completed a touchdown pass to Gates with 11 seconds left to tie the game. The Chargers won the overtime toss, and after an exchange of punts, the Chargers drove 47 yards in 13 plays to set up Kaeding's 40-yard field-goal attempt, which sailed wide right. Pennington completed passes to Moss and Justin McCareins, and LaMont Jordan had a 19-yard run to the Chargers' 15 to set up Brien's game-winning kick with five seconds remaining. Pennington was 23 of 33 for 279 yards and 2 touchdowns, and Moss had 4 catches for 100 yards. Brees was 31 of 42 for 319 yards and 2 touchdowns, with 1 interception.

N.Y. Jets	0	7	10	0	3	—	20
San Diego	0	7	0	10	0	—	17

SD— McCardell 26 pass from Brees (Kaeding kick)
NYJ— Becht 13 pass from Pennington (Brien kick)
NYJ— Moss 47 pass from Pennington (Brien kick)
NYJ— FG Brien 42
SD— FG Kaeding 35
SD— Gates 1 pass from Brees (Kaeding kick)
NYJ— FG Brien 28

NFC WILD CARD PLAYOFF GAMES RESULTS

Season	Date	Winner (Share)	Loser (Share)	Score	Site	Attendance
2004	Jan. 9	Minnesota ($15,000)	Green Bay ($18,000)	31-17	Green Bay	71,075
	Jan. 8	St. Louis ($15,000)	Seattle ($18,000)	27-20	Seattle	65,397
2003	Jan. 4	Green Bay ($18,000)	Seattle ($15,000)	33-27*	Green Bay	71,457
	Jan. 3	Carolina ($18,000)	Dallas ($15,000)	29-10	Charlotte	73,014
2002	Jan. 5	San Francisco ($17,000)	N.Y. Giants ($12,500)	39-38	San Francisco	66,318
	Jan. 4	Atlanta ($12,500)	Green Bay ($17,000)	27-7	Green Bay	65,358
2001	Jan. 13	Green Bay ($12,500)	San Francisco ($12,500)	25-15	Green Bay	59,825
	Jan. 12	Philadelphia ($17,000)	Tampa Bay ($12,500)	31-9	Philadelphia	65,847
2000	Dec. 31	Philadelphia ($12,500)	Tampa Bay ($12,500)	21-3	Philadelphia	65,813
	Dec. 30	New Orleans ($16,000)	St. Louis ($12,500)	31-28	New Orleans	64,900
1999	Jan. 9	Minnesota ($10,000)	Dallas ($10,000)	27-10	Minneapolis	64,056
	Jan. 8	Washington ($16,000)	Detroit ($10,000)	27-13	Washington	79,411
1998	Jan. 3	San Francisco ($10,000)	Green Bay ($10,000)	30-27	San Francisco	66,506
	Jan. 2	Arizona ($10,000)	Dallas ($15,000)	20-7	Dallas	62,969
1997	Dec. 28	Tampa Bay ($10,000)	Detroit ($10,000)	20-10	Tampa	73,361
	Dec. 27	Minnesota ($10,000)	N.Y. Giants ($15,000)	23-22	East Rutherford	77,497
1996	Dec. 29	San Francisco ($10,000)	Philadelphia ($10,000)	14-0	San Francisco	56,460
	Dec. 28	Dallas ($14,000)	Minnesota ($10,000)	40-15	Dallas	64,682
1995	Dec. 31	Green Bay ($13,000)	Atlanta ($7,500)	37-20	Green Bay	60,453
	Dec. 30	Philadelphia ($7,500)	Detroit ($7,500)	58-37	Philadelphia	66,099
1994	Jan. 1	Chicago ($7,500)	Minnesota ($12,000)	35-18	Minnesota	60,347
	Dec. 31	Green Bay ($7,500)	Detroit ($7,500)	16-12	Green Bay	58,125

Season	Date	Winner (Share)	Loser (Share)	Score	Site	Attendance
1993	Jan. 9	N.Y. Giants ($7,500)	Minnesota ($7,500)	17-10	East Rutherford	75,089
	Jan. 8	Green Bay ($7,500)	Detroit ($12,000)	28-24	Detroit	68,479
1992	Jan. 3	Philadelphia ($6,000)	New Orleans ($6,000)	36-20	New Orleans	68,893
	Jan. 2	Washington ($6,000)	Minnesota ($10,000)	24-7	Minnesota	57,353
1991	Dec. 29	Dallas ($6,000)	Chicago ($6,000)	17-13	Chicago	62,594
	Dec. 28	Atlanta ($6,000)	New Orleans ($10,000)	27-20	New Orleans	68,794
1990	Jan. 6	Chicago ($10,000)	New Orleans ($6,000)	16-6	Chicago	60,767
	Jan. 5	Washington ($6,000)	Philadelphia ($6,000)	20-6	Philadelphia	65,287
1989	Dec. 31	L.A. Rams ($6,000)	Philadelphia ($6,000)	21-7	Philadelphia	65,479
1988	Dec. 26	Minnesota ($6,000)	L.A. Rams ($6,000)	28-17	Minnesota	61,204
1987	Jan. 3	Minnesota ($6,000)	New Orleans ($6,000)	44-10	New Orleans	68,546
1986	Dec. 28	Washington ($6,000)	L.A. Rams ($6,000)	19-7	Washington	54,567
1985	Dec. 29	N.Y. Giants ($6,000)	San Francisco ($6,000)	17-3	East Rutherford	75,131
1984	Dec. 23	N.Y. Giants ($6,000)	L.A. Rams ($6,000)	16-13	Anaheim	67,037
1983	Dec. 26	L.A. Rams ($6,000)	Dallas ($6,000)	24-17	Dallas	62,118
1982	Jan. 9	Dallas ($6,000)	Tampa Bay ($6,000)	30-17	Dallas	65,042
	Jan. 9	Minnesota ($6,000)	Atlanta ($6,000)	30-24	Minnesota	60,560
	Jan. 8	Green Bay ($6,000)	St. Louis ($6,000)	41-16	Green Bay	54,282
	Jan. 8	Washington ($6,000)	Detroit ($6,000)	31-7	Washington	55,045
1981	Dec. 27	N.Y. Giants ($3,000)	Philadelphia ($3,000)	27-21	Philadelphia	71,611
1980	Dec. 28	Dallas ($3,000)	Los Angeles ($3,000)	34-13	Dallas	63,052
1979	Dec. 23	Philadelphia ($3,000)	Chicago ($3,000)	27-17	Philadelphia	69,397
1978	Dec. 24	Atlanta ($3,000)	Philadelphia ($3,000)	14-13	Atlanta	59,403

*Sudden death overtime

2004 NFC WILD CARD PLAYOFF GAMES
Lambeau Field, Green Bay, Wisconsin
January 9, 2005, Attendance: 71,075
MINNESOTA 31, GREEN BAY 17—Daunte Culpepper passed for 4 touchdowns and the Vikings' defense intercepted 4 passes to defeat the Packers in the first postseason matchup between the two rivals. Culpepper's 68-yard touchdown pass to Moe Williams three plays into the game set the tone. Following a three-and-out, the Vikings needed just 4 plays to take a 14-0 lead on Randy Moss' 20-yard scoring catch. Antoine Winfield intercepted Brett Favre's pass three plays later to set up Morten Andersen's field goal to give the Vikings a 17-0 lead just 8:54 into the game. The Packers scored on their next two possessions to pull within 17-10, and the Packers blocked Andersen's 27-yard field-goal attempt to swing the momentum. However, on the next play Brian Russell intercepted Favre's pass and Nate Burleson caught a 19-yard touchdown pass two plays later for a 24-10 lead. Ryan Longwell missed a 28-yard attempt wide left just before halftime, but the Packers rallied and drove 78 yards, capped by Najeh Davenport's 1-yard run with 13:37 to play, to cut the deficit to 24-17. On the next possession, Culpepper completed a 8-yard pass to Burleson on third-and-6, and three plays later Moss broke free for a 34-yard touchdown catch with 10:18 remaining. The Vikings' defense forced a punt with 8:21 left, and the offense ran out the clock, with Onterrio Smith's 16-yard catch on third down and Culpepper's 1-yard sneak on fourth-and-1 keeping the drive alive. Culpepper was 19 of 29 for 284 yards and 4 touchdowns. Favre was 22 of 33 for 216 yards and 1 touchdown, with 4 interceptions.

Minnesota	17	7	0	7	—	31
Green Bay	3	7	0	7	—	17

Minn— M. Williams 68 pass from Culpepper (Andersen kick)
Minn— Moss 20 pass from Culpepper (Andersen kick)
Minn— FG Andersen 35
GB— FG Longwell 43
GB— Franks 4 pass from Favre (Longwell kick)
Minn— Burleson 19 pass from Culpepper (Andersen kick)
GB— Davenport 1 run (Longwell kick)
Minn— Moss 34 pass from Culpepper (Andersen kick)

Qwest Field, Seattle, Washington
January 8, 2005, Attendance: 65,397
ST. LOUIS 27, SEATTLE 20—Cam Cleeland caught a 17-yard touchdown pass from Marc Bulger with 2:11 remaining, and Bobby Engram could not hold onto a pass in the end zone in the waning seconds, as the Rams advanced. The Rams had a pair of 75-yard touchdown drives in the first half en route to a 14-10 halftime lead. Darrell Jackson capped a 76-yard drive with a 23-yard touchdown catch to give Seattle a 20-17 lead with 13:43 to play. The Rams responded with an 11-play, 60-yard drive that consumed 6:53 and was capped by Jeff Wilkins' tying 27-yard field goal with 8:07 remaining. The Rams forced a punt, and on third-and-2 from their own 32, Bulger completed a short pass to Shaun McDonald who raced 31 yards down the right side. Four plays later, on third-and-3 from the Seahawks' 17, Bulger found Cleeland, who only had 7 catches all season, open in the seam at the goal line for a touchdown. The Seahawks needed just four plays to reach the Rams' 11. Following a Jimmy Kennedy sack and an incompletion, Matt Hasselbeck completed a 12-yard pass to Engram to the Rams' 5 to set up fourth-and-4 with 27 seconds left. Hasselbeck scrambled within the pocket and threw sidearm and low to Engram cutting across the middle of the end zone, who got his hands on the pass but was unable to hold on. Bulger was 18 of 32 for 313 yards and 2 touchdowns, with 1 interception. Torry Holt had 6 catches for 108 yards, and Kevin Curtis added 4 receptions for 107 yards. Hasselbeck was 27 of 43 for 341 yards and 2 touchdowns, with 1 interception. Jackson had 12 catches for 128 yards.

St. Louis	7	7	3	10	—	27
Seattle	3	7	3	7	—	20

StL— Holt 15 pass from Bulger (Wilkins kick)
Sea— FG J. Brown 47
StL— Faulk 1 run (Wilkins kick)
Sea— Engram 19 passf rom Hasselbeck (J. Brown kick)
Sea— FG J. Brown 30
StL— FG Wilkins 38
Sea— Jackson 23 pass from Hasselbeck (J. Brown kick)
StL— FG Wilkins 27
StL— Cleeland 17 pass from Bulger (Wilkins kick)

AFC-NFC PRO BOWL RESULTS (1971-2005)

AFC leads series, 18-17

Year	Date	Winner (Share)	Loser (Share)	Score	Site	Attendance
2005	Feb. 13	AFC ($35,000)	NFC ($17,500)	38-27	Honolulu	50,225
2004	Feb. 8	NFC ($35,000)	AFC ($17,500)	55-52	Honolulu	50,127
2003	Feb. 2	AFC ($30,000)	NFC ($15,000)	45-20	Honolulu	50,125
2002	Feb. 9	AFC ($30,000)	NFC ($15,000)	38-30	Honolulu	50,301
2001	Feb. 4	AFC ($30,000)	NFC ($15,000)	38-17	Honolulu	50,128
2000	Feb. 6	NFC ($25,000)	AFC ($12,500)	51-31	Honolulu	50,112
1999	Feb. 7	AFC ($25,000)	NFC ($12,500)	23-10	Honolulu	50,075
1998	Feb. 1	AFC ($25,000)	NFC ($12,500)	29-24	Honolulu	49,995
1997	Feb. 2	AFC ($20,000)	NFC ($10,000)	26-23 (OT)	Honolulu	50,031
1996	Feb. 4	NFC ($20,000)	AFC ($10,000)	20-13	Honolulu	50,034
1995	Feb. 5	AFC ($20,000)	NFC ($10,000)	41-13	Honolulu	50,529
1994	Feb. 6	NFC ($20,000)	AFC ($10,000)	17-3	Honolulu	50,026
1993	Feb. 7	AFC ($10,000)	NFC ($5,000)	23-20 (OT)	Honolulu	50,007
1992	Feb. 2	NFC ($10,000)	AFC ($5,000)	21-15	Honolulu	50,209
1991	Feb. 3	AFC ($10,000)	NFC ($5,000)	23-21	Honolulu	50,345
1990	Feb. 4	NFC ($10,000)	AFC ($5,000)	27-21	Honolulu	50,445
1989	Jan. 29	NFC ($10,000)	AFC ($5,000)	34-3	Honolulu	50,113
1988	Feb. 7	AFC ($10,000)	NFC ($5,000)	15-6	Honolulu	50,113
1987	Feb. 1	AFC ($10,000)	NFC ($5,000)	10-6	Honolulu	50,101
1986	Feb. 2	NFC ($10,000)	AFC ($5,000)	28-24	Honolulu	50,101
1985	Jan. 27	AFC ($10,000)	NFC ($5,000)	22-14	Honolulu	50,385
1984	Jan. 29	NFC ($10,000)	AFC ($5,000)	45-3	Honolulu	50,445
1983	Feb. 6	NFC ($10,000)	AFC ($5,000)	20-19	Honolulu	49,883
1982	Jan. 31	AFC ($5,000)	NFC ($2,500)	16-13	Honolulu	50,402
1981	Feb. 1	NFC ($5,000)	AFC ($2,500)	21-7	Honolulu	50,360
1980	Jan. 27	NFC ($5,000)	AFC ($2,500)	37-27	Honolulu	49,800
1979	Jan. 29	NFC ($5,000)	AFC ($2,500)	13-7	Los Angeles	46,281
1978	Jan. 23	NFC ($5,000)	AFC ($2,500)	14-13	Tampa	51,337
1977	Jan. 17	AFC ($2,000)	NFC ($1,500)	24-14	Seattle	64,752
1976	Jan. 26	NFC ($2,000)	AFC ($1,500)	23-20	New Orleans	30,546
1975	Jan. 20	NFC ($2,000)	AFC ($1,500)	17-10	Miami	26,484
1974	Jan. 20	AFC ($2,000)	NFC ($1,500)	15-13	Kansas City	66,918
1973	Jan. 21	AFC ($2,000)	NFC ($1,500)	33-28	Dallas	37,091
1972	Jan. 23	AFC ($2,000)	NFC ($1,500)	26-13	Los Angeles	53,647
1971	Jan. 24	NFC ($2,000)	AFC ($1,500)	27-6	Los Angeles	48,222

2005 AFC-NFC PRO BOWL

Aloha Stadium, Honolulu, Hawaii
February 13, 2005, Attendance: 50,225
AFC 38, NFC 27—Peyton Manning passed for 130 yards and 3 touchdowns as the AFC won for the fourth time in five years. The NFC outgained the AFC 492-343, but committed 3 turnovers and allowed an onside kick for a touchdown. David Akers missed a 43-yard field goal in the first quarter, and the AFC responded with touchdowns on its next four possessions. Manning completed 3 touchdown passes in the stretch, and Hines Ward registered the first onside kick returned for a touchdown in Pro Bowl history. Manning's final scoring pass, a 12-yard toss to Antonio Gates, was set up by Takeo Spikes' interception near midfield, to take a 28-7 lead with 5:50 left in the half. Michael Vick began the second half for the NFC, and engineered a 73-yard drive, capped by Torry Holt's 27-yard touchdown catch. Lito Sheppard intercepted Tom Brady's pass four plays later, and Vick culminated a 69-yard drive with a 3-yard run to cut the deficit to 28-24 with 3:53 left in the third quarter. An exchange of field goals made the score 31-27 with

9:04 remaining, but Drew Brees connected on a 33-yard pass to Gates on a flea-flicker, and LaDainian Tomlinson scored on third-and-goal from the NFC's 4 with 5:15 to play. Nate Clements' interception of Vick's pass with 2:00 remaining clinched the victory. Manning was 6 of 10 for 130 yards and 3 touchdowns to earn the game's most valuable player award. Brady was 4 of 9 for 48 yards, with 1 interception, and Brees was 2 of 2 for 58 yards. Donovan McNabb was 1 of 8 for 24 yards, with 1 interception. Daunte Culpepper was 9 of 15 for 124 yards, with 1 interception. Vick was 14 of 24 for 205 yards and 1 touchdown, with 1 interception, and became the first player to pass and run for a touchdown in the same Pro Bowl game.

NFC (27)	Offense	AFC (38)
Muhsin Muhammad (Carolina)	WR	Marvin Harrison (Indianapolis)
Walter Jones (Seattle)	LT	Jonathan Ogden (Baltimore)
Larry Allen (Dallas)	LG	Alan Faneca (Pittsburgh)
Olin Kreutz (Chicago)	C	Kevin Mawae (N.Y. Jets)
Marco Rivera (Green Bay)	RG	Will Shields (Kansas City)
Orlando Pace (St. Louis)	RT	Tarik Glenn (Indianapolis)
Alge Crumpler (Atlanta)	TE	Antonio Gates (San Diego)
Javon Walker (Green Bay)	WR	Chad Johnson (Cincinnati)
Donovan McNabb (Philadelphia)	QB	Peyton Manning (Indianapolis)
William Henderson (Green Bay)	FB	Tony Richardson (Kansas City)
Tiki Barber (N.Y. Giants)	RB	LaDainian Tomlinson (San Diego)

	Defense	
Bertrand Berry (Arizona)	DE	Jason Taylor (Miami)
La'Roi Glover (Dallas)	DT	Sam Adams (Buffalo)
Kevin Williams (Minnesota)	DT	Marcus Stroud (Jacksonville)
Julius Peppers (Carolina)	DE	Dwight Freeney (Indianapolis)
Keith Brooking (Atlanta)	LOLB	Takeo Spikes (Buffalo)
Dan Morgan (Carolina)	ILB	James Farrior (Pittsburgh)
Marcus Washington (Washington)	ROLB	Terrell Suggs (Baltimore)

Ronde Barber — LCB — Champ Bailey (Tampa Bay) — (Denver)
Dré Bly — RCB — Tory James (Detroit) — (Cincinnati)
Michael Lewis — SS — Ed Reed (Philadelphia) — (Baltimore)
Brian Dawkins — FS — John Lynch (Philadelphia) — (Denver)

SUBSTITUTIONS
NFC—Specialists: K—David Akers (Philadelphia). P—Mitch Berger (New Orleans). KR—Allen Rossum (Atlanta). LS—Brian Jennings (San Francisco). ST—Ike Reese (Philadelphia). Offense: QB—Michael Vick (Atlanta), Daunte Culpepper (Minnesota). RB—Ahman Green (Green Bay), Brian Westbrook (Philadelphia). WR—Torry Holt (St. Louis), Joe Horn (New Orleans). TE—Jason Witten (Dallas). G—Steve Hutchinson (Seattle). C—Matt Birk (Minnesota). Defense: DL—Shaun Rogers (Detroit). DE—Patrick Kearney (Atlanta). LB—Jeremiah Trotter (Philadelphia), Mark Fields (Carolina). CB—Lito Sheppard (Philadelphia). S—Roy Williams (Dallas). Did Not Play: T—Flozell Adams (Dallas). Not Active: KR—Eddie Drummond (Detroit). RB—Shaun Alexander (Seattle). WR—Terrell Owens (Philadelphia). T—Tra Thomas (Philadelphia). LB—Derrick Brooks (Tampa Bay).
AFC—Specialists: K—Adam Vinatieri (New England). P—Shane Lechler (Oakland). KR—Terrence McGee (Buffalo). LS—Kendall Gammon (Kansas City). ST—Larry Izzo (New England). Offense: QB—Tom Brady (New England), Drew Brees (San Diego). RB—Jerome Bettis (Pittsburgh), Rudi Johnson (Cincinnati). WR—Andre Johnson (Houston), Hines Ward (Pittsburgh). TE—Tony Gonzalez (Kansas City). G—Brian Waters (Kansas City). T—Marvel Smith (Pittsburgh). C—Jeff Hartings (Pittsburgh). Defense: DL—John Henderson (Jacksonville). DE—Aaron Smith (Pittsburgh). LB—Tedy Bruschi (New England), Joey Porter (Pittsburgh). CB—Nate Clements (Buffalo). S—Troy Polamalu (Pittsburgh). Not Active: RB—Edgerrin James (Indianapolis), Curtis Martin (N.Y. Jets). T—Willie Anderson (Cincinnati), William Roaf (Kansas City). DE—John Abraham (N.Y. Jets), Richard Seymour (New England). LB—Ray Lewis (Baltimore). CB—Chris McAlister (Baltimore).

HEAD COACHES
AFC—Bill Cowher (Pittsburgh)
NFC—Jim Mora (Atlanta)

OFFICIALS
Referee—Bernie Kukar. Umpire—Roy Ellison. Side Judge—Joe Larrew. Head Linesman—Ed Camp. Back Judge—Jim Howey. Field Judge—Scott Edwards. Line Judge—Charles Stewart.

NFC	0	10	14	3	—	27
AFC	14	14	0	10	—	38

AFC — Harrison 62 pass from Manning (Vinatieri kick)
AFC — Ward 41 pass from Manning (Vinatieri kick)
NFC — Westbrook 12 run (Akers kick)
AFC — Ward 39 kickoff return (Vinatieri kick)
AFC — Gates 12 pass from Manning (Vinatieri kick)
NFC — FG Akers 33
NFC — Holt 27 pass from Vick (Akers kick)
AFC — Vick 3 run (Akers kick)
AFC — FG Vinatieri 44
NFC — FG Akers 29
AFC — Tomlinson 4 run (Vinatieri kick)

TEAM STATISTICS	NFC	AFC
Total First Downs	26	15
Rushing	7	5
Passing	19	9
Penalty	0	1
Total Net Yardage	492	343
Total Offensive Plays	77	51
Avg. Gain Per Offensive Play	6.4	6.7
Rushes	27	27
Yards Gained Rushing (Net)	155	120
Avg. Yards per Rush	5.7	4.4
Passes Attempted	48	22
Passes Completed	24	12
Had Intercepted	3	1
Tackled Attempting to Pass	2	2
Yards Lost Attempting to Pass	16	13
Yards Gained Passing (Net)	337	223
Punts	1	2
Avg. Distance	59.0	42.5
Punt Returns	0	1
Punt Return Yardage	0	7
Kickoff Returns	5	6
Kickoff Return Yardage	136	165
Interception Return Yardage	1	3
Total Return Yardage	1	51
Fumbles	1	1
Fumbles Lost	0	1
Own Fumbles Recovered	1	0
Opponent Fumbles Recovered	1	0
Penalties	3	2
Yards Penalized	28	10
Field Goals	2	1
Field Goals Attempted	3	2
Third-Down Efficiency	10/16	3/10
Fourth-Down Efficiency	0/1	2/2
Time of Possession	35:34	24:26

INDIVIDUAL STATISTICS
RUSHING: NFC: Barber 9-70-0, Westbrook 7-39-1, Green 5-25-0, Vick 3-10-1, Culpepper 2-8-0, McNabb 1-3-0. AFC: R. Johnson 6-33-0, Tomlinson 7-28-1, Izzo 1-27-0, Bettis 5-23-0, Richardson 3-6-0, Ward 1-4-0, Brady 1-2-0, Brees 3-(-3)-0.
PASSING: NFC: Vick 24-14-205-1-1, Culpepper 15-9-124-0-1, McNabb 8-1-24-0-1, Horn 1-0-0-0-0. AFC: Manning 10-6-130-3-0, Brady 9-4-48-0-1, Brees 2-2-58-0-0, Tomlinson 1-0-0-0-0.
RECEIVING: NFC: Holt 5-99-1,

Horn 4-60-0, Muhammad 4-54-0, Walker 4-53-0, Witten 3-50-0, Westbrook 2-7-0, Crumpler 1-24-0, Barber 1-6-0. AFC: Ward 3-63-1, Gates 3-51-1, Harrison 2-66-1, Richardson 2-7-0, Gonzalez 1-25-0, A. Johnson 1-24-0.
KICKOFF RETURNS: NFC: Rossum 5-136-0. AFC: McGee 5-126-0, Ward 1-39-1.
PUNT RETURNS: NFC: Rossum 0-0-0. AFC: Clements 1-7-0.
PUNTING: NFC: Berger 1-59-59.0. AFC: Lechler 2-85-42.5.
INTERCEPTIONS: NFC: Sheppard 1-0-0. AFC: Porter 1-48-0, Clements 1-4-0, Spikes 1-(-1)-0.
SACKS: NFC: Berry, K. Williams. AFC: Henderson, A. Smith.

2004 AFC-NFC PRO BOWL
Aloha Stadium, Honolulu, Hawaii
February 8, 2004, Attendance: 50,127
NFC 55, AFC 52—Marc Bulger passed for a Pro Bowl-record 4 touchdowns as the NFC rallied from a 25-point deficit to win the highest scoring game in Pro Bowl history. The AFC set a record with 626 yards, but committed 6 turnovers which led to 35 points. Steve McNair fired a 90-yard touchdown pass to Chad Johnson on the AFC's first play, and Ed Reed blocked Todd Sauerbrun's punt and returned it 23 yards for a touchdown for a 14-0 lead 3:58 into the game. The AFC led 17-13 in the second quarter when Peyton Manning fired a 50-yard touchdown pass to Marvin Harrison, and his 9-yard scoring pass to Tony Gonzalez on the next possession gave the AFC a 31-13 lead. Jamal Lewis' 22-yard touchdown run gave the AFC a 38-13 lead with 11:08 left in the third quarter. The comeback started when Trent Green fumbled and Leonard Little recovered. Bulger completed a 12-yard touchdown pass to Torry Holt two plays later with 8:08 left in the third quarter. Two plays later, Derrick Mason fumbled and Jerry Azumah returned it 36 yards to the AFC's 7 to set up Bulger's 2-yard touchdown toss to Keenan McCardell. But following an exchange of punts, Green completed a 23-yard touchdown pass to Clinton Portis to give the AFC a 45-27 lead with 13:14 left. The NFC scored 28 points in the next 9:42, set up by Azumah's 60-yard kickoff return, Champ Bailey's interception of a pass by Harrison, and interception returns by Dre' Bly, 32 yards for a touchdown, and Corey Chavous, 39 yards to set up Shaun Alexander's 2-yard touchdown run with 3:32 left, for a 55-45 NFC lead. Manning's 10-yard touchdown pass to Hines Ward with 1:54 left pulled the AFC within three points, and Bulger was intercepted by Brock Marion on fourth-and-10 from the AFC's 28-yard line with 1:15 left. The AFC drove to the NFC 21, but Kris Jenkins sacked Manning for a 12-yard loss, forcing Vanderjagt, who was 37-for-37 on the

season but missed from 52 yards just before halftime, to attempt a 51-yard field goal as time expired. But the kick sailed wide right and the NFC prevailed. Bulger was 12 of 21 for 152 yards and 4 touchdowns, with 1 interception, and was selected as the player of the game. Holt had 7 receptions for 128 yards. Manning was 22 of 41 for 342 yards and 3 touchdowns, with 2 interceptions. Mason had 6 catches for 113 yards, and Johnson had 5 receptions for 156 yards.

AFC	17	14	7	14 —	52
NFC	10	3	14	28 —	55

AFC — C. Johnson 90 pass from McNair (Vanderjagt kick)
AFC — Reed 23 return of blocked punt (Vanderjagt kick)
NFC — Alexander 12 run (Wilkins kick)
NFC — FG Wilkins 28
AFC — FG Vanderjagt 27
NFC — FG Wilkins 38
AFC — Harrison 50 pass from Manning (Vanderjagt kick)
AFC — Gonzalez 9 pass from Manning (Vanderjagt kick)
AFC — J. Lewis 22 run (Vanderjagt kick)
NFC — Holt 12 pass from Bulger (Wilkins kick)
NFC — McCardell 2 pass from Bulger (Wilkins kick)
AFC — Portis 23 pass from Green (Vanderjagt kick)
NFC — Crumpler 33 pass from Bulger (Wilkins kick)
NFC — Alexander 5 pass from Bulger (pass failed)
NFC — Bly 32 interception return (Green run)
NFC — Alexander 2 run (Wilkins kick)
AFC — Ward 10 pass from Manning (Vanderjagt kick)

2003 AFC-NFC PRO BOWL
Aloha Stadium, Honolulu, Hawaii
February 2, 2003, Attendance: 50,125
AFC 45, NFC 20—Ricky Williams rushed for a game-high 56 yards, scored 2 touchdowns, and forced a fumble on special teams to earn player of the game honors. The AFC, which led by as many as 39 points, won for the third consecutive time. Jason Taylor's interception three plays into the game set up Williams' first touchdown run, and Rich Gannon's 11-yard touchdown pass to Tony Gonzalez capped a 71-yard drive on the AFC's next possession to take a 14-3 lead. Rod Woodson's interception early in the second quarter led to Gannon's 13-yard touchdown pass to Travis Henry, and Williams capped another 71-yard drive with a 1-yard run with 47 seconds left in the half to give the AFC a 28-6 lead. Brad Johnson entered the game in the fourth quarter, and Ty Law intercepted a pass and returned it 43 yards for a touchdown on his first possession, and Sam Madison intercepted

Johnson during his second drive to set up Peyton Manning's 32-yard touchdown pass to Hines Ward, which gave the AFC a 45-6 lead with 7:31 left. Johnson guided the NFC to touchdowns on its next two possessions, with the help of Julian Peterson's onside kick recovery, for the game's final points. All three AFC quarterbacks passed for at least 100 yards, led by Drew Bledsoe's 9 of 18 for 122-yard performance. Gonzalez had 5 receptions for 98 yards to lead all receivers. The AFC's defense had 6 interceptions, 3 of which were thrown by NFC starter Jeff Garcia.

NFC	3	3	0	14 —	20
AFC	14	14	3	14 —	45

AFC — R. Williams 1 run (Vinatieri kick)
NFC — FG Akers 45
AFC — Gonzalez 11 pass from Gannon (Vinatieri kick)
AFC — Henry 13 pass from Gannon (Vinatieri kick)
NFC — FG Akers 53
AFC — R. Williams 1 run (Vinatieri kick)
AFC — FG Vinatieri 20
AFC — Law 43 interception return (Vinatieri kick)
AFC — Ward 32 pass from Manning (Vinatieri kick)
NFC — Horn 12 pass from B. Johnson (Akers kick)
NFC — Alstott 4 pass from B. Johnson (Akers kick)

2002 AFC-NFC PRO BOWL
Aloha Stadium, Honolulu, Hawaii
February 9, 2002, Attendance: 50,301
AFC 38, NFC 30—Rich Gannon passed for 137 yards and 2 touchdowns to become the first player to earn back-to-back Pro Bowl player of the game honors. The game had an inauspicious beginning for Gannon, who fumbled the game's first snap. Hugh Douglas recovered the fumble and returned the ball to the AFC's 2-yard line to set up Ahman Green's touchdown 27 seconds into the game. After a three-and-out series, Kurt Warner's 23-yard pass to David Boston set up David Akers' 29-yard field goal to give the NFC a 10-0 lead. Gannon responded two plays later with a 55-yard touchdown pass to Marvin Harrison. Deltha O'Neal's 24-yard interception return to the NFC's 6-yard line moments later set up Curtis Martin's 4-yard touchdown run and gave the AFC a 14-10 lead. After the NFC went three-and-out, the AFC needed just five plays, keyed by Gannon's 30-yard pass to Troy Brown, and capped by Priest Holmes' 39-yard touchdown run to give the AFC its third touchdown in less than six minutes and a 21-10 lead. A 10-play NFC drive led to Akers' second field goal, but Jermaine Lewis' 54-yard kickoff return set up Gannon's 18-yard touchdown pass to Ken Dilger and gave the AFC a 28-10 lead with 12:03 left in the first half. The NFC overcame Shane Lechler's Pro Bowl-

record 73-yard punt with Akers' 49-yard field goal just before halftime to cut the deficit to 28-16. Junior Seau's interception at the AFC's 5-yard line early in the fourth quarter thwarted one NFC rally, but Champ Bailey's interception led to Donovan McNabb's 8-yard touchdown pass to Terrell Owens to cut the deficit to 28-23 with 8:12 left. Runs of 29 and 16 yards by Corey Dillon led to Jason Elam's 38-yard field goal and, two plays later, Ty Law intercepted McNabb at the NFC 44-yard line, returned the ball to the NFC 13 before lateralling to Ray Lewis, who dragged three players into the end zone for a 38-23 lead with 2:49 remaining. McNabb's 15-yard touchdown pass to Garrison Hearst with 1:32 left cut the deficit to 38-30, but Rod Woodson recovered the ensuing onside kick to clinch the victory. Gannon was 8 of 10 for 137 yards and 2 touchdowns. McNabb was 12 of 25 for 149 yards and 2 touchdowns, with 2 interceptions, to lead the NFC. Owens had 8 receptions for 122 yards and 1 touchdown.

AFC	21	7	0	10 —	38
NFC	13	3	0	14 —	30

NFC — Green 2 run (Akers kick)
NFC — FG Akers 29
AFC — Harrison 55 pass from Gannon (Elam kick)
AFC — Martin 4 run (Elam kick)
AFC — Holmes 39 run (Elam kick)
NFC — FG Akers 41
AFC — Dilger 18 pass from Gannon (Elam kick)
NFC — FG Akers 49
NFC — Owens 8 pass from McNabb (Akers kick)
AFC — FG Elam 38
AFC — R. Lewis 13 lateral from Law (Elam kick)
NFC — Hearst 15 pass from McNabb (Akers kick)

2001 AFC-NFC PRO BOWL
Aloha Stadium, Honolulu, Hawaii
February 4, 2001, Attendance: 50,128
AFC 38, NFC 17—Rich Gannon completed 12 of 14 passes for 160 yards during the game's first two possessions to win player of the game honors and lead the AFC to victory. Gannon's touchdown passes capped 87- and 90-yard drives and staked the AFC to a 14-0 lead. Gannon, who was still recovering from a separated non-throwing shoulder suffered in the AFC Championship Game, was replaced by Peyton Manning. The Colts' quarterback engineered a scoring drive, capped by Matt Stover's field goal, to give the AFC a 17-0 lead early in the second quarter. At that point, the AFC had 14 first downs and 231 yards of offense while limiting the NFC to no first downs and 6 yards. Jimmy Smith caught a 2-yard touchdown pass 54 seconds before halftime to give the AFC a 24-3 lead. Third-quarter touchdown passes by Donovan McNabb and Daunte Culpepper trimmed

the AFC's lead to 31-17, but Jason Taylor batted down Culpepper's fourth-and-1 pass early in the fourth quarter, and Edgerrin James' 20-yard touchdown run a few plays later iced the game. The NFC attempted a Pro Bowl record 56 pass attempts, and the two teams combined for a Pro Bowl record 98 pass attempts. Tony Gonzalez had 6 receptions for 108 yards, all in the first half, for the AFC. Torry Holt had 7 receptions for 103 yards. Smith's touchdown reception gives him 5 for his career, an AFC-NFC Pro Bowl record.

NFC	0	3	14	0	—	17
AFC	14	10	7	7	—	38

AFC — Gonzalez 8 pass from Gannon (Stover kick)
AFC — Harrison 16 pass from Gannon (Stover kick)
AFC — FG Stover 29
NFC — FG Gramatica 48
AFC — J. Smith 2 pass from Manning (Stover kick)
NFC — Owens 17 pass from McNabb (Gramatica kick)
AFC — Harrison 24 pass from Manning (Stover kick)
NFC — Holt 20 pass from Culpepper (Gramatica kick)
AFC — James 20 run (Stover kick)

2000 AFC-NFC PRO BOWL
Aloha Stadium, Honolulu, Hawaii
February 6, 2000, Attendance: 50,112
NFC 51, AFC 31—Randy Moss earned player of the game honors by setting records with 9 receptions for 212 yards as the NFC defeated the AFC in the highest-scoring Pro Bowl ever. Aeneas Williams intercepted Peyton Manning's pass and raced 62 yards down the left sideline to give the NFC an early 7-0 lead. Kurt Warner's 48-yard pass to Moss on the NFC's first possession set up Jason Hanson's first field goal. Mike Alstott and Jimmy Smith each scored twice in the first half, and Michael Bates' 66-yard kickoff return led to Hanson's Pro Bowl-record tying 51-yard field goal as the half expired to give the NFC a 27-21 lead. Alstott's third touchdown increased the NFC's lead to 37-21, and Derrick Brooks' interception of Mark Brunell and 20-yard return staked the NFC to a 44-24 lead with 11:12 left. The AFC responded with Manning's 52-yard touchdown pass to Smith with 6:30 remaining, but Steve Beuerlein found Moss with a 25-yard scoring pass with 1:05 left to finish the scoring. Warner led the three NFC quarterbacks by completing 8 of 11 passes for 123 yards. Alstott led all rushers with 13 carries for 67 yards. The NFC forced 6 turnovers. Manning was 17 of 23 for 270 yards and 2 touchdowns, with 2 interceptions. Smith had 8 receptions for 119 yards. The previous record, 64 points, was set in 1980.

AFC	7	14	0	10	—	31
NFC	10	17	10	14	—	51

NFC — A. Williams 62 interception return (Hanson kick)
NFC — FG Hanson 21
AFC — J. Smith 5 pass from Brunell (Mare kick)
NFC — Alstott 1 run (Hanson kick)
AFC — Gonzalez 10 pass from Gannon (Mare kick)
NFC — Alstott 3 run (Hanson kick)
AFC — J. Smith 21 pass from Manning (Mare kick)
NFC — FG Hanson 51
NFC — Alstott 1 run (Hanson kick)
NFC — FG Hanson 23
AFC — FG Mare 33
NFC — Brooks 20 interception return (Hanson kick)
AFC — J. Smith 52 pass from Manning (Mare kick)
NFC — Moss 25 pass from Beuerlein (Hanson kick)

1999 AFC-NFC PRO BOWL
Aloha Stadium, Honolulu, Hawaii
February 7, 1999, Attendance: 50,075
AFC 23, NFC 10—John Elway, appearing in uniform on a football field for the final time, drove the AFC to its initial touchdown and then watched a strong defensive effort as the AFC won the Pro Bowl for the third consecutive season. Elway capped a game-opening 61-yard drive with a touchdown pass to Sam Gash. The AFC led 10-3 late in the first half when Deion Sanders intercepted a Vinny Testaverde pass at the NFC's 10 and raced downfield, only to be caught by Ed McCaffrey at the AFC 3-yard line as the half expired. The NFC drove into AFC territory early in the second half, but Ty Law thwarted the NFC's spirits with a 67-yard interception return for a touchdown to give the AFC a 17-3 lead with 9:42 left in the third quarter. The NFC reached the end zone three minutes later as Emmitt Smith scored, but the AFC responded with a field goal on its ensuing possession. Jason Elam's third field goal with 1:02 remaining finished the scoring. Elway played just one drive and was 4 of 5 for 55 yards and 1 touchdown. Keyshawn Johnson had 7 catches for 87 yards and shared player of the game honors with Law. Chandler completed 9 of 25 passes for 133 yards en route to leading the NFC to its only touchdown. Randy Moss had 7 catches for 108 yards.

NFC	3	0	7	0	—	10
AFC	7	3	10	3	—	23

AFC — Gash 3 pass from Elway (Elam kick)
NFC — FG Anderson 23
AFC — FG Elam 23
AFC — Law 67 interception return (Elam kick)
NFC — E. Smith 3 run (Anderson kick)
AFC — FG Elam 46
AFC — FG Elam 26

1998 AFC-NFC PRO BOWL
Aloha Stadium, Honolulu, Hawaii
February 1, 1998, Attendance: 49,995
AFC 29, NFC 24—Warren Moon guided the AFC to points on all three of his drives, including the winning touchdown from 1 yard with 1:49 left as the AFC scored the game's final 15 points to beat the NFC. Steve Young threw a 22-yard touchdown pass to Herman Moore to cap the game's opening drive and give the NFC a 7-0 lead. Late in the first quarter, Mark Brunell threw a 17-yard touchdown pass to Andre Rison to tie the game. Both touchdown passes came on third-and-8 plays. The NFC responded with a 7-play, 71-yard drive capped by Young's 36-yard touchdown pass to Rob Moore. Trent Dilfer guided the NFC to its third touchdown, keyed by a 21-yard pass to Irving Fryar and 23-yard pass to Mike Alstott, and capped by Dorsey Levens' 12-yard touchdown run with 1:36 left in the half to give the NFC a 21-7 lead. The NFC had a chance to pad its lead on its first possession of the second half, but Jason Hanson missed a 44-yard field goal. The AFC bounced back with a 10-play, 65-yard drive that culminated with Drew Bledsoe's 14-yard touchdown pass to Jimmy Smith late in the third quarter. After Hanson's 35-yard field goal gave the NFC a 24-14 lead with 13:42 left, Moon entered the game and drove the AFC into field-goal range, where Mike Hollis drilled a 48-yard attempt with 8:51 left. Attempting to grind out the clock, Warrick Dunn fumbled, and Darryl Williams recovered at the AFC's 49 with 3:03 remaining. After a holding penalty moved the AFC back 10 yards, Moon fired a 57-yard pass to Tim Brown to set up Eddie George's 4-yard run with 2:31 left. The AFC went for the tie instead of a tie, but Moon's pass to Rison fell incomplete. However, the AFC got the ball back when Chris Chandler fumbled the snap on the NFC's first play, and Michael Sinclair recovered at the NFC's 16 with 2:19 left. Three runs by George set up Moon's winning sneak with 1:49 remaining. Moon's 2-point conversion pass to Brown was incomplete, keeping the AFC's lead at 29-24. The NFC was unable to move beyond its own 31-yard line in the final moments, and the AFC prevailed. Tim Brown had 5 receptions for 129 yards. Moon, who was 4 of 8 for 89 yards, earned player of the game honors.

AFC	7	0	7	15	—	29
NFC	7	14	0	3	—	24

NFC — H. Moore 22 pass from Young (Hanson kick)
AFC — Rison 17 pass from Brunell (Hollis kick)
NFC — R. Moore 36 pass from Young (Hanson kick)
NFC — Levens 12 run (Hanson kick)
AFC — J. Smith 14 pass from Bledsoe (Hollis kick)
NFC — FG Hanson 35

AFC — FG Hollis 48
AFC — George 4 run (pass failed)
AFC — Moon 1 run (pass failed)

1997 AFC-NFC PRO BOWL

Aloha Stadium, Honolulu, Hawaii
February 2, 1997, Attendance: 50,031

AFC 26, NFC 23 (OT)—Cary Blanchard's 37-yard field goal 8:16 into overtime gave the AFC a 26-23 victory. The field goal was an ironic ending to a game that saw Blanchard and NFC kicker John Kasay, who each broke the previous single-season record of 35 field goals, combine to miss 5 of 8 field-goal attempts. The NFC scored on its first two possessions, with Vikings guard Randall McDaniel, who lined up as a fullback, scoring his first professional touchdown to give the NFC a 9-0 lead. However, the follies of the kicking unit began as holder Matt Turk muffed the snap on the extra point attempt. Blanchard booted a 28-yard field goal with 27 seconds left in the half to cut the NFC's lead to 9-3. In the third quarter, Barry Sanders scored from 6 yards out, but Kerry Collins was sacked on the 2-point attempt. A 41-yard pass from Drew Bledsoe to Tony Martin led to Curtis Martin's 3-yard run, and after Ashley Ambrose ran an interception back 54 yards for a touchdown 11 seconds into the fourth quarter, the AFC found itself with a 16-15 lead. The NFC drove for more than six minutes, only to have Kasay miss a 40-yard field goal attempt. After an AFC punt, Cris Carter caught a 47-yard touchdown bomb from Gus Frerotte to put the NFC ahead 23-16. After each team punted, the AFC got the ball on its own 20-yard line with 55 seconds left. Mark Brunell hit Tim Brown with an 80-yard bomb down the right sideline to tie the game with 44 seconds left. Wesley Walls caught a 33-yard pass to give the NFC a chance to win in regulation, but Kasay missed a 39-yard attempt and the game went to overtime. The AFC won the overtime toss, but Blanchard missed a 41-yard field goal attempt. The NFC had to punt after three plays, and Brunell hit Ben Coates with a 43-yard pass on the AFC's first play. After three running plays failed to gain a first down, Blanchard trotted onto the field and made the game-winning kick. The teams combined for a Pro Bowl record 962 total yards. Brunell, who completed 12 of 22 pass attempts for 236 yards, was selected as the player of the game.

AFC	0	3	7	13	3	— 26
NFC	9	0	6	8	0	— 23

NFC — FG Kasay 20
NFC — R. McDaniel 5 pass from Favre (muffed snap)
AFC — FG Blanchard 28
NFC — Sanders 6 run (pass failed)
AFC — Martin 3 run (Blanchard kick)
AFC — Ambrose 54 interception return (pass failed)

NFC — Carter 53 pass from Frerotte (Walls pass from Frerotte)
AFC — T. Brown 80 pass from Brunell (Blanchard kick)
AFC — FG Blanchard 37

1996 AFC-NFC PRO BOWL

Aloha Stadium, Honolulu, Hawaii
February 4, 1996, Attendance: 50,034

NFC 20, AFC 13—Jerry Rice had 6 receptions for 82 yards and 1 touchdown to earn player of the game honors in the NFC's victory. The 49ers' wide receiver, who was named to the Pro Bowl for the tenth consecutive year, caught a 1-yard touchdown pass from Packers quarterback Brett Favre 1:41 into the second quarter to cap an 80-yard drive and give the NFC the lead for good at 10-7. The AFC had taken a 7-0 lead 2:26 into the game when Bengals quarterback Jeff Blake connected with Steelers wide receiver Yancey Thigpen on a Pro Bowl-record 93-yard touchdown pass. The NFC increased its advantage to 20-7 at halftime on Redskins linebacker Ken Harvey's 36-yard interception return for a touchdown and Falcons kicker Morten Andersen's 24-yard field goal. The AFC trimmed its deficit to 20-13 when Colts quarterback Jim Harbaugh teamed with Patriots running back Curtis Martin on a 17-yard touchdown pass in the final minute of the third quarter, but its bid to win or tie was rebuffed twice in the final minutes of the fourth quarter. First, 49ers safety Tim McDonald intercepted Harbaugh's pass in the end zone with 1:50 remaining. Then, after the AFC forced a punt and got the ball back near midfield, Harbaugh drove his team to the NFC's 9-yard line in the closing seconds. But he spiked the ball once to stop the clock and threw 3 consecutive incompletions as time ran out. The AFC outgained the NFC 390 total yards to 287, but its quarterbacks suffered 4 interceptions, including 3 off Harbaugh, the NFL's leading passer during the regular season. The NFC raised its edge to 15-11 in Pro Bowl games since the AFL-NFL merger in 1970.

NFC	3	17	0	0	— 20
AFC	7	0	6	0	— 13

AFC — Thigpen 93 pass from Blake (Elam kick)
NFC — FG Andersen 36
NFC — Rice 1 pass from Favre (Andersen kick)
NFC — Harvey 36 interception return (Andersen kick)
NFC — FG Andersen 24
AFC — Martin 17 pass from Harbaugh (kick failed)

1995 AFC-NFC PRO BOWL

Aloha Stadium, Honolulu, Hawaii
February 5, 1995, Attendance: 50,529

AFC 41, NFC 13—Colts rookie Marshal Faulk rushed for a Pro Bowl-record 180 yards to key the AFC's rout of the NFC.

Faulk, who earned the Dan McGuire Trophy as the player of the game, averaged nearly 14 yards on his 13 carries and shattered the previous rushing mark of 112 yards set by O.J. Simpson in the 1973 game. Faulk's 49-yard touchdown run from punt formation in the fourth quarter was the longest in Pro Bowl history. The Seahawks' Chris Warren added 127 yards on 14 carries as the AFC amassed records for rushing yards (400) and total yards (552). Steelers tight end Eric Green caught 2 touchdown passes for the victors. The NFC managed only 196 total yards, a large chunk coming when 49ers quarterback Steve Young and Vikings wide receiver Cris Carter teamed on a 51-yard touchdown pass in the first quarter. That gave the NFC a 10-0 advantage, but the AFC rallied in the second quarter and took the lead for good when the Browns' Leroy Hoard scored on a 4-yard touchdown run 2:07 before halftime.

AFC	0	17	3	21	— 41
NFC	10	0	3	0	— 13

NFC — FG Reveiz 28
NFC — Carter 51 pass from Young (Reveiz kick)
AFC — Green 22 pass from Elway (Carney kick)
AFC — FG Carney 22
AFC — Hoard 4 run (Carney kick)
NFC — FG Reveiz 49
AFC — FG Carney 23
AFC — Warren 11 run (Carney kick)
AFC — Green 16 pass from Hostetler (Carney kick)
AFC — Faulk 49 run (Carney kick)

1994 AFC-NFC PRO BOWL

Aloha Stadium, Honolulu, Hawaii
February 6, 1994, Attendance: 50,026

NFC 17, AFC 3—The NFC converted a blocked punt and a fumble recovery into touchdowns just 2:20 apart in the second half of its victory over the AFC. With the score tied 3-3 late in the third quarter, Saints linebacker Renaldo Turnbull deflected a punt by the Oilers' Greg Montgomery, and the NFC took possession at the AFC's 48-yard line. A 32-yard pass from Bobby Hebert to Falcons teammate Andre Rison positioned Rams running back Jerome Bettis for a 4-yard touchdown run with 1:27 left in the third quarter. Moments later, Rams defensive tackle Sean Gilbert recovered a fumble by Oilers quarterback Warren Moon at the AFC's 19. Hebert then teamed with the Vikings' Cris Carter on a 15-yard touchdown pass 53 seconds into the fourth period. The NFC kept the AFC out of the end zone by maintaining possession for more than 38 minutes and forcing 6 turnovers. Rison earned the Dan McGuire Trophy as the player of the game by catching 6 passes for 86 yards. The victory was the fourth in the last six years for the NFC, which leads the series 14-10.

| NFC | 3 | 0 | 7 | 7 | — | 17 |
| AFC | 0 | 3 | 0 | 0 | — | 3 |

NFC — FG Johnson 35
AFC — FG Anderson 25
NFC — Bettis 4 run (Johnson kick)
NFC — Carter 15 pass from Hebert
       (Johnson kick)

1993 AFC-NFC PRO BOWL
Aloha Stadium, Honolulu, Hawaii
February 7, 1993, Attendance: 50,007
AFC 23, NFC 20—Nick Lowery's 33-yard field goal 4:09 into overtime gave the American Conference all-stars an unlikely 23-20 victory over the National Conference. Despite being overwhelmed by the NFC in first downs (30-9), and total yards (471-114), the AFC won because it forced 6 turnovers, blocked a pair of field goals (1 of which was returned for a touchdown), and returned an interception for a score. Special-teams star Steve Tasker of the Bills earned the Dan McGuire Trophy as the player of the game for making 4 tackles, forcing a fumble, and blocking a field goal. The block came with eight minutes left in regulation and the game tied at 13-13. The Raiders' Terry McDaniel picked up the loose ball and ran 28 yards for a touchdown and a 20-13 AFC lead. The NFC rallied behind 49ers quarterback Steve Young, whose fourth-down, 23-yard touchdown pass to Giants running back Rodney Hampton tied the game at 20-20 with 10 seconds left in regulation. Young completed 18 of 32 passes for 196 yards but was intercepted 3 times and lost a fumble when sacked in overtime. Raiders defensive end Howie Long fell on that fumble at the NFC 28-yard line, and five plays later, Lowery converted the winning field goal.

| AFC | 0 | 10 | 3 | 7 | 3 | — | 23 |
| NFC | 3 | 10 | 0 | 7 | 0 | — | 20 |

NFC — FG Andersen 27
AFC — Seau 31 interception return
       (Lowery kick)
NFC — FG Andersen 37
NFC — Irvin 9 pass from Aikman
       (Andersen kick)
AFC — FG Lowery 42
AFC — FG Lowery 29
AFC — McDaniel 28 blocked field goal
       return (Lowery kick)
NFC — Hampton 23 pass from Young
       (Andersen kick)
AFC — FG Lowery 33

1992 AFC-NFC PRO BOWL
Aloha Stadium, Honolulu, Hawaii
February 2, 1992, Attendance: 50,209
NFC 21, AFC 15—Atlanta's Chris Miller threw an 11-yard touchdown pass to San Francisco's Jerry Rice with 4:04 remaining in the game to lift the NFC over the AFC. It was the NFC's thirteenth win in the 22-game series. The AFC had taken a 15-14 lead when the Raiders' Jeff Jaeger kicked a 27-yard field goal 1:49 into the fourth quarter. But the NFC, aided by a key

roughing-the-passer penalty on a third-down incompletion from the AFC 24-yard line, drove 85 yards to the winning score. The Cowboys' Michael Irvin, playing in his first Pro Bowl, caught 8 passes for 125 yards, including a 13-yard touchdown in the first quarter, and was named the player of the game. Rice had 7 catches for 77 yards. Mark Rypien of Washington, the Super Bowl most valuable player one week earlier, completed 11 of 18 passes for 165 yards and 2 touchdowns for the NFC, including a 35-yard pass to Redskins teammate Gary Clark just 26 seconds before halftime. Miller completed 7 of his 10 attempts for 85 yards.

| NFC | 7 | 7 | 0 | 7 | — | 21 |
| AFC | 7 | 5 | 0 | 3 | — | 15 |

AFC — Clayton 4 pass from Kelly
       (Jaeger kick)
NFC — Irvin 13 pass from Rypien
       (Lohmiller kick)
AFC — Safety, Townsend tackled
       Byner in end zone
AFC — FG Jaeger 48
NFC — Clark 35 pass from Rypien
       (Lohmiller kick)
AFC — FG Jaeger 27
NFC — Rice 11 pass from Miller
       (Lohmiller kick)

1991 AFC-NFC PRO BOWL
Aloha Stadium, Honolulu, Hawaii
February 3, 1991, Attendance: 50,345
AFC 23, NFC 21—Buffalo's Jim Kelly and Houston's Ernest Givins combined for a 13-yard scoring pass late in the fourth quarter to rally the AFC over the NFC. Phoenix rookie Johnny Johnson scored on runs of 1 and 9 yards to put the NFC ahead 14-3 in the third quarter. Buffalo's Andre Reed, who led all receivers with 4 catches for 80 yards, caught a 20-yard scoring reception from Kelly early in the fourth quarter to move the AFC to within 1 point. Barry Sanders ran 22 yards for a touchdown to increase the NFC's lead to 21-13. Miami's Jeff Cross blocked a 46-yard field-goal attempt by New Orleans' Morten Andersen with seven seconds remaining to preserve the win. Buffalo's Bruce Smith recorded 3 sacks and also had a blocked field goal. Kelly, who completed 13 of 19 passes for 210 yards and 2 touchdowns, was presented the Dan McGuire Award as player of the game. The AFC's victory narrowed the NFC's Pro Bowl series lead to 12-9.

| AFC | 3 | 0 | 3 | 17 | — | 23 |
| NFC | 0 | 7 | 7 | 7 | — | 21 |

AFC — FG Lowery 26
NFC — J. Johnson 1 run
       (Andersen kick)
AFC — FG Lowery 43
NFC — J. Johnson 9 run
       (Andersen kick)
AFC — Reed 20 pass from Kelly
       (Lowery kick)
NFC — Sanders 22 run
       (Andersen kick)

AFC — FG Lowery 34
AFC — Givins 13 pass from Kelly
       (Lowery kick)

1990 AFC-NFC PRO BOWL
Aloha Stadium, Honolulu, Hawaii
February 4, 1990, Attendance: 50,445
NFC 27, AFC 21—The NFC captured its second straight Pro Bowl as the defense accounted for a pair of touchdowns and forced 5 turnovers before the eleventh consecutive sellout crowd at Aloha Stadium. The AFC held a 7-6 halftime edge on a 1-yard scoring run by Christian Okoye of the Chiefs. The NFC then rallied with 21 unanswered points in the third quarter. David Meggett of the Giants began the comeback with an 11-yard touchdown reception from Philadelphia's Randall Cunningham. The Rams' Jerry Gray followed with a 51-yard interception return for a score and the Vikings' Keith Millard added an 8-yard fumble return for a touchdown four minutes later to give the NFC a commanding 27-7 lead. Seattle's Dave Krieg rallied the AFC with a 5-yard touchdown pass to Miami's Ferrell Edmunds. Cleveland's Mike Johnson then returned an interception 22 yards for a score to pull the AFC to within 27-21. Gray, who was credited with 7 tackles, was given the Dan McGuire Award as player of the game. Krieg led all quarterbacks by completing 15 of 23 for 148 yards and 1 touchdown. Buffalo's Thurman Thomas topped all receivers with 5 catches for 47 yards, while Indianapolis' Eric Dickerson led all rushers with 46 yards on 15 carries. The win gave the NFC a 12-8 advantage in Pro Bowl games since 1971.

| NFC | 3 | 3 | 21 | 0 | — | 27 |
| AFC | 0 | 7 | 0 | 14 | — | 21 |

NFC — FG Murray 23
NFC — FG Murray 41
AFC — Okoye 1 run (Treadwell kick)
NFC — Meggett 11 pass from
       Cunningham (Murray kick)
NFC — Gray 51 interception return
       (Murray kick)
NFC — Millard 8 fumble recovery
       return (Murray kick)
AFC — Edmunds 5 pass from Krieg
       (Treadwell kick)
AFC — M. Johnson 22 interception
       return (Treadwell kick)

1989 AFC-NFC PRO BOWL
Aloha Stadium, Honolulu, Hawaii
January 29, 1989, Attendance: 50,113
NFC 34, AFC 3—The NFC scored 34 unanswered points to snap a two-game losing streak to the AFC before the tenth straight sellout crowd in Honolulu's Aloha Stadium. Bills kicker Scott Norwood provided the AFC's only points on a 38-yard field goal 6:23 into the game. Touchdown runs by Dallas' Herschel Walker (4 yards) and Atlanta's John Settle (1) brought the NFC a 14-3 halftime lead. Walker added a

7-yard scoring run, the Saints' Morten Andersen kicked field goals of 27 and 51 yards, and Los Angeles Rams' wide receiver Henry Ellard caught an 8-yard scoring pass from Minnesota quarterback Wade Wilson in the second half to complete the scoring. Chicago running back Neal Anderson and Philadelphia quarterback Randall Cunningham, who were both appearing in their first Pro Bowl, also played major roles in the NFC's victory. Anderson rushed 13 times for 85 yards and had 2 receptions for 17. Cunningham, who was voted the game's outstanding player, completed 10 of 14 passes for 63 yards and rushed for 49 yards. The NFC, which had 5 takeaways, outgained the AFC 355 yards to 167 and held a time-of-possession advantage of 35:18 to 24:42. Houston quarterback Warren Moon completed 13 of 25 passes for 134 yards for the AFC. The win gave the NFC an 11-8 advantage in Pro Bowl games.

AFC	3	0	0	0	— 3
NFC	7	7	10	10	— 34

AFC — FG Norwood 38
NFC — Walker 4 run (Andersen kick)
NFC — Settle 1 run (Andersen kick)
NFC — FG Andersen 27
NFC — Walker 7 run (Andersen kick)
NFC — FG Andersen 51
NFC — Ellard 8 pass from Wilson (Andersen kick)

1988 AFC-NFC PRO BOWL
Aloha Stadium, Honolulu, Hawaii
February 7, 1988, Attendance: 50,113
AFC 15, NFC 6—Led by a tenacious pass rush, the AFC defeated the NFC for the second consecutive year before the ninth straight sellout crowd in Honolulu's Aloha Stadium. Buffalo quarterback Jim Kelly scored the game's lone touchdown on a 1-yard run for a 7-6 halftime lead. Colts kicker Dean Biasucci added field goals from 37 and 30 yards to complete the AFC's scoring. Saints kicker Morten Andersen had 25- and 36-yard field goals to account for the NFC's points. AFC defenders held the NFC to 213 yards and recorded 8 sacks. Bills defensive end Bruce Smith, who had 2 sacks among his 5 tackles, was voted the game's outstanding player. Oilers running back Mike Rozier led all rushers with 49 yards on 9 carries. Jets wide receiver Al Toon had 5 receptions for 75 yards. The AFC generated 341 yards total offense and held a time-of-possession advantage of 34:14 to 25:46. By winning, the AFC cut the NFC's lead in the Pro Bowl series to 10-8.

NFC	0	6	0	0	— 6
AFC	0	7	6	2	— 15

NFC — FG Andersen 25
AFC — Kelly 1 run (Biasucci kick)
NFC — FG Andersen 36
AFC — FG Biasucci 37
AFC — FG Biasucci 30
AFC — Safety, Montana forced out of end zone

1987 AFC-NFC PRO BOWL
Aloha Stadium, Honolulu, Hawaii
February 1, 1987, Attendance: 50,101
AFC 10, NFC 6—The AFC defeated the NFC in the lowest-scoring game in AFC-NFC Pro Bowl history. The AFC took a 10-0 halftime lead on Broncos quarterback John Elway's 10-yard touchdown pass to Raiders tight end Todd Christensen and Patriots kicker Tony Franklin's 26-yard field goal. The AFC defense made the lead stand by forcing the NFC to settle for a pair of field goals from 38 and 19 yards by Saints kicker Morten Andersen after the NFC had first downs at the AFC 31-, 7-, 16-, 15-, 5-, and 7-yard lines. Both AFC scores were set up by fumble recoveries by Seahawks linebacker Fredd Young and Dolphins linebacker John Offerdahl, respectively. Eagles defensive end Reggie White, who tied a Pro Bowl record with 4 sacks among his 7 solo tackles, was voted the game's outstanding player. The AFC victory cut the NFC's lead in the Pro Bowl series to 10-7.

AFC	7	3	0	0	— 10
NFC	0	0	3	3	— 6

AFC — Christensen 10 pass from Elway (Franklin kick)
AFC — FG Franklin 26
NFC — FG Andersen 38
NFC — FG Andersen 19

1986 AFC-NFC PRO BOWL
Aloha Stadium, Honolulu, Hawaii
February 2, 1986, Attendance: 50,101
NFC 28, AFC 24—New York Giants quarterback Phil Simms brought the NFC back from a 24-7 halftime deficit to defeat the AFC. Simms, who completed 15 of 27 passes for 212 yards and 3 touchdowns, was named the most valuable player of the game. The AFC had taken its first-half lead behind a 2-yard run by Los Angeles Raiders running back Marcus Allen, who also threw a 51-yard scoring pass to San Diego wide receiver Wes Chandler, an 11-yard touchdown catch by Pittsburgh wide receiver Louis Lipps, and a 34-yard field goal by Steelers kicker Gary Anderson. Minnesota's Joey Browner accounted for the NFC's only score before halftime with a 48-yard interception return. After intermission, the NFC blanked the AFC while scoring 3 touchdowns via a 15-yard catch by Washington wide receiver Art Monk, a 2-yard reception by Dallas tight end Doug Cosbie, and a 15-yard catch by Tampa Bay tight end Jimmie Giles with 2:47 remaining in the game. The victory gave the NFC a 10-6 Pro Bowl record against the AFC.

NFC	0	7	7	14	— 28
AFC	7	17	0	0	— 24

AFC — Allen 2 run (Anderson kick)
NFC — Browner 48 interception return (Anderson kick)
AFC — Chandler 51 pass from Allen (Anderson kick)
AFC — FG Anderson 34

AFC — Lipps 11 pass from O'Brien (Anderson kick)
NFC — Monk 15 pass from Simms (Andersen kick)
NFC — Cosbie 2 pass from Simms (Andersen kick)
NFC — Giles 15 pass from Simms (Andersen kick)

1985 AFC-NFC PRO BOWL
Aloha Stadium, Honolulu, Hawaii
January 27, 1985, Attendance: 50,385
AFC 22, NFC 14—Defensive end Art Still of the Kansas City Chiefs recovered a fumble and returned it 83 yards for a touchdown to clinch the AFC's victory over the NFC. Still's touchdown came in the fourth period with the AFC trailing 14-12 and was one of several outstanding defensive plays in a Pro Bowl dominated by two record-breaking defenses. The teams combined for a Pro Bowl-record 17 sacks, including 4 by New York Jets defensive end Mark Gastineau, who was named the game's outstanding player. AFC's first score came on a safety when Gastineau tackled running back Eric Dickerson of the Los Angeles Rams in the end zone. The AFC's second score, a 6-yard pass from Miami's Dan Marino to Los Angeles Raiders running back Marcus Allen, was set up by a partial block of a punt by Seahawks linebacker Fredd Young. The NFC leads the series 9-6.

AFC	0	9	0	13	— 22
NFC	0	0	7	7	— 14

AFC — Safety, Gastineau tackled Dickerson in end zone
AFC — Allen 6 pass from Marino (Johnson kick)
NFC — Lofton 13 pass from Montana (Stenerud kick)
NFC — Payton 1 run (Stenerud kick)
AFC — FG Johnson 33
AFC — Still 83 fumble recovery return (Johnson kick)
AFC — FG Johnson 22

1984 AFC-NFC PRO BOWL
Aloha Stadium, Honolulu, Hawaii
January 29, 1984, Attendance: 50,445
NFC 45, AFC 3—The NFC won its sixth Pro Bowl in the last seven seasons by routing the AFC. The NFC was led by the passing of most valuable player Joe Theismann of Washington, who completed 21 of 27 passes for 242 yards and 3 touchdowns. Theismann set Pro Bowl records for completions and touchdown passes. The NFC established Pro Bowl marks for most points scored and fewest points allowed. Running back William Andrews of Atlanta had 6 carries for 43 yards and caught 4 passes for 49 yards, including scoring receptions of 16 and 2 yards. Los Angeles Rams rookie Eric Dickerson gained 46 yards on 11 carries, including a 14-yard touchdown run, and had 45 yards on 5 catches. Rams safety Nolan Cromwell had a 44-yard intercep-

tion return for a touchdown early in the third period to give the NFC a commanding 24-3 lead. Green Bay wide receiver James Lofton caught an 8-yard touchdown pass, while tight end teammate Paul Coffman had a 6-yard scoring catch.

NFC	3	14	14	14	—	45
AFC	0	3	0	0	—	3

NFC — FG Haji-Sheikh 23
NFC — Andrews 16 pass from Theismann (Haji-Sheikh kick)
NFC — Andrews 2 pass from Montana (Haji-Sheikh kick)
AFC — FG Anderson 43
NFC — Cromwell 44 interception return (Haji-Sheikh kick)
NFC — Lofton 8 pass from Theismann (Haji-Sheikh kick)
NFC — Coffman 6 pass from Theismann (Haji-Sheikh kick)
NFC — Dickerson 14 run (Haji-Sheikh kick)

1983 AFC-NFC PRO BOWL
Aloha Stadium, Honolulu, Hawaii
February 6, 1983, Attendance: 49,883
NFC 20, AFC 19—Dallas' Danny White threw an 11-yard touchdown pass to the Packers' John Jefferson with 35 seconds remaining to rally the NFC over the AFC. White, who completed 14 of 26 passes for 162 yards, kept the winning 65-yard drive alive with a 14-yard completion to Jefferson on a fourth-and-7 play at the AFC 25. The AFC was ahead 12-10 at halftime and increased the lead to 19-10 in the third period, when Marcus Allen scored on a 1-yard run. San Diego's Dan Fouts, who attempted 30 passes, set Pro Bowl records for most completions (17) and yards (274). Pittsburgh's John Stallworth was the AFC's leading receiver with 7 catches for 67 yards. William Andrews topped the NFC with 5 receptions for 48 yards. Fouts and Jefferson were co-winners of the player of the game award.

AFC	9	3	7	0	—	19
NFC	0	10	0	10	—	20

AFC — Walker 34 pass from Fouts (Benirschke kick)
AFC — Safety, Still tackled Theismann in end zone
NFC — Andrews 3 run (Moseley kick)
NFC — FG Moseley 35
AFC — FG Benirschke 29
AFC — Allen 1 run (Benirschke kick)
NFC — FG Moseley 41
NFC — Jefferson 11 pass from D. White (Moseley kick)

1982 AFC-NFC PRO BOWL
Aloha Stadium, Honolulu, Hawaii
January 31, 1982, Attendance: 50,402
AFC 16, NFC 13—Nick Lowery of Kansas City kicked a 23-yard field goal with three seconds remaining to give the AFC a last-second victory over the NFC. Lowery's kick climaxed a 69-yard drive directed by quarterback Dan Fouts. The NFC gained a 13-13 tie with 2:43 to go when Dallas'

Tony Dorsett ran 4 yards for a touchdown. In the drive to the winning field goal, Fouts completed 3 passes, including a 23-yard toss to San Diego teammate Kellen Winslow that put the ball on the NFC's 5-yard line. Two plays later, Lowery kicked the field goal. Winslow, who caught 6 passes for 86 yards, was named co-player of the game along with Tampa Bay defensive end Lee Roy Selmon.

NFC	0	6	0	7	—	13
AFC	0	0	13	3	—	16

NFC — Giles 4 pass from Montana (kick blocked)
AFC — Muncie 2 run (kick failed)
AFC — Campbell 1 run (Lowery kick)
NFC — Dorsett 4 run (Septien kick)
AFC — FG Lowery 23

1981 AFC-NFC PRO BOWL
Aloha Stadium, Honolulu, Hawaii
February 1, 1981, Attendance: 50,360
NFC 21, AFC 7—Eddie Murray kicked 4 field goals and Steve Bartkowski fired a 55-yard scoring pass to Alfred Jenkins to lead the NFC to its fourth straight victory over the AFC and a 7-4 edge in the series. Murray was named the game's most valuable player and missed tying Garo Yepremian's Pro Bowl record of 5 field goals when a 37-yard attempt hit the crossbar with 22 seconds left. The AFC's only score came on a 9-yard pass from Brian Sipe to Stanley Morgan. Bartkowski completed 9 of 21 passes for 173 yards, while Sipe connected on 10 of 15 for 142 yards. Ottis Anderson led all rushers with 70 yards on 10 carries. Earl Campbell, the NFL's leading rusher in 1980, was limited to 24 yards on 8 attempts.

AFC	0	7	0	0	—	7
NFC	3	6	0	12	—	21

NFC — FG Murray 31
AFC — Morgan 9 pass from Sipe (J. Smith kick)
NFC — FG Murray 31
NFC — FG Murray 34
NFC — Jenkins 55 pass from Bartkowski (Murray kick)
NFC — FG Murray 39
NFC — Safety, Shell called for holding in end zone

1980 AFC-NFC PRO BOWL
Aloha Stadium, Honolulu, Hawaii
January 27, 1980, Attendance: 49,800
NFC 37, AFC 27—Chuck Muncie ran for 2 touchdowns and threw a 25-yard option pass for another score to give the NFC its third consecutive victory over the AFC. The Saints' Muncie, who was selected the game's most valuable player, snapped a 3-3 tie on a 1-yard touchdown run at 1:41 of the second quarter, then scored on an 11-yard run in the fourth quarter for the NFC's final touchdown. Two scoring records were set in the game—37 points by the NFC, eclipsing the 33 by the AFC in 1973, and the 64 points by both teams, surpassing the 61 scored in 1973.

NFC	3	20	7	7	—	37
AFC	3	7	10	7	—	27

NFC — FG Moseley 37
AFC — FG Fritsch 19
NFC — Muncie 1 run (Moseley kick)
AFC — Pruitt 1 pass from Bradshaw (Fritsch kick)
NFC — D. Hill 13 pass from Manning (kick failed)
NFC — T. Hill 25 pass from Muncie (Moseley kick)
NFC — Henry 86 punt return (Moseley kick)
AFC — Campbell 2 run (Fritsch kick)
AFC — FG Fritsch 29
NFC — Muncie 11 run (Moseley kick)
AFC — Campbell 1 run (Fritsch kick)

1979 AFC-NFC PRO BOWL
Memorial Coliseum, Los Angeles, CA
January 29, 1979, Attendance: 46,281
NFC 13, AFC 7—Roger Staubach completed 9 of 15 passes for 125 yards, including the winning touchdown on a 19-yard strike to Dallas Cowboys teammate Tony Hill in the third period. The winning drive began at the AFC's 45-yard line after a shanked punt. Staubach hit Ahmad Rashad with passes of 15 and 17 yards to set up Hill's decisive catch. The victory gave the NFC a 5-4 advantage in Pro Bowl games. Rashad, who accounted for 89 yards on 5 receptions, was named the player of the game. The AFC led 7-6 at halftime on Bob Griese's 8-yard scoring toss to Steve Largent late in the second quarter. Largent had 5 receptions for 75 yards. The NFC scored first as Archie Manning marched his team 70 yards in 11 plays, capped by Wilbert Montgomery's 2-yard touchdown run. The AFC's Earl Campbell was the game's leading rusher with 66 yards on 12 carries.

AFC	0	7	0	0	—	7
NFC	0	6	7	0	—	13

NFC — Montgomery 2 run (kick failed)
AFC — Largent 8 pass from Griese (Yepremian kick)
NFC — T. Hill 19 pass from Staubach (Corral kick)

1978 AFC-NFC PRO BOWL
Tampa Stadium, Tampa, Florida
January 23, 1978, Attendance: 51,337
NFC 14, AFC 13—Walter Payton, the NFL's leading rusher in 1977, sparked a second-half comeback to give the NFC the win and tie the series between the two conferences at four victories each. Payton, who was the game's most valuable player, gained 77 yards on 13 carries and scored the tying touchdown on a 1-yard burst with 7:37 left in the game. Efren Herrera kicked the winning extra point. The AFC dominated the first half of the game, taking a 13-0 lead on field goals of 21 and 39 yards by Toni Linhart and a 10-yard touchdown pass from Ken Stabler to Oakland teammate Cliff Branch. On the

NFC's first possession of the second half, Pat Haden put together the first touchdown drive after Eddie Brown returned a punt to the AFC 46-yard line. Haden connected on all 4 of his passes on that drive, finally hitting Terry Metcalf with a 4-yard scoring toss. The NFC continued to rally and, with Jim Hart at quarterback, moved 63 yards in 12 plays for the go-ahead score. During the winning drive, Hart completed 5 of 6 passes for 38 yards and Payton picked up 20 more on the ground.

AFC	3	10	0	0	—	13
NFC	0	0	7	7	—	14

AFC — FG Linhart 21
AFC — Branch 10 pass from Stabler (Linhart kick)
AFC — FG Linhart 39
NFC — Metcalf 4 pass from Haden (Herrera kick)
NFC — Payton 1 run (Herrera kick)

1977 AFC-NFC PRO BOWL
Kingdome, Seattle, Washington
January 17, 1977, Attendance: 64,752
AFC 24, NFC 14—O.J. Simpson's 3-yard touchdown burst at 7:03 of the first quarter gave the AFC a lead it would not surrender, breaking a two-game NFC win streak and giving the AFC stars a 4-3 series lead. The AFC took a 17-7 lead midway through the second period on the first of 2 Ken Anderson touchdown passes, a 12-yard toss to Charlie Joiner. But the NFC mounted a 73-yard drive capped by Lawrence McCutcheon's 1-yard touchdown plunge to pull within 17-14 at the half. Following a scoreless third quarter, player of the game Mel Blount thwarted a possible NFC score when he intercepted Jim Hart's pass in the end zone. Less than three minutes later, Blount again picked off a Hart pass. That set up Anderson's 27-yard touchdown strike to Cliff Branch for the final score.

NFC	0	14	0	0	—	14
AFC	10	7	0	7	—	24

AFC — Simpson 3 run (Linhart kick)
AFC — FG Linhart 31
NFC — Thomas 15 run (Bakken kick)
AFC — Joiner 12 pass from Anderson (Linhart kick)
NFC — McCutcheon 1 run (Bakken kick)
AFC — Branch 27 pass from Anderson (Linhart kick)

1976 AFC-NFC PRO BOWL
Superdome, New Orleans, Louisiana
January 26, 1976, Attendance: 30,546
NFC 23, AFC 20—Mike Boryla, a late substitute who did not enter the game until 5:39 remained, lifted the National Football Conference to the victory over the American Football Conference with 2 touchdown passes in the final minutes. It was the second straight NFC win, squaring the series at 3-3. Until Boryla started firing the ball the AFC was in control, leading 13-0 at the half. Boryla entered the game after

Billy Johnson had raced 90 yards with a punt to give the AFC a 20-9 lead. He floated a 14-yard touchdown pass to Terry Metcalf and later fired an 8-yard scoring pass to Mel Gray for the winner.

AFC	0	13	0	7	—	20
NFC	0	0	9	14	—	23

AFC — FG Stenerud 20
AFC — FG Stenerud 35
AFC — Burrough 64 pass from Pastorini (Stenerud kick)
NFC — FG Bakken 42
NFC — Foreman 4 pass from Hart (kick blocked)
AFC — Johnson 90 punt return (Stenerud kick)
NFC — Metcalf 14 pass from Boryla (Bakken kick)
NFC — Gray 8 pass from Boryla (Bakken kick)

1975 AFC-NFC PRO BOWL
Orange Bowl, Miami, Florida
January 20, 1975, Attendance: 26,484
NFC 17, AFC 10—Los Angeles quarterback James Harris, who took over the NFC offense after Jim Hart of St. Louis suffered a laceration above his right eye in the second period, threw 2 touchdown passes early in the fourth period to pace the NFC to its second victory in the five-game Pro Bowl series. The NFC win snapped a three-game AFC victory string. Harris, who was named the player of the game, connected with St. Louis' Mel Gray for an 8-yard touchdown 2:03 into the final period. One minute and 24 seconds later, following a fumble recovery by Washington's Ken Houston, Harris tossed another 8-yard scoring pass to Washington's Charley Taylor for the decisive points.

NFC	0	3	0	14	—	17
AFC	0	0	10	0	—	10

NFC — FG Marcol 33
AFC — Warfield 32 pass from Griese (Gerela kick)
AFC — FG Gerela 33
NFC — Gray 8 pass from J. Harris (Marcol kick)
NFC — Taylor 8 pass from J. Harris (Marcol kick)

1974 AFC-NFC PRO BOWL
Arrowhead Stadium, Kansas City, MO
January 20, 1974, Attendance: 66,918
AFC 15, NFC 13—Miami's Garo Yepremian's fifth field goal—a 42-yard kick with 21 seconds remaining—gave the AFC its third straight victory since the NFC won the inaugural game following the 1970 season. The field goal by Yepremian, who was voted the game's outstanding player, offset a 21-yard field goal by Atlanta's Nick Mike-Mayer that had given the NFC a 13-12 advantage with 1:41 remaining. The only touchdown in the game was scored by the NFC on a 14-yard pass from Philadelphia's Roman Gabriel to the Rams' Lawrence McCutcheon.

NFC	0	10	0	3	—	13
AFC	3	3	3	6	—	15

AFC — FG Yepremian 16
NFC — FG Mike-Mayer 27
NFC — McCutcheon 14 pass from Gabriel (Mike-Mayer kick)
AFC — FG Yepremian 37
AFC — FG Yepremian 27
AFC — FG Yepremian 41
NFC — FG Mike-Mayer 21
AFC — FG Yepremian 42

1973 AFC-NFC PRO BOWL
Texas Stadium, Irving, Texas
January 21, 1973, Attendance: 37,091
AFC 33, NFC 28—Paced by the rushing and receiving of player of the game O.J. Simpson, the AFC erased a 14-0 first period deficit and built a commanding 33-14 lead midway through the fourth period before the NFC managed 2 touchdowns in the final minute of play. Simpson rushed for 112 yards and caught 3 passes for 58 more to gain unanimous recognition in the balloting for player of the game. Green Bay Packers running back John Brockington scored 3 touchdowns for the NFC.

AFC	0	10	10	13	—	33
NFC	14	0	0	14	—	28

NFC — Brockington 1 run (Marcol kick)
NFC — Brockington 3 pass from Kilmer (Marcol kick)
AFC — Simpson 7 run (Gerela kick)
AFC — FG Gerela 18
AFC — FG Gerela 22
AFC — Hubbard 11 run (Gerela kick)
AFC — O. Taylor 5 pass from Lamonica (kick failed)
AFC — Bell 12 interception return (Gerela kick)
NFC — Brockington 1 run (Marcol kick)
NFC — Kwalick 12 pass from Snead (Marcol kick)

1972 AFC-NFC PRO BOWL
Memorial Coliseum, Los Angeles, CA
January 23, 1972, Attendance: 53,647
AFC 26, NFC 13—Kansas City's Jan Stenerud kicked 4 field goals to lead the AFC from a 6-0 deficit to victory. The AFC defense picked off 3 passes. Stenerud was selected as the outstanding offensive player and his Kansas City teammate, linebacker Willie Lanier, was the game's outstanding defensive player.

AFC	0	3	13	10	—	26
NFC	0	6	0	7	—	13

NFC — Grim 50 pass from Landry (kick failed)
AFC — FG Stenerud 25
AFC — FG Stenerud 23
AFC — FG Stenerud 48
AFC — Morin 5 pass from Dawson (Stenerud kick)
AFC — FG Stenerud 42
NFC — V. Washington 2 run (Knight kick)
AFC — F. Little 6 run (Stenerud kick)

1971 AFC-NFC PRO BOWL
Memorial Coliseum, Los Angeles, CA
January 24, 1971, Attendance: 48,222
NFC 27, AFC 6—Mel Renfro of Dallas
broke open the first meeting between the
American Football Conference and National Football Conference all-star teams as
he returned a pair of punts 82 and 56
yards for touchdowns in the final period to
clinch the NFC victory over the AFC. Renfro was voted the game's outstanding
back and linebacker Fred Carr of Green
Bay the outstanding lineman.

AFC	0	3	3	0 —	6
NFC	0	3	10	14 —	27

AFC — FG Stenerud 37
NFC — FG Cox 13
NFC — Osborn 23 pass from Brodie
　　　(Cox kick)
NFC — FG Cox 35
AFC — FG Stenerud 16
NFC — Renfro 82 punt return (Cox
　　　kick)
NFC — Renfro 56 punt return (Cox
　　　kick)

Includes AFL All-Star Game played after the 1961-69 seasons.

Date	Result/Honored players	Site (attendance)
Jan. 15, 1939	New York Giants 13, Pro All-Stars 10	Wrigley Field, Los Angeles (20,000)
Jan. 14, 1940	Green Bay 16, NFL All-Stars 7	Gilmore Stadium, Los Angeles (18,000)
Dec. 29, 1940	Chicago Bears 28, NFL All-Stars 14	Gilmore Stadium, Los Angeles (21,624)
Jan. 4, 1942	Chicago Bears 35, NFL All-Stars 24	Polo Grounds, New York (17,725)
Dec. 27, 1942	NFL All-Stars 17, Washington 14	Shibe Park, Philadelphia (18,671)
Jan. 14, 1951	American Conf. 28, National Conf. 27	Los Angeles Memorial Coliseum (53,676)
	Otto Graham, Cleveland, player of the game	
Jan. 12, 1952	National Conf. 30, American Conf. 13	Los Angeles Memorial Coliseum (19,400)
	Dan Towler, Los Angeles, player of the game	
Jan. 10, 1953	National Conf. 27, American Conf. 7	Los Angeles Memorial Coliseum (34,208)
	Don Doll, Detroit, player of the game	
Jan. 17, 1954	East 20, West 9	Los Angeles Memorial Coliseum (44,214)
	Chuck Bednarik, Philadelphia, player of the game	
Jan. 16, 1955	West 26, East 19	Los Angeles Memorial Coliseum (43,972)
	Billy Wilson, San Francisco, player of the game	
Jan. 15, 1956	East 31, West 30	Los Angeles Memorial Coliseum (37,867)
	Ollie Matson, Chi. Cardinals, player of the game	
Jan. 13, 1957	West 19, East 10	Los Angeles Memorial Coliseum (44,177)
	Bert Rechichar, Baltimore, outstanding back	
	Ernie Stautner, Pittsburgh, outstanding lineman	
Jan. 12, 1958	West 26, East 7	Los Angeles Memorial Coliseum (66,634)
	Hugh McElhenny, San Francisco, outstanding back	
	Gene Brito, Washington, outstanding lineman	
Jan. 11, 1959	East 28, West 21	Los Angeles Memorial Coliseum (72,250)
	Frank Gifford, N.Y. Giants, outstanding back	
	Doug Atkins, Chi. Bears, outstanding lineman	
Jan. 17, 1960	West 38, East 21	Los Angeles Memorial Coliseum (56,876)
	Johnny Unitas, Baltimore, outstanding back	
	Gene (Big Daddy) Lipscomb, Baltimore, outstanding lineman	
Jan. 15, 1961	West 35, East 31	Los Angeles Memorial Coliseum (62,971)
	Johnny Unitas, Baltimore, outstanding back	
	Sam Huff, N.Y. Giants, outstanding lineman	
Jan. 7, 1962	AFL West 47, East 27	Balboa Stadium, San Diego (20,973)
	Cotton Davidson, Dallas Texans, player of the game	
Jan. 14, 1962	NFL West 31, East 30	Los Angeles Memorial Coliseum (57,409)
	Jim Brown, Cleveland, outstanding back	
	Henry Jordan, Green Bay, outstanding lineman	
Jan. 13, 1963	AFL West 21, East 14	Balboa Stadium, San Diego (27,641)
	Curtis McClinton, Dallas Texans, outstanding offensive player	
	Earl Faison, San Diego, outstanding defensive player	
Jan. 13, 1963	NFL East 30, West 20	Los Angeles Memorial Coliseum (61,374)
	Jim Brown, Cleveland, outstanding back	
	Gene (Big Daddy) Lipscomb, Pittsburgh, outstanding lineman	
Jan. 12, 1964	NFL West 31, East 17	Los Angeles Memorial Coliseum (67,242)
	Johnny Unitas, Baltimore, player of the game	
	Gino Marchetti, Baltimore, outstanding lineman	
Jan. 19, 1964	AFL West 27, East 24	Balboa Stadium, San Diego (20,016)
	Keith Lincoln, San Diego, outstanding offensive player	
	Archie Matsos, Oakland, outstanding defensive player	
Jan. 10, 1965	NFL West 34, East 14	Los Angeles Memorial Coliseum (60,598)
	Fran Tarkenton, Minnesota, outstanding back	
	Terry Barr, Detroit, outstanding lineman	
Jan. 16, 1965	AFL West 38, East 14	Jeppesen Stadium, Houston (15,446)
	Keith Lincoln, San Diego, outstanding offensive player	
	Willie Brown, Denver, outstanding defensive player	
Jan. 15, 1966	AFL All-Stars 30, Buffalo 19	Rice Stadium, Houston (35,572)
	Joe Namath, N.Y. Jets, most valuable player, offense	
	Frank Buncom, San Diego, most valuable player, defense	
Jan. 15, 1966	NFL East 36, West 7	Los Angeles Memorial Coliseum (60,124)
	Jim Brown, Cleveland, outstanding back	
	Dale Meinert, St. Louis, outstanding lineman	
Jan. 21, 1967	AFL East 30, West 23	Oakland-Alameda County Coliseum (18,876)
	Babe Parilli, Boston, outstanding offensive player	
	Verlon Biggs, N.Y. Jets, outstanding defensive player	
Jan. 22, 1967	NFL East 20, West 10	Los Angeles Memorial Coliseum (15,062)
	Gale Sayers, Chicago, outstanding back	
	Floyd Peters, Philadelphia, outstanding lineman	

Jan. 21, 1968   AFL East 25, West 24 ....Gator Bowl, Jacksonville, Fla. (40,103)
    Joe Namath and Don Maynard, N.Y. Jets, out. off. players
    Leslie (Speedy) Duncan, San Diego, out. def. player

Jan. 21, 1968   NFL West 38, East 20 ....Los Angeles Memorial Coliseum (53,289)
    Gale Sayers, Chicago, outstanding back
    Dave Robinson, Green Bay, outstanding lineman

Jan. 19, 1969   AFL West 38, East 25 ....Gator Bowl, Jacksonville, Fla. (41,058)
    Len Dawson, Kansas City, outstanding offensive player
    George Webster, Houston, outstanding defensive player

Jan. 19, 1969   NFL West 10, East 7 ....Los Angeles Memorial Coliseum (32,050)
    Roman Gabriel, Los Angeles, outstanding back
    Merlin Olsen, Los Angeles, outstanding lineman

Jan. 17, 1970   AFL West 26, East 3 ....Astrodome, Houston (30,170)
    John Hadl, San Diego, player of the game

Jan. 18, 1970   NFL West 16, East 13 ....Los Angeles Memorial Coliseum (57,786)
    Gale Sayers, Chicago, outstanding back
    George Andrie, Dallas, outstanding lineman

Jan. 24, 1971   NFC 27, AFC 6 ....Los Angeles Memorial Coliseum (48,222)
    Mel Renfro, Dallas, outstanding back
    Fred Carr, Green Bay, outstanding lineman

Jan. 23, 1972   AFC 26, NFC 13 ....Los Angeles Memorial Coliseum (53,647)
    Jan Stenerud, Kansas City, outstanding offensive player
    Willie Lanier, Kansas City, outstanding defensive player

Jan. 21, 1973   AFC 33, NFC 28 ....Texas Stadium, Irving (37,091)
    O.J. Simpson, Buffalo, player of the game

Jan. 20, 1974   AFC 15, NFC 13 ....Arrowhead Stadium, Kansas City (66,918)
    Garo Yepremian, Miami, player of the game

Jan. 20, 1975   NFC 17, AFC 10 ....Orange Bowl, Miami (26,484)
    James Harris, Los Angeles, player of the game

Jan. 26, 1976   NFC 23, AFC 20 ....Louisiana Superdome, New Orleans (30,546)
    Billy Johnson, Houston, player of the game

Jan. 17, 1977   AFC 24, NFC 14 ....Kingdome, Seattle (64,752)
    Mel Blount, Pittsburgh, player of the game

Jan. 23, 1978   NFC 14, AFC 13 ....Tampa Stadium (51,337)
    Walter Payton, Chicago, player of the game

Jan. 29, 1979   NFC 13, AFC 7 ....Los Angeles Memorial Coliseum (46,281)
    Ahmad Rashad, Minnesota, player of the game

Jan. 27, 1980   NFC 37, AFC 27 ....Aloha Stadium, Honolulu (49,800)
    Chuck Muncie, New Orleans, player of the game

Feb. 1, 1981   NFC 21, AFC 7 ....Aloha Stadium, Honolulu (50,360)
    Eddie Murray, Detroit, player of the game

Jan. 31, 1982   AFC 16, NFC 13 ....Aloha Stadium, Honolulu (50,402)
    Kellen Winslow, San Diego, and Lee Roy Selmon, Tampa Bay, players of the game

Feb. 6, 1983   NFC 20, AFC 19 ....Aloha Stadium, Honolulu (49,883)
    Dan Fouts, San Diego, and John Jefferson, Green Bay, players of the game

Jan. 29, 1984   NFC 45, AFC 3 ....Aloha Stadium, Honolulu (50,445)
    Joe Theismann, Washington, player of the game

Jan. 27, 1985   AFC 22, NFC 14 ....Aloha Stadium, Honolulu (50,385)
    Mark Gastineau, N.Y. Jets, player of the game

Feb. 2, 1986   NFC 28, AFC 24 ....Aloha Stadium, Honolulu (50,101)
    Phil Simms, N.Y. Giants, player of the game

Feb. 1, 1987   AFC 10, NFC 6 ....Aloha Stadium, Honolulu (50,101)
    Reggie White, Philadelphia, player of the game

Feb. 7, 1988   AFC 15, NFC 6 ....Aloha Stadium, Honolulu (50,113)
    Bruce Smith, Buffalo, player of the game

Jan. 29, 1989   NFC 34, AFC 3 ....Aloha Stadium, Honolulu (50,113)
    Randall Cunningham, Philadelphia, player of the game

Feb. 4, 1990   NFC 27, AFC 21 ....Aloha Stadium, Honolulu (50,445)
    Jerry Gray, L.A. Rams, player of the game

Feb. 3, 1991   AFC 23, NFC 21 ....Aloha Stadium, Honolulu (50,345)
    Jim Kelly, Buffalo, player of the game

Feb. 2, 1992   NFC 21, AFC 15 ....Aloha Stadium, Honolulu (50,209)
    Michael Irvin, Dallas, player of the game

Feb. 7, 1993   AFC 23, NFC 20 (OT) ....Aloha Stadium, Honolulu (50,007)
    Steve Tasker, Buffalo, player of the game

Feb. 6, 1994   NFC 17, AFC 3 ....Aloha Stadium, Honolulu (50,026)
    Andre Rison, Atlanta, player of the game

Feb. 5, 1995   AFC 41, NFC 13 ....Aloha Stadium, Honolulu (50,529)
    Marshall Faulk, Indianapolis, player of the game

Feb. 4, 1996	NFC 20, AFC 13	Aloha Stadium, Honolulu (50,034)
	Jerry Rice, San Francisco, player of the game	
Feb. 2, 1997	AFC 26, NFC 23 (OT)	Aloha Stadium, Honolulu (50,031)
	Mark Brunell, Jacksonville, player of the game	
Feb. 1, 1998	AFC 29, NFC 24	Aloha Stadium, Honolulu (49,995)
	Warren Moon, Seattle, player of the game	
Feb. 7, 1999	AFC 23, NFC 10	Aloha Stadium, Honolulu (50,075)
	Keyshawn Johnson, N.Y. Jets and Ty Law, New England, co-players of the game	
Feb. 6, 2000	NFC 51, AFC 31	Aloha Stadium, Honolulu (50,112)
	Randy Moss, Minnesota, player of the game	
Feb. 4, 2001	AFC 38, NFC 17	Aloha Stadium, Honolulu (50,128)
	Rich Gannon, Oakland, player of the game	
Feb. 9, 2002	AFC 38, NFC 30	Aloha Stadium, Honolulu (50,301)
	Rich Gannon, Oakland, player of the game	
Feb. 2, 2003	AFC 45, NFC 20	Aloha Stadium, Honolulu (50,125)
	Ricky Williams, Miami, player of the game	
Feb. 8, 2004	NFC 55, AFC 52	Aloha Stadium, Honolulu (50,127)
	Marc Bulger, St. Louis, player of the game	
Feb. 13, 2005	AFC 38, NFC 27	Aloha Stadium, Honolulu (50,225)
	Peyton Manning, Indianapolis, player of the game	

AFC VS. NFC (REGULAR SEASON), 1970-2004

	Balt	Buff	Cin	Cle	Den	Hou	Ind	Jax	KC	Mia
1970		0-3	1-2	0-3	2-2		3-0		0-2-1	2-1
1971		0-3	1-2	2-1	1-3		2-1		2-1	3-0
1972		2-0-1	2-1	1-2	1-3		0-3		2-1	3-0
1973		2-1	2-1	1-2	0-3-1		2-1		1-1-1	3-0
1974		2-1	2-1	1-2	2-2		1-2		1-2	2-1
1975		1-2	3-0	1-3	2-1		2-1		2-1	3-0
1976		0-2	2-0	2-0	2-0		0-2		1-1	0-2
1977		1-1	2-1	1-1	1-1		1-1		1-1	2-0
1978		1-1	2-2	4-0	2-2		2-2		0-2	3-1
1979		2-2	2-2	3-1	3-1		1-1		0-2	4-0
1980		3-1	2-2	3-1	3-1		1-1		2-0	4-0
1981		1-3	2-2	3-1	3-1		0-4		2-2	3-1
1982		1-2	1-0	0-2	2-1		0-1-1		0-3	1-1
1983		1-3	3-1	2-2	0-2		2-0		2-2	3-1
1984		1-3	2-2	1-3	3-1		0-4		1-1	4-0
1985		0-2	2-2	1-3	3-1		3-1		2-2	3-1
1986		1-1	3-1	2-2	3-1		1-3		1-1	2-2
1987		1-2	1-2	2-2	2-1-1		1-0		1-2	3-0
1988		2-2	4-0	4-0	3-1		2-2		0-2	3-1
1989		1-3	2-2	3-1	2-2		1-3		2-0	2-0
1990		3-1	1-3	1-3	1-3		2-2		4-0	2-2
1991		3-1	1-3	0-4	2-0		0-4		2-2	3-1
1992		4-0	1-3	2-2	1-3		2-0		2-2	2-2
1993		4-0	2-2	3-1	1-3		0-4		2-2	3-1
1994		1-3	1-3	3-1	1-3		0-2		3-1	2-2
1995		3-1	2-2	1-3	2-2		2-2	0-4	3-1	2-2
1996	2-2	4-0	2-2		3-1		3-1	2-2	4-0	1-3
1997	2-1-1	1-3	2-2		3-1		1-3	2-2	4-0	1-3
1998	1-3	3-1	1-3		3-1		0-4	3-1	3-1	3-1
1999	2-1	3-1	1-2	1-2	2-2		4-0	4-0	2-2	2-2
2000	2-1	2-2	1-2	0-3	3-1		2-2	2-2	2-2	2-2
2001	2-2	1-3	1-2	1-2	3-1		1-3	1-2	1-3	2-2
2002	0-4	3-1	1-3	2-2	4-0	2-2	2-2	2-2	2-2	2-2
2003	3-1	2-2	2-2	2-2	1-3	2-2	3-1	2-2	3-1	3-1
2004	3-1	4-0	4-0	1-3	3-1	1-3	4-0	3-1	1-3	2-2
Total	17-16-1	64-57-1	64-60	54-60	73-55-2	5-7	51-63-1	21-18	61-51-2	85-40

	NE	NYJ	Oak	Pitt	SD	Sea	TB	Tenn	TOTALS
1970	0-3	2-1	1-2	0-3	1-2			0-3	12-27-1
1971	0-3	0-3	1-1-1	1-2	2-1			0-2-1	15-23-2
1972	3-0	1-2	3-0	2-1	0-3			0-3	20-19-1
1973	2-1	0-3	2-1	3-0	1-2			0-3	19-19-2
1974	3-0	2-1	3-0	3-0	1-2			0-3	23-17
1975	1-2	0-3	3-0	2-1	0-3			3-0	23-17
1976	1-1	0-2	3-0	1-1	2-0	0-1		2-0	16-12
1977	2-0	1-1	1-1	2-0	1-1	1-0		2-0	19-9
1978	2-2	1-3	4-0	3-1	2-2	3-1		2-2	31-21
1979	3-1	3-1	4-0	3-1	3-1	3-1		2-2	36-16
1980	1-3	1-3	2-2	4-0	2-2	1-3		4-0	33-19
1981	0-4	2-0	2-2	3-1	2-2	0-2		1-3	24-28
1982	0-1	4-0	3-0	1-0	1-0	1-0		0-3	15-14-1
1983	2-2	3-1	2-2	2-2	2-2	1-3		1-3	26-26
1984	0-4	0-2	3-1	3-1	4-0	4-0		0-4	26-26
1985	3-1	2-2	3-1	1-3	1-1	2-2		1-3	27-25
1986	3-1	2-2	1-3	2-2	0-4	3-1		2-2	26-26
1987	0-3	0-4	2-2	2-2	2-0	4-0		2-2	23-22-1
1988	2-2	2-0	1-3	1-3	2-2	1-3		3-1	30-22
1989	0-4	1-3	2-2	3-1	2-2	0-4		3-1	24-28
1990	0-4	2-0	3-1	3-1	1-1	2-2		1-3	26-26
1991	1-1	2-2	2-2	0-4	1-3	1-3		1-3	19-33
1992	0-4	0-4	2-2	1-3	2-0	0-4		3-1	22-30
1993	1-1	2-2	3-1	2-2	2-2	0-2		2-2	27-25
1994	4-0	1-3	3-1	2-2	2-2	2-0		0-4	25-27
1995	0-4	0-4	3-1	2-2	3-1	3-1		1-3	27-33
1996	2-2	1-3	1-3	2-2	1-3	2-2		2-2	32-28
1997	1-3	3-1	2-2	2-2	1-3	2-2		4-0	31-28-1
1998	2-2	2-2	3-1	2-2	1-3	3-1		1-3	31-29
1999	3-1	2-2	3-1	3-0	1-3	2-2		3-1	38-22
2000	0-4	3-1	4-0	1-2	0-4	2-2		4-0	30-30
2001	3-1	2-2	3-1	3-0	2-2	1-3		3-1	30-30
2002	3-1	3-1	2-2	2-1-1	2-2			2-2	34-29-1
2003	3-1	0-4	1-3	1-3	2-2			4-0	34-30
2004	4-0	3-1	2-2	4-0	3-1			2-2	44-20
Total	55-67	53-69	83-46-1	72-51-1	55-64	44-44	0-1	61-67-1	918-836-10

NFC VS. AFC (REGULAR SEASON), 1970-2004

	Ariz	Atl	Car	Chi	Dall	Det	GB	Minn	NO
1970	2-0-1	1-2		1-2	3-0	3-0	2-1	2-1	0-3
1971	2-1	3-0		1-2	3-0	4-0	2-1	2-1	0-1-2
1972	1-2	2-2		1-2	3-0	2-0-1	2-1	1-2	0-3
1973	0-2-1	2-1		2-2	2-1	0-3	1-1-1	2-1	1-2
1974	2-1	0-3		0-3	2-1	1-2	2-1	2-1	0-3
1975	2-1	1-2		0-3	2-1	1-2	0-3	4-0	0-3
1976	1-1	0-2		0-2	2-0	2-0	0-2	2-0	1-2
1977	0-2	0-2		1-1	1-1	2-0	0-3	1-1	0-2
1978	0-4	1-3		0-4	3-1	2-2	2-2	1-3	1-3
1979	1-3	1-3		2-2	1-3	0-4	1-3	1-3	0-4
1980	1-1	2-2		0-4	3-1	0-2	1-3	1-3	1-3
1981	3-1	1-3		4-0	4-0	2-2	1-1	1-3	2-2
1982		1-1		1-1	2-1	0-1	1-1-1	1-3	1-0
1983	3-1	3-1		1-1	2-2	1-3	2-2	4-0	1-3
1984	3-1	1-3		2-2	2-2	0-4	0-4	0-4	3-1
1985	2-2	0-4		3-1	3-1	2-2	0-4	2-0	0-4
1986	1-1	1-3		4-0	1-3	1-3	1-3	1-3	1-3
1987	0-1	0-4		2-2	2-1	0-4	1-2-1	2-1	4-0
1988	1-3	1-3		3-1	0-4	1-1	1-3	2-2	4-0
1989	1-3	2-2		2-2	0-2	1-3	0-2	2-2	4-0
1990	2-2	2-2		2-2	1-1	1-3	1-3	2-2	2-2
1991	1-1	3-1		2-2	3-1	4-0	1-3	0-2	3-1
1992	0-2	2-2		1-3	4-0	2-2	3-1	3-1	3-1
1993	1-1	1-3		2-2	2-2	2-0	3-1	2-2	2-2
1994	3-1	1-3		3-1	3-1	2-2	1-3	2-2	1-3
1995	1-3	2-2	3-1	2-2	4-0	3-1	4-0	3-1	4-0
1996	0-4	0-4	3-1	2-2	2-2	1-3	3-1	1-3	1-3
1997	1-3	2-2	2-2	2-2	2-2	2-2	3-1	3-1	2-2
1998	1-3	3-1	1-3	2-2	1-3	1-3	3-1	4-0	1-3
1999	0-4	0-4	2-2	2-2	1-3	1-3	2-2	2-2	0-4
2000	1-3	1-3	2-2	2-2	1-3	2-2	1-3	3-1	1-3
2001	3-1	1-3	0-4	3-1	0-4	0-4	3-1	1-3	2-2
2002	0-4	2-1-1	3-1	1-3	2-2	0-4	3-1	1-3	2-2
2003	1-3	1-3	2-2	3-1	2-2	1-3	3-1	2-2	1-3
2004	1-3	3-1	1-3	1-3	1-3	1-3	1-3	3-1	2-2
Total	42-69-2	47-81-1	19-21	60-67	70-54	48-73-1	55-68-3	66-60	51-75-2

	NYG	Phil	StL	SF	Sea	TB	Wash	TOTALS
1970	3-0	2-1	2-1	4-0			2-1	27-12-1
1971	1-2	1-2	1-2	2-1			1-2	23-15-2
1972	1-2	2-1	1-2	2-1			1-2	19-20-1
1973	1-2	2-1	3-0	1-2			2-1	19-19-2
1974	1-2	2-1	3-1	0-3			2-1	17-23
1975	2-1	0-3	3-0	1-2			1-2	17-23
1976	0-2	0-2	1-1	1-1	1-0		1-1	12-16
1977	0-2	1-1	2-0	0-2		0-1	1-1	9-19
1978	1-1	3-1	2-2	1-3		2-0	2-2	21-31
1979	1-1	2-2	2-2	0-4		2-0	2-2	16-36
1980	1-3	3-1	2-2	2-2		1-3	1-3	19-33
1981	1-1	3-1	1-3	3-1		0-4	2-2	28-24
1982	1-0	2-1	1-2	1-3		2-1		14-15-1
1983	0-4	1-1	1-3	2-2		1-3	4-0	26-26
1984	2-0	3-1	3-1	3-1		1-1	3-1	26-26
1985	2-2	1-1	3-1	3-1		0-4	4-0	25-27
1986	3-1	2-2	2-2	4-0		1-1	3-1	26-26
1987	2-1	3-1	1-2	3-1		0-2	2-1	22-23-1
1988	1-1	2-2	2-2	2-2		1-3	1-3	22-30
1989	4-0	3-1	3-1	4-0		0-4	2-2	28-24
1990	3-1	1-3	2-2	4-0		0-2	3-1	26-26
1991	3-1	4-0	1-3	3-1		1-3	4-0	33-19
1992	2-2	3-1	2-2	3-1		0-2	2-2	30-22
1993	2-2	2-2	2-2	2-2		1-3	1-3	25-27
1994	3-1	1-3	2-2	3-1		1-1	1-1	27-25
1995	0-4	1-3	1-3	3-1		2-2	0-4	33-27
1996	2-2	2-2	2-2	4-0		2-2	3-1	28-32
1997	1-3	2-1-1	0-4	2-2		3-1	1-3	28-31-1
1998	3-1	0-4	3-1	2-2		2-2	2-2	29-31
1999	2-2	1-3	3-1	1-3		3-1	2-2	22-38
2000	3-1	3-1	3-1	2-2		3-1	2-2	30-30
2001	2-2	3-1	4-0	4-0		2-2	2-2	30-30
2002	2-2	1-3	2-2	2-2	2-2	3-1	3-1	29-34-1
2003	1-3	3-1	4-0	1-3	2-2	1-3	2-2	30-34
2004	1-3	2-2	1-3	0-4	1-3	1-3	0-4	20-44
Total	58-58	67-57-1	71-58	75-56	6-7	36-56	65-58	836-918-10

2004 INTERCONFERENCE GAMES
(Home Team in capital letters)
AFC 44, NFC 20

AFC Victories
New England 23, ARIZONA 12
INDIANAPOLIS 45, Green Bay 31
OAKLAND 30, Tampa Bay 20
CLEVELAND 17, Washington 13
Denver 16, TAMPA BAY 13
DENVER 20, Carolina 17
Baltimore 17, WASHINGTON 10
Tennessee 48, GREEN BAY 27
NEW ENGLAND 30, Seattle 20
NEW YORK JETS 22, San Francisco 14
Pittsburgh 24, DALLAS 20
San Diego 17, CAROLINA 6
KANSAS CITY 56, Atlanta 10
MIAMI 31, St. Louis 14
BUFFALO 38, Arizona 14
Oakland 27, CAROLINA 24
CINCINNATI 26, Dallas 3
PITTSBURGH 27, Philadelphia 3
SAN DIEGO 43, New Orleans 17
New England 40, ST. LOUIS 22
INDIANAPOLIS 31, Minnesota 28
JACKSONVILLE 23, Detroit 17 (OT)
Cincinnati 17, WASHINGTON 10
BALTIMORE 30, Dallas 10
BUFFALO 37, St. Louis 17
Indianapolis 41, CHICAGO 10
Denver 34, NEW ORLEANS 13
Indianapolis 41, DETROIT 9
PITTSBURGH 16, Washington 7
New York Jets 13, ARIZONA 3
Miami 24, SAN FRANCISCO 17
Buffalo 38, SEATTLE 9
BALTIMORE 37, New York Giants 14
JACKSONVILLE 22, Chicago 3
SAN DIEGO 31, Tampa Bay 24
Pittsburgh 33, NEW YORK GIANTS 30
Houston 24, CHICAGO 5
Jacksonville 28, GREEN BAY 25
NEW YORK JETS 37, Seattle 14
CINCINNATI 23, New York Giants 22
Buffalo 41, SAN FRANCISCO 7
NEW ENGLAND 21, San Francisco 7
Cincinnati 38, PHILADELPHIA 10
TENNESSEE 24, Detroit 19

NFC Victories
DETROIT 28, Houston 16
Carolina 28, KANSAS CITY 17
DALLAS 19, Cleveland 12
NEW YORK GIANTS 27, Cleveland 10
Minnesota 34, HOUSTON 28 (OT)
ATLANTA 21, San Diego 20
Philadelphia 34, CLEVELAND 31 (OT)
New Orleans 31, OAKLAND 26
MINNESOTA 20, Tennessee 3
PHILADELPHIA 15, Baltimore 10
Atlanta 41, DENVER 28
Arizona 24, MIAMI 23
TAMPA BAY 34, Kansas City 31
NEW ORLEANS 27, Kansas City 20
Chicago 19, TENNESSEE 17 (OT)
SEATTLE 24, Miami 17
Green Bay 16, HOUSTON 13
MINNESOTA 27, Jacksonville 16
ATLANTA 35, Oakland 10
ST. LOUIS 32, New York Jets 29 (OT)

REGULAR SEASON INTERCONFERENCE RECORDS, 1970-2004

AMERICAN FOOTBALL CONFERENCE

East	W	L	T	Pct.
Miami	85	40	0	.680
Buffalo	64	57	1	.529
New England	55	67	0	.451
New York Jets	53	69	0	.434
North	**W**	**L**	**T**	**Pct.**
Pittsburgh	72	51	1	.585
Cincinnati	64	60	0	.516
Baltimore	17	16	1	.515
Cleveland	54	60	0	.474
South	**W**	**L**	**T**	**Pct.**
Jacksonville	21	18	0	.538
Tennessee	61	67	1	.477
Indianapolis	51	63	1	.448
Houston	5	7	0	.417
West	**W**	**L**	**T**	**Pct.**
Oakland	83	46	1	.643
Denver	73	55	2	.569
Kansas City	61	51	2	.544
San Diego	55	64	0	.462

NATIONAL FOOTBALL CONFERENCE

East	W	L	T	Pct.
Dallas	70	54	0	.565
Philadelphia	67	57	1	.540
Washington	65	58	0	.528
New York Giants	58	58	0	.500
North	**W**	**L**	**T**	**Pct.**
Minnesota	66	60	0	.524
Chicago	60	67	0	.472
Green Bay	55	68	3	.448
Detroit	48	73	1	.398
South	**W**	**L**	**T**	**Pct.**
Carolina	19	21	0	.475
New Orleans	51	75	2	.405
Tampa Bay*	36	56	0	.391
Atlanta	47	81	1	.368
West	**W**	**L**	**T**	**Pct.**
San Francisco	75	56	0	.573
St. Louis	71	58	0	.550
Seattle* #	50	51	0	.495
Arizona	42	69	2	.379

* Records include one game played between Seattle and Tampa Bay, won by the Seahawks 13-10, in their inaugural season (1976) when Seattle competed in the NFC and Tampa Bay in the AFC.

\# Seattle was a member of the AFC from 1977-2001.

INTERCONFERENCE VICTORIES, 1970-2004

REGULAR SEASON				PRESEASON			
	AFC	NFC	Tie		AFC	NFC	Tie
1970	12	27	1	1970	21	28	1
1971	15	23	2	1971	28	28	3
1972	20	19	1	1972	27	25	4
1973	19	19	2	1973	23	35	2
1974	23	17	0	1974	35	25	0
1975	23	17	0	1975	30	26	1
1976	16	12	0	1976	30	31	0
1977	19	9	0	1977	38	25	0
1978	31	21	0	1978	20	19	0
1979	36	16	0	1979	25	18	0
1980	33	19	0	1980	22	20	1
1981	24	28	0	1981	18	19	0
1982	15	14	1	1982	25	16	0
1983	26	26	0	1983	15	24	0
1984	26	26	0	1984	16	19	0
1985	27	25	0	1985	10	22	1
1986	26	26	0	1986	22	17	0
1987	23	22	1	1987	22	22	0
1988	30	22	0	1988	23	16	1
1989	24	28	0	1989	16	27	0
1990	26	26	0	1990	15	29	0
1991	19	33	0	1991	19	27	0
1992	22	30	0	1992	30	22	0
1993	27	25	0	1993	17	22	0
1994	25	27	0	1994	22	16	0
1995	27	33	0	1995	19	26	0
1996	32	28	0	1996	27	19	0
1997	31	28	1	1997	26	17	0
1998	31	29	0	1998	34	16	0
1999	38	22	0	1999	22	25	0
2000	30	30	0	2000	34	17	0
2001	30	30	0	2001	28	23	0
2002	34	29	1	2002	25	24	0
2003	34	30	0	2003	25	21	0
2004	44	20	0	2004	21	18	0
Total	918	836	10	Total	830	784	14

PRO FOOTBALL HALL OF FAME GAME (42)

Date	Winner	Loser	Attendance
August 11, 1962	New York Giants 21	St. Louis Cardinals 21	14,000
September 8, 1963	Pittsburgh Steelers 16	Cleveland Browns 7	18,462
September 6, 1964	Baltimore Colts 48	Pittsburgh Steelers 17	11,479
September 12, 1965	Washington Redskins 20	Detroit Lions 3	14,416
1966	No game was played		
August 5, 1967	Philadelphia Eagles 28	Cleveland Browns 13	17,304
August 3, 1968	Chicago Bears 30	Dallas Cowboys 24	14,578
September 13, 1969	Green Bay Packers 38	Atlanta Falcons 24	17,411
August 8, 1970	New Orleans Saints 14	Minnesota Vikings 13	17,932
July 31, 1971	Los Angeles Rams (NFC) 17	Houston Oilers (AFC) 6	19,384
July 29, 1972	Kansas City Chiefs (AFC) 23	New York Giants (NFC) 17	19,304
July 28, 1973	San Francisco 49ers (NFC) 20	New England Patriots (AFC) 7	19,685
July 27, 1974	St. Louis Cardinals (NFC) 21	Buffalo Bills (AFC) 13	17,286
August 2, 1975	Washington Redskins (NFC) 17	Cincinnati Bengals (AFC) 9	19,360
July 24, 1976	Denver Broncos (AFC) 10	Detroit Lions (NFC) 7	17,639
July 30, 1977	Chicago Bears (NFC) 20	New York Jets (AFC) 6	19,057
July 29, 1978	Philadelphia Eagles (NFC) 17	Miami Dolphins (AFC) 3	19,255
July 28, 1979	Oakland Raiders (AFC) 20	Dallas Cowboys (NFC) 13	20,648
August 2, 1980*	San Diego Chargers (AFC) 0	Green Bay Packers (NFC) 0	19,972
August 1, 1981	Cleveland Browns (AFC) 24	Atlanta Falcons (NFC) 10	23,921
August 7, 1982	Minnesota Vikings (NFC) 30	Baltimore Colts (AFC) 14	23,379
July 30, 1983	Pittsburgh Steelers (AFC) 27	New Orleans Saints (NFC) 14	23,909
July 28, 1984	Seattle Seahawks (AFC) 38	Tampa Bay Buccaneers (NFC) 0	22,250
August 3, 1985	New York Giants (NFC) 21	Houston Oilers (AFC) 20	23,940
August 2, 1986	New England Patriots (AFC) 21	St. Louis Cardinals (NFC) 16	22,739
August 8, 1987	San Francisco 49ers (NFC) 20	Kansas City Chiefs (AFC) 7	23,826
July 30, 1988	Cincinnati Bengals (AFC) 14	Los Angeles Rams (NFC) 7	23,801
August 5, 1989	Washington Redskins (NFC) 31	Buffalo Bills (AFC) 6	23,948
August 4, 1990	Chicago Bears (NFC) 13	Cleveland Browns (AFC) 0	23,952
July 27, 1991	Detroit Lions (NFC) 14	Denver Broncos (AFC) 3	23,815
August 1, 1992	New York Jets (AFC) 41	Philadelphia Eagles (NFC) 14	23,853
July 31, 1993	Los Angeles Raiders (AFC) 19	Green Bay Packers (NFC) 3	23,863
July 30, 1994	Atlanta Falcons (NFC) 21	San Diego Chargers (AFC) 17	23,185
July 29, 1995	Carolina Panthers (NFC) 20	Jacksonville Jaguars (AFC) 14	24,625
July 27, 1996	Indianapolis Colts (AFC) 10	New Orleans Saints (NFC) 3	23,376
July 26, 1997	Minnesota Vikings (NFC) 28	Seattle Seahawks (AFC) 26	23,846
August 1, 1998	Tampa Bay Buccaneers (NFC) 30	Pittsburgh Steelers (AFC) 6	23,875
August 9, 1999	Cleveland Browns (AFC) 20	Dallas Cowboys (NFC) 17 (OT)	25,156
July 31, 2000	New England Patriots (AFC) 20	San Francisco 49ers (NFC) 0	22,840
August 6, 2001	St. Louis Rams (NFC) 17	Miami Dolphins (AFC) 10	22,736
August 5, 2002	New York Giants (NFC) 34	Houston Texans (AFC) 17	22,461
August 4, 2003**	Kansas City Chiefs (AFC) 9	Green Bay Packers (NFC) 0	22,385
August 9, 2004	Washington Redskins (NFC) 20	Denver Broncos (AFC) 17	22,177

*Game called with 5:29 remaining because of severe thunder and lightning.
**Game called with 5:49 remaining in the third quarter because of lightning and torrential rain.

NFL INTERNATIONAL GAMES (55)

Date	Site	Teams
August 12, 1950	Ottawa, Canada	N.Y. Giants 27, Ottawa Rough Riders 6
August 11, 1951	Ottawa, Canada	N.Y. Giants 41, Ottawa Rough Riders 18
August 5, 1959	Toronto, Canada	Chi. Cardinals 55, Tor. Argonauts 26
August 3, 1960	Toronto, Canada	Pittsburgh 43, Toronto Argonauts 16
August 15, 1960	Toronto, Canada	Chicago 16, N.Y. Giants 7
August 2, 1961	Toronto, Canada	St. Louis 36, Toronto Argonauts 7
August 5, 1961	Montreal, Canada	Chicago 34, Montreal Allouettes 16
August 8, 1961	Hamilton, Canada	Hamilton Tiger-Cats 38, Buffalo 21
Sept. 11, 1969	Montreal, Canada	Pittsburgh 17, N.Y. Giants 13
August 25, 1969	Montreal, Canada	Detroit 22, Boston 9
August 16, 1976	Tokyo, Japan	St. Louis 20, San Diego 10
August 5, 1978	Mexico City, Mexico	New Orleans 14, Philadelphia 7
August 6, 1983	London, England	Minnesota 28, St. Louis 10
* August 3, 1986	London, England	Chicago 17, Dallas 6
* August 9, 1987	London, England	L.A. Rams 28, Denver 27
* July 31, 1988	London, England	Miami 27, San Francisco 21
August 14, 1988	Goteborg, Sweden	Minnesota 28, Chicago 21
August 18, 1988	Montreal, Canada	N.Y. Jets 11, Cleveland 7
* August 5, 1989	Tokyo, Japan	L.A. Rams 16, San Francisco 13 (OT)
* August 6, 1989	London, England	Philadelphia 17, Cleveland 13
* August 4, 1990	Tokyo, Japan	Denver 10, Seattle 7
* August 5, 1990	London, England	New Orleans 17, L.A. Raiders 10
* August 9, 1990	Montreal, Canada	Pittsburgh 30, New England 14
* August 11, 1990	Berlin, Germany	L.A. Rams 19, Kansas City 3
* July 28, 1991	London, England	Buffalo 17, Philadelphia 13
* August 3, 1991	Berlin, Germany	San Francisco 21, Chicago 7
* August 3, 1991	Tokyo, Japan	Miami 19, L.A. Raiders 17
* August 1, 1992	Tokyo, Japan	Houston 34, Dallas 23
* August 15, 1992	Berlin, Germany	Miami 31, Denver 27
* August 16, 1992	London, England	San Francisco 17, Washington 15
* July 31, 1993	Tokyo, Japan	New Orleans 28, Philadelphia 16
* August 1, 1993	Barcelona, Spain	San Francisco 21, Pittsburgh 14
* August 7, 1993	Berlin, Germany	Minnesota 20, Buffalo 6
* August 8, 1993	London, England	Dallas 13, Detroit 13 (OT)
August 14, 1993	Toronto, Canada	Cleveland 12, New England 9
* July 31, 1994	Barcelona, Spain	L.A. Raiders 25, Denver 22
* August 6, 1994	Tokyo, Japan	Minnesota 17, Kansas City 9
* August 13, 1994	Berlin, Germany	N.Y. Giants 28, San Diego 20
* August 15, 1994	Mexico City, Mexico	Houston 6, Dallas 0
* August 5, 1995	Tokyo, Japan	Denver 24, San Francisco 10
* August 12, 1995	Toronto, Canada	Buffalo 9, Dallas 7
* July 27, 1996	Tokyo, Japan	San Diego 20, Pittsburgh 10
* August 5, 1996	Monterrey, Mexico	Kansas City 32, Dallas 6
* July 27, 1997	Dublin, Ireland	Pittsburgh 30, Chicago 17
* August 4, 1997	Mexico City, Mexico	Miami 38, Denver 19
* August 16, 1997	Toronto, Canada	Green Bay 35, Buffalo 3
* August 1, 1998	Tokyo, Japan	Green Bay 27, Kansas City 24 (OT)
* August 15, 1998	Vancouver, Canada	San Francisco 24, Seattle 21
* August 17, 1998	Mexico City, Mexico	New England 21, Dallas 3
* August 7, 1999	Sydney, Australia	Denver 20, San Diego 17
* August 5, 2000	Tokyo, Japan	Atlanta 20, Dallas 9
* August 19, 2000	Mexico City, Mexico	Indianapolis 24, Pittsburgh 23
* August 27, 2001	Mexico City, Mexico	Dallas 21, Oakland 6
* August 3, 2002	Osaka, Japan	Washington 38, San Francisco 7
* August 2, 2003	Tokyo, Japan	Tampa Bay 30, N.Y. Jets 14

*American Bowl Game

CHICAGO ALL-STAR GAME

Pro teams won 31, lost 9, and tied 2. The game was discontinued after 1976.

Date	Winner	Loser	Attendance
August 31, 1934	Chicago Bears 0	All-Stars 0 (tie)	79,432
August 29, 1935	Chicago Bears 5	All-Stars 0	77,450
September 3, 1936	Detroit Lions 7	All-Stars 7 (tie)	76,000
September 1, 1937	All-Stars 6	Green Bay Packers 0	84,560
August 31, 1938	All-Stars 28	Washington Redskins 16	74,250
August 30, 1939	N.Y. Giants 9	All-Stars 0	81,456
August 29, 1940	Green Bay Packers 45	All-Stars 28	84,567
August 28, 1941	Chicago Bears 37	All-Stars 13	98,203
August 28, 1942	Chicago Bears 21	All-Stars 0	101,100
August 25, 1943	All-Stars 27	Washington Redskins 7	48,471
August 30, 1944	Chicago Bears 24	All-Stars 21	48,769
August 30, 1945	Green Bay Packers 19	All-Stars 7	92,753
August 23, 1946	All-Stars 16	Los Angeles Rams 0	97,380
August 22, 1947	All-Stars 16	Chicago Bears 0	105,840
August 20, 1948	Chicago Cardinals 28	All-Stars 0	101,220
August 12, 1949	Philadelphia Eagles 38	All-Stars 0	93,780
August 11, 1950	All-Stars 17	Philadelphia Eagles 7	88,885
August 17, 1951	Cleveland Browns 33	All-Stars 0	92,180
August 15, 1952	Los Angeles Rams 10	All-Stars 7	88,316
August 14, 1953	Detroit Lions 24	All-Stars 10	93,818
August 13, 1954	Detroit Lions 31	All-Stars 6	93,470
August 12, 1955	All-Stars 30	Cleveland Browns 27	75,000
August 10, 1956	Cleveland Browns 26	All-Stars 0	75,000
August 9, 1957	N.Y. Giants 22	All-Stars 12	75,000
August 15, 1958	All-Stars 35	Detroit Lions 19	70,000
August 14, 1959	Baltimore Colts 29	All-Stars 0	70,000
August 12, 1960	Baltimore Colts 32	All-Stars 7	70,000
August 4, 1961	Philadelphia Eagles 28	All-Stars 14	66,000
August 3, 1962	Green Bay Packers 42	All-Stars 20	65,000
August 2, 1963	All-Stars 20	Green Bay Packers 17	65,000
August 7, 1964	Chicago Bears 28	All-Stars 17	65,000
August 6, 1965	Cleveland Browns 24	All-Stars 16	68,000
August 5, 1966	Green Bay Packers 38	All-Stars 0	72,000
August 4, 1967	Green Bay Packers 27	All-Stars 0	70,934
August 2, 1968	Green Bay Packers 34	All-Stars 17	69,917
August 1, 1969	N.Y. Jets 26	All-Stars 24	74,208
July 31, 1970	Kansas City Chiefs 24	All-Stars 3	69,940
July 30, 1971	Baltimore Colts 24	All-Stars 17	52,289
July 28, 1972	Dallas Cowboys 20	All-Stars 7	54,162
July 27, 1973	Miami Dolphins 14	All-Stars 3	54,103
1974	No game was played		
August 1, 1975	Pittsburgh Steelers 21	All-Stars 14	54,103
July 23, 1976*	Pittsburgh Steelers 24	All-Stars 0	52,895

Game shortened because of thunderstorms.

NFL PLAYOFF BOWL

Consolation game that matched conference runners-up.
Western Conference won 8, Eastern Conference won 2.
All games played at Miami's Orange Bowl.

January 7, 1961	Detroit Lions 17, Cleveland Browns 16
January 6, 1962	Detroit Lions 38, Philadelphia Eagles 10
January 6, 1963	Detroit Lions 17, Pittsburgh Steelers 10
January 5, 1964	Green Bay Packers 40, Cleveland Browns 23
January 3, 1965	St. Louis Cardinals 24, Green Bay Packers 17
January 9, 1966	Baltimore Colts 35, Dallas Cowboys 3
January 8, 1967	Baltimore Colts 20, Philadelphia Eagles 14
January 7, 1968	Los Angeles Rams 30, Cleveland Browns 6
January 5, 1969	Dallas Cowboys 17, Minnesota Vikings 13
January 3, 1970	Los Angeles Rams 31, Dallas Cowboys 0

Compiled by Elias Sports Bureau
*NFL record.

MONDAY NIGHT RECORDS

SCORING
TOUCHDOWNS
Most Touchdowns, Career
36 Jerry Rice, San Francisco, 1985-2000;
    Oakland, 2001-04; Seattle 2004
24 Emmitt Smith, Dallas, 1990-2002; Arizona 2003-04
19 Marcus Allen, L.A. Raiders, 1982-1992;
    Kansas City, 1993-97
Most Touchdowns, Game
4   Ron Johnson, N.Y. Giants at Philadelphia,
    Oct. 2, 1972
    Earl Campbell, Houston vs. Miami, Nov. 20, 1978
    Marcus Allen, L.A. Raiders vs. San Diego,
    Sept. 24, 1984
    Eric Dickerson, Indianapolis vs. Denver,
    Oct. 31, 1988
    Emmitt Smith, Dallas at N.Y. Giants, Sept. 4, 1995
    Marshall Faulk, St. Louis at Tampa Bay,
    Dec. 18, 2000

FIELD GOALS
Most Field Goals, Career
51 Gary Anderson, Pittsburgh, 1982-1994; Philadelphia,
    1995-96; San Francisco, 1997;
    Minnesota, 1998-2002; Tennessee, 2003-04
38 Jason Elam, Denver, 1993-2004
34 Morten Andersen, New Orleans 1982-1994; Atlanta,
    1995-2000; N.Y. Giants, 2001; Kansas City,
    2002-03; Minnesota, 2004
Most Field Goals, Game
7   Chris Boniol, Dallas vs. Green Bay, Nov. 18, 1996*
    Billy Cundiff, Dallas at N.Y. Giants, Sept. 15, 2003 (OT)*
5   Tim Mazzetti, Atlanta vs. Los Angeles, Oct. 30, 1978
    Roger Ruzek, Dallas at L.A. Rams, Dec. 21, 1987
    Rich Karlis, Minnesota vs. Cincinnati, Dec. 25, 1989
    Nick Lowery, Kansas City vs. Denver, Sept. 20, 1993
    Chris Jacke, Green Bay vs. San Francisco,
    Oct. 14, 1996 (OT)
    Richie Cunningham, Dallas vs. Philadelphia,
    Sept. 15, 1997

RUSHING
YARDS GAINED
Most Yards Gained, Career
2,434 Emmitt Smith, Dallas, 1990-2002; Arizona, 2003-04
1,897 Tony Dorsett, Dallas, 1977-1987; Denver, 1988
1,769 Thurman Thomas, Buffalo, 1988-1999; Miami, 2000
Most Yards Gained, Game
221 Bo Jackson, L.A. Raiders at Seattle, Nov. 30, 1987
216 Ricky Williams, Miami vs. Chicago, Dec. 9, 2002
214 Thurman Thomas, Buffalo at N.Y. Jets,
     Sept. 24, 1990
Longest Run From Scrimage, Game
99 Tony Dorsett, Dallas at Minnesota,
    Jan. 3, 1983 (TD)*
91 Bo Jackson, L.A. Raiders at Seattle,
    Nov. 30, 1987 (TD)
83 James Lofton, Green Bay at N.Y. Giants,
    Sept. 20, 1982 (TD)
TOUCHDOWNS
Most Rushing Touchdowns, Career
23 Emmitt Smith, Dallas, 1990-2002; Arizona, 2003-04
17 Marcus Allen, L.A. Raiders, 1982-1992;
    Kansas City, 1993-97
14 Eric Dickerson, L.A. Rams, 1983-87; Indianapolis,
    1987-1991; L.A. Raiders, 1992; Atlanta, 1993

Most Rushing Touchdowns, Game
4   Earl Campbell, Houston vs. Miami, Nov. 20, 1978
    Eric Dickerson, Indianapolis vs. Denver,
    Oct. 31, 1988
    Emmitt Smith, Dallas at N.Y. Giants, Sept. 4, 1995

PASSING
YARDS GAINED
Most Yards Gained, Career
9,654 Dan Marino, Miami, 1983-1999
6,402 Brett Favre, Atlanta, 1991; Green Bay, 1992-2004
5,148 Joe Montana, San Francisco, 1979-1992;
       Kansas City, 1993-94
Most Yards Gained, Game
458 Joe Montana, San Francisco at L.A. Rams,
     Dec. 11, 1989
448 Marc Bulger, St. Louis at Green Bay, Nov. 29, 2004
447 Ken Anderson, Cincinnati vs. Buffalo, Nov. 17, 1975
Longest Pass Play
99 Brett Favre to Robert Brooks, Green Bay at Chicago,
    Sept. 11, 1995 (TD)*
97 Bernie Kosar to Webster Slaughter, Cleveland vs.
    Chicago, Oct. 23, 1989 (TD)
95 Joe Montana to John Taylor, San Francisco at
    L.A. Rams, Dec. 11, 1989 (TD)
TOUCHDOWNS
Most Touchdown Passes, Career
74 Dan Marino, Miami, 1983-1999
48 Brett Favre, Atlanta, 1991; Green Bay, 1992-2004
42 Steve Young, Tampa Bay, 1985-86; San Francisco,
    1987-1999
Most Touchdown Passes, Game
5   Dave Krieg, Seattle vs. L.A. Raiders, Nov. 28, 1988
    Jim Kelly, Buffalo vs. Cincinnati, Oct. 21, 1991
    Vinny Testaverde, N.Y. Jets vs. Miami,
    Oct. 23, 2000 (OT)

RECEIVING
PASS RECEPTIONS
Most Pass Receptions, Career
254 Jerry Rice, San Francisco, 1985-2000;
     Oakland, 2001-04; Seattle, 2004
124 Andre Reed, Buffalo, 1985-1999; Washington, 2000
123 Cris Carter, Philadelphia, 1987-89; Minnesota,
     1990-2001; Miami, 2002
Most Pass Receptions, Game
14 Herman Moore, Detroit vs. Chicago, Dec. 4, 1995
    Jerry Rice, San Francisco vs. Minnesota,
    Dec. 18, 1995
13 Andre Reed, Buffalo vs. Denver, Sept. 18, 1989
    Terrell Owens, San Francisco vs. Philadelphia,
    Nov. 25, 2002
YARDS GAINED
Most Yards Gained, Career
4,029 Jerry Rice, San Francisco, 1985-2000;
       Oakland, 2001-04; Seattle, 2004
1,783 Andre Reed, Buffalo, 1985-1999; Washington, 2000
1,537 Art Monk, Washington, 1980-1993; N.Y. Jets, 1994;
       Philadelphia, 1995
Most Yards Gained, Game
289 Jerry Rice, San Francisco vs. Minnesota,
     Dec. 18, 1995
286 John Taylor, San Francisco at L.A. Rams,
     Dec. 11, 1989
260 Wes Chandler, San Diego vs. Cincinnati,
     Dec. 20, 1982

TOUCHDOWNS
Most Receiving Touchdowns, Career
- 34 Jerry Rice, San Francisco, 1985-2000; Oakland, 2001-04; Seattle, 2004
- 15 Mark Clayton, Miami, 1983-1992; Green Bay, 1993
   Terrell Owens, San Francisco, 1996-2003; Philadelphia, 2004
- 13 Andre Reed, Buffalo, 1985-1999; Washington, 2000

Most Receiving Touchdowns, Game
- 3 Ron Johnson, N.Y. Giants at Philadelphia, Oct. 2, 1972
   Wesley Walker, N.Y. Jets at Detroit, Dec. 6, 1982
   Steve Largent, Seattle at San Diego, Oct. 29, 1984
   Mark Clayton, Miami vs. Dallas, Dec. 17, 1984
   Jerry Rice, San Francisco vs. Chicago, Dec. 14, 1987
   Jerry Rice, San Francisco vs. Minnesota, Dec. 18, 1995
   Lamar Thomas, Miami vs. Denver, Dec. 21, 1998
   Ed McCaffrey, Denver vs. Miami, Sept. 13, 1999
   Randy Moss, Minnesota vs. N.Y. Giants, Nov. 19, 2001
   Isaac Bruce, St. Louis at New Orleans, Dec. 17, 2001
   Terrell Owens, Philadelphia at Dallas, Nov. 15, 2004
   Drew Bennett, Tennessee vs. Kansas City, Dec. 13, 2004

YARDS FROM SCRIMMAGE
Most Scrimmage Yards, Career
- 4,116 Jerry Rice, San Francisco, 1985-2000; Oakland, 2001-04; Seattle, 2004
- 2,836 Emmitt Smith, Dallas, 1990-2002; Arizona, 2003-04
- 2,567 Tony Dorsett, Dallas, 1977-1987; Denver, 1988

INTERCEPTIONS BY
Most Interceptions, Career
- 11 Everson Walls, Dallas, 1981-89; N.Y. Giants, 1990-92; Cleveland, 1992-93
- 9 Merton Hanks, San Francisco, 1991-98; Seattle, 1999
- 8 Emmitt Thomas, Kansas City, 1966-1978

Most Interceptions, Game
- 4 Dick Anderson, Miami vs. Pittsburgh, Dec. 3, 1973*
- 3 Johnny Robinson, Kansas City at Baltimore, Sept. 28, 1970
   Charlie Babb, Miami vs. Oakland, Sept. 22, 1975
   Charles Phillips, Oakland vs. Denver, Dec. 8, 1975
   Mark Murphy, Washington at San Diego, Oct. 31, 1983
   Ken Easley, Seattle at San Diego, Oct. 29, 1984
   Dwayne Harper, San Diego vs. Oakland, Nov. 27, 1995
   Marcus Coleman, N.Y. Jets vs. Miami, Oct. 23, 2000 (OT)

Longest Interception Return
- 102 Eddie Anderson, L.A. Raiders at Miami, Dec. 14, 1992 (TD)
- 101 Lito Sheppard, Philadelphia at Dallas, Nov. 15, 2004 (TD)
- 98 Marcus Coleman, N.Y. Jets vs. Miami, Dec. 27, 1999 (TD)
   Rod Woodson, Oakland at Denver, Nov. 11, 2002 (TD)

SACKS
Most Sacks, Career
- 24.5 Bruce Smith, Buffalo, 1985-1999; Washington, 2000-03
- 20.0 Richard Dent, Chicago, 1983-1993, 1995; San Francisco, 1994; Indianapolis, 1996; Philadelphia, 1997
- 18.0 Kevin Greene, L.A. Rams, 1985-1992; Pittsburgh, 1993-95; Carolina, 1996, 1998-99; San Francisco, 1997

PUNTING
Highest Punt Average, Career (Minimum: 25 Punts)
- 47.3 Shane Lechler, Oakland, 2000-04
- 45.3 Hunter Smith, Indianapolis, 1999-2004
- 44.5 Tom Tupa, Phoenix, 1988-1991; Indianapolis, 1992; Cleveland, 1994-95; New England, 1996-98; N.Y. Jets, 1999-2001; Tampa Bay, 2002-03; Washington, 2004

Longest Punt
- 90 Rodney Williams, N.Y. Giants at Denver, Sept. 10, 2001
- 83 Bryan Barker, Jacksonville vs. N.Y. Jets, Oct. 11, 1999
- 74 Craig Colquitt, Pittsburgh vs. Oakland, Dec. 7, 1981

PUNT RETURNS
Longest Punt Return
- 95 John Taylor, San Francisco vs. Washington, Nov. 21, 1988 (TD)
- 94 Dennis McKinnon, Chicago vs. N.Y. Giants, Sept. 14, 1987 (TD)
- 91 JoJo Townsell, N.Y. Jets vs. Seattle, Nov. 9, 1987 (TD)
   Nate Burleson, Minnesota at Indianapolis, Nov. 8, 2004 (TD)

KICKOFF RETURNS
Longest Kickoff Return
- 105 Terry Fair, Detroit vs. Tampa Bay, Sept. 28, 1998 (TD)
- 102 Harold Hart, Oakland at Miami, Sept. 22, 1975 (TD)
- 101 Roell Preston, Green Bay vs. Minnesota, Oct. 5, 1998 (TD)

FUMBLES
Longest Fumble Return
- 99 Don Griffin, San Francisco vs. Chicago, Dec. 23, 1991 (TD)
- 96 Joe Lavender, Philadelphia vs. Dallas, Sept. 23, 1974 (TD)
- 93 Adam Archuleta, St. Louis vs. Tampa Bay, Oct. 18, 2004 (TD)

MONDAY NIGHT FOOTBALL, 1970-2004

(Home Team in capitals, games listed in chronological order.)

2004
Green Bay 24, CAROLINA 14
PHILADELPHIA 27, Minnesota 16
Dallas 21, WASHINGTON 18
Kansas City 27, BALTIMORE 24
Tennessee 48, GREEN BAY 27
ST. LOUIS 28, Tampa Bay 21
CINCINNATI 23, Denver 10
N.Y. JETS 41, Miami 14
INDIANAPOLIS 31, Minnesota 28
Philadelphia 49, DALLAS 21
New England 27, KANSAS CITY 19
GREEN BAY 45, St. Louis 17
Dallas 43, SEATTLE 39
Kansas City 49, TENNESSEE 38
MIAMI 29, New England 28
ST. LOUIS 20, Philadelphia 7

2003
Tampa Bay 17, PHILADELPHIA 0
Dallas 35, N.Y. GIANTS 32 (OT)
DENVER 31, Oakland 10
Green Bay 38, CHICAGO 23
Indianapolis 38, TAMPA BAY 35 (OT)
ST. LOUIS 36, Atlanta 0
Kansas City 17, OAKLAND 10
Miami 26, SAN DIEGO 10
New England 30, DENVER 26
Philadelphia 17, GREEN BAY 14
SAN FRANCISCO 30, Pittsburgh 14
TAMPA BAY 19, New York Giants 13
NEW YORK JETS 24, Tennessee 17
St. Louis 26, CLEVELAND 20
Philadelphia 34, MIAMI 27
Green Bay 41, OAKLAND 7

2002
NEW ENGLAND 30, Pittsburgh 14
Philadelphia 37, WASHINGTON 7
TAMPA BAY 26, St. Louis 14
BALTIMORE 34, Denver 23
Green Bay 34, CHICAGO 21
San Francisco 28, SEATTLE 21
PITTSBURGH 28, Indianapolis 10
PHILADELPHIA 17, N.Y. Giants 3
GREEN BAY 24, Miami 10
Oakland 34, DENVER 10
ST. LOUIS 21, Chicago 16
Philadelphia 38, SAN FRANCISCO 17
OAKLAND 26, N.Y. Jets 20
MIAMI 27, Chicago 9
TENNESSEE 24, New England 7
Pittsburgh 17, TAMPA BAY 7
ST. LOUIS 31, San Francisco 20

2001
DENVER 31, N.Y. Giants 20
GREEN BAY 37, Washington 0
San Francisco 19, N.Y. JETS 17
St. Louis 35, DETROIT 0
DALLAS 9, Washington 7
Philadelphia 10, N.Y. GIANTS 9
PITTSBURGH 34, Tennessee 7
OAKLAND 38, Denver 28
Baltimore 16, TENNESSEE 10
MINNESOTA 28, N.Y. Giants 16
Tampa Bay 24, ST. LOUIS 17
Green Bay 28, JACKSONVILLE 21
MIAMI 41, Indianapolis 6
St. Louis 34, NEW ORLEANS 21
BALTIMORE 19, Minnesota 3

2000
ST. LOUIS 41, Denver 36
N.Y. JETS 20, New England 19
Dallas 27, WASHINGTON 21
INDIANAPOLIS 43, Jacksonville 14
KANSAS CITY 24, Seattle 17
MINNESOTA 30, Tampa Bay 23
TENNESSEE 27, Jacksonville 13
N.Y. JETS 40, Miami 37 (OT)
Tennessee 27, WASHINGTON 21
GREEN BAY 26, Minnesota 20 (OT)
DENVER 27, Oakland 24
Washington 33, ST. LOUIS 20
CAROLINA 31, Green Bay 14
NEW ENGLAND 30, Kansas City 24
INDIANAPOLIS 44, Buffalo 20
TAMPA BAY 38, St. Louis 35
TENNESSEE 31, Dallas 0

1999
Miami 38, DENVER 21
DALLAS 24, Atlanta 7
San Francisco 24, ARIZONA 10
Buffalo 23, MIAMI 18
Jacksonville 16, N.Y. JETS 6
N.Y. GIANTS 13, Dallas 10
PITTSBURGH 13, Atlanta 9
Seattle 27, GREEN BAY 7
MINNESOTA 27, Dallas 17
N.Y. Jets 24, NEW ENGLAND 17
DENVER 27, Oakland 21 (OT)
Green Bay 20, SAN FRANCISCO 3
TAMPA BAY 24, Minnesota 17
JACKSONVILLE 27, Denver 24
MINNESOTA 24, Green Bay 20
N.Y. Jets 38, MIAMI 31
ATLANTA 34, San Francisco 29

1998
DENVER 27, New England 21
San Francisco 45, WASHINGTON 10
Dallas 31, N.Y. GIANTS 7
DETROIT 27, Tampa Bay 6
Minnesota 37, GREEN BAY 24
JACKSONVILLE 28, Miami 21
N.Y. Jets 24, NEW ENGLAND 14
Pittsburgh 20, KANSAS CITY 13
Dallas 34, PHILADELPHIA 0
PITTSBURGH 27, Green Bay 20
Denver 30, KANSAS CITY 7
NEW ENGLAND 26, Miami 23
SAN FRANCISCO 31, N.Y. Giants 7
TAMPA BAY 24, Green Bay 22
SAN FRANCISCO 35, Detroit 13
MIAMI 31, Denver 21
JACKSONVILLE 21, Pittsburgh 3

1997
GREEN BAY 38, Chicago 24
Kansas City 28, OAKLAND 27
DALLAS 21, Philadelphia 20
JACKSONVILLE 30, Pittsburgh 21
San Francisco 34, CAROLINA 21
DENVER 34, New England 13
WASHINGTON 21, Dallas 16
Buffalo 9, INDIANAPOLIS 6
Green Bay 28, NEW ENGLAND 10
Chicago 36, MIAMI 33 (OT)
KANSAS CITY 13, Pittsburgh 10
San Francisco 24, PHILADELPHIA 12
MIAMI 36, Buffalo 13
DENVER 31, Oakland 3
Green Bay 27, MINNESOTA 11
Carolina 23, DALLAS 13
SAN FRANCISCO 34, Denver 17
New England 14, MIAMI 12

1996
CHICAGO 22, Dallas 6
GREEN BAY 39, Philadelphia 13
PITTSBURGH 24, Buffalo 6
INDIANAPOLIS 10, Miami 6
Dallas 23, PHILADELPHIA 19
Pittsburgh 17, KANSAS CITY 7
GREEN BAY 23, San Francisco 20 (OT)
Oakland 23, SAN DIEGO 14
Chicago 15, MINNESOTA 13
Denver 22, OAKLAND 21
SAN DIEGO 27, Detroit 21
DALLAS 21, Green Bay 6
Pittsburgh 24, MIAMI 17
San Francisco 34, ATLANTA 10
OAKLAND 26, Kansas City 7
MIAMI 16, Buffalo 14
SAN FRANCISCO 24, Detroit 14

1995
Dallas 35, N.Y. GIANTS 0
Green Bay 27, CHICAGO 24
MIAMI 23, Pittsburgh 10
DETROIT 27, San Francisco 24
Buffalo 22, CLEVELAND 19
KANSAS CITY 29, San Diego 23 (OT)
DENVER 27, Oakland 0
NEW ENGLAND 27, Buffalo 14
Chicago 14, MINNESOTA 6
DALLAS 34, Philadelphia 12
PITTSBURGH 20, Cleveland 3
San Francisco 44, MIAMI 20
SAN DIEGO 12, Oakland 6
DETROIT 27, Chicago 7
MIAMI 13, Kansas City 6
SAN FRANCISCO 37, Minnesota 30
Dallas 37, ARIZONA 13

1994
SAN FRANCISCO 44, L.A. Raiders 14
PHILADELPHIA 30, Chicago 22
Detroit 20, DALLAS 17 (OT)
BUFFALO 27, Denver 20
PITTSBURGH 30, Houston 14
Minnesota 27, N.Y. GIANTS 10
Kansas City 31, DENVER 28
PHILADELPHIA 21, Houston 6
Green Bay 33, CHICAGO 6
DALLAS 38, N.Y. Giants 10
PITTSBURGH 23, Buffalo 10
N.Y. Giants 13, HOUSTON 10
San Francisco 35, NEW ORLEANS 14
L.A. Raiders 24, SAN DIEGO 17
MIAMI 45, Kansas City 28
Dallas 24, NEW ORLEANS 16
MINNESOTA 21, San Francisco 14

1993
WASHINGTON 35, Dallas 16
CLEVELAND 23, San Francisco 13
KANSAS CITY 15, Denver 7
Pittsburgh 45, ATLANTA 17
MIAMI 17, Washington 10
BUFFALO 35, Houston 7
L.A. Raiders 23, DENVER 20
Minnesota 19, CHICAGO 12
BUFFALO 24, Washington 10
KANSAS CITY 23, Green Bay 16
PITTSBURGH 23, Buffalo 0
SAN FRANCISCO 42, New Orleans 7
San Diego 31, INDIANAPOLIS 0
DALLAS 23, Philadelphia 17
Pittsburgh 21, MIAMI 20
N.Y. Giants 24, NEW ORLEANS 14
SAN DIEGO 45, Miami 20
Philadelphia 37, SAN FRANCISCO 34 (OT)

1992
DALLAS 23, Washington 10
Miami 27, CLEVELAND 23
N.Y. Giants 27, CHICAGO 14
KANSAS CITY 27, L.A. Raiders 7
PHILADELPHIA 31, Dallas 7
WASHINGTON 34, Denver 3
PITTSBURGH 20, Cincinnati 0
Buffalo 24, N.Y. JETS 20
Minnesota 38, CHICAGO 10
San Francisco 41, ATLANTA 3
Buffalo 26, MIAMI 20
NEW ORLEANS 20, Washington 3
SEATTLE 16, Denver 13 (OT)
HOUSTON 24, Chicago 7
MIAMI 20, L.A. Raiders 7
Dallas 41, ATLANTA 17
SAN FRANCISCO 24, Detroit 6

1991
N.Y. GIANTS 16, San Francisco 14
Washington 33, DALLAS 31
HOUSTON 17, Kansas City 7
CHICAGO 19, N.Y. Jets 13 (OT)
WASHINGTON 23, Philadelphia 0
KANSAS CITY 33, Buffalo 6
N.Y. Giants 23, PITTSBURGH 20
BUFFALO 35, Cincinnati 16
KANSAS CITY 24, L.A. Raiders 21
PHILADELPHIA 30, N.Y. Giants 7
Chicago 34, MINNESOTA 17
Buffalo 41, MIAMI 27
San Francisco 33, L.A. RAMS 10
Philadelphia 13, HOUSTON 6
MIAMI 37, Cincinnati 13
NEW ORLEANS 27, L.A. Raiders 0
SAN FRANCISCO 52, Chicago 14

1990
San Francisco 13, NEW ORLEANS 12
DENVER 24, Kansas City 23
Buffalo 30, N.Y. JETS 7
SEATTLE 31, Cincinnati 16
Cleveland 30, DENVER 29
PHILADELPHIA 32, Minnesota 24
Cincinnati 34, CLEVELAND 13
PITTSBURGH 41, L.A. Rams 10
N.Y. Giants 24, INDIANAPOLIS 7
PHILADELPHIA 28, Washington 14
L.A. Raiders 13, MIAMI 10
HOUSTON 27, Buffalo 24
SAN FRANCISCO 7, N.Y. Giants 3
L.A. Raiders 38, DETROIT 31
San Francisco 26, L.A. RAMS 10
NEW ORLEANS 20, L.A. Rams 17

1989
N.Y. Giants 27, WASHINGTON 24
Denver 28, BUFFALO 14
CINCINNATI 21, Cleveland 14
CHICAGO 27, Philadelphia 13
L.A. Raiders 14, N.Y. JETS 7
BUFFALO 23, L.A. Rams 20
CLEVELAND 27, Chicago 7
N.Y. GIANTS 24, Minnesota 14
SAN FRANCISCO 31, New Orleans 13
HOUSTON 26, Cincinnati 24
Denver 14, WASHINGTON 10
SAN FRANCISCO 34, N.Y. Giants 24
SEATTLE 17, Buffalo 16
San Francisco 30, L.A. RAMS 27
NEW ORLEANS 30, Philadelphia 20
MINNESOTA 29, Cincinnati 21

1988
N.Y. GIANTS 27, Washington 20
Dallas 17, PHOENIX 14
CLEVELAND 23, Indianapolis 17
L.A. Raiders 30, DENVER 27 (OT)
NEW ORLEANS 20, Dallas 17
PHILADELPHIA 24, N.Y. Giants 13
Buffalo 37, N.Y. JETS 14
CHICAGO 10, San Francisco 9
INDIANAPOLIS 55, Denver 23
HOUSTON 24, Cleveland 17
Buffalo 31, MIAMI 6
SAN FRANCISCO 37, Washington 21
SEATTLE 35, L.A. Raiders 27
L.A. RAMS 23, Chicago 3
MIAMI 38, Cleveland 31
MINNESOTA 28, Chicago 27

1987
CHICAGO 34, N.Y. Giants 19
N.Y. JETS 43, New England 24
San Francisco 41, N.Y. GIANTS 21
DENVER 30, L.A. Raiders 14
Washington 13, DALLAS 7
CLEVELAND 30, L.A. Rams 17
MINNESOTA 34, Denver 27
DALLAS 33, N.Y. Giants 24
N.Y. JETS 30, Seattle 14
DENVER 31, Chicago 29
L.A. Rams 30, WASHINGTON 26
L.A. Raiders 37, SEATTLE 14
MIAMI 37, N.Y. Jets 28
SAN FRANCISCO 41, Chicago 0
Dallas 29, L.A. RAMS 21
New England 24, MIAMI 10

1986
DALLAS 31, N.Y. Giants 28
Denver 21, PITTSBURGH 10
Chicago 25, GREEN BAY 12
Dallas 31, ST. LOUIS 7
SEATTLE 33, San Diego 7
CINCINNATI 24, Pittsburgh 22
N.Y. JETS 22, Denver 10
N.Y. GIANTS 27, Washington 20
L.A. Rams 20, CHICAGO 17
CLEVELAND 26, Miami 16
WASHINGTON 14, San Francisco 6
MIAMI 45, N.Y. Jets 3
N.Y. Giants 21, SAN FRANCISCO 17
SEATTLE 37, L.A. Raiders 0
Chicago 16, DETROIT 13
New England 34, MIAMI 27

1985
DALLAS 44, Washington 14
CLEVELAND 17, Pittsburgh 7
L.A. Rams 35, SEATTLE 24
Cincinnati 37, PITTSBURGH 24
WASHINGTON 27, St. Louis 10
N.Y. JETS 23, Miami 7
CHICAGO 23, Green Bay 7
L.A. RAIDERS 34, San Diego 21
ST. LOUIS 21, Dallas 10
DENVER 17, San Francisco 16
WASHINGTON 23, N.Y. Giants 21
SAN FRANCISCO 19, Seattle 6
MIAMI 38, Chicago 24
L.A. Rams 27, SAN FRANCISCO 20
MIAMI 30, New England 27
L.A. Raiders 16, L.A. RAMS 6

1984
Dallas 20, L.A. RAMS 13
SAN FRANCISCO 37, Washington 31
Miami 21, BUFFALO 17
L.A. RAIDERS 33, San Diego 30
PITTSBURGH 38, Cincinnati 17
San Francisco 31, N.Y. GIANTS 10
DENVER 17, Green Bay 14
L.A. Rams 24, ATLANTA 10
Seattle 24, SAN DIEGO 0
WASHINGTON 27, Atlanta 14
SEATTLE 17, L.A. Raiders 14
NEW ORLEANS 27, Pittsburgh 24
MIAMI 28, N.Y. Jets 17
SAN DIEGO 20, Chicago 7
L.A. Raiders 24, DETROIT 3
MIAMI 28, Dallas 21

1983
Dallas 31, WASHINGTON 30
San Diego 17, KANSAS CITY 14
L.A. RAIDERS 27, Miami 14
N.Y. GIANTS 27, Green Bay 3
N.Y. Jets 34, BUFFALO 10
Pittsburgh 24, CINCINNATI 14
GREEN BAY 48, Washington 47
ST. LOUIS 20, N.Y. Giants 20 (OT)
Washington 27, SAN DIEGO 24
DETROIT 15, N.Y. Giants 9
L.A. Rams 36, ATLANTA 13
N.Y. Jets 31, NEW ORLEANS 28
MIAMI 38, Cincinnati 14
DETROIT 13, Minnesota 2
Green Bay 12, TAMPA BAY 9 (OT)
SAN FRANCISCO 42, Dallas 17

1982
Pittsburgh 36, DALLAS 28
Green Bay 27, N.Y. GIANTS 19
L.A. RAIDERS 28, San Diego 24
TAMPA BAY 23, Miami 17
N.Y. Jets 28, DETROIT 13
Dallas 37, HOUSTON 7
SAN DIEGO 50, Cincinnati 34
MIAMI 27, Buffalo 10
MINNESOTA 31, Dallas 27

1981
San Diego 44, CLEVELAND 14
Oakland 36, MINNESOTA 10
Dallas 35, NEW ENGLAND 21
Los Angeles 24, CHICAGO 7
PHILADELPHIA 16, Atlanta 13
BUFFALO 31, Miami 21
DETROIT 48, Chicago 17
PITTSBURGH 26, Houston 13
DENVER 19, Minnesota 17
DALLAS 27, Buffalo 14
SEATTLE 44, San Diego 23
ATLANTA 31, Minnesota 30
MIAMI 13, Philadelphia 10
OAKLAND 30, Pittsburgh 27
LOS ANGELES 21, Atlanta 16
SAN DIEGO 23, Oakland 10

1980
Dallas 17, WASHINGTON 3
Houston 16, CLEVELAND 7
PHILADELPHIA 35, N.Y. Giants 3
NEW ENGLAND 23, Denver 14
CHICAGO 23, Tampa Bay 0
DENVER 20, Washington 17
Oakland 45, PITTSBURGH 34
N.Y. JETS 17, Miami 14
CLEVELAND 27, Chicago 21
HOUSTON 38, New England 34
Oakland 19, SEATTLE 17
Los Angeles 27, NEW ORLEANS 7
OAKLAND 9, Denver 3
MIAMI 16, New England 13 (OT)
LOS ANGELES 38, Dallas 14
SAN DIEGO 26, Pittsburgh 17

1979
Pittsburgh 16, NEW ENGLAND 13 (OT)
Atlanta 14, PHILADELPHIA 10
WASHINGTON 27, N.Y. Giants 0
CLEVELAND 26, Dallas 7
GREEN BAY 27, New England 14
OAKLAND 13, Miami 3
N.Y. JETS 14, Minnesota 7
PITTSBURGH 42, Denver 7
Seattle 31, ATLANTA 28
Houston 9, Miami 6
Philadelphia 31, DALLAS 21
LOS ANGELES 20, Atlanta 14
SEATTLE 30, N.Y. Jets 7
Oakland 42, NEW ORLEANS 35
HOUSTON 20, Pittsburgh 17
SAN DIEGO 17, Denver 7

1978
DALLAS 38, Baltimore 0
MINNESOTA 12, Denver 9 (OT)
Baltimore 34, NEW ENGLAND 27
Minnesota 24, CHICAGO 20
WASHINGTON 9, Dallas 5
MIAMI 21, Cincinnati 0
DENVER 16, Chicago 7
Houston 24, PITTSBURGH 17
ATLANTA 15, Los Angeles 7
BALTIMORE 21, Washington 17
Oakland 34, CINCINNATI 21
HOUSTON 35, Miami 30
Pittsburgh 24, SAN FRANCISCO 7
SAN DIEGO 40, Chicago 7
Cincinnati 20, LOS ANGELES 19
MIAMI 23, New England 3

1977
PITTSBURGH 27, San Francisco 0
CLEVELAND 30, New England 27 (OT)
Oakland 37, KANSAS CITY 28
CHICAGO 24, Los Angeles 23
PITTSBURGH 20, Cincinnati 14
LOS ANGELES 35, Minnesota 3
ST. LOUIS 28, N.Y. Giants 0
BALTIMORE 10, Washington 3
St. Louis 24, DALLAS 17
WASHINGTON 10, Green Bay 9
OAKLAND 34, Buffalo 13
MIAMI 17, Baltimore 6
Dallas 42, SAN FRANCISCO 35

1976
Miami 30, BUFFALO 21
Oakland 24, KANSAS CITY 21
Washington 20, PHILADELPHIA 17 (OT)
MINNESOTA 17, Pittsburgh 6
San Francisco 16, LOS ANGELES 0
NEW ENGLAND 41, N.Y. Jets 7
WASHINGTON 20, St. Louis 10
BALTIMORE 38, Houston 14
CINCINNATI 20, Los Angeles 12
DALLAS 17, Buffalo 10
Baltimore 17, MIAMI 16
SAN FRANCISCO 20, Minnesota 16
OAKLAND 35, Cincinnati 20

1975
Oakland 31, MIAMI 21
DENVER 23, Green Bay 13
Dallas 36, DETROIT 10
WASHINGTON 27, St. Louis 17
N.Y. Giants 17, BUFFALO 14
Minnesota 13, CHICAGO 9
Los Angeles 42, PHILADELPHIA 3
Kansas City 34, DALLAS 31
CINCINNATI 33, Buffalo 24
Pittsburgh 32, HOUSTON 9
MIAMI 20, New England 7
OAKLAND 17, Denver 10
SAN DIEGO 24, N.Y. Jets 16

1974
BUFFALO 21, Oakland 20
PHILADELPHIA 13, Dallas 10
WASHINGTON 30, Denver 3
MIAMI 21, N.Y. Jets 17
DETROIT 17, San Francisco 13
CHICAGO 10, Green Bay 9
PITTSBURGH 24, Atlanta 17
Los Angeles 15, SAN FRANCISCO 13
Minnesota 28, ST. LOUIS 24
Kansas City 42, DENVER 34
Pittsburgh 28, NEW ORLEANS 7
MIAMI 24, Cincinnati 3
Washington 23, LOS ANGELES 17

1973
GREEN BAY 23, N.Y. Jets 7
DALLAS 40, New Orleans 3
DETROIT 31, Atlanta 6
WASHINGTON 14, Dallas 7
Miami 17, CLEVELAND 9
DENVER 23, Oakland 23
BUFFALO 23, Kansas City 14
PITTSBURGH 21, Washington 16
KANSAS CITY 19, Chicago 7
ATLANTA 20, Minnesota 14
SAN FRANCISCO 20, Green Bay 6
MIAMI 30, Pittsburgh 26
LOS ANGELES 40, N.Y. Giants 6

1972
Washington 24, MINNESOTA 21
Kansas City 20, NEW ORLEANS 17
N.Y. Giants 27, PHILADELPHIA 12
Oakland 34, HOUSTON 0
Green Bay 24, DETROIT 23
CHICAGO 13, Minnesota 10
DALLAS 28, Detroit 24
Baltimore 24, NEW ENGLAND 17
Cleveland 21, SAN DIEGO 17
WASHINGTON 24, Atlanta 13
MIAMI 31, St. Louis 10
Los Angeles 26, SAN FRANCISCO 16
OAKLAND 24, N.Y. Jets 16

1971
Minnesota 16, DETROIT 13
ST. LOUIS 17, N.Y. Jets 10
Oakland 34, CLEVELAND 20
DALLAS 20, N.Y. Giants 13
KANSAS CITY 38, Pittsburgh 16
MINNESOTA 10, Baltimore 3
GREEN BAY 14, Detroit 14
BALTIMORE 24, Los Angeles 17
SAN DIEGO 20, St. Louis 17
ATLANTA 28, Green Bay 21
MIAMI 34, Chicago 3
Kansas City 26, SAN FRANCISCO 17
Washington 38, LOS ANGELES 24

1970
CLEVELAND 31, N.Y. Jets 21
Kansas City 44, BALTIMORE 24
DETROIT 28, Chicago 14
Green Bay 22, SAN DIEGO 20
OAKLAND 34, Washington 20
MINNESOTA 13, Los Angeles 3
PITTSBURGH 21, Cincinnati 10
Baltimore 13, GREEN BAY 10
St. Louis 38, DALLAS 0
PHILADELPHIA 23, N.Y. Giants 20
Miami 20, ATLANTA 7
Cleveland 21, HOUSTON 10
Detroit 28, LOS ANGELES 23

MONDAY NIGHT WON-LOST RECORDS, 1970-2004

AMERICAN FOOTBALL CONFERENCE

	Balt.	Buff.	Cin.	Cle.	Den.	Hou.	Ind.	Jax.	K.C.	Mia.	N.E.	N.Y.J.	Oak.	Pitt.	S.D.	Tenn.
Total	3-1	17-20	8-16	13-12	22-29-1	0-0	14-10	5-3	20-14	39-32	11-20	16-19	36-21-1	31-20	14-13	16-15
2004	0-1	1-0		0-1			1-0		2-1	1-1	1-1	1-0				1-1
2003			0-1	1-1			1-0		1-0	1-1	1-0	1-0	0-3	0-1	0-1	0-1
2002	1-0			0-2	0-1					1-1	1-1	0-1	2-0	2-1		1-0
2001	2-0			1-1	0-1			0-1		1-0		0-1	1-0	1-0		0-2
2000		0-1		1-1			2-0	0-2	1-1	0-1	1-1	2-0	0-1			3-0
1999		1-0		1-2			2-0		1-2	0-1	2-1	0-1	1-0			
1998				2-1			2-0	0-2	1-2	1-2	1-0			2-1		
1997		1-1		2-1	0-1		1-0		2-0	1-2	1-2		0-2	0-2		
1996		0-2		1-0	1-0				0-2	1-2			2-1	3-0	1-1	
1995		1-1	0-2	1-0					1-1	2-1	1-0		0-2	1-1	1-1	
1994		1-1		0-2					1-1	1-0			1-1	2-0	0-1	0-3
1993		2-1	1-0	0-2	0-1				2-0	1-2			1-0	3-0	2-0	0-1
1992	2-0	0-1	0-1	0-2					1-0	2-1		0-1	0-2	1-0		1-0
1991	2-1	0-2							2-1	1-1		0-1	0-2	0-1		1-1
1990	1-1	1-1	1-1	1-1	0-1				0-1			0-1	2-0	1-0		1-0
1989	1-2	1-2	1-1	2-0									0-1	1-0		1-0
1988	2-0		1-2	0-2	1-1					1-1		1-1		1-1		1-0
1987			1-0	2-1					1-1		1-1	2-1	1-1			
1986		1-0	1-0	1-1					1-2	1-0	1-1		0-1	0-2	0-1	
1985		1-0	1-0	1-0					2-1	0-1	1-0		2-0	0-2	0-1	
1984	0-1	0-1		1-0					3-0		0-1		2-1	1-1	1-2	
1983	0-1	0-2					0-1		1-1		2-0		1-0	1-0	1-1	
1982	0-1	0-1							1-1		1-0		1-0	1-0	1-1	0-1
1981	1-1								1-1	0-1			2-1	1-1	2-1	0-1
1980			1-1	1-2					1-1	1-2	1-0		3-0	0-2	1-0	2-0
1979			1-0	0-2					0-2	0-2	1-1		2-0	2-1	1-0	2-0
1978		1-2		1-1	2-1				2-1	0-2			1-0	1-1	1-0	2-0
1977	0-1	0-1	1-0				1-1		0-1	1-0	0-1		2-0	2-0		
1976		0-2	1-1				2-0		0-1	1-1	1-0	0-1	2-0	0-1		0-1
1975		0-2	1-0		1-1				1-0	1-1	0-1	0-1	2-0	1-0	1-0	0-1
1974	1-0	0-1		0-2	1-0				2-0			0-1	0-1	2-0		
1973	1-0		0-1	0-0-1					1-1	2-0		0-1	0-0-1	1-1		
1972		1-0					1-0		1-0	1-0	0-1	0-1	2-0		0-1	0-1
1971		0-1							1-1	2-0		0-1	1-0	0-1	1-0	
1970		0-1	2-0		1-1				1-0	1-0		0-1	1-0	1-0	0-1	0-1

MONDAY NIGHT FOOTBALL ALL-TIME STANDINGS

AMERICAN FOOTBALL CONFERENCE

East	W	L	T	Pct.	South	W	L	T	Pct.
Miami	39	32	0	.549	Jacksonville	5	3	0	.625
Buffalo	17	20	0	.459	Indianapolis	14	10	0	.583
New York Jets	16	19	0	.457	Tennessee	16	15	0	.516
New England	11	20	0	.355	Houston	0	0	0	.000

North	W	L	T	Pct.	West	W	L	T	Pct.
Baltimore	3	1	0	.750	Oakland	36	21	1	.629
Pittsburgh	31	20	0	.608	Kansas City	20	14	0	.588
Cleveland	13	12	0	.520	San Diego	14	13	0	.519
Cincinnati	8	16	0	.333	Denver	22	29	1	.433

MONDAY NIGHT WON-LOST RECORDS, 1970-2004
NATIONAL FOOTBALL CONFERENCE

	Ariz.	Atl.	Car.	Chi.	Dall.	Det.	G.B.	Minn.	N.O.	N.Y.G.	Phil.	St.L.	S.F.	Sea.	T.B.	Wash.
Total	5-10-1	6-18	2-2	16-32	38-27	11-13-1	24-20-1	21-22	6-13	15-29-1	22-17	26-25	37-22	12-8	8-7	24-28
2004		0-1		2-1			2-1	0-2				2-1	2-1	0-1	0-1	0-1
2003			0-1	1-0			2-1			0-2	2-1	2-0	1-0		2-1	
2002				0-3			2-0			0-1	3-0	2-1	1-2	0-1	1-1	0-1
2001				1-0	0-1		2-0	1-1	0-1	0-3	1-0	2-1	1-0		1-0	0-2
2000			1-0	1-1			1-1	1-1				1-2		0-1	1-1	1-2
1999	0-1	1-2		1-2			1-2	2-1		1-0			1-2	1-0	1-0	
1998				2-0		1-1	0-3	1-0		0-2	0-1		3-0		1-1	0-1
1997			1-1	1-1	1-2		3-0	0-1				0-2	3-0			1-0
1996		0-1		2-0	2-1	0-2	2-1	0-1				0-2	2-1			
1995	0-1			1-2	3-0	2-0	1-0	0-2		0-1	0-1		2-1			
1994		0-2		2-1	1-0		1-0	2-0	0-2	1-2	2-0		2-1			
1993		0-1		0-1	1-1	0-1	1-0	0-2	1-0	1-1		1-2				1-2
1992		0-2		0-3	2-1	0-1		1-0	1-0	1-0	1-0		2-0	1-0		1-2
1991		2-1		0-1				0-1	1-0	2-1	2-1	0-1	2-1			2-0
1990						0-1		0-1	1-1	1-1	2-0	0-3	3-0	1-0		0-1
1989		1-1						1-1	1-1	2-1	0-2	0-2	3-0	1-0		0-2
1988	0-1			1-2	1-1			1-0	1-0	1-1	1-0	1-0	1-1	1-0		0-2
1987		1-2		2-1				1-0		0-3		1-2	2-0	0-2		1-1
1986	0-1			2-1	2-0	0-1	0-1			2-1		1-0	0-2	2-0		1-1
1985	1-1			1-1	1-1		0-1			0-1		2-1	1-2	0-2		2-1
1984		0-2		0-1	1-1	0-1	0-1		1-0			1-1	2-0	2-0		1-1
1983	0-0-1	0-1		1-1	2-0	2-1	0-1		0-1	1-1-1		1-0	1-0		0-1	1-2
1982				1-2	0-1	1-0	1-0			0-1					1-0	
1981		1-2		0-2	2-0	1-0		0-3			1-1	2-0	1-0			
1980		1-1		1-1					0-1	0-1	1-0	2-0		0-1	0-1	0-2
1979		1-2		0-2			1-0	0-1	0-1	0-1	1-1	1-0	2-0			1-0
1978		1-0		0-3	1-1		2-0					0-2	0-1			1-1
1977	2-0			1-0		0-1	0-1		0-1			1-1	0-2			1-1
1976	0-1			1-0					1-1		0-1		0-2	2-0		
1975	0-1			1-1	0-1	0-1	1-0			1-0	0-1	1-0				1-0
1974	0-1	0-1		1-0	0-1	1-0	0-1			1-0	1-0	1-1	0-2			2-0
1973		1-1		0-1	1-1	1-0	1-1	0-1	0-1			1-0	1-0			1-1
1972	0-1	0-1		1-0	1-0	0-2	1-0	0-2	0-1	1-0	0-1	1-0	0-1			2-0
1971	1-1	1-0		0-1	1-0	0-1-1	0-1-1	2-0		0-1		0-2	0-1			1-0
1970	1-0	0-1		0-1	0-1	2-0	1-1	1-0		0-1	1-0	0-2				0-1

MONDAY NIGHT FOOTBALL ALL-TIME STANDINGS
NATIONAL FOOTBALL CONFERENCE

East	W	L	T	Pct.	South	W	L	T	Pct.
Dallas	38	27	0	.585	Tampa Bay	8	7	0	.533
Philadelphia	22	17	0	.564	Carolina	2	2	0	.500
Washington	24	28	0	.462	New Orleans	6	13	0	.316
New York Giants	15	29	1	.344	Atlanta	6	18	0	.250

North	W	L	T	Pct.	West	W	L	T	Pct.
Green Bay	24	20	1	.546	San Francisco	37	22	0	.627
Minnesota	21	22	0	.488	Seattle	12	8	0	.600
Detroit	11	13	1	.458	St. Louis	26	25	0	.510
Chicago	16	32	0	.333	Arizona	5	10	1	.344

THURSDAY-SUNDAY NIGHT FOOTBALL, 1974-2004
(Home Team in capitals, games listed in chronological order.)

2004
NEW ENGLAND 27, Indianapolis 24 (Thurs.)
DENVER 34, Kansas City 24 (Sun.)
CINCINNATI 16, Miami 13 (Sun.)
OAKLAND 30, Tampa Bay 20 (Sun.)
Pittsburgh 13, MIAMI 3 (Sun.)
St. Louis 24, SAN FRANCISCO 14 (Sun.)
Baltimore 17, WASHINGTON 10 (Sun.)
Minnesota 38, NEW ORLEANS 31 (Sun.)
CHICAGO 23, San Francisco 13 (Sun.)
BALTIMORE 27, Cleveland 13 (Sun.)
NEW ENGLAND 29, Buffalo 6 (Sun.)
Green Bay 16, HOUSTON 13 (Sun.)
Oakland 25, DENVER 24 (Sun.)
Pittsburgh 17, JACKSONVILLE 16 (Sun.)
Philadelphia 17, WASHINGTON 14 (Sun.)
ATLANTA 34, Carolina 31 (OT) (Sat.)
INDIANAPOLIS 20, Baltimore 10 (Sun.)
Denver 37, TENNESSEE 16 (Sat.)
MIAMI 10, Cleveland 7 (Sun.)
NEW YORK GIANTS 28, Dallas 24 (Sun.)

2003
WASHINGTON 16, New York Jets 13 (Thurs.)
TENNESSEE 25, Oakland 20 (Sun.)
MINNESOTA 24, Chicago 13 (Sun.)
MIAMI 17, Buffalo 7 (Sun.)
Indianapolis 55, NEW ORLEANS 21 (Sun.)
Cleveland 33, PITTSBURGH 13 (Sun.)
SEATTLE 20, San Francisco 19 (Sun.)
KANSAS CITY 38, Buffalo 5 (Sun.)
Green Bay 30, MINNESOTA 27 (Sun.)
ST. LOUIS 33, Baltimore 22 (Sun.)
NEW ENGLAND 12, Dallas 0 (Sun.)
MIAMI 24, Washington 23 (Sun.)
JACKSONVILLE 17, Tampa Bay 10 (Sun.)
ATLANTA 20, Carolina 14 (OT) (Sun.)
NEW ORLEANS 45, New York Giants 7 (Sun.)
New England 21, NEW YORK JETS 16 (Sat.)
Denver 31, INDIANAPOLIS 17 (Sun.)
Philadelphia 31, WASHINGTON 7 (Sat.)
BALTIMORE 13, Pittsburgh 10 (OT) (Sun.)

2002
San Francisco 16, NEW YORK GIANTS 13 (Thurs.)
HOUSTON 19, Dallas 10 (Sun.)
Oakland 30, PITTSBURGH 17 (Sun.)
ATLANTA 30, Cincinnati 3 (Sun.)
SEATTLE 48, Minnesota 23 (Sun.)
Baltimore 26, CLEVELAND 21 (Sun.)
Miami 24, DENVER 22 (Sun.)
WASHINGTON 26, Indianapolis 21 (Sun.)
NEW YORK GIANTS 24, Jacksonville 17 (Sun.)
NEW YORK JETS 13, Miami 10 (Sun.)
OAKLAND 27, New England 20 (Sun.)
Indianapolis 23, DENVER 20 (OT) (Sun.)
NEW ORLEANS 23, Tampa Bay 20 (Sun.)
GREEN BAY 26, Minnesota 22 (Sun.)
ST. LOUIS 30, Arizona 28 (Sun.)
Philadelphia 27, DALLAS 3 (Sat.)
New York Jets 30, NEW ENGLAND 17 (Sun.)
Tampa Bay 15, CHICAGO 0 (Sun.)

2001
Miami 31, TENNESSEE 23 (Sun.)
Denver 38, ARIZONA 17 (Sun.)
PHILADELPHIA 40, Dallas 18 (Sun.)
SAN FRANCISCO 24, Carolina 14 (Sun.)
Oakland 23, INDIANAPOLIS 18 (Sun.)
Buffalo 13, JACKSONVILLE 10 (Sun.)
Indianapolis 35, KANSAS CITY 28 (Thurs.)
New York Jets 16, NEW ORLEANS 9 (Sun.)
SEATTLE 34, Oakland 27 (Sun.)
St. Louis 24, NEW ENGLAND 17 (Sun.)
Chicago 13, MINNESOTA 6 (Sun.)
SAN FRANCISCO 35, Buffalo 0 (Sun.)
DENVER 20, Seattle 7 (Sun.)
Pittsburgh 26, BALTIMORE 21 (Sun.)
Tennessee 13, OAKLAND 10 (Sat.)
New York Jets 29, INDIANAPOLIS 28 (Sun.)
TAMPA BAY 22, Baltimore 10 (Sat.)
Washington 40, NEW ORLEANS 10 (Sun.)
Philadelphia 17, TAMPA BAY 13 (Sun.)

2000
BUFFALO 16, Tennessee 13 (Sun.)
ARIZONA 32, Dallas 31 (Sun.)
MIAMI 19, Baltimore 6 (Sun.)
Washington 16, NEW YORK GIANTS 6 (Sun.)
PHILADELPHIA 38, Atlanta 10 (Sun.)
Baltimore 13, JACKSONVILLE 10 (Sun.)
Minnesota 28, CHICAGO 16 (Sun.)
Detroit 28, TAMPA BAY 14 (Thurs.)
Oakland 15, SAN DIEGO 13 (Sun.)
Carolina 27, ST. LOUIS 24 (Sun.)
INDIANAPOLIS 23, New York Jets 15 (Sun.)
Jacksonville 34, PITTSBURGH 24 (Sun.)
New York Giants 31, ARIZONA 7 (Sun.)
MINNESOTA 24, Detroit 17 (Thurs.)
Green Bay 28, CHICAGO 6 (Sun.)
OAKLAND 31, New York Jets 7 (Sun.)
New York Giants 17, DALLAS 13 (Sun.)
Buffalo 42, SEATTLE 23 (Sat.)

1999
Pittsburgh 43, CLEVELAND 0 (Sun.)
BUFFALO 17, N.Y. Jets 3 (Sun.)
NEW ENGLAND 16, N.Y. Giants 14 (Sun.)
SEATTLE 22, Oakland 21 (Sun.)
GREEN BAY 26, Tampa Bay 23 (Sun.)
Washington 24, ARIZONA 10 (Sun.)
Kansas City 35, BALTIMORE 8 (Thurs.)
DETROIT 20, Tampa Bay 3 (Sun.)
MIAMI 17, Tennessee 0 (Sun.)
SEATTLE 20, Denver 17 (Sun.)
JACKSONVILLE 41, New Orleans 23 (Sun.)
CAROLINA 34, Atlanta 28 (Sun.)
JACKSONVILLE 20, Pittsburgh 6 (Thurs.)
NEW ENGLAND 13, Dallas 6 (Sun.)
TENNESSEE 21, Oakland 14 (Thurs.)
KANSAS CITY 31, Minnesota 28 (Sun.)
Buffalo 31, ARIZONA 21 (Sun.)
Washington 26, SAN FRANCISCO 20 (OT) (Sun.)

1998
KANSAS CITY 28, Oakland 8 (Sun.)
NEW ENGLAND 29, Indianapolis 6 (Sun.)
ARIZONA 17, Philadelphia 3 (Sun.)
BALTIMORE 31, Cincinnati 24 (Sun.)
KANSAS CITY 17, Seattle 6 (Sun.)
Atlanta 34, NEW YORK GIANTS 20 (Sun.)
DETROIT 27, Green Bay 20 (Thurs.)
Buffalo 30, CAROLINA 14 (Sun.)
Oakland 31, SEATTLE 18 (Sun.)
Tennessee 31, TAMPA BAY 22 (Sun.)
DETROIT 26, Chicago 3 (Sun.)
SAN FRANCISCO 31, New Orleans 20 (Sun.)
Denver 31, SAN DIEGO 16 (Sun.)
PHILADELPHIA 17, St. Louis 14 (Thurs.)
MINNESOTA 48, Chicago 22 (Sun.)
New York Jets 21, MIAMI 16 (Sun.)
MINNESOTA 50, Jacksonville 10 (Sun.)
DALLAS 23, Washington 7 (Sun.)

1997
Washington 24, CAROLINA 10 (Sun.)
ARIZONA 25, Dallas 22 (OT) (Sun.)
NEW ENGLAND 27, New York Jets 24 (OT) (Sun.)
TAMPA BAY 31, Miami 21 (Sun.)
MINNESOTA 28, Philadelphia 19 (Sun.)
New Orleans 20, CHICAGO 17 (Sun.)
PITTSBURGH 24, Indianapolis 22 (Sun.)
KANSAS CITY 31, San Diego 3 (Thurs.)
CAROLINA 21, Atlanta 12 (Sun.)
GREEN BAY 20, Detroit 10 (Sun.)
PITTSBURGH 37, Baltimore 0 (Sun.)
Oakland 38, SAN DIEGO 13 (Sun.)
WASHINGTON 7, New York Giants 7 (OT) (Sun.)
Denver 38, SAN DIEGO 28 (Sun.)
CINCINNATI 41, Tennessee 14 (Thurs.)
MIAMI 33, Detroit 30 (Sun.)
Chicago 13, ST. LOUIS 10 (Sun.)
SEATTLE 38, San Francisco 9 (Sun.)

1996
Buffalo 23, NEW YORK GIANTS 20 (OT) (Sun.)
Miami 38, ARIZONA 10 (Sun.)
DENVER 27, Tampa Bay 23 (Sun.)
Philadelphia 33, ATLANTA 18 (Sun.)
WASHINGTON 31, New York Jets 16 (Sun.)
Houston 30, CINCINNATI 27 (OT) (Sun.)
INDIANAPOLIS 26, Baltimore 21 (Sun.)
KANSAS CITY 34, Seattle 16 (Thurs.)
NEW ENGLAND 28, Buffalo 25 (Sun.)
San Francisco 24, NEW ORLEANS 17 (Sun.)
CAROLINA 27, New York Giants 17 (Sun.)
Minnesota 16, OAKLAND 13 (OT) (Sun.)
Green Bay 24, ST. LOUIS 9 (Sun.)
New England 45, SAN DIEGO 7 (Sun.)
INDIANAPOLIS 37, Philadelphia 10 (Thurs.)
Minnesota 24, DETROIT 22 (Sun.)
JACKSONVILLE 20, Seattle 13 (Sun.)
SAN DIEGO 16, Denver 10 (Sun.)

1995
DENVER 22, Buffalo 7 (Sun.)
Philadelphia 31, ARIZONA 19 (Sun.)
Dallas 23, MINNESOTA 17 (OT) (Sun.)
Green Bay 24, JACKSONVILLE 14 (Sun.)
Oakland 47, NEW YORK JETS 10 (Sun.)
Denver 37, NEW ENGLAND 3 (Sun.)
ST. LOUIS 21, Atlanta 19 (Thurs.)
Cincinnati 27, PITTSBURGH 9 (Thurs.)
New York Giants 24, WASHINGTON 15 (Sun.)
Miami 24, SAN DIEGO 14 (Sun.)
PHILADELPHIA 31, Denver 13 (Sun.)
KANSAS CITY 20, Houston 13 (Sun.)
NEW ORLEANS 34, Carolina 26 (Sun.)
New York Giants 10, ARIZONA 6 (Thurs.)
SAN FRANCISCO 27, Buffalo 17 (Sun.)
TAMPA BAY 13, Green Bay 10 (OT) (Sun.)
SEATTLE 44, Oakland 10 (Sun.)
Indianapolis 10, New England 7 (Sat.)

1994
San Diego 17, DENVER 34 (Sun.)
New York Giants 20, ARIZONA 17 (Sun.)
Kansas City 30, ATLANTA 10 (Sun.)
Chicago 19, NEW YORK JETS 7 (Sun.)
Miami 23, CINCINNATI 7 (Sun.)
PHILADELPHIA 21, Washington 17 (Sun.)
Cleveland 11, HOUSTON 8 (Thurs.)
MINNESOTA 13, Green Bay 10 (OT) (Thurs.)
ARIZONA 20, Pittsburgh 17 (OT) (Sun.)
KANSAS CITY 13, Los Angeles Raiders 3 (Sun.)
DETROIT 14, Tampa Bay 9 (Sun.)
SAN FRANCISCO 31, Los Angeles Rams 27 (Sun.)
New England 12, INDIANAPOLIS 10 (Sun.)
MINNESOTA 33, Chicago 27 (OT) (Thurs.)
Buffalo 42, MIAMI 31 (Sun.)
New Orleans 29, ATLANTA 20 (Sun.)
Los Angeles Raiders 17, SEATTLE 16 (Sun.)
MIAMI 27, Detroit 20 (Sun.)

1993
NEW ORLEANS 33, Houston 21 (Sun.)
Los Angeles Raiders 17, SEATTLE 13 (Sun.)
Dallas 17, PHOENIX 10 (Sun.)
NEW YORK JETS 45, New England 7 (Sun.)
BUFFALO 17, New York Giants 14 (Sun.)
GREEN BAY 30, Denver 27 (Sun.)
ATLANTA 30, Los Angeles Rams 24 (Thurs.)
MIAMI 41, Indianapolis 27 (Sun.)
Detroit 30, MINNESOTA 27 (Sun.)
WASHINGTON 30, Indianapolis 24 (Sun.)
Chicago 16, SAN DIEGO 13 (Sun.)
TAMPA BAY 23, Minnesota 10 (Sun.)
HOUSTON 23, Pittsburgh 3 (Sun.)
SAN FRANCISCO 21, Cincinnati 8 (Sun.)
Green Bay 20, SAN DIEGO 13 (Sun.)
Philadelphia 20, INDIANAPOLIS 10 (Sun.)
MINNESOTA 30, Kansas City 10 (Sun.)
HOUSTON 24, New York Jets 0 (Sun.)

1992
DENVER 17, Los Angeles Raiders 13 (Sun.)
Philadelphia 31, PHOENIX 14 (Sun.)
BUFFALO 38, Indianapolis 0 (Sun.)
San Francisco 16, NEW ORLEANS 10 (Sun.)
NEW YORK JETS 30, New England 21 (Sun.)
NEW ORLEANS 13, Los Angeles Rams 10 (Sun.)
MINNESOTA 31, Detroit 14 (Thurs.)
Pittsburgh 27, KANSAS CITY 3 (Sun.)
New York Giants 24, WASHINGTON 7 (Sun.)
Cincinnati 31, CHICAGO 28 (OT) (Sun.)
DENVER 27, New York Giants 13 (Sun.)
Kansas City 24, SEATTLE 14 (Sun.)
SAN DIEGO 27, Los Angeles Raiders 3 (Sun.)
NEW ORLEANS 22, Atlanta 14 (Thurs.)
Los Angeles Rams 31, TAMPA BAY 27 (Sun.)
Green Bay 16, HOUSTON 14 (Sun.)
MIAMI 19, New York Jets 17 (Sun.)
HOUSTON 27, Buffalo 3 (Sun.)

1991
WASHINGTON 45, Detroit 0 (Sun.)
Houston 30, CINCINNATI 7 (Sun.)
NEW ORLEANS 24, Los Angeles Rams 7 (Sun.)
Dallas 17, PHOENIX 9 (Sun.)
Denver 13, MINNESOTA 6 (Sun.)
Pittsburgh 21, INDIANAPOLIS 3 (Sun.)
Los Angeles Raiders 23, SEATTLE 20 (Sun.)
Chicago 10, GREEN BAY 0 (Thurs.)
Washington 17, NEW YORK GIANTS 13 (Sun.)
DENVER 20, Pittsburgh 13 (Sun.)
MIAMI 30, New England 20 (Sun.)
HOUSTON 28, Cleveland 24 (Sun.)
Atlanta 23, NEW ORLEANS 20 (OT) (Sun.)
Los Angeles Raiders 9, SAN DIEGO 7 (Sun.)
Minnesota 26, TAMPA BAY 24 (Sun.)
Buffalo 35, INDIANAPOLIS 7 (Sun.)
SEATTLE 23, Los Angeles Rams 9 (Sun.)

1990
NEW YORK GIANTS 27, Philadelphia 20 (Sun.)
PITTSBURGH 20, Houston 9 (Sun.)
TAMPA BAY 23, Detroit 20 (Sun.)
Washington 38, PHOENIX 10 (Sun.)
BUFFALO 38, Los Angeles Raiders 24 (Sun.)
CHICAGO 38, Los Angeles Rams 9 (Sun.)
MIAMI 17, New England 10 (Thurs.)
ATLANTA 38, Cincinnati 17 (Sun.)
MINNESOTA 27, Denver 22 (Sun.)
San Francisco 24, DALLAS 6 (Sun.)
CINCINNATI 27, Pittsburgh 3 (Sun.)
Seattle 13, SAN DIEGO 10 (Sun.)
MINNESOTA 23, Green Bay 7 (Sun.)
MIAMI 23, Philadelphia 20 (Sun.)
DETROIT 38, Chicago 21 (Sun.)
INDIANAPOLIS 35, Washington 28 (Sat.)
SEATTLE 17, Denver 12 (Sun.)
HOUSTON 34, Pittsburgh 14 (Sun.)

1989
Dallas 13, WASHINGTON 3 (Sun.)
SAN DIEGO 14, Los Angeles Raiders 12 (Sun.)
INDIANAPOLIS 27, New York Jets 10 (Sun.)
Los Angeles Rams 20, NEW ORLEANS 17 (Sun.)
MINNESOTA 27, Chicago 16 (Sun.)
MIAMI 31, New England 10 (Sun.)
SEATTLE 23, Los Angeles Raiders 17 (Sun.)
Cleveland 24, HOUSTON 20 (Sat.)

1988
HOUSTON 41, Washington 17 (Sun.)
Los Angeles Raiders 13, SAN DIEGO 3 (Sun.)
Minnesota 43, DALLAS 3 (Sun.)
New England 6, MIAMI 3 (Sun.)
New York Giants 13, NEW ORLEANS 12 (Sun.)
Pittsburgh 37, HOUSTON 34 (Sun.)
SEATTLE 42, Denver 14 (Sun.)
Los Angeles Rams 38, SAN FRANCISCO 16 (Sun.)

1987
NEW YORK GIANTS 17, New England 10 (Sun.)
SAN DIEGO 16, Los Angeles Raiders 14 (Sun.)
Miami 20, DALLAS 14 (Sun.)
SAN FRANCISCO 38, Cleveland 24 (Sun.)
Chicago 30, MINNESOTA 24 (Sun.)
SEATTLE 28, Denver 21 (Sun.)
MIAMI 23, Washington 21 (Sun.)
SAN FRANCISCO 48, Los Angeles Rams 0 (Sun.)

1986
New England 20, NEW YORK JETS 6 (Thurs.)
Cincinnati 30, CLEVELAND 13 (Thurs.)
Los Angeles Raiders 37, SAN DIEGO 31 (OT) (Thurs.)
LOS ANGELES RAMS 29, Dallas 10 (Sun.)
SAN FRANCISCO 24, Los Angeles Rams 14 (Fri.)

1985
KANSAS CITY 36, Los Angeles Raiders 20 (Thurs.)
Chicago 33, MINNESOTA 24 (Thurs.)
Dallas 30, NEW YORK GIANTS 29 (Sun.)
SAN DIEGO 54, Pittsburgh 44 (Sun.)
Denver 27, SEATTLE 24 (Fri.)

1984
Pittsburgh 23, NEW YORK JETS 17 (Thurs.)
Denver 24, CLEVELAND 14 (Sun.)
DALLAS 30, New Orleans 27 (Sun.)
Washington 31, MINNESOTA 17 (Thurs.)
SAN FRANCISCO 19, Los Angeles Rams 16 (Fri.)
1983
San Francisco 48, MINNESOTA 17 (Thurs.)
CLEVELAND 17, Cincinnati 7 (Thurs.)
Los Angeles Raiders 40, DALLAS 38 (Sun.)
Los Angeles Raiders 42, SAN DIEGO 10 (Thurs.)
MIAMI 34, New York Jets 14 (Fri.)

1982
BUFFALO 23, Minnesota 22 (Thurs.)
SAN FRANCISCO 30, Los Angeles Rams 24 (Thurs.)
ATLANTA 17, San Francisco 7 (Sun.)

1981
MIAMI 30, Pittsburgh 10 (Thurs.)
Philadelphia 20, BUFFALO 14 (Thurs.)
DALLAS 29, Los Angeles 17 (Sun.)
HOUSTON 17, Cleveland 13 (Thurs.)

1980
TAMPA BAY 10, Los Angeles 9 (Thurs.)
DALLAS 42, San Diego 31 (Sun.)
San Diego 27, MIAMI 24 (OT) (Thurs.)
HOUSTON 6, Pittsburgh 0 (Thurs.)

1979
Los Angeles 13, DENVER 9 (Thurs.)
DALLAS 30, Los Angeles 6 (Sun.)
OAKLAND 45, San Diego 22 (Thurs.)
MIAMI 39, New England 24 (Thurs.)

1978
New England 21, OAKLAND 14 (Sun.)
Minnesota 21, DALLAS 10 (Thurs.)
LOS ANGELES 10, Pittsburgh 7 (Sun.)
Denver 21, OAKLAND 6 (Sun.)

1977
Minnesota 30, DETROIT 21 (Sat.)

1976
Los Angeles 20, DETROIT 17 (Sat.)

1975
LOS ANGELES 10, Pittsburgh 3 (Sat.)

1974
OAKLAND 27, Dallas 23 (Sat.)

THANKSGIVING DAY FOOTBALL, 1920-2004

(Home Team in capitals, games listed in chronological order.)

(AFL)-American Football League, 1960-69.

Nov. 25, 1920	AKRON PROS 7, Canton Bulldogs 0 Decatur Staleys 6, CHICAGO TIGERS 0 ELYRIA (OH) ATHLETICS* 0, Columbus Panhandles 0 DAYTON TRIANGLES 28, Detroit Heralds 0 CHICAGO BOOSTERS* 27, Hammond Pros 0 All-Tonawanda (NY) 14, ROCHESTER JEFFERSONS 3 * Non league team. Games between league teams and non league teams counted in standings in 1920.
Nov. 24, 1921	Canton Bulldogs 14, AKRON PROS 0 Buffalo All-Americans 7, CHICAGO STALEYS 6
Nov. 30, 1922	Buffalo All-Americans 21, ROCHESTER JEFFERSONS 0 CHICAGO CARDINALS 6, Chicago Bears 0 RACINE LEGION 3, Milwaukee Badgers 0 Oorang Indians 18, COLUMBUS PANHANDLES 6 CANTON BULLDOGS 14, Akron Pros 0
Nov. 29, 1923	CANTON BULLDOGS 28, Toledo Maroons 0 CHICAGO BEARS 3, Chicago Cardinals 0 GREEN BAY PACKERS 19, Hammond Pros 0 Milwaukee Badgers 16, RACINE LEGION 0 AKRON PROS 2, Buffalo All-Americans 0
Nov. 27, 1924	AKRON PROS 22, Buffalo Bisons 0 Chicago Bears 21, CHICAGO CARDINALS 0 FRANKFORD YELLOWJACKETS 32, Dayton Triangles 7 CLEVELAND BULLDOGS 53, Milwaukee Badgers 10 (at Canton, Ohio) Green Bay Packers 17, KANSAS CITY BLUES 6
Nov. 26, 1925	CHICAGO BEARS 0, Chicago Cardinals 0 Kansas City Cowboys 17, CLEVELAND BULLDOGS 0 (at Hartford, Connecticut) Rock Island Independents 6, DETROIT PANTHERS 3 POTTSVILLE MAROONS 31, Green Bay Packers 0
Nov. 25, 1926	New York Giants 17, BROOKLYN LIONS 0 Los Angeles Buccaneers 9, DETROIT PANTHERS 6 CHICAGO BEARS 0, Chicago Cardinals 0 FRANKFORD YELLOWJACKETS 20, Green Bay Packers 14 POTTSVILLE MAROONS 8, Providence Steam Roller 0 CANTON BULLDOGS 0, Akron Pros 0
Nov. 24, 1927	Chicago Cardinals 3, CHICAGO BEARS 0 POTTSVILLE MAROONS 6, Providence Steam Roller 0 Green Bay Packers 17, FRANKFORD YELLOWJACKETS 9 Cleveland Bulldogs 30, NEW YORK YANKEES 19
Nov. 29, 1928	Providence Steam Roller 7, POTTSVILLE MAROONS 0 DETROIT WOLVERINES 33, Dayton Triangles 7 FRANKFORD YELLOWJACKETS 2, Green Bay Packers 0 CHICAGO BEARS 34, Chicago Cardinals 0
Nov. 28, 1929	New York Giants 21, STATEN ISLAND STAPLETONS 7 FRANKFORD YELLOWJACKETS 0, Green Bay Packers 0 Chicago Cardinals 40, CHICAGO BEARS 6
Nov. 27, 1930	STATEN ISLAND STAPLETONS 7, New York Giants 6 BROOKLYN DODGERS 33, Providence Steam Roller 12 Green Bay Packers 25, FRANKFORD YELLOWJACKETS 7 CHICAGO BEARS 6, Chicago Cardinals 0
Nov. 26, 1931	Green Bay Packers 38, PROVIDENCE STEAM ROLLER 7 STATEN ISLAND STAPLETONS 9, New York Giants 6 CHICAGO BEARS 18, Chicago Cardinals 7
Nov. 24, 1932	CHICAGO BEARS 34, Chicago Cardinals 0 Green Bay Packers 7, BROOKLYN DODGERS 0 STATEN ISLAND STAPLETONS 13, New York Giants 13

Nov. 30, 1933	Chicago Bears 22, CHICAGO CARDINALS 6
	New York Giants 10, BROOKLYN DODGERS 0
Nov. 29, 1934	CHICAGO CARDINALS 6, Green Bay Packers 0
	Chicago Bears 19, DETROIT LIONS 16
	New York Giants 27, BROOKLYN DODGERS 0
Nov. 28, 1935	New York Giants 21, BROOKLYN DODGERS 0
	CHICAGO CARDINALS 9, Green Bay Packers 7
	DETROIT LIONS 14, Chicago Bears 2
Nov. 26, 1936	DETROIT LIONS 13, Chicago Bears 7
	New York Giants 14, BROOKLYN DODGERS 0
Nov. 25, 1937	Chicago Bears 13, DETROIT LIONS 0
	BROOKLYN DODGERS 13, New York Giants 13
Nov. 24, 1938	DETROIT LIONS 14, Chicago Bears 7
	BROOKLYN DODGERS 7, New York Giants 7
Nov. 23, 1939#	PHILADELPHIA EAGLES 17, Pittsburgh Steelers 14
Nov. 28, 1940#	Pittsburgh Steelers 7, PHILADELPHIA EAGLES 0

In 1939 and 1940, President Roosevelt moved Thanksgiving one week earlier. Various states celebrated on the date declared by the President, while other states recognized the traditional fourth Thursday of the month. In 1941, Thanksgiving was sanctioned by Congress to be celebrated on the fourth Thursday of November, which it has been ever since.

Nov. 22, 1945	Cleveland Rams 28, DETROIT LIONS 21
Nov. 28, 1946	Boston Yanks 34, DETROIT LIONS 10
Nov. 27, 1947	Chicago Bears 34, DETROIT LIONS 14
Nov. 25, 1948	Chicago Cardinals 28, DETROIT LIONS 14
Nov. 24, 1949	Chicago Bears 28, DETROIT LIONS 7
Nov. 23, 1950	DETROIT LIONS 49, New York Yanks 14
	Pittsburgh Steelers 28, CHICAGO CARDINALS 17
Nov. 22, 1951	DETROIT LIONS 52, Green Bay Packers 35
Nov. 27, 1952	DETROIT LIONS 48, Green Bay Packers 24
	DALLAS TEXANS 27, Chicago Bears 23 (at Akron, Ohio)
Nov. 26, 1953	DETROIT LIONS 34, Green Bay Packers 15
Nov. 25, 1954	DETROIT LIONS 28, Green Bay Packers 24
Nov. 24, 1955	DETROIT LIONS 24, Green Bay Packers 10
Nov. 22, 1956	Green Bay Packers 24, DETROIT LIONS 20
Nov. 28, 1957	DETROIT LIONS 18, Green Bay Packers 6
Nov. 27, 1958	DETROIT LIONS 24, Green Bay Packers 14
Nov. 26, 1959	Green Bay Packers 24, DETROIT LIONS 17
Nov. 24, 1960	DETROIT LIONS 23, Green Bay Packers 10
	(AFL) - NEW YORK TITANS 41, Dallas Texans 35
Nov. 23, 1961	Green Bay Packers 17, DETROIT LIONS 9
	(AFL) - NEW YORK TITANS 21, Buffalo Bills 14
Nov. 22, 1962	DETROIT LIONS 26, Green Bay Packers 14
	(AFL) - New York Titans 46, DENVER BRONCOS 45
Nov. 28, 1963	DETROIT LIONS 13, Green Bay Packers 13
	(AFL) - Oakland Raiders 26, DENVER BRONCOS 10
Nov. 26, 1964	Chicago Bears 27, DETROIT LIONS 24
	(AFL) - Buffalo Bills 27, SAN DIEGO CHARGERS 24
Nov. 25, 1965	DETROIT LIONS 24, Baltimore Colts 24
	(AFL) - SAN DIEGO CHARGERS 20, Buffalo Bills 20

Nov. 24, 1966	San Francisco 49ers 41, DETROIT LIONS 14
	DALLAS COWBOYS 26, Cleveland Browns 14
	(AFL) - Buffalo Bills 31, OAKLAND RAIDERS 10
Nov. 23, 1967	Los Angeles Rams 31, DETROIT LIONS 7
	DALLAS COWBOYS 46, St. Louis Cardinals 21
	(AFL) - Oakland Raiders 44, KANSAS CITY CHIEFS 22
	(AFL) - SAN DIEGO CHARGERS 24, Denver Broncos 20
Nov. 28, 1968	Philadelphia Eagles 12, DETROIT LIONS 0
	DALLAS COWBOYS 29, Washington Redskins 20
	(AFL) - OAKLAND RAIDERS 13, Buffalo Bills 10
	(AFL) - KANSAS CITY CHIEFS 24, Houston Oilers 10
Nov. 27, 1969	Minnesota Vikings 27, DETROIT LIONS 0
	DALLAS COWBOYS 24, San Francisco 49ers 24
	(AFL) - KANSAS CITY CHIEFS 31, Denver Broncos 17
	(AFL) - San Diego Chargers 21, HOUSTON OILERS 17
Nov. 26, 1970	DETROIT LIONS 28, Oakland Raiders 14
	DALLAS COWBOYS 16, Green Bay Packers 3
Nov. 25, 1971	DETROIT LIONS 32, Kansas City Chiefs 21
	DALLAS COWBOYS 28, Los Angeles Rams 21
Nov. 23, 1972	DETROIT LIONS 37, New York Jets 20
	San Francisco 49ers 31, DALLAS COWBOYS 10
Nov. 22, 1973	Washington Redskins 20, DETROIT LIONS 0
	Miami Dolphins 14, DALLAS COWBOYS 7
Nov. 28, 1974	Denver Broncos 31, DETROIT LIONS 27
	DALLAS COWBOYS 24, Washington Redskins 23
Nov. 27, 1975	Los Angeles Rams 20, DETROIT LIONS 0
	Buffalo Bills 32, ST. LOUIS CARDINALS 14
Nov. 25, 1976	DETROIT LIONS 27, Buffalo Bills 14
	DALLAS COWBOYS 19, St. Louis Cardinals 14
Nov. 24, 1977	Chicago Bears 31, DETROIT LIONS 14
	Miami Dolphins 55, ST. LOUIS CARDINALS 14
Nov. 23, 1978	DETROIT LIONS 17, Denver Broncos 14
	DALLAS COWBOYS 37, Washington Redskins 10
Nov. 22, 1979	DETROIT LIONS 20, Chicago Bears 0
	Houston Oilers 30, DALLAS COWBOYS 24
Nov. 27, 1980	Chicago Bears 23, DETROIT LIONS 17 (OT)
	DALLAS COWBOYS 51, Seattle Seahawks 7
Nov. 26, 1981	DETROIT LIONS 27, Kansas City Chiefs 10
	DALLAS COWBOYS 10, Chicago Bears 9
Nov. 25, 1982	New York Giants 13, DETROIT LIONS 6
	DALLAS COWBOYS 31, Cleveland Browns 14
Nov. 24, 1983	DETROIT LIONS 45, Pittsburgh Steelers 3
	DALLAS COWBOYS 35, St. Louis Cardinals 17
Nov. 22, 1984	DETROIT LIONS 31, Green Bay Packers 28
	DALLAS COWBOYS 20, New England Patriots 17
Nov. 28, 1985	DETROIT LIONS 31, New York Jets 20
	DALLAS COWBOYS 35, St. Louis Cardinals 17
Nov. 27, 1986	Green Bay Packers 44, DETROIT LIONS 40
	Seattle Seahawks 31, DALLAS COWBOYS 14
Nov. 26, 1987	Kansas City Chiefs 27, DETROIT LIONS 20
	Minnesota Vikings 44, DALLAS COWBOYS 38 (OT)
Nov. 24, 1988	Minnesota Vikings 23, DETROIT LIONS 0
	Houston Oilers 25, DALLAS COWBOYS 17

Nov. 23, 1989	DETROIT LIONS 13, Cleveland Browns 10
	Philadelphia Eagles 27, DALLAS COWBOYS 0
Nov. 22, 1990	DETROIT LIONS 40, Denver Broncos 27
	DALLAS COWBOYS 27, Washington Redskins 17
Nov. 28, 1991	DETROIT LIONS 16, Chicago Bears 6
	DALLAS COWBOYS 20, Pittsburgh Steelers 10
Nov. 26, 1992	Houston Oilers 24, DETROIT LIONS 21
	DALLAS COWBOYS 30, New York Giants 3
Nov. 25, 1993	Chicago Bears 10, DETROIT LIONS 6
	Miami Dolphins 16, DALLAS COWBOYS 14
Nov. 24, 1994	DETROIT LIONS 35, Buffalo Bills 21
	DALLAS COWBOYS 42, Green Bay Packers 31
Nov. 23, 1995	DETROIT LIONS 44, Minnesota Vikings 38
	DALLAS COWBOYS 24, Kansas City Chiefs 12
Nov. 28, 1996	Kansas City Chiefs 28, DETROIT LIONS 24
	DALLAS COWBOYS 21, Washington Redskins 10
Nov. 27, 1997	DETROIT LIONS 55, Chicago Bears 20
	Tennessee Titans 27, DALLAS COWBOYS 14
Nov. 26, 1998	DETROIT LIONS 19, Pittsburgh Steelers 16 (OT)
	Minnesota Vikings 46, DALLAS COWBOYS 36
Nov. 25, 1999	DETROIT LIONS 21, Chicago Bears 17
	DALLAS COWBOYS 20, Miami Dolphins 0
Nov. 23, 2000	DETROIT LIONS 34, New England Patriots 9
	Minnesota Vikings 27, DALLAS COWBOYS 15
Nov. 22, 2001	Green Bay Packers 29, DETROIT LIONS 27
	Denver Broncos 26, DALLAS COWBOYS 24
Nov. 28, 2002	New England Patriots 20, DETROIT LIONS 12
	DALLAS COWBOYS 27, Washington Redskins 20
Nov. 27, 2003	DETROIT LIONS 22, Green Bay Packers 14
	Miami Dolphins 40, DALLAS COWBOYS 21
Nov. 25, 2004	Indianapolis Colts 41, DETROIT LIONS 9
	DALLAS COWBOYS 21, Chicago Bears 7

THANKSGIVING DAY RECORDS
*NFL record; stats compiled by Elias Sports Bureau.

SCORING / Most Touchdowns, Game
- 6 Ernie Nevers, Chi. Cardinals vs. Chi. Bears, Nov. 28, 1929*
- 4 Sterling Sharpe, Green Bay at Dallas, Nov. 24, 1994
- 3 By many players

RUSHING / Most Yards Rushing, Game
- 273 O.J. Simpson, Buffalo at Detroit, Nov. 25, 1976
- 198 Bob Hoernschemeyer, Detroit vs. N.Y. Yankees, Nov. 23, 1950
- 195 Earl Campbell, Houston at Dallas, Nov. 22, 1979

PASSING / Most Yards Passing, Game
- 455 Troy Aikman, Dallas vs. Minnesota, Nov. 26, 1998
- 410 Scott Mitchell, Detroit vs. Minnesota, Nov. 23, 1995
- 384 Warren Moon, Minnesota at Detroit, Nov. 23, 1995

PASS RECEIVING
RECEPTIONS / Most Pass Receptions, Game
- 12 Brett Perriman, Detroit vs. Minnesota, Nov. 23, 1995
-    Marvin Harrison, Indianapolis at Detroit, Nov. 25, 2004
- 11 Daryl Johnston, Dallas vs. Miami, Nov. 25, 1993
-    Michael Irvin, Dallas vs. Kansas City, Nov. 23, 1995
YARDS GAINED / Most Yards on Pass Receptions, Game
- 303 Jim Benton, Cleveland at Detroit, Nov. 22, 1945
- 185 Lance Alworth, San Diego vs. Buffalo, Nov. 26, 1964
- 184 Anthony Carter, Minnesota at Dallas, Nov. 26, 1987 (OT)

HISTORY OF OVERTIME GAMES
PRESEASON

Aug. 28, 1955	Los Angeles 23, New York Giants 17, at Portland, Oregon
Aug. 24, 1962	Denver 27, Dallas Texans 24, at Fort Worth, Texas
Aug. 10, 1974	San Diego 20, New York Jets 14, at San Diego
Aug. 17, 1974	Pittsburgh 33, Philadelphia 30, at Philadelphia
Aug. 17, 1974	Dallas 19, Houston 13, at Dallas
Aug. 17, 1974	Cincinnati 13, Atlanta 7, at Atlanta
Sept. 6, 1974	Buffalo 23, New York Giants 17, at Buffalo
Aug. 9, 1975	Baltimore 23, Denver 20, at Denver
Aug. 30, 1975	New England 20, Green Bay 17, at Milwaukee
Sept. 13, 1975	Minnesota 14, San Diego 14, at San Diego
Aug. 1, 1976	New England 13, New York Giants 7, at New England
Aug. 2, 1976	Kansas City 9, Houston 3, at Kansas City
Aug. 20, 1976	New Orleans 26, Baltimore 20, at Baltimore
Sept. 4, 1976	Dallas 26, Houston 20, at Dallas
Aug. 13, 1977	Seattle 23, Dallas 17, at Seattle
Aug. 28, 1977	New England 13, Pittsburgh 10, at New England
Aug. 28, 1977	New York Giants 24, Buffalo 21, at East Rutherford, N.J.
Aug. 2, 1979	Seattle 12, Minnesota 9, at Minnesota
Aug. 4, 1979	Los Angeles 20, Oakland 14, at Los Angeles
Aug. 24, 1979	Denver 20, New England 17, at Denver
Aug. 23, 1980	Tampa Bay 20, Cincinnati 14, at Tampa Bay
Aug. 5, 1981	San Francisco 27, Seattle 24, at Seattle
Aug. 29, 1981	New Orleans 20, Detroit 17, at New Orleans
Aug. 28, 1982	Miami 17, Kansas City 17, at Kansas City
Sept. 3, 1982	Miami 16, New York Giants 13, at Miami
Aug. 6, 1983	L.A. Raiders 26, San Francisco 23, at Los Angeles
Aug. 6, 1983	Atlanta 13, Washington 10, at Atlanta
Aug. 13, 1983	St. Louis 27, Chicago 24, at St. Louis
Aug. 18, 1983	New York Jets 20, Cincinnati 17, at Cincinnati
Aug. 27, 1983	Chicago 20, Kansas City 17, at Chicago
Aug. 11, 1984	Pittsburgh 20, Philadelphia 17, at Pittsburgh
Aug. 9, 1985	Buffalo 10, Detroit 10, at Pontiac, Mich.
Aug. 10, 1985	Minnesota 16, Miami 13, at Miami
Aug. 17, 1985	Dallas 27, San Diego 24, at San Diego
Aug. 24, 1985	N.Y. Giants 34, N.Y. Jets 31, at East Rutherford, N.J.
Aug. 15, 1986	Washington 27, Pittsburgh 24, at Washington
Aug. 15, 1986	Detroit 30, Seattle 27, at Detroit
Aug. 23, 1986	Los Angeles Rams 20, San Diego 17, at Anaheim
Aug. 30, 1986	Minnesota 23, Indianapolis 20, at Indianapolis
Aug. 23, 1987	Philadelphia 19, New England 13, at New England
Sept. 5, 1987	Cleveland 30, Green Bay 24, at Milwaukee
Sept. 6, 1987	Kansas City 13, St. Louis 10, at Memphis, Tenn.
Aug. 11, 1988	Seattle 16, Detroit 13, at Detroit
Aug. 19, 1988	Miami 16, Denver 13, at Miami
Aug. 19, 1988	Green Bay 21, Kansas City 21, at Milwaukee
Aug. 20, 1988	Houston 20, Los Angeles Rams 17, at Anaheim
Aug. 21, 1988	Minnesota 19, Phoenix 16, at Phoenix
Aug. 5, 1989	Los Angeles Rams 16, San Francisco 13, at Tokyo, Japan
Aug. 26, 1989	Denver 24, Dallas 21, at Denver
Sept. 1, 1989	N.Y. Jets 15, Kansas City 13, at Kansas City
Aug. 24, 1990	Cincinnati 13, New England 10, at New England
Aug. 16, 1991	Cleveland 24, Washington 21, at Washington
Aug. 17, 1991	Cincinnati 27, Minnesota 24, at Cincinnati
Aug. 23, 1991	Dallas 20, Atlanta 17, at Dallas
Aug. 24, 1991	Cincinnati 19, Green Bay 16, at Green Bay

Aug. 22, 1992	Los Angeles Rams 16, Green Bay 13, at Anaheim
Aug. 8, 1993	Dallas 13, Detroit 13, at London, England
Aug. 12, 1995	Washington 16, Houston 13, at Knoxville, Tenn.
Aug. 19, 1995	Indianapolis 20, Green Bay 17, at Green Bay
Aug. 3, 1996	Minnesota 23, San Diego 20, at Minnesota
Aug. 10, 1996	San Francisco 16, San Diego 13, at San Francisco
Aug. 1, 1998	Green Bay 27, Kansas City 24, at Tokyo, Japan
Aug. 7, 1998	Detroit 13, Arizona 10, at Pontiac, Mich.
Aug. 22, 1998	Minnesota 25, Carolina 22, at Charlotte, N.C.
Aug. 9, 1999	Cleveland 20, Dallas 17, at Canton, Ohio
Aug. 4, 2001	Chicago 16, Cincinnati 13, at Chicago
Aug. 18, 2001	San Diego 23, Miami 20, at Miami
Aug. 18, 2001	Arizona 16, Seattle 13, at Seattle
Aug. 25, 2001	San Diego 13, St. Louis 10, at San Diego
Aug. 10, 2002	Kansas City 17, San Francisco 14, at San Francisco

indicates Monday-night game
 # indicates Thursday/Saturday/Sunday-night game
+ indicates Thanksgiving Day game

REGULAR SEASON

Sept. 22, 1974—Pittsburgh 35, Denver 35, at Denver; Steelers win toss. Gilliam's pass intercepted and returned by Rowser to Denver's 42. Turner misses 41-yard field goal. Walden punts and Greer returns to Broncos' 39. Van Heusen punts and Edwards returns to Steelers' 16. Game ends with Steelers on own 26.

Nov. 10, 1974—New York Jets 26, New York Giants 20, at New Haven, Conn.; Giants win toss. Gogolak misses 42-yard field goal. Namath passes to Boozer for five yards and touchdown at 6:53.

Sept. 28, 1975—Dallas 37, St. Louis 31, at Dallas; Cardinals win toss. Hart's pass intercepted and returned by Jordan to Cardinals' 37. Staubach passes to DuPree for three yards and touchdown at 7:53.

Oct. 12, 1975—Los Angeles 13, San Diego 10, at San Diego; Chargers win toss. Partee punts to Rams' 14. Dempsey kicks 22-yard field goal at 9:27.

Nov. 2, 1975—Washington 30, Dallas 24, at Washington; Cowboys win toss. Staubach's pass intercepted and returned by Houston to Cowboys' 35. Kilmer runs one yard for touchdown at 6:34.

Nov. 16, 1975—St. Louis 20, Washington 17, at St. Louis; Cardinals win toss. Bakken kicks 37-yard field goal at 7:00.

Nov. 23, 1975—Kansas City 24, Detroit 21, at Kansas City; Lions win toss. Chiefs take over on downs at own 38. Stenerud kicks 26-yard field goal at 6:44.

Nov. 23, 1975—Oakland 26, Washington 23, at Washington; Redskins win toss. Bragg punts to Raiders' 42. Blanda kicks 27-yard field goal at 7:13.

Nov. 30, 1975—Denver 13, San Diego 10, at Denver; Broncos win toss. Turner kicks 25-yard field goal at 4:13.

Nov. 30, 1975—Oakland 37, Atlanta 34, at Oakland; Falcons win toss. James punts to Raiders' 16. Guy punts and Herron returns to Falcons' 41. Nick Mike-Mayer misses 45-yard field goal. Guy punts into Falcons' end zone. James punts to Raiders' 39. Blanda kicks 36-yard field goal at 15:00.

Dec. 14, 1975—Baltimore 10, Miami 7, at Baltimore; Dolphins win toss. Seiple punts to Colts' 4. Linhart kicks 31-yard field goal at 12:44.

Sept. 19, 1976—Minnesota 10, Los Angeles 10, at Minnesota; Vikings win toss. Tarkenton's pass intercepted by Monte Jackson and returned to Minnesota 16. Allen blocks Dempsey's 30-yard field goal attempt, ball rolls into end zone for touchback. Clabo punts and Scribner returns to Rams' 20. Rusty Jackson punts to Vikings' 35. Tarkenton's pass intercepted by Kay at Rams' 1, no return. Game ends with Rams on own 3.

Sept. 27, 1976—Washington 20, Philadelphia 17, at Philadelphia; Eagles win toss. Jones punts and E. Brown loses one yard on return to Redskins' 40. Bragg punts 51 yards into end zone for touchback. Jones punts and E. Brown returns to Redskins' 42. Bragg punts and Marshall returns to Eagles' 41. Boryla's pass intercepted by Dusek at Redskins' 37, no return. Bragg punts and Bradley returns. Philadelphia holding penalty moves ball back to Eagles' 8. Boryla pass intercepted by E. Brown and returned to Eagles' 22. Moseley kicks 29-yard field goal at 12:49.

Oct. 17, 1976—Kansas City 20, Miami 17, at Miami; Chiefs win toss. Wilson punts into end zone for touchback. Bulaich fumbles into Kansas City end zone, Collier recovers for touchback. Stenerud kicks 34-yard field goal at 14:48.

Oct. 31, 1976—St. Louis 23, San Francisco 20, at St. Louis; Cardinals win toss. Joyce punts and Leonard fumbles on return, Jones recovers at 49ers' 43. Bakken kicks 21-yard field goal at 6:42.

Dec. 5, 1976—San Diego 13, San Francisco 7, at San Diego; Chargers win toss. Morris runs 13 yards for touchdown at 5:12.

Sept. 18, 1977—Dallas 16, Minnesota 10, at Minnesota; Vikings win toss. Dallas starts on Vikings' 47 after a punt early in the overtime period. Staubach scores seven plays later on a four-yard run at 6:14.

*Sept. 26, 1977—Cleveland 30, New England 27,** at Cleveland; Browns win toss. Sipe throws a 22-yard pass to Logan at Patriots' 19. Cockroft kicks 35-yard field goal at 4:45.

Oct. 16, 1977—Minnesota 22, Chicago 16, at Minnesota; Bears win toss. Parsons punts 53 yards to Vikings' 18. Minnesota drives to Bears' 11. On a first-and-10, Vikings fake a field goal and holder Krause hits Voigt with a touchdown pass at 6:45.

Oct. 30, 1977—Cincinnati 13, Houston 10, at Cincinnati; Bengals win toss. Bahr kicks a 22-yard field goal at 5:51.

Nov. 13, 1977—San Francisco 10, New Orleans 7, at New Orleans; Saints win toss. Saints fail to move ball and Blanchard punts to 49ers' 41. Wersching kicks a 33-yard field goal at 6:33.

Dec. 18, 1977—Chicago 12, New York Giants 9, at East Rutherford, N.J.; Giants win toss. The ball changes hands eight times before Thomas kicks a 28-yard field goal at 14:51.

Sept. 10, 1978—Cleveland 13, Cincinnati 10, at Cleveland; Browns win toss. Collins returns kickoff 41 yards to Browns' 47. Cockroft kicks 27-yard field goal at 4:30.

*Sept. 11, 1978—Minnesota 12, Denver 9,** at Minnesota; Vikings win toss. Danmeier kicks 44-yard field goal at 2:56.

Sept. 24, 1978—Pittsburgh 15, Cleveland 9, at Pittsburgh; Steelers win toss. Cunningham scores on a 37-yard "gadget" pass from Bradshaw at 3:43. Steelers start winning drive on their 21.

Sept. 24, 1978—Denver 23, Kansas City 17, at Kansas City; Broncos win toss. Dilts punts to Kansas City. Chiefs advance to Broncos' 40 where Reed fails to make first down on fourth-and-one situation. Broncos march downfield. Preston scores two-yard touchdown at 10:28.

Oct. 1, 1978—Oakland 25, Chicago 19, at Chicago; Bears win toss. Both teams punt on first possession. On Chicago's second offensive series, Colzie intercepts Avellini's pass and returns it to Bears' 3. Three plays later, Whittington runs two yards for a touchdown at 5:19.

Oct. 15, 1978—Dallas 24, St. Louis 21, at St. Louis; Cowboys win toss. Dallas drives from its 23 into field goal range. Septien kicks 27-yard field goal at 3:28.

Oct. 29, 1978—Denver 20, Seattle 17, at Seattle; Broncos win toss. Ball changes hands four times before Turner kicks 18-yard field goal at 12:59.

Nov. 12, 1978—San Diego 29, Kansas City 23, at San Diego; Chiefs win toss. Fouts hits Jefferson for decisive 14-yard touchdown pass on the last play (15:00) of overtime period.

Nov. 12, 1978—Washington 16, New York Giants 13, at Washington; Redskins win toss. Moseley kicks winning 45-yard field goal at 8:32 after missing first down field goal attempt of 35 yards at 4:50.

Nov. 26, 1978—Green Bay 10, Minnesota 10, at Green Bay; Packers win toss. Both teams have possession of the ball four times.

Dec. 9, 1978—Cleveland 37, New York Jets 34, at Cleveland; Browns win toss. Cockroft kicks 22-yard field goal at 3:07.

Sept. 2, 1979—Atlanta 40, New Orleans 34, at New Orleans; Falcons win toss. Bartkowski's pass intercepted by Myers and returned to Falcons' 46. Erxleben punts to Falcons' 4. James punts to Chandler and Saints' 43. Erxleben punts and Ryckman returns to Falcons' 28. James punts and Chandler returns to Saints' 36. Erxleben retrieves punt snap on Saints' 1 and attempts pass. Mayberry intercepts and returns six yards for touchdown at 8:22.

Sept. 2, 1979—Cleveland 25, New York Jets 22, at New York;

Jets win toss. Leahy's 43-yard field goal attempt goes wide right at 4:41. Evans's punt blocked by Dykes is recovered by Newton. Ramsey punts into end zone for touchback. Evans punts and Harper returns to Jets' 24. Robinson's pass intercepted by Davis and returned 33 yards to Jets' 31. Cockroft kicks 27-yard field goal at 14:45.

* **Sept. 3, 1979—Pittsburgh 16, New England 13**, at Foxboro; Patriots win toss. Hare punts to Swann at Steelers' 31. Bahr kicks 41-yard field goal at 5:10.

Sept. 9, 1979—Tampa Bay 29, Baltimore 26, at Baltimore; Colts win toss. Landry fumbles, recovered by Kollar at Colts' 14. O'Donoghue kicks 31-yard, first-down field goal at 1:41.

Sept. 16, 1979—Denver 20, Atlanta 17, at Atlanta; Broncos win toss. Broncos march 65 yards to Falcons' 7. Turner kicks 24-yard field goal at 6:15.

Sept. 23, 1979—Houston 30, Cincinnati 27, at Cincinnati; Oilers win toss. Parsley punts and Lusby returns to Bengals' 33. Bahr's 32-yard field goal attempt is wide right at 8:05. Parsley's punt downed on Bengals' 5. McInally punts and Ellender returns to Bengals' 42. Fritsch's third down, 29-yard field goal attempt hits left upright and bounces through at 14:28.

Sept. 23, 1979—Minnesota 27, Green Bay 21, at Minnesota; Vikings win toss. Kramer throws 50-yard touchdown pass to Rashad at 3:18.

Oct. 28, 1979—Houston 27, New York Jets 24, at Houston; Oilers win toss. Oilers march 58 yards to Jets' 18. Fritsch kicks 35-yard field goal at 5:10.

Nov. 18, 1979—Cleveland 30, Miami 24, at Cleveland; Browns win toss. Sipe passes 39 yards to Rucker for touchdown at 1:59.

Nov. 25, 1979—Pittsburgh 33, Cleveland 30, at Pittsburgh; Browns win toss. Sipe's pass intercepted by Blount on Steelers' 4. Bradshaw pass intercepted by Bolton on Browns' 12. Evans punts and Bell returns to Steelers' 17. Bahr kicks 37-yard field goal at 14:51.

Nov. 25, 1979—Buffalo 16, New England 13, at Foxboro; Patriots win toss. Hare's punt downed on Bills' 38. Jackson punts and Morgan returns to Patriots' 20. Grogan's pass intercepted by Haslett and returned to Bills' 42. Ferguson's 51-yard pass to Butler sets up N. Mike-Mayer's 29-yard field goal at 9:15.

Dec. 2, 1979—Los Angeles 27, Minnesota 21, at Los Angeles; Rams win toss. Clark punts and Miller returns to Vikings' 25. Kramer's pass intercepted by Brown and returned to Rams' 40. Cromwell, holding for 22-yard field goal attempt, runs around left end untouched for winning score at 6:53.

Sept. 7, 1980—Green Bay 12, Chicago 6, at Green Bay; Bears win toss. Parsons punts and Nixon returns 16 yards. Five plays later, Marcol returns own blocked field goal attempt 24 yards for touchdown at 6:00.

Sept. 14, 1980—San Diego 30, Oakland 24, at San Diego; Raiders win toss. Pastorini's first-down pass intercepted by Edwards. Millen intercepts Fouts' first-down pass and returns to San Diego 46. Bahr's 50-yard field goal attempt partially blocked by Williams and recovered on Chargers' 32. Eight plays later, Fouts throws 24-yard touchdown pass to Jefferson at 8:09.

Sept. 14, 1980—San Francisco 24, St. Louis 21, at San Francisco; Cardinals win toss. Swider punts and Robinson returns to 49ers' 32. San Francisco drives 52 yards to St. Louis 16, where Wersching kicks 33-yard field goal at 4:12.

Oct. 12, 1980—Green Bay 14, Tampa Bay 14, at Tampa Bay; Packers win toss. Teams trade punts twice. Lee returns second Tampa Bay punt to Green Bay 42. Dickey completes three passes to Buccaneers' 18, where Birney's 36-yard field goal attempt is wide left as time expires.

Nov. 9, 1980—Atlanta 33, St. Louis 27, at St. Louis; Falcons win toss. Strong runs 21 yards for touchdown at 4:20.

Nov. 20, 1980—San Diego 27, Miami 24, at Miami; Chargers win toss. Partridge punts into end zone, Dolphins take over on their own 20. Woodley's pass for Nathan intercepted by Lowe

and returned 28 yards to Dolphins' 12. Benirschke kicks 28-yard field goal at 7:14.

Nov. 23, 1980—New York Jets 31, Houston 28, at New York; Jets win toss. Leahy kicks 38-yard field goal at 3:58.

+ **Nov. 27, 1980—Chicago 23, Detroit 17**, at Detroit; Bears win toss. Williams returns kickoff 95 yards for touchdown at 0:21.

Dec. 7, 1980—Buffalo 10, Los Angeles 7, at Buffalo; Rams win toss. Corral punts and Hooks returns to Bills' 34. Ferguson's 30-yard pass to Lewis sets up N. Mike-Mayer's 30-yard field goal at 5:14.

Dec. 7, 1980—San Francisco 38, New Orleans 35, at San Francisco; Saints win toss. Erxleben's punt downed by Hardy on 49ers' 27. Wersching kicks 36-yard field goal at 7:40.

* **Dec. 8, 1980—Miami 16, New England 13**, at Miami; Dolphins win toss. Von Schamann kicks 23-yard field goal at 3:20.

Dec. 14, 1980—Cincinnati 17, Chicago 14, at Chicago; Bengals win toss. Breech kicks 28-yard field goal at 4:23.

Dec. 21, 1980—Los Angeles 20, Atlanta 17, at Los Angeles; Rams win toss. Corral's punt downed at Rams' 37. James punts into end zone for touchback. Corral's punt downed on Falcons' 17. Bartkowski fumbles when hit by Harris, recovered by Delaney. Corral kicks 23-yard field goal on first play of possession at 7:00.

Sept. 27, 1981—Cincinnati 27, Buffalo 24, at Cincinnati; Bills win toss. Cater punts into end zone for touchback. Bengals drive to the Bills' 10 where Breech kicks 28-yard field goal at 9:33.

Sept. 27, 1981—Pittsburgh 27, New England 21, at Pittsburgh; Patriots win toss. Hubach punts and Smith returns five yards to midfield. Four plays later Bradshaw throws 24-yard touchdown pass to Swann at 3:19.

Oct. 4, 1981—Miami 28, New York Jets 28, at Miami; Jets win toss. Teams trade punts twice. Leahy's 48-yard field goal attempt is wide right as time expires.

Oct. 25, 1981—New York Giants 27, Atlanta 24, at Atlanta; Giants win toss. Jennings' punt goes out of bounds at New York 47. Bright returns Atlanta punt to Giants' 14. Woerner fair catches punt at own 28. Andrews fumbles on first play, recovered by Van Pelt. Danelo kicks 40-yard field goal four plays later at 9:20.

Oct. 25, 1981—Chicago 20, San Diego 17, at Chicago; Bears win toss. Teams trade punts. Bears' second punt returned by Brooks to Chargers' 33. Fouts pass intercepted by Fencik and returned 32 yards to San Diego 27. Roveto kicks 27-yard field goal seven plays later at 9:30.

Nov. 8, 1981—Chicago 16, Kansas City 13, at Kansas City; Bears win toss. Teams trade punts. Kansas City takes over on downs on its own 38. Fuller's fumble recovered by Harris on Chicago 36. Roveto's 37-yard field goal wide, but Chiefs penalized for leverage. Roveto's 22-yard field goal attempt three plays later is good at 13:07.

Nov. 8, 1981—Denver 23, Cleveland 20, at Denver; Browns win toss. D. Smith recovers Hill's fumble at Denver 48. Morton's 33-yard pass to Upchurch and 6-yard run by Preston set up Steinfort's 30-yard field goal at 4:10.

Nov. 8, 1981—Miami 30, New England 27, at New England; Dolphins win toss. Orosz punts and Morgan returns six yards to New England 26. Grogan's pass intercepted by Brudzinski who returns 19 yards to Patriots' 26. Von Schamann kicks 30-yard field goal on first down at 7:09.

Nov. 15, 1981—Washington 30, New York Giants 27, at New York; Giants win toss. Nelms returns Giants' punt 26 yards to New York 47. Five plays later Moseley kicks 48-yard field goal at 3:44.

Dec. 20, 1981—New York Giants 13, Dallas 10, at New York; Cowboys win toss and kick off. Jennings punts to Dallas 40. Taylor recovers Dorsett's fumble on second down. Danelo's 33-yard field goal attempt hits right upright and bounces back. White's pass for Pearson intercepted by Hunt and returned seven yards to Dallas 24. Four plays later Danelo kicks 35-yard field goal at 6:19.

Sept. 12, 1982—Washington 37, Philadelphia 34, at Philadelphia; Redskins win toss. Theismann completes five passes for 63 yards to set up Moseley's 26-yard field goal at 4:47.

Sept. 19, 1982—Pittsburgh 26, Cincinnati 20, at Pittsburgh; Bengals win toss. Anderson's pass intended for Kreider intercepted by Woodruff and returned 30 yards to Cincinnati 2. Bradshaw completes two-yard touchdown pass to Stallworth on first down at 1:08.

Dec. 19, 1982—Baltimore 20, Green Bay 20, at Baltimore; Packers win toss. K. Anderson intercepts Dickey's first-down pass and returns to Packers' 42. Miller's 44-yard field goal attempt blocked by G. Lewis. Teams trade punts before Stenerud's 47-yard field goal attempt is wide right. Teams trade punts again before time expires in Colts possession.

Jan. 2, 1983—Tampa Bay 26, Chicago 23, at Tampa; Bears win toss. Parsons punts to T. Bell at Buccaneers' 40. Capece kicks 33-yard field goal at 3:14.

Sept. 4, 1983—Baltimore 29, New England 23, at New England; Patriots win toss. Cooks runs 52 yards with fumble recovery three plays into overtime at 0:30.

Sept. 4, 1983—Green Bay 41, Houston 38, at Houston; Packers win toss. Stenerud kicks 42-yard field goal at 5:55.

Sept. 11, 1983—New York Giants 16, Atlanta 13, at Atlanta; Giants win toss. Dennis returns kickoff 54 yards to Atlanta 41. Haji-Sheikh kicks 30-yard field goal at 3:38.

Sept. 18, 1983—New Orleans 34, Chicago 31, at New Orleans; Bears win toss. Parsons punts and Groth returns five yards to New Orleans 34. Stabler pass intercepted by Schmidt at Chicago 47. Parsons punt downed by Gentry at New Orleans 2. Stabler gains 36 yards in four passes; Wilson 38 on six carries. Andersen kicks 41-yard field goal at 10:57.

Sept. 18, 1983—Minnesota 19, Tampa Bay 16, at Tampa; Vikings win toss. Coleman punts and Bell returns eight yards to Tampa Bay 47. Capece's 33-yard field goal attempt sails wide at 7:26. Dils and Young combine for 48-yard gain to Tampa Bay 27. Ricardo kicks 42-yard field goal at 9:27.

Sept. 25, 1983—Baltimore 22, Chicago 19, at Baltimore; Colts win toss. Allegre kicks 33-yard field goal nine plays later at 4:51.

Sept. 25, 1983—Cleveland 30, San Diego 24, at San Diego; Browns win toss. Walker returns kickoff 33 yards to Cleveland 37. Sipe completes 48-yard touchdown pass to Holt four plays later at 1:53.

Sept. 25, 1983—New York Jets 27, Los Angeles Rams 24, at New York; Jets win toss. Ramsey punts to Irvin who returns to 25 but penalty puts Rams on own 13. Holmes 30-yard interception return sets up Leahy's 26-yard field goal at 3:22.

Oct. 9, 1983—Buffalo 38, Miami 35, at Miami; Dolphins win toss. Von Schamann's 52-yard field goal attempt goes wide at 12:36. Cater punts to Clayton who loses 11 to own 13. Von Schamann's 43-yard field goal attempt sails wide at 5:15. Danelo kicks 36-yard field goal nine plays later at 1:58.

Oct. 9, 1983—Dallas 27, Tampa Bay 24, at Dallas; Cowboys win toss. Septien's 51-yard field-goal attempt goes wide but Buccaneers penalized for roughing kicker. Septien kicks 42-yard field goal at 4:38.

Oct. 23, 1983—Kansas City 13, Houston 10, at Houston; Chiefs win toss. Lowery kicks 41-yard field goal 13 plays later at 7:41.

Oct. 23, 1983—Minnesota 20, Green Bay 17, at Green Bay; Packers win toss. Scribner's punt downed on Vikings' 42. Ricardo kicks 32-yard field goal eight plays later at 5:05.

* **Oct. 24, 1983—New York Giants 20, St. Louis 20,** at St. Louis; Cardinals win toss. Teams trade punts before O'Donoghue's 44-yard field goal attempt is wide left. Jennings' punt returned by Bird to St. Louis 21. Lomax pass intercepted by Haynes who loses six yards to New York 33. Jennings' punt downed on St. Louis 17. O'Donoghue's 19-yard field goal

attempt is wide right. Rutledge's pass intercepted by L. Washington who returns 25 yards to New York 25. O'Donoghue's 42-yard field goal attempt is wide right. Rutledge's pass intercepted by W. Smith at St. Louis 33 to end game.

Oct. 30, 1983—Cleveland 25, Houston 19, at Cleveland; Oilers win toss. Teams trade punts. Nielsen's pass intercepted by Whitwell who returns to Houston 20. Green runs 20 yards for touchdown on first down at 6:34.

Nov. 20, 1983—Detroit 23, Green Bay 20, at Milwaukee; Packers win toss. Scribner punts and Jenkins returns 14 yards to Green Bay 45. Murray's 33-yard field goal attempt is wide left at 9:32. Whitehurst's pass intercepted by Watkins and returned to Green Bay 27. Murray kicks 37-yard field goal four plays later at 8:30.

Nov. 27, 1983—Atlanta 47, Green Bay 41, at Atlanta; Packers win toss. K. Johnson returns interception 31 yards for touchdown at 2:13.

Nov. 27, 1983—Seattle 51, Kansas City 48, at Seattle; Seahawks win toss. Dixon's 47-yard kickoff return sets up N. Johnson's 42-yard field goal at 1:36.

Dec. 11, 1983—New Orleans 20, Philadelphia 17, at Philadelphia; Eagles win toss. Runager punts to Groth who fair catches on New Orleans 32. Stabler completes two passes for 36 yards to Goodlow to set up Andersen's 50-yard field goal at 5:30.

* **Dec. 12, 1983—Green Bay 12, Tampa Bay 9,** at Tampa; Packers win toss. Stenerud kicks 23-yard field goal 11 plays later at 4:07.

Sept. 9, 1984—Detroit 27, Atlanta 24, at Atlanta; Lions win toss. Murray kicks 48-yard field goal nine plays later at 5:06.

Sept. 30, 1984—Tampa Bay 30, Green Bay 27, at Tampa; Packers win toss. Scribner punts 44 yards to Tampa Bay 2. Epps returns Garcia's punt three yards to Green Bay 27. Scribner's punt downed on Buccaneers' 33. Ariri kicks 46-yard field goal 11 plays later at 10:32.

Oct. 14, 1984—Detroit 13, Tampa Bay 7, at Detroit; Buccaneers win toss. Tampa Bay drives to Lions' 39 before Wilder fumbles. Five plays later Danielson hits Thompson with 37-yard touchdown pass at 4:34.

Oct. 21, 1984—Dallas 30, New Orleans 27, at Dallas; Cowboys win toss. Septien kicks 41-yard field goal eight plays later at 3:42.

Oct. 28, 1984—Denver 22, Los Angeles Raiders 19, at Los Angeles; Raiders win toss. Hawkins fumble recovered by Foley at Denver 7. Teams trade punts. Karlis's 42-yard field goal attempt is wide left. Teams trade punts. Manor pass intercepted by R. Jackson at Los Angeles 45, returned 23 yards to Los Angeles 22. Karlis kicks 35-yard field goal two plays later at 15:00.

Nov. 4, 1984—Philadelphia 23, Detroit 23, at Detroit; Lions win toss. Lions drive to Eagles' 3 in eight plays. Murray's 21-yard field goal attempt hits right upright and bounces back. Jaworski's pass intercepted by Watkins at Detroit 5. Teams trade punts. Cooper returns Black's punt five yards to Eagles' 14. Time expires four plays later with Eagles on own 21.

Nov. 18, 1984—San Diego 34, Miami 28, at San Diego; Chargers win toss. McGee scores eight plays later on a 25-yard run at 3:17.

Dec. 2, 1984—Cincinnati 20, Cleveland 17, at Cleveland; Browns win toss. Simmons returns Cox's punt 30 yards to Cleveland 35. Breech kicks 35-yard field goal seven plays later at 4:34.

Dec. 2, 1984—Houston 23, Pittsburgh 20, at Houston; Oilers win toss. Cooper kicks 30-yard field goal 16 plays later at 5:53.

Sept. 8, 1985—St. Louis 27, Cleveland 24, at Cleveland; Cardinals win toss. O'Donoghue kicks 35-yard field goal nine plays later at 5:27.

Sept. 29, 1985—New York Giants 16, Philadelphia 10, at Philadelphia; Eagles win toss. Jaworski's pass tipped by Quick and intercepted by Patterson who returns 29 yards for touchdown at 0:55.

Oct. 20, 1985—Denver 13, Seattle 10, at Denver; Seahawks win toss. Krieg's pass intercepted by Hunter and returned to Seahawks' 15. Karlis kicks 24-yard field goal four plays later at 9:19.

Nov. 10, 1985—Philadelphia 23, Atlanta 17, at Philadelphia; Falcons win toss. Archer's 62-yard punt goes out of bounds at Eagles' 1. Jaworski completes 99-yard touchdown pass to Quick two plays later at 1:49.

Nov. 10, 1985—San Diego 40, Los Angeles Raiders 34, at San Diego; Chargers win toss. James scores on 17-yard run seven plays later at 3:44.

Nov. 17, 1985—Denver 30, San Diego 24, at Denver; Chargers win toss. Thomas' 40-yard field goal attempt blocked by Smith and returned 60 yards by Wright for touchdown at 4:45.

Nov. 24, 1985—New York Jets 16, New England 13, at New York; Jets win toss. Teams trade punts twice. Patriots' second punt returned 46 yards by Sohn to Patriots' 15. Leahy kicks 32-yard field goal one play later at 10:05.

Nov. 24, 1985—Tampa Bay 19, Detroit 16, at Tampa; Lions win toss. Teams trade punts. Lions' punt downed on Buccaneers' 38. Igwebuike kicks 24-yard field goal 11 plays later at 12:31.

Nov. 24, 1985—Los Angeles Raiders 31, Denver 28, at Los Angeles; Raiders win toss. Bahr kicks 32-yard field goal six plays later at 2:42.

Dec. 8, 1985—Los Angeles Raiders 17, Denver 14, at Denver; Broncos win toss. Teams trade punts twice. Elway's fumble recovered by Townsend at Broncos' 8. Bahr kicks 26-yard field goal one play later at 4:55.

Sept. 14, 1986—Chicago 13, Philadelphia 10, at Chicago; Eagles win toss. Crawford's fumble of kickoff recovered by Jackson at Eagles' 35. Butler kicks 23-yard field goal 10 plays later at 5:56.

Sept. 14, 1986—Cincinnati 36, Buffalo 33, at Cincinnati; Bills win toss. Zander intercepts Kelly's first-down pass and returns it to Bills' 17. Breech kicks 20-yard field goal two plays later at 0:56.

Sept. 21, 1986—New York Jets 51, Miami 45, at New York; Jets win toss. O'Brien completes 43-yard touchdown pass to Walker five plays later at 2:35.

Sept. 28, 1986—Pittsburgh 22, Houston 16, at Houston; Oilers win toss. Johnson's punt returned 41 yards by Woods to Oilers' 15. Abercrombie scores on three-yard run three plays later at 2:35.

Sept. 28, 1986—Atlanta 23, Tampa Bay 20, at Tampa; Falcons win toss. Teams trade punts. Luckhurst kicks 34-yard field goal 10 plays later at 12:35.

Oct. 5, 1986—Los Angeles Rams 26, Tampa Bay 20, at Anaheim; Rams win toss. Dickerson scores four plays later on 42-yard run at 2:16.

Oct. 12, 1986—Minnesota 27, San Francisco 24, at San Francisco; Vikings win toss. C. Nelson kicks 28-yard field goal nine plays later at 4:27.

Oct. 19, 1986—San Francisco 10, Atlanta 10, at Atlanta; Falcons win toss. Teams trade punts twice. Donnelly punts to 49ers' 27. The following play Wilson recovers Rice's fumble at 49ers' 46 as time expires.

Nov. 2, 1986—Washington 44, Minnesota 38, at Washington; Redskins win toss. Schroeder completes 38-yard touchdown pass to Clark four plays later at 1:46.

#Nov. 20, 1986—Los Angeles Raiders 37, San Diego 31, at San Diego; Raiders win toss. Teams trade punts. Allen scores five plays later on 28-yard run at 8:33.

Nov. 23, 1986—Cleveland 37, Pittsburgh 31, at Cleveland; Browns win toss. Teams trade punts. Six plays later Kosar hits Slaughter with 36-yard touchdown pass at 6:37.

Nov. 30, 1986—Chicago 13, Pittsburgh 10, at Chicago; Bears win toss and kick off. Newsome's punt returned by Barnes to Chicago 49. Butler kicks 42-yard field goal five plays later at 3:55.

Nov. 30, 1986—Philadelphia 33, Los Angeles Raiders 27, at Los Angeles; Eagles win toss. Teams trade punts. Long recovers Cunningham's fumble at Philadelphia 42. Waters returns Allen's fumble 81 yards to Los Angeles 4. Cunningham scores on one-yard run two plays later at 6:53.

Nov. 30, 1986—Cleveland 13, Houston 10, at Cleveland; Oilers win toss and kick off. Gossett punts to Houston 39. Luck's pass intercepted by Minnifield at Cleveland 21. Gossett punts to Houston 34. Luck's pass intercepted by Minnifield at Cleveland 43 who returns 20 yards to Houston 37. Moseley kicks 29-yard field goal nine plays later at 14:44.

Dec. 7, 1986—St. Louis 10, Philadelphia 10, at Philadelphia; Cardinals win toss. White blocks Schubert's 40-yard field goal attempt. Teams trade punts. McFadden's 43-yard field goal attempt is wide left. Schubert's 37-yard field goal attempt is wide right. Cavanaugh's pass intercepted by Carter and returned to Eagles' 48 to end game.

Dec. 14, 1986—Miami 37, Los Angeles Rams 31, at Anaheim; Dolphins win toss. Marino completes 20-yard touchdown pass to Duper six plays later at 3:04.

Sept. 20, 1987—Denver 17, Green Bay 17, at Milwaukee; Packers win toss. Del Greco's 47-yard field goal attempt is short. Teams trade punts. Elway intercepted by Noble who returns 10 yards to Green Bay 34. Davis fumbles on next play and Smith recovers. Two plays later, Karlis's 40-yard field goal attempt is wide left. Time expires two plays later with Packers on own 23.

Oct. 11, 1987—Detroit 19, Green Bay 16, at Green Bay; Lions win toss. Prindle's 42-yard field goal attempt is wide left. Packers punt downed on Detroit 17. Prindle kicks 31-yard field goal 16 plays later at 12:26.

Oct. 18, 1987—New York Jets 37, Miami 31, at New York; Jets win toss. Teams trade punts. Ryan intercepted by Hooper at Jets' 47 who returns 11 yards. Mackey intercepted by Haslett at Jets' 37 who returns 9 yards. Jets punt. Mackey intercepted by Radachowsky who returns 45 yards to Miami 24. Ryan completes eight-yard touchdown pass to Hunter five plays later at 14:26.

Oct. 18, 1987—Green Bay 16, Philadelphia 10, at Green Bay; Packers win toss. Hargrove scores on seven-yard run 10 plays later at 5:04.

Oct. 18, 1987—Buffalo 6, New York Giants 3, at Buffalo; Bills win toss. Schlopy's 28-yard field goal attempt is wide left. Teams trade punts. Rutledge intercepted by Clark who returns 23 yards to Buffalo 40. Schlopy kicks 27-yard field goal nine plays later at 14:41.

Oct. 25, 1987—Buffalo 34, Miami 31, at Miami; Bills win toss. Norwood kicks 27-yard field goal seven plays later at 4:12.

Nov. 1, 1987—San Diego 27, Cleveland 24, at San Diego; Browns win toss. Kosar intercepted by Glenn who returns 20 yards to Browns' 25. Abbott kicks 33-yard field goal three plays later at 2:16.

Nov. 15, 1987—Dallas 23, New England 17, at New England; Cowboys win toss. Walker scores on 60-yard run four plays later at 1:50.

+Nov. 26, 1987—Minnesota 44, Dallas 38, at Dallas; Vikings win toss. Coleman's punt downed by Hilton at Cowboys' 37. White intercepted by Studwell who returns 12 yards to Vikings' 37. D. Nelson scores on 24-yard run seven plays later at 7:51.

Nov. 29, 1987—Philadelphia 34, New England 31, at New England; Patriots win toss. Ramsey intercepted by Joyner who returns 29 yards to Eagles' 32. Fryar fair catches Teltschik's punt at Patriots' 13. Franklin's 46-yard field-goal attempt is short. McFadden's 39-yard field goal attempt is wide left. Tatupu fumbles on next play and Cobb recovers. McFadden kicks 38-yard field goal four plays later at 12:16.

Dec. 6, 1987—New York Giants 23, Philadelphia 20, at New York; Giants win toss and kick off. Teams trade punts twice.

Teltschik's punt is returned 16 yards by McConkey to Eagles' 33. Three plays later, Allegre's 50-yard field goal attempt is blocked by Joyner and returned 25 yards by Hoage to Eagles' 30. McConkey returns Teltschik's punt four yards to Giants' 44. Allegre kicks 28-yard field goal four plays later at 10:42.

Dec. 6, 1987—Cincinnati 30, Kansas City 27, at Cincinnati; Bengals win toss. Teams trade punts. Breech kicks 32-yard field goal 16 plays later at 9:44.

Dec. 26, 1987—Washington 27, Minnesota 24, at Minnesota; Redskins win toss. Haji-Sheikh kicks 26-yard field goal six plays later at 2:09.

Sept. 4, 1988—Houston 17, Indianapolis 14, at Indianapolis; Colts win toss. Dickerson fumble recovered by Lyles who returns six yards to Colts' 42. Zendejas kicks 35-yard field goal six plays later at 3:51.

* **Sept. 26, 1988—Los Angeles Raiders 30, Denver 27,** at Denver; Broncos win toss. Teams trade punts twice. Elway intercepted by Lee who returns 20 yards to Broncos' 31. Bahr kicks 35-yard field goal four plays later at 12:35.

Oct. 2, 1988—New York Jets 17, Kansas City 17, at New York; Chiefs win toss. Chiefs punt goes into end zone for touchback. Leahy's 44-yard field goal attempt is wide right. Chiefs punt is returned by Townsell to Jets' 26. Burruss recovers McNeil's fumble at Chiefs' 11. DeBerg intercepted by Humphery at Jets' 49. Three plays later, time expires.

Oct. 9, 1988—Denver 16, San Francisco 13, at San Francisco; Broncos win toss and kick off. Young intercepted by Haynes at Broncos' 32. Denver punt downed at 49ers' 5. Young intercepted by Wilson who returns seven yards to 49ers' 5. Karlis kicks 22-yard field goal two plays later at 8:11.

Oct. 30, 1988—New York Giants 13, Detroit 10, at Detroit; Lions win toss. James's fumble recovered by Taylor at Lions' 22. Three plays later, McFadden kicks 33-yard field goal at 1:13.

Nov. 20, 1988—Buffalo 9, New York Jets 6, at Buffalo; Jets win toss. Vick's fumble recovered by Bennett at Bills' 32. Norwood kicks 30-yard field goal five plays later at 3:47.

Nov. 20, 1988—Philadelphia 23, New York Giants 17, at New York; Eagles win toss. Philadelphia punt goes into end zone for touchback. Hostetler intercepted by Hoage who returns 11 yards to Giants' 41. Six plays later, Zendejas's 30-yard field-goal attempt is blocked and ball is recovered behind line of scrimmage by Eagles' Simmons, who runs 15 yards for touchdown at 3:09.

Dec. 11, 1988—New England 10, Tampa Bay 7, at New England; Buccaneers win toss and kick off. Staurovsky kicks 27-yard field goal six plays later at 3:08.

Dec. 17, 1988—Cincinnati 20, Washington 17, at Cincinnati; Bengals win toss. Cincinnati's punt returned by Oliphant to Redskins' 16. Grant recovers Williams's fumble at Redskins' 17. Breech kicks 20-yard field goal three plays later at 7:01.

Sept. 24, 1989—Buffalo 47, Houston 41, at Houston; Oilers win toss. Johnson returns Brady's kickoff 17 yards to Oilers' 19. Oilers drive to Buffalo 25, Zendejas's 37-yard field goal blocked, but Bills offsides and Zendejas's second attempt is wide left. Bills' ball and Kelly completes series of passes, including 28-yard game-winner to Andre Reed, at 8:42.

Oct. 8, 1989—Miami 13, Cleveland 10, at Miami; Browns win toss. Metcalf returns Stoyanovich's kickoff 20 yards to Browns' 28. Browns drive ball 46 yards in eight plays; Bahr wide left on 44-yard field goal attempt. Dolphins ball. Browns called for pass interference on Marino pass to Banks at Cleveland 47. Two plays later, Banks's 20-yard reception at Browns' 23 sets up winning 35-yard field goal by Stoyanovich at 6:23.

Oct. 22, 1989—Denver 24, Seattle 21, at Seattle; Seahawks win toss. Treadwell's 56-yard kickoff returned 18 yards by Jefferson to Seahawks' 27. Seahawks drive to Broncos' 22 in 10 plays, but Johnson's 40-yard field goal attempt wide left. Smith intercepts a Krieg pass and returns it 28 yards to Seahawks' 10. Treadwell kicks winning 27-yard field goal at 7:46.

Oct. 29, 1989—New England 23, Indianapolis 20, at Indianapolis; Patriots win toss. Biasucci kickoff returned 13 yards to Patriots' 23 by Martin. Holding penalty brings ball back to Patriots' 13. After six plays, Feagles punt returned 11 yards by Verdin to Colts' 28. Six plays later, Colts punt to Martin at Patriots' 12. Grogan completes three straight passes to Patriots' 44. Five consecutive runs put New England on Colts' 33. Davis kicks a 51-yard winning field goal for Patriots at 9:46.

Oct. 29, 1989—Green Bay 23, Detroit 20, at Milwaukee; Lions win toss. Sanders touchback on Jacke kickoff. On first play, Murphy intercepts Lions' Peete and returns it three yards to Lions' 26. Fullwood gains five yards on three plays to set up Jacke's 38-yard field goal at 2:14.

Nov. 5, 1989—Minnesota 23, Los Angeles Rams 21, at Minneapolis; Rams win toss. Karlis's kick returned 18 yards by Delpino to Rams' 19. Drive stops at Rams' 28. Merriweather blocks Hatcher's punt at 12. Ball rolls out of end zone for safety.

Nov. 19, 1989—Cleveland 10, Kansas City 10, at Cleveland; Browns win toss. Browns punt three times; Chiefs twice; before Kansas City's Lowery misses 47-yard field goal with 17 seconds remaining in overtime. Kosar's pass intercepted as time expires.

Nov. 26, 1989—Los Angeles Rams 20, New Orleans 17, at New Orleans; Saints win toss. Lansford's kickoff returned 27 yards by Saints to Saints' 30. After four plays, Barnhardt punts to Rams' 15. Saints penalized 35 yards for interference to Rams' 43. Three plays later, Everett hits Anderson with 14-yard pass to Saints' 40, then 26-yarder to put Rams in field goal position. Lansford kicks 31-yard field goal at 6:38.

Dec. 3, 1989—Los Angeles Raiders 16, Denver 13, at Los Angeles; Broncos win toss. Bell returns Jaeger kickoff 14 yards to Broncos' 18. Broncos' penalized for illegal block to Broncos' 9. Elway completes three passes for two first downs. On third and eight Elway sacked for 10-yard loss. Horan punts, Adams calls for fair catch at Raiders' 29. Dyal's 26-yard reception moves Raiders to Denver 43. Raiders move ball 34 yards in three plays to set up Jaeger's 26-yard field goal at 7:02.

Dec. 10, 1989—Indianapolis 23, Cleveland 17, at Indianapolis; Browns win toss. Teams trade punts. McNeil returns Colts' punt 42 yards to 42. Seven plays later, Bahr misses 35-yard field goal attempt. Three plays later, Stark punts and McNeil returns ball to 50-yard line. Two plays later, Prior intercepts Kosar's pass at Colts' 42 and returns it 58 yards for touchdown at 10:54.

Dec. 17, 1989—Cleveland 23, Minnesota 17, at Cleveland; Browns win toss. Browns punt to Vikings' 18. Six plays later, Vikings punt to Browns' 22. Nine plays later, Bahr lines up to attempt 31-yard field goal. Holder Pagel takes snap and passes 14 yards to Waiters for touchdown at 9:30.

Sept. 23, 1990—Denver 34, Seattle 31, at Denver; Seahawks win toss. Loville returns kickoff 19 yards to Seahawks' 27. Seahawks drive to Broncos' 26, where Johnson misses 44-yard field goal wide right. Broncos take over and Elway completes series of passes to set up Treadwell's 25-yard field goal at 9:14.

Sept. 30, 1990—Tampa Bay 23, Minnesota 20, at Minnesota; Vikings win toss. Vikings drive to Buccaneers' 31; Igwebuike's 48-yard field goal attempt wide left. Buccaneers drive to Vikings' 43 and punt. Gannon's pass is intercepted at Vikings' 26 by Wayne Haddix. Buccaneers drive to Vikings' 19 to set up Christie's 36-yard field goal at 9:11.

Oct. 7, 1990—Cincinnati 34, Los Angeles Rams 31, at Anaheim; Rams win toss. Berry returns kickoff to Rams' 21. After 3 plays, English punts and Green downs ball at Bengals' 25. After 3 plays, Johnson punts and Sutton downs ball at Rams' 29-yard line. After 3 plays, English punts and Price signals fair catch at Bengals' 47. Esiason completes series of passes to 26-yard line to set up Breech's 44-yard field goal at 11:56.

Nov. 4, 1990—Washington 41, Detroit 38, at Detroit; Redskins win toss. Howard downs kickoff on Redskins' 15. After 3 plays, Mojsiejenko punts to Redskins' 45. After 3 plays, Arnold punts to Redskins' 10. Rutledge completes series of passes to set up

Lohmiller's 34-yard field goal at 9:10.

Nov. 18, 1990—Chicago 16, Denver 13, at Denver; Broncos win toss. Ezor returns kickoff to Broncos' 12. Both teams have ball twice and have to punt after each possession. Broncos punt after third possession of overtime and Bailey returns 20 yards to Broncos' 34. Harbaugh completes 10-yard pass to Thornton to set up Butler's 44-yard field goal at 13:14.

Nov. 25, 1990—Seattle 13, San Diego 10, at San Diego; Chargers win toss. Lewis returns kickoff to Chargers' 22. After 2 plays, Cox fumbles and ball is recovered by Porter at Chargers' 23. After two plays, Johnson kicks 40-yard field goal at 3:01.

Dec. 2, 1990—Chicago 23, Detroit 17, at Chicago; Lions win toss. Gray returns kickoff to Lions' 35. After 10 plays, Murray misses 35-yard field goal. Bears take possession at Chicago 20. Harbaugh completes 50-yard game-winning pass to Anderson at 10:57.

Dec. 2, 1990—Seattle 13, Houston 10, at Seattle; Seahawks win toss. Warren returns kickoff to Seahawks' 13. After 5 plays, Donnelly punts to Oilers' 23-yard line. Ford's fumble recovered by Wyman. Seahawks take possession at Oilers' 27. After 2 plays, Johnson kicks 42-yard field goal at 4:25.

Dec. 9, 1990—Miami 23, Philadelphia 20, at Miami; Eagles win toss. After 11 plays, Feagles punts to Dolphins' 26. After 6 plays, Roby punts to Eagles' 14 and Harris returns to 25. After 3 plays, Feagles punts to Dolphins' 43. Marino completes series of passes to Eagles' 22. Stoyanovich kicks 39-yard field goal at 12:32.

Dec. 9, 1990—San Francisco 20, Cincinnati 17, at Cincinnati; 49ers win toss. Carter returns kickoff to 49ers' 19. After 10 plays, Cofer kicks 23-yard field goal at 6:12.

* **Sept. 23, 1991—Chicago 19, New York Jets 13,** at Chicago; Jets win toss. Mathis returns kickoff seven yards to New York's 12. Jets drive to New York 26; Bailey returns punt to Chicago 39. Bears drive to Jets' 44-yard line and punt into the end zone. Jets drive to Bears' 11 where Leahy's 28-yard field goal attempt is wide left. Bears drive from 20 to Jets' 1 where Harbaugh runs for touchdown at 14:42.

Oct. 13, 1991—Los Angeles Raiders 23, Seattle 20, at Seattle; Seahawks win toss. Seahawks begin on 20. After 5 plays, Tuten punts and Brown signals fair catch at Raiders' 24. After 3 plays, Gossett punts and Land downs ball at Seattle 9. After 1 play, Lott intercepts at Seahawks' 19 to set up Jaeger's game-winning 37-yard field goal at 6:37.

Oct. 20, 1991—Cleveland 30, San Diego 24, at San Diego; Chargers win toss. After kickoff, Chargers drive to Browns' 45 and punt to Browns' 6 where Hendrickson downs ball. Browns drive to 38 and punt; Taylor fair catches on Chargers' 14. After 3 plays, Brandon intercepts at Chargers' 30 and scores at 5:58.

Oct. 20, 1991—New England 26, Minnesota 23, at New England; Patriots win toss. Martin returns kickoff 18 yards to New England 22. Patriots drive to Minnesota 19. Staurovsky's 36-yard field goal attempt is wide left. Minnesota drives to the 50 where Newsome punts into end zone. On first play, McMillian intercepts at the 40 for Minnesota. After 2 plays, Marion causes Jordan fumble and Pool recovers at New England 24. New England drives to Minnesota 24 where Staurovsky kicks 42-yard field goal as time expires.

Nov. 3, 1991—New York Jets 19, Green Bay 16, at New York; Packers win toss. Thompson returns kickoff 30 yards to Packers' 39. Green Bay drives to New York 24 where Jacke's 42-yard field-goal attempt is wide right. Jets drive to 50. Aguiar's punt is fumbled by Sikahema and recovered by New York at Packers' 23. After 2 plays, Leahy kicks 37-yard field goal at 9:40.

Nov. 3, 1991—Washington 16, Houston 13, at Washington; Redskins win toss. Mitchell returns kickoff 9 yards to Washington 14. After 4 plays, Goodburn punts and Givins returns to Houston 31. After 1 play, Moon's pass is intercepted by Green at Oilers' 35. After 3 plays, Lohmiller kicks 41-yard field goal at 4:01.

Nov. 10, 1991—Houston 26, Dallas 23, at Houston; Oilers win

toss. Pinkett returns kickoff 20 yards to Houston 24. After 6 plays, Montgomery punts and Martin returns to Dallas 24. Cowboys drive to Oilers' 24 where Smith fumbles and McDowell recovers at Oilers' 15. Houston drives to Dallas 5 where Del Greco kicks 23-yard field goal at 14:31.

Nov. 10, 1991—Pittsburgh 33, Cincinnati 27, at Cincinnati; Steelers wins toss. Woodson downs kickoff for touchback. After 3 plays, Stryzinski punts and Barber returns 7 yards to Cincinnati 38. Bengals drive to Pittsburgh 37 where Woods fumbles and Lloyd returns recovery to Cincinnati 44. After 2 plays, O'Donnell passes to Green for 26-yard touchdown at 6:32.

#**Nov. 24, 1991—Atlanta 23, New Orleans 20,** at New Orleans; Falcons win toss. Falcons begin at 20. After 3 plays, Fulhage punts and Fenerty signals fair catch at New Orleans 43. After 3 plays, Barnhardt punts and Thompson downs ball at Atlanta 23. After 3 plays, Fulhage punts and Fenerty fair catches at New Orleans 25. Saints drive to Atlanta 38 where Andersen misses 55-yard field-goal attempt. After 1 play, Rozier fumbles and Martin recovers on 50. Saints drive to Atlanta 38 where Barnhardt punts to Falcons' 2. Atlanta drives to New Orleans 33 where Johnson kicks 50-yard field goal at 13:03.

Nov. 24, 1991—Miami 16, Chicago 13, at Chicago; Dolphins wins toss. Butler kicks to Miami 20 where Paige returns kickoff 15 yards to 35. Miami drives to Chicago 9 where Stoyanovich kicks 27-yard field goal at 4:11.

Dec. 8, 1991—Buffalo 30, Los Angeles Raiders 27, at Los Angeles; Raiders win toss. Daluiso kicks into end zone for touchback. On third play, Kelso intercepts for Buffalo and returns ball to Bills' 36. Bills drive to Los Angeles 24 where Norwood kicks 42-yard field goal at 2:34.

Dec. 8, 1991—Kansas City 20, San Diego 17, at Kansas City; Chiefs win toss. Carney kicks to Kansas City 10 where Stradford returns 23 yards to 33. After 3 plays, Barker punts to San Diego 4. Chargers drive to 40 where Kidd punts 60 yards into end zone for touchdown. Kansas City drives to San Diego 39 where Barker punts 38 yards to 1. After 3 plays, Kidd punts 41 yards to San Diego 42 where Stradford returns 12 yards to 30. Chiefs drive to San Diego 1 where Lowery kicks 18-yard field goal at 11:26.

Dec. 8, 1991—New England 23, Indianapolis 17, at New England; Colts wins toss. Baumann kicks off to Indianapolis 2 where Martin returns 23 yards to 25. After 3 downs, Stark punts to New England 17 where Henderson returns 8 yards to 25. New England drives to 50 where McCarthy punts and Prior signals fair catch at Indianapolis 15. After 3 plays, Stark punts to New England 40 where Henderson returns 7 yards to 47. After 2 plays, Millen passes to Timpson for 45-yard touchdown at 8:55.

Dec. 22, 1991—Detroit 17, Buffalo 14, at Buffalo; Lions wins toss. Daluiso kicks off to Detroit 20 where Dozier returns 15 yards to Lions 35. Lions drive to Bills' 3 where Murray kicks 21-yard field goal at 4:23.

Dec. 22, 1991—New York Jets 23, Miami 20, at Miami; Jets win toss. Aguiar kicks to Miami's 30 where Logan returns 3 yards to the 33. After 4 downs, Stoyanovich punts to Jets' 15 where Baty returns 8 yards to 23. Jets drive to Miami 12 where Allegre kicks 30-yard field goal at 6:33.

Sept. 6, 1992—Minnesota 23, Green Bay 20, at Green Bay; Vikings win toss. Nelson returns kickoff 14 yards to the Minnesota 23. After 5 plays, Newsome punts 49 yards to Green Bay 21 where Brooks returns 12 yards to the 33. After 2 plays, Glenn intercepts pass at the Vikings' 48. On first play, Allen fumbles and Billups recovers at Green Bay 35. After 3 plays, McJulien punts 33 yards to Vikings' 35. Vikings drive to Minnesota 48; Newsome punts 52 yards for touchback. After 3 plays, McJulien punts and Parker returns 10 yards to Green Bay 48. Vikings drive to Packers' 9 where Reveiz kicks 26-yard field goal at 10:20.

Sept. 13, 1992—Cincinnati 24, Los Angeles Raiders 21, at Cincinnati; Raiders win toss. Land returns kickoff 13 yards but fumbles at Los Angeles' 20; ball recovered by Bengals' Bennett at Raiders' 21. After 1 play, Breech kicks 34-yard field goal at

1:01.

Sept. 20, 1992—Houston 23, Kansas City 20, at Houston; Chiefs win toss. Carter returns kickoff 25 yards to Kansas City 28. On third play of drive, Birden fumbles at Kansas City 34; ball recovered by Houston's D. Smith at Chiefs' 23. After one play, Del Greco kicks 39-yard field goal at 1:55.

Oct. 11, 1992—Indianapolis 6, New York Jets 3, at Indianapolis; Colts win toss. Verdin returns kickoff 33 yards to Colts' 36. Colts drive to Jets' 30 where Biasucci kicks 47-yard field goal at 3:01.

#Nov. 8, 1992—Cincinnati 31, Chicago 28, at Chicago; Bears win toss. Lewis returns kickoff 22 yards to Chicago's 29. Bears drive to Chicago's 46 where Gardocki punts; fair catch by Wright at the Cincinnati 17. Bengals drive to Bears' 18 where Breech kicks 36-yard field goal at 8:39.

Nov. 15, 1992—New England 37, Indianapolis 34, at Indianapolis; Colts win toss. Verdin returns kickoff 10 yards to Colts' 20; holding penalty brings ball back to Colts' 10. After two plays, Henderson intercepts pass at Colts' 38 and returns it 9 yards to the 29. In three plays, Patriots drive to 1 where Baumann kicks 18-yard field goal at 3:25.

Nov. 29, 1992—Indianapolis 16, Buffalo 13, at Indianapolis; Colts win toss. Verdin returns kickoff 24 yards to Colts' 22. Colts drive to Buffalo 22 where Biasucci kicks 40-yard field goal at 3:51.

* Nov. 30, 1992—Seattle 16, Denver 13, at Seattle; Seahawks win toss. Daluiso kicks through end zone for touchback. After three plays, Tuten punts 53 yards to Denver 18 where Marshall returns for no gain. After three plays, Rodriguez punts 29 yards to Seattle 45 where Warren signals fair catch. Seahawks drive to Denver 15 where Kasay's 33-yard field goal attempt misses. Broncos take over at Denver 20. After three plays, Rodriguez punts 43 yards to Seattle 38 where Warren signals for fair catch. After four plays, Tuten punts 39 yards to Denver 4 where Daniels downs punt. After three plays, Rodriguez punts 46 yards to Denver 48 where Warren returns 10 yards to the 38. Seahawks drive to Denver 14 where Kasay kicks 32-yard field goal at 11:10.

Dec. 13, 1992—Philadelphia 20, Seattle 17, at Seattle; Eagles win toss. Sydner returns kick 12 yards to Eagles' 16; illegal block penalty brings ball back to 8. Eagles drive to Philadelphia 45 where Feagles punts for a touchback. After 6 plays, Tuten punts 45 yards to Philadelphia 22 where Sydner returns 7 yards to 29. After 6 plays, Feagles punts 44 yards to Seattle 26 where Warren returns 5 yards to 31. After 5 plays, Tuten punts 32 yards to Philadelphia 20 where Sydner signals for fair catch. Eagles drive to Seattle 27 where Ruzek kicks 44-yard field goal with no time remaining.

Dec. 27, 1992—Miami 16, New England 13, at New England; Patriots win toss. Lockwood returns kickoff 15 yards to Patriots' 21. After three plays, McCarthy punts 39 yards to Miami 33 where Miller returns 2 yards to the 35. Miami drives to New England 18 where Stoyanovich kicks 35-yard field goal at 8:17.

Sept. 12, 1993—Detroit 19, New England 16, at New England; Patriots win toss. Patriots begin at 20. After 3 plays, Saxon punts 42 yards to Detroit 29 where Gray returns 12 yards to the 41. After 3 plays, Arnold punts 41 yards to New England 12 where Brown returns 16 yards to the 28. Patriots drive to Detroit 44 where Saxon punts into the end zone for a touchback. Detroit drives to New England 20 where Hanson kicks 38-yard field goal at 11:04.

Nov. 7, 1993—Buffalo 13, New England 10, at New England; Patriots win toss. T. Brown returns kickoff 27 yards to Patriots 30. Patriots drive to Buffalo 48 where Bills take over on downs. Bills drive to New England 25 where Metzelaars fumbles, and C. Brown recovers. After 3 plays, Saxon punts 46 yards to Buffalo 24 where Copeland returns 11 yards to the 35. Bills drive to New England 14 where Christie kicks 32-yard field goal at 9:22.

Dec. 19, 1993—Phoenix 30, Seattle 27, at Seattle; Cardinals win toss. Bailey returns kickoff 14 yards to Cardinals 20. Cardinals drive to Seattle 23 where Davis kicks 41-yard field goal at

6:45.

Jan. 2, 1994—Dallas 16, New York Giants 13, at New York; Giants win toss. Meggett returns kickoff 19 yards to Giants 19. After 6 plays, Horan punts 45 yards to Cowboys 25 where Widmer downs punt. Cowboys drive to Giants' 23 where Murray kicks 41-yard field goal at 10:44.

Jan. 2, 1994—New England 33, Miami 27, at New England; Dolphins win toss. McDuffie returns kickoff 21 yards to Miami 27. After 3 plays, Hatcher punts 43 yards to New England 29 where Harris returns 6 yards to the 35. After 2 plays, Brown intercepts pass from Bledsoe and returns 3 yards to Miami 49. After 3 plays, Hatcher punts 3 yards to New England 14 where Harris returns 18 yards to the 32. After 2 plays, Bledsoe passes 36 yards to Timpson for touchdown at 4:44.

Jan. 2, 1994—Los Angeles Raiders 33, Denver 30, at Los Angeles; Broncos win toss. Delpino returns kickoff 12 yards to Denver 25. Broncos drive to Los Angeles 22 where Elam's 40-yard field goal attempt is wide left. Raiders drive to Denver 29 where Jaeger kicks 47-yard field goal at 7:10.

* Jan. 3, 1994—Philadelphia 37, San Francisco 34, at San Francisco; 49ers win toss. Walker returns kickoff, 19 yards to San Francisco 27. 49ers drive to Philadelphia 14 where Cofer misses 32-yard field goal. Eagles start at their 20-yard line, and, after 3 plays, Feagles punts 48 yards to San Francisco 36 where Carter fumbles and 49ers recover. After 7 plays, Wilmsmeyer punts 57 yards to Philadelphia 6 where Sikahema returns 16 yards to the 22. Eagles drive to San Francisco 10 where Ruzek kicks 28-yard field goal with no time remaining.

Sept. 4, 1994—Detroit 31, Atlanta 28, at Detroit; Falcons win toss. Falcons start at their own 16 after holding penalty on kickoff. After 3 plays, Alexander punts 41 yards to Detroit 39 where Clay returns 12 yards to Atlanta 49. Detroit drives to Atlanta 20 where Hanson kicks 37-yard field goal at 5:14.

Sept. 11, 1994—New York Jets 25, Denver 22, at New York; Jets win toss. Murrell returns kickoff 24 yards to New York 33. Jets drive to Denver 22 where Lowery kicks 39-yard field goal at 3:57.

* Sept. 19, 1994—Detroit 20, Dallas 17, at Dallas; Lions win toss. Gray returns kickoff 24 yards to Detroit 32. Lions drive to Dallas 34 where Hanson's 51-yard field-goal attempt is blocked by Lett. Cowboys take possession at Dallas 42. Cowboys drive to Detroit 37 where Kennard fumbles and Swilling recovers. Lions take possession at Detroit 45. After 6 plays, Montgomery punts 31 yards to Dallas 16. Cowboys drive to Dallas 49 where Aikman fumbles and Thomas recovers at Dallas 43. Lions drive to Dallas 26 where Hanson kicks 44-yard field goal at 14:33.

Oct. 16, 1994—Arizona 19, Washington 16, at Washington; Redskins win toss. Mitchell returns kickoff 27 yards to Washington 41. Redskins drive to Arizona 34 where Lohmiller's 51-yard field-goal attempt is blocked by Joyner and recovered by Williams who returns it to the Washington 37. After 5 plays, Peterson's 45-yard field-goal attempt is wide right. Redskins take possession at the Washington 36. After 3 plays, Roby punts 36 yards to the Arizona 37 where Robinson returns 3 yards to the 40. After 3 plays, Feagles punts 51 yards for a touchback. After 1 play, Shuler's pass is intercepted by Hoage who returns it to the Washington 12. Peterson kicks 29-yard field goal at 10:00.

Oct. 16, 1994—Miami 20, Los Angeles Raiders 17, at Miami; Dolphins win toss. McDuffie returns kickoff 19 yards to Miami 23. Dolphins drive to Los Angeles 12 where Stoyanovich kicks 29-yard field goal at 5:46.

 # Oct. 20, 1994—Minnesota 13, Green Bay 10, at Minnesota; Vikings win toss. Ismail returns kickoff 22 yards to Minnesota 29. Vikings drive to Green Bay 9 where Fuad Reveiz kicks 27-yard field goal at 4:26.

Oct. 30, 1994—Detroit 28, New York Giants 25, at New York; Giants win toss. Lewis returns kickoff 16 yards to New York 27. After 3 plays, Horan punts 42 yards to Detroit 24 where Gray calls for fair catch. Detroit drives to New York 6 where Hanson kicks 24-yard field goal at 6:43.

#Oct. 30, 1994—Arizona 20, Pittsburgh 17, at Arizona; Steelers win toss. Johnson returns kickoff 24 yards to Pittsburgh 30 where he fumbles and Arizona's Merritt recovers at Pittsburgh 32. After 3 plays, Davis kicks 51-yard field goal at 1:40.

Nov. 6, 1994—Cincinnati 20, Seattle 17, at Seattle; Seahawks win toss. Warren returns kickoff 32 yards to Seattle 33. After 3 plays, Tuten punts 37 yards to Cincinnati 28 where Sawyer calls for fair catch. After 3 plays, Johnson punts 64 yards to Seattle 2 where Truitt downs ball. Seahawks drive to Seattle 38 where Tuten punts 50 yards to Cincinnati 12 and Sawyer returns 5 yards to 17. Blake passes to Scott for 76 yards to Seattle 7. Pelfrey kicks 26-yard field goal at 8:14.

Nov. 6, 1994—Pittsburgh 12, Houston 9, at Houston; Steelers win toss. Stone returns kickoff 15 yards to Pittsburgh 28. After 3 plays, Royals punts 53 yards to Houston 13 where Givins downs ball. After 3 plays, Camarillo punts 57 yards to Pittsburgh 31 where Woodson returns 20 yards to Houston 49. After 3 plays, Royals punts 43 yards to Houston 15 where Coleman returns 3 yards to 18. After 5 plays, Camarillo punts 57 yards to Pittsburgh 12 where Hastings returns 12 yards to 24. Steelers drive to Houston 41 where Royals punts 29 yards to Houston 12, and Coleman calls for fair catch. Brown fumbles on first play and Jones recovers at Houston 22. After 1 play, Anderson kicks 40-yard field goal at 11:24.

Nov. 13, 1994—New England 26, Minnesota 20, at New England; Patriots win toss. Thompson returns kickoff 27 yards to New England 33. Patriots drive to Minnesota 14 where Bledsoe passes 14 yards to Turner for touchdown at 4:10.

Nov. 20, 1994—Pittsburgh 16, Miami 13, at Pittsburgh; Steelers win toss. Stone returns kickoff 15 yards to Pittsburgh 16. Steelers drive to Miami 39 where they lose possession on downs. Dolphins drive to Pittsburgh 47 where Arnold punts 35 yards to Pittsburgh 12 and Oliver downs ball. Steelers drive to Miami 21 where Anderson kicks 39-yard field goal at 10:19.

Nov. 27, 1994—Chicago 19, Arizona 16, at Arizona; Cardinals win toss. Levy returns kickoff 31 yards to Arizona 45. After 5 plays, Feagles punts 38 yards to the end zone for a touchback. Bears drive to Arizona 10 where Butler kicks 27-yard field goal at 8:11.

Nov. 27, 1994—Tampa Bay 20, Minnesota 17, at Minnesota; Buccaneers win toss. Harris returns kickoff 12 yards to Tampa Bay 38. After 6 plays, Stryzinski punts 40 yards to Minnesota 4 where Guliford muffs punt and Buccaneers' Brady recovers. Husted kicks 22-yard field goal at 2:08.

 # Dec. 1, 1994—Minnesota 33, Chicago 27, at Minnesota; Bears win toss. Lewis returns kickoff 23 yards to Chicago 33. Bears drive to Minnesota 22 where Butler's 40-yard field goal attempt is wide left. After 1 play, Moon passes 65 yards to Carter for touchdown at 5:46.

Dec. 4, 1994—Denver 20, Kansas City 17, at Kansas City; Broncos win toss. Milburn returns kickoff 24 yards to Denver 29. After 3 plays, Millen fumbles and Phillips recovers at Denver 35. After 4 plays, Allen fumbles and Smith recovers at Denver 27. After 6 plays, Rouen punts 45 yards to Kansas City 25 where Hughes calls for fair catch. After 3 plays, Aguiar punts 33 yards to Denver 42 where Chiefs down ball. Broncos drive to Kansas City 17 where Elam kicks 34-yard field goal at 12:12.

Sept. 3, 1995—Cincinnati 24, Indianapolis 21, at Indianapolis; Bengals win toss. Dunn returns kickoff 15 yards to Bengals' 17. Cincinnati drives to Indianapolis 29 where Pelfrey kicks 47-yard field goal at 2:36.

Sept. 3, 1995—Atlanta 23, Carolina 20, at Atlanta; Panthers win toss. Baldwin downs kickoff for touchback. Panthers drive to Carolina 42 where Reich fumbles and ball is recovered by Archambeau at Carolina 31. Falcons drive to Panthers' 16 where Andersen kicks 35-yard field goal at 6:17.

Sept. 10, 1995—Indianapolis 27, New York Jets 24, at New York; Jets win toss. Carter downs kickoff for touchback. Jets punt downed at Colts' 37. Colts drive to Jets' 35 where Cofer

kicks 52-yard field goal at 4:27.

Sept. 10, 1995—Kansas City 20, New York Giants 17, at Kansas City; Chiefs win toss. Vanover returns kickoff 30 yards to Chiefs' 28. Aguiar punts to Giants' 3. Horan punts to Chiefs' 49. Chiefs drive to Giants' 6 where Elliott kicks 23-yard field goal at 7:49.

Sept. 17, 1995—Kansas City 23, Oakland 17, at Kansas City; Chiefs win toss. Vanover returns kickoff 28 yards to Chiefs' 41. M. Allen fumbles, ball recovered by Robbins at Raiders' 38. Hasty intercepts pass at Chiefs' 36 and returns it 64 yards for touchdown at 4:27.

Sept. 17, 1995—Atlanta 27, New Orleans 24, at Atlanta; Saints win toss. Hughes returns kickoff 21 yards to Saints' 17. Metcalf returns Wilsmeyer's punt 18 yards to Saints' 39. Stryzinski punts, fair catch by Hughes at Saints' 14. Wilsmeyer punt downed at Falcons' 6. Falcons drive to Saints' 3 where Andersen kicks 21-yard field goal at 7:58.

#Sept. 17, 1995—Dallas 23, Minnesota 17, at Minnesota; Cowboys win toss. K. Williams returns kickoff 23 yards to Cowboys' 27. E. Smith scores on 31-yard run at 2:26.

Oct. 8, 1995—Indianapolis 27, Miami 24, at Miami; Colts win toss. Warren returns kickoff 25 yards to Colts' 33. Colts drive to Dolphins' 10 where Blanchard kicks 27-yard field goal at 4:58.

Oct. 8, 1995—New York Giants 27, Arizona 21, at New York; Cardinals win toss. Terry returns kickoff 20 yards to Cardinals' 23. Hamilton recovers Krieg's fumble at Cardinals' 36. Lynch recovers Brown's fumble at Cardinals' 38. Armstead intercepts pass at Giants' 42 and returns it 58 yards for touchdown at 4:05.

Oct. 8, 1995—Minnesota 23, Houston 17, at Minnesota; Vikings win toss. Palmer returns kickoff 10 yards to Vikings' 15. Saxon's punt downed at Oilers' 8. Washington intercepts pass at Vikings' 47 and returns it 25 yards to Oilers' 28. R. Smith scores on 20-yard run at 7:10.

Oct. 8, 1995—Philadelphia 37, Washington 34, at Philadelphia; Redskins win toss. Redskins take possession at their 20 after touchback. Turk punt out of bounds at Eagles' 9. Eagles drive to Redskins' 18 where Anderson kicks 35-yard field goal at 10:06.

* **Oct. 9, 1995—Kansas City 29, San Diego 23,** at Kansas City; Chargers win toss. Coleman returns kickoff 24 yards to Chargers' 28. Vanover makes fair catch of Bennett's punt at Chiefs' 15. Coleman makes fair catch of Aguiar's punt at Chargers' 43. Vanover returns Bennett's punt 86 yards for a touchdown at 7:27.

Oct. 15, 1995—Tampa Bay 20, Minnesota 17, at Tampa Bay; Buccaneers win toss. Edmonds returns kickoff 19 yards to Buccaneers' 22. A. Lee returns Roby's punt to Vikings' 48. Vikings drive to Tampa Bays' 35 where Reveiz's 53-yard field-goal attempt is wide right. Buccaneers take over at own 43 and drive to Vikings' 33 where Husted kicks 51-yard field goal at 6:23.

Oct. 22, 1995—Washington 36, Detroit 30, at Washington; Redskins win toss. B. Mitchell returns kickoff 16 yards to Redskins' 27. Turk's punt downed at Lions' 4. D. Green intercepts S. Mitchell's pass and returns it 7 yards for touchdown at 3:41.

Oct. 29, 1995—Carolina 20, New England 14, at New England; Panthers win toss. Baldwin returns kickoff 22 yards to Panthers' 25. Meggett makes fair catch of Barnhardt's punt at Patriots' 9. Guliford returns O'Neill's punt 9 yards to Patriots' 32. Panthers drive to Patriots' 12 where Kasay kicks 29-yard field goal at 7:08.

Oct. 29, 1995—Cleveland 29, Cincinnati 26, at Cincinnati; Browns win toss. Hunter returns kickoff 31 yards to Browns' 31. Bieniemy returns Tupa's punt 9 yards to Bengals' 37. McCardell makes fair catch of Johnson's punt at Browns' 12. Bieniemy returns Tupa's punt 0 yards to Bengals' 38. Hall intercepts Blake's pass and returns it 5 yards to Bengals' 45. Browns drive to Bengals' 11 where Stover kicks 28-yard field goal at 6:30.

Oct. 29, 1995—Arizona 20, Seattle 14, at Arizona; Cardinals win toss. Dowdell returns kickoff 16 yards to Cardinals' 25. Cardinals drive to Seahawks' 10 where G. Davis' 27-yard field goal attempt is blocked. L. Lynch intercepts Friesz's pass at Cardinals' 28 and returns it 72 yards for a touchdown at 11:16.

Nov. 5, 1995—Pittsburgh 37, Chicago 34, at Chicago; Bears win toss. Timpson returns kickoff 23 yards to Bears' 33. Hastings returns Sauerbrun's punt 2 yards to Steelers' 31. Steelers drive to Bears' 6 where N. Johnson kicks 24-yard field goal at 8:19.

Nov. 12, 1995—Minnesota 30, Arizona 24, at Arizona; Vikings win toss. A. Lee returns kickoff 20 yards to Vikings' 25. Moon throws 50-yard touchdown pass to Ismail at 2:16.

Nov. 26, 1995—Arizona 40, Atlanta 37, at Arizona; Falcons win toss. J. Anderson returns kickoff 20 yards to Falcons' 20. Stryzinski fumbles punt snap. Recovered by England at Falcons' 10 where G. Davis kicks 28-yard field goal at 1:43.

#Dec. 10, 1995—Tampa Bay 13, Green Bay 10, at Tampa Bay; Buccaneers win toss. Edmonds returns kickoff 24 yards to Buccaneers' 23. Tampa Bay drives to Packers' 29 where Husted kicks 47-yard field goal at 3:46.

#Sept. 1, 1996—Buffalo 23, New York Giants 20, at New York; Bills win toss. Daluiso kick is a touchback. Bills drive to Buffalo 46. Toomer returns Mohr's punt to Giants' 16. Dave Brown's fumble recovered by Spielman at Giants' 33. Bills drive to Giants' 16 where Christie kicks 34-yard field goal at 9:08.

Sept. 22, 1996—New England 28, Jacksonville 25, at New England; Patriots win toss. T. Brown returns kickoff 18 yards to Patriots' 29. Patriots drive to Jaguars' 22 where Vinatieri kicks 40-yard field goal at 2:36.

Sept. 29, 1996—Arizona 31, St. Louis 28, at Arizona; Cardinals win toss. Lohmiller kick is a touchback. Cardinals drive to Rams' 7 where G. Davis kicks 24-yard field goal at 1:54.

Oct. 6, 1996—Buffalo 16, Indianapolis 13, at Buffalo; Colts win toss. Christie kick is a touchback. Colts drive to Indianapolis 32. Burris returns Gardocki's punt to Bills' 35. Bills drive to Colts' 48. Mohr puts out of bounds at Colts' 14. Colts drive to Indianapolis 9. Burris returns Gardocki's punt to Colts' 48. Bills drive to Colts' 22 where Christie kicks 39-yard field goal at 9:22.

#Oct. 6, 1996—Houston 30, Cincinnati 27, at Cincinnati; Bengals win toss. Dunn returns kickoff 23 yards to Bengals' 34. Bengals drive to Cincinnati 36. Floyd returns L. Johnson's punt to Oilers' 18. Oilers drive to Bengals' 31 where Del Greco kicks 49-yard field goal at 7:07.

* Oct. 14, 1996—Green Bay 23, San Francisco 20, at Green Bay; 49ers win toss. D. Carter returns kickoff 23 yards to 49ers' 22. 49ers' drive to San Francisco 25. Howard makes fair catch of Thompson's punt at Packers' 44. Packers drive to 49ers' 35 where Jacke kicks 53-yard field goal at 3:41.

Oct. 27, 1996—Baltimore 37, St. Louis 31, at Baltimore; Rams win toss. J. Thomas returns kickoff 17 yard to Rams' 17. Rams drive to Ravens' 15. F. Miller fumble in field goal formation recovered by S. Moore at Ravens' 17. Ravens drive to Baltimore 49 and turn ball over on downs. Rams drive to Ravens' 40 and turn ball over on downs. Testaverde throws 22-yard scoring pass to M. Jackson at 14:50.

Nov. 10, 1996—Dallas 20, San Francisco 17, at San Francisco; Cowboys win toss. H. Walker returns kickoff 10 yards to Cowboys' 23. Cowboys drive to 49ers' 11 where Boniol kicks 29-yard field goal at 6:17.

Nov. 10, 1996—Arizona 37, Washington 34, at Washington; Cardinals win toss. Blanton's kickoff is a touchback. Cardinals drive to Redskins' 15 where Butler misses 32-yard field goal. Redskins drive to Cardinals' 43 where Turk punts for touchback. L. Johnson fumble returned by Morrison to Cardinals' 27. Redskins drive to Cardinals' 31 where Blanton misses 48-yard field goal. Cardinals drive to Redskins' 15 where Butler kicks 32-yard field goal at 14:27.

Nov. 10, 1996—Tampa Bay 20, Oakland 17, at Tampa Bay; Buccaneers win toss. M. Marshall returns kickoff 15 yards to Bucs' 17. Bucs drive to Tampa Bay 36. T. Brown returns Barnhardt's punt four yards to Raiders' 22. Raiders drive to Oakland

25. M. Marshall returns Gossett's punt nine yards to Bucs' 39. Bucs drive to Raiders' 4 where Husted kicks 23-yard field goal at 11:56.

#Nov. 17, 1996—Minnesota 16, Oakland 13, at Oakland; Raiders win toss. Kaufman returns kickoff 32 yards to Raiders' 27. Raiders drive to Oakland 46 where Gossett punts to Vikings' 17. Vikings drive to Raiders' 12 where Sisson kicks 31-yard field goal at 11:53.

Nov. 24, 1996—Jacksonville 28, Baltimore 25, at Baltimore; Jaguars win toss. Jordon returns kickoff 16 yards to Jaguars' 30. Jaguars drive to Jacksonville 37. Barker's punt is downed at Ravens' 6. Ravens drive to Jaguars' 37 where Pritchett recovers Byner's fumble. Jaguars drive to Ravens' 15 where Hollis kicks 34-yard field goal at 9:06.

Nov. 24, 1996—San Francisco 19, Washington 16, at Washington; 49ers win toss. D. Carter returns kickoff 20 yards to 49ers' 32. 49ers drive to Redskins' 20 where Wilkins kicks 38-yard field goal at 3:24.

Dec. 1, 1996—Indianapolis 13, Buffalo 10, at Indianapolis; Bills win toss. Moulds returns kickoff 26 yards to Bills' 25. Bills drive to Buffalo 49. Stock returns Mohr's punt one yard to Colts' 16. Colts drive to Bills' 32 where Blanchard kicks 49-yard field goal at 10:46.

Aug. 31, 1997—Tennessee 24, Oakland 21, at Tennessee; Oilers win toss. Gray returns kickoff 32 yards to Tennessee 33. Oilers drive to Tennessee 38. Roby's punt is downed at the Oakland 33. Raiders drive to Oakland 32. Gray returns Araguz punt to Tennessee 35. Oilers drive to Oakland 15 where Del Greco kicks 33-yard field goal at 6:57.

Sept. 7, 1997—Miami 16, Tennessee 13, at Miami; Dolphins win toss. Spikes returns kickoff 48 yards to Tennessee 45. Dolphins drive to Tennessee 11 where Mare kicks 29-yard field goal at 2:15.

#Sept. 7, 1997— Arizona 25, Dallas 22, at Arizona; Cowboys win toss. Walker returns kickoff 21 yards to Dallas 25. Cowboys drive to Arizona 43. Gowin punts 43 yards for a touchback. Cardinals drive to Dallas 44. Graham fumbles. Cowboys drive to Arizona 42. Williams fumbles. Cardinals drive to Dallas 3 where Butler kicks 20-yard field goal at 8:30.

Sept. 14, 1997—Washington 19, Arizona 13, at Washington; Cardinals win toss. K. Williams returns kickoff 27 yards to Arizona 34. Cardinals drive to Arizona 40. McElroy fumbles. Redskins drive to Arizona 40. Westbrook catches 40-yard touchdown pass from Frerotte at 1:36.

#Sept. 14, 1997—New England 27, New York Jets 24, at New England; Patriots win toss. Hall's kickoff is a touchback. Patriots drive to New England 15. Bledsoe pass intercepted by O. Smith. Jets drive to New York 46. Hansen punts 47 yards. Meggett returns to New England 21. Patriots drive to New York 17 where Vinatieri kicks 34-yard field goal at 8:03.

Sept. 28, 1997—Kansas City 20, Seattle 17, at Kansas City; Seahawks win toss. Broussard returns kickoff 12 yards to Seattle 14. Seahawks drive to Seattle 17. Vanover returns Tuten punt 8 yards to Kansas City 26. Chiefs drive to Seattle 44. Aguiar punt downed at Seattle 11. Seahawks drive to Seattle 26. Moon pass intercepted by Woods and returned 13 yards to 50. Chiefs drive to Seattle 23 where Stoyanovich kicks 41-yard field goal at 13:04.

Oct. 19, 1997—Philadelphia 13, Arizona 10, at Philadelphia; Cardinals win toss. K. Williams returns kickoff 28 yards to Arizona 42. Cardinals drive to Philadelphia 48. Feagles punts 48 yards for touchdown. Eagles drive to Arizona 7 where Boniol kicks 24-yard field goal at 4:02.

Oct. 19, 1997—New York Giants 26, Detroit 20, at Detroit; Giants win toss. Pegram returns kickoff 16 yards to New York 18. Giants drive to New York 32. Calloway catches 68-yard touchdown pass from Kanell at 1:40.

Oct. 26, 1997—Denver 23, Buffalo 20, at Buffalo; Broncos win toss and elects to kickoff. Holmes returns kickoff 20 yards to Buffalo 25. Bills drive to Buffalo 23. Mohr punt downed at

Denver 40. Broncos drive to Buffalo 48. Rouen punt downed at Buffalo 1. Bills drive to Buffalo 20. Gordon returns Mohr punt to Denver 42. Broncos drive to Buffalo 15 where Elam kicks 33-yard field goal at 13:04.

Oct. 26, 1997—Pittsburgh 23, Jacksonville 17, at Pittsburgh; Steelers win toss. Coleman returns kickoff 23 yards to Pittsburgh 23. Steelers drive to Jacksonville 17. Bettis catches 17-yard touchdown pass from Stewart at 3:47.

* **Oct. 27, 1997—Chicago 36, Miami 33**, at Miami; Dolphins win toss. McPhail returns kickoff 23 yards to Miami 27. Dolphins drive to Miami 36. Kidd punts out of bounds at Chicago 10. Bears drive to the Chicago 39. Sauerbrun punt out of bounds at Miami 27. Reeves recovers Marino fumble at Miami 17. Bears drive to Miami 17 where Jaeger kicks 35-yard field goal at 9:25.

Nov. 2, 1997—New York Jets 19, Baltimore 16, at New York; Jets win toss. Stover's kickoff is a touchback. Jets drive to Baltimore 20 where Hall kicks 37-yard field goal at 4:58.

Nov. 16, 1997—Philadelphia 10, Baltimore 10, at Baltimore; Eagles win toss. Stover's kickoff is a touchback. Eagles drive to Philadelphia 19. Hutton punts 36 yards to Baltimore 45. Ravens drive to Baltimore 36 where Eagles take over on downs. Eagles drive to Baltimore 33 where Ravens take over on downs. Ravens drive to Baltimore 37. Montgomery punts 55 yards, and Solomon returns to Philadelphia 22. Eagles drive to Philadelphia 16. Hutton punts 41 yards, and Roe returns to Baltimore 46. Ravens drive to Philadelphia 35 where Stover's 53-yard field-goal attempt is no good. Eagles drive to Baltimore 22 where Boniol's 40-yard field-goal is no good as time expires.

Nov. 16, 1997—New Orleans 20, Seattle 17, at New Orleans; Seahawks win toss. Brien's kickoff is a touchback. Seahawks start at Seattle 20 where Moon's pass intercepted by Tubbs who returns 15 yards to Seattle 20. Saints Brien kicks 38-yard field goal at 17 seconds.

\# **Nov. 23, 1997—New York Giants 7, Washington 7**, at Washington; Redskins win toss. Davis returns kickoff 28 yards to Washington 39. Redskins drive to Washington 36 where Hostetler's pass intercepted by Sehorn who returns minus–2 yards before lateralling to Wooten who returns 5 yards to New York 41. Giants drive to New York 26 where Maynard punts 37 yards to Washington 37. Redskins drive to Washington 39 where Hostetler fumble is recovered by Harris at New York 40. Giants drive to New York 43 where Maynard punts 57 yards for a touchback. Washington drives to New York 41. Giants take over on downs at New York 40. Giants drive to Washington 36 where Daluiso's 54-yard field-goal attempt is no good. Redskins drive to Washington 45 where Hostetler's pass intercepted by Sparks at New York 49. Giants drive to Washington 36 where Maynard punts 36 yards for a touchback. Redskins drive to New York 36 where Blanton's 54-yard field-goal attempt is no good. Giants drive to New York 45 where Kanell's pass intercepted by Patton who laterals to Pounds who returns 11 yards to Washington 24 as time expires.

Nov. 30, 1997—Pittsburgh 26, Arizona 20, at Arizona; Cardinals win toss. K. Williams returns kickoff 11 yards to Arizona 23. Cardinals drive to Arizona 18 where Feagles punts 43 yards. Hawkins returns punt 9 yards to Pittsburgh 48. Steelers drive to Arizona 10 where Bettis scores on a 10-yard touchdown run at 5:34.

Dec. 13, 1997—Pittsburgh 24, New England 21, at New England; Steelers win toss. Coleman returns kickoff 19 yards to Pittsburgh 20. Steelers drive to New England 13 where Johnson kicks a 31-yard field goal at 4:43.

Sept. 6, 1998—San Francisco 36, New York Jets 30, at San Francisco; Jets win toss. Richey's kickoff is a touchback. Jets drive to New York 11. Gallery punts 48 yards. McQuarters returns punt 36 yards for a touchdown. 49ers drive to New York 44. Howard punts 23 yards to New York 21. Johnson calls fair catch. Jets drive to New York 47. Gallery's 49-yard punt downed at San Francisco 4. Hearst runs for a 96-yard touchdown at 4:08.

Sept. 13, 1998—Cincinnati 34, Detroit 28, at Detroit; Lions win toss. Johnson's kickoff is a touchback. Lions drive to Detroit 47 where Mitchell's pass is intercepted by Sawyer and returned for a 58-yard touchdown at 2:06.

Sept. 27, 1998—New Orleans 19, Indianapolis 13, at Indianapolis; Saints win toss. Gardocki's kickoff is returned by Ismail to New Orleans 28. Saints drive to New Orleans 30. Royals punts 64 yards. Poole returns to Indianapolis 12. Colts drive to Indianapolis 20. Gardocki punts 58 yards. Hastings returns to New Orleans 29. Saints drive to New Orleans 32. Royals punts 59 yards. Punt downed at Indianapolis 9. Colts drive to Indianapolis 44 where Manning's pass is intercepted by Drakeford and returned to Indianapolis 36. Saints drive to Indianapolis 33. Wuerffel throws 33-yard touchdown pass to Cleeland at 6:10.

Oct. 25, 1998—Miami 12, New England 9, at Miami; Dolphins win toss. Vinatieri's kickoff is returned by Avery to Miami 15. Dolphins drive to New England 26 where Mare kicks 43-yard field goal at 4:36.

+ **Nov. 26, 1998—Detroit 19, Pittsburgh 16**, at Detroit; Lions win toss. Johnson's kickoff is returned by Fair to Detroit 35. Lions drive to Pittsburgh 24 where Hanson kicks 42-yard field goal at 2:52.

Dec. 6, 1998—San Francisco 31, Carolina 28, at Carolina; Panthers win toss. Richey's kickoff is returned by Floyd to Carolina 36. Panthers drive to Carolina 38 where Beuerlein's fumble is recovered by Doleman at Carolina 30. 49ers drive to Carolina 5 where Richey kicks 23-yard field goal at 4:16.

Dec. 13, 1998—Arizona 20, Philadelphia 17, at Philadelphia; Cardinals win toss. Boniol's kickoff is returned by Metcalf to Arizona 28. Cardinals drive to Philadelphia 15 where Jacke kicks 32-yard field goal at 4:30.

Sept. 12, 1999—Dallas 41, Washington 35, at Washington; Redskins win toss. Gowin's kickoff is returned by B. Mitchell to Washington 24. Redskins drive to Washington 47. M. Turk punts 48 yards. Punt downed at Dallas 5. Cowboys drive to Dallas 24. Aikman passes 76-yard touchdown to R. Ismail at 4:09.

Oct. 3, 1999—Baltimore 19, Atlanta 13, at Atlanta; Falcons win toss. Stover's kickoff is returned by Oliver to Atlanta 18. Falcons drive to Atlanta 23. Stryzinski punts 41 yards, out of bounds at Baltimore 36. Baltimore drives to Baltimore 46. Case passes 54-yard touchdown to Armour at 2:29.

Oct. 31, 1999—New York Giants 23, Philadelphia 17, at Philadelphia; Giants win toss. Akers' kickoff is returned by Levingston to New York 27. New York drives to Giants 31. Maynard punts 43 yards to Philadelphia 26. Rossum returns to Eagles 28. Pederson drives to New York 45. Pederson's pass is intercepted by Strahan at Philadelphia 44. Giants' Peter batted ball up in the air as Pederson backpedaled. Strahan for 44 yards and touchdown at 4:24.

Nov. 14, 1999—Minnesota 27, Chicago 24, at Chicago; Vikings win toss. Boniol kicks to Minnesota 2, Williams touchback. Minnesota starts from own 20. George's pass is intercepted by Harris at Minnesota 29 for -1 yard. Chicago starts at Minnesota 29 and moves to Minnesota 23. Boniol's 41-yard field goal is no good. Minnesota starts from own 31 and drives to Chicago 20. Anderson kicks 38-yard field goal at 9:02.

Nov. 21, 1999—Chicago 23, San Diego 20, at San Diego; Bears win toss. Chicago starts from own 22. Miller completes four consecutive passes and Bears drive to San Diego 22. Enis rushes twice to San Diego 19. Boniol kicks 36-yard field goal at 4:58.

* **Nov. 22, 1999—Denver 27, Oakland 21**, at Denver; Broncos win toss. Denver starts from own 33 and drives to Broncos' 35. Rouen punts 46 yards to Oakland 19. Oakland starts at own 19 and drives to Raiders' 25. Gannon fumbles and Broncos' Pryce recovers at Oakland 25. Denver running back Gary scores on 24-yard run at 2:40.

Nov. 28, 1999—Washington 20, Philadelphia 17, at Washington; Redskins win toss. Akers' kickoff is returned by Thrash for 48 yards to Philadelphia 46. Johnson completes 20-yard pass to Connell to Philadelphia 26. Johnson completes 9-yard pass to Mitchell to Philadelphia 9. Mitchell runs for seven yards to Philadelphia 2. On third down, Washington attempts field goal from Philadelphia 2. Johnson fumbles and recovers at Philadelphia 9. Conway kicks 27-yard field goal at 4:34.

Dec. 19, 1999—Denver 36, Seattle 30, at Denver; Broncos win toss. Peterson kicks to Denver 8. Watson returns kick to Denver 27 for 19 yards. Broncos do not convert a first down. Rouen punts 46 yards, out of bounds at Seattle 25. Kitna passes to Dawkins for 17 yards at Seattle 47. Watters runs for 6 yards to Denver 47. Kitna sacked for 11-yard loss by Crockett. Kitna fumbles, forced by Crockett, recovered by Cadrez at Seattle 37. Cadrez for 37 yards and touchdown at 2:34.

Dec. 26, 1999—Buffalo 13, New England 10, at New England; Patriots win toss. New England's Vinatieri misses 44-yard field goal from Buffalo 26. Buffalo takes over at Bills 34. Flutie passes to Moulds to New England 21 for 17 yards. Moulds fumbles, recovered by Bruschi at Patriots 21. New England drives to own 34. Johnson punts from New England 34 to Buffalo 42. Flutie passes to Price for 7 yards to New England 44. Flutie passes to Moulds for 11 yards to New England 27. Thomas runs for 9 yards to New England 6. Christie kicks 23-yard field goal at 13:12.

#Dec. 26, 1999—Washington 26, San Francisco 20, at San Francisco; Redskins win toss. Richey kicks to Washington 9, Thrash returns 13 yards to Washington 22. Johnson passes to Hicks for 25 yards to Washington 47. Centers runs for 12 yards to San Francisco 33. Johnson passes to Centers for 33 yards and touchdown at 2:00.

Jan. 2, 2000—Oakland 41, Kansas City 38, at Kansas City; Raiders win toss. Baker kicks 69 yards from Kansas City 30 to Oakland 1 and out of bounds. Oakland starts at Raiders 40. Gannon passes to Dudley for 21 yards to Kansas City 40. Gannon passes to Brown at Kansas City 16 for 24 yards. Crockett runs to Kansas City 15 for 1 yard. Nedney kicks 33-yard field goal at 3:13.

Sept. 10, 2000—Tennessee 17, Kansas City 14, at Tennessee; Titans win toss. Mason returns kickoff 28 yards to Tennessee 29. Face-mask penalty on Kansas City, 5 yards, enforced at 29. Titans drive to Kansas City 18 where Del Greco kicks 36-yard field goal at 2:58.

Oct. 1, 2000—Dallas 16, Carolina 13, at Carolina; Cowboys win toss. Tucker returns kickoff 20 yards to Dallas 26. Dallas drives to Carolina 6 where Seder kicks 24-yard field goal at 3:52.

Oct. 1, 2000—Washington 20, Tampa Bay 17, at Washington; Redskins win toss. Thrash returns kickoff 32 yards to Washington 30. Washington gains five yards where Barnhardt punts 52 yards to Tampa Bay 13. Green returns for one yard to Tampa Bay 14. Buccaneers gain one yard to Tampa Bay 15 where Royals punts 50 yards to Washington 35. Sanders returns punt 57 yards to Tampa Bay 8. Davis rushes three times and gets to Tampa Bay 2 where Husted kicks 20-yard field goal at 4:09.

Oct. 8, 2000—Oakland 34, San Francisco 28, at San Francisco; Raiders win toss. Dunn returns kickoff 20 yards to Oakland 19. Raiders drive to San Francisco 17 where Janikowski misses 35-yard field-goal attempt wide right. San Francisco drives to Oakland 11 where Richey's 29-yard field-goal attempt is blocked by Dorsett. Raiders recover at Oakland 16. Oakland drives to San Francisco 31 where Gannon passes to Brown for 31-yard touchdown at 10:15.

Oct. 15, 2000—Buffalo 27, San Diego 24, at Buffalo; Bills win toss. Bills drive to Buffalo 47. Mohr punts 42 yards to San Diego 11. Chargers drive to San Diego 38 where Harbaugh is intercepted at Buffalo 41. Flutie in for injured Johnson. Bills drive to San Diego 28. Christie kicks 46-yard field goal at 8:26.

* **Oct. 23, 2000—New York Jets 40, Miami 37,** at New York; Dolphins win toss. Marion returns kickoff 31 yards to Miami 37. Fielder is intercepted at Miami 46 by Coleman, who returns ball to 39 where he fumbles. Gadsden recovers ball for Dolphins and runs out of bounds at Miami 34. Dolphins drive to New York 43 where Fielder is intercepted again by Coleman at the Jets 34. Jets drive to Miami 23 where Hall kicks 40-yard field goal at 6:47.

Oct. 29, 2000—Jacksonville 23, Dallas 17, at Dallas; Jaguars win toss. Stith returns kickoff 24 yards to Jacksonville 34. Jaguars drive to Dallas 37 where Brunell passes to Whitted for a 37-yard touchdown at 3:02.

Nov. 5, 2000—Buffalo 16, New England 13, at New England; Patriots win toss. Faulk returns kickoff 38 yards to New England 43. Penalty on New England for offensive holding, 10 yards, enforced at New England 33. Patriots lose one yard on three plays. Johnson punts 43 yards to Buffalo 35. Bills drive to New England 13 where Christie kicks 32-yard field goal at 4:21.

Nov. 5, 2000—Philadelphia 16, Dallas 13, at Philadelphia; Eagles win toss. Mitchell returns kickoff 30 yards to Philadelphia 34. Eagles drive to Dallas 36 where McNabb is intercepted by Wortham at Dallas 30. Wortham returns interception to Dallas 31. Cowboys drive to Dallas 48 where Thomas fumbles. Recovered by Hauck at Dallas 48. Eagles drive to Dallas 13 where Akers kicks 32-yard field goal at 7:52.

* **Nov. 6, 2000—Green Bay 26, Minnesota 20,** at Green Bay; Packers win toss. Rossum returns kickoff 13 yards to Green Bay 18. Packers drive to Minnesota 43 where Favre passes to Freeman for a 43-yard touchdown at 3:27.

Nov. 12, 2000—Philadelphia 26, Pittsburgh 23, at Pittsburgh; Eagles win toss. Mitchell returns kickoff 24 yards to Philadelphia 37. Eagles drive to Pittsburgh 24 where Akers kicks 42-yard field goal at 4:09.

Dec. 17, 2000—New England 13, Buffalo 10, at Buffalo; Bills win toss and elect to defend the South goal. Patriots elect to receive. Jackson returns kickoff 38 yards to New England 48. Patriots drive to Buffalo 31 where they turn the ball over on downs. Bills drive to New England 12 where Christie's 30-yard field goal attempt is blocked by Eaton. Patriots recover at New England 11. Patriots drive to Buffalo 6 where Vinatieri kicks 24-yard field goal at 14:37.

Dec. 24, 2000—Green Bay 17, Tampa Bay 14, at Green Bay; Packers win toss. Rossum returns kickoff 29 yards to Green Bay 38. Packers drive to Tampa Bay 4 where Longwell kicks 22-yard field goal at 6:28.

Sept. 9, 2001—St. Louis 20, Philadelphia 17, at Philadelphia; Eagles win toss. Wilkins' kickoff is a touchback. Eagles drive to Philadelphia 30. Landeta punts 34 yards to St. Louis 36. Rams drive to Philadelphia 8. Wilkins kicks 26-yard field goal at 7:56.

Sept. 9, 2001—San Francisco 16, Atlanta 13, at San Francisco; 49ers win toss. Feely's kickoff is a touchback. 49ers drive to Atlanta 9. Cortez kicks 24-yard field goal at 4:04.

Oct. 14, 2001—New England 29, San Diego 26, at New England; Chargers win toss. Jenkins returns kickoff 39 yards to San Diego 40. Chargers drive to San Diego 45. Bennett punts 32 yards to New England 23. Patriots drive to San Diego 26. Vinatieri kicks 44-yard field goal at 4:00.

Oct. 14, 2001—San Francisco 37, Atlanta 31, at Atlanta; 49ers win toss. Sutherland returns kickoff 24 yards to San Francisco 24. 49ers drive to Atlanta 14. Garcia fumbles, Hall recovers at Atlanta 23. Falcons drive to Atlanta 23. Mohr punts 44 yards to San Francisco 33. Garcia throws 52-yard touchdown to Owens at 8:34.

Oct. 14, 2001—Tennessee 31, Tampa Bay 28, at Tennessee; Buccaneers win toss. D. Smith returns kickoff 17 yards to Tampa Bay 18. Buccaneers forced back to Tampa Bay 9. Royals punts 45 yards to Tennessee 46. Titans drive to Tampa Bay 32. Nedney kicks 49-yard field goal at 1:52.

Oct. 21, 2001—Washington 17, Carolina 14, at Washington; Redskins win toss. Bates returns kickoff 17 yards to Washington 14. Redskins drive to Carolina 5. Conway kicks 23-yard field goal at 1:47.

Oct. 28, 2001—Chicago 37, San Francisco 31, at Chicago; 49ers win toss. Edinger's kickoff is a touchback. M. Brown intercepts Garcia pass and returns it 33 yards for touchdown at 16 seconds.

Nov. 4, 2001—Chicago 27, Cleveland 21, at Chicago; Bears win toss. L. Johnson returns kickoff 31 yards to Chicago 32. Bears drive to Chicago 40. Maynard punts 52 yards to Cleveland 8. M. Brown intercepts Couch pass and returns it 16 yards for touchdown at 2:50.

Nov. 4, 2001—New York Giants 27, Dallas 24, at New York; Cowboys win toss. Swinton returns kickoff 21 yards to Dallas 29. Cowboys drive to New York 48. Knorr punts 33 yards to New York 15. Giants drive to Dallas 24. Andersen kicks 42-yard field goal at 7:12.

Nov. 11, 2001—Pittsburgh 15, Cleveland 12, at Cleveland; Steelers win toss. T. Edwards returns kickoff 21 yards to Pittsburgh 28. Steelers drive to Cleveland 14. Brown kicks 32-yard field goal at 5:22.

Nov. 18, 2001—San Francisco 25, Carolina 22, at Carolina; 49ers win toss. Sutherland returns kickoff 24 yards to San Francisco 26. 49ers drive to Carolina 8. Cortez kicks 26-yard field goal at 4:41.

Dec. 2, 2001—Arizona 34, Oakland 31, at Oakland; Raiders win toss. Gramatica's kickoff is a touchback. Raiders drive to Oakland 40. Lechler punts 37 yards to Arizona 23. Cardinals drive to Arizona 48. Stanley punts 29 yards to Oakland 23. Woods recovers Dunn fumble on Oakland 25. Arizona drives to Oakland 18. Gramatica kicks 36-yard field goal at 7:29.

Dec. 2, 2001—Seattle 13, San Diego 10, at Seattle; Seahawks win toss. Rogers returns kickoff 33 yards to Seattle 32. Seahawks drive to San Diego 6. Lindell kicks 24-yard field goal at 6:23.

Dec. 2, 2001—Tampa Bay 16, Cincinnati 13, at Cincinnati; Buccaneers win toss. F. Murphy returns kickoff 20 yards to Tampa Bay 38. Buccaneers drive to Cincinnati 35. Royals punts 31 yards to Cincinnati 4. Lynch recovers Dillon fumble on Cincinnati 3. Gramatica kicks 21-yard field goal at 5:06.

Dec. 16, 2001—Kansas City 26, Denver 23, at Kansas City; Broncos win toss. Carter returns kickoff 24 yards to Denver 41. Broncos drive to Denver 35. Rouen punts 35 yards to Kansas City 30. Chiefs drive to Denver 23. T. Peterson misses 41-yard field-goal attempt. Broncos drive to Denver 32. Rouen punts 38 yards to Kansas City 30. Chiefs drive to Denver 14. T. Peterson kicks 32-yard field goal at 9:04.

Dec. 16, 2001—New England 12, Buffalo 9, at Buffalo; Bills win toss. Bryson returns kickoff 23 yards to Buffalo 28. Bills drive to Buffalo 48. Moorman punts 52 yards to end zone. Patriots drive to Buffalo 5. Vinatieri kicks 23-yard field goal at 5:45.

Dec. 30, 2001—Cincinnati 26, Pittsburgh 23, at Cincinnati; Steelers win toss. Geason returns kickoff and laterals to Logan who carries ball 9 yards to Pittsburgh 38. Steelers drive to Cincinnati 39. Miller punts 38 yards to Cincinnati 1. Bengals drive to Pittsburgh 13. Rackers kicks 31-yard field goal at 10:52.

Sept. 8, 2002—New York Jets 37, Buffalo 31, at Buffalo; Jets win toss. Morton returns kickoff 96 yards for touchdown at 14 seconds.

Sept. 8, 2002—Green Bay 37, Atlanta 34, at Green Bay; Packers win toss. J. Walker returns kickoff 26 yards to Green Bay 34. Packers drive to Atlanta 39. Bidwell punts 27 yards to Atlanta 12. Falcons drive to Atlanta 14. Mohr punts 46 yards to Green Bay 40. Packers drive to Atlanta 19. Longwell kicks 34-yard field goal at 9:40.

Sept. 8, 2002—New Orleans 26, Tampa Bay 20, at Tampa Bay; Tampa Bay wins toss. Stecker returns kickoff 31 yards to

Tampa Bay 42. Buccaneers drive to New Orleans 39. Tupa punts 39 yards into end zone. Saints drive to New Orleans 20. Williams returns Johnson's punt 4 yards to Tampa Bay 46. Buccaneers drive to Tampa Bay 48. Tupa punts 52 yards into end zone. Saints drive to New Orleans 41. Williams returns Johnson's punt -4 yards to Tampa Bay 6. Buccaneers drive to Tampa Bay 5. Tupa pass intercepted by Allen in Tampa Bay end zone at 12:01.

Sept. 15, 2002—Buffalo 45, Minnesota 39, at Minnesota; Buffalo wins toss. Rodgers returns kickoff 22 yards to Buffalo 22. Bills drive to Buffalo 48. Moorman punts 27 yards, downed at Minnesota 25. Vikings drive to Minnesota 32. Richardson punts 45 yards. Downed at Buffalo 23. Bills drive to Minnesota 26. Hollis' 44-yard field-goal attempt is no good. Vikings take over on Minnesota 35. Drive to Minnesota 41. Richardson punts 52 yards. Returned by Rogers 16 yards to Buffalo 24. Bills drive to Minnesota 48. Bledsoe throws 48-yard pass to Price for touchdown at 10:12.

Sept. 22, 2002—Cleveland 31, Tennessee 28, at Tennessee; Cleveland wins toss. White returns kickoff 6 yards to Cleveland 26. Browns drive to Tennessee 15. Dawson kicks 33-yard field goal at 4:09.

Sept. 22, 2002—New England 41, Kansas City 38, at New England; New England wins toss. Branch returns kickoff 30 yards to New England 30. Patriots drive to Kansas City 17. Vinatieri kicks 35-yard field goal at 4:36.

Sept. 29, 2002—Buffalo 33, Chicago 27, at Buffalo; Chicago wins toss. Johnson returns kickoff 19 yards to Chicago 20. Bears drive to Chicago 25. Maynard punts 31 yards to Buffalo 44. Fair catch by Mannelly. Buffalo drives to Chicago 26. Bledsoe throws 26-yard pass to Henry for touchdown at 2:48.

Sept. 29, 2002—Pittsburgh 16, Cleveland 13, at Pittsburgh; Pittsburgh wins toss. Mays returns kickoff 32 yards to Pittsburgh 32. Maddox's pass intercepted by Davis at Pittsburgh 34, returned for no gain. Cleveland drives to Pittsburgh 27. Dawson's 45-yard field-goal attempt no good, tipped at line of scrimmage by Flowers. Steelers take over at Pittsburgh 35. Steelers drive to Cleveland 6, and 24-yard field-goal attempt by Peterson blocked by McKinley, recovered by Peterson, fumbles, recovered by Fiala. Peterson's 31-yard field goal is good at 6:58.

Oct. 20, 2002—Denver 37, Kansas City 34, at Denver; Denver wins toss. Kasper returns kickoff 15 yards to Denver 24. Broncos drive to Denver 33. Rouen punts 43 yards to Kansas City 24. Hall returns punt 13 yards to Kansas City 37. Chiefs drive to Kansas City 43. Stryzinski's punt is blocked and recovered by Burns at Kansas City 32. Denver drives to Kansas City 7. Elam's 25-yard field goal is good at 2:52.

Oct. 20, 2002—Detroit 23, Chicago 20, at Detroit; Detroit wins toss. Edinger's kickoff goes out of bounds at Detroit 2. Lions take over at Detroit 40. Lions drive to Chicago 30. Hanson's 48-yard field goal is good at 4:42.

Oct. 20, 2002—San Diego 27, Oakland 21, at Oakland; San Diego wins toss. Chargers start at San Diego 20 after touchback. Chargers drive to Oakland 19. Tomlinson runs 19 yards for touchdown at 3:33.

Oct. 20, 2002—Arizona 9, Dallas 6, at Arizona; Dallas wins toss. Swinton returns kickoff 26 yards to Dallas 24. Cowboys drive to Dallas 29. Knorr punts 45 yards to Arizona 26. Jackson returns 5 yards to Arizona 31. Cardinals drive to Dallas 38. Player punts 38 yards into end zone. Cowboys take over at Dallas 20. Cowboys drive to Arizona 49. Knorr punts 31 yards to Arizona 18. Fair catch by Jackson. Cardinals drive to Dallas 22. Gramatica's 40-yard field goal is good at 11:45.

Nov. 3, 2002—San Francisco 23, Oakland 20, at Oakland; San Francisco wins toss. Janikowski's kickoff returned to SF 22 by J. Williams. 49ers drive to Oakland 5. Cortez's 23-yard field goal at 8:41.

Nov. 10, 2002—Atlanta 34, Pittsburgh 34, at Pittsburgh; Pittsburgh wins toss. Touchback on Feely kickoff. Pittsburgh starts at own 20, drives to Atlanta 30. Peterson's 48-yard field-goal attempt blocked by Finneran. Atlanta takes over at own 47, drives to Atlanta 33. Mohr punts 47 yards to Randle El, who returns to Pittsburgh 18. Steelers drive to Atlanta 33. Miller punts 22 yards to Atlanta 12, no return. Falcons drive to Atlanta 23. Mohr punts 52 yards. Randle El returns 1 yard to Pittsburgh 26. Steelers drive to Pittsburgh 44. Maddox intercepted by Mathis at Atlanta 43. Mathis returns to Pittsburgh 44. Atlanta drives to Pittsburgh 37. Feely's 56-yard field-goal attempt blocked by Farrior. Pittsburgh takes over on own 49. Maddox pass to Burress downed at Atlanta 1 as time expires.

Nov. 17, 2002—San Diego 20, San Francisco 17, at San Diego; San Diego wins toss. Jenkins returns Cortez kickoff 39 yards to San Diego 38. Chargers drive to San Diego 38. Bennett punts 47 yards to San Francisco 15. Williams returns 9 yards to San Francisco 24. 49ers drive to San Diego 23. Cortez's 41-yard field-goal attempt is no good. San Diego takes over on San Diego 31. Chargers drive to San Francisco 22. Christie's 40-yard field goal is good at 10:49.

Nov. 24, 2002—Chicago 20, Detroit 17, at Chicago; Detroit wins toss. Elects to defend the north goal. Hanson kicks 72 yards. Kick returned 37 yards to Chicago 35. Chicago drives to Detroit 22. Edinger's 40-yard field-goal attempt is good at 6:02.

#**Nov. 24, 2002—Indianapolis 23, Denver 20**, at Denver; Indianapolis wins toss. Knorr kicks 66 yards. Returned by Walters 28 yards to Indianapolis 32. Colts drive to Denver 33. Vanderjagt's 51-yard field-goal attempt is good at 5:38.

Dec. 1, 2002—Atlanta 30, Minnesota 24, at Minnesota; Minnesota wins toss. Feely kicks 60 yards. Returned by Carter 10 yards to Minnesota 20. Vikings drive to Minnesota 11. Richardson punts 47 yards to Atlanta 42. Returned by Rossum 10 yards to Minnesota 48. Falcons drive to Minnesota 46. Vick runs 46 yards for touchdown at 2:25.

Dec. 1, 2002—Tennessee 32, New York Giants 29, at New York; New York wins toss. Nedney kicks 68 yards. Returned by Joyce 38 yards to New York 40. Giants drive to New York 46. Allen punts 34 yards to Tennessee 20. Fair catch by O'Leary. Titans drive to New York 20. Nedney's 38-yard field goal good at 5:00.

Dec. 1, 2002—San Diego 30, Denver 27, at San Diego; Denver wins toss. Christie kicks 65 yards. Droughns returns 27 yards to Denver 32. Broncos drive to Denver 23. Knorr punts 36 yards to San Diego 41. Fair catch by Dwight. Chargers drive to Denver 19. Christie's 38-yard field-goal attempt blocked. Denver takes over on own 27. Broncos drive to San Diego 34. Elam's 53-yard field-goal attempt is no good. San Diego takes over on own 43. Chargers drive to Denver 9. Christie's field goal is good from 27 yards at 11:59.

Dec. 8, 2002—Arizona 23, Detroit 20, at Arizona; Arizona wins toss. Hanson kicks 64 yards. Kasper returns 19 yards to Arizona 30. Cardinals drive to Detroit 24. Gramatica's 42-yard field-goal attempt is good at 4:12.

Dec. 15, 2002—Seattle 30, Atlanta 24, at Atlanta; Seattle wins toss. Lindell kicks 69 yards. Returned 17 yards to Atlanta 18 by Rossum. Atlanta drives to Seattle 18. Feely's 36-yard field-goal attempt wide right. Seattle takes over at own 26. Seahawks drive to Atlanta 27. Alexander runs 27 yards for a touchdown at 10:36.

Dec. 29, 2002—New York Giants 10, Philadelphia 7, at N.Y. Giants; Philadelphia wins toss. Bryant kicks 57 yards. Returned by Mitchell 32 yards to Philadelphia 45. Eagles drive to mid-field. Feeley's pass intercepted by Williams at New York 37, returned for no gain. Giants drive to Philadelphia 22. Bryant's 39-yard field-goal attempt is good at 5:10.

Dec. 29, 2002—New England 27, Miami 24, at New England; New England wins toss. Mare kicks 68 yards out of bounds. Patriots begin at own 40. New England drives to Miami 17. Vinatieri's 35-yard field goal is good at 2:03.

Dec. 29, 2002—Seattle 31, San Diego 28, at San Diego;

Seattle wins toss. Christie kicks 64 yards. Returned by Williams 26 yards to Seattle 32. Seahawks drive to San Diego 28. Hasselbeck's pass is intercepted by Molden at San Diego 20 and returned 1 yard to the 21. Chargers drive to San Diego 12. Bennett punts 48 yards to Seattle 40. Returned by Engram 8 yards to Seattle 48. Seahawks drive to San Diego 6. Lindell's 24-yard field goal is good at 9:58.

Sept. 14, 2003—St. Louis 27, San Francisco 24, at St. Louis; Rams win the toss. Harris returns kick 42 yards to St. Louis 48. Rams drive to San Francisco 10. Wilkins kicks 28-yard field goal at 1:56.

Sept. 14, 2003—Carolina 12, Tampa Bay 9, at Tampa Bay; Panthers win toss. Touchback. Carolina starts at own 20, drives to own 37. Sauerbrun punts 45 yards to Tampa Bay 18. Buccaneers drive to Carolina 42. Tupa punts 34 yards to Carolina 8. Smith returns punt 52 yards to Tampa Bay 40. Panthers drive to Tampa Bay 29. Kasay kicks 47-yard field goal at 11:26.

* **Sept. 15, 2003—Dallas 35, New York Giants 32**, at New York; Cowboys win toss. Smith returns kickoff 21 yards to Dallas 29. Cowboys drive to Dallas 48. Gowin punts 32 yards to Giants 20. Giants drive to New York 15. Feagles punts 42 yards to Dallas 43. Cowboys drive to New York 6. Cundiff kicks 25-yard field goal at 9:04.

Sept. 21, 2003—New York Giants 24, Washington 21, at Washington; Giants win toss. Begin drive on New York 6 due to penalty on kickoff return. Giants drive to Washington 11. Bryant kicks 29-yard field goal at 4:15.

Sept. 28, 2003—Oakland 34, San Diego 31, at Oakland; Chargers win toss. Johnson returns kickoff to San Diego 24. Chargers drive to San Diego 36. Bennett punts 46 yards to Oakland 18. Raiders drive to Oakland 8. Lechler punts 49 yards to San Diego 43. Chargers drive to San Diego 39. Bennett punts to Oakland 8. Raiders drive to San Diego 28. Janikowski kicks 46-yard field goal at 9:59.

Oct. 5, 2003—Buffalo 22, Cincinnati 16, at Buffalo; Bengals win toss. Begin drive on Cincinnati 20 after touchback. Bengals drive to Cincinnati 28. Harris punts 29 yards to Buffalo 43. Bills drive to Cincinnati 2. Henry scores on 2-yard touchdown run at 3:53.

* **Oct. 6, 2003—Indianapolis 38, Tampa Bay 35**, at Tampa Bay; Buccaneers win toss. Barlow returns kickoff 30 yards to Tampa Bay 30. Buccaneers drive to Indianapolis 41. Tupa punts to Indianapolis 13. Colts drive to Tampa Bay 11. Vanderjagt kicks 29-yard field goal at 11:13.

Oct. 12, 2003—Carolina 23, Indianapolis 20, at Indianapolis; Panthers win toss. Smart returns kickoff to Carolina 27. Panthers drive to Indianapolis 30. Kasay kicks 47-yard field goal at 5:39.

Oct. 12, 2003—Kansas City 40, Green Bay 34, at Green Bay; Chiefs win toss. Hall returns kick to Kansas City 29. Chiefs drive to Green Bay 30. Andersen misses 48-yard field goal (ball tipped at line). Packers take over possession at Green Bay 39. A. Green fumbles after eight-yard run. Chiefs recover at Kansas City 49. T. Green throws 51-yard touchdown pass to Kennison at 6:18.

Oct. 19, 2003—New England 19, Miami 13, at Miami; Dolphins win toss. Rogers returns kickoff 24 yards to Miami 26. Dolphins drive to New England 17. Mare's 35-yard field-goal attempt no good. Patriots take over on New England 26. Patriots drive to New England 40. Walter punts to Miami 21. Returned by Rogers to Miami 30. Dolphins drive to Miami 45. Fiedler pass intercepted by Poole at New England 18. Brady passes 82 yards to Brown for touchdown at 9:15.

Oct. 26, 2003—Carolina 23, New Orleans 20, at New Orleans; Saints win toss. Lewis returns kickoff 53 yards to Carolina 46. Saints drive to Carolina 37. McAllister fumbles on fourth-and-one. Panthers take over at Carolina 38 and drive to New Orleans 12. Kasay kicks 31-yard field goal at 4:36.

Oct. 26, 2003—Arizona 16, San Francisco 13, at Arizona; Cardinals win toss. 49ers' Pochman kicks out of bounds. Cardinals take possession at Arizona 40 and drive to San Francisco 22. Duncan kicks 39-yard field goal at 4:59.

Nov. 2, 2003—New York Giants 31, New York Jets 28, at New York Jets; Giants win toss. Mitchell returns kick 26 yards to Giants 34. Giants drive to Jets 21. Conway misses 39-yard field-goal attempt. Jets take over on own 30. Drive to Giants 49. Stryzinski's punt returned by Mitchell two yards to Giants 18. Giants drive to own 35. Feagles' punt returned six yards by Moss to Jets 29. Jets drive to Giants 32. Brien's 51-yard field goal attempt is blocked by Allen. Giants take over on own 36, drive to Jets 11. Conway kicks 29-yard field goal at 14:56.

Nov. 9, 2003—New York Jets 27, Oakland 24, at Oakland; Jets win toss. Jordan returns kick 12 yards to New York 25. Jets drive to Oakland 21. Brien kicks 38-yard field goal at 5:56.

Nov. 16, 2003—Miami 9, Baltimore 6, at Miami; Dolphins win toss. Dolphins start at Miami 20 after touchback, drive to Baltimore 45. Turk punts 36 yards to Baltimore 9. Ravens drive to Baltimore 36. Lewis fumbles, recovered by Dolphins' Thomas. Dolphins drive to Baltimore 25. Mare kicks 43-yard field goal at 6:12.

Nov. 16, 2003—New Orleans 23, Atlanta 20, at New Orleans; Saints win toss. Lewis returns kick 39 yards to New Orleans 38. Saints drive to New Orleans 40. McAllister fumbles on Atlanta 2 after 58-yard run. Ball recovered by Falcons' Stewart for touchback. Falcons drive to New Orleans 37. Feely's 54-yard field-goal attempt no good. Saints take over on New Orleans 45. Drive to Atlanta 18. Carney kicks 36-yard field goal at 3:59.

Nov. 23, 2003—New England 23, Houston 20, at Houston; Texans win toss, take over possession at own 13 after penalty on Hollings' return. Patriots intercept Texans at Houston 23. Patriots drive to Houston 19. Vinatieri's 37-yard field-goal attempt blocked. Texans take over at own 27, drive to New England 40. Stanley punts 31 yards to New England 9. Patriots drive to New England 4. Walter punts 31 yards to New England 35. Texans drive to New England 40. Stanley punts 26 yards to New England 14. Patriots drive to Houston 10. Vinatieri kicks 28-yard field goal at 14:19.

Nov. 23, 2003—Baltimore 44, Seattle 41, at Baltimore; Seahawks win toss. Morris returns kick to Seattle 27. Seahawks drive to Seattle 30. Rouen punts 50 yards to Baltimore 20, returned 1 yard by Brightful to Baltimore 21. Ravens drive to Seattle 24. Stover kicks 42-yard field goal at 8:28.

Nov. 23, 2003—St. Louis 30, Arizona 27, at Arizona; Rams win toss. Harris returns kick to St. Louis 14. Rams drive to Arizona 31. Wilkins kicks 49-yard field goal at 3:38.

 # Dec. 7, 2003—Atlanta 20, Carolina 14, at Atlanta; Panthers win toss. Smart returns kickoff 19 yards to Carolina 22. Panthers drive to Carolina 29. Delhomme's pass intercepted by Mathis at Carolina 32 and returned for touchdown at 1:19.

Dec. 14, 2003—Denver 23, Cleveland 20, at Cleveland; Browns win toss, start on Cleveland 20 after touchback. Browns drive to Cleveland 17. Gardocki punts 42 yards, returned by O'Neal 6 yards to Denver 47. Broncos drive to Cleveland 7. Elam kicks 25-yard field goal at 5:10.

Dec. 21, 2003—San Francisco 31, Philadelphia 28, at Philadelphia; Eagles win toss, start on Philadelphia 21 after penalty on Thrash's return. McNabb's pass intercepted by 49ers' Parrish and returned 29 yards to Philadelphia 4. On second down, Peterson kicks 22-yard field goal at 1:05.

 # Dec. 28, 2003—Baltimore 13, Pittsburgh 10, at Baltimore; Steelers win toss. Mays returns kick to Pittsburgh 20. Steelers drive to Pittsburgh 27. Miller punts 43 yards, returned 6 yards by Brightful to Baltimore 36. Ravens drive to Pittsburgh 29. Stover kicks 47-yard field goal at 3:28.

Sept. 26, 2004—New Orleans 28, St. Louis 25, at St. Louis; Rams win toss. Furrey returns kick 23 yards to St. Louis 32. Rams drive to own 41. Landeta punts 41 yards to New Orleans 18. Lewis returns punt 15 yards to New Orleans 33. Saints drive to St. Louis 13. Carney kicks 31-yard field goal at 7:04.

Oct. 10, 2004—Minnesota 34, Houston 28, at Houston; Vikings win the toss. Burleson returns kick 29 yards to Minnesota 30. Vikings drive to own 35. Bennett punts 47 yards to Houston 18. Houston drives to own 38. Stanley punts 43 yards to Minnesota 19. Minnesota drives to the 50. Culpepper passes to Robinson for 50-yard touchdown at 7:55.

Oct. 10, 2004—St. Louis 33, Seattle 27, at Seattle; Rams win the toss. Harris returns kick 17 yards to St. Louis 29. Rams drive to own 48. Bulger passes to McDonald for 52-yard touchdown at 3:02.

Oct. 10, 2004—San Francisco 31, Arizona 28, at San Francisco; 49ers win the toss. Jackson returns kick 14 yards to San Francisco 39. 49ers drive to Arizona 14. Peterson kicks 32-yard field goal at 3:23.

Oct. 24, 2004—Philadelphia 34, Cleveland 31, at Cleveland; Eagles win the toss. Reed returns kick 27 yards to Philadelphia 30. Eagles drive to Cleveland 37. Johnson returns 47 yards for touchback. Cleveland drives to own 47. Frost punts 30 yards to Eagles 22. Philadelphia drives to Cleveland 32. Akers kicks 50-yard field goal at 9:58.

Nov. 14, 2004—Jacksonville 23, Detroit 17, at Jacksonville; Jaguars win the toss. Lewis returns kick 17 yards to the Jacksonville 24. Jaguars drive to the Detroit 38. Garrard passes to Smith for 38-yard touchdown at 5:28.

Nov. 14, 2004—Chicago 19, Tennessee 17, at Tennessee; Bears win the toss. Azumarh returns kick 22 yards to Chicago 26. Bears drive to own 48. Maynard punts 43 yards to Tennessee. Fair catch by Mason. Volek sacked at Tennessee 0 and fumble is recovered by Miller who is tackled in the end zone for safety at 3:17.

Nov. 14, 2004—Baltimore 20, New York Jets 17, at New York; Jets win the toss. Touchback. Jets drive to own 24. Gowin punts to Baltimore 35. Sams returns punt 9 yards to Baltimore 44. Ravens drive to own 49. Stewart punts 42 yards and ball is downed at the New York 9. Jets drive to own 16. Gowin punts 43 yards to Baltimore 41. Sams returns punt to Baltimore 44. Baltimore drives to New York 24. Stover kicks 42-yard field goal at 7:25.

Dec. 12, 2004—San Francisco 31, Arizona 28, at Arizona; 49ers win the toss. Touchback. 49ers drive to Arizona 37. Lee punts to 34 yards and is downed at Arizona 3. Cardinals drive to own 7. Player punts 51 yards and is returned to Arizona 49. 49ers drive to own 13. Peterson kicks 31-yard field goal at 6:22.

 # Dec. 18, 2004—Atlanta 34, Carolina 31, at Atlanta; Panthers win the toss. Broussard returns kick 16 yards to Carolina 19. Delhomme intercepted by Beasley returns pass 30 yards to Carolina 23. Atlanta drives to Carolina 20. Feely kicks 38-yard field goal at 2:25.

Dec. 26, 2004—Indianapolis 34, San Diego 31, at Indianapolis; Colts win the toss. Rhodes returns kick 17 yards to Indianapolis 27. Colts drive to San Diego 17. Vanderjagt kicks 30-yard field goal at 2:47.

Jan. 2, 2005—St. Louis 32, New York Jets 29, at St. Louis; Rams win the toss. Cason returns kick to St. Louis 24. Rams drive to New York 44. Stemke punts into endzone for touchback. Jets drive to own 44. Gowin punts 33 yards. Fair catch at St. Louis 23. Rams drive to own 31. Stemke punts to New York 27 and returned by McCareins two yards. Jets drive to St. Louis 35. Brien misses 53-yard field goal wide right. Rams begin drive from own 43. Rams drive to Jets 13. Wilkins kicks 31-yard field goal at 11:58.

POSTSEASON

Dec. 28, 1958—Baltimore 23, New York Giants 17, at New York in NFL Championship Game; Giants win toss. Maynard returns kickoff to Giants' 20. Chandler punts and Taseff returns one yard to Colts' 20. Ameche scores on 1-yard run at 8:15.

Dec. 23, 1962—Dallas Texans 20, Houston Oilers 17, at Houston in AFL Championship Game; Texans win toss and kick off. Jancik returns kickoff to Oilers' 33. Norton punts and Jackson makes fair catch on Texans' 22. Wilson punts and Jancik makes fair catch on Oilers' 45. Robinson intercepts Blanda's pass and returns 13 yards to Oilers' 47. Wilson's punt rolls dead at Oilers' 12. Hull intercepts Blanda's pass and returns 23 yards to midfield. Brooker kicks 25-yard field goal at 17:54.

Dec. 26, 1965—Green Bay 13, Baltimore 10, at Green Bay in NFL Divisional Playoff Game; Packers win toss. Moore returns kickoff to Packers' 22. Chandler punts and Haymond returns nine yards to Colts' 41. Gilburg punts and Wood makes fair catch at Packers' 21. Chandler punts and Haymond returns one yard to Colts' 41. Michaels misses 47-yard field goal. Chandler kicks 25-yard field goal at 13:39.

Dec. 25, 1971—Miami 27, Kansas City 24, at Kansas City in AFC Divisional Playoff Game; Chiefs win toss. Podolak, after a lateral from Buchanan, returns kickoff to Chiefs' 46. Stenerud's 42-yard field goal is blocked. Seiple punts and Podolak makes fair catch at Chiefs' 17. Wilson punts and Scott returns 18 yards to Dolphins' 39. Yepremian misses 62-yard field goal. Scott intercepts Dawson's pass and returns 13 yards to Dolphins' 46. Seiple punts and Podolak loses one yard to Chiefs' 15. Wilson punts and Scott makes fair catch on Dolphins' 30. Yepremian kicks 37-yard field goal at 22:40.

Dec. 24, 1977—Oakland 37, Baltimore 31, at Baltimore in AFC Divisional Playoff Game; Colts win toss. Raiders start on own 42 following a punt late in the first overtime. Oakland works way into field-goal range on Stabler's 19-yard pass to Branch at Colts' 26. Four plays later, on the second play of the second overtime, Stabler hits Casper with a 10-yard touchdown pass at 15:43.

Jan. 2, 1982—San Diego 41, Miami 38, at Miami in AFC Divisional Playoff Game; Chargers win toss. San Diego drives from its 13 to Miami 8. On second-and-goal, Benirschke misses 27-yard field goal attempt wide left at 9:15. Miami has the ball twice and San Diego twice more before the Dolphins get their third possession. Miami drives from the San Diego 46 to Chargers' 17 and on fourth-and-two, von Schamann's 34-yard field goal attempt is blocked by San Diego's Winslow after 11:27. Fouts then completes four of five passes, including a 39-yarder to Joiner that puts the ball on Dolphins' 10. On first down, Benirschke kicks a 29-yard field goal at 13:52.

Jan. 3, 1987—Cleveland 23, New York Jets 20, at Cleveland in AFC Divisional Playoff Game; Jets win toss. Jets' punt downed at Browns' 26. Moseley's 23-yard field goal attempt is wide right. Teams trade punts. Jets' second punt downed at Browns' 31. First overtime period expires eight plays later with Browns in possession at Jets' 42. Moseley kicks 27-yard field goal four plays into second overtime at 17:02.

Jan. 11, 1987—Denver 23, Cleveland 20, at Cleveland in AFC Championship Game; Browns win toss. Broncos hold Browns on four downs. Browns' punt returned four yards to Denver's 25. Elway completes 22- and 28-yard passes to set up Karlis's 33-yard field goal nine plays into drive at 5:38.

Jan. 3, 1988—Houston 23, Seattle 20, at Houston in AFC Wild Card Game; Seahawks win toss. Rodriguez punts to K. Johnson who returns one yard to Houston 15. Zendejas kicks 32-yard field goal 12 plays later at 8:05.

Dec. 31, 1989—Pittsburgh 26, Houston 23, at Houston in AFC Wild Card Playoff Game; Steelers win toss. Steelers punt to Oilers. Oilers' fumble recovered by Woodson and returned three yards. Four plays and 13 yards later, Anderson kicks a 50-yard field goal at 3:26.

Jan. 7, 1990—Los Angeles Rams 19, New York Giants 13, at New York in NFC Divisional Game; Rams win toss. Everett completes two passes to move ball to Giants' 48. White called for pass interference; ball spotted on Giants' 25. Everett hits Anderson with a 30-yard touchdown pass at 1:06.

Jan. 3, 1993—Buffalo 41, Houston 38, at Buffalo in AFC Wild Card Game; Oilers win toss. Oilers begin at 20. After 2 plays, Moon's pass is intercepted by Odomes who returns ball 2 yards to Houston 35. After 2 plays, Christie kicks 32-yard field

goal at 3:06.

Jan. 8, 1994—Kansas City 27, Pittsburgh 24, at Kansas City in AFC Wild Card Game; Chiefs win toss. Hughes returns kickoff 20 yards to Kansas City 25. After 3 plays, Barker punts 48 yards to Pittsburgh 18 where Woodson returns 8 yards to the 26. After 6 plays, Royals punts 30 yards to Kansas City 20. Kansas City drives to Pittsburgh 14 where Lowery kicks 32-yard field goal at 11:03.

Jan. 17, 1999—Atlanta 30, Minnesota 27, at Minnesota in NFC Championship Game; Vikings win toss. Palmer returns kickoff 30 yards to Minnesota 29. After four plays, Berger punts 51 yards to Atlanta 7 where Dwight returns 8 yards to Atlanta 15. Falcons drive to Atlanta 36. Stryzinski punts 37 yards to Vikings' 27. Palmer calls fair catch. Vikings drive to Minnesota 39. Berger punts 52 yards to Atlanta 9. Downed by Vikings. Atlanta drives to Minnesota 21 where Andersen kicks 38-yard field goal at 11:52.

Dec. 30, 2000—Miami 23, Indianapolis 17, at Miami in AFC Wild Card Game; Dolphins win toss. Williams returns kickoff 18 yards to Miami 20. Offensive holding penalty on Freeman, 10 yards, ball spotted on Miami 10. Dolphins drive to Miami 29 where Turk punts 53 yards to Indianapolis 18. Colts drive to Miami 31 where Vanderjagt misses 49-yard field-goal attempt wide right. Dolphins drive to Indianapolis 17 where Smith rushes for a 17-yard touchdown at 11:16.

Jan. 19, 2002—New England 16, Oakland 13, at New England in AFC Divisional Playoff Game; Patriots win toss. Pass returns kickoff 24 yards to New England 34. Patriots drive to Oakland 5. Vinatieri kicks 23-yard field goal at 8:29.

Jan. 11, 2003—Tennessee 34, Pittsburgh 31, at Tennessee in AFC Divisional Playoff Game; Tennessee wins toss. Reed kicks 60 yards. Returned by Simon 21 yards to Tennessee 31. Titans drive to Pittsburgh 8. Nedney's 26-yard field goal is good at 2:15.

Jan. 4, 2004—Green Bay 33, Seattle 27, at Green Bay in NFC Wild Card Game; Seahawks win toss. Morris returns kick to Seattle 33. Seahawks drive to Seattle 42. Rouen's 44-yard punt returned by Chatman to Green Bay 26. Packers drive to Green Bay 31. Bidwell punts 35 yards to Seattle 34. Seahawks drive to Seattle 45. Hasselbeck's pass to Bannister intercepted by Packers' Harris and returned 52 yards for touchdown at 4:25.

Jan. 10, 2004—Carolina 29, St. Louis 23, at St. Louis in NFC Divisional Game; Panthers win toss. Smart returns kick to Carolina 32. Panthers drive to St. Louis 27. Kasay's 45-yard field-goal attempt no good. Rams take over at own 35 and drive to Carolina 5. Wilkins' 53-yard field-goal attempt no good. Panthers take over at Carolina 43, drive to Carolina 47. Sauerbrun punts 40 yards to St. Louis 13. Rams drive to Carolina 38. Bulger's pass intercepted by Manning at Carolina 35. Panthers drive to Carolina 31. First overtime ends. On first play of second overtime, Delhomme passes to Smith for 69-yard touchdown at 15:10.

Jan. 11, 2004—Philadelphia 20, Green Bay 17, at Philadelphia in NFC Divisional Game; Eagles win toss. Thrash returns kick to Philadelphia 28. Eagles drive to Philadelphia 24. Johnson punts 49 yards and Packers start at own 32 after holding penalty. Favre's pass intercepted by Dawkins at Philadelphia 31 and returned to Green Bay 34. Eagles drive to Green Bay 13. Akers kicks 31-yard field goal at 4:48.

Jan. 8, 2005—New York Jets 20, San Diego 17, at San Diego in AFC Wild Card Game; Chargers win toss. Dwight returns kick to San Diego 26. Chargers drive to San Diego 35. Scifres punts 39 yards and ball is downed at the New York 26. Jets gain no yards. Gowin punts 41 yards. Parker loses 3 yards on return. San Diego starts on own 30. Chargers drive to New York 22. Kaeding's 40-yard field-goal attempt no good. Jets drive to San Diego 10. Brien kicks 28-yard field goal at 14:55.

Jan. 15, 2005—Pittsburgh 20, New York Jets 17, at Pittsburgh in AFC Divisional Game; Jets win toss. Cotchery returns kick to New York 31. Jets drive to New York 41. Gowin punts

54 yards. Randle El returns 8 yards to Pittsburgh 13. Steelers drive to New York 15. Reed kicks 33-yard field goal at 11:04.

NFL POSTSEASON OVERTIME GAMES
(BY LENGTH OF GAME)

Dec. 25, 1971	Miami 27, KANSAS CITY 24	82:40
Dec. 23, 1962	Dallas Texans 20, HOUSTON 17	77:54
Jan. 3 1987	CLEVELAND 23, N.Y. Jets 20	77:02
Dec. 24, 1977	Oakland 37, BALTIMORE 31	75:43
Jan. 10, 2004	Carolina 29, ST. LOUIS 23	75:10
Jan. 8, 2005	New York Jets 20, SAN DIEGO 17	74:55
Jan 2, 1982	San Diego 41, MIAMI 38	73:52
Dec. 26, 1965	GREEN BAY 13, Baltimore 10	73:39
Jan 17, 1999	Atlanta 30, MINNESOTA 27	71:52
Dec. 30, 2000	MIAMI 23, Indianapolis 17	71:16
Jan. 15, 2005	PITTSBURGH 20, New York Jets 17	71:04
Jan 8, 1994	KANSAS CITY 27, Pittsburgh 24	71:03
Jan. 19, 2002	NEW ENGLAND 16, Oakland 13	68:29
Dec. 28, 1958	Baltimore 23, N.Y. GIANTS 17	68:15
Jan. 3, 1988	HOUSTON 23, Seattle 20	68:05
Jan. 11, 1987	Denver 23, CLEVELAND 20	65:38
Jan. 11, 2004	PHILADELPHIA 20, Green Bay 17	64:48
Jan. 4, 2004	GREEN BAY 33, Seattle 27	64:25
Dec. 31, 1989	Pittsburgh 26, HOUSTON 23	63:26
Jan. 3, 1993	BUFFALO 41, Houston 38	63:06
Jan. 11, 2003	TENNESSEE 34, Pittsburgh 31	62:15
Jan. 7, 1990	L.A. Rams 19, N.Y. GIANTS 13	61:06

Home team in CAPS

There have been 22 overtime postseason games dating back to 1958. In 19 cases, both teams have had at least one possession. Last time: 1/15/05, PITTSBURGH 20, New York Jets 17.

OVERTIME WON-LOST RECORDS, 1974-2004
(REGULAR SEASON)

Team	Win	Loss	Tie	Pct.
AFC				
Baltimore	5	3	1	.611
Buffalo	17	9	0	.654
Cincinnati	14	9	0	.609
Cleveland	13	13	1	.500
Denver	17	12	2	.581
Houston	0	2	0	.000
Indianapolis	12	9	1	.568
Jacksonville	2	2	0	.500
Kansas City	10	11	2	.478
Miami	11	17	1	.397
New England	16	18	0	.471
New York Jets	13	12	2	.519
Oakland	13	16	0	.448
Pittsburgh	15	8	2	.640
San Diego	10	17	0	.370
Tennessee	11	15	0	.423
NFC				
Arizona	16	13	2	.566
Atlanta	10	15	2	.407
Carolina	4	7	0	.363
Chicago	16	14	0	.533
Dallas	12	10	0	.545
Detroit	11	13	1	.460
Green Bay	9	11	4	.458
Minnesota	15	15	2	.500
New Orleans	7	8	0	.466
New York Giants	13	12	2	.519
Philadelphia	11	14	3	.446
St. Louis	11	8	1	.575
San Francisco	14	13	1	.518
Seattle	7	14	0	.333
Tampa Bay	10	13	1	.438
Washington	15	9	1	.620

OVERTIME GAMES BY YEAR
(REGULAR SEASON)

2004-12	1996-14	1988- 9	1980-13
2003-23	1995-21	1987-13	1979-12
2002-25*	1994-16	1986-16	1978-11
2001-17	1993-7	1985-10	1977-6
2000-13	1992-10	1984- 9	1976-5
1999-11	1991-15	1983-19	1975-9
1998-7	1990-10	1982- 4	1974-2
1997-17	1989-11	1981-10	

*Record

OVERTIME GAME SUMMARY—1974-2004

There have been 377 overtime games in regular season play since the rule was adopted in 1974 (12 in 2004 season). Breakdown follows:

RESULTS

198 (9) times the team which won the toss won the game (52.5%)

163 (3) times the team which lost the toss won the game (43.4%)

16 (0) games ended tied (4.4%). Last time: Nov. 10, 2002, Atlanta 34 at Pittsburgh 34.

POSSESSIONS

261 (8) times both teams had at least one possession (69.2%)

104 (4) times the team which won the toss drove for winning score (76 FG, 29 TD) (27.7%)

8 (0) times the defense or special teams won without registering an official possession (5 interceptions, 1 fumble recovery, 1 blocked punt, 1 blocked field goal) (2.1%)

1 (0) times the special teams forced a fumble on the opening kickoff and drove for the winning score (0.27%)

1 (0) times the punting team recovered a muffed punt and drove for winning score with team muffing punt having no official possessions (0.27%)

2 (0) times the team that won the toss elected to kick and the team receiving the ball drove for winning score (0.54%)

SCORING

263 (8) games were decided by a field goal (69.8%)

96 (3) games were decided by a touchdown (25.7%)

2 (1) games were decided by a safety (0.54%)

16 (0) games ended tied (4.4%). Last time: Nov. 10, 2002, Atlanta 34 at Pittsburgh 34.

COIN TOSS

368(12) times the team which won the toss elected to receive (97.6%)

9 (0) times the team whichwon the toss elected to kick off (4 wins) (2.5%)

Note: The number in parentheses represents 2004 Season Total in each category.

MOST OVERTIME GAMES, SEASON

5	Green Bay Packers, 1983
4	Denver Broncos, 1985
	Cleveland Browns, 1989
	Minnesota Vikings, 1994
	Arizona Cardinals, 1995
	Minnesota Vikings, 1995
	Arizona Cardinals, 1997
	San Francisco 49ers, 2001
	Atlanta Falcons, 2002
	San Diego Chargers, 2002
	Carolina Panthers, 2003

LONGEST CONSECUTIVE GAME STREAKS
WITHOUT OVERTIME (Current)

30   Dallas Cowboys (Last OT Game, 9/15/03
        at New York Giants)
(Record: 110, St. Louis/Phoenix Cardinals, 12/7/86-12/19/93)

SHORTEST OVERTIME GAMES

0:14	New York Jets 37, BUFFALO 31; 9/8/02
0:16	CHICAGO 37, San Francisco 31; 10/28/01
0:17	NEW ORLEANS 20, Seattle 17; 11/16/97
0:21	Chicago 23, DETROIT 17; 11/27/80
0:30	Baltimore 29, NEW ENGLAND 23; 9/4/83
0:55	New York Giants 16, PHILADELPHIA 10; 9/29/85

LONGEST OVERTIME GAMES
(ALL POSTSEASON GAMES)

22:40	Miami 27, KANSAS CITY 24; 12/25/71
17:54	Dallas Texans 20, HOUSTON 17; 12/23/62
17:02	CLEVELAND 23, New York Jets 20; 1/3/87
15:43	Oakland 37, BALTIMORE 31; 12/24/77
15:10	Carolina 29, ST. LOUIS 23; 1/10/04

Home team in CAPS
There have been 22 overtime postseason games dating back to 1958. In 19 cases, both teams have had at least one possession. Last time: 1/15/05, PITTSBURGH 20, New York Jets 17.

OVERTIME SCORING SUMMARY

263	were decided by a field goal
44	were decided by a touchdown pass
26	were decided by a touchdown run
15	were decided by an interception (Atlanta 40, New Orleans 34, 9/2/79; Atlanta 47, Green Bay 41, 11/27/83; New York Giants 16, Philadelphia 10, 9/29/85; Indianapolis 23, Cleveland 17, 12/10/89; Cleveland 30, San Diego 24, 10/20/91; Kansas City 23, Oakland 17, 9/17/95; New York Giants 27, Arizona 21, 10/8/95; Washington 36, Detroit 30, 10/22/95; Arizona 20, Seattle 14, 10/29/95; Cincinnati 34, Detroit 28, 9/13/98; New York Giants 23, Philadelphia 17, 10/31/99; Chicago 37, San Francisco 31, 10/28/01; Chicago 27, Cleveland 21, 11/4/01; New Orleans 26, Tampa Bay 20, 9/8/02; Atlanta 20, Carolina 14, 12/7/03)
2	were decided on a fake field goal/touchdown pass (Minnesota 22, Chicago 16, 10/16/77; Cleveland 23, Minnesota 17, 12/17/89)
2	were decided by a fumble recovery (Baltimore 29, New England 23, 9/4/83; Denver 36, Seattle 30, 12/19/99)
2	were decided by a kickoff return (Chicago 23, Detroit 17, 11/27/80; New York Jets 37, Buffalo 31, 9/8/02)
2	was decided by a safety (Minnesota 23, Los Angeles Rams 21, 11/5/89; Chicago 19, Tennessee 17, 11/14/04)
1	was decided by a punt return (Kansas City 29, San Diego 23, 10/9/95)
1	was decided on a fake field goal/touchdown run (Los Angeles Rams 27, Minnesota 21, 12/2/79)
1	was decided on a blocked field goal (Denver 30, San Diego 24, 11/17/85)
1	was decided on a blocked field goal/recovery by kicker (Green Bay 12, Chicago 6, 9/7/80)
1	was decided on a blocked field goal/recovery by kicking team (Philadelphia 23, New York Giants 17, 11/20/88)
16	ended tied

OVERTIME RECORDS
Longest Touchdown Pass
99 Yards — Ron Jaworski to Mike Quick, Philadelphia 23, Atlanta 17 (11/10/85)
82 Yards — Tom Brady to Troy Brown, New England 19, Miami 13 (10/19/03)
76 Yards — Troy Aikman to Raghib Ismail, Dallas 41, Washington 35 (9/12/99)
Longest Touchdown Run
96 Yards — Garrison Hearst, San Francisco 36, New York Jets 30 (9/6/98)
60 Yards — Herschel Walker, Dallas 23, New England 17 (11/15/87)
46 Yards — Michael Vick, Atlanta 30, Minnesota 24 (12/1/02)
Longest Field Goal
53 Yards — Chris Jacke, Green Bay 23, San Francisco 20 (10/4/96)
52 Yards — Mike Cofer, Indianapolis 27, New York Jets 24 (9/10/95)
51 Yards — Greg Davis, New England 23, Indianapolis 20 (10/29/89); Greg Davis, Arizona 20, Pittsburgh 17 (10/30/94); Michael Husted, Tampa Bay 20, Minnesota 17 (10/15/95); Mike Vanderjagt, Indianapolis 23, Denver 20 (11/24/02)
Longest Touchdown Plays
99 Yards — (Pass) Ron Jaworski to Mike Quick, Philadelphia 23, Atlanta 17 (11/10/85)
96 Yards — (Run) Garrison Hearst, San Francisco 36, New York Jets 30 (9/6/98)
96 Yards — (Kickoff return) Chad Morton, New York Jets 37, Buffalo 31 (9/8/02)
95 Yards — (Kickoff return) Dave Williams, Chicago 23, Detroit 17 (11/27/80)
86 Yards — (Punt return) Tamarick Vanover, Kansas City 29, San Diego 23 (10/9/95)

NUMBER-ONE DRAFT CHOICES

Season	Date	Team	Player	Position	College
2005	April 23-24	San Francisco	Alex Smith	QB	Utah
2004	April 24-25	San Diego	Eli Manning	QB	Mississippi
2003	April 26-27	Cincinnati	Carson Palmer	QB	Southern California
2002	April 20-21	Houston	David Carr	QB	Fresno State
2001	April 21-22	Atlanta	Michael Vick	QB	Virginia Tech
2000	April 15-16	Cleveland	Courtney Brown	DE	Penn State
1999	April 17-18	Cleveland	Tim Couch	QB	Kentucky
1998	April 18-19	Indianapolis	Peyton Manning	QB	Tennessee
1997	April 19-20	St. Louis	Orlando Pace	T	Ohio State
1996	April 20-21	New York Jets	Keyshawn Johnson	WR	Southern California
1995	April 22-23	Cincinnati	Ki-Jana Carter	RB	Penn State
1994	April 24-25	Cincinnati	Dan Wilkinson	DT	Ohio State
1993	April 25-26	New England	Drew Bledsoe	QB	Washington State
1992	April 26-27	Indianapolis	Steve Emtman	DT	Washington
1991	April 21-22	Dallas	Russell Maryland	DT	Miami
1990	April 22-23	Indianapolis	Jeff George	QB	Illinois
1989	April 23-24	Dallas	Troy Aikman	QB	UCLA
1988	April 24-25	Atlanta	Aundray Bruce	LB	Auburn
1987	April 28-29	Tampa Bay	Vinny Testaverde	QB	Miami
1986	April 29-30	Tampa Bay	Bo Jackson	RB	Auburn
1985	April 30-May 1	Buffalo	Bruce Smith	DE	Virginia Tech
1984	May 1-2	New England	Irving Fryar	WR	Nebraska
1983	April 26-27	Baltimore	John Elway	QB	Stanford
1982	April 27-28	New England	Kenneth Sims	DT	Texas
1981	April 28-29	New Orleans	George Rogers	RB	South Carolina
1980	April 29-30	Detroit	Billy Sims	RB	Oklahoma
1979	May 3-4	Buffalo	Tom Cousineau	LB	Ohio State
1978	May 2-3	Houston	Earl Campbell	RB	Texas
1977	May 3-4	Tampa Bay	Ricky Bell	RB	Southern California
1976	April 8-9	Tampa Bay	Lee Roy Selmon	DE	Oklahoma
1975	January 28-29	Atlanta	Steve Bartkowski	QB	California
1974	January 29-30	Dallas	Ed Jones	DE	Tennessee State
1973	January 30-31	Houston	John Matuszak	DE	Tampa
1972	February 1-2	Buffalo	Walt Patulski	DE	Notre Dame
1971	January 28-29	New England	Jim Plunkett	QB	Stanford
1970	January 27-28	Pittsburgh	Terry Bradshaw	QB	Louisiana Tech
1969	January 28-29	Buffalo (AFL)	O.J. Simpson	RB	Southern California
1968	January 30-31	Minnesota	Ron Yary	T	Southern California
1967	March 14	Baltimore	Bubba Smith	DT	Michigan State
1966	November 27, 1965	Atlanta	Tommy Nobis	LB	Texas
	November 28, 1965	Miami (AFL)	Jim Grabowski	RB	Illinois
1965	November 28, 1964	New York Giants	Tucker Frederickson	RB	Auburn
	November 28, 1964	Houston (AFL)	Lawrence Elkins	E	Baylor
1964	December 2, 1963	San Francisco	Dave Parks	E	Texas Tech
	November 30, 1963	Boston (AFL)	Jack Concannon	QB	Boston College
1963	December 3, 1962	Los Angeles	Terry Baker	QB	Oregon State
	December 1, 1962	Kansas City (AFL)	Buck Buchanan	DT	Grambling
1962	December 4, 1961	Washington	Ernie Davis	RB	Syracuse
	December 2, 1961	Oakland (AFL)	Roman Gabriel	QB	North Carolina State
1961	December 27-28, 1960	Minnesota	Tommy Mason	RB	Tulane
	November 23, 1960	Buffalo (AFL)	Ken Rice	G	Auburn
1960	Secret Draft	Los Angeles	Billy Cannon	RB	Louisiana State
	November 22, December 2, 1959	(AFL had no formal first pick)			
1959	December 2, 1958	Green Bay	Randy Duncan	QB	Iowa
1958	December 2, 1957	Chicago Cardinals	King Hill	QB	Rice
1957	November 27, 1956	Green Bay	Paul Hornung	HB	Notre Dame
1956	November 29, 1955	Pittsburgh	Gary Glick	DB	Colorado A&M
1955	January 27-28	Baltimore	George Shaw	QB	Oregon
1954	January 28	Cleveland	Bobby Garrett	QB	Stanford
1953	January 22	San Francisco	Harry Babcock	E	Georgia
1952	January 17	Los Angeles	Bill Wade	QB	Vanderbilt

Season	Date	Team	Player	Position	College
1951	January 18-19	New York Giants	Kyle Rote	HB	Southern Methodist
1950	January 21-22	Detroit	Leon Hart	E	Notre Dame
1949	December 21, 1948	Philadelphia	Chuck Bednarik	C	Pennsylvania
1948	December 19, 1947	Washington	Harry Gilmer	QB	Alabama
1947	December 16, 1946	Chicago Bears	Bob Fenimore	HB	Oklahoma A&M
1946	January 14	Boston	Frank Dancewicz	QB	Notre Dame
1945	April 6	Chicago Cardinals	Charley Trippi	HB	Georgia
1944	April 19	Boston	Angelo Bertelli	QB	Notre Dame
1943	April 8	Detroit	Frank Sinkwich	HB	Georgia
1942	December 22, 1941	Pittsburgh	Bill Dudley	HB	Virginia
1941	December 10, 1940	Chicago Bears	Tom Harmon	HB	Michigan
1940	December 9, 1939	Chicago Cardinals	George Cafego	HB	Tennessee
1939	December 8, 1938	Chicago Cardinals	Ki Aldrich	C	Texas Christian
1938	December 12, 1937	Cleveland	Corbett Davis	FB	Indiana
1937	December 12, 1936	Philadelphia	Sam Francis	FB	Nebraska
1936	February 8	Philadelphia	Jay Berwanger	HB	Chicago

Note: From 1947 through 1958, the first selection in the draft was a Bonus pick, awarded to the winner of a random draw. That club, in turn, forfeited its last-round draft choice. The winner of the Bonus choice was eliminated from future draws. The system was abolished after 1958, by which time all clubs had received a Bonus choice.

NUMBER-ONE DRAFT CHOICES BY POSITION

Quarterbacks:	26
Running Backs:	23
Defenisve Linemen:	12
Wide Receivers:	6
Offensive Linemen:	5
Linebackers:	3
Defensive Backs:	1

FIRST-ROUND SELECTIONS

If club had no first-round selection, first player drafted is listed with round in parentheses.

ARIZONA CARDINALS
Year Player, College, Position
1936 Jim Lawrence, Texas Christian, B
1937 Ray Buivid, Marquette, B
1938 Jack Robbins, Arkansas, B
1939 Charles (Ki) Aldrich, TCU, C
1940 George Cafego, Tennessee, B
1941 John Kimbrough, Texas A&M, B
1942 Steve Lach, Duke, B
1943 Glenn Dobbs, Tulsa, B
1944 Pat Harder, Wisconsin, B
1945 Charley Trippi, Georgia, B
1946 Dub Jones, Louisiana State, B
1947 DeWitt (Tex) Coulter, Army, T
1948 Jim Spavital, Oklahoma A&M, B
1949 Bill Fischer, Notre Dame, G
1950 Jack Jennings, Ohio State, T (2)
1951 Jerry Groom, Notre Dame, C
1952 Ollie Matson, San Francisco, B
1953 Johnny Olszewski, California, B
1954 Lamar McHan, Arkansas, B
1955 Max Boydston, Oklahoma, E
1956 Joe Childress, Auburn, B
1957 Jerry Tubbs, Oklahoma, C
1958 King Hill, Rice, B
      John David Crow, Texas A&M, B
1959 Bill Stacy, Mississippi State, B
1960 George Izo, Notre Dame, QB
1961 Ken Rice, Auburn, T
1962 Fate Echols, Northwestern, DT
      Irv Goode, Kentucky, C
1963 Jerry Stovall, Louisiana State, S
      Don Brumm, Purdue, DE
1964 Ken Kortas, Louisville, DT
1965 Joe Namath, Alabama, QB
1966 Carl McAdams, Oklahoma, LB
1967 Dave Williams, Washington, WR
1968 MacArthur Lane, Utah State, RB
1969 Roger Wehrli, Missouri, DB
1970 Larry Stegent, Texas A&M, RB
1971 Norm Thompson, Utah, CB
1972 Bobby Moore, Oregon, RB-WR
1973 Dave Butz, Purdue, DT
1974 J.V. Cain, Colorado, TE
1975 Tim Gray, Texas A&M, DB
1976 Mike Dawson, Arizona, DT
1977 Steve Pisarkiewicz, Missouri, QB
1978 Steve Little, Arkansas, K
      Ken Greene, Washington State, DB
1979 Ottis Anderson, Miami, RB
1980 Curtis Greer, Michigan, DE
1981 E.J. Junior, Alabama, LB
1982 Luis Sharpe, UCLA, T
1983 Leonard Smith, McNeese St., DB
1984 Clyde Duncan, Tennessee, WR
1985 Freddie Joe Nunn, Mississippi, LB
1986 Anthony Bell, Michigan State, LB
1987 Kelly Stouffer, Colorado State, QB
1988 Ken Harvey, California, LB
1989 Eric Hill, Louisiana State, LB
      Joe Wolf, Boston College, G
1990 Anthony Thompson, Indiana, RB (2)
1991 Eric Swann, No College, DE
1992 Tony Sacca, Penn State, QB (2)

1993 Garrison Hearst, Georgia, RB
      Ernest Dye, South Carolina, T
1994 Jamir Miller, UCLA, LB
1995 Frank Sanders, Auburn, WR (2)
1996 Simeon Rice, Illinois, DE
1997 Tom Knight, Iowa, DB
1998 Andre Wadsworth, Florida St., DE
1999 David Boston, Ohio State, WR
      L.J. Shelton, Eastern Michigan, T
2000 Thomas Jones, Virginia, RB
2001 Leonard Davis, Texas, T
2002 Wendell Bryant, Wisconsin, DT
2003 Bryant Johnson, Penn State, WR
      Calvin Pace, Wake Forest, DE
2004 Larry Fitzgerald, Pittsburgh, WR
2005 Antrel Rolle, Miami, DB

ATLANTA FALCONS
Year Player, College, Position
1966 Tommy Nobis, Texas, LB
      Randy Johnson, Texas A&I, QB
1967 Leo Carroll, San Diego St., DE (2)
1968 Claude Humphrey, Tennessee St., DE
1969 George Kunz, Notre Dame, T
1970 John Small, Citadel, LB
1971 Joe Profit, Northeast Louisiana, RB
1972 Clarence Ellis, Notre Dame, DB
1973 Greg Marx, Notre Dame, DT (2)
1974 Gerald Tinker, Kent State, WR (2)
1975 Steve Bartkowski, California, QB
1976 Bubba Bean, Texas A&M, RB
1977 Warren Bryant, Kentucky, T
      Wilson Faumuina, San Jose St., DT
1978 Mike Kenn, Michigan, T
1979 Don Smith, Miami, DE
1980 Junior Miller, Nebraska, TE
1981 Bobby Butler, Florida State, DB
1982 Gerald Riggs, Arizona State, RB
1983 Mike Pitts, Alabama, DE
1984 Rick Bryan, Oklahoma, DT
1985 Bill Fralic, Pittsburgh, T
1986 Tony Casillas, Oklahoma, NT
      Tim Green, Syracuse, LB
1987 Chris Miller, Oregon, QB
1988 Aundray Bruce, Auburn, LB
1989 Deion Sanders, Florida State, DB
      Shawn Collins, No. Arizona, WR
1990 Steve Broussard, Washington St., RB
1991 Bruce Pickens, Nebraska, DB
      Mike Pritchard, Colorado, WR
1992 Bob Whitfield, Stanford, T
      Tony Smith, So. Mississippi, RB
1993 Lincoln Kennedy, Washington, T
1994 Bert Emanuel, Rice, WR (2)
1995 Devin Bush, Florida State, DB
1996 Shannon Brown, Alabama, DT (3)
1997 Michael Booker, Nebraska, DB
1998 Keith Brooking, Georgia Tech, LB
1999 Patrick Kerney, Virginia, DE
2000 Travis Claridge, So. California, T (2)
2001 Michael Vick, Virginia Tech, QB
2002 T.J. Duckett, Michigan State, RB
2003 Bryan Scott, Penn State, DB (2)
2004 DeAngelo Hall, Virginia Tech, DB
      Michael Jenkins, Ohio State, WR
2005 Roddy White, Ala.-Birmingham, WR

BALTIMORE RAVENS
Year Player, College, Position
1996 Jonathan Ogden, UCLA, T

      Ray Lewis, Miami, LB
1997 Peter Boulware, Florida State, DE
1998 Duane Starks, Miami, DB
1999 Chris McAlister, Arizona, DB
2000 Jamal Lewis, Tennessee, RB
      Travis Taylor, Florida, WR
2001 Todd Heap, Arizona State, TE
2002 Ed Reed, Miami, DB
2003 Terrell Suggs, Arizona State, DE
      Kyle Boller, California, QB
2004 Dwan Edwards, Oregon St., DT (2)
2005 Mark Clayton, Oklahoma, WR

BUFFALO BILLS
Year Player, College, Position
1960 Richie Lucas, Penn State, QB
1961 Ken Rice, Auburn, T
1962 Ernie Davis, Syracuse, RB
1963 Dave Behrman, Michigan State, C
1964 Carl Eller, Minnesota, DE
1965 Jim Davidson, Ohio State, T
1966 Mike Dennis, Mississippi, RB
1967 John Pitts, Arizona State, S
1968 Haven Moses, San Diego St., WR
1969 O.J. Simpson, So. California, RB
1970 Al Cowlings, So. California, DE
1971 J.D. Hill, Arizona State, WR
1972 Walt Patulski, Notre Dame, DE
1973 Paul Seymour, Michigan, TE
      Joe DeLamielleure, Michigan St., G
1974 Reuben Gant, Oklahoma State, TE
1975 Tom Ruud, Nebraska, LB
1976 Mario Clark, Oregon, DB
1977 Phil Dokes, Oklahoma State, DT
1978 Terry Miller, Oklahoma State, RB
1979 Tom Cousineau, Ohio State, LB
      Jerry Butler, Clemson, WR
1980 Jim Ritcher, North Carolina St., C
1981 Booker Moore, Penn State, RB
1982 Perry Tuttle, Clemson, WR
1983 Tony Hunter, Notre Dame, TE
      Jim Kelly, Miami, QB
1984 Greg Bell, Notre Dame, RB
1985 Bruce Smith, Virginia Tech, DE
      Derrick Burroughs, Memphis St., DB
1986 Ronnie Harmon, Iowa, RB
      Will Wolford, Vanderbilt, T
1987 Shane Conlan, Penn State, LB
1988 Thurman Thomas, Oklahoma St., RB (2)
1989 Don Beebe, Chadron, Neb., WR (3)
1990 James Williams, Fresno State, DB
1991 Henry Jones, Illinois, DB
1992 John Fina, Arizona, T
1993 Thomas Smith, North Carolina, DB
1994 Jeff Burris, Notre Dame, DB
1995 Ruben Brown, Pittsburgh, G
1996 Eric Moulds, Mississippi St., WR
1997 Antowain Smith, Houston, RB
1998 Sam Cowart, Florida State, LB (2)
1999 Antoine Winfield, Ohio State, DB
2000 Erik Flowers, Arizona State, DE
2001 Nate Clements, Ohio State, DB
2002 Mike Williams, Texas, T
2003 Willis McGahee, Miami, RB
2004 Lee Evans, Wisconsin, WR
      J.P. Losman, Tulane, QB
2005 Roscoe Parrish, Miami, WR (2)

CAROLINA PANTHERS
Year Player, College, Position
1995 Kerry Collins, Penn State, QB
    Tyrone Poole, Ft. Valley State, DB
    Blake Brockermeyer, Texas, T
1996 Tim Biakabutuka, Michigan, RB
1997 Rae Carruth, Colorado, WR
1998 Jason Peter, Nebraska, DT
1999 Chris Terry, Georgia, T (2)
2000 Rashard Anderson, Jackson St., DB
2001 Dan Morgan, Miami, LB
2002 Julius Peppers, North Carolina, DE
2003 Jordan Gross, Utah, T
2004 Chris Gamble, Ohio State, DB
2005 Thomas Davis, Georgia, DB

CHICAGO BEARS
Year Player, College, Position
1936 Joe Stydahar, West Virginia, T
1937 Les McDonald, Nebraska, E
1938 Joe Gray, Oregon State, B
1939 Sid Luckman, Columbia, QB
    Bill Osmanski, Holy Cross, B
1940 Clyde (Bulldog) Turner, Hardin-Simmons, C
1941 Tom Harmon, Michigan, B
    Norm Standlee, Stanford, B
    Don Scott, Ohio State, B
1942 Frankie Albert, Stanford, B
1943 Bob Steber, Missouri, B
1944 Ray Evans, Kansas, B
1945 Don Lund, Michigan, B
1946 Johnny Lujack, Notre Dame, QB
1947 Bob Fenimore, Oklahoma State, B
    Don Kindt, Wisconsin, B
1948 Bobby Layne, Texas, QB
    Max Bumgardner, Texas, E
1949 Dick Harris, Texas, C
1950 Chuck Hunsinger, Florida, B
    Fred Morrison, Ohio State, B
1951 Bob Williams, Notre Dame, B
    Billy Stone, Bradley, B
    Gene Schroeder, Virginia, E
1952 Jim Dooley, Miami, B
1953 Billy Anderson, Compton (Calif.) J.C., B
1954 Stan Wallace, Illinois, B
1955 Ron Drzewiecki, Marquette, B
1956 Menan (Tex) Schriewer, Texas, E
1957 Earl Leggett, Louisiana State, T
1958 Chuck Howley, West Virginia, G
1959 Don Clark, Ohio State, B
1960 Roger Davis, Syracuse, G
1961 Mike Ditka, Pittsburgh, E
1962 Ronnie Bull, Baylor, RB
1963 Dave Behrman, Michigan State, C
1964 Dick Evey, Tennessee, DT
1965 Dick Butkus, Illinois, LB
    Gale Sayers, Kansas, RB
    Steve DeLong, Tennessee, T
1966 George Rice, Louisiana State, DT
1967 Loyd Phillips, Arkansas, DE
1968 Mike Hull, Southern California, RB
1969 Rufus Mayes, Ohio State, T
1970 George Farmer, UCLA, WR (3)
1971 Joe Moore, Missouri, RB
1972 Lionel Antoine, Southern Illinois, T
    Craig Clemons, Iowa, DB
1973 Wally Chambers, Eastern Kentucky, DE
1974 Waymond Bryant, Tennessee St., LB
    Dave Gallagher, Michigan, DT
1975 Walter Payton, Jackson State, RB

1976 Dennis Lick, Wisconsin, T
1977 Ted Albrecht, California, T
1978 Brad Shearer, Texas, DT (3)
1979 Dan Hampton, Arkansas, DT
    Al Harris, Arizona State, DE
1980 Otis Wilson, Louisville, LB
1981 Keith Van Horne, So. California, T
1982 Jim McMahon, Brigham Young, QB
1983 Jim Covert, Pittsburgh, T
    Willie Gault, Tennessee, WR
1984 Wilber Marshall, Florida, LB
1985 William Perry, Clemson, DT
1986 Neal Anderson, Florida, RB
1987 Jim Harbaugh, Michigan, QB
1988 Brad Muster, Stanford, RB
    Wendell Davis, Louisiana St., WR
1989 Donnell Woolford, Clemson, DB
    Trace Armstrong, Florida, DE
1990 Mark Carrier, So. California, DB
1991 Stan Thomas, Texas, T
1992 Alonzo Spellman, Ohio State, DE
1993 Curtis Conway, So. California, WR
1994 John Thierry, Alcorn State, DE
1995 Rashaan Salaam, Colorado, RB
1996 Walt Harris, Mississippi State, DB
1997 John Allred, So. California, TE (2)
1998 Curtis Enis, Penn State, RB
1999 Cade McNown, UCLA, QB
2000 Brian Urlacher, New Mexico, LB
2001 David Terrell, Michigan, WR
2002 Marc Colombo, Boston College, T
2003 Michael Haynes, Penn State, DE
    Rex Grossman, Florida, QB
2004 Tommie Harris, Oklahoma, DT
2005 Cedric Benson, Texas, RB

CINCINNATI BENGALS
Year Player, College, Position
1968 Bob Johnson, Tennessee, C
1969 Greg Cook, Cincinnati, QB
1970 Mike Reid, Penn State, DT
1971 Vernon Holland, Tennessee St., T
1972 Sherman White, California, DE
1973 Isaac Curtis, San Diego State, WR
1974 Bill Kollar, Montana State, DT
1975 Glenn Cameron, Florida, LB
1976 Billy Brooks, Oklahoma, WR
    Archie Griffin, Ohio State, RB
1977 Eddie Edwards, Miami, DT
    Wilson Whitley, Houston, DT
    Mike Cobb, Michigan State, TE
1978 Ross Browner, Notre Dame, DT
    Blair Bush, Washington, C
1979 Jack Thompson, Washington St., QB
    Charles Alexander, Louisiana St., RB
1980 Anthony Muñoz, So. California, T
1981 David Verser, Kansas, WR
1982 Glen Collins, Mississippi State, DE
1983 Dave Rimington, Nebraska, C
1984 Ricky Hunley, Arizona, LB
    Pete Koch, Maryland, DE
    Brian Blados, North Carolina, T
1985 Eddie Brown, Miami, WR
    Emanuel King, Alabama, LB
1986 Joe Kelly, Washington, LB
    Tim McGee, Tennessee, WR
1987 Jason Buck, Brigham Young, DE
1988 Rickey Dixon, Oklahoma, DB
1989 Eric Ball, UCLA, RB (2)
1990 James Francis, Baylor, LB

1991 Alfred Williams, Colorado, LB
1992 David Klingler, Houston, QB
    Darryl Williams, Miami, DB
1993 John Copeland, Alabama, DE
1994 Dan Wilkinson, Ohio State, DT
1995 Ki-Jana Carter, Penn State, RB
1996 Willie Anderson, Auburn, T
1997 Reinard Wilson, Florida State, LB
1998 Takeo Spikes, Auburn, LB
    Brian Simmons, North Carolina, LB
1999 Akili Smith, Oregon, QB
2000 Peter Warrick, Florida State, WR
2001 Justin Smith, Missouri, DE
2002 Levi Jones, Arizona State, T
2003 Carson Palmer, Southern California, QB
2004 Chris Perry, Michigan, RB
2005 David Pollack, Georgia, LB

CLEVELAND BROWNS
Year Player, College, Position
1950 Ken Carpenter, Oregon State, B
1951 Ken Konz, Louisiana State, B
1952 Bert Rechichar, Tennessee, DB
    Harry Agganis, Boston U., QB
1953 Doug Atkins, Tennessee, DE
1954 Bobby Garrett, Stanford, QB
    John Bauer, Illinois, G
1955 Kurt Burris, Oklahoma, C
1956 Preston Carpenter, Arkansas, B
1957 Jim Brown, Syracuse, RB
1958 Jim Shofner, Texas Christian, DB
1959 Rich Kreitling, Illinois, DE
1960 Jim Houston, Ohio State, DE
1961 Bobby Crespino, Mississippi, TE
1962 Gary Collins, Maryland, WR
    Leroy Jackson, Western Illinois, RB
1963 Tom Hutchinson, Kentucky, WR
1964 Paul Warfield, Ohio State, WR
1965 James Garcia, Purdue, T (2)
1966 Milt Morin, Massachusetts, TE
1967 Bob Matheson, Duke, LB
1968 Marvin Upshaw, Trinity, Tex., DT-DE
1969 Ron Johnson, Michigan, RB
1970 Mike Phipps, Purdue, QB
    Bob McKay, Texas, T
1971 Clarence Scott, Kansas State, CB
1972 Thom Darden, Michigan, DB
1973 Steve Holden, Arizona State, WR
    Pete Adams, Southern California, T
1974 Billy Corbett, Johnson C. Smith, T (2)
1975 Mack Mitchell, Houston, DE
1976 Mike Pruitt, Purdue, RB
1977 Robert Jackson, Texas A&M, LB
1978 Clay Matthews, So. California, LB
    Ozzie Newsome, Alabama, TE
1979 Willis Adams, Houston, WR
1980 Charles White, So. California, RB
1981 Hanford Dixon, So. Mississippi, DB
1982 Chip Banks, So. California, LB
1983 Ron Brown, Arizona State, WR (2)
1984 Don Rogers, UCLA, DB
1985 Greg Allen, Florida State, RB (2)
1986 Webster Slaughter, San Diego St., WR (2)
1987 Mike Junkin, Duke, LB
1988 Clifford Charlton, Florida, LB
1989 Eric Metcalf, Texas, RB
1990 Leroy Hoard, Michigan, RB (2)
1991 Eric Turner, UCLA, DB
1992 Tommy Vardell, Stanford, RB
1993 Steve Everitt, Michigan, C

1994 Antonio Langham, Alabama, DB
     Derrick Alexander, Michigan, WR
1995 Craig Powell, Ohio State, LB
1999 Tim Couch, Kentucky, QB
2000 Courtney Brown, Penn State, DE
2001 Gerard Warren, Florida, DT
2002 William Green, Boston College, RB
2003 Jeff Faine, Norte Dame, C
2004 Kellen Winslow, Miami, TE
2005 Braylon Edwards, Michigan, WR

DALLAS COWBOYS
Year Player, College, Position
1960 None
1961 Bob Lilly, Texas Christian, DT
1962 Sonny Gibbs, TCU, QB (2)
1963 Lee Roy Jordan, Alabama, LB
1964 Scott Appleton, Texas, DT
1965 Craig Morton, California, QB
1966 John Niland, Iowa, G
1967 Phil Clark, Northwestern, DB (3)
1968 Dennis Homan, Alabama, WR
1969 Calvin Hill, Yale, RB
1970 Duane Thomas, West Texas St., RB
1971 Tody Smith, So. California, DE
1972 Bill Thomas, Boston College, RB
1973 Billy Joe DuPree, Michigan St., TE
1974 Ed (Too Tall) Jones, Tennessee St., DE
     Charley Young, North Carolina St., RB
1975 Randy White, Maryland, LB
     Thomas Henderson, Langston, LB
1976 Aaron Kyle, Wyoming, DB
1977 Tony Dorsett, Pittsburgh, RB
1978 Larry Bethea, Michigan State, DE
1979 Robert Shaw, Tennessee, C
1980 Bill Roe, Colorado, LB (3)
1981 Howard Richards, Missouri, T
1982 Rod Hill, Kentucky State, DB
1983 Jim Jeffcoat, Arizona State, DE
1984 Billy Cannon, Jr., Texas A&M, LB
1985 Kevin Brooks, Michigan, DE
1986 Mike Sherrard, UCLA, WR
1987 Danny Noonan, Nebraska, DT
1988 Michael Irvin, Miami, WR
1989 Troy Aikman, UCLA, QB
1990 Emmitt Smith, Florida, RB
1991 Russell Maryland, Miami, DT
     Alvin Harper, Tennessee, WR
     Kelvin Pritchett, Mississippi, DT
1992 Kevin Smith, Texas A&M, DB
     Robert Jones, East Carolina, LB
1993 Kevin Williams, Miami, WR (2)
1994 Shante Carver, Arizona State, DE
1995 Sherman Williams, Alabama, RB (2)
1996 Kavika Pittman, McNeese St., DE (2)
1997 David LaFleur, Louisiana State, TE
1998 Greg Ellis, North Carolina, DE
1999 Ebenezer Ekuban, North Carolina, DE
2000 Dwayne Goodrich, Tennessee, DB (2)
2001 Quincy Carter, Georgia, QB (2)
2002 Roy Williams, Oklahoma, DB
2003 Terence Newman, Kansas State, DB
2004 Julius Jones, RB, Notre Dame (2)
2005 Demarcus Ware, DE, Troy
     Marcus Spears, DE, Louisiana St.

DENVER BRONCOS
Year Player, College, Position
1960 Roger LeClerc, Trinity, Conn., C
1961 Bob Gaiters, New Mexico St., RB

1962 Merlin Olsen, Utah State, DT
1963 Kermit Alexander, UCLA, CB
1964 Bob Brown, Nebraska, T
1965 Dick Butkus, Illinois, LB (2)
1966 Jerry Shay, Purdue, DT
1967 Floyd Little, Syracuse, RB
1968 Curley Culp, Arizona State, DE (2)
1969 Grady Cavness, Texas-El Paso, DB (2)
1970 Bob Anderson, Colorado, RB
1971 Marv Montgomery, So. California, T
1972 Riley Odoms, Houston, TE
1973 Otis Armstrong, Purdue, RB
1974 Randy Gradishar, Ohio State, LB
1975 Louis Wright, San Jose State, DB
1976 Tom Glassic, Virginia, G
1977 Steve Schindler, Boston College, G
1978 Don Latimer, Miami, DT
1979 Kelvin Clark, Nebraska, T
1980 Rulon Jones, Utah State, DE (2)
1981 Dennis Smith, So. California, DB
1982 Gerald Willhite, San Jose St., RB
1983 Chris Hinton, Northwestern, G
1984 Andre Townsend, Mississippi, DE (2)
1985 Steve Sewell, Oklahoma, RB
1986 Jim Juriga, Illinois, T (4)
1987 Ricky Nattiel, Florida, WR
1988 Ted Gregory, Syracuse, NT
1989 Steve Atwater, Arkansas, DB
1990 Alton Montgomery, Houston, DB (2)
1991 Mike Croel, Nebraska, LB
1992 Tommy Maddox, UCLA, QB
1993 Dan Williams, Toledo, DE
1994 Allen Aldridge, Houston, LB (2)
1995 Jamie Brown, Florida A&M, T (4)
1996 John Mobley, Kutztown, LB
1997 Trevor Pryce, Clemson, DT
1998 Marcus Nash, Tennessee, WR
1999 Al Wilson, Tennessee, LB
2000 Deltha O'Neal, California, DB
2001 Willie Middlebrooks, Minnesota, DB
2002 Ashley Lelie, Hawaii, WR
2003 George Foster, Georgia, T
2004 D.J. Williams, Miami, LB
2005 Darrent Wiliams, Oklahoma St., DB (2)

DETROIT LIONS
Year Player, College, Position
1936 Sid Wagner, Michigan State, G
1937 Lloyd Cardwell, Nebraska, B
1938 Alex Wojciechowicz, Fordham, C
1939 John Pingel, Michigan State, B
1940 Doyle Nave, Southern California, B
1941 Jim Thomason, Texas A&M, B
1942 Bob Westfall, Michigan, B
1943 Frank Sinkwich, Georgia, B
1944 Otto Graham, Northwestern, B
1945 Frank Szymanski, Notre Dame, C
1946 Bill Dellastatious, Missouri, B
1947 Glenn Davis, Army, B
1948 Y.A. Tittle, Louisiana State, B
1949 John Rauch, Georgia, B
1950 Leon Hart, Notre Dame, E
     Joe Watson, Rice, C
1951 Dick Stanfel, San Francisco, G (2)
1952 Yale Lary, Texas A&M, B (3)
1953 Harley Sewell, Texas, G
1954 Dick Chapman, Rice, T
1955 Dave Middleton, Auburn, B
1956 Hopalong Cassady, Ohio State, B
1957 Bill Glass, Baylor, G

1958 Alex Karras, Iowa, T
1959 Nick Pietrosante, Notre Dame, B
1960 John Robinson, Louisiana State, S
1961 Danny LaRose, Missouri, T (2)
1962 John Hadl, Kansas, QB
1963 Daryl Sanders, Ohio State, T
1964 Pete Beathard, So. California, QB
1965 Tom Nowatzke, Indiana, RB
1966 Nick Eddy, Notre Dame, RB (2)
1967 Mel Farr, UCLA, RB
1968 Greg Landry, Massachusetts, QB
     Earl McCullouch, So. California, WR
1969 Altie Taylor, Utah State, RB (2)
1970 Steve Owens, Oklahoma, RB
1971 Bob Bell, Cincinnati, DT
1972 Herb Orvis, Colorado, DE
1973 Ernie Price, Texas A&I, DE
1974 Ed O'Neil, Penn State, LB
1975 Lynn Boden, South Dakota St., G
1976 James Hunter, Grambling, DB
     Lawrence Gaines, Wyoming, RB
1977 Walt Williams, New Mexico St., DB (2)
1978 Luther Bradley, Notre Dame, DB
1979 Keith Dorney, Penn State, T
1980 Billy Sims, Oklahoma, RB
1981 Mark Nichols, San Jose State, WR
1982 Jimmy Williams, Nebraska, LB
1983 James Jones, Florida, RB
1984 David Lewis, California, TE
1985 Lomas Brown, Florida, T
1986 Chuck Long, Iowa, QB
1987 Reggie Rogers, Washington, DE
1988 Bennie Blades, Miami, DB
1989 Barry Sanders, Oklahoma St., RB
1990 Andre Ware, Houston, QB
1991 Herman Moore, Virginia, WR
1992 Robert Porcher, South Carolina St., DE
1993 Ryan McNeil, Miami, DB (2)
1994 Johnnie Morton, So. California, WR
1995 Luther Elliss, Utah, DT
1996 Reggie Brown, Texas A&M, LB
     Jeff Hartings, Penn State, G
1997 Bryant Westbrook, Texas, DB
1998 Terry Fair, Tennessee, DB
1999 Chris Claiborne, So. California, LB
     Aaron Gibson, Wisconsin, T
2000 Stockar McDougle, Oklahoma, T
2001 Jeff Backus, Michigan, T
2002 Joey Harrington, Oregon, QB
2003 Charles Rogers, Michigan State, WR
2004 Roy Williams, Texas, WR
     Kevin Jones, Virginia Tech, RB
2005 Mike Wiliams, So. California, WR

GREEN BAY PACKERS
Year Player, College, Position
1936 Russ Letlow, San Francisco, G
1937 Eddie Jankowski, Wisconsin, B
1938 Cecil Isbell, Purdue, B
1939 Larry Buhler, Minnesota, B
1940 Harold Van Every, Minnesota, B
1941 George Paskvan, Wisconsin, B
1942 Urban Odson, Minnesota, B
1943 Dick Wildung, Minnesota, T
1944 Merv Pregulman, Michigan, G
1945 Walt Schlinkman, Texas Tech, B
1946 Johnny Strzykalski, Marquette, B
1947 Ernie Case, UCLA, B
1948 Earl (Jug) Girard, Wisconsin, B
1949 Stan Heath, Nevada, B

1950 Clayton Tonnemaker, Minnesota, C
1951 Bob Gain, Kentucky, T
1952 Babe Parilli, Kentucky, QB
1953 Al Carmichael, So. California, B
1954 Art Hunter, Notre Dame, T
     Veryl Switzer, Kansas State, B
1955 Tom Bettis, Purdue, G
1956 Jack Losch, Miami, B
1957 Paul Hornung, Notre Dame, B
     Ron Kramer, Michigan, E
1958 Dan Currie, Michigan State, C
1959 Randy Duncan, Iowa, B
1960 Tom Moore, Vanderbilt, RB
1961 Herb Adderley, Michigan State, CB
1962 Earl Gros, Louisiana State, RB
1963 Dave Robinson, Penn State, LB
1964 Lloyd Voss, Nebraska, DT
1965 Donny Anderson, Texas Tech, RB
     Lawrence Elkins, Baylor, E
1966 Jim Grabowski, Illinois, RB
     Gale Gillingham, Minnesota, T
1967 Bob Hyland, Boston College, C
     Don Horn, San Diego State, QB
1968 Fred Carr, Texas-El Paso, LB
     Bill Lueck, Arizona, G
1969 Rich Moore, Villanova, DT
1970 Mike McCoy, Notre Dame, DT
     Rich McGeorge, Elon, TE
1971 John Brockington, Ohio State, RB
1972 Willie Buchanon, San Diego St., DB
     Jerry Tagge, Nebraska, QB
1973 Barry Smith, Florida State, WR
1974 Barty Smith, Richmond, RB
1975 Bill Bain, So. California, G (2)
1976 Mark Koncar, Colorado, T
1977 Mike Butler, Kansas, DE
     Ezra Johnson, Morris Brown, DE
1978 James Lofton, Stanford, WR
     John Anderson, Michigan, LB
1979 Eddie Lee Ivery, Georgia Tech, RB
1980 Bruce Clark, Penn State, DE
     George Cumby, Oklahoma, LB
1981 Rich Campbell, California, QB
1982 Ron Hallstrom, Iowa, G
1983 Tim Lewis, Pittsburgh, DB
1984 Alphonso Carreker, Florida St., DE
1985 Ken Ruettgers, So. California, T
1986 Kenneth Davis, TCU, RB (2)
1987 Brent Fullwood, Auburn, RB
1988 Sterling Sharpe, South Carolina, WR
1989 Tony Mandarich, Michigan State, T
1990 Tony Bennett, Mississippi, LB
     Darrell Thompson, Minnesota, RB
1991 Vinnie Clark, Ohio State, DB
1992 Terrell Buckley, Florida State, DB
1993 Wayne Simmons, Clemson, LB
     George Teague, Alabama, DB
1994 Aaron Taylor, Notre Dame, T
1995 Craig Newsome, Arizona State, DB
1996 John Michels, Southern California, T
1997 Ross Verba, Iowa, T
1998 Vonnie Holliday, North Carolina, DT
1999 Antuan Edwards, Clemson, DB
2000 Bubba Franks, Miami, TE
2001 Jamal Reynolds, Florida State, DE
2002 Javon Walker, Florida State, WR
2003 Nick Barnett, Oregon State, LB
2004 Ahmad Carroll, Arkansas, DB
2005 Aaron Rodgers, California, QB

HOUSTON TEXANS
Year Player, College, Position
2002 David Carr, Fresno State, QB
2003 Andre Johnson, Miami, WR
2004 Dunta Robinson, South Carolina, DB
     Jason Babin, Western Michigan, LB
2005 Travis Johnson, Florida State, DE

INDIANAPOLIS COLTS
Year Player, College, Position
1953 Billy Vessels, Oklahoma, B
1954 Cotton Davidson, Baylor, B
1955 George Shaw, Oregon, B
     Alan Ameche, Wisconsin, FB
1956 Lenny Moore, Penn State, B
1957 Jim Parker, Ohio State, G
1958 Lenny Lyles, Louisville, B
1959 Jackie Burkett, Auburn, C
1960 Ron Mix, Southern California, T
1961 Tom Matte, Ohio State, RB
1962 Wendell Harris, Louisiana State, S
1963 Bob Vogel, Ohio State, T
1964 Marv Woodson, Indiana, CB
1965 Mike Curtis, Duke, LB
1966 Sam Ball, Kentucky, T
1967 Bubba Smith, Michigan State, DT
     Jim Detwiler, Michigan, RB
1968 John Williams, Minnesota, G
1969 Eddie Hinton, Oklahoma, WR
1970 Norman Bulaich, Texas Christian, RB
1971 Don McCauley, North Carolina, RB
     Leonard Dunlap, North Texas St., DB
1972 Tom Drougas, Oregon, T
1973 Bert Jones, Louisiana State, QB
     Joe Ehrmann, Syracuse, DT
1974 John Dutton, Nebraska, DE
     Roger Carr, Louisiana Tech, WR
1975 Ken Huff, North Carolina, G
1976 Ken Novak, Purdue, DT
1977 Randy Burke, Kentucky, WR
1978 Reese McCall, Auburn, TE
1979 Barry Krauss, Alabama, LB
1980 Curtis Dickey, Texas A&M, RB
     Derrick Hatchett, Texas, DB
1981 Randy McMillan, Pittsburgh, RB
     Donnell Thompson, North Carolina, DT
1982 Johnie Cooks, Mississippi St., LB
     Art Schlichter, Ohio State, QB
1983 John Elway, Stanford, QB
1984 Leonard Coleman, Vanderbilt, DB
     Ron Solt, Maryland, G
1985 Duane Bickett, So. California, LB
1986 Jon Hand, Alabama, DE
1987 Cornelius Bennett, Alabama, LB
1988 Chris Chandler, Washington, QB (3)
1989 Andre Rison, Michigan State, WR
1990 Jeff George, Illinois, QB
1991 Shane Curry, Miami, DE (2)
1992 Steve Emtman, Washington, DT
     Quentin Coryatt, Texas A&M, LB
1993 Sean Dawkins, California, WR
1994 Marshall Faulk, San Diego St., RB
     Trev Alberts, Nebraska, LB
1995 Ellis Johnson, Florida, DT
1996 Marvin Harrison, Syracuse, WR
1997 Tarik Glenn, California, T
1998 Peyton Manning, Tennessee, QB
1999 Edgerrin James, Miami, RB
2000 Rob Morris, Brigham Young, LB
2001 Reggie Wayne, Miami, WR

2002 Dwight Freeney, Syracuse, DE
2003 Dallas Clark, Iowa, TE
2004 Bob Sanders, Iowa, DB (2)
2005 Marlin Jackson, Michigan, DB

JACKSONVILLE JAGUARS
Year Player, College, Position
1995 Tony Boselli, Southern California, T
     James Stewart, Tennessee, RB
1996 Kevin Hardy, Illinois, LB
1997 Renaldo Wynn, Notre Dame, DT
1998 Fred Taylor, Florida, RB
     Donovin Darius, Syracuse, DB
1999 Fernando Bryant, Alabama, DB
2000 R. Jay Soward, So. California, WR
2001 Marcus Stroud, Georgia, DT
2002 John Henderson, Tennessee, DT
2003 Byron Leftwich, Marshall, QB
2004 Reggie Williams, Washington, WR
2005 Matt Jones, Arkansas, WR

KANSAS CITY CHIEFS
Year Player, College, Position
1960 Don Meredith, So. Methodist, QB
1961 E.J. Holub, Texas Tech, C
1962 Ronnie Bull, Baylor, RB
1963 Buck Buchanan, Grambling, DT
     Ed Budde, Michigan State, G
1964 Pete Beathard, So. California, QB
1965 Gale Sayers, Kansas, RB
1966 Aaron Brown, Minnesota, DE
1967 Gene Trosch, Miami, DE-DT
1968 Mo Moorman, Texas A&M, G
     George Daney, Texas-El Paso, G
1969 Jim Marsalis, Tennessee State, CB
1970 Sid Smith, Southern California, T
1971 Elmo Wright, Houston, WR
1972 Jeff Kinney, Nebraska, RB
1973 Gary Butler, Rice, TE (2)
1974 Woody Green, Arizona State, RB
1975 Elmore Stephens, Kentucky, TE (2)
1976 Rod Walters, Iowa, G
1977 Gary Green, Baylor, DB
1978 Art Still, Kentucky, DE
1979 Mike Bell, Colorado State, DE
     Steve Fuller, Clemson, QB
1980 Brad Budde, Southern California, G
1981 Willie Scott, South Carolina, TE
1982 Anthony Hancock, Tennessee, WR
1983 Todd Blackledge, Penn State, QB
1984 Bill Maas, Pittsburgh, DT
     John Alt, Iowa, T
1985 Ethan Horton, North Carolina, RB
1986 Brian Jozwiak, West Virginia, T
1987 Paul Palmer, Temple, RB
1988 Neil Smith, Nebraska, DE
1989 Derrick Thomas, Alabama, LB
1990 Percy Snow, Michigan State, LB
1991 Harvey Williams, Louisiana St., RB
1992 Dale Carter, Tennessee, DB
1993 Will Shields, Nebraska, G (3)
1994 Greg Hill, Texas A&M, RB
1995 Trezelle Jenkins, Michigan, T
1996 Jerome Woods, Memphis, DB
1997 Tony Gonzalez, California, TE
1998 Victor Riley, Auburn, T
1999 John Tait, Brigham Young, T
2000 Sylvester Morris, Jackson St., WR
2001 Eric Downing, Syracuse, DT (3)
2002 Ryan Sims, North Carolina, DT

2003 Larry Johnson, Penn State, RB
2004 Junior Siavii, Oregon, DT (2)
2005 Derrick Johnson, Texas, LB

MIAMI DOLPHINS
Year Player, College, Position
1966 Jim Grabowski, Illinois, RB
    Rick Norton, Kentucky, QB
1967 Bob Griese, Purdue, QB
1968 Larry Csonka, Syracuse, RB
    Doug Crusan, Indiana, T
1969 Bill Stanfill, Georgia, DE
1970 Jim Mandich, Michigan, TE (2)
1971 Otto Stowe, Iowa State, WR (2)
1972 Mike Kadish, Notre Dame, DT
1973 Chuck Bradley, Oregon, C (2)
1974 Donald Reese, Jackson State, DE
1975 Darryl Carlton, Tampa, T
1976 Larry Gordon, Arizona State, LB
    Kim Bokamper, San Jose State, LB
1977 A.J. Duhe, Louisiana State, DT
1978 Guy Benjamin, Stanford, QB (2)
1979 Jon Giesler, Michigan, T
1980 Don McNeal, Alabama, DB
1981 David Overstreet, Oklahoma, RB
1982 Roy Foster, Southern California, G
1983 Dan Marino, Pittsburgh, QB
1984 Jackie Shipp, Oklahoma, LB
1985 Lorenzo Hampton, Florida, RB
1986 John Offerdahl, Western Michigan, LB (2)
1987 John Bosa, Boston College, DE
1988 Eric Kumerow, Ohio State, DE
1989 Sammie Smith, Florida State, RB
    Louis Oliver, Florida, DB
1990 Richmond Webb, Texas A&M, T
1991 Randal Hill, Miami, WR
1992 Troy Vincent, Wisconsin, DB
    Marco Coleman, Georgia Tech, LB
1993 O.J. McDuffie, Penn State, WR
1994 Tim Bowens, Mississippi, DT
1995 Billy Milner, Houston, T
1996 Daryl Gardener, Baylor, DT
1997 Yatil Green, Miami, WR
1998 John Avery, Mississippi, RB
1999 J.J. Johnson, Mississippi St., RB (2)
2000 Todd Wade, Mississippi, T (2)
2001 Jamar Fletcher, Wisconsin, DB
2002 Seth McKinney, Texas A&M, C (3)
2003 Eddie Moore, Tennessee, LB (2)
2004 Vernon Carey, Miami, T
2005 Ronnie Brown, Auburn, RB

MINNESOTA VIKINGS
Year Player, College, Position
1961 Tommy Mason, Tulane, RB
1962 Bill Miller, Miami, WR (3)
1963 Jim Dunaway, Mississippi, T
1964 Carl Eller, Minnesota, DE
1965 Jack Snow, Notre Dame, WR
1966 Jerry Shay, Purdue, DT
1967 Clint Jones, Michigan State, RB
    Gene Washington, Michigan St., WR
    Alan Page, Notre Dame, DT
1968 Ron Yary, Southern California, T
1969 Ed White, California, G (2)
1970 John Ward, Oklahoma State, DT
1971 Leo Hayden, Ohio State, RB
1972 Jeff Siemon, Stanford, LB
1973 Chuck Foreman, Miami, RB
1974 Fred McNeill, UCLA, LB

Steve Riley, Southern California, T
1975 Mark Mullaney, Colorado State, DE
1976 James White, Oklahoma State, DT
1977 Tommy Kramer, Rice, QB
1978 Randy Holloway, Pittsburgh, DE
1979 Ted Brown, North Carolina St., RB
1980 Doug Martin, Washington, DT
1981 Mardye McDole, Mississippi St., WR (2)
1982 Darrin Nelson, Stanford, RB
1983 Joey Browner, So. California, DB
1984 Keith Millard, Washington St., DE
1985 Chris Doleman, Pittsburgh, LB
1986 Gerald Robinson, Auburn, DE
1987 D.J. Dozier, Penn State, RB
1988 Randall McDaniel, Arizona State, G
1989 David Braxton, Wake Forest, LB (2)
1990 Mike Jones, Texas A&M, TE (3)
1991 Carlos Jenkins, Michigan St., LB (3)
1992 Robert Harris, Southern Univ., DE (2)
1993 Robert Smith, Ohio State, RB
1994 DeWayne Washington, N. Carolina St., DB
    Todd Steussie, California, T
1995 Derrick Alexander, Florida St., DE
    Korey Stringer, Ohio State, T
1996 Duane Clemons, California, DE
1997 Dwayne Rudd, Alabama, LB
1998 Randy Moss, Marshall, WR
1999 Daunte Culpepper, Central Florida, QB
    Dimitrius Underwood, Michigan St., DE
2000 Chris Hovan, Boston College, DT
2001 Michael Bennett, Wisconsin, RB
2002 Bryant McKinnie, Miami, T
2003 Kevin Williams, Oklahoma State, DT
2004 Kenechi Udeze, Southern California, DE
2005 Troy Williamson, South Carolina, WR
    Erasmus James, Wisconsin, DE

NEW ENGLAND PATRIOTS
Year Player, College, Position
1960 Ron Burton, Northwestern, RB
1961 Tommy Mason, Tulane, RB
1962 Gary Collins, Maryland, WR
1963 Art Graham, Boston College, WR
1964 Jack Concannon, Boston College, QB
1965 Jerry Rush, Michigan State, WR
1966 Karl Singer, Purdue, T
1967 John Charles, Purdue, S
1968 Dennis Byrd, North Carolina St., DE
1969 Ron Sellers, Florida State, WR
1970 Phil Olsen, Utah State, DE
1971 Jim Plunkett, Stanford, QB
1972 Tom Reynolds, San Diego St., WR (2)
1973 John Hannah, Alabama, G
    Sam Cunningham, So. California, RB
    Darryl Stingley, Purdue, WR
1974 Steve Corbett, Boston College, G (2)
1975 Russ Francis, Oregon, TE
1976 Mike Haynes, Arizona State, DB
    Pete Brock, Colorado, C
    Tim Fox, Ohio State, DB
1977 Raymond Clayborn, Texas, DB
    Stanley Morgan, Tennessee, WR
1978 Bob Cryder, Alabama, G
1979 Rick Sanford, South Carolina, DB
1980 Roland James, Tennessee, DB
    Vagas Ferguson, Notre Dame, RB
1981 Brian Holloway, Stanford, T
1982 Kenneth Sims, Texas, DT
    Lester Williams, Miami, DT
1983 Tony Eason, Illinois, QB

1984 Irving Fryar, Nebraska, WR
1985 Trevor Matich, Brigham Young, C
1986 Reggie Dupard, So. Methodist, RB
1987 Bruce Armstrong, Louisville, T
1988 John Stephens, Northwestern St., La., RB
1989 Hart Lee Dykes, Oklahoma St., WR
1990 Chris Singleton, Arizona, LB
    Ray Agnew, North Carolina St., DE
1991 Pat Harlow, Southern California, T
    Leonard Russell, Arizona St., RB
1992 Eugene Chung, Virginia Tech, T
1993 Drew Bledsoe, Washington St., QB
1994 Willie McGinest, So. California, DE
1995 Ty Law, Michigan, DB
1996 Terry Glenn, Ohio State, WR
1997 Chris Canty, Kansas State, DB
1998 Robert Edwards, Georgia, RB
    Tebucky Jones, Syracuse, DB
1999 Damien Woody, Boston College, C
    Andy Katzenmoyer, Ohio State, LB
2000 Adrian Klemm, Hawaii, T (2)
2001 Richard Seymour, Georgia, DT
2002 Daniel Graham, Colorado, TE
2003 Ty Warren, Texas A&M, DT
2004 Vince Wilfork, Miami, DT
    Ben Watson, Georgia, TE
2005 Logan Mankins, Fresno State, G

NEW ORLEANS SAINTS
Year Player, College, Position
1967 Les Kelley, Alabama, RB
1968 Kevin Hardy, Notre Dame, DE
1969 John Shinners, Xavier, G
1970 Ken Burrough, Texas Southern, WR
1971 Archie Manning, Mississippi, QB
1972 Royce Smith, Georgia, G
1973 Derland Moore, Oklahoma, DE (2)
1974 Rick Middleton, Ohio State, LB
1975 Larry Burton, Purdue, WR
    Kurt Schumacher, Ohio State, T
1976 Chuck Muncie, California, RB
1977 Joe Campbell, Maryland, DE
1978 Wes Chandler, Florida, WR
1979 Russell Erxleben, Texas, P-K
1980 Stan Brock, Colorado, T
1981 George Rogers, South Carolina, RB
1982 Lindsay Scott, Georgia, WR
1983 Steve Korte, Arkansas, G (2)
1984 James Geathers, Wichita State, DE
1985 Alvin Toles, Tennessee, LB
1986 Jim Dombrowski, Virginia, T
1987 Shawn Knight, Brigham Young, DT
1988 Craig Heyward, Pittsburgh, RB
1989 Wayne Martin, Arkansas, DE
1990 Renaldo Turnbull, West Virginia, DE
1991 Wesley Carroll, Miami, WR (2)
1992 Vaughn Dunbar, Indiana, RB
1993 Willie Roaf, Louisiana Tech, T
    Irv Smith, Notre Dame, TE
1994 Joe Johnson, Louisville, DE
1995 Mark Fields, Washington State, LB
1996 Alex Molden, Oregon, DB
1997 Chris Naeole, Colorado, G
1998 Kyle Turley, San Diego State, T
1999 Ricky Williams, Texas, RB
2000 Darren Howard, Kansas St., DE (2)
2001 Deuce McAllister, Mississippi, RB
2002 Donte' Stallworth, Tennessee, WR
    Charles Grant, Georgia, DE
2003 Johnathan Sullivan, Georgia, DT

2004 Will Smith, Ohio State, DE
2005 Jammal Brown, Oklahoma, T

NEW YORK GIANTS
Year Player, College, Position
1936 Art Lewis, Ohio U., T
1937 Ed Widseth, Minnesota, T
1938 George Karamatic, Gonzaga, B
1939 Walt Neilson, Arizona, B
1940 Grenville Lansdell, So. California, B
1941 George Franck, Minnesota, B
1942 Merle Hapes, Mississippi, B
1943 Steve Filipowicz, Fordham, B
1944 Billy Hillenbrand, Indiana, B
1945 Elmer Barbour, Wake Forest, B
1946 George Connor, Notre Dame, T
1947 Vic Schwall, Northwestern, B
1948 Tony Minisi, Pennsylvania, B
1949 Paul Page, Southern Methodist, B
1950 Travis Tidwell, Auburn, B
1951 Kyle Rote, Southern Methodist, B
       Jim Spavital, Oklahoma A&M, B
1952 Frank Gifford, Southern California, B
1953 Bobby Marlow, Alabama, B
1954 Ken Buck, Pacific, C (2)
1955 Joe Heap, Notre Dame, B
1956 Henry Moore, Arkansas, B (2)
1957 Sam DeLuca, South Carolina, T (2)
1958 Phil King, Vanderbilt, B
1959 Lee Grosscup, Utah, B
1960 Lou Cordileone, Clemson, G
1961 Bruce Tarbox, Syracuse, G (2)
1962 Jerry Hillebrand, Colorado, LB
1963 Frank Lasky, Florida, T (2)
1964 Joe Don Looney, Oklahoma, RB
1965 Tucker Frederickson, Auburn, RB
1966 Francis Peay, Missouri, T
1967 Louis Thompson, Alabama, DT (4)
1968 Dick Buzin, Penn State, T (2)
1969 Fred Dryer, San Diego State, DE
1970 Jim Files, Oklahoma, LB
1971 Rocky Thompson, West Texas St., WR
1972 Eldridge Small, Texas A&I, DB
       Larry Jacobson, Nebraska, DE
1973 Brad Van Pelt, Michigan St., LB (2)
1974 John Hicks, Ohio State, G
1975 Al Simpson, Colorado State, T (2)
1976 Troy Archer, Colorado, DE
1977 Gary Jeter, Southern California, DT
1978 Gordon King, Stanford, T
1979 Phil Simms, Morehead State, QB
1980 Mark Haynes, Colorado, DB
1981 Lawrence Taylor, North Carolina, LB
1982 Butch Woolfolk, Michigan, RB
1983 Terry Kinard, Clemson, DB
1984 Carl Banks, Michigan State, LB
       William Roberts, Ohio State, T
1985 George Adams, Kentucky, RB
1986 Eric Dorsey, Notre Dame, DE
1987 Mark Ingram, Michigan State, WR
1988 Eric Moore, Indiana, T
1989 Brian Williams, Minnesota, C-G
1990 Rodney Hampton, Georgia, RB
1991 Jarrod Bunch, Michigan, RB
1992 Derek Brown, Notre Dame, TE
1993 Michael Strahan, Texas Southern, DE (2)
1994 Thomas Lewis, Indiana, WR
1995 Tyrone Wheatley, Michigan, RB
1996 Cedric Jones, Oklahoma, DE
1997 Ike Hilliard, Florida, WR

1998 Shaun Williams, UCLA, DB
1999 Luke Petitgout, Notre Dame, T
2000 Ron Dayne, Wisconsin, RB
2001 Will Allen, Syracuse, DB
2002 Jeremy Shockey, Miami, TE
2003 William Joseph, Miami, DT
2004 Philip Rivers, North Carolina St., QB
2005 Corey Webster, Louisiana St., DB (2)

NEW YORK JETS
Year Player, College, Position
1960 George Izo, Notre Dame, QB
1961 Tom Brown, Minnesota, G
1962 Sandy Stephens, Minnesota, QB
1963 Jerry Stovall, Louisiana State, S
1964 Matt Snell, Ohio State, RB
1965 Joe Namath, Alabama, QB
       Tom Nowatzke, Indiana, RB
1966 Bill Yearby, Michigan, DT
1967 Paul Seiler, Notre Dame, T
1968 Lee White, Weber State, RB
1969 Dave Foley, Ohio State, T
1970 Steve Tannen, Florida, CB
1971 John Riggins, Kansas, RB
1972 Jerome Barkum, Jackson St., WR
       Mike Taylor, Michigan, LB
1973 Burgess Owens, Miami, DB
1974 Carl Barzilauskas, Indiana, DT
1975 Anthony Davis, So. California, RB (2)
1976 Richard Todd, Alabama, QB
1977 Marvin Powell, So. California, T
1978 Chris Ward, Ohio State, T
1979 Marty Lyons, Alabama, DE
1980 Johnny (Lam) Jones, Texas, WR
1981 Freeman McNeil, UCLA, RB
1982 Bob Crable, Notre Dame, LB
1983 Ken O'Brien, Cal-Davis, QB
1984 Russell Carter, So. Methodist, DB
       Ron Faurot, Arkansas, DE
1985 Al Toon, Wisconsin, WR
1986 Mike Haight, Iowa, T
1987 Roger Vick, Texas A&M, RB
1988 Dave Cadigan, So. California, T
1989 Jeff Lageman, Virginia, LB
1990 Blair Thomas, Penn State, RB
1991 Browning Nagle, Louisville, QB (2)
1992 Johnny Mitchell, Nebraska, TE
1993 Marvin Jones, Florida State, LB
1994 Aaron Glenn, Texas A&M, DB
1995 Kyle Brady, Penn State, TE
       Hugh Douglas, Central St., Ohio, DE
1996 Keyshawn Johnson, So. California, WR
1997 James Farrior, Virginia, LB
1998 Dorian Boose, Washington St., DE (2)
1999 Randy Thomas, Mississippi St., G (2)
2000 Shaun Ellis, Tennessee, DE
       John Abraham, South Carolina, LB
       Chad Pennington, Marshall, QB
       Anthony Becht, West Virginia, TE
2001 Santana Moss, Miami, WR
2002 Bryan Thomas, Ala.-Birmingham, DE
2003 Dewayne Robertson, Kentucky, DT
2004 Jonathan Vilma, Miami, LB
2005 Mike Nugent, Ohio State, K (2)

OAKLAND RAIDERS
Year Player, College, Position
1960 Dale Hackbart, Wisconsin, CB
1961 Joe Rutgens, Illinois, DT
1962 Roman Gabriel, North Carolina St., QB

1963 George Wilson, Alabama, RB (6)
1964 Tony Lorick, Arizona State, RB
1965 Harry Schuh, Memphis State, T
1966 Rodger Bird, Kentucky, S
1967 Gene Upshaw, Texas A&I, G
1968 Eldridge Dickey, Tennessee St., QB
1969 Art Thoms, Syracuse, DT
1970 Raymond Chester, Morgan St., TE
1971 Jack Tatum, Ohio State, S
1972 Mike Siani, Villanova, WR
1973 Ray Guy, Southern Mississippi, P
1974 Henry Lawrence, Florida A&M, T
1975 Neal Colzie, Ohio State, DB
1976 Charles Philyaw, Texas Southern, DT (2)
1977 Mike Davis, Colorado, DB (2)
1978 Dave Browning, Washington, DE (2)
1979 Willie Jones, Florida State, DE (2)
1980 Marc Wilson, Brigham Young, QB
1981 Ted Watts, Texas Tech, DB
       Curt Marsh, Washington, T
1982 Marcus Allen, So. California, RB
1983 Don Mosebar, So. California, T
1984 Sean Jones, Northeastern, DE (2)
1985 Jessie Hester, Florida State, WR
1986 Bob Buczkowski, Pittsburgh, DE
1987 John Clay, Missouri, T
1988 Tim Brown, Notre Dame, WR
       Terry McDaniel, Tennessee, DB
       Scott Davis, Illinois, DE
1989 Jeff Francis, Tennessee, QB (6)
1990 Anthony Smith, Arizona, DE
1991 Todd Marinovich, So. California, QB
1992 Chester McGlockton, Clemson, DE
1993 Patrick Bates, Texas A&M, DB
1994 Rob Fredrickson, Michigan St., LB
1995 Napoleon Kaufman, Washington, RB
1996 Rickey Dudley, Ohio State, TE
1997 Darrell Russell, Southern
       California, DT
1998 Charles Woodson, Michigan, DB
       Mo Collins, Florida, T
1999 Matt Stinchcomb, Georgia, T
2000 Sebastian Janikowski, Florida St., K
2001 Derrick Gibson, Florida State, DB
2002 Phillip Buchanon, Miami, DB
       Napoleon Harris, Northwestern, LB
2003 Nnamdi Asomugha, California, DB
       Tyler Brayton, Colorado, DE
2004 Robert Gallery, Iowa, T
2005 Fabian Washington, Nebraska, DB

PHILADELPHIA EAGLES
Year Player, College, Position
1936 Jay Berwanger, Chicago, B
1937 Sam Francis, Nebraska, B
1938 Jim McDonald, Ohio State, B
1939 Davey O'Brien, Texas Christian, B
1940 George McAfee, Duke, B
1941 Art Jones, Richmond, B (2)
1942 Pete Kmetovic, Stanford, B
1943 Joe Muha, Virginia Military, B
1944 Steve Van Buren, Louisiana St., B
1945 John Yonaker, Notre Dame, E
1946 Leo Riggs, Southern California, B
1947 Neill Armstrong, Oklahoma A&M, E
1948 Clyde (Smackover) Scott, Arkansas, B
1949 Chuck Bednarik, Pennsylvania, C
       Frank Tripucka, Notre Dame, B
1950 Harry (Bud) Grant, Minnesota, E
1951 Ebert Van Buren, Louisiana St., B

Chet Mutryn, Xavier, B
1952 Johnny Bright, Drake, B
1953 Al Conway, Army, B (2)
1954 Neil Worden, Notre Dame, B
1955 Dick Bielski, Maryland, B
1956 Bob Pellegrini, Maryland, C
1957 Clarence Peaks, Michigan State, B
1958 Walt Kowalczyk, Michigan State, B
1959 J.D. Smith, Rice, T (2)
1960 Ron Burton, Northwestern, RB
1961 Art Baker, Syracuse, RB
1962 Pete Case, Georgia, G (2)
1963 Ed Budde, Michigan State, G
1964 Bob Brown, Nebraska, T
1965 Ray Rissmiller, Georgia, T (2)
1966 Randy Beisler, Indiana, DE
1967 Harry Jones, Arkansas, RB
1968 Tim Rossovich, So. California, DE
1969 Leroy Keyes, Purdue, RB
1970 Steve Zabel, Oklahoma, TE
1971 Richard Harris, Grambling, DE
1972 John Reaves, Florida, QB
1973 Jerry Sisemore, Texas, T
     Charle Young, So. California, TE
1974 Mitch Sutton, Kansas, DT (3)
1975 Bill Capraun, Miami, T (7)
1976 Mike Smith, Florida, DE (4)
1977 Skip Sharp, Kansas, DB (5)
1978 Reggie Wilkes, Georgia Tech, LB (3)
1979 Jerry Robinson, UCLA, LB
1980 Roynell Young, Alcorn State, DB
1981 Leonard Mitchell, Houston, DE
1982 Mike Quick, North Carolina St., WR
1983 Michael Haddix, Mississippi St., RB
1984 Kenny Jackson, Penn State, WR
1985 Kevin Allen, Indiana, T
1986 Keith Byars, Ohio State, RB
1987 Jerome Brown, Miami, DT
1988 Keith Jackson, Oklahoma, TE
1989 Jessie Small, Eastern Kentucky, LB (2)
1990 Ben Smith, Georgia, DB
1991 Antone Davis, Tennessee, T
1992 Siran Stacy, Alabama, RB (2)
1993 Lester Holmes, Jackson State, T
     Leonard Renfro, Colorado, DT
1994 Bernard Williams, Georgia, T
1995 Mike Mamula, Boston College, DE
1996 Jermane Mayberry, Texas A&M-Kingsville, T
1997 Jon Harris, Virginia, DE
1998 Tra Thomas, Florida State, T
1999 Donovan McNabb, Syracuse, QB
2000 Corey Simon, Florida State, DT
2001 Freddie Mitchell, UCLA, WR
2002 Lito Sheppard, Florida, DB
2003 Jerome McDougle, Miami, DE
2004 Shawn Andrews, Arkansas, T
2005 Mike Patterson, So. California, DT

PITTSBURGH STEELERS
Year Player, College, Position
1936 Bill Shakespeare, Notre Dame, B
1937 Mike Basrak, Duquesne, C
1938 Byron (Whizzer) White, Colorado, B
1939 Bill Patterson, Baylor, B (3)
1940 Kay Eakin, Arkansas, B
1941 Chet Gladchuk, Boston College, C (2)
1942 Bill Dudley, Virginia, B
1943 Bill Daley, Minnesota, B
1944 Johnny Podesto, St. Mary's, Calif., B
1945 Paul Duhart, Florida, B

1946 Felix (Doc) Blanchard, Army, B
1947 Hub Bechtol, Texas, E
1948 Dan Edwards, Georgia, E
1949 Bobby Gage, Clemson, B
1950 Lynn Chandnois, Michigan St., B
1951 Butch Avinger, Alabama, B
1952 Ed Modzelewski, Maryland, B
1953 Ted Marchibroda, St. Bonaventure, B
1954 Johnny Lattner, Notre Dame, B
1955 Frank Varrichione, Notre Dame, T
1956 Gary Glick, Colorado A&M, B
     Art Davis, Mississippi State, B
1957 Len Dawson, Purdue, B
1958 Larry Krutko, West Virginia, B (2)
1959 Tom Barnett, Purdue, B (8)
1960 Jack Spikes, Texas Christian, RB
1961 Myron Pottios, Notre Dame, LB (2)
1962 Bob Ferguson, Ohio State, RB
1963 Frank Atkinson, Stanford, T (8)
1964 Paul Martha, Pittsburgh, S
1965 Roy Jefferson, Utah, WR (2)
1966 Dick Leftridge, West Virginia, RB
1967 Don Shy, San Diego State, RB (2)
1968 Mike Taylor, Southern California, T
1969 Joe Greene, North Texas State, DT
1970 Terry Bradshaw, Louisiana Tech, QB
1971 Frank Lewis, Grambling, WR
1972 Franco Harris, Penn State, RB
1973 J.T. Thomas, Florida State, DB
1974 Lynn Swann, So. California, WR
1975 Dave Brown, Michigan, DB
1976 Bennie Cunningham, Clemson, TE
1977 Robin Cole, New Mexico, LB
1978 Ron Johnson, Eastern Michigan, DB
1979 Greg Hawthorne, Baylor, RB
1980 Mark Malone, Arizona State, QB
1981 Keith Gary, Oklahoma, DE
1982 Walter Abercrombie, Baylor, RB
1983 Gabriel Rivera, Texas Tech, DT
1984 Louis Lipps, So. Mississippi, WR
1985 Darryl Sims, Wisconsin, DE
1986 John Rienstra, Temple, G
1987 Rod Woodson, Purdue, DB
1988 Aaron Jones, Eastern Kentucky, DE
1989 Tim Worley, Georgia, RB
     Tom Ricketts, Pittsburgh, T
1990 Eric Green, Liberty, TE
1991 Huey Richardson, Florida, DE
1992 Leon Searcy, Miami, T
1993 Deon Figures, Colorado, DB
1994 Charles Johnson, Colorado, WR
1995 Mark Bruener, Washington, TE
1996 Jamain Stephens, North Carolina A&T, T
1997 Chad Scott, Maryland, DB
1998 Alan Faneca, Louisiana State, G
1999 Troy Edwards, Lousiana Tech, WR
2000 Plaxico Burress, Michigan St., WR
2001 Casey Hampton, Texas, DT
2002 Kendall Simmons, Auburn, G
2003 Troy Polamalu, Southern California, DB
2004 Ben Roethlisberger, Miami (OH), QB
2005 Heath Miller, Virginia, TE

ST. LOUIS RAMS
Year Player, College, Position
1937 Johnny Drake, Purdue, B
1938 Corbett Davis, Indiana, B
1939 Parker Hall, Mississippi, B
1940 Ollie Cordill, Rice, B
1941 Rudy Mucha, Washington, C

1942 Jack Wilson, Baylor, B
1943 Mike Holovak, Boston College, B
1944 Tony Butkovich, Illinois, B
1945 Elroy (Crazylegs) Hirsch, Wisconsin, B
1946 Emil Sitko, Notre Dame, B
1947 Herman Wedemeyer, St. Mary's, Calif., B
1948 Tom Keane, West Virginia, B (2)
1949 Bobby Thomason, Virginia Military, B
1950 Ralph Pasquariello, Villanova, B
     Stan West, Oklahoma, G
1951 Bud McFadin, Texas, G
1952 Bill Wade, Vanderbilt, QB
     Bob Carey, Michigan State, E
1953 Donn Moomaw, UCLA, C
     Ed Barker, Washington State, E
1954 Ed Beatty, Cincinnati, C
1955 Larry Morris, Georgia Tech, C
1956 Joe Marconi, West Virginia, B
     Charles Horton, Vanderbilt, B
1957 Jon Arnett, Southern California, B
     Del Shofner, Baylor, E
1958 Lou Michaels, Kentucky, T
     Jim Phillips, Auburn, E
1959 Dick Bass, Pacific, B
     Paul Dickson, Baylor, T
1960 Billy Cannon, Louisiana State, RB
1961 Marlin McKeever, So. California, E-LB
1962 Roman Gabriel, North Carolina St., QB
     Merlin Olsen, Utah State, DT
1963 Terry Baker, Oregon State, QB
     Rufus Guthrie, Georgia Tech, G
1964 Bill Munson, Utah State, QB
1965 Clancy Williams, Washington St., CB
1966 Tom Mack, Michigan, G
1967 Willie Ellison, Texas Southern, RB (2)
1968 Gary Beban, UCLA, QB (2)
1969 Larry Smith, Florida, RB
     Jim Seymour, Notre Dame, WR
     Bob Klein, Southern California, TE
1970 Jack Reynolds, Tennessee, LB
1971 Isiah Robertson, Southern, LB
     Jack Youngblood, Florida, DE
1972 Jim Bertelsen, Texas, RB (2)
1973 Cullen Bryant, Colorado, DB (2)
1974 John Cappelletti, Penn State, RB
1975 Mike Fanning, Notre Dame, DT
     Dennis Harrah, Miami, T
     Doug France, Ohio State, T
1976 Kevin McLain, Colorado State, LB
1977 Bob Brudzinski, Ohio State, LB
1978 Elvis Peacock, Oklahoma, RB
1979 George Andrews, Nebraska, LB
     Kent Hill, Georgia Tech, T
1980 Johnnie Johnson, Texas, DB
1981 Mel Owens, Michigan, LB
1982 Barry Redden, Richmond, RB
1983 Eric Dickerson, So. Methodist, RB
1984 Hal Stephens, East Carolina, DE (5)
1985 Jerry Gray, Texas, DB
1986 Mike Schad, Queen's Univ., Canada, T
1987 Donald Evans, Winston-Salem, DE (2)
1988 Gaston Green, UCLA, RB
     Aaron Cox, Arizona State, WR
1989 Bill Hawkins, Miami, DE
     Cleveland Gary, Miami, RB
1990 Bern Brostek, Washington, C
1991 Todd Lyght, Notre Dame, DB
1992 Sean Gilbert, Pittsburgh, DE
1993 Jerome Bettis, Notre Dame, RB
1994 Wayne Gandy, Auburn, T

1995 Kevin Carter, Florida, DE
1996 Lawrence Phillips, Nebraska, RB
   Eddie Kennison, Louisiana St., WR
1997 Orlando Pace, Ohio State, T
1998 Grant Wistrom, Nebraska, DE
1999 Torry Holt, North Carolina St., WR
2000 Trung Canidate, Arizona, RB
2001 Damione Lewis, Miami, DT
   Adam Archuleta, Arizona State, DB
   Ryan Pickett, Ohio State, DT
2002 Robert Thomas, UCLA, LB
2003 Jimmy Kennedy, Penn State, DT
2004 Steven Jackson, Oregon State, RB
2005 Alex Barron, Florida State, T

SAN DIEGO CHARGERS
Year Player, College, Position
1960 Monty Stickles, Notre Dame, E
1961 Earl Faison, Indiana, DE
1962 Bob Ferguson, Ohio State, RB
1963 Walt Sweeney, Syracuse, G
1964 Ted Davis, Georgia Tech, LB
1965 Steve DeLong, Tennessee, DE
1966 Don Davis, Cal St.-Los Angeles, DT
1967 Ron Billingsley, Wyoming, DE
1968 Russ Washington, Missouri, DT
   Jimmy Hill, Texas A&I, DB
1969 Marty Domres, Columbia, QB
   Bob Babich, Miami, Ohio, LB
1970 Walker Gillette, Richmond, WR
1971 Leon Burns, Long Beach State, RB
1972 Pete Lazetich, Stanford, DE (2)
1973 Johnny Rodgers, Nebraska, WR
1974 Bo Matthews, Colorado, RB
   Don Goode, Kansas, LB
1975 Gary Johnson, Grambling, DT
   Mike Williams, Louisiana State, DB
1976 Joe Washington, Oklahoma, RB
1977 Bob Rush, Memphis State, C
1978 John Jefferson, Arizona State, WR
1979 Kellen Winslow, Missouri, TE
1980 Ed Luther, San Jose State, QB (4)
1981 James Brooks, Auburn, RB
1982 Hollis Hall, Clemson, DB (7)
1983 Billy Ray Smith, Arkansas, LB
   Gary Anderson, Arkansas, WR
   Gill Byrd, San Jose State, DB
1984 Mossy Cade, Texas, DB
1985 Jim Lachey, Ohio State, G
1986 Leslie O'Neal, Oklahoma State, DE
   James FitzPatrick, So. California, T
1987 Rod Bernstine, Texas A&M, TE
1988 Anthony Miller, Tennessee, WR
1989 Burt Grossman, Pittsburgh, DE
1990 Junior Seau, So. California, LB
1991 Stanley Richard, Texas, DB
1992 Chris Mims, Tennessee, DE
1993 Darrien Gordon, Stanford, DB
1994 Isaac Davis, Arkansas, G (2)
1995 Terrance Shaw, Stephen F. Austin, DB (2)
1996 Bryan Still, Virginia Tech, WR (2)
1997 Freddie Jones, North Carolina, TE (2)
1998 Ryan Leaf, Washington State, QB
1999 Jermaine Fazande, Oklahoma, RB (2)
2000 Rogers Beckett, Marshall, DB (2)
2001 LaDainian Tomlinson, TCU, RB
2002 Quentin Jammer, Texas, DB
2003 Sammy Davis, Texas A&M, DB
2004 Eli Manning, Mississippi, QB

2005 Shawne Merriman, Maryland, LB
   Luis Castillo, Northwestern, DT

SAN FRANCISCO 49ERS
Year Player, College, Position
1950 Leo Nomellini, Minnesota, T
1951 Y.A. Tittle, Louisiana State, B
1952 Hugh McElhenny, Washington, B
1953 Harry Babcock, Georgia, E
   Tom Stolhandske, Texas, E
1954 Bernie Faloney, Maryland, B
1955 Dickie Moegle, Rice, B
1956 Earl Morrall, Michigan State, B
1957 John Brodie, Stanford, B
1958 Jim Pace, Michigan, B
   Charlie Krueger, Texas A&M, T
1959 Dave Baker, Oklahoma, B
   Dan James, Ohio State, C
1960 Monty Stickles, Notre Dame, E
1961 Jimmy Johnson, UCLA, CB
   Bernie Casey, Bowling Green, WR
   Bill Kilmer, UCLA, QB
1962 Lance Alworth, Arkansas, WR
1963 Kermit Alexander, UCLA, CB
1964 Dave Parks, Texas Tech, WR
1965 Ken Willard, North Carolina, RB
   George Donnelly, Illinois, DB
1966 Stan Hindman, Mississippi, DE
1967 Steve Spurrier, Florida, QB
   Cas Banaszek, Northwestern, T
1968 Forrest Blue, Auburn, C
1969 Ted Kwalick, Penn State, TE
   Gene Washington, Stanford, WR
1970 Cedrick Hardman, North Texas St., DE
   Bruce Taylor, Boston U., DB
1971 Tim Anderson, Ohio State, DB
1972 Terry Beasley, Auburn, WR
1973 Mike Holmes, Texas Southern, DB
1974 Wilbur Jackson, Alabama, RB
   Bill Sandifer, UCLA, DT
1975 Jimmy Webb, Mississippi St., DT
1976 Randy Cross, UCLA, C (2)
1977 Elmo Boyd, Eastern Kentucky, WR (3)
1978 Ken MacAfee, Notre Dame, TE
   Dan Bunz, Cal St.-Long Beach, LB
1979 James Owens, UCLA, WR (2)
1980 Earl Cooper, Rice, RB
   Jim Stuckey, Clemson, DT
1981 Ronnie Lott, So. California, DB
1982 Bubba Paris, Michigan, T (2)
1983 Roger Craig, Nebraska, RB (2)
1984 Todd Shell, Brigham Young, LB
1985 Jerry Rice, Mississippi Valley St., WR
1986 Larry Roberts, Alabama, DE (2)
1987 Harris Barton, North Carolina, T
   Terrence Flagler, Clemson, RB
1988 Danny Stubbs, Miami, DE (2)
1989 Keith DeLong, Tennessee, LB
1990 Dexter Carter, Florida State, RB
1991 Ted Washington, Louisville, DT
1992 Dana Hall, Washington, DB
1993 Dana Stubblefield, Kansas, DT
   Todd Kelly, Tennessee, DE
1994 Bryant Young, Notre Dame, DT
   William Floyd, Florida State, RB
1995 J.J. Stokes, UCLA, WR
1996 Israel Ifeanyi, So.California, DE (2)
1997 Jim Druckenmiller, Virginia Tech, QB
1998 R.W. McQuarters, Oklahoma St., DB
1999 Reggie McGrew, Florida, DT

2000 Julian Peterson, Michigan St., LB
   Ahmed Plummer, Ohio State, DB
2001 Andre Carter, California, DE
2002 Mike Rumph, Miami, DB
2003 Kwame Harris, Stanford, T
2004 Rashaun Woods, Oklahoma St., WR
2005 Alex Smith, Utah, QB

SEATTLE SEAHAWKS
Year Player, College, Position
1976 Steve Niehaus, Notre Dame, DT
1977 Steve August, Tulsa, G
1978 Keith Simpson, Memphis St., DB
1979 Manu Tuiasosopo, UCLA, DT
1980 Jacob Green, Texas A&M, DE
1981 Ken Easley, UCLA, DB
1982 Jeff Bryant, Clemson, DE
1983 Curt Warner, Penn State, RB
1984 Terry Taylor, Southern Illinois, DB
1985 Owen Gill, Iowa, RB (2)
1986 John L. Williams, Florida, RB
1987 Tony Woods, Pittsburgh, LB
1988 Brian Blades, Miami, WR (2)
1989 Andy Heck, Notre Dame, T
1990 Cortez Kennedy, Miami, DT
1991 Dan McGwire, San Diego St., QB
1992 Ray Roberts, Virginia, T
1993 Rick Mirer, Notre Dame, QB
1994 Sam Adams, Texas A&M, DT
1995 Joey Galloway, Ohio State, WR
1996 Pete Kendall, Boston College, T
1997 Shawn Springs, Ohio State, DB
   Walter Jones, Florida State, T
1998 Anthony Simmons, Clemson, LB
1999 Lamar King, Saginaw Valley St., DE
2000 Shaun Alexander, Alabama, RB
   Chris McIntosh, Wisconsin, T
2001 Koren Robinson, North Carolina St., WR
   Steve Hutchinson, Michigan, G
2002 Jerramy Stevens, Washington, TE
2003 Marcus Trufant, Washington State, DB
2004 Marcus Tubbs, Texas, DT
2005 Chris Spencer, Mississippi, C

TAMPA BAY BUCCANEERS
Year Player, College, Position
1976 Lee Roy Selmon, Oklahoma, DT
1977 Ricky Bell, Southern California, RB
1978 Doug Williams, Grambling, QB
1979 Greg Roberts, Oklahoma, G (2)
1980 Ray Snell, Wisconsin, G
1981 Hugh Green, Pittsburgh, LB
1982 Sean Farrell, Penn State, G
1983 Randy Grimes, Baylor, C (2)
1984 Keith Browner, So. California, LB (2)
1985 Ron Holmes, Washington, DE
1986 Bo Jackson, Auburn, RB
   Roderick Jones, So. Methodist, DB
1987 Vinny Testaverde, Miami, QB
1988 Paul Gruber, Wisconsin, T
1989 Broderick Thomas, Nebraska, LB
1990 Keith McCants, Alabama, LB
1991 Charles McRae, Tennessee, T
1992 Courtney Hawkins, Michigan St., WR (2)
1993 Eric Curry, Alabama, DE
1994 Trent Dilfer, Fresno State, QB
1995 Warren Sapp, Miami, DT
   Derrick Brooks, Florida State, LB
1996 Regan Upshaw, California, DE
   Marcus Jones, North Carolina, DT

1997 Warrick Dunn, Florida State, RB
Reidel Anthony, Florida, WR
1998 Jacquez Green, Florida, WR (2)
1999 Anthony McFarland, Louisiana St., DT
2000 Cosey Coleman, Tennessee, G (2)
2001 Kenyatta Walker, Florida, T
2002 Marquise Walker, Michigan, WR (3)
2003 Dewayne White, Louisville, DE (2)
2004 Michael Clayton, Louisiana St., WR
2005 Carnell Williams, Auburn, RB

TENNESSEE TITANS
Year Player, College, Position
1960 Billy Cannon, Louisiana State, RB
1961 Mike Ditka, Pittsburgh, E
1962 Ray Jacobs, Howard Payne, DT
1963 Danny Brabham, Arkansas, LB
1964 Scott Appleton, Texas, DT
1965 Lawrence Elkins, Baylor, WR
1966 Tommy Nobis, Texas, LB
1967 George Webster, Michigan St., LB
Tom Regner, Notre Dame, G
1968 Mac Haik, Mississippi, WR (2)
1969 Ron Pritchard, Arizona State, LB
1970 Doug Wilkerson, N. Carolina Central, G
1971 Dan Pastorini, Santa Clara, QB
1972 Greg Sampson, Stanford, DE
1973 John Matuszak, Tampa, DE
George Amundson, Iowa State, RB
1974 Steve Manstedt, Nebraska, LB (4)
1975 Robert Brazile, Jackson State, LB
Don Hardeman, Texas A&I, RB
1976 Mike Barber, Louisiana Tech, TE (2)
1977 Morris Towns, Missouri, T
1978 Earl Campbell, Texas, RB
1979 Mike Stensrud, Iowa State, DE (2)
1980 Angelo Fields, Michigan St., T (2)
1981 Michael Holston, Morgan St., WR (3)
1982 Mike Munchak, Penn State, G
1983 Bruce Matthews, So. California, T
1984 Dean Steinkuhler, Nebraska, T
1985 Ray Childress, Texas A&M, DE
Richard Johnson, Wisconsin, DB
1986 Jim Everett, Purdue, QB
1987 Alonzo Highsmith, Miami, RB
Haywood Jeffires, North Carolina St., WR
1988 Lorenzo White, Michigan State, RB
1989 David Williams, Florida, T
1990 Lamar Lathon, Houston, LB
1991 Mike Dumas, Indiana, DB (2)
1992 Eddie Robinson, Alabama St., LB (2)
1993 Brad Hopkins, Illinois, T
1994 Henry Ford, Arkansas, DE
1995 Steve McNair, Alcorn State, QB
1996 Eddie George, Ohio State, RB
1997 Kenny Holmes, Miami, DE
1998 Kevin Dyson, Utah, WR
1999 Jevon Kearse, Florida, DE
2000 Keith Bulluck, Syracuse, LB
2001 Andre Dyson, Utah, DB (2)
2002 Albert Haynesworth, Tennessee, DT
2003 Andre Woolfolk, Oklahoma, DB
2004 Ben Troupe, Florida, TE (2)
2005 Adam Jones, West Virginia, DB

WASHINGTON REDSKINS
Year Player, College, Position
1936 Riley Smith, Alabama, B
1937 Sammy Baugh, Texas Christian, B
1938 Andy Farkas, Detroit, B

1939 I.B. Hale, Texas Christian, T
1940 Ed Boell, New York U., B
1941 Forest Evashevski, Michigan, B
1942 Orban (Spec) Sanders, Texas, B
1943 Jack Jenkins, Missouri, B
1944 Mike Micka, Colgate, B
1945 Jim Hardy, Southern California, B
1946 Cal Rossi, UCLA, B*
1947 Cal Rossi, UCLA, B
1948 Harry Gilmer, Alabama, B
Lowell Tew, Alabama, B
1949 Rob Goode, Texas A&M, B
1950 George Thomas, Oklahoma, B
1951 Leon Heath, Oklahoma, B
1952 Larry Isbell, Baylor, B
1953 Jack Scarbath, Maryland, B
1954 Steve Meilinger, Kentucky, E
1955 Ralph Guglielmi, Notre Dame, B
1956 Ed Vereb, Maryland, B
1957 Don Bosseler, Miami, B
1958 Mike Sommer, George
Washington, B (2)
1959 Don Allard, Boston College, B
1960 Richie Lucas, Penn State, QB
1961 Norman Snead, Wake Forest, QB
Joe Rutgens, Illinois, DT
1962 Ernie Davis, Syracuse, RB
1963 Pat Richter, Wisconsin, TE
1964 Charley Taylor, Arizona St., RB-WR
1965 Bob Breitenstein, Tulsa, T (2)
1966 Charlie Gogolak, Princeton, K
1967 Ray McDonald, Idaho, RB
1968 Jim Smith, Oregon, DB
1969 Eugene Epps, Texas-El Paso, DB (2)
1970 Bill Bundige, Colorado, DT (2)
1971 Cotton Speyrer, Texas, WR (2)
1972 Moses Denson, Maryland St., RB (8)
1973 Charles Cantrell, Lamar, G (5)
1974 Jon Keyworth, Colorado, TE (6)
1975 Mike Thomas, Nevada-Las Vegas, RB (6)
1976 Mike Hughes, Baylor, G (5)
1977 Duncan McColl, Stanford, DE (4)
1978 Tony Green, Florida, RB (6)
1979 Don Warren, San Diego St., TE (4)
1980 Art Monk, Syracuse, WR
1981 Mark May, Pittsburgh, T
1982 Vernon Dean, San Diego St., DB (2)
1983 Darrell Green, Texas A&I, DB
1984 Bob Slater, Oklahoma, DT (2)
1985 Tory Nixon, San Diego St., DB (2)
1986 Markus Koch, Boise State, DE (2)
1987 Brian Davis, Nebraska, DB (2)
1988 Chip Lohmiller, Minnesota, K (2)
1989 Tracy Rocker, Auburn, DT (3)
1990 Andre Collins, Penn State, LB (2)
1991 Bobby Wilson, Michigan State, DT
1992 Desmond Howard, Michigan, WR
1993 Tom Carter, Notre Dame, DB
1994 Heath Shuler, Tennessee, QB
1995 Michael Westbrook, Colorado, WR
1996 Andre Johnson, Penn State, T
1997 Kenard Lang, Miami, DE
1998 Stephen Alexander, Oklahoma, TE (2)
1999 Champ Bailey, Georgia, DB
2000 LaVar Arrington, Penn State, LB
Chris Samuels, Alabama, T
2001 Rod Gardner, Clemson, WR
2002 Patrick Ramsey, Tulane, QB
2003 Taylor Jacobs, Florida, WR (2)
2004 Sean Taylor, Miami, DB

2005 Carlos Rogers, Auburn, DB
Jason Campbell, Auburn, QB
Choice lost because of ineligibility

WALTER PAYTON NFL MAN OF THE YEAR

The Walter Payton NFL Man of the Year Award is the only NFL award that recognizes a player for his community service activities as well as his excellence on the field. Renamed in 1999 for the legendary Chicago Bears Pro Football Hall of Fame running back, the Walter Payton NFL Man of the Year Award has been given annually since 1970.

YEAR	PLAYER	POS.	TEAM
1970	Johnny Unitas	QB	Baltimore Colts
1971	John Hadl	QB	San Diego Chargers
1972	Willie Lanier	LB	Kansas City Chiefs
1973	Len Dawson	QB	Kansas City Chiefs
1974	George Blanda	QB	Oakland Raiders
1975	Ken Anderson	QB	Cincinnati Bengals
1976	Franco Harris	RB	Pittsburgh Steelers
1977	Walter Payton	RB	Chicago Bears
1978	Roger Staubach	QB	Dallas Cowboys
1979	Joe Greene	DT	Pittsburgh Steelers
1980	Harold Carmichael	WR	Philadelphia Eagles
1981	Lynn Swann	WR	Pittsburgh Steelers
1982	Joe Theismann	QB	Washington Redskins
1983	Rolf Benirschke	K	San Diego Chargers
1984	Marty Lyons	T	New York Jets
1985	Dwight Stephenson	C	Miami Dolphins
1986	Reggie Williams	LB	Cincinnati Bengals
1987	Dave Duerson	S	Chicago Bears
1988	Steve Largent	WR	Seattle Seahawks
1989	Warren Moon	QB	Houston Oilers
1990	Mike Singletary	LB	Chicago Bears
1991	Anthony Muñoz	T	Cincinnati Bengals
1992	John Elway	QB	Denver Broncos
1993	Derrick Thomas	LB	Kansas City Chiefs
1994	Junior Seau	LB	San Diego Chargers
1995	Boomer Esiason	QB	New York Jets
1996	Darrell Green	CB	Washington Redskins
1997	Troy Aikman	QB	Dallas Cowboys
1998	Dan Marino	QB	Miami Dolphins
1999	Cris Carter	WR	Minnesota Vikings
2000*	Derrick Brooks	LB	Tampa Bay Buccaneers
	Jim Flanigan	DT	Chicago Bears
2001	Jerome Bettis	RB	Pittsburgh Steelers
2002	Troy Vincent	CB	Philadelphia Eagles
2003	Will Shields	G	Kansas City Chiefs
2004	Warrick Dunn	RB	Atlanta Falcons

* The award was shared in 2000.

ASSOCIATED PRESS NFL AWARDS

THE FOLLOWING AWARDS WERE NAMED BY *ASSOCIATED PRESS* IN BALLOTING BY A NATIONWIDE PANEL OF MEDIA.

NFL MOST VALUABLE PLAYER AWARD

YEAR	PLAYER	POS.	TEAM	ACCOMPLISHMENTS
1957	Jim Brown	RB	Cleveland Browns	Rushed for league-leading 942 yards and added 9 TDs as a rookie.
1958	Gino Marchetti	DE	Baltimore Colts	Leader of defense that permitted league-low 1,291 rushing yards and division-low 203 points.
1959	Charley Conerly	QB	New York Giants	Passed for 14 TDs and only 4 interceptions. Led offense to division-leading 284 points.
1960*	Norm Van Brocklin	QB	Philadelphia Eagles	Guided Eagles to first division title since 1949. Passed for 2,471 yards and 24 TDs.
	Joe Schmidt	LB	Detroit Lions	After 0-3 start, team went 7-2 when he returned from injury. Scored 2 defensive TDs.
1961	Paul Hornung	RB	Green Bay Packers	Led league in scoring for second straight season with 146 points (10 TD, 15 FG, 41 PAT).
1962	Jim Taylor	RB	Green Bay Packers	League rushing champion with 1,474 yards. Scored then all-time record 19 touchdowns.
1963	Y.A. Tittle	QB	New York Giants	Set then all-time season record with 36 TD passes. Guided league's top offense (5,024 yards).
1964	Johnny Unitas	QB	Baltimore Colts	Guided Colts to NFL's best record (12-2) and league's top offensive attack (4,779 yards).
1965	Jim Brown	RB	Cleveland Browns	Leader of NFL's top rushing attack. Led league with 1,544 yards, added 21 total TDs.
1966	Bart Starr	QB	Green Bay Packers	Passed for 14 touchdowns and only 3 interceptions. Led Packers to league-best 12-2 record.
1967	Johnny Unitas	QB	Baltimore Colts	Passed for 3,428 yards and 20 touchdowns. Led Colts to 11-1-2 record.
1968	Earl Morrall	QB	Baltimore Colts	Guided Colts to NFL-best 13-1 record. Led league with 26 touchdown passes.
1969	Roman Gabriel	QB	Los Angeles Rams	Led NFL with 24 touchdown passes. Guided Rams to 11-3 record.
1970	John Brodie	QB	San Francisco 49ers	Took 49ers to first division title. Threw NFL-best 24 TD passes.
1971	Alan Page	DT	Minnesota Vikings	Led defense that allowed NFL-low 139 points. Vikings won fourth straight NFC Central title.
1972	Larry Brown	RB	Washington Redskins	Led conference with 1,216 rushing yards. Redskins had NFC-best 11-3 record.
1973	O.J. Simpson	RB	Buffalo Bills	Rushed for then all-time record 2,003 yards, including three 200-yard performances.
1974	Ken Stabler	QB	Oakland Raiders	Led league with 26 touchdown passes and only 12 interceptions. Raiders had NFL-best 12-2 record.
1975	Fran Tarkenton	QB	Minnesota Vikings	Tied for league-best 12-2 record. Led NFC with 91.7 passer rating.
1976	Bert Jones	QB	Baltimore Colts	Threw 24 touchdowns and only 9 interceptions for 102.5 passer rating.
1977	Walter Payton	RB	Chicago Bears	Rushed for league-leading 1,852 yards and 16 total touchdowns.
1978	Terry Bradshaw	QB	Pittsburgh Steelers	Led Steelers to league-leading 14-2 mark. Set club record with 28 TD passes.
1979	Earl Campbell	RB	Houston Oilers	Led league with 1,697 rushing yards and 19 touchdowns.
1980	Brian Sipe	QB	Cleveland Browns	NFL-best 91.4 passer rating. Set Browns' records with 30 TD passes and 4,132 yards.
1981	Ken Anderson	QB	Cincinnati Bengals	Led Bengals to first division title since 1973. NFL-high 98.5 passer rating.
1982	Mark Moseley	K	Washington Redskins	Converted 20 of 21 FGs. Set then consecutive field-goal record at 23 (including last three in '81).
1983	Joe Theismann	QB	Washington Redskins	Leader of offense that scored then-NFL record 541 points. Redskins had NFL-best 14-2 record.
1984	Dan Marino	QB	Miami Dolphins	Set NFL records with 5,084 yards and 48 TD passes. Led Dolphins to AFC-best 14-2 mark.
1985	Marcus Allen	RB	Los Angeles Raiders	Rushed for league-leading 1,759 yards. Tied for AFC lead with 11 rushing touchdowns.
1986	Lawrence Taylor	LB	New York Giants	Recorded league-high 20.5 sacks, and led Giants' second-ranked defense (297.3).
1987	John Elway	QB	Denver Broncos	In 12 games, passed for 19 TDs and 3,198 yards, including four 300-yard games.
1988	Boomer Esiason	QB	Cincinnati Bengals	Led NFL with 97.4 passer rating. Tied for AFC lead with 28 TD passes.
1989	Joe Montana	QB	San Francisco 49ers	Set then-NFL record with 112.4 passer rating, including 70.2 completion percentage.
1990	Joe Montana	QB	San Francisco 49ers	Led 49ers to league-best 14-2 record. Completed NFC-high 61.7 percent of passes.
1991	Thurman Thomas	RB	Buffalo Bills	Recorded league-high 2,038 yards from scrimmage (1,407 rushing, 631 receiving).

1992	Steve Young	QB	San Francisco 49ers	NFL's top passer with 107.0 rating. Led 49ers to league-best 14-2 record.
1993	Emmitt Smith	RB	Dallas Cowboys	Led league in rushing (1,486 yards) for third straight year despite missing first two games.
1994	Steve Young	QB	San Francisco 49ers	Compiled NFL all-time best 112.8 passer rating. Completed more than 70 percent of his passes.
1995	Brett Favre	QB	Green Bay Packers	Led league with 38 touchdown passes and NFC with 99.5 passer rating.
1996	Brett Favre	QB	Green Bay Packers	Led Packers to top conference record (13-3). Threw NFL-best 39 TD passes.
1997*	Brett Favre	QB	Green Bay Packers	Led league with 35 touchdown passes. Led NFC with 3,867 passing yards.
	Barry Sanders	RB	Detroit Lions	Rushed for all-time second-best 2,053 yards, including record 14 straight 100-yard games.
1998	Terrell Davis	RB	Denver Broncos	Rushed for 2,008 yards and scored league-best 23 total touchdowns.
1999	Kurt Warner	QB	St. Louis Rams	Became the second QB in history to have 40 touchdown passes in a season (41).
2000	Marshall Faulk	RB	St. Louis Rams	Set NFL record with 26 touchdowns and led NFC with 2,189 yards from scrimmage.
2001	Kurt Warner	QB	St. Louis Rams	Led NFL with 4,830 passing yards, 36 touchdowns, 68.7 completion percentage, and 101.4 passer rating.
2002	Rich Gannon	QB	Oakland Raiders	Set single-season records with 10 300-yard passing games and 418 completions, and led NFL with 4,689 passing yards.
2003*	Peyton Manning	QB	Indianapolis Colts	Led NFL with 4,267 passing yards, had AFC-best 29 touchdown passes, and posted 99.0 passer rating.
	Steve McNair	QB	Tennessee Titans	Posted NFL-best 100.4 passer rating, passing for 3,215 yards with 24 touchdowns against 7 interceptions.
2004	Peyton Manning	QB	Indianapolis Colts	Set NFL records with 49 touchdown passes and 121.1 passer rating while passing for 4,557 yards.

Total *Associated Press* NFL MVPs: 51
Two-time Winners: Jim Brown, Brett Favre (3), Peyton Manning, Joe Montana, Johnny Unitas, Kurt Warner, Steve Young
* The award was shared in 1960, 1997, and 2003.

ASSOCIATED PRESS MVPs WHO WON SUPER BOWL/ NFL CHAMPIONSHIP IN SAME SEASON: 15

1958	Gino Marchetti	Baltimore Colts
1960	Norm Van Brocklin	Philadelphia Eagles
1961	Paul Hornung	Green Bay Packers
1962	Jim Taylor	Green Bay Packers
1966	Bart Starr	Green Bay Packers
1968	Earl Morrall	Baltimore Colts
1978	Terry Bradshaw	Pittsburgh Steelers
1982	Mark Moseley	Washington Redskins
1986	Lawrence Taylor	New York Giants
1989	Joe Montana	San Francisco 49ers
1993	Emmitt Smith	Dallas Cowboys
1994	Steve Young	San Francisco 49ers
1996	Brett Favre	Green Bay Packers
1998	Terrell Davis	Denver Broncos
1999	Kurt Warner	St. Louis Rams

ASSOCIATED PRESS NFL MVP BY POSITION

Quarterback:	32	Defensive End:	1
Running Back:	14	Defensive Tackle:	1
Linebacker:	2	Kicker:	1

ASSOCIATED PRESS MVPs BY TEAM

7	Indianapolis/Baltimore Colts	1	Chicago Bears
			Dallas Cowboys
6	Green Bay Packers		Houston Oilers
			Miami Dolphins
5	San Francisco 49ers		Philadelphia Eagles
			Pittsburgh Steelers
4	St. Louis/Los Angeles Rams		Tennessee Titans
3	Cleveland Browns		
	New York Giants		
	Oakland/Los Angeles Raiders		
	Washington Redskins		
2	Buffalo Bills		
	Cincinnati Bengals		
	Denver Broncos		
	Detroit Lions		
	Minnesota Vikings		

AP OFFENSIVE PLAYER OF THE YEAR

Year	Player	Pos	Team
1973	O.J. Simpson	RB	Buffalo Bills
1974	Ken Stabler	QB	Oakland Raiders
1975	Fran Tarkenton	QB	Minnesota Vikings
1976	Bert Jones	QB	Baltimore Colts
1977	Walter Payton	RB	Chicago Bears
1978	Earl Campbell	RB	Houston Oilers
1979	Earl Campbell	RB	Houston Oilers
1980	Earl Campbell	RB	Houston Oilers
1981	Ken Anderson	QB	Cincinnati Bengals
1982	Dan Fouts	QB	San Diego Chargers
1983	Joe Theismann	QB	Washington Redskins
1984	Dan Marino	QB	Miami Dolphins
1985	Marcus Allen	RB	Los Angeles Raiders
1986	Eric Dickerson	RB	Los Angeles Rams
1987	Jerry Rice	WR	San Francisco 49ers
1988	Roger Craig	RB	San Francisco 49ers
1989	Joe Montana	QB	San Francisco 49ers
1990	Warren Moon	QB	Houston Oilers
1991	Thurman Thomas	RB	Buffalo Bills
1992	Steve Young	QB	San Francisco 49ers
1993	Jerry Rice	WR	San Francisco 49ers
1994	Barry Sanders	RB	Detroit Lions
1995	Brett Favre	QB	Green Bay Packers
1996	Terrell Davis	RB	Denver Broncos
1997	Barry Sanders	RB	Detroit Lions
1998	Terrell Davis	RB	Denver Broncos
1999	Marshall Faulk	RB	St. Louis Rams
2000	Marshall Faulk	RB	St. Louis Rams
2001	Marshall Faulk	RB	St. Louis Rams
2002	Priest Holmes	RB	Kansas City Chiefs
2003	Jamal Lewis	RB	Baltimore Ravens
2004	Peyton Manning	QB	Indianapolis Colts

AP OFFENSIVE ROOKIE OF THE YEAR

1957	Jim Brown	RB	Cleveland Browns
1958	Jimmy Orr	WR	Pittsburgh Steelers
1959	Nick Pietrosante	RB	Detroit Lions
1960	Gail Cogdill	WR	Detroit Lions
1961	Mike Ditka	TE	Chicago Bears
1962	Ron Bull	RB	Chicago Bears
1963	Paul Flatley	WR	Minnesota Vikings
1964	Charley Taylor	WR	Washington Redskins
1965	Gale Sayers	RB	Chicago Bears
1966	Johnny Roland	RB	St. Louis Cardinals
1967	Mel Farr	RB	Detroit Lions
1968	Earl McCullouch	WR	Detroit Lions
1969	Calvin Hill	RB	Dallas Cowboys
1970	Duane Thomas	RB	Dallas Cowboys
1971	John Brockington	RB	Green Bay Packers
1972	Franco Harris	RB	Pittsburgh Steelers
1973	Chuck Foreman	RB	Minnesota Vikings
1974	Don Woods	RB	San Diego Chargers
1975	Mike Thomas	RB	Washington Redskins
1976	Sammy White	WR	Minnesota Vikings
1977	Tony Dorsett	RB	Dallas Cowboys
1978	Earl Campbell	RB	Houston Oilers
1979	Ottis Anderson	RB	St. Louis Cardinals
1980	Billy Sims	RB	Detroit Lions
1981	George Rogers	RB	New Orleans Saints
1982	Marcus Allen	RB	Los Angeles Raiders
1983	Eric Dickerson	RB	Los Angeles Rams
1984	Louis Lipps	WR	Pittsburgh Steelers
1985	Eddie Brown	WR	Cincinnati Bengals
1986	Rueben Mayes	RB	New Orleans Saints
1987	Troy Stradford	RB	Miami Dolphins
1988	John Stephens	RB	New England Patriots
1989	Barry Sanders	RB	Detroit Lions

Year	Player	Pos	Team
1990	Emmitt Smith	RB	Dallas Cowboys
1991	Leonard Russell	RB	New England Patriots
1992	Carl Pickens	WR	Cincinnati Bengals
1993	Jerome Bettis	RB	Los Angeles Rams
1994	Marshall Faulk	RB	Indianapolis Colts
1995	Curtis Martin	RB	New England Patriots
1996	Eddie George	RB	Houston Oilers
1997	Warrick Dunn	RB	Tampa Bay Buccaneers
1998	Randy Moss	WR	Minnesota Vikings
1999	Edgerrin James	RB	Indianapolis Colts
2000	Mike Anderson	RB	Denver Broncos
2001	Anthony Thomas	RB	Chicago Bears
2002	Clinton Portis	RB	Denver Broncos
2003	Anquan Boldin	WR	Arizona Cardinals
2004	Ben Roethlisberger	QB	Pittsburgh Steelers

AP DEFENSIVE PLAYER OF THE YEAR

1971	Alan Page	DT	Minnesota Vikings
1972	Joe Greene	DT	Pittsburgh Steelers
1973	Dick Anderson	S	Miami Dolphins
1974	Joe Greene	DT	Pittsburgh Steelers
1975	Mel Blount	CB	Pittsburgh Steelers
1976	Jack Lambert	LB	Pittsburgh Steelers
1977	Harvey Martin	DE	Dallas Cowboys
1978	Randy Gradishar	LB	Denver Broncos
1979	Lee Roy Selmon	DE	Tampa Bay Buccaneers
1980	Lester Hayes	CB	Oakland Raiders
1981	Lawrence Taylor	LB	New York Giants
1982	Lawrence Taylor	LB	New York Giants
1983	Doug Betters	DE	Miami Dolphins
1984	Kenny Easley	S	Seattle Seahawks
1985	Mike Singletary	LB	Chicago Bears
1986	Lawrence Taylor	LB	New York Giants
1987	Reggie White	DT	Philadelphia Eagles
1988	Mike Singletary	LB	Chicago Bears
1989	Keith Millard	DT	Minnesota Vikings
1990	Bruce Smith	DE	Buffalo Bills
1991	Pat Swilling	LB	New Orleans Saints
1992	Cortez Kennedy	DT	Seattle Seahawks
1993	Rod Woodson	CB	Pittsburgh Steelers
1994	Deion Sanders	CB	San Francisco 49ers
1995	Bryce Paup	LB	Buffalo Bills
1996	Bruce Smith	DE	Buffalo Bills
1997	Dana Stubblefield	DT	San Francisco 49ers
1998	Reggie White	DE	Green Bay Packers
1999	Warren Sapp	DT	Tampa Bay Buccaneers
2000	Ray Lewis	LB	Baltimore Ravens
2001	Michael Strahan	DE	New York Giants
2002	Derrick Brooks	LB	Tampa Bay Buccaneers
2003	Ray Lewis	LB	Baltimore Ravens
2004	Ed Reed	S	Baltimore Ravens

AP DEFENSIVE ROOKIE OF THE YEAR

1967	Lem Barney	CB	Detroit Lions
1968	Claude Humphrey	DE	Atlanta Falcons
1969	Joe Greene	DT	Pittsburgh Steelers
1970	Bruce Taylor	CB	San Franicsco 49ers
1971	Isiah Robertson	LB	Los Angeles Rams
1972	Willie Buchanon	CB	Green Bay Packers
1973	Wally Chambers	DT	Chicago Bears
1974	Jack Lambert	LB	Pittsburgh Steelers
1975	Robert Brazile	LB	Houston Oilers
1976	Mike Haynes	S	New England Patriots
1977	A.J. Duhe	DT	Miami Dolphins
1978	Al Baker	DE	Detroit Lions
1979	Jim Haslett	LB	Buffalo Bills
1980*	Buddy Curry	LB	Atlanta Falcons
	Al Richardson	LB	Atlanta Falcons

Year	Player	Pos	Team		Year	Player	Team
1981	Lawrence Taylor	LB	New York Giants		1988	Mike Ditka	Chicago Bears
1982	Chip Banks	LB	Cleveland Browns		1989	Lindy Infante	Green Bay Packers
1983	Vernon Maxwell	LB	Baltimore Colts		1990	Jimmy Johnson	Dallas Cowboys
1984	Bill Maas	NT	Kansas City Chiefs		1991	Wayne Fontes	Detroit Lions
1985	Duane Bickett	LB	Indianapolis Colts		1992	Bill Cowher	Pittsburgh Steelers
1986	John Offerdahl	LB	Miami Dolphins		1993	Dan Reeves	New York Giants
1987	Shane Conlan	LB	Buffalo Bills		1994	Bill Parcells	New England Patriots
1988	Erik McMillan	S	New York Jets		1995	Ray Rhodes	Philadelphia Eagles
1989	Derrick Thomas	LB	Kansas City Chiefs		1996	Dom Capers	Carolina Panthers
1990	Mark Carrier	S	Chicago Bears		1997	Jim Fassel	New York Giants
1991	Mike Croel	LB	Denver Broncos		1998	Dan Reeves	Atlanta Falcons
1992	Dale Carter	CB	Kansas City Chiefs		1999	Dick Vermeil	St. Louis Rams
1993	Dana Stubblefield	DT	San Francisco 49ers		2000	Jim Haslett	New Orleans Saints
1994	Tim Bowens	DT	Miami Dolphins		2001	Dick Jauron	Chicago Bears
1995	Hugh Douglas	DE	New York Jets		2002	Andy Reid	Philadelphia Eagles
1996	Simeon Rice	DE	Arizona Cardinals		2003	Bill Belichick	New England Patriots
1997	Peter Boulware	LB	Baltimore Ravens		2004	Marty Schottenheimer	San Diego Chargers
1998	Charles Woodson	CB	Oakland Raiders				
1999	Jevon Kearse	DE	Tennessee Titans				
2000	Brian Urlacher	LB	Chicago Bears				
2001	Kendrell Bell	LB	Pittsburgh Steelers				
2002	Julius Peppers	DE	Carolina Panthers				
2003	Terrell Suggs	LB	Baltimore Ravens				
2004	Jonathan Vilma	LB	New York Jets				

*The award was shared in 1980.

*The award was shared in 1967.

AP COMEBACK PLAYER OF THE YEAR

1998	Doug Flutie	QB	Buffalo Bills
1999	Bryant Young	DT	San Francisco 49ers
2000	Joe Johnson	DE	New Orleans Saints
2001	Garrison Hearst	RB	San Francisco 49ers
2002	Tommy Maddox	QB	Pittsburgh Steelers
2003	Jon Kitna	QB	Cincinnati Bengals
2004	Drew Brees	QB	San Diego Chargers

AP COACH OF THE YEAR

1957	George Wilson	Detroit Lions
1958	Weeb Ewbank	Baltimore Colts
1959	Vince Lombardi	Green Bay Packers
1960	Buck Shaw	Philadelphia Eagles
1961	Allie Sherman	New York Giants
1962	Allie Sherman	New York Giants
1963	George Halas	Chicago Bears
1964	Don Shula	Baltimore Colts
1965	George Halas	Chicago Bears
1966	Tom Landry	Dallas Cowboys
1967*	George Allen	Los Angeles Rams
	Don Shula	Baltimore Colts
1968	Don Shula	Baltimore Colts
1969	Bud Grant	Minnesota Vikings
1970	Paul Brown	Cincinnati Bengals
1971	George Allen	Washington Redskins
1972	Don Shula	Miami Dolphins
1973	Chuck Knox	Los Angeles Rams
1974	Don Coryell	St. Louis Cardinals
1975	Ted Marchibroda	Baltimore Colts
1976	Forrest Gregg	Cleveland Browns
1977	Red Miller	Denver Broncos
1978	Jack Patera	Seattle Seahawks
1979	Jack Pardee	Washington Redskins
1980	Chuck Knox	Buffalo Bills
1981	Bill Walsh	San Francisco 49ers
1982	Joe Gibbs	Washington Redskins
1983	Joe Gibbs	Washington Redskins
1984	Chuck Knox	Seattle Seahawks
1985	Mike Ditka	Chicago Bears
1986	Bill Parcells	New York Giants
1987	Jim Mora	New Orleans Saints

NFL'S 10 HIGHEST SCORING WEEKENDS

Point Total	Date	Weekend
788	December 5-6, 2004	13th
788	September 5, 8-9, 2002	1st
762	November 10-11, 1996	11th
761	October 16-17, 1983	7th
753	December 8-9, 2002	14th
748	December 18-20, 2004	15th
740	November 29-30, 1998	13th
739	November 23, 26-27, 1995	13th
736	October 25-26, 1987	7th
734	November 19-20, 1995	12th

TOP 10 TELEVISED SPORTS EVENTS OF ALL-TIME
(Based on A.C. Nielsen Figures)

Program	Date	Network	Share	Rating
Super Bowl XVI	1/24/82	CBS	73%	49.1
Super Bowl XVII	1/30/83	NBC	69%	48.6
Winter Olympics	2/23/94	CBS	64%	48.5
Super Bowl XX	1/26/86	NBC	70%	48.3
Super Bowl XII	1/15/78	CBS	67%	47.2
Super Bowl XIII	1/21/79	NBC	74%	47.1
Super Bowl XVIII	1/22/84	CBS	71%	46.4
Super Bowl XIX	1/20/85	ABC	63%	46.4
Super Bowl XIV	1/20/80	CBS	67%	46.3
Super Bowl XXX	1/28/96	NBC	68%	46.0

TEN MOST WATCHED TV PROGRAMS & ESTIMATED TOTAL NUMBER OF VIEWERS
(Based on A.C. Nielsen Figures)

Program	Date	Network	*Total Viewers
Super Bowl XXXVIII	Feb. 1, 2004	CBS	144,400,000
Super Bowl XXXVII	Jan. 26, 2003	ABC	138,900,000
Super Bowl XXX	Jan. 28, 1996	NBC	138,488,000
Super Bowl XXVIII	Jan. 30, 1994	NBC	134,800,000
Super Bowl XXXIX	Feb. 6, 2005	FOX	133,700,000
Super Bowl XXXII	Jan. 25, 1998	NBC	133,400,000
Super Bowl XXVII	Jan. 31, 1993	NBC	133,400,000
Super Bowl XXXVI	Feb. 3, 2002	FOX	131,700,000
Super Bowl XXXV	Jan. 28, 2001	CBS	131,200,000
Super Bowl XXXIV	Jan. 30, 2000	ABC	130,744,800

Watched some portion of the broadcast

NFL'S TOP FIVE PAID ATTENDANCE TOTALS FOR ALL GAMES

Year	Preseason	Regular Season	Postseason	All Games
2004	3,918,848	17,000,811	788,965	21,708,624
2003	3,919,910	16,913,584	805,546	21,639,040
2002	3,889,884	16,833,310	781,944	21,505,138
2000	3,757,231	16,387,289	809,132	20,953,652
1999	3,762,331	16,206,640	793,759	20,762,730

TEN HIGHEST-RATED ABC *NFL MONDAY NIGHT FOOTBALL* GAMES OF ALL-TIME
(Based on A.C. Nielsen Figures)

Game	Date	Share	Rating
Chicago at Miami	12/2/85	46%	29.6
N.Y. Giants at San Francisco	12/3/90	42%	26.9
Dallas at Washington	10/2/78	43%	26.8
Pittsburgh at San Diego	12/22/80	40%	25.3
Philadelphia at Miami	11/30/81	40%	25.3
Pittsburgh at Houston	12/10/79	40%	25.1
Dallas at Miami	12/17/84	40%	25.1
Pittsburgh at Dallas	9/13/82	42%	24.9
Cincinnati at Oakland	12/6/76	40%	24.7
Dallas at Washington	10/8/73	40%	24.6
Minnesota at Atlanta	11/19/73	40%	24.6

NFL'S 10 BIGGEST SINGLE-GAME ATTENDANCE TOTALS

Date	Site	Game	Teams	Attendance
August 15, 1994	Azteca Stadium	American Bowl (Mexico City)	Cowboys vs. Oilers	112,376
August 17, 1998	Azteca Stadium	American Bowl (Mexico City)	Cowboys vs. Patriots	106,424
August 22, 1947	Soldier Field	College All-Star	Bears vs. All-Stars	105,840
August 4, 1997	Estadio Guillermo Canedo	American Bowl (Mexico City)	Broncos vs. Dolphins	104,629
January 20, 1980	Rose Bowl	Super Bowl XIV	Steelers vs. Rams	103,985
January 30, 1983	Rose Bowl	Super Bowl XVII	Redskins vs. Dolphins	103,667
January 9, 1977	Rose Bowl	Super Bowl XI	Raiders vs. Vikings	103,438
November 10, 1957	L.A. Coliseum	Regular Season	49ers vs. Rams	102,368
January 25, 1987	Rose Bowl	Super Bowl XXI	Giants vs. Broncos	101,643
August 20, 1948	Soldier Field	College All-Star	Cardinals vs. All-Stars	101,220

NFL'S TOP 10 PAID ATTENDANCE WEEKENDS

Weekend	Games	Attendance
December 27-28, 2003	16	1,106,818
September 9, 12-13, 2004	16	1,101,332
September 4, 7-8, 2003	16	1,095,720
November 23-24, 2003	16	1,087,869
September 15-16, 2002	16	1,081,206
December 7-8, 2003	16	1,078,229
November 24-25, 2002	16	1,078,011
December 12-13, 2004	16	1,072,137
November 27, 30-December 1, 2003	16	1,070,451
September 5, 8-9, 2002	16	1,067,957

NFL'S TOP 10 TEAM SINGLE-SEASON HOME PAID ATTENDANCE TOTALS

Year	Club	Games	Attendance
2004	Washington Redskins	8	707,920
2003	Washington Redskins	8	667,033
2002	Washington Redskins	8	663,536
2001	Washington Redskins	8	661,970
2000	Washington Redskins	8	656,599
1980	Detroit Lions	8	634,204
1988	Buffalo Bills	8	631,818
1991	Buffalo Bills	8	631,786
1992	Buffalo Bills	8	630,978
2004	New York Giants	8	629,874

NFL PAID ATTENDANCE

For detailed 2004 attendance, see page 346.

Year	Regular Season			Average	Postseason	Total
2004	#17,000,811	(256 games)		#66,409	788,965 (12)	#17,789,776
2003	16,913,584	(255 games***)		66,328	805,546 (12)	17,719,130
2002	16,833,310	(256 games)		65,755	781,944 (12)	17,615,254
2001	16,166,258	(248 games)		65,187	766,905 (12)	16,933,163
2000	16,387,289	(248 games)		66,078	809,132 (12)	17,196,421
1999	16,206,640	(248 games)		65,349	793,759 (12)	17,000,399
1998	15,364,873	(240 games)		64,020	822,885 (12)	16,187,758
1997	14,967,314	(240 games)		62,364	801,879 (12)	15,769,193
1996	14,612,417	(240 games)		60,885	769,310 (12)	15,381,727
1995	15,043,562	(240 games)		62,682	790,906 (12)	15,834,468
1994	14,030,435	(224 games)		62,636	779,738 (12)	14,810,173
1993	13,966,843	(224 games)		62,352	814,607 (12)	14,781,450
1992	13,828,887	(224 games)		61,736	815,910 (12)	14,644,797
1991	13,841,459	(224 games)		61,792	813,247 (12)	14,654,706
1990	13,959,896	(224 games)		62,321	847,543 (12)	14,807,439
1989	13,625,662	(224 games)		60,829	685,771 (10)	14,311,433
1988	13,539,848	(224 games)		60,446	658,317 (10)	14,198,165
1987	11,406,166	(210 games**)		54,315	656,977 (10)	12,063,143
1986	13,588,551	(224 games)		60,663	734,002 (10)	14,322,553
1985	13,345,047	(224 games)		59,567	710,768 (10)	14,055,815
1984	13,398,112	(224 games)		59,813	665,194 (10)	14,063,306
1983	13,277,222	(224 games)		59,273	675,513 (10)	13,952,735
1982	7,367,438	(126 games*)		58,472	1,033,153 (16)	8,400,591
1981	13,606,990	(224 games)		60,745	637,763 (10)	14,244,753
1980	13,392,230	(224 games)		59,787	624,430 (10)	14,016,660
1979	13,182,039	(224 games)		58,848	630,326 (10)	13,812,365
1978	12,771,800	(224 games)		57,017	624,388 (10)	13,396,188
1977	11,018,632	(196 games)		56,218	534,925 (8)	11,553,557
1976	11,070,543	(196 games)		56,482	492,884 (8)	11,563,427
1975	10,213,193	(182 games)		56,116	475,919 (8)	10,689,112
1974	10,236,322	(182 games)		56,244	438,664 (8)	10,674,986
1973	10,730,933	(182 games)		58,961	525,433 (8)	11,256,366
1972	10,445,827	(182 games)		57,395	483,345 (8)	10,929,172
1971	10,076,035	(182 games)		55,363	483,891 (8)	10,559,926
1970	9,533,333	(182 games)		52,381	458,493 (8)	9,991,826
1969	6,096,127	(112 games)	NFL	54,430	162,279 (3)	6,258,406
	2,843,373	(70 games)	AFL	40,620	167,088 (3)	3,010,461
1968	5,882,313	(112 games)	NFL	52,521	215,902 (3)	6,098,215
	2,635,004	(70 games)	AFL	37,643	114,438 (2)	2,749,442
1967	5,938,924	(112 games)	NFL	53,026	166,208 (3)	6,105,132
	2,295,697	(63 games)	AFL	36,439	53,330 (1)	2,349,027
1966	5,337,044	(105 games)	NFL	50,829	74,152 (1)	5,411,196
	2,160,369	(63 games)	AFL	34,291	42,080 (1)	2,202,449
1965	4,634,021	(98 games)	NFL	47,286	100,304 (2)	4,734,325
	1,782,384	(56 games)	AFL	31,828	30,361 (1)	1,812,745
1964	4,563,049	(98 games)	NFL	46,562	79,544 (1)	4,642,593
	1,447,875	(56 games)	AFL	25,855	40,242 (1)	1,488,117
1963	4,163,643	(98 games)	NFL	42,486	45,801 (1)	4,209,444
	1,208,697	(56 games)	AFL	21,584	63,171 (2)	1,271,868
1962	4,003,421	(98 games)	NFL	40,851	64,892 (1)	4,068,313
	1,147,302	(56 games)	AFL	20,487	37,981 (1)	1,185,283

PAID ATTENDANCE

Year	Regular Season			Average	Postseason	Total
1961	3,986,159	(98 games)	NFL	40,675	39,029 (1)	4,025,188
	1,002,657	(56 games)	AFL	17,904	29,556 (1)	1,032,213
1960	3,128,296	(78 games)	NFL	40,106	67,325 (1)	3,195,621
	926,156	(56 games)	AFL	16,538	32,183 (1)	958,339
1959	3,140,000	(72 games)		43,617	57,545 (1)	3,197,545
1958	3,006,124	(72 games)		41,752	123,659 (2)	3,129,783
1957	2,836,318	(72 games)		39,393	119,579 (2)	2,955,897
1956	2,551,263	(72 games)		35,434	56,836 (1)	2,608,099
1955	2,521,836	(72 games)		35,026	85,693 (1)	2,607,529
1954	2,190,571	(72 games)		30,425	43,827 (1)	2,234,398
1953	2,164,585	(72 games)		30,064	54,577 (1)	2,219,162
1952	2,052,126	(72 games)		28,502	97,507 (2)	2,149,633
1951	1,913,019	(72 games)		26,570	57,522 (1)	1,970,541
1950	1,977,753	(78 games)		25,356	136,647 (3)	2,114,400
1949	1,391,735	(60 games)		23,196	27,980 (1)	1,419,715
1948	1,525,243	(60 games)		25,421	36,309 (1)	1,561,552
1947	1,837,437	(60 games)		30,624	66,268 (2)	1,903,705
1946	1,732,135	(55 games)		31,493	58,346 (1)	1,790,481
1945	1,270,401	(50 games)		25,408	32,178 (1)	1,302,579
1944	1,019,649	(50 games)		20,393	46,016 (1)	1,065,665
1943	969,128	(40 games)		24,228	71,315 (2)	1,040,443
1942	887,920	(55 games)		16,144	36,006 (1)	923,926
1941	1,108,615	(55 games)		20,157	55,870 (2)	1,164,485
1940	1,063,025	(55 games)		19,328	36,034 (1)	1,099,059
1939	1,071,200	(55 games)		19,476	32,279 (1)	1,103,479
1938	937,197	(55 games)		17,040	48,120 (1)	985,317
1937	963,039	(55 games)		17,510	15,878 (1)	978,917
1936	816,007	(54 games)		15,111	29,545 (1)	845,552
1935	638,178	(53 games)		12,041	15,000 (1)	653,178
1934	492,684	(60 games)		8,211	35,059 (1)	527,743

 # Record
  *Players' 57-day strike reduced 224-game schedule to 126 games.
  **Players' 24-day strike reduced 224-game schedule to 210 games.
  ***The Week 8 Miami at San Diego game is not included. The game was moved to Arizona due to the San Diego wildfires and tickets were distributed at no charge.

75TH ANNIVERSARY ALL-TIME TEAM
Chosen by a selection committee of media and league personnel in 1994.

Position	Name	Team(s)	Ht.	Wt.	College
OFFENSE					
QB	Sammy Baugh	Washington Redskins (1937-52)	6-2	180	Texas Christian
QB	Otto Graham	Cleveland Browns (1946-55)	6-1	195	Northwestern
QB	Joe Montana	San Francisco 49ers (1979-92), Kansas City Chiefs (1993-94)	6-2	195	Notre Dame
QB	Johnny Unitas	Baltimore Colts (1956-72), San Diego Chargers (1973)	6-1	195	Louisville
RB	Jim Brown	Cleveland Browns (1957-65)	6-2	232	Syracuse
RB	Marion Motley	Cleveland Browns (1946-53), Pittsburgh Steelers (1955)	6-1	238	Nevada-Reno
RB	Bronko Nagurski	Chicago Bears (1930-37, 1943)	6-2	225	Minnesota
RB	Walter Payton	Chicago Bears (1975-87)	5-10	202	Jackson State
RB	Gale Sayers	Chicago Bears (1965-71)	6-0	200	Kansas
RB	O.J. Simpson	Buffalo Bills (1969-77), San Francisco 49ers (1978-79)	6-1	212	Southern California
RB	Steve Van Buren	Philadelphia Eagles (1944-51)	6-1	200	Louisiana State
WR	Lance Alworth	San Diego Chargers (1962-70), Dallas Cowboys (1971-72)	6-0	184	Arkansas
WR	Raymond Berry	Baltimore Colts (1955-67)	6-2	187	Southern Methodist
WR	Don Hutson	Green Bay Packers (1935-45)	6-1	180	Alabama
WR	Jerry Rice	San Francisco 49ers (1985-2000), Oakland Raiders (2001-04), Seattle Seahawks (2004)	6-2	200	Miss. Valley State
TE	Mike Ditka	Chicago Bears (1961-66), Philadelphia Eagles (1967-68), Dallas Cowboys (1969-72)	6-3	225	Pittsburgh
TE	Kellen Winslow	San Diego Chargers (1979-87)	6-5	250	Missouri
T	Roosevelt Brown	New York Giants (1953-65)	6-3	255	Morgan State
T	Forrest Gregg	Green Bay Packers (1956, 1958-70)	6-4	250	Southern Methodist
T	Anthony Muñoz	Cincinnati Bengals (1980-92)	6-6	285	Southern California
G	John Hannah	New England Patriots (1973-85)	6-3	265	Alabama
G	Jim Parker	Baltimore Colts (1957-67)	6-3	273	Ohio State
G	Gene Upshaw	Oakland Raiders (1967-81)	6-5	255	Texas A&I
C	Mel Hein	New York Giants (1931-45)	6-2	225	Washington State
C	Mike Webster	Pittsburgh Steelers (1974-88), Kansas City Chiefs (1989-90)	6-2	250	Wisconsin
DEFENSE					
DE	David (Deacon) Jones	Los Angeles Rams (1961-71), San Diego Chargers (1972-73), Washington Redskins (1974)	6-5	250	Miss. Vocational-South Carolina St.
DE	Gino Marchetti	Dallas Texans (1952), Baltimore Colts (1953-64, 1966)	6-4	245	San Francisco
DE	Reggie White	Philadelphia Eagles (1985-92), Green Bay Packers (1993-1998), Carolina Panthers (2000)	6-5	290	Tennessee
DT	Joe Greene	Pittsburgh Steelers (1969-81)	6-4	260	North Texas State
DT	Bob Lilly	Dallas Cowboys (1961-74)	6-5	260	Texas Christian
DT	Merlin Olsen	Los Angeles Rams (1962-76)	6-5	270	Utah State
LB	Dick Butkus	Chicago Bears (1965-73)	6-3	245	Illinois
LB	Jack Ham	Pittsburgh Steelers (1971-82)	6-1	225	Penn State
LB	Ted Hendricks	Baltimore Colts (1969-73), Green Bay Packers (1974), Oakland/L.A. Raiders (1975-83)	6-7	235	Miami
LB	Jack Lambert	Pittsburgh Steelers (1974-84)	6-4	220	Kent State
LB	Willie Lanier	Kansas City Chiefs (1967-77)	6-1	245	Morgan State
LB	Ray Nitschke	Green Bay Packers (1958-72)	6-3	235	Illinois
LB	Lawrence Taylor	New York Giants (1981-93)	6-3	243	North Carolina
CB	Mel Blount	Pittsburgh Steelers (1970-83)	6-3	205	Southern
CB	Mike Haynes	New England Patriots (1976-82), Los Angeles Raiders (1983-89)	6-2	190	Arizona State
CB	Dick (Night Train) Lane	Los Angeles Rams (1952-53), Chicago Cardinals (1954-59), Detroit Lions (1960-65)	6-2	210	Scottsbluff JC
CB	Rod Woodson	Pittsburgh Steelers (1987-96), San Francisco 49ers (1997), Baltimore Ravens (1998-2001), Oakland Raiders (2002-2003)	6-0	200	Purdue
S	Ken Houston	Houston Oilers (1967-72), Washington Redskins (1973-80)	6-3	198	Prairie View A&M
S	Ronnie Lott	San Francisco 49ers (1981-90), Los Angeles Raiders (1991-92), New York Jets (1993-94)	6-0	200	Southern California
S	Larry Wilson	St. Louis Cardinals (1960-72)	6-0	190	Utah
SPECIAL TEAMS					
P	Ray Guy	Oakland/L.A. Raiders (1973-86)	6-3	190	Southern Mississippi
K	Jan Stenerud	Kansas City Chiefs (1967-79), Green Bay Packers (1980-83), Minnesota Vikings (1984-85)	6-2	190	Montana State
PR	Billy (White Shoes) Johnson	Houston Oilers (1974-80), Atlanta Falcons (1982-87), Washington Redskins (1988)	5-9	170	Widener
KR	Gale Sayers	Chicago Bears (1965-71)	6-0	200	Kansas

75TH ANNIVERSARY ALL-TWO-WAY TEAM

Positions

Quarterback, Defensive Halfback, Punter	Sammy Baugh
Center, Linebacker	Chuck Bednarik
Quarterback, Defensive Halfback, Punter	Earl (Dutch) Clark
Tackle, Defensive Tackle	George Connor
Guard, Defensive Tackle	Danny Fortmann
Center, Defensive Tackle	Mel Hein
Tackle, Defensive Tackle, Punter	Wilbur (Pete) Henry
Back, Defensive Halfback	Bill Hewitt
Fullback, Linebacker, Kicker	Clarke Hinkle
Tackle, Defensive Tackle	Cal Hubbard
End, Defensive Halfback	Don Hutson
Back, Defensive Back	George McAfee
Fullback, Linebacker	Marion Motley
Guard-Tackle, Defensive Tackle	George Musso
Fullback, Linebacker	Bronko Nagurski
Halfback, Defensive Halfback	Ernie Nevers
End, Defensive Back	Pete Pihos
Tackle, Defensive Tackle	Joe Stydahar
Running Back, Defensive Back	Steve Van Buren

50TH ANNIVERSARY TEAM

Chosen by the Hall of Fame Selection Committee in 1969.

Offense

Split End	Don Hutson
Tight End	John Mackey
Tackle	Cal Hubbard
Guard	Jerry Kramer
Center	Chuck Bednarik
Flanker	Elroy Hirsch
Quarterback	Johnny Unitas
Halfback	Jim Thorpe
Halfback	Gale Sayers
Fullback	Jim Brown
Kicker	Lou Groza

Defense

End	Gino Marchetti
Tackle	Leo Nomellini
Linebacker	Ray Nitschke
Cornerback	Dick (Night Train) Lane
Safety	Emlen Tunnell

SUPER BOWL SILVER ANNIVERSARY TEAM

Chosen by the fans in 1990 prior to Super Bowl XXV.

Head Coach	Vince Lombardi

Offense

Quarterback	Joe Montana
Running Back	Franco Harris
Running Back	Larry Csonka
Wide Receiver	Lynn Swann
Wide Receiver	Jerry Rice
Tight End	Dave Casper
Tackle	Art Shell
Tackle	Forrest Gregg
Guard	Gene Upshaw
Guard	Jerry Kramer
Center	Mike Webster

Defense

Defensive End	L.C. Greenwood
Defensive End	Ed (Too Tall) Jones
Defensive Tackle	Joe Greene
Defensive Tackle	Randy White
Inside Linebacker	Jack Lambert
Inside Linebacker	Mike Singletary
Outside Linebacker	Jack Ham
Outside Linebacker	Ted Hendricks
Cornerback	Ronnie Lott
Cornerback	Mel Blount
Safety	Donnie Shell
Safety	Willie Wood

Special Teams

Punter	Ray Guy
Kicker	Jan Stenerud
Kick Returner	John Taylor

All-Decade teams chosen by the Hall of Fame Selection Committee members.

1920s ALL-DECADE TEAM

End	Guy Chamberlin
End	Lavern Dilweg
End	George Halas
Tackle	Ed Healey
Tackle	Wilbur (Pete) Henry
Tackle	Cal Hubbard
Tackle	Steve Owen
Guard	Hunk Anderson
Guard	Walt Kiesling
Guard	Mike Michalske
Center	George Trafton
Quarterback	Jimmy Conzelman
Quarterback	John (Paddy) Driscoll
Halfback	Harold (Red) Grange
Halfback	Joe Guyon
Halfback	Earl (Curly) Lambeau
Halfback	Jim Thorpe
Fullback	Ernie Nevers

1930s ALL-DECADE TEAM

End	Bill Hewitt
End	Don Hutson
End	Wayne Millner
End	Gaynell Tinsley
Tackle	George Christensen
Tackle	Frank Cope
Tackle	Glen (Turk) Edwards
Tackle	Bill Lee
Tackle	Joe Stydahar
Guard	Grover (Ox) Emerson
Guard	Dan Fortmann
Guard	Charles (Buckets) Goldenberg
Guard	Russ Letlow
Center	Mel Hein
Center	George Svendsen
Quarterback	Earl (Dutch) Clark
Quarterback	Arnie Herber
Quarterback	Cecil Isbell
Halfback	Cliff Battles
Halfback	Johnny (Blood) McNally
Halfback	Beattie Feathers
Halfback	Alphonse (Tuffy) Leemans
Halfback	Ken Strong
Fullback	Clarke Hinkle
Fullback	Bronko Nagurski

1940s ALL-DECADE TEAM

End	Jim Benton
End	Jack Ferrante
End	Ken Kavanaugh
End	Dante Lavelli
End	Pete Pihos
End	Mac Speedie
End	Ed Sprinkle
Tackle	Al Blozis
Tackle	George Connor
Tackle	Frank (Bucko) Kilroy
Tackle	Buford (Baby) Ray
Tackle	Vic Sears
Tackle	Al Wistert
Guard	Bruno Banducci
Guard	Bill Edwards
Guard	Garrard (Buster) Ramsey
Guard	Bill Willis
Guard	Len Younce
Center	Charley Brock
Center	Clyde (Bulldog) Turner
Center	Alex Wojciechowicz
Quarterback	Sammy Baugh
Quarterback	Sid Luckman
Quarterback	Bob Waterfield
Halfback	Tony Canadeo
Halfback	Bill Dudley
Halfback	George McAfee
Halfback	Charley Trippi
Halfback	Steve Van Buren
Halfback	Byron (Whizzer) White
Fullback	Pat Harder
Fullback	Marion Motley
Fullback	Bill Osmanski

1950s ALL-DECADE TEAM

Offense

End	Raymond Berry
End	Tom Fears
End	Bobby Walston
Halfback-End	Elroy (Crazylegs) Hirsch
Tackle	Roosevelt Brown
Tackle	Bob St. Clair
Guard	Dick Barwegan
Guard	Jim Parker
Guard	Dick Stanfel
Center	Chuck Bednarik
Quarterback	Otto Graham
Quarterback	Bobby Layne
Quarterback	Norm Van Brocklin
Halfback	Frank Gifford
Halfback	Ollie Matson
Halfback	Hugh McElhenny
Halfback	Lenny Moore
Fullback	Alan Ameche
Fullback	Joe Perry
Kicker	Lou Groza

Defense

End	Len Ford
End	Gino Marchetti
Tackle	Art Donovan
Tackle	Leo Nomellini
Tackle	Ernie Stautner
Linebacker	Joe Fortunato
Linebacker	Bill George
Linebacker	Sam Huff
Linebacker	Joe Schmidt
Halfback	Jack Butler
Halfback	Dick (Night Train) Lane
Safety	Jack Christiansen
Safety	Yale Lary
Safety	Emlen Tunnell

1960s ALL-DECADE TEAM

Offense

Split End	Del Shofner
Split End	Charley Taylor
Flanker	Gary Collins
Flanker	Boyd Dowler
Tight End	John Mackey
Tackle	Bob Brown
Tackle	Forrest Gregg
Tackle	Ralph Neely
Guard	Gene Hickerson
Guard	Jerry Kramer
Guard	Howard Mudd
Center	Jim Ringo
Quarterback	Sonny Jurgensen
Quarterback	Bart Starr
Quarterback	Johnny Unitas
Halfback	John David Crow
Halfback	Paul Hornung
Halfback	Leroy Kelly
Halfback	Gale Sayers
Fullback	Jim Brown
Fullback	Jim Taylor
Kicker	Jim Bakken

Defense

End	Doug Atkins
End	Willie Davis
End	David (Deacon) Jones
Tackle	Alex Karras
Tackle	Bob Lilly
Tackle	Merlin Olsen
Linebacker	Dick Butkus
Linebacker	Larry Morris
Linebacker	Ray Nitschke
Linebacker	Tommy Nobis
Linebacker	Dave Robinson
Cornerback	Herb Adderley
Cornerback	Lem Barney
Cornerback	Bobby Boyd
Safety	Eddie Meador
Safety	Larry Wilson
Safety	Willie Wood
Punter	Don Chandler

1970s ALL-DECADE TEAM

Offense

Wide Receiver	Harold Carmichael
Wide Receiver	Drew Pearson
Wide Receiver	Lynn Swann
Wide Receiver	Paul Warfield
Tight End	Dave Casper
Tight End	Charlie Sanders
Tackle	Dan Dierdorf
Tackle	Art Shell
Tackle	Rayfield Wright
Tackle	Ron Yary
Guard	Joe DeLamielleure
Guard	John Hannah
Guard	Larry Little
Guard	Gene Upshaw
Center	Jim Langer
Center	Mike Webster
Quarterback	Terry Bradshaw
Quarterback	Ken Stabler
Quarterback	Roger Staubach
Running Back	Earl Campbell
Running Back	Franco Harris
Running Back	Walter Payton
Running Back	O.J. Simpson
Kicker	Garo Yepremian

Defense

End	Carl Eller
End	L.C. Greenwood
End	Harvey Martin
End	Jack Youngblood
Tackle	Joe Greene
Tackle	Bob Lilly
Tackle	Merlin Olsen
Tackle	Alan Page
Linebacker	Bobby Bell
Linebacker	Robert Brazile
Linebacker	Dick Butkus
Linebacker	Jack Ham
Linebacker	Ted Hendricks
Linebacker	Jack Lambert
Cornerback	Willie Brown
Cornerback	Jimmy Johnson
Cornerback	Roger Wehrli
Cornerback	Louis Wright
Safety	Dick Anderson
Safety	Cliff Harris
Safety	Ken Houston
Safety	Larry Wilson
Punter	Ray Guy

1980s ALL-DECADE TEAM

Offense

Wide Receiver	Jerry Rice
Wide Receiver	Steve Largent
Wide Receiver	James Lofton
Wide Receiver	Art Monk
Tight End	Kellen Winslow
Tight End	Ozzie Newsome
Tackle	Anthony Munoz
Tackle	Jim Covert
Tackle	Gary Zimmerman
Tackle	Joe Jacoby
Guard	John Hannah
Guard	Russ Grimm
Guard	Bill Fralic
Guard	Mike Munchak
Center	Dwight Stephenson
Center	Mike Webster
Quarterback	Joe Montana
Quarterback	Dan Fouts
Running Back	Walter Payton
Running Back	Eric Dickerson
Running Back	Roger Craig
Running Back	John Riggins

Defense

End	Reggie White
End	Howie Long
End	Lee Roy Selmon
End	Bruce Smith
Tackle	Randy White
Tackle	Dan Hampton
Tackle	Keith Millard
Tackle	Dave Butz
Linebacker	Mike Singletary
Linebacker	Lawrence Taylor
Linebacker	Ted Hendricks
Linebacker	Jack Lambert
Linebacker	Andre Tippett
Linebacker	John Anderson
Linebacker	Carl Banks
Cornerback	Mike Haynes
Cornerback	Mel Blount
Cornerback	Frank Minnifield
Cornerback	Lester Hayes
Safety	Ronnie Lott
Safety	Kenny Easley
Safety	Deron Cherry
Safety	Joey Browner
Safety	Nolan Cromwell

Specialists

Punter	Sean Landeta
Punter	Reggie Roby
Kicker	Morten Andersen
Kicker	Gary Anderson
Kicker	Eddie Murray
Punt Returner	Billy (White Shoes) Johnson
Punt Returner	John Taylor
Kick Returner	Mike Nelms
Kick Returner	Rick Upchurch
Coach	Bill Walsh
Coach	Chuck Noll

1990s ALL-DECADE TEAM

Offense

Wide Receiver	Cris Carter
Wide Receiver	Jerry Rice
Wide Receiver	Tim Brown
Wide Receiver	Michael Irvin
Tight End	Shannon Sharpe
Tight End	Ben Coates
Tackle	William Roaf
Tackle	Gary Zimmerman
Tackle	Tony Boselli
Tackle	Richmond Webb
Guard	Bruce Matthews
Guard	Randall McDaniel
Guard	Larry Allen
Guard	Steve Wisniewski
Center	Dermontti Dawson
Center	Mark Stepnoski
Quarterback	John Elway
Quarterback	Brett Favre
Running Back	Barry Sanders
Running Back	Emmitt Smith
Running Back	Terrell Davis
Running Back	Thurman Thomas

Defense

End	Bruce Smith
End	Reggie White
End	Chris Doleman
End	Neil Smith
Tackle	Cortez Kennedy
Tackle	John Randle
Tackle	Warren Sapp
Tackle	Bryant Young
Linebacker	Kevin Greene
Linebacker	Junior Seau
Linebacker	Derrick Thomas
Linebacker	Cornelius Bennett
Linebacker	Hardy Nickerson
Linebacker	Levon Kirkland
Cornerback	Deion Sanders
Cornerback	Rod Woodson
Cornerback	Darrell Green
Cornerback	Aeneas Williams
Safety	Steve Atwater
Safety	LeRoy Butler
Safety	Carnell Lake
Safety	Ronnie Lott

Specialists

Punter	Darren Bennett
Punter	Sean Landeta
Kicker	Morten Andersen
Kicker	Gary Anderson
Punt Returner	Deion Sanders
Punt Returner	Mel Gray
Kick Returner	Michael Bates
Kick Returner	Mel Gray
Coach	Bill Parcells
Coach	Marv Levy

ALL-TIME AFL TEAM

Chosen by 1969 AFL Hall of Fame Selection Committee members.

Offense

Flanker	Lance Alworth
End	Don Maynard
Tight End	Fred Arbanas
Tackle	Ron Mix
Tackle	Jim Tyrer
Guard	Ed Budde
Guard	Billy Shaw
Center	Jim Otto
Quarterback	Joe Namath
Running Back	Clem Daniels
Running Back	Paul Lowe

Defense

End	Jerry Mays
End	Gerry Philbin
Tackle	Houston Antwine
Tackle	Tom Sestak
Linebacker	Bobby Bell
Linebacker	George Webster
Linebacker	Nick Buoniconti
Cornerback	Willie Brown
Cornerback	Dave Grayson
Safety	Johnny Robinson
Safety	George Saimes

Special Teams

Kicker	George Blanda
Punter	Jerrel Wilson

ALL-TIME NFL TEAM

Chosen by members of the Hall of Fame Selection Committee in 2000 for the book NFL's Greatest.

Offense

Wide Receiver	Don Hutson
Wide Receiver	Jerry Rice
Tight End	John Mackey
Tackle	Roosevelt Brown
Tackle	Anthony Muñoz
Guard	John Hannah
Guard	Jim Parker
Center	Mike Webster
Quarterback	Johnny Unitas
Running Back	Jim Brown
Running Back	Walter Payton

Defense

End	Deacon Jones
End	Reggie White
Tackle	Joe Greene
Tackle	Bob Lilly
Middle Linebacker	Dick Butkus
Outside Linebacker	Jack Ham
Outside Linebacker	Lawrence Taylor
Cornerback	Mel Blount
Cornerback	Dick (Night Train) Lane
Safety	Ronnie Lott
Safety	Larry Wilson

Special Teams

Kicker	Jan Stenerud
Punter	Ray Guy
Kick Returner	Gale Sayers
Punt Returner	Deion Sanders
Special Teams	Steve Tasker

AFL-NFL 1960-1984 ALL-STAR TEAM

Chosen by the Hall of Fame Selection Committee in 1985.

Offense

Quarterback	Johnny Unitas
Running Back	Jim Brown
Running Back	O.J. Simpson
Wide Receiver	Lance Alworth
Wide Receiver	Raymond Berry
Tight End	Kellen Winslow
Tight End	Forrest Gregg
Tight End	Ron Mix
Guard	Jim Parker
Guard	John Hannah
Center	Jim Otto

Defense

End	Gino Marchetti
End	Willie Davis
Tackle	Bob Lilly
Tackle	Merlin Olsen
Linebacker	Dick Butkus
Linebacker	Jack Lambert
Linebacker	Ray Nitschke
Cornerback	Willie Brown
Cornerback	Dick (Night Train) Lane
Safety	Larry Wilson
Safety	Yale Lary

Special Teams

Punter	Ray Guy
Kicker	Jan Stenerud
Kick Returner	Gale Sayers
Kick Returner	Rick Upchurch
Coach	Don Shula
Coach	Vince Lombardi

Records

Compiled by Elias Sports Bureau

The following records reflect all available official information on the National Football League from its formation in 1920 to date. Also included are all applicable records from the American Football League, 1960-69.

Individuals eligible for Rookie records are players who were in their first season of professional football and had not been on the roster of another professional football team, including teams in other leagues, for any regular-season or postseason games in a previous season. Eligible players, therefore, include those who were under contract to a National Football League club for a previous season but were terminated prior to their club's first regular-season game and not re-signed, or who were placed on Reserve/Injured (or another category of the Reserve List) prior to their club's first regular-season game and were not activated during the rest of the regular season or postseason.

INDIVIDUAL RECORDS

SERVICE
Most Seasons
- 26   George Blanda, Chi. Bears, 1949, 1950-58; Baltimore, 1950; Houston, 1960-66; Oakland, 1967-1975
- 23   Morten Andersen, New Orleans, 1982-1994; Atlanta, 1995-2000; N.Y. Giants, 2001; Kansas City, 2002-03; Minnesota, 2004
-     Gary Anderson, Pittsburgh, 1982-1994; Philadelphia, 1995-96; San Francisco, 1997; Minnesota, 1998-2002; Tennessee, 2003-04
- 21   Earl Morrall, San Francisco, 1956; Pittsburgh, 1957-58; Detroit, 1958-1964; N.Y. Giants, 1965-67; Baltimore, 1968-1971; Miami, 1972-76

Most Seasons, One Club
- 20   Jackie Slater, L.A. Rams, 1976-1994; St. Louis, 1995
-     Darrell Green, Washington, 1983-2002
- 19   Jim Marshall, Minnesota, 1961-1979
-     Bruce Matthews, Houston, 1983-1996; Tennessee, 1997-2001
- 18   Jim Hart, St. Louis, 1966-1983
-     Jeff Van Note, Atlanta, 1969-1986
-     Pat Leahy, N.Y. Jets, 1974-1991

Most Games Played, Career
- 354   Morten Andersen, New Orleans, 1982-1994; Atlanta, 1995-2000; N.Y. Giants, 2001; Kansas City, 2002-03; Minnesota, 2004
- 353   Gary Anderson, Pittsburgh, 1982-1994; Philadelphia, 1995-96; San Francisco, 1997; Minnesota, 1998-2002; Tennessee, 2003-04
- 340   George Blanda, Chi. Bears, 1949, 1950-58; Baltimore, 1950; Houston, 1960-66; Oakland, 1967-1975

Most Consecutive Games Played, Career
- 282   Jim Marshall, Cleveland, 1960; Minnesota, 1961-1979
- 272   Jeff Feagles, New England, 1988-89; Philadelphia, 1990-93; Arizona, 1994-97; Seattle, 1998-2002; N.Y. Giants, 2003-04 (current)
- 248   Morten Andersen, New Orleans, 1987-1994; Atlanta, 1995-2000; N.Y. Giants, 2001; Kansas City, 2002

SCORING
Most Seasons Leading League
- 5   Don Hutson, Green Bay, 1940-44
-    Gino Cappelletti, Boston, 1961, 1963-66
- 3   Earl (Dutch) Clark, Portsmouth, 1932; Detroit, 1935-36
-    Pat Harder, Chi. Cardinals, 1947-49
-    Paul Hornung, Green Bay, 1959-1961
- 2   Jack Manders, Chi. Bears, 1934, 1937
-    Gordy Soltau, San Francisco, 1952-53
-    Doak Walker, Detroit, 1950, 1955
-    Gene Mingo, Denver, 1960, 1962

-    Jim Turner, N.Y. Jets, 1968-69
-    Fred Cox, Minnesota, 1969-1970
-    Chester Marcol, Green Bay, 1972, 1974
-    John Smith, New England, 1979-1980
-    Marshall Faulk, St. Louis, 2000-01

Most Consecutive Seasons Leading League
- 5   Don Hutson, Green Bay, 1940-44
- 4   Gino Cappelletti, Boston, 1963-66
- 3   Pat Harder, Chi. Cardinals, 1947-49
-    Paul Hornung, Green Bay, 1959-1961

POINTS
Most Points, Career
- 2,434   Gary Anderson, Pittsburgh, 1982-1994; Philadelphia 1995-96; San Francisco, 1997; Minnesota, 1998-2002; Tennessee, 2003-04 (820-pat, 538-fg)
- 2,358   Morten Andersen, New Orleans, 1982-1994; Atlanta, 1995-2000; N.Y. Giants, 2001; Kansas City, 2002-03; Minnesota, 2004 (798-pat, 520-fg)
- 2,002   George Blanda, Chi. Bears, 1949, 1950-58; Baltimore, 1950; Houston, 1960-66; Oakland, 1967-1975 (9-td, 943-pat, 335-fg)

Most Points, Season
- 176   Paul Hornung, Green Bay, 1960 (15-td, 41-pat, 15-fg)
- 164   Gary Anderson, Minnesota, 1998 (59-pat, 35-fg)
- 163   Jeff Wilkins, St. Louis, 2003 (46-pat, 39-fg)

Most Points, No Touchdowns, Season
- 164   Gary Anderson, Minnesota, 1998 (59-pat, 35-fg)
- 163   Jeff Wilkins, St. Louis, 2003 (46-pat, 39-fg)
- 161   Mark Moseley, Washington, 1983 (62-pat, 33-fg)

Most Seasons, 100 or More Points
- 14   Gary Anderson, Pittsburgh, 1982-1994; Philadelphia 1995-96; San Francisco, 1997; Minnesota, 1998-2002; Tennessee, 2003
-    Morten Andersen, New Orleans, 1982-1994; Atlanta, 1995-2000; N.Y. Giants, 2001; Kansas City, 2002-03
- 12   Jason Elam, Denver, 1993-2004
- 11   Nick Lowery, Kansas City, 1981, 1983-86, 1988-1993

Most Points, Rookie, Season
- 144   Kevin Butler, Chicago, 1985 (51-pat, 31-fg)
- 132   Gale Sayers, Chicago, 1965 (22-td)
- 128   Doak Walker, Detroit, 1950 (11-td, 38-pat, 8-fg)
-    Chester Marcol, Green Bay, 1972 (29-pat, 33-fg)

Most Points, Game
- 40   Ernie Nevers, Chi. Cardinals vs. Chi. Bears, Nov. 28, 1929 (6-td, 4-pat)
- 36   Dub Jones, Cleveland vs. Chi. Bears, Nov. 25, 1951 (6-td)
-    Gale Sayers, Chicago vs. San Francisco, Dec. 12, 1965 (6-td)
- 33   Paul Hornung, Green Bay vs. Baltimore, Oct. 8, 1961 (4-td, 6-pat, 1-fg)

Most Consecutive Games Scoring
- 332   Morten Andersen, New Orleans, 1983-1994; Atlanta, 1995-2000; N.Y. Giants, 2001; Kansas City, 2002-03; Minnesota, 2004 (current)
- 188   Jason Elam, Denver, 1993-2004 (current)
- 186   Jim Breech, Oakland, 1979; Cincinnati, 1980-1992

TOUCHDOWNS
Most Seasons Leading League
- 8   Don Hutson, Green Bay, 1935-38, 1941-44
- 3   Jim Brown, Cleveland, 1958-59, 1963
-    Lance Alworth, San Diego, 1964-66
-    Emmitt Smith, Dallas, 1992, 1994-95
- 2   By many players

Most Consecutive Seasons Leading League
- 4   Don Hutson, Green Bay, 1935-38, 1941-44

3   Lance Alworth, San Diego, 1964-66
2   By many players

Most Touchdowns, Career

208   Jerry Rice, San Francisco, 1985-2000;
       Oakland, 2001-04; Seattle, 2004
       (10-r, 197-p, 1-ret)

175   Emmitt Smith, Dallas, 1990-2002; Arizona, 2003-04
       (164-r, 11-p)

145   Marcus Allen, L.A. Raiders, 1982-1992; Kansas City,
       1993-97 (123-r, 21-p, 1-ret)

Most Touchdowns, Season

27   Priest Holmes, Kansas City, 2003 (27-r)
26   Marshall Faulk, St. Louis, 2000 (18-r, 8-p)
25   Emmitt Smith, Dallas, 1995 (25-r)

Most Touchdowns, Rookie, Season

22   Gale Sayers, Chicago, 1965 (14-r, 6-p, 2-ret)
20   Eric Dickerson, L.A. Rams, 1983 (18-r, 2-p)
17   Randy Moss, Minnesota, 1998 (17-p)
      Fred Taylor, Jacksonville, 1998 (14-r, 3-p)
      Edgerrin James, Indianapolis, 1999 (13-r, 4-p)
      Clinton Portis, Denver, 2002 (15-r, 2-p)

Most Touchdowns, Game

6   Ernie Nevers, Chi. Cardinals vs. Chi. Bears,
      Nov. 28, 1929 (6-r)
      Dub Jones, Cleveland vs. Chi. Bears, Nov. 25, 1951
      (4-r, 2-p)
      Gale Sayers, Chicago vs. San Francisco, Dec. 12, 1965
      (4-r, 1-p, 1-ret)
5   Jimmy Conzelman, Rhode Island vs. Evansville,
      Oct. 15, 1922 (5-r)
      Bob Shaw, Chi. Cardinals vs. Baltimore, Oct. 2, 1950
      (5-p)
      Jim Brown, Cleveland vs. Baltimore, Nov. 1, 1959 (5-r)
      Abner Haynes, Dall. Texans vs. Oakland,
      Nov. 26, 1961 (4-r, 1-p)
      Billy Cannon, Houston vs. N.Y. Titans, Dec. 10, 1961
      (3-r, 2-p)
      Cookie Gilchrist, Buffalo vs. N.Y. Jets, Dec. 8, 1963 (5-r)
      Paul Hornung, Green Bay vs. Baltimore,
      Dec. 12, 1965 (3-r, 2-p)
      Kellen Winslow, San Diego vs. Oakland,
      Nov. 22, 1981 (5-p)
      Jerry Rice, San Francisco vs. Atlanta, Oct. 14, 1990
      (5-p)
      James Stewart, Jacksonville vs. Philadelphia,
      Oct. 12, 1997 (5-r)
      Shaun Alexander, Seattle vs. Minnesota,
      Sept. 29, 2002 (4-r, 1-p)
      Clinton Portis, Denver vs. Kansas City, Dec. 7, 2003
      (5-r)
4   By many players. Last time: T.J. Duckett,
      Atlanta vs. Oakland, Dec. 12, 2004

Most Consecutive Games Scoring Touchdowns

18   Lenny Moore, Baltimore, 1963-65
14   O.J. Simpson, Buffalo, 1975
13   John Riggins, Washington, 1982-83
      George Rogers, Washington, 1985-86
      Jerry Rice, San Francisco, 1986-87

POINTS AFTER TOUCHDOWN

Most Seasons Leading League

8   George Blanda, Chi. Bears, 1956; Houston,
      1961-62; Oakland, 1967-69, 1972, 1974
4   Bob Waterfield, Cleveland, 1945; Los Angeles, 1946,
      1950, 1952
3   Earl (Dutch) Clark, Portsmouth, 1932; Detroit,
      1935-36 Jack Manders, Chi. Bears, 1933-35
      Don Hutson, Green Bay, 1941-42, 1945

Most (Kicking) Points After Touchdown Attempted, Career

959   George Blanda, Chi. Bears, 1949, 1950-58; Baltimore,
       1950; Houston, 1960-66; Oakland, 1967-1975
827   Gary Anderson, Pittsburgh, 1982-1994; Philadelphia
       1995-96; San Francisco, 1997; Minnesota,
       1998-2002; Tennessee, 2003-04
808   Morten Andersen, New Orleans, 1982-1994;
       Atlanta, 1995-2000; N.Y. Giants, 2001;
       Kansas City, 2002-03; Minnesota, 2004

Most (Kicking) Points After Touchdown Attempted, Season

70   Uwe von Schamann, Miami, 1984
65   George Blanda, Houston, 1961
64   Jeff Wilkins, St. Louis, 1999

Most (Kicking) Points After Touchdown Attempted, Game

10   Charlie Gogolak, Washington vs. N.Y. Giants,
      Nov. 27, 1966
9   Pat Harder, Chi. Cardinals vs. N.Y. Giants,
      Oct. 17, 1948; vs. N.Y. Bulldogs, Nov. 13, 1949
      Bob Waterfield, Los Angeles vs. Baltimore,
      Oct. 22, 1950
      Bob Thomas, Chicago vs. Green Bay, Dec. 7, 1980
8   By many players

Most (One-Point) Points After Touchdown, Career

943   George Blanda, Chi. Bears, 1949, 1950-58; Baltimore,
       1950; Houston, 1960-66; Oakland, 1967-1975
820   Gary Anderson, Pittsburgh, 1982-1994; Philadelphia
       1995-96; San Francisco, 1997; Minnesota,
       1998-2002; Tennessee, 2003-04
798   Morten Andersen, New Orleans, 1982-1994; Atlanta,
       1995-2000; N.Y. Giants, 2001; Kansas City,
       2002-03; Minnesota, 2004

Most (One-Point) Points After Touchdown, Season

66   Uwe von Schamann, Miami, 1984
64   George Blanda, Houston, 1961
      Jeff Wilkins, St. Louis, 1999
62   Mark Moseley, Washington, 1983

Most (One-Point) Points After Touchdown, Game

9   Pat Harder, Chi. Cardinals vs. N.Y. Giants,
      Oct. 17, 1948
      Bob Waterfield, Los Angeles vs. Baltimore,
      Oct. 22, 1950
      Charlie Gogolak, Washington vs. N.Y. Giants,
      Nov. 27, 1966
8   By many players

Most Consecutive (Kicking) Points After Touchdown

371   Jason Elam, Denver, 1993-2002
301   Norm Johnson, Atlanta, 1991-94; Pittsburgh,
       1995-98; Philadelphia, 1999
275   Jeff Wilkins, St. Louis, 1999-2004 (current)

Highest (Kicking) Points After Touchdown Percentage, Career
(200 points after touchdown)

99.59 Jason Elam, Denver, 1993-2004 (493-491)
99.43 Tommy Davis, San Francisco, 1959-1969 (350-348)
99.32 Mike Vanderjagt, Indianapolis, 1998-2004 (294-292)

Most (Kicking) Points After Touchdown, No Misses, Season

64   Jeff Wilkins, St. Louis, 1999
59   Gary Anderson, Minnesota, 1998
58   Jason Elam, Denver, 1998
      Jeff Wilkins, St. Louis, 2001

Most (Kicking) Points After Touchdown, No Misses, Game

9   Pat Harder, Chi. Cardinals vs. N.Y. Giants,
      Oct. 17, 1948
      Bob Waterfield, Los Angeles vs. Baltimore,
      Oct. 22, 1950
8   By many players

Most Two-Point Conversions, Career

Two-point conversions include AFL (1960-69) and NFL (since 1994).
6   Terance Mathis, Atlanta, 1994-2001; Pittsburgh, 2002
      Marshall Faulk, Indianapolis, 1994-98; St. Louis,
      1999-2004

5 Cris Carter, Minnesota, 1994-2001; Miami, 2002
    Rob Moore, N.Y. Jets, 1994; Arizona, 1995-99
    Willie Jackson, Jacksonville, 1995-97; Cincinnati,
      1998-99; New Orleans, 2000-01; Washington,
      2002
    Keenan McCardell, Cleveland, 1994-95; Jacksonville,
      1996-2001; Tampa Bay, 2002-03; San Diego,
      2004
    Marvin Harrison, Indianapolis, 1996-2004
    Marcus Pollard, Indianapolis, 1995-2004
    Todd Heap, Baltimore, 2001-04
4 Gino Cappelletti, Boston, 1960-69
    Jerry Rice, San Francisco, 1994-2000; Oakland,
      2001-04; Seattle, 2004
    Lamar Smith, Seattle, 1994-97; New Orleans,
      1998-99; Miami, 2000-01; Carolina, 2002;
      New Orleans, 2003
    Floyd Turner, Indianapolis, 1994-95; Baltimore,
      1996, 1998
    Jackie Harris, Tampa Bay, 1994-97; Tennessee,
      1998-99; Dallas, 2000-01
    Marshall Faulk, Indianapolis, 1994-98; St. Louis,
      1999-2003
    Frank Sanders, Arizona, 1995-2002; Baltimore, 2003
    Hines Ward, Pittsburgh, 1998-2004
    Kerry Collins, Carolina, 1995-98; New Orleans,
      1998; N.Y. Giants, 1999-2003; Oakland, 2004
    Daunte Culpepper, Minnesota, 1999-2004
    Edgerrin James, Indianapolis, 1999-2004

Most Two-Point Conversions, Season
4 Todd Heap, Baltimore, 2003
3 Gino Cappelletti, Boston, 1960
    Richie Lucas, Buffalo, 1961
    Ronnie Harmon, San Diego, 1994
    Haywood Jeffires, Houston, 1994
    Tom Tupa, Cleveland, 1994
    Terance Mathis, Atlanta, 1995
    Lamar Smith, Seattle, 1996
    Cris Carter, Minnesota, 1997
    Terrell Davis, Denver, 1997
    James Stewart, Detroit, 2000
    Hines Ward, Pittsburgh, 2002
2 By many players

Most Two-Point Conversions, Game
2 Brett Perriman, Detroit vs. Green Bay, Nov. 6, 1994
    Michael Jackson, Baltimore vs. New England,
      Oct. 6, 1996
    Terrell Davis, Denver vs. Atlanta, Sept. 28, 1997
    Charles Johnson, Pittsburgh vs. Tennessee,
      Nov. 1, 1998
    Marshall Faulk, St. Louis vs. Atlanta, Oct. 15, 2000
    Todd Heap, Baltimore vs. Cincinnati, Oct. 19, 2003

FIELD GOALS
Most Seasons Leading League
5 Lou Groza, Cleveland, 1950, 1952-54, 1957
4 Jack Manders, Chi. Bears, 1933-34, 1936-37
    Ward Cuff, N.Y. Giants, 1938-39, 1943; Green Bay,
      1947
    Mark Moseley, Washington, 1976-77, 1979, 1982
3 Bob Waterfield, Los Angeles, 1947, 1949, 1951
    Gino Cappelletti, Boston, 1961, 1963-64
    Fred Cox, Minnesota, 1965, 1969-1970
    Jan Stenerud, Kansas City, 1967, 1970, 1975

Most Consecutive Seasons Leading League
3 Lou Groza, Cleveland, 1952-54
2 Jack Manders, Chi. Bears, 1933-34
    Armand Niccolai, Pittsburgh, 1935-36
    Jack Manders, Chi. Bears, 1936-37
    Ward Cuff, N.Y. Giants, 1938-39

    Clark Hinkle, Green Bay, 1940-41
    Cliff Patton, Philadelphia, 1948-49
    Gino Cappelletti, Boston, 1963-64
    Jim Turner, N.Y. Jets, 1968-69
    Fred Cox, Minnesota, 1969-1970
    Mark Moseley, Washington, 1976-77
    Chip Lohmiller, Washington, 1991-92
    Pete Stoyanovich, Miami, 1991-92

Most Field Goals Attempted, Career
672 Gary Anderson, Pittsburgh, 1982-1994; Philadelphia
      1995-96; San Francisco, 1997; Minnesota,
      1998-2002; Tennessee, 2003-04
658 Morten Andersen, New Orleans, 1982-1994;
      Atlanta, 1995-2000; N.Y. Giants, 2001;
      Kansas City, 2002-03; Minnesota, 2004
637 George Blanda, Chi. Bears, 1949, 1950-58; Baltimore,
      1950; Houston, 1960-66; Oakland, 1967-1975

Most Field Goals Attempted, Season
49 Bruce Gossett, Los Angeles, 1966
    Curt Knight, Washington, 1971
48 Chester Marcol, Green Bay, 1972
47 Jim Turner, N.Y. Jets, 1969
    David Ray, Los Angeles, 1973
    Mark Moseley, Washington, 1983

Most Field Goals Attempted, Game
9 Jim Bakken, St. Louis vs. Pittsburgh, Sept. 24, 1967
8 Lou Michaels, Pittsburgh vs. St. Louis, Dec. 2, 1962
    Garo Yepremian, Detroit vs. Minnesota, Nov. 13, 1966
    Jim Turner, N.Y. Jets vs. Buffalo, Nov. 3, 1968
    Billy Cundiff, Dallas vs. N.Y. Giants, Sept. 15, 2003 (OT)
7 By many players

Most Field Goals, Career
538 Gary Anderson, Pittsburgh, 1982-1994; Philadelphia,
      1995-96; San Francisco, 1997; Minnesota,
      1998-2002; Tennessee, 2003-04
520 Morten Andersen, New Orleans, 1982-1994;
      Atlanta, 1995-2000; N.Y. Giants, 2001;
      Kansas City, 2002-03; Minnesota, 2004
383 Nick Lowery, New England, 1978; Kansas City,
      1980-1993; N.Y. Jets, 1994-1996

Most Field Goals, Season
39 Olindo Mare, Miami, 1999
    Jeff Wilkins, St. Louis, 2003
37 John Kasay, Carolina, 1996
    Mike Vanderjagt, Indianapolis, 2003
36 Cary Blanchard, Indianapolis, 1996
    Al Del Greco, Tennessee, 1998

Most Field Goals, Rookie, Season
35 Ali Haji-Sheikh, N.Y. Giants, 1983
34 Richie Cunningham, Dallas, 1997
33 Chester Marcol, Green Bay, 1972

Most Field Goals, Game
7 Jim Bakken, St. Louis vs. Pittsburgh, Sept. 24, 1967
    Rich Karlis, Minnesota vs. L.A. Rams, Nov. 5, 1989
      (OT)
    Chris Boniol, Dallas vs. Green Bay, Nov. 18, 1996
    Billy Cundiff, Dallas vs. N.Y. Giants, Sept. 15, 2003 (OT)
6 Gino Cappelletti, Boston vs. Denver, Oct. 4, 1964
    Garo Yepremian, Detroit vs. Minnesota, Nov. 13, 1966
    Jim Turner, N.Y. Jets vs. Buffalo, Nov. 3, 1968
    Tom Dempsey, Philadelphia vs. Houston,
      Nov. 12, 1972
    Bobby Howfield, N.Y. Jets vs. New Orleans,
      Dec. 3, 1972
    Jim Bakken, St. Louis vs. Atlanta, Dec. 9, 1973
    Joe Danelo, N.Y. Giants vs. Seattle, Oct. 18, 1981
    Ray Wersching, San Francisco vs. New Orleans,
      Oct. 16, 1983
    Gary Anderson, Pittsburgh vs. Denver, Oct. 23, 1988
    John Carney, San Diego vs. Seattle, Sept. 5, 1993

John Carney, San Diego vs. Houston, Sept. 19, 1993
Doug Pelfrey, Cincinnati vs. Seattle, Nov. 6, 1994 (OT)
Norm Johnson, Atlanta vs. New Orleans, Nov. 13, 1994
Jeff Wilkins, San Francisco vs. Atlanta, Sept. 29, 1996
Steve Christie, Buffalo vs. N.Y. Jets, Oct. 20, 1996
Greg Davis, San Diego vs. Oakland, Oct. 5, 1997
Gary Anderson, Minnesota vs. Baltimore, Dec. 13, 1998
Olindo Mare, Miami vs. New England, Oct. 17, 1999
Jason Hanson, Detroit vs. Minnesota, Oct. 17, 1999
Jeff Reed, Pittsburgh vs. Jacksonville, Dec. 1, 2002
John Kasay, Carolina vs. New Orleans, Dec. 5, 2004
5   By many players

Most Field Goals, One Quarter
4   Garo Yepremian, Detroit vs. Minnesota, Nov. 13, 1966
      (second quarter)
      Curt Knight, Washington vs. N.Y. Giants, Nov. 15, 1970
      (second quarter)
      Roger Ruzek, Dallas vs. N.Y. Giants, Nov. 2, 1987
      (fourth quarter)
      Cary Blanchard, Indianapolis vs. Buffalo,
      Sept. 21 1997 (second quarter)
      Sebastian Janikowski, Oakland vs. Chicago,
      Oct. 5, 2003 (second quarter)
      Jeff Wilkins, St. Louis vs. Baltimore, Nov. 9, 2003
      (fourth quarter)
3   By many players

Most Consecutive Games Scoring Field Goals
38   Matt Stover, Baltimore, 1999-2001
31   Fred Cox, Minnesota, 1968-1970
28   Jim Turner, N.Y. Jets, 1970; Denver, 1971-72
      Chip Lohmiller, Washington, 1988-1990

Most Consecutive Field Goals
42   Mike Vanderjagt, Indianapolis, 2002-04
40   Gary Anderson, San Francisco, 1997; Minnesota, 1998
31   Fuad Reveiz, Minnesota, 1994-95

Longest Field Goal
63   Tom Dempsey, New Orleans vs. Detroit, Nov. 8, 1970
      Jason Elam, Denver vs. Jacksonville, Oct. 25, 1998
60   Steve Cox, Cleveland vs. Cincinnati, Oct. 21, 1984
      Morten Andersen, New Orleans vs. Chicago, Oct. 27, 1991
59   Tony Franklin, Philadelphia vs. Dallas, Nov. 12, 1979
      Pete Stoyanovich, Miami vs. N.Y. Jets, Nov. 12, 1989
      Steve Christie, Buffalo vs. Miami, Sept. 26, 1993
      Morten Andersen, Atlanta vs. San Francisco, Dec. 24, 1995

Highest Field Goal Percentage, Career (100 field goals)
87.00   Mike Vanderjagt, Indianapolis, 1998-2004
83.23   David Akers, Washington, 1998; Philadelphia, 1999-2004
82.74   Matt Stover, Cleveland, 1991-95; Baltimore, 1996-2004

Highest Field Goal Percentage, Season (Qualifiers)
100.00   Tony Zendejas, L.A. Rams, 1991 (17-17)
      Gary Anderson, Minnesota, 1998 (35-35)
      Jeff Wilkins, St. Louis, 2000 (17-17)
      Mike Vanderjagt, Indianapolis, 2003 (37-37)
96.43   Chris Boniol, Dallas, 1995 (28-27)
96.30   Norm Johnson, Atlanta, 1993 (27-26)
      Pete Stoyanovich, Kansas City, 1997 (27-26)

Most Field Goals, No Misses, Game
7   Rich Karlis, Minnesota vs. L.A. Rams, Nov. 5, 1989 (OT)
      Chris Boniol, Dallas vs. Green Bay, Nov. 18, 1996
6   Gino Cappelletti, Boston vs. Denver, Oct. 4, 1964
      Joe Danelo, N.Y. Giants vs. Seattle, Oct. 18, 1981
      Ray Wersching, San Francisco vs. New Orleans, Oct. 16, 1983

Gary Anderson, Pittsburgh vs. Denver, Oct. 23, 1988
John Carney, San Diego vs. Seattle, Sept. 5, 1993
John Carney, San Diego vs. Houston, Sept. 19, 1993
Doug Pelfrey, Cincinnati vs. Seattle, Nov. 6, 1994 (OT)
Norm Johnson, Atlanta vs. New Orleans, Nov. 13, 1994
Jeff Wilkins, San Francisco vs. Atlanta, Sept. 29, 1996
Greg Davis, San Diego vs. Oakland, Oct. 5, 1997
Gary Anderson, Minnesota vs. Baltimore, Dec. 13, 1998
Olindo Mare, Miami vs. New England, Oct. 17, 1999
Jeff Reed, Pittsburgh vs. Jacksonville, Dec. 1, 2002
John Kasay, Carolina vs. New Orleans, Dec. 5, 2004
5   By many players

Most Field Goals, 50 or More Yards, Career
40   Morten Andersen, New Orleans, 1982-1994;
      Atlanta, 1995-2000; N.Y. Giants, 2001;
      Kansas City, 2002-03; Minnesota, 2004
34   Jason Elam, Denver, 1993-2004
26   John Kasay, Seattle, 1991-94; Carolina, 1995-2004

Most Field Goals, 50 or More Yards, Season
8   Morten Andersen, Atlanta, 1995
6   Dean Biasucci, Indianapolis, 1988
      Chris Jacke, Green Bay, 1993
      Tony Zendejas, L.A. Rams, 1993
      Mike Vanderjagt, Indianapolis, 1998
5   Fred Steinfort, Denver, 1980
      Norm Johnson, Seattle, 1986
      Kevin Butler, Chicago, 1993
      Jason Elam, Denver, 1995
      Cary Blanchard, Indianapolis, 1996
      Jason Elam, Denver, 1999
      Martín Gramatica, Tampa Bay, 2000, 2002
      Paul Edinger, Chicago, 2002
      Neil Rackers, Arizona, 2004

Most Field Goals, 50 or More Yards, Game
3   Morten Andersen, Atlanta vs. New Orleans, Dec. 10, 1995
      Neil Rackers, Arizona vs. Seattle, Oct. 24, 2004
2   By many players. Last time: Jeff Wilkins, St. Louis, vs. San Francisco, Dec. 5, 2004

SAFETIES
Most Safeties, Career
4   Ted Hendricks, Baltimore, 1969-1973; Green Bay, 1974; Oakland, 1975-1981; L.A. Raiders, 1982-83
      Doug English, Detroit, 1975-79, 1981-85
3   Bill McPeak, Pittsburgh, 1949-1957
      Charlie Krueger, San Francisco, 1959-1973
      Ernie Stautner, Pittsburgh, 1950-1963
      Jim Katcavage, N.Y. Giants, 1956-1968
      Roger Brown, Detroit, 1960-66; Los Angeles, 1967-69
      Bruce Maher, Detroit, 1960-67; N.Y. Giants, 1968-69
      Ron McDole, St. Louis, 1961; Houston, 1962; Buffalo, 1963-1970; Washington, 1971-78
      Alan Page, Minnesota, 1967-1978; Chicago, 1979-1981
      Lyle Alzado, Denver, 1971-78; Cleveland, 1979-1981; L.A. Raiders, 1982-85
      Rulon Jones, Denver, 1980-88
      Steve McMichael, New England, 1980; Chicago, 1981-1993; Green Bay, 1994
      Kevin Greene, L.A. Rams, 1985-1992; Pittsburgh, 1993-95; Carolina, 1996, 1998-99; San Francisco, 1997
      Burt Grossman, San Diego, 1989-1993; Philadelphia, 1994

Eric Swann, Phoenix, 1991-93; Arizona, 1994-99;
Carolina, 2000
Dan Saleaumua, Detroit, 1987-88; Kansas City,
1989-1996; Seattle, 1997-98
Derrick Thomas, Kansas City, 1989-1999
Bryant Young, San Francisco, 1994-2004
2   By many players

Most Safeties, Season
2   Tom Nash, Green Bay, 1932
Roger Brown, Detroit, 1962
Ron McDole, Buffalo, 1964
Alan Page, Minnesota, 1971
Fred Dryer, Los Angeles, 1973
Benny Barnes, Dallas, 1973
James Young, Houston, 1977
Doug English, Detroit, 1983
Don Blackmon, New England, 1985
Tim Harris, Green Bay, 1988
Brian Jordan, Atlanta, 1991
Burt Grossman, San Diego, 1992
Rod Stephens, Seattle, 1993
Bryant Young, San Francisco, 1996

Most Safeties, Game
2   Fred Dryer, Los Angeles vs. Green Bay,
Oct. 21, 1973

RUSHING
Most Seasons Leading League
8   Jim Brown, Cleveland, 1957-1961, 1963-65
4   Steve Van Buren, Philadelphia, 1945, 1947-49
O.J. Simpson, Buffalo, 1972-73, 1975-76
Eric Dickerson, L.A. Rams, 1983-84, 1986;
Indianapolis, 1988
Emmitt Smith, Dallas, 1991-93, 1995
Barry Sanders, Detroit, 1990, 1994, 1996-97
3   Earl Campbell, Houston, 1978-1980

Most Consecutive Seasons Leading League
5   Jim Brown, Cleveland, 1957-1961
3   Steve Van Buren, Philadelphia, 1947-49
Jim Brown, Cleveland, 1963-65
Earl Campbell, Houston, 1978-1980
Emmitt Smith, Dallas, 1991-93
2   Bill Paschal, N.Y. Giants, 1943-44
Joe Perry, San Francisco, 1953-54
Jim Nance, Boston, 1966-67
Leroy Kelly, Cleveland, 1967-68
O.J. Simpson, Buffalo, 1972-73; 1975-76
Eric Dickerson, L.A. Rams, 1983-84
Barry Sanders, Detroit, 1996-97
Edgerrin James, Indianapolis, 1999-2000

ATTEMPTS
Most Seasons Leading League
6   Jim Brown, Cleveland, 1958-59, 1961, 1963-65
4   Steve Van Buren, Philadelphia, 1947-1950
Walter Payton, Chicago, 1976-79
3   Cookie Gilchrist, Buffalo, 1963-64; Denver, 1965
Jim Nance, Boston, 1966-67, 1969
O.J. Simpson, Buffalo, 1973-75
Eric Dickerson, L.A. Rams, 1983, 1986;
Indianapolis, 1988
Emmitt Smith, Dallas, 1991, 1994-95

Most Consecutive Seasons Leading League
4   Steve Van Buren, Philadelphia, 1947-1950
Walter Payton, Chicago, 1976-79
3   Jim Brown, Cleveland, 1963-65
Cookie Gilchrist, Buffalo, 1963-64; Denver, 1965
O.J. Simpson, Buffalo, 1973-75
2   By many players

Most Attempts, Career
4,409   Emmitt Smith, Dallas, 1990-2002; Arizona, 2003-04
3,838   Walter Payton, Chicago, 1975-1987
3,369   Jerome Bettis, L.A. Rams, 1993-94; St. Louis, 1995;
Pittsburgh, 1996-2004

Most Attempts, Season
410   Jamal Anderson, Atlanta, 1998
407   James Wilder, Tampa Bay, 1984
404   Eric Dickerson, L.A. Rams, 1986

Most Attempts, Rookie, Season
390   Eric Dickerson, L.A. Rams, 1983
378   George Rogers, New Orleans, 1981
369   Edgerrin James, Indianapolis, 1999

Most Attempts, Game
45   Jamie Morris, Washington vs. Cincinnati,
Dec. 17, 1988 (OT)
43   Butch Woolfolk, N.Y. Giants vs. Philadelphia,
Nov. 20, 1983
James Wilder, Tampa Bay vs. Green Bay,
Sept. 30, 1984 (OT)
Rudi Johnson, Cincinnati vs. Houston, Nov. 9, 2003
42   James Wilder, Tampa Bay vs. Pittsburgh,
Oct. 30, 1983
Terrell Davis, Denver vs. Buffalo, Oct. 26, 1997 (OT)
Ricky Williams, Miami vs. Buffalo, Sept. 21, 2003

YARDS GAINED
Most Yards Gained, Career
18,355   Emmitt Smith, Dallas, 1990-2002; Arizona, 2003-04
16,726   Walter Payton, Chicago, 1975-1987
15,269   Barry Sanders, Detroit, 1989-1998

Most Seasons, 1,000 or More Yards Rushing
11   Emmitt Smith, Dallas, 1991-2001
10   Walter Payton, Chicago, 1976-1981, 1983-86
Barry Sanders, Detroit, 1989-1998
Curtis Martin, New England, 1995-97; N.Y. Jets,
1998-2004
8   Franco Harris, Pittsburgh, 1972, 1974-79, 1983
Tony Dorsett, Dallas, 1977-1981, 1983-85
Thurman Thomas, Buffalo, 1989-1996
Jerome Bettis, L.A. Rams, 1993-94; Pittsburgh,
1996-2001

Most Consecutive Seasons, 1,000 or More Yards Rushing
11   Emmitt Smith, Dallas, 1991-2001
10   Barry Sanders, Detroit, 1989-1998
Curtis Martin, New England, 1995-97; N.Y. Jets,
1998-2004 (current)
8   Thurman Thomas, Buffalo, 1989-1996

Most Yards Gained, Season
2,105   Eric Dickerson, L.A. Rams, 1984
2,066   Jamal Lewis, Baltimore, 2003
2,053   Barry Sanders, Detroit, 1997

Most Yards Gained, Rookie, Season
1,808   Eric Dickerson, L.A. Rams, 1983
1,674   George Rogers, New Orleans, 1981
1,605   Ottis Anderson, St. Louis, 1979

Most Yards Gained, Game
295   Jamal Lewis, Baltimore vs. Cleveland, Sept. 14, 2003
278   Corey Dillon, Cincinnati vs. Denver, Oct. 22, 2000
275   Walter Payton, Chicago vs. Minnesota,
Nov. 20, 1977

Most Games, 200 or More Yards Rushing, Career
6   O.J. Simpson, Buffalo, 1969-1977; San Francisco,
1978-79
4   Jim Brown, Cleveland, 1957-1965
Earl Campbell, Houston, 1978-1984; New Orleans,
1984-85
Barry Sanders, Detroit, 1989-1998
LaDainian Tomlinson, San Diego, 2001-04

3   Eric Dickerson, L.A. Rams, 1983-87; Indianapolis, 1987-1991; L.A. Raiders, 1992; Atlanta, 1993
Greg Bell, Buffalo, 1984-87; L.A. Rams, 1987-89; L.A. Raiders, 1990
Terrell Davis, Denver, 1995-2001
Corey Dillon, Cincinnati, 1997-2003; New England, 2004
Marshall Faulk, Indianapolis, 1994-98; St. Louis, 1999-2004

Most Games, 200 or More Yards Rushing, Season
4   Earl Campbell, Houston, 1980
3   O.J. Simpson, Buffalo, 1973
2   Jim Brown, Cleveland, 1963
     O.J. Simpson, Buffalo, 1976
     Walter Payton, Chicago, 1977
     Eric Dickerson, L.A. Rams, 1984
     Greg Bell, L.A. Rams, 1989
     Terrell Davis, Denver, 1997
     Barry Sanders, Detroit, 1997
     Corey Dillon, Cincinnati, 2000
     Marshall Faulk, St. Louis, 2000
     LaDainian Tomlinson, San Diego, 2002
     Ricky Williams, Miami, 2002
     Jamal Lewis, Baltimore, 2003
     LaDainian Tomlinson, San Diego, 2003

Most Consecutive Games, 200 or More Yards Rushing
2   O.J. Simpson, Buffalo, 1973, 1976
     Earl Campbell, Houston, 1980
     Ricky Williams, Miami, 2002

Most Games, 100 or More Yards Rushing, Career
78   Emmitt Smith, Dallas, 1990-2002; Arizona, 2003-04
77   Walter Payton, Chicago, 1975-1987
76   Barry Sanders, Detroit, 1989-1998

Most Games, 100 or More Yards Rushing, Season
14   Barry Sanders, Detroit, 1997
12   Eric Dickerson, L.A. Rams, 1984
     Barry Foster, Pittsburgh, 1992
     Jamal Anderson, Atlanta, 1998
     Jamal Lewis, Baltimore, 2003
11   O.J. Simpson, Buffalo, 1973
     Earl Campbell, Houston, 1979
     Marcus Allen, L.A. Raiders, 1985
     Eric Dickerson, L.A. Rams, 1986
     Emmitt Smith, Dallas, 1995
     Terrell Davis, Denver, 1998

Most Consecutive Games, 100 or More Yards Rushing
14   Barry Sanders, Detroit, 1997
11   Marcus Allen, L.A. Raiders, 1985-86
9   Walter Payton, Chicago, 1985
     Fred Taylor, Jacksonville, 2000
     Deuce McAllister, New Orleans, 2003

Longest Run From Scrimmage
99   Tony Dorsett, Dallas vs. Minnesota, Jan. 3, 1983 (TD)
98   Ahman Green, Green Bay vs. Denver, Dec. 28, 2003 (TD)
97   Andy Uram, Green Bay vs. Chi. Cardinals, Oct. 8, 1939 (TD)
     Bob Gage, Pittsburgh vs. Chi. Bears, Dec. 4, 1949 (TD)

AVERAGE GAIN
Highest Average Gain, Career (750 attempts)
6.36   Randall Cunningham, Philadelphia, 1985-1995; Minnesota, 1997-99; Dallas, 2000; Baltimore, 2001 (775-4,928)
5.22   Jim Brown, Cleveland, 1957-1965 (2,359-12,312)
5.14   Eugene (Mercury) Morris, Miami, 1969-1975; San Diego, 1976 (804-4,133)

Highest Average Gain, Season (Qualifiers)
8.44   Beattie Feathers, Chi. Bears, 1934 (119-1,004)
7.98   Randall Cunningham, Philadelphia, 1990 (118-942)
7.52   Michael Vick, Atlanta, 2004 (120-902)

Highest Average Gain, Game (10 attempts)
17.30   Michael Vick, Atlanta vs. Minnesota, Dec. 1, 2002 (OT) (10-173)
17.09   Marion Motley, Cleveland vs. Pittsburgh, Oct. 29, 1950 (11-188)
16.70   Bill Grimes, Green Bay vs. N.Y. Yanks, Oct. 8, 1950 (10-167)

TOUCHDOWNS
Most Seasons Leading League
5   Jim Brown, Cleveland, 1957-59, 1963, 1965
4   Steve Van Buren, Philadelphia, 1945, 1947-49
3   Abner Haynes, Dall. Texans, 1960-62
     Cookie Gilchrist, Buffalo, 1962-64
     Paul Lowe, L.A. Chargers, 1960; San Diego, 1961, 1965
     Leroy Kelly, Cleveland, 1966-68
     Emmitt Smith, Dallas, 1992, 1994-95

Most Consecutive Seasons Leading League
3   Steve Van Buren, Philadelphia, 1947-49
     Jim Brown, Cleveland, 1957-59
     Abner Haynes, Dall. Texans, 1960-62
     Cookie Gilchrist, Buffalo, 1962-64
     Leroy Kelly, Cleveland, 1966-68

Most Touchdowns, Career
164   Emmitt Smith, Dallas, 1990-2002; Arizona, 2003-04
123   Marcus Allen, L.A. Raiders, 1982-1992; Kansas City, 1993-97
110   Walter Payton, Chicago, 1975-1987

Most Touchdowns, Season
27   Priest Holmes, Kansas City, 2003
25   Emmitt Smith, Dallas, 1995
24   John Riggins, Washington, 1983

Most Touchdowns, Rookie, Season
18   Eric Dickerson, L.A. Rams, 1983
15   Ickey Woods, Cincinnati, 1988
     Mike Anderson, Denver, 2000
     Clinton Portis, Denver, 2002
14   Gale Sayers, Chicago, 1965
     Barry Sanders, Detroit, 1989
     Curtis Martin, New England, 1995
     Fred Taylor, Jacksonville, 1998

Most Touchdowns, Game
6   Ernie Nevers, Chi. Cardinals vs. Chi. Bears, Nov. 28, 1929
5   Jimmy Conzelman, Rhode Island vs. Evansville, Oct. 15, 1922
     Jim Brown, Cleveland vs. Baltimore, Nov. 1, 1959
     Cookie Gilchrist, Buffalo vs. N.Y. Jets, Dec. 8, 1963
     James Stewart, Jacksonville vs. Philadelphia, Oct. 12, 1997
     Clinton Portis, Denver vs. Kansas City, Dec. 7, 2003
4   By many players

Most Consecutive Games Rushing for Touchdowns
13   John Riggins, Washington, 1982-83
     George Rogers, Washington, 1985-86
12   LaDainian Tomlinson, San Diego, 2004 (current)
11   Lenny Moore, Baltimore, 1963-64
     Emmitt Smith, Dallas, 1994-95
     Emmitt Smith, Dallas, 1995
     Priest Holmes, Kansas City, 2002

PASSING
Most Seasons Leading League
6   Sammy Baugh, Washington, 1937, 1940, 1943, 1945, 1947, 1949

    Steve Young San Francisco, 1991-94, 1996-97
- 4 Len Dawson, Dall. Texans; 1962; Kansas City, 1964, 1966, 1968
    Roger Staubach, Dallas, 1971, 1973, 1978-79
    Ken Anderson, Cincinnati, 1974-75, 1981-82
- 3 Arnie Herber, Green Bay, 1932, 1934, 1936
    Norm Van Brocklin, Los Angeles, 1950, 1952, 1954
    Bart Starr, Green Bay, 1962, 1964, 1966

Most Consecutive Seasons Leading League
- 4 Steve Young, San Francisco, 1991-94
- 2 Cecil Isbell, Green Bay, 1941-42
    Milt Plum, Cleveland, 1960-61
    Ken Anderson, Cincinnati, 1974-75, 1981-82
    Roger Staubach, Dallas, 1978-79
    Steve Young, San Francisco, 1996-97

PASSER RATING
Highest Passer Rating, Career (1,500 attempts)
- 96.8 Steve Young, Tampa Bay, 1985-86; San Francisco, 1987-1999
- 95.7 Kurt Warner, St. Louis, 1998-2003; N.Y. Giants, 2004
- 93.2 Daunte Culpepper, Minnesota, 1999-2004

Highest Passer Rating, Season (Qualifiers)
- 121.1 Peyton Manning, Indianapolis, 2004
- 112.8 Steve Young, San Francisco, 1994
- 112.4 Joe Montana, San Francisco, 1989

Highest Passer Rating, Rookie, Season (Qualifiers)
- 98.1 Ben Roethlisberger, Pittsburgh, 2004
- 96.0 Dan Marino, Miami, 1983
- 88.2 Greg Cook, Cincinnati, 1969

ATTEMPTS
Most Seasons Leading League
- 5 Dan Marino, Miami, 1984, 1986, 1988, 1992, 1997
- 4 Sammy Baugh, Washington, 1937, 1943, 1947-48
    Johnny Unitas, Baltimore, 1957, 1959-1961
    George Blanda, Chi. Bears, 1953; Houston, 1963-65
- 3 Arnie Herber, Green Bay, 1932, 1934, 1936
    Sonny Jurgensen, Washington, 1966-67, 1969
    Drew Bledsoe, New England, 1994-96

Most Consecutive Seasons Leading League
- 3 Johnny Unitas, Baltimore, 1959-1961
    George Blanda, Houston, 1963-65
    Drew Bledsoe, New England, 1994-96
- 2 By many players

Most Passes Attempted, Career
- 8,358 Dan Marino, Miami, 1983-1999
- 7,250 John Elway, Denver, 1983-1998
- 7,003 Brett Favre, Atlanta, 1991; Green Bay, 1992-2004

Most Passes Attempted, Season
- 691 Drew Bledsoe, New England, 1994
- 655 Warren Moon, Houston, 1991
- 636 Drew Bledsoe, New England, 1995

Most Passes Attempted, Rookie, Season
- 575 Peyton Manning, Indianapolis, 1998
- 540 Chris Weinke, Carolina, 2001
- 486 Rick Mirer, Seattle, 1993

Most Passes Attempted, Game
- 70 Drew Bledsoe, New England vs. Minnesota, Nov. 13, 1994 (OT)
- 69 Vinny Testaverde, N.Y. Jets vs. Baltimore, Dec. 24, 2000
- 68 George Blanda, Houston vs. Buffalo, Nov. 1, 1964
    Jon Kitna, Cincinnati vs. Pittsburgh, Dec. 30, 2001 (OT)

COMPLETIONS
Most Seasons Leading League
- 6 Dan Marino, Miami, 1984-86, 1988, 1992, 1997

- 5 Sammy Baugh, Washington, 1937, 1943, 1945, 1947-48
- 4 George Blanda, Chi. Bears, 1953; Houston, 1963-65
    Sonny Jurgensen, Philadelphia, 1961; Washington, 1966-67, 1969

Most Consecutive Seasons Leading League
- 3 George Blanda, Houston, 1963-65
    Dan Marino, Miami, 1984-86
- 2 By many players

Most Passes Completed, Career
- 4,967 Dan Marino, Miami, 1983-1999
- 4,306 Brett Favre, Atlanta, 1991; Green Bay, 1992-2004
- 4,123 John Elway, Denver, 1983-1998

Most Passes Completed, Season
- 418 Rich Gannon, Oakland, 2002
- 404 Warren Moon, Houston, 1991
- 400 Drew Bledsoe, New England, 1994

Most Passes Completed, Rookie, Season
- 326 Peyton Manning, Indianapolis, 1998
- 293 Chris Weinke, Carolina, 2001
- 274 Rick Mirer, Seattle, 1993

Most Passes Completed, Game
- 45 Drew Bledsoe, New England vs. Minnesota, Nov. 13, 1994 (OT)
- 43 Rich Gannon, Oakland vs. Pittsburgh, Sept. 15, 2002
- 42 Richard Todd, N.Y. Jets vs. San Francisco, Sept. 21, 1980
    Vinny Testaverde, N.Y. Jets vs. Seattle, Dec. 6, 1998

Most Consecutive Passes Completed
- 24 Donovan McNabb, Philadelphia vs. N.Y. Giants (10), Nov. 28, 2004; vs. Green Bay (14), Dec. 5, 2004
- 22 Joe Montana, San Francisco vs. Cleveland (5), Nov. 29, 1987; vs. Green Bay (17), Dec. 6, 1987
- 21 Rich Gannon, Oakland vs. Denver, Nov. 11, 2002

COMPLETION PERCENTAGE
Most Seasons Leading League
- 8 Len Dawson, Dall. Texans, 1962; Kansas City, 1964-69, 1975
- 7 Sammy Baugh, Washington, 1940, 1942-43, 1945, 1947-49
- 5 Joe Montana, San Francisco, 1980-81, 1985, 1987, 1989
    Steve Young, San Francisco, 1992, 1994-97

Most Consecutive Seasons Leading League
- 6 Len Dawson, Kansas City, 1964-69
- 4 Steve Young, San Francisco, 1994-97
- 3 Sammy Baugh, Washington, 1947-49
    Otto Graham, Cleveland, 1953-55
    Milt Plum, Cleveland, 1959-1961
    Kurt Warner, St. Louis, 1999-2001

Highest Completion Percentage, Career (1,500 attempts)
- 65.90 Kurt Warner, St. Louis, 1998-2003; N.Y. Giants, 2004 (1,965-1,295)
- 64.37 Daunte Culpepper, Minnesota, 1999-2004 (2,391-1,539)
- 64.28 Steve Young, Tampa Bay, 1985-86; San Francisco, 1987-1999 (4,149-2,667)

Highest Completion Percentage, Season (Qualifiers)
- 70.55 Ken Anderson, Cincinnati, 1982 (309-218)
- 70.33 Sammy Baugh, Washington, 1945 (182-128)
- 70.28 Steve Young, San Francisco, 1994 (461-324)

Highest Completion Percentage, Rookie, Season (Qualifiers)
- 66.44 Ben Roethlisberger, Pittsburgh, 2004 (295-196)
- 58.45 Dan Marino, Miami, 1983 (296-173)
- 57.18 Byron Leftwich, Jacksonville, 2003 (418-239)

Highest Completion Percentage, Game (20 attempts)
- 91.30 Vinny Testaverde, Cleveland vs. L.A. Rams, Dec. 26, 1993 (23-21)

90.91 Ken Anderson, Cincinnati vs. Pittsburgh,
       Nov. 10, 1974 (22-20)
90.48 Lynn Dickey, Green Bay vs. New Orleans,
       Dec. 13, 1981 (21-19)

YARDS GAINED
Most Seasons Leading League
5   Sonny Jurgensen, Philadelphia, 1961-62;
    Washington, 1966-67, 1969
    Dan Marino, Miami, 1984-86, 1988, 1992
4   Sammy Baugh, Washington, 1937, 1940, 1947-48
    Johnny Unitas, Baltimore, 1957, 1959-1960, 1963
    Dan Fouts, San Diego, 1979-1982
3   Arnie Herber, Green Bay, 1932, 1934, 1936
    Sid Luckman, Chi. Bears, 1943, 1945-46
    John Brodie, San Francisco, 1965, 1968, 1970
    John Hadl, San Diego, 1965, 1968, 1971
    Joe Namath, N.Y. Jets, 1966-67, 1972
Most Consecutive Seasons Leading League
4   Dan Fouts, San Diego, 1979-1982
3   Dan Marino, Miami, 1984-86
2   By many players
Most Yards Gained, Career
61,361 Dan Marino, Miami, 1983-1999
51,475 John Elway, Denver, 1983-1998
49,734 Brett Favre, Atlanta, 1991; Green Bay, 1992-2004
Most Seasons, 3,000 or More Yards Passing
13 Dan Marino, Miami, 1984-1992, 1994-95, 1997-98
    Brett Favre, Green Bay, 1992-2004
12 John Elway, Denver, 1985-1991, 1993-97
9   Warren Moon, Houston, 1984,1986, 1989-1991,
    1993; Minnesota, 1994-95; Seattle, 1997
Most Yards Gained, Season
5,084 Dan Marino, Miami, 1984
4,830 Kurt Warner, St. Louis, 2001
4,802 Dan Fouts, San Diego, 1981
Most Yards Gained, Rookie, Season
3,739 Peyton Manning, Indianapolis, 1998
2,931 Chris Weinke, Carolina, 2001
2,833 Rick Mirer, Seattle, 1993
Most Yards Gained, Game
554 Norm Van Brocklin, Los Angeles vs. N.Y. Yanks,
     Sept. 28, 1951
527 Warren Moon, Houston vs. Kansas City,
     Dec. 16, 1990
522 Boomer Esiason, Arizona vs. Washington,
     Nov. 10, 1996
Most Games, 400 or More Yards Passing, Career
13 Dan Marino, Miami, 1983-1999
7   Joe Montana, San Francisco, 1979-1990, 1992;
    Kansas City, 1993-94
    Warren Moon, Houston, 1984-1993; Minnesota,
    1994-96; Seattle, 1997-98; Kansas City,
    1999-2000
6   Dan Fouts, San Diego, 1973-1987
    Drew Bledsoe, New England, 1993-2001; Buffalo,
    2002-03
    Peyton Manning, Indianapolis, 1998-2004
Most Games, 400 or More Yards Passing, Season
4   Dan Marino, Miami, 1984
3   Dan Marino, Miami, 1986
2   By many players
Most Consecutive Games, 400 or More Yards Passing
2   Dan Fouts, San Diego, 1982
    Dan Marino, Miami, 1984
    Phil Simms, N.Y. Giants, 1985
    Billy Volek, Tennessee, 2004
Most Games, 300 or More Yards Passing, Career
63 Dan Marino, Miami, 1983-1999
51 Dan Fouts, San Diego, 1973-1987

49 Warren Moon, Houston, 1984-1993; Minnesota,
    1994-96; Seattle, 1997-98; Kansas City,
    1999-2000
Most Games, 300 or More Yards Passing, Season
10 Rich Gannon, Oakland, 2002
9   Dan Marino, Miami, 1984
    Warren Moon, Houston, 1990
    Kurt Warner, St. Louis, 1999
    Kurt Warner, St. Louis, 2001
8   Dan Fouts, San Diego, 1980
    Kurt Warner, St. Louis, 2000
    Trent Green, Kansas City, 2004
Most Consecutive Games, 300 or More Yards Passing
6   Steve Young, San Francisco, 1998
    Kurt Warner, St. Louis, 2000
    Rich Gannon, Oakland, 2002
5   Joe Montana, San Francisco, 1982
    Kerry Collins, N.Y. Giants, 2001-02
4   Dan Fouts, San Diego, 1979
    Dan Fouts, San Diego, 1980-81
    Bill Kenney, Kansas City, 1983
    Joe Montana, San Francisco, 1985-86
    Joe Montana, San Francisco, 1990
    Warren Moon, Houston, 1990
    Drew Bledsoe, New England, 1993-94
    Kurt Warner, St. Louis, 1999
    Brian Griese, Denver, 2002
    Daunte Culpepper, Minnesota, 2004
    Trent Green, Kansas City, 2004
Longest Pass Completion (All TDs except as noted)
99 Frank Filchock (to Farkas), Washington vs.
    Pittsburgh, Oct. 15, 1939
    George Izo (to Mitchell), Washington vs. Cleveland,
    Sept. 15, 1963
    Karl Sweetan (to Studstill), Detroit vs. Baltimore,
    Oct. 16, 1966
    Sonny Jurgensen (to Allen), Washington vs.
    Chicago, Sept. 15, 1968
    Jim Plunkett (to Branch), L.A. Raiders vs.
    Washington, Oct. 2, 1983
    Ron Jaworski (to Quick), Philadelphia vs. Atlanta,
    Nov. 10, 1985
    Stan Humphries (to Martin), San Diego vs. Seattle,
    Sept. 18, 1994
    Brett Favre (to Brooks), Green Bay vs. Chicago,
    Sept. 11, 1995
    Trent Green (to Boerigter), Kansas City vs.
    San Diego, Dec. 22, 2002
    Jeff Garcia, (to Davis), Cleveland vs. Cincinnati,
    Oct. 17, 2004
98 Doug Russell (to Tinsley), Chi. Cardinals vs.
    Cleveland, Nov. 27, 1938
    Ogden Compton (to Lane), Chi. Cardinals vs.
    Green Bay, Nov. 13, 1955
    Bill Wade (to Farrington), Chicago Bears vs. Detroit,
    Oct. 8, 1961
    Jacky Lee (to Dewveall), Houston vs. San Diego,
    Nov. 25, 1962
    Earl Morrall (to Jones), N.Y. Giants vs. Pittsburgh,
    Sept. 11, 1966
    Jim Hart (to Moore), St. Louis vs. Los Angeles,
    Dec. 10, 1972 (no TD)
    Bobby Hebert (to Haynes), Atlanta vs. New Orleans,
    Sept. 12, 1993
    Charlie Batch (to Morton), Detroit vs. Chicago,
    Oct. 4, 1998
97 Pat Coffee (to Tinsley), Chi. Cardinals vs. Chi. Bears,
    Dec. 5, 1937
    Bobby Layne (to Box), Detroit vs. Green Bay,
    Nov. 26, 1953

George Shaw (to Tarr), Denver vs. Boston,
  Sept. 21, 1962
Bernie Kosar (to Slaughter), Cleveland vs. Chicago,
  Oct. 23, 1989
Steve Young (to Taylor), San Francisco vs. Atlanta,
  Nov. 3, 1991

AVERAGE GAIN
Most Seasons Leading League
7   Sid Luckman, Chi. Bears, 1939-1943, 1946-47
5   Steve Young, San Francisco, 1991-94, 1997
3   Arnie Herber, Green Bay, 1932, 1934, 1936
    Norm Van Brocklin, Los Angeles, 1950, 1952, 1954
    Len Dawson, Dall. Texans, 1962; Kansas City, 1966,
     1968
    Bart Starr, Green Bay, 1966-68
    Kurt Warner, St. Louis, 1999-2001
Most Consecutive Seasons Leading League
5   Sid Luckman, Chi. Bears, 1939-1943
4   Steve Young, San Francisco, 1991-94
3   Bart Starr, Green Bay, 1966-68
    Kurt Warner, St. Louis, 1999-2001
Highest Average Gain, Career (1,500 attempts)
8.63 Otto Graham, Cleveland, 1950-55 (1,565-13,499)
8.42 Sid Luckman, Chi. Bears, 1939-1950
      (1,744-14,686)
8.40 Kurt Warner, St. Louis, 1998-2003; N.Y. Giants,
      2004 (1,965-16,501)
Highest Average Gain, Season (Qualifiers)
11.17 Tommy O'Connell, Cleveland, 1957 (110-1,229)
10.86 Sid Luckman, Chi. Bears, 1943 (202-2,194)
10.55 Otto Graham, Cleveland, 1953 (258-2,722)
Highest Average Gain, Rookie, Season (Qualifiers)
9.411 Greg Cook, Cincinnati, 1969 (197-1,854)
9.409 Bob Waterfield, Cleveland, 1945 (171-1,609)
8.88 Ben Roethlisberger, Pittsburgh, 2004 (295-2,621)
Highest Average Gain, Game (20 attempts)
18.58 Sammy Baugh, Washington vs. Boston,
       Oct. 31, 1948 (24-446)
18.50 Johnny Unitas, Baltimore vs. Atlanta, Nov. 12, 1967
       (20-370)
17.71 Joe Namath, N.Y. Jets vs. Baltimore, Sept. 24, 1972
       (28-496)

TOUCHDOWNS
Most Seasons Leading League
4   Johnny Unitas, Baltimore, 1957-1960
    Len Dawson, Dall. Texans, 1962; Kansas City, 1963,
     1965-66
    Steve Young, San Francisco, 1992-94, 1998
    Brett Favre, Green Bay, 1995-97, 2003
3   Arnie Herber, Green Bay, 1932, 1934, 1936
    Sid Luckman, Chi. Bears, 1943, 1945-46
    Y.A. Tittle, San Francisco, 1955; N.Y. Giants, 1962-63
    Dan Marino, Miami, 1984-86
2   By many players
Most Consecutive Seasons Leading League
4   Johnny Unitas, Baltimore, 1957-1960
3   Dan Marino, Miami, 1984-86
    Steve Young, San Francisco, 1992-94
    Brett Favre, Green Bay, 1995-97
2   By many players
Most Touchdown Passes, Career
420 Dan Marino, Miami, 1983-1999
376 Brett Favre, Atlanta, 1991; Green Bay, 1992-2004
342 Fran Tarkenton, Minnesota, 1961-66, 1972-78;
     N.Y. Giants, 1967-1971
Most Touchdown Passes, Season
49 Peyton Manning, Indianapolis, 2004
48 Dan Marino, Miami, 1984

44 Dan Marino, Miami, 1986
Most Touchdown Passes, Rookie, Season
26 Peyton Manning, Indianapolis, 1998
22 Charlie Conerly, N.Y. Giants, 1948
20 Dan Marino, Miami, 1983
Most Touchdown Passes, Game
7   Sid Luckman, Chi. Bears vs. N.Y. Giants,
     Nov. 14, 1943
    Adrian Burk, Philadelphia vs. Washington,
     Oct. 17, 1954
    George Blanda, Houston vs. N.Y. Titans,
     Nov. 19, 1961
    Y.A. Tittle, N.Y. Giants vs. Washington, Oct. 28, 1962
    Joe Kapp, Minnesota vs. Baltimore, Sept. 28, 1969
6   By many players. Last time:
    Peyton Manning, Indianapolis vs. Detroit,
     Nov. 25, 2004
Most Games, Four or More Touchdown Passes, Career
21 Dan Marino, Miami, 1983-1999
18 Brett Favre, Atlanta, 1991; Green Bay, 1992-2004
17 Johnny Unitas, Baltimore, 1956-1972; San Diego,
     1973
Most Games, Four or More Touchdown Passes, Season
6   Dan Marino, Miami, 1984
    Peyton Manning, Indianapolis, 2004
5   Dan Marino, Miami, 1986
    Brett Favre, Green Bay, 1996
    Donovan McNabb, Philadelphia, 2004
4   George Blanda, Houston, 1961
    Vince Ferragamo, Los Angeles, 1980
    Steve Young, San Francisco, 1994
    Randall Cunningham, Minnesota, 1998
    Daunte Culpepper, Minnesota, 2004
Most Consecutive Games, Four or More Touchdown Passes
5   Peyton Manning, Indianapolis, 2004
4   Dan Marino, Miami, 1984
2   By many players
Most Consecutive Games, Touchdown Passes
47 Johnny Unitas, Baltimore, 1956-1960
36 Brett Favre, Green Bay, 2002-2004
30 Dan Marino, Miami, 1985-87

HAD INTERCEPTED
Most Consecutive Passes Attempted, None Intercepted
308 Bernie Kosar, Cleveland, 1990-91
294 Bart Starr, Green Bay, 1964-65
279 Jeff George, Indianapolis, 1993; Atlanta, 1994
Most Passes Had Intercepted, Career
277 George Blanda, Chi. Bears, 1949, 1950-58; Baltimore,
     1950; Houston, 1960-66; Oakland, 1967-1975
268 John Hadl, San Diego, 1962-1972; Los Angeles,
     1973-74; Green Bay, 1974-75; Houston, 1976-77
266 Fran Tarkenton, Minnesota, 1961-66, 1972-78;
     N.Y. Giants, 1967-1971
Most Passes Had Intercepted, Season
42 George Blanda, Houston, 1962
35 Vinny Testaverde, Tampa Bay, 1988
34 Frank Tripucka, Denver, 1960
Most Passes Had Intercepted, Game
8   Jim Hardy, Chi. Cardinals vs. Philadelphia,
     Sept. 24, 1950
7   Parker Hall, Cleveland vs. Green Bay, Nov. 8, 1942
    Frank Sinkwich, Detroit vs. Green Bay, Oct. 24, 1943
    Bob Waterfield, Los Angeles vs. Green Bay,
     Oct. 17, 1948
    Zeke Bratkowski, Chicago vs. Baltimore,
     Oct. 2, 1960
    Tommy Wade, Pittsburgh vs. Philadelphia,
     Dec. 12, 1965
    Ken Stabler, Oakland vs. Denver, Oct. 16, 1977

       Steve DeBerg, Tampa Bay vs. San Francisco,
          Sept. 7, 1986
       Ty Detmer, Detroit vs. Cleveland, Sept. 23, 2001
   6   By many players

Most Attempts, No Interceptions, Game
  70   Drew Bledsoe, New England vs. Minnesota,
         Nov. 13, 1994 (OT)
  63   Rich Gannon, Minnesota vs. New England,
         Oct. 20, 1991 (OT)
  60   Davey O'Brien, Philadelphia vs. Washington,
         Dec. 1, 1940

LOWEST PERCENTAGE, PASSES HAD INTERCEPTED
Most Seasons Leading League, Lowest Percentage, Passes Had Intercepted
   5   Sammy Baugh, Washington, 1940, 1942, 1944-45,
        1947
   3   Charlie Conerly, N.Y. Giants, 1950, 1956, 1959
        Bart Starr, Green Bay, 1962, 1964, 1966
        Roger Staubach, Dallas, 1971, 1977, 1979
        Ken Anderson, Cincinnati, 1972, 1981-82
        Ken O'Brien, N.Y. Jets, 1985, 1987-88
   2   By many players

Lowest Percentage, Passes Had Intercepted, Career (1,500 attempts)
  2.11   Neil O'Donnell, Pittsburgh, 1991-95; N.Y. Jets,
         1996-97; Cincinnati, 1998; Tennessee,
         1999-2003 (3,229-68)
  2.20   Donovan McNabb, Philadelphia, 1999-2004
         (2,586-57)
  2.37   Mark Brunell, Green Bay, 1994; Jacksonville,
         1995-2003; Washginton, 2004 (3,880-92)

Lowest Percentage, Passes Had Intercepted, Season (Qualifiers)
  0.66   Joe Ferguson, Buffalo, 1976 (151-1)
  0.90   Steve DeBerg, Kansas City, 1990 (444-4)
  1.16   Steve Bartkowski, Atlanta, 1983 (432-5)

Lowest Percentage, Passes Had Intercepted, Rookie, Season (Qualifiers)
  1.98   Charlie Batch, Detroit, 1998 (303-6)
  2.03   Dan Marino, Miami, 1983 (296-6)
  2.10   Gary Wood, N.Y. Giants, 1964 (143-3)

TIMES SACKED
Times Sacked has been compiled since 1963.
Most Times Sacked, Career
  516   John Elway, Denver, 1983-1998
  494   Dave Krieg, Seattle, 1980-1991; Kansas City,
         1992-93; Detroit, 1994; Arizona, 1995;
         Chicago, 1996; Tennessee, 1997-98
  484   Randall Cunningham, Philadelphia, 1985-1995;
         Minnesota, 1997-99; Dallas, 2000; Baltimore,
         2001

Most Times Sacked, Season
  76   David Carr, Houston, 2002
  72   Randall Cunningham, Philadelphia, 1986
  62   Ken O'Brien, N.Y. Jets, 1985
      Steve Beuerlein, Carolina, 2000

Most Times Sacked, Game
  12   Bert Jones, Baltimore vs. St. Louis, Oct. 26, 1980
      Warren Moon, Houston vs. Dallas, Sept. 29, 1985
  11   Charley Johnson, St. Louis vs. N.Y. Giants,
         Nov. 1, 1964
      Bart Starr, Green Bay vs. Detroit, Nov. 7, 1965
      Jack Kemp, Buffalo vs. Oakland, Oct. 15, 1967
      Bob Berry, Atlanta vs. St. Louis, Nov. 24, 1968
      Greg Landry, Detroit vs. Dallas, Oct. 6, 1975
      Ron Jaworski, Philadelphia vs. St. Louis,
         Dec. 18, 1983

       Paul McDonald, Cleveland vs. Kansas City,
          Sept. 30, 1984
       Archie Manning, Minnesota vs. Chicago,
          Oct. 28, 1984
       Steve Pelluer, Dallas vs. San Diego, Nov. 16, 1986
       Randall Cunningham, Philadelphia vs. L.A. Raiders,
          Nov. 30, 1986 (OT)
       David Norrie, N.Y. Jets vs. Dallas, Oct. 4, 1987
       Troy Aikman, Dallas vs. Philadelphia, Sept. 15, 1991
       Bernie Kosar, Cleveland vs. Indianapolis,
          Sept. 6, 1992
  10   By many players

RECEIVING
Most Seasons Leading League
   8   Don Hutson, Green Bay, 1936-37, 1939, 1941-45
   5   Lionel Taylor, Denver, 1960-63, 1965
   3   Tom Fears, Los Angeles, 1948-1950
      Pete Pihos, Philadelphia, 1953-55
      Billy Wilson, San Francisco, 1954, 1956-57
      Raymond Berry, Baltimore, 1958-1960
      Lance Alworth, San Diego, 1966, 1968-69
      Sterling Sharpe, Green Bay, 1989, 1992-93

Most Consecutive Seasons Leading League
   5   Don Hutson, Green Bay, 1941-45
   4   Lionel Taylor, Denver, 1960-63
   3   Tom Fears, Los Angeles, 1948-1950
      Pete Pihos, Philadelphia, 1953-55
      Raymond Berry, Baltimore, 1958-1960

Most Pass Receptions, Career
  1,549   Jerry Rice, San Francisco, 1985-2000; Oakland,
         2001-04; Seattle, 2004
  1,101   Cris Carter, Philadelphia, 1987-89; Minnesota,
         1990-2001; Miami, 2002
  1,094   Tim Brown, L.A. Raiders, 1988-1994; Oakland,
         1995-2003; Tampa Bay, 2004

Most Seasons, 50 or More Pass Receptions
  17   Jerry Rice, San Francisco, 1986-1996, 1998-2000;
         Oakland, 2001-03
  13   Andre Reed, Buffalo, 1986-1994, 1996-99
  11   Cris Carter, Minnesota, 1991-2001
      Tim Brown, L.A. Raiders, 1993-1994; Oakland,
         1995-2003
      Shannon Sharpe, Denver 1992-98; Baltimore,
         2000-01; Denver, 2002-03

Most Pass Receptions, Season
  143   Marvin Harrison, Indianapolis, 2002
  123   Herman Moore, Detroit, 1995
  122   Cris Carter, Minnesota, 1994
      Cris Carter, Minnesota, 1995
      Jerry Rice, San Francisco, 1995

Most Pass Receptions, Rookie, Season
  101   Anquan Boldin, Arizona, 2003
  90   Terry Glenn, New England, 1996
  83   Earl Cooper, San Francisco, 1980

Most Pass Receptions, Game
  20   Terrell Owens, San Francisco vs. Chicago,
         Dec. 17, 2000
  18   Tom Fears, Los Angeles vs. Green Bay, Dec. 3, 1950
  17   Clark Gaines, N.Y. Jets vs. San Francisco,
         Sept. 21, 1980

Most Consecutive Games, Pass Receptions
  274   Jerry Rice, San Francisco, 1985-2000; Oakland,
         2001-04
  183   Art Monk, Washington, 1983-1993; N.Y. Jets, 1994;
         Philadelphia, 1995
  179   Tim Brown, L.A. Raiders, 1993-94; Oakland,
         1995-2003; Tampa Bay, 2004

YARDS GAINED

Most Seasons Leading League

7   Don Hutson, Green Bay, 1936, 1938-39, 1941-44
6   Jerry Rice, San Francisco, 1986, 1989-1990, 1993-95
3   Raymond Berry, Baltimore, 1957, 1959-1960
    Lance Alworth, San Diego, 1965-66, 1968

Most Consecutive Seasons Leading League

4   Don Hutson, Green Bay, 1941-44
3   Jerry Rice, San Francisco, 1993-95
2   By many players

Most Yards Gained, Career

22,895   Jerry Rice, San Francisco, 1985-2000; Oakland, 2001-04; Seattle, 2004
14,934   Tim Brown, L.A. Raiders, 1988-1994; Oakland, 1995-2003; Tampa Bay, 2004
14,004   James Lofton, Green Bay, 1978-1986; L.A. Raiders, 1987-88; Buffalo, 1989-1992; L.A. Rams, 1993; Philadelphia, 1993

Most Seasons, 1,000 or More Yards, Pass Receiving

14   Jerry Rice, San Francisco, 1986-1996, 1998; Oakland, 2001-02
9   Tim Brown, L.A. Raiders, 1993-94; Oakland, 1995-2001
8   Steve Largent, Seattle, 1978-1981, 1983-86
    Cris Carter, Minnesota, 1993-2000
    Jimmy Smith, Jacksonville, 1996-2002, 2004

Most Yards Gained, Season

1,848   Jerry Rice, San Francisco, 1995
1,781   Isaac Bruce, St. Louis, 1995
1,746   Charley Hennigan, Houston, 1961

Most Yards Gained, Rookie, Season

1,473   Bill Groman, Houston, 1960
1,377   Anquan Boldin, Arizona, 2003
1,313   Randy Moss, Minnesota, 1998

Most Yards Gained, Game

336   Willie Anderson, L.A. Rams vs. New Orleans, Nov. 26, 1989 (OT)
309   Stephone Paige, Kansas City vs. San Diego, Dec. 22, 1985
303   Jim Benton, Cleveland vs. Detroit, Nov. 22, 1945

Most Games, 200 or More Yards Pass Receiving, Career

5   Lance Alworth, San Diego, 1962-1970; Dallas, 1971-72
4   Don Hutson, Green Bay, 1935-45
    Charley Hennigan, Houston, 1960-66
    Jerry Rice, San Francisco, 1985-2000; Oakland, 2001-04; Seattle, 2004
3   Don Maynard, N.Y. Giants, 1958; N.Y. Jets, 1960-1972; St. Louis, 1973
    Wes Chandler, New Orleans, 1978-1981; San Diego, 1981-87; San Francisco, 1988
    Isaac Bruce, L.A. Rams, 1994; St. Louis, 1995-2004

Most Games, 200 or More Yards Pass Receiving, Season

3   Charley Hennigan, Houston, 1961
2   Don Hutson, Green Bay, 1942
    Gene Roberts, N.Y. Giants, 1949
    Lance Alworth, San Diego, 1963
    Don Maynard, N.Y. Jets, 1968

Most Games, 100 or More Yards Pass Receiving, Career

76   Jerry Rice, San Francisco, 1985-2000; Oakland, 2001-04; Seattle, 2004
50   Don Maynard, N.Y. Giants, 1958; N.Y. Jets, 1960-1972; St. Louis, 1973
47   Michael Irvin, Dallas, 1988-1999
    Marvin Harrison, Indianapolis, 1996-2004

Most Games, 100 or More Yards Pass Receiving, Season

11   Michael Irvin, Dallas, 1995
10   Charley Hennigan, Houston, 1961
    Herman Moore, Detroit, 1995

    Marvin Harrison, Indianapolis, 2002
    Torry Holt, St. Louis, 2003
9   Elroy (Crazylegs) Hirsch, Los Angeles, 1951
    Bill Groman, Houston, 1960
    Lance Alworth, San Diego, 1965
    Don Maynard, N.Y. Jets, 1967
    Stanley Morgan, New England, 1986
    Mark Carrier, Tampa Bay, 1989
    Robert Brooks, Green Bay, 1995
    Isaac Bruce, St. Louis, 1995
    Jerry Rice, San Francisco, 1995
    Marvin Harrison, Indianapolis, 1999
    Jimmy Smith, Jacksonville, 1999
    David Boston, Arizona, 2001

Most Consecutive Games, 100 or More Yards Pass Receiving

7   Charley Hennigan, Houston, 1961
    Michael Irvin, Dallas, 1995
6   Raymond Berry, Baltimore, 1960
    Bill Groman, Houston, 1961
    Pat Studstill, Detroit, 1966
    Isaac Bruce, St. Louis, 1995
5   Elroy (Crazylegs) Hirsch, Los Angeles, 1951
    Bob Boyd, Los Angeles, 1954
    Terry Barr, Detroit, 1963
    Lance Alworth, San Diego, 1966
    Don Maynard, N.Y. Jets, 1968-69
    Harold Jackson, Philadelphia, 1971-72
    Patrick Jeffers, Carolina, 1999
    Terrell Owens, Philadelphia, 2004

Longest Pass Reception (All TDs except as noted)

99   Andy Farkas (from Filchock), Washington vs. Pittsburgh, Oct. 15, 1939
    Bobby Mitchell (from Izo), Washington vs. Cleveland, Sept. 15, 1963
    Pat Studstill (from Sweetan), Detroit vs. Baltimore, Oct. 16, 1966
    Gerry Allen (from Jurgensen), Washington vs. Chicago, Sept. 15, 1968
    Cliff Branch (from Plunkett), L.A. Raiders vs. Washington, Oct. 2, 1983
    Mike Quick (from Jaworski), Philadelphia vs. Atlanta, Nov. 10, 1985
    Tony Martin (from Humphries), San Diego vs. Seattle, Sept. 18, 1994
    Robert Brooks (from Favre), Green Bay vs. Chicago, Sept. 11, 1995
    Marc Boerigter (from Green), Kansas City vs. San Diego, Dec. 22, 2002
    Andre Davis (from Garcia), Cleveland vs. Cincinnati, Oct. 17, 2004
98   Gaynell Tinsley (from Russell), Chi. Cardinals vs. Cleveland, Nov. 17, 1938
    Dick (Night Train) Lane (from Compton), Chi. Cardinals vs. Green Bay, Nov. 13, 1955
    John Farrington (from Wade), Chicago vs. Detroit, Oct. 8, 1961
    Willard Dewveall (from Lee), Houston vs. San Diego, Nov. 25, 1962
    Homer Jones (from Morrall), N.Y. Giants vs. Pittsburgh, Sept. 11, 1966
    Bobby Moore (from Hart), St. Louis vs. Los Angeles, Dec. 10, 1972 (no TD)
    Michael Haynes (from Hebert), Atlanta vs. New Orleans, Sept. 12, 1993
    Johnnie Morton (from Batch), Detroit vs. Chicago, Oct. 4, 1998
97   Gaynell Tinsley (from Coffee), Chi. Cardinals vs. Chi. Bears, Dec. 5, 1937

Cloyce Box (from Layne), Detroit vs. Green Bay, Nov. 26, 1953
Jerry Tarr (from Shaw), Denver vs. Boston, Sept. 21, 1962
Webster Slaughter (from Kosar), Cleveland vs. Chicago, Oct. 23, 1989
John Taylor (from Young), San Francisco vs. Atlanta, Nov. 3, 1991

AVERAGE GAIN
Highest Average Gain, Career (200 receptions)
22.26 Homer Jones, N.Y. Giants, 1964-69; Cleveland, 1970 (224-4,986)
20.83 Buddy Dial, Pittsburgh, 1959-1963; Dallas, 1964-66 (261-5,436)
20.24 Harlon Hill, Chi. Bears, 1954-1961; Pittsburgh, 1962; Detroit, 1962 (233-4,717)
Highest Average Gain, Season (24 receptions)
32.58 Don Currivan, Boston, 1947 (24-782)
31.44 Bucky Pope, Los Angeles, 1964 (25-786)
28.60 Bobby Duckworth, San Diego, 1984 (25-715)
Highest Average Gain, Game (3 receptions)
63.00 Torry Holt, St. Louis vs. Atlanta, Sept. 24, 2000 (3-189)
60.67 Bill Groman, Houston vs. Denver, Nov. 20, 1960 (3-182)
       Homer Jones, N.Y. Giants vs. Washington, Dec. 12, 1965 (3-182)
60.33 Don Currivan, Boston vs. Washington, Nov. 30, 1947 (3-181)

TOUCHDOWNS
Most Seasons Leading League
9 Don Hutson, Green Bay, 1935-38, 1940-44
6 Jerry Rice, San Francisco, 1986-87, 1989-1991, 1993
3 Lance Alworth, San Diego, 1964-66
   Cris Carter, Minnesota, 1995, 1997, 1999
   Randy Moss, Minnesota, 1998, 2000, 2003
Most Consecutive Seasons Leading League
5 Don Hutson, Green Bay, 1940-44
4 Don Hutson, Green Bay, 1935-38
3 Lance Alworth, San Diego, 1964-66
   Jerry Rice, San Francisco, 1989-1991
Most Touchdowns, Career
197 Jerry Rice, San Francisco, 1985-2000; Oakland, 2001-04; Seattle, 2004
130 Cris Carter, Philadelphia, 1987-89; Minnesota, 1990-2001; Miami, 2002
100 Steve Largent, Seattle, 1976-1989
     Tim Brown, L.A. Raiders, 1988-1994; Oakland, 1995-2003; Tampa Bay, 2004
Most Touchdowns, Season
22 Jerry Rice, San Francisco, 1987
18 Mark Clayton, Miami, 1984
    Sterling Sharpe, Green Bay, 1994
17 Don Hutson, Green Bay, 1942
    Elroy (Crazylegs) Hirsch, Los Angeles, 1951
    Bill Groman, Houston, 1961
    Jerry Rice, San Francisco, 1989
    Cris Carter, Minnesota, 1995
    Carl Pickens, Cincinnati, 1995
    Randy Moss, Minnesota, 1998
    Randy Moss, Minnesota, 2003
Most Touchdowns, Rookie, Season
17 Randy Moss, Minnesota, 1998
13 Bill Howton, Green Bay, 1952
    John Jefferson, San Diego, 1978
12 Harlon Hill, Chi. Bears, 1954
    Bill Groman, Houston, 1960

Mike Ditka, Chicago, 1961
Bob Hayes, Dallas, 1965
Most Touchdowns, Game
5 Bob Shaw, Chi. Cardinals vs. Baltimore, Oct. 2, 1950
   Kellen Winslow, San Diego vs. Oakland, Nov. 22, 1981
   Jerry Rice, San Francisco vs. Atlanta, Oct. 14, 1990
4 By many players. Last time: Joe Horn, New Orleans vs. N.Y. Giants, Dec. 14, 2003
Most Consecutive Games, Touchdowns
13 Jerry Rice, San Francisco, 1986-87
11 Elroy (Crazylegs) Hirsch, Los Angeles, 1950-51
    Buddy Dial, Pittsburgh, 1959-1960
10 Carl Pickens, Cincinnati, 1994-95
    Randy Moss, Minnesota, 2003-04

YARDS FROM SCRIMMAGE
Most Scrimmage Yards, Career
23,540 Jerry Rice, San Francisco 1985-2000; Oakland, 2001-04; Seattle, 2004
21,579 Emmitt Smith, Dallas, 1990-2002; Arizona, 2003-04
21,264 Walter Payton, Chicago, 1975-1987
Most Scrimmage Yards, Season
2,429 Marshall Faulk, St. Louis, 1999 (1,381 rush., 1,048 rec.)
2,370 LaDainian Tomlinson, San Diego, 2003 (1,645 rush., 725 rec.)
2,358 Barry Sanders, Detroit, 1997 (2,053 rush., 305 rec.)
Most Scrimmage Yards, Rookie, Season
2,212 Eric Dickerson, L.A. Rams, 1983 (1,808 rush., 404 rec.)
2,139 Edgerrin James, Indianapolis, 1999 (1,553 rush., 586 rec.)
1,924 Billy Sims, Detroit, 1980 (1,303 rush., 621 rec.)
Most Scrimmage Yards, Game
336 Flipper Anderson, L.A. Rams vs. New Orleans, Nov. 26, 1989 (OT) (336 rec.)
330 Billy Cannon, Houston vs. N.Y. Titans, Dec. 10, 1961 (216 rush., 114 rec.)
309 Stephone Paige, Kansas City vs. San Diego, Dec. 22, 1985 (309 rec.)

INTERCEPTIONS BY
Most Seasons Leading League
3 Everson Walls, Dallas, 1981-82, 1985
2 Dick (Night Train) Lane, Los Angeles, 1952; Chi. Cardinals, 1954
   Jack Christiansen, Detroit, 1953, 1957
   Milt Davis, Baltimore, 1957, 1959
   Dick Lynch, N.Y. Giants, 1961, 1963
   Johnny Robinson, Kansas City, 1966, 1970
   Bill Bradley, Philadelphia, 1971-72
   Emmitt Thomas, Kansas City, 1969, 1974
   Ronnie Lott, San Francisco, 1986; L.A. Raiders, 1991
   Rod Woodson, Baltimore, 1999; Oakland, 2002
Most Interceptions By, Career
81 Paul Krause, Washington, 1964-67; Minnesota, 1968-1979
79 Emlen Tunnell, N.Y. Giants, 1948-1958; Green Bay, 1959-1961
71 Rod Woodson, Pittsburgh, 1987-1996; San Francisco, 1997; Baltimore, 1998-2001; Oakland, 2002-03
Most Interceptions By, Season
14 Dick (Night Train) Lane, Los Angeles, 1952
13 Dan Sandifer, Washington, 1948
    Orban (Spec) Sanders, N.Y. Yanks, 1950
    Lester Hayes, Oakland, 1980
12 By nine players
Most Interceptions By, Rookie, Season
14 Dick (Night Train) Lane, Los Angeles, 1952
13 Dan Sandifer, Washington, 1948

12 Woodley Lewis, Los Angeles, 1950
    Paul Krause, Washington, 1964

Most Interceptions By, Game

4 Sammy Baugh, Washington vs. Detroit, Nov. 14, 1943
   Dan Sandifer, Washington vs. Boston, Oct. 31, 1948
   Don Doll, Detroit vs. Chi. Cardinals, Oct. 23, 1949
   Bob Nussbaumer, Chi. Cardinals vs. N.Y. Bulldogs,
    Nov. 13, 1949
   Russ Craft, Philadelphia vs. Chi. Cardinals,
    Sept. 24, 1950
   Bobby Dillon, Green Bay vs. Detroit, Nov. 26, 1953
   Jack Butler, Pittsburgh vs. Washington, Dec. 13, 1953
   Austin (Goose) Gonsoulin, Denver vs. Buffalo,
    Sept. 18, 1960
   Jerry Norton, St. Louis vs. Washington,
    Nov. 20, 1960; vs. Pittsburgh, Nov. 26, 1961
   Dave Baker, San Francisco vs. L.A. Rams,
    Dec. 4, 1960
   Bobby Ply, Dall. Texans vs. San Diego, Dec. 16, 1962
   Bobby Hunt, Kansas City vs. Houston, Oct. 4, 1964
   Willie Brown, Denver vs. N.Y. Jets, Nov. 15, 1964
   Dick Anderson, Miami vs. Pittsburgh, Dec. 3, 1973
   Willie Buchanon, Green Bay vs. San Diego,
    Sept. 24, 1978
   Deron Cherry, Kansas City vs. Seattle, Sept. 29, 1985
   Kwamie Lassiter, Arizona vs. San Diego,
    Dec. 27, 1998
   Deltha O'Neal, Denver vs. Kansas City, Oct. 7, 2001

Most Consecutive Games, Passes Intercepted By

8 Tom Morrow, Oakland, 1962-63
7 Tom Landry, N.Y. Giants, 1950-51
   Paul Krause, Washington, 1964
   Larry Wilson, St. Louis, 1966
   Ben Davis, Cleveland, 1968
6 By many players.
    Last time: Brian Russell, Minnesota, 2003

YARDS GAINED

Most Seasons Leading League

2 Dick (Night Train) Lane, Los Angeles, 1952;
    Chi. Cardinals, 1954
   Herb Adderley, Green Bay, 1965, 1969
   Dick Anderson, Miami, 1968, 1970

Most Yards Gained, Career

1,483 Rod Woodson, Pittsburgh, 1987-1996; San Francisco,
    1997; Baltimore, 1998-2001; Oakland, 2002-03
1,282 Emlen Tunnell, N.Y. Giants, 1948-1958; Green Bay,
    1959-1961
1,274 Deion Sanders, Atlanta, 1989-1993; San Francisco,
    1994; Dallas, 1995-99; Washington, 2000;
    Baltimore, 2004

Most Yards Gained, Season

358 Ed Reed, Balitmore, 2004
349 Charlie McNeil, San Diego, 1961
303 Deion Sanders, San Francisco, 1994

Most Yards Gained, Rookie, Season

301 Don Doll, Detroit, 1949
298 Dick (Night Train) Lane, Los Angeles, 1952
275 Woodley Lewis, Los Angeles, 1950

Most Yards Gained, Game

177 Charlie McNeil, San Diego vs. Houston,
    Sept. 24, 1961
170 Louis Oliver, Miami vs. Buffalo, Oct. 4, 1992
167 Dick Jauron, Detroit vs. Chicago, Nov. 18, 1973

Longest Return (All TDs)

106 Ed Reed, Baltimore vs. Cleveland, Nov. 7, 2004
103 Vencie Glenn, San Diego vs. Denver, Nov. 29, 1987
   Louis Oliver, Miami vs. Buffalo, Oct. 4, 1992

102 Bob Smith, Detroit vs. Chi. Bears, Nov. 24, 1949
   Erich Barnes, N.Y. Giants vs. Dall. Cowboys,
    Oct. 15, 1961
   Gary Barbaro, Kansas City vs. Seattle, Dec. 11, 1977
   Louis Breeden, Cincinnati vs. San Diego, Nov. 8, 1981
   Eddie Anderson, L.A. Raiders vs. Miami, Dec. 14, 1992
   Donald Frank, San Diego vs. L.A. Raiders,
    Oct. 31, 1993
   Artrell Hawkins, Cincinnati vs. Houston, Nov. 3, 2002
   Marcus Coleman, Houston vs. Kansas City,
    Sept. 26, 2004

TOUCHDOWNS

Most Touchdowns, Career

12 Rod Woodson, Pittsburgh, 1987-1996; San Francisco,
    1997; Baltimore, 1998-2001; Oakland, 2002-03
9 Ken Houston, Houston, 1967-1972; Washington,
    1973-1980
   Aeneas Williams, Phoenix, 1991-93; Arizona,
    1994-2000; St. Louis, 2001-04
   Deion Sanders, Atlanta, 1989-1993; San Francisco,
    1994; Dallas, 1995-99; Washington, 2000;
    Baltimore, 2004
8 Eric Allen, Philadelphia, 1988-1994; New Orleans,
    1995-97; Oakland, 1998-2001

Most Touchdowns, Season

4 Ken Houston, Houston, 1971
   Jim Kearney, Kansas City, 1972
   Eric Allen, Philadelphia, 1993
3 Dick Harris, San Diego, 1961
   Dick Lynch, N.Y. Giants, 1963
   Herb Adderley, Green Bay, 1965
   Lem Barney, Detroit, 1967
   Miller Farr, Houston, 1967
   Monte Jackson, Los Angeles, 1976
   Rod Perry, Los Angeles, 1978
   Ronnie Lott, San Francisco, 1981
   Lloyd Burruss, Kansas City, 1986
   Wayne Haddix, Tampa Bay, 1990
   Robert Massey, Phoenix, 1992
   Ray Buchanan, Indianapolis, 1994
   Deion Sanders, San Francisco, 1994
   Mark McMillian, Kansas City, 1997
   Otis Smith, N.Y. Jets, 1997
   Jimmy Hitchcock, Minnesota, 1998
   Eric Allen, Oakland, 2000
   Derrick Brooks, Tampa Bay, 2002
2 By many players

Most Touchdowns, Rookie, Season

3 Lem Barney, Detroit, 1967
   Ronnie Lott, San Francisco, 1981
2 By many players

Most Touchdowns, Game

2 Bill Blackburn, Chi. Cardinals vs. Boston,
    Oct. 24, 1948
   Dan Sandifer, Washington vs. Boston, Oct. 31, 1948
   Bob Franklin, Cleveland vs. Chicago, Dec. 11, 1960
   Bill Stacy, St. Louis vs. Dall. Cowboys, Nov. 5, 1961
   Jerry Norton, St. Louis vs. Pittsburgh, Nov. 26, 1961
   Miller Farr, Houston vs. Buffalo, Dec. 7, 1968
   Ken Houston, Houston vs. San Diego, Dec. 19, 1971
   Jim Kearney, Kansas City vs. Denver, Oct. 1, 1972
   Lemar Parrish, Cincinnati vs. Houston, Dec. 17, 1972
   Dick Anderson, Miami vs. Pittsburgh, Dec. 3, 1973
   Prentice McCray, New England vs. N.Y. Jets,
    Nov. 21, 1976
   Kenny Johnson, Atlanta vs. Green Bay,
    Nov. 27, 1983 (OT)
   Mike Kozlowski, Miami vs. N.Y. Jets, Dec. 16, 1983
   Dave Brown, Seattle vs. Kansas City, Nov. 4, 1984

Lloyd Burruss, Kansas City vs. San Diego,
Oct. 19, 1986
Henry Jones, Buffalo vs. Indianapolis, Sept. 20, 1992
Robert Massey, Phoenix vs. Washington, Oct. 4, 1992
Eric Allen, Philadelphia vs. New Orleans,
Dec. 26, 1993
Ken Norton, San Francisco vs. St. Louis,
Oct. 22, 1995
Otis Smith, N.Y. Jets vs. Tampa Bay, Dec. 14, 1997
Dewayne Washington, Pittsburgh vs. Jacksonville,
Nov. 22, 1998
Aaron Glenn, Houston vs. Pittsburgh, Dec. 8, 2002

PUNTING
Most Seasons Leading League
4   Sammy Baugh, Washington, 1940-43
     Jerrel Wilson, Kansas City, 1965, 1968, 1972-73
3   Yale Lary, Detroit, 1959, 1961, 1963
     Jim Fraser, Denver, 1962-64
     Ray Guy, Oakland, 1974-75, 1977
     Rohn Stark, Baltimore, 1983; Indianapolis, 1985-86
2   By many players
Most Consecutive Seasons Leading League
4   Sammy Baugh, Washington, 1940-43
3   Jim Fraser, Denver, 1962-64
2   By many players

PUNTS
Most Punts, Career
1,367   Sean Landeta, N.Y. Giants, 1985-1993; L.A. Rams,
     1993-94; St. Louis, 1995-96; Tampa Bay, 1997;
     Green Bay, 1998; Philadelphia, 1999-2002;
     St. Louis, 2003-04
1,364   Jeff Feagles, New England, 1988-89; Philadelphia,
     1990-93; Arizona, 1994-97; Seattle, 1998-2002;
     N.Y. Giants, 2003-04
1,226   Lee Johnson, Houston, 1985-87; Cleveland, 1987-
     88; Cincinnati, 1988-1998; New England, 1999-
     2001; Minnesota, 2001; Philadelphia, 2002
Most Punts, Season
114   Bob Parsons, Chicago, 1981
     Chad Stanley, Houston, 2002
111   Brad Maynard, N.Y. Giants, 1997
109   John James, Atlanta, 1978
Most Punts, Rookie, Season
111   Brad Maynard, N.Y. Giants, 1997
108   John Teltschik, Philadelphia, 1986
101   Daniel Pope, Kansas City, 1999
Most Punts, Game
16   Leo Araguz, Oakland vs. San Diego, Oct. 11, 1998
15   John Teltschik, Philadelphia vs. N.Y. Giants,
     Dec. 6, 1987 (OT)
14   Dick Nesbitt, Chi. Cardinals vs. Chi. Bears,
     Nov. 30, 1933
     Keith Molesworth, Chi. Bears vs. Green Bay,
     Dec. 10, 1933
     Sammy Baugh, Washington vs. Philadelphia,
     Nov. 5, 1939
     Carl Kinscherf, N.Y. Giants vs. Detroit, Nov. 7, 1943
     George Taliaferro, N.Y. Yanks vs. Los Angeles,
     Sept. 28, 1951
Longest Punt
98   Steve O'Neal, N.Y. Jets vs. Denver, Sept. 21, 1969
94   Joe Lintzenich, Chi. Bears vs. N.Y. Giants, Nov. 16, 1931
93   Shawn McCarthy, New England vs. Buffalo,
     Nov. 3, 1991

AVERAGE YARDAGE
Highest Average, Punting, Career (250 punts)
45.89   Shane Lechler, Oakland, 2000-04 (360-16,522)

45.10   Sammy Baugh, Washington, 1937-1952
     (338-15,245)
44.68   Tommy Davis, San Francisco, 1959-1969
     (511-22,833)
Highest Average, Punting, Season (Qualifiers)
51.40   Sammy Baugh, Washington, 1940 (35-1,799)
48.94   Yale Lary, Detroit, 1963 (35-1,713)
48.73   Sammy Baugh, Washington, 1941 (30-1,462)
Highest Average, Punting, Rookie, Season (Qualifiers)
45.92   Frank Sinkwich, Detroit, 1943 (12-551)
45.91   Shane Lechler, Oakland, 2000 (65-2,984)
45.66   Tommy Davis, San Francisco, 1959 (59-2,694)
Highest Average, Punting, Game (4 punts)
61.75   Bob Cifers, Detroit vs. Chi. Bears, Nov. 24, 1946
     (4-247)
61.60   Roy McKay, Green Bay vs. Chi. Cardinals,
     Oct. 28, 1945 (5-308)
59.50   Darren Bennett, San Diego vs. Pittsburgh,
     Oct. 1, 1995 (4-238)

PUNTS HAD BLOCKED
Most Consecutive Punts, None Blocked
1,045   Chris Gardocki, Chicago, 1992-94; Indianapolis,
     1995-98; Cleveland, 1999-2003; Pittsburgh,
     2004 (current)
828   Bryan Barker, Kansas City, 1993; Philadelphia, 1994;
     Jacksonville, 1995-2000; Washington, 2001-03
     Green Bay, 2004 (current)
638   Tom Tupa, New England, 1997-98; N.Y. Jets,
     1999-2001; Tampa Bay, 2002-03;
     Washington, 2004
Most Punts Had Blocked, Career
14   Herman Weaver, Detroit, 1970-76; Seattle, 1977-1980
     Harry Newsome, Pittsburgh, 1985-89; Minnesota,
     1990-93
12   Jerrel Wilson, Kansas City, 1963-1977;
     New England, 1978
     Tom Blanchard, N.Y. Giants, 1971-73; New Orleans,
     1974-78; Tampa Bay, 1979-1981
11   David Lee, Baltimore, 1966-1978
     Jeff Feagles, New England, 1988-89; Philadelphia,
     1990-93; Arizona, 1994-97; Seattle, 1998-2002;
     N.Y. Giants, 2003-04
Most Punts Had Blocked, Season
6   Harry Newsome, Pittsburgh, 1988
4   Bryan Wagner, Cleveland, 1990
3   By many players

PUNTS INSIDE THE 20
Punts Inside the 20 have been compiled since 1976.
Most Punts Inside the 20, Career
430   Jeff Feagles, New England, 1988-89; Philadelphia,
     1990-93; Arizona, 1994-97; Seattle, 1998-2002;
     N.Y. Giants, 2003-04
374   Sean Landeta, N.Y. Giants, 1985-1993; L.A. Rams,
     1993-94; St. Louis, 1995-96; Tampa Bay, 1997;
     Green Bay, 1998; Philadelphia, 1999-2002;
     St. Louis, 2003-04
318   Lee Johnson, Houston, 1985-87; Cleveland, 1987-
     88; Cincinnati, 1988-1998; New England, 1999-
     2001; Minnesota, 2001; Philadelphia, 2002
Most Punts Inside the 20, Season
39   Kyle Richardson, Baltimore, 1999
36   Brad Maynard, Chicago, 2001
     Chad Stanley, Houston, 2002
     Chad Stanley, Houston, 2003
35   Rich Camarillo, Houston, 1994
     Mark Royals, Pittsburgh, 1994
     Craig Hentrich, Tennessee, 1999
     Kyle Richardson, Baltimore, 2000

Todd Sauerbrun, Carolina, 2001

Most Punts Inside the 20, Game

8   Mark Royals, Pittsburgh vs. Houston, Nov. 6, 1994 (OT)

    Bryan Barker, Jacksonville vs. Baltimore, Nov. 14, 1999

7   Josh Miller, Pittsburgh vs. Cincinnati, Dec. 20, 1998

6   By many players

PUNT RETURNS

Most Seasons Leading League

3   Les (Speedy) Duncan, San Diego, 1965-66; Washington, 1971

    Rick Upchurch, Denver, 1976, 1978, 1982

2   Dick Christy, N.Y. Titans, 1961-62

    Claude Gibson, Oakland, 1963-64

    Billy (White Shoes) Johnson, Houston, 1975, 1977

    Mel Gray, New Orleans, 1987; Detroit, 1991

    Jermaine Lewis, Baltimore, 1997, 2000

PUNT RETURNS

Most Punt Returns, Career

463   Brian Mitchell, Washington, 1990-99; Philadelphia, 2000-02; N.Y. Giants, 2003

351   Eric Metcalf, Cleveland, 1989-1994; Atlanta, 1995-96; San Diego, 1997; Arizona, 1998; Carolina, 1999; Washington, 2001; Green Bay, 2002

349   David Meggett, N.Y. Giants, 1989-1994; New England, 1995-97; N.Y. Jets, 1998

Most Punt Returns, Season

70   Danny Reece, Tampa Bay, 1979

62   Fulton Walker, Miami-L.A. Raiders, 1985

58   J.T. Smith, Kansas City, 1979

    Greg Pruitt, L.A. Raiders, 1983

    Leo Lewis, Minnesota, 1988

    Desmond Howard, Green Bay, 1996

Most Punt Returns, Rookie, Season

57   Lew Barnes, Chicago, 1986

55   B.J. Sams, Baltimore, 2004

54   James Jones, Dallas, 1980

Most Punt Returns, Game

11   Eddie Brown, Washington vs. Tampa Bay, Oct. 9, 1977

10   Theo Bell, Pittsburgh vs. Buffalo, Dec. 16, 1979

    Mike Nelms, Washington vs. New Orleans, Dec. 26, 1982

    Ronnie Harris, New England vs. Pittsburgh, Dec. 5, 1993

9   Rodger Bird, Oakland vs. Denver, Sept. 10, 1967

    Ralph McGill, San Francisco vs. Atlanta, Oct. 29, 1972

    Ed Podolak, Kansas City vs. San Diego, Nov. 10, 1974

    Anthony Leonard, San Francisco vs. New Orleans, Oct. 17, 1976

    Butch Johnson, Dallas vs. Buffalo, Nov. 15, 1976

    Larry Marshall, Philadelphia vs. Tampa Bay, Sept. 18, 1977

    Nesby Glasgow, Baltimore vs. Kansas City, Sept. 2, 1979

    Mike Nelms, Washington vs. St. Louis, Dec. 21, 1980

    Leon Bright, N.Y. Giants vs. Philadelphia, Dec. 11, 1982

    Pete Shaw, N.Y. Giants vs. Philadelphia, Nov. 20, 1983

    Cleotha Montgomery, L.A. Raiders vs. Detroit, Dec. 10, 1984

    Phil McConkey, N.Y. Giants vs. Philadelphia, Dec. 6, 1987 (OT)

Andre Hastings, Pittsburgh vs. Cleveland, Nov. 13, 1995

Steve Smith, Carolina vs. Detroit, Sept. 15, 2002

FAIR CATCHES

Most Fair Catches, Career

231   Brian Mitchell, Washington, 1990-99; Philadelphia, 2000-02; N.Y. Giants, 2003

162   Tim Brown, L.A. Raiders, 1988-1994; Oakland, 1995-2003; Tampa Bay, 2004

144   Glyn Milburn, Denver, 1993-95; Detroit, 1996-97; Chicago, 1998-2001; San Diego, 2001

Most Fair Catches, Season

33   Brian Mitchell, Philadelphia, 2000

27   Leo Lewis, Minnesota, 1989

    Antonio Chatman, Green Bay, 2004

26   Eric Guliford, New Orleans, 1997

    Glyn Milburn, Detroit, 1997

    Glyn Milburn, Chicago, 2000

Most Fair Catches, Game

7   Bake Turner, N.Y. Jets vs. Miami, Nov. 20, 1966

    Lem Barney, Detroit vs. Chicago, Nov. 21, 1976

    Bobby Morse, Philadelphia vs. Buffalo, Dec. 27, 1987

6   Jake Scott, Miami vs. Buffalo, Dec. 20, 1970

    Greg Pruitt, L.A. Raiders vs. Seattle, Oct. 7, 1984

    Phil McConkey, San Diego vs. Kansas City, Dec. 17, 1989

    Gerald McNeil, Houston vs. Pittsburgh, Sept. 16, 1990

    Bobby Engram, Chicago vs. Minnesota, Sept. 15, 1996

    Eddie Kennison, New Orleans vs. Baltimore, Dec. 19, 1999

5   By many players

YARDS GAINED

Most Seasons Leading League

3   Alvin Haymond, Baltimore, 1965-66; Los Angeles, 1969

2   Bill Dudley, Pittsburgh, 1942, 1946

    Emlen Tunnell, N.Y. Giants, 1951-52

    Dick Christy, N.Y. Titans, 1961-62

    Claude Gibson, Oakland, 1963-64

    Rodger Bird, Oakland, 1966-67

    J.T. Smith, Kansas City, 1979-1980

    Vai Sikahema, St. Louis, 1986-87

    David Meggett, N.Y. Giants, 1989-1990

    Tamarick Vanover, Kansas City, 1995, 1999

Most Yards Gained, Career

4,999   Brian Mitchell, Washington, 1990-99; Philadelphia, 2000-02; N.Y. Giants, 2003

3,708   David Meggett, N.Y. Giants, 1989-1994; New England, 1995-97; N.Y. Jets, 1998

3,601   Darrien Gordon, San Diego, 1993-94, 1996; Denver, 1997-98; Oakland, 1999-2000; Atlanta, 2001; Green Bay, 2002

Most Yards Gained, Season

875   Desmond Howard, Green Bay, 1996

692   Fulton Walker, Miami-L.A. Raiders, 1985

666   Greg Pruitt, L.A. Raiders, 1983

Most Yards Gained, Rookie, Season

656   Louis Lipps, Pittsburgh, 1984

655   Neal Colzie, Oakland, 1975

619   Leon Johnson, N.Y. Jets, 1997

Most Yards Gained, Game

207   LeRoy Irvin, Los Angeles vs. Atlanta, Oct. 11, 1981

205   George Atkinson, Oakland vs. Buffalo, Sept. 15, 1968

199   Eddie Drummond, Detroit vs. Jacksonville, Nov. 14, 2004 (OT)

Longest Punt Return (All TDs)
- 103 Robert Bailey, L.A. Rams vs. New Orleans, Oct. 23, 1994
- 98 Gil LeFebvre, Cincinnati vs. Brooklyn, Dec. 3, 1933
  Charlie West, Minnesota vs. Washington, Nov. 3, 1968
  Dennis Morgan, Dallas vs. St. Louis, Oct. 13, 1974
  Terance Mathis, N.Y. Jets vs. Dallas, Nov. 4, 1990
- 97 Greg Pruitt, L.A. Raiders vs. Washington, Oct. 2, 1983

AVERAGE YARDAGE
Highest Average, Career (75 returns)
- 12.78 George McAfee, Chi. Bears, 1940-41, 1945-1950 (112-1,431)
- 12.75 Jack Christiansen, Detroit, 1951-58 (85-1,084)
- 12.55 Claude Gibson, San Diego, 1961-62; Oakland, 1963-65 (110-1,381)

Highest Average, Season (Qualifiers)
- 23.00 Herb Rich, Baltimore, 1950 (12-276)
- 21.47 Jack Christiansen, Detroit, 1952 (15-322)
- 21.28 Dick Christy, N.Y. Titans, 1961 (18-383)

Highest Average, Rookie, Season (Qualifiers)
- 23.00 Herb Rich, Baltimore, 1950 (12-276)
- 20.88 Jerry Davis, Chi. Cardinals, 1948 (16-334)
- 20.73 Frank Sinkwich, Detroit, 1943 (11-228)

Highest Average, Game (3 returns)
- 51.00 Steve Smith, Carolina vs. Cincinnati, Dec. 8, 2002 (3-153)
- 47.67 Chuck Latourette, St. Louis vs. New Orleans, Sept. 29, 1968 (3-143)
- 47.33 Johnny Roland, St. Louis vs. Philadelphia, Oct. 2, 1966 (3-142)

TOUCHDOWNS
Most Touchdowns, Career
- 10 Eric Metcalf, Cleveland, 1989-1994; Atlanta, 1995-96; San Diego, 1997; Arizona, 1998; Carolina, 1999; Washington, 2001; Green Bay, 2002
- 9 Brian Mitchell, Washington, 1990-99; Philadelphia 2000-02; N.Y. Giants, 2003
- 8 Jack Christiansen, Detroit, 1951-58
  Rick Upchurch, Denver, 1975-1983
  Desmond Howard, Washington, 1992-94; Jacksonville, 1995; Green Bay, 1996, 1999; Oakland, 1997-98; Detroit, 1999-2002

Most Touchdowns, Season
- 4 Jack Christiansen, Detroit, 1951
  Rick Upchurch, Denver, 1976
- 3 Emlen Tunnell, N.Y. Giants, 1951
  Billy (White Shoes) Johnson, Houston, 1975
  LeRoy Irvin, Los Angeles, 1981
  Desmond Howard, Green Bay, 1996
  Darrien Gordon, Denver, 1997
  Eric Metcalf, San Diego, 1997
- 2 By many players

Most Touchdowns, Rookie, Season
- 4 Jack Christiansen, Detroit, 1951
- 2 By many players

Most Touchdowns, Game
- 2 Jack Christiansen, Detroit vs. Los Angeles, Oct. 14, 1951; vs. Green Bay, Nov. 22, 1951
  Dick Christy, N.Y. Titans vs. Denver, Sept. 24, 1961
  Rick Upchurch, Denver vs. Cleveland, Sept. 26, 1976
  LeRoy Irvin, Los Angeles vs. Atlanta, Oct. 11, 1981
  Vai Sikahema, St. Louis vs. Tampa Bay, Dec. 21, 1986
  Todd Kinchen, L.A. Rams vs. Atlanta, Dec. 27, 1992
  Eric Metcalf, Cleveland vs. Pittsburgh, Oct. 24, 1993; San Diego vs. Cincinnati, Nov. 2, 1997
  Darrien Gordon, Denver vs. Carolina, Nov. 9, 1997

Jermaine Lewis, Baltimore vs. Seattle, Dec. 7, 1997; Baltimore vs. N.Y. Jets, Dec. 24, 2000
Steve Smith, Carolina vs. Cincinnati, Dec. 8, 2002
Eddie Drummond, Detroit vs. Jacksonville, Nov. 14, 2004 (OT)

KICKOFF RETURNS
Most Seasons Leading League
- 3 Abe Woodson, San Francisco, 1959, 1962-63
- 2 Lynn Chandnois, Pittsburgh, 1951-52
  Bobby Jancik, Houston, 1962-63
  Travis Williams, Green Bay, 1967; Los Angeles, 1971
  Mel Gray, Detroit, 1991, 1994
  Michael Bates, Carolina, 1996-97

KICKOFF RETURNS
Most Kickoff Returns, Career
- 607 Brian Mitchell, Washington, 1990-99; Philadelphia 2000-02; N.Y. Giants, 2003
- 421 Mel Gray, New Orleans, 1986-88; Detroit, 1989-1994; Houston, 1995-96; Tennessee, 1997; Philadelphia, 1997
- 407 Glyn Milburn, Denver, 1993-95; Detroit, 1996-97; Chicago, 1998-2001; San Diego, 2001

Most Kickoff Returns, Season
- 82 MarTay Jenkins, Arizona, 2000
- 73 Josh Scobey, Arizona, 2003
- 70 Tyrone Hughes, New Orleans, 1996
  Michael Lewis, New Orleans, 2002

Most Kickoff Returns, Rookie, Season
- 73 Josh Scobey, Arizona, 2003
- 67 Ronney Jenkins, San Diego, 2000
- 61 Wes Welker, San Diego-Miami, 2004

Most Kickoff Returns, Game
- 10 Desmond Howard, Oakland vs. Seattle, Oct. 26, 1997
  Richard Alston, Cleveland vs. Cincinnati, Nov. 28, 2004
- 9 Noland Smith, Kansas City vs. Oakland, Nov. 23, 1967
  Dino Hall, Cleveland vs. Pittsburgh, Oct. 7, 1979
  Paul Palmer, Kansas City vs. Seattle, Sept. 20, 1987
  Eric Metcalf, Atlanta vs. San Francisco, Sept. 29, 1996; vs. St. Louis, Nov. 10, 1996
  Michael Bates, Carolina vs. Atlanta, Oct. 4, 1998
  Nate Jacquet, Minnesota vs. Philadelphia, Nov. 11, 2001
  Ahmad Merritt, Chicago vs. San Francisco, Sept. 7, 2003
  Josh Scobey, Arizona vs. Cleveland, Nov. 16, 2003
- 8 By many players

YARDS GAINED
Most Seasons Leading League
- 3 Bruce Harper, N.Y. Jets, 1977-79
  Tyrone Hughes, New Orleans, 1994-96
- 2 Marshall Goldberg, Chi. Cardinals, 1941-42
  Woodley Lewis, Los Angeles, 1953-54
  Al Carmichael, Green Bay, 1956-57
  Timmy Brown, Philadelphia, 1961, 1963
  Bobby Jancik, Houston, 1963, 1966
  Ron Smith, Atlanta, 1966-67

Most Yards Gained, Career
- 14,014 Brian Mitchell, Washington, 1990-99; Philadelphia 2000-02; N.Y. Giants, 2003
- 10,250 Mel Gray, New Orleans, 1986-88; Detroit, 1989-1994; Houston, 1995-96; Tennessee, 1997; Philadelphia, 1997
- 9,788 Glyn Milburn, Denver, 1993-95; Detroit, 1996-97; Chicago, 1998-2001; San Diego, 2001

Most Yards Gained, Season
- 2,186 MarTay Jenkins, Arizona, 2000

1,807 Michael Lewis, New Orleans, 2002
1,791 Tyrone Hughes, New Orleans, 1996
Most Yards Gained, Rookie, Season
1,684 Josh Scobey, Arizona, 2003
1,531 Ronney Jenkins, San Diego, 2000
1,431 Steve Smith, Carolina, 2001
Most Yards Gained, Game
304 Tyrone Hughes, New Orleans vs. L.A. Rams,
Oct. 23, 1994
294 Wally Triplett, Detroit vs. Los Angeles, Oct. 29, 1950
278 Chad Morton, N.Y. Jets vs. Buffalo, Sept. 8, 2002
(OT)
Longest Kickoff Return (All TDs)
106 Al Carmichael, Green Bay vs. Chi. Bears, Oct. 7, 1956
Noland Smith, Kansas City vs. Denver, Dec. 17, 1967
Roy Green, St. Louis vs. Dallas, Oct. 21, 1979
105 Frank Seno, Chi. Cardinals vs. N.Y. Giants,
Oct. 20, 1946
Ollie Matson, Chi. Cardinals vs. Washington,
Oct. 14, 1956
Abe Woodson, San Francisco vs. Los Angeles,
Nov. 8, 1959
Timmy Brown, Philadelphia vs. Cleveland,
Sept. 17, 1961
Jon Arnett, Los Angeles vs. Detroit, Oct. 29, 1961
Eugene (Mercury) Morris, Miami vs. Cincinnati,
Sept. 14, 1969
Travis Williams, Los Angeles vs. New Orleans,
Dec. 5, 1971
Terry Fair, Detroit vs. Tampa Bay, Sept. 28, 1998
104 By many players

AVERAGE YARDAGE
Highest Average, Career (75 returns)
30.56 Gale Sayers, Chicago, 1965-1971 (91-2,781)
29.57 Lynn Chandnois, Pittsburgh, 1950-56 (92-2,720)
28.69 Abe Woodson, San Francisco, 1958-1964; St. Louis,
1965-66 (193-5,538)
Highest Average, Season (Qualifiers)
41.06 Travis Williams, Green Bay, 1967 (18-739)
37.69 Gale Sayers, Chicago, 1967 (16-603)
35.50 Ollie Matson, Chi. Cardinals, 1958 (14-497)
Highest Average, Rookie, Season (Qualifiers)
41.06 Travis Williams, Green Bay, 1967 (18-739)
33.08 Tom Moore, Green Bay, 1960 (12-397)
32.88 Duriel Harris, Miami, 1976 (17-559)
Highest Average, Game (3 returns)
73.50 Wally Triplett, Detroit vs. Los Angeles, Oct. 29, 1950
(4-294)
67.33 Lenny Lyles, San Francisco vs. Baltimore,
Dec. 18, 1960 (3-202)
65.33 Ken Hall, Houston vs. N.Y. Titans, Oct. 23, 1960
(3-196)

TOUCHDOWNS
Most Touchdowns, Career
6 Ollie Matson, Chi. Cardinals, 1952, 1954-58;
L.A. Rams, 1959-1962; Detroit, 1963;
Philadelphia, 1964
Gale Sayers, Chicago, 1965-1971
Travis Williams, Green Bay, 1967-1970;
Los Angeles, 1971
Mel Gray, New Orleans, 1986-88; Detroit,
1989-1994; Houston, 1995-96; Tennessee,
1997; Philadelphia, 1997
5 Bobby Mitchell, Cleveland, 1958-1961; Washington,
1962-68
Abe Woodson, San Francisco, 1958-1964; St. Louis,
1965-66

Timmy Brown, Green Bay, 1959; Philadelphia,
1960-67; Baltimore, 1968
Michael Bates, Seattle, 1993-94; Cleveland, 1995;
Carolina, 1996-2000, 2002; Washington, 2001;
N.Y. Jets, 2003; Dallas, 2003
Dante Hall, Kansas City, 2000-04
4 Cecil Turner, Chicago, 1968-1973
Ron Brown, L.A. Rams, 1984-89, 1991;
L.A. Raiders, 1990
Jon Vaughn, New England, 1991-92; Seattle,
1993-94; Kansas City, 1994
Andre Coleman, San Diego, 1994-96; Seattle, 1997;
Pittsburgh, 1997-98
Tamarick Vanover, Kansas City, 1995-99, San Diego,
2002
Tony Horne, St. Louis, 1998-2000
Brian Mitchell, Washington, 1990-99; Philadelphia,
2000-02; N.Y. Giants, 2003
Darrick Vaughn, Atlanta, 2000-01; Houston, 2003
Most Touchdowns, Season
4 Travis Williams, Green Bay, 1967
Cecil Turner, Chicago, 1970
3 Verda (Vitamin T) Smith, Los Angeles, 1950
Abe Woodson, San Francisco, 1963
Gale Sayers, Chicago, 1967
Raymond Clayborn, New England, 1977
Ron Brown, L.A. Rams, 1985
Mel Gray, Detroit, 1994
Darrick Vaughn, Atlanta, 2000
Terrence McGee, Buffalo, 2004
2 By many players
Most Touchdowns, Rookie, Season
4 Travis Williams, Green Bay, 1967
3 Raymond Clayborn, New England, 1977
Darrick Vaughn, Atlanta, 2000
2 By many players
Most Touchdowns, Game
2 Timmy Brown, Philadelphia vs. Dallas, Nov. 6, 1966
Travis Williams, Green Bay vs. Cleveland,
Nov. 12, 1967
Ron Brown, L.A. Rams vs. Green Bay, Nov. 24, 1985
Tyrone Hughes, New Orleans vs. L.A. Rams,
Oct. 23, 1994
Chad Morton, N.Y. Jets vs. Buffalo, Sept. 8, 2002 (OT)

COMBINED KICK RETURNS
Most Combined Kick Returns, Career
1,070 Brian Mitchell, Washington, 1990-99; Philadelphia,
2000-02; N.Y. Giants, 2003 (p-463, k-607)
711 Glyn Milburn, Denver, 1993-95; Detroit, 1996-97;
Chicago, 1998-2001; San Diego, 2001 (p-304,
k-407)
673 Mel Gray, New Orleans, 1986-88; Detroit,
1989-1994; Houston, 1995-96; Tennessee,
1997; Philadelphia, 1997 (p-252, k-421)
Most Combined Kick Returns, Season
114 Michael Lewis, New Orleans, 2002 (p-44, k-70)
B.J. Sams, Baltimore, 2004 (p-55, k-59)
104 Wes Welker, San Diego-Miami, 2004 (p-43, k-61)
103 Brian Mitchell, Washington, 1998 (p-44, k-59)
Most Combined Kick Returns, Game
13 Stump Mitchell, St. Louis vs. Atlanta, Oct. 18, 1981
(p-6, k-7)
Ronnie Harris, New England vs. Pittsburgh,
Dec. 5, 1993 (p-10, k-3)
12 Mel Renfro, Dallas vs. Green Bay, Nov. 29, 1964
(p-4, k-8)
Larry Jones, Washington vs. Dallas, Dec. 13, 1975
(p-6, k-6)

Eddie Brown, Washington vs. Tampa Bay,
Oct. 9, 1977 (p-11, k-1)
Nesby Glasgow, Baltimore vs. Denver, Sept. 2, 1979
(p-9, k-3)
Tim Dwight, Atlanta vs. Detroit, Nov. 12, 2000
(p-8, k-4)
Wes Welker, Miami vs. Buffalo, Dec. 5, 2004
(p-6, k-6)
11   By many players

YARDS GAINED
Most Yards Returned, Career
19,013   Brian Mitchell, Washington, 1990-99; Philadelphia,
2000-02; N.Y. Giants, 2003 (p-4,999; k-14,014)
13,003   Mel Gray, New Orleans, 1986-88; Detroit,
1989-1994; Houston, 1995-96; Tennessee,
1997; Philadelphia, 1997 (p-2,753; k-10,250)
12,772   Glyn Milburn, Denver, 1993-95; Detroit, 1996-97;
Chicago, 1998-2001; San Diego, 2001
(p-2,984; k-9,788)
Most Yards Returned, Season
2,432   Michael Lewis, New Orleans, 2002 (p-625, k-1,807)
2,187   MarTay Jenkins, Arizona, 2000 (p-1, k-2,186)
1,992   Charlie Rogers, Seattle, 2000 (p-363, k-1,629)
Most Yards Returned, Game
347   Tyrone Hughes, New Orleans vs. L.A. Rams,
Oct. 23, 1994 (p-43, k-304)
294   Wally Triplett, Detroit vs. Los Angeles, Oct. 29, 1950
(k-294)
Woodley Lewis, Los Angeles vs. Detroit,
Oct. 18, 1953 (p-120, k-174)
289   Eddie Payton, Detroit vs. Minnesota, Dec. 17, 1977
(p-105, k-184)

TOUCHDOWNS
Most Touchdowns, Career
13   Brian Mitchell, Washington, 1990-99; Philadelphia,
2000-02; N.Y. Giants, 2003 (p-9, k-4)
12   Eric Metcalf, Cleveland, 1989-1994; Atlanta,
1995-96; San Diego, 1997; Arizona, 1998;
Carolina, 1999; Washington, 2001; Green Bay,
2002 (p-10, k-2)
9   Ollie Matson, Chi. Cardinals, 1952, 1954-58;
Los Angeles, 1959-1962; Detroit, 1963;
Philadelphia, 1964-66 (p-3, k-6)
Mel Gray, New Orleans, 1986-88; Detroit,
1989-1994; Houston, 1995-96; Tennessee,
1997; Philadelphia, 1997 (p-3, k-6)
Deion Sanders, Atlanta, 1989-1993; San Francisco,
1994; Dallas, 1995-99; Washington, 2000;
Baltimore, 2004 (p-6, k-3)
Dante Hall, Kansas City, 2000-04 (p-4, k-5)
Most Touchdowns, Season
4   Jack Christiansen, Detroit, 1951 (p-4)
Emlen Tunnell, N.Y. Giants, 1951 (p-3, k-1)
Gale Sayers, Chicago, 1967 (p-1, k-3)
Travis Williams, Green Bay, 1967 (k-4)
Cecil Turner, Chicago, 1970 (k-4)
Billy Johnson, Houston, 1975 (p-3, k-1)
Rick Upchurch, Denver, 1976 (p-4)
Dante Hall, Kansas City, 2003 (p-2, r-2)
Eddie Drummond, Detroit, 2004 (p-2, k-2)
3   Verda (Vitamin T) Smith, Los Angeles, 1950 (k-3)
Abe Woodson, San Francisco, 1963 (k-3)
Raymond Clayborn, New England, 1977 (k-3)
Billy Johnson, Houston, 1977 (p-2, k-1)
LeRoy Irvin, Los Angeles, 1981 (p-3)
Ron Brown, L.A. Rams, 1985 (k-3)
Tyrone Hughes, New Orleans, 1993 (p-2, k-1)
Mel Gray, Detroit, 1994 (k-3)

Andre Coleman, San Diego, 1995 (p-2; k-1)
Tamarick Vanover, Kansas City, 1995 (p-1, k-2)
Desmond Howard, Green Bay, 1996 (p-3)
Darrien Gordon, Denver, 1997 (p-3)
Eric Metcalf, San Diego, 1997 (p-3)
Glyn Milburn, Chicago, 1998 (p-2, k-1)
Roell Preston, Green Bay, 1998 (p-2, k-1)
Darrick Vaughn, Atlanta, 2000 (k-3)
Steve Smith, Carolina, 2001 (p-1, k-2)
Michael Lewis, New Orleans, 2002 (p-1, k-2)
Dante Hall, Kansas City, 2002 (p-2, k-1)
Terrence McGee, Buffalo, 2004 (k-3)
2   By many players
Most Touchdowns, Game
2   Jack Christiansen, Detroit vs. Los Angeles,
Oct. 14, 1951 (p-2); vs. Green Bay,
Nov. 22, 1951 (p-2)
Jim Patton, N.Y. Giants vs. Washington,
Oct. 30, 1955 (p-1, k-1)
Bobby Mitchell, Cleveland vs. Philadelphia,
Nov. 23, 1958 (p-1, k-1)
Dick Christy, N.Y. Titans vs. Denver, Sept. 24, 1961
(p-2)
Al Frazier, Denver vs. Boston, Dec. 3, 1961 (p-1, k-1)
Timmy Brown, Philadelphia vs. Dallas, Nov. 6, 1966
(k-2)
Travis Williams, Green Bay vs. Cleveland,
Nov. 12, 1967 (k-2); vs. Pittsburgh,
Nov. 2, 1969 (p-1, k-1)
Gale Sayers, Chicago vs. San Francisco,
Dec. 3, 1967 (p-1, k-1)
Rick Upchurch, Denver vs. Cleveland,
Sept. 26, 1976 (p-2)
Eddie Payton, Detroit vs. Minnesota, Dec. 17, 1977
(p-1, k-1)
LeRoy Irvin, Los Angeles vs. Atlanta, Oct. 11, 1981
(p-2)
Ron Brown, L.A. Rams vs. Green Bay,
Nov. 24, 1985 (k-2)
Vai Sikahema, St. Louis vs. Tampa Bay,
Dec. 21, 1986 (p-2)
Todd Kinchen, L.A. Rams vs. Atlanta, Dec. 27, 1992
(p-2)
Eric Metcalf, Cleveland vs. Pittsburgh, Oct. 24, 1993
(p-2); San Diego vs. Cincinnati, Nov. 2, 1997
(p-2)
Tyrone Hughes, New Orleans vs. L.A. Rams,
Oct. 23, 1994 (k-2)
Darrien Gordon, Denver vs. Carolina, Nov. 9, 1997
(p-2)
Jermaine Lewis, Baltimore vs. Seattle, Dec. 7, 1997
(p-2); Baltimore vs. N.Y. Jets, Dec. 24, 2000
(p-2)
Chad Morton, N.Y. Jets vs. Buffalo, Sept. 8, 2002
(OT) (k-2)
Michael Lewis, New Orleans vs. Washington,
Oct. 13, 2002 (p-1, k-1)
Dante Hall, Kansas City vs. St. Louis, Dec. 8, 2002
(p-1, k-1)
Steve Smith, Carolina vs. Cincinnati, Dec. 8, 2002
(p-2)
Eddie Drummond, Detroit vs. Jacksonville,
Nov. 14, 2004 (OT) (p-2)

FUMBLES
Most Fumbles, Career
161   Warren Moon, Houston, 1984-1993; Minnesota,
1994-96; Seattle, 1997-98; Kansas City,
1999-2000

153 Dave Krieg, Seattle, 1980-1991; Kansas City,
     1992-93; Detroit, 1994; Arizona, 1995;
     Chicago, 1996; Tennessee, 1997-98
137 John Elway, Denver, 1983-1998

Most Fumbles, Season
23   Kerry Collins, N.Y. Giants, 2001
     Daunte Culpepper, Minnesota, 2002
21   Tony Banks, St. Louis, 1996
     David Carr, Houston, 2002
18   Dave Krieg, Seattle, 1989
     Warren Moon, Houston, 1990

Most Fumbles, Game
7   Len Dawson, Kansas City vs. San Diego,
     Nov. 15, 1964
6   Sam Etcheverry, St. Louis vs. N.Y. Giants,
     Sept. 17, 1961
     Dave Krieg, Seattle vs. Kansas City, Nov. 5, 1989
     Brett Favre, Green Bay vs. Tampa Bay, Dec. 7, 1998
     Kurt Warner, St. Louis vs. N.Y. Giants, Sept. 7, 2003
5   Paul Christman, Chi. Cardinals vs. Green Bay,
     Nov. 10, 1946
     Charlie Conerly, N.Y. Giants vs. San Francisco,
     Dec. 1, 1957
     Jack Kemp, Buffalo vs. Houston, Oct. 29, 1967
     Roman Gabriel, Philadelphia vs. Oakland,
     Nov. 21, 1976
     Randall Cunningham, Philadelphia vs. L.A. Raiders,
     Nov. 30, 1986 (OT)
     Willie Totten, Buffalo vs. Indianapolis, Oct. 4, 1987
     Dave Walter, Cincinnati vs. Seattle, Oct. 11, 1987
     Dave Krieg, Seattle vs. San Diego, Nov. 25, 1990 (OT)
     Andre Ware, Detroit vs. Green Bay, Dec. 6, 1992
     Steve Beuerlein, Carolina vs. San Francisco,
     Nov. 8, 1998
     Patrick Ramsey, Washington vs. Green Bay,
     Oct. 20, 2002

FUMBLES RECOVERED
Most Fumbles Recovered, Career, Own and Opponents'
56   Warren Moon, Houston, 1984-1993; Minnesota,
     1994-96; Seattle, 1997-98; Kansas City,
     1999-2000 (56 own)
47   Dave Krieg, Seattle, 1980-1991; Kansas City,
     1992-93; Detroit, 1994; Arizona, 1995; Chica-
     go, 1996; Tennessee, 1997-98 (47 own)
45   Boomer Esiason, Cincinnati, 1984-1992, 1997;
     N.Y. Jets, 1993-95; Arizona, 1996 (45 own)

Most Fumbles Recovered, Season, Own and Opponents'
12   David Carr, Houston, 2002 (12 own)
9   Don Hultz, Minnesota, 1963 (9 opp)
     Dave Krieg, Seattle, 1989 (9 own)
     Brian Griese, Denver, 1999 (9 own)
     Jon Kitna, Seattle, 2000 (9 own)
8   Paul Christman, Chi. Cardinals, 1945 (8 own)
     Joe Schmidt, Detroit, 1955 (8 opp)
     Bill Butler, Minnesota, 1963 (8 own)
     Kermit Alexander, San Francisco, 1965
     (4 own, 4 opp)
     Jack Lambert, Pittsburgh, 1976 (1 own, 7 opp)
     Danny White, Dallas, 1981 (8 own)
     Dan Marino, Miami, 1988 (7 own, 1 opp)
     Tony Banks, St. Louis, 1998 (8 own)

Most Fumbles Recovered, Game, Own and Opponents'
4   Otto Graham, Cleveland vs. N.Y. Giants,
     Oct. 25, 1953 (4 own)
     Sam Etcheverry, St. Louis vs. N.Y. Giants,
     Sept. 17, 1961 (4 own)
     Roman Gabriel, Los Angeles vs. San Francisco,
     Oct. 12, 1969 (4 own)

     Joe Ferguson, Buffalo vs. Miami, Sept. 18, 1977
     (4 own)
     Randall Cunningham, Philadelphia vs. L.A. Raiders,
     Nov. 30, 1986 (OT) (4 own)
3   By many players

OWN FUMBLES RECOVERED
Most Own Fumbles Recovered, Career
56   Warren Moon, Houston, 1984-1993; Minnesota,
     1994-96; Seattle, 1997-98; Kansas City,
     1999-2000
47   Dave Krieg, Seattle, 1980-1991; Kansas City,
     1992-93; Detroit, 1994; Arizona, 1995;
     Chicago, 1996; Tennessee, 1997-98
45   Boomer Esiason, Cincinnati, 1984-1992, 1997;
     N.Y. Jets, 1993-95; Arizona, 1996

Most Own Fumbles Recovered, Season
12   David Carr, Houston, 2002
9   Dave Krieg, Seattle, 1989
     Brian Griese, Denver, 1999
     Jon Kitna, Seattle, 2000
8   Paul Christman, Chi. Cardinals, 1945
     Bill Butler, Minnesota, 1963
     Danny White, Dallas, 1981
     Tony Banks, St. Louis, 1998

Most Own Fumbles Recovered, Game
4   Otto Graham, Cleveland vs. N.Y. Giants, Oct. 25, 1953
     Sam Etcheverry, St. Louis vs. N.Y. Giants,
     Sept. 17, 1961
     Roman Gabriel, Los Angeles vs. San Francisco,
     Oct. 12, 1969
     Joe Ferguson, Buffalo vs. Miami, Sept. 18, 1977
     Randall Cunningham, Philadelphia vs. L.A. Raiders,
     Nov. 30, 1986 (OT)
3   By many players

OPPONENTS' FUMBLES RECOVERED
Most Opponents' Fumbles Recovered, Career
29   Jim Marshall, Cleveland, 1960; Minnesota, 1961-1979
28   Rickey Jackson, New Orleans, 1981-1993;
     San Francisco, 1994-95
26   Kevin Greene, L.A. Rams, 1985-1992; Pittsburgh,
     1993-95; Carolina, 1996, 1998-99;
     San Francisco, 1997
     Cornelius Bennett, Buffalo, 1987-1995; Atlanta,
     1996-98; Indianapolis, 1999-2000

Most Opponents' Fumbles Recovered, Season
9   Don Hultz, Minnesota, 1963
8   Joe Schmidt, Detroit, 1955
7   Alan Page, Minnesota, 1970
     Jack Lambert, Pittsburgh, 1976
     Ray Childress, Houston, 1988
     Rickey Jackson, New Orleans, 1990

Most Opponents' Fumbles Recovered, Game
3   Corwin Clatt, Chi. Cardinals vs. Detroit, Nov. 6, 1949
     Vic Sears, Philadelphia vs. Green Bay, Nov. 2, 1952
     Ed Beatty, San Francisco vs. Los Angeles,
     Oct. 7, 1956
     Ron Carroll, Houston vs. Cincinnati, Oct. 27, 1974
     Maurice Spencer, New Orleans vs. Atlanta,
     Oct. 10, 1976
     Steve Nelson, New England vs. Philadelphia,
     Oct. 8, 1978
     Charles Jackson, Kansas City vs. Pittsburgh,
     Sept. 6, 1981
     Willie Buchanon, San Diego vs. Denver,
     Sept. 27, 1981
     Joey Browner, Minnesota vs. San Francisco,
     Sept. 8, 1985
     Ray Childress, Houston vs. Washington, Oct. 30, 1988

John Thierry, Chicago vs. Houston, Oct. 22, 1995
Stephen Boyd, Detroit vs. Chicago, Oct. 4, 1998
Darryl Williams, Seattle vs. Kansas City, Oct. 4, 1998
Rod Woodson, Oakland vs. Pittsburgh, Sept. 15, 2002
Brian Young, St. Louis vs. Baltimore, Nov. 9, 2003
  2   By many players

YARDS RETURNING FUMBLES
Longest Fumble Run (All TDs)
 104   Jack Tatum, Oakland vs. Green Bay, Sept. 24, 1972
      Aeneas Williams, Arizona vs. Washington,
        Nov. 5, 2000
 102   Travis Davis, Pittsburgh vs. Carolina, Dec. 26, 1999
 100   Chris Martin, Kansas City vs. Miami, Oct. 13, 1991

TOUCHDOWNS
Most Touchdowns, Career (Total)
  5   Jessie Tuggle, Atlanta, 1987-2000
  4   Bill Thompson, Denver, 1969-1981
     Derrick Thomas, Kansas City, 1989-1999
     Jason Taylor, Miami, 1997-2004
  3   By many players

Most Touchdowns, Season (Total)
  2   Harold McPhail, Boston, 1934
     Harry Ebding, Detroit, 1937
     John Morelli, Boston, 1944
     Frank Maznicki, Boston, 1947
     Fred (Dippy) Evans, Chi. Bears, 1948
     Ralph Heywood, Boston, 1948
     Art Tait, N.Y. Yanks, 1951
     John Dwyer, Los Angeles, 1952
     Leo Sugar, Chi. Cardinals, 1957
     Doug Cline, Houston, 1961
     Jim Bradshaw, Pittsburgh, 1964
     Royce Berry, Cincinnati, 1970
     Ahmad Rashad, Buffalo, 1974
     Tim Gray, Kansas City, 1977
     Charles Phillips, Oakland, 1978
     Kenny Johnson, Atlanta, 1981
     George Martin, N.Y. Giants, 1981
     Del Rodgers, Green Bay, 1982
     Mike Douglass, Green Bay, 1983
     Shelton Robinson, Seattle, 1983
     Erik McMillan, N.Y. Jets, 1989
     Les Miller, San Diego, 1990
     Seth Joyner, Philadelphia, 1991
     Robert Goff, New Orleans, 1992
     Willie Clay, Detroit, 1993
     Tyrone Hughes, New Orleans, 1994
     Chad Brown, Seattle, 1997
     Marcus Robertson, Tennessee, 1997
     Dwayne Rudd, Minnesota, 1998
     Keith McKenzie, Green Bay, 1999
     Ronde Barber, Tampa Bay, 2004
     Leonard Little, St. Louis, 2004

Most Touchdowns, Career (Own recovered)
  2   Ken Kavanaugh, Chi. Bears, 1940-41, 1945-1950
     Mike Ditka, Chicago, 1961-66; Philadelphia,
       1967-68; Dallas, 1969-1972
     Gail Cogdill, Detroit, 1960-68; Baltimore, 1968;
       Atlanta, 1969-1970
     Ahmad Rashad, St. Louis, 1972-73; Buffalo, 1974;
       Minnesota, 1976-1982
     Jim Mitchell, Atlanta, 1969-1979
     Drew Pearson, Dallas, 1973-1983
     Del Rodgers, Green Bay, 1982, 1984; San Francisco,
       1987-88
     Alan Ricard, Baltimore, 2001-04

Most Touchdowns, Season (Own recovered)
  2   Ahmad Rashad, Buffalo, 1974

Del Rodgers, Green Bay, 1982
  1   By many players

Most Touchdowns, Career (Opponents' recovered)
  5   Jessie Tuggle, Atlanta, 1987-2000
  4   Derrick Thomas, Kansas City, 1989-1999
     Jason Taylor, Miami, 1997-2004
  3   By many players

Most Touchdowns, Season (Opponents' recovered)
  2   Harold McPhail, Boston, 1934
     Harry Ebding, Detroit, 1937
     John Morelli, Boston, 1944
     Frank Maznicki, Boston, 1947
     Fred (Dippy) Evans, Chi. Bears, 1948
     Ralph Heywood, Boston, 1948
     Art Tait, N.Y. Yanks, 1951
     John Dwyer, Los Angeles, 1952
     Leo Sugar, Chi. Cardinals, 1957
     Doug Cline, Houston, 1961
     Jim Bradshaw, Pittsburgh, 1964
     Royce Berry, Cincinnati, 1970
     Tim Gray, Kansas City, 1977
     Charles Phillips, Oakland, 1978
     Kenny Johnson, Atlanta, 1981
     George Martin, N.Y. Giants, 1981
     Mike Douglass, Green Bay, 1983
     Shelton Robinson, Seattle, 1983
     Erik McMillan, N.Y. Jets, 1989
     Les Miller, San Diego, 1990
     Seth Joyner, Philadelphia, 1991
     Robert Goff, New Orleans, 1992
     Willie Clay, Detroit, 1993
     Tyrone Hughes, New Orleans, 1994
     Chad Brown, Seattle, 1997
     Marcus Robertson, Tennessee, 1997
     Dwayne Rudd, Minnesota, 1998
     Keith McKenzie, Green Bay, 1999
     Ronde Barber, Tampa Bay, 2004
     Leonard Little, St. Louis, 2004

Most Touchdowns, Game (Opponents' recovered)
  2   Fred (Dippy) Evans, Chi. Bears vs. Washington,
       Nov. 28, 1948

COMBINED NET YARDS GAINED
Rushing, receiving, interception returns, punt returns, kickoff returns, and fumble returns

Most Seasons Leading League
  5   Jim Brown, Cleveland, 1958-1961, 1964
  4   Brian Mitchell, Washington, 1994-96, 1998
  3   Cliff Battles, Boston, 1932-33; Washington, 1937
     Gale Sayers, Chicago, 1965-67
     Eric Dickerson, L.A. Rams, 1983-84, 1986
     Thurman Thomas, Buffalo, 1989, 1991-92

Most Consecutive Seasons Leading League
  4   Jim Brown, Cleveland, 1958-1961
  3   Gale Sayers, Chicago, 1965-67
     Brian Mitchell, Washington, 1994-96
  2   Cliff Battles, Boston, 1932-33
     Charley Trippi, Chi. Cardinals, 1948-49
     Timmy Brown, Philadelphia, 1962-63
     Floyd Little, Denver, 1967-68
     James Brooks, San Diego, 1981-82
     Eric Dickerson, L.A. Rams, 1983-84
     Thurman Thomas, Buffalo, 1991-92
     Dante Hall, Kansas City, 2003-04

ATTEMPTS
Most Attempts, Career
4,939   Emmitt Smith, Dallas, 1990-2002; Arizona, 2003-04
4,368   Walter Payton, Chicago, 1975-1987

3,770   Curtis Martin, New England, 1995-97; N.Y. Jets, 1998-2004

Most Attempts, Season
496   James Wilder, Tampa Bay, 1984
455   Eddie George, Tennessee, 2000
451   LaDainian Tomlinson, San Diego, 2002

Most Attempts, Rookie, Season
442   Eric Dickerson, L.A. Rams, 1983
433   Edgerrin James, Indianapolis, 1999
401   Curtis Martin, New England, 1995

Most Attempts, Game
48   James Wilder, Tampa Bay vs. Pittsburgh, Oct. 30, 1983
     LaDainian Tomlinson, San Diego vs. Denver, Dec. 1, 2002 (OT)
47   James Wilder, Tampa Bay vs. Green Bay, Sept. 30, 1984 (OT)
     Terrell Davis, Denver vs. Buffalo, Oct. 26, 1997 (OT)
46   Gerald Riggs, Atlanta vs. L.A. Rams, Nov. 17, 1985

YARDS GAINED
Most Yards Gained, Career
23,546   Jerry Rice, San Francisco, 1985-2000; Oakland, 2001-04; Seattle, 2004
23,330   Brian Mitchell, Washington, 1990-99; Philadelphia, 2000-02; N.Y. Giants, 2003
21,803   Walter Payton, Chicago, 1975-1987

Most Yards Gained, Season
2,690   Derrick Mason, Tennessee, 2000
2,647   Michael Lewis, New Orleans, 2002
2,535   Lionel James, San Diego, 1985

Most Yards Gained, Rookie, Season
2,317   Tim Brown, L.A. Raiders, 1988
2,272   Gale Sayers, Chicago, 1965
2,212   Eric Dickerson, L.A. Rams, 1983

Most Yards Gained, Game
404   Glyn Milburn, Denver vs. Seattle, Dec. 10, 1995
373   Billy Cannon, Houston vs. N.Y. Titans, Dec. 10, 1961
356   Michael Lewis, New Orleans vs. Washington, Oct. 13, 2002

SACKS
Sacks have been compiled since 1982.

Most Seasons Leading League
2   Mark Gastineau, N.Y. Jets, 1983-84
    Reggie White, Philadelphia, 1987-88
    Kevin Greene, Pittsburgh, 1994; Carolina, 1996
    Michael Strahan, N.Y. Giants, 2001, 2003

Most Sacks, Career
200.0   Bruce Smith, Buffalo, 1985-1999; Washington, 2000-03
198.0   Reggie White, Philadelphia, 1985-1992; Green Bay, 1993-98; Carolina, 2000
160.0   Kevin Greene, L.A. Rams, 1985-1992; Pittsburgh, 1993-95; Carolina, 1996, 1998-99; San Francisco, 1997

Most Sacks, Season
22.5   Michael Strahan, N.Y. Giants, 2001
22.0   Mark Gastineau, N.Y. Jets, 1984
21.0   Reggie White, Philadelphia, 1987
       Chris Doleman, Minnesota, 1989

Most Sacks, Rookie, Season
14.5   Jevon Kearse, Tennessee, 1999
13.0   Dwight Freeney, Indianapolis, 2002
12.5   Leslie O'Neal, San Diego, 1986
       Simeon Rice, Arizona, 1996

Most Sacks, Game
7.0   Derrick Thomas, Kansas City vs. Seattle, Nov. 11, 1990
6.0   Fred Dean, San Francisco vs. New Orleans, Nov. 13, 1983

     Derrick Thomas, Kansas City vs. Oakland, Sept. 6, 1998
5.5   William Gay, Detroit vs. Tampa Bay, Sept. 4, 1983

Most Seasons, 10 or More Sacks
13   Bruce Smith, Buffalo, 1986-1990, 1992-98; Washington, 2000
12   Reggie White, Philadelphia, 1985-1992; Green Bay, 1993, 1995, 1997-98
10   Kevin Greene, L.A. Rams, 1988-1990, 1992; Pittsburgh, 1993-94; Carolina, 1996, 1998-99; San Francisco, 1997

Most Consecutive Seasons, 10 or More Sacks
9   Reggie White, Philadelphia, 1985-1992; Green Bay, 1993
8   John Randle, Minnesota, 1992-99
7   Lawrence Taylor, N.Y. Giants, 1984-1990
    Bruce Smith, Buffalo, 1992-98

Most Consecutive Games, Sack
10   Simon Fletcher, Denver, Nov. 15, 1992-Sept. 20, 1993
9   Bruce Smith, Buffalo, Nov. 16, 1986-Oct. 25, 1987
    Kevin Greene, San Francisco-Carolina, Dec. 7, 1997-Oct. 18, 1998
8   By many players

MISCELLANEOUS
Longest Return of Missed Field Goal (All TDs)
107   Chris McAlister, Baltimore vs. Denver, Sept. 30, 2002
104   Aaron Glenn, N.Y. Jets vs. Indianapolis, Nov. 15, 1998
101   Al Nelson, Philadelphia vs. Dallas, Sept. 26, 1971

TEAM RECORDS

CHAMPIONSHIPS
Most Seasons League Champion
12   Green Bay, 1929-1931, 1936, 1939, 1944, 1961-62, 1965-67, 1996
9   Chi. Bears, 1921, 1932-33, 1940-41, 1943, 1946, 1963, 1985
6   N.Y. Giants, 1927, 1934, 1938, 1956, 1986, 1990

Most Consecutive Seasons League Champion
3   Green Bay, 1929-1931
    Green Bay, 1965-67
2   Canton, 1922-23
    Chi. Bears, 1932-33
    Chi. Bears, 1940-41
    Philadelphia, 1948-49
    Detroit, 1952-53
    Cleveland, 1954-55
    Baltimore, 1958-59
    Houston, 1960-61
    Green Bay, 1961-62
    Buffalo, 1964-65
    Miami, 1972-73
    Pittsburgh, 1974-75
    Pittsburgh, 1978-79
    San Francisco, 1988-89
    Dallas, 1992-93
    Denver, 1997-98
    New England, 2003-04

Most Times Finishing First, Regular Season
20   N.Y. Giants, 1927, 1933-35, 1938-39, 1941, 1944, 1946, 1956, 1958-59, 1961-63, 1986, 1989-1990, 1997, 2000
     Green Bay, 1929-1931, 1936, 1938-39, 1944, 1960-62, 1965-67, 1972, 1995-97, 2002-04
19   Dallas, 1966-1971, 1973, 1976-79, 1981, 1985, 1992-96, 1998
     Chi. Bears, 1921, 1932-34, 1937, 1940-43, 1946, 1956, 1963, 1984-88, 1990, 2001

18 Cle. Browns, 1950-55, 1957, 1964-65, 1967-69, 1971, 1980, 1985-87, 1989

Cleveland/L.A./St. Louis Rams, 1945, 1949-1951, 1955, 1967, 1969, 1973-79, 1985, 1999, 2001, 2003

Most Consecutive Times Finishing First, Regular Season

7 Los Angeles, 1973-79

6 Cleveland, 1950-55

  Dallas, 1966-1971

  Minnesota, 1973-78

  Pittsburgh, 1974-79

5 Oakland, 1972-76

  Chicago, 1984-88

  San Francisco, 1986-1990

  Dallas, 1992-96

GAMES WON

Most Consecutive Games Won

18 New England, 2003-04

17 Chi. Bears, 1933-34

16 Chi. Bears, 1941-42

  Miami, 1971-73

  Miami, 1983-84

Most Consecutive Games Without Defeat

25 Canton, 1921-23 (won 22, tied 3)

24 Chi. Bears, 1941-43 (won 23, tied 1)

23 Green Bay, 1928-1930 (won 21, tied 2)

Most Games Won, Season

15 San Francisco, 1984

  Chicago, 1985

  Minnesota, 1998

  Pittsburgh, 2004

14 Frankford, 1926

  Miami, 1972

  Pittsburgh, 1978

  Washington, 1983

  Miami, 1984

  Chicago, 1986

  N.Y. Giants, 1986

  San Francisco, 1989

  San Francisco, 1990

  Washington, 1991

  San Francisco, 1992

  Atlanta, 1998

  Denver, 1998

  Jacksonville, 1999

  St. Louis, 2001

  New England, 2003

  New England, 2004

13 By many teams

Most Consecutive Games Won, Season

14 Miami, 1972

  Pittsburgh, 2004

13 Chi. Bears, 1934

  Denver, 1998

12 Minnesota, 1969

  Chicago, 1985

  New England, 2003

Most Consecutive Games Won, Start of Season

14 Miami, 1972, entire season

13 Chi. Bears, 1934, entire season

  Denver, 1998

12 Chicago, 1985

Most Consecutive Games Won, End of Season

14 Miami, 1972, entire season

  Pittsburgh, 2004

13 Chi. Bears, 1934, entire season

12 New England, 2003

Most Consecutive Games Without Defeat, Season

14 Miami, 1972 (won 14)

Pittsburgh, 2004 (won 14)

13 Chi. Bears, 1926 (won 11, tied 2)

  Green Bay, 1929 (won 12, tied 1)

  Chi. Bears, 1934 (won 13)

  Baltimore, 1967 (won 11, tied 2)

  Denver, 1998 (won 13)

12 Canton, 1922 (won 10, tied 2)

  Canton, 1923 (won 11, tied 1)

  Minnesota, 1969 (won 12)

  Chicago, 1985 (won 12)

  New England, 2003 (won 12)

Most Consecutive Games Without Defeat, Start of Season

14 Miami, 1972 (won 14), entire season

13 Chi. Bears, 1926 (won 11, tied 2)

  Green Bay, 1929 (won 12, tied 1), entire season

  Chi. Bears, 1934 (won 13), entire season

  Baltimore, 1967 (won 11, tied 2)

  Denver, 1998 (won 13)

12 Canton, 1922 (won 10, tied 2), entire season

  Canton, 1923 (won 11, tied 1), entire season

  Chicago, 1985 (won 12)

Most Consecutive Games Without Defeat, End of Season

14 Miami, 1972 (won 14), entire season

  Pittsburgh, 2004 (won 14)

13 Green Bay, 1929 (won 12, tied 1), entire season

  Chi. Bears, 1934 (won 13), entire season

12 Canton, 1922 (won 10, tied 2), entire season

  Canton, 1923 (won 11, tied 1), entire season

  New England, 2003 (won 12)

Most Consecutive Home Games Won

27 Miami, 1971-74

25 Green Bay, 1995-98

24 Denver, 1996-98

Most Consecutive Home Games Without Defeat

30 Green Bay, 1928-1933 (won 27, tied 3)

27 Miami, 1971-74 (won 27)

25 Chi. Bears, 1923-25 (won 19, tied 6)

  Green Bay, 1995-98 (won 25)

Most Consecutive Road Games Won

18 San Francisco, 1988-1990

11 L.A. Chargers/San Diego, 1960-61

  San Francisco, 1987-88

10 Chi. Bears, 1941-42

  Dallas, 1968-69

  New Orleans, 1987-88

Most Consecutive Road Games Without Defeat

18 San Francisco, 1988-1990 (won 18)

13 Chi. Bears, 1941-43 (won 12, tied 1)

12 Green Bay, 1928-1930 (won 10, tied 2)

Most Shutout Games Won or Tied, Season

10 Pottsville, 1926 (won 9, tied 1)

  N.Y. Giants, 1927 (won 9, tied 1)

9 Akron, 1921 (won 8, tied 1)

  Canton, 1922 (won 7, tied 2)

  Frankford, 1926 (won 9)

  Frankford, 1929 (won 6, tied 3)

8 By many teams

Most Consecutive Shutout Games Won or Tied

13 Akron, 1920-21 (won 10, tied 3)

7 Pottsville, 1926 (won 6, tied 1)

  Detroit, 1934 (won 7)

6 Buffalo, 1920-21 (won 5, tied 1)

  Frankford, 1926 (won 6)

  Detroit, 1926 (won 4, tied 2)

  N.Y. Giants, 1926-27 (won 5, tied 1)

GAMES LOST

Most Consecutive Games Lost

26 Tampa Bay, 1976-1977

19 Chi. Cardinals, 1942-43, 1945

Oakland, 1961-62
18   Houston, 1972-73

Most Consecutive Games Without Victory
26   Tampa Bay, 1976-77 (lost 26)
23   Rochester, 1922-25 (lost 21, tied 2)
     Washington, 1960-61 (lost 20, tied 3)
19   Dayton, 1927-29 (lost 18, tied 1)
     Chi. Cardinals, 1942-43, 1945 (lost 19)
     Oakland, 1961-62 (lost 19)

Most Games Lost, Season
15   New Orleans, 1980
     Dallas, 1989
     New England, 1990
     Indianapolis, 1991
     N.Y. Jets, 1996
     San Diego, 2000
     Carolina, 2001
14   By many teams

Most Consecutive Games Lost, Season
15   Carolina, 2001
14   Tampa Bay, 1976
     New Orleans, 1980
     Baltimore, 1981
     New England, 1990
13   Oakland, 1962
     Pittsburgh, 1969
     Indianapolis, 1986

Most Consecutive Games Lost, Start of Season
14   Tampa Bay, 1976, entire season
     New Orleans, 1980
13   Oakland, 1962
     Indianapolis, 1986
12   Tampa Bay, 1977
     Detroit, 2001

Most Consecutive Games Lost, End of Season
15   Carolina, 2001
14   Tampa Bay, 1976, entire season
     New England, 1990
13   Pittsburgh, 1969

Most Consecutive Games Without Victory, Season
15   Carolina, 2001 (lost 15)
14   Tampa Bay, 1976 (lost 14), entire season
     New Orleans, 1980 (lost 14)
     Baltimore, 1981 (lost 14)
     New England, 1990 (lost 14)
13   Washington, 1961 (lost 12, tied 1)
     Oakland, 1962 (lost 13)
     Pittsburgh, 1969 (lost 13)
     Indianapolis, 1986 (lost 13)

Most Consecutive Games Without Victory, Start of Season
14   Tampa Bay, 1976 (lost 14), entire season
     New Orleans, 1980 (lost 14)
13   Washington, 1961 (lost 12, tied 1)
     Oakland, 1962 (lost 13)
     Indianapolis, 1986 (lost 13)
12   Dall. Cowboys, 1960 (lost 11, tied 1), entire season
     Tampa Bay, 1977 (lost 12)
     Detroit, 2001 (lost 12)

Most Consecutive Games Without Victory, End of Season
15   Carolina, 2001
14   Tampa Bay, 1976, (lost 14), entire season
     New England, 1990 (lost 14)
13   Pittsburgh, 1969 (lost 13)

Most Consecutive Home Games Lost
14   Dallas, 1988-89
13   Houston, 1972-73
     Tampa Bay, 1976-77
     N.Y. Jets, 1995-97
11   Oakland, 1961-62
     Los Angeles, 1961-63

Cincinnati, 1998-99

Most Consecutive Home Games Without Victory
14   Dallas, 1988-89 (lost 14)
13   Houston, 1972-73 (lost 13)
     Tampa Bay, 1976-77 (lost 13)
     N.Y. Jets, 1995-97 (lost 13)
12   Philadelphia, 1936-38 (lost 11, tied 1)

Most Consecutive Road Games Lost
24   Detroit, 2001-03
23   Houston, 1981-84
22   Buffalo, 1983-86

Most Consecutive Road Games Without Victory
24   Detroit, 2001-03 (lost 24)
23   Houston, 1981-84 (lost 23)
22   Buffalo, 1983-86 (lost 22)

Most Shutout Games Lost or Tied, Season
8   Frankford, 1927 (lost 6, tied 2)
     Brooklyn, 1931 (lost 8)
7   Dayton, 1925 (lost 6, tied 1)
     Orange, 1929 (lost 4, tied 3)
     Frankford, 1931 (lost 6, tied 1)
6   By many teams

Most Consecutive Shutout Games Lost or Tied
8   Rochester, 1922-24 (lost 8)
7   Hammond, 1922-23 (lost 6, tied 1)
6   Providence, 1926-27 (lost 5, tied 1)
     Brooklyn, 1942-43 (lost 6)

TIE GAMES
Most Tie Games, Season
6   Chi. Bears, 1932
5   Frankford, 1929
4   Chi. Bears, 1924
     Orange, 1929
     Portsmouth, 1932

Most Consecutive Tie Games
3   Chi. Bears, 1932
2   By many teams

SCORING
Most Seasons Leading League
10   Chi. Bears, 1932, 1934-35, 1939, 1941-43,
     1946-47, 1956
9   San Francisco, 1953, 1965, 1970, 1987, 1989,
     1992-95
     L.A./St. Louis Rams, 1950-52, 1957, 1967, 1973,
     1999-2001
7   Green Bay, 1931, 1936-38, 1961-62, 1996

Most Consecutive Seasons Leading League
4   San Francisco, 1992-1995
3   Green Bay, 1936-38
     Chi. Bears, 1941-43
     Los Angeles, 1950-52
     Oakland, 1967-69
     St. Louis, 1999-2001
2   By many teams

POINTS
Most Points, Season
556   Minnesota, 1998
541   Washington, 1983
540   St. Louis, 2000

Fewest Points, Season (Since 1932)
37   Cincinnati/St. Louis, 1934
38   Cincinnati, 1933
     Detroit, 1942
51   Pittsburgh, 1934
     Philadelphia, 1936

Most Points, Game
72   Washington vs. N.Y. Giants, Nov. 27, 1966

70 Los Angeles vs. Baltimore, Oct. 22, 1950
65 Chi. Cardinals vs. N.Y. Bulldogs, Nov. 13, 1949
     Los Angeles vs. Detroit, Oct. 29, 1950

Most Points, Both Teams, Game
113 Washington (72) vs. N.Y. Giants (41), Nov. 27, 1966
106 Cincinnati (58) vs. Cleveland (48), Nov. 28, 2004
101 Oakland (52) vs. Houston (49), Dec. 22, 1963

Fewest Points, Both Teams, Game
  0 In many games. Last time: N.Y. Giants vs. Detroit, Nov. 7, 1943

Most Points, Shutout Victory, Game
64 Philadelphia vs. Cincinnati, Nov. 6, 1934
62 Akron vs. Oorang, Oct. 29, 1922
60 Rock Island vs. Evansville, Oct. 15, 1922
     Chi. Cardinals vs. Rochester, Oct. 7, 1923

Fewest Points, Shutout Victory, Game
  2 Green Bay vs. Chi. Bears, Oct. 16, 1932
     Chi. Bears vs. Green Bay, Sept. 18, 1938

Most Points Overcome to Win Game
28 San Francisco vs. New Orleans, Dec. 7, 1980 (OT)
     (trailed 7-35, won 38-35)
26 Buffalo vs. Indianapolis, Sept., 21, 1997
     (trailed 0-26, won 37-35)
25 St. Louis vs. Tampa Bay, Nov. 8, 1987
     (trailed 3-28, won 31-28)

Most Points Overcome to Tie Game
31 Denver vs. Buffalo, Nov. 27, 1960
     (trailed 7-38, tied 38-38)
28 Los Angeles vs. Philadelphia, Oct. 3, 1948
     (trailed 0-28, tied 28-28)

Most Points, Each Half
1st: 49 Green Bay vs. Tampa Bay, Oct. 2, 1983
     48 Buffalo vs. Miami, Sept. 18, 1966
     45 Green Bay vs. Cleveland, Nov. 12, 1967
          Indianapolis vs. Denver, Oct. 31, 1988
          Houston vs. Cleveland, Dec. 9, 1990
          Seattle vs. Minnesota, Sept. 29, 2002
2nd: 49 Chi. Bears vs. Philadelphia, Nov. 30, 1941
     48 Chi. Cardinals vs. Baltimore, Oct. 2, 1950
          N.Y. Giants vs. Baltimore, Nov. 19, 1950
     45 Cincinnati vs. Houston, Dec. 17, 1972

Most Points, Both Teams, Each Half
1st: 70 Houston (35) vs. Oakland (35), Dec. 22, 1963
     62 N.Y. Jets (41) vs. Tampa Bay (21), Nov. 17, 1985
     59 St. Louis (31) vs. Philadelphia (28), Dec. 16, 1962
2nd: 66 Cleveland (35) vs. Cincinnati (31), Nov. 28, 2004
     65 Washington (38) vs. N.Y. Giants (27), Nov. 27, 1966
     62 L.A. Raiders (31) vs. San Diego (31), Jan. 2, 1983
          Baltimore (38) vs. Seattle (24), Nov. 23, 2003

Most Points, One Quarter
41 Green Bay vs. Detroit, Oct. 7, 1945 (second quarter)
     Los Angeles vs. Detroit, Oct. 29, 1950
     (third quarter)
37 Los Angeles vs. Green Bay, Sept. 21, 1980
     (second quarter)
35 Chi. Cardinals vs. Boston, Oct. 24, 1948
     (third quarter)
     Green Bay vs. Cleveland, Nov. 12, 1967 (first quarter)
     Green Bay vs. Tampa Bay, Oct. 2, 1983
     (second quarter)

Most Points, Both Teams, One Quarter
49 Oakland (28) vs. Houston (21), Dec. 22, 1963
     (second quarter)
48 Green Bay (41) vs. Detroit (7), Oct. 7, 1945
     (second quarter)
     Los Angeles (41) vs. Detroit (7), Oct. 29, 1950
     (third quarter)
47 St. Louis (27) vs. Philadelphia (20), Dec. 13, 1964
     (second quarter)

Most Points, Each Quarter
1st: 35 Green Bay vs. Cleveland, Nov. 12, 1967
     31 Buffalo vs. Kansas City, Sept. 13, 1964
     28 By eight teams
2nd: 41 Green Bay vs. Detroit, Oct. 7, 1945
     37 Los Angeles vs. Green Bay, Sept. 21, 1980
     35 Green Bay vs. Tampa Bay, Oct. 2, 1983
3rd: 41 Los Angeles vs. Detroit, Oct. 29, 1950
     35 Chi. Cardinals vs. Boston, Oct. 24, 1948
     28 By 10 teams
4th: 31 Oakland vs. Denver, Dec. 17, 1960
          Oakland vs. San Diego, Dec. 8, 1963
          Atlanta vs. Green Bay, Sept. 13, 1981
     30 N.Y. Jets vs. Miami, Oct. 23, 2000
     28 By many teams

Most Points, Both Teams, Each Quarter
1st: 42 Green Bay (35) vs. Cleveland (7), Nov. 12, 1967
     41 Tennessee (24) vs. Indianapolis (17), Dec. 5, 2004
     35 Dall. Texans (21) vs. N.Y. Titans (14), Nov. 11, 1962
          Dallas (28) vs. Philadelphia (7), Oct. 19, 1969
          Kansas City (21) vs. Seattle (14), Dec. 11, 1977
          Detroit (21) vs. L.A. Raiders (14), Dec. 10, 1990
          Dallas (21) vs. Atlanta (14), Dec. 22, 1991
          Indianapolis (21) vs. Green Bay (14), Sept 26, 2004
          Miami (21) vs. Buffalo (14), Dec. 5, 2004
2nd: 49 Oakland (28) vs. Houston (21), Dec. 22, 1963
     48 Green Bay (41) vs. Detroit (7), Oct. 7, 1945
     47 St. Louis (27) vs. Philadelphia (20), Dec. 13, 1964
3rd: 48 Los Angeles (41) vs. Detroit (7), Oct. 29, 1950
     42 Washington (28) vs. Philadelphia (14), Oct. 1, 1955
     41 Green Bay (21) vs. N.Y. Yanks (20), Oct. 8, 1950
4th: 42 Chi. Cardinals (28) vs. Philadelphia (14), Dec. 7, 1947
          Green Bay (28) vs. Chi. Bears (14), Nov. 6, 1955
          N.Y. Jets (28) vs. Boston (14), Oct. 27, 1968
          Pittsburgh (21) vs. Cleveland (21), Oct. 18, 1969
          New England (21) vs. Kansas City (21), Sept. 22, 2002
     41 Baltimore (27) vs. New England (14), Sept. 18, 1978
          New England (27) vs. Baltimore (14), Nov. 23, 1980
     40 Chicago (21) vs. Tampa Bay (19), Nov. 19, 1989

Most Consecutive Games Scoring
420 San Francisco, 1977-2004 (current)
274 Cleveland, 1950-1971
220 Minnesota, 1991-2004 (current)

TOUCHDOWNS
Most Seasons Leading League, Touchdowns
13 Chi. Bears, 1932, 1934-35, 1939, 1941-44, 1946-48, 1956, 1965
  7 Dallas, 1966, 1968, 1971, 1973, 1977-78, 1980
     San Francisco, 1953, 1970, 1987, 1992-95
     L.A./St. Louis Rams, 1949-1952, 1999-2001
  6 Oakland, 1967-69, 1972, 1974, 1977
     San Diego, 1963, 1965, 1979, 1981-82, 1985
     Green Bay, 1932, 1937-38, 1961-62, 1996
     Baltimore/Indianapolis Colts, 1957-59, 1964, 1976, 2004

Most Consecutive Seasons Leading League, Touchdowns
4 Chi. Bears, 1941-44
    Los Angeles, 1949-1952
    San Francisco, 1992-95
3 Chi. Bears, 1946-48
    Baltimore, 1957-59
    Oakland, 1967-69
    St. Louis, 1999-2001
2 By many teams

Most Touchdowns, Season
70 Miami, 1984
67 St. Louis, 2000

66 Houston, 1961
    San Francisco, 1994
    St. Louis, 1999
    Indianapolis, 2004

Fewest Touchdowns, Season (Since 1932)
3 Cincinnati, 1933
4 Cincinnati/St. Louis, 1934
5 Detroit, 1942

Most Touchdowns, Game
10 Philadelphia vs. Cincinnati, Nov. 6, 1934
    Los Angeles vs. Baltimore, Oct. 22, 1950
    Washington vs. N.Y. Giants, Nov. 27, 1966
9 Chi. Cardinals vs. Rochester, Oct. 7, 1923
    Chi. Cardinals vs. N.Y. Giants, Oct. 17, 1948
    Chi. Cardinals vs. N.Y. Bulldogs, Nov. 13, 1949
    Los Angeles vs. Detroit, Oct. 29, 1950
    Pittsburgh vs. N.Y. Giants, Nov. 30, 1952
    Chicago vs. San Francisco, Dec. 12, 1965
    Chicago vs. Green Bay, Dec. 7, 1980
8 By many teams

Most Touchdowns, Both Teams, Game
16 Washington (10) vs. N.Y. Giants (6), Nov. 27, 1966
14 Chi. Cardinals (9) vs. N.Y. Giants (5), Oct. 17, 1948
    Los Angeles (10) vs. Baltimore (4), Oct. 22, 1950
    Houston (7) vs. Oakland (7), Dec. 22, 1963
13 New Orleans (7) vs. St. Louis (6), Nov. 2, 1969
    Kansas City (7) vs. Seattle (6), Nov. 27, 1983 (OT)
    San Diego (8) vs. Pittsburgh (5), Dec. 8, 1985
    N.Y. Jets (7) vs. Miami (6), Sept. 21, 1986 (OT)
    Cincinnati (7) vs. Cleveland (6), Nov. 28, 2004

Most Consecutive Games Scoring Touchdowns
166 Cleveland, 1957-1969
97 Oakland, 1966-1973
    Minnesota, 1995-2001
96 Kansas City, 1963-1970

POINTS AFTER TOUCHDOWN

Most (One-Point) Points After Touchdown, Season
66 Miami, 1984
65 Houston, 1961
64 St. Louis, 1999
    Indianapolis, 2004

Fewest (One-Point) Points After Touchdown, Season
2 Chi. Cardinals, 1933
3 Cincinnati, 1933
    Pittsburgh, 1934
4 Cincinnati/St. Louis, 1934

Most (One-Point) Points After Touchdown, Game
10 Los Angeles vs. Baltimore, Oct. 22, 1950
9 Chi. Cardinals vs. N.Y. Giants, Oct. 17, 1948
    Pittsburgh vs. N.Y. Giants, Nov. 30, 1952
    Washington vs. N.Y. Giants, Nov. 27, 1966
8 By many teams

Most (One-Point) Points After Touchdown, Both Teams, Game
14 Chi. Cardinals (9) vs. N.Y. Giants (5), Oct. 17, 1948
    Houston (7) vs. Oakland (7), Dec. 22, 1963
    Washington (9) vs. N.Y. Giants (5), Nov. 27, 1966
13 Los Angeles (10) vs. Baltimore (3), Oct. 22, 1950
    Cincinnati (7) vs. Cleveland (6), Nov. 28, 2004
12 In many games

Most Two-Point Conversions, Season
6 Miami, 1994
    Minnesota, 1997
5 Arizona, 1995
    Baltimore, 1996
    Jacksonville, 1996
    Chicago, 1997
    San Francisco, 1998
    Pittsburgh, 2002
4 By many teams

Most Two-Point Conversions, Game
4 St. Louis vs. Atlanta, Oct. 15, 2000
3 Baltimore vs. New England, Oct. 6, 1996
    Pittsburgh vs. Tennessee, Nov. 1, 1998
2 By many teams

Most Two-Point Conversions, Both Teams, Game
5 Baltimore (3) vs. New England (2), Oct. 6, 1996
    St. Louis (4) vs. Atlanta (1), Oct. 15, 2000
3 Seattle (2) vs. Kansas City (1), Oct. 23, 1994
    Minnesota (2) vs. Seattle (1), Nov. 10, 1996
    Pittsburgh (3) vs. Tennessee (0), Nov. 1, 1998
2 In many games

FIELD GOALS

Most Seasons Leading League, Field Goals
11 Green Bay, 1935-36, 1940-43, 1946-47, 1955, 1972, 1974
8 Washington, 1945, 1956, 1971, 1976-77, 1979, 1982, 1992
7 N.Y. Giants, 1933, 1937, 1939, 1941, 1944, 1959, 1983
    L.A./St. Louis Rams, 1949, 1951, 1958, 1966, 1973, 1978, 2003

Most Consecutive Seasons Leading League, Field Goals
4 Green Bay, 1940-43
3 Cleveland, 1952-54
2 By many teams

Most Field Goals Attempted, Season
49 Los Angeles, 1966
    Washington, 1971
48 Green Bay, 1972
47 N.Y. Jets, 1969
    Los Angeles, 1973
    Washington, 1983

Fewest Field Goals Attempted, Season (Since 1938)
0 Chi. Bears, 1944
2 Cleveland, 1939
    Card-Pitt, 1944
    Boston, 1946
    Chi. Bears, 1947
3 Chi. Bears, 1945
    Cleveland, 1945

Most Field Goals Attempted, Game
9 St. Louis vs. Pittsburgh, Sept. 24, 1967
8 Pittsburgh vs. St. Louis, Dec. 2, 1962
    Detroit vs. Minnesota, Nov. 13, 1966
    N.Y. Jets vs. Buffalo, Nov. 3, 1968
    Dallas vs. N.Y. Giants, Sept. 15, 2003 (OT)
7 By many teams

Most Field Goals Attempted, Both Teams, Game
11 St. Louis (6) vs. Pittsburgh (5), Nov. 13, 1966
    Washington (6) vs. Chicago (5), Nov. 14, 1971
    Green Bay (6) vs. Detroit (5), Sept. 29, 1974
    Washington (6) vs. N.Y. Giants (5), Nov. 14, 1976
10 In many games

Most Field Goals, Season
39 Miami, 1999
    St. Louis, 2003
37 Carolina, 1996
    Indianapolis, 2003
36 Indianapolis, 1996
    Tennessee, 1998

Fewest Field Goals, Season (Since 1932)
0 Boston, 1932, 1935
    Chi. Cardinals, 1932, 1945
    Green Bay, 1932, 1944
    N.Y. Giants, 1932
    Brooklyn, 1944
    Card-Pitt, 1944
    Chi. Bears, 1944, 1947

Boston, 1946
Baltimore, 1950
Dallas, 1952

Most Field Goals, Game

7 St. Louis vs. Pittsburgh, Sept. 24, 1967
   Minnesota vs. L.A. Rams, Nov. 5, 1989 (OT)
   Dallas vs. Green Bay, Nov. 18, 1996
   Dallas vs. N.Y. Giants, Sept. 15, 2003 (OT)

6 Boston vs. Denver, Oct. 4, 1964
   Detroit vs. Minnesota, Nov. 13, 1966
   N.Y. Jets vs. Buffalo, Nov. 3, 1968
   Philadelphia vs. Houston, Nov. 12, 1972
   N.Y. Jets vs. New Orleans, Dec. 3, 1972
   St. Louis vs. Atlanta, Dec. 9, 1973
   N.Y. Giants vs. Seattle, Oct. 18, 1981
   San Francisco vs. New Orleans, Oct. 16, 1983
   Pittsburgh vs. Denver, Oct. 23, 1988
   San Diego vs. Seattle, Sept. 5, 1993
   San Diego vs. Houston, Sept. 19, 1993
   Cincinnati vs. Seattle, Nov. 6, 1994
   Atlanta vs. New Orleans, Nov. 13, 1994
   San Francisco vs. Atlanta, Sept. 29, 1996
   Buffalo vs. N.Y. Jets, Oct. 20, 1996
   San Diego vs. Oakland, Oct. 5, 1997
   Minnesota vs. Baltimore, Dec. 13, 1998
   Detroit vs. Minnesota, Oct. 17, 1999
   Miami vs. New England, Oct. 17, 1999
   Pittsburgh vs. Jacksonville, Dec. 1, 2002
   Carolina vs. New Orleans, Dec. 5, 2004

5 By many teams

Most Field Goals, Both Teams, Game

9 San Diego (5) vs. Kansas City (4), Sept. 29, 1996
   Miami (6) vs. New England (3), Oct. 17, 1999

8 Cleveland (4) vs. St. Louis (4), Sept. 20, 1964
   Chicago (5) vs. Philadelphia (3), Oct. 20, 1968
   Washington (5) vs. Chicago (3), Nov. 14, 1971
   Kansas City (5) vs. Buffalo (3), Dec. 19, 1971
   Detroit (4) vs. Green Bay (4), Sept. 29, 1974
   Cleveland (5) vs. Denver (3), Oct. 19, 1975
   New England (4) vs. San Diego (4), Nov. 9, 1975
   San Francisco (6) vs. New Orleans (2), Oct. 16, 1983
   Seattle (5) vs. L.A. Raiders (3), Dec. 18, 1988
   Atlanta (6) vs. New Orleans (2), Nov. 13, 1994
   Indianapolis (4) vs. San Diego (4), Nov. 3, 1996
   Dallas (7) vs. N.Y. Giants (1), Sept. 15, 2003 (OT)
   Oakland (5) vs. Chicago (3), Oct. 5, 2003

7 In many games

Most Consecutive Games Scoring Field Goals

38 Baltimore, 1999-2001
31 Minnesota, 1968-1970
28 Washington, 1988-1990

SAFETIES

Most Safeties, Season

4 Cleveland, 1927
   Detroit, 1962
   Seattle, 1993
   San Francisco, 1996
   Tennessee, 1999

3 By many teams

Most Safeties, Game

3 L.A. Rams vs. N.Y. Giants, Sept. 30, 1984

2 N.Y. Giants vs. Pottsville, Oct. 30, 1927
   Chi. Bears vs. Pottsville, Nov. 13, 1927
   Detroit vs. Brooklyn, Dec. 1, 1935
   N.Y. Giants vs. Pittsburgh, Sept. 17, 1950
   N.Y. Giants vs. Washington, Nov. 5, 1961
   Chicago vs. Pittsburgh, Nov. 9, 1969
   Dallas vs. Philadelphia, Nov. 19, 1972
   Los Angeles vs. Green Bay, Oct. 21, 1973

Oakland vs. San Diego, Oct. 26, 1975
Denver vs. Seattle, Jan. 2, 1983
New Orleans vs. Cleveland, Sept. 13, 1987
Buffalo vs. Denver, Nov. 8, 1987
San Francisco vs. St. Louis, Sept. 8, 1996
Jacksonville vs. Pittsburgh, Oct. 3, 1999
Minnesota vs. Atlanta, Oct. 5, 2003
Dallas vs. Arizona, Oct. 5, 2003
Buffalo vs. Houston, Nov. 16, 2003

Most Safeties, Both Teams, Game

3 L.A. Rams (3) vs. N.Y. Giants (0), Sept. 30, 1984

2 Chi. Cardinals (1) vs. Frankford (1), Nov. 19, 1927
   Chi. Cardinals (1) vs. Cincinnati (1), Nov. 12, 1933
   Chi. Bears (1) vs. San Francisco (1), Oct. 19, 1952
   Cincinnati (1) vs. Los Angeles (1), Oct. 22, 1972
   Chi. Bears (1) vs. San Francisco (1), Sept. 19, 1976
   Baltimore (1) vs. Miami (1), Oct. 29, 1978
   Atlanta (1) vs. Detroit (1), Oct. 5, 1980
   Houston (1) vs. Philadelphia (1), Oct. 2, 1988
   Cleveland (1) vs. Seattle (1), Nov. 14, 1993
   Arizona (1) vs. Houston (1), Dec. 4, 1994
   (Also see previous record)

FIRST DOWNS

Most Seasons Leading League

9 Chi. Bears, 1935, 1939, 1941, 1943, 1945,
   1947-49, 1955

7 San Diego, 1965, 1969, 1980-83, 1985
   L.A./St. Louis Rams, 1946, 1950-51, 1954, 1957,
   1973, 2001

6 San Francisco, 1965, 1987, 1989, 1993-94, 1998

Most Consecutive Seasons Leading League

4 San Diego, 1980-83
3 Chi. Bears, 1947-49
2 By many teams

Most First Downs, Season

398 Kansas City, 2004
387 Miami, 1984
383 Denver, 2000

Fewest First Downs, Season

51 Cincinnati, 1933
64 Pittsburgh, 1935
67 Philadelphia, 1937

Most First Downs, Game

39 N.Y. Jets vs. Miami, Nov. 27, 1988
   Washington vs. Detroit, Nov. 4, 1990 (OT)
38 Los Angeles vs. N.Y. Giants, Nov. 13, 1966
37 Green Bay vs. Philadelphia, Nov. 11, 1962

Fewest First Downs, Game

0 N.Y. Giants vs. Green Bay, Oct. 1, 1933
   Pittsburgh vs. Boston, Oct. 29, 1933
   Philadelphia vs. Detroit, Sept. 20, 1935
   N.Y. Giants vs. Washington, Sept. 27, 1942
   Denver vs. Houston, Sept. 3, 1966

Most First Downs, Both Teams, Game

64 Seattle (32) vs. Kansas City (32), Nov. 24, 2002
62 San Diego (32) vs. Seattle (30), Sept. 15, 1985
   Oakland (31) vs. Kansas City (31), Nov. 5, 2000
59 Miami (31) vs. Buffalo (28), Oct. 9, 1983 (OT)
   Seattle (33) vs. Kansas City (26), Nov. 27, 1983 (OT)
   N.Y. Jets (32) vs. Miami (27), Sept. 21, 1986 (OT)
   N.Y. Jets (39) vs. Miami (20), Nov. 27, 1988
   Oakland (31) vs. San Francisco (28), Oct. 8, 2000 (OT)

Fewest First Downs, Both Teams, Game

7 Chi. Cardinals (2) vs. Detroit (5), Sept. 15, 1940
9 Pittsburgh (1) vs. Boston (8), Oct. 27, 1935
   Boston (4) vs. Brooklyn (5), Nov. 24, 1935
   N.Y. Giants (3) vs. Detroit (6), Nov. 7, 1943
   Pittsburgh (4) vs. Chi. Cardinals (5), Nov. 11, 1945
   N.Y. Bulldogs (1) vs. Philadelphia (8), Sept. 22, 1949

  10 N.Y. Giants (4) vs. Washington (6), Dec. 11, 1960

Most First Downs, Rushing, Season
- 181 New England, 1978
- 177 Los Angeles, 1973
- 176 Chicago, 1985

Fewest First Downs, Rushing, Season
- 36 Cleveland, 1942
-     Boston, 1944
- 39 Brooklyn, 1943
- 40 Philadelphia, 1940
-     Detroit, 1945

Most First Downs, Rushing, Game
- 25 Philadelphia vs. Washington, Dec. 2, 1951
- 23 St. Louis vs. New Orleans, Oct. 5, 1980
- 21 Cleveland vs. Philadelphia, Dec. 13, 1959
-     Green Bay vs. Philadelphia, Nov. 11, 1962
-     Los Angeles vs. New Orleans, Nov. 25, 1973
-     Pittsburgh vs. Kansas City, Nov. 7, 1976
-     New England vs. Denver, Nov. 28, 1976
-     Oakland vs. Green Bay, Sept. 17, 1978
-     Buffalo vs. Washington, Nov. 3, 1996
-     San Francisco vs. Detroit, Dec. 14, 1998
-     Kansas City vs. Atlanta, Oct. 24, 2004

Fewest First Downs, Rushing, Game
- 0 By many teams. Last time: Chicago vs. Jacksonville, Dec. 12, 2004

Most First Downs, Rushing, Both Teams, Game
- 36 Philadelphia (25) vs. Washington (11), Dec. 2, 1951
- 31 Detroit (18) vs. Washington (13), Sept. 30, 1951
- 30 Los Angeles (17) vs. Minnesota (13), Nov. 5, 1961
-     New Orleans (17) vs. Green Bay (13), Sept. 9, 1979
-     New Orleans (16) vs. San Francisco (14), Nov. 11, 1979
-     New England (16) vs. Kansas City (14), Oct. 4, 1981

Fewest First Downs, Rushing, Both Teams, Game
- 1 Oakland (0) vs. Tennessee (1), Sept. 7, 2003
- 2 Houston (0) vs. Denver (2), Dec. 2, 1962
-     N.Y. Jets, (1) vs. St. Louis (1), Dec. 3, 1995
-     Miami (1) vs. San Diego (1), Dec. 19, 1999
-     New Orleans (0) vs. Baltimore (2), Dec. 19, 1999
- 3 In many games

Most First Downs, Passing, Season
- 259 San Diego, 1985
- 251 Houston, 1990
- 250 Miami, 1986

Fewest First Downs, Passing, Season
- 18 Pittsburgh, 1941
- 23 Brooklyn, 1942
-     N.Y. Giants, 1944
- 24 N.Y. Giants, 1943

Most First Downs, Passing, Game
- 29 N.Y. Giants vs. Cincinnati, Oct. 13, 1985
- 28 Tennessee vs. Oakland, Dec. 19, 2004
- 27 San Diego vs. Seattle, Sept. 15, 1985

Fewest First Downs, Passing, Game
- 0 By many teams. Last time: Cleveland vs. Jacksonville, Dec. 3, 2000

Most First Downs, Passing, Both Teams, Game
- 43 San Diego (23) vs. Cincinnati (20), Dec. 20, 1982
-     Miami (24) vs. N.Y. Jets (19), Sept. 21, 1986 (OT)
-     Tennessee (28) vs. Oakland (15), Dec. 19, 2004
- 42 San Francisco (22) vs. San Diego (20), Dec. 11, 1982
- 41 San Diego (27) vs. Seattle (14), Sept. 15, 1985
-     Miami (26) vs. Cleveland (15), Dec. 12, 1988
-     Kansas City (23) vs. Oakland (18), Nov. 5, 2000

Fewest First Downs, Passing, Both Teams, Game
- 0 Brooklyn vs. Pittsburgh, Nov. 29, 1942
- 1 Green Bay (0) vs. Cleveland (1), Sept. 21, 1941
-     Pittsburgh (0) vs. Brooklyn (1), Oct. 11, 1942
-     N.Y. Giants (0) vs. Detroit (1), Nov. 7, 1943
-     Pittsburgh (0) vs. Chi. Cardinals (1), Nov. 11, 1945

    N.Y. Bulldogs (0) vs. Philadelphia (1), Sept. 22, 1949
    Chicago (0) vs. Buffalo (1), Oct. 7, 1979
- 2 In many games

Most First Downs, Penalty, Season
- 47 Buffalo, 2002
-     Indianapolis, 2004
- 43 Denver, 1994
- 42 Chicago, 1987
-     Arizona, 2004

Fewest First Downs, Penalty, Season
- 2 Brooklyn, 1940
- 4 Chi. Cardinals, 1940
-     N.Y. Giants, 1942, 1944
-     Washington, 1944
-     Cleveland, 1952
-     Kansas City, 1969
- 5 Brooklyn, 1939
-     Chi. Bears, 1939
-     Detroit, 1953
-     Los Angeles, 1953
-     Houston, 1982

Most First Downs, Penalty, Game
- 11 Denver vs. Houston, Oct. 6, 1985
- 9 Chi. Bears vs. Cleveland, Nov. 25, 1951
-     Baltimore vs. Pittsburgh, Oct. 30, 1977
-     N.Y. Jets vs. Houston, Sept. 18, 1988
- 8 Philadelphia vs. Detroit, Dec. 2, 1979
-     Cincinnati vs. N.Y. Jets, Oct. 6, 1985
-     Buffalo vs. Houston, Sept. 20, 1987
-     Houston vs. Atlanta, Sept. 9, 1990
-     Kansas City vs. L.A. Raiders, Oct. 3, 1993
-     San Francisco vs. New Orleans, Oct. 11, 1998
-     Oakland vs. San Francisco, Oct. 8, 2000 (OT)
-     Philadelphia vs. Chicago, Nov. 3, 2002

Most First Downs, Penalty, Both Teams, Game
- 12 Buffalo (7) vs. San Francisco (5), Oct. 4, 1998
- 11 Chi. Bears (9) vs. Cleveland (2), Nov. 25, 1951
-     Cincinnati (8) vs. N.Y. Jets (3), Oct. 6, 1985
-     Denver (11) vs. Houston (0), Oct. 6, 1985
-     Detroit (6) vs. Dallas (5), Nov. 8, 1987
-     N.Y. Jets (9) vs. Houston (2), Sept. 18, 1988
-     Kansas City (8) vs. L.A. Raiders (3), Oct. 3, 1993
-     Detroit (6) vs. San Diego (5), Nov. 11, 1996
-     Philadelphia (8) vs. Chicago (3), Nov. 3, 2002
- 10 In many games

NET YARDS GAINED RUSHING AND PASSING

Most Seasons Leading League
- 12 Chi. Bears, 1932, 1934-35, 1939, 1941-44, 1947, 1949, 1955-56
- 9 L.A./St. Louis Rams, 1946, 1950-51, 1954, 1957, 1973, 1999-2001
- 7 San Diego, 1963, 1965, 1980-83, 1985

Most Consecutive Seasons Leading League
- 4 Chi. Bears, 1941-44
-     San Diego, 1980-83
- 3 Baltimore, 1958-1960
-     Houston, 1960-62
-     Oakland, 1968-1970
-     St. Louis, 1999-2001
- 2 By many teams

Most Yards Gained, Season
- 7,075 St. Louis, 2000
- 6,936 Miami, 1984
- 6,800 San Francisco, 1998

Fewest Yards Gained, Season
- 1,150 Cincinnati, 1933
- 1,443 Chi. Cardinals, 1934
- 1,486 Chi. Cardinals, 1933

Most Yards Gained, Game
735 Los Angeles vs. N.Y. Yanks, Sept. 28, 1951
683 Pittsburgh vs. Chi. Cardinals, Dec. 13, 1958
682 Chi. Bears vs. N.Y. Giants, Nov. 14, 1943

Fewest Yards Gained, Game
−7 Seattle vs. Los Angeles, Nov. 4, 1979
−5 Denver vs. Oakland, Sept. 10, 1967
14 Chi. Cardinals vs. Detroit, Sept. 15, 1940

Most Yards Gained, Both Teams, Game
1,133 Los Angeles (636) vs. N.Y. Yanks (497), Nov. 19, 1950
1,102 San Diego (661) vs. Cincinnati (441), Dec. 20, 1982
1,095 Kansas City (590) vs. Indianapolis (505), Oct. 31, 2004

Fewest Yards Gained, Both Teams, Game
30 Chi. Cardinals (14) vs. Detroit (16), Sept. 15, 1940
136 Chi. Cardinals (50) vs. Green Bay (86), Nov. 18, 1934
154 N.Y. Giants (51) vs. Washington (103), Dec. 11, 1960

Most Consecutive Games, 400 or More Yards Gained
11 San Diego, 1982-83
8 St. Louis, 1999-2000
6 Houston, 1961-62
San Diego, 1981
San Francisco, 1987

Most Consecutive Games, 300 or More Yards Gained
36 Minnesota, 2002-04
30 Minnesota, 1999-2000
St. Louis, 2000-02
29 Los Angeles, 1949-1951

RUSHING

Most Seasons Leading League
16 Chi. Bears, 1932, 1934-35, 1939-1942, 1951, 1955-56, 1968, 1977, 1983-86
7 Buffalo, 1962, 1964, 1973, 1975, 1982, 1991-92
6 Cleveland, 1958-59, 1963, 1965-67
San Francisco, 1952-54, 1987, 1998-99

Most Consecutive Seasons Leading League
4 Chi. Bears, 1939-1942
Chi. Bears, 1983-86
3 Detroit, 1936-38
San Francisco, 1952-54
Cleveland, 1965-67
2 By many teams

ATTEMPTS

Most Rushing Attempts, Season
681 Oakland, 1977
674 Chicago, 1984
671 New England, 1978

Fewest Rushing Attempts, Season
211 Philadelphia, 1982
219 San Francisco, 1982
225 Houston, 1982

Most Rushing Attempts, Game
72 Chi. Bears vs. Brooklyn, Oct. 20, 1935
70 Chi. Cardinals vs. Green Bay, Dec. 5, 1948
69 Chi. Cardinals vs. Green Bay, Dec. 6, 1936
Kansas City vs. Cincinnati, Sept. 3, 1978

Fewest Rushing Attempts, Game
6 Chi. Cardinals vs. Boston, Oct. 29, 1933
New England vs. Pittsburgh, Oct. 31, 2004
7 Oakland vs. Buffalo, Oct. 15, 1963
Houston vs. N.Y. Giants, Dec. 8, 1985
Seattle vs. L.A. Raiders, Nov. 17, 1991
Green Bay vs. Miami, Sept. 11, 1994
8 Denver vs. Oakland, Dec. 17, 1960
Buffalo vs. St. Louis, Sept. 9, 1984
Detroit vs. San Francisco, Oct. 20, 1991
Atlanta vs. Detroit, Sept. 5, 1993
St. Louis vs. San Francisco, Nov. 2, 2003

Most Rushing Attempts, Both Teams, Game
108 Chi. Cardinals (70) vs. Green Bay (38), Dec. 5, 1948
105 Oakland (62) vs. Atlanta (43), Nov. 30, 1975 (OT)
104 Chi. Bears (64) vs. Pittsburgh (40), Oct. 18, 1936

Fewest Rushing Attempts, Both Teams, Game
34 Atlanta (12) vs. Houston (22), Dec. 5, 1993
Atlanta (15) vs. San Francisco (19), Dec. 24, 1995
35 Seattle (15) vs. New Orleans (20), Sept. 1, 1991
Oakland (17) vs. Pittsburgh (18), Sept. 15, 2002
36 Houston (15) vs. N.Y. Jets (21), Oct. 13, 1991
St. Louis (16) vs. Detroit (20), Nov. 7, 1999
Detroit (15) vs. Washington (21), Dec. 5, 1999
Tennessee (14) vs. Baltimore (22), Dec. 5, 1999
Tampa Bay (16) vs. St. Louis (20), Sept. 23, 2002
Oakland (14) vs. Denver (22), Nov. 11, 2002
Philadelphia (17) vs. Minnesota (19), Sept. 20, 2004

YARDS GAINED

Most Yards Gained Rushing, Season
3,165 New England, 1978
3,088 Buffalo, 1973
2,986 Kansas City, 1978

Fewest Yards Gained Rushing, Season
298 Philadelphia, 1940
467 Detroit, 1946
471 Boston, 1944

Most Yards Gained Rushing, Game
426 Detroit vs. Pittsburgh, Nov. 4, 1934
423 N.Y. Giants vs. Baltimore, Nov. 19, 1950
420 Boston vs. N.Y. Giants, Oct. 8, 1933

Fewest Yards Gained Rushing, Game
−53 Detroit vs. Chi. Cardinals, Oct. 17, 1943
−36 Philadelphia vs. Chi. Bears, Nov. 19, 1939
−33 Phil-Pitt vs. Brooklyn, Oct. 2, 1943

Most Yards Gained Rushing, Both Teams, Game
595 Los Angeles (371) vs. N.Y. Yanks (224), Nov. 18, 1951
574 Chi. Bears (396) vs. Pittsburgh (178), Oct. 10, 1934
558 Boston (420) vs. N.Y. Giants (138), Oct. 8, 1933

Fewest Yards Gained Rushing, Both Teams, Game
−15 Detroit (−53) vs. Chi. Cardinals (38), Oct. 17, 1943
4 Detroit (−10) vs. Chi. Cardinals (14), Sept. 15, 1940
62 L.A. Rams (15) vs. San Francisco (47), Dec. 6, 1964

AVERAGE GAIN

Highest Average Gain, Rushing, Season
5.74 Cleveland, 1963
5.65 San Francisco, 1954
5.56 San Diego, 1963

Lowest Average Gain, Rushing, Season
0.94 Philadelphia, 1940
1.45 Boston, 1944
1.55 Pittsburgh, 1935

TOUCHDOWNS

Most Touchdowns, Rushing, Season
36 Green Bay, 1962
33 Pittsburgh, 1976
32 Kansas City, 2003

Fewest Touchdowns, Rushing, Season
1 Brooklyn, 1934
2 Chi. Cardinals, 1933
Cincinnati, 1933
Pittsburgh, 1934
Philadelphia, 1935
Philadelphia, 1936
Philadelphia, 1937
Philadelphia, 1938
Pittsburgh, 1940
Philadelphia, 1972

N.Y. Jets, 1995
3   By many teams

Most Touchdowns, Rushing, Game
9   Rock Island vs. Evansville, Oct. 15, 1922
    Racine vs. Louisville, Nov. 5, 1922
8   Chi. Cardinals vs. Rochester, Oct. 7, 1923
    Kansas City vs. Atlanta, Oct. 24, 2004
7   By many teams

Most Touchdowns, Rushing, Both Teams, Game
9   Rock Island (9) vs. Evansville (0), Oct. 15, 1922
    Racine (9) vs. Louisville (0), Nov. 5, 1922
8   Chi. Cardinals (8) vs. Rochester (0), Oct. 7, 1923
    Canton (7) vs. Cleveland (1), Nov. 25, 1923
    Los Angeles (6) vs. N.Y. Yanks (2), Nov. 18, 1951
    Chi. Bears (5) vs. Green Bay (3), Nov. 6, 1955
    Denver (5) vs. Kansas City (3), Dec. 7, 2003
    Kansas City (8) vs. Atlanta (0), Oct. 24, 2004
7   In many games

PASSING
ATTEMPTS
Most Passes Attempted, Season
709   Minnesota, 1981
699   New England, 1994
686   New England, 1995

Fewest Passes Attempted, Season
102   Cincinnati, 1933
106   Boston, 1933
120   Detroit, 1937

Most Passes Attempted, Game
70   New England vs. Minnesota, Nov. 13, 1994 (OT)
69   N.Y. Jets vs. Baltimore, Dec. 24, 2000
68   Houston vs. Buffalo, Nov 1, 1964
    Cincinnati vs. Pittsburgh, Dec. 30, 2001 (OT)

Fewest Passes Attempted, Game
0   Green Bay vs. Portsmouth, Oct. 8, 1933
    Detroit vs. Cleveland, Sept. 10, 1937
    Pittsburgh vs. Brooklyn, Nov. 16, 1941
    Pittsburgh vs. Los Angeles, Nov. 13, 1949
    Cleveland vs. Philadelphia, Dec. 3, 1950

Most Passes Attempted, Both Teams, Game
112   New England (70) vs. Minnesota (42), Nov. 13, 1994
104   Miami (55) vs. N.Y. Jets (49), Oct. 18, 1987 (OT)
    N.Y. Jets (58) vs. San Francisco (46), Sept. 6, 1998 (OT)
103   Cincinnati (68) vs. Pittsburgh (35), Dec. 30, 2001 (OT)
    Seattle (53) vs. San Diego (50), Dec. 29, 2002 (OT)

Fewest Passes Attempted, Both Teams, Game
4   Chi. Cardinals (1) vs. Detroit (3), Nov. 3, 1935
    Detroit (0) vs. Cleveland (4), Sept. 10, 1937
6   Chi. Cardinals (2) vs. Detroit (4), Sept. 15, 1940
8   Brooklyn (2) vs. Philadelphia (6), Oct. 1, 1939

COMPLETIONS
Most Passes Completed, Season
432   San Francisco, 1995
418   Oakland, 2002
411   Houston, 1991

Fewest Passes Completed, Season
25   Cincinnati, 1933
33   Boston, 1933
34   Chi. Cardinals, 1934
    Detroit, 1934

Most Passes Completed, Game
45   New England vs. Minnesota, Nov. 13, 1994 (OT)
43   Washington vs. Detroit, Nov. 4, 1990 (OT)
    Oakland vs. Pittsburgh, Sept. 15, 2002
42   N.Y. Jets vs. San Francisco, Sept. 21, 1980
    N.Y. Jets vs. Seattle, Dec. 6, 1998

Fewest Passes Completed, Game
0   By many teams. Last time: Buffalo vs. N.Y. Jets,

Sept. 29, 1974
Most Passes Completed, Both Teams, Game
71   New England (45) vs. Minnesota (26), Nov. 13, 1994
68   San Francisco (37) vs. Atlanta (31), Oct. 6, 1985
    Denver (34) vs. Oakland (34), Nov. 11, 2002
66   Cincinnati (40) vs. San Diego (26), Dec. 20, 1982

Fewest Passes Completed, Both Teams, Game
1   Chi. Cardinals (0) vs. Philadelphia (1), Nov. 8, 1936
    Detroit (0) vs. Cleveland (1), Sept. 10, 1937
    Chi. Cardinals (0) vs. Detroit (1), Sept. 15, 1940
    Brooklyn (0) vs. Pittsburgh (1), Nov. 29, 1942
2   Chi. Cardinals (0) vs. Detroit (2), Nov. 3, 1935
    Buffalo (0) vs. N.Y. Jets (2), Sept. 29, 1974
    Chi. Cardinals (0) vs. Green Bay (2), Nov. 18, 1934
3   In seven games

YARDS GAINED
Most Seasons Leading League, Passing Yardage
10   San Diego, 1965, 1968, 1971, 1978-1983, 1985
8   Chi. Bears, 1932, 1939, 1941, 1943, 1945, 1949,
    1954, 1964
    Washington, 1938, 1940, 1944, 1947-48, 1967,
    1974, 1989
7   Houston, 1960-61, 1963-64, 1990-92
    L.A./St. Louis Rams, 1946, 1950-51, 1956,
    1999-2001
    Balt./Indianapolis, 1957, 1959, 1960, 1963, 1976,
    2003-04

Most Consecutive Seasons Leading League, Passing Yardage
6   San Diego, 1978-1983
4   Green Bay, 1934-37
3   Miami, 1986-88
    Houston, 1990-92
    St. Louis, 1999-2001

Most Yards Gained, Passing, Season
5,232   St. Louis, 2000
5,018   Miami, 1984
4,870   San Diego, 1985

Fewest Yards Gained, Passing, Season
302   Chi. Cardinals, 1934
357   Cincinnati, 1933
459   Boston, 1934

Most Yards Gained, Passing, Game
554   Los Angeles vs. N.Y. Yanks, Sept. 28, 1951
530   Minnesota vs. Baltimore, Sept. 28, 1969
521   Miami vs. N.Y. Jets, Oct. 23, 1988

Fewest Yards Gained, Passing, Game
−53   Denver vs. Oakland, Sept. 10, 1967
−52   Cincinnati vs. Houston, Oct. 31, 1971
−39   Atlanta vs. San Francisco, Oct. 23, 1976

Most Yards Gained, Passing, Both Teams, Game
884   N.Y. Jets (449) vs. Miami (435), Sept. 21, 1986 (OT)
883   San Diego (486) vs. Cincinnati (397), Dec. 20, 1982
874   Miami (456) vs. New England (418), Sept. 4, 1994

Fewest Yards Gained, Passing, Both Teams, Game
−11   Green Bay (−10) vs. Dallas (−1), Oct. 24, 1965
1   Chi. Cardinals (0) vs. Philadelphia (1), Nov. 8, 1936
7   Brooklyn (0) vs. Pittsburgh (7), Nov. 29, 1942

TIMES SACKED
Most Seasons Leading League, Fewest Times Sacked
10   Miami, 1973, 1982-1990
5   N.Y. Jets, 1965-66, 1968, 1993, 2000
4   San Diego, 1963-64, 1967-68
    San Francisco, 1964-65, 1970-71

Most Consecutive Seasons Leading League, Fewest Times Sacked
9   Miami, 1982-1990
3   St. Louis, 1974-76
2   By many teams

Most Times Sacked, Season
- 104 Philadelphia, 1986
- 78 Arizona, 1997
- 76 Houston, 2002

Fewest Times Sacked, Season
- 7 Miami, 1988
- 8 San Francisco, 1970
- St. Louis, 1975
- 9 N.Y. Jets, 1966
- Washington, 1991

Most Times Sacked, Game
- 12 Pittsburgh vs. Dallas, Nov. 20, 1966
- Baltimore vs. St. Louis, Oct. 26, 1980
- Detroit vs. Chicago, Dec. 16, 1984
- Houston vs. Dallas, Sept. 29, 1985
- 11 St. Louis vs. N.Y. Giants, Nov. 1, 1964
- Los Angeles vs. Baltimore, Nov. 22, 1964
- Denver vs. Buffalo, Dec. 13, 1964
- Green Bay vs. Detroit, Nov. 7, 1965
- Buffalo vs. Oakland, Oct. 15, 1967
- Denver vs. Oakland, Nov. 5, 1967
- Atlanta vs. St. Louis, Nov. 24, 1968
- Detroit vs. Dallas, Oct. 6, 1975
- Philadelphia vs. St. Louis, Dec. 18, 1983
- Cleveland vs. Kansas City, Sept. 30, 1984
- Minnesota vs. Chicago, Oct. 28, 1984
- Atlanta vs. Cleveland, Nov. 18, 1984
- Dallas vs. San Diego, Nov. 16, 1986
- Philadelphia vs. Detroit, Nov. 16, 1986
- Philadelphia vs. L.A. Raiders, Nov. 30, 1986 (OT)
- L.A. Raiders vs. Seattle, Dec. 8, 1986
- N.Y. Jets vs. Dallas, Oct. 4, 1987
- Philadelphia vs. Chicago, Oct. 4, 1987
- Dallas vs. Philadelphia, Sept. 15, 1991
- Cleveland vs. Indianapolis, Sept. 6, 1992
- 10 By many teams

Most Times Sacked, Both Teams, Game
- 18 Green Bay (10) vs. San Diego (8), Sept. 24, 1978
- 17 Buffalo (10) vs. N.Y. Titans (7), Nov. 23, 1961
- Pittsburgh (12) vs. Dallas (5), Nov. 20, 1966
- Atlanta (9) vs. Philadelphia (8), Dec. 16, 1984
- Philadelphia (11) vs. L.A. Raiders (6), Nov. 30, 1986 (OT)
- 16 Los Angeles (11) vs. Baltimore (5), Nov. 22, 1964
- Buffalo (11) vs. Oakland (5), Oct. 15, 1967

COMPLETION PERCENTAGE

Most Seasons Leading League, Completion Percentage
- 14 San Francisco, 1952, 1957-58, 1965, 1981, 1983, 1987, 1989, 1992-97
- 11 Washington, 1937, 1939-1940, 1942-45, 1947-48, 1969-1970
- 8 Green Bay, 1936, 1941, 1961-62, 1964, 1966, 1968, 1998

Most Consecutive Seasons Leading League, Completion Percentage
- 6 San Francisco, 1992-97
- 4 Washington, 1942-45
- Kansas City, 1966-69
- 3 Cleveland, 1953-55
- St. Louis, 1999-2001

Highest Completion Percentage, Season
- 70.65 Cincinnati, 1982 (310-219)
- 70.25 San Francisco, 1994 (511-359)
- 70.19 San Francisco, 1989 (483-339)

Lowest Completion Percentage, Season
- 22.9 Philadelphia, 1936 (170-39)
- 24.5 Cincinnati, 1933 (102-25)
- 25.0 Pittsburgh, 1941 (168-42)

TOUCHDOWNS

Most Touchdowns, Passing, Season
- 51 Indianapolis, 2004
- 49 Miami, 1984
- 48 Houston, 1961

Fewest Touchdowns, Passing, Season
- 0 Cincinnati, 1933
- Pittsburgh, 1945
- 1 Boston, 1932
- Boston, 1933
- Chi. Cardinals, 1934
- Cincinnati/St. Louis, 1934
- Detroit, 1942
- 2 Chi. Cardinals, 1932
- Stapleton, 1932
- Chi. Cardinals, 1935
- Brooklyn, 1936
- Pittsburgh, 1942

Most Touchdowns, Passing, Game
- 7 Chi. Bears vs. N.Y. Giants, Nov. 14, 1943
- Philadelphia vs. Washington, Oct. 17, 1954
- Houston vs. N.Y. Titans, Nov. 19, 1961
- Houston vs. N.Y. Titans, Oct. 14, 1962
- N.Y. Giants vs. Washington, Oct. 28, 1962
- Minnesota vs. Baltimore, Sept. 28, 1969
- San Diego vs. Oakland, Nov. 22, 1981
- 6 By many teams

Most Touchdowns, Passing, Both Teams, Game
- 12 New Orleans (6) vs. St. Louis (6), Nov. 2, 1969
- 11 N.Y. Giants (7) vs. Washington (4), Oct. 28, 1962
- Oakland (6) vs. Houston (5), Dec. 22, 1963
- 10 San Diego (5) vs. Seattle (5), Sept. 15, 1985
- Miami (6) vs. N.Y. Jets (4), Sept. 21, 1986 (OT)
- San Francisco (6) vs. Atlanta (4), Oct. 14, 1990

PASSES HAD INTERCEPTED

Most Passes Had Intercepted, Season
- 48 Houston, 1962
- 45 Denver, 1961
- 41 Card-Pitt, 1944

Fewest Passes Had Intercepted, Season
- 5 Cleveland, 1960
- Green Bay, 1966
- Kansas City, 1990
- N.Y. Giants, 1990
- 6 Green Bay, 1964
- St. Louis, 1982
- Dallas, 1993
- 7 Los Angeles, 1969

Most Passes Had Intercepted, Game
- 9 Detroit vs. Green Bay, Oct. 24, 1943
- Pittsburgh vs. Philadelphia, Dec. 12, 1965
- 8 Green Bay vs. N.Y. Giants, Nov. 21, 1948
- Chi. Cardinals vs. Philadelphia, Sept. 24, 1950
- N.Y. Yanks vs. N.Y. Giants, Dec. 16, 1951
- Denver vs. Houston, Dec. 2, 1962
- Chi. Bears vs. Detroit, Sept. 22, 1968
- Baltimore vs. N.Y. Jets, Sept. 23, 1973
- 7 By many teams. Last time: Detroit vs. Cleveland, Sept. 23, 2001

Most Passes Had Intercepted, Both Teams, Game
- 13 Denver (8) vs. Houston (5), Dec. 2, 1962
- 11 Philadelphia (7) vs. Boston (4), Nov. 3, 1935
- Boston (6) vs. Pittsburgh (5), Dec. 1, 1935
- Cleveland (7) vs. Green Bay (4), Oct. 30, 1938
- Green Bay (7) vs. Detroit (4), Oct. 20, 1940
- Detroit (7) vs. Chi. Bears (4), Nov. 22, 1942
- Detroit (7) vs. Cleveland (4), Nov. 26, 1944
- Chi. Cardinals (8) vs. Philadelphia (3), Sept. 24, 1950
- Washington (7) vs. N.Y. Giants (4), Dec. 8, 1963

Pittsburgh (9) vs. Philadelphia (2), Dec 12, 1965
10 In many games

PUNTING

Most Seasons Leading League (Average Distance)
7 Denver 1962-64, 1966-67, 1982, 1999
6 Washington, 1940-43, 1945, 1958
   Kansas City, 1968, 1971-73, 1979, 1984
   Oakland, 1974-75, 1977-78, 2003-04
5 L.A. Rams, 1946, 1949, 1955-56, 1994

**Most Consecutive Seasons Leading League
(Average Distance)**
4 Washington, 1940-43
3 Cleveland, 1950-52
   Denver, 1962-64
   Kansas City, 1971-73

Most Punts, Season
116 Houston, 2002
114 Chicago, 1981
113 Boston, 1934
     Brooklyn, 1934
     Dallas, 2002

Fewest Punts, Season
23 San Diego, 1982
31 Cincinnati, 1982
32 Chi. Bears, 1941

Most Punts, Game
17 Chi. Bears vs. Green Bay, Oct. 22, 1933
    Cincinnati vs. Pittsburgh, Oct. 22, 1933
16 Cincinnati vs. Portsmouth, Sept. 17, 1933
    Chi. Cardinals vs. Chi. Bears, Nov. 30, 1933
    Chi. Cardinals vs. Detroit, Sept. 15, 1940
    Oakland vs. San Diego, Oct. 11, 1998
15 N.Y. Giants vs. Chi. Bears, Nov. 17, 1935
    Philadelphia vs. N.Y. Giants, Dec. 6, 1987 (OT)

Fewest Punts, Game
0 By many teams. Last time:
    Pittsburgh vs. Baltimore, Dec. 26, 2004

Most Punts, Both Teams, Game
31 Chi. Bears (17) vs. Green Bay (14), Oct. 22, 1933
    Cincinnati (17), vs. Pittsburgh (14), Oct. 22, 1933
29 Chi. Cardinals (15) vs. Cincinnati (14), Nov. 12, 1933
    Chi. Cardinals (16) vs. Chi. Bears (13), Nov. 30, 1933
    Chi. Cardinals (16) vs. Detroit (13), Sept. 15, 1940
28 Philadelphia (14) vs. Washington (14), Nov. 5, 1939

Fewest Punts, Both Teams, Game
0 Buffalo vs. San Francisco, Sept. 13, 1992
1 Baltimore (0) vs. Cleveland (1), Nov. 1, 1959
   Dall. Cowboys (0) vs. Cleveland (1), Dec. 3, 1961
   Chicago (0) vs. Detroit (1), Oct. 1, 1972
   San Francisco (0) vs. N.Y. Giants (1), Oct. 15, 1972
   Green Bay (0) vs. Buffalo (1), Dec. 5, 1982
   Miami (0) vs. Buffalo (1), Oct. 12, 1986
   Green Bay (0) vs. Chicago (1), Dec. 17, 1989
   Oakland (0) vs. Seattle (1), Dec. 5, 1999
   Tampa Bay (0) vs. Minnesota (1), Oct. 29, 2000
   New Orleans (0) vs. San Francisco (1), Oct. 20, 2002
2 In many games

AVERAGE YARDAGE

Highest Average Distance, Punting, Season
47.6 Detroit, 1961 (56-2,664)
47.2 Tennessee, 1998 (69-3,258)
47.0 Carolina, 2001 (94-4,419)

Lowest Average Distance, Punting, Season
32.7 Card-Pitt, 1944 (60-1,964)
33.8 Cincinnati, 1986 (59-1,996)
33.9 Detroit, 1969 (74-2,510)

PUNT RETURNS

Most Seasons Leading League (Average Return)
9 Detroit, 1943-45, 1951-52, 1962, 1966, 1969, 1991
7 Chi. Cardinals/St. Louis, 1948-49, 1955-56, 1959, 1986-87
6 Green Bay, 1950, 1953-54, 1961, 1972, 1996
   Dallas/Kansas City, 1960, 1968, 1970, 1979-1980, 2003

Most Consecutive Seasons Leading League (Average Return)
3 Detroit, 1943-45
2 By many teams

Most Punt Returns, Season
71 Pittsburgh, 1976
    Tampa Bay, 1979
    L.A. Raiders, 1985
67 Pittsburgh, 1974
    Los Angeles, 1978
    L.A. Raiders, 1984
65 San Francisco, 1976

Fewest Punt Returns, Season
12 Baltimore, 1981
    San Diego, 1982
14 Los Angeles, 1961
    Philadelphia, 1962
    Baltimore, 1982
15 Houston, 1960
    Washington, 1960
    Oakland, 1961
    N.Y. Giants, 1969
    Philadelphia, 1973
    Kansas City, 1982

Most Punt Returns, Game
12 Philadelphia vs. Cleveland, Dec. 3, 1950
11 Chi. Bears vs. Chi. Cardinals, Oct. 8, 1950
    Washington vs. Tampa Bay, Oct. 9, 1977
10 Philadelphia vs. N.Y. Giants, Nov. 26, 1950
    Philadelphia vs. Tampa Bay, Sept. 18, 1977
    Pittsburgh vs. Buffalo, Dec. 16, 1979
    Washington vs. New Orleans, Dec. 26, 1982
    Philadelphia vs. Seattle, Dec. 13, 1992 (OT)
    New England vs. Pittsburgh, Dec. 5, 1993

Most Punt Returns, Both Teams, Game
17 Philadelphia (12) vs. Cleveland (5), Dec. 3, 1950
16 N.Y. Giants (9) vs. Philadelphia (7), Dec. 12, 1954
    Washington (11) vs. Tampa Bay (5), Oct. 9, 1977
    Oakland (8) vs. San Diego (8), Oct. 11, 1998
15 Detroit (8) vs. Cleveland (7), Sept. 27, 1942
    Los Angeles (8) vs. Baltimore (7), Nov. 27, 1966
    Pittsburgh (8) vs. Houston (7), Dec. 1, 1974
    Philadelphia (10) vs. Tampa Bay (5), Sept. 18, 1977
    Baltimore (9) vs. Kansas City (6), Sept. 2, 1979
    Washington (10) vs. New Orleans (5), Dec. 26, 1982
    L.A. Raiders (8) vs. Cleveland (7), Nov. 16, 1986

FAIR CATCHES

Most Fair Catches, Season
34 Baltimore, 1971
33 Philadelphia, 2000
32 San Diego, 1969
    Oakland, 2001

Fewest Fair Catches, Season
0 San Diego, 1975
   New England, 1976
   Tampa Bay, 1976
   Pittsburgh, 1977
   Dallas, 1982
1 Cleveland, 1974
   San Francisco, 1975
   Kansas City, 1976

      St. Louis, 1976
      San Diego, 1976
      L.A. Rams, 1982
      St. Louis, 1982
      Tampa Bay, 1982
      Arizona, 2001
  2 By many teams

Most Fair Catches, Game
  7 Minnesota vs. Dallas, Sept. 25, 1966
      N.Y. Jets vs. Miami, Nov. 20, 1966
      Detroit vs. Chicago, Nov. 21, 1976
      Philadelphia vs. Buffalo, Dec. 27, 1987
  6 By many teams

YARDS GAINED

Most Yards, Punt Returns, Season
  875 Green Bay, 1996
  785 L.A. Raiders, 1985
  781 Chi. Bears, 1948

Fewest Yards, Punt Returns, Season
  27 St. Louis, 1965
  35 N.Y. Giants, 1965
  37 New England, 1972

Most Yards, Punt Returns, Game
  231 Detroit vs. San Francisco, Oct. 6, 1963
  225 Oakland vs. Buffalo, Sept. 15, 1968
  219 Los Angeles vs. Atlanta, Oct. 11, 1981

Fewest Yards, Punt Returns, Game
  -28 Washington vs. Dallas, Dec. 11, 1966
  -23 N.Y. Giants vs. Buffalo, Oct. 20, 1975
      Pittsburgh vs. Houston, Sept. 20, 1970
  -20 New Orleans vs. Pittsburgh, Oct. 20, 1968

Most Yards, Punt Returns, Both Teams, Game
  282 Los Angeles (219) vs. Atlanta (63), Oct. 11, 1981
  245 Detroit (231) vs. San Francisco (14), Oct. 6, 1963
  244 Oakland (225) vs. Buffalo (19), Sept. 15, 1968

Fewest Yards, Punt Returns, Both Teams, Game
  -18 Buffalo (-18) vs. Pittsburgh (0), Oct. 29, 1972
  -14 Miami (-14) vs. Boston (0), Nov. 30, 1969
      Tennessee (-14) vs. New Orleans (0),
        Sept. 21, 2003
  -13 N.Y. Giants (-13) vs. Cleveland (0), Nov. 14, 1965

AVERAGE YARDS RETURNING PUNTS

Highest Average, Punt Returns, Season
  20.2 Chi. Bears, 1941 (27-546)
  19.1 Chi. Cardinals, 1948 (35-669)
  18.2 Chi. Cardinals, 1949 (30-546)

Lowest Average, Punt Returns, Season
  1.2 St. Louis, 1965 (23-27)
  1.5 N.Y. Giants, 1965 (24-35)
  1.7 Washington, 1970 (27-45)

TOUCHDOWNS RETURNING PUNTS

Most Touchdowns, Punt Returns, Season
  5 Chi. Cardinals, 1959
  4 Chi. Cardinals, 1948
    Detroit, 1951
    N.Y. Giants, 1951
    Denver, 1976
  3 Washington, 1941
    Detroit, 1952
    Pittsburgh, 1952
    Houston, 1975
    Los Angeles, 1981
    Cleveland, 1993
    Green Bay, 1996
    Denver, 1997
    San Diego, 1997

Most Touchdowns, Punt Returns, Game
  2 Detroit vs. Los Angeles, Oct. 14, 1951
    Detroit vs. Green Bay, Nov. 22, 1951
    Chi. Cardinals vs. Pittsburgh, Nov. 1, 1959
    Chi. Cardinals vs. N.Y. Giants, Nov. 22, 1959
    N.Y. Titans vs. Denver, Sept. 24, 1961
    Denver vs. Cleveland, Sept. 26, 1976
    Los Angeles vs. Atlanta, Oct. 11, 1981
    St. Louis vs. Tampa Bay, Dec. 21, 1986
    L.A. Rams vs. Atlanta, Dec. 27, 1992
    Cleveland vs. Pittsburgh, Oct. 24, 1993
    San Diego vs. Cincinnati, Nov. 2, 1997
    Denver vs. Carolina, Nov. 9, 1997
    Baltimore vs. Seattle, Dec. 7, 1997
    Baltimore vs. N.Y. Jets, Dec. 24, 2000
    Oakland vs. Tennessee, Sept. 29, 2002
    Carolina vs. Cincinnati, Dec. 8, 2002
    Detroit at Jacksonville, Nov. 14, 2004 (OT)

Most Touchdowns, Punt Returns, Both Teams, Game
  2 Philadelphia (1) vs. Washington (1), Nov. 9, 1952
    Kansas City (1) vs. Buffalo (1), Sept. 11, 1966
    Baltimore (1) vs. New England (1), Nov. 18, 1979
    L.A. Raiders (1) vs. Philadelphia (1),
      Nov. 30, 1986 (OT)
    Cincinnati (1) vs. Green Bay (1), Sept. 20, 1992
    Oakland (1) vs. Seattle (1), Nov. 15, 1998
    Atlanta (1) vs. Tennessee (1), Nov. 23, 2003
(Also see previous record)

KICKOFF RETURNS

Most Seasons Leading League (Average Return)
  8 Washington, 1942, 1947, 1962-63, 1973-74, 1981,
    1995
  6 Chicago Bears, 1943, 1948, 1958, 1966, 1972, 1985
    N.Y. Giants, 1944, 1946, 1949, 1951, 1953, 2004
  5 Green Bay, 1954, 1964, 1967, 1993, 1998

Most Consecutive Seasons Leading League (Average Return)
  3 Denver, 1965-67
  2 By many teams

Most Kickoff Returns, Season
  89 Cleveland, 1999
  88 New Orleans, 1980
  87 Atlanta, 1996
      New Orleans, 2001

Fewest Kickoff Returns, Season
  17 N.Y. Giants, 1944
  20 N.Y. Giants, 1941, 1943
      Chi. Bears, 1942
  23 Washington, 1942

Most Kickoff Returns, Game
  12 N.Y. Giants vs. Washington, Nov. 27, 1966
  10 By many teams

Most Kickoff Returns, Both Teams, Game
  19 N.Y. Giants (12) vs. Washington (7), Nov. 27, 1966
    Cleveland (10) vs. Cincinnati (9), Nov. 28, 2004
  18 Houston (10) vs. Oakland (8), Dec. 22, 1963
  17 Washington (9) vs. Green Bay (8), Oct. 17, 1983
    San Diego (9) vs. Pittsburgh (8), Dec. 8, 1985
    Detroit (9) vs. Green Bay (8), Nov. 27, 1986
    L.A. Raiders (9) vs. Seattle (8), Dec. 18, 1988
    Oakland (10) vs. Seattle (7), Oct. 26, 1997
    Buffalo (9) vs. Minnesota (8), Sept. 15, 2002 (OT)

YARDS GAINED

Most Yards, Kickoff Returns, Season
  2,296 Arizona, 2000
  2,039 Detroit, 2002
  2,027 New Orleans, 2001

Fewest Yards, Kickoff Returns, Season
  282 N.Y. Giants, 1940

381   Green Bay, 1940
424   Chicago, 1963

Most Yards, Kickoff Returns, Game
367   Baltimore vs. Minnesota, Dec. 13, 1998
362   Detroit vs. Los Angeles, Oct. 29, 1950
304   Chi. Bears vs. Green Bay, Nov. 9, 1952
     New Orleans vs. L.A. Rams, Oct. 23, 1994

Most Yards, Kickoff Returns, Both Teams, Game
560   Detroit (362) vs. Los Angeles (198), Oct. 29, 1950
511   Baltimore (367) vs. Minnesota (144), Dec. 13, 1998
501   New Orleans (304) vs. L.A. Rams (197),
     Oct. 23, 1994

AVERAGE YARDAGE

Highest Average, Kickoff Returns, Season
29.4   Chicago, 1972 (52-1,528)
28.9   Pittsburgh, 1952 (39-1,128)
28.2   Washington, 1962 (61-1,720)

Lowest Average, Kickoff Returns, Season
14.7   N.Y. Jets, 1993 (46-675)
15.8   N.Y. Giants, 1993 (32-507)
15.9   Tampa Bay, 1993 (58-922)

TOUCHDOWNS

Most Touchdowns, Kickoff Returns, Season
4   Green Bay, 1967
  Chicago, 1970
  Detroit, 1994
3   Los Angeles, 1950
  Chi. Cardinals, 1954
  San Francisco, 1963
  Denver, 1966
  Chicago, 1967
  New England, 1977
  L.A. Rams, 1985
  Atlanta, 2000
  Buffalo, 2004
2   By many teams

Most Touchdowns, Kickoff Returns, Game
2   Chi. Bears vs. Green Bay, Sept. 22, 1940
  Chi. Bears vs. Green Bay, Nov. 9, 1952
  Philadelphia vs. Dallas, Nov. 6, 1966
  Green Bay vs. Cleveland, Nov. 12, 1967
  L.A. Rams vs. Green Bay, Nov. 24, 1985
  New Orleans vs. L.A. Rams, Oct. 23, 1994
  Baltimore vs. Minnesota, Dec. 13, 1998
  N.Y. Jets vs. Buffalo, Sept. 8, 2002 (OT)

Most Touchdowns, Kickoff Returns, Both Teams, Game
3   Baltimore (2) vs. Minnesota (1), Dec. 13, 1998
2   In many games

FUMBLES

Most Fumbles, Season
56   Chi. Bears, 1938
   San Francisco, 1978
54   Philadelphia, 1946
51   New England, 1973

Fewest Fumbles, Season
7   Kansas City, 2002
8   Cleveland, 1959
10   Indianapolis, 1998
   Minnesota, 1998

Most Fumbles, Game
10   Phil-Pitt vs. N.Y. Giants, Oct. 9, 1943
   Detroit vs. Minnesota, Nov. 12, 1967
   Kansas City vs. Houston, Oct. 12, 1969
   San Francisco vs. Detroit, Dec. 17, 1978
9   Philadelphia vs. Green Bay, Oct. 13, 1946
  Boston at Oakland, Dec. 16, 1962
  Kansas City vs. San Diego, Nov. 15, 1964

N.Y. Giants vs. Buffalo, Oct. 20, 1975
St. Louis vs. Washington, Oct. 25, 1976
San Diego vs. Green Bay, Sept. 24, 1978
Pittsburgh vs. Cincinnati, Oct. 14, 1979
Cleveland vs. Seattle, Dec. 20, 1981
Cleveland vs. Pittsburgh, Dec. 23, 1990
Oakland vs. Seattle, Dec. 22, 1996
8   By many teams

Most Fumbles, Both Teams, Game
14   Washington (8) vs. Pittsburgh (6), Nov. 14, 1937
   Chi. Bears (7) vs. Cleveland (7), Nov. 24, 1940
   St. Louis (8) vs. N.Y. Giants (6), Sept. 17, 1961
   Kansas City (10) vs. Houston (4), Oct. 12, 1969
13   Washington (8) vs. Pittsburgh (5), Nov. 14, 1937
   Philadelphia (7) vs. Boston (6), Dec. 8, 1946
   N.Y. Giants (7) vs. Washington (6), Nov. 5, 1950
   Kansas City (9) vs. San Diego (4), Nov. 15, 1964
   Buffalo (7) vs. Denver (6), Dec. 13, 1964
   N.Y. Jets (7) vs. Houston (6), Sept. 12, 1965
   Cleveland (7) vs. New Orleans (6), Dec. 12, 1971
   Houston (8) vs. Pittsburgh (5), Dec. 9, 1973
   St. Louis (9) vs. Washington (4), Oct. 25, 1976
   Cleveland (9) vs. Seattle (4), Dec. 20, 1981
   Green Bay (7) vs. Detroit (6), Oct. 6, 1985
12   In many games

FUMBLES LOST

Most Fumbles Lost, Season
36   Chi. Cardinals, 1959
31   Green Bay, 1952
29   Chi. Cardinals, 1946
   Pittsburgh, 1950
   Cleveland, 1978

Fewest Fumbles Lost, Season
2   Kansas City, 2002
3   Philadelphia, 1938
  Minnesota, 1980
4   San Francisco, 1960
  Kansas City, 1982
  Minnesota, 1998
  Detroit, 2003

Most Fumbles Lost, Game
8   St. Louis vs. Washington, Oct. 25, 1976
  Cleveland vs. Pittsburgh, Dec. 23, 1990
7   Cincinnati vs. Buffalo, Nov. 30, 1969
  Pittsburgh vs. Cincinnati, Oct. 14, 1979
  Cleveland vs. Seattle, Dec. 20, 1981
6   By many teams

FUMBLES RECOVERED

Most Fumbles Recovered, Season, Own and Opponents'
58   Minnesota, 1963 (27 own, 31 opp)
51   Chi. Bears, 1938 (37 own, 14 opp)
   San Francisco, 1978 (24 own, 27 opp)
50   Philadelphia, 1987 (23 own, 27 opp)

Fewest Fumbles Recovered, Season, Own and Opponents'
9   San Francisco, 1982 (5 own, 4 opp)
11   Cincinnati, 1982 (5 own, 6 opp)
12   Washington, 1994 (6 own, 6 opp)
   Arizona, 1997 (7 own, 5 opp)

Most Fumbles Recovered, Game, Own and Opponents'
10   Denver vs. Buffalo, Dec. 13, 1964 (5 own, 5 opp)
   Pittsburgh vs. Houston, Dec. 9, 1973 (5 own, 5 opp)
   Washington vs. St. Louis, Oct. 25, 1976
   (2 own, 8 opp)
9   St. Louis vs. N.Y. Giants, Sept. 17, 1961
  (6 own, 3 opp)
  Houston vs. Cincinnati, Oct. 27, 1974 (4 own, 5 opp)
  Kansas City vs. Dallas, Nov. 10, 1975 (4 own, 5 opp)
  Green Bay vs. Detroit, Oct. 6, 1985 (5 own, 4 opp)

Pittsburgh vs. Cleveland, Dec. 23, 1990
(1 own, 8 opp)
8 By many teams

Most Own Fumbles Recovered, Season
37 Chi. Bears, 1938
28 Pittsburgh, 1987
27 Philadelphia, 1946
Minnesota, 1963

Fewest Own Fumbles Recovered, Season
2 Washington, 1958
Miami, 2000
3 Detroit, 1956
Cleveland, 1959
Houston, 1982
4 By many teams

Most Opponents' Fumbles Recovered, Season
31 Minnesota, 1963
29 Cleveland, 1951
28 Green Bay, 1946
Houston, 1977
Seattle, 1983

Fewest Opponents' Fumbles Recovered, Season
3 Los Angeles, 1974
Green Bay, 1995
4 Philadelphia, 1944
San Francisco, 1982
5 Baltimore, 1982
Arizona, 1997
Baltimore, 1998
Chicago, 2003

Most Opponents' Fumbles Recovered, Game
8 Washington vs. St. Louis, Oct. 25, 1976
Pittsburgh vs. Cleveland, Dec. 23, 1990
7 Buffalo vs. Cincinnati, Nov. 30, 1969
Cincinnati vs. Pittsburgh, Oct. 14, 1979
Seattle vs. Cleveland, Dec. 20, 1981
6 By many teams

TOUCHDOWNS

Most Touchdowns, Fumbles Recovered, Season, Own and Opponents'
5 Chi. Bears, 1942 (1 own, 4 opp)
Los Angeles, 1952 (1 own, 4 opp)
San Francisco, 1965 (1 own, 4 opp)
Oakland, 1978 (2 own, 3 opp)
4 Chi. Bears, 1948 (1 own, 3 opp)
Boston, 1948 (4 opp)
Denver, 1979 (1 own, 3 opp)
Atlanta, 1981 (1 own, 3 opp)
Denver, 1984 (4 opp)
St. Louis, 1987 (4 opp)
Minnesota, 1989 (4 opp)
Atlanta, 1991 (4 opp)
Philadelphia, 1995 (4 opp)
Atlanta, 1998 (4 opp)
New Orleans, 1998 (4 opp)
Kansas City, 1999 (4 opp)
3 By many teams

Most Touchdowns, Own Fumbles Recovered, Season
2 Chi. Bears, 1953
New England, 1973
Buffalo, 1974
Denver, 1975
Oakland, 1978
Green Bay, 1982
New Orleans, 1983
Cleveland, 1986
Green Bay, 1989
Miami, 1996
Buffalo, 2000

Most Touchdowns, Opponents' Fumbles Recovered, Season
4 Detroit, 1937
Chi. Bears, 1942
Boston, 1948
Los Angeles, 1952
San Francisco, 1965
Denver, 1984
St. Louis, 1987
Minnesota, 1989
Atlanta, 1991
Philadelphia, 1995
Atlanta, 1998
New Orleans, 1998
Kansas City, 1999
3 By many teams

Most Touchdowns, Fumbles Recovered, Game, Own and Opponents'
2 By many teams

Most Touchdowns, Fumbles Recovered, Game, Both Teams, Own and Opponents'
3 Detroit (2) vs. Minnesota (1), Dec. 9, 1962
(2 own, 1 opp)
Green Bay (2) vs. Dallas (1), Nov. 29, 1964 (3 opp)
Oakland (2) vs. Buffalo (1), Dec. 24, 1967 (3 opp)
Oakland (2) vs. Philadelphia (1), Sept. 24, 1995
(3 opp)
Tennessee (2) vs. Pittsburgh (1), Jan. 2, 2000
(3 opp)

Most Touchdowns, Own Fumbles Recovered, Game
2 Miami vs. New England, Sept.1, 1996

Most Touchdowns, Opponents' Fumbles Recovered, Game
2 Many times. Last time:
Green Bay vs. St. Louis, Nov. 29, 2004

Most Touchdowns, Opponents' Fumbles Recovered, Game, Both Teams
3 Green Bay (2) vs. Dallas (1), Nov. 29, 1964
Oakland (2) vs. Buffalo (1), Dec. 24, 1967
Oakland (2) vs. Philadelphia (1), Sept. 24, 1995
Tennessee (2) vs. Pittsburgh (1), Jan. 2, 2000

TURNOVERS
(Number of times losing the ball on interceptions and fumbles.)

Most Turnovers, Season
65 Denver, 1961
63 San Francisco, 1978
58 Chi. Bears, 1947
Pittsburgh, 1950
N.Y. Giants, 1983

Fewest Turnovers, Season
12 Kansas City, 1982
14 N.Y. Giants, 1943
Cleveland, 1959
N.Y. Giants, 1990
15 Dallas, 1998
Jacksonville, 2002
Kansas City, 2002

Most Turnovers, Game
12 Detroit vs. Chi. Bears, Nov. 22, 1942
Chi. Cardinals vs. Philadelphia, Sept. 24, 1950
Pittsburgh vs. Philadelphia, Dec. 12, 1965
11 San Diego vs. Green Bay, Sept. 24, 1978
10 Washington vs. N.Y. Giants, Dec. 4, 1938
Pittsburgh vs. Green Bay, Nov. 23, 1941
Detroit vs. Green Bay, Oct. 24, 1943
Chi. Cardinals vs. Green Bay, Nov. 10, 1946
Chi. Cardinals vs. N.Y. Giants, Nov. 2, 1952
Minnesota vs. Detroit, Dec. 9, 1962
Houston vs. Oakland, Sept. 7, 1963
Washington vs. N.Y. Giants, Dec. 8, 1963
Chicago vs. Detroit, Sept. 22, 1968

St. Louis vs. Washington, Oct. 25, 1976
N.Y. Jets vs. New England, Nov. 21, 1976
San Francisco vs. Dallas, Oct. 12, 1980
Cleveland vs. Seattle, Dec. 20, 1981
Detroit vs. Denver, Oct. 7, 1984

Most Turnovers, Both Teams, Game
17 Detroit (12) vs. Chi. Bears (5), Nov. 22, 1942
Boston (9) vs. Philadelphia (8), Dec. 8, 1946
16 Chi. Cardinals (12) vs. Philadelphia (4),
Sept. 24, 1950
Chi. Cardinals (8) vs. Chi. Bears (8), Dec. 7, 1958
Minnesota (10) vs. Detroit (6), Dec. 9, 1962
Houston (9) vs. Kansas City (7), Oct. 12, 1969
15 Philadelphia (8) vs. Chi. Cardinals (7), Oct. 3, 1954
Denver (9) vs. Houston (6), Dec. 2, 1962
Washington (10) vs. N.Y. Giants (5), Dec. 8, 1963
St. Louis (9) vs. Kansas City (6), Oct. 2, 1983

PENALTIES

Most Seasons Leading League, Fewest Penalties
13 Miami, 1968, 1976-1984, 1986, 1990-91
9 Pittsburgh, 1946-47, 1950-52, 1954, 1963, 1965,
1968
7 Boston/New England, 1962, 1964-65, 1973, 1987,
1989, 1993
Most Consecutive Seasons Leading League, Fewest Penalties
9 Miami, 1976-1984
3 Pittsburgh, 1950-52
2 By many teams
Most Seasons Leading League, Most Penalties
16 Chi. Bears, 1941-44, 1946-49, 1951, 1959-1961,
1963, 1965, 1968, 1976
14 Oakland/L.A. Raiders, 1963, 1966, 1968-69, 1975,
1982, 1984, 1991, 1993-96, 2003-04
7 L.A./St. Louis Rams, 1950, 1952, 1962, 1969,
1978, 1980, 1997
Most Consecutive Seasons Leading League, Most Penalties
4 Chi. Bears, 1941-44, 1946-49
Oakland/L.A. Raiders, 1993-96
3 Chi. Cardinals, 1954-56
Chi. Bears, 1959-1961
Fewest Penalties, Season
19 Detroit, 1937
21 Boston, 1935
24 Philadelphia, 1936
Most Penalties, Season
158 Kansas City, 1998
156 L.A. Raiders, 1994
Oakland, 1996
149 Houston, 1989
Fewest Penalties, Game
0 By many teams. Last time:
Washington vs. Carolina, Nov. 16, 2003
Most Penalties, Game
22 Brooklyn vs. Green Bay, Sept. 17, 1944
Chi. Bears vs. Philadelphia, Nov. 26, 1944
San Francisco vs. Buffalo, Oct. 4, 1998
21 Cleveland vs. Chi. Bears, Nov. 25, 1951
20 Tampa Bay vs. Seattle, Oct. 17, 1976
Oakland vs. Denver, Dec. 15, 1996
Fewest Penalties, Both Teams, Game
0 Brooklyn vs. Pittsburgh, Oct. 28, 1934
Brooklyn vs. Boston, Sept. 28, 1936
Cleveland vs. Chi. Bears, Oct. 9, 1938
Pittsburgh vs. Philadelphia, Nov. 10, 1940
Most Penalties, Both Teams, Game
37 Cleveland (21) vs. Chi. Bears (16), Nov. 25, 1951
35 Tampa Bay (20) vs. Seattle (15), Oct. 17, 1976
34 San Francisco (22) vs. Buffalo (12), Oct. 4, 1998

YARDS PENALIZED
Most Seasons Leading League, Fewest Yards Penalized
13 Miami, 1967-68, 1973, 1977-1984, 1990-91
10 Boston/Washington, 1935, 1953-54, 1956-58,
1970, 1985, 1995, 1997
7 Pittsburgh, 1946-47, 1950, 1952, 1962, 1965, 1968
Boston/New England, 1962, 1964-66, 1987, 1989,
1993
Most Consecutive Seasons Leading League, Fewest Yards Penalized
8 Miami, 1977-1984
3 Washington, 1956-58
Boston, 1964-66
2 By many teams
Most Seasons Leading League, Most Yards Penalized
15 Chi. Bears, 1935, 1937, 1939-1944, 1946-47,
1949, 1951, 1961-62, 1968
12 Oakland/L.A. Raiders, 1963-64, 1968-69, 1975,
1982, 1984, 1991, 1993-94, 1996, 2003
6 Buffalo, 1962, 1967, 1970, 1972, 1981, 1983
Houston, 1961, 1985-86, 1988-1990
Most Consecutive Seasons Leading League, Most Yards Penalized
6 Chi. Bears, 1939-1944
3 Houston, 1988-1990
2 By many teams
Fewest Yards Penalized, Season
139 Detroit, 1937
146 Philadelphia, 1937
159 Philadelphia, 1936
Most Yards Penalized, Season
1,304 Kansas City, 1998
1,274 Oakland, 1969
1,266 Oakland, 1996
Fewest Yards Penalized, Game
0 By many teams. Last time:
Washington vs. Carolina, Nov. 16, 2003
Most Yards Penalized, Game
212 Tennessee vs. Baltimore, Oct. 10, 1999
209 Cleveland vs. Chi. Bears, Nov. 25, 1951
191 Philadelphia vs. Seattle, Dec. 13, 1992 (OT)
Fewest Yards Penalized, Both Teams, Game
0 Brooklyn vs. Pittsburgh, Oct. 28, 1934
Brooklyn vs. Boston, Sept. 28, 1936
Cleveland vs. Chi. Bears, Oct. 9, 1938
Pittsburgh vs. Philadelphia, Nov. 10, 1940
Most Yards Penalized, Both Teams, Game
374 Cleveland (209) vs. Chi. Bears (165), Nov. 25, 1951
310 Tampa Bay (190) vs. Seattle (120), Oct. 17, 1976
309 Green Bay (184) vs. Boston (125), Oct. 21, 1945

DEFENSE

SCORING
Most Seasons Leading League, Fewest Points Allowed
11 N.Y. Giants, 1927, 1935, 1938-39, 1941, 1944,
1958-59, 1961, 1990, 1993
10 Chi. Bears, 1932, 1936-37, 1942, 1948, 1963,
1985-86, 1988, 2001
7 Cleveland, 1951, 1953-57, 1994
Green Bay, 1929, 1935, 1947, 1962, 1965-66, 1996
Most Consecutive Seasons Leading League, Fewest Points Allowed
5 Cleveland, 1953-57
3 Buffalo, 1964-66
Minnesota, 1969-1971
2 By many teams
Fewest Points Allowed, Season (Since 1932)
44 Chi. Bears, 1932
54 Brooklyn, 1933

59   Detroit, 1934
Most Points Allowed, Season
533   Baltimore, 1981
501   N.Y. Giants, 1966
487   New Orleans, 1980
Fewest Touchdowns Allowed, Season (Since 1932)
6   Chi. Bears, 1932
    Brooklyn, 1933
7   Detroit, 1934
8   Green Bay, 1932
Most Touchdowns Allowed, Season
68   Baltimore, 1981
66   N.Y. Giants, 1966
63   Baltimore, 1950

FIRST DOWNS
Fewest First Downs Allowed Season
77   Detroit, 1935
79   Boston, 1935
82   Washington, 1937
Most First Downs Allowed, Season
406   Baltimore, 1981
371   Seattle, 1981
368   Cleveland, 1999
Fewest First Downs Allowed, Rushing, Season
35   Chi. Bears, 1942
40   Green Bay, 1939
41   Brooklyn, 1944
Most First Downs Allowed, Rushing, Season
179   Detroit, 1985
178   New Orleans, 1980
175   Seattle, 1981
Fewest First Downs Allowed, Passing, Season
33   Chi. Bears, 1943
34   Pittsburgh, 1941
    Washington, 1943
35   Detroit, 1940
    Philadelphia, 1940, 1944
Most First Downs Allowed, Passing, Season
230   Atlanta, 1995
227   Kansas City, 2002
221   Detroit, 2002
Fewest First Downs Allowed, Penalty, Season
1   Boston, 1944
3   Philadelphia, 1940
    Pittsburgh, 1945
    Washington, 1957
4   Cleveland, 1940
    Green Bay, 1943
    N.Y. Giants, 1943
Most First Downs Allowed, Penalty, Season
56   Kansas City, 1998
48   Houston, 1985
46   Houston, 1986

NET YARDS ALLOWED RUSHING AND PASSING
Most Seasons Leading League, Fewest Yards Allowed
8   Chi. Bears, 1942-43, 1948, 1958, 1963, 1984-86
6   N.Y. Giants, 1938, 1940-41, 1951, 1956, 1959
    Philadelphia, 1944-45, 1949, 1953, 1981, 1991
    Minnesota, 1969-1970, 1975, 1988-89, 1993
    Pittsburgh, 1957, 1974, 1976, 1990, 2001, 2004
5   Boston/Washington, 1935-37, 1939, 1946
**Most Consecutive Seasons Leading League,
Fewest Yards Allowed**
3   Boston/Washington, 1935-37
    Chicago, 1984-86
2   By many teams
Fewest Yards Allowed, Season
1,539   Chi. Cardinals, 1934

1,703   Chi. Bears, 1942
1,789   Brooklyn, 1933
Most Yards Allowed, Season
6,793   Baltimore, 1981
6,403   Green Bay, 1983
6,391   Seattle, 2000

RUSHING
Most Seasons Leading League, Fewest Yards Allowed
10   Chi. Bears, 1937, 1939, 1942, 1946, 1949, 1963,
     1984-85, 1987-88
7   Detroit, 1938, 1950, 1952, 1962, 1970, 1980-81
    Philadelphia, 1944-45, 1947-48, 1953, 1990-91
    Dallas, 1966-69, 1972, 1978, 1992
    Pittsburgh, 1961, 1976, 1982, 1997, 2001-02, 2004
5   N.Y. Giants, 1940, 1951, 1956, 1959, 1986
    L.A./St. Louis Rams, 1964-65, 1973-74, 1999
Most Consecutive Seasons Leading League, Fewest Yards Allowed
4   Dallas, 1966-69
2   By many teams
Fewest Yards Allowed, Rushing, Season
519   Chi. Bears, 1942
558   Philadelphia, 1944
762   Pittsburgh, 1982
Most Yards Allowed, Rushing, Season
3,228   Buffalo, 1978
3,106   New Orleans, 1980
3,010   Baltimore, 1978
Fewest Touchdowns Allowed, Rushing, Season
2   Detroit, 1934
    N.Y. Giants, 1944
    Dallas, 1968
    Minnesota, 1971
3   By many teams
Most Touchdowns Allowed, Rushing, Season
36   Oakland, 1961
31   N.Y. Giants, 1980
    Tampa Bay, 1986
30   Baltimore, 1981

PASSING
Most Seasons Leading League, Fewest Yards Allowed
9   Green Bay, 1947-48, 1962, 1964-68, 1996
7   Washington, 1939, 1942, 1945, 1952-53, 1980,
    1985
    Philadelphia 1934, 1936, 1940, 1949, 1981, 1991,
    1998
6   Chi. Bears, 1938, 1943-44, 1958, 1960, 1963
    Minnesota, 1969-1970, 1972, 1975-76, 1989
    Pittsburgh, 1941, 1946, 1951, 1955, 1974, 1990
**Most Consecutive Seasons Leading League, Fewest Yards
Allowed**
5   Green Bay, 1964-68
2   By many teams
Fewest Yards Allowed, Passing, Season
545   Philadelphia, 1934
558   Portsmouth, 1933
585   Chi. Cardinals, 1934
Most Yards Allowed, Passing, Season
4,541   Atlanta, 1995
4,389   N.Y. Jets, 1986
4,311   San Diego, 1981
Fewest Touchdowns Allowed, Passing, Season
1   Portsmouth, 1932
    Philadelphia, 1934
2   Brooklyn, 1933
    Chi. Bears, 1934
3   Chi. Bears, 1932
    Green Bay, 1932
    Green Bay, 1934

Chi. Bears, 1936
New York, 1939
New York, 1944

Most Touchdowns Allowed, Passing, Season
40   Denver, 1963
38   St. Louis, 1969
37   Washington, 1961
     Baltimore, 1981

SACKS
Most Seasons Leading League
5   Oakland/L.A. Raiders, 1966-68, 1982, 1986
4   New England/Boston, 1961, 1963, 1977, 1979
    Dallas, 1966, 1968-69, 1978
    Dallas/Kansas City, 1960, 1965, 1969, 1990
    L.A./St. Louis Rams, 1968, 1970, 1988, 1999
3   San Francisco, 1967, 1972, 1976
    N.Y. Giants, 1963, 1985, 1998
    New Orleans, 1992, 1997, 2000
    Pittsburgh, 1974, 1994, 2001

Most Consecutive Seasons Leading League
3   Oakland, 1966-68
2   Dallas, 1968-69

Most Sacks, Season
72   Chicago, 1984
71   Minnesota, 1989
70   Chicago, 1987

Fewest Sacks, Season
11   Baltimore, 1982
12   Buffalo, 1982
13   Baltimore, 1981

Most Sacks, Game
12   Dallas vs. Pittsburgh, Nov. 20, 1966
     St. Louis vs. Baltimore, Oct. 26, 1980
     Chicago vs. Detroit, Dec. 16, 1984
     Dallas vs. Houston, Sept. 29, 1985
11   N.Y. Giants vs. St. Louis, Nov. 1, 1964
     Baltimore vs. Los Angeles, Nov. 22, 1964
     Buffalo vs. Denver, Dec. 13, 1964
     Detroit vs. Green Bay, Nov. 7, 1965
     Oakland vs. Buffalo, Oct. 15, 1967
     Oakland vs. Denver, Nov. 5, 1967
     St. Louis vs. Atlanta, Nov. 24, 1968
     Dallas vs. Detroit, Oct. 6, 1975
     St. Louis vs. Philadelphia, Dec. 18, 1983
     Kansas City vs. Cleveland, Sept. 30, 1984
     Chicago vs. Minnesota, Oct. 28, 1984
     Cleveland vs. Atlanta, Nov. 18, 1984
     Detroit vs. Philadelphia, Nov. 16, 1986
     San Diego vs. Dallas, Nov. 16, 1986
     L.A. Raiders vs. Philadelphia, Nov. 30, 1986 (OT)
     Seattle vs. L.A. Raiders, Dec. 8, 1986
     Chicago vs. Philadelphia, Oct. 4, 1987
     Dallas vs. N.Y. Jets, Oct. 4, 1987
     Philadelphia vs. Dallas, Sept. 15, 1991
     Indianapolis vs. Cleveland, Sept. 6, 1992
10   By many teams

Most Opponents Yards Lost Attempting to Pass, Season
666   Oakland, 1967
583   Chicago, 1984
573   San Francisco, 1976

Fewest Opponents Yards Lost Attempting to Pass, Season
72   Jacksonville, 1995
75   Green Bay, 1956
77   N.Y. Bulldogs, 1949

INTERCEPTIONS BY
Most Seasons Leading League
10   N.Y. Giants, 1933, 1937-39, 1944, 1948, 1951,
     1954, 1961, 1997

8   Green Bay, 1940, 1942-43, 1947, 1955, 1957,
    1962, 1965
    Chi. Bears, 1935-36, 1941-42, 1946, 1963, 1985,
    1990
6   Kansas City, 1966-1970, 1974

Most Consecutive Seasons Leading League
5   Kansas City, 1966-1970
3   N.Y. Giants, 1937-39
2   By many teams

Most Passes Intercepted By, Season
49   San Diego, 1961
42   Green Bay, 1943
41   N.Y. Giants, 1951

Fewest Passes Intercepted By, Season
3   Houston, 1982
5   Baltimore, 1982
6   Houston, 1972
    St. Louis, 1982
    Atlanta, 1996
    St. Louis, 2004

Most Passes Intercepted By, Game
9   Green Bay vs. Detroit, Oct. 24, 1943
    Philadelphia vs. Pittsburgh, Dec. 12, 1965
8   N.Y. Giants vs. Green Bay, Nov. 21, 1948
    Philadelphia vs. Chi. Cardinals, Sept. 24, 1950
    N.Y. Giants vs. N.Y. Yanks, Dec. 16, 1951
    Houston vs. Denver, Dec. 2, 1962
    Detroit vs. Chicago, Sept. 22, 1968
    N.Y. Jets vs. Baltimore, Sept. 23, 1973
7   By many teams. Last time:
    Cleveland vs. Detroit, Sept. 23, 2001

Most Consecutive Games, One or More Interceptions By
46   L.A. Chargers/San Diego, 1960-63
37   Detroit, 1960-63
36   Boston, 1944-47

Most Yards Returning Interceptions, Season
929   San Diego, 1961
712   Los Angeles, 1952
700   Baltimore, 2004

Fewest Yards Returning Interceptions, Season
5   Los Angeles, 1959
37   Dallas, 1989
39   Denver, 2003

Most Yards Returning Interceptions, Game
325   Seattle vs. Kansas City, Nov. 4, 1984
314   Los Angeles vs. San Francisco, Oct. 18, 1964
245   Houston vs. N.Y. Jets, Oct. 15, 1967

Most Yards Returning Interceptions, Both Teams, Game
356   Seattle (325) vs. Kansas City (31), Nov. 4, 1984
338   Los Angeles (314) vs. San Francisco (24),
      Oct. 18, 1964
308   Dallas (182) vs. Los Angeles (126), Nov. 2, 1952

Most Touchdowns, Returning Interceptions, Season
9   San Diego, 1961
8   Seattle, 1998
7   Seattle, 1984
    St. Louis, 1999

Most Touchdowns Returning Interceptions, Game
4   Seattle vs. Kansas City, Nov. 4, 1984
3   Baltimore vs. Green Bay, Nov. 5, 1950
    Cleveland vs. Chicago, Dec. 11, 1960
    Philadelphia vs. Pittsburgh, Dec. 12, 1965
    Baltimore vs. Pittsburgh, Sept. 29, 1968
    Buffalo vs. N.Y. Jets, Sept. 29, 1968
    Houston vs. San Diego, Dec. 19, 1971
    Cincinnati vs. Houston, Dec. 17, 1972
    Tampa Bay vs. New Orleans, Dec. 11, 1977
2   By many teams

Most Touchdown Returning Interceptions, Both Teams, Game
4   Philadelphia (3) vs. Pittsburgh (1), Dec. 12, 1965

         Seattle (4) vs. Kansas City (0), Nov. 4, 1984
  3 Los Angeles (2) vs. Detroit (1), Nov. 1, 1953
       Cleveland (2) vs. N.Y. Giants (1), Dec. 18, 1960
       Pittsburgh (2) vs. Cincinnati (1), Oct. 10, 1983
       Kansas City (2) vs. San Diego (1), Oct. 19, 1986
       (Also see previous record)

PUNT RETURNS
Fewest Opponents Punt Returns, Season
   7 Washington, 1962
      San Diego, 1982
  10 Buffalo, 1982
  11 Boston, 1962
Most Opponents Punt Returns, Season
  71 Tampa Bay, 1976, 1977
  69 N.Y. Giants, 1953
      Cleveland, 2000
  68 Cleveland, 1974
      Cleveland, 1999
Fewest Yards Allowed, Punt Returns, Season
  22 Green Bay, 1967
  30 Buffalo, 1982
  34 Washington, 1962
Most Yards Allowed, Punt Returns, Season
 932 Green Bay, 1949
 913 Boston, 1947
 906 New Orleans, 1974
Lowest Average Allowed, Punt Returns, Season
 1.20 Chi. Cardinals, 1954 (46-55)
 1.22 Cleveland, 1959 (32-39)
 1.55 Chi. Cardinals, 1953 (44-68)
Highest Average Allowed, Punt Returns, Season
 18.6 Green Bay, 1949 (50-932)
 18.0 Cleveland, 1977 (31-558)
 17.9 Boston, 1960 (20-357)
Most Touchdowns Allowed, Punt Returns, Season
  4 New York, 1959
     Atlanta, 1992
  3 Green Bay, 1949
     Chi. Cardinals, 1951
     L.A. Rams, 1951, 1994
     Washington, 1952
     Dallas, 1952
     Pittsburgh, 1959, 1993
     N.Y. Jets, 1968
     Cleveland, 1977
     Atlanta, 1986
     Tampa Bay, 1986
     Arizona, 2002
     Cincinnati, 2002
     Tennessee, 2002
  2 By many teams

KICKOFF RETURNS
Fewest Opponents Kickoff Returns, Season
  10 Brooklyn, 1943
  13 Denver, 1992
  15 Detroit, 1942
      Brooklyn, 1944
Most Opponents Kickoff Returns, Season
  93 Indianapolis, 2003
  92 Indianapolis, 2004
  91 Washington, 1983
Fewest Yards Allowed, Kickoff Returns, Season
 225 Brooklyn, 1943
 254 Denver, 1992
 293 Brooklyn, 1944
Most Yards Allowed, Kickoff Returns, Season
 2,194 St. Louis, 2001
 2,115 St. Louis, 1999

 2,045 Kansas City, 1966
Lowest Average Allowed, Kickoff Returns, Season
 14.3 Cleveland, 1980 (71-1,018)
 14.9 Indianapolis, 1993 (37-551)
 15.0 Seattle, 1982 (24-361)
Highest Average Allowed, Kickoff Returns, Season
 29.5 N.Y. Jets, 1972 (47-1,386)
 29.4 Los Angeles, 1950 (48-1,411)
 29.1 New England, 1971 (49-1,427)
Most Touchdowns Allowed, Kickoff Returns, Season
  4 Minnesota, 1998
  3 Minnesota, 1963, 1970
     Dallas, 1966
     Detroit, 1980
     Pittsburgh, 1986
     Buffalo, 1997
     Atlanta, 2000
  2 By many teams

FUMBLES
Fewest Opponents Fumbles, Season
  11 Cleveland, 1956
     Baltimore, 1982
     Tennessee, 1998
  12 Green Bay, 1995
     Cincinnati, 1998
  13 Los Angeles, 1956
     Chicago, 1960
     Cleveland, 1963
     Cleveland, 1965
     Detroit, 1967
     San Diego, 1969
Most Opponents Fumbles, Season
  50 Minnesota, 1963
     San Francisco, 1978
  48 N.Y. Giants, 1980
     N.Y. Jets, 1986
  47 N.Y. Giants, 1977
     Seattle, 1984

TURNOVERS
(Number of times losing the ball on interceptions and fumbles.)
Fewest Opponents Turnovers, Season
  11 Baltimore, 1982
  13 San Francisco, 1982
  15 St. Louis, 1982
     Green Bay, 2004
     St. Louis, 2004
Most Opponents Turnovers, Season
  66 San Diego, 1961
  63 Seattle, 1984
  61 Washington, 1983
Most Opponents Turnovers, Game
  12 Chi. Bears vs. Detroit, Nov. 22, 1942
     Philadelphia vs. Chi. Cardinals, Sept. 24, 1950
     Philadelphia vs. Pittsburgh, Dec. 12, 1965
  11 Green Bay vs. San Diego, Sept. 24, 1978
  10 By 14 teams

1,000 YARDS RUSHING IN A SEASON

Year	Player, Team	Att.	Yards	Avg.	Long	TD
2004	Curtis Martin, N.Y. Jets[10]	371	1,697	4.6	25	12
	Shaun Alexander, Seattle[4]	353	1,696	4.8	44	16
	Corey Dillon, New England[7]	345	1,635	4.7	44	12
	Edgerrin James, Indianapolis[4]	334	1,548	4.6	40	9
	Tiki Barber, N.Y. Giants[4]	322	1,518	4.7	72	13
	Rudi Johnson, Cincinnati	361	1,454	4.0	52	12
	LaDainian Tomlinson, San Diego[4]	339	1,335	3.9	42	17
	Clinton Portis, Washington[3]	343	1,315	3.8	64	5
	Reuben Droughns, Denver	275	1,240	4.5	51	6
	Fred Taylor, Jacksonville[5]	260	1,224	4.7	46	2
	Domanick Davis, Houston[2]	302	1,188	3.9	44	13
	Ahman Green, Green Bay[5]	259	1,163	4.5	90	7
	*Kevin Jones, Detroit	241	1,133	4.7	74	5
	Willis McGahee, Buffalo	284	1,128	4.0	41	13
	Warrick Dunn, Atlanta[3]	265	1,106	4.2	60	9
	Deuce McAllister, New Orleans[3]	269	1,074	4.0	71	9
	Chris Brown, Tennessee	220	1,067	4.9	52	6
	Jamal Lewis, Baltimore[4]	235	1,006	4.3	75	7
2003	Jamal Lewis, Baltimore[3]	387	2,066	5.3	82	14
	Ahman Green, Green Bay[4]	355	1,883	5.3	98	15
	LaDainian Tomlinson, San Diego[3]	313	1,645	5.3	73	13
	Deuce McAllister, New Orleans[2]	351	1,641	4.7	76	8
	Clinton Portis, Denver[2]	290	1,591	5.5	65	14
	Fred Taylor, Jacksonville[4]	345	1,572	4.6	62	6
	Stephen Davis, Carolina[4]	318	1,444	4.5	40	8
	Shaun Alexander, Seattle[3]	326	1,435	4.4	55	14
	Priest Holmes, Kansas City[4]	320	1,420	4.4	31	27
	Ricky Williams, Miami[4]	392	1,372	3.5	45	9
	Travis Henry, Buffalo[2]	331	1,356	4.1	64	10
	Curtis Martin, N.Y. Jets[9]	323	1,308	4.1	56	2
	Edgerrin James, Indianapolis[3]	310	1,259	4.1	43	11
	Tiki Barber, N.Y. Giants[3]	278	1,216	4.4	27	2
	*Domanick Davis, Houston	238	1,031	4.3	51	8
	Eddie George, Tennessee[7]	312	1,031	3.3	27	5
	Kevan Barlow, San Francisco	201	1,024	5.1	78	6
	Anthony Thomas, Chicago[2]	244	1,024	4.2	67	6
2002	Ricky Williams, Miami[3]	383	1,853	4.8	63	16
	LaDainian Tomlinson, San Diego[2]	372	1,683	4.5	76	14
	Priest Holmes, Kansas City[3]	313	1,615	5.2	56	21
	*Clinton Portis, Denver	273	1,508	5.5	59	15
	Travis Henry, Buffalo	325	1,438	4.4	34	13
	Deuce McAllister, New Orleans	325	1,388	4.3	62	13
	Tiki Barber, N.Y. Giants[2]	304	1,387	4.6	70	11
	Jamal Lewis, Baltimore[2]	308	1,327	4.3	75	6
	Fred Taylor, Jacksonville[3]	287	1,314	4.6	63	8
	Corey Dillon, Cincinnati[6]	314	1,311	4.2	67	7
	Michael Bennett, Minnesota	255	1,296	5.1	85	5
	Ahman Green, Green Bay[3]	286	1,240	4.3	43	7
	Shaun Alexander, Seattle[2]	295	1,175	4.0	58	16
	Eddie George, Tennessee[6]	343	1,165	3.4	35	12
	Curtis Martin, N.Y. Jets[8]	261	1,094	4.2	35	7
	Duce Staley, Philadelphia[3]	269	1,029	3.8	57	5
	James Stewart, Detroit[2]	231	1,021	4.4	56	4
2001	Priest Holmes, Kansas City[2]	327	1,555	4.8	41	8
	Curtis Martin, N.Y. Jets[7]	333	1,513	4.5	47	10
	Stephen Davis, Washington[3]	356	1,432	4.0	32	5
	Ahman Green, Green Bay[2]	304	1,387	4.6	83	9
	Marshall Faulk, St. Louis[7]	260	1,382	5.3	71	12
	Shaun Alexander, Seattle	309	1,318	4.3	88	14
	Corey Dillon, Cincinnati[5]	340	1,315	3.9	96	10
	Ricky Williams, New Orleans[2]	313	1,245	4.0	46	6
	*LaDainian Tomlinson, San Diego	339	1,236	3.6	54	10
	Garrison Hearst, San Francisco[4]	252	1,206	4.8	43	4
	*Anthony Thomas, Chicago	278	1,183	4.3	46	7
	Antowain Smith, New England[2]	287	1,157	4.0	44	12
	*Dominic Rhodes, Indianapolis	233	1,104	4.7	77	9
	Jerome Bettis, Pittsburgh[8]	225	1,072	4.8	48	4
	Emmitt Smith, Dallas[11]	261	1,021	3.9	44	3

Year	Player, Team	Att.	Yards	Avg.	Long	TD
2000	Edgerrin James, Indianapolis[2]	387	1,709	4.4	30	13
	Robert Smith, Minnesota[4]	295	1,521	5.2	72	7
	Eddie George, Tennessee[5]	403	1,509	3.7	35	14
	*Mike Anderson, Denver	297	1,487	5.0	80	15
	Corey Dillon, Cincinnati[4]	315	1,435	4.6	80	7
	Fred Taylor, Jacksonville[2]	292	1,399	4.8	71	12
	*Jamal Lewis, Baltimore	309	1,364	4.4	45	6
	Marshall Faulk, St. Louis[6]	253	1,359	5.4	36	18
	Jerome Bettis, Pittsburgh[7]	355	1,341	3.8	30	8
	Stephen Davis, Washington[2]	332	1,318	4.0	50	11
	Ricky Watters, Seattle[7]	278	1,242	4.5	55	7
	Curtis Martin, N.Y. Jets[6]	316	1,204	3.8	55	9
	Emmitt Smith, Dallas[10]	294	1,203	4.1	52	9
	James Stewart, Detroit	339	1,184	3.5	34	10
	Ahman Green, Green Bay	263	1,175	4.5	39	10
	Charlie Garner, San Francisco[2]	258	1,142	4.4	42	7
	Lamar Smith, Miami	309	1,139	3.7	68	14
	Warrick Dunn, Tampa Bay[2]	248	1,133	4.6	70	8
	James Allen, Chicago	290	1,120	3.9	29	2
	Tyrone Wheatley, Oakland	232	1,046	4.5	80	9
	Jamal Anderson, Atlanta[4]	282	1,024	3.6	42	6
	Tiki Barber, N.Y. Giants	213	1,006	4.7	78	8
	Ricky Williams, New Orleans	248	1,000	4.0	26	8
1999	*Edgerrin James, Indianapolis	369	1,553	4.2	72	13
	Curtis Martin, N.Y. Jets[5]	367	1,464	4.0	50	5
	Stephen Davis, Washington	290	1,405	4.8	76	17
	Emmitt Smith, Dallas[9]	329	1,397	4.3	63	11
	Marshall Faulk, St. Louis[5]	253	1,381	5.5	58	7
	Eddie George, Tennessee[4]	320	1,304	4.1	40	9
	Duce Staley, Philadelphia[2]	325	1,273	3.9	29	4
	Charlie Garner, San Francisco	241	1,229	5.1	53	4
	Ricky Watters, Seattle[6]	325	1,210	3.7	45	5
	Corey Dillon, Cincinnati[3]	263	1,200	4.6	50	5
	*Olandis Gary, Denver	276	1,159	4.2	71	7
	Jerome Bettis, Pittsburgh[6]	299	1,091	3.7	35	7
	Dorsey Levens, Green Bay[2]	279	1,034	3.7	36	9
	Robert Smith, Minnesota[3]	221	1,015	4.6	70	2
1998	Terrell Davis, Denver[4]	392	2,008	5.1	70	21
	Jamal Anderson, Atlanta[3]	410	1,846	4.5	48	14
	Garrison Hearst, San Francisco[3]	310	1,570	5.1	96	7
	Barry Sanders, Detroit[10]	343	1,491	4.3	73	4
	Emmitt Smith, Dallas[8]	319	1,332	4.2	32	13
	Marshall Faulk, Indianapolis[4]	324	1,319	4.1	68	6
	Eddie George, Tennessee[3]	348	1,294	3.7	37	5
	Curtis Martin, N.Y. Jets[4]	369	1,287	3.5	60	8
	Ricky Watters, Seattle[5]	319	1,239	3.9	39	9
	*Fred Taylor, Jacksonville	264	1,223	4.6	77	14
	Robert Smith, Minnesota[2]	249	1,187	4.8	74	6
	Jerome Bettis, Pittsburgh[5]	316	1,185	3.8	42	3
	Corey Dillon, Cincinnati[2]	262	1,130	4.3	66	4
	Antowain Smith, Buffalo	300	1,124	3.7	30	8
	*Robert Edwards, New England	291	1,115	3.8	53	9
	Duce Staley, Philadelphia	258	1,065	4.1	64	5
	Gary Brown, N.Y. Giants[2]	247	1,063	4.3	45	5
	Adrian Murrell, Arizona[3]	274	1,042	3.8	32	8
	Warrick Dunn, Tampa Bay	245	1,026	4.2	50	2
	Priest Holmes, Baltimore	233	1,008	4.3	56	7
1997	Barry Sanders, Detroit[9]	335	2,053	6.1	82	11
	Terrell Davis, Denver[3]	369	1,750	4.7	50	15
	Jerome Bettis, Pittsburgh[4]	375	1,665	4.4	34	7
	Dorsey Levens, Green Bay	329	1,435	4.4	52	7
	Eddie George, Tennessee[2]	357	1,399	3.9	30	6
	Napoleon Kaufman, Oakland	272	1,294	4.8	83	6
	Robert Smith, Minnesota	232	1,266	5.5	78	6
	Curtis Martin, New England[3]	274	1,160	4.2	70	4
	*Corey Dillon, Cincinnati	233	1,129	4.8	71	10
	Ricky Watters, Philadelphia[4]	285	1,110	3.9	28	7
	Adrian Murrell, N.Y. Jets[2]	300	1,086	3.6	43	7
	Emmitt Smith, Dallas[7]	261	1,074	4.1	44	4

Year	Player, Team	Att.	Yards	Avg.	Long	TD
	Marshall Faulk, Indianapolis[3]	264	1,054	4.0	45	7
	Raymont Harris, Chicago	275	1,033	3.8	68	10
	Garrison Hearst, San Francisco[2]	234	1,019	4.4	51	4
	Jamal Anderson, Atlanta[2]	290	1,002	3.5	39	7
1996	Barry Sanders, Detroit[8]	307	1,553	5.1	54	11
	Terrell Davis, Denver[2]	345	1,538	4.5	71	13
	Jerome Bettis, Pittsburgh[3]	320	1,431	4.5	50	11
	Ricky Watters, Philadelphia[3]	353	1,411	4.0	56	13
	*Eddie George, Houston	335	1,368	4.1	76	8
	Terry Allen, Washington[4]	347	1,353	3.9	49	21
	Adrian Murrell, N.Y. Jets	301	1,249	4.1	78	6
	Emmitt Smith, Dallas[6]	327	1,204	3.7	42	12
	Curtis Martin, New England[2]	316	1,152	3.6	57	14
	Anthony Johnson, Carolina	300	1,120	3.7	29	6
	*Karim Abdul-Jabbar, Miami	307	1,116	3.6	29	11
	Jamal Anderson, Atlanta	232	1,055	4.5	32	5
	Thurman Thomas, Buffalo[8]	281	1,033	3.7	36	8
1995	Emmitt Smith, Dallas[5]	377	1,773	4.7	60	25
	Barry Sanders, Detroit[7]	314	1,500	4.8	75	11
	James Brooks, Cincinnati[2]	221	1,239	5.6	65	7
	*Bobby Humphrey, Denver	294	1,151	3.9	40	7
	Greg Bell, L.A. Rams[3]	272	1,137	4.2	47	15
	Roger Craig, San Francisco[3]	271	1,054	3.9	27	6
	Ottis Anderson, N.Y. Giants[6]	325	1,023	3.1	36	14
	*Curtis Martin, New England	368	1,487	4.0	49	14
	Chris Warren, Seattle[4]	310	1,346	4.3	52	15
	Terry Allen, Washington[3]	338	1,309	3.9	28	10
	Ricky Watters, Philadelphia[2]	337	1,273	3.8	57	11
	Errict Rhett, Tampa Bay[2]	332	1,207	3.6	21	11
	Rodney Hampton, N.Y. Giants[5]	306	1,182	3.9	32	10
	*Terrell Davis, Denver	237	1,117	4.7	60	7
	Harvey Williams, Oakland	255	1,114	4.4	60	9
	Craig Heyward, Atlanta	236	1,083	4.6	31	6
	Marshall Faulk, Indianapolis[2]	289	1,078	3.7	40	11
	*Rashaan Salaam, Chicago	296	1,074	3.6	42	10
	Garrison Hearst, Arizona	284	1,070	3.8	38	1
	Edgar Bennett, Green Bay	316	1,067	3.4	23	3
	Thurman Thomas, Buffalo[7]	267	1,005	3.8	49	6
1994	Barry Sanders, Detroit[6]	331	1,883	5.7	85	7
	Chris Warren, Seattle[3]	333	1,545	4.6	41	9
	Emmitt Smith, Dallas[4]	368	1,484	4.0	46	21
	Natrone Means, San Diego	343	1,350	3.9	25	12
	*Marshall Faulk, Indianapolis	314	1,282	4.1	52	11
	Thurman Thomas, Buffalo[6]	287	1,093	3.8	29	7
	Rodney Hampton, N.Y. Giants[4]	327	1,075	3.3	27	6
	Terry Allen, Minnesota[2]	255	1,031	4.0	45	8
	Jerome Bettis, L.A. Rams[2]	319	1,025	3.2	19	3
	*Errict Rhett, Tampa Bay	284	1,011	3.6	27	7
1993	Emmitt Smith, Dallas[3]	283	1,486	5.3	62	9
	*Jerome Bettis, L.A. Rams	294	1,429	4.9	71	7
	Thurman Thomas, Buffalo[5]	355	1,315	3.7	27	6
	Erric Pegram, Atlanta	292	1,185	4.1	29	3
	Barry Sanders, Detroit[5]	243	1,115	4.6	42	3
	Leonard Russell, New England	300	1,088	3.6	21	7
	Rodney Hampton, N.Y. Giants[3]	292	1,077	3.7	20	5
	Chris Warren, Seattle[2]	273	1,072	3.9	45	7
	*Reggie Brooks, Washington	223	1,063	4.8	85	3
	*Ron Moore, Phoenix	263	1,018	3.9	20	9
	Gary Brown, Houston	195	1,002	5.1	26	6
1992	Emmitt Smith, Dallas[2]	373	1,713	4.6	68	18
	Barry Foster, Pittsburgh	390	1,690	4.3	69	11
	Thurman Thomas, Buffalo[4]	312	1,487	4.8	44	9
	Barry Sanders, Detroit[4]	312	1,352	4.3	55	9
	Lorenzo White, Houston	265	1,226	4.6	44	7
	Terry Allen, Minnesota	266	1,201	4.5	51	13
	Reggie Cobb, Tampa Bay	310	1,171	3.8	25	9
	Harold Green, Cincinnati	265	1,170	4.4	53	2
	Rodney Hampton, N.Y. Giants[2]	257	1,141	4.4	63	14
	Cleveland Gary, L.A. Rams	279	1,125	4.0	63	7

Year	Player, Team	Att.	Yards	Avg.	Long	TD
	Herschel Walker, Philadelphia[2]	267	1,070	4.0	38	8
	Chris Warren, Seattle	223	1,017	4.6	52	3
	Ricky Watters, San Francisco	206	1,013	4.9	43	9
1991	Emmitt Smith, Dallas	365	1,563	4.3	75	12
	Barry Sanders, Detroit[3]	342	1,548	4.5	69	16
	Thurman Thomas, Buffalo[3]	288	1,407	4.9	33	7
	Rodney Hampton, N.Y. Giants	256	1,059	4.1	44	10
	Earnest Byner, Washington[3]	274	1,048	3.8	32	5
	Gaston Green, Denver	261	1,037	4.0	63	4
	Christian Okoye, Kansas City[2]	225	1,031	4.6	48	9
1990	Barry Sanders, Detroit[2]	255	1,304	5.1	45	13
	Thurman Thomas, Buffalo[2]	271	1,297	4.8	80	11
	Marion Butts, San Diego	265	1,225	4.6	52	8
	Earnest Byner, Washington[2]	297	1,219	4.1	22	6
	Bobby Humphrey, Denver[2]	288	1,202	4.2	37	7
	Neal Anderson, Chicago[3]	260	1,078	4.1	52	10
	Barry Word, Kansas City	204	1,015	5.0	53	4
	James Brooks, Cincinnati[3]	195	1,004	5.1	56	5
1989	Christian Okoye, Kansas City	370	1,480	4.0	59	12
	*Barry Sanders, Detroit	280	1,470	5.3	34	14
	Eric Dickerson, Indianapolis[7]	314	1,311	4.2	21	7
	Neal Anderson, Chicago[2]	274	1,275	4.7	73	11
	Dalton Hilliard, New Orleans	344	1,262	3.7	40	13
	Thurman Thomas, Buffalo	298	1,244	4.2	38	6
	James Allen, Chicago	290	1,120	3.9	29	2
	Tyrone Wheatley, Oakland	232	1,046	4.5	80	9
	Jamal Anderson, Atlanta[4]	282	1,024	3.6	42	6
	Tiki Barber, N.Y. Giants	213	1,006	4.7	78	8
	Ricky Williams, New Orleans	248	1,000	4.0	26	8
1988	Eric Dickerson, Indianapolis[6]	388	1,659	4.3	41	14
	Herschel Walker, Dallas	361	1,514	4.2	38	5
	Roger Craig, San Francisco[2]	310	1,502	4.8	46	9
	Greg Bell, L.A. Rams[2]	288	1,212	4.2	44	16
	*John Stephens, New England	297	1,168	3.9	52	4
	Gary Anderson, San Diego	225	1,119	5.0	36	3
	Neal Anderson, Chicago	249	1,106	4.4	80	12
	Joe Morris, N.Y. Giants[3]	307	1,083	3.5	27	5
	*Ickey Woods, Cincinnati	203	1,066	5.3	56	15
	Curt Warner, Seattle[4]	266	1,025	3.9	29	10
	John Settle, Atlanta	232	1,024	4.4	62	7
	Mike Rozier, Houston	251	1,002	4.0	28	10
1987	Charles White, L.A. Rams	324	1,374	4.2	58	11
	Eric Dickerson, L.A. Rams-Indianapolis[5]	283	1,288	4.6	57	6
1986	Eric Dickerson, L.A. Rams[4]	404	1,821	4.5	42	11
	Joe Morris, N.Y. Giants[2]	341	1,516	4.4	54	14
	Curt Warner, Seattle[3]	319	1,481	4.6	60	13
	*Rueben Mayes, New Orleans	286	1,353	4.7	50	8
	Walter Payton, Chicago[10]	321	1,333	4.2	41	8
	Gerald Riggs, Atlanta[3]	343	1,327	3.9	31	9
	George Rogers, Washington[4]	303	1,203	4.0	42	18
	James Brooks, Cincinnati	205	1,087	5.3	56	5
1985	Marcus Allen, L.A. Raiders[3]	390	1,759	4.6	61	11
	Gerald Riggs, Atlanta[2]	397	1,719	4.3	50	10
	Walter Payton, Chicago[9]	324	1,551	4.8	40	9
	Joe Morris, N.Y. Giants	294	1,336	4.5	65	21
	Freeman McNeil, N.Y. Jets[2]	294	1,331	4.5	69	3
	Tony Dorsett, Dallas[8]	305	1,307	4.3	60	7
	James Wilder, Tampa Bay[2]	365	1,300	3.6	28	10
	Eric Dickerson, L.A. Rams[3]	292	1,234	4.2	43	12
	Craig James, New England	263	1,227	4.7	65	5
	Kevin Mack, Cleveland	222	1,104	5.0	61	7
	Curt Warner, Seattle[2]	291	1,094	3.8	38	8
	George Rogers, Washington[3]	231	1,093	4.7	35	7
	Roger Craig, San Francisco	214	1,050	4.9	62	9
	Earnest Jackson, Philadelphia[2]	282	1,028	3.6	59	5
	Stump Mitchell, St. Louis	183	1,006	5.5	64	7
	Earnest Byner, Cleveland	244	1,002	4.1	36	8
1984	Eric Dickerson, L.A. Rams[2]	379	2,105	5.6	66	14
	Walter Payton, Chicago[8]	381	1,684	4.4	72	11

Year	Player, Team	Att.	Yards	Avg.	Long	TD
	James Wilder, Tampa Bay	407	1,544	3.8	37	13
	Gerald Riggs, Atlanta	353	1,486	4.2	57	13
	Wendell Tyler, San Francisco[3]	246	1,262	5.1	40	7
	John Riggins, Washington[5]	327	1,239	3.8	24	14
	Tony Dorsett, Dallas[7]	302	1,189	3.9	31	6
	Earnest Jackson, San Diego	296	1,179	4.0	32	8
	Ottis Anderson, St. Louis[5]	289	1,174	4.1	24	6
	Marcus Allen, L.A. Raiders[2]	275	1,168	4.2	52	13
	Sammy Winder, Denver	296	1,153	3.9	24	4
	*Greg Bell, Buffalo	262	1,100	4.2	85	7
	Freeman McNeil, N.Y. Jets	229	1,070	4.7	53	5
1983	*Eric Dickerson, L.A. Rams	390	1,808	4.6	85	18
	William Andrews, Atlanta[4]	331	1,567	4.7	27	7
	*Curt Warner, Seattle	335	1,449	4.3	60	13
	Walter Payton, Chicago[7]	314	1,421	4.5	49	6
	John Riggins, Washington[4]	375	1,347	3.6	44	24
	Tony Dorsett, Dallas[6]	289	1,321	4.6	77	8
	Earl Campbell, Houston[5]	322	1,301	4.0	42	12
	Ottis Anderson, St. Louis[4]	296	1,270	4.3	43	5
	Mike Pruitt, Cleveland[4]	293	1,184	4.0	27	10
	George Rogers, New Orleans[2]	256	1,144	4.5	76	5
	Joe Cribbs, Buffalo[3]	263	1,131	4.3	45	3
	Curtis Dickey, Baltimore	254	1,122	4.4	56	4
	Tony Collins, New England	219	1,049	4.8	50	10
	Billy Sims, Detroit[3]	220	1,040	4.7	41	7
	Marcus Allen, L.A. Raiders	266	1,014	3.8	19	9
	Franco Harris, Pittsburgh[8]	279	1,007	3.6	19	5
1981	*George Rogers, New Orleans	378	1,674	4.4	79	13
	Tony Dorsett, Dallas[5]	342	1,646	4.8	75	4
	Billy Sims, Detroit[2]	296	1,437	4.9	51	13
	Wilbert Montgomery, Philadelphia[3]	286	1,402	4.9	41	8
	Ottis Anderson, St. Louis[3]	328	1,376	4.2	28	9
	Earl Campbell, Houston[4]	361	1,376	3.8	43	10
	William Andrews, Atlanta[3]	289	1,301	4.5	29	10
	Walter Payton, Chicago[6]	339	1,222	3.6	39	6
	Chuck Muncie, San Diego[2]	251	1,144	4.6	73	19
	*Joe Delaney, Kansas City	234	1,121	4.8	82	3
	Mike Pruitt, Cleveland[3]	247	1,103	4.5	21	7
	Joe Cribbs, Buffalo[2]	257	1,097	4.3	35	3
	Pete Johnson, Cincinnati	274	1,077	3.9	39	12
	Wendell Tyler, Los Angeles[2]	260	1,074	4.1	69	12
	Ted Brown, Minnesota	274	1,063	3.9	34	6
1980	Earl Campbell, Houston[3]	373	1,934	5.2	55	13
	Walter Payton, Chicago[5]	317	1,460	4.6	69	6
	Ottis Anderson, St. Louis[2]	301	1,352	4.5	52	9
	William Andrews, Atlanta[2]	265	1,308	4.9	33	4
	*Billy Sims, Detroit	313	1,303	4.2	52	13
	Tony Dorsett, Dallas[4]	278	1,185	4.3	56	11
	*Joe Cribbs, Buffalo	306	1,185	3.9	48	11
	Mike Pruitt, Cleveland[2]	249	1,034	4.2	56	6
1979	Earl Campbell, Houston[2]	368	1,697	4.6	61	19
	Walter Payton, Chicago[4]	369	1,610	4.4	43	14
	*Ottis Anderson, St. Louis	331	1,605	4.8	76	8
	Wilbert Montgomery, Philadelphia[2]	338	1,512	4.5	62	9
	Mike Pruitt, Cleveland	264	1,294	4.9	77	9
	Ricky Bell, Tampa Bay	283	1,263	4.5	49	7
	Chuck Muncie, New Orleans	238	1,198	5.0	69	11
	Franco Harris, Pittsburgh[7]	267	1,186	4.4	71	11
	John Riggins, Washington[3]	260	1,153	4.4	66	9
	Wendell Tyler, Los Angeles	218	1,109	5.1	63	9
	Tony Dorsett, Dallas[3]	250	1,107	4.4	41	6
	*William Andrews, Atlanta	239	1,023	4.3	23	3
1978	*Earl Campbell, Houston	302	1,450	4.8	81	13
	Walter Payton, Chicago[3]	333	1,395	4.2	76	11
	Tony Dorsett, Dallas[2]	290	1,325	4.6	63	7
	Delvin Williams, Miami[2]	272	1,258	4.6	58	8
	Wilbert Montgomery, Philadelphia	259	1,220	4.7	47	9
	Terdell Middleton, Green Bay	284	1,116	3.9	76	11
	Franco Harris, Pittsburgh[6]	310	1,082	3.5	37	8

Year	Player, Team	Att.	Yards	Avg.	Long	TD
	Mark van Eeghen, Oakland[3]	270	1,080	4.0	34	9
	*Terry Miller, Buffalo	238	1,060	4.5	60	7
	Tony Reed, Kansas City	206	1,053	5.1	62	5
	John Riggins, Washington[2]	248	1,014	4.1	31	5
1977	Walter Payton, Chicago[2]	339	1,852	5.5	73	14
	Mark van Eeghen, Oakland[2]	324	1,273	3.9	27	7
	Lawrence McCutcheon, Los Angeles[4]	294	1,238	4.2	48	7
	Franco Harris, Pittsburgh[5]	300	1,162	3.9	61	11
	Lydell Mitchell, Baltimore[3]	301	1,159	3.9	64	3
	Chuck Foreman, Minnesota[3]	270	1,112	4.1	51	6
	Greg Pruitt, Cleveland[3]	236	1,086	4.6	78	3
	Sam Cunningham, New England	270	1,015	3.8	31	4
	*Tony Dorsett, Dallas	208	1,007	4.8	84	12
1976	O.J. Simpson, Buffalo[5]	290	1,503	5.2	75	8
	Walter Payton, Chicago	311	1,390	4.5	60	13
	Delvin Williams, San Francisco	248	1,203	4.9	80	7
	Lydell Mitchell, Baltimore[2]	289	1,200	4.2	43	5
	Lawrence McCutcheon, Los Angeles[3]	291	1,168	4.0	40	9
	Chuck Foreman, Minnesota[2]	278	1,155	4.2	46	13
	Franco Harris, Pittsburgh[4]	289	1,128	3.9	30	14
	Mike Thomas, Washington	254	1,101	4.3	28	5
	Rocky Bleier, Pittsburgh	220	1,036	4.7	28	5
	Mark van Eeghen, Oakland	233	1,012	4.3	21	3
	Otis Armstrong, Denver[2]	247	1,008	4.1	31	5
	Greg Pruitt, Cleveland[2]	209	1,000	4.8	64	4
1975	O.J. Simpson, Buffalo[4]	329	1,817	5.5	88	16
	Franco Harris, Pittsburgh[3]	262	1,246	4.8	36	10
	Lydell Mitchell, Baltimore	289	1,193	4.1	70	11
	Jim Otis, St. Louis	269	1,076	4.0	30	5
	Chuck Foreman, Minnesota	280	1,070	3.8	31	13
	Greg Pruitt, Cleveland	217	1,067	4.9	50	8
	John Riggins, N.Y. Jets	238	1,005	4.2	42	8
	Dave Hampton, Atlanta	250	1,002	4.0	22	5
1974	Otis Armstrong, Denver	263	1,407	5.3	43	9
	*Don Woods, San Diego	227	1,162	5.1	56	7
	O.J. Simpson, Buffalo[3]	270	1,125	4.2	41	3
	Lawrence McCutcheon, Los Angeles[2]	236	1,109	4.7	23	3
	Franco Harris, Pittsburgh[2]	208	1,006	4.8	54	5
1973	O.J. Simpson, Buffalo[2]	332	2,003	6.0	80	12
	John Brockington, Green Bay[3]	265	1,144	4.3	53	3
	Calvin Hill, Dallas[2]	273	1,142	4.2	21	6
	Lawrence McCutcheon, Los Angeles	210	1,097	5.2	37	2
	Larry Csonka, Miami[3]	219	1,003	4.6	25	5
1972	O.J. Simpson, Buffalo	292	1,251	4.3	94	6
	Larry Brown, Washington[2]	285	1,216	4.3	38	8
	Ron Johnson, N.Y. Giants[2]	298	1,182	4.0	35	9
	Larry Csonka, Miami[2]	213	1,117	5.2	45	6
	Marv Hubbard, Oakland	219	1,100	5.0	39	4
	*Franco Harris, Pittsburgh	188	1,055	5.6	75	10
	Calvin Hill, Dallas	245	1,036	4.2	26	6
	Mike Garrett, San Diego[2]	272	1,031	3.8	41	6
	John Brockington, Green Bay[2]	274	1,027	3.7	30	8
	Eugene (Mercury) Morris, Miami	190	1,000	5.3	33	12
1971	Floyd Little, Denver	284	1,133	4.0	40	6
	*John Brockington, Green Bay	216	1,105	5.1	52	4
	Larry Csonka, Miami	195	1,051	5.4	28	7
	Steve Owens, Detroit	246	1,035	4.2	23	8
	Willie Ellison, Los Angeles	211	1,000	4.7	80	4
1970	Larry Brown, Washington	237	1,125	4.7	75	5
	Ron Johnson, N.Y. Giants	263	1,027	3.9	68	8
1969	Gale Sayers, Chicago[2]	236	1,032	4.4	28	8
1968	Leroy Kelly, Cleveland[3]	248	1,239	5.0	65	16
	*Paul Robinson, Cincinnati	238	1,023	4.3	87	8
1967	Jim Nance, Boston[2]	269	1,216	4.5	53	7
	Leroy Kelly, Cleveland[2]	235	1,205	5.1	42	11
	Hoyle Granger, Houston	236	1,194	5.1	67	6
	Mike Garrett, Kansas City	236	1,087	4.6	58	9
1966	Jim Nance, Boston	299	1,458	4.9	65	11
	Gale Sayers, Chicago	229	1,231	5.4	58	8

Year	Player, Team	Att.	Yards	Avg.	Long	TD
	Leroy Kelly, Cleveland	209	1,141	5.5	70	15
	Dick Bass, Los Angeles[2]	248	1,090	4.4	50	8
1965	Jim Brown, Cleveland[7]	289	1,544	5.3	67	17
	Paul Lowe, San Diego[2]	222	1,121	5.0	59	7
1964	Jim Brown, Cleveland[6]	280	1,446	5.2	71	7
	Jim Taylor, Green Bay[5]	235	1,169	5.0	84	12
	John Henry Johnson, Pittsburgh[2]	235	1,048	4.5	45	7
1963	Jim Brown, Cleveland[5]	291	1,863	6.4	80	12
	Clem Daniels, Oakland	215	1,099	5.1	74	3
	Jim Taylor, Green Bay[4]	248	1,018	4.1	40	9
	Paul Lowe, San Diego	177	1,010	5.7	66	8
1962	Jim Taylor, Green Bay[3]	272	1,474	5.4	51	19
	John Henry Johnson, Pittsburgh	251	1,141	4.5	40	7
	Cookie Gilchrist, Buffalo	214	1,096	5.1	44	13
	Abner Haynes, Dall. Texans	221	1,049	4.7	71	13
	Dick Bass, Los Angeles	196	1,033	5.3	57	6
	Charlie Tolar, Houston	244	1,012	4.1	25	7
1961	Jim Brown, Cleveland[4]	305	1,408	4.6	38	8
	Jim Taylor, Green Bay[2]	243	1,307	5.4	53	15
1960	Jim Brown, Cleveland[3]	215	1,257	5.8	71	9
	Jim Taylor, Green Bay	230	1,101	4.8	32	11
	John David Crow, St. Louis	183	1,071	5.9	57	6
1959	Jim Brown, Cleveland[2]	290	1,329	4.6	70	14
	J.D. Smith, San Francisco	207	1,036	5.0	73	10
1958	Jim Brown, Cleveland	257	1,527	5.9	65	17
1956	Rick Casares, Chi. Bears	234	1,126	4.8	68	12
1954	Joe Perry, San Francisco[2]	173	1,049	6.1	58	8
1953	Joe Perry, San Francisco	192	1,018	5.3	51	10
1949	Steve Van Buren, Philadelphia[2]	263	1,146	4.4	41	11
	Tony Canadeo, Green Bay	208	1,052	5.1	54	4
1947	Steve Van Buren, Philadelphia	217	1,008	4.6	45	13
1934	*Beattie Feathers, Chi. Bears	119	1,004	8.4	82	8

*First season of professional football.

200 YARDS RUSHING IN A GAME

Date	Player, Team, Opponent	Att.	Yards	TD
Nov. 28, 2004	Rudi Johnson, Cincinnati vs. Cleveland	26	202	2
Nov. 21, 2004	Edgerrin James, Indianapolis vs. Chicago	23	204	1
Dec. 28, 2003	Ahman Green, Green Bay vs. Denver	20	218	2
Dec. 28, 2003	LaDainian Tomlinson, San Diego vs. Oakland	31	243	2
Dec. 21, 2003	Jamal Lewis, Baltimore vs. Cleveland	22	205	2
Dec. 7, 2003	Clinton Portis, Denver vs. Kansas City	22	218	5
Oct. 19, 2003	LaDainian Tomlinson, San Diego vs. Cleveland	26	200	1
Sept. 14, 2003	Jamal Lewis, Baltimore vs. Cleveland	30	295	2
Dec. 29, 2002	*Clinton Portis, Denver vs. Arizona	24	228	2
Dec. 28, 2002	Tiki Barber, N.Y. Giants vs. Philadelphia	32	203	0
Dec. 9, 2002	Ricky Williams, Miami vs. Chicago	31	216	2
Dec. 1, 2002	LaDainian Tomlinson, San Diego vs. Denver	37	220	3
Dec. 1, 2002	Ricky Williams, Miami vs. Buffalo	27	228	2
Sept. 29, 2002	LaDainian Tomlinson, San Diego vs. New England	27	217	2
Dec. 23, 2001	Marshall Faulk, St. Louis vs. Carolina	30	202	2
Nov. 11, 2001	Shaun Alexander, Seattle vs. Oakland	35	266	3
Dec. 24, 2000	Marshall Faulk, St. Louis vs. New Orleans	32	220	2
Dec. 3, 2000	Corey Dillon, Cincinnati vs. Arizona	35	216	1
Dec. 3, 2000	Warrick Dunn, Tampa Bay vs. Dallas	22	210	1
Dec. 3, 2000	*Mike Anderson, Denver vs. New Orleans	37	251	4
Dec. 3, 2000	Curtis Martin, N.Y. Jets vs. Indianapolis	30	203	1
Nov. 19, 2000	Fred Taylor, Jacksonville vs. Pittsburgh	30	234	3
Oct. 22, 2000	Corey Dillon, Cincinnati vs. Denver	22	278	2
Oct. 15, 2000	Marshall Faulk, St. Louis vs. Atlanta	25	208	1
Oct. 15, 2000	Edgerrin James, Indianapolis vs. Seattle	38	219	3
Sept. 24, 2000	Charlie Garner, San Francisco vs. Dallas	36	201	1
Sept. 3, 2000	Duce Staley, Philadelphia vs. Dallas	26	201	1
Nov. 22, 1998	Priest Holmes, Baltimore vs. Cincinnati	36	227	1
Oct. 11, 1998	Terrell Davis, Denver vs. Seattle	30	208	1
Dec. 4, 1997	*Corey Dillon, Cincinnati vs. Tennessee	39	246	4
Nov. 23, 1997	Barry Sanders, Detroit vs. Indianapolis	24	216	2
Oct. 26, 1997	Terrell Davis, Denver vs. Buffalo (OT)	42	207	1
Oct. 19, 1997	Napoleon Kaufman, Oakland vs. Denver	28	227	1
Oct. 12, 1997	Barry Sanders, Detroit vs. Tampa Bay	24	215	2

Date	Player, Team, Opponent	Att.	Yards	TD
Sept. 21, 1997	Terrell Davis, Denver vs. Cincinnati	27	215	1
Aug. 31, 1997	Eddie George, Tennessee vs. Oakland (OT)	35	216	1
Sept. 22, 1996	LeShon Johnson, Arizona vs. New Orleans	21	214	2
Nov. 13, 1994	Barry Sanders, Detroit vs. Tampa Bay	26	237	0
Dec. 12, 1993	*Jerome Bettis, L.A. Rams vs. New Orleans	28	212	1
Oct. 31, 1993	Emmitt Smith, Dallas vs. Philadelphia	30	237	1
Nov. 24, 1991	Barry Sanders, Detroit vs. Minnesota	23	220	4
Dec. 23, 1990	James Brooks, Cincinnati vs. Houston	20	201	1
Oct. 14, 1990	Barry Word, Kansas City vs. Detroit	18	200	2
Sept. 24, 1990	Thurman Thomas, Buffalo vs. N.Y. Jets	18	214	0
Dec. 24, 1989	Greg Bell, L.A. Rams vs. New England	26	210	1
Sept. 24, 1989	Greg Bell, L.A. Rams vs. Green Bay	28	221	2
Sept. 17, 1989	Gerald Riggs, Washington vs. Philadelphia	29	221	1
Dec. 18, 1988	Gary Anderson, San Diego vs. Kansas City	34	217	1
Nov. 30, 1987	*Bo Jackson, L.A. Raiders vs. Seattle	18	221	2
Nov. 15, 1987	Charles White, L.A. Rams vs. St. Louis	34	213	1
Dec. 7, 1986	Rueben Mayes, New Orleans vs. Miami	28	203	2
Oct. 5, 1986	Eric Dickerson, L.A. Rams vs. Tampa Bay (OT)	30	207	2
Dec. 21, 1985	George Rogers, Washington vs. St. Louis	34	206	1
Dec. 21, 1985	Joe Morris, N.Y. Giants vs. Pittsburgh	36	202	3
Dec. 9, 1984	Eric Dickerson, L.A. Rams vs. Houston	27	215	2
Nov. 18, 1984	*Greg Bell, Buffalo vs. Dallas	27	206	1
Nov. 4, 1984	Eric Dickerson, L.A. Rams vs. St. Louis	21	208	0
Sept. 2, 1984	Gerald Riggs, Atlanta vs. New Orleans	35	202	2
Nov. 27, 1983	*Curt Warner, Seattle vs. Kansas City (OT)	32	207	3
Nov. 6, 1983	James Wilder, Tampa Bay vs. Minnesota	31	219	1
Sept. 18, 1983	Tony Collins, New England vs. N.Y. Jets	23	212	3
Sept. 4, 1983	George Rogers, New Orleans vs. St. Louis	24	206	2
Dec. 21, 1980	Earl Campbell, Houston vs. Minnesota	29	203	1
Nov. 16, 1980	Earl Campbell, Houston vs. Chicago	31	206	0
Oct. 26, 1980	Earl Campbell, Houston vs. Cincinnati	27	202	2
Oct. 19, 1980	Earl Campbell, Houston vs. Tampa Bay	33	203	0
Nov. 26, 1978	*Terry Miller, Buffalo vs. N.Y. Giants	21	208	2
Dec. 4, 1977	*Tony Dorsett, Dallas vs. Philadelphia	23	206	2
Nov. 20, 1977	Walter Payton, Chicago vs. Minnesota	40	275	1
Oct. 30, 1977	Walter Payton, Chicago vs. Green Bay	23	205	2
Dec. 5, 1976	O.J. Simpson, Buffalo vs. Miami	24	203	1
Nov. 25, 1976	O.J. Simpson, Buffalo vs. Detroit	29	273	2
Oct. 24, 1976	Chuck Foreman, Minnesota vs. Philadelphia	28	200	2
Dec. 14, 1975	Greg Pruitt, Cleveland vs. Kansas City	26	214	3
Sept. 28, 1975	O.J. Simpson, Buffalo vs. Pittsburgh	28	227	1
Dec. 16, 1973	O.J. Simpson, Buffalo vs. N.Y. Jets	34	200	1
Dec. 9, 1973	O.J. Simpson, Buffalo vs. New England	22	219	1
Sept. 16, 1973	O.J. Simpson, Buffalo vs. New England	29	250	2
Dec. 5, 1971	Willie Ellison, Los Angeles vs. New Orleans	26	247	1
Dec. 20, 1970	John (Frenchy) Fuqua, Pittsburgh vs. Philadelphia	20	218	2
Nov. 3, 1968	Gale Sayers, Chicago vs. Green Bay	24	205	0
Oct. 30, 1966	Jim Nance, Boston vs. Oakland	38	208	2
Oct. 10, 1964	John Henry Johnson, Pittsburgh vs. Cleveland	30	200	3
Dec. 8, 1963	Cookie Gilchrist, Buffalo vs. N.Y. Jets	36	243	5
Nov. 3, 1963	Jim Brown, Cleveland vs. Philadelphia	28	223	1
Oct. 20, 1963	Clem Daniels, Oakland vs. N.Y. Jets	27	200	2
Sept. 22, 1963	Jim Brown, Cleveland vs. Dallas	20	232	2
Dec. 10, 1961	Billy Cannon, Houston vs. N.Y. Titans	25	216	3
Nov. 19, 1961	Jim Brown, Cleveland vs. Philadelphia	34	237	4
Dec. 18, 1960	John David Crow, St. Louis vs. Pittsburgh	24	203	0
Nov. 15, 1959	Bobby Mitchell, Cleveland vs. Washington	14	232	3
Nov. 24, 1957	*Jim Brown, Cleveland vs. Los Angeles	31	237	4
Dec. 16, 1956	*Tom Wilson, Los Angeles vs. Green Bay	23	223	0
Nov. 22, 1953	Dan Towler, Los Angeles vs. Baltimore	14	205	1
Nov. 12, 1950	Gene Roberts, N.Y. Giants vs. Chi. Cardinals	26	218	2
Nov. 27, 1949	Steve Van Buren, Philadelphia vs. Pittsburgh	27	205	0
Oct. 8, 1933	Cliff Battles, Boston vs. N.Y. Giants	16	215	1

*First season of professional football.

TIMES 200 OR MORE

97 times by 63 players…Simpson 6; Brown, Campbell, Sanders, Tomlinson 4; Bell, Davis, Dickerson, Dillon, Faulk 3; James, Lewis, Payton, Portis, Riggs, Rogers, Williams 2.

4,000 YARDS PASSING IN A SEASON

Year	Player, Team	Att.	Comp.	Pct.	Yards	TD	Int.
2004	Daunte Culpepper, Minnesota	548	379	69.2	4,717	39	11
	Trent Green, Kansas City[2]	556	369	66.4	4,591	27	17
	Peyton Manning, Indianapolis[6]	497	336	67.6	4,557	49	10
	Jake Plummer, Denver	521	303	58.2	4,089	27	20
	Brett Favre, Green Bay[4]	540	346	64.1	4,088	30	17
2003	Peyton Manning, Indianapolis[5]	566	379	67.0	4,267	29	10
	Trent Green, Kansas City	523	330	63.1	4,039	24	12
2002	Rich Gannon, Oakland	618	418	67.6	4,689	26	10
	Drew Bledsoe, Buffalo[3]	610	375	61.5	4,359	24	15
	Peyton Manning, Indianapolis[4]	591	392	66.3	4,200	27	19
	Kerry Collins, N.Y. Giants	545	335	61.5	4,073	19	14
2001	Kurt Warner, St. Louis[2]	546	375	68.7	4,830	36	22
	Peyton Manning, Indianapolis[3]	547	343	62.7	4,131	26	23
2000	Peyton Manning, Indianapolis[2]	571	357	62.5	4,413	33	15
	Jeff Garcia, San Francisco	561	355	63.3	4,278	31	10
	Elvis Grbac, Kansas City	547	326	59.6	4,169	28	14
1999	Steve Beuerlein, Carolina	571	343	60.1	4,436	36	15
	Kurt Warner, St. Louis	499	325	65.1	4,353	41	13
	Peyton Manning, Indianapolis	533	331	62.1	4,135	26	15
	Brett Favre, Green Bay[3]	595	341	57.3	4,091	22	23
	Brad Johnson, Washington	519	316	60.9	4,005	24	13
1998	Brett Favre, Green Bay[2]	551	347	63.0	4,212	31	23
	Steve Young, San Francisco[2]	517	322	62.3	4,170	36	12
1996	Mark Brunell, Jacksonville	557	353	63.4	4,367	19	20
	Vinny Testaverde, Baltimore	549	325	59.2	4,177	33	19
	Drew Bledsoe, New England[2]	623	373	59.9	4,086	27	15
1995	Brett Favre, Green Bay	570	359	63.0	4,413	38	13
	Scott Mitchell, Detroit	583	346	59.3	4,338	32	12
	Warren Moon, Minnesota[4]	606	377	62.2	4,228	33	14
	Jeff George, Atlanta	557	336	60.3	4,143	24	11
1994	Drew Bledsoe, New England	691	400	57.9	4,555	25	27
	Dan Marino, Miami[6]	615	385	62.6	4,453	30	17
	Warren Moon, Minnesota[3]	601	371	61.7	4,264	18	19
1993	John Elway, Denver	551	348	63.2	4,030	25	10
	Steve Young, San Francisco	462	314	68.0	4,023	29	16
1992	Dan Marino, Miami[5]	554	330	59.6	4,116	24	16
1991	Warren Moon, Houston[2]	655	404	61.7	4,690	23	21
1990	Warren Moon, Houston	584	362	62.0	4,689	33	13
1989	Don Majkowski, Green Bay	599	353	58.9	4,318	27	20
	Jim Everett, L.A. Rams	518	304	58.7	4,310	29	17
1988	Dan Marino, Miami[4]	606	354	58.4	4,434	28	23
1986	Dan Marino, Miami[3]	623	378	60.7	4,746	44	23
	Jay Schroeder, Washington	541	276	51.0	4,109	22	22
1985	Dan Marino, Miami[2]	567	336	59.3	4,137	30	21
1984	Dan Marino, Miami	564	362	64.2	5,084	48	17
	Neil Lomax, St. Louis	560	345	61.6	4,614	28	16
	Phil Simms, N.Y. Giants	533	286	53.7	4,044	22	18
1983	Lynn Dickey, Green Bay	484	289	59.7	4,458	32	29
	Bill Kenney, Kansas City	603	346	57.4	4,348	24	18
1981	Dan Fouts, San Diego[3]	609	360	59.1	4,802	33	17
1980	Dan Fouts, San Diego[2]	589	348	59.1	4,715	30	24
	Brian Sipe, Cleveland	554	337	60.8	4,132	30	14
1979	Dan Fouts, San Diego	530	332	62.6	4,082	24	24
1967	Joe Namath, N.Y. Jets	491	258	52.5	4,007	26	28

400 YARDS PASSING IN A GAME

Date	Player, Team, Opponent	Att.	Comp.	Yards	TD
Jan. 2, 2005	Marc Bulger, St. Louis vs. N.Y. Jets (OT)	39	29	450	3
Dec. 19, 2004	Daunte Culpepper, Minnesota vs. Detroit	35	25	404	3
Dec. 19, 2004	Billy Volek, Tennessee vs. Oakland	60	40	492	4
Dec. 13, 2004	Billy Volek, Tennessee vs. Kansas City	43	29	426	4
Dec. 6, 2004	Matt Hasselbeck, Seattle vs. Dallas	40	28	414	3
Dec. 5, 2004	Peyton Manning, Indianapolis vs. Tennessee	33	25	425	3
Dec. 5, 2004	Donovan McNabb, Philadelphia vs. Green Bay	43	32	464	5
Nov. 29, 2004	Marc Bulger, St. Louis vs. Green Bay	53	35	448	2
Nov. 28, 2004	Kelly Holcomb, Cleveland vs. Cincinnati	39	30	413	5
Oct. 31, 2004	Peyton Manning, Indianapolis vs. Kansas City	44	25	472	5
Oct. 31, 2004	Jake Plummer, Denver vs. Atlanta	55	31	499	4

Date	Player, Team, Opponent	Att.	Comp.	Yards	TD
Oct. 17, 2004	Daunte Culpepper, Minnesota vs. New Orleans	37	26	425	5
Oct. 10. 2004	Tim Rattay, San Francisco vs. Arizona (OT)	57	38	417	2
Nov. 16, 2003	Peyton Manning, Indianapolis vs. N.Y. Jets	36	27	401	1
Oct. 12, 2003	Trent Green, Kansas City vs. Green Bay (OT)	45	27	400	3
Oct. 12, 2003	Steve McNair, Tennessee vs. Houston	27	18	421	3
Dec. 29, 2002	Matt Hasselbeck, Seattle vs. San Diego (OT)	53	36	449	2
Dec. 1, 2002	Matt Hasselbeck, Seattle vs. San Francisco	55	30	427	3
Nov. 10, 2002	Marc Bulger, St. Louis vs. San Diego	48	36	453	4
Nov. 10, 2002	Tommy Maddox, Pittsburgh vs. Atlanta (OT)	41	28	473	4
Oct. 6, 2002	Drew Bledsoe, Buffalo vs. Oakland	53	32	417	2
Sept. 22, 2002	Tom Brady, New England vs. Kansas City (OT)	54	39	410	4
Sept. 15, 2002	Drew Bledsoe, Buffalo vs. Minnesota (OT)	49	35	463	3
Sept. 15, 2002	Rich Gannon, Oakland vs. Pittsburgh	64	43	403	1
Dec. 30, 2001	Jon Kitna, Cincinnati vs. Pittsburgh	68	35	411	2
Dec. 23, 2001	Chris Chandler, Atlanta vs. Buffalo	40	28	431	2
Nov. 18, 2001	Charlie Batch, Detroit vs. Arizona	62	36	436	3
Nov. 18, 2001	Kurt Warner, St. Louis vs. New England	42	30	401	3
Sept. 23, 2001	Peyton Manning, Indianapolis vs. Buffalo	29	23	421	4
Dec. 24, 2000	Vinny Testaverde, N.Y. Jets vs. Baltimore	69	36	481	2
Dec. 17, 2000	Jeff Garcia, San Francisco vs. Chicago	44	36	402	2
Dec. 3, 2000	Aaron Brooks, New Orleans vs. Denver	48	30	441	2
Nov. 19, 2000	Gus Frerotte, Denver vs. San Diego	58	36	462	5
Nov. 5, 2000	Elvis Grbac, Kansas City vs. Oakland	53	39	504	2
Nov. 5, 2000	Trent Green, St. Louis vs. Carolina	42	29	431	2
Sept. 25, 2000	Peyton Manning, Indianapolis vs. Jacksonville	36	23	440	4
Sept. 4, 2000	Kurt Warner, St. Louis vs. Denver	35	25	441	3
Dec. 26, 1999	Brad Johnson, Washington vs. San Francisco (OT)	47	32	471	2
Dec. 5, 1999	Jeff Garcia, San Francisco vs. Cincinnati	49	33	437	3
Nov. 28, 1999	Jim Harbaugh, San Diego vs. Minnesota	39	25	404	1
Nov. 14, 1999	Jim Miller, Chicago vs. Minnesota (OT)	48	34	422	3
Sept. 26, 1999	Peyton Manning, Indianapolis vs. San Diego	54	29	404	2
Dec. 6, 1998	Vinny Testaverde, N.Y. Jets vs. Seattle	63	42	418	2
Dec. 6, 1998	John Elway, Denver vs. Kansas City	32	22	400	2
Nov. 26, 1998	Troy Aikman, Dallas vs. Minnesota	57	34	455	1
Nov. 23, 1998	Drew Bledsoe, New England vs. Miami	54	28	423	2
Nov. 15, 1998	Jake Plummer, Arizona vs. Dallas	56	31	465	3
Oct. 5, 1998	Randall Cunningham, Minnesota vs. Green Bay	32	20	442	4
Sept. 6, 1998	Glenn Foley, N.Y. Jets vs. San Francisco (OT)	58	30	415	3
Nov. 2, 1997	Tony Banks, St. Louis vs. Atlanta	34	23	401	2
Oct. 26, 1997	Warren Moon, Seattle vs. Oakland	44	28	409	5
Nov. 10, 1996	Boomer Esiason, Arizona vs. Washington (OT)	59	35	522	3
Nov. 3, 1996	Drew Bledsoe, New England vs. Miami	41	30	419	3
Oct. 27, 1996	Vinny Testaverde, Baltimore vs. St. Louis (OT)	51	31	429	3
Oct. 20, 1996	Mark Brunell, Jacksonville vs. St. Louis	52	37	421	0
Sept. 22, 1996	Mark Brunell, Jacksonville vs. New England (OT)	39	23	432	3
Dec. 18, 1995	Steve Young, San Francisco vs. Minnesota	49	30	425	3
Nov. 26, 1995	Dave Krieg, Arizona vs. Atlanta (OT)	43	27	413	4
Nov. 23, 1995	Scott Mitchell, Detroit vs. Minnesota	45	30	410	4
Oct. 1, 1995	Dan Marino, Miami vs. Cincinnati	48	33	450	2
Nov. 20, 1994	Warren Moon, Minnesota vs. N.Y. Jets	50	33	400	2
Nov. 13, 1994	Drew Bledsoe, New England vs. Minnesota (OT)	70	45	426	3
Nov. 6, 1994	Warren Moon, Minnesota vs. New Orleans	57	33	420	3
Sept. 25, 1994	Dan Marino, Miami vs. Minnesota	54	29	431	3
Sept. 4, 1994	Dan Marino, Miami vs. New England (OT)	42	23	473	5
Sept. 4, 1994	Drew Bledsoe, New England vs. Miami (OT)	51	32	421	4
Dec. 19, 1993	Steve Beuerlein, Phoenix vs. Seattle	53	34	431	4
Dec. 5, 1993	Brett Favre, Green Bay vs. Chicago	54	36	402	2
Nov. 28, 1993	Steve Young, San Francisco vs. L.A. Rams	32	26	462	4
Oct. 31, 1993	Jeff Hostetler, L.A. Raiders vs. San Diego	32	20	424	2
Sept. 13, 1992	Steve Young, San Francisco vs. Buffalo	37	26	449	3
Sept. 13, 1992	Jim Kelly, Buffalo vs. San Francisco	33	22	403	3
Nov. 10, 1991	Warren Moon, Houston vs. Dallas (OT)	56	41	432	0
Nov. 10, 1991	Mark Rypien, Washington vs. Atlanta	31	16	442	6
Oct. 13, 1991	Warren Moon, Houston vs. N.Y. Jets	50	35	423	2
Dec. 16, 1990	Warren Moon, Houston vs. Kansas City	45	27	527	3
Nov. 4, 1990	Joe Montana, San Francisco vs. Green Bay	40	25	411	3
Oct. 14, 1990	Joe Montana, San Francisco vs. Atlanta	49	32	476	6
Oct. 7, 1990	Boomer Esiason, Cincinnati vs. L.A. Rams (OT)	45	31	490	3
Dec. 23, 1989	Warren Moon, Houston vs. Cleveland	51	32	414	2

Date	Player, Team, Opponent	Att.	Comp.	Yards	TD
Dec. 11, 1989	Joe Montana, San Francisco vs. L.A. Rams	42	30	458	3
Nov. 26, 1989	Jim Everett, L.A. Rams vs. New Orleans (OT)	51	29	454	1
Nov. 26, 1989	Mark Rypien, Washington vs. Chicago	47	30	401	4
Oct. 2, 1989	Randall Cunningham, Philadelphia vs. Chicago	62	32	401	1
Sept. 24, 1989	Joe Montana, San Francisco vs. Philadelphia	34	25	428	5
Sept. 24, 1989	Dan Marino, Miami vs. N.Y. Jets	55	33	427	3
Sept. 17, 1989	Randall Cunningham, Philadelphia vs. Washington	46	34	447	5
Dec. 18, 1988	Dave Krieg, Seattle vs. L.A. Raiders	32	19	410	4
Dec. 12, 1988	Dan Marino, Miami vs. Cleveland	50	30	404	4
Oct. 23, 1988	Dan Marino, Miami vs. N.Y. Jets	60	35	521	3
Oct. 16, 1988	Vinny Testaverde, Tampa Bay vs. Indianapolis	42	25	469	2
Sept. 11, 1988	Doug Williams, Washington vs. Pittsburgh	52	30	430	2
Nov. 29, 1987	Tom Ramsey, New England vs. Philadelphia	53	34	402	3
Nov. 22, 1987	Boomer Esiason, Cincinnati vs. Pittsburgh	53	30	409	0
Sept. 20, 1987	Neil Lomax, St. Louis vs. San Diego	61	32	457	3
Dec. 21, 1986	Boomer Esiason, Cincinnati vs. N.Y. Jets	30	23	425	5
Dec. 14, 1986	Dan Marino, Miami vs. L.A. Rams (OT)	46	29	403	5
Nov. 23, 1986	Bernie Kosar, Cleveland vs. Pittsburgh (OT)	46	28	414	2
Nov. 17, 1986	Joe Montana, San Francisco vs. Washington	60	33	441	0
Nov. 16, 1986	Dan Marino, Miami vs. Buffalo	54	39	404	4
Nov. 10, 1986	Bernie Kosar, Cleveland vs. Miami	50	32	401	0
Nov. 2, 1986	Tommy Kramer, Minnesota vs. Washington (OT)	35	20	490	4
Nov. 2, 1986	Ken O'Brien, N.Y. Jets vs. Seattle	32	26	431	4
Oct. 27, 1986	Jay Schroeder, Washington vs. N.Y. Giants	40	22	420	1
Oct. 12, 1986	Steve Grogan, New England vs. N.Y. Jets	42	23	401	3
Sept. 21, 1986	Ken O'Brien, N.Y. Jets vs. Miami (OT)	43	29	479	4
Sept. 21, 1986	Dan Marino, Miami vs. N.Y. Jets (OT)	50	30	448	6
Sept. 21, 1986	Tony Eason, New England vs. Seattle	45	26	414	3
Dec. 20, 1985	John Elway, Denver vs. Seattle	42	24	432	1
Nov. 10, 1985	Dan Fouts, San Diego vs. L.A. Raiders (OT)	41	26	436	4
Oct. 13, 1985	Phil Simms, N.Y. Giants vs. Cincinnati	62	40	513	1
Oct. 13, 1985	Dave Krieg, Seattle vs. Atlanta	51	33	405	4
Oct. 6, 1985	Phil Simms, N.Y. Giants vs. Dallas	36	18	432	3
Oct. 6, 1985	Joe Montana, San Francisco vs. Atlanta	57	37	429	5
Sept. 19, 1985	Tommy Kramer, Minnesota vs. Chicago	55	28	436	3
Sept. 15, 1985	Dan Fouts, San Diego vs. Seattle	43	29	440	4
Dec. 16, 1984	Neil Lomax, St. Louis vs. Washington	46	37	468	2
Dec. 9, 1984	Dan Marino, Miami vs. Indianapolis	41	29	404	4
Dec. 2, 1984	Dan Marino, Miami vs. L.A. Raiders	57	35	470	4
Nov. 25, 1984	Dave Krieg, Seattle vs. Denver	44	30	406	3
Nov. 4, 1984	Dan Marino, Miami vs. N.Y. Jets	42	23	422	2
Oct. 21, 1984	Dan Fouts, San Diego vs. L.A. Raiders	45	24	410	3
Sept. 30, 1984	Dan Marino, Miami vs. St. Louis	36	24	429	3
Sept. 2, 1984	Phil Simms, N.Y. Giants vs. Philadelphia	30	23	409	4
Dec. 11, 1983	Bill Kenney, Kansas City vs. San Diego	41	31	411	4
Nov. 20, 1983	Dave Krieg, Seattle vs. Denver	42	31	418	3
Oct. 9, 1983	Joe Ferguson, Buffalo vs. Miami (OT)	55	38	419	5
Oct. 2, 1983	Joe Theismann, Washington vs. L.A. Raiders	39	23	417	3
Sept. 25, 1983	Richard Todd, N.Y. Jets vs. L.A. Rams (OT)	50	37	446	2
Dec. 26, 1982	Vince Ferragamo, L.A. Rams vs. Chicago	46	30	509	3
Dec. 20, 1982	Dan Fouts, San Diego vs. Cincinnati	40	25	435	1
Dec. 20, 1982	Ken Anderson, Cincinnati vs. San Diego	56	40	416	2
Dec. 11, 1982	Dan Fouts, San Diego vs. San Francisco	48	33	444	5
Nov. 21, 1982	Joe Montana, San Francisco vs. St. Louis	39	26	408	3
Nov. 15, 1981	Steve Bartkowski, Atlanta vs. Pittsburgh	50	33	416	2
Oct. 25, 1981	Brian Sipe, Cleveland vs. Baltimore	41	30	444	4
Oct. 25, 1981	David Woodley, Miami vs. Dallas	37	21	408	3
Oct. 11, 1981	Tommy Kramer, Minnesota vs. San Diego	43	27	444	4
Dec. 14, 1980	Tommy Kramer, Minnesota vs. Cleveland	49	38	456	4
Nov. 16, 1980	Doug Williams, Tampa Bay vs. Minnesota	55	30	486	4
Oct. 19, 1980	Dan Fouts, San Diego vs. N.Y. Giants	41	26	444	3
Oct. 12, 1980	Lynn Dickey, Green Bay vs. Tampa Bay (OT)	51	35	418	1
Sept. 21, 1980	Richard Todd, N.Y. Jets vs. San Francisco	60	42	447	3
Oct. 3, 1976	James Harris, Los Angeles vs. Miami	29	17	436	2
Nov. 17, 1975	Ken Anderson, Cincinnati vs. Buffalo	46	30	447	2
Nov. 18, 1974	Charley Johnson, Denver vs. Kansas City	42	28	445	2
Dec. 11, 1972	Joe Namath, N.Y. Jets vs. Oakland	46	25	403	1
Sept. 24, 1972	Joe Namath, N.Y. Jets vs. Baltimore	28	15	496	6
Dec. 21, 1969	Don Horn, Green Bay vs. St. Louis	31	22	410	5

Date	Player, Team, Opponent	Att.	Comp.	Yards	TD
Sept. 28, 1969	Joe Kapp, Minnesota vs. Baltimore	43	28	449	7
Sept. 9, 1968	Pete Beathard, Houston vs. Kansas City	48	23	413	2
Nov. 26, 1967	Sonny Jurgensen, Washington vs. Cleveland	50	32	418	3
Oct. 1, 1967	Joe Namath, N.Y. Jets vs. Miami	39	23	415	3
Sept. 17, 1967	Johnny Unitas, Baltimore vs. Atlanta	32	22	401	2
Nov. 13, 1966	Don Meredith, Dallas vs. Washington	29	21	406	2
Nov. 28, 1965	Sonny Jurgensen, Washington vs. Dallas	43	26	411	3
Oct. 24, 1965	Fran Tarkenton, Minnesota vs. San Francisco	35	21	407	3
Nov. 1, 1964	Len Dawson, Kansas City vs. Denver	38	23	435	6
Oct. 25, 1964	Cotton Davidson, Oakland vs. Denver	36	23	427	5
Oct. 16, 1964	Babe Parilli, Boston vs. Oakland	47	25	422	4
Dec. 22, 1963	Tom Flores, Oakland vs. Houston	29	17	407	6
Nov. 17, 1963	Norm Snead, Washington vs. Pittsburgh	40	23	424	2
Nov. 10, 1963	Don Meredith, Dallas vs. San Francisco	48	30	460	3
Oct. 13, 1963	Charley Johnson, St. Louis vs. Pittsburgh	41	20	428	2
Dec. 16, 1962	Sonny Jurgensen, Philadelphia vs. St. Louis	34	15	419	5
Nov. 18, 1962	Bill Wade, Chicago vs. Dall. Cowboys	46	28	466	2
Oct. 28, 1962	Y.A. Tittle, N.Y. Giants vs. Washington	39	27	505	7
Sept. 15, 1962	Frank Tripucka, Denver vs. Buffalo	56	29	447	2
Dec. 17, 1961	Sonny Jurgensen, Philadelphia vs. Detroit	42	27	403	3
Nov. 19, 1961	George Blanda, Houston vs. N.Y. Titans	32	20	418	7
Oct. 29, 1961	George Blanda, Houston vs. Buffalo	32	18	464	4
Oct. 29, 1961	Sonny Jurgensen, Philadelphia vs. Washington	41	27	436	3
Oct. 13, 1961	Jacky Lee, Houston vs. Boston	41	27	457	2
Dec. 13, 1958	Bobby Layne, Pittsburgh vs. Chi. Cardinals	49	23	409	2
Nov. 8, 1953	Bobby Thomason, Philadelphia vs. N.Y. Giants	44	22	437	4
Oct. 4, 1952	Otto Graham, Cleveland vs. Pittsburgh	49	21	401	3
Sept. 28, 1951	Norm Van Brocklin, Los Angeles vs. N.Y. Yanks	41	27	554	5
Dec. 11, 1949	Johnny Lujack, Chi. Bears vs. Chi. Cardinals	39	24	468	6
Oct. 31, 1948	Sammy Baugh,Washington vs. Boston	24	17	446	4
Oct. 31, 1948	Jim Hardy, Los Angeles vs. Chi. Cardinals	53	28	406	3
Nov. 14, 1943	Sid Luckman, Chi. Bears vs. N.Y. Giants	32	21	433	7

TIMES 400 OR MORE

181 times by 95 players…Marino 13; Montana, Moon 7; Bledsoe, Fouts, Manning 6; Jurgensen, Krieg 5; Esiason, Kramer, Testaverde 4; Bulger, Cunningham, Hasselbeck, Namath, Simms, Young 3; Anderson, Blanda, Brunell, Culpepper, Elway, Garcia, Green, Johnson, Kosar, Lomax, Meredith, O'Brien, Plummer, Rypien, Todd, Volek, Warner, Williams 2.

100 PASS RECEPTIONS IN A SEASON

Year	Player, Team	No.	Yards	Avg.	Long	TD
2004	Tony Gonzalez, Kansas City	102	1,258	12.3	32	7
2003	Torry Holt, St. Louis	117	1,696	14.5	48	12
	Randy Moss, Minnesota[2]	111	1,632	14.7	72	17
	*Anquan Boldin, Arizona	101	1,377	13.6	71	8
	LaDainian Tomlinson, San Diego	100	725	7.3	73	4
2002	Marvin Harrison, Indianapolis[4]	143	1,722	12.0	69	11
	Hines Ward, Pittsburgh	112	1,329	11.9	72	12
	Randy Moss, Minnesota	106	1,347	12.7	60	7
	Eric Moulds, Buffalo	100	1,292	12.9	70	10
	Terrell Owens, San Francisco	100	1,300	13.0	76	13
2001	Rod Smith, Denver[2]	113	1,343	11.9	65	11
	Jimmy Smith, Jacksonville[2]	112	1,373	12.3	35	8
	Marvin Harrison, Indianapolis[3]	109	1,524	14.0	68	15
	Keyshawn Johnson, Tampa Bay	106	1,266	11.9	47	1
	Troy Brown, New England	101	1,199	11.9	60	5
	Marty Booker, Chicago	100	1,071	10.7	66	8
2000	Marvin Harrison, Indianapolis[2]	102	1,413	13.9	78	14
	Muhsin Muhammad, Carolina	102	1,183	11.6	36	6
	Ed McCaffrey, Denver	101	1,317	13.0	61	9
	Rod Smith, Denver	100	1,602	16.0	49	8
1999	Jimmy Smith, Jacksonville	116	1,636	14.1	62	6
	Marvin Harrison, Indianapolis	115	1,663	14.5	57	12
1997	Tim Brown, Oakland	104	1,408	13.5	59	5
	Herman Moore, Detroit[3]	104	1,293	12.4	79	8
1996	Jerry Rice, San Francisco[4]	108	1,254	11.6	39	8
	Herman Moore, Detroit[2]	106	1,296	12.2	50	9

Year	Player, Team	No.	Yards	Avg.	Long	TD
	Carl Pickens, Cincinnati	100	1,180	11.8	61	12
1995	Herman Moore, Detroit	123	1,686	13.7	69	14
	Jerry Rice, San Francisco[3]	122	1,848	15.1	81	15
	Cris Carter, Minnesota[2]	122	1,371	11.2	60	17
	Isaac Bruce, St. Louis	119	1,781	15.0	72	13
	Michael Irvin, Dallas	111	1,603	14.4	50	10
	Brett Perriman, Detroit	108	1,488	13.8	91	9
	Eric Metcalf, Atlanta	104	1,189	11.4	62	8
	Robert Brooks, Green Bay	102	1,497	14.7	99	13
	Larry Centers, Arizona	101	962	9.5	32	2
1994	Cris Carter, Minnesota	122	1,256	10.3	65	7
	Jerry Rice, San Francisco[2]	112	1,499	13.4	69	13
	Terance Mathis, Atlanta	111	1,342	12.1	81	11
1993	Sterling Sharpe, Green Bay[2]	112	1,274	11.4	54	11
1992	Sterling Sharpe, Green Bay	108	1,461	13.5	76	13
1991	Haywood Jeffires, Houston	100	1,181	11.8	44	7
1990	Jerry Rice, San Francisco	100	1,502	15.0	64	13
1984	Art Monk, Washington	106	1,372	12.9	72	7
1964	Charley Hennigan, Houston	101	1,546	15.3	53	8
1961	Lionel Taylor, Denver	100	1,176	11.8	52	4

1,000 YARDS PASS RECEIVING IN A SEASON

Year	Player, Team	No.	Yards	Avg.	Long	TD
2004	Muhsin Muhammad, Carolina[3]	93	1,405	15.1	51	16
	Joe Horn, New Orleans[4]	94	1,399	14.9	57	11
	Javon Walker, Green Bay	89	1,382	15.5	79	12
	Torry Holt, St. Louis[5]	94	1,372	14.6	75	10
	Isaac Bruce, St. Louis[7]	89	1,292	14.5	56	6
	Chad Johnson, Cincinnati[3]	95	1,274	13.4	53	9
	Tony Gonzalez, Kansas City[2]	102	1,258	12.3	32	7
	Drew Bennett, Tennessee	80	1,247	15.6	48	11
	Reggie Wayne, Indianapolis	77	1,210	15.7	71	12
	Donald Driver, Green Bay[2]	84	1,208	14.4	50	9
	Terrell Owens, Philadelphia[6]	77	1,200	15.6	59	14
	Darrell Jackson, Seattle[3]	87	1,199	13.8	56	7
	*Michael Clayton, Tampa Bay	80	1,193	14.9	75	7
	Jimmy Smith, Jacksonville[6]	74	1,172	15.8	65	6
	Derrick Mason, Tennessee[4]	96	1,168	12.2	37	7
	Rod Smith, Denver[7]	79	1,144	14.5	85	7
	Andre Johnson, Houston	79	1,142	14.5	54	6
	Marvin Harrison, Indianapolis[6]	86	1,113	12.9	59	15
	Eddie Kennison, Kansas City	62	1,086	17.5	70	8
	Ashley Lelie, Denver	54	1,084	20.1	58	7
	Brandon Stokley, Indianapolis	68	1,077	15.8	69	10
	Eric Moulds, Buffalo[4]	88	1,043	11.9	49	5
	Nate Burleson, Minnesota	68	1,006	14.8	68	9
	Hines Ward, Pittsburgh[4]	80	1,004	12.6	58	4
2003	Torry Holt, St. Louis[4]	117	1,696	14.5	48	12
	Randy Moss, Minnesota[6]	111	1,632	14.7	72	17
	*Anquan Boldin, Arizona	101	1,377	13.6	71	8
	Chad Johnson, Cincinnati[2]	90	1,355	15.1	82	10
	Derrick Mason, Tennessee[3]	95	1,303	13.7	50	8
	Marvin Harrison, Indianapolis[5]	94	1,272	13.5	79	10
	Laveranues Coles, Washington[2]	82	1,204	14.7	64	6
	Keenan McCardell, Tampa Bay[5]	84	1,174	14.0	76	8
	Hines Ward, Pittsburgh[3]	95	1,163	12.2	50	10
	Darrell Jackson, Seattle[2]	68	1,137	16.7	80	9
	Steve Smith, Carolina	88	1,110	12.6	67	7
	Santana Moss, N.Y. Jets	74	1,105	14.9	65	10
	Terrell Owens, San Francisco[5]	80	1,102	13.8	75	9
	Amani Toomer, N.Y. Giants[5]	63	1,057	16.8	77	5
2002	Marvin Harrison, Indianapolis[4]	143	1,722	12.0	69	11
	Randy Moss, Minnesota[5]	106	1,347	12.7	60	7
	Amani Toomer, N.Y. Giants[4]	82	1,343	16.4	82	8
	Hines Ward, Pittsburgh[2]	112	1,329	11.9	72	12
	Plaxico Burress, Pittsburgh[2]	78	1,325	17.0	62	7
	Joe Horn, New Orleans[3]	88	1,312	14.9	63	7
	Torry Holt, St. Louis[3]	91	1,302	14.3	58	4
	Terrell Owens, San Francisco[4]	100	1,300	13.0	76	13

Year	Player, Team	No.	Yards	Avg.	Long	TD
	Eric Moulds, Buffalo[3]	100	1,292	12.9	70	10
	Laveranues Coles, N.Y. Jets	89	1,264	14.2	43	5
	Peerless Price, Buffalo	94	1,252	13.3	73	9
	Koren Robinson, Seattle	78	1,240	15.9	83	5
	Jerry Rice, Oakland[14]	92	1,211	13.2	75	7
	Marty Booker, Chicago[2]	97	1,189	12.3	54	6
	Chad Johnson, Cincinnati	69	1,166	16.9	72	5
	Keyshawn Johnson, Tampa Bay[4]	76	1,088	14.3	76	5
	Isaac Bruce, St. Louis[6]	79	1,075	13.6	34	7
	Donald Driver, Green Bay	70	1,064	15.2	85	9
	Jimmy Smith, Jacksonville[7]	80	1,027	12.8	47	7
	Rod Smith, Denver[6]	89	1,027	11.5	46	5
	Derrick Mason, Tennessee[2]	79	1,012	12.8	40	5
	Rod Gardner, Washington	71	1,006	14.2	43	8
2001	David Boston, Arizona[2]	98	1,598	16.3	61	8
	Marvin Harrison, Indianapolis[3]	109	1,524	14.0	68	15
	Terrell Owens, San Francisco[3]	93	1,412	15.2	60	16
	Jimmy Smith, Jacksonville[6]	112	1,373	12.3	35	8
	Torry Holt, St. Louis[2]	81	1,363	16.8	51	7
	Rod Smith, Denver[5]	113	1,343	11.9	65	11
	Keyshawn Johnson, Tampa Bay[3]	106	1,266	11.9	47	1
	Joe Horn, New Orleans[2]	83	1,265	15.2	56	9
	Randy Moss, Minnesota[4]	82	1,233	15.0	73	10
	Troy Brown, New England	101	1,199	11.9	60	5
	Tim Brown, Oakland[9]	91	1,165	12.8	46	9
	Johnnie Morton, Detroit[4]	77	1,154	15.0	76	4
	Jerry Rice, Oakland[13]	83	1,139	13.7	40	9
	Derrick Mason, Tennessee	73	1,128	15.5	71	9
	Curtis Conway, San Diego[3]	71	1,125	15.8	72	6
	Keenan McCardell, Jacksonville[4]	93	1,110	11.9	45	6
	Isaac Bruce, St. Louis[5]	64	1,106	17.3	51	6
	Kevin Johnson, Cleveland	84	1,097	13.1	55	9
	Darrell Jackson, Seattle	70	1,081	15.4	64	8
	Marty Booker, Chicago	100	1,071	10.7	66	8
	Qadry Ismail, Baltimore[2]	74	1,059	14.3	77	7
	Amani Toomer, N.Y. Giants[3]	72	1,054	14.6	60	5
	Willie Jackson, New Orleans	81	1,046	12.9	63	5
	Plaxico Burress, Pittsburgh	66	1,008	15.3	43	6
	Hines Ward, Pittsburgh	94	1,003	10.7	34	4
2000	Torry Holt, St. Louis	82	1,635	19.9	85	6
	Rod Smith, Denver[4]	100	1,602	16.0	49	8
	Isaac Bruce, St. Louis[4]	87	1,471	16.9	78	9
	Terrell Owens, San Francisco[2]	97	1,451	15.0	69	13
	Randy Moss, Minnesota[3]	77	1,437	18.7	78	15
	Marvin Harrison, Indianapolis[2]	102	1,413	13.9	78	14
	Derrick Alexander, Kansas City[3]	78	1,391	17.8	81	10
	Joe Horn, New Orleans	94	1,340	14.3	52	8
	Eric Moulds, Buffalo[2]	94	1,326	14.1	52	5
	Ed McCaffrey, Denver[3]	101	1,317	13.0	61	9
	Cris Carter, Minnesota[8]	96	1,274	13.3	53	9
	Jimmy Smith, Jacksonville[5]	91	1,213	13.3	65	8
	Keenan McCardell, Jacksonville[3]	94	1,207	12.8	67	5
	Tony Gonzalez, Kansas City	93	1,203	12.9	39	9
	Muhsin Muhammad, Carolina[2]	102	1,183	11.6	36	6
	David Boston, Arizona	71	1,156	16.3	70	7
	Tim Brown, Oakland[8]	76	1,128	14.8	45	11
	Amani Toomer, N.Y. Giants[2]	78	1,094	14.0	54	7
1999	Marvin Harrison, Indianapolis	115	1,663	14.5	57	12
	Jimmy Smith, Jacksonville[4]	116	1,636	14.1	62	6
	Randy Moss, Minnesota[2]	80	1,413	17.7	67	11
	Marcus Robinson, Chicago	84	1,400	16.7	80	9
	Tim Brown, Oakland[7]	90	1,344	14.9	47	6
	Germane Crowell, Detroit	81	1,338	16.5	77	7
	Muhsin Muhammad, Carolina	96	1,253	13.1	60	8
	Cris Carter, Minnesota[7]	90	1,241	13.8	68	13
	Michael Westbrook, Washington	65	1,191	18.3	65	9
	Amani Toomer, N.Y. Giants	79	1,183	15.0	80	6
	Keyshawn Johnson, N.Y. Jets[2]	89	1,170	13.2	65	8
	Isaac Bruce, St. Louis[3]	77	1,165	15.1	60	12

Year	Player, Team	No.	Yards	Avg.	Long	TD
	Terry Glenn, New England[2]	69	1,147	16.6	67	4
	Albert Connell, Washington	62	1,132	18.3	62	7
	Johnnie Morton, Detroit[3]	80	1,129	14.1	48	5
	Qadry Ismail, Baltimore	68	1,105	16.3	76	6
	Raghib Ismail, Dallas[2]	80	1,097	13.7	76	6
	Patrick Jeffers, Carolina	63	1,082	17.2	88	12
	Antonio Freeman, Green Bay[3]	74	1,074	14.5	51	6
	Bill Schroeder, Green Bay	74	1,051	14.2	51	5
	Marshall Faulk, St. Louis	87	1,048	12.1	57	5
	Tony Martin, Miami[4]	67	1,037	15.5	69	5
	Darnay Scott, Cincinnati	68	1,022	15.0	76	7
	Rod Smith, Denver[3]	79	1,020	12.9	71	4
	Ed McCaffrey, Denver[2]	71	1,018	14.3	78	7
	Terance Mathis, Atlanta[4]	81	1,016	12.5	52	6
1998	Antonio Freeman, Green Bay[2]	84	1,424	17.0	84	14
	Eric Moulds, Buffalo	67	1,368	20.4	84	9
	*Randy Moss, Minnesota	69	1,313	19.0	61	17
	Rod Smith, Denver[2]	86	1,222	14.2	58	6
	Jimmy Smith, Jacksonville[3]	78	1,182	15.2	72	8
	Tony Martin, Atlanta[3]	66	1,181	17.9	62	6
	Jerry Rice, San Francisco[12]	82	1,157	14.1	75	9
	Frank Sanders, Arizona[2]	89	1,145	12.9	42	3
	Terance Mathis, Atlanta[3]	64	1,136	17.8	78	11
	Keyshawn Johnson, N.Y. Jets	83	1,131	13.6	41	10
	Terrell Owens, San Francisco	67	1,097	16.4	79	14
	Wayne Chrebet, N.Y. Jets	75	1,083	14.4	63	8
	Michael Irvin, Dallas[7]	74	1,057	14.3	51	1
	Ed McCaffrey, Denver	64	1,053	16.5	48	10
	O.J. McDuffie, Miami	90	1,050	11.7	61	7
	Joey Galloway, Seattle[3]	65	1,047	16.1	81	10
	Johnnie Morton, Detroit[2]	69	1,028	14.9	98	2
	Raghib Ismail, Carolina	69	1,024	14.8	62	8
	Carl Pickens, Cincinnati[4]	82	1,023	12.5	67	5
	Tim Brown, Oakland[6]	81	1,012	12.5	49	9
	Cris Carter, Minnesota[6]	78	1,011	13.0	54	12
1997	Rob Moore, Arizona[3]	97	1,584	16.3	47	8
	Tim Brown, Oakland[5]	104	1,408	13.5	59	5
	Yancey Thigpen, Pittsburgh[2]	79	1,398	17.7	69	7
	Jimmy Smith, Jacksonville[2]	82	1,324	16.1	75	4
	Irving Fryar, Philadelphia[5]	86	1,316	15.3	72	6
	Herman Moore, Detroit[4]	104	1,293	12.4	79	8
	Antonio Freeman, Green Bay	81	1,243	15.3	58	12
	Michael Irvin, Dallas[6]	75	1,180	15.7	55	9
	Rod Smith, Denver	70	1,180	16.9	78	12
	Keenan McCardell, Jacksonville[2]	85	1,164	13.7	60	5
	Jake Reed, Minnesota[4]	68	1,138	16.7	56	6
	Shannon Sharpe, Denver[3]	72	1,107	15.4	68	3
	Andre Rison, Kansas City[5]	72	1,092	15.2	45	7
	Cris Carter, Minnesota[5]	89	1,069	12.0	43	13
	Johnnie Morton, Detroit	80	1,057	13.2	73	6
	Joey Galloway, Seattle[2]	72	1,049	14.6	53	12
	Frank Sanders, Arizona	75	1,017	13.6	70	4
	Robert Brooks, Green Bay[2]	60	1,010	16.8	48	7
	Derrick Alexander, Baltimore[2]	65	1,009	15.5	92	9
1996	Isaac Bruce, St. Louis[2]	84	1,338	15.9	70	7
	Jake Reed, Minnesota[3]	72	1,320	18.3	82	7
	Herman Moore, Detroit[3]	106	1,296	12.2	50	9
	Jerry Rice, San Francisco[11]	108	1,254	11.6	39	8
	Jimmy Smith, Jacksonville	83	1,244	15.0	62	7
	Michael Jackson, Baltimore	76	1,201	15.8	86	14
	Irving Fryar, Philadelphia[4]	88	1,195	13.6	42	11
	Carl Pickens, Cincinnati[3]	100	1,180	11.8	61	12
	Tony Martin, San Diego[2]	85	1,171	13.8	55	14
	Cris Carter, Minnesota[4]	96	1,163	12.1	43	10
	*Terry Glenn, New England	90	1,132	12.6	37	6
	Keenan McCardell, Jacksonville	85	1,129	13.3	52	3
	Tim Brown, Oakland[4]	90	1,104	12.3	42	9
	Derrick Alexander, Baltimore	62	1,099	17.7	64	9
	Shannon Sharpe, Denver[2]	80	1,062	13.3	51	10

Year	Player, Team	No.	Yards	Avg.	Long	TD
	Curtis Conway, Chicago[2]	81	1,049	13.0	58	7
	Andre Reed, Buffalo[4]	66	1,036	15.7	67	6
	Brett Perriman, Detroit[2]	94	1,021	10.9	44	5
	Rob Moore, Arizona[2]	58	1,016	17.5	69	4
	Henry Ellard, Washington[7]	52	1,014	19.5	51	2
	Charles Johnson, Pittsburgh	60	1,008	16.8	70	3
1995	Jerry Rice, San Francisco[10]	122	1,848	15.1	81	15
	Isaac Bruce, St. Louis	119	1,781	15.0	72	13
	Herman Moore, Detroit[2]	123	1,686	13.7	69	14
	Michael Irvin, Dallas[5]	111	1,603	14.4	50	10
	Robert Brooks, Green Bay	102	1,497	14.7	99	13
	Brett Perriman, Detroit	108	1,488	13.8	91	9
	Cris Carter, Minnesota[3]	122	1,371	11.2	60	17
	Tim Brown, Oakland[3]	89	1,342	15.1	80	10
	Yancey Thigpen, Pittsburgh	85	1,307	15.4	43	5
	Jeff Graham, Chicago	82	1,301	15.9	51	4
	Carl Pickens, Cincinnati[2]	99	1,234	12.5	68	17
	Tony Martin, San Diego	90	1,224	13.6	51	6
	Eric Metcalf, Atlanta	104	1,189	11.4	62	8
	Jake Reed, Minnesota[2]	72	1,167	16.2	55	9
	Quinn Early, New Orleans	81	1,087	13.4	70	8
	Anthony Miller, Denver[5]	59	1,079	18.3	62	14
	Bert Emanuel, Atlanta	74	1,039	14.0	52	5
	*Joey Galloway, Seattle	67	1,039	15.5	59	7
	Terance Mathis, Atlanta[2]	78	1,039	13.3	54	9
	Curtis Conway, Chicago	62	1,037	16.7	76	12
	Henry Ellard, Washington[6]	56	1,005	17.9	59	5
	Mark Carrier, Carolina[2]	66	1,002	15.2	66	3
	Brian Blades, Seattle[4]	77	1,001	13.0	49	4
1994	Jerry Rice, San Francisco[9]	112	1,499	13.4	69	13
	Henry Ellard, Washington[5]	74	1,397	18.9	73	6
	Terance Mathis, Atlanta	111	1,342	12.1	81	11
	Tim Brown, L.A. Raiders[2]	89	1,309	14.7	77	9
	Andre Reed, Buffalo[3]	90	1,303	14.5	83	8
	Irving Fryar, Miami[3]	73	1,270	17.4	54	7
	Cris Carter, Minnesota[2]	122	1,256	10.3	65	7
	Michael Irvin, Dallas[4]	79	1,241	15.7	65	6
	Jake Reed, Minnesota	85	1,175	13.8	59	4
	Ben Coates, New England	96	1,174	12.2	62	7
	Herman Moore, Detroit	72	1,173	16.3	51	11
	Fred Barnett, Philadelphia[2]	78	1,127	14.4	54	5
	Carl Pickens, Cincinnati	71	1,127	15.9	70	11
	Sterling Sharpe, Green Bay[4]	94	1,119	11.9	49	18
	Anthony Miller, Denver[4]	60	1,107	18.5	76	5
	Andre Rison, Atlanta[3]	81	1,088	13.4	69	8
	Brian Blades, Seattle[3]	81	1,088	13.4	45	4
	Rob Moore, N.Y. Jets	78	1,010	12.9	41	6
	Shannon Sharpe, Denver	87	1,010	11.6	44	4
1993	Jerry Rice, San Francisco[8]	98	1,503	15.3	80	15
	Michael Irvin, Dallas[3]	88	1,330	15.1	61	7
	Sterling Sharpe, Green Bay[4]	112	1,274	11.4	54	11
	Andre Rison, Atlanta[3]	86	1,242	14.4	53	15
	Tim Brown, L.A. Raiders	80	1,180	14.8	71	7
	Anthony Miller, San Diego[3]	84	1,162	13.8	66	7
	Cris Carter, Minnesota	86	1,071	12.5	58	9
	Reggie Langhorne, Indianapolis	85	1,038	12.2	72	3
	Irving Fryar, Miami[2]	64	1,010	15.8	65	5
1992	Sterling Sharpe, Green Bay[3]	108	1,461	13.5	76	13
	Michael Irvin, Dallas[2]	78	1,396	17.9	87	7
	Jerry Rice, San Francisco[7]	84	1,201	14.3	80	10
	Andre Rison, Atlanta[2]	93	1,119	12.0	71	11
	Fred Barnett, Philadelphia	67	1,083	16.2	71	6
	Anthony Miller, San Diego[2]	72	1,060	14.7	67	7
	Eric Martin, New Orleans[3]	68	1,041	15.3	52	5
1991	Michael Irvin, Dallas	93	1,523	16.4	66	8
	Gary Clark, Washington[5]	70	1,340	19.1	82	10
	Jerry Rice, San Francisco[6]	80	1,206	15.1	73	14
	Haywood Jeffires, Houston[2]	100	1,181	11.8	44	7
	Michael Haynes, Atlanta	50	1,122	22.4	80	11

Year	Player, Team	No.	Yards	Avg.	Long	TD
	Andre Reed, Buffalo[2]	81	1,113	13.7	55	10
	Drew Hill, Houston[5]	90	1,109	12.3	61	4
	Mark Duper, Miami[4]	70	1,085	15.5	43	5
	James Lofton, Buffalo[6]	57	1,072	18.8	77	8
	Mark Clayton, Miami[5]	70	1,053	15.0	43	12
	Henry Ellard, L.A. Rams[4]	64	1,052	16.4	38	3
	Art Monk, Washington[5]	71	1,049	14.8	64	8
	Irving Fryar, New England	68	1,014	14.9	56	3
	John Taylor, San Francisco[2]	64	1,011	15.8	97	9
	Brian Blades, Seattle[2]	70	1,003	14.3	52	2
1990	Jerry Rice, San Francisco[5]	100	1,502	15.0	64	13
	Henry Ellard, L.A. Rams[3]	76	1,294	17.0	50	4
	Andre Rison, Atlanta	82	1,208	14.7	75	10
	Gary Clark, Washington[4]	75	1,112	14.8	53	8
	Sterling Sharpe, Green Bay[2]	67	1,105	16.5	76	6
	Willie Anderson, L.A. Rams[2]	51	1,097	21.5	55	4
	Haywood Jeffires, Houston	74	1,048	14.2	87	8
	Stephone Paige, Kansas City	65	1,021	15.7	86	5
	Drew Hill, Houston[4]	74	1,019	13.8	57	5
	Anthony Carter, Minnesota[3]	70	1,008	14.4	56	8
1989	Jerry Rice, San Francisco[4]	82	1,483	18.1	68	17
	Sterling Sharpe, Green Bay	90	1,423	15.8	79	12
	Mark Carrier, Tampa Bay	86	1,422	16.5	78	9
	Henry Ellard, L.A. Rams[2]	70	1,382	19.7	53	8
	Andre Reed, Buffalo	88	1,312	14.9	78	9
	Anthony Miller, San Diego	75	1,252	16.7	69	10
	Webster Slaughter, Cleveland	65	1,236	19.0	97	6
	Gary Clark, Washington[3]	79	1,229	15.6	80	9
	Tim McGee, Cincinnati	65	1,211	18.6	74	8
	Art Monk, Washington[4]	86	1,186	13.8	60	8
	Willie Anderson, L.A. Rams	44	1,146	26.0	78	5
	Ricky Sanders, Washington[2]	80	1,138	14.2	68	4
	Vance Johnson, Denver	76	1,095	14.4	69	7
	Richard Johnson, Detroit	70	1,091	15.6	75	8
	Eric Martin, New Orleans[2]	68	1,090	16.0	53	8
	John Taylor, San Francisco	60	1,077	18.0	95	10
	Mervyn Fernandez, L.A. Raiders	57	1,069	18.8	75	9
	Anthony Carter, Minnesota[2]	65	1,066	16.4	50	4
	Brian Blades, Seattle	77	1,063	13.8	60	5
	Mark Clayton, Miami[4]	64	1,011	15.8	78	9
1988	Henry Ellard, L.A. Rams	86	1,414	16.4	68	10
	Jerry Rice, San Francisco[3]	64	1,306	20.4	96	9
	Eddie Brown, Cincinnati	53	1,273	24.0	86	9
	Anthony Carter, Minnesota	72	1,225	17.0	67	6
	Ricky Sanders, Washington	73	1,148	15.7	55	12
	Drew Hill, Houston[3]	72	1,141	15.8	57	10
	Mark Clayton, Miami[3]	86	1,129	13.1	45	14
	Roy Green, Phoenix[3]	68	1,097	16.1	52	7
	Eric Martin, New Orleans	85	1,083	12.7	40	7
	Al Toon, N.Y. Jets[2]	93	1,067	11.5	42	5
	Bruce Hill, Tampa Bay	58	1,040	17.9	42	9
	Lionel Manuel, N.Y. Giants	65	1,029	15.8	46	4
1987	J.T. Smith, St. Louis[2]	91	1,117	12.3	38	8
	Jerry Rice, San Francisco[2]	65	1,078	16.6	57	22
	Gary Clark, Washington[2]	56	1,066	19.0	84	7
	Carlos Carson, Kansas City[3]	55	1,044	19.0	81	7
1986	Jerry Rice, San Francisco	86	1,570	18.3	66	15
	Stanley Morgan, New England[3]	84	1,491	17.8	44	10
	Mark Duper, Miami[3]	67	1,313	19.6	85	11
	Gary Clark, Washington	74	1,265	17.1	55	7
	Al Toon, N.Y. Jets	85	1,176	13.8	62	8
	Todd Christensen, L.A. Raiders[3]	95	1,153	12.1	35	8
	Mark Clayton, Miami[2]	60	1,150	19.2	68	10
	*Bill Brooks, Indianapolis	65	1,131	17.4	84	8
	Drew Hill, Houston[2]	65	1,112	17.1	81	5
	Steve Largent, Seattle[8]	70	1,070	15.3	38	9
	Art Monk, Washington[3]	73	1,068	14.6	69	4
	*Ernest Givins, Houston	61	1,062	17.4	60	3
	Cris Collinsworth, Cincinnati[4]	62	1,024	16.5	46	10

Year	Player, Team	No.	Yards	Avg.	Long	TD
	Wesley Walker, N.Y. Jets[2]	49	1,016	20.7	83	12
	J.T. Smith, St. Louis	80	1,014	12.7	45	6
	Mark Bavaro, N.Y. Giants	66	1,001	15.2	41	4
1985	Steve Largent, Seattle[7]	79	1,287	16.3	43	6
	Mike Quick, Philadelphia[3]	73	1,247	17.1	99	11
	Art Monk, Washington[2]	91	1,226	13.5	53	2
	Wes Chandler, San Diego[4]	67	1,199	17.9	75	10
	Drew Hill, Houston	64	1,169	18.3	57	9
	James Lofton, Green Bay[5]	69	1,153	16.7	56	4
	Louis Lipps, Pittsburgh	59	1,134	19.2	51	12
	Cris Collinsworth, Cincinnati[3]	65	1,125	17.3	71	5
	Tony Hill, Dallas[3]	74	1,113	15.0	53	7
	Lionel James, San Diego	86	1,027	11.9	67	6
	Roger Craig, San Francisco	92	1,016	11.0	73	6
1984	Roy Green, St. Louis[2]	78	1,555	19.9	83	12
	John Stallworth, Pittsburgh[3]	80	1,395	17.4	51	11
	Mark Clayton, Miami	73	1,389	19.0	65	18
	Art Monk, Washington	106	1,372	12.9	72	7
	James Lofton, Green Bay[4]	62	1,361	22.0	79	7
	Mark Duper, Miami[2]	71	1,306	18.4	80	8
	Steve Watson, Denver[3]	69	1,170	17.0	73	7
	Steve Largent, Seattle[6]	74	1,164	15.7	65	12
	Tim Smith, Houston[2]	69	1,141	16.5	75	4
	Stacey Bailey, Atlanta	67	1,138	17.0	61	6
	Carlos Carson, Kansas City[2]	57	1,078	18.9	57	4
	Mike Quick, Philadelphia[2]	61	1,052	17.2	90	9
	Todd Christensen, L.A. Raiders[2]	80	1,007	12.6	38	7
	Kevin House, Tampa Bay[2]	76	1,005	13.2	55	5
	Ozzie Newsome, Cleveland[2]	89	1,001	11.2	52	5
1983	Mike Quick, Philadelphia	69	1,409	20.4	83	13
	Carlos Carson, Kansas City	80	1,351	16.9	50	7
	James Lofton, Green Bay[3]	58	1,300	22.4	74	8
	Todd Christensen, L.A. Raiders	92	1,247	13.6	45	12
	Roy Green, St. Louis	78	1,227	15.7	71	14
	Charlie Brown, Washington	78	1,225	15.7	75	8
	Tim Smith, Houston	83	1,176	14.2	47	6
	Kellen Winslow, San Diego[3]	88	1,172	13.3	46	8
	Earnest Gray, N.Y. Giants	78	1,139	14.6	62	5
	Steve Watson, Denver[2]	59	1,133	19.2	78	5
	Cris Collinsworth, Cincinnati[2]	66	1,130	17.1	63	5
	Steve Largent, Seattle[5]	72	1,074	14.9	46	11
	Mark Duper, Miami	51	1,003	19.7	85	10
1982	Wes Chandler, San Diego[3]	49	1,032	21.1	66	9
1981	Alfred Jenkins, Atlanta[2]	70	1,358	19.4	67	13
	James Lofton, Green Bay[2]	71	1,294	18.2	75	8
	Steve Watson, Denver	60	1,244	20.7	95	13
	Frank Lewis, Buffalo[2]	70	1,244	17.8	33	4
	Steve Largent, Seattle[4]	75	1,224	16.3	57	9
	Charlie Joiner, San Diego[4]	70	1,188	17.0	57	7
	Kevin House, Tampa Bay	56	1,176	21.0	84	9
	Wes Chandler, N.O.-San Diego[2]	69	1,142	16.6	51	6
	Dwight Clark, San Francisco	85	1,105	13.0	78	4
	John Stallworth, Pittsburgh[2]	63	1,098	17.4	55	5
	Kellen Winslow, San Diego[2]	88	1,075	12.2	67	10
	Pat Tilley, St. Louis	66	1,040	15.8	75	3
	Stanley Morgan, New England[2]	44	1,029	23.4	76	6
	Harold Carmichael, Philadelphia[3]	61	1,028	16.9	85	6
	Freddie Scott, Detroit	53	1,022	19.3	48	5
	*Cris Collinsworth, Cincinnati	67	1,009	15.1	74	8
	Joe Senser, Minnesota	79	1,004	12.7	53	8
	Ozzie Newsome, Cleveland	69	1,002	14.5	62	6
	Sammy White, Minnesota	66	1,001	15.2	53	3
1980	John Jefferson, San Diego[3]	82	1,340	16.3	58	13
	Kellen Winslow, San Diego	89	1,290	14.5	65	9
	James Lofton, Green Bay	71	1,226	17.3	47	4
	Charlie Joiner, San Diego[3]	71	1,132	15.9	51	4
	Ahmad Rashad, Minnesota[2]	69	1,095	15.9	76	5
	Steve Largent, Seattle[3]	66	1,064	16.1	67	6
	Tony Hill, Dallas[2]	60	1,055	17.6	58	8

Year	Player, Team	No.	Yards	Avg.	Long	TD
	Alfred Jenkins, Atlanta	57	1,026	18.0	57	6
1979	Steve Largent, Seattle[2]	66	1,237	18.7	55	9
	John Stallworth, Pittsburgh	70	1,183	16.9	65	8
	Ahmad Rashad, Minnesota	80	1,156	14.5	52	9
	John Jefferson, San Diego[2]	61	1,090	17.9	65	10
	Frank Lewis, Buffalo	54	1,082	20.0	55	2
	Wes Chandler, New Orleans	65	1,069	16.4	85	6
	Tony Hill, Dallas	60	1,062	17.7	75	10
	Drew Pearson, Dallas[2]	55	1,026	18.7	56	8
	Wallace Francis, Atlanta	74	1,013	13.7	42	8
	Harold Jackson, New England[3]	45	1,013	22.5	59	7
	Charlie Joiner, San Diego[2]	72	1,008	14.0	39	4
	Stanley Morgan, New England	44	1,002	22.8	63	12
1978	Wesley Walker, N.Y. Jets	48	1,169	24.4	77	8
	Steve Largent, Seattle	71	1,168	16.5	57	8
	Harold Carmichael, Philadelphia[2]	55	1,072	19.5	56	8
	*John Jefferson, San Diego	56	1,001	17.9	46	13
1976	Roger Carr, Baltimore	43	1,112	25.9	79	11
	Cliff Branch, Oakland[2]	46	1,111	24.2	88	12
	Charlie Joiner, San Diego	50	1,056	21.1	81	7
1975	Ken Burrough, Houston	53	1,063	20.1	77	8
1974	Cliff Branch, Oakland	60	1,092	18.2	67	13
	Drew Pearson, Dallas	62	1,087	17.5	50	2
1973	Harold Carmichael, Philadelphia	67	1,116	16.7	73	9
1972	Harold Jackson, Philadelphia[2]	62	1,048	16.9	77	4
	John Gilliam, Minnesota	47	1,035	22.0	66	7
1971	Otis Taylor, Kansas City[2]	57	1,110	19.5	82	7
1970	Gene Washington, San Francisco	53	1,100	20.8	79	12
	Marlin Briscoe, Buffalo	57	1,036	18.2	48	8
	Dick Gordon, Chicago	71	1,026	14.5	69	13
	Gary Garrison, San Diego[2]	44	1,006	22.9	67	12
1969	Warren Wells, Oakland[2]	47	1,260	26.8	80	14
	Harold Jackson, Philadelphia	65	1,116	17.2	65	9
	Roy Jefferson, Pittsburgh[2]	67	1,079	16.1	63	9
	Dan Abramowicz, New Orleans	73	1,015	13.9	49	7
	Lance Alworth, San Diego[7]	64	1,003	15.7	76	4
1968	Lance Alworth, San Diego[6]	68	1,312	19.3	80	10
	Don Maynard, N.Y. Jets[5]	57	1,297	22.8	87	10
	George Sauer, N.Y. Jets[3]	66	1,141	17.3	43	3
	Warren Wells, Oakland	53	1,137	21.5	94	11
	Gary Garrison, San Diego	52	1,103	21.2	84	10
	Roy Jefferson, Pittsburgh	58	1,074	18.5	62	11
	Paul Warfield, Cleveland	50	1,067	21.3	65	12
	Homer Jones, N.Y. Giants[3]	45	1,057	23.5	84	7
	Fred Biletnikoff, Oakland	61	1,037	17.0	82	6
	Lance Rentzel, Dallas	54	1,009	18.7	65	6
1967	Don Maynard, N.Y. Jets[4]	71	1,434	20.2	75	10
	Ben Hawkins, Philadelphia	59	1,265	21.4	87	10
	Homer Jones, N.Y. Giants[2]	49	1,209	24.7	70	13
	Jackie Smith, St. Louis	56	1,205	21.5	76	9
	George Sauer, N.Y. Jets[2]	75	1,189	15.9	61	6
	Lance Alworth, San Diego[5]	52	1,010	19.4	71	9
1966	Lance Alworth, San Diego[4]	73	1,383	18.9	78	13
	Otis Taylor, Kansas City	58	1,297	22.4	89	8
	Pat Studstill, Detroit	67	1,266	18.9	99	5
	Bob Hayes, Dallas[2]	64	1,232	19.3	95	13
	Charlie Frazier, Houston	57	1,129	19.8	79	12
	Charley Taylor, Washington	72	1,119	15.5	86	12
	George Sauer, N.Y. Jets	63	1,081	17.2	77	5
	Homer Jones, N.Y. Giants	48	1,044	21.8	98	8
	Art Powell, Oakland[5]	53	1,026	19.4	46	11
1965	Lance Alworth, San Diego[3]	69	1,602	23.2	85	14
	Dave Parks, San Francisco	80	1,344	16.8	53	12
	Don Maynard, N.Y. Jets[3]	68	1,218	17.9	56	14
	Pete Retzlaff, Philadelphia	66	1,190	18.0	78	10
	Lionel Taylor, Denver[4]	85	1,131	13.3	63	6
	Tommy McDonald, Los Angeles[3]	67	1,036	15.5	51	9
	*Bob Hayes, Dallas	46	1,003	21.8	82	12
1964	Charley Hennigan, Houston[3]	101	1,546	15.3	53	8

Year	Player, Team	No.	Yards	Avg.	Long	TD
	Art Powell, Oakland[4]	76	1,361	17.9	77	11
	Lance Alworth, San Diego[2]	61	1,235	20.2	82	13
	Johnny Morris, Chicago	93	1,200	12.9	63	10
	Elbert Dubenion, Buffalo	42	1,139	27.1	72	10
	Terry Barr, Detroit[2]	57	1,030	18.1	58	9
1963	Bobby Mitchell, Washington[2]	69	1,436	20.8	99	7
	Art Powell, Oakland[3]	73	1,304	17.9	85	16
	Buddy Dial, Pittsburgh[2]	60	1,295	21.6	83	9
	Lance Alworth, San Diego	61	1,205	19.8	85	11
	Del Shofner, N.Y. Giants[4]	64	1,181	18.5	70	9
	Lionel Taylor, Denver[3]	78	1,101	14.1	72	10
	Terry Barr, Detroit	66	1,086	16.5	75	13
	Charley Hennigan, Houston[2]	61	1,051	17.2	83	10
	Sonny Randle, St. Louis[2]	51	1,014	19.9	68	12
	Bake Turner, N.Y. Jets	71	1,009	14.2	53	6
1962	Bobby Mitchell, Washington	72	1,384	19.2	81	11
	Sonny Randle, St. Louis	63	1,158	18.4	86	7
	Tommy McDonald, Philadelphia[2]	58	1,146	19.8	60	10
	Del Shofner, N.Y. Giants[3]	53	1,133	21.4	69	12
	Art Powell, N.Y. Titans[2]	64	1,130	17.7	80	8
	Frank Clarke, Dall. Cowboys	47	1,043	22.2	66	14
	Don Maynard, N.Y. Titans[2]	56	1,041	18.6	86	8
1961	Charley Hennigan, Houston	82	1,746	21.3	80	12
	Lionel Taylor, Denver[2]	100	1,176	11.8	52	4
	Bill Groman, Houston[2]	50	1,175	23.5	80	17
	Tommy McDonald, Philadelphia	64	1,144	17.9	66	13
	Del Shofner, N.Y. Giants[2]	68	1,125	16.5	46	11
	Jim Phillips, Los Angeles	78	1,092	14.0	69	5
	*Mike Ditka, Chicago	56	1,076	19.2	76	12
	Dave Kocourek, San Diego	55	1,055	19.2	76	4
	Buddy Dial, Pittsburgh	53	1,047	19.8	88	12
	R.C. Owens, San Francisco	55	1,032	18.8	54	5
1960	*Bill Groman, Houston	72	1,473	20.5	92	12
	Raymond Berry, Baltimore	74	1,298	17.5	70	10
	Don Maynard, N.Y. Titans	72	1,265	17.6	65	6
	Lionel Taylor, Denver	92	1,235	13.4	80	12
	Art Powell, N.Y. Titans	69	1,167	16.9	76	14
1958	Del Shofner, Los Angeles	51	1,097	21.5	92	8
1956	Bill Howton, Green Bay[2]	55	1,188	21.6	66	12
	Harlon Hill, Chi. Bears[2]	47	1,128	24.0	79	11
1954	Bob Boyd, Los Angeles	53	1,212	22.9	80	6
	*Harlon Hill, Chi. Bears	45	1,124	25.0	76	12
1953	Pete Pihos, Philadelphia	63	1,049	16.7	59	10
1952	*Bill Howton, Green Bay	53	1,231	23.2	90	13
1951	Elroy (Crazylegs) Hirsch, Los Angeles	66	1,495	22.7	91	17
1950	Tom Fears, Los Angeles[2]	84	1,116	13.3	53	7
	Cloyce Box, Detroit	50	1,009	20.2	82	11
1949	Bob Mann, Detroit	66	1,014	15.4	64	4
	Tom Fears, Los Angeles	77	1,013	13.2	51	9
1945	Jim Benton, Cleveland	45	1,067	23.7	84	8
1942	Don Hutson, Green Bay	74	1,211	16.4	73	17

*First season of professional football.

250 YARDS PASS RECEIVING IN A GAME

Date	Player, Team, Opponent	No.	Yards	TD
Nov. 10, 2002	Plaxico Burress, Pittsburgh vs. Atlanta (OT)	9	253	2
Dec. 17, 2000	Terrell Owens, San Francisco vs. Chicago	20	283	1
Sept. 10, 2000	Jimmy Smith, Jacksonville vs. Baltimore	15	291	3
Dec. 12, 1999	Qadry Ismail, Baltimore vs. Pittsburgh	6	258	3
Dec. 18, 1995	Jerry Rice, San Francisco vs. Minnesota	14	289	3
Dec. 11, 1989	John Taylor, San Francisco vs. L.A. Rams	11	286	2
Nov. 26, 1989	Willie Anderson, L.A. Rams vs. New Orleans (OT)	15	336	1
Oct. 18, 1987	Steve Largent, Seattle vs. Detroit	15	261	3
Oct. 4, 1987	Anthony Allen, Washington vs. St. Louis	7	255	3
Dec. 22, 1985	Stephone Paige, Kansas City vs. San Diego	8	309	2
Dec. 20, 1982	Wes Chandler, San Diego vs. Cincinnati	10	260	2
Sept. 23, 1979	*Jerry Butler, Buffalo vs. N.Y. Jets	10	255	4
Nov. 4, 1962	Sonny Randle, St. Louis vs. N.Y. Giants	16	256	1
Oct. 28, 1962	Del Shofner, N.Y. Giants vs. Washington	11	269	1

Date	Player, Team, Opponent	No.	Yards	TD
Oct. 13, 1961	Charley Hennigan, Houston vs. Boston	13	272	1
Oct. 21, 1956	Billy Howton, Green Bay vs. Los Angeles	7	257	2
Dec. 3, 1950	Cloyce Box, Detroit vs. Baltimore	12	302	4
Nov. 22, 1945	Jim Benton, Cleveland vs. Detroit	10	303	1

*First season of professional football.

2,000 COMBINED NET YARDS GAINED IN A SEASON

Year	Player, Team	Rushing Att.-Yds.	Pass Rec.	Punt Ret.	Kickoff Ret.	Fum. Ret.	Total Yds.
2004	Dante Hall, Kansas City[3]	8-56	25-230	23-232	68-1,718	0-0	124-2,236
	Tiki Barber, N.Y. Giants[2]	322-1,518	52-578	0-0	0-0	2-0	376-2,096
	Edgerrin James, Indianapolis[3]	334-1,548	51-483	0-0	0-0	1-0	386-2,031
2003	Dante Hall, Kansas City[2]	16-73	40-423	29-472	57-1,478	0-0	142-2,446
	LaDainian Tomlinson, San Diego[2]	313-1,645	100-725	0-0	0-0	2-0	415-2,370
	Jamal Lewis, Baltimore	387-2,066	26-205	0-0	0-0	1-0	414-2,271
	Ahman Green, Green Bay	355-1,883	50-367	0-0	0-0	2-0	407-2,250
	Deuce McAllister, New Orleans	351-1,641	69-516	0-0	0-0	3-(-3)	423-2,154
	Priest Holmes, Kansas City[3]	320-1,420	74-690	0-0	0-0	0-0	394-2,110
2002	Michael Lewis, New Orleans	1-15	8-200	44-625	70-1,807	2-0	125-2,647
	Priest Holmes, Kansas City[2]	313-1,615	70-672	0-0	0-0	0-0	383-2,287
	Ricky Williams, Miami	383-1,853	47-363	0-0	0-0	1-0	431-2,216
	LaDainian Tomlinson, San Diego	372-1,683	79-489	0-0	0-0	0-0	451-2,172
	Dante Hall, Kansas City	11-54	20-322	29-390	57-1,354	1-0	118-2,120
2001	Priest Holmes, Kansas City	327-1,555	62-614	0-0	0-0	0-0	389-2,169
	Marshall Faulk, St. Louis[4]	260-1,382	83-765	0-0	0-0	2-0	345-2,147
	Derrick Mason, Tennessee[2]	0-0	73-1,128	20-128	34-748	1-0	128-2,004
2000	Derrick Mason, Tennessee	1-1	63-895	51-662	42-1,132	1-0	158-2,690
	MarTay Jenkins, Arizona	1-(-4)	17-219	1-1	82-2,186	0-0	101-2,402
	Edgerrin James, Indianapolis[2]	387-1,709	63-594	0-0	0-0	0-0	450-2,303
	Marshall Faulk, St. Louis[3]	253-1,359	81-830	0-0	1-18	2-0	337-2,207
	Tiki Barber, N.Y. Giants	213-1,006	70-719	39-332	1-28	5-0	328-2,085
1999	Marshall Faulk, St. Louis[2]	253-1,381	87-1,048	0-0	0-0	0-0	340-2,429
	*Edgerrin James, Indianapolis	369-1,553	62-586	0-0	0-0	2-0	433-2,139
	*Terrence Wilkins, Indianapolis	1-2	42-565	41-388	51-1,134	1-0	136-2,089
	Glyn Milburn, Chicago[2]	16-102	20-151	30-346	61-1,426	2-0	129-2,025
1998	Brian Mitchell, Washington[4]	39-208	44-306	44-506	59-1,337	0-0	186-2,357
	Marshall Faulk, Indianapolis	324-1,319	86-908	0-0	0-0	2-13	412-2,240
	Terrell Davis, Denver[2]	392-2,008	25-217	0-0	0-0	1-0	418-2,225
	Jamal Anderson, Atlanta	410-1,846	27-319	0-0	0-0	1-0	438-2,165
	Garrison Hearst, San Francisco[2]	310-1,570	39-535	0-0	0-0	1-0	350-2,105
1997	Barry Sanders, Detroit[2]	335-2,053	33-305	0-0	0-0	1-0	369-2,358
	Kevin Williams, Arizona	1-(-2)	20-273	40-462	59-1,458	1-0	121-2,191
	Brian Mitchell, Washington[3]	23-107	36-438	38-442	47-1,094	0-0	144-2,081
	Terrell Davis, Denver	369-1,750	42-287	0-0	0-0	2-(-7)	413-2,030
	Jermaine Lewis, Baltimore	3-35	42-648	28-437	41-905	2-0	116-2,025
1995	Brian Mitchell, Washington[2]	46-301	38-324	25-315	55-1,408	0-0	164-2,348
	Emmitt Smith, Dallas[2]	377-1,773	62-375	0-0	0-0	0-0	439-2,148
	Glyn Milburn, Denver	49-266	22-191	31-354	47-1,269	0-0	149-2,080
	Ernie Mills, Pittsburgh	5-39	39-679	0-0	54-1,306	0-0	98-2,024
1994	Brian Mitchell, Washington	78-311	26-236	32-452	58-1,478	0-0	194-2,477
	Barry Sanders, Detroit	331-1,883	44-283	0-0	0-0	0-0	375-2,166
1992	Thurman Thomas, Buffalo[2]	312-1,487	58-626	0-0	0-0	1-0	371-2,113
	Emmitt Smith, Dallas	373-1,713	59-335	0-0	0-0	1-0	433-2,048
	Barry Foster, Pittsburgh	390-1,690	36-344	0-0	0-0	2-(-20)	428-2,014
1991	Thurman Thomas, Buffalo	288-1,407	62-631	0-0	0-0	0-0	350-2,038
1990	Herschel Walker, Minnesota[2]	184-770	35-315	0-0	44-966	4-0	267-2,051
1988	*Tim Brown, L.A. Raiders	14-50	43-725	49-444	41-1,098	7-0	154-2,317
	Roger Craig, San Francisco[2]	310-1,502	76-534	0-0	2-32	2-0	390-2,068
	Eric Dickerson, Indianapolis[4]	388-1,659	36-377	0-0	0-0	1-0	425-2,036
	Herschel Walker, Dallas	361-1,514	53-505	0-0	0-0	3-0	417-2,019
1986	Eric Dickerson, L.A. Rams[3]	404-1,821	26-205	0-0	0-0	2-0	432-2,026
	Gary Anderson, San Diego	127-442	80-871	25-227	24-482	2-0	258-2,022
1985	Lionel James, San Diego	105-516	86-1,027	25-213	36-779	1-0	253-2,535
	Marcus Allen, L.A. Raiders	380-1,759	67-555	0-0	0-0	2-(-6)	449-2,308
	Roger Craig, San Francisco	214-1,050	92-1,016	0-0	0-0	0-0	306-2,066
	Walter Payton, Chicago[4]	324-1,551	49-483	0-0	0-0	1-0	374-2,034
1984	Eric Dickerson, L.A. Rams[2]	379-2,105	21-139	0-0	0-0	4-15	404-2,259
	James Wilder, Tampa Bay	407-1,544	85-685	0-0	0-0	4-0	496-2,229
	Walter Payton, Chicago[3]	381-1,684	45-368	0-0	0-0	1-0	427-2,052

Year	Player, Team	Rushing Att.-Yds.	Pass Rec.	Punt Ret.	Kickoff Ret.	Fum. Ret.	Total Yds.
1983	*Eric Dickerson, L.A. Rams	390-1,808	51-404	0-0	0-0	1-0	442-2,212
	William Andrews, Atlanta[2]	331-1,567	59-609	0-0	0-0	2-0	392-2,176
	Walter Payton, Chicago[2]	314-1,421	53-607	0-0	0-0	2-0	369-2,028
1981	*James Brooks, San Diego	109-525	46-329	22-290	40-949	2-0	219-2,093
	William Andrews, Atlanta	289-1,301	81-735	0-0	0-0	0-0	370-2,036
1980	Bruce Harper, N.Y. Jets[2]	45-126	50-634	28-242	49-1,070	3-0	175-2,072
1979	Wilbert Montgomery, Philadelphia	338-1,512	41-494	0-0	1-6	2-0	382-2,012
1978	Bruce Harper, N.Y. Jets	58-303	13-196	30-378	55-1,280	1-0	157-2,157
1977	Walter Payton, Chicago	339-1,852	27-269	0-0	2-95	5-0	373-2,216
	Terry Metcalf, St. Louis[3]	149-739	34-403	14-108	32-772	1-0	230-2,022
1975	Terry Metcalf, St. Louis[2]	165-816	43-378	23-285	35-960	2-23	268-2,462
	O.J. Simpson, Buffalo[2]	329-1,817	28-426	0-0	0-0	1-0	358-2,243
1974	Mack Herron, New England	231-824	38-474	35-517	28-629	3-0	335-2,444
	Otis Armstrong, Denver	263-1,407	38-405	0-0	16-386	1-0	318-2,198
	Terry Metcalf, St. Louis	152-718	50-377	26-340	20-623	7-0	255-2,058
1973	O.J. Simpson, Buffalo	332-2,003	6-70	0-0	0-0	0-0	338-2,073
1966	Gale Sayers, Chicago[2]	229-1,231	34-447	6-44	23-718	3-0	295-2,440
	Leroy Kelly, Cleveland	209-1,141	32-366	13-104	19-403	0-0	273-2,014
1965	*Gale Sayers, Chicago	166-867	29-507	16-238	21-660	4-0	236-2,272
1963	Timmy Brown, Philadelphia[2]	192-841	36-487	16-152	33-945	2-3	279-2,428
	Jim Brown, Cleveland	291-1,863	24-268	0-0	0-0	0-0	315-2,131
1962	Timmy Brown, Philadelphia	137-545	52-849	6-81	30-831	4-0	229-2,306
	Dick Christy, N.Y. Titans	114-535	62-538	15-250	38-824	2-0	231-2,147
1961	Billy Cannon, Houston	200-948	43-586	9-70	18-439	2-0	272-2,043
1960	*Abner Haynes, Dallas Texans	156-875	55-576	14-215	19-434	4-0	248-2,100

*First season of professional football.

300 COMBINED NET YARDS GAINED IN A GAME

Date	Player, Team, Opponent	No.	Yards	TD
Dec. 14, 2003	Derrick Mason, Tennessee vs. Buffalo	21	302	0
Nov. 16, 2003	Jonathan Carter, N.Y. Jets vs. Indianapolis	7	304	2
Dec. 8, 2002	Steve Smith, Carolina vs. Cincinnati	9	313	3
Nov. 24, 2002	Priest Holmes, Kansas City vs. Seattle	30	307	3
Oct. 13, 2002	Michael Lewis, New Orleans vs. Washington	8	356	2
Dec. 24, 1999	Jason Tucker, Dallas vs. New Orleans	13	331	1
Dec. 7, 1997	Jermaine Lewis, Baltimore vs. Seattle	10	308	3
Dec. 25, 1995	Kevin Williams, Dallas vs. Arizona	16	307	2
Dec. 10, 1995	Glyn Milburn, Denver vs. Seattle	33	404	0
Oct. 23, 1994	Tyrone Hughes, New Orleans vs. L.A. Rams	11	347	2
Dec. 11, 1989	John Taylor, San Francisco vs. L.A. Rams	14	321	2
Nov. 26, 1989	Willie Anderson, L.A. Rams vs. New Orleans (OT)	15	336	1
Nov. 28, 1988	*Tim Brown, L.A. Raiders vs. Seattle	12	308	1
Dec. 22, 1985	Stephone Paige, Kansas City vs. San Diego	8	309	2
Nov. 10, 1985	Lionel James, San Diego vs. L.A. Raiders (OT)	23	345	0
Sept. 22, 1985	Lionel James, San Diego vs. Cincinnati	20	316	2
Dec. 21, 1975	*Walter Payton, Chicago vs. New Orleans	32	300	1
Nov. 23, 1975	Greg Pruitt, Cleveland vs. Cincinnati	28	304	2
Nov. 1, 1970	Eugene (Mercury) Morris, Miami vs. Baltimore	17	302	0
Oct. 4, 1970	O.J. Simpson, Buffalo vs. N.Y. Jets	26	303	2
Dec. 6, 1969	Jerry LeVias, Houston vs. N.Y. Jets	18	329	1
Nov. 2, 1969	Travis Williams, Green Bay vs. Pittsburgh	11	314	3
Dec. 18, 1966	Gale Sayers, Chicago vs. Minnesota	20	339	2
Dec. 12, 1965	*Gale Sayers, Chicago vs. San Francisco	17	336	6
Nov. 17, 1963	Gary Ballman, Pittsburgh vs. Washington	12	320	2
Dec. 16, 1962	Timmy Brown, Philadelphia vs. St. Louis	19	341	2
Dec. 10, 1961	Billy Cannon, Houston vs. N.Y. Titans	32	373	5
Nov. 19, 1961	Jim Brown, Cleveland vs. Philadelphia	38	313	4
Dec. 3, 1950	Cloyce Box, Detroit vs. Baltimore	13	302	4
Oct. 29, 1950	Wally Triplett, Detroit vs. Los Angeles	11	331	1
Nov. 22, 1945	Jim Benton, Cleveland vs. Detroit	10	303	1

*First season of professional football.

2,000 SCRIMMAGE YARDS GAINED IN A SEASON

Year	Player, Team	Att.	Rushing Yards	Receptions	Receiving Yards	Scrimm. Yards
2004	Tiki Barber, N.Y. Giants	322	1,518	52	578	2,096
	Edgerrin James, Indianapolis[3]	334	1,548	51	483	2,031
2003	LaDainian Tomlinson, San Diego[2]	313	1,645	100	725	2,370
	Jamal Lewis, Baltimore	387	2,066	26	205	2,271
	Ahman Green, Green Bay	355	1,883	50	367	2,250

Year	Player, Team	Att.	Rushing Yards	Receptions	Receiving Yards	Scrimm. Yards
	Deuce McAllister, New Orleans	351	1,641	69	516	2,157
	Priest Holmes, Kansas City[3]	320	1,420	74	690	2,110
2002	Priest Holmes, Kansas City[2]	313	1,615	70	672	2,287
	Ricky Williams, Miami	383	1,853	47	363	2,216
	LaDainian Tomlinson, San Diego	372	1,683	79	489	2,172
2001	Priest Holmes, Kansas City	327	1,555	62	614	2,169
	Marshall Faulk, St. Louis[4]	260	1,382	83	765	2,147
2000	Edgerrin James, Indianapolis[2]	387	1,709	63	594	2,303
	Marshall Faulk, St. Louis[3]	253	1,359	81	830	2,189
1999	Marshall Faulk, St. Louis[2]	253	1,381	87	1,048	2,429
	*Edgerrin James, Indianapolis	369	1,553	62	586	2,139
1998	Marshall Faulk, Indianapolis	324	1,319	86	908	2,227
	Terrell Davis, Denver[2]	392	2,008	25	217	2,225
	Jamal Anderson, Atlanta	410	1,846	27	319	2,165
	Garrison Hearst, San Francisco	310	1,570	39	535	2,105
1997	Barry Sanders, Detroit[2]	335	2,053	33	305	2,358
	Terrell Davis, Denver	369	1,750	42	287	2,037
1995	Emmitt Smith, Dallas[2]	377	1,773	62	375	2,148
1994	Barry Sanders, Detroit	331	1,883	44	283	2,166
1992	Thurman Thomas, Buffalo[2]	312	1,487	58	626	2,113
	Emmitt Smith, Dallas	373	1,713	59	335	2,048
	Barry Foster, Pittsburgh	390	1,690	36	344	2,034
1991	Thurman Thomas, Buffalo	288	1,407	62	631	2,038
1988	Roger Craig, San Francisco[2]	310	1,502	76	534	2,036
	Eric Dickerson, Indianapolis[4]	388	1,659	36	377	2,036
	Herschel Walker, Dallas	361	1,514	53	505	2,019
1986	Eric Dickerson, L.A. Rams[3]	404	1,821	26	205	2,026
1985	Marcus Allen, L.A. Raiders	380	1,759	67	555	2,314
	Roger Craig, San Francisco	214	1,050	92	1,016	2,066
	Walter Payton, Chicago[4]	324	1,551	49	483	2,034
1984	Eric Dickerson, L. A. Rams[2]	379	2,105	21	139	2,244
	James Wilder, Tampa Bay	407	1,544	85	685	2,229
	Walter Payton, Chicago[3]	381	1,684	45	368	2,052
1983	*Eric Dickerson, L.A. Rams	390	1,808	51	404	2,212
	William Andrews, Atlanta[2]	331	1,567	59	609	2,176
	Walter Payton, Chicago[2]	314	1,421	53	607	2,028
1981	William Andrews, Atlanta	289	1,301	81	735	2,036
1979	Wilbert Montgomery, Philadelphia	338	1,512	41	494	2,006
1977	Walter Payton, Chicago	339	1,852	27	269	2,121
1975	O.J. Simpson, Buffalo[2]	329	1,817	28	426	2,243
1973	O.J. Simpson, Buffalo	332	2,003	6	70	2,073
1963	Jim Brown, Cleveland	91	1,863	24	268	2,131

First season of professional football.

300 SCRIMMAGE YARDS GAINED IN A GAME

Date	Player, Team, Opponent	Att.	Yards	TD
Nov. 24, 2002	Priest Holmes, Kansas City vs. Seattle	30	307	3
Nov. 26, 1989	Flipper Anderson, L.A. Rams vs. New Orleans (OT)	15	336	1
Dec. 22, 1985	Stephone Paige, Kansas City vs. San Diego	8	309	2
Dec. 10, 1961	Billy Cannon, Houston vs. N.Y. Titans	30	330	5
Dec. 3, 1950	Cloyce Box, Detroit vs. Baltimore	12	302	4
Nov. 22, 1945	Jim Benton, Cleveland vs. Detroit	10	303	1

TOP 20 SCORERS

Player	Years	TD	FG	PAT	TP
Gary Anderson	23	0	538	820	2,434
Morten Andersen	23	0	520	798	2,358
George Blanda	26	9	335	942	2,002
Norm Johnson	18	0	366	638	1,736
Nick Lowery	18	0	383	562	1,711
Jan Stenerud	19	0	373	580	1,699
Eddie Murray	19	0	352	538	1,594
Al Del Greco	17	0	347	543	1,584
John Carney	17	0	365	442	1,537
Matt Stover	14	0	350	431	1,481
Steve Christie	15	0	336	468	1,476
Pat Leahy	18	0	304	558	1,470
Jason Elam	12	0	317	491	1,442
Jim Turner	16	1	304	521	1,439
Matt Bahr	17	0	300	522	1,422
Mark Moseley	16	0	300	482	1,382
Jim Bakken	17	0	282	534	1,380
Fred Cox	15	0	282	519	1,365
Lou Groza	17	1	234	641	1,349
Jason Hanson	13	0	308	412	1,336

TOP 20 TOUCHDOWN SCORERS

Player	Years	Rush	Rec.	Total Returns	TD
Jerry Rice	20	10	197	1	208
Emmitt Smith	15	164	11	0	175
Marcus Allen	16	123	21	1	145
Marshal Faulk	11	100	35	0	135
Cris Carter	16	0	130	1	131
Jim Brown	9	106	20	0	126
Walter Payton	13	110	15	0	125
John Riggins	14	104	12	0	116
Lenny Moore	12	63	48	2	113
Barry Sanders	10	99	10	0	109
Tim Brown	17	1	100	4	105
Don Hutson	11	3	99	3	105
Steve Largent	14	1	100	0	101
Franco Harris	13	91	9	0	100
Marvin Harrison	9	0	98	0	98
Terrell Owens	9	2	95	0	97
Eric Dickerson	11	90	6	0	96
Curtis Martin	10	85	10	0	95
Jim Taylor	10	83	10	0	93
Four tied					91

TOP 20 RUSHERS

Player	Years	Att.	Yards	Avg.	Long	TD
Emmitt Smith	15	4,409	18,355	4.2	75	164
Walter Payton	13	3,838	16,726	4.4	76	110
Barry Sanders	10	3,062	15,269	5.0	85	99
Curtis Martin	10	3,298	13,366	4.1	70	85
Jerome Bettis	12	3,369	13,294	3.9	71	82
Eric Dickerson	11	2,996	13,259	4.4	85	90
Tony Dorsett	12	2,936	12,739	4.3	99	77
Jim Brown	9	2,359	12,312	5.2	80	106
Marcus Allen	16	3,022	12,243	4.1	61	123
Franco Harris	13	2,949	12,120	4.1	75	91
Thurman Thomas	13	2,877	12,074	4.2	80	65
Marshall Faulk	11	2,771	11,987	4.3	71	100
John Riggins	14	2,916	11,352	3.9	66	104
O.J. Simpson	11	2,404	11,236	4.7	94	61
Ricky Watters	10	2,622	10,643	4.1	57	78
Eddie George	9	2,865	10,441	3.6	76	68
Ottis Anderson	14	2,562	10,273	4.0	76	81
Corey Dillon	8	2,210	9,696	4.4	96	57
Earl Campbell	9	2,187	9,407	4.3	81	74
Terry Allen	10	2,152	8,614	4.0	55	73

TOP 20 COMBINED YARDS GAINED

Player	Years	Tot.	Rush.	Rec.	Int. Ret.	Punt Ret.	Kickoff Ret.	Fumble Ret.
Jerry Rice	20	23,546	645	22,895	0	0	6	0
Brian Mitchell	14	23,330	1,967	2,336	0	4,999	14,014	14
Walter Payton	13	21,803	16,726	4,538	0	0	539	0
Emmitt Smith	15	21,564	18,355	3,224	0	0	0	-15
Tim Brown	17	19,682	190	14,934	0	3,320	1,235	3
Marshall Faulk	11	18,607	11,987	6,584	0	0	18	18
Barry Sanders	10	18,308	15,269	2,921	0	0	118	0
Herschel Walker	12	18,168	8,225	4,859	0	0	5,084	0
Marcus Allen	16	17,648	12,243	5,411	0	0	0	-6
Eric Metcalf	13	17,230	2,392	5,572	0	3,453	5,813	0
Curtis Martin	10	16,568	13,366	3,211	0	0	0	-9
Thurman Thomas	13	16,532	12,074	4,458	0	0	0	0
Tony Dorsett	12	16,326	12,739	3,554	0	0	0	54
Henry Ellard	16	15,718	50	13,777	0	1,527	364	0
Irving Fryar	17	15,594	242	12,785	0	2,055	505	7
Jim Brown	9	15,459	12,312	2,499	0	0	648	0
Eric Dickerson	11	15,411	13,259	2,137	0	0	0	15
Glyn Milburn	9	14,911	817	1,322	0	2,984	9,788	0
James Brooks	12	14,910	7,962	3,621	0	565	2,762	0
Ricky Watters	10	14,891	10,643	4,248	0	0	0	0

TOP 20 YARDS FROM SCRIMMAGE

Player	Years	Scrimmage Yards	Rushing Yards	Receiving Yards
Jerry Rice	20	23,540	645	22,895
Emmitt Smith	15	21,579	18,355	3,224
Walter Payton	13	21,264	16,726	4,538
Marshall Faulk	11	18,571	11,987	6,584
Barry Sanders	10	18,190	15,269	2,921
Marcus Allen	16	17,654	12,243	5,411
Curtis Martin	10	16,577	13,366	3,211
Thurman Thomas	13	16,532	12,074	4,458
Tony Dorsett	12	16,293	12,739	3,554
Eric Dickerson	11	15,396	13,259	2,137
Tim Brown	17	15,124	190	14,934
Ricky Watters	10	14,891	10,643	4,248
Jim Brown	9	14,811	12,312	2,499
Jerome Bettis	12	14,703	13,294	1,409
Franco Harris	13	14,407	12,120	2,287
James Lofton	16	14,250	246	14,004
Cris Carter	16	13,940	41	13,899
Henry Ellard	16	13,827	50	13,777
Andre Reed	16	13,698	500	13,198
John Riggins	14	13,442	11,352	2,090

TOP 20 PASSERS

Player	Years	Att.	Comp.	Pct. Comp.	Yards	Avg. Gain	TD	Pct. TD	Int.	Pct. Int.	Rating
Steve Young	15	4,149	2,667	64.3	33,124	7.98	232	5.6	107	2.6	96.8
Kurt Warner	7	1,965	1,295	65.9	16,501	8.40	108	5.5	69	3.5	95.7
Daunte Culpepper	6	2,391	1,539	64.4	18,598	7.78	129	5.4	74	3.1	93.2
Peyton Manning	7	3,880	2,464	63.5	29,442	7.59	216	5.6	120	3.1	92.3
Joe Montana	15	5,391	3,409	63.2	40,551	7.52	273	5.1	139	2.6	92.3
Trent Green	7	2,822	1,705	60.4	21,607	7.66	133	4.7	82	2.9	87.9
Tom Brady	5	2,018	1,243	61.6	13,925	6.90	97	4.8	52	2.6	87.5
Brett Favre	14	7,003	4,306	61.5	49,734	7.10	376	5.4	226	3.2	87.4
Jeff Garcia	6	2,612	1,593	61.0	18,139	6.94	123	4.7	65	2.5	87.2
Dan Marino	17	8,358	4,967	59.4	61,361	7.34	420	5.0	252	3.0	86.4
Brian Griese	7	2,144	1,351	63.0	15,208	7.09	96	4.5	71	3.3	85.3
Rich Gannon	16	4,206	2,533	60.2	28,743	6.83	180	4.3	104	2.5	84.7
Jim Kelly	11	4,779	2,874	60.1	35,467	7.42	237	5.0	175	3.7	84.4
Brad Johnson	11	3,504	2,166	61.8	23,913	6.82	143	4.1	98	2.8	84.0
Donovan McNabb	6	2,586	1,507	58.3	16,926	6.55	118	4.6	57	2.2	83.9
Mark Brunell	11	3,880	2,314	59.6	26,987	6.96	151	3.9	92	2.4	83.9
Matt Hasselbeck	6	1,756	1,048	59.7	12,466	7.10	72	4.1	48	2.7	83.7
Roger Staubach	11	2,958	1,685	57.0	22,700	7.67	153	5.2	109	3.7	83.4
Steve McNair	10	3,395	2,013	59.3	23,980	7.06	140	4.1	92	2.7	83.4
Neil Lomax	8	3,153	1,817	57.6	22,771	7.22	136	4.3	90	2.9	82.7

1,500 or more attempts. The passing ratings are based on performance standards established for completion percentage, interception percentage, touchdown percentage, and average gain. Please consult page 364 for more information.

TOP 20 LEADERS IN PASSES COMPLETED

Dan Marino	4,967
Brett Favre	4,306
John Elway	4,123
Warren Moon	3,988
Fran Tarkenton	3,686
Vinny Testaverde	3,631
Drew Bledsoe	3,449
Joe Montana	3,409
Dan Fouts	3,297
Dave Krieg	3,105
Boomer Esiason	2,969
Troy Aikman	2,898
Steve DeBerg	2,874
Jim Kelly	2,874
Jim Everett	2,841
Johnny Unitas	2,830
Steve Young	2,667
Ken Anderson	2,654
Jim Hart	2,593
Phil Simms	2,576

TOP 20 LEADERS IN PASSING YARDS

Dan Marino	61,361
John Elway	51,475
Brett Favre	49,734
Warren Moon	49,325
Fran Tarkenton	47,003
Vinny Testaverde	44,475
Dan Fouts	43,040
Joe Montana	40,551
Johnny Unitas	40,239
Drew Bledsoe	39,808
Dave Krieg	38,147
Boomer Esiason	37,920
Jim Kelly	35,467
Jim Everett	34,837
Jim Hart	34,665
Steve DeBerg	34,241
John Hadl	33,503
Phil Simms	33,462
Steve Young	33,124
Troy Aikman	32,942

TOP 20 LEADERS IN TOUCHDOWN PASSES

Dan Marino	420
Brett Favre	376
Fran Tarkenton	342
John Elway	300
Warren Moon	291
Johnny Unitas	290
Joe Montana	273
Vinny Testaverde	268
Dave Krieg	261
Sonny Jurgensen	255
Dan Fouts	254
Boomer Esiason	247
John Hadl	244
Len Dawson	239
Jim Kelly	237
George Blanda	236
Steve Young	232
Drew Bledsoe	221
Peyton Manning	216
John Brodie	214

TOP 20 LEADERS IN RECEPTION YARDS

Jerry Rice	22,895
Tim Brown	14,934
James Lofton	14,004
Cris Carter	13,899
Henry Ellard	13,777
Andre Reed	13,198
Steve Largent	13,089
Irving Fryar	12,785
Art Monk	12,721
Charlie Joiner	12,146
Michael Irvin	11,904
Don Maynard	11,834
Isaac Bruce	11,753
Jimmy Smith	11,264
Marvin Harrison	11,185
Gary Clark	10,856
Stanley Morgan	10,716
Harold Jackson	10,372
Lance Alworth	10,266
Andre Rison	10,205

TOP 20 PASS RECEIVERS

Player	Years	No.	Yards	Avg.	Long	TD
Jerry Rice	20	1,549	22,895	14.8	96	197
Cris Carter	16	1,101	13,899	12.6	80	130
Tim Brown	17	1,094	14,934	13.7	80	100
Andre Reed	16	951	13,198	13.9	83	87
Art Monk	16	940	12,721	13.5	79	68
Irving Fryar	17	851	12,785	15.0	80	84
Marvin Harrison	9	845	11,185	13.2	79	98
Larry Centers	14	827	6,797	8.2	54	28
Steve Largent	14	819	13,089	16.0	74	100
Shannon Sharpe	14	815	10,060	12.3	82	62
Henry Ellard	16	814	13,777	16.9	81	65
Jimmy Smith	11	792	11,264	14.2	75	61
Isaac Bruce	11	777	11,753	15.1	80	74
James Lofton	16	764	14,004	18.3	80	75
Keenan McCardell	13	755	9,763	12.9	76	53
Michael Irvin	12	750	11,904	15.9	87	65
Charlie Joiner	18	750	12,146	16.2	87	65
Andre Rison	12	743	10,205	13.7	80	84
Marshall Faulk	11	723	6,584	9.1	85	35
Rod Smith	10	712	9,772	13.7	85	59

TOP 20 INTERCEPTORS

Player	Years	No.	Yards	Avg.	Long	TD
Paul Krause	16	81	1,185	14.6	81	3
Emlen Tunnell	14	79	1,282	16.2	55	4
Rod Woodson	17	71	1,483	20.9	98	12
Dick (Night Train) Lane	14	68	1,207	17.8	80	5
Ken Riley	15	65	596	9.2	66	5
Ronnie Lott	14	63	730	11.6	83	5
Dave Brown	15	62	698	11.3	90	5
Dick LeBeau	14	62	762	12.3	70	3
Emmitt Thomas	13	58	937	16.2	73	5
Mel Blount	14	57	736	12.9	52	2
Bobby Boyd	9	57	994	17.4	74	4
Eugene Robinson	16	57	762	13.4	49	1
Johnny Robinson	12	57	741	13.0	57	1
Everson Walls	13	57	504	8.8	40	1
Lem Barney	11	56	1,077	19.2	71	7
Pat Fischer	17	56	941	16.8	69	4
Aeneas Williams	14	55	807	14.7	65	9
Eric Allen	14	54	826	15.3	94	8
Willie Brown	16	54	472	8.7	45	2
Darrell Green	20	54	621	11.5	83	6

TOP 20 PUNTERS (MINIMUM 250 PUNTS)

Player	Years	No.	Yards	Avg.	Long	Blk.
Shane Lechler	5	360	16,522	45.9	73	2
Sammy Baugh	16	338	15,245	45.1	85	9
Tommy Davis	11	511	22,833	44.7	82	2
Yale Lary	11	503	22,279	44.3	74	4
Todd Sauerbrun	10	760	33,443	44.0	73	6
Bob Scarpitto	8	283	12,408	43.8	87	4
Horace Gillom	7	385	16,872	43.8	80	5
Jerry Norton	11	358	15,671	43.8	78	2
Dave Lewis	4	285	12,447	43.7	63	0
Tom Rouen	11	749	32,650	43.6	76	9
Greg Montgomery	9	524	22,831	43.6	77	8
Darren Bennett	10	828	36,016	43.5	66	3
Chris Hanson	5	274	11,910	43.5	69	1
Don Chandler	12	660	28,678	43.5	90	4
Rick Tuten	11	741	32,190	43.4	73	2
Tom Tupa	16	873	37,862	43.4	73	1
Rohn Stark	16	1,141	49,471	43.4	72	7
Sean Landeta	20	1,367	59,224	43.3	77	5
Reggie Roby	16	992	42,951	43.3	77	5
Hunter Smith	6	373	16,128	43.2	69	4

TOP 20 KICKOFF RETURNERS (MINIMUM 75 RETURNS)

Player	Years	No.	Yards	Avg.	Long	TD
Gale Sayers	7	91	2,781	30.6	103	6
Lynn Chandnois	7	92	2,720	29.6	93	3
Abe Woodson	9	193	5,538	28.7	105	5
Buddy Young	6	90	2,514	27.9	104	2
Travis Williams	5	102	2,801	27.5	105	6
Joe Arenas	7	139	3,798	27.3	96	1
Clarence Davis	8	79	2,140	27.1	76	0
Steve Van Buren	8	76	2,030	26.7	98	3
Lenny Lyles	12	81	2,161	26.7	103	3
Mercury Morris	8	111	2,947	26.5	105	3
Bobby Jancik	6	158	4,185	26.5	61	0
Mel Renfro	14	85	2,246	26.4	100	2
Bobby Mitchell	14	102	2,690	26.4	98	5
Ollie Matson	14	143	3,746	26.2	105	6
Alvin Haymond	10	170	4,438	26.1	98	2
Noland Smith	3	82	2,137	26.1	106	1
Al Nelson	9	101	2,625	26.0	78	0
Timmy Brown	11	184	4,781	26.0	105	5
Vic Washington	6	129	3,341	25.9	98	1
Dave Hampton	8	113	2,923	25.9	101	3

TOP 20 PUNT RETURNERS (MINIMUM 75 RETURNS)

Player	Years	No.	Yards	Avg.	Long	TD
George McAfee	8	112	1,431	12.8	74	2
Jack Christiansen	8	85	1,084	12.8	89	8
Claude Gibson	5	110	1,381	12.6	85	3
Bill Dudley	9	124	1,515	12.2	96	3
Rick Upchurch	9	248	3,008	12.1	92	8
Santana Moss	4	88	1,052	12.0	63	2
Desmond Howard	11	244	2,895	11.9	95	8
Billy Johnson	14	282	3,317	11.8	87	6
Mack Herron	3	84	982	11.7	66	0
Billy Thompson	13	157	1,814	11.6	60	0
Az-Zahir Hakim	7	131	1,513	11.5	86	3
Dante Hall	5	119	1,366	11.5	93	4
Darrien Gordon	9	314	3,601	11.5	94	6
Henry Ellard	16	135	1,527	11.3	83	4
Rodger Bird	3	94	1,063	11.3	78	0
Bosh Pritchard	6	95	1,072	11.3	81	2
Michael Lewis	4	122	1,363	11.2	83	1
Terry Metcalf	6	84	936	11.1	69	1
Bob Hayes	11	104	1,158	11.1	90	3
Jermaine Lewis	9	295	3,282	11.1	89	6

TOP 20 LEADERS IN SACKS

Player	*Years	No.
Bruce Smith	19	200.0
Reggie White	15	198.0
Kevin Greene	15	160.0
Chris Doleman	15	150.5
Richard Dent	15	137.5
John Randle	14	137.5
Leslie O'Neal	13	132.5
Lawrence Taylor	12	132.5
Rickey Jackson	14	128.0
Derrick Thomas	11	126.5
Clyde Simmons	15	121.5
Michael Strahan	12	118.0
Sean Jones	13	113.0
Greg Townsend	13	109.5
Pat Swilling	12	107.5
Trace Armstrong	15	106.0
Simeon Rice	9	105.0
Neil Smith	13	104.5
Jim Jeffcoat	15	102.5
William Fuller	13	100.5
Charles Haley	12	100.5

*Years played since 1982 when sacks became an official statistic.

POSTSEASON LEADERS
TOP 10 POSTSEASON RUSHERS

Player	Att.	Yards	Avg.	Long	TD
Emmitt Smith	349	1,586	4.5	65	19
Franco Harris	400	1,556	3.9	50	16
Thurman Thomas	339	1,442	4.3	40	16
Tony Dorsett	302	1,383	4.6	53	9
Marcus Allen	267	1,347	5.0	74	11
Terrell Davis	204	1,140	5.6	62	12
John Riggins	251	996	4.0	43	12
Larry Csonka	225	891	4.0	49	9
Chuck Foreman	229	860	3.8	62	7
Roger Craig	208	841	4.0	80	7

TOP 10 POSTSEASON PASSERS

Player	Att.	Comp.	Pct. Comp.	Yards	Avg. Gain	TD	Pct. TD	Int.	Pct. Int.	Rating
Bart Starr	213	130	61.0	1,753	8.23	15	7.0	3	1.4	104.8
Joe Montana	734	460	62.7	5,772	7.86	45	6.1	21	2.9	95.6
Ken Anderson	166	110	66.3	1,321	7.96	9	5.4	6	3.6	93.5
Kurt Warner	268	169	63.1	2,221	8.29	15	5.6	10	3.7	92.3
Joe Theismann	211	128	60.7	1,782	8.45	11	5.2	7	3.3	91.4
Peyton Manning	283	171	60.4	2,172	7.67	14	4.9	8	2.8	89.1
Tom Brady	304	190	62.5	1,951	6.42	11	3.6	3	1.0	88.9
Troy Aikman	502	320	63.7	3,849	7.67	23	4.6	17	3.4	88.3
Steve Young	471	292	62.0	3,326	7.06	20	4.2	13	3.5	84.9
Warren Moon	403	259	64.3	2,870	7.12	17	4.2	14	3.5	84.9

TOP 10 POSTSEASON PASS RECEIVERS

Player	No.	Yards	Avg.	Long	TD
Jerry Rice	151	2,245	14.9	72	22
Micahel Irvin	87	1,315	15.1	53	8
Andre Reed	85	1,229	14.5	72	9
Thurman Thomas	76	672	8.8	27	5
Cliff Branch	73	1,289	17.7	72	5
Fred Biletnikoff	70	1,167	16.7	57	10
Art Monk	69	1,062	15.4	48	7
Drew Pearson	67	1,105	16.5	83	8
Tony Nathan	65	649	10.0	39	2
Cris Carter	63	870	13.8	66	8
Roger Craig	63	606	9.6	40	2

TOP 10 POSTSEASON INTERCEPTION LEADERS

Player	Interceptions
Ronnie Lott	9
Bill Simpson	9
Charlie Waters	9
Lester Hayes	8
Willie Brown	7
Dennis Thurman	7
Bobby Bryant	6
Eric Davis	6
Glen Edwards	6
Darrell Green	6
Cliff Harris	6
Rodney Harrison	6
Vernon Perry	6
Aeneas Williams	6

TOP 10 POSTSEASON SACK LEADERS

Player	Sacks
Bruce Smith	14.5
Reggie White	12.0
Willie McGinest	11.5
Charles Haley	11.0
Richard Dent	10.5
Trace Armstrong	10.0
Charles Mann	10.0
Tony Tolbert	10.0
Neil Smith	9.5
Jeff Wright	9.0

*Sacks became an official statistic in 1982.

ANNUAL SCORING LEADERS

Year	Player, Team	TD	FG	PAT	TP
2004	Adam Vinatieri, New England, AFC	0	31	48	141
	David Akers, Philadelphia, NFC	0	27	41	122
2003	Jeff Wilkins, St. Louis, NFC	0	39	46	163
	Priest Holmes, Kansas City, AFC	27	0	0	162
2002	Priest Holmes, Kansas City, AFC	24	0	0	144
	Jay Feely, Atlanta, NFC	0	32	42	138
2001	Marshall Faulk, St. Louis, NFC	21	0	0	#128
	Mike Vanderjagt, Indianapolis, AFC	0	28	41	125
2000	Marshall Faulk, St. Louis, NFC	26	0	0	##160
	Matt Stover, Baltimore, AFC	0	35	30	135
1999	Mike Vanderjagt, Indianapolis, AFC	0	34	43	145
	Jeff Wilkins, St. Louis, NFC	0	20	64	124
1998	Gary Anderson, Minnesota, NFC	0	35	59	164
	Steve Christie, Buffalo, AFC	0	33	41	140
1997	Mike Hollis, Jacksonville, AFC	0	31	41	134
	Richie Cunningham, Dallas, NFC	0	34	24	126
1996	John Kasay, Carolina, NFC	0	37	34	145
	Cary Blanchard, Indianapolis, AFC	0	36	27	135
1995	Emmitt Smith, Dallas, NFC	25	0	0	150
	Norm Johnson, Pittsburgh, AFC	0	34	39	141
1994	John Carney, San Diego, AFC	0	34	33	135
	Fuad Reveiz, Minnesota, NFC	0	34	30	132
1993	Jeff Jaeger, L.A. Raiders, AFC	0	35	27	132
	Jason Hanson, Detroit, NFC	0	34	28	130
1992	Pete Stoyanovich, Miami, AFC	0	30	34	124
	Morten Andersen, New Orleans, NFC	0	29	33	120
	Chip Lohmiller, Washington, NFC	0	30	30	120
1991	Chip Lohmiller, Washington, NFC	0	31	56	149
	Pete Stoyanovich, Miami, AFC	0	31	28	121
1990	Nick Lowery, Kansas City, AFC	0	34	37	139
	Chip Lohmiller, Washington, NFC	0	30	41	131
1989	Mike Cofer, San Francisco, NFC	0	29	49	136
	*David Treadwell, Denver, AFC	0	27	39	120
1988	Scott Norwood, Buffalo, AFC	0	32	33	129
	Mike Cofer, San Francisco, NFC	0	27	40	121
1987	Jerry Rice, San Francisco, NFC	23	0	0	138
	Jim Breech, Cincinnati, AFC	0	24	25	97
1986	Tony Franklin, New England, AFC	0	32	44	140
	Kevin Butler, Chicago, NFC	0	28	36	120
1985	*Kevin Butler, Chicago, NFC	0	31	51	144
	Gary Anderson, Pittsburgh, AFC	0	33	40	139
1984	Ray Wersching, San Francisco, NFC	0	25	56	131
	Gary Anderson, Pittsburgh, AFC	0	24	45	117
1983	Mark Moseley, Washington, NFC	0	33	62	161
	Gary Anderson, Pittsburgh, AFC	0	27	38	119
1982	*Marcus Allen, L.A. Raiders, AFC	14	0	0	84
	Wendell Tyler, L.A. Rams, NFC	13	0	0	78
1981	Ed Murray, Detroit, NFC	0	25	46	121
	Rafael Septien, Dallas, NFC	0	27	40	121
	Jim Breech, Cincinnati, AFC	0	22	49	115
	Nick Lowery, Kansas City, AFC	0	26	37	115
1980	John Smith, New England, AFC	0	26	51	129
	*Ed Murray, Detroit, NFC	0	27	35	116
1979	John Smith, New England, AFC	0	23	46	115
	Mark Moseley, Washington, NFC	0	25	39	114
1978	*Frank Corral, Los Angeles, NFC	0	29	31	118
	Pat Leahy, N.Y. Jets, AFC	0	22	41	107
1977	Errol Mann, Oakland, AFC	0	20	39	99
	Walter Payton, Chicago, NFC	16	0	0	96
1976	Toni Linhart, Baltimore, AFC	0	20	49	109
	Mark Moseley, Washington, NFC	0	22	31	97
1975	O.J. Simpson, Buffalo, AFC	23	0	0	138
	Chuck Foreman, Minnesota, NFC	22	0	0	132
1974	Chester Marcol, Green Bay, NFC	0	25	19	94
	Roy Gerela, Pittsburgh, AFC	0	20	33	93
1973	David Ray, Los Angeles, NFC	0	30	40	130
	Roy Gerela, Pittsburgh, AFC	0	29	36	123

Year	Player, Team	TD	FG	PAT	TP
1972	*Chester Marcol, Green Bay, NFC	0	33	29	128
	Bobby Howfield, N.Y. Jets, AFC	0	27	40	121
1971	Garo Yepremian, Miami, AFC	0	28	33	117
	Curt Knight, Washington, NFC	0	29	27	114
1970	Fred Cox, Minnesota, NFC	0	30	35	125
	Jan Stenerud, Kansas City, AFC	0	30	26	116
1969	Jim Turner, N.Y. Jets, AFL	0	32	33	129
	Fred Cox, Minnesota, NFL	0	26	43	121
1968	Jim Turner, N.Y. Jets, AFL	0	34	43	145
	Leroy Kelly, Cleveland, NFL	20	0	0	120
1967	Jim Bakken, St. Louis, NFL	0	27	36	117
	George Blanda, Oakland, AFL	0	20	56	116
1966	Gino Cappelletti, Boston, AFL	6	16	35	119
	Bruce Gossett, Los Angeles, NFL	0	28	29	113
1965	*Gale Sayers, Chicago, NFL	22	0	0	132
	Gino Cappelletti, Boston, AFL	9	17	27	132
1964	Gino Cappelletti, Boston, AFL	7	25	36	#155
	Lenny Moore, Baltimore, NFL	20	0	0	120
1963	Gino Cappelletti, Boston, AFL	2	22	35	113
	Don Chandler, N.Y. Giants, NFL	0	18	52	106
1962	Gene Mingo, Denver, AFL	4	27	32	137
	Jim Taylor, Green Bay, NFL	19	0	0	114
1961	Gino Cappelletti, Boston, AFL	8	17	48	147
	Paul Hornung, Green Bay, NFL	10	15	41	146
1960	Paul Hornung, Green Bay, NFL	15	15	41	176
	*Gene Mingo, Denver, AFL	6	18	33	123
1959	Paul Hornung, Green Bay	7	7	31	94
1958	Jim Brown, Cleveland	18	0	0	108
1957	Sam Baker, Washington	1	14	29	77
	Lou Groza, Cleveland	0	15	32	77
1956	Bobby Layne, Detroit	5	12	33	99
1955	Doak Walker, Detroit	7	9	27	96
1954	Bobby Walston, Philadelphia	11	4	36	114
1953	Gordy Soltau, San Francisco	6	10	48	114
1952	Gordy Soltau, San Francisco	7	6	34	94
1951	Elroy (Crazylegs) Hirsch, Los Angeles	17	0	0	102
1950	*Doak Walker, Detroit	11	8	38	128
1949	Pat Harder, Chi. Cardinals	8	3	45	102
	Gene Roberts, N.Y. Giants	17	0	0	102
1948	Pat Harder, Chi. Cardinals	6	7	53	110
1947	Pat Harder, Chi. Cardinals	7	7	39	102
1946	Ted Fritsch, Green Bay	10	9	13	100
1945	Steve Van Buren, Philadelphia	18	0	2	110
1944	Don Hutson, Green Bay	9	0	31	85
1943	Don Hutson, Green Bay	12	3	36	117
1942	Don Hutson, Green Bay	17	1	33	138
1941	Don Hutson, Green Bay	12	1	20	95
1940	Don Hutson, Green Bay	7	0	15	57
1939	Andy Farkas, Washington	11	0	2	68
1938	Clarke Hinkle, Green Bay	7	3	7	58
1937	Jack Manders, Chi. Bears	5	8	15	69
1936	Earl (Dutch) Clark, Detroit	7	4	19	73
1935	Earl (Dutch) Clark, Detroit	6	1	16	55
1934	Jack Manders, Chi. Bears	3	10	31	79
1933	Ken Strong, N.Y. Giants	6	5	13	64
	Glenn Presnell, Portsmouth	6	6	10	64
1932	Earl (Dutch) Clark, Portsmouth	6	3	10	55

*First season of professional football.
#Cappelletti's total and Faulk's total in 2001 include a two-point conversion.
##Faulk's total in 2000 includes 2 two-point conversions.

ANNUAL TOUCHDOWN LEADERS

Year	Player, Team	TD	Rush	Pass	Ret.
2004	Shaun Alexander, Seattle, NFC	20	16	4	0
	LaDainian Tomlinson, San Diego, AFC	18	17	1	0
2003	Priest Holmes, Kansas City, AFC	27	27	0	0
	Ahman Green, Green Bay, NFC	20	15	5	0
2002	Priest Holmes, Kansas City, AFC	24	21	3	0
	Shaun Alexander, Seattle, NFC	18	16	2	0

Year	Player, Team	TD	Rush	Pass	Ret.
2001	Marshall Faulk, St. Louis, NFC	21	12	9	0
	Shaun Alexander, Seattle, AFC	16	14	2	0
2000	Marshall Faulk, St. Louis, NFC	26	18	8	0
	Edgerrin James, Indianapolis, AFC	18	13	5	0
1999	Stephen Davis, Washington, NFC	17	17	0	0
	*Edgerrin James, Indianapolis, AFC	17	13	4	0
1998	Terrell Davis, Denver, AFC	23	21	2	0
	*Randy Moss, Minnesota, NFC	17	0	17	0
1997	Karim Abdul-Jabbar, Miami, AFC	16	15	1	0
	Barry Sanders, Detroit, NFC	14	11	3	0
1996	Terry Allen, Washington, NFC	21	21	0	0
	Curtis Martin, New England, AFC	17	14	3	0
1995	Emmitt Smith, Dallas, NFC	25	25	0	0
	Carl Pickens, Cincinnati, AFC	17	0	17	0
1994	Emmitt Smith, Dallas, NFC	22	21	1	0
	*Marshall Faulk, Indianapolis, AFC	12	11	1	0
	Natrone Means, San Diego, AFC	12	12	0	0
1993	Jerry Rice, San Francisco, NFC	16	1	15	0
	Marcus Allen, Kansas City, AFC	15	12	3	0
1992	Emmitt Smith, Dallas, NFC	19	18	1	0
	Thurman Thomas, Buffalo, AFC	12	9	3	0
1991	Barry Sanders, Detroit, NFC	17	16	1	0
	Mark Clayton, Miami, AFC	12	0	12	0
	Thurman Thomas, Buffalo, AFC	12	7	5	0
1990	Barry Sanders, Detroit, NFC	16	13	3	0
	Derrick Fenner, Seattle, AFC	15	14	1	0
1989	Dalton Hilliard, New Orleans, NFC	18	13	5	0
	Christian Okoye, Kansas City, AFC	12	12	0	0
	Thurman Thomas, Buffalo, AFC	12	6	6	0
1988	Greg Bell, L.A. Rams, NFC	18	16	2	0
	Eric Dickerson, Indianapolis, AFC	15	14	1	0
	*Ickey Woods, Cincinnati, AFC	15	15	0	0
1987	Jerry Rice, San Francisco, NFC	23	1	22	0
	Johnny Hector, N.Y. Jets, AFC	11	11	0	0
1986	George Rogers, Washington, NFC	18	18	0	0
	Sammy Winder, Denver, AFC	14	9	5	0
1985	Joe Morris, N.Y. Giants, NFC	21	21	0	0
	Louis Lipps, Pittsburgh, AFC	15	1	12	2
1984	Marcus Allen, L.A. Raiders, AFC	18	13	5	0
	Mark Clayton, Miami, AFC	18	0	18	0
	Eric Dickerson, L.A. Rams, NFC	14	14	0	0
	John Riggins, Washington, NFC	14	14	0	0
1983	John Riggins, Washington, NFC	24	24	0	0
	Pete Johnson, Cincinnati, AFC	14	14	0	0
	*Curt Warner, Seattle, AFC	14	13	1	0
1982	*Marcus Allen, L.A. Raiders, AFC	14	11	3	0
	Wendell Tyler, L.A. Rams, NFC	13	9	4	0
1981	Chuck Muncie, San Diego, AFC	19	19	0	0
	Wendell Tyler, Los Angeles, NFC	17	12	5	0
1980	*Billy Sims, Detroit, NFC	16	13	3	0
	Earl Campbell, Houston, AFC	13	13	0	0
	*Curtis Dickey, Baltimore, AFC	13	11	2	0
	John Jefferson, San Diego, AFC	13	0	13	0
1979	Earl Campbell, Houston, AFC	19	19	0	0
	Walter Payton, Chicago, NFC	16	14	2	0
1978	David Sims, Seattle, AFC	15	14	1	0
	Terdell Middleton, Green Bay, NFC	12	11	1	0
1977	Walter Payton, Chicago, NFC	16	14	2	0
	Nat Moore, Miami, AFC	13	1	12	0
1976	Chuck Foreman, Minnesota, NFC	14	13	1	0
	Franco Harris, Pittsburgh, AFC	14	14	0	0
1975	O.J. Simpson, Buffalo, AFC	23	16	7	0
	Chuck Foreman, Minnesota, NFC	22	13	9	0
1974	Chuck Foreman, Minnesota, NFC	15	9	6	0
	Cliff Branch, Oakland, AFC	13	0	13	0
1973	Larry Brown, Washington, NFC	14	8	6	0
	Floyd Little, Denver, AFC	13	12	1	0
1972	Emerson Boozer, N.Y. Jets, AFC	14	11	3	0
	Ron Johnson, N.Y. Giants, NFC	14	9	5	0

Year	Player, Team	TD	Rush	Pass	Ret.
1971	Duane Thomas, Dallas, NFC	13	11	2	0
	Leroy Kelly, Cleveland, AFC	12	10	2	0
1970	Dick Gordon, Chicago, NFC	13	0	13	0
	MacArthur Lane, St. Louis, NFC	13	11	2	0
	Gary Garrison, San Diego, AFC	12	0	12	0
1969	Warren Wells, Oakland, AFL	14	0	14	0
	Tom Matte, Baltimore, NFL	13	11	2	0
	Lance Rentzel, Dallas, NFL	13	0	12	1
1968	Leroy Kelly, Cleveland, NFL	20	16	4	0
	Warren Wells, Oakland, AFL	12	1	11	0
1967	Homer Jones, N.Y. Giants, NFL	14	1	13	0
	Emerson Boozer, N.Y. Jets, AFL	13	10	3	0
1966	Leroy Kelly, Cleveland, NFL	16	15	1	0
	Dan Reeves, Dallas, NFL	16	8	8	0
	Lance Alworth, San Diego, AFL	13	0	13	0
1965	*Gale Sayers, Chicago, NFL	22	14	6	2
	Lance Alworth, San Diego, AFL	14	0	14	0
	Don Maynard, N.Y. Jets, AFL	14	0	14	0
1964	Lenny Moore, Baltimore, NFL	20	16	3	1
	Lance Alworth, San Diego, AFL	15	2	13	0
1963	Art Powell, Oakland, AFL	16	0	16	0
	Jim Brown, Cleveland, NFL	15	12	3	0
1962	Abner Haynes, Dallas, AFL	19	13	6	0
	Jim Taylor, Green Bay, NFL	19	19	0	0
1961	Bill Groman, Houston, AFL	18	1	17	0
	Jim Taylor, Green Bay, NFL	16	15	1	0
1960	Paul Hornung, Green Bay, NFL	15	13	2	0
	Sonny Randle, St. Louis, NFL	15	0	15	0
	Art Powell, N.Y. Titans, AFL	14	0	14	0
1959	Raymond Berry, Baltimore	14	0	14	0
	Jim Brown, Cleveland	14	14	0	0
1958	Jim Brown, Cleveland	18	17	1	0
1957	Lenny Moore, Baltimore	11	3	7	1
1956	Rick Casares, Chi. Bears	14	12	2	0
1955	*Alan Ameche, Baltimore	9	9	0	0
	Harlon Hill, Chi. Bears	9	0	9	0
1954	*Harlon Hill, Chi. Bears	12	0	12	0
1953	Joseph Perry, San Francisco	13	10	3	0
1952	Cloyce Box, Detroit	15	0	15	0
1951	Elroy (Crazylegs) Hirsch, Los Angeles	17	0	17	0
1950	Bob Shaw, Chi. Cardinals	12	0	12	0
1949	Gene Roberts, N.Y. Giants	17	9	8	0
1948	Mal Kutner, Chi. Cardinals	15	1	14	0
1947	Steve Van Buren, Philadelphia	14	13	0	1
1946	Ted Fritsch, Green Bay	10	9	1	0
1945	Steve Van Buren, Philadelphia	18	15	2	1
1944	Don Hutson, Green Bay	9	0	9	0
	Bill Paschal, N.Y. Giants	9	9	0	0
1943	Don Hutson, Green Bay	12	0	11	1
	*Bill Paschal, N.Y. Giants	12	10	2	0
1942	Don Hutson, Green Bay	17	0	17	0
1941	Don Hutson, Green Bay	12	2	10	0
	George McAfee, Chi. Bears	12	6	3	3
1940	John Drake, Cleveland	9	9	0	0
	Richard Todd, Washington	9	4	4	1
1939	Andrew Farkas, Washington	11	5	5	1
1938	Don Hutson, Green Bay	9	0	9	0
1937	Cliff Battles, Washington	7	5	1	1
	Clarke Hinkle, Green Bay	7	5	2	0
	Don Hutson, Green Bay	7	0	7	0
1936	Don Hutson, Green Bay	9	0	8	1
1935	*Don Hutson, Green Bay	7	0	6	1
1934	*Beattie Feathers, Chi. Bears	9	8	1	0
1933	*Charlie (Buckets) Goldenberg, Green Bay	7	4	1	2
	John (Shipwreck) Kelly, Brooklyn	7	2	3	2
	*Elvin (Kink) Richards, N.Y. Giants	7	4	3	0
1932	Earl (Dutch) Clark, Portsmouth	6	3	3	0
	Red Grange, Chi. Bears	6	3	3	0

First season of professional football.

ANNUAL LEADERS—MOST FIELD GOALS MADE

Year	Player, Team	Att.	Made	Pct.
2004	Adam Vinatieri, New England, AFC	33	31	93.9
	David Akers, Philadelphia, NFC	32	27	84.4
2003	Jeff Wilkins, St. Louis, NFC	42	39	92.9
	Mike Vanderjagt, Indianapolis, AFC	37	37	100.0
2002	Jay Feely, Atlanta, NFC	40	32	80.0
	Martín Gramatica, Tampa Bay, NFC	39	32	82.1
	Adam Vinatieri, New England, AFC	30	27	90.0
2001	Jason Elam, Denver, AFC	36	31	86.1
	*Jay Feely, Atlanta, NFC	37	29	78.4
2000	Matt Stover, Baltimore, AFC	39	35	89.7
	Ryan Longwell, Green Bay, NFC	38	33	86.8
1999	Olindo Mare, Miami, AFC	46	39	84.8
	*Martin Gramatica, Tampa Bay, NFC	32	27	84.4
1998	Al Del Greco, Tennessee, AFC	39	36	92.3
	Gary Anderson, Minnesota, NFC	35	35	100.0
1997	Richie Cunningham, Dallas, NFC	37	34	91.9
	Cary Blanchard, Indianapolis, AFC	41	32	78.1
1996	John Kasay, Carolina, NFC	45	37	82.2
	Cary Blanchard, Indianapolis, AFC	40	36	90.0
1995	Norm Johnson, Pittsburgh, AFC	41	34	82.9
	Morten Andersen, Atlanta, NFC	37	31	83.8
1994	John Carney, San Diego, AFC	38	34	89.5
	Fuad Reveiz, Minnesota, NFC	39	34	87.2
1993	Jeff Jaeger, L.A. Raiders, AFC	44	35	79.5
	Jason Hanson, Detroit, NFC	43	34	79.1
1992	Pete Stoyanovich, Miami, AFC	37	30	81.1
	Chip Lohmiller, Washington, NFC	40	30	75.0
1991	Pete Stoyanovich, Miami, AFC	37	31	83.8
	Chip Lohmiller, Washington, NFC	43	31	72.1
1990	Nick Lowery, Kansas City, AFC	37	34	91.9
	Chip Lohmiller, Washington, NFC	40	30	75.0
1989	Rich Karlis, Minnesota, NFC	39	31	79.5
	*David Treadwell, Denver, AFC	33	27	81.8
1988	Scott Norwood, Buffalo, AFC	37	32	86.5
	Mike Cofer, San Francisco, NFC	38	27	71.1
1987	Morten Andersen, New Orleans, NFC	36	28	77.8
	Dean Biasucci, Indianpolis, AFC	27	24	88.9
	Jim Breech, Cincinnati, AFC	30	24	80.0
1986	Tony Franklin, New England, AFC	41	32	78.0
	Kevin Butler, Chicago, NFC	41	28	68.3
1985	Gary Anderson, Pittsburgh, AFC	42	33	78.6
	Morten Andersen, New Orleans, NFC	35	31	88.6
	*Kevin Butler, Chicago, NFC	37	31	83.8
1984	*Paul McFadden, Philadelphia, NFC	37	30	81.1
	Gary Anderson, Pittsburgh, AFC	32	24	75.0
	Matt Bahr, Cleveland, AFC	32	24	75.0
1983	*Ali-Haji-Sheikh, N.Y. Giants, NFC	42	35	83.3
	*Raul Allegre, Baltimore, AFC	35	30	85.7
1982	Mark Moseley, Washington, NFC	21	20	95.2
	Nick Lowery, Kansas City, AFC	24	19	79.2
1981	Rafael Septien, Dallas, NFC	35	27	77.1
	Nick Lowery, Kansas City, AFC	36	26	72.2
1980	*Ed Murray, Detroit, NFC	42	27	64.3
	John Smith, New England, AFC	34	26	76.5
	Fred Steinfort, Denver, AFC,	34	26	76.5
1979	Mark Moseley, Washington, NFC	33	25	75.8
	John Smith, New England, AFC	33	23	69.7
1978	*Frank Corral, Los Angeles, NFC	43	29	67.4
	Pat Leahy, N.Y. Jets, AFC	30	22	73.3
1977	Mark Moseley, Washington, NFC	37	21	56.8
	Errol Mann, Oakland, AFC	28	20	71.4
1976	Mark Moseley, Washington, NFC	34	22	64.7
	Jan Stenerud, Kansas City, AFC	38	21	55.3
1975	Jan Stenerud, Kansas City, AFC	32	22	68.8
	Toni Fritsch, Dallas, NFC	35	22	62.9
1974	Chester Marcol, Green Bay, NFC	39	25	64.1
	Roy Gerela, Pittsburgh, AFC	29	20	69.0

Year	Player, Team	Att.	Made	Pct.
1973	David Ray, Los Angeles, NFC	47	30	63.8
	Roy Gerela, Pittsburgh, AFC	43	29	67.4
1972	*Chester Marcol, Green Bay, NFC	48	33	68.8
	Roy Gerela, Pittsburgh, AFC	41	28	68.3
1971	Curt Knight, Washington, NFC	49	29	59.2
	Garo Yepremian, Miami, AFC	40	28	70.0
1970	Jan Stenerud, Kansas City, AFC	42	30	71.4
	Fred Cox, Minnesota, NFC	46	30	65.2
1969	Jim Turner, N.Y. Jets, AFL	47	32	68.1
	Fred Cox, Minnesota, NFL	37	26	70.3
1968	Jim Turner, N.Y. Jets, AFL	46	34	73.9
	Mac Percival, Chicago, NFL	36	25	69.4
1967	Jim Bakken, St. Louis, NFL	39	27	69.2
	Jan Stenerud, Kansas City, AFL	36	21	58.3
1966	Bruce Gossett, Los Angeles, NFL	49	28	57.1
	Mike Mercer, Oakland-Kansas City, AFL	30	21	70.0
1965	Pete Gogolak, Buffalo, AFL	46	28	60.9
	Fred Cox, Minnesota, NFL	35	23	65.7
1964	Jim Bakken, St. Louis, NFL	38	25	65.8
	Gino Cappelletti, Boston, AFL	39	25	64.1
1963	Jim Martin, Baltimore, NFL	39	24	61.5
	Gino Cappelletti, Boston, AFL	38	22	57.9
1962	Gene Mingo, Denver, AFL	39	27	69.2
	Lou Michaels, Pittsburgh, NFL	42	26	61.9
1961	Steve Myhra, Baltimore, NFL	39	21	53.8
	Gino Cappelletti, Boston, AFL	32	17	53.1
1960	Tommy Davis, San Francisco, NFL	32	19	59.4
	*Gene Mingo, Denver, AFL	28	18	64.3
1959	Pat Summerall, N.Y. Giants	29	20	69.0
1958	Paige Cothren, Los Angeles	25	14	56.0
	*Tom Miner, Pittsburgh	28	14	50.0
1957	Lou Groza, Cleveland	22	15	68.2
1956	Sam Baker, Washington	25	17	68.0
1955	Fred Cone, Green Bay	24	16	66.7
1954	Lou Groza, Cleveland	24	16	66.7
1953	Lou Groza, Cleveland	26	23	88.5
1952	Lou Groza, Cleveland	33	19	57.6
1951	Bob Waterfield, Los Angeles	23	13	56.5
1950	Lou Groza, Cleveland	19	13	68.4
1949	Cliff Patton, Philadelphia	18	9	50.0
	Bob Waterfield, Los Angeles	16	9	56.3
1948	Cliff Patton, Philadelphia	12	8	66.7
1947	Ward Cuff, Green Bay	16	7	43.8
	Pat Harder, Chi. Cardinals	10	7	70.0
	Bob Waterfield, Los Angeles	16	7	43.8
1946	Ted Fritsch, Green Bay	17	9	52.9
1945	Joe Aguirre, Washington	13	7	53.8
1944	Ken Strong, N.Y. Giants	12	6	50.0
1943	Ward Cuff, N.Y. Giants	9	3	33.3
	Don Hutson, Green Bay	5	3	60.0
1942	Bill Daddio, Chi. Cardinals	10	5	50.0
1941	Clarke Hinkle, Green Bay	14	6	42.9
1940	Clarke Hinkle, Green Bay	14	9	64.3
1939	Ward Cuff, N.Y. Giants	16	7	43.8
1938	Ward Cuff, N.Y. Giants	9	5	55.6
	Ralph Kercheval, Brooklyn	13	5	38.5
1937	Jack Manders, Chi. Bears		8	
1936	Jack Manders, Chi. Bears		7	
	Armand Niccolai, Pittsburgh		7	
1935	Armand Niccolai, Pittsburgh		6	
	Bill Smith, Chi. Cardinals		6	
1934	Jack Manders, Chi. Bears		10	
1933	*Jack Manders, Chi. Bears		6	
	Glenn Presnell, Portsmouth		6	
1932	Earl (Dutch) Clark, Portsmouth		3	

*First season of professional football.

ANNUAL RUSHING LEADERS

Year	Player, Team	Att.	Yards	Avg.	TD
2004	Curtis Martin, N.Y. Jets, AFC	371	1,697	4.6	12
	Shaun Alexander, Seattle, NFC	353	1,696	4.8	16
2003	Jamal Lewis, Baltimore, AFC	387	2,066	5.3	14
	Ahman Green, Green Bay, NFC	355	1,883	5.3	15
2002	Ricky Williams, Miami, AFC	383	1,853	4.8	16
	Deuce McAllister, New Orleans, NFC	325	1,388	4.3	13
2001	Priest Holmes, Kansas City, AFC	327	1,555	4.8	8
	Stephen Davis, Washington, NFC	356	1,432	4.0	5
2000	Edgerrin James, Indianapolis, AFC	387	1,709	4.4	13
	Robert Smith, Minnesota, NFC	295	1,521	5.2	7
1999	*Edgerrin James, Indianapolis, AFC	369	1,553	4.2	13
	Stephen Davis, Washington, NFC	290	1,405	4.8	17
1998	Terrell Davis, Denver, AFC	392	2,008	5.1	21
	Jamal Anderson, Atlanta, NFC	410	1,846	4.5	14
1997	Barry Sanders, Detroit, NFC	335	2,053	6.1	11
	Terrell Davis, Denver, AFC	369	1,750	4.7	15
1996	Barry Sanders, Detroit, NFC	307	1,553	5.1	11
	Terrell Davis, Denver, AFC	345	1,538	4.5	13
1995	Emmitt Smith, Dallas, NFC	377	1,773	4.7	25
	*Curtis Martin, New England, AFC	368	1,487	4.0	14
1994	Barry Sanders, Detroit, NFC	331	1,883	5.7	7
	Chris Warren, Seattle, AFC	333	1,545	4.6	9
1993	Emmitt Smith, Dallas, NFC	283	1,486	5.3	9
	Thurman Thomas, Buffalo, AFC	355	1,315	3.7	6
1992	Emmitt Smith, Dallas, NFC	373	1,713	4.6	18
	Barry Foster, Pittsburgh, AFC	390	1,690	4.3	11
1991	Emmitt Smith, Dallas, NFC	365	1,563	4.3	12
	Thurman Thomas, Buffalo, AFC	288	1,407	4.9	7
1990	Barry Sanders, Detroit, NFC	255	1,304	5.1	13
	Thurman Thomas, Buffalo, AFC	271	1,297	4.8	11
1989	Christian Okoye, Kansas City, AFC	370	1,480	4.0	12
	*Barry Sanders, Detroit, NFC	280	1,470	5.3	14
1988	Eric Dickerson, Indianapolis, AFC	388	1,659	4.3	14
	Herschel Walker, Dallas, NFC	361	1,514	4.2	5
1987	Charles White, L.A. Rams, NFC	324	1,374	4.2	11
	Eric Dickerson, Indianapolis, AFC	223	1,011	4.5	5
1986	Eric Dickerson, L.A. Rams, NFC	404	1,821	4.5	11
	Curt Warner, Seattle, AFC	319	1,481	4.6	13
1985	Marcus Allen, L.A. Raiders, AFC	380	1,759	4.6	11
	Gerald Riggs, Atlanta, NFC	397	1,719	4.3	10
1984	Eric Dickerson, L.A. Rams, NFC	379	2,105	5.6	14
	Earnest Jackson, San Diego, AFC	296	1,179	4.0	8
1983	*Eric Dickerson, L.A. Rams, NFC	390	1,808	4.6	18
	*Curt Warner, Seattle, AFC	335	1,449	4.3	13
1982	Freeman McNeil, N.Y. Jets, AFC	151	786	5.2	6
	Tony Dorsett, Dallas, NFC	177	745	4.2	5
1981	*George Rogers, New Orleans, NFC	378	1,674	4.4	13
	Earl Campbell, Houston, AFC	361	1,376	3.8	10
1980	Earl Campbell, Houston, AFC	373	1,934	5.2	13
	Walter Payton, Chicago, NFC	317	1,460	4.6	6
1979	Earl Campbell, Houston, AFC	368	1,697	4.6	19
	Walter Payton, Chicago, NFC	369	1,610	4.4	14
1978	*Earl Campbell, Houston, AFC	302	1,450	4.8	13
	Walter Payton, Chicago, NFC	333	1,395	4.2	11
1977	Walter Payton, Chicago, NFC	339	1,852	5.5	14
	Mark van Eeghen, Oakland, AFC	324	1,273	3.9	7
1976	O.J. Simpson, Buffalo, AFC	290	1,503	5.2	8
	Walter Payton, Chicago, NFC	311	1,390	4.5	13
1975	O.J. Simpson, Buffalo, AFC	329	1,817	5.5	16
	Jim Otis, St. Louis, NFC	269	1,076	4.0	5
1974	Otis Armstrong, Denver, AFC	263	1,407	5.3	9
	Lawrence McCutcheon, Los Angeles, NFC	236	1,109	4.7	3
1973	O.J. Simpson, Buffalo, AFC	332	2,003	6.0	12
	John Brockington, Green Bay, NFC	265	1,144	4.3	3
1972	O.J. Simpson, Buffalo, AFC	292	1,251	4.3	6
	Larry Brown, Washington, NFC	285	1,216	4.3	8
1971	Floyd Little, Denver, AFC	284	1,133	4.0	6
	*John Brockington, Green Bay, NFC	216	1,105	5.1	4

Year	Player, Team	Att.	Yards	Avg.	TD
1970	Larry Brown, Washington, NFC	237	1,125	4.7	5
	Floyd Little, Denver, AFC	209	901	4.3	3
1969	Gale Sayers, Chicago, NFL	236	1,032	4.4	8
	Dickie Post, San Diego, AFL	182	873	4.8	6
1968	Leroy Kelly, Cleveland, NFL	248	1,239	5.0	16
	*Paul Robinson, Cincinnati, AFL	238	1,023	4.3	8
1967	Jim Nance, Boston, AFL	269	1,216	4.5	7
	Leroy Kelly, Cleveland, NFL	235	1,205	5.1	11
1966	Jim Nance, Boston, AFL	299	1,458	4.9	11
	Gale Sayers, Chicago, NFL	229	1,231	5.4	8
1965	Jim Brown, Cleveland, NFL	289	1,544	5.3	17
	Paul Lowe, San Diego, AFL	222	1,121	5.0	7
1964	Jim Brown, Cleveland, NFL	280	1,446	5.2	7
	Cookie Gilchrist, Buffalo, AFL	230	981	4.3	6
1963	Jim Brown, Cleveland, NFL	291	1,863	6.4	12
	Clem Daniels, Oakland, AFL	215	1,099	5.1	3
1962	Jim Taylor, Green Bay, NFL	272	1,474	5.4	19
	Cookie Gilchrist, Buffalo, AFL	214	1,096	5.1	13
1961	Jim Brown, Cleveland, NFL	305	1,408	4.6	8
	Billy Cannon, Houston, AFL	200	948	4.7	6
1960	Jim Brown, Cleveland, NFL	215	1,257	5.8	9
	*Abner Haynes, Dall. Texans, AFL	156	875	5.6	9
1959	Jim Brown, Cleveland	290	1,329	4.6	14
1958	Jim Brown, Cleveland	257	1,527	5.9	17
1957	*Jim Brown, Cleveland	202	942	4.7	9
1956	Rick Casares, Chi. Bears	234	1,126	4.8	12
1955	*Alan Ameche, Baltimore	213	961	4.5	9
1954	Joe Perry, San Francisco	173	1,049	6.1	8
1953	Joe Perry, San Francisco	192	1,018	5.3	10
1952	Dan Towler, Los Angeles	156	894	5.7	10
1951	Eddie Price, N.Y. Giants	271	971	3.6	7
1950	Marion Motley, Cleveland	140	810	5.8	3
1949	Steve Van Buren, Philadelphia	263	1,146	4.4	11
1948	Steve Van Buren, Philadelphia	201	945	4.7	10
1947	Steve Van Buren, Philadelphia	217	1,008	4.6	13
1946	Bill Dudley, Pittsburgh	146	604	4.1	3
1945	Steve Van Buren, Philadelphia	143	832	5.8	15
1944	Bill Paschal, N.Y. Giants	196	737	3.8	9
1943	*Bill Paschal, N.Y. Giants	147	572	3.9	10
1942	*Bill Dudley, Pittsburgh	162	696	4.3	5
1941	Clarence (Pug) Manders, Brooklyn	111	486	4.4	5
1940	Byron (Whizzer) White, Detroit	146	514	3.5	5
1939	*Bill Osmanski, Chicago	121	699	5.8	7
1938	*Byron (Whizzer) White, Pittsburgh	152	567	3.7	4
1937	Cliff Battles, Washington	216	874	4.0	5
1936	*Alphonse (Tuffy) Leemans, N.Y. Giants	206	830	4.0	2
1935	Doug Russell, Chi. Cardinals	140	499	3.6	0
1934	*Beattie Feathers, Chi. Bears	119	1,004	8.4	8
1933	Jim Musick, Boston	173	809	4.7	5
1932	*Cliff Battles, Boston	148	576	3.9	3

*First season of professional football.

ANNUAL PASSING LEADERS

(Current rating system implemented in 1973)

Year	Player, Team	Att.	Comp.	Yards	TD	Int.	Rating
2004	Peyton Manning, Indianapolis, AFC	497	336	4,557	49	10	121.1
	Daunte Culpepper, Minnesota, NFC	548	379	4,717	39	11	110.9
2003	Steve McNair, Tennessee, AFC	400	250	3,215	24	7	100.4
	Daunte Culpepper, Minnesota, NFC	454	295	3,479	25	11	96.4
2002	Chad Pennington, N.Y. Jets, AFC	399	275	3,120	22	6	104.2
	Brad Johnson, Tampa Bay, NFC	451	281	3,049	22	6	92.9
2001	Kurt Warner, St. Louis, NFC	546	375	4,830	36	22	101.4
	Rich Gannon, Oakland, AFC	549	361	3,828	27	9	95.5
2000	Brian Griese, Denver, AFC	336	216	2,688	19	4	102.9
	Trent Green, St. Louis, NFC	240	145	2,063	16	5	101.8
1999	Kurt Warner, St. Louis, NFC	499	325	4,353	41	13	109.2
	Peyton Manning, Indianapolis, AFC	533	331	4,135	26	15	90.7
1998	Randall Cunningham, Minnesota, NFC	425	259	3,704	34	10	106.0
	Vinny Testaverde, N.Y. Jets, AFC	421	259	3,256	29	7	101.6

Year	Player, Team	Att.	Comp.	Yards	TD	Int.	Rating
1997	Steve Young, San Francisco, NFC	356	241	3,029	19	6	104.7
	Mark Brunell, Jacksonville, AFC	435	264	3,281	18	7	91.2
1996	Steve Young, San Francisco NFC	316	214	2,410	14	6	97.2
	John Elway, Denver, AFC	466	287	3,328	26	14	89.2
1995	Jim Harbaugh, Indianapolis, AFC	314	200	2,575	17	5	100.7
	Brett Favre, Green Bay, NFC	570	359	4,413	38	13	99.5
1994	Steve Young, San Francisco, NFC	461	324	3,969	35	10	112.8
	Dan Marino, Miami, AFC	615	385	4,453	30	17	89.2
1993	Steve Young, San Francisco, NFC	462	314	4,023	29	16	101.5
	John Elway, Denver, AFC	551	348	4,030	25	10	92.8
1992	Steve Young, San Francisco, NFC	402	268	3,465	25	7	107.0
	Warren Moon, Houston, AFC	346	224	2,521	18	12	89.3
1991	Steve Young, San Francisco, NFC	279	180	2,517	17	8	101.8
	Jim Kelly, Buffalo, AFC	474	304	3,844	33	17	97.6
1990	Jim Kelly, Buffalo, AFC	346	219	2,829	24	9	101.2
	Phil Simms, N.Y. Giants, NFC	311	184	2,284	15	4	92.7
1989	Joe Montana, San Francisco, NFC	386	271	3,521	26	8	112.4
	Boomer Esiason, Cincinnati, AFC	455	258	3,525	28	11	92.1
1988	Boomer Esiason, Cincinnati, AFC	388	223	3,572	28	14	97.4
	Wade Wilson, Minnesota, NFC	332	204	2,746	15	9	91.5
1987	Joe Montana, San Francisco, NFC	398	266	3,054	31	13	102.1
	Bernie Kosar, Cleveland, AFC	389	241	3,033	22	9	95.4
1986	Tommy Kramer, Minnesota, NFC	372	208	3,000	24	10	92.6
	Dan Marino, Miami, AFC	623	378	4,746	44	23	92.5
1985	Ken O'Brien, N.Y. Jets, AFC	488	297	3,888	25	8	96.2
	Joe Montana, San Francisco, NFC	494	303	3,653	27	13	91.3
1984	Dan Marino, Miami, AFC	564	362	5,084	48	17	108.9
	Joe Montana, San Francisco, NFC	432	279	3,630	28	10	102.9
1983	Steve Bartkowski, Atlanta, NFC	432	274	3,167	22	5	97.6
	*Dan Marino, Miami, AFC	296	173	2,210	20	6	96.0
1982	Ken Anderson, Cincinnati, AFC	309	218	2,495	12	9	95.3
	Joe Theismann, Washington, NFC	252	161	2,033	13	9	91.3
1981	Ken Anderson, Cincinnati, AFC	479	300	3,754	29	10	98.4
	Joe Montana, San Francisco, NFC	488	311	3,565	19	12	88.4
1980	Brian Sipe, Cleveland, AFC	554	337	4,132	30	14	91.4
	Ron Jaworski, Philadelphia, NFC	451	257	3,529	27	12	91.0
1979	Roger Staubach, Dallas, NFC	461	267	3,586	27	11	92.3
	Dan Fouts, San Diego, AFC	530	332	4,082	24	24	82.6
1978	Roger Staubach, Dallas, NFC	413	231	3,190	25	16	84.9
	Terry Bradshaw, Pittsburgh, AFC	368	207	2,915	28	20	84.7
1977	Bob Griese, Miami, AFC	307	180	2,252	22	13	87.8
	Roger Staubach, Dallas, NFC	361	210	2,620	18	9	87.0
1976	Ken Stabler, Oakland, AFC	291	194	2,737	27	17	103.4
	James Harris, Los Angeles, NFC	158	91	1,460	8	6	89.6
1975	Ken Anderson, Cincinnati, AFC	377	228	3,169	21	11	93.9
	Fran Tarkenton, Minnesota, NFC	425	273	2,994	25	13	91.8
1974	Ken Anderson, Cincinnati, AFC	328	213	2,667	18	10	95.7
	Sonny Jurgensen, Washington, NFC	167	107	1,185	11	5	94.5
1973	Roger Staubach, Dallas, NFC	286	179	2,428	23	15	94.6
	Ken Stabler, Oakland, AFC	260	163	1,997	14	10	88.3
1972	Norm Snead, N.Y. Giants, NFC	325	196	2,307	17	12	
	Earl Morrall, Miami, AFC	150	83	1,360	11	7	
1971	Roger Staubach, Dallas, NFC	211	126	1,882	15	4	
	Bob Griese, Miami, AFC	263	145	2,089	19	9	
1970	John Brodie, San Francisco, NFC	378	223	2,941	24	10	
	Daryle Lamonica, Oakland, AFC	356	179	2,516	22	15	
1969	Sonny Jurgensen, Washington, NFL	442	274	3,102	22	15	
	*Greg Cook, Cincinnati, AFL	197	106	1,854	15	11	
1968	Len Dawson, Kansas City, AFL	224	131	2,109	17	9	
	Earl Morrall, Baltimore, NFL	317	182	2,909	26	17	
1967	Sonny Jurgensen, Washington, NFL	508	288	3,747	31	16	
	Daryle Lamonica, Oakland, AFL	425	220	3,228	30	20	
1966	Bart Starr, Green Bay, NFL	251	156	2,257	14	3	
	Len Dawson, Kansas City, AFL	284	159	2,527	26	10	
1965	Rudy Bukich, Chicago, NFL	312	176	2,641	20	9	
	John Hadl, San Diego, AFL	348	174	2,798	20	21	
1964	Len Dawson, Kansas City, AFL	354	199	2,879	30	18	
	Bart Starr, Green Bay, NFL	272	163	2,144	15	4	

Year	Player, Team	Att.	Comp.	Yards	TD	Int.	Rating
1963	Y.A. Tittle, N.Y. Giants, NFL	367	221	3,145	36	14	
	Tobin Rote, San Diego, AFL	286	170	2,510	20	17	
1962	Len Dawson, Dallas Texans, AFL	310	189	2,759	29	17	
	Bart Starr, Green Bay, NFL	285	178	2,438	12	9	
1961	George Blanda, Houston, AFL	362	187	3,330	36	22	
	Milt Plum, Cleveland, NFL	302	177	2,416	18	10	
1960	Milt Plum, Cleveland, NFL	250	151	2,297	21	5	
	Jack Kemp, L.A. Chargers, AFL	406	211	3,018	20	25	
1959	Charlie Conerly, N.Y. Giants	194	113	1,706	14	4	
1958	Eddie LeBaron, Washington	145	79	1,365	11	10	
1957	Tommy O'Connell, Cleveland	110	63	1,229	9	8	
1956	Ed Brown, Chicago Bears	168	96	1,667	11	12	
1955	Otto Graham, Cleveland	185	98	1,721	15	8	
1954	Norm Van Brocklin, Los Angeles	260	139	2,637	13	21	
1953	Otto Graham, Cleveland	258	167	2,722	11	9	
1952	Norm Van Brocklin, Los Angeles	205	113	1,736	14	17	
1951	Bob Waterfield, Los Angeles	176	88	1,566	13	10	
1950	Norm Van Brocklin, Los Angeles	233	127	2,061	18	14	
1949	Sammy Baugh, Washington	255	145	1,903	18	14	
1948	Tommy Thompson, Philadelphia	246	141	1,965	25	11	
1947	Sammy Baugh, Washington	354	210	2,938	25	15	
1946	Bob Waterfield, Los Angeles	251	127	1,747	18	17	
1945	Sammy Baugh, Washington	182	128	1,669	11	4	
	Sid Luckman, Chicago Bears	217	117	1,725	14	10	
1944	Frank Filchock, Washington	147	84	1,139	13	9	
1943	Sammy Baugh, Washington	239	133	1,754	23	19	
1942	Cecil Isbell, Green Bay	268	146	2,021	24	14	
1941	Cecil Isbell, Green Bay	206	117	1,479	15	11	
1940	Sammy Baugh, Washington	177	111	1,367	12	10	
1939	*Parker Hall, Cleveland	208	106	1,227	9	13	
1938	Ed Danowski, N.Y. Giants	129	70	848	7	8	
1937	*Sammy Baugh, Washington	171	81	1,127	8	14	
1936	Arnie Herber, Green Bay	173	77	1,239	11	13	
1935	Ed Danowski, N.Y. Giants	113	57	794	10	9	
1934	Arnie Herber, Green Bay	115	42	799	8	12	
1933	*Harry Newman, N.Y. Giants	136	53	973	11	17	
1932	Arnie Herber, Green Bay	101	37	639	9	9	

First season of professional football.

ANNUAL PASSING TOUCHDOWN LEADERS

Year	Player, Team	TD
2004	Peyton Manning, Indianapolis, AFC	49
	Daunte Culpepper, Minnesota, NFC	39
2003	Brett Favre, Green Bay, NFC	32
	Peyton Manning, Indianapolis, AFC	29
2002	Tom Brady, New England, AFC	28
	Aaron Brooks, New Orleans, NFC	27
	Brett Favre, Green Bay, NFC	27
2001	Kurt Warner, St. Louis, NFC	36
	Rich Gannon, Oakland, AFC	27
2000	Daunte Culpepper, Minnesota, NFC	33
	Peyton Manning, Indianapolis, AFC	33
1999	Kurt Warner, St. Louis, NFC	41
	Peyton Manning, Indianapolis, AFC	26
1998	Steve Young, San Francisco, NFC	36
	Vinny Testaverde, N.Y. Jets, AFC	29
1997	Brett Favre, Green Bay, NFC	35
	Jeff George, Oakland, AFC	29
1996	Brett Favre, Green Bay, NFC	39
	Vinny Testaverde, Baltimore, AFC	33
1995	Brett Favre, Green Bay, NFC	38
	Jeff Blake, Cincinnati, AFC	28
1994	Steve Young, San Francisco, NFC	35
	Dan Marino, Miami, AFC	30
1993	Steve Young, San Francisco, NFC	29
	John Elway, Denver, AFC	25
1992	Steve Young, San Francisco, NFC	25
	Dan Marino, Miami, AFC	24

Year	Player, Team	TD
1991	Jim Kelly, Buffalo, AFC	33
	Mark Rypien, Washington, NFC	28
1990	Warren Moon, Houston, AFC	33
	Randall Cunningham, Philadelphia, NFC	30
1989	Jim Everett, L.A. Rams, NFC	29
	Boomer Esiason, Cincinnati, AFC	28
1988	Jim Everett, L.A. Rams, NFC	31
	Boomer Esiason, Cincinnati, AFC	28
	Dan Marino, Miami, AFC	28
1987	Joe Montana, San Francisco, NFC	31
	Dan Marino, Miami, AFC	26
1986	Dan Marino, Miami, AFC	44
	Tommy Kramer, Minnesota, NFC	24
1985	Dan Marino, Miami, AFC	30
	Joe Montana, San Francisco, NFC	27
1984	Dan Marino, Miami, AFC	48
	Neil Lomax, St. Louis, NFC	28
	Joe Montana, San Francisco, NFC	28
1983	Lynn Dickey, Green Bay, NFC	32
	Joe Ferguson, Buffalo, AFC	26
	Brian Sipe, Cleveland, AFC	26
1982	Terry Bradshaw, Pittsburgh, AFC	17
	Dan Fouts, San Diego, AFC	17
	Joe Montana, San Francisco, NFC	17
1981	Dan Fouts, San Diego, AFC	33
	Steve Bartkowski, Atlanta, NFC	30
1980	Steve Bartkowski, Atlanta, NFC	31
	Dan Fouts, San Diego, AFC	30
	Brian Sipe, Cleveland, AFC	30

Year	Player, Team	TD	Year	Player, Team	TD
1979	Steve Grogan, New England, AFC	28	1962	Y.A. Tittle, N.Y. Giants, NFL	33
	Brian Sipe, Cleveland, AFC	28		Len Dawson, Dallas, AFL	29
	Roger Staubach, Dallas, NFC	27	1961	George Blanda, Houston, AFL	36
1978	Terry Bradshaw, Pittsburgh, AFC	28		Sonny Jurgensen, Philadelphia, NFL	32
	Roger Staubach, Dallas, NFC	25	1960	Al Dorow, N.Y. Titans, AFL	26
	Fran Tarkenton, Minnesota, NFC	25		Johnny Unitas, Baltimore, NFL	25
1977	Bob Griese, Miami, AFC	22	1959	Johnny Unitas, Baltimore	32
	Ron Jaworski, Philadelphia, NFC	18	1958	Johnny Unitas, Baltimore	19
	Roger Staubach, Dallas, NFC	18	1957	Johnny Unitas, Baltimore	24
1976	Ken Stabler, Oakland, AFC	27	1956	Tobin Rote, Green Bay	18
	Jim Hart, St. Louis, NFC	18	1955	Tobin Rote, Green Bay	17
1975	Joe Ferguson, Buffalo, AFC	25		Y.A. Tittle, San Francisco	17
	Fran Tarkenton, Minnesota, NFC	25	1954	Adrian Burk, Philadelphia	23
1974	Ken Stabler, Oakland, AFC	26	1953	Robert Thomason, Philadelphia	21
	Jim Hart, St. Louis, NFC	20	1952	Jim Finks, Pittsburgh	20
1973	Roman Gabriel, Philadelphia, NFC	23		Otto Graham, Cleveland	20
	Roger Staubach, Dallas, NFC	23	1951	Bobby Layne, Detroit	26
	Charley Johnson, Denver, AFC	20	1950	George Ratterman, N.Y. Yanks	22
1972	Billy Kilmer, Washington, NFC	19	1949	Johnny Lujack, Chi. Bears	23
	Joe Namath, N.Y. Jets, AFC	19	1948	Tommy Thompson, Philadelphia	25
1971	John Hadl, San Diego, AFC	21	1947	Sammy Baugh, Washington	25
	John Brodie, San Francisco, NFC	18	1946	Sid Luckman, Chi. Bears	17
1970	John Brodie, San Francisco, NFC	24		Bob Waterfield, Los Angeles	17
	John Hadl, San Diego, AFC	22	1945	Sid Luckman, Chi. Bears	14
	Daryle Lamonica, Oakland, AFC	22		*Bob Waterfield, Cleveland	14
1969	Daryle Lamonica, Oakland, AFL	34	1944	Frank Filchock, Washington	13
	Roman Gabriel, Los Angeles, NFL	24	1943	Sid Luckman, Chi. Bears	28
1968	John Hadl, San Diego, AFL	27	1942	Cecil Isbell, Green Bay	24
	Earl Morrall, Baltimore, NFL	26	1941	Cecil Isbell, Green Bay	15
1967	Sonny Jurgensen, Washington, NFL	31	1940	Sammy Baugh, Washington	12
	Daryle Lamonica, Oakland, AFL	30	1939	Frank Filchock, Washington	11
1966	Frank Ryan, Cleveland, NFL	29	1938	Bob Monnett, Green Bay	9
	Len Dawson, Kansas City, AFL	26	1937	Bernie Masterson, Chi. Bears	9
1965	John Brodie, San Francisco, NFL	30	1936	Arnie Herber, Green Bay	11
	Len Dawson, Kansas City, AFL	21	1935	Ed Danowski, N.Y. Giants	10
1964	Babe Parilli, Boston, AFL	31	1934	Arnie Herber, Green Bay	8
	Frank Ryan, Cleveland, NFL	25	1933	*Harry Newman, N.Y. Giants	11
1963	Y.A. Tittle, N.Y. Giants, NFL	36	1932	Arnie Herber, Green Bay	9
	Len Dawson, Kansas City, AFL	26		*First season of professional football.	

ANNUAL PASS RECEIVING LEADERS

Year	Player, Team	No.	Yards	Avg.	TD
2004	Tony Gonzalez, Kansas City, AFC	102	1,258	12.3	7
	Joe Horn, New Orleans, NFC	94	1,399	14.9	11
	Torry Holt, St. Louis, NFC	94	1,372	14.6	10
2003	Torry Holt, St. Louis, NFC	117	1,696	14.5	12
	LaDainian Tomlinson, San Diego, AFC	100	725	7.3	4
2002	Marvin Harrison, Indianapolis, AFC	143	1,722	12.0	11
	Randy Moss, Minnesota, NFC	106	1,347	12.7	7
2001	Rod Smith, Denver, AFC	113	1,343	11.9	11
	Keyshawn Johnson, Tampa Bay, NFC	106	1,266	11.9	1
2000	Marvin Harrison, Indianapolis, AFC	102	1,413	13.9	14
	Muhsin Muhammad, Carolina, NFC	102	1,183	11.6	6
1999	Jimmy Smith, Jacksonville, AFC	116	1,636	14.1	6
	Muhsin Muhammad, Carolina, NFC	96	1,253	13.1	8
1998	O.J. McDuffie, Miami, AFC	90	1,050	11.7	7
	Frank Sanders, Arizona, NFC	89	1,145	12.9	3
1997	Tim Brown, Oakland, AFC	104	1,408	13.5	5
	Herman Moore, Detroit, NFC	104	1,293	12.4	8
1996	Jerry Rice, San Francisco, NFC	108	1,254	11.6	8
	Carl Pickens, Cincinnati, AFC	100	1,180	11.8	12
1995	Herman Moore, Detroit, NFC	123	1,686	13.7	14
	Carl Pickens, Cincinnati, AFC	99	1,234	12.5	17
1994	Cris Carter, Minnesota, NFC	122	1,256	10.3	7
	Ben Coates, New England, AFC	96	1,174	12.2	7
1993	Sterling Sharpe, Green Bay, NFC	112	1,274	11.4	11
	Reggie Langhorne, Indianapolis, AFC	85	1,038	12.2	3
1992	Sterling Sharpe, Green Bay, NFC	108	1,461	13.5	13
	Haywood Jeffires, Houston, AFC	90	913	10.1	9

Year	Player, Team	No.	Yards	Avg.	TD
1991	Haywood Jeffries, Houston, AFC	100	1,181	11.8	7
	Michael Irvin, Dallas, NFC	93	1,523	16.4	8
1990	Jerry Rice, San Francisco, NFC	100	1,502	15.0	13
	Haywood Jeffries, Houston, AFC	74	1,048	14.2	8
	Drew Hill, Houston, AFC	74	1,019	13.8	5
1989	Sterling Sharpe, Green Bay, NFC	90	1,423	15.8	12
	Andre Reed, Buffalo, AFC	88	1,312	14.9	9
1988	Al Toon, N.Y. Jets, AFC	93	1,067	11.5	5
	Henry Ellard, L.A. Rams, NFC	86	1,414	16.4	10
1987	J.T. Smith, St. Louis, NFC	91	1,117	12.3	8
	Al Toon, N.Y. Jets, AFC	68	976	14.4	5
1986	Todd Christensen, L.A. Raiders, AFC	95	1,153	12.1	8
	Jerry Rice, San Francisco, NFC	86	1,570	18.3	15
1985	Roger Craig, San Francisco, NFC	92	1,016	11.0	6
	Lionel James, San Diego, AFC	86	1,027	11.9	6
1984	Art Monk, Washington, NFC	106	1,372	12.9	7
	Ozzie Newsome, Cleveland, AFC	89	1,001	11.2	5
1983	Todd Christensen, L.A. Raiders, AFC	92	1,247	13.6	12
	Roy Green, St. Louis, NFC	78	1,227	15.7	14
	Charlie Brown, Washington, NFC	78	1,225	15.7	8
	Earnest Gray, N.Y. Giants, NFC	78	1,139	14.6	5
1982	Dwight Clark, San Francisco, NFC	60	913	15.2	5
	Kellen Winslow, San Diego, AFC	54	721	13.4	6
1981	Kellen Winslow, San Diego, AFC	88	1,075	12.2	10
	Dwight Clark, San Francisco, NFC	85	1,105	13.0	4
1980	Kellen Winslow, San Diego, AFC	89	1,290	14.5	9
	*Earl Cooper, San Francisco, NFC	83	567	6.8	4
1979	Joe Washington, Baltimore, AFC	82	750	9.1	3
	Ahmad Rashad, Minnesota, NFC	80	1,156	14.5	9
1978	Rickey Young, Minnesota, NFC	88	704	8.0	5
	Steve Largent, Seattle, AFC	71	1,168	16.5	8
1977	Lydell Mitchell, Baltimore, AFC	71	620	8.7	4
	Ahmad Rashad, Minnesota, NFC	51	681	13.4	2
1976	MacArthur Lane, Kansas City, AFC	66	686	10.4	1
	Drew Pearson, Dallas, NFC	58	806	13.9	6
1975	Chuck Foreman, Minnesota, NFC	73	691	9.5	9
	Reggie Rucker, Cleveland, AFC	60	770	12.8	3
	Lydell Mitchell, Baltimore, AFC	60	544	9.1	4
1974	Lydell Mitchell, Baltimore, AFC	72	544	7.6	2
	Charles Young, Philadelphia, NFC	63	696	11.0	3
1973	Harold Carmichael, Philadelphia, NFC	67	1,116	16.7	9
	Fred Willis, Houston, AFC	57	371	6.5	1
1972	Harold Jackson, Philadelphia, NFC	62	1,048	16.9	4
	Fred Biletnikoff, Oakland, AFC	58	802	13.8	7
1971	Fred Biletnikoff, Oakland, AFC	61	929	15.2	9
	Bob Tucker, N.Y. Giants, NFC	59	791	13.4	4
1970	Dick Gordon, Chicago, NFC	71	1,026	14.5	13
	Marlin Briscoe, Buffalo, AFC	57	1,036	18.2	8
1969	Dan Abramowicz, New Orleans, NFL	73	1,015	13.9	7
	Lance Alworth, San Diego, AFL	64	1,003	15.7	4
1968	Clifton McNeil, San Francisco, NFL	71	994	14.0	7
	Lance Alworth, San Diego, AFL	68	1,312	19.3	10
1967	George Sauer, N.Y. Jets, AFL	75	1,189	15.9	6
	Charley Taylor, Washington, NFL	70	990	14.1	9
1966	Lance Alworth, San Diego, AFL	73	1,383	18.9	13
	Charley Taylor, Washington, NFL	72	1,119	15.5	12
1965	Lionel Taylor, Denver, AFL	85	1,131	13.3	6
	Dave Parks, San Francisco, NFL	80	1,344	16.8	12
1964	Charley Hennigan, Houston, AFL	101	1,546	15.3	8
	Johnny Morris, Chicago, NFL	93	1,200	12.9	10
1963	Lionel Taylor, Denver, AFL	78	1,101	14.1	10
	Bobby Joe Conrad, St. Louis, NFL	73	967	13.2	10
1962	Lionel Taylor, Denver, AFL	77	908	11.8	4
	Bobby Mitchell, Washington, NFL	72	1,384	19.2	11
1961	Lionel Taylor, Denver, AFL	100	1,176	11.8	4
	Jim (Red) Phillips, Los Angeles, NFL	78	1,092	14.0	5
1960	Lionel Taylor, Denver, AFL	92	1,235	13.4	12
	Raymond Berry, Baltimore, NFL	74	1,298	17.5	10

Year	Player, Team	No.	Yards	Avg.	TD
1959	Raymond Berry, Baltimore	66	959	14.5	14
1958	Raymond Berry, Baltimore	56	794	14.2	9
	Pete Retzlaff, Philadelphia	56	766	13.7	2
1957	Billy Wilson, San Francisco	52	757	14.6	6
1956	Billy Wilson, San Francisco	60	889	14.8	5
1955	Pete Pihos, Philadelphia	62	864	13.9	7
1954	Pete Pihos, Philadelphia	60	872	14.5	10
	Billy Wilson, San Francisco	60	830	13.8	5
1953	Pete Pihos, Philadelphia	63	1,049	16.7	10
1952	Mac Speedie, Cleveland	62	911	14.7	5
1951	Elroy (Crazylegs) Hirsch, Los Angeles	66	1,495	22.7	17
1950	Tom Fears, Los Angeles	84	1,116	13.3	7
1949	Tom Fears, Los Angeles	77	1,013	13.2	9
1948	*Tom Fears, Los Angeles	51	698	13.7	4
1947	Jim Keane, Chi. Bears	64	910	14.2	10
1946	Jim Benton, Los Angeles	63	981	15.6	6
1945	Don Hutson, Green Bay	47	834	17.7	9
1944	Don Hutson, Green Bay	58	866	14.9	9
1943	Don Hutson, Green Bay	47	776	16.5	11
1942	Don Hutson, Green Bay	74	1,211	16.4	17
1941	Don Hutson, Green Bay	58	738	12.7	10
1940	*Don Looney, Philadelphia	58	707	12.2	4
1939	Don Hutson, Green Bay	34	846	24.9	6
1938	Gaynell Tinsley, Chi. Cardinals	41	516	12.6	1
1937	Don Hutson, Green Bay	41	552	13.5	7
1936	Don Hutson, Green Bay	34	536	15.8	8
1935	*Tod Goodwin, N.Y. Giants	26	432	16.6	4
1934	Joe Carter, Philadelphia	16	238	14.9	4
	Morris (Red) Badgro, N.Y. Giants	16	206	12.9	1
1933	John (Shipwreck) Kelly, Brooklyn	22	246	11.2	3
1932	Ray Flaherty, N.Y. Giants	21	350	16.7	3

*First season of professional football.

ANNUAL PASS RECEIVING LEADERS (YARDS)

Year	Player, Team	No.	Yards	Avg.	TD
2004	Muhsin Muhammad, Carolina, NFC	93	1,405	15.1	16
	Chad Johnson, Cincinnati, AFC	95	1,274	13.4	9
2003	Torry Holt, St. Louis, NFC	117	1,696	14.5	12
	Chad Johnson, Cincinnati, AFC	90	1,355	15.1	10
2002	Marvin Harrison, Indianapolis, AFC	143	1,722	12.0	11
	Randy Moss, Minnesota, NFC	106	1,347	12.7	7
2001	David Boston, Arizona, NFC	98	1,598	16.3	8
	Marvin Harrison, Indianapolis, AFC	109	1,524	14.0	15
2000	Torry Holt, St. Louis, NFC	82	1,635	19.9	6
	Rod Smith, Denver, AFC	100	1,602	16.0	8
1999	Marvin Harrison, Indianapolis, AFC	115	1,663	14.5	12
	Randy Moss, Minnesota, NFC	80	1,413	17.7	11
1998	Antonio Freeman, Green Bay, NFC	84	1,424	17.0	14
	Eric Moulds, Buffalo, AFC	67	1,368	20.4	9
1997	Rob Moore, Arizona, NFC	97	1,584	16.3	8
	Tim Brown, Oakland, AFC	104	1,408	13.5	5
1996	Isaac Bruce, St. Louis, NFC	84	1,338	15.9	7
	Jimmy Smith, Jacksonville, AFC	83	1,244	15.0	7
1995	Jerry Rice, San Francisco, NFC	122	1,848	15.1	15
	Tim Brown, Oakland, AFC	89	1,342	15.1	10
1994	Jerry Rice, San Francisco, NFC	112	1,499	13.4	13
	Tim Brown, L.A. Raiders, AFC	89	1,309	14.7	9
1993	Jerry Rice, San Francisco, NFC	98	1,503	15.3	15
	Tim Brown, L.A. Raiders, AFC	80	1,180	14.8	7
1992	Sterling Sharpe, Green Bay, NFC	108	1,461	13.5	13
	Anthony Miller, San Diego, AFC	72	1,060	14.7	7
1991	Michael Irvin, Dallas, NFC	93	1,523	16.4	8
	Haywood Jeffires, Houston, AFC	100	1,181	11.8	7
1990	Jerry Rice, San Francisco, NFC	100	1,502	15.0	13
	Haywood Jeffires, Houston, AFC	74	1,048	14.2	8
1989	Jerry Rice, San Francisco, NFC	82	1,483	18.1	17
	Andre Reed, Buffalo, AFC	88	1,312	14.9	9
1988	Henry Ellard, L.A. Rams, NFC	86	1,414	16.4	10
	Eddie Brown, Cincinnati, AFC	53	1,273	24.0	9

Year	Player, Team	No.	Yards	Avg.	TD
1987	J.T. Smith, St. Louis, NFC	91	1,117	12.3	8
	Carlos Carson, Kansas City, AFC	55	1,044	19.0	7
1986	Jerry Rice, San Francisco, NFC	86	1,570	18.3	15
	Stanley Morgan, New England, AFC	84	1,491	17.8	10
1985	Steve Largent, Seattle, AFC	79	1,287	16.3	6
	Mike Quick, Philadelphia, NFC	73	1,247	17.1	11
1984	Roy Green, St. Louis, NFC	78	1,555	19.9	12
	John Stallworth, Pittsburgh, AFC	80	1,395	17.4	11
1983	Mike Quick, Philadelphia, NFC	69	1,409	20.4	13
	Carlos Carson, Kansas City, AFC	80	1,351	16.9	7
1982	Wes Chandler, San Diego, AFC	49	1,032	21.1	9
	Dwight Clark, San Francisco, NFC	60	913	15.2	5
1981	Alfred Jenkins, Atlanta, NFC	70	1,358	19.4	13
	Frank Lewis, Buffalo, AFC	70	1,244	17.8	4
	Steve Watson, Denver, AFC	60	1,244	20.7	13
1980	John Jefferson, San Diego, AFC	82	1,340	16.3	13
	James Lofton, Green Bay, NFC	71	1,226	17.3	4
1979	Steve Largent, Seattle, AFC	66	1,237	18.7	9
	Ahmad Rashad, Minnesota, NFC	80	1,156	14.5	9
1978	Wesley Walker, N.Y. Jets, AFC	48	1,169	24.4	8
	Harold Carmichael, Philadelphia, NFC	55	1,072	19.5	8
1977	Drew Pearson, Dallas, NFC	48	870	18.1	2
	Ken Burrough, Houston, AFC	43	816	19.0	8
1976	Roger Carr, Baltimore, AFC	43	1,112	25.9	11
	*Sammy White, Minnesota, NFC	51	906	17.8	10
1975	Ken Burrough, Houston, AFC	53	1,063	20.1	8
	Mel Gray, St. Louis, NFC	48	926	19.3	11
1974	Cliff Branch, Oakland, AFC	60	1,092	18.2	13
	Drew Pearson, Dallas, NFC	62	1,087	17.5	2
1973	Harold Carmichael, Philadelphia, NFC	67	1,116	16.7	9
	*Isaac Curtis, Cincinnati, AFC	45	843	18.7	9
1972	Harold Jackson, Philadelphia, NFC	62	1,048	16.9	4
	Rich Caster, N.Y. Jets, AFC	39	833	21.4	10
1971	Otis Taylor, Kansas City, AFC	57	1,110	19.5	7
	Gene Washington, San Francisco, NFC	46	884	19.2	4
1970	Gene Washington, San Francisco, NFC	53	1,100	20.8	12
	Marlin Briscoe, Buffalo, AFC	57	1,036	18.2	8
1969	Warren Wells, Oakland, AFL	47	1,260	26.8	14
	Harold Jackson, Philadelphia, NFL	65	1,116	17.2	9
1968	Lance Alworth, San Diego, AFL	68	1,312	19.3	10
	Roy Jefferson, Pittsburgh, NFL	58	1,074	18.5	11
1967	Don Maynard, N.Y. Jets, AFL	71	1,434	20.3	10
	Ben Hawkins, Philadelphia, NFL	59	1,265	21.4	10
1966	Lance Alworth, San Diego, AFL	73	1,383	18.9	13
	Pat Studstill, Detroit, NFL	67	1,266	18.9	5
1965	Lance Alworth, San Diego, AFL	69	1,602	23.2	14
	Dave Parks, San Francisco, NFL	80	1,344	16.8	12
1964	Charley Hennigan, Houston, AFL	101	1,546	15.3	8
	Johnny Morris, Chicago, NFL	93	1,200	12.9	10
1963	Bobby Mitchell, Washington, NFL	69	1,436	20.8	7
	Art Powell, Oakland, AFL	73	1,304	17.8	16
1962	Bobby Mitchell, Washington, NFL	72	1,384	19.2	11
	Art Powell, N.Y. Titans, AFL	64	1,130	17.6	8
1961	Charley Hennigan, Houston, AFL	82	1,746	21.3	12
	Tommy McDonald, Philadelphia, NFL	64	1,144	17.9	13
1960	*Bill Groman, Houston, AFL	72	1,473	20.5	12
	Raymond Berry, Baltimore, NFL	74	1,298	17.5	10
1959	Raymond Berry, Baltimore	66	959	14.5	14
1958	Del Shofner, Los Angeles	51	1,097	21.5	8
1957	Raymond Berry, Baltimore	47	800	17.0	6
1956	Billy Howton, Green Bay	55	1,188	21.6	12
1955	Pete Pihos, Philadelphia	62	864	13.9	7
1954	Bob Boyd, Los Angeles	53	1,212	22.9	6
1953	Pete Pihos, Philadelphia	63	1,049	16.7	10
1952	*Bill Howton, Green Bay	53	1,231	23.2	13
1951	Elroy (Crazylegs) Hirsch, Los Angeles	66	1,495	22.7	17
1950	Tom Fears, Los Angeles	84	1,116	13.3	7
1949	Bob Mann, Detroit	66	1,014	15.4	4
1948	Mal Kutner, Chi. Cardinals	41	943	23.0	14

Year	Player, Team	No.	Yards	Avg.		TD
1947	Mal Kutner, Chi. Cardinals	43	944	21.9		7
1946	Jim Benton, Los Angeles	63	981	15.5		6
1945	Jim Benton, Cleveland	45	1,067	23.7		8
1944	Don Hutson, Green Bay	58	866	14.6		9
1943	Don Hutson, Green Bay	47	776	16.5		11
1942	Don Hutson, Green Bay	74	1,211	16.4		17
1941	Don Hutson, Green Bay	58	738	12.7		10
1940	*Don Looney, Philadelphia	58	707	12.2		4
1939	Don Hutson, Green Bay	34	846	24.9		6
1938	Don Hutson, Green Bay	32	548	17.1		9
1937	*Gaynell Tinsley, Chi. Cardinals	36	675	18.8		5
1936	Don Hutson, Green Bay	34	526	15.5		8
1935	Charley Malone, Boston	22	433	19.7		2
1934	Harry Ebding, Detroit	9	257	28.6		2
1933	*Paul Moss, Pittsburgh	18	383	21.3		2
1932	Johnny (Blood) McNally, Green Bay	19	326	17.2		3

*First season of professional football.

ANNUAL PUNT RETURN LEADERS

Year	Player, Team	No.	Yards	Avg.	Long	TD
2004	Eddie Drummond, Detroit, NFC	24	316	13.2	83	2
	Dennis Northcutt, Cleveland, AFC	36	432	12.0	44	0
2003	Dante Hall, Kansas City, AFC	29	472	16.3	93	2
	Brian Westbrook, Philadelphia, NFC	20	306	15.3	84	2
2002	Jimmy Williams, San Francisco, NFC	20	336	16.8	89	1
	Santana Moss, N.Y. Jets, AFC	25	413	16.5	63	2
2001	Troy Brown, New England, AFC	29	413	14.2	85	2
	Darrien Gordon, Atlanta, NFC	31	437	14.1	74	0
2000	Jermaine Lewis, Baltimore, AFC	36	578	16.1	89	2
	Az-Zahir Hakim, St. Louis, NFC	32	489	15.3	86	1
1999	*Charlie Rogers, Seattle, AFC	22	318	14.5	94	1
	*Mac Cody, Arizona, NFC	32	373	11.7	31	0
1998	Deion Sanders, Dallas, NFC	24	375	15.6	69	2
	Reggie Barlow, Jacksonville, AFC	43	555	12.9	85	1
1997	Jermaine Lewis, Baltimore, AFC	28	437	15.6	89	2
	David Palmer, Minnesota, NFC	34	444	13.1	57	0
1996	Desmond Howard, Green Bay, NFC	58	875	15.1	92	3
	Darrien Gordon, San Diego, AFC	36	537	14.9	81	1
1995	David Palmer, Minnesota, NFC	26	342	13.2	74	1
	Andre Coleman, San Diego, AFC	28	326	11.6	88	1
1994	Brian Mitchell, Washington, NFC	32	452	14.1	78	2
	Darrien Gordon, San Diego, AFC	36	475	13.2	90	2
1993	*Tyrone Hughes, New Orleans, NFC	37	503	13.6	83	2
	Eric Metcalf, Cleveland, AFC	36	464	12.9	91	2
1992	Johnny Bailey, Phoenix, NFC	20	263	13.2	65	0
	Rod Woodson, Pittsburgh, AFC	32	364	11.4	80	1
1991	Mel Gray, Detroit, NFC	25	385	15.4	78	1
	Rod Woodson, Pittsburgh, AFC	28	320	11.4	40	0
1990	Clarence Verdin, Indianapolis, AFC	31	396	12.8	36	0
	*Johnny Bailey, Chicago, NFC	36	399	11.1	95	1
1989	Walter Stanley, Detroit, NFC	36	496	13.8	74	0
	Clarence Verdin, Indianapolis, AFC	23	296	12.9	49	1
1988	John Taylor, San Francisco, NFC	44	556	12.6	95	2
	JoJo Townsell, N.Y. Jets, AFC	35	409	11.7	59	1
1987	Mel Gray, New Orleans, NFC	24	352	14.7	80	0
	Bobby Joe Edmonds, Seattle, AFC	20	251	12.6	40	0
1986	*Bobby Joe Edmonds, Seattle, AFC	34	419	12.3	75	1
	*Vai Sikahema, St. Louis, NFC	43	522	12.1	71	2
1985	Irving Fryar, New England, AFC	37	520	14.1	85	2
	Henry Ellard, L.A. Rams, NFC	37	501	13.5	80	1
1984	Mike Martin, Cincinnati, AFC	24	376	15.7	55	0
	Henry Ellard, L.A. Rams, NFC	30	403	13.4	83	2
1983	*Henry Ellard, L.A. Rams, NFC	16	217	13.6	72	1
	Kirk Springs, N.Y. Jets, AFC	23	287	12.5	76	1
1982	Rick Upchurch, Denver, AFC	15	242	16.1	78	2
	Billy Johnson, Atlanta, NFC	24	273	11.4	71	0
1981	LeRoy Irvin, Los Angeles, NFC	46	615	13.4	84	3
	*James Brooks, San Diego, AFC	22	290	13.2	42	0

Year	Player, Team	No.	Yards	Avg.	Long	TD
1980	J.T. Smith, Kansas City, AFC	40	581	14.5	75	2
	*Kenny Johnson, Atlanta, NFC	23	281	12.2	56	0
1979	John Sciarra, Philadelphia, NFC	16	182	11.4	38	0
	*Tony Nathan, Miami, AFC	28	306	10.9	86	1
1978	Rick Upchurch, Denver, AFC	36	493	13.7	75	1
	Jackie Wallace, Los Angeles, NFC	52	618	11.9	58	0
1977	Billy Johnson, Houston, AFC	35	539	15.4	87	2
	Larry Marshall, Philadelphia, NFC	46	489	10.6	48	0
1976	Rick Upchurch, Denver, AFC	39	536	13.7	92	4
	Eddie Brown, Washington, NFC	48	646	13.5	71	1
1975	Billy Johnson, Houston, AFC	40	612	15.3	83	3
	Terry Metcalf, St. Louis, NFC	23	285	12.4	69	1
1974	Lemar Parrish, Cincinnati, AFC	18	338	18.8	90	2
	Dick Jauron, Detroit, NFC	17	286	16.8	58	0
1973	Bruce Taylor, San Francisco, NFC	15	207	13.8	61	0
	Ron Smith, San Diego, AFC	27	352	13.0	84	2
1972	Ken Ellis, Green Bay, NFC	14	215	15.4	80	1
	Chris Farasopoulos, N.Y. Jets, AFC	17	179	10.5	65	1
1971	Les (Speedy) Duncan, Washington, NFC.	22	233	10.6	33	0
	Leroy Kelly, Cleveland, AFC	30	292	9.7	74	0
1970	Ed Podolak, Kansas City, AFC	23	311	13.5	60	0
	*Bruce Taylor, San Francisco, NFC	43	516	12.0	76	0
1969	Alvin Haymond, Los Angeles, NFL	33	435	13.2	52	0
	*Bill Thompson, Denver, AFL	25	288	11.5	40	0
1968	Bob Hayes, Dallas, NFL	15	312	20.8	90	2
	Noland Smith, Kansas City, AFL	18	270	15.0	80	1
1967	Floyd Little, Denver, AFL	16	270	16.9	72	1
	Ben Davis, Cleveland, NFL	18	229	12.7	52	1
1966	Les (Speedy) Duncan, San Diego, AFL	18	238	13.2	81	1
	Johnny Roland, St. Louis, NFL	20	221	11.1	86	1
1965	Leroy Kelly, Cleveland, NFL	17	265	15.6	67	2
	Les (Speedy) Duncan, San Diego, AFL	30	464	15.5	66	2
1964	Bobby Jancik, Houston, AFL	12	220	18.3	82	1
	Tommy Watkins, Detroit, NFL	16	238	14.9	68	2
1963	Dick James, Washington, NFL	16	214	13.4	39	0
	Claude (Hoot) Gibson, Oakland, AFL	26	307	11.8	85	2
1962	Dick Christy, N.Y. Titans, AFL	15	250	16.7	73	2
	Pat Studstill, Detroit, NFL	29	457	15.8	44	0
1961	Dick Christy, N.Y. Titans, AFL	18	383	21.3	70	2
	Willie Wood, Green Bay, NFL	14	225	16.1	72	2
1960	*Abner Haynes, Dall. Texans, AFL	14	215	15.4	46	0
	Abe Woodson, San Francisco, NFL	13	174	13.4	48	0
1959	Johnny Morris, Chi. Bears	14	171	12.2	78	1
1958	Jon Arnett, Los Angeles	18	223	12.4	58	0
1957	Bert Zagers, Washington	14	217	15.5	76	2
1956	Ken Konz, Cleveland	13	187	14.4	65	1
1955	Ollie Matson, Chi. Cardinals	13	245	18.8	78	2
1954	*Veryl Switzer, Green Bay	24	306	12.8	93	1
1953	Charley Trippi, Chi. Cardinals	21	239	11.4	38	0
1952	Jack Christiansen, Detroit	15	322	21.5	79	2
1951	Claude (Buddy) Young, N.Y. Yanks	12	231	19.3	79	1
1950	*Herb Rich, Baltimore	12	276	23.0	86	1
1949	Verda (Vitamin T) Smith, Los Angeles	27	427	15.8	85	1
1948	George McAfee, Chi. Bears	30	417	13.9	60	1
1947	*Walt Slater, Pittsburgh	28	435	15.5	33	0
1946	Bill Dudley, Pittsburgh	27	385	14.3	52	0
1945	*Dave Ryan, Detroit	15	220	14.7	56	0
1944	*Steve Van Buren, Philadelphia	15	230	15.3	55	1
1943	Andy Farkas, Washington	15	168	11.2	33	0
1942	Merlyn Condit, Brooklyn	21	210	10.0	23	0
1941	Byron (Whizzer) White, Detroit	19	262	13.8	64	0

First season of professional football.

ANNUAL KICKOFF RETURN LEADERS

Year	Player, Team	No.	Yards	Avg.	Long	TD
2004	Willie Ponder, N.Y. Giants, NFC	36	967	26.9	91	1
	Terrence McGee, Buffalo, AFC	52	1,370	26.3	104	3
2003	Jerry Azumah, Chicago, NFC	41	1,191	29.0	89	2
	*Bethel Johnson, New England, AFC	30	847	28.2	92	1

Year	Player, Team	No.	Yards	Avg.	Long	TD
2002	MarTay Jenkins, Arizona, NFC	20	559	28.0	95	1
	Kevin Faulk, New England, AFC	26	725	27.9	87	2
2001	Ronney Jenkins, San Diego, AFC	58	1,541	26.6	93	2
	*Steve Smith, Carolina, NFC	56	1,431	25.6	99	2
2000	*Darrick Vaughn, Atlanta, NFC	39	1,082	27.7	100	3
	Derrick Mason, Tennessee, AFC	42	1,132	27.0	66	0
1999	Tony Horne, St. Louis, NFC	30	892	29.7	101	2
	Tremain Mack, Cincinnati, AFC	51	1,382	27.1	99	1
1998	*Terry Fair, Detroit, NFC	51	1,428	28.0	105	2
	Corey Harris, Baltimore, AFC	35	965	27.6	95	1
1997	Michael Bates, Carolina, NFC	47	1,281	27.3	56	0
	Aaron Glenn, N.Y. Jets, AFC	28	741	26.5	96	1
1996	Michael Bates, Carolina, NFC	33	998	30.2	93	1
	Tamarick Vanover, Kansas City, AFC	33	854	25.9	97	1
1995	Ron Carpenter, N.Y. Jets, AFC	20	553	27.7	58	0
	Brian Mitchell, Washington, NFC	55	1,408	25.6	59	0
1994	Mel Gray, Detroit, NFC	45	1,276	28.4	102	3
	Randy Baldwin, Cleveland, AFC	28	753	26.9	85	1
1993	Robert Brooks, Green Bay, NFC	23	611	26.6	95	1
	*Raghib Ismail, L.A. Raiders, AFC	25	605	24.2	66	0
1992	Jon Vaughn, New England, AFC	20	564	28.2	100	1
	Deion Sanders, Atlanta, NFC	40	1,067	26.7	99	2
1991	Mel Gray, Detroit, NFC	36	929	25.8	71	0
	Nate Lewis, San Diego, AFC	23	578	25.1	95	1
1990	Kevin Clark, Denver, AFC	20	505	25.3	75	0
	David Meggett, N.Y. Giants, NFC	21	492	23.4	58	0
1989	Rod Woodson, Pittsburgh, AFC	36	982	27.3	84	1
	Mel Gray, Detroit, NFC	24	640	26.7	57	0
1988	*Tim Brown, L.A. Raiders, AFC	41	1,098	26.8	97	1
	Donnie Elder, Tampa Bay, NFC	34	772	22.7	51	0
1987	Sylvester Stamps, Atlanta, NFC	24	660	27.5	97	1
	Paul Palmer, Kansas City, AFC	38	923	24.3	95	2
1986	Dennis Gentry, Chicago, NFC	20	576	28.8	91	1
	Lupe Sanchez, Pittsburgh, AFC	25	591	23.6	64	0
1985	Ron Brown, L.A. Rams, NFC	28	918	32.8	98	3
	Glen Young, Cleveland, AFC	35	898	25.7	63	0
1984	*Bobby Humphery, N.Y. Jets, AFC	22	675	30.7	97	1
	Barry Redden, L.A. Rams, NFC	23	530	23.0	40	0
1983	Fulton Walker, Miami, AFC	36	962	26.7	78	0
	Darrin Nelson, Minnesota, NFC	18	445	24.7	50	0
1982	*Mike Mosley, Buffalo, AFC	18	487	27.1	66	0
	Alvin Hall, Detroit, NFC	16	426	26.6	96	1
1981	Mike Nelms, Washington, NFC	37	1,099	29.7	84	0
	Carl Roaches, Houston, AFC	28	769	27.5	96	1
1980	Horace Ivory, New England, AFC	36	992	27.6	98	1
	Rich Mauti, New Orleans, NFC	31	798	25.7	52	0
1979	Larry Brunson, Oakland, AFC	17	441	25.9	89	0
	Jimmy Edwards, Minnesota, NFC	44	1,103	25.1	83	0
1978	Steve Odom, Green Bay, NFC	25	677	27.1	95	1
	*Keith Wright, Cleveland, AFC	30	789	26.3	86	0
1977	*Raymond Clayborn, New England, AFC	28	869	31.0	101	3
	*Wilbert Montgomery, Philadelphia, NFC	23	619	26.9	99	1
1976	*Duriel Harris, Miami, AFC	17	559	32.9	69	0
	Cullen Bryant, Los Angeles, NFC	16	459	28.7	90	1
1975	*Walter Payton, Chicago, NFC	14	444	31.7	70	0
	Harold Hart, Oakland, AFC	17	518	30.5	102	1
1974	Terry Metcalf, St. Louis, NFC	20	623	31.2	94	1
	Greg Pruitt, Cleveland, AFC	22	606	27.5	88	1
1973	Carl Garrett, Chicago, NFC	16	486	30.4	67	0
	*Wallace Francis, Buffalo, AFC	23	687	29.9	101	2
1972	Ron Smith, Chicago, NFC	30	924	30.8	94	1
	*Bruce Laird, Baltimore, AFC	29	843	29.1	73	0
1971	Travis Williams, Los Angeles, NFC	25	743	29.7	105	1
	Eugene (Mercury) Morris, Miami, AFC	15	423	28.2	94	1
1970	Jim Duncan, Baltimore, AFC	20	707	35.4	99	1
	Cecil Turner, Chicago, NFC	23	752	32.7	96	4
1969	Bobby Williams, Detroit, NFL	17	563	33.1	96	1
	*Bill Thompson, Denver, AFL	18	513	28.5	63	0

Year	Player, Team	No.	Yards	Avg.	Long	TD
1968	Preston Pearson, Baltimore, NFL	15	527	35.1	102	2
	*George Atkinson, Oakland, AFL	32	802	25.1	60	0
1967	*Travis Williams, Green Bay, NFL	18	739	41.1	104	4
	*Zeke Moore, Houston, AFL	14	405	28.9	92	1
1966	Gale Sayers, Chicago, NFL	23	718	31.2	93	2
	*Goldie Sellers, Denver, AFL	19	541	28.5	100	2
1965	Tommy Watkins, Detroit, NFL	17	584	34.4	94	0
	Abner Haynes, Denver, AFL	34	901	26.5	60	0
1964	*Clarence Childs, N.Y. Giants, NFL	34	987	29.0	100	1
	Bo Roberson, Oakland, AFL	36	975	27.1	59	0
1963	Abe Woodson, San Francisco, NFL	29	935	32.2	103	3
	Bobby Jancik, Houston, AFL	45	1,317	29.3	53	0
1962	Abe Woodson, San Francisco, NFL	37	1,157	31.3	79	0
	*Bobby Jancik, Houston, AFL	24	826	30.3	61	0
1961	Dick Bass, Los Angeles, NFL	23	698	30.3	64	0
	*Dave Grayson, Dall. Texans, AFL	16	453	28.3	73	0
1960	*Tom Moore, Green Bay, NFL	12	397	33.1	84	0
	Ken Hall, Houston, AFL	19	594	31.3	104	1
1959	Abe Woodson, San Francisco	13	382	29.4	105	1
1958	Ollie Matson, Chi. Cardinals	14	497	35.5	101	2
1957	*Jon Arnett, Los Angeles	18	504	28.0	98	1
1956	*Tom Wilson, Los Angeles	15	477	31.8	103	1
1955	Al Carmichael, Green Bay	14	418	29.9	100	1
1954	Billy Reynolds, Cleveland	14	413	29.5	51	0
1953	Joe Arenas, San Francisco	16	551	34.4	82	0
1952	Lynn Chandnois, Pittsburgh	17	599	35.2	93	2
1951	Lynn Chandnois, Pittsburgh	12	390	32.5	55	0
1950	Verda (Vitamin T) Smith, Los Angeles	22	742	33.7	97	3
1949	*Don Doll, Detroit	21	536	25.5	56	0
1948	*Joe Scott, N.Y. Giants	20	569	28.5	99	1
1947	Eddie Saenz, Washington	29	797	27.5	94	2
1946	Abe Karnofsky, Boston	21	599	28.5	97	1
1945	Steve Van Buren, Philadelphia	13	373	28.7	98	1
1944	Bob Thurbon, Card.-Pitt.	12	291	24.3	55	0
1943	Ken Heineman, Brooklyn	16	444	27.8	69	0
1942	Marshall Goldberg, Chi. Cardinals	15	393	26.2	95	1
1941	Marshall Goldberg, Chi. Cardinals	12	290	24.2	41	0

*First season of professional football.

ANNUAL INTERCEPTION LEADERS

Year	Player, Team	No.	Yards	TD
2004	Ed Reed, Baltimore, AFC	9	358	1
	Ken Lucas, Seattle, NFC	6	46	1
	*Chris Gamble, Carolina, NFC	6	15	0
2003	Tony Parrish, San Francisco, NFC	9	202	0
	Brian Russell, Minnesota, NFC	9	185	0
	Ed Reed, Baltimore, AFC	7	132	1
	Marcus Coleman, Houston, AFC	7	95	0
	Patrick Surtain, Miami, AFC	7	59	0
2002	Rod Woodson, Oakland, AFC	8	225	2
	Brian Kelly, Tampa Bay, NFC	8	68	0
2001	*Anthony Henry, Cleveland, AFC	10	177	1
	Ronde Barber, Tampa Bay, NFC	10	86	1
2000	Darren Sharper, Green Bay, NFC	9	109	0
	Samari Rolle, Tennessee, AFC	7	140	1
	Brian Walker, Miami, AFC	7	80	0
1999	Rod Woodson, Baltimore, AFC	7	195	2
	Sam Madison, Miami, AFC	7	164	1
	James Hasty, Kansas City, AFC	7	98	2
	Donnie Abraham, Tampa Bay, NFC	7	115	2
	Troy Vincent, Philadelphia, NFC	7	91	0
1998	Ty Law, New England, AFC	9	133	1
	Kwamie Lassiter, Arizona, NFC	9	80	0
1997	Ryan McNeil, St. Louis, NFC	9	127	1
	Mark McMillian, Kansas City, AFC	8	274	3
	Darryl Williams, Seattle, AFC	8	172	1
1996	Tyrone Braxton, Denver, AFC	9	128	1
	Keith Lyle, St. Louis, NFC	9	152	0
1995	*Orlando Thomas, Minnesota, NFC	9	108	1
	Willie Williams, Pittsburgh, AFC	7	122	1
1994	Eric Turner, Cleveland, AFC	9	199	1
	Aeneas Williams, Arizona, NFC	9	89	0
1993	Eugene Robinson, Seattle, AFC	9	80	0
	Nate Odomes, Buffalo, AFC	9	65	0
	Deion Sanders, Atlanta, NFC	7	91	0
1992	Henry Jones, Buffalo, AFC	8	263	2
	Audray McMillian, Minnesota, NFC	8	157	2
1991	Ronnie Lott, L.A. Raiders, AFC	8	52	0
	Ray Crockett, Detroit, NFC	6	141	1
	Deion Sanders, Atlanta, NFC	6	119	1
	*Aeneas Williams, Phoenix, NFC	6	60	0
	Tim McKyer, Atlanta, NFC	6	24	0
1990	*Mark Carrier, Chicago, NFC	10	39	0
	Richard Johnson, Houston, AFC	8	100	1
1989	Felix Wright, Cleveland, AFC	9	91	1
	Eric Allen, Philadelphia, NFC	8	38	0
1988	Scott Case, Atlanta, NFC	10	47	0
	Erik McMillan, N.Y. Jets, AFC	8	168	2
1987	Barry Wilburn, Washington, NFC	9	135	1
	Mike Prior, Indianapolis, AFC	6	57	0
	Mark Kelso, Buffalo, AFC	6	25	0
	Keith Bostic, Houston, AFC	6	-14	0
1986	Ronnie Lott, San Francisco, NFC	10	134	1
	Deron Cherry, Kansas City, AFC	9	150	0
1985	Everson Walls, Dallas, NFC	9	31	0
	Albert Lewis, Kansas City, AFC	8	59	0
	Eugene Daniel, Indianapolis, AFC	8	53	0

Year	Player, Team	No.	Yards	TD
1984	Ken Easley, Seattle, AFC	10	126	2
	*Tom Flynn, Green Bay, NFC	9	106	0
1983	Mark Murphy, Washington, NFC	9	127	0
	Ken Riley, Cincinnati, AFC	8	89	2
	Vann McElroy, L.A. Raiders, AFC	8	68	0
1982	Everson Walls, Dallas, NFC	7	61	0
	Ken Riley, Cincinnati, AFC	5	88	1
	Bobby Jackson, N.Y Jets, AFC	5	84	1
	Dwayne Woodruff, Pittsburgh, AFC	5	53	0
	Donnie Shell, Pittsburgh, AFC	5	27	0
1981	*Everson Walls, Dallas, NFC	11	133	0
	John Harris, Seattle, AFC	10	155	2
1980	Lester Hayes, Oakland, AFC	13	273	1
	Nolan Cromwell, Los Angeles, NFC	8	140	1
1979	Mike Reinfeldt, Houston, AFC	12	205	0
	Lemar Parrish, Washiongton, NFC	9	65	0
1978	Thom Darden, Cleveland, AFC	10	200	0
	Ken Stone, St. Louis, NFC	9	139	0
	Willie Buchanon, Green Bay, NFC	9	93	1
1977	Lyle Blackwood, Baltimore, AFC	10	163	0
	Rolland Lawrence, Atlanta, NFC	7	138	0
1976	Monte Jackson, Los Angeles, NFC	10	173	3
	Ken Riley, Cincinnati, AFC	9	141	1
1975	Mel Blount, Pittsburgh, AFC	11	121	1
	Paul Krause, Minnesota, NFC	10	201	0
1974	Emmitt Thomas, Kansas City, AFC	12	214	2
	Ray Brown, Atlanta, NFC	8	164	1
1973	Dick Anderson, Miami, AFC	8	163	2
	Mike Wagner, Pittsburgh, AFC	8	134	0
	Bobby Bryant, Minnesota, NFC	7	105	1
1972	Bill Bradley, Philadelphia, NFC	9	73	0
	Mike Sensibaugh, Kansas City, AFC	8	65	0
1971	Bill Bradley, Philadelphia, NFC	11	248	0
	Ken Houston, Houston, AFC	9	220	4
1970	Johnny Robinson, Kansas City, AFC	10	155	0
	Dick LeBeau, Detroit, NFC	9	96	0
1969	Mel Renfro, Dallas, NFL	10	118	0
	Emmitt Thomas, Kansas City, AFL	9	146	1
1968	Dave Grayson, Oakland, AFL	10	195	1
	Willie Williams, N.Y. Giants, NFL	10	103	0
1967	Miller Farr, Houston, AFL	10	264	3
	*Lem Barney, Detroit, NFL	10	232	3
	Tom Janik, Buffalo, AFL	10	222	2
	Dave Whitsell, New Orleans, NFL	10	178	2
	Dick Westmoreland, Miami, AFL	10	127	1
1966	Larry Wilson, St. Louis, NFL	10	180	2
	Johnny Robinson, Kansas City, AFL	10	136	1
	Bobby Hunt, Kansas City, AFL	10	113	0
1965	W.K. Hicks, Houston, AFL	9	156	0
	Bobby Boyd, Baltimore, NFL	9	78	1
1964	Dainard Paulson, N.Y. Jets, AFL	12	157	1
	*Paul Krause, Washington, NFL	12	140	1
1963	Fred Glick, Houston, AFL	12	180	1
	Dick Lynch, N.Y. Giants, NFL	9	251	3
	Roosevelt Taylor, Chicago, NFL	9	172	1
1962	Lee Riley, N.Y. Titans, AFL	11	122	0
	Willie Wood, Green Bay, NFL	9	132	0
1961	Billy Atkins, Buffalo, AFL	10	158	0
	Dick Lynch, N.Y. Giants, NFL	9	60	0
1960	*Austin (Goose) Gonsoulin, Denver, AFL	11	98	0
	Dave Baker, San Francisco, NFL	10	96	0
	Jerry Norton, St. Louis, NFL	10	96	0
1959	Dean Derby, Pittsburgh	7	127	0
	Milt Davis, Baltimore	7	119	1
	Don Shinnick, Baltimore	7	70	0
1958	Jim Patton, N.Y. Giants	11	183	0
1957	Milt Davis, Baltimore	10	219	2
	Jack Christiansen, Detroit	10	137	1
	Jack Butler, Pittsburgh	10	85	0

Year	Player, Team	No.	Avg.	Long
1956	Linden Crow, Chi. Cardinals	11	170	0
1955	Will Sherman, Los Angeles	11	101	0
1954	Dick (Night Train) Lane, Chi. Cardinals	10	181	0
1953	Jack Christiansen, Detroit	12	238	1
1952	*Dick (Night Train) Lane, Los Angeles	14	298	2
1951	Otto Schnellbacher, N.Y. Giants	11	194	2
1950	Orban (Spec) Sanders, N.Y. Yanks	13	199	0
1949	Bob Nussbaumer, Chi. Cardinals	12	157	0
1948	*Dan Sandifer, Washington	13	258	2
1947	Frank Reagan, N.Y. Giants	10	203	0
	Frank Seno, Boston	10	100	0
1946	Bill Dudley, Pittsburgh	10	242	1
1945	Roy Zimmerman, Philadelphia	7	90	0
1944	*Howard Livingston, N.Y. Giants	9	172	1
1943	Sammy Baugh, Washington	11	112	0
1942	Clyde (Bulldog) Turner, Chi. Bears	8	96	1
1941	Marshall Goldberg, Chi. Cardinals	7	54	0
	*Art Jones, Pittsburgh	7	35	0
1940	Clarence (Ace) Parker, Brooklyn	6	146	1
	Kent Ryan, Detroit	6	65	0
	Don Hutson, Green Bay	6	24	0

*First season of professional football.

ANNUAL PUNTING LEADERS

Year	Player, Team	No.	Avg.	Long
2004	Shane Lechler, Oakland, AFC	73	46.7	67
	Tom Tupa, Washington, NFC	103	44.1	61
2003	Shane Lechler, Oakland, AFC	96	46.9	73
	Todd Sauerbrun, Carolina, NFC	77	44.6	64
2002	Todd Sauerbrun, Carolina, NFC	104	45.5	67
	Chris Hanson, Jacksonville, AFC	81	44.2	64
2001	Todd Sauerbrun, Carolina, NFC	93	47.5	73
	Shane Lechler, Oakland, AFC	73	46.2	65
2000	Darren Bennett, San Diego, AFC	92	46.2	66
	Mitch Berger, Minnesota, NFC	62	44.7	60
1999	Tom Rouen, Denver, AFC	84	46.5	65
	Mitch Berger, Minnesota, NFC	61	45.4	75
1998	Craig Hentrich, Tennessee, AFC	69	47.2	71
	Mark Royals, New Orleans, NFC	88	45.6	64
1997	Mark Royals, New Orleans, NFC	88	45.9	66
	Tom Tupa, New England, AFC	78	45.8	73
1996	John Kidd, Miami, AFC	78	46.3	63
	Matt Turk, Washington, NFC	75	45.1	63
1995	Rick Tuten, Seattle, AFC	83	45.0	73
	Sean Landeta, St. Louis, NFC	83	44.3	63
1994	Sean Landeta, L.A. Rams, NFC	78	44.8	62
	Jeff Gossett, L.A. Raiders, AFC	77	43.9	65
1993	Greg Montgomery, Houston, AFC	54	45.6	77
	Jim Arnold, Detroit, NFC	72	44.5	68
1992	Greg Montgomery, Houston, AFC	53	46.9	66
	Harry Newsome, Minnesota, NFC	72	45.0	84
1991	Reggie Roby, Miami, AFC	54	45.7	64
	Harry Newsome, Minnesota, NFC	68	45.5	65
1990	Mike Horan, Denver, AFC	58	44.4	67
	Sean Landeta, N.Y. Giants, NFC	75	44.1	67
1989	Rich Camarillo, Phoenix, NFC	76	43.4	58
	Greg Montgomery, Houston, AFC	56	43.3	63
1988	Harry Newsome, Pittsburgh, AFC	65	45.4	62
	Jim Arnold, Detroit, NFC	97	42.4	69
1987	Rick Donnelly, Atlanta, NFC	61	44.0	62
	Ralf Mojsiejenko, San Diego, AFC	67	42.9	57
1986	Rohn Stark, Indianapolis, AFC	76	45.2	63
	Sean Landeta, N.Y. Giants, NFC	79	44.8	61
1985	Rohn Stark, Indianapolis, AFC	78	45.9	68
	*Rick Donnelly, Atlanta, NFC	59	43.6	68
1984	Jim Arnold, Kansas City, AFC	98	44.9	63
	*Brian Hansen, New Orleans, NFC	69	43.8	66
1983	Rohn Stark, Baltimore, AFC	91	45.3	68
	Frank Garcia, Tampa Bay, NFC	95	42.2	64

Year	Player, Team	No.	Avg.	Long
1982	Luke Prestridge, Denver, AFC	45	45.0	65
	Carl Birdsong, St. Louis, NFC	54	43.8	65
1981	Pat McInally, Cincinnati, AFC	72	45.4	62
	Tom Skladany, Detroit, NFC	64	43.5	74
1980	Dave Jennings, N.Y. Giants, NFC	94	44.8	63
	Luke Prestridge, Denver, AFC	70	43.9	57
1979	*Bob Grupp, Kansas City, AFC	89	43.6	74
	Dave Jennings, N.Y. Giants, NFC	104	42.7	72
1978	Pat McInally, Cincinnati, AFC	91	43.1	65
	*Tom Skladany, Detroit, NFC	86	42.5	63
1977	Ray Guy, Oakland, AFC	59	43.3	74
	Tom Blanchard, New Orleans, NFC	82	42.4	66
1976	Marv Bateman, Buffalo, AFC	86	42.8	78
	John James, Atlanta, NFC	101	42.1	67
1975	Ray Guy, Oakland, AFC	68	43.8	64
	Herman Weaver, Detroit, NFC	80	42.0	61
1974	Ray Guy, Oakland, AFC	74	42.2	66
	Tom Blanchard, New Orleans, NFC	88	42.1	71
1973	Jerrel Wilson, Kansas City, AFC	80	45.5	68
	*Tom Wittum, San Francisco, NFC	79	43.7	62
1972	Jerrel Wilson, Kansas City, AFC	66	44.8	69
	Dave Chapple, Los Angeles, NFC	53	44.2	70
1971	Dave Lewis, Cincinnati, AFC	72	44.8	56
	Tom McNeill, Philadelphia, NFC	73	42.0	64
1970	Dave Lewis, Cincinnati, AFC	79	46.2	63
	*Julian Fagan, New Orleans, NFC	77	42.5	64
1969	David Lee, Baltimore, NFL	57	45.3	66
	Dennis Partee, San Diego, AFL	71	44.6	62
1968	Jerrel Wilson, Kansas City, AFL	63	45.1	70
	Billy Lothridge, Atlanta, NFL	75	44.3	70
1967	Bob Scarpitto, Denver, AFL	105	44.9	73
	Billy Lothridge, Atlanta, NFL	87	43.7	62
1966	Bob Scarpitto, Denver, AFL	76	45.8	70
	*David Lee, Baltimore, NFL	49	45.6	64
1965	Gary Collins, Cleveland, NFL	65	46.7	71
	Jerrel Wilson, Kansas City, AFL	69	45.4	64
1964	Bobby Walden, Minnesota, NFL	72	46.4	73
	Jim Fraser, Denver, AFL	73	44.2	67
1963	Yale Lary, Detroit, NFL	35	48.9	73
	Jim Fraser, Denver, AFL	81	44.4	66
1962	Tommy Davis, San Francisco, NFL	48	45.6	82
	Jim Fraser, Denver, AFL	55	43.6	75
1961	Yale Lary, Detroit, NFL	52	48.4	71
	Billy Atkins, Buffalo, AFL	85	44.5	70
1960	Jerry Norton, St. Louis, NFL	39	45.6	62
	*Paul Maguire, L.A. Chargers, AFL	43	40.5	61
1959	Yale Lary, Detroit	45	47.1	67
1958	Sam Baker, Washington	48	45.4	64
1957	Don Chandler, N.Y. Giants	60	44.6	61
1956	Norm Van Brocklin, Los Angeles	48	43.1	72
1955	Norm Van Brocklin, Los Angeles	60	44.6	61
1954	Pat Brady, Pittsburgh	66	43.2	72
1953	Pat Brady, Pittsburgh	80	46.9	64
1952	Horace Gillom, Cleveland	61	45.7	73
1951	Horace Gillom, Cleveland	73	45.5	66
1950	*Fred (Curly) Morrison, Chi. Bears	57	43.3	65
1949	*Mike Boyda, N.Y. Bulldogs	56	44.0	61
1948	Joe Muha, Philadelphia	57	47.3	82
1947	Jack Jacobs, Green Bay	57	43.5	74
1946	Roy McKay, Green Bay	64	42.7	64
1945	Roy McKay, Green Bay	44	41.2	73
1944	Frank Sinkwich, Detroit	45	41.0	73
1943	Sammy Baugh, Washington	50	45.9	81
1942	Sammy Baugh, Washington	37	48.2	74
1941	Sammy Baugh, Washington	30	48.7	75
1940	Sammy Baugh, Washington	35	51.4	85
1939	*Parker Hall, Cleveland	58	40.8	80

*First season of professional football.

ANNUAL LEADERS IN SACKS (SINCE 1982)

Year	Player, Team	Sacks
2004	Dwight Freeney, Indianapolis, AFC	16.0
	Bertrand Berry, Arizona, NFC	14.5
2003	Michael Strahan, N.Y. Giants, NFC	18.5
	Adewale Ogunleye, Miami, AFC	15.0
2002	Jason Taylor, Miami, AFC	18.5
	Simeon Rice, Tampa Bay, NFC	15.5
2001	Michael Strahan, N.Y. Giants, NFC	22.5
	Peter Boulware, Baltimore, AFC	15.0
2000	La'Roi Glover, New Orleans, NFC	17.0
	Trace Armstrong, Miami, AFC	16.5
1999	Kevin Carter, St. Louis, NFC	17.0
	*Jevon Kearse, Tennessee, AFC	14.5
1998	Michael Sinclair, Seattle, AFC	16.5
	Reggie White, Green Bay, NFC	16.0
1997	John Randle, Minnesota, NFC	15.5
	Bruce Smith, Buffalo, AFC	14.0
1996	Kevin Greene, Carolina, NFC	14.5
	Michael McCrary, Seattle, AFC	13.5
	Bruce Smith, Buffalo, AFC	13.5
1995	Bryce Paup, Buffalo, AFC	17.5
	William Fuller, Philadelphia, NFC	13.0
	Wayne Martin, New Orleans, NFC	13.0
1994	Kevin Greene, Pittsburgh, AFC	14.0
	Ken Harvey, Washington, NFC	13.5
	John Randle, Minnesota, NFC	13.5
1993	Neil Smith, Kansas City, AFC	15.0
	Renaldo Turnbull, New Orleans, NFC	13.0
	Reggie White, Green Bay, NFC	13.0
1992	Clyde Simmons, Philadelphia, NFC	19.0
	Leslie O'Neal, San Diego, AFC	17.0
1991	Pat Swilling, New Orleans, NFC	17.0
	William Fuller, Houston, AFC	15.0
1990	Derrick Thomas, Kansas City, AFC	20.0
	Charles Haley, San Francisco, NFC	16.0
1989	Chris Doleman, Minnesota, NFC	21.0
	Lee Williams, San Diego, AFC	14.0
1988	Reggie White, Philadelphia, NFC	18.0
	Greg Townsend, L.A. Raiders, AFC	11.5
1987	Reggie White, Philadelphia, NFC	21.0
	Andre Tippett, New England, AFC	12.5
1986	Lawrence Taylor, N.Y. Giants, NFC	20.5
	Sean Jones, L.A. Raiders, AFC	15.5
1985	Richard Dent, Chicago, NFC	17.0
	Andre Tippett, New England, AFC	16.5
1984	Mark Gastineau, N.Y. Jets, AFC	22.0
	Richard Dent, Chicago, NFC	17.5
1983	Mark Gastineau, N.Y. Jets, AFC	19.0
	Fred Dean, San Francisco, NFC	17.5
1982	Doug Martin, Minnesota, NFC	11.5
	Jesse Baker, Houston, AFC	7.5

*First season of professional football.

POINTS SCORED

Year	Team	Points
2004	Indianapolis, AFC	522
	Green Bay, NFC	424
2003	Kansas City, AFC	484
	St. Louis, NFC	447
2002	Kansas City, AFC	467
	New Orleans, NFC	432
2001	St. Louis, NFC	503
	Indianapolis, AFC	413
2000	St. Louis, NFC	540
	Denver, AFC	485
1999	St. Louis, NFC	526
	Indianapolis, AFC	423
1998	Minnesota, NFC	556
	Denver, AFC	501

Year	Team	Points	Year	Team	Points
1997	Denver, AFC	472	1963	N.Y. Giants, NFL	448
	Green Bay, NFC	422		San Diego, AFL	399
1996	Green Bay, NFC	456	1962	Green Bay, NFL	415
	New England, AFC	418		Dall. Texans, AFL	389
1995	San Francisco, NFC	457	1961	Houston, AFL	513
	Pittsburgh, AFC	407		Green Bay, NFL	391
1994	San Francisco, NFC	505	1960	N.Y. Titans, AFL	382
	Miami, AFC	389		Cleveland, NFL	362
1993	San Francisco, NFC	473	1959	Baltimore	374
	Denver, AFC	373	1958	Baltimore	381
1992	San Francisco, NFC	431	1957	Los Angeles	307
	Buffalo, AFC	381	1956	Chi. Bears	363
1991	Washington, NFC	485	1955	Cleveland	349
	Buffalo, AFC	458	1954	Detroit	337
1990	Buffalo, AFC	428	1953	San Francisco	372
	Philadelphia, NFC	396	1952	Los Angeles	349
1989	San Francisco, NFC	442	1951	Los Angeles	392
	Buffalo, AFC	409	1950	Los Angeles	466
1988	Cincinnati, AFC	448	1949	Philadelphia	364
	L.A. Rams, NFC	407	1948	Chi. Cardinals	395
1987	San Francisco, NFC	459	1947	Chi. Bears	363
	Cleveland, AFC	390	1946	Chi. Bears	289
1986	Miami, AFC	430	1945	Philadelphia	272
	Minnesota, NFC	398	1944	Philadelphia	267
1985	San Diego, AFC	467	1943	Chi. Bears	303
	Chicago, NFC	456	1942	Chi. Bears	376
1984	Miami, AFC	513	1941	Chi. Bears	396
	San Francisco, NFC	475	1940	Washington	245
1983	Washington, NFC	541	1939	Chi. Bears	298
	L.A. Raiders, AFC	442	1938	Green Bay	223
1982	San Diego, AFC	288	1937	Green Bay	220
	Dallas, NFC	226	1936	Green Bay	248
	Green Bay, NFC	226	1935	Chi. Bears	192
1981	San Diego, AFC	478	1934	Chi. Bears	286
	Atlanta, NFC	426	1933	N.Y. Giants	244
1980	Dallas, NFC	454	1932	Chi. Bears	160
	New England, AFC	441			
1979	Pittsburgh, AFC	416			
	Dallas, NFC	371	**TOTAL YARDS GAINED**		
1978	Dallas, NFC	384	Year	Team	Yards
	Miami, AFC	372	2004	Kansas City, AFC	6,695
1977	Oakland, AFC	351		Green Bay, NFC	6,357
	Dallas, NFC	345	2003	Minnesota, NFC	6,294
1976	Baltimore, AFC	417		Kansas City, AFC	5,910
	Los Angeles, NFC	351	2002	Oakland, AFC	6,237
1975	Buffalo, AFC	420		Minnesota, NFC	6,192
	Minnesota, NFC	377	2001	St. Louis, NFC	6,690
1974	Oakland, AFC	355		Indianapolis, AFC	5,955
	Washington, NFC	320	2000	St. Louis, NFC	7,075
1973	Los Angeles, NFC	388		Denver, AFC	6,554
	Denver, AFC	354	1999	St. Louis, NFC	6,412
1972	Miami, AFC	385		Indianapolis, AFC	5,726
	San Francisco, NFC	353	1998	San Francisco, NFC	6,800
1971	Dallas, NFC	406		Denver, AFC	6,092
	Oakland, AFC	344	1997	Denver, AFC	5,872
1970	San Francisco, NFC	352		Detroit, NFC	5,798
	Baltimore, AFC	321	1996	Denver, AFC	5,791
1969	Minnesota, NFL	379		Philadelphia, NFC	5,627
	Oakland, AFL	377	1995	Detroit, NFC	6,113
1968	Oakland, AFL	453		Denver, AFC	6,040
	Dallas, NFL	431	1994	Miami, AFC	6,078
1967	Oakland, AFL	468		San Francisco, NFC	6,060
	Los Angeles, NFL	398	1993	San Francisco, NFC	6,435
1966	Kansas City, AFL	448		Miami, AFC	5,812
	Dallas, NFL	445	1992	San Francisco, NFC	6,195
1965	San Francisco, NFL	421		Buffalo, AFC	5,893
	San Diego, AFL	340	1991	Buffalo, AFC	6,252
1964	Baltimore, NFL	428		San Francisco, NFC	5,858
	Buffalo, AFL	400			

Year	Team	Yards
1990	Houston, AFC	6,222
	San Francisco, NFC	5,895
1989	San Francisco, NFC	6,268
	Cincinnati, AFC	6,101
1988	Cincinnati, AFC	6,057
	San Francisco, NFC	5,900
1987	San Francisco, NFC	5,987
	Denver, AFC	5,624
1986	Cincinnati, AFC	6,490
	San Francisco, NFC	6,082
1985	San Diego, AFC	6,535
	San Francisco, NFC	5,920
1984	Miami, AFC	6,936
	San Francisco, NFC	6,366
1983	San Diego, AFC	6,197
	Green Bay, NFC	6,172
1982	San Diego, AFC	4,048
	San Francisco, NFC	3,242
1981	San Diego, AFC	6,744
	Detroit, NFC	5,933
1980	San Diego, AFC	6,410
	Los Angeles, NFC	6,006
1979	Pittsburgh, AFC	6,258
	Dallas, NFC	5,968
1978	New England, AFC	5,965
	Dallas, NFC	5,959
1977	Dallas, NFC	4,812
	Oakland, AFC	4,736
1976	Baltimore, AFC	5,236
	St. Louis, NFC	5,136
1975	Buffalo, AFC	5,467
	Dallas, NFC	5,025
1974	Dallas, NFC	4,983
	Oakland, AFC	4,718
1973	Los Angeles, NFC	4,906
	Oakland, AFC	4,773
1972	Miami, AFC	5,036
	N.Y. Giants, NFC	4,483
1971	Dallas, NFC	5,035
	San Diego, AFC	4,738
1970	Oakland, AFC	4,829
	San Francisco, NFC	4,503
1969	Dallas, NFL	5,122
	Oakland, AFL	5,036
1968	Oakland, AFL	5,696
	Dallas, NFL	5,117
1967	N.Y. Jets, AFL	5,152
	Baltimore, NFL	5,008
1966	Dallas, NFL	5,145
	Kansas City, AFL	5,114
1965	San Francisco, NFL	5,270
	San Diego, AFL	5,188
1964	Buffalo, AFL	5,206
	Baltimore, NFL	4,779
1963	San Diego, AFL	5,153
	N.Y. Giants, NFL	5,024
1962	N.Y. Giants, NFL	5,005
	Houston, AFL	4,971
1961	Houston, AFL	6,288
	Philadelphia, NFL	5,112
1960	Houston, AFL	4,936
	Baltimore, NFL	4,245
1959	Baltimore	4,458
1958	Baltimore	4,539
1957	Los Angeles	4,143
1956	Chi. Bears	4,537
1955	Chi. Bears	4,316
1954	Los Angeles	5,187
1953	Philadelphia	4,811

Year	Team	Yards
1952	Cleveland	4,352
1951	Los Angeles	5,506
1950	Los Angeles	5,420
1949	Chi. Bears	4,873
1948	Chi. Cardinals	4,705
1947	Chi. Bears	5,053
1946	Los Angeles	3,793
1945	Washington	3,549
1944	Chi. Bears	3,239
1943	Chi. Bears	4,045
1942	Chi. Bears	3,900
1941	Chi. Bears	4,265
1940	Green Bay	3,400
1939	Chi. Bears	3,988
1938	Green Bay	3,037
1937	Green Bay	3,201
1936	Detroit	3,703
1935	Chi. Bears	3,454
1934	Chi. Bears	3,900
1933	N.Y. Giants	2,973
1932	Chi. Bears	2,755

YARDS RUSHING

Year	Team	Yards
2004	Atlanta, NFC	2,672
	Pittsburgh, AFC	2,464
2003	Baltimore, AFC	2,674
	Green Bay, NFC	2,558
2002	Minnesota, NFC	2,507
	Miami, AFC	2,502
2001	Pittsburgh, AFC	2,774
	San Francisco, NFC	2,244
2000	Oakland, AFC	2,470
	Minnesota, NFC	2,129
1999	San Francisco, NFC	2,095
	Jacksonville, AFC	2,091
1998	San Francisco, NFC	2,544
	Denver, AFC	2,468
1997	Pittsburgh, AFC	2,479
	Detroit, NFC	2,464
1996	Denver, AFC	2,362
	Washington, NFC	1,910
1995	Kansas City, AFC	2,222
	Dallas, NFC	2,201
1994	Pittsburgh, AFC	2,180
	Detroit, NFC	2,080
1993	N.Y. Giants, NFC	2,210
	Seattle, AFC	2,015
1992	Buffalo, AFC	2,436
	Philadelphia, NFC	2,388
1991	Buffalo, AFC	2,381
	Minnesota, NFC	2,201
1990	Philadelphia, NFC	2,556
	San Diego, AFC	2,257
1989	Cincinnati, AFC	2,483
	Chicago, NFC	2,287
1988	Cincinnati, AFC	2,710
	San Francisco, NFC	2,523
1987	San Francisco, NFC	2,237
	L.A. Raiders, AFC	2,197
1986	Chicago, NFC	2,700
	Cincinnati, AFC	2,533
1985	Chicago, NFC	2,761
	Indianapolis, AFC	2,439
1984	Chicago, NFC	2,974
	N.Y. Jets, AFC	2,189
1983	Chicago, NFC	2,727
	Baltimore, AFC	2,695

Year	Team	Yards
1982	Buffalo, AFC	1,371
	Dallas, NFC	1,313
1981	Detroit, NFC	2,795
	Kansas City, AFC	2,633
1980	Los Angeles, NFC	2,799
	Houston, AFC	2,635
1979	N.Y. Jets, AFC	2,646
	St. Louis, NFC	2,582
1978	New England, AFC	3,165
	Dallas, NFC	2,783
1977	Chicago, NFC	2,811
	Oakland, AFC	2,627
1976	Pittsburgh, AFC	2,971
	Los Angeles, NFC	2,528
1975	Buffalo, AFC	2,974
	Dallas, NFC	2,432
1974	Dallas, NFC	2,454
	Pittsburgh, AFC	2,417
1973	Buffalo, AFC	3,088
	Los Angeles, NFC	2,925
1972	Miami, AFC	2,960
	Chicago, NFC	2,360
1971	Miami, AFC	2,429
	Detroit, NFC	2,376
1970	Dallas, NFC	2,300
	Miami, AFC	2,082
1969	Dallas, NFL	2,276
	Kansas City, AFL	2,220
1968	Chicago, NFL	2,377
	Kansas City, AFL	2,227
1967	Cleveland, NFL	2,139
	Houston, AFL	2,122
1966	Kansas City, AFL	2,274
	Cleveland, NFL	2,166
1965	Cleveland, NFL	2,331
	San Diego, AFL	2,085
1964	Green Bay, NFL	2,276
	Buffalo, AFL	2,040
1963	Cleveland, NFL	2,639
	San Diego, AFL	2,203
1962	Buffalo, AFL	2,480
	Green Bay, NFL	2,460
1961	Green Bay, NFL	2,350
	Dall. Texans, AFL	2,189
1960	St. Louis, NFL	2,356
	Oakland, AFL	2,056
1959	Cleveland	2,149
1958	Cleveland	2,526
1957	Los Angeles	2,142
1956	Chi. Bears	2,468
1955	Chi. Bears	2,388
1954	San Francisco	2,498
1953	San Francisco	2,230
1952	San Francisco	1,905
1951	Chi. Bears	2,408
1950	N.Y. Giants	2,336
1949	Philadelphia	2,607
1948	Chi. Cardinals	2,560
1947	Los Angeles	2,171
1946	Green Bay	1,765
1945	Cleveland	1,714
1944	Philadelphia	1,661
1943	Phil-Pitt	1,730
1942	Chi. Bears	1,881
1941	Chi. Bears	2,263
1940	Chi. Bears	1,818
1939	Chi. Bears	2,043
1938	Detroit	1,893
1937	Detroit	2,074

Year	Team	Yards
1936	Detroit	2,885
1935	Chi. Bears	2,096
1934	Chi. Bears	2,847
1933	Boston	2,260
1932	Chi. Bears	1,770

YARDS PASSING

Leadership in this category has been based on net yards since 1952.

Year	Team	Yards
2004	Indianapolis, AFC	4,623
	Minnesota, NFC	4,516
2003	Indianapolis, AFC	4,179
	St. Louis, NFC	3,961
2002	Oakland, AFC	4,475
	St. Louis, NFC	4,154
2001	St. Louis, NFC	4,663
	Indianapolis, AFC	3,989
2000	St. Louis, NFC	5,232
	Indianapolis, AFC	4,282
1999	St. Louis, NFC	4,353
	Indianapolis, AFC	4,066
1998	Minnesota, NFC	4,328
	N.Y. Jets, AFC	3,836
1997	Seattle, AFC	3,959
	Green Bay, NFC	3,705
1996	Jacksonville, AFC	4,110
	Philadelphia, NFC	3,745
1995	San Francisco, NFC	4,608
	Miami, AFC	4,210
1994	New England, AFC	4,444
	Minnesota, NFC	4,324
1993	Miami, AFC	4,353
	San Francisco, NFC	4,302
1992	Houston, AFC	4,029
	San Francisco, NFC	3,880
1991	Houston, AFC	4,621
	San Francisco, NFC	3,997
1990	Houston, AFC	4,805
	San Francisco, NFC	4,177
1989	Washington, NFC	4,349
	Miami, AFC	4,216
1988	Miami, AFC	4,516
	Washington, NFC	4,136
1987	Miami, AFC	3,876
	San Francisco, NFC	3,750
1986	Miami, AFC	4,779
	San Francisco, NFC	4,096
1985	San Diego, AFC	4,870
	Dallas, NFC	3,861
1984	Miami, AFC	5,018
	St. Louis, NFC	4,257
1983	San Diego, AFC	4,661
	Green Bay, NFC	4,365
1982	San Diego, AFC	2,927
	San Francisco, NFC	2,502
1981	San Diego, AFC	4,739
	Minnesota, NFC	4,333
1980	San Diego, AFC	4,531
	Minnesota, NFC	3,688
1979	San Diego, AFC	3,915
	San Francisco, NFC	3,641
1978	San Diego, AFC	3,375
	Minnesota, NFC	3,243
1977	Buffalo, AFC	2,530
	St. Louis, NFC	2,499
1976	Baltimore, AFC	2,933
	Minnesota, NFC	2,855

Year	Team	Yards
1975	Cincinnati, AFC	3,241
	Washington, NFC	2,917
1974	Washington, NFC	2,978
	Cincinnati, AFC	2,804
1973	Philadelphia, NFC	2,998
	Denver, AFC	2,519
1972	N.Y. Jets, AFC	2,777
	San Francisco, NFC	2,735
1971	San Diego, AFC	3,134
	Dallas, NFC	2,786
1970	San Francisco, NFC	2,923
	Oakland, AFC	2,865
1969	Oakland, AFL	3,271
	San Francisco, NFL	3,158
1968	San Diego, AFL	3,623
	Dallas, NFL	3,026
1967	N.Y. Jets, AFL	3,845
	Washington, NFL	3,730
1966	N.Y. Jets, AFL	3,464
	Dallas, NFL	3,023
1965	San Francisco, NFL	3,487
	San Diego, AFL	3,103
1964	Houston, AFL	3,527
	Chicago, NFL	2,841
1963	Baltimore, NFL	3,296
	Houston, AFL	3,222
1962	Denver, AFL	3,404
	Philadelphia, NFL	3,385
1961	Houston, AFL	4,392
	Philadelphia, NFL	3,605
1960	Houston, AFL	3,203
	Baltimore, NFL	2,956
1959	Baltimore	2,753
1958	Pittsburgh	2,752
1957	Baltimore	2,388
1956	Los Angeles	2,419
1955	Philadelphia	2,472
1954	Chi. Bears	3,104
1953	Philadelphia	3,089
1952	Cleveland	2,566
1951	Los Angeles	3,296
1950	Los Angeles	3,709
1949	Chi. Bears	3,055
1948	Washington	2,861
1947	Washington	3,336
1946	Los Angeles	2,080
1945	Chi. Bears	1,857
1944	Washington	2,021
1943	Chi. Bears	2,310
1942	Green Bay	2,407
1941	Chi. Bears	2,002
1940	Washington	1,887
1939	Chi. Bears	1,965
1938	Washington	1,536
1937	Green Bay	1,398
1936	Green Bay	1,629
1935	Green Bay	1,449
1934	Green Bay	1,165
1933	N.Y. Giants	1,348
1932	Chi. Bears	1,013

FEWEST POINTS ALLOWED

Year	Team	Points
2004	Pittsburgh, AFC	251
	Philadelphia, NFC	260
2003	New England, AFC	238
	Dallas, NFC	260
2002	Tampa Bay, NFC	196
	Miami, AFC	301

Year	Team	Points
2001	Chicago, NFC	203
	Pittsburgh, AFC	212
2000	Baltimore, AFC	165
	Philadelphia, NFC	245
1999	Jacksonville, AFC	217
	Tampa Bay, NFC	235
1998	Miami, AFC	265
	Dallas, NFC	275
1997	Kansas City, AFC	232
	Tampa Bay, NFC	263
1996	Green Bay, NFC	210
	Pittsburgh, AFC	257
1995	Kansas City, AFC	241
	San Francisco, NFC	258
1994	Cleveland, AFC	204
	Dallas, NFC	248
1993	N.Y. Giants, NFC	205
	Houston, AFC	238
1992	New Orleans, NFC	202
	Pittsburgh, AFC	225
1991	New Orleans, NFC	211
	Denver, AFC	235
1990	N.Y. Giants, NFC	211
	Pittsburgh, AFC	240
1989	Denver, AFC	226
	N.Y. Giants, NFC	252
1988	Chicago, NFC	215
	Buffalo, AFC	237
1987	Indianapolis, AFC	238
	San Francisco, NFC	253
1986	Chicago, NFC	187
	Seattle, AFC	293
1985	Chicago, NFC	198
	N.Y. Jets, AFC	264
1984	San Francisco, NFC	227
	Denver, AFC	241
1983	Miami, AFC	250
	Detroit, NFC	286
1982	Washington, NFC	128
	Miami, AFC	131
1981	Philadelphia, NFC	221
	Miami, AFC	275
1980	Philadelphia, NFC	222
	Houston, AFC	251
1979	Tampa Bay, NFC	237
	San Diego, AFC	246
1978	Pittsburgh, AFC	195
	Dallas, NFC	208
1977	Atlanta, NFC	129
	Denver, AFC	148
1976	Pittsburgh, AFC	138
	Minnesota, NFC	176
1975	Los Angeles, NFC	135
	Pittsburgh, AFC	162
1974	Los Angeles, NFC	181
	Pittsburgh, AFC	189
1973	Miami, AFC	150
	Minnesota, NFC	168
1972	Miami, AFC	171
	Washington, NFC	218
1971	Minnesota, NFC	139
	Baltimore, AFC	140
1970	Minnesota, NFC	143
	Miami, AFC	228
1969	Minnesota, NFL	133
	Kansas City, AFL	177
1968	Baltimore, NFL	144
	Kansas City, AFL	170

Year	Team	Yards
1967	Los Angeles, NFL	196
	Houston, AFL	199
1966	Green Bay, NFL	163
	Buffalo, AFL	255
1965	Green Bay, NFL	224
	Buffalo, AFL	226
1964	Baltimore, NFL	225
	Buffalo, AFL	242
1963	Chicago, NFL	144
	San Diego, AFL	255
1962	Green Bay, NFL	148
	Dall. Texans, AFL	233
1961	San Diego, AFL	219
	N.Y. Giants, NFL	220
1960	San Francisco, NFL	205
	Dall. Texans, AFL	253
1959	N.Y. Giants	170
1958	N.Y. Giants	183
1957	Cleveland	172
1956	Cleveland	177
1955	Cleveland	218
1954	Cleveland	162
1953	Cleveland	162
1952	Detroit	192
1951	Cleveland	152
1950	Philadelphia	141
1949	Philadelphia	134
1948	Chi. Bears	151
1947	Green Bay	210
1946	Pittsburgh	117
1945	Washington	121
1944	N.Y. Giants	75
1943	Washington	137
1942	Chi. Bears	84
1941	N.Y. Giants	114
1940	Brooklyn	120
1939	N.Y. Giants	85
1938	N.Y. Giants	79
1937	Chi. Bears	100
1936	Chi. Bears	94
1935	Green Bay	96
	N.Y. Giants	96
1934	Detroit	59
1933	Brooklyn	54
1932	Chi. Bears	44

FEWEST TOTAL YARDS ALLOWED

Year	Team	Yards
2004	Pittsburgh, AFC	4,134
	Washington, NFC	4,281
2003	Dallas, NFC	4,056
	Buffalo, AFC	4,313
2002	Tampa Bay, NFC	4,044
	Miami, AFC	4,656
2001	Pittsburgh, AFC	4,137
	St. Louis, NFC	4,471
2000	Tennessee, AFC	3,813
	Washington, NFC	4,474
1999	Buffalo, AFC	4,045
	Tampa Bay, NFC	4,280
1998	San Diego, AFC	4,208
	Tampa Bay, NFC	4,345
1997	San Francisco, NFC	4,013
	Denver, AFC	4,671
1996	Green Bay, NFC	4,156
	Pittsburgh, AFC	4,362
1995	San Francisco, NFC	4,398
	Kansas City, AFC	4,549
1994	Dallas, NFC	4,313
	Pittsburgh, AFC	4,326
1993	Minnesota, NFC	4,406
	Pittsburgh, AFC	4,531
1992	Dallas, NFC	3,931
	Houston, AFC	4,211
1991	Philadelphia, NFC	3,549
	Denver, AFC	4,549
1990	Pittsburgh, AFC	4,115
	N.Y. Giants, NFC	4,206
1989	Minnesota, NFC	4,184
	Kansas City, AFC	4,293
1988	Minnesota, NFC	4,091
	Buffalo, AFC	4,578
1987	San Francisco, NFC	4,095
	Cleveland, AFC	4,264
1986	Chicago, NFC	4,130
	L.A. Raiders, AFC	4,804
1985	Chicago, NFC	4,135
	L.A. Raiders, AFC	4,603
1984	Chicago, NFC	3,863
	Cleveland, AFC	4,641
1983	Cincinnati, AFC	4,327
	New Orleans, NFC	4,691
1982	Miami, AFC	2,312
	Tampa Bay, NFC	2,442
1981	Philadelphia, NFC	4,447
	N.Y. Jets, AFC	4,871
1980	Buffalo, AFC	4,101
	Philadelphia, NFC	4,443
1979	Tampa Bay, NFC	3,949
	Pittsburgh, AFC	4,270
1978	Los Angeles, NFC	3,893
	Pittsburgh, AFC	4,168
1977	Dallas, NFC	3,213
	New England, AFC	3,638
1976	Pittsburgh, AFC	3,323
	San Francisco, NFC	3,562
1975	Minnesota, NFC	3,153
	Oakland, AFC	3,629
1974	Pittsburgh, AFC	3,074
	Washington, NFC	3,285
1973	Los Angeles, NFC	2,951
	Oakland, AFC	3,160
1972	Miami, AFC	3,297
	Green Bay, NFC	3,474
1971	Baltimore, AFC	2,852
	Minnesota, NFC	3,406
1970	Minnesota, NFC	2,803
	N.Y. Jets, AFC	3,655
1969	Minnesota, NFL	2,720
	Kansas City, AFL	3,163
1968	Los Angeles, NFL	3,118
	N.Y. Jets, AFL	3,363
1967	Oakland, AFL	3,294
	Green Bay, NFL	3,300
1966	St. Louis, NFL	3,492
	Oakland, AFL	3,910
1965	San Diego, AFL	3,262
	Detroit, NFL	3,557
1964	Green Bay, NFL	3,179
	Buffalo, AFL	3,878
1963	Chicago, NFL	3,176
	Boston, AFL	3,834
1962	Detroit, NFL	3,217
	Dall. Texans, AFL	3,951
1961	San Diego, AFL	3,726
	Baltimore, NFL	3,782

Year	Team	Yards
1960	St. Louis, NFL	3,029
	Buffalo, AFL	3,866
1959	N.Y. Giants	2,843
1958	Chi. Bears	3,066
1957	Pittsburgh	2,791
1956	N.Y. Giants	3,081
1955	Cleveland	2,841
1954	Cleveland	2,658
1953	Philadelphia	2,998
1952	Cleveland	3,075
1951	N.Y. Giants	3,250
1950	Cleveland	3,154
1949	Philadelphia	2,831
1948	Chi. Bears	2,931
1947	Green Bay	3,396
1946	Washington	2,451
1945	Philadelphia	2,073
1944	Philadelphia	1,943
1943	Chi. Bears	2,262
1942	Chi. Bears	1,703
1941	N.Y. Giants	2,368
1940	N.Y. Giants	2,219
1939	Washington	2,116
1938	N.Y. Giants	2,029
1937	Washington	2,123
1936	Boston	2,181
1935	Boston	1,996
1934	Chi. Cardinals	1,539
1933	Brooklyn	1,789

FEWEST RUSHING YARDS ALLOWED

Year	Team	Yards
2004	Pittsburgh, AFC	1,299
	Washington, NFC	1,304
2003	Tennessee, AFC	1,295
	Dallas, NFC	1,425
2002	Pittsburgh, AFC	1,375
	Tampa Bay, NFC	1,554
2001	Pittsburgh, AFC	1,195
	Chicago, NFC	1,313
2000	Baltimore, AFC	970
	N.Y. Giants, NFC	1,156
1999	St. Louis, NFC	1,189
	Baltimore, AFC	1,231
1998	San Diego, AFC	1,140
	Atlanta, NFC	1,203
1997	Pittsburgh, AFC	1,318
	San Francisco, NFC	1,366
1996	Denver, AFC	1,331
	Green Bay, NFC	1,416
1995	San Francisco, NFC	1,061
	Pittsburgh, AFC	1,321
1994	Minnesota, NFC	1,090
	San Diego, AFC	1,404
1993	Houston, AFC	1,273
	Minnesota, NFC	1,536
1992	Dallas, NFC	1,244
	Buffalo, AFC	1,395
	San Diego, AFC	1,395
1991	Philadelphia, NFC	1,136
	N.Y. Jets, AFC	1,442
1990	Philadelphia, NFC	1,169
	San Diego, AFC	1,515
1989	New Orleans, NFC	1,326
	Denver, AFC	1,580
1988	Chicago, NFC	1,326
	Houston, AFC	1,592
1987	Chicago, NFC	1,413
	Cleveland, AFC	1,433

Year	Team	Yards
1986	N.Y. Giants, NFC	1,284
	Denver, AFC	1,651
1985	Chicago, NFC	1,319
	N.Y. Jets, AFC	1,516
1984	Chicago, NFC	1,377
	Pittsburgh, AFC	1,617
1983	Washington, NFC	1,289
	Cincinnati, AFC	1,499
1982	Pittsburgh, AFC	762
	Detroit, NFC	854
1981	Detroit, NFC	1,623
	Kansas City, AFC	1,747
1980	Detroit, NFC	1,599
	Cincinnati, AFC	1,680
1979	Denver, AFC	1,693
	Tampa Bay, NFC	1,873
1978	Dallas, NFC	1,721
	Pittsburgh, AFC	1,774
1977	Denver, AFC	1,531
	Dallas, NFC	1,651
1976	Pittsburgh, AFC	1,457
	Los Angeles, NFC	1,564
1975	Minnesota, NFC	1,532
	Houston, AFC	1,680
1974	Los Angeles, NFC	1,302
	New England, AFC	1,587
1973	Los Angeles, NFC	1,270
	Oakland, AFC	1,470
1972	Dallas, NFC	1,515
	Miami, AFC	1,548
1971	Baltimore, AFC	1,113
	Dallas, NFC	1,144
1970	Detroit, NFC	1,152
	N.Y. Jets, AFC	1,283
1969	Dallas, NFL	1,050
	Kansas City, AFL	1,091
1968	Dallas, NFL	1,195
	N.Y. Jets, AFL	1,195
1967	Dallas, NFL	1,081
	Oakland, AFL	1,129
1966	Buffalo, AFL	1,051
	Dallas, NFL	1,176
1965	San Diego, AFL	1,094
	Los Angeles, NFL	1,409
1964	Buffalo, AFL	913
	Los Angeles, NFL	1,501
1963	Boston, AFL	1,107
	Chicago, NFL	1,442
1962	Detroit, NFL	1,231
	Dall. Texans, AFL	1,250
1961	Boston, AFL	1,041
	Pittsburgh, NFL	1,463
1960	St. Louis, NFL	1,212
	Dall. Texans, AFL	1,338
1959	N.Y. Giants	1,261
1958	Baltimore	1,291
1957	Baltimore	1,174
1956	N.Y. Giants	1,443
1955	Cleveland	1,189
1954	Cleveland	1,050
1953	Philadelphia	1,117
1952	Detroit	1,145
1951	N.Y. Giants	913
1950	Detroit	1,367
1949	Chi. Bears	1,196
1948	Philadelphia	1,209
1947	Philadelphia	1,329
1946	Chi. Bears	1,060
1945	Philadelphia	817

Year	Team	Yards
1944	Philadelphia	558
1943	Phil-Pitt	793
1942	Chi. Bears	519
1941	Washington	1,042
1940	N.Y. Giants	977
1939	Chi. Bears	812
1938	Detroit	1,081
1937	Chi. Bears	933
1936	Boston	1,148
1935	Boston	998
1934	Chi. Cardinals	954
1933	Brooklyn	964

FEWEST PASSING YARDS ALLOWED

Leadership in this category has been based on net yards since 1952.

Year	Team	Yards
2004	Tampa Bay, NFC	2,579
	Miami, AFC	2,592
2003	Dallas, NFC	2,631
	Buffalo, AFC	2,707
2002	Tampa Bay, NFC	2,490
	Indianapolis, AFC	2,917
2001	Miami, AFC	2,829
	Philadelphia, NFC	2,864
2000	Tennessee, AFC	2,423
	Washington, NFC	2,621
1999	Buffalo, AFC	2,675
	Tampa Bay, NFC	2,873
1998	Philadelphia, NFC	2,720
	Oakland, AFC	2,876
1997	Dallas, NFC	2,522
	Indianapolis, AFC	2,820
1996	Green Bay, NFC	2,740
	Pittsburgh, AFC	2,947
1995	N.Y. Jets, AFC	2,740
	Philadelphia, NFC	2,816
1994	Dallas, NFC	2,752
	Houston, AFC	2,795
1993	New Orleans, NFC	2,606
	Cincinnati, AFC	2,798
1992	New Orleans, NFC	2,470
	Kansas City, AFC	2,537
1991	Philadelphia, NFC	2,413
	Denver, AFC	2,755
1990	Pittsburgh, AFC	2,500
	Dallas, NFC	2,639
1989	Minnesota, NFC	2,501
	Kansas City, AFC	2,527
1988	Kansas City, AFC	2,434
	Minnesota, NFC	2,489
1987	San Francisco, NFC	2,484
	L.A. Raiders, AFC	2,727
1986	St. Louis, NFC	2,637
	New England, AFC	2,978
1985	Washington, NFC	2,746
	Pittsburgh, AFC	2,783
1984	New Orleans, NFC	2,453
	Cleveland, AFC	2,696
1983	New Orleans, NFC	2,691
	Cincinnati, AFC	2,828
1982	Miami, AFC	1,027
	Tampa Bay, NFC	1,384
1981	Philadelphia, NFC	2,696
	Buffalo, AFC	2,870
1980	Washington, NFC	2,171
	Buffalo, AFC	2,282
1979	Tampa Bay, NFC	2,076
	Buffalo, AFC	2,530

Year	Team	Yards
1978	Buffalo, AFC	1,960
	Los Angeles, NFC	2,048
1977	Atlanta, NFC	1,384
	San Diego, AFC	1,725
1976	Minnesota, NFC	1,575
	Cincinnati, AFC	1,758
1975	Minnesota, NFC	1,621
	Cincinnati, AFC	1,729
1974	Pittsburgh, AFC	1,466
	Atlanta, NFC	1,572
1973	Miami, AFC	1,290
	Atlanta, NFC	1,430
1972	Minnesota, NFC	1,699
	Cleveland, AFC	1,736
1971	Atlanta, NFC	1,638
	Baltimore, AFC	1,739
1970	Minnesota, NFC	1,438
	Kansas City, AFC	2,010
1969	Minnesota, NFL	1,631
	Kansas City, AFL	2,072
1968	Houston, AFL	1,671
	Green Bay, NFL	1,796
1967	Green Bay, NFL	1,377
	Buffalo, AFL	1,825
1966	Green Bay, NFL	1,959
	Oakland, AFL	2,118
1965	Green Bay, NFL	1,981
	San Diego, AFL	2,168
1964	Green Bay, NFL	1,647
	San Diego, AFL	2,518
1963	Chicago, NFL	1,734
	Oakland, AFL	2,589
1962	Green Bay, NFL	1,746
	Oakland, AFL	2,306
1961	Baltimore, NFL	1,913
	San Diego, AFL	2,363
1960	Chicago, NFL	1,388
	Buffalo, AFL	2,124
1959	N.Y. Giants	1,582
1958	Chi. Bears	1,769
1957	Cleveland	1,300
1956	Cleveland	1,103
1955	Pittsburgh	1,295
1954	Cleveland	1,608
1953	Washington	1,751
1952	Washington	1,580
1951	Pittsburgh	1,687
1950	Cleveland	1,581
1949	Philadelphia	1,607
1948	Green Bay	1,626
1947	Green Bay	1,790
1946	Pittsburgh	939
1945	Washington	1,121
1944	Chi. Bears	1,052
1943	Chi. Bears	980
1942	Washington	1,093
1941	Pittsburgh	1,168
1940	Philadelphia	1,012
1939	Washington	1,116
1938	Chi. Bears	897
1937	Detroit	804
1936	Philadelphia	853
1935	Chi. Cardinals	793
1934	Philadelphia	545
1933	Portsmouth	558

Compiled by Elias Sports Bureau

Super Bowl I, 1/15/67
Super Bowl II, 1/14/68
Super Bowl III, 1/12/69
Super Bowl IV, 1/11/70
Super Bowl V, 1/17/71
Super Bowl VI, 1/16/72
Super Bowl VII, 1/14/73
Super Bowl VIII, 1/13/74
Super Bowl IX, 1/12/75
Super Bowl X, 1/18/76
Super Bowl XI, 1/9/77
Super Bowl XII, 1/15/78
Super Bowl XIII, 1/21/79
Super Bowl XIV, 1/20/80
Super Bowl XV, 1/25/81
Super Bowl XVI, 1/24/82
Super Bowl XVII, 1/30/83
Super Bowl XVIII, 1/22/84
Super Bowl XIX, 1/20/85
Super Bowl XX, 1/26/86

Super Bowl XXI, 1/25/87
Super Bowl XXII, 1/31/88
Super Bowl XXIII, 1/22/89
Super Bowl XXIV, 1/28/90
Super Bowl XXV, 1/27/91
Super Bowl XXVI, 1/26/92
Super Bowl XXVII, 1/31/93
Super Bowl XXVIII, 1/30/94
Super Bowl XXIX, 1/29/95
Super Bowl XXX, 1/28/96
Super Bowl XXXI, 1/26/97
Super Bowl XXXII, 1/25/98
Super Bowl XXXIII, 1/31/99
Super Bowl XXXIV, 1/30/00
Super Bowl XXXV, 1/28/01
Super Bowl XXXVI, 2/3/02
Super Bowl XXXVII, 1/26/03
Super Bowl XXXVIII, 2/1/04
Super Bowl XXXIX, 2/6/05

INDIVIDUAL RECORDS

SERVICE
Most Games
- 6 Mike Lodish, Buffalo, XXV-XXVIII; Denver, XXXII-XXXIII
- 5 Marv Fleming, Green Bay, I-II; Miami, VI-VIII
  - Larry Cole, Dallas, V-VI, X, XII-XIII
  - Cliff Harris, Dallas, V-VI, X, XII-XIII
  - Charles Haley, San Francisco, XXIII-XXIV; Dallas, XXVII-XXVIII, XXX
  - D.D. Lewis, Dallas, V-VI, X, XII-XIII
  - Preston Pearson, Baltimore, III; Pittsburgh, IX; Dallas, X, XII-XIII
  - Charlie Waters, Dallas, V-VI, X, XII-XIII
  - Rayfield Wright, Dallas, V-VI, X, XII-XIII
  - Cornelius Bennett, Buffalo, XXV-XXVIII; Atlanta, XXXIII
  - John Elway, Denver, XXI-XXII, XXIV, XXXII-XXXIII
  - Glenn Parker, Buffalo, XXV-XXVIII; N.Y. Giants, XXXV
  - Bill Romanowski, San Francisco, XXIII-XXIV; Denver, XXXII-XXXIII; Oakland, XXXVII
- 4 By many players

Most Games, Winning Team
- 5 Charles Haley, San Francisco, XXIII-XXIV; Dallas, XXVII-XXVIII, XXX
- 4 By many players

Most Games, Coach
- 6 Don Shula, Baltimore, III; Miami, VI-VIII, XVII, XIX
- 5 Tom Landry, Dallas, V-VI, X, XII-XIII
- 4 Bud Grant, Minnesota, IV, VIII-IX, XI
  - Chuck Noll, Pittsburgh, IX-X, XIII-XIV
  - Joe Gibbs, Washington, XVII-XVIII, XXII, XXVI
  - Marv Levy, Buffalo, XXV-XXVIII
  - Dan Reeves, Denver, XXI-XXII, XXIV; Atlanta, XXXIII

Most Games, Winning Team, Coach
- 4 Chuck Noll, Pittsburgh, IX-X, XIII-XIV
- 3 Bill Walsh, San Francisco, XVI, XIX, XXIII
  - Joe Gibbs, Washington, XVII, XXII, XXVI
  - Bill Belichick, New England, XXXVI, XXXVIII-XXXIX
- 2 Vince Lombardi, Green Bay, I-II
  - Tom Landry, Dallas, VI, XII
  - Don Shula, Miami, VII-VIII
  - Tom Flores, Oakland, XV; L.A. Raiders, XVIII
  - Bill Parcells, N.Y. Giants, XXI, XXV
  - Jimmy Johnson, Dallas, XXVII-XXVIII
  - George Seifert, San Francisco, XXIV, XXIX
  - Mike Shanahan, Denver, XXXII-XXXIII

Most Games, Losing Team, Coach
- 4 Bud Grant, Minnesota, IV, VIII-IX, XI

-    Don Shula, Baltimore, III; Miami, VI, XVII, XIX
-    Marv Levy, Buffalo, XXV-XXVIII
-    Dan Reeves, Denver, XXI-XXII, XXIV; Atlanta, XXXIII
- 3 Tom Landry, Dallas, V, X, XIII

SCORING
POINTS
Most Points, Career
- 48 Jerry Rice, San Francisco-Oakland, 4 games (8-td)
- 30 Emmitt Smith, Dallas, 3 games (5-td)
- 24 Franco Harris, Pittsburgh, 4 games (4-td)
  - Roger Craig, San Francisco, 3 games (4-td)
  - Thurman Thomas, Buffalo, 4 games (4-td)
  - John Elway, Denver, 5 games (4-td)

Most Points, Game
- 18 Roger Craig, San Francisco vs. Miami, XIX (3-td)
  - Jerry Rice, San Francisco vs. Denver, XXIV (3-td); vs. San Diego, XXIX (3-td)
  - Ricky Watters, San Francisco vs. San Diego, XXIX (3-td)
  - Terrell Davis, Denver vs. Green Bay, XXXII (3-td)
- 15 Don Chandler, Green Bay vs. Oakland, II (3-pat, 4-fg)
- 14 Ray Wersching, San Francisco vs. Cincinnati, XVI (2-pat, 4-fg)
  - Kevin Butler, Chicago vs. New England, XX (5-pat, 3-fg)

TOUCHDOWNS
Most Touchdowns, Career
- 8 Jerry Rice, San Francisco-Oakland, 4 games (8-p)
- 5 Emmitt Smith, Dallas, 3 games (5-r)
- 4 Franco Harris, Pittsburgh, 4 games (4-r)
  - Roger Craig, San Francisco, 3 games (2-r, 2-p)
  - Thurman Thomas, Buffalo, 4 games (4-r)
  - John Elway, Denver, 5 games (4-r)

Most Touchdowns, Game
- 3 Roger Craig, San Francisco vs. Miami, XIX (1-r, 2-p)
  - Jerry Rice, San Francisco. vs. Denver, XXIV (3-p); vs. San Diego, XXIX (3-p)
  - Ricky Watters, San Francisco vs. San Diego, XXIX (1-r, 2-p)
  - Terrell Davis, Denver vs. Green Bay, XXXII (3-r)
- 2 Max McGee, Green Bay vs. Kansas City, I (2-p)
  - Elijah Pitts, Green Bay vs. Kansas City, I (2-r)
  - Bill Miller, Oakland vs. Green Bay, II (2-p)
  - Larry Csonka, Miami vs. Minnesota, VIII (2-r)
  - Pete Banaszak, Oakland vs. Minnesota, XI (2-r)
  - John Stallworth, Pittsburgh vs. Dallas, XIII (2-p)
  - Franco Harris, Pittsburgh vs. Los Angeles, XIV (2-r)
  - Cliff Branch, Oakland vs. Philadelphia, XV (2-p)
  - Dan Ross, Cincinnati vs. San Francisco, XVI (2-p)
  - Marcus Allen, L.A. Raiders vs. Washington, XVIII (2-r)
  - Jim McMahon, Chicago vs. New England, XX (2-r)
  - Ricky Sanders, Washington vs. Denver, XXII (2-p)
  - Timmy Smith, Washington vs. Denver, XXII (2-r)
  - Tom Rathman, San Francisco vs. Denver, XXIV (2-r)
  - Gerald Riggs, Washington vs. Buffalo, XXVI (2-r)
  - Michael Irvin, Dallas vs. Buffalo, XXVII (2-p)
  - Emmitt Smith, Dallas vs. Buffalo, XXVIII (2-r)
  - Emmitt Smith, Dallas vs. Pittsburgh, XXX (2-r)
  - Antonio Freeman, Green Bay vs. Denver, XXXII (2-p)
  - Howard Griffith, Denver vs. Atlanta, XXXIII (2-r)
  - Eddie George, Tennessee vs. St. Louis, XXXIV (2-r)
  - Keenan McCardell, Tampa Bay vs. Oakland, XXXVII (2-r)
  - Dwight Smith, Tampa Bay vs. Oakland, XXXVII (2-ret)

POINTS AFTER TOUCHDOWN
Most (One-Point) Points After Touchdown, Career
- 11 Adam Vinatieri, New England, 4 games (11 att)

9 Mike Cofer, San Francisco, 2 games (10 att)
8 Don Chandler, Green Bay, 2 games (8 att)
   Roy Gerela, Pittsburgh, 3 games (9 att)
   Chris Bahr, Oakland-L.A. Raiders, 2 games (8 att)
   Jason Elam, Denver, 2 games (8 att)

Most (One-Point) Points After Touchdown, Game
7 Mike Cofer, San Francisco vs. Denver, XXIV (8 att)
   Lin Elliott, Dallas vs. Buffalo, XXVII (7 att)
   Doug Brien, San Francisco vs. San Diego, XXIX (7 att)
6 Ali Hají-Sheikh, Washington vs. Denver, XXII (6 att)
   Martín Gramatica, Tampa Bay vs. Oakland, XXXVII
      (6 att)
5 Don Chandler, Green Bay vs. Kansas City, I (5 att)
   Roy Gerela, Pittsburgh vs. Dallas, XIII (5 att)
   Chris Bahr, L.A. Raiders vs. Washington, XVIII (5 att)
   Ray Wersching, San Francisco vs. Miami, XIX (5 att)
   Kevin Butler, Chicago vs. New England, XX (5 att)

Most Two-Point Conversions, Game
1 Mark Seay, San Diego vs. San Francisco, XXIX
   Alfred Pupunu, San Diego vs. San Francisco, XXIX
   Mark Chmura, Green Bay vs. New England, XXXI
   Kevin Faulk, New England vs. Carolina, XXXVIII

FIELD GOALS
Field Goals Attempted, Career
6 Jim Turner, N.Y. Jets-Denver, 2 games
   Roy Gerela, Pittsburgh, 3 games
   Rich Karlis, Denver, 2 games
   Jeff Wilkins, St. Louis, 2 games
   Adam Vinatieri, New England, 4 games
5 Efren Herrera, Dallas, 1 game
   Ray Wersching, San Francisco, 2 games
   Jason Elam, Denver, 2 games

Most Field Goals Attempted, Game
5 Jim Turner, N.Y. Jets vs. Baltimore, III
   Efren Herrera, Dallas vs. Denver, XII
4 Don Chandler, Green Bay vs. Oakland, II
   Roy Gerela, Pittsburgh vs. Dallas, X
   Ray Wersching, San Francisco vs. Cincinnati, XVI
   Rich Karlis, Denver vs. N.Y. Giants, XXI
   Mike Cofer, San Francisco vs. Cincinnati, XXIII
   Jason Elam, Denver vs. Atlanta, XXXIII
   Jeff Wilkins, St. Louis vs. Tennessee, XXXIV

Most Field Goals, Career
5 Ray Wersching, San Francisco, 2 games (5 att)
4 Don Chandler, Green Bay, 2 games (4 att)
   Jim Turner, N.Y. Jets-Denver, 2 games (6 att)
   Uwe von Schamann, Miami, 2 games (4 att)
   Jeff Wilkins, St. Louis, 2 games (6 att)
   Adam Vinatieri, New England, 4 games (6 att)
3 Mike Clark, Dallas, 2 games (3 att)
   Jan Stenerud, Kansas City, 1 game (3 att)
   Chris Bahr, Oakland-L.A. Raiders, 2 games (4 att)
   Mark Moseley, Washington, 2 games (4 att)
   Kevin Butler, Chicago, 1 game (3 att)
   Rich Karlis, Denver, 2 games (6 att)
   Jim Breech, Cincinnati, 2 games (3 att)
   Matt Bahr, Pittsburgh-N.Y. Giants, 2 games (3 att)
   Chip Lohmiller, Washington, 1 game (3 att)
   Steve Christie, Buffalo, 2 games (3 att)
   Eddie Murray, Dallas, 1 game (3 att)
   Jason Elam, Denver, 2 games (5 att)

Most Field Goals, Game
4 Don Chandler, Green Bay vs. Oakland, II
   Ray Wersching, San Francisco vs. Cincinnati, XVI
3 Jim Turner, N.Y. Jets vs. Baltimore, III
   Jan Stenerud, Kansas City vs. Minnesota, IV
   Uwe von Schamann, Miami vs. San Francisco, XIX
   Kevin Butler, Chicago vs. New England, XX
   Jim Breech, Cincinnati vs. San Francisco, XXIII

Chip Lohmiller, Washington vs. Buffalo, XXVI
Eddie Murray, Dallas vs. Buffalo, XXVIII
Jeff Wilkins, St. Louis vs. Tennessee, XXXIV

Longest Field Goal
54 Steve Christie, Buffalo vs. Dallas, XXVIII
51 Jason Elam, Denver vs. Green Bay, XXXII
50 Jeff Wilkins, St. Louis vs. New England, XXXVI
    John Kasay, Carolina vs. New England, XXXVIII

SAFETIES
Most Safeties, Game
1 Dwight White, Pittsburgh vs. Minnesota, IX
   Reggie Harrison, Pittsburgh vs. Dallas, X
   Henry Waechter, Chicago vs. New England, XX
   George Martin, N.Y. Giants vs. Denver, XXI
   Bruce Smith, Buffalo vs. N.Y. Giants, XXV

RUSHING
ATTEMPTS
Most Attempts, Career
101 Franco Harris, Pittsburgh, 4 games
 70 Emmitt Smith, Dallas, 3 games
 64 John Riggins, Washington, 2 games

Most Attempts, Game
38 John Riggins, Washington vs. Miami, XVII
34 Franco Harris, Pittsburgh vs. Minnesota, IX
33 Larry Csonka, Miami vs. Minnesota, VIII

YARDS GAINED
Most Yards Gained, Career
354 Franco Harris, Pittsburgh, 4 games
297 Larry Csonka, Miami, 3 games
289 Emmitt Smith, Dallas, 3 games

Most Yards Gained, Game
204 Timmy Smith, Washington vs. Denver, XXII
191 Marcus Allen, L.A. Raiders vs. Washington, XVIII
166 John Riggins, Washington vs. Miami, XVII

Longest Run From Scrimmage
74 Marcus Allen, L.A. Raiders vs. Washington, XVIII (TD)
58 Tom Matte, Baltimore vs. N.Y. Jets, III
    Timmy Smith, Washington vs. Denver, XXII (TD)
49 Larry Csonka, Miami vs. Washington, VII

AVERAGE GAIN
Highest Average Gain, Career (20 attempts)
9.6 Marcus Allen, L.A. Raiders, 1 game (20-191)
9.3 Timmy Smith, Washington, 1 game (22-204)
5.3 Walt Garrison, Dallas, 2 games (26-139)

Highest Average Gain, Game (10 attempts)
10.5 Tom Matte, Baltimore vs. N.Y. Jets, III (11-116)
 9.6 Marcus Allen, L.A. Raiders vs. Washington, XVIII
      (20-191)
 9.3 Timmy Smith, Washington vs. Denver, XXII (22-204)

TOUCHDOWNS
Most Touchdowns, Career
5 Emmitt Smith, Dallas, 3 games
4 Franco Harris, Pittsburgh, 4 games
   Thurman Thomas, Buffalo, 4 games
   John Elway, Denver, 5 games
3 Terrell Davis, Denver, 2 games

Most Touchdowns, Game
3 Terrell Davis, Denver vs. Green Bay, XXXII
2 Elijah Pitts, Green Bay vs. Kansas City, I
   Larry Csonka, Miami vs. Minnesota, VIII
   Pete Banaszak, Oakland vs. Minnesota, XI
   Franco Harris, Pittsburgh vs. Los Angeles, XIV
   Marcus Allen, L.A. Raiders vs. Washington, XVIII
   Jim McMahon, Chicago vs. New England, XX
   Timmy Smith, Washington vs. Denver, XXII

Tom Rathman, San Francisco vs. Denver, XXIV
Gerald Riggs, Washington vs. Buffalo, XXVI
Emmitt Smith, Dallas vs. Buffalo, XXVIII
Emmitt Smith, Dallas vs. Pittsburgh, XXX
Howard Griffith, Denver vs. Atlanta, XXXIII
Eddie George, Tennessee vs. St. Louis, XXXIV

PASSING
PASSER RATING
Highest Passer Rating, Career (40 attempts)
127.8 Joe Montana, San Francisco, 4 games
122.8 Jim Plunkett, Oakland-L.A. Raiders, 2 games
112.8 Terry Bradshaw, Pittsburgh, 4 games

ATTEMPTS
Most Passes Attempted, Career
152 John Elway, Denver, 5 games
145 Jim Kelly, Buffalo, 4 games
122 Joe Montana, San Francisco, 4 games
Most Passes Attempted, Game
58 Jim Kelly, Buffalo vs. Washington, XXVI
51 Donovan McNabb, Philadelphia vs. New England, XXXIX
50 Dan Marino, Miami vs. San Francisco, XIX
Jim Kelly, Buffalo vs. Dallas, XXVIII

COMPLETIONS
Most Passes Completed, Career
83 Joe Montana, San Francisco, 4 games
81 Jim Kelly, Buffalo, 4 games
76 John Elway, Denver, 5 games
Most Passes Completed, Game
32 Tom Brady, New England vs. Carolina, XXXVIII
31 Jim Kelly, Buffalo vs. Dallas, XXVIII
30 Donovan McNabb, Philadelphia vs. New England, XXXIX
Most Consecutive Completions, Game
13 Joe Montana, San Francisco vs. Denver, XXIV
10 Phil Simms, N.Y. Giants vs. Denver, XXI
Troy Aikman, Dallas vs. Pittsburgh, XXX
9 Jim Kelly, Buffalo vs. Dallas, XXVIII
Neil O'Donnell, Pittsburgh vs. Dallas, XXX
Steve McNair, Tennessee vs. St. Louis, XXXIV

COMPLETION PERCENTAGE
Highest Completion Percentage, Career (40 attempts)
70.0 Troy Aikman, Dallas, 3 games, (80-56)
68.0 Joe Montana, San Francisco, 4 games (122-83)
65.7 Tom Brady, New England, 3 games (108-71)
Highest Completion Percentage, Game (20 attempts)
88.0 Phil Simms, N.Y. Giants vs. Denver, XXI (25-22)
75.9 Joe Montana, San Francisco vs. Denver, XXIV (29-22)
73.5 Ken Anderson, Cincinnati vs. San Francisco, XVI (34-25)

YARDS GAINED
Most Yards Gained, Career
1,142 Joe Montana, San Francisco, 4 games
1,128 John Elway, Denver, 5 games
932 Terry Bradshaw, Pittsburgh, 4 games
Most Yards Gained, Game
414 Kurt Warner, St. Louis vs. Tennessee, XXXIV
365 Kurt Warner, St. Louis vs. New England, XXXVI
357 Joe Montana, San Francisco vs. Cincinnati, XXIII
Donovan McNabb, Philadelphia vs. New England, XXXIX
Longest Pass Completion
85 Jake Delhomme (to Muhammad), Carolina vs. New England, XXXVIII (TD)

81 Brett Favre (to Freeman), Green Bay vs. New England, XXXI (TD)
80 Jim Plunkett (to King), Oakland vs. Philadelphia, XV (TD)
Doug Williams (to Sanders), Washington vs. Denver, XXII (TD)
John Elway (to R. Smith), Denver vs. Atlanta, XXXIII (TD)

AVERAGE GAIN
Highest Average Gain, Career (40 attempts)
11.10 Terry Bradshaw, Pittsburgh, 4 games (84-932)
9.62 Bart Starr, Green Bay, 2 games (47-452)
9.41 Jim Plunkett, Oakland-L.A. Raiders, 2 games (46-433)
Highest Average Gain, Game (20 attempts)
14.71 Terry Bradshaw, Pittsburgh vs. Los Angeles, XIV (21-309)
12.80 Jim McMahon, Chicago vs. New England, XX (20-256)
12.43 Jim Plunkett, Oakland vs. Philadelphia, XV (21-261)

TOUCHDOWNS
Most Touchdown Passes, Career
11 Joe Montana, San Francisco, 4 games
9 Terry Bradshaw, Pittsburgh, 4 games
8 Roger Staubach, Dallas, 4 games
Most Touchdown Passes, Game
6 Steve Young, San Francisco vs. San Diego, XXIX
5 Joe Montana, San Francisco vs. Denver, XXIV
4 Terry Bradshaw, Pittsburgh vs. Dallas, XIII
Doug Williams, Washington vs. Denver, XXII
Troy Aikman, Dallas vs. Buffalo, XXVII

HAD INTERCEPTED
Lowest Percentage, Passes Had Intercepted, Career (40 attempts)
0.00 Jim Plunkett, Oakland-L.A. Raiders, 2 games (46-0)
Joe Montana, San Francisco, 4 games (122-0)
0.93 Tom Brady, New England, 3 games (108-1)
1.25 Troy Aikman, Dallas, 3 games (80-1)
Most Attempts, Without Interception, Game
45 Kurt Warner, St. Louis vs. Tennessee, XXXIV
36 Joe Montana, San Francisco vs. Cincinnati, XXIII
Steve Young, San Francisco vs. San Diego, XXIX
Steve McNair, Tennessee vs. St. Louis, XXXIV
35 Joe Montana, San Francisco vs. Miami, XIX
Most Passes Had Intercepted, Career
8 John Elway, Denver, 5 games
7 Craig Morton, Dallas-Denver, 2 games
Jim Kelly, Buffalo, 4 games
6 Fran Tarkenton, Minnesota, 3 games
Most Passes Had Intercepted, Game
5 Rich Gannon, Oakland vs. Tampa Bay, XXXVII
4 Craig Morton, Denver vs. Dallas, XII
Jim Kelly, Buffalo vs. Washington, XXVI
Drew Bledsoe, New England vs. Green Bay, XXXI
Kerry Collins, N.Y. Giants vs. Baltimore, XXXV
3 By 11 players

PASS RECEIVING
RECEPTIONS
Most Receptions, Career
33 Jerry Rice, San Francisco-Oakland, 4 games
27 Andre Reed, Buffalo, 4 games
20 Roger Craig, San Francisco, 3 games
Thurman Thomas, Buffalo, 4 games
Most Receptions, Game
11 Dan Ross, Cincinnati vs. San Francisco, XVI
Jerry Rice, San Francisco vs. Cincinnati, XXIII
Deion Branch, New England vs. Philadelphia, XXXIX
10 Tony Nathan, Miami vs. San Francisco, XIX
Jerry Rice, San Francisco vs. San Diego, XXIX

Andre Hastings, Pittsburgh vs. Dallas, XXX
Deion Branch, New England vs. Carolina, XXXVIII
9   Ricky Sanders, Washington vs. Denver, XXII
Antonio Freeman, Green Bay vs. Denver, XXXII
Terrell Owens, Philadelphia vs. New England, XXXIX

YARDS GAINED
Most Yards Gained, Career
589   Jerry Rice, San Francisco-Oakland, 4 games
364   Lynn Swann, Pittsburgh, 4 games
323   Andre Reed, Buffalo, 4 games
Most Yards Gained, Game
215   Jerry Rice, San Francisco vs. Cincinnati, XXIII
193   Ricky Sanders, Washington vs. Denver, XXII
162   Isaac Bruce, St. Louis vs. Tennessee, XXXIV
Longest Reception
85   Muhsin Muhammad (from Delhomme), Carolina vs.
New England, XXXVIII
81   Antonio Freeman (from Favre), Green Bay vs.
New England, XXXI (TD)
80   Kenny King (from Plunkett), Oakland vs.
Philadelphia, XV (TD)
Ricky Sanders (from Williams), Washington vs.
Denver, XXII (TD)
Rod Smith (from Elway), Denver vs. Atlanta, XXXIII

AVERAGE GAIN
Highest Average Gain, Career (8 receptions)
24.4   John Stallworth, Pittsburgh, 4 games (11-268)
23.4   Ricky Sanders, Washington, 2 games (10-234)
22.8   Lynn Swann, Pittsburgh, 4 games (16-364)
Highest Average Gain, Game (3 receptions)
40.33   John Stallworth, Pittsburgh vs. Los Angeles, XIV
(3-121)
40.25   Lynn Swann, Pittsburgh vs. Dallas, X (4-161)
38.33   John Stallworth, Pittsburgh vs. Dallas, XIII (3-115)

TOUCHDOWNS
Most Touchdowns, Career
8   Jerry Rice, San Francisco-Oakland, 4 games
3   John Stallworth, Pittsburgh, 4 games
Lynn Swann, Pittsburgh, 4 games
Cliff Branch, Oakland-L.A. Raiders, 3 games
Antonio Freeman, Green Bay, 2 games
2   Max McGee, Green Bay, 2 games
Bill Miller, Oakland, 1 game
Butch Johnson, Dallas, 2 games
Dan Ross, Cincinnati, 1 game
Roger Craig, San Francisco, 3 games
Ricky Sanders, Washington, 2 games
John Taylor, San Francisco, 3 games
Gary Clark, Washington, 2 games
Don Beebe, Buffalo-Green Bay, 4 games
Michael Irvin, Dallas, 3 games
Ricky Watters, San Francisco, 1 game
Jay Novacek, Dallas, 3 games
Keenan McCardell, Tampa Bay, 1 game
Ricky Proehl, St. Louis-Carolina, 3 games
David Givens, New England, 2 games
Mike Vrabel, New England, 3 games
Most Touchdowns, Game
3   Jerry Rice, San Francisco vs. Denver, XXIV; vs.
San Diego, XXIX
2   Max McGee, Green Bay vs. Kansas City, I
Bill Miller, Oakland vs. Green Bay, II
John Stallworth, Pittsburgh vs. Dallas, XIII
Cliff Branch, Oakland vs. Philadelphia, XV
Dan Ross, Cincinnati vs. San Francisco, XVI
Roger Craig, San Francisco vs. Miami, XIX
Ricky Sanders, Washington vs. Denver, XXII

Michael Irvin, Dallas vs. Buffalo, XXVII
Ricky Watters, San Francisco vs. San Diego, XXIX
Antonio Freeman, Green Bay vs. Denver, XXXII
Keenan McCardell, Tampa Bay vs. Oakland, XXXVII

INTERCEPTIONS BY
Most Interceptions By, Career
3   Chuck Howley, Dallas, 2 games
Rod Martin, Oakland-L.A. Raiders, 2 games
Larry Brown, Dallas, 3 games
2   Randy Beverly, N.Y. Jets, 1 game
Jake Scott, Miami, 3 games
Mike Wagner, Pittsburgh, 3 games
Mel Blount, Pittsburgh, 4 games
Eric Wright, San Francisco, 4 games
Barry Wilburn, Washington, 1 game
Brad Edwards, Washington, 1 game
Thomas Everett, Dallas, 2 games
James Washington, Dallas, 2 games
Darrien Gordon, San Diego-Denver-Oakland,
4 games
Dexter Jackson, Tampa Bay, 1 game
Dwight Smith, Tampa Bay, 1 game
Rodney Harrison, San Diego-New England, 3 games
Most Interceptions By, Game
3   Rod Martin, Oakland vs. Philadelphia, XV
2   Randy Beverly, N.Y. Jets vs. Baltimore, III
Chuck Howley, Dallas vs. Baltimore, V
Jake Scott, Miami vs. Washington, VII
Barry Wilburn, Washington vs. Denver, XXII
Brad Edwards, Washington vs. Buffalo, XXVI
Thomas Everett, Dallas vs. Buffalo, XXVII
Larry Brown, Dallas vs. Pittsburgh, XXX
Darrien Gordon, Denver vs. Atlanta, XXXIII
Dexter Jackson, Tampa Bay vs. Oakland, XXXVII
Dwight Smith, Tampa Bay vs. Oakland, XXXVII
Rodney Harrison, New England vs. Philadelphia,
XXXIX

YARDS GAINED
Most Yards Gained, Career
108   Darrien Gordon, San Diego-Denver-Oakland,
4 games
94   Dwight Smith, Tampa Bay, 1 game
77   Larry Brown, Dallas, 3 games
Most Yards Gained, Game
108   Darrien Gordon, Denver vs. Atlanta, XXXIII
94   Dwight Smith, Tampa Bay vs. Oakland, XXXVII
77   Larry Brown, Dallas vs. Pittsburgh, XXX
Longest Return
75   Willie Brown, Oakland vs. Minnesota, XI (TD)
60   Herb Adderley, Green Bay vs. Oakland, II (TD)
58   Darrien Gordon, Denver vs. Atlanta, XXXIII

TOUCHDOWNS
Most Touchdowns, Game
2   Dwight Smith, Tampa Bay vs. Oakland, XXXVII
1   Herb Adderley, Green Bay vs. Oakland, II
Willie Brown, Oakland vs. Minnesota, XI
Jack Squirek, L.A. Raiders vs. Washington, XVIII
Reggie Phillips, Chicago vs. New England, XX
Duane Starks, Baltimore vs. N.Y. Giants, XXXV
Ty Law, New England vs. St. Louis, XXXVI
Derrick Brooks, Tampa Bay vs. Oakland, XXXVII

PUNTING
Most Punts, Career
17   Mike Eischeid, Oakland-Minnesota, 3 games
Mike Horan, Denver-St. Louis, 4 games
15   Larry Seiple, Miami, 3 games

14 Ron Widby, Dallas, 2 games
      Ray Guy, Oakland-L.A. Raiders, 3 games
      Chris Mohr, Buffalo, 3 games
      Craig Hentrich, Green Bay-Tennessee, 3 games

Most Punts, Game

11 Brad Maynard, N.Y. Giants vs. Baltimore, XXXV
10 Kyle Richardson, Baltimore vs. N.Y. Giants, XXXV
 9 Ron Widby, Dallas vs. Baltimore, V

Longest Punt

63 Lee Johnson, Cincinnati vs. San Francisco, XXIII
62 Rich Camarillo, New England vs. Chicago, XX
61 Jerrel Wilson, Kansas City vs. Green Bay, I

AVERAGE YARDAGE

Highest Average, Punting, Career (10 punts)

46.5 Jerrel Wilson, Kansas City, 2 games (11-511)
43.0 Kyle Richardson, Baltimore, 1 game (10-430)
      Tom Tupa, New England-Tampa Bay, 2 games
      (12-516)
41.9 Ray Guy, Oakland-L.A. Raiders, 3 games (14-587)

Highest Average, Punting, Game (4 punts)

48.8 Bryan Wagner, San Diego vs. San Francisco, XXIX
      (4-195)
48.5 Jerrel Wilson, Kansas City vs. Minnesota, IV (4-194)
46.3 Jim Miller, San Francisco vs. Cincinnati, XVI (4-185)

PUNT RETURNS

Most Punt Returns, Career

8 Troy Brown, New England, 3 games
6 Willie Wood, Green Bay, 2 games
   Jake Scott, Miami, 3 games
   Theo Bell, Pittsburgh, 2 games
   Mike Nelms, Washington, 1 game
   John Taylor, San Francisco, 3 games
   Desmond Howard, Green Bay, 1 game
   David Meggett, N.Y. Giants-New England, 2 games
   Darrien Gordon, San Diego-Denver-Oakland,
     4 games
5 Dana McLemore, San Francisco, 1 game

Most Punt Returns, Game

6 Mike Nelms, Washington vs. Miami, XVII
   Desmond Howard, Green Bay vs. New England, XXXI
5 Willie Wood, Green Bay vs. Oakland, II
   Dana McLemore, San Francisco vs. Miami, XIX
4 By eight players

Most Fair Catches, Game

4 Jermaine Lewis, Baltimore vs. N.Y. Giants, XXXV
   Karl Williams, Tampa Bay vs. Oakland, XXXVII
3 Ron Gardin, Baltimore vs. Dallas, V
   Golden Richards, Dallas vs. Pittsburgh, X
   Greg Pruitt, L.A. Raiders vs. Washington, XVIII
   Al Edwards, Buffalo vs. N.Y. Giants, XXV
   David Meggett, N.Y. Giants vs. Buffalo, XXV

YARDS GAINED

Most Yards Gained, Career

94 John Taylor, San Francisco, 3 games
90 Desmond Howard, Green Bay, 1 game
67 David Meggett, N.Y. Giants-New England, 2 games

Most Yards Gained, Game

90 Desmond Howard, Green Bay vs. New England, XXXI
56 John Taylor, San Francisco vs. Cincinnati, XXIII
52 Mike Nelms, Washington vs. Miami, XVII

Longest Return

45 John Taylor, San Francisco vs. Cincinnati, XXIII
34 Darrell Green, Washington vs. L.A. Raiders, XVIII
   Desmond Howard, Green Bay vs. New England, XXXI
   Jermaine Lewis, Baltimore vs. N.Y. Giants, XXXV
32 Desmond Howard, Green Bay vs. New England, XXXI

AVERAGE YARDAGE

Highest Average, Career (4 returns)

15.7 John Taylor, San Francisco, 3 games (6-94)
15.0 Desmond Howard, Green Bay, 1 game (6-90)
11.2 David Meggett, N.Y. Giants-New England, 2 games
      (6-67)

Highest Average, Game (3 returns)

18.7 John Taylor, San Francisco vs. Cincinnati, XXIII (3-56)
15.0 Desmond Howard, Green Bay vs. New England, XXXI
      (6-90)
12.7 John Taylor, San Francisco vs. Denver, XXIV (3-38)

TOUCHDOWNS

Most Touchdowns, Game

   None

KICKOFF RETURNS

Most Kickoff Returns, Career

10 Ken Bell, Denver, 3 games
 8 Larry Anderson, Pittsburgh, 2 games
    Fulton Walker, Miami, 2 games
    Andre Coleman, San Diego, 1 game
    Marcus Knight, Oakland, 1 game
 7 Preston Pearson, Baltimore-Pittsburgh-Dallas, 5 games
    Stephen Starring, New England, 1 game
    David Meggett, N.Y. Giants-New England, 2 games

Most Kickoff Returns, Game

8 Andre Coleman, San Diego vs. San Francisco, XXIX
   Marcus Knight, Oakland vs. Tampa Bay, XXXVII
7 Stephen Starring, New England vs. Chicago, XX
6 Darren Carrington, Denver vs. San Francisco, XXIV
   Antonio Freeman, Green Bay vs. Denver, XXXII
   Ron Dixon, N.Y. Giants vs. Baltimore, XXXV

YARDS GAINED

Most Yards Gained, Career

283 Fulton Walker, Miami, 2 games
244 Andre Coleman, San Diego, 1 game
210 Tim Dwight, Atlanta, 1 game

Most Yards Gained, Game

244 Andre Coleman, San Diego vs. San Francisco, XXIX
210 Tim Dwight, Atlanta vs. Denver, XXXIII
190 Fulton Walker, Miami vs. Washington, XVII

Longest Return

99 Desmond Howard, Green Bay vs. New England, XXXI
   (TD)
98 Fulton Walker, Miami vs. Washington, XVII (TD)
   Andre Coleman, San Diego vs. San Francisco, XXIX
   (TD)
97 Ron Dixon, N.Y. Giants vs. Baltimore, XXXV (TD)

AVERAGE YARDAGE

Highest Average, Career (4 returns)

42.0 Tim Dwight, Atlanta, 1 game (5-210)
38.5 Desmond Howard, Green Bay, 1 game (4-154)
35.4 Fulton Walker, Miami, 2 games (8-283)

Highest Average, Game (3 returns)

47.5 Fulton Walker, Miami vs. Washington, XVII (4-190)
42.0 Tim Dwight, Atlanta vs. Denver, XXXIII (5-210)
38.5 Desmond Howard, Green Bay vs. New England, XXXI
      (4-154)

TOUCHDOWNS

Most Touchdowns, Game

1 Fulton Walker, Miami vs. Washington, XVII
   Stanford Jennings, Cincinnati vs. San Francisco, XXIII
   Andre Coleman, San Diego vs. San Francisco, XXIX
   Desmond Howard, Green Bay vs. New England, XXXI
   Tim Dwight, Atlanta vs. Denver, XXXIII
   Ron Dixon, N.Y. Giants vs. Baltimore, XXXV

Jermaine Lewis, Baltimore vs. N.Y. Giants, XXXV

FUMBLES
Most Fumbles, Career
- 5   Roger Staubach, Dallas, 4 games
- 4   Jim Kelly, Buffalo, 4 games
- 3   Franco Harris, Pittsburgh, 4 games
  - Terry Bradshaw, Pittsburgh, 4 games
  - John Elway, Denver, 5 games
  - Frank Reich, Buffalo, 4 games
  - Thurman Thomas, Buffalo, 4 games

Most Fumbles, Game
- 3   Roger Staubach, Dallas vs. Pittsburgh, X
  - Jim Kelly, Buffalo vs. Washington, XXVI
  - Frank Reich, Buffalo vs. Dallas, XXVII
- 2   Franco Harris, Pittsburgh vs. Minnesota, IX
  - Butch Johnson, Dallas vs. Denver, XII
  - Terry Bradshaw, Pittsburgh vs. Dallas, XIII
  - Joe Montana, San Francisco vs. Cincinnati, XXIII
  - John Elway, Denver vs. San Francisco, XXIV
  - Thurman Thomas, Buffalo vs. Dallas, XXVIII

RECOVERIES
Most Fumbles Recovered, Career
- 2   Jake Scott, Miami, 3 games (1 own, 1 opp)
  - Fran Tarkenton, Minnesota, 3 games (2 own)
  - Franco Harris, Pittsburgh, 4 games (2 own)
  - Roger Staubach, Dallas, 4 games (2 own)
  - Bobby Walden, Pittsburgh, 2 games (2 own)
  - John Fitzgerald, Dallas, 4 games (2 own)
  - Randy Hughes, Dallas, 3 games (2 opp)
  - Butch Johnson, Dallas, 2 games (2 own)
  - Mike Singletary, Chicago, 1 game (2 opp)
  - John Elway, Denver, 5 games (2 own)
  - Jimmie Jones, Dallas, 2 games (2 opp)
  - Kenneth Davis, Buffalo, 4 games (2 own)
  - Kurt Warner, St. Louis, 2 games (2 own)

Most Fumbles Recovered, Game
- 2   Jake Scott, Miami vs. Minnesota, VIII (1 own, 1 opp)
  - Roger Staubach, Dallas vs. Pittsburgh, X (2 own)
  - Randy Hughes, Dallas vs. Denver, XII (2 opp)
  - Butch Johnson, Dallas vs. Denver, XII (2 own)
  - Mike Singletary, Chicago vs. New England, XX (2 opp)
  - Jimmie Jones, Dallas vs. Buffalo, XXVII (2 opp)

YARDS GAINED
Most Yards Gained, Game
- 64   Leon Lett, Dallas vs. Buffalo, XXVII (opp)
- 49   Mike Bass, Washington vs. Miami, VII (opp)
- 46   James Washington, Dallas vs. Buffalo, XXVIII (opp)

Longest Return
- 64   Leon Lett, Dallas vs. Buffalo, XXVII
- 49   Mike Bass, Washington vs. Miami, VII (TD)
- 46   James Washington, Dallas vs. Buffalo, XXVIII (TD)

TOUCHDOWNS
Most Touchdowns, Game
- 1   Mike Bass, Washington vs. Miami, VII (opp 49 yds)
  - Mike Hegman, Dallas vs. Pittsburgh, XIII (opp 37 yds)
  - Jimmie Jones, Dallas vs. Buffalo, XXVII (opp 2 yds)
  - Ken Norton, Dallas vs. Buffalo, XXVII (opp 9 yds)
  - James Washington, Dallas vs. Buffalo, XXVIII (opp 46 yds)

COMBINED NET YARDS GAINED
(Rushing, receiving, interception returns, punt returns, kickoff returns, and fumble returns)
ATTEMPTS
Most Attempts, Career
- 108   Franco Harris, Pittsburgh, 4 games

- 81   Emmitt Smith, Dallas, 3 games
- 72   Roger Craig, San Francisco, 3 games
  - Thurman Thomas, Buffalo, 4 games

Most Attempts, Game
- 39   John Riggins, Washington vs. Miami, XVII
- 35   Franco Harris, Pittsburgh vs. Minnesota, IX
- 34   Matt Snell, N.Y. Jets vs. Baltimore, III
  - Emmitt Smith, Dallas vs. Buffalo, XXVIII

YARDS GAINED
Most Yards Gained, Career
- 604   Jerry Rice, San Francisco-Oakland, 4 games
- 468   Franco Harris, Pittsburgh, 4 games
- 410   Roger Craig, San Francisco, 3 games

Most Yards Gained, Game
- 244   Andre Coleman, San Diego vs. San Francisco, XXIX
  - Desmond Howard, Green Bay vs. New England, XXXI
- 235   Ricky Sanders, Washington vs. Denver, XXII
- 230   Antonio Freeman, Green Bay vs. Denver, XXXII

SACKS
Sacks have been compiled since XVII.
Most Sacks, Career
- 4.5   Charles Haley, San Francisco-Dallas, 5 games
- 3.0   Danny Stubbs, San Francisco, 2 games
  - Leonard Marshall, N.Y. Giants, 2 games
  - Jeff Wright, Buffalo, 4 games
  - Reggie White, Green Bay, 2 games
  - Willie McGinest, New England, 4 games
  - Tedy Bruschi, New England, 4 games
  - Mike Vrabel, New England, 3 games
- 2.5   Dexter Manley, Washington, 3 games

Most Sacks, Game
- 3.0   Reggie White, Green Bay vs. New England, XXXI
- 2.0   Dwaine Board, San Francisco vs. Miami, XIX
  - Dennis Owens, New England vs. Chicago, XX
  - Otis Wilson, Chicago vs. New England, XX
  - Leonard Marshall, N.Y. Giants vs. Denver, XXI
  - Alvin Walton, Washington vs. Denver, XXII
  - Charles Haley, San Francisco vs. Cincinnati, XXIII
  - Danny Stubbs, San Francisco vs. Denver, XXIV
  - Jeff Wright, Buffalo vs. Dallas, XXVIII
  - Raylee Johnson, San Diego vs. San Francisco, XXIX
  - Chad Hennings, Dallas vs. Pittsburgh, XXX
  - Tedy Bruschi, New England vs. Green Bay, XXXI
  - Michael McCrary, Baltimore vs. N.Y. Giants, XXXV
  - Simeon Rice, Tampa Bay vs. Oakland, XXXVII
  - Mike Vrabel, New England vs. Carolina, XXXVIII

TEAM RECORDS

GAMES, VICTORIES, DEFEATS
Most Games
- 8   Dallas, V-VI, X, XII-XIII, XXVII-XXVIII, XXX
- 6   Denver, XII, XXI-XXII, XXIV, XXXII-XXXIII
- 5   Miami, VI-VIII, XVII, XIX
  - Washington, VII, XVII-XVIII, XXII, XXVI
  - San Francisco, XVI, XIX, XXIII-XXIV, XXIX
  - Pittsburgh, IX-X, XIII-XIV, XXX
  - Oakland/L.A. Raiders, II, XI, XV, XVIII, XXXVII
  - New England, XX, XXXI, XXXVI, XXXVIII-XXXIX

Most Consecutive Games
- 4   Buffalo, XXV-XXVIII
- 3   Miami, VI-VIII
- 2   Green Bay, I-II; XXXI-XXXII
  - Dallas, V-VI; XII-XIII; XXVII-XXVIII
  - Minnesota, VIII-IX
  - Pittsburgh, IX-X; XIII-XIV
  - Washington, XVII-XVIII
  - Denver, XXI-XXII; XXXII-XXXIII

San Francisco, XXIII-XXIV
New England, XXXVIII-XXXIX

Most Games Won

5 San Francisco, XVI, XIX, XXIII-XXIV, XXIX
Dallas, VI, XII, XXVII-XXVIII, XXX
4 Pittsburgh, IX-X, XIII-XIV
3 Oakland/L.A. Raiders, XI, XV, XVIII
Washington, XVII, XXII, XXVI
Green Bay, I-II, XXXI
New England, XXXVI, XXXVIII-XXXIX

Most Consecutive Games Won

2 Green Bay, I-II
Miami, VII-VIII
Pittsburgh, IX-X, XIII-XIV
San Francisco, XXIII-XXIV
Dallas, XXVII-XXVIII
Denver, XXXII-XXXIII
New England, XXXVIII-XXXIX

Most Games Lost

4 Minnesota, IV, VIII-IX, XI
Denver, XII, XXI-XXII, XXIV
Buffalo, XXV-XXVIII
3 Dallas, V, X, XIII
Miami, VI, XVII, XIX
2 Washington, VII, XVIII
Cincinnati, XVI, XXIII
New England, XX, XXXI
L.A./St. Louis Rams, XIV, XXXVI
Oakland/L.A. Raiders, II, XXXVII
Philadelphia, XV, XXXIX

Most Consecutive Games Lost

4 Buffalo, XXV-XXVIII
2 Minnesota, VIII-IX
Denver, XXI-XXII

SCORING

Most Points, Game

55 San Francisco vs. Denver, XXIV
52 Dallas vs. Buffalo, XXVII
49 San Francisco vs. San Diego, XXIX

Fewest Points, Game

3 Miami vs. Dallas, VI
6 Minnesota vs. Pittsburgh, IX
7 By five teams

Most Points, Both Teams, Game

75 San Francisco (49) vs. San Diego (26), XXIX
69 Dallas (52) vs. Buffalo (17), XXVII
Tampa Bay (48) vs. Oakland (21), XXXVII
66 Pittsburgh (35) vs. Dallas (31), XIII

Fewest Points, Both Teams, Game

21 Washington (7) vs. Miami (14), VII
22 Minnesota (6) vs. Pittsburgh (16), IX
23 Baltimore (7) vs. N.Y. Jets (16), III

Largest Margin of Victory, Game

45 San Francisco vs. Denver, XXIV (55-10)
36 Chicago vs. New England, XX (46-10)
35 Dallas vs. Buffalo, XXVII (52-17)

Most Points, Each Half

1st: 35 Washington vs. Denver, XXII
2nd: 30 N.Y. Giants vs. Denver, XXI

Most Points, Each Quarter

1st: 14 Miami vs. Minnesota, VIII
Oakland vs. Philadelphia, XV
Dallas vs. Buffalo, XXVII
San Francisco vs. San Diego, XXIX
New England vs. Green Bay, XXXI
2nd: 35 Washington vs. Denver, XXII
3rd: 21 Chicago vs. New England, XX
4th: 21 Dallas vs. Buffalo, XXVII

Most Points, Both Teams, Each Half

1st: 45 Washington (35) vs. Denver (10), XXII
2nd: 46 Tampa Bay (28) vs. Oakland (18), XXXVII

Fewest Points, Both Teams, Each Half

1st: 2 Minnesota (0) vs. Pittsburgh (2), IX
2nd: 7 Miami (0) vs. Washington (7), VII
Denver (0) vs. Washington (7), XXII

Most Points, Both Teams, Each Quarter

1st: 24 New England (14) vs. Green Bay (10), XXXI
2nd: 35 Washington (35) vs. Denver (0), XXII
3rd: 24 Washington (14) vs. Buffalo (10), XXVI
4th: 37 Carolina (19) vs. New England (18), XXXVIII

TOUCHDOWNS

Most Touchdowns, Game

8 San Francisco vs. Denver, XXIV
7 Dallas vs. Buffalo, XXVII
San Francisco vs. San Diego, XXIX
6 Washington vs. Denver, XXII
Tampa Bay vs. Oakland, XXXVII

Fewest Touchdowns, Game

0 Miami vs. Dallas, VI
1 By 18 teams

Most Touchdowns, Both Teams, Game

10 San Francisco (7) vs. San Diego (3), XXIX
9 Pittsburgh (5) vs. Dallas (4), XIII
San Francisco (8) vs. Denver (1), XXIV
Dallas (7) vs. Buffalo (2), XXVII
Tampa Bay (6) vs. Oakland (3), XXXVII
8 Carolina (4) vs. New England (4), XXXVIII

Fewest Touchdowns, Both Teams, Game

2 Baltimore (1) vs. N.Y. Jets (1), III
3 In six games

POINTS AFTER TOUCHDOWN

Most (One-Point) Points After Touchdown, Game

7 San Francisco vs. Denver, XXIV
Dallas vs. Buffalo, XXVII
San Francisco vs. San Diego, XXIX
6 Washington vs. Denver, XXII
Tampa Bay vs. Oakland, XXXVII
5 Green Bay vs. Kansas City, I
Pittsburgh vs. Dallas, XIII
L.A. Raiders vs. Washington, XVIII
San Francisco vs. Miami, XIX
Chicago vs. New England, XX

Most (One-Point) Points After Touchdown, Both Teams, Game

9 Pittsburgh (5) vs. Dallas (4), XIII
Dallas (7) vs. Buffalo (2), XXVII
8 San Francisco (7) vs. Denver (1), XXIV
San Francisco (7) vs. San Diego (1), XXIX
7 Washington (6) vs. Denver (1), XXII
Washington (4) vs. Buffalo (3), XXVI
Denver (4) vs. Green Bay (3), XXXII

Fewest (One-Point) Points After Touchdown, Both Teams, Game

2 Baltimore (1) vs. N.Y. Jets (1), III
Baltimore (1) vs. Dallas (1), V
Minnesota (0) vs. Pittsburgh (2), IX

Most Two-Point Conversions, Game

2 San Diego vs. San Francisco, XXIX

Most Two-Point Conversions, Both Teams, Game

2 San Diego (2) vs. San Francisco (0), XXIX

FIELD GOALS

Most Field Goals Attempted, Game

5 N.Y. Jets vs. Baltimore, III
Dallas vs. Denver, XII
4 Green Bay vs. Oakland, II
Pittsburgh vs. Dallas, XX
San Francisco vs. Cincinnati, XVI; XXIII

Denver vs. N.Y. Giants, XXI
Denver vs. Atlanta, XXXIII
St. Louis vs. Tennessee, XXXIV

Most Field Goals Attempted, Both Teams, Game
7   N.Y. Jets (5) vs. Baltimore (2), III
    San Francisco (4) vs. Cincinnati (3), XXIII
    St. Louis (4) vs. Tennessee (3), XXXIV
    Denver (4) vs. Atlanta (3), XXXIII
6   Dallas (5) vs. Denver (1), XII
5   Green Bay (4) vs. Oakland (1), II
    Pittsburgh (4) vs. Dallas (1), X
    Oakland (3) vs. Philadelphia (2), XV
    Denver (4) vs. N.Y. Giants (1), XXI
    Dallas (3) vs. Buffalo (2), XXVIII

Fewest Field Goals Attempted, Both Teams, Game
1   Minnesota (0) vs. Miami (1), VIII
    San Francisco (0) vs. Denver (1), XXIV
    Philadelphia (0) vs. New England (1), XXXIX
2   Green Bay (0) vs. Kansas City (2), I
    Miami (1) vs. Washington (1), VII
    Minnesota (1) vs. Pittsburgh (1), IX
    Dallas (1) vs. Pittsburgh (1), XIII
    Dallas (1) vs. Buffalo (1), XXVII
    San Diego (1) vs. San Francisco (1), XXIX
    Denver (1) vs. Green Bay (1), XXXII

Most Field Goals, Game
4   Green Bay vs. Oakland, II
    San Francisco vs. Cincinnati, XVI
3   N.Y. Jets vs. Baltimore, III
    Kansas City vs. Minnesota, IV
    Miami vs. San Francisco, XIX
    Chicago vs. New England, XX
    Cincinnati vs. San Francisco, XXIII
    Washington vs. Buffalo, XXVI
    Dallas vs. Buffalo, XXVIII
    St. Louis vs. Tennessee, XXXIV

Most Field Goals, Both Teams, Game
5   Cincinnati (3) vs. San Francisco (2), XXIII
    Dallas (3) vs. Buffalo (2), XXVIII
4   Green Bay (4) vs. Oakland (0), II
    San Francisco (4) vs. Cincinnati (0), XVI
    Miami (3) vs. San Francisco (1), XIX
    Chicago (3) vs. New England (1), XX
    Washington (3) vs. Buffalo (1), XXVI
    Atlanta (2) vs. Denver (2), XXXIII
    St. Louis (3) vs. Tennessee (1), XXXIV
3   In 13 games

Fewest Field Goals, Both Teams, Game
0   Miami vs. Washington, VII
    Pittsburgh vs. Minnesota, IX
1   Green Bay (0) vs. Kansas City (1), I
    Minnesota (0) vs. Miami (1), VIII
    Pittsburgh (0) vs. Dallas (1), XIII
    Washington (0) vs. Denver (1), XXII
    San Francisco (0) vs. Denver (1), XXIV
    San Francisco (0) vs. San Diego (1), XXIX
    Philadelphia (0) vs. New England (1), XXXIX

SAFETIES
Most Safeties, Game
1   Pittsburgh vs. Minnesota, IX; vs. Dallas, X
    Chicago vs. New England, XX
    N.Y. Giants vs. Denver, XXI
    Buffalo vs. N.Y. Giants, XXV

FIRST DOWNS
Most First Downs, Game
31 San Francisco vs. Miami, XIX
29 New England vs. Carolina, XXXVIII
28 San Francisco vs. Denver, XXIV

San Francisco vs. San Diego, XXIX

Fewest First Downs, Game
9   Minnesota vs. Pittsburgh, IX
    Miami vs. Washington, XVII
10 Dallas vs. Baltimore, V
    Miami vs. Dallas, VI
11 Denver vs. Dallas, XII
    N.Y. Giants vs. Baltimore, XXXV
    Oakland vs. Tampa Bay, XXXVII

Most First Downs, Both Teams, Game
50 San Francisco (31) vs. Miami (19), XIX
    Tennessee (27) vs. St. Louis (23), XXXIV
49 Buffalo (25) vs. Washington (24), XXVI
48 San Francisco (28) vs. San Diego (20), XXIX

Fewest First Downs, Both Teams, Game
24 Dallas (10) vs. Baltimore (14), V
    N.Y. Giants (11) vs. Baltimore (13), XXXV
26 Minnesota (9) vs. Pittsburgh (17), IX
27 Pittsburgh (13) vs. Dallas (14), X

RUSHING
Most First Downs, Rushing, Game
16 San Francisco vs. Miami, XIX
15 Dallas vs. Miami, VI
14 Washington vs. Miami, XVII
    San Francisco vs. Denver, XXIV
    Denver vs. Green Bay, XXXII

Fewest First Downs, Rushing, Game
1   New England vs. Chicago, XX
    St. Louis vs. Tennessee, XXXIV
    Oakland vs. Tampa Bay, XXXVII
2   Minnesota vs. Kansas City, IV; vs. Pittsburgh, IX;
        vs. Oakland, XI
    Pittsburgh vs. Dallas, XIII
    Miami vs. San Francisco, XIX
    N.Y. Giants vs. Baltimore, XXXV
3   Miami vs. Dallas, VI
    Philadelphia vs. Oakland, XV
    New England vs. Green Bay, XXXI
    Carolina vs. New England, XXXVIII

Most First Downs, Rushing, Both Teams, Game
21 Washington (14) vs. Miami (7), XVII
19 Washington (13) vs. Denver (6), XXII
    San Francisco (14) vs. Denver (5), XXIV
18 Dallas (15) vs. Miami (3), VI
    Miami (13) vs. Minnesota (5), VIII
    San Francisco (16) vs. Miami (2), XIX
    N.Y. Giants (10) vs. Buffalo (8), XXV
    Denver (14) vs. Green Bay (4), XXXII

Fewest First Downs, Rushing, Both Teams, Game
7   Oakland (1) vs. Tampa Bay (6), XXXVII
8   Baltimore (4) vs. Dallas (4), V
    Pittsburgh (2) vs. Dallas (6), XIII
    N.Y. Giants (2) vs. Baltimore (6), XXXV
9   Philadelphia (3) vs. Oakland (6), XV

PASSING
Most First Downs, Passing, Game
19 New England vs. Carolina, XXXVIII
18 Buffalo vs. Washington, XXVI
    St. Louis vs. Tennessee, XXXIV
    Philadelphia vs. New England, XXXIX
17 Miami vs. San Francisco, XIX
    San Francisco vs. San Diego, XXIX

Fewest First Downs, Passing, Game
1   Denver vs. Dallas, XII
2   Miami vs. Washington, XVII
4   Miami vs. Minnesota, VIII

Most First Downs, Passing, Both Teams, Game
- 32   Miami (17) vs. San Francisco (15), XIX
  - Philadelphia (18) vs. New England (14), XXXIX
- 31   San Francisco (17) vs. San Diego (14), XXIX
  - St. Louis (18) vs. Tennessee (13), XXXIV
  - New England (19) vs. Carolina (12), XXXVIII
- 30   Buffalo (18) vs. Washington (12), XXVI

Fewest First Downs, Passing, Both Teams, Game
- 9   Denver (1) vs. Dallas (8), XII
- 10   Minnesota (5) vs. Pittsburgh (5), IX
- 11   Dallas (5) vs. Baltimore (6), V
  - Miami (2) vs. Washington (9), XVII

PENALTY

Most First Downs, Penalty, Game
- 4   Baltimore vs. Dallas, V
  - Miami vs. Minnesota, VIII
  - Cincinnati vs. San Francisco, XVI
  - Buffalo vs. Dallas, XXVII
  - St. Louis vs. Tennessee, XXXIV
- 3   Kansas City vs. Minnesota, IV
  - Minnesota vs. Oakland, XI
  - Buffalo vs. Washington, XXVI
  - Green Bay vs. Denver, XXXII
  - N.Y. Giants vs. Baltimore, XXXV
  - St. Louis vs. New England, XXXVI
  - Tampa Bay vs. Oakland, XXXVII
  - New England vs. Carolina, XXXVIII

Most First Downs, Penalty, Both Teams, Game
- 6   Cincinnati (4) vs. San Francisco (2), XVI
  - St. Louis (4) vs. Tennessee (2), XXXIV
- 5   Baltimore (4) vs. Dallas (1), V
  - Miami (4) vs. Minnesota (1), VIII
  - Buffalo (3) vs. Washington (2), XXVI
  - Green Bay (3) vs. Denver (2), XXXII
  - New England (3) vs. Carolina (2), XXXVIII
- 4   Kansas City (3) vs. Minnesota (1), IV
  - Buffalo (4) vs. Dallas (0), XXVII
  - N.Y. Giants (3) vs. Baltimore (1), XXXV
  - St. Louis (3) vs. New England (1), XXXVI
  - Tampa Bay (3) vs Oakland (1), XXXVII

Fewest First Downs, Penalty, Both Teams, Game
- 0   Dallas vs. Miami, VI
  - Miami vs. Washington, VII
  - Dallas vs. Pittsburgh, X
  - Miami vs. San Francisco, XIX
- 1   Green Bay (0) vs. Kansas City (1), I
  - Miami (0) vs. Washington (1), XVII
  - Cincinnati (0) vs. San Francisco (1), XXIII
  - San Francisco (0) vs. Denver (1), XXIV
  - Dallas (0) vs. Buffalo (1), XXVIII
  - Dallas (0) vs. Pittsburgh (1), XXX
  - Denver (0) vs. Atlanta (1), XXXIII

NET YARDS GAINED RUSHING AND PASSING

Most Yards Gained, Game
- 602   Washington vs. Denver, XXII
- 537   San Francisco vs. Miami, XIX
- 481   New England vs. Carolina, XXXVIII

Fewest Yards Gained, Game
- 119   Minnesota vs. Pittsburgh, IX
- 123   New England vs. Chicago, XX
- 152   N.Y. Giants vs. Baltimore, XXXV

Most Yards Gained, Both Teams, Game
- 929   Washington (602) vs. Denver (327), XXII
- 868   New England (481) vs. Carolina (387), XXXVIII
- 851   San Francisco (537) vs. Miami (314), XIX

Fewest Yards Gained, Both Teams, Game
- 396   N.Y. Giants (152) vs. Baltimore (244), XXXV
- 452   Minnesota (119) vs. Pittsburgh (333), IX

- 481   Washington (228) vs. Miami (253), VII
  - Denver (156) vs. Dallas (325), XII

RUSHING
ATTEMPTS

Most Attempts, Game
- 57   Pittsburgh vs. Minnesota, IX
- 53   Miami vs. Minnesota, VIII
- 52   Oakland vs. Minnesota, XI
  - Washington vs. Miami, XVII

Fewest Attempts, Game
- 9   Miami vs. San Francisco, XIX
- 11   New England vs. Chicago, XX
  - Oakland vs. Tampa Bay, XXXVII
- 13   New England vs. Green Bay, XXXI
  - St. Louis vs. Tennessee, XXXIV

Most Attempts, Both Teams, Game
- 81   Washington (52) vs. Miami (29), XVII
- 78   Pittsburgh (57) vs. Minnesota (21), IX
  - Oakland (52) vs. Minnesota (26), XI
- 77   Miami (53) vs. Minnesota (24), VIII
  - Pittsburgh (46) vs. Dallas (31), X

Fewest Attempts, Both Teams, Game
- 45   Philadelphia (17) vs. New England (28), XXXIX
- 47   St. Louis (22) vs. New England (25), XXXVI
- 49   Miami (9) vs. San Francisco (40), XIX
  - New England (13) vs. Green Bay (36), XXXI
  - St. Louis (13) vs. Tennessee (36), XXXIV
  - N.Y. Giants (16) vs. Baltimore (33), XXXV

YARDS GAINED

Most Yards Gained, Game
- 280   Washington vs. Denver, XXII
- 276   Washington vs. Miami, XVII
- 266   Oakland vs. Minnesota, XI

Fewest Yards Gained, Game
- 7   New England vs. Chicago, XX
- 17   Minnesota vs. Pittsburgh, IX
- 19   Oakland vs. Tampa Bay, XXXVII

Most Yards Gained, Both Teams, Game
- 377   Washington (280) vs. Denver (97), XXII
- 372   Washington (276) vs. Miami (96), XVII
- 338   N.Y. Giants (172) vs. Buffalo (166), XXV

Fewest Yards Gained, Both Teams, Game
- 157   Philadelphia (45) vs. New England (112), XXXIX
- 158   New England (43) vs. Green Bay (115), XXXI
- 159   Dallas (56) vs. Pittsburgh (103), XXX

AVERAGE GAIN
Highest Average Gain, Game
- 7.00   L.A. Raiders vs. Washington, XVIII (33-231)
  - Washington vs. Denver, XXII (40-280)
- 6.64   Buffalo vs. N.Y. Giants, XXV (25-166)
- 6.22   Baltimore vs. N.Y. Jets, III (23-143)

Lowest Average Gain, Game
- 0.64   New England vs. Chicago, XX (11-7)
- 0.81   Minnesota vs. Pittsburgh, IX (21-17)
- 1.73   Oakland vs. Tampa Bay, XXXVII (11-19)

TOUCHDOWNS
Most Touchdowns, Game
- 4   Chicago vs. New England, XX
  - Denver vs. Green Bay, XXXII
- 3   Green Bay vs. Kansas City, I
  - Miami vs. Minnesota, VIII
  - San Francisco vs. Denver, XXIV
  - Denver vs. Atlanta, XXXIII
- 2   Oakland vs. Minnesota, XI
  - Pittsburgh vs. Los Angeles, XIV
  - L.A. Raiders vs. Washington, XVIII

San Francisco vs. Miami, XIX
N.Y. Giants vs. Denver, XXI
Washington vs. Denver, XXII; vs. Buffalo, XXVI
Buffalo vs. N.Y. Giants, XXV
Dallas vs. Buffalo, XXVIII; vs. Pittsburgh, XXX
Tennessee vs. St. Louis, XXXIV

Fewest Touchdowns, Game
0   By 25 teams

Most Touchdowns, Both Teams, Game
4   Miami (3) vs. Minnesota (1), VIII
     Chicago (4) vs. New England (0), XX
     San Francisco (3) vs. Denver (1), XXIV
     Denver (4) vs. Green Bay (0), XXXII
3   In nine games

Fewest Touchdowns, Both Teams, Game
0   Pittsburgh vs. Dallas, X
     Oakland vs. Philadelphia, XV
     Cincinnati vs. San Francisco, XXIII
1   In 11 games

PASSING
ATTEMPTS
Most Passes Attempted, Game
59   Buffalo vs. Washington, XXVI
55   San Diego vs. San Francisco, XXIX
51   Philadelphia vs. New England, XXXIX

Fewest Passes Attempted, Game
7   Miami vs. Minnesota, VIII
11   Miami vs. Washington, VII
14   Pittsburgh vs. Minnesota, IX

Most Passes Attempted, Both Teams, Game
93   San Diego (55) vs. San Francisco (38), XXIX
92   Buffalo (59) vs. Washington (33), XXVI
85   Miami (50) vs. San Francisco (35), XIX

Fewest Passes Attempted, Both Teams, Game
35   Miami (7) vs. Minnesota (28), VIII
39   Miami (11) vs. Washington (28), VII
40   Pittsburgh (14) vs. Minnesota (26), IX
     Miami (17) vs. Washington (23), XVII

COMPLETIONS
Most Passes Completed, Game
32   New England vs. Carolina, XXXVIII
31   Buffalo vs. Dallas, XXVIII
30   Philadelphia vs. New England, XXXIX

Fewest Passes Completed, Game
4   Miami vs. Washington, XVII
6   Miami vs. Minnesota, VIII
8   Miami vs. Washington, VII
     Denver vs. Dallas, XII

Most Passes Completed, Both Teams, Game
53   Miami (29) vs. San Francisco (24), XIX
     Philadelphia (30) vs. New England (23), XXXIX
52   San Diego (27) vs. San Francisco (25), XXIX
50   Buffalo (31) vs. Dallas (19), XXVIII

Fewest Passes Completed, Both Teams, Game
19   Miami (4) vs. Washington (15), XVII
20   Pittsburgh (9) vs. Minnesota (11), IX
22   Miami (8) vs. Washington (14), VII

COMPLETION PERCENTAGE
Highest Completion Percentage, Game (20 attempts)
88.0   N.Y. Giants vs. Denver, XXI (25-22)
75.0   San Francisco vs. Denver, XXIV (32-24)
73.5   Cincinnati vs. San Francisco, XVI (34-25)

Lowest Completion Percentage, Game (20 attempts)
32.0   Denver vs. Dallas, XII (25-8)
37.9   Denver vs. San Francisco, XXIV (29-11)
38.5   Denver vs. Washington, XXII (39-15)
     N.Y. Giants vs. Baltimore, XXXV (39-15)

YARDS GAINED
Most Yards Gained, Game
407   St. Louis vs. Tennessee, XXXIV
354   New England vs. Carolina, XXXVIII
341   San Francisco vs. Cincinnati, XXIII

Fewest Yards Gained, Game
35   Denver vs. Dallas, XII
63   Miami vs. Minnesota, VIII
69   Miami vs. Washington, VII

Most Yards Gained, Both Teams, Game
649   New England (354) vs. Carolina (295), XXXVIII
615   San Francisco (326) vs. Miami (289), XIX
     St. Louis (407) vs. Tennessee (208), XXXIV
603   San Francisco (316) vs. San Diego (287), XXIX

Fewest Yards Gained, Both Teams, Game
156   Miami (69) vs. Washington (87), VII
186   Pittsburgh (84) vs. Minnesota (102), IX
204   Miami (80) vs. Washington (124), XVII

TIMES SACKED
Most Times Sacked, Game
7   Dallas vs. Pittsburgh, X
     New England vs. Chicago, XX
6   Kansas City vs. Green Bay, I
     Washington vs. L.A. Raiders, XVIII
     Denver vs. San Francisco, XXIV
5   Dallas vs. Denver, XII; vs. Pittsburgh, XIII
     Cincinnati vs. San Francisco, XVI; XXIII
     Denver vs. Washington, XXII
     Buffalo vs. Washington, XXVI
     Green Bay vs. New England, XXXI
     New England vs. Green Bay, XXXI
     Oakland vs. Tampa Bay, XXXVII

Fewest Times Sacked, Game
0   Baltimore vs. N.Y. Jets, III; vs. Dallas, V
     Minnesota vs. Pittsburgh, IX
     Pittsburgh vs. Los Angeles, XIV
     Philadelphia vs. Oakland, XV
     Washington vs. Buffalo, XXVI
     Denver vs. Green Bay, XXXII; vs. Atlanta, XXXIII
     Tampa Bay vs. Oakland, XXXVII
     New England vs. Carolina, XXXVIII
1   By 13 teams

Most Times Sacked, Both Teams, Game
10   New England (7) vs. Chicago (3), XX
     Green Bay (5) vs. New England (5), XXXI
9   Kansas City (6) vs. Green Bay (3), I
     Dallas (7) vs. Pittsburgh (2), X
     Dallas (5) vs. Denver (4), XII
     Dallas (5) vs. Pittsburgh (4), XIII
     Cincinnati (5) vs. San Francisco (4), XXIII
8   Washington (6) vs. L.A. Raiders (2), XVIII

Fewest Times Sacked, Both Teams, Game
1   Philadelphia (0) vs. Oakland (1), XV
     Denver (0) vs. Green Bay (1), XXXII
2   Baltimore (0) vs. N.Y. Jets (2), III
     Baltimore (0) vs. Dallas (2), V
     Minnesota (0) vs. Pittsburgh (2), IX
     Denver (0) vs. Atlanta (2), XXXIII
3   In five games

TOUCHDOWNS
Most Touchdowns, Game
6   San Francisco vs. San Diego, XXIX
5   San Francisco vs. Denver, XXIV
4   Pittsburgh vs. Dallas, XIII
     Washington vs. Denver, XXII
     Dallas vs. Buffalo, XXVII

Fewest Touchdowns, Game
0   By 19 teams

Most Touchdowns, Both Teams, Game
- 7 Pittsburgh (4) vs. Dallas (3), XIII
  San Francisco (6) vs. San Diego (1), XXIX
- 6 Carolina (3) vs. New England (3), XXXVIII
- 5 Washington (4) vs. Denver (1), XXII
  San Francisco (5) vs. Denver (0), XXIV
  Dallas (4) vs. Buffalo (1), XXVII
  Philadelphia (3) vs. New England (2), XXXIX

Fewest Touchdowns, Both Teams, Game
- 0 N.Y. Jets vs. Baltimore, III
  Miami vs. Minnesota, VIII
  Buffalo vs. Dallas, XXVIII
- 1 In seven games

INTERCEPTIONS BY
Most Interceptions By, Game
- 5 Tampa Bay vs. Oakland, XXXVII
- 4 N.Y. Jets vs. Baltimore, III
  Dallas vs. Denver, XII
  Washington vs. Buffalo, XXVI
  Dallas vs. Buffalo, XXVII
  Green Bay vs. New England, XXXI
  Baltimore vs. N.Y. Giants, XXXV
- 3 By 13 teams

Most Interceptions By, Both Teams, Game
- 6 Baltimore (3) vs. Dallas (3), V
  Tampa Bay (5) vs. Oakland (1), XXXVII
- 5 Washington (4) vs. Buffalo (1), XXVI
- 4 In 10 games

Fewest Interceptions By, Both Teams, Game
- 0 Buffalo vs. N.Y. Giants, XXV
  St. Louis vs. Tennessee, XXXIV
- 1 Oakland (0) vs. Green Bay (1), II
  Miami (0) vs. Dallas (1), VI
  Minnesota (0) vs. Miami (1), VIII
  N.Y. Giants (0) vs. Denver (1), XXI
  Cincinnati (0) vs. San Francisco (1), XXIII
  New England (0) vs. Carolina (1), XXXVIII

YARDS GAINED
Most Yards Gained, Game
- 172 Tampa Bay vs. Oakland (12), XXXVII
- 136 Denver vs. Atlanta, XXXIII
- 95 Miami vs. Washington, VII

Most Yards Gained, Both Teams, Game
- 184 Tampa Bay (172) vs. Oakland (12), XXXVII
- 137 Denver (136) vs. Atlanta (1), XXXIII
- 95 Miami (95) vs. Washington (0), VII

TOUCHDOWNS
Most Touchdowns, Game
- 3 Tampa Bay vs. Oakland, XXXVII
- 1 Green Bay vs. Oakland, II
  Oakland vs. Minnesota, XI
  L.A. Raiders vs. Washington, XVIII
  Chicago vs. New England, XX
  Baltimore vs. N.Y. Giants, XXXV
  New England vs. St. Louis, XXXVI

PUNTING
Most Punts, Game
- 11 N.Y. Giants vs. Baltimore, XXXV
- 10 Baltimore vs. N.Y. Giants, XXXV
- 9 Dallas vs. Baltimore, V

Fewest Punts, Game
- 1 Atlanta vs. Denver, XXXIII
  Denver vs. Atlanta, XXXIII
- 2 Pittsburgh vs. Los Angeles, XIV
  Denver vs. N.Y. Giants, XXI
  St. Louis vs. Tennessee, XXXIV

- 3 By 11 teams

Most Punts, Both Teams, Game
- 21 N.Y. Giants (11) vs. Baltimore (10), XXXV
- 15 Washington (8) vs. L.A. Raiders (7), XVIII
  New England (8) vs. Green Bay (7), XXXI
- 13 Dallas (9) vs. Baltimore (4), V
  Pittsburgh (7) vs. Minnesota (6), IX

Fewest Punts, Both Teams, Game
- 2 Atlanta (1) vs. Denver (1), XXXIII
- 5 Denver (2) vs. N.Y. Giants (3), XXI
  St. Louis (2) vs. Tennessee (3), XXXIV
- 6 Oakland (3) vs. Philadelphia (3), XV

AVERAGE YARDAGE
Highest Average, Game (4 punts)
- 48.75 San Diego vs. San Francisco, XXIX (4-195)
- 48.50 Kansas City vs. Minnesota, IV (4-194)
- 46.25 San Francisco vs. Cincinnati, XVI (4-185)

Lowest Average, Game (4 punts)
- 31.00 Tampa Bay vs. Oakland, XXXVII (5-155)
- 31.20 Washington vs. Miami, VII (5-156)
- 32.38 Washington vs. L.A. Raiders, XVIII (8-259)

PUNT RETURNS
Most Punt Returns, Game
- 6 Washington vs. Miami, XVII
  Green Bay vs. New England, XXXI
- 5 By seven teams

Fewest Punt Returns, Game
- 0 Minnesota vs. Miami, VIII
  Buffalo vs. N.Y. Giants, XXV
  Washington vs. Buffalo, XXVI
  Denver vs. Green Bay, XXXII
  Green Bay vs. Denver, XXXII
  Atlanta vs. Denver, XXXIII
  Denver vs. Atlanta, XXXIII
- 1 By 19 teams

Most Punt Returns, Both Teams, Game
- 10 Green Bay (6) vs. New England (4), XXXI
- 9 Pittsburgh (5) vs. Minnesota (4), IX
- 8 Green Bay (5) vs. Oakland (3), II
  Baltimore (5) vs. Dallas (3), V
  Washington (6) vs. Miami (2), XVII
  N.Y. Giants (5) vs. Baltimore (3), XXXV

Fewest Punt Returns, Both Teams, Game
- 0 Denver vs. Green Bay, XXXII
  Atlanta vs. Denver, XXXIII
- 2 Dallas (1) vs. Miami (1), VI
  Denver (1) vs. N.Y. Giants (1), XXI
  Buffalo (0) vs. N.Y. Giants (2), XXV
  Buffalo (1) vs. Dallas (1), XXVIII
- 3 Kansas City (1) vs. Minnesota (2), IV
  Minnesota (0) vs. Miami (3), VIII
  Washington (1) vs. Denver (2), XXII
  Washington (0) vs. Buffalo (3), XXVI
  Dallas (1) vs. Pittsburgh (2), XXX
  Tennessee (1) vs. St. Louis (2), XXXIV

YARDS GAINED
Most Yards Gained, Game
- 90 Green Bay vs. New England, XXXI
- 56 San Francisco vs. Cincinnati, XXIII
- 52 Washington vs. Miami, XVII

Fewest Yards Gained, Game
- −1 Dallas vs. Miami, VI
  Tennessee vs. St. Louis, XXXIV
- 0 By 12 teams

Most Yards Gained, Both Teams, Game
- 120 Green Bay (90) vs. New England (30), XXXI
- 80 N.Y. Giants (46) vs. Baltimore (34), XXXV

74   Washington (52) vs. Miami (22), XVII
Fewest Yards Gained, Both Teams, Game
  0   Denver vs. Green Bay, XXXII
       Atlanta vs. Denver, XXXIII
  7   Tennessee (-1) vs. St. Louis (8), XXXIV
  9   Washington (0) vs. Bufffalo (9), XXVI

AVERAGE RETURN
Highest Average, Game (3 returns)
 18.7   San Francisco vs. Cincinnati, XXIII (3-56)
 15.0   Green Bay vs. New England, XXXI (6-90)
 12.7   San Francisco vs. Denver, XXIV (3-38)

TOUCHDOWNS
Most Touchdowns, Game
       None

KICKOFF RETURNS
Most Kickoff Returns, Game
  9   Denver vs. San Francisco, XXIV
       Oakland vs. Tampa Bay, XXXVII
  8   San Diego vs. San Francisco, XXIX
  7   By eight teams
Fewest Kickoff Returns, Game
  1   N.Y. Jets vs. Baltimore, III
       L.A. Raiders vs. Washington, XVIII
       Washington vs. Buffalo, XXVI
  2   By eight teams
Most Kickoff Returns, Both Teams, Game
 13   Oakland (9) vs. Tampa Bay (4), XXXVII
 12   Denver (9) vs. San Francisco (3), XXIV
       San Diego (8) vs. San Francisco (4), XXIX
 11   Los Angeles (6) vs. Pittsburgh (5), XIV
       Miami (7) vs. San Francisco (4), XIX
       New England (7) vs. Chicago (4), XX
       Green Bay (6) vs. Denver (5), XXXII
Fewest Kickoff Returns, Both Teams, Game
  5   N.Y. Jets (1) vs. Baltimore (4), III
       Miami (2) vs. Washington (3), VII
       Washington (1) vs. Buffalo (4), XXVI
  6   In three games

YARDS GAINED
Most Yards Gained, Game
 244   San Diego vs. San Francisco, XXIX
 227   Atlanta vs. Denver, XXXIII
 222   Miami vs. Washington, XVII
Fewest Yards Gained, Game
 16   Washington vs. Buffalo, XXVI
 17   L.A. Raiders vs. Washington, XVIII
 25   N.Y. Jets vs. Baltimore, III
Most Yards Gained, Both Teams, Game
 292   San Diego (244) vs. San Francisco (48), XXIX
 289   Green Bay (154) vs. New England (135), XXXI
 281   N.Y. Giants (170) vs. Baltimore (111), XXXV
Fewest Yards Gained, Both Teams, Game
 78   Miami (33) vs. Washington (45), VII
 82   Pittsburgh (32) vs. Minnesota (50), IX
 92   San Francisco (40) vs. Cincinnati (52), XVI

AVERAGE GAIN
Highest Average, Game (3 returns)
 44.0   Cincinnati vs. San Francisco, XXIII (3-132)
 38.5   Green Bay vs. New England, XXXI (4-154)
 37.0   Miami vs. Washington, XVII (6-222)

TOUCHDOWNS
Most Touchdowns, Game
  1   Miami vs. Washington, XVII
       Cincinnati vs. San Francisco, XXIII

San Diego vs. San Francisco, XXIX
Green Bay vs. New England, XXXI
Atlanta vs. Denver, XXXIII
Baltimore vs. N.Y. Giants, XXXV
N.Y. Giants vs. Baltimore, XXXV
Most Touchdowns, Both Teams, Game
  2   Baltimore (1) vs. N.Y. Giants (1), XXXV

PENALTIES
Most Penalties, Game
 12   Dallas vs. Denver, XII
       Carolina vs. New England, XXXVIII
 10   Dallas vs. Baltimore, V
  9   Dallas vs. Pittsburgh, XIII
       Green Bay vs. Denver, XXXII
       Baltimore vs. N.Y. Giants, XXXV
Fewest Penalties, Game
  0   Miami vs. Dallas, VI
       Pittsburgh vs. Dallas, X
       Denver vs. San Francisco, XXIV
       Atlanta vs. Denver, XXXIII
  1   Green Bay vs. Oakland, II
       Miami vs. Minnesota, VIII; vs. San Francisco, XIX
       Buffalo vs. Dallas, XXVIII
  2   By six teams
Most Penalties, Both Teams, Game
 20   Dallas (12) vs. Denver (8), XII
       Carolina (12) vs. New England (8), XXXVIII
 16   Cincinnati (8) vs. San Francisco (8), XVI
       Green Bay (9) vs. Denver (7), XXXII
 15   St. Louis (8) vs. Tennessee (7), XXXIV
       Baltimore (9) vs. N.Y. Giants (6), XXXV
Fewest Penalties, Both Teams, Game
  2   Pittsburgh (0) vs. Dallas (2), X
  3   Miami (0) vs. Dallas (3), VI
       Miami (1) vs. San Francisco (2), XIX
  4   Denver (0) vs. San Francisco (4), XXIV
       Atlanta (0) vs. Denver (4), XXXIII

YARDS PENALIZED
Most Yards Penalized, Game
 133   Dallas vs. Baltimore, X
 122   Pittsburgh vs. Minnesota, IX
 94   Dallas vs. Denver, XII
Fewest Yards Penalized, Game
  0   Miami vs. Dallas, VI
       Pittsburgh vs. Dallas, X
       Denver vs. San Francisco, XXIV
       Atlanta vs. Denver, XXXIII
  4   Miami vs. Minnesota, VIII
 10   Miami vs. San Francisco, XIX
       San Francisco vs. Miami, XIX
       Buffalo vs. Dallas, XXVIII
Most Yards Penalized, Both Teams, Game
 164   Dallas (133) vs. Baltimore (31), V
 154   Dallas (94) vs. Denver (60), XII
 140   Pittsburgh (122) vs. Minnesota (18), IX
Fewest Yards Penalized, Both Teams, Game
 15   Miami (0) vs. Dallas (15), VI
 20   Pittsburgh (0) vs. Dallas (20), X
       Miami (10) vs. San Francisco (10), XIX
 38   Denver (0) vs. San Francisco (38), XXIV

FUMBLES
Most Fumbles, Game
  8   Buffalo vs. Dallas, XXVII
  6   Dallas vs. Denver, XII
       Buffalo vs. Washington, XXVI
  5   Baltimore vs. Dallas, V

Fewest Fumbles, Game
- 0 By 17 teams

Most Fumbles, Both Teams, Game
- 12 Buffalo (8) vs. Dallas (4), XXVII
- 10 Dallas (6) vs. Denver (4), XII
- 8 Dallas (4) vs. Pittsburgh (4), X

Fewest Fumbles, Both Teams, Game
- 0 Los Angeles vs. Pittsburgh, XIV
   Green Bay vs. New England, XXXI
- 1 Oakland (0) vs. Minnesota (1), XI
   Oakland (0) vs. Philadelphia (1), XV
   Denver (0) vs. Washington (1), XXII
   N.Y. Giants (0) vs. Buffalo (1), XXV
   Denver (0) vs. Atlanta (1), XXXIII
- 2 In eight games

Most Fumbles Lost, Game
- 5 Buffalo vs. Dallas, XXVII
- 4 Baltimore vs. Dallas, V
   Denver vs. Dallas, XII
   New England vs. Chicago, XX
- 2 In many games

Most Fumbles Lost, Both Teams, Game
- 7 Buffalo (5) vs. Dallas (2), XXVII
- 6 Denver (4) vs. Dallas (2), XII
   New England (4) vs. Chicago (2), XX
- 5 Baltimore (4) vs. Dallas (1), V

Fewest Fumbles Lost, Both Teams, Game
- 0 Green Bay vs. Kansas City, I
   Dallas vs. Pittsburgh, X
   Los Angeles vs. Pittsburgh, XIV
   Denver vs. N.Y. Giants, XXI; vs. Washington, XXII
   Buffalo vs. N.Y. Giants, XXV
   San Diego vs. San Francisco, XXIX
   Dallas vs. Pittsburgh, XXX
   Green Bay vs. New England, XXXI
   St. Louis vs. Tennessee, XXXIV
   Oakland vs. Tampa Bay, XXXVII

Most Fumbles Recovered, Game
- 8 Dallas vs. Denver, XII (4 own, 4 opp.)
- 6 Dallas vs. Buffalo, XXVII (1 own, 5 opp.)
- 5 Chicago vs. New England, XX (1 own, 4 opp.)

TURNOVERS
(Number of times losing the ball on interceptions and fumbles.)

Most Turnovers, Game
- 9 Buffalo vs. Dallas, XXVII
- 8 Denver vs. Dallas, XII
- 7 Baltimore vs. Dallas, V

Fewest Turnovers, Game
- 0 Green Bay vs. Oakland, II
   Miami vs. Minnesota, VIII
   Pittsburgh vs. Dallas, X
   Oakland vs. Minnesota, XI; vs. Philadelphia, XV
   N.Y. Giants vs. Denver, XXI; vs. Buffalo, XXV
   San Francisco vs. Denver, XXIV; vs. San Diego, XXIX
   Buffalo vs. N.Y. Giants, XXV
   Dallas vs. Pittsburgh, XXX
   Green Bay vs. New England, XXXI
   St. Louis vs. Tennessee, XXXIV
   Tennessee vs. St. Louis, XXXIV
   Baltimore vs. N.Y. Giants, XXXV
   New England vs. St. Louis, XXXVI
- 1 By many teams

Most Turnovers, Both Teams, Game
- 11 Baltimore (7) vs. Dallas (4), V
   Buffalo (9) vs. Dallas (2), XXVII
- 10 Denver (8) vs. Dallas (2), XII
- 8 New England (6) vs. Chicago (2), XX

Fewest Turnovers, Both Teams, Game
- 0 Buffalo vs. N.Y. Giants, XXV

St. Louis vs. Tennessee, XXXIV
- 1 N.Y. Giants (0) vs. Denver (1), XXI
- 2 Green Bay (1) vs. Kansas City (1), I
   Miami (0) vs. Minnesota (2), VIII
   Cincinnati (1) vs. San Francisco (1), XXIII
   Carolina (1) vs. New England (1), XXXVIII

Compiled by Elias Sports Bureau

Throughout this all-time postseason record section, the following abbreviations are used to indicate various levels of postseason games:

SB Super Bowl (1966 to date)

AFC AFC Championship Game (1970 to date) or AFL Championship Game (1960-69)

NFC NFC Championship Game (1970 to date) or NFL Championship Game (1933-69)

AFC-D AFC Divisional Playoff Game (1970 to date), AFC Second-Round Playoff Game (1982), AFL Inter-Divisional Playoff Game (1969), or special playoff game to break tie for AFL Division Championship (1963, 1968)

NFC-D NFC Divisional Playoff Game (1970 to date), NFC Second-Round Playoff Game (1982), NFL Conference Championship Game (1967-69), or special playoff game to break tie for NFL Division or Conference Championship (1941, 1943, 1947, 1950, 1952, 1957, 1958, 1965)

AFC-FR AFC First-Round Playoff Game (1978 to date)

NFC-FR NFC First-Round Playoff Game (1978 to date)

Year indicates season in which game took place and does not necessarily reflect calendar year.

POSTSEASON GAME COMPOSITE STANDINGS

	W	L	PCT.	PTS.	OP
Baltimore Ravens	5	2	.714	142	73
Carolina Panthers	4	2	.667	140	115
Green Bay Packers	24	14	.632	888	723
New England Patriots#	16	10	.615	528	512
San Francisco 49ers	25	17	.595	1,044	853
Washington Redskins*	22	15	.595	778	642
Dallas Cowboys	32	22	.593	1,281	1,008
Oakland Raiders**	25	18	.581	1,028	797
Pittsburgh Steelers	24	18	.571	959	866
Denver Broncos	16	14	.533	650	747
Miami Dolphins	20	19	.513	780	848
Jacksonville Jaguars	4	4	.500	208	200
Philadelphia Eagles	16	16	.500	606	561
Buffalo Bills	14	15	.483	681	658
Chicago Bears	14	15	.483	598	585
Indianapolis Colts***	13	15	.464	538	581
Tampa Bay Buccaneers	6	7	.462	206	238
Tennessee Titans†	14	17	.452	563	732
New York Jets	8	10	.444	372	352
St. Louis Rams††	19	24	.442	770	944
New York Giants	16	21	.432	647	699
Atlanta Falcons	6	8	.429	298	331
Minnesota Vikings	18	24	.429	824	957
Cincinnati Bengals	5	7	.417	246	257
Detroit Lions	7	10	.412	365	404
Kansas City Chiefs****	8	12	.400	332	422
San Diego Chargers†††	7	12	.368	349	448
Cleveland Browns	11	20	.355	629	728
Seattle Seahawks	3	7	.300	192	219
Arizona Cardinals††††	2	5	.286	122	182
New Orleans Saints	1	5	.167	103	185

* *One game played when franchise was in Boston (lost 21-6).*

** *12 games played when franchise was in Los Angeles (won 6, lost 6, 268 points scored, 224 points allowed).*

*** *15 games played when franchise was in Baltimore (won 8, lost 7, 264 points scored, 262 points allowed).*

**** *One game played when franchise was Dallas Texans (won 20-17).*

Two games played when franchise was in Boston (won 26-8, lost 51-10).

† *22 games played when franchise was in Houston and known as the Oilers (won 9, lost 13, 371 points scored, 533 points allowed).*

†† *One game played when franchise was in Cleveland (won 15-14), 32 games played when franchise was in Los Ange-*

les (won 12, lost 20, 486 points scored, 683 points allowed).

††† *One game played when franchise was in Los Angeles (lost 24-16).*

†††† *Two games played when franchise was in Chicago (won 28-21, lost 7-0), three games played when franchise was in St. Louis (lost 30-14, lost 35-23, lost 41-16).*

INDIVIDUAL RECORDS

SERVICE

Most Games, Career

29 Jerry Rice, San Francisco-Oakland-Seattle (SB 4, NFC 6, AFC 1, NFC-D 11, AFC-D 2, NFC-FR 4, AFC-FR 1)

27 D.D. Lewis, Dallas (SB 5, NFC 9, NFC-D 12, NFC-FR 1)

26 Larry Cole, Dallas (SB 5, NFC 8, NFC-D 12, NFC-FR 1)

Bill Romanowski, San Francisco-Philadelphia-Denver-Oakland (SB 5, NFC 5, AFC 3, NFC-D 6, AFC-D 4, NFC-FR 1, AFC-FR 2)

Most Games, Head Coach

36 Tom Landry, Dallas

Don Shula, Baltimore-Miami

24 Chuck Noll, Pittsburgh

22 Bud Grant, Minnesota

Most Games Won, Head Coach

20 Tom Landry, Dallas

19 Don Shula, Baltimore-Miami

16 Chuck Noll, Pittsburgh

Joe Gibbs, Washington

Most Games Lost, Head Coach

17 Don Shula, Baltimore-Miami

16 Tom Landry, Dallas

12 Bud Grant, Minnesota

Marty Schottenheimer, Cleveland-Kansas City-San Diego

SCORING

POINTS

Most Points, Career

153 Gary Anderson, Pittsburgh-Philadelphia-San Francisco-Minnesota-Tennessee, (57-pat, 32-fg)

132 Jerry Rice, San Francisco-Oakland-Seattle, 29 games (22-td)

126 Thurman Thomas, Buffalo, 21 games (21-td)

Emmitt Smith, Dallas, 17 games (21-td)

Most Points, Game

30 Ricky Watters, NFC-D: San Francisco vs. N.Y. Giants, 1993 (5-td)

19 Pat Harder, NFC-D: Detroit vs. Los Angeles, 1952 (2-td, 4-pat, 1-fg)

Paul Hornung, NFC: Green Bay vs. N.Y. Giants, 1961 (1-td, 4-pat, 3-fg)

18 By many players

Most Consecutive Games Scoring

19 George Blanda, Chi. Bears-Houston-Oakland, 1956-1975

16 Norm Johnson, Seattle-Atlanta-Pittsburgh, 1983-1997

15 Roy Gerela, Houston-Pittsburgh, 1969-1978

Adam Vinatieri, New England, 1996-2004 (current)

TOUCHDOWNS

Most Touchdowns, Career

22 Jerry Rice, San Francisco-Oakland-Seattle, 29 games (22-p)

21 Thurman Thomas, Buffalo, 21 games (16-r, 5-p)

Emmitt Smith, Dallas, 17 games (19-r, 2-p)

17 Franco Harris, Pittsburgh, 19 games (16-r, 1-p)

Most Touchdowns, Game

5 Ricky Watters, NFC-D: San Francisco vs. N.Y. Giants, 1993 (5-r)

3 Andy Farkas, NFC-D: Washington vs. N.Y. Giants, 1943 (3-r)

Tom Fears, NFC-D: Los Angeles vs. Chi. Bears, 1950 (3-p)
Otto Graham, NFC: Cleveland vs. Detroit, 1954 (3-r)
Gary Collins, NFC: Cleveland vs. Baltimore, 1964 (3-p)
Craig Baynham, NFC-D: Dallas vs. Cleveland, 1967
    (2-r, 1-p)
Fred Biletnikoff, AFC-D: Oakland vs. Kansas City, 1968 (3-p)
Tom Matte, NFC: Baltimore vs. Cleveland, 1968 (3-r)
Larry Schreiber, NFC-D: San Francisco vs. Dallas, 1972 (3-r)
Larry Csonka, AFC: Miami vs. Oakland, 1973 (3-r)
Franco Harris, AFC-D: Pittsburgh vs. Buffalo, 1974 (3-r)
Preston Pearson, NFC: Dallas vs. Los Angeles, 1975 (3-p)
Dave Casper, AFC-D: Oakland vs. Baltimore, 1977 (OT) (3-p)
Alvin Garrett, NFC-FR: Washington vs. Detroit, 1982 (3-p)
John Riggins, NFC-D: Washington vs. L.A. Rams, 1983 (3-r)
Roger Craig, SB: San Francisco vs. Miami, 1984 (1-r, 2-p)
Jerry Rice, NFC-D: San Francisco vs. Minnesota, 1988 (3-p)
Jerry Rice, SB: San Francisco vs. Denver, 1989 (3-p)
Kenneth Davis, AFC: Buffalo vs. L.A. Raiders, 1990 (3-r)
Andre Reed, AFC-FR: Buffalo vs. Houston, 1992 (OT)
    (3-p)
Sterling Sharpe, NFC-FR: Green Bay vs. Detroit, 1993 (3-p)
Napoleon McCallum, AFC-FR: L.A. Raiders vs. Denver,
    1993 (3-r)
Thurman Thomas, AFC: Buffalo vs. Kansas City, 1993 (3-r)
William Floyd, NFC-D: San Francisco vs. Chicago, 1994 (3-r)
Ricky Watters, SB: San Francisco vs. San Diego, 1994
    (1-r, 2-p)
Jerry Rice, SB: San Francisco vs. San Diego, 1994 (3-p)
Emmitt Smith, NFC: Dallas vs. Green Bay, 1995 (3-r)
Curtis Martin, AFC-D: New England vs. Pittsburgh, 1996 (3-r)
Terrell Davis, SB: Denver vs. Green Bay, 1997 (3-r)
Mario Bates, NFC-D: Arizona vs. Minnesota, 1998 (3-r)
Leroy Hoard, NFC-D: Minnesota vs. Arizona, 1998 (2-r, 1-p)
Willie Jackson, NFC-FR: New Orleans vs. St. Louis, 2000
    (3-p)
Amani Toomer, NFC-FR: N.Y. Giants vs. San Francisco,
    2002 (3-p)
Shaun Alexander, NFC-FR: Seattle vs. Green Bay, 2003
    (OT) (3-r)

Most Consecutive Games Scoring Touchdowns
9   Thurman Thomas, Buffalo, 1992-98
8   John Stallworth, Pittsburgh, 1978-1983
    Emmitt Smith, Dallas, 1993-96
7   John Riggins, Washington, 1982-84
    Marcus Allen, L.A. Raiders, 1982-85
    Terrell Davis, Denver, 1996-98

POINTS AFTER TOUCHDOWN
Most (One-Point) Points After Touchdown, Career
57 Gary Anderson, Pittsburgh-Philadelphia-San Francisco-
    Minnesota-Tennessee, 22 games (57 att)
49 George Blanda, Chi. Bears-Houston-Oakland, 19 games
    (49 att)
42 Mike Cofer, San Francisco, 12 games (46 att)
Most (One-Point) Points After Touchdown, Game
8   Lou Groza, NFC: Cleveland vs. Detroit, 1954 (8 att)
    Jim Martin, NFC: Detroit vs. Cleveland, 1957 (8 att)
    George Blanda, AFC-D: Oakland vs. Houston, 1969 (8 att)
    Mike Hollis, AFC-D: Jacksonville vs. Miami, 1999 (8 att)
7   Danny Villanueva, NFC-D: Dallas vs. Cleveland, 1967 (7 att)
    Raul Allegre, NFC-D: N.Y. Giants vs. San Francisco, 1986
    (7 att)
    Mike Cofer, SB: San Francisco vs. Denver, 1989 (8 att)
    Lin Elliott, SB: Dallas vs. Buffalo, 1992 (7 att)
    Doug Brien, SB: San Francisco vs. San Diego, 1994 (7 att)
    Gary Anderson, NFC-FR: Philadelphia vs. Detroit, 1995 (7 att)
    Jeff Wilkins, NFC-D: St. Louis vs. Minnesota, 1999 (7 att)
    Mike Vanderjagt, AFC-FR: Indianapolis vs. Denver, 2004
    (7 att)
6   George Blair, AFC: San Diego vs. Boston, 1963 (6 att)

Mark Moseley, NFC-D: Washington vs. L.A. Rams, 1983 (6 att)
Uwe von Schamann, AFC: Miami vs. Pittsburgh, 1984 (6 att)
Ali Haji-Sheikh, SB: Washington vs. Denver, 1987 (6 att)
Scott Norwood, AFC: Buffalo vs. L.A. Raiders, 1990 (7 att)
Jeff Jaeger, AFC-FR: L.A. Raiders vs. Denver, 1993 (6 att)
Jason Elam, AFC-FR: Denver vs. Jacksonville, 1997 (6 att)
Jeff Wilkins, NFC-D: St. Louis vs. Green Bay, 2001 (6 att)
Martin Gramatica, SB: Tampa Bay vs. Oakland, 2002 (6 att)
Jay Feely, NFC-D: Atlanta vs. St. Louis, 2004 (6 att)
Most (Kicking) Points After Touchdown, No Misses, Career
57 Gary Anderson, Pittsburgh-Philadelphia-San Francisco-
    Minnesota-Tennessee, 22 games
49 George Blanda, Chi. Bears-Houston-Oakland, 19 games
41 Rafael Septien, L.A. Rams-Dallas, 15 games
Most Two-Point Conversions, Career
2   Terrell Owens, San Francisco-Philadelphia, 10 games
Most Two-Point Conversions, Game
2   Terrell Owens, NFC-FR: San Francisco vs. N.Y. Giants,
    2002

FIELD GOALS
Most Field Goals Attempted, Career
40 Gary Anderson, Pittsburgh-Philadelphia-San Francisco-
    Minnesota-Tennessee, 22 games
39 George Blanda, Chi. Bears-Houston-Oakland, 19 games
31 Mark Moseley, Washington-Cleveland, 11 games
    Adam Vinatieri, New England, 15 games
Most Field Goals Attempted, Game
6   George Blanda, AFC: Oakland vs. Houston, 1967
    David Ray, NFC-D: Los Angeles vs. Dallas, 1973
    Mark Moseley, AFC-D: Cleveland vs. N.Y. Jets, 1986 (OT)
    Matt Bahr, NFC: N.Y. Giants vs. San Francisco, 1990
    Steve Christie, AFC: Buffalo vs. Miami, 1992
    Jeff Wilkins, NFC-D: St. Louis vs. Carolina, 2003 (2 OT)
5   By many players
Most Field Goals, Career
32 Gary Anderson, Pittsburgh-Philadelphia-San Francisco-
    Minnesota-Tennessee, 22 games
24 Adam Vinatieri, New England, 15 games
22 George Blanda, Chi. Bears-Houston-Oakland, 19 games
    Steve Christie, Buffalo, 12 games
Most Field Goals, Game
5   Chuck Nelson, NFC-D: Minnesota vs. San Francisco, 1987
    Matt Bahr, NFC: N.Y. Giants vs. San Francisco, 1990
    Steve Christie, AFC: Buffalo vs. Miami, 1992
    Brad Daluiso, NFC-FR: N.Y. Giants vs. Minnesota, 1997
    John Kasay, NFC-FR: Carolina vs. Dallas, 2003
    Jeff Wilkins, NFC-D: St. Louis vs. Carolina, 2003 (2 OT)
    Adam Vinatieri, AFC: New England vs. Indianapolis, 2003
4   Gino Cappelletti, AFC-D: Boston vs. Buffalo, 1963
    George Blanda, AFC: Oakland vs. Houston, 1967
    Don Chandler, SB: Green Bay vs. Oakland, 1967
    Curt Knight, NFC: Washington vs. Dallas, 1972
    George Blanda, AFC-D: Oakland vs. Pittsburgh, 1973
    Ray Wersching, SB: San Francisco vs. Cincinnati, 1981
    Tony Franklin, AFC-FR: New England vs. N.Y. Jets, 1985
    Jess Atkinson, NFC-FR: Washington vs. L.A. Rams, 1986
    Luis Zendejas, NFC-D: Philadelphia vs. Chicago, 1988
    Gary Anderson, AFC-FR: Pittsburgh vs. Houston, 1989 (OT)
    Norm Johnson, AFC-D: Pittsburgh vs. Buffalo, 1995
    Chris Boniol, NFC-FR: Dallas vs. Minnesota, 1996
    John Kasay, NFC-D: Carolina vs. Dallas, 1996
    Mike Hollis, AFC-D: Jacksonville vs. New England, 1998
    Al Del Greco, AFC-FR: Tennessee vs. Indianapolis, 1999
    David Akers, NFC-D: Philadelphia vs. Chicago, 2001
3   By many players
Most Consecutive Games Scoring Field Goals
13 Toni Fritsch, Dallas-Houston, 1972-79
12 Adam Vinatieri, New England, 1997-2004 (current)
10 David Akers, Philadelphia, 2000-04

Morten Andersen, New Orleans-Atlanta-Kansas City-
Minnesota, 1987-2004

Most Consecutive Field Goals

16   Gary Anderson, Pittsburgh-Philadelphia, 1989-1995
15   Rafael Septien, Dallas, 1978-1982
14   Mike Hollis, Jacksonville, 1996-99
      John Kasay, Carolina, 1996-2003

Longest Field Goal

58   Pete Stoyanovich, AFC-FR: Miami vs. Kansas City, 1990
55   Jeff Wilkins, NFC-D: St. Louis vs. Atlanta, 2004
54   Ed Murray, NFC-D: Detroit vs. San Francisco, 1983
      Steve Christie, SB: Buffalo vs. Dallas, 1993
      John Carney, AFC-FR: San Diego vs. Indianapolis, 1995

Highest Field Goal Percentage, Career (10 field goals)

91.7   Martin Gramatica, Tampa Bay-Indianapolis, 8 games
         (12-11)
90.9   Chuck Nelson, L.A. Rams-Minnesota, 6 games (11-10)
88.9   Mike Hollis, Jacksonville, 8 games (18-16)

SAFETIES
Most Safeties, Game

1   Bill Willis, NFC-D: Cleveland vs. N.Y. Giants, 1950
     Carl Eller, NFC-D: Minnesota vs. Los Angeles, 1969
     George Andrie, NFC-D: Dallas vs. Detroit, 1970
     Alan Page, NFC-D: Minnesota vs. Dallas, 1971
     Dwight White, SB: Pittsburgh vs. Minnesota, 1974
     Reggie Harrison, SB: Pittsburgh vs. Dallas, 1975
     Jim Jensen, NFC-D: Dallas vs. Los Angeles, 1976
     Ted Washington, AFC: Houston vs. Pittsburgh, 1978
     Randy White, NFC-D: Dallas vs. Los Angeles, 1979
     Henry Waechter, SB: Chicago vs. New England, 1985
     Rulon Jones, AFC-FR: Denver vs. New England, 1986
     George Martin, SB: N.Y. Giants vs. Denver, 1986
     D.D. Hoggard, AFC: Cleveland vs. Denver, 1987
     Bruce Smith, SB: Buffalo vs. N.Y. Giants, 1990
     Reggie White, AFC-FR: Philadelphia vs. New Orleans, 1992
     Willie Clay, NFC-FR: Detroit vs. Green Bay, 1994
     Carnell Lake, AFC-D: Pittsburgh vs. Cleveland, 1994
     Reuben Davis, AFC-D: San Diego vs. Miami, 1994
     Jevon Kearse, AFC-FR: Tennessee vs. Buffalo, 1999
     Brady Smith, NFC-D: Atlanta vs. St. Louis, 2004

RUSHING
ATTEMPTS
Most Attempts, Career

400   Franco Harris, Pittsburgh, 19 games
349   Emmitt Smith, Dallas, 17 games
339   Thurman Thomas, Buffalo, 21 games

Most Attempts, Game

40   Lamar Smith, AFC-FR: Miami vs. Indianapolis, 2000 (OT)
38   Ricky Bell, NFC-D: Tampa Bay vs. Philadelphia, 1979
      John Riggins, SB: Washington vs. Miami, 1982
37   Lawrence McCutcheon, NFC-D: Los Angeles vs. St. Louis,
      1975
      John Riggins, NFC-D: Washington vs. Minnesota, 1982

YARDS GAINED
Most Yards Gained, Career

1,586   Emmitt Smith, Dallas, 17 games
1,556   Franco Harris, Pittsburgh, 19 games
1,442   Thurman Thomas, Buffalo, 21 games

Most Yards Gained, Game

248   Eric Dickerson, NFC-D: L.A. Rams vs. Dallas, 1985
209   Lamar Smith, AFC-FR: Miami vs. Indianapolis, 2000 (OT)
206   Keith Lincoln, AFC: San Diego vs. Boston, 1963

Most Games, 100 or More Yards Rushing, Career

7   Emmitt Smith, Dallas, 17 games
     Terrell Davis, Denver, 8 games
6   John Riggins, Washington, 9 games
     Thurman Thomas, Buffalo, 21 games

5   Franco Harris, Pittsburgh, 19 games
     Marcus Allen, L.A. Raiders-Kansas City, 16 games

Most Consecutive Games, 100 or More Yards Rushing

7   Terrell Davis, Denver, 1997-98
6   John Riggins, Washington, 1982-83
4   Thurman Thomas, Buffalo, 1990-91

Longest Run From Scrimmage

90   Fred Taylor, AFC-D: Jacksonville vs. Miami, 1999 (TD)
80   Roger Craig, NFC-D: San Francisco vs. Minnesota, 1988 (TD)
      Charlie Garner, AFC-FR: Oakland vs. N.Y. Jets, 2001 (TD)
78   Curtis Martin, AFC-D: New England vs. Pittsburgh, 1996 (TD)

AVERAGE GAIN
Highest Average Gain, Career (100 attempts)

5.59   Terrell Davis, Denver, 8 games (204-1,140)
5.04   Marcus Allen, L.A. Raiders-Kansas City, 16 games
         (267-1,347)
4.89   Eric Dickerson, L.A. Rams-Indianapolis, 7 games (148-724)

Highest Average Gain, Game (10 attempts)

15.90   Elmer Angsman, NFC: Chi. Cardinals vs. Philadelphia,
           1947 (10-159)
15.85   Keith Lincoln, AFC: San Diego vs. Boston, 1963 (13-206)
11.31   Zack Crockett, AFC-FR: Indianapolis vs. San Diego, 1995
           (13-147)

TOUCHDOWNS
Most Touchdowns, Career

19   Emmitt Smith, Dallas, 17 games
16   Franco Harris, Pittsburgh, 19 games
      Thurman Thomas, Buffalo, 21 games
12   John Riggins, Washington, 9 games
      Terrell Davis, Denver, 8 games

Most Touchdowns, Game

5   Ricky Watters, NFC-D: San Francisco vs. N.Y. Giants, 1993
3   Andy Farkas, NFC-D: Washington vs. N.Y. Giants, 1943
     Otto Graham, NFC: Cleveland vs. Detroit, 1954
     Tom Matte, NFC: Baltimore vs. Cleveland, 1968
     Larry Schreiber, NFC-D: San Francisco vs. Dallas, 1972
     Larry Csonka, AFC: Miami vs. Oakland, 1973
     Franco Harris, AFC-D: Pittsburgh vs. Buffalo, 1974
     John Riggins, NFC-D: Washington vs. L.A. Rams, 1983
     Kenneth Davis, AFC: Buffalo vs. L.A. Raiders, 1990
     Napoleon McCallum, AFC-FR: L.A. Raiders vs. Denver, 1993
     Thurman Thomas, AFC: Buffalo vs. Kansas City, 1993
     William Floyd, NFC-D: San Francisco vs. Chicago, 1994
     Emmitt Smith, NFC: Dallas vs. Green Bay, 1995
     Curtis Martin, AFC-D: New England vs. Pittsburgh, 1996
     Terrell Davis, SB: Denver vs. Green Bay, 1997
     Mario Bates, NFC-D: Arizona vs. Minnesota, 1998
     Shaun Alexander, NFC-FR: Seattle vs. Green Bay, 2003 (OT)

Most Consecutive Games Rushing for Touchdowns

8   Emmitt Smith, Dallas, 1993-96
     Thurman Thomas, Buffalo, 1992-98
7   John Riggins, Washington, 1982-84
     Terrell Davis, Denver, 1996-98
5   Franco Harris, Pittsburgh, 1974-75
     Franco Harris, Pittsburgh, 1977-79
     Curtis Martin, New England-N.Y. Jets, 1996-98

PASSING
PASSER RATING
Highest Passer Rating, Career (150 attempts)

104.8   Bart Starr, Green Bay, 10 games
95.6   Joe Montana, San Francisco-Kansas City, 23 games
93.5   Ken Anderson, Cincinnati, 6 games

ATTEMPTS
Most Passes Attempted, Career

734   Joe Montana, San Francisco-Kansas City, 23 games
687   Dan Marino, Miami, 18 games

663   Brett Favre, Green Bay, 20 games

Most Passes Attempted, Game

65   Steve Young, NFC-D: San Francisco vs. Green Bay, 1995
64   Bernie Kosar, AFC-D: Cleveland vs. N.Y. Jets, 1986 (OT)
      Dan Marino, AFC-FR: Miami vs. Buffalo, 1995
58   Jim Kelly, SB: Buffalo vs. Washington, 1991

COMPLETIONS

Most Passes Completed, Career

460   Joe Montana, San Francisco-Kansas City, 23 games
401   Brett Favre, Green Bay, 20 games
385   Dan Marino, Miami, 18 games

Most Passes Completed, Game

36   Warren Moon, AFC-FR: Houston vs. Buffalo, 1992 (OT)
33   Dan Fouts, AFC-D: San Diego vs. Miami, 1981 (OT)
      Bernie Kosar, AFC-D: Cleveland vs. N.Y. Jets, 1986 (OT)
      Dan Marino, AFC-FR: Miami vs. Buffalo, 1995
32   Neil Lomax, NFC-FR: St. Louis vs. Green Bay, 1982
      Danny White, NFC-FR: Dallas vs. L.A. Rams, 1983
      Warren Moon, AFC-D: Houston vs. Kansas City, 1993
      Neil O'Donnell, AFC: Pittsburgh vs. San Diego, 1994
      Steve Young, NFC-D: San Francisco vs. Green Bay, 1995
      Tom Brady, AFC-D: New England vs. Oakland, 2001 (OT)
      Tom Brady, SB: New England vs. Carolina, 2003

COMPLETION PERCENTAGE

Highest Completion Percentage, Career (150 attempts)

66.3   Ken Anderson, Cincinnati, 6 games (166-110)
64.3   Warren Moon, Houston-Minnesota, 10 games (403-259)
64.2   Rich Gannon, Minnesota-Kanas City-Oakland, 10 games
       (240-154)

Highest Completion Percentage, Game (15 completions)

88.0   Phil Simms, SB: N.Y. Giants vs. Denver, 1986 (25-22)
86.7   Joe Montana, NFC: San Francisco vs. L.A. Rams, 1989
       (30-26)
84.6   Peyton Manning, AFC-FR: Indianapolis vs. Denver, 2003
       (26-22)

YARDS GAINED

Most Yards Gained, Career

5,772   Joe Montana, San Francisco-Kansas City, 23 games
4,964   John Elway, Denver, 22 games
4,902   Brett Favre, Green Bay, 20 games

Most Yards Gained, Game

489   Bernie Kosar, AFC-D: Cleveland vs. N.Y. Jets, 1986 (OT)
458   Peyton Manning, AFC-FR: Indianapolis vs. Denver, 2004
433   Dan Fouts, AFC-D: San Diego vs. Miami, 1981 (OT)

Most Games, 300 or More Yards Passing, Career

6   Joe Montana, San Francisco-Kansas City, 23 games
5   Dan Fouts, San Diego, 7 games
4   Warren Moon, Houston-Minnesota, 10 games
    Troy Aikman, Dallas, 16 games
    Dan Marino, Miami, 18 games
    John Elway, Denver, 22 games
    Kurt Warner, St. Louis, 7 games

Most Consecutive Games, 300 or More Yards Passing

4   Dan Fouts, San Diego, 1979-1981
3   Jim Kelly, Buffalo, 1989-1990
    Warren Moon, Houston, 1991-93
2   Daryle Lamonica, Oakland, 1968
    Ken Anderson, Cincinnati, 1981-82
    Terry Bradshaw, Pittsburgh, 1979-1982
    Joe Montana, San Francisco, 1983-84
    Dan Marino, Miami, 1984
    Troy Aikman, Dallas, 1994
    Steve Young, San Francisco, 1994-95
    Kurt Warner, St. Louis, 1999-2000
    Peyton Manning, Indianapolis, 2003
    Marc Bulger, St. Louis, 2003-04
    Matt Hasselbeck, Seattle, 2003-04 (current)

Longest Pass Completion

96   Trent Dilfer (to Sharpe), AFC: Baltimore vs. Oakland, 2000 (TD)
94   Troy Aikman (to Harper), NFC-D: Dallas vs. Green Bay,
     1994 (TD)
93   Daryle Lamonica (to Dubenion), AFC-D: Buffalo vs. Boston,
     1963 (TD)

AVERAGE GAIN

Highest Average Gain, Career (150 attempts)

8.45   Joe Theismann, Washington, 10 games (211-1,782)
8.43   Jim Plunkett, Oakland/L.A.Raiders, 10 games (272-2,293)
8.41   Terry Bradshaw, Pittsburgh, 19 games (456-3,833)

Highest Average Gain, Game (20 attempts)

14.71   Terry Bradshaw, SB: Pittsburgh vs. Los Angeles, 1979 (21-309)
14.50   Peyton Manning, AFC-FR: Indianapolis vs. Denver, 2003
       (26-377)
13.88   Peyton Manning, AFC-FR: Indianapolis vs. Denver, 2004
       (33-458)

TOUCHDOWNS

Most Touchdown Passes, Career

45   Joe Montana, San Francisco-Kansas City, 23 games
34   Brett Favre, Green Bay, 20 games
32   Dan Marino, Miami, 18 games

Most Touchdown Passes, Game

6   Daryle Lamonica, AFC-D: Oakland vs. Houston, 1969
    Steve Young, SB: San Francisco vs. San Diego, 1994
5   Sid Luckman, NFC: Chi. Bears vs. Washington, 1943
    Daryle Lamonica, AFC-D: Oakland vs. Kansas City, 1968
    Joe Montana, SB: San Francisco vs. Denver, 1989
    Kurt Warner, NFC-D: St. Louis vs. Minnesota, 1999
    Kerry Collins, NFC: N.Y. Giants vs. Minnesota, 2000
    Peyton Manning, AFC-FR: Indianapolis vs. Denver, 2003
4   Otto Graham, NFC: Cleveland vs. Los Angeles, 1950
    Tobin Rote, NFC: Detroit vs. Cleveland, 1957
    Bart Starr, NFC: Green Bay vs. Dallas, 1966
    Ken Stabler, AFC-D: Oakland vs. Miami, 1974
    Roger Staubach, NFC: Dallas vs. Los Angeles, 1975
    Terry Bradshaw, SB: Pittsburgh vs. Dallas, 1978
    Don Strock, AFC-D: Miami vs. San Diego, 1981 (OT)
    Lynn Dickey, NFC-FR: Green Bay vs. St. Louis, 1982
    Dan Marino, AFC: Miami vs. Pittsburgh, 1984
    Phil Simms, NFC-D: N.Y. Giants vs. San Francisco, 1986
    Doug Williams, SB: Washington vs. Denver, 1987
    Jim Kelly, AFC-D: Buffalo vs. Cleveland, 1989
    Joe Montana, NFC-D: San Francisco vs. Minnesota, 1989
    Warren Moon, AFC-FR: Houston vs. Buffalo, 1992 (OT)
    Frank Reich, AFC-FR: Buffalo vs. Houston, 1992 (OT)
    Troy Aikman, SB: Dallas vs. Buffalo, 1992
    Jeff George, NFC-D: Minnesota vs. St. Louis, 1999
    Aaron Brooks, NFC-FR: New Orleans vs. St. Louis, 2000
    Kerry Collins, NFC-FR: N.Y. Giants vs. San Francisco, 2002
    Peyton Manning, AFC-FR: Indianapolis vs. Denver, 2004
    Daunte Culpepper, NFC-FR: Minnesota vs. Green Bay, 2004

Most Consecutive Games, Touchdown Passes

16   Brett Favre, Green Bay, 1995-2004 (current)
13   Dan Marino, Miami, 1983-1995
10   Ken Stabler, Oakland, 1973-77
    Joe Montana, San Francisco-Kansas City, 1988-1993

HAD INTERCEPTED

Lowest Percentage, Passes Had Intercepted, Career (150 attempts)

0.99   Tom Brady, New England, 9 games (304-3)
1.41   Bart Starr, Green Bay, 10 games (213-3)
2.15   Phil Simms, N.Y. Giants, 10 games (279-6)

Most Attempts Without Interception, Game

54   Neil O'Donnell, AFC: Pittsburgh vs. San Diego, 1994
48   Warren Moon, AFC-FR: Houston vs. Pittsburgh, 1989 (OT)
    Randall Cunningham, NFC: Minnesota vs. Atlanta, 1998 (OT)
47   Daryle Lamonica, AFC: Oakland vs. N.Y. Jets, 1968

Most Passes Had Intercepted, Career
   28   Jim Kelly, Buffalo, 17 games
   26   Terry Bradshaw, Pittsburgh, 19 games
         Brett Favre, Green Bay, 20 games
   24   Dan Marino, Miami, 18 games

Most Passes Had Intercepted, Game
    6   Frank Filchock, NFC: N.Y. Giants vs. Chi. Bears, 1946
        Bobby Layne, NFC: Detroit vs. Cleveland, 1954
        Norm Van Brocklin, NFC: Los Angeles vs. Cleveland, 1955
        Brett Favre, NFC-D: Green Bay vs. St. Louis, 2001
    5   Frank Filchock, NFC: Washington vs. Chi. Bears, 1940
        George Blanda, AFC: Houston vs. San Diego, 1961
        George Blanda, AFC: Houston vs. Dall. Texans, 1962 (OT)
        Y.A. Tittle, NFC: N.Y. Giants vs. Chicago, 1963
        Mike Phipps, AFC-D: Cleveland vs. Miami, 1972
        Dan Pastorini, AFC: Houston vs. Pittsburgh, 1978
        Dan Fouts, AFC-D: San Diego vs. Houston, 1979
        Tommy Kramer, NFC-D: Minnesota vs. Philadelphia, 1980
        Dan Fouts, AFC-D: San Diego vs. Miami, 1982
        Richard Todd, AFC: N.Y. Jets vs Miami, 1982
        Gary Danielson, NFC-D: Detroit vs. San Francisco, 1983
        Jay Schroeder, AFC: L.A. Raiders vs. Buffalo, 1990
        Rich Gannon, SB: Oakland vs. Tampa Bay, 2002
    4   By many players

PASS RECEIVING
RECEPTIONS
Most Receptions, Career
  151   Jerry Rice, San Francisco-Oakland-Seattle, 29 games
   87   Michael Irvin, Dallas, 16 games
   85   Andre Reed, Buffalo, 21 games

Most Receptions, Game
   13   Kellen Winslow, AFC-D: San Diego vs. Miami, 1981 (OT)
        Thurman Thomas, AFC-D: Buffalo vs. Cleveland, 1989
        Shannon Sharpe, AFC-FR: Denver vs. L.A. Raiders, 1993
        Chad Morton, NFC-D: New Orleans vs. Minnesota, 2000
   12   Raymond Berry, NFC: Baltimore vs. N.Y. Giants, 1958
        Michael Irvin, NFC: Dallas vs. San Francisco, 1994
        Darrell Jackson, NFC-FR: Seattle vs. St. Louis, 2004
   11   Dante Lavelli, NFC: Cleveland vs. Los Angeles, 1950
        Dan Ross, SB: Cincinnati vs. San Francisco, 1981
        Franco Harris, AFC-FR: Pittsburgh vs. San Diego, 1982
        Steve Watson, AFC-D: Denver vs. Pittsburgh, 1984
        John L. Williams, AFC-D: Seattle vs. Cincinnati, 1988
        Jerry Rice, SB: San Francisco vs. Cincinnati, 1988
        Ernest Givins, AFC-FR: Houston vs. Pittsburgh, 1989 (OT)
        Amp Lee, NFC-D: Minnesota vs. Chicago, 1994
        Jay Novacek, NFC-D: Dallas vs. Green Bay, 1994
        O.J. McDuffie, AFC-FR: Miami vs. Buffalo, 1995
        Jerry Rice, NFC-C: San Francisco vs. Green Bay, 1995
        Hines Ward, AFC-FR: Pittsburgh vs. Cleveland, 2002
        Deion Branch, SB: New England vs. Philadelphia, 2004

Most Consecutive Games, Pass Receptions
   28   Jerry Rice, San Francisco-Oakland, 1985-2002
   22   Drew Pearson, Dallas, 1973-1983
   18   Paul Warfield, Cleveland-Miami, 1964-1974
        Cliff Branch, Oakland/L.A. Raiders, 1974-1983
        Thurman Thomas, Buffalo, 1989-1998
        Shannon Sharpe, Denver-Baltimore-Denver, 1991-2003

YARDS GAINED
Most Yards Gained, Career
 2,245   Jerry Rice, San Francisco-Oakland-Seattle, 29 games
 1,315   Michael Irvin, Dallas, 16 games
 1,289   Cliff Branch, Oakland/L.A. Raiders, 22 games

Most Yards Gained, Game
  240   Eric Moulds, AFC-FR: Buffalo vs. Miami, 1998
  227   Anthony Carter, NFC-D: Minnesota vs. San Francisco, 1987
  221   Reggie Wayne, AFC-FR: Indianapolis vs. Denver, 2004

Most Games, 100 or More Yards Receiving, Career
    8   Jerry Rice, San Francisco-Oakland-Seattle, 29 games
    6   Michael Irvin, Dallas, 16 games
    5   John Stallworth, Pittsburgh, 18 games
        Andre Reed, Buffalo, 21 games

Most Consecutive Games, 100 or More Yards Receiving, Career
    3   Tom Fears, Los Angeles, 1950-51
        Jerry Rice, San Francisco, 1988-89
        Randy Moss, Minnesota, 1999-2000
    2   By many players

Longest Reception
   96   Shannon Sharpe (from Dilfer), AFC: Baltimore vs. Oakland,
          2000 (TD)
   94   Alvin Harper (from Aikman), NFC-D: Dallas vs. Green Bay,
          1994 (TD)
   93   Elbert Dubenion (from Lamonica), AFC-D: Buffalo vs.
          Boston, 1963 (TD)

AVERAGE GAIN
Highest Average Gain, Career (20 receptions)
  27.3   Alvin Harper, Dallas, 10 games (24-655)
  23.7   Willie Gault, Chicago-L.A. Raiders, 12 games (21-497)
  22.8   Harold Jackson, L.A. Rams-New England-Minnesota-Seattle,
         14 games (24-548)

Highest Average Gain, Game (3 receptions)
  46.3   Harold Jackson, NFC: Los Angeles vs. Minnesota, 1974 (3-139)
  42.7   Billy Cannon, AFC: Houston vs. L.A. Chargers, 1960 (3-128)
  42.0   Lenny Moore, NFC: Baltimore vs. N.Y. Giants, 1959 (3-126)

TOUCHDOWNS
Most Touchdowns, Career
   22   Jerry Rice, San Francisco-Oakland-Seattle, 29 games
   12   John Stallworth, Pittsburgh, 18 games
   10   Fred Biletnikoff, Oakland, 19 games
        Antonio Freeman, Green Bay-Philadelphia-Green Bay,
         16 games

Most Touchdowns, Game
    3   Tom Fears, NFC-D: Los Angeles vs. Chi. Bears, 1950
        Gary Collins, NFC: Cleveland vs. Baltimore, 1964
        Fred Biletnikoff, AFC-D: Oakland vs. Kansas City, 1968
        Preston Pearson, NFC: Dallas vs. Los Angeles, 1975
        Dave Casper, AFC-D: Oakland vs. Baltimore, 1977 (OT)
        Alvin Garrett, NFC-FR: Washington vs. Detroit, 1982
        Jerry Rice, NFC-D: San Francisco vs. Minnesota, 1988
        Jerry Rice, SB: San Francisco vs. Denver, 1989
        Andre Reed, AFC-FR: Buffalo vs. Houston, 1992 (OT)
        Sterling Sharpe, NFC-FR: Green Bay vs. Detroit, 1993
        Jerry Rice, SB: San Francisco vs. San Diego, 1994
        Willie Jackson, NFC-FR: New Orleans vs. St. Louis, 2000
        Amani Toomer, NFC-FR: N.Y. Giants vs. San Francisco, 2002

Most Consecutive Games, Touchdown Passes Caught
    8   John Stallworth, Pittsburgh, 1978-1983
    5   James Lofton, Green Bay-Buffalo, 1982-1990
        Randy Moss, Minnesota, 1998-2000
        Antonio Freeman, Green Bay, 1997-2001
        David Givens, New England, 2003-04 (current)
    4   Lynn Swann, Pittsburgh, 1978-79
        Harold Carmichael, Philadelphia, 1978-1980
        Fred Solomon, San Francisco, 1983-84
        Jerry Rice, San Francisco, 1988-89
        John Taylor, San Francisco, 1988-89
        Hines Ward, Pittsburgh, 2002-04 (current)

INTERCEPTIONS BY
Most Interceptions, Career
    9   Charlie Waters, Dallas, 25 games
        Bill Simpson, Los Angeles-Buffalo, 11 games
        Ronnie Lott, San Francisco-L.A. Raiders, 20 games
    8   Lester Hayes, Oakland/L.A. Raiders, 13 games
    7   Willie Brown, Oakland, 17 games

Dennis Thurman, Dallas, 14 games

Most Interceptions, Game
- 4 Vernon Perry, AFC-D: Houston vs. San Diego, 1979
- 3 Joe Laws, NFC: Green Bay vs. N.Y. Giants, 1944
  Charlie Waters, NFC-D: Dallas vs. Chicago, 1977
  Rod Martin, SB: Oakland vs. Philadelphia, 1980
  Dennis Thurman, NFC-D: Dallas vs. Green Bay, 1982
  A.J. Duhe, AFC: Miami vs. N.Y. Jets, 1982
  Ty Law, AFC: New England vs. Indianapolis, 2003
  Ricky Manning Jr., NFC: Carolina vs. Philadelphia, 2003
- 2 By many players

Most Consecutive Games, Interceptions
- 4 Aeneas Williams, Arizona-St. Louis, 1998-2001
- 3 By many players. Last time:
  Rodney Harrison, New England, 2004 (current)

YARDS GAINED

Most Yards Gained, Career
- 196 Willie Brown, Oakland, 17 games
- 187 Ronnie Lott, San Francisco-L.A.-Raiders, 20 games
- 160 George Teague, Green Bay-Dallas-Miami-Dallas, 12 games

Most Yards Gained, Game
- 108 Darrien Gordon, SB: Denver vs. Atlanta, 1998
- 101 George Teague, NFC-FR: Green Bay vs. Detroit, 1993
- 98 Darrol Ray, AFC-FR: N.Y. Jets vs. Cincinnati, 1982
  Tory James, AFC-D: Oakland vs. Miami, 2000

Longest Return
- 101 George Teague, NFC-FR: Green Bay vs. Detroit, 1993 (TD)
- 98 Darrol Ray, AFC-FR: N.Y. Jets vs. Cincinnati, 1982 (TD)
- 94 LeRoy Irvin, NFC-FR: L.A. Rams vs. Dallas, 1983

TOUCHDOWNS

Most Touchdowns, Career
- 3 Willie Brown, Oakland, 17 games
- 2 Lester Hayes, Oakland/L.A. Raiders, 13 games
  Ronnie Lott, San Francisco-L.A. Raiders, 20 games
  Darrell Green, Washington, 18 games
  Melvin Jenkins, Seattle-Detroit, 5 games
  George Teague, Green Bay-Dallas-Miami-Dallas, 12 games
  Aeneas Williams, Arizona-St. Louis, 6 games
  Dwight Smith, Tampa Bay, 4 games

Most Touchdowns, Game
- 2 Aeneas Williams, NFC-D: St. Louis vs. Green Bay, 2001
  Dwight Smith, SB: Tampa Bay vs. Oakland, 2002
- 1 By many players

PUNTING

Most Punts, Career
- 111 Ray Guy, Oakland/L.A. Raiders, 22 games
- 92 Craig Hentrich, Green Bay-Tennessee, 20 games
- 84 Danny White, Dallas, 18 games
  Sean Landeta, N.Y. Giants-Tampa Bay-Green Bay-Philadelphia-St. Louis, 18 games

Most Punts, Game
- 14 Dave Jennings, AFC-D: N.Y. Jets vs. Cleveland, 1986 (OT)
- 12 David Lee, AFC-D: Baltimore vs. Oakland, 1977 (OT)
- 11 Ken Strong, NFC: N.Y. Giants vs. Chi. Bears, 1933
  Jim Norton, AFC: Houston vs. Oakland, 1967
  Ode Burrell, AFC-D: Houston vs. Oakland, 1969
  Dale Hatcher, NFC: L.A. Rams vs. Chicago, 1985
  Brad Maynard, SB: N.Y. Giants vs. Baltimore, 2000

Longest Punt
- 76 Ed Danowski, NFC: N.Y. Giants vs. Detroit, 1935
  Mike Horan, AFC: Denver vs. Buffalo, 1991
- 72 Charlie Conerly, NFC-D: N.Y. Giants vs. Cleveland, 1950
  Yale Lary, NFC: Detroit vs. Cleveland, 1953
- 71 Ray Guy, AFC: Oakland vs. San Diego, 1980

AVERAGE YARDAGE

Highest Average, Career (25 punts)
- 44.5 Rich Camarillo, New England, 6 games (35-1,559)
- 44.3 Jeff Feagles, Philadelphia-Seattle, 4 games (26-1,151)
- 43.4 Jerrel Wilson, Kansas City-New England, 8 games (43-1,866)

Highest Average, Game (4 punts)
- 56.0 Ray Guy, AFC: Oakland vs. San Diego, 1980 (4-224)
- 52.5 Sammy Baugh, NFC: Washington vs. Chi. Bears, 1942 (6-315)
- 52.0 Craig Hentrich, AFC-D: Tennessee vs. Indianapolis, 1999 (5-260)

PUNT RETURNS

Most Punt Returns, Career
- 34 David Meggett, N.Y. Giants-New England-N.Y. Jets, 13 games
  Brian Mitchell, Washington-Philadelphia, 16 games
- 29 Troy Brown, New England, 15 games
- 25 Theo Bell, Pittsburgh-Tampa Bay, 10 games

Most Punt Returns, Game
- 7 Ron Gardin, AFC-D: Baltimore vs. Cincinnati, 1970
  Carl Roaches, AFC-FR: Houston vs. Oakland, 1980
  Gerald McNeil, AFC-D: Cleveland vs. N.Y. Jets, 1986 (OT)
  Phil McConkey, NFC-D: N.Y. Giants vs. San Francisco, 1986
  David Meggett, AFC-D: New England vs. Pittsburgh, 1996
  Reggie Barlow, AFC-FR: Jacksonville vs. New England, 1998
- 6 George McAfee, NFC-D: Chi. Bears vs. Los Angeles, 1950
  Eddie Brown, NFC-D: Washington vs. Minnesota, 1976
  Theo Bell, AFC: Pittsburgh vs. Houston, 1978
  Eddie Brown, NFC: Los Angeles vs. Tampa Bay, 1979
  John Sciarra, NFC: Philadelphia vs. Dallas, 1980
  Kurt Sohn, AFC: N.Y. Jets vs. Miami, 1982
  Mike Nelms, SB: Washington vs. Miami, 1982
  Anthony Carter, NFC-FR: Minnesota vs. New Orleans, 1987
  Desmond Howard, SB: Green Bay vs. New England, 1996
  Nate Jacquet, AFC-FR: Miami vs. Seattle, 1999
  Derrick Mason, AFC-FR: Tennessee vs. Baltimore, 2003
  Antonio Chatman, AFC-D: Green Bay vs. Philadelphia, 2003
- 5 By many players

YARDS GAINED

Most Yards Gained, Career
- 339 Brian Mitchell, Washington-Philadelphia, 16 games
- 312 David Meggett, N.Y. Giants-New England-N.Y. Jets, 13 games
- 276 Troy Brown, New England, 15 games

Most Yards Gained, Game
- 152 Allen Rossum, NFC-D: Atlanta vs. St. Louis, 2004
- 143 Anthony Carter, NFC-FR: Minnesota vs. New Orleans, 1987
- 141 Bob Hayes, NFC-D: Dallas vs. Cleveland, 1967

Longest Return
- 88 Jermaine Lewis, AFC-D: Baltimore vs. Pittsburgh, 2001 (TD)
- 84 Anthony Carter, NFC-FR: Minnesota vs. New Orleans, 1987 (TD)
- 81 Hugh Gallarneau, NFC-D: Chi. Bears vs. Green Bay, 1941 (TD)

AVERAGE YARDAGE

Highest Average, Career (10 returns)
- 23.9 Allen Rossum, Green Bay-Atlanta, 6 games (10-239)
- 15.3 Robert Brooks, Green Bay, 11 games (14-214)
- 15.2 Anthony Carter, Minnesota-Detroit, 9 games (17-259)

Highest Average Gain, Game (3 returns)

- 50.7 Allen Rossum, NFC-D: Atlanta vs. St. Louis, 2004 (3-152)
- 47.0 Bob Hayes, NFC-D: Dallas vs. Cleveland, 1967 (3-141)
- 33.0 Jermaine Lewis, AFC-D: Baltimore vs. Pittsburgh, 2001 (3-99)
- 29.0 George (Butch) Byrd, AFC: Buffalo vs. San Diego, 1965 (3-87)

TOUCHDOWNS
Most Touchdowns
- 1 Hugh Gallarneau, NFC-D: Chicago Bears vs. Green Bay, 1941
- Bosh Pritchard, NFC-D: Philadelphia vs. Pittsburgh, 1947
- Charley Trippi, NFC: Chicago Cardinals vs. Philadelphia, 1947
- Verda (Vitamin T) Smith, NFC-D: Los Angeles vs. Detroit, 1952
- George (Butch) Byrd, AFC: Buffalo vs. San Diego, 1965
- Golden Richards, NFC: Dallas vs. Minnesota, 1973
- Wes Chandler, AFC-D: San Diego vs. Miami, 1981 (OT)
- Shaun Gayle, NFC-D: Chicago vs. N.Y. Giants, 1985
- Anthony Carter, NFC-FR: Minnesota vs. New Orleans, 1987
- Darrell Green, NFC-D: Washington vs. Chicago, 1987
- Antonio Freeman, NFC-FR: Green Bay vs. Atlanta, 1995
- Desmond Howard, NFC-D: Green Bay vs. San Francisco, 1996
- Jermaine Lewis, AFC-D: Baltimore vs. Pittsburgh, 2001
- Troy Brown, AFC: New England vs. Pittsburgh, 2001
- Antwaan Randle El, AFC-FR: Pittsburgh vs. Cleveland, 2002
- Santana Moss, AFC-D: N.Y. Jets vs. Pittsburgh, 2004 (OT)
- Allen Rossum, NFC-D: Atlanta vs. St. Louis, 2004

KICKOFF RETURNS
Most Kickoff Returns, Career
- 36 Brian Mitchell, Washington-Philadelphia, 16 games
- 31 Kevin Williams, Dallas-Buffalo, 12 games
- 29 Fulton Walker, Miami-L.A. Raiders, 10 games

Most Kickoff Returns, Game
- 8 Marc Logan, AFC-D: Miami vs. Buffalo, 1990
- Andre Coleman, SB: San Diego vs. San Francisco, 1994
- Marcus Knight, SB: Oakland vs. Tampa Bay, 2002
- 7 Don Bingham, NFC: Chi. Bears vs. N.Y. Giants, 1956
- Reggie Brown, NFC-FR: Atlanta vs. Minnesota, 1982
- David Verser, AFC-FR: Cincinnati vs. N.Y. Jets, 1982
- Del Rodgers, NFC-D: Green Bay vs. Dallas, 1982
- Henry Ellard, NFC-D: L.A. Rams vs. Washington, 1983
- Stephen Starring, SB: New England vs. Chicago, 1985
- Darick Holmes, AFC-D: Buffalo vs. Pittsburgh, 1995
- Antonio Freeman, NFC: Green Bay vs. Dallas, 1995
- Roell Preston, NFC-FR: Green Bay vs. San Francisco, 1998
- Robert Tate, NFC-D: Minnesota vs. St. Louis, 1999
- Fred McAfee, NFC-D: New Orleans vs. Minnesota, 2000
- Michael Bates, NFC-FR: Dallas vs. Carolina, 2003
- Dante Hall, AFC-D: Kansas City vs. Indianapolis, 2003
- 6 By many players

YARDS GAINED
Most Yards Gained, Career
- 875 Brian Mitchell, Washington-Philadelphia, 16 games
- 677 Fulton Walker, Miami-L.A. Raiders, 10 games
- 632 Kevin Williams, Dallas-Buffalo, 12 games

Most Yards Gained, Game
- 244 Andre Coleman, SB: San Diego vs. San Francisco, 1994
- 210 Tim Dwight, SB: Atlanta vs. Denver, 1998
- 208 Dante Hall, AFC-D: Kansas City vs. Indianapolis, 2003

Longest Return
- 100 Brian Mitchell, NFC-D: Washington vs. Tampa Bay, 1999 (TD)

- 99 Desmond Howard, SB: Green Bay vs. New England, 1996 (TD)
- 98 Fulton Walker, SB: Miami vs. Washington, 1982 (TD)
- Andre Coleman, SB: San Diego vs. San Francisco, 1994 (TD)

AVERAGE YARDAGE
Highest Average, Career (10 returns)
- 30.1 Carl Garrett, Oakland, 5 games (16-481)
- 30.0 Reggie Barlow, Jacksonville, 8 games (12-360)
- 28.9 Derrick Mason, Tennessee, 9 games (17-492)

Highest Average, Game (3 returns)
- 56.7 Les (Speedy) Duncan, NFC-D: Washington vs. San Francisco, 1971 (3-170)
- 51.3 Ed Podolak, AFC-D: Kansas City vs. Miami, 1971 (OT) (3-154)
- 49.0 Les (Speedy) Duncan, AFC: San Diego vs. Buffalo, 1964 (3-147)

TOUCHDOWNS
Most Touchdowns, Career
- 2 Ron Dixon, N.Y. Giants, 4 games
- 1 By many players

Most Touchdowns, Game
- 1 Vic Washington, NFC-D: San Francisco vs. Dallas, 1972
- Nat Moore, AFC-D: Miami vs. Oakland, 1974
- Marshall Johnson, AFC-D: Baltimore vs. Oakland, 1977 (OT)
- Fulton Walker, SB: Miami vs. Washington, 1982
- Stanford Jennings, SB: Cincinnati vs. San Francisco, 1988
- Eric Metcalf, AFC-D: Cleveland vs. Buffalo, 1989
- Andre Coleman, SB: San Diego vs. San Francisco, 1994
- Desmond Howard, SB: Green Bay vs. New England, 1996
- Chuck Levy, NFC: San Franisco vs. Green Bay, 1997
- Tim Dwight, SB: Atlanta vs. Denver, 1998
- Kevin Dyson, AFC-FR: Tennessee vs. Buffalo, 1999
- Charlie Rogers, AFC-FR: Seattle vs. Miami, 1999
- Brian Mitchell, NFC-D: Washington vs. Tampa Bay, 1999
- Tony Horne, NFC-D: St. Louis vs. Minnesota, 1999
- Derrick Mason, AFC: Tennessee vs. Jacksonville, 1999
- Ron Dixon, NFC-D: N.Y. Giants vs. Philadelphia, 2000; SB: N.Y. Giants vs. Baltimore, 2000
- Jermaine Lewis, SB: Baltimore vs. N.Y. Giants, 2000
- Dante Hall, AFC-D: Kansas City vs. Indianapolis, 2003

FUMBLES
Most Fumbles, Career
- 16 Warren Moon, Houston-Minnesota, 10 games
- 14 John Elway, Denver, 22 games
- 13 Tony Dorsett, Dallas, 17 games

Most Fumbles, Game
- 5 Warren Moon, AFC-D: Houston vs. Kansas City, 1993
- 4 Brian Sipe, AFC-D: Cleveland vs. Oakland, 1980
- Randall Cunningham, NFC-FR: Minnesota vs. N.Y. Giants, 1997
- 3 By many players

RECOVERIES
Most Own Fumbles Recovered, Career
- 8 Warren Moon, Houston-Minnesota, 10 games
- 7 John Elway, Denver, 22 games
- 6 Jim Kelly, Buffalo, 17 games

Most Opponents' Fumbles Recovered, Career
- 4 Cliff Harris, Dallas, 21 games
- Harvey Martin, Dallas, 21 games
- Ted Hendricks, Baltimore-Oakland/L.A. Raiders, 21 games
- Alvin Walton, Washington, 9 games
- Monte Coleman, Washington, 21 games
- Dave Thomas, Dallas-Jacksonville-N.Y. Giants, 13 games
- 3 Paul Krause, Minnesota, 19 games

Jack Lambert, Pittsburgh, 18 games
Fred Dryer, Los Angeles, 14 games
Charlie Waters, Dallas, 25 games
Jack Ham, Pittsburgh, 16 games
Mike Hegman, Dallas, 16 games
Tom Jackson, Denver, 10 games
Rich Milot, Washington, 13 games
Mike Singletary, Chicago, 12 games
Darryl Grant, Washington, 16 games
Wes Hopkins, Philadelphia, 3 games
Wilber Marshall, Chicago-Washington, 15 games
Tyrone Braxton, Denver-Miami-Denver, 19 games
Neil Smith, Kansas City-Denver, 16 games
Tony Brackens, Jacksonville, 7 games
Phil Hansen, Buffalo, 14 games
Carnell Lake, Pittsburgh-Jacksonville-Baltimore, 17 games
Jason Gildon, Pittsburgh, 13 games
Tedy Bruschi, New England, 15 games
   2   By many players

Most Fumbles Recovered, Game, Own and Opponents'
   3   Jack Lambert, AFC: Pittsburgh vs. Oakland, 1975 (3 opp)
       Ron Jaworski, NFC-FR: Philadelphia vs. N.Y. Giants, 1981 (3 own)
   2   By many players

YARDS GAINED
Longest Return
  93 Andy Russell, AFC-D: Pittsburgh vs. Baltimore, 1975 (opp, TD)
  79 Neil Smith, AFC-D: Denver vs. Miami, 1998 (opp, TD)
  64 Leon Lett, SB: Dallas vs. Buffalo, 1992 (opp)

TOUCHDOWNS
Most Touchdowns
   1   By many players

COMBINED NET YARDS GAINED
Rushing, receiving, interception returns, punt returns, kickoff returns, and fumble returns.

ATTEMPTS
Most Attempts, Career
 454 Franco Harris, Pittsburgh, 19 games
 417 Thurman Thomas, Buffalo, 21 games
 397 Emmitt Smith, Dallas, 17 games

Most Attempts, Game
  43 Lamar Smith, AFC-FR: Miami vs. Indianapolis, 2000 (OT)
  42 Curtis Martin, AFC-D: N.Y. Jets vs. Jacksonville, 1998
  40 Lawrence McCutcheon, NFC-D: Los Angeles vs. St. Louis, 1975

YARDS GAINED
Most Yards Gained, Career
2,289 Jerry Rice, San Francisco-Oakland-Seattle, 29 games
2,124 Thurman Thomas, Buffalo, 21 games
2,060 Franco Harris, Pittsburgh, 19 games

Most Yards Gained, Game
 350 Ed Podolak, AFC-D: Kansas City vs. Miami, 1971 (OT)
 329 Keith Lincoln, AFC: San Diego vs. Boston, 1963
 285 Bob Hayes, NFC-D: Dallas vs. Cleveland, 1967

SACKS
Sacks have been compiled since 1982.
Most Sacks, Career
14.5 Bruce Smith, Buffalo, 20 games
12.0 Reggie White, Philadelphia-Green Bay, 19 games
11.5 Willie McGinest, New England, 16 games

Most Sacks, Game
 3.5 Rich Milot, NFC-D: Washington vs. Chicago, 1984
     Richard Dent, NFC-D: Chicago vs. N.Y. Giants, 1985
 3.0 Richard Dent, NFC-D: Chicago vs. Washington, 1984

Garin Veris, AFC-FR: New England vs. N.Y. Jets, 1985
Gary Jeter, NFC-D: L.A. Rams vs. Dallas, 1985
Carl Hairston, AFC-D: Cleveland vs. N.Y. Jets, 1986 (OT)
Charles Mann, NFC-D: Washington vs. Chicago, 1987
Kevin Greene, NFC-FR: L.A. Rams vs. Minnesota, 1988
Greg Townsend, AFC-D: L.A. Raiders vs. Cincinnati, 1990
Wilber Marshall, NFC: Washington vs. Detroit, 1991
Fred Stokes, NFC-FR: Washington vs. Minnesota, 1992
Pierce Holt, NFC-D: San Francisco vs. Washington, 1992
Tony Casillas, NFC: Dallas vs. San Francisco, 1992
Gerald Williams, AFC-FR: Pittsburgh vs. Kansas City, 1993
Chad Brown, AFC-FR: Pittsburgh vs. Indianapolis, 1996
Reggie White, SB: Green Bay vs. New England, 1996
Warren Sapp, NFC-D: Tampa Bay vs. Green Bay, 1997
Trace Armstrong, AFC-FR: Miami vs. Seattle, 1999
Michael McCrary, AFC-FR: Baltimore vs. Denver, 2000
Willie McGinest, AFC-D: New England vs. Tennessee, 2003
 2.5 Lyle Alzado, AFC-D: L.A. Raiders vs. Pittsburgh, 1983
     Jacob Green, AFC-FR: Seattle vs. L.A. Raiders, 1984
     Larry Roberts, NFC-D: San Francisco vs. Minnesota, 1988
     Leslie O'Neal, AFC-FR: San Diego vs. Kansas City, 1992
     Bruce Smith, AFC-FR: Buffalo vs. Tennessee, 1999
     Jarvis Green, AFC: New England vs. Indianapolis, 2003

TEAM RECORDS

GAMES, VICTORIES, DEFEATS
Most Seasons Participating in Postseason Games
  27 Dallas, 1966-1973, 1975-1983, 1985, 1991-96, 1998-99, 2003
     Cleveland/L.A./St. Louis Rams, 1945, 1949-1952, 1955, 1967, 1969, 1973-1980, 1983-86, 1988-89, 1999-2001, 2003-04
  26 N.Y. Giants, 1933-35, 1938-39, 1941, 1943-44, 1946, 1950, 1956, 1958-59, 1961-63, 1981, 1984-86, 1989-1990, 1993, 1997, 2000, 2002
  24 Cleveland, 1950-55, 1957-58, 1964-65, 1967-69, 1971-72, 1980, 1982, 1985-89, 1994, 2002
     Minnesota, 1968-1971, 1973-78, 1980, 1982, 1987-89, 1992-94, 1996-2000, 2004

Most Consecutive Seasons Participating in Postseason Games
   9 Dallas, 1975-1983
   8 Dallas, 1966-1973
     Pittsburgh, 1972-79
     Los Angeles, 1973-1980
     San Francisco, 1983-1990
   7 Houston, 1987-1993
     San Francisco, 1992-98

Most Games
  54 Dallas, 1966-1973, 1975-1983, 1985, 1991-96, 1998-99, 2003
  43 Oakland/L.A. Raiders, 1967-1970, 1972-77, 1980, 1982-85, 1990-91, 1993, 2000-02
     Cleveland/L.A./St. Louis Rams, 1945, 1949-1952, 1955, 1967, 1969, 1973-1980, 1983-86, 1988-89, 1999-2001, 2003-04
  42 San Francisco, 1957, 1970-72, 1981, 1983-1990, 1992-98, 2001-02
     Minnesota, 1968-1971, 1973-78, 1980, 1982, 1987-89, 1992-94, 1996-2000, 2004
     Pittsburgh, 1947, 1972-79, 1982-84, 1989, 1992-97, 2001-02, 2004

Most Games Won
  32 Dallas, 1967, 1970-73, 1975, 1977-78, 1980-82, 1991-96
  25 Oakland/L.A. Raiders, 1967-1970, 1973-77, 1980, 1982-83, 1990, 1993, 2000-02
     San Francisco, 1970-71, 1981, 1983-84, 1988-1990, 1992-94, 1996-98, 2002

24 Green Bay, 1936, 1939, 1944, 1961-62, 1965-67, 1982,
    1993-97, 2001, 2003
    Pittsburgh, 1972, 1974-76, 1978-79, 1984, 1989,
    1994-97, 2001-02, 2004

Most Consecutive Games Won
9   Green Bay, 1961-62, 1965-67
    New England, 2001, 2003-04 (current)
7   Pittsburgh, 1974-76
    San Francisco, 1988-1990
    Dallas, 1992-94
    Denver, 1997-98
6   Miami, 1972-73
    Pittsburgh, 1978-79
    Washington, 1982-83

Most Games Lost
24 Minnesota, 1968-1971, 1973-78, 1980, 1982, 1987-89,
    1992-94, 1996-2000, 2004
    L.A./St. Louis Rams, 1949-1950, 1952, 1955, 1967,
    1969, 1973-1980, 1983-86, 1988-89, 2000-01,
    2003-04
22 Dallas, 1966-1970, 1972-73, 1975-76, 1978-1983, 1985,
    1991, 1994, 1996, 1998-99, 2003
21 N.Y. Giants, 1993, 1935, 1939, 1941, 1943-44, 1946,
    1950, 1958-59, 1961-63, 1981, 1984-85, 1989,
    1993, 1997, 2000, 2002

Most Consecutive Games Lost
6   N.Y. Giants, 1939, 1941, 1943-44, 1946, 1950
    Cleveland, 1969, 1971-72, 1980, 1982, 1985
    Minnesota, 1988-89, 1992-94, 1996
    Detroit, 1991, 1993-95, 1997, 1999 (current)
    Seattle, 1984, 1987-88, 1999, 2003-04 (current)
5   N.Y. Giants, 1958-59, 1961-63
    Los Angeles, 1952, 1955, 1967, 1969, 1973
    Denver, 1977-79, 1983-84
    Baltimore/Indianapolis, 1971, 1975-77, 1987
    Philadelphia, 1980-81, 1988-1990
    Indianapolis, 1995-96, 1999-2000, 2002
    Kansas City, 1993-95, 1997, 2003 (current)
4   Washington, 1972-74, 1976
    Miami, 1974, 1978-79, 1981
    Chi. Cardinals/St. Louis, 1948, 1974-75, 1982
    Boston/New England, 1963, 1976, 1978, 1982
    New Orleans, 1987, 1990-92
    Buffalo, 1995-96, 1998-99 (current)
    Dallas, 1996, 1998-99, 2003 (current)

SCORING
Most Points, Game
73 NFC: Chi. Bears vs. Washington, 1940
62 AFC-D: Jacksonville vs. Miami, 1999
59 NFC: Detroit vs. Cleveland, 1957

Most Points, Both Teams, Game
95 NFC-FR: Philadelphia (58) vs. Detroit (37), 1995
86 NFC-D: St. Louis (49) vs. Minnesota (37), 1999
79 AFC-D: San Diego (41) vs. Miami (38), 1981 (OT)
    AFC-FR: Buffalo (41) vs. Houston (38), 1992 (OT)

Fewest Points, Both Teams, Game
5   NFC-D: Detroit (0) vs. Dallas (5), 1970
7   NFC: Chi. Cardinals (0) vs. Philadelphia (7), 1948
9   NFC: Tampa Bay (0) vs. Los Angeles (9), 1979

Largest Margin of Victory, Game
73 NFC: Chi. Bears vs. Washington, 1940 (73-0)
55 AFC-D: Jacksonville vs. Miami, 1999 (62-7)
49 AFC-D: Oakland vs. Houston, 1969 (56-7)

Most Points, Shutout Victory, Game
73 NFC: Chi. Bears vs. Washington, 1940
41 NFC: N.Y. Giants vs. Minnesota, 2000
    AFC-FR: N.Y. Jets vs. Indianapolis, 2002
38 NFC-D: Dallas vs. Tampa Bay, 1981

Most Points Overcome to Win Game
32 AFC-FR: Buffalo vs. Houston, 1992 (trailed 3-35,
    won 41-38) (OT)
24 NFC-FR: San Francisco vs. N.Y. Giants, 2002 (trailed
    14-38, won 39-38)
20 NFC-D: Detroit vs. San Francisco, 1957 (trailed 7-27,
    won 31-27)

Most Points, Each Half
1st: 41 AFC: Buffalo vs. L.A. Raiders, 1990
          AFC-FR: Jacksonville vs. Miami, 1999
      38 NFC-D: Washington vs. L.A. Rams, 1983
          NFC-FR: Philadelphia vs. Detroit, 1995
      35 NFC: Cleveland vs. Detroit, 1954
          AFC-D: Oakland vs. Houston, 1969
          SB: Washington vs. Denver, 1987
          AFC-FR: Indianapolis vs. Denver, 2004
2nd: 45 NFC: Chi. Bears vs. Washington, 1940
      35 AFC-FR: Buffalo vs. Houston, 1992
          NFC-D: St. Louis vs. Minnesota, 1999
      30 SB: N.Y. Giants vs. Denver, 1986
          AFC: Cleveland vs. Denver, 1987
          NFC-FR: Detroit vs. Philadelphia, 1995

Most Points, Each Quarter
1st: 28 AFC-D: Oakland vs. Houston, 1969
      24 AFC-D: San Diego vs. Miami, 1981
          AFC-D: Jacksonville vs. Miami, 1999
      21 NFC: Chi. Bears vs. Washington, 1940
          AFC: San Diego vs. Boston, 1963
          AFC-D: Oakland vs. Kansas City, 1968
          AFC: Oakland vs. San Diego, 1980
          AFC: Buffalo vs. L.A. Raiders, 1990
          NFC: San Francisco vs. Dallas, 1994
2nd: 35 SB: Washington vs. Denver, 1987
      31 NFC-FR: Philadelphia vs. Detroit, 1995
      26 AFC-D: Pittsburgh vs. Buffalo, 1974
3rd: 28 AFC-FR: Buffalo vs. Houston, 1992
      26 NFC: Chi. Bears vs. Washington, 1940
      21 NFC-D: Dallas vs. Cleveland, 1967
          NFC-D: Dallas vs. Tampa Bay, 1981
          AFC-D: L.A. Raiders vs. Pittsburgh, 1983
          SB: Chicago vs. New England, 1985
          NFC-D: N.Y. Giants vs. San Francisco, 1986
          AFC: Cleveland vs. Denver, 1987
          AFC: Cleveland vs. Denver, 1989
          NFC-D: St. Louis vs. Minnesota, 1999
4th: 27 NFC: N.Y. Giants vs. Chi. Bears, 1934
      26 NFC-FR: Philadelphia vs. New Orleans, 1992
      24 NFC: Baltimore vs. N.Y. Giants, 1959
OT: 6   NFC: Baltimore vs. N.Y. Giants, 1958
          AFC-D: Oakland vs. Baltimore, 1977
          NFC-D: L.A. Rams vs. N.Y. Giants, 1989
          AFC-FR: Miami vs. Indianapolis, 2000
          NFC-FR: Green Bay vs. Seattle, 2003
          NFC-D: Carolina vs. St. Louis, 2003

TOUCHDOWNS
Most Touchdowns, Game
11 NFC: Chi. Bears vs. Washington, 1940
8   NFC: Cleveland vs. Detroit, 1954
    NFC: Detroit vs. Cleveland, 1957
    AFC-D: Oakland vs. Houston, 1969
    SB: San Francisco vs. Denver, 1989
    AFC-D: Jacksonville vs. Miami, 1999
7   AFC: San Diego vs. Boston, 1963
    NFC-D: Dallas vs. Cleveland, 1967
    NFC-D: N.Y. Giants vs. San Francisco, 1986
    AFC: Buffalo vs. L.A. Raiders, 1990
    SB: Dallas vs. Buffalo, 1992
    SB: San Francisco vs. San Diego, 1994
    NFC-FR: Philadelphia vs. Detroit, 1995

NFC-D: St. Louis vs. Minnesota, 1999
AFC-FR: Indianapolis vs. Denver, 2004

Most Touchdowns, Both Teams, Game
- 12 NFC-FR: Philadelphia (7) vs. Detroit (5), 1995
  NFC-D: St. Louis (7) vs. Minnesota (5), 1999
- 11 NFC: Chi. Bears (11) vs. Washington (0), 1940
- 10 NFC: Detroit (8) vs. Cleveland (2), 1957
  AFC-D: Miami (5) vs. San Diego (5), 1981 (OT)
  AFC: Miami (6) vs. Pittsburgh (4), 1984
  AFC-FR: Buffalo (5) vs. Houston (5), 1992 (OT)
  SB: San Francisco (7) vs. San Diego (3), 1994
  NFC-FR: San Francisco (5) vs. N.Y. Giants (5), 2002
  AFC-FR: Indianapolis (7) vs. Denver (3), 2004

Fewest Touchdowns, Both Teams, Game
- 0 NFC-D: N.Y. Giants vs. Cleveland, 1950
  NFC-D: Dallas vs. Detroit, 1970
  NFC: Los Angeles vs. Tampa Bay, 1979
- 1 NFC: Chi. Cardinals (0) vs. Philadelphia (1), 1948
  NFC-D: Cleveland (0) vs. N.Y. Giants (1), 1958
  AFC: San Diego (0) vs. Houston (1), 1961
  AFC-D: N.Y. Jets (0) vs. Kansas City (1), 1969
  NFC-D: Green Bay (0) vs. Washington (1), 1972
  NFC-FR: New Orleans (0) vs. Chicago (1), 1990
  NFC: N.Y. Giants (0) vs. San Francisco (1), 1990
  AFC-FR: L.A. Raiders (0) vs. Kansas City (1), 1991
  AFC-D: New England (0) vs. Pittsburgh (1), 1997
  NFC: Tampa Bay (0) vs. St. Louis (1), 1999
  AFC: Oakland (0) vs. Baltimore (1), 2000
- 2 In many games

POINTS AFTER TOUCHDOWN
Most (One-Point) Points After Touchdown, Game
- 8 NFC: Cleveland vs. Detroit, 1954
  NFC: Detroit vs. Cleveland, 1957
  AFC-D: Oakland vs. Houston, 1969
  AFC-D: Jacksonville vs. Miami, 1999
- 7 NFC: Chi. Bears vs. Washington, 1940
  NFC-D: Dallas vs. Cleveland, 1967
  NFC-D: N.Y. Giants vs. San Francisco, 1986
  SB: San Francisco vs. Denver, 1989
  SB: Dallas vs. Buffalo, 1992
  SB: San Francisco vs. San Diego, 1994
  NFC-FR: Philadelphia vs. Detroit, 1995
  NFC-D: St. Louis vs. Minnesota, 1999
  AFC-FR: Indianapolis vs. Denver, 2004
- 6 AFC: San Diego vs. Boston, 1963
  NFC-D: Washington vs. L.A. Rams, 1983
  AFC: Miami vs. Pittsburgh, 1984
  SB: Washington vs. Denver, 1987
  AFC: Buffalo vs. L.A. Raiders, 1990
  AFC-FR: L.A. Raiders vs. Denver, 1993
  AFC-FR: Denver vs. Jacksonville, 1997
  NFC-D: St. Louis vs. Green Bay, 2001
  SB: Tampa Bay vs. Oakland, 2002
  NFC-D: Atlanta vs. St. Louis, 2004

Most (One-Point) Points After Touchdown, Both Teams, Game
- 10 NFC: Detroit (8) vs. Cleveland (2), 1957
  AFC-D: Miami (5) vs. San Diego (5), 1981 (OT)
  AFC: Miami (6) vs. Pittsburgh (4), 1984
  AFC-FR: Buffalo (5) vs. Houston (5), 1992 (OT)
  NFC-FR: Philadelphia (7) vs. Detroit (3), 1995
  AFC-FR: Indianapolis (7) vs. Denver (3), 2004
- 9 In many games

Fewest (One-Point) Points After Touchdown, Both Teams, Game
- 0 NFC-D: N.Y. Giants vs. Cleveland, 1950
  NFC-D: Dallas vs. Detroit, 1970
  NFC: Los Angeles vs. Tampa Bay, 1979
  NFC: St. Louis vs. Tampa Bay, 1999

Most Two-Point Conversions, Game
- 2 SB: San Diego vs. San Francisco, 1994

NFC-FR: Detroit vs. Philadelphia, 1995
NFC-FR: San Francisco vs.. N.Y. Giants, 2002
- 1 By many teams

FIELD GOALS
Most Field Goals, Game
- 5 NFC-D: Minnesota vs. San Francisco, 1987
  NFC: N.Y. Giants vs. San Francisco, 1990
  AFC: Buffalo vs. Miami, 1992
  NFC-FR: N.Y. Giants vs. Minnesota, 1997
  NFC-FR: Carolina vs. Dallas, 2003
  NFC-D: St. Louis vs. Carolina, 2003 (2 OT)
  AFC: New England vs. Indianapolis, 2003
- 4 AFC-D: Boston vs. Buffalo, 1963
  AFC: Oakland vs. Houston, 1967
  SB: Green Bay vs. Oakland, 1967
  NFC: Washington vs. Dallas, 1972
  AFC-D: Oakland vs. Pittsburgh, 1973
  SB: San Francisco vs. Cincinnati, 1981
  AFC-FR: New England vs. N.Y. Jets, 1985
  NFC-FR: Washington vs. L.A. Rams, 1986
  NFC-D: Philadelphia vs. Chicago, 1988
  AFC-FR: Pittsburgh vs. Houston, 1989 (OT)
  AFC: Pittsburgh vs. Buffalo, 1995
  NFC-D: Dallas vs. Minnesota, 1996
  NFC-D: Carolina vs. Dallas, 1996
  AFC-FR: Jacksonville vs. New England, 1998
  AFC-D: Tennessee vs. Indianapolis, 1999
  NFC-D: Philadelphia vs. Chicago, 2001
- 3 By many teams

Most Field Goals, Both Teams, Game
- 8 NFC-FR: N.Y. Giants (5) vs. Minnesota (3), 1997
  NFC-D: St. Louis (5) vs. Carolina (3), 2003 (2 OT)
- 7 AFC-FR: Pittsburgh (4) vs. Houston (3), 1989 (OT)
  NFC: N.Y. Giants (5) vs. San Francisco (2), 1990
  NFC-D: Carolina (4) vs. Dallas (3), 1996
  AFC-D: Tennessee (4) vs. Indianapolis (3), 1999
- 6 NFC-D: Minnesota (5) vs. San Francisco (1), 1987
  NFC-D: Philadelphia (4) vs. Chicago (2), 1988
  AFC: Buffalo (5) vs. Miami (1), 1992
  NFC-FR: Carolina (5) vs. Dallas (1), 2003

Most Field Goals Attempted, Game
- 6 AFC: Oakland vs. Houston, 1967
  NFC-D: Los Angeles vs. Dallas, 1973
  AFC-D: Cleveland vs. N.Y. Jets, 1986 (OT)
  NFC: N.Y. Giants vs. San Francisco, 1990
  AFC: Buffalo vs. Miami, 1992
  NFC-D: St. Louis vs. Carolina, 2003 (2 OT)
- 5 By many teams

Most Field Goals Attempted, Both Teams, Game
- 11 NFC-D: St. Louis (6) vs. Carolina (5), 2003 (2 OT)
- 9 NFC-D: Philadelphia (5) vs. Chicago (4), 1988
  NFC-FR: N.Y. Giants (5) vs. Minnesota (4), 1997
- 8 NFC-D: Los Angeles (6) vs. Dallas (2), 1973
  NFC-D: Detroit (5) vs. San Francisco (3), 1983
  AFC-D: Cleveland (6) vs. N.Y. Jets (2), 1986 (OT)
  NFC-D: Minnesota (5) vs. San Francisco (3), 1987
  AFC-FR: Houston (4) vs. Pittsburgh (4), 1989 (OT)
  NFC-FR: Chicago (4) vs. New Orleans (4), 1990
  NFC: N.Y. Giants (6) vs. San Francisco (2), 1990

SAFETIES
Most Safeties, Game
- 1 By many teams

Most Safeties, Both Teams, Game
- 1 In many games

FIRST DOWNS
Most First Downs, Game
- 34 AFC-D: San Diego vs. Miami, 1981 (OT)

33 AFC-D: Cleveland vs. N.Y. Jets, 1986 (OT)
31 SB: San Francisco vs. Miami, 1984
    NFC-D: San Francisco vs. Minnesota, 1997
    NFC: N.Y. Giants vs. Minnesota, 2000

Fewest First Downs, Game

6 NFC: N.Y. Giants vs. Green Bay, 1961
   AFC-D: Baltimore vs. Tennessee, 2000
7 NFC: Green Bay vs. Boston, 1936
   NFC-D: Pittsburgh vs. Philadelphia, 1947
   NFC: Chi. Cardinals vs. Philadelphia, 1948
   NFC: Los Angeles vs. Philadelphia, 1949
   NFC-D: Cleveland vs. N.Y. Giants, 1958
   AFC-D: Cincinnati vs. Baltimore, 1970
   NFC-D: Detroit vs. Dallas, 1970
   NFC: Tampa Bay vs. Los Angeles, 1979
   AFC-D: Baltimore vs. Pittsburgh, 2001
8 By many teams

Most First Downs, Both Teams, Game

59 AFC-D: San Diego (34) vs. Miami (25), 1981 (OT)
55 AFC-FR: San Diego (29) vs. Pittsburgh (26), 1982
54 AFC-FR: Buffalo (28) vs. Miami (26), 1995

Fewest First Downs, Both Teams, Game

15 NFC: Green Bay (7) vs. Boston (8), 1936
19 NFC: N.Y. Giants (9) vs. Green Bay (10), 1939
    NFC: Washington (9) vs. Chi. Bears (10), 1942
20 NFC-D: Cleveland (9) vs. N.Y. Giants (11), 1950

RUSHING

Most First Downs, Rushing, Game

19 NFC-FR: Dallas vs. Los Angeles, 1980
18 AFC-D: Miami vs. Cincinnati, 1973
    AFC: Miami vs. Oakland, 1973
    AFC-D: Pittsburgh vs. Buffalo, 1974
    AFC-FR: Buffalo vs. Miami, 1995
    AFC-FR: Denver vs. Jacksonville, 1997
17 AFC-D: Cincinnati vs. Seattle, 1988
    AFC: Buffalo vs. Kansas City, 1993

Fewest First Downs, Rushing, Game

0 NFC: Los Angeles vs. Philadelphia, 1949
   AFC-D: Buffalo vs. Boston, 1963
   AFC: Oakland vs. Pittsburgh, 1974
   NFC-FR: New Orleans vs. Minnesota, 1987
   NFC: L.A. Rams vs. San Francisco, 1989
   NFC-D: Chicago vs. N.Y. Giants, 1990
   AFC-D: Indianapolis vs. Pittsburgh, 1996
   AFC-FR: Seattle vs. Miami, 1999
   AFC-D: Miami vs. Jacksonville, 1999
   AFC-D: Miami vs. Oakland, 2000
   AFC-D: Baltimore vs. Pittsburgh, 2001
   AFC-D: Indianapolis vs. New England, 2004
1 By many teams

Most First Downs, Rushing, Both Teams, Game

26 AFC: Buffalo (14) vs. L.A. Raiders (12), 1990
25 NFC-FR: Dallas (19) vs. Los Angeles (6), 1980
23 NFC: Cleveland (15) vs. Detroit (8), 1952
    AFC-D: Miami (18) vs. Cincinnati (5), 1973
    AFC-D: Pittsburgh (18) vs. Buffalo (5), 1974
    AFC-FR: Buffalo (18) vs. Miami (5), 1995

Fewest First Downs, Rushing, Both Teams, Game

2 NFC-FR: New Orleans (1) vs. St. Louis (1), 2000
5 AFC-D: Buffalo (0) vs. Boston (5), 1963
   NFC-D: Washington (1) vs. Tampa Bay (4), 1999
   AFC-FR: Cleveland (2) vs. Pittsburgh (3), 2002
6 NFC: Green Bay (2) vs. Boston (4), 1936
   NFC-D: Baltimore (2) vs. Minnesota (4), 1968
   AFC-D: Houston (1) vs. Oakland (5), 1969
   AFC-FR: N.Y. Jets (1) vs. Houston (5), 1991
   AFC-FR: Denver (1) vs. Baltimore (5), 2000

PASSING

Most First Downs, Passing, Game

24 AFC-FR: Pittsburgh vs. Cleveland, 2002
21 AFC-D: Miami vs. San Diego, 1981 (OT)
    AFC-D: San Diego vs. Miami, 1981 (OT)
    AFC-D: Cleveland vs. N.Y. Jets, 1986 (OT)
    NFC-D: Philadelphia vs. Chicago, 1988
20 NFC-FR: Dallas vs. L.A. Rams, 1983
    AFC-D: Buffalo vs. Cleveland, 1989
    AFC-FR: Miami vs. Buffalo, 1995
    NFC-FR: Detroit vs. Philadelphia, 1995
    AFC-FR: San Diego vs. Indianapolis, 1995
    NFC-D: Minnesota vs. St. Louis, 1999

Fewest First Downs, Passing, Game

0 NFC: Philadelphia vs. Chi. Cardinals, 1948
1 NFC-D: N.Y. Giants vs. Washington, 1943
   NFC: Cleveland vs. Detroit, 1953
   SB: Denver vs. Dallas, 1977
2 By many teams

Most First Downs, Passing, Both Teams, Game

42 AFC-D: Miami (21) vs. San Diego (21), 1981 (OT)
    AFC-FR: Pittsburgh (24) vs. Cleveland (18), 2002
38 AFC-FR: Pittsburgh (19) vs. San Diego (19), 1982
    NFC-D: Minnesota (20) vs. St. Louis (18), 1999
36 NFC: Minnesota (19) vs. Atlanta (17), 1998 (OT)

Fewest First Downs, Passing, Both Teams, Game

2 NFC: Philadelphia (0) vs. Chi. Cardinals (2), 1948
4 NFC-D: Cleveland (2) vs. N.Y. Giants (2), 1950
5 NFC: Detroit (2) vs. N.Y. Giants (3), 1935
   NFC: Green Bay (2) vs. N.Y. Giants (3), 1939

PENALTY

Most First Downs, Penalty, Game

7 AFC-D: New England vs. Oakland, 1976
   AFC: Tennessee vs. Oakland, 2002
6 AFC-D: Cleveland vs. N.Y. Jets, 1986 (OT)
5 AFC-FR: Cleveland vs. L. A. Raiders, 1982
   NFC-D: San Francisco vs. Minnesota, 1997
   AFC-FR: Miami vs. Buffalo, 1998
   NFC-D: Arizona vs. Minnesota, 1998
   AFC: Pittsburgh vs. New England, 2001
   AFC-D: Pittsburgh vs. Tennessee, 2002 (OT)

Most First Downs, Penalty, Both Teams, Game

10 AFC: Tennessee (7) vs. Oakland (3), 2002
9 AFC-D: New England (7) vs. Oakland (2), 1976
8 NFC-FR: Atlanta (4) vs. Minnesota (4), 1982
   AFC-FR: Miami (5) vs. Buffalo (3), 1998

NET YARDS GAINED RUSHING AND PASSING

Most Yards Gained, Game

610 AFC: San Diego vs. Boston, 1963
602 SB: Washington vs. Denver, 1987
569 AFC: Miami vs. Pittsburgh, 1984

Fewest Yards Gained, Game

86 NFC-D: Cleveland vs. N.Y. Giants, 1958
99 NFC: Chi. Cardinals vs. Philadelphia, 1948
114 NFC-D: N.Y. Giants vs. Washington, 1943
     NFC: Minnesota vs. N.Y. Giants, 2000

Most Yards Gained, Both Teams, Game

1,038 AFC-FR: Buffalo (536) vs. Miami (502), 1995
1,036 AFC-D: San Diego (564) vs. Miami (472), 1981 (OT)
1,024 AFC: Miami (569) vs. Pittsburgh (455), 1984

Fewest Yards Gained, Both Teams, Game

331 NFC: Chi. Cardinals (99) vs. Philadelphia (232), 1948
332 NFC-D: N.Y. Giants (150) vs. Cleveland (182), 1950
336 NFC: Boston (116) vs. Green Bay (220), 1936

RUSHING

ATTEMPTS

Most Attempts, Game
- 65 NFC: Detroit vs. N.Y. Giants, 1935
- 61 NFC: Philadelphia vs. Los Angeles, 1949
- 59 AFC: New England vs. Miami, 1985

Fewest Attempts, Game
- 8 AFC-D: Miami vs. San Diego, 1994
- 9 SB: Miami vs. San Francisco, 1984
  - NFC: Minnesota vs. N.Y. Giants, 2000
- 10 NFC: L.A. Rams vs. San Francisco, 1989
  - NFC-FR: Atlanta vs. Green Bay, 1995
  - NFC-FR: Detroit vs. Washington, 1999

Most Attempts, Both Teams, Game
- 109 NFC: Detroit (65) vs. N.Y. Giants (44), 1935
- 97 AFC-D: Baltimore (50) vs. Oakland (47), 1977 (OT)
- 91 NFC: Philadelphia (57) vs. Chi. Cardinals (34), 1948

Fewest Attempts, Both Teams, Game
- 32 AFC-D: Houston (14) vs. Kansas City (18), 1993
- 38 NFC-D: Detroit (16) vs. Dallas (22), 1991
- 39 NFC-FR: Atlanta (10) vs. Green Bay (29), 1995

YARDS GAINED

Most Yards Gained, Game
- 382 NFC: Chi. Bears vs. Washington, 1940
- 341 AFC-FR: Buffalo vs. Miami, 1995
- 338 NFC-D: Dallas vs. Los Angeles, 1980

Fewest Yards Gained, Game
- – 4 NFC-FR: Detroit vs. Green Bay, 1994
- 7 AFC-D: Buffalo vs. Boston, 1963
  - SB: New England vs. Chicago, 1985
- 14 AFC-D: Miami vs. Denver, 1998
  - AFC: N.Y. Jets vs. Denver, 1998

Most Yards Gained, Both Teams, Game
- 430 NFC-FR: Dallas (338) vs. Los Angeles (92), 1980
- 426 NFC: Cleveland (227) vs. Detroit (199), 1952
- 411 AFC-FR: Buffalo (341) vs. Miami (70), 1995

Fewest Yards Gained, Both Teams, Game
- 77 NFC-FR: Detroit (–4) vs. Green Bay (81), 1994
- 84 NFC-FR: St. Louis (34) vs. New Orleans (50), 2000
- 90 AFC-D: Buffalo (7) vs. Boston (83), 1963
  - NFC-D: Tampa Bay (44) vs. Washington (46), 1999

AVERAGE GAIN

Highest Average Gain, Game
- 9.94 AFC: San Diego vs. Boston, 1963 (32-318)
- 9.29 NFC-D: Green Bay vs. Dallas, 1982 (17-158)
- 8.18 NFC-D: Atlanta vs. St. Louis, 2004 (40-327)

Lowest Average Gain, Game
- – 0.27 NFC-FR: Detroit vs. Green Bay, 1994 (15-(– 4))
- 0.58 AFC-D: Buffalo vs. Boston, 1963 (12-7)
- 0.64 SB: New England vs. Chicago, 1985 (11-7)

TOUCHDOWNS

Most Touchdowns, Game
- 7 NFC: Chi. Bears vs. Washington, 1940
- 6 NFC-D: San Francisco vs. N.Y. Giants, 1993
- 5 NFC: Cleveland vs. Detroit, 1954
  - NFC-D: San Francisco vs. Chicago, 1994
  - AFC-FR: Pittsburgh vs. Indianapolis, 1996
  - AFC-FR: Denver vs. Jacksonville, 1997

Most Touchdowns, Both Teams, Game
- 7 NFC: Chi. Bears (7) vs. Washington (0), 1940
- 6 NFC: Cleveland (5) vs. Detroit (1), 1954
  - NFC-D: San Francisco (6) vs. N.Y. Giants (0), 1993
  - NFC-D: San Francisco (5) vs. Chicago (1), 1994
  - AFC-FR: Denver (5) vs. Jacksonville (1), 1997
- 5 NFC: Chi. Cardinals (3) vs. Philadelphia (2), 1947
  - AFC: San Diego (4) vs. Boston (1), 1963

- AFC-D: Cincinnati (3) vs. Buffalo (2), 1981
- AFC-FR: Pittsburgh (5) vs. Indianapolis (0), 1996
- NFC-D: Arizona (3) vs. Minnesota (2), 1998
- NFC-FR: Seattle (3) vs. Green Bay (2), 2003 (OT)

PASSING

ATTEMPTS

Most Attempts, Game
- 66 AFC-FR: Miami vs. Buffalo, 1995
- 65 AFC-D: Cleveland vs. N.Y. Jets, 1986 (OT)
  - NFC-D: San Francisco vs. Green Bay, 1995
- 61 NFC-FR: Minnesota vs. Chicago, 1994

Fewest Attempts, Game
- 5 NFC: Detroit vs. N.Y. Giants, 1935
- 6 AFC: Miami vs. Oakland, 1973
- 7 SB: Miami vs. Minnesota, 1973

Most Attempts, Both Teams, Game
- 102 AFC-D: San Diego (54) vs. Miami (48), 1981 (OT)
- 96 AFC: N.Y. Jets (49) vs. Oakland (47), 1968
- 95 AFC-D: Cleveland (65) vs. N.Y. Jets (30), 1986 (OT)

Fewest Attempts, Both Teams, Game
- 18 NFC: Detroit (5) vs. N.Y. Giants (13), 1935
- 23 NFC: Chi. Cardinals (11) vs. Philadelphia (12), 1948
- 24 NFC-D: Cleveland (9) vs. N.Y. Giants (15), 1950

COMPLETIONS

Most Completions, Game
- 36 AFC-FR: Houston vs. Buffalo, 1992 (OT)
- 34 AFC-D: Cleveland vs. N.Y. Jets, 1986 (OT)
  - AFC-FR: Miami vs. Buffalo, 1995
- 33 AFC-D: San Diego vs. Miami, 1981 (OT)
  - NFC-FR: Minnesota vs. Chicago, 1994

Fewest Completions, Game
- 2 NFC: Detroit vs. N.Y. Giants, 1935
  - NFC: Philadelphia vs. Chi. Cardinals, 1948
- 3 NFC: N.Y. Giants vs. Chi. Bears, 1941
  - NFC: Green Bay vs. N.Y. Giants, 1944
  - NFC: Chi. Cardinals vs. Philadelphia, 1947
  - NFC: Chi. Cardinals vs. Philadelphia, 1948
  - NFC-D: Cleveland vs. N.Y. Giants, 1950
  - NFC-D: N.Y. Giants vs. Cleveland, 1950
  - NFC: Cleveland vs. Detroit, 1953
  - AFC: Miami vs. Oakland, 1973
- 4 NFC: N.Y. Giants vs. Detroit, 1935
  - NFC: N.Y. Giants vs. Washington, 1943
  - NFC-D: Pittsburgh vs. Philadelphia, 1947
  - NFC-D: Dallas vs. Detroit, 1970
  - AFC: Miami vs. Baltimore, 1971
  - SB: Miami vs. Washington, 1982
  - AFC-FR: Seattle vs. L.A. Raiders, 1984

Most Completions, Both Teams, Game
- 64 AFC-D: San Diego (33) vs. Miami (31), 1981 (OT)
- 57 AFC-FR: Houston (36) vs. Buffalo (21), 1992 (OT)
  - NFC-FR: N.Y. Giants (29) vs. San Francisco (28), 2002
- 56 NFC-D: Dallas (28) vs. Green Bay (28), 1993
  - NFC: Minnesota (29) vs. Atlanta (27), 1998 (OT)
  - NFC-D: Minnesota (29) vs. St. Louis (27), 1999
  - AFC-FR: Pittsburgh (30) vs. Cleveland (26), 2002

Fewest Completions, Both Teams, Game
- 5 NFC: Philadelphia (2) vs. Chi. Cardinals (3), 1948
- 6 NFC: Detroit (2) vs. N.Y. Giants (4), 1935
  - NFC-D: Cleveland (3) vs. N.Y. Giants (3), 1950
- 11 NFC: Green Bay (3) vs. N.Y. Giants (8), 1944
  - NFC-D: Dallas (4) vs. Detroit (7), 1970

COMPLETION PERCENTAGE

Highest Completion Percentage, Game (20 attempts)
- 88.0 SB: N.Y. Giants vs. Denver, 1986 (25-22)
- 87.1 NFC: San Francisco vs. L.A. Rams, 1989 (31-27)
- 83.9 AFC-FR: Indianapolis vs. Denver, 2003

Lowest Completion Percentage, Game (20 attempts)
- 18.5 NFC: Tampa Bay vs. Los Angeles, 1979 (27-5)
- 20.0 NFC-D: N.Y. Giants vs. Washington, 1943 (20-4)
- 25.8 NFC: Chi. Bears vs. Washington, 1937 (31-8)

YARDS GAINED
Most Yards Gained, Game
- 483 AFC-D: Cleveland vs. N.Y. Jets, 1986 (OT)
- 454 AFC-FR: Indianapolis vs. Denver, 2004
- 435 AFC: Miami vs. Pittsburgh, 1984

Fewest Yards Gained, Game
- 3 NFC: Chi. Cardinals vs. Philadelphia, 1948
- 7 Philadelphia vs. Chi. Cardinals, 1948
- 9 NFC-D: N.Y. Giants vs. Cleveland, 1950
-   NFC: Cleveland vs. Detroit, 1953

Most Yards Gained, Both Teams, Game
- 809 AFC-D: San Diego (415) vs. Miami (394), 1981 (OT)
- 762 NFC-D: Minnesota (388) vs. St. Louis (374), 1999
- 752 AFC-FR: Cleveland (409) vs. Pittsburgh (343), 2002

Fewest Yards Gained, Both Teams, Game
- 10 NFC: Chi. Cardinals (3) vs. Philadelphia (7), 1948
- 38 NFC-D: N.Y. Giants (9) vs. Cleveland (29), 1950
- 102 NFC-D: Dallas (22) vs. Detroit (80), 1970

TIMES SACKED
Most Times Sacked, Game
- 9 AFC: Kansas City vs. Buffalo, 1966
-   NFC: Chicago vs. San Francisco, 1984
-   AFC-D: N.Y. Jets vs. Cleveland, 1986 (OT)
-   AFC-D: Houston vs. Kansas City, 1993
- 8 NFC: Green Bay vs. Dallas, 1967
-   NFC: Minnesota vs. Washington, 1987
-   NFC-D: Philadelphia vs. Green Bay, 2003 (OT)
- 7 NFC-D: Dallas vs. Los Angeles, 1973
-   SB: Dallas vs. Pittsburgh, 1975
-   AFC-FR: Houston vs. Oakland, 1980
-   NFC-D: Washington vs. Chicago, 1984
-   SB: New England vs. Chicago, 1985
-   AFC-FR: Kansas City vs. San Diego, 1992
-   AFC-D: Pittsburgh vs. Buffalo, 1992

Most Times Sacked, Both Teams, Game
- 13 AFC: Kansas City (9) vs. Buffalo (4), 1966
-   AFC-D: N.Y. Jets (9) vs. Cleveland (4), 1986 (OT)
- 12 NFC-D: Dallas (7) vs. Los Angeles (5), 1973
-   NFC-D: Washington (7) vs. Chicago (5), 1984
-   NFC: Chicago (9) vs. San Francisco (3), 1984
-   AFC-FR: Kansas City (7) vs. San Diego (5), 1992
- 11 AFC-D: Houston (9) vs. Kansas City (2), 1993

Fewest Times Sacked, Both Teams, Game
- 0 AFC-D: Buffalo vs. Pittsburgh, 1974
-   AFC-FR: Pittsburgh vs. San Diego, 1982
-   AFC: Miami vs. Pittsburgh, 1984
-   AFC-D: Buffalo vs. Miami, 1990
-   AFC-D: Denver vs. Houston, 1991
-   AFC-FR: Buffalo vs. Miami, 1995
-   AFC-D: Indianapolis vs. Tennessee, 1999
- 1 In many games

TOUCHDOWNS
Most Touchdowns, Game
- 6 AFC-D: Oakland vs. Houston, 1969
-   SB: San Francisco vs. San Diego, 1994
- 5 NFC: Chi. Bears vs. Washington, 1943
-   NFC: Detroit vs. Cleveland, 1957
-   AFC-D: Oakland vs. Kansas City, 1968
-   SB: San Francisco vs. Denver, 1989
-   NFC-D: St. Louis vs. Minnesota, 1999
-   NFC: N.Y. Giants vs. Minnesota, 2000
-   AFC-FR: Indianapolis vs. Denver, 2003
- 4 By many teams

Most Touchdowns, Both Teams, Game
- 9 NFC-D: St. Louis (5) vs. Minnesota (4), 1999
- 8 AFC-FR: Buffalo (4) vs. Houston (4), 1992 (OT)
- 7 NFC: Chi. Bears (5) vs. Washington (2), 1943
-   AFC-D: Oakland (6) vs. Houston (1), 1969
-   SB: Pittsburgh (4) vs. Dallas (3), 1978
-   AFC-D: Miami (4) vs. San Diego (3), 1981 (OT)
-   AFC: Miami (4) vs. Pittsburgh (3), 1984
-   AFC-D: Buffalo (4) vs. Cleveland (3), 1989
-   SB: San Francisco (6) vs. San Diego (1), 1994
-   NFC-FR: Detroit (4) vs. Philadelphia (3), 1995
-   NFC-FR: New Orleans (4) vs. St. Louis (3), 2000
-   NFC-FR: N.Y. Giants (4) vs. San Francisco (3), 2002

INTERCEPTIONS BY
Most Interceptions By, Game
- 8 NFC: Chi. Bears vs. Washington, 1940
- 7 NFC: Cleveland vs. Los Angeles, 1955
- 6 NFC: Green Bay vs. N.Y. Giants, 1939
-   NFC: Chi. Bears vs. N.Y. Giants, 1946
-   NFC: Cleveland vs. Detroit, 1954
-   AFC: San Diego vs. Houston, 1961
-   AFC: Buffalo vs. L.A. Raiders, 1990
-   NFC-FR: Philadelphia vs. Detroit, 1995
-   NFC-D: St. Louis vs. Green Bay, 2001

Most Interceptions By, Both Teams, Game
- 10 NFC: Cleveland (7) vs. Los Angeles (3), 1955
-   AFC: San Diego (6) vs. Houston (4), 1961
- 9 NFC: Green Bay (6) vs. N.Y. Giants (3), 1939
- 8 NFC: Chi. Bears (8) vs. Washington (0), 1940
-   NFC: Chi. Bears (6) vs. N.Y. Giants (2), 1946
-   NFC: Cleveland (6) vs. Detroit (2), 1954
-   AFC-FR: Buffalo (4) vs. N.Y. Jets (4), 1981
-   AFC: Miami (5) vs. N.Y. Jets (3), 1982

YARDS GAINED
Most Yards Gained, Game
- 172 SB: Tampa Bay vs. Oakland, 2002
- 161 NFC-D: St. Louis vs. Green Bay, 2001
- 138 AFC-FR: N.Y. Jets vs. Cincinnati, 1982

Most Yards Gained, Both Teams, Game
- 184 SB: Tampa Bay (172) vs. Oakland (12), 2002
- 161 NFC-D: St. Louis (161) vs. Green Bay (0), 2001
- 156 NFC: Green Bay (123) vs. N.Y. Giants (33), 1939

TOUCHDOWNS
Most Touchdowns, Game
- 3 NFC: Chi. Bears vs. Washington, 1940
-   NFC-D: St. Louis vs. Green Bay, 2001
-   SB: Tampa Bay vs. Oakland, 2002
- 2 NFC-D: Los Angeles vs. St. Louis, 1975
-   NFC-FR: Philadelphia vs. Detroit, 1995
- 1 In many games

Most Touchdowns, Both Teams, Game
- 3 NFC: Chi. Bears (3) vs. Washington (0), 1940
-   NFC-D: St. Louis (3) vs. Green Bay (0), 2001
-   SB: Tampa Bay (3) vs. Oakland (0), 2002
- 2 NFC-D: Los Angeles (2) vs. St. Louis(0), 1975
-   NFC-D: Dallas (1) vs. Green Bay (1), 1982
-   NFC-D: Minnesota (1) vs. San Francisco (1), 1987
-   NFC-FR: Detroit (1) vs. Green Bay (1), 1993
-   NFC-FR: Philadelphia (2) vs. Detroit (0), 1995
-   AFC-FR: Buffalo (1) vs. Jacksonville (1), 1996
- 1 In many games

PUNTING
Most Punts, Game
- 14 AFC-D: N.Y. Jets vs. Cleveland, 1986 (OT)
- 13 NFC: N.Y. Giants vs. Chi. Bears, 1933
-   AFC-D: Baltimore vs. Oakland, 1977 (OT)

11 AFC: Houston vs. Oakland, 1967
AFC-D: Houston vs. Oakland, 1969
NFC: L.A. Rams vs. Chicago, 1985
SB: N.Y. Giants vs. Baltimore, 2000

Fewest Punts, Game
0 NFC-FR: St. Louis vs. Green Bay, 1982
AFC-FR: N.Y. Jets vs. Cincinnati, 1982
AFC-FR: Indianapolis vs. Denver, 2003
AFC-D: Kansas City vs. Indianapolis, 2003
AFC-D: Indianapolis vs. Kansas City, 2003
1 By many teams

Most Punts, Both Teams, Game
23 NFC: N.Y. Giants (13) vs. Chi. Bears (10), 1933
22 AFC: N.Y. Jets (14) vs. Cleveland (8), 1986 (OT)
21 AFC-D: Baltimore (13) vs. Oakland (8), 1977 (OT)
NFC: L.A. Rams (11) vs. Chicago (10), 1985
SB: N.Y. Giants (11) vs. Baltimore (10), 2000

Fewest Punts, Both Teams, Game
0 AFC-D: Kansas City vs. Indianapolis, 2003
1 NFC-FR: St. Louis (0) vs. Green Bay (1), 1982
2 AFC-FR: N.Y. Jets (0) vs. Cincinnati (2), 1982
SB: Atlanta (1) vs. Denver (1), 1998
AFC-FR: Indianapolis (0) vs. Denver (2), 2003

AVERAGE YARDAGE
Highest Average, Punting, Game (4 punts)
56.0 AFC: Oakland vs. San Diego, 1980
52.5 NFC: Washington vs. Chi. Bears, 1942
52.0 AFC-D: Tennessee vs. Indianapolis, 1999

Lowest Average, Punting, Game (4 punts)
24.9 NFC: Washington vs. Chi. Bears, 1937
25.3 AFC-FR: Pittsburgh vs. Houston, 1989
25.5 NFC: Green Bay vs. N.Y. Giants, 1962

PUNT RETURNS
Most Punt Returns, Game
8 NFC: Green Bay vs. N.Y. Giants, 1944
7 by many teams

Most Punt Returns, Both Teams, Game
13 AFC-FR: Houston (7) vs. Oakland (6), 1980
12 AFC-D: New England (7) vs. Pittsburgh (5), 1996
11 NFC: Green Bay (8) vs. N.Y. Giants (3), 1944
NFC-D: Green Bay (6) vs. Baltimore (5), 1965
AFC-FR: Jacksonville (7) vs. New England (4), 1998

Fewest Punt Returns, Both Teams, Game
0 NFC: Chi. Bears vs. N.Y. Giants, 1941
AFC: Boston vs. San Diego, 1963
NFC-FR: Green Bay vs. St. Louis, 1982
AFC-FR: Houston vs. N.Y. Jets, 1991
AFC-D: Denver vs. Houston, 1991
NFC-D: San Francisco vs. Washington, 1992
SB: Denver vs. Green Bay, 1997
SB: Atlanta vs. Denver, 1998
AFC-FR: Oakland vs. N.Y. Jets, 2001
AFC-D: N.Y. Jets vs. Oakland, 2002
AFC-FR: Denver vs. Indianapolis, 2003
NFC-D: Carolina vs. St. Louis, 2003
AFC-D: Indianapolis vs. Kansas City, 2003
1 In many games

YARDS GAINED
Most Yards Gained, Game
155 NFC-D: Dallas vs. Cleveland, 1967
152 NFC-D: Atlanta vs. St. Louis, 2004
150 NFC: Chi. Cardinals vs. Philadelphia, 1947

Fewest Yards Gained, Game
−10 NFC: Green Bay vs. Cleveland, 1965
−9 NFC: Dallas vs. Green Bay, 1966
AFC-D: Kansas City vs. Oakland, 1968
−7 NFC-D: San Francisco vs. Atlanta, 1998

Most Yards Gained, Both Teams, Game
166 NFC-D: Dallas (155) vs. Cleveland (11), 1967
AFC-D: Baltimore (99) vs. Pittsburgh (67), 2001
160 NFC: Chi. Cardinals (150) vs. Philadelphia (10), 1947
152 NFC-D: Atlanta (152) vs. St. Louis (0), 2004

Fewest Yards Gained, Both Teams, Game
−9 NFC: Dallas (−9) vs. Green Bay (0), 1966
−6 AFC-D: Miami (−5) vs. Oakland (−1), 1970
−3 NFC-D: San Francisco (−5) vs. Dallas (2), 1972

TOUCHDOWNS
Most Touchdowns, Game
1 By 17 teams

KICKOFF RETURNS
Most Kickoff Returns, Game
10 AFC-D: L.A. Rams vs. Washington, 1983
NFC-FR: Detroit vs. Philadelphia, 1995
9 NFC: Chi. Bears vs. N.Y. Giants, 1956
AFC: Boston vs. San Diego, 1963
AFC: Houston vs. Oakland, 1967
SB: Denver vs. San Francisco, 1989
AFC-D: Miami vs. Buffalo, 1990
AFC: L.A. Raiders vs. Buffalo, 1990
AFC-D: Miami vs. Jacksonville, 1999
SB: Oakland vs. Tampa Bay, 2002
8 By many teams

Most Kickoff Returns, Both Teams, Game
15 AFC-D: Miami (9) vs. Buffalo (6), 1990
14 NFC-FR: Detroit (10) vs. Philadelphia (4), 1995
13 NFC-D: Green Bay (7) vs. Dallas (6), 1982
NFC-FR: Green Bay (7) vs. San Francisco (6), 1998
AFC-FR: N.Y. Jets (8) vs. Oakland (5), 2001
NFC-FR: San Francisco (7) vs. N.Y. Giants (6), 2002
AFC-D: Tennessee (7) vs. Pittsburgh (6), 2002
SB: Oakland (9) vs. Tampa Bay (4), 2002
NFC-FR: Seattle (7) vs. Green Bay (6), 2003 (OT)
AFC-D: Kansas City (7) vs. Indianapolis (6), 2003
AFC: Pittsburgh (8) vs. New England (5), 2004

Fewest Kickoff Returns, Both Teams, Game
1 NFC: Green Bay (0) vs. Boston (1), 1936
AFC-FR: San Diego (0) vs. Kansas City (1), 1992
2 NFC-D: Los Angeles (0) vs. Chi. Bears (2), 1950
AFC: Houston (0) vs. San Diego (2), 1961
AFC-D: Oakland (1) vs. Pittsburgh (1), 1972
AFC-D: N.Y. Jets (0) vs. L.A. Raiders (2), 1982
AFC: Miami (1) vs. N.Y. Jets (1), 1982
NFC: N.Y. Giants (0) vs. Washington (2), 1986
3 In many games

YARDS GAINED
Most Yards Gained, Game
244 SB: San Diego vs. San Francisco, 1994
227 SB: Atlanta vs. Denver, 1998
225 NFC: Washington vs. Chi. Bears, 1940

Most Yards Gained, Both Teams, Game
379 AFC-D: Baltimore (193) vs. Oakland (186), 1977 (OT)
348 NFC-D: Minnesota (174) vs. St. Louis (174), 1999
322 NFC-D: Green Bay (194) vs. San Francisco (128), 1998

Fewest Yards Gained, Both Teams, Game
5 AFC-FR: San Diego (0) vs. Kansas City (5), 1992
15 NFC: N.Y. Giants (0) vs. Washington (15), 1986
31 NFC-D: Los Angeles (0) vs. Chi. Bears (31), 1950

TOUCHDOWNS
Most Touchdowns, Game
1 NFC-D: San Francisco vs. Dallas, 1972
AFC-D: Miami vs. Oakland, 1974
AFC-D: Baltimore vs. Oakland, 1977 (OT)
SB: Miami vs. Washington, 1982

SB: Cincinnati vs. San Francisco, 1988
AFC-D: Cleveland vs. Buffalo, 1989
SB: San Diego vs. San Francisco, 1994
SB: Green Bay vs. New England, 1996
NFC: San Francisco vs. Green Bay, 1997
SB: Atlanta vs. Denver, 1998
AFC-FR: Tennessee vs. Buffalo, 1999
AFC-FR: Seattle vs. Miami, 1999
NFC-D: Washington vs. Tampa Bay, 1999
NFC-D: St. Louis vs. Minnesota, 1999
AFC: Tennessee vs. Jacksonville, 1999
NFC-D: N.Y. Giants vs. Philadelphia, 2000
SB: Baltimore vs. N.Y. Giants, 2000
SB: N.Y. Giants vs. Baltimore, 2000
AFC-D: Kansas City vs. Indianapolis, 2003

Most Touchdowns, Both Teams, Game
  2 SB: Baltimore (1) vs. N.Y. Giants (1), 2000

PENALTIES
Most Penalties, Game
 17 AFC-FR: L.A. Raiders vs. Denver, 1993
 14 AFC-FR: Oakland vs. Houston, 1980
      NFC-D: San Francisco vs. N.Y. Giants, 1981
      AFC: Oakland vs. Tennessee, 2002
 13 AFC-FR: Houston vs. Cleveland, 1988
      AFC-D: Houston vs. Denver, 1991
      NFC-D: Arizona vs. Minnesota, 1998
      NFC-D: Carolina vs. St. Louis, 2003 (2 OT)

Fewest Penalties, Game
  0 NFC: Philadelphia vs. Green Bay, 1960
      NFC-D: Detroit vs. Dallas, 1970
      AFC-D: Miami vs. Oakland, 1970
      SB: Miami vs. Dallas, 1971
      NFC-D: Washington vs. Minnesota, 1973
      SB: Pittsburgh vs. Dallas, 1975
      NFC: San Francisco vs. Chicago, 1988
      SB: Denver vs. San Francisco, 1989
      AFC-D: L.A. Raiders vs. Cincinnati, 1990
      AFC-D: Miami vs. San Diego, 1992
      SB: Atlanta vs. Denver, 1998
      AFC-FR: N.Y. Jets vs. Oakland, 2001
      NFC-FR: Carolina vs. Dallas, 2003
  1 By many teams

Most Penalties, Both Teams, Game
 27 AFC-FR: L.A. Raiders (17) vs. Denver (10), 1993
 22 AFC-FR: Oakland (14) vs. Houston (8), 1980
      NFC-D: San Francisco (14) vs. N.Y. Giants (8), 1981
      AFC-FR: Houston (13) vs. Cleveland (9), 1988
      NFC-D: Arizona (13) vs. Minnesota (9), 1998
 21 AFC-D: Oakland (14) vs. New England (7), 1976
      AFC: Oakland (14) vs. Tennessee (7), 2002

Fewest Penalties, Both Teams, Game
  1 AFC-D: L.A. Raiders (0) vs. Cincinnati (1), 1990
  2 NFC: Washington (1) vs. Chi. Bears (1), 1937
      NFC-D: Washington (0) vs. Minnesota (2), 1973
      SB: Pittsburgh (0) vs. Dallas (2), 1975
      NFC-FR: Carolina (0) vs. Dallas (2), 2003
  3 AFC: Miami (1) vs. Baltimore (2), 1971
      NFC: San Francisco (1) vs. Dallas (2), 1971
      SB: Miami (0) vs. Dallas (3), 1971
      AFC-D: Pittsburgh (1) vs. Oakland (2), 1972
      AFC-D: Miami (1) vs. Cincinnati (2), 1973
      SB: Miami (1) vs. San Francisco (2), 1984
      NFC: San Francisco (0) vs. Chicago (3), 1988
      AFC: New England (1) vs. Pittsburgh (2), 2004

YARDS PENALIZED
Most Yards Penalized, Game
 145 NFC-D: San Francisco vs. N.Y. Giants, 1981
 133 SB: Dallas vs. Baltimore, 1970
 130 AFC-FR: L.A. Raiders vs. Denver, 1993

Fewest Yards Penalized, Game
  0 By many teams

Most Yards Penalized, Both Teams, Game
 227 AFC-FR: L.A. Raiders (130) vs. Denver (97), 1993
 206 NFC-D: San Francisco (145) vs. N.Y. Giants (61), 1981
 201 NFC-FR: Detroit (126) vs. Washington (75), 1999

Fewest Yards Penalized, Both Teams, Game
  5 AFC-D: L.A. Raiders (0) vs. Cincinnati (5), 1990
  9 NFC-D: Washington (0) vs. Minnesota (9), 1973
 11 NFC-FR: Carolina (0) vs. Dallas (11), 2003

FUMBLES
Most Fumbles, Game
  8 SB: Buffalo vs. Dallas, 1992
  7 AFC-D: Houston vs. Kansas City, 1993
  6 By 12 teams

Most Fumbles, Both Teams, Game
 12 AFC: Houston (6) vs. Pittsburgh (6), 1978
      SB: Buffalo (8) vs. Dallas (4), 1992
 10 NFC: Chi. Bears (5) vs. N.Y. Giants (5), 1934
      SB: Dallas (6) vs. Denver (4), 1977
      AFC: Jacksonville (5) vs. Tennessee (5), 1999
  9 NFC-D: San Francisco (6) vs. Detroit (3), 1957
      NFC-D: San Francisco (5) vs. Dallas (4), 1972
      NFC: Dallas (5) vs. Philadelphia (4), 1980

Most Fumbles Lost, Game
  5 SB: Buffalo vs. Dallas, 1992
      AFC-D: Miami vs. Jacksonville, 1999
  4 NFC: N.Y. Giants vs. Baltimore, 1958 (OT)
      AFC: Kansas City vs. Oakland, 1969
      SB: Baltimore vs. Dallas, 1970
      AFC: Pittsburgh vs. Oakland, 1975
      SB: Denver vs. Dallas, 1977
      AFC: Houston vs. Pittsburgh, 1978
      AFC: Miami vs. New England, 1985
      SB: New England vs. Chicago, 1985
      NFC-FR: L.A. Rams vs. Washington, 1986
      NFC-FR: Minnesota vs. Dallas, 1996
      AFC-FR: Buffalo vs. Miami, 1998
      AFC: N.Y. Jets vs. Denver, 1998
      AFC: Jacksonville vs. Tennessee, 1999
  3 By many teams

Fewest Fumbles, Both Teams, Game
  0 NFC: Green Bay vs. Cleveland, 1965
      AFC-D: Houston vs. San Diego, 1979
      NFC-D: Dallas vs. Los Angeles, 1979
      SB: Los Angeles vs. Pittsburgh, 1979
      AFC-D: Buffalo vs. Cincinnati, 1981
      NFC: Minnesota vs. Washington, 1987
      NFC-D: San Francisco vs. Washington, 1990
      NFC: Dallas vs. Green Bay, 1995
      AFC-D: New England vs. Pittsburgh, 1996
      SB: Green Bay vs. New England, 1996
      AFC-FR: Miami vs. Seattle, 1999
      AFC-FR: Miami vs. Indianapolis, 2000 (OT)
      AFC-D: Baltimore vs. Tennessee, 2000
  1 In many games

RECOVERIES
Most Total Fumbles Recovered, Game
  8 SB: Dallas vs. Denver, 1977 (4 own, 4 opp)
  7 NFC: Chi. Bears vs. N.Y. Giants, 1934 (5 own, 2 opp)
      NFC-D: San Francisco vs. Detroit, 1957 (4 own, 3 opp)
      NFC-D: San Francisco vs. Dallas, 1972 (4 own, 3 opp)
      AFC: Pittsburgh vs. Houston, 1978 (3 own, 4 opp)
  6 AFC: Houston vs. San Diego, 1961 (4 own, 2 opp)
      AFC-D: Cleveland vs. Baltimore, 1971 (4 own, 2 opp)
      AFC-D: Cleveland vs. Oakland, 1980 (5 own, 1 opp)
      NFC: Philadelphia vs. Dallas, 1980 (3 own, 3 opp)

SB: Dallas vs. Buffalo, 1992 (1 own, 5 opp)
NFC-D: Green Bay vs. San Francisco, 1996
 (4 own, 2 opp)
AFC: Denver vs. N.Y. Jets, 1998 (2 own, 4 opp)
AFC: Tennessee vs. Jacksonville, 1999 (2 own, 4 opp)

Most Own Fumbles Recovered, Game
5 NFC: Chi. Bears vs. N.Y. Giants, 1934
 AFC-D: Cleveland vs. Oakland, 1980
4 By many teams

TOUCHDOWNS
Most Touchdowns, Game
2 SB: Dallas vs. Buffalo, 1992

TURNOVERS
Numbers of times losing the ball on interceptions and fumbles.

Most Turnovers, Game
9 NFC: Washington vs. Chi. Bears, 1940
 NFC: Detroit vs. Cleveland, 1954
 AFC: Houston vs. Pittsburgh, 1978
 SB: Buffalo vs. Dallas, 1992
8 NFC: N.Y. Giants vs. Chi. Bears, 1946
 NFC: Los Angeles vs. Cleveland, 1955
 NFC: Cleveland vs. Detroit, 1957
 SB: Denver vs. Dallas, 1977
 NFC-D: Minnesota vs. Philadelphia, 1980
 NFC-D: Green Bay vs. St. Louis, 2001
7 In many games

Fewest Turnovers, Game
0 By many teams

Most Turnovers, Both Teams, Game
14 AFC: Houston (9) vs. Pittsburgh (5), 1978
13 NFC: Detroit (9) vs. Cleveland (4), 1954
 AFC: Houston (7) vs. San Diego (6), 1961
12 AFC: Pittsburgh (7) vs. Oakland (5), 1975

Fewest Turnovers, Both Teams, Game
0 SB: Buffalo vs. N.Y. Giants, 1990
 AFC-FR: Kansas City vs Pittsburgh, 1993 (OT)
 NFC-FR: Detroit vs. Green Bay, 1994
 AFC-FR: Denver vs. Jacksonville, 1996
 SB: St. Louis vs. Tennessee, 1999
1 AFC-D: Baltimore (0) vs. Cincinnati (1), 1970
 AFC-D: Pittsburgh (0) vs. Buffalo (1), 1974
 AFC: Oakland (0) vs. Pittsburgh (1), 1976
 NFC-D: Minnesota (0) vs. Washington (1), 1982
 NFC-D: Chicago (0) vs. N.Y. Giants (1), 1985
 SB: N.Y. Giants (0) vs. Denver (1), 1986
 NFC: Washington (0) vs. Minnesota (1), 1987
 AFC-D: Cincinnati (0) vs. L.A. Raiders (1), 1990
 NFC: N.Y. Giants (0) vs. San Francisco (1), 1990
 NFC-FR: N.Y. Giants (0) vs. Minnesota (1), 1993
 AFC-FR: L.A. Raiders (0) vs. Denver (1), 1993
 NFC: Dallas (0) vs. San Francisco (1), 1993
 AFC: Indianapolis (0) vs. Pittsburgh (1), 1995
 NFC-D: San Francisco (0) vs. Minnesota (1), 1997
 AFC-D: Indianapolis (0) vs. Tennessee (1), 1999
 AFC-FR: Baltimore (0) vs. Denver (1), 2000
 AFC-D: Baltimore (0) vs. Tennessee (1), 2000
 AFC-D: Oakland (0) vs. New England (1), 2001
 NFC-FR: Green Bay (0) vs. Seattle (1), 2003 (OT)
 AFC-D: Indianapolis (0) vs. Kansas City (1), 2003
 AFC-FR: N.Y. Jets (0) vs. San Diego (1), 2004 (OT)
 NFC: Philadelphia (0) vs. Atlanta (1), 2004
2 In many games

Includes records of AFC-NFC Pro Bowls, 1971-2005
Compiled by Elias Sports Bureau

INDIVIDUAL RECORDS

SERVICE
Most Games
- 12 Randall McDaniel, Minnesota 1990-2000; Tampa Bay 2001
- 11 *Reggie White, Philadelphia, 1987-1993; Green Bay, 1994, 1996-97, 1999
  Junior Seau, San Diego, 1992-2002
  Rod Woodson, Pittsburgh, 1990-95, 1997; Baltimore, 2000-02; Oakland, 2003
- 10 Lawrence Taylor, N.Y. Giants, 1982-1991
  Ronnie Lott, San Francisco, 1982-85, 1987-1991; L.A. Raiders 1992
  Mike Singletary, Chicago, 1984-1993
  **Bruce Matthews, Houston, 1989-1995, 1997; Tennessee, 2000, 2002
  ***Jerry Rice, San Francisco, 1987-88, 1990-94, 1996, 1999; Oakland, 2003
  Will Shields, Kansas City, 1996-2005

*Also selected, but did not play, in two additional games
**Also selected, but did not play, in four additional games
***Also selected but did not play, in three additional games

SCORING
POINTS
Most Points, Career
- 45 Morten Andersen, New Orleans, 1986-89, 1991, 1993; Atlanta, 1996 (15-pat, 10-fg)
- 30 Jan Stenerud, Kansas City, 1971-72, 1976; Minnesota, 1985 (6-pat, 8-fg)
  Jimmy Smith, Jacksonville, 1998-2001 (5-td)
  Marvin Harrison, Indianapolis, 2000-05 (5-td)
- 29 David Akers, Philadelphia, 2002-03, 2005 (8-pat, 7-fg)

Most Points, Game
- 18 John Brockington, Green Bay, 1973 (3-td)
  Mike Alstott, Tampa Bay, 2000 (3-td)
  Jimmy Smith, Jacksonville, 2000 (3-td)
  Shaun Alexander, Seattle, 2004 (3-td)
- 15 Garo Yepremian, Miami, 1974 (5-fg)
  Jason Hanson, Detroit, 2000 (6-pat, 3-fg)
- 14 Jan Stenerud, Kansas City, 1972 (2-pat, 4-fg)

TOUCHDOWNS
Most Touchdowns, Career
- 5 Jimmy Smith, Jacksonville, 1998-2001 (5-p)
  Marvin Harrison, Indianapolis, 2000-05 (5-p)
- 4 Mike Alstott, Tampa Bay, 1998-2003 (3-r, 1-p)
  Tony Gonzalez, Kansas City, 2000-01, 2003-05 (4-p)
  Hines Ward, Pittsburgh, 2002-05 (3-p, 1-ret)
- 3 John Brockington, Green Bay, 1972-74 (2-r, 1-p)
  Earl Campbell, Houston, 1979-1982, 1984 (3-r)
  Chuck Muncie, New Orleans, 1980; San Diego, 1982-83 (3-r)
  William Andrews, Atlanta, 1981-84 (1-r, 2-p)
  Marcus Allen, L.A. Raiders, 1983, 1985-86, 1988; Kansas City, 1994 (2-r, 1-p)
  Cris Carter, Minnesota, 1994-2001 (3-p)
  Curtis Martin, New England, 1996-97; N.Y. Jets, 1999, 2002 (2-r, 1-p)
  Shaun Alexander, Seattle, 2004 (2-r, 1-p)
  Torry Holt, St. Louis, 2001-02, 2004-05 (3-p)

Most Touchdowns, Game
- 3 John Brockington, Green Bay, 1973 (2-r, 1-p)
  Mike Alstott, Tampa Bay, 2000 (3-r)

  Jimmy Smith, Jacksonville, 2000 (3-p)
  Shaun Alexander, Seattle, 2004 (2-r, 1-p)
- 2 Mel Renfro, Dallas, 1971 (2-ret)
  Earl Campbell, Houston, 1980 (2-r)
  Chuck Muncie, New Orleans, 1980 (2-r)
  William Andrews, Atlanta, 1984 (2-p)
  Herschel Walker, Dallas, 1989 (2-r)
  Johnny Johnson, Phoenix, 1991 (2-r)
  Eric Green, Pittsburgh, 1995 (2-p)
  Marvin Harrison, Indianapolis, 2001 (2-p)
  Ricky Wiilliams, Miami, 2003 (2-r)
  Hines Ward, Pittsburgh, 2005 (1-p, 1-ret)

POINTS AFTER TOUCHDOWN
Most Points After Touchdown, Career
- 15 Morten Andersen, New Orleans, 1986-89, 1991, 1993; Atlanta, 1996 (15 att)
- 11 Adam Vinatieri, New England, 2003, 2005 (11 att)
- 9 Jason Hanson, Detroit, 1998, 2000 (9 att)

Most Points After Touchdown, Game
- 7 Mike Vanderjagt, Indianapolis, 2004 (7 att)
- 6 Ali Haji-Sheikh, N.Y. Giants, 1984 (6 att)
  Jason Hanson, Detroit, 2000 (6 att)
  Adam Vinatieri, New England, 2003 (6 att)
- 5 John Carney, San Diego, 1995 (5 att)
  Matt Stover, Baltimore, 2001 (5 att)
  Jason Elam, Denver, 2002 (5 att)
  Jeff Wilkins, St. Louis, 2004 (5 att)
  Adam Vinatieri, New England, 2005 (5 att)

FIELD GOALS
Most Field Goals Attempted, Career
- 18 Morten Andersen, New Orleans, 1986-89, 1991, 1993; Atlanta, 1996
- 15 Jan Stenerud, Kansas City, 1971-72, 1976; Minnesota, 1985
- 10 Nick Lowery, Kansas City, 1982, 1991, 1993

Most Field Goals Attempted, Game
- 6 Jan Stenerud, Kansas City, 1972
  Eddie Murray, Detroit, 1981
  Mark Moseley, Washington, 1983
- 5 Garo Yepremian, Miami, 1974
- 4 Jan Stenerud, Kansas City, 1976
  Nick Lowery, Kansas City, 1991, 1993
  Morten Andersen, New Orleans, 1993
  Cary Blanchard, Indianapolis, 1997
  John Kasay, Carolina, 1997
  David Akers, Philadelphia, 2002
  Jeff Wilkins, St. Louis, 2004

Most Field Goals, Career
- 10 Morten Andersen, New Orleans, 1986-89, 1991, 1993; Atlanta, 1996
- 8 Jan Stenerud, Kansas City, 1971-72, 1976; Minnesota, 1985
- 7 Nick Lowery, Kansas City, 1982, 1991, 1993
  David Akers, Philadelphia, 2002-03, 2005

Most Field Goals, Game
- 5 Garo Yepremian, Miami, 1974 (5 att)
- 4 Jan Stenerud, Kansas City, 1972 (6 att)
  Eddie Murray, Detroit, 1981 (6 att)
- 3 Nick Lowery, Kansas City, 1991 (4 att)
  Nick Lowery, Kansas City, 1993 (4 att)
  Jason Elam, Denver, 1999 (3 att)
  Jason Hanson, Detroit, 2000 (3 att)
  David Akers, Philadelphia, 2002 (4 att)

Longest Field Goal
- 53 David Akers, Philadelphia, 2003
- 51 Morten Andersen, New Orleans, 1989
  Jason Hanson, Detroit, 2000

49 Fuad Reveiz, Minnesota, 1995
      David Akers, Philadelphia, 2002

SAFETIES
Most Safeties, Game
1 Art Still, Kansas City, 1983
    Mark Gastineau, N.Y. Jets, 1985
    Greg Townsend, L.A. Raiders, 1992

RUSHING
ATTEMPTS
Most Attempts, Career
81 Walter Payton, Chicago, 1977-1981, 1984-87
68 O.J. Simpson, Buffalo, 1973-77
66 Barry Sanders, Detroit, 1990-93, 1995-98
Most Attempts, Game
19 O.J. Simpson, Buffalo, 1974
17 Marv Hubbard, Oakland, 1974
16 O.J. Simpson, Buffalo, 1973
    Marcus Allen, L.A. Raiders, 1986

YARDS GAINED
Most Yards Gained, Career
368 Walter Payton, Chicago, 1977-1981, 1984-87
356 O.J. Simpson, Buffalo, 1973-77
271 Marshall Faulk, Indianapolis, 1995-96, 1999;
      St. Louis, 2000, 2002-03
Most Yards Gained, Game
180 Marshall Faulk, Indianapolis, 1995
127 Chris Warren, Seattle, 1995
112 O. J. Simpson, Buffalo, 1973
Longest Run From Scrimmage
49 Marshall Faulk, Indianapolis, 1995 (TD)
41 Lawrence McCutcheon, Los Angeles, 1976
    Natrone Means, San Diego, 1995
    Marshall Faulk, Indianapolis, 1995
39 Chris Warren, Seattle, 1994
    Priest Holmes, Kansas City, 2002

AVERAGE GAIN
Highest Average Gain, Career (20 attempts)
9.36 Chris Warren, Seattle, 1994-96, (25-234)
6.45 Marshall Faulk, Indianapolis, 1995-96, 1999;
      St. Louis, 2000, 2002-03 (42-271)
5.81 Marv Hubbard, Oakland, 1972-74 (36-209)
Highest Average Gain, Game (10 attempts)
13.85 Marshall Faulk, Indianapolis, 1995 (13-180)
9.07 Chris Warren, Seattle, 1995 (14-127)
7.00 O.J. Simpson, Buffalo, 1973 (16-112)
    Ottis Anderson, St. Louis, 1981 (10-70)

TOUCHDOWNS
Most Touchdowns, Career
3 Earl Campbell, Houston, 1979-1982, 1984
   Chuck Muncie, New Orleans, 1980; San Diego,
     1982-83
   Mike Alstott, Tampa Bay, 1998-2003
2 John Brockington, Green Bay, 1972-74
   O.J. Simpson, Buffalo, 1973-77
   Walter Payton, Chicago, 1977-1981, 1984-87
   Marcus Allen, L.A. Raiders, 1983, 1985-86, 1988;
     Kansas City, 1994
   Herschel Walker, Dallas, 1988-89
   Johnny Johnson, Phoenix, 1991
   Barry Sanders, Detroit, 1990-93, 1995-98
   Curtis Martin, New England, 1996-97; N.Y. Jets,
     1999, 2002
   Ricky Williams, Miami, 2003
   Shaun Alexander, Seattle, 2004

Most Touchdowns, Game
3 Mike Alstott, Tampa Bay, 2000
2 John Brockington, Green Bay, 1973
   Earl Campbell, Houston, 1980
   Chuck Muncie, New Orleans, 1980
   Herschel Walker, Dallas, 1989
   Johnny Johnson, Phoenix, 1991
   Ricky Williams, Miami, 2003
   Shaun Alexander, Seattle, 2004

PASSING
ATTEMPTS
Most Attempts, Career
120 Dan Fouts, San Diego, 1980-84, 1986
108 Peyton Manning, Indianapolis, 2000-01, 2003-05
101 Steve Young, San Francisco, 1993-96, 1998-99
Most Attempts, Game
41 Peyton Manning, Indianapolis, 2004
32 Bill Kenney, Kansas City, 1984
    Steve Young, San Francisco, 1993
30 Dan Fouts, San Diego, 1983

COMPLETIONS
Most Completions, Career
66 Peyton Manning, Indianapolis, 2000-01, 2003-05
63 Dan Fouts, San Diego, 1980-84, 1986
48 Steve Young, San Francisco, 1993-96, 1998-99
Most Completions, Game
22 Peyton Manning, Indianapolis, 2004
21 Joe Theismann, Washington, 1984
18 Steve Young, San Francisco, 1993

COMPLETION PERCENTAGE
Highest Completion Percentage, Career (40 attempts)
68.9 Joe Theismann, Washington, 1983-84 (45-31)
67.9 Rich Gannon, Oakland, 2000-03 (53-36)
64.4 Jim Kelly, Buffalo, 1988, 1991-92 (45-29)
Highest Completion Percentage, Game (10 attempts)
90.0 Archie Manning, New Orleans, 1980 (10-9)
85.7 Rich Gannon, Oakland, 2001 (14-12)
80.0 Rich Gannon, Oakland, 2002 (10-8)

YARDS GAINED
Most Yards Gained, Career
992 Peyton Manning, Indianapolis, 2000-01, 2003-05
890 Dan Fouts, San Diego, 1980-84, 1986
614 Steve Young, San Francisco, 1993-96, 1998-99
Most Yards Gained, Game
342 Peyton Manning, Indianapolis, 2004
274 Dan Fouts, San Diego, 1983
270 Peyton Manning, Indianapolis, 2000
Longest Completion
93 Jeff Blake, Cincinnati (to Thigpen, Pittsburgh),
    1996 (TD)
90 Steve McNair, Tennessee (to Johnson, Cincinnati),
    2004 (TD)
80 Mark Brunell, Jacksonville (to Brown, Oakland),
    1997 (TD)

AVERAGE GAIN
Highest Average Gain, Career (40 attempts)
9.19 Peyton Manning, Indianapolis, 2000-01,
     2003-05 (108-992)
8.19 Rich Gannon, Oakland, 2000-03 (53-434)
8.12 Brett Favre, Green Bay, 1993-94, 1996-97 (57-463)
Highest Average Gain, Game (10 attempts)
15.27 Randall Cunningham, Philadelphia, 1991 (11-168)
13.70 Rich Gannon, Oakland, 2002 (10-137)
13.00 Brett Favre, Green Bay, 1997 (11-143)

TOUCHDOWNS
Most Touchdowns, Career
- 11 Peyton Manning, Indianapolis, 2000-01, 2003-05
- 7 Rich Gannon, Oakland, 2000-03
- 4 Steve Young, San Francisco, 1993-96, 1998-99
   Marc Bulger, St. Louis, 2004

Most Touchdowns, Game
- 4 Marc Bulger, St. Louis, 2004
- 3 Joe Theismann, Washington, 1984
   Phil Simms, N.Y. Giants, 1986
   Peyton Manning, Indianapolis, 2004
   Peyton Manning, Indianapolis, 2005
- 2 James Harris, Los Angeles, 1975
   Mike Boryla, Philadelphia, 1976
   Ken Anderson, Cincinnati, 1977
   Jim Kelly, Buffalo, 1991
   Mark Rypien, Washington, 1992
   Steve Young, San Francisco, 1998
   Peyton Manning, Indianapolis, 2000
   Rich Gannon, Oakland, 2001
   Peyton Manning, Indianapolis, 2001
   Rich Gannon, Oakland, 2002
   Donovan McNabb, Philadelphia, 2002
   Rich Gannon, Oakland, 2003
   Brad Johnson, Tampa Bay, 2003

HAD INTERCEPTED
Most Passes Had Intercepted, Career
- 8 Dan Fouts, San Diego, 1980-84, 1986
- 6 Jim Hart, St. Louis, 1975-78
- 5 Ken Stabler, Oakland, 1974-75, 1978
   Peyton Manning, Indianapolis, 2000-01, 2003-05
   Donovan McNabb, Philadelphia, 2001-03, 2005

Most Passes Had Intercepted, Game
- 5 Jim Hart, St. Louis, 1977
- 4 Ken Stabler, Oakland, 1974
- 3 Dan Fouts, San Diego, 1986
   Mark Rypien, Washington, 1990
   Steve Young, San Francisco, 1993
   Jim Harbaugh, Indianapolis, 1996
   Vinny Testaverde, N.Y. Jets, 1999
   Jeff Garcia, San Francisco, 2003

Most Attempts, Without Interception, Game
- 27 Joe Theismann, Washington, 1984
   Phil Simms, N.Y. Giants, 1986
- 26 John Brodie, San Francisco, 1971
   Danny White, Dallas, 1983
- 23 Dave Krieg, Seattle, 1990

PERCENTAGE, PASSES HAD INTERCEPTED
Lowest Percentage, Passes Had Intercepted, Career
(40 attempts)
- 0.00 Joe Theismann, Washington, 1983-84 (45-0)
- 1.89 Rich Gannon, Oakland, 2000-03 (53-1)
- 2.13 Dave Krieg, Seattle, 1985, 1989-1990 (47-1)

PASS RECEIVING
RECEPTIONS
Most Receptions, Career
- 37 Jerry Rice, San Francisco, 1987-88, 1990-94, 1996, 1999; Oakland, 2003
- 27 Cris Carter, Minnesota, 1994-2001
- 26 Marvin Harrison, Indianapolis, 2000-05

Most Receptions, Game
- 9 Randy Moss, Minnesota, 2000
- 8 Steve Largent, Seattle, 1986
   Michael Irvin, Dallas, 1992
   Andre Rison, Atlanta, 1993
   Jimmy Smith, Jacksonville, 2000

   Marvin Harrison, Indianapolis, 2001
   Terrell Owens, San Francisco, 2002
- 7 John Stallworth, Pittsburgh, 1983
   Jerry Rice, San Francisco, 1992
   Isaac Bruce, St. Louis, 1997
   Keyshawn Johnson, N.Y. Jets, 1999
   Randy Moss, Minnesota, 1999
   Warrick Dunn, Tampa Bay, 2001
   Torry Holt, St. Louis, 2001
   Torry Holt, St. Louis, 2004

YARDS GAINED
Most Yards Gained, Career
- 495 Jerry Rice, San Francisco, 1987-88, 1990-94, 1996, 1999; Oakland, 2003
- 408 Tim Brown, L.A. Raiders, 1989, 1992, 1994-95; Oakland, 1996-98, 2002
- 388 Marvin Harrison, Indianapolis, 2000-05

Most Yards Gained, Game
- 212 Randy Moss, Minnesota, 2000
- 156 Chad Johnson, Cincinnati, 2004
- 137 Tim Brown, Oakland, 1997

Longest Reception
- 93 Yancey Thigpen, Pittsburgh (from Blake, Cincinnati), 1996 (TD)
- 90 Chad Johnson, Cincinnati (from McNair, Tennessee), 2004 (TD)
- 80 Tim Brown, Oakland (from Brunell, Jacksonville), 1997 (TD)

TOUCHDOWNS
Most Touchdowns, Career
- 5 Jimmy Smith, Jacksonville, 1998-2001
   Marvin Harrison, Indianapolis, 2000-05
- 4 Tony Gonzalez, Kansas City, 2000-01, 2003-05
- 3 Cris Carter, Minnesota, 1994-2001
   Torry Holt, St. Louis, 2001-02, 2004-05
   Hines Ward, Pittsburgh, 2002-05

Most Touchdowns, Game
- 3 Jimmy Smith, Jacksonville, 2000
- 2 William Andrews, Atlanta, 1984
   Eric Green, Pittsburgh, 1995
   Marvin Harrison, Indianapolis, 2001

INTERCEPTIONS BY
Most Interceptions By, Career
- 4 Everson Walls, Dallas, 1982-84, 1986
   Deion Sanders, Atlanta, 1992-94; San Francisco, 1995; Dallas, 1999
- 3 Ken Houston, Houston, 1971-73; Washington, 1974-79
   Jack Lambert, Pittsburgh, 1976-1984
   Ted Hendricks, Baltimore, 1972-74; Green Bay, 1975; Oakland, 1981-82; L.A. Raiders, 1983-84
   Mike Haynes, New England, 1978-1981, 1983; L.A. Raiders, 1985-87
   Ty Law, New England, 1999, 2002-04
   Champ Bailey, Washington, 2001-04; Denver, 2005
- 2 By 16 players

Most Interceptions By, Game
- 2 Mel Blount, Pittsburgh, 1977
   Everson Walls, Dallas, 1982, 1983
   LeRoy Irvin, L.A. Rams, 1986
   David Fulcher, Cincinnati, 1990
   Brian Dawkins, Philadelphia, 2000
   Rod Woodson, Oakland, 2003

YARDS GAINED
Most Yards Gained, Career
- 147   Ty Law, New England, 1999, 2002-04
- 103   Deion Sanders, Atlanta, 1992-94; San Francisco, 1995; Dallas, 1999
- 88   Rod Woodson, Pittsburgh, 1990-95, 1997; Baltimore, 2000-02; Oakland, 2003

Most Yards Gained, Game
- 87   Deion Sanders, Dallas, 1999
- 73   Rod Woodson, Pittsburgh, 1994
- 67   Ty Law, New England, 1999

Longest Gain
- 87   Deion Sanders, Dallas, 1999
- 73   Rod Woodson, Pittsburgh, 1994 (lateral)
- 67   Ty Law, New England, 1999 (TD)

TOUCHDOWNS
Most Touchdowns, Career
- 2   Ty Law, New England, 1999, 2002-04
- 1   By many

Most Touchdowns, Game
- 1   Bobby Bell, Kansas City, 1973
  Nolan Cromwell, L.A. Rams, 1984
  Joey Browner, Minnesota, 1986
  Jerry Gray, L.A. Rams, 1990
  Mike Johnson, Cleveland, 1990
  Junior Seau, San Diego, 1993
  Ken Harvey, Washington, 1996
  Ashley Ambrose, Cincinnati, 1997
  Ty Law, New England, 1999
  Derrick Brooks, Tampa Bay, 2000
  Aeneas Williams, Arizona, 2000
  Ray Lewis, Baltimore, 2002
  Ty Law, New England, 2003
  Dre' Bly, Detroit, 2004

PUNTING
Most Punts, Career
- 33   Ray Guy, Oakland, 1974-79, 1981
- 23   Rohn Stark, Indianapolis, 1986-87, 1991, 1993
- 22   Reggie Roby, Miami, 1985, 1990; Washington, 1995

Most Punts, Game
- 10   Reggie Roby, Miami, 1985
- 9   Tom Wittum, San Francisco, 1974
  Rohn Stark, Indianapolis, 1987
- 8   Jerrel Wilson, Kansas City, 1971
  Tom Skladany, Detroit, 1982
  Reggie Roby, Washington, 1995

Longest Punt
- 73   Shane Lechler, Oakland, 2002
- 70   Shane Lechler, Oakland, 2002
- 64   Tom Wittum, San Francisco, 1974
  Darren Bennett, San Diego, 1996

AVERAGE YARDAGE
Highest Average, Career (10 punts)
- 46.73   Reggie Roby, Miami, 1985, 1990; Washington, 1995 (22-1,028)
- 45.27   Matt Turk, Washington, 1997-99 (15-679)
- 45.25   Jerrel Wilson, Kansas City, 1971-73 (16-724)

Highest Average, Game (4 punts)
- 60.75   Shane Lechler, Oakland, 2002 (4-243)
- 55.50   Darren Bennett, San Diego, 1996 (4-222)
- 52.00   Matt Turk, Washington, 1999 (4-208)

PUNT RETURNS
Most Punt Returns, Career
- 13   Rick Upchurch, Denver, 1977, 1979-1980, 1983
- 11   Vai Sikahema, St. Louis, 1987-88
  Eric Metcalf, Cleveland 1994-95; San Diego 1998
- 10   Mike Nelms, Washington, 1981-83

Most Punt Returns, Game
- 7   Vai Sikahema, St. Louis, 1987
- 6   Henry Ellard, L.A. Rams, 1985
  Gerald McNeil, Cleveland, 1988
  Eric Metcalf, Cleveland, 1995
- 5   Rick Upchurch, Denver, 1980
  Mike Nelms, Washington, 1981
  Carl Roaches, Houston, 1982
  Johnny Bailey, Phoenix, 1993

Most Fair Catches, Game
- 2   Jerry Logan, Baltimore, 1971
  Dick Anderson, Miami, 1974
  Henry Ellard, L.A. Rams, 1985
  Isaac Bruce, St. Louis, 1997
  Desmond Howard, Detroit, 2001

YARDS GAINED
Most Yards Gained, Career
- 183   Billy Johnson, Houston, 1976, 1978; Atlanta, 1984
- 138   Mel Renfro, Dallas, 1971-72, 1974
  Rick Upchurch, Denver, 1977, 1979-1980, 1983
- 135   Eric Metcalf, Cleveland, 1994-95; San Diego 1998

Most Yards Gained, Game
- 159   Billy Johnson, Houston, 1976
- 138   Mel Renfro, Dallas, 1971
- 117   Wally Henry, Philadelphia, 1980

Longest Punt Return
- 90   Billy Johnson, Houston, 1976 (TD)
- 86   Wally Henry, Philadelphia, 1980 (TD)
- 82   Mel Renfro, Dallas, 1971 (TD)

AVERAGE YARDAGE
Highest Average, Career (4 returns)
- 22.88   Billy Johnson, Houston, 1976, 1978; Atlanta, 1984 (8-183)
- 21.50   Tony Green, Washington, 1979 (4-86)
- 15.67   David Meggett, N.Y. Giants, 1990; New England, 1997

Highest Average, Game (3 returns)
- 39.75   Billy Johnson, Houston, 1976 (4-159)
- 39.00   Wally Henry, Philadelphia, 1980 (3-117)
- 21.50   Tony Green, Washington, 1979 (4-86)

TOUCHDOWNS
Most Touchdowns, Game
- 2   Mel Renfro, Dallas, 1971
- 1   Billy Johnson, Houston, 1976
  Wally Henry, Philadelphia, 1980

KICKOFF RETURNS
Most Kickoff Returns, Career
- 17   Michael Bates, Carolina, 1997-2001
- 14   Mel Gray, Detroit, 1991-92, 1995
- 11   Eric Metcalf, Cleveland, 1994-95; San Diego, 1998
  Derrick Mason, Tennessee, 2001, 2004

Most Kickoff Returns, Game
- 8   Derrick Mason, Tennessee, 2004
- 7   Mel Gray, Detroit, 1995
  Jerry Azumah, Chicago, 2004
- 6   Greg Pruitt, L.A. Raiders, 1984
  David Meggett, New England, 1997
  Michael Bates, Carolina, 1998
  Steve Smith, Carolina, 2002

YARDS GAINED
Most Yards Gained, Career
- 488   Michael Bates, Carolina, 1997-2001
- 309   Greg Pruitt, Cleveland, 1974-75, 1977-78; L.A. Raiders, 1984

294   Mel Gray, Detroit, 1991-92, 1995
Most Yards Gained, Game
228   Jerry Azumah, Chicago, 2004
217   Michael Lewis, New Orleans, 2003
192   Greg Pruitt, L.A. Raiders, 1984
Longest Kickoff Return
66   Michael Bates, Carolina, 2000
62   Greg Pruitt, L.A. Raiders, 1984
61   Eugene (Mercury) Morris, Miami, 1972

AVERAGE YARDAGE
Highest Average, Career (4 returns)
43.40   Michael Lewis, New Orleans, 2003 (5-217)
35.00   Les (Speedy) Duncan, Washington, 1972 (5-175)
32.57   Jerry Azumah, Chicago, 2004 (7-228)
Highest Average, Game (3 returns)
43.40   Michael Lewis, New Orleans, 2003 (5-217)
42.00   Michael Bates, Carolina, 2000 (4-168)
35.00   Les (Speedy) Duncan, Washington, 1972 (5-175)

TOUCHDOWNS
Most Touchdowns, Game
1   Hines Ward, Pittsburgh, 2005

FUMBLES
Most Fumbles, Career
6   Dan Fouts, San Diego, 1980-84, 1986
4   Lawrence McCutcheon, Los Angeles, 1974-78
Franco Harris, Pittsburgh, 1973-76, 1978-1981
Jay Schroeder, Washington, 1987
Vai Sikahema, St. Louis, 1987-88
Trent Green, Kansas City, 2004
3   O.J. Simpson, Buffalo, 1973-77
William Andrews, Atlanta, 1981-84
Joe Montana, San Francisco, 1982, 1984-85, 1988
Walter Payton, Chicago, 1977-1981, 1984-87
Neil Lomax, St. Louis, 1985, 1988
Jim Kelly, Buffalo, 1988, 1991-92
Chris Chandler, Atlanta, 1998-99
Peyton Manning, Indianapolis, 2000-01, 2003-05
Most Fumbles, Game
4   Jay Schroeder, Washington, 1987
Trent Green, Kansas City, 2004
3   Dan Fouts, San Diego, 1982
Vai Sikahema, St. Louis, 1987
2   By 14 players

RECOVERIES
Most Fumbles Recovered, Career
3   Harold Jackson, Philadelphia, 1973; Los Angeles, 1974, 1976, 1978 (3-own)
Dan Fouts, San Diego, 1980-84, 1986 (3-own)
Randy White, Dallas, 1978, 1980-86 (3-opp)
Trent Green, Kansas City, 2004 (3-own)
2   By many players
Most Fumbles Recovered, Game
3   Trent Green, Kansas City, 2004 (3-own)
2   Dick Anderson, Miami, 1974 (1-own, 1-opp)
Harold Jackson, Los Angeles, 1974 (2-own)
Dan Fouts, San Diego, 1982 (2-own)
Joey Browner, Minnesota, 1990 (2-opp)
Jessie Armstead, N.Y. Giants, 1999 (1-own, 1-opp)
Steve Beuerlein, Carolina, 2000 (2-own)

YARDAGE
Longest Fumble Return
83   Art Still, Kansas City, 1985 (TD, opp)
51   Phil Villapiano, Oakland, 1974 (opp)
37   Sam Mills, New Orleans, 1988 (opp)

TOUCHDOWNS
Most Touchdowns, Game
1   Art Still, Kansas City, 1985
Keith Millard, Minnesota, 1990

SACKS
Sacks have been compiled since 1983.
Most Sacks, Career
9.5   Reggie White, Philadelphia, 1987-1993; Green Bay, 1994, 1996-97, 1999
9.0   Howie Long, L.A. Raiders, 1984-88, 1990, 1993-1994
7.5   Bruce Smith, Buffalo, 1988-1991, 1995-96, 1998-99
Most Sacks, Game
4   Mark Gastineau, N.Y. Jets, 1985
Reggie White, Philadelphia, 1987
3   Richard Dent, Chicago, 1985
Bruce Smith, Buffalo, 1991
2.5   Bruce Smith, Buffalo, 1998

TEAM RECORDS

SCORING
Most Points, Game
55   NFC, 2004
Fewest Points, Game
3   AFC, 1984, 1989, 1994
Most Points, Both Teams, Game
107   NFC (55) vs. AFC (52), 2004
Fewest Points, Both Teams, Game
16   NFC (6) vs. AFC (10), 1987

TOUCHDOWNS
Most Touchdowns, Game
7   AFC, 2004
NFC, 2004
Fewest Touchdowns, Game
0   AFC, 1971, 1974, 1984, 1989, 1994
NFC, 1987, 1988
Most Touchdowns, Both Teams, Game
14   AFC (7) vs. NFC (7), 2004
Fewest Touchdowns, Both Teams, Game
1   AFC (0) vs. NFC (1), 1974
NFC (0) vs. AFC (1), 1987
NFC (0) vs. AFC (1), 1988

POINTS AFTER TOUCHDOWN
Most Points After Touchdown, Game
7   AFC, 2004
Most Points After Touchdown, Both Teams, Game
12   AFC (7) vs. NFC (5), 2004

FIELD GOALS
Most Field Goals Attempted, Game
6   AFC, 1972
NFC, 1981, 1983
Most Field Goals Attempted, Both Teams, Game
9   NFC (6) vs. AFC (3), 1983
Most Field Goals, Game
5   AFC, 1974
Most Field Goals, Both Teams, Game
7   AFC (5) vs. NFC (2), 1974

NET YARDS GAINED RUSHING AND PASSING
Most Yards Gained, Game
626   AFC, 2004
Fewest Yards Gained, Game
114   AFC, 1993
Most Yards Gained, Both Teams, Game
1,022   AFC (626) vs. NFC (396), 2004

Fewest Yards Gained, Both Teams, Game
424 AFC (202) vs. NFC (222), 1987

RUSHING
ATTEMPTS
Most Attempts, Game
50 AFC, 1974
Fewest Attempts, Game
9 NFC, 2001
Most Attempts, Both Teams, Game
80 AFC (50) vs. NFC (30), 1974
Fewest Attempts, Both Teams, Game
32 NFC (9) vs. AFC (23), 2001

YARDS GAINED
Most Yards Gained, Game
400 AFC, 1995
Fewest Yards Gained, Game
28 NFC, 1992
Most Yards Gained, Both Teams, Game
441 AFC (400) vs. NFC (41), 1995
Fewest Yards Gained, Both Teams, Game
119 NFC (36) vs. AFC (83), 2001

TOUCHDOWNS
Most Touchdowns, Game
3 NFC, 1989, 1991, 2000
AFC, 1995
Most Touchdowns, Both Teams, Game
4 AFC (2) vs. NFC (2), 1973
AFC (2) vs. NFC (2), 1980

PASSING
ATTEMPTS
Most Attempts, Game
58 NFC, 2002
Fewest Attempts, Game
17 NFC, 1972
Most Attempts, Both Teams, Game
101 NFC (54) vs. AFC (47), 2003
Fewest Attempts, Both Teams, Game
42 NFC (17) vs. AFC (25), 1972

COMPLETIONS
Most Completions, Game
32 NFC, 1993
AFC, 2001
Fewest Completions, Game
7 NFC, 1972, 1982
Most Completions, Both Teams, Game
60 AFC (32) vs. NFC (28), 2001
Fewest Completions, Both Teams, Game
18 NFC (7) vs. AFC (11), 1972

YARDS GAINED
Most Yards Gained, Game
515 AFC, 2004
Fewest Yards Gained, Game
42 NFC, 1982
Most Yards Gained, Both Teams, Game
775 AFC (515) vs. NFC (260), 2004
Fewest Yards Gained, Both Teams, Game
215 NFC (89) vs. AFC (126), 1972

TIMES SACKED
Most Times Sacked, Game
9 NFC, 1985
Fewest Times Sacked, Game
0 AFC, 1998, 1999, 2000, 2003
NFC, 1971, 1997, 2001

Most Times Sacked, Both Teams, Game
17 NFC (9) vs. AFC (8), 1985
Fewest Times Sacked, Both Teams, Game
1 NFC (0) vs. AFC (1), 1997

TOUCHDOWNS
Most Touchdowns, Game
5 AFC, 2004
Most Touchdowns, Both Teams, Game
9 AFC (5) vs. NFC (4), 2004

INTERCEPTIONS BY
Most Interceptions By, Game
6 AFC, 1977, 2003
Most Interceptions By, Both Teams, Game
8 AFC (6) vs. NFC (2), 2003

YARDS GAINED
Most Yards Gained, Game
113 AFC, 2003
Most Yards Gained, Both Teams, Game
172 NFC (102) vs. AFC (70), 1999

TOUCHDOWNS
Most Touchdowns, Game
2 NFC, 2000

PUNTING
Most Punts, Game
10 AFC, 1985
Fewest Punts, Game
0 NFC, 1989
Most Punts, Both Teams, Game
16 AFC (10) vs. NFC (6), 1985
Fewest Punts, Both Teams, Game
3 NFC (1) vs. AFC (2), 2005

PUNT RETURNS
Most Punt Returns, Game
7 NFC, 1985, 1987
AFC, 1995
Fewest Punt Returns, Game
0 AFC, 1984, 1989
NFC, 2005
Most Punt Returns, Both Teams, Game
11 NFC (7) vs. AFC (4), 1985
Fewest Punt Returns, Both Teams, Game
1 NFC (0) vs. AFC (1), 2005

YARDS GAINED
Most Yards Gained, Game
177 AFC, 1976
Fewest Yards Gained, Game
–1 NFC, 1991
Most Yards Gained, Both Teams, Game
263 AFC (177) vs. NFC (86), 1976
Fewest Yards Gained, Both Teams, Game
7 NFC (0) vs. AFC (7), 2005

TOUCHDOWNS
Most Touchdowns, Game
2 NFC, 1971

KICKOFF RETURNS
Most Kickoff Returns, Game
10 AFC, 2004
Fewest Kickoff Returns, Game
1 NFC, 1971, 1984, 1994
AFC, 1988, 1991

Most Kickoff Returns, Both Teams, Game
  18 AFC (10) vs. NFC (8), 2004
Fewest Kickoff Returns, Both Teams, Game
   5 NFC (2) vs. AFC (3), 1979
         AFC (1) vs. NFC (4), 1988
         NFC (2) vs. AFC (3), 1992
         NFC (1) vs. AFC (4), 1994

YARDS GAINED
Most Yards Gained, Game
  247 NFC, 2004
Fewest Yards Gained, Game
    6 NFC, 1971
Most Yards Gained, Both Teams, Game
  461 NFC (247) vs. AFC (214), 2004
Fewest Yards Gained, Both Teams, Game
   99 NFC (48) vs. AFC (51), 1987

TOUCHDOWNS
Most Touchdowns, Game
    1 AFC, 2005

FUMBLES
Most Fumbles, Game
  10 NFC, 1974
Most Fumbles, Both Teams, Game
  15 NFC (10) vs. AFC (5), 1974

RECOVERIES
Most Fumbles Recovered, Game
  10 NFC, 1974 (6 own, 4 opp)
Most Fumbles Lost, Game
    4 AFC, 1974, 1988
         NFC, 1974

YARDS GAINED
Most Yards Gained, Game
  87 AFC, 1985

TOUCHDOWNS
Most Touchdowns, Game
    1 AFC, 1985
         NFC, 1990

TURNOVERS
(Number of times losing the ball on interceptions and fumbles.)
Most Turnovers, Game
    8 AFC, 1974
Fewest Turnovers, Game
    0 AFC, 1991, 1997
         NFC, 1991, 1995, 1996, 2001
Most Turnovers, Both Teams, Game
  12 AFC (8) vs. NFC (4), 1974
Fewest Turnovers, Both Teams, Game
    0 AFC vs. NFC, 1991

Rules

2005 NFL ROSTER OF OFFICIALS

Mike Pereira, Director of Officiating
Larry Upson, Director of Officiating Operations
Ron Baynes, Supervisor of Officials
Jim Daopoulos, Supervisor of Officials
Neely Dunn, Supervisor of Officials

No.	Name	Position	College	No.	Name	Position	College
66	Anderson, Walt	Referee	Texas	92	Madsen, Carl	Umpire	Washington
108	Arthur, Gary	Line Judge	Wright State	77	McAulay, Terry	Referee	Louisiana State
34	Austin, Gerald	Referee	Western Carolina	120	McGrath, John	Head Linesman	Kentucky
26	Baltz, Mark	Head Linesman	Ohio University	110	McKinnely, Phil	Head Linesman	UCLA
72	Banks, Michael	Side Judge	Illinois State	48	Mello, Jim	Head Linesman	Northeastern
55	Barnes, Tom	Line Judge	Minnesota	78	Meyer, Greg	Side Judge	TCU
32	Bergman, Jeff	Line Judge	Robert Morris	115	Michalek, Tony	Umpire	Indiana
91	Bergman, Jerry	Head Linesman	Robert Morris	135	Morelli, Pete	Referee	St. Mary's College
7	Blum, Ron	Line Judge	Marin College	20	Nemmers, Larry	Referee	Upper Iowa
109	Boger, Jerome	Line Judge	Morehouse College	124	Paganelli, Carl	Umpire	Michigan State
18	Boston, Byron	Line Judge	Austin	46	Paganelli, Perry	Back Judge	Hope College
74	Bowers, Derick	Line Judge	Oklahoma	132	Parry, John	Side Judge	Purdue
31	Brown, Chad	Umpire	East Texas State	15	Patterson, Rick	Side Judge	Wofford
134	Camp, Ed	Head Linesman	William Paterson	9	Perlman, Mark	Line Judge	Salem
126	Carey, Don	Back Judge	UC Riverside	10	Phares, Ron	Head Linesman	Virginia Tech
94	Carey, Mike	Referee	Santa Clara	38	Powers, Eddy	Field Judge	Tennessee
39	Carlsen, Don	Side Judge	Cal State-Chico	5	Quirk, Jim	Umpire	Delaware
63	Carollo, Bill	Referee	Wisconsin-Milwaukee	83	Reels, Richard	Back Judge	Chicago State
11	Carroll, Duke	Field Judge	Ithaca	44	Rice, Jeff	Umpire	Northwestern
60	Cavaletto, Gary	Field Judge	Hancock	57	Riveron, Alberto	Side Judge	Miami
41	Cheek, Boris	Field Judge	Morgan State	121	Rivers, Sanford	Head Linesman	Youngstown State
51	Cheffers, Carl	Side Judge	UC Irvine	128	Rose, Larry	Side Judge	Florida
65	Coleman, Walt	Referee	Arkansas	67	Rosenbaum, Doug	Field Judge	Illinois Wesleyan
99	Corrente, Tony	Referee	Cal State-Fullerton	58	Saracino, Jim	Field Judge	Northern Colorado
71	Coukart, Ed	Umpire	Northwestern	21	Schleyer, John	Head Linesman	Millersville
70	Dawson, Scott	Umpire	Virginia Tech	122	Schmitz, Bill	Back Judge	Colorado State
53	DeFelice, Garth	Umpire	San Diego State	129	Schuster, Blll	Umpire	Alfred
113	Dorkowski, Don	Back Judge	Cal State-Los Angeles	45	Seeman, Jeff	Line Judge	Minnesota
6	Dornan, Kirk	Back Judge	Central Washington	118	Sifferman, Tom	Field Judge	Seattle
27	Dyer, Lee	Field Judge	Tennessee-Chattanooga	30	Slaughter, Gary	Head Linesman	East Texas State
3	Edwards, Scott	Field Judge	Alabama	2	Smith, Billy	Back Judge	East Carolina
81	Ellison, Roy	Umpire	Savannah State	90	Spanier, Michael	Line Judge	St. Cloud State
61	Ferguson, Keith	Back Judge	San Jose State	8	Spyksma, Bill	Line Judge	South Dakota
64	Ferrell, Dan	Umpire	Cal State-Fullerton	24	Stabile, Tom	Head Linesman	Slippery Rock
47	Fincken, Tom	Side Judge	Kansas State	12	Steed, Greg	Back Judge	Howard
133	Freeman, Steve	Back Judge	Mississippi State	88	Steenson, Scott	Field Judge	North Texas
80	Gautreaux, Greg	Field Judge	Southwestern Louisiana	84	Steinkerchner, Mark	Line Judge	Akron
19	Green, Scott	Referee	Delaware	22	Stelljes, Steve	Head Linesman	Friends University
49	Hall, Rich	Umpire	Arizona	68	Stephan, Tom	Line Judge	Pittsburg State
40	Hannah, Butch	Umpire	Middle Tennessee State	114	Steratore, Gene	Field Judge	Kent State
125	Hayes, Laird	Side Judge	Princeton	112	Steratore, Tony	Back Judge	California (Penn.)
54	Hayward, George	Head Linesman	Missouri Western	62	Stewart, Charles	Line Judge	Long Beach State
93	Helverson, Scott	Back Judge	Iowa	4	Toole, Doug	Side Judge	Utah State
97	Hill, Tom	Side Judge	Carson-Newman	42	Triplette, Jeff	Referee	Wake Forest
28	Hittner, Mark	Head Linesman	Pittsburg State	75	Vernatchi, Rob	Side Judge	UC Riverside
85	Hochuli, Ed	Referee	Texas-El Paso	36	Veteri, Tony	Head Linesman	Manhattan College
82	Horton, Buddy	Field Judge	Oregon State	52	Vinovich, Bill	Referee	San Diego
37	Howey, Jim	Back Judge	Erskine College	25	Waggoner, Bob	Back Judge	Juniata College
35	Hussey, John	Line Judge	Idaho State	96	Wash, Undrey	Umpire	Texas-Arlington
76	Jenkins, Darrell	Umpire	San Jose State	116	Weatherford, Mike	Side Judge	Oklahoma State
101	Johnson, Carl	Line Judge	Nicholls State	87	Weidner, Paul	Head Linesman	Cincinnati
106	Jury, Al	Field Judge	San Bernardino Valley	50	Weir, Mike	Field Judge	Missouri
86	Kukar, Bernie	Referee	St. John's	123	White, Tom	Referee	Temple
103	Lamberth, Jeff	Side Judge	Texas A&M	43	Wilson, James	Head Linesman	Eastern Kentucky
73	Larrew, Joe	Side Judge	St. Louis University	29	Wilson, Steve	Umpire	Whitworth College
17	Lawing, Bob	Back Judge	North Carolina State	14	Winter, Ron	Referee	Michigan State
127	Leavy, Bill	Referee	San Jose State	89	Wrolstad, Craig	Field Judge	Washington
130	Lewis, Darryll	Line Judge	Dartmouth	16	Wyant, David	Side Judge	Virginia
98	Lovett, Bill	Field Judge	Maryland	33	Zimmer, Steve	Field Judge	Hofstra
59	Luckett, Phil	Back Judge	Texas-El Paso				

Roster as of May 2005

NUMERICAL ROSTER

No.	Name	Position
2	Billy Smith	BJ
3	Scott Edwards	FJ
4	Doug Toole	SJ
5	Jim Quirk	U
6	Kirk Dornan	BJ
7	Ron Blum	LJ
8	Bill Spyksma	LJ
9	Mark Perlman	LJ
10	Ron Phares	HL
11	Duke Carroll	FJ
12	Greg Steed	BJ
14	Ron Winter	R
15	Rick Patterson	SJ
16	David Wyant	SJ
17	Bob Lawing	BJ
18	Byron Boston	LJ
19	Scott Green	R
20	Larry Nemmers	R
21	John Schleyer	HL
22	Steve Stelljes	HL
24	Tom Stabile	HL
25	Bob Waggoner	BJ
26	Mark Baltz	HL
27	Lee Dyer	FJ
28	Mark Hittner	HL
29	Steve Wilson	U
30	Gary Slaughter	HL
31	Chad Brown	U
32	Jeff Bergman	LJ
33	Steve Zimmer	FJ
34	Gerry Austin	R
35	John Hussey	LJ
36	Tony Veteri	HL
37	Jim Howey	BJ
38	Eddy Powers	FJ
39	Don Carlsen	SJ
40	Butch Hannah	U
41	Boris Cheek	FJ
42	Jeff Triplette	R
43	James Wilson	HL
44	Jeff Rice	U
45	Jeff Seeman	LJ
46	Perry Paganelli	BJ
47	Tom Fincken	SJ
48	Jim Mello	HL
49	Rich Hall	U
50	Mike Weir	FJ
51	Carl Cheffers	SJ
52	Bill Vinovich	R
53	Garth DeFelice	U
54	George Hayward	HL
55	Tom Barnes	LJ
57	Alberto Riveron	SJ
58	Jim Saracino	FJ
59	Phil Luckett	BJ
60	Gary Cavaletto	FJ
61	Keith Ferguson	BJ
62	Charles Stewart	LJ
63	Bill Carollo	R
64	Dan Ferrell	U
65	Walt Coleman	R
66	Walt Anderson	R
67	Doug Rosenbaum	FJ
68	Tom Stephan	LJ
70	Scott Dawson	U
71	Ed Coukart	U
72	Michael Banks	SJ
73	Joe Larrew	SJ
74	Derick Bowers	LJ
75	Rob Vernatchi	SJ
76	Darrell Jenkins	U
77	Terry McAulay	R
78	Greg Meyer	SJ
80	Greg Gautreaux	FJ
81	Roy Ellison	U
82	Buddy Horton	FJ
83	Richard Reels	BJ
84	Mark Steinkerchner	LJ
85	Ed Hochuli	R
86	Bernie Kukar	R
87	Paul Weidner	HL
88	Scott Steenson	FJ
89	Craig Wrolstad	FJ
90	Michael Spanier	LJ
91	Jerry Bergman	HL
92	Carl Madsen	U
93	Scott Helverson	BJ
94	Mike Carey	R
96	Undrey Wash	U
97	Tom Hill	SJ
98	Bill Lovett	FJ
99	Tony Corrente	R
101	Carl Johnson	LJ
103	Jeff Lamberth	SJ
106	Al Jury	FJ
107	Ron Marinucci	LJ
108	Gary Arthur	LJ
109	Jerome Boger	LJ
110	Phil McKinnely	HL
112	Tony Steratore	BJ
113	Don Dorkowski	BJ
114	Gene Steratore	FJ
115	Tony Michalek	U
116	Mike Weatherford	SJ
118	Tom Sifferman	FJ
120	John McGrath	HL
121	Sanford Rivers	HL
122	Bill Schmitz	BJ
123	Tom White	R
124	Carl Paganelli	U
125	Laird Hayes	SJ
126	Don Carey	BJ
127	Bill Leavy	R
128	Larry Rose	SJ
129	Bill Schuster	U
130	Darryll Lewis	LJ
132	John Parry	SJ
133	Steve Freeman	BJ
134	Ed Camp	HL
135	Pete Morelli	R

Roster as of May 2005

2005 OFFICIALS AT A GLANCE
REFEREES
Walt Anderson, No. **66,** Texas, dentist, orthodontics, 10th year.
Gerry Austin, No. **34,** Western Carolina, president, leadership development group, 24th year.
Mike Carey, No. **94,** Santa Clara, owner, skiing accessories, 16th year.
Bill Carollo, No. **63,** Wisconsin-Milwaukee, marketing executive, 17th year.
Walt Coleman, No. **65,** Arkansas, manager, dairy processor, 17th year.
Tony Corrente, No. **99,** Cal State-Fullerton, educator, 11th year.
Scott Green, No. **19,** Delaware, vice-president, government relations, 15th year.
Ed Hochuli, No. **85,** Texas-El Paso, attorney, 16th year.
Bernie Kukar, No. **86,** St. John's, sales representative, employees benefit plan, 22nd year.
Bill Leavy, No. **127,** San Jose State, retired firefighter, 11th year.
Terry McAulay, No. **77,** Louisiana State, senior computer scientist, 8th year.
Pete Morelli, No. **135,** St. Mary's, high school principal, 9th year.
Larry Nemmers, No. **20,** Upper Iowa, motivational speaker, 21st year.
Jeff Triplette, No. **42,** Wake Forest, vice president, world-wide energy company, 10th year.
Bill Vinovich, No. **52,** San Diego, certified public accountant, 5th year.
Tom White, No. **123,** Temple, consultant, 17th year.
Ron Winter, No. **14,** Michigan State, university professor, 11th year.

UMPIRES
Chad Brown, No. **31,** East Texas State, manager, intramural/sports clubs, 14th year.
Ed Coukart, No. **71,** Northwestern, vice-president, commercial bank, 17th year.
Scott Dawson, No. **70,** Virginia Tech, president/owner, commercial construction company, 11th year.
Garth DeFelice, No. **53,** San Diego State, director of distributing, beverage company, 8th year.
Roy Ellison, No. **81,** Savannah State, technical staff member, 3rd year.
Dan Ferrell, No. **64,** Cal State-Fullerton, regional manager, parts distribution and logistics, 3rd year.
Rich Hall, No. **49,** Arizona, custom cabinetry, 2nd year.
Butch Hannah, No. **40,** Middle Tennessee State, federal probation officer, 7th year.
Darrell Jenkins, No. **76,** San Jose State, retired, 4th year.
Carl Madsen, No. **92,** Washington, partner/owner, office furniture dealership, 9th year.
Tony Michalek, No. **115,** Indiana, eurodollar future trader, 4th year.
Carl Paganelli, No. **124,** Michigan State, federal probation officer, 7th year.
Jim Quirk, No. **5,** Delaware, consultant, 18th year.
Jeff Rice, No. **44,** Northwestern, attorney, 11th year.
Bill Schuster, No. **129,** Alfred, insurance broker, 6th year.
Undrey Wash, No. **96,** Texas-Arlington, claims manager, 6th year.
Steve Wilson, No. **29,** Whitworth College, church administrator, 7th year.

HEAD LINESMEN
Mark Baltz, No. **26,** Ohio University, sales consultant, 17th year.
Jerry Bergman, No. **91,** Robert Morris, sales executive, 4th year.
Ed Camp, No. **134,** William Paterson, teacher, 6th year.
George Hayward, No. **54,** Missouri Western, vice-president and manager, warehouse company, 15th year.
Mark Hittner, No. **28,** Pittsburg State, investment banker, 9th year.
John McGrath, No. **120,** Kentucky, senior account executive, 4th year.
Phil McKinnely, No. **110,** UCLA, inventory control, former NFL player, 3rd year.
Jim Mello, No. **48,** Northeastern, facilities management, 2nd year.
Ron Phares, No. **10,** Virginia Tech, president, construction company, 21st year.
Sanford Rivers, No. **121,** Youngstown State, university vice-president, 16th year.
John Schleyer, No. **21,** Millersville, medical sales, 16th year.
Gary Slaughter, No. **30,** East Texas State, general manager, 10th year.
Tom Stabile, No. **24,** Slippery Rock, secondary educational administrator, 11th year.
Steve Stelljes, No. **22,** Friends University, business planning manager, 4th year.
Tony Veteri, No. **36,** Manhattan, director of athletics, 14th year.
Paul Weidner, No. **87,** Cincinnati, marketing manager, 20th year.
James Wilson, No. **43,** Eastern Kentucky, area sales manager, 8th year.

LINE JUDGES
Gary Arthur, No. **108,** Wright State, president, commercial printing company, 9th year.
Tom Barnes, No. **55,** Minnesota, manufacturing representative, 20th year.
Jeff Bergman, No. **32,** Robert Morris, president and chief executive officer, medical services, 14th year.
Ron Blum, No. **7,** Marin College, professional golfer, 21st year.
Jerome Boger, No. **109,** Morehouse College, commercial insurance underwriter, 2nd year.
Byron Boston, No. **18,** Austin, tax consultant, 11th year.
Derick Bowers, No. **74,** East Central University, purchasing supervisor, 3rd year.
John Hussey, No. **35,** Idaho State, sales representative, retail logistics group, 4th year.
Carl Johnson, No. **101,** Nicholls State, district sales manager, 5th year.
Darryll Lewis, No. **130,** Dartmouth, associate professor, 7th year.
Mark Perlman, No. **9,** Salem, teacher, 5th year.
Jeff Seeman, No. **45,** Minnesota, brokerage sales, 4th year.
Mike Spanier, No. **90,** St. Cloud State, middle school principal, 7th year.
Bill Spyksma, No. **8,** South Dakota, managing partner, marina, 11th year.
Mark Steinkerchner, No. **84,** Akron, vice-president, 12th year.
Tom Stephan, No. **68,** Pittsburg State, business broker, 7th year.
Charles Stewart, No. **62,** Long Beach State, retired human services administrator, 14th year.

Roster as of May 2005

FIELD JUDGES

Duke Carroll, No. **11,** Ithaca, insurance sales, 11th year.
Gary Cavaletto, No. **60,** Hancock, general manager, agricultural operations, 3rd year.
Boris Cheek, No. **41,** Morgan State, director of operations and management, 10th year.
Lee Dyer, No. **27,** Tennessee-Chattanooga, sales manager, 3rd year.
Scott Edwards, No. **3,** Alabama, environmental engineer, 7th year.
Greg Gautreaux, No. **80,** Southwestern Louisiana, athletic programs manager, 4th year.
Buddy Horton, No. **82,** Oregon State, water service worker, 7th year.
Al Jury, No. **106,** San Bernardino Valley, state traffic officer, 28th year.
Bill Lovett, No. **98,** Maryland, managing partner, financial sales, 16th year.
Eddy Powers, No. **38,** Tennessee, sales/design office supply, 4th year.
Doug Rosenbaum, No. **67,** Illinois Wesleyan, financial advisor, 5th year.
Jim Saracino, No. **58,** Northern Colorado, secondary educator, 11th year.
Tom Sifferman, No. **118,** Seattle, manufacturer's representative, 20th year.
Scott Steenson, No. **88,** North Texas, commercial real estate broker, 15th year.
Gene Steratore, No. **114,** Kent State, co-owner, supply company, 3rd year.
Mike Weir, No. **50,** Missouri, owner, sporting goods store, 4th year.
Craig Wrolstad, No. **89,** Washington, education, 3rd year.
Steve Zimmer, No. **33,** Hofstra, attorney, 9th year.

SIDE JUDGES

Michael Banks, No. **72,** Illinois State, carpenter foreman, 4th year.
Don Carlsen, No. **39,** Cal State-Chico, retired county school superintendent, 17th year.
Carl Cheffers, No. **51,** UC Irvine, sales manager, 6th year.
Tom Fincken, No. **47,** Emporia State, retired educational administrator, 22nd year.
Laird Hayes, No. **125,** Princeton, professor, physical education & athletics, 11th year.
Tom Hill, No. **97,** Carson Newman, teacher, 7th year.
Jeff Lamberth, No. **103,** Texas A&M, attorney, 4th year.
Joe Larrew, No. **73,** St. Louis University, attorney, 4th year.
Greg Meyer, No. **78,** TCU, banker, 4th year.
John Parry, No. **132,** Purdue, corporate pilot, 6th year.
Rick Patterson, No. **15,** Wofford, banker, 10th year.
Alberto Riveron, No. **57,** Miami, commercial restaurant equipment, 2nd year.
Larry Rose, No. **128,** Florida, financial planner, 9th year.
Doug Toole, No. **4,** Utah State, physical therapist, 18th year.
Rob Vernatchi, No. **75,** UC Riverside, enforcement investigator, 2nd year.
Mike Weatherford, No. **116,** Oklahoma State, energy trader, 4th year.
David Wyant, No. **16,** Virginia, consulting engineer, 15th year.

BACK JUDGES

Don Carey, No. **126,** UC Riverside, contract manager, 11th year.
Don Dorkowski, No. **113,** Cal State-Los Angeles, pump manufacturer, 20th year.
Kirk Dornan, No. **6,** Central Washington, purchasing manager, 12th year.
Keith Ferguson, No. **61,** San Jose State, sales, 6th year.
Steve Freeman, No. **133,** Mississippi State, custom home builder, 5th year.
Scott Helverson, No. **93,** Iowa, sales, printing and promotions, 3rd year.
Jim Howey, No. **37,** Erskine College, director of adult education, 7th year.
Bob Lawing, No. **17,** North Carolina State, real estate management, 9th year.
Phil Luckett, No. **59,** Texas-El Paso, computer program analyst, federal civil services, 15th year.
Perry Paganelli, No. **46,** Hope College, high school administrator, 8th year.
Richard Reels, No. **83,** Chicago State, director of security, court services, 13th year.
Bill Schmitz, No. **122,** Colorado State, general sales manager, 17th year.
Billy Smith, No. **2,** East Carolina, federal government, 11th year.
Greg Steed, No. **12,** Howard, computer systems analyst, 3rd year.
Tony Steratore, No. **112,** California (Penn.), co-owner, supply company, 6th year.
Bob Waggoner, No. **25,** Juniata College, probation officer, 9th year.

Roster as of May 2005

1

**TOUCHDOWN, FIELD GOAL,
or SUCCESSFUL TRY**
Both arms extended above head.

2

SAFETY
Palms together above head.

3

FIRST DOWN
Arm pointed toward defensive
team's goal.

4

**CROWD NOISE,
DEAD BALL, or NEUTRAL
ZONE ESTABLISHED**
One arm above head
with an open hand.
With fist closed: **Fourth Down.**

5

**BALL ILLEGALLY
TOUCHED, KICKED,
or BATTED**
Fingertips tap both shoulders.

6

TIME OUT
Hands crisscrossed above head.
Same signal followed by placing one
hand on top of cap: **Referee's Time Out.**
Same signal followed by arm swung at
side: **Touchback.**

7

**NO TIME OUT or
TIME IN WITH WHISTLE**
Full arm circled to
simulate moving clock.

8

**DELAY OF GAME
or EXCESS TIME OUT**
Folded arms.

9

**FALSE START,
ILLEGAL FORMATION, or
KICKOFF or SAFETY KICK
OUT OF BOUNDS or
KICKING TEAM PLAYER
VOLUNTARILY OUT OF BOUNDS
DURING A PUNT**
Forearms rotated over and over
in front of body.

10

PERSONAL FOUL
One wrist striking the other above head.
Same signal followed by swinging leg:
Roughing the Kicker.
Same signal followed by raised arm
swinging forward:
Roughing the Passer.
Same signal followed by grasping
facemask: **Major Facemask.**

11

HOLDING
Grasping one wrist,
the fist clenched,
in front of chest.

12

**ILLEGAL USE OF HANDS,
ARMS, or BODY**
Grasping one wrist,
the hand open and facing
forward, in front of chest.

13

PENALTY REFUSED, INCOMPLETE PASS, PLAY OVER, or MISSED FIELD GOAL or EXTRA POINT
Hands shifted in horizontal plane.

14

PASS JUGGLED INBOUNDS AND CAUGHT OUT OF BOUNDS
Hands up and down in front of chest (following incomplete pass signal).

15

ILLEGAL FORWARD PASS
One hand waved behind back followed by loss of down signal (23), when appropriate.

16

INTENTIONAL GROUNDING OF PASS
Parallel arms waved in a diagonal plane across body. Followed by loss of down signal (23).

17

INTERFERENCE WITH FORWARD PASS or FAIR CATCH
Hands open and extended forward from shoulders with hands vertical.

18

INVALID FAIR-CATCH SIGNAL
One hand waved above head.

19

**INELIGIBLE RECEIVER
or INELIGIBLE
MEMBER OF KICKING TEAM
DOWNFIELD**
Right hand touching top of cap.

20

ILLEGAL CONTACT
One open hand extended forward.

21

**OFFSIDE, ENCROACHMENT, or
NEUTRAL ZONE INFRACTION**
Hands on hips.

22

ILLEGAL MOTION AT SNAP
Horizontal arc with one hand.

23

LOSS OF DOWN
Both hands held behind head.

24

**INTERLOCKING
INTERFERENCE, PUSHING, or
HELPING RUNNER**
Pushing movement of hands
to front with arms downward.

25

**TOUCHING A FORWARD
PASS or SCRIMMAGE KICK**
Diagonal motion of
one hand across another.

26

**UNSPORTSMANLIKE
CONDUCT**
Arms outstretched,
palms down.

27

ILLEGAL CUT
Hand striking front of thigh.
ILLEGAL BLOCK BELOW THE WAIST
One hand striking front of thigh
preceded by personal-foul signal (10).
CHOP BLOCK
Both hands striking side of thighs
preceded by personal-foul signal (10).
CLIPPING
One hand striking back of calf
preceded by personal-foul signal (10).

28

ILLEGAL CRACKBACK
Strike of an
open right hand
against the right mid-thigh
preceded by personal foul
signal (10).

29

PLAYER DISQUALIFIED
Ejection signal.

30

TRIPPING
Repeated action of right foot
in back of left heel.

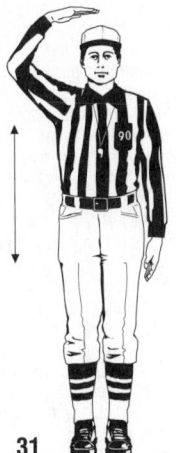

31

**UNCATCHABLE
FORWARD PASS**
Palm of right hand held
parallel to ground above head
and moved back and forth.

32

**TWELVE MEN IN OFFENSIVE HUDDLE
or TOO MANY MEN
ON THE FIELD**
Both hands on top of head.

33

FACEMASK
Grasping facemask with one
hand.

34

ILLEGAL SHIFT
Horizontal arcs with two hands.

35

**RESET PLAY CLOCK–
25 SECONDS**
Pump one arm vertically.

36

**RESET PLAY CLOCK–
40 SECONDS**
Pump two arms vertically.

NFL DIGEST OF RULES

This Digest of Rules of the National Football League has been prepared to aid players, fans, and members of the press, radio, and television media in their understanding of the game.

It is not meant to be a substitute for the official rule book. In any case of conflict between these explanations and the official rules, the rules always have precedence.

In order to make it easier to coordinate the information in this digest, the topics discussed generally follow the order of the rule book.

OFFICIALS' JURISDICTIONS, POSITIONS, AND DUTIES

Referee—General oversight and control of game. Gives signals for all fouls and is final authority for rule interpretations. Takes a position in backfield 10 to 12 yards behind line of scrimmage, favors right side (if quarterback is right-handed passer). Determines legality of snap, observes deep back(s) for legal motion. On running plays, observes quarterback during and after handoff, remains with him until action has cleared away, then proceeds downfield, checking on runner and contact behind him. When runner is downed, Referee determines forward progress from wing official and, if necessary, adjusts final position of ball.

On pass plays, drops back as quarterback begins to fade back, picks up legality of tackle on Head Linesman's side. Changes to complete concentration on quarterback as defenders approach. Primarily responsible to rule on possible roughing action on passer and if ball becomes loose, rules whether ball is free on a fumble or dead on an incomplete pass. Shares responsibility with Umpire, Linesman, and Line Judge on intentional grounding.

During kicking situations, Referee has primary responsibility to rule on kicker's actions and whether or not any subsequent contact by a defender is legal. During punt plays, Referee's position is parallel to kicker and wide. The Referee will announce on the microphone when each period is ended, penalties, a charged team time out, and when the two-minute warning for each half is reached.

Umpire—Primary responsibilities are to rule on players' conduct and actions on scrimmage line, as well as check on their equipment. Lines up approximately four to five yards downfield, varying position from the outside shoulder of one guard to outside shoulder of opposite guard. Looks for possible false start by offensive linemen. Observes legality of contact by both offensive linemen while blocking and by defensive players while they attempt to ward off blockers. Is prepared to call rule infractions if they occur on offense or defense. Moves forward to line of scrimmage when pass play develops in order to insure that interior linemen do not move illegally downfield. If offensive linemen indicate screen pass is to be attempted, Umpire shifts his attention toward screen side, picks up potential receiver in order to insure that he will legally be permitted to run his pattern and continues to rule on action of blockers. Umpire is to assist in ruling on incomplete or trapped passes when ball is thrown overhead or short. On field goal and try-kick attempts, he will become a second umpire with the Side Judge.

Head Linesman—Primarily responsible for ruling on offside, encroachment, and actions pertaining to scrimmage line prior to or at snap. Takes a position straddling the line of scrimmage. Keys on closest setback on his side of the field. On pass plays, Linesman is responsible to clear his receiver approximately seven yards downfield as he moves to a point five yards beyond the line. Linesman's secondary responsibility is to rule on any illegal action taken by defenders on any delay receiver moving downfield. Has full responsibility for ruling on sideline plays on his side, e.g., pass receiver or runner in or out of bounds. Together with Referee, Linesman is responsible for keeping track of number of downs and is in charge of mechanics of his chain crew in connection with its duties.

Linesman must be prepared to assist in determining forward progress by a runner on play directed toward middle or into his side zone. He, in turn, is to signal Referee or Umpire what forward

point ball has reached. Linesman is also responsible to rule on legality of action involving any receiver who approaches his side zone. He is to call pass interference when the infraction occurs and is to rule on legality of blockers and defenders on plays involving ball carriers, whether it is entirely a running play, a combination pass and run, or a play involving a kick. Also assists referee with intentional grounding.

Line Judge—Straddles line of scrimmage on side of field opposite Linesman. Keeps time of game as a backup for official clock operator. However, should official clock malfunction or be operated improperly, the time kept by the Line Judge is official. Along with Linesman is responsible for offside, encroachment, and actions pertaining to scrimmage line prior to or at snap. Line Judge keys on closest setback on his side of field. Line Judge is to observe his receiver until he moves at least seven yards downfield. He then moves toward backfield side, being especially alert to rule on any back in motion and on flight of ball when pass is made (he must rule whether forward or backward). Line Judge has primary responsibility to rule whether or not passer is behind or beyond line of scrimmage when pass is made. He also assists in observing actions by blockers and defenders who are on his side of field. After pass is thrown, Line Judge directs attention toward activities that occur in back of Umpire. During punting situations, Line Judge remains at line of scrimmage to be sure that only the end men move downfield until kick has been made. He also rules whether or not the kick crossed line and then observes action by members of the kicking team who are moving downfield to cover the kick. The Line Judge will advise the Referee when time has expired at the end of each period.

Field Judge—Operates on same side of field as Line Judge, 20 yards deep. Keys on widest receiver on his side. Concentrates on path of end or back, observing legality of his potential block(s) or of actions taken against him. Is prepared to rule from deep position on holding or illegal use of hands by end or back or on defensive infractions committed by player guarding him. Has primary responsibility to make decisions involving sideline on his side of field, e.g., pass receiver or runner in or out of bounds.

Field Judge makes decisions involving catching, recovery, or illegal touching of a loose ball beyond line of scrimmage. Rules on plays involving pass receiver, including legality of catch or pass interference. Assists in covering actions of runner, including blocks by teammates and that of defenders. Rules on blocking during punt returns and, together with Back Judge, rules whether or not field goal and try-kick attempts are successful.

Side Judge—Operates on same side of field as Linesman, 20 yards deep. Keys on widest receiver on his side. Concentrates on path of this receiver, observing legality of his potential block(s) or of actions taken against him. Is prepared to rule from deep position on holding or illegal use of hands by the receiver or on defensive infractions committed by player defending him. Has primary responsibility to make decisions involving sideline on his side of field, e.g., pass receiver or runner in or out of bounds.

Side Judge makes decisions involving catching, recovery, or illegal touching of a loose ball beyond line of scrimmage. Rules on plays involving pass receiver, including legality of catch or pass interference. Assists in covering actions of runner, including blocks by teammates and that of defenders and rules on blocking during punt returns. On field goals and try-kick attempts, he becomes a second umpire.

Back Judge—Takes a position 25 yards downfield. In general, favors the tight end's side of field. Usually keys on tight end, concentrates on his path and observes legality of tight end's potential block(s) or of actions taken against him. Is prepared to rule from deep position on holding or illegal use of hands by end or back or on defensive infractions committed by player defending him.

Back Judge times interval between plays on 40/25-second clock plus intermission between two periods of each half. Makes decisions involving catching, recovery, or illegal touching of a loose ball beyond line of scrimmage. Is responsible to rule on plays involving end line. Calls pass interference, fair-catch infractions, and blocking during kick returns and, together with Field Judge, rules whether or not field goal and try-kick attempts are successful.

DEFINITIONS

1. **Chucking:** Warding off an opponent who is in front of a defender by contacting him with a quick extension of arm or arms, followed by the return of arm(s) to a flexed position, thereby breaking the original contact.
2. **Clipping:** Throwing the body across the back of an opponent's leg or hitting him from the back below the waist while moving up from behind unless the opponent is a runner or the contact is above the knee in close line play.
3. **Close Line Play:** The area between the positions normally occupied by the offensive tackles, extending three yards on each side of the line of scrimmage. It is legal to clip above the knee.
4. **Crackback:** Eligible receivers who take or move to a position more than two yards outside the tackle or a player in a backfiel position may not block an opponent below the waist toward the ball at the snap and within five yards of the line of scrimmage.
5. **Dead Ball:** Ball not in play.
6. **Double Foul:** A foul by each team during the same down.
7. **Down:** The period of action that starts when the ball is put in play and ends when it is dead.
8. **Encroachment:** When a defensive player enters the neutral zone and makes contact with an opponent before the ball is snapped.
9. **Fair Catch:** An unhindered catch of a kick by a member of the receiving team who must raise one arm a full length above his head and wave his arm from side to side while the kick is in flight.
10. **Foul:** Any violation of a playing rule.
11. **Free Kick:** A kickoff or safety kick. It may be a placekick, dropkick, or punt, except a punt may not be used on a kick-off following a touchdown, successful field goal, or to begin each half or overtime period. A tee cannot be used on a fair-catch or safety kick.
12. **Fumble:** The unintentional loss of player possession of the ball.
13. **Game Clock:** Scoreboard game clock.
14. **Impetus:** The action of a player that gives momentum to the ball and sends it into the end zone.
15. **Live Ball:** A ball legally free-kicked or snapped. It continues in play until the down ends.
16. **Loose Ball:** A live ball not in possession of any player.
17. **Muff:** The touching of a loose ball by a player in an unsuccessful attempt to obtain possession.
18. **Neutral Zone:** The space the length of a ball between the two scrimmage lines. The offensive team and defensive team must remain behind their end of the ball.
    Exception: The offensive player who snaps the ball.
19. **Offside:** A player is offside when any part of his body is beyond his scrimmage or free kick line when the ball is snapped or kicked. Exception: Snapper, holder of placekick or kicker.
20. **Own Goal:** The goal a team is defending.
21. **Play Clock:** 40/25 second clock.
22. **Pocket Area:** Applies from a point two yards outside of either offensive tackle and includes the tight end if he drops off the line of scrimmage to pass protect. Pocket extends longitudinally behind the line back to offensive team's own end line. For purposes of intentional grounding, the pocket is considered tackle to tackle.
23. **Possession of a Pass:** When a player controls the ball throughout the act of clearly touching both feet, or any other part of his body other than his hand(s), to the ground inbounds.

24. **Post-Possession Foul:** A foul by the receiving team that occurs after a ball is legally kicked from scrimmage prior to possession changing. The ball must cross the line of scrimmage and the receiving team must retain the kicked ball unless it is part of a double foul.
25. **Punt:** A kick made when a player drops the ball and kicks it while it is in flight.
26. **Safety:** The situation in which the ball is dead on or behind a team's own goal if the impetus comes from a player on that team. Two points are scored for the opposing team.
27. **Shift:** The movement of two or more offensive players at the same time before the snap.
28. **Striking:** The act of swinging, clubbing, or propelling the arm or forearm in contacting an opponent.
29. **Sudden Death:** The continuation of a tied game into sudden death overtime in which the team scoring first (by safety, field goal, or touchdown) wins.
30. **Touchback:** When a ball is dead on or behind a team's own goal line, provided the impetus came from an opponent and provided it is not a touchdown or a missed field goal attempt when the ball was kicked outside the 20-yard line.
31. **Touchdown:** When any part of the ball, legally in possession of a player inbounds, breaks the plane of the opponent's goal line, provided it is not a touchback.
32. **Unsportsmanlike Conduct:** Any act contrary to the generally understood principles of sportsmanship.

SUMMARY OF PENALTIES
Automatic First Down
1. Awarded to offensive team on all defensive fouls with these exceptions:
   (a) Offside.
   (b) Encroachment.
   (c) Delay of game.
   (d) Illegal substitution.
   (e) Excessive time out(s).
   (f) Incidental grasp of facemask.
   (g) Neutral zone infraction.
   (h) Running into the kicker.
   (i) More than 11 players on the field at the snap for either team.

Five Yards
1. Defensive holding or illegal use of hands (automatic first down).
2. Delay of game on offense or defense.
3. Delay of kickoff.
4. Encroachment.
5. Excessive time out(s).
6. False start.
7. Illegal formation.
8. Illegal shift.
9. Illegal motion.
10. Illegal substitution.
11. First onside kickoff out of bounds between goal lines and untouched or last touched by kickers.
12. Invalid fair catch signal.
13. More than 11 players on the field at snap for either team.
14. Less than seven men on offensive line at snap.
15. Offside.
16. Failure to pause one second after shift or huddle.
17. Running into kicker.
18. More than one man in motion at snap.
19. Grasping facemask of the ball carrier or quarterback.
20. Player out of bounds at snap.
21. Ineligible member(s) of kicking team going beyond line of scrimmage before ball is kicked.
22. Illegal return.
23. Failure to report change of eligibility.
24. Neutral zone infraction.

25. Loss of team time out(s) or five-yard penalty on the defense for excessive crowd noise. Offensive team's quarterback can be penalized if he does not make every effort to put the ball in play.
26. Ineligible player downfield during passing down.
27. Second forward pass behind the line.
28. Forward pass is first touched by eligible receiver who has gone out of bounds and returned.
29. Forward pass touches or is caught by an ineligible receiver on or behind line.
30. Forward pass thrown from behind line of scrimmage after ball once crossed the line.
31. Kicking team player voluntarily out of bounds during a punt.
32. Twelve (12) men in the huddle.

Ten Yards
1. Offensive pass interference.
2. Holding, illegal use of hands, arms, or body by offense.
3. Tripping by a member of either team.
4. Helping the runner.
5. Deliberately batting or punching a loose ball.
6. Deliberately kicking a loose ball.
7. Illegal block above the waist.

Fifteen Yards
1. Chop block.
2. Clipping below the waist.
3. Fair catch interference.
4. Illegal crackback block by offense.
5. Piling on.
6. Roughing the kicker.
7. Roughing the passer.
8. Twisting, turning, or pulling an opponent by the facemask.
9. Unnecessary roughness.
10. Unsportsmanlike conduct.
11. Delay of game at start of either half.
12. Illegal low block.
13. A tackler using his helmet to butt, spear, or ram an opponent.
14. Any player who uses the top of his helmet unnecessarily.
15. A punter, placekicker, or holder who simulates being roughed by a defensive player.
16. Leaping.
17. Leverage.
18. Any player who removes his helmet after a play while on the field.
19. Taunting.

Five Yards and Loss of Down (Combination Penalty)
1. Forward pass thrown from beyond line of scrimmage.

Ten Yards and Loss of Down (Combination Penalty)
1. Intentional grounding of forward pass (safety if passer is in own end zone). If foul occurs more than 10 yards behind line, play results in loss of down at spot of foul.

Fifteen Yards and Loss of Coin Toss Option
1. Team's late arrival on the field prior to scheduled kickoff.
2. Captains not appearing for coin toss.

Fifteen Yards (and disqualification if flagrant)
1. Striking opponent with fist.
2. Kicking or kneeing opponent.
3. Striking opponent on head or neck with forearm, elbow, or hands whether or not the initial contact is made below the neck area.
4. Roughing kicker.
5. Roughing passer.
6. Malicious unnecessary roughness.
7. Unsportsmanlike conduct.
8. Palpably unfair act. (Distance penalty determined by the Referee after consultation with other officials.)

Fifteen Yards and Automatic Disqualification
1. Using a helmet (not worn) as a weapon.
2. Striking or purposely shoving a game official.

Suspension From Game For One Down
1. Illegal equipment. (Player may return after one down when legally equipped.)

Touchdown Awarded (Palpably Unfair Act)
1. When Referee determines a palpably unfair act deprived a team of a touchdown. (Example: Player comes off bench and tackles runner apparently en route to touchdown.)

FIELD
1. Sidelines and end lines are out of bounds. The goal line is actually in the end zone. A player with the ball in his possession scores a touchdown when the ball is on, above, or over the goal line.
2. The field is rimmed by a white border, six feet wide, along the sidelines. All of this is out of bounds.
3. The hashmarks (inbound lines) are 70 feet, 9 inches from each sideline.
4. Goal posts must be single-standard type, offset from the end line and painted bright gold. The goal posts must be 18 feet, 6 inches wide and the top face of the crossbar must be 10 feet above the ground. Vertical posts extend at least 30 feet above the crossbar. A ribbon 4 inches by 42 inches long is to be attached to the top of each post. The actual goal is the plane extending indefinitely above the crossbar and between the outer edges of the posts.
5. The field is 360 feet long and 160 feet wide. The end zones are 30 feet deep. The line used in try-for-point plays is two yards out from the goal line.
6. Chain crew members and ball boys must be uniformly identifiable.
7. All clubs must use standardized sideline markers. Pylons must be used for goal line and end line markings.
8. End zone markings and club identification at 50 yard line must be approved by the Commissioner to avoid any confusion as to delineation of goal lines, sidelines, and end lines.

BALL
1. The home club shall have 36 balls for outdoor games and 24 for indoor games available for testing with a pressure gauge by the referee two hours prior to the starting time of the game to meet with League requirements. Twelve (12) new footballs, sealed in a special box and shipped by the manufacturer, will be opened in the officials' locker room two hours prior to the starting time of the game. These balls are to be specially marked with the letter "k" and used exclusively for the kicking game.

COIN TOSS
1. The toss of coin will take place within three minutes of kickoff in center of field. The toss will be called by the visiting captain before the coin is flipped. The winner may choose one of two privileges and the loser gets the other:
   (a) Receive or kick
   (b) Goal his team will defend
2. Immediately prior to the start of the second half, the captains of both teams must inform the officials of their respective choices. The loser of the original coin toss gets first choice.

TIMING
1. The stadium game clock is official. In case it stops or is operating incorrectly, the Line Judge takes over the official timing on the field.
2. Each period is 15 minutes. The intermission between the periods is two minutes. Halftime is 12 minutes, unless otherwise specified.
3. On charged team time outs, the Back Judge starts watch and blows whistle after 1 minute 50 seconds, unless television does not utilize the time for commercial. In this case the length of the time out is reduced to 30 seconds.

4. The Referee will allow necessary time to attend to an injured player, or repair a legal player's equipment.
5. Each team is allowed three time outs each half.
6. Time between plays will be 40 seconds from the end of a given play until the snap of the ball for the next play, or a 25-second interval after certain administrative stoppages and game delays.
7. Clock will start running when ball is snapped following all changes of team possession.
8. With the exception of the last two minutes of the first half and the last five minutes of the second half, the game clock will be restarted following a player going out of bounds on a play from scrimmage, or after declined penalties when appropriate on the referee's signal.
9. Consecutive team time outs can be taken by opposing teams but the length of the second time out will be reduced to 30 seconds.
10. When, in the judgment of the Referee, the level of crowd noise prevents the offense from hearing its signals, he can institute a series of procedures which can result in a loss of team time outs or a five-yard penalty against the defensive team.
11. On kickoff, clock does not start until the ball has been legally touched by player of either team in the field of play.

SUDDEN DEATH

1. The sudden death system of determining the winner shall prevail when score is tied at the end of the regulation playing time of all NFL games. The team scoring first during overtime play shall be the winner and the game automatically ends upon any score (by safety, field goal, or touchdown) or when a score is awarded by Referee for a palpably unfair act.
2. At the end of regulation time the Referee will immediately toss coin at center of field in accordance with rules pertaining to the usual pregame toss. The captain of the visiting team will call the toss prior to the coin being flipped.
3. Following a three-minute intermission after the end of the regulation game, play will be continued in 15-minute periods or until there is a score. There is a two-minute intermission between subsequent periods. The teams change goals at the start of each period. Each team has three time outs per half and all general timing provisions apply as during a regular game. Disqualified players are not allowed to return.
   Exception: In preseason and regular season games there shall be a maximum of 15 minutes of sudden death with two time outs instead of three. General provisions that apply for the fourth quarter will prevail. Try not attempted if touchdown scored.

TIMING IN FINAL TWO MINUTES OF EACH HALF

1. A team cannot buy an excess time out for a penalty. However, a fourth time out is allowed without penalty for an injured player, who must be removed immediately. A fifth time out or more is allowed for an injury and a five-yard penalty is assessed. Additionally, if the clock was running and the score is tied or the team in possession is losing, the ball cannot be put in play for at least 10 seconds on the fourth or more time out. The half or game can end while those 10 seconds are run off on the clock.
2. If the defensive team is behind in the score and commits a foul when it has no time outs left in the final 40 seconds of either half, the offensive team can decline the penalty for the foul and have the time on the clock expire.
3. Fouls that occur in the last five minutes of the fourth quarter as well as the last two minutes of the first half will result in the clock starting on the snap.

TRY

1. After a touchdown, the scoring team is allowed a try during one scrimmage down. The ball may be spotted anywhere between the inbounds lines, two or more yards from the goal

line. The successful conversion counts one point by kick; two points for a successful conversion by touchdown; or one point for a safety.
2. The defensive team never can score on a try. As soon as defense gets possession or the kick is blocked or a touchdown is not scored, the try is over.
3. Any distance penalty for fouls committed by the defense that prevent the try from being attempted can be enforced on the succeeding try or succeeding kickoff. Any foul committed on a successful try will result in a distance penalty being assessed on the ensuing kickoff.
4. Only the fumbling player can recover and advance a fumble during a try.

PLAYERS-SUBSTITUTIONS

1. Each team is permitted 11 men on the field at the snap.
2. Unlimited substitution is permitted. However, players may enter the field only when the ball is dead. Players who have been substituted for are not permitted to linger on the field. Such lingering will be interpreted as unsportsmanlike conduct.
3. Players leaving the game must be out of bounds on their own side, clearing the field between the end lines, before a snap or free kick. If player crosses end line leaving field, it is delay of game (five-yard penalty).
4. Offensive substitutes who remain in the game must move onto the field as far as the inside of the field numerals before moving to a wide position.
5. With the exception of the last two minutes of either half, the offensive team, while in the process of substitution or simulated substitution, is prohibited from rushing quickly to the line and snapping the ball with the obvious attempt to cause a defensive foul; i.e., too many men on the field.
6. There never can be 12 or more players in the offensive huddle.

KICKOFF

1. The kickoff shall be from the kicking team's 30-yard line at the start of each half and after a field goal and try. A kickoff is one type of free kick.
2. A one-inch tee may be used (no tee permitted for field goal, safety kick, or try attempt) on a kickoff. The ball is put in play by a placekick.
3. A kickoff may not score a field goal.
4. A kickoff is illegal unless it travels 10 yards OR is touched by the receiving team. Once the ball is touched by the receiving team or has gone 10 yards, it is a free ball. Receivers may recover and advance. Kicking team may recover but NOT advance UNLESS receiver had possession and lost the ball.
5. When a kickoff goes out of bounds between the goal lines without being touched by the receiving team, the ball belongs to the receivers 30 yards from the spot of the kick or at the out-of-bounds spot unless the ball went out-of-bounds the first time an onside kick was attempted. In this case, the kicking team is penalized five yards and the ball must be kicked again.
6. When a kickoff goes out of bounds between the goal lines and is touched last by receiving team, it is receiver's ball at out-of-bounds spot.
7. If the kicking team either illegally kicks off out of bounds or is guilty of a short free kick on two or more consecutive onside kicks, receivers may take possession of the ball at the dead ball spot, out-of-bounds spot, or spot of illegal touch.

SAFETY

1. In addition to a kickoff, the other free kick is a kick after a safety (safety kick). A punt may be used (a punt may not be used on a kickoff).
2. On a safety kick, the team scored upon puts ball in play by a punt, dropkick, or placekick without tee. No score can be

made on a free kick following a safety, even if a series of penalties places team in position. (A field goal can be scored only on a play from scrimmage or a free kick after a fair catch.)

FAIR CATCH KICK

1. After a fair catch, the receiving team has the option to put the ball in play by a snap or a fair catch kick (field goal attempt), with fair catch kick lines established ten yards apart. All general rules apply as for a field goal attempt from scrimmage. The clock starts when the ball is kicked. (No tee permitted.)

FIELD GOAL

1. All field goals attempted (kicker) and missed from beyond the 20-yard line will result in the defensive team taking possession of the ball at the spot of the kick. On any field goal attempted and missed where the spot of the kick is on or inside the 20-yard line, ball will revert to defensive team at the 20-yard line.

SAFETY

1. The important factor in a safety is impetus. Two points are scored for the opposing team when the ball is dead on or behind a team's own goal line if the impetus came from a player on that team.

Examples of Safety:

(a) Blocked punt goes out of kicking team's end zone. Impetus was provided by punting team. The block only changes direction of ball, not impetus.

(b) Ball carrier retreats from field of play into his own end zone and is downed. Ball carrier provides impetus.

(c) Offensive team commits a foul and spot of enforcement is behind its own goal line.

(d) Player on receiving team muffs punt and, trying to get ball, forces or illegally kicks (creating new impetus) it into end zone where it goes out of the end zone or is recovered by a member of the receiving team in the end zone.

Examples of Non-Safety:

(a) Player intercepts a pass with both feet inbounds in the field of play and his momentum carries him into his own end zone. Ball is put in play at spot of interception.

(b) Player intercepts a pass in his own end zone and is downed in the end zone, even after recovering in the end zone. Impetus came from passing team, not from defense. (Touchback)

(c) Player passes from behind his own goal line. Opponent bats down ball in end zone. (Incomplete pass)

MEASURING

1. The forward point of the ball is used when measuring.

POSITION OF PLAYERS AT SNAP

1. Offensive team must have at least seven players on line.
2. Offensive players, not on line, must be at least one yard back at snap.
   (Exception: player who takes snap.)
3. No interior lineman may move abruptly after taking or simulating a three-point stance.
4. No player of either team may enter neutral zone before snap.
5. No player of offensive team may charge or move abruptly, after assuming set position, in such manner as to lead defense to believe snap has started. No player of the defensive team within one yard of the line of scrimmage may make an abrupt movement in an attempt to cause the offense to false start.
6. If a player changes his eligibility, the Referee must alert the defensive captain after player has reported to him.

7. All players of offensive team must be stationary at snap, except one back who may be in motion parallel to scrimmage line or backward (not forward).
8. After a shift or huddle all players on offensive team must come to an absolute stop for at least one second with no movement of hands, feet, head, or swaying of body.
9. Quarterbacks can be called for a false start penalty (five yards) if their actions are judged to be an obvious attempt to draw an opponent offside.
10. Offensive linemen are permitted to interlock legs.

USE OF HANDS, ARMS, AND BODY

1. No player on offense may assist a runner except by blocking for him. There shall be no interlocking interference.
2. A runner may ward off opponents with his hands and arms but no other player on offense may use hands or arms to obstruct an opponent by grasping with hands, pushing, or encircling any part of his body during a block. Hands (open or closed) can be thrust forward to initially contact an opponent on or outside the opponent's frame, but the blocker immediately must work to bring his hands on or inside the frame.
   Note: Pass blocking: Hand(s) thrust forward that slip outside the body of the defender will be legal if blocker immediately worked to bring them back inside. Hand(s) or arm(s) that encircle a defender—i.e., hook an opponent—are to be considered illegal and officials are to call a foul for holding. Blocker cannot use his hands or arms to push from behind, hang onto, or encircle an opponent in a manner that restricts his movement as the play develops.
3. Hands cannot be thrust forward above the frame to contact an opponent on the neck, face or head.
   Note: The frame is defined as the part of the opponent's body below the neck that is presented to the blocker.
4. A defensive player may not tackle or hold an opponent other than a runner. Otherwise, he may use his hands, arms, or body only:
   (a) To defend or protect himself against an obstructing opponent.
   Exception: An eligible receiver is considered to be an obstructing opponent ONLY to a point five yards beyond the line of scrimmage unless the player who receives the snap clearly demonstrates no further intention to pass the ball. Within this five-yard zone, a defensive player may chuck an eligible player in front of him. A defensive player is allowed to maintain continuous and unbroken contact within the five-yard zone until a point when the receiver is even with the defender. The defensive player cannot use his hands or arms to push from behind, hang onto, or encircle an eligible receiver in a manner that restricts movement as the play develops. Beyond this five-yard limitation, a defender may use his hands or arms ONLY to defend or protect himself against impending contact caused by a receiver. In such reaction, the defender may not contact a receiver who attempts to take a path to evade him.
   (b) To push or pull opponent out of the way on line of scrimmage.
   (c) In actual attempt to get at or tackle runner.
   (d) To push or pull opponent out of the way in a legal attempt to recover a loose ball.
   (e) During a legal block on an opponent who is not an eligible pass receiver.
   (f) When legally blocking an eligible pass receiver above the waist.
   Exception: Eligible receivers lined up within two yards of the tackle, whether on or immediately behind the line, may be blocked below the waist at or behind the line of scrimmage. NO eligible receiver may be blocked below the waist after he goes beyond the line. (Illegal cut)

Note: Once the quarterback hands off or pitches the ball to a back, or if the quarterback leaves the pocket area, the restrictions (illegal chuck, illegal cut) on the defensive team relative to the offensive receivers will end, provided the ball is not in the air.

5. A defensive player may not contact an opponent above the shoulders with the palm of his hand except to ward him off on the line. This exception is permitted only if it is not a repeated act against the same opponent during any one contact. In all other cases the palms may be used on head, neck, or face only to ward off or push an opponent in legal attempt to get at the ball.

6. Any offensive player who pretends to possess the ball or to whom a teammate pretends to give the ball may be tackled provided he is crossing his scrimmage line between the ends of a normal tight offensive line.

7. An offensive player who lines up more than two yards outside his own tackle or a player who, at the snap, is in a backfield position and subsequently takes a position more than two yards outside a tackle may not clip an opponent anywhere nor may he contact an opponent below the waist if the blocker is moving toward the ball and if contact is made within an area five yards on either side of the line. (crackback)

8. A player of either team may block at any time provided it is not pass interference, fair catch interference, or unnecessary roughness.

9. A player may not bat or punch:
   (a) A loose ball (in field of play) toward his opponent's goal line or in any direction in either end zone.
   (b) A ball in player possession.
   Note: If there is any question as to whether a defender is stripping or batting a ball in player possession, the official(s) will rule the action as a legal act (stripping the ball).
   Exception: A forward or backward pass may be batted, tipped, or deflected in any direction at any time by either the offense or the defense.
   Note: A pass in flight that is controlled or caught may only be thrown backward, if it is thrown forward it is considered an illegal bat.

10. No player may deliberately kick any ball except as a punt, dropkick, or placekick.

FORWARD PASS

1. A forward pass may be touched or caught by any eligible receiver. All members of the defensive team are eligible. Eligible receivers on the offensive team are players on either end of line (other than center, guard, or tackle) or players at least one yard behind the line at the snap. A T-formation quarterback is not eligible to receive a forward pass during a play from scrimmage.
   Exception: T-formation quarterback becomes eligible if pass is previously touched by an eligible receiver.

2. An offensive team may make only one forward pass during each play from scrimmage (Loss of 5 yards).

3. The passer must be behind his line of scrimmage (Loss of down and five yards, enforced from the spot of pass).

4. Any eligible offensive player may catch a forward pass. If a pass is touched by one eligible offensive player and touched or caught by a second offensive player, pass completion is legal. Further, all offensive players become eligible once a pass is touched by an eligible receiver or any defensive player.

5. The rules concerning a forward pass and ineligible receivers:
   (a) If ball is touched accidentally by an ineligible receiver on or behind his line: loss of five yards.
   (b) If ineligible receiver is illegally downfield: loss of five yards.
   (c) If touched or caught (intentionally or accidentally) by ineligible receiver beyond the line: loss of 5 yards.

6. The player who first controls and continues to maintain control of a pass will be awarded the ball even though his opponent later establishes joint control of the ball.

7. Any forward pass becomes incomplete and ball is dead if:
   (a) Pass hits the ground or goes out of bounds.
   (b) Pass hits the goal post or the crossbar of either team.

8. A forward pass is complete when a receiver clearly possesses the pass and touches the ground with both feet inbounds while in possession of the ball. If a receiver would have landed inbounds with both feet but is carried or pushed out of bounds while maintaining possession of the ball, pass is complete at the out-of-bounds spot.

9. If a personal foul is committed by the defense prior to the completion of a pass, the penalty is 15 yards from the spot where ball becomes dead.

10. If a personal foul is committed by the offense prior to the completion of a pass, the penalty is 15 yards from the previous line of scrimmage.

INTENTIONAL GROUNDING OF FORWARD PASS

1. Intentional grounding of a forward pass is a foul: loss of down and 10 yards from previous spot if passer is in the field of play or loss of down at the spot of the foul if it occurs more than 10 yards behind the line or safety if passer is in his own end zone when ball is released.

2. Intentional grounding will be called when a passer, facing an imminent loss of yardage due to pressure from the defense, throws a forward pass without a realistic chance of completion.

3. Intentional grounding will not be called when a passer, while out of the pocket and facing an imminent loss of yardage, throws a pass that lands at or beyond the line of scrimmage, even if no offensive player(s) have a realistic chance to catch the ball (including if the ball lands out of bounds over the sideline or end line).

PROTECTION OF PASSER

1. By interpretation, a pass begins when the passer—with possession of ball—starts to bring his hand forward. If ball strikes ground after this action has begun, play is ruled an incomplete pass. If passer loses control of ball prior to his bringing his hand forward, play is ruled a fumble.

2. When a passer is holding the ball to pass it forward, any intentional forward movement of his hand starts a forward pass. If a defensive player contacts the passer or the ball after forward movement begins, and the ball leaves the passer's hand, a forward pass is ruled, regardless of where the ball strikes the ground or a player.

3. No defensive player may run into a passer of a legal forward pass after the ball has left his hand (15 yards). The Referee must determine whether opponent had a reasonable chance to stop his momentum during an attempt to block the pass or tackle the passer while he still had the ball.

4. No defensive player who has an unrestricted path to the quarterback may hit him flagrantly in the area of the knee(s) or below when approaching in any direction.

5. Officials are to blow the play dead as soon as the quarterback is clearly in the grasp and control of any tackler, and his safety is in jeopardy.

6. No defensive player may hit the quarterback in the head, face, or neck.

PASS INTERFERENCE

1. There shall be no interference with a forward pass thrown from behind the line. The restriction for the passing team starts with the snap. The restriction on the defensive team starts when the ball leaves the passer's hand. Both restrictions end when the ball is touched by anyone.

2. The penalty for defensive pass interference is an automatic first down at the spot of the foul. If interference is in the end

zone, it is first down for the offense on the defense's 1-yard line. If previous spot was inside the defense's 1-yard line, penalty is half the distance to the goal line.

3. The penalty for <u>offensive</u> pass interference is 10 yards from the previous spot.

4. It is pass interference by either team when any player movement beyond the line of scrimmage significantly hinders the progress of an eligible player of such player's opportunity to catch the ball. Offensive pass interference rules apply from the time the ball is snapped until the ball is touched. Defensive pass interference rules apply from the time the ball is thrown until the ball is touched.

Actions that constitute defensive pass interference include but are not limited to:

(a) Contact by a defender who is not playing the ball and such contact restricts the receiver's opportunity to make the catch.

(b) Playing through the back of a receiver in an attempt to make a play on the ball.

(c) Grabbing a receiver's arm(s) in such a manner that restricts his opportunity to catch a pass.

(d) Extending an arm across the body of a receiver thus restricting his ability to catch a pass, regardless of whether the defender is playing the ball.

(e) Cutting off the path of a receiver by making contact with him without playing the ball.

(f) Hooking a receiver in an attempt to get to the ball in such a manner that it causes the receiver's body to turn prior to the ball arriving.

<u>Actions that do not constitute pass interference include but are not limited to:</u>

(a) Incidental contact by a defender's hands, arms, or body when both players are competing for the ball, or neither player is looking for the ball. If there is any question whether contact is incidental, the ruling shall be no interference.

(b) Inadvertent tangling of feet when both players are playing the ball or neither player is playing the ball.

(c) Contact that would normally be considered pass interference, but the ball is clearly uncatchable by the involved players.

(d) Laying a hand on a receiver that does not restrict the receiver in an attempt to make a play on the ball.

(e) Contact by a defender who has gained position on a receiver in an attempt to catch the ball.

<u>Actions that constitute offensive pass interference include but are not limited to:</u>

(a) Blocking downfield by an offensive player prior to the ball being touched.

(b) Initiating contact with a defender by shoving or pushing off thus creating a separation in an attempt to catch a pass.

(c) Driving through a defender who has established a position on the field.

<u>Actions that do not constitute offensive pass interference include but are not limited to:</u>

(a) Incidental contact by a receiver's hands, arms, or body when both players are competing for the ball or neither player is looking for the ball.

(b) Inadvertent touching of feet when both players are playing the ball or neither player is playing the ball.

(c) Contact that would normally be considered pass interference, but the ball is clearly uncatchable by involved players.

Note 1: If there is any question whether player contact is incidental, the ruling should be no interference.

Note 2: Defensive players have as much right to the path of the ball as eligible offensive players.

Note 3: Pass interference for both teams ends when the pass is touched.

Note 4: There can be no pass interference at or behind the line of scrimmage, but defensive actions such as tackling a receiver can still result in a 5-yard penalty for defensive holding, if accepted.

Note 5: Whenever a team presents an apparent punting formation, defensive pass interference is not to be called for action on the end man on the line of scrimmage, or an eligible receiver behind the line of scrimmage who is aligned or in motion more than one yard outside the end man on the line. Defensive holding, such as tackling a receiver, still can be called and result in a 5-yard penalty and automatic first down from the previous spot, if accepted. Offensive pass interference rules still apply.

BACKWARD PASS

1. Any pass not forward is regarded as a backward pass. A pass parallel to the line is a backward pass. A runner may pass backward at any time.

2. A backward pass that strikes the ground can be recovered and advanced by either team.

3. A backward pass <u>caught in the air</u> can be <u>advanced</u> by <u>either team</u>.

4. A backward pass in flight may not be batted forward by an offensive player.

FUMBLE

1. The distinction between a <u>fumble</u> and a <u>muff</u> should be kept in mind in considering rules about fumbles. A <u>fumble</u> is the <u>loss of player possession</u> of the ball. A muff is the touching of a loose ball by a player in an <u>unsuccessful attempt to obtain possession</u>.

2. A fumble may be advanced by any player on either team regardless of whether recovered before or after ball hits the ground.

3. A fumble that goes forward and out of bounds will return to the fumbling team at the spot of the fumble unless the ball goes out of bounds in the opponent's end zone. In this case, it is a touchback.

4. On a play from scrimmage, if an offensive player fumbles anywhere on the field during fourth down, only the fumbling player is permitted to recover and/or advance the ball. If any player fumbles after the two-minute warning in a half, only the fumbling player is permitted to recover and/or advance the ball. If recovered by any other offensive player, the ball is dead at the spot of the fumble unless it is recovered behind the spot of the fumble. In that case, the ball is dead at the spot of recovery. Any defensive player may recover and/or advance any fumble at any time.

5. A muffed hand-to-hand snap from center is treated as a fumble.

KICKS FROM SCRIMMAGE

1. Any kick from scrimmage must be made from behind the line to be legal.

2. Any punt or missed field goal that touches a goal post is dead.

3. During a kick from scrimmage, <u>only the end men</u>, as eligible receivers on the line of scrimmage at the time of the snap, are permitted to go beyond the line before the ball is kicked.
Exception: An eligible receiver who, at the snap, is aligned or in motion behind the line and more than one yard outside the end man on his side of the line, clearly making him the outside receiver, replaces that end man as the player eligible to go downfield after the snap. All other members of the kicking team must remain at the line of scrimmage until the ball has been kicked.

4. Any punt that is blocked and does <u>not</u> cross the line of scrimmage can be recovered and advanced by either team. However, if offensive team recovers it must make the yardage necessary for its first down to retain possession if punt was

on fourth down.

5. The kicking team may never advance its own kick even though legal recovery is made beyond the line of scrimmage. Possession only.

6. A member of the receiving team may not run into or rough a kicker who kicks from behind his line unless contact is:
   (a) Incidental to and after he had touched ball in flight.
   (b) Caused by kicker's own motions.
   (c) Occurs during a quick kick, or a kick made after a run behind the line, or after kicker recovers a loose ball on the ground. Ball is loose when kicker muffs snap or snap hits ground.
   (d) Defender is blocked into kicker.
   The penalty for running into the kicker is 5 yards. For roughing the kicker: 15 yards, an automatic first down and disqualification if flagrant.

7. If a member of the kicking team attempting to down the ball on or inside opponent's 5-yard line carries the ball into the end zone, it is a touchback.

8. Fouls during a punt are enforced from the previous spot (line of scrimmage).
   Exception: Illegal touching, fair-catch interference, invalid fair-catch signal, or personal foul (blocking after a fair-catch signal).

9. While the ball is in the air or rolling on the ground following a punt or field-goal attempt and receiving team commits a foul only before or after gaining possession, receiving team will retain possession and will be penalized for its foul.

10. It will be illegal for a defensive player to jump or stand on any player, or be picked up by a teammate or to use a hand or hands on a teammate to gain additional height in an attempt to block a kick (Penalty: 15 yards, unsportsmanlike conduct).

11. A punted ball remains a kicked ball until it is declared dead or in possession of either team.

12. Any member of the punting team may down the ball anywhere in the field of play. However, it is illegal touching (Official's time out and receiver's ball at spot of illegal touching). This foul does not offset any foul by receivers during the down.

13. Defensive team may advance all kicks from scrimmage (including unsuccessful field goal) whether or not ball crosses defensive team's goal line. Rules pertaining to kicks from scrimmage apply until defensive team gains possession.

14. When a team presents a punt formation, defensive pass interference is not to be called for actions on the widest player eligible to go beyond line. Defensive holding may be called.

FAIR CATCH

1. The member of the receiving team must raise one arm a full length above his head and wave it from side to side while kick is in flight. (Failure to give proper sign: receivers' ball five yards behind spot of signal.) **Note:** It is legal for the receiver to shield his eyes from the sun by raising one hand no higher than the helmet.

2. No opponent may interfere with the fair catcher, the ball, or his path to the ball. Penalty: 15 yards from spot of foul and fair catch is awarded.

3. A player who signals for a fair catch is not required to catch the ball. However, if a player signals for a fair catch, he may not block or initiate contact with any player on the kicking team until the ball touches a player. Penalty: snap 15 yards.

4. If ball is touched by member of kicking team in flight, fair catch signal is off and all rules for a kicked ball apply.

5. Any undue advance by a fair catch receiver is delay of game. No specific distance is specified for undue advance as ball is dead at spot of catch. If player comes to a reasonable stop, no penalty. For penalty, five yards.

6. If time expires while ball is in play and a fair catch is awarded,

receiving team may choose to extend the period with one fair catch kick down. However, placekicker may not use tee.

FOUL ON LAST PLAY OF HALF OR GAME

1. On a foul by defense on last play of half or game, the down is replayed if penalty is accepted.

2. On a foul by the offense on last play of half or game, the down is not replayed and the play in which the foul is committed is nullified.
   Exception: Fair catch interference, foul following change of possession, illegal touching. No score by offense counts.

SPOT OF ENFORCEMENT OF FOUL

1. There are four basic spots at which a penalty for a foul is enforced:
   (a) Spot of foul: The spot where the foul is committed.
   (b) Previous spot: The spot where the ball was put in play.
   (c) Spot of snap, backward pass or fumble: The spot where the foul occurred or the spot where the penalty is to be enforced.
   (d) Succeeding spot: The spot where the ball next would be put in play if no distance penalty were to be enforced.
      Exception: If foul occurs after a touchdown and before the whistle for a try, succeeding spot is spot of next kickoff.

2. All fouls committed by offensive team behind the line of scrimmage (except in the end zone) shall be penalized from the previous spot. If the foul is in the end zone, it is a safety.

3. When spot of enforcement for fouls involving defensive holding or illegal use of hands by the defense is behind the line of scrimmage, any penalty yardage to be assessed on that play shall be measured from the line if the foul occurred beyond the line.

DOUBLE FOUL

1. If there is a double foul during a down in which there is a change of possession, the team last gaining possession may keep the ball unless its foul was committed prior to the change of possession.

2. If double foul occurs after a change of possession, the defensive team retains the ball at the spot of its foul or dead ball spot.

3. If one of the fouls of a double foul involves disqualification, that player must be removed, but no penalty yardage is to be assessed.

4. If the kickers foul during a kickoff, punt, safety kick, or field-goal attempt before possession changes, the receivers will have the option of replaying the down at the previous spot (offsetting fouls), or keeping the ball after enforcement for its fouls.

PENALTY ENFORCED ON FOLLOWING KICKOFF

1. When a team scores by touchdown, field goal, extra point, or safety and either team commits a personal foul, unsportsmanlike conduct, or obvious unfair act during the down, the penalty will be assessed on the following kickoff.

EMERGENCIES AND UNFAIR ACTS
Emergencies—Policy

The National Football League requires all League personnel, including game officials, League office employees, players, coaches, and other club employees to use best effort to see that each game—preseason, regular season, and postseason—is played to its conclusion. The League recognizes, however, that emergencies may arise that make a game's completion impossible or inadvisable. Such circumstances may include, but are not limited to, severely inclement weather, natural or manmade disaster, power failure, and spectator interference. Games should be suspended, cancelled, postponed, or terminated when circumstances exist such that comencement or continuation of play would pose a threat to the safety of participants or spectators.

Authority of Commissioner's Office

1. Authority to cancel, postpone, or terminate games is vested only in the Commissioner and the League President (other League office representatives and referees may suspend play temporarily; see point No. 3 under this section and point No. 1 under "Authority of Referee" below). The following definitions apply:
    *   **Cancel.** To cancel a game is to nullify it either before or after it begins and to make no provision for rescheduling it or for including its score or other performance statistics in League records.
    *   **Postpone.** To postpone a game is (a) to defer its starting time to a later date, or (b) to suspend it after play has begun and to make provision to resume at a later date with all scores and other performance statistics up to the point of postponement added to those achieved in the resumed portion of the game.
    *   **Terminate.** To terminate a game is to end it short of a full 60 minutes of play, to record it officially as a completed game, and to make no provision to resume it at a later date. The Commissioner or League President may terminate a game in an emergency if, in his opinion, it is reasonable to project that its resumption (a) would not change its ultimate result or (b) would not adversely affect any other interteam competitive issue.
    *   **Forfeit.** The Commissioner, (except in cases of disciplinary action; see last section on "Removing Team from Field"), League President, and their representatives, including referees, are not authorized unilaterally to declare forfeits. A forfeit occurs only when a game is not played because of the failure or refusal of *one* team to participate. In that event, the other team, if ready and willing to play, is the winner by a score of 2-0.
2. If an emergency arises that may require cancellation, postponement, or termination (see above), the highest ranking representative from the Commissioner's office working the game in a "control" capacity will consult with the Commissioner, League President, or game-day duty officer designated by the League (by telephone, if that person is not in attendance) concerning such decision. If circumstances warrant, the League representative should also attempt to consult with the weather bureau and with appropriate security personnel of the League, club, stadium, and local authorities. If no representative from the Commissioner's office is working the game in a "control" capacity, the referee will be in charge (see "Authority of Referee" below).
3. In circumstances where safety is of immediate concern, the Commissioner's office representative may, after consulting with the referee, authorize a temporary suspension in play and, if warranted, removal of the participants from the playing field. The representative should be mindful of the safety of spectators, players, game officials, nonplayer personnel in the bench areas, and other field-level personnel such as photographers and cheerleaders.
4. If possible, the League-office representative should consult with authorized representatives of the two participating clubs before any decision involving cancellation, postponement, or termination is made by the Commissioner or League President.
5. If the Commissioner or League President decides to cancel, postpone, or terminate a game, his representative at the game or the game-day duty officer will then determine the method(s) for announcing such decision, e.g., by public-address announcement over referee's wireless microphone, by public-address announcement by home club, or by communication to radio, television, and other news media.

Authority of Referee

1. If a referee determines that an emergency warrants immediate removal of participants from the playing field for

safety reasons, he may do so on his own authority. If, however, circumstances allow him the time, he must reach the highest ranking full-time League office representative working at the game in a "control" capacity or the game-day duty officer designated by the League (by telephone, if that person is not in attendance) and discuss the actual or potential emergency with such representative or duty officer. That representative or duty officer then will make the final decision on removal of participants from the field or obtain a decision from the Commissioner or League President.
2. If a referee removes participants from the playing field under No. 1 above, he may order them to their respective bench areas or to their locker rooms, whichever is appropriate in the circumstances.
3. After appropriate consultation under No. 1 above, the referee must advise the two participating head coaches of the nature of the emergency and the action contemplated (if the decision has not yet been reached) or of the final decision.
4. The referee must *not*, before a decision is reached, make an announcement on his microphone concerning the possibility of a cancellation, postponement, or termination unless instructed to do so by an appropriate representative of the Commissioner's office.
5. The referee must *not* discuss a forfeit with head coaches or club personnel and must *not* use that term over the referee's microphone (see definition of *forfeit* under No. 1 of "Authority of Commissioner's Office" above).
6. The referee must *not* assess an unsportsmanlike-conduct penalty on the home team for actions of fans that cause or contribute to an emergency.
7. The referee should be mindful of the safety of not only players and officials, but also of the spectators and other nonparticipants.
8. If an emergency involves spectator interference (for example, nonparticipants on the field or thrown objects), the referee immediately should contact the appropriate club or League representative for additional security assistance, including, if applicable, involvement of the League's security representative(s) assigned to the game.
9. The referee may order the resumption of play when he deems conditions safe for all concerned and, if circumstances warrant, after consultation with appropriate representatives of the Commissioner's office.
10. Under no circumstances is the referee authorized to cancel, postpone, terminate, or declare forfeiture of a game unilaterally.

Procedures for Starting and Resuming Games

Subject to the points of authority listed above, League personnel and referees will be guided by the following procedures for starting and resuming games that are affected by emergencies.

1. If, because of an emergency, a regular-season or postseason game is not started at its scheduled time and cannot be played at any later time that same day, the game nevertheless must be played on a subsequent date to be determined by the Commissioner.
2. If an emergency threatens to occur during the playing of a game (for example, an incoming tropical storm), the starting time of the game will not be moved to an earlier time unless there is clearly sufficient time to make an orderly change.
3. All games that are suspended temporarily and resumed on the same day, and all suspended games that are postponed to a later date, will be resumed at the point of suspension. On suspension, the referee will call timeout and make a record of the following: team possessing the ball, direction in which its offense was headed, position of the ball on the field, down, distance, period, time remaining in the period, and any other pertinent information required for an orderly and equitable resumption of play.
4. For regular-season postponements, the Commissioner will make every effort to set the game for no later than two days

after its originally scheduled date and at the same site. If unable to schedule at the same site, he will select an appropriate alternative site. If it is impossible to schedule the game within two days after its original date, the Commissioner will attempt to schedule it on the Tuesday of the next calendar week. The Commissioner will keep in mind the potential for competitive inequities if one or both of the involved clubs has already been scheduled for a game close to the Tuesday of that week (for example, a Thursday game).

5. For postseason postponements, the Commissioner will make every effort to set the game as soon as possible after its originally scheduled date and at the same site. If unable to schedule at the same site, he will select an appropriate alternative site.

6. Whenever postponement is attributable to negligence by a club, the negligent club is responsible for all home club costs and expenses, including, subject to approval by the Commissioner, gate receipts and television-contract income. [See Section 19.11 (C) of the NFL Constitution and Bylaws.]

7. Each home club is strictly responsible for having the playing surface of its stadium well maintained and suitable for NFL play.

UNFAIR ACTS
Commissioner's Authority
The Commissioner has sole authority to investigate and to take appropriate disciplinary or corrective measures if any club action, nonparticipant interference, or emergency occurs in an NFL game which he deems so unfair or outside the accepted tactics encountered in professional football that such action has a major effect on the result of a game.

No Club Protests
The authority and measures provided for in this section (UNFAIR ACTS) do not constitute a protest machinery for NFL clubs to dispute the result of a game. The Commissioner will conduct an investigation under this section only to review an act or occurrence that he deems so unfair that the result of the game in question may be inequitable to one of the participating teams. The Commissioner will not apply his authority under this section when a club registers a complaint concerning judgmental errors or routine errors of omission by game officials. Games involving such complaints will continue to stand as completed.

Penalties for Unfair Acts
The Commissioner's powers under this section (UNFAIR ACTS) include the imposition of monetary fines and draft choice forfeitures, suspension of persons involved, and, if appropriate, the reversal of a game's result or the rescheduling of a game, either from the beginning or from the point at which the extraordinary act occurred. In the event of rescheduling a game, the Commissioner will be guided by the procedures specified above ("Procedures for Starting and Resuming Games" under EMERGENCIES). In all cases, the Commissioner will conduct a full investigation, including the opportunity for hearings, use of game videotape, and any other procedures he deems appropriate.

REMOVING TEAM FROM FIELD
No player, coach, or other person affiliated with a club may remove that club's team from the playing of any game, including preseason, except at the direction of the referee. Any club violating this rule will be subject to disciplinary action by the Commissioner, including possible game forfeiture and sole liability for financial losses suffered by the opposing club and any other affected member clubs of the League. [See Section 9.1 (E) of the NFL Constitution and Bylaws.]

General Information

AMERICAN FOOTBALL CONFERENCE

BALTIMORE RAVENS
1 Winning Drive
Owings Mills, MD 21117
410/701-4000

BUFFALO BILLS
One Bills Drive
Orchard Park, NY 14127
716/648-1800

CINCINNATI BENGALS
One Paul Brown Stadium
Cincinnati, OH 45202
513/621-3550

CLEVELAND BROWNS
76 Lou Groza Boulevard
Berea, OH 44017
440/891-5000

DENVER BRONCOS
13655 Broncos Parkway
Englewood, CO 80112
303/649-9000

HOUSTON TEXANS
Two Reliant Park
Houston, TX 77054
832/667-2000

INDIANAPOLIS COLTS
P.O. Box 535000
Indianapolis, IN 46253
317/297-2658

JACKSONVILLE JAGUARS
ALLTEL Stadium
One ALLTEL Stadium Place
Jacksonville, FL 32202
904/633-6000

KANSAS CITY CHIEFS
One Arrowhead Drive
Kansas City, MO 64129
816/920-9300

MIAMI DOLPHINS
7500 S.W. 30th Street
Davie, FL 33314
954/452-7000

NEW ENGLAND PATRIOTS
Gillette Stadium
One Patriot Place
Foxborough, MA 02035
508/543-8200

NEW YORK JETS
1000 Fulton Avenue
Hempstead, NY 11550
516/560-8100

OAKLAND RAIDERS
1220 Harbor Bay Parkway
Alameda, CA 94502
510/864-5000

PITTSBURGH STEELERS
3400 South Water Street
Pittsburgh, PA 15203
412/432-7800

SAN DIEGO CHARGERS
P.O. Box 609609
San Diego, CA 92160
858/874-4500

TENNESSEE TITANS
460 Great Circle Road
Nashville, TN 37228
615/565-4000

NATIONAL FOOTBALL CONFERENCE

ARIZONA CARDINALS
P.O. Box 888
Phoenix, AZ 85001
602/379-0101

ATLANTA FALCONS
4400 Falcon Parkway
Flowery Branch, GA 30542
770/965-3115

CAROLINA PANTHERS
800 South Mint Street
Charlotte, NC 28202
704/358-7000

CHICAGO BEARS
Halas Hall at Conway Park
1000 Football Drive
Lake Forest, IL 60045
847/295-6600

DALLAS COWBOYS
Cowboys Center
One Cowboys Parkway
Irving, TX 75063
972/556-9900

DETROIT LIONS
Detroit Lions Practice & Training Facility
222 Republic Drive
Allen Park, MI 48101
313/216-4000

GREEN BAY PACKERS
Lambeau Field Atrium
1265 Lombardi Avenue
Green Bay, WI 54304
920/569-7500

MINNESOTA VIKINGS
9520 Viking Drive
Eden Prairie, MN 55344
952/828-6500

NEW ORLEANS SAINTS
5800 Airline Drive
Metairie, LA 70003
504/733-0255

NEW YORK GIANTS
Giants Stadium
East Rutherford, NJ 07073
201/935-8111

PHILADELPHIA EAGLES
NovaCare Complex
One NovaCare Way
Philadelphia, PA 19145
215/463-2500

ST. LOUIS RAMS
One Rams Way
St. Louis, MO 63045
314/982-7267

SAN FRANCISCO 49ERS
4949 Centennial Boulevard
Santa Clara, CA 95054
408/562-4949

SEATTLE SEAHAWKS
11220 N.E. 53rd Street
Kirkland, WA 98033
425/827-9777

TAMPA BAY BUCCANEERS
One Buccaneer Place
Tampa, FL 33607
813/870-2700

WASHINGTON REDSKINS
Redskin Park
21300 Redskin Park Drive
Ashburn, VA 20147
703/726-7000

AMERICAN FOOTBALL CONFERENCE

BALTIMORE RAVENS
Stadium: M&T Bank Stadium
   (opened in 1998)
   •**Capacity:** 69,084
   1101 Russell Street
   Baltimore, MD 21230
Playing Surface: Sportexe Momentum

BUFFALO BILLS
Stadium: Ralph Wilson Stadium
   (opened in 1973)
   •**Capacity:** 73,967
   One Bills Drive
   Orchard Park, NY 14127
Playing Surface: AstroPlay

CINCINNATI BENGALS
Stadium: Paul Brown Stadium
   (opened in 2000)
   •**Capacity:** 65,326
   One Paul Brown Stadium
   Cincinnati, OH 45202
Playing Surface: Synthetic

CLEVELAND BROWNS
Stadium: Cleveland Browns Stadium
   (opened in 1999)
   •**Capacity:** 73,300
   100 Alfred Lerner Way
   Cleveland, OH 44114
Playing Surface: Grass

DENVER BRONCOS
Stadium: INVESCO Field at Mile High
   (opened in 2001)
   •**Capacity:** 76,125
   1701 Bryant Street
   Denver, CO 80204
Playing Surface: Grass (PAT)

HOUSTON TEXANS
Stadium: Reliant Stadium
   (opened in 2002)
   •**Capacity:** 71,054
   Houston, TX 77054
Playing Surface: Grass

INDIANAPOLIS COLTS
Stadium: RCA Dome
   (opened in 1983)
   •**Capacity:** 55,506
   100 South Capitol Avenue
   Indianapolis, IN 46225
Playing Surface: FieldTurf

JACKSONVILLE JAGUARS
Stadium: ALLTEL Stadium
   (opened in 1995)
   •**Capacity:** 67,164
   One ALLTEL Stadium Place
   Jacksonville, FL 32202
Playing Surface: Grass

KANSAS CITY CHIEFS
Stadium: Arrowhead Stadium
   (opened in 1972)
   •**Capacity:** 79,451
   One Arrowhead Drive
   Kansas City, MO 64129
Playing Surface: Grass

MIAMI DOLPHINS
Stadium: Dolphins Stadium
   (opened in 1987)
   •**Capacity:** 75,192
   2269 Dan Marino Blvd.
   Miami, FL 33056
Playing Surface: Grass (PAT)

NEW ENGLAND PATRIOTS
Stadium: Gillette Stadium
   (opened in 2002)
   •**Capacity:** 68,756
   One Patriot Place
   Foxborough, MA 02035
Playing Surface: Grass

NEW YORK JETS
Stadium: Meadowlands
   (opened in 1976)
   •**Capacity:** 79,466
   East Rutherford, NJ 07073
Playing Surface: FieldTurf

OAKLAND RAIDERS
Stadium: McAfee Coliseum
   (opened in 1966)
   •**Capacity:** 63,132
   7000 Coliseum Way
   Oakland, CA 94621
Playing Surface: Grass

PITTSBURGH STEELERS
Stadium: Heinz Field
   (opened in 2001)
   •**Capacity:** 64,350
   100 Art Rooney Avenue
   Pittsburgh, PA 15212
Playing Surface: DD GrassMaster

SAN DIEGO CHARGERS
Stadium: Qualcomm Stadium
   (opened in 1967)
   •**Capacity:** 70,000
   9449 Friars Road
   San Diego, CA 92108
Playing Surface: Grass

TENNESSEE TITANS
Stadium: The Coliseum
   (opened in 1999)
   •**Capacity:** 68,809
   One Titans Way
   Nashville, TN 37213
Playing Surface: Natural Grass

NATIONAL FOOTBALL CONFERENCE

ARIZONA CARDINALS
Stadium: Sun Devil Stadium
(opened in 1958)
• **Capacity:** 73,014
Fifth Street
Tempe, AZ 85287
Playing Surface: Grass

ATLANTA FALCONS
Stadium: Georgia Dome
(opened in 1992)
• **Capacity:** 71,228
One Georgia Dome Drive
Atlanta, GA 30313
Playing Surface: FieldTurf

CAROLINA PANTHERS
Stadium: Bank of America Stadium
(opened in 1996)
• **Capacity:** 73,298
Charlotte, NC 28202
Playing Surface: Grass

CHICAGO BEARS
Stadium: Soldier Field
(opened in 1924)
• **Capacity:** 61,500
1410 S. Museum Campus Dr.
Chicago, IL 60605
Playing Surface: Natural Grass

DALLAS COWBOYS
Stadium: Texas Stadium
(opened in 1971)
• **Capacity:** 65,529
2401 E. Airport Freeway
Irving, TX 75062
Playing Surface: Sportfield Realgrass

DETROIT LIONS
Stadium: Ford Field
(opened in 2002)
• **Capacity:** 64,500
2000 Brush Street
Detroit, MI 48226
Playing Surface: FieldTurf

GREEN BAY PACKERS
Stadium: Lambeau Field
(opened in 1957)
• **Capacity:** 72,601
1265 Lombardi Avenue
Green Bay, WI 54304
Playing Surface: Grass

MINNESOTA VIKINGS
Stadium: Hubert H. Humphrey Metrodome
(opened in 1982)
• **Capacity:** 64,121
500 11th Avenue South
Minneapolis, MN 55415
Playing Surface: FieldTurf

NEW ORLEANS SAINTS
Stadium: Louisiana Superdome
(opened in 1975)
• **Capacity:** 64,900
1500 Poydras Street
New Orleans, LA 70112
Playing Surface: Sportexe Momentum

NEW YORK GIANTS
Stadium: Giants Stadium
(opened in 1976)
• **Capacity:** 80,242
East Rutherford, NJ 07073
Playing Surface: FieldTurf

PHILADELPHIA EAGLES
Stadium: Lincoln Financial Field
(opened in 2003)
• **Capacity:** 68,400
One Lincoln Financial Field Way
Philadelphia, PA 19148
Playing Surface: Natural Grass

ST. LOUIS RAMS
Stadium: Edward Jones Dome
(opened in 1995)
• **Capacity:** 66,000
701 Convention Plaza
St. Louis, MO 63101
Playing Surface: FieldTurf

SAN FRANCISCO 49ERS
Stadium: Monster Park
(opened in 1958)
• **Capacity:** 69,732
San Francisco, CA 94124
Playing Surface: Natural Grass

SEATTLE SEAHAWKS
Stadium: Qwest Field
(opened in 2002)
• **Capacity:** 67,000
800 Occidental Ave South, #200
Seattle, WA 98134
Playing Surface: FieldTurf

TAMPA BAY BUCCANEERS
Stadium: Raymond James Stadium
(opened in 1998)
• **Capacity:** 65,657
Tampa, FL 33607
Playing Surface: Grass

WASHINGTON REDSKINS
Stadium: FedExField
(opened in 1997)
• **Capacity:** 91,665
1600 FedEx Way
Landover, MD 20785
Playing Surface: Natural Grass

280 Park Avenue, New York, New York 10017 (212) 450-2000

NFL Internet Network: www.NFL.com

Commissioner: Paul Tagliabue

Executive Vice President/Chief Operating Officer: Roger Goodell

Executive Vice President/Chief Administrative Officer-Counsel: Jeff Pash

Executive Vice President of Labor Relations/Chairman NFLMC: Harold Henderson

Executive Vice President of Communications and Public Affairs: Joe Browne

Executive Vice President of Media/President and
Chief Executive Officer of NFL Network: Steve Bornstein

Executive Vice President of Finance and Strategic Transactions: Eric Grubman